wwnorton.com/nael

Use the code below to register for a password for the
FREE StudySpace site and Supplemental Ebook that accompany
The Norton Anthology of English Literature. (The password is
needed to give you access to copyrighted materials.)

BRIT-BOOK

The Middle Ages • SIMPSON / DAVID

The Sixteenth Century • GREENBLATT / LOGAN

The Early Seventeenth Century
MAUS / LEWALSKI

The Restoration and the Eighteenth Century
NOGGLE / LIPKING

The Romantic Period • LYNCH / STILLINGER

The Victorian Age • ROBSON / CHRIST

The Twentieth Century and After
RAMAZANI / STALLWORTHY

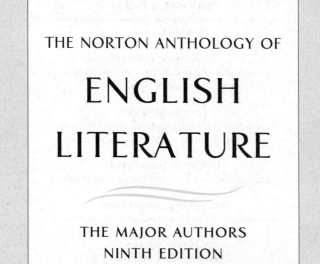

THE NORTON ANTHOLOGY OF

ENGLISH

LITERATURE

THE MAJOR AUTHORS
NINTH EDITION

VOLUME 1

THE NORTON ANTHOLOGY OF
ENGLISH
LITERATURE

THE MAJOR AUTHORS
NINTH EDITION

Stephen Greenblatt, *General Editor*

COGAN UNIVERSITY PROFESSOR OF THE HUMANITIES
HARVARD UNIVERSITY

VOLUME 1

W · W · NORTON & COMPANY
NEW YORK · LONDON

W. W. Norton & Company has been independent since its founding in 1923, when William Warder Norton and Mary D. Herter Norton first published lectures delivered at the People's Institute, the adult education division of New York City's Cooper Union. The firm soon expanded its program beyond the Institute, publishing books by celebrated academics from America and abroad. By midcentury, the two major pillars of Norton's publishing program—trade books and college texts—were firmly established. In the 1950s, the Norton family transferred control of the company to its employees, and today—with a staff of four hundred and a comparable number of trade, college, and professional titles published each year—W. W. Norton & Company stands as the largest and oldest publishing house owned wholly by its employees.

Editor: Julia Reidhead
Associate Editor: Carly Fraser Doria
Managing Editor, College: Marian Johnson
Manuscript Editors: Susan Joseph, Jennifer Harris, Katharine Ings, Pam Lawson, and Jack Borrebach
Project Editor: Rachel Mayer
Electronic Media Editor: Eileen Connell
Editorial Assistant(s): Hannah Blaisdell, Jennifer Barnhardt
Marketing Manager, Literature: Kimberly Bowers
Production Manager: Sean Mintus
Photo Editor: Michael Fodera
Permissions Manager: Megan Jackson
Permissions Clearing: Nancy J. Rodwan
Text Design: Jo Anne Metsch
Art Director: Rubina Yeh
Composition: The Westchester Book Group
Manufacturing: LSC—Crawfordsville, IN

The text of this book is composed in Fairfield Medium with the display set in Aperto.

Since this page cannot legibly accommodate all the copyright notices, the Permissions Acknowledgments constitute an extension of the copyright page.

Library of Congress Cataloging-in-Publication Data has been applied for.

ISBN 978-0-393-91964-6

W. W. Norton & Company, Inc., 500 Fifth Avenue, New York, NY 10110-0017
wwnorton.com

W. W. Norton & Company Ltd., 15 Carlisle Street, London W1D 3BS

Contents*

The Middle Ages (to ca. 1485)

---

* To explore the table of contents of the supplemental ebook, visit wwnorton.com/nael.

The Sixteenth Century (1485–1603)

The Early Seventeenth Century (1603–1660)

The Restoration and
the Eighteenth Century (1660–1785)

Preface to the Ninth Edition

A great anthology of English literature is a compact library for life. Its goal is to bring together works of enduring value and to make them accessible, comprehensible, and pleasurable to a wide range of readers. Its success depends on earning the reader's trust: trust in the wisdom of the choices, the accuracy of the texts, and the usefulness and good sense of the apparatus. It is not a place for the display of pedantry, the pushing of cherished theories, or the promotion of a narrow ideological agenda. If it succeeds, if it manages to give its readers access to many of the most remarkable works written in English during centuries of restless creative effort, then it furthers a worthwhile democratic cause, that of openness. What might have been a closed pleasure ground, jealously guarded as the preserve of a privileged elite, becomes open to all. Over fifty years and nine editions, *The Norton Anthology of English Literature* has served this important goal.

The works anthologized here generally form the core of courses that are designed to introduce students to English literature. The selections reach back to the earliest moments of literary creativity in English, when the language itself was still molten, and extend to some of the most recent experiments, when, once again, English seems remarkably fluid and open. That openness—a recurrent characteristic of a language that has never been officially regulated and that has constantly renewed itself—helps to account for the sense of freshness that characterizes the works brought together here.

One of the joys of literature in English is its spectacular abundance. Even within the geographical confines of England, Scotland, Wales, and Ireland, where the majority of texts in this collection originated, one can find more than enough distinguished and exciting works to fill the pages of this anthology many times over. But English literature is not confined to the British Isles; it is a global phenomenon. This border-crossing is not a consequence of modernity alone. It is fitting that among the first works here is *Beowulf*, a powerful epic written in the Germanic language known as Old English about a singularly restless Scandinavian hero. *Beowulf*'s remarkable translator in *The Norton Anthology of English Literature*, Seamus Heaney, was one of the great contemporary masters of English literature—he was awarded the Nobel Prize for Literature in 1995—but it would be potentially misleading to call him an "English poet" for he was born in Northern Ireland and was not in fact English. It would be still more misleading to call him a "British poet," as if the British Empire were the most salient fact about the language he spoke and wrote in or the culture by which he was shaped. What matters is that the language in which Heaney wrote is English, and this fact links him powerfully with the authors assembled in this edition, a linguistic community that stubbornly refuses to fit comfortably within any firm geographical or ethnic or national boundaries. So too, to glance at other authors and writings in the anthology, in the twelfth century, the noblewoman Marie de France wrote her short stories in an Anglo-Norman dialect at home on both sides of the channel; in the sixteenth century William Tyndale, in exile in the Low Countries and inspired by German religious reformers, translated the New Testament from Greek and thereby changed the course of the English language; in the seventeenth century Aphra Behn touched readers with a story that moves from Africa, where its hero is born, to South America, where Behn herself may have witnessed some of the tragic events she describes; and early in the twentieth century Joseph Conrad, born in Ukraine of Polish parents, wrote in eloquent English a celebrated novella whose ironic vision of European empire gave way by the century's end to the voices of those over whom the empire, now in ruins, had once hoped to rule: the Caribbean-born Derek Walcott; the African-born Chinua Achebe and J. M. Coetzee; and the Indian-born Salman Rushdie.

A vital literary culture is always on the move. This principle was the watchword of M. H. Abrams, the distinguished literary critic who first conceived *The Norton Anthology of English Literature,* brought together the original team of editors, and, with characteristic insight, diplomacy, and humor, oversaw seven editions and has graciously offered counsel on subsequent editions. Abrams wisely understood that new scholarly discoveries and the shifting interests of readers constantly alter the landscape of literary history. To stay vital, the anthology, therefore, would need to undergo a process of periodic revision, guided by advice from teachers, as well as students, who view the anthology with a loyal but critical eye. As with past editions, we have benefited from detailed information on the works actually assigned and suggestions for improvements from 133 reviewers. Their participation has been crucial as the editors grapple with the task of strengthening the selection of more traditional texts while adding texts that reflect the expansion of the field of English studies.

The great challenge (and therefore the interest) of the task is inevitably linked to space constraints. The virtually limitless resources of the Web make some of the difficult choices less vexing: in addition to the print anthology, we have created for our readers a supplemental ebook, with more than one thousand texts from the Middle Ages to the turn of the twentieth century. The expansion of the anthology's range by means of this ebook is breathtaking: at no additional cost, readers have access to remarkable works, edited, glossed, and annotated with the sensitivity to classroom use for which the Norton Anthology is renowned. Hence teachers who wish to extend the selections from major authors included in the print anthology will find hundreds of further readings—Milton's *Comus* and *Samson Agonistes,* for example, or Conrad's *Youth*—in the supplemental ebook. At the same time, the ebook contains marvelous works that might otherwise be lost from view: among them, to cite several of my personal favorites, Gascoigne's "Woodmanship," Wycherley's *The Country Wife,* Mary Robinson's "The Camp," and Edward Lear's "The Jumblies." In addition, there are many fascinating topical clusters—"The First Crusade: Sanctifying War," "Genius," "Romantic Literature and Wartime," "Victorian Issues: Education," "Imagining Ireland," to name only a few—all designed to draw readers into larger cultural contexts and to expose them to a wide spectrum of voices.

With each edition, *The Norton Anthology of English Literature* has offered a broadened canon without sacrificing major writers and a selection of complete longer texts in which readers can immerse themselves. Perhaps the most emblematic of these great texts is the epic *Beowulf*. Among the many other complete longer works in the Major Authors Edition are four new selections—*Sir Gawain and the Green Knight* (new in Simon Armitage's spectacular translation) and, much requested by instructors, William Shakespeare's *Othello*, Virginia Woolf's *Mrs. Dalloway*, and Samuel Beckett's *Waiting for Godot*—as well as Aphra Behn's *Oroonoko*, Robert Louis Stevenson's *The Strange Case of Dr. Jekyll and Mr. Hyde*, Rudyard Kipling's *The Man Who Would Be King*, and Joseph Conrad's *Heart of Darkness*. To augment the number of complete longer works instructors can assign, and—a special concern—better to represent the achievements of novelists, the publisher is making available the full list of Norton Critical Editions, more than 220 titles, including such frequently assigned novels as Jane Austen's *Pride and Prejudice*, Mary Shelley's *Frankenstein*, Charles Dickens's *Hard Times*, and Chinua Achebe's *Things Fall Apart*. A Norton Critical Edition may be packaged with the one-volume version, two-splits package, or either individual paperback-split volume for free.

In The Major Authors, Ninth Edition, we have continued to expand the selection of writing by women in several historical periods. The sustained work of scholars in recent years has recovered dozens of significant authors who had been marginalized or neglected by a male-dominated literary tradition and has deepened our understanding of those women writers who had managed, against considerable odds, to claim a place in that tradition. The First Edition of the Major Authors *Norton Anthology* included no women writers; this Ninth Edition includes twenty-seven, of whom two are newly added and four are reselected or expanded. Poets and dramatists whose names were scarcely mentioned even in the specialized literary histories of earlier generations—Aemilia Lanyer, Lady Mary Wroth, Margaret Cavendish, Anna Letitia Barbauld, Charlotte Smith, and many others—now appear in the company of their male contemporaries. There are in addition two complete long prose works by women—Aphra Behn's *Oroonoko* and Virginia Woolf's *Mrs. Dalloway*—along with new selections from such celebrated fiction writers as Jean Rhys, Katherine Mansfield, Margaret Atwood, and Zadie Smith.

Now, as in the past, cultures define themselves by the songs they sing and the stories they tell. But the central importance of visual media in contemporary culture has heightened our awareness of the ways in which songs and stories have always been closely linked to the images that societies have fashioned and viewed. The Major Authors Edition features sixty pages of color plates and more than 90 black-and-white illustrations throughout this edition. In selecting visual material—from the Sutton Hoo treasure of the seventh century to Yinka Shonibare's *Nelson's Ship in a Bottle* in the twenty-first century—the editors sought to provide images that conjure up, whether directly or indirectly, the individual writers in each section; that relate specifically to individual works in the anthology; and that shape and illuminate the culture of a particular literary period. We have tried to choose visually striking images that will interest students and provoke discussion, and our captions draw attention to important details and cross-reference related texts in the anthology.

Period-by-Period Revisions

The Middle Ages, edited by James Simpson and Alfred David, has taken on a striking new look, with a major revision and expansion of its selections. The heart of the Anglo-Saxon portion is the great epic *Beowulf,* in an acclaimed translation, specially commissioned for *The Norton Anthology of English Literature,* by Seamus Heaney. The array of Anglo-Saxon texts includes Alfred David's new verse translations of the poignant, visionary *Dream of the Rood* and the elegiac *Wanderer,* and *The Wife's Lament.* A new Irish Literature selection features a tale from *The Tain* and a group of vivid ninth-century lyrics. The Anglo-Norman section—a key bridge between the Anglo-Saxon period and the time of Chaucer—includes a story by Marie de France. The Middle English section centers, as always, on Chaucer, with a generous selection of texts carefully glossed and annotated so as to heighten their accessibility. New to the Major Authors Edition is a brilliant, specially revised verse translation of *Sir Gawain and the Green Knight* by Simon Armitage, one of the foremost poets and translators of our time. Among the highlights of the revised and expanded medieval section of the ebook—too extensive to enumerate here—is a new, fully annotated edition of the great fifteenth-century morality play, *Mankind.*

The Sixteenth Century, edited by Stephen Greenblatt and George Logan, features two complete longer texts: Marlowe's *Doctor Faustus* and Shakespeare's *Othello,* the latter included for the first time in the Major Authors Edition. New to the ebook are the originals (in Italian and modern English translation) of key Petrarchan poems by Wyatt and Surrey, Skelton's brooding, paranoidal vision of life in the orbit of Henry VIII, "The Bowge of Court," and a greatly expanded cluster of texts of exploration and discovery in "The Wider World."

The Early Seventeenth Century. At the heart of this section, edited by Katharine Eisaman Maus and Barbara Lewalski, is the substantial selection from John Milton's *Paradise Lost.* Complete longer works include John Donne's soul-searching *Satire* 3; Aemilia Lanyer's country-house poem "The Description of Cookham"; and Milton's "Lycidas." Significant additions have been made to the works of Donne, Ben Jonson, George Herbert, and Robert Herrick. Headnotes, introductions, and bibliographies have all been revised. And among the highlights of the ebook are a selection from Donne's startling defense of suicide, the *Biathanatos*; Ben Jonson's *Masque of Blackness*; and the complete text of the first tragedy in English from the pen of a woman, Elizabeth Cary's *The Tragedy of Mariam.*

The Restoration and the Eighteenth Century. The impressive array of complete longer texts in this section, edited by James Noggle and Lawrence Lipking, includes Dryden's satires *Absalom and Achitophel* and *Mac Flecknoe*; Aphra Behn's novel *Oroonoko*; Pope's *Essay on Criticism, The Rape of the Lock,* and *Epistle to Dr. Arbuthnot*; Hogarth's graphic satire "Marriage A-la-Mode"; Johnson's *Vanity of Human Wishes*; and Gray's "Elegy Written in a Country Churchyard." There are new texts by Samuel Johnson, and Christopher Smart is represented for the first time. The Major Authors Edition continues to include such distinguished women writers as Aphra Behn,

Lady Mary Wortley Montagu (with a new selection of Turkish Embassy letters), and Frances Burney. Among the many features of the corresponding ebook section are extensive readings in eighteenth-century aesthetics (with texts on grace, on the general and the particular, and on genius); topical clusters on daily life in London, slavery and the slave trade, the plurality of worlds, and travel, trade, and the expansion of empire; and the complete text of William Wycherley's scandalous Restoration comedy *The Country Wife*.

The Romantic Period, edited by Deidre Shauna Lynch and Jack Stillinger, has been extensively revised; every text, headnote, and annotation has been reconsidered. The result is a dramatic reimagining of the entire period. There are new works in this edition for almost every author, including Felicia Hemans's ambitious and exciting dramatic monologue "Properzia Rossi." But the revision of this period in the anthology is not only a matter of strong additions. The facing-page comparison in the new section on "Versions of *The Prelude*" allows readers to see Wordsworth as a reviser and to gauge the significance of the changes he wrought. By replacing the 1850 *Prelude* with the 1805 *Prelude*, the Norton Anthology provides a text that shows Wordsworth immediately engaged with his Romantic contemporaries. This sense of engagement—as if windows in an ornate room had been thrown open to the world outside—extends to the new ebook topic, "Reviewer vs. Poet in the Romantic Period," conveys the rough-and-tumble of literary battles, while another new ebook topic, "Romantic Literature and Wartime," documents Romantic writers' pointed efforts to make literature do justice to the wider world.

The Victorian Age, edited by Catherine Robson and Carol Christ, opens with a revised introduction that features expanded discussions of fiction and the cultural role of poetry. Among the many complete longer works included here are major poems by Elizabeth Barrett Browning, Alfred, Lord Tennyson, Robert Browning, Christina Rossetti, and Gerard Manley Hopkins. The distinguished array of complete prose works, includes Oscar Wilde's *The Importance of Being Earnest*, Elizabeth Gaskell's *The Old Nurse's Story*, Robert Louis Stevenson's *The Strange Case of Dr. Jekyll and Mr. Hyde*, and Rudyard Kipling's *The Man Who Would Be King*. The extensive ebook section includes a new topic on Victorian education that brings together powerful reflections by Newman, Mill, and others with key passages from such works as *Hard Times*, *Alice's Adventures in Wonderland*, and *Jude the Obscure*.

The Twentieth Century and After. The editors, Jahan Ramazani and Jon Stallworthy, have undertaken a root-and-branch reconsideration, leading to a dramatic revision of the entire section. Its spine, as it were, consists of two modernist masterpieces: Virginia Woolf's *Mrs. Dalloway*, and Samuel Beckett's *Waiting for Godot*. These complete works are surrounded by a dazzling choice of other fiction and drama, including, among others, Joseph Conrad's *Heart of Darkness* and powerful stories by D. H. Lawrence, Katherine Mansfield, Jean Rhys, and Nadine Gordimer. A generous representation of poetry centers on a substantial selection of key works by Thomas Hardy, William Butler Yeats, and T. S. Eliot, and extends out to a wide array of other poets, from W. H. Auden and Dylan Thomas to Philip Larkin, Derek Walcott, and Seamus Heaney. Other new fiction includes works by Jean Rhys, Chinua

Achebe, Margaret Atwood, Ian McEwan, and Zadie Smith. There are also new images and new nonfiction selections, including a text by Salman Rushdie.

Editorial Procedures and Format

The Major Authors, Ninth Edition, adheres to the principles that have always characterized *The Norton Anthology of English Literature*. Period introductions, headnotes, and annotations are designed to enhance students' reading and, without imposing an interpretation, to give students the information they need to understand each text. The aim of these editorial materials is to make the anthology self-sufficient, so that it can be read anywhere—in a coffee shop, on a bus, under a tree.

The Norton Anthology of English Literature prides itself on both the scholarly accuracy and the readability of its texts. To ease students' encounter with some works, we have normalized spelling and capitalization in texts up to and including the Romantic period—for the most part they now follow the conventions of modern English. We leave unaltered, however, texts in which such modernizing would change semantic or metrical qualities. From the Victorian period onward, we have used the original spelling and punctuation. We continue other editorial procedures that have proved useful in the past. After each work, we cite the date of first publication on the right; in some instances, this date is followed by the date of a revised edition for which the author was responsible. Dates of composition, when they differ from those of publication and when they are known, are provided on the left. We have used square brackets to indicate titles supplied by the editors for the convenience of readers. Whenever a portion of a text has been omitted, we have indicated that omission with three asterisks. If the omitted portion is important for following the plot or argument, we have provided a brief summary within the text or in a footnote. Finally, we have reconsidered annotations throughout and increased the number of marginal glosses for archaic, dialect, or unfamiliar words.

Thanks to the thorough work of James Simpson, with help from Lara Bovilsky of the University of Oregon, The Major Authors, Ninth Edition, provides a more useful "Literary Terminology" appendix, recast as a quick-reference alphabetical glossary with examples from works in the anthology. We have also overhauled and updated the General Bibliography that appears in the print edition, as well as the period and author bibliographies, which now appear in the supplemental ebook, where they can be more easily searched and updated.

Additional Resources from the Publisher

For students using *The Norton Anthology of English Literature*, the publisher provides a wealth of resources on the free StudySpace website (wwnorton.com/nael). Students who activate the free password included in each new copy of the anthology gain access both to the supplemental ebook and to StudySpace, where they will find approximately fifty multiple-choice reading-comprehension quizzes on widely taught individual works with extensive feedback; summaries of the period introductions; period review quizzes with feedback; a new "Literary Places" feature that uses images, maps, and Google Tours tools to offer students a practical way to (virtually) visit the Lake District, Dover Beach, Canterbury, and other literary places; art galleries—one per period—including author portraits, interactive timelines, and over three hours of spoken-word and musical recordings. The rich gathering of content on StudySpace is designed to help students understand individual works and appreciate the places, sounds, and sights of literature.

The publisher also provides extensive instructor-support materials. Designed to enhance large or small lecture environments, the Instructor Resource Disc, expanded for the Ninth Edition, features more than 300 images with explanatory captions; PowerPoint slides for each period introduction and for most topic clusters; and audio recordings (MP3). Much praised by both new and experienced instructors, *Teaching with* The Norton Anthology of English Literature: *A Guide for Instructors* by Sondra Archimedes (University of California–Santa Cruz), Laura Runge (University of South Florida), Philip Schwyzer (University of Exeter), Leslie Ritchie (Queen's University), and Scott-Morgan Straker (Queen's University) provides extensive help, from planning a course and developing a syllabus and course objectives to preparing exams. Guide entries provide a "hook" to start class discussion; a Quick Read section to refresh instructors on essential information about a text or author; Teaching Suggestions that call out interesting textual or contextual features; Teaching Clusters of suggested groups or pairs of texts; and Discussion Questions. To help instructors integrate the anthology's rich supplemental ebook, the Guide features new entries for online texts and clusters. The Guide also offers revised material on using technology in the classroom, with suggestions for teaching the anthology's multimedia with the texts and for incorporating the media into traditional or distance-learning courses. For the first time, the Guide will also be made available in a searchable online format. Finally, Norton Coursepacks bring high-quality Norton digital media into a new or existing online course. The coursepacks include all content from the StudySpace website, short-answer questions with suggested answers, and a bank of discussion questions adapted from the Guide. Norton's Coursepacks are available in a variety of formats, including Blackboard/WebCT, Desire2Learn, Angel, and Moodle at no cost to instructors or students.

The editors are deeply grateful to the hundreds of teachers worldwide who have helped us to improve the Major Edition of *The Norton Anthology of English Literature*. A list of the instructors who replied to a detailed questionnaire follows, under Acknowledgments. The editors would like to express appreciation for their assistance to Elizabeth Anker (University of Virginia), Paul B. Armstrong (Brown University), Derek Attridge (University of York, UK), Homi Bhabha (Harvard University), Glenn Black (Oriel College, Oxford), Gordon Braden (University of Virginia), Mary Ellen Brown (Indiana University), Sandie Byrne (Oxford University), Sarita Cargas (University of New Mexico), Joseph W. Childers (University of California, Riverside), Jason Coats (University of Virginia), Kathleen Coleman (Harvard University), Daniel Cook (University of California, Davis), Guy Cuthbertson (University of St. Andrews), Pamela Dalziel (University of British Columbia, Vancouver), Linda David, Roy Davids (Oxford University), Jed Esty (University of Pennsylvania), Christopher Fanning (Queen's University), Laura Farwell Blake (Harvard University Library, who provided invaluable and expert help with the General Bibliography), Jamie H. Ferguson (University of Houston), Anne Fernald

(Fordham University), William Flesch (Brandeis University), Robert Folkenflik (University of California, Irvine), Ryan Fong (University of California, Davis), Robert D. Fulk (Indiana University), Hans Walter Gabler (University of Munich), Kevis Goodman (University of California, Berkeley), Susannah Gottlieb (Northwestern University), Omaar Hena (University of Virginia), Heather Jackson (University of Toronto), Anuj Kapoor (University of Virginia), Tom Keirstead (University of Toronto), Theresa Kelley (University of Wisconsin, Madison), Tim Kendall (University of Exeter), Shayna Kessel (University of Southern California), Scott Klein (Wake Forest University), Cara Lewis (University of Virginia), Joanna Lipking (Northwestern University), Ian Little (Liverpool University), Tricia Lootens (University of Georgia), Lynne Magnusson (University of Toronto), Laura Mandell (Texas A & M University), Steven Matthews (Oxford Brookes University), Peter McDonald (Oxford University), Tara McDonald (University of Toronto), Edward Mendelson (Columbia University), Erin Minear (Harvard University), Andrew Motion, Elaine Musgrave (University of California, Davis), J. Morgan Myers (University of Virginia), Kate Nash (University of Virginia), Bernard O'Donoghue (Oxford University), Paul O'Prey (Roehampton University), Daniel O'Quinn (University of Guelph), Ruth Perry (M.I.T.), Emily Peterson (Harvard University), Kate Pilson (Harvard University), Adela Pinch (University of Michigan), Jane Potter (Oxford Brookes University), Leah Price (Harvard University), Mark Rankin (James Madison University), Angelique Richardson (Exeter University), Ronald Schuchard (Emory University), Philip Schwyzer (Exeter University), John W. Sider (Westmont College), Claire Marie Stancek (University of California, Berkeley), Paul Stevens (University of Toronto), Ramie Targoff (Brandeis University), Elisa Tersigni (University of Toronto), and Daniel White (University of Toronto). We also thank the many people at Norton who contributed to the Ninth Edition: Julia Reidhead, who served not only as the inhouse supervisor but also as an unfailingly wise and effective collaborator in every aspect of planning and accomplishing this Ninth Edition; Marian Johnson, managing editor for college books; Carly Fraser, associate editor and Course Guide editor; Eileen Connell, electronic media editor; Rachel Mayer, Susan Joseph, Jennifer Harris, Pam Lawson, Jack Borrebach, and Katharine Ings, manuscript editors; Ben Reynolds, senior production manager; Sean Mintus, production manager; Nancy Rodwan, permissions; Jo Anne Metsch, designer; Mike Fodera, photo editor; and Hannah Blaisdell and Jennifer Barnhardt, editorial assistants. All these friends provided the editors with indispensable help in meeting the challenge of representing the unparalleled range and variety of English literature.

STEPHEN GREENBLATT

Acknowledgments

The editors would like to express appreciation and thanks to the hundreds of teachers who provided reviews:

John Achorn (New England College); Robert Aguirre (Wayne State University); Maureen Amos (Keiser University); Rhonda Armstrong (Paris Junior College); Edmondson O. Asgill (Bethune-Cookman University); Brenda Ayres (Liberty University); George H. Bailey (Northern Essex Community College); Eric Ball (Langara College); John Baxter (Dalhousie University); John Black (Moravian College); Deborah Blacklock (Langara College); Elizabeth Bobo (University of Louisiana at Lafayette); Alan Brown (University of West Alabama); Douglas Bruster (University of Texas at Austin); Karen Budra (Langara College); Sarah Burns (Virginia Western Community College); Eric R. Carlson (University of South Carolina, Aiken); Glynis Carr (Bucknell University); Elvira Casal (Middle Tennessee State University); Youngjeen Choe (Chung-Ang University); Lynn Childress (Clemson University); Tim Conley (Brock University); Carl Curtis (Liberty University); Phillip Dale Davis (Northwest Mississippi Community College); Wayne G. Deahl (Eastern Wyoming College); Mary J. Dengler (Dordt College); Michael John DiSanto (Algoma University); Elizabeth Evans (Penn State University-DuBois); Joshua Everett (Central Texas College); Paula R. Feldman (University of South Carolina); John Flood (University of Groningen); James Flynn (Western Kentucky University); Beverly Forsyth (Odessa College); Pamela J. Francis (Northwestern State University); Joel Fredell (Southeastern Louisiana University); Anne Frey (Texas Christian University); LaDonna Friesen (Central Bible College); David Galef (Montclair State University); David Gay (University of Alberta); Stephen Geller (Savannah College of Art and Design); Michael Gilmour (Providence College); Sunithi Gnanadoss (Germanna Community College); Eva Gold (English Southeastern Louisiana University); Richard J. Grande (Penn State University, Abington College); David A. Grant (Columbus State Community College); Elissa S. Guralnick (University of Colorado at Boulder); Corrinne Harol (University of Alberta); Licia Hendriks (The Citadel); Teshie Herbert (Keiser University); David Ingham (St. Thomas University); Randy R. James (Florida Memorial University); Suzanne James (University of British Columbia); Yvonne Jocks (Tarrant County College South East); John Kerrigan (Rockhurst University); Mark Knockemus (Northeastern Technical College); Seunghyeok Kweon (Seoul Women's University); Sean Lawrence (University of British Columbia, Okanagan); Anne Lockwood (Limestone College); Paul Lumsden (Grant MacEwan University); Kim Manganelli (Clemson University); Ami Massengill (Nashville

State Community College); Jeannine McDevitt (Pennsylvania Highlands Community College); Howard Gene Melton II (North Carolina State University); L. Adam Mekler (Morgan State University); Terry L. Meyers (College of William and Mary); Gregg Neikirk (Westfield State University); Meg Pearson (University of West Georgia); John Pekins (Tallahassee Community College); Jenny Perkins (Tallahassee Community College); Curtis Perry (University of Illinois); Kate Pilhuj (The Citadel); Kendrick Prewitt (University of West Alabama); Helaine Razovsky (Northwestern State University of Louisiana); Wayne A. Rebhorn (University of Texas); Joseph Register (Harrisburg Area Community College); Stephen R. Reimer (University of Alberta); Chris Roark (John Carroll University); Catherine Ross (University of Texas at Tyler); Marilyn Sandidge (Westfield State University); Lisa Schnell (University of Vermont); Dr. M.P.A. Sheaffer (Millersville University); Paul Sheneman (Warner University); Lisa Shoemaker (State Fair Community College); Mary Simpson (Central Texas College); Stephen Slimp (University of West Alabama); Isabel Stanley (East Tennessee State University); Claire Strasbaugh (Bethany University); Kathryn Strong (The Citadel); Kim Trainor (University of British Columbia); Martin Trapp (Northwestern Michigan College); Michael E. Travers (The College at Southeastern, Southeastern Baptist Theological Seminary); J.K. Van Dover (Lincoln University); Lisa Vargo (University of Saskatchewan); Jennifer Vaught (University of Louisiana at Lafayette); Deborah Vause (York College of Pennsylvania); Preston L. Waller (McLennan Community College); Ellen Weir (Belmont Abbey College); Steve Werkmeister (Johnson County Community College); Mary Kathleen Whitaker (East Georgia College); Gwen Whitehead (Lamar State College-Orange); Lance Wilder (University of Georgia); Ed Wiltse (Nazareth College); Rita Wisdom (Tarrant County College-Northeast); Stefanie Wortman (University of Missouri); James F. Wurtz (Indiana State University)

Congratulations to Shelton J. Handy (University of Maryland Eastern Shore), Elizabeth Scoville (Bradley University), and Jakia Propst (St. Stephens High School), winners of the 2012 Norton Anthology Student Recitation Contest.

THE NORTON ANTHOLOGY OF

ENGLISH

LITERATURE

THE MAJOR AUTHORS
NINTH EDITION

The Middle Ages
to ca. 1485

43–ca. 420:	Roman invasion and occupation of Britain
ca. 450:	Anglo-Saxon Conquest
597:	St. Augustine arrives in Kent; beginning of Anglo-Saxon conversion to Christianity
871–899:	Reign of King Alfred
1066:	Norman Conquest
1154–1189:	Reign of Henry II
ca. 1200:	Beginnings of Middle English literature
1360–1400:	Geoffrey Chaucer; *Piers Plowman*; *Sir Gawain and the Green Knight*
1485:	William Caxton's printing of Sir Thomas Malory's *Morte Darthur*, one of the first books printed in England

The Middle Ages designates the time span roughly from the collapse of the Roman Empire to the Renaissance and Reformation. The adjective "medieval," coined from Latin *medium* (middle) and *aevum* (age), refers to whatever was made, written, or thought during the Middle Ages. The Renaissance was so named by nineteenth-century historians and critics because they associated it with an outburst of creativity attributed to a "rebirth" or revival of Latin and, especially, of Greek learning and literature. The word "Reformation" designates the powerful religious movement that began in the early sixteenth century and repudiated the supreme authority of the Roman Catholic Church. The Renaissance was seen as spreading from Italy in the fourteenth and fifteenth centuries to the rest of Europe, whereas the Reformation began in Germany and quickly affected all of Europe to a greater or lesser degree. The very idea of a Renaissance or rebirth, however, implies something dormant or lacking in the preceding era. More recently, there have been two nonexclusive tendencies in our understanding of the medieval period and what follows. Some scholars emphasize the continuities between the Middle Ages and the later time now often called

Pilgrims leaving Canterbury, ca. 1420. For more information about this image, see the color insert in this volume.

the Early Modern Period. Others emphasize the ways in which sixteenth-century writers in some sense "created" the Middle Ages, in order to highlight what they saw as the brilliance of their own time. Medieval authors, of course, did not think of themselves as living in the "middle"; they sometimes expressed the idea that the world was growing old and that theirs was a declining age, close to the end of time. Yet art, literature, and science flourished during the Middle Ages, rooted in the Christian culture that preserved, transmitted, and transformed classical tradition.

The works covered in this section of the anthology encompass a period of more than eight hundred years, from Cædmon's *Hymn* at the end of the seventh century to Morte Darthur in the fifteenth. The date 1485, the year of the accession of Henry VII and the beginning of the Tudor dynasty, is an arbitrary but convenient one to mark the "end" of the Middle Ages in England.

Although the Roman Catholic Church provided continuity, the period was one of enormous historical, social, and linguistic change. To emphasize these changes and the events underlying them, we have divided the period into three primary sections: Anglo-Saxon Literature, Anglo-Norman Literature, and Middle English Literature in the Fourteenth and Fifteenth Centuries. The Anglo-Saxon invaders, who began their conquest of the southeastern part of Britain around 450, spoke an early form of the language we now call Old English. Old English displays its kinship with other Germanic languages (German or Dutch, for example) much more clearly than does contemporary British and American English, of which Old English is the ancestor. As late as the tenth century, part of an Old Saxon poem written on the Continent was transcribed and transliterated into the West Saxon dialect of Old English without presenting problems to its English readers. In form and content Old English literature also has much in common with other Germanic literatures with which it shared a body of heroic as well as Christian stories. The major characters in *Beowulf* are pagan Danes and Geats, and the only connection to England is an obscure allusion to the ancestor of one of the kings of the Angles.

The changes already in progress in the language and culture of Anglo-Saxon England were greatly accelerated by the Norman Conquest of 1066. The ascendancy of a French-speaking ruling class had the effect of adding a vast number of French loan words to the English vocabulary. The conquest resulted in new forms of political organization and administration, architecture, and literary expression. In the twelfth century, through the interest of the Anglo-Normans in British history before the Anglo-Saxon Conquest, not only England but all of Western Europe became fascinated with a legendary hero named Arthur who makes his earliest appearances in Celtic literature. King Arthur and his knights became a staple subject of medieval French, English, and German literature. Selections from Latin, French, and Old Irish, as well as from Early Middle English have been included here to give a sense of the cross-currents of languages and literatures in Anglo-Norman England and to provide background for later English literature in all periods.

Literature in English was performed orally and written throughout the Middle Ages, but the awareness of and pride in a uniquely *English* literature did not actually exist before the late fourteenth century. In 1336 Edward III began a war to enforce his claims to the throne of France; the war continued intermittently for more than one hundred years until finally the English were driven from all their French territories, except for the port of Calais, in 1453. One result of the war and these losses was a keener sense on the part of England's nobility of their English heritage and identity. Toward the close of the fourteenth century English finally began to displace French as the language for conducting business in Parliament and much official correspondence. Although the high nobility continued to speak French by preference, they were certainly bilingual, whereas some of the earlier Norman kings had known no English at all. It was becoming possible to obtain patronage for literary achievement in English. The decision of Chaucer (d. 1400) to emulate French and Italian poetry in his own vernacular is an indication of the change taking place in the status of English, and Chaucer's works were greatly to enhance the prestige of English as a vehicle for literature of high ambition. He was acclaimed by fifteenth-century poets as the embellisher of the English tongue; later writers called him the English Homer and the father of English poetry. His friend John Gower (ca. 1330–1408) wrote long poems in French and Latin before producing his last major work, the *Confessio Amantis* (The Lover's Confession), which in spite of its Latin title is composed in English.

The third and longest of the three primary sections, Middle English Literature in the Fourteenth and Fifteenth Centuries, is thus not only a chronological and linguistic division but implies a new sense of English as a literary medium that could compete with French and Latin in elegance and seriousness.

Book production throughout the medieval period was an expensive process. Until the invention of moveable type in the mid-fifteenth century (introduced into England by Caxton in 1476), medieval books were reproduced by hand in manuscript (literally "written by hand"). While paper became increasingly common for less expensive manuscripts in the fifteenth century, manuscripts were until then written on carefully prepared animal (usually calf or sheep) skin, known as parchment or vellum. More expensive books could be illuminated both by colored and calligraphic lettering, and by visual images.

The institutions of book production developed across the period. In the Anglo-Saxon period monasteries were the main centers of book production and storage. Until their dissolution in the 1530s, monastic and other religious houses continued to produce books, but from the early fourteenth century, particularly in London, commercial book-making enterprises came into being. These were loose organizations of various artisans such as parchmentmakers, scribes, flourishers, illuminators, and binders, who usually lived in the same neighborhoods in towns. A bookseller or dealer (usually a member of one of these trades) would coordinate the production of books to order for wealthy patrons, sometimes distributing the work of copying to different scribes, who would be responsible for different gatherings, or quires, of the same book. Such shops could call upon the services of professional scribes working in the bureaucracies of the royal court.

The market for books also changed across the period: while monasteries, other religious houses, and royal courts continued to fund the production of books, from the Anglo-Norman period books were also produced for (and sometimes by) noble and gentry households. From the fourteenth century the market was widened yet further, with wealthy urban patrons also ordering books. Some of these books were dedicated to single works, some largely to single genres; most were much more miscellaneous, containing texts of many kinds and (particularly in the Anglo-Norman period) written in different languages (especially Latin, French, and English). Only a small proportion of medieval books survive; large numbers were destroyed at the time of the dissolution of the monasteries in the 1530s.

Texts in Old English, Early Middle English, the more difficult texts in later Middle English (*Sir Gawain and the Green Knight*), and those in other languages are given in translation. Chaucer and other Middle English works may be read in the original, even by the beginner, with the help of marginal glosses and notes. These texts have been spelled in a way that is intended to aid the reader. Analyses of the sounds and grammar of Middle English and of Old and Middle English prosody are presented on pages 19–25.

ANGLO-SAXON LITERATURE

From the first to the fifth century, England was a province of the Roman Empire and was named Britannia after its Celtic-speaking inhabitants, the Britons. The Britons adapted themselves to Roman civilization, of which the ruins survived to impress the poet of *The Wanderer*, who refers to them as "the ancient works of giants." The withdrawal of the Roman legions during the fifth century, in a vain attempt to protect Rome itself from the threat of Germanic conquest, left the island vulnerable to seafaring Germanic invaders. These belonged primarily to three related tribes, the Angles, the Saxons, and the Jutes. The name *English* derives from the Angles, and the names of the counties Essex, Sussex, and Wessex refer to the territories occupied by the East, South, and West Saxons.

The Anglo-Saxon occupation was no sudden conquest but extended over decades of fighting against the native Britons. The latter were, finally, largely confined to the mountainous region of Wales, where the modern form of their language is spoken alongside English to this day. The Britons had become Christians in the fourth century after the conversion of Emperor Constantine along with most of the rest of the Roman Empire, but for about 150 years after the beginning of the invasion, Christianity was maintained only in the remoter regions where the as yet pagan Anglo-Saxons failed to penetrate. In the year 597, however, a Benedictine monk (afterward St. Augustine of Canterbury) was sent by Pope Gregory as a missionary to King Ethelbert of Kent, the most southerly of the kingdoms into which England was then divided, and about the same time missionaries from Ireland began to preach Christianity in the north. Within 75 years the island was once more predominantly Christian. Before Christianity there had been no books. The impact of Christianity on literacy is evident from the fact that the first extended written specimen of the Old English (Anglo-Saxon) language is a code of laws promulgated by Ethelbert, the first English Christian king.

In the centuries that followed the conversion, England produced many distinguished churchmen. One of the earliest of these was Bede, whose Latin *Ecclesiastical History of the English People*, which tells the story of the conversion and of the English church, was completed in 731; this remains one of our most important sources of knowledge about the period. In the next generation Alcuin (735–804), a man of wide culture, became the friend and adviser of the Frankish emperor Charlemagne, whom he assisted in making the Frankish court a great center of learning; thus by the year 800 English culture had developed so richly that it overflowed its insular boundaries.

In the ninth century the Christian Anglo-Saxons were themselves subjected to new Germanic invasions by the Danes who in their longboats repeatedly ravaged the coast, sacking Bede's monastery among others. Such a raid late in the tenth century inspired *The Battle of Maldon*, the last of the Old English heroic poems. The Danes also occupied the northern part of the island, threatening to overrun the rest. They were stopped by Alfred, king of the West Saxons from 871 to 899, who for a time united all the kingdoms of southern England. This most active

Lindisfarne Gospels. Opening of Gospel of St. Matthew, ca. 698. The veil of mysteries is drawn aside, and the author of the gospel text copies his book as if by divine dictation.

king was also an enthusiastic patron of literature. He himself translated various works from Latin, the most important of which was Boethius's *Consolation of Philosophy*, a sixth-century Roman work also translated in the fourteenth century by Chaucer. Alfred probably also instigated a translation of Bede's *History* and the beginning of the *Anglo-Saxon Chronicle*: this year-by-year record in Old English of important events in England was maintained at one monastery until the middle of the twelfth century. Practically all of Old English poetry is preserved in copies made in the West Saxon dialect after the reign of Alfred.

Old English Poetry

The Anglo-Saxon invaders brought with them a tradition of oral poetry (see "Bede and Cædmon's *Hymn*," p. 29). Because nothing was written down before the conversion to Christianity, we have only circumstantial evidence of what that poetry must have been like. Aside from a few short inscriptions on small artifacts, the earliest records in the English language are in manuscripts produced at monasteries and other religious establishments, beginning in the seventh century. Literacy was mainly restricted to servants of the church, and so it is natural that the bulk of Old English literature deals with religious subjects and is mostly drawn from Latin sources. Under the expensive conditions of manuscript production, few texts were written down that did not pertain directly to the work of the church. Most of Old English poetry is contained in just four manuscripts.

Germanic heroic poetry continued to be performed orally in alliterative verse and was at times used to describe current events. *The Battle of Brunanburh*, which celebrates an English victory over the Danes in traditional alliterative verse, is preserved in the *Anglo-Saxon Chronicle*. *The Battle of Maldon* (in the supplemental ebook) commemorates a Viking victory in which the Christian English invoke the ancient code of honor that obliges a warrior to avenge his slain lord or to die beside him.

These poems show that the aristocratic heroic and kinship values of Germanic society continued to inspire both clergy and laity in the Christian era. As represented in the relatively small body of Anglo-Saxon heroic poetry that survives, this world shares many characteristics with the heroic world described by Homer. Nations are reckoned as groups of people related by kinship rather than by geographical areas, and kinship is the basis of the heroic code. The tribe is ruled by a chieftain who is called *king*, a word that has "kin" for its root. The *lord* (a word derived from Old English *hlaf*, "loaf," plus *weard*, "protector") surrounds himself with a band of retainers (many of them his blood kindred) who are members of his household. He leads his men in battle and rewards them with the spoils; royal generosity was one of the most important aspects of heroic behavior. In return, the retainers are obligated to fight for their lord to the death, and if he is slain, to avenge him or die in the attempt. Blood vengeance is regarded as a sacred duty, and in poetry, everlasting shame awaits those who fail to observe it.

Even though the heroic world of poetry could be invoked to rally resistance to the Viking invasions, it was already remote from the Christian world of Anglo-Saxon England. Nevertheless, Christian writers like the *Beowulf* poet were fascinated by the distant culture of their pagan ancestors and by the inherent conflict between the heroic code and a religion that teaches that we should "forgive those who trespass against us" and that "all they that take the sword shall perish with the sword." The *Beowulf* poet looks back on that ancient world with admiration for the courage of which it was capable and at the same time with elegiac sympathy for its inevitable doom.

For Anglo-Saxon poetry, it is difficult and probably futile to draw a line between "heroic" and "Christian," for the best poetry crosses that boundary. Much of the Christian poetry is also cast in the heroic mode: although the Anglo-Saxons adapted themselves readily to the ideals of Christianity, they did not do so without adapting Christianity to their own heroic ideal. Thus Moses and St. Andrew, Christ and God the Father are represented in the style of heroic verse. In *The Dream of the Rood*, the Cross speaks of Christ as "this young man, . . . strong and courageous." In Cædmon's *Hymn* the creation of heaven and earth is seen as a mighty deed, an "establishment of wonders." Anglo-Saxon heroines, too, are portrayed in the heroic manner. St. Helena, who leads an expedition to the Holy Land to discover the true Cross, is described as a "battle-queen." The biblical narrative related in the Anglo-Saxon poem *Judith* is recast in the terms of Germanic heroic poetry. Christian and heroic ideals are poignantly blended in *The Wanderer*, which laments the separation from one's lord and kinsmen and the transience of all earthly treasures. Love between man and woman, as described by the female speaker of *The Wife's Lament*, is disrupted by separation, exile, and the malice of kinfolk.

The world of Old English poetry is often elegiac. Men are said to be cheerful in the mead hall, but even there they think of war, of possible triumph but more possible failure. Romantic love—one of the principal topics of later literature—appears hardly at all. Even so, at some of the bleakest moments, the poets powerfully recall the return of spring. The blade of the magic sword with which Beowulf has killed Grendel's mother in her sinister underwater lair begins to melt, "as ice melts / when the Father eases the fetters off the frost / and unravels the water ropes, He who wields power."

The poetic diction, formulaic phrases, and repetitions of parallel syntactic structures, which are determined by the versification, are difficult to reproduce in modern translation. A few features may be anticipated here and studied in the text of Cædmon's *Hymn*, printed below (pp. 29–32) with interlinear translation.

Poetic language is created out of a special vocabulary that contains a multiplicity of terms for *lord, warrior, spear, shield*, and so on. Synecdoche and metonymy are common figures of speech, as when "keel" is used for *ship* or "iron" for *sword*. A particularly striking effect is achieved by the kenning, a compound of two words in place of another as when *sea* becomes "whale-road" or *body* is called "life-house." The figurative use of language finds playful expression in poetic riddles, of which about one hundred survive. Common (and sometimes uncommon) creatures, objects, or phenomena are described in an enigmatic passage of alliterative verse, and the reader must guess their identity. Sometimes they are personified and ask, "What is my name?"

Because special vocabulary and compounds are among the chief poetic effects, the verse is constructed in such a way as to show off such terms by creating a series of them in apposition. In the second sentence of Cædmon's *Hymn*, for example, God is referred to five times appositively as "he," "holy Creator," "mankind's Guardian," "eternal Lord," and "Master Almighty." This use of parallel and appositive expressions, known as *variation*, gives the verse a highly structured and musical quality.

The overall effect of the language is to formalize and elevate speech. Instead of being straightforward, it moves at a slow and stately pace with steady indirection. A favorite mode of this indirection is irony. A grim irony pervades heroic poetry even at the level of diction where *fighting* is called "battle-play." A favorite device, known by the rhetorical term *litotes*, is ironic understatement. After the monster Grendel has slaughtered the Danes in the great hall Heorot, it stands deserted. The poet observes, "It was easy then to meet with a man / shifting himself to a safer distance."

More than a figure of thought, irony is also a mode of perception in Old English poetry. In a famous passage, the Wanderer articulates the theme of *Ubi sunt?* (where are they now?): "Where did the steed go? Where the young warrior? Where the treasure-giver? . . ." *Beowulf* is full of ironic balances and contrasts—between the aged Danish king and the youthful Beowulf, and between Beowulf, the high-spirited young warrior at the beginning, and Beowulf, the gray-haired king at the end, facing the dragon and death.

The formal and dignified speech of Old English poetry was always distant from the everyday language of the Anglo-Saxons, and this poetic idiom remained remarkably uniform throughout the roughly three hundred years that separate Cædmon's *Hymn* from *The Battle of Maldon*. This clinging to old forms—grammatical and orthographic as well as literary—by the Anglo-Saxon church and aristocracy conceals from us the enormous changes that were taking place in the English language and the diversity of its dialects. The dramatic changes between Old and Middle English did not happen overnight or over the course of a single century. The Normans displaced the English ruling class with their own barons and clerics, whose native language was a dialect of Old French that we call Anglo-Norman. Without a ruling literate class to preserve English traditions, the custom of transcribing vernacular texts in an earlier form of the West-Saxon dialect was abandoned, and both language and literature were allowed to develop unchecked in new directions.

For examples of Irish medieval literature, see the excerpt from the Old Irish epic *Táin Bó Cuailnge* (The Cattle Raid of Cooley) and some delightful monastic lyrics.

ANGLO-NORMAN LITERATURE

The Normans, who took possession of England after the decisive Battle of Hastings (1066), were, like the Anglo-Saxons, descendants of Germanic adventurers, who at the beginning of the tenth century had seized a wide part of northern France. Their name is actually a contraction of "Norsemen." A highly adaptable people, they had adopted the French language of the land they had settled in and its Christian religion. Both in Normandy and in Britain they were great builders of castles, with which they enforced their political dominance, and magnificent churches. Norman bishops, who held land and castles like the barons, wielded both political and spiritual authority. The earlier Norman kings of England, however, were often absentee rulers, as much concerned with defending their Continental possessions as with ruling over their English holdings. The English Crown's French territories were enormously increased in 1154 when Henry II, the first of England's Plantagenet kings, ascended the throne. Through his marriage with Eleanor of Aquitaine, the divorced wife of Louis VII of France, Henry had acquired vast provinces in the southwest of France.

The presence of a French-speaking ruling class in England created exceptional opportunities for linguistic and cultural exchange. Four languages coexisted in the realm of Anglo-Norman England: Latin, as it had been for Bede, remained the international language of learning, used for theology, science, and history. It was not by any means a written language only but also a lingua franca by which different nationalities communicated in the church and the newly founded universities. The Norman aristocracy for the most part spoke French, but intermarriage with the native English nobility and the business of daily life between masters and servants encouraged bilingualism. Different branches of the Celtic language group were spoken in Scotland, Ireland, Wales, Cornwall, and Brittany.

Inevitably, there was also literary intercourse among the different languages. The Latin Bible and Latin saints' lives provided subjects for a great deal of Old English as well as Old French poetry and prose. The first medieval drama in the vernacular, *The Play of Adam*, with elaborate stage directions in Latin and realistic dialogue in the Anglo-Norman dialect of French, was probably produced in England during the twelfth century.

The Anglo-Norman aristocracy was especially attracted to Celtic legends and tales that had been circulating orally for centuries. The twelfth-century poets Thomas of England, Marie de France, and Chrétien de Troyes each claim to have obtained their narratives from Breton storytellers, who were probably bilingual performers of native tales for French audiences. *Sir Orfeo* may represent the kind of lay that served as a model for Marie. "Breton" may indicate that they came from Brittany, or it may have been a generic term for a Celtic bard. Marie speaks respectfully of

King Harold Fatally Struck in the Eye. Bayeux Tapestry, textile,
ca. 1070–80. The decisive historical moment is captured as Harold
falls victim to irrepressible horizontal attack. Note the dead being
stripped of their armor, in the margins.

the storytellers, while Thomas expresses caution about their tendency to
vary narratives; Chrétien accuses them of marring their material, which, he
boasts, he has retold with an elegant fusion of form and meaning. Marie
wrote a series of short romances, which she refers to as "lays" originally told
by Bretons. Her versions are the most original and sophisticated examples of
the genre that came to be known as the Breton lay, represented here by
Marie's *Lanval*. It is very likely that Henry II is the "noble king" to whom she
dedicated her lays and that they were written for his court. Thomas composed a moving, almost operatic version of the adulterous passion of Tristran and Ysolt, very different from the powerful version of the same story by
Beroul, also composed in the last half of the twelfth century. Chrétien is the
principal creator of the romance of chivalry in which knightly adventures
are a means of exploring psychological and ethical dilemmas that the
knights must solve, in addition to displaying martial prowess in saving ladies
from monsters, giants, and wicked knights. Chrétien, like Marie, is thought
to have spent time in England at the court of Henry II.

Thomas, Marie, and Chrétien de Troyes were innovators of the genre that
has become known as "romance." The word *roman* was initially applied in
French to a work written in the French vernacular. Thus the thirteenth-
century *Roman de Troie* is a long poem about the Trojan War in French.
While this work deals mainly with the siege of Troy, it also includes stories
about the love of Troilus for Cressida and of Achilles for the Trojan princess
Polyxena. Eventually, "romance" acquired the generic associations it has for
us as a story about love and adventure.

Romance was the principal narrative genre for late medieval readers. Insofar as it was centrally concerned with love, it developed ways of representing
psychological interiority with great subtlety. That subtlety itself provoked a
sub-genre of questions about love. Thus in the late twelfth century, Andreas
Capellanus (Andrew the Chaplain) wrote a Latin treatise, the title of which
may be translated *The Art of Loving Correctly* [*honeste*]. In one part, Eleanor of Aquitaine, her daughter, the countess Marie de Champagne, and other

noble women are cited as a supreme court rendering decisions on difficult questions of love—for example, whether there is greater passion between lovers or between married couples. Whether such "courts of love" were purely imaginary or whether they represent some actual court entertainment, they imply that the literary taste and judgment of women had a significant role in fostering the rise of romance in France and Anglo-Norman England.

In Marie's *Lanval* and in Chrétien's romances, the court of King Arthur had already acquired for French audiences a reputation as the most famous center of chivalry. That eminence is owing in large measure to a remarkable book in Latin, *The History of the Kings of Britain*, completed by Geoffrey of Monmouth, ca. 1136–38. Geoffrey claimed to have based his "history" on a book in the British tongue (i.e., Welsh), but no one has ever found such a book. He drew on a few earlier Latin chronicles, but the bulk of his history was probably fabricated from Celtic oral tradition, his familiarity with Roman history and literature, and his own fertile imagination. The climax of the book is the reign of King Arthur, who defeats the Roman armies but is forced to turn back to Britain to counter the treachery of his nephew Mordred. In 1155 Geoffrey's Latin was rendered into French rhyme by an Anglo-Norman poet called Wace, and fifty or so years later Wace's poem was turned by Layamon, an English priest, into a much longer poem that combines English alliterative verse with sporadic rhyme.

Layamon's work is one of many instances where English receives new material directly through French sources, which may be drawn from Celtic or Latin sources. There are two Middle English versions of Marie's *Lanval*, and the English romance called *Yvain and Gawain* is a cruder version of Chrétien's *Le Chevalier au Lion* (The Knight of the Lion). A marvelous English lay, *Sir Orfeo*, is a version of the Orpheus story in which Orpheus succeeds in rescuing his wife from the other world, for which a French original, if there was one, has never been found. Romance, stripped of its courtly, psychological, and ethical subtleties, had an immense popular appeal for English readers and listeners. Many of these romances are simplified adaptations of more aristocratic French poems and recount in a rollicking and rambling style the adventures of heroes like Guy of Warwick, a poor steward who must prove his knightly worth to win the love of Fair Phyllis. The ethos of many romances, aristocratic and popular alike, involves a knight proving his worthiness through nobility of character and brave deeds rather than through high birth. In this respect romances reflect the aspirations of a lower order of the nobility to rise in the world, as historically some of these nobles did. William the Marshall, for example, the fourth son of a baron of middle rank, used his talents in war and in tournaments to become tutor to the oldest son of Henry II and Eleanor of Aquitaine. He married a great heiress and became one of the most powerful nobles in England and the subject of a verse biography in French, which often reads like a romance.

Of course, not all writing in Early Middle English depends on French sources or intermediaries. The *Anglo-Saxon Chronicle* continued to be written at the monastery of Peterborough. It is an invaluable witness for the changes taking place in the English language and allows us to see Norman rule from an English point of view. *The Owl and the Nightingale* (?late twelfth century) is a witty and entertaining poem in which these two female birds engage in a fierce debate about the benefits their singing brings to humankind. The owl grimly reminds her rival of the sinfulness of the human condition, which her mournful song is intended to amend; the nightingale sings about the pleasures of life and love when lord and lady are in bed together. The poet, who was certainly a cleric, is well aware of the fashionable new romance literature; he specifically has the nightingale allude to Marie de France's lay *Laüstic*, the Breton word, she says, for "rossignol" in French and "nightingale" in English. The poet does not side with either bird; rather he has amusingly created the sort of dialectic between the discourses of religion and romance that is carried on throughout medieval literature.

There is also a body of Early Middle English religious prose aimed at women. Three saints' lives celebrate the heroic combats of virgin martyrs who suffer dismemberment and death; a tract entitled *Holy Maidenhead* paints the woes of marriage not from the point of view of the husband, as in standard medieval antifeminist writings, but from that of the wife. Related to these texts, named the Katherine Group after one of the virgin martyrs, is a religious work also written for women but in a very different spirit. The *Ancrene Wisse* (Anchoresses' Guide) is one of the finest works of English religious prose in any period. It is a manual of instruction written at the request of three sisters who have chosen to live as religious recluses. The author, who may have been their personal confessor, addresses them with affection, and, at times, with kindness and humor. He is also profoundly serious in his analyses of sin, penance, and love.

MIDDLE ENGLISH LITERATURE IN THE FOURTEENTH AND FIFTEENTH CENTURIES

The styles of *The Owl and the Nightingale* and *Ancrene Wisse* show that around the year 1200 both poetry and prose were being written for sophisticated and well-educated readers whose primary language was English. Throughout the thirteenth and early fourteenth centuries, there are many

The City. Ambrogio Lorenzetti, *Effects of Good Government in the City*, 1338–39. The extraordinary energies of urban culture are set in a dynamic relation of peace and competition: the external walls of the city protect against outside invasion, even as the skyscrapers compete for space and power within the city.

kinds of evidence that, although French continued to be the principal language of Parliament, law, business, and high culture, English was gaining ground. Several authors of religious and didactic works in English state that they are writing for the benefit of those who do not understand Latin or French. Anthologies were made of miscellaneous works adapted from French for English readers and original pieces in English. Most of the nobility were by now bilingual, and the author of an English romance written early in the fourteenth century declares that he has seen many nobles who cannot speak French. Children of the nobility and the merchant class were now learning French as a second language. By the 1360s the linguistic, political, and cultural climate had been prepared for the flowering of Middle English literature in the writings of Chaucer, Gower, Langland, and the *Gawain* poet.

The Fourteenth Century

War and disease were prevalent throughout the Middle Ages but never more devastatingly than during the fourteenth century. In the wars against France, the gains of two spectacular English victories, at Crécy in 1346 and Poitiers in 1356, were gradually frittered away in futile campaigns that ravaged the French countryside without obtaining any clear advantage for the English. In 1348 the first and most virulent epidemic of the bubonic plague—the Black Death—swept Europe, wiping out a quarter to a third of the population. The toll was higher in crowded urban centers. Giovanni Boccaccio's description of the plague in Florence, with which he introduces the *Decameron*, vividly portrays its ravages: "So many corpses would arrive in front of a church every day and at every hour that the amount of holy ground for burials was certainly insufficient for the ancient custom of giving each body its individual place; when all the graves were full, huge trenches were dug in all of the cemeteries of the churches and into them the new arrivals were dumped by the hundreds; and they were packed in there with dirt, one on top of another, like a ship's cargo, until the trench was filled." The resulting scarcity of labor and a sudden expansion of the possibilities for social mobility fostered popular discontent. In 1381 attempts to enforce wage controls and to collect oppressive new taxes provoked a rural uprising in Essex and Kent that dealt a profound shock to the English ruling class. The participants were for the most part tenant farmers, day laborers, apprentices, and rural workers not attached to the big manors. A few of the lower clergy sided with the rebels against their wealthy church superiors; the priest John Ball was among the leaders. The movement was quickly suppressed, but not before sympathizers in London had admitted the rebels through two city gates, which had been barred against them. The insurgents burned down the palace of the hated duke of Lancaster, and they summarily beheaded the archbishop of Canterbury and the treasurer of England, who had taken refuge in the Tower of London. The church had become the target of popular resentment because it was among the greatest of the oppressive landowners and because of the wealth, worldliness, and venality of many of the higher clergy.

These calamities and upheavals nevertheless did not stem the growth of international trade and the influence of the merchant class. In the portrait of Geoffrey Chaucer's merchant, we see the budding of capitalism based on credit and interest. Cities like London ran their own affairs under politically powerful mayors and aldermen. Edward III, chronically in need of money to finance his wars, was obliged to negotiate for revenues with the Commons in the English Parliament, an institution that became a major political force during this period. A large part of the king's revenues depended on taxing the profitable export of English wool to the Continent. The Crown thus became involved in the country's economic affairs, and this involvement led to a need for capable administrators. These were no longer drawn mainly from the church, as in the past, but from a newly educated laity that occupied a rank somewhere between that of the lesser nobility and the upper bourgeoisie. The career of Chaucer, who served Edward III and his successor Richard II in a number of civil posts, is typical of this class—with the exception that Chaucer was also a great poet.

In the fourteenth century, a few poets and intellectuals achieved the status and respect formerly accorded only to the ancients. Marie de France and Chrétien de Troyes had dedicated their works to noble patrons and, in their role as narrators, address themselves as entertainers and sometimes as instructors to court audiences. Dante (1265–1321) made himself the protagonist of *The Divine Comedy*, the sacred poem, as he called it, in which he revealed the secrets of the afterlife. After his death, manuscripts of the work were provided with lengthy commentaries as though it were Scripture, and public readings and lectures were devoted to it. Francis Petrarch (1304–1374) won an international reputation as a man of letters. He wrote primarily in Latin and contrived to have himself crowned "poet laureate" in emulation of the Roman poets whose works he imitated, but his most famous work is the sonnet sequence he wrote in Italian. Giovanni Boccaccio (1313–1375) was among Petrarch's most ardent admirers and carried on a literary correspondence with him.

Chaucer read these authors along with the ancient Roman poets and drew on them in his own works. Chaucer's *Clerk's Tale* is based on a Latin version Petrarch made from the last tale in Boccaccio's *Decameron*; in his prologue, the Clerk refers to Petrarch as "lauriat poete" whose sweet rhetoric illuminated all Italy with his poetry. Yet in his own time, the English poet Chaucer never attained the kind of laurels that he and others accorded to Petrarch. In his earlier works, Chaucer portrayed himself comically as a diligent reader of old books, as an aspiring apprentice writer, and as an eager spectator on the fringe of a fashionable world of courtiers and poets. In *The House of Fame*, he relates a dream of being snatched up by a huge golden eagle (the eagle and many other things in this work were inspired by Dante), who transports him to the palace of the goddess Fame. There he gets to see phantoms, like the shades in Dante's poem, of all the famous authors of antiquity. At the end of his romance *Troilus and Criseyde*, Chaucer asks his "litel book" to kiss the footsteps where the great ancient poets had passed before. Like Dante and Petrarch, Chaucer had an ideal of great poetry and, in his *Troilus* at least, strove to emulate it. But in *The House of Fame* and in his final work, *The Canterbury Tales*, he also views that ideal ironically and distances himself from it. The many surviving documents that record Geoffrey Chaucer's career as a civil servant do not contain a single word to show that he was also a poet. Only in the following centuries would he be canonized as the father of English poetry.

Chaucer is unlikely to have known his contemporary William Langland, who says in an autobiographical passage, added to the third and last version of his great poem *Piers Plowman*, that he lived in London on Cornhill (a poor area of the city) among "lollers." "Loller" was a slang term for the unemployed and transients; it was later applied to followers of the religious and social reformer John Wycliffe, some of whom were burned at the stake for heresy in the next century. Langland assailed corruption in church and state, but he was certainly no radical. It is thought that he may have written the third version of *Piers Plowman*, which tones down his attacks on the church, after the rebels of 1381 invoked Piers as one of their own. Although Langland does not condone rebellion and his religion is not revolutionary, he nevertheless presents the most clear-sighted vision of social and religious issues in the England of his day. *Piers Plowman* is also a painfully honest search for the right way that leads to salvation. Though learned himself, Langland and the dreamer who represents him in the poem arrive at the insight that learning can be one of the chief obstacles on that way.

Langland came from the west of England, and his poem belongs to the "Alliterative Revival," a final flowering in the late fourteenth century of the verse form that goes all the way back to Anglo-Saxon England. Anglo-Saxon traditions held out longest in the west and north, away from London, where Chaucer and his audience were more open to literary fashions from the Continent.

John Gower is a third major late fourteenth-century English poet. While his first and second large works are written in French and Latin verse respectively, his *Confessio Amantis* (1390) is written in English four-stress couplets. Gower's first two works are severe satires; the *Confessio*, by contrast, broaches political and ethical issues from an oblique angle. Its primary narrative concerns the treatment of a suffering lover. His therapy consists of listening to, and understanding, many other narratives, many of which are drawn from classical sources. Like Chaucer, Gower anglicizes and absorbs classical Latin literature.

Admiration for the poetry of both Chaucer and Gower and the controversial nature of Langland's writing assured the survival of their work in many manuscripts. The work of a fourth major fourteenth-century English poet, who remains anonymous, is known only through a single manuscript, which contains four poems all thought to be by a single author: *Cleanness* and *Patience*, two biblical narratives in alliterative verse; *Pearl*, a moving dream vision in which a grief-stricken father is visited and consoled by his dead child, who has been transformed into a queen in the kingdom of heaven; and *Sir Gawain and the Green Knight*, the finest of all English romances. The plot of *Gawain* involves a folklore motif of a challenge by a supernatural visitor, first found in an Old Irish tale. The poet has made this motif a challenge to King Arthur's court and has framed the tale with allusions at the beginning and end to the legends that link Arthur's reign with the Trojan War and the founding of Rome and of Britain. The poet has a sophisticated awareness of romance as a literary genre and plays a game with both the hero's and the reader's expectations of what is supposed to happen in a romance. One could say that the broader subject of *Sir Gawain and the Green Knight* is "romance" itself, and in this respect the poem resembles Chaucer's *Canterbury Tales* in its author's interest in literary form.

Julian of Norwich is a fifth major writer of this period. The first known woman writer in the English vernacular, the anchoress Julian participates in a Continental tradition of visionary writings, often by women. She spent a good deal of her life meditating and writing about a series of visions, which she called "showings," that she had received in 1373, when she was thirty

years old. While very carefully negotiating the dangers of writing as a
woman, and of writing sophisticated
theology in the vernacular, Julian
manages to produce visionary writing that is at once penetrating and
serene.

The Fifteenth Century

In 1399 Henry Bolingbroke, the
duke of Lancaster, deposed his
cousin Richard II, who was murdered in prison. As Henry IV, he
successfully defended his crown
against several insurrections and
passed it on to Henry V, who briefly
united the country once more and
achieved one last apparently decisive victory over the French at the
Battle of Agincourt (1415). The pre-
mature death of Henry V in 1422,
however, left England exposed to
the civil wars known as the Wars of
the Roses, the red rose being the
emblem of the house of Lancaster;
the white, of York. These wars did
not end until 1485, when Henry
Tudor defeated Richard III at Bosworth Field and acceded to the
throne as Henry VII.

The Seasons. Limbourg Brothers, "February," from *Les Très Riches Heures du Duc de
Berry* (ca. 1411–16). The calm inevitability of
cosmic, seasonal change is set above the
uncertain yet inventive struggle of peasants,
for heat and food, in the main frame.

The most prolific poet of the fif-
teenth century was the monk John Lydgate (1371?–1449), who produced
dream visions; a life of the Virgin; translations of French religious allegories;
a *Troy Book*; *The Siege of Thebes*, which he framed as a "new" Canterbury
tale; and a thirty-six-thousand-line poem called *The Fall of Princes*, a free
translation of a French work, itself based on a Latin work by Boccaccio. The
last illustrates the late medieval idea of tragedy, namely that emperors, kings,
and other famous men enjoy power and fortune only to be cast down in misery. Lydgate shapes these tales as a "mirror" for princes, i.e., as object lessons
to the powerful men of his own day, several of whom were his patrons. A self-
styled imitator of Chaucer, Lydgate had a reputation almost equal to Chaucer's in the fifteenth century. The other significant poet of the first half of the
fifteenth century is Thomas Hoccleve (1367?–1426). Like Lydgate, Hoccleve
also wrote for powerful Lancastrian patrons, but his poetry is strikingly private, painfully concerned as it often is with his penury and mental instability.
The searing poem *My Compleinte* is an example of his work.

Religious works of all kinds continued to be produced in the fifteenth
century, but under greater surveillance. The Lancastrian authorities
responded to the reformist religious movement known as "Lollardy" in
draconian ways. They introduced a statute for the burning of heretics (the
first such statute) in 1401, and a series of measures designed to survey and

censor theology in English in 1409. Despite this, many writers continued to produce religious works in the vernacular. Perhaps the most remarkable of these writers is Margery Kempe (who records her visit to Julian of Norwich in about 1413). Kempe made pilgrimages to the Holy Land, Rome, Santiago, and to shrines in Northern Europe. These she records, in the context of her often fraught and painful personal life, in her *Book of Margery Kempe*. Both Julian of Norwich and Margery Kempe, in highly individual ways, allow us to see the medieval church and its doctrines from female points of view.

Social, economic, and literary life continued as they had throughout all of the previously mentioned wars. The prosperity of the towns was shown by performances of the mystery plays—a sequence or "cycle" of plays based on the Bible and produced by the city guilds, the organizations representing the various trades and crafts. The cycles of several towns are lost, but those of York and Chester have been preserved, along with two other complete cycles, one possibly from Wakefield in Yorkshire, and the other titled the "N-Town" Cycle. Under the guise of dramatizing biblical history, playwrights such as the Wakefield Master manage to comment satirically on the social ills of the times. The century also saw the development of the morality play, in which personified vices and virtues struggle for the soul of "Mankind" or "Everyman." Performed by professional players, the morality plays were precursors of the professional theater in the reign of Elizabeth I.

The best of Chaucer's imitators was Robert Henryson, who, in the last quarter of the fifteenth century, wrote *The Testament of Cresseid*, a continuation of Chaucer's great poem *Troilus and Criseyde*. He also wrote the *Moral Fabilis of Esope*, among which *The Cock and the Fox* is a remake of Chaucer's *Nun's Priest's Tale*.

The works of Sir Thomas Malory (d. 1471) gave the definitive form in English to the legend of King Arthur and his knights. Malory spent years in prison Englishing a series of Arthurian romances that he translated and abridged chiefly from several enormously long thirteenth-century French prose romances. Malory was a passionate devotee of chivalry, which he personified in his hero Sir Lancelot. In the jealousies and rivalries that finally break up the round table and destroy Arthur's kingdom, Malory saw a distant image of the civil wars of his own time. A manuscript of Malory's works fell into the hands of William Caxton (1422?–1492), who had introduced the new art of printing by movable type to England in 1476. Caxton divided Malory's tales into the chapters and books of a single long work, as though it were a chronicle history, and gave it the title *Morte Darthur*, which has stuck to it ever since. Caxton also printed *The Canterbury Tales*, some of Chaucer's earlier works, and Gower's *Confessio Amantis*. Caxton himself translated many of the works he printed for English readers: a history of Troy, a book on chivalry, Aesop's fables, *The History of Reynard the Fox*, and *The Game and Playe of Chesse*. The new technology extended literacy and made books more easily accessible to new classes of readers. Printing made the production of literature a business and made possible the bitter political and doctrinal disputes that, in the sixteenth century, were waged in print as well as on the field of battle.

Doubled vowels and terminal vowels are always long, whereas single vowels before two consonants other than *th, ch* are always short. The vowels *a, e,* and *o* are long before a single consonant followed by a vowel: *nāmë, sēkë* (sick), *hōly*. In general, words that have descended into Modern English reflect their original Middle English quantity: *līven* (to live), but *līf* (life).

The close and open sounds of long *e* and long *o* may often be identified by the Modern English spellings of the words in which they appear. Original long close *e* is generally represented in Modern English by *ee*: "sweet," "knee," "teeth," "see" have close *e* in Middle English, but so does "be"; original long open *e* is generally represented in Modern English by *ea*: "meat," "heath," "sea," "great," "breath" have open *e* in Middle English. Similarly, original long close *o* is now generally represented by *oo*: "soon," "food," "good," but also "do," "to"; original long open *o* is represented either by *oa* or by *o*: "coat," "boat," "moan," but also "go," "bone," "foe," "home." Notice that original close *o* is now almost always pronounced like the *oo* in "goose," but that original open *o* is almost never so pronounced; thus it is often possible to identify the Middle English vowels through Modern English sounds.

The nonphonetic Middle English spelling of *o* for short *u* has been preserved in a number of Modern English words ("love," "son," "come"), but in others *u* has been restored: "sun" (*sonne*), "run" (*ronne*).

For the treatment of final *e*, see "General Rules," "Final *e*."

2. DIPHTHONGS

Sound	Pronunciation	Example
ai, ay, ei, ay	between *ai* in "aisle" and *ay* in "day"	*saide, day, veine, preye*
au, aw	*ou* in "out"	*chaunge, bawdy*
eu, ew	*ew* in "few"	*newe*
oi, oy	*oy* in "joy"	*joye, point*
ou, ow	*ou* in "thought"	*thought, lowe*

Note that in words with *ou, ow* that in Modern English are sounded with the *ou* of "about," the combination indicates not the diphthong but the simple vowel long *u* (see "Simple Vowels").

3. CONSONANTS

In general, all consonants except *h* were always sounded in Middle English, including consonants that have become silent in Modern English, such as the *g* in *gnaw*, the *k* in *knight*, the *l* in *folk*, and the *w* in *write*. In noninitial *gn*, however, the *g* was silent as in Modern English "sign." Initial *h* was silent in short common English words and in words borrowed from French and may have been almost silent in all words. The combination *gh* as in *night* or *thought* was sounded like the *ch* of German *ich* or *nach*. Note that Middle English *gg* represents both the hard sound of "dagger" and the soft sound of "bridge."

III. Parts of Speech and Grammar

1. NOUNS

The plural and possessive of nouns end in *es*, formed by adding *s* or *es* to the singular: *knight, knightes; roote, rootes;* a final consonant is frequently doubled before *es: bed, beddes*. A common irregular plural is *yën*, from *yë*, eye.

2. PRONOUNS

The chief comparisons with Modern English are as follows:

Modern English	East Midlands Middle English
I	*I, ich* (*ik* is a northern form)
you (singular)	*thou* (subjective); *thee* (objective)
her	*hir(e), her(e)*
its	*his*
you (plural)	*ye* (subjective); *you* (objective)
they	*they*
their	*hir* (*their* is a Northern form)
them	*hem* (*them* is a Northern form)

In formal speech, the second-person plural is often used for the singular. The possessive adjectives *my, thy* take *n* before a word beginning with a vowel or *h: thyn yë, myn host.*

3. ADJECTIVES

Adjectives ending in a consonant add final *e* when they stand before the noun they modify and after another modifying word such as *the, this, that,* or nouns or pronouns in the possessive: *a good hors,* but *the* (*this, my, the kinges*) *goode hors.* They also generally add *e* when standing before and modifying a plural noun, a noun in the vocative, or any proper noun: *goode men, oh goode man, faire Venus.*

Adjectives are compared by adding *er(e)* for the comparative, *est(e)* for the superlative. Sometimes the stem vowel is shortened or altered in the process: *sweete, swettere, swettest; long, lenger, lengest.*

4. ADVERBS

Adverbs are formed from adjectives by adding *e, ly,* or *liche*; the adjective *fair* thus yields *faire, fairly, fairliche.*

5. VERBS

Middle English verbs, like Modern English verbs, are either "weak" or "strong." Weak verbs form their preterites and past participles with a *t* or *d* suffix and preserve the same stem vowel throughout their systems, although it is sometimes shortened in the preterite and past participle: *love, loved; bend, bent; hear, heard; meet, met.* Strong verbs do not use the *t* or *d* suffix, but vary their stem vowel in the preterite and past participle: *take, took, taken; begin, began, begun; find, found, found.*

The inflectional endings are the same for Middle English strong verbs and weak verbs except in the preterite singular and the imperative singular. In the following paradigms, the weak verbs *loven* (to love) and *heeren* (to hear), and the strong verbs *taken* (to take) and *ginnen* (to begin) serve as models.

	Present Indicative	Preterite Indicative
I	*love, heere*	*loved(e), herde*
	take, ginne	*took, gan*
thou	*lovest, heerest*	*lovedest, herdest*
	takest, ginnest	*tooke, gonne*
he, she, it	*loveth, heereth*	*loved(e), herde*

	taketh, ginneth	took, gan
we, ye, they	love(n) (th), heere(n) (th)	loved(e) (en), herde(n)
	take(n) (th), ginne(n) (th)	tooke(n), gonne(n)

The present plural ending *eth* is southern, whereas the *e(n)* ending is Midland and characteristic of Chaucer. In the north, *s* may appear as the ending of all persons of the present. In the weak preterite, when the ending *e* gave a verb three or more syllables, it was frequently dropped. Note that in certain strong verbs like *ginnen* there are two distinct stem vowels in the preterite; even in Chaucer's time, however, one of these had begun to replace the other, and Chaucer occasionally writes *gan* for all persons of the preterite.

	Present Subjunctive	Preterite Subjunctive
Singular	love, heere	lovede, herde
	take, ginne	tooke, gonne
Plural	love(n), heere(n)	lovede(n), herde(n)
	take(n), ginne(n)	tooke(n), gonne(n)

In verbs like *ginnen*, which have two stem vowels in the indicative preterite, it is the vowel of the plural and of the second person singular that is used for the preterite subjunctive.

The imperative singular of most weak verbs is *e*: *(thou) love*, but of some weak verbs and all strong verbs, the imperative singular is without termination: *(thou) heer, taak, gin*. The imperative plural of all verbs is either *e* or *eth*: *(ye) love(th), heere(th), take(th), ginne(th)*.

The infinitive of verbs is *e* or *en*: *love(n), heere(n), take(n), ginne(n)*.

The past participle of weak verbs is the same as the preterite without inflectional ending: *loved, herd*. In strong verbs the ending is either *e* or *en*: *take(n), gonne(n)*. The prefix *y* often appears on past participles: *yloved, yherd, ytake(n)*.

OLD AND MIDDLE ENGLISH PROSODY

All the poetry of Old English is in the same verse form. The verse unit is the single line, because rhyme was not used to link one line to another, except very occasionally in late Old English. The organizing device of the line is alliteration, the beginning of several words with the same sound ("Foemen fled"). The Old English alliterative line contains, on the average, four principal stresses and is divided into two half-lines of two stresses each by a strong medial caesura, or pause. These two half-lines are linked to each other by the alliteration; at least one of the two stressed words in the first half-line, and often both of them, begin with the same sound as the first stressed word of the second half-line (the second stressed word is generally nonalliterative). The fourth line of *Beowulf* is an example (*sc* has the value of modern *sh*; þ is a runic symbol with the value of modern *th*):

Oft Scyld Scefing   sceaþena þreatum.

For further examples, see Cædmon's *Hymn*. It will be noticed that any vowel alliterates with any other vowel. In addition to the alliteration, the length of the unstressed syllables and their number and pattern is governed by a highly complex set of rules. When sung or intoned—as it was—to the rhythmic strumming of a harp, Old English poetry must have been wonderfully impressive in the dignified, highly formalized way that aptly fits both its subject matter and tone.

The majority of Middle English verse is either in alternately stressed rhyming verse, adapted from French after the conquest, or in alliterative verse that is descended from Old English. The latter preserves the caesura of Old English and in its purest form the same alliterative system, the two stressed words of the first half-line (or at least one of them) alliterating with the first stressed word in the second half-line. But most of the alliterative poets allowed themselves a number of deviations from the norm. All four stressed words may alliterate, as in the first line of *Piers Plowman:*

> In a summer season   when soft was the sun.

Or the line may contain five, six, or even more stressed words, of which all or only the basic minimum may alliterate:

> A *fair field full* of   *folk found* I there between.

There is no rule determining the number of unstressed syllables, and at times some poets seem to ignore alliteration entirely. As in Old English, any vowel may alliterate with any other vowel; furthermore, since initial *h* was silent or lightly pronounced in Middle English, words beginning with *h* are treated as though they began with the following vowel.

There are two general types of stressed verse with rhyme. In the more common, unstressed and stressed syllables alternate regularly as x X x X x X or, with two unstressed syllables intervening as x x X x x X x x X or a combination of the two as x x X x X x x X (of the reverse patterns, only X x X x X x is common in English). There is also a line that can only be defined as containing a predetermined number of stressed syllables but an irregular number and pattern of unstressed syllables. Much Middle English verse has to be read without expectation of regularity; some of this was evidently composed in the irregular meter, but some was probably originally composed according to a strict metrical system that has been obliterated by scribes careless of fine points. One receives the impression that many of the lyrics—as well as the *Second Shepherds' Play*—were at least composed with regular syllabic alternation. In the play *Everyman*, only the number of stresses is generally predetermined but not the number or placement of unstressed syllables.

In pre-Chaucerian verse the number of stresses, whether regularly or irregularly alternated, was most often four, although sometimes the number was three and rose in some poems to seven. Rhyme in Middle English (as in Modern English) may be either between adjacent or alternate lines, or may occur in more complex patterns. Most of the *Canterbury Tales* are in rhymed couplets, the line containing five stresses with regular alternation— technically known as iambic pentameter, the standard English poetic line, perhaps introduced into English by Chaucer. In reading Chaucer and much pre-Chaucerian verse, one must remember that the final *e,* which is silent in Modern English, could be pronounced at any time to provide a needed unstressed syllable. Evidence seems to indicate that it was also pronounced at the end of the line, even though it thus produced a line with eleven syllables. Although he was a very regular metricist, Chaucer used various conventional devices that are apt to make the reader stumble until he or she understands them. Final *e* is often not pronounced before a word beginning with a vowel or *h,* and may be suppressed whenever metrically convenient.

The same medial and terminal syllables that are slurred in Modern English are apt to be suppressed in Chaucer's English: *Canterb'ry* for *Canterbury*; *ev'r* (perhaps *e'er*) for *evere*. The plural in *es* may either be syllabic or reduced to *s* as in Modern English. Despite these seeming irregularities, Chaucer's verse is not difficult to read if one constantly bears in mind the basic pattern of the iambic pentameter line.

THE MIDDLE AGES

TEXTS	CONTEXTS
	43–ca. 420 Romans conquer Britons; Brittania a province of the Roman Empire
	307–37 Reign of Constantine the Great leads to adoption of Christianity as official religion of the Roman Empire
ca. 405 St. Jerome completes *Vulgate*, Latin translation of the Bible that becomes standard for the Roman Catholic Church	
	432 St. Patrick begins mission to convert Ireland
	ca. 450 Anglo-Saxon conquest of Britons begins
523 Boethius, *Consolation of Philosophy* (Latin)	
	597 St. Augustine of Canterbury's mission to Kent begins conversion of Anglo-Saxons to Christianity
ca. 658–80 Cædmon's *Hymn*, earliest poem recorded in English	
731 Bede completes *Ecclesiastical History of the English People*	
? ca. 750 *Beowulf* composed	
	ca. 787 First Viking raids on England
871–99 Texts written or commissioned by Alfred	**871–99** Reign of King Alfred
ca. 1000 Unique manuscript of *Beowulf* and *Judith*	
	1066 Norman Conquest by William I establishes French-speaking ruling class in England
	1095–1221 Crusades
ca. 1135–38 Geoffrey of Monmouth's Latin *History of the Kings of Britain* gives pseudohistorical status to Arthurian and other legends	
	1152 Future Henry II marries Eleanor of Aquitaine, bringing vast French territories to the English crown
1154 End of *Peterborough Chronicle*, last branch of the *Anglo-Saxon Chronicle*	
? ca. 1165–80 Marie de France, *Lais* in Anglo-Norman French from Breton sources	
ca. 1170–91 Chrétien de Troyes, chivalric romances about knights of the Round Table	**1170** Archbishop Thomas Becket murdered in Canterbury Cathedral
? ca. 1200 Layamon's *Brut*	**1182** Birth of St. Francis of Assisi

TEXTS	CONTEXTS
? ca. 1215–25 *Ancrene Wisse*	1215 Fourth Lateran Council requires annual confession. English barons force King John to seal Magna Carta (the Great Charter) guaranteeing baronial rights
ca. 1304–21 Dante Alighieri writing *Divine Comedy*	*1290 – Expulsion of Jews*
ca. 1340–1374 Giovanni Boccaccio active as writer in Naples and Florence	ca. 1337–1453 Hundred Years' War
	1348 Black Death ravages Europe
ca. 1340–1374 Francis Petrarch active as writer	1362 English first used in law courts and Parliament
1368 Chaucer, *Book of the Duchess*	
	1372 Chaucer's first journey to Italy
1373–93 Julian of Norwich, *Book of Showings*	
ca. 1375–1400 *Sir Gawain and the Green Knight*	
	1376 Earliest record of performance of cycle drama at York
1377–79 William Langland, *Piers Plowman* (B-Text)	
ca. 1380 Followers of John Wycliffe begin first complete translation of the Bible into English	
	1381 People's uprising briefly takes control of London before being suppressed
ca. 1385–87 Chaucer, *Troilus and Criseyde*	
ca. 1387–99 Chaucer working on *The Canterbury Tales*	
ca. 1390–92 John Gower, *Confessio Amantis*	
	1399 Richard II deposed by his cousin, who succeeds him as Henry IV
	1400 Richard II murdered
	1401 Execution of William Sawtre, first Lollard burned at the stake under new law against heresy
ca. 1410–49 John Lydgate active	
ca. 1420 Thomas Hoccleve, *My Compleinte*	1415 Henry V defeats French at Agincourt
ca. 1425 *York Play of the Crucifixion*	
	1431 English burn Joan of Arc at Rouen
ca. 1432–38 Margery Kempe, *The Book of Margery Kempe*	
ca. 1450–75 Wakefield mystery cycle, *Second Shepherds' Play*	
	1455–85 Wars of the Roses

TEXTS	CONTEXTS
ca. 1470 Sir Thomas Malory in prison working on *Morte Darthur*	
ca. 1475 Robert Henryson active	
	1476 William Caxton sets up first printing press in England
1485 Caxton publishes *Morte Darthur,* one of the first books in English to be printed	**1485** The earl of Richmond defeats the Yorkist king, Richard III, at Bosworth Field and succeeds him as Henry VII, founder of the Tudor dynasty
ca. 1510 *Everyman*	
	1575 Last performance of mystery plays at Chester

Anglo-Saxon Literature

BEDE (ca. 673–735) and CÆDMON'S *HYMN*

The Venerable Bede (the title by which he is known to posterity) became a novice at the age of seven and spent the rest of his life at the neighboring monasteries of Wearmouth and Jarrow. Although he may never have traveled beyond the boundaries of his native district of Northumbria, he achieved an international reputation as one of the greatest scholars of his age. Writing in Latin, the learned language of the era, Bede produced many theological works as well as books on science and rhetoric, but his most popular and enduring work is the *Ecclesiastical History of the English People* (completed 731). The *History* tells about the Anglo-Saxon conquest and the vicissitudes of the petty kingdoms that comprised Anglo-Saxon England; Bede's main theme, however, is the spread of Christianity and the growth of the English church. The latter were the great events leading up to Bede's own time, and he regarded them as the unfolding of God's providence. The *History* is, therefore, also a moral work and a hagiography—that is, it contains many stories of saints and miracles meant to testify to the grace and glory of God.

The story we reprint preserves what is probably the earliest extant Old English poem (composed sometime between 658 and 680) and the only biographical information, outside of what is said in the poems themselves, about any Old English poet. Bede tells how Cædmon, an illiterate cowherd employed by the monastery of Whitby, miraculously received the gift of song, entered the monastery, and became the founder of a school of Christian poetry. Cædmon was clearly an oral-formulaic poet, one who created his work by combining and varying formulas—units of verse developed in a tradition transmitted by one generation of singers to another. In this respect he resembles the singers of the Homeric poems and oral-formulaic poets recorded in the twentieth century, especially in the Balkan countries. Although Bede tells us that Cædmon had never learned the art of song, we may suspect that he concealed his skill from his fellow workmen and from the monks because he was ashamed of knowing "vain and idle" songs, the kind Bede says Cædmon never composed. Cædmon's inspiration and the true miracle, then, was to apply the meter and language of such songs, presumably including pagan heroic verse, to Christian themes.

Although most Old English poetry was written by lettered poets, they continued to use the oral-formulaic style. The *Hymn* is, therefore, a good short example of the way Old English verse, with its traditional poetic diction and interwoven formulaic expressions, is constructed. Eight of the poem's eighteen half-lines contain epithets describing various aspects of God: He is *Weard* (Guardian), *Meotod* (Measurer), *Wuldor-Fæder* (Glory-Father), *Drihten* (Lord), *Scyppend* (Creator), and *Frea* (Master). God is *heofonrices Weard* or *mancynnes Weard* (heaven's or mankind's Guardian), depending on the alliteration required. This formulaic style provides a richness of texture and meaning difficult to convey in translation. As Bede said about his own Latin paraphrase of the *Hymn*, no literal translation of poetry from one language to another is possible without sacrifice of some poetic quality.

Several manuscripts of Bede's *History* contain the Old English text in addition to Bede's Latin version. The poem is given here in a West Saxon form with a literal interlinear translation. In Old English spelling, æ (as in Cædmon's name and line 3) is a vowel symbol that represents the vowel of Modern English *cat*; þ (line 2) and ð (line 7) both represented the sound *th*. The spelling *sc* (line 1)=*sh*; ġ (line 1)=*y* in *yard*; ċ (line 1)=*ch* in *chin*; *c* (line 2)=*k*. The large space in the middle of the line indicates the caesura. The alliterating sounds that connect the half-lines are printed in bold italics.

From An Ecclesiastical History of the English People

[THE STORY OF CÆDMON]

Heavenly grace had especially singled out a certain one of the brothers in the monastery ruled by this abbes[1] for he used to compose devout and religious songs. Whatever he learned of holy Scripture with the aid of interpreters, he quickly turned into the sweetest and most moving poetry in his own language, that is to say English. It often happened that his songs kindled a contempt for this world and a longing for the life of Heaven in the hearts of many men. Indeed, after him others among the English people tried to compose religious poetry, but no one could equal him because he was not taught the art of song by men or by human agency but received this gift through heavenly grace. Therefore, he was never able to compose any vain and idle songs but only such as dealt with religion and were proper for his religious tongue to utter. As a matter of fact, he had lived in the secular estate until he was well advanced in age without learning any songs. Therefore, at feasts, when it was decided to have a good time by taking turns singing, whenever he would see the harp getting close to his place,[2] he got up in the middle of the meal and went home.

Once when he left the feast like this, he went to the cattle shed, which he had been assigned the duty of guarding that night. And after he had stretched himself out and gone to sleep, he dreamed that someone was standing at his side and greeted him, calling out his name. "Cædmon," he said, "sing me something."

And he replied, "I don't know how to sing; that is why I left the feast to come here—because I cannot sing."

"All the same," said the one who was speaking to him, "you have to sing for me."

"What must I sing?" he said.

And he said, "Sing about the Creation."

At this, Cædmon immediately began to sing verses in praise of God the Creator, which he had never heard before and of which the sense is this:

Nu sculon *h*eriġean	*h*eofonriċes Weard
Now we must praise	heaven-kingdom's Guardian,
*M*eotodes *m*eahte	and his *m*odġeþanc
the Measurer's might	and his mind-plans,

---

1. Abbess Hilda (614–680), a grandniece of the first Christian king of Northumbria, founded Whitby, a double house for monks and nuns, in 657 and ruled over it for twenty-two years.

2. Oral poetry was performed to the accompaniment of a harp; here the harp is being passed from one participant of the feast to another, each being expected to perform in turn.

*w*eorc Wuldor-Fæder	swa he *w*undra ġehwæs
the work of the Glory-Father,	when he of wonders of every one,
*e*ċe Drihten	*or o*nstealde
eternal Lord,	the beginning established.[3]
He ærest sceop	*i*elda[4] bearnum
He first created	for men's sons
*h*eofon to *h*rofe	*h*aliġ Scyppend
heaven as a roof,	holy Creator;
ða *m*iddanġeard	*m*oncynnes Weard
then middle-earth	mankind's Guardian,
*e*ċe Drihten	æfter teode
eternal Lord,	afterwards made—
*f*irum *f*oldan	Frea ælmihtiġ
for men earth,	Master almighty.

This is the general sense but not the exact order of the words that he sang in his sleep;[5] for it is impossible to make a literal translation, no matter how well-written, of poetry into another language without losing some of the beauty and dignity. When he woke up, he remembered everything that he had sung in his sleep, and to this he soon added, in the same poetic measure, more verses praising God.

The next morning he went to the reeve,[6] who was his foreman, and told him about the gift he had received. He was taken to the abbess and ordered to tell his dream and to recite his song to an audience of the most learned men so that they might judge what the nature of that vision was and where it came from. It was evident to all of them that he had been granted the heavenly grace of God. Then they expounded some bit of sacred story or teaching to him, and instructed him to turn it into poetry if he could. He agreed and went away. And when he came back the next morning, he gave back what had been commissioned to him in the finest verse.

Therefore, the abbess, who cherished the grace of God in this man, instructed him to give up secular life and to take monastic vows. And when she and all those subject to her had received him into the community of brothers, she gave orders that he be taught the whole sequence of sacred history. He remembered everything that he was able to learn by listening, and turning it over in his mind like a clean beast that chews the cud,[7] he converted it into sweetest song, which sounded so delightful that he made his teachers, in their turn, his listeners. He sang about the creation of the world and the origin of the human race and all the history of Genesis; about the exodus of Israel out of Egypt and entrance into the promised land; and about many other stories

---

3. I.e., established the beginning of every one of the wonders.

4. The later manuscript copies read *eorpan*, "earth," for *ælda* (West Saxon *ielda*), "men's."

5. Bede is referring to his Latin translation, for which we have substituted the Old English text with interlinear translation.

6. Superintendent of the farms belonging to the monastery.

7. In Mosaic law "clean" animals, those that may be eaten, are those that both chew the cud and have a cloven hoof (cf. Leviticus 11.3 and Deuteronomy 14.6).

of sacred Scripture, about the Lord's incarnation, and his passion,[8] resurrection, and ascension into Heaven; about the advent of the Holy Spirit and the teachings of the apostles. He also made many songs about the terror of the coming judgment and the horror of the punishments of hell and the sweetness of heavenly kingdom; and a great many others besides about divine grace and justice in all of which he sought to draw men away from the love of sin and to inspire them with delight in the practice of good works.[9] * * *

8. The suffering of Christ between the night of the Last Supper and his death.
9. The great majority of extant Old English poems are on religious subjects like those listed here, but most are thought to be later than Cædmon.

THE DREAM OF THE ROOD

*T*he Dream of the Rood (i.e., of the Cross) is considered the finest of a large number of religious poems in Anglo-Saxon. Neither the author nor its date of composition is known. It appears in a late tenth-century manuscript located in Vercelli in northern Italy, a manuscript made up of Old English religious poems and sermons. The poem may antedate its manuscript, because some passages from the Rood's speech were carved, with some variations, in runes on a stone cross at some time after its construction early in the eighth century; this is the famous Ruthwell Cross, preserved near Dumfries in southern Scotland. The precise relation of the poem to this cross is, however, uncertain.

The experience of the Rood, often called "tree" in the poem—its humiliation at the hands of those who cut it down and made it into an instrument of punishment for criminals and its humility when the young hero Christ mounts it—has a suggestive relevance to the condition of the Dreamer. His isolation and melancholy is typical of exile figures in Anglo-Saxon poetry. For the Rood, however, glory has replaced torment, and at the end, the Dreamer's description of Christ's entry into heaven with the souls he has liberated from Hades reflects the Dreamer's response to the hope that has been brought to him. Christ and the Rood both act in keeping with, and yet diametrically opposed to, a code of heroic action: Christ is both heroic in mounting and passive in suffering on the Rood, while the Rood is loyal to its lord, yet must participate in his death.

Ruthwell Cross, Ruthwell, Scotland, ca. 8th century. Not only is the cross sculpted with Christian images; it also has lines from *The Dream of the Rood* inscribed in runic letters. They may have been added at a later date.

The Dream of the Rood[1]

Attend to what   I intend to tell you
a marvelous dream   that moved me at night
when human voices   are veiled in sleep.
In my dream I espied   the most splendid tree.
looming aloft   with light all around,
the most brilliant beam.   That bright tree was
covered with gold; gemstones gleamed
fairly fashioned down to its foot,   yet another five were standing[2]
high up on the crossbeam   —the Lord's angel beheld them—[3]
cast by eternal decree.   Clearly this was no criminal's gallows,[4]
but holy spirits   were beholding it there,
men on this earth,   all that mighty creation.
That tree was triumphant   and I tarnished by sin,
begrimed with evil.   I beheld Glory's trunk
garnished with grandeur,   gleaming in bliss,
all plated with gold;   precious gemstones
had gloriously graced   the Lord God's tree.
Yet I could see   signs of ancient strife:
beneath that gold   it had begun
bleeding on the right side.[5]   I was all bereft with sorrows;
that splendid sight made me afraid.   I beheld the sign rapidly
changing clothing and colors.   Now it was covered with moisture,
drenched with streaming blood,   now decked in treasure.
Yet I, lying there   for a long time,
sorrowfully beheld   the tree of our Savior
until I could hear it   call out to me,
the best of all wood   began speaking words:
    "That was years ago   —I yet remember—
that I was cut down   at the edge of the forest
torn up from my trunk.   There powerful enemies took me,
put me up to make a circus-play to lift   up and parade their criminals.
Soldiers bore me on their shoulders   till they set me up on a mountain;
more than enough foes made me stand fast.   I saw the lord of mankind
coming with great haste   so that he might climb up on me.
    Then I did not dare   act against the Lord's word
bow down or fall to pieces   when I felt the surface
of the earth trembling.[6]   Although I might
have destroyed the foes,   I stood in place.
Then this young man stripped himself   —that was God Almighty—
strong and courageous;   he climbed up on the high gallows,
brave in the sight of many,   as he set out to redeem mankind.

---

1. The translation by Alfred David is based on *Eight Old English Poems*, 3rd ed., edited by John C. Pope, revised by R. D. Fulk (2000).
2. This longer line and the two following, as well as lines 20–23, 30–34, 39–43, 46–49, 59–70, 75–76, and 133, contain additional stresses and are designated as "hypermetric." Less than 500 such lines survive in the corpus of Anglo-Saxon poetry.
3. The translation follows R. D. Fulk's emendation: "beheold on þam engel dryhtnes."
4. Constantine the Great, emperor from 306 to 337, erected a jeweled cross at the site of the crucifixion, transforming the Roman "felon's gallows" from a symbol of shame into a universal icon of Christian art.
5. According to biblical tradition, following John 19.34, Christ was wounded by the centurion's lance on the right side.
6. According to Matthew 27.51, the earth quaked at the crucifixion.

I trembled when the man embraced me;   I dared not bow down to earth,
stoop to the surface of the ground,   but I had to stand fast.
　　I was reared a rood;   I raised up a mighty king,
45　　the heavens' lord;   I dared not bow in homage.
They drove dark nails into me;   the dints of those wounds can still be seen,
open marks of malice;   but I did not dare maul any of them in return.
They mocked both of us.   I was moistened all over with blood,
shed from the man's side   after he had sent up his spirit.
50　　On that mountain   I have endured many
　　cruel happenings.   I saw the God of hosts
　　direly stretched out.   Shades of darkness
　　had clouded over   the corpse of the Lord,
　　the shining radiance;   shadows went forth
55　　dark under clouds.   All creation wept,
　　mourning the king's fall: Christ was on the cross.
　　　　"Yet from afar   fervent men came
　　to that sovereign.   I saw all that.
I was badly burdened with grief   yet bowed down to their hands,
60　　submissive with most resolve.   There they took up almighty God,
lifted him from that cruel torment.   Then the warriors left me there
standing, blood all over me,   pierced everywhere with arrows.
They laid him there, limb-wearied;   they stood at the head of his lifeless
　　　body.
65　　There they beheld the lord of heaven,   and he rested there for a while,
spent after that great struggle.   Then they set about to construct a sepulcher
warriors in the slayer's[7] sight.   Out of bright stone they carved it;
they laid the lord of victories into it.   They began singing a lay of sorrow,
warriors sad as night was falling,   when they wished to journey back
70　　wearily far from that famous lord;   he rested there with few followers.[8]
　　　We,[9]grieving there   for a good while,
　　stood still in place;   the soldiers' voices
　　faded away.   Finally men brought axes
　　to fell us to earth.   That was a frightful destiny!
75　　They buried us in a deep pit.   But thanes° of the Lord,　　　　　　retainers
friends learned about me[1]* * *
　　　　* * *adorned me   with gold and silver.
　　　"Now, man so dear to me,   you may understand
　　that I have gone through   grievous sufferings,
80　　terrible sorrows.   Now the time has come
　　so that far and wide   men worship me
　　everywhere on earth,   and all creation,
　　pray to this sign.   On me the son of God
　　suffered a time;   therefore I now tower
85　　in glory under heaven,   and I may heal
　　any one of those   in awe of me.
　　Long ago I became   the most cruel punishment,
　　most hated by men,   until I made open
　　the right way of life   to language-bearers.

7. I.e., the Cross. See John 19.41–42.
8. An example of Anglo-Saxon litotes, ironically
expressing something by its contrary. In fact,
Christ's tomb is now deserted.
9. I.e, Christ's Cross and those on which the two

thieves had been crucified.
1. The reference in this gap in the manuscript
must be to the discovery of the Cross by St.
Helena.

90 So the lord of glory,   guardian of Heaven,
exalted me then   over all forest-trees,
as Almighty God   before all humankind
exalted over   all the race of women
His own mother,   Mary herself.
95   "Now I command you,   my man so dear,
to tell others   the events you have seen;
find words to tell   it was the tree of glory
Almighty God   suffered upon
for mankind's   so many sins
100 and for that ancient   offense of Adam.
There he tasted death;   yet the Redeemer arose
with his great might   to help mankind.
Then he rose to Heaven.   He will come again
to this middle-earth   to seek out mankind
105 on Judgment Day,   the Redeemer himself,
God Almighty   and his angels with him,
so that He will judge,   He who has power of the Judgment,
all humanity   as to the merits each
has brought about   in this brief life.
110 Nor may anyone   be unafraid
of the last question   the Lord will ask.
Before the multitude   he will demand
where a soul might be   who in the Savior's name
would suffer the death   He suffered on that tree.
115 But they shall fear   and few shall think
what to contrive   to say to Christ.
But no one there   need be afraid
who bears the best   sign on his breast.
And on this earth   each soul that longs
120 to exist with its savior   forevermore
must seek His kingdom   through that cross."
        Then compelled by joy,   I prayed to that tree
with ardent zeal,   where I was alone
with few followers.   Then my heart felt
125 an urge to set forth;   I have suffered
much longing since.   Now I live in hope,
venturing after   that victory-tree,
alone more often   than all other men,
to worship it well.   The will to do so
130 is much in my heart;   my protection
depends on the rood.   I possess but few
friends on this earth.   But forth from here
they have set out from worldly joys   to seek the King of Glory.
They dwell in Heaven now   with the High-father
135 living in glory,   and I look forward
constantly toward   that time the Lord's rood
which I beheld before   here on this earth
shall fetch me away   from this fleeting life
and bring me then   where bliss is eternal
140 to joy in Paradise   where the Lord's people
are joined at that feast   where joy lasts forever
and seat me there   where evermore

I shall dwell in glory,   together with the saints
share in their delights.   May the Lord be my friend,
145   who on earth long ago   on the gallows-tree
suffered agony   for the sins of men:
he redeemed us   and gave us life,
a home in Heaven.   Hope was made new
and blossomed with bliss   to those burning in fire.[2]
150   The Son was victorious   in venturing forth,
mighty and triumphant   when he returned with many,
a company of souls   to the Kingdom of God,
the Almighty Ruler,   to the joy of angels,
and all those holy ones   come to Heaven before.[3]
155   to live in glory,   when their Lord returned,
the Eternal King   to His own country.

2. This line and those following refer to the so-called Harrowing of Hell. After his death on the Cross, Christ descended into hell, from which he released the souls of certain patriarchs and prophets, conducting them into heaven (see *Piers Plowman*, Passus 18). The analogy is to the triumphal procession of a Roman emperor returning from war.

3. The line probably refers to a belief that God had sanctified a chosen few before the crucifixion.

BEOWULF

*B*eowulf, the oldest of the great long poems written in English, may have been composed more than twelve hundred years ago, in the first half of the eighth century, although some scholars would place it as late as the tenth century. As is the case with most Old English poems, the title has been assigned by modern editors, for the manuscripts do not normally give any indication of title or authorship. Linguistic evidence shows that the poem was originally composed in the dialect of what was then Mercia, the Midlands of England today. But in the unique late-tenth-century manuscript preserving the poem, it has been converted into the West-Saxon dialect of the southwest in which most of Old English literature survives. In 1731, before any modern transcript of the text had been made, the manuscript was seriously damaged in a fire that destroyed the building in London that housed the extraordinary collection of medieval English manuscripts made by Sir Robert Bruce Cotton (1571–1631). As a result of the fire and subsequent deterioration, a number of lines and words have been lost from the poem.

It is possible that *Beowulf* may be the lone survivor of a genre of Old English long epics, but it must have been a remarkable and difficult work even in its own day. The poet was reviving the heroic language, style, and pagan world of ancient Germanic oral poetry, a world that was already remote for his contemporaries and that is stranger to the modern reader, in many respects, than the epic world of Homer and Virgil. With the help of *Beowulf* itself, a few shorter heroic poems in Old English, and later poetry and prose in Old Saxon, Old Icelandic, and Middle High German, we can only conjecture what Germanic oral epic must have been like when performed by the Germanic *scop*, or bard. The *Beowulf* poet himself imagines such oral performances by having King Hrothgar's court poet recite a heroic lay at a feast celebrating Beowulf's defeat of Grendel. Many of the words and formulaic expressions in *Beowulf* can be found in other Old English poems, but there are also an extraordinary number of what linguists call *hapax legomena*—that is, words recorded only once in a language. The poet may have found them elsewhere, but the high incidence of such words suggests that he was an original wordsmith in his own right.

Although the poem itself is English in language and origin, it deals not with native Englishmen but with their Germanic forebears, especially with two south Scandinavian tribes, the Danes and the Geats, who lived on the Danish island of Zealand and in southern Sweden. Thus the historical period the poem concerns—insofar as it may be said to refer to history at all—is some centuries before it was written—that is, a time after the initial invasion of England by Germanic tribes in the middle of the fifth century but before the Anglo-Saxon migration was completed. The one datable fact of history mentioned in the poem is a raid on the Franks in which Hygelac, the king of the Geats and Beowulf's lord, was killed, and this raid occurred in the year 520. Yet the poet's elliptical references to quasihistorical and legendary material show that his audience was still familiar with many old stories, the outlines of which we can only infer, sometimes with the help of later analogous tales in other Germanic languages. This knowledge was probably kept alive by other heroic poetry, of which little has been preserved in English, although much may once have existed.

It is now widely believed that *Beowulf* is the work of a single poet who was a Christian and that his poem reflects well-established Christian tradition. The conversion of the Germanic settlers in England had been largely completed during the seventh century. The Danish king Hrothgar's poet sings a song about the Creation (lines 87–98) reminiscent of Cædmon's *Hymn*. The monster Grendel is said to be a descendant of Cain. There are allusions to God's judgment and to fate (*wyrd*) but none to pagan deities. References to the New Testament are notably absent, but Hrothgar and Beowulf often speak of God as though their religion is monotheistic. With sadness the poet relates that, made desperate by Grendel's attacks, the Danes pray for help at heathen shrines—apparently backsliding as the children of Israel had sometimes lapsed into idolatry.

Although Hrothgar and Beowulf are portrayed as morally upright and enlightened pagans, they fully espouse and frequently affirm the values of Germanic heroic poetry. In the poetry depicting this warrior society, the most important of human relationships was that which existed between the warrior—the thane—and his lord, a relationship based less on subordination of one man's will to another's than on mutual trust and respect. When a warrior vowed loyalty to his lord, he became not so much his servant as his voluntary companion, one who would take pride in defending him and fighting in his wars. In return, the lord was expected to take care of his thanes and to reward them richly for their valor; a good king, one like Hrothgar or Beowulf, is referred to by such poetic epithets as "ring-giver" and as the "helmet" and "shield" of his people.

The relationship between kinsmen was also of deep significance to this society. If one of his kinsmen had been slain, a man had a moral obligation

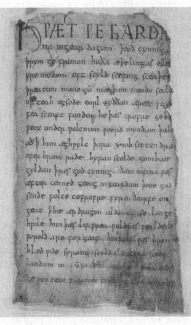

Beowulf. The opening page. Note the charred edges, caused by a fire in 1731.

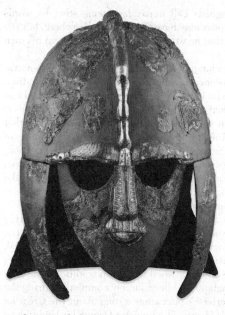

Anglo-Saxon helmet, 6th to 7th centuries. Excavated at Sutton Hoo, Suffolk.

either to kill the slayer or to exact the payment of *wergild* (man-price) in compensation. Each rank of society was evaluated at a definite price, which had to be paid to the dead man's kin by the killer if he wished to avoid their vengeance—even if the killing had been an accident. In the absence of any legal code other than custom or any body of law enforcement, it was the duty of the family (often with the lord's support) to execute justice. The payment itself had less significance as wealth than as proof that the kinsmen had done what was right. The failure to take revenge or to exact compensation was considered shameful. Hrothgar's anguish over the murders committed by Grendel is not only for the loss of his men but also for the shame of his inability either to kill Grendel or to exact a "death-price" from the killer. "It is always better / to avenge dear ones than to indulge in mourning" (lines 1384–85), Beowulf says to Hrothgar, who has been thrown back into despair by the revenge-slaying of his old friend Aeschere by Grendel's mother.

Yet the young Beowulf's attempt to comfort the bereaved old king by invoking the code of vengeance may be one of several instances of the poet's ironic treatment of the tragic futility of the never-ending blood feuds. The most graphic example in the poem of that irony is the Finnsburg episode, the lay sung by Hrothgar's hall-poet. The Danish princess Hildeburh, married to the Frisian king Finn—probably to put an end to a feud between those peoples—loses both her brother and her son when a bloody fight breaks out in the hall between a visiting party of Danes and her husband's men. The bodies are cremated together on a huge funeral pyre: "The glutton element flamed and consumed / the dead of both sides. Their great days were gone" (lines 1124–25).

Such feuds, the staple subject of Germanic epic and saga, have only a peripheral place in the poem. Instead, the poem turns on Beowulf's three great fights against preternatural evil, which inhabits the dangerous and demonic space surrounding human society. He undertakes the fight against Grendel to save the Danes from the monster and to exact vengeance for the men Grendel has slain. Another motive is to demonstrate his strength and courage and thereby to enhance his personal glory. Hrothgar's magnificent gifts become the material emblems of that glory. Revenge and glory also motivate Beowulf's slaying of Grendel's mother. He undertakes his last battle against the dragon, however, only because there is no other way to save his own people.

A somber and dignified elegiac mood pervades *Beowulf*. The poem opens and closes with the description of a funeral and is filled with laments for the dead. Our first view of Beowulf is of an ambitious young hero. At the end, he has become an old king, facing the dragon and death. His people mourn him and praise him, as does the poet, for his nobility, generosity, courage, and, what is less common in Germanic heroes, kindness to his people. The poet's elegiac tone may be informed by something more than the duty to "praise a prince whom he holds dear / and cherish his memory when that moment comes / when he has to be convoyed from his bodily home" (lines 3175–77). The entire poem could be viewed as the poet's lament for heroes like Beowulf who went into the darkness without the light of the poet's own Christian faith.

The present verse translation is by the Irish poet Seamus Heaney, who received the Nobel Prize for literature in 1995. Selections from Heaney's own poems appear in the Twentieth Century and After section of the anthology.

TRIBES AND GENEALOGIES

1. The Danes (Bright-, Half-, Ring-, Spear-, North-, East-, South-, West-Danes; Shield-ings, Honor-, Victor-, War-Shieldings; Ing's friends)

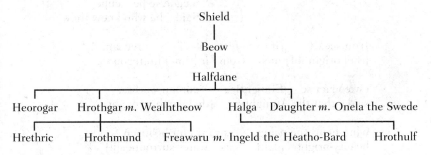

2. The Geats (Sea-, War-, Weather-Geats)

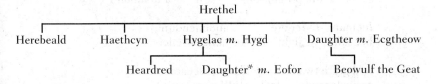

3. The Swedes

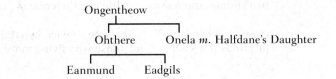

4. *Miscellaneous*

A. The Half-Danes (also called Shieldings) involved in the fight at Finnsburg may represent a different tribe from the Danes *described above*. Their king Hoc had a son, Hnaef, who succeeded him, and a daughter Hildeburh, who married Finn, king of the Jutes.

B. The Jutes or Frisians are represented as enemies of the Danes in the fight at Finnsburg and as allies of the Franks or Hugas at the time Hygelac the Geat made the attack in which he lost his life and from which Beowulf swam home. Also allied with the Franks at this time were the Hetware.

C. The Heatho-Bards (i.e., "Battle-Bards") are represented as inveterate enemies of the Danes. Their king Froda had been killed in an attack on the Danes, and

---

*The daughter of Hygelac who was given to Eofor may have been born to him by a former wife, older than Hygd.

Hrothgar's attempt to make peace with them by marrying his daughter Freawaru to Froda's son Ingeld failed when the latter attacked Heorot. The attack was repulsed, although Heorot was burned.

The Poet's Song in Heorot

To give the reader a sample of the language, style, and texture of *Beowulf* in the original we print the following passage, lines 90–98, in Old English with interlinear glosses. One may compare these lines with Cædmon's *Hymn* (pp. 29–32) on the same theme. See the headnote there for the pronunciation of Old English characters.

Sægde se þe   cuþe
Said   he who knew [how]

*f*rumsceaft   *f*ira   *f*eorran   reccan,
[the] origin [of] men   from far [time] [to]recount,

cwæð þæt se   Ælmightiga   *eo*rðan worhte,
said   that the Almighty   [the] earth wrought

*w*lite-beorhtne *w*ang,   swa *w*æter bebugeð,
beauty-bright   plain   as   water surrounds[it]

gesette sige-hreþig   sunnan ond monan,
    set   triumph-glorious   sun   and moon

*l*eoman   to *l*eohte   *l*andbuendum,
beacons   as light   [for] land-dwellers

ond gefrætwade   *f*oldan   sceatas
and adorned   [of]earth[the]grounds

*l*eomum ond *l*eafum,   *l*if   eac gesceop
[with]limbs and leaves,   life also[he]created

*c*ynna   gehwylcum*   þara ðe   cwice hwyrfaþ.
[of]kinds [for]each   [of]those who living move about

A NOTE ON NAMES

Old English, like Modern German, contained many compound words, most of which have been lost in Modern English. Most of the names in *Beowulf* are compounds. Hrothgar is a combination of words meaning "glory" and "spear"; the name of his older brother, Heorogar, comes from "army" and "spear"; Hrothgar's sons Hrethric and Hrothmund contain the first elements of their father's name combined, respectively, with *ric* (kingdom, empire; Modern German *Reich*) and *mund* (hand, protection). As in the case of the Danish dynasty, family names often alliterate. Masculine names of the warrior class have military associations. The importance of family and the demands of alliteration frequently lead to the designation of characters by formulas identifying them in terms of relationships. Thus Beowulf is referred to as "son of Ecgtheow" or "kinsman of Hygelac" (his uncle and lord).

---

*Modern syntax would be "for each of kinds." In Old English, the endings *-a* and *-um* indicate that *gewylcum* is an indirect object and *cynna*, a possessive plural.

The Old English spellings of names are mostly preserved in the translation. A few rules of pronunciation are worth keeping in mind. Initial *H* before *r* was sounded, and so Hrothgar's name alliterates with that of his brother Heorogar. The combination *cg* has the value of *dg* in words like "edge." The first element in the name of Beowulf's father "Ecgtheow" is the same word as "edge," and, by the figure of speech called synecdoche (a part of something stands for the whole), *ecg* stands for *sword* and Ecgtheow means "sword-servant."

For more information about *Beowulf*, see "The Linguistic and Literary Contexts of *Beowulf*," in the supplemental ebook.

Beowulf

[PROLOGUE: THE RISE OF THE DANISH NATION]

So. The Spear-Danes[1] in days gone by
and the kings who ruled them had courage and greatness.
We have heard of those princes' heroic campaigns.
There was Shield Sheafson,[2] scourge of many tribes,
5   a wrecker of mead-benches, rampaging among foes.
This terror of the hall-troops had come far.
A foundling to start with, he would flourish later on
as his powers waxed and his worth was proved.
In the end each clan on the outlying coasts
10   beyond the whale-road had to yield to him
and begin to pay tribute. That was one good king.
    Afterward a boy-child was born to Shield,
a cub in the yard, a comfort sent
by God to that nation. He knew what they had tholed,[3]
15   the long times and troubles they'd come through
without a leader; so the Lord of Life,
the glorious Almighty, made this man renowned.
Shield had fathered a famous son:
Beow's name was known through the north.
20   And a young prince must be prudent like that,
giving freely while his father lives
so that afterward in age when fighting starts
steadfast companions will stand by him
and hold the line. Behavior that's admired
25   is the path to power among people everywhere.
    Shield was still thriving when his time came
and he crossed over into the Lord's keeping.
His warrior band did what he bade them
when he laid down the law among the Danes:
30   they shouldered him out to the sea's flood,
the chief they revered who had long ruled them.

1. There are different compound names for tribes, often determined by alliteration in Old English poetry. Line 1 reads, *"Hwæt, we Gar-dena in gear-dagum,"* where alliteration falls on *Gar* (spear) and *gear* (year). Old English hard and soft g (spelled *y* in Modern English) alliterate. The compound *geardagum* derives from "year," used in the special sense of "long ago," and "days" and survives in the archaic expression "days of yore."

2. Shield is the name of the founder of the Danish royal line. Sheafson translates *Scefing*, i.e., *sheaf* + the patronymic suffix-*ing*. Because Sheaf was a "foundling" (line 7: *feasceaft funden*, i.e., found destitute) who arrived by sea (lines 45–46), it is likely that as a child Shield brought with him only a sheaf, a symbol of fruitfulness.

3. Suffered, endured.

A ring-whorled prow rode in the harbor,
ice-clad, outbound, a craft for a prince.
They stretched their beloved lord in his boat,
35 laid out by the mast, amidships,
the great ring-giver. Far-fetched treasures
were piled upon him, and precious gear.
I never heard before of a ship so well furbished
with battle-tackle, bladed weapons
40 and coats of mail. The massed treasure
was loaded on top of him: it would travel far
on out into the ocean's sway.
They decked his body no less bountifully
with offerings than those first ones did
45 who cast him away when he was a child
and launched him alone out over the waves.[4]
And they set a gold standard up
high above his head and let him drift
to wind and tide, bewailing him
50 and mourning their loss. No man can tell,
no wise man in hall or weathered veteran
knows for certain who salvaged that load.

    Then it fell to Beow to keep the forts.
He was well regarded and ruled the Danes
55 for a long time after his father took leave
of his life on earth. And then his heir,
the great Halfdane,[5] held sway
for as long as he lived, their elder and warlord.
He was four times a father, this fighter prince:
60 one by one they entered the world,
Heorogar, Hrothgar, the good Halga,
and a daughter, I have heard, who was Onela's queen,
a balm in bed to the battle-scarred Swede.
    The fortunes of war favored Hrothgar.
65 Friends and kinsmen flocked to his ranks,
young followers, a force that grew
to be a mighty army. So his mind turned
to hall-building: he handed down orders
for men to work on a great mead-hall
70 meant to be a wonder of the world forever;
it would be his throne-room and there he would dispense
his God-given goods to young and old—
but not the common land or people's lives.[6]
Far and wide through the world, I have heard,
75 orders for work to adorn that wallstead
were sent to many peoples. And soon it stood there
finished and ready, in full view,
the hall of halls. Heorot was the name[7]

---

4. See n. 2, p. 41. Since Shield was found destitute, "no less bountifully" is litotes or understatement; the ironic reminder that he came with
nothing (line 43) emphasizes the reversal of his
fortunes.
5. Probably named so because, according to one

source, his mother was a Swedish princess.
6. The king could not dispose of land used by all,
such as a common pasture, or of slaves.
7. I.e., "Hart," from antlers fastened to the gables
or because the crossed gable-ends resembled a
stag's antlers; the hart was also an icon of royalty.

he had settled on it, whose utterance was law.
80   Nor did he renege, but doled out rings
and torques at the table. The hall towered,
its gables wide and high and awaiting
a barbarous burning.[8] That doom abided,
but in time it would come: the killer instinct
85   unleashed among in-laws, the blood-lust rampant.[9]

[HEOROT IS ATTACKED]

Then a powerful demon,[1] a prowler through the dark,
nursed a hard grievance. It harrowed him
to hear the din of the loud banquet
every day in the hall, the harp being struck
90   and the clear song of a skilled poet
telling with mastery of man's beginnings,
how the Almighty had made the earth
a gleaming plain girdled with waters;
in His splendor He set the sun and the moon
95   to be earth's lamplight, lanterns for men,
and filled the broad lap of the world
with branches and leaves; and quickened life
in every other thing that moved.
So times were pleasant for the people there
100   until finally one, a fiend out of hell,
began to work his evil in the world.
Grendel was the name of this grim demon
haunting the marches, marauding round the heath
and the desolate fens; he had dwelt for a time
105   in misery among the banished monsters,
Cain's clan, whom the Creator had outlawed
and condemned as outcasts.[2] For the killing of Abel
the Eternal Lord had exacted a price:
Cain got no good from committing that murder
110   because the Almighty made him anathema
and out of the curse of his exile there sprang
ogres and elves and evil phantoms
and the giants too who strove with God
time and again until He gave them their reward.
115   So, after nightfall, Grendel set out
for the lofty house, to see how the Ring-Danes
were settling into it after their drink,
and there he came upon them, a company of the best
asleep from their feasting, insensible to pain
120   and human sorrow. Suddenly then
the God-cursed brute was creating havoc:
greedy and grim, he grabbed thirty men
from their resting places and rushed to his lair,

---

8. An allusion to the future destruction of Heorot
by fire, probably in a raid by the Heatho-Bards.
9. As told later (lines 2020–69), Hrothgar plans to
marry a daughter to Ingeld, chief of the Heatho-
Bards, in hopes of resolving a long-standing feud.

See previous note.
1. The poet withholds the name for several lines.
He does the same with the name of the hero as
well as others.
2. See Genesis 4.9–12.

flushed up and inflamed from the raid,
125   blundering back with the butchered corpses.
      Then as dawn brightened and the day broke,
Grendel's powers of destruction were plain:
their wassail was over, they wept to heaven
and mourned under morning. Their mighty prince,
130   the storied leader, sat stricken and helpless,
humiliated by the loss of his guard,
bewildered and stunned, staring aghast
at the demon's trail, in deep distress.
He was numb with grief, but got no respite
135   for one night later merciless Grendel
struck again with more gruesome murders.
Malignant by nature, he never showed remorse.
It was easy then to meet with a man
shifting himself to a safer distance
140   to bed in the bothies[3] for who could be blind
to the evidence of his eyes, the obviousness
of the hall-watcher's hate? Whoever escaped
kept a weather-eye open and moved away.
      So Grendel ruled in defiance of right,
145   one against all, until the greatest house
in the world stood empty, a deserted wallstead.
For twelve winters, seasons of woe,
the lord of the Shieldings[4] suffered under
his load of sorrow; and so, before long,
150   the news was known over the whole world.
Sad lays were sung about the beset king,
the vicious raids and ravages of Grendel,
his long and unrelenting feud,
nothing but war; how he would never
155   parley or make peace with any Dane
nor stop his death-dealing nor pay the death-price.[5]
No counselor could ever expect
fair reparation from those rabid hands.
All were endangered; young and old
160   were hunted down by that dark death-shadow
who lurked and swooped in the long nights
on the misty moors; nobody knows
where these reavers from hell roam on their errands.
      So Grendel waged his lonely war,
165   inflicting constant cruelties on the people,
atrocious hurt. He took over Heorot,
haunted the glittering hall after dark,
but the throne itself, the treasure-seat,
he was kept from approaching; he was the Lord's outcast.
170   These were hard times, heartbreaking
for the prince of the Shieldings; powerful counselors,
the highest in the land, would lend advice,

---

3. Huts, outlying buildings. Evidently Grendel wants only to dominate the hall.
4. The descendants of Shield, another name for the Danes.

5. I.e., *wergild* (man-price); monetary compensation for the life of the slain man is the only way, according to Germanic law, to settle a feud peacefully.

plotting how best the bold defenders
might resist and beat off sudden attacks.
175 Sometimes at pagan shrines they vowed
offerings to idols, swore oaths
that the killer of souls[6] might come to their aid
and save the people. That was their way,
their heathenish hope; deep in their hearts
180 they remembered hell. The Almighty Judge
of good deeds and bad, the Lord God,
Head of the Heavens and High King of the World,
was unknown to them. Oh, cursed is he
who in time of trouble has to thrust his soul
185 in the fire's embrace, forfeiting help;
he has nowhere to turn. But blessed is he
who after death can approach the Lord
and find friendship in the Father's embrace.

[THE HERO COMES TO HEOROT]

So that troubled time continued, woe
190 that never stopped, steady affliction
for Halfdane's son, too hard an ordeal.
There was panic after dark, people endured
raids in the night, riven by the terror.
When he heard about Grendel, Hygelac's thane
195 was on home ground, over in Geatland.
There was no one else like him alive.
In his day, he was the mightiest man on earth,
highborn and powerful. He ordered a boat
that would ply the waves. He announced his plan:
200 to sail the swan's road and seek out that king,
the famous prince who needed defenders.
Nobody tried to keep him from going,
no elder denied him, dear as he was to them.
Instead, they inspected omens and spurred
205 his ambition to go, whilst he moved about
like the leader he was, enlisting men,
the best he could find; with fourteen others
the warrior boarded the boat as captain,
a canny pilot along coast and currents.
210 Time went by, the boat was on water,
in close under the cliffs.
Men climbed eagerly up the gangplank,
sand churned in surf, warriors loaded
a cargo of weapons, shining war-gear
215 in the vessel's hold, then heaved out,
away with a will in their wood-wreathed ship.
Over the waves, with the wind behind her
and foam at her neck, she flew like a bird
until her curved prow had covered the distance,
220 and on the following day, at the due hour,

6. I.e., the devil. Heathen gods were thought to be devils.

those seafarers sighted land,
sunlit cliffs, sheer crags
and looming headlands, the landfall they sought.
It was the end of their voyage and the Geats vaulted
225   over the side, out on to the sand,
and moored their ship. There was a clash of mail
and a thresh of gear. They thanked God
for that easy crossing on a calm sea.
     When the watchman on the wall, the Shieldings' lookout
230   whose job it was to guard the sea-cliffs,
saw shields glittering on the gangplank
and battle-equipment being unloaded
he had to find out who and what
the arrivals were. So he rode to the shore,
235   this horseman of Hrothgar's, and challenged them
in formal terms, flourishing his spear:
"What kind of men are you who arrive
rigged out for combat in your coats of mail,
sailing here over the sea-lanes
240   in your steep-hulled boat? I have been stationed
as lookout on this coast for a long time.
My job is to watch the waves for raiders,
any danger to the Danish shore.
Never before has a force under arms
245   disembarked so openly—not bothering to ask
if the sentries allowed them safe passage
or the clan had consented. Nor have I seen
a mightier man-at-arms on this earth
than the one standing here: unless I am mistaken,
250   he is truly noble. This is no mere
hanger-on in a hero's armor.
So now, before you fare inland
as interlopers, I have to be informed
about who you are and where you hail from.
255   Outsiders from across the water,
I say it again: the sooner you tell
where you come from and why, the better."
     The leader of the troop unlocked his word-hoard;
the distinguished one delivered this answer:
260   "We belong by birth to the Geat people
and owe allegiance to Lord Hygelac.
In his day, my father was a famous man,
a noble warrior-lord named Ecgtheow.
He outlasted many a long winter
265   and went on his way. All over the world
men wise in counsel continue to remember him.
We come in good faith to find your lord
and nation's shield, the son of Halfdane.
Give us the right advice and direction.
270   We have arrived here on a great errand
to the lord of the Danes, and I believe therefore
there should be nothing hidden or withheld between us.
So tell us if what we have heard is true

about this threat, whatever it is,
275 this danger abroad in the dark nights,
this corpse-maker mongering death
in the Shieldings' country. I come to proffer
my wholehearted help and counsel.
I can show the wise Hrothgar a way
280 to defeat his enemy and find respite—
if any respite is to reach him, ever.
I can calm the turmoil and terror in his mind.
Otherwise, he must endure woes
and live with grief for as long as his hall
285 stands at the horizon on its high ground."
    Undaunted, sitting astride his horse,
the coast-guard answered: "Anyone with gumption
and a sharp mind will take the measure
of two things: what's said and what's done.
290 I believe what you have told me, that you are a troop
loyal to our king. So come ahead
with your arms and your gear, and I will guide you.
What's more, I'll order my own comrades
on their word of honor to watch your boat
295 down there on the strand—keep her safe
in her fresh tar, until the time comes
for her curved prow to preen on the waves
and bear this hero back to Geatland.
May one so valiant and venturesome
300 come unharmed through the clash of battle."
    So they went on their way. The ship rode the water,
broad-beamed, bound by its hawser
and anchored fast. Boar-shapes[7] flashed
above their cheek-guards, the brightly forged
305 work of goldsmiths, watching over
those stern-faced men. They marched in step,
hurrying on till the timbered hall
rose before them, radiant with gold.
Nobody on earth knew of another
310 building like it. Majesty lodged there,
its light shone over many lands.
So their gallant escort guided them
to that dazzling stronghold and indicated
the shortest way to it; then the noble warrior
315 wheeled on his horse and spoke these words:
"It is time for me to go. May the Almighty
Father keep you and in His kindness
watch over your exploits. I'm away to the sea,
back on alert against enemy raiders."
320   It was a paved track, a path that kept them
in marching order. Their mail-shirts glinted,
hard and hand-linked; the high-gloss iron
of their armor rang. So they duly arrived

---

7. Carved images of boars were placed on helmets, probably as charms to protect the warriors.

in their grim war-graith[8] and gear at the hall,
325   and, weary from the sea, stacked wide shields
of the toughest hardwood against the wall,
then collapsed on the benches; battle-dress
and weapons clashed. They collected their spears
in a seafarers' stook, a stand of grayish
330   tapering ash. And the troops themselves
were as good as their weapons.
                            Then a proud warrior
questioned the men concerning their origins:
"Where do you come from, carrying these
decorated shields and shirts of mail,
335   these cheek-hinged helmets and javelins?
I am Hrothgar's herald and officer.
I have never seen so impressive or large
an assembly of strangers. Stoutness of heart,
bravery not banishment, must have brought you to Hrothgar."
340   The man whose name was known for courage,
the Geat leader, resolute in his helmet,
answered in return: "We are retainers
from Hygelac's band. Beowulf is my name.
If your lord and master, the most renowned
345   son of Halfdane, will hear me out
and graciously allow me to greet him in person,
I am ready and willing to report my errand."
    Wulfgar replied, a Wendel chief
renowned as a warrior, well known for his wisdom
350   and the temper of his mind: "I will take this message,
in accordance with your wish, to our noble king,
our dear lord, friend of the Danes,
the giver of rings. I will go and ask him
about your coming here, then hurry back
355   with whatever reply it pleases him to give."
    With that he turned to where Hrothgar sat,
an old man among retainers;
the valiant follower stood foursquare
in front of his king: he knew the courtesies.
360   Wulfgar addressed his dear lord:
"People from Geatland have put ashore.
They have sailed far over the wide sea.
They call the chief in charge of their band
by the name of Beowulf. They beg, my lord,
365   an audience with you, exchange of words
and formal greeting. Most gracious Hrothgar,
do not refuse them, but grant them a reply.
From their arms and appointment, they appear well born
and worthy of respect, especially the one
370   who has led them this far: he is formidable indeed."
    Hrothgar, protector of Shieldings, replied:
"I used to know him when he was a young boy.
His father before him was called Ecgtheow.

---

8. "Graith": archaic for apparel.

Hrethel the Geat[9] gave Ecgtheow
375   his daughter in marriage. This man is their son,
here to follow up an old friendship.
A crew of seamen who sailed for me once
with a gift-cargo across to Geatland
returned with marvelous tales about him:
380   a thane, they declared, with the strength of thirty
in the grip of each hand. Now Holy God
has, in His goodness, guided him here
to the West-Danes, to defend us from Grendel.
This is my hope; and for his heroism
385   I will recompense him with a rich treasure.
Go immediately, bid him and the Geats
he has in attendance to assemble and enter.
Say, moreover, when you speak to them,
they are welcome to Denmark."
                            At the door of the hall,
390   Wulfgar duly delivered the message:
"My lord, the conquering king of the Danes,
bids me announce that he knows your ancestry;
also that he welcomes you here to Heorot
and salutes your arrival from across the sea.
395   You are free now to move forward
to meet Hrothgar in helmets and armor,
but shields must stay here and spears be stacked
until the outcome of the audience is clear."
    The hero arose, surrounded closely
400   by his powerful thanes. A party remained
under orders to keep watch on the arms;
the rest proceeded, led by their prince
under Heorot's roof. And standing on the hearth
in webbed links that the smith had woven,
405   the fine-forged mesh of his gleaming mail-shirt,
resolute in his helmet, Beowulf spoke:
"Greetings to Hrothgar. I am Hygelac's kinsman,
one of his hall-troop. When I was younger,
I had great triumphs. Then news of Grendel,
410   hard to ignore, reached me at home:
sailors brought stories of the plight you suffer
in this legendary hall, how it lies deserted,
empty and useless once the evening light
hides itself under heaven's dome.
415   So every elder and experienced councilman
among my people supported my resolve
to come here to you, King Hrothgar,
because all knew of my awesome strength.
They had seen me boltered[1] in the blood of enemies
420   when I battled and bound five beasts,
raided a troll-nest and in the night-sea
slaughtered sea-brutes. I have suffered extremes
and avenged the Geats (their enemies brought it

9. Hygelac's father and Beowulf's grandfather.   1. Clotted, sticky.

upon themselves; I devastated them).

⁴²⁵ Now I mean to be a match for Grendel,
settle the outcome in single combat.
And so, my request, O king of Bright-Danes,
dear prince of the Shieldings, friend of the people
and their ring of defense, my one request
⁴³⁰ is that you won't refuse me, who have come this far,
the privilege of purifying Heorot,
with my own men to help me, and nobody else.
I have heard moreover that the monster scorns
in his reckless way to use weapons;
⁴³⁵ therefore, to heighten Hygelac's fame
and gladden his heart, I hereby renounce
sword and the shelter of the broad shield,
the heavy war-board: hand-to-hand
is how it will be, a life-and-death
⁴⁴⁰ fight with the fiend. Whichever one death fells
must deem it a just judgment by God.
If Grendel wins, it will be a gruesome day;
he will glut himself on the Geats in the war-hall,
swoop without fear on that flower of manhood
⁴⁴⁵ as on others before. Then my face won't be there
to be covered in death: he will carry me away
as he goes to ground, gorged and bloodied;
he will run gloating with my raw corpse
and feed on it alone, in a cruel frenzy
⁴⁵⁰ fouling his moor-nest. No need then
to lament for long or lay out my body:[2]
if the battle takes me, send back
this breast-webbing that Weland[3] fashioned
and Hrethel gave me, to Lord Hygelac.
⁴⁵⁵ Fate goes ever as fate must."
    Hrothgar, the helmet of Shieldings, spoke:
"Beowulf, my friend, you have traveled here
to favor us with help and to fight for us.
There was a feud one time, begun by your father.
⁴⁶⁰ With his own hands he had killed Heatholaf
who was a Wulfing; so war was looming
and his people, in fear of it, forced him to leave.
He came away then over rolling waves
to the South-Danes here, the sons of honor.
⁴⁶⁵ I was then in the first flush of kingship,
establishing my sway over the rich strongholds
of this heroic land. Heorogar,
my older brother and the better man,
also a son of Halfdane's, had died.
⁴⁷⁰ Finally I healed the feud by paying:
I shipped a treasure-trove to the Wulfings,
and Ecgtheow acknowledged me with oaths of allegiance.

2. I.e., for burial. Hrothgar will not need to give
Beowulf an expensive funeral.

3. Famed blacksmith in Germanic legend.

"It bothers me to have to burden anyone
with all the grief that Grendel has caused

475 and the havoc he has wreaked upon us in Heorot,
our humiliations. My household guard
are on the wane, fate sweeps them away
into Grendel's clutches—but God can easily
halt these raids and harrowing attacks!

480 "Time and again, when the goblets passed
and seasoned fighters got flushed with beer
they would pledge themselves to protect Heorot
and wait for Grendel with their whetted swords.
But when dawn broke and day crept in

485 over each empty, blood-spattered bench,
the floor of the mead-hall where they had feasted
would be slick with slaughter. And so they died,
faithful retainers, and my following dwindled.
Now take your place at the table, relish

490 the triumph of heroes to your heart's content."

[FEAST AT HEOROT]

Then a bench was cleared in that banquet hall
so the Geats could have room to be together
and the party sat, proud in their bearing,
strong and stalwart. An attendant stood by

495 with a decorated pitcher, pouring bright
helpings of mead. And the minstrel sang,
filling Heorot with his head-clearing voice,
gladdening that great rally of Geats and Danes.
From where he crouched at the king's feet,

500 Unferth, a son of Ecglaf's, spoke
contrary words. Beowulf's coming,
his sea-braving, made him sick with envy:
he could not brook or abide the fact
that anyone else alive under heaven

505 might enjoy greater regard than he did:
"Are you the Beowulf who took on Breca
in a swimming match on the open sea,
risking the water just to prove that you could win?
It was sheer vanity made you venture out

510 on the main deep. And no matter who tried,
friend or foe, to deflect the pair of you,
neither would back down: the sea-test obsessed you.
You waded in, embracing water,
taking its measure, mastering currents,

515 riding on the swell. The ocean swayed,
winter went wild in the waves, but you vied
for seven nights; and then he outswam you,
came ashore the stronger contender.
He was cast up safe and sound one morning

520 among the Heatho-Reams, then made his way
to where he belonged in Branding country,
home again, sure of his ground

in strongroom and bawn.[4] So Breca made good
his boast upon you and was proved right.
525 No matter, therefore, how you may have fared
in every bout and battle until now,
this time you'll be worsted; no one has ever
outlasted an entire night against Grendel."
     Beowulf, Ecgtheow's son, replied:
530 "Well, friend Unferth, you have had your say
about Breca and me. But it was mostly beer
that was doing the talking. The truth is this:
when the going was heavy in those high waves,
I was the strongest swimmer of all.
535 We'd been children together and we grew up
daring ourselves to outdo each other,
boasting and urging each other to risk
our lives on the sea. And so it turned out.
Each of us swam holding a sword,
540 a naked, hard-proofed blade for protection
against the whale-beasts. But Breca could never
move out farther or faster from me
than I could manage to move from him.
Shoulder to shoulder, we struggled on
545 for five nights, until the long flow
and pitch of the waves, the perishing cold,
night falling and winds from the north
drove us apart. The deep boiled up
and its wallowing sent the sea-brutes wild.
550 My armor helped me to hold out;
my hard-ringed chain-mail, hand-forged and linked,
a fine, close-fitting filigree of gold,
kept me safe when some ocean creature
pulled me to the bottom. Pinioned fast
555 and swathed in its grip, I was granted one
final chance: my sword plunged
and the ordeal was over. Through my own hands,
the fury of battle had finished off the sea-beast.
     "Time and again, foul things attacked me,
560 lurking and stalking, but I lashed out,
gave as good as I got with my sword.
My flesh was not for feasting on,
there would be no monsters gnawing and gloating
over their banquet at the bottom of the sea.
565 Instead, in the morning, mangled and sleeping
the sleep of the sword, they slopped and floated
like the ocean's leavings. From now on
sailors would be safe, the deep-sea raids
were over for good. Light came from the east,
570 bright guarantee of God, and the waves
went quiet; I could see headlands
and buffeted cliffs. Often, for undaunted courage,

---

4. Fortified outwork of a court or castle. The word was used by English planters in Ulster to describe
fortified dwellings they erected on lands confiscated from the Irish [Translator's note].

fate spares the man it has not already marked.
However it occurred, my sword had killed
575 nine sea-monsters. Such night dangers
and hard ordeals I have never heard of
nor of a man more desolate in surging waves.
But worn out as I was, I survived,
came through with my life. The ocean lifted
580 and laid me ashore, I landed safe
on the coast of Finland.
                         Now I cannot recall
any fight you entered, Unferth,
that bears comparison. I don't boast when I say
that neither you nor Breca were ever much
585 celebrated for swordsmanship
or for facing danger on the field of battle.
You killed your own kith and kin,
so for all your cleverness and quick tongue,
you will suffer damnation in the depths of hell.
590 The fact is, Unferth, if you were truly
as keen or courageous as you claim to be
Grendel would never have got away with
such unchecked atrocity, attacks on your king,
havoc in Heorot and horrors everywhere.
595 But he knows he need never be in dread
of your blade making a mizzle of his blood
or of vengeance arriving ever from this quarter—
from the Victory-Shieldings, the shoulderers of the spear.
He knows he can trample down you Danes
600 to his heart's content, humiliate and murder
without fear of reprisal. But he will find me different.
I will show him how Geats shape to kill
in the heat of battle. Then whoever wants to
may go bravely to mead, when the morning light,
605 scarfed in sun-dazzle, shines forth from the south
and brings another daybreak to the world."
    Then the gray-haired treasure-giver was glad;
far-famed in battle, the prince of Bright-Danes
and keeper of his people counted on Beowulf,
610 on the warrior's steadfastness and his word.
So the laughter started, the din got louder
and the crowd was happy. Wealhtheow came in,
Hrothgar's queen, observing the courtesies.
Adorned in her gold, she graciously saluted
615 the men in the hall, then handed the cup
first to Hrothgar, their homeland's guardian,
urging him to drink deep and enjoy it
because he was dear to them. And he drank it down
like the warlord he was, with festive cheer.
620 So the Helming woman went on her rounds,
queenly and dignified, decked out in rings,
offering the goblet to all ranks,
treating the household and the assembled troop,
until it was Beowulf's turn to take it from her hand.

625 With measured words she welcomed the Geat
and thanked God for granting her wish
that a deliverer she could believe in would arrive
to ease their afflictions. He accepted the cup,
a daunting man, dangerous in action
630 and eager for it always. He addressed Wealhtheow;
Beowulf, son of Ecgtheow, said:
"I had a fixed purpose when I put to sea.
As I sat in the boat with my band of men,
I meant to perform to the uttermost
635 what your people wanted or perish in the attempt,
in the fiend's clutches. And I shall fulfill that purpose,
prove myself with a proud deed
or meet my death here in the mead-hall."
This formal boast by Beowulf the Geat
640 pleased the lady well and she went to sit
by Hrothgar, regal and arrayed with gold.
    Then it was like old times in the echoing hall,
proud talk and the people happy,
loud and excited; until soon enough
645 Halfdane's heir had to be away
to his night's rest. He realized
that the demon was going to descend on the hall,
that he had plotted all day, from dawn light
until darkness gathered again over the world
650 and stealthy night-shapes came stealing forth
under the cloud-murk. The company stood
as the two leaders took leave of each other:
Hrothgar wished Beowulf health and good luck,
named him hall-warden and announced as follows:
655 "Never, since my hand could hold a shield
have I entrusted or given control
of the Danes' hall to anyone but you.
Ward and guard it, for it is the greatest of houses.
Be on your mettle now, keep in mind your fame,
660 beware of the enemy. There's nothing you wish for
that won't be yours if you win through alive."

[THE FIGHT WITH GRENDEL]

    Hrothgar departed then with his house-guard.
The lord of the Shieldings, their shelter in war,
left the mead-hall to lie with Wealhtheow,
665 his queen and bedmate. The King of Glory
(as people learned) had posted a lookout
who was a match for Grendel, a guard against monsters,
special protection to the Danish prince.
And the Geat placed complete trust
670 in his strength of limb and the Lord's favor.
He began to remove his iron breast-mail,
took off the helmet and handed his attendant
the patterned sword, a smith's masterpiece,
ordering him to keep the equipment guarded.

675 And before he bedded down, Beowulf,
that prince of goodness, proudly asserted:
"When it comes to fighting, I count myself
as dangerous any day as Grendel.
So it won't be a cutting edge I'll wield
680 to mow him down, easily as I might.
He has no idea of the arts of war,
of shield or sword-play, although he does possess
a wild strength. No weapons, therefore,
for either this night: unarmed he shall face me
685 if face me he dares. And may the Divine Lord
in His wisdom grant the glory of victory
to whichever side He sees fit."
    Then down the brave man lay with his bolster
under his head and his whole company
690 of sea-rovers at rest beside him.
None of them expected he would ever see   → The Geats
his homeland again or get back
to his native place and the people who reared him. They're still loyal
They knew too well the way it was before,
695 how often the Danes had fallen prey
to death in the mead-hall. But the Lord was weaving
a victory on His war-loom for the Weather-Geats.
Through the strength of one they all prevailed;
they would crush their enemy and come through
700 in triumph and gladness. The truth is clear:
Almighty God rules over mankind
and always has.
                Then out of the night
came the shadow-stalker, stealthy and swift.
The hall-guards were slack, asleep at their posts,
705 all except one; it was widely understood
that as long as God disallowed it,
the fiend could not bear them to his shadow-bourne.
One man, however, was in fighting mood,
awake and on edge, spoiling for action.
710   In off the moors, down through the mist-bands
God-cursed Grendel came greedily loping.
The bane of the race of men roamed forth,
hunting for a prey in the high hall.
Under the cloud-murk he moved toward it
715 until it shone above him, a sheer keep
of fortified gold. Nor was that the first time
he had scouted the grounds of Hrothgar's dwelling—
‹jected although never in his life, before or since,
did he find harder fortune or hall-defenders.
720 Spurned and joyless, he journeyed on ahead
and arrived at the bawn.[5] The iron-braced door
turned on its hinge when his hands touched it.
Then his rage boiled over, he ripped open
the mouth of the building, maddening for blood,

5. See p. 52, n. 4.

725 pacing the length of the patterned floor
with his loathsome tread, while a baleful light,
flame more than light, flared from his eyes.
He saw many men in the mansion, sleeping,
a ranked company of kinsmen and warriors
730 quartered together. And his glee was demonic,
picturing the mayhem: before morning
he would rip life from limb and devour them,
feed on their flesh; but his fate that night
was due to change, his days of ravening
735 had come to an end.
                Mighty and canny,
Hygelac's kinsman was keenly watching
for the first move the monster would make.
Nor did the creature keep him waiting
but struck suddenly and started in;
740 he grabbed and mauled a man on his bench, — *Drinking*
bit into his bone-lappings, bolted down his blood
and gorged on him in lumps, leaving the body
utterly lifeless, eaten up
hand and foot. Venturing closer,

Image

745 his talon was raised to attack Beowulf
where he lay on the bed, he was bearing in
with open claw when the alert hero's
comeback and armlock forestalled him utterly.
The captain of evil discovered himself
750 in a handgrip harder than anything
he had ever encountered in any man
on the face of the earth. Every bone in his body
quailed and recoiled, but he could not escape.
He was desperate to flee to his den and hide
755 with the devil's litter, for in all his days
he had never been clamped or cornered like this.
Then Hygelac's trusty retainer recalled
his bedtime speech, sprang to his feet
and got a firm hold. Fingers were bursting,
760 the monster back-tracking, the man overpowering.
The dread of the land was desperate to escape,
to take a roundabout road and flee
to his lair in the fens. The latching power
in his fingers weakened; it was the worst trip
765 the terror-monger had taken to Heorot.
And now the timbers trembled and sang,
a hall-session[6] that harrowed every Dane
inside the stockade: stumbling in fury,
the two contenders crashed through the building.
770 The hall clattered and hammered, but somehow
survived the onslaught and kept standing:
it was handsomely structured, a sturdy frame
braced with the best of blacksmith's work
inside and out. The story goes

---

6. In Hiberno-English the word "session" (*seissiún* in Irish) can mean a gathering where musicians and singers perform for their own enjoyment [Translator's note].

775   that as the pair struggled, mead-benches were smashed
and sprung off the floor, gold fittings and all.
Before then, no Shielding elder would believe
there was any power or person upon earth
capable of wrecking their horn-rigged hall
780   unless the burning embrace of a fire
engulf it in flame. Then an extraordinary
wail arose, and bewildering fear
came over the Danes. Everyone felt it
who heard that cry as it echoed off the wall,
785   a God-cursed scream and strain of catastrophe,
the howl of the loser, the lament of the hell-serf
keening his wound. He was overwhelmed,
manacled tight by the man who of all men
was foremost and strongest in the days of this life.
790   But the earl-troop's leader was not inclined] *understatement*
to allow his caller to depart alive:
he did not consider that life of much account
to anyone anywhere. Time and again,
Beowulf's warriors worked to defend
795   their lord's life, laying about them
as best they could, with their ancestral blades.
Stalwart in action, they kept striking out
on every side, seeking to cut
straight to the soul. When they joined the struggle
800   there was something they could not have known at the time,
that no blade on earth, no blacksmith's art
could ever damage their demon opponent.
He had conjured the harm from the cutting edge
of every weapon.[7] But his going away
805   out of this world and the days of his life
would be agony to him, and his alien spirit
would travel far into fiends' keeping.
       Then he who had harrowed the hearts of men
with pain and affliction in former times
810   and had given offense also to God
found that his bodily powers failed him.
Hygelac's kinsman kept him helplessly
locked in a handgrip. As long as either lived,
he was hateful to the other. The monster's whole
815   body was in pain; a tremendous wound
appeared on his shoulder. Sinews split
and the bone-lappings burst. Beowulf was granted
the glory of winning; Grendel was driven
under the fen-banks, fatally hurt,
820   to his desolate lair. His days were numbered,
the end of his life was coming over him,
he knew it for certain; and one bloody clash
had fulfilled the dearest wishes of the Danes.
The man who had lately landed among them,
825   proud and sure, had purged the hall,
kept it from harm; he was happy with his nightwork

---

7. Grendel is protected by a charm against metals.

and the courage he had shown. The Geat captain
had boldly fulfilled his boast to the Danes:
he had healed and relieved a huge distress,
830   unremitting humiliations,
the hard fate they'd been forced to undergo,
no small affliction. Clear proof of this
could be seen in the hand the hero displayed
high up near the roof: the whole of Grendel's
835   shoulder and arm, his awesome grasp.

[CELEBRATION AT HEOROT]

Then morning came and many a warrior
gathered, as I've heard, around the gift-hall,
clan-chiefs flocking from far and near
down wide-ranging roads, wondering greatly
840   at the monster's footprints. His fatal departure
was regretted by no one who witnessed his trail,
the ignominious marks of his flight
where he'd skulked away, exhausted in spirit
and beaten in battle, bloodying the path,
845   hauling his doom to the demons' mere.[8]
The bloodshot water wallowed and surged,
there were loathsome upthrows and overturnings
of waves and gore and wound-slurry.
With his death upon him, he had dived deep
850   into his marsh-den, drowned out his life
and his heathen soul: hell claimed him there.
Then away they rode, the old retainers
with many a young man following after,
a troop on horseback, in high spirits
855   on their bay steeds. Beowulf's doings
were praised over and over again.
Nowhere, they said, north or south
between the two seas or under the tall sky
on the broad earth was there anyone better
860   to raise a shield or to rule a kingdom.
Yet there was no laying of blame on their lord,
the noble Hrothgar; he was a good king.
At times the war-band broke into a gallop,
letting their chestnut horses race
865   wherever they found the going good
on those well-known tracks. Meanwhile, a thane
of the king's household, a carrier of tales,
a traditional singer deeply schooled
in the lore of the past, linked a new theme
870   to a strict meter.[9] The man started
to recite with skill, rehearsing Beowulf's
triumphs and feats in well-fashioned lines,
entwining his words.
            He told what he'd heard

---

8. A lake or pool, although we learn later that it
has an outlet to the sea. Grendel's habitat.

9. I.e., an extemporaneous heroic poem in alliterative verse about Beowulf's deeds.

repeated in songs about Sigemund's exploits,[1]
875 all of those many feats and marvels,
the struggles and wanderings of Waels's son,[2]
things unknown to anyone
except to Fitela, feuds and foul doings
confided by uncle to nephew when he felt
880 the urge to speak of them: always they had been
partners in the fight, friends in need.
They killed giants, their conquering swords
had brought them down.

After his death
Sigemund's glory   grew and grew
885 because of his courage   when he killed the dragon,
the guardian of the hoard.   Under gray stone
he had dared to enter   all by himself
to face the worst   without Fitela.
But it came to pass   that his sword plunged
890 right through   those radiant scales
and drove into the wall.   The dragon died of it.
His daring had given him   total possession
of the treasure-hoard,   his to dispose of
however he liked.   He loaded a boat:
895 Waels's son   weighted her hold
with dazzling spoils.   The hot dragon melted.
    Sigemund's name   was known everywhere.
He was utterly valiant   and venturesome,
a fence round his fighters   and flourished therefore
900 after King Heremod's[3]   prowess declined
and his campaigns slowed down.   The king was betrayed,
ambushed in Jutland,   overpowered
and done away with.   The waves of his grief
had beaten him down,   made him a burden,
905 a source of anxiety   to his own nobles:
that expedition   was often condemned
in those earlier times   by experienced men,
men who relied   on his lordship for redress,
who presumed that the part   of a prince was to thrive
910 on his father's throne   and defend the nation,
the Shielding land   where they lived and belonged,
its holdings and strongholds.   Such was Beowulf
in the affection of his friends   and of everyone alive.
But evil entered   into Heremod.
915   They kept racing each other, urging their mounts
down sandy lanes. The light of day
broke and kept brightening. Bands of retainers
galloped in excitement to the gabled hall
to see the marvel; and the king himself,
920 guardian of the ring-hoard, goodness in person,

1. Tales about Sigemund, his nephew Sinfjotli (Fitela), and his son Sigurth are found in a 13th-century Old Icelandic collection of legends known as the *Volsung Saga*. Analogous stories must have been known to the poet and his audi-ence, though details differ.
2. Waels is the father of Sigemund.
3. Heremod was a bad king, held up by the bard as the opposite of Beowulf, as Sigemund is held up as a heroic prototype of Beowulf.

walked in majesty from the women's quarters
with a numerous train, attended by his queen
and her crowd of maidens, across to the mead-hall.
    When Hrothgar arrived at the hall, he spoke,
925 standing on the steps, under the steep eaves,
gazing toward the roofwork and Grendel's talon:
"First and foremost, let the Almighty Father
be thanked for this sight. I suffered a long
harrowing by Grendel. But the Heavenly Shepherd
930 can work His wonders always and everywhere.
Not long since, it seemed I would never
be granted the slightest solace or relief
from any of my burdens: the best of houses
glittered and reeked and ran with blood.
935 This one worry outweighed all others—
a constant distress to counselors entrusted
with defending the people's forts from assault
by monsters and demons. But now a man,
with the Lord's assistance, has accomplished something
940 none of us could manage before now
for all our efforts. Whoever she was
who brought forth this flower of manhood,
if she is still alive, that woman can say
that in her labor the Lord of Ages
945 bestowed a grace on her. So now, Beowulf,
I adopt you in my heart as a dear son.
Nourish and maintain this new connection,
you noblest of men; there'll be nothing you'll want for,
no worldly goods that won't be yours.
950 I have often honored smaller achievements,
recognized warriors not nearly as worthy,
lavished rewards on the less deserving.
But you have made yourself immortal
by your glorious action. May the God of Ages
955 continue to keep and requite you well."
    Beowulf, son of Ecgtheow, spoke:
"We have gone through with a glorious endeavor
and been much favored in this fight we dared
against the unknown. Nevertheless,
960 if you could have seen the monster himself
where he lay beaten, I would have been better pleased.
My plan was to pounce, pin him down
in a tight grip and grapple him to death—
have him panting for life, powerless and clasped
965 in my bare hands, his body in thrall.
But I couldn't stop him from slipping my hold.
The Lord allowed it, my lock on him
wasn't strong enough; he struggled fiercely
and broke and ran. Yet he bought his freedom
970 at a high price, for he left his hand
and arm and shoulder to show he had been here,
a cold comfort for having come among us.
And now he won't be long for this world.
He has done his worst but the wound will end him.

975 He is hasped and hooped and hirpling with pain,
limping and looped in it. Like a man outlawed
for wickedness, he must await
the mighty judgment of God in majesty."
      There was less tampering and big talk then
980 from Unferth the boaster, less of his blather
as the hall-thanes eyed the awful proof
of the hero's prowess, the splayed hand
up under the eaves. Every nail,
claw-scale and spur, every spike
985 and welt on the hand of that heathen brute
was like barbed steel. Everybody said
there was no honed iron hard enough
to pierce him through, no time-proofed blade
that could cut his brutal, blood-caked claw.
990   Then the order was given for all hands
to help to refurbish Heorot immediately:
men and women thronging the wine-hall,
getting it ready. Gold thread shone
in the wall-hangings, woven scenes
995 that attracted and held the eye's attention.
But iron-braced as the inside of it had been,
that bright room lay in ruins now.
The very doors had been dragged from their hinges.
Only the roof remained unscathed
1000 by the time the guilt-fouled fiend turned tail
in despair of his life. But death is not easily
escaped from by anyone:
all of us with souls, earth-dwellers
and children of men, must make our way
1005 to a destination already ordained
where the body, after the banqueting,
sleeps on its deathbed.
                              Then the due time arrived
for Halfdane's son to proceed to the hall.
The king himself would sit down to feast.
1010 No group ever gathered in greater numbers
or better order around their ring-giver.
The benches filled with famous men
who fell to with relish; round upon round
of mead was passed; those powerful kinsmen,
1015 Hrothgar and Hrothulf, were in high spirits
in the raftered hall. Inside Heorot
there was nothing but friendship. The Shielding nation
was not yet familiar with feud and betrayal.[4]
      Then Halfdane's son presented Beowulf
1020 with a gold standard as a victory gift,
an embroidered banner; also breast-mail
and a helmet; and a sword carried high,
that was both precious object and token of honor.
So Beowulf drank his drink, at ease;

4. Probably an ironic allusion to the future usurpation of the throne from Hrothgar's sons by Hrothulf,
although no such treachery is recorded of Hrothulf, who is the hero of other Germanic stories.

1025   it was hardly a shame to be showered with such gifts
      in front of the hall-troops. There haven't been many
      moments, I am sure, when men exchanged
      four such treasures at so friendly a sitting.
      An embossed ridge, a band lapped with wire
1030   arched over the helmet: head-protection
      to keep the keen-ground cutting edge
      from damaging it when danger threatened
      and the man was battling behind his shield.
      Next the king ordered eight horses
1035   with gold bridles to be brought through the yard
      into the hall. The harness of one
      included a saddle of sumptuous design,
      the battle-seat where the son of Halfdane
      rode when he wished to join the sword-play:
1040   wherever the killing and carnage were the worst,
      he would be to the fore, fighting hard.
      Then the Danish prince, descendant of Ing,
      handed over both the arms and the horses,
      urging Beowulf to use them well.
1045   And so their leader, the lord and guard
      of coffer and strongroom, with customary grace
      bestowed upon Beowulf both sets of gifts.
      A fair witness can see how well each one behaved.
      The chieftain went on to reward the others:
1050   each man on the bench who had sailed with Beowulf
      and risked the voyage received a bounty,
      some treasured possession. And compensation,
      a price in gold, was settled for the Geat
      Grendel had cruelly killed earlier—
1055   as he would have killed more, had not mindful God
      and one man's daring prevented that doom.
      Past and present, God's will prevails.
      Hence, understanding is always best
      and a prudent mind. Whoever remains
1060   for long here in this earthly life
      will enjoy and endure more than enough.
         They sang then and played to please the hero,
      words and music for their warrior prince,
      harp tunes and tales of adventure:
1065   there were high times on the hall benches,
      and the king's poet performed his part
      with the saga of Finn and his sons, unfolding
      the tale of the fierce attack in Friesland
      where Hnaef, king of the Danes, met death.[5]

---

5. The bard's lay is known as the Finnsburg Episode. Its allusive style makes the tale obscure in many details, although some can be filled in from a fragmentary Old English lay, which modern editors have entitled *The Fight at Finnsburg*. Hildeburh, the daughter of the former Danish king Hoc, was married to Finn, king of Friesland, presumably to help end a feud between their peoples. As the episode opens, the feud has already broken out again when a visiting party of Danes, led by Hildeburh's brother Hnaef, who has succeeded their father, is attacked by a tribe called the Jutes. The Jutes are subject to Finn but may be a clan distinct from the Frisians, and Finn does not seem to have instigated the attack. In the ensuing battle, both Hnaef and the son of Hildeburh and Finn are killed, and both sides suffer heavy losses.

1070　Hildeburh
　　　　　　had little cause
　　to credit the Jutes:
　　　　　　　　son and brother,
　　she lost them both
　　　　　　　　on the battlefield.
　　She, bereft
　　　　　　and blameless, they
　　foredoomed, cut down
　　　　　　　　and spear-gored. She,
1075　the woman in shock,
　　　　　　　　waylaid by grief,
　　Hoc's daughter—
　　　　　　how could she not
　　lament her fate
　　　　　　when morning came
　　and the light broke
　　　　　　　　on her murdered dears?
　　And so farewell
　　　　　　delight on earth,
1080　war carried away
　　　　　　　　Finn's troop of thanes
　　all but a few.
　　　　　　How then could Finn
　　hold the line
　　　　　　or fight on
　　to the end with Hengest,
　　　　　　　　how save
　　the rump of his force
　　　　　　　　from that enemy chief?
1085　So a truce was offered
　　　　　　　　as follows:[6] first
　　separate quarters
　　　　　　　　to be cleared for the Danes,
　　hall and throne
　　　　　　　　to be shared with the Frisians.
　　Then, second:
　　　　　　　every day
　　at the dole-out of gifts
　　　　　　　　Finn, son of Focwald,
1090　should honor the Danes,
　　　　　　　　bestow with an even
　　hand to Hengest
　　　　　　　and Hengest's men
　　the wrought-gold rings,
　　　　　　　　bounty to match
　　the measure he gave
　　　　　　　his own Frisians—
　　to keep morale
　　　　　　　in the beer-hall high.

---

6. The truce was offered by Finn to Hengest, who succeeded Hnaef as leader of the Danes.

1095 Both sides then
　　　　　　sealed their agreement.
　　With oaths to Hengest
　　　　　　　　　Finn swore
　　openly, solemnly,
　　　　　　　　that the battle survivors
　　would be guaranteed
　　　　　　　　honor and status.
　　No infringement
　　　　　　　by word or deed,
1100 no provocation
　　　　　　　would be permitted.
　　Their own ring-giver
　　　　　　　　after all
　　was dead and gone,
　　　　　　　　they were leaderless,
　　in forced allegiance
　　　　　　　to his murderer.
　　So if any Frisian
　　　　　　　stirred up bad blood
1105 with insinuations
　　　　　　　or taunts about this,
　　the blade of the sword
　　　　　　　　would arbitrate it.
　　A funeral pyre
　　　　　　　was then prepared,
　　effulgent gold
　　　　　　　brought out from the hoard.
　　The pride and prince
　　　　　　　of the Shieldings lay
1110 awaiting the flame.
　　　　　　　Everywhere
　　there were blood-plastered
　　　　　　　　　coats of mail.
　　The pyre was heaped
　　　　　　　with boar-shaped helmets
　　forged in gold,
　　　　　　　with the gashed corpses
　　of wellborn Danes—
　　　　　　　many had fallen.
1115 Then Hildeburh
　　　　　　　ordered her own
　　son's body
　　　　　　　be burnt with Hnaef's,
　　the flesh on his bones
　　　　　　　to sputter and blaze
　　beside his uncle's.
　　　　　　　The woman wailed
　　and sang keens,
　　　　　　　the warrior went up.[7]

7. The meaning may be that the warrior was placed up on the pyre, or went up in smoke. "Keens":
lamentations or dirges for the dead.

1120 Carcass flame
                    swirled and fumed,
      they stood round the burial
                           mound and howled
      as heads melted,
                    crusted gashes
      spattered and ran
                    bloody matter.
      The glutton element
                    flamed and consumed
1125 the dead of both sides.
                           Their great days were gone.
      Warriors scattered
                    to homes and forts
      all over Friesland,
                    fewer now, feeling
      loss of friends.
                    Hengest stayed,
      lived out that whole
                    resentful, blood-sullen
1130 winter with Finn,
                    homesick and helpless.
      No ring-whorled prow
                    could up then
      and away on the sea.
                    Wind and water
      raged with storms,
                    wave and shingle
      were shackled in ice
                    until another year
1135 appeared in the yard
                    as it does to this day,
      the seasons constant,
                    the wonder of light
      coming over us.
                    Then winter was gone,
      earth's lap grew lovely,
                    longing woke
      in the cooped-up exile
                    for a voyage home—
1140 but more for vengeance,
                    some way of bringing
      things to a head:
                    his sword arm hankered
      to greet the Jutes.
                    So he did not balk
      once Hunlafing
                    placed on his lap
      Dazzle-the-Duel,
                    the best sword of all,[8]

---

8. Hunlafing may be the son of a Danish warrior called Hunlaf. The placing of the sword in Hengest's lap is a symbolic call for revenge.

1145   *whose edges Jutes*
                        knew only too well.
    Thus blood was spilled,
                      the gallant Finn
    slain in his home
                    after Guthlaf and Oslaf[9]
    back from their voyage
                      made old accusation:
    the brutal ambush,
                    the fate they had suffered,
1150   *all blamed on Finn.*
                    The wildness in them
    had to brim over.
                  The hall ran red
    with blood of enemies.
                  Finn was cut down,
    the queen brought away
                    and everything
    the Shieldings could find
                  inside Finn's walls—
1155   *the Frisian king's*
                  gold collars and gemstones—
    swept off to the ship.
                  Over sea-lanes then
    back to Daneland
                  the warrior troop
    bore that lady home.

                The poem was over,
the poet had performed, a pleasant murmur
1160 started on the benches, stewards did the rounds
with wine in splendid jugs, and Wealhtheow came to sit
in her gold crown between two good men,
uncle and nephew, each one of whom
still trusted the other;[1] and the forthright Unferth,
1165 admired by all for his mind and courage
although under a cloud for killing his brothers,
reclined near the king.
                The queen spoke:
"Enjoy this drink, my most generous lord;
raise up your goblet, entertain the Geats
1170 duly and gently, discourse with them,
be open-handed, happy and fond.
Relish their company, but recollect as well
all of the boons that have been bestowed on you.
The bright court of Heorot has been cleansèd
1175 and now the word is that you want to adopt
this warrior as a son. So, while you may,
bask in your fortune, and then bequeath

---

9. It is not clear whether the Danes have traveled home and then returned to Friesland with reinforcements, or whether the Danish survivors attack once the weather allows them to take ship.
1. See n. 4, p. 61.

kingdom and nation to your kith and kin,
before your decease. I am certain of Hrothulf.
He is noble and will use the young ones well.
He will not let you down. Should you die before him,
he will treat our children truly and fairly.
He will honor, I am sure, our two sons,
repay them in kind, when he recollects
all the good things we gave him once,
the favor and respect he found in his childhood."
She turned then to the bench where her boys sat,
Hrethric and Hrothmund, with other nobles' sons,
all the youth together; and that good man,
Beowulf the Geat, sat between the brothers.
     The cup was carried to him, kind words
spoken in welcome and a wealth of wrought gold
graciously bestowed: two arm bangles,
a mail-shirt and rings, and the most resplendent
torque of gold I ever heard tell of
anywhere on earth or under heaven.
There was no hoard like it since Hama snatched
the Brosings' neck-chain and bore it away
with its gems and settings to his shining fort,
away from Eormenric's wiles and hatred,[2]
and thereby ensured his eternal reward.
Hygelac the Geat, grandson of Swerting,
wore this neck-ring on his last raid;[3]
at bay under his banner, he defended the booty,
treasure he had won. Fate swept him away
because of his proud need to provoke
a feud with the Frisians. He fell beneath his shield,
in the same gem-crusted, kingly gear
he had worn when he crossed the frothing wave-vat.
So the dead king fell into Frankish hands.
They took his breast-mail, also his neck-torque,
and punier warriors plundered the slain
when the carnage ended; Geat corpses
covered the field.
                    Applause filled the hall.
Then Wealhtheow pronounced in the presence of the company:
"Take delight in this torque, dear Beowulf,
wear it for luck and wear also this mail
from our people's armory: may you prosper in them!
Be acclaimed for strength, for kindly guidance
to these two boys, and your bounty will be sure.
You have won renown: you are known to all men
far and near, now and forever.
Your sway is wide as the wind's home,

1180
1185
1190
1195
1200
1205
1210
1215
1220

2. The necklace presented to Beowulf is compared to one worn by the goddess Freya in Germanic mythology. In another story it was stolen
by Hama from the Gothic king Eormenric, who
is treated as a tyrant in Germanic legend, but
how Eormenric came to possess it is not known.
3. Later we learn that Beowulf gave the necklace
to Hygd, the queen of his lord Hygelac. Hygelac
is here said to have been wearing it on his last
expedition. This is the first of several allusions to
Hygelac's death on a raid up the Rhine, the one
incident in the poem that can be connected to a
historical event documented elsewhere.

as the sea around cliffs. And so, my prince,
1225 I wish you a lifetime's luck and blessings
to enjoy this treasure. Treat my sons
with tender care, be strong and kind.
Here each comrade is true to the other,
loyal to lord, loving in spirit.
1230 The thanes have one purpose, the people are ready:
having drunk and pledged, the ranks do as I bid."
    She moved then to her place. Men were drinking wine
at that rare feast; how could they know fate,
the grim shape of things to come,
1235 the threat looming over many thanes
as night approached and King Hrothgar prepared
to retire to his quarters? Retainers in great numbers
were posted on guard as so often in the past.
Benches were pushed back, bedding gear and bolsters
1240 spread across the floor, and one man
lay down to his rest, already marked for death.
At their heads they placed their polished timber
battle-shields; and on the bench above them,
each man's kit was kept to hand:
1245 a towering war-helmet, webbed mail-shirt
and great-shafted spear. It was their habit
always and everywhere to be ready for action,
at home or in the camp, in whatever case
and at whatever time the need arose
1250 to rally round their lord. They were a right people.

[ANOTHER ATTACK]

    They went to sleep. And one paid dearly
for his night's ease, as had happened to them often,
ever since Grendel occupied the gold-hall,
committing evil until the end came,
1255 death after his crimes. Then it became clear,
obvious to everyone once the fight was over,
that an avenger lurked and was still alive,
grimly biding time. Grendel's mother,
monstrous hell-bride, brooded on her wrongs.
1260 She had been forced down into fearful waters,
the cold depths, after Cain had killed
his father's son, felled his own
brother with a sword. Branded an outlaw,
marked by having murdered, he moved into the wilds,
1265 shunned company and joy. And from Cain there sprang
misbegotten spirits, among them Grendel,
the banished and accursed, due to come to grips
with that watcher in Heorot waiting to do battle.
The monster wrenched and wrestled with him,
1270 but Beowulf was mindful of his mighty strength,
the wondrous gifts God had showered on him:
he relied for help on the Lord of All,
on His care and favor. So he overcame the foe,

brought down the hell-brute. Broken and bowed,
1275 outcast from all sweetness, the enemy of mankind
made for his death-den. But now his mother
had sallied forth on a savage journey,
grief-racked and ravenous, desperate for revenge.
    She came to Heorot. There, inside the hall,
1280 Danes lay asleep, earls who would soon endure
a great reversal, once Grendel's mother
attacked and entered. Her onslaught was less
only by as much as an amazon warrior's
strength is less than an armed man's
1285 when the hefted sword, its hammered edge
and gleaming blade slathered in blood,
razes the sturdy boar-ridge off a helmet.
Then in the hall, hard-honed swords
were grabbed from the bench, many a broad shield
1290 lifted and braced; there was little thought of helmets
or woven mail when they woke in terror.
    The hell-dam was in panic, desperate to get out,
in mortal terror the moment she was found.
She had pounced and taken one of the retainers
1295 in a tight hold, then headed for the fen.
To Hrothgar, this man was the most beloved
of the friends he trusted between the two seas.
She had done away with a great warrior,
ambushed him at rest.
                  Beowulf was elsewhere.
1300 Earlier, after the award of the treasure,
the Geat had been given another lodging.
    There was uproar in Heorot. She had snatched their trophy,
Grendel's bloodied hand. It was a fresh blow
to the afflicted bawn. The bargain was hard,
1305 both parties having to pay
with the lives of friends. And the old lord,
the gray-haired warrior, was heartsore and weary
when he heard the news: his highest-placed adviser,
his dearest companion, was dead and gone.
1310 Beowulf was quickly brought to the chamber:
the winner of fights, the arch-warrior,
came first-footing in with his fellow troops
to where the king in his wisdom waited,
still wondering whether Almighty God
1315 would ever turn the tide of his misfortunes.
So Beowulf entered with his band in attendance
and the wooden floorboards banged and rang
as he advanced, hurrying to address
the prince of the Ingwins, asking if he'd rested
1320 since the urgent summons had come as a surprise.
    Then Hrothgar, the Shieldings' helmet, spoke:
"Rest? What is rest? Sorrow has returned.
Alas for the Danes! Aeschere is dead.
He was Yrmenlaf's elder brother
1325 and a soul-mate to me, a true mentor,

my right-hand man when the ranks clashed
and our boar-crests had to take a battering
in the line of action. Aeschere was everything
the world admires in a wise man and a friend.
1330   Then this roaming killer came in a fury
and slaughtered him in Heorot. Where she is hiding,
glutting on the corpse and glorying in her escape,
I cannot tell; she has taken up the feud
because of last night, when you killed Grendel,
1335   wrestled and racked him in ruinous combat
since for too long he had terrorized us
with his depredations. He died in battle,
paid with his life; and now this powerful
other one arrives, this force for evil
1340   driven to avenge her kinsman's death.
Or so it seems to thanes in their grief,
in the anguish every thane endures
at the loss of a ring-giver, now that the hand
that bestowed so richly has been stilled in death.
1345   "I have heard it said by my people in hall,
counselors who live in the upland country,
that they have seen two such creatures
prowling the moors, huge marauders
from some other world. One of these things,
1350   as far as anyone ever can discern,
looks like a woman; the other, warped
in the shape of a man, moves beyond the pale
bigger than any man, an unnatural birth
called Grendel by the country people
1355   in former days. They are fatherless creatures,
and their whole ancestry is hidden in a past
of demons and ghosts. They dwell apart
among wolves on the hills, on windswept crags
and treacherous keshes, where cold streams
1360   pour down the mountain and disappear
under mist and moorland.
                            A few miles from here
a frost-stiffened wood waits and keeps watch
above a mere; the overhanging bank
is a maze of tree-roots mirrored in its surface.
1365   At night there, something uncanny happens:
the water burns. And the mere bottom
has never been sounded by the sons of men.
On its bank, the heather-stepper halts:
the hart in flight from pursuing hounds
1370   will turn to face them with firm-set horns
and die in the wood rather than dive
beneath its surface. That is no good place.
When wind blows up and stormy weather
makes clouds scud and the skies weep,
1375   out of its depths a dirty surge
is pitched toward the heavens. Now help depends
again on you and on you alone.

[handwritten annotations: "All the more monstrous" and "Buck / Male Deer"]

The gap of danger where the demon waits
is still unknown to you. Seek it if you dare.
1380 I will compensate you for settling the feud
as I did the last time with lavish wealth,
coffers of coiled gold, if you come back."

[BEOWULF FIGHTS GRENDEL'S MOTHER]

Beowulf, son of Ecgtheow, spoke:
"Wise sir, do not grieve. It is always better
1385 to avenge dear ones than to indulge in mourning.
For every one of us, living in this world
means waiting for our end. Let whoever can
win glory before death. When a warrior is gone,
that will be his best and only bulwark.
1390 So arise, my lord, and let us immediately
set forth on the trail of this troll-dam.
I guarantee you: she will not get away,
not to dens under ground nor upland groves
nor the ocean floor. She'll have nowhere to flee to.
1395 Endure your troubles today. Bear up
and be the man I expect you to be."
    With that the old lord sprang to his feet
and praised God for Beowulf's pledge.
Then a bit and halter were brought for his horse
1400 with the plaited mane. The wise king mounted
the royal saddle and rode out in style
with a force of shield-bearers. The forest paths
were marked all over with the monster's tracks,
her trail on the ground wherever she had gone
1405 across the dark moors, dragging away
the body of that thane, Hrothgar's best
counselor and overseer of the country.
So the noble prince proceeded undismayed
up fells and screes, along narrow footpaths
1410 and ways where they were forced into single file,
ledges on cliffs above lairs of water-monsters.
He went in front with a few men,
good judges of the lie of the land,
and suddenly discovered the dismal wood,
1415 mountain trees growing out at an angle
above gray stones: the bloodshot water
surged underneath. It was a sore blow
to all of the Danes, friends of the Shieldings,
a hurt to each and every one
1420 of that noble company when they came upon
Aeschere's head at the foot of the cliff.
    Everybody gazed as the hot gore
kept wallowing up and an urgent war-horn
repeated its notes: the whole party
1425 sat down to watch. The water was infested
with all kinds of reptiles. There were writhing sea-dragons
and monsters slouching on slopes by the cliff,

serpents and wild things such as those that often
surface at dawn to roam the sail-road
1430   and doom the voyage. Down they plunged,
lashing in anger at the loud call
of the battle-bugle. An arrow from the bow
of the Geat chief got one of them
as he surged to the surface: the seasoned shaft
1435   stuck deep in his flank and his freedom in the water
got less and less. It was his last swim.
He was swiftly overwhelmed in the shallows,
prodded by barbed boar-spears,
cornered, beaten, pulled up on the bank,
1440   a strange lake-birth, a loathsome catch
men gazed at in awe.
                        Beowulf got ready,
donned his war-gear, indifferent to death;
his mighty, hand-forged, fine-webbed mail
would soon meet with the menace underwater.
1445   It would keep the bone-cage of his body safe:
no enemy's clasp could crush him in it,
no vicious armlock choke his life out.
To guard his head he had a glittering helmet
that was due to be muddied on the mere bottom
1450   and blurred in the upswirl. It was of beaten gold,
princely headgear hooped and hasped
by a weapon-smith who had worked wonders
in days gone by and adorned it with boar-shapes;
since then it had resisted every sword.
1455   And another item lent by Unferth
at that moment of need was of no small importance:
the brehon[4] handed him a hilted weapon,
a rare and ancient sword named Hrunting.
The iron blade with its ill-boding patterns
1460   had been tempered in blood. It had never failed
the hand of anyone who hefted it in battle,
anyone who had fought and faced the worst
in the gap of danger. This was not the first time
it had been called to perform heroic feats.
1465   When he lent that blade to the better swordsman,
Unferth, the strong-built son of Ecglaf,
could hardly have remembered the ranting speech
he had made in his cups. He was not man enough
to face the turmoil of a fight under water
1470   and the risk to his life. So there he lost
fame and repute. It was different for the other
rigged out in his gear, ready to do battle.
      Beowulf, son of Ecgtheow, spoke:
"Wisest of kings, now that I have come
1475   to the point of action, I ask you to recall
what we said earlier: that you, son of Halfdane

---

4. One of an ancient class of lawyers in Ireland [Translator's note]. The Old English word for Unferth's
office, *thyle*, has been interpreted as "orator" and "spokesman."

and gold-friend to retainers, that you, if I should fall
and suffer death while serving your cause,
would act like a father to me afterward.
1480 If this combat kills me, take care
of my young company, my comrades in arms.
And be sure also, my beloved Hrothgar,
to send Hygelac the treasures I received.
Let the lord of the Geats gaze on that gold,
1485 let Hrethel's son take note of it and see
that I found a ring-giver of rare magnificence
and enjoyed the good of his generosity.
And Unferth is to have what I inherited:
to that far-famed man I bequeath my own
1490 sharp-honed, wave-sheened wonder-blade.
With Hrunting I shall gain glory or die."
     After these words, the prince of the Weather-Geats
was impatient to be away and plunged suddenly:
without more ado, he dived into the heaving
1495 depths of the lake. It was the best part of a day
before he could see the solid bottom.
     Quickly the one who haunted those waters,
who had scavenged and gone her gluttonous rounds
for a hundred seasons, sensed a human
1500 observing her outlandish lair from above.
So she lunged and clutched and managed to catch him
in her brutal grip; but his body, for all that,
remained unscathed: the mesh of the chain-mail
saved him on the outside. Her savage talons
1505 failed to rip the web of his war-shirt.
Then once she touched bottom, that wolfish swimmer
carried the ring-mailed prince to her court
so that for all his courage he could never use
the weapons he carried; and a bewildering horde
1510 came at him from the depths, droves of sea-beasts
who attacked with tusks and tore at his chain-mail
in a ghastly onslaught. The gallant man
could see he had entered some hellish turn-hole
and yet the water there did not work against him
1515 because the hall-roofing held off
the force of the current; then he saw firelight,
a gleam and flare-up, a glimmer of brightness.
     The hero observed that swamp-thing from hell,
the tarn-hag in all her terrible strength,
1520 then heaved his war-sword and swung his arm:
the decorated blade came down ringing
and singing on her head. But he soon found
his battle-torch extinguished; the shining blade
refused to bite. It spared her and failed
1525 the man in his need. It had gone through many
hand-to-hand fight, had hewed the armor
and helmets of the doomed, but here at last
the fabulous powers of that heirloom failed.
     Hygelac's kinsman kept thinking about

1530 his name and fame: he never lost heart.
Then, in a fury, he flung his sword away.
The keen, inlaid, worm-loop-patterned steel
was hurled to the ground: he would have to rely
on the might of his arm. So must a man do
1535 who intends to gain enduring glory
in a combat. Life doesn't cost him a thought.
Then the prince of War-Geats, warming to this fight
with Grendel's mother, gripped her shoulder
and laid about him in a battle frenzy:
1540 he pitched his killer opponent to the floor
but she rose quickly and retaliated,
grappled him tightly in her grim embrace.
The sure-footed fighter felt daunted,
the strongest of warriors stumbled and fell.
1545 So she pounced upon him and pulled out
a broad, whetted knife: now she would avenge
her only child. But the mesh of chain-mail
on Beowulf's shoulder shielded his life,
turned the edge and tip of the blade.
1550 The son of Ecgtheow would have surely perished
and the Geats lost their warrior under the wide earth
had the strong links and locks of his war-gear
not helped to save him: holy God
decided the victory. It was easy for the Lord,
1555 the Ruler of Heaven, to redress the balance
once Beowulf got back up on his feet.
Then he saw a blade that boded well,
a sword in her armory, an ancient heirloom
from the days of the giants, an ideal weapon,
1560 one that any warrior would envy,
but so huge and heavy of itself
only Beowulf could wield it in a battle.
So the Shieldings' hero hard-pressed and enraged,
took a firm hold of the hilt and swung
1565 the blade in an arc, a resolute blow
that bit deep into her neck-bone
and severed it entirely, toppling the doomed
house of her flesh; she fell to the floor.
The sword dripped blood, the swordsman was elated.
1570   A light appeared and the place brightened
the way the sky does when heaven's candle
is shining clearly. He inspected the vault:
with sword held high, its hilt raised
to guard and threaten, Hygelac's thane
1575 scouted by the wall in Grendel's wake.
Now the weapon was to prove its worth.
The warrior determined to take revenge
for every gross act Grendel had committed—
and not only for that one occasion
1580 when he'd come to slaughter the sleeping troops,
fifteen of Hrothgar's house-guards
surprised on their benches and ruthlessly devoured,

and as many again carried away,
a brutal plunder. Beowulf in his fury
1585 now settled that score: he saw the monster
in his resting place, war-weary and wrecked,
a lifeless corpse, a casualty
of the battle in Heorot. The body gaped
at the stroke dealt to it after death:
1590 Beowulf cut the corpse's head off.
    Immediately the counselors keeping a lookout
with Hrothgar, watching the lake water,
saw a heave-up and surge of waves
and blood in the backwash. They bowed gray heads,
1595 spoke in their sage, experienced way
about the good warrior, how they never again
expected to see that prince returning
in triumph to their king. It was clear to many
that the wolf of the deep had destroyed him forever.
1600   The ninth hour of the day arrived.
The brave Shieldings abandoned the cliff-top
and the king went home; but sick at heart,
staring at the mere, the strangers held on.
They wished, without hope, to behold their lord,
Beowulf himself.
1605   Meanwhile, the sword
began to wilt into gory icicles
to slather and thaw. It was a wonderful thing,
the way it all melted as ice melts
when the Father eases the fetters off the frost
1610 and unravels the water-ropes, He who wields power
over time and tide: He is the true Lord.
    The Geat captain saw treasure in abundance
but carried no spoils from those quarters
except for the head and the inlaid hilt
1615 embossed with jewels; its blade had melted
and the scrollwork on it burned, so scalding was the blood
of the poisonous fiend who had perished there.
Then away he swam, the one who had survived
the fall of his enemies, flailing to the surface.
1620 The wide water, the waves and pools,
were no longer infested once the wandering fiend
let go of her life and this unreliable world.
    The seafarers' leader made for land,
resolutely swimming, delighted with his prize,
1625 the mighty load he was lugging to the surface.
His thanes advanced in a troop to meet him,
thanking God and taking great delight
in seeing their prince back safe and sound.
Quickly the hero's helmet and mail-shirt
1630 were loosed and unlaced. The lake settled,
clouds darkened above the bloodshot depths.
    With high hearts they headed away
along footpaths and trails through the fields,
roads that they knew, each of them wrestling

1635 with the head they were carrying from the lakeside cliff,
men kingly in their courage and capable
of difficult work. It was a task for four
to hoist Grendel's head on a spear
and bear it under strain to the bright hall.
1640 But soon enough they neared the place,
fourteen Geats in fine fettle,
striding across the outlying ground
in a delighted throng around their leader.
  In he came then, the thanes' commander,
1645 the arch-warrior, to address Hrothgar:
his courage was proven, his glory was secure.
Grendel's head was hauled by the hair,
dragged across the floor where the people were drinking,
a horror for both queen and company to behold.
1650 They stared in awe. It was an astonishing sight.

[ANOTHER CELEBRATION AT HEOROT]

  Beowulf, son of Ecgtheow, spoke:
"So, son of Halfdane, prince of the Shieldings,
we are glad to bring this booty from the lake.
It is a token of triumph and we tender it to you.
1655 I barely survived the battle under water.
It was hard-fought, a desperate affair
that could have gone badly; if God had not helped me,
the outcome would have been quick and fatal.
Although Hrunting is hard-edged,
1660 I could never bring it to bear in battle.
But the Lord of Men allowed me to behold—
for He often helps the unbefriended—
an ancient sword shining on the wall,
a weapon made for giants, there for the wielding.
1665 Then my moment came in the combat and I struck
the dwellers in that den. Next thing the damascened
sword blade melted; it bloated and it burned
in their rushing blood. I have wrested the hilt
from the enemies' hand, avenged the evil
1670 done to the Danes; it is what was due.
And this I pledge, O prince of the Shieldings:
you can sleep secure with your company of troops
in Heorot Hall. Never need you fear
for a single thane of your sept or nation,
1675 young warriors or old, that laying waste of life
that you and your people endured of yore."
  Then the gold hilt was handed over
to the old lord, a relic from long ago
for the venerable ruler. That rare smithwork
1680 was passed on to the prince of the Danes
when those devils perished; once death removed
that murdering, guilt-steeped, God-cursed fiend,
eliminating his unholy life
and his mother's as well, it was willed to that king

1685 who of all the lavish gift-lords of the north
was the best regarded between the two seas.
 Hrothgar spoke; he examined the hilt,
that relic of old times. It was engraved all over
and showed how war first came into the world
1690 and the flood destroyed the tribe of giants.
They suffered a terrible severance from the Lord;
the Almighty made the waters rise,
drowned them in the deluge for retribution.
In pure gold inlay on the sword-guards
1695 there were rune-markings correctly incised,
stating and recording for whom the sword
had been first made and ornamented
with its scrollworked hilt. Then everyone hushed
as the son of Halfdane spoke this wisdom:
1700 "A protector of his people, pledged to uphold
truth and justice and to respect tradition,
is entitled to affirm that this man
was born to distinction. Beowulf, my friend,
your fame has gone far and wide,
1705 you are known everywhere. In all things you are even-tempered,
prudent and resolute. So I stand firm by the promise of friendship
we exchanged before. Forever you will be
your people's mainstay and your own warriors'
helping hand.
 Heremod was different,
1710 the way he behaved to Ecgwela's sons.
His rise in the world brought little joy
to the Danish people, only death and destruction.
He vented his rage on men he caroused with,
killed his own comrades, a pariah king
1715 who cut himself off from his own kind,
even though Almighty God had made him
eminent and powerful and marked him from the start
for a happy life. But a change happened,
he grew bloodthirsty, gave no more rings
1720 to honor the Danes. He suffered in the end
for having plagued his people for so long:
his life lost happiness.
 So learn from this
and understand true values. I who tell you
have wintered into wisdom.
 It is a great wonder
1725 how Almighty God in His magnificence
favors our race with rank and scope
and the gift of wisdom; His sway is wide.
Sometimes He allows the mind of a man
of distinguished birth to follow its bent,
1730 grants him fulfillment and felicity on earth
and forts to command in his own country.
He permits him to lord it in many lands
until the man in his unthinkingness
forgets that it will ever end for him.

1735 He indulges his desires; illness and old age
mean nothing to him; his mind is untroubled
by envy or malice or the thought of enemies
with their hate-honed swords. The whole world
conforms to his will, he is kept from the worst
1740 until an element of overweening
enters him and takes hold
while the soul's guard, its sentry, drowses,
grown too distracted. A killer stalks him,
an archer who draws a deadly bow.
1745 And then the man is hit in the heart,
the arrow flies beneath his defenses,
the devious promptings of the demon start.
His old possessions seem paltry to him now.
He covets and resents; dishonors custom
1750 and bestows no gold; and because of good things
that the Heavenly Powers gave him in the past
he ignores the shape of things to come.
Then finally the end arrives
when the body he was lent collapses and falls
1755 prey to its death; ancestral possessions
and the goods he hoarded are inherited by another
who lets them go with a liberal hand.
    "O flower of warriors, beware of that trap.
Choose, dear Beowulf, the better part,
1760 eternal rewards. Do not give way to pride.
For a brief while your strength is in bloom
but it fades quickly; and soon there will follow
illness or the sword to lay you low,
or a sudden fire or surge of water
1765 or jabbing blade or javelin from the air
or repellent age. Your piercing eye
will dim and darken; and death will arrive,
dear warrior, to sweep you away.
    "Just so I ruled the Ring-Danes' country
1770 for fifty years, defended them in wartime
with spear and sword against constant assaults
by many tribes: I came to believe
my enemies had faded from the face of the earth.
Still, what happened was a hard reversal
1775 from bliss to grief. Grendel struck
after lying in wait. He laid waste to the land
and from that moment my mind was in dread
of his depredations. So I praise God
in His heavenly glory that I lived to behold
1780 this head dripping blood and that after such harrowing
I can look upon it in triumph at last.
Take your place, then, with pride and pleasure,
and move to the feast. Tomorrow morning
our treasure will be shared and showered upon you."
1785   The Geat was elated and gladly obeyed
the old man's bidding; he sat on the bench.
And soon all was restored, the same as before.

Happiness came back, the hall was thronged,
and a banquet set forth; black night fell
1790   and covered them in darkness.
                          Then the company rose
for the old campaigner: the gray-haired prince
was ready for bed. And a need for rest
came over the brave shield-bearing Geat.
He was a weary seafarer, far from home,
1795   so immediately a house-guard guided him out,
one whose office entailed looking after
whatever a thane on the road in those days
might need or require. It was noble courtesy.

[BEOWULF RETURNS HOME]

    That great heart rested. The hall towered,
1800   gold-shingled and gabled, and the guest slept in it
until the black raven with raucous glee
announced heaven's joy, and a hurry of brightness
overran the shadows. Warriors rose quickly,
impatient to be off: their own country
1805   was beckoning the nobles; and the bold voyager
longed to be aboard his distant boat.
Then that stalwart fighter ordered Hrunting
to be brought to Unferth, and bade Unferth
take the sword and thanked him for lending it.
1810   He said he had found it a friend in battle
and a powerful help; he put no blame
on the blade's cutting edge. He was a considerate man.
    And there the warriors stood in their war-gear,
eager to go, while their honored lord
1815   approached the platform where the other sat.
The undaunted hero addressed Hrothgar.
Beowulf, son of Ecgtheow, spoke:
"Now we who crossed the wide sea
have to inform you that we feel a desire
1820   to return to Hygelac. Here we have been welcomed
and thoroughly entertained. You have treated us well.
If there is any favor on earth I can perform
beyond deeds of arms I have done already,
anything that would merit your affections more,
1825   I shall act, my lord, with alacrity.
If ever I hear from across the ocean
that people on your borders are threatening battle
as attackers have done from time to time,
I shall land with a thousand thanes at my back
1830   to help your cause. Hygelac may be young
to rule a nation, but this much I know
about the king of the Geats: he will come to my aid
and want to support me by word and action
in your hour of need, when honor dictates
1835   that I raise a hedge of spears around you.
Then if Hrethric should think about traveling

as a king's son to the court of the Geats,
he will find many friends. Foreign places
yield more to one who is himself worth meeting."
1840   Hrothgar spoke and answered him:
"The Lord in his wisdom sent you those words
and they came from the heart. I have never heard
so young a man make truer observations.
You are strong in body and mature in mind,
1845   impressive in speech. If it should come to pass
that Hrethel's descendant dies beneath a spear,
if deadly battle or the sword blade or disease
fells the prince who guards your people
and you are still alive, then I firmly believe
1850   the seafaring Geats won't find a man
worthier of acclaim as their king and defender
than you, if only you would undertake
the lordship of your homeland. My liking for you
deepens with time, dear Beowulf.
1855   What you have done is to draw two peoples,
the Geat nation and us neighboring Danes,
into shared peace and a pact of friendship
in spite of hatreds we have harbored in the past.
For as long as I rule this far-flung land
1860   treasures will change hands and each side will treat
the other with gifts; across the gannet's bath,
over the broad sea, whorled prows will bring
presents and tokens. I know your people
are beyond reproach in every respect,
1865   steadfast in the old way with friend or foe."
    Then the earls' defender furnished the hero
with twelve treasures and told him to set out,
sail with those gifts safely home
to the people he loved, but to return promptly.
1870   And so the good and gray-haired Dane,
that highborn king, kissed Beowulf
and embraced his neck, then broke down
in sudden tears. Two forebodings
disturbed him in his wisdom, but one was stronger:
1875   nevermore would they meet each other
face to face. And such was his affection
that he could not help being overcome:
his fondness for the man was so deep-founded,
it warmed his heart and wound the heartstrings
1880   tight in his breast.
             The embrace ended
and Beowulf, glorious in his gold regalia,
stepped the green earth. Straining at anchor
and ready for boarding, his boat awaited him.
So they went on their journey, and Hrothgar's generosity
1885   was praised repeatedly. He was a peerless king
until old age sapped his strength and did him
mortal harm, as it has done so many.
    Down to the waves then, dressed in the web
of their chain-mail and war-shirts the young men marched

1890 in high spirits. The coast-guard spied them,
thanes setting forth, the same as before.
His salute this time from the top of the cliff
was far from unmannerly; he galloped to meet them
and as they took ship in their shining gear,
1895 he said how welcome they would be in Geatland.
Then the broad hull was beached on the sand
to be cargoed with treasure, horses and war-gear.
The curved prow motioned; the mast stood high
above Hrothgar's riches in the loaded hold.
1900 The guard who had watched the boat was given
a sword with gold fittings, and in future days
that present would make him a respected man
at his place on the mead-bench.
                                Then the keel plunged
and shook in the sea; and they sailed from Denmark.
1905 Right away the mast was rigged with its sea-shawl;
sail-ropes were tightened, timbers drummed
and stiff winds kept the wave-crosser
skimming ahead; as she heaved forward,
her foamy neck was fleet and buoyant,
1910 a lapped prow loping over currents,
until finally the Geats caught sight of coastline
and familiar cliffs. The keel reared up,
wind lifted it home, it hit on the land.
     The harbor guard came hurrying out
1915 to the rolling water: he had watched the offing
long and hard, on the lookout for those friends.
With the anchor cables, he moored their craft
right where it had beached, in case a backwash
might catch the hull and carry it away.
1920 Then he ordered the prince's treasure-trove
to be carried ashore. It was a short step
from there to where Hrethel's son and heir,
Hygelac the gold-giver, makes his home
on a secure cliff, in the company of retainers.
1925 The building was magnificent, the king majestic,
ensconced in his hall; and although Hygd, his queen,
was young, a few short years at court,
her mind was thoughtful and her manners sure.
Haereth's daughter behaved generously
1930 and stinted nothing when she distributed
bounty to the Geats.
                    Great Queen Modthryth
perpetrated terrible wrongs.[5]
If any retainer ever made bold
to look her in the face, if an eye not her lord's[6]

---

5. The story of Queen Modthryth's vices is abruptly introduced as a foil to Queen Hygd's virtues. A transitional passage may have been lost, but the poet's device is similar to that of using the earlier reference to the wickedness of King Heremod to contrast with the good qualities of Sigemund and Beowulf.

6. This could refer to her husband or her father before her marriage. The story resembles folktales about a proud princess whose unsuccessful suitors are all put to death, although the unfortunate victims in this case seem to be guilty only of looking at her.

1935 stared at her directly during daylight,
     the outcome was sealed: he was kept bound,
     in hand-tightened shackles, racked, tortured
     until doom was pronounced—death by the sword,
     slash of blade, blood-gush, and death-qualms
1940 in an evil display. Even a queen
     outstanding in beauty must not overstep like that.
     A queen should weave peace, not punish the innocent
     with loss of life for imagined insults.
     But Hemming's kinsman[7] put a halt to her ways
1945 and drinkers round the table had another tale:
     she was less of a bane to people's lives,
     less cruel-minded, after she was married
     to the brave Offa, a bride arrayed
     in her gold finery, given away
1950 by a caring father, ferried to her young prince
     over dim seas. In days to come
     she would grace the throne and grow famous
     for her good deeds and conduct of life,
     her high devotion to the hero king
1955 who was the best king, it has been said,
     between the two seas or anywhere else
     on the face of the earth. Offa was honored
     far and wide for his generous ways,
     his fighting spirit and his farseeing
1960 defense of his homeland; from him there sprang Eomer,
     Garmund's grandson, kinsman of Hemming,[8]
     his warriors' mainstay and master of the field.
         Heroic Beowulf and his band of men
     crossed the wide strand, striding along
1965 the sandy foreshore; the sun shone,
     the world's candle warmed them from the south
     as they hastened to where, as they had heard,
     the young king, Ongentheow's killer
     and his people's protector,[9] was dispensing rings
1970 inside his bawn. Beowulf's return
     was reported to Hygelac as soon as possible,
     news that the captain was now in the enclosure,
     his battle-brother back from the fray
     alive and well, walking to the hall.
1975 Room was quickly made, on the king's orders,
     and the troops filed across the cleared floor.
         After Hygelac had offered greetings
     to his loyal thane in a lofty speech,
     he and his kinsman, that hale survivor,
1980 sat face to face. Haereth's daughter

---

7. I.e., Offa I, a legendary king of the Angles. We know nothing about Hemming other than that Offa was related to him. Offa II (757–96) was king of Mercia, and although the story is about the second Offa's ancestor on the Continent, this is the only English connection in the poem and has been taken as evidence to date its origins to 8th-century Mercia.

8. I.e., Eomer, Offa's son. See previous note.

Garmund was presumably the name of Offa's father.

9. I.e., Hygelac. Ongentheow was king of the Swedish people called the Shylfings. This is the first of the references to wars between the Geats and the Swedes. One of Hygelac's war party named Eofer was the actual slayer of Ongentheow.

moved about with the mead-jug in her hand,
taking care of the company, filling the cups
that warriors held out. Then Hygelac began
to put courteous questions to his old comrade
1985 in the high hall. He hankered to know
every tale the Sea-Geats had to tell:
"How did you fare on your foreign voyage,
dear Beowulf, when you abruptly decided
to sail away across the salt water
1990 and fight at Heorot? Did you help Hrothgar
much in the end? Could you ease the prince
of his well-known troubles? Your undertaking
cast my spirits down, I dreaded the outcome
of your expedition and pleaded with you
1995 long and hard to leave the killer be,
let the South-Danes settle their own
blood-feud with Grendel. So God be thanked
I am granted this sight of you, safe and sound."
　　Beowulf, son of Ecgtheow, spoke:
2000 　"What happened, Lord Hygelac, is hardly a secret
any more among men in this world—
myself and Grendel coming to grips
on the very spot where he visited destruction
on the Victory-Shieldings and violated
2005 life and limb, losses I avenged
so no earthly offspring of Grendel's
need ever boast of that bout before dawn,
no matter how long the last of his evil
family survives.
　　　　　　　When I first landed
2010 I hastened to the ring-hall and saluted Hrothgar.
Once he discovered why I had come,
the son of Halfdane sent me immediately
to sit with his own sons on the bench.
It was a happy gathering. In my whole life
2015 I have never seen mead enjoyed more
in any hall on earth. Sometimes the queen
herself appeared, peace-pledge between nations,
to hearten the young ones and hand out
a torque to a warrior, then take her place.
2020 Sometimes Hrothgar's daughter distributed
ale to older ranks, in order on the benches:
I heard the company call her Freawaru
as she made her rounds, presenting men
with the gem-studded bowl, young bride-to-be
2025 to the gracious Ingeld,[1] in her gold-trimmed attire.
The friend of the Shieldings favors her betrothal:
the guardian of the kingdom sees good in it
and hopes this woman will heal old wounds
and grievous feuds.
　　　　　　　But generally the spear

Freawaru marries Ingeld to stop a feud

Similar to Finnsburg Episode

---

1. King of the Heatho-Bards; his father, Froda, was killed by the Danes.

2030 is prompt to retaliate when a prince is killed,
no matter how admirable the bride may be.
 "Think how the Heatho-Bards are bound to feel,
their lord, Ingeld, and his loyal thanes,
when he walks in with that woman to the feast:
2035 Danes are at the table, being entertained,
honored guests in glittering regalia,
burnished ring-mail that was their hosts' birthright,
looted when the Heatho-Bards could no longer wield
their weapons in the shield-clash, when they went down
2040 with their beloved comrades and forfeited their lives.
Then an old spearman will speak while they are drinking,
having glimpsed some heirloom that brings alive
memories of the massacre; his mood will darken
and heart-stricken, in the stress of his emotion,
2045 he will begin to test a young man's temper
and stir up trouble, starting like this:
'Now, my friend, don't you recognize
your father's sword, his favorite weapon,
the one he wore when he went out in his war-mask
2050 to face the Danes on that final day?
After Withergeld[2] died and his men were doomed,
the Shieldings quickly claimed the field;
and now here's a son of one or other
of those same killers coming through our hall
2055 overbearing us, mouthing boasts,
and rigged in armor that by right is yours.'
And so he keeps on, recalling and accusing,
working things up with bitter words
until one of the lady's retainers lies
2060 spattered in blood, split open
on his father's account.[3] The killer knows
the lie of the land and escapes with his life.
Then on both sides the oath-bound lords
will break the peace, a passionate hate
2065 will build up in Ingeld, and love for his bride
will falter in him as the feud rankles.
I therefore suspect the good faith of the Heatho-Bards,
the truth of their friendship and the trustworthiness
of their alliance with the Danes.
                                    But now, my lord,
2070 I shall carry on with my account of Grendel,
the whole story of everything that happened
in the hand-to-hand fight.
                            After heaven's gem
had gone mildly to earth, that maddened spirit,
the terror of those twilights, came to attack us
2075 where we stood guard, still safe inside the hall.
There deadly violence came down on Hondscio
and he fell as fate ordained, the first to perish,

[handwritten marginal note: only Geat killed]

---

2. One of the Heatho-Bard leaders.
3. I.e., the young Danish attendant is killed because
his father killed the father of the young Heatho-

Bard who has been egged on by the old veteran of
that campaign.

rigged out for the combat. A comrade from our ranks
had come to grief in Grendel's maw:
2080 he ate up the entire body.
There was blood on his teeth, he was bloated and dangerous,
all roused up, yet still unready
to leave the hall empty-handed;
renowned for his might, he matched himself against me,
2085 wildly reaching. He had this roomy pouch,
a strange accoutrement, intricately strung
and hung at the ready, a rare patchwork
of devilishly fitted dragon-skins.
I had done him no wrong, yet the raging demon
2090 wanted to cram me and many another
into this bag—but it was not to be
once I got to my feet in a blind fury.
It would take too long to tell how I repaid
the terror of the land for every life he took
2095 and so won credit for you, my king,
and for all your people. And although he got away
to enjoy life's sweetness for a while longer,
his right hand stayed behind him in Heorot,
evidence of his miserable overthrow
2100 as he dived into murk on the mere bottom.
    "I got lavish rewards from the lord of the Danes
for my part in the battle, beaten gold
and much else, once morning came
and we took our places at the banquet table.
2105 There was singing and excitement: an old reciter,
a carrier of stories, recalled the early days.
At times some hero made the timbered harp
tremble with sweetness, or related true
and tragic happenings; at times the king
2110 gave the proper turn to some fantastic tale;
or a battle-scarred veteran, bowed with age,
would begin to remember the martial deeds
of his youth and prime and be overcome
as the past welled up in his wintry heart.
2115   "We were happy there the whole day long
and enjoyed our time until another night
descended upon us. Then suddenly
the vehement mother avenged her son
and wreaked destruction. Death had robbed her,
2120 Geats had slain Grendel, so his ghastly dam
struck back and with bare-faced defiance
laid a man low. Thus life departed
from the sage Aeschere, an elder wise in counsel.
But afterward, on the morning following,
2125 the Danes could not burn the dead body
nor lay the remains of the man they loved
on his funeral pyre. She had fled with the corpse
and taken refuge beneath torrents on the mountain.
It was a hard blow for Hrothgar to bear,
2130 harder than any he had undergone before.
And so the heartsore king beseeched me

in your royal name to take my chances
underwater, to win glory
and prove my worth. He promised me rewards.
2135　Hence, as is well known, I went to my encounter
with the terror-monger at the bottom of the tarn.
For a while it was hand-to-hand between us,
then blood went curling along the currents
and I beheaded Grendel's mother in the hall
2140　with a mighty sword. I barely managed
to escape with my life; my time had not yet come.
But Halfdane's heir, the shelter of those earls,
again endowed me with gifts in abundance.
　　　"Thus the king acted with due custom.
2145　I was paid and recompensed completely,
given full measure and the freedom to choose
from Hothgar's treasures by Hrothgar himself.
These, King Hygelac, I am happy to present
to you as gifts. It is still upon your grace
2150　that all favor depends. I have few kinsmen
who are close, my king, except for your kind self."
Then he ordered the boar-framed standard to be brought,
the battle-topping helmet, the mail-shirt gray as hoar-frost,
and the precious war-sword; and proceeded with his speech:
2155　"When Hrothgar presented this war-gear to me
he instructed me, my lord, to give you some account
of why it signifies his special favor.
He said it had belonged to his older brother,
King Heorogar, who had long kept it,
2160　but that Heorogar had never bequeathed it
to his son Heoroward, that worthy scion,
loyal as he was. Enjoy it well."
　　　I heard four horses were handed over next.
Beowulf bestowed four bay steeds
2165　to go with the armor, swift gallopers,
all alike. So ought a kinsman act,
instead of plotting and planning in secret
to bring people to grief, or conspiring to arrange
the death of comrades. The warrior king
2170　was uncle to Beowulf and honored by his nephew:
each was concerned for the other's good.
　　　I heard he presented Hygd with a gorget,
the priceless torque that the prince's daughter,
Wealhtheow, had given him; and three horses,
2175　supple creatures brilliantly saddled.
The bright necklace would be luminous on Hygd's breast.
　　　Thus Beowulf bore himself with valor;
he was formidable in battle yet behaved with honor
and took no advantage; never cut down
2180　a comrade who was drunk, kept his temper
and, warrior that he was, watched and controlled
his God-sent strength and his outstanding
natural powers. He had been poorly regarded
for a long time, was taken by the Geats

2185 for less than he was worth:[4] and their lord too
    had never much esteemed him in the mead-hall.
    They firmly believed that he lacked force,
    that the prince was a weakling; but presently
    every affront to his deserving was reversed.
2190   The battle-famed king, bulwark of his earls,
    ordered a gold-chased heirloom of Hrethel's[5]
    to be brought in; it was the best example
    of a gem-studded sword in the Geat treasury.
    This he laid on Beowulf's lap
2195 and then rewarded him with land as well,
    seven thousand hides; and a hall and a throne.
    Both owned land by birth in that country,
    ancestral grounds; but the greater right
    and sway were inherited by the higher born.

[THE DRAGON WAKES]

2200 A lot was to happen in later days
    in the fury of battle. Hygelac fell
    and the shelter of Heardred's shield proved useless
    against the fierce aggression of the Shylfings:[6]
    ruthless swordsmen, seasoned campaigners,
2205 they came against him and his conquering nation,
    and with cruel force cut him down
    so that afterwards
                   the wide kingdom
    reverted to Beowulf. He ruled it well
    for fifty winters, grew old and wise
2210 as warden of the land
               until one began
    to dominate the dark, a dragon on the prowl
    from the steep vaults of a stone-roofed barrow
    where he guarded a hoard; there was a hidden passage,
    unknown to men, but someone[7] managed
2215 to enter by it and interfere
    with the heathen trove. He had handled and removed
    a gem-studded goblet; it gained him nothing,

4. There is no other mention of Beowulf's unpromising youth. This motif of the "Cinderella hero" and others, such as Grendel's magic pouch, are examples of folklore material, probably circulating orally, that made its way into the poem.
5. Hygelac's father and Beowulf's grandfather.
6. There are several references, some of them lengthy, to the wars between the Geats and the Swedes. Because these are highly allusive and not in chronological order, they are difficult to follow and keep straight. This outline, along with the Genealogies (p. 39), may serve as a guide. *Phase 1*: After the death of the Geat patriarch, King Hrethel (lines 2462–70), Ohthere and Onela, the sons of the Swedish king Ongentheow, invade Geat territory and inflict heavy casualties in a battle at Hreosnahill (lines 2472–78). *Phase 2*: The Geats invade Sweden under Haethcyn, King Hrethel's son who has succeeded him. At the battle of Ravenswood, the Geats capture Ongentheow's queen, but Ongen

theow counterattacks, rescues the queen, and kills Haethcyn. Hygelac, Haethcyn's younger brother, arrives with reinforcements; Ongentheow is killed in savage combat with two of Hygelac's men; and the Swedes are routed (lines 2479–89 and 2922–90). *Phase 3*: Eanmund and Eadgils, the sons of Ohthere (presumably dead), are driven into exile by their uncle Onela, who is now king of the Swedes. They are given refuge by Hygelac's son Heardred, who has succeeded his father. Onela invades Geatland and kills Heardred; his retainer Weohstan kills Eanmund; and after the Swedes withdraw, Beowulf becomes king (lines 2204–8, which follow, and 2379–90). *Phase 4*: Eadgils, supported by Beowulf, invades Sweden and kills Onela (lines 2391–96).
7. The following section was damaged by fire. In lines 2215–31 entire words and phrases are missing or indicated by only a few letters. Editorial attempts to reconstruct the text are conjectural and often disagree.

though with a thief's wiles he had outwitted
the sleeping dragon. That drove him into rage,
2220 as the people of that country would soon discover.
    The intruder who broached the dragon's treasure
and moved him to wrath had never meant to.
It was desperation on the part of a slave
fleeing the heavy hand of some master,
2225 guilt-ridden and on the run,
going to ground. But he soon began
to shake with terror;[8] . . . . . . in shock
the wretch . . . .
. . . . panicked and ran
2230 away with the precious . . . . . .
metalwork. There were many other
heirlooms heaped inside the earth-house,
because long ago, with deliberate care,
some forgotten person had deposited the whole
2235 rich inheritance of a highborn race
in this ancient cache. Death had come
and taken them all in times gone by
and the only one left to tell their tale,
the last of their line, could look forward to nothing
2240 but the same fate for himself: he foresaw that his joy
in the treasure would be brief.
                        A newly constructed
barrow stood waiting, on a wide headland
close to the waves, its entryway secured.
Into it the keeper of the hoard had carried
2245 all the goods and golden ware
worth preserving. His words were few:
"Now, earth, hold what earls once held
and heroes can no more; it was mined from you first
by honorable men. My own people
2250 have been ruined in war; one by one
they went down to death, looked their last
on sweet life in the hall. I am left with nobody
to bear a sword or to burnish plated goblets,
put a sheen on the cup. The companies have departed.
2255 The hard helmet, hasped with gold,
will be stripped of its hoops; and the helmet-shiner
who should polish the metal of the war-mask sleeps;
the coat of mail that came through all fights,
through shield-collapse and cut of sword,
2260 decays with the warrior. Nor may webbed mail
range far and wide on the warlord's back
beside his mustered troops. No trembling harp,
no tuned timber, no tumbling hawk
swerving through the hall, no swift horse
2265 pawing the courtyard. Pillage and slaughter
have emptied the earth of entire peoples."
And so he mourned as he moved about the world,
deserted and alone, lamenting his unhappiness

---

8. Lines 2227–30 are so damaged that they defy guesswork to reconstruct them.

day and night, until death's flood
2270 brimmed up in his heart.
                          Then an old harrower of the dark
happened to find the hoard open,
the burning one who hunts out barrows,
the slick-skinned dragon, threatening the night sky
with streamers of fire. People on the farms
2275 are in dread of him. He is driven to hunt out
hoards under ground, to guard heathen gold
through age-long vigils, though to little avail.
For three centuries, this scourge of the people
had stood guard on that stoutly protected
2280 underground treasury, until the intruder
unleashed its fury; he hurried to his lord
with the gold-plated cup and made his plea
to be reinstated. Then the vault was rifled,
the ring-hoard robbed, and the wretched man
2285 had his request granted. His master gazed
on that find from the past for the first time.
    When the dragon awoke, trouble flared again.
He rippled down the rock, writhing with anger
when he saw the footprints of the prowler who had stolen
2290 too close to his dreaming head.
So may a man not marked by fate
easily escape exile and woe
by the grace of God.
                    The hoard-guardian
scorched the ground as he scoured and hunted
2295 for the trespasser who had troubled his sleep.
Hot and savage, he kept circling and circling
the outside of the mound. No man appeared
in that desert waste, but he worked himself up
by imagining battle; then back in he'd go
2300 in search of the cup, only to discover
signs that someone had stumbled upon
the golden treasures. So the guardian of the mound,
the hoard-watcher, waited for the gloaming
with fierce impatience; his pent-up fury
2305 at the loss of the vessel made him long to hit back
and lash out in flames. Then, to his delight,
the day waned and he could wait no longer
behind the wall, but hurtled forth
in a fiery blaze. The first to suffer
2310 were the people on the land, but before long
it was their treasure-giver who would come to grief.
    The dragon began to belch out flames
and burn bright homesteads; there was a hot glow
that scared everyone, for the vile sky-winger
2315 would leave nothing alive in his wake.
Everywhere the havoc he wrought was in evidence.
Far and near, the Geat nation
bore the brunt of his brutal assaults
and virulent hate. Then back to the hoard
2320 he would dart before daybreak, to hide in his den.

He had swinged the land, swathed it in flame,
in fire and burning, and now he felt secure
in the vaults of his barrow; but his trust was unavailing.
    Then Beowulf was given bad news,
2325   the hard truth: his own home,
the best of buildings, had been burned to a cinder,
the throne-room of the Geats. It threw the hero
into deep anguish and darkened his mood:
the wise man thought he must have thwarted
2330   ancient ordinance of the eternal Lord,
broken His commandment. His mind was in turmoil,
unaccustomed anxiety and gloom
confused his brain; the fire-dragon
had razed the coastal region and reduced
2335   forts and earthworks to dust and ashes,
so the war-king planned and plotted his revenge.
The warriors' protector, prince of the hall-troop,
ordered a marvelous all-iron shield
from his smithy works. He well knew
2340   that linden boards would let him down
and timber burn. After many trials,
he was destined to face the end of his days,
in this mortal world, as was the dragon,
for all his long leasehold on the treasure.
2345   Yet the prince of the rings was too proud
to line up with a large army
against the sky-plague. He had scant regard
for the dragon as a threat, no dread at all
of its courage or strength, for he had kept going
2350   often in the past, through perils and ordeals
of every sort, after he had purged
Hrothgar's hall, triumphed in Heorot
and beaten Grendel. He outgrappled the monster
and his evil kin.
                One of his crudest
2355   hand-to-hand encounters had happened
when Hygelac, king of the Geats, was killed
in Friesland: the people's friend and lord,
Hrethel's son, slaked a swordblade's
thirst for blood. But Beowulf's prodigious
2360   gifts as a swimmer guaranteed his safety:
he arrived at the shore, shouldering thirty
battle-dresses, the booty he had won.
There was little for the Hetware[9] to be happy about
as they shielded their faces and fighting on the ground
2365   began in earnest. With Beowulf against them,
few could hope to return home.
    Across the wide sea, desolate and alone,
the son of Ecgtheow swam back to his people.
There Hygd offered him throne and authority
2370   as lord of the ring-hoard: with Hygelac dead,
she had no belief in her son's ability

---

9. A tribe of the Franks allied with the Frisians.

to defend their homeland against foreign invaders.
Yet there was no way the weakened nation
could get Beowulf to give in and agree
2375 to be elevated over Heardred as his lord
or to undertake the office of kingship.
But he did provide support for the prince,
honored and minded him until he matured
as the ruler of Geatland.
                      Then over sea-roads
2380 exiles arrived, sons of Ohthere.[1]
They had rebelled against the best of all
the sea-kings in Sweden, the one who held sway
in the Shylfing nation, their renowned prince,
lord of the mead-hall. That marked the end
2385 for Hygelac's son: his hospitality
was mortally rewarded with wounds from a sword.
Heardred lay slaughtered and Onela returned
to the land of Sweden, leaving Beowulf
to ascend the throne, to sit in majesty
2390 and rule over the Geats. He was a good king.
    In days to come, he contrived to avenge
the fall of his prince; he befriended Eadgils
when Eadgils was friendless, aiding his cause
with weapons and warriors over the wide sea,
2395 sending him men. The feud was settled
on a comfortless campaign when he killed Onela.
    And so the son of Ecgtheow had survived
every extreme, excelling himself
in daring and in danger, until the day arrived
2400 when he had to come face to face with the dragon.
The lord of the Geats took eleven comrades
and went in a rage to reconnoiter.
By then he had discovered the cause of the affliction
being visited on the people. The precious cup
2405 had come to him from the hand of the finder,
the one who had started all this strife
and was now added as a thirteenth to their number.
They press-ganged and compelled this poor creature
to be their guide. Against his will
2410 he led them to the earth-vault he alone knew,
an underground barrow near the sea-billows
and heaving waves, heaped inside
with exquisite metalwork. The one who stood guard
was dangerous and watchful, warden of the trove
2415 buried under earth: no easy bargain
would be made in that place by any man.
    The veteran king sat down on the cliff-top.
He wished good luck to the Geats who had shared
his hearth and his gold. He was sad at heart,
2420 unsettled yet ready, sensing his death.
His fate hovered near, unknowable but certain:
it would soon claim his coffered soul,

1. See p. 87, n. 6, Phases 3 and 4.

part life from limb. Before long
the prince's spirit would spin free from his body.
2425 Beowulf, son of Ecgtheow, spoke:
"Many a skirmish I survived when I was young
and many times of war: I remember them well.
At seven, I was fostered out by my father,
left in the charge of my people's lord.
2430 King Hrethel kept me and took care of me,
was openhanded, behaved like a kinsman.
While I was his ward, he treated me no worse
as a wean[2] about the place than one of his own boys,
Herebeald and Haethcyn, or my own Hygelac.
2435 For the eldest, Herebeald, an unexpected
deathbed was laid out, through a brother's doing,
when Haethcyn bent his horn-tipped bow
and loosed the arrow that destroyed his life.
He shot wide and buried a shaft
2440 in the flesh and blood of his own brother.
That offense was beyond redress; a wrongfooting
of the heart's affections; for who could avenge
the prince's life or pay his death-price?
It was like the misery endured by an old man
2445 who has lived to see his son's body
swing on the gallows. He begins to keen
and weep for his boy, watching the raven
gloat where he hangs: he can be of no help.
The wisdom of age is worthless to him.
2450 Morning after morning, he wakes to remember
that his child is gone; he has no interest
in living on until another heir
is born in the hall, now that his first-born
has entered death's dominion forever.
2455 He gazes sorrowfully at his son's dwelling,
the banquet hall bereft of all delight,
the windswept hearthstone; the horsemen are sleeping,
the warriors under ground; what was is no more.
No tunes from the harp, no cheer raised in the yard.
2460 Alone with his longing, he lies down on his bed
and sings a lament; everything seems too large,
the steadings and the fields.
                              Such was the feeling
of loss endured by the lord of the Geats
after Herebeald's death. He was helplessly placed
2465 to set to rights the wrong committed,
could not punish the killer in accordance with the law
of the blood-feud, although he felt no love for him.
Heartsore, wearied, he turned away
from life's joys, chose God's light
2470 and departed, leaving buildings and lands
to his sons, as a man of substance will.
    "Then over the wide sea Swedes and Geats
battled and feuded and fought without quarter.

2. A young child [Northern Ireland; Translator's note].

Hostilities broke out when Hrethel died.[3]
2475 Ongentheow's sons were unrelenting,
refusing to make peace, campaigning violently
from coast to coast, constantly setting up
terrible ambushes around Hreosnahill.
My own kith and kin avenged
2480 these evil events, as everybody knows,
but the price was high: one of them paid
with his life. Haethcyn, lord of the Geats,
met his fate there and fell in the battle.
Then, as I have heard, Hygelac's sword
2485 was raised in the morning against Ongentheow,
his brother's killer. When Eofor cleft
the old Swede's helmet, halved it open,
he fell, death-pale: his feud-calloused hand
could not stave off the fatal stroke.
2490   "The treasures that Hygelac lavished on me
I paid for when I fought, as fortune allowed me,
with my glittering sword. He gave me land
and the security land brings, so he had no call
to go looking for some lesser champion,
2495 some mercenary from among the Gifthas
or the Spear-Danes or the men of Sweden.
I marched ahead of him, always there
at the front of the line; and I shall fight like that
for as long as I live, as long as this sword
2500 shall last, which has stood me in good stead
late and soon, ever since I killed
Dayraven the Frank in front of the two armies.
He brought back no looted breastplate
to the Frisian king but fell in battle,
2505 their standard-bearer, highborn and brave.
No sword blade sent him to his death:
my bare hands stilled his heartbeats
and wrecked the bone-house. Now blade and hand,
sword and sword-stroke, will assay the hoard."

[BEOWULF ATTACKS THE DRAGON]

2510   Beowulf spoke, made a formal boast
for the last time: "I risked my life
often when I was young. Now I am old,
but as king of the people I shall pursue this fight
for the glory of winning, if the evil one will only
2515 abandon his earth-fort and face me in the open."
    Then he addressed each dear companion
one final time, those fighters in their helmets,
resolute and highborn: "I would rather not
use a weapon if I knew another way
2520 to grapple with the dragon and make good my boast
as I did against Grendel in days gone by.
But I shall be meeting molten venom
in the fire he breathes, so I go forth

3. See p. 87, n. 6, Phases 1 and 2.

in mail-shirt and shield. I won't shift a foot
2525 when I meet the cave-guard: what occurs on the wall
between the two of us will turn out as fate,
overseer of men, decides. I am resolved.
I scorn further words against this sky-borne foe.
    "Men-at-arms, remain here on the barrow,
2530 safe in your armor, to see which one of us
is better in the end at bearing wounds
in a deadly fray. This fight is not yours,
nor is it up to any man except me
to measure his strength against the monster
2535 or to prove his worth. I shall win the gold
by my courage, or else mortal combat,
doom of battle, will bear your lord away."
    Then he drew himself up beside his shield.
The fabled warrior in his war-shirt and helmet
2540 trusted in his own strength entirely
and went under the crag. No coward path.
    Hard by the rock-face that hale veteran,
a good man who had gone repeatedly
into combat and danger and come through,
2545 saw a stone arch and a gushing stream
that burst from the barrow, blazing and wafting
a deadly heat. It would be hard to survive
unscathed near the hoard, to hold firm
against the dragon in those flaming depths.
2550 Then he gave a shout. The lord of the Geats
unburdened his breast and broke out
in a storm of anger. Under gray stone
his voice challenged and resounded clearly.
Hate was ignited. The hoard-guard recognized
2555 a human voice, the time was over
for peace and parleying. Pouring forth
in a hot battle-fume, the breath of the monster
burst from the rock. There was a rumble under ground.
Down there in the barrow, Beowulf the warrior
2560 lifted his shield: the outlandish thing
writhed and convulsed and viciously
turned on the king, whose keen-edged sword,
an heirloom inherited by ancient right,
was already in his hand. Roused to a fury,
2565 each antagonist struck terror in the other.
Unyielding, the lord of his people loomed
by his tall shield, sure of his ground,
while the serpent looped and unleashed itself.
Swaddled in flames, it came gliding and flexing
2570 and racing toward its fate. Yet his shield defended
the renowned leader's life and limb
for a shorter time than he meant it to:
that final day was the first time
when Beowulf fought and fate denied him
2575 glory in battle. So the king of the Geats
raised his hand and struck hard

at the enameled scales, but scarcely cut through:
the blade flashed and slashed yet the blow
was far less powerful than the hard-pressed king
2580 had need of at that moment. The mound-keeper
went into a spasm and spouted deadly flames:
when he felt the stroke, battle-fire
billowed and spewed. Beowulf was foiled
of a glorious victory. The glittering sword,
2585 infallible before that day,
failed when he unsheathed it, as it never should have.
For the son of Ecgtheow, it was no easy thing
to have to give ground like that and go
unwillingly to inhabit another home
2590 in a place beyond; so every man must yield
the leasehold of his days.
                    Before long
the fierce contenders clashed again.
The hoard-guard took heart, inhaled and swelled up
and got a new wind; he who had once ruled
2595 was furled in fire and had to face the worst.
No help or backing was to be had then
from his highborn comrades; that hand-picked troop
broke ranks and ran for their lives
to the safety of the wood. But within one heart
2600 sorrow welled up: in a man of worth
the claims of kinship cannot be denied.
   His name was Wiglaf, a son of Weohstan's,
a well-regarded Shylfing warrior
related to Aelfhere.[4] When he saw his lord
2605 tormented by the heat of his scalding helmet,
he remembered the bountiful gifts bestowed on him,
how well he lived among the Waegmundings,
the freehold he inherited from his father[5] before him.
He could not hold back: one hand brandished
2610 the yellow-timbered shield, the other drew his sword—
an ancient blade that was said to have belonged
to Eanmund, the son of Ohthere, the one
Weohstan had slain when he was an exile without friends.
He carried the arms to the victim's kinfolk,
2615 the burnished helmet, the webbed chain-mail
and that relic of the giants. But Onela returned
the weapons to him, rewarded Weohstan
with Eanmund's war-gear. He ignored the blood-feud,
the fact that Eanmund was his brother's son.[6]
2620   Weohstan kept that war-gear for a lifetime,
the sword and the mail-shirt, until it was the son's turn

4. Although Wiglaf is here said to be a Shylfing (i.e., a Swede), in line 2607 we are told his family are Waegmundings, a clan of the Geats, which is also Beowulf's family. It was possible for a family to owe allegiance to more than one nation and to shift sides as a result of feuds. Nothing is known of Aelfhere.
5. I.e., Weohstan, who, as explained below, was the slayer of Onela's nephew Eanmund. Possibly,

Weohstan joined the Geats under Beowulf after Eanmund's brother, with Beowulf's help, avenged Eanmund's death on Onela and became king of the Shylfings. See p. 87, n. 6, Phase 2.
6. An ironic comment: since Onela wanted to kill Eanmund, he rewarded Weohstan for killing his nephew instead of exacting compensation or revenge.

to follow his father and perform his part.
Then, in old age, at the end of his days
among the Weather-Geats, he bequeathed to Wiglaf
2625 innumerable weapons.
                    And now the youth
was to enter the line of battle with his lord,
his first time to be tested as a fighter.
His spirit did not break and the ancestral blade
would keep its edge, as the dragon discovered
2630 as soon as they came together in the combat.
    Sad at heart, addressing his companions,
Wiglaf spoke wise and fluent words:
"I remember that time when mead was flowing,
how we pledged loyalty to our lord in the hall,
2635 promised our ring-giver we would be worth our price,
make good the gift of the war-gear,
those swords and helmets, as and when
his need required it. He picked us out
from the army deliberately, honored us and judged us
2640 fit for this action, made me these lavish gifts—
and all because he considered us the best
of his arms-bearing thanes. And now, although
he wanted this challenge to be one he'd face
by himself alone—the shepherd of our land,
2645 a man unequaled in the quest for glory
and a name for daring—now the day has come
when this lord we serve needs sound men
to give him their support. Let us go to him,
help our leader through the hot flame
2650 and dread of the fire. As God is my witness,
I would rather my body were robed in the same
burning blaze as my gold-giver's body
than go back home bearing arms.
That is unthinkable, unless we have first
2655 slain the foe and defended the life
of the prince of the Weather-Geats. I well know
the things he has done for us deserve better.
Should he alone be left exposed
to fall in battle? We must bond together,
2660 shield and helmet, mail-shirt and sword."
Then he waded the dangerous reek and went
under arms to his lord, saying only:
"Go on, dear Beowulf, do everything
you said you would when you were still young
2665 and vowed you would never let your name and fame
be dimmed while you lived. Your deeds are famous,
so stay resolute, my lord, defend your life now
with the whole of your strength. I shall stand by you."
    After those words, a wildness rose
2670 in the dragon again and drove it to attack,
heaving up fire, hunting for enemies,
the humans it loathed. Flames lapped the shield,
charred it to the boss, and the body armor
on the young warrior was useless to him.

2675 But Wiglaf did well under the wide rim
Beowulf shared with him once his own had shattered
in sparks and ashes.
                    Inspired again
by the thought of glory, the war-king threw
his whole strength behind a sword stroke
2680 and connected with the skull. And Naegling snapped.
Beowulf's ancient iron-gray sword
let him down in the fight. It was never his fortune
to be helped in combat by the cutting edge
of weapons made of iron. When he wielded a sword,
2685 no matter how blooded and hard-edged the blade,
his hand was too strong, the stroke he dealt
(I have heard) would ruin it. He could reap no advantage.
     Then the bane of that people, the fire-breathing dragon,
was mad to attack for a third time.
2690 When a chance came, he caught the hero
in a rush of flame and clamped sharp fangs
into his neck. Beowulf's body
ran wet with his life-blood: it came welling out.
     Next thing, they say, the noble son of Weohstan
2695 saw the king in danger at his side
and displayed his inborn bravery and strength.
He left the head alone,[7] but his fighting hand
was burned when he came to his kinsman's aid.
He lunged at the enemy lower down
2700 so that his decorated sword sank into its belly
and the flames grew weaker.
                         Once again the king
gathered his strength and drew a stabbing knife
he carried on his belt, sharpened for battle.
He stuck it deep in the dragon's flank.
2705 Beowulf dealt it a deadly wound.
They had killed the enemy, courage quelled his life;
that pair of kinsmen, partners in nobility,
had destroyed the foe. So every man should act,
be at hand when needed; but now, for the king,
2710 this would be the last of his many labors
and triumphs in the world.
                         Then the wound
dealt by the ground-burner earlier began
to scald and swell; Beowulf discovered
deadly poison suppurating inside him,
2715 surges of nausea, and so, in his wisdom,
the prince realized his state and struggled
toward a seat on the rampart. He steadied his gaze
on those gigantic stones, saw how the earthwork
was braced with arches built over columns.
2720 And now that thane unequaled for goodness
with his own hands washed his lord's wounds,
swabbed the weary prince with water,
bathed him clean, unbuckled his helmet.

7. I.e., he avoided the dragon's flame-breathing head.

Beowulf spoke: in spite of his wounds,
2725 mortal wounds, he still spoke
for he well knew his days in the world
had been lived out to the end—his allotted time
was drawing to a close, death was very near.
  "Now is the time when I would have wanted
2730 to bestow this armor on my own son,
had it been my fortune to have fathered an heir
and live on in his flesh. For fifty years
I ruled this nation. No king
of any neighboring clan would dare
2735 face me with troops, none had the power
to intimidate me. I took what came,
cared for and stood by things in my keeping,
never fomented quarrels, never
swore to a lie. All this consoles me,
2740 doomed as I am and sickening for death;
because of my right ways, the Ruler of mankind
need never blame me when the breath leaves my body
for murder of kinsmen. Go now quickly,
dearest Wiglaf, under the gray stone
2745 where the dragon is laid out, lost to his treasure;
hurry to feast your eyes on the hoard.
Away you go: I want to examine
that ancient gold, gaze my fill
on those garnered jewels; my going will be easier
2750 for having seen the treasure, a less troubled letting-go
of the life and lordship I have long maintained."
  And so, I have heard, the son of Weohstan
quickly obeyed the command of his languishing
war-weary lord; he went in his chain-mail
2755 under the rock-piled roof of the barrow,
exulting in his triumph, and saw beyond the seat
a treasure-trove of astonishing richness,
wall-hangings that were a wonder to behold,
glittering gold spread across the ground,
2760 the old dawn-scorching serpent's den
packed with goblets and vessels from the past,
tarnished and corroding. Rusty helmets
all eaten away. Armbands everywhere,
artfully wrought. How easily treasure
2765 buried in the ground, gold hidden
however skillfully, can escape from any man!
  And he saw too a standard, entirely of gold,
hanging high over the hoard,
a masterpiece of filigree; it glowed with light
2770 so he could make out the ground at his feet
and inspect the valuables. Of the dragon there was no
remaining sign: the sword had dispatched him.
Then, the story goes, a certain man
plundered the hoard in that immemorial howe,
2775 filled his arms with flagons and plates,
anything he wanted; and took the standard also,
most brilliant of banners.

              Already the blade
of the old king's sharp killing-sword
had done its worst: the one who had for long
2780   minded the hoard, hovering over gold,
unleashing fire, surging forth
midnight after midnight, had been mown down.
    Wiglaf went quickly, keen to get back,
excited by the treasure. Anxiety weighed
2785   on his brave heart—he was hoping he would find
the leader of the Geats alive where he had left him
helpless, earlier, on the open ground.
    So he came to the place, carrying the treasure
and found his lord bleeding profusely,
2790   his life at an end; again he began
to swab his body. The beginnings of an utterance
broke out from the king's breast-cage.
The old lord gazed sadly at the gold.
    "To the everlasting Lord of all,
2795   to the King of Glory, I give thanks
that I behold this treasure here in front of me,
that I have been allowed to leave my people
so well endowed on the day I die.
Now that I have bartered my last breath
2800   to own this fortune, it is up to you
to look after their needs. I can hold out no longer.
Order my troop to construct a barrow
on a headland on the coast, after my pyre has cooled.
It will loom on the horizon at Hronesness[8]
2805   and be a reminder among my people—
so that in coming times crews under sail
will call it Beowulf's Barrow, as they steer
ships across the wide and shrouded waters."
    Then the king in his great-heartedness unclasped
2810   the collar of gold from his neck and gave it
to the young thane, telling him to use
it and the war-shirt and gilded helmet well.
"You are the last of us, the only one left
of the Waegmundings. Fate swept us away,
2815   sent my whole brave highborn clan
to their final doom. Now I must follow them."
    That was the warrior's last word.
He had no more to confide. The furious heat
of the pyre would assail him. His soul fled from his breast
2820   to its destined place among the steadfast ones.

[BEOWULF'S FUNERAL]

    It was hard then on the young hero,
having to watch the one he held so dear
there on the ground, going through
his death agony. The dragon from underearth,
2825   his nightmarish destroyer, lay destroyed as well,

---

8. A headland by the sea. The name means "Whalesness."

utterly without life. No longer would his snakefolds
ply themselves to safeguard hidden gold.
Hard-edged blades, hammered out
and keenly filed, had finished him
2830 so that the sky-roamer lay there rigid,
brought low beside the treasure-lodge.
    Never again would he glitter and glide
and show himself off in midnight air,
exulting in his riches: he fell to earth
2835 through the battle-strength in Beowulf's arm.
There were few, indeed, as far as I have heard,
big and brave as they may have been,
few who would have held out if they had had to face
the outpourings of that poison-breather
2840 or gone foraging on the ring-hall floor
and found the deep barrow-dweller
on guard and awake.
                The treasure had been won,
bought and paid for by Beowulf's death.
Both had reached the end of the road
2845 through the life they had been lent.
                        Before long
the battle-dodgers abandoned the wood,
the ones who had let down their lord earlier,
the tail-turners, ten of them together.
When he needed them most, they had made off.
2850 Now they were ashamed and came behind shields,
in their battle-outfits, to where the old man lay.
They watched Wiglaf, sitting worn out,
a comrade shoulder to shoulder with his lord,
trying in vain to bring him round with water.
2855 Much as he wanted to, there was no way
he could preserve his lord's life on earth
or alter in the least the Almighty's will.
What God judged right would rule what happened
to every man, as it does to this day.
2860   Then a stern rebuke was bound to come
from the young warrior to the ones who had been cowards.
Wiglaf, son of Weohstan, spoke
disdainfully and in disappointment:
"Anyone ready to admit the truth
2865 will surely realize that the lord of men
who showered you with gifts and gave you the armor
you are standing in—when he would distribute
helmets and mail-shirts to men on the mead-benches,
a prince treating his thanes in hall
2870 to the best he could find, far or near—
was throwing weapons uselessly away.
It would be a sad waste when the war broke out.
Beowulf had little cause to brag
about his armed guard; yet God who ordains
2875 who wins or loses allowed him to strike
with his own blade when bravery was needed.
There was little I could do to protect his life

in the heat of the fray, but I found new strength
welling up when I went to help him.

2880 Then my sword connected and the deadly assaults
of our foe grew weaker, the fire coursed
less strongly from his head. But when the worst happened
too few rallied around the prince.

"So it is good-bye now to all you know and love
2885 on your home ground, the open-handedness,
the giving of war-swords. Every one of you
with freeholds of land, our whole nation,
will be dispossessed, once princes from beyond
get tidings of how you turned and fled
2890 and disgraced yourselves. A warrior will sooner
die than live a life of shame."

Then he ordered the outcome of the fight to be reported
to those camped on the ridge, that crowd of retainers
who had sat all morning, sad at heart,
2895 shield-bearers wondering about
the man they loved: would this day be his last
or would he return? He told the truth
and did not balk, the rider who bore
news to the cliff-top. He addressed them all:
2900 "Now the people's pride and love,
the lord of the Geats, is laid on his deathbed,
brought down by the dragon's attack.
Beside him lies the bane of his life,
dead from knife-wounds. There was no way
2905 Beowulf could manage to get the better
of the monster with his sword. Wiglaf sits
at Beowulf's side, the son of Weohstan,
the living warrior watching by the dead,
keeping weary vigil, holding a wake
2910 for the loved and the loathed.

                           Now war is looming
over our nation, soon it will be known
to Franks and Frisians, far and wide,
that the king is gone. Hostility has been great
among the Franks since Hygelac sailed forth
2915 at the head of a war-fleet into Friesland:
there the Hetware harried and attacked
and overwhelmed him with great odds.
The leader in his war-gear was laid low,
fell among followers: that lord did not favor
2920 his company with spoils. The Merovingian king
has been an enemy to us ever since.

"Nor do I expect peace or pact-keeping
of any sort from the Swedes. Remember:
at Ravenswood,[9] Ongentheow
2925 slaughtered Haethcyn, Hrethel's son,
when the Geat people in their arrogance
first attacked the fierce Shylfings.

---

9. The messenger describes in greater detail the Battle of Ravenswood. See the outline of the Swedish wars on p. 87 n. 6.

The return blow was quickly struck
by Ohthere's father.[1] Old and terrible,
2930   he felled the sea-king and saved his own
aged wife, the mother of Onela
and of Ohthere, bereft of her gold rings.
Then he kept hard on the heels of the foe
and drove them, leaderless, lucky to get away
2935   in a desperate rout into Ravenswood.
His army surrounded the weary remnant
where they nursed their wounds; all through the night
he howled threats at those huddled survivors,
promised to axe their bodies open
2940   when dawn broke, dangle them from gallows
to feed the birds. But at first light
when their spirits were lowest, relief arrived.
They heard the sound of Hygelac's horn,
his trumpet calling as he came to find them,
2945   the hero in pursuit, at hand with troops.
    "The bloody swathe that Swedes and Geats
cut through each other was everywhere.
No one could miss their murderous feuding.
Then the old man made his move,
2950   pulled back, barred his people in:
Ongentheow withdrew to higher ground.
Hygelac's pride and prowess as a fighter
were known to the earl; he had no confidence
that he could hold out against that horde of seamen,
2955   defend his wife and the ones he loved
from the shock of the attack. He retreated for shelter
behind the earthwall. Then Hygelac swooped
on the Swedes at bay, his banners swarmed
into their refuge, his Geat forces
2960   drove forward to destroy the camp.
There in his gray hairs, Ongentheow
was cornered, ringed around with swords.
And it came to pass that the king's fate
was in Eofor's hands,[2] and in his alone.
2965   Wulf, son of Wonred, went for him in anger,
split him open so that blood came spurting
from under his hair. The old hero
still did not flinch, but parried fast,
hit back with a harder stroke:
2970   the king turned and took him on.
Then Wonred's son, the brave Wulf,
could land no blow against the aged lord.
Ongentheow divided his helmet
so that he buckled and bowed his bloodied head
2975   and dropped to the ground. But his doom held off.
Though he was cut deep, he recovered again.

---

1. I.e., Ongentheow.
2. I.e., he was at Eofor's mercy. Eofor's slaying of Ongentheow was described in lines 2486–89, where no mention is made of his brother Wulf's part in the battle. They are the sons of Wonred. *Eofor* means boar; *Wulf* is the Old English spelling of wolf.

"With his brother down, the undaunted Eofor,
Hygelac's thane, hefted his sword
and smashed murderously at the massive helmet
2980   past the lifted shield. And the king collapsed,
the shepherd of people was sheared of life.
Many then hurried to help Wulf,
bandaged and lifted him, now that they were left
masters of the blood-soaked battle-ground.
2985   One warrior stripped the other,
looted Ongentheow's iron mail-coat,
his hard sword-hilt, his helmet too,
and carried the graith[3] to King Hygelac,
he accepted the prize, promised fairly
2990   that reward would come, and kept his word.
For their bravery in action, when they arrived home,
Eofor and Wulf were overloaded
by Hrethel's son, Hygelac the Geat,
with gifts of land and linked rings
2995   that were worth a fortune. They had won glory,
so there was no gainsaying his generosity.
And he gave Eofor his only daughter
to bide at home with him, an honor and a bond.
    "So this bad blood between us and the Swedes,
3000   this vicious feud, I am convinced,
is bound to revive; they will cross our borders
and attack in force when they find out
that Beowulf is dead. In days gone by
when our warriors fell and we were undefended,
3005   he kept our coffers and our kingdom safe.
He worked for the people, but as well as that
he behaved like a hero.
                  We must hurry now
to take a last look at the king
and launch him, lord and lavisher of rings,
3010   on the funeral road. His royal pyre
will melt no small amount of gold:
heaped there in a hoard, it was bought at heavy cost,
and that pile of rings he paid for at the end
with his own life will go up with the flame,
3015   be furled in fire: treasure no follower
will wear in his memory, nor lovely woman
link and attach as a torque around her neck—
but often, repeatedly, in the path of exile
they shall walk bereft, bowed under woe,
3020   now that their leader's laugh is silenced,
high spirits quenched. Many a spear
dawn-cold to the touch will be taken down
and waved on high; the swept harp
won't waken warriors, but the raven winging
3025   darkly over the doomed will have news,
tidings for the eagle of how he hoked and ate,

---

3. Possessions, apparel.

how the wolf and he made short work of the dead."[4]
    Such was the drift of the dire report
that gallant man delivered. He got little wrong
3030 in what he told and predicted.
                                    The whole troop
rose in tears, then took their way
to the uncanny scene under Earnaness.[5]
There, on the sand, where his soul had left him,
they found him at rest, their ring-giver
3035 from days gone by. The great man
had breathed his last. Beowulf the king
had indeed met with a marvelous death.
    But what they saw first was far stranger:
the serpent on the ground, gruesome and vile,
3040 lying facing him. The fire-dragon
was scaresomely burned, scorched all colors.
From head to tail, his entire length
was fifty feet. He had shimmered forth
on the night air once, then winged back
3045 down to his den; but death owned him now,
he would never enter his earth-gallery again.
Beside him stood pitchers and piled-up dishes,
silent flagons, precious swords
eaten through with rust, ranged as they had been
3050 while they waited their thousand winters under ground.
That huge cache, gold inherited
from an ancient race, was under a spell—
which meant no one was ever permitted
to enter the ring-hall unless God Himself,
3055 mankind's Keeper, True King of Triumphs,
allowed some person pleasing to Him—
and in His eyes worthy—to open the hoard.
    What came about brought to nothing
the hopes of the one who had wrongly hidden
3060 riches under the rock-face. First the dragon slew
that man among men, who in turn made fierce amends
and settled the feud. Famous for his deeds
a warrior may be, but it remains a mystery
where his life will end, when he may no longer
3065 dwell in the mead-hall among his own.
So it was with Beowulf, when he faced the cruelty
and cunning of the mound-guard. He himself was ignorant
of how his departure from the world would happen.
The highborn chiefs who had buried the treasure
3070 declared it until doomsday so accursed
that whoever robbed it would be guilty of wrong
and grimly punished for their transgression,
hasped in hell-bonds in heathen shrines.
Yet Beowulf's gaze at the gold treasure
3075 when he first saw it had not been selfish.
    Wiglaf, son of Weohstan, spoke:

---

4. The raven, eagle, and wolf—the scavengers who
will feed on the slain—are "the beasts of battle," a
common motif in Germanic war poetry. "Hoked":

rooted about [Northern Ireland, Translator's note].
5. The site of Beowulf's fight with the dragon.
The name means "Eaglesness."

"Often when one man follows his own will
many are hurt. This happened to us.
Nothing we advised could ever convince
3080 the prince we loved, our land's guardian,
not to vex the custodian of the gold,
let him lie where he was long accustomed,
lurk there under earth until the end of the world.
He held to his high destiny. The hoard is laid bare,
3085 but at a grave cost; it was too cruel a fate
that forced the king to that encounter.
I have been inside and seen everything
amassed in the vault. I managed to enter
although no great welcome awaited me
3090 under the earthwall. I quickly gathered up
a huge pile of the priceless treasures
handpicked from the hoard and carried them here
where the king could see them. He was still himself,
alive, aware, and in spite of his weakness
3095 he had many requests. He wanted me to greet you
and order the building of a barrow that would crown
the site of his pyre, serve as his memorial,
in a commanding position, since of all men
to have lived and thrived and lorded it on earth
3100 his worth and due as a warrior were the greatest.
Now let us again go quickly
and feast our eyes on that amazing fortune
heaped under the wall. I will show the way
and take you close to those coffers packed with rings
3105 and bars of gold. Let a bier be made
and got ready quickly when we come out
and then let us bring the body of our lord,
the man we loved, to where he will lodge
for a long time in the care of the Almighty."
3110   Then Weohstan's son, stalwart to the end,
had orders given to owners of dwellings,
many people of importance in the land,
to fetch wood from far and wide
for the good man's pyre:
                         "Now shall flame consume
3115 our leader in battle, the blaze darken
round him who stood his ground in the steel-hail,
when the arrow-storm shot from bowstrings
pelted the shield-wall. The shaft hit home.
Feather-fledged, it finned the barb in flight."
3120   Next the wise son of Weohstan
called from among the king's thanes
a group of seven: he selected the best
and entered with them, the eighth of their number,
under the God-cursed roof; one raised
3125 a lighted torch and led the way.
No lots were cast for who should loot the hoard
for it was obvious to them that every bit of it
lay unprotected within the vault,
there for the taking. It was no trouble

3130   to hurry to work and haul out
the priceless store. They pitched the dragon
over the cliff-top, let tide's flow
and backwash take the treasure-minder.
Then coiled gold was loaded on a cart

3135   in great abundance, and the gray-haired leader,
the prince on his bier, borne to Hronesness.
    The Geat people built a pyre for Beowulf,
stacked and decked it until it stood foursquare,
hung with helmets, heavy war-shields

3140   and shining armor, just as he had ordered.
Then his warriors laid him in the middle of it,
mourning a lord far-famed and beloved.
On a height they kindled the hugest of all
funeral fires; fumes of woodsmoke

3145   billowed darkly up, the blaze roared
and drowned out their weeping, wind died down
and flames wrought havoc in the hot bone-house,
burning it to the core. They were disconsolate
and wailed aloud for their lord's decease.

3150   A Geat woman too sang out in grief;
with hair bound up, she unburdened herself
of her worst fears, a wild litany
of nightmare and lament: her nation invaded,
enemies on the rampage, bodies in piles,

3155   slavery and abasement. Heaven swallowed the smoke.
    Then the Geat people began to construct
a mound on a headland, high and imposing,
a marker that sailors could see from far away,
and in ten days they had done the work.

3160   It was their hero's memorial; what remained from the fire
they housed inside it, behind a wall
as worthy of him as their workmanship could make it.
And they buried torques in the barrow, and jewels
and a trove of such things as trespassing men

3165   had once dared to drag from the hoard.
They let the ground keep that ancestral treasure,
gold under gravel, gone to earth,
as useless to men now as it ever was.
Then twelve warriors rode around the tomb,

3170   chieftains' sons, champions in battle,
all of them distraught, chanting in dirges,
mourning his loss as a man and a king.
They extolled his heroic nature and exploits
and gave thanks for his greatness; which was the proper thing,

3175   for a man should praise a prince whom he holds dear
and cherish his memory when that moment comes
when he has to be convoyed from his bodily home.
So the Geat people, his hearth-companions,
sorrowed for the lord who had been laid low.

3180   They said that of all the kings upon earth
he was the man most gracious and fair-minded,
kindest to his people and keenest to win fame.

THE WANDERER

The lament of *The Wanderer* is an excellent example of the elegiac mood so common in Anglo-Saxon poetry. Such poems look back to a time when oral poets performed heroic songs in the meter preserved, practiced, and recorded in original works by their Christian descendants. In celebration of Beowulf's victory over Grendel, Hrothgar's court poet performs a heroic lay about the Germanic hero Sigemund (lines 883–914). The elegiac tone common to *Beowulf* and these later poems, however, expresses the poets' profound feelings toward their ancestors who lived before St. Augustine brought the "good news" to Kent and initiated the conversion. Nowhere are those feelings expressed more poignantly than in *The Wanderer*.

As is true of most Anglo-Saxon elegiac laments, both the language and the structure of *The Wanderer* are difficult. At the beginning, the speaker (whom the poet identifies as an "earth-treader") voices hope of finding comfort after his many tribulations. After the poet's interruption, the Wanderer continues to speak—to himself—of his long search for a new home, describing how he must keep his thoughts locked within him while he makes that search. But these thoughts form the most vivid and moving part of his soliloquy—how, floating on the sea, dazed with sorrow and fatigue, he imagines that he sees his old companions, and how, as he wakens to reality, they vanish on the water like seabirds. The second part of the poem, beginning "Therefore I don't know why," expands the theme from one man to all human beings in a world wasted by war and time. He derives such cold comfort as he can from asking the old question, Where are they now, who were once so glad in the mead-hall?

The Wanderer is preserved only in the Exeter Book, a manuscript of about 975 (although the poem may be much earlier), which contains the largest surviving collection of Anglo-Saxon poetry.

The Wanderer [1]

"Often the lone-dweller[2]   longs for relief,
the Almighty's mercy,   though melancholy,
his hands turning   time and again
the ocean's currents,   the ice-cold seas,
5   following paths of exile.   Fate is firmly set."
   So spoke the Wanderer,[3]   weary of hardships,
cruel combats,   the death of kinsmen.
   "Often alone,   always at daybreak
I must lament my cares;   not one remains alive
10   to whom I could utter   the thoughts in my heart,
tell him my sorrows.   In truth, I know that
for any eorl[4]   an excellent virtue

---

1. The translation by Alfred David is based on *Eight Old English Poems*, 3rd ed., edited by John C. Pope, revised by R. D. Fulk. The translation is also indebted to comments by Professor Fulk.
2. Old English *an-haga* = one + hedge, enclosure—i.e., one who dwells alone in some sort of confinement.
3. Old English *eard-stapa* = earth + treader. The modern title—there is no title in the manuscript—derives from this compound noun.
4. *Eorl* = warrior. Only later did the Old English word come to designate a member of the British nobility.

is to lock tight   the treasure chest
within one's heart,   howsoever he may think.
15 A downcast heart   won't defy destiny,
nor the sad spirit   give sustenance.
And therefore those   who thirst for fame
often bind fast   their breast chamber.
      "So I must hold in   the thoughts of my heart—
20 though often wretched,   bereft of my homeland,
far from kinfolk—   bind them with fetters,
since in days long past   with darkness of earth
I covered my gold-friend,[5]   and I fared from there
over the waves' bed,   winter-weary,
25 longing for a hall   and a lord of rings,
where near or far   I might find one
in the mead-hall   remembering me and my kin,
or else show favor   to a friendless man,
requite me with comfort.   One acquainted with pain
30 understands how cruel   a traveling companion
sorrow is for someone   with few friends at his side.
Exile attends him,   not twisted gold rings,
Heart-freezing frost,   not fruits of the earth.
He recalls tablemates   and treasure distributed,
35 how from the first   his friend and lord
helped him to the feast.   That happy time is no more.
      "This, indeed, anyone forced to   forgo for long
the beloved counsel   of his lord knows well.
Often when sorrow   and sleep together
40 bind the poor lone-dweller   in their embrace,
he dreams he clasps   and that he kisses
his liege-lord again,   lays head and hands
on the lord's knees   as he did long ago,
enjoyed the gift-giving   in days gone by.
45 Then the warrior, friendless,   awakens again,
sees before him   the fallow waves,
seabirds on the water   spreading their wings,
snow and hail falling   and sleet as well.
Then the heart's wounds   grow heavier,
50 sadness for dear ones.   Sorrow returns.
Then through his mind   pass memories of kinsmen—
joyfully he greets them,   eagerly gazes—
his fellow warriors,   the floating spirits,
fade on their way.   They fail to bring
55 much familiar talk   —trouble is renewed—
for any man   who must often send
his weary spirit   over the waves' bed.
      "Therefore I don't know why   my woeful heart
should not wax dark   in this wide world
60 when I look back on   the life of eorls,
how quickly they   quit the mead-hall's floor,
brave young men.   So this middle-earth

---

5. Old English *gold-wine*=gold-friend, one of the many formulas applied to the lord, here in his role as dispenser of treasure to his retainers.

from day to day   dwindles and fails;
therefore no one is wise   without his share of winters
65 in the world's kingdom.   A wise man must be patient,
not too hot of heart   nor hasty of speech,
not reluctant to fight   nor too reckless,
not too timid nor too glad,   not too greedy,
and never eager to commit   until he can be sure.
70 A man should hold back   his boast until
that time has come   when he truly knows
to direct his heart   on the right path.
    "A wise man must know   the misery of that time
when the world's wealth   shall all stand waste,
75 just as in our own day   all over middle-earth
walls are standing   wind-swept and wasted,
downed by frost,   and dwellings covered with snow.
The mead-hall crumbles,   its master lies dead,
bereft of pleasures,   all the warrior-band[6] perished,
80 boldly by the wall.   Battle took some,
bore them away;   a bird carried one
above the high waves;   the gray wolf took another,
divided him with death;   dreary-spirited
an eorl buried another   in an earthen pit.
85   "Mankind's Creator   laid waste this middle-earth
till the clamor of city-dwellers   ceased to be heard
and ancient works of giants   stood empty.
He who wisely   contemplates this wall-stead,
and considers deeply   the darkness of this life,
90 mature in years,   remembers many
bloody battlegrounds   and so begins:
    'Where did the steed go? Where the young warrior?   Where the
        treasure-giver?
Where the seats of fellowship?   Where the hall's festivity?
Alas bright beaker!   Alas burnished warrior!
95 Alas pride of princes!   How the time has passed,
gone under night-helm   as if it never was!
A towering wall,   traced with serpent shapes,[7]
endures instead   of the dear warrior-band.
Strength of ash-spears   destroyed warriors,
100 slaughter-greedy weapons,   overwhelming fate,
and storms beat against   these stone-faced cliffs,
snow descending   seals up the ground,
drumming of winter   when darkness falls,
night shadows darken,   from the north send down
105 fierce hail-showers   in hatred of men.
All is wretchedness   in the realm of earth;
fate's work lays low   the world under heaven.
Here wealth is fleeting,   here friend is fleeting,
here family is fleeting,   here humankind is fleeting.
110 All this resting-place Earth   shall become empty.'"
    So said the wise man   as he sat in meditation.

---

6. Old English *duguth* = generally something that affords benefit or advantage, but here it specifically applies to a band of warriors.

7. The reference is to a kind of serpentine ornamentation; examples from Roman times survive in Britain.

A good man holds his words back,   tells his woes not too soon,
baring his inner heart   before knowing the best way,
an eorl who acts with courage.   All shall be well for him who seeks
    grace,
115   help from our Father in heaven   where a fortress stands for us all.

THE WIFE'S LAMENT

In modern English translation, the speaker of this poem sounds much like the
speaker in *The Wanderer*, lamenting his exile, isolation, and the loss of his lord. But
in Old English the grammatical gender of the pronouns reveals that this speaker is a
woman; the man she refers to as "my lord" must, therefore, be her husband. The story
behind the lament remains obscure. All that can be made out for certain is that the
speaker was married to a nobleman of another country; that her husband has left her
(possibly forced into exile as a result of a feud); that his kinsmen are hostile to her;
and that she is now living alone in a wilderness. Although the circumstances are
shadowy, it is reasonable to conjecture that the wife may have been a "peace-weaver"
(a woman married off to make peace between warring tribes), like Hildeburh and
Freawaru, whose politically inspired marriages only result in further bloodshed (see
Beowulf, pp. 63 and 83). The obscurity of the Old English text has led to diametrically opposed interpretations of the husband's feeling toward his wife. One interpretation holds that, for unexplained reasons, possibly because of his kinsmen's hostility
to her, he has turned against her. The other, which is adopted in this translation,
is that, in her mind at least, they share the suffering of his exile and their separation.
Thus in the line here rendered "I must suffer the feud of my much-beloved," *fæhðu*
(feud) is read by some as the technical term for a blood feud—the way it is used in
Beowulf when Hrothgar says he settled a great feud started by Beowulf's father with
feo (fee), i.e., monetary compensation (p. 50). Others take the word in a more general
sense as referring to the man's enmity toward his wife. In either case, the woman's
themes and language resemble those of male "wræccas" (outcasts or exiles; the Old
English root survives in modern *wretch* and *wretched*) in the Old English poems
called "elegies" because of their elegiac content and mood.

The Wife's Lament[1]

Full of sorrow,   I shall make this song
about me, my own fate.   Surely I can tell
what sufferings I endured   since I came of age,
both the new and old,   never more than now.
5   I must endure without end   the misery of exile.
    First my lord[2] departed   from his people

---

1. The translation by Alfred David is based on
Eight Old English Poems, 3rd ed., edited by John
C. Pope, revised by R. D. Fulk (2000). I am
indebted to Professor Fulk for his advice on my
translation.
2. A woman would refer to her husband as her
"lord."

over tossing waves;   I worried when day came
in what land   my liege-lord could be.
Then I set out,   a friendless exile,
10   to seek a place   for my sore need.
My husband's kin   had hatched a plot,
conspiring secretly   to separate us,
so that we[3] widest apart   in the world's realms
lived in most misery,   and I languished.
15   My lord commanded me   to keep house here;
in this dwelling-place;   I had few dear ones,
devoted friends.   Therefore I feel downcast.
Then I learned my lord   was like myself—
down on his luck,   dreary-spirited,
20   secretly minding   murder in his heart.
A happy pair   we had promised each other,
that death alone   would ever divide us,
and nothing else.   All that is changed;
our nearness once   is now as though
25   it never had been.   Now, far or near, I must
bear the malice   of the man I loved.
        I was told to live   in a grove of trees,
under an oak   in an earthen cave.
That earth-hall is old;   yearning overcomes me.
30   These dales are dark   and the dunes high,
bitter bulwarks   overgrown with briers,
a joyless place.   Here my lord's departure
afflicts me cruelly.   Friends here on earth,
lovers lying together,   lounge in bed,
35   while at daybreak   I abandon
this earthen-pit   under the oak
to sit alone   the summer-long day.
There I may bewail   my many woes,
suffering of exile,   for I can never
40   obtain comfort   for all my cares
nor all the longing   this life brought me.
        If ever anyone   should feel anguish,
harsh pain at heart,   she[4] should put on
a happy appearance   while enduring
45   endless sorrows—   should she possess
all the world's bliss,   or be banished far away
from her homeland.   I believe my lord sits
by a stony   storm-beaten cliff,
that water-tossed   my weary friend
50   sits in a desolate home.   He must suffer
much in his mind,   remembering too often
a happier place.   Woe unto him
who languishing   waits for a loved one.

3. Old English *wit*, an example of the dual form, used for two persons.
4. Old English *geong-man*. The identity of the speaker has been debated, but most recent opinion holds it to be the wife herself, speaking impersonally. The translation takes the liberty of using "she" in reference to the speaker.

IRISH LITERATURE

The changes European literature underwent during the twelfth and thirteenth centuries were greatly indebted to Celtic influences. The legends about King Arthur and his knights, although they were assimilated to the feudal culture of the Anglo-Normans and transmitted by texts written in Latin, French, and English (see p. 12), were originally products of Celtic myth and legend. The folkloric otherworld elements and the major role played by women in those stories profoundly shaped and colored the literature we now think of as "romance." The French Tristran romances, the romances of Marie de France and Chrétien de Troyes, and even the legends of the Holy Grail could not have been imagined without their Celtic components.

The Celts overran central Europe, Spain, and the British Isles during the first millennium B.C.E. On the Continent and in Great Britain, south of the wall built by the emperor Hadrian (see the map inside the front cover), they were absorbed into the Roman Empire. However, the Celtic vernacular continued to be spoken as the native language, and Ireland never became a Roman province. The Anglo-Saxon invasions in the fifth and early sixth centuries, and the Danish invasions after the eighth, displaced Celts in England, but Celtic language and culture continued to flourish in Wales (Welsh), in Cornwall (Cornish), across the English Channel in Brittany (Breton), and, of course, in Ireland (Gaelic). While still part of the Roman Empire, Britain and, in consequence, Ireland had been converted to Christianity. As portrayed in the Arthurian legend, the Christian Britons fought against barbaric Germanic invaders. Irish and Welsh missionaries, along with Roman ones, brought about the conversion of the Anglo-Saxons.

The earliest Celtic literature, like that of the Anglo-Saxons, was transmitted orally and little was copied down before the twelfth century. Nevertheless, the surviving monuments indicate its richness and its significance for the development of French and English medieval literature.

What follows are two examples of Irish literature, an excerpt from the Old Irish epic *Táin Bó Cuailnge* (The Cattle Raid of Cooley) and some delightful monastic lyrics written between the sixth and the ninth centuries.

CÚCHULAINN'S BOYHOOD DEEDS

Cúchulainn (koo-chúll-in), nephew of Ulster's king Conchobor, is the hero of the Old Irish epic *Táin Bó Cuailnge* (The Cattle Raid of Cooley), which tells of a great war between the kingdoms of Connacht and Ulster. The cause of the war that gives this epic work its title is the desire of Queen Medb of Connacht to obtain possession of the brown bull of Ulster to match one owned by her husband, King Ailill. The tales go back to ancient oral literature; the best surviving manuscript, pieced together in the twelfth century from different sources, although seriously defective, nevertheless tells powerful tales. This excerpt is part of the answer Medb and Ailill, leading the invading army, are given to the query "What sort of man . . . is this Hound of Ulster?"

Cúchulainn's Boyhood Deeds[1]

'There was another deed he did,' Fiacha Mac Fir Febe said. 'Cathbad the druid was staying with his son, Conchobor mac Nesa. He had one hundred studious men learning druid lore from him—this was always the number that Cathbad taught.

'One day a pupil asked him what that day would be lucky for. Cathbad said if a warrior took up arms for the first time that day his name would endure in Ireland as a word signifying mighty acts, and stories about him would last forever.

'Cúchulainn overheard this. He went to Conchobor and claimed his weapons. Conchobor said:

"By whose instruction?"

"My friend Cathbad's," Cúchulainn said.

"We have heard of him," Conchobor said, and gave him shield and spear. Cúchulainn brandished them in the middle of the house, and not one piece survived of the fifteen sets that Conchobor kept in store for new warriors or in case of breakage. He was given Conchobor's own weapons at last, and these survived. He made a flourish and saluted their owner the king and said:

"Long life to their seed and breed, who have for their king the man who owns these weapons."

'It was then that Cathbad came in and said:

"Do I see a young boy newly armed?"

"Yes," Conchobor said.

"Then woe to his mother's son," he said:

"What is this? Wasn't it by your own direction he came?" Conchobor said.

"Certainly not," Cathbad said.

"Little demon, why did you lie to me?" Conchobor said to Cúchulainn.

"It was no lie, king of warriors," Cúchulainn said. "I happened to hear him instructing his pupils this morning south of Emain, and I came to you then."

"Well," Cathbad said, "the day has this merit: he who arms for the first time today will achieve fame and greatness. But his life is short."

"That is a fair bargain," Cúchulainn said. "If I achieve fame I am content, though I had only one day on earth."

'Another day came and another druid asked what that day would be lucky for.

"Whoever mounts his first chariot today," Cathbad said, "his name will live forever in Ireland."

Cúchulainn overheard this also, and went to Conchobor and said:

"Friend Conchobor, my chariot!"

'A chariot was given to him. He clapped his hand to the chariot between the shafts, and the frame broke at his touch. In the same way he broke twelve chariots. At last they gave him Conchobor's chariot and that survived him.

'He mounted the chariot beside Conchobor's charioteer. This charioteer, Ibor by name, turned the chariot round where it stood.

---

1. The translation is by Thomas Kinsella, *The Táin* (1969). For "The Exile of the Sons of Uisliu," see the supplemental ebook.

"You can get out of the chariot now," the charioteer said.

"You think your horses are precious," Cúchulainn said, "but so am I, my friend. Drive round Emain now, and you won't lose by it."

The charioteer set off.

'Cúchulainn urged him to take the road to the boy-troop, to greet them and get their blessing in return. After this he asked him to go further along the road. Cúchulainn said to the charioteer as they drove onward:

"Use your goad on the horses now."

"Which direction?" the charioteer said.

"As far as the road will take us!" Cúchulainn said.

They came to Sliab Fuait. They met Conall Cernach there—for to Conall Cernach had fallen the care of the province boundary that day. Each of Ulster's heroic warriors had his day on Sliab Fuait, to take care of every man who came that way with poetry, and to fight any others. In this way everyone was challenged and no one slipped past to Emain unnoticed.

"May you prosper," Conall said. "I wish you victory and triumph."

"Conall, go back to the fort," Cúchulainn said, "and let me keep watch here a little."

"You would do for looking after men of poetry," Conall said. "But you are a little young still for dealing with men of war."

"It might never happen at all," Cúchulainn said. "Let us wander off, meanwhile," he said, "to view the shore of Loch Echtra. Warriors are often camped there."

"It is a pleasant thought," Conall said.

They set off. Suddenly Cúchulainn let fly a stone from his sling and smashed the shaft of Conall Cernach's chariot.

"Why did you cast that stone, boy?" Conall said.

"To test my hand and the straightness of my aim," Cúchulainn said. "Now, since it is your Ulster custom not to continue a dangerous journey, go back to Emain, friend Conall, and leave me here on guard."

"If I must," Conall said.

'Conall Cernach wouldn't go beyond that point.

'Cúchulainn went on to Loch Echtra but found no one there. The charioteer said to Cúchulainn that they ought to go back to Emain, that they might get there for the drinking.

"No," Cúchulainn said. "What is that peak there?"

"Sliab Mondairn," the charioteer said.

"Take me there," Cúchulainn said.

They travelled on until they got there. On arriving at the mountain, Cúchulainn asked:

"That white heap of stones on the mountain-top, what is it called?"

"The look-out place, Finncarn, the white cairn," the charioteer said.

"That plain there before us?" Cúchulainn said.

"Mag mBreg, Breg Plain," the charioteer said.

'In this way he gave the name of every fort of any size between Temair and Cenannos. And he recited to him also all fields and fords, all habitations and places of note, and every fastness and fortress. He pointed out at last the fort of the three sons of Nechta Scéne, who were called Foill (for deceitfulness) and Fannall (the Swallow) and Tuachell (the Cunning). They came from the mouth of the river Scéne. Fer Ulli, Lugaid's son, was their father and Nechta Scéne their mother. Ulstermen had killed their father and this is why they were at enmity with them.

"Is it these who say," Cúchulainn said, "that they have killed as many Ulstermen as are now living?"

"They are the ones," the charioteer said.

"Take me to meet them," Cúchulainn said.

"That is looking for danger," the charioteer said.

"We're not going there to avoid it," Cúchulainn said.

'They travelled on, and turned their horses loose where bog and river met, to the south and upstream of their enemies' stronghold. He took the spancel-hoop of challenge from the pillar-stone at the ford and threw it as far as he could out into the river and let the current take it—thus challenging the ban of the sons of Nechta Scéne.

'They took note of this and started out to find him.

'Cúchulainn, after sending the spancel-hoop downstream, lay down by the pillar-stone to rest, and said to his charioteer:

"If only one man comes, or two, don't wake me, but wake me if they all come."

'The charioteer waited meanwhile in terror. He yoked the chariot and pulled off the skins and coverings that were over Cúchulainn, trying not to wake him, since Cúchulainn had told him not to wake him for only one.

'Then the sons of Nechta Scéne came up.

"Who is that there?" said one.

"A little boy out in his chariot today for the first time," the charioteer said.

"Then his luck has deserted him," the warrior said. "This is a bad beginning in arms for him. Get out of our land. Graze your horses here no more."

"I have the reins in my hand," the charioteer said.

Then Ibor said to the warrior:

"Why should you earn enmity? Look, the boy is asleep."

"A boy with a difference!" cried Cúchulainn. "A boy who came here to look for fight!"

"It will be a pleasure," the warrior said.

"You may have that pleasure now, in the ford there," Cúchulainn said.

"You would be wise," the charioteer said, "to be careful of the man who is coming against you. Foill is his name," he said. "If you don't get him with your first thrust, you may thrust away all day."

"I swear the oath of my people that he won't play that trick on an Ulsterman again when my friend Conchobor's broad spear leaves my hand to find him. He'll feel it like the hand of an outlaw!"

'He flung the spear at him, and it pierced him and broke his back. He removed the trophies, and the head with them.

"Watch this other one," the charioteer said. "Fannall is his name, and he treads the water no heavier than swan or swallow."

"I swear he won't use that trick on an Ulsterman again," Cúchulainn said. "You have seen how I foot the pool in Emain."

'They met in the ford, and he killed the man and took away the trophies and the head.

"Watch this next one advancing against you," the charioteer said. "Tuachell is his name, and he wasn't named in vain. He has never fallen to any weapon."

"I have the *del chliss* for him, a wily weapon to churn him up and red-riddle him," Cúchulainn said.

'He threw the spear at him and tore him asunder where he stood. He went up and cut off his head. He gave the head and trophies to his charioteer.

'Then a scream rose up behind them from the mother, Nechta Scéne. Cúchulainn lifted the trophies off the ground and brought the three heads with him into the chariot, saying:

"I won't let go of these trophies until we reach Emain Macha."

'They set out for Emain Macha with all his spoils. Cúchulainn said to his charioteer:

"You promised us great driving. We'll need it now after our fight, with this chase after us."

'They travelled onward to Sliab Fuait. So fleet their haste across Breg Plain, as he hurried the charioteer, that the chariot-horses overtook the wind and the birds in flight, and Cúchulainn could catch the shot from his sling before it hit the earth.

'When they got to Sliab Fuait they found a herd of deer before them.

"What are those nimble beasts there?" Cúchulainn said.

"Wild deer," the charioteer said.

Cúchulainn said:

"Which would the men of Ulster like brought in, a dead one or a live one?"

"A live one would startle them more," the charioteer said. "It isn't every-one who could do it. Every man there has brought home a dead one. You can't catch them alive."

"I can," Cúchulainn said. "Use your goad on the horses, over the marsh."

'The charioteer did so until the horses bogged down. Cúchulainn got out and caught the deer nearest to him, the handsomest of all. He lashed the horses free of the bog and calmed the deer quickly. Then he tethered it between the rear shafts of the chariot.

'The next thing they saw before them was a flock of swans.

"Would the men of Ulster prefer to have these brought in alive or dead?" Cúchulainn said.

"The quickest and the most expert take them alive," the charioteer said.

'Cúchulainn immediately flung a little stone at the birds and brought down eight of them. Then he flung a bigger stone that brought down twelve more. He did this with his feat of the stunning-shot.

"Gather in our birds now," Cúchulainn said to his charioteer. "If I go out to them this wild stag will turn on you."

"But it's no easier if I go," the charioteer said. "The horses are so mad-dened that I can't get past them. I can't get over the two iron rims of the chariot wheels, they are so sharp. And I can't get past the stag; his antlers fill all the space between the chariot's shafts."

"Step out onto the antlers," Cúchulainn said. "I swear the oath of Ulster's people, I'll turn my head on him with such a stare, I'll fix him with such an eye, that he won't dare to stir or budge his head at you."

'He did this. Cúchulainn tied the reins and the charioteer gathered up the birds. Then Cúchulainn fastened the birds to the cords and thongs of the chariot. It was in this manner that they came back to Emain Macha: a wild stag behind the chariot, a swan-flock fluttering above, and the three heads of Nechta Scéne's sons inside the chariot.

'They came to Emain.

"A man in a chariot advancing upon us," cried the watcher in Emain Macha. "He'll spill the blood of the whole court unless you see to him and send naked women to meet him."

'Cúchulainn turned the left chariot-board toward Emain in insult, and he said:

"I swear by the oath of Ulster's people that if a man isn't found to fight me, I'll spill the blood of everyone in this court."

"Naked women to him!" Conchobor said.

'The women of Emain went forth, with Mugain the wife of Conchobor mac Nesa at their head, and they stripped their breasts at him.

"These are the warriors you must struggle with today," Mugain said.

'He hid his countenance. Immediately the warriors of Emain seized him and plunged him in a vat of cold water. The vat burst asunder about him. Then he was thrust in another vat and it boiled with bubbles the size of fists. He was placed at last in a third vat and warmed it till its heat and cold were equal. Then he got out and Mugain the queen gave him a blue cloak to go round him with a silver brooch in it, and a hooded tunic. And he sat on Conchobor's knee, and that was his seat ever after.

'What wonder,' Fiacha mac Fir Febe said, 'that the one who did this in his seventh year should triumph against odds and beat his match today, when he is fully seventeen years old?'

EARLY IRISH LYRICS

Monastic Irish scribes were also composers of beautiful lyrics, inspired by both the study and what could be seen from the study.

The Scholar and His Cat

I and white Pangur practice each of us his special art: his mind is set on hunting, my mind on my special craft.

I love (it is better than all fame) to be quiet beside my book, diligently pursuing knowledge. White Pangur does not envy me: he loves his childish craft.

When the two of us (this tale never wearies us) are alone together in our house, we have something to which we may apply our skill, an endless sport.

It is usual, at times, for a mouse to stick in his net, as a result of warlike battlings. For my part, into my net falls some difficult rule of hard meaning.

He directs his bright perfect eye against an enclosing wall. Though my clear eye is very weak I direct it against keenness of knowledge.

He is joyful with swift movement when a mouse sticks in his sharp paw. I too am joyful when I understand a dearly loved difficult problem.

Though we be thus at any time, neither of us hinders the other: each of us likes his craft, severally rejoicing in them.

He it is who is master for himself of the work which he does every day. I can perform my own work directed at understanding clearly what is difficult.

The Scribe in the Woods

A hedge of trees overlooks me; a blackbird's lay sings to me (an announcement which I shall not conceal); above my lined book the birds' chanting sings to me.

A clear-voiced cuckoo sings to me (goodly utterance) in a grey cloak from bush fortresses. The Lord is indeed good to me: well do I write beneath a forest of woodland.

The Lord of Creation

Let us adore the Lord, maker of wondrous works, great bright Heaven with its angels, the white-waved sea on earth.

My Hand Is Weary with Writing

My hand is weary with writing; my sharp great point is not thick; my slender-beaked pen juts forth a beetle-hued draft of bright blue ink.

A steady stream of wisdom springs from my well-colored neat fair hand; on the page it pours its draft of ink of the green-skinned holly.

I send my little dripping pen unceasingly over an assemblage of books of great beauty, to enrich the possessions of men of art—whence my hand is weary with writing.

Anglo-Norman Literature

ROMANCE

R omances satisfy our deepest imaginative desires. If we most fear loss of identity in separation from what we hold dearest and from what makes us what we are, romances allay that fear. As they imagine narratives of separation, errancy, and loss, they therapeutically deliver endings of reintegration, recovery, and return. That which was lost is found.

The word *romans* was originally a simple linguistic designation, meaning "French," since French was derived from Latin, the language of Rome. In the twelfth century, however, the word narrowed in meaning, coming to designate narrative (forms of *roman* still mean "novel" in French, Italian, and German). The word then became particularly associated with a genre of narrative. It came to designate stories of separation and return, disintegration and reintegration.

Certainly classical Greek literature has examples of "romance" narrative, stories that involve separation, testing, and travel, all the prelude to, and premise of, a final homecoming and recognition. Homer's *Odyssey* is fundamentally a romance; five later Greek narratives of this kind also survive (first to fourth centuries CE). The broader modal commitment of romance to "comedy" (a story with a happy ending) also has classical roots. Romances are "comic" stories not because they make us laugh but, rather, like Shakespeare's comedies, they make us feel good through happy endings.

The dynamic French-speaking court cultures of twelfth-century France and England gave the genre its most powerful, undying impetus. Chrétien de Troyes (fl. 1160–90) is its greatest exponent in his Arthurian romances, but the rich set of Tristran materials, and the lais of Marie de France, are also of exceptional importance. The genre, once deeply planted in the twelfth century in French, flourishes anew in all European vernacular languages and in each historical period of European and American culture. It remains energetically immune to the literary plant killers of moralistic objection, high literary disdain for escapist entertainment, and satire.

The fundamental characteristic of romances is structural, not stylistic. They can be short or long, oral or literary, but to be romances they must have, or adapt, a particular story structure. Romances classically have a tripartite structure: integration (or implied integration); disintegration; and reintegration. They

The Dance of Mirth. *The Romance of the Rose*, ca. 1500. The scene illustrates a moment in the thirteenth-century French poem. Note the splendor and circularity of this aristocratic performance of amorous ritual.

begin in, or at least imply, a protected, civilized state of some integrated social unit (e.g., family). That state is disrupted, expelling a member of the unit (the hero or heroine of the story, who is usually young) into a wild place. Undergoing the tests of that wild place is the premise of return to the integrated, civilized state of familial and/or social unity. Successfully undergoing tests in the wild often results in marriage, in which case return to home and family is also return to an enlarged home and family.

This story pattern is characteristic of many fairy stories, medieval romances, Shakespearean comedies, novels, and popular movies. It not only represents desire but activates desire in its readers: the pleasure we take in such stories derives from our desire for the reintegration of lives in a coherent and constructive narrative. The desired pattern can also, of course, be adapted in many variations. In particular, it can be activated in order to be frustrated: some protagonists, particularly adulterous ones like Tristan and Ysolt, never reach home, forever needing to defer that unreachable happy ending of recognition.

Romances, then, are symbolic stories, replaying and allaying the fears of the young as they face the apparently insuperable challenges of the adult world. Their deepest wisdom is this: civilization is not a unitary concept. To enter and remain in the world of civilized order, we must, say romances, have commerce with all that threatens it. To regain Rome at the center, we must first be tested in the marginal wilds of romance. To be recognized and found, we must first be lost.

The romances offered here exemplify different possibilities derived from this story structure. *Lanval*, *Sir Gawain and the Green Knight*, and Chaucer's *Wife of Bath's Tale* each play fascinating games with the classic structure; they each pull against that structure in different ways.

MARIE DE FRANCE

M uch of twelfth-century French literature was composed in England in the Anglo-Norman dialect (see p. 10). Prominent among the earliest poets writing in the French vernacular, who shaped the genres, themes, and styles of later medieval European poetry, is the author who, in an epilogue to her *Fables*, calls herself Marie de France. That signature tells us only that her given name was Marie and that she was born in France, but circumstantial evidence from her writings shows that she spent much of her life in England. A reference to her in a French poem written in England around 1180 speaks of "dame Marie" who wrote "lais" much loved and praised, read, and heard by counts, barons, and knights and indicates that her poems also appealed to ladies who listened to them gladly and joyfully.

Three works can be safely attributed to Marie, probably written in the following order: the *Lais* [English "lay" refers to a short narrative poem in verse], the *Fables*, and *St. Patrick's Purgatory*. Marie's twelve lays are short romances (they range from 118 to 1,184 lines), each of which deals with a single event or crisis in the affairs of noble lovers. In her prologue, Marie tells us that she had heard these *performed*, and in several of the lays she refers to the Breton language and Breton storytellers—that is, professional minstrels from the French province of Brittany or the Celtic parts of Great Britain. Marie's lays provide the basis of the genre that came to be known as the "Breton lay." In the prologue Marie dedicates the work to a "noble king," who is most likely to have been Henry II of England, who reigned from 1154 to 1189.

The portrait of the author that emerges from the combination of these works is of a highly educated noblewoman, proficient in Latin and English as well as her native French, with ideas of her own and a strong commitment to writing. Scholars have proposed several Maries of the period who fit this description to identify the author. A likely candidate is Marie, abbess of Shaftesbury, an illegitimate daughter of Geoffrey of Anjou and thus half-sister of Henry II. Correct or not, such an identification points to the milieu in which Marie moved and to the kind of audience she was addressing.

Many of Marie's lays contain elements of magic and mystery. Medieval readers would recognize that *Lanval* is about a mortal lover and a fairy bride, although the word "fairy" is not used in the tale. In the Middle Ages fairies were not thought of as the small creatures they became in Elizabethan and later literature. Fairies are supernatural, sometimes dangerous, beings who possess magical powers and inhabit another world. Their realm in some respects resembles the human (fairies have kings and queens), and fairies generally keep to themselves and disappear when humans notice them. But the tales are often about crossovers between the human and fairy worlds. Chaucer's *Wife of Bath's Tale* is such a story.

Marie's narrative *Milun* has a tight family unit at its core, but that unit is divided in time and space by an oppressive marital system. Testing consists of long deferral; ability to recognize signs; and intergenerational violence, between father and son, that turns out to be constructive.

Chevrefoil, the shortest of Marie's lays, tells of a brief encounter between Tristran and Ysolt. The lay exemplifies the pain of their separation as well as the stratagems by which the lovers are forced to communicate and meet. The title refers to an image from the natural world that serves as a symbol of the inextricable and fatal character of the love that binds them to one another.

Marie wrote in eight-syllable couplets, which was the standard form of French narrative verse, employed also by Wace and Chrétien de Troyes. Here is what the beginning of Marie's prologue to the *Lais* says about her view of a writer's duty and, implicitly, of her own talent:

Ki Deu ad duné escïence	He to whom God has given knowledge
E de parler bon' eloquence	And the gift of speaking eloquently,
Ne s'en deit taisir ne celer,	Must not keep silent nor conceal the gift.
Ainz se deit volunters mustrer.	But he must willingly display it.

This translation of Marie's *Lanval* is by Robert Hanning and Joan Ferrante.

Lanval

I shall tell you the adventure of another *lai,*
just as it happened:
it was composed about a very noble vassal;
in Breton, they call him Lanval.
5   Arthur, the brave and the courtly king,
was staying at Cardoel,
because the Scots and the Picts
were destroying the land.
They invaded Logres[1]
10   and laid it waste.

1. England.

At Pentecost, in summer,[2]
the king stayed there.
He gave out many rich gifts:
to counts and barons,
15   members of the Round Table—
such a company had no equal[3] in all the world—
he distributed wives and lands,
to all but one who had served him.
That was Lanval; Arthur forgot him,
20   and none of his men favored him either.
For his valor, for his generosity,
his beauty and his bravery,
most men envied him;
some feigned the appearance of love
25   who, if something unpleasant happened to him,
would not have been at all disturbed.
He was the son of a king of high degree
but he was far from his heritage.
He was of the king's household
30   but he had spent all his wealth,
for the king gave him nothing
nor did Lanval ask.
Now Lanval was in difficulty,
depressed and very worried.
35   My lords, don't be surprised:
a strange man, without friends,
is very sad in another land,
when he doesn't know where to look for help.
The knight of whom I speak,
40   who had served the king so long,
one day mounted his horse
and went off to amuse himself.
He left the city
and came, all alone, to a field;
45   he dismounted by a running stream
but his horse trembled badly.
He removed the saddle and went off,
leaving the horse to roll around in the meadow.
He folded his cloak beneath his head
50   and lay down.
He worried about his difficulty,
he could see nothing that pleased him.
As he lay there
he looked down along the bank
55   and saw two girls approaching;
he had never seen any lovelier.
They were richly dressed,
tightly laced,
in tunics of dark purple;
60   their faces were very lovely.

2. In medieval poetry the feast of Pentecost is frequently the starting point of an Arthurian adventure.
3. Equal in number as well as in worth.

The older one carried basins,
golden, well made, and fine;
I shall tell you the truth about it, without fail.[4]
The other carried a towel.
65 They went straight
to where the knight was lying.
Lanval, who was very well bred,
got up to meet them.
They greeted him first
70 and gave him their message:
"Sir Lanval, my lady,
who is worthy and wise and beautiful,
sent us for you.
Come with us now.
75 We shall guide you there safely.
See, her pavilion is nearby!"
The knight went with them;
giving no thought to his horse
who was feeding before him in the meadow.
80 They led him up to the tent,
which was quite beautiful and well placed.
Queen Semiramis,
however much more wealth,
power, or knowledge she had,
85 or the emperor Octavian
could not have paid for one of the flaps.
There was a golden eagle on top of it,
whose value I could not tell,
nor could I judge the value of the cords or the poles
90 that held up the sides of the tent;
there is no king on earth who could buy it,
no matter what wealth he offered.
The girl was inside the tent:
the lily and the young rose
95 when they appear in the summer
are surpassed by her beauty.
She lay on a beautiful bed—
the bedclothes were worth a castle—
dressed only in her shift.
100 Her body was well shaped and elegant;
for the heat, she had thrown over herself,
a precious cloak of white ermine,
covered with purple alexandrine,
but her whole side was uncovered,
105 her face, her neck and her bosom;
she was whiter than the hawthorn flower.
The knight went forward
and the girl addressed him.
He sat before the bed.
110 "Lanval," she said, "sweet love,

---

4. Cf. lines 178–79, where these articles are used. Washing one's hands before meals indicates aristocratic luxury and refinement. Marie makes a mock pretense that her listeners could hardly imagine these splendors of the other world.

because of you I have come from my land;
I came to seek you from far away.
If you are brave and courtly,
no emperor or count or king
115   will ever have known such joy or good;
for I love you more than anything."
He looked at her and saw that she was beautiful;
Love stung him with a spark
that burned and set fire to his heart.
120   He answered her in a suitable way.
"Lovely one," he said, "if it pleased you,
if such joy might be mine
that you would love me,
there is nothing you might command,
125   within my power, that I would not do,
whether foolish or wise.
I shall obey your command;
for you, I shall abandon everyone.
I want never to leave you.
130   That is what I most desire."
When the girl heard the words
of the man who could love her so,
she granted him her love and her body.
Now Lanval was on the right road!
135   Afterward, she gave him a gift:
he would never again want anything,
he would receive as he desired;
however generously he might give and spend,
she would provide what he needed.
140   Now Lanval is well cared for.
The more lavishly he spends,
the more gold and silver he will have.
"Love," she said, "I admonish you now,
I command and beg you,
145   do not let any man know about this.
I shall tell you why:
you would lose me for good
if this love were known;
you would never see me again
150   or possess my body."
He answered that he would do
exactly as she commanded.
He lay beside her on the bed;
now Lanval is well cared for.
155   He remained with her
that afternoon, until evening
and would have stayed longer, if he could,
and if his love had consented.
"Love," she said, "get up.
160   You cannot stay any longer.
Go away now; I shall remain
but I will tell you one thing:
when you want to talk to me

there is no place you can think of
165 where a man might have his mistress
without reproach or shame,
that I shall not be there with you
to satisfy all your desires.
No man but you will see me
170 or hear my words."
When he heard her, he was very happy,
he kissed her, and then got up.
The girls who had brought him to the tent
dressed him in rich clothes;
175 when he was dressed anew,
there wasn't a more handsome youth in all the world;
he was no fool, no boor.
They gave him water for his hands
and a towel to dry them,
180 and they brought him food.
He took supper with his love;
it was not to be refused.
He was served with great courtesy,
he received it with great joy.
185 There was an entremet[5]
that vastly pleased the knight
for he kissed his lady often
and held her close.
When they finished dinner,
190 his horse was brought to him.
The horse had been well saddled;
Lanval was very richly served.
The knight took his leave, mounted,
and rode toward the city,
195 often looking behind him.
Lanval was very disturbed;
he wondered about his adventure
and was doubtful in his heart;
he was amazed, not knowing what to believe;
200 he didn't expect ever to see her again.
He came to his lodging
and found his men well dressed.
That night, his accommodations were rich
but no one knew where it came from.
205 There was no knight in the city
who really needed a place to stay
whom he didn't invite to join him
to be well and richly served.
Lanval gave rich gifts,
210 Lanval released prisoners,
Lanval dressed jongleurs,[6]
Lanval offered great honors.

---

5. French *entremès*: a side dish served between main courses; an interlude between acts. Marie may well intend a double-entendre involving both meanings.
6. Performers.

There was no stranger or friend
to whom Lanval didn't give.
215 Lanval's joy and pleasure were intense;
in the daytime or at night,
he could see his love often;
she was completely at his command.

In that same year, it seems to me,
220 after the feast of St. John,
about thirty knights
were amusing themselves
in an orchard beneath the tower
where the queen was staying.
225 Gawain was with them
and his cousin, the handsome Yvain;
Gawain, the noble, the brave,
who was so loved by all, said:
"By God, my lords, we wronged
230 our companion Lanval,
who is so generous and courtly,
and whose father is a rich king,
when we didn't bring him with us."
They immediately turned back,
235 went to his lodging
and prevailed on Lanval to come along with them.
At a sculpted window
the queen was looking out;
she had three ladies with her.
240 She saw the king's retinue,
recognized Lanval and looked at him.
Then she told one of her ladies
to send for her maidens,
the loveliest and the most refined;
245 together they went to amuse themselves
in the orchard where the others were.
She brought thirty or more with her;
they descended the steps.
The knights came to meet them,
250 because they were delighted to see them.
The knights took them by the hand;
their conversation was in no way vulgar.
Lanval went off to one side,
far from the others; he was impatient
255 to hold his love,
to kiss and embrace and touch her;
he thought little of others' joys
if he could not have his pleasure.
When the queen saw him alone,
260 she went straight to the knight.
She sat beside him and spoke,
revealing her whole heart:
"Lanval, I have shown you much honor,
I have cherished you, and loved you.

265 You may have all my love;
just tell me your desire.
I promise you my affection.
You should be very happy with me."
"My lady," he said, "let me be!
270 I have no desire to love you.
I've served the king a long time;
I don't want to betray my faith to him.
Never, for you or for your love,
will I do anything to harm my lord."
275 The queen got angry;
in her wrath, she insulted him:
"Lanval," she said, "I am sure
you don't care for such pleasure;
people have often told me
280 that you have no interest in women.
You have fine-looking boys
with whom you enjoy yourself.
Base coward, lousy cripple,
my lord made a bad mistake
285 when he let you stay with him.
For all I know, he'll lose God because of it."
When Lanval heard her, he was quite disturbed;
he was not slow to answer.
He said something out of spite
290 that he would later regret.
"Lady," he said, "of that activity
I know nothing,
but I love and I am loved
by one who should have the prize
295 over all the women I know.
And I shall tell you one thing;
you might as well know all:
any one of those who serve her,
the poorest girl of all,
300 is better than you, my lady queen,
in body, face, and beauty,
in breeding and in goodness."
The queen left him
and went, weeping, to her chamber.
305 She was upset and angry
because he had insulted her.
She went to bed sick;
never, she said, would she get up
unless the king gave her satisfaction
310 for the offense against her.
The king returned from the woods,
he'd had a very good day.
He entered the queen's chambers.
When she saw him, she began to complain.
315 She fell at his feet, asked his mercy,
saying that Lanval had dishonored her;
he had asked for her love,

and because she refused him
he insulted and offended her:
320 he boasted of a love
who was so refined and noble and proud
that her chambermaid,
the poorest one who served her,
was better than the queen.
325 The king got very angry;
he swore an oath:
if Lanval could not defend himself in court
he would have him burned or hanged.
The king left her chamber
330 and called for three of his barons;
he sent them for Lanval
who was feeling great sorrow and distress.
He had come back to his dwelling,
knowing very well
335 that he'd lost his love,
he had betrayed their affair.
He was all alone in a room,
disturbed and troubled;
he called on his love, again and again,
340 but it did him no good.
He complained and sighed,
from time to time he fainted;
then he cried a hundred times for her to have mercy
and speak to her love.
345 He cursed his heart and his mouth;
it's a wonder he didn't kill himself.
No matter how much he cried and shouted,
ranted and raged,
she would not have mercy on him,
350 not even let him see her.
How will he ever contain himself?
The men the king sent
arrived and told him
to appear in court without delay:
355 the king had summoned him
because the queen had accused him.
Lanval went with his great sorrow;
they could have killed him, for all he cared.
He came before the king;
360 he was very sad, thoughtful, silent;
his face revealed great suffering.
In anger the king told him:
"Vassal, you have done me a great wrong!
This was a base undertaking,
365 to shame and disgrace me
and to insult the queen.
You have made a foolish boast:
your love is much too noble
if her maid is more beautiful,
370 more worthy, than the queen."

Lanval denied that he'd dishonored
or shamed his lord,
word for word, as the king spoke:
he had not made advances to the queen;
375 but of what he had said,
he acknowledged the truth,
about the love he had boasted of,
that now made him sad because he'd lost her.
About that he said he would do
380 whatever the court decided.
The king was very angry with him;
he sent for all his men
to determine exactly what he ought to do
so that no one could find fault with his decision.[7]
385 They did as he commanded,
whether they liked it or not.
They assembled,
judged, and decided,
than Lanval should have his day;
390 but he must find pledges for his lord
to guarantee that he would await the judgment,
return, and be present at it.
Then the court would be increased,
for now there were none but the king's household.[8]
395 The barons came back to the king
and announced their decision.
The king demanded pledges.
Lanval was alone and forlorn,
he had no relative, no friend.
400 Gawain went and pledged himself for him,
and all his companions followed.
The king addressed them: "I release him to you
on forfeit of whatever you hold from me,
lands and fiefs, each one for himself."
405 When Lanval was pledged, there was nothing else to do.
He returned to his lodging.
The knights accompanied him,
they reproached and admonished him
that he give up his great sorrow;
410 they cursed his foolish love.
Each day they went to see him,
because they wanted to know
whether he was drinking and eating;
they were afraid that he'd kill himself.
415 On the day that they had named,
the barons assembled.
The king and the queen were there
and the pledges brought Lanval back.
They were all very sad for him:

7. The trial of Lanval shows precise knowledge
of 12th-century legal procedure concerning the
respective rights of the king and his barons.
8. The case is important enough to require judgment by all of Arthur's vassals, not just the imme-

420 I think there were a hundred
who would have done all they could
to set him free without a trial
where he would be wrongly accused.
The king demanded a verdict
425 according to the charge and rebuttal.
Now it all fell to the barons.
They went to the judgment,
worried and distressed
for the noble man from another land
430 who'd gotten into such trouble in their midst.
Many wanted to condemn him
in order to satisfy their lord.
The Duke of Cornwall said:
"No one can blame us;
435 whether it makes you weep or sing
justice must be carried out.
The king spoke against his vassal
whom I have heard named Lanval;
he accused him of felony,
440 charged him with a misdeed—
a love that he had boasted of,
which made the queen angry.
No one but the king accused him:
by the faith I owe you,
445 if one were to speak the truth,
there should have been no need for defense,
except that a man owes his lord honor
in every circumstance.[9]
He will be bound by his oath,
450 and the king will forgive us our pledges
if he can produce proof;
if his love would come forward,
if what he said,
what upset the queen, is true,
455 then he will be acquitted,
because he did not say it out of malice.
But if he cannot get his proof,
we must make it clear to him
that he will forfeit his service to the king;
460 he must take his leave."
They sent to the knight,
told and announced to him
that he should have his love come
to defend and stand surety for him.
465 He told them that he could not do it:
he would never receive help from her.
They went back to the judges,
not expecting any help from Lanval.

diate household. Hence the delay of the trial.
9. Lanval's denial of the queen's accusation of
improper advances (lines 371–74) is accepted,
but he is nevertheless guilty of dishonoring his
lord unless he can prove the claims about his
mistress to which he has admitted.

The king pressed them hard
470 because of the queen who was waiting.
When they were ready to give their verdict
they saw two girls approaching,
riding handsome palfreys.
They were very attractive,
475 dressed in purple taffeta,
over their bare skin.
The men looked at them with pleasure.
Gawain, taking three knights with him,
went to Lanval and told him;
480 he pointed out the two girls.
Gawain was extremely happy, and begged him
to tell if his love were one of them.
Lanval said he didn't know who they were,
where they came from or where they were going.
485 The girls proceeded
still on horseback;
they dismounted before the high table
at which Arthur, the king, sat.
They were of great beauty,
490 and spoke in a courtly manner:
"King, clear your chambers,
have them hung with silk
where my lady may dismount;
she wishes to take shelter with you."
495 He promised it willingly
and called two knights
to guide them up to the chambers.
On that subject no more was said.
The king asked his barons
500 for their judgment and decision;
he said they had angered him very much
with their long delay.
"Sire," they said, "we have decided.
Because of the ladies we have just seen
505 we have made no judgment.
Let us reconvene the trial."
Then they assembled, everyone was worried;
there was much noise and strife.
While they were in that confusion,
510 two girls in noble array,
dressed in Phrygian silks
and riding Spanish mules,
were seen coming down the street.
This gave the vassals great joy;
515 to each other they said that now
Lanval, the brave and bold, was saved.
Gawain went up to him,
bringing his companions along.
"Sire," he said, "take heart.
520 For the love of God, speak to us.
Here come two maidens,

well adorned and very beautiful;
one must certainly be your love."
Lanval answered quickly
525 that he did not recognize them,
he didn't know them or love them.
Meanwhile they'd arrived,
and dismounted before the king.
Most of those who saw them praised them
530 for their bodies, their faces, their coloring;
each was more impressive
than the queen had ever been.
The older one was courtly and wise,
she spoke her message fittingly:
535 "King, have chambers prepared for us
to lodge my lady according to her need;
she is coming here to speak with you."
He ordered them to be taken
to the others who had preceded them.
540 There was no problem with the mules.
When he had seen to the girls,
he summoned all his barons
to render their judgment;
it had already dragged out too much.
545 The queen was getting angry
because she had fasted so long.
They were about to give their judgment
when through the city came riding
a girl on horseback:
550 there was none more beautiful in the world.
She rode a white palfrey,
who carried her handsomely and smoothly:
he was well apportioned in the neck and head,
no finer beast in the world.
555 The palfrey's trappings were rich;
under heaven there was no count or king
who could have afforded them all
without selling or mortgaging lands.
She was dressed in this fashion:
560 in a white linen shift
that revealed both her sides
since the lacing was along the side.
Her body was elegant, her hips slim,
her neck whiter than snow on a branch,
565 her eyes bright, her face white,
a beautiful mouth, a well-set nose,
dark eyebrows and an elegant forehead,
her hair curly and rather blond;
golden wire does not shine
570 like her hair in the light.
Her cloak, which she had wrapped around her,
was dark purple.
On her wrist she held a sparrow hawk,
a greyhound followed her.

575 In the town, no one, small or big,
old man or child,
failed to come look.
As they watched her pass,
there was no joking about her beauty.
580 She proceeded at a slow pace.
The judges who saw her
marveled at the sight;
no one who looked at her
was not warmed with joy.
585 Those who loved the knight
came to him and told him
of the girl who was approaching,
if God pleased, to rescue him.
"Sir companion, here comes one
590 neither tawny nor dark;
this is, of all who exist,
the most beautiful woman in the world."
Lanval heard them and lifted his head;
he recognized her and sighed.
595 The blood rose to his face;
he was quick to speak.
"By my faith," he said, "that is my love.
Now I don't care if I am killed,
if only she forgives me.
600 For I am restored, now that I see her."
The lady entered the palace;
no one so beautiful had ever been there.
She dismounted before the king
so that she was well seen by all.
605 And she let her cloak fall
so they could see her better.
The king, who was well bred,
rose and went to meet her;
all the others honored her
610 and offered to serve her.
When they had looked at her well,
when they had greatly praised her beauty,
she spoke in this way,
she didn't want to wait:
615 "I have loved one of your vassals:
you see him before you—Lanval.
He has been accused in your court—
I don't want him to suffer
for what he said; you should know
620 that the queen was in the wrong.
He never made advances to her.
And for the boast that he made,
if he can be acquitted through me,
let him be set free by your barons."
625 Whatever the barons judged by law
the king promised would prevail.
To the last man they agreed

that Lanval had successfully answered the charge.
He was set free by their decision
630 and the girl departed.
The king could not detain her,
though there were enough people to serve her.
Outside the hall stood
a great stone of dark marble
635 where heavy men mounted
when they left the king's court;
Lanval climbed on it.
When the girl came through the gate
Lanval leapt, in one bound,
640 onto the palfrey, behind her.
With her he went to Avalun,
so the Bretons tell us,
to a very beautiful island;
there the youth was carried off.
645 No man heard of him again,
and I have no more to tell.

1154–89

Middle English Literature in the Fourteenth and Fifteenth Centuries

SIR GAWAIN AND THE GREEN KNIGHT
ca. 1375–1400

Between the *Ancrene Wisse* and the later fourteenth century, writers deployed English for many genres, especially for saints' lives and romances. The finest Arthurian romance in English survives in only one manuscript, which also contains three religious poems—*Pearl, Patience,* and *Purity*—generally believed to be by the same poet. Nothing is known about the author except what can be inferred from the works. The dialect of the poems locates them in a remote corner of the northwest midlands between Cheshire and Staffordshire, and details of Sir Gawain's journey north show that the author was familiar with the geography of that region. But if author and audience were provincials, *Sir Gawain* and the other poems in the manuscript reveal them to have been highly sophisticated and well acquainted both with the international culture of the high Middle Ages and with ancient insular traditions.

Sir Gawain belongs to the so-called Alliterative Revival. After the Norman Conquest, alliterative verse doubtless continued to be recited by oral poets. At the beginning, the *Gawain* poet pretends that this romance is an oral poem and asks the audience to "listen" to a story, which he has "heard." Alliterative verse also continued to appear in Early Middle English texts. Layamon's *Brut* is the outstanding example. During the late fourteenth century there was a renewed flowering of alliterative poetry, especially in the north and west of Britain, which includes *Piers Plowman* and a splendid poem known as *The Alliterative Morte Darthur*.

The *Gawain* poet's audience evidently valued the kind of alliterative verse that Chaucer's Parson caricatures as "Rum-Ram-Ruf by lettre". They would also have understood archaic poetic diction surviving from Old English poetry such as *athel* (noble) and words of Scandinavian origin such as *skete* (quickly) and *skifted* (alternated). They were well acquainted with French Arthurian romances and the latest fashions in clothing, armor, and castle building. In making Sir Gawain, Arthur's sister's son, the preeminent knight of the Round Table, the poet was faithful to an older tradition. The thirteenth-century French romances, which in the next century became the main sources of Sir Thomas Malory, had made Sir Lancelot the best of Arthur's knights and Lancelot's adultery with Queen Guinevere the central event on which the fate of Arthur's kingdom turns. In *Sir Gawain* Lancelot is only one name in a list of Arthur's knights. Arthur is still a youth, and the court is in its springtime. Sir Gawain epitomizes this first blooming of Arthurian chivalry, and the reputation of the court rests upon his shoulders.

Ostensibly, Gawain's head is what is at stake. The main plot belongs to a type folklorists classify as the "Beheading Game," in which a supernatural challenger offers to let his head be cut off in exchange for a return blow. The earliest written occurrence of this motif is in the Middle Irish tale of *Bricriu's Feast*. The *Gawain* poet could have

Baronial Feasting. Limbourg Brothers, "January," from *Les Très Riches Heures du Duc de Berry*, ca. 1411–16. This wall hanging depicts the Trojan War as if it were invading the protected space of the duke's feast.

encountered it in several French romances as well as in oral tradition. But the outcome of the game here does not turn only on the champion's courage as it does in *Bricriu's Feast*. The *Gawain* poet has devised another series of tests for the hero that link the beheading with his truth, the emblem of which is the pentangle—a five-pointed star—displayed on Gawain's coat of arms and shield. The word *truth* in Middle English means not only what it still means now—a fact, belief, or idea held to be "true"—but what is conveyed by the old-fashioned variant from the same root: *troth*—that is, faith pledged by one's word and owed to a lord, a spouse, or anyone who puts someone else under an obligation. In this respect, Sir Gawain is being measured against a moral and Christian ideal of chivalry. Whether or not he succeeds in that contest is a question carefully left unresolved—perhaps as a challenge for the reader.

The poet has framed Gawain's adventure with references in the first and last stanzas to what are called the "Brutus books," the foundation stories that trace the origins of Rome and Britain back to the destruction of Troy. A cyclical sense of history as well as of the cycles of the seasons of the year, the generations of humankind, and of individual lives runs through *Sir Gawain and the Green Knight*.

The poem is written in stanzas that contain a group of alliterative lines (the number of lines in a stanza varies). The line is longer and does not contain a fixed number or pattern of stresses like the classical alliterative measure of Old English poetry. Each stanza closes with five short lines rhyming *a b a b a*. The first of these rhyming lines contains just one stress and is called the "bob"; the four three-stress lines that follow are called the "wheel." For details on alliterative verse, see "Old and Middle English Prosody" (pp. 23–25). The opening stanza is printed below in Middle English with an interlinear translation. The stressed alliterating sounds have been italicized.

> *Si*then the *se*ge and the *a*ssaut was *se*sed at *Troye*,
> After the siege and the assault was ceased at Troy,
>
> The *b*orgh *b*rittened and *b*rent to *b*rondes and askes,
> The city destroyed and burned to brands and ashes,
>
> The *t*ulk that the *t*rammes of *t*resoun ther wroght
> The man who the plots of treason there wrought
>
> Was *t*ried for his *t*richerie, the *t*rewest on erthe.
> Was tried for his treachery, the truest on earth.

Hit was *E*nnias the *a*thel and his *h*ighe kynde,
It was Aeneas the noble and his high race,

That sithen de*p*reced *p*rovinces, and *p*atrounes bicome
Who after subjugated provinces, and lords became

*W*elneghe of al the *w*ele in the *w*est iles.
Wellnigh of all the wealth in the west isles.

Fro *r*iche *R*omulus to *R*ome *r*icchis hym swythe,
Then noble Romulus to Rome proceeds quickly,

With gret *b*obbaunce that *b*urghe he *b*iges upon fyrst
With great pride that city he builds at first

And *n*evenes hit his aune *n*ome, as hit *n*ow hat;
And names it his own name, as it now is called;

*T*icius to *T*uskan and *t*eldes bigynnes,
Ticius (goes) to Tuscany and houses begins,

*L*angaberde in *L*umbardie *l*yftes up homes,
Longbeard in Lombardy raises up homes,

And *f*er over the *F*rench *f*lod, Felix Brutus
And far over the English Channel, Felix Brutus

On mony *b*onkkes ful *b*rode Bretayn he settes
On many banks very broad Brittain he sets

*Wyth *w*ynne,*
With joy,

*W*here *w*erre and *w*rake and *w*onder
Where war and revenge and wondrous happenings

Bi sythes has wont therinne,
On occasions have dwelled therein

And oft *b*othe *b*lysse and *b*lunder
And often both joy and strife

Ful *sk*ete has *sk*yfted synne.
Very swiftly have alternated since.

Sir Gawain and the Green Knight[1]

FITT i

Once the siege and assault of Troy had ceased,
with the city a smoke-heap of cinders and ash,

---

1. This translation is by Simon Armitage.

the traitor who contrived such betrayal there
was tried for his treachery, the truest on earth;[2]
5 Aeneas, it was, with his noble warriors
who went conquering abroad, laying claim to the crowns
of the wealthiest kingdoms in the western world.
Mighty Romulus[3] quickly careered towards Rome
and conceived a city in magnificent style
10 which from then until now has been known by his name.
Ticius constructed townships in Tuscany
and Langobard[4] did likewise building homes in Lombardy.
And further afield, over the Sea of France,
Felix Brutus[5] founds Britain on broad banks
15   most grand.
         And wonder, dread and war
         have lingered in that land
         where loss and love in turn
         have held the upper hand.

20 After Britain was built by this founding father
a bold race bred there, battle-happy men
causing trouble and torment in turbulent times,
and through history more strangeness has happened here
than anywhere else I know of on Earth.
25 But most regal of rulers in the royal line
was Arthur, who I heard is honored above all,
and the inspiring story I intend to spin
has moved the hearts and minds of many—
an awesome episode in the legends of Arthur.
30 So listen a little while to my tale if you will
and I'll tell it as it's told in the town where it trips from
                    the tongue;
         and as it has been inked
         in stories bold and strong,
35   where loyal letters linked
         have lasted loud and long.

It was Christmas at Camelot—King Arthur's court,
where the great and the good of the land had gathered,
the right noble lords of the ranks of the Round Table
40 all roundly carousing and reveling in pleasure.
Time after time, in tournaments of joust,
they had lunged at each other with leveled lances
then returned to the castle to carry on their caroling,
for the feasting lasted a full fortnight and one day,
45 with more food and drink than a fellow could dream of.
The hubbub of their humor was heavenly to hear:
pleasant dialogue by day and dancing after dusk,

---

2. The treacherous knight is Aeneas, who was a
traitor to his city, Troy, according to medieval
tradition, but Aeneas was actually tried by the
Greeks for his refusal to hand his sister Polyxena
over to them.
3. Like Aeneas, the legendary founder of Rome

is here given Trojan ancestry.
4. The reputed founder of Lombardy. Ticius is
not otherwise known.
5. Great-grandson of Aeneas and legendary
founder of Britain, not elsewhere given the name
Felix (Latin, "happy").

so house and hall were lit with happiness
and lords and ladies were luminous with joy.
50 With all the wonder in the world they gathered there as one:
the most chivalrous and courteous knights known to Christendom;
the most wonderful women to have walked in this world;
the handsomest king to be crowned at court.
All these fair folk in their first age, together in
55   that hall:
        most fortunate under heaven,
        with Arthur, that man of high will;
        no bolder band could ever
        be found on field or hill.

60 With New Year so young it still yawned and stretched
helpings were doubled on the dais that day.
And as king and company were coming to the hall
the choir in the chapel fell suddenly quiet,
then a chorus erupted from the courtiers and clerks:
65 "Noel," they cheered, then "Noel, Noel,"
"New Year Gifts!" the knights cried next
as they pressed forwards to offer their presents,
teasing with frivolous favors and forfeits,
till those ladies who lost couldn't help but laugh,
70 and the undefeated were far from forlorn.[6]
Their merrymaking rolled on in this manner until mealtime,
when, worthily washed, they went to the table,
and were seated in order of honor, as was apt,
with Guinevere in their gathering, gloriously framed
75 at her place on the platform, pricelessly curtained
by silk to each side, and canopied across
with tasteful tapestries of Toulouse and Tharsia,
studded with stones and stunning gems
beyond pocket or purse, beyond what pennies
80   could buy.
        But not one stone outshone
        the quartz of the queen's eyes;
        with hand on heart, no one
        could argue otherwise.

85 But Arthur would not eat until all were served.
He brimmed with ebullience, being almost boyish
in his love of life, and what he liked the least
was to sit still watching the seasons slip by.
His blood was busy and he buzzed with thoughts,
90 and the matter which played on his mind at that moment
was his pledge to take no portion from his plate
on such a special day until a story was told:
some far-fetched yarn or outrageous fable,
the tallest of tales, yet one ringing with truth,
95 like the action-packed epics of men-at-arms.
Or till some chancer had challenged his chosen knight,

---

6. The forfeit that made the ladies who lost laugh was in all likelihood a kiss.

dared him, with a lance, to lay life on the line,
to stare death face-to-face and accept defeat
should fortune or fate smile more favorably on his foe.
100 Within Camelot's castle this was the custom,
and at feasts and festivals when the fellowship
would meet.
With features proud and fine
he stood there tall and straight,
105 a king at Christmastime
amid great merriment.

And still he stands there just being himself,
chatting away charmingly, exchanging views.
Good Sir Gawain is seated by Guinevere,
110 and on his other side Agravain the Hard Hand sits,
both nephews of the king and notable knights.
At the head of the board sat Bishop Baldwin,
with Ywain, son of Urien, to eat beside him.
First those sitting on the dais[7] were splendidly served,
115 then those stalwarts seated on the benches to the sides.
The first course comes in to the fanfare and clamor
of blasting trumpets hung with trembling banners,
then pounding double-drums and dinning pipes,
weird sounds and wails of such warbled wildness
120 that to hear and feel them made the heart float free.
Flavorsome delicacies of flesh were fetched in
and the freshest of foods, so many in fact
there was scarcely space to present the stews
or to set the soups in the silver bowls on
125 the cloth.
Each guest received his share
of bread or meat or broth;
a dozen plates per pair—
plus beer or wine, or both.

130 Now, on the subject of supper I'll say no more
as it's obvious to everyone that no one went without.
Because another sound, a new sound, suddenly drew near,
which might signal the king to sample his supper,
for barely had the horns finished blowing their breath
135 and with starters just spooned to the seated guests,
a fearful form appeared, framed in the door:
a mountain of a man, immeasurably high,
a hulk of a human from head to hips,
so long and thick in his loins and his limbs
140 I should genuinely judge him to be a half giant,
or a most massive man, the mightiest of mortals.
But handsome, too, like any horseman worth his horse,
for despite the bulk and brawn of his body
his stomach and waist were slender and sleek.

---

7. A raised platform. Although the Round Table is referred to (line 39), the king and queen, along with the most prominent members of the court, are seated above the rest.

145 In fact in all features he was finely formed
    it seemed.
   Amazement seized their minds,
   no soul had ever seen
   a knight of such a kind—
150   entirely emerald green.

And his gear and garments were green as well:
a tight fitting tunic, tailored to his torso,
and a cloak to cover him, the cloth fully lined
with smoothly shorn fur clearly showing, and faced
155 with all-white ermine, as was the hood,
worn shawled on his shoulders, shucked from his head.
On his lower limbs his leggings were also green,
wrapped closely round his calves, and his sparkling spurs
were green-gold, strapped with stripy silk,
160 and were set on his stockings, for this stranger was shoeless.
In all vestments he revealed himself veritably verdant!
From his belt hooks and buckle to the baubles and gems
arrayed so richly around his costume
and adorning the saddle, stitched onto silk.
165 All the details of his dress are difficult to describe,
embroidered as it was with butterflies and birds,
green beads emblazoned on a background of gold.
All the horse's tack—harness strap, hind strap,
the eye of the bit, each alloy and enamel
170 and the stirrups he stood in were similarly tinted,
and the same with the cantle and the skirts of the saddle,
all glimmering and glinting with the greenest jewels.
And the horse: every hair was green, from hoof
    to mane.
175   A steed of pure green stock.
   Each snort and shudder strained
   the hand-stitched bridle, but
   his rider had him reined.

The fellow in green was in fine fettle.
180 The hair of his head was as green as his horse,
fine flowing locks which fanned across his back,
plus a bushy green beard growing down to his breast,
which hung with the splendid hair from his head
and was lopped in a line at elbow length
185 so half his arms were gowned in green growth,
crimped at the collar, like a king's cape.
The mane of his mount was groomed to match,
combed and knotted into curlicues
then tinseled with gold, tied and twisted
190 green over gold, green over gold.
The fetlocks were finished in the same fashion
with bright green ribbon braided with beads,
as was the tail—to its tippety-tip!
And a long, tied thong lacing it tight
195 where bright and burnished gold bells chimed clearly.

No waking man had witnessed such a warrior
or weird warhorse—otherworldly, yet flesh
        and bone.
     His look was lightning bright
200   said those who glimpsed its glow.
     It seemed no man there might
     survive his violent blow.

Yet he wore no helmet and no hauberk either,
no armored apparel or plate was apparent,
205   and he swung no sword nor sported any shield,
but held in one hand a sprig of holly—
of all the evergreens the greenest ever—
and in the other hand held the mother of all axes,
a cruel piece of kit I kid you not:
210   the head was an ell in length at least
and forged in green steel with a gilt finish;
its broad-edged blade brightly burnished,
it could shear a man's scalp and shave him to boot.
The handle which fitted that fiend's great fist
215   was inlaid with iron, end to end,
with green pigment picking out impressive designs.
From stock to neck, where it stopped with a knot,
a lace was looped the length of the haft,
trimmed with tassels and tails of string
220   fastened firmly in place by forest-green buttons.
And he kicks on, canters through that crowded hall
towards the top table, not the least bit timid,
cocksure of himself, sitting high in the saddle.
"And who," he bellows, without breaking breath,
225   "is governor of this gaggle? I'll be glad to know.
It's with him and no one else that I'll hold
        a pact."
     He held them with his eyes,
     and looked from right to left,
230   not knowing, of those knights,
     which person to respect.

The guests looked on. They gaped and they gawked
and were mute with amazement: what did it mean
that human and horse could develop this hue,
235   should grow to be grass-green or greener still,
like green enamel emboldened by bright gold?
Some stood and stared then stepped a little closer,
drawn near to the knight to know his next move;
they'd seen some sights, but this was something special,
240   a miracle or magic, or so they imagined.
Yet several of the lords were like statues in their seats,
left speechless and rigid, not risking a response.
The hall fell hushed, as if all who were present
had slipped into sleep or some trancelike state.
245   No doubt
     not all were stunned and stilled

by dread, but duty bound
to hold their tongues until
their sovereign could respond.

250 Then the king acknowledged this curious occurrence,
cordially addressed him, keeping his cool.
"A warm welcome, sir, this winter's night.
My name is Arthur, I am head of this house.
Won't you slide from that saddle and stay awhile,
255 and the business which brings you we shall learn of later."
"No," said the knight, "by Him in highest heaven,
I'm not here to idle in your hall this evening.
But because your acclaim is so loudly chorused,
and your castle and brotherhood are called the best,
260 the strongest men to ever mount the saddle,
the worthiest knights ever known to the world,
both in competition and true combat,
and since courtesy, so it's said, is championed here,
I'm intrigued, and attracted to your door at this time.
265 Be assured by this holly stem here in my hand
that I mean no menace. So expect no malice,
for if I'd slogged here tonight to slay and slaughter
my helmet and hauberk wouldn't be at home
and my sword and spear would be here at my side,
270 and more weapons of war, as I'm sure you're aware;
I'm clothed for peace, not kitted out for conflict.
But if you're half as honorable as I've heard folk say
you'll gracefully grant me this game which I ask for
                    by right."
275   Then Arthur answered, "Knight
            most courteous, if you claim
            a fair, unarmored fight,
            we'll see you have the same."

"I'm spoiling for no scrap, I swear. Besides,
280 the bodies on these benches are just bum-fluffed bairns.
If I'd ridden to your castle rigged out for a ruck
these lightweight men wouldn't last a minute.
But it's Yuletide—a time of youthfulness, yes?
So at Christmas in this court I lay down a challenge:
285 if a person here present, within these premises,
is big or bold or red-blooded enough
to strike me one stroke and be struck in return,
I shall give him as a gift this gigantic cleaver
and the axe shall be his to handle how he likes.
290 I'll kneel, bare my neck and take the first knock.
So who has the gall? The gumption? The guts?
Who'll spring from his seat and snatch this weapon?
I offer the axe—who'll have it as his own?
I'll afford one free hit from which I won't flinch,
295 and promise that twelve months will pass in peace,
                    then claim
            the duty I deserve

in one year and one day.
Does no one have the nerve
300   to wager in this way?"

If flustered at first, now totally foxed
were the household and the lords, both the highborn and
      the low.
Still stirruped, the knight swiveled round in his saddle
looking left and right, his red eyes rolling
305   beneath the bristles of his bushy green brows,
his beard swishing from side to side.
When the court kept its counsel he cleared his throat
and stiffened his spine. Then he spoke his mind:
"So here is the House of Arthur," he scoffed,
310   "whose virtues reverberate across vast realms.
Where's the fortitude and fearlessness you're so famous for?
And the breathtaking bravery and the big-mouth bragging?
The towering reputation of the Round Table,
skittled and scuppered by a stranger—what a scandal!
315   You flap and you flinch and I've not raised a finger!"
Then he laughed so loud that their leader saw red.
Blood flowed to his fine-featured face and he raged
                inside.
            His men were also hurt—
320   those words had pricked their pride.
            But born so brave at heart
            the king stepped up one stride.

"Your request," he countered, "is quite insane,
and folly finds the man who flirts with the fool.
325   No warrior worth his salt would be worried by your words,
so in heaven's good name hand over the axe
and I'll happily fulfill the favor you ask."
He strides to him swiftly and seizes his arm;
the man dismounts in one mighty leap.
330   Then Arthur grips the axe, grabs it by its haft
and takes it above him, intending to attack.
Yet the stranger before him stands up straight,
highest in the house by at least a head.
He stands there sternly, stroking his beard
335   drawing down his coat, countenance undaunted,
about to be bludgeoned, but no more bothered
than a guest at the table being given a goblet
                of wine.
            By Guinevere, Gawain
340   now to his king inclines
            and says, "I stake my claim.
            May this melee be mine."

"Should you call me, courteous lord," said Gawain to
      his king,
"to rise from my seat and stand at your side,
345   politely take leave of my place at the table
and quit without causing offence to my queen,

then I would come to your counsel before this great court.
For I find it unfitting, as my fellow knights would,
when a deed of such daring is dangled before us
350 that you take on this trial—tempted as you are—
when brave, bold men are seated on these benches,
men never matched in the mettle of their minds,
never beaten or bettered in the field of battle.
I am weakest of your warriors and feeblest of wit;
355 loss of my life would be least lamented.
Were I not your nephew my life would mean nothing;
to be born of your blood is my body's only claim.
Such a foolish affair is unfitting for a king,
so; being first to come forward, it should fall to me.
360 And if my proposal is improper, let no other person
    stand blame."
   The knighthood then unites
   and each knight says the same:
   their king can stand aside
365   and give Gawain the game.

So the sovereign instructed his knight to stand.
Getting to his feet he moved graciously forward
and knelt before Arthur, taking hold of the axe.
Letting go of it, Arthur then held up his hand
370 to give young Gawain the blessing of God
and hope he finds firmness in heart and fist.
"Take care, young cousin, to catch him cleanly,
use full-blooded force then you needn't fear
the blow which he threatens to trade in return."
375 Gawain, with the weapon, walked towards the warrior,
and they stood face-to-face, not one man afraid.
Then the green knight spoke, growled at Gawain:
"Before we compete, repeat what we've promised.
And start by saying your name to me, sir,
380 and tell me the truth so I can take it on trust."
"In good faith," said the knight, "Gawain is my name.
I heave this axe, and whatever happens after,
in twelvemonth's time I'll be struck in return
with any weapon you wish, and by you and you
385   alone."
   The green man speaks again:
   "I swear on all I know,
   I'm glad it's you, Gawain,
   who'll drive the axe-head home."

390 "Gawain," said the green knight, "by God, I'm glad
the favor I've called for will fall from your fist.
You've perfectly repeated the promise we made
and the terms of the contest are crystal clear.
Except for one thing: you must solemnly swear
395 that you'll seek me yourself; that you'll search me out
to the ends of the earth to earn the same blow
as you'll dole out today in this decorous hall."
"But where will you be? Where's your abode?

You're a man of mystery, as God is my maker.
400 Which court do you come from and what are you called?
There is knowledge I need, including your name,
then I shall use all my wit to work out the way,
and keep to our contract, so cross my heart."
"But enough at New Year. It needs nothing more,"
405 said the warrior in green to worthy Gawain.
"I could tell you the truth once you've taken the blow;
if you smite me smartly I could spell out the facts
of my house and home and my name, if it helps,
then you'll pay me a visit and vouch for our pact.
410 Or if I keep quiet you might cope all the better,
loafing and lounging here, looking no further. But
        we stall!
        Now grasp that gruesome axe
        and show your striking style."
415   He answered, "Since you ask,"
        and touched the tempered steel.

The green knight took his stance, prepared to be struck,
bent forward, revealing a flash of green flesh
as he heaped his hair to the crown of his head,
420 the nape of his neck now naked and ready.
Gawain grips the axe and heaves it heavenwards,
plants his left foot firmly on the floor in front,
then swings it swiftly towards the bare skin.
The cleanness of the strike cleaved the spinal cord
425 and parted the fat and the flesh so far
that the bright steel blade took a bite from the floor.
The handsome head tumbles onto the earth
and the king's men kick it as it clatters past.
Blood gutters brightly against his green gown,
430 yet the man doesn't shudder or stagger or sink
but trudges towards them on those tree-trunk legs
and rummages around, reaches at their feet
and cops hold of his head and hoists it high,
and strides to his steed, snatches the bridle,
435 steps into the stirrup and swings into the saddle
still gripping his head by a handful of hair.
Then he settles himself in his seat with the ease
of a man unmarked, never mind being minus
        his head!
440   He wheeled his bulk about,
        that body which still bled.
        They cowered in the court
        before his speech was said.

For that scalp and skull now swung from his fist;
445 to the noblest at the table he turned the face
and it opened its eyelids, stared straight ahead
and spoke this speech, which you'll hear for yourselves:
"Sir Gawain, be wise enough to keep your word
and faithfully follow me until you find me,
450 as you vowed in this hall within hearing of these horsemen.

You're charged with getting to the Green Chapel,
to reap what you've sown. You'll rightfully receive
that what is due to be dealt to you as New Year dawns.
Men know my name as the Green Chapel knight,
455 and even a fool couldn't fail to find me.
So come, or be called a coward forever."
With a tug of the reins he twisted around
and, head still in hand, galloped out of the hall,
so the hooves brought fire from the flame in the flint.
460 Which kingdom he came from they hadn't a clue,
no more than they knew where he made for next.
       And then?
       Well, with the green man gone
       they laughed and grinned again.
465   And yet such goings-on
       were magic to those men.

And although King Arthur was awestruck at heart
no sign of it showed. Instead he spoke
to his exquisite queen with courteous words:
470 "Dear lady, don't be daunted by this deed today,
it's in keeping that such strangeness should occur at Christmas
between sessions of banter and seasonal song,
amid the lively pastimes of ladies and lords.
And at least I'm allowed to eat at last,
475 having witnessed such wonder, wouldn't you say?"
Then he glanced at Gawain and spoke gracefully:
"Now hang up your axe[8]—one hack is enough."
So it dangled from the drape behind the dais
so that men who saw it would be mesmerized and amazed,
480 and give voice, on its evidence, to that stunning event.
Then the two of them turned and walked to the table,
the monarch and his knight, and men served the meal—
double dishes apiece, rare delicacies,
all manner of food—and the music of minstrels.
485 And they danced and sang till the sun went down
       that day.
       But mind your mood, Gawain,
       lest dread make you delay,
       or lose this lethal game
490   you've promised you will play.

FITT ii

This happening was a gift—just as Arthur had asked for
and had yearned to hear of while the year was young.
And if guests had no subject as they strolled to their seats,
now this serious concern sustained their chatter.
495 And Gawain had been glad to begin the game,
but don't be so shocked should the plot turn pear-shaped:
for men might be merry when addled with mead
but each year, short lived, is unlike the last

---

8. A colloquial expression equivalent to "bury the hatchet," but here with an ironic literal sense.

and rarely resolves in the style it arrived.
500 So the festival finishes and a new year follows
in eternal sequence, season by season.
After lavish Christmas come the lean days of Lent
when the flesh is tested with fish and simple food.
Then the world's weather wages war on winter:
505 cold shrinks earthwards and the clouds climb;
sun-warmed, shimmering rain comes showering
onto meadows and fields where flowers unfurl;
woods and grounds wear a wardrobe of green;
birds burble with life and build busily
510 as summer spreads, settling on slopes as
                    it should.
            Now every hedgerow brims
            with blossom and with bud,
            and lively songbirds sing
515   from lovely, leafy woods.

So summer comes in season with its subtle airs,
when the west wind sighs among shoots and seeds,
and those plants which flower and flourish are a pleasure
as their leaves let drip their drink of dew
520 and they sparkle and glitter when glanced by sunlight.
Then autumn arrives to harden the harvest
and with it comes a warning to ripen before winter.
The drying airs arrive, driving up dust
from the face of the earth to the heights of heaven,
525 and wild sky wrestles the sun with its winds,
and the leaves of the lime lie littered on the ground,
and grass that was green turns withered and gray.
Then all which had risen over-ripens and rots
and yesterday on yesterday the year dies away,
530 and winter returns, as is the way of the world
                    through time.
            At Michaelmas⁹ the moon
            stands like that season's sign,
            a warning to Gawain
535   to rouse himself and ride.

Yet he stayed until All Saints' Day by his sovereign's side,
and they feasted in the name of their noble knight
with the revels and riches of the Round Table.
The lords of that hall and their loving ladies
540 were sad and concerned for the sake of their knight,
but nevertheless they made light of his load.
Those joyless at his plight made jokes and rejoiced.
Then sorrowfully, after supper, he spoke with his uncle,
and openly talked of the trip he must take:
545 "Now, lord of my life, I must ask for your leave.
You were witness to my wager. I have no wish
to retell you the terms—they're nothing but a trifle.
I must set out tomorrow to receive that stroke

9. September 29.   1. November 1.

from the knight in green, and let God be my guide."
550 Then the cream of Camelot crowded around:
Ywain and Eric and others of that ilk,
Sir Dodinal the Dreaded, the Duke of Clarence,
Lancelot, Lionel, Lucan the Good,
and Sir Bors and Sir Bedevere—both big names,
555 and powerful men such as Mador de la Port.
This courtly committee approaches the king
to offer up heartfelt advice to our hero.
And sounds of sadness and sorrow were heard
that one as worthy and well liked as Gawain
560 should suffer that strike but offer no stroke in
reply.
Yet keeping calm the knight
just quipped, "Why should I shy
away. If fate is kind.
565 or cruel, man still must try."

He remained all that day and in the morning he dressed,
asked early for his arms and all were produced.
First a rug of rare cloth was unrolled on the floor,
heaped with gear which glimmered and gleamed,
570 and the stout knight steps onto it and handles the steel.
He tries on his tunic of extravagant silk,
then the neatly cut cloak, closed at the neck,
its lining finished with a layer of white fur.
Then they settled his feet into steel shoes
575 and clad his calves, clamped them with greaves,
then hinged and highly polished plates
were knotted with gold thread to the knight's knees.
Then leg guards were fitted, lagging the flesh,
attached with thongs to his thick-set thighs.
580 Then comes the suit of shimmering steel rings
encasing his body and his costly clothes:
well burnished braces to both of his arms,
good elbow guards and glinting metal gloves,
all the trimmings and trappings of a knight tricked out
585 to ride:
a metal suit that shone;
gold spurs which gleam with pride;
a keen sword swinging from
the silk belt to his side.

590 Fastened in his armor he seemed fabulous, famous,
every link looking golden to the very last loop.
Yet for all that metal he still made it to mass,
honored the Almighty before the high altar.
After which he comes to the king and his consorts
595 and asks to take leave of the ladies and lords;
they escort and kiss him and commended him to Christ.
Now Gringolet is rigged out and ready to ride
with a saddle which flickered with fine gold fringes
and was set with new studs for the special occasion.
600 The bridle was bound with stripes of bright gold,

the apparel of the panels was matched in appearance
to the color of the saddlebows and cropper and cover,
and nails of red gold were arrayed all around,
shining splendidly like splintered sunlight.
605 Then he holds up his helmet and hastily kisses it;
it was strongly stapled and its lining was stuffed,
and sat high on his head, fastened behind
with a colorful cloth to cover his neck
embroidered and bejeweled with brilliant gems
610 on the broad silk border, and with birds on the seams
such as painted parrots perched among periwinkles
and turtle doves and true lover's knots, tightly entwined
as if women had worked at it seven winters
    at least.
615   The diamond diadem
   was greater still. It gleamed
   with flawless, flashing gems
   both clear and smoked, it seemed.

Then they showed him the shining scarlet shield
620 with its pentangle painted in pure gold.[2]
He seized it by its strap and slung it round his neck;
he looked well in what he wore, and was worthy of it.
And why the pentangle was appropriate to that prince
I intend to say, though it will stall our story.
625 It is a symbol that Solomon once set in place
and is taken to this day as a token of fidelity,
for the form of the figure is a five-pointed star
and each line overlaps and links with the last
so is ever eternal, and when spoken of in England
630 is known by the name of the endless knot.
So it suits this soldier in his spotless armor,
fully faithful in five ways five times over.
For Gawain was as good as the purest gold—
devoid of vices but virtuous, loyal
635   and kind,
   so bore that badge on both
   his shawl and shield alike.
   A prince who talked the truth:
   known as the noblest knight.

2. A five-pointed star, formed by five lines drawn without lifting the pencil from the paper; as Solomon's sign (line 625), a mystical significance was attributed to it.

640 First he was deemed flawless in his five senses;
and secondly his five fingers were never at fault;
and thirdly his faith was founded in the five wounds
Christ received on the cross, as the creed recalls.
And fourthly, if that soldier struggled in skirmish
645 one thought pulled him through above all other things:
the fortitude he found in the five joys
which Mary had conceived in her son, our Savior.[3]
For precisely that reason the princely rider
had the shape of her image inside his shield,
650 so by catching her eye his courage would not crack.
The fifth set of five which I heard the knight followed
included friendship and fraternity with fellow men,
purity and politeness that impressed at all times,
and pity, which surpassed all pointedness. Five things
655 which meant more to Gawain than to most other men.
So these five sets of five were fixed in this knight,
each linked to the last through the endless line,
a five-pointed form which never failed,
never stronger to one side or slack at the other,
660 but unbroken in its being from beginning to end
however its trail is tracked and traced.
So the star on the spangling shield he sported
shone royally, in gold, on a ruby red background,
the pure pentangle as people have called it
665   for years.
      Then, lance in hand, held high,
      and got up in his gear
      he bids them all good-bye
      one final time, he fears.

670 Spiked with the spurs the steed sped away
with such force that the fire-stones sparked underfoot.
All sighed at the sight, and with sinking hearts
they whispered their worries to one another,
concerned for their comrade. "A pity, by Christ,
675 if a lord so noble should lose his life.
To find his equal on earth would be far from easy.
Cleverer to have acted with caution and care,
deemed him a duke—a title he was due—
a leader of men, lord of many lands;
680 better that than being battered into oblivion,
beheaded by an ogre, through headstrong pride.
Whoever knew any king to take counsel of a knight
in the grip of an engrossing Christmas game?"
Warm tears welled up in their weepy eyes
685 as gallant Sir Gawain galloped from court
        that day.
      He sped from home and hearth
      and went his winding way

---

3. The Annunciation, Nativity, Resurrection, Ascension, and Assumption. These overlap but are not similar to the Five Joyful Mysteries of the Rosary, which were not formally established until the 16th century.

on steep and snaking paths,
690   just as the story says.

Now through England's realm he rides and rides,
Sir Gawain, God's servant, on his grim quest,
passing long dark nights unloved and alone,
foraging to feed, finding little to call food,
695 with no friend but his horse through forests and hills
and only our Lord in heaven to hear him.
He wanders near to the north of Wales
with the Isles of Anglesey off to the left.
He keeps to the coast, fording each course,
700 crossing at Holy Head and coming ashore
in the wilds of the Wirral, whose wayward people
both God and good men have quite given up on.[4]
And he constantly enquires of those he encounters
if they know, or not, in this neck of the woods,
705 of a great green man or a Green Chapel.
No, they say, never. Never in their lives.
They know of neither a chap nor a chapel
        so strange.
    He trails through bleak terrain.
710   His mood and manner change
        at every twist and turn
        towards that chosen church.

In a strange region he scales steep slopes;
far from his friends he cuts a lonely figure.
715 Where he bridges a brook or wades through a waterway
it's no surprise to find that he faces a foe
so foul or fierce he is bound to use force.
So momentous are his travels among the mountains
to tell just a tenth would be a tall order.
720 Here he scraps with serpents and snarling wolves,
here he tangles with wodwos causing trouble in the crags,
or with bulls and bears and the odd wild boar.
Hard on his heels through the highlands come giants.
Only diligence and faith in the face of death
725 will keep him from becoming a corpse or carrion.
And the wars were one thing, but winter was worse:
clouds shed their cargo of crystallized rain
which froze as it fell to the frost-glazed earth.
Nearly slain by sleet he slept in his armor,
730 bivouacked in the blackness amongst bare rocks
where meltwater streamed from the snow-capped summits
and high overhead hung chandeliers of ice.
So in peril and pain Sir Gawain made progress,
crisscrossing the countryside until Christmas
735   Eve. Then
        at that time of tiding,

---

4. Gawain travels from Camelot north to the northern coast of Wales, opposite the islands of Anglesey, where he turns east across the Dee to the forest of Wirral in Cheshire.

he prayed to highest heaven.
Let Mother Mary guide him
towards some house or haven.

740   That morning he moves on, skirts the mountainside,
descends a deep forest, densely overgrown,
with vaulting hills to each half of the valley
and ancient oaks in huddles of hundreds.
Hazel and hawthorn are interwoven,
745   decked and draped in damp, shaggy moss,
and bedraggled birds on bare, black branches
pipe pitifully into the piercing cold.
Under cover of the canopy he girded Gringolet
through mud and marshland, a man all alone,
750   concerned and afraid in case he should fail
in the worship of our Deity, who, on that date
was born the Virgin's son to save our souls.
He prayed with heavy heart. "Father, hear me,
and Lady Mary, our mother most mild,
755   let me happen on some house where mass might be heard,
and matins in the morning; meekly I ask,
and here I utter my pater, ave
              and creed."
       He rides the path and prays,
760   dismayed by his misdeeds,
       and signs Christ's cross and says,
       "Be near me in my need."

No sooner had he signed himself three times
than he became aware, in those woods, of high walls
765   in a moat, on a mound, bordered by the boughs
of thick-trunked timber which trimmed the water.
The most commanding castle a knight ever kept,
positioned in a site of sweeping parkland
with a palisade of pikes pitched in the earth
770   in the midst of tall trees for two miles or more.
He stopped and stared at one side of that stronghold
as it sparkled and shone within shimmering oaks,
and with helmet in hand he offered up thanks
to Jesus and Saint Julian,[5] both gentle and good,
775   who had courteously heard him and heeded his cry.
"A lodging at last. So allow it, my Lord."
Then he girded Gringolet with his gilded spurs,
and purely by chance chose the principal approach
to the building, which brought him to the end of the bridge
780   with haste.
       The drawbridge stood withdrawn,
       the front gates were shut fast.
       Such well-constructed walls
       would blunt the storm wind's blast.

---

5. Patron saint of hospitality.

785   In the saddle of his steed he halts on the slope
       of the delving moat with its double ditch.
       Out of water of wondrous depth, the walls
       then loomed overhead to a huge height,
       course after course of crafted stone,
790   then battlements embellished in the boldest style
       and turrets arranged around the ramparts
       with lockable loopholes set into the lookouts.
       The knight had not seen a more stunning structure.
       Further in, his eye was drawn to a hall
795   attended, architecturally, by many tall towers
       with a series of spires spiking the air
       all crowned by carvings exquisitely cut.
       Uncountable chimneys the color of chalk
       sprutted from the roof and sparkled in the sun.
800   So perfect was that vision of painted pinnacles
       clustered within the castle's enclosure
       it appeared that the place was cut from paper.[6]
       Then a notion occurred to that noble knight:
       to seek a visit, get invited inside,
805   to be hosted and housed, and all the holy days
              remain.
              Responding to his call
              a pleasant porter came,
              a watchman on the wall,
810   who welcomed Sir Gawain.

       "Good morning," said Gawain, "will you go with a message
       to the lord of this house to let me have lodging?"
       "By Saint Peter," said the porter, "it'll be my pleasure,
       and I'll warrant you'll be welcome for as long as you wish."
815   Then he went on his way, but came back at once
       with a group who had gathered to greet the stranger;
       the drawbridge came down and they crossed the ditch
       and knelt in the frost in front of the knight
       to welcome this man in a way deemed worthy.
820   Then they yielded to their guest, yanked open the gate,
       and bidding them to rise he rode across the bridge.
       He was assisted from the saddle by several men
       and the strongest amongst them stabled his steed.
       Then knights, and the squires of knights, drew near,
825   to escort him, with courtesy, into the castle.
       As he took off his helmet, many hasty hands
       stretched to receive it and to serve this noble knight,
       and his sword and his shield were taken aside.
       Then he made himself known to nobles and knights
830   and proud fellows pressed forwards to confer their respects.
       Still heavy with armor he was led to the hall
       where a fire burned bright with the fiercest flames.
       Then the master of the manor emerged from his chamber,
       to greet him in the hall with all due honor,

---

6. Paper castles were a common table decoration at feasts.

835   saying, "Behave in my house as your heart pleases.
To whatever you want you are welcome, do what
         you will."
    "My thanks," Gawain exclaimed,
    "May Christ reward you well."
840   Then firmly, like good friends,
    arm into arm they fell.

Gawain gazed at the lord who greeted him so gracefully,
the great one who governed that grand estate,
powerful and large, in the prime of his life,
845   with a bushy beard as red as a beaver's,
steady in his stance, solid of build,
with a fiery face and fine conversation:
and it suited him well, so it seemed to Gawain,
to keep such a castle and captain his knights.
850   Escorted to his quarters the lord quickly orders
that a servant be assigned to assist Gawain,
and many were willing to wait on his word.
They brought him to a bedroom, beautifully furnished
with fine silken fabrics finished in gold
855   and curious coverlets lavishly quilted
in bright ermine and embroidered to each border.
Curtains ran on cords through red-gold rings,
tapestries from Toulouse and Turkistan
were fixed against walls and fitted underfoot.
860   With humorous banter Gawain was helped out
of his chain-mail coat and costly clothes,
then they rushed to bring him an array of robes
of the choicest cloth. He chose, and changed,
and as soon as he stood in that stunning gown
865   with its flowing skirts which suited his shape
it almost appeared to the persons present
that spring, with its spectrum of colors, had sprung;
so alive and lean were that young man's limbs
a nobler creature Christ had never created, they declared.
870   This knight,
    whose country was unclear,
    now seemed to them by sight
    a prince without a peer
    in fields where fierce men fight.

875   In front of a flaming fireside a chair
was pulled into place for Gawain, and padded
with covers and quilts all cleverly stitched,
then a cape was cast across the knight
of rich brown cloth with embroidered borders,
880   finished inside with the finest furs,
ermine, to be exact, and a hood which echoed it.
Resplendently dressed he settled in his seat;
as his limbs thawed, so his thoughts lightened.
Soon a table was set on sturdy trestles
885   covered entirely with a clean white cloth

and cruets of salt and silver spoons.
In a while he washed and went to his meal.
Staff came quickly and served him in style
with several soups all seasoned to taste,
890 double helpings as was fitting, and a feast of fish,
some baked in bread, some browned over flames,
some boiled or steamed, some stewed in spices
and subtle sauces which the knight savored.
Four or five times he called it a feast,
895 and the courteous company happily cheered him
along:
"On penance plates you dine—[7]
there's better board to come."
The warming, heady wine
900 then freed his mind for fun.

Now through tactful talk and tentative enquiry
polite questions are put to this prince;
he responds respectfully, and speaks of his journey
from the Court of Arthur, King of Camelot,
905 the royal ruler of the Round Table,
and he says they now sit with Gawain himself,
who has come here at Christmastime quite by chance.
Once the lord has gathered that his guest is Gawain
he likes it so well that he laughs out loud.
910 All the men of that manor were of the same mind,
being happy to appear promptly in his presence,
this person famed for prowess and purity,
whose noble skills were sung to the skies,
whose life was the stuff of legend and lore.
915 Then knight spoke softly to knight, saying
"Watch now, we'll witness his graceful ways,
hear the faultless phrasing of flawless speech;
if we listen we will learn the merits of language
since we have in our hall a man of high honor.
920 Ours is a graceful and giving God
to grant that we welcome Gawain as our guest
as we sing of His birth who was born to save us.
We few
shall learn a lesson here
925 in tact and manners true,
and hopefully we'll hear
love's tender language, too."

Once dinner was done Gawain drew to his feet
and darkness neared as day became dusk.
930 Chaplains went off to the castle's chapels
to sound the bells hard, to signal the hour
of evensong, summoning each and every soul.
The lord goes alone, then his lady arrives,
concealing herself in a private pew.

7. "Penance" because, although sumptuous, the meal consists of fish dishes appropriate to a fasting day.

935 Gawain attends, too; tugged by his sleeve
he is steered to a seat, led by the lord
who greets Gawain by name as his guest.
No man in the world is more welcome, are his words.
For that he is thanked. And they hug there and then,
940 and sit as a pair through the service in prayer.
Then she who desired to see this stranger
came from her closet with her sisterly crew.
She was fairest amongst them—her face, her flesh,
her complexion, her quality, her bearing, her body,
945 more glorious than Guinevere, or so Gawain thought,
and in the chancel of the church they exchanged courtesies.
She was hand in hand with a lady to her left,
someone altered by age, an ancient dame,
well respected, it seemed, by the servants at her side.
950 Those ladies were not the least bit alike:
one woman was young, one withered by years.
The body of the beauty seemed to bloom with blood,
the cheeks of the crone were wattled and slack.
One was clothed in a kerchief clustered with pearls
955 which shone like snow—snow on the slopes
of her upper breast and bright bare throat.
The other was noosed and knotted at the neck,
her chin enveloped in chalk-white veils,
her forehead fully enfolded in silk
960 with detailed designs at the edges and hems;
nothing bare, except for the black of her brows
and the eyes and nose and naked lips
which were chapped and bleared and a sorrowful sight.
A grand old mother, a matriarch she might
965   be hailed.
          Her trunk was square and squat,
          her buttocks bulged and swelled.
          Most men would sooner squint
          at her whose hand she held.

970 Then Gawain glanced at the gracious-looking woman,
and by leave of the lord he approached those ladies
saluting the elder with a long, low bow,
holding the other for a moment in his arms,
kissing her respectfully and speaking with courtesy.
975 They request his acquaintance, and quickly he offers
to serve them unswervingly should they say the word.
They take him between them and talk as they walk
to a hearth full of heat, and hurriedly ask
for specially spiced cakes, which are speedily fetched,
980 and wine filled each goblet again and again.
Frequently the lord would leap to his feet
insisting that mirth and merriment be made:
hauling off his hood he hoisted it on a spear—
a prize, he promised, to the person providing
985 most comfort and cheer at Christmastime.
"And my fellows and friends shall help in my fight

to see that it hangs from no head but my own."
So the laughter of that lord lights up the room,
and Gawain and the gathering are gladdened by games
990   till late.
   So late, his lordship said,
   that lamps should burn with light.
   Then, blissful, bound for bed,
   Sir Gawain waved good night.

995 So the morning dawns when man remembers
the day our Redeemer was born to die,
and every house on earth is joyful for Lord Jesus.
Their day was no different, being a diary of delights:
banquets and buffets were beautifully cooked
1000 and dutifully served to diners at the dais.
The ancient elder sat highest at the table
with the lord, I believe, in the chair to her left;
the sweeter one and Gawain took seats in the center
and were first at the feast to dine; then food
1005 was carried around as custom decrees
and served to each man as his status deserved.
There was feasting, there was fun, and such feelings of joy
as could not be conveyed by quick description,
yet to tell it in detail would take too much time.
1010 But I'm aware that Gawain and the beautiful woman
found such comfort and closeness in each other's company
through warm exchanges of whispered words
and refined conversation free from foulness
that their pleasure surpassed all princely sports
1015   by far.
   Beneath the din of drums
   men followed their affairs,
   and trumpets thrilled and thrummed
   as those two tended theirs.

1020 They drank and danced all day and the next
and danced and drank the day after that,
then Saint John's Day[8] passed with a gentler joy
as the Christmas feasting came to a close.
Guests were to go in the grayness of dawn,
1025 so they laughed and dined as the dusk darkened,
swaying and swirling to music and song.
Then at last, in the lateness, they upped and left
toward distant parts along different paths.
Gawain offered his good-byes, but was ushered by his host
1030 to his host's own chamber and the heat of its chimney,
waylaid by the lord so the lord might thank him
profoundly and profusely for the favor he had shown
in honoring his house at that hallowed season
and lighting every corner of the castle with his character.
1035 "For as long as I live my life shall be better

---

8. December 27.

that Gawain was my guest at God's own feast."
"By God," said Gawain, "but the gratitude goes to you.
May the High King of Heaven repay your honor.
Your requests are now this knight's commands.
1040   I am bound by your bidding, no boon is too high
                    to say."
                At length his lordship tried
                to get his guest to stay.
                But proud Gawain replied
1045   he must now make his way.

Then the lord of the castle inquired courteously
of what desperate deed in the depth of winter
should coax him from Camelot, so quickly and alone,
before Christmas was over in his king's court.
1050   "What you ask," said the knight, "you shall now know.
A most pressing matter prized me from that place:
I myself am summoned to seek out a site
and I have not the faintest idea where to find it.
But find it I must by the first of the year, and not fail
1055   for all the acres in England, so the Lord help me.
Consequently this inquiry I come to ask of you:
that you tell me, in truth, if you have heard the tale
of a green chapel and the ground where it stands,
or the guardian of those grounds who is colored green.
1060   For I am bound by a bond agreed by us both
to link up with him there, should I live that long.
As dawn on New Year's Day draws near,
if God sees fit, I shall face that freak
more happily than I would the most wondrous wealth!
1065   With your blessing, therefore, I must follow my feet.
In three short days my destiny is due,
and I would rather drop dead than default from duty."
Then laughing the lord of the house said, "Stay longer.
I'll direct you to your rendezvous when the time is right,
1070   you'll get to the green chapel, so give up your grieving.
You can bask in your bed, bide your time,
save your fond farewells till the first of the year
and still meet him by midmorning to do as you might.
                    So stay.
1075   A guide will get you there
                at dawn on New Year's Day.
                The place you need is near,
                two miles at most away."

Then Gawain was giddy with gladness, and declared,
1080   "For this more than anything I thank you thoroughly,
and shall work to do well at whatever you wish,
until that time, attending every task."
The lord squeezed Gawain's arm and seated him at his side,
and called for the ladies to keep them company.
1085   There was pleasure aplenty in their private talk,
the lord delighting in such lively language,

like man who might well be losing his mind.
Then speaking to Gawain, he suddenly shouted:
"You have sworn to serve me, whatever I instruct.
1090 Will you hold to that oath right here and now?"
"You may trust my tongue," said Gawain, in truth,
"for within these walls I am servant to your will."
The lord said warmly, "You were weary and worn,
hollow with hunger, harrowed by tiredness,
1095 yet joined in my reveling right royally every night.
You relax as you like, lie in your bed
until mass tomorrow, then go to your meal
where my wife will be waiting; she will sit at your side
to accompany and comfort you in my absence from court.
1100   So lounge:
    at dawn I'll rise and ride
    to hunt with horse and hound."
    The gracious knight agreed
    and, bending low, he bowed.

1105 "Furthermore," said the master, "let's make a pact.
Here's a wager: what I win in the woods will be yours,
and what you gain while I'm gone you will give to me.
Young sir, let's swap, and strike a bond,
1110 let a bargain be a bargain, for better or worse."
"By God," said Gawain, "I agree to the terms,
and I find it pleasing that you favor such fun."
"Let drink be served and we'll seal the deal,"
the lord cried loudly, and everyone laughed.
1115 So they reveled and caroused uproariously,
those lords and ladies, for as long as they liked;
then with immaculate exchanges of manners and remarks
they slowed and they stood and they spoke softly.
And with parting kisses the party dispersed,
1120 footmen going forward with flaring torches,
and everybody was brought to their bed at long last,
       to dream.
    Before they part the pair
    repeat their pact again.
1125   That lord was well aware
    of how to host a game.

FITT iii

Well before sunrise the servants were stirring;
the guests who were going had called for their grooms,
and they scurried to the stables to strap on the saddles,
trussing and tying all the trammel and tack.
1130 The high-ranking nobles got ready to ride,
jumped stylishly to their saddles and seized the reins,
then cantered away on their chosen courses.
The lord of that land was by no means last
to be rigged out for riding with the rest of his men.
1135 After mass he wolfed down a meal, then made

**The Temptation of Sir Gawain by Bertilak's
Wife.** Gawain may think he is protected, but
bedrooms are dangerous places.

for the hills in a hurry with his hunting horn.
So as morning was lifting its lamp to the land
his lordship and his huntsmen were high on horseback,
and the canny kennel men had coupled the hounds
1140 and opened the cages and called them out.
On the bugles they blew three long, bare notes
to a din of baying and barking, and any dogs
which wandered at will where whipped back into line
by a hundred hunters, or so I heard tell,
1145   at least.
         The handlers hold their hounds,
         the huntsmen's hounds run free.
         Each bugle blast rebounds
         between the trunks of trees.

1150 As the cry went up the wild creatures quaked.
The deer in the dale, quivering with dread
hurtled to high ground, but were headed off
by the ring of beaters who bellowed boisterously.
The stags of the herd with their high-branched heads
1155 and the broad-horned bucks were allowed to pass by,
for the lord of the land had laid down a law
that man should not maim the male in close season.
But the hinds were halted with hollers and whoops
and the din drove the does to sprint for the dells.
1160 Then the eye can see that the air is all arrows:
all across the forest they flashed and flickered,
biting through hides with their broad heads.
What! They bleat as they bleed and they die on the banks,
and always the hounds are hard on their heels,
1165 and the hunters on horseback come hammering behind

with stone-splitting cries, as if cliffs had collapsed.
And those animals which escaped the aim of the archers
were steered from the slopes down to rivers and streams
and set upon and seized at the stations below.
1170 So perfect and practiced were the men at their posts
and so great were the greyhounds which grappled with the deer
that prey was pounced on and dispatched with speed
                    and force.
            The lord's heart leaps with life.
1175   Now on, now off his horse
            all day he hacks and drives.
            And dusk comes in due course.

So through a lime-leaf border the lord led the hunt,
while good Gawain lay slumbering in his sheets,
1180 dozing as the daylight dappled the walls,
under a splendid cover, enclosed by curtains.
And while snoozing he heard a slyly made sound,
the sigh of a door swinging slowly aside.
From below the bedding he brings up his head
1185 and lifts the corner of the curtain a little
wondering warily what it might be.
It was she, the lady, looking her loveliest,
most quietly and craftily closing the door,
nearing the bed. The knight felt nervous;
1190 lying back he assumed the shape of sleep
as she stole towards him with silent steps,
then cast up the curtain and crept inside,
then sat down softly at the side of his bed.
And awaited his wakening for a good long while.
1195 Gawain lay still, in his state of false sleep,
turning over in his mind what this matter might mean,
and where the lady's unlikely visit might lead.
Yet he said to himself, "Instead of this stealth
I should openly ask what her actions imply."
1200 So he stirred and stretched, turned on his side,
lifted his eyelids and, looking alarmed,
crossed himself hurriedly with his hand, as if saving
                    his life.
            Her chin is pale, her cheeks
1205   are ruddy red with health;
            her smile is sweet, she speaks
            with lips that love to laugh:

"Good morning, Sir Gawain," said the graceful lady,
"You sleep so soundly one might sidle in here.
1210 You're tricked and trapped! But let's make a truce,
or I'll bind you in your bed, and you'd better believe me."
The lady laughed, making light of his quandary.
"Good morning, madam," Gawain said merrily.
I'll contentedly attend whatever task you set,
1215 and in serving your desires I shall seek your mercy,
which seems my best plan, in the circumstances!"
And he loaded his light-hearted words with laughter.

"But my gracious lady, if you grant me leave,
will you pardon this prisoner and prompt him to rise,
1220   then I'll quit these covers and pull on my clothes,
and our words will flow more freely back and forth."
"Not so, beautiful sir," the sweet lady said.
"Bide in your bed—my own plan is better.
I'll tuck in your covers corner to corner,
1225   then playfully parley with the man I have pinned.
Because I know your name—the knight Sir Gawain,
famed through all realms whichever road he rides,
whose princely honor is highly praised
amongst lords and ladies and everyone alive.
1230   And right here you lie. And we are left all alone,
with my husband and his huntsmen away in the hills
and the servants snoring and my maids asleep
and the door to this bedroom barred with a bolt.
I have in my house an honored guest
1235   so I'll make the most of my time and stay talking
> a while.
> > You're free to have my all,
> > do with me what you will.
> > I'll come just as you call
1240   and swear to serve you well."

"In-good faith," said Gawain, "such gracious flattery,
though I am not him of whom you speak.
I don't dare to receive the respect you describe
and in no way warrant such worthy words.
1245   By God, I would be glad, if you agreed it fitting,
to devote myself through speech or deed
to the prize of your praise—my joy in it would be pure."
Said the gracious lady, "Sir Gawain, in good faith,
how improper on my part if I were to imply
1250   any slur or slight on your status as a knight.
But what lady in this land wouldn't latch the door,
wouldn't rather hold you as I do here—
in the company of your clever conversation,
forgetting all grief and engaging in joy—
1255   than hang on to half the gold that she owns?
I praise the Lord who upholds the high heavens,
for I have what I hoped for above all else by
> His grace."
> > That lovely looking maid,
1260   she charmed him and she chased.
> > But every move she made
> > he countered, case by case.

"Madam," said our man, "may Mary reward you,
in good faith, I have found your fairness noble.
1265   Some fellows are praised for the feats they perform;
I hardly deserve to receive such respect.
It is you who is genuinely joyful and generous."
"By Mary," she declared, "it's quite the contrary.
Were I the wealthiest woman in the world

1270 with priceless pearls in the palm of my hand
to bargain with and buy the best of all men,
then for all the signs you have shown me, sir,
of kindness, courtesy and exquisite looks—
a picture of perfection now proved to be true—
1275 no person on this planet would be picked before you."
"In fairness," said Gawain, "you found far better.
But I'm proud of the price you would pay from your purse,
and will swear to serve you as my sovereign lady.
Let Gawain be your servant and Christ your Savior."
1280 Then they muse on many things through morning and midday,
and the lady stares with a loving look,
but Gawain acts graciously and remains on guard,
and although no woman could be warmer or more winning,
he is cool in his conduct, on account of the scene he
1285   foresees:
            the strike he must receive,
            as cruel fate decrees.
            The lady begs her leave—
            at once Gawain agrees.

1290 She glanced at him, laughed and gave her good-bye,
then stood, and stunned him with astounding words:
"May the Lord repay you for your prize performance.
But I know that Gawain could never be your name."
"But why not?" the knight asked nervously,
1295 afraid that some fault in his manners had failed him.
The beautiful woman blessed him, then rebuked him:
"A good man like Gawain, so greatly regarded,
the embodiment of courtliness to the bones of his being,
could never have lingered so long with a lady
1300 without craving a kiss, as politeness requires,
or coaxing a kiss with his closing words."
"Very well," said Gawain, "Let it be as you wish.
I shall kiss at your command, as becomes a knight,
and further, should it please you, so press me no more."
1305 The lady comes close, cradles him in her arms,
leans nearer and nearer, then kisses the knight.
Then they courteously commend one another to Christ,
and without one more word the woman is away.
Rapidly he rises and makes himself ready,
1310 calls for his chamberlain, chooses his clothes,
makes himself ready then marches off to mass.
Then he went to a meal which was made and waiting,
and was merry and amused till the moon had silvered
            the view.
1315   No man felt more at home
            tucked in between those two,
            the cute one and the crone.
            Their gladness grew and grew.

And the lord of the land still led the hunt,
1320 driving hinds to their death through holts and heaths,
and by the setting of the sun had slaughtered so many

of the does and other deer that it beggared belief.
Then finally the folk came flocking to one spot
and quickly they collected and counted the kill.
1325   Then the leading lords and their loyal men
chose the finest deer—those fullest with fat—
and ordered them cut open by those skilled in the art.
They assessed and sized every slain creature
and even on the feeblest found two fingers worth of fat.
1330   Through the sliced-open throat they seized the stomach
and the butchered innards were bound in a bundle.
Next they lopped off the legs and peeled back the pelt
and hooked out the bowels through the broken belly,
but carefully, being cautious not to cleave the knot.
1335   Then they clasped the throat, and clinically they cut
the gullet from the windpipe, then garbaged the guts.
Then the shoulder blades were severed with sharp knives
and slotted through a slit so the hide stayed whole.
Then the beasts were prized apart at the breast,
1340   and they went to work on the gralloching again,
riving open the front as far as the hind fork,
fetching out the offal, then with further purpose
filleting the ribs in the recognized fashion.
And the spine was subject to a similar process,
1345   being pared to the haunch so it held as one piece
then hoisting it high and hacking it off.
And its name is the numbles, as far as I know, and
                    just that.
              Its hind legs pulled apart
1350   they slit the fleshy flaps,
              then cleave and quickly start
              to break it down its back.

Then the heads and necks of hinds were hewn off,
and the choice meat of the flanks chopped away from the chine,
1355   and a fee for the crows was cast into the copse.
Then each side was skewered, stabbed through the ribs
and heaved up high, hung by its hocks,
and every person was paid with appropriate portions.
Using pelts for plates, the dogs pogged out
1360   on liver and lights and stomach linings
and a blended sop of blood and bread.
The kill horn was blown and the bloodhounds bayed.
Then hauling their meat they headed for home,
sounding howling wails on their hunting horns,
1365   and as daylight died they had covered the distance
and had come to the castle where the knight was ensconced,
                    adjourned
              in peace, with fires aflame.
              The huntsman has returned,
1370   and when he greets Gawain
              warm feelings are confirmed.

Then the whole of the household was ordered to the hall,
and the women as well with their maids in waiting.

And once assembled he instructs the servants
1375   that the venison be revealed in full view,
and in excellent humor he asked that Gawain
should see for himself the size of the kill,
and showed him the side slabs sliced from the ribs.
"Are you pleased with this pile? Have I won your praise?
1380   Does my skill at this sport deserve your esteem?"
"Yes indeed," said the other. "It's the hugest haul
I have seen this seven years in the winter season."
"And I give it all to you, Gawain," said the master,
"for according to our contract it is yours to claim."
1385   "Just so," said Gawain, "and I'll say the same,
for whatever I've won within these walls
such gains will be graciously given to you."
So he held out his arms and hugged the lord
and kissed him in the comeliest way he could.
1390   "You're welcome to my winnings—to my one profit,
though I'd gladly have given you any greater prize."
"I'm grateful," said the lord, "and Gawain, this gift
would carry more worth if you cared to confess
by what wit you won it. And when. And where."
1395   "That wasn't our pact," he replied. "So don't pry.
You'll be given nothing greater, the agreement we have
        holds good!"
      They laugh aloud and trade
      wise words which match their mood.
1400   When supper's meal is made
      they dine on dainty food.

Later, they lounged by the lord's fire,
and were served unstintingly with subtle wines
and agreed to the game again next morning
1405   and to play by the rules already in place:
any takings to be traded between the two men
at night when they met, no matter what the merchandise.
They concurred on this contract in front of the court,
and drank on the deal, and went on drinking
1410   till late, when they took their leave at last,
and every person present departed to bed.
By the third cackle of the crowing cock
the lord and his liegemen are leaping from their beds,
so that mass and the morning meal are taken,
1415   and riders are rigged out ready to run as
        day dawns.
      They leave the levels, loud
      with howling hunting horns.
      The huntsmen loose the hounds
1420   through thickets and through thorns.

Soon they picked up a scent at the side of a swamp,
and the hounds which first found it were urged ahead
by wild words and shrill shouting.
The pack responded with vigor and pace,
1425   alert to the trail, forty lurchers at least.

Then such a raucous din rose up all around them
it ricocheted and rang through the rocky slopes.
The hounds were mushed with hollers and the horn,
then suddenly they swerved and swarmed together
1430   in a wood, between a pool and a precipice.
On a mound, near a cliff, on the margins of a marsh
where toppled stones lay scattered and strewn,
they coursed towards their quarry with huntsmen at heel.
Then a crew of them ringed the hillock and the cliff,
1435   until they were certain that inside their circle
was the beast whose being three bloodhounds had sensed.
Then they riled the creature with their rowdy ruckus,
and suddenly he breaks the barrier of beaters,
—the biggest of wild boars has bolted from his cover—
1440   ancient in years and estranged from the herd,
savage and strong, a most massive swine,
truly grim when he grunted. And the group were aggrieved,
for three were thrown down by the first of his thrusts;
then he fled away fast without further damage.
1445   The other huntsmen bawled "hi" and "hay, hay,"
blasted on their bugles, blew to regroup,
so the dogs and the men made a merry din,
tracking him nosily, testing him time and time
                again.
1450   The boar would stand at bay
           and aim to maul and maim
           the thronging dogs, and they
           would yelp and yowl in pain.

Then the archers advanced with their bows and took aim,
1455   shooting arrows at him which were often on target,
but their points could not pierce his impenetrable shoulders
and bounced away from his bristly brow.
The smooth, slender shafts splintered into pieces,
and the heads glanced away from wherever they hit.
1460   Battered and baited by such bombardment,
in frenzied fury he flies at the men,
hurts them horribly as he hurtles past
so that many grew timid and retreated a tad.
But the master of the manor gave chase on his mount,
1465   the boldest of beast hunters, his bugle blaring,
trumpeting the tally-ho and tearing through thickets
till the setting sun slipped from the western sky.
So the day was spent in pursuits of this style,
while our lovable young lord had not left his bed,
1470   and, cosseted in costly quilted covers, there he
             remained.
           The lady, at first light,
           did not neglect Gawain,
           but went to wake the knight
1475   and meant to change his mind.

She approaches the curtains, parts them and peeps in,
at which Sir Gawain makes her welcome at once,

and with prompt speech she replies to the prince,
settling by his side and laughing sweetly,
1480 looking at him lovingly before launching her words.
"Sir, if you truly are Gawain it seems wondrous to me
that a man so dedicated to doing his duty
cannot heed the first rule of honorable behavior,
which has entered through one ear and exited the other;
1485 you have already lost what yesterday you learned
in the truest lesson my tongue could teach."
"What lesson?" asked the knight. "I know of none,
though if discourtesy has occurred then blame me, of course."
"I encouraged you to kiss," the lady said kindly,
1490 "and to claim one quickly when one is required,
an act which ennobles any knight worth the name."
"Dear lady," said the other, "don't think such a thing,
I dare not kiss in case I am turned down.
If refused, I'd be at fault for offering in the first place."
1495 "In truth," she told him, "you cannot be turned down.
If someone were so snooty as to snub your advance,
a man like you has the means of his muscles."
"Yes, by God," said Gawain, "what you say holds good.
But such heavy-handedness is frowned on in my homeland,
1500 and so is any gift not given with grace.
What kiss you command I will courteously supply,
have what you want or hold off, whichever
                    the case."
            So bending from above
1505   the fair one kissed his face.
            The two then talk of love:
            its grief; also its grace.

"I would like to learn," said the noble lady,
"and please find no offence, but how can it follow
1510 that a lord so lively and young in years,
a champion in chivalry across the country—
and in chivalry, the chiefmost aspect to choose,
as all knights acknowledge, is loyalty in love,
for when tales of truthful knights are told
1515 in both title and text the topic they describe
is how lords have laid down their lives for love,
endured for many days love's dreadful ordeal,
then vented their feelings with avenging valor
by bringing great bliss to a lady's bedroom—
1520 and you the most notable knight who is known,
whose fame goes before him . . . yes, how can it follow
that twice I have taken this seat at your side
yet you have not spoken the smallest syllable
which belongs to love or anything like it.
1525 A knight so courteous and considerate in his service
really ought to be eager to offer this pupil
some lessons in love, and to lead by example.
Why, are you, whom all men honor, actually ignorant,
or do you deem me too dull to hear of dalliances?

1530   I come
   to learn of love and more,
   a lady all alone.
   Perform for me before
   my husband heads for home."

1535 "In faith," said Gawain, "may God grant you fortune.
It gives me great gladness and seems a good game
that a woman so worthy should want to come here
and take pains to play with your poor knight,
unfit for her favors—I am flattered indeed.
1540 But to take on the task of explaining true love
or touch on the topics those love tales tell of,
with yourself, who I sense has more insight and skill
in the art than I have, or even a hundred
of the likes of me, on earth where I live,
1545 would be somewhat presumptuous, I have to say.
But to the best of my ability I'll do your bidding,
bound as I am to honor you forever
and to serve you, so let our Savior preserve me!"
So the lady tempted and teased him, trying
1550 to entice him to wherever her intentions might lie.
But fairly and without fault he defended himself,
no sin on either side transpiring, only happiness
   that day.
   At length, when they had laughed,
1555   the woman kissed Gawain.
   Politely then she left
   and went her own sweet way.

Roused and risen he was ready for mass,
and then men sumptuously served the morning meal.
1560 Then he loitered with the ladies the length of the day
while the lord of the land ranged left and right
in pursuit of that pig which stampeded through the uplands,
breaking his best hounds with its back-snapping bite
when it stood embattled . . . then bowmen would strike,
1565 goading it to gallop into open ground
where the air was alive with the huntsman's arrows.
That boar made the best men flinch and bolt,
till at last his legs were like lead beneath him,
and he hobbled away to hunker in a hole
1570 by a stony rise at the side of a stream.
With the bank at his back he scrapes and burrows,
frothing and foaming foully at the mouth,
whetting his white tusks. The hunters waited,
irked by the effort of aiming from afar
1575 but daunted by the danger of daring to venture
   too near.
   So many men before
   had fallen prey. They feared
   that fierce and frenzied boar
1580   whose tusks could slash and tear.

Till his lordship hacks up, urging on his horse,
spots the swine at standstill encircled by men,
then handsomely dismounts and unhands his horse,
brandishes a bright sword and goes bounding onwards,
1585 wades through the water to where the beast waits.
Aware that the man was wafting a weapon
the hog's hairs stood on end, and its howling grunt
made the fellows there fear for their master's fate.
Then the boar burst forward, bounded at the lord,
1590 so that beast and hunter both went bundling
into white water, and the swine came off worst,
because the moment they clashed the man found his mark,
knifing the boar's neck, nailing his prey,
hammering it to the hilt, bursting the hog's heart.
1595 Screaming, it was swept downstream, almost slipping
beneath.
At least a hundred hounds
latch on with tearing teeth.
Then, dragged to drier ground,
1600 the dogs complete its death.

The kill was blown on many blaring bugle
and the unhurt hunters hollered and whooped.
The chief amongst them, in charge of the chase,
commanded the bloodhounds to bay at the boar,
1605 then one who was wise in woodland ways
began carefully to cut and carve up the carcass.
First he hacks off its head and hoists it aloft,
then roughly rives it right along the spine;
he gouges out the guts and grills them over coals,
1610 and blended with bread they are tidbits for the bloodhounds.
Next he fetches out the fillets of glimmering flesh
and retrieves the intestines in time-honored style,
then the two sides are stitched together intact
and proudly displayed on a strong pole.
1615 So with the swine swinging they swagger home,
the head of the boar being borne before the lord
who had fought so fiercely in the ford till the beast
was slain.
The day then dragged, it seemed,
1620 before he found Gawain,
who comes when called, most keen
to countenance the claim.

Now the lord is loud with words and laughter
and speaks excitedly when he sees Sir Gawain;
1625 he calls for the ladies and the company of the court
and he shows off the meat slabs and shares the story
of the boar's hulking hugeness, and the full horror
of the fight to the finish as it fled through the forest.
And Gawain is quick to compliment the conquest,
1630 praising it as proof of the lord's prowess,
for such prime pieces of perfect pork

and such sides of swine were a sight to be seen.
Then admiringly he handles the boar's huge head,
feigning fear to flatter the master's feelings.
1635 "Now Gawain," said the lord, "I give you this game,
as our wager warranted, as well you remember."
"Certainly," said Sir Gawain. "It shall be so.
And graciously I shall give you my gains in exchange."
He catches him by the neck and courteously kisses him,
1640 then a second time kisses him in a similar style.
"Now we're even," said Gawain, "at this eventide;
the clauses of our contract have been kept and you have what
            I owe."
        "By Saint Giles," the just lord says,
1645   "You're now the best I know.
        By wagering this way
        your gains will grow and grow."

Then the trestle tables were swiftly assembled
and cast with fine cloths. A clear, living light
1650 from the waxen torches awakened the walls.
Places were set and supper was served,
and a din arose as they reveled in a ring
around the fire on the floor, and the feasting party
made much pleasant music at the meal and after,
1655 singing seasonal songs and carol dancing
with as much amusement as a mouth could mention.
The young woman and Gawain sat together all the while.
And so loving was that lady towards the young lord,
with stolen glances and secret smiles
1660 that the man himself was maddened and amazed,
but his breeding forbade him rebuking a lady,
and though tongues might wag he returned her attention
                all night.
        Before his friends retire
1665   his lordship leads the knight,
        heads for his hearth and fire
        to linger by its light.

They supped and swapped stories, and spoke again
of the night to come next, which was New Year's Eve.
1670 Gawain pleaded politely to depart by morning,
so in two days' time he might honor his treaty.
But the lord was unswerving, insisting that he stayed:
"As an honest soul I swear on my heart,
you shall find the Green Chapel to finish your affairs
1675 long before dawn on New Year's Day.
So lie in your room and laze at your leisure
while I ride my estate, and, as our terms dictate,
we'll trade our trophies when the hunt returns.
I have tested you twice and found you truthful.
1680 But think tomorrow *third time throw best*.
Now, a lord can feel low whenever he likes,
so let's chase cheerfulness while we have the chance."

So those gentlemen agreed that Gawain would stay,
and they took more drink, then by torchlight retired to
1685   their beds.
        Our man then sleeps, a most
        reposed and peaceful rest.
        As hunters must, his host
        is up at dawn and dressed.

1690 After mass the master grabs a meal with his men
and asks for his mount on that marvelous morning.
All those grooms engaged to go with their lord
were high on their horses before the hall gates.
The fields were dazzling, fixed with frost,
1695 and the crown of sunrise rose scarlet and crimson,
scalding and scattering cloud from the sky.
At the fringe of the forest the dogs were set free
and the rumpus of the horns went ringing through the rocks.
They fall on the scent of a fox, and follow,
1700 turning and twisting as they sniff out the trail.
A young harrier yowls and a huntsman yells,
then the pack come panting to pick up the scent,
running as a rabble along the right track.
The fox scurries ahead, they scamper behind,
1705 and pursue him at speed when he comes within sight,
haranguing him with horrific ranting howls.
Now and then he doubles back through thorny thickets,
or halts and harkens in the hem of a hedge,
until finally, by a hollow, he hurdles a fence,
1710 and carefully he creeps by the edge of a copse,
convinced that his cunning has conned those canines!
But unawares he wanders where they lie in wait,
where greyhounds are gathered together, a group
              of three.
1715   He springs back with a start,
        then twists and turns and flees.
        With heavy, heaving heart
        he tracks towards the trees.

It was one of life's delights to listen to those hounds
1720 as they massed to meet him, marauding together.
They bayed bloodily at the sight of his being,
as if clustering cliffs had crashed to the ground.
Here he was ambushed by bushwhacking huntsmen
waiting with a welcome of wounding words;
1725 there he was threatened and branded a thief,
and the team on his tail gave him no time to tarry.
Often, in the open, the pack tried to pounce,
then that crafty Reynard would creep into cover.
So his lordship and his lords were merrily led
1730 in this manner through the mountains until midafternoon,
while our handsome hero snoozed contentedly at home,
kept from the cold of the morning by curtains.
But love would not let her ladyship sleep

nor suppress the purpose which possessed her heart.
1735 She rose from her rest and rushed to his room
in a flowing robe that reached to the floor
and was finished inside with fine-trimmed furs.
Her head went unhooded, but heavenly gems
were entwined in her tresses in clusters of twenty.
1740 She wore nothing on her face; her neck was naked,
and her shoulders were bare to both back and breast.
She comes into his quarters and closes the door,
throws the window wide open and wakes Gawain,
right away rouses him with ringing words for
1745   his ear.
    "Oh, sir, how can you sleep
    when morning comes so clear?"
    And though his dreams are deep
    he cannot help but hear.

1750 Yes he dozes in a daze, dreams and mutters
like a mournful man with his mind on dark matters—
how destiny might deal him a death blow on the day
when he grapples with the guardian of the Green Chapel;
of how the strike of the axe must be suffered without struggle.
1755 But sensing her presence there he surfaces from sleep,
comes quickly from the depths of his dreams to address her.
Laughing warmly she walks towards him
and finds his face with the friendliest kiss.
In a worthy style he welcomes the woman
1760 and seeing her so lovely and alluringly dressed,
every feature so faultless, her complexion so fine,
a passionate heat takes hold in his heart.
They traded smiles and speech tripped from their tongues,
and a bond of friendship was forged there, all blissful
1765   and bright.
    They talk with tenderness
    and pride, and yet their plight
    is perilous unless
    sweet Mary minds her knight.

1770 For that noble princess pushed him and pressed him,
nudged him ever nearer to a limit where he needed
to allow her love or impolitely reject it.
He was careful to be courteous and avoid uncouthness,
and more so for the sake of his soul should he sin
1775 and be counted a betrayer by the keeper of the castle.
"I shall not succumb," he swore to himself.
With affectionate laughter he fenced and deflected
all the loving phrases which leapt from her lips.
"You shall bear the blame," said the beautiful one,
1780 "if you feel no love for the lady you lie with,
and wound her, more than anyone on earth, to the heart.
Unless, of course, there is a lady in your life
to whom you are tied and so tightly attached
that the bond will not break, as I must now believe.

1785   So in honesty and trust now tell me the truth;
       for all the love alive, do not lessen the truth
                   with guile."
               "You judge wrong, by Saint John,"
               he said to her, and smiled.
1790   "There is no other one
               nor will be for this while!"

       "Those words," said the woman, "are the worst of all.
       But I asked, and you answered, and now I ache.
       Kiss me as I wish and I shall walk away
1795   in mourning like a lady who loved too much."
       Stooping and sighing she kisses him sweetly,
       then withdraws from his side, saying as she stands,
       "But before we part will you find me some small favor?
       Give me some gift—a glove at least,
1800   that might leaven my loss when we meet in my memory."
       "Well it were," said Gawain. "I wish I had here
       my most precious possession as a present for your love,
       for over and over you deserve and are owed
       the highest prize I could hope to offer.
1805   But I would not wish on you a worthless token,
       and it strikes me as unseemly that you should receive
       nothing greater than a glove as a keepsake from Gawain.
       I am here on an errand in an unknown land
       without men bearing bags of beautiful things,
1810   which my regard for you, lady, makes me regret;
       but man must live by his means, and neither mope
                   nor moan."
               The pretty one replies:
               "Nay, knight, since you decline
1815   to pass to me a prize,
               you must have one of mine."

       She offers him a ring of rich, red gold,
       and the stunning stone set upon it stood proud,
       beaming and burning with the brightness of the sun;
1820   what wealth it was worth you can well imagine.
       But he would not accept it, and said straight away,
       "By God, no tokens will I take at this time;
       I have nothing to give, so nothing will I gain."
       She insists he receive it but still he resists,
1825   and swears, on his name as a knight, not to swerve.
       Snubbed by his decision, she said to him then,
       "You refuse my ring because you find it too fine,
       and don't care to be deeply indebted to me;
       so I give you my girdle, a lesser thing to gain."
1830   From around her body she unbuckled the belt
       which fastened the frock beneath her fair mantle,
       a green silk girdle trimmed with gold,
       exquisitely edged and hemmed by hand.
       And she sweetly beseeched Sir Gawain to receive it,
1835   in spite of its slightness, and hoped he would accept.

But still he maintained he intended to take
neither gold nor girdle, until by God's grace
the challenge he had chosen was finally achieved.
"With apologies I pray you be not displeased,
1840   but end all your offers, for always against them
            I am.
        For all your grace I owe
        a thousand thank-you's, ma'am.
        I shall through sun and snow
1845   remain your loyal man."

"And now he spurns my silk," the lady responded,
"so simple in itself, or so it appears,
so little and unlikely, worth nothing, or less.
But the knight who knew of the power knitted in it
1850   would pay a high price to possess it, perhaps.
For the body which is bound within this green belt,
as long as it is buckled robustly about him,
will be safe against anyone who seeks to strike him,
and all the slyness on earth wouldn't see him slain."
1855   The man mulled it over, and it entered his mind
it might just be the jewel for the jeopardy he faced
and save him from the strike in his challenge at the chapel.
With luck, it might let him escape with his life.
So relenting at last he let her speak,
1860   and promptly she pressed him to take the present,
and he granted her wish, and she gave with good grace,
though went on to beg him not to whisper a word
of this gift to her husband, and Gawain agreed;
those words of theirs within those walls
1865   should stay.
        His thanks are heartfelt, then.
        No sooner can he say
        how much it matters, when
        the third kiss comes his way.

1870   Then the lady departed, leaving him alone,
for no more merriment could be had from that man.
And once she has quit he clothes himself quickly,
rises and dresses in the richest of robes,
stowing the love-lace safely aside,
1875   hiding it away from all hands and eyes.
Then he went at once to the chapel of worship,
privately approached the priest and implored him
to allow his confession, and to lead him in life
so his soul might be saved when he goes to his grave.
1880   Then fully and frankly he spoke of his sins,
no matter how small, always seeking mercy,
beseeching the counselor that he receive absolution.
The priest declares him so clean and so pure
that the Day of Doom could dawn in the morning.
1885   Then in merrier mood he mingled with the ladies,
caroling and carousing and carrying on

as never before, until nightfall. Folk feel
        and hear
      and see his boundless bliss
1890   and say, "Such charm and cheer;
      he's at his happiest
      since his arrival here."

And long let him loiter there, looked after by love.
Now the lord of the land was still leading his men,
1895 finishing off the fox he had followed for so long.
He vaults a fence to flush out the victim,
hearing that the hounds are harrying hard.
Then Reynard scoots from a section of scrub
and the rabble of the pack rush right at his heels.
1900 Aware of its presence the wary lord waits,
then bares his bright sword and swishes at the beast,
which shirks from its sharpness, and would have shot away
but a hound flew forward before it could flee
and under the hooves of the horses they have him,
1905 worrying the wily one with wrathful baying.
The lord hurtles from his horse and heaves the fox up,
wrestles it from the reach of those ravenous mouths,
holds it high over head and hurrahs manfully
while the bloodthirsty bloodhounds bay and howl.
1910 And the other huntsmen hurried with their horns
to catch sight of the slaughter and celebrate the kill.
And when the courtly company had come together
the buglers blew with one mighty blast,
and the others hallooed with open throats.
1915 It was the merriest music ever heard by men,
that rapturous roar which for Reynard's soul
        was raised.
     The dogs, due their reward,
     are patted, stroked and praised.
1920   Then red fur rips—Reynard
    out of his pelt is prised.

Then with night drawing near they headed homewards,
blaring their bugles with the fullness of their breath.
And at last the lord lands at his lovely home,
1925 to find, by the heat of the fireside, his friend
the good Sir Gawain, in glad spirits
on account of the company he had kept with the ladies.
His blue robe flowed as far as the floor,
his soft-furred surcoat suited him well,
1930 and the hood which echoed it hung from his shoulders.
Both hood and coat were edged in ermine.
He meets the master in the middle of the room,
greets him graciously, with Gawain saying:
"I shall first fulfill our formal agreement
1935 which we fixed in words when the drink flowed freely."
He clasps him tight and kisses him three times
with as much emotion as a man could muster.

"By the Almighty," said the master, "you must have had luck
to profit such a prize—if the price was right."
1940 "Oh fiddlesticks to the fee," said the other fellow.
"As long as I have given the goods which I gained."
"By Mary," said the master, "mine's a miserable match.
I've hunted for hours with nothing to my name
but this foul-stinking fox—fling its fur to the devil—
1945 so poor in comparison with such priceless things,
these presents you impart, three kisses perfect
          and true."
      "Enough!" the knight entreats,
      "I thank you through and through."
1950   The standing lord then speaks
      of how the fox fur flew!

And with meals and mirth and minstrelsy
they made as much amusement as any mortal could,
and among those merry men and laughing ladies
1955 Gawain and his host got giddy together;
only lunatics and drunkards could have looked more delirious.
Every person present performed party pieces
till the hour arrived when revelers must rest,
and the company in that court heard the call of their beds.
1960 And lastly, in the hall, humbly to his host,
our knight says good night and renews his gratitude.
"Your uncountable courtesies have kept me here
this Christmas—be honored by the High King's kindness.
If it suits, I submit myself as your servant.
1965 But tomorrow morning I must make a move;
if you will, as you promised, please appoint some person
to guide me, God willing, towards the Green Chapel,
where my destiny will dawn on New Year's Day."
"On my honor," he replied. "With hand on heart,
1970 every promise I made shall be put into practice."
He assigns him a servant to steer his course,
to lead him through the land without losing time,
to ride the fastest route between forest
          and fell.
1975   Gawain will warmly thank
      his host in terms that tell;
      towards the womenfolk
      the knight then waves farewell.

It's with a heavy heart that guests in the hall
1980 are kissed and thanked for their care and kindness,
and they respond with speeches of the same sort,
commending him to our Savior with sorrowful sighs.
Then politely he leaves the lord and his household,
and to each person he passes he imparts his thanks
1985 for taking such trouble in their service and assistance
and such attention to detail in attendance of duty.
And every guest is grieved at the prospect of his going,
as if honorable Gawain were one of their own.

By tapering torchlight he was taken to his room
1990 and brought to his bed to be at his rest.
But if our knight sleeps soundly I couldn't say,
for the matter in the morning might be muddying
        his thoughts.
      So let him lie and think,
1995   in sight of what he sought.
      In time I'll tell if tricks
      work out the way they ought.

              FITT iv

Now night passes and New Year draws near,
drawing off darkness as our Deity decrees.
2000 But wild-looking weather was about in the world:
clouds decanted their cold rain earthwards;
the nithering north needled man's very nature;
creatures were scattered by the stinging sleet.
Then a whip-cracking wind comes whistling between hills
2005 driving snow into deepening drifts in the dales.
Alert and listening, Gawain lies in his bed;
his lids are lowered but he sleeps very little
as each crow of the cock brings his destiny closer.
Before day had dawned he was up and dressed
2010 for the room was livened by the light of a lamp.
To suit him in his metal and to saddle his mount
he called for a servant, who came quickly,
bounded from his bedsheets bringing his garments.
He swathes Sir Gawain in glorious style,
2015 first fastening clothes to fend off the frost,
then his armor, looked after all the while by the household:
the buffed and burnished stomach and breastplates,
and the rings of chain mail, raked free of rust,
all gleaming good as new, for which he is grateful
2020   indeed.
      With every polished piece
      no man shone more, it seemed
      from here to ancient Greece.
      He sent then for his steed.

2025 He clothes himself in the costliest costume:
his coat with the brightly emblazoned badge
mounted on velvet; magical minerals
inside and set about it; embroidered seams;
a lining finished with fabulous furs.
2030 And he did not leave off the lady's lace girdle;
for his own good, Gawain won't forget that gift.
Then with his sword sheathed at his shapely hips
he bound himself twice about with the belt,
touchingly wrapped it around his waist.
2035 That green silk girdle truly suited Sir Gawain
and went well with the rich red weaves that he wore.
But our man bore the belt not merely for its beauty,

or the appeal of its pennants, polished though they were,
or the gleam of its edges which glimmered with gold,
2040 but to save his skin when presenting himself,
without shield or sword, to the fatal swing of
the axe.
Now in his gear and gown
he turns towards those ranks
2045 who served with such renown
and offers thorough thanks.

Then his great horse Gringolet was got up ready.
The steed had been stabled in comfort and safety
and snorted and stamped in readiness for the ride.
2050 Gawain comes closer to examine his coat,
saying soberly to himself, swearing on his word:
"There are folk in this castle who keep courtesy to the forefront;
their master maintains them—happiness to them all.
And let his lordship's lady be loved all her life.
2055 If they choose, out of charity, to cherish a guest,
showing kindness and care, then may heaven's King
who reigns over all reward them handsomely.
For as long as I live in the lands of this world
I shall practice every means in my power to repay him."
2060 Then he steps in the stirrup and vaults to the saddle
and his servant lifts his shield which he slings on his shoulder,
then he girds on Gringolet with his golden spurs
who clatters from the courtyard, not stalling to snort
or prance.
2065 His man was mounted, too,
who lugged the spear and lance.
"Christ keep this castle true,"
he chanted. "Grant good chance."

The drawbridge was dropped, and the double-fronted gates
2070 were unbarred and each half was heaved wide open.
As he clears the planking he crosses himself quickly,
and praises the porter, who kneels before the prince
and prays that God be good to Gawain.
Then he went on his way with the one whose task
2075 was to point out the road to that perilous place
where the knight would receive the sorry stroke.
They scrambled up bankings where branches were bare,
clambered up cliff faces where the cold clings.
The clouds which had climbed now cooled and dropped
2080 so the moors and the mountains were muzzy with mist
and every hill wore a hat of mizzle on its head.
The streams on the slopes seemed to fume and foam,
whitening the wayside with spume and spray.
They wandered onwards through the wildest woods
2085 till the sun, at that season, came skyward, showing
its hand.
On hilly heights they ride,
snow littering the land.

The servant at his side
2090   then has them slow and stand.

"I have accompanied you across this countryside, my lord,
and now you are near the site you have named
and have steered and searched for with such singleness of mind.
But there's something I should like to share with you, sir,
2095 because upon my life, you're a lord that I love,
so if you value your health you'll hear my advice:
the place you proceed to is held to be perilous.
In that wilderness lives a wildman, the worst in the world,
he is brooding and brutal and loves bludgeoning people.
2100 He's more powerful than any person alive on this earth
and four times the figure of any fighting knight
in Arthur's house, or Hector or any other hero.
He chooses the green chapel for his grim goings-on,
and to pass through that place unscathed is impossible,
2105 for he deals out death blows by dint of his hands,
a man without measure who shows no mercy.
Be it chaplain or churl who rides by the chapel,
monk or priest, whatever man or person,
he loves murdering more than he loves his own life.
2110 So I say, just as sure as you sit in your saddle,
if you come there you'll be killed, of that there's no question.
Trust me, he could trample you twenty times over
        or more.
    He's lurked about too long
2115   engaged in grief and gore.
    His hits are swift and strong—
    he'll fell you to the floor."

"Therefore, good Sir Gawain, let the man go,
and for God's sake travel an alternate track,
2120 ride another road, and be rescued by Christ.
I'll head off home, and with hand on heart
I shall swear by God and all his good saints,
and on all earthly holiness, and other such oaths,
that your secret is safe, and not a soul will know
2125 that you fled in fear from the fellow I described."
"Many thanks," said Gawain, in a terse tone of voice,
"and for having my interests at heart, be lucky.
I'm certain such a secret would be silent in your keep.
But as faithful as you are, if I failed to find him
2130 and were to flee in fear in the fashion you urge,
I'd be christened a coward, and could not be excused.
So I'll trek to the chapel and take my chances,
say my piece to that person, speak with him plainly,
whether fairness or foulness follows, however fate
2135   behaves.
    He may be stout and stern
    and standing armed with stave,
    but those who strive to serve
    our Lord, our Lord will save."

2140 "By Mary," said the servant, "you seem to be saying
you're hell-bent on heaping harm on yourself
and losing your life, so I'll delay you no longer.
Set your helmet on your head and your lance in your hand
and ride a route through that rocky ravine
2145 till you're brought to the bottom of that foreboding valley,
then look towards a glade a little to the left
and you'll see in the clearing the site itself,
and the hulking person who inhabits the place.
Now God bless and good-bye, brave Sir Gawain;
2150 for all the wealth in the world I wouldn't walk with you
or go further in this forest by a single footstep."
With a wrench on the reins he reeled around
and heel-kicked the horse as hard as he could,
and was gone from Gawain, galloping hard
2155   for home.
  "By Christ, I will not cry,"
  announced the knight, "or groan,
  but find my fortune by
  the grace of God alone."

2160 Then he presses ahead, picks up a path,
enters a steep-sided grove on his steed
then goes by and by to the bottom of a gorge
where he wonders and watches—it looks a wild place:
no sign of a settlement anywhere to be seen
2165 but heady heights to both halves of the valley
and set with saber-toothed stones of such sharpness
no cloud in the sky could escape unscratched.
He stalls and halts, holds the horse still,
glances side to side to glimpse the green chapel
2170 but sees no such thing, which he thinks is strange,
except at mid-distance what might be a mound,
a sort of bald knoll on the bank of a brook
where fell water surged with frenzied force,
bursting with bubbles as if it had boiled.
2175 He heels the horse, heads for that mound,
grounds himself gracefully and tethers Gringolet,
looping the reins to the limb of a lime.
Then he strides forwards and circles the feature,
baffled as to what that bizarre hill could be:
2180 it had a hole at one end and at either side,
and its walls, matted with weeds and moss,
enclosed a cavity, like a kind of old cave
or crevice in the crag—it was all too unclear to
   declare.
2185   "Green Church?" chunters the knight.
  "More like the devil's lair
  where at the nub of night
  he dabbles in dark prayers."

"For certain," he says, "this is a soulless spot,
2190 a ghostly cathedral overgrown with grass,

the kind of kirk where that camouflaged man
might deal in devotions on the devil's behalf.
My five senses inform me that Satan himself
has tricked me in this tryst, intending to destroy me.
2195 This is a haunted house—may it go to hell.
I never came across a church so cursed."
With head helmeted and lance in hand
he scrambled towards skylight in that strange abyss.
Then he heard on the hillside, from behind a hard rock
2200 and beyond the brook, a blood-chilling noise.
What! It cannoned though the cliffs as if they might crack,
like the scream of a scythe being ground on a stone.
What! It whined and wailed, like a waterwheel.
What! It rasped and rang, raw on the ear.
2205 "My God," cried Gawain, "that grinding is a greeting.
My arrival is honored with the honing of an axe
up there.
Then let the Lord decide.
'Oh well,' won't help me here.
2210 I might well lose my life
but freak sounds hold no fear."

Then Gawain called as loudly as his lungs would allow,
"Who has power in this place to honor his pact?
Because good Gawain now walks on this ground.
2215 If anyone wants anything then hurry and appear
to do what he needs—it's now or it's never."
"Abide," came a voice from above the bank.
"You'll cop for what's coming to you quickly enough."
Yet he went at his work, whetting the blade,
2220 not showing until it was sharpened and stropped.
Then out of the crags he comes, through the cave mouth,
whirling into view with a wondrous weapon,
a Danish-style axe for dealing the dint,
with a brute of a blade curving back to the haft
2225 filed on a stone, a four footer at least
by the look of the length of its shining lace.
And again he was green, as a year ago,
with green flesh, hair and beard, and a fully green face,
and firmly on green feet he came stomping forwards,
2230 the handle of that axe like a staff in his hand.
At the edge of the water, he will not wade
but vaults the stream with the shaft, and strides
with an ominous face onto earth covered over
with snow.
2235 Our brave knight bowed, his head
hung low—but not too low!
"Sweet Sir," the green man said,
"Your visit keeps your vow."

The green knight spoke again, "God guard you, Gawain.
2240 Welcome to my world after all your wandering.
You have timed your arrival like a true traveller,

honouring the terms that entwine us together.
Twelvemonths ago at this time you took what was yours,
and with New Year come you are called to account.
2245 We're very much alone, beyond view in this valley,
no person to part us—we can do as we please.
Pull your helmet from your head and take what you're owed.
Show no more struggle than I showed myself
when you severed my head with a single smite."
2250 "No," said good Gawain, "by my life-giving God,
I won't gripe or begrudge the grimness to come,
so keep to one stroke and I'll stand stock-still,
won't whisper a word of unwillingness, or one
        complaint."
2255   He bowed to take the blade
        and bared his neck and nape,
        but, loath to look afraid,
        he feigned a fearless state.

Suddenly the green knight summons up his strength,
2260 hoists the axe high over Gawain's head,
lifts it aloft with every fiber of his life
and begins to bring home a bone-splitting blow.
Had he seen it through as thoroughly as threatened
the knight, being brave, would have died from the blow.
2265 But glimpsing the axe at the edge of his eye
bringing death earthwards as it arced through the air,
and sensing its sharpness, Gawain shrank at the shoulders.
The swinging axman swerved from his stroke,
and reproached the young prince with some proud words:
2270 "You are not Gawain," he goaded, "with his good name,
who faced down every foe in the field of battle
but now flinches with fear at the foretaste of harm.
Never could I hear of such cowardice from that knight.
Did I budge or even blink when you aimed the axe,
2275 or carp or quibble in King Arthur's castle,
or flap when my head went flying to my feet?
But entirely untouched, you are terror struck.
I'll be found the better fellow, since you were so feeble
        and frail."
2280   Gawain confessed, "I flinched
        at first, but will not fail.
        Though once my head's unhitched
        it's off once and for all!"

"So be brisk with the blow, bring on the blade.
2285 Deal me my destiny and do it out of hand,
and I'll stand the stroke without shiver or shudder
and be wasted by your weapon. You have my word."
"Take this then," said the other, throwing up the axe,
with a menacing glare like the gaze of a maniac.
2290 Then he launches his swing but leaves him unscathed,
withholds his arm before harm could be done.
And Gawain was motionless, never moved a muscle,

but stood stone-still, or as still as a tree stump
anchored in the earth by a hundred roots.
2295 Then the warrior in green mocked Gawain again:
"Now you've plucked up your courage I'll dispatch you properly.
May the honorable knighthood heaped on you by Arthur—
if it proves to be powerful—protect your neck."
That insulting slur drew a spirited response:
2300 "Thrash away then, thug, your threats are hollow.
Such huffing and fussing—you'll frighten your own heart."
"By God," said the green man, "since you speak so grandly
there'll be no more shilly-shallying, I shall shatter you,
         I vow."
2305   He stands to strike, a sneer
        comes over lip and brow.
        Gawain is gripped by fear,
        no hope of rescue now.

Hoisted and aimed, the axe hurtled downwards,
2310 the blade bearing down on the knight's bare neck,
a ferocious blow, but far from being fatal
it skewed to one side, just skimming the skin
and finely snicking the fat of the flesh
so that bright red blood shot from body to earth
2315 Seeing it shining on the snowy ground
Gawain leapt forward a spear's length at least,
grabbed hold of his helmet and rammed it on his head,
brought his shield to his side with a shimmy of his shoulder,
then brandished his sword before blurting out brave words,
2320 because never since birth, as his mother's babe,
was he half as happy as here and now.
"Enough swiping, sir, you've swung your swing.
I've borne one blow without backing out,
go for me again and you'll get some by return,
2325 with interest! Hit out, and be hit in an instant,
         and hard.
        One axe attack—that's all.
        Now keep the covenant
        agreed in Arthur's hall
2330   and hold the axe in hand."

The warrior steps away and leans on his weapon,
props the handle in the earth and slouches on the head
and studies how Gawain is standing his ground,
bold in his bearing, brave in his actions,
2335 armed and ready. In his heart he admires him.
Then remarking merrily, but in a mighty voice,
with reaching words he rounded on the knight:
"Be a mite less feisty, fearless young fellow,
you've suffered no insulting or heinous incident
2340 beyond the game we agreed on in the court of your king.
One strike was promised—consider yourself well paid!
From any lingering loyalties you are hereby released.
Had I mustered all my muscles into one mighty blow

I would have hit more harshly and done you great harm.
2345 But my first strike fooled you—a feint, no less—
not fracturing your flesh, which was only fair
in keeping with the contract we declared that first night,
for with truthful behavior you honored my trust
and gave up your gains as a good man should.
2350 Then I missed you once more, and this for the morning
when you kissed my pretty wife then kindly kissed me.
So twice you were truthful, therefore twice I left
        no scar.
      The person who repays
2355   will live to feel no fear.
      The third time, though, you strayed,
      and felt my blade therefore."

"Because the belt you are bound with belongs to me;
it was woven by my wife so I know it very well.
2360 And I know of your courtesies, and conduct, and kisses,
and the wooing of my wife—for it was all my work!
I sent her to test you—and in truth it turns out
you're by the far the most faultless fellow on earth.
As a pearl is more prized than a pea which is white,
2365 in good faith, so is Gawain, amongst gallant knights.
But a little thing more—it was loyalty that you lacked:
not because you're wicked, or a womanizer, or worse,
but you loved your own life; so I blame you less."
Gawain stood speechless for what seemed a great while,
2370 so shocked and ashamed that he shuddered inside.
The fire of his blood brought flames to his face
and he shrank out of shame at what the other had said.
Then he tried to talk, and finding his tongue, said:
"A curse upon cowardice and covetousness.
2375 They breed villainy and vice, and destroy all virtue."
Then he grabbed the girdle and ungathered its knot
and flung it in fury at the man before him.
"My downfall and undoing; let the devil take it.
Dread of the death blow and cowardly doubts
2380 meant I gave in to greed, and in doing so forgot
the freedom and fidelity every knight knows to follow.
And now I am found to be flawed and false,
through treachery and untruth I have totally failed," said
        Gawain.
2385   "Such terrible mistakes,
      and I shall bear the blame.
      But tell me what it takes
      to clear my clouded name."

The green lord laughed, and leniently replied:
2390 "The harm which you caused me is wholly healed.
By confessing your failings you are free from fault
and have openly paid penance at the point of my axe.
I declare you purged, as polished and as pure
as the day you were born, without blemish or blame.

2395 And this gold-hemmed girdle I present as a gift,
which is green like my gown. It's yours, Sir Gawain,
a reminder of our meeting when you mix and mingle
with princes and kings. And this keepsake will be proof
to all chivalrous knights of your challenge in this chapel.
2400 But follow me home. New Year's far from finished—
we'll resume our reveling with supper and song.
What's more
my wife is waiting there
who flummoxed you before.
2405 This time you'll have in her
a friend and not a foe."

"Thank you," said the other, taking helmet from head,
holding it in hand as he offered his thanks.
"But I've loitered long enough. The Lord bless your life
2410 and bestow on you such honor as you surely deserve.
And mind you commend me to your fair wife,
both to her and the other, those honorable ladies
who kidded me so cleverly with their cunning tricks.
But no wonder if a fool finds his way into folly
2415 and be wiped of his wits by womanly guile—
it's the way of the world. Adam fell because of a woman,
and Solomon because of several, and as for Samson,
Delilah was his downfall, and afterwards David
was bamboozled by Bathsheba and bore the grief.
2420 All wrecked and ruined by their wrongs; if only
we could love our ladies without believing their lies.
And those were foremost of all whom fortune favored,
excellent beyond all others existing under heaven,"
he cried.
2425 "Yet all were charmed and changed
by wily womankind.
I suffered just the same,
but clear me of my crime."

"But the girdle," he went on, "God bless you for this gift.
2430 And I shall wear it with good will, but not for its gold,
nor its silks and streamers, and not for the sake
of its wonderful workmanship or even its worth,
but as a sign of my sin—I'll see it as such
when I swagger in the saddle—a sad reminder
2435 that the frailty of his flesh is man's biggest fault,
how the touch of filth taints his tender frame.
So when praise for my prowess in arms swells my pride,
one look at this love-lace will lessen my ardor.
But I will ask one thing, if it won't offend:
2440 since I stayed so long in your lordship's land
and was hosted in your house—let Him reward you
who upholds the heavens and sits upon high—
will you make known your name? And I'll ask nothing else."
"Then I'll treat you to the truth," the other told him,
2445 "Here in my homelands they call me Bertilak de Hautdesert.
And in my manor lives the mighty Morgan le Fay,

so adept and adroit in the dark arts,
who learned magic from Merlin—the master of mystery—
for in earlier times she was intimately entwined
2450 with that knowledgeable man, as all you knights know
                    back home.
          Yes, 'Morgan the Goddess'—
          I will announce her name.
          There is no nobleness
2455   she cannot take and tame."

"She guided me in this guise to your great hall
to put pride on trial, and to test with this trick
what distinction and trust the Round Table deserves.
She imagined this mischief would muddle your minds
2460 and that grieving Guinevere would go to her grave
at the sight of a specter making ghostly speeches
with his head in his hands before the high table.
So that ancient woman who inhabits my home
is also your aunt—Arthur's half sister,
2465 the daughter of the duchess of Tintagel; the duchess
who through Uther, was mother to Arthur, your king.
So I ask you again, come and greet your aunt
and make merry in my house; you're much loved there,
and, by my faith, I am as fond of you my friend
2470 as any man under God, for your great truth."
But Gawain would not. No way would he go.
So they clasped and kissed and made kind commendations
to the Prince of Paradise, and then parted in the cold,
                    that pair.
2475   Our man, back on his mount
          now hurtles home from there.
          The green knight leaves his ground
          to wander who-knows-where.

So he winds through the wilds of the world once more,
2480 Gawain on Gringolet, by the grace of God,
under a roof sometimes and sometimes roughing it,
and in valleys and vales had adventures and victories
but time is too tight to tell how they went.
The nick to his neck was healed by now;
2485 thereabouts he had bound the belt like a baldric—
slantwise, as a sash, from shoulder to side,
laced in a knot looped below his left arm,
as a sign that his honor was stained by sin.
So safe and sound he sets foot in court,
2490 and great joy came to the king in his castle
when tidings of Gawain's return had been told.
The king kissed his knight and so did the queen,
and Gawain was embraced by his band of brothers,
who made eager enquiries, and he answered them all
2495 with the tale of his trial and tribulations,
and the challenge at the chapel, and the great green chap,
and the love of the lady, which led to the belt.
And he showed them the scar at the side of his neck,

confirming his breach of faith, like a badge
2500 of blame.
He grimaced with disgrace,
he writhed in rage and pain.
Blood flowed towards his face
and showed his smarting shame.

2505 "Regard," said Gawain, as he held up the girdle,
"the symbol of sin, for which my neck bears the scar;
a sign of my fault and offence and failure,
of the cowardice and covetousness I came to commit.
I was tainted by untruth. This, its token,
2510 I will drape across my chest till the day I die.
For man's crimes can be covered but never made clean;
once sin is entwined it is attached for all time."
The king gave comfort, then the whole of the court
allow, as they laugh in lovely accord,
2515 that the lords and ladies who belong to the Table,
every knight in the brotherhood, should bear such a belt,
a bright green belt worn obliquely to the body,
crosswise, like a sash, for the sake of this man.
So that slanting green stripe was adopted as their sign,
2520 and each knight who held it was honored ever after,
as all the best books on romance remind us:
an adventure which happened in Arthur's era,
as the chronicles of this country have stated clearly.
Since fearless Brutus first set foot
2525 on these shores, once the siege land assault at Troy
had ceased,
our coffers have been crammed
with stories such as these.
Now let our Lord, thorn-crowned,
2530 bring us to perfect peace. AMEN.

HONY SOYT QUI MAL PENCE[9]

---

9. "Shame be to the man who has evil in his mind." This is the motto of the Order of the Garter, founded
ca. 1350; apparently a copyist of the poem associated this order with the one founded to honor Gawain.

GEOFFREY CHAUCER
ca. 1343–1400

Medieval social theory held that society was made up of three "estates": the nobility, composed of a small hereditary aristocracy, whose mission on earth was to rule over and defend the body politic; the church, whose duty was to look after the spiritual welfare of that body; and everyone else, the large mass of commoners who were supposed to do the work that provided for its physical needs. By the late fourteenth century, however, these basic categories were layered into complex, interrelated, and unstable social strata among which birth, wealth, profession, and personal ability all played a part in determining one's status in a world that was rapidly changing economically, politically, and socially. Chaucer's life and his works, especially *The Canterbury Tales*, were profoundly influenced by these forces. A growing and prosperous middle class was beginning to play increasingly important roles in church and state, blurring the traditional class boundaries, and it was into this middle class that Chaucer was born.

Chaucer was the son of a prosperous wine merchant and probably spent his boyhood in the mercantile atmosphere of London's Vintry, where ships docked with wines from France and Spain. Here he would have mixed daily with people of all sorts, heard several languages spoken, become fluent in French, and

Middle-class Prosperity. Jan van Eyck, *The Arnolfini Portrait*, 1434. Note the way the religious elements of the scene are secondary to the fine, rich qualities of fabric represented here.

received schooling in Latin. Instead of apprenticing Chaucer to the family business, however, his father was apparently able to place him, in his early teens, as a page in one of the great aristocratic households of England, that of the countess of Ulster who was married to Prince Lionel, the second son of Edward III. There Chaucer would have acquired the manners and skills required for a career in the service of the ruling class, not only in the role of personal attendant in royal households but in a series of administrative posts. (For Chaucer's portrait, see the color insert in this volume.)

We can trace Chaucer's official and personal life in a considerable number of surviving historical documents, beginning with a reference, in Elizabeth of Ulster's household accounts, to an outfit he received as a page (1357). He was captured by the French and ransomed in one of Edward III's campaigns during the Hundred Years War (1359). He was a member of King Edward's personal household (1367) and took part in several diplomatic missions to Spain (1366), France (1368), and Italy (1372). As controller of customs on wool, sheepskins, and leather for the port of London (1374–85), Chaucer audited and kept books on the export taxes, which were one of the Crown's main sources of revenue. During this period he was living in a rent-free apartment over one of the gates in the city wall, probably as a perquisite of the customs job. He served as a justice of the peace and knight of the shire (the title given to members of Parliament) for the county of Kent (1385–86) where he moved after giving up the controllership. As clerk of the king's works (1389–91), Chaucer was responsible for the maintenance of numerous royal residences, parks, and other holdings; his duties included supervision of the construction of the nave of Westminster Abbey and of stands and lists for a celebrated tournament staged by Richard II. While the records show Chaucer receiving many grants and annuities in addition to his salary for these services, they also show that at times he was being pressed by creditors and obliged to borrow money.

These activities brought Chaucer into association with the ruling nobility of the kingdom, with Prince Lionel and his younger brother John of Gaunt, duke of Lancaster, England's most powerful baron during much of Chaucer's lifetime; with their father, King Edward; and with Edward's grandson, who succeeded to the throne as Richard II. Near the end of his life Chaucer addressed a comic *Complaint to His Purse* to Henry IV—John of Gaunt's son, who had usurped the crown from his cousin Richard—as a reminder that the treasury owed Chaucer his annuity. Chaucer's wife, Philippa, served in the households of Edward's queen and of John of Gaunt's second wife, Constance, daughter of the king of Castile. A Thomas Chaucer, who was probably Chaucer's son, was an eminent man in the next generation, and Thomas's daughter Alice was married successively to the earl of Salisbury and the duke of Suffolk. The gap between the commoners and the aristocracy would thus have been bridged by Chaucer's family in the course of three generations.

None of these documents contains any hint that this hardworking civil servant wrote poetry, although poetry would certainly have been among the diversions cultivated at English courts in Chaucer's youth. That poetry, however, would have been in French, which still remained the fashionable language and literature of the English aristocracy, whose culture in many ways had more in common with that of the French nobles with whom they warred than with that of their English subjects. Chaucer's earliest models, works by Guillaume de Machaut (1300?–1377) and Jean Froissart (1333?–1400?), the leading French poets of the day, were lyrics and narratives about courtly love, often cast in the form of a dream in which the poet acted as a protagonist or participant in some aristocratic love affair. The poetry of Machaut and Froissart derives from the thirteenth-century *Romance of the Rose*, a long dream allegory in which the dreamer suffers many agonies and trials for the love of a symbolic rosebud. Chaucer's apprentice work may well have been a partial translation of the twenty-one-thousand-line *Romance*. His first important original poem is *The Book of the Duchess*, an elegy in the form of a dream vision commemorating John of Gaunt's first wife, the young duchess of Lancaster, who died in 1368.

The diplomatic mission that sent Chaucer to Italy in 1372 was in all likelihood a milestone in his literary development. Although he may have acquired some knowledge of the language and literature from Italian merchants and bankers posted in London, this visit and a subsequent one to Florence (1378) brought him into direct contact with the Italian Renaissance. Probably he acquired manuscripts of works by Dante, Petrarch, and Boccaccio—the last two still alive at the time of Chaucer's visit, although he probably did not meet them. These writers provided him with models of new verse forms, new subject matter, and new modes of representation. *The House of Fame*, still a dream vision, takes the poet on a journey in the talons of a gigantic eagle to the celestial palace of the goddess Fame, a trip that at many points affectionately parodies Dante's journey in the *Divine Comedy*. In his dream vision *The Parliament of Fowls*, all the birds meet on St. Valentine's Day to choose their mates; their "parliament" humorously depicts the ways in which different classes in human society think and talk about love. Boccaccio provided sources for two of Chaucer's finest poems—although Chaucer never mentions his name. *The Knight's Tale*, the first of *The Canterbury Tales*, is based on Boccaccio's romance *Il Teseida* (The Story of Theseus). His longest completed poem, *Troilus and Criseyde* (ca. 1385), which tells the story of how Trojan Prince Troilus loved and finally lost Criseyde to the Greek warrior Diomede, is an adaptation of Boccaccio's *Il Filostrato* (The Love-Stricken). Chaucer reworked the latter into one of the greatest love poems in any language. Even if he had never written *The Canterbury Tales*, *Troilus* would have secured Chaucer a place among the major English poets.

A final dream vision provides the frame for Chaucer's first experiment with a series of tales, the unfinished *Legend of Good Women*. In the dream, Chaucer is accused of heresy and antifeminism by Cupid, the god of love himself, and ordered to do penance by writing a series of "legends," i.e., saints' lives, of Cupid's martyrs, women who were betrayed by false men and died for love. Perhaps a noble patron, possibly Queen Anne, asked the poet to write something to make up for telling about Criseyde's betrayal of Troilus.

Throughout his life Chaucer also wrote moral and religious works, chiefly translations. Besides French, which was a second language for him, and Italian, Chaucer also read Latin. He made a prose translation of the Latin *Consolation of Philosophy*, written by the sixth-century Roman statesman Boethius while in prison awaiting execution for crimes for which he had been unjustly condemned. The *Consolation* became a favorite book for the Middle Ages, providing inspiration and comfort through its lesson that worldly fortune is deceitful and ephemeral and through the platonic doctrine that the body itself is only a prison house for the soul that aspires to eternal things. The influence of Boethius is deeply ingrained in *The Knight's Tale* and *Troilus*. The ballade *Truth* compresses the Boethian and Christian teaching into three stanzas of homely moral advice.

Thus long before Chaucer conceived of *The Canterbury Tales*, his writings were many faceted: they embrace prose and poetry; human and divine love; French, Italian, and Latin sources; secular and religious influences; comedy and philosophy. Moreover, different elements are likely to mix in the same work, often making it difficult to extract from Chaucer simple, direct, and certain meanings.

This Chaucerian complexity owes much to the wide range of Chaucer's learning and his exposure to new literary currents on the Continent but perhaps also to the special social position he occupied as a member of a new class of civil servants. Born into the urban middle class, Chaucer, through his association with the court and service of the Crown, had attained the rank of "esquire," roughly equivalent to what would later be termed a "gentleman." His career brought him into contact with overlapping bourgeois and aristocratic social worlds, without his being securely anchored in either. Although he was born a commoner and continued to associate with commoners in his official life, he did not live as a commoner; and although his training and service at court, his wife's connections, and probably his poetry brought him into contact with the nobility, he must always have been conscious of the fact that he did not really belong to that society of which birth alone could make one a true member. Situated at the intersection of these social worlds, Chaucer had the gift of being able to view with both sympathy and humor the behaviors, beliefs, and pretensions of the diverse people who comprised the levels of society. Chaucer's art of being at once involved in and detached from a given situation is peculiarly his own, but that art would have been appreciated by a small group of friends close to Chaucer's social position—men like Sir Philip de la Vache, to whom Chaucer addressed the humorous envoy to *Truth*. Chaucer belongs to an age when poetry was read aloud. A beautiful frontispiece to a manuscript of *Troilus* pictures the poet's public performance before a magnificently dressed royal audience, and he may well have been invited at times to read his poems at court. But besides addressing a listening audience, to whose allegedly superior taste and sensibility the poet often ironically defers (for example, *The General Prologue*, lines 745–48), Chaucer has in mind discriminating readers whom he might expect to share his sense of humor and his complex attitudes toward the company of "sondry folk" who make the pilgrimage to Canterbury.

The text given here is from E. T. Donaldson's *Chaucer's Poetry: An Anthology for the Modern Reader* (1958, 1975) with some modifications. For *The Canterbury Tales* the Hengwrt Manuscript has provided the textual basis. The spelling has been altered to improve consistency and has been modernized in so far as is possible without distorting the phonological values of the Middle English. A discussion of Middle English pronunciation, grammar, and prosody is included in the introduction to "The Middle Ages" (pp. 19–25).

The Canterbury Tales   Chaucer's original plan for *The Canterbury Tales*—
if we assume it to be the same as that which the fictional Host proposes at the end

of *The General Prologue*—projected about one hundred twenty stories, two for each pilgrim to tell on the way to Canterbury and two more on the way back. Chaucer actually completed only twenty-two and the beginnings of two others. He did write an ending, for the Host says to the Parson, who tells the last tale, that everyone except him has told "his tale." Indeed, the pilgrims never even get to Canterbury. The work was probably first conceived in 1386, when Chaucer was living in Greenwich, some miles east of London. From his house he might have been able to see the pilgrim road that led toward the shrine of the famous English saint, Thomas Becket, the archbishop of Canterbury who was murdered in his cathedral in 1170. Medieval pilgrims were notorious tale tellers, and the sight and sound of the bands riding toward Canterbury may well have suggested to Chaucer the idea of using a fictitious pilgrimage as a framing device for a number of stories. Collections of stories linked by such a device were common in the later Middle Ages. Chaucer's contemporary John Gower had used one in his *Confessio Amantis*. The most famous medieval framing tale besides Chaucer's is Boccaccio's *Decameron*, in which ten different narrators each tell a tale a day for ten days. Chaucer could have known the *Decameron*, which contains tales with plots analogous to plots found also in *The Canterbury Tales*, but these stories were widespread, and there is no proof that Chaucer got them from Boccaccio.

Chaucer's artistic exploitation of the device is, in any case, altogether his own. Whereas in Gower a single speaker relates all the stories, and in Boccaccio the ten speakers—three young gentlemen and seven young ladies—all belong to the same sophisticated social elite, Chaucer's pilgrim narrators represent a wide spectrum of ranks and occupations. This device, however, should not be mistaken for "realism." It is highly unlikely that a group like Chaucer's pilgrims would ever have joined together and communicated on such seemingly equal terms. That is part of the fiction, as is the tacit assumption that a group so large could have ridden along listening to one another tell tales in verse. The variety of tellers is matched by the diversity of their tales: tales are assigned to appropriate narrators and juxtaposed to bring out contrasts in genre, style, tone, and values. Thus the Knight's courtly romance about the rivalry of two noble lovers for a lady is followed by the Miller's fabliau of the seduction of an old carpenter's young wife by a student. In several of *The Canterbury Tales* there is a fascinating accord between the narrators and their stories, so that the story takes on rich overtones from what we have learned of its teller in *The General Prologue* and elsewhere, and the character itself grows and is revealed by the story. Chaucer conducts two fictions simultaneously—that of the individual tale and that of the pilgrim to whom he has assigned it. He develops the second fiction not only through *The General Prologue* but also through the "links," the interchanges among pilgrims connecting the stories. These interchanges sometimes lead to quarrels. Thus *The Miller's Tale* offends the Reeve, who takes the figure of the Miller's foolish, cuckolded carpenter as directed personally at himself, and he retaliates with a story satirizing an arrogant miller very much like the pilgrim Miller. The antagonism of the two tellers provides comedy in the links and enhances the comedy of their tales. The links also offer interesting literary commentary on the tales by members of the pilgrim audience, especially the Host, whom the pilgrims have declared "governour" and "juge" of the storytelling. Further dramatic interest is created by the fact that several tales respond to topics taken up by previous tellers. The Wife of Bath's thesis that women should have sovereignty over men in marriage gets a reply from the Clerk, which in turn elicits responses from the Merchant and the Franklin. The tales have their own logic and interest quite apart from the framing fiction; no other medieval framing fiction, however, has such varied and lively interaction between the frame and the individual stories.

The composition of none of the tales can be accurately dated; most of them were written during the last fourteen years of Chaucer's life, although a few were probably written earlier and inserted into *The Canterbury Tales*. The popularity of the poem in late medieval England is attested by the number of surviving manuscripts:

more than eighty, none from Chaucer's lifetime. It was also twice printed by William Caxton, who introduced printing to England in 1476, and often reprinted by Caxton's early successors. The manuscripts reflect the unfinished state of the poem—the fact that when he died Chaucer had not made up his mind about a number of details and hence left many inconsistencies. The poem appears in the manuscripts as nine or ten "fragments" or blocks of tales; the order of the poems within each fragment is generally the same, but the order of the fragments themselves varies widely. The fragment containing *The General Prologue,* the Knight's, Miller's, and Reeve's tales; and the Cook's unfinished tale, always comes first, and the fragment consisting of *The Parson's Tale* and *The Retraction* always comes last. But the others, such as that containing the Wife of Bath, the Friar, and the Summoner or that consisting of the Physician and Pardoner or the longest fragment, consisting of six tales concluding with the Nun's Priest's, are by no means stable in relation to one another. The order followed here, that of the Ellesmere manuscript, has been adopted as the most nearly satisfactory.

THE GENERAL PROLOGUE

Chaucer did not need to make a pilgrimage himself to meet the types of people that his fictitious pilgrimage includes, because most of them had long inhabited literature as well as life: the ideal Knight, who had taken part in all the major expeditions and battles of the crusades during the last half-century; his fashionably dressed son, the Squire, a typical young lover; the lady Prioress, the hunting Monk, and the flattering Friar, who practice the little vanities and larger vices for which such ecclesiastics were conventionally attacked; the prosperous Franklin; the fraudulent Doctor; the lusty and domineering Wife of Bath; the austere Parson; and so on down through the lower orders to that spellbinding preacher and mercenary, the Pardoner, peddling his paper indulgences and phony relics. One meets all these types throughout medieval literature, but particularly in a genre called estates satire, which sets out to expose and pillory typical examples of corruption at all levels of society. (For more information on estates satire, see the "Medieval Estates and Orders" topic in the supplemental ebook.) A remarkable number of details in *The General Prologue* could have been taken straight out of books as well as drawn from life. Although it has been argued that some of the pilgrims are portraits of actual people, the impression that they are drawn from life is more likely to be a function of Chaucer's art, which is able to endow types with a reality we generally associate only with people we know. The salient features of each pilgrim leap out randomly at the reader, as they might to an observer concerned only with what meets the eye. This imitation of the way our minds actually perceive reality may make us fail to notice the care with which Chaucer has selected his details to give an integrated sketch of the person being described. Most of these details give something more than mere verisimilitude to the description. The pilgrims' facial features, the clothes they wear, the foods they like to eat, the things they say, the work they do are all clues not only to their social rank but to their moral and spiritual condition and, through the accumulation of detail, to the condition of late-medieval society, of which, collectively, they are representative. What uniquely distinguishes Chaucer's prologue from more conventional estates satire, such as the *Prologue* to *Piers Plowman,* is the suppression in all but a few flagrant instances of overt moral judgment. The narrator, in fact, seems to be expressing chiefly admiration and praise at the superlative skills and accomplishments of this particular group, even such dubious ones as the Friar's begging techniques or the Manciple's success in cheating the learned lawyers who employ him. The reader is left free to draw out the ironic implications of details presented with such seeming artlessness, even while falling in with the easygoing mood of "felaweship" that pervades Chaucer's prologue to the pilgrimage.

FROM THE CANTERBURY TALES

The General Prologue

    Whan that April with his° showres soote°   *its / fresh*
The droughte of March hath perced to the roote,
And bathed every veine[1] in swich° licour,°   *such / liquid*
Of which vertu[2] engendred is the flowr;
5 Whan Zephyrus eek° with his sweete breeth   *also*
Inspired[3] hath in every holt° and heeth°   *grove / field*
The tendre croppes,° and the yonge sonne[4]   *shoots*
Hath in the Ram his halve cours yronne,
And smale fowles° maken melodye   *birds*
10 That sleepen al the night with open yë°—   *eye*
So priketh hem° Nature in hir corages[5]—   *them*
Thanne longen folk to goon° on pilgrimages,   *go*
And palmeres for to seeken straunge strondes
To ferne halwes,[6] couthe° in sondry° londes;   *known / various*
15 And specially from every shires ende
Of Engelond to Canterbury they wende,
The holy blisful martyr[7] for to seeke
That hem hath holpen° whan that they were seke.°   *helped / sick*
    Bifel° that in that seson on a day,   *It happened*
20 In Southwerk[8] at the Tabard as I lay,
Redy to wenden on my pilgrimage,
To Canterbury with ful° devout corage,   *very*
At night was come into that hostelrye
Wel nine and twenty in a compaignye
25 Of sondry folk, by aventure° yfalle   *chance*
In felaweshipe, and pilgrimes were they alle
That toward Canterbury wolden° ride.   *would*
The chambres and the stables weren wide,
And wel we weren esed° at the beste.[9]   *accommodated*
30 And shortly,° whan the sonne was to reste,[1]   *in brief*
So hadde I spoken with hem everichoon°   *every one*
That I was of hir felaweshipe anoon,°   *at once*
And made forward[2] erly for to rise,
To take oure way ther as[3] I you devise.°   *describe*
35   But nathelees,° whil I have time and space,[4]   *nevertheless*
Er° that I ferther in this tale pace,°   *before / proceed*
Me thinketh it accordant to resoun[5]
To telle you al the condicioun
Of eech of hem, so as it seemed me,

---

1. I.e., in plants.
2. By the power of which.
3. Breathed into. "Zephyrus": the west wind.
4. The sun is young because it has run only halfway through its course in Aries, the Ram—the first sign of the zodiac in the solar year.
5. Their hearts.
6. Far-off shrines. "Palmeres": palmers, wide-ranging pilgrims—especially those who sought out the "straunge strondes" (foreign shores) of the Holy Land.

7. St. Thomas à Becket, murdered in Canterbury Cathedral in 1170.
8. Southwark, site of the Tabard Inn, was then a suburb of London, south of the Thames River.
9. In the best possible way.
1. Had set.
2. I.e., (we) made an agreement.
3. Where.
4. I.e., opportunity.
5. It seems to me according to reason.

40	And whiche they were, and of what degree,°	*social rank*
	And eek° in what array that they were inne:	*also*
	And at a knight thanne° wol I first biginne.	*then*
	A Knight ther was, and that a worthy man,	
	That fro the time that he first bigan	
45	To riden out, he loved chivalrye,	
	Trouthe and honour, freedom and curteisye.[6]	
	Ful worthy was he in his lordes werre,°	*war*
	And therto hadde he riden, no man ferre,°	*farther*
	As wel in Cristendom as hethenesse,[7]	
50	And[8] evere honoured for his worthinesse.	
	At Alisandre[9] he was whan it was wonne;	
	Ful ofte time he hadde the boord bigonne[1]	
	Aboven alle nacions in Pruce;	
	In Lettou had he reised,° and in Ruce,	*campaigned*
55	No Cristen man so ofte of his degree;	
	In Gernade° at the sege eek hadde he be	*Granada*
	Of Algezir, and riden in Belmarye;	
	At Lyeis was he, and at Satalye,	
	Whan they were wonne; and in the Grete See°	*Mediterranean*
60	At many a noble arivee° hadde he be.	*military landing*
	At mortal batailes[2] hadde he been fifteene,	
	And foughten for oure faith at Tramissene	
	In listes[3] thries,° and ay° slain his fo.	*thrice / always*
	This ilke° worthy Knight hadde been also	*same*
65	Sometime with the lord of Palatye[4]	
	Again° another hethen in Turkye;	*against*
	And everemore he hadde a soverein pris.°	*reputation*
	And though that he were worthy, he was wis,[5]	
	And of his port° as meeke as is a maide.	*demeanor*
70	He nevere yit no vilainye° ne saide	*rudeness*
	In al his lif unto no manere wight:[6]	
	He was a verray,° parfit,° gentil° knight.	*true / perfect / noble*
	But for to tellen you of his array,	
	His hors° were goode, but he was nat gay.[7]	*horses*
75	Of fustian° he wered° a gipoun[8]	*thick cloth / wore*
	Al bismotered with his haubergeoun,[9]	

6. Courtesy. "Trouthe": integrity. "Freedom": generosity of spirit.
7. Heathen lands. "Cristendom" here designates specifically only crusades waged by the nations of Roman Catholic Western Europe in lands under other dispensations, primarily Arabic, Turkish, and Moorish Islam but also, as indicated in the list of the Knight's campaigns given below, the Christian Eastern Orthodox Church. Conspicuous by absence is any reference to major battles in the Hundred Years War, fought between French and English Catholics. For excerpts from Christian, Jewish, and Arabic texts on the First Crusade, see the supplemental ebook.
8. I.e., and he was.
9. The capture of Alexandria in Egypt (1365) was considered a famous victory, although the Crusaders abandoned the city after a week of looting. Below: "Pruce" (Prussia), "Lettow" (Lithuania), and "Ruce" (Russia) refer to campaigns by the Teutonic Order of Knights on the shores of the

Baltic Sea in northern Europe against the Eastern Orthodox Church, "Gernada" (Granada), "Algezir" (Algeciras), and "Belmarye" (Belmarin), to northern Spain and Morocco; "Lyeis" (Ayash, seaport near Antioch, modern Syria), "Satalye," "Palatye" (Antalya and Balat, modern Turkey), "Tramyssene" (Tlemcen, modern Algeria).
1. Sat in the seat of honor at military feasts.
2. Tournaments fought to the death.
3. Lists, tournament grounds.
4. A Moslem: alliances of convenience were often made during the Crusades between Christians and Moslems.
5. I.e., he was wise as well as bold.
6. Any sort of person. In Middle English, negatives are multiplied for emphasis, as in these two lines: "nevere," "no," "ne," "no."
7. I.e., gaily dressed.
8. Tunic worn underneath the coat of mail.
9. All rust-stained from his hauberk (coat of mail).

For he was late° come from his viage,°   *lately / expedition*
And wente for to doon his pilgrimage.
    With him ther was his sone, a yong Squier,[1]
80 A lovere and a lusty bacheler,
With lokkes crulle° as° they were laid in presse.   *curly / as if*
Of twenty yeer of age he was, I gesse.
Of his stature he was of evene° lengthe,   *moderate*
And wonderly delivere,° and of greet° strengthe.   *agile / great*
85 And he hadde been som time in chivachye[2]
In Flandres, in Artois, and Picardye,
And born him wel as of so litel space,[3]
In hope to stonden in his lady° grace.   *lady's*
    Embrouded° was he as it were a mede,[4]   *embroidered*
90 Al ful of fresshe flowres, white and rede;°   *red*
Singing he was, or floiting,° al the day: *whistling*
He was as fressh as is the month of May.
Short was his gowne, with sleeves longe and wide.
Wel coude he sitte on hors, and faire ride;
95 He coude songes make, and wel endite,°   *compose verse*
Juste[5] and eek° daunce, and wel portraye° and write. *also / sketch*
So hote° he loved that by nightertale[6]   *hotly*
He slepte namore than dooth a nightingale.
Curteis he was, lowely,° and servisable,   *humble*
100 And carf biforn his fader at the table.[7]
    A Yeman hadde he[8] and servants namo°   *no more*
At that time, for him liste[9] ride so;
And he[1] was clad in cote and hood of greene.
A sheef of pecok arwes,° bright and keene,   *arrows*
105 Under his belt he bar° ful thriftily;°   *bore / properly*
Wel coude he dresse° his takel° yemanly:[2]   *tend to / gear*
His arwes drouped nought with fetheres lowe.
And in his hand he bar a mighty bowe.
A not-heed° hadde he with a brown visage.   *close-cut head*
110 Of wodecraft wel coude° he al the usage.   *knew*
Upon his arm he bar a gay bracer,[3]
And by his side a swerd° and a bokeler,[4]   *sword*
And on that other side a gay daggere,
Harneised° wel and sharp as point of spere;   *mounted*
115 A Cristophre[5] on his brest of silver sheene;°   *bright*
An horn he bar, the baudrik[6] was of greene.
A forster° was he soothly,° as I gesse.   *forester / truly*
    Ther was also a Nonne, a Prioresse,
That of hir smiling was ful simple and coy.[7]

---

1. The vague term "Squier" (Squire) here seems to be the equivalent of "bacheler" (line 80), a young knight still in the service of an older one.
2. On cavalry expeditions. The places in the next line are sites of skirmishes in the constant warfare between the English and the French.
3. I.e., considering the little time he had been in service.
4. Mead, meadow.
5. Joust, fight in a tournament.
6. At night.
7. It was a squire's duty to carve his lord's meat.

8. I.e., the Knight. The "Yeman" (Yeoman) is an independent commoner who acts as the Knight's military servant.
9. It pleased him to.
1. I.e., the Yeoman.
2. In a workmanlike way.
3. Wrist guard for archers.
4. Buckler (a small shield).
5. St. Christopher medal.
6. Baldric (a supporting strap).
7. Sincere and shy. The Prioress is the mother superior of her nunnery.

120	Hir gretteste ooth was but by sainte Loy!°	*Eloi*
	And she was cleped° Madame Eglantine.	*named*
	Ful wel she soong° the service divine,	*sang*
	Entuned° in hir nose ful semely;[8]	*chanted*
	And Frenssh she spak ful faire and fetisly,°	*elegantly*
125	After the scole° of Stratford at the Bowe[9]—	*school*
	For Frenssh of Paris was to hire unknowe.	
	At mete° wel ytaught was she withalle:°	*meals / besides*
	She leet° no morsel from hir lippes falle,	*let*
	Ne wette hir fingres in hir sauce deepe;	
130	Wel coude she carye a morsel, and wel keepe°	*take care*
	That no drope ne fille° upon hir brest.	*should fall*
	In curteisye was set ful muchel hir lest.[1]	
	Hir over-lippe° wiped she so clene	*upper lip*
	That in hir coppe° ther was no ferthing° seene	*cup / bit*
135	Of grece,° whan she dronken hadde hir draughte;	*grease*
	Ful semely after hir mete she raughte.°	*reached*
	And sikerly° she was of greet disport,[2]	*certainly*
	And ful plesant, and amiable of port,°	*mien*
	And pained hire to countrefete cheere[3]	
140	Of court, and to been statlich° of manere,	*dignified*
	And to been holden digne[4] of reverence.	
	But, for to speken of hir conscience,	
	She was so charitable and so pitous°	*merciful*
	She wolde weepe if that she saw a mous	
145	Caught in a trappe, if it were deed° or bledde.	*dead*
	Of[5] smale houndes hadde she that she fedde	
	With rosted flessh, or milk and wastelbreed;°	*fine white bread*
	But sore wepte she if oon of hem were deed,	
	Or if men smoot it with a yerde smerte;[6]	
150	And al was conscience and tendre herte.	
	Ful semely hir wimpel° pinched° was,	*headdress / pleated*
	Hir nose tretis,° hir yën° greye as glas,	*well-formed / eyes*
	Hir mouth ful smal, and therto° softe and reed,°	*moreover / red*
	But sikerly° she hadde a fair forheed:	*certainly*
155	It was almost a spanne brood,[7] I trowe,°	*believe*
	For hardily,° she was nat undergrowe.	*assuredly*
	Ful fetis° was hir cloke, as I was war;°	*becoming / aware*
	Of smal° coral aboute hir arm she bar	*dainty*
	A paire of bedes, gauded all with greene,[8]	
160	And theron heeng° a brooch of gold ful sheene,°	*hung / bright*
	On which ther was first writen a crowned A,[9]	
	And after, *Amor vincit omnia.*[1]	
	Another Nonne with hire hadde she	
	That was hir chapelaine,° and preestes three.[2]	*secretary*
165	A Monk ther was, a fair for the maistrye,[3]	

8. In a seemly, proper manner.
9. The French learned in a convent school in Stratford-at-the-Bow, a suburb of London, was evidently not up to the Parisian standard.
1. I.e., her chief delight lay in good manners.
2. Of great good cheer.
3. And took pains to imitate the behavior.
4. And to be considered worthy.
5. I.e., some.

6. If someone struck it with a rod sharply.
7. A handsbreadth wide.
8. Provided with green beads to mark certain prayers. "A paire": string (i.e., a rosary).
9. An A with an ornamental crown on it.
1. "Love conquers all."
2. The three get reduced to just one nun's priest.
3. I.e., a superlatively fine one.

An outridere[4] that loved venerye,°   *hunting*
A manly man, to been an abbot able.°   *worthy*
Ful many a daintee° hors hadde he in stable,   *fine*
And whan he rood,° men mighte his bridel heere   *rode*
170 Ginglen° in a whistling wind as clere   *jingle*
And eek° as loude as dooth the chapel belle   *also*
Ther as this lord was kepere of the celle.[5]
The rule of Saint Maure or of Saint Beneit,
By cause that it was old and somdeel strait[6]—
175 This ilke° Monk leet olde thinges pace,°   *same / pass away*
And heeld° after the newe world the space.°   *held / course*
He yaf° nought of that text a pulled hen[7]   *gave*
That saith that hunteres been° nought holy men,   *are*
Ne that a monk, whan he is recchelees,[8]
180 Is likned til° a fissh that is waterlees—   *to*
This is to sayn, a monk out of his cloistre;
But thilke° text heeld he nat worth an oystre.   *that same*
And I saide his opinion was good:
What° sholde he studye and make himselven wood°   *why / crazy*
185 Upon a book in cloistre alway to poure,°   *pore*
Or swinke° with his handes and laboure,   *work*
As Austin bit?[9] How shal the world be served?
Lat Austin have his swink to him reserved!
Therefore he was a prikasour° aright.   *hard rider*
190 Grehoundes he hadde as swift as fowl in flight.
Of priking° and of hunting for the hare   *riding*
Was al his lust,° for no cost wolde he spare.   *pleasure*
I sawgh his sleeves purfiled° at the hand   *fur lined*
With gris,° and that the fineste of a land;   *gray fur*
195 And for to festne his hood under his chin
He hadde of gold wrought a ful curious[1] pin:
A love-knotte in the grettere° ende ther was.   *greater*
His heed was balled,° that shoon as any glas,   *bald*
And eek his face, as he hadde been anoint:
200 He was a lord ful fat and in good point;[2]
His yën steepe,° and rolling in his heed,   *protruding*
That stemed as a furnais of a leed,[3]
His bootes souple,° his hors in greet estat°   *supple / condition*
Now certainly he was a fair prelat.[4]
205 He was nat pale as a forpined° gost: *wasted away*
A fat swan loved he best of any rost.
His palfrey° was as brown as is a berye.   *saddle horse*
  A Frere ther was, a wantoune° and a merye,   *jovial*
A limitour,[5] a ful solempne° man.   *ceremonious*

---

4. A monk charged with supervising property distant from the monastery. Monasteries obtained income from large landholdings.
5. Prior of an outlying cell (branch) of the monastery.
6. Somewhat strict. St. Maurus and St. Benedict were authors of monastic rules.
7. He didn't give a plucked hen for that text.
8. Reckless, careless of rule.
9. I.e., as St. Augustine bids. St. Augustine had written that monks should perform manual labor.
1. Of careful workmanship.
2. In good shape, plump.
3. That glowed like a furnace with a pot in it.
4. Prelate (an important churchman).
5. The "Frere" (Friar) is a member of one of the four religious orders whose members live by begging; as a "limitour" he has been granted by his order exclusive begging rights within a certain limited area.

<table>
<tr><td>210</td><td>In alle the ordres foure is noon that can°</td><td>knows</td></tr>
<tr><td></td><td>So muche of daliaunce° and fair langage:</td><td>sociability</td></tr>
<tr><td></td><td>He hadde maad ful many a mariage</td><td></td></tr>
<tr><td></td><td>Of yonge wommen at his owene cost;</td><td></td></tr>
<tr><td></td><td>Unto his ordre he was a noble post.[6]</td><td></td></tr>
<tr><td>215</td><td>Ful wel biloved and familier was he</td><td></td></tr>
<tr><td></td><td>With frankelains over al[7] in his contree,</td><td></td></tr>
<tr><td></td><td>And with worthy wommen of the town—</td><td></td></tr>
<tr><td></td><td>For he hadde power of confessioun,</td><td></td></tr>
<tr><td></td><td>As saide himself, more than a curat,°</td><td>parish priest</td></tr>
<tr><td>220</td><td>For of° his ordre he was licenciat.[8]</td><td>by</td></tr>
<tr><td></td><td>Ful swetely herde he confessioun,</td><td></td></tr>
<tr><td></td><td>And plesant was his absolucioun.</td><td></td></tr>
<tr><td></td><td>He was an esy man to yive penaunce</td><td></td></tr>
<tr><td></td><td>Ther as he wiste to have[9] a good pitaunce;°</td><td>donation</td></tr>
<tr><td>225</td><td>For unto a poore ordre for to yive</td><td></td></tr>
<tr><td></td><td>Is signe that a man is wel yshrive,[1]</td><td></td></tr>
<tr><td></td><td>For if he yaf, he dorste make avaunt°</td><td>boast</td></tr>
<tr><td></td><td>He wiste° that a man was repentaunt;</td><td>knew</td></tr>
<tr><td></td><td>For many a man so hard is of his herte</td><td></td></tr>
<tr><td>230</td><td>He may nat weepe though him sore smerte:[2]</td><td></td></tr>
<tr><td></td><td>Therfore, in stede of weeping and prayeres,</td><td></td></tr>
<tr><td></td><td>Men mote° yive silver to the poore freres.[3]</td><td>may</td></tr>
<tr><td></td><td>His tipet° was ay farsed° ful of knives</td><td>hood / stuffed</td></tr>
<tr><td></td><td>And pinnes, for to yiven faire wives;</td><td></td></tr>
<tr><td>235</td><td>And certainly he hadde a merye note;</td><td></td></tr>
<tr><td></td><td>Wel coude he singe and playen on a rote;°</td><td>fiddle</td></tr>
<tr><td></td><td>Of yeddinges he bar outrely the pris.[4]</td><td></td></tr>
<tr><td></td><td>His nekke whit was as the flowr-de-lis;°</td><td>lily</td></tr>
<tr><td></td><td>Therto he strong was as a champioun.</td><td></td></tr>
<tr><td>240</td><td>He knew the tavernes wel in every town,</td><td></td></tr>
<tr><td></td><td>And every hostiler° and tappestere,°</td><td>innkeeper / barmaid</td></tr>
<tr><td></td><td>Bet° than a lazar or a beggestere.[5]</td><td>better</td></tr>
<tr><td></td><td>For unto swich a worthy man as he</td><td></td></tr>
<tr><td></td><td>Accorded nat, as by his facultee,[6]</td><td></td></tr>
<tr><td>245</td><td>To have with sike° lazars aquaintaunce:</td><td>sick</td></tr>
<tr><td></td><td>It is nat honeste,° it may nought avaunce,°</td><td>dignified / profit</td></tr>
<tr><td></td><td>For to delen with no swich poraile,[7]</td><td></td></tr>
<tr><td></td><td>But al with riche, and selleres of vitaile;°</td><td>foodstuffs</td></tr>
<tr><td></td><td>And over al ther as[8] profit sholde arise,</td><td></td></tr>
<tr><td>250</td><td>Curteis he was, and lowely of servise.</td><td></td></tr>
<tr><td></td><td>Ther was no man nowher so vertuous:°</td><td>effective</td></tr>
<tr><td></td><td>He was the beste beggere in his hous.°</td><td>friary</td></tr>
</table>

6. I.e., pillar, a staunch supporter.
7. I.e., with franklins everywhere. Franklins were well-to-do country men.
8. I.e., licensed to hear confessions.
9. Where he knew he would have.
1. Shriven, absolved.
2. Although he is sorely grieved.
3. Before granting absolution, the confessor must be sure the sinner is contrite; moreover, the absolution is contingent on the sinner's performance of an act of satisfaction. In the case of

Chaucer's Friar, a liberal contribution served both as proof of contrition and as satisfaction.
4. He absolutely took the prize for ballads.
5. "Beggestere": female beggar. "Lazar:" leper.
6. It was not suitable because of his position.
7. I.e., poor trash. The oldest order of friars had been founded by St. Francis to administer to the spiritual needs of precisely those classes the Friar avoids.
8. Everywhere.

And yaf a certain ferme for the graunt;[9]
Noon of his bretheren cam ther in his haunt.[1]

255 For though a widwe° hadde nought a sho,°   widow / shoe
So plesant was his *In principio*[2]
Yit wolde he have a ferthing° er he wente;   small coin
His purchas was wel bettre than his rente.[3]
And rage he coude as it were right a whelpe;[4]

260 In love-dayes[5] ther coude he muchel° helpe,   much
For ther he was nat lik a cloisterer,
With a thredbare cope, as is a poore scoler,
But he was lik a maister[6] or a pope.
Of double worstede was his semicope,°   short robe

265 And rounded as a belle out of the presse.°   bell mold
Somwhat he lipsed° for his wantounesse°   lisped / affectation
To make his Englissh sweete upon his tonge;
And in his harping, whan he hadde songe,°   sung
His yën twinkled in his heed aright

270 As doon the sterres° in the frosty night.   stars
This worthy limitour was cleped Huberd.
  A Marchant was ther with a forked beerd,
In motelee,[7] and hye on hors he sat,
Upon his heed a Flandrissh° bevere hat,   Flemish

275 His bootes clasped faire and fetisly.°   elegantly
His resons° he spak ful solempnely,   opinions
Souning° alway th' encrees of his winning.°   implying / profit
He wolde the see were kept for any thing[8]
Bitwixen Middelburgh and Orewelle.

280 Wel coude he in eschaunge sheeldes[9] selle.
This worthy man ful wel his wit bisette:°   employed
Ther wiste° no wight° that he was in dette,   knew / person
So statly° was he of his governaunce,[1]   dignified
With his bargaines,° and with his chevissaunce.°   bargainings / borrowing

285 Forsoothe° he was a worthy man withalle;   in truth
But, sooth to sayn, I noot° how men him calle.   don't know
  A Clerk[2] ther was of Oxenforde also
That unto logik hadde longe ygo.[3]
As lene was his hors as is a rake,

290 And he was nought right fat, I undertake,
But looked holwe,° and therto sobrely.   hollow
Ful thredbare was his overeste courtepy,
For he hadde geten him yit no benefice,[4]
Ne was so worldly for to have office.°   secular employment

---

9. And he paid a certain rent for the privilege of begging.
1. Assigned territory.
2. A friar's usual salutation: "In the beginning [was the Word]" (John 1.1).
3. I.e., the money he got through such activity was more than his proper income.
4. And he could flirt wantonly, as if he were a puppy.
5. Days appointed for the settlement of lawsuits out of court.
6. A man of recognized learning.
7. Motley, a cloth of mixed color.
8. I.e., he wished the sea to be guarded at all costs. The sea route between Middelburgh (in the Netherlands) and Orwell (in Suffolk) was vital to the Merchant's export and import of wool—the basis of England's chief trade at the time.
9. Shields were units of transfer in international credit, which he exchanged at a profit.
1. The management of his affairs.
2. The Clerk is a student at Oxford; to become a student, he would have had to signify his intention of becoming a cleric, but he was not bound to proceed to a position of responsibility in the church.
3. Who had long since matriculated in philosophy.
4. Ecclesiastical living, such as the income a parish priest receives. "Courtepy": outer cloak.

295 For him was levere⁵ have at his beddes heed
Twenty bookes, clad in blak or reed,
Of Aristotle and his philosophye,
Than robes riche, or fithele,° or gay sautrye.⁶   *fiddle*
But al be that he was a philosophre⁷
300 Yit hadde he but litel gold in cofre;°   *coffer*
But al that he mighte of his freendes hente,°   *take*
On bookes and on lerning he it spente,
And bisily gan for the soules praye
Of hem that yaf him wherwith to scoleye.°   *study*
305 Of studye took he most cure° and most heede.   *care*
Nought oo° word spak he more than was neede,   *one*
And that was said in forme⁸ and reverence,
And short and quik,° and ful of heigh sentence:⁹   *lively*
Souning° in moral vertu was his speeche,   *resounding*
310 And gladly wolde he lerne, and gladly teche.
    A Sergeant of the Lawe, war and wis,¹
That often hadde been at the Parvis²
Ther was also, ful riche of excellence.
Discreet he was, and of greet reverence—
315 He seemed swich, his wordes weren so wise.
Justice he was ful often in assise°   *circuit courts*
By patente³ and by plein° commissioun.   *full*
For his science° and for his heigh renown   *knowledge*
Of fees and robes hadde he many oon.
320 So greet a purchasour° was nowher noon;   *speculator in land*
Al was fee simple⁴ to him in effect—
His purchasing mighte nat been infect.⁵
Nowher so bisy a man as he ther nas;°   *was not*
And yit he seemed bisier than he was.
325 In termes hadde he caas and doomes⁶ alle
That from the time of King William⁷ were falle.
Therto he coude endite and make a thing,⁸
Ther coude no wight pinchen° at his writing;   *cavil*
And every statut coude° he plein° by rote.⁹   *knew / entire*
330 He rood but hoomly° in a medlee cote,¹   *unpretentiously*
Girt with a ceint° of silk, with barres² smale.   *belt*
Of his array telle I no lenger tale.
    A Frankelain³ was in his compaignye:
Whit was his beerd as is the dayesye;°   *daisy*
335 Of his complexion he was sanguin.⁴

---

5. He would rather.
6. Psaltery (a kind of harp).
7. The word may also mean alchemist, someone who tries to turn base metals into gold. The Clerk's "philosophy" does not pay either way.
8. With decorum.
9. Elevated thought.
1. Wary and wise. The Sergeant is not only a practicing lawyer but one of the high justices of the nation.
2. The Paradise, the porch of St. Paul's Cathedral, a meeting place for lawyers and their clients.
3. Royal warrant.
4. Owned outright without legal impediments.
5. Invalidated on a legal technicality.

6. Law cases and decisions. "By termes": i.e., by heart.
7. I.e., the Conqueror (reigned 1066–87).
8. Compose and draw up a deed.
9. By heart.
1. A coat of mixed color.
2. Transverse stripes.
3. The "Frankelain" (Franklin) is a prosperous country man, whose lower-class ancestry is no impediment to the importance he has attained in his county.
4. A reference to the fact that the Franklin's temperament, "humor," is dominated by blood as well as by his red face (see p. 204, n. 8).

Wel loved he by the morwe a sop in win.[5]
To liven in delit° was evere his wone,°   *sensual delight / wont*
For he was Epicurus[6] owene sone,
That heeld opinion that plein° delit   *full*
340 Was verray° felicitee parfit.°   *true / perfect*
An housholdere and that a greet was he:
Saint Julian[7] he was in his contree.
His breed, his ale, was always after oon;[8]
A bettre envined° man was nevere noon.   *wine-stocked*
345 Withouten bake mete was nevere his hous,
Of fissh and flessh, and that so plentevous°   *plenteous*
It snewed° in his hous of mete° and drinke,   *snowed / food*
Of alle daintees that men coude thinke.
After° the sondry sesons of the yeer   *according to*
350 So chaunged he his mete° and his soper.°   *dinner / supper*
Ful many a fat partrich hadde he in mewe,°   *cage*
And many a breem,° and many a luce° in stewe[9]   *carp / pike*
Wo was his cook but if his sauce were
Poinant° and sharp, and redy all his gere.   *spicy*
355 His table dormant in his halle alway
Stood redy covered all the longe day.[1]
At sessions ther was he lord and sire.
Ful ofte time he was Knight of the Shire.[2]
An anlaas° and a gipser° al of silk   *dagger / purse*
360 Heeng at his girdel,[3] whit as morne° milk.   *morning*
A shirreve° hadde he been, and countour.[4]   *sheriff*
Was nowhere swich a worthy vavasour.[5]

    An Haberdasshere and a Carpenter,
A Webbe,° a Dyere, and a Tapicer°—   *weaver / tapestry maker*
365 And they were clothed alle in oo liveree[6]
Of a solempne and greet fraternitee.
Ful fresshe and newe hir gere apiked° was;   *trimmed*
Hir knives were chaped° nought with bras,   *mounted*
But al with silver; wrought ful clene and weel
370 Hir girdles and hir pouches everydeel.°   *altogether*
Wel seemed eech of hem a fair burgeis°   *burgher*
To sitten in a yeldehalle° on a dais.   *guildhall*
Everich, for the wisdom that he can,[7]
Was shaply° for to been an alderman.   *suitable*
375 For catel° hadde they ynough and rente,°   *property / income*
And eek hir wives wolde it wel assente—
And elles certain were they to blame:
It is ful fair to been ycleped° "Madame,"   *called*
And goon to vigilies all bifore,[8]

---

5. I.e., in the morning he was very fond of a piece of bread soaked in wine.
6. The Greek philosopher whose teaching is popularly believed to make pleasure the chief goal of life.
7. The patron saint of hospitality.
8. Always of the same high quality.
9. Fishpond.
1. Tables were usually dismounted when not in use, but the Franklin kept his mounted and set ("covered"), hence "dormant."
2. County representative in Parliament. "Ses-

sions": i.e., sessions of the justices of the peace.
3. Hung at his belt.
4. Auditor of county finances.
5. Feudal landholder of lowest rank; a provincial gentleman.
6. In one livery, i.e., the uniform of their "fraternitee" or guild, a partly religious, partly social organization.
7. Was capable of.
8. I.e., at the head of the procession. "Vigiles": feasts held on the eve of saints' days.

380 And have a mantel royalliche ybore.[9]
    A Cook they hadde with hem for the nones,[1]
To boile the chiknes with the marybones,°   *marrowbones*
And powdre-marchant tart and galingale.[2]
Wel coude he knowe° a draughte of London ale.   *recognize*
385 He coude roste, and seethe,° and broile, and frye,   *boil*
Maken mortreux,° and wel bake a pie.   *stews*
But greet harm was it, as it thoughte° me,   *seemed to*
That on his shine a mormal° hadde he,   *ulcer*
For blankmanger,[3] that made he with the beste.
390   A Shipman was ther, woning° fer by weste—°   *dwelling / in the west*
For ought I woot,° he was of Dertemouthe.[4]   *know*
He rood upon a rouncy° as he couthe,[5]   *large nag*
In a gowne of falding° to the knee.   *heavy wool*
A daggere hanging on a laas° hadde he   *strap*
395 Aboute his nekke, under his arm adown.
The hote somer hadde maad his hewe° al brown;   *color*
And certainly he was a good felawe.
Ful many a draughte of win hadde he drawe[6]
Fro Burdeuxward, whil that the chapman sleep:[7]
400 Of nice° conscience took he no keep;°   *fastidious / heed*
If that he faught and hadde the hyer° hand,   *upper*
By water he sente hem hoom to every land.[8]
But of his craft, to rekene wel his tides,
His stremes° and his daungers° him bisides,[9]   *currents / hazards*
405 His herberwe° and his moone, his lodemenage,[1]   *anchorage*
There was noon swich from Hulle to Cartage.[2]
Hardy he was and wis to undertake;[3]
With many a tempest hadde his beerd been shake;
He knew alle the havenes° as they were   *harbors*
410 Fro Gotlond to the Cape of Finistere,[4]
And every crike° in Britaine° and in Spaine.   *inlet / Brittany*
His barge ycleped was the Maudelaine.°   *Magdalene*
    With us ther was a Doctour of Physik:°   *medicine*
In al this world ne was ther noon him lik
415 To speken of physik and of surgerye.
For° he was grounded in astronomye,°   *because / astrology*
He kepte° his pacient a ful greet deel[5]   *tended to*
In houres by his magik naturel.[6]
Wel coude he fortunen the ascendent
420 Of his images[7] for his pacient.
He knew the cause of every maladye,

9. Royally carried.
1. For the occasion.
2. "Powdre-marchant" and "galingale" are flavoring materials.
3. A white stew or mousse.
4. Dartmouth, a port in the southwest of England.
5. As best he could.
6. Drawn, i.e., stolen.
7. Merchant slept. "Fro Burdeuxward": from Bordeaux; i.e., while carrying wine from Bordeaux (the wine center of France).
8. He drowned his prisoners.
9. Around him.
1. Pilotage, art of navigation.
2. From Hull (in northern England) to Carta-

gena (in Spain).
3. Shrewd in his undertakings.
4. From Gotland (an island in the Baltic) to Finisterre (the westernmost point in Spain).
5. Closely.
6. Natural—as opposed to black—magic. "In houres": i.e., the astrologically important hours (when conjunctions of the planets might help his recovery).
7. Assign the propitious time, according to the position of stars, for using talismanic images. Such images, representing either the patient himself or points in the zodiac, were thought to be influential on the course of the disease.

Were it of hoot or cold or moiste or drye,
And where engendred and of what humour:[8]
He was a verray parfit praktisour.[9]
425 The cause yknowe,° and of his° harm the roote,   *known / its*
Anoon he yaf the sike man his boote.°   *remedy*
    Ful redy hadde he his apothecaries
To senden him drogges° and his letuaries,°   *drugs / medicines*
For eech of hem made other for to winne:
430 Hir frendshipe was nought newe to biginne.
Wel knew he the olde Esculapius.[1]
And Deiscorides and eek Rufus,
Olde Ipocras, Hali, and Galien,
Serapion, Razis, and Avicen,
435 Averrois, Damascien, and Constantin,
Bernard, and Gatesden, and Gilbertin.
Of his diete mesurable° was he,   *moderate*
For it was of no superfluitee,
But of greet norissing° and digestible.   *nourishment*
440 His studye was but litel on the Bible.
In sanguin° and in pers° he clad was al,   *blood red / blue*
Lined with taffata and with sendal;°   *silk*
And yit he was but esy of dispence;°   *expenditure*
He kepte that he wan in pestilence.[2]
445 For° gold in physik is a cordial,[3]   *because*
Therfore he loved gold in special.
    A good Wif was ther of biside Bathe,
But she was somdeel deef,° and that was scathe.°   *a bit deaf / a pity*
Of cloth-making she hadde swich an haunt,°   *skill*
450 She passed° hem of Ypres and of Gaunt.[4]   *surpassed*
In al the parissh wif ne was ther noon
That to the offring[5] bifore hire sholde goon,
And if ther dide, certain so wroth° was she   *angry*
That she was out of alle charitee.
455 Hir coverchiefs° ful fine were of ground°—   *headcovers / texture*
I dorste° swere they weyeden° ten pound   *dare / weighed*
That on a Sonday weren° upon hir heed.   *were*
Hir hosen° weren of fin scarlet reed,°   *leggings / red*
Ful straite yteyd,[6] and shoes ful moiste° and newe.   *supple*
460 Bold was hir face and fair and reed of hewe.
She was a worthy womman al hir live:

---

8. Diseases were thought to be caused by a disturbance of one or another of the four bodily "humors," each of which, like the four elements, was a compound of two of the elementary qualities mentioned in line 422: the melancholy humor, seated in the black bile, was cold and dry (like earth); the sanguine, seated in the blood, hot and moist (like air); the choleric, seated in the yellow bile, hot and dry (like fire); the phlegmatic, seated in the phlegm, cold and moist (like water).
9. True perfect practitioner.
1. The Doctor is familiar with the treatises that the Middle Ages attributed to the "great names" of medical history, whom Chaucer names: the purely legendary Greek demigod Aesculapius; the Greeks Dioscorides, Rufus, Hippocrates, Galen, and Serapion; the Persians Hali and Rhazes; the Arabians Avicenna and Averroës; the early Christians John (?) of Damascus and Constantine Afer; the Scotsman Bernard Gordon; the Englishmen John of Gatesden and Gilbert, the former an early contemporary of Chaucer.
2. He saved the money he made during the plague time.
3. A stimulant. Gold was thought to have some medicinal properties.
4. Ypres and Ghent ("Gaunt") were Flemish clothmaking centers.
5. The offering in church, when the congregation brought its gifts forward.
6. Tightly laced.

Housbondes at chirche dore[7] she hadde five,
Withouten° other compaignye in youthe—   *not counting*
But therof needeth nought to speke as nouthe.°   *now*
465 And thries hadde she been at Jerusalem;
She hadde passed many a straunge° streem;   *foreign*
At Rome she hadde been, and at Boloigne,
In Galice at Saint Jame, and at Coloigne:[8]
She coude° muchel of wandring by the waye: *knew*
470 Gat-toothed[9] was she, soothly for to saye.
Upon an amblere[1] esily she sat,
Ywimpled° wel, and on hir heed an hat   *veiled*
As brood as is a bokeler or a targe,[2]
A foot-mantel° aboute hir hipes large,   *riding skirt*
475 And on hir feet a paire of spores° sharpe.   *spurs*
In felaweshipe wel coude she laughe and carpe:°   *talk*
Of remedies of love she knew parchaunce,°   *as it happened*
For she coude of that art the olde daunce.[3]
    A good man was ther of religioun,
480 And was a poore Person° of a town,   *parson*
But riche he was of holy thought and werk.
He was also a lerned man, a clerk,
That Cristes gospel trewely° wolde preche;   *faithfully*
His parisshens° devoutly wolde he teche.   *parishioners*
485 Benigne he was, and wonder° diligent,   *wonderfully*
And in adversitee ful pacient,
And swich he was preved° ofte sithes.°   *proved / times*
Ful loth were him to cursen for his tithes,[4]
But rather wolde he yiven, out of doute,[5]
490 Unto his poore parisshens aboute
Of his offring[6] and eek of his substaunce:°   *property*
He coude in litel thing have suffisaunce.°   *sufficiency*
Wid was his parissh, and houses fer asonder,
But he ne lafte° nought for rain ne thonder,   *neglected*
495 In siknesse nor in meschief,° to visite   *misfortune*
The ferreste° in his parissh, muche and lite,[7]   *farthest*
Upon his feet, and in his hand a staf.
This noble ensample° to his sheep he yaf   *example*
That first he wroughte,[8] and afterward he taughte.
500 Out of the Gospel he tho° wordes caughte,°   *those / took*
And this figure° he added eek therto: *metaphor*
That if gold ruste, what shal iren do?
For if a preest be foul, on whom we truste,
No wonder is a lewed° man to ruste.   *uneducated*
505 And shame it is, if a preest take keep,°   *heed*
A shiten° shepherde and a clene sheep.   *befouled*

---

7. In medieval times, weddings were performed at the church door.
8. Rome, Boulogne (in France), St. James (of Compostella) in Galicia (Spain), and Cologne (in Germany) were all sites of shrines much visited by pilgrims.
9. Gap-toothed, thought to be a sign of amorousness.
1. Horse with an easy gait.

2. "Bokeler" and "targe": small shields.
3. I.e., she knew all the tricks of that trade.
4. He would be most reluctant to invoke excommunication in order to collect his tithes.
5. Without doubt.
6. The offering made by the congregation of his church was at the Parson's disposal.
7. Great and small.
8. I.e., he practiced what he preached.

Wel oughte a preest ensample for to yive
By his clennesse how that his sheep sholde live.
He sette nought his benefice[9] to hire
510 And leet° his sheep encombred in the mire   *left*
And ran to London, unto Sainte Poules,[1]
To seeken him a chaunterye[2] for soules,
Or with a bretherhede to been withholde,[3]
But dwelte at hoom and kepte wel his folde,
515 So that the wolf ne made it nought miscarye:[4]
He was a shepherde and nought a mercenarye.
And though he holy were and vertuous,
He was to sinful men nought despitous,°   *scornful*
Ne of his speeche daungerous° ne digne,°   *disdainful / haughty*
520 But in his teching discreet and benigne,
To drawen folk to hevene by fairnesse
By good ensample—this was his bisinesse.
But it° were any persone obstinat,   *if there*
What so he were, of heigh or lowe estat,
525 Him wolde he snibben° sharply for the nones:[5]   *scold*
A bettre preest I trowe° ther nowher noon is.   *believe*
He waited after[6] no pompe and reverence,
Ne maked him a spiced conscience,[7]
But Cristes lore° and his Apostles twelve   *teaching*
530 He taughte, but first he folwed it himselve.
    With him ther was a Plowman, was his brother,
That hadde ylad° of dong° ful many a fother[8]   *carried / dung*
A trewe swinkere° and a good was he,   *worker*
Living in pees° and parfit charitee.   *peace*
535 God loved he best with al his hoole° herte   *whole*
At alle times, though him gamed or smerte,[9]
And thanne his neighebor right as himselve.[1]
He wolde thresshe, and therto dike° and delve,°   *work hard / dig*
For Cristes sake, for every poore wight,
540 Withouten hire, if it laye in his might.
His tithes payed he ful faire and wel,
Bothe of his propre swink[2] and his catel.°   *property*
In a tabard° he rood upon a mere.°   *workman's smock / mare*
    Ther was also a Reeve° and a Millere,   *estate manager*
545 A Somnour, and a Pardoner[3] also,
A Manciple,° and myself—ther were namo.   *steward*
    The Millere was a stout carl° for the nones.   *fellow*
Ful big he was of brawn° and eek of bones—   *muscle*
That preved[4] wel, for overal ther he cam

---

9. I.e., his parish. A priest might rent his parish to another and take a more profitable position.
1. St. Paul's Cathedral.
2. Chantry, i.e., a foundation that employed priests for the sole duty of saying masses for the souls of wealthy deceased persons. St. Paul's had many of them.
3. Or to be employed by a brotherhood; i.e., to take a lucrative and fairly easy position as chaplain with a parish guild (see p. 205, n. 6).
4. See John 10.11–13.
5. On the spot, promptly.

6. I.e., expected.
7. Nor did he assume an overfastidious conscience, a holier-than-thou attitude.
8. Load.
9. Whether he was pleased or grieved.
1. Matthew 22.36–40.
2. His own work.
3. "Somnour" (Summoner): server of summonses to the ecclesiastical court. "Pardoner": dispenser of papal pardons (see p. 209, 2nd n. 7).
4. Proved, i.e., was evident.

550   At wrastling he wolde have alway the ram.[5]
He was short-shuldred, brood,° a thikke knarre.[6]   *broad*
Ther was no dore that he nolde heve of harre,[7]
Or breke it at a renning° with his heed.°   *running / head*
His beerd as any sowe or fox was reed,°   *red*
555   And therto brood, as though it were a spade;
Upon the cop right[8] of his nose he hade
A werte,° and theron stood a tuft of heres,   *wart*
Rede as the bristles of a sowes eres;°   *ears*
His nosethirles° blake were and wide.   *nostrils*
560   A swerd and a bokeler° bar° he by his side.   *shield / bore*
His mouth as greet was as a greet furnais.°   *furnace*
He was a janglere° and a Goliardais,[9]   *chatterer*
And that was most of sinne and harlotries.°   *obscenities*
Wel coude he stelen corn and tollen thries[1]—
565   And yit he hadde a thombe[2] of gold, pardee.°   *by heaven*
A whit cote and a blew hood wered° he.   *wore*
A baggepipe wel coude he blowe and soune,°   *sound*
And therwithal° he broughte us out of towne.   *therewith*
    A gentil Manciple[3] was ther of a temple,
570   Of which achatours° mighte take exemple   *buyers of food*
For to been wise in bying of vitaile;°   *victuals*
For wheither that he paide or took by taile,[4]
Algate he waited so in his achat[5]
That he was ay biforn and in good stat.[6]
575   Now is nat that of God a ful fair grace
That swich a lewed° mannes wit shal pace° *uneducated / surpass*
The wisdom of an heep of lerned men?
Of maistres° hadde he mo than thries ten   *masters*
That weren of lawe expert and curious,°   *cunning*
580   Of whiche ther were a dozeine in that hous
Worthy to been stiwardes of rente° and lond   *income*
Of any lord that is in Engelond,
To make him live by his propre good[7]
In honour dettelees but if he were wood,[8]
585   Or live as scarsly° as him list° desire, *economically / it pleases*
And able for to helpen al a shire
In any caas° that mighte falle° or happe,   *event / befall*
And yit this Manciple sette hir aller cappe![9]
    The Reeve was a sclendre° colerik[1] man;   *slender*
590   His beerd was shave as neigh° as evere he can;   *close*
His heer was by his eres ful round yshorn;
His top was dokked[2] lik a preest biforn;°   *in front*

---

5. A ram was frequently offered as the prize in wrastling, a village sport.
6. Sturdy fellow.
7. He would not heave off (its) hinge.
8. Right on the tip.
9. Goliard, teller of ribald stories.
1. Take toll thrice—i.e., deduct from the grain far more than the lawful percentage.
2. Thumb. Ironic allusion to a proverb: "An honest miller has a golden thumb."
3. The Manciple is the business agent of a community of lawyers in London (a "temple").
4. By tally, i.e., on credit.

5. Always he was on the watch in his purchasing.
6. Financial condition. "Ay biforn": i.e., ahead of the game.
7. His own money.
8. Out of debt unless he were crazy.
9. This Manciple made fools of them all.
1. Choleric describes a person whose dominant humor is yellow bile (choler)—i.e., a hot-tempered person. The Reeve is the superintendent of a large farming estate.
2. Cut short; the clergy wore the head partially shaved.

Ful longe were his legges and ful lene,
Ylik a staf, ther was no calf yseene.°   *visible*
Wel coude he keepe° a gerner° and a binne—   *guard / granary*
Ther was noon auditour coude on him winne.[3]
Wel wiste° he by the droughte and by the rain   *knew*
The yeelding of his seed and of his grain.
His lordes sheep, his neet,° his dayerye,°   *cattle / dairy herd*
600   His swin, his hors, his stoor,° and his pultrye   *stock*
Was hoolly° in this Reeves governinge,   *wholly*
And by his covenant yaf[4] the rekeninge,
Sin° that his lord was twenty-yeer of age.   *since*
There coude no man bringe him in arrerage.[5]
605   Ther nas baillif, hierde, nor other hine,
That he ne knew his sleighte and his covine[6]
They were adrad° of him as of the deeth.°   *afraid / plague*
His woning° was ful faire upon an heeth;°   *dwelling / meadow*
With greene trees shadwed was his place.
610   He coude bettre than his lord purchace.°   *acquire goods*
Ful riche he was astored° prively.°   *stocked / secretly*
His lord wel coude he plesen subtilly,
To yive and lene° him of his owene good,°   *lend / property*
And have a thank, and yit a cote and hood.
615   In youthe he hadde lerned a good mister:°   *occupation*
He was a wel good wrighte, a carpenter.
This Reeve sat upon a ful good stot°   *stallion*
That was a pomely° grey and highte° Scot.   *dapple / was named*
A long surcote° of pers° upon he hade,[7]   *overcoat / blue*
620   And by his side he bar° a rusty blade.   *bore*
Of Northfolk was this Reeve of which I telle,
Biside a town men clepen Baldeswelle.°   *Bawdswell*
Tukked[8] he was as is a frere aboute,
And evere he rood the hindreste of oure route.[9]
625   A Somnour[1] was ther with us in that place
That hadde a fir-reed° cherubinnes[2] face,   *fire-red*
For saucefleem° he was, with yën narwe,   *pimply*
And hoot° he was, and lecherous as a sparwe,°   *hot / sparrow*
With scaled° browes blake and piled[3] beerd: *scabby*
630   Of his visage children were aferd.°   *afraid*
Ther nas quiksilver, litarge, ne brimstoon,
Boras, ceruce, ne oile of tartre noon,[4]
Ne oinement that wolde dense and bite,
That him mighte helpen of his whelkes° white,   *pimples*
635   Nor of the knobbes° sitting on his cheekes.   *lumps*
Wel loved he garlek, oinons, and eek leekes,

---

3. I.e., find him in default.
4. And according to his contract he gave.
5. Convict him of being in arrears financially.
6. There was no bailiff (i.e., foreman), shepherd, or other farm laborer whose craftiness and plots he didn't know.
7. He had on.
8. With clothing tucked up like a friar.
9. Hindmost of our group.
1. The "Somnour" (Summoner) is an employee of the ecclesiastical court, whose duty is to bring to court persons whom the archdeacon—the justice of the court—suspects of offenses against canon law. By this time, however, summoners had generally transformed themselves into corrupt detectives who spied out offenders and blackmailed them by threats of summonses.
2. Cherubs, often depicted in art with red faces.
3. Uneven, partly hairless.
4. These are all ointments for diseases affecting the skin, probably diseases of venereal origin.

And for to drinke strong win reed as blood.
Thanne wolde he speke and crye as he were wood;°   *mad*
And whan that he wel dronken hadde the win,
640 Thanne wolde he speke no word but Latin:
A fewe termes hadde he, two or three,
That he hadde lerned out of som decree;
No wonder is—he herde it al the day,
And eek ye knowe wel how that a jay°   *parrot*
645 Can clepen "Watte"[5] as wel as can the Pope—
But whoso coude in other thing him grope,°   *examine*
Thanne hadde he spent all his philosophye;[6]
Ay *Questio quid juris*[7] wolde he crye.
    He was a gentil harlot° and a kinde;   *rascal*
650 A bettre felawe sholde men nought finde:
He wolde suffre,° for a quart of win,   *permit*
A good felawe to have his concubin
A twelfmonth, and excusen him at the fulle;[8]
Ful prively° a finch eek coude he pulle.[9]   *secretly*
655 And if he foond° owher° a good felawe   *found / anywhere*
He wolde techen him to have noon awe
In swich caas of the Ercedekenes curs,[1]
But if[2] a mannes soule were in his purs,
For in nis purs he sholde ypunisshed be.
660 "Purs is the Ercedekenes helle," saide he.
    But wel I woot he lied right in deede:
Of cursing° oughte eech gilty man him drede,   *excommunication*
For curs wol slee° right as assoiling° savith—   *slay / absolution*
And also war him of a *significavit*.[3]
665   In daunger[4] hadde he at his owene gise°   *disposal*
The yonge girles of the diocise,
And knew hir conseil,° and was al hir reed.[5]   *secrets*
A gerland hadde he set upon his heed
As greet as it were for an ale-stake,[6]
670 A bokeler hadde he maad him of a cake.
    With him ther rood a gentil Pardoner[7]
Of Rouncival, his freend and his compeer,°   *comrade*
That straight was comen fro the Court of Rome.[8]
Ful loude he soong,° "Com hider, love, to me."   *sang*
675 This Somnour bar to him a stif burdoun:[9]
Was nevere trompe° of half so greet a soun.   *trumpet*

5. Call out: "Walter"—like modern parrots' "Polly."
6. I.e., learning.
7. "What point of law does this investigation involve?" A phrase frequently used in ecclesiastical courts.
8. Fully. Ecclesiastical courts had jurisdiction over many offenses that today would come under civil law, including sexual offenses.
9. "To pull a finch" (pluck a bird) is to have sexual relations with a woman.
1. Archdeacon's sentence of excommunication.
2. Unless.
3. And also one should be careful of a *significavit* (the writ that transferred the guilty offender from the ecclesiastical to the civil arm for pun-

ishment).
4. Under his domination.
5. Was their chief source of advice.
6. A tavern was signalized by a pole ("ale-stake"), rather like a modern flagpole, projecting from its front wall; on this hung a garland, or "bush."
7. A Pardoner dispensed papal pardon for sins to those who contributed to the charitable institution that he was licensed to represent; this Pardoner purported to be collecting for the hospital of Roncesvalles ("Rouncival") in Spain, which had a London branch.
8. The papal court.
9. I.e., provided him with a strong bass accompaniment.

This Pardoner hadde heer as yelow as wex,
But smoothe it heeng° as dooth a strike° of flex;°   *hung / hank / flax*
By ounces[1] heenge his lokkes that he hadde,
680 And therwith he his shuldres overspradde,°   *overspread*
But thinne it lay, by colpons,° oon by oon;   *strands*
But hood for jolitee° wered° he noon,   *nonchalance / wore*
For it was trussed up in his walet:°   *pack*
Him thoughte he rood al of the newe jet.°   *fashion*
685 Dischevelee° save his cappe he rood al bare.   *with hair down*
Swiche glaring yën hadde he as an hare.
A vernicle[2] hadde he sowed upon his cappe,
His walet biforn him in his lappe,
Bretful° of pardon, come from Rome al hoot.°   *brimful / hot*
690 A vois he hadde as smal° as hath a goot;°   *high-pitched / goat*
No beerd hadde he, ne nevere sholde have;
As smoothe it was as it were late yshave:
I trowe° he were a gelding[3] or a mare.   *believe*
But of his craft, fro Berwik into Ware,[4]
695 Ne was ther swich another pardoner;
For in his male° he hadde a pilwe-beer°   *bag / pillowcase*
Which that he saide was Oure Lady veil;
He saide he hadde a gobet° of the sail   *piece*
That Sainte Peter hadde whan that he wente
700 Upon the see, til Jesu Crist him hente.°   *seized*
He hadde a crois° of laton,° ful of stones,   *cross / brassy metal*
And in a glas he hadde pigges bones,
But with thise relikes[5] whan that he foond°   *found*
A poore person° dwelling upon lond,[6]   *parson*
705 Upon° a day he gat° him more moneye   *in / got*
Than that the person gat in monthes twaye;
And thus with feined° flaterye and japes°   *false / tricks*
He made the person and the peple his apes.°   *dupes*
But trewely to tellen at the laste,
710 He was in chirche a noble ecclesiaste;
Wel coude he rede a lesson and a storye,°   *liturgical narrative*
But alderbest° he soong an offertorye,[7]   *best of all*
For wel he wiste° whan that song was songe,   *knew*
He moste° preche and wel affile° his tonge   *must / sharpen*
715 To winne silver, as he ful wel coude—
Therefore he soong the merierly° and loude.   *more merrily*
    Now have I told you soothly in a clause[8]
Th'estaat, th'array, the nombre, and eek the cause
Why that assembled was this compaignye
720 In Southwerk at this gentil hostelrye
That highte the Tabard, faste° by the Belle;[9]   *close*
But now is time to you for to telle

---

1. I.e., thin strands.
2. Portrait of Christ's face as it was said to have
been impressed on St. Veronica's handkerchief,
i.e., a souvenir reproduction of a famous relic in
Rome.
3. A neutered stallion, i.e., a eunuch.
4. I.e., from one end of England to the other.

5. Relics, i.e., the pigs' bones that the Pardoner
represented as saints' bones.
6. Upcountry.
7. Part of the mass sung before the offering of
alms.
8. I.e., in a short space.
9. Another tavern in Southwark.

How that we baren us[1] that ilke° night   *same*
Whan we were in that hostelrye alight;
725 And after wol I telle of oure viage,°   *trip*
And al the remenant of oure pilgrimage.
But first I praye you of youre curteisye
That ye n'arette it nought my vilainye[2]
Though that I plainly speke in this matere
730 To telle you hir wordes and hir cheere,°   *behavior*
Ne though I speke hir wordes proprely;°   *accurately*
For this ye knowen also wel as I:
Who so shal telle a tale after a man
He moot° reherce,° as neigh as evere he can,   *must / repeat*
735 Everich a word, if it be in his charge,°   *responsibility*
Al speke he[3] nevere so rudeliche and large,°   *broadly*
Or elles he moot telle his tale untrewe,
Or feine° thing, or finde° wordes newe;   *make up / devise*
He may nought spare[4] although he were his brother:
740 He moot as wel saye oo word as another.
Crist spak himself ful brode° in Holy Writ,   *broadly*
And wel ye woot no vilainye° is it;   *rudeness*
Eek Plato saith, who so can him rede,
The wordes mote be cosin to the deede.
745   Also I praye you to foryive it me
Al° have I nat set folk in hir degree   *although*
Here in this tale as that they sholde stonde:
My wit is short, ye may wel understonde.
    Greet cheere made oure Host[5] us everichoon,
750 And to the soper sette he us anoon.°   *at once*
He served us with vitaile° at the beste.   *food*
Strong was the win, and wel to drinke us leste.°   *it pleased*
A semely man oure Hoste was withalle
For to been a marchal[6] in an halle;
755 A large man he was, with yën steepe,°   *prominent*
A fairer burgeis° was ther noon in Chepe[7]—   *burgher*
Bold of his speeche, and wis, and wel ytaught,
And of manhood him lakkede right naught.
Eek therto he was right a merye man,
760 And after soper playen he bigan,
And spak of mirthe amonges othere thinges—
Whan that we hadde maad oure rekeninges[8]—
And saide thus, "Now, lordinges, trewely,
Ye been to me right welcome, hertely.°   *heartily*
765 For by my trouthe, if that I shal nat lie,
I sawgh nat this yeer so merye a compaignye
At ones in this herberwe° as is now.   *inn*
Fain° wolde I doon you mirthe, wiste I[9] how.   *gladly*
And of a mirthe I am right now bithought,
770 To doon you ese, and it shal coste nought.

---

1. Bore ourselves.   6. Marshal, one who was in charge of feasts.
2. That you do not attribute it to my boorishness.   7. Cheapside, business center of London.
3. Although he speak.   8. Had paid our bills.
4. I.e., spare anyone.   9. If I knew.
5. The landlord of the Tabard Inn.

"Ye goon to Canterbury—God you speede;
The blisful martyr quite you youre meede.[1]
And wel I woot as ye goon by the waye
Ye shapen you[2] to talen° and to playe,   *converse*
775 For trewely, confort ne mirthe is noon
To ride by the waye domb as stoon;°   *stone*
And therefore wol I maken you disport
As I saide erst,° and doon you som confort;   *before*
And if you liketh alle, by oon assent,
780 For to stonden at[3] my juggement,
And for to werken as I shall you saye,
Tomorwe whan ye riden by the waye—
Now by my fader° soule that is deed,   *father's*
But° ye be merye I wol yive you myn heed!°   *unless / head*
785 Holde up youre handes withouten more speeche."
    Oure counseil was nat longe for to seeche;°   *seek*
Us thought it was not worth to make it wis,[4]
And graunted him withouten more avis,°   *deliberation*
And bade him saye his voirdit° as him leste.[5]   *verdict*
790   "Lordinges," quod he, "now herkneth for the beste;
But taketh it nought, I praye you, in desdain.
This is the point, to speken short and plain,
That eech of you, to shorte° with oure waye   *shorten*
In this viage, shal tellen tales twaye°—   *two*
795 To Canterburyward, I mene it so,
And hoomward he shal tellen othere two,
Of aventures that whilom° have bifalle;   *once upon a time*
And which of you that bereth him best of alle—
That is to sayn, that telleth in this cas
800 Tales of best sentence° and most solas°—   *meaning / delight*
Shal have a soper at oure aller cost,[6]
Here in this place, sitting by this post,
Whan that we come again fro Canterbury.
And for to make you the more mury°   *merry*
805 I wol myself goodly° with you ride—   *kindly*
Right at myn owene cost—and be youre gide.
And who so wol my juggement withsaye°   *contradict*
Shal paye al that we spende by the waye.
And if ye vouche sauf that it be so,
810 Telle me anoon, withouten wordes mo,°   *more*
And I wol erly shape me[7] therefore."
    This thing was graunted and oure othes swore
With ful glad herte, and prayden[8] him also
That he wolde vouche sauf for to do so,
815 And that he wolde been oure governour,
And of oure tales juge and reportour,°   *accountant*
And sette a soper at a certain pris,°   *price*
And we wol ruled been at his devis,°   *disposal*

---

1. Pay you your reward.
2. Intend.
3. Abide by.
4. We didn't think it worthwhile to make an issue of it.
5. It pleased.
6. At the cost of us all.
7. Prepare myself.
8. I.e., we prayed.

In heigh and lowe; and thus by oon assent
820　We been accorded to his juggement.
　　And therupon the win was fet° anoon;　　　　　　　　　　*fetched*
　　We dronken and to reste wente eechoon°　　　　　　　　*each one*
　　Withouten any lenger° taryinge.　　　　　　　　　　　　*longer*
　　　Amorwe° whan that day bigan to springe　　　*in the morning*
825　Up roos oure Host and was oure aller cok,[9]
　　And gadred us togidres in a flok,
　　And forth we riden, a litel more than pas,°　　　　*walking pace*
　　Unto the watering of Saint Thomas;[1]
　　And ther oure Host bigan his hors arreste,°　　　　　　　*halt*
830　And saide, "Lordes, herkneth if you leste:°　　　　　*it please*
　　　Ye woot youre forward° and it you recorde:[2]　　　*agreement*
　　If evensong and morwesong° accorde,°　　*morning song / agree*
　　Lat see now who shal telle the firste tale.
　　As evere mote° I drinken win or ale,　　　　　　　　　　　*may*
835　Who so be rebel to my juggement
　　Shal paye for al that by the way is spent.
　　Now draweth cut er that we ferrer twinne:[3]
　　He which that hath the shorteste shal biginne.
　　　"Sire Knight," quod he, "my maister and my lord,
840　Now draweth cut, for that is myn accord.°　　　　　　　　*will*
　　Cometh neer," quod he, "my lady Prioresse,
　　And ye, sire Clerk, lat be youre shamefastnesse°—　　　*modesty*
　　Ne studieth nought. Lay hand to, every man!"
　　　Anoon to drawen every wight bigan,
845　And shortly for to tellen as it was
　　Were it by aventure, or sort, or cas,[4]
　　The soothe° is this, the cut fil° to the Knight;　　*truth / fell*
　　Of which ful blithe and glad was every wight,
　　And telle he moste° his tale, as was resoun,　　　　　　　*must*
850　By forward and by composicioun,[5]
　　As ye han herd. What needeth wordes mo?
　　And whan this goode man sawgh that it was so,
　　As he that wis was and obedient
　　To keepe his forward by his free assent,
855　He saide, "Sin° I shal biginne the game,　　　　　　　　　*since*
　　What, welcome be the cut, in Goddes name!
　　Now lat us ride, and herkneth what I saye."
　　And with that word we riden forth oure waye,
　　And he bigan with right a merye cheere°　　　　　*countenance*
860　His tale anoon, and saide as ye may heere.

Summary　[*The Knight's Tale* is a romance of 2,350 lines, which Chaucer had written before beginning *The Canterbury Tales*—one of several works assumed to be earlier that he inserted into the collection. It is probably the same story, with only minor revisions, that Chaucer referred to in *The Legend of Good Women* as "al the love of Palamon and Arcite." These are the names of the two heroes of *The Knight's*

---

9. Was rooster for us all.
1. A watering place near Southwark.
2. You recall it.

3. Go farther. "Draweth cut": i.e., draw straws.
4. Whether it was luck, fate, or chance.
5. By agreement and compact.

Tale, kinsmen and best friends who are taken prisoner at the siege and destruction of ancient Thebes by Theseus, the ruler of Athens. Gazing out from their prison cell in a tower, they fall in love at first sight and almost at the same moment with Theseus's sister-in-law, Emily, who is taking an early-morning walk in a garden below their window. After a bitter rivalry, they are at last reconciled through a tournament in which Emily is the prize. Arcite wins the tournament but, as he lies dying after being thrown by his horse, he makes a noble speech encouraging Palamon and Emily to marry. The tale is an ambitious combination of classical setting and mythology, romance plot, and themes of fortune and destiny.]

The Miller's Prologue and Tale

The Miller's Tale belongs to a genre known as the "fabliau": a short story in verse that deals satirically, often grossly and fantastically as well as hilariously, with intrigues and deceptions about sex or money (and often both these elements in the same story). These are the tales Chaucer is anticipating in *The General Prologue* when he warns his presumably genteel audience that they must expect some rude speaking (see lines 727–44). An even more pointed apology follows at the end of *The Miller's Prologue*. Fabliau tales exist everywhere in oral literature; as a literary form they flourished in France, especially in the thirteenth century. By having Robin the Miller tell a fabliau to "quit" (to requite or pay back) the Knight's aristocratic romance, Chaucer sets up a dialectic between classes, genres, and styles that he exploits throughout *The Canterbury Tales*.

The Prologue

Whan that the Knight hadde thus his tale ytold,
In al the route° nas° ther yong ne old   *group / was not*
That he ne saide it was a noble storye,
And worthy for to drawen° to memorye,   *recall*
5 And namely° the gentils everichoon.   *especially*
  Oure Hoste lough° and swoor, "So mote I goon,[1]   *laughed*
This gooth aright: unbokeled is the male.°   *pouch*
Lat see now who shal telle another tale.
For trewely the game is wel bigonne.
10 Now telleth ye, sire Monk, if that ye conne,°   *can*
Somwhat to quite° with the Knightes tale."   *repay*
  The Millere, that for dronken[2] was al pale,
So that unnethe° upon his hors he sat,   *with difficulty*
He nolde° avalen° neither hood ne hat,   *would not / take off*
15 Ne abiden no man for his curteisye,
But in Pilates vois[3] he gan to crye,
And swoor, "By armes[4] and by blood and bones,
I can° a noble tale for the nones,   *know*
With which I wol now quite the Knightes tale."
20 Oure Hoste sawgh that he was dronke of ale,
And saide, "Abide, Robin, leve° brother,   *dear*
Som bettre man shal telle us first another.

---

1. So might I walk—an oath.
2. I.e., drunkenness.
3. The harsh voice usually associated with the character of Pontius Pilate in the mystery plays.
4. I.e., by God's arms, a blasphemous oath.

Abide, and lat us werken thriftily."°   *with propriety*
    "By Goddes soule," quod he, "that wol nat I,
25 For I wol speke or elles go my way."
    Oure Host answerde, "Tel on, a devele way!⁵
Thou art a fool; thy wit is overcome."
    "Now herkneth," quod the Millere, "alle and some.⁶
But first I make a protestacioun°   *public affirmation*
30 That I am dronke: I knowe it by my soun.°   *tone of voice*
And therfore if that I misspeke° or saye,   *speak or say wrongly*
Wite it⁷ the ale of Southwerk, I you praye;
For I wol telle a legende° and a lif   *saint's life*
Bothe of a carpenter and of his wif,
35 How that a clerk hath set the wrightes cappe."⁸
    The Reeve answerde and saide, "Stint thy clappe!⁹
Lat be thy lewed° dronken harlotrye.°   *ignorant / obscenity*
It is a sinne and eek° a greet folye   *also*
To apairen° any man or him defame,   *injure*
40 And eek to bringen wives in swich fame.°   *reputation*
Thou maist ynough of othere thinges sayn."
    This dronken Millere spak ful soone again,
And saide, "Leve° brother Osewold,   *dear*
Who hath no wif, he is no cokewold.°   *cuckold*
45 But I saye nat therfore that thou art oon.
Ther ben ful goode wives many oon,°   *a one*
And evere a thousand goode ayains oon badde.
That knowestou wel thyself but if thou madde.°   *rave*
Why artou angry with my tale now?
50 I have a wif, pardee,° as wel as thou,   *by God*
Yit nolde° I, for the oxen in my plough,   *would not*
Take upon me more than ynough°   *enough*
As deemen of myself that I were oon:¹
I wol bileve wel that I am noon.
55 An housbonde shal nought been inquisitif
Of Goddes privetee,° nor of his wif.   *secrets*
So² he may finde Goddes foison° there,   *plenty*
Of the remenant° needeth nought enquere."°   *rest / inquire*
    What sholde I more sayn but this Millere
60 He nolde his wordes for no man forbere,
But tolde his cherles tale in his manere.
M'athinketh° that I shal reherce° it here,   *I regret / repeat*
And therefore every gentil wight I praye,
Deemeth nought, for Goddes love, that I saye
65 Of yvel entente, but for° I moot reherse   *because*
Hir tales alle, be they bet° or werse,   *better*
Or elles falsen° som of my matere.   *falsify*
And therfore, whoso list it nought yheere°   *hear*
Turne over the leef,° and chese° another tale,   *page / choose*
70 For he shal finde ynowe,° grete and smale,   *enough*
Of storial³ thing that toucheth gentilesse,°   *gentility*

---

5. I.e., in the devil's name.   9. Stop your chatter.
6. Each and every one.   1. To think that I were one (a cuckold).
7. Blame it on.   2. Provided that.
8. I.e., how a clerk made a fool of a carpenter.   3. Historical, i.e., true.

And eek moralitee and holinesse:
Blameth nought me if that ye chese amis.
The Millere is a cherl, ye knowe wel this,
75 So was the Reeve eek, and othere mo,
And harlotrye° they tolden bothe two.   *ribaldry*
Aviseth you,[4] and putte me out of blame:
And eek men shal nought maken ernest of game.

The Tale

Whilom° ther was dwelling at Oxenforde   *once upon a time*
80 A riche gnof° that gestes heeld to boorde,[5]   *churl*
And of his craft he was a carpenter.
With him ther was dwelling a poore scoler,
Hadde lerned art[6] but al his fantasye°   *desire*
Was turned for to lere° astrologye,   *learn*
85 And coude a certain of conclusiouns,
To deemen by interrogaciouns,[7]
If that men axed° him in certain houres   *asked*
Whan that men sholde have droughte or elles showres,
Or if men axed him what shal bifalle
90 Of every thing—I may nat rekene hem alle.
This clerk was cleped° hende[8] Nicholas.   *called*
Of derne love he coude, and of solas,[9]
And therto he was sly and ful privee,°   *secretive*
And lik a maide meeke for to see.
95 A chambre hadde he in that hostelrye
Allone, withouten any compaignye,
Ful fetisly ydight[1] with herbes swoote,°   *sweet*
And he himself as sweete as is the roote
Of licoris or any setewale.[2]
100 His *Almageste*[3] and bookes grete and smale,
His astrelabye, longing for[4] his art,
His augrim stones,[5] layen faire apart
On shelves couched° at his beddes heed;   *set*
His presse° ycovered with a falding reed;[6]   *storage chest*
105 And al above ther lay a gay sautrye,°   *psaltery (harp)*
On which he made a-nightes melodye
So swetely that al the chambre roong,°   *rang*
And *Angelus ad Virginem*[7] he soong,
And after that he soong the *Kinges Note*.[8]
110 Ful often blessed was his merye throte.
And thus this sweete clerk his time spente

4. Take heed.
5. I.e., took in boarders.
6. Who had completed the first stage of university education (the trivium).
7. I.e., and he knew a number of propositions on which to base astrological analyses (which would reveal the matters in the next three lines).
8. Courteous, handy, attractive.
9. I.e., he knew about secret love and pleasurable practices.
1. Elegantly furnished.

2. Setwall, a spice.
3. The 2nd-century treatise by Ptolemy, still the standard astronomy textbook.
4. Belonging to. "Astrelabye": astrolabe, an astronomical instrument.
5. Counters used in arithmetic.
6. Red coarse woolen cloth.
7. "The Angel to the Virgin," an Annunciation hymn.
8. Probably a popular song of the time.

After his freendes finding and his rente.[9]
    This carpenter hadde wedded newe° a wif   *lately*
Which that he loved more than his lif.
115 Of eighteteene yeer she was of age;
Jalous he was, and heeld hire narwe in cage,
For she was wilde and yong, and he was old,
And deemed himself been lik a cokewold[1]
He knew nat Caton,[2] for his wit was rude,
120 That bad men sholde wedde his similitude:[3]
Men sholde wedden after hir estat,[4]
For youthe and elde° is often at debat.   *age*
But sith that he was fallen in the snare,
He moste endure, as other folk, his care.
125   Fair was this yonge wif, and therwithal
As any wesele° hir body gent and smal.[5]   *weasel*
A ceint she wered, barred[6] al of silk;
A barmcloth° as whit as morne° milk   *apron / morning*
Upon hir lendes,° ful of many a gore;°   *loins / flounce*
130 Whit was hir smok,° and broiden° al bifore   *undergarment / embroidered*
And eek bihinde, on hir coler° aboute,   *collar*
Of° col-blak silk, withinne and eek withoute;   *with*
The tapes° of hir white voluper°   *ribbons / cap*
Were of the same suite of[7] hir coler;
135 Hir filet° brood° of silk ana set ful hye;   *headband / broad*
And sikerly° she hadde a likerous° yë;   *certainly / wanton*
Ful smale ypulled[8] were hir browes two,
And tho were bent,° and blake as any slo.°   *arching / sloeberry*
She was ful more blisful on to see
140 Than is the newe perejonette° tree,   *pear*
And softer than the wolle° is of a wether;°   *wool / ram*
And by hir girdel° heeng° a purs of lether,   *belt / hung*
Tasseled with silk and perled with latoun.[9]
In al this world, to seeken up and down,
145 Ther nis no man so wis that coude thenche°   *imagine*
So gay a popelote° or swich° a wenche.   *doll / such*
Ful brighter was the shining of hir hewe
Than in the Towr[1] the noble° yforged newe.   *gold coin*
But of hir song, it was as loud and yerne°   *lively*
150 As any swalwe° sitting on a berne.°   *swallow / barn*
Therto she coude skippe and make game°   *play*
As any kide or calf folwing his dame.°   *mother*
Hir mouth was sweete as bragot or the meeth,[2]
Or hoord of apples laid in hay or heeth.°   *heather*
155 Winsing° she was as is a joly° colt,   *skittish / high-spirited*
Long as a mast, and upright° as a bolt.°   *straight / arrow*
A brooch she bar upon hir lowe coler

---

9. In accordance with his friends' provision and his own income.
1. I.e., suspected of himself that he was like a cuckold.
2. Dionysius Cato, the supposed author of a book of maxims used in elementary education.
3. Commanded that one should wed his equal.
4. Men should marry according to their condition.
5. Slender and delicate.
6. A belt she wore, with transverse stripes.
7. The same kind as, i.e., black.
8. Delicately plucked.
9. I.e., with brassy spangles on it.
1. The Tower of London, the Mint.
2. "Bragot" and "meeth" are honey drinks.

As brood as is the boos° of a bokeler;°   *boss / shield*
Hir shoes were laced on hir legges hye.
160   She was a primerole,° a piggesnye,[3]   *primrose*
For any lord to leggen° in his bedde,   *lay*
Or yit for any good yeman to wedde.
    Now sire, and eft° sire, so bifel the cas   *again*
That on a day this hende Nicholas
165   Fil° with this yonge wif to rage° and playe,   *happened / flirt*
Whil that hir housbonde was at Oseneye[4]
(As clerkes been ful subtil and ful quainte),°   *clever*
And prively he caughte hire by the queinte,[5]
And saide, "Ywis,° but° if ich° have my wille,   *truly / unless / I*
170   For derne° love of thee, lemman, I spille,"°   *secret / die*
And heeld hire harde by the haunche-bones,°   *thighs*
And saide, "Lemman,° love me al atones,[6]   *sweetheart*
Or I wol dien, also° God me save."   *so*
And she sproong° as a colt dooth in a trave,[7]   *sprang*
175   And with hir heed she wried° faste away;   *twisted*
She saide, "I wol nat kisse thee, by my fay.°   *faith*
Why, lat be," quod she, "lat be, Nicholas!
Or I wol crye 'Out, harrow,° and allas!'   *help*
Do way youre handes, for your curteisye!"
180   This Nicholas gan mercy for to crye,
And spak so faire, and profred him so faste,[8]
That she hir love him graunted atte laste,
And swoor hir ooth by Saint Thomas of Kent[9]
That she wolde been at his comandement,
185   Whan that she may hir leiser[1] wel espye.
"Myn housbonde is so ful of jalousye
That but ye waite° wel and been privee   *be on guard*
I woot right wel I nam but deed,"[2] quod she.
"Ye moste been ful derne° as in this cas."   *secret*
190   "Nay, therof care thee nought," quod Nicholas.
"A clerk hadde litherly biset his while,[3]
But if he coude a carpenter bigile."
And thus they been accorded and ysworn
To waite° a time, as I have told biforn.   *watch for*
195   Whan Nicholas hadde doon this everydeel,°   *every bit*
And thakked° hire upon the lendes° weel,   *patted / loins*
He kiste hire sweete, and taketh his sautrye,
And playeth faste, and maketh melodye.
    Thanne fil° it thus, that to the parissh chirche,   *befell*
200   Cristes owene werkes for to wirche,°   *perform*
This goode wif wente on an haliday:°   *holy day*
Hir forheed shoon as bright as any day,
So was it wasshen whan she leet° hir werk.   *left*
Now was ther of that chirche a parissh clerk,[4]

---

3. A pig's eye, a name for a common flower.
4. A town near Oxford.
5. Elegant (thing); a euphemism for the female genitals.
6. Right now.
7. Frame for holding a horse to be shod.
8. I.e., made such vigorous advances.

9. Thomas à Becket.
1. I.e., opportunity.
2. I am no more than dead, I am done for.
3. Poorly employed his time.
4. Assistant to the parish priest, not a cleric or student.

205	The which that was ycleped° Absolon:	*called*
	Crul° was his heer, and as the gold it shoon,	*curly*
	And strouted° as a fanne⁵ large and brode;	*spread out*
	Ful straight and evene lay his joly shode.⁶	
	His rode° was reed, his yën greye as goos.°	*complexion / goose*
210	With Poules window corven⁷ on his shoos,	
	In hoses° rede he wente fetisly.°	*stockings / elegantly*
	Yclad he was ful smale° and propely,	*finely*
	Al in a kirtel° of a light waget°—	*tunic / blue*
	Ful faire and thikke been the pointes⁸ set—	
215	And therupon he hadde a gay surplis,°	*surplice*
	As whit as is the blosme upon the ris.°	*bough*
	A merye child° he was, so God me save.	*young man*
	Wel coude he laten blood, and clippe,⁹ and shave,	
	And maken a chartre of land, or acquitaunce;¹	
220	In twenty manere° coude he trippe and daunce	*ways*
	After the scole of Oxenforde tho,°	*then*
	And with his legges casten° to and fro,	*prance*
	And playen songes on a smal rubible;°	*fiddle*
	Therto he soong somtime a loud quinible,²	
225	And as wel coude he playe on a giterne:°	*guitar*
	In al the town nas brewhous ne taverne	
	That he ne visited with his solas,°	*entertainment*
	Ther any gailard tappestere³ was.	
	But sooth to sayn, he was somdeel squaimous°	*a bit squeamish*
230	Of° farting, and of speeche daungerous.⁴	*about*
	This Absolon, that joly° was and gay,	*pretty, amorous*
	Gooth with a cencer° on the haliday,	*incense burner*
	Cencing the wives of the parissh faste,	
	And many a lovely look on hem he caste,	
235	And namely° on this carpenteres wif:	*especially*
	To looke on hire him thoughte a merye lif.	
	She was so propre° and sweete and likerous,⁵	*neat*
	I dar wel sayn, if she hadde been a mous,	
	And he a cat, he wolde hire hente° anoon.	*pounce on*
240	This parissh clerk, this joly Absolon,	
	Hath in his herte swich a love-longinge°	*lovesickness*
	That of no wif ne took he noon offringe—	
	For curteisye he saide he wolde noon.	
	The moone, whan it was night, ful brighte shoon,°	*shone*
245	And Absolon his giterne° hath ytake—	*guitar*
	For paramours° he thoughte for to wake—	*love*
	And forth he gooth, jolif° and amorous,	*pretty*
	Til he cam to the carpenteres hous,	
	A litel after cokkes hadde ycrowe,	
250	And dressed him up by a shot-windowe⁶	

---

5. Wide-mouthed basket for separating grain from chaff.
6. Parting of the hair.
7. Carved with intricate designs, like the tracery in the windows of St. Paul's.
8. Laces for fastening the tunic and holding up the hose.
9. Let blood and give haircuts. Bleeding was a

medical treatment performed by barbers.
1. Legal release. "Chartre": deed.
2. Part requiring a very high voice.
3. Gay barmaid.
4. Prudish about (vulgar) talk.
5. Wanton, appetizing.
6. Took his position by a hinged window.

That was upon the carpenteres wal.
He singeth in his vois gentil and smal,°   *dainty*
"Now dere lady, if thy wille be,
I praye you that ye wol rewe° on me,"   *have pity*
255 Ful wel accordant to his giterninge.[7]
This carpenter awook and herde him singe,
And spak unto his wif, and saide anoon,
"What, Alison, heerestou nought Absolon
That chaunteth thus under oure bowres° wal?"   *bedroom's*
260 And she answerde hir housbonde therwithal,
"Yis, God woot, John, I heere it everydeel."°   *every bit*
   This passeth forth. What wol ye bet than weel?[8]
Fro day to day this joly Absolon
So woweth° hire that him is wo-bigoon: *woos*
265 He waketh° al the night and al the day;   *stays awake*
He kembed° his lokkes brode[9] and made him gay;   *combed*
He woweth hire by menes and brocage,[1]
And swoor he wolde been hir owene page°   *personal servant*
He singeth, brokking° as a nightingale;   *trilling*
270 He sente hire piment,° meeth,° and spiced ale,   *spiced wine / mead*
And wafres° piping hoot out of the gleede;°   *pastries / coals*
And for she was of towne,[2] he profred meede°—   *money*
For som folk wol be wonnen for richesse,
And som for strokes,° and som for gentilesse.   *blows (force)*
275 Somtime to shewe his lightnesse and maistrye,[3]
He playeth Herodes[4] upon a scaffold° hye.   *platform, stage*
But what availeth him as in this cas?
She loveth so this hende Nicholas
That Absolon may blowe the bukkes horn;[5]
280 He ne hadde for his labour but a scorn.
And thus she maketh Absolon hir ape,[6]
And al his ernest turneth til° a jape.°   *to / joke*
Ful sooth is this proverbe, it is no lie;
Men saith right thus: "Alway the nye slye
285 Maketh the ferre leve to be loth."[7]
For though that Absolon be wood° or wroth,   *furious*
By cause that he fer was from hir sighte,
This nye° Nicholas stood in his lighte.   *nearby*
   Now beer° thee wel, thou hende Nicholas,   *bear*
290 For Absolon may waile and singe allas.
   And so bifel it on a Saterday
This carpenter was goon til Oseney,
And hende Nicholas and Alisoun
Accorded been to this conclusioun,
295 That Nicholas shal shapen° hem a wile°   *arrange / trick*
This sely[8] jalous housbonde to bigile,
And if so be this game wente aright,

7. In harmony with his guitar playing.
8. Better than well.
9. I.e., wide-spreading.
1. By go-betweens and agents.
2. Because she was a town woman.
3. Facility and virtuosity.
4. Herod, a role traditionally played as a bully in the mystery plays.
5. Blow the buck's horn, i.e., go whistle, waste his time.
6. I.e., thus she makes a monkey out of Absolon.
7. Always the sly man at hand makes the distant dear one hated.
8. Poor innocent.

She sholden sleepen in his arm al night—
For this was his desir and hire° also.   *hers*
300 And right anoon, withouten wordes mo,
This Nicholas no lenger wolde tarye,
But dooth ful softe unto his chambre carye
Bothe mete and drinke for a day or twaye,
And to hir housbonde bad hire for to saye,
305 If that he axed after Nicholas,
She sholde saye she niste° wher he was—   *didn't know*
Of al that day she sawgh him nought with yë:
She trowed° that he was in maladye,   *believed*
For for no cry hir maide coude him calle,
310 He nolde answere for no thing that mighte falle.°   *happen*
      This passeth forth al thilke° Saterday   *this*
That Nicholas stille in his chambre lay,
And eet,° and sleep,° or dide what him leste,[9]   *ate / slept*
Til Sonday that the sonne gooth to reste.
315   This sely carpenter hath greet mervaile
Of Nicholas, or what thing mighte him aile,
And saide, "I am adrad,° by Saint Thomas,   *afraid*
It stondeth nat aright with Nicholas.
God shilde° that he deide sodeinly!   *forbid*
320 This world is now ful tikel,° sikerly: *precarious*
I sawgh today a corps yborn to chirche
That now a° Monday last I sawgh him wirche.°   *on / work*
Go up," quod he unto his knave° anoon,   *manservant*
"Clepe° at his dore or knokke with a stoon.°   *call / stone*
325 Looke how it is and tel me boldely."
      This knave gooth him up ful sturdily,
And at the chambre dore whil that he stood
He cride and knokked as that he were wood,°   *mad*
"What? How? What do ye, maister Nicholay?"
330 How may ye sleepen al the longe day?"
But al for nought: he herde nat a word.
An hole he foond ful lowe upon a boord,
Ther as the cat was wont in for to creepe,
And at that hole he looked in ful deepe,
335 And atte laste he hadde of him a sighte.
      This Nicholas sat evere caping° uprighte   *gaping*
As he hadde kiked° on the newe moone.   *gazed*
Adown he gooth and tolde his maister soone
In what array° he saw this ilke° man.   *condition / same*
340   This carpenter to blessen him[1] bigan,
And saide, "Help us, Sainte Frideswide![2]
A man woot litel what him shal bitide.
This man is falle, with his astromye,°   *astronomy*
In som woodnesse° or in som agonye.   *madness*
345 I thoughte ay° wel how that it sholde be: *always*
Men sholde nought knowe of Goddes privetee.°   *secrets*
Ye, blessed be alway a lewed° man   *ignorant*

9. He wanted.   2. Patron saint of Oxford.
1. Cross himself.

That nought but only his bileve° can.°   *creed / knows*
So ferde° another clerk with astromye: *fared*
350   He walked in the feeldes for to prye°   *gaze*
Upon the sterres,° what ther sholde bifalle,   *stars*
Til he was in a marle-pit[3] yfalle—
He saw nat that. But yit, by Saint Thomas,
Me reweth sore[4] for hende Nicholas.
355   He shal be rated of[5] his studying,
If that I may, by Jesus, hevene king!
Get me a staf that I may underspore,°   *pry up*
Whil that thou, Robin, hevest° up the dore.   *heave*
He shal[6] out of his studying, as I gesse."
360   And to the chambre dore he gan him dresse.[7]
His knave was a strong carl° for the nones,°   *fellow / purpose*
And by the haspe he haaf° it up atones: *heaved*
Into° the floor the dore fil° anoon.   *on / fell*
This Nicholas sat ay as stille as stoon,
365   And evere caped up into the air.
This carpenter wende° he were in despair,   *thought*
And hente° him by the shuldres mightily,   *seized*
And shook him harde, and cride spitously,°   *vehemently*
"What, Nicholay, what, how! What! Looke adown!
370   Awaak and thenk on Cristes passioun![8]
I crouche[9] thee from elves and fro wightes."°   *wicked creatures*
Therwith the nightspel saide he anoonrightes[1]
On foure halves° of the hous aboute,   *sides*
And on the thresshfold° on the dore withoute: *threshold*
375   "Jesu Crist and Sainte Benedight,°   *Benedict*
Blesse this hous from every wikked wight!
For nightes nerye the White Pater Noster.[2]
Where wentestou,° thou Sainte Petres soster?°   *did you go / sister*
And at the laste this hende Nicholas
380   Gan for to sike° sore, and saide, "Allas,   *sigh*
Shal al the world be lost eftsoones° now?"   *again*
    This carpenter answerde, "What saistou?
What, thenk on God as we doon, men that swinke."°   *work*
    This Nicholas answerde, "Fecche me drinke,
385   And after wol I speke in privetee
Of certain thing that toucheth me and thee.
I wol telle it noon other man, certain."
    This carpenter gooth down and comth again,
And broughte of mighty° ale a large quart,   *strong*
390   And when that eech of hem hadde dronke his part,
This Nicholas his dore faste shette,°   *shut*
And down the carpenter by him he sette,

---

3. Pit from which a fertilizing clay is dug.
4. I sorely pity.
5. Scolded for.
6. I.e., shall come.
7. Took his stand.
8. I.e., the Crucifixion.
9. Make the sign of the cross on.
1. The night-charm he said right away (to ward off evil spirits).

2. Pater Noster is Latin for "Our Father," the beginning of the Lord's Prayer. The line is obscure, but a conjectural reading would be, "May the White 'Our Father' (or 'Our White Father') [either a prayer or the personification of a protecting power] defend [*nerye*] (us) against nights." The "nightspel" is a jumble of Christian references and pagan superstition.

And saide, "John, myn hoste lief° and dere,   *beloved*
Thou shalt upon thy trouthe° swere me here   *word of honor*
395   That to no wight thou shalt this conseil° wraye;°   *secret / disclose*
For it is Cristes conseil that I saye,
And if thou telle it man,[3] thou art forlore,°   *lost*
For this vengeance thou shalt have therfore,
That if thou wraye me, thou shalt be wood."[4]
400   "Nay, Crist forbede it, for his holy blood,"
Quod tho this sely° man. "I nam no labbe,°   *innocent / tell-tale*
And though I saye, I nam nat lief to gabbe.[5]
Say what thou wilt, I shal it nevere telle
To child ne wif, by him that harwed helle."[6]
405   "Now John," quod Nicholas, "I wol nought lie.
I have yfounde in myn astrologye,
As I have looked in the moone bright,
That now a Monday next, at quarter night,[7]
Shal falle a rain, and that so wilde and wood,°   *furious*
410   That half so greet was nevere Noees° flood.   *Noah's*
This world," he saide, "in lasse° than an hour   *less*
Shal al be dreint,° so hidous is the showr.   *drowned*
Thus shal mankinde drenche° and lese° hir lif."   *drown / lose*
    This carpenter answerde, "Allas, my wif!
415   And shal she drenche? Allas, myn Alisoun!"
For sorwe of this he fil almost[8] adown,
And saide, "Is there no remedye in this cas?"
    "Why yis, for[9] Gode," quod hende Nicholas,
"If thou wolt werken after lore and reed[1]—
420   Thou maist nought werken after thyn owene heed;°   *head*
For thus saith Salomon that was ful trewe,
'Werk al by conseil and thou shalt nought rewe.'°   *be sorry*
And if thou werken wolt by good conseil,
I undertake, withouten mast or sail,
425   Yit shal I save hire and thee and me.
Hastou nat herd how saved was Noee
Whan that oure Lord hadde warned him biforn
That al the world with water sholde be lorn?"°   *lost*
    "Yis," quod this carpenter, "ful yore° ago."   *long*
430   "Hastou nat herd," quod Nicholas, "also
The sorwe of Noee with his felaweshipe?
Er° that he mighte gete his wif to shipe,   *before*
Him hadde levere,[2] I dar wel undertake,
At thilke time than alle his wetheres[3] blake
435   That she hadde had a ship hirself allone.[4]
And therfore woostou,° what is best to doone?   *do you know*
This axeth° haste, and of an hastif° thing   *requires / urgent*
Men may nought preche or maken tarying.
Anoon go gete us faste into this in°   *lodging*

---

3. To anyone.   1. Act according to learning and advice.
4. Go mad.   2. He had rather.
5. And though I say it myself, I don't like to gossip.   3. Rams. I.e., he'd have given all the black rams
6. By Him that despoiled hell—i.e., Christ.   he had.
7. I.e., shortly before dawn.   4. The reluctance of Noah's wife to board the ark
8. Almost fell.   is a traditional comic theme in the mystery plays.
9. I.e., by.

440 A kneeding trough or elles a kimelin°   *brewing tub*
    For eech of us, but looke that they be large,°   *wide*
    In whiche we mowen swimme as in a barge,[5]
    And han therinne vitaile suffisaunt[6]
    But for a day—fy° on the remenaunt!   *fie*
445 The water shal aslake° and goon away   *diminish*
    Aboute prime[7] upon the nexte day.
    But Robin may nat wite° of this, thy knave,   *know*
    Ne eek thy maide Gille I may nat save.
    Axe nought why, for though thou axe me,
450 I wol nought tellen Goddes privetee.°   *secrets*
    Suffiseth thee, but if thy wittes madde,°   *go mad*
    To han° as greet a grace as Noee hadde.   *have*
    Thy wif shal I wel saven, out of doute.
    Go now thy way, and speed thee heraboute.
455 But whan thou hast for hire° and thee and me   *her*
    Ygeten us thise kneeding-tubbes three,
    Thanne shaltou hangen hem in the roof ful hye,
    That no man of oure purveyance° espye.   *preparations*
    And whan thou thus hast doon as I have said,
460 And hast oure vitaile faire in hem ylaid,
    And eek an ax to smite the corde atwo,
    Whan that the water comth that we may go,
    And broke an hole an heigh[8] upon the gable
    Unto the gardinward,[9] over the stable,
465 That we may freely passen forth oure way,
    Whan that the grete showr is goon away,
    Thanne shaltou swimme as merye, I undertake,
    As dooth the white doke° after hir drake.   *duck*
    Thanne wol I clepe,° 'How, Alison? How, John?   *call*
470 Be merye, for the flood wol passe anoon.'
    And thou wolt sayn, 'Hail, maister Nicholay!
    Good morwe, I see thee wel, for it is day!'
    And thanne shal we be lordes al oure lif
    Of al the world, as Noee and his wif.
475 But of oo thing I warne thee ful right:
    Be wel avised° on that ilke night   *warned*
    That we been entred into shippes boord
    That noon of us ne speke nought a word,
    Ne clepe, ne crye, but been in his prayere,
480 For it is Goddes owene heeste dere[1]
    Thy wif and thou mote hange fer atwinne,[2]
    For that bitwixe you shal be no sinne—
    Namore in looking than ther shal in deede.
    This ordinance is said: go, God thee speede.
485 Tomorwe at night whan men been alle asleepe,
    Into oure kneeding-tubbes wol we creepe,
    And sitten there, abiding Goddes grace.
    Go now thy way, I have no lenger space°   *time*

5. In which we can float as in a vessel.   9. Toward the garden.
6. Sufficient food.   1. Precious commandment.
7. 9 A.M.   2. Far apart.
8. On high.

To make of this no lenger sermoning.
490 Men sayn thus: 'Send the wise and say no thing.'
Thou art so wis it needeth thee nat teche:
Go save oure lif, and that I thee biseeche."
   This sely carpenter gooth forth his way:
Ful ofte he saide allas and wailaway,
495 And to his wif he tolde his privetee,
And she was war,° and knew it bet° than he,   *aware / better*
What al this quainte cast was for to saye.³
But nathelees she ferde° as she wolde deye,   *acted*
And saide, "Allas, go forth thy way anoon.
500 Help us to scape,° or we been dede eechoon.   *escape*
I am thy trewe verray wedded wif:
Go, dere spouse, and help to save oure lif."
   Lo, which a greet thing is affeccioun!°   *emotion*
Men may dien of imaginacioun,
505 So deepe° may impression be take.   *deeply*
This sely carpenter biginneth quake;
Him thinketh verrailiche° that he may see   *truly*
Noees flood come walwing° as the see   *rolling*
To drenchen° Alison, his hony dere.   *drown*
510 He weepeth, waileth, maketh sory cheere;
He siketh° with ful many a sory swough,°   *sighs / groan*
And gooth and geteth him a kneeding-trough,
And after a tubbe and a kimelin,
And prively he sente hem to his in,°   *dwelling*
515 And heeng° hem in the roof in privetee;   *hung*
His° owene hand he made laddres three,   *with his*
To climben by the ronges° and the stalkes°   *rungs / uprights*
Unto the tubbes hanging in the balkes,°   *rafters*
And hem vitailed,° bothe trough and tubbe,   *victualed*
520 With breed and cheese and good ale in a jubbe,°   *jug*
Suffising right ynough as for a day.
But er° that he hadde maad al this array,   *before*
He sente his knave, and eek his wenche also,
Upon his neede⁴ to London for to go.
525 And on the Monday whan it drow to⁵ nighte,
He shette° his dore withouten candel-lighte,   *shut*
And dressed° alle thing as it sholde be,   *arranged*
And shortly up they clomben° alle three.   *climbed*
They seten° stille wel a furlong way⁶   *sat*
530   "Now, Pater Noster, clum,"⁷ saide Nicholay,
And "Clum" quod John, and "Clum" saide Alisoun.
This carpenter saide his devocioun,
And stille he sit° and biddeth° his prayere,   *sits / prays*
Awaiting on the rain, if he it heere.°   *might hear*
535   The dede sleep, for wery bisinesse,
Fil° on this carpenter right as I gesse   *fell*
Aboute corfew time,⁸ or litel more.

---

3. What all this clever plan meant.
4. On an errand for him.
5. Drew toward.
6. The time it takes to go a furlong (i.e., a few minutes).
7. Hush (?). "Pater Noster": Our Father.
8. Probably about 8 P.M.

For travailing of his gost[9] he groneth sore,
And eft° he routeth,° for his heed mislay.[1]   *then / snores*
540   Down of the laddre stalketh Nicholay,
And Alison ful softe adown she spedde:
Withouten wordes mo they goon to bedde
Ther as the carpenter is wont to lie.
Ther was the revel and the melodye,
545   And thus lith° Alison and Nicholas   *lies*
In bisinesse of mirthe and of solas,°   *pleasure*
Til that the belle of Laudes[2] gan to ringe,
And freres° in the chauncel° gonne singe.   *friars / chancel*
    This parissh clerk, this amorous Absolon,
550   That is for love alway so wo-bigoon,
Upon the Monday was at Oseneye,
With compaignye him to disporte and playe,
And axed upon caas a cloisterer[3]
Ful prively after John the carpenter;
555   And he drow him apart out of the chirche,
And saide, "I noot:[4] I sawgh him here nought wirche°   *work*
Sith Saterday. I trowe that he be went
For timber ther oure abbot hath him sent.
For he is wont for timber for to go,
560   And dwellen atte grange[5] a day or two.
Or elles he is at his hous, certain.
Where that he be I can nought soothly sayn."
    This Absolon ful jolif was and light,[6]
And thoughte, "Now is time to wake al night,
565   For sikerly,° I sawgh him nought stiringe   *certainly*
Aboute his dore sin day bigan to springe.
So mote° I thrive, I shal at cokkes crowe   *may*
Ful prively knokken at his windowe
That stant° ful lowe upon his bowres° wal.   *stands / bedroom's*
570   To Alison now wol I tellen al
My love-longing,° for yet I shal nat misse   *lovesickness*
That at the leeste way[7] I shal hire kisse.
Som manere confort shal I have, parfay.°   *in faith*
My mouth hath icched al this longe day:
575   That is a signe of kissing at the leeste.
Al night me mette[8] eek I was at a feeste.
Therfore I wol go sleepe an hour or twaye,
And al the night thanne wol I wake and playe."
    Whan that the firste cok hath crowe, anoon
580   Up rist° this joly lovere Absolon,   *rises*
And him arrayeth gay at point devis.[9]
But first he cheweth grain[1] and licoris,
To smellen sweete, er he hadde kembd° his heer.   *combed*
Under his tonge a trewe-love[2] he beer,°   *bore*

---

9. Affliction of his spirit.
1. Lay in the wrong position.
2. The first church service of the day, before daybreak.
3. Here a member of the religious order of Osney Abbey. "Upon caas": by chance.
4. Don't know.

5. The outlying farm belonging to the abbey.
6. Was very amorous and cheerful.
7. I.e., at least.
8. I dreamed.
9. To perfection.
1. Grain of paradise; a spice.
2. Sprig of a cloverlike plant.

585 For therby wende° he to be gracious.°   *supposed / pleasing*
He rometh° to the carpenteres hous,   *strolls*
And stille he stant° under the shot-windowe—   *stands*
Unto his brest it raughte,° it was so lowe—   *reached*
And ofte he cougheth with a semisoun.°   *small sound*
590 "What do ye, hony-comb, sweete Alisoun,
My faire brid,[3] my sweete cinamome?°   *cinnamon*
Awaketh, lemman° myn, and speketh to me.   *sweetheart*
Wel litel thinken ye upon my wo
That for your love I swete° ther I go.   *sweat*
595 No wonder is though that I swelte° and swete: *melt*
I moorne as doth a lamb after the tete.°   *teat*
Ywis, lemman, I have swich love-longinge,
That lik a turtle° trewe is my moorninge: *dove*
I may nat ete namore than a maide."
600   "Go fro the windowe, Jakke fool," she saide.
"As help me God, it wol nat be com-pa-me.°   *come-kiss-me*
I love another, and elles I were to blame,
Wel bet° than thee, by Jesu, Absolon.   *better*
Go forth thy way or I wol caste a stoon,
605 And lat me sleepe, a twenty devele way."[4]
    "Allas," quod Absolon, "and wailaway,
That trewe love was evere so yvele biset.[5]
Thanne kis me, sin that it may be no bet,
For Jesus love and for the love of me."
610   "Woltou thanne go thy way therwith?" quod she.
"Ye, certes, lemman," quod this Absolon.
"Thanne maak thee redy," quod she. "I come anoon."
And unto Nicholas she saide stille,°   *quietly*
"Now hust,° and thou shalt laughen al thy fille."   *hush*
615   This Absolon down sette him on his knees,
And said, "I am a lord at alle degrees,[6]
For after this I hope ther cometh more.
Lemman, thy grace, and sweete brid, thyn ore!"°   *mercy*
    The windowe she undooth, and that in haste.
620 "Have do," quod she, "come of and speed thee faste,
Lest that oure neighebores thee espye."
    This Absolon gan wipe his mouth ful drye:
Derk was the night as pich or as the cole,
And at the windowe out she putte hir hole,
625 And Absolon, him fil no bet ne wers,[7]
But with his mouth he kiste hir naked ers,
Ful savourly,° er he were war of this.   *with relish*
Abak he sterte,° and thoughte it was amis,   *started*
For wel he wiste a womman hath no beerd.°   *beard*
630 He felte a thing al rough and longe yherd,°   *haired*
And saide, "Fy, allas, what have I do?"
    "Teehee," quod she, and clapte the windowe to.
And Absolon gooth forth a sory pas.[8]

---

3. Bird or bride.   6. In every way.
4. In the name of twenty devils.   7. It befell him neither better nor worse.
5. Ill-used.   8. I.e., walking sadly.

"A beerd, a beerd!"[9] quod hende Nicholas,
635 "By Goddes corpus,° this gooth faire and weel."   body
This sely Absolon herde everydeel,°   every bit
And on his lippe he gan for anger bite,
And to himself he saide, "I shal thee quite."°   repay
Who rubbeth now, who froteth° now his lippes   wipes
640 With dust, with sond,° with straw, with cloth, with chippes,   sand
But Absolon, that saith ful ofte allas?
"My soule bitake° I unto Satanas,°   commit / Satan
But me were levere[1] than all this town," quod he,
"Of this despit° awroken° for to be.   insult / avenged
645 Allas," quod he, "allas I ne hadde ybleint!"°   turned aside
His hote love was cold and al yqueint,°   quenched
For fro that time that he hadde kist hir ers
Of paramours he sette nought a kers,[2]
For he was heled° of his maladye.   cured
650 Ful ofte paramours he gan defye,°   renounce
And weep° as dooth a child that is ybete.   wept
A softe paas[3] he wente over the streete
Until° a smith men clepen daun Gervais,[4]   to
That in his forge smithed plough harneis:°   equipment
655 He sharpeth shaar and cultour[5] bisily.
This Absolon knokketh al esily,°   quietly
And saide, "Undo, Gervais, and that anoon."°   at once
"What, who artou?" "It am I, Absolon."
"What, Absolon? What, Cristes sweete tree!°   cross
660 Why rise ye so rathe?° Ey, benedicite,°   early / bless me
What aileth you? Som gay girl, God it woot,
Hath brought you thus upon the viritoot.[6]
By Sainte Note, ye woot wel what I mene."
This Absolon ne roughte nat a bene[7]
665 Of al his play. No word again he yaf:
He hadde more tow on his distaf[8]
Than Gervais knew, and saide, "Freend so dere,
This hote cultour in the chimenee° here,   fireplace
As lene[9] it me: I have therwith to doone.
670 I wol bringe it thee again ful soone."
Gervais answerde, "Certes, were it gold,
Or in a poke nobles alle untold,[1]
Thou sholdest have, as I am trewe smith.
Ey, Cristes fo,[2] what wol ye do therwith?"
675 "Therof," quod Absolon, "be as be may.
I shal wel telle it thee another day."
And caughte the cultour by the colde stele.°   handle
Ful softe out at the dore he gan to stele,
And wente unto the carpenteres wal:
680 He cougheth first and knokketh therwithal

9. A trick (slang), but with a play on line 629.
1. I had rather.
2. He didn't care a piece of cress for woman's love.
3. I.e., quiet walk.
4. Master Gervais.
5. He sharpens plowshare and coulter (the turf cutter on a plow).
6. I.e., on the prowl.
7. Didn't care a bean.
8. I.e., more on his mind.
9. I.e., please lend.
1. Or gold coins all uncounted in a bag.
2. Foe, i.e., Satan.

Upon the windowe, right as he dide er.°   *before*
  This Alison answerde, "Who is ther
That knokketh so? I warante[3] it a thief."
  "Why, nay," quod he, "God woot, my sweete lief,°   *dear*
685 I am thyn Absolon, my dereling.°   *darling*
Of gold," quod he, "I have thee brought a ring—
My moder yaf it me, so God me save;
Ful fin it is and therto wel ygrave:°   *engraved*
This wol I yiven thee if thou me kisse."
690   This Nicholas was risen for to pisse,
And thoughte he wolde amenden[4] al the jape:°   *joke*
He sholde kisse his ers er that he scape.
And up the windowe dide he hastily,
And out his ers he putteth prively,
695 Over the buttok to the haunche-boon.
  And therwith spak this clerk, this Absolon,
"Speek, sweete brid, I noot nought wher thou art."
This Nicholas anoon leet flee[5] a fart
As greet as it hadde been a thonder-dent°   *thunderbolt*
700 That with the strook he was almost yblent,°   *blinded*
And he was redy with his iren hoot,°   *hot*
And Nicholas amidde the ers he smoot:°   *smote*
Of° gooth the skin an hande-brede° aboute;   *off / handsbreadth*
The hote cultour brende so his toute°   *buttocks*
705 That for the smert° he wende for to[6] die;   *pain*
As he were wood° for wo he gan to crye,   *crazy*
"Help! Water! Water! Help, for Goddes herte!"
  This carpenter out of his slomber sterte,
And herde oon cryen "Water!" as he were wood,
710 And thoughte, "Allas, now cometh Noweles[7] flood!"
He sette him up[8] withoute wordes mo,
And with his ax he smoot the corde atwo,
And down gooth al: he foond neither to selle
Ne breed ne ale til he cam to the celle,[9]
715 Upon the floor, and ther aswoune° he lay.   *in a faint*
  Up sterte hire[1] Alison and Nicholay,
And criden "Out" and "Harrow" in the streete.
The neighebores, bothe smale and grete,
In ronnen for to gauren° on this man   *gape*
720 That aswoune lay bothe pale and wan,
For with the fal he brosten° hadde his arm;   *broken*
But stonde he moste° unto his owene harm,   *must*
For whan he spak he was anoon bore down[2]
With° hende Nicholas and Alisoun: *by*
725 They tolden every man that he was wood—
He was agast so of Noweles flood,
Thurgh fantasye, that of his vanitee°   *folly*

---

3. I.e., wager.
4. Improve on.
5. Let fly.
6. Thought he would.
7. The carpenter is confusing Noah and Noel (Christmas).

8. Got up.
9. He found time to sell neither bread nor ale until he arrived at the foundation, i.e., he did not take time out.
1. Started.
2. Refuted.

He hadde ybought him kneeding-tubbes three,
And hadde hem hanged in the roof above,
730 And that he prayed hem, for Goddes love,
To sitten in the roof, *par compaignye*.³
    The folk gan laughen at his fantasye.
Into the roof they kiken° and they cape,°   *peer / gape*
And turned al his harm unto a jape,°   *joke*
735 For what so that this carpenter answerde,
It was for nought: no man his reson° herde;   *argument*
With othes grete he was so sworn adown,
That he was holden° wood in al the town,   *considered*
For every clerk anoonright heeld with other:
740 They saide, "The man was wood, my leve brother,"
And every wight gan laughen at this strif.°   *fuss*
Thus swived⁴ was the carpenteres wif
For al his keeping° and his jalousye,   *guarding*
And Absolon hath kist hir nether° yë,   *lower*
745 And Nicholas is scalded in the toute:
This tale is doon, and God save al the route!°   *company*

The Wife of Bath's Prologue and Tale

In creating the Wife of Bath, Chaucer drew upon a centuries-old tradition of misogynist writing that was particularly nurtured by the medieval church. In their conviction that the rational, intellectual, spiritual, and, therefore, higher side of human nature predominated in men, whereas the irrational, material, earthly, and,

The Wife of Bath. Illumination from the Ellesmere Manuscript of *The Canterbury Tales*, ca. 1400–1405. Note the whip and the spurs.

therefore, lower side of human nature predominated in women, St. Paul and the early Church fathers exalted celibacy and virginity above marriage, although they were also obliged to concede the necessity and sanctity of matrimony. In the fourth century, a monk called Jovinian wrote a tract in which he apparently presented marriage as a positive good rather than as a necessary evil. That tract is known only through St. Jerome's extreme attack upon it. Jerome's diatribe and other antifeminist and antimatrimonial literature provided Chaucer with a rich body of bookish male "auctoritee" (authority) against which the Wife of Bath asserts her female "experience" and defends her rights and justifies her life as a five-time married woman. In her polemical wars with medieval clerks and her matrimonial wars with her five husbands, the last of whom was once a clerk of Oxenford, the Wife of Bath seems ironically to confirm the accusations of the clerks, but at the same time she succeeds in satirizing the shallowness of the stereotypes of women and marriage in antifeminist writings and in demonstrating how much the largeness and complexity of her own character rise above that stereotype.

---

3. For company's sake.

4. The vulgar verb for having sexual intercourse.

The Prologue

Experience, though noon auctoritee
Were in this world, is right ynough for me
To speke of wo that is in mariage:
For lordinges,° sith I twelf yeer was of age—   *gentlemen*
5   Thanked be God that is eterne on live—
Housbondes at chirche dore[1] I have had five
(If I so ofte mighte han wedded be),
And alle were worthy men in hir degree.
But me was told, certain, nat longe agoon is,
10 That sith that Crist ne wente nevere but ones°   *once*
To wedding in the Cane[2] of Galilee,
That by the same ensample° taughte he me   *example*
That I ne sholde wedded be but ones.
Herke eek,° lo, which° a sharp word for the nones,[3]   *also / what*
15 Biside a welle, Jesus, God and man,
Spak in repreve° of the Samaritan: *reproof*
"Thou hast yhad five housbondes," quod he,
"And that ilke° man that now hath thee   *same*
Is nat thyn housbonde." Thus saide he certain.
20 What that he mente therby I can nat sayn,
But that I axe° why the fifthe man   *ask*
Was noon housbonde to the Samaritan?[4]
How manye mighte she han in mariage?
Yit herde I nevere tellen in myn age
25 Upon this nombre diffinicioun.°   *definition*
Men may divine° and glosen° up and down,   *guess / interpret*
But wel I woot,° expres,° withouten lie,   *know / expressly*
God bad us for to wexe[5] and multiplye:
That gentil text can I wel understonde.
30 Eek wel I woot° he saide that myn housbonde   *know*
Sholde lete° fader and moder and take to me,[6]   *leave*
But of no nombre mencion made he—
Of bigamye or of octogamye?[7]
Why sholde men thanne speke of it vilainye?
35 Lo, here the wise king daun° Salomon: *master*
I trowe° he hadde wives many oon,[8]   *believe*
As wolde God it leveful° were to me   *permissible*
To be refresshed half so ofte as he.
Which yifte[9] of God hadde he for alle his wives!
40 No man hath swich° that in this world alive is.   *such*
God woot this noble king, as to my wit,°   *knowledge*
The firste night hadde many a merye fit°   *bout*
With eech of hem, so wel was him on live.[1]
Blessed be God that I have wedded five,

---

1. The actual wedding ceremony was celebrated at the church door, not in the chancel.
2. Cana (see John 2.1).
3. To the purpose.
4. Christ was actually referring to a sixth man who was not married to the Samaritan woman (cf. John 4.6ff.).
5. I.e., increase (see Genesis 1.28).
6. See Matthew 19.5.
7. I.e., of two or even eight marriages. The Wife of Bath is referring to successive, rather than simultaneous, marriages.
8. Solomon had seven hundred wives and three hundred concubines (1 Kings 11.3).
9. What a gift.
1. I.e., so pleasant a life he had.

45   Of whiche I have piked out the beste,[2]
    Bothe of hir nether purs[3] and of hir cheste.°   *money box*
    Diverse scoles maken parfit° clerkes,   *perfect*
    And diverse practikes[4] in sondry werkes
    Maken the werkman parfit sikerly:°   *certainly*
50   Of five housbondes scoleying° am I.   *schooling*
    Welcome the sixte whan that evere he shal![5]
    For sith I wol nat kepe me chast° in al,   *celibate*
    Whan my housbonde is fro the world agoon,
    Som Cristen man shal wedde me anoon.°   *right away*
55   For thanne th'Apostle[6] saith that I am free
    To wedde, a Goddes half, where it liketh me.[7]
    He saide that to be wedded is no sinne:
    Bet is to be wedded than to brinne.[8]
    What rekketh me[9] though folk saye vilainye
60   Of shrewed° Lamech[1] and his bigamye?   *cursed*
    I woot wel Abraham was an holy man,
    And Jacob eek, as fer as evere I can,°   *know*
    And eech of hem hadde wives mo than two,
    And many another holy man also.
65   Where can ye saye in any manere age
    That hye God defended° mariage   *prohibited*
    By expres word? I praye you, telleth me.
    Or where comanded he virginitee?
    I woot as wel as ye, it is no drede,°   *doubt*
70   Th'Apostle, whan he speketh of maidenhede,°   *virginity*
    He saide that precept therof hadde he noon:
    Men may conseile a womman to be oon,°   *single*
    But conseiling nis° no comandement.   *is not*
    He putte it in oure owene juggement.
75   For hadde God comanded maidenhede,
    Thanne hadde he dampned° wedding with the deede;[2]   *condemned*
    And certes, if there were no seed ysowe,
    Virginitee, thanne wherof sholde it growe?
    Paul dorste nat comanden at the leeste
80   A thing of which his maister yaf° no heeste.°   *gave / command*
    The dart[3] is set up for virginitee:
    Cacche whoso may, who renneth° best lat see.   *runs*
    But this word is nought take of[4] every wight,°   *person*
    But ther as[5] God list° yive it of his might.   *it pleases*
85   I woot wel that th'Apostle was a maide,°   *virgin*
    But nathelees, though that he wroot and saide
    He wolde that every wight were swich° as he,   *such*
    Al nis but conseil to virginitee;
    And for to been a wif he yaf me leve

---

2. Whom I have cleaned out of everything worth while.
3. Lower purse, i.e., testicles.
4. Practical experiences.
5. I.e., shall come along.
6. St. Paul.
7. I please. "A Goddes half": on God's behalf.
8. "It is better to marry than to burn" (1 Corinthians 7.9). Many of the Wife's citations of St. Paul are from this chapter, often secondhand from St.

Jerome's tract *Against Jovinian*.
9. What do I care.
1. The first man whom the Bible mentions as having two wives (Genesis 4.19–24); he is cursed, however, not for his marriages but for murder.
2. I.e., at the same time.
3. I.e., prize in a race.
4. Understood for, i.e., applicable to.
5. Where.

90　Of indulgence; so nis it no repreve°　　　　　　　　　　*disgrace*
　　To wedde me[6] if that my make° die,　　　　　　　　　*mate*
　　Withouten excepcion of bigamy[7]—
　　Al° were it good no womman for to touche[8]　　　　*although*
　　(He mente as in his bed or in his couche,
95　For peril is bothe fir° and tow° t'assemble—　　　　　*fire / flax*
　　Ye knowe what this ensample may resemble).[9]
　　This al and som,[1] he heeld virginitee
　　More parfit than wedding in freletee.°　　　　　　　　　*frailty*
　　(Freletee clepe I but if[2] that he and she
100　Wolde leden al hir lif in chastitee.)
　　I graunte it wel, I have noon envye
　　Though maidenhede preferre° bigamye:°　　　*excel / remarriage*
　　It liketh hem to be clene in body and gost.°　　　　　　*spirit*
　　Of myn estaat ne wol I make no boost;
105　For wel ye knowe, a lord in his houshold
　　Ne hath nat every vessel al of gold:
　　Some been of tree,° and doon hir lord servise.　　　　*wood*
　　God clepeth° folk to him in sondry wise,　　　　　　　*calls*
　　And everich hath of God a propre yifte,[3]
110　Som this, som that, as him liketh shifte.°　　　　　　*ordain*
　　Virginitee is greet perfeccioun,
　　And continence eek with devocioun,
　　But Crist, that of perfeccion is welle,°　　　　　　　　*source*
　　Bad nat every wight he sholde go selle
115　Al that he hadde and yive it to the poore,
　　And in swich wise folwe him and his fore:°[4]　　　*footsteps*
　　He spak to hem that wolde live parfitly°—　　　　　*perfectly*
　　And lordinges, by youre leve, that am nat I.
　　I wol bistowe the flour of al myn age
120　In th'actes and in fruit of mariage.
　　　　Telle me also, to what conclusioun°　　　　　　　　*end*
　　Were membres maad of generacioun
　　And of so parfit wis a wrighte ywrought?[5]
　　　　Trusteth right wel, they were nat maad for nought.
125　Glose° whoso wol, and saye bothe up and down　　*interpret*
　　That they were maked for purgacioun
　　Of urine, and oure bothe thinges smale
　　Was eek° to knowe a femele from a male,　　　　　　　*also*
　　And for noon other cause—saye ye no?
130　Th'experience woot it is nought so.
　　So that the clerkes be nat with me wrothe,
　　I saye this, that they been maad for bothe—
　　That is to sayn, for office° and for ese°　　　　*use / pleasure*
　　Of engendrure,° ther we nat God displese.　　　*procreation*
135　Why sholde men elles in hir bookes sette
　　That man shal yeelde[6] to his wif hir dette?°　　*(marital) debt*

---

6. For me to marry.
7. I.e., without there being any legal objection on the score of remarriage.
8. "It is good for a man not to touch a woman" (1 Corinthians 7.1).
9. I.e., what this metaphor may apply to.

1. This is all there is to it.
2. Frailty I call it unless.
3. See 1 Corinthians 7.7.
4. Matthew 19.21
5. And wrought by so perfectly wise a maker.
6. I.e., pay. See 1 Corinthians 7.4–5.

Now wherwith sholde he make his payement
If he ne used his sely° instrument?   innocent
Thanne were they maad upon a creature
140   To purge urine, and eek for engendrure.
But I saye nought that every wight is holde,°   bound
That hath swich harneis° as I to you tolde,   equipment
To goon and usen hem in engendrure:
Thanne sholde men take of chastitee no cure.°   heed
145   Crist was a maide° and shapen as a man,   virgin
And many a saint sith that the world bigan,
Yit lived they evere in parfit chastitee.
I nil° envye no virginitee: will not
Lat hem be breed° of pured° whete seed,   bread / refined
150   And lat us wives hote° barly breed—   be called
And yit with barly breed, Mark telle can,
Oure Lord Jesu refresshed many a man.[7]
In swich estaat as God hath cleped us
I wol persevere: I nam nat precious.°   fastidious
155   In wifhood wol I use myn instrument
As freely° as my Makere hath it sent.   generously
If I be daungerous,[8] God yive me sorwe:
Myn housbonde shal it han both eve and morwe,°   morning
      Whan that him list[9] come forth and paye his dette.
160   An housbonde wol I have, I wol nat lette,[1]
Which shal be bothe my dettour° and my thral,°   debtor / slave
And have his tribulacion withal°   as well
Upon his flessh whil that I am his wif.
I have the power during al my lif
165   Upon his propre° body, and nat he: own
Right thus th'Apostle tolde it unto me,
And bad oure housbondes for to love us weel.
Al this sentence° me liketh everydeel.°   sense / entirely

[AN INTERLUDE]

Up sterte° the Pardoner and that anoon:°   started / at once
170   "Now dame," quod he, "by God and by Saint John,
Ye been a noble prechour in this cas.
I was aboute to wedde a wif: allas,
What° sholde I bye° it on my flessh so dere?   why / purchase
Yit hadde I levere° wedde no wif toyere."°   rather / this year
175   "Abid," quod she, "my tale is nat bigonne.
Nay, thou shalt drinken of another tonne,°   tun, barrel
Er° that I go, shal savoure wors than ale.   before
And whan that I have told thee forth my tale
Of tribulacion in mariage,
180   Of which I am expert in al myn age—
This is to saye, myself hath been the whippe—

7. In the descriptions of the miracle of the
loaves and fishes, it is actually John, not Mark,
who mentions barley bread (6.9).
8. In romance *dangerous* is a term for disdain-
fulness with which a woman rejects a lover. The

Wife means she will not withhold sexual favors,
in emulation of God's generosity (line 156).
9. When he wishes to.
1. I will not leave off, desist.

Thanne maistou chese° wheither thou wolt sippe   *choose*
Of thilke° tonne that I shal abroche;°   *this same / open*
Be war of it, er thou too neigh approche,
185 For I shal telle ensamples mo than ten.
'Whoso that nil° be war by othere men,   *will not*
By him shal othere men corrected be.'
Thise same wordes writeth Ptolomee:
Rede in his *Almageste* and take it there."[2]
190 "Dame, I wolde praye you if youre wil it were,"
Saide this Pardoner, "as ye bigan,
Telle forth youre tale; spareth for no man,
And teche us yonge men of youre practike."°   *mode of operation*
"Gladly," quod she, "sith it may you like;°   *please*
195 But that I praye to al this compaignye,
If that I speke after my fantasye,[3]
As taketh nat agrief° of that I saye,   *amiss*
For myn entente nis but for to playe."

[THE WIFE CONTINUES]

Now sire, thanne wol I telle you forth my tale.
200 As evere mote I drinke win or ale,
I shal saye sooth: tho° housbondes that I hadde,   *those*
As three of hem were goode, and two were badde.
The three men were goode, and riche, and olde;
Unnethe° mighte they the statut holde   *scarcely*
205 In which they were bounden unto me—
Ye woot wel what I mene of this, pardee.
As help me God, I laughe whan I thinke
How pitously anight I made hem swinke;°   *work*
And by my fay,° I tolde of it no stoor:[4]   *faith*
210 They hadde me yiven hir land and hir tresor;
Me needed nat do lenger diligence
To winne hir love or doon hem reverence.
They loved me so wel, by God above,
That I ne tolde no daintee of[5] hir love.
215 A wis womman wol bisye hire evere in oon[6]
To gete hire love, ye, ther as she hath noon.
But sith I hadde hem hoolly in myn hand,
And sith that they hadde yiven me al hir land,
What° sholde I take keep° hem for to plese,   *why / care*
220 But it were for my profit and myn ese?
I sette hem so awerke,° by my fay,   *awork*
That many a night they songen° wailaway.   *sang*
The bacon was nat fet° for hem, I trowe,   *brought back*
That some men han in Essexe at Dunmowe.[7]
225 I governed hem so wel after° my lawe   *according to*

---

2. "He who will not be warned by the example of others shall become an example to others." The *Almagest*, an astronomical work by the Greek astronomer and mathematician Ptolemy (2nd century C.E.), contains no such aphorism.
3. If I speak according to my fancy.
4. I set no store by it.

5. Set no value on.
6. Busy herself constantly.
7. At Dunmow, a side of bacon was awarded to the couple who after a year of marriage could claim no quarrels, no regrets, and the desire, if freed, to remarry one another.

That eech of hem ful blisful was and fawe° *glad*
To bringe me gaye thinges fro the faire;
They were ful glade whan I spak hem faire,
For God it woot, I chidde° hem spitously.° *chided / cruelly*
230 Now herkneth how I bar me° proprely: *bore myself, behaved*
Ye wise wives, that conne understonde,
Thus sholde ye speke and bere him wrong on honde[8]—
For half so boldely can ther no man
Sweren and lyen as a woman can.
235 I saye nat this by wives that been wise,
But if it be whan they hem misavise.[9]
A wis wif, if that she can hir good,[1]
Shal bere him on hande the cow is wood,[2]
And take witnesse of hir owene maide
240 Of hir assent.[3] But herkneth how I saide:
    "Sire olde cainard,° is this thyn array?[4] *sluggard*
Why is my neighebores wif so gay?
She is honoured overal° ther she gooth: *wherever*
I sitte at hoom; I have no thrifty° cloth. *decent*
245 What doostou at my neighebores hous?
Is she so fair? Artou so amorous?
What roune° ye with oure maide, benedicite.[5] *whisper*
Sire olde lechour, lat thy japes° be. *tricks, intrigues*
And if I have a gossib° or a freend *confidant*
250 Withouten gilt, ye chiden as a feend,
If that I walke or playe unto his hous.
Thou comest hoom as dronken as a mous,
And prechest on thy bench, with yvel preef.[6]
Thou saist to me, it is a greet mischief° *misfortune*
255 To wedde a poore womman for costage.[7]
And if that she be riche, of heigh parage,° *descent*
Thanne saistou that it is a tormentrye
To suffre hir pride and hir malencolye.° *bad humor*
And if that she be fair, thou verray knave,
260 Thou saist that every holour° wol hire have: *lecher*
She may no while in chastitee abide[8]
That is assailed upon eech a side.
    "Thou saist som folk desiren us for richesse,
Som[9] for oure shap, and som for oure fairnesse,
265 And som for she can outher° singe or daunce, *either*
And som for gentilesse and daliaunce,° *flirtatiousness*
Som for hir handes and hir armes smale°— *slender*
Thus gooth al to the devel by thy tale![1]
Thou saist men may nat keepe[2] a castel wal,
270 It may so longe assailed been overal.° *everywhere*

8. Accuse him falsely.
9. Unless it happens that they make a mistake.
1. If she knows what's good for her.
2. Shall persuade him the chough has gone crazy. The chough, a talking bird, was popularly supposed to tell husbands of their wives' infidelity.
3. And call as a witness her maid, who is on her side.
4. I.e., is this how you behave?

5. The Lord bless you.
6. I.e., (may you have) bad luck.
7. Because of the expense.
8. Remain faithful to her husband.
9. "Som," in this and the following lines, means "one."
1. I.e., according to your story.
2. I.e., keep safe.

And if that she be foul,° thou saist that she   *ugly*
Coveiteth° every man that she may see;   *desires*
For as a spaniel she wol on him lepe,
Til that she finde som man hire to chepe.°   *bargain for*
275 Ne noon so grey goos gooth ther in the lake,
As, saistou, wol be withoute make;°   *mate*
And saist it is an hard thing for to weelde°   *possess*
A thing that no man wol, his thankes, heelde³
Thus saistou, lorel,° whan thou goost to bedde,   *wretch*
280 And that no wis man needeth for to wedde,
Ne no man that entendeth° unto hevene—   *aims*
With wilde thonder-dint° and firy levene°   *thunderbolt / lightning*
Mote thy welked nekke be tobroke!⁴
Thou saist that dropping° houses and eek smoke   *leaking*
285 And chiding wives maken men to flee
Out of hir owene hous: a, benedicite,
What aileth swich an old man for to chide?
Thou saist we wives wil oure vices hide
Til we be fast,⁵ and thanne we wol hem shewe—
290 Wel may that be a proverbe of a shrewe!°   *rascal*
Thou saist that oxen, asses, hors,° and houndes,   *horses*
They been assayed° at diverse stoundes;°   *tried out / times*
Bacins, lavours,° er that men hem bye,°   *washbowls / buy*
Spoones, stooles, and al swich housbondrye,°   *household goods*
295 And so be° pottes, clothes, and array°—   *are / clothing*
But folk of wives maken noon assay
Til they be wedded—olde dotard shrewe!
And thanne, saistou, we wil oure vices shewe.
Thou saist also that it displeseth me
300 But if° that thou wolt praise my beautee,   *unless*
And but thou poure° alway upon my face,   *gaze*
And clepe me 'Faire Dame' in every place,
And but thou make a feeste on thilke day
That I was born, and make me fressh and gay,
305 And but thou do to my norice° honour,   *nurse*
And to my chamberere within my bowr,⁶
And to my fadres folk, and his allies⁷—
Thus saistou, olde barel-ful of lies.
And yit of our apprentice Janekin,
310 For his crispe° heer, shining as gold so fin,   *curly*
And for° he squiereth me bothe up and down,   *because*
Yit hastou caught a fals suspecioun;
I wil° him nat though thou were deed° tomorwe.   *want / dead*
    "But tel me this, why hidestou with sorwe⁸
315 The keyes of thy cheste° away fro me?   *money box*
It is my good° as wel as thyn, pardee.   *property*
What, weenestou° make an idiot of oure dame?⁹   *do you think to*
Now by that lord that called is Saint Jame,
Thou shalt nought bothe, though thou were wood,°   *furious*

---

3. No man would willingly hold.   7. Relatives by marriage.
4. May thy withered neck be broken!   8. I.e., with sorrow to you.
5. I.e., married.   9. I.e., me, the mistress of the house.
6. And to my chambermaid within my bedroom.

320   Be maister of my body and of my good:
       That oon thou shalt forgo, maugree thine yën.[1]
          "What helpeth it of me enquere° and spyen?   inquire
       I trowe thou woldest loke° me in thy cheste.   lock
       Thou sholdest saye, 'Wif, go wher thee leste.°   it may please
325   Taak youre disport[2]—I nil leve° no tales: believe
       I knowe you for a trewe wif, dame Alis.'
       We love no man that taketh keep or charge[3]
       Wher that we goon: we wol been at oure large.[4]
       Of alle men yblessed mote he be
330   The wise astrologen° daun Ptolomee,   astronomer
       That saith this proverbe in his *Almageste*:
       'Of alle men his wisdom is the hyeste
       That rekketh° nat who hath the world in honde.[5]   cares
       By this proverbe thou shalt understonde,
335   Have thou[6] ynough, what thar° thee rekke or care   need
       How merily that othere folkes fare?
       For certes, olde dotard, by youre leve,
       Ye shal han queinte[7] right ynough at eve:
       He is too greet a nigard that wil werne°   refuse
340   A man to lighte a candle at his lanterne;
       He shal han nevere the lasse° lighte, pardee.   less
       Have thou ynough, thee thar nat plaine thee.[8]
          "Thou saist also that if we make us gay
       With clothing and with precious array,
345   That it is peril of oure chastitee,
       And yit, with sorwe, thou moste enforce thee,[9]
       And saye thise wordes in th' Apostles[1] name:
       'In habit° maad with chastitee and shame   clothing
       Ye wommen shal apparaile you,' quod he,
350   'And nat in tressed heer[2] and gay perree,°   jewelry
       As perles, ne with gold ne clothes riche.'[3]
       After thy text, ne after thy rubriche,[4]
       I wol nat werke as muchel as a gnat.
       Thou saidest this, that I was lik a cat:
355   For whoso wolde senge° a cattes skin,   singe
       Thanne wolde the cat wel dwellen in his in;°   lodging
       And if the cattes skin be slik° and gay,   sleek
       She wol nat dwelle in house half a day,
       But forth she wol, er any day be dawed,[5]
360   To shewe her skin and goon a-caterwawed.°   caterwauling
       This is to saye, if I be gay, sire shrewe,
       I wol renne° out, my borel° for to shewe.   run / clothing
       Sir olde fool, what helpeth[6] thee t'espyen?
       Though thou praye Argus with his hundred yën[7]

1. Despite your eyes, i.e., despite anything you
can do about it.
2. Enjoy yourself.
3. Notice or interest.
4. I.e., liberty.
5. Who rules the world.
6. If you have.
7. Elegant, pleasing thing; a euphemism for sexual enjoyment.
8. I.e., you need not complain.

9. Strengthen your position.
1. I.e., St. Paul's.
2. I.e., elaborate hairdo.
3. See 1 Timothy 2.9.
4. Rubric, i.e., direction.
5. Has dawned.
6. What does it help.
7. Argus was a monster whom Juno set to watch over one of Jupiter's mistresses. Mercury put all one hundred of his eyes to sleep and slew him.

365 To be my wardecors,° as he can best,   *bodyguard*
In faith, he shal nat keepe° me but me lest:[8]   *guard*
Yit coude I make his beerd,[9] so mote I thee.°   *prosper*
    "Thou saidest eek that ther been thinges three,
The whiche thinges troublen al this erthe,
370 And that no wight may endure the ferthe.°   *fourth*
O leve° sire shrewe, Jesu shorte° thy lif!   *dear / shorten*
Yit prechestou and saist an hateful wif
Yrekened° is for oon of thise meschaunces.[1]   *is counted*
Been ther nat none othere resemblaunces
375 That ye may likne youre parables to,[2]
But if° a sely° wif be oon of tho?   *unless / innocent*
    "Thou liknest eek wommanes love to helle,
To bareine° land ther water may nat dwelle;   *barren*
Thou liknest it also to wilde fir—
380 The more it brenneth,° the more it hath desir   *burns*
To consumen every thing that brent° wol be;   *burned*
Thou saist right° as wormes shende° a tree,   *just / destroy*
Right so a wif destroyeth hir housbonde—
This knowen they that been to wives bonde."°   *bound*
385   Lordinges, right thus, as ye han understonde,
Bar I stifly mine olde housbondes on honde[3]
That thus they saiden in hir dronkenesse—
And al was fals, but that I took witnesse
On Janekin and on my nece also.
390 O Lord, the paine I dide hem and the wo,
Ful giltelees, by Goddes sweete pine!°   *suffering*
For as an hors I coude bite and whine;°   *whinny*
I coude plaine° and° I was in the gilt,   *complain / if*
Or elles often time I hadde been spilt.°   *ruined*
395 Whoso that first to mille comth first grint.°   *grinds*
I plained first: so was oure werre stint.[4]
They were ful glade to excusen hem ful blive°   *quickly*
Of thing of which they nevere agilte hir live.[5]
Of wenches wolde I beren hem on honde,[6]
400 Whan that for sik[7] they mighte unnethe° stonde,   *scarcely*
Yit tikled I his herte for that he
Wende° I hadde had of him so greet cheertee.°   *thought / affection*
I swoor that al my walking out by nighte
Was for to espye wenches that he dighte.[8]
405 Under that colour[9] hadde I many a mirthe.
For al swich wit is yiven us in oure birthe:
Deceite, weeping, spinning God hath yive
To wommen kindely° whil they may live.   *naturally*
And thus of oo thing I avaunte me:[1]
410 At ende I hadde the bet° in eech degree,   *better*
By sleighte or force, or by som manere thing,

8. Unless I please.
9. I.e., deceive him.
1. For the other three misfortunes see Proverbs 30.21–23.
2. Are there no other (appropriate) similitudes to which you might draw analogies?
3. I rigorously accused my old husbands.
4. Our war brought to an end.
5. Of which they were never guilty in their lives.
6. Falsely accuse them.
7. I.e., sickness.
8. Had intercourse with.
9. I.e., pretense.
1. Boast.

As by continuel murmur° or grucching;°   *complaint / grumbling*
Namely° abedde hadden they meschaunce: *especially*
Ther wolde I chide and do hem no plesaunce;[2]
415 I wolde no lenger in the bed abide
If that I felte his arm over my side,
Til he hadde maad his raunson° unto me;   *ransom*
Thanne wolde I suffre him do his nicetee.°   *foolishness (sex)*
And therfore every man this tale I telle:
420 Winne whoso may, for al is for to selle;
With empty hand men may no hawkes lure.
For winning° wolde I al his lust endure,   *profit*
And make me a feined° appetit—   *pretended*
And yit in bacon[3] hadde I nevere delit.
425 That made me that evere I wolde hem chide;
For though the Pope hadde seten° hem biside,   *sat*
I wolde nought spare hem at hir owene boord.°   *table*
For by my trouthe, I quitte° hem word for word.   *repaid*
As help me verray God omnipotent,
430 Though I right now sholde make my testament,
I ne owe hem nat a word that it nis quit.
I broughte it so aboute by my wit
That they moste yive it up as for the beste,
Or elles hadde we nevere been in reste;
435 For though he looked as a wood° leoun,   *furious*
Yit sholde he faile of his conclusioun.°   *object*
  Thanne wolde I saye, "Goodelief, taak keep,[4]
How mekely looketh Wilekin,[5] oure sheep!
Com neer my spouse, lat me ba° thy cheeke—   *kiss*
440 Ye sholden be al pacient and meeke,
And han a sweete-spiced° conscience,   *mild*
Sith ye so preche of Jobes pacience;
Suffreth alway, sin ye so wel can preche;
And but ye do, certain, we shal you teche
445 That it is fair to han a wif in pees.
Oon of us two moste bowen, doutelees,
And sith a man is more resonable
Than womman is, ye mosten been suffrable.°   *patient*
What aileth you to grucche° thus and grone?   *grumble*
450 Is it for ye wolde have my queinte° allone?   *sexual organ*
Why, taak it al—lo, have it everydeel.°   *all of it*
Peter,[6] I shrewe° you but ye° love it weel.   *curse / if you don't*
For if I wolde selle my bele chose,[7]
I coude walke as fressh as is a rose;
455 But I wol keepe it for youre owene tooth.°   *taste*
Ye be to blame. By God, I saye you sooth!"°   *the truth*
Swiche manere° wordes hadde we on honde.   *kind of*
Now wol I speke of my ferthe° housbonde.   *fourth*
  My ferthe housbonde was a revelour°   *reveler*
460 This is to sayn, he hadde a paramour°   *mistress*

---

2. Give them no pleasure.
3. I.e., old meat.
4. Good friend, take notice.
5. I.e., Willie.

6. By St. Peter.
7. French for "beautiful thing"; a euphemism for sexual organs.

And I was yong and ful of ragerye,°   *passion*
Stibourne° and strong and joly as a pie:°   *untamable / magpie*
How coude I daunce to an harpe smale,°   *gracefully*
And singe, ywis,° as any nightingale,   *indeed*
465   Whan I hadde dronke a draughte of sweete win.
Metellius, the foule cherl, the swin,
That with a staf birafte° his wif hir lif   *deprived*
For° she drank win, though I hadde been his wif,   *because*
Ne sholde nat han daunted° me fro drinke;   *frightened*
470   And after win on Venus moste° I thinke,   *must*
For also siker° as cold engendreth hail,   *sure*
A likerous° mouth moste han a likerous° tail: *greedy / lecherous*
In womman vinolent° is no defence—   *who drinks*
This knowen lechours by experience.
475   But Lord Crist, whan that it remembreth me[8]
Upon my youthe and on my jolitee,
It tikleth me aboute myn herte roote—
Unto this day it dooth myn herte boote°   *good*
That I have had my world as in my time.
480   But age, allas, that al wol envenime,°   *poison*
Hath me biraft[9] my beautee and my pith°—   *vigor*
Lat go, farewel, the devel go therwith!
The flour is goon, ther is namore to telle:
The bren° as I best can now moste I selle;   *bran*
485   But yit to be right merye wol I fonde.°   *strive*
Now wol I tellen of my ferthe housbonde.
    I saye I hadde in herte greet despit
That he of any other hadde delit,
But he was quit,° by God and by Saint Joce: *paid back*
490   I made him of the same wode a croce[1]—
Nat of my body in no foul manere—
But, certainly, I made folk swich cheere[2]
That in his owene grece I made him frye,
For angre and for verray jalousye.
495   By God, in erthe I was his purgatorye,
For which I hope his soule be in glorye.
For God it woot, he sat ful ofte and soong°   *sang*
Whan that his sho ful bitterly him wroong.°   *pinched*
Ther was no wight save God and he that wiste°   *knew*
500   In many wise how sore I him twiste.
He deide whan I cam fro Jerusalem,
And lith ygrave under the roode-beem,[3]
Al° is his tombe nought so curious[4]   *although*
As was the sepulcre of him Darius,
505   Which that Apelles wroughte subtilly:[5]
It nis but wast to burye him preciously.°   *expensively*
Lat him fare wel, God yive his soule reste;

---

8. When I look back.
9. Has taken away from me.
1. I made him a cross of the same wood. The proverb has much the same sense as the one quoted in line 493.
2. Pretended to be in love with others.

3. And lies buried under the rood beam (the crucifix beam running between nave and chancel).
4. Carefully wrought.
5. Accordingly to medieval legend, the artist Apelles decorated the tomb of Darius, king of the Persians.

He is now in his grave and in his cheste.°   *coffin*
    Now of my fifthe housbonde wol I telle—
510 God lete his soule nevere come in helle—
And yit he was to me the moste shrewe:[6]
That feele I on my ribbes al by rewe,[7]
And evere shal unto myn ending day.
But in oure bed he was so fressh and gay,
515 And therwithal so wel coulde he me glose°   *flatter, coax*
Whan that he wolde han my bele chose,
That though he hadde me bet° on every boon,°   *beaten / bone*
He coude winne again my love anoon.°   *immediately*
I trowe I loved him best for that he
520 Was of his love daungerous[8] to me.
We wommen han, if that I shal nat lie,
In this matere a quainte fantasye:[9]
Waite what[1] thing we may nat lightly° have,   *easily*
Therafter wol we crye al day and crave;
525 Forbede us thing, and that desiren we;
Preesse on us faste, and thanne wol we flee.
With daunger oute we al oure chaffare:[2]
Greet prees° at market maketh dere° ware,   *crowd / expensive*
And too greet chepe is holden at litel pris.[3]
530 This knoweth every womman that is wis.
    My fifthe housbonde—God his soule blesse!—
Which that I took for love and no richesse,
He somtime was a clerk at Oxenforde,
And hadde laft° scole and wente at hoom to boorde   *left*
535 With my gossib,° dwelling in oure town   *confidante*
God have hir soule!—hir name was Alisoun;
She knew myn herte and eek my privetee°   *secrets*
Bet° than oure parissh preest, as mote I thee.° *better / prosper*
To hire biwrayed° I my conseil° al,   *disclosed / secrets*
540 For hadde myn housbonde pissed on a wal,
Or doon a thing that sholde han cost his lif,
To hire,° and to another worthy wif,   *her*
And to my nece which I loved weel,
I wolde han told his conseil everydeel;°   *entirely*
545 And so I dide ful often, God it woot,
That made his face often reed° and hoot°   *red / hot*
For verray shame, and blamed himself for he
Hadde told to me so greet a privetee.
    And so bifel that ones° in a Lente—   *once*
550 So often times I to my gossib wente,
For evere yit I loved to be gay,
And for to walke in March, Averil, and May,
From hous to hous, to heere sondry tales—
That Janekin clerk and my gossib dame Alis
555 And I myself into the feeldes wente.
Myn housbonde was at London al that Lente:

---

6. Worst rascal.
7. In a row.
8. I.e., he played hard to get.
9. Strange fancy.

1. Whatever.
2. (Meeting) with reserve, we spread out our merchandise.
3. Too good a bargain is held at little value.

I hadde the better leiser for to playe,
And for to see, and eek for to be seye°   *seen*
Of lusty folk—what wiste I wher my grace°   *luck*
560 Was shapen° for to be, or in what place?   *destined*
Therfore I made my visitaciouns
To vigilies[4] and to processiouns,
To preching eek, and to thise pilgrimages,
To playes of miracles and to mariages,
565 And wered upon[5] my gaye scarlet gites°—   *gowns*
Thise wormes ne thise motthes ne thise mites,
Upon my peril[6] frete° hem neveradeel: *ate*
And woostou why? For they were used weel.
    Now wol I tellen forth what happed me.
570 I saye that in the feeldes walked we,
Til trewely we hadde swich daliaunce,°   *flirtation*
This clerk and I, that of my purveyaunce°   *foresight*
I spak to him and saide him how that he,
If I were widwe, sholde wedde me.
575 For certainly, I saye for no bobaunce,°   *boast*
Yit was I nevere withouten purveyaunce
Of mariage n'of othere thinges eek:
I holde a mouses herte nought worth a leek
That hath but oon hole for to sterte° to,   *run*
580 And if that faile thanne is al ydo.[7]
I bar him on hand[8] he hadde enchaunted me
(My dame° taughte me that subtiltee);   *mother*
And eek I saide I mette° of him al night: *dreamed*
He wolde han slain me as I lay upright,°   *on my back*
585 And al my bed was ful of verray blood—
"But yit I hope that ye shul do me good;
For blood bitokeneth° gold, as me was taught."   *signifies*
And al was fals, I dremed of it right naught,
But as I folwed ay my dames° lore°   *mother's / teaching*
590 As wel of that as othere thinges more.
But now sire—lat me see, what shal I sayn?
Aha, by God, I have my tale again.
    Whan that my ferthe housbonde was on beere,°   *funeral bier*
I weep,° algate,° and made sory cheere,   *wept / anyhow*
595 As wives moten,° for it is usage,°   *must / custom*
And with my coverchief covered my visage;
But for I was purveyed° of a make.°   *provided / mate*
I wepte but smale, and that I undertake.°   *guarantee*
    To chirche was myn housbonde born amorwe;[9]
600 With neighebores that for him maden sorwe,
And Janekin oure clerk was oon of tho.
As help me God, whan that I saw him go
After the beere, me thoughte he hadde a paire
Of legges and of feet so clene[1] and faire,
605 That al myn herte I yaf unto his hold.°   *possession*

4. Evening service before a religious holiday.
5. Wore.
6. On peril (to my soul), an oath.
7. I.e., the game is up.

8. I pretended to him.
9. In the morning.
1. I.e., neat.

He was, I trowe,° twenty winter old,   *believe*
And I was fourty, if I shal saye sooth—
But yit I hadde alway a coltes tooth:[2]
Gat-toothed[3] was I, and that bicam me weel;
610 I hadde the prente[4] of Sainte Venus seel.°   *seal*
As help me God, I was a lusty oon,
And fair and riche and yong and wel-bigoon,°   *well-situated*
And trewely, as mine housbondes tolde me,
I hadde the beste quoniam[5] mighte be.
615 For certes I am al Venerien
In feeling, and myn herte is Marcien:[6]
Venus me yaf my lust, my likerousnesse,°   *amorousness*
And Mars yaf me my sturdy hardinesse.
Myn ascendent was Taur[7] and Mars therinne—
620 Allas, allas, that evere love was sinne!
I folwed ay° my inclinacioun   *ever*
By vertu of my constellacioun;[8]
That made me I coude nought withdrawe
My chambre of Venus from a good felawe.
625 Yit have I Martes° merk upon my face,   *Mars's*
And also in another privee place.
For God so wis° be my savacioun,°   *surely / salvation*
I loved nevere by no discrecioun,°   *moderation*
But evere folwede myn appetit,
630 Al were he short or long or blak or whit;
I took no keep,° so that he liked° me,   *heed / pleased*
How poore he was, ne eek of what degree.
What sholde I saye but at the monthes ende
This joly clerk Janekin that was so hende°   *courteous, nice*
635 Hath wedded me with greet solempnitee,°   *splendor*
And to him yaf I al the land and fee°   *property*
That evere was me yiven therbifore—
But afterward repented me ful sore:
He nolde suffre no thing of my list.°   *wish*
640 By God, he smoot° me ones on the list°   *struck / ear*
For that I rente° out of his book a leef,   *tore*
That of the strook° myn ere weex° al deef.   *blow / grew*
Stibourne° I was as is a leonesse,   *stubborn*
And of my tonge a verray jangleresse,°   *chatterbox*
645 And walke I wolde, as I hadde doon biforn,
From hous to hous, although he hadde it[9] sworn;
For which he often times wolde preche,
And me of olde Romain geestes° teche,   *stories*
How he Simplicius Gallus lafte° his wif,   *left*
650 And hire forsook for terme of al his lif,
Nought but for open-heveded he hire sey[1]
Looking out at his dore upon a day.

---

2. I.e., youthful appetites.
3. Gap-toothed women were considered to be amorous.
4. Print, i.e., a birthmark.
5. Latin for "because"; another euphemism for a sexual organ.
6. Influenced by Mars. "Venerien": astrologically influenced by Venus.
7. My birth sign was the constellation Taurus, a sign in which Venus is dominant.
8. I.e., horoscope.
9. I.e., the contrary.
1. Just because he saw her bareheaded.

Another Romain tolde he me by name
That, for his wif was at a someres° game   *summer's*
655 Withouten his witing,° he forsook hire eke;   *knowledge*
And thanne wolde he upon his Bible seeke
That ilke proverbe of Ecclesiaste[2]
Where he comandeth and forbedeth faste°   *strictly*
Man shal nat suffre his wif go roule° aboute;   *roam*
660 Thanne wolde he saye right thus withouten doute:
"Whoso that buildeth his hous al of salwes,°   *willow sticks*
And priketh° his blinde hors over the falwes,[3]   *rides*
And suffreth° his wif to go seeken halwes,°   *allows / shrines*
Is worthy to be hanged on the galwes."°   *gallows*
665 But al for nought—I sette nought an hawe[4]
Of his proverbes n'of his olde sawe;
N' I wolde nat of him corrected be:
I hate him that my vices telleth me,
And so doon mo, God woot, of us than I.
670 This made him with me wood al outrely:°   *entirely*
I nolde nought forbere° him in no cas.   *submit to*
Now wol I saye you sooth, by Saint Thomas,
Why that I rente° out of his book a leef,   *tore*
For which he smoot me so that I was deef.
675 He hadde a book that gladly night and day
For his disport° he wolde rede alway.   *entertainment*
He cleped it *Valerie*[5] *and Theofraste*,
At which book he lough° alway ful faste;   *laughed*
And eek ther was somtime a clerk at Rome,
680 A cardinal, that highte Saint Jerome,
That made a book[6] again° Jovinian;   *against*
In which book eek ther was Tertulan,
Crysippus, Trotula, and Helouis,[7]
That was abbesse nat fer fro Paris;
685 And eek the Parables of Salomon,
Ovides *Art*,[8] and bookes many oon—
And alle thise were bounden in oo volume.
And every night and day was his custume,
Whan he hadde leiser and vacacioun°   *free time*
690 From other worldly occupacioun,
To reden in this book of wikked wives.
He knew of hem mo legendes and lives
Than been of goode wives in the Bible.
For trusteth wel, it is an impossible°   *impossibility*
695 That any clerk wol speke good of wives,
But if it be of holy saintes lives,
N'of noon other womman nevere the mo—

---

2. Ecclesiasticus (25.25).
3. Plowed land.
4. I did not rate at the value of a hawthorn berry.
5. "*Valerie*": i.e., the *Letter of Valerius Concerning Not Marrying*, by Walter Map; "*Theofraste*": Theophrastus's *Book Concerning Marriage*. Medieval manuscripts often contained a number of different works, sometimes, as here, dealing with the same subject.

6. St. Jerome's misogynist *Against Jovinian*.
7. "Tertulan": i.e., Tertullian, author of treatises on sexual modesty. "Crysippus": mentioned by Jerome as an antifeminist. "Trotula": a female doctor whose presence here is unexplained. "Helouis": i.e., Eloise, whose love affair with the great scholar Abelard was a medieval scandal.
8. Ovid's *Art of Love*. "Parables of Salomon": the biblical Book of Proverbs.

Who painted the leon, tel me who?[9]
By God, if wommen hadden writen stories,
700 As clerkes han within hir oratories,°   *chapels*
They wolde han writen of men more wikkednesse
Than al the merk[1] of Adam may redresse.
The children of Mercurye and Venus[2]
Been in hir werking° ful contrarious:°   *operation / opposed*
705 Mercurye loveth wisdom and science,
And Venus loveth riot° and dispence;°   *revelry / spending*
And for hir diverse disposicioun
Each falleth in otheres exaltacioun,[3]
And thus, God woot, Mercurye is desolat
710 In Pisces wher Venus is exaltat,[4]
And Venus falleth ther Mercurye is raised:
Therfore no womman of no clerk is praised.
The clerk, whan he is old and may nought do
Of Venus werkes worth his olde sho,°   *shoe*
715 Thanne sit° he down and writ° in his dotage   *sits / writes*
That wommen can nat keepe hir mariage.
   But now to purpose why I tolde thee
That I was beten for a book, pardee:
Upon a night Janekin, that was our sire,[5]
720 Redde on his book as he sat by the fire
Of Eva first, that for hir wikkednesse
Was al mankinde brought to wrecchednesse,
For which that Jesu Crist himself was slain
That boughte° us with his herte blood again—   *redeemed*
725 Lo, heer expres of wommen may ye finde
That womman was the los° of al mankinde.[6]   *ruin*
   Tho° redde he me how Sampson loste his heres: *then*
Sleeping his lemman° kitte° it with hir sheres,   *lover / cut*
Thurgh which treson loste he both his yën.
730   Tho redde he me, if that I shal nat lien,
Of Ercules and of his Dianire,[7]
That caused him to sette himself afire.
No thing forgat he the sorwe and wo
That Socrates hadde with his wives two—
735 How Xantippa caste pisse upon his heed:
This sely° man sat stille as he were deed;   *poor, hapless*
He wiped his heed, namore dorste° he sayn   *dared*
But "Er that thonder stinte,° comth a rain."   *stops*
   Of Pasipha[8] that was the queene of Crete—
740 For shrewednesse° him thoughte the tale sweete—   *malice*
Fy, speek namore, it is a grisly thing
Of hir horrible lust and hir liking.°   *pleasure*

9. In one of Aesop's fables, the lion, shown a picture of a man killing a lion, asked who painted the picture. Had a lion been the artist, of course, the roles would have been reversed.
1. Mark, sex.
2. I.e., clerks and women, astrologically ruled by Mercury and Venus, respectively.
3. Because of their contrary positions (as planets), each one descends (in the belt of the zodiac) as the other rises, hence one loses its power as the other becomes dominant.
4. I.e., Mercury is deprived of power in Pisces (the sign of the Fish), where Venus is most powerful.
5. My husband.
6. The stories of wicked women Chaucer drew mainly from St. Jerome and Walter Map.
7. Deianira unwittingly gave Hercules a poisoned shirt, which hurt him so much that he committed suicide by fire.
8. Pasiphaë, who had intercourse with a bull.

Of Clytermistra[9] for hir lecherye
That falsly made hir housbonde for to die,
745 He redde it with ful good devocioun.
    He tolde me eek for what occasioun
Amphiorax[1] at Thebes loste his lif:
Myn housbonde hadde a legende of his wif
Eriphylem, that for an ouche° of gold   *trinket*
750 Hath prively unto the Greekes told
Wher that hir housbonde hidde him in a place,
For which he hadde at Thebes sory grace.
    Of Livia tolde he me and of Lucie:[2]
They bothe made hir housbondes for to die,
755 That oon for love, that other was for hate;
Livia hir housbonde on an even late
Empoisoned hath for that she was his fo;
Lucia likerous° loved hir housbonde so   *lecherous*
That for° he sholde alway upon hire thinke,   *in order that*
760 She yaf him swich a manere love-drinke
That he was deed er it were by the morwe.[3]
And thus algates° housbondes han sorwe.   *in every way*
    Thanne tolde he me how oon Latumius
Complained unto his felawe Arrius
765 That in his garden growed swich a tree,
On which he saide how that his wives three
Hanged hemself for herte despitous.[4]
    "O leve° brother," quod this Arrius,   *dear*
"Yif me a plante of thilke blessed tree,
770 And in my gardin planted shal it be."
    Of latter date of wives hath he red
That some han slain hir housbondes in hir bed
And lete hir lechour dighte[5] hire al the night,
Whan that the cors° lay in the floor upright;°   *corpse / on his back*
775 And some han driven nailes in hir brain
Whil that they sleepe, and thus they han hem slain;
Some han hem yiven poison in hir drinke.
He spak more harm than herte may bithinke,°   *imagine*
And therwithal he knew of mo proverbes
780 Than in this world ther growen gras or herbes:
"Bet° is," quod he, "thyn habitacioun   *better*
Be with a leon or a foul dragoun
Than with a womman using° for to chide."   *accustomed*
"Bet is," quod he, "hye in the roof abide
785 Than with an angry wif down in the hous:
They been so wikked° and contrarious,   *perverse*
They haten that hir housbondes loveth ay."
He saide, "A womman cast° hir shame away   *casts*
When she cast of° hir smok,"[6] and ferthermo,   *off*

---

9. Clytemnestra, who, with her lover, Aegisthus, slew her husband, Agamemnon.
1. Amphiaraus, betrayed by his wife, Eriphyle, and forced to go to the war against Thebes.
2. Livia murdered her husband on behalf of her lover, Sejanus. "Lucie": i.e., Lucilla, who was said to have poisoned her husband, the poet Lucretius, with a potion designed to keep him faithful.
3. He was dead before it was near morning.
4. For malice of heart.
5. Have intercourse with.
6. Undergarment.

790 "A fair womman, but she be chast also,
Is like a gold ring in a sowes nose."
Who wolde weene,° or who wolde suppose   *think*
The wo that in myn herte was and pine?°   *suffering*
   And whan I sawgh he wolde nevere fine°   *end*
795 To reden on this cursed book al night,
Al sodeinly three leves have I plight°   *snatched*
Out of his book right as he redde, and eke
I with my fist so took[7] him on the cheeke
That in oure fir he fil° bakward adown.   *fell*
800 And up he sterte as dooth a wood° leoun,   *raging*
And with his fist he smoot me on the heed°   *head*
That in the floor I lay as I were deed.°   *dead*
And whan he sawgh how stille that I lay,
He was agast, and wolde have fled his way,
805 Til atte laste out of my swough° I braide:°   *swoon / started*
"O hastou slain me, false thief?" I saide,
"And for my land thus hastou mordred° me?   *murdered*
Er I be deed yit wol I kisse thee."
And neer he cam and kneeled faire adown,
810 And saide, "Dere suster Alisoun,
As help me God, I shal thee nevere smite.
That I have doon, it is thyself to wite.°   *blame*
Foryif it me, and that I thee biseeke."°   *beseech*
And yit eftsoones° I hitte him on the cheeke,   *another time*
815 And saide, "Thief, thus muchel am I wreke.°   *avenged*
Now wol I die: I may no lenger speke."
   But at the laste with muchel care and wo
We fille[8] accorded by us selven two.
He yaf me al the bridel° in myn hand,   *bridle*
820 To han the governance of hous and land,
And of his tonge and his hand also;
And made[9] him brenne° his book anoonright tho.   *burn*
And whan that I hadde geten unto me
By maistrye° al the sovereinetee,°   *skill / dominion*
825 And that he saide, "Myn owene trewe wif,
Do as thee lust° the terme of al thy lif;   *it pleases*
Keep thyn honour, and keep eek myn estat,"
After that day we hadde nevere debat.
God help me so, I was to him as kinde
830 As any wif from Denmark unto Inde,°   *India*
And also trewe, and so was he to me.
I praye to God that sit° in majestee,   *sits*
So blesse his soule for his mercy dere.
Now wol I saye my tale if ye wol heere.

[ANOTHER INTERRUPTION]

835   The Frere lough° when he hadde herd all this: *laughed*
"Now dame," quod he, "so have I joye or blis,

---

7. I.e., hit.   9. I.e., I made.
8. I.e., became.

This is a long preamble of a tale."
And whan the Somnour herde the Frere gale,°   *exclaim*
"Lo," quod the Somnour, "Goddes armes two,
840 A frere wol entremette him[1] everemo!
Lo, goode men, a flye and eek a frere
Wol falle in every dissh and eek matere.
What spekestou of preambulacioun?
What, amble or trotte or pisse or go sitte down!
845 Thou lettest° oure disport in this manere."   *hinder*
    "Ye, woltou so, sire Somnour?" quod the Frere.
"Now by my faith, I shal er that I go
Telle of a somnour swich a tale or two
That al the folk shal laughen in this place."
850   'Now elles, Frere, I wol bishrewe° thy face,"   *curse*
Quod this Somnour, "and I bishrewe me,
But if I telle tales two or three
Of freres, er I come to Sidingborne,[2]
That I shal make thyn herte for to moorne°—   *mourn*
855 For wel I woot thy pacience is goon."
    Oure Hoste cride, "Pees, and that anoon!"
And saide, "Lat the womman telle hir tale:
Ye fare as folk that dronken been of ale.
Do, dame, tel forth youre tale, and that is best."
860   "Al redy, sire," quod she, "right as you lest°—   *it pleases*
If I have licence of this worthy Frere."
"Yis, dame," quod he, "tel forth and I wol heere."

The Tale

Chaucer may have originally written the fabliau that became *The Shipman's Tale*
for the Wife of Bath. If so, then he replaced it with a tale that is not simply appropriate to her character but that develops it even beyond the complexity already
revealed in her *Prologue*. The story survives in two other versions in which the hero
is Sir Gawain, whose courtesy contrasts sharply with the behavior of the knight in
the Wife's tale. (For excerpts from *The Marriage of Sir Gawain and Dame Ragnell*,
see the "King Arthur" topic in the supplemental ebook.) As Chaucer has the Wife
tell it, the tale expresses her views about the relations of the sexes, her wit and
humor, and her fantasies. Like Marie de France's lay *Lanval* (see p. 121), the Wife's
tale is about a fairy bride who seeks out and tests a mortal lover.

    In th'olde dayes of the King Arthour,
    Of which that Britouns speken greet honour,
865 Al was this land fulfild of faïrye:[3]
The elf-queene° with hir joly compaignye   *queen of the fairies*
Daunced ful ofte in many a greene mede°—   *meadow*
This was the olde opinion as I rede;
I speke of many hundred yeres ago.
870 But now can no man see none elves mo,
For now the grete charitee and prayeres
Of limitours,[4] and othere holy freres,

---

1. Intrude himself.
2. Sittingbourne (a town forty miles from
London).

3. I.e., filled full of supernatural creatures.
4. Friars licensed to beg in a certain territory.

That serchen every land and every streem,
As thikke as motes° in the sonne-beem,   dust particles
875   Blessing halles, chambres, kichenes, bowres,
Citees, burghes,° castels, hye towres,   townships
Thropes, bernes, shipnes,[5] dayeries—
This maketh that ther been no fairies.
For ther as wont to walken was an elf
880   Ther walketh now the limitour himself,
In undermeles° and in morweninges,°   afternoons / mornings
And saith his Matins and his holy thinges,
As he gooth in his limitacioun.[6]
Wommen may go saufly° up and down: safely
885   In every bussh or under every tree
Ther is noon other incubus[7] but he,
And he ne wol doon hem but[8] dishonour.
      And so bifel it that this King Arthour
Hadde in his hous a lusty bacheler,°   young knight
890   That on a day cam riding fro river,[9]
And happed° that, allone as he was born,   it happened
He sawgh a maide walking him biforn;
Of which maide anoon, maugree hir heed,[1]
By verray force he rafte° hir maidenheed;   deprived her of
895   For which oppression° was swich clamour,   rape
And swich pursuite° unto the King Arthour,   petitioning
That dampned was this knight for to be deed[2]
By cours of lawe, and sholde han lost his heed—
Paraventure° swich was the statut tho—   perchance
900   But that the queene and othere ladies mo
So longe prayeden the king of grace,
Til he his lif him graunted in the place,
And yaf him to the queene, al at hir wille,
To chese° wheither she wolde him save or spille.[3]   choose
905   The queene thanked the king with al hir might,
And after this thus spak she to the knight,
Whan that she saw hir time upon a day:
"Thou standest yit," quod she, "in swich array°   condition
That of thy lif yit hastou no suretee.°   guarantee
910   I graunte thee lif if thou canst tellen me
What thing it is that wommen most desiren:
Be war and keep thy nekke boon° from iren.   bone
And if thou canst nat tellen me anoon,°   right away
Yit wol I yive thee leve for to goon
915   A twelfmonth and a day to seeche° and lere°   search / learn
An answere suffisant° in this matere,   satisfactory
And suretee wol I han er that thou pace,°   pass
Thy body for to yeelden in this place."
      Wo was this knight, and sorwefully he siketh.°   sighs

5. Thorps (villages), barns, stables.
6. I.e., the friar's assigned area. His "holy thinges"
are prayers.
7. An evil spirit that seduces mortal women.
8. "Ne . . . but": only.
9. Hawking, usually carried out on the banks of

a stream.
1. Despite her head, i.e., despite anything she
could do.
2. This knight was condemned to death.
3. Put to death.

920 But what, he may nat doon al as him liketh,
And atte laste he chees° him for to wende,　　　　　　　　　*chose*
And come again right at the yeres ende,
With swich answere as God wolde him purveye,°　　　　*provide*
And taketh his leve and wendeth forth his waye.
925 He seeketh every hous and every place
Wher as he hopeth for to finde grace,
To lerne what thing wommen love most.
But he ne coude arriven in no coost[4]
Wher as he mighte finde in this matere
930 Two creatures according in fere.[5]
　　Some saiden wommen loven best richesse;
Some saide honour, some saide jolinesse;°　　　　　　*pleasure*
Some riche array, some saiden lust abedde,
And ofte time to be widwe and wedde.
935 Some saide that oure herte is most esed
Whan that we been yflatered and yplesed—
He gooth ful neigh the soothe, I wol nat lie:
A man shal winne us best with flaterye,
And with attendance° and with bisinesse°　　*attention / solicitude*
940 Been we ylimed,° bothe more and lesse.　　　　　　*ensnared*
　　And some sayen that we loven best
For to be free, and do right as us lest,°　　　　　　*it pleases*
And that no man repreve° us of oure vice,　　　　　　*reprove*
But saye that we be wise and no thing nice.°　　　　*foolish*
945 For trewely, ther is noon of us alle,
If any wight wol clawe° us on the galle,°　　　*rub / sore spot*
That we nil kike° for° he saith us sooth:　　　*kick / because*
Assaye° and he shal finde it that so dooth.　　　　　　*try*
For be we nevere so vicious withinne,
950 We wol be holden° wise and clene of sinne.　　*considered*
　　And some sayn that greet delit han we
For to be holden stable and eek secree,[6]
And in oo° purpos stedefastly to dwelle,　　　　　　　*one*
And nat biwraye° thing that men us telle—　　　　　*disclose*
955 But that tale is nat worth a rake-stele.°　　　　*rake handle*
Pardee,° we wommen conne no thing hele:°　　*by God / conceal*
Witnesse on Mida.° Wol ye heere the tale?　　　　　　*Midas*
　　Ovide, amonges othere thinges smale,
Saide Mida hadde under his longe heres,
960 Growing upon his heed, two asses eres,
The whiche vice° he hidde as he best mighte　　　　　*defect*
Ful subtilly from every mannes sighte,
That save his wif ther wiste° of it namo.　　　　　　*knew*
He loved hire most and trusted hire also.
965 He prayed hire that to no creature
She sholde tellen of his disfigure.°　　　　　　　*deformity*
　　She swoor him nay, for al this world to winne,
She nolde do that vilainye or sinne
To make hir housbonde han so foul a name:

---

4. I.e., country.
5. Agreeing together.

6. Reliable and also closemouthed.

970 She nolde nat telle it for hir owene shame.
But nathelees, hir thoughte that she dyde°   would die
That she so longe sholde a conseil° hide;   secret
Hire thoughte it swal° so sore about hir herte   swelled
That nedely som word hire moste asterte,[7]
975 And sith she dorste nat telle it to no man,
Down to a mareis° faste° by she ran—   marsh / close
Til she cam there hir herte was afire—
And as a bitore bombleth[8] in the mire,
She laide hir mouth unto the water doun:
980 "Biwray° me nat, thou water, with thy soun,"°   betray / sound
Quod she. "To thee I telle it and namo:°   to no one else
Myn housbonde hath longe asses eres two.
Now is myn herte al hool,[9] now is it oute.
I mighte no lenger keep it, out of doute."
985 Here may ye see, though we a time abide,
Yit oute it moot:° we can no conseil hide.   must
The remenant of the tale if ye wol heere,
Redeth Ovide, and ther ye may it lere.[1]
    This knight of which my tale is specially,
990 Whan that he sawgh he mighte nat come thereby—
This is to saye what wommen loven most—
Within his brest ful sorweful was his gost,°   spirit
But hoom he gooth, he mighte nat sojourne:°   delay
The day was come that hoomward moste° he turne.   must
995 And in his way it happed him to ride
In al this care under° a forest side,   by
Wher as he sawgh upon a daunce go
Of ladies foure and twenty and yit mo;
Toward the whiche daunce he drow ful yerne,[2]
1000 In hope that som wisdom sholde he lerne.
But certainly, er he cam fully there,
Vanisshed was this daunce, he niste° where.   knew not
No creature sawgh he that bar° lif,   bore
Save on the greene he sawgh sitting a wif°—   woman
1005 A fouler wight ther may no man devise.°   imagine
Again[3] the knight this olde wif gan rise,
And saide, "Sire knight, heer forth lith° no way.°   lies / road
Telle me what ye seeken, by youre fay.°   faith
Paraventure it may the better be:
1010 Thise olde folk conne° muchel thing," quod she.   know
    "My leve moder,"° quod this knight, "certain,   mother
I nam but deed but if that I can sayn
What thing it is that wommen most desire.
Coude ye me wisse,° I wolde wel quite youre hire."[4]   teach
1015   "Plight° me thy trouthe here in myn hand," quod she,   pledge
"The nexte thing that I requere° thee,   require of
Thou shalt it do, if it lie in thy might,

---

7. Of necessity some word must escape her.
8. Makes a booming noise. "Bitore": bittern, a heron.
9. I.e., sound.
1. Learn. The reeds disclosed the secret by whispering *"aures aselli"* (ass's ears).
2. Drew very quickly.
3. I.e., to meet.
4. Repay your trouble.

And I wol telle it you er it be night."
"Have heer my trouthe," quod the knight. "I graunte."
1020 "Thanne," quod she, "I dar me wel avaunte°   boast
Thy lif is sauf,° for I wol stande therby.   safe
Upon my lif the queene wol saye as I.
Lat see which is the pruddeste° of hem alle   proudest
That wereth on⁵ a coverchief or a calle°   headdress
1025 That dar saye nay of that I shal thee teche.
Lat us go forth withouten lenger speeche."
Tho rouned° she a pistel° in his ere,   whispered / message
And bad him to be glad and have no fere.
      Whan they be comen to the court, this knight
1030 Saide he hadde holde his day as he hadde hight,°   promised
And redy was his answere, as he saide.
Ful many a noble wif, and many a maide,
And many a widwe—for that they been wise—
The queene hirself sitting as justise,
1035 Assembled been this answere for to heere,
And afterward this knight was bode° appere.   bidden to
To every wight comanded was silence,
And that the knight sholde telle in audience°   open hearing
What thing that worldly wommen loven best.
1040 This knight ne stood nat stille as dooth a best,°   beast
But to his question anoon answerde
With manly vois that al the court it herde.
      "My lige° lady, generally," quod he,   liege
"Wommen desire to have sovereinetee°   dominion
1045 As wel over hir housbonde as hir love,
And for to been in maistrye him above.
This is youre moste desir though ye me kille.
Dooth as you list:° I am here at youre wille."   please
      In al the court ne was ther wif ne maide
1050 Ne widwe that contraried° that he saide,   contradicted
But saiden he was worthy han° his lif.   to have
      And with that word up sterte° that olde wif,   started
Which that the knight sawgh sitting on the greene;
"Mercy," quod she, "my soverein lady queene,
1055 Er that youre court departe, do me right.
I taughte this answere unto the knight,
For which he plighte me his trouthe there
The firste thing I wolde him requere°   require
He wolde it do, if it laye in his might.
1060 Bifore the court thanne praye I thee, sire knight,"
Quod she, "that thou me take unto thy wif,
For wel thou woost that I have kept° thy lif.   saved
If I saye fals, say nay, upon thy fay."
      This knight answerde, "Allas and wailaway,
1065 I woot right wel that swich was my biheeste.°   promise
For Goddes love, as chees° a newe requeste: choose
Taak al my good and lat my body go."
      "Nay thanne," quod she, "I shrewe° us bothe two.   curse

5. That wears.

For though that I be foul and old and poore,
1070 I nolde for al the metal ne for ore
That under erthe is grave° or lith° above,   *buried / lies*
But if thy wif I were and eek thy love."
  "My love," quod he. "Nay, my dampnacioun!° *damnation*
Allas, that any of my nacioun[6]
1075 Sholde evere so foule disparaged° be."   *degraded*
But al for nought, th'ende is this, that he
Constrained was: he needes moste hire wedde,
And taketh his olde wif and gooth to bedde.
  Now wolden some men saye, paraventure,
1080 That for my necligence I do no cure[7]
To tellen you the joye and al th'array
That at the feeste was that ilke day.
To which thing shortly answere I shal:
I saye ther nas no joye ne feeste at al;
1085 Ther nas but hevinesse and muche sorwe.
For prively he wedded hire on morwe,[8]
And al day after hidde him as an owle,
So wo was him, his wif looked so foule.
  Greet was the wo the knight hadde in his thought:
1090 Whan he was with his wif abedde brought,
He walweth° and he turneth to and fro.   *tosses*
His olde wif lay smiling everemo,
And saide, "O dere housbonde, benedicite,° *bless me*
Fareth° every knight thus with his wif as ye? *behaves*
1095 Is this the lawe of King Arthures hous?
Is every knight of his thus daungerous?°   *standoffish*
I am youre owene love and youre wif;
I am she which that saved hath youre lif;
And certes yit ne dide I you nevere unright.
1100 Why fare ye thus with me this firste night?
Ye faren like a man hadde lost his wit.
What is my gilt? For Goddes love, telle it,
And it shal been amended if I may."
  "Amended!" quod this knight. "Allas, nay, nay,
1105 It wol nat been amended neveremo.
Thou art so lothly° and so old also,   *hideous*
And therto comen of so lowe a kinde,°   *lineage*
That litel wonder is though I walwe and winde.° *turn*
So wolde God myn herte wolde breste!"° *break*
1110 "Is this," quod she, "the cause of youre unreste?"
"Ye, certainly," quod he. "No wonder is."
"Now sire," quod she, "I coude amende al this,
If that me liste, er it were dayes three,
So° wel ye mighte bere you[9] unto me.   *provided that*
1115 "But for ye speken of swich gentilesse°   *nobility*
As is descended out of old richesse—
That therfore sholden ye be gentilmen—
Swich arrogance is nat worth an hen.

---

6. I.e., family.
7. I do not take the trouble.
8. In the morning.
9. Behave.

Looke who that is most vertuous alway,
1120 Privee and apert,[1] and most entendeth° ay°   *tries / always*
To do the gentil deedes that he can,
Taak him for the gretteste° gentilman.   *greatest*
Crist wol° we claime of him oure gentilesse,   *desires that*
Nat of oure eldres for hir 'old richesse.'
1125 For though they yive us al hir heritage,
For which we claime to been of heigh parage,°   *descent*
Yit may they nat biquethe for no thing
To noon of us hir vertuous living,
That made hem gentilmen ycalled be,
1130 And bad[2] us folwen hem in swich degree.
   "Wel can the wise poete of Florence,
That highte Dant,[3] speken in this sentence;°   *topic*
Lo, in swich manere rym is Dantes tale:
'Ful selde° up riseth by his braunches[4] smale   *seldom*
1135 Prowesse° of man, for God of his prowesse   *excellence*
Wol that of him we claime oure gentilesse.'
For of oure eldres may we no thing claime
But temporel thing that man may hurte and maime.
Eek every wight woot this as wel as I,
1140 If gentilesse were planted natureelly
Unto a certain linage down the line,
Privee and apert, thanne wolde they nevere fine°   *cease*
To doon of gentilesse the faire office°—   *function*
They mighte do no vilainye or vice.
1145   "Taak fir and beer° it in the derkeste hous   *bear*
Bitwixe this and the Mount of Caucasus,
And lat men shette° the dores and go thenne,°   *shut / thence*
Yit wol the fir as faire lye° and brenne°   *blaze / burn*
As twenty thousand men mighte it biholde:
1150 His° office natureel ay wol it holde,   *its*
Up° peril of my lif, til that it die.   *upon*
Heer may ye see wel how that genterye°   *gentility*
Is nat annexed° to possessioun,[5]   *related*
Sith folk ne doon hir operacioun
1155 Alway, as dooth the fir, lo, in his kinde.°   *nature*
For God it woot, men may wel often finde
A lordes sone do shame and vilainye;
And he that wol han pris of his gentrye,[6]
For he was boren° of a gentil° hous,   *born / noble*
1160 And hadde his eldres noble and vertuous,
And nil himselven do no gentil deedes,
Ne folwen his gentil auncestre that deed° is,   *dead*
He nis nat gentil, be he due or erl—
For vilaines sinful deedes maken a cherl.
1165 Thy gentilesse[7] nis but renomee°   *renown*
Of thine auncestres for hir heigh bountee,°   *magnanimity*
Which is a straunge° thing for thy persone.   *external*

---

1. Privately and publicly.
2. I.e., they bade.
3. Dante (see his *Convivio*).
4. I.e., by the branches of a man's family tree.
5. I.e., inheritable property.
6. Have credit for his noble birth.
7. I.e., the gentility you claim.

For gentilesse[8] cometh fro God allone.
Thanne comth oure verray gentilesse of grace:
1170 It was no thing biquethe us with oure place,
Thenketh how noble, as saith Valerius,[9]
Was thilke Tullius Hostilius
That out of poverte° roos to heigh noblesse.   poverty
Redeth Senek° and redeth eek Boece:°   Seneca / Boethius
1175 Ther shul ye seen expres that no drede° is   doubt
That he is gentil that dooth gentil deedes.
And therfore, leve housbonde, I thus conclude:
Al° were it that mine auncestres weren rude,[1]   although
Yit may the hye God—and so hope I—
1180 Graunte me grace to liven vertuously.
Thanne am I gentil whan that I biginne
To liven vertuously and waive° sinne.   avoid
    "And ther as ye of poverte me repreve,°   reprove
The hye God, on whom that we bileve,
1185 In wilful° poverte chees° to live his lif;   voluntary / chose
And certes every man, maiden, or wif
May understonde that Jesus, hevene king,
Ne wolde nat chese° a vicious living.   choose
Glad poverte is an honeste° thing, certain;   honorable
1190 This wol Senek and othere clerkes sayn.
Whoso that halt him paid of[2] his poverte,
I holde him riche al hadde he nat a sherte.°   shirt
He that coveiteth[3] is a poore wight,
For he wolde han that is nat in his might;
1195 But he that nought hath, ne coveiteth° have,   desires to
Is riche, although we holde him but a knave.°   peasant
Verray° poverte it singeth proprely.°   true / appropriately
Juvenal saith of poverte, 'Merily
The poore man, whan he gooth by the waye,
1200 Biforn the theves he may singe and playe.'
Poverte is hateful good, and as I gesse,
A ful greet bringere out of bisinesse;[4]
A greet amendere eek of sapience°   wisdom
To him that taketh it in pacience;
1205 Poverte is thing, although it seeme elenge,°   wretched
Possession that no wight wol chalenge;[5]
Poverte ful often, whan a man is lowe,
Maketh[6] his God and eek himself to knowe;
Poverte a spectacle° is, as thinketh me,   pair of spectacles
1210 Thurgh which he may his verray° freendes see.   true
And therfore, sire, sin that I nought you greve,
Of my poverte namore ye me repreve.°   reproach
    "Now sire, of elde° ye repreve me: old age
And certes sire, though noon auctoritee
1215 Were in no book, ye gentils of honour
Sayn that men sholde an old wight doon favour,
And clepe him fader for youre gentilesse—

8. I.e., true gentility.
9. A Roman historian.
1. I.e., low born.
2. Considers himself satisfied with.

3. I.e., suffers desires.
4. I.e., remover of cares.
5. Claim as his property.
6. I.e., makes him.

And auctours[7] shal I finde, as I gesse.

   "Now ther ye saye that I am foul° and old: *ugly*

1220 Thanne drede you nought to been a cokewold,°   *cuckold*

For filthe° and elde, also mote I thee,[8]   *ugliness*

Been grete wardeins° upon chastitee.   *guardians*

But nathelees, sin I knowe your delit,

I shal fulfille youre worldly appetit.

1225   "Chees° now," quod she, "oon of thise thinges twaye: *choose*

To han me foul and old til that I deye

And be to you a trewe humble wif,

And nevere you displese in al my lif,

Or elles ye wol han me yong and fair,

1230 And take youre aventure° of the repair[9]   *chance*

That shal be to youre hous by cause of me—

Or in some other place, wel may be.

Now chees youreselven wheither° that you liketh."   *whichever*

   This knight aviseth him[1] and sore siketh;°   *sighs*

1235 But atte laste he saide in this manere:

"My lady and my love, and wif so dere,

I putte me in youre wise governaunce:

Cheseth° yourself which may be most plesaunce°   *choose / pleasure*

And most honour to you and me also.

1240 I do no fors the wheither[2] of the two,

For as you liketh it suffiseth° me."   *satisfies*

   "Thanne have I gete° of you maistrye," quod she,   *got*

"Sin I may chese and governe as me lest?"°   *it pleases*

   "Ye, certes, wif," quod he. "I holde it best."

1245   "Kisse me," quod she. "We be no lenger wrothe.

For by my trouthe, I wol be to you bothe—

This is to sayn, ye, bothe fair and good.

I praye to God that I mote sterven wood.[3]

But° I to you be al so good and trewe   *unless*

1250 As evere was wif sin that the world was newe.

And but I be tomorn° as fair to seene   *tomorrow morning*

As any lady, emperisse, or queene,

That is bitwixe the eest and eek the west,

Do with my lif and deeth right as you lest:

1255 Caste up the curtin,[4] looke how that it is."

   And whan the knight sawgh verraily al this,

That she so fair was and so yong therto,

For joye he hente° hire in his armes two;   *took*

His herte bathed in a bath of blisse;

1260 A thousand time arewe° he gan hire kisse,   *in a row*

And she obeyed him in every thing

That mighte do him plesance or liking.°   *pleasure*

And thus they live unto hir lives ende

In parfit° joye. And Jesu Crist us sende   *perfect*

1265 Housbondes meeke, yonge, and fresshe abedde—

And grace t'overbide° hem that we wedde.   *outlive*

And eek I praye Jesu shorte° hir lives   *shorten*

---

7. I.e., authorities.   2. I do not care whichever.

8. So may I prosper.   3. Die mad.

9. I.e., visits.   4. The curtain around the bed.

1. Considers.

That nought wol be governed by hir wives,
And olde and angry nigardes° of dispence°—   misers / spending
1270 God sende hem soone a verray° pestilence!   veritable

The Pardoner's Prologue and Tale

As with *The Wife of Bath's Prologue* and *Tale, The Pardoner's Prologue* and *Tale*
develop in profound and surprising ways the portrait sketched in *The General
Prologue.* In his *Prologue* the Pardoner boasts to his fellow pilgrims about his
own depravity and the ingenuity with which he abuses his office and extracts
money from poor and ignorant
people.

The Power of Money. Quinten Metsys, *The
Money Lender and His Wife,* 1514. Note the gaze
of the wife: she has turned away from her book of
devotions toward the more fascinating sight of
money being weighed.

The medieval pardoner's job
was to collect money for the charitable enterprises, such as hospitals, supported by the church. In
return for donations he was
licensed by the pope to award
token remission of sins that the
donor should have repented and
confessed. By canon law pardoners were permitted to work only
in a prescribed area; within that
area they might visit churches
during Sunday service, briefly
explain their mission, receive
contributions, and in the pope's
name issue indulgence, which
was not considered to be a sale
but a gift from the infinite
treasury of Christ's mercy made
in return for a gift of money. In
practice, pardoners ignored the
restrictions on their office, made
their way into churches at will,
preached emotional sermons, and claimed extraordinary power for their pardons.

The Pardoner's Tale is a bombastic sermon against gluttony, gambling, and swearing, which he preaches to the pilgrims to show off his professional skills. The sermon
is framed by a narrative that is supposed to function as an *exemplum* (that is, an illustration) of the scriptural text, the one on which the Pardoner, as he tells the pilgrims,
always preaches: *"Radix malorum est cupiditas"* (Avarice is the root of evil).

The Introduction

Oure Hoste gan to swere as he were wood°   insane
"Harrow,"° quod he, "by nailes and by blood,[1]   help
This was a fals cherl and a fals justise.[2]
As shameful deeth as herte may devise

---

1. I.e., God's nails and blood.
2. The Host has been affected by the Physician's
sad tale of the Roman maiden Virginia, whose
great beauty caused a judge to attempt to obtain

her person by means of a trumped-up lawsuit in
which he connived with a "churl" who claimed
her as his slave; in order to preserve her chastity,
her father killed her.

5   Come to thise juges and hir advocats.
      Algate° this sely° maide is slain, allas!   *at any rate / innocent*
      Allas, too dere boughte she beautee!
      Wherfore I saye alday° that men may see   *always*
      The yiftes of Fortune and of Nature
10   Been cause of deeth to many a creature.
      As bothe yiftes that I speke of now,
      Men han ful ofte more for harm than prow.°   *benefit*
        "But trewely, myn owene maister dere,
      This is a pitous tale for to heere.
15   But nathelees, passe over, is no fors:[3]
      I praye to God to save thy gentil cors,°   *body*
      And eek thine urinals and thy jurdones,[4]
      Thyn ipocras and eek thy galiones,[5]
      And every boiste° ful of thy letuarye°—   *box / medicine*
20   God blesse hem, and oure lady Sainte Marye.
      So mote I theen,[6] thou art a propre man,
      And lik a prelat, by Saint Ronian![7]
      Saide I nat wel? I can nat speke in terme.[8]
      But wel I woot, thou doost° myn herte to erme°   *make / grieve*
25   That I almost have caught a cardinacle.[9]
      By corpus bones,[1] but if° I have triacle,°   *unless / medicine*
      Or elles a draughte of moiste° and corny° ale,   *fresh / malty*
      Or but I here anoon° a merye tale,   *at once*
      Myn herte is lost for pitee of this maide.
30   "Thou bel ami,[2] thou Pardoner," he saide,
      "Tel us som mirthe or japes° right anoon."   *jokes*
        "It shal be doon," quod he, "by Saint Ronion.
      But first," quod he, "here at this ale-stake[3]
      I wol bothe drinke and eten of a cake."°   *flat loaf of bread*
35   And right anoon thise gentils gan to crye,
      "Nay, lat him telle us of no ribaudye.°   *ribaldry*
      Tel us som moral thing that we may lere,°   *learn*
      Som wit,[4] and thanne wol we gladly heere."
        "I graunte, ywis,"° quod he, "but I moot thinke   *certainly*
40   Upon som honeste° thing whil that I drinke."   *decent*

The Prologue

      Lordinges—quod he—in chirches whan I preche,
      I paine me[5] to han° an hautein° speeche,   *have / loud*
      And ringe it out as round as gooth a belle,
      For I can al by rote[6] that I telle.
45   My theme is alway oon,[7] and evere was:

3. I.e., never mind.
4. Jordans (chamberpots): the Host is somewhat confused in his endeavor to use technical medical terms. "Urinals": vessels for examining urine.
5. A medicine, probably invented on the spot by the Host, named after Galen. "Ipocras": a medicinal drink named after Hippocrates.
6. So might I prosper.
7. St. Ronan or St. Ninian, with a possible play on "runnion" (sexual organ).
8. Speak in technical idiom.

9. Apparently a cardiac condition, confused in the Host's mind with a cardinal.
1. An illiterate oath, mixing "God's bones" with *corpus dei* ("God's body").
2. Fair friend.
3. Sign of a tavern.
4. I.e., something with significance.
5. Take pains.
6. I know all by heart.
7. I.e., the same. "Theme": biblical text on which the sermon is based.

Radix malorum est cupiditas.[8]
First I pronounce whennes° that I come,   whence
And thanne my bulles shewe I alle and some:[9]
Oure lige lordes seel on my patente,[1]
50   That shewe I first, my body to warente,°   keep safe
That no man be so bold, ne preest ne clerk,
Me to destourbe of Cristes holy werk.
And after that thanne telle I forth my tales[2]—
Bulles of popes and of cardinales,
55   Of patriarkes and bisshopes I shewe,
And in Latin I speke a wordes fewe,
To saffron with[3] my predicacioun,°   preaching
And for to stire hem to devocioun.
     Thanne shewe I forth my longe crystal stones,°   jars
60   Ycrammed ful of cloutes° and of bones   rags
Relikes been they, as weenen° they eechoon.   suppose
Thanne have I in laton° a shulder-boon   brass
Which that was of an holy Jewes sheep.
"Goode men," I saye, "take of my wordes keep:°   notice
65   If that this boon be wasshe° in any welle,   dipped
If cow, or calf, or sheep, or oxe swelle,
That any worm hath ete or worm ystonge,[4]
Take water of that welle and wassh his tonge,
And it is hool[5] anoon. And ferthermoor,
70   Of pokkes° and of scabbe and every soor°   pox, pustules / sore
Shal every sheep be hool that of this welle
Drinketh a draughte. Take keep eek° that I telle: also
If that the goode man that the beestes oweth°   owns
Wol every wike,° er° that the cok him croweth,   week / before
75   Fasting drinken of this welle a draughte—
As thilke° holy Jew oure eldres taughte—   that same
His beestes and his stoor° shal multiplye.   stock
     "And sire, also it heleth jalousye:
For though a man be falle in jalous rage,
80   Lat maken with this water his potage,°   soup
And nevere shal he more his wif mistriste,°   mistrust
Though he the soothe of hir defaute wiste,[6]
Al hadde she[7] taken preestes two or three.
     "Here is a mitein° eek that ye may see: mitten
85   He that his hand wol putte in this mitein
He shal have multiplying of his grain,
Whan he hath sowen, be it whete or otes—
So that he offre pens or elles grotes.[8]
     "Goode men and wommen, oo thing warne I you:
90   If any wight be in this chirche now
That hath doon sinne horrible, that he
Dar nat for shame of it yshriven° be,   confessed

---

8. Avarice is the root of evil (1 Timothy 6.10).
9. Each and every one. "Bulles": papal bulls, official documents.
1. I.e., the pope's or bishop's seal on my papal license.
2. I go on with my yarn.
3. To add spice to.

4. That has eaten any worm or been bitten by any snake.
5. I.e., sound.
6. Knew the truth of her infidelity.
7. Even if she had.
8. Pennies, groats, coins.

Or any womman, be she yong or old,
That hath ymaked hir housbonde cokewold,°   *cuckold*
95   Swich° folk shal have no power ne no grace   *such*
To offren to[9] my relikes in this place;
And whoso findeth him out of swich blame,
He wol come up and offre in Goddes name,
And I assoile° him by the auctoritee   *absolve*
100   Which that by bulle ygraunted was to me."
     By this gaude° have I wonne, yeer by yeer,   *trick*
An hundred mark[1] sith° I was pardoner.   *since*
I stonde lik a clerk in my pulpet,
And whan the lewed° peple is down yset,   *ignorant*
105   I preche so as ye han herd bifore,
And telle an hundred false japes° more.   *tricks*
Thanne paine I me[2] to strecche forth the nekke,
And eest and west upon the peple I bekke°   *nod*
As dooth a douve,° sitting on a berne;°   *dove / barn*
110   Mine handes and my tonge goon so yerne°   *fast*
That it is joye to see my bisinesse.
Of avarice and of swich cursednesse°   *sin*
Is al my preching, for to make hem free°   *generous*
To yiven hir pens, and namely° unto me,   *especially*
115   For myn entente is nat but for to winne,[3]
And no thing for correccion of sinne:
I rekke° nevere whan that they been beried°   *care / buried*
Though that hir soules goon a-blakeberied.[4]
For certes, many a predicacioun°   *sermon*
120   Comth ofte time of yvel entencioun:
Som for plesance of folk and flaterye,
To been avaunced° by ypocrisye,   *promoted*
And som for vaine glorye, and som for hate;
For whan I dar noon otherways debate,°   *fight*
125   Thanne wol I stinge him[5] with my tonge smerte°   *sharply*
In preching, so that he shal nat asterte°   *escape*
To been defamed falsly, if that he
Hath trespassed to my bretheren[6] or to me.
For though I telle nought his propre name,
130   Men shal wel knowe that it is the same
By signes and by othere circumstaunces.
Thus quite° I folk that doon us displesaunces;[7]   *pay back*
Thus spete° I out my venim under hewe°   *spit / false colors*
Of holinesse, to seeme holy and trewe.
135   But shortly myn entente I wol devise:°   *explain*
I preche of no thing but for coveitise;°   *covetousness*
Therfore my theme is yit and evere was
Radix malorum est cupiditas.
     Thus can I preche again that same vice
140   Which that I use, and that is avarice.
But though myself be gilty in that sinne,

---

9. To make gifts in reverence of.
1. Marks (pecuniary units).
2. I take pains.
3. My intent is only to make money.

4. Go blackberrying, i.e., go to hell.
5. An adversary critical of pardoners.
6. Injured my fellow pardoners.
7. Make trouble for us.

Yit can I make other folk to twinne°   *separate*
From avarice, and sore to repente—
But that is nat my principal entente:
145 I preche no thing but for coveitise.
Of this matere it oughte ynough suffise.
  Thanne telle I hem ensamples[8] many oon
Of olde stories longe time agoon,
For lewed° peple loven tales olde—   *ignorant*
150 Swiche° thinges can they wel reporte and holde.[9]   *such*
What, trowe° ye that whiles I may preche,   *believe*
And winne gold and silver for° I teche,   *because*
That I wol live in poverte wilfully?°   *voluntarily*
Nay, nay, I thoughte° it nevere, trewely,   *intended*
155 For I wol preche and begge in sondry landes;
I wol nat do no labour with mine handes,
Ne make baskettes and live therby,
By cause I wol nat beggen idelly.[1]
I wol none of the Apostles countrefete:°   *imitate*
160 I wol have moneye, wolle,° cheese, and whete, *wool*
Al were it[2] yiven of the pooreste page,
Or of the pooreste widwe in a village—
Al sholde hir children sterve[3] for famine.
Nay, I wol drinke licour of the vine
165 And have a joly wenche in every town.
But herkneth, lordinges, in conclusioun,
Youre liking° is that I shal telle a tale: *pleasure*
Now have I dronke a draughte of corny ale,
By God, I hope I shal you telle a thing
170 That shal by reson been at youre liking;
For though myself be a ful vicious man,
A moral tale yit I you telle can,
Which I am wont to preche for to winne.
Now holde youre pees, my tale I wol biginne.

The Tale

175 In Flandres whilom° was a compaignye   *once*
Of yonge folk that haunteden° folye—   *practiced*
As riot, hasard, stewes,[4] and tavernes,
Wher as with harpes, lutes, and giternes°   *guitars*
They daunce and playen at dees° bothe day and night, *dice*
180 And ete also and drinke over hir might,[5]
Thurgh which they doon the devel sacrifise
Within that develes temple in cursed wise
By superfluitee° abhominable.   *overindulgence*
Hir othes been so grete and so dampnable
185 That it is grisly for to heere hem swere:
Oure blessed Lordes body they totere[6]—

---

8. Exempla (stories illustrating moral principles).
9. Repeat and remember.
1. I.e., without profit.
2. Even though it were.
3. Even though her children should die.

4. Wild parties, gambling, brothels.
5. Beyond their capacity.
6. Tear apart (a reference to oaths sworn by parts of His body, such as "God's bones!" or "God's teeth!").

	Hem thoughte that Jewes rente° him nought ynough.	*tore*
	And eech of hem at otheres sinne lough.°	*laughed*
	And right anoon thanne comen tombesteres,°	*dancing girls*
190	Fetis° and smale,° and yonge frutesteres,[7]	*shapely / slender*
	Singeres with harpes, bawdes,° wafereres[8]—	*pimps*
	Whiche been the verray develes officeres,	
	To kindle and blowe the fir of lecherye	
	That is annexed unto glotonye:[9]	
195	The Holy Writ take I to my witnesse	
	That luxure° is in win and dronkenesse.	*lechery*
	Lo, how that dronken Lot[1] unkindely°	*unnaturally*
	Lay by his doughtres two unwitingly:	
	So dronke he was he niste° what he wroughte.°	*didn't know / did*
200	Herodes, who so wel the stories soughte,[2]	
	Whan he of win was repleet° at his feeste,	*filled*
	Right at his owene table he yaf his heeste°	*command*
	To sleen° the Baptist John, ful giltelees.	*slay*
	Senek[3] saith a good word doutelees:	
205	He saith he can no difference finde	
	Bitwixe a man that is out of his minde	
	And a man which that is dronkelewe,°	*drunken*
	But that woodnesse, yfallen in a shrewe,[4]	
	Persevereth lenger than dooth dronkenesse.	
210	O glotonye, ful of cursednesse!°	*wickedness*
	O cause first of oure confusioun!°	*downfall*
	O original of oure dampnacioun,°	*damnation*
	Til Crist hadde bought° us with his blood again!	*redeemed*
	Lo, how dere, shortly for to sayn,	
215	Abought° was thilke° cursed vilainye;	*paid for / that same*
	Corrupt was al this world for glotonye:	
	Adam oure fader and his wif also	
	Fro Paradis to labour and to wo	
	Were driven for that vice, it is no drede.°	*doubt*
220	For whil that Adam fasted, as I rede,	
	He was in Paradis; and whan that he	
	Eet° of the fruit defended° on a tree,	*ate / forbidden*
	Anoon he was out cast to wo and paine.	
	O glotonye, on thee wel oughte us plaine!°	*complain*
225	O, wiste a man[5] how manye maladies	
	Folwen of excesse and of glotonies,	
	He wolde been the more mesurable°	*moderate*
	Of his diete, sitting at his table.	
	Allas, the shorte throte, the tendre mouth,	
230	Maketh that eest and west and north and south,	
	In erthe, in air, in water, men to swinke,°	*work*
	To gete a gloton daintee mete° and drinke.	*food*
	Of this matere, O Paul, wel canstou trete:	
	"Mete unto wombe,° and wombe eek unto mete,	*belly*

---

7. Fruit-selling girls.
8. Girl cake vendors.
9. I.e., closely related to gluttony.
1. See Genesis 19.30–36.
2. For the story of Herod and St. John the Bap-

tist, see Mark 6.17–29. "Who so . . . soughte": i.e., whoever looked it up in the Gospel would find.
3. Seneca, the Roman Stoic philosopher.
4. But that madness, occurring in a wicked man.
5. If a man knew.

235 Shal God destroyen bothe," as Paulus saith.[6]
     Allas, a foul thing is it, by my faith,
     To saye this word, and fouler is the deede
     Whan man so drinketh of the white and rede[7]
     That of his throte he maketh his privee°   *toilet*
240 Thurgh thilke cursed superfluitee.°   *overindulgence*
        The Apostle[8] weeping saith ful pitously,
     "Ther walken manye of which you told have I—
     I saye it now weeping with pitous vois—
     They been enemies of Cristes crois,°   *cross*
245 Of whiche the ende is deeth—wombe is hir god!"[9]
     O wombe,° O bely, O stinking cod,°   *belly / bag*
     Fulfilled° of dong° and of corrupcioun!   *filled full / dung*
     At either ende of thee foul is the soun.°   *sound*
     How greet labour and cost is thee to finde!°   *provide for*
250 Thise cookes, how they stampe° and straine and grinde,   *pound*
     And turnen substance into accident[1]
     To fulfillen al thy likerous° talent!°   *greedy / appetite*
     Out of the harde bones knokke they
     The mary,° for they caste nought away   *marrow*
255 That may go thurgh the golet[2] softe and soote.°   *sweetly*
     Of spicerye° of leef and bark and roote   *spices*
     Shal been his sauce ymaked by delit,
     To make him yit a newer appetit.
     But certes, he that haunteth swiche delices°   *pleasures*
260 Is deed° whil that he liveth in tho° vices.   *dead / those*
        A lecherous thing is win, and dronkenesse
     Is ful of striving° and of wrecchednesse.   *quarreling*
     O dronke man, disfigured is thy face!
     Sour is thy breeth, foul artou to embrace!
265 And thurgh thy dronke nose seemeth the soun
     As though thou saidest ay,° "Sampsoun, Sampsoun."   *always*
     And yit, God woot,° Sampson drank nevere win.[3]   *knows*
     Thou fallest as it were a stiked swin;°   *stuck pig*
     Thy tonge is lost, and al thyn honeste cure,[4]
270 For dronkenesse is verray sepulture°   *burial*
     Of mannes wit° and his discrecioun.   *intelligence*
     In whom that drinke hath dominacioun
     He can no conseil° keepe, it is no drede.°   *secrets / doubt*
     Now keepe you fro the white and fro the rede—
275 And namely° fro the white win of Lepe[5]   *particularly*
     That is to selle in Fisshstreete or in Chepe:[6]
     The win of Spaine creepeth subtilly
     In othere wines growing faste° by,   *close*
     Of which ther riseth swich fumositee°   *heady fumes*
280 That whan a man hath dronken draughtes three

6. See 1 Corinthians 6.13.
7. I.e., white and red wines.
8. I.e., St. Paul.
9. See Philippians 3.18.
1. A philosophic joke, depending on the distinction between inner reality (substance) and outward appearance (accident).
2. Through the gullet.

3. Before Samson's birth an angel told his mother that he would be a Nazarite throughout his life; persons who took this vow took no strong drink.
4. Care for self-respect.
5. A town in Spain.
6. Fishstreet and Cheapside in the London market district.

And weeneth° that he be at hoom in Chepe, *supposes*
He is in Spaine, right at the town of Lepe,
Nat at The Rochele ne at Burdeux town;[7]
And thanne wol he sayn, "Sampsoun, Sampsoun."
285 But herkneth, lordinges, oo° word I you praye, *one*
That alle the soverein actes,[8] dar I saye,
Of victories in the Olde Testament,
Thurgh verray God that is omnipotent,
Were doon in abstinence and in prayere:
290 Looketh° the Bible and ther ye may it lere.° *behold / learn*
 Looke Attila, the grete conquerour,[9]
Deide° in his sleep with shame and dishonour, *died*
Bleeding at his nose in dronkenesse:
A capitain sholde live in sobrenesse.
295 And overal this, aviseth you[1] right wel
What was comanded unto Lamuel[2]—
Nat Samuel, but Lamuel, saye I—
Redeth the Bible and finde it expresly,
Of win-yiving° to hem that har[3] justise: *wine-serving*
300 Namore of this, for it may wel suffise.
 And now that I have spoken of glotonye,
Now wol I you defende° hasardrye:° *prohibit / gambling*
Hasard is verray moder° of lesinges,° *mother / lies*
And of deceite and cursed forsweringes,° *perjuries*
305 Blaspheme of Crist, manslaughtre, and wast° also *waste*
Of catel° and of time; and ferthermo, *property*
It is repreve° and contrarye of honour *disgrace*
For to been holden a commune hasardour,° *gambler*
And evere the hyer he is of estat
310 The more is he holden desolat.[4]
If that a prince useth hasardrye,
In alle governance and policye
He is, as by commune opinioun,
Yholde the lasse° in reputacioun. *less*
315 Stilbon, that was a wis embassadour,
Was sent to Corinthe in ful greet honour
Fro Lacedomye° to make hir alliaunce, *Sparta*
And whan he cam him happede° parchaunce *it happened*
That alle the gretteste° that were of that lond *greatest*
320 Playing at the hasard he hem foond,° *found*
For which as soone as it mighte be
He stal him[5] hoom again to his contree,
And saide, "Ther wol I nat lese° my name, *lose*
N'I wol nat take on me so greet defame° *dishonor*
325 You to allye unto none hasardours:
Sendeth othere wise embassadours,
For by my trouthe, me were levere[6] die

---

7. The Pardoner is joking about the illegal custom of adulterating fine wines of Bordeaux and La Rochelle with strong Spanish wine.
8. Distinguished deeds.
9. Attila was the leader of the Huns who almost captured Rome in the 5th century.
1. Consider.

2. Lemuel's mother told him that kings should not drink (Proverbs 31.4–5).
3. I.e., administer.
4. I.e., dissolute.
5. He stole away.
6. I had rather.

Than I you sholde to hasardours allye.
For ye that been so glorious in honours
330 Shal nat allye you with hasardours
As by my wil, ne as by my tretee."°   *treaty*
This wise philosophre, thus saide he.
    Looke eek that to the king Demetrius
The King of Parthes,° as the book[7] saith us,   *Parthians*
335 Sente him a paire of dees° of gold in scorn,   *dice*
For he hadde used hasard therbiforn,
For which he heeld his glorye or his renown
At no value or reputacioun.
Lordes may finden other manere play
340 Honeste° ynough to drive the day away.   *honorable*
    Now wol I speke of othes false and grete
A word or two, as olde bookes trete:
    Greet swering is a thing abhominable,
And fals swering is yit more reprevable.°   *reprehensible*
345 The hye God forbad swering at al—
Witnesse on Mathew.[8] But in special
Of swering saith the holy Jeremie,[9]
"Thou shalt swere sooth thine othes and nat lie,
And swere in doom° and eek in rightwisnesse,°   *equity / righteousness*
350 But idel swering is a cursednesse."°   *wickedness*
    Biholde and see that in the firste Table[1]
Of hye Goddes heestes° honorable   *commandments*
How that the seconde heeste of him is this:
"Take nat my name in idel or amis."
355 Lo, rather° he forbedeth swich swering   *sooner*
Than homicide, or many a cursed thing.
I saye that as by ordre thus it stondeth—
This knoweth that[2] his heestes understondeth
How that the seconde heeste of God is that.
360 And fertherover,° I wol thee telle al plat°   *moreover / plain*
That vengeance shal nat parten° from his hous   *depart*
That of his othes is too outrageous.
"By Goddes precious herte!" and "By his nailes!"°   *fingernails*
And "By the blood of Crist that is in Hailes,[3]
365 Sevene is my chaunce,° and thyn is cink and traye!"[4]   *winning number*
"By Goddes armes, if thou falsly playe
This daggere shal thurghout thyn herte go!"
This fruit cometh of the bicche bones[5] two—
Forswering, ire, falsnesse, homicide.
370 Now for the love of Crist that for us dyde,°   *died*
Lete° youre othes bothe grete and smale.   *leave*
But sires, now wol I telle forth my tale.
    Thise riotoures° three of whiche I telle,   *revelers*
Longe erst er prime[6] ronge of any belle,

---

7. The book that relates this and the previous incident is the *Policraticus* of the 12th-century Latin writer John of Salisbury.
8. "But I say unto you, Swear not at all" (Matthew 5.34).
9. Jeremiah 4.2.
1. I.e., the first four of the Ten Commandments, which specify duties humankind owes to God.
2. I.e., he that.
3. An abbey in Gloucestershire supposed to possess some of Christ's blood.
4. Five and three.
5. I.e., damned dice.
6. Long before 9 A.M.

375 Were set hem in a taverne to drinke,
And as they sat they herde a belle clinke
Biforn a cors° was caried to his grave.   *corpse*
That oon of hem gan callen to his knave:°   *servant*
Go bet,"[7] quod he, "and axe° redily°   *ask / promptly*
380 What cors is this that passeth heer forby,
And looke° that thou reporte his name weel."°   *be sure / well*
    "Sire," quod this boy, "it needeth neveradeel.[8]
It was me told er ye cam heer two houres.
He was, pardee,° an old felawe of youres,   *by God*
385 And sodeinly he was yslain tonight,°   *last night*
Fordronke° as he sat on his bench upright;   *very drunk*
Ther cam a privee° thief men clepeth° Deeth,   *stealthy / call*
That in this contree al the peple sleeth,°   *slays*
And with his spere he smoot his herte atwo,
390 And wente his way withouten wordes mo.
He hath a thousand slain this° pestilence.   *during this*
And maister, er ye come in his presence,
Me thinketh that it were necessarye
For to be war of swich an adversarye;
395 Beeth redy for to meete him everemore:
Thus taughte me my dame.° I saye namore."   *mother*
    "By Sainte Marye," saide this taverner,
"The child saith sooth, for he hath slain this yeer,
Henne° over a mile, within a greet village,   *hence*
400 Bothe man and womman, child and hine[9] and page.
I trowe° his habitacion be there.   *believe*
To been avised° greet wisdom it were   *wary*
Er that he dide a man a dishonour."
    "Ye, Goddes armes," quod this riotour,
405 "Is it swich peril with him for to meete?
I shal him seeke by way and eek by streete,[1]
I make avow to Goddes digne° bones.   *worthy*
Herkneth, felawes, we three been alle ones:°   *of one mind*
Lat eech of us holde up his hand to other
410 And eech of us bicome otheres brother,
And we wol sleen this false traitour Deeth.
He shal be slain, he that so manye sleeth,
By Goddes dignitee, er it be night."
    Togidres han thise three hir trouthes plight[2]
415 To live and dien eech of hem with other,
As though he were his owene ybore° brother.   *born*
And up they sterte,° al dronken in this rage,   *started*
And forth they goon towardes that village
Of which the taverner hadde spoke biforn,
420 And many a grisly ooth thanne han they sworn,
And Cristes blessed body they torente:°   *tore apart*
Deeth shal be deed° if that they may him hente.°   *dead / catch*
    Whan they han goon nat fully half a mile,

7. Better, i.e., quick.   1. By highway and byway.
8. It isn't a bit necessary.   2. Pledged their words of honor.
9. Farm laborer.

Right as they wolde han treden° over a stile, *stepped*
425 An old man and a poore with hem mette;
This olde man ful mekely hem grette,° *greeted*
And saide thus, "Now lordes, God you see."[3]

  The pruddeste° of thise riotoures three *proudest*
Answerde again, "What, carl° with sory grace, *fellow*
430 Why artou al forwrapped° save thy face? *muffled up*
Why livestou so longe in so greet age?"

  This olde man gan looke in his visage,
And saide thus, "For° I ne can nat finde *because*
A man, though that I walked into Inde,° *India*
435 Neither in citee ne in no village,
That wolde chaunge his youthe for myn age;
And therefore moot° I han myn age stille, *must*
As longe time as it is Goddes wille.

  "Ne Deeth, allas, ne wol nat have my lif.
440 Thus walke I lik a resteleees caitif,° *wretch*
And on the ground which is my modres° gate *mother's*
I knokke with my staf bothe erly and late,
And saye, 'Leve° moder, leet me in: *dear*
Lo, how I vanisshe, flessh and blood and skin.
445 Allas, whan shal my bones been at reste?
Moder, with you wolde I chaunge° my cheste[4] *exchange*
That in my chambre longe time hath be,
Ye, for an haire-clour[5] to wrappe me.'
But yit to me she wol nat do that grace,
450 For which ful pale and welked° is my face. *withered*
But sires, to you it is no curteisye
To speken to an old man vilainye,° *rudeness*
But° he trespasse° in word or elles in deede. *unless / offend*
In Holy Writ ye may yourself wel rede,
455 'Agains[6] an old man, hoor° upon his heed, *hoar*
Ye shall arise.'[7] Wherfore I yive you reed,° *advice*
Ne dooth unto an old man noon harm now,
Namore than that ye wolde men dide to you
In age, if that ye so longe abide.[8]
460 And God be with you wher ye go° or ride: *walk*
I moot go thider as I have to go."

  "Nay, olde cherl, by God thou shalt nat so,"
Saide this other hasardour anoon.
"Thou partest nat so lightly,° by Saint John! *easily*
465 Thou speke° right now of thilke traitour Deeth, *spoke*
That in this contree alle oure freendes sleeth:
Have here my trouthe, as thou art his espye,° *spy*
Tel wher he is, or thou shalt it abye,° *pay for*
By God and by the holy sacrament!
470 For soothly thou art oon of his assent[9]
To sleen us yonge folk, thou false thief."

  "Now sires," quod he, "if that ye be so lief° *anxious*

---

3. May God protect you.
4. Chest for one's belongings, used here as the symbol for life—or perhaps a coffin.
5. Haircloth, for a winding sheet.

6. In the presence of.
7. Cf. Leviticus 19.32.
8. I.e., if you live so long.
9. I.e., one of his party.

To finde Deeth, turne up this crooked way,
For in that grove I lafte° him, by my fay,°   *left / faith*
475 Under a tree, and ther he wol abide:
Nat for youre boost° he wol him no thing hide.   *boast*
See ye that ook?° Right ther ye shal him finde.   *oak*
God save you, that boughte again[1] mankinde,
And you amende." Thus saide this olde man.
480 And everich of thise riotoures ran
Til he cam to that tree, and ther they founde
Of florins° fine of gold ycoined rounde   *coins*
Wel neigh an eighte busshels as hem thoughte—
Ne lenger thanne after Deeth they soughte,
485 But eech of hem so glad was of the sighte,
For that the florins been so faire and brighte,
That down they sette hem by this precious hoord.
The worste of hem he spak the firste word:
 "Bretheren," quod he, "take keep° what that I saye: *heed*
490 My wit is greet though that I bourde° and playe.   *joke*
This tresor hath Fortune unto us yiven
In mirthe and jolitee oure lif to liven,
And lightly° as it cometh so wol we spende.   *easily*
Ey, Goddes precious dignitee, who wende[2]
495 Today that we sholde han so fair a grace?
But mighte this gold be caried fro this place
Hoom to myn hous—or elles unto youres—
For wel ye woot that al this gold is oures—
Thanne were we in heigh felicitee.
500 But trewely, by daye it mighte nat be:
Men wolde sayn that we were theves stronge,°   *flagrant*
And for oure owene tresor doon us honge.[3]
This tresor moste ycaried be by nighte,
As wisely and as slyly as it mighte.
505 Therefore I rede° that cut° amonges us alle   *advise / straws*
Be drawe, and lat see wher the cut wol falle;
And he that hath the cut with herte blithe
Shal renne° to the town, and that ful swithe,°   *run / quickly*
And bringe us breed and win ful prively;
510 And two of us shal keepen° subtilly   *guard*
This tresor wel, and if he wol nat tarye,
Whan it is night we wol this tresor carye
By oon assent wher as us thinketh best."
That oon of hem the cut broughte in his fest°   *fist*
515 And bad hem drawe and looke wher it wol falle;
And it fil° on the yongeste of hem alle,   *fell*
And forth toward the town he wente anoon.
And also° soone as that he was agoon,°   *as / gone away*
That oon of hem spak thus unto that other:
520 "Thou knowest wel thou art my sworen brother;
Thy profit wol I telle thee anoon:
Thou woost wel that oure felawe is agoon,

1. Redeemed.   3. Have us hanged.
2. Who would have supposed.

And here is gold, and that ful greet plentee,
That shall departed° been among us three. *divided*
525 But nathelees, if I can shape° it so *arrange*
That it departed were among us two,
Hadde I nat doon a freendes turn to thee?"
   That other answerde, "I noot[4] how that may be:
He woot that the gold is with us twaye.
530 What shal we doon? What shal we to him saye?"
   "Shal it be conseil?"[5] saide the firste shrewe.° *villain*
"And I shal telle in a wordes fewe
What we shul doon, and bringe it wel aboute."
   "I graunte," quod that other, "out of doute,
535 That by my trouthe I wol thee nat biwraye."° *expose*
   "Now," quod the firste, "thou woost wel we be twaye,
And two of us shal strenger° be than oon: *stronger*
Looke whan that he is set that right anoon
Aris as though thou woldest with him playe,
540 And I shal rive° him thurgh the sides twaye, *pierce*
Whil that thou strugelest with him as in game,
And with thy daggere looke thou do the same;
And thanne shal al this gold departed be,
My dere freend, bitwixe thee and me.
545 Thanne we may bothe oure lustes° al fulfille, *desires*
And playe at dees° right at oure owene wille." *dice*
And thus accorded been thise shrewes twaye
To sleen the thridde, as ye han herd me saye.
   This yongeste, which that wente to the town,
550 Ful ofte in herte he rolleth up and down
The beautee of thise florins newe and brighte.
"O Lord," quod he, "if so were that I mighte
Have al this tresor to myself allone,
Ther is no man that liveth under the trone° *throne*
555 Of God that sholde live so merye as I."
And at the laste the feend oure enemy
Putte in his thought that he sholde poison beye,° *buy*
With which he mighte sleen his felawes twaye—
Forwhy° the feend° foond him in swich livinge *because / devil*
560 That he hadde leve° him to sorwe bringe:[6] *permission*
For this was outrely° his fulle entente, *plainly*
To sleen hem bothe, and nevere to repente.
   And forth he gooth—no lenger wolde he tarye—
Into the town unto a pothecarye,° *apothecary*
565 And prayed him that he him wolde selle
Som poison that he mighte, his rattes quelle,° *kill*
And eek ther was a polcat[7] in his hawe° *yard*
That, as he saide, his capons hadde yslawe,° *slain*
And fain he wolde wreke him[8] if he mighte
570 On vermin that destroyed him[9] by nighte.
   The pothecarye answerde, "And thou shalt have

---

4. Don't know.
5. A secret.
6. Christian doctrine teaches that the devil may not tempt people except with God's permission.
7. A weasellike animal.
8. He would gladly avenge himself.
9. I.e., were ruining his farming.

A thing that, also° God my soule save,   *as*

In al this world there is no creature

That ete or dronke hath of this confiture°   *mixture*

575 Nat but the mountance° of a corn° of whete—   *amount / grain*

That he ne shal his lif anoon forlete.°   *lose*

Ye, sterve° he shal, and that in lasse° while   *die / less*

Than thou wolt goon a paas[1] nat but a mile,

The poison is so strong and violent."

580 This cursed man hath in his hand yhent°   *taken*

This poison in a box and sith° he ran   *then*

Into the nexte streete unto a man

And borwed of him large botels three,

And in the two his poison poured he—

585 The thridde he kepte clene for his drinke,

For al the night he shoop him[2] for to swinke°   *work*

In carying of the gold out of that place.

And whan this riotour with sory grace

Hadde filled with win his grete botels three,

590 To his felawes again repaireth he.

    What needeth it to sermone of it more?

For right as they had cast° his deeth bifore,   *plotted*

Right so they han him slain, and that anoon.

And whan that this was doon, thus spak that oon:

595 "Now lat us sitte and drinke and make us merye,

And afterward we wol his body berye."°   *bury*

And with that word it happed him par cas[3]

To take the botel ther the poison was,

And drank, and yaf his felawe drinke also,

600 For which anoon they storven° bothe two.   *died*

    But certes I suppose that Avicen

Wroot nevere in no canon ne in no *fen*[4]

Mo wonder signes[5] of empoisoning

Than hadde thise wrecches two er hir ending:

605 Thus ended been thise homicides two,

And eek the false empoisonere also.

    O cursed sinne of alle cursednesse!

O traitours homicide, O wikkednesse!

O glotonye, luxure,° and hasardrye!   *lechery*

610 Thou blasphemour of Crist with vilainye

And othes grete of usage° and of pride!   *habit*

Allas, mankinde, how may it bitide

That to thy Creatour which that thee wroughte,

And with his precious herte blood thee boughte,°   *redeemed*

615 Thou art so fals and so unkinde,° allas?   *unnatural*

    Now goode men, God foryive you youre trespas,

And ware° you fro the sinne of avarice: *guard*

Myn holy pardon may you alle warice°—   *save*

So that ye offre nobles or sterlinges,[6]

620 Or elles silver brooches, spoones, ringes.

---

1. Take a walk.
2. He was preparing.
3. By chance.
4. The *Canon of Medicine*, by Avicenna, an

11th-century Arabic philosopher, was divided
into sections called "fens."
5. More wonderful symptoms.
6. "Nobles" and "sterlinges" were valuable coins.

Boweth your heed under this holy bulle!
Cometh up, ye wives, offreth of youre wolle!°   wool
Youre name I entre here in my rolle: anoon
Into the blisse of hevene shul ye goon.
625   I you assoile° by myn heigh power—   absolve
Ye that wol offre—as clene and eek as cleer
As ye were born.—And lo, sires, thus I preche.
And Jesu Crist that is oure soules leeche°   physician
So graunte you his pardon to receive,
630   For that is best—I wol you nat deceive.

The Epilogue

"But sires, oo word forgat I in my tale:
I have relikes and pardon in my male°   bag
As faire as any man in Engelond,
Whiche were me yiven by the Popes hond.
635   If any of you wol of devocioun
Offren and han myn absolucioun,
Come forth anoon, and kneeleth here adown,
And mekely receiveth my pardoun,
Or elles taketh pardon as ye wende,°   ride along
640   Al newe and fressh at every miles ende—
So that ye offre alway newe and newe[7]
Nobles or pens whiche that be goode and trewe.
It is an honour to everich° that is heer   everyone
That ye have a suffisant° pardoner   competent
645   T'assoile you in contrees as ye ride,
For aventures° whiche that may bitide: accidents
Paraventure ther may falle oon or two
Down of his hors and breke his nekke atwo;
Looke which a suretee° is it to you alle   safeguard
650   That I am in youre felaweshipe yfalle
That may assoile you, bothe more and lasse,[8]
Whan that the soule shal fro the body passe.
I rede° that oure Hoste shal biginne,   advise
For he is most envoluped° in sinne.   involved
655   Com forth, sire Host, and offre first anoon,
And thou shalt kisse the relikes everichoon,°   each one
Ye, for a grote: unbokele° anoon thy purs."   unbuckle
"Nay, nay," quod he, "thanne have I Cristes curs!
Lat be," quod he, "it shal nat be, so theech!°   may I prosper
660   Thou woldest make me kisse thyn olde breech°   breeches
And swere it were a relik of a saint,
Though it were with thy fundament° depeint.°   anus / stained
But, by the crois which that Sainte Elaine foond,[9]
I wolde I hadde thy coilons° in myn hond,   testicles
665   In stede of relikes or of saintuarye.°   relic-box
Lat cutte hem of: I wol thee helpe hem carye.

---

7. Over and over.
8. Both high and low (i.e., everybody).
9. I.e., by the cross that St. Helena found. Helena, mother of Constantine the Great, was
reputed to have found the cross on which Christ
was crucified.

They shal be shrined in an hogges tord."°   turd
This Pardoner answerde nat a word:
So wroth he was no word ne wolde he saye.
670   "Now," quod oure Host, "I wol no lenger playe
With thee, ne with noon other angry man."
But right anoon the worthy Knight bigan,
Whan that he sawgh that al the peple lough,°   laughed
"Namore of this, for it is right ynough.
675   Sire Pardoner, be glad and merye of cheere,
And ye, sire Host that been to me so dere,
I praye you that ye kisse the Pardoner,
And Pardoner, I praye thee, draw thee neer,
And as we diden lat us laughe and playe."
680   Anoon they kiste and riden forth hir waye.

The Nun's Priest's Tale

In the framing story, *The Nun's Priest's Tale* is linked to a dramatic exchange that follows *The Monk's Tale*. The latter consists of brief tragedies, the common theme of which is the fall of famous men and one woman, most of whom are rulers, through the reversals of Fortune. Like *The Knight's Tale*, this was probably an earlier work of Chaucer's, one that he never finished. As the Monk's tragedies promise to go on and on monotonously, the Knight interrupts and politely tells the Monk that his tragedies are too painful. The Host chimes in to say that the tragedies are "nat worth a botterflye" and asks the Monk to try another subject, but the Monk is offended and refuses. The Host then turns to the Nun's Priest, that is, the priest who is accompanying the Prioress. The three priests said in *The General Prologue* to have been traveling with her have apparently been reduced to one.

The Nun's Priest's Tale is an example of the literary genre known as the "animal fable," familiar from the fables of Aesop in which animals, behaving like human beings, point to a moral. In the Middle Ages fables often functioned as elementary texts to teach boys Latin. Marie de France's fables in French are the earliest known vernacular translations. This particular fable derives from an episode in the French *Roman de Renard*, a "beast epic," which satirically represents a feudal animal society ruled over by Noble the Lion. Reynard the Fox is a wily trickster hero who is constantly preying upon and outwitting the other animals, although sometimes Reynard himself is outwitted by one of his victims.

In *The Nun's Priest's Tale*, morals proliferate: both the priest-narrator and his hero, Chauntecleer the rooster, spout examples, learned allusions, proverbs, and sententious generalizations, often in highly inflated rhetoric. The simple beast fable is thus inflated into a delightful satire of learning and moralizing and of the pretentious rhetoric by which medieval writers sometimes sought to elevate their works. Among them, we may include Chaucer himself, who in this tale seems to be making affectionate fun of some of his own works, like the tragedies which became *The Monk's Tale*.

A poore widwe somdeel stape° in age   *advanced*
Was whilom° dwelling in a narwe¹ cotage,   *once upon a time*
Biside a grove, stonding in a dale:
This widwe of which I telle you my tale,
5   Sin thilke° day that she was last a wif,   *that same*

---

1. I.e., small.

In pacience ladde° a ful simple lif.　　　　　　　　　　*led*
For litel was hir catel° and hir rente,°　　　*property / income*
By housbondrye° of swich as God hire sente　　　*economy*
She foond° hirself and eek hir doughtren two.　　　*provided for*
10　Three large sowes hadde she and namo,
Three kin,° and eek a sheep that highte° Malle.　　*cows / was called*
Ful sooty² was hir bowr° and eek hir halle.　　　*bedroom*
In which she eet ful many a sclendre° meel;　　　*scanty*
Of poinant° sauce hire needed neveradeel:°　　*pungent / not a bit*
15　No daintee morsel passed thurgh hir throte—
Hir diete was accordant to hir cote.°　　　　　　　*cottage*
Repleccioun° ne made hire nevere sik:　　　　　　*overeating*
Attempre° diete was al hir physik,°　　　*moderate / medicine*
And exercise and hertes suffisaunce.°　　　　　*contentment*
20　The goute lette hire nothing for to daunce,³
N'apoplexye shente° nat hir heed.°　　　　　　　*hurt / head*
No win ne drank she, neither whit ne reed:°　　　　*red*
Hir boord° was served most with whit and blak,⁴　　　*table*
Milk and brown breed, in which she foond no lak;°　　*found no fault*
25　Seind° bacon, and somtime an ey° or twaye,　　*Broiled / egg*
For she was as it were a manere daye.⁵
A yeerd° she hadde, enclosed al withoute　　　　　　*yard*
With stikkes, and a drye dich aboute,
In which she hadde a cok heet° Chauntecleer:　　　*named*
30　In al the land of crowing nas° his peer.　　　　*was not*
His vois was merier than the merye orgon
On massedayes that in the chirche goon;⁶
Wel sikerer⁷ was his crowing in his logge°　　　　*dwelling*
Than is a clok or an abbeye orlogge;°　　　　　*timepiece*
35　By nature he knew eech ascensioun
Of th'equinoxial⁸ in thilke town:
For whan degrees fifteene were ascended,
Thanne crew° he that it mighte nat been amended.°　*crowed / improved*
His comb was redder than the fin coral,
40　And batailed° as it were a castel wal;　　　　*battlemented*
His bile° was blak, and as the jeet° it shoon;　　　*bill / jet*
Like asure⁹ were his legges and his toon;°　　　　*toes*
His nailes whitter° than the lilye flowr,　　　　　*whiter*
And lik the burned° gold was his colour.　　　　*burnished*
45　This gentil° cok hadde in his governaunce　　　*noble*
Sevene hennes for to doon al his plesaunce,°　　　*pleasure*
Whiche were his sustres and his paramours,¹
And wonder like to him as of colours;
Of whiche the faireste hewed° on hir throte　　　*colored*
50　Was cleped° faire damoisele Pertelote:　　　　*called*
Curteis she was, discreet, and debonaire,°　　　　*meek*
And compaignable,° and bar° hirself so faire,　*companionable / bore*

2. I.e., her cottage lacked a chimney.
3. The gout didn't hinder her at all from dancing.
4. I.e., milk and bread.
5. I.e., a kind of dairywoman.
6. I.e., is played.
7. More reliable.
8. I.e., he knew by instinct each step in the pro-

gression of the celestial equator. The celestial equator was thought to make a 360° rotation around the earth every twenty-four hours; therefore, a progression of 15° would be equal to the passage of an hour (line 37).
9. Blue (lapis lazuli).
1. His sisters and his mistresses.

Sin thilke day that she was seven night old,
That trewely she hath the herte in hold
55 Of Chauntecleer, loken° in every lith.°   *locked / limb*
He loved hire so that wel was him therwith.[2]
But swich a joye was it to heere hem singe,
Whan that the brighte sonne gan to springe,
In sweete accord *My Lief is Faren in Londe*[3]—
60 For thilke time, as I have understonde,
Beestes and briddes couden speke and singe.
   And so bifel that in a daweninge,
As Chauntecleer among his wives alle
Sat on his perche that was in the halle,
65 And next him sat this faire Pertelote,
This Chauntecleer gan gronen in his throte,
As man that in his dreem is drecched° sore.   *troubled*
   And whan that Pertelote thus herde him rore,°   *roar*
She was agast, and saide, "Herte dere,
70 What aileth you to grone in this manere?
Ye been a verray slepere,[4] fy, for shame!"
   And he answerde and saide thus, "Madame,
I praye you that ye take it nat agrief.°   *amiss*
By God, me mette I was in swich meschief[5]
75 Right now, that yit myn herte is sore afright.
Now God," quod he, "my swevene recche aright,[6]
And keepe my body out of foul prisoun!
Me mette° how that I romed up and down   *dreamed*
Within oure yeerd, wher as I sawgh a beest,
80 Was lik an hound and wolde han maad arrest[7]
Upon my body, and han had me deed.[8]
His colour was bitwixe yelow and reed,
And tipped was his tail and bothe his eres
With blak, unlik the remenant° of his heres;°   *rest / hairs*
85 His snoute smal, with glowing yën twaye.
Yit of his look for fere almost I deye:°   *die*
This caused me my groning, doutelees."
   "Avoi,"° quod she, "fy on you, hertelees!°   *fie / coward*
Allas," quod she, "for by that God above,
90 Now han ye lost myn herte and al my love!
I can nat love a coward, by my faith.
For certes, what so any womman saith,
We alle desiren, if it mighte be,
To han housbondes hardy, wise, and free,°   *generous*
95 And secree,° and no nigard,° ne no fool,   *discreet / miser*
Ne him that is agast of every tool,°   *weapon*
Ne noon avauntour.° By that God above,   *boaster*
How dorste° ye sayn for shame unto youre love   *dare*
That any thing mighte make you aferd?
100 Have ye no mannes herte and han a beerd?°   *beard*

---

2. That he was well contented.
3. "My Love Has Gone Away," a popular song of
the time.
4. Sound sleeper.
5. I dreamed that I was in such misfortune.

6. Interpret my dream correctly (i.e., in an auspicious manner).
7. Would have laid hold.
8. I.e., killed me.

Allas, and conne° ye been agast of swevenes?°   *can / dreams*
No thing, God woot, but vanitee⁹ in swevene is!
Swevenes engendren of replexiouns,¹
And ofte of fume° and of complexiouns,° *gas / bodily humors*
105 Whan humours been too habundant in a wight.²
Certes, this dreem which ye han met° tonight   *dreamed*
Comth of the grete superfluitee
Of youre rede colera,³ pardee,
Which causeth folk to dreden° in hir dremes   *fear*
110 Of arwes,° and of fir with rede lemes,° *arrows / flames*
Of rede beestes, that they wol hem bite,
Of contek,° and of whelpes grete and lite⁴—   *strife*
Right° as the humour of malencplye⁵   *just*
Causeth ful many a man in sleep to crye
115 For fere of blake beres° or boles° blake, *bears / bulls*
Or elles blake develes wol hem take.
Of othere humours coude I tell also
That werken many a man in sleep ful wo,
But I wol passe as lightly° as I can.   *quickly*
120 Lo, Caton,⁶ which that was so wis a man,
Saide he nat thus? 'Ne do no fors of⁷ dremes.'
Now, sire," quod she, "whan we flee fro the bemes,⁸
For Goddes love, as take som laxatif.
Up° peril of my soule and of my lif,   *upon*
125 I conseile you the beste, I wol nat lie,
That bothe of colere and of malencolye
Ye purge you; and for° ye shal nat tarye, *in order that*
Though in this town is noon apothecarye,
I shal myself to herbes techen you,
130 That shal been for youre hele° and for youre prow,° *health / benefit*
And in oure yeerd tho° herbes shal I finde,   *those*
The whiche han of hir propretee by kinde°   *nature*
To purge you binethe and eek above.
Foryet° nat this, for Goddes owene love.   *forget*
135 Ye been ful colerik° of complexioun;   *bilious*
Ware° the sonne in his ascencioun   *beware that*
Ne finde you nat repleet° of humours hote;° *filled / hot*
And if it do, I dar wel laye° a grote   *bet*
That ye shul have a fevere terciane,⁹
140 Or an agu° that may be youre bane.° *ague / death*
A day or two ye shul han digestives
Of wormes, er° ye take youre laxatives   *before*
Of lauriol, centaure, and fumetere,¹
Or elles of ellebor° that groweth there,   *hellebore*
145 Of catapuce, or of gaitres beries,²

9. I.e., empty illusion.
1. Dreams have their origin in overeating.
2. I.e., when humors (bodily fluids) are too abundant in a person. Pertelote's diagnosis is based on the familiar concept that an excess of one of the bodily humors in a person affected his or her temperament (see p. 204, n. 8).
3. Red bile.
4. And of big and little dogs.
5. I.e., black bile.

6. Dionysius Cato, supposed author of a book of maxims used in elementary education.
7. Pay no attention to.
8. Fly down from the rafters.
9. Tertian (recurring every other day).
1. Of laureole, centaury, and fumitory. These, and the herbs mentioned in the next lines, were all common medieval medicines used as cathartics.
2. Of caper berry or of gaiter berry.

Of herb-ive° growing in oure yeerd ther merye is[3]—   *herb ivy*
Pekke hem right up as they growe and ete hem in.
Be merye, housbonde, for youre fader° kin!   *father's*
Dredeth no dreem: I can saye you namore."
150   "Madame," quod he, "graunt mercy of youre lore,[4]
But nathelees, as touching daun° Catoun,   *master*
That hath of wisdom swich a greet renown,
Though that he bad no dremes for to drede,
By God, men may in olde bookes rede
155   Of many a man more of auctoritee°   *authority*
Than evere Caton was, so mote I thee,°   *prosper*
That al the revers sayn of his sentence,°   *opinion*
And han wel founden by experience
That dremes been significaciouns
160   As wel of joye as tribulaciouns
That folk enduren in this lif present.
Ther needeth make of this noon argument:
The verray preve[5] sheweth it in deede.
     "Oon of the gretteste auctour[6] that men rede
165   Saith thus, that whilom two felawes wente
On pilgrimage in a ful good entente,
And happed so they comen in a town,
Wher as ther was swich congregacioun
Of peple, and eek so strait of herbergage,[7]
170   That they ne founde as muche as oo cotage
In which they bothe mighte ylogged° be;   *lodged*
Wherfore they mosten° of necessitee   *must*
As for that night departe° compaignye.   *part*
And eech of hem gooth to his hostelrye,
175   And took his logging as it wolde falle.°   *befall*
That oon of hem was logged in a stalle,
Fer° in a yeerd, with oxen of the plough;   *far away*
That other man was logged wel ynough,
As was his aventure° or his fortune,   *lot*
180   That us governeth alle as in commune.
And so bifel that longe er it were day,
This man mette° in his bed, ther as he lay,   *dreamed*
How that his felawe gan upon him calle,
And saide, 'Allas, for in an oxes stalle
185   This night I shal be mordred° ther I lie!   *murdered*
Now help me, dere brother, or I die!
In alle haste com to me,' he saide.
     "This man out of his sleep for fere abraide,°   *started up*
But whan that he was wakened of his sleep,
190   He turned him and took of this no keep:°   *heed*
Him thoughte his dreem nas but a vanitee.°   *illusion*
Thus twies in his sleeping dremed he,
And atte thridde time yit his felawe.
Cam, as him thoughte, and saide, 'I am now slawe:°   *slain*

---

3. Where it is pleasant.
4. Many thanks for your instruction.
5. Actual experience.

6. I.e., one of the greatest authors (perhaps Cicero or Valerius Maximus).
7. And also such a shortage of lodging.

195 Bihold my bloody woundes deepe and wide.
Axis up erly in the morwe tide,[8]
And atte west gate of the town,' quod he,
'A carte ful of dong° ther shaltou see,   *dung*
In which my body is hid ful prively:
200 Do thilke carte arresten boldely.[9]
My gold caused my mordre, sooth to sayn'
—And tolde him every point how he was slain,
With a ful pitous face, pale of hewe.
And truste wel, his dreem he foond° ful trewe,   *found*
205 For on the morwe° as soone as it was day,   *morning*
To his felawes in° he took the way,   *lodging*
And whan that he cam to this oxes stalle,
After his felawe he bigan to calle.
  "The hostiler° answerde him anoon,   *innkeeper*
210 And saide, 'Sire, youre felawe is agoon:°   *gone away*
As soone as day he wente out of the town.'
  "This man gan fallen in suspecioun,
Remembring on his dremes that he mette;°   *dreamed*
And forth he gooth, no lenger wolde he lette,°   *tarry*
215 Unto the west gate of the town, and foond
A dong carte, wente as it were to donge° lond,   *put manure on*
That was arrayed in that same wise
As ye han herd the dede° man devise;   *dead*
And with an hardy herte he gan to crye,
220 'Vengeance and justice of this felonye!
My felawe mordred is this same night,
And in this carte he lith° gaping upright!°   *lies / on his back*
I crye out on the ministres,' quod he,
'That sholde keepe and rulen this citee.
225 Harrow,° allas, here lith my felawe slain!'   *help*
What sholde I more unto this tale sayn?
The peple up sterte° and caste the carte to grounde,   *started*
And in the middel of the dong they founde
The dede man that mordred was al newe.[1]
230   "O blisful God that art so just and trewe,
Lo, how that thou biwrayest° mordre alway!   *disclose*
Mordre wol out, that see we day by day:
Mordre is so wlatsom° and abhominable   *loathsome*
To God that is so just and resonable,
235 That he ne wol nat suffre it heled° be,   *concealed*
Though it abide a yeer or two or three.
Mordre wol out: this my conclusioun.
And right anoon ministres of that town
Han hent° the cartere and so sore him pined,[2]   *seized*
240 And eek the hostiler so sore engined,°   *racked*
That they biknewe° hir wikkednesse anoon,   *confessed*
And were anhanged° by the nekke boon.   *hanged*
Here may men seen that dremes been to drede.[3]

---

8. In the morning.
9. Boldly have this same cart seized.
1. Recently.

2. Tortured.
3. Worthy of being feared.

"And certes, in the same book I rede—
245 Right in the nexte chapitre after this—
I gabbe° nat, so have I joye or blis—   *lie*
Two men that wolde han passed over see
For certain cause into a fer contree,
If that the wind ne hadde been contrarye
250 That made hem in a citee for to tarye,
That stood ful merye upon an haven° side—   *harbor's*
But on a day again° the even-tide   *toward*
The wind gan chaunge, and blewe right as hem leste:[4]
Jolif° and glad they wenten unto reste,   *merry*
255 And casten° hem ful erly for to saile.   *determined*
     "But to that oo man fil° a greet mervaile;   *befell*
That oon of hem, in sleeping as he lay,
Him mette[5] a wonder dreem again the day:
Him thoughte a man stood by his beddes side,
260 And him comanded that he sholde abide,
And saide him thus, 'If thou tomorwe wende,
Thou shalt be dreint:° my tale is at an ende.'   *drowned*
     "He wook and tolde his felawe what he mette,
And prayed him his viage° to lette;°   *voyage / delay*
265 As for that day he prayed him to bide.
     "His felawe that lay by his beddes side
Gan for to laughe, and scorned him ful faste.°   *hard*
'No dreem,' quod he, 'may so myn herte agaste°   *terrify*
That I wol lette for to do my thinges.°   *business*
270 I sette nat a straw by thy dreminges,[6]
For swevenes been but vanitees and japes:[7]
Men dreme alday° of owles or of apes,[8]   *constantly*
And of many a maze° therwithal—   *delusion*
Men dreme of thing that nevere was ne shal.[9]
275 But sith I see that thou wolt here abide,
And thus forsleuthen° wilfully thy tide,°   *waste / time*
God woot, it reweth me,[1] and have good day.'
And thus he took his leve and wente his way.
But er that he hadde half his cours ysailed—
280 Noot I nat why ne what meschaunce it ailed—
But casuelly the shippes botme rente,[2]
And ship and man under the water wente,
In sighte of othere shippes it biside,
That with hem sailed at the same tide.
285 And therfore, faire Pertelote so dere,
By swiche ensamples olde maistou lere°   *learn*
That no man sholde been too recchelees°   *careless*
Of dremes, for I saye thee doutelees
That many a dreem ful sore is for to drede.
290   "Lo, in the lif of Saint Kenelm[3] I rede—

---

4. Just as they wished.
5. He dreamed.
6. I don't care a straw for your dreamings.
7. Dreams are but illusions and frauds.
8. I.e., of absurdities.
9. I.e., shall be.

1. I'm sorry.
2. I don't know why nor what was the trouble with it—but accidentally the ship's bottom split.
3. Kenelm succeeded his father as king of Mercia at the age of seven, but was slain by his aunt (in 821).

That was Kenulphus sone, the noble king
Of Mercenrike°—how Kenelm mette a thing   *Mercia*
A lite° er he was mordred on a day.   *little*
His mordre in his avision° he sey.°   *dream / saw*
295 His norice° him expounded everydeel°   *nurse / every bit*
His swevene, and bad him for to keepe him[4] weel
For traison, but he nas but seven yeer old,
And therfore litel tale hath he told
Of any dreem,[5] so holy was his herte.
300 By God, I hadde levere than my sherte[6]
That ye hadde rad° his legende as have I.   *read*
    "Dame Pertelote, I saye you trewely,
Macrobeus,[7] that writ the *Avisioun*
In Affrike of the worthy Scipioun,
305 Affermeth° dremes, and saith that they been   *confirms*
Warning of thinges that men after seen.
    "And ferthermore, I praye you looketh wel
In the Olde Testament of Daniel,
If he heeld° dremes any vanitee.[8]   *considered*
310   "Rede eek of Joseph[9] and ther shul ye see
Wher° dremes be somtime—I saye nat alle—   *whether*
Warning of thinges that shul after falle.
    "Looke of Egypte the king daun Pharao,
His bakere and his botelere° also,   *butler*
315 Wher they ne felte noon effect in dremes.[1]
Whoso wol seeke actes of sondry remes°   *realms*
May rede of dremes many a wonder thing.
    "Lo Cresus, which that was of Lyde° king,   *Lydia*
Mette° he nat that he sat upon a tree,   *dreamed*
320 Which signified he sholde anhanged° be?   *hanged*
    "Lo here Andromacha, Ectores° wif,   *Hector's*
That day that Ector sholde lese° his lif,   *lose*
She dremed on the same night biforn
How that the lif of Ector sholde be lorn,°   *lost*
325 If thilke° day he wente into bataile;   *that same*
She warned him, but it mighte nat availe:°   *do any good*
He wente for to fighte nathelees,
But he was slain anoon° of Achilles.   *right away*
But thilke tale is al too long to telle,
330 And eek it is neigh day, I may nat dwelle.
Shortly I saye, as for conclusioun,
That I shal han of this avisioun[2]
Adversitee, and I saye ferthermoor
That I ne telle of[3] laxatives no stoor,
335 For they been venimes,° I woot it weel: *poisons*
I hem defye, I love hem neveradeel.°   *not a bit*
    "Now lat us speke of mirthe and stinte° al this.   *stop*

---

4. Guard himself.
5. Therefore he has set little store by any dream.
6. I.e., I'd give my shirt.
7. Macrobius wrote a famous commentary on Cicero's account in *De Republica* of the dream of Scipio Africanus Minor; the commentary came to be regarded as a standard authority on dream lore.

8. See Daniel 7.
9. See Genesis 37.
1. See Genesis 39–41.
2. Divinely inspired dream (as opposed to the more ordinary "swevene" or "dreem").
3. Set by.

Madame Pertelote, so have I blis,
Of oo thing God hath sente me large grace:
340 For whan I see the beautee of youre face—
Ye been so scarlet reed° aboute youre yën—   *red*
It maketh al my drede for to dien.
For also siker° as *In principio*,[4]   *certain*
Mulier est hominis confusio,[5]
345 Madame, the sentence° of this Latin is,   *meaning*
'Womman is mannes joye and al his blis.'
For whan I feele anight youre softe side—
Al be it that I may nat on you ride,
For that oure perche is maad so narwe, allas—
350 I am so ful of joye and of solas°   *delight*
That I defye bothe swevene and dreem."
And with that word he fleigh° down fro the beem,   *flew*
For it was day, and eek his hennes alle,
And with a "chuk" he gan hem for to calle,
355 For he hadde founde a corn° lay in the yeerd.   *grain*
Real° he was, he was namore aferd:°   *regal / afraid*
He fethered[6] Pertelote twenty time,
And trad hire as ofte er it was prime.[7]
He looketh as it were a grim leoun,
360 And on his toes he rometh up and down:
Him deined[8] nat to sette his foot to grounde.
He chukketh whan he hath a corn yfounde,
And to him rennen° thanne his wives alle.   *run*
Thus royal, as a prince is in his halle,
365 Leve I this Chauntecleer in his pasture,
And after wol I telle his aventure.
    Whan that the month in which the world bigan,
That highte° March, whan God first maked man,   *is called*
Was compleet, and passed were also,
370 Sin March biran,° thritty days and two,[9]   *passed by*
Bifel that Chauntecleer in al his pride,
His sevene wives walking him biside,
Caste up his yën to the brighte sonne,
That in the signe of Taurus hadde yronne
375 Twenty degrees and oon and somwhat more,
And knew by kinde,° and by noon other lore,   *nature*
That it was prime, and crew with blisful stevene.°   *voice*
"The sonne," he saide, "is clomben[1] up on hevene
Fourty degrees and oon and more, ywis.°   *indeed*
380 Madame Pertelote, my worldes blis,
Herkneth thise blisful briddes° how they singe,   *birds*
And see the fresshe flowers how they springe:
Ful is myn herte of revel and solas."
But sodeinly him fil° a sorweful cas,°   *befell / chance*
385 For evere the latter ende of joye is wo—

---

4. Beginning of the Gospel of St. John that gives the essential premises of Christianity: "In the beginning was the Word."
5. Woman is man's ruination.
6. I.e., embraced.
7. 9 A.M. "Trad": trod, copulated with.
8. He deigned.
9. The rhetorical time telling yields May 3.
1. Has climbed.

God woot that worldly joye is soone ago,
And if a rethor° coude faire endite,°   *rhetorician / compose*
He in a cronicle saufly° mighte it write,   *safely*
As for a soverein notabilitee.[2]
390 Now every wis man lat him herkne me:
This storye is also° trewe, I undertake,   *as*
As is the book of *Launcelot de Lake*,[3]
That wommen holde in ful greet reverence.
Now wol I turne again to my sentence.°   *main point*
395   A colfox[4] ful of sly iniquitee,
That in the grove hadde woned° yeres three,   *dwelled*
By heigh imaginacion forncast,[5]
The same night thurghout the hegges° brast°   *hedges / burst*
Into the yeerd ther Chauntecleer the faire
400 Was wont, and eek his wives, to repaire;
And in a bed of wortes° stille he lay   *cabbages*
Til it was passed undren° of the day,   *midmorning*
Waiting his time on Chauntecleer to falle,
As gladly doon thise homicides alle,
405 That in await liggen to mordre[6] men.
O false mordrour, lurking in thy den!
O newe Scariot! Newe Geniloun![7]
False dissimilour!° O Greek Sinoun,[8]   *dissembler*
That broughtest Troye al outrely° to sorwe!   *utterly*
410 O Chauntecleer, accursed be that morwe°   *morning*
That thou into the yeerd flaugh° fro the bemes!   *flew*
Thou were ful wel ywarned by thy dremes
That thilke day was perilous to thee;
But what that God forwoot° moot° needes be,   *foreknows / must*
415 After° the opinion of certain clerkes: *according to*
Witnesse on him that any parfit° clerk is   *perfect*
That in scole is greet altercacioun
In this matere, and greet disputisoun,°   *disputation*
And hath been of an hundred thousand men.
420 But I ne can nat bulte it to the bren,[9]
As can the holy doctour Augustin,
Or Boece, or the bisshop Bradwardin[1]—
Wheither that Goddes worthy forwiting°   *foreknowledge*
Straineth me nedely[2] for to doon a thing
425   ("Nedely" clepe I simple necessitee),
Or elles if free chois be graunted me
To do that same thing or do it naught,
Though God forwoot° it er that I was wrought;   *foreknew*
Or if his wiring° straineth neveradeel,   *knowledge*

2. Indisputable fact.
3. Romances of the courteous knight Lancelot of the Lake were very popular.
4. Fox with black markings.
5. Having planned with great cunning.
6. That lie in ambush to murder.
7. I.e., Ganelon, who betrayed Roland to the Saracens (in the medieval French epic *The Song of Roland*). "Scariot": Judas Iscariot.
8. Sinon, who persuaded the Trojans to take the Greeks' wooden horse into their city—with, of course, the result that the city was destroyed.
9. Sift it to the bran, i.e., get to the bottom of it.
1. St. Augustine, Boethius (6th-century Roman philosopher, whose *Consolation of Philosophy* was translated by Chaucer), and Thomas Bradwardine (archbishop of Canterbury, d. 1349) were all concerned with the interrelationship between people's free will and God's foreknowledge.
2. Constrains me necessarily.

430 But by necessitee condicionel[3]—
   I wol nat han to do of swich matere:
   My tale is of a cok, as ye may heere,
   That took his conseil of his wif with sorwe,
   To walken in the yeerd upon that morwe
435 That he hadde met° the dreem that I you tolde.   *dreamed*
   Wommenes conseils been ful ofte colde,[4]
   Wommanes conseil broughte us first to wo,
   And made Adam fro Paradis to go,
   Ther as he was ful merye and wel at ese.
440 But for I noot° to whom it mighte displese   *don't know*
   If I conseil of wommen wolde blame,
   Passe over, for I saide it in my game°—   *sport*
   Rede auctours where they trete of swich matere,
   And what they sayn of wommen ye may heere—
445 Thise been the cokkes wordes and nat mine:
   I can noon harm of no womman divine.°   *guess*
      Faire in the sond° to bathe hire merily   *sand*
   Lith° Pertelote, and alle hir sustres by,   *lies*
   Again° the sonne, and Chauntecleer so free°   *in / noble*
450 Soong° merier than the mermaide in the see—   *sang*
   For Physiologus[5] saith sikerly
   How that they singen wel and merily.
      And so bifel that as he caste his yë
   Among the wortes on a boterflye,°   *butterfly*
455 He was war of this fox that lay ful lowe.
   No thing ne liste him[6] thanne for to crowe,
   But cride anoon "Cok cok!" and up he sterte,°   *started*
   As man that[7] was affrayed in his herte—
   For naturelly a beest desireth flee
460 Fro his contrarye[8] if he may it see,
   Though he nevere erst° hadde seen it with his yë.   *before*
   This Chauntecleer, whan he gan him espye,
   He wolde han fled, but that the fox anoon
   Saide, "Gentil sire, allas, wher wol ye goon?
465 Be ye afraid of me that am youre freend?
   Now certes, I were worse than a feend
   If I to you wolde° harm or vilainye.   *meant*
   I am nat come youre conseil° for t'espye,   *secrets*
   But trewely the cause of my cominge
470 Was only for to herkne how ye singe:
   For trewely, ye han as merye a stevene°   *voice*
   As any angel hath that is in hevene.
   Therwith ye han in musik more feelinge
   Than hadde Boece,[9] or any that can singe.
475 My lord your fader—God his soule blesse!—
   And eek youre moder, of hir gentilesse,°   *gentility*
   Han in myn hous ybeen, to my grete ese.

---

3. Boethius's "conditional necessity" permitted a large measure of free will.
4. I.e., baneful.
5. Supposed author of a bestiary, a book of moralized zoology describing both natural and supernatural animals (including mermaids).
6. He wished.
7. Like one who.
8. I.e., his natural enemy.
9. Boethius also wrote a treatise on music.

And certes sire, ful fain° wolde I you plese.   *gladly*
 "But for men speke of singing, I wol saye,
480 So mote I brouke[1] wel mine yën twaye,
Save ye, I herde nevere man to singe
As dide youre fader in the morweninge.
Certes, it was of herte° al that he soong.°   *heartfelt / sang*
And for to make his vois the more strong,
485 He wolde so paine him[2] that with bothe his yën
He moste winke,[3] so loude wolde he cryen;
And stonden on his tiptoon therwithal,
And strecche forth his nekke long and smal;
And eek he was of swich discrecioun
490 That ther nas no man in no regioun
That him in song or wisdom mighte passe.
I have wel rad° in *Daun Burnel the Asse*[4]   *read*
Among his vers how that ther was a cok,
For a preestes sone yaf him a knok[5]
495 Upon his leg whil he was yong and nice,°   *foolish*
He made him for to lese° his benefice.[6]   *lose*
But certain, ther nis no comparisoun
Bitwixe the wisdom and discrecioun
Of youre fader and of his subtiltee.[7]
500 Now singeth, sire, for sainte° charitee!   *holy*
Lat see, conne° ye youre fader countrefete?"°   *can / imitate*
 This Chauntecleer his winges gan to bete,
As man that coude his traison nat espye,
So was he ravisshed with his flaterye.
505 Allas, ye lordes, many a fals flatour°   *flatterer*
Is in youre court, and many a losengeour°   *deceiver*
That plesen you wel more, by my faith,
Than he that soothfastnesse° unto you saith!   *truth*
Redeth Ecclesiaste[8] of flaterye.
510 Beeth war, ye lordes, of hir trecherye.
 This Chauntecleer stood hye upon his toos,
Strecching his nekke, and heeld his yën cloos,
And gan to crowe loude for the nones;°   *occasion*
And daun Russel the fox sterte° up atones,   *jumped*
515 And by the gargat° hente° Chauntecleer,   *throat / seized*
And on his bak toward the wode him beer,°   *bore*
For yit ne was ther no man that him sued.°   *followed*
 O destinee that maist nat been eschued!°   *eschewed*
Allas that Chauntecleer fleigh° fro the bemes!   *flew*
520 Allas his wif ne roughte nat of[9] dremes!
And on a Friday fil° al this meschaunce!   *befell*
 O Venus that art goddesse of plesaunce,
Sin that thy servant was this Chauntecleer,
And in thy service dide al his power—

1. So might I enjoy the use of.
2. Take pains.
3. He had to shut his eyes.
4. Master Brunellus, a discontented donkey, was the hero of a 12th-century satirical poem by Nigel Wireker.
5. Because a priest's son gave him a knock.

6. The offended cock neglected to crow so that his master, now grown to manhood, overslept, missing his ordination and losing his benefice.
7. His (the cock in the story) cleverness.
8. The Book of Ecclesiasticus, in the Apocrypha.
9. Didn't care for.

525 More for delit than world¹ to multiplye—
Why woldestou suffre him on thy day² to die?
O Gaufred,³ dere maister soverein,
That, whan thy worthy king Richard was slain
With shot,⁴ complainedest his deeth so sore,
530 Why ne hadde I now thy sentence and thy lore,⁵
The Friday for to chide as diden ye?
For on a Friday soothly slain was he.
Thanne wolde I shewe you how that I coude plaine°   *lament*
For Chauntecleres drede and for his paine.
535 Certes, swich cry ne lamentacioun
Was nevere of ladies maad when Ilioun°   *Ilium, Troy*
Was wonne, and Pyrrus⁶ with his straite° swerd,   *drawn*
Whan he hadde hent° King Priam by the beerd   *seized*
And slain him, as saith us *Eneidos*,⁷
540 As maden alle the hennes in the cloos,°   *yard*
Whan they hadde seen of Chauntecleer the sighte.
But sovereinly° Dame Pertelote shrighte°   *supremely / shrieked*
Ful louder than dide Hasdrubales⁸ wif
Whan that hir housbonde hadde lost his lif,
545 And that the Romains hadden brend° Cartage: *burned*
She was so ful of torment and of rage°   *madness*
That wilfully unto the fir she sterte,°   *jumped*
And brende hirselven with a stedefast herte.
O woful hennes, right so criden ye
550 As, whan that Nero brende the citee
Of Rome, criden senatoures wives
For that hir housbondes losten alle hir lives:⁹
Withouten gilt this Nero hath hem slain.
Now wol I turne to my tale again.
555 The sely° widwe and eek hir doughtres two   *innocent*
Herden thise hennes crye and maken wo,
And out at dores sterten° they anoon,   *leapt*
And sien° the fox toward the grove goon,   *saw*
And bar upon his bak the cok away,
560 And criden, "Out, harrow,° and wailaway,   *help*
Ha, ha, the fox," and after him they ran,
And eek with staves many another man;
Ran Colle oure dogge, and Talbot and Gerland,¹
And Malkin with a distaf in hir hand,
565 Ran cow and calf, and eek the verray hogges,
Sore aferd° for berking of the dogges   *frightened*
And shouting of the men and wommen eke.
They ronne° so hem thoughte hir herte breke;²   *ran*
They yelleden as feendes doon in helle;

---

1. I.e., population.
2. Friday is Venus's day.
3. Geoffrey of Vinsauf, a famous medieval rhetorician, who wrote a lament on the death of Richard I in which he scolded Friday, the day on which the king died.
4. I.e., a missile.
5. Thy wisdom and thy learning.
6. Pyrrhus was the Greek who slew Priam, king

of Troy.
7. As the *Aeneid* tells us.
8. Hasdrubal was king of Carthage when it was destroyed by the Romans.
9. According to the legend, Nero not only set fire to Rome (in 64 c.e.) but also put many senators to death.
1. Two other dogs.
2. Would break.

570 The dokes° criden as men wolde hem quelle;°   *ducks / kill*
The gees for fere flowen° over the trees;   *flew*
Out of the hive cam the swarm of bees;
So hidous was the noise, a, benedicite,°   *bless me*
Certes, he Jakke Straw[3] and his meinee°   *company*
575 Ne made nevere shoutes half so shrille
Whan that they wolden any Fleming kille,
As thilke day was maad upon the fox:
Of bras they broughten bemes° and of box,°   *trumpets / boxwood*
Of horn, of boon,° in whiche they blewe and pouped,°   *bone / tooted*
580 And therwithal they skriked° and they houped°—   *shrieked / whooped*
It seemed as that hevene sholde falle.
    Now goode men, I praye you herkneth alle:
Lo, how Fortune turneth° sodeinly   *reverses, overturns*
The hope and pride eek of hir enemy.
585 This cok that lay upon the foxes bak,
In al his drede unto the fox he spak,
And saide, "Sire, if that I were as ye,
Yit sholde I sayn, as wis° God helpe me,   *surely*
'Turneth ayain, ye proude cherles alle!
590 A verray pestilence upon you falle!
Now am I come unto this wodes side,
Maugree your heed,[4] the cok shal here abide.
I wol him ete, in faith, and that anoon.'"
    The fox answerde, "In faith, it shal be doon."
595 And as he spak that word, al sodeinly
The cok brak from his mouth deliverly,°   *nimbly*
And hye upon a tree he fleigh° anoon.   *flew*
    And whan the fox sawgh that he was agoon,
"Allas," quod he, "O Chauntecleer, allas!
600 I have to you," quod he, "ydoon trespas,
In as muche as I maked you aferd
Whan I you hente° and broughte out of the yeerd.   *seized*
But sire, I dide it in no wikke° entente: *wicked*
Come down, and I shal telle you what I mente.
605 I shal saye sooth to you, God help me so."
    "Nay thanne," quod he, "I shrewe° us bothe two: *curse*
But first I shrewe myself, bothe blood and bones,
If thou bigile me ofter than ones;
Thou shalt namore thurgh thy flaterye
610 Do° me to singe and winken with myn yë.   *cause*
For he that winketh° whan he sholde see,   *closes both eyes*
Al wilfully, God lat him nevere thee."°   *prosper*
    "Nay," quod the fox, "but God yive him meschaunce
That is so undiscreet of governaunce°   *self-control*
615 That jangleth° whan he sholde holde his pees."   *chatters*
    Lo, swich it is for to be reccheless°   *careless*
And necligent and truste on flaterye.
But ye that holden this tale a folye
As of a fox, or of a cok and hen,

---

3. One of the leaders of the Uprising of 1381, which was partially directed against the Flemings living in London.

4. Despite your head—i.e., despite anything you can do.

620 Taketh the moralitee, goode men.
For Saint Paul saith that al that writen is
To oure doctrine° it is ywrit, ywis:[5]   *teaching*
Taketh the fruit, and lat the chaf be stille.[6]
Now goode God, if that it be thy wille,
625 As saith my lord, so make us alle goode men,
And bringe us to his hye blisse. Amen.

Close of Canterbury Tales   At the end of *The Canterbury Tales*, Chaucer
invokes a common allegorical theme, that life on earth is a pilgrimage. As Chaucer
puts it in his moral ballade *Truth*, "*Here* in noon home . . . / Forth, pilgrim, forth!" In
the final fragment, he makes explicit a metaphor that has been implicit all along in
the journey to Canterbury. The pilgrims never arrive at the shrine of St. Thomas,
but in the short introduction to the final tale, *The Parson's Tale*, and the "Retraction" that follows it, Chaucer seems to be making an end for two pilgrimages that
had become one, that of his fiction and that of his life.

   In the introduction to the tale we find the twenty-nine pilgrims moving through
a nameless little village as the sun sinks to within twenty-nine degrees of the horizon. The atmosphere contains something of both the chill and the urgency of a late
autumn afternoon, and we are surprised to find that the pilgrimage is almost over,
that there is need for haste to make that "good end" that every medieval Christian
hoped for. This delicately suggestive passage, rich with allegorical overtones, introduces an extremely long penitential treatise, translated by Chaucer from Latin or
French sources. Although often assumed to be an earlier work, it may well have
been written by Chaucer to provide the ending for *The Canterbury Tales*.

   In the "Retraction" that follows *The Parson's Tale*, Chaucer acknowledges, lists,
revokes, and asks forgiveness for his "giltes" (that is, his sins), which consist of having
written most of the works on which his reputation as a great poet depends. He thanks
Christ and Mary for his religious and moral works. One need not take this as evidence of a spiritual crisis or conversion at the end of his life. The "Retraction" seems
to have been written to appear at the end of *The Canterbury Tales*, without censoring
any of the tales deemed to be sinful. At the same time, one need not question Chaucer's sincerity. A readiness to deny his own reality before the reality of his God is
implicit in many of Chaucer's works, and the placement of the "Retraction" within or
just outside the border of the fictional pilgrimage suggests that although Chaucer
finally rejected his fictions, he recognized that he and they were inseparable.

Chaucer's Retraction

Here taketh the makere of this book his leve[1]

Now praye I to hem alle that herkne this litel tretis[2] or rede, that if ther be
any thing in it that liketh[3] hem, that therof they thanken oure Lord Jesu
Crist, of whom proceedeth al wit[4] and al goodnesse. And if ther be any thing

---

5. See Romans 15.4.
6. The "fruit" refers to the kernel of moral or doctrinal meaning; the "chaf," or husk, is the narrative containing that meaning. The metaphor was
commonly applied to scriptural interpretation.
1. "Chaucer's Retraction" is the title given to
this passage by modern editors. The heading,

"*Here . . . leve*," which does appear in all manuscripts, may be by Chaucer himself or by a
scribe.
2. Hear this little treatise, i.e., *The Parson's Tale*.
3. Pleases.
4. Understanding.

that displese hem, I praye hem also that they arrette it to the defaute of myn unconning,[5] and nat to my wil, that wolde ful fain[6] have said bettre if I hadde had conning. For oure book saith, "Al that is writen is writen for oure doctrine,"[7] and that is myn entente. Wherfore I biseeke[8] you mekely, for the mercy of God, that ye praye for me that Crist have mercy on me and foryive me my giltes, and namely of my translacions and enditinges[9] of worldly vanitees, the whiche I revoke in my retraccions: as is the *Book of Troilus*; the Book also of *Fame*; the *Book of the Five and Twenty Ladies*;[1] the *Book of the Duchesse*; the *Book of Saint Valentines Day of the Parlement of Briddes*; the *Tales of Canterbury*, thilke that sounen into[2] sinne; the *Book of the Leon*;[3] and many another book, if they were in my remembrance, and many a song and many a leccherous lay:[4] that Crist for his grete mercy foryive me the sinne. But of the translacion of Boece[5] *De Consolatione*, and othere bookes of legendes of saintes, and omelies,[6] and moralitee, and devocion, that thanke I oure Lord Jesu Crist and his blisful Moder and alle the saintes of hevene, biseeking hem that they from hennes[7] forth unto my lives ende sende me grace to biwaile my giltes and to studye to the salvacion of my soule, and graunte me grace of verray[8] penitence, confession, and satisfaccion to doon in this present lif, thurgh the benigne grace of him that is king of kinges and preest over alle preestes, that boughte[9] us with the precious blood of his herte, so that I may been oon of hem at the day of doom[1] that shulle be saved. *Qui cum patre et Spiritu Sancto vivit et regnas Deus per omnia saecula.*[2] *Amen.*

1386–1400

5. Ascribe it to the defect of my lack of skill.
6. Gladly.
7. Romans 15.4.
8. Beseech.
9. Compositions. "Namely": especially.
1. I.e., the *Legend of Good Women.*
2. Those that tend toward.
3. The *Book of the Lion* has not been preserved.
4. Lyric poem.

5. Boethius.
6. Homilies.
7. Hence.
8. True.
9. Redeemed.
1. Judgment.
2. Who with the Father and the Holy Spirit livest and reignest God forever.

CHRIST'S HUMANITY

The literary and visual representation of the godhead is necessarily, in any religion, a powerful index of religious culture. In some religions, indeed, visual representation of God is such a sensitive issue that it is forbidden altogether. Christian culture has experienced moments of severe hostility to visual representation (for example, in the Reformation period of the sixteenth century), but has, in general, permitted images of God (and especially of God-become-man, Christ). In the later Middle Ages in Europe the bodily representation of Christ became a central preoccupation for writers, readers, and visual artists.

In the late eleventh century St. Anselm of Canterbury (1033–1099) developed a new conception of the Atonement ("at-one-ment"), the act whereby humans are reconciled with God after the separation caused by Original Sin. An earlier theory had posited that the Atonement was the solution to a dispute between God and the Devil concerning property rights over Mankind. In his tract *Why Did Christ Become Man?* Anselm argued instead that the real center of the Atonement was Mankind's moral responsibility to pay God back. Humanity needed to repay God for the sin committed, but was unable to do so. Faced with this impasse, God could either simply abolish the debt, or else *become human*, in order to repay Himself, as it were. God chose this latter route, allowing Christ to suffer and die as a human in order to clear the debt.

Earlier representations of the Crucifixion had tended to place the accent on Christ as impassive King, standing erect on the Cross, come to claim His property of mankind. In *The Dream of the Rood* (see pp. 33–36), for example, Christ's suffering is for the most part absorbed by the Cross itself, while Christ is represented as a conquering, royal hero. Later medieval representations of Christ, by contrast, accentuate the suffering, sagging, lacerated body of a very human God. In this newly conceived theology, Christ's suffering humanity takes center stage. The artistic significance of this massively influential development was itself massive. Certainly the older tradition survived in vital form: Langland's Christ, too, comes to claim his property as a conquering hero. It was, nonetheless, the tradition of Christ suffering in His humanity that dominated literary and visual art from the thirteenth century until the Reformation initiated in 1517.

These theological developments had forceful artistic and stylistic consequences. Because the theology was best expressed through visual or verbal images, it fed readily into both painting and a highly pictorial literature. In both painting and literature, a humble style, focusing on the particularities of bodily pain and grief, became the bearer of high theological significance. The painting of Giotto (1266?–1337), for example, broke with a prior tradition of painting that represented an elegant Christ against a splendid gold background; Giotto's inelegant and crucified Christ suffers under the pull of his own weight. Spiritual experience was, in the first instance, something *seen* more than something *thought*. It was also a spirituality rooted in the dramatic present: as one saw Christ, one saw Him in the here and now. Thus works in this almost cinematic mode foreshorten historical and geographical distance: such texts encourage readers, that is, to imagine that they are physically and emotionally present at the crucial scenes of Christ's life. In some examples of the tradition, viewers are encouraged to imagine those around Christ (especially Romans and Jews) as wholly responsible for the infliction of pain; in others, viewers are made to realize that they are themselves responsible for the continued suffering of Christ.

As deployed by the Church, this movement discouraged abstract thought. It did nevertheless have the effect of widening access to spiritual experience, and, in ways unforeseen by official sponsors of such piety, could be the springboard for very sophisticated theology. As the Church attempted to deepen the spiritual literacy of its members from the late twelfth century, emphasis on Christ's humanity in art and literature opened powerful spiritual experience to a much wider audience of readers and viewers. To engage in this spirituality, a public did not need to be versed in detailed matters of doctrine. Instead, a reader or viewer had to develop the capacity for sympathetic response to physical suffering. Such spirituality gained official impetus through the foundation of the Franciscan order of friars (1223), who promoted earthly poverty in imitation of, and emotional response to, Christ's sufferings. The centrality of Christ's living presence in the liturgy was, furthermore, reaffirmed and extended with the establishment, throughout Christendom, of the Feast of Corpus Christi (the Feast of the Body of Christ), first proclaimed by the pope in 1264 and again in 1311. This feast celebrated the Eucharistic host, or wafer, as Christ's body. It grew steadily in popularity and came to involve outdoor processions depicting the biblical foreshadowings of the Eucharist, as a prelude to display of the Eucharist itself. In some medieval English cities this was the day also chosen for the performance of cycle plays, sometimes known as the plays of Corpus Christi.

Female readers in particular, who had been excluded from the Latin-based, textual traditions of theology, discovered fertile ground in this tradition of so-called "affective," or emotional, piety. Through such emotive imagining, one gained an apparently unmediated, and potentially authoritative, relation with Christ. Women working in this tradition did not necessarily remain, however, within its visual, imaginative terms: Julian of Norwich is, for example, capable of developing very subtle and abstract thought, holding the incarnate image in view all the while.

This powerfully emotional piety also provoked wider social applications of the Christian narrative. Whereas "The Parable of the Christ Knight" in the *Ancrene Wisse* (supplemental ebook) presents a suffering Christ as an aristocratic lover for a very select spiritual elite of women, the Christ of Margery Kempe is very much the "homely" husband of a bourgeois woman (see in particular Book I, Chapter 36). On a much larger scale, the mystery plays mark the moment in which urban institutions represent Christ for themselves. In this drama, both Old and New Testament narrative is inflected by the trials of domestic and urban experience (on the origins, civic sponsorship, and production of these plays, see the introduction to "Mystery Plays," p. 299).

JULIAN OF NORWICH
1342–ca. 1416

The "Showings," or "Revelations" as they are also called, were sixteen mystical visions received by the woman known as Julian of Norwich. The name may be one that she adopted when she became an anchoress in a cell attached to the church of St. Julian that still stands in that city in East Anglia, then one of the most important English cities. An anchorite (m.) or anchoress (f.) is a religious recluse confined to an enclosure, which he or she has vowed never to leave. At the time of such an enclosing the burial service was performed, signifying that the enclosed person was dead to the world and that the enclosure corresponded to a grave. The point of this confinement was, of course, to pursue more actively the contemplative or spiritual life.

Julian may well have belonged to a religious order at the time that her visions led her to choose the life of an anchoress. We know little about her except what she tells us in her writings. She is, however, very precise about the date of her visions. They occurred, she tells us, at the age of thirty and a half on May 13, 1373. Four extant wills bequeath sums for Julian's maintenance in her anchorage. The most important document witnessing her life is *The Book of Margery Kempe*. Kempe asked Julian whether there might be any deception in Kempe's own visions, "for the anchoress," she says, "was expert in such things." Kempe's description of Julian's conversation accords well with the doctrines and personality that emerge from Julian's own book.

A *Book of Showings* survives in a short and a long version. The longer text, from which the following excerpts are taken, was the product of fifteen and more years of meditation on the meaning of the visions in which much had been obscure to Julian. Apparently the mystical experiences were never repeated, but through constant study and contemplation the showings acquired a greater clarity, richness, and profundity as they continued to be turned over in a mind both gifted with spiritual insight and learned in theology. Her editors document her extensive use of the Bible and her familiarity with medieval religious writings in both English and Latin.

Julian's sixteen revelations are each treated in uneven numbers of Chapters; these groupings of chapters form an extended meditation on a given vision. Each vision is treated with an unpredictable combination of visual description of what Julian saw, the words she was offered, and the meanings she "saw." Her visions are, in her words, "ghostly" (that is, spiritual), "bodily," and subtle combinations of the two. They embrace powerful visual phenomena such as blood drops running from the crown of thorns and revelations that take place in pure mind. All are, nevertheless, "seen"; the spiritualized meanings do not render bodily sights redundant.

The selections here, Chapters 5 and 7, are from Julian's First Vision. This vision is provoked by Julian's own bodily approximation to the bodily pains of Christ, as she thinks she is dying. The crucifix offered for her comfort provokes a kinetic, fresh response, as it seems to move into life, bleeding and persuading Julian that the vision is God's unmediated gift to her. Julian moves well beyond this initial sight, however; she

Reading and Vision. *The Hours of Mary of Burgundy*, ca. 1475. This extraordinary and utterly impossible view makes perfect sense as a vision of what the woman envisions from her reading.

sees a sequence of created things: the Virgin Mary as the best creature that God made, and, lower down the scale, the entire world in her palm, "the quantity of an hazelnut." Such a vision might lead away from created things altogether, into a realm of pure essence; significantly, it does not, precisely because Julian never leaves the sight of the wounded, bodily Christ, whose very physical suffering is somehow simultaneous with these almost immaterial visions. Julian strains the tradition of affective piety to its limits, but ends by transforming rather than rejecting it.

The serene optimism Julian's visions express for the material, created world and for fallen creatures extends into the most daring and surprising realms of speculation. "Sin is behovely": these are (Julian's) Christ's own words. They are expressed in the Thirteenth Vision for the first time (Chapter 27), but only in the extended, daring meditation of the Fourteenth Vision (not included in the Shorter Version) are they given their deepest sense. At the heart of Julian's profoundly optimistic theology is a transformative understanding of Christ's Humanity. She develops, without ever mentioning it explicitly, the idea of the felix culpa, the notion that, given its happy consequence in Christ's redemption of mankind, Adam's sin, or culpa, was somehow, "happy" (felix). Christ is so much a part of us, by Julian's account, that He is "the ground of our kind [natural/kind] making" (Chapter 59). He is our Mother, who strains and suffers as He gives birth to our salvation. Julian's concept of Jesus as mother has antecedents in both Old and New Testaments, in medieval theology, and in the writings of medieval mystics (both men and women), but nowhere else in Middle English writing is the concept so subtly and resonantly explored.

Julian was clearly aware of the dangers of expressing such high mysteries as a woman writer. She participates, it is true, in a late medieval tradition of visionary writing, often by women, such as the *Dialogue* of Catherine of Siena (translated into Middle English as the *Orchard of Syon*) and the *Revelations* of St. Bridget of Sweden (also translated into Middle English). Julian, however, does not refer to these figures; instead, she negotiates the difficulties and dangers of writing as a woman with enormous tact and shrewdness, both disclaiming and creating exceptional authority. Part of her strategy is to write with calm lucidity; part is to claim that the vision is not particular to her alone. Precisely by virtue of a common humanity, the visions are common property: "We are all one, and I am sure I saw it for the profit of many other."

From A Book of Showings to the Anchoress Julian of Norwich[1]

Chapter 5

[ALL CREATION AS A HAZELNUT]

In this same time that I saw this sight of the head bleeding, our good Lord showed a ghostly sight of his homely loving. I saw that he is to us all thing that is good and comfortable to our help. He is our clothing that for love wrappeth us and windeth us, halseth us[1] and all becloses us, hangeth about us for tender love that[2] he may never leave us. And so in this sight I saw that he is all thing that is good, as to my understanding.

And in this he showed a little thing, the quantity of an hazelnut, lying in the palm of my hand, as me seemed, and it was as round as a ball. I looked thereon with the eye of my understanding, and thought: What may this be? And it was answered generally thus: It is all that is made. I marvelled how it might last, for me thought it might suddenly have fallen to nought for[3] littleness. And I was answered in my understanding: It lasteth and ever shall, for God loveth it; and so hath all thing being by the love of God.

In this little thing I saw three properties. The first is that God made it, the second that God loveth it, the third that God keepeth[4] it. But what beheld I therein? Verily, the maker, the keeper, the lover. For till I am substantially united to him[5] I may never have full rest ne very[6] bliss; that is to say that I be so fastened to him that there be right nought that is made between my God and me.

This little thing that is made, me thought it might have fallen to nought for littleness. Of this needeth us to have knowledge, that us liketh nought all thing that is made, for to love and have God that is unmade.[7] For this is the cause why we be not all in ease of heart and of soul, for we seek here rest in this thing that is so little, where no rest is in, and we know not our God, that is almighty, all wise and all good, for he is very rest. God will be known, and him liketh that we rest us in him; for all that is beneath him suffiseth not to us. And this is the cause why that no soul is in rest till it is noughted of all things that is made.[8] When she is wilfully[9] noughted for love, to have him that is all, then is she able to receive ghostly rest.

---

1. Envelops us and embraces us.
2. So that.
3. Because of.
4. Looks after.
5. Joined to him in "substance," which Julian regards as the eternal essence of being.
6. True.

7. I.e., we need to know that we should not be attracted to earthly things, which are made, to love and possess God, who is not made, who exists eternally.
8. Emptied of (its attachment to) all created things.
9. Of its free will.

And also our good Lord showed that it is full great pleasance to him that a sely[1] soul come to him naked, plainly and homely. For this is the kind[2] yearning of the soul by the touching of the Holy Ghost, as by the understanding that I have in this showing: God of thy goodness gave me thyself, for thou art enough to me, and I may ask nothing that is less that may be full worship to thee. And if I ask any thing that is less, ever me wanteth;[3] but only in thee I have all.

And these words of the goodness of God be full lovesome to the soul and full near touching the will of our Lord, for his goodness fulfilleth all his creatures and all his blessed works and overpasseth[4] without end. For he is the endlesshead and he made us only to himself and restored us by his precious passion,[5] and ever keepeth us in his blessed love; and all this is of his goodness.

*　*　*

Chapter 7

[CHRIST AS HOMELY AND COURTEOUS]

And in all that time that he showed this that I have now said in ghostly sight, I saw the bodily sight lasting of the plenteous bleeding of the head. The great drops of blood fell down fro under the garland like pellets, seeming as it had come out of the veins. And in the coming out they were brown red, for the blood was full thick; and in the spreading abroad they were bright red. And when it came at the brows, there they vanished; and not withstanding the bleeding continued till many things were seen and understood. Nevertheless the fairhead and livelihead continued in the same beauty and liveliness.

The plenteoushead is like to the drops of water that fall of the evesing[6] of an house after a great shower of rain, that fall so thick that no man may number them with no bodily wit.[7] And for the roundness they were like to the scale of herring in the spreading of the forehead.

These three things came to my mind in the time: pellets for the roundhead[8] in the coming out of the blood, the scale of the herring for the roundhead in the spreading, the drops of the evesing of a house for the plenteoushead unnumerable. This showing was quick[9] and lively and hideous and dreadful and sweet and lovely; and of all the sight that I saw this was most comfort to me, that our good Lord, that is so reverend and dreadful, is so homely and so courteous, and this most fulfilled me with liking and sickerness[1] in soule.

And to the understanding of this he showed this open example. It is the most worship[2] that a solemn king or a great lord may do to a poor servant if he will be homely with him; and namely if he show it himself of a full true meaning[3] and with a glad cheer both in private and openly. Then thinketh this poor creature thus: "Lo, what might this noble lord do more worship and joy to me than to show to me that am so little this marvelous homeliness? Verily, it is more joy and liking to me than if he gave me great gifts and were

1. Innocent.
2. Natural.
3. I am forever lacking.
4. Surpasses.
5. Suffering.
6. Eaves.
7. Intelligence.
8. Roundness.
9. Vivid.
1. Security.
2. Honor.
3. Intent.

himself strange in manner." This bodily example was showed so high that this man's heart might be ravished and almost forget himself for joy of this great homeliness.

Thus it fareth by our Lord Jesu and by us, for verily it is the most joy that may be, as to my sight, that he that is highest and mightiest, noblest and worthiest, is lowest and meekest, homeliest and courteousest. And truly and verily this marvelous joy shall be show us all when we shall see him. And this will our good Lord that we believe and trust, joy and like, comfort us and make solace as we may with his grace and with his help, into[4] the time that we see it verily. For the most fullhead of joy that we shall have, as to my sight, is this marvelous courtesy and homeliness of our fader, that is our maker, in our Lord Jesu Christ, that is our brother and oure saviour. But this marvelous homeliness may no man know in this life, but if he have it by special showing of our Lord, or of great plenty of grace inwardly given of the Holy Ghost. But faith and belief with charity deserve the meed,[5] and so it is had by grace. For in faith with hope and charity our life is grounded. The showing is made to whom that God will, plainly teacheth the same opened and declared, with many privy points belonging to our faith and belief which be worshipful to be known. And when the showing which is given for a time is passed and hid, then faith keepeth it by grace of the Holy Ghost into our life's end. And thus by the showing it is none other than the faith, ne less ne more, as it may be seen by our Lord's meaning in the same matter, by then[6] it come to the last end.

4. Until.
5. Reward. "Charity": love. See 1 Corinthians
13.13.
6. By the time that.

MARGERY KEMPE
ca. 1373–1438

*T*he *Book of Margery Kempe* is the spiritual autobiography of a medieval laywoman, telling of her struggles to carry out instructions for a holy life that she claimed to have received in personal visions from Christ and the Virgin Mary. The assertion of such a mission by a married woman, the mother of fourteen children, was in itself sufficient grounds for controversy; in addition, Kempe's outspoken defense of her visions as well as her highly emotional style of religious expression embroiled her with fellow citizens and pilgrims and with the Church, although she also won both lay and clerical supporters. Ordered by the archbishop of York to swear not to teach in his diocese, she courageously stood up for her freedom to speak her conscience.

Margery Kempe was the daughter of John Burnham, five-time mayor of King's Lynn, a thriving commercial town in Norfolk. At about the age of twenty she married John Kempe, a well-to-do fellow townsman. After the traumatic delivery of her first child—the rate of maternal mortality in childbirth was high—she sought to confess to a priest whose harsh, censorious response precipitated a mental breakdown, from which she eventually recovered through the first of her visions. Her subsequent conversion and strict religious observances generated a good deal of domestic strife, but she continued to share her husband's bed until, around the age of forty, she negotiated a vow of celibacy with him, which was confirmed before the bishop and left her free to undertake a pilgrimage to the Holy Land. There she experienced visions of Christ's passion and of the sufferings of the Virgin. These visions recurred during the rest of her life, and her noisy weeping at such times made her the object of much scorn and hostility. Her orthodoxy was several times examined, but her unquestioning acceptance of the Church's doctrines and authority, and perhaps also her status as a former mayor's daughter, shielded her against charges of heresy.

Kempe was unable to read or write, but acquired her command of Scripture and theology from sermons and other oral sources. Late in her life, she dictated her story in two parts to two different scribes; the latter of these was a priest who revised the whole text. Nevertheless, it seems likely that the work retains much of the characteristic form and expression of its author.

Kempe's text offers a perspective on the tradition of "affective piety" unlike any other: here that visionary tradition comes to life in the context of vividly realized, often painful psychological and bodily experience. Kempe's own marriage, and her often troubled worldly relations, inform and are informed by her "homely" and sometimes erotic spiritual relations. Her imitation of Christ moves her to travel vast distances to be present at the scenes of Christ's suffering, just as she sees Christ present in male babies or good-looking young men. She sees the living divine presence in the Eucharistic host. "Sir," she says to a skeptic, "His death is as fresh to me as He had died this same day." This form of intensely sympathetic vision has, however, its negative obverse. As in Chaucer's *Prioress's Tale*, where tender feeling for the Blessed Virgin is complemented by hatred for the "cursed Jewes," Christian pathos can produce an anti-Semitic reflex.

From The Book of Margery Kempe[1]

[MARGERY'S MARRIAGE TO AND INTIMACY WITH CHRIST]

* * *

[Book 1.35] As this creature was in the Apostle's Church at Rome on St. John Lateran's Day,[2] the Father of Heaven said to her, "Daughter, I am well pleased with you, inasmuch as you believe in all the sacraments of Holy Church and in all faith that pertains to it, and specially because you believe in the manhood of my son and because of the great compassion that you have for his bitter Passion."

Also the Father said to this creature, "Daughter, I will have you wedded to my Godhead, for I shall show you my secrets and my counsels,[3] for you shall dwell with me without end."

Then the creature kept silence in her soul and answered not thereto, for she was full sore afraid of the Godhead, and she had no knowledge of the dalliance of the Godhead, for all her love and all her affection was set on the manhood of Christ and thereof had she good knowledge, and she would for no thing have parted therefrom. She was so much affected by the manhood of Christ that when she saw women in Rome bearing children in their arms, if she might learn that there were any men children, she should then cry,

---

1. The text is based on the unique manuscript, first discovered in 1934, edited by Lynn Staley. Spelling and inflexional forms have in many cases been modernized. Some archaic words have also been silently translated.
2. Saint John Lateran's Day, November 9.
3. Private deliberations.

roar, and weep as though she had seen Christ in his childhood. And, if she might have had her will, oftentimes she would have taken the children out from the mother's arms and have kissed them in the place of Christ. And, if she saw a handsome man, she had great pain to look on him in case she might have seen him who was both God and man. And therefore she cried many times and often when she met a seemly man and wept and sobbed full sorely in the manhood of Christ as she went in the streets at Rome, so that those who saw her wondered full much on her, for they knew not the cause.

And therefore it was no wonder if she were silent and answered not the Father of Heaven when he told her that she should be wedded to his Godhead. Then said the second person, Christ Jesus, whose manhood she loved so much, to her, "What say you, Margery, daughter, to my Father of these words that he speaks to you? Are you well pleased that it is so?"

And then she would not answer the second person but wept wonder sore, desiring to have still himself and in no way to be parted from him.

Then the second person in the Trinity answered to his Father for her and said, "Father, have her excused, for she is yet but young and not fully instructed as to how she should answer."

And then the Father took her by the hand in her soul before the Son and the Holy Ghost and the Mother of Jesus and all the twelve apostles and Saint Katherine and Saint Margaret and many other saints and holy virgins, with a great multitude of angels, saying to her soul, "I take you, Margery, for my wedded wife, for fairer, for fouler, for richer, for poorer, as long as you be buxom[4] and obedient to do what I bid you do. For, daughter, there was never a child so buxom to the mother as I shall be to you, both in well and in woe, to help you and comfort you. And thereto I make you surety."

And then the Mother of God and all the saints that were there present in her soul prayed that they might have much joy together. And then the creature with high devotion, with great plenty of tears, thanked God for this ghostly[5] comfort, considering herself in her own feeling right unworthy of any such grace as she felt, for she felt many great comforts, both ghostly comforts and bodily comforts. Sometimes she felt sweet smells with her nose; it was sweeter, she thought, than ever was any sweet earthly thing that she smelled before, nor might she ever tell how sweet it was, for she thought she might have lived thereby if they would have lasted.

Sometimes she heard with her bodily ears such sounds and melodies that she might not well hear what a man said to her in that time unless he spoke the louder. These sounds and melodies had she heard nearly every day for the term of twenty-five years when this book was written, and especially when she was in devout prayer, also many times while she was at Rome and in England both.

She saw with her bodily eye many white things flying all about her on every side, as thick in a manner as motes[6] in the sun; they were right delicate and comfortable, and the brighter that the sun shone, the better she might see them. She saw them many different times and in many different places, both in church and in her chamber, at her meal and in her prayers, in field and in

4. Submissive.
5. Spiritual.

6. Specks of dust.

town, both going and sitting. And many times she was afraid what they might be, for she saw them as well in nights in darkness as in daylight. Then, when she was afraid of them, our Lord said unto her, "By this token, daughter, believe it is God that speaks in you, for whereso God is, heaven is, and where God is there are many angels, and God is in you and you are in him. And therefore be not afraid, daughter, for this betokens that you have many angels about you to keep you both day and night so that no devil shall have power over you nor no evil man harm you."

Then from that time forward she used to say when she saw them come, "*Benedictus qui venit in nomine domini.*"[7]

Also our Lord gave her another token, which endured about sixteen years, and it increased ever more and more, and that was a flame of fire wonderfully hot and delectable and right comfortable, not wasting but ever increasing of flame, for, though the weather was never so cold, she felt the heat burning in her breast and at her heart, as verily as a man should feel the material fire if he put his hand or his finger therein.

When she felt first the fire of love burning in her breast, she was afraid thereof, and then our Lord answered to her mind and said, "Daughter, be not afraid, for this heat is the heat of the Holy Ghost, which shall burn away all your sins, for the fire of love quenches all sins. And you shall understand by this token that the Holy Ghost is in you, and you know well wherever the Holy Ghost is, there is the Father, and where the Father is, there is the Son, and so you have fully in your soul all the Holy Trinity. Therefore you have great cause to love me right well, and yet you shall have greater cause than ever you had to love me, for you shall hear what you never heard, and you shall see what you never saw, and you shall feel what you never felt.

For, daughter, you are sure of the love of God as God is God. Your soul is more sure of the love of God than of your own body, for your soul shall part from your body, but God shall never part from your soul, for they are joined together without end. Therefore, daughter, you have as great cause to be merry as any lady in this world, and, if you knew, daughter, how much you please me when you suffer me willfully to speak in you, you should never do otherwise, for this is a holy life, and the time is right well spent. For, daughter, this life pleases me more than wearing of the jacket of mail or of the hair shirt or fasting on bread and water, for, if you said every day a thousand Pater Nosters[8] you should not please me as well as you do when you are in silence and suffer me to speak in your soul.

[Book 1.36] "Fasting, daughter, is good for young beginners and discreet penance, especially that which their ghostly father gives them or enjoins them to do. And to bid many beads,[9] it is good to those who can do no better, and yet it is not perfect. But it is a good way toward perfection. For I tell you, daughter, those who are great fasters and great doers of penance, they desire that it should be considered the best life; also those who give themselves to say many devotions, they would have that the best life, and those who give many alms, they would that that was held the best life. And I have oftentimes, daughter, told you that thinking, weeping, and high contemplation is the

---

7. "Blessed is he who comes in the name of the Lord" (Matthew 21.9). A blessing used in the Mass as part of the consecration.

8. "Our Father," i.e., the Lord's Prayer.
9. Prayers (the original sense of the word "bedes," applied by association to beads in a rosary).

best life on earth. And you shall have more merit in heaven for one year of thinking in your mind than for a hundred years of praying with your mouth, and yet you will not believe me, for you will bid many beads whether I will or not.

"And yet, daughter, I will not be displeased with you whatever you think, say, or speak, for I am always pleased with you. And, if I were on earth as bodily as I was before I died on the cross, I should not be ashamed of you as many other men are, for I should take you by the hand among the people and make you great welcome so that they should well know that I loved you right well. For it is suitable for the wife to be homely with her husband. Be he never so great a lord and she so poor a woman when he wedded her, yet they must lie together and rest together in joy and peace. Right so must it be between you and me, for I take no heed what you have been but what you wish to be. And oftentimes have I told you that I have clean forgiven you all your sins. Therefore must I needs be homely with you and lie in your bed with you. Daughter, you desire greatly to see me, and you may boldly, when you are in your bed, take me to you as your wedded husband, as your most worthy darling, and as your sweet son, for I will be loved as a son should be loved by the mother and will that you love me, daughter, as a good wife ought to love her husband. And therefore you may boldly take me in the arms of your soul and kiss my mouth, my head, and my feet as sweetly as you will.

"And, as often as you think on me or would do any good deed to me, you shall have the same reward in heaven as if you did it to my own precious body which is in heaven, for I ask no more of you but your heart to love what loves you, for my love is ever ready for you."

Then she gave thanks and praise to our Lord Jesus Christ for the high grace and mercy that he showed unto her, an unworthy wretch.

This creature had divers tokens in her bodily hearing. One was a manner of sound as if it had been a pair of bellows blowing in her ear. She, being confounded thereof, was warned in her soul no fear to have, for it was the sound of the Holy Ghost. And then our Lord turned that sound into the voice of a dove, and afterward he turned it into the voice of a little bird which is called a red breast that sang full merrily oftentimes in her right ear. And then should she evermore have great grace after she heard such a token. And she had been used to such tokens about twenty-five years at the writing of this book.

Then our Lord Jesus Christ said to his creature, "By these tokens may you well know that I love you, for you are to me a very mother, and to all the world, because of that great charity that is in you, and yet I myself am the cause of that charity, and you shall have great reward therefore in Heaven.

MYSTERY PLAYS

The increasing prosperity and importance of the towns was shown by performances of the mystery plays—a sequence or "cycle" of plays based on the Bible
and produced by the city guilds, the organizations representing the various trades
and crafts. The cycles of several towns are lost. Those of York and Chester have
been preserved, the latter in a post-Reformation form. The Towneley plays, sometimes connected with Wakefield (Yorkshire), and those that constitute the so-
called N-town plays from East Anglia treat comparable material, as do fragmentary
survivals from elsewhere.

Medieval mystery plays had an immensely confident reach in both space and time.
In York, for example, the theatrical space and time of this urban, amateur drama
was that of the entire city, lasting from sunrise throughout the entire long summer
holiday. The time represented ran from the Fall of the Angels and the Creation of
the World right through to the end of time, in the Last Judgment. Between these
extremities of the beginning and end of time, each cycle presents key episodes of
Old Testament narrative, such as the Fall and the Flood, before presenting a concentrated sequence of freely interpreted New Testament plays focused on the life and
Passion of Christ.

The church had its own drama in Latin, dating back to the tenth century, which
developed through the dramatization and elaboration of the liturgy—the regular
service—for certain holidays, the Easter morning service in particular. The vernacular drama was once thought to have evolved from the liturgical, passing by
stages from the church into the streets of the town. However, even though the vernacular plays at times echo their Latin counterparts and although their authors may
have been clerics, the mysteries represent an old and largely independent tradition
of vernacular religious drama. As early as the twelfth century a *Play of Adam* in
Anglo-Norman French was performed in England, a dramatization of the Fall with
highly sophisticated dialogue, characterization, and stagecraft.

During the late fourteenth and the fifteenth centuries, the great English mystery
cycles were formed in provincial, yet increasingly powerful and independent cities.
They were the production of the city itself, with particular responsibility for staging
and performance devolving onto the city guilds. A guild was also known as a "mystery,"
from Latin *ministerium,* whence the phrase "mystery plays." A guild combined the
functions of modern trade union, club, religious society, and political action group.
The performance and staging required significant investments of time and money
from amateur performers, the status of whose mystery might be at stake in the quality
of their performance. Often the subject of the play corresponded to the function of the
guild (thus the Pinners, or nail-makers, performed the York Crucifixion, for example).

Most of our knowledge of the plays, apart from the texts themselves, comes
through municipal and guild records, which tell us a great deal about the evolution,
staging, and all aspects of the production of the cycles. In some of the cities each
guild had a wagon that served as a stage. The wagon proceeded from one strategic
point in the city to another, and the play would be performed a number of times on
the same day. In other towns, plays were probably acted out in sequence on a platform erected at a single location such as the main city square.

The cycles were performed every year at the time of one of two great early sum-
mer festivals—Whitsuntide, the week following the seventh Sunday after Easter, or
Corpus Christi, a week later (falling somewhere between May 21 and June 24).
They served as both religious instruction and entertainment for wide audiences,

including unlearned folk like the carpenter in *The Miller's Tale* (lines 405–74), who recalls from them the trouble Noah had getting his wife aboard the ark, but also educated laypeople and clerics, who besides enjoying the sometimes boisterous comedy would find the plays acting out traditional interpretations of Scripture such as the ark as a type, or prefiguration, of the church.

Thus the cycles were public spectacles watched by every layer of society, and they paved the way for the professional theater in the age of Elizabeth I. The rainbow in *Noah's Flood* (lines 356–71; for the text of *Noah's Flood* see the supplemental ebook) and the Angel's *Gloria* in the *Shepherds' Play*, with their messages of mercy and hope, unite actors and audience in a common faith. Yet the first shepherd's opening speech, complaining of taxation and the insolent exploitation of farmers by "gentlery-men," shows how the plays also served as vehicles of social criticism and reveal many of the rifts and tensions in the late-medieval social fabric.

The particular intersection of religious and civic institutions that made the cycles possible was put under strain from the beginning of the Reformation in England from the 1530s. Given the strength of civic institutions, the cycles survived into the reign of Elizabeth, but partly because they were identified with the Catholic Church, were suppressed by local ecclesiastical pressures in each city in the late 1560s and 1570s. The last performance of the York Cycle in 1569 is very nearly coincident with the opening of the first professional theater in Whitechapel (London) in 1567.

The Wakefield Second Shepherds' Play

In putting on the stage biblical shepherds and soldiers, medieval playwrights inevitably and often quite deliberately gave them the appearance and characters of contemporary men and women. No play better illustrates this aspect of the drama than the *Second Shepherds' Play*, included in the Towneley collection of mystery plays and imaginatively based on scriptural material typical of the cycles. As the play opens, the shepherds complain about the cold, the taxes, and the high-handed treatment they get from the gentry—evils closer to shepherds on the Yorkshire moors than to those keeping their flocks near Bethlehem. The sophisticated dramatic intelligence at work in this and several other of the Wakefield plays belonged undoubtedly to one individual, who probably revised older, more traditional plays some time during the last quarter of the fifteenth century. His identity is not known, but because of his achievement scholars refer to him as the Wakefield Master. He was probably a highly educated cleric stationed in the vicinity of Wakefield. The Wakefield Master had a genius for combining comedy, including broad farce, with religion in ways that make them enhance one another. In the *Second Shepherds' Play*, by linking the comic subplot of Mak and Gill with the solemn story of Christ's nativity, the Wakefield Master has produced a dramatic parable of what the Nativity means in Christian history and in Christian hearts. No one will fail to observe the parallelism between the stolen sheep, ludicrously disguised as Mak's latest heir, lying in the cradle, and the real Lamb of God, born in the stable among beasts. A complex of relationships based on this relationship suggests itself. But perhaps the most important point is that the charity twice shown by the shepherds—in the first instance to the supposed son of Mak and in the second instance to Mak and Gill when they decide to let them off with only the mildest of punishments—is rewarded when they are invited to visit the Christ Child, the embodiment of charity. The bleak beginning of the play, with its series of individual complaints, is ultimately balanced by the optimistic ending, which sees the shepherds once again singing together in harmony.

The *Second Shepherds' Play* is exceptional among the mystery plays in its development of plot and character. There is no parallel to its elaboration of the comic subplot and no character quite like Mak, who has doubtless been imported into religious drama from popular farce. Mak is perhaps the best humorous character outside of Chaucer's works in this period. A braggart of the worst kind, he has something of

Falstaff's charm; and he resembles Falstaff also in his grotesque attempts to maintain the last shreds of his dignity when he is caught in a lie. Most readers will be glad that the shepherds do not carry out their threat to have the death penalty invoked for his crime.

Following the 1994 edition of the Early English Text Society, the stanza, traditionally printed as nine lines (with an opening quatrain of four long lines, the first halves of which rhyme with one another) is rendered here as "thirteeners," rhyming *a b a b a b a b c d d d c*.

The Second Shepherds' Play[1]

CAST OF CHARACTERS

COLL	GILL
GIB	ANGEL
DAW	MARY
MAK	

[A field.]

[Enter COLL]

COLL	Lord, what° these weathers are cold,	*how*
	And I am ill happed;°	*badly covered*
	I am nearhand dold,°	*numb*
	So long have I napped;	
	My legs they fold,°	*give way*
	My fingers are chapped.	
	It is not as I wold,°	*would (wish)*
	For I am all lapped°	*wrapped*
	In sorrow:	
	In storms and tempest,	
	Now in the east, now in the west,	
	Woe is him that has never rest	
	Midday nor morrow!	
	But we sely° husbands[2]	*hapless*
	That walks on the moor,	
	In faith we are nearhands°	*nearly*
	Out of the door.°	*homeless*
	No wonder, as it stands	
	If we be poor,	
	For the tilth of our lands	
	Lies fallow as the floor,[3]	
	As ye ken.°	*know*

---

1. The text is based on the (1994) edition by A. C. Cawley and Martin Stevens, but has been freely edited. Spelling has been normalized except where rhyme makes changes impossible. Because the original text has no indications of scenes and only four stage directions, written in Latin, appropriate scenes of action and additional stage directions have been added; the four original stage directions are identified in the notes.
2. Farmers. The shepherds are also tenant farmers.
3. The arable part of our land lies fallow (as flat) as the floor. Landowners were converting farmland to pasture for sheep.

We are so hammed,
Fortaxed, and rammed,
25   We are made hand-tamed
    With these gentlery-men.[4]

Thus they reave° us our rest—   *rob*
Our Lady them wary!°   *curse*
These men that are lord-fest,[5]
30   They cause the plow tarry.[6]
That, men say, is for the best—
We find it contrary.
Thus are husbands oppressed
In point to miscarry.
35   On live.[7]
Thus hold they us under,
Thus they bring us in blunder,°   *trouble*
It were a great wonder
    And° ever should we thrive.   *if*

40 For may he get a paint-sleeve[8]
Or brooch nowadays,
Woe is him that him grieve
Or once again-says.°   *gainsays*
Dare no man him reprieve,°   *reprove*
45   What mastery he maes.[9]
And yet may no man lieve°   *believe*
One word that he says,
    No letter.
He can make purveyance[1]
50   With boast and bragance,°   *bragging*
And all is through maintenance[2]
    Of men that are greater.

There shall come a swain°   *fellow*
As proud as a po:°   *peacock*
55   He must borrow my wain,°   *wagon*
My plow also;
Then I am full fain°   *glad*
To grant ere he go.
Thus live we in pain,
60   Anger, and woe,
    By night and by day.
He must have if he lang° it,   *wants*
If I should forgang it.[3]

---

4. We are so hamstrung, overtaxed, and beaten down [that] we are made to obey these gentry folk. Coll is here complaining about the peasants' hard lot, at the mercy of retainers of the wealthy landowners.
5. Attached to lords.
6. Hold up the plow, i.e., interfere with the farm work.
7. In life. "In point to miscarry": to the point of ruin.
8. An embroidered sleeve, part of the livery worn by the landlord's officers as a badge of authority.
9. No matter what force he uses.
1. Requisition (of private property).
2. Practice of retaining servants under a nobleman's protection with the power to lord it over his tenants.
3. Even if I have to do without it.

I were better be hanged
   Than once say him nay.

It does me good, as I walk
Thus by mine one,°   *self*
Of this world for to talk
In manner of moan.
To my sheep I will stalk,
And hearken anon,
There abide on a balk,[4]
Or sit on a stone,
   Full soon;
For I trow,° pardie,°   *think / by God*
True men if they be,
We get more company
   Ere it be noon.[5]

[*Enter* GIB, *who at first does not see* COLL.]

GIB   Bensté and Dominus,[6]
   What may this bemean?°   *mean*
   Why fares this world thus?
   Oft have we not seen.
   Lord, these weathers are spiteous°   *cruel*
   And the winds full keen,
   And the frosts so hideous
   They water mine een,°   *eyes*
      No lie.
   Now in dry, now in wet,
   Now in snow, now in sleet,
   When my shoon° freeze to my feet   *shoes*
      It is not all easy.

   But as far as I ken,°   *see*
   Or yet as I go,°   *walk*
   We sely° wedmen°   *hapless / married men*
   Dree° mickle° woe;   *suffer / much*
   We have sorrow then and then°—   *constantly*
   It falls oft so.
   Sely Copple, our hen,[7]
   Both to and fro
      She cackles;
   But begin she to croak,
   To groan or to cluck,
   Woe is him is our cock,
      For he is in the shackles.

---

4. A raised strip of grassland dividing parts of a field.
5. I.e., if the other shepherds keep their promise to meet Coll.
6. Bless us and Lord.
7. Silly Copple, our hen, i.e., Gib's wife, who henpecks him.

105 These men that are wed
    Have not all their will:
    When they are full hard stead°   *beset*
    They sigh full still;°   *constantly*
    God wot° they are led   *knows*
110 Full hard and full ill;
    In bower nor in bed
    They say nought theretill.°   *against that*
      This tide°   *time*
    My part have I fun;°   *found, learned*
115 I know my lesson:
    Woe is him that is bun,°   *bound (in wedlock)*
      For he must abide.

    But now late in our lives—
    A marvel to me,
120 That I think my heart rives°   *splits*
    Such wonders to see;
    What that destiny drives
    It should so be[8]—
    Some men will have two wives,
125 And some men three
      In store.[9]
    Some are woe° that has any,   *miserable*
    But so far can° I,   *know*
    Woe is him that has many,
130   For he feels sore.

    But young men a-wooing,
    For God that you bought,°   *redeemed*
    Be well ware of wedding
    And think in your thought:
135 "Had I wist"° is a thing   *known*
    That serves of nought.
    Mickle° still° mourning   *much / continual*
    Has wedding home brought,
      And griefs,
140 With many a sharp shower,°   *fight*
    For thou may catch in an hour
    That° shall sow° thee full sour° *that which / vex / bitterly*
      As long as thou lives.

    For as ever read I 'pistle,[1]
145 I have one to my fere[2]
    As sharp as a thistle,
    As rough as a brere;°   *briar*
    She is browed like a bristle,
    With a sour-loten cheer;[3]

---

8. What destiny causes must occur.
9. I.e., by remarrying after being widowed.
1. Epistle, i.e., part of the church service.

2. As my mate.
3. She has brows like pig's bristles and a sour-looking face.

Had she once wet her whistle
She could sing full clear
   Her Pater Noster.[4]
She is great as a whale;
She has a gallon of gall:
By him that died for us all,
   I would I had run to° I lost her.   *till*

COLL   God look over the raw![5]
[*to* GIB] Full deafly ye stand!
GIB   Yea, the devil in thy maw°   *guts*
So tariand![6]
Saw thou awhere° of Daw?   *anywhere*
COLL   Yea, on a lea-land°   *pasture land*
Heard I him blaw.°   *blow (his horn)*
He comes here at hand,
   Not far.
Stand still.
GIB   Why?

COLL   For he comes, hope° I.   *think*
GIB   He will make us both a lie
   But if° we be ware.   *unless*

      [*Enter* DAW,[7] *who does not see the others.*]

DAW   Christ's cross me speed
And Saint Nicholas![8]
Thereof had I need:
It is worse than it was.
Whoso could take heed
And let the world pass,
It is ever in dread°   *doubt*
And brickie° as glass,   *brittle*
   And slithes.°   *slips away*
This world foor° never so,   *behaved*
With marvels mo° and mo,   *more*
Now in weal, now in woe,
   And all thing writhes.°   *changes*

Was never sin° Noah's flood   *since*
Such floods seen,
Winds and rains so rude
And storms so keen:
Some stammered, some stood
In doubt,[9] as I ween.°   *suppose*
Now God turn all to good!
I say as I mean.

4. "Our Father," or the Lord's Prayer.
5. I.e., God watch over the audience! Coll has been trying to get Gib's attention as the latter harangues the audience.
6. For being so late.
7. Daw (Davy) is a boy working for the older shepherds.
8. May Christ's cross and St. Nicholas help me.
9. Probably refers to people's consternation at the time of Noah's Flood.

For ponder:°   *consider (this)*
These floods so they drown
Both in fields and in town,
And bears all down,
195   And that is a wonder.

We that walk on the nights
Our cattle to keep,°   *keep watch over*
We see sudden° sights   *startling*
When other men sleep.
200   Yet methink my heart lights:°   *feels lighter*
I see shrews peep.[1]

     [*He sees the others, but does not hail them*]

Ye are two tall wights.°   *creatures*
I will give my sheep
    A turn.
205   But full ill have I meant:[2]
As I walk on this bent°   *field*
I may lightly° repent,   *quickly*
    My toes if I spurn.°   *stub*

Ah, sir, God you save,
210   And master mine!
A drink fain° would I have,   *gladly*
And somewhat to dine.

COLL   Christ's curse, my knave,
Thou art a lither° hine!°   *lazy / servant*
215 GIB What, the boy list rave!
Abide unto sine.[3]
    We have made it.°   *had dinner*
Ill thrift on thy pate![4]
Though the shrew° came late   *rascal*
220   Yet is he in state
    To dine—if he had it.

DAW   Such servants as I,
That° sweats and swinks,°   *who / toil*
Eats our bread full dry,
225   And that me forthinks.°   *angers*
We are oft wet and weary
When master-men winks,°   *sleep*
Yet comes full lately°   *tardily*
Both dinners and drinks.
230   But nately°   *profitably*
Both our dame and our sire,[5]

---

1. I see rascals peeping. Daw is relieved to recognize the other shepherds aren't monstrous apparitions.
2. But that's a very poor idea (to give the sheep a turn).
3. The boy must be crazy! Wait till later.
4. Bad luck on thy head!
5. I.e., mistress and master.

When we have run in the mire,
They can nip at our hire,[6]
  And pay us full lately.

But here my troth, master,
For the fare° that ye make°   *food / provide*
I shall do thereafter:
Work as I take.[7]
I shall do a little, sir,
And among° ever lake,°   *betweentimes / play*
For yet lay my supper
Never on my stomach[8]
  In fields.
Whereto should I threap?°   *haggle*
With my staff can I leap,°   *run away*
And men say, "Light cheap
  Litherly foryields."[9]

COLL   Thou were an ill lad
To ride a-wooing
With a man that had
But little of spending.[1]
GIB   Peace, boy, I bade—
No more jangling,
Or I shall make thee full rad,°   *quickly (stop)*
By the heaven's King!
        With thy gauds°—   *tricks*
Where are our sheep, boy?—we scorn.[2]
DAW   Sir, this same day at morn
I left them in the corn°   *wheat*
  When they rang Lauds.[3]

They have pasture good,
They cannot go wrong.
COLL   That is right. By the rood,°   *cross*
These nights are long!
Yet I would, ere we yode,°   *went*
One° gave us a song.   *someone*
GIB   So I thought as I stood,
To mirth° us among.°   *cheer / meanwhile*
DAW   I grant.
COLL   Let me sing the tenory.°   *tenor*
GIB   And I the treble so hee.°   *high*
DAW   Then the mean° falls to me.   *middle part*
Let see how you chant.   *[They sing.]*

    [Enter MAK *with a cloak over his clothes.]*[4]

---

6. They can deduct from our wages.
7. I.e., work (as little) as I am paid.
8. I.e., a full stomach has never weighed me down.
9. A cheap bargain repays badly (a proverb).
1. You would be a bad servant to take wooing for

a man with little money to spend.
2. We scorn (your tricks).
3. The first church service of the day (morn) but
performed while it is still dark.
4. Stage direction in the original manuscript.

MAK   Now, Lord, for thy names seven,
275   That made both moon and starns°   *stars*
      Well mo than I can neven,°   *name*
      Thy will, Lord, of me tharns.[5]
      I am all uneven°—   *at odds*
      That moves oft my harns.[6]
280   Now would God I were in heaven,
      For there weep no barns°   *children*
         So still.°   *continually*
COLL   Who is that pipes so poor?
MAK   [*aside*] Would God ye wist° how I foor!°   *knew / fared*
285   [*aloud*] Lo, a man that walks on the moor
      And has not all his will.

GIB   Mak, where has thou gane?°   *gone*
      Tell us tiding.
DAW.   Is he come? Then ilkane
290   Take heed to his thing.[7]

      [*Snatches the cloak from him.*]

MAK   What! Ich[8] be a yeoman,
      I tell you, of the king,
      The self and the same,
      Sond° from a great lording   *messenger*
295   And sich.°   *suchlike*
      Fie on you! Goth° hence   *go*
      Out of my presence:
      I must have reverence.
         Why, who be ich?

300   COLL   Why make ye it so quaint?[9]
      Mak, ye do wrang.°   *wrong*
GIB   But, Mak, list ye saint?
      I trow that ye lang.[1]
DAW   I trow the shrew can paint[2]—
305   The devil might him hang!
MAK   Ich shall make complaint
      And make you all to thwang°   *be flogged*
         At a word,
      And tell even° how ye doth.   *exactly*
310   COLL   But Mak, is that sooth?
      Now take out that Southern tooth,[3]
      And set in a turd![4]

5. Thy will, Lord, falls short in regard to me.
6. That often disturbs my brains.
7. Each one look to his possessions (lest Mak steal them). The stage direction below is in the manuscript.
8. I (a southern dialect form in contrast with the northern dialect spoken by the Yorkshire shepherds). Mak pretends to be an important person from the south.
9. Why are you putting on such airs?
1. Do you want to play the saint? I guess you long (to do so).
2. I think the rascal knows how to put on false colors.
3. I.e., now stop pretending to speak like a southerner.
4. I.e., shut up!

GIB   Mak, the devil in your ee!°   *eye*
  A stroke would I lean° you!   *give*
DAW   Mak, know ye not me?
  By God, I could teen° you.   *vex*
MAK   God look° you all three: *guard*
  Methought I had seen you.
  Ye are a fair company.
COLL   Can ye now mean you?[5]
GIB   Shrew, peep![6]
  Thus late as thou goes,
  What will men suppose?
  And thou has an ill nose[7]
    Of stealing sheep.

MAK   And I am true as steel,
  All men wate.°   *know*
  But a sickness I feel
  That holds me full hate:°   *hot, feverish*
  My belly fares not weel,
  It is out of estate.
DAW   Seldom lies the de'el°   *devil*
  Dead by the gate.[8]
MAK   Therefore[9]
  Full sore am I and ill
  If I stand stone-still,
  I eat not a needill[1]
    This month and more.

COLL   How fares thy wife? By my hood,
  How fares sho?°   *she*
MAK   Lies waltering,° by the rood,   *sprawling*
  By the fire, lo!
  And a house full of brood.°   *children*
  She drinks well, too:
  Ill speed other good
  That she will do![2]
    But sho
  Eats as fast as she can;
  And ilk° year that comes to man   *every*
  She brings forth a lakan°—   *baby*
    And some years two.

  But were I now more gracious°   *prosperous*
  And richer by far,
  I were eaten out of house
  And of harbar.°   *home*
  Yet is she a foul douce,°   *sweetheart*

---

5. Can you now remember (who you are)?
6. Rascal, watch out.
7. Noise, i.e., reputation.
8. Road, i.e., the devil is always on the move.
9. Mak ignores Daw and continues his speech

from line 331.
1. As sure as I'm standing here as still as a stone, I haven't eaten a needle (i.e., a tiny bit).
2. I.e., that (drinking) is the only good she does.

If ye come nar:³
There is none that trows°   imagines
Nor knows a war°   worse
360   Than ken° I.   know
Now will ye see what I proffer:
To give all in my coffer
Tomorn at next° to offer   tomorrow
  Her head-masspenny.⁴

365 GIB I wot° so forwaked⁵   know
Is none in this shire.
I would sleep if° I taked   even if
Less to my hire.⁶
DAW I am cold and naked
370 And would have a fire.
COLL I am weary forraked°   from walking
And run in the mire.
  Wake thou!⁷   [Lies down.]
GIB Nay, I will lie down by,
375 For I must sleep, truly.   [Lies down beside him.]
DAW As good a man's son was I
  As any of you.

[Lies down and motions to MAK to lie between them.]

But Mak, come hither, between
Shall thou lie down.
380 MAK Then might I let you bedeen
Of that ye would rown,⁸
  No dread.°   doubt
From my top to my toe,   [Lies down and prays.]
Manus tuas commendo
385 Pontio Pilato⁹
  Christ's cross me speed!° help

[He gets up as the others sleep and speaks.]¹

Now were time for a man
That lacks what he wold°   would, wants
To stalk privily than°   then
390 Unto a fold,°   sheepfold
And nimbly to work than,
And be not too bold,
For he might abuy° the bargan°   pay for / bargain
If it were told
395   At the ending.

3. I.e., near the truth.
4. The penny paid to sing a mass for her soul; i.e., I wish she were dead.
5. Exhausted from lack of sleep.
6. I should take a cut in wages.
7. Keep watch.
8. Then I might be in the way if you wanted to whisper together.
9. "Thy hands I commend to Pontius Pilate." A parody of Luke 23.46, "Into thy hands I commend my spirit."
1. One of the original stage directions.

Now were time for to reel:°   *move fast*
But he needs good counseel°   *counsel*
That fain would fare weel°   *well*
  And has but little spending.°   *money*

> [*He draws a magic circle around the shepherds and recites
> a spell.*]

But about you a circill,°   *circle*
As round as a moon,
To° I have done that° I will,   *until / what*
Till that it be noon,
That ye lie stone-still
To° that I have done;   *until*
And I shall say theretill°   *thereto*
Of good words a foon:°   *few*
  "On hight,
Over your heads my hand I lift.
Out go your eyes! Fordo your sight!"[2]
But yet I must make better shift
  And it be right.[3]

Lord, what° they sleep hard—   *how*
That may ye all hear.
Was I never a shephard,
But now will I lear.°   *learn*
If the flock be scar'd,
Yet shall I nip near.[4]
How! Draws hitherward![5]   [*He catches one.*]
Now mends our cheer
  From sorrow.
A fat sheep, I dare say!
A good fleece, dare I lay!°   *bet*
Eft-quit° when I may,   *repay*
But this will I borrow.

> [*Moves with the sheep to his cottage and calls from outside.*]

How, Gill, art thou in?
Get us some light.
GILL [*inside*]   Who makes such a din
This time of the night?
I am set for to spin;
I hope not I might
Rise a penny to win[6]—
I shrew° them on height!   *curse*
  So fares

---

2. May your sight be rendered powerless.
3. If it is to turn out all right.
4. Even if the flock is alarmed, yet shall I grip (a sheep) close.

5. Stop! come this way.
6. I don't think I can earn a penny by getting up (from my work).

435　　A housewife that has been
　　　　To be raised thus between:
　　　　Here may no note be seen
　　　　For such small chares.[7]

　　MAK　Good wife, open the hek!°　　　　　　　　　　　　door
440　　Sees thou not what I bring?
　　GILL　I may thole thee draw the sneck.[8]
　　　　Ah, come in, my sweeting.°　　　　　　　　　　　sweetheart
　　MAK　Yea, thou thar not reck
　　　　Of my long standing.[9]

　　　　　　[*She opens the door.*]

445　　GILL　By the naked neck
　　　　Art thou like for to hing.°　　　　　　　　　　　hang
　　MAK　Do way!°　　　　　　　　　　　　　　　　　　　let it be
　　　　I am worthy° my meat,　　　　　　　　　　　　worthy of
　　　　For in a strait° I can get　　　　　　　　　　　pinch
450　　More than they that swink° and sweat　　　　　work
　　　　All the long day.

　　　　Thus it fell to my lot,
　　　　Gill, I had such grace.°　　　　　　　　　　　　luck
　　GILL　It were a foul blot
455　　To be hanged for the case.°　　　　　　　　　　deed
　　MAK　I have 'scaped,° Jelot,°　　　　　　　escaped / Gill
　　　　Of as hard a glase.°　　　　　　　　　　　　　blow
　　GILL　But "So long goes the pot
　　　　To the water," men says,
460　　　　"At last
　　　　Comes it home broken."
　　MAK　Well know I the token,°　　　　　　　　　　saying
　　　　But let it never be spoken!
　　　　　　But come and help fast.

465　　I would he were flain,°　　　　　　　　　　　skinned
　　　　I list° well eat:　　　　　　　　　　　　　　　wish
　　　　This twelvemonth was I not so fain
　　　　Of one sheep-meat.
　　GILL　Come they ere he be slain,
470　　And hear the sheep bleat—
　　MAK　Then might I be ta'en°—　　　　　　　　　taken
　　　　That were a cold sweat!
　　　　　　Go spar°　　　　　　　　　　　　　　　fasten
　　　　The gate-door.°　　　　　　　　　　　　street door
　　GILL　　　　　　Yes, Mak,
475　　For and° they come at thy back—　　　　　　　if

7. So it goes with anyone who has been a housewife—to be interrupted like this: no work gets
done here because of such petty chores.
8. I'll let you draw the latch.
9. Sure, you needn't care about keeping me
standing a long time.

MAK   Then might I buy, for all the pack,
    The devil of the war.[1]

GILL   A good bourd° have I spied,   *trick*
    Sin° thou can° none.   *since / know*
    Here shall we him hide
    To° they be gone,   *until*
    In my cradle. Abide!
    Let me alone,
    And I shall lie beside
    In childbed and groan.
MAK   Thou red,°   *get ready*
    And I shall say thou was light°   *delivered*
    Of a knave-child° this night.   *boy child*
GILL   Now well is me day bright
    That ever I was bred.[2]

    This is a good guise°   *method*
    And a far-cast:°   *clever trick*
    Yet a woman's advice
    Helps at the last.
    I wot° never who spies: *know*
    Again° go thou fast.   *back*
MAK   But° I come ere they rise,   *unless*
    Else blows a cold blast.
      I will go sleep.   *[Returns to the shepherds.]*
    Yet sleeps all this meny,°   *company*
    And I shall go stalk privily,
    As it had never been I
      That carried their sheep.   *[Lies down among them.]*

     [The shepherds are waking.]

COLL   *Resurrex a mortruus!*[3]
    Have hold my hand!
    Judas carnas dominus![4]
    I may not well stand.
    My foot sleeps, by Jesus,
    And I waiter° fastand.°   *stagger / (from) fasting*
    I thought we had laid us
    Full near England.
GIB   Ah; yea?
    Lord, what° I have slept weel!°   *how / well*
    As fresh as an eel,
    As light I me feel
      As leaf on a tree.

1. Then I might have to pay the devil the worse
on account of the whole pack of them.
2. Now lucky for me the bright day I was born.

3. A garbled form of "resurrexit a mortuis" (he
arose from the dead) from the Creed.
4. Judas, (in?)carnate lord.

DAW Bensté° be herein!   *(God's) blessing*
   So my body quakes,
   My heart is out of skin,
520   What-so° it makes.°   *whatever / causes*
   Who makes all this din?
   So my brows blakes,[5]
   To the door will I win.[6]
   Hark, fellows, wakes!
525   We were four:
   See ye aywhere of Mak now?
COLL   We were up ere thou.
GIB   Man, I give God avow
   Yet-yede he naw're.[7]

530 DAW   Methought he was lapped°   *covered*
   In a wolfskin.
COLL   So are many happed°   *clad*
   Now, namely° within.   *especially*
DAW   When we had long napped,
535   Methought with a gin°   *snare*
   A fat sheep he trapped,
   But he made no din.
GIB   Be still!
   Thy dream makes thee wood.°   *crazy*
540   It is but phantom, by the rood.°   *cross*
COLL   Now God turn all to good,
   If it be his will.

[They wake up MAK *who pretends to have been asleep.]*

GIB   Rise, Mak, for shame!
   Thou lies right lang.°   *long*
545 MAK   Now Christ's holy name
   Be us amang!°   *among*
   What is this? For Saint Jame,
   I may not well gang.°   *walk*
   I trow° I be the same.   *think*
550   Ah, my neck has lain wrang.°   *wrong*
     [One of them twists his neck.]
    Enough!
   Mickle° thank! Sin° yestereven   *much / since*
   Now, by Saint Stephen,
   I was flayed with a sweven—
555   My heart out of slough.[8]

   I thought Gill began to croak
   And travail° full sad,°   *labor / hard*

---

5. My brow turns pale (with fear).
6. I'll head for the door. Still half-asleep, Daw thinks he's inside.
7. He's gone nowhere yet.
8. I was terrified by a dream—my heart [jumped] out of [my] skin.

Well-near at the first cock,[9]
Of a young lad,
For to mend° our flock—   *increase*
Then be I never glad:
I have tow on my rock[1]
More than ever I had.
   Ah, my head!
A house full of young tharms!°   *bellies*
The devil knock out their harns!°   *brains*
Woe is him has many barns,°   *children*
   And thereto little bread.

I must go home, by your leave,
To Gill, as I thought.°   *intended*
I pray you look° my sleeve,   *examine*
That I steal nought.
I am loath you to grieve
Or from you take aught.
DAW Go forth! Ill might thou chieve!°   *prosper*
  Now would I we sought
    This morn,
That we had all our store.[2]
COLL But I will go before.
  Let us meet.
GIB   Whore?°   *where*
DAW At the crooked thorn.

     [MAK's *house.* MAK *at the door.*]

MAK Undo this door!
GILL   Who is here?
MAK How long shall I stand?
GILL Who makes such a bere?°   *clamor*
  Now walk in the weniand!°[3]
MAK Ah, Gill, what cheer?
  It is I, Mak, your husband.
GILL Then may we see here
  The devil in a band,[4]
    Sir Guile!
  Lo, he comes with a lote°   *sound*
  As° he were holden in° the throat: *as if / by*
  I may not sit at my note°   *work*
    A hand-long° while.   *short*

MAK Will ye hear what fare° she makes   *fuss*
  To get her a glose?°   *excuse*
  And does nought but lakes°   *plays*

---

9. First cockcrow, i.e., midnight.
1. Flax on my distaff (i.e., trouble, mouths to feed).
2. Now I want us to make sure . . . we have all
our stock.

3. Waning of the moon (an unlucky time), i.e.,
"Go with bad luck!"
4. In a noose (?) Gill perhaps continues to remind
Mak that sheep stealing is a hanging offense.

And claws° her toes? *scratches*

GILL Why, who wanders? Who wakes?
600   Who comes? Who goes?
      Who brews? Who bakes?
      What makes me thus hose?⁵
         And than°   *then*
      It is ruth° to behold,   *pity*
605   Now in hot, now in cold,
      Full woeful is the household
         That wants° a woman.   *lacks*

      But what end has thou made
      With the herds,° Mak?   *shepherds*
610 MAK The last word that they said
      When I turned my back,
      They would look that they had
      Their sheep all the pack.
      I hope they will not be well paid⁶
615   When they their sheep lack.
         Pardie!°   *by God*
      But how-so the game goes,
      To me they will suppose,⁷
         And make a foul nose,°   *noise*
620   And cry out upon me.
      But thou must do as thou hight.°   *promised*
GILL I accord me theretill.⁸
      I shall swaddle him right
      In my cradill.

      [*She wraps up the sheep and puts it in the cradle.*]

625   If it were a greater sleight,
      Yet could I help till.⁹
      I will lie down straight.°   *immediately*
      Come hap° me.   *cover*
MAK   I will.
         [*Covers her.*]
GILL Behind
630   Come Coll and his marrow,¹
      They will nip° us full narrow.°   *pinch / closely*
MAK But I may cry "Out, harrow,"²
      The sheep if they find.

GILL Hearken ay when they call—
635   They will come anon.
      Come and make ready all,

5. Hoarse (from shouting at her husband and children).
6. I expect they won't be well pleased.
7. They will suspect me.
8. I agree to that.
9. Even if it were a greater trick, I could still help with it.
1. Coll and his mate are coming on your tracks.
2. A cry of distress.

And sing by thine one.°   self
Sing "lullay"° thou shall,   lullaby
For I must groan
And cry out by the wall
On Mary and John
     For sore.°   pain
Sing "lullay" on fast
When thou hears at the last,[3]
And but I play a false cast,[4]
     Trust me no more.

   [*The shepherds meet again.*]

DAW   Ah, Coll, good morn.
   Why sleeps thou not?
COLL   Alas, that ever I was born!
   We have a foul blot:
   A fat wether° have we lorn.°   ram / lost
DAW   Marry, God's forbot!°   God forbid
GIB   Who should do us that scorn?
   That were a foul spot!°   disgrace
COLL   Some shrew.°   rascal
   I have sought with my dogs
   All Horbury[5] shrogs,°   thickets
   And of fifteen hogs
      Found I but one ewe.[6]

DAW   Now trow° me, if ye will,   believe
   By Saint Thomas of Kent,
   Either Mak or Gill
   Was at that assent.[7]
COLL   Peace, man, be still!
   I saw when he went.
   Thou slanders him ill—
   Thou ought to repent
      Good speed.°   speedily
GIB   Now as ever might I thee,°   thrive
   If I should even here dee,°   die
   I would say it were he
      That did that same deed.

DAW   Go we thither, I read,°   advise
   And run on our feet.
   Shall I never eat bread
   The sooth to I weet.[8]
COLL   Nor drink in my head,
   With him till I meet.[9]

3. When at last you hear (them coming).   (i.e., the wether [ram] was missing).
4. Unless I play a false trick.   7. Was a party to it.
5. A village near Wakefield.   8. Until I know the truth.
6. And with fifteen lambs I found only a ewe   9. Nor take a drink till I meet with him.

GIB   I will rest in no stead°   *place*
680   Till that I him greet,
          My brother.
       One I will hight:[1]
       Till I see him in sight
       Shall I never sleep one night
685   There I do another.[2]

          [*The shepherds approach* MAK's *house.* MAK *and* GILL *within, she in bed, groaning, he singing a lullaby.*]

DAW   Will ye hear how they hack?[3]
       Our sire list° croon.   *wants to*
COLL   Heard I never none crack°   *sing loudly*
       So clear out of tune.
       Call on him.
690 GIB   Mak!
       Undo your door soon!°   *at once*
MAK   Who is that spake,
          As° it were noon,   *as if*
          On loft?°   *loudly*
695   Who is that, I say?
DAW   Good fellows, were it day.[4]
MAK   As far as ye may,
          [*opening*] Good,° speaks soft   *good men*

       Over a sick woman's head
700   That is at malease.[5]
       I had liefer° be dead   *rather*
       Ere she had any disease.°   *distress*
GILL   Go to another stead!°   *place*
       I may not well wheeze:°   *breathe*
705   Each foot that ye tread
       Goes through my nese.°   *nose*
          So, hee![6]
COLL   Tell us, Mak, if you may,
       How fare ye, I say?
710 MAK   But are ye in this town today?[7]
          Now how fare ye?

       Ye have run in the mire
       And are wet yit.
       I shall make you a fire
715   If you will sit.
       A nurse would I hire.

---

1. One thing will I promise.
2. I'll never sleep in the same place two nights in a row.
3. Trill; a musical term used sarcastically, as also "crack" below.
4. Good friends, if it were daylight (i.e., not friends, since it's still night).
5. Who feels badly.
6. So loudly, i.e., your tramping goes right through my head.
7. I.e., what brings you to this neighborhood today?

THE SECOND SHEPHERDS' PLAY | 319

Think ye on yit?[8]
Well quit is my hire—
My dream this is it—
　　A season.[9]
I have barns,° if ye knew,   *children*
Wel mo° than enew:°   *more / enough*
But we must drink as we brew,
　　And that is but reason.

I would ye dined ere ye yode.°   *went*
Methink that ye sweat.
GIB Nay, neither mends our mood,
　　Drink nor meat.[1]
MAK Why sir, ails you aught but good?[2]
DAW Yea, our sheep that we get°   *tend*
Are stolen as they yode:°   *wandered*
Our loss is great.
MAK Sirs, drinks!
　　Had I been thore,°   *there*
Some should have bought° it full sore.   *paid for*
COLL Marry, some men trows° that ye wore,°   *think / were*
　　And that us forthinks.°   *displeases*

GIB Mak, some men trows,
　　That it should be ye.
DAW Either ye or your spouse,
　　So say we.
MAK Now if you have suspouse°   *suspicion*
　　To Gill or to me,
Come and ripe° the house   *ransack*
And then may ye see
　　Who had her[3]—
If I any sheep fot,°   *fetched, stole*
Either cow or stot[4]—
And Gill my wife rose not
　　Here sin she laid her.°   *lay down*

As I am true and leal,°   *honest*
To God here I pray
That this be the first meal
That I shall eat this day.
COLL Mak, as I have sele,[5]
　　Advise thee, I say:
He learned timely to steal
That could not say nay.[6]   [*They begin to search.*]

---

8. Do you still remember (my dream)?
9. Ironic: my season's wages are well paid—my
dream (that Gill was giving birth) has come true.
1. Neither food nor drink will improve our mood.
2. Does anything other than good trouble you?
I.e., what's wrong?

3. I.e., the sheep.
4. Either female or male.
5. As I hope to have salvation.
6. He learned early to steal who could not say no
(proverbial).

GILL I swelt!°   *die*

760   Out, thieves, from my wones!°   *dwelling*
      Ye come to rob us for the nones.[7]
   MAK Hear ye not how she groans?
      Your hearts should melt.

   GILL Out, thieves, from my barn!°   *child*
765   Nigh him not thore![8]
   MAK Wist ye how she had farn,[9]
      Your hearts would be sore.
      You do wrong, I you warn,
      That thus comes before°   *in the presence*
770   To a woman that has farn°—   *been in labor*
      But I say no more.
   GILL Ah, my middill!°   *middle*
      I pray to God so mild,
      If ever I you beguiled,
775   That I eat this child
        That lies in this cradill.
   MAK Peace, woman, for God's pain,
      And cry not so!

      Thou spills° thy brain   *harm*
780   And makes me full woe.
   GIB I trow our sheep be slain.
      What find ye two?
   DAW All work we in vain;
      As well may we go.
785   But hatters![1]
      I can find no flesh,
      Hard nor nesh,°   *soft*
      Salt nor fresh,
       But two tome° platters.   *empty*

790   Quick cattle but this,[2]
      Tame nor wild,
      None, as I have bliss,
      As loud as he smiled.[3]   *[Approaches the cradle.]*
   GILL No, so God me bliss,°   *bless*
795   And give me joy of my child!
   COLL We have marked° amiss— *aimed*
      I hold° us beguiled.   *consider*
   GIB Sir, don!°   *totally*
      [to MAK] Sir—Our Lady him save!—
800   Is your child a knave?[4]
   MAK Any lord might him have,
      This child, to° his son.   *as*

---

7. You come for the purpose of robbing us.
8. Don't come close to him there.
9. If you knew how she had fared (in labor).
1. An expression of consternation.

2. Livestock other than this (the baby).
3. Smelled as strongly as he (the missing ram).
4. Boy (although Mak takes the alternate meaning of "rascal").

When he wakens he kips,°   snatches, grabs
  That joy is to see.
DAW   In good time to his hips,
  And in sely.[5]
  But who were his gossips,°   godparents
  So soon ready?
MAK   So fair fall their lips[6]—
COLL   Hark, now, a lee,°   lie
MAK   So God them thank,
  Perkin, and Gibbon Waller, I say,
  And gentle John Horne, in good fay°—   faith
  He made all the garray°   quarrel
    With the great shank.[7]

GIB   Mak, friends will we be,
  For we are all one.°   in accord
MAK   We? Now I hold for me,
  For mends get I none.[8]
  Farewell all three,
  All glad[9] were ye gone.
DAW   Fair words may there be,
  But love is there none
    This year.   [They go out the door.]
COLL   Gave ye the child anything?
GIB   I trow not one farthing.
DAW   Fast again will I fling.°   dash
  Abide ye me there.   [He runs back.]

  Mak, take it no grief
  If I come to thy barn.°   child
MAK   Nay, thou does me great reprief,°   shame
  And foul has thou farn.°   behaved
DAW   The child it will not grief,
  That little day-starn.°   day star
  Mak, with your leaf,°   permission
  Let me give your barn
    But sixpence.
MAK   Nay, do way! He sleeps.
DAW   Methinks he peeps.°   opens his eyes
MAK   When he wakens he weeps.
  I pray you go hence.

    [The other shepherds reenter.]

DAW   Give me leave him to kiss,
  And lift up the clout.°   cover

---

5. Good luck and happiness to him.
6. May good luck befall them.
7. An allusion to a dispute among the shepherds in the author's *First Shepherds' Play.*
8. I'll look out for myself, for I'll get no compensation.
9. I.e., I would be glad.

[lifts the cover]
What the devil is this?
845 He has a long snout!
COLL He is marked amiss.
We wot ill about.[1]
GIB Ill-spun weft, ywis,
Ay comes foul out.[2]
850 Aye, so!
He is like to our sheep.
DAW How, Gib, may I peep?
COLL I trow kind will creep
Where it may not go.[3]

855 GIB This was a quaint gaud
And a far-cast.[4]
It was high fraud.
DAW Yea, sirs, was't.°   *it was*
Let bren° this bawd°   *burn / evildoer*
860 And bind her fast.
A false scaud°   *scold*
Hang at the last:[5]
So shall thou.
Will you see how they swaddle
865 His four feet in the middle?
Saw I never in the cradle
A horned lad ere now.

MAK Peace bid I! What,
Let be your fare!°   *fuss*
870 I am he that him gat.°   *begot*
And yond woman him bare.
COLL What devil shall he hat?[6]
Lo, God, Mak's heir!
GIB Let be all that!
875 Now God give him care°—   *sorrow*
I sawgh!°   *saw*
GILL A pretty child is he
As sits on a woman's knee,
A dillydown,° pardie,° *darling / by God*
880 To gar° a man laugh.   *make*

DAW I know him by the earmark—
That is a good token.
MAK I tell you, sirs, hark,
His nose was broken.

1. He is deformed. We know something fishy is
going on around here.
2. An ill-spun web, indeed, always comes out
badly (proverbial), i.e., ill work always comes to a
bad end.

3. Nature will creep where it can't walk (proverbial), i.e., nature will reveal itself by hook or crook.
4. This was a cunning trick and a clever ruse.
5. Will hang in the end.
6. What the devil shall he be named?

Sithen° told me a clerk   *later*
That he was forspoken.°   *bewitched*
COLL   This is a false wark.°   *work*
  I would fain be wroken.°   *avenged*
    Get wapen.°   *weapon*
GILL   He was taken with an elf[7]
  I saw it myself—
  When the clock struck twelf
    Was he forshapen.°   *transformed*

GIB   Ye two are well feft
  Sam in a stead.[8]
DAW   Sin° they maintain their theft,   *since*
  Let do° them to dead.°   *put / death*
MAK   If I trespass eft,°   *again*
  Gird° off my head.   *chop*
  With you will I be left.[9]
COLL   Sirs, do my read:°   *advice*
  For this trespass
  We will neither ban° ne flite,°   *curse / quarrel*
  Fight nor chite,°   *chide*
  But have done as tite,°   *quickly*
    And cast him in canvas.

[*They toss* MAK *in a blanket.*]

[*The fields*]

COLL   Lord, what° I am sore,   *how*
  In point for to brist!°   *burst*
  In faith, I may no more—
  Therefore will I rist.°   *rest*
GIB   As a sheep of seven score[1]
  He weighed in my fist:
  For to sleep aywhore°   *anywhere*
  Methink that I list.°   *want*
DAW   Now I pray you
  Lie down on this green.
COLL   On the thieves yet I mean.°   *think*
DAW   Whereto should ye teen?°   *be angry*
  Do as I say you.   [*They lie down.*]

[*An* ANGEL *sings* Gloria in Excelsis *and then speaks.*][2]

ANGEL   Rise, herdmen hend,°   *gracious*
  For now is he born
  That shall take fro the fiend°   *devil*

---

7. He was stolen by a fairy, i.e., the baby is a changeling.
8. You two are well endowed in the same place, i.e., you are two of a kind.
9. I put myself at your mercy.
1. I.e., 140 pounds.
2. This is an original stage direction; "Glory [to God] in the highest" (see Luke 2.14).

That Adam had lorn;³
That warlock° to shend,°   *devil / destroy*
925 This night is he born.
God is made your friend
Now at this morn,
    He behestys.°   *promises*
At Bedlem° go see: *Bethlehem*
930 There lies that free,°   *noble one*
In a crib full poorly,
    Betwixt two bestys.°   *beasts*

      [*The* ANGEL *withdraws.*]

COLL   This was a quaint° steven°   *marvelous / voice*
   That ever yet I hard.°   *heard*
935 It is a marvel to neven°   *tell of*
   Thus to be scar'd.°   *scared*
GIB Of God's Son of heaven
   He spake upward.°   *on high*
All the wood on a leven
940 Methought that he gard
      Appear.⁴
DAW He spake of a barn°   *child*
   In Bedlem, I you warn.°   *tell*
COLL   That betokens yond starn.⁵
945   Let us seek him there.

GIB Say, what was his song?
   Heard ye not how he cracked it?⁶
   Three breves° to a long?   *in triple rhythm*
DAW Yea, marry, he hacked it.
950 Was no crochet⁷ wrong,
   Nor nothing that lacked it.⁸
COLL   For to sing us among,
   Right as he knacked it,
      I can.°   *know how*
955 GIB Let see how ye croon!
   Can ye bark at the moon?
DAW Hold your tongues! Have done!
COLL   Hark after, than!   [*Sings.*]

GIB To Bedlem he bade
960 That we should gang:°   *go*
   I am full fard°   *afraid*
   That we tarry too lang.°   *long*

3. That [which] Adam had brought to ruin.
4. I thought he made the whole woods appear in
a flash of light.
5. That's what yonder star means.
6. Trilled it; a technical musical term, close in
meaning to *hacked* and *knacked*: to break (notes),
to sing in a lively or ornate manner (cf. lines 685
and 687).
7. A very short note, requiring quick and skillful
execution.
8. That it lacked.

DAW Be merry and not sad;
  Of mirth is our sang:
  Everlasting glad°   *joy*
  To meed° may we fang.°   *reward / get*
COLL Without nose°   *noise*
  Hie we thither forthy°   *therefore*
  To that child and that lady;
  If° we be wet and weary,   *though*
    We have it not to lose.[9]

GIB We find by the prophecy—
  Let be your din!—
  Of David and Isay,
  And mo than I min,[1]
  That prophesied by clergy°   *learning*
  That in a virgin
  Should he light° and lie,   *alight*
  To sloken° our sin   *quench*
    And slake° it,   *relieve*
  Our kind,° from woe,   *humankind*
  For Isay said so:
  Ecce virgo
    Concipiet[2] a child that is naked.

DAW Full glad may we be
  And° we abide that day   *if*
  That lovely to see,
  That all mights may.[3]
  Lord, well were me
  For once and for ay
  Might I kneel on my knee,
  Some word for to say
    To that child.
  But the angel said
  In a crib was he laid,
  He was poorly arrayed,
    Both meaner° and mild.   *very humbly*

COLL Patriarchs that has been,
  And prophets beforn,°   *before (our time)*
  That desired to have seen
  This child that is born,
  They are gone full clean—
  That have they lorn.[4]
  We shall see him, I ween,°   *think*
  Ere it be morn,
    To token.[5]

---

9. We must not neglect it.
1. Of David and Isaiah and more than I remember.
2. Behold, a virgin shall conceive (Isaiah 7.14).
3. I.e., when we see that lovely one who is all-
powerful.
4. That (sight) have they lost. See Matthew 13.17.
5. As a sign.

When I see him and feel,
Then wot° I full weel°   *know / well*
It is true as steel
1010   That° prophets have spoken: *what*

To so poor as we are
That he would appear,
First find and declare⁶
By his messenger.
1015   GIB   Go we now, let us fare,
The place is us near.
DAW   I am ready and yare;°   *eager*
Go we in fere°   *together*
To that bright.°   *glorious one*
1020   Lord, if thy wills be—
We are lewd° all three—   *ignorant*
Thou grant us some kins glee⁷
To comfort thy wight.°   *child*

[*They go to Bethlehem and enter the stable.*]

COLL   Hail, comely and clean!°   *pure*
1025   Hail, young child!
Hail Maker, as I mean,°   *believe*
Of° a maiden so mild!   *born of*
Thou has waried,° I ween,°   *cursed / think*
The warlock° so wild.   *devil*
1030   The false guiler of teen,⁸
Now goes he beguiled.
Lo, he merries!°   *is merry*
Lo, he laughs, my sweeting!
A well fair meeting!
1035   I have holden my heting:°   *promise*
Have a bob° of cherries.   *bunch*

GIB   Hail, sovereign Saviour,
For thou has us sought!
Hail freely food° and flour,°   *noble child / flower*
1040   That all thing has wrought!°   *created*
Hail, full of favour,
That made all of nought!
Hail! I kneel and I cower.°   *crouch*
A bird have I brought
1045   To my barn.°   *child*
Hail, little tiny mop!°   *baby*
Of our creed thou art crop.°   *head*
I would drink on thy cup,
Little day-starn.°   *day star*

---

6. Find (us) first (of all), and make known (his   7. Some kind of cheer.
birth).   8. The false grievous deceiver, i.e., the devil.

DAW   Hail, darling dear,
   Full of Godhead!
   I pray thee be near
   When that I have need.
   Hail, sweet is thy cheer°—   *face*
   My heart would bleed
   To see thee sit here
   In so poor weed,°   *clothing*
      With no pennies.
   Hail, put forth thy dall!°   *hand*
   I bring thee but a ball:
   Have and play thee withal,
      And go to the tennis.
MARY   The Father of heaven,
   God omnipotent,
   That set all on seven,[9]
   His Son has he sent.
   My name could he neven,
   And light ere he went.[1]
   I conceived him full even
   Through might as he meant.[2]
   And now is he born.
   He° keep you from woe!   *(may) he*
   I shall pray him so.
   Tell forth as ye go,
      And min on° this morn.   *remember*

COLL   Farewell, lady,
   So fair to behold,
   With thy child on thy knee.
GIB   But he lies full cold.
   Lord, well is me.
   Now we go, thou behold.
DAW   Forsooth, already
   It seems to be told
      Full oft.
COLL   What grace we have fun!°   *received*
GIB   Come forth, now are we won!°   *redeemed*
DAW   To sing are we bun:°   *bound*
   Let take on loft.[3]
      [*They sing.*]

9. Who created everything in seven (days).   2. I conceived him, indeed, through his power,
1. My name did he name, and alighted (in me)   just as he intended.
before he went (see Luke 1.28).   3. Let's raise our voices.

SIR THOMAS MALORY
ca. 1405–1471

*M*orte Darthur (Death of Arthur) is the title that William Caxton, the first English printer, gave to Malory's volume, which Caxton described more accurately in his Preface as "the noble histories of * * * King Arthur and of certain of his knights." The volume begins with the mythical story of Arthur's birth. King Uther Pendragon falls in love with the wife of one of his barons. Merlin's magic transforms Uther into the likeness of her husband, and Arthur is born of this union. The volume ends with the destruction of the Round Table and the deaths of Arthur, Queen Guinevere, and Sir Lancelot, who is Arthur's best knight and the queen's lover. The bulk of the work is taken up with the separate adventures of the knights of the Round Table.

During the thirteenth century the stories about Arthur and his knights had been turned into a series of enormously long prose romances in French, and it was these, as Caxton informed his readers, "Sir Thomas Malory did take out of certain books of French and reduced into English." For Caxton's Preface and excerpts from a modern translation of the French *Prose Vulgate Cycle* (Malory's "French books"), see the "King Arthur" topic in the supplemental ebook.

Little was known about the author until the early twentieth century when scholars began to unearth the criminal record of a Sir Thomas Malory of Newbold Revell in Warwickshire. In 1451 he was arrested for the first time to prevent his doing injury—presumably further injury—to a priory in Lincolnshire, and shortly thereafter he was accused of a number of criminal acts. These included escaping from prison after his first arrest, twice breaking into and plundering the Abbey of Coombe, extorting money from various persons, and committing rape. Malory pleaded innocent of all charges. The Wars of the Roses—in which Malory, like the formidable earl of Warwick (the "kingmaker"), whom he seems to have followed, switched sides from Lancaster to York and back again—may account for some of his troubles with the law. After a failed Lancastrian revolt, the Yorkist king, Edward IV, specifically excluded Malory from four amnesties he granted to the Lancastrians.

The identification of this Sir Thomas Malory (there is another candidate with the same name) as the author of the *Morte* was strengthened by the discovery in 1934 of a manuscript that differed from Caxton's text, the only version previously known. The manuscript contained eight separate romances. Caxton, in order to give the impression of a continuous narrative, had welded these together into twenty-one books, subdivided into short chapters with summary chapter headings. Caxton suppressed all but the last of the personal remarks the author had appended to individual tales in the manuscript. At the very end of the book Malory asks "all gentlemen and gentlewomen that readeth this book * * * pray for me while I am alive that God send me good deliverance." The discovery of the manuscript revealed that at the close of the first tale he had written: "this was drawyn by a knight presoner Sir Thomas Malleoré, that God sende him good recover." There is strong circumstantial evidence, therefore, that the book from which the Arthurian legends were passed on to future generations to be adapted in literature, art, and film was written in prison by a man whose violent career might seem at odds with the chivalric ideals he professes.

Such a contradiction—if it really is one—should not be surprising. Nostalgia for an ideal past that never truly existed is typical of much historical romance. Like the slave-owning plantation society of Margaret Mitchell's *Gone with the Wind*, whose southern gentlemen cultivate chivalrous manners and respect for gentlewomen, Malory's Arthurian world is a fiction. In our terms, it cannot even be labeled "historical," although the distinction between romance and history is not one that Malory would have made. Only rarely does he voice skepticism about the historicity of his tale; one such example is his questioning of the myth of Arthur's return. Much of the tragic power of his romance lies in his sense of the irretrievability of past glory in comparison with the sordidness of his own age.

The success of Malory's retelling owes much to his development of a terse and direct prose style, especially the naturalistic dialogue that keeps his narrative close to earth. And both he and many of his characters are masters of understatement who express themselves, in moments of great emotional tension, with a bare minimum of words.

In spite of its professed dedication to service of women, Malory's chivalry is primarily devoted to the fellowship and competitions of aristocratic men. Fighting consists mainly of single combats in tournaments, chance encounters, and battles, which Malory never tires of describing in professional detail. Commoners rarely come into view; when they do, the effect can be chilling—as when pillagers by moonlight plunder the corpses of the knights left on the field of Arthur's last battle. Above all, Malory cherishes an aristocratic male code of honor for which his favorite word is "worship." Men win or lose "worship" through their actions in war and love.

The most "worshipful" of Arthur's knights is Sir Lancelot, the "head of all Christian knights," as he is called in a moving eulogy by his brother, Sir Ector. But Lancelot is compromised by his fatal liaison with Arthur's queen and torn between the incompatible loyalties that bind him as an honorable knight, on the one hand, to his lord Arthur and, on the other, to his lady Guinevere. Malory loves his character Lancelot even to the point of indulging in the fleeting speculation, after Lancelot has been admitted to the queen's chamber, that their activities might have been innocent, "for love that time was not as love is nowadays." But when the jealousy and malice of two wicked knights force the affair into the open, nothing can avert a mighty civil war; the breaking up of the fellowship of the Round Table; and the death of Arthur himself, which Malory relates with somber magnificence as the passing of a great era.

From Morte Darthur[1]

[THE CONSPIRACY AGAINST LANCELOT AND GUINEVERE]

In May, when every lusty[2] heart flourisheth and burgeoneth, for as the season is lusty to behold and comfortable,[3] so man and woman rejoiceth and gladdeth of summer coming with his fresh flowers; for winter with his rough winds and blasts causeth lusty men and women to cower and to sit fast by the fire—so this season it befell in the month of May a great anger and unhap that stinted not[4] till the flower of chivalry of all the world was destroyed and slain. And all was long upon two unhappy[5] knights which were named Sir Agravain and Sir Mordred that were brethren unto Sir Gawain.[6] For this

1. The selections here are from the section that Caxton called book 20, chaps. 1–4, 8–10, and book 21, chaps. 3–7, 10–12, with omissions. In the Winchester manuscript this section is titled "The Most Piteous Tale of the Morte Arthur Saunz Guerdon" (i.e., the death of Arthur without reward or compensation). The text is based on Winchester, with some readings introduced from the Caxton edition; spelling has been modernized and modern punctuation added.
2. Merry.
3. Pleasant.
4. Misfortune that ceased not.
5. On account of two ill-fated.
6. Gawain and Agravain are sons of King Lot of Orkney and his wife, Arthur's half-sister Morgause. Mordred is the illegitimate son of Arthur and Morgause.

Sir Agravain and Sir Mordred had ever a privy[7] hate unto the Queen, Dame Guinevere, and to Sir Lancelot, and daily and nightly they ever watched upon Sir Lancelot.

So it misfortuned Sir Gawain and all his brethren were in King Arthur's chamber, and then Sir Agravain said thus openly, and not in no counsel,[8] that many knights might hear: "I marvel that we all be not ashamed both to see and to know how Sir Lancelot lieth daily and nightly by the Queen. And all we know well that it is so, and it is shamefully suffered of us all[9] that we should suffer so noble a king as King Arthur is to be shamed."

Then spoke Sir Gawain and said, "Brother, Sir Agravain, I pray you and charge you, move no such matters no more afore[1] me, for wit you well, I will not be of your counsel."[2]

"So God me help," said Sir Gaheris and Sir Gareth,[3] "we will not be known of your deeds."[4]

"Then will I!" said Sir Mordred.

"I lieve[5] you well," said Sir Gawain, "for ever unto all unhappiness, sir, ye will grant.[6] And I would that ye left all this and make you not so busy, for I know," said Sir Gawain, "what will fall of it."[7]

"Fall whatsoever fall may," said Sir Agravain, "I will disclose it to the King."

"Not by my counsel," said Sir Gawain, "for and[8] there arise war and wrack betwixt[9] Sir Lancelot and us, wit you well, brother, there will many kings and great lords hold with Sir Lancelot. Also, brother, Sir Agravain," said Sir Gawain, "ye must remember how often times Sir Lancelot hath rescued the King and the Queen. And the best of us all had been full cold at the heart-root[1] had not Sir Lancelot been better than we, and that has he proved himself full oft. And as for my part," said Sir Gawain, "I will never be against Sir Lancelot for[2] one day's deed, when he rescued me from King Carados of the Dolorous[3] Tower and slew him and saved my life. Also, brother, Sir Agravain and Sir Mordred, in like wise Sir Lancelot rescued you both and three score and two[4] from Sir Tarquin. And therefore, brother, methinks such noble deeds and kindness should be remembered."

"Do as ye list,"[5] said Sir Agravain, "for I will layne[6] it no longer."

So with these words came in Sir Arthur.

"Now, brother," said Sir Gawain, "stint your noise."[7]

"That will I not," said Sir Agravain and Sir Mordred.

"Well, will ye so?" said Sir Gawain. "Then God speed you, for I will not hear of your tales, neither be of your counsel."

"No more will I," said Sir Gaheris.

"Neither I," said Sir Gareth, "for I shall never say evil by[8] that man that made me knight." And therewithal they three departed making great dole.[9]

---

7. Secret.
8. Secret manner.
9. Put up with by all of us.
1. Before. "Move": propose.
2. On your side. "Wit you well": know well, i.e., give you to understand.
3. Sons of King Lot and Gawain's brothers.
4. A party to your doings.
5. Believe.
6. You will consent to all mischief.
7. Come of it.

8. If.
9. Strife between.
1. Would have been dead.
2. On account of.
3. Dismal.
4. I.e., sixty two.
5. You please.
6. Conceal.
7. Stop making scandal.
8. About.
9. Lamentation.

"Alas!" said Sir Gawain and Sir Gareth, "now is this realm wholly destroyed and mischieved,[1] and the noble fellowship of the Round Table shall be disparbeled."[2]

So they departed, and then King Arthur asked them what noise[3] they made. "My lord," said Sir Agravain, "I shall tell you, for I may keep[4] it no longer. Here is I and my brother Sir Mordred broke[5] unto my brother Sir Gawain, Sir Gaheris, and to Sir Gareth—for this is all, to make it short—how that we know all that Sir Lancelot holdeth your queen, and hath done long; and we be your sister[6] sons, we may suffer it no longer. And all we woot[7] that ye should be above Sir Lancelot, and ye are the king that made him knight, and therefore we will prove it that he is a traitor to your person."

"If it be so," said the King, "wit[8] you well, he is none other. But I would be loath to begin such a thing but[9] I might have proofs of it, for Sir Lancelot is an hardy knight, and all ye know that he is the best knight among us all. And but if he be taken with the deed,[1] he will fight with him that bringeth up the noise, and I know no knight that is able to match him. Therefore, and[2] it be sooth as ye say, I would that he were taken with the deed."

For, as the French book saith, the King was full loath that such a noise should be upon Sir Lancelot and his queen. For the King had a deeming[3] of it, but he would not hear of it, for Sir Lancelot had done so much for him and for the Queen so many times that, wit you well, the King loved him passingly[4] well.

"My lord," said Sir Agravain, "ye shall ride tomorn[5] on hunting, and doubt ye not, Sir Lancelot will not go with you. And so when it draweth toward night, ye may send the Queen word that ye will lie out all that night, and so may ye send for your cooks. And then, upon pain of death, that night we shall take him with the Queen, and we shall bring him unto you, quick[6] or dead."

"I will well," said the King. "Then I counsel you to take with you sure fellowship."

"Sir," said Sir Agravain, "my brother, Sir Mordred, and I will take with us twelve knights of the Round Table."

"Beware," said King Arthur, "for I warn you, ye shall find him wight."[8]

"Let us deal!"[9] said Sir Agravain and Sir Mordred.

So on the morn King Arthur rode on hunting and sent word to the Queen that he would be out all that night. Then Sir Agravain and Sir Mordred got to them[1] twelve knights and hid themself in a chamber in the castle of Carlisle. And these were their names: Sir Colgrevance, Sir Mador de la Porte, Sir Guingalen, Sir Meliot de Logres, Sir Petipace of Winchelsea, Sir Galeron of Galway, Sir Melion de la Mountain, Sir Ascamore, Sir Gromore Somyr Jour, Sir Curselayne, Sir Florence, and Sir Lovell. So these twelve knights were with Sir Mordred and Sir Agravain, and all they were of Scotland, or else of Sir Gawain's kin, or well-willers[2] to his brother.

1. Put to shame.
2. Dispersed.
3. Rumor.
4. Conceal.
5. Revealed.
6. Sister's.
7. Know.
8. Know.
9. Unless
1. Unless he is caught in the act.

2. If.
3. Suspicion.
4. Exceedingly.
5. Tomorrow.
6. Alive.
7. Readily agree.
8. Strong.
9. Leave it to us.
1. Gathered to themselves.
2. Partisans.

So when the night came, Sir Lancelot told Sir Bors[3] how he would go that night and speak with the Queen.

"Sir," said Sir Bors, "ye shall not go this night by my counsel."

"Why?" said Sir Lancelot.

"Sir," said Sir Bors, "I dread me[4] ever of Sir Agravain that waiteth upon[5] you daily to do you shame and us all. And never gave my heart against no going that ever ye went[6] to the queen so much as now, for I mistrust[7] that the King is out this night from the Queen because peradventure he hath lain[8] some watch for you and the Queen. Therefore, I dread me sore of some treason."

"Have ye no dread," said Sir Lancelot, "for I shall go and come again and make no tarrying."

"Sir," said Sir Bors, "that me repents,[9] for I dread me sore that your going this night shall wrath[1] us all."

"Fair nephew," said Sir Lancelot, "I marvel me much why ye say thus, sithen[2] the Queen hath sent for me. And wit you well, I will not be so much a coward, but she shall understand I will[3] see her good grace."

"God speed you well," said Sir Bors, "and send you sound and safe again!"

So Sir Lancelot departed and took his sword under his arm, and so he walked in his mantel,[4] that noble knight, and put himself in great jeopardy. And so he passed on till he came to the Queen's chamber, and so lightly he was had[5] into the chamber. And then, as the French book saith, the Queen and Sir Lancelot were together. And whether they were abed or at other manner of disports, me list[6] not thereof make no mention, for love that time[7] was not as love is nowadays.

But thus as they were together there came Sir Agravain and Sir Mordred with twelve knights with them of the Round Table, and they said with great crying and scaring[8] voice: "Thou traitor, Sir Lancelot, now are thou taken!" And thus they cried with a loud voice that all the court might hear it. And these fourteen knights all were armed at all points, as[9] they should fight in a battle.

"Alas!" said Queen Guinevere, "now are we mischieved[1] both!"

"Madam," said Sir Lancelot, "is there here any armor within your chamber that I might cover my body withal? And if there be any, give it me, and I shall soon stint[2] their malice, by the grace of God!"

"Now, truly," said the Queen, "I have none armor neither helm, shield, sword, neither spear, wherefore I dread me sore our long love is come to a mischievous end. For I hear by their noise there be many noble knights, and well I woot they be surely[3] armed, and against them ye may make no resistance. Wherefore ye are likely to be slain, and then shall I be burned! For and[4] ye might escape them," said the Queen, "I would not doubt but that ye would rescue me in what danger that ever I stood in."

3. Nephew and confidant of Sir Lancelot.
4. I am afraid.
5. Lies in wait.
6. Never misgave my heart against any visit you made.
7. Suspect.
8. Perhaps he has set.
9. I regret.
1. Cause injury to.
2. Since.
3. Wish to.

4. Cloak. Lancelot goes without armor.
5. Quickly he was received.
6. I care. "Disports": pastimes.
7. At that time.
8. Terrifying.
9. Completely, as if.
1. Come to grief.
2. Stop.
3. Securely.
4. If.

"Alas!" said Sir Lancelot, "in all my life thus was I never bestead[5] that I should be thus shamefully slain for lack of mine armor."

But ever in one[6] Sir Agravain and Sir Mordred cried: "Traitor knight, come out of the Queen's chamber! For wit thou well thou art beset so that thou shalt not escape."

"Ah, Jesu mercy!" said Sir Lancelot, "this shameful cry and noise I may not suffer, for better were death at once than thus to endure this pain." Then he took the Queen in his arms and kissed her and said, "Most noblest Christian queen, I beseech you, as ye have been ever my special good lady, and I at all times your poor knight and true unto[7] my power, and as I never failed you in right nor in wrong sithen the first day King Arthur made me knight, that ye will pray for my soul if that I be slain. For well I am assured that Sir Bors, my nephew, and all the remnant of my kin, with Sir Lavain and Sir Urry,[8] that they will not fail you to rescue you from the fire. And therefore, mine own lady, recomfort yourself,[9] whatsoever come of me, that ye go with Sir Bors, my nephew, and Sir Urry and they all will do you all the pleasure that they may, and ye shall live like a queen upon my lands."

"Nay, Sir Lancelot, nay!" said the Queen. "Wit thou well that I will not live long after thy days. But and[1] ye be slain I will take my death as meekly as ever did martyr take his death for Jesu Christ's sake."

"Well, Madam," said Sir Lancelot, "sith it is so that the day is come that our love must depart,[2] wit you well I shall sell my life as dear as I may. And a thousandfold," said Sir Lancelot, "I am more heavier[3] for you than for myself! And now I had liefer[4] than to be lord of all Christendom that I had sure armor upon me, that men might speak of my deeds ere ever I were slain."

"Truly," said the Queen, "and[5] it might please God, I would that they would take me and slay me and suffer[6] you to escape."

"That shall never be," said Sir Lancelot. "God defend me from such a shame! But, Jesu Christ, be Thou my shield and mine armor!" And therewith Sir Lancelot wrapped his mantel about his arm well and surely; and by then they had gotten a great form[7] out of the hall, and therewith they all rushed at the door. "Now, fair lords," said Sir Lancelot, "leave[8] your noise and your rushing, and I shall set open this door, and then may ye do with me what it liketh you."[9]

"Come off,[1] then," said they all, "and do it, for it availeth thee not to strive against us all. And therefore let us into this chamber, and we shall save thy life until thou come to King Arthur."

Then Sir Lancelot unbarred the door, and with his left hand he held it open a little, that but one man might come in at once. And so there came striding a good knight, a much[2] man and a large, and his name was called Sir Colgrevance of Gore. And he with a sword struck at Sir Lancelot mightily. And he put aside[3] the stroke and gave him such a buffet[4] upon the helmet that he fell groveling dead within the chamber door. Then Sir Lancelot

5. Beset.
6. In unison.
7. To the utmost of.
8. The brother of Elaine, the Fair Maid of Astolat, and a knight miraculously healed of his wound by Sir Lancelot. "Remnant": rest.
9. Take heart again.
1. If.
2. Come to an end.
3. More grieved.

4. Rather.
5. If.
6. Allow.
7. Bench.
8. Stop.
9. Pleases you.
1. Go ahead.
2. Big.
3. Fended off.
4. Blow.

with great might drew the knight within[5] the chamber door. And then Sir Lancelot, with help of the Queen and her ladies, he was lightly[6] armed in Colgrevance's armor. And ever stood Sir Agravain and Sir Mordred, crying, "Traitor knight! Come forth out of the Queen's chamber!"

"Sirs, leave[7] your noise," said Sir Lancelot, "for wit you well, Sir Agravain, ye shall not prison me this night. And therefore, and[8] ye do by my counsel, go ye all from this chamber door and make you no such crying and such manner of slander as ye do. For I promise you by my knighthood, and ye will depart and make no more noise, I shall as tomorn appear afore you all and before the King, and then let it be seen which of you all, other else ye all,[9] that will deprove[1] me of treason. And there shall I answer you, as a knight should, that hither I came to the Queen for no manner of mal engine,[2] and that will I prove and make it good upon you with my hands."

"Fie upon thee, traitor," said Sir Agravain and Sir Mordred, "for we will have thee malgré thine head[3] and slay thee, and we list.[4] For we let thee wit we have the choice of[5] King Arthur to save thee other slay thee."

"Ah, sirs," said Sir Lancelot, "is there none other grace with you? Then keep[6] yourself!" And then Sir Lancelot set all open the chamber door and mightily and knightly he strode in among them. And anon[7] at the first stroke he slew Sir Agravain, and after twelve of his fellows. Within a little while he had laid them down cold to the earth, for there was none of the twelve knights might stand Sir Lancelot one buffet.[8] And also he wounded Sir Mordred, and therewithal he fled with all his might.

And then Sir Lancelot returned again unto the Queen and said, "Madam, now wit you well, all our true love is brought to an end, for now will King Arthur ever be my foe. And therefore, Madam, and it like you[9] that I may have you with me, I shall save you from all manner adventurous[1] dangers."

"Sir, that is not best," said the Queen, "me seemeth, for[2] now ye have done so much harm, it will be best that ye hold you still with this. And if ye see that as tomorn they will put me unto death, then may ye rescue me as ye think best."

"I will well,"[3] said Sir Lancelot, "for have ye no doubt, while I am a man living I shall rescue you." And then he kissed her, and either of them gave other a ring, and so there he left the Queen and went until[4] his lodging.

[WAR BREAKS OUT BETWEEN ARTHUR AND LANCELOT][5]

Then said King Arthur unto Sir Gawain, "Dear nephew, I pray you make ready in your best armor with your brethren, Sir Gaheris and Sir Gareth, to bring my Queen to the fire, there to have her judgment and receive the death."

---

5. Inside.
6. Quickly.
7. Stop.
8. If.
9. Or else all of you.
1. Accuse.
2. Evil design.
3. In spite of you.
4. If we please.
5. From.
6. Defend.
7. Right away.
8. Withstand Sir Lancelot one blow.

9. If it please you.
1. Perilous.
2. Because.
3. Agree.
4. To.
5. Lancelot and Sir Bors mobilize their friends for the rescue of Guinevere. In the morning Mordred reports the events of the night to Arthur who, against Gawain's strong opposition, condemns the queen to be burned, for "the law was such in those days that whatsoever they were, of what estate or degree, if they were found guilty of treason there should be none other remedy but death."

"Nay, my most noble king," said Sir Gawain, "that will I never do, for wit you well I will never be in that place where so noble a queen as is my lady Dame Guinevere shall take such a shameful end. For wit you well," said Sir Gawain, "my heart will not serve me for to see her die, and it shall never be said that ever I was of your counsel for her death."

"Then," said the King unto Sir Gawain, "suffer[6] your brethren Sir Gaheris and Sir Gareth to be there."

"My lord," said Sir Gawain, "wit you well they will be loath to be there present because of many adventures[7] that is like to fall, but they are young and full unable to say you nay."

Then spake Sir Gaheris and the good knight Sir Gareth unto King Arthur: "Sir, ye may well command us to be there, but wit you well it shall be sore against our will. But and[8] we be there by your strait commandment, ye shall plainly[9] hold us there excused—we will be there in peaceable wise and bear none harness of war[1] upon us."

"In the name of God," said the King, "then make you ready, for she shall have soon[2] her judgment."

"Alas," said Sir Gawain, "that ever I should endure[3] to see this woeful day." So Sir Gawain turned him and wept heartily, and so he went into his chamber.

And then the Queen was led forth without[4] Carlisle, and anon she was dispoiled into[5] her smock. And then her ghostly father[6] was brought to her to be shriven of her misdeeds.[7] Then was there weeping and wailing and wringing of hands of many lords and ladies, but there were but few in comparison that would bear any armor for to strengthen[8] the death of the Queen.

Then was there one that Sir Lancelot had sent unto that place, which went to espy what time the Queen should go unto her death. And anon as[9] he saw the Queen dispoiled into her smock and shriven, then he gave Sir Lancelot warning. Then was there but spurring and plucking up[1] of horses, and right so they came unto the fire. And who[2] that stood against them, there were they slain—there might none withstand Sir Lancelot. So all that bore arms and withstood them, there were they slain, full many a noble knight. * * * And so in this rushing and hurling, as Sir Lancelot thrang[3] here and there, it misfortuned him[4] to slay Sir Gaheris and Sir Gareth, the noble knight, for they were unarmed and unwares.[5] As the French book saith, Sir Lancelot smote Sir Gaheris and Sir Gareth upon the brain-pans, wherethrough[6] that they were slain in the field, howbeit[7] Sir Lancelot saw them not. And so were they found dead among the thickest of the press.[8]

Then when Sir Lancelot had thus done, and slain and put to flight all that would withstand him, then he rode straight unto Queen Guinevere and made a kirtle[9] and a gown to be cast upon her, and then he made her to be set behind him and prayed her to be of good cheer. Now wit you well the

---

6. Allow.
7. Chance occurrences.
8. If.
9. "Strait": strict; "plainly": openly.
1. Armor.
2. Right away.
3. Live.
4. Outside.
5. Undressed down to.
6. Spiritual father, i.e., her priest.
7. For her to be confessed of her sins.

8. Secure.
9. As soon as.
1. Urging forward.
2. Whoever.
3. Pressed. "Hurling": turmoil.
4. He had the misfortune.
5. Unaware.
6. Through which.
7. Although.
8. Crowd.
9. Petticoat.

Queen was glad that she was escaped from death, and then she thanked God and Sir Lancelot.

And so he rode his way with the Queen, as the French book saith, unto Joyous Garde,[1] and there he kept her as a noble knight should. And many great lords and many good knights were sent him, and many full noble knights drew unto him. When they heard that King Arthur and Sir Lancelot were at debate,[2] many knights were glad, and many were sorry of their debate.

Now turn we again unto King Arthur, that when it was told him how and in what manner the Queen was taken away from the fire, and when he heard of the death of his noble knights, and in especial Sir Gaheris and Sir Gareth, then he swooned for very pure[3] sorrow. And when he awoke of his swoon, then he said: "Alas, that ever I bore crown upon my head! For now have I lost the fairest fellowship of noble knights that ever held Christian king[4] together. Alas, my good knights be slain and gone away from me. Now within these two days I have lost nigh forty knights and also the noble fellowship of Sir Lancelot and his blood,[5] for now I may nevermore hold them together with my worship.[6] Alas, that ever this war began!

"Now, fair fellows," said the King, "I charge you that no man tell Sir Gawain of the death of his two brethren, for I am sure," said the King, "when he heareth tell that Sir Gareth is dead, he will go nigh out of his mind. Mercy Jesu," said the King, "why slew he Sir Gaheris and Sir Gareth? For I dare say, as for Sir Gareth, he loved Sir Lancelot above all men earthly."[7]

"That is truth," said some knights, "but they were slain in the hurling,[8] as Sir Lancelot thrang in the thickest of the press. And as they were unarmed, he smote them and wist[9] not whom that he smote, and so unhappily[1] they were slain."

"Well," said Arthur, "the death of them will cause the greatest mortal war that ever was, for I am sure that when Sir Gawain knoweth hereof that Sir Gareth is slain, I shall never have rest of him[2] till I have destroyed Sir Lancelot's kin and himself both, other else he to destroy me. And therefore," said the King, "wit you well, my heart was never so heavy as it is now. And much more I am sorrier for my good knights' loss[3] than for the loss of my fair queen; for queens I might have enough, but such a fellowship of good knights shall never be together in no company. And now I dare say," said King Arthur, "there was never Christian king that ever held such a fellowship together. And alas, that ever Sir Lancelot and I should be at debate. Ah, Agravain, Agravain!" said the King, "Jesu forgive it thy soul, for thine evil will that thou and thy brother Sir Mordred haddest unto Sir Lancelot hath caused all this sorrow." And ever among these complaints the King wept and swooned.

Then came there one to Sir Gawain and told him how the Queen was led away with[4] Sir Lancelot, and nigh a four-and-twenty knights slain. "Ah, Jesu, save me my two brethren!" said Sir Gawain. "For full well wist I," said Sir Gawain, "that Sir Lancelot would rescue her, other else he would die in that field. And to say the truth he were not of worship but if he had[5] rescued the

---

1. Lancelot's castle in England.
2. Strife.
3. Sheer.
4. That Christian king ever held.
5. Kin.
6. Keep both them and my dignity.
7. Earthly men.

8. Turmoil.
9. Knew.
1. Unluckily.
2. He will never give me any peace.
3. The loss of my good knights.
4. By.
5. Of honor if he had not.

Queen, insomuch as she should have been burned for his sake. And as in that," said Sir Gawain, "he hath done but knightly, and as I would have done myself and I had stood in like case. But where are my brethren?" said Sir Gawain. "I marvel that I hear not of them."

Then said that man, "Truly, Sir Gaheris and Sir Gareth be slain."

"Jesu defend!"[6] said Sir Gawain. "For all this world I would not that they were slain, and in especial my good brother Sir Gareth."

"Sir," said the man, "he is slain, and that is great pity."

"Who slew him?" said Sir Gawain.

"Sir Lancelot," said the man, "slew them both."

"That may I not believe," said Sir Gawain, "that ever he slew my good brother Sir Gareth, for I dare say my brother loved him better than me and all his brethren and the King both. Also I dare say, an[7] Sir Lancelot had desired my brother Sir Gareth with him, he would have been with him against the King and us all. And therefore I may never believe that Sir Lancelot slew my brethren."

"Verily, sir," said the man, "it is noised[8] that he slew him."

"Alas," said Sir Gawain, "now is my joy gone." And then he fell down and swooned, and long he lay there as he had been dead. And when he arose out of his swoon, he cried out sorrowfully and said, "Alas!" And forthwith he ran unto the King, crying and weeping, and said, "Ah, mine uncle King Arthur! My good brother Sir Gareth is slain, and so is my brother Sir Gaheris, which were two noble knights."

Then the King wept and he both, and so they fell on swooning. And when they were revived, then spake Sir Gawain and said, "Sir, I will go and see my brother Sir Gareth."

"Sir, ye may not see him," said the King, "for I caused him to be interred and Sir Gaheris both, for I well understood that ye would make overmuch sorrow, and the sight of Sir Gareth should have caused your double sorrow."

"Alas, my lord," said Sir Gawain, "how slew he my brother Sir Gareth? Mine own good lord, I pray you tell me."

"Truly," said the King, "I shall tell you as it hath been told me—Sir Lancelot slew him and Sir Gaheris both."

"Alas," said Sir Gawain, "they bore none arms against him, neither of them both."

"I woot not how it was," said the King, "but as it is said, Sir Lancelot slew them in the thickest of the press and knew them not. And therefore let us shape a remedy for to revenge their deaths."

"My king, my lord, and mine uncle," said Sir Gawain, "wit you well, now I shall make you a promise which I shall hold by my knighthood, that from this day forward I shall never fail[9] Sir Lancelot until that one of us have slain the other. And therefore I require you, my lord and king, dress[1] you unto the wars, for wit you well, I will be revenged upon Sir Lancelot; and therefore, as ye will have my service and my love, now haste you thereto and assay[2] your friends. For I promise unto God," said Sir Gawain, "for the death of my brother Sir Gareth I shall seek Sir Lancelot throughout seven kings' realms, but I shall slay him, other else he shall slay me."

6. Forbid.
7. If.
8. Reported.

9. Give up the pursuit of.
1. Prepare.
2. Appeal to.

"Sir, ye shall not need to seek him so far," said the King, "for as I hear say, Sir Lancelot will abide me and us all within the castle of Joyous Garde. And much people draweth unto him, as I hear say."

"That may I right well believe," said Sir Gawain, "but my lord," he said, "assay your friends and I will assay mine."

"It shall be done," said the King, "and as I suppose I shall be big[3] enough to drive him out of the biggest tower of his castle."

So then the King sent letters and writs throughout all England, both the length and the breadth, for to summon all his knights. And so unto King Arthur drew many knights, dukes, and earls, that he had a great host, and when they were assembled the King informed them how Sir Lancelot had bereft him his Queen. Then the King and all his host made them ready to lay siege about Sir Lancelot where he lay within Joyous Garde.

[THE DEATH OF ARTHUR][4]

So upon Trinity Sunday at night King Arthur dreamed a wonderful dream, and in his dream him seemed that he saw upon a chafflet[5] a chair, and the chair was fast to a wheel, and thereupon sat King Arthur in the richest cloth of gold that might be made. And the King thought there was under him, far from him, an hideous deep black water, and therein was all manner of serpents, and worms, and wild beasts, foul and horrible. And suddenly the King thought that the wheel turned upside down, and he fell among the serpents, and every beast took him by a limb. And then the King cried as he lay in his bed, "Help, help!"

And then knights, squires, and yeomen awaked the King, and then he was so amazed[6] that he wist[7] not where he was. And then so he awaked[8] until it was nigh day, and then he fell on slumbering again, not sleeping nor thoroughly waking. So the King seemed[9] verily that there came Sir Gawain unto him with a number of fair ladies with him. So when King Arthur saw him, he said, "Welcome, my sister's son. I weened ye had been dead. And now I see thee on-live, much am I beholden unto Almighty Jesu. Ah, fair nephew and my sister's son, what been these ladies that hither be come with you?"

"Sir," said Sir Gawain, "all these be ladies for whom I have foughten for when I was man living. And all these are tho[1] that I did battle for in righteous quarrels, and God hath given them that grace, at their great prayer, because I did battle for them for their right, that they should bring me hither unto you. Thus much hath given me leave God, for to warn you of your death. For and ye fight as tomorn[2] with Sir Mordred, as ye both have assigned,[3] doubt ye not ye must be slain, and the most party of your people on both parties. And for the great grace and goodness that Almighty Jesu hath unto you, and for

---

3. Strong.
4. The pope arranges a truce, Guinevere is returned to Arthur, and Lancelot and his kin leave England to become rulers of France. At Gawain's instigation Arthur invades France to resume the war against Lancelot. Word comes to the king that Mordred has seized the kingdom, and Arthur leads his forces back to England. Mordred attacks them upon their landing, and Gawain is mortally wounded and dies, although not before he has repented for having insisted that Arthur fight

Lancelot and has written Lancelot to come to the aid of his former lord.
5. Scaffold. "Him seemed": it seemed to him.
6. Confused.
7. Knew.
8. Lay awake.
9. It seemed to the king.
1. Those.
2. If you fight tomorrow.
3. Decided.

pity of you and many mo other good men there[4] shall be slain, God hath sent me to you of his special grace to give you warning that in no wise ye do battle as tomorn, but that ye take a treatise for a month-day.[5] And proffer you largely,[6] so that tomorn ye put in a delay. For within a month shall come Sir Lancelot with all his noble knights and rescue you worshipfully and slay Sir Mordred and all that ever will hold with him."

Then Sir Gawain and all the ladies vanished. And anon the King called upon his knights, squires, and yeomen, and charged them wightly[7] to fetch his noble lords and wise bishops unto him. And when they were come the King told them of his avision,[8] that Sir Gawain had told him and warned him that, and he fought on the morn, he should be slain. Then the King commanded Sir Lucan the Butler[9] and his brother Sir Bedivere the Bold, with two bishops with them, and charged them in any wise to take a treatise for a month-day[1] with Sir Mordred. "And spare not: proffer him lands and goods as much as ye think reasonable."

So then they departed and came to Sir Mordred where he had a grim host of an hundred thousand, and there they entreated[2] Sir Mordred long time. And at the last Sir Mordred was agreed for to have Cornwall and Kent by King Arthur's days,[3] and after that, all England, after the days of King Arthur.

Then were they condescended[4] that King Arthur and Sir Mordred should meet betwixt both their hosts, and everich[5] of them should bring fourteen persons. And so they came with this word unto Arthur. Then said he, "I am glad that this is done," and so he went into the field.

And when King Arthur should depart, he warned all his host that, and[6] they, see any sword drawn, "Look ye come on fiercely and slay that traitor Sir Mordred, for I in no wise trust him." In like wise Sir Mordred warned his host that "And ye see any manner of sword drawn, look that ye come on fiercely, and so slay all that ever before you standeth, for in no wise I will not trust for this treatise." And in the same wise said Sir Mordred unto his host, "For I know well my father will be avenged upon me."

And so they met as their pointment[7] was and were agreed and accorded thoroughly. And wine was fetched and they drank together. Right so came an adder out of a little heath-bush, and it stung a knight in the foot. And so when the knight felt him so stung, he looked down and saw the adder. And anon he drew his sword to slay the adder, and thought[8] none other harm. And when the host on both parties saw that sword drawn, then they blew beams,[9] trumpets, and horns, and shouted grimly. And so both hosts dressed them[1] together. And King Arthur took his horse and said, "Alas, this unhappy day!" and so rode to his party, and Sir Mordred in like wise.

And never since was there never seen a more dolefuller battle in no Christian land, for there was but rushing and riding, foining[2] and striking; and

4. I.e., who there. "Mo": more.
5. For a month from today. "Treatise": treaty, truce.
6. Make generous offers.
7. Quickly.
8. Dream.
9. "Butler" here is probably only a title of high rank, although it was originally used to designate the officer who had charge of wine for the king's table.
1. By any means necessary to make a treaty for

the period of a month.
2. Dealt with.
3. During King Arthur's lifetime.
4. Agreed.
5. Each.
6. If.
7. Arrangement.
8. Meant.
9. A kind of trumpet.
1. Prepared to come.
2. Lunging.

many a grim word was there spoken of either to other, and many a deadly stroke. But ever King Arthur rode throughout the battle[3] of Sir Mordred many times and did full nobly, as a noble king should do, and at all times he fainted[4] never. And Sir Mordred did his devoir[5] that day and put himself in great peril.

And thus they fought all the long day, and never stinted[6] till the noble knights were laid to the cold earth. And ever they fought still till it was near night, and by then was there an hundred thousand laid dead upon the down.[7] Then was King Arthur wood-wroth[8] out of measure when he saw his people so slain from him. And so he looked about him and could see no mo[9] of all his host, and good knights left no mo on-live, but two knights: the t'one[1] was Sir Lucan the Butler and [the other] his brother Sir Bedivere. And yet they were full sore wounded.

"Jesu, mercy," said the King, "where are all my noble knights become?[2] Alas that ever I should see this doleful day! For now," said King Arthur, "I am come to mine end. But would to God," said he, "that I wist[3] now where were that traitor Sir Mordred that has caused all this mischief."

Then King Arthur looked about and was ware where stood Sir Mordred leaning upon his sword among a great heap of dead men.

"Now give me my spear," said King Arthur unto Sir Lucan, "for yonder I have espied the traitor that all this woe hath wrought."

"Sir, let him be," said Sir Lucan, "for he is unhappy.[4] And if ye pass this unhappy day ye shall be right well revenged upon him. And, good lord, remember ye of your night's dream, and what the spirit of Sir Gawain told you tonight, and yet God of his great goodness hath preserved you hitherto. And for God's sake, my lord, leave off by this,[5] for, blessed be God, ye have won the field: for yet we been here three on-live, and with Sir Mordred is not one on-live. And therefore if ye leave off now, this wicked day of destiny is past."

"Now, tide[6] me death, tide me life," said the King, "now I see him yonder alone, he shall never escape mine hands. For at a better avail[7] shall I never have him."

"God speed you well!" said Sir Bedivere.

Then the King got his spear in both his hands and ran toward Sir Mordred, crying and saying, "Traitor, now is thy deathday come!"

And when Sir Mordred saw King Arthur he ran until him with his sword drawn in his hand, and there King Arthur smote Sir Mordred under the shield, with a foin[8] of his spear, throughout the body more than a fathom.[9] And when Sir Mordred felt that he had his death's wound, he thrust himself with the might that he had up to the burr[1] of King Arthur's spear, and right so he smote his father King Arthur with his sword holden in both his hands, upon the side of the head, that the sword pierced the helmet and the tay[2] of the brain. And therewith Sir Mordred dashed down stark dead to the earth.

3. Battalion.
4. Lost heart.
5. Knightly duty.
6. Stopped.
7. Upland.
8. Mad with rage.
9. Others.
1. That one, i.e., the first.
2. What has become of all my noble knights?

3. Knew.
4. I.e., unlucky for you.
5. I.e., with this much accomplished.
6. Betide.
7. Advantage.
8. Thrust.
9. I.e., six feet.
1. Hand guard.
2. Outer membrane.

And noble King Arthur fell in a swough[3] to the earth, and there he swooned oftentimes, and Sir Lucan and Sir Bedivere ofttimes heaved him up. And so, weakly betwixt them, they led him to a little chapel not far from the seaside, and when the King was there, him thought him reasonably eased. Then heard they people cry in the field. "Now go thou, Sir Lucan," said the King, "and do me to wit[4] what betokens that noise in the field."

So Sir Lucan departed, for he was grievously wounded in many places. And so as he yede[5] he saw and harkened by the moonlight how that pillers[6] and robbers were come into the field to pill and to rob many a full noble knight of brooches and bees[7] and of many a good ring and many a rich jewel. And who that were not dead all out there they slew them for their harness[8] and their riches. When Sir Lucan understood this work, he came to the King as soon as he might and told him all what he had heard and seen. "Therefore by my read,"[9] said Sir Lucan, "it is best that we bring you to some town."

"I would it were so," said the King, "but I may not stand, my head works[1] so. Ah, Sir Lancelot," said King Arthur, "this day have I sore missed thee. And alas that ever I was against thee, for now have I my death, whereof Sir Gawain me warned in my dream."

Then Sir Lucan took up the King the t'one party[2] and Sir Bedivere the other party; and in the lifting up the King swooned and in the lifting Sir Lucan fell in a swoon that part of his guts fell out of his body, and therewith the noble knight's heart burst. And when the King awoke he beheld Sir Lucan how he lay foaming at the mouth and part of his guts lay at his feet.

"Alas," said the King, "this is to me a full heavy[3] sight to see this noble duke so die for my sake, for he would have holpen[4] me that had more need of help than I. Alas that he would not complain him for[5] his heart was so set to help me. Now Jesu have mercy upon his soul."

Then Sir Bedivere wept for the death of his brother.

"Now leave this mourning and weeping, gentle knight," said the King, "for all this will not avail me. For wit thou well, and[6] I might live myself, the death of Sir Lucan would grieve me evermore. But my time passeth on fast," said the King. "Therefore," said King Arthur unto Sir Bedivere, "take thou here Excalibur[7] my good sword and go with it to yonder water's side; and when thou comest there I charge thee throw my sword in that water and come again and tell me what thou sawest there."

"My lord," said Sir Bedivere, "your commandment shall be done, and [I shall] lightly[8] bring you word again."

So Sir Bedivere departed. And by the way he beheld that noble sword, that the pommel and the haft[9] was all precious stones. And then he said to himself, "If I throw this rich sword in the water, thereof shall never come good, but harm and loss." And then Sir Bedivere hid Excalibur under a tree. And so, as soon as he might, he came again unto the King and said he had been at the water and had thrown the sword into the water.

---

3. Swoon.
4. Let me know.
5. Walked.
6. Plunderers.
7. Bracelets.
8. Armor. "All out": entirely.
9. Advice.
1. Aches.
2. On one side.
3. Sorrowful.

4. Helped.
5. Because.
6. If.
7. The sword that Arthur had received as a young man from the Lady of the Lake; it is presumably she who catches it when Bedivere finally throws it into the water.
8. Quickly.
9. Handle. "Pommel": rounded knob on the hilt.

"What saw thou there?" said the King.

"Sir," he said, "I saw nothing but waves and winds."

"That is untruly said of thee," said the King. "And therefore go thou lightly again and do my commandment; as thou art to me lief[1] and dear, spare not, but throw it in."

Then Sir Bedivere returned again and took the sword in his hand. And yet him thought[2] sin and shame to throw away that noble sword. And so eft[3] he hid the sword and returned again and told the King that he had been at the water and done his commandment.

"What sawest thou there?" said the King.

"Sir," he said, "I saw nothing but waters wap and waves wan."[4]

"Ah, traitor unto me and untrue," said King Arthur, "now hast thou betrayed me twice. Who would have weened that thou that has been to me so lief and dear, and thou art named a noble knight, and would betray me for the riches of this sword. But now go again lightly, for thy long tarrying putteth me in great jeopardy of my life, for I have taken cold. And but if thou do now as I bid thee, if ever I may see thee I shall slay thee mine[5] own hands, for thou wouldest for my rich sword see me dead."

Then Sir Bedivere departed and went to the sword and lightly took it up, and so he went to the water's side; and there he bound the girdle[6] about the hilts, and threw the sword as far into the water as he might. And there came an arm and an hand above the water and took it and clutched it, and shook it thrice and brandished; and then vanished away the hand with the sword into the water. So Sir Bedivere came again to the King and told him what he saw.

"Alas," said the King, "help me hence, for I dread me I have tarried overlong."

Then Sir Bedivere took the King upon his back and so went with him to that water's side. And when they were at the water's side, even fast[7] by the bank hoved[8] a little barge with many fair ladies in it; and among them all was a queen; and all they had black hoods, and all they wept and shrieked when they saw King Arthur.

"Now put me into that barge," said the King; and so he did softly. And there received him three ladies with great mourning, and so they set them[9] down. And in one of their laps King Arthur laid his head, and then the queen said, "Ah, my dear brother, why have ye tarried so long from me? Alas, this wound on your head hath caught overmuch cold." And anon they rowed fromward the land, and Sir Bedivere beheld all tho ladies go froward him.

Then Sir Bedivere cried and said, "Ah, my lord Arthur, what shall become of me, now ye go from me and leave me here alone among mine enemies?"

"Comfort thyself," said the King, "and do as well as thou mayest, for in me is no trust for to trust in. For I must into the vale of Avilion[1] to heal me of my grievous wound. And if thou hear nevermore of me, pray for my soul."

But ever the queen and ladies wept and shrieked that it was pity to hear. And as soon as Sir Bedivere had lost the sight of the barge he wept and

---

1. Beloved.
2. It seemed to him.
3. Again.
4. The phrase seems to mean "waters wash the shore and waves grow dark."
5. I.e., with mine.

6. Sword belt.
7. Close.
8. Waited.
9. I.e., they sat.
1. A legendary island, sometimes identified with the earthly paradise.

wailed and so took the forest, and went[2] all that night. And in the morning he was ware betwixt two holts hoar[3] of a chapel and an hermitage.[4]

* * *

Thus of Arthur I find no more written in books that been authorized,[5] neither more of the very certainty of his death heard I never read,[6] but thus was he led away in a ship wherein were three queens: that one was King Arthur's sister, Queen Morgan la Fée,[7] the t'other[8] was the Queen of North Wales, and the third was the Queen of the Waste Lands. * * *

Now more of the death of King Arthur could I never find but that these ladies brought him to his burials,[9] and such one was buried there that the hermit bore witness that sometime was Bishop of Canterbury.[1] But yet the hermit knew not in certain that he was verily the body of King Arthur, for this tale Sir Bedivere, a Knight of the Table Round, made it to be written. Yet some men say in many parts of England that King Arthur is not dead, but had[2] by the will of our Lord Jesu into another place. And men say that he shall come again and he shall win the Holy Cross. Yet I will not say that it shall be so, but rather I will say, Here in this world he changed his life. And many men say that there is written upon his tomb this verse: *Hic iacet Arthurus, rex quondam, rexque futurus.*[3]

[THE DEATHS OF LANCELOT AND GUINEVERE][4]

And thus upon a night there came a vision to Sir Lancelot and charged him, in remission[5] of his sins, to haste him unto Amesbury: "And by then[6] thou come there, thou shalt find Queen Guinevere dead. And therefore take thy fellows with thee, and purvey them of an horse-bier,[7] and fetch thou the corse[8] of her, and bury her by her husband, the noble King Arthur. So this avision[9] came to Lancelot thrice in one night. Then Sir Lancelot rose up ere day and told the hermit.

"It were well done," said the hermit, "that ye made you ready and that ye disobey not the avision."

Then Sir Lancelot took his eight fellows with him, and on foot they yede[1] from Glastonbury to Amesbury, the which is little more than thirty mile, and thither they came within two days, for they were weak and feeble to go. And when Sir Lancelot was come to Amesbury within the nunnery, Queen Guinevere died but half an hour afore. And the ladies told Sir Lancelot that

2. Walked. "Took": took to.
3. Ancient thickets of small trees.
4. In the passage here omitted, Sir Bedivere meets the former bishop of Canterbury, now a hermit, who describes how on the previous night a company of ladies had brought to the chapel a dead body, asking that it be buried. Sir Bedivere exclaims that the dead man must have been King Arthur and vows to spend the rest of his life there in the chapel as a hermit.
5. That have authority.
6. Tell.
7. The fairy.
8. The second.
9. Grave.
1. Of whom the hermit, who was formerly bishop of Canterbury, bore witness.

2. Conveyed.
3. "Here lies Arthur, who was once king and king will be again."
4. Guinevere enters a convent at Amesbury, where Lancelot, returned with his companions to England, visits her, but she commands him never to see him again. Emulating her example, Lancelot joins the bishop of Canterbury and Bedivere in their hermitage, where he takes holy orders and is joined in turn by seven of his fellow knights.
5. For the remission.
6. By the time.
7. Provide them with a horse-drawn hearse.
8. Body.
9. Dream.
1. Went.

Queen Guinevere told them all ere she passed that Sir Lancelot had been priest near a twelve-month:[2] "and hither he cometh as fast as he may to fetch my corse, and beside my lord King Arthur he shall bury me." Wherefore the Queen said in hearing of them all, "I beseech Almighty God that I may never have power to see Sir Lancelot with my worldly eyes."

"And thus," said all the ladies, "was ever her prayer these two days till she was dead."

Then Sir Lancelot saw her visage, but he wept not greatly, but sighed. And so he did all the observance of the service himself, both the *dirige*[3] and on the morn he sang mass. And there was ordained[4] an horse-bier, and so with an hundred torches ever burning about the corse of the Queen, and ever Sir Lancelot with his eight fellows went about[5] the horse-bier, singing and reading many an holy orison,[6] and frankincense upon the corse incensed.[7]

Thus Sir Lancelot and his eight fellows went on foot from Amesbury unto Glastonbury, and when they were come to the chapel and the hermitage, there she had a *dirige* with great devotion.[8] And on the morn the hermit that sometime[9] was Bishop of Canterbury sang the mass of requiem with great devotion, and Sir Lancelot was the first that offered, and then als[1] his eight fellows. And then she was wrapped in cered cloth of Rennes, from the top[2] to the toe, in thirtyfold, and after she was put in a web[3] of lead, and then in a coffin of marble.

And when she was put in the earth Sir Lancelot swooned and lay long still, while[4] the hermit came and awaked him, and said, "Ye be to blame, for ye displease God with such manner of sorrow-making."

"Truly," said Sir Lancelot, "I trust I do not displease God, for He knoweth mine intent—for my sorrow was not, nor is not, for any rejoicing of sin, but my sorrow may never have end. For when I remember of her beaulté and of her noblesse[5] that was both with her king and with her,[6] so when I saw his corse and her corse so lie together, truly mine heart would not serve to sustain my careful[7] body. Also when I remember me how by my defaute and mine orgule[8] and my pride that they were both laid full low, that were peerless that ever was living of Christian people, wit you well," said Sir Lancelot, "this remembered, of their kindness and mine unkindness, sank so to mine heart that I might not sustain myself." So the French book maketh mention.

Then Sir Lancelot never after ate but little meat,[9] nor drank, till he was dead, for then he sickened more and more and dried and dwined[1] away. For the Bishop nor none of his fellows might not make him to eat, and little he drank, that he was waxen by a kibbet[2] shorter than he was, that the people could not know him. For evermore, day and night, he prayed, but sometime he slumbered a broken sleep. Ever he was lying groveling on the tomb of King Arthur and Queen Guinevere, and there was no comfort that the Bishop nor Sir Bors, nor none of his fellows could make him—it availed not.

2. Nearly twelve months.
3. *Dirige* (modern "dirge"): the first word of the anthem beginning the funeral service.
4. Prepared.
5. Around.
6. Reciting many a prayer.
7. Burned frankincense over the body.
8. Earnest reverence.
9. Once.
1. Also. "Offered": made his donation.
2. Head. "Cloth of Rennes": A shroud made of fine linen smeared with wax, produced at Rennes.
3. Afterward she was put in a sheet.
4. Until.
5. Her beauty and nobility.
6. That she and her king both had.
7. Sorrowful.
8. My fault and my haughtiness.
9. Food.
1. Wasted.
2. Grown by a cubit.

So within six weeks after, Sir Lancelot fell sick and lay in his bed. And then he sent for the Bishop that there was hermit, and all his true fellows. Then Sir Lancelot said with dreary steven,[3] "Sir Bishop, I pray you give to me all my rights that longeth[4] to a Christian man."

"It shall not need you,"[5] said the hermit and all his fellows. "It is but heaviness of your blood. Ye shall be well mended by the grace of God tomorn."

"My fair lords," said Sir Lancelot, "wit you well my careful body will into the earth; I have warning more than now I will say. Therefore give me my rights."

So when he was houseled and annealed[6] and had all that a Christian man ought to have, he prayed the Bishop that his fellows might bear his body to Joyous Garde. (Some men say it was Alnwick, and some men say it was Bamborough.) "Howbeit," said Sir Lancelot, "me repenteth[7] sore, but I made mine avow sometime that in Joyous Garde I would be buried. And because of breaking[8] of mine avow, I pray you all, lead me thither." Then there was weeping and wringing of hands among his fellows.

So at a season of the night they all went to their beds, for they all lay in one chamber. And so after midnight, against[9] day, the Bishop that was hermit, as he lay in his bed asleep, he fell upon a great laughter. And therewith all the fellowship awoke and came to the Bishop and asked him what he ailed.[1]

"Ah, Jesu mercy," said the Bishop, "why did ye awake me? I was never in all my life so merry and so well at ease."

"Wherefore?" said Sir Bors.

"Truly," said the Bishop, "here was Sir Lancelot with me, with mo[2] angels than ever I saw men in one day. And I saw the angels heave[3] up Sir Lancelot unto heaven, and the gates of heaven opened against him."

"It is but dretching of swevens,"[4] said Sir Bors, "for I doubt not Sir Lancelot aileth nothing but good."[5]

"It may well be," said the Bishop. "Go ye to his bed and then shall ye prove the sooth."

So when Sir Bors and his fellows came to his bed, they found him stark dead. And he lay as he had smiled, and the sweetest savor[6] about him that ever they felt. Then was there weeping and wringing of hands, and the greatest dole they made that ever made men. And on the morn the Bishop did his mass of Requiem, and after the Bishop and all the nine knights put Sir Lancelot in the same horse-bier that Queen Guinevere was laid in tofore that she was buried. And so the Bishop and they all together went with the body of Sir Lancelot daily, till they came to Joyous Garde. And ever they had an hundred torches burning about him.

And so within fifteen days they came to Joyous Garde. And there they laid his corse in the body of the choir,[7] and sang and read many psalters[8] and prayers over him and about him. And ever his visage was laid open and naked, that all folks might behold him; for such was the custom in tho[9]

---

3. Sad voice.
4. Pertains. "Rights": last sacrament.
5. You shall not need it.
6. Given communion and extreme unction.
7. I am sorry.
8. In order not to break.
9. Toward.
1. Ailed him.
2. More.

3. Lift.
4. Illusion of dreams.
5. Has nothing wrong with him.
6. Odor. A sweet scent is a conventional sign in saints' lives of a sanctified death.
7. The center of the chancel, the place of honor.
8. Psalms.
9. Those.

days that all men of worship should so lie with open visage till that they were buried.

And right thus as they were at their service, there came Sir Ector de Maris that had seven year sought all England, Scotland, and Wales, seeking his brother, Sir Lancelot. And when Sir Ector heard such noise and light in the choir of Joyous Garde, he alight and put his horse from him and came into the choir. And there he saw men sing and weep, and all they knew Sir Ector, but he knew not them. Then went Sir Bors unto Sir Ector and told him how there lay his brother, Sir Lancelot, dead. And then Sir Ector threw his shield, sword, and helm from him, and when he beheld Sir Lancelot's visage, he fell down in a swoon. And when he waked, it were hard any tongue to tell the doleful complaints that he made for his brother.

"Ah, Lancelot!" he said, "thou were head of all Christian knights. And now I dare say," said Sir Ector, "thou Sir Lancelot, there thou liest, that thou were never matched of earthly knight's hand. And thou were the courteoust[1] knight that ever bore shield. And thou were the truest friend to thy lover that ever bestrode horse, and thou were the truest lover, of a sinful man,[2] that ever loved woman, and thou were the kindest man that ever struck with sword. And thou were the goodliest person that ever came among press of knights, and thou was the meekest man and the gentlest that ever ate in hall among ladies, and thou were the sternest knight to thy mortal foe that ever put spear in the rest."[3]

Then there was weeping and dolor out of measure.

Thus they kept Sir Lancelot's corse aloft fifteen days, and then they buried it with great devotion. And then at leisure they went all with the Bishop of Canterbury to his hermitage, and there they were together more than a month.

Then Sir Constantine that was Sir Cador's son of Cornwall was chosen king of England, and he was a full noble knight, and worshipfully he ruled this realm. And then this King Constantine sent for the Bishop of Canterbury, for he heard say where he was. And so he was restored unto his bishopric and left that hermitage, and Sir Bedivere was there ever still hermit to his life's end.

Then Sir Bors de Ganis, Sir Ector de Maris, Sir Gahalantine, Sir Galihud, Sir Galihodin, Sir Blamour, Sir Bleoberis, Sir Villiars le Valiant, Sir Clarrus of Clermount, all these knights drew them to their countries.[4] Howbeit[5] King Constantine would have had them with him, but they would not abide in this realm. And there they all lived in their countries as holy men.

And some English books make mention that they went never out of England after the death of Sir Lancelot—but that was but favor of makers.[6] For the French book maketh mention—and is authorized—that Sir Bors, Sir Ector, Sir Blamour, and Sir Bleoberis went into the Holy Land, thereas Jesu Christ was quick[7] and dead, and anon as they had stablished their lands;[8] for the book saith so Sir Lancelot commanded them for to do ere ever he passed out of this world. There these four knights did many battles upon

1. Most courteous.
2. Of any man born in original sin.
3. Support for the butt of the lance.
4. Withdrew themselves to their home districts.

5. However.
6. The authors' bias.
7. Living. "Thereas": where.
8. As soon as they had put their lands in order.

the miscreaunts,[9] or Turks, and there they died upon a Good Friday for God's sake.

Here is the end of the whole book of King Arthur and of his noble knights of the Round Table, that when they were whole together there was ever an hundred and forty. And here is the end of *The Death of Arthur*.[1]

I pray you all gentlemen and gentlewomen that readeth this book of Arthur and his knights from the beginning to the ending, pray for me while I am alive that God send me good deliverance. And when I am dead, I pray you all pray for my soul.

For this book was ended the ninth year of the reign of King Edward the Fourth, by Sir Thomas Malory, knight, as Jesu help him for His great might, as he is the servant of Jesu both day and night.

1469–70   1485

---

9. Infidels.
1. By the "whole book" Malory refers to the entire work; the *Death of Arthur*, which Caxton

made the title of the entire work, refers to the last part of Malory's book.

The Sixteenth Century 1485–1603

handwritten: 1511 - Desiderius Erasmus
handwritten: Utopia
handwritten: 1516 - Thomas More
handwritten: 1519 - Cortez invades Mexico

1485: Accession of Henry VII inaugurates the Tudor dynasty

1509: Accession of Henry VIII

1517: Martin Luther's Wittenberg Theses; beginning of the Reformation

1534: Henry VIII declares himself head of the English church

1557: Publication of Tottel's *Songs and Sonnets*, containing poems by Sir Thomas Wyatt; Henry Howard, earl of Surrey; and others

1558: Accession of Elizabeth I

1576: Building of The Theater, the first permanent structure in England for the presentation of plays

1588: Defeat of the Spanish Armada

1603: Death of Elizabeth I and accession of James I, the first of the Stuart kings

The ancient Roman poet Virgil characterized Britain as a wild, remote place set apart from all the world, and it must still have seemed so in the early sixteenth century to the inhabitants of cities like Venice, Madrid, and Paris. To be sure, some venturesome Continental travelers crossed the Channel and visited London, Oxford, or Cambridge, bringing home reports of bustling markets, impressive universities, and ambitious nobles vying for position at an increasingly powerful royal court. But these visitors were but a trickle compared with the flood of wealthy young Englishmen (and, to a lesser extent, Englishwomen) who embarked at the first opportunity for the Continent. English travelers were virtually obliged to learn some French, Italian, or Spanish, for

The Life and Death of Sir Henry Unton (detail), anonymous, ca. 1597. For more information about this painting, see the color insert in this volume.

they would encounter very few people who knew their language. On returning home, they would frequently wear foreign fashions—much to the disgust of moralists—and would pepper their speech with foreign phrases.

At the beginning of the sixteenth century, the English language had almost no prestige abroad, and there were those at home who doubted that it could serve as a suitable medium for serious, elevated, or elegant discourse. It is no accident that one of the first works in this selection of English Renaissance literature, Thomas More's *Utopia*, was not written in English: More, who began his great book in 1515 when he was on a diplomatic mission in the Netherlands, was writing for an international intellectual community, and as such his language of choice was Latin. His work quickly became famous throughout Europe, but it was not translated into English until the 1550s. Evidently, neither More himself nor the London printers and booksellers thought it imperative to publish a vernacular *Utopia*. Yet by the century's end there were signs of a great increase in what we might call linguistic self-confidence, signs that at least some contemporary observers were aware that something extraordinary was happening to their language. Though in 1600 England still remained somewhat peripheral to the Continent, English had been fashioned into an immensely powerful expressive medium, one whose cadences in the works of Marlowe, Shakespeare, and the translators of the Bible continue after more than four centuries to thrill readers.

How did it come about that by the century's end so many remarkable poems, plays, and prose works were written in English? The answer lies in part in the spectacular creativity of a succession of brilliant writers, the best of whom are represented in these pages. Still, a vital literary culture is the product of a complex process, involving thousands of more modest, half-hidden creative acts sparked by a wide range of motives, some of which we will briefly explore.

THE COURT AND THE CITY

The development of the English language in the sixteenth century is linked at least indirectly to the consolidation and strengthening of the English state. Preoccupied by violent clashes between the thuggish feudal retainers of rival barons, the English, through most of the fifteenth century, had rather limited time and inclination to cultivate rhetorical skills. The social and economic health of the nation had been severely damaged by the so-called Wars of the Roses, a vicious, decades-long struggle for royal power between the noble houses of York and Lancaster. The struggle was resolved by the establishment of the Tudor dynasty that ruled England from 1485 to 1603. The family name derives from Owen Tudor, an ambitious Welshman who himself had no claim to the throne but who married Catherine of Valois, widow of the Lancastrian king Henry V. Their grandson, the earl of Richmond, who also inherited Lancastrian blood on his mother's side, became the first Tudor monarch: he won the crown by leading the army that defeated and killed the reigning Yorkist king, Richard III, at the battle of Bosworth Field. The victorious Richmond, crowned King Henry VII in 1485, promptly consolidated his rather shaky claim to the throne by marrying Elizabeth of the house of York, hence effectively uniting the two rival factions.

England's barons, impoverished and divided by the dynastic wars, could not effectively oppose the new power of the Crown, and the leaders of the Church also generally supported royal power. The wily Henry VII was therefore able to counter the multiple and competing power structures characteristic of feudal society and to impose a much stronger central authority and order on the nation. Initiated by the first Tudor sovereign, this consolidation progressed throughout the sixteenth century; by the reign of the last Tudor—Henry's granddaughter, Elizabeth I—though the ruler still needed the consent of Parliament on crucial matters (including the all-important one of levying taxes), the royal court had concentrated in itself much of the nation's power.

The court was a center of culture as well as power: court entertainments such as theater and masque (a sumptuous, elaborately costumed performance of dance, song, and poetry); court fashions in dress and speech; court tastes in painting, music, and poetry—all shaped the taste and the imagination of the country as a whole. Culture and power were not, in any case, easily separable in Tudor England. In a society with no freedom of speech as we understand it and with relatively limited means of mass communication, important public issues were often aired indirectly, through what we might now regard as entertainment, and lyrics that to us seem slight and nonchalant could serve as carefully designed manifestations of rhetorical agility by aspiring courtiers.

Whereas in the Middle Ages noblemen had guarded their power by keeping their distance from London and the king, ruling over semi-independent fiefdoms, in the Tudor era the route to power lay in proximity to the royal body. (One of the coveted positions in the court of Henry VIII was Groom of the Stool, "close stool" being the Tudor term for toilet.) The monarch's chief ministers and favorites were the primary channels through which patronage was dispensed to courtiers who competed for offices in the court, the government bureaucracies, the royal household, the army, the church, and the universities, or who sought titles, grants of land, leases, or similar favors. But if proximity held out the promise of wealth and power, it also harbored danger. Festive evenings with the likes of the ruthless Henry VIII were not occasions for relaxation. The court fostered paranoia, and an attendant obsession with secrecy, spying, duplicity, and betrayal.

Tudor courtiers were torn between the need to protect themselves and the equally pressing need to display themselves. For lessons in the art of intrigue, many no doubt turned to Machiavelli's notorious *Il Principe* (The Prince), with its cool guidance on how power may be gained and kept. For advice on the cultivation and display of the self, they could resort to the still more influential *Il Cortegiano* (The Courtier) by Count Baldassare Castiglione. It was particularly important, Castiglione wrote, to conceal the effort that lay behind elegant accomplishments, so that they would seem natural. In this anxious atmosphere, courtiers became highly practiced at crafting and deciphering graceful words with double or triple meanings. Poets had much to learn from courtiers, the Elizabethan critic George Puttenham observed; indeed many of the best poets in the period, Sir Thomas Wyatt, Sir Philip Sidney, Sir Walter Ralegh, and others, *were* courtiers.

If court culture fostered performances for a small coterie audience, other forces in Tudor England pulled toward a more public sphere. Markets expanded significantly, international trade flourished, and cities throughout the realm experienced a rapid surge in size and importance. London's population in particular soared, from 60,000 in 1520, to 120,000 in 1550, to 375,000 a century later, making it the largest and fastest-growing city not only in England but in all of Europe. Every year in the first half of the seventeenth century about 10,000 people migrated to London from other parts of England—wages in London tended to be around 50 percent higher than in the rest of the country—and it is estimated that one in eight English people lived in London at some point in their lives. Elderly Londoners in the 1590s could barely recognize the city of their childhood; London's boom was one factor among many contributing to the sense of a culture moving at increasing velocity away from its historical roots.

About a decade before Henry VII won his throne, the art of printing from movable metal type, a German invention, had been introduced into England by William Caxton (ca. 1422–1491), who had learned and practiced it in the Low Countries. Though reliable statistics are impossible to come by, literacy seems to have increased during the fifteenth century and still more during the sixteenth, when Protestantism encouraged a direct encounter with the Bible. Printing made books cheaper and more plentiful, providing more opportunity to read and more incentive to learn. The greater availability of books may also have reinforced the trend toward silent reading, a practice that gradually transformed what had been a communal experience into a more intimate encounter with a text.

Yet it would be a mistake to imagine these changes as sudden and dramatic. Manuscripts retained considerable prestige among the elite; throughout the sixteenth century and well into the seventeenth, court poets in particular were wary of the "stigma of print" that might mark their verse as less exclusive. Although Caxton, who was an author and translator as well as a printer, introduced printed books, he attempted to cater to courtly tastes by translating works whose tone was more medieval than modern. Fascination with the old chivalric code of behavior is reflected as well in the jousts and tournaments that continued at court for a century, long after gunpowder had rendered them obsolete. As often in an age of alarming novelty, many people looked back to an idealized past. Indeed the great innovations of the Tudor era—intellectual, governmental, and religious—were all presented, at the time, as attempts to restore lost links with ancient traditions.

RENAISSANCE HUMANISM

During the fifteenth century a few English clerics and government officials had journeyed to Italy and had seen something of the extraordinary cultural and intellectual movement flourishing in the city-states there. That movement, generally known as the Renaissance, involved a rebirth of letters and arts stimulated by the recovery of texts and artifacts from classical antiquity, the development of techniques such as linear perspective, and the creation of powerful new aesthetic practices based on classical models. It also unleashed new ideas and new social, political, and economic forces that gradually displaced the spiritual and communal values of the Middle Ages. To Renaissance intellectuals and artists, the achievements of the pagan philosophers of ancient Greece and Rome came to seem more compelling than the subtle distinctions drawn by medieval Christian theologians. In the brilliant, intensely competitive, and vital world of Leonardo da Vinci and Michelangelo, the submission of the human spirit to penitential discipline gave way to unleashed curiosity, individual self-assertion, and a powerful conviction that man was the measure of all things. Yet the superb human figure placed at the center of the Renaissance worldview was also seen as remarkably malleable. "We have made thee neither of heaven nor of earth, neither mortal nor immortal," God tells Adam, in the Florentine Pico della Mirandola's *Oration on the Dignity of Man* (1486), "so that with freedom of choice and with honor, as though the maker and molder of thyself, thou mayest fashion thyself in whatever shape thou shalt prefer." "As though the maker and molder of thyself": this vision of self-fashioning may be glimpsed in the poetry of Petrarch, the sculpture of Donatello, and the statecraft of Lorenzo de' Medici. But in England it was not until Henry VII's reign brought some measure of political stability that the Renaissance could take root, and it was not until the accession of Henry VIII that it began to flower.

This flowering, when it occurred, came not, as in Italy, in painting, sculpture, and architecture. It came rather in the intellectual program and literary vision known as humanism. More's *Utopia* (1516), with its dream of human existence entirely transformed by a radical change in institutional arrangements, is an extreme instance of a general humanist interest in education: in England and elsewhere, humanism was bound up with struggles over the purposes of education and curriculum reform. The great Dutch humanist Erasmus, who spent some time in England and developed a close friendship with More, was a leader in the assault on what he and others regarded as a hopelessly narrow and outmoded intellectual culture based on scholastic hairsplitting and a dogmatic adherence to the philosophy of Aristotle. English humanists, including John Colet (who, as dean of St. Paul's Cathedral, recast its grammar school on humanist principles), Roger Ascham (tutor to Princess Elizabeth), and Sir Thomas Elyot, wrote treatises on education to promote the kind of learning they regarded as the most suitable preparation for public service. That education—predominantly male and conducted by tutors in wealthy families or in grammar schools—was still ordered according to the subjects of the medieval *trivium* (grammar, logic, and rhetoric) and *quadrivium* (arithmetic, geometry, astronomy, and music), but its focus shifted from training for the Church to the general acquisition of "literature," in the sense both of literacy and of cultural knowledge. For some of the more intellectually ambitious humanists, that knowledge extended to ancient Greek, whose enthusiastic adherents began to challenge the entrenched preeminence of Latin.

Still, at the core of the curriculum remained the study of Latin, the mastery of which was in effect a prolonged male puberty rite involving pain as well as pleasure. Though some educators counseled mildness, punishment was an established part of the pedagogy of the age, and even gifted students could rarely escape recurrent flogging. The purpose was to train the sons of the nobility and gentry to speak and write good Latin, the language of diplomacy, of the professions, and of all higher learning. Their sisters were always educated at home or in other noble houses. They chiefly learned modern languages, religion, music, and needlework, but they very seldom received the thorough training in the ancient languages and classical literature so central to the dominant culture. Through this training, Elizabethan schoolmasters sought to impart facility and rhetorical elegance, but the books their students laboriously pored over were not considered mere exhibitions of literary style: from the *Sententiae Pueriles* (Maxims for Children) for beginners on up through the dramatists Terence, Plautus, and Seneca, the poets Virgil and Horace, and the orator Cicero, the classics were also studied for the moral, political, and philosophical truths they contained. Though originating in pagan times, those truths could, in the opinion of many humanists, be reconciled to the moral vision of Christianity. The result, perplexing for some modern readers, is that pagan gods and goddesses flourish on the pages of even such a devoutly Christian poem as Edmund Spenser's *Faerie Queene*.

Humanists committed to classical learning were faced with the question of whether to write their own works in Latin or in English. To many learned men, influenced both by the humanist exaltation of the classical languages and by the characteristic Renaissance desire for eternal fame, the national languages seemed relatively unstable and ephemeral. Intellectuals had long shared a pan-European world of scientific inquiry, so that works by such English scientists as William Gilbert, William Harvey, and Francis Bacon easily joined those by Nicolaus Copernicus, Johannes Kepler, and Andreas Vesalius in the common linguistic medium of Latin. But throughout Europe nationalism and the expansion of the reading public were steadily strengthening the power and allure of the vernaculars. The famous schoolmaster

Tudor schoolroom. In this lithograph from the sixteenth century, the pupils sit on "forms," or benches, with few if any desks. As an early school statute explains, "When they have to write, let them use their knees for a table." All the lessons, for the different age groups, are taught in the same room: the younger boys (left) are learning their letters, while the students at the upper right are studying music. The schoolmaster, seated, holds a birch, while the usher, or assistant master, is beating a student. The windows of the schoolroom are set high in the walls, to cut down on distractions. Next to the far pillar is an hourglass used in marking time for various lessons. The school's valuable books are kept in a locked chest, behind the schoolmaster.

Richard Mulcaster (ca. 1530–1611), Spenser's teacher, captured this emergent sense of national identity in singing the praises of his native tongue:

> Is it not indeed a marvelous bondage, to become servants to one tongue for learning's sake the most of our time, with loss of most time, whereas we may have the very same treasure in our own tongue, with the gain of more time? our own bearing the joyful title of our liberty and freedom, the Latin tongue remembering us of our thralldom and bondage? I love Rome, but London better; I favor Italy, but England more; I honor the Latin, but I worship the English.

These two impulses—humanist reverence for the classics and English pride in the vernacular language—gave rise to many distinguished translations throughout the century: Homer's *Iliad* and *Odyssey* by George Chapman, Plutarch's *Lives of the Noble Grecians and Romans* by Sir Thomas North, and Ovid's *Metamorphoses* by Arthur Golding. Translators also sought to make available in English the most notable literary works in the modern languages: Castiglione's *Il Cortegiano* by Sir Thomas Hoby, Ariosto's *Orlando furioso* (Orlando mad) by Sir John Harington, and Montaigne's *Essais* by John Florio. The London book trade of the sixteenth century was a thoroughly international affair.

THE REFORMATION

There had long been serious ideological and institutional tensions in the religious life of England, but officially, at least, England in the early sixteenth century had a single religion, Catholicism, whose acknowledged head was the pope in Rome. For its faithful adherents the Roman Catholic Church was the central institution in their lives, a universal and infallible guide to human existence from cradle to grave and on into the life to come. They were instructed by its teachings, corrected by its discipline, sustained by its sacraments, and comforted by its promises. At Mass, its most sacred ritual, the congregation could witness a miracle, as the priest held aloft the Host and uttered the words that transformed the bread and wine into the body and blood of God incarnate. A vast system of confession, pardons, penance, absolution, indulgences, sacred relics, and ceremonies gave the unmarried male clerical hierarchy great power, at once spiritual and material, over their largely illiterate flock. The Bible, the liturgy, and most of the theological discussions were in Latin, which few laypeople could understand; however, religious doctrine and spirituality were mediated to them by the priests, by beautiful church art and music, and by the liturgical ceremonies of daily life—festivals, holy days, baptisms, marriages, exorcisms, and funerals.

Several of the key doctrines and practices of the Catholic Church had been challenged in fourteenth-century England by the teachings of John Wycliffe and his followers, known as Lollards. But the heretical challenge had been ruthlessly suppressed, and the embers of dissent lay largely dormant until they were ignited once again in Germany by Martin Luther, an Augustinian monk and professor of theology at the University of Wittenberg. What began in November 1517 as an academic disputation grew with amazing speed into a bitter, far-reaching, and bloody revolt that forever ruptured the unity of Western Christendom.

The Pope as Antichrist. In this satirical woodcut, the pope, riding the seven-headed Beast of the Apocalypse, holds in his hand a banner on which he urges his followers to be traitors and kill their princes. His message, carried by three froglike devils, flies into the gaping mouths of a knight, a bishop, and a monk. The devils are a reference to Revelation 16.13: "And I saw three unclean spirits like frogs come out of the mouth of the dragon, and out of the mouth of the beast, and out of the mouth of the false prophet." From *Fierie Tryall of God's Saints* (1611; author unknown).

When Luther rose up against the ancient church, he did so in the name of private conscience enlightened by a personal reading of the Scriptures. A person of formidable intellectual energy, eloquence, and rhetorical violence, Luther charged that the pope and his hierarchy were the servants of Satan and that the Church had degenerated into a corrupt, worldly conspiracy designed to bilk the credulous and subvert secular authority. Salvation depended upon destroying this conspiracy and enabling all of the people to regain direct access to the word of God by means of vernacular translations of the Bible. The common watchwords of the Reformation, as the movement Luther sparked came to be known, were *sola scriptura* and *sola fide*: only the Scriptures (not the Church or tradition or the clerical hierarchy) have authority in matters of religion and should determine what an individual must believe and practice; only the faith of the individual (not good works or the scrupulous observance of religious rituals) can effect a Christian's salvation.

These tenets, heretical in the eyes of the Catholic Church, spread and gathered force, especially in northern Europe, where major leaders like the Swiss pastor Ulrich Zwingli in Zurich and the French theologian John Calvin in Geneva, elaborating various and sometimes conflicting doctrinal principles, organized the populace to overturn the existing church and established new institutional structures. In England, however, the Reformation began less with popular discontent and theological disputation than with dynastic politics and royal greed. Henry VIII, who had received from Pope Leo X the title Defender of the Faith for writing a diatribe against Luther, craved a legitimate son to succeed to the throne, and his queen, Catherine of Aragon, failed to give him one. (Catherine had borne six children, but only a daughter, Mary, survived infancy.) After lengthy negotiations, the pope, under pressure from Catherine's powerful Spanish family, refused to grant the king the divorce he sought in order to marry Anne Boleyn.

A series of momentous events followed, as England lurched away from the Church of Rome. In 1531 Henry forced the entire clergy of England to beg pardon for having usurped royal authority in the administration of canon law (the law that governed such matters as divorce). Two years later Henry's marriage to Catherine was officially declared null and void and Anne Boleyn was crowned queen. The king was promptly excommunicated by the pope, Clement VII. In the following year, a parliamentary Act of Succession required an oath from all adult male subjects confirming the new dynastic settlement. Thomas More and John Fisher, the bishop of Rochester, were among the small number who refused. The Act of Supremacy, passed later in the year, formally declared the king to be "Supreme Head of the Church in England" and again required an oath to this effect. In 1535 and 1536 further acts made it treasonous to refuse the oath of royal supremacy or, as More had tried to do, to remain silent. The first victims were three Carthusian monks who rejected the oath—"How could the king, a layman," said one of them, "be Head of the Church of England?"—and in May 1535 were duly hanged, drawn, and quartered. A few weeks later Fisher and More were convicted and beheaded. Between 1536 and 1539, under the direction of Henry's powerful secretary of state, Thomas Cromwell, England's monasteries were suppressed. Their vast wealth was seized by the Crown and transferred, by either gift or sale, to the king's followers.

Royal defiance of the authority of Rome was a key element in the Reformation but did not by itself constitute the establishment of Protestantism in England. On the contrary, in the same year that Fisher and More were martyred for their adherence to Roman Catholicism, twenty-five Protestants, members of a sect known as Anabaptists, were burned for heresy on a single day. Through most of his reign, Henry remained an equal-opportunity persecutor, pitiless to Catholics loyal to Rome and hostile to many of those who espoused Reformation ideas, though these ideas, aided greatly by the printing press, gradually established themselves on English soil.

Upon Henry's death, in 1547, his son, Edward (by his third wife, Jane Seymour), came to the throne. Both the ten-year-old Edward and his successive Protectors, the dukes of Somerset and Northumberland, were staunch Protestants, and reformers hastened to transform the English Church accordingly. During Edward's brief reign, Thomas Cranmer, the archbishop of Canterbury, formulated the forty-two articles of religion which became the core of Anglican orthodoxy and wrote the first *Book of Common Prayer*, which was officially adopted in 1549 as the basis of English worship services.

The sickly Edward died in 1553, only six years after his accession to the throne, and was succeeded by his half-sister Mary (Henry VIII's daughter by his first wife, Catherine), who immediately took steps to return her kingdom to Roman Catholicism. Though she was unable to get Parliament to agree to return church lands seized under Henry VIII, she restored the Catholic Mass, once again affirmed the authority of the pope, and put down a rebellion that sought to depose her. Seconded by her ardently Catholic husband, Philip II, king of Spain, she initiated a series of religious persecutions that earned her (from her enemies) the name Bloody Mary. Hundreds of Protestants took refuge abroad in cities like Calvin's Geneva; almost three hundred less-fortunate Protestants were condemned as heretics and burned at the stake.

Yet for thousands of English men and women, Mary's reign came as a liberation; the rapid restoration of old Catholic ornaments to parish churches all over England indicates that they had not in fact been confiscated or destroyed as ordered, but simply hidden away, in hopes of better times.

Mary died childless in 1558, and her younger half-sister, Elizabeth, became queen. Elizabeth's succession had been by no means assured. For if Protestants regarded as invalid Henry VIII's marriage to Catherine and hence deemed Mary illegitimate, so Catholics regarded as invalid his marriage to Anne Boleyn and hence deemed *her* daughter illegitimate. Henry himself seemed to support both views, since only three years after divorcing Catherine he beheaded Anne on charges of treason and adultery and urged Parliament to invalidate the marriage. Moreover, though during her sister's reign Elizabeth outwardly complied with the official Catholic religious observances, Mary and her advisers rightly suspected her of Protestant leanings, and the young princess's life was in grave danger. Poised and circumspect, Elizabeth warily evaded the traps that were set for her. When she ascended the throne, her actions were scrutinized for some indication of the country's future course. During her coronation procession, when a girl in an allegorical pageant presented her with a Bible in English translation—banned under Mary's reign—Elizabeth kissed the book, held it up reverently, and laid it to her breast. By this simple yet profound (and carefully choreographed) gesture, Elizabeth signaled England's return to the Reformation.

Many English men and women, of all classes, remained loyal to the old Catholic faith, but English authorities under Elizabeth moved steadily, if cautiously, toward ensuring at least an outward conformity to the official Protestant settlement. Recusants, those who refused to attend regular Sunday services in their parish churches, were heavily fined. Anyone who wished to receive a university degree, to be ordained as a priest in the Church of England, or to be named as an officer of the state had to swear an oath to the royal supremacy. Commissioners were sent throughout the land to confirm that religious services were following the officially approved liturgy and to investigate any reported backsliding into Catholic practice or, alternatively, any attempts to introduce reforms more radical than the queen and her bishops had chosen to embrace. For the Protestant exiles who streamed back were eager not only to undo the damage Mary had done but also to carry the Reformation much further than it had gone. A minority, who would come to be known as Puritans, sought to dismantle the church hierarchy, to purge the calendar of folk customs deemed pagan and the church service of ritual practices deemed superstitious, to dress the clergy in simple garb, and, at the extreme edge, to smash "idolatrous" statues, crucifixes, and altarpieces. Throughout her long reign, however, Elizabeth remained cautiously conservative and determined to hold religious zealotry in check.

In the space of a single lifetime, England had gone officially from Roman Catholicism, to Catholicism under the supreme headship of the English king, to a guarded Protestantism, to a more radical Protestantism, to a renewed and aggressive Roman Catholicism, and finally to Protestantism again. Each of these shifts was accompanied by danger, persecution, and death. It was enough to make people wary. Or skeptical. Or extremely agile.

A FEMALE MONARCH IN A MALE WORLD

In the last year of Mary's reign, the Scottish Calvinist minister John Knox thundered against what he called "the monstrous regiment of women." After the Protestant Elizabeth came to the throne the following year, Knox and his religious brethren were less inclined to denounce all female rulers, but in England, as elsewhere in Europe, there remained a widespread conviction that women were unsuited to wield power over men. Many men seem to have regarded the capacity for rational thought as exclusively male; women, they assumed, were led only by their passions. While gentlemen mastered the arts of rhetoric and warfare, gentlewomen were expected to display the virtues of silence and good housekeeping. Among upper-class males, the will to dominate others was acceptable and indeed admired; the same will in women was condemned as a grotesque and dangerous aberration.

Apologists for the queen countered these prejudices by appealing to historical precedent and legal theory. History offered inspiring examples of just female rulers, notably Deborah, the biblical prophetess who had judged Israel. In the legal sphere, Crown lawyers advanced the theory of "the king's two bodies." As England's crowned head, Elizabeth's person was mystically divided between her mortal "body natural" and the immortal "body politic." While the queen's natural body was inevitably subject to the failings of human flesh, the body politic was timeless and perfect. In political terms, therefore, Elizabeth's sex was a matter of no consequence, a thing indifferent.

Elizabeth, who had received a fine humanist education and an extended, dangerous lesson in the art of survival, made it immediately clear that she intended to rule in more than name only. She assembled a group of trustworthy advisers, foremost among them William Cecil (later created Lord Burghley), but she insisted on making many of the crucial decisions herself. Like many Renaissance monarchs, Elizabeth was drawn to the idea of royal absolutism, the theory that ultimate power was quite properly concentrated in her person and indeed that God had appointed her to be His deputy in the kingdom. Opposition to her rule, in this view, was not only a political act but also a kind of impiety, a blasphemous grudging against the will of God. Supporters of absolutism contended that God commands obedience even to manifestly wicked rulers whom He has sent to punish the sinfulness of humankind. Such arguments were routinely made in speeches and political tracts and from the pulpits of churches, where they were incorporated into the *Book of Homilies* that clergymen were required to read out to their congregations.

In reality, Elizabeth's power was not absolute. The government had a network of spies, informers, and *agents provocateurs*, but it lacked a standing army, a national police force, an efficient system of communication, and an extensive bureaucracy. Above all, the queen had limited financial resources and needed to turn periodically to an independent and often recalcitrant Parliament, which by long tradition had the sole right to levy taxes and to grant subsidies. Members of the House of Commons were elected from their boroughs, not appointed by the monarch, and though the queen had considerable influence over their decisions, she could by no means dictate policy. Under these constraints, Elizabeth ruled through a combination of adroit political maneuvering and imperious command, all the while enhancing her authority in the eyes of both court and country by means of an extraordinary cult of love.

"We all loved her," Elizabeth's godson Sir John Harington wrote, with just a touch of irony, a few years after the queen's death, "for she said she loved us." Ambassadors, courtiers, and parliamentarians all submitted to Elizabeth's cult of love, in which the queen's gender was transformed from a potential liability into a significant asset. Those who approached her generally did so on their knees and were expected to address her with the most extravagant compliments; she in turn spoke, when it suited her to do so, in a comparable language of love. The court moved in an atmosphere of romance, with music, dancing, plays, and the elaborate, fancy-dress entertainments called masques. The queen adorned herself in dazzling clothes and rich jewels. When she went on one of her summer "progresses," ceremonial journeys through her land, she looked like an exotic, sacred image in a religious cult of love, and her noble hosts virtually bankrupted themselves to lavish upon her the costliest pleasures. England's leading artists, such as the poet Edmund Spenser and the painter Nicholas Hilliard, enlisted themselves in the celebration of Elizabeth's mystery, likening her to the goddesses of mythology and the heroines of the Bible: Diana, Astraea, Cynthia, Deborah. The cultural sources of the cult of Elizabeth were both secular (her courtiers could pine for her as the cruelly chaste mistress celebrated in Petrarchan love poetry) and sacred (the veneration that under Catholicism had been due to the Virgin Mary could now be directed toward England's semi-divine queen).

There was a sober, even grim aspect to these poetical fantasies: Elizabeth was brilliant at playing off one dangerous faction against another, now turning her gracious smiles on one favorite, now honoring his hated rival, now suddenly looking elsewhere and raising an obscure upstart to royal favor. And when she was disobeyed or when she felt that her prerogatives had been challenged, she was capable of an anger that, as Harington put it, "left no doubtings whose daughter she was." Thus when Sir Walter Ralegh, one of the queen's glittering favorites, married without her knowledge and consent, he found himself promptly imprisoned in the Tower of London. Or when the Protestant polemicist John Stubbes ventured to publish a pamphlet stridently denouncing the queen's proposed marriage to the French Catholic duke of Anjou, Stubbes and his publisher were arrested and had their right hands chopped off. (After receiving the blow, the now prudent Stubbes lifted his hat with his remaining hand and cried, "God save the Queen!")

THE KINGDOM IN DANGER

Beset by Catholic and Protestant extremists, Elizabeth contrived to forge a moderate compromise that enabled her realm to avert the massacres and civil wars that poisoned France and other countries on the Continent. But menace was never far off, and there were continual fears of conspiracy, rebellion, and assassination. Suspicion swirled around Elizabeth's second cousin Mary, Queen of Scots, who had been driven from her own kingdom in 1568 and had taken refuge in England. The presence, under a kind of house arrest, of a Catholic queen with a plausible claim to the English throne was the source of widespread anxiety and helped generate recurrent rumors of plots. Some of these were real enough, others imaginary, still others fabricated by the secret agents of the government's intelligence service under the direction of Sir Francis Walsingham. Fears of Catholic conspiracies intensified greatly after Spanish imperial armies invaded the Netherlands in order to stamp out Protestant rebels (1567), after the St. Bartholomew's Day Massacre of Protestants (Huguenots) in France (1572), and after the assassination of Europe's other major Protestant leader, William of Orange (1584).

The queen's life seemed to be in even greater danger after Pope Gregory XIII's proclamation in 1580 that the assassination of the great heretic Elizabeth (who had been excommunicated a decade before) would not constitute a mortal sin. The immediate effect of the proclamation was to make life more difficult for English Catholics, most of whom were loyal to the queen but who fell under grave suspicion. Suspicion was heightened by the clandestine presence of English Jesuits, trained at seminaries abroad and smuggled back into England to serve the Roman Catholic cause. When, after several botched conspiracies had been disclosed, Elizabeth's spymaster Walsingham unearthed another assassination plot, in the correspondence between the Queen of Scots and the Catholic Anthony Babington, the wretched Mary's fate was sealed. After a public display of vacillation and perhaps with genuine regret, Elizabeth signed the death warrant, and her cousin was beheaded.

The long-anticipated military confrontation with Catholic Spain was now unavoidable. Elizabeth learned that Philip II, her former brother-in-law and one-time suitor, was preparing to send an enormous fleet against her island realm. The Armada was to sail first to the Netherlands, where a Spanish army would be waiting to embark and invade England. Barring its way was England's small fleet of well-armed and highly maneuverable fighting vessels, backed up by ships from the merchant navy. The Invincible Armada reached English waters in July 1588, only to be routed in one of the most famous and decisive naval battles in European history. Then, in what many viewed as an act of God on behalf of Protestant England, the Spanish fleet was dispersed and all but destroyed by violent storms.

As England braced itself to withstand the land invasion that never materialized, Elizabeth appeared in person to review a detachment of soldiers assembled at Tilbury, on the Thames estuary. Dressed in a white gown and a silver breastplate, she declared that though some among her councilors had urged her not to appear before a large crowd of armed men, she would never fail to trust the loyalty of her faithful and loving subjects. Nor did she fear the Spanish armies. "I know I have the body but of a weak and feeble woman," Elizabeth declared, "but I have the heart and stomach [i.e., valor] of a king, and of a king of England too." In this celebrated, carefully publicized speech, Elizabeth displayed many of her most memorable qualities: her self-consciously theatrical command of grand public occasions, her subtle blending of magniloquent rhetoric and the language of love, her strategic appropriation of traditionally masculine qualities, and her great personal courage. "We princes," she once remarked, "are set on stages in the sight and view of all the world."

Armada Portrait. This portrait of Queen Elizabeth, painted ca. 1588–89, is attributed to George Gower. Through the windows to the left and right can be glimpsed the arrival and then the defeat of the Spanish Armada, wrecked in violent storms. The queen, glowing with the pearls that symbolized her chastity, rests her hand on a globe, her fingers in effect claiming the Americas for her empire.

THE ENGLISH AND OTHERNESS

In 1485, most English people would have devoted little thought to their national identity. If asked to describe their sense of belonging, they would probably have spoken of the international community of Christendom and of their local region, such as Kent or Cornwall. The extraordinary events of the Tudor era, from the encounter with the New World to the break with Rome, made many people newly aware and proud of their Englishness. At the same time, they began to perceive those who lay outside the national community in new (and often negative) ways. Like most national communities, the English defined themselves largely in terms of what or who they were not. In the wake of the Reformation, the most prominent "others" were those who had until recently been more or less the same, that is, the Catholics of western Christendom. But other groups were also instrumental in the project of English self-definition.

Elizabethan London had a large population of resident aliens, mainly artisans and merchants and their families, from Portugal, Italy, Spain, Germany, and, above all, France and the Netherlands. Many of these people were Protestant refugees, and they were accorded some legal and economic protection by the government. But they were not always welcome to the local populace. Throughout the sixteenth century, London was the site of repeated demonstrations and, on occasion, bloody riots against the communities of foreign artisans, who were accused of taking jobs away from Englishmen. There was widespread hostility as well toward the Welsh, the Scots, and above all the Irish, whom the English had for centuries been struggling unsuccessfully to subdue. The kings of England claimed to be rulers of Ireland, but in reality they effectively controlled only a small area known as the Pale, extending north from Dublin. The great majority of the Irish population remained stubbornly Catholic and, despite endlessly reiterated English repression, burning of villages, destruction of crops, seizure of land, and massacres, incorrigibly independent.

Medieval England's Jewish population, the recurrent object of persecution, extortion, and massacre, had been officially expelled by King Edward I in 1290—the earliest such mass expulsion in Europe—but Elizabethan England harbored a tiny number of Jews or Jewish converts to Christianity. They were the objects of suspicion and hostility. Elizabethans appear to have been fascinated by Jews and Judaism but quite uncertain whether the terms referred to a people, a foreign nation, a set of strange practices, a living faith, a defunct religion, a villainous conspiracy, or a messianic inheritance. Protestant Reformers brooded deeply on the Hebraic origins of Christianity; government officials ordered the arrest of those "suspected to be Jews"; villagers paid pennies to itinerant fortune-tellers who claimed to be descended from Abraham or masters of kabbalistic mysteries; and London playgoers enjoyed the spectacle of the downfall of the wicked Barabas in Christopher Marlowe's *The Jew of Malta* and the forced conversion of Shylock in Shakespeare's *The Merchant of Venice*. Jews were not officially permitted to resettle in England until the middle of the seventeenth century, and even then their legal status was ambiguous.

Sixteenth-century England also had a small African population, whose skin color was the subject of pseudoscientific speculation and theological debate. Some Elizabethans believed that Africans' blackness resulted from the climate of the regions where they lived, where, as one traveler put it, they were "so scorched and vexed with the heat of the sun, that in many places they curse it when it riseth." Others held that blackness was a curse inherited from their forefather Cush, the son of Ham (who had, according to Genesis, wickedly exposed the nakedness of his drunken father,

Etching of a black woman, 1645, by Wenceslaus Hollar. The Bohemian-born Hollar lived and worked for most of his career in Antwerp and in London. He drew portraits of many men and women, including this sympathetic depiction of a black woman, probably a servant.

Noah). George Best, a proponent of this theory of inherited skin color, reported that "I myself have seen an Ethiopian as black as coal brought into England, who taking a fair English woman to wife, begat a son in all respects as black as the father was, although England were his native country, and an English woman his mother: whereby it seemeth this blackness proceedeth rather of some natural infection of that man."

As the word "infection" suggests, Elizabethans frequently regarded blackness as a physical defect, though the black people who lived in England and Scotland throughout the sixteenth century were also treated as exotic curiosities. At his marriage to Anne of Denmark, James VI of Scotland (the son of Mary, Queen of Scots; as James I of England, he succeeded Elizabeth, in 1603) entertained his bride and her family by commanding four naked black youths to dance before him in the snow. (The youths died of exposure shortly afterward.) In 1594, in the festivities celebrating the baptism of James's son, a "Black-Moor" entered pulling an elaborately decorated chariot that was, in the original plan, supposed to be pulled by a lion. In England there was a black trumpeter in the courts of Henry VII and Henry VIII, while Elizabeth had at least two black servants, one an entertainer, the other a page. Africans became increasingly fashionable as servants in aristocratic and gentle households in the last decades of the sixteenth century.

Some of these Africans were almost certainly slaves, though the legal status of slavery in England was ambiguous. In Cartwright's Case (1569), the court ruled "that England was too Pure an Air for Slaves to breathe in," but there is evidence that black slaves were owned in Elizabethan and Jacobean England. Moreover, by the mid-sixteenth century the English had become involved in the profitable trade that carried African slaves to the New World. In 1562 John Hawkins embarked on his first slaving voyage, transporting some three hundred Africans from the Guinea coast to Hispaniola, where they were sold for ten thousand pounds. Elizabeth is reported to have said that this venture was "detestable, and would call down the Vengeance of Heaven upon the Undertakers." Nevertheless, she invested profitably in Hawkins's subsequent voyages and loaned him ships.

Elizabeth also invested in other enterprises that combined aggressive nationalism and the pursuit of profit. In 1493 the pope had divided the New World between the Spanish and the Portuguese by drawing a line from pole to pole (hence Brazil speaks Portuguese today and the rest of Latin America speaks Spanish): the English were not in the picture. But by the end of Edward VI's reign the Company of Merchant Adventurers was founded, and Englishmen began to explore Asia and North America. Some of these adventurers turned to piracy, preying on Spanish ships that were returning laden with wealth extracted from Spain's New World possessions. (The pope had ruled that the Indians were human beings—and hence could be converted to Christianity—but the ruling did nothing to prevent their enslavement and brutal exploitation.) English acts of piracy soon became a private undeclared war, with the queen and her courtiers covertly investing in the raids but accepting no responsibility for them. The greatest of many astounding exploits was the voyage of Francis Drake (1577–80): he sailed through the Strait of Magellan, pillaged Spanish towns on the Pacific, reached as far north as San Francisco, crossed to the Philippines, and returned around the Cape of Good Hope; he came back with a million pounds in treasure, and his investors earned a dividend of 5,000 percent. Queen Elizabeth knighted him on the deck of his ship, *The Golden Hind.*

WRITERS, PRINTERS, AND PATRONS

The association between literature and print, so natural to us, was less immediate in the sixteenth century. Poetry in particular frequently circulated in manuscript, copied by reader after reader into personal anthologies— commonplace books—or reproduced by professional scribes for a fee. The texts that have come down to us in printed form often bear an uncertain relation to authorial manuscripts, and were frequently published only posthumously. The career of professional writer in sixteenth-century England was almost impossible: there was no such thing as author's copyright, no royalties paid to an author according to the sales of his book, and virtually no notion that anyone could make a decent living through the creation of works of literature. Writers sold their manuscripts to the printer or bookseller outright, for what now seem like ridiculously low prices. The churchyard of St. Paul's Cathedral in London was lined with booksellers' shops: dissolved chantries were taken over by bookshops in the 1540s, church officials leased out their residences near the church's north door to members of the Stationers' Company (the guild whose members had the exclusive right to own printing presses), and eventually bookstores two stories high and more filled the bays between the cathedral's buttresses. St. Paul's was the main center of business in the capital, with the church itself serving as a meeting place, and its columns as bulletin boards; publishers would post there, and elsewhere in the city, the title pages of new books as advertisements. Those title pages listed the wholesaler for the work, but customers could have bought popular books at most of the shops in St. Paul's Yard. The publishing business was not entirely contained in that busy space. Some stationers were only printers, merely working as contractors for publishers, and their printshops were located all over the city, often in the owner's residence.

Freedom of the press did not exist. Before Elizabeth's reign, state control of printed books was poorly organized, although licensing efforts had been underway since 1538. In 1557, however, the Stationers' Company received its charter, and became responsible for the licensing of books. Two years later, the government commanded the stationers to license only books that had been approved by either six privy councilors or the archbishop of Canterbury and the bishop of London. Despite these seemingly strict regulations, "scandalous, malicious, schismatical, and heretical" works were never effectively suppressed. Though there were occasional show trials and horrendous punishments—the printer William Carter was hanged for treason in 1584 because he had published a Catholic pamphlet; the Protestant separatists John Penry, Henry Barrow, and John Greenwood were executed in 1593 under a statute that made it a capital offense to "devise and write, print or set forth, any manner of book . . . letter, or writing containing false, seditious, and slanderous matter to the defamation of the Queen's Majesty"—active censorship was not as frequent or thorough as we might expect.

The censors largely focused their attention on works of history, which often had political implications for the present, and on religious treatises. In this, they shared the public's taste. Plays and secular poetry occasionally sold well (Shakespeare's *Henry IV, Part 1* was printed 7 times in 25 years), but they could not compete with publishing blockbusters such as *The Plain Man's Pathway* (16 editions in 25 years), let alone *The Psalms in English Meter*, published 124 times between 1583 and 1608. Publishers were largely interested in profit margins, and the predominance of devotional texts among the surviving books from the period attests to their greater marketability. The format in which works of literature were usually published is also telling. We normally find plays and poetry in quartos (or octavos), small volumes which had four (or eight) pages printed on each side of a sheet which was then folded twice (or three times) and stitched together with other such folded sheets to form the book. The more imposing folio format (in which the paper was folded only once, at two pages per side of a sheet) tended to be reserved not just for longer works but for those regarded as meriting especially respectful treatment. In 1577, Raphael Holinshed's massive history *The Chronicles of England, Scotlande, and Irelande* appeared in a woodcut-illustrated folio; ten years later, a second edition was published, again in the large format. In contrast, Edmund Spenser's huge poem *The Faerie Queene* was printed as a quarto both in 1590 and in 1596. A decade after his death, though, as the poet's reputation grew, his epic appeared again (1609), this time as a folio.

Elizabethan writers of exalted social standing, like the earl of Surrey or Sir Philip Sidney, thought of themselves as courtiers, statesmen, and landowners; poetry was for them an indispensable social grace and a deeply pleasurable, exalted form of play. Writers of lower rank, such as Samuel Daniel and Michael Drayton, sought careers as civil servants, secretaries, tutors, and clerics; they might take up more or less permanent residence in a noble household, or, more casually, offer their literary work to actual or prospective patrons, in the hope of protection, career advancement, or financial reward. Ambitious authors eager to rise from threadbare obscurity often looked to the court for livelihood, notice, and encouragement, but their great expectations generally proved chimerical. "A thousand hopes, but all nothing," wailed John Lyly, alluding to his long wait for the office of Master of the Revels, "a hundred promises but yet nothing."

Financial rewards for writing prose or poetry came mostly in the form of gifts from wealthy patrons, who sought to enhance their status and gratify their vanity through the achievements and lavish praises of their clients. Some Elizabethan patrons, though, were well-educated humanists motivated by aesthetic interests, and with them, patronage extended beyond financial support to the creation of lively literary and intellectual circles. Poems by Daniel, Ben Jonson, Aemilia Lanyer, and others bear witness to the sustaining intelligence and sophistication, as well as the generosity, of their benefactors. But the experience of Robert Greene is perhaps equally revealing: the fact that he had sixteen different patrons for seventeen books suggests that he did not find much favor or support from any one of them. Indeed, a practice grew up of printing off several dedications to be inserted into particular copies of a book, so that an impecunious author could deceive each of several patrons into thinking that he or she was the uniquely fortunate person to be honored by the volume.

In addition to the court and great families as dispensers of patronage, the city of London and the two universities also had a substantial impact on the period's literature. London was the center of the book trade, the nursery of a fledgling middle-class reading public, and, most important, the home of the public theaters. Before Elizabeth's time, the universities were mainly devoted to educating the clergy, and that remained an important part of their function. But in the second half of the century, the sons of the gentry and the aristocracy were going in increasing numbers to the universities and the Inns of Court (law schools), not in order to take religious orders or to practice law but to prepare for public service or the management of their estates. Other, less affluent students, such as Marlowe and Spenser, attended Oxford or Cambridge on scholarship. A group of graduates, including Thomas Nashe, Robert Greene, and George Peele, enlivened the literary scene in London in the 1590s, but the precarious lives of these so-called "university wits" testify to the difficulties they encountered in their quixotic attempt to survive by their writing skill. The diary of Philip Henslowe, a leading theatrical manager, has entry after entry showing university graduates in prison or in debt or at best eking out a miserable existence patching plays.

Women had no access to grammar schools, the universities, or the Inns of Court. While Protestantism, with its emphasis on reading Scripture, certainly helped to improve female literacy in the sixteenth century, girls were rarely encouraged to pursue their studies. Indeed, while girls were increasingly taught to read, they were not necessarily taught to write, for the latter skill in women was considered to be at the very least useless, at the worst dangerous. When the prominent humanist Sir Thomas Smith thought of how he should describe his country's social order, he declared that "we do reject women, as those whom nature hath made to keep home and to nourish their family and children, and not to meddle with matters abroad, nor to bear office in a city or commonwealth." Then, with a kind of nervous glance over his shoulder, he made an exception of those few in whom "the blood is respected, not the age nor the sex": for example, the queen. Every piece of writing by a woman from this period is a triumph over nearly impossible odds.

TUDOR STYLE: ORNAMENT, PLAINNESS, AND WONDER

Renaissance literature is the product of a rhetorical culture, a culture steeped in the arts of persuasion and trained to process complex verbal signals. (The contemporary equivalent would be the ease with which we deal with complex visual signals, effortlessly processing such devices as fade-out, montage, crosscutting, and morphing.) In 1512, Erasmus published a work called *De copia* that taught its readers how to cultivate "copiousness," verbal richness, in discourse. The work obligingly provides, as a sample, a list of 144 different ways of saying "Thank you for your letter."

In Renaissance England, certain syntactic forms or patterns of words known as "figures" (also called "schemes") were shaped and repeated in order to confer beauty or heighten expressive power. Figures were usually known by their Greek and Latin names, though in an Elizabethan rhetorical manual, *The Arte of English Poesie*, George Puttenham made a valiant if short-lived attempt to give them English equivalents, such as "Hyperbole, or the Overreacher" and "Ironia, or the Dry Mock." Those who received a grammar-school education throughout Europe at almost any point between the Roman Empire and the eighteenth century probably knew by heart the names of up to one hundred such figures, just as they knew by heart their multiplication tables. According to one scholar's count, William Shake-speare knew and made use of about two hundred.

As certain grotesquely inflated Renaissance texts attest, lessons from *De copia* and similar rhetorical guides could encourage prolixity and verbal self-display. Elizabethans had a taste for elaborate ornament in language as in clothing, jewelry, and furniture, and, if we are to appreciate their accomplishments, it helps to set aside the modern preference, particularly in prose, for unadorned simplicity and directness. When, in one of the age's most fashionable works of prose fiction, John Lyly wishes to explain that the vices of his young hero, Euphues, are tarnishing his virtues, he offers a small flood of synonymous images: "The freshest colors soonest fade, the teenest [i.e., keenest] razor soonest turneth his edge, the finest cloth is soonest eaten with moths." Lyly's multiplication of balanced rhetorical figures sparked a small literary craze known as "Euphuism," which was soon ridiculed by Shakespeare and others for its formulaic excesses. Yet the multiplication of figures was a source of deep-rooted pleasure in rhetorical culture, and most of the greatest Renaissance writers used it to extraordinary effect. Consider, for example, the succession of images in Shakespeare's sonnet 73:

> That time of year thou mayst in me behold
> When yellow leaves, or none, or few, do hang
> Upon those boughs which shake against the cold,
> Bare ruined choirs, where late the sweet birds sang.
> In me thou seest the twilight of such day
> As after sunset fadeth in the west;
> Which by and by black night doth take away,
> Death's second self that seals up all in rest.
> In me thou seest the glowing of such fire
> That on the ashes of his youth doth lie,
> As the deathbed whereon it must expire,
> Consumed with that which it was nourished by.
>   This thou perceiv'st, which makes thy love more strong,
>   To love that well, which thou must leave ere long.

What seems merely repetitious in Lyly here becomes a subtle, poignant amplification of the perception of decay, through the succession of images from winter (or late fall) to twilight to the last glow of a dying fire. Each of these images is in turn sensitively explored, so that, for example, the season is figured by bare boughs that shiver, as if they were human, and then these anthropomorphized tree branches in turn are figured as the ruined choirs of a church where services were once sung. No sooner is the image of singers in a church choir evoked than these singers are instantaneously transmuted back into the songbirds who, in an earlier season, had sat upon the boughs, while these sweet birds in turn conjure up the poet's own vanished youth. And this nostalgic gaze extends, at least glancingly, to the chancels of the Catholic abbeys reduced to ruins by Protestant iconoclasm and the dissolution of the monasteries. All of this within the first four lines: here and elsewhere Shakespeare, along with other poets of his time, contrives to freight the small compass and tight formal constraints of the sonnet—fourteen lines of rhymed iambic pentameter—with remarkable emotional intensity, psychological nuance, and imagistic complexity. The effect is what Christopher Marlowe called "infinite riches in a little room."

Elizabethans were certainly capable of admiring plainness of speech—in *King Lear* Shakespeare contrasts the severe directness of the virtuous Cordelia to the "glib and oily art" of her wicked sisters—and such poets as George Gascoigne, Thomas Nashe, and, in the early seventeenth century, Ben Jonson wrote restrained, aphoristic, moralizing lyrics in a plain style whose power depends precisely on the avoidance of richly figurative verbal pyrotechnics. This power is readily apparent in the wintry spareness of Nashe's "A Litany in Time of Plague," with its grim refrain:

> Wit with his wantonness
> Tasteth death's bitterness;
> Hell's executioner
> Hath no ears for to hear
> What vain art can reply.
> I am sick, I must die.
> Lord, have mercy on us!

Here the linguistic playfulness beloved by Elizabethan culture is scorned as an ineffectual "vain art" to which the executioner, death, is utterly indifferent.

But here and in other plain-style poetry, the somber, lapidary effect depends on a tacit recognition of the allure of the suppleness, grace, and sweet harmony that the dominant literary artists of the period so assiduously cultivated. Poetry, writes Puttenham, is "more delicate to the ear than prose is, because it is more current and slipper upon the tongue [i.e., flowing and easily pronounced], and withal tunable and melodious, as a kind of Music, and therefore may be termed a musical speech or utterance." The sixteenth century was an age of superb vocal music. The renowned composers William Byrd, Thomas Morley, John Dowland, and others scarcely less distinguished, wrote a rich profusion of madrigals (part songs for two to eight voices, unaccompanied) and airs (songs for solo voice, generally accompanied by the lute). These works, along with hymns, popular ballads, rounds, catches, and other forms of song, enjoyed immense popularity, not only in the royal court, where musical skill was regarded as an important accomplishment, and in aristocratic households, where professional musicians were employed as entertainers, but also in less exalted social circles. In his *Plain and Easy Introduction to Practical Music* (1597), Morley tells a story of social humiliation at a failure to perform that suggests that a well-educated Elizabethan was expected to be able to sight-sing. Even if this is an exaggeration in the interest of book sales, there is evidence of impressively widespread musical literacy, a literacy reflected in a splendid array of music for the lute, viol, recorder, harp, and virginal, as well as vocal music.

Many sixteenth-century poems were written to be set to music, but even those that were not often aspire in their metrical and syllabic virtuosity to the complex pleasures of madrigals or to the sweet fluency of airs. In poetry and music, as in gardens, architecture, and dance, Elizabethans had a taste for elaborate, intricate, but perfectly regular designs. They admired form, valued the artist's manifest control of the medium, and took pleasure in the highly patterned surfaces of things. Modern responses to art often evidence a suspicion of surfaces, impatience with order, the desire to rip away the mask in order to discover a hidden core of experiential truth: these responses are far less evident in Renaissance aesthetics than is a delight in pattern. Indeed many writers of the time expressed the faith that the universe itself had in its basic construction the beauty, concord, and harmonious order of a poem or a piece of music. "The world is made by Symmetry and proportion," wrote Thomas Campion, who was both a poet and a composer, "and is in that respect compared to Music, and Music to Poetry." The design of an exquisite work of art is deeply linked in this view to the design of the cosmos.

Such an emphasis on conspicuous pattern might seem to encourage an art as stiff as the starched ruffs that ladies and gentlemen wore around their necks, but the period's fascination with order was conjoined with a profound interest in persuasively conveying the movements of the mind and heart. Syntax in the sixteenth century was looser, more flexible than our own and punctuation less systematic. If the effect is sometimes confusing, it also enabled writers to follow the twists and turns of thought or perception. Consider, for example, Roger Ascham's account, in his book on archery, of a day in which he saw the wind blowing the new-fallen snow:

> That morning the sun shone bright and clear, the wind was whistling aloft, and sharp according to the time of the year. The snow in the highway lay loose and trodden with horse feet: so as the wind blew, it took the loose snow with it, and made it so slide upon the snow in the field which was hard and crusted by reason of the frost overnight, that thereby I might see very well, the whole nature of the wind as it blew that day. And I had a great delight and pleasure to mark it, which maketh me now far better to remember it. Sometime the wind would be not past two yards broad, and so it would carry the snow as far as I could see. Another time the snow would blow over half the field at once. Sometime the snow would tumble softly, by and by it would fly wonderful fast. And this I perceived also, that the wind goeth by streams and not whole together. . . . And that which was the most marvel of all, at one time two drifts of snow flew, the one of the West into the East, the other out of the North into the East: And I saw two winds by reason of the snow the one cross over the other, as it had been two highways. . . . The more uncertain and deceivable the wind is, the more heed must a wise Archer give to know the guiles of it.

What is delightful here is not only the author's moment of sharpened perception but his confidence that this moment—a glimpse of baffling complexity and uncertainty—can be captured in the restless succession of sentences and then neatly summed up in the pithy conclusion. (This effect parallels that of the couplet that sums up the complexities of a Shakespearean sonnet.) A similar confidence emanates from Sir Walter Ralegh's deeply melancholy, deeply ironic apostrophe to Death at the close of *The History of the World*, written when he was a prisoner in the Tower of London:

> O eloquent, just, and mighty Death! Whom none could advise, thou hast persuaded; what none hath dared, thou hast done; and whom all the world hath flattered, thou only hast cast out of the world and despised; thou hast drawn together all the far-stretched greatness, all the pride, cruelty, and ambition of man, and covered it all over with these two narrow words: *Hic jacet!* [Here lies]

Death is triumphant here, but so is Ralegh's eloquent, just, and mighty language.

The sense of *wonder* that animates both of these exuberant prose passages—as if the world were being seen clearly and distinctly for the first time—characterizes much of the period's poetry as well. The mood need not always be solemn. One can sense laughter, for example, rippling just below the surface of Marlowe's admiring description of the beautiful maiden Hero's boots:

> Buskins of shells all silvered usèd she,
> And branched with blushing coral to the knee,
> Where sparrows perched, of hollow pearl and gold,
> Such as the world would wonder to behold;
> Those with sweet water oft her handmaid fills;
> Which, as she went, would chirrup through the bills.

Seashells were beloved by Renaissance collectors because their intricate designs, functionally inexplicable, seemed the works of an ingenious, infinitely playful craftsman. Typically, the shells did not simply stand by themselves in cabinets but were gilded or silvered and then turned into other objects: cups, miniature ships, or, in Marlowe's fantasy, boots further decorated with coral and mechanical sparrows made of conspicuously precious materials and designed, as he puts it deliciously, to "chirrup." The poet knows perfectly well that the boots would be implausible footwear in the real world, but he invites us into an imaginary world of passion, a world in which the heroine's costume includes a skirt "whereon was many a stain, / Made with the blood of wretched lovers slain" and a veil of "artificial flowers and leaves, / Whose workmanship both man and beast deceives." The veil reflects an admiration for an art of successful imitation—after all, bees are said to look in vain for honey amidst the artificial flowers—but it is cunning illusion rather than realism that excites Marlowe's wonder. Renaissance poetry is interested not in representational accuracy but in the magical power of exquisite workmanship to draw its readers into fabricated worlds.

In his *Defense of Poesy*, the most important work of literary criticism in sixteenth-century England, Sidney claims that this magical power is also a moral power. All other arts, he argues, are subjected to fallen, imperfect nature, but the poet alone is free to range "within the zodiac of his own wit" and create a second nature, superior to the one we are condemned to inhabit: "Her world is brazen, the poets only deliver a golden." The poet's golden world in this account is not an escapist fantasy; it is a model to be emulated in actual life, an ideal to be brought into reality as completely as possible. It is difficult to say, of course, how seriously this project of realization was taken—though the circumstances of Sidney's own death suggest that he may have been attempting to enact on the battlefield an ideal image of Protestant chivalry. A didactic role for poetry is, in any case, urged not by Sidney alone but by most Elizabethan poets. Human sinfulness has corrupted life, robbing it of the sweet wholesomeness that it had once possessed in Eden, but poetry can mark the way back to a more virtuous and fulfilled existence. And not only mark the way: poetry, Sidney and others argue, has a unique persuasive force that shatters inertia and impels readers toward the good they glimpse in its ravishing lines.

This force, attributed to the energy and vividness of figurative language, made poetry a fitting instrument not only for such high-minded enterprises as moral exhortation, prayer, and praise, and for such uplifting narratives as the legends of religious and national heroes, but also for such verbal actions as cursing, lamenting, flattering, and seducing. The almost inexhaustible range of motives was given some order by literary conventions that functioned as shared cultural codes, enabling poets to elicit particular responses from readers and to relate their words to other times, other languages, and other cultures. Among the most prominent of the clusters of conventions in the period were those that defined the major literary modes (or "kinds," as Sidney terms them): pastoral, heroic, lyric, satiric, elegiac, tragic, and comic. They helped to shape subject matter, attitude, tone, and values, and in some cases—sonnet, verse epistle, epigram, funeral elegy, and masque, to name a few—they also governed formal structure, meter, style, length, and occasion. We can glimpse some of the ways in which these literary codes worked by looking briefly at two that are, for modern readers, among the least familiar: pastoral and heroic.

The conventions of the pastoral mode present a world inhabited by shepherds and shepherdesses who are concerned not just to tend their flocks but to fall in love and to engage in friendly singing contests. The mode celebrated leisure, humility, and contentment, exalting the simple country life over the city and its business, the military camp and its violence, the court and its burdens of rule. Pastoral motifs could be deployed in different genres. Pastoral songs commonly expressed the joys of the shepherd's life or his disappointment in love. Pastoral dialogues between shepherds might conceal serious, satiric comment on abuses in the great world under the guise of homely, local concerns. There were pastoral funeral elegies, pastoral dramas, pastoral romances (prose fiction), and even pastoral episodes within epics. The most famous pastoral poem of the period is Marlowe's "The Passionate Shepherd to His Love," an erotic invitation whose promise of gold buckles, coral clasps, and amber studs serves to remind us that, however much it sings of naïve innocence, the mode is ineradicably sophisticated and urban.

With its rustic characters, simple concerns, and modest scope, the pastoral mode was regarded as situated at the opposite extreme from heroic, with its values of honor, martial courage, loyalty, leadership, and endurance, and its glorification of a nation or people. The chief genre here was the epic, typically a long, ambitious poem in the high style, based on a heroic story from the nation's distant past and imitating Homer and Virgil in structure and motifs. Renaissance poets throughout Europe undertook to honor their nations and their vernacular languages by writing this most prestigious kind of poetry. In sixteenth-century England the major success in heroic poetry is Spenser's *Faerie Queene*. Yet the success of *The Faerie Queene* owes much to the fact that the poem is a generic hybrid, in which the conventions of classical epic mingle with those of romance, medieval allegory, pastoral, satire, mythological narrative, comedy, philosophical meditation, and many others in a strange, wonderful blend. The spectacular mixing of genres in Spenser's poem is only an extreme instance of a general Elizabethan indifference to the generic purity admired by writers, principally on the Continent, who adhered to Aristotle's *Poetics*. Where such neoclassicists attempted to observe rigid stylistic boundaries, English poets tended to approach the different genres in the spirit of Sidney's inclusivism: "if severed they be good, the conjunction cannot be hurtful."

THE ELIZABETHAN THEATER

If Sidney welcomed the experimental intertwining of genres in both poetry and prose—and his own *Arcadia*, a prose romance incorporating both pastoral and heroic elements, confirms that he did—there was one place where he found it absurd: the theater. He condemned the conjunction of high and low characters in "mongrel" tragicomedies that mingled "kings and clowns." Moreover, in the spirit of neoclassical advocacy of the "dramatic unities," Sidney disliked the ease with which the action on the bare stage ("where you shall have Asia of the one side, and Afric of the other") violated the laws of time and space. "Now you shall have three ladies walk to gather flowers," he writes in *The Defense of Poesy*, "and then we must believe the stage to be a garden. By and by we hear news of shipwreck in the same place: and then we are to blame if we accept it not for a rock." The irony is that this mocking account, written probably in 1579, anticipates by a few years the stupendous achievements of Marlowe and Shakespeare, whose plays joyously break every rule that Sidney thought it essential to observe.

A permanent, freestanding public theater in England dates only from Shakespeare's own lifetime. A London playhouse, the Red Lion, is first mentioned in 1567, and James Burbage's playhouse, The Theater, was built in 1576. But it is quite misleading to identify English drama exclusively with the new, specially constructed playhouses, for in fact there was a rich and vital theatrical tradition in England stretching back for centuries. Townspeople in late medieval England mounted elaborate cycles of plays (sometimes called "mystery plays") depicting the great biblical stories, from the creation of the world to Christ's Passion and its miraculous aftermath. Many of these plays have been lost, but those that survive, as the selection in this anthology demonstrates, include magnificent and complex works of art. At once civic and religious festivals, the cycles continued to be performed into the reign of Elizabeth, but their close links to popular Catholic piety led Protestant authorities in the later sixteenth century to suppress them.

Early English theater was not restricted to these annual festivals. Performers acted in town halls and the halls of guilds and aristocratic mansions, on scaffolds erected in town squares and marketplaces, on pageant wagons in the streets, and in innyards. By the fifteenth century, and probably earlier, there were organized companies of players traveling under noble patronage. Such companies earned a precarious living providing amusement, while enhancing the prestige of the patron whose livery they wore and whose protection they enjoyed. (Otherwise, by statutes enjoining productive labor, actors without another, ordinary trade could have been classified as vagabonds and whipped or branded.) This practice explains why the professional acting companies of Shakespeare's time, including Shakespeare's own, attached themselves to a nobleman and were technically his servants (the Lord Chamberlain's Men, the Lord Admiral's Men, etc.), even though virtually all their time was devoted to entertaining the public, from whom most of their income derived.

Before the construction of the public theaters, the playing companies often performed short plays called "interludes" that were, in effect, staged dialogues on religious, moral, and political themes. Henry Medwall's *Fulgens and Lucrece* (ca. 1490–1501), for example, pits a wealthy but dissolute

The **"Long View" of London,** 1647, by Wenceslaus Hollar. In this detail from Hollar's engraving of London, one can glimpse, on the south bank of the Thames, the Globe Theater and an arena for bearbaiting. The labels were accidentally transposed in the original: the Globe is the round structure on the left.

nobleman against a virtuous public servant of humble origins, while John Heywood's *The Play of the Weather* (ca. 1525–33) stages a debate among social rivals, including a gentleman, a merchant, a forest ranger, and two millers. The structure of such plays reflects the training in argumentation that students received in Tudor schools and, in particular, the sustained practice in examining both sides of a difficult question. Some of Shakespeare's amazing ability to look at critical issues from multiple perspectives may be traced back to this practice and the dramatic interludes it helped to inspire.

Another major form of theater that flourished in England in the fifteenth century and continued on into the sixteenth was the morality play, a dramatization of the spiritual struggle of the Christian soul. These dramas derived their power from the poignancy and terror of an individual's encounter with death. Often this somber power was supplemented by the extraordinary comic vitality of the evil character, or Vice.

If such plays sound more than a bit like sermons, it is because they were. The Church was a profoundly different institution from the theater, but its professionals shared some of the same rhetorical skills. It would be grossly misleading to regard churchgoing and playgoing as comparable entertainments, but clerical attacks on the theater sometimes make it sound as if ministers thought themselves to be in direct competition with professional players. The players, for their part, were generally too discreet to present themselves in a similar light, yet they almost certainly understood their craft as relating to sermons, with an uneasy blend of emulation and rivalry. When, in 1610, the theater manager Philip Rosseter was reported to have declared that plays were as good as sermons, he was summoned before the bishop of London to recant; but Rosseter had said no more than what many players must have privately thought.

By the later sixteenth century, many churchmen, particularly those with Puritan leanings, were steadfastly opposed to the theater, but some early Protestant Reformers, such as John Bale, tried their hand at writing plays. Thomas Norton, who with a fellow lawyer, Thomas Sackville, wrote the first English tragedy in blank verse, *Gorboduc, or Ferrex and Porrex* (1561), was also a translator of the great Reformer John Calvin. There is no evidence that Norton felt a tension between his religious convictions and his theatrical interests, nor was his play a private exercise. The five-act tragedy, a grim vision of Britain descending into civil war, was performed at the Inner Temple (one of London's law schools) and subsequently acted before the queen.

Gorboduc was closely modeled on the works of the Roman playwright Seneca, and Senecan influence—including violent plots, resounding rhetorical speeches, and ghosts thirsting for blood—remained pervasive in the Elizabethan theater, giving rise to the subgenre of revenge tragedy, in which a wronged protagonist plots and executes revenge, destroying himself (or herself) in the process. An early, highly influential example is Thomas Kyd's *Spanish Tragedy* (1592), and, despite its unprecedented psychological complexity, Shakespeare's *Hamlet* clearly participates in this kind. A related but distinct kind is the villain tragedy, in which the protagonist is blatantly evil: in his *Poetics*, Aristotle had advised against attempting to use a wicked person as the hero of a tragedy, but Shakespeare's *Richard III* and *Macbeth* amply justify the general English indifference to classical rules. Some Elizabethan tragedies, such as the fine *Arden of Feversham* (whose author is unknown), are concerned not with the fall of great men but with domestic violence; others, such as Christopher Marlowe's *Tamburlaine*, are concerned with "overreachers," larger-than-life heroes who challenge the limits of human possibility. Certain tragedies in the period, such as *Richard III*, intersect with another Elizabethan genre, the history play, in which dramatists staged the great events, most often conspiracies, rebellions, and wars, of the nation. Not all of the events commemorated in history plays were tragic, but they tend to circle back again and again to the act that epitomized what for this period was the ultimate challenge to authority: the killing of a king. When the English cut off the head of their king in 1649, they were performing a deed which they had been rehearsing, literally, for most of a century.

English schoolboys would read and occasionally perform comedies by the great Roman playwrights Plautus and Terence. Shortly before mid-century a schoolmaster, Nicholas Udall, used these as a model for a comedy in English, *Ralph Roister Doister*. At about the same time, another comedy, *Gammar Gurton's Needle*, which put vivid, native English material into classical form, was amusing the students at Cambridge. From the classical models English playwrights derived some elements of structure and content: plots based on intrigue, division into acts and scenes, and type characters such as the rascally servant and the *miles gloriosus* (cowardly braggart soldier). The latter type appears in *Ralph Roister Doister* and is a remote ancestor of Shakespeare's Sir John Falstaff in the two parts of *Henry IV* and *The Merry Wives of Windsor*.

Early plays such as *Gorboduc* and *Ralph Roister Doister* are rarely performed or read today, and with good reason. In terms of both dramatic structure and style, they are comparatively crude. Take, for example, this clumsy expression of passionate love by the title character in *Cambyses, King of Persia*, a popular play written around 1560 by a Cambridge graduate, Thomas Preston:

> For Cupid he, that eyeless boy, my heart hath so enflamed
> With beauty, you me to content the like cannot be named;
> For since I entered in this place and on you fixed mine eyes,
> Most burning fits about my heart in ample wise did rise.
> The heat of them such force doth yield, my corpse they scorch, alas!
> And burns the same with wasting heat as Titan doth the grass.
> And sith this heat is kindled so and fresh in heart of me,
> There is no way but of the same the quencher you must be.

Around 1590, an extraordinary change overcame the English drama, transforming it almost overnight into a vehicle for unparalleled poetic and dramatic expression. Many factors contributed to this transformation, but probably the chief was the eruption onto the scene of Christopher Marlowe. Compare Preston's couplets, written in a meter called "fourteeners," with the lines in Marlowe's *Doctor Faustus* (ca. 1592–93) with which Faustus greets the conjured figure of Helen of Troy:

> Was this the face that launched a thousand ships,
> And burnt the topless towers of Ilium?
> Sweet Helen, make me immortal with a kiss:
> Her lips sucks forth my soul, see where it flies!
> Come Helen, come, give me my soul again.
> Here will I dwell, for heaven be in these lips,
> And all is dross that is not Helena! (Scene 12, lines 81–87)

Marlowe has created and mastered a theatrical language—a superb unrhymed iambic pentameter, or blank verse—far more expressive than anything that anyone accustomed to the likes of Preston could have imagined.

Play-acting, whether of tragedies, comedies, or any of the other Elizabethan genres, took its place alongside other forms of public expression and entertainment as well. Perhaps the most important, from the perspective of the theater, were music and dance, since these were directly and repeatedly incorporated into plays. Moreover, virtually all plays in the period, including Shakespeare's, apparently ended with a dance. Brushing off the theatrical gore and changing their expressions from woe to pleasure, the actors in plays like *Doctor Faustus* and *King Lear* would presumably have received the audience's applause and then bid for a second round by performing a stately pavane or a lively jig.

Plays, music, and dancing were by no means the only shows in town. There were jousts, tournaments, royal entries, religious processions, pageants in honor of newly installed civic officials or ambassadors arriving from abroad; wedding masques, court masques, and costumed entertainments known as Disguisings or Mummings; juggling acts, fortune-tellers, exhibitions of swordsmanship, mountebanks, folk healers, storytellers, magic shows; bearbaiting, bullbaiting, cockfighting, and other blood sports; folk festivals such as Maying, the Feast of Fools, Carnival, and Whitsun Ales. For several years,

Elizabethan Londoners were delighted by a trained animal—Banks's Horse—that could, it was thought, do arithmetic and answer questions. And there was always the grim but compelling spectacle of public shaming, mutilation, and execution.

Most English towns had stocks and whipping posts. Drunks, fraudulent merchants, adulterers, and quarrelers could be placed in carts or mounted backward on asses and paraded through the streets for crowds to jeer and throw refuse at. Women accused of being scolds could be publicly muzzled by an iron device called a brank or tied to a "cucking stool" and dunked in the river. Convicted criminals could have their ears cut off, their noses slit, their foreheads branded. Public beheadings and hangings were common. In the worst cases, felons were sentenced to be "hanged by the neck, and being alive cut down, and your privy members to be cut off, and your bowels to be taken out of your belly and there burned, you being alive." In the dismemberment with which Marlowe's *Doctor Faustus* ends, the audience was witnessing the theatrical equivalent of the execution of criminals and traitors that they could have also watched in the flesh, as it were, nearby.

Doctor Faustus was performed by the Lord Admiral's Men at the Rose Theater, one of four major public playhouses that by the mid-1590s were feverishly competing for crowds of spectators. These playhouses (including

Scold's bridle, or brank. First recorded in Scotland, the scold's bridle was a device to humiliate and torture women who were regarded as "riotous" or "troublesome" in speech. The metal gag was designed to inflict maximum pain if the victim attempted to speak. In England, unruly women were also humiliated by being dragged through the streets in chairs known as "cucking stools," to be dunked.

Shakespeare's famous Globe Theater, which opened in 1599) each accommodated some two thousand spectators and generally followed the same design: they were oval in shape, with an unroofed yard in the center where stood the groundlings (apprentices, servants, and others of the lower classes) and three rising tiers around the yard for men and women able to pay a higher price for places to sit and a roof over their heads. A large platform stage jutted out into the yard, surrounded on three sides by spectators (see the conjectural drawing of an Elizabethan playhouse in the appendices to this volume). These financially risky ventures relied on admission charges—it was an innovation of this period to have money advanced in the expectation of pleasure rather than offered to servants afterward as a reward—and counted on habitual playgoing fueled by a steady supply of new plays. The public playhouses were all located outside the limits of the city of London and, accordingly, beyond the jurisdiction of the city authorities, who were generally hostile to dramatic spectacles. Eventually, indoor theaters, artificially lighted and patronized by a more select audience, were also built inside the city, secured under conditions that would allow them some protection from those who wished to shut them down.

Why should what we now regard as one of the undisputed glories of the age have aroused so much hostility? One answer, curiously enough, is traffic: plays drew large audiences, and nearby residents objected to the crowds, the noise, and the crush of carriages. Other, more serious concerns were public health and crime. It was thought that many diseases, including the dreaded bubonic plague, were spread by noxious odors, and the packed playhouses were obvious breeding grounds for infection. (Patrons often tried to protect themselves by sniffing nosegays or stuffing cloves in their nostrils.) The large crowds drew pickpockets, cutpurses, and other scoundrels. On one memorable afternoon a pickpocket was caught in the act and tied for the duration of the play to one of the posts that held up the canopy above the stage. The theater was, moreover, a well-known haunt of prostitutes, and, it was alleged, a place where innocent maids were seduced and respectable matrons corrupted. It was darkly rumored that "chambers and secret places" adjoined the theater galleries, and, in any case, taverns, disreputable inns, and brothels were close at hand.

There were other charges as well. Plays were performed in the afternoon and therefore drew people, especially the young, away from their work. They were schools of idleness, luring apprentices from their trades, law students from their studies, housewives from their kitchens, and potentially pious souls from the sober meditations to which they might otherwise devote themselves. Moralists warned that the theaters were nests of sedition, and religious polemicists, especially Puritans, obsessively focusing on the use of boy actors to play the female parts, charged that theatrical transvestism excited illicit sexual desires, both heterosexual and homosexual.

But the playing companies had powerful allies, including Queen Elizabeth herself, and continuing popular support. One theater historian has estimated that between the late 1560s and 1642, when the playhouses were shut down by the English Civil War, well over fifty million visits were paid to the London theater, an astonishing figure for a city that had, by our standards, a very modest population. Plays were performed without the scene breaks and intermissions to which we are accustomed; there was no scenery and few props, but costumes were usually costly and elaborate. The players formed what would now be called repertory companies—that is, they filled the roles of each play from members of their own group, not employing outsiders. They performed a number of different plays on consecutive days, and the principal actors were shareholders in the profits of the company. Boys were apprenticed to actors just as they were apprenticed to master craftsmen in the guilds; they took the women's parts in plays until their voices changed. The plays might be bought for the company from freelance writers, or, as in Shakespeare's company, the group might include an actor-playwright who could supply it with some (though by no means all) of its plays. The script remained the property of the company, but a popular play was eagerly sought by the printers, and the companies, which generally tried to keep their plays from appearing in print, sometimes had trouble guarding their rights. The editors of the earliest collected edition of Shakespeare, the First Folio (1623), complained about the prior publication of "divers stolen and surreptitious copies" of his plays, "maimed and deformed by the frauds and stealths of injurious imposters."

SURPRISED BY TIME

All of the ways we cut up time into units are inevitably distortions. The dividing line between centuries was not, as far as we can tell, a highly significant one for people in the Renaissance, and many of the most important literary careers cross into the seventeenth century without a self-conscious moment of reflection. But virtually everyone must have been aware, by the end of the 1590s, that the long reign of England's Queen Elizabeth was nearing its end, and this impending closure occasioned considerable anxiety. Childless, the last of her line, Elizabeth had steadfastly refused to name a successor. She continued to make brilliant speeches, to receive the extravagant compliments of her flatterers, and to exercise her authority—in 1601, she had her favorite, the headstrong earl of Essex, executed for attempting to raise an insurrection. But, as her seventieth birthday approached, she was clearly, as Ralegh put it, "a lady surprised by time." She suffered from bouts of ill health and melancholy; her godson Sir John Harington was dismayed to see her pacing through the rooms of her palace, striking at the tapestries with a sword. Her more astute advisers—among them Lord Burghley's son, Sir Robert Cecil, who had succeeded his father as her principal councillor—secretly entered into correspondence with the likeliest claimant to the throne, James VI of Scotland. Though the English queen had executed his Catholic mother, Mary, Queen of Scots, the Protestant James had continued to exchange polite letters with Elizabeth. It was at least plausible, as officially claimed, that in her dying breath, on March 24, 1603, Elizabeth designated James as her successor. A jittery nation that had feared a possible civil war at her death lit bonfires to welcome its new king. But in just a very few years, the English began to express nostalgia for the rule of "Good Queen Bess" and to look back on her reign as a magnificent high point in the history and culture of their nation.

THE SIXTEENTH CENTURY

TEXTS	CONTEXTS
	1485 Accession of Henry VII inaugurates Tudor dynasty
	ca. 1504 Leonardo da Vinci paints the *Mona Lisa*
ca. 1505–07 Amerigo Vespucci, *New World* and *Four Voyages*	1508–12 Michaelangelo paints Sistine Chapel ceiling
	1509 Death of Henry VII; accession of Henry VIII
1511 Desiderius Erasmus, *Praise of Folly*	
	1513 James IV of Scotland killed at Battle of Flodden; succeeded by James V
1516 Thomas More, *Utopia*. Ludovico Ariosto, *Orlando furioso*	
ca. 1517 John Skelton, "The Tunning of Elinour Rumming"	1517 Martin Luther's Ninety-Five Theses; beginning of the Reformation in Germany
	1519 Cortés invades Mexico. Magellen begins his voyage around the world
	1521 Pope Leo X names Henry VIII "Defender of the Faith"
1520s–30s Thomas Wyatt's poems circulating in manuscript	
1525 William Tyndale's English translation of the New Testament	
1528 Baldassare Castiglione, *The Courtier*	1529–32 More is Lord Chancellor
1532 Niccolò Machiavelli, *The Prince* (written 1513)	1532–34 Henry VIII divorces Catherine of Aragon to marry Anne Boleyn; Elizabeth I born; Henry declares himself head of the Church of England
	1535 More beheaded
1537 John Calvin, *The Institution of Christian Religion*	1537 Establishment of Calvin's theocracy at Geneva
	1542 Roman Inquisition. James V of Scotland dies; succeeded by infant daughter, Mary
1543 Copernicus, *On the Revolution of the Spheres*	
1547 *Book of Homilies*	1547 Death of Henry VIII; accession of Protestant Edward VI
1549 *Book of Common Prayer*	
	1553 Death of Edward VI; failed attempt to put Protestant Lady Jane Grey on throne; accession of Catholic Queen Mary, daughter of Catherine of Aragon
	1555–56 Archbishop Cranmer and former bishops Latimer and Ridley burned at the stake
1557 Tottel's *Songs and Sonnets* (printing poems by Wyatt, Surrey, and others)	
	1558 Mary dies; succeeded by Protestant Elizabeth I

TEXTS	CONTEXTS
1563 John Foxe, *Acts and Monuments*	
1565 Thomas Norton and Thomas Sackville, *Gorboduc*, first English blank-verse tragedy (acted in 1561)	
1567 Arthur Golding, translation of Ovid's *Metamorphoses*	**1567–68** Mary, Queen of Scots, forced to abdicate; succeeded by her son James VI; Mary imprisoned in England
	1570 Elizabeth I excommunicated by Pope Pius V
	1572 St. Bartholomew's Day Massacre of French Protestants
	1576 James Burbage's playhouse, The Theater, built in London
	1577–80 Drake's circumnavigation of the globe
1578 John Lyly, *Euphues*	
1579 Edmund Spenser, *The Shepheardes Calender*	
1580 Montaigne, *Essais*	
	1583 Irish rebellion crushed
	1584–87 Sir Walter Ralegh's earliest attempts to colonize Virginia
	1586–87 Mary, Queen of Scots, tried for treason and executed
ca. 1587–90 Marlowe's *Tamburlaine* acted. Shakespeare begins career as actor and playwright	
1588 Thomas Hariot, *A Brief and True Report of . . . Virginia*	**1588** Failed invasion of the Spanish Armada
1589 Richard Hakluyt, *The Principal Navigations . . . of the English Nation*	
1590 Sir Philip Sidney, *Arcadia* (posthumously published); Spenser, *The Faerie Queene*, Books 1–3	
1591 Sidney, *Astrophil and Stella* published	
ca. 1592 John Donne's earliest poems circulating in manuscript	
1595 Sidney, *The Defense of Poesy* published	**1595** Ralegh's voyage to Guiana
1596 Spenser, *The Faerie Queene*, Books 4–6 (with Books 1–3)	
1598 Ben Jonson, *Every Man in His Humor*	
	1599 Globe Theater opens
	1603 Elizabeth I dies; succeeded by James VI of Scotland (as James I), inaugurating the Stuart dynasty

SIR THOMAS WYATT THE ELDER
1503–1542

Thomas Wyatt made his career in the shifting, dangerous currents of Renaissance courts, and court culture, with its power struggles, sexual intrigues, and sophisticated tastes, shaped his remarkable achievements as a poet. Educated at St. John's College, Cambridge, Wyatt entered the service of Henry VIII, becoming clerk of the king's jewels, a member of diplomatic missions to France and the Low Countries, and, in 1537–39, ambassador to Spain at the court of the Holy Roman Emperor, Charles V. The years he spent abroad as a diplomat had a significant impact upon his writing, most obvious in his translations and imitations of poems by the Italian Renaissance writers Serafino, Aretino, Sannazaro, Alamanni, and, above all, Petrarch. Diplomacy, with its veiled threats, rhetorical manipulation, and cynical role-playing, may have had a more indirect impact as well, reinforcing the lessons in self-presentation and self-concealment that Wyatt would have received at the English court.

Life in the orbit of the ruthless, unpredictable Henry VIII was competitive and risky. When, in the late 1530s, Wyatt wrote to his son of the "thousand dangers and hazards, enmities, hatreds, prisonments, despites, and indignations" he had faced, he was not exaggerating. He probably came closest to the executioner's axe when in 1536 he was imprisoned in the Tower of London along with several others accused of having committed adultery with the queen, Anne Boleyn. As his poem "Who list his wealth and ease retain" suggests, Wyatt may have watched from his cell the execution of the queen and her alleged lovers; but he himself was spared, as he was spared a few years later, when he was again imprisoned in the Tower on charges of high treason brought by his enemies at court. His death, at the age of thirty-nine, came from a fever.

It is not surprising, given his career, that many of Wyatt's poems, including his satires and his psalm translations, express an intense longing for "steadfastness" and an escape from the corruption, anxiety, and duplicity of the court. The praise, in his verse epistle to John Poins, of a quiet retired life in the country and the harsh condemnation of courtly hypocrisy derive from his own experience. But of course the eloquent celebration of simplicity and truthfulness can itself be a cunning strategy. Wyatt was a master of the game of poetic self-display. Again and again he represents himself as a plain-speaking and steadfast man, betrayed by the "doubleness" of a fickle mistress or the instability of fortune. At this distance it is impossible to know how much this account corresponds to reality, but we can admire, as Wyatt's contemporaries did, the rhetorical deftness of the performance.

In a move with momentous consequences for English poetry, Wyatt introduced into English the sonnet, a fourteen-line poem in iambic pentameter with a complex, intertwining rhyme scheme. For the most part, he took his subject matter from Petrarch's sonnets, but his rhyme schemes make a significant departure. Petrarch's sonnets consist of an "octave," rhyming *abba abba*, followed, after a turn (*volta*) in the sense, by a "sestet" with various rhyme schemes (such as *cd cd cd* and *cde cde*) that have in common their avoidance of a rhyming couplet at the end. Wyatt employs the Petrarchan octave, but his most common sestet scheme is *cddc ee*: the Petrarchan sonnet was already beginning to change into the characteristic "English" structure for the sonnet, three quatrains and a closing couplet.

In his freest translations of Petrarchan sonnets, such as "Whoso list to hunt," Wyatt tends to turn the idealizing of the woman into disillusionment and complaint.

For the lover in Petrarch's poems, love is a transcendent experience, extending beyond the boundaries of life itself; for the lover in Wyatt's poems, it is all too transient, and embittering. The tone of bitterness carries over to many poems less closely linked to Italian and French models, poems with short stanzas and refrains that associate them with the native English song tradition. Some of Wyatt's songs, to be sure, strike a note of jaunty independence, often tinged with misogyny; but melancholy complaint is rarely very distant. Perhaps the poem that most brilliantly captures his blend of passion, anger, cynicism, longing, and pain is "They flee from me."

Though Wyatt's representations of women are often cynical, it is clear that aristocratic women played a key role in the reception and preservation of his poetry. Women were not excluded from the courtly game of lyric-making. The Devonshire Manuscript, one of the chief sources for Wyatt's poetry, contains a number of poems that were probably by women, many more transcribed by female hands, and some male-authored poems written in a female voice, as well as any number of misogynist verses, by Wyatt and others.

Wyatt never published a collection of his own poems, and very little of his verse appeared in print during his lifetime. In 1557 (fifteen years after his death), the printer Richard Tottel included 97 poems attributed to Wyatt among the 271 poems in his miscellany, *Songs and Sonnets*. Wyatt was not primarily concerned with regularity of accent and smoothness of rhythm. By the time Tottel's collection was published, Wyatt's deliberately rough, vigorous, and expressive metrical practice was felt to be crude, and Tottel (or perhaps some intermediary) smoothed out the versification. We reprint "They flee from me" both in Tottel's "improved" version and in the version found in the Egerton Manuscript, which contains poems in Wyatt's own hand and corrections he made to scribal copies of his poems. Unlike the Egerton Manuscript (E. MS.), the Devonshire Manuscript (D. MS.) was not apparently in the poet's possession, but some of its texts seem earlier than Egerton's, and it furnishes additional poems, as do the Blage Manuscript (B. MS.) and the Arundel Manuscript (A. MS.).

In the following selections we have indicated the manuscript from which each of the poems derives.*

The long love that in my thought doth harbor[1]

> The long love that in my thought doth harbor,
> And in mine heart doth keep his residence,
> Into my face presseth with bold pretense
> And therein campeth, spreading his banner.[2]
> 5 She that me learneth° to love and suffer   *teaches me*
> And will that my trust and lust's negligence[3]
> Be reined by reason, shame, and reverence,
> With his hardiness taketh displeasure.
> Wherewithal° unto the heart's forest he fleeth, *because of which*
> 10 Leaving his enterprise with pain and cry,

---

* For the Italian originals of the Petrarchan sonnets translated in our selection, as well as additional poems by Wyatt, see the supplemental ebook.

1. Wyatt's version of poem 140 of Petrarch's *Rime sparse* (Scattered rhymes); his younger friend the earl of Surrey also translated it (p. 387).

2. I.e., the speaker's blush. The first four lines of this sonnet introduce the "conceit" (elaborately

sustained metaphor) of Love as a warrior who, "with bold pretense" (i.e., making bold claim), flaunts his presence by means of the "banner." Elaborate metaphors of this kind are common in Petrarchan (and Elizabethan) love poetry, and often, as in this instance, an entire sonnet will turn on a single conceit.

3. I.e., my open and careless revelation of my love.

And there him hideth, and not appeareth.
What may I do, when my master feareth,
But in the field with him to live and die?
For good is the life ending faithfully.

E. MS.

Petrarch, Rima 140

A MODERN PROSE TRANSLATION[4]

Love, who lives and reigns in my thought and keeps his principal seat in my heart, sometimes comes forth all in armor into my forehead, there camps, and there sets up his banner.

She who teaches us to love and to be patient, and wishes my great desire, my kindled hope, to be reined in by reason, shame, and reverence, at our boldness is angry within herself.

Wherefore Love flees terrified to my heart, abandoning his every enterprise, and weeps and trembles; there he hides and no more appears outside.

What can I do, when my lord is afraid, except stay with him until the last hour? For he makes a good end who dies loving well.

Whoso list to hunt[1]

Whoso list° to hunt, I know where is an hind,°   cares / female deer
But as for me, alas, I may no more.
The vain travail° hath wearied me so sore,°   labor / sorely, seriously
I am of them that farthest cometh behind.
5   Yet may I, by no means, my wearied mind
Draw from the deer, but as she fleeth afore,
Fainting I follow. I leave off, therefore,
Since in a net I seek to hold the wind.
Who list her hunt, I put him out of doubt,°   assure him
10   As well as I, may spend his time in vain.
And graven with diamonds in letters plain
There is written, her fair neck round about,
"*Noli me tangere*, for Caesar's I am,
And wild for to hold, though I seem tame."

E. MS.

---

4. This and the prose translation of Rime 190 are by Robert K. Durling.
1. An adaptation of Petrarch's Rima 190, perhaps influenced by commentators on Petrarch, who said that *Noli me tangere quia Caesaris sum* ("Touch me not, for I am Caesar's") was inscribed on the collars of Caesar's hinds, which were then set free and were presumably safe from hunters. Wyatt's sonnet is usually supposed to refer to Anne Boleyn, in whom Henry VIII became interested in 1526.

Petrarch, Rima 190

A MODERN PROSE TRANSLATION

A white doe on the green grass appeared to me, with two golden horns, between two rivers, in the shade of a laurel, when the sun was rising in the unripe season.

Her look was so sweet and proud that to follow her I left every task, like the miser who as he seeks treasure sweetens his trouble with delight.

"Let no one touch me," she bore written with diamonds and topazes around her lovely neck. "It has pleased my Caesar to make me free."

And the sun had already turned at midday; my eyes were tired by looking but not sated, when I fell into the water, and she disappeared.

They flee from me

They flee from me, that sometime did me seek
With naked foot stalking° in my chamber.   *walking softly*
I have seen them gentle, tame, and meek
That now are wild and do not remember
5   That sometime they put themself in danger
To take bread at my hand; and now they range,
Busily seeking with a continual change.

Thanked be fortune it hath been otherwise
Twenty times better; but once in special,
10   In thin array, after a pleasant guise,
When her loose gown from her shoulders did fall,
And she me caught in her arms long and small,°   *slender*
Therewithal° sweetly did me kiss   *with that*
And softly said, "Dear heart, how like you this?"

15   It was no dream, I lay broad waking.
But all is turned, thorough° my gentleness,   *through*
Into a strange fashion of forsaking;
And I have leave to go, of her goodness,
And she also to use newfangleness.°   *fickleness*
20   But since that I so kindely[1] am served,
I fain would° know what she hath deserved.   *would like to*

E. MS.

---

1. Naturally (from *kind*: "nature," but with an ironic suggestion of the modern meaning of "kindly"). In Wyatt's spelling, the word should presumably be pronounced as three syllables.

Stand whoso list[1]

Stand whoso list° upon the slipper° top   *cares to / slippery*
Of court's estates,° and let me here rejoice   *high positions*
And use me quiet without let or stop,[2]
Unknown in court, that hath such brackish[3] joys.
5   In hidden place so let my days forth pass
That when my years be done withouten noise,
I may die aged after the common trace.°   *way*
For him death grippeth right hard by the crop°   *throat*
That is much known of other, and of himself, alas,
10   Doth die unknown, dazed, with dreadful° face.   *fearful*

A. MS.

1. A translation of Seneca, *Thyestes*, lines 391–403. For a literal translation of this famous passage, and other verse translations of it, see the supplemental ebook.

2. Comport myself quietly without hindrance or impediment.
3. Spoiled by mixture, as of seawater with fresh.

HENRY HOWARD, EARL OF SURREY
1517–1547

The axe that decapitated Surrey at the age of thirty had been hanging over his head for much of his life. In the court of Henry VIII, it was dangerous to be a potential claimant to the throne, and Surrey was descended from kings on both sides of his family. He was brought up at Windsor Castle as the close companion of Henry VIII's illegitimate son, the duke of Richmond, who married Surrey's sister. As the eldest son of the duke of Norfolk, the chief bulwark of the old Catholic aristocracy against the rising tide of "new men" and the reformed religion, Surrey was the heir not only to the Howard family's great wealth but also to their immense pride, their sense at once of noble privilege and of obligation. Like his father and grandfather, he was a brave and able soldier, serving in Henry VIII's French wars as "Lieutenant General of the King on Sea and Land." He was also repeatedly imprisoned for rash behavior, on one occasion for striking a courtier, on another for wandering through the streets of London breaking the windows of sleeping townspeople. In 1541 Surrey used his family connections—his first cousin, Catherine Howard, was queen—to secure the release from the Tower of his close friend the poet Thomas Wyatt, who had been accused of treason. But a year later, Catherine Howard was executed for adultery, like Anne Boleyn before her. Power returned to the rival family of the former queen Jane Seymour, who had died in childbirth giving a son and heir to the aging Henry VIII. Surrey's situation was already precarious, and his vocal opposition to the Seymours, with their strong Protestant leanings, sealed his fate. Convicted of treason, he had the grim distinction of being Henry's last victim.

Poets and critics of the later sixteenth century, fascinated by Surrey's noble rank and his tragic fate, routinely praised him as one of the very greatest English poets.

The full title of Tottel's influential miscellany, published in 1557 (ten years after Surrey's death), is *Songs and Sonnets Written by the Right Honorable Lord Henry Howard Late Earl of Surrey and Other*. The principal "other" here is his older friend Wyatt, with whose poetry Surrey's is closely linked. Poets who circulated their verse in manuscript in a courtly milieu, the two shared a passion for French and Italian poetry, especially for Petrarch's sonnets. Surrey established a form for these that was used by Shakespeare and that has become known as the English sonnet: three quatrains and a couplet, all in iambic pentameter and rhyming *abab cdcd efef gg*. Even more significant, he was the first English poet to publish in blank verse—unrhymed iambic pentameter—a verse form so popular in the succeeding centuries that it has come to seem almost indigenous to the language. The work in which he used his "strange meter," as the publisher called it, was a translation of part of Virgil's *Aeneid*. Managing the five-stress line with exceptional skill, Surrey initiated the rhythmic fluency that distinguishes so many Elizabethan lyrics. It is striking that his two great literary innovations, the English sonnet and blank verse, should emerge in the same period that saw radical upheavals in traditional religious and social life. It is possible that he was drawn to Virgil's epic because it offered a model of continuity in the face of disaster. Aeneas cannot prevent the fall of Troy, but he goes on to establish a new world without abandoning his old values.[*]

Love, that doth reign and live within my thought[1]

> Love, that doth reign and live within my thought,
> And built his seat within my captive breast,
> Clad in the arms wherein with me he fought,
> Oft in my face he doth his banner rest.
> 5 But she that taught me love and suffer pain,
> My doubtful hope and eke° my hot desire   *also*
> With shamefast° look to shadow and refrain,°   *modest / restrain*
> Her smiling grace converteth straight to ire.
> And coward Love then to the heart apace°   *at once*
> 10 Taketh his flight, where he doth lurk and plain,°   *complain*
> His purpose lost, and dare not show his face.
> For my lord's guilt thus faultless bide° I pain,   *endure*
> Yet from my lord shall not my foot remove:
> Sweet is the death that taketh end by love.

1557

---

[*] For additional lyrics by Surrey, as well as two excerpts from his partial translation of Virgil's *Aeneid* and the Italian originals of some of his sonnets, see the supplemental ebook.

1. Cf. Surrey's version of Petrarch's Rima 140 with Wyatt's translation of the same original (pp. 383–84; with a modern prose translation).

THE ENGLISH BIBLE

Protestant insistence that true belief must be based on the Holy Scriptures alone made the translation and dissemination of the Bible in English and other vernacular languages a matter of utmost urgency. Prior to the Reformation, the Roman Catholic Church had not always and everywhere opposed vernacular translations of the Bible, but it generally preferred that the populace encounter the Scriptures through the interpretations of its priests, trained to read the Latin translation known as the Vulgate. In times of great conflict this preference for clerical mediation hardened into outright prohibition of vernacular translation and into persecution and book burning. It was in the face of fierce opposition that zealous Protestants all over Europe set out to put the Bible into the hands of the laity. A remarkable translation of the New Testament by an English Lutheran named William Tyndale was printed on the Continent and smuggled into England in 1525; Tyndale's translation of the Pentateuch, the first five books of the Hebrew Bible, followed in 1530. Many copies of these translations were seized and destroyed, as was the translator himself, but the printing press made it extremely difficult for authorities to eradicate books for which there was a passionate demand.

Tyndale's translation was completed by an associate, Miles Coverdale, whose rendering of the Psalms proved to be particularly influential. Their joint labor was the basis for the Great Bible (1539), a copy of which was ordered to be placed in every church in the kingdom. Four years later, as Henry VIII sought to halt the tide of reform, a law was passed forbidding women, craftsmen, servants, and laborers from reading the Bible either in public or in private. Yet nothing could be done at this stage to take the Scriptures out of the hands of the populace. Though there would be further opposition in years to come—innumerable Bibles were printed under Edward VI, only to be burned during the reign of his sister Mary—the English Bible was a force that could not be suppressed, and it became, in its various forms, the single most important book of the sixteenth century.

Marian persecution was indirectly responsible for what would become the most scholarly Protestant English Bible, the translation known as the Geneva Bible, prepared, with extensive, learned, and often fiercely polemical marginal notes, by English exiles in Calvin's Geneva and widely diffused in England after Elizabeth came to the throne. In addition, Elizabethan church authorities ordered a careful revision of the Great Bible, and this version, known as the Bishops' Bible, was the one read in the churches. The success of the Geneva Bible in particular prompted those Elizabethan Catholics who now in turn found themselves in exile to bring out a vernacular translation of their own, the Douay-Rheims version, in order to counter the Protestant readings and glosses.

After Elizabeth's death, in 1603, King James I and his bishops ordered that a revised translation of the entire Bible be undertaken by a group of forty-seven scholars. The result, published in 1611, was the Authorized Version, more popularly known as the King James Bible.

In the passage selected here, 1 Corinthians 13, Tyndale's use of the word "love," echoed by the Geneva Bible, is set against the Catholic "charity." The latter term gestures toward the religious doctrine of "works," against the Protestant insistence on salvation by faith alone. It is a sign of the conservative, moderate Protestantism of the King James version that it too opts for "charity."

1 Corinthians 13[1]

From *Tyndale's Translation*

Though I spake with the tongues of men and angels, and yet had no love, I were even as sounding brass: or as a tinkling cymbal. And though I could prophesy, and understood all secrets, and all knowledge: yea, if I had all faith, so that I could move mountains out of their places, and yet had no love, I were nothing. And though I bestowed all my goods to feed the poor, and though I gave my body even that I burned, and yet had no love, it profiteth me nothing.

Love suffereth long, and is courteous. Love envieth not. Love doth not forwardly,[2] swelleth not, dealeth not dishonestly, seeketh not her own, is not provoked to anger, thinketh not evil, rejoiceth not in iniquity: but rejoiceth in the truth, suffereth all things, believeth all things, hopeth all things, endureth in all things. Though that prophesying fail, other[3] tongues shall cease, or knowledge vanish away, yet love falleth never away.

For our knowledge is unperfect and our prophesying is unperfect. But when that which is perfect is come, then that which is unperfect shall be done away. When I was a child, I spake as a child, I understood as a child, I imagined as a child. But as soon as I was a man, I put away childishness. Now we see in a glass, even in a dark[4] speaking: but then shall we see face to face. Now I know unperfectly: but then shall I know even as I am known. Now abideth faith, hope, and love, even these three: but the chief of these is love.

1525, 1535

From *The Geneva Bible*

Though I speak with the tongues of men and Angels, and have not love, I am as sounding brass, or a tinkling cymbal. And though I had the gift of prophecy, and knew all secrets and all knowledge, yea, if I had all faith, so that I could remove mountains, and had not love, I were nothing. And though I feed the poor with all my goods, and though I give my body, that I be burned, and have not love, it profiteth me nothing. Love suffereth long: it is bountiful: love envieth not: love doth not boast itself: it is not puffed up: It disdaineth not: it seeketh not her own things: it is not provoked to anger: it thinketh not evil: It rejoiceth not in iniquity, but rejoiceth in the truth: It suffereth all things: it believeth all things: it hopeth all things: it endureth all things. Love doth never fall away, though that prophesyings be abolished, or the tongues cease, or knowledge vanish away. For we know in part, and we prophesy in part. But when that which is perfect is come, then that which is in part shall be abolished. When I was a child, I spake as a child, I understood as a child, I thought as a child: but when I became a man, I put away childish things. For now we see through a glass darkly:[5] but

---

1. For two additional sets of passages from 16th-century English Bibles (Psalm 23, Isaiah 53.3–6), see the supplemental ebook.
2. Perversely, evilly.
3. Or.

4. Obscure, unclear. "Glass": mirror. The metaphor of indirect and imperfect sight seems to derive from Plato's Allegory of the Cave (*Republic* 7).
5. By means of a mirror, obscurely.

A page from the Geneva Bible, with commentary; 1583 edition. The Geneva Bible includes elaborate marginal notes, often with a sharply Protestant inflection. Some Elizabethan Catholics may have detected such a perspective in the note's anticipation of a redeemed state "where we shal neither nede scholes nor teachers."

then shall we see face to face. Now I know in part: but then shall I know even as I am known. And now abideth faith, hope, and love, even these three: but the chiefest of these is love.

1560, 1602

From *The Douay-Rheims Version*

If I speak with the tongues of men and of Angels, and have not charity,[6] I am become as sounding brass, or a tinkling cymbal. And if I should have prophecy, and knew all mysteries, and all knowledge, and if I should have all faith so that I could remove mountains, and have not charity, I am nothing. And if I should distribute all my goods to be meat[7] for the poor, and if I should deliver my body so that I burn, and have not charity, it doth profit me nothing.

Charity is patient, is benign: charity envieth not, dealeth not perversely: is not puffed up, is not ambitious, seeketh not her own, is not provoked to anger, thinketh not evil: rejoiceth not upon iniquity, but rejoiceth with the truth: suffereth all things, believeth all things, hopeth all things, beareth all things. Charity never falleth away: whether prophecies shall be made void, or tongues shall cease, or knowledge shall be destroyed. For in part we know, and in part we prophesy. But when that shall come that is perfect, that shall be made void that is in part. When I was a little one, I spake as a little one, I understood as a little one, I thought as a little one. But when I was made a man, I did away the things that belonged to a little one. We see now by a glass in a dark sort: but then face to face. Now I know in part: but then I shall know as also I am known. And now there remain faith, hope, charity, these three, but the greater of these is charity.

1582

From *The Authorized (King James) Version*

Though I speak with the tongues of men and of angels, and have not charity, I am become as sounding brass, or a tinkling cymbal. And though I have the gift of prophecy, and understand all mysteries, and all knowledge; and though I have all faith, so that I could remove mountains, and have no charity, I am nothing. And though I bestow all my goods to feed the poor, and though I give my body to be burned, and have not charity, it profiteth me nothing. Charity suffereth long, and is kind; charity envieth not; charity vaunteth not itself, is not puffed up, doth not behave itself unseemly, seeketh not her own, is not easily provoked, thinketh no evil; rejoiceth not in iniquity, but rejoiceth in the truth; beareth all things, believeth all things, hopeth all things, endureth all things. Charity never faileth: but whether there be prophecies, they shall fail; whether there be tongues, they shall cease; whether there be knowledge, it shall vanish away. For we know in part, and we prophesy in part. But when that which is perfect is come, then that which is in part shall be done away. When I was a child, I spake as a child, I understood as a child, I thought as a child: but when I became a man, I put away childish things. For now we see through a glass, darkly; but then face to face: now I know in part; but then shall I know even as also I am known. And now abideth faith, hope, charity, these three; but the greatest of these is charity.

1611

6. From Latin *caritas*, love; but also carrying the modern sense.
7. Food (in general).

ELIZABETH I
1533–1603

Elizabeth I, queen of England from 1558 to her death, set her mark indelibly on the age that has come to bear her name. Endowed with intelligence, courage, cunning, and a talent for self-display, she managed to survive and flourish in a world that would easily have crushed a weaker person. Her birth was a disappointment to her father, Henry VIII, who had hoped for a male heir to the throne, and her prospects were further dimmed when her mother, Anne Boleyn, was executed a few years later on charges of adultery and treason. At six years old, observers noted, Elizabeth had as much gravity as if she had been forty.

Under distinguished tutors, including the Protestant humanist Roger Ascham, the young princess received a rigorous education, with training in classical and modern languages, history, rhetoric, theology, and moral philosophy. Her own religious orientation was also Protestant, which put her in great danger during the reign of her Catholic older half-sister, Mary. Imprisoned in the Tower of London, interrogated and constantly spied upon, Elizabeth steadfastly professed innocence, loyalty, and a pious abhorrence of heresy. Upon Mary's death, she ascended the throne and quickly made clear that the official religion of the land would be Protestantism.

When she came to the throne, at twenty-five, speculation about a suitable match, already widespread, intensified. It remained for decades at a fever pitch, for the stakes were high. If Elizabeth died childless, the Tudor line would come to an end. The nearest heir was her cousin Mary, Queen of Scots, a Catholic whose claim was supported by France and by the papacy, and whose penchant for sexual and political intrigue soon confirmed the worst fears of English Protestants. The obvious way to avert the nightmare was for Elizabeth to marry and produce an heir, and the pressure upon her to do so was intense.

More than the royal succession hinged on the question of the queen's marriage; Elizabeth's perceived eligibility was a vital factor in the complex machinations of international diplomacy. A dynastic marriage between the queen of England and a foreign ruler could forge an alliance sufficient to alter the balance of power in Europe. The English court hosted a steady stream of ambassadors from kings and princelings eager to win the hand of the royal maiden, and Elizabeth played her romantic part with exemplary skill, sighing and spinning the negotiations out for months and even years. Most probably, she never meant to marry any of her numerous foreign (and domestic) suitors. Such a decisive act would have meant the end of her independence, as well as the end of the marriage game by which she played one power off against another. One day she would seem to be on the verge of accepting a proposal; the next, she would vow never to forsake her virginity. "She is a princess," the French ambassador remarked, "who can act any part she pleases." Ultimately she refused all offers and declared repeatedly that she was wedded to her country.

In the face of deep skepticism about the ability of any woman to rule, Elizabeth strategically blended imperiousness with an elaborate cult of love. Quickly making it clear that she would not be a figurehead, she gathered around her an able group of advisers, but she held firmly to the reins of power, subtly manipulating factional disputes, conducting diplomacy, and negotiating with an often contentious Parliament. Her courtiers and advisers, on their knees, approached the queen, glittering in jewels and gorgeous gowns, and addressed her in extravagant terms that conjoined romantic passion and religious veneration. Artists and poets celebrated her in mythological guise—as Diana, the chaste goddess of the moon;

Astraea, the goddess of justice; Gloriana, the queen of the fairies. Though she could suddenly veer, whenever she chose, toward bluntness and anger, Elizabeth often contrived to transform the language of politics into the language of love. "We all loved her," her godson John Harington wrote with a touch of irony, "for she said she loved us."

Throughout her life, Elizabeth took pride in her command of languages (she spoke fluent French and Italian and read Latin and Greek) and in her felicity of expression. Her own writing includes carefully crafted letters and speeches on several state occasions; a number of prayers; prose and verse translations, including works of Horace, Seneca, Plutarch, Boethius, Calvin, and the French Protestant Queen Margaret of Navarre; and a few original poems. The original poems known to be hers deal with actual events in her life. They show her to be an exceptionally agile, poised, and self-conscious writer, a gifted role-player fully in control of the rhetorical as well as political situation in which she found herself. The texts printed here, occasionally altered in light of variant versions, are from *Elizabeth I: Collected Works*, ed. Leah Marcus, Janel Mueller, and Mary Beth Rose (2000).*

The doubt of future foes[1]

The doubt° of future foes exiles my present joy,	*fear*
And wit° me warns to shun such snares as threatens mine	*intelligence*
annoy.[2]	
For falsehood now doth flow, and subjects' faith doth ebb,[3]	
Which should not be, if reason ruled or wisdom weaved the web.	
5 But clouds of toys untried do cloak aspiring minds,	
Which turns to rain of late repent, by course of changèd winds.[4]	
The top of hope supposed, the root of rue° shall be,	*regret*
And fruitless all their grafted guile, as shortly you shall see.[5]	
Their dazzled eyes with pride, which great ambition blinds,	
10 Shall be unsealed° by worthy wights° whose foresight	*opened / men*
falsehood finds.	
The daughter of debate,[6] that discord aye° doth sow,	*continually*
Shall reap no gain where former rule[7] still° peace hath taught	*stable*
to grow.	
No foreign banished wight shall anchor in this port:	
Our realm brooks no seditious sects—let them elsewhere resort.	
15 My rusty sword through rest[8] shall first his edge employ	
To poll their tops[9] who seek such change or gape for future joy.	

Vivat Regina[1]

ca. 1571   1589

---

* See the supplemental ebook for an additional letter from Elizabeth—to Henry III of France, furiously objecting to his intervention on behalf of Mary, Queen of Scots. For a painting of the queen in procession, see the color insert in this volume.
1. The poem concerns Mary, Queen of Scots, who in 1568 sought refuge in England from her rebellious subjects.
2. I.e., threaten to do me harm ("annoy").
3. I.e., the tide of faith (loyalty) is ebbing, yielding to the rising tide of falsehood.
4. Clouds of tricks ("toys") not yet tested or detected hide the "aspiring minds" of ambitious foes, but those clouds will turn at last into rains of repentance.
5. The deception ("guile") grafted into them will not bear fruit.
6. Strife. Mary Stuart also was sometimes called "Mother of Debate," because she was constantly the focus of conspiracies and plots.
7. "Former rule": either the reign of Henry VIII or that of Edward VI, which established the Reformation in England.
8. Sword rusty from disuse.
9. Strike off their heads.
1. Long live the queen.

On Monsieur's Departure[1]

I grieve and dare not show my discontent,
I love and yet am forced to seem to hate,
I do, yet dare not say I ever meant,
I seem stark mute but inwardly do prate.°   chatter
     I am and not, I freeze and yet am burned,   5
     Since from myself another self I turned.

My care is like my shadow in the sun,
Follows me flying, flies when I pursue it,
Stands and lies by me, doth what I have done.[2]
His too familiar care[3] doth make me rue° it.   regret
     No means I find to rid him from my breast,
     Till by the end of things it be suppressed.

Some gentler passion slide into my mind,
For I am soft and made of melting snow;
Or be more cruel, love, and so be kind.   15
Let me or° float or sink, be high or low.   either
     Or let me live with some more sweet content,
     Or die and so forget what love e'er° meant.   ever

ca. 1582   1823

Verse Exchange between Elizabeth and Sir Walter Ralegh[1]

[RALEGH TO ELIZABETH]

Fortune hath taken away my love,
My life's joy and my soul's heaven above.
Fortune hath taken thee away, my princess,
My world's joy and my true fantasy's mistress.

     Fortune hath taken thee away from me;   5
Fortune hath taken all by taking thee.
Dead to all joys, I only live to woe:
So is Fortune become my fantasy's foe.

In vain, my eyes, in vain ye waste your tears;
In vain, my sights,[2] the smoke of my despairs,   10
In vain you search the earth and heaven above.
In vain you search, for Fortune keeps my love.

---

1. The heading, present in a 17th-century manuscript, identifies the occasion of this poem as the breaking off of marriage negotiations between Elizabeth and the French duke of Anjou, in 1582.
2. Does everything I do.
3. I.e., my own care, which he caused.

1. This exchange, which exemplifies the poetic banter that sometimes passed between the queen and her favorites, took place about 1587, when Ralegh believed that the rapid rise of the earl of Essex in Elizabeth's favor entailed a diminution of his own standing with her.
2. Sighs?

Then will I leave my love in Fortune's hand;
Then will I leave my love in worldlings' band,[3]
15 And only love the sorrows due to me—
Sorrow, henceforth, that shall my princess be—

And only joy that Fortune conquers kings.
Fortune, that rules the earth and earthly things,
Hath taken my love in spite of virtue's might:
20 So blind a goddess did never virtue right.

With wisdom's eyes had but blind Fortune seen,
Then had my love, my love forever been.
But love, farewell—though Fortune conquer thee,
No fortune base nor frail shall alter me.

[ELIZABETH TO RALEGH]

Ah, silly Pug,[4] wert thou so sore afraid?
Mourn not, my Wat,[5] nor be thou so dismayed.
It passeth fickle Fortune's power and skill
To force my heart to think thee any ill.
5 No Fortune base, thou sayest, shall alter thee?
And may so blind a witch so conquer me?
No, no, my Pug, though Fortune were not blind,
Assure thyself she could not rule my mind.
Fortune, I know, sometimes doth conquer kings,
10 And rules and reigns on earth and earthly things,
But never think Fortune can bear the sway
If virtue watch, and will her not obey.
Ne chose I thee by fickle Fortune's rede,[6]
Ne she shall force me alter with such speed
15 But if to try this mistress' jest with thee.[7]
Pull up thy heart, suppress thy brackish tears,
Torment thee not, but put away thy fears.
Dead to all joys and living unto woe,
Slain quite by her that ne'er gave wise men blow,
20 Revive again and live without all dread,
The less afraid, the better thou shalt speed.[8]

ca. 1587   ca. 1600?

---

3. Bond.
4. An endearment, which Elizabeth used as her pet name for Ralegh.
5. Short for Walter.
6. Decision. "Ne": nor.

7. Since "thee" has nothing to rhyme with, and since the line is hard to construe, it seems likely that there is a line missing before or after this one. "But if": unless I do it.
8. Succeed.

Speech to the Troops at Tilbury[1]

My loving people, I have been persuaded by some that are careful of[2] my safety, to take heed how I committed myself to armed multitudes, for fear of treachery. But I tell you that I would not desire to live to distrust my faithful and loving people. Let tyrants fear! I have so behaved myself that, under God, I have placed my chiefest strength and safeguard in the loyal hearts and goodwill of my subjects. Wherefore I am come among you at this time but for my recreation and pleasure, being resolved in the midst and heat of the battle to live and die amongst you all,[3] to lay down for my God and for my kingdom and for my people mine honor and my blood even in the dust. I know I have the body but of a weak and feeble woman; but I have the heart and stomach of a king, and of a king of England too[4]—and take foul scorn that Parma[5] or any prince of Europe should dare to invade the borders of my realm. To the which, rather than any dishonor shall grow by me, I myself will venter[6] my royal blood; I myself will be your general, judge, and rewarder of your virtue in the field. I know that already for your forwardness you have deserved rewards and crowns,[7] and I assure you in the word of a prince you shall not fail of them. In the meantime, my lieutenant general[8] shall be in my stead, than whom never prince commanded a more noble or worthy subject; not doubting but by your concord in the camp and valor in the field, and your obedience to myself and my general, we shall shortly have a famous victory over these enemies of my God and of my kingdom.

1588   1654

The "Golden Speech"   A speech to Elizabeth's last Parliament, delivered November 30, 1601, and here given as recorded by one of the members. The designation "Golden Speech" stems from the headnote to a version of the speech printed near the end of the Puritan interregnum (1659?): "This speech ought to be set in letters of gold, that as well the majesty, prudence, and virtue of this royal queen might in general most exquisitely appear, as also that her religious love and tender respect which she particularly and constantly did bear to her Parliament in unfeigned sincerity might (to the shame and perpetual disgrace and infamy of some of her successors) be nobly and truly vindicated."

1. Delivered by Elizabeth on August 9, 1588, to the land forces assembled at Tilbury (in Essex) to repel the anticipated invasion of the Spanish Armada, a fleet of warships sent by Philip II. The Armada was defeated at sea and never reached England, a miraculous deliverance and sign of God's special favor to Elizabeth and to England, in the general view.

2. Anxious about.

3. In another version of the speech (based, like this one, on an auditor's memory), the sentence up to this point reads: "And therefore I am come amongst you, as you see at this time, not for my recreation and disport, but being resolved in the midst and heat of the battle to live or die amongst you all."

4. An allusion to the concept of the king's (or queen's) two bodies, the one natural and mortal, the other an ideal and enduring political construct. "Stomach": valor.

5. Alessandro Farnese, duke of Parma, allied with the king of Spain and expected to join with him in the invasion of England.

6. Venture, risk.

7. The crown was an English coin. "Forwardness": eagerness.

8. The earl of Leicester led the English troops. Elizabeth's great and powerful favorite, he died just a month later.

The royal prerogatives included the right to grant or sell "letters patent," which gave the recipient monopoly control of some branch of commerce. (Sir Walter Ralegh, for example, was given the exclusive right, for a period of thirty years, to license all taverns.) Discontent with the monopolies— which had resulted in higher prices for a wide range of commodities, including such basic ones as salt and starch—came to a head in the Parliament of 1601. Under parliamentary pressure (and in return for a subsidy granted to her treasury), Elizabeth agreed to revoke some of the most obnoxious patents and to allow the courts to rule freely on charges brought against the holders of others. She invited members of Parliament who wished to offer thanks for this largesse to come to her in a body, and on November 30 received about 150 of them at Whitehall Palace. After effusive remarks by the speaker of the House of Commons (Sir John Croke), the queen responded more or less as recorded here. (Elizabeth revised the speech for publication; and none of the surviving versions of it—which differ considerably—was printed earlier than about 1628.)

The "Golden Speech"[1]

Mr. Speaker, we have heard your declaration and perceive your care of our estate,[2] by falling into the consideration of a grateful acknowledgment of such benefits as you have received; and that your coming is to present thanks unto us, which I accept with no less joy than your loves can have desire to offer such a present.

I do assure you that there is no prince that loveth his subjects better, or whose love can countervail[3] our loves. There is no jewel, be it of never so rich a price, which I set before this jewel—I mean your loves. For I do more esteem it than any treasure or riches: for that we know how to prize, but love and thanks I count unvaluable.[4] And though God hath raised me high, yet this I count the glory of my crown, that I have reigned with your loves. This makes me that I do not so much rejoice that God hath made me to be a queen, as to be a queen over so thankful a people. Therefore I have cause to wish nothing more than to content the subjects, and that is a duty which I owe. Neither do I desire to live longer days than that I may see your prosperity, and that is my only desire. And as I am that person that still,[5] yet under God, hath delivered you, so I trust, by the almighty power of God, that I shall be His instrument to preserve you from envy, peril, dishonor, shame, tyranny, and oppression, partly by means of your intended helps, which we take very acceptable because it manifesteth the largeness of your loves and loyalties unto your sovereign.

Of myself I must say this: I never was any greedy, scraping grasper, nor a strait, fast-holding prince, nor yet a waster. My heart was never set on worldly goods, but only for my subjects' good. What you bestow on me, I will not hoard it up, but receive it to bestow on you again. Yea, my own properties I account yours to be expended for your good, and your eyes shall see the bestowing of

---

1. We print only the words of the queen, omitting various interpolations, as well as opening remarks by the speaker of the Parliament.
2. Rank, position.
3. Match.
4. Invaluable.
5. Continually.

all for your good. Therefore render unto them from me, I beseech you, Mr. Speaker, such thanks as you imagine my heart yieldeth but my tongue cannot express.

Mr. Speaker, I would wish you and the rest to stand up, for I shall yet trouble you with longer speech.[6]

Mr. Speaker, you give me thanks, but I doubt[7] me that I have more cause to thank you all than you me; and I charge you to thank them of the Lower House[8] from me. For had I not received a knowledge from you, I might have fallen into the lapse of an error only for lack of true information.

Since I was queen yet did I never put my pen to any grant but that upon pretext and semblance made unto me, it was both good and beneficial to the subject in general, though a private profit to some of my ancient servants who had deserved well. But the contrary being found by experience, I am exceedingly beholding to such subjects as would move the same at the first.[9] And I am not so simple to suppose but that there be some of the Lower House whom these grievances never touched; and for them I think they speak out of zeal to their countries[1] and not out of spleen or malevolent affection, as being parties grieved. And I take it exceedingly gratefully from them, because it gives us to know that no respects or interests had moved them other than the minds they bear to suffer[2] no diminution of our honor and our subjects' love unto us, the zeal of which affection, tending to ease my people and knit their hearts unto me, I embrace with a princely care.

For above all earthly treasures I esteem my people's love, more than which I desire not to merit. That my grants should be grievous to my people and oppressions to be privileged under color[3] of our patents, our kingly dignity shall not suffer it. Yea, when I heard it I could give no rest unto my thoughts until I had reformed it.[4] Shall they (think you) escape unpunished that have thus oppressed you and have been respectless of their duty and regardless of our honor? No, no, Mr. Speaker, I assure you were it not more for conscience' sake than for any glory or increase of love that I desire, these errors, troubles, vexations, and oppressions done by these varlets and low persons (not worthy the name of subjects) should not escape without condign punishment. But I perceive they dealt with me like physicians who, ministering a drug, make it more acceptable by giving it a good aromatical savor; or when they give pills, do gild them all over.

I have ever used[5] to set the Last Judgment Day before my eyes and so to rule as I shall be judged, to answer before a higher Judge. To whose judgment seat I do appeal that never thought was cherished in my heart that tended not unto my people's good. And now if my kingly bounties have been abused and my grants turned to the hurts of my people, contrary to my will and meaning, or if any in authority under me have neglected or perverted what I have committed to them, I hope God will not lay their culps[6] and offenses to my charge. Who, though there were danger in repealing our grants, yet what

6. Up to this point, the assemblage had been kneeling.
7. Fear.
8. The House of Commons.
9. I.e., those members of the House of Commons who had raised the issue of monopolies in previous sessions.
1. Their constituents.

2. Permit. "Minds": intentions.
3. Pretext.
4. In fact Elizabeth was extremely slow to respond to the grievances, which had, for example, previously been raised in the Parliament of 1597.
5. Been accustomed.
6. Sins.

danger would I not rather incur for your good than I would suffer them still to continue?

I know the title of a king is a glorious title, but assure yourself that the shining glory of princely authority hath not so dazzled the eyes of our understanding but that we well know and remember that we also are to yield an account of our actions before the great Judge. To be a king and wear a crown is more glorious to them that see it than it is pleasant to them that bear it. For myself, I was never so much enticed with the glorious name of a king or royal authority of a queen as delighted that God hath made me His instrument to maintain His truth and glory, and to defend this kingdom (as I said) from peril, dishonor, tyranny, and oppression.

There will never queen sit in my seat with more zeal to my country, care to my subjects, and that will sooner with willingness venture her life for your good and safety, than myself. For it is not my desire to live nor reign longer than my life and reign shall be for your good. And though you have had and may have many princes more mighty and wise sitting in this seat, yet you never had or shall have any that will be more careful and loving.

Shall I ascribe anything to myself and my sexly[7] weakness? I were not worthy to live then, and of all most unworthy of the mercies I have had from God, who hath ever yet given me a heart which yet never feared any foreign or home enemy. I speak it to give God the praise as a testimony before you, and not to attribute anything unto myself. For I, O Lord, what am I, whom practices and perils past should not fear?[8] O, what can I do, that I should speak for any glory? God forbid!

This, Mr. Speaker, I pray you deliver unto the House, to whom heartily recommend me. And so I commit you all to your best fortunes and further counsels. And I pray you, Mr. Comptroller, Mr. Secretary,[9] and you of my council, that before these gentlemen depart into their countries,[1] you bring them all to kiss my hand.

1601   1601 (in a summary version)

---

7. Characteristic of my sex. "Ascribe": attribute.
8. Frighten. "Practices": treacherous schemes.
9. William Knollys, earl of Banbury, and Robert

Cecil, earl of Salisbury.
1. Districts.

EDMUND SPENSER
1552?–1599

Edmund Spenser set out, consciously and deliberately, to become the great English poet of his age. In a culture in which most accomplished poetry was written by those who were, or at least professed to be, principally interested in something else—advancement at court, diplomacy, statecraft, or the church—Spenser's ambition was altogether remarkable, and it is still more remarkable that he succeeded in reaching his goal. Unlike such poets as Wyatt, Surrey, and Sidney, born to privilege and social distinction, Spenser was born to parents of modest means and station, in

London, probably in 1552. He nonetheless received an impressive education, first at the Merchant Taylors' School, under its demanding headmaster, the humanist Richard Mulcaster, then at Pembroke College, Cambridge, where he was enrolled as a "sizar," or poor (meaning impoverished) scholar. At Cambridge, which harbored many Puritans, Spenser started as a poet by translating some poems for a volume of anti-Catholic propaganda. He also began his friendship with Gabriel Harvey, an eccentric Cambridge don, humanist, and pamphleteer. Their correspondence shows that they shared a passionate and patriotic interest in the reformation of English verse. In a 1580 letter to Harvey, Spenser demanded, "Why a God's name may not we, as else the Greeks, have the kingdom of our own language?"

After receiving the B.A. degree in 1573 and the M.A. in 1576, Spenser served as personal secretary and aide to several prominent men, including the earl of Leicester, the queen's principal favorite. During his employment in Leicester's household he came to know Sir Philip Sidney and Sir Edward Dyer, courtiers who sought to promote a new English poetry. Spenser's contribution to the movement was *The Shepheardes Calender*, published in 1579 and dedicated to Sidney.

In *The Shepheardes Calender* Spenser used a deliberately archaic language, partly in homage to Chaucer, whose work he praised as a "well of English undefiled," and partly to achieve a rustic effect, in keeping with the feigned simplicity of pastoral poetry's shepherd singers. Sidney did not entirely approve, and another contemporary, Ben Jonson, growled that Spenser "writ no language." In the eighteenth century, Samuel Johnson described the language of *The Shepheardes Calender* as "studied barbarity." Johnson's characterization is, in a way, quite accurate, for Spenser was attempting to conjure up a native English style to which he could wed the classical mode of the pastoral. Moreover, since pastoral was traditionally viewed as the prelude in a great national poet's career to more ambitious undertakings, Spenser was also in effect announcing his extravagant ambition.

Spenser was a prolific and daring experimenter: the poems of *The Shepheardes Calender* use no fewer than thirteen different metrical schemes. In his later poems, he went on to make further innovations: the best-known of these are the special rhyme scheme of the Spenserian sonnet; the remarkably beautiful adaptation of the Italian *canzone* forms for the *Epithalamion* and *Prothalamion*; and the nine-line, or "Spenserian," stanza of *The Faerie Queene*, with its hexameter (six-stress) line at the end. Spenser is sometimes called the "poet's poet," because so many later English poets learned the art of versification from him. In the nineteenth century alone his influence may be seen in Shelley's *Revolt of Islam*, Byron's *Childe Harold's Pilgrimage*, Keats's *Eve of St. Agnes*, and Tennyson's "The Lotos-Eaters."

The year after the publication of *The Shepheardes Calender*, Spenser went to Ireland as secretary and aide to Lord Grey of Wilton, lord deputy of Ireland. Although he tried continually to obtain appointments in England and to secure the patronage of the queen, he spent the rest of his career in Ireland, holding various minor government posts and hence participating actively in the English struggle against those who resisted colonial domination. The grim realities of that struggle—massacre, the burning of miserable hovels and of crops with the deliberate intention of starving the inhabitants, the forced relocation of whole communities, the manipulation of treason charges so as to facilitate the seizure of lands, the endless repetition of acts of military "justice" calculated to intimidate and break the spirit—may be glimpsed in distorted and on occasion direct form throughout Spenser's writings, along with dreamlike depictions of the beauty of the Irish landscape. Those writings include an anonymously published political tract, *A View of the Present State of Ireland*, which was unusual in its time both for its genuine fascination with Irish culture and for the ruthlessness of the policies it recommended.

Spenser's attitudes toward Ireland and his conduct there raise difficult questions concerning the relationship between literature and colonialism. Are the harsh policies of the *View* echoed, allegorically, in *The Faerie Queene*? What does it mean to admire a poet who might, by modern standards, be judged a war criminal (as his master, Lord Grey, was judged to be, even by notoriously brutal Elizabethan standards)? Does Spenser use his Irish vantage point to launch daring criticisms of Queen Elizabeth and the English form of government? In addition to sharpening racial chauvinism, the experience of Ireland seems to have given English settlers a new perspective on events back home. As one of Spenser's contemporaries remarked, words that would be considered treasonous in England were common table talk among the Irish settlers.

Spenser was rewarded for his efforts in Ireland with a castle and 3,028 acres of expropriated land at Kilcolman, in the province of Munster. There he was visited by another colonist and poet, the powerful and well-connected Sir Walter Ralegh, to whom Spenser showed the great chivalric epic on which he was at work. With Ralegh's influential backing, Spenser traveled to England and published, in 1590, the first three books of The Faerie Queene, which made a strong bid for the queen's favor and patronage. He was rewarded with a handsome pension of fifty pounds a year for life, though the queen's principal councillor, Lord Burghley, is said to have complained that it was a lot for a song. Soon after, Spenser published a volume of poems called Complaints; a pastoral called Colin Clouts Come Home Againe (1595), commenting on the courtiers and ladies at the center of English court life at the time of his 1590 visit; his sonnet cycle, Amoretti; and two wedding poems, Epithalamion and Prothalamion. The six-book Faerie Queene was published in 1596, with some revisions in the first part and a changed ending to Book 3 to provide a bridge to the added books; the two so-called Mutability Cantos and two stanzas of a third—perhaps part of an intended seventh book—appeared posthumously, in the edition of 1609.

In 1598 there was an uprising in Munster, and rebels burned down the house in which Spenser lived. The poet fled with his wife; their newborn baby is said to have died in the flames. Spenser was sent to England with messages from the besieged English garrison. He died on January 13, 1599, and was buried near his beloved Chaucer in what is now called the Poets' Corner of Westminster Abbey.

Spenser cannot be put into neatly labeled categories. His work is steeped in Renaissance Neoplatonism but is also earthy and practical. He is a lover and celebrator of physical beauty yet also a profound analyst of good and evil in all their perplexing shapes and complexities. Strongly influenced by Puritanism in his early days, he remained a thoroughgoing Protestant all his life, and portrayed the Roman Catholic Church as a demonic villain in The Faerie Queene; yet his understanding of faith and of sin owes much to Catholic thinkers. He is a poet of sensuous images yet also something of an iconoclast, deeply suspicious of the power of images (material and verbal) to turn into idols. He is an idealist, drawn to courtesy, gentleness, and exquisite moral refinement, yet also a celebrant of English nationalism, empire, and martial power. He is the author of the most memorable literary idealization of Elizabeth I, yet he fills his poem with coded criticisms of the queen. He is in some ways a backward-looking poet, who paid homage to Chaucer, used archaic language, and compared his own age unfavorably with the feudal past. Yet as a British epic poet and poet-prophet, he points forward to the poetry of the Romantics and especially Milton—who himself paid homage to the "sage and serious" Spenser as "a better teacher than Scotus or Aquinas."

Because it was a deliberate choice on Spenser's part that his language should seem antique, his poetry is always printed in the original spelling and punctuation; a few of the most confusing punctuation marks have, however, been altered in the present text. Spenser also spells words variably, in such a way as to suggest rhymes to the eye or to suggest etymologies (often incorrect ones). This inconsistency in his spelling is typical of his time; in the sixteenth century, people varied even the spelling of their own names.*

---

* For additional writings by Spenser—"Aprill" from The Shepheardes Calender, four more sonnets from the Amoretti (nos. 15, 35, 59, 70), "A Hymne in Honour of Beautie," and, from The Faerie Queene, the Cave of Mammon canto from Book 2, exten- sive excerpts from Book 3, and the Mutabilitie Cantos—see the supplemental ebook. For excerpts from A View of the Present State of Ireland and a portrait of Spenser, see "Island Nations" in the ebook.

The Faerie Queene   In a letter to Sir Walter Ralegh, appended to the first, 1590, edition of *The Faerie Queene*, Spenser describes his exuberant, multifaceted poem as an allegory—an extended metaphor or "dark conceit"—and invites us to interpret the characters and adventures in its several books in terms of the particular virtues and vices they enact or come to embody. Thus the Redcrosse Knight in Book 1 is the knight of Holiness (and also St. George, the patron saint of England); Sir Guyon in Book 2 is the knight of Temperance; the female knight Britomart in Book 3 is the knight of Chastity (chastity here meaning chaste love leading to marriage). The heroes of Books 4, 5, and 6 represent Friendship, Justice, and Courtesy. The poem's general end, Spenser writes, is "to fashion a gentleman or noble person in vertuous and gentle discipline," and the individual moral qualities, taken together, constitute the ideal human being.

However, Spenser's allegory is not as simple as the letter to Ralegh might suggest, and the fashioning of identity proves to be anything but straightforward. Far from being the static embodiments of abstract moral precepts, the knights have a surprisingly complex, altogether human relation to their allegorical identities, identities into which they grow only through painful trial and error in the course of their adventures. These adventures repeatedly take the form of mortal combat with sworn enemies—hence the Redcrosse Knight of Holiness smites the "Saracen" (that is, Muslim) Sansfoy (literally, "without faith")—but the enemies are revealed more often than not to be weirdly dissociated aspects of the knights themselves: when he encounters Sansfoy, Redcrosse has just been faithless to his lady, Una, and his most dangerous enemy ultimately proves to be his own despair. Accordingly, the meaning of the various characters, episodes, and places is richly complex, revealed to us (and to the characters themselves) only by degrees.

The complexity is heightened by the inclusion, in addition to the moral allegory, of a historical allegory to which Spenser calls attention, in the letter to Ralegh, by observing that both the Faerie Queene and Belphoebe are personifications of Queen Elizabeth. (In fact, they are only two among many oblique representations of Elizabeth in the poem, some of them far from complimentary.) Throughout the poem there is a dense network of allusions to events, issues, and particular persons in England and Ireland—for example, the queen, her rival Mary, Queen of Scots, the Spanish Armada, the English Reformation, the controversies over religious images, and the bitter colonial struggles against Irish rebellion. Some of Spenser's characters are identified by conventional symbols and attributes that would have been obvious to readers of his time. For example, they would know immediately that a woman who wears a miter and scarlet clothes and dwells near the river Tiber represents (in one sense at least) the Roman Catholic Church, which had often been identified by Protestant preachers with the Whore of Babylon in the Book of Revelation. Marginal notes jotted in early copies of *The Faerie Queene* suggest, however, that there was no consensus among Spenser's contemporaries about the precise historical referents of others of the poem's myriad figures. (Sir Walter Ralegh's wife, Bess, for example, seems to have identified many of the virtuous female characters as allegorical representations of herself.) Spenser's poem may be enjoyed as a fascinating story with multiple meanings, a story that works on several levels at once and continually eludes the full and definitive allegorical explanation it constantly promises to deliver.

The poem is also an epic. In moving from *The Shepheardes Calender* to *The Faerie Queene* Spenser deliberately fashioned himself after the great Roman poet Virgil, who began his poetic career with pastoral poetry and moved on to his epic poem, the *Aeneid*. Spenser was acutely conscious that poets elsewhere in Europe, such as Ariosto and Tasso in Italy, and Camoens in Portugal, had already produced works modeled on Virgil's, in celebration of their respective nations. In weaving together classical and medieval sources, drawing on pictorial traditions, and adapting whole episodes from Ariosto and Tasso, he was providing his country with the epic it had hitherto lacked. Like Virgil, Spenser is deeply concerned with the dangerous struggles and painful renunciations required to achieve the highest values of human civilization. The heroic deeds of Spenser's brave knights are the achievements of individual aristocratic men and women, not the triumphs of armies or communities united in serving a common purpose, not even the triumph of the virtually invisible royal court of Gloriana, the Faerie Queene. Yet, taken together, the disjointed adventures of these solitary warriors constitute in Spenser's fervent vision the glory of Britain, the collective memory of its heroic past and the promise of a still more glorious future. And if the Faerie Queene herself is consigned to the margins of the poem that bears her name, she nonetheless is the symbolic embodiment of a shared national destiny, a destiny that reaches beyond mere political success to participate in the ultimate, millennial triumph of good over evil.

If *The Faerie Queene* is thus an epic celebration of Queen Elizabeth, the Protestant faith, and the English nation, it is also a chivalric romance, full of jousting knights and damsels in distress, dragons, witches, enchanted trees, wicked magicians, giants, dark caves, shining castles, and "paynims" (with French names). A clear, pleasant stream may be dangerous to drink from because to do so produces loss of strength. A pious hermit may prove to be a cunningly disguised villain. Houses, castles, and gardens are often places of education and challenge or of especially dense allegorical significance, as if they possess special, half-hidden keys to the meaning of the books in which they appear. As a romance, Spenser's poem is designed to produce wonder, to enthrall its readers with sprawling plots, marvelous adventures, heroic characters, ravishing descriptions, and esoteric mysteries.

In addition to enthralling readers, the poem habitually entraps, misleads, and deludes them. Like Spenser's protagonists, readers are constantly in danger of mistaking hypocritical evil for good, or cunningly disguised foulness for true beauty. *The Faerie Queene* demands vigilance from readers, and many passages must be reread in light of what follows after. In some sections, such as the dialogue between Redcrosse and Despaire (Book 1, canto 9), the repeated use of pronouns instead of proper names can lead to confusion as to who is speaking; the effect is intentional, for the promptings of evil are not always easy to disentangle from the voice of conscience.

The whole of *The Faerie Queene* is written in a remarkable nine-line stanza of closely interlocking rhymes (*ababbcbcc*), the first eight lines with five stresses each (iambic pentameter) and the final line with six stresses (iambic hexameter, or Alexandrine). The stanza gives the work a certain formal regularity, but the various books are composed on quite different structural principles. Book 1 is almost entirely self-contained; it has been called a miniature epic in itself, centering on the adventures of one principal hero, Redcrosse, who at length achieves the quest he undertakes at Una's behest: killing the dragon who has imprisoned her parents and thereby winning her as his bride. The spiritual allegory is similarly self-contained; it presents the Christian struggling heroically against many evils and temptations—doctrinal error, hypocrisy, the Seven Deadly Sins, and despair—to some of which he succumbs before finally emerging triumphant. It shows him separated from the one true faith and, aided by interventions of divine grace, at length reunited with it. Then it treats his purgation from sin, his education in the House of Holinesse, and his final salvation. By contrast, the structure of Book 3 is more romancelike, with its multiplicity of principal characters (who present, allegorically, several varieties of chaste and unchaste love), its interwoven stories, its heightened attention to women, and its conspicuous lack of closure.

To some degree a lack of closure characterizes all of *The Faerie Queene*, including the more self-contained of the six finished books, and it is fitting that there survives the fragment of another book, the cantos of Mutabilitie, in which Spenser broods on the tension in nature between systematic order and ceaseless change. The poem as a whole is built around principles that pull tautly against one another:

a commitment to a life of constant struggle and a profound longing for rest; a celebration of human heroism and a perception of ineradicable human sinfulness; a vision of evil as a terrifyingly potent force and a vision of evil as mere emptiness and filth; a faith in the supreme value of visionary art and a recurrent suspicion that art is dangerously allied to graven images and deception. That Spenser's knights never quite reach the havens they seek may reflect irresolvable tensions to which we owe much of the power and beauty of this great, unfinished work.

FROM THE FAERIE QUEENE

The First Booke of The Faerie Queene

Contayning
The Legende of the
Knight of the Red Crosse, or
Of Holinesse

1

Lo I the man, whose Muse whilome did maske,
    As time her taught, in lowly Shepheards weeds,[1]
    Am now enforst a far unfitter taske,
    For trumpets sterne to chaunge mine Oaten reeds,[2]
    And sing of Knights and Ladies gentle° deeds;   *noble*
    Whose prayses having slept in silence long,[3]
    Me, all too meane,° the sacred Muse areeds°   *low / counsels*
    To blazon° broad emongst her learned throng: *proclaim*
Fierce warres and faithfull loves shall moralize[4] my song.

2

Helpe then, O holy Virgin chiefe of nine,[5]
    Thy weaker° Novice to performe thy will,   *too weak*
    Lay forth out of thine everlasting scryne° *a chest for papers*
    The antique rolles, which there lye hidden still,
    Of Faerie knights and fairest Tanaquill,°   *i.e., Gloriana*
    Whom that most noble Briton Prince[6] so long
    Sought through the world, and suffered so much ill,
    That I must rue° his undeserved wrong: *pity*
O helpe thou my weake wit, and sharpen my dull tong.

3

And thou most dreaded impe° of highest Jove,   *offspring*
    Faire Venus sonne,° that with thy cruell dart   *Cupid*
    At that good knight so cunningly didst rove,°   *shoot*

---

1. Garb. The poet appeared before ("whilome") as a writer of humble pastoral (i.e., *The Shepheardes Calender*). These lines are imitated from the verses prefixed to Renaissance editions of Virgil's *Aeneid*.
2. To write heroic poetry, of which the trumpet is a symbol, instead of pastoral poetry symbolized by the humble shepherd's pipe ("Oaten reeds").
3. This and the preceding line are imitated from the opening of Ariosto's *Orlando furioso*.
4. Provide subjects for moralizing.
5. Scholars have debated whether the reference is to Clio, the Muse of history, or to Calliope, the Muse of epic.
6. I.e., Arthur, named in canto 9, stanza 6.

That glorious fire it kindled in his hart,
Lay now thy deadly Heben° bow apart,   ebony
And with thy mother milde come to mine ayde:
Come both, and with you bring triumphant Mart,[7]
In loves and gentle jollities arrayd,
After his murdrous spoiles and bloudy rage allayd.

4

And with them eke,° O Goddesse heavenly bright,   also
    Mirrour of grace and Majestie divine,
    Great Lady of the greatest Isle, whose light
    Like Phoebus lampe throughout the world doth shine,
    Shed thy faire beames into my feeble eyne,°   eyes
    And raise my thoughts too humble and too vile,°   lowly
    To thinke of that true glorious type[8] of thine,
    The argument° of mine afflicted stile:°   subject / humble work
The which to heare, vouchsafe, O dearest dred° a-while.   object of awe

Canto 1

The Patron of true Holinesse,
Foule Errour doth defeate:
Hypocrisie him to entrappe,
Doth to his home entreate.

1

A Gentle Knight was pricking° on the plaine,   spurring
    Ycladd[9] in mightie armes and silver shielde,
    Wherein old dints of deepe wounds did remaine,
    The cruell markes of many a bloudy fielde;
    Yet armes till that time did he never wield:
    His angry steede did chide his foming bitt,
    As much disdayning to the curbe to yield:
    Full jolly° knight he seemd, and faire did sitt,   gallant
As one for knightly giusts° and fierce encounters fitt.   jousts, tourneys

2

But on his brest a bloudie Crosse he bore,
    The deare remembrance of his dying Lord,
    For whose sweete sake that glorious badge he wore,
    And dead as living ever him adored:[1]
    Upon his shield the like was also scored,°   incised
    For soveraine[2] hope, which in his helpe he had:
    Right faithfull true[3] he was in deede and word,

---

7. Mars, god of war and lover of Venus.
8. I.e., Gloriana is the "type" (prefiguration) of Queen Elizabeth.
9. Imitating Chaucerian English, Spenser sometimes uses the prefix *y* as the sign of a past participle.
1. A compressed reference to Revelation 1.18:

"I am he that liveth, and was dead; and, behold, I am alive for evermore."
2. Having greatest power (often applied to medical remedies).
3. Compare Revelation 19.11: "And I saw heaven opened; and behold a white horse; and he that sat upon him was called Faithful and True."

But of his cheere⁴ did seeme too solemne sad;°   *grave*
Yet nothing did he dread, but ever was ydrad.°   *dreaded, feared*

3

Upon a great adventure he was bond,
    That greatest Gloriana to him gave,
    That greatest Glorious Queene of Faerie Lond,
    To winne him worship,° and her grace to have,   *honor*
    Which of all earthly things he most did crave;
    And ever as he rode, his hart did earne°   *yearn*
    To prove his puissance° in battell brave   *might*
    Upon his foe, and his new force to learne;
Upon his foe, a Dragon horrible and stearne.

4

A lovely Ladie rode him faire beside,
    Upon a lowly Asse more white then° snow,   *than*
    Yet she much whiter, but the same did hide
    Under a vele, that wimpled° was full low,   *lying in folds*
    And over all a blacke stole she did throw,
    As one that inly mournd: so was she sad,
    And heavie sat upon her palfrey slow:
Seemèd in heart some hidden care she had,
And by her in a line° a milke white lambe she lad.   *on a leash*

5

So pure an innocent, as that same lambe,
    She was in life and every vertuous lore,
    And by descent from Royall lynage came
    Of ancient Kings and Queenes, that had of yore
    Their scepters stretcht from East to Westerne shore,
    And all the world in their subjection held;
    Till that infernall feend with foule uprore
    Forwasted° all their land, and them expeld: *laid waste*
Whom to avenge, she had this Knight from far compeld.°   *summoned*

6

Behind her farre away a Dwarfe did lag,
    That lasie seemd in being ever last,
    Or wearièd with bearing of her bag
    Of needments at his backe. Thus as they past,
    The day with cloudes was suddeine overcast,
    And angry Jove an hideous storme of raine
    Did poure into his Lemans⁵ lap so fast,
    That every wight° to shrowd° it did constrain,   *creature / take shelter*
And this faire couple eke° to shroud themselves were fain.°   *also / eager*

---

4. Facial expression; mood.
5. His lover's, i.e., the earth's.

7

Enforst to seeke some covert nigh at hand,
  A shadie grove not far away they spide,
  That promist ayde the tempest to withstand:
  Whose loftie trees yclad with sommers pride,
  Did spred so broad, that heavens light did hide,
  Not perceable° with power of any starre: *penetrable*
  And all within were pathes and alleies wide,
  With footing worne, and leading inward farre:
Faire harbour that them seemes; so in they entred arre.

8

And foorth they passe, with pleasure forward led,
  Joying to heare the birdes sweete harmony,
  Which therein shrouded from the tempest dred,°   *fearful*
  Seemd in their song to scorne the cruell sky.
  Much can° they prayse the trees, so straight and hy,   *did*
  The sayling Pine, the Cedar proud and tall,
  The vine-prop Elme, the Poplar never dry,
  The builder Oake, sole king of forrests all,
The Aspine good for staves, the Cypresse funerall.°   *funereal*

9

The Laurell, meed° of mightie Conquerours   *reward*
  And Poets sage, the Firre that weepeth still,[6]
  The Willow worne of forlorne Paramours,
  The Eugh° obedient to the benders will,   *yew*
  The Birch for shaftes, the Sallow° for the mill,   *willow*
  The Mirrhe sweete bleeding in the bitter wound,
  The warlike Beech, the Ash for nothing ill,
  The fruitfull Olive, and the Platane° round,   *plane-tree*
The carver Holme,[7] the Maple seeldom inward sound.

10

Led with delight, they thus beguile the way,
  Untill the blustring storme is overblowne;
  When weening° to returne, whence they did stray,   *thinking*
  They cannot finde that path, which first was showne,
  But wander too and fro in wayes unknowne,
  Furthest from end then, when they neerest weene,
  That makes them doubt, their wits be not their owne:
  So many pathes, so many turnings seene,
That which of them to take, in diverse doubt they been.

---

6. I.e., exudes resin continuously. Spenser in these stanzas imitates Chaucer's catalog of trees in the *Parliament of Fowls*; the convention goes back to Ovid.
7. Holly or holm-oak, both suitable for carving.

11

At last resolving forward still to fare,
  Till that some end they finde or° in or out,   *either*
  That path they take, that beaten seemed most bare,
  And like to lead the labyrinth about°   *out of*
  Which when by tract they hunted had throughout,
  At length it brought them to a hollow cave,
  Amid the thickest woods. The Champion stout
  Eftsoones° dismounted from his courser brave,   *at once*
And to the Dwarfe a while his needlesse spere[8] he gave.

12

"Be well aware,"° quoth then that Ladie milde,   *watchful*
  "Least suddaine mischiefe° ye too rash provoke: *misfortune*
  The danger hid, the place unknowne and wilde,
  Breedes dreadfull doubts: Oft fire is without smoke,
  And perill without show: therefore your stroke
  Sir knight with-hold, till further triall made."
  "Ah Ladie," said he, "shame were to revoke°   *draw back*
  The forward footing for° an hidden shade: *because of*
Vertue gives her selfe light, through darkenesse for to wade."

13

"Yea but," quoth she, "the perill of this place
  I better wot then° you, though now too late   *know than*
  To wish you backe returne with foule disgrace,
  Yet wisedome warnes, whilest foot is in the gate,
  To stay the stepe, ere forcèd to retrate.
  This is the wandring wood, this Errours den,
  A monster vile, whom God and man does hate:
  Therefore I read° beware." "Fly fly," quoth then   *advise*
The fearefull Dwarfe: "this is no place for living men."

14

But full of fire and greedy hardiment,°   *boldness*
  The youthfull knight could not for ought° be staide,   *anything*
  But forth unto the darksome hole he went,
  And lookèd in: his glistring° armor made   *shining*
  A litle glooming light, much like a shade,
  By which he saw the ugly monster plaine,
  Halfe like a serpent horribly displaide,
  But th' other halfe did womans shape retaine,
Most lothsom, filthie, foule, and full of vile disdaine.°[9]   *loathsomeness*

8. "Needlesse" because the spear is used only on horseback. "By tract" (line 5): by following the track.

9. The description echoes both classical and biblical monsters (cf. Revelation 9.7–10).

15

And as she lay upon the durtie ground,
 Her huge long taile her den all overspred,
 Yet was in knots and many boughtes° upwound,   *coils*
 Pointed with mortall sting. Of her there bred
A thousand yong ones, which she dayly fed,
 Sucking upon her poisonous dugs, eachone
 Of sundry shapes, yet all ill favorèd:
 Soone as that uncouth° light upon them shone,   *unfamiliar*
Into her mouth they crept, and suddain all were gone.

16

Their dam upstart, out of her den effraide,°   *alarmed*
 And rushèd forth, hurling her hideous taile
 About her cursèd head, whose folds displaid°   *extended*
 Were stretcht now forth at length without entraile.° *coiling*
She lookt about, and seeing one in mayle
 Armèd to point,° sought backe to turne againe; *i.e., completely*
 For light she hated as the deadly bale,°   *injury*
 Ay wont° in desert darknesse to remain,   *ever accustomed*
Where plaine none might her see, nor she see any plaine.

17

Which when the valiant Elfe[1] perceived, he lept
 As Lyon fierce upon the flying pray,
 And with his trenchand° blade her boldly kept   *cutting*
 From turning backe, and forcèd her to stay:
Therewith enraged she loudly gan to bray,
 And turning fierce, her speckled taile advaunst;
 Threatning her angry sting, him to dismay:°   *defeat*
 Who nought aghast, his mightie hand enhaunst:° *lifted up*
The stroke down from her head unto her shoulder glaunst.

18

Much daunted with that dint,° her sence was dazd,   *blow*
 Yet kindling rage, her selfe she gathered round,
 And all attonce her beastly body raizd
 With doubled forces high above the ground:
Tho° wrapping up her wrethèd sterne arownd,   *then*
 Lept fierce upon his shield, and her huge traine°   *tail*
 All suddenly about his body wound,
 That hand or foot to stirre he strove in vaine:
God helpe the man so wrapt in Errours endlesse traine.

19

His Lady sad to see his sore constraint,
 Cride out, "Now now Sir knight, shew what ye bee,

---

1. I.e., knight of Faerie Land.

Add faith unto your force, and be not faint:
Strangle her, else she sure will strangle thee."
That when he heard, in great perplexitie,[2]
His gall did grate[3] for griefe° and high disdaine,   *wrath*
And knitting all his force got one hand free,
Wherewith he grypt her gorge° with so great paine,   *throat*
That soone to loose her wicked bands did her constraine.

20

Therewith she spewd out of her filthy maw
A floud of poyson horrible and blacke,
Full of great lumpes of flesh and gobbets raw,
Which stunck so vildly, that it forst him slacke
His grasping hold, and from her turne him backe:
Her vomit full of bookes and papers was,[4]
With loathly frogs and toades, which eyes did lacke,
And creeping sought way in the weedy gras:
Her filthy parbreake° all the place defilèd has.[5]   *vomit*

21

As when old father Nilus gins to swell
With timely° pride above the Aegyptian vale,   *in season*
His fattie° waves do fertile slime outwell,   *rich*
And overflow each plaine and lowly dale:
But when his later spring gins to avale,°   *subside*
Huge heapes of mudd he leaves, wherein there breed
Ten thousand kindes of creatures, partly male
And partly female of his fruitfull seed;
Such ugly monstrous shapes elswhere may no man reed.°   *see*

22

The same so sore annoyed° has the knight,   *injuriously affected*
That welnigh chokèd with the deadly stinke,
His forces faile, ne° can no longer fight.   *nor*
Whose corage when the feend perceived to shrinke,
She pourèd forth out of her hellish sinke[6]
Her fruitfull cursèd spawne of serpents small,
Deformèd monsters, fowle, and blacke as inke,
Which swarming all about his legs did crall,
And him encombred sore, but could not hurt at all.

23

As gentle Shepheard in sweete even-tide,
When ruddy Phoebus gins to welke° in west,   *sink*

---

2. In both the usual sense and the sense of "entangled condition."
3. I.e., his gallbladder (considered the seat of anger) was violently disturbed.
4. Alluding (at one level) to books and pamphlets of Catholic propaganda, notably attacks on Queen Elizabeth.
5. Revelation 16.13: "And I saw three unclean spirits like frogs come out of the mouth of the dragon, and out of the mouth of the beast, and out of the mouth of the false prophet."
6. Cesspool (i.e., her womb or organ of excretion).

High on an hill, his flocke to vewen wide,
Markes° which do byte their hasty supper best;   *observes*
A cloud of combrous° gnattes do him molest,   *encumbering*
All striving to infixe their feeble stings,
That from their noyance he no where can rest,
But with his clownish° hands their tender wings   *rustic*
He brusheth oft, and oft doth mar their murmurings.

24

Thus ill bestedd,° and fearful more of shame,   *situated*
Then of the certaine perill he stood in,
Halfe furious unto his foe he came,
Resolved in minde all suddenly to win,
Or soone to lose, before he once would lin;°   *cease*
And strooke at her with more then manly force,
That from her body full of filthie sin
He raft° her hatefull head without remorse;   *cut away*
A streame of cole black bloud forth gushèd from her corse.

25

Her scattred brood, soone as their Parent deare
They saw so rudely° falling to the ground,   *with great force*
Groning full deadly, all with troublous feare,
Gathred themselves about her body round,
Weening° their wonted entrance to have found   *thinking*
At her wide mouth: but being there withstood
They flockèd all about her bleeding wound,
And suckèd up their dying mothers blood,
Making her death their life, and eke° her hurt their good.   *also*

26

That detestable sight him much amazde,°   *stunned*
To see th'unkindly Impes° of heaven accurst,   *unnatural offspring*
Devoure their dam; on whom while so he gazd,
Having all satisfide their bloudy thurst,
Their bellies swolne he saw with fulnesse burst,
And bowels gushing forth: well worthy end
Of such as drunke her life, the which them nurst;
Now needeth him no lenger° labour spend,   *longer*
His foes have slaine themselves, with whom he should contend.

27

His Ladie seeing all, that chaunst, from farre
Approcht in hast to greet° his victorie,   *congratulate*
And said, "Faire knight, borne under happy starre,
Who see your vanquisht foes before you lye;
Well worthy be you of that Armorie,°   *armor*
Wherein ye have great glory wonne this day,
And prooved your strength on a strong enimie,
Your first adventure: many such I pray,
And henceforth ever wish, that like succeed it may."

28

Then mounted he upon his Steede againe,
  And with the Lady backward sought to wend;°   *go*
  That path he kept, which beaten was most plaine,
  Ne ever would to any by-way bend,
  But still did follow one unto the end,
  The which at last out of the wood them brought.
  So forward on his way (with God to frend)°   *with God as friend*
  He passèd forth, and new adventure sought;
Long way he travelèd, before he heard of ought.°   *aught, anything*

29

At length they chaunst to meet upon the way
  An agèd Sire, in long blacke weedes yclad,[7]
  His feete all bare, his beard all hoarie gray,
  And by his belt his booke he hanging had;
  Sober he seemde, and very sagely sad,°   *grave*
  And to the ground his eyes were lowly bent,
  Simple in shew,° and voyde of malice bad,   *show*
  And all the way he prayèd, as he went,
And often knockt his brest, as one that did repent.

30

He faire the knight saluted, louting° low,   *bowing*
  Who faire him quited,° as that courteous was: *responded*
  And after askèd him, if he did know
  Of straunge adventures, which abroad did pas.
  "Ah my deare Sonne," quoth he, "how should, alas,
  Silly° old man, that lives in hidden cell,   *simple*
  Bidding his beades° all day for his trespas,   *saying his prayers*
  Tydings of warre and worldly trouble tell?
With holy father sits not with such things to mell.[8]

31

"But if of daunger which hereby doth dwell,
  And homebred evill ye desire to heare,
  Of a straunge man I can you tidings tell,
  That wasteth all this countrey farre and neare."
  "Of such," said he, "I chiefly do inquere,
  And shall you well reward to shew the place,
  In which that wicked wight his dayes doth weare.°   *spend*
  For to all knighthood it is foule disgrace,
That such a cursèd creature lives so long a space."

32

"Far hence," quoth he, "in wastfull° wildernesse   *desolate*
  His dwelling is, by which no living wight°   *creature*

---

7. Dressed in long black garments.
8. I.e., it is not fitting for a holy hermit to meddle ("mell") with such things.

May ever passe, but thorough° great distresse."   *through*
"Now," sayd the Lady, "draweth toward night,
And well I wote, that of your later° fight   *recent*
Ye all forwearied be: for what so strong,
But wanting° rest will also want of might?   *lacking*
The Sunne that measures heaven all day long,
At night doth baite° his steedes the Ocean waves emong. *feed; refresh*

33

"Then with the Sunne take Sir, your timely rest,
And with new day new worke at once begin:
Untroubled night they say gives counsell best."
"Right well Sir knight ye have advisèd bin,"
Quoth then that agèd man; "the way to win
Is wisely to advise:° now day is spent; *take thought*
Therefore with me ye may take up your In° *lodging*
For this same night." The knight was well content.
So with that godly father to his home they went.

34

A little lowly Hermitage it was,
Downe in a dale, hard by° a forests side,   *close to*
Far from resort of people, that did pas
In travell to and froe: a little wyde°   *apart*
There was an holy Chappell edifyde,°   *built*
Wherein the Hermite dewly wont° to say *was accustomed*
His holy things° each morne and eventyde: *prayers*
Thereby a Christall streame did gently play,
Which from a sacred fountaine wellèd forth alway.

35

Arrivèd there, the little house they fill,
Ne looke for entertainement,° where none was: *elegant provision*
Rest is their feast, and all things at their will;
The noblest mind the best contentment has.
With faire discourse the evening so they pas:
For that old man of pleasing wordes had store,
And well could file° his tongue as smooth as glas; *polish*
He told of Saintes and Popes, and evermore
He strowd an *Ave-Mary*[9] after and before.

36

The drouping Night thus creepeth on them fast,
And the sad humour° loading their eye liddes, *heavy moisture*
As messenger of Morpheus[1] on them cast
Sweet slombring deaw, the which to sleepe them biddes.
Unto their lodgings then his guestes he riddes:° *leads*

---

9. "Hail Mary"—that is, a Catholic prayer.
1. Here (as often) Morpheus, the classical god of

dreams, is conflated with his father, Somnus, god
of sleep.

Where when all drownd in deadly sleepe° he findes,   *sleep like death*
He to his study goes, and there amiddes
His Magick bookes and artes of sundry kindes,
He seekes out mighty charmes, to trouble sleepy mindes.

37

Then choosing out few wordes most horrible
(Let none them read), thereof did verses frame,
With which and other spelles like terrible,
He bade awake blacke Plutoes griesly Dame,[2]
And cursèd heaven, and spake reprochfull shame
Of highest God, the Lord of life and light;
A bold bad man, that dared to call by name
Great Gorgon,[3] Prince of darknesse and dead night,
At which Cocytus quakes, and Styx is put to flight.

38

And forth he cald out of deepe darknesse dred
Legions of Sprights,° the which like little flyes[4]   *spirits*
Fluttring about his ever damnèd hed,
A-waite whereto their service he applyes,
To aide his friends, or fray° his enimies: *frighten*
Of those he chose out two, the falsest twoo,
And fittest for to forge true-seeming lyes;
The one of them he gave a message too,
The other by him selfe staide other worke to doo.

39

He making speedy way through spersèd° ayre,   *dispersed*
And through the world of waters wide and deepe,
To Morpheus house doth hastily repaire.
Amid the bowels of the earth full steepe,
And low, where dawning day doth never peepe,
His dwelling is; there Tethys° his wet bed   *the wife of Ocean*
Doth ever wash, and Cynthia[5] still° doth steepe   *continually*
In silver deaw his ever-drouping hed,
Whiles sad° Night over him her mantle black doth spred.   *sober*

40

Whose double gates he findeth lockèd fast,
The one faire framed of burnisht Yvory,
The other all with silver overcast;
And wakefull dogges before them farre do lye,
Watching to banish Care their enimy,
Who oft is wont° to trouble gentle Sleepe.   *accustomed*

---

2. Proserpine, as patron of witchcraft.
3. Demogorgon, in some myths the progenitor of all the gods, so powerful that the mention of his name causes hell's rivers (Styx and Cocytus) to tremble.
4. The simile associates him with Beelzebub ("Lord of Flies"), the name given to "the prince of the devils."
5. Diana, as goddess of the moon.

By them the Sprite doth passe in quietly,
And unto Morpheus comes, whom drownèd deepe
In drowsie fit he findes: of nothing he takes keepe.°   *notice*

41

And more, to lulle him in his slumber soft,
  A trickling streame from high rocke tumbling downe
  And ever-drizling raine upon the loft,°   *aloft, above*
  Mixt with a murmuring winde, much like the sowne°   *sound*
  Of swarming Bees, did cast him in a swowne:°   *swoon*
  No other noyse, nor peoples troublous cryes,
  As still° are wont t'annoy the wallèd towne,   *always*
  Might there be heard: but carelesse° Quiet lyes,   *free from care*
Wrapt in eternall silence farre from enemyes.[6]

42

The messenger approching to him spake,
  But his wast° wordes returnd to him in vaine: *wasted*
  So sound he slept, that nought mought° him awake.   *might*
  Then rudely he him thrust, and pusht with paine,°   *effort*
  Whereat he gan to stretch: but he againe
  Shooke him so hard, that forcèd him to speake.
  As one then in a dreame, whose dryer braine[7]
  Is tost with troubled sights and fancies° weake,   *fantasies*
He mumbled soft, but would not all his silence breake.

43

The Sprite then gan more boldly him to wake,
  And threatned unto him the dreaded name
  Of Hecate:° whereat he gan to quake,   *queen of Hades*
  And lifting up his lumpish° head, with blame   *heavy*
  Halfe angry askèd him, for what° he came.   *why*
  "Hither," quoth he, "me Archimago[8] sent,
  He that the stubborne Sprites can wisely tame,
  He bids thee to him send for his intent
A fit false dreame, that can delude the sleepers sent."°   *senses*

44

The God obayde, and calling forth straight way
  A diverse° dreame out of his prison darke,   *diverting, distracting*
  Delivered it to him, and downe did lay
  His heavie head, devoide of carefull carke,°   *anxious concerns*
  Whose sences all were straight benumbd and starke.[9]
  He backe returning by the Yvorie dore,[1]

6. Spenser is imitating descriptions of the caves of Morpheus in Chaucer (*Book of the Duchess*, lines 153–77) and of Somnus in Ovid (*Metamorphoses* 11.592–632).
7. According to the old physiology, elderly people and other light sleepers had too little moisture in the brain.
8. The name can be construed as meaning both "archmagician" and "architect of images."
9. Immediately ("straight") benumbed and paralyzed.
1. According to Homer (*Odyssey* 19.562–67) and Virgil (*Aeneid* 6.893–96), false dreams come through Sleep's ivory gate, true dreams through his gate of horn.

Remounted up as light as chearefull Larke,
And on his litle winges the dreame he bore
In hast unto his Lord, where he him left afore.

45

Who all this while with charmes and hidden artes,
   Had made a Lady of that other Spright,
   And framed of liquid ayre her tender partes
   So lively,° and so like in all mens sight,   *lifelike*
   That weaker° sence it could have ravisht quight: *too weak*
   The maker selfe for all his wondrous witt,
   Was nigh beguilèd° with so goodly sight: *deceived*
   Her all in white he clad, and over it
Cast a blacke stole, most like to seeme for Una² fit.°   *fitting*

46

Now when that ydle dreame was to him brought
   Unto that Elfin knight he bad him fly,
   Where he slept soundly void of evill thought
   And with false shewes abuse his fantasy,°   *imagination*
   In sort as° he him schoolèd privily: *in the way that*
   And that new creature borne without her dew,°   *unnaturally*
   Full of the makers guile, with usage sly
   He taught to imitate that Lady trew,
Whose semblance she did carrie under feignèd hew.°   *form*

47

Thus well instructed, to their worke they hast
   And comming where the knight in slomber lay
   The one upon his hardy head him plast,°   *placed*
   And made him dreame of loves and lustfull play,
   That nigh his manly hart did melt away,
   Bathèd in wanton blis and wicked joy:
   Then seemèd him his Lady by him lay,
   And to him playnd,° how that false wingèd boy°   *complained / Cupid*
Her chast hart had subdewd, to learne Dame pleasures toy.°   *lustful play*

48

And she her selfe of beautie soveraigne Queene,
   Faire Venus seemde unto his bed to bring
   Her, whom he waking evermore did weene°   *think*
   To be the chastest flowre, that ay° did spring   *ever*
   On earthly braunch, the daughter of a king,
   Now a loose Leman° to vile service bound: *paramour*
   And eke° the Graces seemèd all to sing,   *also*

---

2. Her name means "one, unity." Elizabethan readers would know the Latin phrase *Una Vera Fides* ("one true faith") and also the proverb "Truth is one."

Hymen iô Hymen, dauncing all around,
Whilst freshest Flora her with Yvie girlond crownd.[3]

49

In this great passion of unwonted° lust,   *unaccustomed*
   Or wonted feare of doing ought amis,
He started up, as seeming to mistrust°   *suspect*
Some secret ill, or hidden foe of his:
Lo there before his face his Lady is,
Under blake stole hyding her bayted hooke,
And as halfe blushing offred him to kis,
With gentle blandishment and lovely° looke,   *loving*
Most like that virgin true, which for her knight him took.

50

All cleane dismayd to see so uncouth° sight,   *strange; unseemly*
   And halfe enragèd at her shamelesse guise,
He thought have slaine her in his fierce despight:°   *indignation*
But hasty heat tempring with sufferance° wise,   *patience*
He stayde his hand, and gan himselfe advise
To prove his sense, and tempt° her faignèd truth.   *test*
Wringing her hands in wemens pitteous wise,
Tho can° she weepe, to stirre up gentle ruth,°   *then did / pity*
Both for her noble bloud, and for her tender youth.

51

And said, "Ah Sir, my liege Lord and my love,
   Shall I accuse the hidden cruell fate,
And mightie causes wrought in heaven above,
Or the blind God, that doth me thus amate,°   *dismay*
For° hopèd love to winne me certaine hate?   *instead of*
Yet thus perforce° he bids me do, or die.   *forcibly*
Die is my dew:[4] yet rew° my wretched state   *pity*
You, whom my hard avenging destinie
Hath made judge of my life or death indifferently.°   *impartially*

52

"Your owne deare sake forst me at first to leave
   My Fathers kingdome," There she stopt with teares;
Her swollen hart her speach seemd to bereave,
And then againe begun, "My weaker yeares
Captived to fortune and frayle worldly feares,
Fly to your faith for succour and sure ayde:
Let me not dye in languor° and long teares.   *sorrow*
"Why Dame," quoth he, "what hath ye thus dismayd?
What frayes° ye, that were wont to comfort me affrayd?"   *frightens*

3. The Three Graces of classical mythology were personifications of grace and beauty; here they sing a call to the pleasures of the marriage bed (Hymen was god of marriage). In the March eclogue of *The Shepheardes Calender*, E. K. glossed Flora as "the Goddesse of flowres, but indede (as saith Tacitus) a famous harlot."
4. I.e., I deserve to die.

53

"Love of your selfe," she said, "and deare° constraint   *dire*
  Lets me not sleepe, but wast the wearie night
  In secret anguish and unpittied plaint,
  Whiles you in carelesse sleepe are drownèd quight."
  Her doubtfull words made that redoubted[5] knight
  Suspect her truth: yet since no'untruth he knew,
  Her fawning love with foule disdainefull spight
  He would not shend,° but said, "Deare dame I rew,   *reject*
That for my sake unknowne such griefe unto you grew.

54

"Assure your selfe, it fell not all to ground;
  For all so deare as life is to my hart,
  I deeme your love, and hold me to you bound;
  Ne let vaine feares procure your needlesse smart,°   *pain*
  Where cause is none, but to your rest depart."
  Not all content, yet seemd she to appease°   *cease*
  Her mournefull plaintes, beguilèd of her art,°   *foiled in her cunning*
  And fed with words, that could not chuse° but please,   *choose*
So slyding softly forth, she turnd° as to her ease.   *returned*

55

Long after lay he musing at her mood,
  Much grieved to thinke that gentle Dame so light,°   *frivolous; wanton*
  For whose defence he was to shed his blood.
  At last dull wearinesse of former fight
  Having yrockt a sleepe his irkesome spright,
  That troublous dreame gan freshly tosse his braine,
  With bowres and beds, and Ladies deare delight:
  But when he saw his labour all was vaine,
With that misformèd spright[6] he backe returnd againe.

From *Canto 2*

[REDCROSSE WINS FIDESSA]

The guilefull great Enchaunter parts
  The Redcrosse Knight from Truth:
Into whose stead faire falshood steps,
  And workes him wofull ruth.°   *mischief*

I

By this the Northerne wagoner had set
  His seven fold teame behind the stedfast starre,[7]
  That was in Ocean waves yet never wet,
  But firme is fixt, and sendeth light from farre

---

5. Dreaded, but also "doubting again." "Doubt-full": fearful; also questionable, arousing doubt.
6. I.e., with the spirit impersonating Una.

7. I.e., by this time the Big Dipper had set, behind the North Star.

To all, that in the wide deepe wandring arre:
And chearefull Chaunticlere with his note shrill
Had warnèd once, that Phoebus fiery carre[8]
In hast was climbing up the Easterne hill,
Full envious that night so long his roome° did fill.　　　　*place*

2

When those accursèd messengers of hell,
　　That feigning dreame, and that faire-forgèd Spright
　　Came to their wicked maister, and gan tell
　　Their bootelesse° paines, and ill succeeding night:　　　*useless*
　　Who all in rage to see his skilfull might
　　Deluded so, gan threaten hellish paine
　　And sad Proserpines wrath, them to affright.
But when he saw his threatning was but vaine,
He cast about, and searcht his balefull° bookes againe.　　*deadly*

3

Eftsoones° he tooke that miscreated faire,　　　　*immediately*
　　And that false other Spright, on whom he spred
　　A seeming body of the subtile° aire,　　　　*rarefied*
　　Like a young Squire, in loves and lusty-hed
　　His wanton dayes that ever loosely led,
　　Without regard of armes and dreaded fight:
　　Those two he tooke, and in a secret bed,
　　Covered with darknesse and misdeeming° night,　　*misleading*
Them both together laid, to joy in vaine delight.

4

Forthwith he runnes with feignèd faithfull hast
　　Unto his guest, who after troublous sights
　　And dreames, gan now to take more sound repast,°　　*rest*
　　Whom suddenly he wakes with fearefull frights,
　　As one aghast with feends or damnèd sprights,
　　And to him cals, "Rise rise unhappy Swaine,°　　*youth; rustic*
　　That here wex° old in sleepe, whiles wicked wights　*grow*
　　Have knit themselves in Venus shamefull chaine;
Come see, where your false Lady doth her honour staine."

5

All in amaze he suddenly up start
　　With sword in hand, and with the old man went;
　　Who soone him brought into a secret part,
　　Where that false couple were full closely ment°　　*mingled*
　　In wanton lust and lewd embracèment:
　　Which when he saw, he burnt with gealous fire,
　　The eye of reason was with rage yblent,°　　*blinded*

---

8. Chariot of the sun god, Phoebus Apollo. "Chaunticlere": Chanticleer—generic name for a rooster.

And would have slaine them in his furious ire,
But hardly° was restreinèd of° that agèd sire.   *with difficulty / by*

6

Returning to his bed in torment great,
  And bitter anguish of his guiltie sight,
  He could not rest, but did his stout heart eat,
  And wast his inward gall with deepe despight,°   *malice*
  Yrkesome° of life, and too long lingring night.   *tired*
  At last faire Hesperus[9] in highest skie
  Had spent his lampe, and brought forth dawning light,
  Then up he rose, and clad him hastily;
The Dwarfe him brought his steed: so both away do fly.

7

Now when the rosy-fingred Morning faire,
  Weary of aged Tithones[1] saffron bed,
  Had spred her purple robe through deawy aire,
  And the high hils Titan° discoverèd,°   *the sun / revealed*
  The royall virgin shooke off drowsy-hed,
  And rising forth out of her baser° bowre,   *too lowly*
  Lookt for her knight, who far away was fled,
  And for her Dwarfe, that wont° to wait each houre: *was accustomed*
Then gan she waile and weepe, to see that woefull stowre.°   *affliction*

8

And after him she rode with so much speede
  As her slow beast could make; but all in vaine:
  For him so far had borne his light-foot steede,
  Prickèd with wrath and fiery fierce disdaine,°   *indignation*
  That him to follow was but fruitlesse paine;
  Yet she her weary limbes would never rest,
  But every hill and dale, each wood and plaine
  Did search, sore grievèd in her gentle brest,
He so ungently left her, whom she lovèd best.

9

But subtill° Archimago, when his guests   *cunning*
  He saw divided into double parts,
  And Una wandring in woods and forrests,
  Th' end of his drift,° he praisd his divelish arts   *plot*
  That had such might over true meaning harts;
  Yet rests not so, but other meanes doth make,
  How he may worke unto her further smarts:°   *pains*
  For her he hated as the hissing snake,
And in her many troubles did most pleasure take.

9. The morning star.
1. Tithonus is the husband of Aurora, goddess of the dawn.

10

He then devisde himselfe how to disguise;
   For by his mightie science° he could take   *knowledge*
   As many formes and shapes in seeming wise,°   *in appearance*
   As ever Proteus[2] to himselfe could make:
   Sometime a fowle, sometime a fish in lake,
   Now like a foxe, now like a dragon fell,°   *fierce*
   That of himselfe he oft for feare would quake,
   And oft would flie away. O who can tell
The hidden power of herbes, and might of Magicke spell?

11

But now seemde best, the person to put on
   Of that good knight, his late beguilèd guest:
   In mighty armes he was yclad anon,
   And silver shield: upon his coward brest
   A bloudy crosse, and on his craven crest
   A bounch of haires discolourd diversly:°   *variously colored*
   Full jolly° knight he seemde, and well addrest,° *gallant / armed*
   And when he sate upon his courser free,°   *high-spirited*
Saint George himself ye would have deemèd him to be.

12

But he the knight, whose semblaunt° he did beare,   *likeness*
   The true Saint George was wandred far away,
   Still flying from° his thoughts and gealous feare; *because of*
   Will was his guide, and griefe led him astray.
   At last him chaunst to meete upon the way
   A faithlesse Sarazin[3] all armed to point,°   *completely*
   In whose great shield was writ with letters gay
   Sans foy:[4] full large of limbe and every joint
He was, and carèd not for God or man a point.°   *at all*

13

He had a faire companion of his way,
   A goodly Lady clad in scarlot red,
   Purfled° with gold and pearle of rich assay,[5]   *decorated*
   And like a Persian mitre on her hed
   She wore, with crownes and owches° garnishèd,   *brooches*
   The which her lavish lovers to her gave;[6]
   Her wanton° palfrey all was overspred   *unruly*
   With tinsell trappings, woven like a wave,
Whose bridle rung with golden bels and bosses brave.° *handsome studs*

2. A sea god who could change his shape at will (*Odyssey* 4.398–424).
3. Saracen, i.e., a Muslim, especially the foes of the Christian knights in the Crusades to the Holy Land; sometimes used generically of any "pagan."
4. Without faith, faithless (French).
5. Proven of rich value.
6. The lady's garb associates her with the biblical Whore of Babylon (Revelation 17.3–4): "And I saw a woman sit upon a scarlet colored beast, full of names of blasphemy, having seven heads and ten horns. And the woman was arrayed in purple and scarlet color, and decked with gold and precious stones and pearls, having a golden cup in her hand full of abominations and filthiness of her fornication."

14

With faire disport° and courting dalliaunce   *diversion*
  She intertainde her lover all the way:
  But when she saw the knight his speare advaunce,
  She soone left off her mirth and wanton play,
  And bad her knight addresse him to the fray:
  His foe was nigh at hand. He prickt with pride
  And hope to winne his Ladies heart that day,
  Forth spurrèd fast: adowne his coursers side
The red bloud trickling staind the way, as he did ride.

15

The knight of the Redcrosse when him he spide,
  Spurring so hote with rage dispiteous,°   *cruel*
  Gan fairely couch° his speare, and towards ride: *lower*
  Soone meete they both, both fell° and furious,   *fierce*
  That daunted° with their forces hideous,   *dazed*
  Their steeds do stagger, and amazèd° stand,   *stunned*
  And eke° themselves too rudely rigorous,°   *also / violent*
  Astonied° with the stroke of their owne hand,   *stunned*
Do backe rebut,° and each to other yeeldeth land.   *recoil*

16

As when two rams stird with ambitious pride,
  Fight for the rule of the rich fleecèd flocke,
  Their hornèd fronts so fierce on either side
  Do meete, that with the terrour of the shocke
  Astonied both, stand sencelesse as a blocke,
  Forgetfull of the hanging° victory: *in the balance*
  So stood these twaine, unmovèd as a rocke,
  Both staring fierce, and holding idely
The broken reliques of their former cruelty.

17

The Sarazin sore daunted with the buffe
  Snatcheth his sword, and fiercely to him flies;
  Who well it wards, and quyteth° cuff with cuff: *requites, repays*
  Each others equall puissaunce envies,°   *power seeks to rival*
  And through their iron sides with cruell spies°   *looks*
  Does seeke to perce: repining courage yields
  No foote to foe. The flashing fier flies
  As from a forge out of their burning shields,
And streames of purple bloud new dies the verdant fields.

18

"Curse on that Crosse," quoth then the Sarazin,
  "That keepes thy body from the bitter fit;°   *death pangs*
  Dead long ygoe I wote° thou haddest bin,   *know*
  Had not that charme from thee forwarnèd° it: *prevented*

But yet I warne thee now assurèd° sitt,   *securely*
    And hide thy head." Therewith upon his crest
    With rigour° so outrageöus he smitt,   *violence*
    That a large share it hewd out of the rest,
And glauncing downe his shield, from blame him fairely blest.[7]

19

Who thereat wondrous wroth, the sleeping spark
    Of native vertue° gan eftsoones° revive,   *strength / again*
    And at his haughtie helmet making mark,°   *taking aim*
    So hugely° stroke, that it the steele did rive,   *mightily*
    And cleft his head. He tumbling downe alive,
    With bloudy mouth his mother earth did kis,
    Greeting his grave: his grudging° ghost did strive   *complaining*
    With the fraile flesh; at last it flitted is,
Whither the soules do fly of men, that live amis.

20

The Lady when she saw her champion fall,
    Like the old ruines of a broken towre,
    Staid not to waile his woefull funerall,°   *death*
    But from him fled away with all her powre;
    Who after her as hastily gan scowre,°   *scurry*
    Bidding the Dwarfe with him to bring away
    The Sarazins shield, signe of the conqueroure.
    Her soone he overtooke, and bad to stay,
For present cause was none of dread her to dismay.

21

She turning backe with ruefull° countenaunce,   *pitiable*
    Cride, "Mercy mercy Sir vouchsafe to show
    On silly° Dame, subject to hard mischaunce,   *helpless*
    And to your mighty will." Her humblesse low
    In so ritch weedes° and seeming glorious show,   *clothes*
    Did much emmove his stout heroicke heart,
    And said, "Deare dame, your suddein overthrow
    Much rueth° me; but now put feare apart,   *grieves*
And tell, both who ye be, and who that tooke your part."

22

Melting in teares, then gan she thus lament;
    "The wretched woman, whom unhappy howre
    Hath now made thrall° to your commandèment,   *slave*
    Before that angry heavens list to lowre,°   *chose to frown*
    And fortune false betraide me to your powre,
    Was (O what now availeth that I was!)
    Borne the sole daughter of an Emperour,

---

7. Preserved him from harm.

He that the wide West under his rule has,
And high hath set his throne, where Tiberis doth pas.[8]

23

"He in the first flowre of my freshest age,
    Betrothèd me unto the onely haire°   *heir*
    Of a most mighty king, most rich and sage;[9]
    Was never Prince so faithfull and so faire,
    Was never Prince so meeke and debonaire;°   *gracious*
    But ere my hopèd day of spousall shone,
    My dearest Lord fell from high honours staire,
    Into the hands of his accursèd fone,°   *foes*
And cruelly was slaine, that shall I ever mone.

24

"His blessèd body spoild of lively breath,
    Was afterward, I know not how, convaid°   *carried away*
    And fro° me hid: of whose most innocent death   *from*
    When tidings came to me unhappy maid,
    O how great sorrow my sad soule assaid.°   *afflicted*
    Then forth I went his woefull corse to find,
    And many yeares throughout the world I straid,
    A virgin widow, whose deepe wounded mind
With love, long time did languish as the striken hind.° *deer*

25

"At last it chauncèd this proud Sarazin
    To meete me wandring, who perforce° me led   *by violence*
    With him away, but yet could never win
    The fort, that Ladies hold in soveraigne dread.° *utmost reverence*
    There lies he now with foule dishonour dead,
    Who whiles he livde, was callèd proud Sans foy,
    The eldest of three brethren, all three bred
    Of one bad sire, whose youngest is Sans joy,
And twixt them both was borne the bloudy bold Sans loy.[1]

26

"In this sad plight, friendlesse, unfortunate,
    Now miserable I Fidessa° dwell,   *Faithful*
    Craving of you in pitty of my state,
    To do none° ill, if please ye not do well."   *no*
    He in great passion all this while did dwell,° *continue*
    More busying his quicke eyes, her face to view,
    Then his dull eares, to heare what she did tell;
    And said, "Faire Lady hart of flint would rew
The undeservèd woes and sorrowes, which ye shew.

8. The Tiber River runs through Rome. The lady is hence associated with the Catholic Church. Her father, she says, is ruler of the west—but Una's father had the rule of both east *and* west (canto 1, stanza 5); historically, the true church once embraced east and west.
9. The lady claims to have been betrothed to Christ, bridegroom of the Church (Matthew 9.15).
1. Without law—lawless.

27

"Henceforth in safe assauraunce may ye rest,
  Having both found a new friend you to aid,
  And lost an old foe, that did you molest:
  Better new friend than an old foe is° said."   *it is*
  With chaunge of cheare° the seeming simple maid   *countenance*
  Let fall her eyen, as shamefast° to the earth,   *as if modestly*
  And yeelding soft, in that she nought gain-said,°   *objected*
  So forth they rode, he feining° seemely merth,   *simulating*
And she coy lookes: so dainty they say maketh derth.[2]

Summary   In the second half of the canto, Redcrosse and his new companion seek relief from the blazing sun in the shade of two trees. Plucking a bough from one of them to make a garland for the lady, he is astonished to hear a groaning voice from within the tree. The voice is that of a knight named Fradubio (Brother Doubt), who explains that he and his beloved have been metamorphosed into trees by a wicked witch named Duessa. Unbeknownst to him, Redcrosse is in the company of this witch.

Canto 3 *Summary*   In search of the knight who has abandoned her, Una encounters a lion who licks her hands and accompanies her in her wanderings. They take refuge for the night in the cottage of a superstitious old woman and her daughter. During the night the daughter's lover, a robber of churches, returns to the cottage with booty for her and is torn to pieces by the lion. Seeking revenge, the old woman encounters Archimago and tells him where to find Una. The magician presents himself to Una disguised as Redcrosse, but his plan backfires when he is attacked by the Saracen Sans loy (brother of the slain Sans foy). Sans loy then kills the faithful lion and abducts Una, leaving Archimago lying wounded.

From *Canto 4*

[THE HOUSE OF PRIDE]

*To sinfull house of Pride, Duessa
  guides the faithfull knight,
Where brothers death to wreak° Sansjoy   avenge
  doth chalenge him to fight.*

I

Young knight, what ever that dost armes professe,
  And through long labours huntest after fame,
  Beware of fraud, beware of ficklenesse,
  In choice, and change of thy deare lovèd Dame,
  Least thou of her beleeve too lightly blame,[3]
  And rash misweening° doe thy hart remove: *misjudgment*
  For unto knight there is no greater shame,

---

2. Proverbial: what's dear is rare; here, coyness
creates unsatisfied desire.

3. Lest you too readily believe accusations about
her.

Then lightnesse and inconstancie in love;
That doth this Redcrosse knights ensample° plainly prove. *example*

2

Who after that he had faire Una lorne,° *forsaken*
  Through light misdeeming° of her loialtie, *misjudging*
  And false Duessa in her sted had borne,° *taken as companion*
  Called Fidess', and so supposd to bee;
  Long with her traveild, till at last they see
  A goodly building, bravely garnishèd,° *adorned*
  The house of mightie Prince it seemd to bee:
  And towards it a broad high way⁴ that led,
All bare through peoples feet, which thither traveilèd.

3

Great troupes of people traveild thitherward
  Both day and night, of each degree and place,° *rank*
  But few returnèd, having scapèd hard,° *with difficulty*
  With balefull° beggerie, or foule disgrace, *wretched*
  Which ever after in most wretched case,
  Like loathsome lazars,° by the hedges lay. *lepers*
  Thither Duessa bad him bend his pace:° *direct his steps*
  For she is wearie of the toilesome way,
And also nigh consumèd is the lingring day.

4

A stately Pallace built of squarèd bricke,
  Which cunningly was without morter laid,
  Whose wals were high, but nothing strong, nor thick,
  And golden foile° all over them displaid, *thin layer of gold*
  That purest skye with brightnesse they dismaid:° *outdid*
  High lifted up were many loftie towres,
  And goodly galleries farre over laid,° *placed above*
  Full of faire windowes, and delightfull bowres;
And on the top a Diall told the timely howres.⁵

5

It was a goodly heape° for to behould, *building*
  And spake the praises of the workmans wit;° *skill*
  But full great pittie, that so faire a mould° *structure*
  Did on so weake foundation ever sit:
  For on a sandie hill,⁶ that still did flit,° *shift*
  And fall away, it mounted was full hie,
  That every breath of heaven shakèd it:
  And all the hinder parts, that few could spie,
Were ruinous and old, but painted cunningly.

---

4. "Broad is the way that leadeth to destruction" (Matthew 7.13).
5. A sundial measured the hours of the day.
6. Matthew 7.26–27: "A foolish man . . . built his house upon the sand: And the rain descended, and the floods came, and the winds blew, and beat upon that house; and it fell; and great was the fall of it."

6

Arrivèd there they passèd in forth right;
  For still° to all the gates stood open wide,   *always*
  Yet charge of them was to a Porter hight°   *committed*
  Cald Malvenù,[7] who entrance none denide:
  Thence to the hall, which was on every side
  With rich array and costly arras dight:[8]
  Infinite sorts of people did abide
  There waiting long, to win the wishèd sight
Of her, that was the Lady of that Pallace bright.

7

By them they passe, all gazing on them round,
  And to the Presence[9] mount; whose glorious vew
  Their frayle amazèd senses did confound:
  In living Princes court none ever knew
  Such endlesse richesse, and so sumptuous shew;°   *show*
  Ne° Persia selfe, the nourse of pompous pride   *nor*
  Like ever saw. And there a noble crew
  Of Lordes and Ladies stood on every side,
Which with their presence faire, the place much beautifide.

8

High above all a cloth of State° was spred,   *canopy*
  And a rich throne, as bright as sunny day,
  On which there sate most brave embellishèd°   *handsomely clad*
  With royall robes and gorgeous array,
  A mayden Queene, that shone as Titans° ray,   *the sun's*
  In glistring gold, and peerelesse pretious stone:
  Yet her bright blazing beautie did assay°   *attempt*
  To dim the brightnesse of her glorious throne,
As envying her selfe, that too exceeding shone.

9

Exceeding shone, like Phoebus fairest childe,
  That did presume° his fathers firie wayne,°   *usurp / chariot*
  And flaming mouthes of steedes unwonted° wilde   *unusually*
  Through highest heaven with weaker° hand to rayne;   *too weak*
  Proud of such glory and advancement vaine,
  While flashing beames do daze his feeble eyen,
  He leaves the welkin° way most beaten plaine,   *heavenly*
  And rapt° with whirling wheeles, inflames the skyen,   *carried away*
With fire not made to burne, but fairely for to shyne.[1]

---

7. "Unwelcome." In courtly love allegories, the porter is often called Bienvenu or Bel-accueil ("welcome").
8. Decorated with costly wall hangings.
9. Presence chamber, where a sovereign receives guests.
1. Phaëthon tried to drive the chariot of his father, Phoebus, the sun god, but set the skies on fire and fell.

10

So proud she shynèd in her Princely state,
  Looking to heaven; for earth she did disdayne,
  And sitting high; for lowly° she did hate: *lowliness*
  Lo underneath her scornefull feete, was layne
  A dreadfull Dragon with an hideous trayne,°   *tail*
  And in her hand she held a mirrhour bright,[2]
  Wherein her face she often vewèd fayne,°   *with pleasure*
  And in her selfe-loved semblance tooke delight;
For she was wondrous faire, as any living wight.

11

Of griesly° Pluto she the daughter was,   *horrid*
  And sad Proserpina the Queene of hell;
  Yet did she thinke her pearelesse worth to pas°   *surpass*
  That parentage, with pride so did she swell,
  And thundring Jove, that high in heaven doth dwell,
  And wield° the world, she claymèd for her syre,   *govern*
  Or if that any else did Jove excell:
  For to the highest she did still aspyre,
Or if ought° higher were then that, did it desyre.   *anything*

12

And proud Lucifera men did her call,
  That made her selfe a Queene, and crownd to be,
  Yet rightfull kingdome she had none at all,
  Ne heritage of native soveraintie,
  But did usurpe with wrong and tyrannie
  Upon the scepter, which she now did hold:
  Ne ruld her Realmes with lawes, but pollicie,°   *political cunning*
  And strong advizement of six wisards old,
That with their counsels bad her kingdome did uphold.

13

Soone as the Elfin knight in presence came,
  And false Duessa seeming Lady faire,
  A gentle Husher,° Vanitie by name   *usher*
  Made rowme, and passage for them did prepaire:
  So goodly° brought them to the lowest staire   *graciously*
  Of her high throne, where they on humble knee
  Making obeyssance,° did the cause declare,   *submission*
  Why they were come, her royall state to see,
To prove° the wide report of her great Majestee.   *verify*

14

With loftie eyes, halfe loth to looke so low,
  She thankèd them in her disdainefull wise,°   *manner*

---

2. Pride and figures associated with her in Renaissance literature and art often hold a mirror, emblematic of self-love.

Ne other grace vouchsafèd them to show
Of Princesse worthy, scarse them bad° arise.   *bade*
Her Lordes and Ladies all this while devise°   *make ready*
Themselves to setten forth to straungers sight:
Some frounce° their curlèd haire in courtly guise,   *frizzle*
Some prancke° their ruffes, and others trimly dight°   *pleat / arrange*
Their gay attire: each others greater pride does spight.³

15

Goodly they all that knight do entertaine,
Right glad with him to have increast their crew:
But to Duess' each one himselfe did paine
All kindnesse and faire courtesie to shew;
For in that court whylome° her well they knew: *formerly*
Yet the stout Faerie mongst the middest° crowd   *thickest*
Thought all their glorie vaine in knightly vew,
And that great Princesse too exceeding prowd,
That to strange° knight no better countenance° allowd.   *stranger / favor*

16

Suddein upriseth from her stately place
The royall Dame, and for her coche doth call:
All hurtlen° forth and she with Princely pace,   *rush*
As faire Aurora in her purple pall,⁴
Out of the East the dawning day doth call:
So forth she comes: her brightnesse brode° doth blaze;   *abroad*
The heapes of people thronging in the hall,
Do ride° each other, upon her to gaze: *climb up on*
Her glorious glitterand° light doth all mens eyes amaze.   *glittering*

17

So forth she comes, and to her coche does clyme,
Adornèd all with gold, and girlonds gay,
That seemd as fresh as Flora° in her prime,   *the goddess of flowers*
And strove to match, in royall rich array,
Great Junos golden chaire,° the which they say   *chariot*
The Gods stand gazing on, when she does ride
To Joves high house through heavens bras-pavèd way
Drawne of faire Pecocks, that excell in pride,
And full of Argus eyes their tailes dispredden wide.⁵

18

But this was drawne of six unequall beasts,
On which her six sage Counsellours did ryde,
Taught to obay their bestiall beheasts,°   *bidding*

---

3. Each despises the others' greater pride.
4. Goddess of dawn, in her crimson robe ("purple pall").
5. Peacocks, with their tails outspread ("dispred-

den wide"), are a symbol of pride. The hundred-eyed monster Argus was set by Juno to watch Io, one of Jupiter's loves. When Mercury killed Argus, his eyes were put in the peacock's tail feathers.

With like conditions to their kinds applyde:[6]
Of which the first, that all the rest did guyde,
Was sluggish Idlenesse the nourse of sin;
Upon a slouthfull Asse he chose to ryde,
Arayd in habit blacke, and amis thin,[7]
Like to an holy Monck, the service to begin.

19

And in his hand his Portesse° still he bare,   *breviary, prayerbook*
That much was worne, but therein little red,
For of devotion he had little care,
Still drownd in sleepe, and most of his dayes ded;
Scarse could he once uphold his heavie hed,
To looken, whether it were night or day:
May seeme the wayne° was very evill led,   *chariot*
When such an one had guiding of the way,
That knew not, whether right he went, or else astray.

20

From worldly cares himselfe he did esloyne,°   *withdraw*
And greatly shunnèd manly exercise,
From every worke he chalengèd essoyne,°   *claimed exemption*
For contemplation sake: yet otherwise,
His life he led in lawlesse riotise;°   *riotous conduct*
By which he grew to grievous malady;
For in his lustlesse° limbs through evill guise°   *feeble / living*
A shaking fever raignd continually:
Such one was Idlenesse, first of this company.

21

And by his side rode loathsome Gluttony,
Deformèd creature, on a filthie swyne,
His belly was up-blowne with luxury,°   *indulgence*
And eke° with fatnesse swollen were his eyne,°   *also / eyes*
And like a Crane his necke was long and fyne,[8]
With which he swallowd up excessive feast,
For want whereof poore people oft did pyne;°   *starve*
And all the way, most like a brutish beast,
He spuèd up his gorge,[9] that° all did him deteast.   *so that*

22

In greene vine leaves he was right fitly clad;
For other clothes he could not weare for heat,

---

6. I.e., each bestial rider gave commands to his beast appropriate to its particular nature: the beasts and riders are suited to each other. This procession of the Seven Deadly Sins—of which Pride is queen—had a long tradition in medieval art and literature (see also Marlowe, *Dr. Faustus*, scene 5, lines 272–328).

7. Idleness wears the gown ("habit") and hood or amice ("amis") of a monk. Traditionally, Idleness led the procession of the deadly sins.

8. The crane is a common symbol of gluttony because its long and thin ("fyne") neck allows extended pleasure in swallowing.

9. Vomited up what he had swallowed.

And on his head an yvie girland had,[1]
  From under which fast trickled downe the sweat:
  Still as he rode, he somewhat° still did eat,   *something*
  And in his hand did beare a bouzing° can,   *drinking*
  Of which he supt so oft, that on his seat
  His dronken corse° he scarse upholden can,   *body*
In shape and life more like a monster, then° a man.   *than*

23

Unfit he was for any worldly thing,
  And eke unhable once° to stirre or go,°   *at all / walk*
  Not meet° to be of counsell to a king,   *fit*
  Whose mind in meat and drinke was drownèd so,
  That from his friend he seldome knew his fo:
  Full of diseases was his carcas blew,
  And a dry dropsie through his flesh did flow,
  Which by misdiet daily greater grew:
Such one was Gluttony, the second of that crew.

24

And next° to him rode lustfull Lechery,   *just after*
  Upon a bearded Goat,[2] whose rugged° haire,   *shaggy*
  And whally° eyes (the signe of gelosy,°)   *glaring / jealousy*
  Was like the person selfe, whom he did beare:
  Who rough, and blacke, and filthy did appeare,
  Unseemely man to please faire Ladies eye;
  Yet he of Ladies oft was lovèd deare,
When fairer faces were bid standen by:°   *away*
O who does know the bent of womens fantasy?°   *caprice, whim*

25

In a greene gowne he clothèd was full faire,
  Which underneath did hide his filthinesse,
  And in his hand a burning hart he bare,
  Full of vaine follies, and new fangleness:°   *fickleness*
  For he was false, and fraught with ficklenesse,
  And learnèd had to love with secret lookes,
  And well could daunce, and sing with ruefulnesse,°   *pathos*
  And fortunes tell, and read in loving bookes,[3]
And thousand other wayes, to bait his fleshly hookes.

26

Inconstant man, that lovèd all he saw,
  And lusted after all, that he did love,
  Ne would his looser life be tide to law,
  But joyd weake wemens hearts to tempt and prove°   *try*
  If from their loyall loves he might them move;

---

1. He resembles the drunken satyr Silenus, foster father of Bacchus, god of wine; ivy is sacred to Bacchus.

2. Traditional symbol of lust.

3. Either manuals on the art of love (e.g., Ovid's *Ars Amatoria*) or more ordinary erotica.

Which lewdnesse fild him with reprochfull paine
Of that fowle evill, which all men reprove,°   *i.e., syphilis*
That rots the marrow, and consumes the braine:
Such one was Lecherie, the third of all this traine.

27

And greedy Avarice by him did ride,
  Upon a Camell loaden all with gold;[4]
  Two iron coffers hong on either side,
  With precious mettall full, as they might hold,
  And in his lap an heape of coine he told:°   *counted*
  For of his wicked pelfe° his God he made,   *money*
  And unto hell him selfe for money sold;
  Accursèd usurie was all his trade,
And right and wrong ylike in equall ballaunce waide.[5]

28

His life was nigh unto deaths doore yplast,
  And thread-bare cote, and cobled° shoes he ware,   *roughly mended*
  Ne scarse good morsell all his life did tast,
  But both from backe and belly still did spare,
  To fill his bags, and richesse to compare;°   *acquire*
  Yet chylde ne° kinsman living had he none   *nor*
  To leave them to; but thorough° daily care   *through*
  To get, and nightly feare to lose his owne,
He led a wretched life unto him selfe unknowne.

29

Most wretched wight, whom nothing might suffise,
  Whose greedy lust° did lacke in greatest store,°   *desire / plenty*
  Whose need had end, but no end covetise,
  Whose wealth was want, whose plenty made him pore,
  Who had enough, yet wishèd ever more;
  A vile disease, and eke in foote and hand
  A grievous gout tormented him full sore,
  That well he could not touch, nor go,° nor stand: *walk*
Such one was Avarice, the fourth of this faire band.

30

And next to him malicious Envie rode,
  Upon a ravenous wolfe, and still° did chaw   *continually*
  Betweene his cankred° teeth a venemous tode,   *infected*
  That all the poison ran about his chaw;°   *jaw*
  But inwardly he chawèd his owne maw°   *entrails*
  At neighbours wealth, that made him ever sad;
  For death it was, when any good he saw,
  And wept, that cause of weeping none he had,
But when he heard of harme, he wexèd° wondrous glad.   *waxed, grew*

4. The camel as a symbol of avarice is based on Matthew 19.24: "It is easier for a camel to go through the eye of a needle, than for a rich man to enter into the kingdom of God."

5. I.e., he made no distinction between right and wrong.

31

All in a kirtle of discolourd say[6]
  He clothèd was, ypainted full of eyes;
And in his bosome secretly there lay
An hatefull Snake,[7] the which his taile uptyes
In many folds, and mortall sting implyes.°   *enfolds*
Still as he rode, he gnasht his teeth, to see
Those heapes of gold with griple Covetyse,°   *grasping Avarice*
  And grudgèd at the great felicitie
Of proud Lucifera, and his owne companie.

32

He hated all good workes and vertuous deeds,
  And him no lesse, that any like did use,°   *perform*
And who with gracious bread the hungry feeds,
His almes for want of faith he doth accuse;[8]
So every good to bad he doth abuse:°   *twist*
And eke the verse of famous Poets witt
He does backebite, and spightfull poison spues
  From leprous mouth on all, that ever writt:
Such one vile Envie was, that fifte in row did sitt.

33

And him beside rides fierce revenging Wrath,
  Upon a Lion, loth for to be led;
And in his hand a burning brond° he hath,   *sword*
The which he brandisheth about his hed;
His eyes did hurle forth sparkles fiery red,
And starèd sterne on all, that him beheld,
As ashes pale of hew and seeming ded;
  And on his dagger still° his hand he held,   *always*
Trembling through hasty rage, when choler° in him sweld.   *anger*

34

His ruffin° raiment all was staind with blood,   *disorderly*
  Which he had spilt, and all to rags yrent,°   *torn*
Through unadvisèd rashnesse woxen wood,°   *grown insane*
For of his hands he had no governement,°   *control*
Ne cared for° bloud in his avengement: *minded*
But when the furious fit was overpast,
His cruell facts° he often would repent;   *actions*
  Yet wilfull man he never would forecast,
How many mischieves should ensue his heedlesse hast.[9]

---

6. Robe or gown of many-colored cloth.
7. Traditional attribute of envy.
8. Envy perversely discounts others' good works by attributing them to a selfish motive: the desire to compensate (in God's eyes) for lack of faith.
9. I.e., he never would foresee ("forecast") the calamities his careless haste caused.

35

Full many mischiefes follow cruell Wrath;
  Abhorrèd bloudshed, and tumultuous strife,
  Unmanly murder, and unthrifty scath,[1]
  Bitter despight,° with rancours rusty knife,   *malice*
  And fretting griefe the enemy of life;
  All these, and many evils moe° haunt ire,°   *more / anger*
  The swelling Splene,[2] and Frenzy raging rife,
  The shaking Palsey, and Saint Fraunces fire:[3]
Such one was Wrath, the last of this ungoldly tire.°   *train*

36

And after all, upon the wagon beame
  Rode Sathan,° with a smarting whip in hand,   *Satan*
  With which he forward lasht the laesie teme,
  So oft as Slowth° still in the mire did stand.   *Idleness*
  Huge routs° of people did about them band,   *crowds*
  Showting for joy, and still before their way
  A foggy mist had covered all the land;
  And underneath their feet, all scattered lay
Dead sculs and bones of men, whose life had gone astray.

Summary   In the remainder of the canto, the third Saracen brother, Sans joy, arrives at the House of Pride and demands to do battle with Redcrosse. Lucifera intervenes and orders them to meet in a formal combat on the following day. Duessa visits Sans joy in the night, warning him of the power of Redcrosse's invulnerable armor, and promising him her secret aid.

Canto 5 *Summary*

Just as Redcrosse is about to slay Sans joy in combat, the Saracen vanishes in a magical cloud created by Duessa. To heal the wounded Sans joy, the witch enlists the help of Night, the queen of darkness who is grandmother of the three Saracen brothers. Together they take Sans joy down to Hades, the classical underworld. There he will be healed by the legendary physician Aesculapius, who has the power to raise the dead and is himself immortal, but doomed to live forever in Hades. Meanwhile, Redcrosse's companion the dwarf discovers Lucifera's dungeon, where the bodies of the proud are cast in heaps. With the dwarf, Redcrosse flees in the night, stumbling over piled-up corpses as he makes his escape, and Duessa returns to find him gone.

Canto 6 *Summary*

Sans loy intends to rape Una, but is frightened away by a band of fauns and satyrs (mythological creatures who are men above the waist and goats below). They take Una and proceed to worship her as a goddess, in spite of her attempts to teach them true religion. She is discovered among them by Satyrane, a wild but virtuous knight born of a human mother and a satyr father.

---

1. I.e., inhuman murder and destructive harm.
2. In Renaissance physiology, the spleen was regarded as the seat of ill-humor.

3. Presumably St. Anthony's fire: erysipelas, or the flaming itch; appropriate to Wrath.

Together they escape her idolators. They then meet with a pilgrim who informs them that Redcrosse has been slain by Sans loy. Satyrane seeks out the Saracen and they do battle. Una flees in terror and is pursued by the pilgrim, who is revealed as Archimago in disguise.

Canto 7 and 8 *Summary*

Still disguised as Fidessa, Duessa pursues and finds Redcrosse. He drinks from a fountain which robs him of strength. The enfeebled knight is discovered lying with Duessa by the giant Orgoglio (Pride), who easily conquers Redcrosse and casts him into his dungeon. The giant pampers Duessa, attiring her as the Whore of Babylon in Revelation (a figure associated by Protestants with the papacy), and mounting her on a seven-headed beast. Meanwhile, the dwarf finds Una and reveals to her what has happened. Una sets out in search of Redcrosse and meets with Prince Arthur—the future king of Britain whose story runs through all the books of *The Faerie Queene*. She tells Arthur her story, explaining that Redcrosse has been assigned by the Faerie Queene to rescue her parents, the king and queen of Eden, from a dragon. Arthur promises to rescue Redcrosse. In an epic fight, he defeats and kills Orgoglio, after stunning the giant and the beast with the divine brightness of his shield. Arthur seizes the keys to Orgoglio's dungeon from the giant's ancient foster-father, Ignaro (Ignorance), and liberates the starving Redcrosse. They strip Duessa, who is revealed as a filthy, bestial hag. She hides herself in the wilderness.

From *Canto 9*

His loves and lignage° Arthur tells: lineage
   The knights knit friendly bands:°   bonds
Sir Trevisan flies from Despayre,
   Whom Redcrosse knight withstands.

Summary

In the first part of the canto, Arthur tells Redcrosse and Una of his past life. Taken from his mother at birth, Arthur is ignorant of his lineage, but has been told by the magician Merlin that he is heir to a king. After being visited by the Faerie Queene in a dream, in which she lay beside him on the grass, he has fallen in love with her. The knights then exchange vows of friendship and gifts. Arthur gives Redcrosse a precious liquid which heals wounds, while Redcrosse gives him the New Testament. Arthur then rides off in search of the Faerie Queene. Una looks with concern at Redcrosse, who remains weak and weary from his recent ordeal.

21

So as they traveild, lo they gan espy
   An armèd knight towards them gallop fast,
   That seemèd from some fearèd foe to fly,
   Or other griesly thing, that him agast.°   *terrified*
Still° as he fled, his eye was backward cast,   *continually*
   As if his feare still followed him behind;
   Als flew his steed, as he his bands had brast,°   *broken*
   And with his wingèd heeles did tread the wind,
As he had beene a fole of Pegasus his kind.[4]

4. I.e., as if he had been a foal of a horse like Pegasus, the flying horse of classical mythology.

22

Nigh as he drew, they might perceive his head
  To be unarmd, and curld uncombèd heares
  Upstaring° stiffe, dismayd with uncouth° dread;   *bristling / strange*
  Nor drop of bloud in all his face appeares
  Nor life in limbe: and to increase his feares,
  In fowle reproch° of knighthoods faire degree,°   *disgrace / condition*
  About his neck an hempen rope he weares,
  That with his glistring armes does ill agree;
But he of rope or armes has now no memoree.

23

The Redcrosse knight toward him crossèd fast,
  To weet,° what mister° wight was so dismayd: *learn / kind of*
  There him he finds all sencelesse and aghast,
  That of him selfe he seemd to be afrayd;
  Whom hardly° he from flying forward stayd,   *with difficulty*
  Till he these wordes to him deliver might;
  "Sir knight, aread° who hath ye thus arayd,   *declare*
  And eke from whom make ye this hasty flight:
For never knight I saw in such misseeming° plight."   *unseemly*

24

He answerd nought at all, but adding new
  Feare to his first amazment, staring wide
  With stony eyes, and hartlesse hollow hew,[5]
  Astonisht stood, as one that had aspide
  Infernall furies, with their chaines untide.
  Him yet againe, and yet againe bespake
  The gentle knight; who nought to him replide,
  But trembling every joynt did inly quake,
And foltring tongue at last these words seemd forth to shake.

25

"For Gods deare love, Sir knight, do me not stay;
  For loe he comes, he comes fast after mee."
  Eft° looking backe would faine have runne away;   *again*
  But he him forst to stay, and tellen free
  The secret cause of his perplexitie:°   *distress*
  Yet nathemore° by his bold hartie speach,   *not at all*
  Could his bloud-frosen hart emboldned bee,
  But through his boldnesse rather feare did reach,
Yet forst, at last he made through silence suddein breach.

26

"And am I now in safetie sure," quoth he,
  "From him, that would have forcèd me to dye?
  And is the point of death now turnd fro mee,

---

5. I.e., with blanched, bloodless countenance.

That I may tell this haplesse history?"° *story of misfortune*
"Feare nought:" quoth he, "no daunger now is nye."
"Then shall I you recount a ruefull cace,"° *pitiable event*
Said he, "the which with this unlucky eye
I late beheld, and had not greater grace
Me reft° from it, had bene partaker of the place.[6] *carried*

27

"I lately chaunst (Would I had never chaunst)
    With a faire knight to keepen companee,
    Sir Terwin[7] hight,° that well himselfe advaunst *named*
    In all affaires, and was both bold and free,
    But not so happie as mote happie bee:
    He loved, as was his lot, a Ladie gent,° *gentle*
    That him againe° loved in the least degree: *in return*
    For she was proud, and of too high intent,° *mind*
And joyd to see her lover languish and lament.

28

"From whom returning sad and comfortlesse,° *desolate*
    As on the way together we did fare,
    We met that villen (God from him me blesse°) *defend*
    That cursèd wight, from whom I scapt whyleare,° *a while before*
    A man of hell, that cals himselfe Despaire;[8]
    Who first us greets, and after faire areedes° *tells*
    Of tydings strange, and of adventures rare:
    So creeping close, as Snake in hidden weedes,
Inquireth of our states, and of our knightly deedes.

29

"Which when he knew, and felt our feeble harts
    Embost° with bale,° and bitter byting griefe, *exhausted / sorrow*
    Which love had launchèd° with his deadly darts, *pierced*
    With wounding words and termes of foule repriefe,° *insult, scorn*
    He pluckt from us all hope of due reliefe,
    That earst° us held in love of lingring life; *formerly*
    Then hopelesse hartlesse, gan the cunning thiefe
    Perswade us die, to stint° all further strife: *end*
To me he lent this rope, to him a rustie° knife. *i.e., bloodstained*

30

"With which sad instrument of hastie death,
    That wofull lover, loathing lenger° light, *longer*
    A wide way made to let forth living breath.
    But I more fearefull, or more luckie wight,
    Dismayd with that deformèd dismall sight,
    Fled fast away, halfe dead with dying feare:° *fear of death*

---

6. I.e., shared the same fate.
7. His name may connote weariness or fatigue ("terwyn").

8. Despair is the ultimate Christian sin, denying the possibility of divine mercy and grace.

Ne yet assur'd of life by you, Sir knight,
 Whose like infirmitie like chaunce may beare:
But God you never let his charmèd speeches heare."[9]

31

"How may a man," said he, "with idle speach
 Be wonne, to spoyle° the Castle of his health?"   *destroy*
"I wote," quoth he, "whom triall° late did teach,   *experience*
 That like would not[1] for all this worldes wealth:
His subtill tongue, like dropping honny, mealt'th°   *melts*
 Into the hart, and searcheth every vaine,
 That ere one be aware, by secret stealth
 His powre is reft, and weaknesse doth remaine.
O never Sir desire to try° his guilefull traine."°   *test / treachery*

32

"Certès,"° said he, "hence shall I never rest,   *surely*
 Till I that treachours art have heard and tride;
And you Sir knight, whose name mote° I request,   *might*
 Of grace° do me unto his cabin° guide."   *favor / cave*
"I that hight° Trevisan,"[2] quoth he, "will ride   *am called*
 Against my liking backe, to doe you grace:°   *a favor*
 But nor for gold nor glee[3] will I abide
 By you, when ye arrive in that same place;
For lever° had I die, then° see his deadly face."   *rather / than*

33

Ere long they come, where that same wicked wight
 His dwelling has, low in an hollow cave,
Farre underneath a craggie clift ypight,°   *placed*
 Darke, dolefull, drearie, like a greedie grave,
 That still° for carrion carcases doth crave: *continually*
On top whereof aye° dwelt the ghastly Owle,[4]   *ever*
 Shrieking his balefull note, which ever drave
 Farre from that haunt all other chearefull fowle;
And all about it wandring ghostes did waile and howle.

34

And all about old stockes° and stubs of trees,   *stumps*
 Whereon nor fruit, nor leafe was ever seene,
 Did hang upon the ragged rocky knees;°   *crags*
 On which had many wretches hangèd beene,
 Whose carcases were scattered on the greene,
 And throwne about the cliffs. Arrivèd there,
 That bare-head knight for dread and dolefull teene,°   *grief*
 Would faine° have fled, ne durst approachen neare,   *gladly*
But th' other forst him stay, and comforted in feare.

---

9. I.e., may God never let you hear his mesmer-
izing ("charmèd") speeches.
1. I.e., would not do the like again.
2. The meaning is uncertain, but may be "flight"
or "dread."
3. Beauty; i.e., not for anything in the world.
4. Traditionally a messenger of death.

35

That darkesome cave they enter, where they find
  That cursèd man, low sitting on the ground,
  Musing full sadly in his sullein° mind;   *morose*
  His griesie° lockes, long growen, and unbound,   *gray*
  Disordred hong about his shoulders round,
  And hid his face; through which his hollow eyne
  Lookt deadly dull, and starèd as astound;°   *as if stunned*
  His raw-bone cheekes through penurie and pine,° *starvation*
Were shronke into his jawes, as° he did never dine. *as if*

36

His garment nought but many ragged clouts,°   *scraps*
  With thornes together pind and patchèd was,
  The which his naked sides he wrapt abouts;
  And him beside there lay upon the gras
  A drearie corse,° whose life away did pas, *bloody corpse*
  All wallowd in his owne yet luke-warme blood,
  That from his wound yet wellèd fresh alas;
  In which a rustie knife fast fixèd stood,
And made an open passage for the gushing flood.

37

Which piteous spectacle, approving° trew   *confirming*
  The wofull tale that Trevisan had told,
  When as the gentle Redcrosse knight did vew,
  With firie zeale he burnt in courage bold,
  Him to avenge, before his bloud were cold,
  And to the villein said, "Thou agèd damnèd wight,
  The author of this fact,° we here behold,   *deed*
  What justice can but judge against thee right,
With thine owne bloud to price° his bloud, here shed in sight?" *pay for*

38

"What franticke fit," quoth he, "hath thus distraught
  Thee, foolish man, so rash a doome° to give? *judgment*
  What justice ever other judgement taught,
  But he should die, who merites not to live?
  None else to death this man despayring drive,° *drove*
  But his owne guiltie mind deserving death.
  Is then unjust to each his due to give?
  Or let him die, that loatheth living breath?
Or let him die at ease, that liveth here uneath?° *in hardship*

39

"Who travels by the wearie wandring way,
  To come unto his wishèd home in haste,
  And meetes a flood, that doth his passage stay,
  Is not great grace to helpe him over past,
  Or free his feet, that in the myre sticke fast?
  Most envious man, that grieves at neighbours good,

And fond,° that joyest in the woe thou hast,   *foolish*
  Why wilt not let him passe, that long hath stood
Upon the banke, yet wilt thy selfe not passe the flood?

40

"He there does now enjoy eternall rest
  And happie ease, which thou doest want and crave,
  And further from it daily wanderest:
  What if some litle paine the passage have,
  That makes fraile flesh to feare the bitter wave?
  Is not short paine well borne, that brings long ease,
  And layes the soule to sleepe in quiet grave?
  Sleepe after toyle, port after stormie seas,
Ease after warre, death after life does greatly please."[5]

41

The knight much wondred at his suddeine wit,°   *quick intelligence*
  And said, "The terme of life is limited,
  Ne may a man prolong, nor shorten it;
  The souldier may not move from watchfull sted,[6]
  Nor leave his stand, untill his Captaine bed."°   *commands*
  "Who life did limit by almightie doome,"
  Quoth he, "knowes best the termes establishèd;
  And he, that points the Centonell his roome,°   *station*
Doth license him depart at sound of morning droome.[7]

42

"Is not his deed, what ever thing is donne,
  In heaven and earth? did not he all create
  To die againe? all ends that was begonne.
  Their times in his eternall booke of fate
  Are written sure, and have their certaine° date.   *fixed*
  Who then can strive with strong necessitie,
  That holds the world in his still chaunging state,
  Or shunne the death ordaynd by destinie?
When houre of death is come, let none aske whence, nor why.

43

"The lenger° life, I wote° the greater sin,   *longer / know*
  The greater sin, the greater punishment:
  All those great battels, which thou boasts to win,
  Through strife, and bloud-shed, and avengement,
  Now praysd, hereafter deare° thou shalt repent: *bitterly*
  For life must life, and bloud must bloud repay.[8]
  Is not enough thy evill life forespent?

---

5. Despaire's arguments on behalf of suicide as against a painful life are derived, like those of Hamlet in his third soliloquy (*Hamlet* 3.1.58–90), principally from Seneca, Marcus Aurelius, other ancient Stoics, and Old Testament statements on divine justice.
6. The sentry post assigned him.
7. Drum, with a pun on *doom*.
8. An echo of Genesis 9.6: "Whoso sheddeth man's blood, by man shall his blood be shed."

For he, that once hath missèd the right way,
The further he doth goe, the further he doth stray.

44

"Then do no further goe, no further stray,
   But here lie downe, and to thy rest betake,
   Th'ill to prevent, that life ensewen may.[9]
   For what hath life, that may it lovèd make,
   And gives not rather cause it to forsake?
   Feare, sicknesse, age, losse, labour, sorrow, strife,
   Paine, hunger, cold, that makes the hart to quake;
   And ever fickle fortune rageth rife,
All which, and thousands mo° do make a loathsome life.   *more*

45

"Thou wretched man, of death hast greatest need,
   If in true ballance thou wilt weigh thy state:
   For never knight, that darèd warlike deede,
   More lucklesse disaventures° did amate:°   *mishaps / daunt*
   Witnesse the dongeon deepe, wherein of late
   Thy life shut up, for death so oft did call;
   And though good lucke prolongèd hath thy date,°   *span of life*
   Yet death then, would the like mishaps forestall,
Into the which hereafter thou maiest happen fall.°   *happen to fall*

46

"Why then doest thou, O man of sin, desire
   To draw thy dayes forth to their last degree?
   Is not the measure of thy sinfull hire°   *service to sin*
   High heapèd up with huge iniquitie,
   Against the day of wrath,° to burden thee?   *Judgment Day*
   Is not enough that to this Ladie milde
   Thou falsèd° hast thy faith with perjurie,°   *betrayed / oath-breaking*
   And sold thy selfe to serve Duessa vilde,°   *vile*
With whom in all abuse thou thast thy selfe defilde?

47

"Is not he just, that all this doth behold
   From highest heaven, and beares an equall° eye?   *impartial*
   Shall he thy sins up in his knowledge fold,
   And guiltie be of thine impietie?
   Is not his law, Let every sinner die:[1]
   Die shall all flesh? what then must needs be donne,
   Is it not better to doe willinglie,
   Then linger, till the glasse° be all out ronne?   *hourglass*
Death is the end of woes: die soone, O faeries sonne."

---

9. I.e., to prevent the evil that will ensue in the rest of your life.
1. Despaire cites only half of the Scripture verse: "The wages of sin is death; but the gift of God is eternal life through Jesus Christ our Lord" (Romans 6.23).

48

The knight was much enmovèd with his speach,
  That as a swords point through his hart did perse,
  And in his conscience made a secret breach,°   *wound*
  Well knowing true all, that he did reherse,°   *recount*
  And to his fresh remembrance did reverse°   *bring back*
  The ugly vew of his deformèd crimes,
  That all his manly powres it did disperse,
As he were charmèd with inchaunted rimes,
That oftentimes he quakt, and fainted° oftentimes.   *lost heart*

49

In which amazement, when the Miscreant°   *misbeliever*
  Perceivèd him to waver weake and fraile,
  Whiles trembling horror did his conscience dant,°   *daunt*
  And hellish anguish° did his soule assaile,   *i.e., fear of hell*
  To drive him to despaire, and quite to quaile,°   *be dismayed*
  He shewed him painted in a table° plaine,   *picture*
  The damnèd ghosts, that doe in torments waile,
  And thousand feends that doe them endlesse paine
With fire and brimstone, which for ever shall remaine.

50

The sight whereof so throughly him dismaid,
  That nought but death before his eyes he saw,
  And ever burning wrath before him laid,
  By righteous sentence of th'Almighties law:
  Then gan the villein him to overcraw,°   *exult over*
  And brought unto him swords, ropes, poison, fire,
  And all that might him to perdition draw;
  And bad him choose, what death he would desire:
For death was due to him, that had provokt Gods ire.

51

But when as none of them he saw him take,
  He to him raught° a dagger sharpe and keene,   *reached*
  And gave it him in hand: his hand did quake,
  And tremble like a leafe of Aspin greene,
  And troubled bloud through his pale face was seene
  To come, and goe with tydings from the hart,
  As it a running messenger had beene.
  At last resolved to worke his finall smart,°   *pain*
He lifted up his hand, that backe againe did start.

52

Which when as Una saw, through every vaine
  The crudled° cold ran to her well of life,°   *congealing / heart*
  As in a swowne: but soone relived° againe,   *revived*
  Out of his hand she snatcht the cursèd knife,
  And threw it to the ground, enragèd rife,°   *deeply*

And to him said, "Fie, fie, faint harted knight,
  What meanest thou by this reprochfull° strife?   *deserving reproach*
  Is this the battell, which thou vauntst to fight
With the fire-mouthèd Dragon, horrible and bright?

53

"Come, come away, fraile, feeble, fleshly wight,
  Ne let vaine words bewitch thy manly hart,
  Ne divelish thoughts dismay thy constant spright.°   *spirit*
  In heavenly mercies hast thou not a part?
  Why shouldst thou then despeire, that chosen[2] art?
  Where justice growes, there grows eke° greater grace,   *also*
  The which doth quench the brond° of hellish smart,   *firebrand*
  And that accurst hand-writing[3] doth deface.°   *blot out*
Arise, Sir knight arise, and leave this cursèd place."

54

So up he rose, and thence amounted° streight.   *mounted his horse*
  Which when the carle° beheld, and saw his guest   *churl*
  Would safe depart, for° all his subtill sleight,   *in spite of*
  He chose an halter° from among the rest,   *noose*
  And with it hung himselfe, unbid° unblest.   *unprayed for*
  But death he could not worke himselfe thereby;
  For thousand times he so himselfe had drest,°   *made ready*
  Yet nathelesse it could not doe° him die,   *make*
Till he should die his last, that is eternally.

From *Canto 10*

Her faithfull knight faire Una brings
to house of Holinesse,
Where he is taught repentance, and
the way to heavenly blesse.°   *bliss*

Summary   In the first part of the canto, Una brings Redcrosse to the House of Holinesse to he healed in body and spirit. The house is kept by Dame Caelia (Heavenly) with her three daughters Fidelia (Faith), Speranza (Hope), and Charissa (Charity, or Love). Redcrosse is welcomed and given counsel by Fidelia and Speranza, but remains wracked by guilt and suicidal impulses. He is entrusted to the doctor Patience and undergoes a painful cure with Penance, Remorse, and Repentance. He next comes to Charissa, who instructs him in love and good deeds and places him in the hands of a godly matron, Mercie. She leads him along a narrow and thorny path to a holy Hospitall (hostel), kept by seven Bead-men (men of prayer), where Redcrosse learns to frame his life in righteousness. Redcrosse and Mercie then continue on their way.

---

2. Cf. 2 Thessalonians 2.13: "God hath from the beginning chosen you to salvation through sanctification of the Spirit and belief of the truth." This is one of several similar passages in the epistles of St. Paul that form the basis of the theological doctrine of predestination.

3. An echo of Colossians 2.14: "Blotting out the handwriting of ordinances [i.e., the Old Testament Law] that was against us, which was contrary to us, and took it out of the way, nailing it to his cross."

46

Thence forward by that painfull way they pas,
  Forth to an hill, that was both steepe and hy;
  On top whereof a sacred chappell was,
  And eke a litle Hermitage thereby,
  Wherein an agèd holy man did lye,°   *live*
  That day and night said his devotiön,
  Ne other worldly busines did apply;[4]
  His name was heavenly Contemplation;
Of God and goodnesse was his meditation.

47

Great grace that old man to him given had;
  For God he often saw from heavens hight,
  All° were his earthly eyen both blunt° and bad,   *although / dim*
  And through great age had lost their kindly° sight,   *natural*
  Yet wondrous quick and persant° was his spright,°   *piercing / spirit*
  As Eagles eye, that can behold the Sunne:
  That hill they scale with all their powre and might,
  That his frayle thighes nigh wearie and fordonne°   *exhausted*
Gan faile, but by her helpe the top at last he wonne.

48

There they do finde that godly agèd Sire,
  With snowy lockes adowne his shoulders shed,
  As hoarie frost with spangles doth attire
  The mossy braunches of an Oke halfe ded.
  Each bone might through his body well be red,°   *seen*
  And every sinew seene through° his long fast: *because of*
  For nought he cared his carcas long unfed;
  His mind was full of spirituall repast,
And pyned° his flesh, to keepe his body low° and chast.   *starved / weak*

49

Who when these two approching he aspide,
  At their first presence grew agrievèd sore,[5]
  That forst him lay his heavenly thoughts aside;
  And had he not that Dame respected more,°   *greatly*
  Whom highly he did reverence and adore,
  He would not once have movèd for the knight.
  They him saluted standing far afore;°   *away*
  Who well them greeting, humbly did requight,°   *respond*
And askèd, to what end they clomb° that tedious height.   *had climbed*

50

"What end," quoth she, "should cause us take such paine,
  But that same end, which every living wight

---

4. I.e., he did not attend to any worldly activities.   5. I.e., he was at first sorely grieved at their arrival.

Should make his marke,° high heaven to attaine?   goal
Is not from hence the way, that leadeth right
To that most glorious house, that glistreth bright
With burning starres, and everliving fire,
Whereof the keyes are to thy hand behight°   entrusted
By wise Fidelia? she doth thee require,
To shew it to this knight, according° his desire."   granting

51

"Thrise happy man," said then the father grave,
    "Whose staggering steps thy° steady hand doth lead,   i.e., Mercy's
And shewes the way, his sinfull soule to save.
Who better can the way to heaven aread°   direct
Then thou thy selfe, that was both borne and bred
In heavenly throne, where thousand Angels shine?
Thou doest the prayers of the righteous sead°   seed
Present before the majestie divine,
And his avenging wrath to clemencie incline.

52

"Yet since thou bidst, thy pleasure shalbe donne.
    Then come thou man of earth,[6] and see the way,
That never yet was seene of Faeries sonne,
That never leads the traveiler astray,
But after labours long, and sad delay,
Brings them to joyous rest and endlesse blis.
But first thou must a season fast and pray,
Till from her bands the spright assoilèd° is,   spirit released
And have her strength recured° from fraile infirmitis."   recovered

53

That done, he leads him to the highest Mount;
    Such one, as that same mighty man of God,
That bloud-red billowes like a wallèd front
On either side disparted° with his rod,   parted asunder
Till that his army dry-foot through them yod,°   went
Dwelt fortie dayes upon; where writ in stone
With bloudy letters by the hand of God,
The bitter doome of death and balefull mone[7]
He did receive, whiles flashing fire about him shone.

54

Or like that sacred hill, whose head full hie,
    Adornd with fruitfull Olives all arownd,
Is, as it were for endlesse memory
Of that deare Lord, who oft thereon was fownd,

---

6. An allusion to humankind's formation from the dust of the earth (Genesis 2.7) and also to the knight's name (see below, stanza 66 and note).
7. I.e., the Ten Commandments ("bloudy let-
ters") carried with them the judgment ("doome") of death and pain (causing sorrowful moans— "balefull mone").

For ever with a flowring girlond crownd:
Or like that pleasaunt Mount, that is for ay
Through famous Poets verse each where° renownd, *everywhere*
On which the thrise three learned Ladies play
Their heavenly notes, and make full many a lovely lay.[8]

55

From thence, far off he unto him did shew
A litle path, that was both steepe and long,
Which to a goodly Citie led his vew;
Whose wals and towres were builded high and strong
Of perle and precious stone, that earthly tong
Cannot describe, nor wit of man can tell;
Too high a ditty° for my simple song; *subject*
The Citie of the great king hight° it well, *is called*
Wherein eternall peace and happinesse doth dwell.

56

As he thereon stood gazing, he might° see *could*
The blessed Angels to and fro descend
From highest heaven, in gladsome companee,
And with great joy into that Citie wend,
As commonly° as friend does with his frend.[9] *familiarly*
Whereat he wondred much, and gan enquere,
What stately building durst so high extend
Her loftie towres unto the starry sphere,
And what unknowen nation there empeopled were.

57

"Faire knight," quoth he, "Hierusalem that is,
The new Hierusalem, that God has built
For those to dwell in, that are chosen his,
His chosen people purged from sinfull guilt,
With pretious bloud, which cruelly was spilt
On cursèd tree, of that unspotted lam,[1]
That for the sinnes of all the world was kilt:
Now are they Saints all in that Citie sam,° *together*
More deare unto their God, then younglings to their dam."[2]

58

"Till now," said then the knight, "I weenèd well,
That great Cleopolis,[3] where I have beene,

---

8. Song. The mountain is successively compared to Mount Sinai, where Moses, after parting the "bloud-red billowes" of the Red Sea, received the tablets of the Ten Commandments; to the Mount of Olives, associated with Christ; and to Mount Parnassus, where the Nine Muses of art and poetry dwelt.
9. Cf. Jacob's ladder, which "reached to heaven; and behold the angels of God ascending and descending on it" (Genesis 28.12).
1. Christ (the lamb of God), whose death on the cross ("cursèd tree") purged the guilt of sin from those "chosen his."
2. The New Jerusalem is described in Revelation 21–22; "the nations of them which are saved shall walk in the light of it" (21.24).
3. "City of Fame"; in the historical allegory, London or Westminster.

In which that fairest Faerie Queene doth dwell,
The fairest Citie was, that might be seene;
And that bright towre all built of christall cleene,°   clear
Panthea,[4] seemd the brightest thing, that was:
But now by proofe° all otherwise I weene;   experience
For this great Citie that[5] does far surpas,
And this bright Angels towre quite dims that towre of glas."

59

"Most trew," then said the holy agèd man;
    "Yet is Cleopolis for earthly frame,°   structure
    The fairest peece,° that eye beholden can: masterpiece
    And well beseemes° all knights of noble name,   becomes
    That covet in th'immortall booke of fame
    To be eternizèd, that same to haunt,°   frequent
    And doen their service to that soveraigne Dame,
    That glorie does to them for guerdon° graunt: reward
For she is heavenly borne, and heaven may justly vaunt.[6]

60

"And thou faire ymp,° sprong out from English race,   youth
    How ever now accompted° Elfins sonne,   accounted
    Well worthy doest thy service for her grace,°   favor
    To aide a virgin desolate foredonne.°   undone
    But when thou famous victorie hast wonne,
    And high emongst all knights hast hong thy shield,
    Thenceforth the suit° of earthly conquest shonne,   pursuit
    And wash thy hands from guilt of bloudy field:
For bloud can nought but sin, and wars but sorrowes yield.

61

"Then seeke this path, that I to thee presage,°   show prophetically
    Which after all to heaven shall thee send;
    Then peaceably thy painefull° pilgrimage   laborious
    To yonder same Hierusalem do bend,
    Where is for thee ordaind a blessèd end:
    For thou emongst those Saints, whom thou doest see,
    Shalt be a Saint, and thine owne nations frend
    And Patrone: thou Saint George shalt callèd bee,
Saint George of mery England, the signe of victoree."[7]

62

"Unworthy wretch," quoth he, "of so great grace,
    How dare I thinke such glory to attaine?"

4. Reminiscent of the temple of glass in Chaucer's *House of Fame*; perhaps intended to allude to Westminster Abbey as pantheon of the English great.
5. I.e., the New Jerusalem far surpasses Cleopolis ("that").
6. I.e., may justly boast ("vaunt") that heaven is her home.
7. Spenser's conception of St. George, patron saint of England, draws on the *Legenda Aurea* (*The Golden Legend*—a medieval manual of ecclesiastical lore, translated into English by William Caxton in 1487) and on pictures, tapestries, pageants, and folklore.

"These that have it attaind, were in like cace,"
Quoth he, "as wretched, and lived in like paine."
"But deeds of armes must I at last be faine,°   *content (to leave)*
And Ladies love to leave so dearely bought?"
"What need of armes, where peace doth ay° remaine,"   *ever*
Said he, "and battailes none are to be fought?
As for loose° loves are° vaine, and vanish into nought." *wanton / i.e., they are*

63

"O let me not," quoth he, "then turne againe
  Backe to the world, whose joyes so fruitlesse are;
  But let me here for aye in peace remaine,
  Or streight way on that last long voyage fare,
  That nothing may my present hope empare."°   *impair*
"That may not be," said he, "ne maist thou yit
  Forgo that royall maides bequeathèd care,°   *charge*
  Who did her cause into thy hand commit,
Till from her cursèd foe thou have her freely quit."°   *released*

64

"Then shall I soone," quoth he, "so God me grace,
  Abet° that virgins cause disconsolate,   *maintain*
  And shortly backe returne unto this place
  To walke this way in Pilgrims poore estate.
  But now aread,° old father, why of late   *declare*
  Didst thou behight° me borne of English blood,   *call*
  Whom all a Faeries sonne doen nominate?"°   *name*
"That word shall I," said he, "avouchen° good,   *prove*
Sith° to thee is unknowne the cradle of thy brood.   *since*

65

"For well I wote,° thou springst from ancient race   *know*
  Of Saxon kings, that have with mightie hand
  And many bloudie battailes fought in place°   *there*
  High reard their royall throne in Britane land,
  And vanquisht them,° unable to withstand: *i.e., the ancient Britons*
  From thence a Faerie thee unweeting reft,°   *secretly stole*
  There as thou slepst in tender swadling band,
  And her base Elfin brood° there for thee left.   *offspring*
Such men do Chaungelings call, so chaungd by Faeries theft.

66

"Thence she thee brought into this Faerie lond,
  And in an heapèd furrow did thee hyde,
  Where thee a Ploughman all unweeting° fond,   *unknowing*
  As he his toylesome teme° that way did guyde,   *team of oxen*
  And brought thee up in ploughmans state to byde,
  Whereof Georgos he thee gave to name;[8]

8. I.e., as a name. *Georgos* is Greek for "farmer" (cf. Virgil's *Georgics*, on farming).

Till prickt° with courage, and thy forces pryde,   *spurred*
   To Faery court thou cam'st to seeke for fame,
And prove thy puissaunt° armes, as seemes thee best became."[9]   *powerful*

67

"O holy Sire," quoth he, "how shall I quight°   *repay*
   The many favours I with thee have found,
   That hast my name and nation red° aright,   *declared*
   And taught the way that does to heaven bound?"°   *go*
   This said, adowne he lookèd to the ground,
   To have returnd, but dazèd° were his eyne,   *dazzled*
   Through passing° brightnesse, which did quite confound   *surpassing*
   His feeble sence, and too exceeding shyne.
So darke are earthly things compard to things divine.

68

At last whenas himselfe he gan to find,°   *recover*
   To Una back he cast him to retire;
   Who him awaited still with pensive° mind.   *anxious*
   Great thankes and goodly meed° to that good syre,   *gift*
   He thence departing gave for his paines hyre.°   *reward*
   So came to Una, who him joyd to see,
   And after litle rest, gan him desire,
   Of her adventure mindfull for to bee.
So leave they take of Caelia, and her daughters three.

Canto 11

The knight with that old Dragon fights
two dayes incessantly:
The third him overthrowes, and gayns
most glorious victory.

1

High time now gan it wex° for Una faire,   *grow*
   To thinke of those her captive Parents deare,
   And their forwasted kingdome to repaire:[1]
   Whereto whenas they now approachèd neare,
   With hartie° words her knight she gan to cheare,   *bold*
   And in her modest manner thus bespake;
   "Deare knight, as deare, as ever knight was deare,
   That all these sorrowes suffer for my sake,
High heaven behold the tedious toyle, ye for me take.

2

"Now are we come unto my native soyle,
   And to the place, where all our perils dwell;

---

9. As best suited you.
1. I.e., to restore their kingdom, laid waste (by the dragon).

Here haunts that feend, and does his dayly spoyle,
Therefore henceforth be at your keeping well,°   *be well on your guard*
And ever ready for your foeman fell.
The sparke of noble courage now awake,
And strive your excellent selfe to excell;
That shall ye evermore renowmèd make,
Above all knights on earth, that batteill undertake."

3

And pointing forth, "lo yonder is," said she,
"The brasen towre in which my parents deare
For dread of that huge feend emprisond be,
Whom I from far see on the walles appeare,
Whose sight my feeble soule doth greatly cheare:
And on the top of all I do espye
The watchman wayting tydings glad to heare,
That O my parents might I happily
Unto you bring, to ease you of your misery."

4

With that they heard a roaring hideous sound,
That all the ayre with terrour fillèd wide,
And seemd uneath° to shake the stedfast ground.   *almost*
Eftsoones° that dreadfull Dragon they espide,   *immediately*
Where stretcht he lay upon the sunny side
Of a great hill, himselfe like a great hill.
But all so soone, as he from far descride
Those glistring armes, that heaven with light did fill,
He rousd himselfe full blith,° and hastned them untill.°   *joyfully / toward*

5

Then bad° the knight his Lady yede° aloofe,   *bade / go*
And to an hill her selfe withdraw aside,
From whence she might behold that battailles proof°   *outcome*
And eke° be safe from daunger far descryde:°   *also / observed from afar*
She him obayd, and turnd a little wyde.°   *aside*
Now O thou sacred Muse, most learnèd Dame,
Faire ympe° of Phoebus, and his agèd bride,[2]   *child*
The Nourse of time, and everlasting fame,
That warlike hands ennoblest with immortall name;

6

O gently come into my feeble brest,
Come gently, but not with that mighty rage,
Wherewith the martiall troupes thou doest infest,°   *arouse*
And harts of great Heroes doest enrage,
That nought their kindled courage may aswage,
Soone as thy dreadfull trompe° begins to sownd;   *trumpet*

2. I.e., Mnemosyne (memory), mother of the Muses.

The God of warre with his fiers equipage
Thou doest awake, sleepe never he so sownd,
And scarèd nations doest with horrour sterne astown.°   *appall*

7

Faire Goddesse lay that furious fit° aside,   *strain*
  Till I of warres and bloudy Mars do sing,[3]
  And Briton fields with Sarazin° bloud bedyde,°   *Saracen / dyed*
  Twixt that great faery Queene and Paynim° king,   *pagan*
  That with their horrour heaven and earth did ring,
  A worke of labour long, and endlesse prayse:
  But now a while let downe that haughtie string,
  And to my tunes thy second tenor rayse,[4]
That I this man of God his godly armes may blaze.°   *proclaim*

8

By this the dreadfull Beast drew nigh to hand,
  Halfe flying, and halfe footing° in his hast,   *walking*
  That with his largenesse measurèd much land,
  And made wide shadow under his huge wast;°   *girth*
  As mountaine doth the valley overcast.
  Approching nigh, he rearèd high afore
  His body monstrous, horrible, and vast,
  Which to increase his wondrous greatnesse more,
Was swolne with wrath, and poyson, and with bloudy gore.

9

And over, all with brasen scales was armd,
  Like plated coate of steele, so couchèd neare,°   *placed so closely*
  That nought mote perce,[5] ne might his corse° be harmd   *body*
  With dint of sword, nor push of pointed speare;
  Which as an Eagle, seeing pray appeare,
  His aery Plumes doth rouze,° full rudely dight,°   *shake / ruggedly arrayed*
  So shakèd he, that horrour was to heare,
  For as the clashing of an Armour bright,
Such noyse his rouzèd scales did send unto the knight.

10

His flaggy° wings when forth he did display,   *drooping*
  Were like two sayles, in which the hollow wynd
  Is gathered full, and worketh speedy way:
  And eke the pennes, that did his pineons bynd,
  Were like mayne-yards, with flying canvas lynd,[6]
  With which whenas him list° the ayre to beat,   *he chose*
  And there by force unwonted° passage find,   *unaccustomed*

---

3. Perhaps a reference to a projected but unwritten book of *The Faerie Queene*.
4. The "haughtie" (high-pitched) mode would be appropriate to a large-scale epic war; the "second tenor" (lower in pitch) to this present battle.

5. Nothing might pierce.
6. I.e., the ribs of his wings were like the massive spars (main yards) to which a ship's mainsail is affixed.

The cloudes before him fled for terrour great,
And all the heavens stood still amazèd with his threat.

II

His huge long tayle wound up in hundred foldes,
  Does overspred his long bras-scaly backe,
  Whose wreathèd boughts° when ever he unfoldes,   coils
  And thicke entangled knots adown does slacke,
  Bespotted as with shields° of red and blacke,   scales
  It sweepeth all the land behind him farre,
  And of three furlongs[7] does but litle lacke;
  And at the point two stings in-fixèd arre,
Both deadly sharpe, that sharpest steele exceeden farre.

12

But stings and sharpest steele did far exceed°   i.e., were far exceeded by
  The sharpnesse of his cruell rending clawes;
  Dead was it sure, as sure as death in deed,°   in its effect
  What ever thing does touch his ravenous pawes,
  Or what within his reach he ever drawes.
  But his most hideous head my toung to tell
  Does tremble: for his deepe devouring jawes
  Wide gapèd, like the griesly° mouth of hell,   horrid
Through which into his darke abisse all ravin° fell.   prey; booty

13

And that° more wondrous was, in either jaw   what
  Three ranckes of yron teeth enraungèd were,
  In which yet trickling bloud and gobbets raw°   chunks of unswallowed food
  Of late° devourèd bodies did appeare,   recently
  That sight thereof bred cold congealèd feare:
  Which to increase, and all at once to kill,
  A cloud of smoothering smoke and sulphur seare°   burning
  Out of his stinking gorge° forth steemèd still,   maw
That all the ayre about with smoke and stench did fill.

14

His blazing eyes, like two bright shining shields,
  Did burne with wrath, and sparkled living fyre;
  As two broad Beacons, set in open fields,
  Send forth their flames farre off to every shyre,°   shire
  And warning give, that enemies conspyre,
  With fire and sword the region to invade;
  So flamed his eyne° with rage and rancorous yre:°   eyes / ire, anger
  But farre within, as in a hollow glade,
Those glaring lampes were set, that made a dreadfull shade.

7. I.e., three-eighths of a mile.

15

So dreadfully he towards him did pas,
    Forelifting up aloft his speckled brest,
    And often bounding on the brusèd gras,
    As for great joyance of his newcome guest.
    Eftsoones he gan advance his haughtie crest,
    As chauffèd° Bore his bristles doth upreare,   *angry*
    And shoke his scales to battell readie drest;°   *prepared*
    That made the Redcrosse knight nigh quake for feare,
As bidding bold defiance to his foeman neare.

16

The knight gan fairely couch° his steadie speare,   *level*
    And fiercely ran at him with rigorous° might: *violent*
    The pointed steele arriving rudely° theare,   *roughly*
    His harder hide would neither perce, nor bight,
    But glauncing by forth passèd forward right;
    Yet sore amovèd with so puissant push,
    The wrathfull beast about him turnèd light,°   *quickly*
    And him so rudely passing by, did brush
With his long tayle, that horse and man to ground did rush.

17

Both horse and man up lightly rose againe,
    And fresh encounter towards him addrest:
    But th'idle stroke yet backe recoyld in vaine,
    And found no place his° deadly point to rest.   *its*
    Exceeding rage enflamed the furious beast,
    To be avengèd of so great despight;°   *outrage*
    For never felt his imperceable brest
    So wondrous force, from hand of living wight;
Yet had he provèd° the powre of many a puissant knight.   *tested*

18

Then with his waving wings displayèd wyde,
    Himselfe up high he lifted from the ground,
    And with strong flight did forcibly divide
    The yielding aire, which nigh° too feeble found   *nearly*
    Her flitting° partes, and element unsound,°   *moving / weak*
    To beare so great a weight: he cutting way
    With his broad sayles, about him soarèd round:
    At last low stouping with unweldie sway,°   *ponderous force*
Snatcht up both horse and man, to beare them quite away.

19

Long he them bore above the subject plaine,°   *i.e., the ground below*
    So farre as Ewghen° bow a shaft may send,   *yewen, of yew*
    Till struggling strong did him at last constraine,
    To let them downe before his flightès end:
    As hagard° hauke presuming to contend   *untamed*

With hardie fowle, above his hable might,°   *able power*
 His wearie pounces° all in vaine doth spend,   *claws*
 To trusse° the pray too heavie for his flight;   *seize*
Which comming downe to ground, does free it selfe by fight.

20

He so disseizèd of his gryping grosse,[8]
 The knight his thrilant° speare againe assayd   *piercing*
 In his bras-plated body to embosse,°   *plunge*
 And three mens strength unto the stroke he layd;
 Wherewith the stiffe beame quakèd, as affrayd,
 And glauncing from his scaly necke, did glyde
 Close under his left wing, then broad displayd.
 The percing steele there wrought a wound full wyde,
That with the uncouth° smart the Monster lowdly cryde. *unfamiliar*

21

He cryde, as raging seas are wont° to rore,   *accustomed*
 When wintry storme his wrathfull wreck° does threat, *ruin*
 The rolling billowes beat the ragged shore,
 As° they the earth would shoulder from her seat,   *as if*
 And greedie gulfe° does gape, as he would eat   *i.e., the sea*
 His neighbour element° in his revenge: *i.e., earth*
 Then gin the blustring brethren° boldly threat,   *the winds*
 To move the world from off his stedfast henge,°   *axis*
And boystrous battell make, each other to avenge.

22

The steely head stucke fast still in his flesh,
 Till with his cruell clawes he snatcht the wood,
 And quite a sunder broke. Forth flowèd fresh
 A gushing river of blacke goarie° blood,   *clotted*
 That drownèd all the land, whereon he stood;
 The stream thereof would drive a water-mill.
 Trebly augmented was his furious mood
 With bitter sense of his deepe rooted ill,°   *injury*
That flames of fire he threw forth from his large nosethrill.° *nostril*

23

His hideous tayle then hurlèd he about,
 And therewith all enwrapt the nimble thyes°   *thighs*
 Of his froth-fomy steed, whose courage stout
 Striving to loose the knot, that fast him tyes,
 Himselfe in streighter° bandes too rash implyes,[9]   *tighter*
 That to the ground he is perforce° constraynd   *of necessity*
 To throw his rider: who can° quickly ryse   *did*
 From off the earth, with durty bloud distaynd,°   *defiled*
For that reprochfull fall right fowly he disdaynd.° *resented*

---

8. Freed from his formidable grip.   9. I.e., too quickly entangles.

24

And fiercely tooke his trenchand° blade in hand, *sharp*
   With which he stroke so furious and so fell,° *fiercely*
   That nothing seemd the puissance could withstand:
   Upon his crest the hardned yron fell,
   But his more hardned crest was armd so well,
   That deeper dint therein it would not make;[1]
   Yet so extremely did the buffe° him quell,° *blow / dismay*
   That from thenceforth he shund the like to take,
But when he saw them come, he did them still forsake.° *avoid*

25

The knight was wrath to see his stroke beguyld,° *foiled*
   And smote againe with more outrageous might;
   But backe againe the sparckling steele recoyld,
   And left not any marke, where it did light;
   As if in Adamant rocke it had bene pight.° *struck against*
   The beast impatient of his smarting wound,
   And of so fierce and forcible despight,° *powerful injury*
   Thought with his wings to stye° above the ground; *mount*
But his late wounded wing unserviceable found.

26

Then full of griefe and anguish vehement,
   He lowdly brayd, that like was never heard,
   And from his wide devouring oven sent
   A flake of fire, that flashing in his beard,
   Him all amazd, and almost made affeard;
   The scorching flame sore swingèd° all his face, *singed*
   And through his armour all his bodie seard,
   That he could not endure so cruell cace,° *plight*
But thought his armes to leave, and helmet to unlace.

27

Not that great Champion of the antique world,
   Whom famous Poetes verse so much doth vaunt,
   And hath for twelve huge labours high extold,
   So many furies and sharpe fits did haunt,
   When him the poysoned garment did enchaunt
   With Centaures bloud, and bloudie verses charmed,
   As did this knight twelve thousand dolours° daunt, *pains*
   Whom fyrie steele now burnt, that earst° him armed, *formerly*
That erst him goodly armed, now most of all him harmed.[2]

28

Faint, wearie, sore, emboylèd, grievèd, brent° *burned*
   With heat, toyle, wounds, armes, smart, and inward fire

---

1. I.e., it could not make a deep gash there.
2. Redcrosse's fire baptism is compared with the burning shirt of Nessus, which killed Hercules,
"that great Champion of the antique world" (line 1). His "twelve huge labours" are paralleled to the knight's "twelve thousand dolours."

That never man such mischiefes° did torment;   *misfortunes*
Death better were, death did he oft desire,
But death will never come, when needes require.
Whom so dismayd when that his foe beheld,
He cast to suffer° him no more respire,°   *allow / live*
But gan his sturdie sterne° about to weld,°   *tail / lash*
And him so strongly stroke, that to the ground him feld.

29

It fortunèd (as faire it then befell)
Behind his backe unweeting,° where he stood,   *unnoticed*
Of auncient time there was a springing well,
From which fast trickled forth a silver flood,
Full of great vertues,° and for med'cine good.   *powers*
Whylome,° before that cursèd Dragon got   *formerly*
That happie land, and all with innocent blood
Defyld those sacred waves, it rightly hot°   *was called*
The Well of Life,[3] ne yet his vertues had forgot.

30

For unto life the dead it could restore,
And guilt of sinfull crimes cleane wash away,
Those that with sicknesse were infected sore,
It could recure, and agèd long decay
Renew, as one were borne that very day.
Both Silo this, and Jordan did excell,
And th'English Bath, and eke the german Spau,
Ne can Cephise, nor Hebrus match this well:
Into the same the knight backe overthrowen, fell.[4]

31

Now gan the golden Phoebus for to steepe
His fierie face in billowes of the west,
And his faint steedes watred in Ocean deepe,
Whiles from their journall° labours they did rest,   *daily*
When that infernall Monster, having kest°   *cast*
His wearie foe into that living well,
Can° high advaunce his broad discoloured brest,   *did*
Above his wonted pitch,° with countenance fell,°   *height / sinister*
And clapt his yron wings, as victor he did dwell.°   *remain*

---

3. An allusion to Revelation 22.1–2: "And he showed me a pure river of water of life, clear as crystal, proceeding out of the throne of God, and of the Lamb. In the midst of the street of it, and on either side of the river, was the tree of life which bare twelve manner of fruits and yielded her fruit every month: and the leaves of the tree were for the healing of the nations."
4. The Well of Life, with its powers of renewal, is successively compared with waters of the Bible, of England and Europe, and of classical antiquity. In the pool of Siloam ("Silo"), a blind man was cured by Christ (John 9.7); water of the river Jordan cured Naaman of leprosy (2 Kings 5.14) and Christ was baptized therein (Matthew 3.16). "Bath" and "Spau" (Spa) were famed for their medicinal waters. "Cephise" and "Hebrus" in Greece were rivers noted for purifying and healing powers.

32

Which when his pensive° Ladie saw from farre,   *anxious*
  Great woe and sorrow did her soule assay,°   *assail*
  As weening° that the sad end of the warre,   *thinking*
  And gan to highest God entirely° pray,   *earnestly*
  That fearèd chaunce° from her to turne away;   *fate*
  With folded hands and knees full lowly bent
  All night she watcht, ne once adowne would lay
  Her daintie limbs in her sad dreriment,°   *dismal condition*
But praying still did wake, and waking did lament.

33

The morrow next gan early to appeare,
  That° Titan° rose to runne his daily race;   *when / the sun god*
  But early ere the morrow next gan reare
  Out of the sea faire Titans deawy face,
  Up rose the gentle virgin from her place,
  And lookèd all about, if she might spy
  Her lovèd knight to move° his manly pace: *i.e., moving*
  For she had great doubt of his safety,
Since late she saw him fall before his enemy.

34

At last she saw, where he upstarted brave
  Out of the well, wherein he drenchèd lay;
  As Eagle fresh out of the Ocean wave,
  Where he hath left his plumes all hoary gray,
  And deckt himselfe with feathers youthly gay,
  Like Eyas hauke° up mounts unto the skies,   *unfledged hawk*
  His newly budded pineons to assay,
  And marveiles at himselfe, still as he flies:
So new this new-borne knight to battell new did rise.

35

Whom when the damnèd feend so fresh did spy,
  No wonder if he wondred at the sight,
  And doubted, whether his late enemy
  It were, or other new supplièd knight.
  He, now to prove° his late renewèd might,   *try*
  High brandishing his bright deaw-burning blade,
  Upon his crested scalpe so sore did smite,
  That to the scull a yawning wound it made:
The deadly dint° his dullèd senses all dismaid.   *blow*

36

I wote° not, whether the revenging steele   *know*
  Were hardnèd with that holy water dew,
  Wherein he fell, or sharper edge did feele,
  Or his baptizèd hands now greater° grew;   *stronger*
  Or other secret vertue° did ensew;   *power*

Else never could the force of fleshly arme,
Ne molten mettall in his bloud embrew:°   *plunge*
For till that stownd° could never wight him harme,   *moment*
By subtilty, nor slight,° nor might, nor mighty charme.   *trickery*

37

The cruell wound enragèd him so sore,
  That loud he yellèd for exceeding paine;
  As hundred ramping° Lyons seemed to rore,   *rearing*
  Whom ravenous hunger did thereto constraine:
  Then gan he tosse aloft his stretchèd traine,°   *tail*
  And therewith scourge the buxome° aire so sore,   *yielding*
  That to his force to yeelden it was faine;°   *obliged*
  Ne ought his sturdie strokes might stand afore,[5]
That high trees overthrew, and rocks in peeces tore.

38

The same advauncing high above his head,
  With sharpe intended° sting so rude° him smot,   *extended / roughly*
  That to the earth him drove, as stricken dead,
  Ne living wight would have him life behot:[6]
  The mortall sting his angry needle shot
  Quite through his shield, and in his shoulder seasd,
  Where fast it stucke, ne would there out be got:
  The griefe° thereof him wondrous sore diseasd,°   *pain / afflicted*
Ne might his ranckling paine with patience be appeasd.

39

But yet more mindfull of his honour deare,
  Then° of the grievous smart, which him did wring,°   *than / torment*
  From loathèd soile he can° him lightly reare,   *did*
  And strove to loose the farre infixèd sting:
  Which when in vaine he tryde with struggeling,
  Inflamed with wrath, his raging blade he heft,°   *heaved*
  And strooke so strongly, that the knotty string
  Of his huge taile he quite a sunder cleft,
Five joynts thereof he hewd, and but the stump him left.

40

Hart cannot thinke, what outrage,° and what cryes,   *violent clamor*
  With foule enfouldred[7] smoake and flashing fire,
  The hell-bred beast threw forth unto the skyes,
  That all was coverèd with darknesse dire:
  Then fraught° with rancour, and engorgèd° ire,   *filled / swollen*
  He cast at once him to avenge for all,
  And gathering up himselfe out of the mire,

---

5. I.e., neither could anything ("ought") stand before his violent ("sturdie") strokes.
6. Promised. I.e., no one would have thought he could survive the blow.
7. Black as a thundercloud.

With his uneven wings did fiercely fall
Upon his sunne-bright shield, and gript it fast withall.

41

Much was the man encombred with his hold,
  In feare to lose his weapon in his paw,
  Ne wist° yet, how his talents° to unfold;   *knew / talons*
  Nor harder was from Cerberus[8] greedie jaw
  To plucke a bone, then from his cruell claw
  To reave° by strength the gripèd gage° away: *seize / prize*
  Thrise he assayd° it from his foot to draw,   *tried*
  And thrise in vaine to draw it did assay,
It booted nought to thinke, to robbe him of his pray.

42

Tho° when he saw no power might prevaile,   *then*
  His trustie sword he cald to his last aid,
  Wherewith he fiercely did his foe assaile,
  And double blowes about him stoutly laid,
  That glauncing fire out of the yron plaid;
  As sparckles from the Andvile° use to fly,   *anvil*
  When heavie hammers on the wedge are swaid;°   *struck*
  Therewith at last he forst him to unty°   *loosen*
One of his grasping feete, him to defend thereby.

43

The other foot, fast fixèd on his shield,
  Whenas no strength, nor stroks mote° him constraine *might*
  To loose, ne yet the warlike pledge to yield,
  He smot thereat with all his might and maine,
  That nought so wondrous puissance might sustaine;
  Upon the joynt the lucky steele did light,
  And made such way, that hewd it quite in twaine;
  The paw yet missèd not his minisht° might,   *lessened*
But hong still on the shield, as it at first was pight.° *placed*

44

For griefe° thereof, and divelish despight,   *pain*
  From his infernall fournace forth he threw
  Huge flames, that dimmèd all the heavens light,
  Enrold in duskish smoke and brimstone blew;
  As burning Aetna from his boyling stew°   *cauldron*
  Doth belch out flames, and rockes in peeces broke,
  And ragged ribs of mountaines molten new
  Enwrapt in coleblacke clouds and filthy smoke,
That all the land with stench, and heaven with horror choke.

---

8. The dog that guards the mouth of Hades.

45

The heate whereof, and harmefull pestilence
  So sore him noyd,° that forst him to retire   *troubled*
  A little backward for his best defence,
  To save his bodie from the scorching fire,
  Which he from hellish entrailes did expire.°   *breathe out*
  It chaunst (eternall God that chaunce did guide)
  As he recoylèd backward, in the mire
  His nigh forwearied° feeble feet did slide,   *exhausted*
And downe he fell, with dread of shame sore terrifide.

46

There grew a goodly tree him faire beside,
  Loaden with fruit and apples rosie red,
  As they in pure vermilion had beene dide,
  Whereof great vertues over all were red:°   *everywhere were told*
  For happie life to all, which thereon fed,
  And life eke everlasting did befall:
  Great God it planted in that blessed sted°   *place*
  With his almightie hand, and did it call
The Tree of Life, the crime of our first fathers fall.[9]

47

In all the world like was not to be found,
  Save in that soile, where all good things did grow,
  And freely sprong out of the fruitfull ground,
  As incorrupted Nature did them sow,
  Till that dread Dragon all did overthrow.
  Another like faire tree eke grew thereby,
  Whereof who so did eat, eftsoones did know
  Both good and ill: O mornefull memory:
That tree through one mans fault hath doen us all to dy.°   *i.e., killed us*

48

From that first tree forth flowd, as from a well,
  A trickling streame of Balme, most soveraine°   *powerful for cures*
  And daintie deare,° which on the ground still fell,   *precious*
  And overflowèd all the fertill plaine,
  As it had deawèd bene with timely° raine: *seasonable*
  Life and long health that gratious° ointment gave,   *full of grace*
  And deadly woundes could heale, and reare° againe   *raise*
  The senselesse corse appointed° for the grave.   *made ready*
Into that same he fell: which did from death him save.[1]

---

9. Genesis 2.9 describes the Tree of Life and also the Tree of Knowledge of Good and Evil, both of which God planted in the Garden of Eden. The "crime of our first fathers fall" is that Adam, in eating of the second and being banished from Eden, separated himself—and (according to Christian doctrine) his descendants—from the first. The Tree of Life appears again in the New Jerusalem (Revelation 22.2).
1. The healing balm flowing from the Tree of Life is understood to be Christ's blood, shed to redeem humankind from eternal damnation.

49

For nigh thereto the ever damnèd beast
   Durst not approch, for he was deadly made,°   *i.e., a child of death*
   And all that life preservèd, did detest:
   Yet he it oft adventured° to invade.   *attempted*
   By this the drouping day-light gan to fade,
   And yeeld his roome° to sad succeeding night,   *its place*
   Who with her sable mantle gan to shade
   The face of earth, and wayes of living wight,
And high her burning torch set up in heaven bright.

50

When gentle Una saw the second fall
   Of her deare knight, who wearie of long fight,
   And faint through losse of bloud, moved not at all,
   But lay as in a dreame of deepe delight,
   Besmeard with pretious Balme, whose vertuous might
   Did heale his wounds, and scorching heat alay,[2]
   Againe she stricken was with sore affright,
   And for his safetie gan devoutly pray;
And watch the noyous° night, and wait for joyous day.   *noxious*

51

The joyous day gan early to appeare,
   And faire Aurora from the deawy bed
   Of agèd Tithone gan her selfe to reare,[3]
   With rosie cheekes, for shame as blushing red;
   Her golden lockes for haste were loosely shed
   About her eares, when Una her did marke
   Clymbe to her charet, all with flowers spred,
   From heaven high to chase the chearelesse darke;
With merry note her loud salutes the mounting larke.

52

Then freshly up arose the doughtie° knight,   *valiant*
   All healèd of his hurts and woundès wide,
   And did himselfe to battell readie dight;°   *prepare*
   Whose early foe awaiting him beside
   To have devourd, so soone as day he spyde,
   When now he saw himselfe so freshly reare,
   As if late fight had nought him damnifyde,°   *injured*
   He woxe° dismayd, and gan his fate to feare;   *grew*
Nathlesse° with wonted rage he him advauncèd neare.   *nevertheless*

2. Cf. Revelation 2.7, 11: "To him that over-cometh will I give to eat of the tree of life" and "He that overcometh shall not be hurt of the second death" (i.e., the eternal death, of the soul).

3. Aurora is goddess of the dawn, Tithonus her husband ("agèd" because he was granted ever-lasting life without everlasting youth).

53

And in his first encounter, gaping wide,
  He thought attonce him to have swallowed quight,
  And rusht upon him with outragious pride;
  Who him r'encountring fierce, as hauke in flight,
  Perforce rebutted° backe. The weapon bright   *drove*
  Taking advantage of his open jaw,
  Ran through his mouth with so importune° might,   *violent*
  That deepe emperst his darksome hollow maw,
And back retyrd,⁴ his life bloud forth with all did draw.

54

So downe he fell, and forth his life did breath,
  That vanisht into smoke and cloudès swift;
  So downe he fell, that th'earth him underneath
  Did grone, as feeble so great load to lift;
  So downe he fell, as an huge rockie clift,
  Whose false° foundation waves have washt away,   *insecure*
  With dreadfull poyse° is from the mayneland rift,°   *falling weight / split*
  And rolling downe, great Neptune doth dismay;
So downe he fell, and like an heapèd mountaine lay.

55

The knight himselfe even trembled at his fall,
  So huge and horrible a masse it seemed;
  And his deare Ladie, that beheld it all,
  Durst not approch for dread, which she misdeemed,°   *misjudged*
  But yet at last, when as the direfull feend
  She saw not stirre, off-shaking vaine affright,
  She nigher drew, and saw that joyous end:
  Then God she praysd, and thankt her faithfull knight,
That had atchiev'd so great a conquest by his might.

Canto 12 *Summary*   The king and queen of Eden emerge from the castle with all their followers and gaze in wonder at the dead dragon. A great banquet is held in the castle, and Redcrosse and Una are betrothed, through Redcrosse must still fulfill his pledge to serve the Faerie Queene in war for six more years. A messenger arrives bearing a letter from Fidessa (Duessa), in which she charges Redcrosse with breach of promise and seeks to prevent his marriage to Una. Redcrosse explains to the king how he was led astray by Duessa's wicked arts. The messenger is revealed by Una as Archimago and thrown into a dungeon. The king then performs the wedding ceremony. They live in happiness for some time, until Redcrosse must return to the Faerie Queene, leaving Una to mourn.

---

4. I.e., on being drawn back.

From The Second Booke of The Faerie Queene

Contayning
The Legend of Sir Guyon,
or
Of Temperaunce

Summary   In Book 2, Sir Guyon represents and becomes the virtue of Temperance, which requires moderation, self-control, and sometimes abstinence in regard to anger, sex, greed, ambition, and the whole spectrum of passions, desires, pleasures, and material goods. In his climactic adventure, he visits and destroys the Bower of Bliss of the witch Acrasia.

From *Canto 12*

[THE BOWER OF BLISS][1]

42

Thence passing forth, they[2] shortly do arrive,
  Whereas the Bowre of Blisse was situate;
  A place pickt out by choice of best alive,°   *the best living artisans*
  That natures worke by art can imitate:
  In which what ever in this worldly state
  Is sweet, and pleasing unto living sense,
  Or that may dayntiest fantasie aggrate,°   *please, satisfy*
  Was pourèd forth with plentifull dispence,°   *liberality*
And made there to abound with lavish affluence.

43

Goodly it was enclosèd round about,
  Aswell their entred guests to keepe within,
  As those unruly beasts to hold without;[3]
  Yet was the fence thereof but weake and thin;
  Nought feard their force, that fortilage° to win,[4]   *fortress*
  But wisedomes powre, and temperaunces might,
  By which the mightiest things efforcèd bin:°   *are compelled*
  And eke° the gate was wrought of substaunce light,   *also*
Rather for pleasure, then° for battery or fight.   *than*

---

1. The Bower of Bliss, perhaps the most famous of Spenser's symbolic places, has been variously interpreted. Some critics emphasize its aspects of sterility and artifice; others, its seductive and threatening eroticism and idolatry akin to that associated, in Spenser's time, with the New World and Ireland.
2. I.e., Guyon and a character called the Palmer, who is his guide throughout Book 2 (and who is usually thought to represent reason). Pilgrims to

the Holy Land were called palmers in token of the palm leaves they often brought back.
3. Just outside the Bower, Guyon and the Palmer had encountered "many beasts, that roard outrageously, / As if that hungers point, or Venus sting / Had them enraged" (stanza 39). The Palmer had used the magical power of his staff to turn their aggression into cringing fear.
4. I.e., it was not at all feared that the physical force of the beasts could breach that fortress.

44

Yt framèd° was of precious yvory,   *made*
   That seemd a worke of admirable wit;°   *marvelous skill*
   And therein all the famous history
   Of Jason and Medaea was ywrit;
   Her mighty charmes, her furious loving fit,
   His goodly conquest of the golden fleece,
   His falsèd° faith, and love too lightly flit,°   *violated / altering*
   The wondred° Argo, which in venturous peece[5]   *admired*
First through the Euxine seas bore all the flowr of Greece.[6]

45

Ye might° have seene the frothy billowes fry°   *could / foam*
   Under the ship, as thorough° them she went,   *through*
   That seemd the waves were into yvory,
   Or yvory into the waves were sent;
   And other where the snowy substaunce sprent°   *sprinkled*
   With vermell,° like the boyes bloud therein shed,[7]   *vermilion*
   A piteous spectacle did represent,
   And otherwhiles° with gold besprinkelèd;   *elsewhere*
Yt seemd th'enchaunted flame, which did Creüsa wed.[8]

46

All this, and more might in that goodly gate
   Be red; that ever open stood to all,
   Which thither came: but in the Porch there sate
   A comely personage of stature tall,
   And semblaunce° pleasing, more then naturall,   *appearance*
   That travellers to him seemd to entize;
   His looser° garment to the ground did fall,   *too loose*
   And flew about his heeles in wanton wize,
Not fit for speedy pace, or manly exercize.

47

They in that place him Genius° did call: *presiding spirit*
   Not that celestiall powre, to whom the care
   Of life, and generatïon of all
   That lives, pertaines in charge particulare,[9]
   Who wondrous things concerning our welfare,
   And strange phantomes doth let us oft forsee,
   And oft of secret ill bids us beware:
   That is our Selfe,[1] whom though we do not see,
Yet each doth in him selfe it well perceive to bee.

---

5. I.e., adventurous vessel.
6. Jason, in his ship the *Argo*, sought the Golden Fleece of the king of Colchis; the sorceress Medea, the king's daughter, fell in love with him and used "her mighty charmes" to help him obtain it.
7. The blood of Absyrtus, Medea's younger brother, whose body she cut into pieces and scattered to delay her father's pursuit.
8. Jason later deserted Medea for Creüsa. In revenge, Medea gave her a dress that burst into flame when she put it on; the flame consumed and thus "wed" her.
9. I.e., not Agdistes (see next stanza), the god of generation. The true Agdistes appears in the Garden of Adonis canto of Book 3 (canto 6, stanzas 31–33).
1. I.e., the *daemon*, or indwelling divine power, that directs the course of our lives.

48

Therefore a God him sage Antiquity
  Did wisely make,[2] and good Agdistes call:
  But this same[3] was to that quite contrary,
  The foe of life, that good envyes° to all,   *grudges*
  That secretly doth us procure° to fall,   *cause*
  Through guilefull semblaunts,° which he makes us see.   *illusions*
  He of this Gardin had the governall,°   *management*
  And Pleasures porter was devizd° to bee,   *appointed*
Holding a staffe in hand for more formalitee.

49

With diverse flowres he daintily was deckt,
  And strowèd round about, and by his side
  A mighty Mazer bowle[4] of wine was set,
  As if it had to him bene sacrifide;°   *consecrated*
  Wherewith all new-come guests he gratifide:
  So did he eke Sir Guyon passing by:
  But he his idle curtesie defide,
  And overthrew his bowle disdainfully;
And broke his staffe, with which he charmèd semblants sly.[5]

50

Thus being entred, they behold around
  A large and spacious plaine, on every side
  Strowed with pleasauns,° whose faire grassy ground *pleasure-grounds*
  Mantled with greene, and goodly beautifide
  With all the ornaments of Floraes° pride,   *goddess of flowers*
  Wherewith her mother Art, as halfe in scorne
  Of niggard° Nature, like a pompous bride   *stingy*
  Did decke her, and too lavishly adorne,
When forth from virgin bowre she comes in th'early morne.

51

Thereto the Heavens alwayes Joviall,[6]
  Lookt on them lovely,° still° in stedfast state,   *lovingly / always*
  Ne° suffred storme nor frost on them to fall,   *nor*
  Their tender buds or leaves to violate,
  Nor scorching heat, nor cold intemperate
  T'afflict the creatures, which therein did dwell,
  But the milde aire with season moderate
  Gently attempred, and disposd so well,
That still it breathèd forth sweet spirit° and holesome smell. *breath*

---

2. I.e., the wise ancients were right to declare this power a god.
3. I.e., the Genius of the Bower.
4. A drinking cup of maple.
5. Raised deceitful apparitions. The rod and bowl are traditional emblems of enchantment (cf. Duessa's cup, Book 1, canto 8, stanza 14).
6. Serene and beneficent, as influenced by the planet Jupiter.

52

More sweet and holesome, then° the pleasaunt hill   *than*
   Of Rhodope, on which the Nimphe, that bore
   A gyaunt babe, her selfe for griefe did kill;
   Or the Thessalian Tempe, where of yore
   Faire Daphne Phoebus hart with love did gore;
   Or Ida, where the Gods lov'd to repaire,°   *resort*
   When ever they their heavenly bowres forlore;°   *deserted*
   Or sweet Parnasse, the haunt of Muses faire;[7]
Or Eden selfe, if ought° with Eden mote compaire.   *aught, anything*

53

Much wondred Guyon at the faire aspect
   Of that sweet place, yet suffred no delight
   To sincke into his sence, nor mind affect,
   But passèd forth, and lookt still forward right,°   *straight ahead*
   Bridling his will, and maistering his might:
   Till that he came unto another gate,
   No gate, but like one, being goodly dight°   *arrayed*
   With boughes and braunches, which did broad dilate° *spread out*
Their clasping armes, in wanton wreathings intricate.

54

So fashionèd a Porch with rare device,°   *design*
   Archt over head with an embracing vine,
   Whose bounches hanging downe, seemed to entice
   All passers by, to tast their lushious wine,
   And did themselves into their hands incline,
   As freely offering to be gatherèd:
   Some deepe empurpled as the Hyacine,[8]
   Some as the Rubine,° laughing sweetly red,   *ruby*
Some like faire Emeraudes, not yet well ripenèd.

55

And them amongst, some were of burnisht gold,
   So made by art, to beautifie the rest,
   Which did themselves emongst the leaves enfold,
   As lurking from the vew of covetous guest,
   That the weake bowes,° with so rich load opprest,   *boughs*
   Did bowe adowne, as over-burdenèd.
   Under that Porch a comely dame did rest,
   Clad in faire weedes,° but fowle disorderèd,   *garments*
And garments loose, that seemd unmeet for womanhed.[9]

---

7. The nymph Rhodope, who had a "gyaunt babe," Athos, by Neptune, was turned into a mountain. Daphne, another nymph, charmed Apollo so much that he pursued her until she prayed for aid and was turned into a laurel tree. Mount Ida was the scene of the rape of Ganymede by Jupiter, the judgment of Paris, and the gods' vantage point for viewing the Trojan War. Mount Parnassus is the home of the Muses.
8. The hyacinth or jacinth, a sapphire-colored stone.
9. Unfitting for womanhood.

56

In her left hand a Cup of gold she held,
 And with her right the riper° fruit did reach,   *overripe*
 Whose sappy liquor, that with fulnesse sweld,
 Into her cup she scruzd,° with daintie breach°   *squeezed / crushing*
 Of her fine fingers, without fowle empeach,°   *injury*
 That so faire wine-presse made the wine more sweet:
 Thereof she usd to give to drinke to each,
 Whom passing by she happenèd to meet:
It was her guise,° all Straungers goodly so to greet.   *custom*

57

So she to Guyon offred it to tast;
 Who taking it out of her tender hond,
 The cup to ground did violently cast,
 That all in peeces it was broken fond,°   *found*
 And with the liquor stainèd all the lond:°   *land*
 Whereat Excesse exceedingly was wroth,
 Yet no'te° the same amend, ne yet withstond,   *knew not how to*
 But suffered° him to passe, all° were she loth;   *allowed / although*
Who nought regarding her displeasure forward goth.

58

There the most daintie Paradise on ground,
 It selfe doth offer to his sober eye,
 In which all pleasures plenteously abound,
 And none does others happinesse envye:
 The painted° flowres, the trees upshooting hye,   *brightly colored*
 The dales for shade, the hilles for breathing space,
 The trembling groves, the Christall° running by;   *clear stream*
 And that, which all faire workes doth most aggrace,°   *add grace to*
The art, which all that wrought, appearèd in no place.

59

One would have thought (so cunningly, the rude,
 And scornèd parts were mingled with the fine)
 That nature had for wantonesse ensude°   *playfulness imitated*
 Art, and that Art at nature did repine;°   *complain*
 So striving each th'other to undermine,
 Each did the others worke more beautifie;
 So diff'ring both in willes, agreed in fine:°   *in the end*
 So all agreed through sweete diversitie,
This Gardin to adorne with all varietie.

60

And in the midst of all, a fountaine stood,
 Of richest substaunce, that on earth might bee,
 So pure and shiny, that the silver flood
 Through every channell running one might see;
 Most goodly it with curious imageree

Was over-wrought, and shapes of naked boyes,
 Of which some seemd with lively jollitee,
 To fly about, playing their wanton toyes,°   *sports*
Whilest others did them selves embay° in liquid joyes. *bathe*

61

And over all, of purest gold was spred,
 A trayle of yvie in his native hew:
 For the rich mettall was so colourèd,
 That wight, who did not well avis'd° it vew,   *carefully*
 Would surely deeme it to be yvie trew:
 Low his lascivious armes adown did creepe,
 That themselves dipping in the silver dew,
 Their fleecy flowres they tenderly did steepe,
Which° drops of Christall seemd for wantones to weepe. *on which*

62

Infinit streames continually did well
 Out of this fountaine, sweet and faire to see,
 The which into an ample laver° fell,   *basin*
 And shortly grew to so great quantitie,
 That like a little lake it seemd to bee;
 Whose depth exceeded not three cubits[1] hight,
 That through the waves one might the bottom see,
 All pav'd beneath with Jaspar shining bright,
That seemd the fountaine in that sea did sayle upright.

63

And all the margent° round about was set,   *border*
 With shady Laurell trees, thence to defend°   *ward off*
 The sunny beames, which on the billowes bet,°   *beat*
 And those which therein bathèd, mote offend.°   *harm*
 As Guyon hapned by the same to wend,
 Two naked Damzelles he therein espyde,
 Which therein bathing, seemèd to contend,
 And wrestle wantonly, ne car'd to hyde,
Their dainty parts from vew of any, which them eyde.

64

Sometimes the one would lift the other quight
 Above the waters, and then downe againe
 Her plong,° as over maisterèd by might,   *plunge*
 Where both awhile would coverèd remaine,
 And each the other from to rise° restraine;   *rising*
 The whiles their snowy limbes, as through a vele,
 So through the Christall waves appearèd plaine:
 Then suddeinly both would themselves unhele,° *uncover*
And th'amarous sweet spoiles° to greedy eyes revele. *booty, plunder*

---

1. A cubit is about twenty inches (thus the depth is no more than five feet).

65

As that faire Starre, the messenger of morne,[2]
  His deawy face out of the sea doth reare:
  Or as the Cyprian goddess,[3] newly borne
  Of th'Oceans fruitfull froth,° did first appeare: *foam*
  Such seemèd they, and so their yellow heare
  Christalline humour° droppèd downe apace.   *clear water*
  Whom such when Guyon saw, he drew him neare,
  And somewhat gan relent his earnest pace,
His stubborne brest gan secret pleasaunce to embrace.

66

The wanton Maidens him espying, stood
  Gazing a while at his unwonted guise;°   *unaccustomed behavior*
  Then th'one her selfe low duckèd in the flood,
  Abasht, that her a straunger did avise:°   *see*
  But th'other rather higher did arise,
  And her two lilly paps aloft displayd,
  And all, that might his melting hart entise
  To her delights, she unto him bewrayed:°   *revealed*
The rest hid underneath, him more desirous made.

67

With that, the other likewise up arose,
  And her faire lockes, which formerly were bownd
  Up in one knot, she low adowne did lose:°   *loosen*
  Which flowing long and thick, her cloth'd arownd,
  And th'yvorie in golden mantle gownd:
  So that faire spectacle from him was reft,°   *taken*
  Yet that, which reft it, no lesse faire was fownd:
  So hid in lockes and waves from lookers theft,
Nought but her lovely face she for his looking left.

68

Withall she laughèd, and she blusht withall,
  That blushing to her laughter gave more grace,
  And laughter to her blushing, as did fall:
  Now when they spide the knight to slacke his pace,
  Them to behold, and in his sparkling face
  The secret signes of kindled lust appeare,
  Their wanton meriments they did encreace,
  And to him beckned, to approch more neare,
And shewd him many sights, that courage cold could reare.[4]

---

2. Unless "his" in the next line is to be taken as neuter, it implies that the reference is not to Venus but to Phosphorus (or Heophorus), the minor male divinity sometimes identified with the morning star.

3. Venus, one of whose principal shrines was on the island of Cyprus.
4. That could arouse sexual desire ("courage") when cold.

69

On which when gazing him the Palmer saw,
    He much rebukt those wandring eyes of his,
    And counseld well, him forward thence did draw.
    Now are they come nigh to the Bowre of blis
    Of her fond° favorites so nam'd amis: *enamored; foolish*
    When thus the Palmer; "Now Sir, well avise;°   *take care*
    For here the end of all our travell° is: *travel; travail*
    Here wonnes° Acrasia, whom we must surprise,   *dwells*
Else she will slip away, and all our drift despise."°   *plan set at nought*

70

Eftsoones° they heard a most melodious sound,   *immediately*
    Of all that mote delight a daintie eare,
    Such as attonce might not on living ground,
    Save in this Paradise, be heard elswhere:
    Right hard it was, for wight,° which did it heare,   *person*
    To read,° what manner musicke that mote bee: *discern*
    For all that pleasing is to living eare,
    Was there consorted in one harmonee,
Birdes, voyces, instruments, windes, waters, all agree.

71

The joyous birdes shrouded in chearefull shade,
    Their notes unto the voyce attempred° sweet;   *attuned*
    Th'Angelicall soft trembling voyces made
    To th'instruments divine respondence meet:°   *fitting*
    The silver sounding instruments did meet°   *join*
    With the base murmure of the waters fall:
    The waters fall with difference discreet,°   *distinct variation*
    Now soft, now loud, unto the wind did call:
The gentle warbling wind low answerèd to all.

72

There, whence that Musick seemèd heard to bee,
    Was the faire Witch her selfe[5] now solacing,°   *taking pleasure*
    With a new Lover, whom through sorceree
    And witchcraft, she from farre did thither bring:
    There she had him now layd a slombering,
    In secret shade, after long wanton joyes:
    Whilst round about them pleasauntly did sing
    Many faire Ladies, and lascivious boyes,
That ever mixt their song with light licentious toyes.°   *amorous play*

---

5. Acrasia—whose name means both "intemperance" and "incontinence"—bears many resemblances to the classical Circe (in *Odyssey* 10 as well as the more witchlike and seductive figure in Ovid's *Metamorphoses* 14) and also to the enchantresses of Italian romance who derive from Circe: Acratia in Trissino's *L'Italia liberata* and Armida in Tasso's *Gerusalemme liberata*. Much of the description in this scene is imitated from Tasso's account of the garden of Armida.

73

And all that while, right over him she hong,
  With her false° eyes fast fixèd in his sight,   *deceitful*
  As seeking medicine, whence she was stong,°   *stung*
  Or greedily depasturing° delight: *feeding on*
  And oft inclining downe with kisses light,
  For feare of waking him, his lips bedewd,
  And through his humid eyes did sucke his spright,°   *spirit*
  Quite molten into lust and pleasure lewd;
Wherewith she sighèd soft, as if his case she rewd.°   *pitied*

74

The whiles some one did chaunt this lovely lay:[6]
  "Ah see, who so faire thing doest faine° to see,   *delight*
  In springing flowre the image of thy day;
  Ah see the Virgin Rose, how sweetly shee
  Doth first peepe forth with bashfull modestee,
  That fairer seemes, the lesse ye see her may;
  Lo see soone after, how more bold and free
  Her barèd bosome she doth broad display;
Loe see soone after, how she fades, and falles away.

75

"So passeth, in the passing of a day,
  Of mortall life the leafe, the bud, the flowre,
  Ne more doth flourish after first decay,
  That earst° was sought to decke both bed and bowre,   *formerly*
  Of many a Ladie, and many a Paramowre:°   *lover*
  Gather therefore the Rose, whilest yet is prime,° *(its) springtime*
  For soone comes age, that will her pride deflowre:
  Gather the Rose of love, whilest yet is time,
Whilest loving thou mayst lovèd be with equal crime."

76

He ceast, and then gan all the quire of birdes
  Their diverse notes t'attune unto his lay,
  As in approvance of his pleasing words.
  The constant paire[7] heard all, that he did say,
  Yet swarvèd not, but kept their forward way,
  Through many covert groves, and thickets close,
  In which they creeping did at last display°   *discover*
  That wanton Ladie, with her lover lose,°   *loose, wanton*
Whose sleepie head she in her lap did soft dispose.

---

6. The song ("lay") of stanzas 74 and 75 imitates that in *Gerusalemme liberata* 16.14–15; this is a classic statement of the *carpe florem* (or *carpe diem*) theme—pick the flower of youth before it fades.
7. I.e., Guyon and the Palmer.

77

Upon a bed of Roses she was layd,
   As faint through heat, or dight to° pleasant sin,   *ready for*
And was arayd, or rather disarayd,
All in a vele of silke and silver thin,
That hid no whit her alablaster skin,
But rather shewd more white, if more might bee:
   More subtile web Arachne° cannot spin,   *the spider*
Nor the fine nets, which oft we woven see
Of scorchèd deaw, do not in th'aire more lightly flee.°   *float*

78

Her snowy brest was bare to readie spoyle
   Of hungry eies, which n'ote° therewith be fild,   *could not*
And yet through languor of her late sweet toyle,
Few drops, more cleare then Nectar, forth distild,
That like pure Orient perles[8] adowne it trild,°   *trickled*
And her faire eyes sweet smyling in delight,
   Moystened their fierie beames, with which she thrild°   *pierced*
Fraile harts, yet quenchèd° not; like starry light   *quenched; killed*
Which sparckling on the silent waves, does seeme more bright.

79

The young man sleeping by her, seemd to bee
   Some goodly swayne of honorable place,°   *rank*
That certès° it great pittie was to see   *certainly*
Him his nobilitie so foule deface;°   *disgrace*
A sweet regard,° and amiable grace,   *demeanor*
Mixèd with manly sternnesse did appeare
   Yet sleeping, in his well proportioned face,
And on his tender lips the downy heare
Did now but freshly spring, and silken blossomes beare.

80

His warlike armes, the idle instruments
   Of sleeping praise,° were hong upon a tree,   *worthiness*
And his brave° shield, full of old moniments,°   *splendid / marks of honor*
Was fowly ra'st,° that none the signes might see;   *erased*
Ne for them, ne for honour carèd hee,
   Ne ought,° that did to his advauncement tend,   *aught, anything*
But in lewd loves, and wastfull luxuree,°   *licentiousness*
His dayes, his goods, his bodie he did spend:
O horrible enchantment, that him so did blend.°   *blind*

81

The noble Elfe,[9] and carefull Palmer drew
   So nigh them, minding nought, but° lustfull game,   *heedful only of*
That suddein forth they on them rusht, and threw

---

8. Lustrous pearls of the East.   9. Knight of Faerie Land, here, Guyon.

A subtile net, which onely for the same
  The skilfull Palmer formally° did frame.[1]   *expressly*
So held them under fast, the whiles the rest
Fled all away from feare of fowler shame.
  The faire Enchauntresse, so unwares opprest,°   *surprised*
Tryde all her arts, and all her sleights, thence out to wrest.

82

And eke° her lover strove: but all in vaine;   *also*
  For that same net so cunningly was wound,
  That neither guile, nor force might it distraine.°   *tear*
They tooke them both, and both them strongly bound
  In captive bandes,° which there they readie found: *bonds*
But her in chaines of adamant[2] he tyde;
  For nothing else might keepe her safe and sound;
But Verdant° (so he hight°) he soone untyde,   *Green / was called*
And counsell sage in steed° thereof to him applyde.   *instead*

83

But all those pleasant bowres and Pallace brave,°   *splendid*
  Guyon broke downe, with rigour pittilesse;
  Ne ought their goodly workmanship might save
Them from the tempest of his wrathfulnesse,
  But that their blisse he turn'd to balefulnesse:°   *distress*
Their groves he feld, their gardins did deface,
  Their arbers spoyle, their Cabinets° suppresse,   *bowers*
Their banket° houses burne, their buildings race,°   *banquet / raze*
And of the fairest late,° now made the fowlest place.   *lately*

84

Then led they her away, and eke that knight
  They with them led, both sorrowfull and sad:
  The way they came, the same retourn'd they right,
Till they arrivèd, where they lately had
  Charm'd those wild-beasts, that rag'd with furie mad.[3]
Which now awaking, fierce at them gan fly,
  As in their mistresse reskew, whom they lad;°   *led*
But them the Palmer soone did pacify.
Then Guyon askt, what meant those beastes, which there did ly.

85

Said he, "These seeming beasts are men indeed,
  Whom this Enchauntresse hath transformèd thus,
  Whylome° her lovers, which her lusts did feed,   *formerly*
Now turnèd into figures hideous,
  According to their mindes like monstruous."[4]

---

1. The episode recalls the capture of Venus and her lover Mars in a net cunningly set around his marriage bed by Venus's husband, Vulcan, the blacksmith god (*Odyssey* 8.272–84).
2. Steel or some other extremely hard substance.
3. See above, stanza 43, note 3.
4. Even as their own minds were similarly monstrous. Circe changed Odysseus's companions into animals, but Odysseus had a charm to release them.

"Sad end," quoth he, "of life intemperate,
And mournefull meed° of joyes delicious: *reward*
But Palmer, if it mote thee so aggrate,°   *please*
Let them returnèd be unto their former state."

86

Streight way he with his vertuous° staffe them strooke,   *powerful*
And streight of beasts they comely men became;
Yet being men they did unmanly looke,
And starèd ghastly, some for inward shame,
And some for wrath, to see their captive Dame:
But one aboye the rest in speciall,
That had an hog beene late, hight° Grille⁵ by name,   *called*
Repinèd° greatly, and did him miscall,°   *complained / revile*
That had from hoggish forme him brought to naturall.

87

Said Guyon, "See the mind of beastly man,
That hath so soone forgot the excellence
Of his creation, when he life began,
That now he chooseth, with vile difference,°   *preference*
To be a beast, and lacke intelligence."
To whom the Palmer thus, "The donghill kind
Delights in filth and foule incontinence:
Let Grill be Grill, and have his hoggish mind,
But let us hence depart, whilest wether serves and wind."

1590, 1596

Amoretti *and* Epithalamion

In the early 1590s the widowed Spenser wooed and won Elizabeth Boyle, whom he married in Ireland in 1594. The next year he published a small volume that included the sonnet sequence *Amoretti* ("little loves" or "little cupids") and the *Epithalamion*. Several of the sonnets explicitly address an "Elizabeth," and the volume's subtitle, "Written not long since," suggests that these poems, taken together, are a portrait of Spenser's recent courtship and marriage. It was unusual to write sonnets about a happy and successful love; traditionally, the sonneteer's love was for someone painfully inaccessible. Spenser rehearses some of the conventional motifs of frustration and longing, but his cycle of polished, eloquent poems leads toward joyous possession. Thus, for example, in sonnet 67 ("Lyke as a huntsman after weary chace"), he transforms a Petrarchan lament into a vision of unexpected fulfillment.

Spenser's great celebration of this fulfillment is the *Epithalamion*. A learned poet, he was acutely conscious that he was writing within a tradition: an epithalamion is a wedding song whose Greek name conveys that it was sung on the threshold of the bridal chamber. The genre, which goes back at least as far as Sappho (ca. 612 B.C.E.), was widely practiced by the Roman poets, particularly Catullus, and imitated in the Renaissance. Its elements typically include an invocation of the Muses, followed by a celebratory description of the procession of the bride, the religious rites, the sing-

---

5. According to one of Plutarch's dialogues, a man named Gryllus ("fierce," "cruel"), having been changed into a hog by Circe, refused to be restored to human form by Odysseus.

ing and dancing at the wedding party, the preparations for the wedding night, and the sexual consummation of the marriage.

In long, flowing stanzas, Spenser follows these conventions closely, adapting them with exquisite delicacy to his small-town Irish setting and native folklore. But his first stanza announces a major innovation: "So I unto myselfe alone will sing." Traditionally, the poet of an epithalamion was an admiring observer, a kind of master of ceremonies; by combining the roles of poet and bridegroom, Spenser transforms a genial social performance into a passionate lyric utterance. Equally remarkable innovations are the complex stanza form, for which no direct model has been discovered, and the still more complex overall structure. That structure is a triumph of symbolic patterning; the more scholars have studied it, the more elaborate the order they seem to have uncovered. This subtle and rich poetic structure conjures up not only a single day of celebration but also, beyond this particular event, an orderly, harmonious universe, with a hidden pattern of coherence and regularity. If the *Epithalamion* goes to remarkable lengths to affirm this pattern, it is perhaps because it also registers so insistently all that threatens the enduring happiness of wedded love and indeed of human life itself. The greatest threat is the force over which the poem exercises its greatest power: time.

From Amoretti

Sonnet 1

Happy ye leaves[1] when as those lilly hands,
   Which hold my life in their dead doing° might,   *killing*
   Shall handle you and hold in loves soft bands,°   *bonds*
   Lyke captives trembling at the victors sight.
5 And happy lines, on which with starry light,
   Those lamping° eyes will deigne sometimes to look   *flashing*
   And reade the sorrowes of my dying spright,°   *spirit*
   Written with teares in harts close° bleeding book.   *secret*
And happy rymes bath'd in the sacred brooke
10   Of Helicon[2] whence she derivèd is,
   When ye behold that Angels blessèd looke,
   My soules long lackèd foode, my heavens blis.
Leaves, lines, and rymes, seeke her to please alone,
   Whom if ye please, I care for other none.

Sonnet 34[3]

Lyke as a ship that through the Ocean wyde,
   By conduct of some star doth make her way,
   Whenas a storme hath dimd her trusty guyde,
   Out of her course doth wander far astray:
5 So I whose star, that wont° with her bright ray   *was accustomed*
   Me to direct, with cloudes is overcast,
   Doe wander now in darknesse and dismay,
   Through hidden perils round about me plast.°   *placed*
Yet hope I well, that when this storme is past
10   My Helice[4] the lodestar° of my lyfe   *guiding star*

1. I.e., of the book: pages.
2. The "sacred brooke" is Hippocrene, which flows from Mount Helicon, the mountain sacred to the Muses.

3. An adaptation of Petrarch's Rima 189.
4. A name for the Big Dipper (after the nymph who, in classical mythology, was transformed into it).

Will shine again, and looke on me at last,
With lovely light to cleare my cloudy grief.
Till then I wander carefull° comfortlesse,   *full of cares*
In secret sorow and sad pensivenesse.

Sonnet 54

Of this worlds Theatre in which we stay,
 My love like the Spectator ydly sits
Beholding me that all the pageants° play,   *dramatic scenes*
 Disguysing diversly my troubled wits.
5 Sometimes I joy when glad occasion fits,
 And mask in myrth lyke to a Comedy:
Soone after when my joy to sorrow flits,
 I waile and make my woes a Tragedy.
Yet she beholding me with constant° eye,   *unmoved*
10 Delights not in my merth nor rues my smart:° *pities my hurt*
But when I laugh she mocks, and when I cry
 She laughes and hardens evermore her hart.
What then can move her? if nor merth nor mone,° *moan*
 She is no woman, but a sencelesse stone.

Sonnet 64[5]

Comming to kisse her lyps (such grace I found)
 Me seemd I smelt a gardin of sweet flowres
That dainty odours from them threw around,
 For damzels fit to decke their lovers bowres.
5 Her lips did smell lyke unto Gillyflowers,°   *carnations*
 Her ruddy cheeks lyke unto Roses red;
Her snowy browes lyke budded Bellamoures,[6]
 Her lovely eyes like Pincks but newly spred,
Her goodly bosome lyke a Strawberry bed,
10 Her neck lyke to a bounch of Cullambynes;
Her brest lyke lillyes, ere theyr leaves be shed,
 Her nipples lyke yong blossomd Jessemynes.°   *jasmines*
Such fragrant flowres doe give most odorous smell,
 But her sweet odour did them all excell.

Sonnet 67[7]

Lyke as a huntsman after weary chace,
 Seeing the game from him escapt away,
Sits downe to rest him in some shady place,
 With panting hounds beguilèd° of their pray: *deluded*
5 So after long pursuit and vaine assay,°   *attempt*
 When I all weary had the chace forsooke,
The gentle deare returnd the selfe-same way,

5. Much of the imagery of this sonnet is imitated from the Song of Solomon 4.10–16.
6. Unidentified flower, evidently white.
7. An imitation of Petrarch's Rima 190, but with a very different ending. Cf. Sir Thomas Wyatt's adaptation ("Whoso list to hunt") of the same sonnet, and the prose translation of the Petrarchan original appended to it: pp. 384–85.

Thinking to quench her thirst at the next° brooke.   *nearby*
There she beholding me with mylder looke,
10   Sought not to fly, but fearelesse still did bide:
Till I in hand her yet halfe trembling tooke,
And with her owne goodwill hir fyrmely tyde.
Strange thing me seemd to see a beast so wyld,
  So goodly wonne with her owne will beguyld.

Sonnet 75

One day I wrote her name upon the strand,°   *shore*
  But came the waves and washèd it away:
  Agayne I wrote it with a second hand,
  But came the tyde, and made my paynes his pray.°   *prey*
5   "Vayne man," sayd she, "that doest in vaine assay,°   *attempt*
  A mortall thing so to immortalize,
  For I my selve shall lyke to this decay,
  And eek° my name bee wypèd out lykewize."   *also*
"Not so," quod° I, "let baser things devize°   *quoth / contrive*
10   To dy in dust, but you shall live by fame:
  My verse your vertues rare shall eternize,
  And in the heavens wryte your glorious name.
Where whenas death shall all the world subdew,
  Our love shall live, and later life renew."

Sonnet 79

Men call you fayre, and you doe credit° it,   *believe*
  For that your selfe ye dayly such doe see:
  But the trew fayre,° that is the gentle wit,°   *beauty / intelligence*
  And vertuous mind, is much more praysd of me.
5   For all the rest, how ever fayre it be,
    Shall turne to nought and loose that glorious hew:°   *form*
    But onely that is permanent and free
    From frayle corruption, that doth flesh ensew.°   *outlast*
  That is true beautie: that doth argue° you   *prove*
10   To be divine and borne of heavenly seed:
    Deriv'd from that fayre Spirit,° from whom al true   *i.e., God*
  And perfect beauty did at first proceed.
He onely fayre, and what he fayre hath made:
  All other fayre, lyke flowres, untymely fade.

1595

Epithalamion

Ye learnèd sisters which have oftentimes
  Beene to me ayding, others to adorne:[1]

---

1. To write poems in praise of others. The "learnèd sisters" are the Muses.

Whom ye thought worthy of your gracefull rymes,
That even the greatest did not greatly scorne
5 To heare theyr names sung in your simple layes,°   *songs*
But joyèd in theyr prayse.
And when ye list° your owne mishaps to mourne,   *chose*
Which death, or love, or fortunes wreck did rayse,
Your string could soone to sadder tenor° turne,   *mood*
10 And teach the woods and waters to lament
Your dolefull dreriment.°   *sorrow*
Now lay those sorrowfull complaints aside,
And having all your heads with girland crownd,
Helpe me mine owne loves prayses to resound,
15 Ne° let the same of° any be envide: *nor / by*
So Orpheus did for his owne bride,[2]
So I unto my selfe alone will sing,
The woods shall to me answer and my eccho ring.

Early before the worlds light giving lampe,
20 His golden beame upon the hils doth spred,
Having disperst the nights unchearefull dampe,
Doe ye awake, and with fresh lustyhed°   *vigor*
Go to the bowre° of my belovèd love,   *bedchamber*
My truest turtle dove,
25 Bid her awake; for Hymen[3] is awake,
And long since ready forth his maske to move,
With his bright Tead[4] that flames with many a flake,°   *spark*
And many a bachelor to waite on him,
In theyr fresh garments trim.
30 Bid her awake therefore and soone her dight,°   *dress*
For lo the wishèd day is come at last,
That shall for al the paynes and sorrowes past,
Pay to her usury° of long delight: *interest*
And whylest she doth her dight,
35 Doe ye to her of joy and solace° sing,   *pleasure*
That all the woods may answer and your Eccho ring.

Bring with you all the Nymphes that you can heare°   *can hear you*
Both of the rivers and the forrests greene:
And of the sea that neighbours to her neare,
40 Al with gay girlands goodly wel beseene.°   *beautified*
And let them also with them bring in hand,
Another gay girland
For my fayre love of lillyes and of roses,
Bound truelove wize° with a blew silke riband.   *i.e., in a love knot*
45 And let them make great store° of bridale poses,°   *abundance / posies*
And let them eeke° bring store of other flowers   *also*
To deck the bridale bowers.
And let the ground whereas° her foot shall tread,   *where*

2. Orpheus, archetype of the poet in classical antiquity, was famous for his love for his wife, Eurydice.
3. The god of marriage, who leads a "maske" or procession at weddings.
4. A ceremonial torch, associated with marriages since classical times.

For feare the stones her tender foot should wrong
50 Be strewed with fragrant flowers all along,
And diapred lyke the discolorèd mead.[5]
Which done, doe at her chamber dore awayt,
For she will waken strayt,°   straightway
The whiles doe ye this song unto her sing,
55 The woods shall to you answer and your Eccho ring.

Ye Nymphes of Mulla[6] which with careful heed,
The silver scaly trouts doe tend full well,
And greedy pikes which use° therein to feed,   are accustomed
(Those trouts and pikes all others doo excell)
60 And ye likewise which keepe the rushy lake,
Where none doo fishes take,
Bynd up the locks the which hang scatterd light,
And in his waters which your mirror make,
Behold your faces as the christall bright,
65 That when you come whereas° my love doth lie,   where
No blemish she may spie.
And eke ye lightfoot mayds which keepe the deere,
That on the hoary mountayne use to towre,[7]
And the wylde wolves which seeke them to devoure,
70 With your steele darts° doo chace from comming neer,   spears
Be also present heere,
To helpe to decke her and to help to sing,
That all the woods may answer and your eccho ring.

Wake now my love, awake; for it is time,
75 The Rosy Morne long since left Tithones bed,[8]
All ready to her silver coche° to clyme,   coach
And Phoebus° gins to shew his glorious hed.   the sun god
Hark how the cheerefull birds do chaunt theyr laies
And carroll of loves praise.
80 The merry Larke hir mattins° sings aloft,   morning prayers
The thrush replyes, the Mavis descant playes,
The Ouzell shrills, the Ruddock warbles soft,[9]
So goodly all agree with sweet consent,
To this dayes merriment.
85 Ah my deere love why doe ye sleepe thus long,
When meeter° were that ye should now awake,   more fitting
T'awayt the comming of your joyous make,°   mate
And hearken to the birds lovelearnèd song,
The deawy leaves among.
90 For they of joy and pleasance to you sing,
That all the woods them answer and theyr eccho ring.

5. Ornamented like the many-colored meadow.
6. A river near Spenser's home in Ireland.
7. A falconry term meaning to occupy heights.
"The deere": all wild animals, kept by the woodland nymphs.
8. See Song of Solomon 2.10–13: "Rise up, my
love, my fair one, and come away. For, lo, the
winter is past, the rain is over and gone; the flowers appear on the earth; the time of the singing

of birds is come." In classical myth, Tithonus is
the aged husband of Aurora, the dawn.
9. The "Mavis" is the song thrush; the "Ouzell,"
the blackbird (which sings in England); and the
"Ruddock," the European robin. The birds' concert is a convention of medieval love poetry. "Descant": a melody or counterpoint written above a
musical theme—a soprano obbligato.

My love is now awake out of her dreame,
And her fayre eyes like stars that dimmèd were
With darksome cloud, now shew° theyr goodly beams   *show*
95   More bright then° Hesperus° his head doth rere.   *than / evening star*
Come now ye damzels, daughters of delight,
Helpe quickly her to dight,°   *attire*
But first come ye fayre houres which were begot
In Joves sweet paradice, of Day and Night,
100   Which doe the seasons of the yeare allot,
And al that ever in this world is fayre
Doe make and still° repayre.   *continuously*
And ye three handmayds of the Cyprian Queene,[1]
The which doe still adorne her beauties pride,
105   Helpe to addorne my beautifullest bride:
And as ye her array, still throw betweene°   *at intervals*
Some graces to be seene,
And as ye use° to Venus, to her sing,   *are accustomed*
The whiles the woods shal answer and your eccho ring.

110   Now is my love all ready forth to come,
Let all the virgins therefore well awayt,
And ye fresh boyes that tend upon her groome
Prepare your selves; for he is comming strayt.°   *straightway*
Set all your things in seemely good aray°   *order*
115   Fit for so joyfull day,
The joyfulst day that ever sunne did see.
Faire Sun, shew forth thy favourable ray,
And let thy lifull° heat not fervent° be   *life-giving / hot*
For feare of burning her sunshyny face,
120   Her beauty to disgrace.°   *mar*
O fayrest Phoebus, father of the Muse,[2]
If ever I did honour thee aright,
Or sing the thing, that mote° thy mind delight,   *might*
Doe not thy servants simple boone° refuse,   *request*
125   But let this day let this one day be myne,
Let all the rest be thine.
Then I thy soverayne prayses loud wil sing,
That all the woods shal answer and theyr eccho ring.

Harke how the Minstrels gin° to shrill aloud   *begin*
130   Their merry Musick that resounds from far,
The pipe, the tabor,° and the trembling Croud,[3]   *small drum*
That well agree withouten breach or jar.°   *discord*
But most of all the Damzels doe delite,
When they their tymbrels° smyte,   *tambourines*
135   And thereunto doe daunce and carrol sweet,
That all the sences they doe ravish quite,
The whyles the boyes run up and downe the street,

---

1. The Graces attending on Venus ("Cyprian Queene"), representing brightness, joy, and bloom.
2. Phoebus Apollo, god of the sun, was also god of music and poetry, but he was not normally regarded as the father of the Nine Muses (Zeus was).
3. Primitive fiddle. Spenser here designates Irish, not classical, instruments and music for the classical masque or ballet.

Crying aloud with strong confusèd noyce,
As if it were one voyce.
140 *Hymen iô Hymen, Hymen*[4] they do shout,
That even to the heavens theyr shouting shrill
Doth reach, and all the firmament doth fill,
To which the people standing all about,
As in approvance doe thereto applaud
145 And loud advaunce her laud,°   *praise*
And evermore they *Hymen Hymen* sing,
That all the woods them answer and theyr eccho ring.

Loe where she comes along with portly° pace,   *stately*
Lyke Phoebe from her chamber of the East,
150 Arysing forth to run her mighty race,[5]
Clad all in white, that seemes° a virgin best.   *beseems, suits*
So well it her beseems that ye would weene°   *think*
Some angell she had beene.
Her long loose yellow locks lyke golden wyre,
155 Sprinckled with perle, and perling° flowres a tweene,   *winding*
Doe lyke a golden mantle her attyre,
And being crownèd with a girland greene,
Seeme lyke some mayden Queene.
Her modest eyes abashèd to behold
160 So many gazers, as on her do stare,
Upon the lowly ground affixèd are.
Ne dare lift up her countenance too bold,
But blush to heare her prayses sung so loud,
So farre from being proud.
165 Nathlesse doe ye still loud her prayses sing,
That all the woods may answer and your eccho ring.

Tell me ye merchants daughters did ye see
So fayre a creature in your towne before,
So sweet, so lovely, and so mild as she,
170 Adornd with beautyes grace and vertues store,
Her goodly eyes lyke Saphyres shining bright,
Her forehead yvory white,
Her cheekes lyke apples which the sun hath rudded,°   *made red*
Her lips lyke cherryes charming men to byte,
175 Her brest like to a bowle of creame uncrudded,°   *uncurdled*
Her paps° lyke lyllies budded,   *breasts*
Her snowie necke lyke to a marble towre,
And all her body like a pallace fayre,
Ascending uppe with many a stately stayre,
180 To honors seat and chastities sweet bowre.[6]
Why stand ye still ye virgins in amaze,
Upon her so to gaze,
Whiles ye forget your former lay to sing,
To which the woods did answer and your eccho ring.

4. The name of the classical god of marriage, used as a conventional exclamation at weddings in ancient Greece.
5. Phoebe is the moon, a virgin like the bride; the reference to her anticipates the night.
6. The head, where the higher faculties are. The catalog of qualities is a convention in love poetry (cf. Song of Solomon 4–8).

185   But if ye saw that which no eyes can see,
    The inward beauty of her lively spright,°   *living spirit, soul*
    Garnisht with heavenly guifts of high degree,
    Much more then would ye wonder at that sight,
    And stand astonisht lyke to those which red°   *saw*
190   Medusaes mazeful hed.[7]
    There dwels sweet love and constant chastity,
    Unspotted fayth° and comely womanhood,   *fidelity*
    Regard of honour and mild modesty,
    There vertue raynes as Queene in royal throne,
195   And giveth lawes alone.
    The which the base° affections doe obay,   *lower*
    And yeeld theyr services unto her will,
    Ne thought of thing uncomely ever may
    Thereto approch to tempt her mind to ill.
200   Had ye once seene these her celestial threasures,
    And unrevealèd pleasures,
    Then would ye wonder and her prayses sing,
    That all the woods should answer and your Echo ring.

    Open the temple gates unto my love,
205   Open them wide that she may enter in,[8]
    And all the postes adorne as doth behove,[9]
    And all the pillours deck with girlands trim,
    For to recyve this Saynt with honour dew,
    That commeth in to you.
210   With trembling steps and humble reverence,
    She commeth in, before th'almighties vew,
    Of her ye virgins learne obedience,
    When so ye come into those holy places,
    To humble your proud faces:
215   Bring her up to th'high altar, that she may
    The sacred ceremonies there partake,
    The which do endless matrimony make,
    And let the roring Organs loudly play
    The praises of the Lord in lively notes,
220   The whiles with hollow throates
    The Choristers the joyous Antheme sing,
    That all the woods may answere and theyr eccho ring.

    Behold whiles she before the altar stands
    Hearing the holy priest that to her speakes
225   And blesseth her with his two happy hands,
    How the red roses flush up in her cheekes,
    And the pure snow with goodly vermill° stayne,   *vermilion*
    Like crimsin dyde in grayne,°   *fast color*
    That even th'Angels which continually,

---

7. Medusa, one of the Gorgons, had serpents instead of hair (hence a "mazeful hed"): the effect on beholders was to turn them to stone.
8. Cf. Psalm 24.7: "Lift up your heads, O ye gates; and be ye lift up, ye everlasting doors; and the

King of glory shall come in."
9. As is proper. The doorposts were trimmed for weddings in classical times, and the custom was often referred to in classical and later love poetry.

230 About the sacred Altare doe remaine,
Forget their service and about her fly,
Ofte peeping in her face that seemes more fayre,
The more they on it stare.
But her sad° eyes still° fastened on the ground,   *serious / ever*
235 Are governèd with goodly modesty,
That suffers° not one looke to glaunce awry,   *permits*
Which may let in a little thought unsownd.
Why blush ye love to give to me your hand,
The pledge of all our band?°   *bond, tie*
240 Sing ye sweet Angels, Alleluya sing,
That all the woods may answere and your eccho ring.

Now al is done; bring home the bride againe,
Bring home the triumph of our victory,
Bring home with you the glory of her gaine,[1]
245 With joyance bring her and with jollity.
Never had man more joyfull day then this,
Whom heaven would heape with blis.
Make feast therefore now all this live long day,
This day for ever to me holy is,
250 Poure out the wine without restraint or stay,
Poure not by cups, but by the belly° full,   *wineskin*
Poure out to all that wull,°   *want it*
And sprinkle all the postes and wals with wine,
That they may sweat, and drunken be withall.
255 Crowne ye God Bacchus° with a coronall,°   *god of wine / garland*
And Hymen also crowne with wreathes of vine,
And let the Graces daunce unto the rest;
For they can doo it best:
The whiles the maydens doe theyr carroll sing,
260 To which the woods shall answer and theyr eccho ring.

Ring ye the bels, ye young men of the towne,
And leave your wonted° labors for this day: *usual*
This day is holy; doe ye write it downe,
That ye for ever it remember may.
265 This day the sunne is in his chiefest hight,
With Barnaby the bright,[2]
From whence declining daily by degrees,
He somewhat loseth of his heat and light,
When once the Crab[3] behind his back he sees.
270 But for this time it ill ordainèd was,
To chose the longest day in all the yeare,
And shortest night, when longest fitter weare:
Yet never day so long, but late° would passe.   *at last*
Ring ye the bels, to make it weare away,
275 And bonefiers° make all day,   *bonfires*

---

1. I.e., the glory of gaining her.
2. St. Barnabas's Day, at the time of the summer solstice.

3. The constellation Cancer between Gemini and Leo. The sun, passing through the zodiac, leaves the Crab behind toward the end of July.

And daunce about them, and about them sing:
That all the woods may answer, and your eccho ring.

Ah when will this long weary day have end,
And lende me leave to come unto my love?
280 How slowly do the houres theyr numbers spend?
How slowly does sad Time his feathers move?
Hast° thee O fayrest Planet to thy home   *haste*
Within the Westerne fome:
Thy tyred steedes long since have need of rest.[4]
285 Long though it be, at last I see it gloome,°   *begin to darken*
And the bright evening star with golden creast°   *crest*
Appeare out of the East.
Fayre childe of beauty, glorious lampe of love
That all the host of heaven in rankes doost lead,
290 And guydest lovers through the nightès dread,
How chearefully thou lookest from above,
And seemst to laugh atweene thy twinkling light
As joying in the sight
Of these glad many which for joy doe sing,
295 That all the woods them answer and theyr echo ring.

Now ceasse ye damsels your delights forepast;
Enough is it, that all the day was youres:
Now day is doen, and night is nighing fast:
Now bring the Bryde into the brydall boures.
300 Now night is come, now soone her disaray,°   *undress*
And in her bed her lay;
Lay her in lillies and in violets,
And silken courteins over her display,°   *spread*
And odourd° sheetes, and Arras° coverlets.   *perfumed / tapestry*
305 Behold how goodly my faire love does ly
In proud humility;
Like unto Maia,[5] when as Jove her tooke,
In Tempe,[6] lying on the flowry gras,
Twixt sleepe and wake, after she weary was,
310 With bathing in the Acidalian brooke.[7]
Now it is night, ye damsels may be gon,
And leave my love alone,
And leave likewise your former lay to sing:
The woods no more shall answere, nor your echo ring.

315 Now welcome night, thou night so long expected,
That long daies labour doest at last defray,°   *pay for*
And all my cares, which cruell love collected,
Hast sumd in one, and cancellèd for aye:°   *forever*
Spread thy broad wing over my love and me,
320 That no man may us see,

4. The sun's chariot completes its daily course in the western sea.
5. The eldest and most beautiful of the seven daughters of Atlas. (They were stellified as the Pleiades.) Jove fathered Mercury on her.
6. The Vale of Tempe in Thessaly (not, however, traditionally the site of Jove's encounter with Maia).
7. The Acidalian brook is associated with Venus.

And in thy sable mantle us enwrap,
From feare of perrill and foule horror free.
Let no false treason seeke us to entrap,
Nor any dread disquiet once annoy°   *interfere with*
325 The safety of our joy:
But let the night be calme and quietsome,
Without tempestuous storms or sad afray:°   *fear*
Lyke as when Jove with fayre Alcmena[8] lay,
When he begot the great Tirynthian groome:
330 Or lyke as when he with thy selfe[9] did lie,
And begot Majesty.
And let the mayds and yongmen cease to sing:
Ne let the woods them answer, nor theyr Eccho ring.

Let no lamenting cryes, nor dolefull teares,
335 Be heard all night within nor yet without:
Ne let false whispers, breeding hidden feares,
Breake gentle sleepe with misconceivèd dout.°   *fear*
Let no deluding dreames, nor dreadful sights
Make sudden sad affrights;
340 Ne let housefyres, nor lightnings helpelesse harmes,
Ne let the Pouke,[1] nor other evill sprights,
Ne let mischivous witches with theyr charmes,
Ne let hob Goblins, names whose sence we see not,
Fray° us with things that be not.   *terrify*
345 Let not the shriech Oule, nor the Storke be heard:
Nor the night Raven that still° deadly yels,[2]   *always*
Nor damnèd ghosts cald up with mighty spels,
Nor griesly° vultures make us once affeard: *horrid*
Ne let th'unpleasant Quyre of Frogs still croking
350 Make us to wish theyr choking.
Let none of these theyr drery accents sing;
Ne let the woods them answer, nor theyr eccho ring.

But let stil Silence trew night watches keepe,
That sacred peace may in assurance rayne,
355 And tymely Sleep, when it is tyme to sleepe,
May poure his limbs forth on your pleasant playne,
The whiles an hundred little wingèd loves,°   *cupids (or amoretti)*
Like divers fethered doves,
Shall fly and flutter round about your bed,
360 And in the secret darke, that none reproves,
Their prety stealthes shal worke, and snares shal spread
To filch away sweet snatches of delight,
Conceald through covert night.
Ye sonnes of Venus, play your sports at will,
365 For greedy pleasure, carelesse of your toyes,°   *amorous dallying*

8. The mother of Hercules ("the great Tirynthian groome"). Jove made that first night last as
long as three.
9. Night. This is Spenser's own myth.
1. Puck, Robin Goodfellow—here more powerful

and evil than Shakespeare made him in *A Midsummer Night's Dream.*
2. The owl and the night raven were birds of ill
omen; the stork, in Chaucer's *Parliament of Fowls,*
is called an avenger of adultery.

Thinks more upon her paradise of joyes,
Then° what ye do, albe it° good or ill.   *than / albeit, although*
All night therefore attend your merry play,
For it will soone be day:
370   Now none doth hinder you, that say or sing,
Ne will the woods now answer, nor your Eccho ring.

Who is the same, which at my window peepes?
Or whose is that faire face, that shines so bright,
Is it not Cinthia,[3] she that never sleepes,
375   But walkes about high heaven al the night?
O fayrest goddesse, do thou not envy
My love with me to spy:
For thou likewise didst love, though now unthought,°   *not thought of*
And for a fleece of woll,° which privily,   *wool*
380   The Latmian shephard[4] once unto thee brought,
His pleasures with thee wrought.
Therefore to us be favorable now;
And sith° of wemens labours thou hast charge,[5]   *since*
And generation goodly dost enlarge,
385   Encline thy will t'effect our wishfull vow,
And the chast wombe informe° with timely seed,   *give life to*
That may our comfort breed:
Till which we cease our hopefull hap° to sing,   *fortune we hope for*
Ne let the woods us answer, nor our Eccho ring.

390   And thou great Juno, which with awful° might   *awesome*
The lawes of wedlock still dost patronize,°   *watch over*
And the religion° of the faith first plight°   *sanctity / pledged*
With sacred rites hast taught to solemnize:
And eeke° for comfort often callèd art   *also*
395   Of women in their smart,°   *(labor) pains*
Eternally bind thou this lovely band,°   *bond*
And all thy blessings unto us impart.
And thou glad Genius,[6] in whose gentle hand,
The bridale bowre and geniall bed remaine,
400   Without blemish or staine,
And the sweet pleasures of theyr loves delight
With secret ayde doest succour° and supply,   *help*
Till they bring forth the fruitfull progeny,
Send us the timely fruit of this same night.
405   And thou fayre Hebe,[7] and thou Hymen free,
Grant that it may so be.
Til which we cease your further prayse to sing,
Ne any woods shall answer, nor your Eccho ring.

And ye high heavens, the temple of the gods,
410   In which a thousand torches flaming bright

3. Cynthia (or Diana) is goddess of the moon.
4. Endymion, beloved of the moon. The "fleece of woll," however, comes from another story—that of Pan's enticement of the moon.
5. Diana is, as Lucina, patroness of births. The

"labours" are, of course, those of childbirth.
6. God of generation and birth. In the next line, "geniall"—having both the usual sense and the sense of "generative"—puns on his name.
7. Goddess of youth and freedom.

Doe burne, that to us wretched earthly clods,
In dreadful darknesse lend desirèd light;
And all ye powers which in the same remayne,
More then we men can fayne,°   *imagine*
415   Poure out your blessing on us plentiously,
And happy influence upon us raine,
That we may raise a large posterity,
Which from the earth, which they may long possesse,
With lasting happinesse,
420   Up to your haughty° pallaces may mount,   *lofty*
And for the guerdon° of theyr glorious merit   *reward*
May heavenly tabernacles there inherit,
Of blessèd Saints for to increase the count.
So let us rest, sweet love, in hope of this,
425   And cease till then our tymely joyes to sing,
The woods no more us answer, nor our eccho ring.

Song made in lieu of many ornaments,
With which my love should duly have bene dect,°   *adorned*
Which cutting off through hasty accidents,
430   Ye would not stay your dew time to expect,°   *await*
But promist both to recompens,
Be unto her a goodly ornament,
And for short time an endlesse moniment.[8]

1595

8. The envoy (brief final stanza addressed to the poem itself) is traditionally apologetic in tone: the poem is offered as a substitute for presents ("ornaments") that did not arrive in time for the wedding. But this elaborate poem is itself a "goodly ornament," for it stands as a timeless monument of art to the passing day that it celebrates.

SIR WALTER RALEGH
1552–1618

The brilliant and versatile Sir Walter Ralegh was a soldier, courtier, philosopher, explorer and colonist, student of science, historian, and poet. Born to West Country gentry of modest means, Ralegh amassed great wealth thanks to his position at court, leading him to be denounced by some as an upstart and hated by others as a rapacious monopolist. He fought ruthlessly in Ireland and Cádiz, directed the colonization of Virginia, introduced the potato to Ireland and tobacco to Europe, brought Spenser from Ireland to the English court, conducted scientific experiments, led expeditions to Guiana in an unsuccessful effort to find gold, and wrote several reports urging England to challenge Spanish dominance in the New World. He was known for his violent temper, his dramatic sense of life, his extravagant dress, his skepticism in religious matters, his bitter hatred of Spain, and his great favor with Queen Elizabeth, interrupted in 1592 when he seduced, and then married, one of her ladies-in-waiting. His long poem to the queen, *The Ocean to Cynthia*, remains in manuscript fragments, one of more than five hundred lines. His best-known shorter poems include the reply to Marlowe's "Passionate Shepherd" and "The Lie," an attack on social classes and institutions which itself provoked many replies. His active resistance to printing his poems—in one case he forced a printer to recall a volume and paste a slip of paper over his initials—makes it very difficult to put the copies that circulated in manuscript in any reliable chronological order.

King James suspected Ralegh of opposing his succession and threw him into the Tower of London in 1603 on trumped-up charges of treason; there he remained for the rest of his life save for an ill-fated last voyage to Guiana in 1617, which again failed to discover gold. In prison he wrote his long, unfinished *History of the World*, which begins with the Creation, emphasizes the providential punishment of evil princes, and projects a treatment of English history—although not of recent events, because, he declared, he who follows truth too closely at the heels might get kicked in the teeth. The work was to have been dedicated to Henry, prince of Wales, Ralegh's most powerful friend and supporter, who declared, "Only my father would keep such a bird in a cage." But Henry died in 1612, and Ralegh broke off his narrative at 168 B.C.E. Six years later James, bowing to Spanish pressure, had Ralegh executed on the old treason charge.*

The Nymph's Reply to the Shepherd[1]

If all the world and love were young,
And truth in every shepherd's tongue,
These pretty pleasures might me move
To live with thee and be thy love.

5   Time drives the flocks from field to fold
When rivers rage and rocks grow cold,
And Philomel° becometh dumb;   *the nightingale*
The rest complains of cares to come.

  The flowers do fade, and wanton fields
10   To wayward winter reckoning yields;°   *renders an account*
A honey tongue, a heart of gall,
Is fancy's spring, but sorrow's fall.

  Thy gowns, thy shoes, thy beds of roses,
Thy cap, thy kirtle,° and thy posies°   *dress / bouquets*
15   Soon break, soon wither, soon forgotten—
In folly ripe, in reason rotten.

  Thy belt of straw and ivy buds,
Thy coral clasps and amber studs,
All these in me no means can move
20   To come to thee and be thy love.

---

* See the supplemental ebook for Ralegh's poem beginning "As you came from the holy land of Walsinghame" and for excerpts from his account of the battle between the *Revenge* and a Spanish fleet.

1. Cf. Marlowe, "The Passionate Shepherd to His Love," pp. 499–500.

But could youth last and love still breed,
Had joys no date° nor age no need,   *ending*
Then these delights my mind might move
To live with thee and be thy love.

1600

From The History of the World

[CONCLUSION: ON DEATH]

It is * * * Death alone that can suddenly make man to know himself. He tells the proud and insolent that they are but abjects,[1] and humbles them at the instant; makes them cry, complain, and repent; yea, even to hate their fore-passed happiness. He takes the account[2] of the rich, and proves him a beggar, a naked beggar, which hath interest in nothing but in the gravel that fills his mouth. He holds a glass[3] before the eyes of the most beautiful, and makes them see therein their deformity and rottenness, and they acknowledge it.

O eloquent, just, and mighty Death! Whom none could advise, thou hast persuaded; what none hath dared, thou hast done; and whom all the world hath flattered, thou only hast cast out of the world and despised; thou hast drawn together all the far-stretched greatness, all the pride, cruelty, and ambition of man, and covered it all over with these two narrow words: *Hic jacet!*[4]

1614

1. Castoffs.
2. Estimate, measure.
3. Mirror.

4. Latin for "Here lies," often carved on tombstones.

SIR PHILIP SIDNEY
1554–1586

Sir Philip Sidney's face was "spoiled with pimples," Ben Jonson remarked in 1619, wryly distancing himself from the virtual Sidney cult that had arisen in the years after his death. Knight, soldier, poet, friend, and patron, Sidney seemed to the Elizabethans to embody all the traits of character and personality they admired: he was Castiglione's perfect courtier come to life. When he was killed in battle in the Low Countries at the age of thirty-two, fighting for the Protestant cause against the hated Spanish, all England mourned. Stories, possibly apocryphal, began immediately to circulate about his gallantry on the battlefield—grievously wounded, he gave his water to a dying foot soldier with the words "Thy necessity is yet greater than mine"—and about his astonishing self-composure as he himself lay dying: suffering from his putrifying, gangrenous wound, Sidney composed a song and had it sung by his deathbed. When his corpse was brought back to England for burial, the spectacular funeral procession, one of the most elaborate ever staged, almost bankrupted his father-in-law, Francis Walsingham, the wealthy head of Queen Elizabeth's secret service.

Philip Sidney's father was Sir Henry Sidney, thrice lord deputy (governor) of Ireland, and his mother was a sister of Robert Dudley, earl of Leicester, the most spectacular and powerful of all the queen's favorites. He entered Shrewsbury School in 1564, at the age of ten, on the same day as Fulke Greville, who became his lifelong friend and his biographer. Greville wrote of Sidney, "though I lived with him and knew him from a child, yet I never knew him other than a man—with such staidness of mind, lovely and familiar gravity, as carried grace and reverence above greater years." He attended Oxford but left without taking a degree and completed his education by extended travels on the Continent. There he met many of the most important people of the time, from kings and queens to philosophers, theologians, and poets. In France he witnessed the Massacre of St. Bartholomew's Day, which began in Paris on August 24, 1572, and raged through France for more than a month, as Catholic mobs incited by Queen Catherine de Médicis slaughtered perhaps 50,000 Huguenots (French Protestants). This experience undoubtedly strengthened Sidney's ardent Protestantism, which had been inculcated by his family background and education. In an intense correspondence with his mentor, the Burgundian humanist Hubert Languet, he brooded on how he could help to save Europe from what he viewed as the Roman Catholic menace.

Languet and his associates clearly hoped that this brilliant and wonderfully well-connected young Englishman would be able to steer royal policy toward active intervention in Europe's wars of religion. Yet when he returned to England, Sidney found the direct path to heroic action blocked by the caution and hard-nosed realism of Queen Elizabeth and her principal advisers. Though she sent him on some diplomatic missions, the queen clearly regarded the zealous young man with considerable skepticism. As a prominent courtier with literary interests, Sidney actively encouraged authors such as Edward Dyer, Greville, and, most important, Edmund Spenser, who dedicated *The Shepheardes Calender* to him as "the president [chief exemplar] of noblesse and of chevalree." But he clearly longed to be something more than an influential patron of letters. In 1580 his Protestant convictions led him publicly to oppose Queen Elizabeth's projected marriage to the Catholic duke of Anjou. The queen, who hated interference with her diplomatic maneuvers, angrily dismissed Sidney from the court.

He retired to Wilton, the estate of his beloved and learned sister, Mary Herbert, countess of Pembroke, and there he wrote a long, elaborate epic romance in prose, called *Arcadia*. Sidney's claim, made with studied nonchalance, that the work was casually tossed off for his sister's private entertainment is belied by its considerable literary, political, and moral ambitions, qualities that were reinforced and intensified in the extensive revisions he began to make to it in 1582. Our selection is from this revised version, termed by scholars the *New Arcadia*.

In addition to *Arcadia*, which inspired many imitations, including the *Urania* of Sidney's niece, Lady Mary Wroth, two other influential works by Sidney have had still more lasting importance. One of these, *The Defense of Poesy*, is the major work of literary criticism produced in the English Renaissance. In this long essay Sidney eloquently defends poetry (his term for all imaginative literature) against its attackers and, in the process, greatly exalts the role of the poet, the freedom of the imagination, and the moral value of fiction. Perhaps Sidney's finest literary achievement is *Astrophil and Stella* (Starlover and Star), the first of the great Elizabethan sonnet cycles. The principal focus of these sonnets is not a sequence of events or an unfolding relationship. Rather, they explore the lover's state of mind and soul, the contradictory impulses, intense desires, and frustrations that haunt him.

In his guise as a Petrarchan sonneteer, Sidney repeatedly insists that the thought of his beloved drives all more mundane matters from his mind. Yet a number of the sonnets betray a continuing preoccupation with matters of politics and foreign policy. Neither love nor literature could distract Sidney for long from what he took to be his destined role. In 1585 he tried to join Sir Francis Drake's West Indian expedition but was prevented by the queen; instead, she appointed him governor of Flushing in the Netherlands, where as a volunteer and knight-errant he engaged in several vicious skirmishes in the war against Spain. At Zutphen on September 13, 1586, leading a charge against great odds, Sidney was wounded in the thigh, shortly after he had thrown away his thigh armor in an ill-fated chivalric gesture. He died after lingering for twenty-six days.

Sidney called poetry his "unelected vocation," and in keeping with the norms of his class, he did not publish any of his major literary works himself. His ambition, continually thwarted, was to be a man of action whose deeds would affect his country's destiny. Yet he was the author of the most ambitious work of prose fiction, the most important piece of literary criticism, and the most influential sonnet cycle of the Elizabethan Age.*

Astrophil and Stella

Sidney was a jealous protector of his privacy. "I assure you before God," he had written once in an angry letter to his father's private secretary, Molyneux, "that if ever I know you do so much as read any letter I write to my father, without his commandment or my consent, I will thrust my dagger into you. And trust to it, for I speak it in earnest." Yet in *Astrophil and Stella* he seems to hold up a mirror to every nuance of his emotional being. For its original coterie audience, Sidney's sonnet sequence must have been an elaborate game of literary masks, psychological risk-taking, and open secrets. The loosely linked succession of 108 sonnets and eleven songs, with its dazzling display of technical virtuosity, provides tantalizing glimpses of identifiable characters and, still more, a sustained and remarkably intimate portrait of the poet's inner life.

Much biographical speculation has centered on Sidney's ambiguous relationship with Penelope Devereux, the supposed original of Stella. A marriage between the two had been proposed in 1576 and was talked about for some years, but in 1581 she married Lord Robert Rich, and two years later Sidney also married. (At their high social rank, marriages were negotiated in the interests of the powerful families involved, not of the individuals.) Some of the sonnets contain sly puns on the name *Rich*, and it seems likely that there are autobiographical elements in the shadowy narrative sketched by the work. At the same time, however, the "plot" of the sequence, full of trials, setbacks, much suffering on the part of the lover and occasional encouragement on the part of the lady, is highly conventional, derived from Petrarch and his many Italian, French, and Spanish imitators.

Poets in this tradition undertook to produce an anatomy of love, displaying its shifting and often contradictory states: hope and despair, tenderness and bitterness, exultation and modesty, bodily desire and spiritual transcendence. Petrarch had deployed a series of ingenious metaphors to describe these states, but by Sidney's time the metaphors—love as a freezing fire, the beloved's glance as an arrow striking the lover's heart, and so forth—had through endless repetition become familiar and predictable, less a revelation than a role. Sidney, in the role of Astrophil, protests that he uses no standard conventional phrases, that his verse is original and comes from his heart. This protest is itself conventional, and yet Sidney manages to infuse his sonnets with an extraordinary vigor and freshness. Certain of the sonnets have, within their narrow fourteen-line bounds, the force of the drama: "Fly, fly, my friends, I have my death-wound, fly" or "What, have I thus betrayed my liberty?" Others, in their grappling with insistent desire, have the probing, psychological resonance of private confession: "With what sharp checks I in myself am shent" or "Who will in fairest book of Nature know." Still others ask crucial questions about the

---

* For additional writings by Sidney—another sonnet from *Astrophil and Stella* (64), four poems from *Certain Sonnets*, and more excerpts from *Arcadia*—see the supplemental ebook.

whole project of self-representation: "Stella oft sees the very face of woe." Virtually all of them manifest the exceptional *energia*—forcibleness—that Sidney, in *The Defense of Poesy*, says is the key ingredient of good love poetry.

From Astrophil and Stella

1[1]

Loving in truth, and fain° in verse my love to show,   *desirous*
That the dear She might take some pleasure of my pain,
Pleasure might cause her read, reading might make her know,
Knowledge might pity win, and pity grace obtain,
5   I sought fit words to paint the blackest face of woe,
Studying inventions fine, her wits to entertain,
Oft turning others' leaves, to see if thence would flow
Some fresh and fruitful showers upon my sunburned brain.
    But words came halting forth, wanting Invention's stay;[2]
10 Invention, Nature's child, fled step-dame Study's blows,
And others' feet still° seemed but strangers in my way.   *continually*
Thus great with child to speak, and helpless in my throes,
    Biting my truant pen, beating myself for spite,
    "Fool," said my Muse to me, "look in thy heart and write."

2

Not at first sight, nor with a dribbèd[3] shot
    Love gave the wound, which while I breathe will bleed,
    But known worth did in mine[4] of time proceed,
Till by degrees it had full conquest got.
5 I saw and liked, I liked but lovèd not,
    I loved, but straight did not[5] what Love decreed;
    At length to Love's decrees, I, forced, agreed,
Yet with repining° at so partial° lot.   *complaining / unfair*
    Now even that footstep of lost liberty
10 Is gone, and now like slave-born Muscovite,[6]
I call it praise to suffer tyranny;
And now employ the remnant of my wit°   *mind*
    To make myself believe that all is well,
    While with a feeling skill I paint my hell.

6

Some lovers speak, when they their muses entertain,
Of hopes begot by fear, of wot° not what desires,   *know*
Of force of heavenly beams infusing hellish pain,
Of living deaths, dear wounds, fair storms, and freezing fires.[7]

---

1. One of six sonnets in the sequence written in hexameters.
2. I.e., lacking the support of Invention, his words moved haltingly.
3. Ineffectual or at random.
4. Tunnel dug to undermine a besieged fortress.

5. Did not immediately do.
6. Inhabitant of Muscovy, Russian principality ruled from Moscow; 16th-century travel books describe Muscovites as contented slaves.
7. Conventional Petrarchan oxymorons.

5   Some one his song in Jove and Jove's strange tales attires,
Bordered with bulls and swans, powdered with golden rain;[8]
Another humbler wit to shepherd's pipe retires,
Yet hiding royal blood full oft in rural vein.[9]
     To some a sweetest plaint a sweetest style affords,[1]
10   While tears pour out his ink, and sighs breathe out his words,
His paper pale Despair, and Pain his pen doth move.
     I can speak what I feel, and feel as much as they,
     But think that all the map of my state I display,
When trembling voice brings forth that I do Stella love.

20

Fly, fly, my friends, I have my death-wound, fly;
See there that boy, that murth'ring° boy, I say,   *murdering*
Who like a thief hid in dark bush doth lie
Till bloody bullet get him wrongful prey.
5   So tyran° he no fitter place could spy,   *tyrant*
Nor so fair level° in so secret stay,°   *aim / stopping place*
As that sweet black° which veils the heav'nly eye;   *i.e., pupil*
There himself with his shot he close° doth lay.   *secretly*
     Poor passenger,° pass now thereby I did,   *passerby*
10 And stayed, pleased with the prospect of the place,
While that black hue from me the bad guest hid:
     But straight I saw motions of lightning grace,
     And then descried° the glist'ring° of his dart;°   *saw / glittering / arrow*
But ere I could fly thence, it pierced my heart.

28

You that with allegory's curious frame°   *intricate contrivance*
     Of others' children changelings use° to make,   *are accustomed*
     With me those pains for God's sake do not take:
I list not° dig so deep for brazen fame.   *I don't care to*
5 When I say Stella, I do mean the same
     Princess of beauty for whose only sake
     The reins of love I love, though never slake,°   *slack*
And joy therein, though nations count it shame.
     I beg no subject to use eloquence,[2]
10 Nor in hid ways to guide philosophy;
Look at my hands for no such quintessence,[3]
But know that I in pure simplicity
     Breathe out the flames which burn within my heart,
     Love only reading unto me this art.

8. Jove courted Europa in the shape of a bull; Leda, as a swan; and Danaë, as a golden shower. For "Bordered," the emendation "Broadred" (embroidered) has been proposed.
9. I.e., in pastoral allegory. By convention, a pastoral poet pipes his songs on an oaten or reed pipe.
1. Parodying the overuse of the word *sweet* in love complaints, with allusion to the very musical *dolce stil nuovo* (sweet new style) associated with Dante and his Italian contemporaries.
2. I.e., I don't ask for a topic simply as an excuse to display my rhetorical skills.
3. The mysterious "fifth element" of matter (supplementary to earth, air, fire, and water), which alchemists labored to extract.

31

With how sad steps, O Moon, thou climb'st the skies,
How silently, and with how wan a face!
What, may it be that even in heavenly place
That busy archer° his sharp arrows tries?   *Cupid*
5   Sure, if that long-with-love-acquainted eyes
Can judge of love, thou feel'st a lover's case;
I read it in thy looks: thy languished grace,
To me that feel the like, thy state descries.°   *reveals*
Then even of fellowship, O Moon, tell me,
10   Is constant love deemed there but want of wit?°   *lack of intelligence*
Are beauties there as proud as here they be?
Do they above love to be loved, and yet
Those lovers scorn whom that love doth possess?
Do they call virtue there ungratefulness?[4]

52

A strife is grown between Virtue and Love,
While each pretends° that Stella must be his: *claims*
Her eyes, her lips, her all, saith Love, do this,
Since they do wear his badge,[5] most firmly prove.
5   But Virtue thus that title doth disprove:
That Stella (O dear name) that Stella is
That virtuous soul, sure heir of heavenly bliss;
Not this fair outside, which our hearts doth move.
And therefore, though her beauty and her grace
10   Be Love's indeed, in Stella's self he may
By no pretence claim any manner° place.   *kind of*
Well, Love, since this demur° our suit[6] doth stay,°   *objection / stop*
Let Virtue have that Stella's self; yet thus,
That Virtue but° that body grant to us.   *only*

71

Who will in fairest book of Nature know
How Virtue may best lodged in beauty be,
Let him but learn of Love to read in thee,
Stella, those fair lines, which true goodness show.
5   There shall he find all vices' overthrow,
Not by rude force, but sweetest sovereignty
Of reason, from whose light those night-birds[7] fly;
That inward sun in thine eyes shineth so.
And not content to be Perfection's heir
10   Thyself, dost strive all minds that way to move,
Who mark° in thee what is in thee most fair.[8]   *perceive*

---

4. I.e., is the lady's ingratitude considered virtue in heaven (as here)? Also, is the lover's virtue (fidelity) considered distasteful in heaven (as here)?
5. Device or livery worn to identify someone's (here, Cupid's) servants.

6. "Courtship," in addition to the legal meaning.
7. The owl, for example, was an emblem of various vices.
8. I.e., her virtue, which is fairer even than her beauty.

So while thy beauty draws the heart to love,
 As fast° thy Virtue bends that love to good;   *at the same rate*
 "But, ah," Desire still cries, "give me some food."

72

Desire, though thou my old companion art,
 And oft so clings to my pure Love that I
 One from the other scarcely can descry,°   *distinguish*
While each doth blow the fire of my heart,
5 Now from thy fellowship I needs must part:
 Venus is taught with Dian's wings to fly;[9]
 I must no more in thy sweet passions lie;
Virtue's gold now must head my Cupid's dart.
 Service and honor, wonder with delight,
10 Fear to offend, will worthy to appear,[1]
 Care shining in mine eyes, faith in my sprite:°   *spirit*
These things are left me by my only dear.
  But thou, Desire, because thou wouldst have all,
  Now banished art. But yet alas how shall?

74

I never drank of Aganippe well,
 Nor ever did in shade of Tempe[2] sit;
 And Muses scorn with vulgar° brains to dwell;   *common*
Poor layman I, for sacred rites unfit.
5 Some do I hear of poets' fury° tell,   *inspiration*
 But God wot,° wot not what they mean by it;   *knows*
 And this I swear by blackest brook of hell,[3]
I am no pick-purse of another's wit.
 How falls it then that with so smooth an ease
10 My thoughts I speak, and what I speak doth flow
 In verse, and that my verse best wits doth please?
Guess we the cause. "What, is it thus?" Fie no.
  "Or so?" Much less. "How then?" Sure thus it is:
  My lips are sweet, inspired with Stella's kiss.[4]

108[5]

When Sorrow (using mine own fire's might)
 Melts down his lead into my boiling breast,
 Through that dark furnace to my heart oppressed
There shines a joy from thee, my only light;

---

9. Diana, goddess of the moon and patron of chastity; Venus, goddess of beauty and love, mother of Cupid.
1. The phrase can mean either "the wish to appear worthy" or "desire that is worthy to appear [i.e., not shameful]."
2. Valley beside Mount Olympus, sacred to Apollo, the god of poetry. "Aganippe well": foun-tain at the foot of Mount Helicon in Greece, sacred to the Muses.
3. The most binding of all oaths were those sworn by the River Styx.
4. A kiss he stole from Stella when he caught her napping (Song 2).
5. In many sonnet sequences, as here, the final poem brings no resolution.

5   But soon as thought of thee breeds my delight,
     And my young soul flutters to thee, his nest,
     Most rude Despair, my daily unbidden guest,

Clips straight° my wings, straight wraps me in his night,   *immediately*
  And makes me then bow down my head and say,
10 "Ah, what doth Phoebus'° gold that wretch avail,   *god of the sun*
  Whom iron doors do keep from use of day?"
So strangely (alas) thy works in me prevail,
    That in my woes for thee thou art my joy,
    And in my joys for thee my only annoy.°   *trouble, pain*

1582?   1591, 1598

MARY (SIDNEY) HERBERT, COUNTESS OF PEMBROKE
1562–1621

When her brother, the celebrated courtier and author Philip Sidney, died, in 1586, Mary Sidney, the countess of Pembroke, became the custodian not only of his writings but also of his last name. Though her marriage in 1577 to Henry Herbert, the second earl of Pembroke, represented a great social advance for her family—her offspring would no longer be members of the gentry but rather would be among the nation's tiny hereditary nobility—yet throughout her life the countess of Pembroke held onto her identity as a Sidney.

She had good reason to do so. The Sidneys were celebrated for their generous support of poets, clergymen, alchemists, naturalists, scientists, and musicians. The Pembroke country estate, Wilton, quickly became a gathering place for thinkers who enjoyed the countess's patronage and shared her staunch Protestant convictions and her literary interests. Books, pamphlets, and scores of poems were dedicated to her in the 1590s and thereafter, as well as to her brother Robert (whose country house, Penshurst, is praised in a well-known poem by Ben Jonson). Nicholas Breton and Samuel Daniel in particular benefited from her support, as did her niece, goddaughter, and frequent companion, Mary Wroth.

In one of the dedicatory poems to *Salve Deus Rex Judaeorum*, Aemilia Lanyer praises Mary Sidney not only for her generosity toward poets but also for those "works that are more deep and more profound." These include her translation of Robert Garnier's neoclassical French tragedy *Antonius* and a translation of the religious tract *A Discourse of Life and Death* by the French Protestant Philippe de Mornay. Her translation of Petrarch's *Triumph of Death* was the first in English to maintain the original *terza rima* (a particularly challenging rhyme scheme for an English versifier). Although translation was considered an especially appropriate genre for women to work in, it is a mistake to assume that Mary Sidney's efforts as a poet are merely derivative: Elizabethans understood that translation offered the opportunity not only for the display of linguistic and technical skills but also for the indirect expression of personal and political concerns. Mary Sidney also expressed these concerns more directly: among her original poems was a powerful elegy for her brother Philip and a short pastoral entertainment for Queen Elizabeth.

Mary Sidney was best known for having prepared a composite edition of Philip Sidney's *Arcadia* and for contributing the larger number (107) of the verse translations of the 150 biblical psalms that her brother had begun. Her very free renderings re-create the psalms as English poems, using an amazing variety of stanzaic and metrical patterns and some strikingly effective images. Widely circulated in manuscript, this influential collection was an important bridge between the many metrical paraphrases of psalms in this period and the works of the great religious lyric poets of the seventeenth century, especially George Herbert. Donne's poem *Upon the Translation of the Psalms by Sir Philip Sidney and the Countess of Pembroke His Sister* testifies to that importance: "They tell us *why*, and teach us *how* to sing."*

Psalm 52

Tyrant, why swell'st thou thus,
    Of mischief vaunting?
Since help from God to us
    Is never wanting.

5 Lewd° lies thy tongue contrives,   *vile*
    Loud lies it soundeth;
Sharper than sharpest knives
    With lies it woundeth.

Falsehood thy wit° approves,   *mind*
10   All truth rejected:
Thy will all vices loves,
    Virtue neglected.

Not words from cursèd thee,
    But gulfs° are pourèd;   *abysses, yawning chasms*
15 Gulfs wherein daily be
    Good men devourèd.

Think'st thou to bear it° so?   *bear it off, triumph*
    God shall displace thee;
God shall thee overthrow,
20   Crush thee, deface° thee.   *destroy*

The just shall fearing see
    These fearful chances,
And laughing shoot at thee
    With scornful glances.

25 Lo, lo, the wretched wight,°   *creature*
    Who, God disdaining,
His mischief made his might,
    His guard his gaining.°   *riches*

---

* For Mary Sidney's elegy on Sir Philip Sidney, her translation of Psalm 58, her "Dialogue between two shepherds," and the King James Bible version of the psalm printed here, see the supplemental ebook.

        I as an olive tree
30   Still green shall flourish:
        God's house the soil shall be
            My roots to nourish.

        My trust on his true love
            Truly attending,
35   Shall never thence remove,
            Never see ending.

        Thee will I honor still,
            Lord, for this justice;
        There fix my hopes I will
40   Where thy saints' trust is.

        Thy saints trust in thy name,
            Therein they joy them:
        Protected by the same,
            Nought° can annoy° them.   *nothing / harm*

ca. 1595   1823

CHRISTOPHER MARLOWE
1564–1593

The son of a Canterbury shoemaker, Christopher Marlowe was born two months before William Shakespeare. In 1580 he went to Corpus Christi College, Cambridge, on a scholarship that was ordinarily awarded to students preparing for the ministry. He held the scholarship for the maximum time, six years, but did not take holy orders. Instead, he began to write plays. When he applied for his Master of Arts degree in 1587, the university was about to deny it to him on the ground that he intended to go abroad to join the dissident English Catholics at Rheims. But the Privy Council intervened and requested that because Marlowe had done the queen "good service" he be granted his degree at the next commencement. "It is not Her Majesty's pleasure," the government officials added, "that anyone employed as he had been in matters touching the benefit of his country should be defamed by those that are ignorant in the affairs he went about." Although much sensational information about Marlowe has been discovered in modern times, we are still largely "ignorant in the affairs he went about." The likeliest possibility is that he served as a spy or an agent provocateur against English Catholics who were conspiring to overthrow the Protestant regime.

Before he left Cambridge, Marlowe had written his tremendously successful play *Tamburlaine* and perhaps also, in collaboration with his younger Cambridge contemporary Thomas Nashe, the tragedy of *Dido, Queen of Carthage*. *Tamburlaine* dramatizes the exploits of a fourteenth-century Mongol warrior who rose from humble origins to conquer a huge territory that extended from the Black Sea to Delhi. In some sixteenth-century chronicles, Tamburlaine is represented as God's scourge, the instrument of divine wrath. In Marlowe's play there are few if any glimpses of a transcendent design. His hero is the vehicle for the expression of boundless energy and ambition, the impulse to strive ceaselessly for absolute dominance. Tamburlaine's conquests are achieved not only by force of arms but also by his extraordinary mastery of language, his "high astounding terms." The English theater audience had never before heard such resonant, immensely energetic blank verse. The great period of Elizabethan drama was launched by what Ben Jonson called "Marlowe's mighty line."

From the time of his first theatrical success, when he was twenty-three, Marlowe had only six years to live. They were not calm years. In 1589 he was involved in a brawl with one William Bradley, in which the poet Thomas Watson intervened and killed Bradley. Both poets were jailed, but Watson got off on a plea of self-defense, and Marlowe was released. In 1591 Marlowe was living in London with the playwright Thomas Kyd, who later, under torture, gave information to the Privy Council accusing him of atheism and treason. On May 30, 1593, an informer named Richard Baines submitted a note to the Council which, on the evidence of Marlowe's own alleged utterances, branded him with atheism, sedition, and homosexuality. Four days later, at an inn in the London suburb of Deptford, Marlowe was killed by a dagger thrust, purportedly in an argument over the bill. Modern scholars have discovered that the murderer and the others present in the room at the inn had connections to the world of spies, double agents, and swindlers to which Marlowe himself was in some way linked. Those who were arrested in connection with the murder were briefly held and then quietly released.

On the bare surface, Marlowe's tragic vision seems for the most part religiously and socially conventional. Tamburlaine at last suffers divine retribution and death at the end of the sequel, *Tamburlaine Part II*; the central character of *The Jew of Malta* is a monstrous anti-Semitic caricature; *Doctor Faustus* and *Edward II* (which treats the tragic fate of a homosexual king) demonstrate the destruction that awaits those who rebel against God or violate the official moral order. Yet there is a force at work in these plays that relentlessly questions and undermines conventional morality. The crime for which Tamburlaine is apparently struck down is the burning of the Muslim Koran; the Jew of Malta turns out to be, if anything, less ruthless and hypocritical than his Christian counterparts; and Edward II's life of homoerotic indulgence seems innocent in comparison with the cynical and violent dealings of the corrupt rebels who turn against him. In a way that goes far beyond the demands of moral instruction, Marlowe seems to revel in the depiction of flamboyant transgression, physical abjection, and brutal punishment. Whether as a radical pursuit of absolute liberty or as an expression of sheer destructive negativity, Marlowe's plays, written in the turbulent years before his murder at the age of twenty-nine, have continued to fascinate and disturb readers and audiences.

The Passionate Shepherd to His Love[1]

Come live with me and be my love,
And we will all the pleasures prove°   *test, experience*
That valleys, groves, hills, and fields,
Woods, or steepy mountain yields.

5 And we will sit upon the rocks,
Seeing the shepherds feed their flocks,

---

1. This pastoral lyric of invitation is one of the most famous of Elizabethan songs, and a few lines from it are sung in Shakespeare's *Merry Wives of Windsor*. Many poets have written replies to it, the best known of which is by Sir Walter Ralegh (pp. 488–89).

By shallow rivers to whose falls
Melodious birds sing madrigals.

And I will make thee beds of roses
10 And a thousand fragrant posies,°   *bouquets (also of poems)*
A cap of flowers, and a kirtle°   *dress*
Embroidered all with leaves of myrtle;

A gown made of the finest wool
Which from our pretty lambs we pull;
15 Fair linèd slippers for the cold,
With buckles of the purest gold;

A belt of straw and ivy buds,
With coral clasps and amber studs:
And if these pleasures may thee move,
20 Come live with me, and be my love.

The shepherd swains shall dance and sing
For thy delight each May morning:
If these delights thy mind may move,
Then live with me and be my love.

1599, 1600

Doctor Faustus

Marlowe's major dramas, *Tamburlaine, The Jew of Malta*, and *Doctor Faustus*, all portray heroes who passionately seek power—the power of rule, the power of money, and the power of knowledge, respectively. Each of the heroes is an overreacher, striving to get beyond the conventional boundaries established to contain the human will.

Unlike Tamburlaine, whose aim and goal is "the sweet fruition of an earthly crown," or Barabas, the Jew of Malta, who lusts for "infinite riches in a little room," Faustus seeks the mastery and voluptuous pleasure that come from forbidden knowledge. To achieve his goal Faustus must make—or chooses to make—a bargain with Lucifer. This is an old folklore motif, but it would have been taken seriously in a time when belief in the reality of devils was almost universal. The story's power over its original audience is vividly suggested by the numerous accounts of uncanny events at performances of the play: strange noises in the theater or extra devils who suddenly appeared among the actors on stage, causing panic.

In the opening soliloquy, Marlowe's Faustus bids farewell to each of his studies—logic, medicine, law, and divinity—as something he has used up. He turns instead to black magic, but the devil exacts a fearful price in exchange: the eternal damnation of Faustus's soul. Faustus aspires to be more than a man: "A sound magician is a mighty god," he declares. His fall is caused by the same pride and ambition that caused the fall of the angels in heaven and of humankind in the Garden of Eden. But it is characteristic of Marlowe that he makes this aspiration nonetheless magnificent.

The immediate source of the play is a German narrative called, in its English translation, *The History of the Damnable Life and Deserved Death of Doctor John Faustus*. That source supplies Marlowe's drama with the scenes of horseplay and low practical joking that contrast so markedly with the passages of huge ambition. It is quite possible that these comic scenes are the work of a collaborator; but no other Elizabethan could have written the first scene (with its brilliant representation of the insatiable aspiring mind of the hero), the ecstatic address to Helen of

Troy, or the searing scene of Faustus's last hour. And though compared with these celebrated passages the comic scenes often seem crude, they too contribute to the overarching vision of Faustus's fate: the half-trivial, half-daring exploits, the alternating states of bliss and despair, the questions that are not answered and the answers that bring no real satisfaction, the heroic wanderings that lead nowhere.

Marlowe's play exists in two very different forms: the A text (1604) and the much longer B text (1616), which probably incorporates additions by other hands and which has also been revised to conform to the severe censorship statutes of 1606. We use Roma Gill's edition, based on the A text.[*]

The Tragical History of Doctor Faustus

Dramatis Personae[1]

CHORUS	THREE SCHOLARS
DR. JOHN FAUSTUS	GOOD ANGEL
WAGNER, *his servant, a student*	EVIL ANGEL
VALDES ⎱ *his friends, magicians*	MEPHASTOPHILIS
CORNELIUS ⎰	LUCIFER
BELZEBUB	*Spirits presenting*
OLD MAN	THE SEVEN DEADLY SINS
CLOWN	PRIDE
ROBIN ⎱ *ostlers at an inn*	COVETOUSNESS
RAFE ⎰	WRATH
VINTNER	ENVY
HORSE-COURSER	GLUTTONY
THE POPE	SLOTH
THE CARDINAL OF LORRAINE	LECHERY
CHARLES V, EMPEROR OF	ALEXANDER THE GREAT *and his*
GERMANY	PARAMOUR
A KNIGHT *at the* EMPEROR'S *court*	HELEN OF TROY
DUKE OF VANHOLT	
DUCHESS OF VANHOLT	ATTENDANTS, FRIARS, *and* DEVILS

Prologue

[*Enter* CHORUS.][2]

CHORUS   Not marching now in fields of Thrasimene,
    Where Mars[3] did mate° the Carthaginians,   *join with*
    Nor sporting in the dalliance of love,
    In courts of kings where state° is overturned,   *political power*
    Nor in the pomp of proud audacious deeds,
    Intends our Muse to vaunt his heavenly verse:
    Only this (Gentlemen) we must perform,

---

[*] For scenes from the B texts and a host of texts and images related to the play, its author, and 16th-century conceptions of sorcery, see "The Magician, the Heretic, and the Playwright" in the supplemental ebook.
1. There is no list of characters in the A text. The one here is an editorial construction.

2. A single actor who recited a prologue to an act or a whole play, and occasionally delivered an epilogue.
3. God of war. The battle of Lake Trasimene (217 B.C.E.) was one of the Carthaginian leader Hannibal's great victories.

The form of Faustus' fortunes good or bad.
To patient judgments we appeal our plaud,°   *applause*
10   And speak for Faustus in his infancy:
Now is he born, his parents base of stock,
In Germany, within a town called Rhodes;
Of riper years to Wittenberg⁴ he went,
Whereas° his kinsmen chiefly brought him up.   *where*
15   So soon he profits in divinity,°   *theology*
The fruitful plot of scholarism graced,
That shortly he was graced with doctor's name,⁵
Excelling all whose sweet delight disputes⁶
In heavenly matters of theology.
20   Till, swollen with cunning,° of a self-conceit,   *knowledge*
His waxen wings did mount above his reach,
And melting heavens conspired his overthrow.⁷
For falling to a devilish exercise,
And glutted more with learning's golden gifts,
25   He surfeits upon cursed necromancy:°   *black magic*
Nothing so sweet as magic is to him,
Which he prefers before his chiefest bliss.⁸
And this the man⁹ that in his study sits.   [*Exit.*]

SCENE 1

[*Enter* FAUSTUS *in his study.*]
FAUSTUS   Settle thy studies, Faustus, and begin
To sound the depth of that thou wilt profess:
Having commenced, be a divine in show,¹
Yet level° at the end of every art,   *aim*
5   And live and die in Aristotle's works.
Sweet *Analytics*, 'tis thou hast ravished me.
*Bene disserere est finis logices.*²
Is to dispute well logic's chiefest end?
Affords this art no greater miracle?
10   Then read no more, thou hast attained the end;
A greater subject fitteth Faustus' wit.°   *intellect*
Bid *on kai me on* farewell;³ Galen come:
Seeing, *ubi desinit philosophus, ibi incipit medicus.*⁴
Be a physician, Faustus, heap up gold,
15   And be eternized for some wondrous cure.

4. The famous university where Martin Luther studied, as did Shakespeare's Hamlet and Horatio. "Rhodes": Roda, or Stadtroda, in Germany.
5. The lines play on two senses of *graced*: he so (1) adorned the place ("plot") of scholarship—i.e., the university—that shortly he was (2) honored with a doctor's degree.
6. Referring to formal disputations, academic exercises that occupied the place now held by examinations.
7. In Greek myth, Icarus flew too near the sun on wings of feathers and wax made by his father, Daedalus; the wax melted, and he fell into the sea and drowned.

8. The salvation of his soul.
9. Apparently a cue for the Chorus to draw aside the curtain to the enclosed space at the rear of the stage.
1. In external appearance. "Commenced": graduated, i.e., received the doctor's degree.
2. "To carry on a disputation well is the end [or purpose] of logic" (Latin). *Analytics*: the title of two treatises on logic by Aristotle.
3. The Greek phrase means "being and not being"; i.e., philosophy.
4. "Where the philosopher leaves off the physician begins" (Latin). Galen: the supreme ancient authority on medicine (2nd century C.E.).

Summmum bonum medicinae sanitas:[5]
The end of physic° is our body's health.   *medicine*
Why Faustus, hast thou not attained that end?
Is not thy common talk found aphorisms?[6]
Are not thy bills° hung up as monuments,   *prescriptions*
Whereby whole cities have escaped the plague,
And thousand desperate maladies been eased?
Yet art thou still but Faustus, and a man.
Couldst thou make men to live eternally,
Or, being dead, raise them to life again,
Then this profession were to be esteemed.
Physic farewell! Where is Justinian?[7]
Si una eademque res legatur duobus,
Alter rem alter valorem rei, etc.[8]
A pretty case of paltry legacies.
Exhereditare filium non potest pater nisi . . . [9]
Such is the subject of the Institute
And universal Body of the Law:
This study fits a mercenary drudge
Who aims at nothing but external trash!
Too servile and illiberal for me.
When all is done, divinity is best.
Jerome's Bible,[1] Faustus, view it well:
Stipendium peccati mors est:[2] ha! *Stipendium, etc.*
The reward of sin is death? That's hard.
Si pecasse negamus, fallimur, et nulla est in nobis veritas:[3]
If we say that we have no sin,
We deceive ourselves, and there's no truth in us.
Why then belike° we must sin,   *in all likelihood*
And so consequently die.
Ay, we must die an everlasting death.
What doctrine call you this? *Che sarà, sarà:*
What will be, shall be? Divinity, adieu!
These metaphysics° of magicians   *occult lore*
And necromantic books are heavenly!
Lines, circles, schemes, letters, and characters!
Ay, these are those that Faustus most desires.
O what a world of profit and delight,
Of power, of honor, of omnipotence
Is promised to the studious artisan![4]
All things that move between the quiet° poles   *unmoving*
Shall be at my command: emperors and kings
Are but obeyed in their several° provinces,   *separate*

---

5. The Latin is translated in the following line.
6. I.e., generally accepted wisdom.
7. Roman emperor and authority on law (483–565 C.E.). The Latin passages that follow paraphrase Justinian's *Institutiones*, a manual included in his *Corpus Iuris* (Body of the Law: cf. below, lines 32–33).
8. "If something is bequeathed to two persons, one shall have the thing itself, the other something of equal value."

9. "A father cannot disinherit his son unless . . ."
1. The Latin translation, or "Vulgate," of St. Jerome (ca. 340–420 C.E.).
2. Romans 6.23. But Faustus reads only part of the Scripture verse: "For the wages of sin is death; but the gift of God is eternal life through Jesus Christ our Lord."
3. I John 1.8 (translated in the following two lines).
4. A practitioner of an art; here, necromancy.

Nor can they raise the wind, or rend the clouds;
60   But his dominion that exceeds in this
Stretcheth as far as doth the mind of man:
A sound magician is a mighty god.
Here, Faustus, try thy brains to gain a deity.
        [*Enter* WAGNER.]
Wagner, commend me to my dearest friends,
65   The German Valdes and Cornelius,
Request them earnestly to visit me.
WAGNER   I will, sir.   [*Exit.*]
FAUSTUS   Their conference will be a greater help to me
Than all my labors, plod I ne'er so fast.
        [*Enter the* GOOD ANGEL *and the* EVIL ANGEL.]
70   GOOD ANGEL   O Faustus, lay that damnèd book aside,
And gaze not on it, lest it tempt thy soul
And heap God's heavy wrath upon thy head:
Read, read the Scriptures; that is blasphemy.
EVIL ANGEL   Go forward, Faustus, in that famous art,
75   Wherein all nature's treasury is contained:
Be thou on earth as Jove⁵ is in the sky,
Lord and commander of these elements.   [*Exeunt.*]
FAUSTUS   How am I glutted with conceit° of this!   *filled with the idea*
Shall I make spirits fetch me what I please,
80   Resolve me of all ambiguities,
Perform what desperate enterprise I will?
I'll have them fly to India for gold,
Ransack the ocean for orient pearl,⁶
And search all corners of the new-found world
85   For pleasant fruits and princely delicates.
I'll have them read me strange philosophy,
And tell the secrets of all foreign kings;
I'll have them wall all Germany with brass,
And make swift Rhine circle fair Wittenberg;⁷
90   I'll have them fill the public schools⁸ with silk,
Wherewith the students shall be bravely° clad.   *splendidly*
I'll levy soldiers with the coin they bring,
And chase the Prince of Parma⁹ from our land,
And reign sole king of all our provinces.
95   Yea, stranger engines for the brunt of war
Than was the fiery keel at Antwerp's bridge,¹
I'll make my servile spirits to invent.
Come German Valdes and Cornelius,
And make me blest with your sage conference.
        [*Enter* VALDES *and* CORNELIUS.]
100   Valdes, sweet Valdes, and Cornelius,

5. God—a common substitution in Elizabethan
drama.
6. Pearl of orient—the especially lustrous pearl
from the seas around India.
7. Wittenberg is in fact on the Elbe River.
8. The university lecture rooms.

9. The duke of Parma was the Spanish governor-
general of the Low Countries, 1579–92.
1. A reference to the burning ship sent by the
Protestant Netherlanders in 1585 against the
barrier on the river Scheldt that Parma had built
as a part of the blockade of Antwerp.

Know that your words have won me at the last
To practise magic and concealèd arts;
Yet not your words only, but mine own fantasy,°   *imagination*
That will receive no object[2] for my head,
But ruminates on necromantic skill.
Philosophy is odious and obscure,
Both law and physic are for petty wits;
Divinity is basest of the three,
Unpleasant, harsh, contemptible, and vile.
'Tis magic, magic that hath ravished me.
Then, gentle friends, aid me in this attempt,
And I, that have with concise syllogisms
Graveled° the pastors of the German church   *confounded*
And made the flowering pride of Wittenberg
Swarm to my problems[3] as the infernal spirits
On sweet Musaeus when he came to hell,
Will be as cunning as Agrippa was,
Whose shadows made all Europe honor him.[4]

VALDES Faustus, these books, thy wit,° and our experience   *intellect*
Shall make all nations to canonize us.
As Indian Moors[5] obey their Spanish lords,
So shall the spirits of every element
Be always serviceable to us three.
Like lions shall they guard us when we please,
Like Almaine rutters° with their horsemen's staves,   *German horsemen*
Or Lapland giants trotting by our sides;
Sometimes like women, or unwedded maids,
Shadowing° more beauty in their airy brows   *harboring*
Than in the white breasts of the Queen of Love.
From Venice shall they drag huge argosies,°   *merchant ships*
And from America the golden fleece
That yearly stuffs old Philip's treasury,[6]
If learnèd Faustus will be resolute.

FAUSTUS Valdes, as resolute am I in this
As thou to live, therefore object it not.[7]

CORNELIUS The miracles that magic will perform
Will make thee vow to study nothing else.
He that is grounded in astrology,
Enriched with tongues,° well seen° in minerals,   *languages / expert*
Hath all the principles magic doth require:
Then doubt not, Faustus, but to be renowned
And more frequented° for this mystery°   *visited / craft*
Than heretofore the Delphian oracle.[8]

2. That will pay no attention to physical reality.
3. Questions posed for public academic disputation.
4. Cornelius Agrippa, German author of *The Vanity and Uncertainty of Arts and Sciences* (1530), was popularly believed to have had the power of calling up the "shadows" or shades of the dead. Musaeus was a legendary singer, supposed son of Orpheus; it was, however, Orpheus who charmed the denizens of hell with his music.

5. Dark-skinned Native Americans. ("India" in the period could refer to either the East Indies or the West Indies.)
6. Comparing the treasures Phillip II of Spain received from the Americas to the Golden Fleece taken, in Greek mythology, from Colchis by Jason and the Argonauts. (Evidently the Venetian argosies put Marlowe in mind of Jason's ship, the *Argo*.)
7. I.e., do not make an issue of my resolve.
8. The oracle of Apollo at Delphi in Greece.

The spirits tell me they can dry the sea,
145 And fetch the treasure of all foreign wrecks,
Ay, all the wealth that our forefathers hid
Within the massy° entrails of the earth.   massive
Then tell me, Faustus, what shall we three want?°   lack
FAUSTUS   Nothing, Cornelius. O this cheers my soul!
150 Come, show me some demonstrations magical,
That I may conjure in some lusty° grove,   pleasant
And have these joys in full possessiön.
VALDES   Then haste thee to some solitary grove,
And bear wise Bacon's and Abanus'⁹ works,
155 The Hebrew Psalter, and New Testament;
And whatsoever else is requisite
We will inform thee ere our conference cease.
CORNELIUS   Valdes, first let him know the words of art,¹
And then, all other ceremonies learned,
160 Faustus may try his cunning by himself.
VALDES   First I'll instruct thee in the rudiments,
And then wilt thou be perfecter° than I.   more accomplished
FAUSTUS   Then come and dine with me, and after meat
We'll canvass every quiddity° thereof: essential feature
165 For ere I sleep, I'll try what I can do.
This night I'll conjure,° though° I die therefore.   call up spirits / even if
                                                           [Exeunt.]

SCENE 2

[Enter two SCHOLARS.]

1 SCHOLAR   I wonder what's become of Faustus, that was wont to make our schools ring with sic probo.²
2 SCHOLAR   That shall we know; for see, here comes his boy.³

[Enter WAGNER.]

1 SCHOLAR   How now, sirra,⁴ where's thy master?
5 WAGNER   God in heaven knows.
2 SCHOLAR   Why, dost not thou know?
WAGNER   Yes I know, but that follows not.
1 SCHOLAR   Go to,⁵ sirra, leave your jesting, and tell us where he is.
WAGNER   That follows not necessary by force of argument, that you,
10 being licentiates,⁶ should stand upon't; therefore acknowledge your error, and be attentive.
2 SCHOLAR   Why, didst thou not say thou knew'st?
WAGNER   Have you any witness on't?
1 SCHOLAR   Yes, sirra, I heard you.
15 WAGNER   Ask my fellow if I be a thief.⁷
2 SCHOLAR   Well, you will not tell us.

---

9. Roger Bacon, the 13th-century friar and scientist popularly thought to be a magician, and Pietro d'Abano, 13th-century alchemist.
1. I.e., the technical terms.
2. Thus I prove; a phrase in scholastic disputation.
3. In this case, a poor student acting as a servant

to earn his living.
4. A variant of "sir," used condescendingly.
5. Come on!
6. Graduate students.
7. I.e., the testimony of your companion ("fellow") is worth no more than one thief's testimony for another.

WAGNER   Yes sir, I will tell you; yet if you were not dunces you would
never ask me such a question. For is not he *corpus naturale*? And is
not that *mobile*?[8] Then wherefore should you ask me such a question? But that I am by nature phlegmatic,[9] slow to wrath and prone
to lechery—to love I would say—it were not for you to come within
forty foot of the place of execution,[1] although I do not doubt to see
you both hanged the next sessions. Thus having triumphed over
you, I will set my countenance like a precisian,[2] and begin to speak
thus: Truly, my dear brethren, my master is within at dinner with
Valdes and Cornelius, as this wine, if it could speak, it would
inform your worships. And so the Lord bless you, preserve you, and
keep you, my dear brethren, my dear brethren.   [*Exit.*]

1 SCHOLAR   Nay then, I fear he is fallen into that damned art, for
which they two are infamous through the world.

2 SCHOLAR   Were he a stranger, and not allied to me, yet should I
grieve for him. But come, let us go and inform the rector,[3] and see
if he by his grave counsel can reclaim him.

1 SCHOLAR   O but I fear me nothing can reclaim him.

2 SCHOLAR   Yet let us try what we can do.   [*Exeunt.*]

SCENE 3

[*Enter* FAUSTUS *to conjure.*]

FAUSTUS   Now that the gloomy shadow of the earth,
Longing to view Orion's drizzling look,[4]
Leaps from th'antarctic world unto the sky,
And dims the welkin° with her pitchy breath,   *sky*
Faustus, begin thine incantations,
And try if devils will obey thy hest,°   *command*
Seeing thou hast prayed and sacrificed to them.
Within this circle[5] is Jehovah's name,
Forward and backward anagrammatized;
Th'bbreviated names of holy saints,
Figures of every adjunct to the heavens,
And characters of signs and erring stars,[6]
By which the spirits are enforced to rise.
Then fear not Faustus, but be resolute,
And try the uttermost magic can perform.
Sint mihi dei Acherontis propitii! Valeat numen triplex Jehovae!
Ignei, aerii, aquatici, terreni spiritus salvete! Orientis princeps, Bel-
zebub inferni ardentis monarcha, et Demogorgon, propitiamus vos
ut appareat et surgat Mephastophilis. Quid tu moraris? Per Jehovam,

8. *Corpus naturale et mobile* ("matter natural and
movable") was a scholastic definition of the subject matter of physics. Wagner is here parodying
the language of learning at the university.
9. Dominated by the phlegm, one of the four
humors (bodily fluids) whose relative proportions
were thought to determine a person's physical
and psychological qualities.
1. I.e., if I were not slow to anger, it would be
fatally dangerous for you to come near me.
2. Puritan. The rest of his speech is in the style of
the Puritans. "Sessions": sittings of a court.

3. The head of a German university.
4. The constellation Orion appears at the beginning of winter. The phrase is a reminiscence of
Virgil.
5. The magic circle drawn on the ground, within
which the magician would be safe from the spirits he conjured.
6. The moving planets. "Adjunct": heavenly body,
thought to be joined to the solid firmament of the
sky. "Characters of signs": signs of the zodiac and
the planets.

20 *Gehennam, et consecratam aquam quam nunc spargo, signumque*
  crucis quod nunc facio, et per vota nostra, ipse nunc surgat nobis
  dicatus Mephastophilis.[7]
       [*Enter a* DEVIL.]
     I charge thee to return and change thy shape,
     Thou art too ugly to attend on me;
25   Go and return an old Franciscan friar,
     That holy shape becomes a devil best.   [*Exit* DEVIL.]
     I see there's virtue° in my heavenly words!   power
     Who would not be proficient in this art?
     How pliant is this Mephastophilis,
30   Full of obedience and humility,
     Such is the force of magic and my spells.
     Now Faustus, thou art conjurer laureate°   preeminent
     That canst command great Mephastophilis.
     Quin redis, Mephastophilis, fratris imagine![8]
       [*Enter* MEPHASTOPHILIS.]
35 MEPHASTOPHILIS   Now Faustus, what would'st thou have me do?
FAUSTUS   I charge thee wait upon me whilst I live,
     To do whatever Faustus shall command,
     Be it to make the moon drop from her sphere,
     Or the ocean to overwhelm the world.
40 MEPHASTOPHILIS   I am a servant to great Lucifer,
     And may not follow thee without his leave;
     No more than he commands must we perform.
FAUSTUS   Did not he charge thee to appear to me?
MEPHASTOPHILIS   No, I came now hither of mine own accord.
45 FAUSTUS   Did not my conjuring speeches raise thee? Speak!
MEPHASTOPHILIS   That was the cause, but yet *per accidens*,[9]
     For when we hear one rack[1] the name of God,
     Abjure° the Scriptures, and his savior Christ,   repudiate
     We fly in hope to get his glorious soul;
50   Nor will we come unless he use such means
     Whereby he is in danger to be damned:
     Therefore the shortest cut for conjuring
     Is stoutly to abjure the Trinity,
     And pray devoutly to the prince of hell.
55 FAUSTUS   So Faustus hath already done, and holds this principle:
     There is no chief but only Belzebub,
     To whom Faustus doth dedicate himself.
     This word damnation terrifies not him,
     For he confounds hell in Elysium:
60   His ghost be with the old philosophers.[2]

7. Faustus's Latin conjures the devils: "May the gods of the lower regions favor me! Farewell to the Trinity! Hail, spirits of fire, air, water, and earth! Prince of the East, Belzebub, monarch of burning hell, and Demogorgon, we pray to you that Mephastophilis may appear and rise. What are you waiting for? By Jehovah, Gehenna, and the holy water that I now sprinkle, and the sign of the cross that I now make, and by our vows, may Mephastophilis himself now rise to serve us." "Beelzebub" ("Lord of Flies"): an ancient Phoeni-

cian deity; in Matthew 12.24, he is called "the prince of the devils." "Demogorgon": in Renaissance versions of classical mythology, a mysterious primeval god.
8. "Return, Mephastophilis, in the shape of a friar."
9. The immediate, not ultimate, cause.
1. Torture (here, by anagrammatizing).
2. Faustus considers hell to be the Elysium of the classical philosophers, not the Christian hell of torment.

But leaving these vain trifles of men's souls,
  Tell me, what is that Lucifer thy lord?
MEPHASTOPHILIS   Arch-regent and commander of all spirits.
FAUSTUS   Was not that Lucifer an angel once?
MEPHASTOPHILIS   Yes Faustus, and most dearly loved of God.
FAUSTUS   How comes it then that he is prince of devils?
MEPHASTOPHILIS   O, by aspiring pride and insolence,
  For which God threw him from the face of heaven.
FAUSTUS   And what are you that live with Lucifer?
MEPHASTOPHILIS   Unhappy spirits that fell with Lucifer,
  Conspired against our God with Lucifer,
  And are forever damned with Lucifer.
FAUSTUS   Where are you damned?
MEPHASTOPHILIS   In hell.
FAUSTUS   How comes it then that thou art out of hell?
MEPHASTOPHILIS   Why this is hell, nor am I out of it.
  Think'st thou that I, who saw the face of God,
  And tasted the eternal joys of heaven,
  Am not tormented with ten thousand hells
  In being deprived of everlasting bliss?[3]
  O Faustus, leave these frivolous demands,°   *questions*
  Which strike a terror to my fainting soul.
FAUSTUS   What, is great Mephastophilis so passionate
  For being deprivèd of the joys of heaven?
  Learn thou of Faustus manly fortitude,
  And scorn those joys thou never shalt possess.
  Go bear these tidings to great Lucifer:
  Seeing Faustus hath incurred eternal death
  By desp'rate thoughts against Jove's deity,
  Say he surrenders up to him his soul,
  So° he will spare him four and twenty years,   *on condition that*
  Letting him live in all voluptuousness,
  Having thee ever to attend on me,
  To give me whatsoever I shall ask,
  To tell me whatsoever I demand,
  To slay mine enemies and aid my friends,
  And always be obedient to my will.
  Go, and return to mighty Lucifer,
  And meet me in my study at midnight
  And then resolve me of thy master's mind.[4]
MEPHASTOPHILIS   I will, Faustus.   [*Exit.*]
FAUSTUS   Had I as many souls as there be stars,
  I'd give them all for Mephastophilis.
  By him I'll be great emperor of the world,
  And make a bridge through the moving air
  To pass the ocean with a band of men;
  I'll join the hills that bind the Afric shore,
  And make that land continent to° Spain,   *connected to*

3. This is the punishment of loss of God's presence, which is supposed to be the greatest torment of hell.
4. I.e., give me his decision.

And both contributory to my crown.
110 The emperor[5] shall not live but by my leave,
Nor any potentate of Germany.
Now that I have obtained what I desire,
I'll live in speculation° of this art   *contemplation*
Till Mephastophilis return again.   [*Exit.*]

SCENE 4

[*Enter* WAGNER *and the* CLOWN.[6]]

WAGNER Sirra boy, come hither.

CLOWN How, boy? Zounds, boy! I hope you have seen many boys with such pickadevants as I have. Boy, quotha![7]

WAGNER Tell me, sirra, hast thou any comings in?[8]

5 CLOWN Ay, and goings out too; you may see else.[9]

WAGNER Alas poor slave, see how poverty jesteth in his nakedness! The villain is bare, and out of service,[1] and so hungry that I know he would give his soul to the devil for a shoulder of mutton, though it were blood raw.

10 CLOWN How, my soul to the devil for a shoulder of mutton though 'twere blood raw? Not so good, friend; by'rlady,[2] I had need have it well roasted, and good sauce to it, if I pay so dear.

WAGNER Well, wilt thou serve me, and I'll make thee go like *qui mihi discipulus?*[3]

15 CLOWN How, in verse?

WAGNER No, sirra; in beaten silk and stavesacre.[4]

CLOWN How, how, knavesacre?[5] Ay, I thought that was all the land his father left him! Do ye hear, I would be sorry to rob you of your living.

20 WAGNER Sirra, I say in stavesacre.

CLOWN Oho, oho, stavesacre! Why then belike, if I were your man, I should be full of vermin.

WAGNER So thou shalt, whether thou be'st with me or no. But sirra, leave your jesting, and bind yourself presently unto me for seven
25 years, or I'll turn all the lice about thee into familiars,[6] and they shall tear thee in pieces.

CLOWN Do you hear, sir? You may save that labor: they are too familiar with me already—zounds, they are as bold with my flesh as if they had paid for my meat and drink.

30 WAGNER Well, do you hear, sirra? Hold, take these guilders.[7]

CLOWN Gridirons; what be they?

WAGNER Why, French crowns.[8]

---

5. The Holy Roman Emperor.

6. Not a court jester (as in some of Shakespeare's plays) but an older stock character, a rustic buffoon.

7. Says he. The point of the clown's retort is that he is a man and wears a beard. "Zounds": an oath, meaning "God's wounds." "Pickadevants": small, pointed beards.

8. Income, but the clown then puns on the literal meaning.

9. I.e., if you don't believe me.

1. Out of a job.

2. An oath: "by Our Lady."

3. "You who are my pupil" (the opening phrase of a poem on how students should behave, from Lily's *Latin Grammar*, ca. 1509). Wagner means "like a proper servant of a learned man."

4. A preparation from delphinium seeds, used for killing vermin.

5. Wordplay, here and below.

6. Familiar spirits, demons. "Bind yourself": i.e., as apprentice. "Presently": immediately.

7. Coins. "Hold": here.

8. French crowns, legal tender in England at this period, were easily counterfeited.

CLOWN   'Mass, but for the name of French crowns a man were as good have as many English counters![9] And what should I do with these?

WAGNER   Why, now, sirra, thou art at an hour's warning whensoever or wheresoever the devil shall fetch thee.

CLOWN   No, no, here take your gridirons again.

WAGNER   Truly I'll none of them.

CLOWN   Truly but you shall.

WAGNER   Bear witness I gave them him.

CLOWN   Bear witness I give them you again.

WAGNER   Well, I will cause two devils presently to fetch thee away. Baliol[1] and Belcher!

CLOWN   Let your Baliol and your Belcher come here, and I'll knock[2] them, they were never so knocked since they were devils! Say I should kill one of them, what would folks say? "Do ye see yonder tall fellow in the round slop?[3] He has killed the devil!" So I should be called "Killdevil" all the parish over.

   [Enter two DEVILS, and the CLOWN runs up and down crying.]

WAGNER   Baliol and Belcher, spirits, away!   [Exeunt DEVILS.]

CLOWN   What, are they gone? A vengeance on them! They have vile long nails. There was a he devil and a she devil. I'll tell you how you shall know them: all he devils has horns,[4] and all she devils has clefts and cloven feet.

WAGNER   Well, sirra, follow me.

CLOWN   But do you hear? If I should serve you, would you teach me to raise up Banios and Belcheos?

WAGNER   I will teach thee to turn thyself to anything, to a dog, or a cat, or a mouse, or a rat, or anything.

CLOWN   How! A Christian fellow to a dog or a cat, a mouse or a rat? No, no, sir, if you turn me into anything, let it be in the likeness of a little pretty frisking flea, that I may be here, and there, and everywhere. O I'll tickle the pretty wenches' plackets! I'll be amongst them, i'faith.[5]

WAGNER   Well, sirra, come.

CLOWN   But do you hear, Wagner . . . ?

WAGNER   How? Baliol and Belcher!

CLOWN   O Lord I pray, sir, let Banio and Belcher go sleep.

WAGNER   Villain, call me Master Wagner; and let thy left eye be diametarily fixed upon my right heel, with *quasi vestigias nostras insistere*.[6]   [Exit.]

CLOWN   God forgive me, he speaks Dutch fustian![7] Well, I'll follow him, I'll serve him; that's flat.   [Exit.]

SCENE 5

   [Enter FAUSTUS in his study.]

FAUSTUS   Now Faustus, must thou needs be damned,
   And canst thou not be saved.

---

9. Worthless tokens. "'Mass": by the Mass.
1. Probably a corruption of Belial.
2. Beat.
3. Baggy pants. "Tall": fine.
4. Traditional mark both of devils and of cuckolded husbands.

5. In faith. "Plackets": slits in garments—but with an obvious sexual allusion.
6. A pedantic way of saying "Follow my footsteps." "Diametarily": diametrically.
7. Gibberish.

What boots° it then to think of God or heaven?   *avails*
Away with such vain fancies, and despair,
5   Despair in God, and trust in Belzebub.
Now go not backward: no, Faustus, be resolute;
Why waverest thou? O, something soundeth in mine ears:
"Abjure this magic, turn to God again."
Ay, and Faustus will turn to God again.
10   To God? He loves thee not:
The god thou servest is thine own appetite,
Wherein is fixed the love of Belzebub.
To him I'll build an altar and a church,
And offer lukewarm blood of newborn babes.
      [*Enter* GOOD ANGEL *and* EVIL.]
15 GOOD ANGEL   Sweet Faustus, leave that execrable° art.   *accursed*
FAUSTUS   Contrition, prayer, repentance: what of them?
GOOD ANGEL   O they are means to bring thee unto heaven.
EVIL ANGEL   Rather illusions, fruits of lunacy,
    That makes men foolish that do trust them most.
20 GOOD ANGEL   Sweet Faustus, think of heaven, and heavenly things.
EVIL ANGEL   No, Faustus, think of honor and of wealth.   [*Exeunt.*]
FAUSTUS   Of wealth!
    Why, the signory° of Emden[8] shall be mine,   *lordship*
    When Mephastophilis shall stand by me.
25 What god can hurt thee, Faustus? Thou art safe,
    Cast no more doubts. Come, Mephastophilis,
    And bring glad tidings from great Lucifer.
    Is't not midnight? Come, Mephastophilis:
    Veni, veni, Mephastophile![9]
      [*Enter* MEPHASTOPHILIS.]
30 Now tell, what says Lucifer thy lord?
MEPHASTOPHILIS   That I shall wait on Faustus whilst he lives,
    So° he will buy my service with his soul.   *provided that*
FAUSTUS   Already Faustus hath hazarded that for thee.
MEPHASTOPHILIS   But Faustus, thou must bequeath it solemnly,
35 And write a deed of gift with thine own blood,
    For that security° craves great Lucifer.   *guarantee*
    If thou deny it, I will back to hell.
FAUSTUS   Stay, Mephastophilis, and tell me,
    What good will my soul do thy lord?
40 MEPHASTOPHILIS   Enlarge his kingdom.
FAUSTUS   Is that the reason he tempts us thus?
MEPHASTOPHILIS   *Solamen miseris socios habuisse doloris.*[1]
FAUSTUS   Have you any pain that tortures others?
MEPHASTOPHILIS   As great as have the human souls of men.
45 But tell me Faustus, shall I have thy soul?
    And I will be thy slave and wait on thee,
    And give thee more than thou hast wit to ask.
FAUSTUS   Ay Mephastophilis, I give it thee.

---

8. A wealthy German trade center.   1. "Misery loves company."
9. "Come, come, Mephastophilis!"

MEPHASTOPHILIS   Then stab thine arm courageously,
  And bind thy soul, that at some certain day
  Great Lucifer may claim it as his own,
  And then be thou as great as Lucifer.
FAUSTUS   Lo Mephastophilis, for love of thee,
  I cut my arm, and with my proper° blood   own
  Assure my soul to be great Lucifer's,
  Chief lord and regent of perpetual night.
  View here the blood that trickles from mine arm,
  And let it be propitious for my wish.
MEPHASTOPHILIS   But Faustus, thou must write it
  In manner of a deed of gift.
FAUSTUS   Ay, so I will; but, Mephastophilis,
  My blood congeals and I can write no more.
MEPHASTOPHILIS   I'll fetch thee fire to dissolve it straight.   [Exit.]
FAUSTUS   What might the staying of my blood portend?
  Is it unwilling I should write this bill?°   contract
  Why streams it not, that I may write afresh:
  "Faustus gives to thee his soul"? Ah, there it stayed!
  Why should'st thou not? Is not thy soul thine own?
  Then write again: "Faustus gives to thee his soul."
        [Enter MEPHASTOPHILIS with a chafer° of coals.]   a portable grate
MEPHASTOPHILIS   Here's fire, come Faustus, set it on.
FAUSTUS   So, now the blood begins to clear again.
  Now will I make an end immediately.
MEPHASTOPHILIS   O what will not I do to obtain his soul!
FAUSTUS   Consummatum est,[2] this bill is ended,
  And Faustus hath bequeathed his soul to Lucifer.
  But what is this inscription on mine arm?
  Homo fuge.° Whither should I fly?   "O man, fly"
  If unto God, he'll throw me down to hell.
  My senses are deceived, here's nothing writ;
  I see it plain, here in this place is writ,
  Homo fuge! Yet shall not Faustus fly.
MEPHASTOPHILIS   I'll fetch him somewhat to delight his mind.   [Exit.]
        [Enter with DEVILS, giving crowns and rich apparel to FAUSTUS, and
        dance, and then depart.]
FAUSTUS   Speak, Mephastophilis, what means this show?
MEPHASTOPHILIS   Nothing, Faustus, but to delight thy mind withal,
  And to show thee what magic can perform.
FAUSTUS   But may I raise up spirits when I please?
MEPHASTOPHILIS   Ay, Faustus, and do greater things than these.
FAUSTUS   Then there's enough for a thousand souls!
  Here, Mephastophilis, receive this scroll,
  A deed of gift of body and of soul:
  But yet conditionally, that thou perform
  All articles prescribed between us both.
MEPHASTOPHILIS   Faustus, I swear by hell and Lucifer
  To effect all promises between us made.

2. "It is finished": a blasphemy, because these are the words of Christ on the Cross (John 19.30).

95 FAUSTUS Then hear me read them. On these conditions following:
First, that Faustus may be a spirit[3] in form and substance.
Secondly, that Mephastophilis shall be his servant, and at his command.
Thirdly, that Mephastophilis shall do for him, and bring him whatso-
100 *ever.*
Fourthly, that he shall be in his chamber or house invisible.
Lastly, that he shall appear to the said John Faustus at all times, in what form or shape soever he please.
I, John Faustus of Wittenberg, doctor, by these presents,[4] do give
105 *both body and soul to Lucifer, Prince of the East, and his minister Mephastophilis; and furthermore grant unto them that, four and twenty years being expired, the articles above-written inviolate, full power to fetch or carry the said John Faustus, body and soul, flesh, blood, or goods, into their habitation wheresoever.*
110   *By me John Faustus.*
MEPHASTOPHILIS Speak, Faustus: do you deliver this as your deed?
FAUSTUS Ay, take it; and the devil give thee good on't.
MEPHASTOPHILIS Now, Faustus, ask what thou wilt.
FAUSTUS First will I question with thee about hell:
115 Tell me, where is the place that men call hell?
MEPHASTOPHILIS Under the heavens.
FAUSTUS Ay, but whereabouts?
MEPHASTOPHILIS Within the bowels of these elements,
Where we are tortured and remain for ever.
120 Hell hath no limits, nor is circumscribed
In one self place; for where we are is hell,
And where hell is, there must we ever be.
And to conclude, when all the world dissolves,
And every creature shall be purified,
125 All places shall be hell that is not heaven.
FAUSTUS Come, I think hell's a fable.
MEPHASTOPHILIS Ay, think so still, till experience change thy mind.
FAUSTUS Why? think'st thou then that Faustus shall be damned?
MEPHASTOPHILIS Ay, of necessity, for here's the scroll
130 Wherein thou hast given thy soul to Lucifer.
FAUSTUS Ay, and body too; but what of that?
Think'st thou that Faustus is so fond° to imagine   foolish
That after this life there is any pain?
Tush, these are trifles and mere old wives' tales.
MEPHASTOPHILIS But Faustus, I am an instance to prove the
135 contrary:
For I am damned, and am now in hell.
FAUSTUS How, now in hell? Nay, and this be hell, I'll willingly be
damned here! What? walking, disputing, etc. . . . But leaving off
this, let me have a wife, the fairest maid in Germany, for I am
140 wanton and lascivious, and cannot live without a wife.

3. I.e., have the supernatural powers of a spirit.
4. Legal articles.

MEPHASTOPHILIS   How, a wife? I prithee Faustus, talk not of a wife.[5]

FAUSTUS   Nay sweet Mephastophilis, fetch me one, for I will have one.

MEPHASTOPHILIS   Well, thou wilt have one; sit there till I come.
I'll fetch thee a wife in the devil's name.   [*Exit.*]
        [*Enter with a* DEVIL *dressed like a woman, with fireworks.*]

MEPHASTOPHILIS   Tell, Faustus, how dost thou like thy wife?

FAUSTUS   A plague on her for a hot whore!

MEPHASTOPHILIS   Tut, Faustus, marriage is but a ceremonial toy;
    If thou lovest me, think no more of it.
    I'll cull thee out the fairest courtesans
    And bring them every morning to thy bed:
    She whom thine eye shall like, thy heart shall have,
    Be she as chaste as was Penelope,
    As wise as Saba,[6] or as beautiful
    As was bright Lucifer before his fall.
    Hold, take this book, peruse it thoroughly:
    The iterating° of these lines brings gold;   *repeating*
    The framing° of this circle on the ground   *drawing*
    Brings whirlwinds, tempests, thunder and lightning.
    Pronounce this thrice devoutly to thyself,
    And men in armor shall appear to thee,
    Ready to execute what thou desirest.

FAUSTUS   Thanks, Mephastophilis, yet fain would I have a book
    wherein I might behold all spells and incantations, that I might
    raise up spirits when I please.

MEPHASTOPHILIS   Here they are in this book.   [*There turn to them.*]

FAUSTUS   Now would I have a book where I might see all characters
    and planets of the heavens, that I might know their motions and
    dispositions.[7]

MEPHASTOPHILIS   Here they are too.   [*Turn to them.*]

FAUSTUS   Nay, let me have one book more, and then I have done,
    wherein I might see all plants, herbs, and trees that grow upon the
    earth.

MEPHASTOPHILIS   Here they be.

FAUSTUS   O thou art deceived!

MEPHASTOPHILIS   Tut, I warrant[8] thee.   [*Turn to them.*]

FAUSTUS   When I behold the heavens, then I repent,
    And curse thee, wicked Mephastophilis,
    Because thou hast deprived me of those joys.

MEPHASTOPHILIS   Why Faustus,
    Think'st thou that heaven is such a glorious thing?
    I tell thee 'tis not half so fair as thou,
    Or any man that breathes on earth.

FAUSTUS   How prov'st thou that?

MEPHASTOPHILIS   It was made for man, therefore is man more excellent.

---

5. Mephastophilis cannot produce a wife for
Faustus because marriage is a sacrament.
6. The queen of Sheba, who tested Solomon's wisdom with "hard questions" (1 Kings 10). "Penelope": the wife of Ulysses, famed for chastity and
fidelity.
7. Relationships to other planets. "Characters":
occult symbols.
8. Assure.

FAUSTUS   If it were made for man, 'twas made for me:
    I will renounce this magic, and repent.
      [*Enter* GOOD ANGEL *and* EVIL ANGEL.]
    GOOD ANGEL   Faustus, repent, yet° God will pity thee.   *still*
    EVIL ANGEL   Thou art a spirit,° God cannot pity thee.   *evil spirit, devil*
190   FAUSTUS   Who buzzeth in mine ears I am a spirit?
      Be I a devil, yet God may pity me.
      Ay, God will pity me if I repent.
    EVIL ANGEL   Ay, but Faustus never shall repent.   [*Exeunt.*]
    FAUSTUS   My heart's so hardened I cannot repent!
195   Scarce can I name salvation, faith, or heaven,
    But fearful echoes thunders in mine ears,
    "Faustus, thou are damned"; then swords and knives,
    Poison, guns, halters,° and envenomed steel   *hangman's nooses*
    Are laid before me to dispatch myself:
200   And long ere this I should have slain myself,
    Had not sweet pleasure conquered deep despair.
    Have I not made blind Homer sing to me
    Of Alexander's[9] love, and Oenon's death?
    And hath not he that built the walls of Thebes
205   With ravishing sound of his melodious harp,[1]
    Made music with my Mephastophilis?
    Why should I die then, or basely despair?
    I am resolved! Faustus shall ne'er repent.
    Come, Mephastophilis, let us dispute again,
210   And argue of divine astrology.
    Tell me, are there many heavens above the moon?
    Are all celestial bodies but one globe,
    As is the substance of this centric earth?[2]
    MEPHASTOPHILIS   As are the elements, such are the spheres,
215   Mutually folded in each other's orb.
    And, Faustus, all jointly move upon one axletree
    Whose terminè° is termed the world's wide pole,   *end*
    Nor are the names of Saturn, Mars, or Jupiter
    Feigned, but are erring stars.[3]
220   FAUSTUS   But tell me, have they all one motion, both *situ et tempore?*[4]
    MEPHASTOPHILIS   All jointly move from east to west in four-and-
    twenty hours upon the poles of the world, but differ in their
    motion upon the poles of the zodiac.[5]
    FAUSTUS   Tush, these slender trifles Wagner can decide!
225   Hath Mephastophilis no greater skill?

---

9. Alexander is another name for Paris, the lover of Oenone; later he deserted her and abducted Helen, causing the Trojan War. Oenone refused to heal the wounds Paris received in battle, and when he died of them, she killed herself in remorse.
1. The legendary musician Amphion, whose harp caused stones, of themselves, to form the walls of Thebes.
2. Faustus asks whether all the apparently different heavenly bodies form really "one globe" like the earth. Mephastophilis answers that like the elements, which are separate but combined, the heavenly bodies are separate but their spheres are enfolded and they move on one axletree.
3. It is appropriate to give individual names to Saturn, Mars, Jupiter, and the other planets—which are called wandering, or "erring" stars. The fixed stars were in the eighth sphere (the firmament, or crystalline sphere).
4. "In position and in time."
5. The common axletree on which all the spheres revolve.

Who knows not the double motion of the planets?
The first is finished in a natural day, the second thus: as Saturn in
thirty years; Jupiter in twelve; Mars in four; the Sun, Venus, and
Mercury in a year; the Moon in twenty-eight days. Tush, these are
freshmen's suppositions. But tell me, hath every sphere a domin-
ion or *intelligentia?*[6]
MEPHASTOPHILIS Ay.
FAUSTUS How many heavens or spheres are there?
MEPHASTOPHILIS Nine: the seven planets, the firmament, and the
empyreal heaven.[7]
FAUSTUS Well, resolve me then in this question: why have we not
conjunctions, oppositions,[8] aspects, eclipses, all at one time, but
in some years we have more, in some less?
MEPHASTOPHILIS *Per inaequalem motum respectu totius.*[9]
FAUSTUS Well, I am answered. Tell me who made the world?
MEPHASTOPHILIS I will not.
FAUSTUS Sweet Mephastophilis, tell me.
MEPHASTOPHILIS Move° me not, for I will not tell thee.   urge
FAUSTUS Villain, have I not bound thee to tell me anything?
MEPHASTOPHILIS Ay, that is not against our kingdom; but this is.
Think thou on hell, Faustus, for thou art damned.
FAUSTUS Think, Faustus, upon God, that made the world.
MEPHASTOPHILIS Remember this.   [*Exit.*]
FAUSTUS Ay, go accursèd spirit, to ugly hell,
'Tis thou hast damned distressèd Faustus' soul:
Is't not too late?
        [*Enter* GOOD ANGEL *and* EVIL.]
EVIL ANGEL Too late.
GOOD ANGEL Never too late, if Faustus will repent.
EVIL ANGEL If thou repent, devils shall tear thee in pieces.
GOOD ANGEL Repent, and they shall never raze° thy skin.   graze
        [*Exeunt.*]
FAUSTUS Ah Christ my Savior! seek to save
Distressèd Faustus' soul!
        [*Enter* LUCIFER, BELZEBUB, *and* MEPHASTOPHILIS.]
LUCIFER Christ cannot save thy soul, for he is just.
There's none but I have interest in the same.
FAUSTUS O who art thou that look'st so terrible?
LUCIFER I am Lucifer, and this is my companion prince in hell.
FAUSTUS O Faustus, they are come to fetch away thy soul!
LUCIFER We come to tell thee thou dost injure us.
Thou talk'st of Christ, contrary to thy promise.
Thou should'st not think of God; think of the devil,
And his dam[1] too.
FAUSTUS Nor will I henceforth: pardon me in this,

6. An angel, or intelligence, thought to be the
source of motion in each sphere.
7. The ninth sphere was the immovable empyrean.
8. "Oppositions": when two planets are most
remote from each other. "Conjunctions": the
apparent joinings of two planets. These are two
of the planetary "aspects" (relative positions)
that figure in astrology.
9. "Because of their unequal movements in
respect of the whole."
1. Mother. "The devil and his dam" was a common colloquial expression.

And Faustus vows never to look to heaven,
Never to name God, or to pray to him,
270 To burn his Scriptures, slay his ministers,
And make my spirits pull his churches down.

LUCIFER Do so, and we will highly gratify thee. Faustus, we are
come from hell to show thee some pastime; sit down, and thou
shalt see all the Seven Deadly Sins[2] appear in their proper shapes.

275 FAUSTUS That sight will be as pleasing unto me as Paradise was to
Adam, the first day of his creation.

LUCIFER Talk not of Paradise, nor creation, but mark this show;
talk of the devil and nothing else. Come away.
[*Enter the* SEVEN DEADLY SINS.]
Now Faustus, examine them of their several names and disposi-
280 tions.

FAUSTUS What art thou, the first?

PRIDE I am Pride: I disdain to have any parents. I am like to Ovid's
flea, I can creep into every corner of a wench: sometimes like a
periwig,[3] I sit upon her brow; or like a fan of feathers, I kiss her lips.
285 Indeed I do—what do I not! But fie, what a scent is here? I'll not
speak another word, except the ground were perfumed and covered
with cloth of arras.[4]

FAUSTUS What art thou, the second?

COVETOUSNESS I am Covetousness, begotten of an old churl in an
290 old leathern bag; and might I have my wish, I would desire that this
house, and all the people in it, were turned to gold, that I might
lock you up in my good chest. O my sweet gold!

FAUSTUS What art thou, the third?

WRATH I am Wrath. I had neither father nor mother: I leaped out of
295 a lion's mouth when I was scarce half an hour old, and ever since
I have run up and down the world with this case of rapiers, wounding myself when I had nobody to fight withal. I was born in hell—
and look to it, for some of you shall be my father.

FAUSTUS What art thou, the fourth?

300 ENVY I am Envy, begotten of a chimney-sweeper and an oyster-wife.
I cannot read, and therefore wish all books were burnt; I am lean
with seeing others eat—O that there would come a famine through
all the world, that all might die, and I live alone; then thou should'st
see how fat I would be! But must thou sit and I stand? Come down,
305 with a vengeance!

FAUSTUS Away, envious rascal! What art thou, the fifth?

GLUTTONY Who, I sir? I am Gluttony. My parents are all dead, and
the devil a penny they have left me but a bare pension, and that is
thirty meals a day and ten bevers[5]—a small trifle to suffice nature.
310 O, I come of a royal parentage: my grandfather was a gammon[6] of
bacon, my grandmother a hogshead of claret wine; my godfathers

2. Pride, avarice, lust, anger, gluttony, envy, and
sloth, called deadly because they lead to spirtual
death. All other sins are said to grow out of them
(cf. the procession of the Seven Deadly Sins in
Spenser's *The Faerie Queene*, Book 1, canto 4,
stanzas 16–37).
3. Wig. "Ovid's flea": a salacious medieval poem

"Carmen de Pulice" (Song of the Flea) was attributed to Ovid.
4. Arras in Flanders exported fine cloth used
for tapestry hangings. "Scent": stink. "Except":
unless.
5. Snacks.
6. The lower side of pork, including the leg.

were these: Peter Pickled-Herring, and Martin Martlemas-Beef.[7] O but my godmother! She was a jolly gentlewoman, and well-beloved in every good town and city; her name was Mistress Margery March-Beer.[8] Now, Faustus, thou hast heard all my progeny;[9] wilt thou bid me to supper?

FAUSTUS   No, I'll see thee hanged; thou wilt eat up all my victuals.

GLUTTONY   Then the devil choke thee!

FAUSTUS   Choke thyself, Glutton. What art thou, the sixth?

SLOTH   I am Sloth; I was begotten on a sunny bank, where I have lain ever since—and you have done me great injury to bring me from thence. Let me be carried thither again by Gluttony and Lechery. I'll not speak another word for a king's ransom.

FAUSTUS   What are you, Mistress Minx, the seventh and last?

LECHERY   Who, I sir? I am one that loves an inch of raw mutton better than an ell of fried stockfish;[1] and the first letter of my name begins with Lechery.

LUCIFER   Away! To hell, to hell!   [Exeunt the SINS.]
Now Faustus, how dost thou like this?

FAUSTUS   O this feeds my soul!

LUCIFER   Tut, Faustus, in hell is all manner of delight.

FAUSTUS   O might I see hell, and return again, how happy were I then!

LUCIFER   Thou shalt; I will send for thee at midnight. In meantime, take this book, peruse it thoroughly, and thou shalt turn thyself into what shape thou wilt.

FAUSTUS   Great thanks, mighty Lucifer; this will I keep as chary[2] as my life.

LUCIFER   Farewell, Faustus; and think on the devil.

FAUSTUS   Farewell, great Lucifer; come, Mephastophilis.

                                        [Exeunt OMNES.]

SCENE 6

[Enter ROBIN the ostler[3] with a book in his hand.]

ROBIN   O this is admirable! here I ha' stolen one of Doctor Faustus' conjuring books, and i'faith I mean to search some circles[4] for my own use: now will I make all the maidens in our parish dance at my pleasure stark naked before me, and so by that means I shall see more than ere I felt or saw yet.

            [Enter RAFE calling ROBIN.]

RAFE   Robin, prithee come away, there's a gentleman tarries to have his horse, and he would have his things rubbed and made clean. He keeps such a chafing[5] with my mistress about it, and she has sent me to look thee out. Prithee, come away.

ROBIN   Keep out, keep out; or else you are blown up, you are dismembered, Rafe. Keep out, for I am about a roaring[6] piece of work.

---

7. Meat, salted to preserve it during the winter, was prepared around Martinmas (November 11).
8. A rich ale, made in March.
9. Lineage.
1. Dried cod. "Mutton": frequently a bawdy term in Elizabethan English; here, the penis. "Ell":

forty-five inches.
2. Carefully.
3. Hostler, stablehand.
4. Magicians' circles, but with a sexual innuendo.
5. Scolding. "Tarries": is waiting.
6. Dangerous.

RAFE   Come, what dost thou with that same book? Thou canst not
        read!
ROBIN   Yes, my master and mistress shall find that I can read—he
15   for his forehead,[7] she for her private study. She's born to bear with
        me,[8] or else my art fails.
RAFE   Why Robin, what book is that?
ROBIN   What book? Why the most intolerable[9] book for conjuring
        that ere was invented by any brimstone devil.
20 RAFE   Canst thou conjure with it?
ROBIN   I can do all these things easily with it: first, I can make thee
        drunk with 'ipocrase[1] at any tavern in Europe for nothing, that's
        one of my conjuring works.
RAFE   Our master parson says that's nothing.
25 ROBIN   True, Rafe! And more, Rafe, if thou hast any mind to Nan
        Spit, our kitchen maid, then turn her and wind her to thy own
        use, as often as thou wilt, and at midnight.
RAFE   O brave Robin! Shall I have Nan Spit, and to mine own use?
        On that condition I'll feed thy devil with horsebread as long as he
30   lives, of free cost.[2]
ROBIN   No more, sweet Rafe; let's go and make clean our boots
        which lie foul upon our hands, and then to our conjuring in the
        devil's name.   [*Exeunt.*]

CHORUS 2

        [*Enter* WAGNER *solus.*]
WAGNER   Learned Faustus,
        To know the secrets of astronomy
        Graven in the book of Jove's high firmament,
        Did mount himself to scale Olympus'[3] top.
5   Being seated in a chariot burning bright,
        Drawn by the strength of yokèd dragons' necks.
        He now is gone to prove cosmography,[4]
        And, as I guess, will first arrive at Rome
        To see the pope, and manner of his court,
10   And take some part of holy Peter's feast,[5]
        That to this day is highly solemnized.   [*Exit* WAGNER.]

SCENE 7

        [*Enter* FAUSTUS *and* MEPHASTOPHILIS.]
FAUSTUS   Having now, my good Mephastophilis,
        Passed with delight the stately town of Trier,[6]
        Environed round with airy mountain tops,
        With walls of flint, and deep entrenchèd lakes,°   moats
5   Not to be won by any conquering prince;
        From Paris next, coasting° the realm of France,   traversing

---

7. That is, Robin intends to give his master
horns—cuckold him.
8. I.e., bear his weight, or bear him a child.
9. Irresistible.
1. Robin's pronunciation of *hippocras*, a spiced
wine.

2. Free of charge. "Horsebread": fodder.
3. The home of the gods in Greek mythology.
4. To test the accuracy of maps.
5. St. Peter's feast is June 29.
6. Treves (in Prussia).

We saw the river Main fall into Rhine,
Whose banks are set with groves of fruitful vines;
Then up to Naples, rich Campania,
With buildings fair and gorgeous to the eye,
The streets straight forth, and paved with finest brick,
Quarters the town in four equivalents;
There saw we learned Maro's[7] golden tomb,
The way° he cut, an English mile in length,   *tunnel*
Thorough° a rock of stone in one night's space.   *through*
From thence to Venice, Padua, and the rest,
In midst of which a sumptuous temple° stands   *St. Mark's in Venice*
That threats the stars with her aspiring top.
Thus hitherto hath Faustus spent his time.
But tell me now, what resting place is this?
Hast thou, as erst° I did command,   *earlier*
Conducted me within the walls of Rome?

MEPHASTOPHILIS   Faustus, I have; and because we will not be unpro-
vided, I have taken up his holiness' privy chamber[8] for our use.

FAUSTUS   I hope his holiness will bid us welcome.

MEPHASTOPHILIS   Tut, 'tis no matter, man, we'll be bold with his good
cheer.[9]
And now, my Faustus, that thou may'st perceive
What Rome containeth to delight thee with,
Know that this city stands upon seven hills
That underprop the groundwork of the same;
Just through the midst runs flowing Tiber's stream,
With winding banks, that cut it in two parts;
Over the which four stately bridges lean,
That makes safe passage to each part of Rome.
Upon the bridge called Ponte Angelo
Erected is a castle passing[1] strong,
Within whose walls such store of ordnance are
And double cannons, framed of carvèd brass,
As match the days within one complete year—
Besides the gates and high pyramides°   *obelisks*
Which Julius Caesar brought from Africa.

FAUSTUS   Now by the kingdoms of infernal rule,
Of Styx, Acheron, and the fiery lake
Of ever-burning Phlegethon,[2] I swear
That I do long to see the monuments
And situation of bright-splendent Rome.
Come therefore, let's away.

MEPHASTOPHILIS   Nay, Faustus, stay. I know you'd fain see the pope,
And take some part of holy Peter's feast,
Where thou shalt see a troop of bald-pate friars,
Whose *summum bonum*[3] is in belly-cheer.

---

7. Virgil's. In medieval legend the Roman poet
Virgil was considered a magician whose powers
produced a tunnel on the promontory of Posilippo
at Naples, near his tomb.
8. Private quarters.

9. Entertainment.
1. Surpassingly. Actually the castle is on the
bank, not the bridge.
2. Classical names for rivers of the underworld.
3. The greatest good; often refers to God.

FAUSTUS   Well, I am content to compass[4] then some sport,
And by their folly make us merriment.

55   Then charm me that I may be invisible, to do what I please
unseen of any whilst I stay in Rome.

MEPHASTOPHILIS *[casts a spell on him].*   So Faustus, now do what
thou wilt, thou shalt not be discerned.

[Sound a sennet;[5] enter the POPE *and the* CARDINAL OF LORRAINE *to the banquet, with* FRIARS *attending.]*

POPE   My lord of Lorraine, will't please you draw near?

60   FAUSTUS   Fall to; and the devil choke you and[6] you spare.

POPE   How now, who's that which spake? Friars, look about.

1 FRIAR   Here's nobody, if it like[7] your holiness.

POPE   My lord, here is a dainty dish was sent to me from the bishop
of Milan.

65   FAUSTUS   I thank you, sir.   *[Snatch it.]*

POPE   How now, who's that which snatched the meat from me? Will
no man look? My lord, this dish was sent me from the cardinal of
Florence.

FAUSTUS   You say true? I'll have't.   *[Snatch it.]*

70   POPE   What, again! My lord, I'll drink to your grace.

FAUSTUS   I'll pledge[8] your grace.   *[Snatch the cup.]*

LORRAINE   My lord, it may be some ghost newly crept out of purgatory come to beg a pardon of your holiness.

POPE   It may be so; friars, prepare a dirge[9] to lay the fury of this ghost.

75   Once again my lord, fall to.   *[The* POPE *crosseth himself.]*

FAUSTUS   What, are you crossing of your self? Well, use that trick
no more, I would advise you.

[Cross again.]

FAUSTUS   Well, there's the second time; aware[1] the third! I give you
fair warning.

[Cross again, and FAUSTUS *hits him a box of the ear, and they all run away.]*

80   Come on, Mephastophilis, what shall we do?

MEPHASTOPHILIS   Nay, I know not; we shall be cursed with bell,
book, and candle.[2]

FAUSTUS   How! Bell, book, and candle; candle, book, and bell,
Forward and backward, to curse Faustus to hell.

85   Anon you shall hear a hog grunt, a calf bleat, and an ass bray,
Because it is St. Peter's holy day.

[Enter all the FRIARS *to sing the Dirge.]*

1 FRIAR   Come brethren, let's about our business with good
devotion.

[Sing this.]

Cursed be he that stole away His Holiness' meat from the table.
Maledicat Dominus.[3]

---

4. Take part in.
5. A set of notes on the trumpet or cornet.
6. If. "Fall to": start eating.
7. Please.
8. Toast.
9. A requiem mass. But what actually follows is

a litany of curses.
1. Beware.
2. The traditional paraphernalia for cursing and excommunication.
3. "May the Lord curse him."

Cursed be he that struck His Holiness a blow on the face.
    Maledicat Dominus.
Cursed be he that took Friar Sandelo a blow on the pate.
    Maledicat Dominus.
Cursed be he that disturbeth our holy dirge.
    Maledicat Dominus.
Cursed be he that took away His Holiness' wine.
    Maledicat dominus.
       Et omnes sancti.[4] Amen.
    [*Beat the* FRIARS, *and fling fireworks among them, and so Exeunt.*]

SCENE 8

    [*Enter* ROBIN *and* RAFE *with a silver goblet.*]

ROBIN   Come, Rafe, did not I tell thee we were forever made by this Doctor Faustus' book? *Ecce signum!*[5] Here's a simple purchase for horsekeepers: our horses shall eat no hay as long as this lasts.
    [*Enter the* VINTNER.]

RAFE   But Robin, here comes the vintner.

ROBIN   Hush, I'll gull him supernaturally! Drawer,[6] I hope all is paid; God be with you. Come, Rafe.

VINTNER   Soft, sir, a word with you. I must yet have a goblet paid from you ere you go.

ROBIN   I, a goblet, Rafe? I, a goblet? I scorn you: and you are but a etc.[7] . . . I, a goblet? Search me.

VINTNER   I mean so, sir, with your favor.   [*Searches* ROBIN.]

ROBIN   How say you now?

VINTNER   I must say somewhat to your fellow; you, sir!

RAFE   Me, sir? Me, sir? Search your fill. Now sir, you may be ashamed to burden honest men with a matter of truth.

VINTNER   [*searches* RAFE] Well, t'one of you hath this goblet about you.

ROBIN   You lie, drawer; 'tis afore me. Sirra you, I'll teach ye to impeach[8] honest men: [*to* RAFE] stand by. [*to the* VINTNER] I'll scour you for a goblet—stand aside, you were best—I charge you in the name of Belzebub—look to the goblet, Rafe!

VINTNER   What mean you, sirra?

ROBIN   I'll tell you what I mean: [*he reads*] *Sanctobulorum Periphrasticon*—nay, I'll tickle you, vintner—look to the goblet, Rafe—*Polypragmos Belseborams framanto pacostiphos tostis Mephastophilis, etc. . . . *[9]
    [*Enter* MEPHASTOPHILIS: *sets squibs*[1] *at their backs: they run about.*]

VINTNER   *O nomine Domine!*[2] What mean'st thou, Robin? Thou hast no goblet.

RAFE   *Peccatum peccatorum!*[3] Here's thy goblet, good vintner.

---

4. "And all the saints (also curse him)."
5. "Behold the proof."
6. Wine-drawer. "Gull": trick.
7. The actor might ad lib abuse at this point.
8. Accuse.
9. Dog-Latin, as Robin attempts to conjure from Faustus's book.

1. Firecrackers. Evidently Mephastophilis is on stage only long enough to set off the firecrackers and is not seen by Robin, Rafe, or the vintner. He then reenters at line 32.
2. "In the name of the Lord"; the Latin invocations are used in swearing.
3. "Sin of sins!"

30 ROBIN *Misericordia pro nobis!*[4] What shall I do? Good devil, forgive
me now, and I'll never rob thy library more.
[*Enter to them* MEPHASTOPHILIS.]
MEPHASTOPHILIS Vanish, villains, th'one like an ape, another like a
bear, the third an ass, for doing this enterprise. [*Exit* VINTNER.]
Monarch of hell, under whose black survey
35 Great potentates do kneel with awful fear;
Upon whose altars thousand souls do lie;
How am I vexèd with these villains' charms!
From Constantinople am I hither come,
Only for pleasure of these damnèd slaves.
40 ROBIN How, from Constantinople? You have had a great journey!
Will you take sixpence in your purse to pay for your supper, and be
gone?
MEPHASTOPHILIS Well, villains, for your presumption, I transform
thee into an ape, and thee into a dog; and so begone! [*Exit.*]
45 ROBIN How, into an ape? That's brave: I'll have fine sport with the
boys; I'll get nuts and apples enow.[5]
RAFE And I must be a dog.
ROBIN I'faith, thy head will never be out of the potage[6] pot.
[*Exeunt.*]

CHORUS 3

[*Enter* CHORUS.[7]]
CHORUS When Faustus had with pleasure ta'en the view
Of rarest things, and royal courts of kings,
He stayed his course, and so returnèd home;
Where such as bare his absence but with grief—
5 I mean his friends and nearest companions—
Did gratulate his safety with kind words.
And in their conference of what befell,
Touching his journey through the world and air,
They put forth questions of astrology,
10 Which Faustus answered with such learnèd skill
As they admired and wondered at his wit.
Now is his fame spread forth in every land:
Amongst the rest the emperor is one,
Carolus the Fifth,[8] at whose palace now
15 Faustus is feasted 'mongst his noblemen.
What there he did in trial° of his art   demonstration
I leave untold: your eyes shall see performed.   [*Exit.*]

SCENE 9

[*Enter* EMPEROR, FAUSTUS, *and a* KNIGHT, *with Attendants.*]
EMPEROR Master Doctor Faustus, I have heard strange report of thy
knowledge in the black art, how that none in my empire, nor in the
whole world, can compare with thee for the rare effects of magic.

4. "Have mercy on us!"
5. Enough. "Brave": splendid.
6. Porridge.
7. I.e., Wagner.
8. The Holy Roman Emperor Charles V (reigned 1519–56).

They say thou hast a familiar spirit, by whom thou canst accomplish what thou list! This therefore is my request: that thou let me see some proof of thy skill, that mine eyes may be witnesses to confirm what mine ears have heard reported. And here I swear to thee, by the honor of mine imperial crown, that whatever thou dost, thou shalt be in no ways prejudiced or endamaged.

KNIGHT [*aside*]   I'faith, he looks much like a conjuror.

FAUSTUS   My gracious sovereign, though I must confess myself far inferior to the report men have published, and nothing answerable to[9] the honor of your imperial majesty, yet for that love and duty binds me thereunto, I am content to do whatsoever your majesty shall command me.

EMPEROR   Then Doctor Faustus, mark what I shall say. As I was sometime solitary set within my closet,[1] sundry thoughts arose about the honor of mine ancestors—how they had won by prowess such exploits, got such riches, subdued so many kingdoms, as we that do succeed, or they that shall hereafter possess our throne, shall (I fear me) never attain to that degree of high renown and great authority. Amongst which kings is Alexander the Great,[2] chief spectacle of the world's pre-eminence:
The bright shining of whose glorious acts
Lightens the world with his reflecting beams;
As when I hear but motion° made of him,   *mention*
It grieves my soul I never saw the man.
If therefore thou, by cunning of thine art,
Canst raise this man from hollow vaults below,
Where lies entombed this famous conqueror,
And bring with him his beauteous paramour,[3]
Both in their right shapes, gesture, and attire
They used to wear during their time of life,
Thou shalt both satisfy my just desire
And give me cause to praise thee whilst I live.

FAUSTUS   My gracious lord, I am ready to accomplish your request, so far forth as by art and power of my spirit I am able to perform.

KNIGHT [*aside*]   I'faith, that's just nothing at all.

FAUSTUS   But, if it like your grace, it is not in my ability to present before your eyes the true substantial bodies of those two deceased princes, which long since are consumed to dust.

KNIGHT [*aside*]   Ay, marry,[4] master doctor, now there's a sign of grace in you, when you will confess the truth.

FAUSTUS   But such spirits as can lively resemble Alexander and his paramour shall appear before your grace, in that manner that they best lived in, in their most flourishing estate: which I doubt not shall sufficiently content your imperial majesty.

EMPEROR   Go to, master doctor, let me see them presently.[5]

KNIGHT   Do you hear, master doctor? You bring Alexander and his paramour before the emperor!

---

9. Not at all deserving of.
1. Private chamber.
2. The emperor traces his ancestry to the world conqueror (356–323 B.C.E.).

3. Probably Roxana, Alexander's wife.
4. To be sure.
5. Immediately. "Estate": condition.

FAUSTUS   How then, sir?

KNIGHT   I'faith, that's as true as Diana turned me to a stag.

FAUSTUS   No sir; but when Actaeon died, he left the horns[6] for you!
Mephastophilis, begone   [*Exit* MEPHASTOPHILIS.]

55 KNIGHT   Nay, and[7] you go to conjuring I'll be gone.   [*Exit* KNIGHT.]

FAUSTUS   I'll meet with you anon[8] for interrupting me so. Here they
are, my gracious lord.

[*Enter* MEPHASTOPHILIS *with* ALEXANDER *and his* PARAMOUR.]

EMPEROR   Master doctor, I heard this lady, while she lived, had a
wart or mole in her neck; how shall I know whether it be so or no?

60 FAUSTUS   Your highness may boldly go and see.

[*The* EMPEROR *examines the lady's neck.*]

EMPEROR   Sure, these are no spirits, but the true substantial bodies
of those two deceased princes.

[*Exit* ALEXANDER (*and his* PARAMOUR).]

FAUSTUS   Will't please your highness now to send for the knight
that was so pleasant with me here of late?

65 EMPEROR   One of you call him forth.

[*Enter the* KNIGHT *with a pair of horns on his head.*]

How now, sir knight? Why, I had thought thou hadst been a bachelor, but now I see thou hast a wife that not only gives thee horns
but makes thee wear them! Feel on thy head.

KNIGHT   Thou damnèd wretch and execrable° dog,   detestable

70 Bred in the concave of some monstrous rock,
How dar'st thou thus abuse a gentleman?
Villain, I say, undo what thou hast done.

FAUSTUS   O not so fast, sir, there's no haste but good. Are you
remembered[9] how you crossed me in my conference with the

75 emperor? I think I have met with you for it.

EMPEROR   Good master doctor, at my entreaty release him; he hath
done penance sufficient.

FAUSTUS   My gracious lord, not so much for the injury he offered me
here in your presence, as to delight you with some mirth, hath Faus-

80 tus worthily requited this injurious knight; which being all I desire,
I am content to release him of his horns. And, sir knight, hereafter
speak well of scholars: Mephastophilis, transform him straight.[1]
Now, my good lord, having done my duty, I humbly take my leave.

EMPEROR   Farewell, master doctor; yet ere you go, expect from me a

85 bounteous reward.

[*Exit* EMPEROR (*and his* ATTENDANTS).]

FAUSTUS   Now, Mephastophilis, the restless course
That time doth run with calm and silent foot,
Shortening my days and thread of vital life,
Calls for the payment of my latest years;

90 Therefore, sweet Mephastophilis, let us make haste to Wittenberg.

---

6. Horns were traditionally a sign of the cuckolded husband (cf. Scene 6, lines 14–15).
"Actaeon": the hunter of classical legend who happened to see the goddess Diana bathing. For punishment he was changed into a stag; he was then
chased and killed by his own hounds.

7. If.
8. Shortly. "Meet with": be revenged on.
9. Have you forgotten. "No haste but good": a
proverb: no point hurrying, unless it's to good
effect.
1. Immediately.

MEPHASTOPHILIS   What, will you go on horseback or on foot?

FAUSTUS   Nay, till I am past this fair and pleasant green, I'll walk on foot.

SCENE *10*

[*Enter a* HORSE-COURSER.[2]]

HORSE-COURSER   I have been all this day seeking one Master Fustian: 'Mass,[3] see where he is! God save you, master doctor.

FAUSTUS   What, horse-courser: you are well met.

HORSE-COURSER   Do you hear, sir; I have brought you forty dollars[4] for your horse.

FAUSTUS   I cannot sell him so: if thou lik'st him for fifty, take him.

HORSE-COURSER   Alas sir, I have no more. I pray you speak for me.

MEPHASTOPHILIS   I pray you let him have him; he is an honest fellow, and he has a great charge[5]—neither wife nor child.

FAUSTUS   Well, come, give me your money; my boy will deliver him to you. But I must tell you one thing before you have him: ride him not into the water at any hand.[6]

HORSE-COURSER   Why sir, will he not drink of all waters?

FAUSTUS   O yes, he will drink of all waters, but ride him not into the water. Ride him over hedge or ditch, or where thou wilt, but not into the water.

HORSE-COURSER   Well sir. Now am I made man forever: I'll not leave my horse for forty! If he had but the quality of hey ding ding, hey ding ding,[7] I'd make a brave living on him! He has a buttock as slick as an eel. Well, God b'y,[8] sir; your boy will deliver him me. But hark ye sir, if my horse be sick, or ill at ease, if I bring his water[9] to you, you'll tell me what it is?

[*Exit* HORSE-COURSER.]

FAUSTUS   Away, you villain! What, dost think I am a horse-doctor?
What art thou, Faustus, but a man condemned to die?
Thy fatal time° doth draw to final end.   *time allotted by fate*
Despair doth drive distrust unto my thoughts.
Confound these passions with a quiet sleep:
Tush, Christ did call the thief upon the cross.[1]
Then rest thee, Faustus, quiet in conceit.°   *in mind*

[*Sleep in his chair.*]

[*Enter* HORSE-COURSER *all wet, crying.*]

HORSE-COURSER   Alas, alas, Doctor Fustian, quotha? 'Mass, Doctor Lopus[2] was never such a doctor! H'as given me a purgation, h'as purged me of forty dollars! I shall never see them more. But yet, like an ass as I was, I would not be ruled by him; for he bade me

---

2. Horse trader, traditionally a sharp bargainer or cheat.
3. By the Mass. "Fustian": the horse-courser's comic mistake for Faustus's name.
4. Common German coins.
5. Burden.
6. On any account.
7. I.e., he wishes his horse were a stallion, not a gelding, so he could put him to stud.
8. Good-bye (contracted from "God be with

you").
9. Urine.
1. In Luke 23.39–43 one of the two thieves crucified with Jesus is promised paradise. "Tush": a scoffing exclamation.
2. In February 1594 Roderigo Lopez, the queen's personal physician, was executed for plotting to poison her. Obviously Marlowe, who died in 1593, did not write the line. "Quotha": he said.

I should ride him into no water. Now I, thinking my horse had had
some rare quality that he would not have had me known of, I, like
a vent'rous youth, rid him into the deep pond at the town's end.
I was no sooner in the middle of the pond, but my horse vanished
away, and I sat upon a bottle[3] of hay, never so near drowning in
my life! But I'll seek out my doctor, and have my forty dollars
again, or I'll make it the dearest[4] horse. O, yonder is his snipper-
snapper! Do you hear, you hey-pass,[5] where's your master?

MEPHASTOPHILIS   Why, sir, what would you? You cannot speak with
him.

HORSE-COURSER   But I will speak with him.

MEPHASTOPHILIS   Why, he's fast asleep; come some other time.

HORSE-COURSER   I'll speak with him now, or I'll break his glasswin-
dows[6] about his ears.

MEPHASTOPHILIS   I tell thee, he has not slept this eight nights.

HORSE-COURSER   And he have not slept this eight weeks I'll speak
with him.

MEPHASTOPHILIS   See where he is, fast asleep.

HORSE-COURSER   Ay, this is he; God save ye, master doctor, master
doctor, master Doctor Fustian, forty dollars, forty dollars for a
bottle of hay!

MEPHASTOPHILIS   Why, thou seest he hears thee not.

HORSE-COURSER   So ho ho; so ho ho.[7] [Halloo in his ear.] No, will you
not wake? I'll make you wake ere I go. [Pull him by the leg, and pull
it away.] Alas, I am undone! What shall I do?

FAUSTUS   O my leg, my leg! Help, Mephastophilis! Call the officers!
My leg, my leg!

MEPHASTOPHILIS   Come villain, to the constable.

HORSE-COURSER   O Lord, sir! Let me go, and I'll give you forty dollars
more.

MEPHASTOPHILIS   Where be they?

HORSE-COURSER   I have none about me: come to my ostry[8] and I'll
give them you.

MEPHASTOPHILIS   Begone quickly!
   [HORSE-COURSER runs away.]

FAUSTUS   What, is he gone? Farewell he: Faustus has his leg again,
and the horse-courser—I take it—a bottle of hay for his labor!
Well, this trick shall cost him forty dollars more.
   [Enter WAGNER.]
How now, Wagner, what's the news with thee?

WAGNER   Sir, the duke of Vanholt doth earnestly entreat your
company.

FAUSTUS   The duke of Vanholt! An honorable gentleman, to whom
I must be no niggard of my cunning.[9] Come, Mephastophilis, let's
away to him.   [Exeunt.]

---

3. Bundle. "Vent'rous": adventurous.
4. Most expensive.
5. A conjurer's phrase. "Snipper-snapper": insignificant youth, whipper-snapper.
6. Spectacles.

7. The huntsman's cry, when he sights the
quarry.
8. Hostelry, inn.
9. I.e., must generously display my skill.

SCENE 11

[FAUSTUS *and* MEPHASTOPHILIS *return to the stage. Enter to them the* DUKE *and the* DUCHESS; *the* DUKE *speaks.*]

DUKE   Believe me, master doctor, this merriment hath much pleased me.

FAUSTUS   My gracious lord, I am glad it contents you so well: but it may be, madam, you take no delight in this; I have heard that great-bellied[1] women do long for some dainties or other—what is it, madam? Tell me, and you shall have it.

DUCHESS   Thanks, good master doctor; and for I see your courteous intent to pleasure me, I will not hide from you the thing my heart desires. And were it now summer, as it is January and the dead of winter, I would desire no better meat than a dish of ripe grapes.

FAUSTUS   Alas madam, that's nothing! Mephastophilis, begone! [*Exit* MEPHASTOPHILIS.] Were it a greater thing than this, so it would content you, you should have it. [*Enter* MEPHASTOPHILIS *with the grapes.*] Here they be, madam; will't please you taste on them?

DUKE   Believe me, master doctor, this makes me wonder above the rest: that being in the dead time of winter, and in the month of January, how you should come by these grapes?

FAUSTUS   If it like your grace, the year is divided into two circles over the whole world, that when it is here winter with us, in the contrary circle it is summer with them, as in India, Saba,[2] and farther countries in the east; and by means of a swift spirit that I have, I had them brought hither, as ye see. How do you like them, madam; be they good?

DUCHESS   Believe me, master doctor, they be the best grapes that ere I tasted in my life before.

FAUSTUS   I am glad they content you so, madam.

DUKE   Come, madam, let us in, where you must well reward this learned man for the great kindness he hath showed to you.

DUCHESS   And so I will, my lord; and whilst I live, rest beholding for this courtesy.

FAUSTUS   I humbly thank your grace.

DUKE   Come, master doctor, follow us, and receive your reward.

[*Exeunt*]

CHORUS 4

[*Enter* WAGNER *solus.*]

WAGNER   I think my master means to die shortly,
    For he hath given to me all his goods.
    And yet methinks, if that death were near,
    He would not banquet, and carouse, and swill
5   Amongst the students, as even now he doth,
    Who are at supper with such belly-cheer°   gluttony
    As Wagner ne'er beheld in all his life.
    See where they come: belike the feast is ended.   [*Exit.*]

---

1. Pregnant.
2. The biblical kingdom of Sheba, in southwestern Arabia. "Like": please.

SCENE 12

[*Enter* FAUSTUS (*and* MEPHASTOPHILIS), *with two or three*
SCHOLARS.]

1 SCHOLAR   Master Doctor Faustus, since our conference about
fair ladies, which was the beautifulest in all the world, we have
determined with ourselves that Helen of Greece was the admira-
blest lady that ever lived. Therefore, master doctor, if you will do
5   us that favor as to let us see that peerless dame of Greece, whom
all the world admires for majesty, we should think ourselves much
beholding unto you.

FAUSTUS   Gentlemen, for that I know your friendship is unfeigned,
And Faustus' custom is not to deny
10   The just requests of those that wish him well,
You shall behold that peerless dame of Greece,
No otherways for pomp and majesty
Than when Sir Paris crossed the seas with her
And brought the spoils to rich Dardania.°   Troy
15   Be silent then, for danger is in words.

[*Music sounds, and* HELEN *passeth over the stage.*]

2 SCHOLAR   Too simple is my wit to tell her praise,
Whom all the world admires for majesty.

3 SCHOLAR   No marvel though the angry Greeks pursued
With ten years' war the rape° of such a queen,   abduction
20   Whose heavenly beauty passeth all compare.

1 SCHOLAR   Since we have seen the pride of Nature's works
And only paragon of excellence,
Let us depart; and for this glorious deed
Happy and blest be Faustus evermore.

25 FAUSTUS   Gentlemen, farewell; the same I wish to you.

[*Exeunt* SCHOLARS.]

[*Enter an* OLD MAN.]

OLD MAN   Ah Doctor Faustus, that I might prevail
To guide thy steps unto the way of life,
By which sweet path thou may'st attain the goal
That shall conduct thee to celestial rest.
30   Break heart, drop blood, and mingle it with tears,
Tears falling from repentant heaviness°   grief
Of thy most vile and loathsome filthiness,
The stench whereof corrupts the inward soul
With such flagitious° crimes of heinous sins,   villainous
35   As no commiseration may expel
But mercy, Faustus, of thy savior sweet,
Whose blood alone must wash away thy guilt.

FAUSTUS   Where art thou, Faustus? Wretch, what hast thou done!
Damned art thou, Faustus, damned; despair and die!
40   Hell calls for right, and with a roaring voice
Says, "Faustus, come: thine hour is come!"

[MEPHASTOPHILIS *gives him a dagger.*]

And Faustus will come to do thee right.

OLD MAN   Ah stay, good Faustus, stay thy desperate steps!
I see an angel hovers o'er thy head

And with a vial full of precious grace
Offers to pour the same into thy soul!
Then call for mercy, and avoid despair.
FAUSTUS   Ah my sweet friend, I feel thy words
   To comfort my distressèd soul;
   Leave me awhile to ponder on my sins.
OLD MAN   I go, sweet Faustus; but with heavy cheer,°   heavy heart
   Fearing the ruin of thy hopeless soul.   [*Exit.*]
FAUSTUS   Accursèd Faustus, where is mercy now?
   I do repent, and yet I do despair:
   Hell strives with grace for conquest in my breast!
   What shall I do to shun the snares of death?
MEPHASTOPHILIS   Thou traitor, Faustus: I arrest thy soul
   For disobedience to my sovereign lord.
   Revolt,³ or I'll in piecemeal tear thy flesh.
FAUSTUS   Sweet Mephastophilis, entreat thy lord
   To pardon my unjust presumptiön;
   And with my blood again I will confirm
   My former vow I made to Lucifer.
MEPHASTOPHILIS   Do it then quickly, with unfeignèd heart,
   Lest greater danger do attend thy drift.°   intent
FAUSTUS   Torment, sweet friend, that base and crooked age°   aged man
   That durst° dissuade me from thy Lucifer,   dared to
   With greatest torments that our hell affords.
MEPHASTOPHILIS   His faith is great, I cannot touch his soul,
   But what I may afflict his body with
   I will attempt—which is but little worth.
FAUSTUS   One thing, good servant, let me crave of thee,
   To glut the longing of my heart's desire:
   That I might have unto° my paramour   for
   That heavenly Helen which I saw of late,
   Whose sweet embracings may extinguish clean
   These thoughts that do dissuade me from my vow,
   And keep mine oath I made to Lucifer.
MEPHASTOPHILIS   Faustus, this, or what else thou shalt desire,
   Shall be performed in twinkling of an eye.
           [*Enter* HELEN.]
FAUSTUS   Was this the face that launched a thousand ships,
   And burnt the topless⁴ towers of Ilium?°   Troy
   Sweet Helen, make me immortal with a kiss:
   Her lips sucks forth my soul, see where it flies!
   Come Helen, come, give me my soul again.
   Here will I dwell, for heaven be in these lips,
   And all is dross that is not Helena!
           [*Enter* OLD MAN.]
   I will be Paris, and for love of thee,
   Instead of Troy shall Wittenberg be sacked;
   And I will combat with weak Menelaus,°   Helen's husband

---

3. Turn back (to your allegiance to Lucifer).   4. Immeasurably high; matchless.

And wear thy colors on my plumèd crest;
Yea, I will wound Achilles in the heel,[5]
And then return to Helen for a kiss.
O thou art fairer than the evening air
95 Clad in the beauty of a thousand stars,
Brighter art thou than flaming Jupiter
When he appeared to hapless Semele;[6]
More lovely than the monarch of the sky
In wanton Arethusa's azured arms;[7]
100 And none but thou shalt be my paramour.

> [*Exeunt* (FAUSTUS *and* HELEN).]

OLD MAN Accursèd Faustus, miserable man,
That from thy soul exclud'st the grace of heaven
And fliest the throne of His tribunal seat!

> [*Enter the* DEVILS.]

Satan begins to sift me with his pride,[8]
105 As in this furnace God shall try my faith.
My faith, vile hell, shall triumph over thee!
Ambitious fiends, see how the heavens smiles
At your repulse, and laughs your state° to scorn.   *royal power*
Hence hell, for hence I fly unto my God.

> [*Exeunt.*]

SCENE 13

[*Enter* FAUSTUS *with the* SCHOLARS.]

FAUSTUS Ah gentlemen!

1 SCHOLAR What ails Faustus?

FAUSTUS Ah my sweet chamber-fellow, had I lived with thee, then
had I lived still;[9] but now I die eternally. Look, comes he not, comes
5 he not?

2 SCHOLAR What means Faustus?

3 SCHOLAR Belike he is grown into some sickness by being over-
solitary.

1 SCHOLAR If it be so, we'll have physicians to cure him; 'tis but a
10 surfeit:[1] never fear, man.

FAUSTUS A surfeit of deadly sin, that hath damned both body and
soul.

2 SCHOLAR Yet Faustus, look up to heaven; remember God's mercies are infinite.

15 FAUSTUS But Faustus' offense can ne'er be pardoned! The serpent
that tempted Eve may be saved, but not Faustus. Ah gentlemen,
hear me with patience, and tremble not at my speeches, though
my heart pants and quivers to remember that I have been a student here these thirty years—O would I had never seen Witten-
20 berg, never read book—and what wonders I have done, all

---

5. Achilles could be wounded only in his heel—
where he was shot by Paris.
6. A Theban girl, loved by Jupiter and destroyed
by the fire of his lightning when he appeared to
her in his full splendor.
7. Arethusa was the nymph of a fountain, as well

as the fountain itself; she excited the passion of
the river god Alpheus, who was by some accounts
related to the sun.
8. To test me with his strength.
9. Always.
1. Indigestion caused by overeating.

Wittenberg can witness—yea, all the world; for which Faustus hath lost both Germany and the world—yea, heaven itself—heaven, the seat of God, the throne of the blessed, the kingdom of joy; and must remain in hell forever—hell, ah, hell forever! Sweet friends, what shall become of Faustus, being in hell forever?

3 SCHOLAR   Yet Faustus, call on God.

FAUSTUS   On God, whom Faustus hath abjured? On God, whom Faustus hath blasphemed? Ah, my God—I would weep, but the devil draws in my tears! Gush forth blood, instead of tears—yea, life and soul! O, he stays my tongue! I would lift up my hands, but see, they hold them, they hold them!

ALL   Who, Faustus?

FAUSTUS   Lucifer and Mephastophilis! Ah gentlemen, I gave them my soul for my cunning.

ALL   God forbid!

FAUSTUS   God forbade it indeed, but Faustus hath done it: for the vain pleasure of four-and-twenty years hath Faustus lost eternal joy and felicity. I writ them a bill[2] with mine own blood, the date is expired, the time will come, and he will fetch me.

1 SCHOLAR   Why did not Faustus tell us of this before, that divines might have prayed for thee?

FAUSTUS   Oft have I thought to have done so, but the devil threatened to tear me in pieces if I named God, to fetch both body and soul if I once gave ear to divinity; and now 'tis too late. Gentlemen, away, lest you perish with me!

2 SCHOLAR   O what shall we do to save Faustus?

3 SCHOLAR   God will strengthen me. I will stay with Faustus.

1 SCHOLAR   Tempt not God, sweet friend, but let us into the next room, and there pray for him.

FAUSTUS   Ay, pray for me, pray for me; and what noise soever ye hear, come not unto me, for nothing can rescue me.

2 SCHOLAR   Pray thou, and we will pray, that God may have mercy upon thee.

FAUSTUS   Gentlemen, farewell. If I live till morning, I'll visit you; if not, Faustus is gone to hell.

ALL   Faustus, farewell.   [*Exeunt* SCHOLARS.]
      [*The clock strikes eleven.*]

FAUSTUS   Ah Faustus,
Now hast thou but one bare hour to live,
And then thou must be damned perpetually.
Stand still, you ever-moving spheres of heaven,
That time may cease, and midnight never come.
Fair Nature's eye, rise, rise again, and make
Perpetual day, or let this hour be but
A year, a month, a week, a natural day,
That Faustus may repent and save his soul.
O lente, lente currite noctis equi![3]

---

2. Document.
3. "Slowly, slowly run, O horses of the night"; adapted from a line in Ovid's *Amores*.

The stars move still, time runs, the clock will strike,
The devil will come, and Faustus must be damned.
O I'll leap up to my God! Who pulls me down?
70 See, see where Christ's blood streams in the firmament!°   *sky*
One drop would save my soul, half a drop: ah my Christ—
Ah, rend not my heart for naming of my Christ;
Yet will I call on him—O spare me, Lucifer!
Where is it now? 'Tis gone: and see where God
75 Stretcheth out his arm, and bends his ireful brows!
Mountains and hills, come, come and fall on me,
And hide me from the heavy wrath of God.
No, no?
Then will I headlong run into the earth:
80 Earth, gape! O no, it will not harbor me.
You stars that reigned at my nativity,
Whose influence hath allotted death and hell,
Now draw up Faustus like a foggy mist
Into the entrails of yon laboring cloud,
85 That when you vomit forth into the air
My limbs may issue from your smoky mouths,
So that my soul may but ascend to heaven.[4]
     [*The watch strikes.*]
Ah, half the hour is past: 'twill all be past anon.°   *shortly*
O God, if thou wilt not have mercy on my soul,
90 Yet for Christ's sake, whose blood hath ransomed me,
Impose some end to my incessant pain:
Let Faustus live in hell a thousand years,
A hundred thousand, and at last be saved.
O no end is limited to damnèd souls!
95 Why wert thou not a creature wanting° soul?   *lacking*
Or why is this immortal that thou hast?
Ah, Pythagoras' *metempsychosis*[5]—were that true,
This soul should fly from me, and I be changed
Unto some brutish beast:
100 All beasts are happy, for when they die,
Their souls are soon dissolved in elements;
But mine must live still° to be plagued in hell.   *always*
Cursed be the parents that engendered me!
No, Faustus, curse thy self, curse Lucifer,
105 That hath deprived thee of the joys of heaven.
     [*The clock striketh twelve.*]
O it strikes, it strikes! Now body, turn to air,
Or Lucifer will bear thee quick° to hell.   *alive*
     [*Thunder and lightning.*]
O soul, be changed into little water drops
And fall into the ocean, ne'er be found.
110 My God, my God, look not so fierce on me!
     [*Enter* DEVILS.]

---

4. Faustus wants to be drawn up into a cloud, which would compact his body into a thunderbolt so that his soul, thus purified, might ascend to heaven.
5. Pythagoras's doctrine of the transmigration of souls.

Adders and serpents, let me breathe awhile!
Ugly hell gape not! Come not, Lucifer!
I'll burn my books—ah, Mephastophilis!
    [*Exeunt with him.*]

Epilogue

[*Enter* CHORUS.]
Cut is the branch that might have grown full straight,
And burnèd is Apollo's laurel bough,[6]
That sometime grew within this learnèd man.
Faustus is gone! Regard his hellish fall,
Whose fiendful fortune° may exhort the wise   *devilish fate*
Only to wonder at[7] unlawful things:
Whose deepness doth entice such forward wits°   *aspiring minds*
To practice more than heavenly power permits.

        [*Exit.*]

    Terminat hora diem, terminat author opus.[8]

1604, 1616

6. The laurel crown of Apollo symbolizes (among other things) learning and wisdom.
7. Be content simply to observe with awe.

8. "The hour ends the day, the author ends his work"; this motto was probably added by the printer.

WILLIAM SHAKESPEARE
1564–1616

William Shakespeare was born in the small market town of Stratford-on-Avon in April (probably April 23) 1564. His father, a successful glovemaker, land-owner, moneylender, and dealer in agricultural commodities, was elected to several important posts in local government but later suffered financial and social reverses, possibly as a result of adherence to the Catholic faith. Shakespeare almost certainly attended the free Stratford grammar school, where he would have acquired a rea-sonably impressive education, including a respectable knowledge of Latin, but he did not proceed to Oxford or Cambridge. There are legends about Shakespeare's youth but no documented facts. Some scholars are tempted to associate him with "William Shakeshafte," a young actor attached to a recusant Catholic circle in Lancashire around 1581; one of Shakespeare's former Stratford schoolmasters belonged to this circle. But the first unambiguous record we have of his life after his christening is that of his marriage, in 1582, at age eighteen, to Anne Hathaway, eight years his senior. A daughter, Susanna, was born six months later, in 1583, and twins, Hamnet and Judith, in 1585. We possess no information about his activities for the next seven years, but by 1592 he was in London as an actor and apparently already well known as a playwright, for a rival dramatist, Robert Greene, refers to him resent-fully in *A Groatsworth of Wit* as "an upstart crow, beautified with our feathers."

Labels on the sketch:
tectum
porticus
orchestia
mimorum
ædes
ingressus
proscænium
planities sive arena

Sketch of the Swan Theater. This drawing by Arend van Buchell (ca. 1596), based on the observations of Johannes De Witt, shows features of the public playhouse in Shakespeare's time. Resembling the courtyard of an Elizabethan inn, the Swan had three galleries for the audience, and probably additional room for audience members in the gallery at the back of the stage, above the tiring-house (dressing-room). The stage itself had two doors for players' entrances and exits, and the roof over the stage was supported by pillars. The flag flying from the roof signals that a play is to be performed that day, and a trumpeter announces the beginning of the performance (though the sketch shows a performance already under way). De Witt labeled parts of the sketch using Latin names derived from the Roman theater.

At this time, there were several companies of professional actors in London and in the provinces. What links Shakespeare had with one or more of them before 1592 is conjectural, but we do know of his long and fruitful connection, established by 1594, with the most successful troupe, the Lord Chamberlain's Men, who later, when James I came to the throne, became the King's Men. Shakespeare not only acted with this company but eventually became a leading shareholder and the principal playwright. Then as now, making a living in the professional theater was not easy: competition among the repertory companies was stiff, civic officials and religious moralists regarded playacting as a sinful, time-wasting nuisance and tried to ban it altogether, government officials exercised censorship over the contents of the plays, and periodic outbreaks of bubonic plague led to temporary closing of the London theaters. But Shakespeare's company, which included some of the most famous actors of the day, nonetheless thrived and in 1599 began to perform in the Globe, a fine, open-air theater that the company built for itself on the south bank of the Thames. The company also performed frequently at court and, after 1608, at Blackfriars, an indoor London theater. Already by 1597 Shakespeare had so prospered that he was able to purchase New Place, a handsome house in Stratford; he could now call himself a gentleman, as his father had (probably with the financial assistance of his successful playwright son) been granted a coat of arms the previous year. Shakespeare's wife and daughters (his son, Hamnet, having died in 1596) resided in Stratford, while the playwright, living in rented rooms in London, pursued his career. Shortly after writing *The Tempest* (ca. 1611), he retired from direct involvement in the theater and returned to Stratford. In March 1616, he signed his will; he died a month later, leaving the bulk of his estate to his daughter Susanna. To his wife of thirty-four years, he left "my second best bed."

Shakespeare began his career as a playwright, probably in the early 1590s, by writing comedies and history plays. The earliest of these histories, generally based on accounts of English kings written by Raphael Holinshed and other sixteenth-century chroniclers, seem theatrically vital but crude, as does an early attempt at tragedy, *Titus Andronicus*. But Shakespeare quickly moved on to create by the later 1590s a sequence of profoundly searching and ambitious history plays—*Richard II*, the first and second parts of *Henry IV*, and *Henry V*—which together explore the death throes of feudal England and the birth of the modern nation-state ruled by a charismatic monarch. In the same years he wrote a succession of romantic comedies (*The Merchant of Venice, The Merry Wives of Windsor, Much Ado About Nothing, As You Like It, Twelfth Night*) whose poetic richness and emotional complexity remain unmatched.

Twelfth Night was probably written in the same year as *Hamlet* (ca. 1601), which initiated an outpouring of great tragic dramas: *Othello, King Lear, Macbeth, Antony and Cleopatra*, and *Coriolanus*. These plays, written from 1601 to 1607, seem to mark a major shift in sensibility, an existential and metaphysical darkening that many readers think must have originated in personal anguish. Whatever the truth of this speculation—and we have no direct, personal testimony either to support or to undermine it—there appears to have occurred in the same period a shift as well in Shakespeare's comic sensibility. The comedies written between 1601 and 1604, *Troilus and Cressida, All's Well That Ends Well*, and *Measure for Measure*, are sufficiently different from the earlier comedies—more biting in tone, more uneasy with comic conventions, more ruthlessly questioning of the values of the characters and the resolutions of the plots—to have led some modern scholars to classify them as "problem plays" or "dark comedies." Another group of plays, among the last that Shakespeare wrote, seem similarly to define a distinct category. *Pericles, Cymbeline, The Winter's Tale*, and *The Tempest*, written between 1608 and 1611, when Shakespeare had developed a remarkably fluid, dream-like sense of plot and a poetic style that could veer, apparently effortlessly, from the tortured to the ineffably sweet, are now commonly known as the "romances." These plays share an interest in the moral and emotional life less of the adolescents who dominate the earlier comedies than of their parents. The "romances" are deeply concerned with patterns of loss and recovery, suffering and redemption, despair and renewal. They have seemed to many critics to constitute a self-conscious conclusion to a career that opened with histories and comedies and passed through the dark and tormented tragedies.

Shakespeare himself apparently had no interest in preserving for posterity the sum of his writings, let alone in clarifying the chronology of his works or in specifying which plays he wrote alone and which with collaborators. He wrote plays for performance by his company, and his scripts existed in his own handwritten manuscripts or in scribal copies, in playhouse prompt books, and probably in pirated texts based on shorthand reports of a performance or on reconstructions from memory by an actor or a spectator. None of these manuscript versions has survived. Eighteen of his plays were published during his lifetime in the small-format, inexpensive books called quartos; to these were added eighteen other plays, never before printed, in the large, expensive folio volume of *Mr. William Shakespeares Comedies, Histories, & Tragedies* (1623), published seven years after his death. This First Folio, edited by two of his friends and fellow actors, John Heminges and Henry Condell, is prefaced by a poem of Ben Jonson's, in which Shakespeare is hailed, presciently, as "not of an age, but for all time."

That Shakespeare is "for all time" does not mean that he did not also belong to his own age. It is possible to see where Shakespeare adapted the techniques of his contemporaries and where, crucially, he differed from them. Shakespeare rarely invented the plots of his dramas, preferring to work, often quite closely, with stories he found ready-made in histories, novellas, narrative poems, or other plays. The religious mystery plays and the allegorical morality plays still popular during his childhood taught him that dramas worth seeing must get at something central to the human condition, that they should embody as well as narrate the crucial actions, and that they could reach not only a coterie of the educated elite but also the great mass of ordinary people. From these and other theatrical models, Shakespeare learned how to construct plays around the struggle for the soul of a protagonist, how to create theatrically compelling and subversive figures of wickedness, and how to focus attention on his characters' psychological, moral, and spiritual lives, as well as on their outward behavior.

The authors of the morality plays thought that they could enhance the broad impact they sought to achieve by stripping their characters of all incidental distinguishing traits and getting to their essences. They believed that their audiences would thereby not be distracted by the irrelevant details of individual identities. Shakespeare grasped that the spectacle of human destiny was in fact vastly more compelling when it was attached not to generalized abstractions but to particular people, people whom he realized with an unprecedented intensity of individuation: [not Evil but Iago, not Everyman but Othello.] No other writer of his time was able to create and enter into the interior worlds of so many characters, conveying again and again a sense of unique and irreducible selfhood. In the plays of Shakespeare's brilliant contemporary Marlowe, the protagonist overwhelms virtually all of the other characters; in Shakespeare, by contrast, even relatively minor characters—Emilia in *Othello*, for example—make astonishingly powerful claims on the audience's attention. The Romantic critic William Hazlitt observed that Shakespeare had the power to multiply himself marvelously. His plays convey the sense of an inexhaustible imaginative generosity.

Shakespeare was singularly alert to the fantastic vitality of the English language. His immense vocabulary bears witness to an uncanny ability to absorb terms from a wide range of pursuits and to transform them into intimate registers of thought and feeling. He had a seemingly boundless capacity to generate metaphors, and he was virtually addicted to wordplay. Double-meanings, verbal echoes, and submerged associations ripple through every passage, deepening the reader's enjoyment and understanding, though sometimes at the expense of a single clear sense. The eighteenth-century critic Samuel Johnson complained with some justice that the quibble, the pun, was "the fatal Cleopatra for which Shakespeare lost the world and was content to lose it." For the power that continually discharges itself throughout his plays and poems, at once constituting and unsettling everything it touches, is the polymorphous power of language.

Anachronism is rarely a concern for Shakespeare. His ancient Romans throw their caps into the air and use Christian oaths: to this extent he pulled everything he touched into his contemporary existence. But at the same time he was not a social realist; other writers in this period are better at conveying the precise details of the daily lives of shoemakers, alchemists, and judges. The settings of his plays were often for Shakespeare not realistic representations of particular historical times and places but rather imaginative displacements into alternative worlds that remain strangely familiar. Venice and Cyprus in *Othello* have some of their historical specificity, but it is striking that this specificity seems to fade in importance as the play continues, finally ceding place to the bedroom in which the tragic climax unfolds.

Though on occasion he depicts ghosts, demons, and other supernatural figures, the universe Shakespeare conjures up seems resolutely human-centered and secular: the torments and joys that most deeply matter are found in this world, not in the next. Attempts to claim him for one or another religious system have proven unconvincing, as have attempts to assign him a specific political label. Activists and ideologues of all political stripes have viewed him as an ally: he has been admiringly quoted by kings and by revolutionaries, by fascists, liberal democrats, socialists, republicans, and communists. At once an agent of civility and an agent of subversion, Shakespeare seems to have been able to view society simultaneously as an insider and as an outsider. His plays can be interpreted and performed—with deep conviction and compelling power—in utterly contradictory ways. The centuries-long accumulation of these interpretations and performances, far from exhausting Shakespeare's aesthetic appeal, seems only to have enhanced its perennial freshness.*

Sonnets

In Elizabethan England aristocratic patronage, with the money, protection, and prestige it alone could provide, was probably a professional writer's most important asset. This patronage, or at least Shakespeare's quest for it, is most visible in his dedication, in 1593 and 1594, of his narrative poems, *Venus and Adonis* and *The Rape of Lucrece*, to the wealthy young nobleman Henry Wriothesley, earl of Southampton. What return the poet got for his exquisite offerings is unknown. We do know that among wits and gallants the narrative poems won Shakespeare a fine reputation as an immensely stylish and accomplished poet. This reputation was enhanced as well by manuscript circulation of his sonnets, which were mentioned admiringly in print more than ten years before they were published in 1609 (apparently without his personal supervision and perhaps without his consent).

Shakespeare's sonnets are quite unlike the other sonnet sequences of his day, notably in his almost unprecedented choice of a beautiful young man (rather than a lady) as the principal object of praise, love, and idealizing devotion and in his portrait of a dark, sensuous, and sexually promiscuous mistress (rather than the usual chaste and aloof blond beauty). Nor are the moods confined to what the Renaissance thought were those of the despairing Petrarchan lover: they include delight, pride, melancholy, shame, disgust, and fear. Shakespeare's sequence suggests a story, although the details are vague, and there is even doubt whether the sonnets as published are in an order established by the poet himself. Certain motifs are evident: an introductory series (1 to 17) celebrates the beauty of a young man and urges him to marry and beget children who will bear his image. The subsequent long sequence (18 to 126), passionately focused on the beloved young man, develops as a dominant motif the

---

* For additional writings by Shakespeare—including the full text of *The First Part of King Henry IV*, Ulysses' speech on degree from *Troilus and Cressida*, a collection of songs from the plays, five additional sonnets (nos. 56, 104, 118, 121, 124), and the philosophical poem "The Phoenix and the Turtle"—see the supplemental ebook. See the color insert in this volume for the "Chandos" portrait of Shakespeare and a portrait of Henry Wriothesley, third earl of Southampton and the dedicatee of Shakespeare's two narrative poems and, possibly, of his *Sonnets*.

transience and destructive power of time, countered only by the force of love and the permanence of poetry. The remaining sonnets focus chiefly on the so-called Dark Lady as an alluring but degrading object of desire. Some sonnets (like 144) intimate a love triangle involving the speaker, the male friend, and the woman; others take note of a rival poet (sometimes identified as George Chapman or Christopher Marlowe). The biographical background of the sonnets has inspired a mountain of speculation, but very little of it has any factual support.

Though there are many variations, Shakespeare's most frequent rhyme scheme in the sonnets is *abab cdcd efef gg*. This so-called Shakespearean pattern often (though not always) calls attention to three distinct quatrains (each of which may develop a separate metaphor), followed by a closing couplet that may either confirm or pull sharply against what has gone before. Startling shifts in direction may occur in lines other than the closing ones; consider, for example, the twists and turns in the opening lines of sonnet 138: "When my love swears that she is made of truth, / I do believe her, though I know she lies." Shakespeare's sonnets as a whole are strikingly intense, conveying a sense of high psychological and moral stakes. They are also remarkably dense, written with a daunting energy, concentration, and compression. Often the main idea of the poem may be grasped quickly, but the precise movement of thought and feeling, the links among the shifting images, the syntax, tone, and rhetorical structure prove immensely challenging. These are poems that famously reward rereading.

Sonnets

To the Only Begetter of
These Ensuing Sonnets
Mr. W. H. All Happiness
and That Eternity
Promised
By
Our Ever-Living Poet
Wisheth
The Well-Wishing
Adventurer in
Setting Forth
T. T.[1]

1

From fairest creatures we desire increase,
That thereby beauty's rose might never die,
But as the riper should by time decease,
His tender heir might bear his memory;
5   But thou, contracted[2] to thine own bright eyes,
Feed'st thy light's flame with self-substantial[3] fuel,
Making a famine where abundance lies,

---

1. This odd dedication bears the initials of the publisher, Thomas Thorpe. The W. H. addressed here may or may not be the male friend addressed in sonnets 1 to 126. Leading candidates for that role are Henry Wriothesley, earl of Southampton, the dedicatee of *Venus and Adonis* (1593) and *The Rape of Lucrece* (1594), and William Herbert, earl of Pembroke, a dedicatee of the First Folio. But there is no hard evidence to support these or other suggested identifications of the male friend or of the so-called Dark Lady; these sonnet personages may or may not have had real-life counterparts.

Since all the sonnets save two were first published in 1609, we do not repeat the date after each one. Numbers 138 and 144 were first published in 1599, in a verse miscellany called *The Passionate Pilgrim.*
2. Betrothed; also, withdrawn into.
3. Of your own substance.

Thyself thy foe, to thy sweet self too cruel.
Thou that art now the world's fresh ornament

10 And only[4] herald to the gaudy spring,
Within thine own bud buriest thy content[5]
And, tender churl,[6] mak'st waste in niggarding.°   *hoarding*
   Pity the world, or else this glutton be,
   To eat the world's due, by the grave and thee.[7]

12

When I do count the clock that tells the time
And see the brave° day sunk in hideous night,   *splendid*
When I behold the violet past prime
And sable curls all silvered o'er with white,

5 When lofty trees I see barren of leaves,
Which erst° from heat did canopy the herd   *formerly*
And summer's green all girded up in sheaves
Borne on the bier with white and bristly beard:
Then of thy beauty do I question make°   *speculate*

10 That thou among the wastes of time must go,
Since sweets and beauties do themselves forsake,
And die as fast as they see others grow,
   And nothing 'gainst Time's scythe can make defense
   Save breed,° to brave° him when he takes thee hence.   *offspring / defy*

15

When I consider every thing that grows
Holds° in perfection but a little moment;   *remains*
That this huge stage presenteth nought but shows
Whereon the stars in secret influence comment;[8]

5 When I perceive that men as plants increase,
Cheered and checked[9] even by the selfsame sky,
Vaunt[1] in their youthful sap, at height decrease,
And wear their brave state out of memory;[2]
Then the conceit° of this inconstant stay   *conception*

10 Sets you most rich in youth before my sight,
Where wasteful Time debateth[3] with Decay
To change your day of youth to sullied° night,   *soiled, blackened*
   And all in war with Time for love of you,
   As he takes from you, I ingraft[4] you new.

18

Shall I compare thee to a summer's day?
Thou art more lovely and more temperate:
Rough winds do shake the darling buds of May,

4. Principal, with overtones of single, solitary.
5. What you contain (potential for fatherhood), also what would content you (marriage and fatherhood).
6. Gentle boor (an oxymoron).
7. "This . . . thee": be a glutton by causing what is owed to the world (your posterity) to be consumed by the grave and within yourself.
8. The stars secretly affect human actions.

"Shows": (1) appearances, (2) performances.
9. Encouraged and reproached or stopped.
1. Exult, display themselves.
2. Wear their showy splendor out and are forgotten.
3. (1)Fights, (2) joins forces.
4. Renew by grafting; implant beauty again (by my verse).

And summer's lease hath all too short a date;
5   Sometime too hot the eye of heaven shines,
And often is his gold complexion dimmed;
And every fair from fair sometime declines,
By chance or nature's changing course untrimmed.[5]
But thy eternal summer shall not fade,
10   Nor lose possession of that fair thou ow'st;°   *ownest*
Nor shall death brag thou wander'st in his shade,
When in eternal lines to time thou grow'st:°   *are grafted*
    So long as men can breathe or eyes can see,
    So long lives this,[6] and this gives life to thee.

19

Devouring Time, blunt thou the lion's paws,
And make the earth devour her own sweet brood;
Pluck the keen teeth from the fierce tiger's jaws,
And burn the long-lived phoenix in her blood;[7]
5   Make glad and sorry seasons as thou fleet'st,
And do whate'er thou wilt, swift-footed Time,
To the wide world and all her fading sweets,
But I forbid thee one most heinous crime:
O carve not with thy hours my love's fair brow,
10   Nor draw no lines there with thine antique[8] pen;
Him in thy course untainted[9] do allow,
For beauty's pattern to succeeding men.
    Yet do thy worst, old Time: despite thy wrong,
    My love shall in my verse ever live young.

20

A woman's face with Nature's own hand painted[1]
Hast thou, the master mistress of my passion;[2]
A woman's gentle heart but not acquainted
With shifting change as is false women's fashion;
5   An eye more bright than theirs, less false in rolling,°   *roving*
Gilding the object whereupon it gazeth;
A man in hue all hues[3] in his controlling,
Which steals men's eyes and women's souls amazeth.
And for a woman wert thou first created,
10   Till Nature as she wrought thee fell a-doting,[4]
And by addition me of thee defeated,
By adding one thing to my purpose nothing.
    But since she pricked[5] thee out for women's pleasure,
    Mine be thy love, and thy love's use[6] their treasure.

---

5. Stripped of gay apparel.
6. I.e., the poem. The boast of immortality for one's verse was a convention going back to the Greek and Roman classics.
7. In full vigor of life (a hunting term). The phoenix was a mythical bird that lived five hundred years, then died in flames to rise again from its ashes.
8. (1) Old, (2) fantastic (antic).
9. (1) Undefiled, (2) untouched by a weapon (a term from jousting).

1. I.e., not made up with cosmetics.
2. (1) Strong feeling, (2) poem.
3. "Hue" probably means appearance or form. In the first edition, "hues" is spelled "*Hews*," which some have taken as indicating a pun on a proper name. It has also been suggested that "man in" is a copyist's or compositor's misreading of "maiden."
4. (1) Crazy, (2) infatuated.
5. Marked, with obvious sexual pun.
6. (1) Sexual enjoyment, (2) interest (as in usury).

23

As an unperfect actor on the stage
Who with his fear is put besides° his part,   *forgets*
Or some fierce thing replete with too much rage
Whose strength's abundance weakens his own heart,
5   So I, for fear of trust,° forget to say   *lack of confidence*
The perfect ceremony of love's rite,[7]
And in mine own love's strength seem to decay,
O'er-charged° with burden of mine own love's might.   *overweighed*
O let my books be then the eloquence
10 And dumb presagers° of my speaking breast,   *mute presenters*
Who plead for love, and look for recompense
More than that tongue that more hath more expressed.[8]
    O learn to read what silent love hath writ;
    To hear with eyes belongs to love's fine wit.°   *intelligence*

29

When, in disgrace° with Fortune and men's eyes,   *disfavor*
I all alone beweep my outcast state,
And trouble deaf heaven with my bootless° cries,   *futile*
And look upon myself and curse my fate,
5   Wishing me like to one more rich in hope,
Featured like him, like him with friends possessed,[9]
Desiring this man's art° and that man's scope,°   *skill / ability*
With what I most enjoy contented least;
Yet in these thoughts myself almost despising,
10 Haply I think on thee, and then my state[1]
(Like to the lark at break of day arising
From sullen earth) sings hymns at heaven's gate;
    For thy sweet love remembered such wealth brings
    That then I scorn to change my state with kings.

30

When to the sessions[2] of sweet silent thought
I summon up remembrance of things past,
I sigh the lack of many a thing I sought,
And with old woes new wail° my dear time's waste: *bewail anew*
5   Then can I drown an eye (unused to flow)
For precious friends hid in death's dateless° night,   *endless*
And weep afresh love's long since canceled woe,
And moan th' expense° of many a vanished sight: *loss*
Then can I grieve at grievances foregone,°   *former*
10 And heavily from woe to woe tell° o'er   *count*
The sad account of fore-bemoanèd moan,
Which I new pay as if not paid before.

7. The first edition has "right," suggesting love's
due as well as love's ritual ("rite").
8. More than that (rival) speaker who has more
often said more.
9. I.e., I wish I had one man's looks, another man's
friends.
1. Condition, state of mind; but in line 14 there
is a pun on *state* meaning chair of state, throne.
2. Sittings of court. "Summon up" (next line) continues the metaphor.

But if the while I think on thee, dear friend,
All losses are restored and sorrows end.

33

Full many a glorious morning have I seen
Flatter the mountain tops with sovereign eye,°   *sunlight*
Kissing with golden face the meadows green,
Gilding pale streams with heavenly alchemy;
5 Anon° permit the basest° clouds to ride   *(but) soon / darkest*
With ugly rack° on his celestial face,   *cloudy mask*
And from the forlorn world his visage hide,
Stealing unseen to west with this disgrace.
Even so my sun one early morn did shine
10 With all triumphant splendor on my brow;
But out, alack,° he was but one hour mine;   *alas*
The region° cloud hath masked him from me now.   *high*
  Yet him for this my love no whit disdaineth:
  Suns of the world may stain° when heaven's sun staineth.   *darken*

55

Not marble nor the gilded monuments
Of princes shall outlive this powerful rhyme;
But you shall shine more bright in these contents
Than unswept stone, besmeared with sluttish time.[3]
5 When wasteful war shall statues overturn,
And broils° root out the work of masonry,   *battles*
Nor Mars his° sword nor war's quick fire shall burn   *neither Mars's*
The living record of your memory.
'Gainst death and all-oblivious enmity[4]
10 Shall you pace forth; your praise shall still find room
Even in the eyes of all posterity
That wear this world out to the ending doom.°   *Judgment Day*
  So, till the judgment that yourself arise,[5]
  You live in this, and dwell in lovers' eyes.

60

Like as the waves make towards the pebbled shore,
So do our minutes hasten to their end;
Each changing place with that which goes before,
In sequent toil all forwards do contend.[6]
5 Nativity, once in the main° of light,   *broad expanse*
Crawls to maturity, wherewith being crowned,
Crooked° eclipses 'gainst his glory fight,   *pernicious*
And Time that gave doth now his gift confound.
Time doth transfix the flourish set on youth,
10 And delves the parallels[7] in beauty's brow,

---

3. I.e., than in a stone tomb or effigy that time wears away and covers with dust. "Sluttish": slovenly.
4. The enmity of oblivion, of being forgotten.
5. Until you rise from the dead on Judgment Day.

6. Toiling and following each other, all struggle to move forward.
7. Digs the parallel furrows (wrinkles). "Transfix the flourish": destroy the embellishment. To "flourish" is also to blossom.

Feeds on the rarities of nature's truth,
And nothing stands but for his scythe to mow.
    And yet to times in hope° my verse shall stand,   *future times*
    Praising thy worth, despite his cruel hand.

62

Sin of self-love possesseth all mine eye,
And all my soul, and all my every part;
And for this sin there is no remedy,
It is so grounded inward in my heart.
5 Methinks no face so gracious° is as mine,   *pleasing*
No shape so true,° no truth of such account,   *perfect*
And for myself mine own worth do define
As° I all other° in all worths surmount.   *as if / others*
But when my glass° shows me myself indeed,   *mirror*
10 Beated and chapped with tanned antiquity,
Mine own self-love quite contrary° I read;   *differently*
Self so self-loving were iniquity.
    'Tis thee, my self,° that for° myself I praise,   *you, my other self / as*
    Painting my age with beauty of thy days.

65

Since[8] brass, nor stone, nor earth, nor boundless sea,
But sad mortality o'ersways their power,
How with this rage° shall beauty hold a plea,   *destructive power*
Whose action is no stronger than a flower?
5 O how shall summer's honey breath hold out
Against the wrackful° siege of batt'ring days,   *destructive*
When rocks impregnable are not so stout,
Nor gates of steel so strong, but Time decays?
O fearful meditation! Where, alack,
10 Shall Time's best jewel from Time's chest[9] he hid?
Or what strong hand can hold his swift foot back?
Or who his spoil° of beauty can forbid?   *ravaging*
    O none, unless this miracle have might,
    That in black ink my love may still shine bright.

71

No longer mourn for me when I am dead
Than you shall hear the surly sullen bell[1]
Give warning to the world that I am fled
From this vile world, with vilest worms to dwell.
5 Nay, if you read this line, remember not
The hand that writ it; for I love you so,
That I in your sweet thoughts would be forgot,
If thinking on me then should make you woe.
O, if, I say, you look upon this verse

8. I.e., since there is neither.
9. I.e., from being coffered up by Time.
1. The bell was tolled to announce the death of a member of the parish—one stroke for each year of his or her life.

10 When I perhaps compounded am with clay,
    Do not so much as my poor name rehearse,°   *repeat*
    But let your love even with my life decay;
        Lest the wise world should look into your moan,
        And mock you with me after I am gone.

73

    That time of year thou may'st in me behold
    When yellow leaves, or none, or few, do hang
    Upon those boughs which shake against the cold,
    Bare ruined choirs,[2] where late° the sweet birds sang.   *lately*
5   In me thou seest the twilight of such day
    As after sunset fadeth in the west;
    Which by and by black night doth take away,
    Death's second self that seals up all in rest.
    In me thou seest the glowing of such fire
10 That on the ashes of his youth doth lie,
    As the deathbed whereon it must expire,
    Consumed with that which it was nourished by.[3]
        This thou perceiv'st, which makes thy love more strong,
        To love that well, which thou must leave ere long.

80

    O, how I faint° when I of you do write,   *get discouraged*
    Knowing a better spirit[4] doth use your name,
    And in the praise thereof spends all his might,
    To make me tongue-tied, speaking of your fame!
5   But since your worth, wide as the ocean is,
    The humble as° the proudest sail doth bear,   *as well as*
    My saucy bark,° inferior far to his,   *impudent boat*
    On your broad main° doth willfully° appear.   *waters / boldly*
    Your shallowest help will hold me up afloat
10 Whilst he upon your soundless° deep doth ride;   *bottomless*
    Or, being wrecked, I am a worthless boat,
    He of tall building[5] and of goodly pride.°   *magnificence*
        Then if he thrive and I be cast away,
        The worst was this: my love was my decay.

85

    My tongue-tied muse in manners holds her still°   *tactfully says nothing*
    While comments of° your praise, richly compiled,   *commentaries in*
    Reserve thy character° with golden quill   *hoard up your features*
    And precious phrase by all the muses filed.°   *polished*
5   I think good thoughts whilst other° write good words,   *others*
    And like unlettered clerk still cry "Amen"
    To every hymn[6] that able spirit affords°   *offers*

---

2. The part of a church where divine service was sung.
3. Choked by the ashes of that which once nourished its flame.
4. A rival poet. See the headnote.

5. Tall, strong build.
6. "Like . . . hymn": like an illiterate parish clerk reflexively approve ("cry 'Amen'" after) every poem ("hymn") of praise.

In polished form of well-refinèd pen.
Hearing you praised I say "'Tis so, 'tis true,"
10 And to the most° of praise add something more;   highest
But that is in my thought,° whose love to you,   *i.e., is unspoken*
Though words come hindmost, holds his rank before.°   *before all others*
   Then others for the breath of words respect,°   regard
   Me for my dumb thoughts, speaking in effect.°   *in reality*

87

Farewell: thou art too dear[7] for my possessing,
And like enough thou know'st thy estimate.°   value
The charter° of thy worth gives thee releasing;[8]   *deed; contract for property*
My bonds in thee are all determinate.°   expired
5 For how do I hold thee but by thy granting,
And for that riches where is my deserving?
The cause of this fair gift in me is wanting,°   absent
And so my patent° back again is swerving.[9]   title
Thy self thou gav'st, thy own worth then not knowing,
10 Or me, to whom thou gav'st it, else mistaking;°   *i.e., overestimating*
So thy great gift, upon misprision growing,°   *based on error*
Comes home again, on better judgment making.[1]
   Thus have I had thee as a dream doth flatter:
   In sleep a king, but waking no such matter.

93

So shall I live supposing thou art true,
Like a deceivèd husband; so love's face°   appearance
May still seem love to me, though altered new—
Thy looks with me, thy heart in other place.
5 For there can live no hatred in thine eye;
Therefore in that I cannot know thy change.
In many's looks the false heart's history
Is writ in moods and frowns and wrinkles strange:[2]
But heaven in thy creation did decree
10 That in thy face sweet love should ever dwell;
Whate'er thy thoughts or thy heart's workings be,
Thy looks should nothing thence but sweetness tell.
   How like Eve's apple doth thy beauty grow°   become
   If thy sweet virtue answer not thy show![3]

94

They that have power to hurt and will do none,
That do not do the thing they most do show,[4]
Who, moving others, are themselves as stone,
Unmovèd, cold, and to temptation slow;
5 They rightly do inherit heaven's graces
And husband nature's riches from expense;[5]

---

7. (1) Expensive, (2) beloved.
8. Releases you (from love's bonds).
9. I.e., reverting to you.
1. I.e., when you realize your error.

2. Unaccustomed. "Moods": moody expressions.
3. Does not correspond to your appearance.
4. Seem to do, or seem capable of doing.
5. I.e., they do not squander nature's gifts.

They are the lords and owners of their faces,
Others but stewards of their excellence.
The summer's flower is to the summer sweet,
10   Though to itself it only live and die,[6]
But if that flower with base infection meet,
The basest weed outbraves° his dignity: *surpasses*
    For sweetest things turn sourest by their deeds;
    Lilies that fester smell far worse than weeds.

97

How like a winter hath my absence been
From thee, the pleasure of the fleeting year!
What freezings have I felt, what dark days seen!
What old December's bareness everywhere!
5   And yet this time removed[7] was summer's time,
The teeming autumn, big with rich increase,
Bearing the wanton burthen of the prime,[8]
Like widowed wombs after their lords' decease.
Yet this abundant issue° seemed to me   *outgrowth*
10 But hope of orphans and unfathered fruit;
For summer and his pleasures wait° on thee,   *attend*
And, thou away, the very birds are mute;
    Or, if they sing, 'tis with so dull a cheer°   *such a dismal mood*
    That leaves look pale, dreading the winter's near.

105

Let not my love be called idolatry,
Nor my belovèd as an idol show,
Since all alike my songs and praises be
To one, of one, still° such, and ever so.   *continually*
5   Kind is my love today, tomorrow kind,
Still constant in a wondrous excellence.
Therefore my verse, to constancy confined,
One thing expressing, leaves out difference.°   *variety*
"Fair, kind, and true" is all my argument,°   *theme*
10 "Fair, kind, and true" varying to other words,
And in this change is my invention spent,[9]
Three themes in one, which wonderous scope affords.
    Fair, kind, and true have often lived alone,°   *separately*
    Which three till now never kept seat° in one.   *dwelt permanently*

106

When in the chronicle of wasted° time   *past*
I see descriptions of the fairest wights,°   *persons*
And beauty making beautiful old rhyme
In praise of ladies dead and lovely knights,

---

6. Even if it lives and dies in apparent isolation (unpollinated).
7. I.e., when I was absent.
8. Spring, which has engendered the lavish crop ("wanton burthen") that autumn is now left to bear.
9. And in varying the words alone my inventiveness is expended.

5   Then, in the blazon[1] of sweet beauty's best,
Of hand, of foot, of lip, of eye, of brow,
I see their antique pen would have expressed
Even such a beauty as you master now.
So all their praises are but prophecies
10 Of this our time, all you prefiguring;
And, for they looked but with divining eyes,[2]
They had not skill enough your worth to sing:
    For we, which now behold these present days,
    Have eyes to wonder, but lack tongues to praise.

116

Let me not to the marriage of true minds
Admit impediments;[3] love is not love
Which alters when it alteration finds,
Or bends with the remover to remove:
5 O, no, it is an ever-fixèd mark,[4]
That looks on tempests and is never shaken;
It is the star to every wand'ring bark,
Whose worth's unknown, although his height[5] be taken.
Love's not Time's fool,° though rosy lips and cheeks   *plaything*
10 Within his[6] bending sickle's compass come;
Love alters not with his brief hours and weeks,
But bears it out even to the edge of doom.°   *brink of Judgment Day*
    If this be error and upon me proved,
    I never writ, nor no man ever loved.

129

Th' expense of spirit in a waste of shame
Is lust in action;[7] and till action, lust
Is perjured, murd'rous, bloody, full of blame,
Savage, extreme, rude,° cruel, not to trust;   *brutal*
5 Enjoyed no sooner but despisèd straight;°   *immediately*
Past reason hunted, and no sooner had,
Past reason hated as a swallowed bait
On purpose laid to make the taker mad:
Mad in pursuit, and in possession so;
10 Had, having, and in quest to have, extreme;
A bliss in proof,[8] and proved, a very° woe;   *true*
Before, a joy proposed; behind, a dream.
    All this the world well knows; yet none knows well
    To shun the heaven that leads men to this hell.

1. Catalog of excellencies.
2. Because ("for") they were able only ("but") to foresee prophetically.
3. From the Anglican marriage service: "If either of you do know any impediment why ye may not be lawfully joined together . . ."
4. Seamark, such as a lighthouse or a beacon.
5. The star's value is incalculable, although its altitude may be known and used for navigation.
6. Time's (as also in line 11).
7. The word order here is inverted and slightly obscures the meaning. Lust, when put into action, expends "spirit" (life, vitality; also semen) in a "waste" (desert; also with a pun on *waist*) of shame.
8. A bliss during the experience.

130

My mistress' eyes are nothing like the sun;[9]
Coral is far more red than her lips' red;
If snow be white, why then her breasts are dun;
If hairs be wires, black wires grow on her head.
5   I have seen roses damasked,° red and white,   *dappled*
But no such roses see I in her cheeks;
And in some perfumes is there more delight
Than in the breath that from my mistress reeks.[1]
I love to hear her speak, yet well I know
10   That music hath a far more pleasing sound;
I grant I never saw a goddess go;°   *walk*
My mistress, when she walks, treads on the ground.
    And yet, by heaven, I think my love as rare°   *admirable; extraordinary*
    As any she belied° with false compare.   *misrepresented*

135

Whoever hath her wish, thou hast thy *Will*,[2]
And *Will* to boot, and *Will* in overplus;
More than enough am I that vex thee still,°   *always*
To thy sweet will making addition thus.
5   Wilt thou, whose will is large and spacious,
Not once vouchsafe° to hide my will in thine?   *consent*
Shall will in others seem right gracious,
And in° my will no fair acceptance shine?   *in the case of*
The sea, all water, yet receives rain still,
10   And in abundance addeth to his store,°   *plenty*
So thou being rich in *Will* add to thy *Will*
One will of mine to make thy large *Will* more.
    Let no unkind, no fair beseechers kill;[3]
    Think all but one, and me in that one *Will*.

138

When my love swears that she is made of truth,
I do believe her, though I know she lies,[4]
That she might think me some untutored youth,
Unlearnèd in the world's false subtleties.
5   Thus vainly thinking that she thinks me young,
Although she knows my days are past the best,[5]
Simply° I credit her false-speaking tongue: *like a simpleton*
On both sides thus is simple truth suppressed.
But wherefore says she not she is unjust?°   *unfaithful*

---

9. An anti-Petrarchan sonnet. All of the details commonly attributed by other Elizabethan sonneteers to their ladies (for example, in Spenser's *Amoretti* 64, p. 476) are here denied to the poet's mistress.
1. Not with our pejorative sense, but simply "emanates."
2. (1) Wishes, (2) carnal desire, (3) the male and female sexual organs, (4) one or more lovers— evidently including Shakespeare—named Will.

This is one of several sonnets punning on the word.
3. I.e., do not kill with unkindness any of your wooers.
4. With the obvious sexual pun (as also in lines 13–14). "Made of truth": (1) is utterly honest, (2) is faithful.
5. Shakespeare was thirty-five or younger when he wrote this sonnet (it first appeared in *The Passionate Pilgrim*, 1599).

10 And wherefore say not I that I am old?
   Oh, love's best habit° is in seeming trust,   *clothing, guise*
   And age in love loves not to have years told.°   *counted*
       Therefore I lie with her and she with me,
       And in our faults by lies we flattered be.

144

Two loves I have of comfort and despair,[6]
Which like two spirits do suggest me still:°   *tempt me constantly*
The better angel is a man right fair,
The worser spirit a woman colored ill.°   *dark*
5 To win me soon to hell, my female evil
  Tempteth my better angel from my side,
  And would corrupt my saint to be a devil,
  Wooing his purity with her foul pride.[7]
  And whether that my angel be turned fiend
10 Suspect I may, yet not directly tell;
   But being both from me, both to each[8] friend,
   I guess one angel in another's hell.
       Yet this shall I ne'er know, but live in doubt,
       Till my bad angel fire my good one out.[9]

146

Poor soul, the center of my sinful earth,
Lord of[1] these rebel powers that thee array,[2]
Why dost thou pine within and suffer dearth,
Painting thy outward walls so costly gay?
5 Why so large cost, having so short a lease,
  Dost thou upon thy fading mansion spend?
  Shall worms, inheritors of this excess,
  Eat up thy charge?[3] Is this thy body's end?°   *destiny; purpose*
  Then, soul, live thou upon thy servant's loss,
10 And let that pine to aggravate thy store;[4]
   Buy terms divine in selling hours of dross;[5]
   Within be fed, without be rich no more.
       So shalt thou feed on death, that feeds on men,
       And death once dead, there's no more dying then.

147

My love is as a fever, longing still°   *continually*
For that which longer nurseth[6] the disease,
Feeding on that which doth preserve the ill,°   *maintain the illness*
Th' uncertain sickly appetite[7] to please.

6. I have two beloveds, one bringing me comfort and the other despair.
7. (1) Vanity, (2) sexuality.
8. Each other. "From": away from.
9. I.e., until she infects him with venereal disease.
1. "Lord of": an emendation. The 1609 edition repeats the last three words of line 1. Other suggestions are "Thrall to," "Starved by," "Pressed by," and leaving the repetition but dropping "that

thee" in line 2.
2. The rebellious body that clothes you.
3. (1) Your expense, (2) the thing you were responsible for (i.e., the body).
4. Let "that" (i.e., the body) deteriorate to increase ("aggravate") the soul's riches ("thy store").
5. Rubbish. "Terms": long periods.
6. (1) Nourishes, (2) takes care of.
7. (1) Desire for food, (2) lust.

5 My reason, the physician to my love,
 Angry that his prescriptions are not kept,
 Hath left me, and I desperate now approve
 Desire is death, which physic did except.[8]
 Past cure I am, now reason is past care,[9]
10 And frantic mad with evermore unrest;
 My thoughts and my discourse as madmen's are,
 At random from the truth, vainly expressed:[1]
  For I have sworn thee fair, and thought thee bright,
  Who art as black as hell, as dark as night.

152

 In loving thee thou know'st I am forsworn,[2]
 But thou art twice forsworn to me love swearing:
 In act thy bed-vow° broke, and new faith torn   *to husband (or lover)*
 In vowing new hate after new love bearing.[3]
5 But why of two oaths' breach do I accuse thee
 When I break twenty? I am perjured most,
 For all my vows are oaths but to misuse° thee,   *deceive; misrepresent*
 And all my honest faith in thee is lost.
 For I have sworn deep oaths of thy deep kindness,
10 Oaths of thy love, thy truth, thy constancy,
 And to enlighten thee gave eyes to blindness,[4]
 Or made them swear against the thing they see.
  For I have sworn thee fair—more perjured eye°   *(punning on "I")*
  To swear against the truth so foul a lie.

1609

Othello

Othello (1603–04), one of a succession of tragic masterpieces that Shakespeare wrote in the early years of the seventeenth century, is unrivaled in its excruciating intensity. The play has for centuries aroused in audiences the paradoxical blend of pleasure and acute discomfort characteristic of the effect of great tragedy. The performance history of *Othello* includes anecdotes of spectators attempting to intervene by angrily denouncing the villain, shouting advice to the deceived hero, or even rushing onstage to save the doomed heroine, and if such stories reveal a fundamental misunderstanding of the nature of theater, they also disclose Shakespeare's brilliant exploitation of the gap between the performers and the audience. We see what is happening; we understand where it is leading; we urgently want to prevent the catastrophe—but we are powerless to do so. *Othello* is a prime instance of what the twentieth-century French writer Antonin Artaud called "the theater of cruelty."

This cruelty is intensified by the fact that the plot of Shakespeare's tragedy is woven from some of the elements of the joyous comedies with which he had already distinguished himself. *Othello* begins with a miniature version of the traditional comedy of sexual fulfillment. Refusing to allow his daughter to elope with the man

---

8. I.e., I learn by experience that desire, which rejected reason's medicine, is death.
9. I.e., medical care (of me). The line is a version of the proverb "past cure, past care."
1. Wide of the mark and senselessly uttered.
2. I.e., am breaking loving vows to another.

3. The object of the "new faith" followed by "new hate" could be either the speaker's young friend or the speaker himself.
4. And to make you fair (or give you insight), I looked blindly on your failings (or pretended to see what I couldn't).

of her choosing, an angry father, well-born, wealthy, and powerful, lodges a formal complaint before the authorities. His daughter, he alleges, has been seduced by means of witchcraft; otherwise, she would never have been attracted to someone so far below her in social class and culture. At first the authorities—the senators of the Venetian Republic—seem inclined to agree, but after hearing testimony from the couple in question, Othello and Desdemona, they dismiss the father's complaint. The rigid hold of the older generation over the desires of the next is broken; paternal possessiveness is defeated; and romantic love triumphs over familial bonds. And lest this triumph should seem to threaten the social order, the romantic couple is legitimated by marriage, the newlywed husband makes clear his devotion to serving the state in its war against the Turks, and the spouse who at first seemed socially unsuitable turns out to be the equal of his amorous conquest. "I fetch my life and being," Othello declares, "From men of royal siege" (1.2.21–22). All's well that ends well.

But, of course, it does not end well. Disturbing hints of other, less benign comic plots have already begun to surface in the first scenes. One of these is a potential resemblance to the familiar farces of January and May, where an old man is married to a much younger wife who is courted by handsome, unscrupulous suitors. Another is to what we might call the comedy of fantastical passion, involving a person who awakens from the trance of love to find that the object of desire is in fact ridiculous. Another is to the comedy of the braggart soldier, the preening, self-promoting hero who is revealed to be an empty shell. And yet another is to the collective mocking of the alien, the ridiculing of an outsider who hopes to be accepted but whom the natives despise as outlandish, gullible, or grotesque.

There is one person who is particularly sensitive to all of these cruel comic undertones: Othello's devious, resentful third-in-command, Iago. Unable to derail Othello's elopement, Iago seizes on potentially destructive versions of Othello and Desdemona's story. Desdemona fell in love with Othello merely for his bragging, he tells the lovesick Roderigo, but she will soon realize her mistake and long for someone younger, more handsome, more appropriate. When Roderigo doubts that Desdemona can be so easily seduced—"I cannot believe that in her; she's full of most blessed condition"—Iago replies with the cynic's tough, deflating realism: "Blessed fig's-end! The wine she drinks is made of grapes" (2.1.246–49).

The initial problem for Iago, though, is that none of these conventional comic designs seems to be going anywhere. Desdemona shows no sign of restlessness with her choice, nor does she register discomfort with the age difference between herself and her husband. Othello's martial heroism is the real thing, attested to by everyone and elegantly manifested in the serene self-confidence with which he greets the armed followers of his irate father-in-law: "Keep up your bright swords, for the dew will rust them" (1.2.59). It is true that he initially allured Desdemona with exotic tales from what he calls "the story of my life" (1.3.128), but the bond between them is anything but superficial: consecrating her "soul and fortunes" to her husband, she declares that her "heart's subdued / Even to the very quality of my lord" (1.3.252, 248–49).

The strongest weapon in Iago's arsenal is the contempt and revulsion with which many Europeans in the Middle Ages and the Renaissance routinely stigmatized dark skin and negroid features. Othello is a "Moor," whether that refers to people of North or sub-Saharan Africa, and this identity is enough to trigger and evidently to allow with impunity the racist abuse Iago and Roderigo shout in the darkness in the first moments of the play. Othello is a "thick-lips," an "old black ram," a "Barbary horse" (1.1.63, 85, 108). But even this weapon seems blunted. Othello is not a religious outsider, but a Christian. He is the valiant commander to whom the state of Venice turns when it needs to defend its strategic outpost Cyprus against the great Muslim enemy, the Turks. Racial slurs in this play are the hallmarks of viciousness, not the collective judgment of the community. As for Desdemona, her declaration that she "saw Othello's visage in his mind" (1.3.250) suggests, among other things, that the color of her husband's skin is not relevant to the great love that unites them.

How then does Iago do it? How does he succeed in undermining Othello's absolute faith in his wife and in shattering what seems an unshakable bond? Shakespeare depicts the destruction in one of the greatest scenes he ever wrote, a quiet conversation between the two men. The Turkish threat has vanished, blown away by a storm; Othello and Desdemona have been safely reunited in Cyprus; and though a drunken brawl in the night (cunningly instigated by Iago) has temporarily disgraced Othello's lieutenant Cassio, all the significant obstacles to harmony both public and private seem to have been resolved. At this moment of almost perfect security, Iago injects the fatal poison of jealousy into Othello by little more than the intonation of the simple word "indeed?" (3.3.101). Without leveling any direct accusation or offering a shred of evidence, with only a succession of apparently naïve questions and broken phrases, Iago manages to insert himself into and remake—ultimately, destroy—Othello's whole world.

Othello is not naïve. He grasps that his ensign's verbal feints and dodges could "in a false disloyal knave" (3.3.124) be tricks designed to take in a gullible person. But he knows Iago well, he thinks, and has confidence in his honesty. Tormented by the unbearable pain of aroused jealousy, Othello demands "ocular proof" (3.3.361) of Desdemona's adultery with Cassio. Iago, who has been promoted to lieutenant in Cassio's place, then embarks on a devious set of deceptions, centered on an embroidered handkerchief, a gift from Othello, that Desdemona has mislaid. "Trifles light as air," Iago gleefully observes, "Are to the jealous confirmations strong / As proofs of holy writ" (3.3.323–25).

What is Iago's motive? Why should he want to destroy both Othello, on whom his livelihood depends, and Desdemona, whom his own wife, Emilia, serves as lady's maid? Early in the play Iago presents himself as someone with an eye only for his own interests: "not I for love and duty, / But seeming so, for my peculiar end" (1.1.56–57). But it is difficult to make out how ruining his commander could possibly help. What is his peculiar—that is, personal—end?

As was his usual practice, Shakespeare did not make up the plot of his play from scratch but instead adapted it from another work; in this case, a short story by the sixteenth-century Italian writer Giraldi Cinthio. In Cinthio's account the villain's pathology is reasonably clear. Having fallen ardently in love with Desdemona, he tried to seduce her. When he did not succeed, the love he felt for the general's wife turned into violent loathing, and he set about to destroy her. Shakespeare discards this motivation. His villain does not dream of possessing Othello's wife, nor is she the particular object of his hatred. To be sure, there is a moment in which Iago seems to be heading in this direction—"Now I do love her too" (2.1.287), he declares in one of his sinister soliloquies—yet he immediately veers away from it toward a farrago of other explanations. Iago's repeated attempts to account for his obsessive, unappeasable hatred of Othello are famously unconvincing. Samuel Taylor Coleridge called them "the motive-hunting of a motiveless malignity." Near the play's end, when he has come to understand that he has been duped into murdering his innocent, loving wife and that his life has been destroyed in the cruelest imaginable way, Othello asks why Iago "hath thus ensnared my soul and body?" Iago's spare, monosyllabic reply—his last utterance in the play—is a refusal to apologize or explain: "What you know, you know. / From this time forth I never will speak word" (5.2.307–09).

But why does Othello succumb? Why should a passion on which he has staked his whole being—"when I love thee not, / Chaos is come again" (3.3.91–92)—prove so fragile? Why should he doubt the faith of a woman so obviously single-minded in her devotion to him and so pure in her love? The answer in part seems to lie in the terrible vulnerability of trust. As Iago coolly observes, "The Moor is of a free and open nature / That thinks men honest that but seem to be so" (1.3.389–90). That openness, that disinclination to suspect treachery and double-dealing, makes it possible for Iago to penetrate Othello's psychic defenses and refashion his perceptions.

Though Iago has a coarse and reductive account of human nature, he is a brilliant improviser, able to employ whatever comes to hand to shape illusions and to manipulate those around him like puppets in a theatrical performance of his making. He bustles about using people without a trace of moral restraint or shame, and he has the peculiar liberty of complete fraudulence: "I am not what I am" (1.1.62). In the end, he is exposed—by the wife whom he despises and finally murders—but not before he has ruined whatever seemed most beautiful and precious around him. Such is the power of cunning lies and twisted hatred over someone "that loved not wisely but too well" (5.2.349).

But perhaps this characterization of himself, offered by Othello just before his suicide, is not quite right, or at least not complete. Perhaps there is something disturbing in his love—some strain of anxiety about the future, about sexual pleasure, about his capacity for happiness—that Iago senses he can exploit. "If it were now to die," Othello has declared at the height of his joy,

> 'Twere now to be most happy; for I fear
> My soul hath her content so absolute
> That not another comfort like to this
> Succeeds in unknown fate. (2.1.188–91)

Desdemona attempts to offer reassurance—"The heavens forbid / But that our loves and comforts should increase / Even as our days do grow" (2.1.191–93)—but the malevolent worm of Iago's doubt is more powerful than her generous embrace. Or, finally, is it? Desdemona struggles in her last breath to commend herself to her "kind lord" (5.2.128), and Othello, desperately attempting to reestablish a moral order by executing himself, dies kissing the wife whose innocence he knows he has fatally wronged. Readers and audiences have, for more than four centuries, pondered how much these final gestures offer a slender glimpse of redemption.

The Tragedy of Othello, the Moor of Venice[*]

The Names of the Actors[1]

Othello, the Moor [and General of the Venetian forces]
Brabantio, father to Desdemona [and a Venetian Senator]
Cassio, an honorable lieutenant [to Othello]
Iago, a villain [and Othello's standard-bearer or ensign]
Roderigo, a gulled° gentleman   deceived
Duke of Venice
Senators
Montano, Governor of Cyprus
Gentlemen of Cyprus
Lodovico and Gratiano, two Noble Venetians [and kinsmen to Brabantio]
Sailors
Clown
Desdemona, wife to Othello
Emilia, wife to Iago
Bianca, a courtesan

---

[*]*Othello* exists in two early texts, both of which have a claim to authority: a version published in the small, inexpensive quarto format in 1622 (Q) and a version published in the great First Folio of 1623 (F). There are many small and some substantial differences between them, including 160 lines that are found only in F. The text in the Major Authors Edition is adapted from the Nor-

ton Critical Edition of *Othello*, edited by Edward Pechter. Like most modern editors of the play, Pechter bases his text on F, corrected by some readings from Q. Significant departures from Pechter's text have been footnoted.
1. The list of characters (with its misleading title) is reproduced from the First Folio, with some bracketed additions.

1.1

Enter RODERIGO *and* IAGO[1]

RODERIGO   Tush, never tell me![2] I take it much unkindly
  That thou, Iago, who hast had my purse
  As if the strings were thine, shouldst know of this.
IAGO   'Sblood,° but you'll not hear me! If ever I did dream   *by Christ's blood*
  Of such a matter, abhor me.
5 RODERIGO   Thou told'st me
  Thou didst hold him in thy hate.
IAGO   Despise me
  If I do not. Three great ones of the city,
  In personal suit to make me his lieutenant,
  Off-capped° to him; and by the faith of man   *took off their caps*
10 I know my price; I am worth no worse a place.
  But he, as loving his own pride and purposes,
  Evades them with a bombast circumstance,[3]
  Horribly stuffed with epithets of war,°   *i.e., military jargon*
  Non-suits° my mediators. For "Certes,"° says he,   *denies / certainly*
15 "I have already chose my officer." And what was he?
  Forsooth, a great arithmetician,[4]
  One Michael Cassio, a Florentine,
  A fellow almost damned in a fair wife,[5]
  That° never set a squadron in the field,   *who*
20 Nor the division° of a battle° knows   *ordering / battalion*
  More than a spinster°—unless the bookish theorick,°   *housewife / learning*
  Wherein the tonguèd consuls can propose[6]
  As masterly as he. Mere prattle without practice
  Is all his soldiership. But he, sir, had th'election
25 And I—of whom his eyes had seen the proof
  At Rhodes, at Cyprus, and on other grounds,
  Christened and heathen—must be beeled° and calmed[7]   *without wind*
  By debitor and creditor. This counter-caster,[8]
  He in good time° must his lieutenant be,   *indeed (scornful)*
30 And I—God bless the mark!° —his Moorship's ancient.[9]   *God help us*
RODERIGO   By heaven, I rather would have been his
    hangman.
IAGO   Why, there's no remedy. 'Tis the curse of service;
  Preferment goes by letter and affection,[1]

1.1 Location: A street in Venice.
1. Iago's name may be related to that of Santiago Matamoros ("St. James the Moor-Slayer"), the patron saint of Spain.
2. "Tush, never tell me": expressive of annoyance, disbelief
3. With an inflated circumlocution. "Bombast": cotton padding in clothes, a metaphor picked up by "stuffed" (line 13) and perhaps "Non-suits" (line 14).
4. Implying that Cassio's knowledge of war is purely theoretical.
5. Obscure. Cassio has not yet met Bianca and is unmarried (although in Shakespeare's source he is married). Perhaps Shakespeare's error, a reference to Cassio as a ladies' man, or an oblique

anticipation of the main plot.
6. In which the glib senators can debate. In Q the senators are not "tonguèd" but "togaed," i.e., toga-wearing.
7. Becalmed.
8. "Debitor and creditor," "counter-caster": pejorative terms for an accountant (Cassio).
9. As "ancient" (a variant form of "ensign"), Iago is something like a standard-bearer or third-in-command. He clearly ranks below "lieutenant" Cassio, the second-in-command. This reference to "his Moorship" is also the first indication about whom Iago has been complaining.
1. Promotion comes through connections and favoritism.

And not by old gradation,° where each second   *traditional seniority*
Stood heir to th'first. Now, sir, be judge yourself
Whether I in any just term am affined°   *am bound in any just way*
To love the Moor.[2]

RODERIGO   I would not follow him then.

IAGO   O, sir, content you.°   *be content*
  I follow him to serve my turn upon him.
  We cannot all be masters, nor all masters
  Cannot be truly followed. You shall mark
  Many a duteous and knee-crooking knave
  That, doting on his own obsequious bondage,
  Wears out his time much like his master's ass,
  For naught but provender;° and when he's old—   *animal feed*
    cashiered.°   *fired*
  Whip me° such honest knaves! Others there are   *the hell with*
  Who, trimmed° in forms and visages of duty,   *outwardly decorated*
  Keep yet their hearts attending on themselves
  And, throwing but shows of service on their lords,
  Do well thrive by them; and when they have lined their
    coats,
  Do themselves homage. These fellows have some soul,
  And such a one do I profess myself. For, sir,
  It is as sure as you are Roderigo,
  Were I the Moor, I would not be Iago.
  In following him, I follow but myself.
  Heaven is my judge, not I for° love and duty,   *I am not driven by*
  But seeming so, for my peculiar° end.   *personal*
  For when my outward action doth demonstrate
  The native act and figure[3] of my heart
  In complement extern,° 'tis not long after   *outward appearance*
  But I will wear my heart upon my sleeve
  For daws° to peck at. I am not what I am.   *crowlike birds*

RODERIGO   What a full fortune does the thick-lips owe°   *own*
  If he can carry't thus!

IAGO   Call up her father,
  Rouse him, make after him, poison his delight.
  Proclaim him in the streets, incense her kinsmen,
  And though he in a fertile climate dwell,
  Plague him with flies. Though that his joy be joy,
  Yet throw such chances of vexation on't,
  As it may lose some color.

RODERIGO   Here is her father's house. I'll call aloud.

IAGO   Do, with like timorous accent° and dire yell   *frightening tone*
  As when, by night and negligence, the fire

---

2. A Moor was a Muslim of the mixed Berber and Arab people inhabiting northwest Africa. This term, like the comparison of Othello to a "Barbary horse" (an Arab, line 108), formerly led to the denial of Othello's blackness. But the passages describing Othello's appearance—"thick-lips," "black ram," "sooty bosom," "black Othello," "I am black," "black / As mine own face" (1.1.63, 1.1.85, 1.2.70, 2.3.29, 3.3.265, 3.3.388–89)— seem to have greater weight. In the Renaissance, "Moor" often meant sub-Saharan African.
3. The innate operation (or motivation) and shape (or nature).

Is spied in populous cities.

75 RODERIGO   What ho, Brabantio! Signor Brabantio, ho!

IAGO   Awake! What ho, Brabantio! Thieves, thieves!
Look to your house, your daughter, and your bags!
Thieves, thieves!

[*Enter*] BRABANTIO *above at a window*

BRABANTIO   What is the reason of this terrible summons?

80   What is the matter there?

RODERIGO   Signor, is all your family within?

IAGO   Are your doors locked?

BRABANTIO   Why? Wherefore ask you this?

IAGO   'Swounds,° sir, you're robbed! For shame, put on   *by Christ's wounds*
your gown!
Your heart is burst, you have lost half your soul.

85   Even now, now, very now, an old black ram
Is tupping° your white ewe. Arise, arise!   *copulating with*
Awake the snorting° citizens with the bell,   *snoring*
Or else the devil will make a grandsire of you.
Arise, I say!

BRABANTIO   What, have you lost your wits?

90 RODERIGO   Most reverend signor, do you know my voice?

BRABANTIO   Not I; what are you?

RODERIGO   My name is Roderigo.

BRABANTIO   The worser welcome!
I have charged thee not to haunt about my doors;
In honest plainness thou hast heard me say

95   My daughter is not for thee. And now in madness,
Being full of supper and distemp'ring° draughts,   *destabilizing*
Upon malicious bravery,° dost thou come   *defiance*
To start° my quiet.   *upset*

RODERIGO   Sir, sir, sir—

BRABANTIO   But thou must needs be sure,

100   My spirits and my place° have in their power   *rank*
To make this bitter to thee.

RODERIGO   Patience, good sir.

BRABANTIO   What tell'st thou me of robbing? This is
Venice;
My house is not a grange.°   *country house*

RODERIGO   Most grave Brabantio,
In simple and pure soul, I come to you.

105 IAGO   'Swounds, sir, you are one of those that will not
serve God if the devil bid you. Because we come to do
you service and you think we are ruffians, you'll have
your daughter covered with a Barbary horse;[4] you'll
have your nephews° neigh to you; you'll have coursers   *grandsons*

110   for cousins and jennets for germans.[5]

---

4. Horse from northwest coastal Africa.   "cousins": kinsmen; "jennets": small Spanish
5. Close relatives. "Coursers": strong horses;   horses.

BRABANTIO   What profane wretch art thou?
IAGO   I am one, sir, that comes to tell you your daughter
   and the Moor are making the beast with two backs.°   *copulating*
BRABANTIO   Thou art a villain.
IAGO   You are a senator.
BRABANTIO   This thou shalt answer.° I know thee,   *account for*
   Roderigo.
RODERIGO   Sir, I will answer anything. But I beseech you,
   If't be your pleasure, and most wise consent—⁶
   As partly I find it is—that your fair daughter,
   At this odd-even° and dull watch o'th' night,   *late (around midnight)*
   Transported with no worse nor better guard
   But with a knave of common° hire, a gondolier,   *public*
   To the gross clasps of a lascivious Moor—
   If this be known to you, and your allowance,°   *allowed by you*
   We then have done you bold and saucy wrongs.
   But if you know not this, my manners tell me
   We have your wrong rebuke. Do not believe
   That from° the sense of all civility   *in opposition to*
   I thus would play and trifle with your reverence.
   Your daughter, if you have not given her leave,
   I say again, hath made a gross revolt,
   Tying her duty, beauty, wit, and fortunes
   In an extravagant and wheeling stranger⁷
   Of here and everywhere. Straight° satisfy yourself.   *immediately*
   If she be in her chamber or your house,
   Let loose on me the justice of the state
   For thus deluding you.
BRABANTIO   Strike on the tinder,° ho!   *a light*
   Give me a taper,° call up all my people!   *candle*
   This accident° is not unlike my dream;   *event*
   Belief of it oppresses me already.
   Light, I say, light!   *Exit [above]*
IAGO   Farewell, for I must leave you.
   It seems not meet° nor wholesome to my place   *proper*
   To be producted°—as, if I stay, I shall—   *presented as witness*
   Against the Moor. For I do know the state,
   However this may gall him with some check,°   *reprimand*
   Cannot with safety cast° him; for he's embarked°   *dismiss / committed*
   With such loud reason° to the Cyprus wars,   *urgent*
   Which even now stands in act,° that, for their souls,   *are taking place*
   Another of his fathom° they have none   *caliber*
   To lead their business. In which regard,
   Though I do hate him as I do hell pains,
   Yet for necessity of present life
   I must show out a flag and sign of love,
   Which is indeed but sign. That you shall surely find
   him,

6. Lines 118–134 do not appear in Q.
7. In a vagrant and vagabond foreigner.

155   Lead to the Sagittary[8] the raisèd search,°   *awakened searchers*
    And there will I be with him. So farewell.   *Exit*
    Enter [below] BRABANTIO *in his nightgown, with*
    servants and torches
BRABANTIO   It is too true an evil. Gone she is,
    And what's to come of my despisèd time°   *lifetime*
    Is naught but bitterness. Now, Roderigo,
160   Where didst thou see her?—O unhappy girl!—
    With the Moor, say'st thou?—Who would be a father?—
    How didst thou know 'twas she?—O, she deceives me
    Past thought!—What said she to you?— *[To servants]* Get
      more tapers,
    Raise all my kindred!   *[Exit one or more]*
    [To RODERIGO*]*   Are they married, think you?
165 RODERIGO   Truly, I think they are.
BRABANTIO   O heaven! How got she out? O treason of
    the blood!
    Fathers, from hence trust not your daughters' minds
    By what you see them act. Is there not charms°   *magic*
    By which the property° of youth and maidhood°   *attribute / virginity*
170   May be abused? Have you not read, Roderigo,
    Of some such thing?
RODERIGO   Yes, sir, I have indeed.
BRABANTIO   *[to servants]* Call up my brother.
    [To RODERIGO*]*   O, would you had had her!
    [To servants] Some one way, some another.
                [Exit one or more]
    [To RODERIGO*]*   Do you know
    Where we may apprehend her and the Moor?
175 RODERIGO   I think I can discover him, if you please
    To get good guard and go along with me.
BRABANTIO   Pray you lead on. At every house I'll call;
    I may command° at most.—Get weapons, ho!   *demand help*
    And raise some special officers of night.—
180   On, good Roderigo; I will deserve° your pains.   *reward*
                Exeunt

1.2

    Enter OTHELLO, IAGO, *[and] attendants with torches*
IAGO   Though in the trade of war I have slain men,
    Yet do I hold it very stuff° o'th' conscience   *essence*
    To do no contrived° murder. I lack iniquity,   *premeditated*
    Sometime, to do me service. Nine or ten times
5   I had thought t'have yerked him° here, under the ribs.   *stabbed (Roderigo)*
OTHELLO   'Tis better as it is.

8. Perhaps indicating an inn named for the astrological sign Sagittarius, where Othello and Desdemona are staying. It may also suggest Othello himself, since Sagittarius is depicted as a centaur (a mythological being part man, part horse), and Iago has already likened Othello to a "Barbary horse."
1.2 Location: Another street in Venice, before Othello's lodgings.

IAGO   Nay, but he prated
　And spoke such scurvy and provoking terms
　Against your honor
　That, with the little godliness I have,
　I did full hard forbear him.¹ But I pray you, sir,
　Are you fast° married? Be assured of this,   *legitimately*
　That the magnifico° is much beloved,   *(Brabantio)*
　And hath in his effect a voice potential°   *powerful*
　As double as the duke's. He will divorce you,
　Or put upon you what restraint or grievance
　The law, with all his might to enforce it on,
　Will give him cable.°   *scope*
OTHELLO   Let him do his spite.
　My services, which I have done the signory,°   *Venetian government*
　Shall out-tongue his complaints. 'Tis yet to know°—   *not publicly known*
　Which, when I know that boasting is an honor,
　I shall promulgate—I fetch my life and being
　From men of royal siege;° and my demerits°   *rank / deserts*
　May speak unbonneted² to as proud a fortune
　As this that I have reached. For know, Iago,
　But that I love the gentle Desdemona,
　I would not my unhousèd° free condition   *unconfined*
　Put into circumscription and confine
　For the seas' worth. But look, what lights come yond?
　　　　Enter CASSIO, *with officers and torches*
IAGO   Those are the raisèd father and his friends.
　You were best go in.
OTHELLO   Not I; I must be found.
　My parts,° my title, and my perfect soul³   *qualities*
　Shall manifest me rightly. Is it they?
IAGO   By Janus,° I think no.   *two-faced Roman god*
OTHELLO   The servants of the duke? And my lieutenant?
　The goodness of the night upon you, friends.
　What is the news?
CASSIO   The duke does greet you, general,
　And he requires your haste-post-haste appearance
　Even on the instant.
OTHELLO   What is the matter, think you?
CASSIO   Something from Cyprus, as I may divine.
　It is a business of some heat.° The galleys   *urgency*
　Have sent a dozen sequent° messengers   *successive*
　This very night at one another's heels,
　And many of the consuls, raised and met,
　Are at the duke's already. You have been hotly called for;
　When, being not at your lodging to be found,
　The senate hath sent about° three several quests   *out*
　To search you out.
OTHELLO   'Tis well I am found by you.

---

1. I barely restrained myself from attacking him.　　3. My clear conscience.
2. Without deference; modestly.

I will but spend a word here in the house
And go with you.   [*Exit*]
CASSIO   Ancient, what makes he here?
50 IAGO   Faith, he tonight hath boarded a land-carrack.[4]
If it prove lawful prize, he's made forever.
CASSIO   I do not understand.
IAGO   He's married.
CASSIO   To who?
IAGO   Marry,° to— [*Enter* OTHELLO]   *By Mary (a mild oath)*
Come, captain, will you go?
OTHELLO   Have with you.°   *let's go*
CASSIO   Here comes another troop to seek for you.
        Enter BRABANTIO [*and*] RODERIGO, *with officers and
        torches*
55 IAGO   It is Brabantio; general, be advised,
He comes to bad intent.
OTHELLO   Holla, stand there!
RODERIGO   Signor, it is the Moor.
BRABANTIO   Down with him, thief!
        [*They draw on both sides*]
IAGO   You, Roderigo? Come, sir, I am for you.
OTHELLO   Keep up° your bright swords, for the dew will   *put away*
rust them.
60 Good signor, you shall more command with years
Than with your weapons.
BRABANTIO   O thou foul thief, where hast thou stowed
my daughter?
Damned as thou art, thou hast enchanted her;
For I'll refer me to all things of sense,[5]
65 If she in chains of magic were not bound,
Whether a maid, so tender, fair, and happy,
So opposite to marriage that she shunned
The wealthy curlèd darlings of our nation,
Would ever have, t'incur a general mock,
70 Run from her guardage to the sooty bosom
Of such a thing as thou—to fear, not to delight.
Judge me the world if 'tis not gross in sense[6]
That thou hast practiced on her with foul charms,
Abused her delicate youth with drugs or minerals
75 That weakens motion.° I'll have't disputed on;[7]   *natural inclination*
'Tis probable and palpable to thinking.
I therefore apprehend and do attach° thee   *arrest*
For an abuser of the world, a practicer
Of arts inhibited and out of warrant.°   *prohibited and illegal*
80 Lay hold upon him; if he do resist,
Subdue him at his peril!
OTHELLO   Hold your hands,
Both you of my inclining° and the rest.   *following*

---

4. A carrack is a large merchant ship.
5. For I'll ask, relying on common sense.
6. If it is not patently obvious. Lines 72–77 do

not appear in Q.
7. Argued by experts.

Were it my cue to fight, I should have known it
Without a prompter. Where will you that I go
To answer this your charge?
BRABANTIO   To prison, till fit time
Of law and course of direct session
Call thee to answer.
OTHELLO   What if I do obey?
How may the duke be therewith satisfied,
Whose messengers are here about my side
Upon some present business of the state
To bring me to him?
OFFICER   'Tis true, most worthy signor.
The duke's in council, and your noble self
I am sure is sent for.
BRABANTIO   How? The duke in council?
In this time of the night? Bring him away.°   along
Mine's not an idle cause. The duke himself,
Or any of my brothers of the state,
Cannot but feel this wrong as 'twere their own;
For if such actions may have passage free,
Bondslaves and pagans shall our statesmen be.

                                                            Exeunt

1.3

Enter DUKE *and* SENATORS *set at a table, with lights
and* OFFICERS
DUKE   There's no composition in this news
That gives them credit.[1]
FIRST SENATOR   Indeed, they are disproportioned;°   *inconsistent*
My letters say a hundred and seven galleys.
DUKE   And mine a hundred forty.
SECOND SENATOR   And mine two hundred.
But though they jump not on a just account°—   *don't exactly agree*
As in these cases where the aim reports
'Tis oft with difference[2]—yet do they all confirm
A Turkish fleet, and bearing up to Cyprus.
DUKE   Nay, it is possible enough to judgment;
I do not so secure me in the error
But the main article I do approve
In fearful sense.[3]
SAILOR (*within*)   What ho! what ho! what ho!
            Enter SAILOR
OFFICER   A messenger from the galleys.
DUKE   Now, what's the business?

1.3 Location: A Venetian council room.
1. The reports lack the consistency that would
make them believable.
2. "Where . . . difference": where the reports are
estimates, there are often discrepancies among

them.
3. "I do not . . . sense": I am not so reassured by
the discrepancies as to dismiss the main
concern—the approach of a Turkish fleet.

SAILOR The Turkish preparation° makes for Rhodes.   *battle-ready fleet*
15   So was I bid report here to the state
     By Signor Angelo.[4]
DUKE How say you by this change?
FIRST SENATOR   This cannot be
     By no assay° of reason. 'Tis a pageant   *test*
     To keep us in false gaze. When we consider
20   Th' importancy of Cyprus to the Turk,
     And let ourselves again but understand
     That, as it more concerns the Turk than Rhodes,
     So may he with more facile question bear it,[5]
     For that it stands not in such warlike brace,
25   But altogether lacks th'abilities
     That Rhodes is dressed in—if we make thought of this,
     We must not think the Turk is so unskillful
     To leave that latest° which concerns him first,   *last*
     Neglecting an attempt of ease and gain
30   To wake and wage° a danger profitless.   *risk*
DUKE Nay, in all confidence, he's not for Rhodes.
OFFICER Here is more news.

                Enter a MESSENGER

MESSENGER The Ottomites,° reverend and gracious,[6]   *Ottoman Turks*
     Steering with due course toward the isle of Rhodes,
35   Have there injointed them with an after° fleet.   *joined with another*
FIRST SENATOR Ay, so I thought. How many, as you guess?
MESSENGER Of thirty sail; and now they do re-stem°   *retrace*
     Their backward course, bearing with frank appearance
     Their purposes toward Cyprus. Signor Montano,
40   Your trusty and most valiant servitor,
     With his free duty recommends you thus,[7]
     And prays you to believe him.
DUKE 'Tis certain then for Cyprus.
     Marcus Luccicos[8]—is not he in town?
45   FIRST SENATOR He's now in Florence.
DUKE Write from us to him post-post-haste. Dispatch!
FIRST SENATOR Here comes Brabantio and the valiant
     Moor.

          Enter BRABANTIO, OTHELLO, CASSIO, IAGO, RODERIGO,
          and officers

DUKE Valiant Othello, we must straight° employ you   *immediately*
     Against the general enemy° Ottoman.   *(of all Christendom)*
     [*To* BRABANTIO] I did not see you; welcome, gentle°   *noble*
50   signor.
     We lacked your counsel and your help tonight.
BRABANTIO So did I yours. Good your grace, pardon me.

---

4. Not mentioned elsewhere in the play, Angelus
Sorianus was a Venetian sea captain who received
the Venetian ambassador bearing from Constantinople the Turkish ultimatum to surrender Cyprus,
shortly before its capture by the Turks in 1571.
5. So also can the Turkish fleet more easily win it.

6. "Reverend and gracious": addressed to the
senators.
7. With his freely given loyalty reports to you
thus.
8. Not mentioned elsewhere in the play.

Neither my place° nor aught I heard of business   *official duty*
Hath raised me from my bed; nor doth the general care
Take hold on me. For my particular grief
Is of so floodgate and o'erbearing nature
That it engluts and swallows other sorrows,
And it is still itself.⁹

DUKE   Why, what's the matter?

BRABANTIO   My daughter, O my daughter!

SENATOR   Dead?

BRABANTIO   Ay, to me.

She is abused,° stol'n from me and corrupted   *deluded*
By spells and medicines bought of mountebanks;°   *quacks*
For nature so preposterously to err,
Being not deficient, blind, or lame of sense,
Sans° witchcraft could not.   *without*

DUKE   Whoe'er he be that in this foul proceeding
Hath thus beguiled your daughter of herself
And you of her, the bloody book of law
You shall yourself read in the bitter letter
After your own sense; yea, though our proper son
Stood in your action.¹

BRABANTIO   Humbly I thank your grace.
Here is the man, this Moor, whom now it seems
Your special mandate for the state affairs
Hath hither brought.

ALL   We are very sorry for't.

DUKE [*to* OTHELLO]   What in your own part can you say
    to this?

BRABANTIO   Nothing, but this is so.

OTHELLO   Most potent, grave, and reverend signors,
My very noble and approved good masters:
That I have ta'en away this old man's daughter
It is most true; true I have married her.
The very head and front° of my offending   *height and breadth*
Hath this extent, no more. Rude° am I in my speech,   *unpolished*
And little blessed with the soft phrase of peace;
For since these arms of mine had seven years' pith°   *strength*
Till now some nine moons wasted,° they have used   *nine months ago*
Their dearest° action in the tented field;   *most valued*
And little of this great world can I speak
More than pertains to feats of broils° and battle,   *combats*
And therefore little shall I grace my cause
In speaking for myself. Yet, by your gracious patience,
I will a round° unvarnished tale deliver,   *plain*
Of my whole course of love: what drugs, what charms,
What conjuration and what mighty magic—
For such proceeding I am charged withal° —   *with*
I won his daughter.

---

9. That it (my grief) can incorporate other sorrows without being affected.

1. I.e., you yourself shall interpret the law as you see fit, even if my own son was the one you accuse.

BRABANTIO   A maiden never bold;
95   Of spirit so still and quiet that her motion
    Blushed at herself[2] and she—in spite of nature,
    Of years, of country, credit,° everything—   *reputation*
    To fall in love with what she feared to look on?
    It is a judgment maimed and most imperfect
100   That will confess perfection so could err
    Against all rules of nature, and must° be driven   *(we therefore) must*
    To find out practices of cunning hell
    Why this should be. I therefore vouch again
    That with some mixtures powerful o'er the blood,°   *passions*
105   Or with some dram conjured° to this effect,   *enchanted dose*
    He wrought upon her.
DUKE   To vouch this is no proof,
    Without more wider and more overt test
    Than these thin habits and poor likelihoods
    Of modern seeming do prefer against him.[3]
110 SENATOR   But, Othello, speak;
    Did you by indirect and forced courses°   *means*
    Subdue and poison this young maid's affections?
    Or came it by request and such fair question°   *conversation*
    As soul to soul affordeth?
OTHELLO   I do beseech you
115   Send for the lady to the Sagittary,
    And let her speak of me before her father.
    If you do find me foul in her report,
    The trust, the office I do hold of you,
    Not only take away, but let your sentence
    Even fall upon my life.
120 DUKE [to OFFICERS]   Fetch Desdemona hither.
OTHELLO   Ancient, conduct them; you best know the
    place.

            *Exit [*IAGO *and] two or three [attendants]*
    And till she come, as truly as to heaven
    I do confess the vices of my blood,°   *sins of passion*
    So justly to your grave ears I'll present
125   How I did thrive in this fair lady's love
    And she in mine.
DUKE   Say it, Othello.
OTHELLO   Her father loved me, oft invited me,
    Still° questioned me the story of my life   *constantly*
    From year to year, the battles, sieges, fortunes
130   That I have past.
    I ran it through, even from my boyish days
    To th'very moment that he bade me tell it;
    Wherein I spoke of most disastrous chances,°   *events*
    Of moving accidents° by flood and field,   *events*

---

2. "Her . . . herself": she blushed at herself at the slightest provocation.
3. "Without . . . him": without fuller and more direct testimony than mere appearances and conjecture based on currently popular beliefs against him.

Of hair-breadth scapes i'th' imminent-deadly breach,[4]
Of being taken by the insolent foe
And sold to slavery, of my redemption thence
And portance° in my traveler's history;   conduct
Wherein of antars° vast and deserts idle,   caves
Rough quarries, rocks, and hills whose heads touch
    heaven,
It was my hint° to speak—such was my process° —   occasion / story
And of the cannibals that each other eat,
The anthropophagi,[5] and men whose heads
Do grow beneath their shoulders. These things to hear
Would Desdemona seriously incline,
But still the house affairs would draw her thence,
Which ever as° she could with haste dispatch   whenever
She'd come again and with a greedy ear
Devour up my discourse; which I, observing,
Took once a pliant° hour and found good means   convenient
To draw from her a prayer of earnest heart
That I would all my pilgrimage dilate,°   relate
Whereof by parcels she had something heard,
But not intentively.° I did consent   continuously
And often did beguile her of her tears
When I did speak of some distressful stroke
That my youth suffered. My story being done,
She gave me for my pains a world of kisses;[6]
She swore in faith 'twas strange, 'twas passing° strange,   exceptionally
'Twas pitiful, 'twas wondrous pitiful.
She wished she had not heard it, yet she wished
That heaven had made her such a man.[7] She thanked me
And bade me, if I had a friend that loved her,
I should but teach him how to tell my story,
And that would woo her. Upon this hint I spake.
She loved me for the dangers I had past,
And I loved her that she did pity them.
This only is the witchcraft I have used.
Here comes the lady; let her witness it.
          Enter DESDEMONA, IAGO, [*and*] *attendants*
DUKE   I think this tale would win my daughter too.
    Good Brabantio, take up this mangled matter at the
        best.°   make the best of this
    Men do their broken weapons rather use,
    Than their bare hands.
BRABANTIO   I pray you hear her speak.
    If she confess that she was half the wooer,
    Destruction on my head if my bad blame

---

4. In the immediately life-threatening gaps in a fortification.
5. Man-eaters. The term is from the ancient Roman writer Pliny the Elder. Shakespeare was also indebted to the travel literature of the Middle Ages (*The Travels of Sir John Mandeville*) and the

Renaissance (Hakluyt's *Principal Navigations*, among others).
6. F reads "kisses," Q "sighs." It is hard to explain "kisses" as a textual error.
7. Made such a man for her; made her into such a man.

Light on the man. Come hither, gentle mistress.
Do you perceive in all this noble company
Where most you owe obedience?

DESDEMONA   My noble father,
I do perceive here a divided duty.
180 To you I am bound for life and education;
My life and education both do learn° me   teach
How to respect you; you are the lord of duty;
I am hitherto your daughter. But here's my husband;
And so much duty as my mother showed
185 To you, preferring you before her father,
So much I challenge° that I may profess   assert
Due to the Moor my lord.

BRABANTIO   God be with you; I have done.
Please it° your grace, on to the state affairs;   if it pleases
I had rather to adopt a child than get° it.   beget
190 Come hither, Moor.
I here do give thee that° with all my heart   that which
Which, but° thou hast already, with all my heart   except that
I would keep from thee. [*To* DESDEMONA] For your sake,
     jewel,
I am glad at soul I have no other child,
195 For thy escape would teach me tyranny
To hang clogs[8] on them. I have done, my lord.

DUKE   Let me speak like yourself and lay a sentence°   draw a moral
Which, as a grise° or step, may help these lovers   step
Into your favor.
200 When remedies are past, the griefs are ended
By seeing the worst, which late on hopes depended.[9]
To mourn a mischief that is past and gone
Is the next way to draw new mischief on.
What cannot be preserved, when fortune takes,
205 Patience her injury a mockery makes.[1]
The robbed that smiles steals something from the thief;
He robs himself that spends a bootless° grief.   pointless

BRABANTIO   So let the Turk of Cyprus us beguile:
We lose it not, so long as we can smile.
210 He bears the sentence° well that nothing bears   saying; judgment
But the free comfort which from thence he hears.
But he bears both the sentence and the sorrow
That, to pay grief, must of poor patience borrow.
These sentences, to sugar or to gall,°   both sweet and bitter
215 Being strong on both sides, are equivocal.
But words are words; I never yet did hear
That the bruised heart was piercèd[2] through the ear.

---

8. Blocks of wood tied to criminals' legs to keep them from escaping.
9. By seeing those things come to pass that caused grief in anticipation. The duke paints the moral in rhyming couplets, to which Brabantio

replies in kind.
1. Patience laughs at what cannot be helped (and thus reduces the "injury").
2. Surgically lanced (and presumably cured).

I humbly beseech you proceed to th'affairs of state.

DUKE   The Turk with a most mighty preparation makes for
Cyprus. Othello, the fortitude of the place is best known
to you; and though we have there a substitute of most
allowed sufficiency,° yet opinion, a more sovereign mis-   *known ability*
tress of effects, throws a more safer voice on you.[3] You
must therefore be content to slubber° the gloss of your   *soil*
new fortunes with this more stubborn° and boisterous   *rougher*
expedition.

OTHELLO   The tyrant custom, most grave senators,
Hath made the flinty and steel couch of war
My thrice-driven° bed of down. I do agnize°   *sifted / acknowledge*
A natural and prompt alacrity
I find in hardness,° and do undertake   *hardship*
This present wars against the Ottomites.
Most humbly, therefore, bending to your state,°   *authority*
I crave fit disposition for my wife,
Due reference of place, and exhibition,[4]
With such accommodation and besort°   *suitable attendance*
As levels with her breeding.

DUKE   Why, at her father's.

BRABANTIO   I will not have it so.

OTHELLO   Nor I.

DESDEMONA   Nor would I there reside,
To put my father in impatient thoughts
By being in his eye. Most gracious duke,
To my unfolding° lend your prosperous° ear,   *proposal / receptive*
And let me find a charter° in your voice   *an authorization*
T'assist my simpleness.

DUKE   What would you, Desdemona?

DESDEMONA   That I love the Moor to live with him,
My downright violence and storm of fortunes[5]
May trumpet to the world. My heart's subdued
Even to the very quality[6] of my lord.
I saw Othello's visage in his mind,
And to his honors and his valiant parts°   *qualities*
Did I my soul and fortunes consecrate;
So that, dear lords, if I be left behind,
A moth of peace, and he go to the war,
The rites° for why I love him are bereft me,   *(of love); (of war?)*
And I a heavy interim shall support
By his dear absence. Let me go with him.

OTHELLO   [*to the* DUKE] Let her have your voice.
Vouch with me, heaven, I therefor beg it not
To please the palate of my appetite,
Nor to comply with heat° (the young affects[7]   *sexual passion*

---

3. "Opinion . . . you": public opinion, which
determines what gets done, finds greater security with you.
4. Proper accommodation and maintenance.
5. My outright defiance of custom.

6. "Very quality": essential nature. In the Quarto,
Desdemona says that her heart is subdued to
Othello's "utmost pleasure."
7. The youthful desires.

In me defunct) and proper° satisfaction,   *personal; fitting*
But to be free° and bounteous to her mind;   *liberal*
And heaven defend your good souls that you think
265 I will your serious and great business scant
When she is with me. No, when light-winged toys°   *diversions*
Of feathered Cupid seel° with wanton dullness   *blind*
My speculative and officed instruments,[8]
That my disports° corrupt and taint my business, *sexual pleasures*
270 Let housewives make a skillet of my helm,
And all indign° and base adversities   *undignified*
Make head against my estimation.[9]
DUKE Be it as you shall privately determine,
Either for her stay or going. Th'affair cries haste,
275 And speed must answer it.
SENATOR You must away tonight.
DESDEMONA Tonight, my lord?
DUKE   This night.[1]
OTHELLO   With all my heart.
DUKE At nine i'th' morning here we'll meet again.
Othello, leave some officer behind,
280 And he shall our commission bring to you,
And such things else of quality and respect° *weight and importance*
As doth import° you.   *concern*
OTHELLO   So please your grace, my ancient;
A man he is of honesty[2] and trust.
To his conveyance I assign my wife,
285 With what else needful your good grace shall think
To be sent after me.
DUKE   Let it be so.
Good night to every one. [*To* BRABANTIO] And, noble
  signor,
If virtue no delighted° beauty lack,   *delightful*
Your son-in-law is far more fair than black.
           [*Exit* DUKE]
290 SENATOR Adieu, brave Moor; use Desdemona well.
BRABANTIO Look to her,° Moor, if thou hast eyes to see: *watch her carefully*
She has deceived her father, and may thee.
    Exeunt [BRABANTIO, CASSIO, SENATORS, *and officers*]
OTHELLO My life upon her faith!—Honest Iago,
My Desdemona must I leave to thee.
295 I prithee let thy wife attend on her,
And bring them after in the best advantage.[3]
Come, Desdemona; I have but an hour
Of love, of worldly matter and direction
To spend with thee. We must obey the time.
    Exeunt [OTHELLO *the*] *Moor and* DESDEMONA
300 RODERIGO Iago?

8. My duty-bound faculties of sense.
9. Raise an army against my good reputation.
1. This exchange between Desdemona and the Duke is only in Q.

2. The first of many references to Iago's "honesty."
3. And bring them along at the most favorable moment.

IAGO What say'st thou, noble heart?

RODERIGO What will I do, think'st thou?

IAGO Why, go to bed and sleep.

RODERIGO I will incontinently° drown myself.   *immediately*

IAGO If thou dost, I shall never love thee after. Why, thou
 silly gentleman?

RODERIGO It is silliness to live when to live is torment; and
 then have we a prescription[4] to die when death is our
 physician.

IAGO O villainous!° I have looked upon the world for four   *absurd*
 times seven years, and since I could distinguish betwixt
 a benefit and an injury, I never found man that knew how
 to love himself. Ere I would say I would drown myself for
 the love of a guinea-hen,° I would change my humanity   *woman*
 with a baboon.

RODERIGO What should I do? I confess it is my shame to
 be so fond, but it is not in my virtue° to amend it.   *native ability*

IAGO Virtue? A fig!° 'Tis in ourselves that we are thus or   *(an obscenity)*
 thus. Our bodies are our gardens, to the which our wills
 are gardeners. So that if we will plant nettles or sow let-
 tuce, set hyssop° and weed up thyme, supply it with one   *mint herb*
 gender° of herbs or distract it with many, either to have it   *kind*
 sterile with idleness° or manured with industry, why, the   *noncultivation*
 power and corrigible authority° of this lies in our wills. If   *ability to decide*
 the balance of our lives had not one scale of reason to
 poise° another of sensuality, the blood and baseness of   *counterweigh*
 our natures would conduct us to most preposterous con-
 clusions. But we have reason to cool our raging motions,°   *appetites*
 our carnal stings or unbitted° lusts; whereof I take this   *unrestrained*
 that you call love to be a sect or scion.°   *offshoot*

RODERIGO It cannot be.

IAGO It is merely a lust of the blood and a permission of
 the will. Come, be a man! Drown thyself? Drown cats and
 blind puppies. I have professed me thy friend, and I confess me knit to thy deserving with cables of perdurable°
 toughness. I could never better stead° thee than now.   *durable / help*
 Put money in thy purse. Follow thou the wars; defeat thy
 favor with an usurped beard.[5] I say, put money in thy
 purse. It cannot be long that Desdemona should continue her love to the Moor—put money in thy purse—
 nor he his to her. It was a violent commencement[6] in
 her, and thou shalt see an answerable sequestration[7]—
 put but money in thy purse. These Moors are changeable in their wills—fill thy purse with money. The food
 that to him now is as luscious as locusts[8] shall be to him
 shortly as bitter as coloquintida.[9] She must change for
 youth: when she is sated with his body, she will find

---

4. Right; doctor's order.
5. Disguise your appearance with a fake beard.
6. An abruptly begun affair.
7. A correspondingly abrupt separation.

8. A sweet, exotic fruit, perhaps carob or honeysuckle.
9. Colocynth, a purgative—one of Iago's many
references to the digestive tract.

the error of her choice. Therefore, put money in thy
purse. If thou wilt needs° damn thyself, do it a more — *if you must*
delicate way than drowning—make all the money thou
canst. If sanctimony° and a frail vow betwixt an erring[1] — *holy rite*
barbarian and a super-subtle° Venetian be not too hard — *highly sensitive*
for my wits and all the tribe of hell, thou shalt enjoy
her. Therefore make money. A pox of drowning thyself;
it is clean out of the way.° Seek thou rather to be hanged — *of no use*
in compassing° thy joy than to be drowned and go with- — *encompassing*
out her.

RODERIGO Wilt thou be fast° to my hopes, if I depend on — *duty-bound*
the issue?° — *outcome*

IAGO Thou art sure of me—go make money. I have told
thee often, and I retell thee again and again, I hate the
Moor. My cause is hearted;° thine hath no less reason. — *heartfelt*
Let us be conjunctive° in our revenge against him. If thou — *joined*
canst cuckold him, thou dost thyself a pleasure, me a
sport. There are many events in the womb of time which
will be delivered. Traverse,° go, provide thy money. We — *go (to arms)*
will have more of this tomorrow. Adieu.

RODERIGO Where shall we meet i'th' morning?

IAGO At my lodging.

RODERIGO I'll be with thee betimes.° — *early*

IAGO Go to, farewell. Do you hear, Roderigo?

RODERIGO I'll sell all my land. *Exit*

IAGO Thus do I ever make my fool my purse;
For I mine own gained knowledge should profane
If I would time expend with such a snipe° — *fool*
But for my sport and profit. I hate the Moor,
And it is thought abroad° that 'twixt my sheets — *rumored*
H'as done my office. I know not if't be true,
But I for mere suspicion in that kind
Will do° as if for surety. He holds° me well; — *act / esteems*
The better shall my purpose work on him.
Cassio's a proper° man. Let me see now . . . — *handsome*
To get his place and to plume up° my will — *gratify*
In double knavery—how? how? Let's see . . .
After some time, to abuse Othello's ears
That he is too familiar with his wife.[2]
He hath a person and a smooth dispose° — *manner*
To be suspected, framed° to make women false. — *formed*
The Moor is of a free° and open nature — *liberal*
That thinks men honest that but seem to be so,
And will as tenderly° be led by th'nose — *easily*
As asses are. . . .
I have't! It is engendered! Hell and night
Must bring this monstrous birth to the world's light. *Exit*

1. A wandering.
2. "He" is Cassio (as in line 387), but "his" refers to Othello.

2.1

Enter MONTANO *and two* GENTLEMEN [*one above*]

MONTANO What from the cape can you discern at sea?

FIRST GENTLEMAN Nothing at all; it is a high-wrought
    flood.°   *very rough sea*

I cannot 'twixt the heaven and the main°   *sea*

Descry° a sail.   *discern*

MONTANO Methinks the wind hath spoke aloud at land;

A fuller blast ne'er shook our battlements

If it hath ruffianed° so upon the sea,   *raged*

What ribs of oak, when mountains melt on them,

Can hold the mortise?[1] What shall we hear of this?

SECOND GENTLEMAN A segregation° of the Turkish fleet: *separation*

For do but stand upon the foaming shore,

The chidden billow[2] seems to pelt the clouds;

The wind-shaked surge, with high and monstrous mane,

Seems to cast water on the burning Bear

And quench the guards of th'ever-fixèd pole.[3]

I never did like molestation view°   *see such a tumult*

On the enchafed° flood.   *raging*

MONTANO   If that the Turkish fleet

Be not ensheltered and embayed, they are drowned;

It is impossible to bear it out.

Enter a THIRD GENTLEMAN

THIRD GENTLEMAN News, lads! Our wars are done.

The desperate tempest hath so banged the Turks

That their designment° halts. A noble ship of Venice   *plan*

Hath seen a grievous wrack and sufferance°   *damage*

On most part of their fleet.

MONTANO How? Is this true?

THIRD GENTLEMAN   The ship is here put in,

A Veronnesa.[4] Michael Cassio,

Lieutenant to the warlike Moor, Othello,

Is come on shore; the Moor himself at sea,

And is in full commission here for Cyprus.

MONTANO I am glad on't—'tis a worthy governor.

THIRD GENTLEMAN But this same Cassio, though he
    speak of comfort

Touching the Turkish loss, yet he looks sadly°   *seriously*

And prays the Moor be safe; for they were parted

With foul and violent tempest.

MONTANO   Pray heavens he be,

For I have served him, and the man commands

Like a full soldier. Let's to the seaside—ho!—

2.1 Location: A seaport in Cyprus; outdoors near
the harbor.
1. "What . . . mortise": what ship (with "ribs of
oak") can hold its joints ("mortise") together when
"mountains" of water pour on it?
2. The surging ocean, rebuked ("chidden") by the
wind (or repulsed by the land).

3. The "burning Bear" is the constellation Ursa
Minor; the "guards" are probably two stars in the
constellation that point in a line to the polestar,
also in Ursa Minor.
4. Meaning unclear: either a ship originally
from Verona, though now used by the Venetians;
on perhaps a particular *kind* of ship.

As well to see the vessel that's come in
As to throw out our eyes for brave Othello,
Even till we make the main and th'aerial blue
An indistinct regard.[5]

40 THIRD GENTLEMAN   Come, let's do so;
For every minute is expectancy
Of more arrivance.

    Enter CASSIO

CASSIO   Thanks, you the valiant of the warlike isle,
That so approve the Moor! O, let the heavens
45 Give him defense against the elements,
For I have lost him on a dangerous sea.

MONTANO   Is he well shipped?

CASSIO   His bark is stoutly timbered, and his pilot
Of very expert and approved allowance;°   *known ability*
50 Therefore my hopes, not surfeited to death,°   *not excessive*
Stand in bold cure.°   *likely to be rewarded*

VOICES *within*   A sail! a sail! a sail!

CASSIO   What noise?

GENTLEMAN   The town is empty; on the brow o'th' sea
Stand ranks of people, and they cry "A sail!"

55 CASSIO   My hopes do shape him for° the governor.   *make it out to be*

    A shot

SECOND GENTLEMAN   They do discharge their shot of
     courtesy—
Our friends, at least.

CASSIO   I pray you, sir, go forth
And give us truth who 'tis that is arrived.

SECOND GENTLEMAN   I shall.   *Exit*

60 MONTANO   But, good lieutenant, is your general wived?

CASSIO   Most fortunately: he hath achieved a maid
That paragons° description and wild fame,   *stands above*
One that excels the quirks of blazoning° pens,   *praise-giving*
And in th'essential vesture of creation
Does tire the ingener.[6]

    Enter SECOND GENTLEMAN

65   How now? Who has put in?

SECOND GENTLEMAN   'Tis one Iago, ancient to the general.

CASSIO   He's had most favorable and happy speed:
Tempests themselves, high seas, and howling winds,
The guttered° rocks and congregated° sands,   *jagged / accumulated*
70 Traitors ensteeped° to enclog the guiltless keel,   *underwater*
As having sense of beauty, do omit°   *forgo*
Their mortal° natures, letting go safely by   *deadly*
The divine Desdemona.

MONTANO   What is she?

CASSIO   She that I spake of, our great captain's captain,
75 Left in the conduct of the bold Iago,

---

5. "Even . . . regard": until we can't distinguish sea from sky.

6. "In . . . engineer": whose natural beauty exhausts the poet's capacity to invent praise.

Whose footing here anticipates our thoughts
A se'night's speed.[7] Great Jove, Othello guard,
And swell his sail with thine own powerful breath,
That he may bless this bay with his tall ship,
Make love's quick pants in Desdemona's arms,
Give renewed fire to our extincted spirits,
And bring all Cyprus comfort!

      Enter DESDEMONA, IAGO, RODERIGO, *and* EMILIA

                  O, behold!
The riches of the ship is come on shore.
You men of Cyprus, let her have your knees.
Hail to thee, lady, and the grace of heaven
Before, behind thee, and on every hand
Enwheel thee round.

DESDEMONA   I thank you, valiant Cassio.
What tidings can you tell me of my lord?

CASSIO   He is not yet arrived, nor know I aught
But that he's well and will be shortly here.

DESDEMONA   O, but I fear!—How lost you company?

CASSIO   The great contention of sea and skies
Parted our fellowship.

VOICES *within*   A sail! a sail!
    [*A shot*]

CASSIO   But hark—a sail.

GENTLEMAN   They give their greeting to the citadel;
This likewise is a friend.

CASSIO   See for the news.

                  [*Exit* GENTLEMAN]

Good ancient, you are welcome. Welcome, mistress.

                  [*Kisses* EMILIA]

Let it not gall your patience, good Iago,
That I extend my manners. 'Tis my breeding
That gives me this bold show of courtesy.

IAGO   Sir, would she give you so much of her lips
As of her tongue she oft bestows on me,
You would have enough.

DESDEMONA   Alas, she has no speech.[8]

IAGO   In faith, too much:
I find it still° when I have leave to sleep.   *always*
Marry, before your ladyship, I grant,
She puts her tongue a little in her heart[9]
And chides with thinking.

EMILIA   You have little cause to say so.

IAGO   Come on! come on! You are pictures out of door,
Bells in your parlors, wildcats in your kitchens,
Saints in your injuries, devils being offended,

---

7. Whose arrival predates our expectations by a week.

8. Perhaps both a defense of Emilia and a prod for her to speak.

9. She keeps her (critical) thoughts to herself.

Players in your huswifery, and huswives in your beds.[1]

DESDEMONA O, fie upon thee, slanderer!

IAGO Nay, it is true, or else I am a Turk:

You rise to play and go to bed to work.

EMILIA You shall not write my praise.

IAGO   No, let me not.

DESDEMONA What wouldst write of me, if thou shouldst
praise me?

IAGO O, gentle lady, do not put me to't,
For I am nothing if not critical.

DESDEMONA Come on, assay.° There's one gone to the   essay, try
harbor?

IAGO Ay, madam.

DESDEMONA I am not merry, but I do beguile°   disguise
The thing I am° by seeming otherwise.—   (worried for Othello)
Come, how wouldst thou praise me?

IAGO I am about it, but indeed my invention
Comes from my pate as birdlime[2] does from frieze.°   coarse wool cloth
It plucks out brains and all. But my muse labors,°   (in childbirth)
And thus she is delivered:
If she be fair and wise, fairness and wit,
The one's for use, the other useth it.[3]

DESDEMONA Well praised! How if she be black and witty?

IAGO *If she be black, and thereto have a wit,*
She'll find a white that shall her blackness fit.[4]

DESDEMONA Worse and worse!

EMILIA How if fair and foolish?

IAGO *She never yet was foolish that was fair,*
For even her folly° helped her to an heir.   foolishness; lechery

DESDEMONA These are old fond° paradoxes, to make fools   foolish
laugh i'th' alehouse. What miserable praise hast thou for
her that's foul° and foolish?   ugly

IAGO *There's none so foul and foolish thereunto,°*   to boot
But does foul° pranks which fair and wise ones do.   lascivious

DESDEMONA O, heavy ignorance! Thou praisest the worst
best. But what praise couldst thou bestow on a deserving woman indeed? One that in the authority of her
merit did justly put on the vouch[5] of very malice itself.

IAGO *She that was ever fair, and never proud,*
Had tongue at will, and yet was never loud,
Never lacked gold, and yet went never gay,°   lavishly clothed
Fled from her wish, and yet said "now I may";[6]
She that, being angered, her revenge being nigh,
Bade her wrong stay° and her displeasure fly;   sense of injury end

---

1. In this speech Iago shifts from Emilia to women
generally. "Pictures": models of silent propriety.
"Bells": i.e., noisy. "Saints": i.e., martyrs. "Players
in your huswifery": deceptive in managing household expenses. "Huswives": pronounced "hussies"
and thus carrying opposed suggestions: wanton;
businesslike, charily husbanding sexual favors (cf.
line 115).

2. Sticky substance used to trap small birds.
3. I.e., intelligence makes use of beauty.
4. With sexual double entendre. "Black": dark-
haired or dark-complexioned. "White": fair-
skinned person ("wight" means "person").
5. Compel the approval.
6. Voluntarily withstood temptation even when
given the choice.

She that in wisdom never was so frail
To change the cod's head for the salmon's tail;[7]
She that could think, and ne'er disclose her mind,
See suitors following, and not look behind:
She was a wight (if ever such wights were) . . .

DESDEMONA To do what?

IAGO *To suckle fools and chronicle small beer.*[8]

DESDEMONA O, most lame and impotent conclusion! Do
not learn of him, Emilia, though he be thy husband.
How say you, Cassio? Is he not a most profane and lib-
eral° counselor?   outspoken

CASSIO He speaks home, madam. You may relish him
more in° the soldier than in the scholar.   as

IAGO [*aside*] He takes her by the palm. Ay, well said,°   well done
whisper! With as little a web as this will I ensnare as
great a fly as Cassio. Ay, smile upon her, do! I will gyve°   shackle
thee in thine own courtship.°—You say true, 'tis so   courtliness
indeed.—If such tricks as these strip you out of your
lieutenantry, it had been better you had not kissed your
three fingers[9] so oft, which now again you are most apt
to play the sir° in. Very good! well kissed and excellent   gentleman
courtesy!—'Tis so indeed.—Yet again, your fingers to
your lips? Would they were clyster pipes° for your sake!   enema tubes

    Trumpets within

The Moor! I know his trumpet.

CASSIO 'Tis truly so.

DESDEMONA Let's meet him and receive him.

CASSIO Lo, where he comes.

    Enter OTHELLO *and attendants*

OTHELLO O, my fair warrior!

DESDEMONA   My dear Othello!

OTHELLO It gives me wonder great as my content
To see you here before me. O! my soul's joy,
If after every tempest come such calms,
May the winds blow till they have wakened death,
And let the laboring bark° climb hills of seas   small ship
Olympus-high,[1] and duck again as low
As hell's from heaven! If it were now to die,[2]
'Twere now to be most happy; for I fear
My soul hath her content so absolute
That not another comfort like to this
Succeeds° in unknown fate.°   will follow / future

DESDEMONA   The heavens forbid
But that our loves and comforts should increase
Even as our days do grow.

OTHELLO   Amen to that, sweet powers!

---

7. To make an unworthy exchange.
8. I.e., to breast-feed babies and keep track of
trivial domestic goods.
9. Kissing one's own hand was a common courtly
gesture from a gentleman to a lady.

1. Mt. Olympus, home of the Greek gods and
hence too high for mortals.
2. To perish, but also evoking the very common
sense "to have an orgasm."

I cannot speak enough of this content;
195 It stops me here; it is too much of joy.
And this, and this—   *They kiss*
         the greatest discords be
That e'er our hearts shall make!

IAGO [*aside*]   O, you are well tuned now;
But I'll set down the pegs that make this music,[3]
As honest as I am.

OTHELLO   Come, let us to the castle.
200 News, friends; our wars are done. The Turks are drowned.
How does my old acquaintance of this isle?—
Honey, you shall be well desired° in Cyprus;   welcomed
I have found great love amongst them. O, my sweet,
I prattle out of fashion, and I dote
205 In mine own comforts. I prithee, good Iago,
Go to the bay and disembark my coffers.°   trunks
Bring thou the master° to the citadel;   captain
He is a good one, and his worthiness
Does challenge° much respect. Come, Desdemona;   deserve
210 Once more well met at Cyprus.
         Exit OTHELLO *and* DESDEMONA [*and all but* IAGO *and*
         RODERIGO]
IAGO   [*to a departing attendant*] Do thou meet me presently at the harbor. [*To* RODERIGO] Come hither. If thou
be'st valiant—as they say base° men, being in love, have   lowly born
then a nobility in their natures more than is native to
215 them—list° me. The lieutenant tonight watches on the   listen to
court of guard.[4] First I must tell thee this: Desdemona is
directly in love with him.
RODERIGO   With him? Why, 'tis not possible.
IAGO   Lay thy finger thus,° and let thy soul be instructed.   be silent
220 Mark me with what violence she first loved the Moor,
but° for bragging and telling her fantastical lies. To love   only
him still for prating, let not thy discreet heart think it.
Her eye must be fed. And what delight shall she have to
look on the devil? When the blood is made dull with the
225 act of sport, there should be—again to enflame it, and
to give satiety a fresh appetite—loveliness in favor,°   looks
sympathy in years, manners, and beauties, all which the
Moor is defective in. Now for want of these required
conveniences,° her delicate tenderness will find itself   compatibilities
230 abused,° begin to heave the gorge,[5] disrelish and abhor   revolted
the Moor. Very nature will instruct her in it and compel
her to some second choice. Now, sir, this granted—as it
is a most pregnant° and unforced position—who stands   obvious; (sexual)
so eminent in the degree of[6] this fortune as Cassio
235 does?—a knave very voluble,° no further conscionable[7]   facile

---

3. I'll untune (by loosening) the "pegs" that hold
the strings of the musical instrument taut.
4. I.e., Cassio is in charge of the watch at the
guardhouse.

5. Feel nausea.
6. As next in line for.
7. No more ethical.

than in putting on the mere form of civil and humane
seeming for the better compass° of his salt[8] and most · achievement
hidden loose affection. Why none! why none! A slipper° · slippery
and subtle knave, a finder of occasion, that has an eye
can stamp and counterfeit advantages,[9] though true
advantage never present itself. A devilish knave! Besides,
the knave is handsome, young, and hath all those requi-
sites in him that folly° and green minds look after. A · wantonness
pestilent° complete knave! And the woman hath found · damnably
him already.

RODERIGO   I cannot believe that in her; she's full of most
blessed condition.

IAGO   Blessed fig's-end!° The wine she drinks is made of · (obscene)
grapes. If she had been blessed, she would never have
loved the Moor. Blessed pudding!° Didst thou not see · sausage
her paddle with the palm of his hand? Didst not mark
that?

RODERIGO   Yes, that I did, but that was but courtesy.

IAGO   Lechery, by this hand! an index and obscure prologue to the history of lust and foul thoughts.[1] They
met so near with their lips that their breaths embraced
together. Villainous thoughts, Roderigo: when these
mutualities so marshal the way, hard at hand comes the
master and main exercise,[2] th'incorporate° conclusion. · in the flesh
Pish! But, sir, be you ruled by me. I have brought you
from Venice. Watch you tonight. For the command, I'll
lay't upon you.[3] Cassio knows you not. I'll not be far from
you. Do you find some occasion to anger Cassio, either by
speaking too loud or tainting° his discipline, or from what · insulting
other course you please, which the time shall more favorably minister.° · provide

RODERIGO   Well.

IAGO   Sir, he's rash and very sudden in choler, and haply° · perhaps
may strike at you. Provoke him that he may; for even out
of that will I cause these of Cyprus to mutiny; whose
qualification shall come into no true taste again[4] but by
the displanting of Cassio. So shall you have a shorter
journey to your desires by the means I shall then have to
prefer° them, and the impediment most profitably · promote
removed without the which there were no expectation of
our prosperity.

RODERIGO   I will do this if you can bring it to any opportunity.

IAGO   I warrant thee. Meet me by and by at the citadel. I
must fetch his necessaries[5] ashore. Farewell.

8. Lewd.
9. Who can (like a counterfeiter) create his own
opportunities.
1. The analogy is to a dirty book. "Index": table
of contents. "Obscure": encoded. "History": story.
2. When these intimacies have cleared the way,

the main event follows close behind. Here, the
analogy is to an official procession.
3. Stand watch tonight. I'll see that you receive
orders.
4. Who will not be adequately appeased.
5. Othello's possessions.

RODERIGO Adieu.   *Exit*
IAGO That Cassio loves her, I do well believ't;
  That she loves him, 'tis apt and of great credit.°   *likely and believable*
  The Moor, howbeit that I endure him not,
285 Is of a constant, loving, noble nature,
  And I dare think he'll prove to Desdemona
  A most dear° husband. Now I do love her too,   *affectionate; costly*
  Not out of absolute lust (though peradventure
  I stand accountant° for as great a sin),   *accountable*
290 But partly led to diet° my revenge,   *feed*
  For that I do suspect the lusty Moor
  Hath leaped into my seat°—the thought whereof   *slept with my wife*
  Doth, like a poisonous mineral, gnaw my inwards,°   *innards*
  And nothing can or shall content my soul
295 Till I am evened with him, wife for wife;
  Or failing so, yet that I put the Moor
  At least into a jealousy so strong
  That judgment cannot cure; which thing to do,
  If this poor trash of Venice, whom I trace
300 For his quick hunting, stand the putting on,[6]
  I'll have our Michael Cassio on the hip,°   *at my mercy*
  Abuse° him to the Moor in the rank garb°   *slander / gross manner*
  (For I fear Cassio with my nightcap° too),   *(as sexual rival)*
  Make the Moor thank me, love me, and reward me
305 For making him egregiously an ass
  And practicing upon° his peace and quiet   *undermining*
  Even to madness. 'Tis here,° but yet confused;   *i.e., my plan is here*
  Knavery's plain face is never seen till used.   *Exit*

2.2

Enter OTHELLO'S HERALD *with a proclamation*
HERALD [*reads*] "It is Othello's pleasure, our noble and
  valiant general, that upon certain tidings now arrived
  importing the mere perdition° of the Turkish fleet, every   *entire loss*
  man put himself into triumph—some to dance, some to
5 make bonfires, each man to what sport and revels his
  addition° leads him. For besides these beneficial news, it   *inclination*
  is the celebration of his nuptial." So much was his plea-
  sure should be proclaimed. All offices° are open, and   *storehouses*
  there is full liberty of feasting from this present hour of
10 five till the bell have told eleven. Heaven bless the isle of
  Cyprus and our noble general Othello!   *Exit*

2.3

Enter OTHELLO, DESDEMONA, CASSIO, *and attendants*
OTHELLO Good Michael, look you to the guard tonight.
  Let's teach ourselves that honorable stop,°   *self-restraint*

6. "If . . . on": if Roderigo, whom I follow (?), harness (?), is successfully set on the hunt when incited.
2.2 Location: A street in Cyprus.
2.3 Location: The citadel at Cyprus.

Not to outsport° discretion.   *pass the limits of*

CASSIO Iago hath direction what to do;
    But notwithstanding, with my personal eye
    Will I look to't.

OTHELLO   Iago is most honest.
    Michael, goodnight. Tomorrow with your earliest
    Let me have speech with you.—Come, my dear love.
    The purchase made, the fruits are to ensue,
    That profit's yet to come 'tween me and you.[1]
    Goodnight.
                    Exit [OTHELLO, DESDEMONA, *and attendants*]
            Enter IAGO

CASSIO Welcome, Iago; we must to the watch.

IAGO   Not this hour, lieutenant; 'tis not yet ten o'th' clock.
    Our general cast° us thus early for the love of his Desde-   *dismissed*
    mona, who let us not therefore blame: he hath not yet
    made wanton the night with her, and she is sport for
    Jove.

CASSIO She's a most exquisite lady.

IAGO   And, I'll warrant her, full of game.

CASSIO Indeed, she's a most fresh and delicate creature.

IAGO   What an eye she has! Methinks it sounds a parley°   *(military) call*
    to provocation.

CASSIO An inviting eye; and yet, methinks, right modest.

IAGO   And when she speaks, is it not an alarum° to love?   *a call (to arms)*

CASSIO She is indeed perfection.

IAGO   Well, happiness to their sheets! Come, lieutenant, I
    have a stoup° of wine, and here without are a brace° of   *two quarts / pair*
    Cyprus gallants that would fain have a measure[2] to the
    health of black Othello.

CASSIO Not tonight, good Iago. I have very poor and
    unhappy brains for drinking. I could well wish courtesy
    would invent some other custom of entertainment.

IAGO   O, they are our friends; but one cup; I'll drink for
    you.

CASSIO I have drunk but one cup tonight, and that was
    craftily qualified° too; and behold what innovation[3] it   *well diluted*
    makes here. I am unfortunate in the infirmity and dare
    not task my weakness with any more.

IAGO   What, man! 'Tis a night of revels—the gallants
    desire it.

CASSIO Where are they?

IAGO   Here at the door; I pray you call them in.

CASSIO I'll do't, but it dislikes me.°   *Exit*   *I don't like it*

IAGO   If I can fasten but one cup upon him
    With that which he hath drunk tonight already,
    He'll be as full of quarrel and offense
    As my young mistress' dog. Now my sick fool, Roderigo,
    Whom love hath turned almost the wrong side out,

---

1. I.e., we haven't yet consummated our marriage.
2. "Would fain have a measure": would like to
drink.
3. Disorder.

To Desdemona hath tonight caroused
50 Potations pottle-deep; and he's to watch.[4]
Three else of Cyprus (noble swelling° spirits,   *proud*
That hold their honors in a wary distance,[5]
The very elements° of this warlike isle)   *typical residents*
Have I tonight flustered with flowing cups,
55 And they watch too. Now, 'mongst this flock of drunkards
Am I to put our Cassio in some action
That may offend the isle. But here they come.
    Enter CASSIO, MONTANO, *and* GENTLEMEN [*with wine*]
If consequence do but approve my dream,[6]
My boat sails freely, both with wind and stream.°   *current*
60 CASSIO 'Fore God, they have given me a rouse° already.   *full draft*
MONTANO Good faith, a little one; not past a pint, as I am
  a soldier.
IAGO Some wine, ho!
    [*Sings*]
      And let me the cannikin° clink, clink,   *drinking vessel*
65   And let me the cannikin clink.
        A soldier's a man,
        O man's life's but a span,
      Why then, let a soldier drink.
  Some wine, boys!
70 CASSIO 'Fore God, an excellent song!
IAGO I learned it in England, where indeed they are most
  potent in potting.[7] Your Dane, your German, and your
  swag°-bellied Hollander—drink, ho!—are nothing to   *hanging*
  your English.
75 CASSIO Is your Englishman so exquisite in his drinking?
IAGO Why, he drinks you with facility your Dane dead
  drunk. He sweats not to overthrow your Almaine.° He   *German*
  gives your Hollander a vomit ere the next pottle° can be   *tankard*
  filled.
80 CASSIO To the health of our general!
MONTANO I am for it, lieutenant, and I'll do you justice.[8]
IAGO O sweet England!
    [*Sings*]
      King Stephen was and-a worthy peer,
        His breeches cost him but a crown;[9]
85   He held them sixpence all too dear,
        With that he called the tailor lown.°   *lout*
      He was a wight of high renown,
        And thou art but of low degree;
      'Tis pride° that pulls the country down,   *ostentatious clothing*
90   And take thy auld cloak about thee.
  Some wine, ho!
CASSIO 'Fore God, this is a more exquisite song than the
  other.

---

4. "Caroused . . . watch": consumed drink to the bottom of the tankard; and he's assigned guard duty.
5. Who are touchy about their honor.
6. If events turn out as I hope.
7. Most adept at drinking.
8. Match your drinking.
9. A coin (worth 60 pence).

IAGO Will you hear't again?

CASSIO No, for I hold him to be unworthy of his place
that does those things. Well, God's above all, and there
be souls must be saved, and there be souls must not be
saved.[1]

IAGO It's true, good lieutenant.

CASSIO For mine own part—no offense to the general,
nor any man of quality°—I hope to be saved.   rank

IAGO And so do I too, lieutenant.

CASSIO Ay; but by your leave, not before me. The lieutenant is to be saved before the ancient. Let's have no more
of this. Let's to our affairs. God forgive us our sins.
Gentlemen, let's look to our business. Do not think,
gentlemen, I am drunk. This is my ancient, this is my
right hand, and this is my left. I am not drunk now. I
can stand well enough, and I speak well enough.

GENTLEMAN Excellent well.

CASSIO Why, very well then. You must not think, then,
that I am drunk.   *Exit*

MONTANO To th'platform, masters; come, let's set the
watch.   [*Exeunt some* GENTLEMEN]

IAGO [*to* MONTANO] You see this fellow that is gone before:
He's a soldier fit to stand by Caesar
And give direction. And do but see his vice:
'Tis to his virtue a just equinox,°   *of equal size*
The one as long as th'other. 'Tis pity of him;
I fear the trust Othello puts him in
On some odd time of his infirmity
Will shake this island.

MONTANO   But is he often thus?

IAGO 'Tis evermore his prologue to his sleep.
He'll watch the horologe a double set[2]
If drink rock not his cradle.

MONTANO   It were well
The general were put in mind of it.
Perhaps he sees it not, or his good nature
Prizes the virtue that appears in Cassio
And looks not on his evils. Is not this true?
     Enter RODERIGO

IAGO [*aside*] How now, Roderigo?
I pray you after the lieutenant—go!   *Exit* RODERIGO

MONTANO And 'tis great pity that the noble Moor
Should hazard such a place as his own second
With one of an ingraft° infirmity.   *ingrained*
It were an honest action to say so
To the Moor.

IAGO   Not I, for this fair island.
I do love Cassio well and would do much

---

1. Referring to the doctrine of predestination, the belief held by Calvinist Protestants that some souls are destined from all eternity to be saved and others to be damned.
2. He'll stay up twice around the clock.

To cure him of this evil.
VOICES (*within*) Help, help!³
                                    But hark, what noise?
            Enter CASSIO, *pursuing* RODERIGO
140 CASSIO 'Swounds, you rogue! you rascal!
     MONTANO   What's the matter, lieutenant?
     CASSIO A knave teach me my duty? I'll beat the knave
          into a twiggen° bottle.   *wicker-cased*
     RODERIGO Beat me?
145 CASSIO Dost thou prate, rogue?   [*Attacks* RODERIGO]
     MONTANO   Nay, good lieutenant! I pray you, sir, hold your
          hand.
     CASSIO   Let me go, sir, or I'll knock you o'er the mazzard.°   *head*
     MONTANO   Come, come; you're drunk!
150 CASSIO Drunk?   [CASSIO *and* MONTANO *fight*]
     IAGO [*aside to* RODERIGO]   Away, I say! Go out and cry a
          mutiny.
                                    [*Exit* RODERIGO]
          Nay, good lieutenant! God's will, gentlemen!
          Help ho! Lieutenant! Sir—Montano—Sir!
155   Help, masters! Here's a goodly watch indeed!
          A bell rung
          Who's that which rings the bell? Diablo,° ho!   *the devil*
          The town will rise. God's will, lieutenant, hold!
          You'll be ashamed forever.
            Enter OTHELLO *and attendants*
     OTHELLO   What is the matter here?
160 MONTANO   'Swounds, I bleed still; I am hurt to th'death.
          [*Attacks* CASSIO] He dies.
     OTHELLO   Hold, for your lives!
     IAGO   Hold, ho! Lieutenant—Sir—Montano—gentlemen!
          Have you forgot all place of sense and duty?
165   Hold! The general speaks to you. Hold, for shame!
     OTHELLO   Why, how now, ho? From whence ariseth this?
          Are we turned Turks? and to ourselves do that
          Which heaven hath forbid the Ottomites?°   *(by raising a storm)*
          For Christian shame, put by this barbarous brawl!
170   He that stirs next, to carve for his own rage,°   *draw a sword in anger*
          Holds his soul light; he dies upon his motion.
          Silence that dreadful bell—it frights the isle
          From her propriety. What is the matter, masters?
          Honest Iago, that looks dead with grieving,
175   Speak. Who began this? On thy love, I charge thee.
     IAGO   I do not know. Friends all, but now, even now,
          In quarter° and in terms like bride and groom   *under control*
          Divesting them° for bed; and then, but now,   *getting undressed*
          As if some planet° had unwitted men,   *astrological influence*
180   Swords out and tilting one at other's breasts
          In opposition bloody. I cannot speak

---

3. The offstage shouts for help are only in Q.

Any beginning to this peevish odds,°   *silly quarrel*
And would in action glorious I had lost
Those legs that brought me to a part of it.
OTHELLO   How comes it, Michael, you are thus forgot?
CASSIO   I pray you pardon me; I cannot speak.
OTHELLO   Worthy Montano, you were wont° to be civil;   *were accustomed*
The gravity and stillness of your youth
The world hath noted, and your name is great
In mouths of wisest censure.° What's the matter,   *judgment*
That you unlace your reputation thus
And spend your rich opinion° for the name   *reputation*
Of a night brawler? Give me answer to it.
MONTANO   Worthy Othello, I am hurt to danger.
Your officer, Iago, can inform you—
While I spare speech, which something now offends me[4]—
Of all that I do know; nor know I aught
By me that's said or done amiss this night,
Unless self-charity° be sometimes a vice,   *care of oneself*
And to defend ourselves it be a sin
When violence assails us.
OTHELLO   Now, by heaven,
My blood begins my safer guides to rule,
And passion, having my best judgment collied,°   *darkened*
Assays° to lead the way. 'Swounds, if I stir   *tries*
Or do but lift this arm, the best of you
Shall sink in my rebuke. Give me to know
How this foul rout began, who set it on;
And he that is approved° in this offense,   *proven guilty*
Though he had twinned with me, both at a birth,
Shall lose me. What! in a town of war,
Yet° wild, the people's hearts brimful of fear,   *still*
To manage° private and domestic quarrel?   *carry on*
In night, and on the court and guard of safety?[5]
'Tis monstrous. Iago, who began't?
MONTANO   If partially affined,° or leagued in office,   *biased (for Cassio)*
Thou dost deliver more or less than truth,
Thou art no soldier.
IAGO   Touch me not so near.
I had rather have this tongue cut from my mouth
Than it should do offense to Michael Cassio;
Yet I persuade myself to speak the truth
Shall nothing wrong him. This it is, general:
Montano and myself being in speech,
There comes a fellow crying out for help,
And Cassio following him with determined sword
To execute upon° him. Sir, this gentleman   *to attack*
Steps in to Cassio and entreats his pause;
Myself the crying fellow did pursue,

---

4. Somewhat now pains me.
5. And at the place where safety and security are at stake (on the night watch).

Lest by his clamor—as it so fell out—
The town might fall in fright. He, swift of foot,
230 Outran my purpose; and I returned, the rather
For that I heard the clink and fall of swords
And Cassio high in oath, which till tonight
I ne'er might say before. When I came back—
For this was brief—I found them close together
235 At blow and thrust, even as again they were
When yourself did part them.
More of this matter cannot I report.
But men are men: the best sometimes forget.
Though Cassio did some little wrong to him,
240 As men in rage strike those that wish them best,
Yet surely Cassio, I believe, received
From him that fled some strange indignity
Which patience could not pass.°   *let pass*

OTHELLO   I know, Iago,
Thy honesty and love doth mince° this matter,   *minimize*
245 Making it light to Cassio. Cassio, I love thee,
But never more be officer of mine.—
       Enter DESDEMONA, *attended*
Look if my gentle love be not raised up!—
I'll make thee an example.

DESDEMONA   What is the matter, dear?

OTHELLO   All's well, sweeting;
250 Come away to bed. [*To* MONTANO] Sir, for your hurts
Myself will be your surgeon. Lead him off.
                 [*Exeunt attendants with* MONTANO]
Iago, look with care about the town,
And silence those whom this vile brawl distracted.
Come, Desdemona; 'tis the soldier's life
255 To have their balmy slumbers waked with strife.
      Exeunt [OTHELLO *the*] *Moor,* DESDEMONA, *and attendants*

IAGO   What, are you hurt, lieutenant?

CASSIO   Ay, past all surgery.

IAGO   Marry, God forbid!

CASSIO   Reputation, reputation, reputation! O, I have lost
260 my reputation! I have lost the immortal part of myself,
and what remains is bestial. My reputation, Iago, my
reputation!

IAGO   As I am an honest man, I had thought you had
received some bodily wound; there is more sense in that
265 than in reputation. Reputation is an idle and most false
imposition,° oft got without merit and lost without   *artificial notion*
deserving. You have lost no reputation at all, unless you
repute yourself such a loser. What, man! there are more
ways to recover the general again. You are but now cast in
270 his mood, a punishment more in policy⁶ than in malice,

---

6. "Cast . . . policy": dismissed in anger—a matter of policy (of public example).

even so as one would beat his offenseless dog to affright
an imperious lion. Sue to° him again, and he's yours.   *petition*

CASSIO   I will rather sue to be despised than to deceive
so good a commander with so slight, so drunken, and so
indiscreet an officer. Drunk? And speak parrot?° And   *rant on*
squabble? Swagger? Swear? And discourse fustian° with   *nonsense*
one's own shadow? O, thou invisible spirit of wine! if
thou hast no name to be known by, let us call thee devil.

IAGO   What was he that you followed with your sword?
What had he done to you?

CASSIO   I know not.

IAGO   Is't possible?

CASSIO   I remember a mass of things, but nothing distinctly; a quarrel, but nothing wherefore.° O God! that   *but not why*
men should put an enemy in their mouths to steal away
their brains! that we should with joy, pleasance, revel,
and applause transform ourselves into beasts!

IAGO   Why, but you are now well enough. How came you
thus recovered?

CASSIO   It hath pleased the devil drunkenness to give
place to the devil wrath; one unperfectness shows me
another, to make me frankly despise myself.

IAGO   Come, you are too severe a moraler. As the time,
the place, and the condition of this country stands, I
could heartily wish this had not befallen; but since it is
as it is, mend it for your own good.

CASSIO   I will ask him for my place again. He shall tell me
I am a drunkard. Had I as many mouths as Hydra,[7] such
an answer would stop them all. To be now a sensible
man, by and by a fool, and presently a beast!—O, strange!
Every inordinate cup is unblessed, and the ingredient is
a devil.

IAGO   Come, come; good wine is a good familiar creature
if it be well used. Exclaim no more against it. And, good
lieutenant, I think you think I love you.

CASSIO   I have well approved° it, sir—I drunk?   *tested*

IAGO   You or any man living may be drunk at a time, man.
I tell you what you shall do. Our general's wife is now
the general. I may say so in this respect, for that he
hath devoted and given up himself to the contemplation,
mark, and devotement° of her parts[8] and graces. Confess   *observation*
yourself freely to her; importune her help to put you in
your place again. She is of so free,° so kind, so apt, so   *generous*
blessed a disposition, she holds it a vice in her goodness
not to do more than she is requested. This broken joint
between you and her husband entreat her to splinter,[9]
and my fortunes against any lay° worth naming, this   *wager*
crack of your love shall grow stronger than it was before.

---

7. A mythical serpent with many heads, who   8. Qualities.
grew two more when one was cut off.   9. Heal with a splint.

CASSIO You advise me well.

320 IAGO I protest,° in the sincerity of love and honest   *insist*
kindness.

CASSIO I think it freely; and betimes° in the morning I   *early*
will beseech the virtuous Desdemona to undertake for
me. I am desperate of my fortunes if they check° me.   *stop*

325 IAGO You are in the right. Good night, lieutenant; I must
to the watch.

CASSIO Good night, honest Iago.   *Exit* CASSIO

IAGO And what's he then that says I play the villain,
When this advice is free I give and honest,

330 Probal° to thinking, and indeed the course   *wise*
To win the Moor again? For 'tis most easy
Th'inclining° Desdemona to subdue   *well-disposed*
In any honest suit: she's framed as fruitful°   *generous*
As the free elements; and then for her

335 To win the Moor, were't to renounce his baptism,
All seals and symbols of redeemèd sin,
His soul is so enfettered to her love
That she may make, unmake, do what she list,
Even as her appetite° shall play the god   *wishes*

340 With his weak function.° How am I then a villain   *faculties*
To counsel Cassio to this parallel° course   *suitable*
Directly to his good? Divinity° of hell!   *theology*
When devils will the blackest sins put on,
They do suggest at first with heavenly shows,

345 As I do now. For whiles this honest fool
Plies Desdemona to repair his fortune,
And she for him pleads strongly to the Moor,
I'll pour this pestilence into his ear:
That she repeals him° for her body's lust,   *appeals for him*

350 And by how much she strives to do him good
She shall undo her credit with the Moor.
So will I turn her virtue into pitch,[1]
And out of her own goodness make the net
That shall enmesh them all.

          Enter RODERIGO

355 How now, Roderigo?

RODERIGO I do follow here in the chase, not like a hound
that hunts, but one that fills up the cry.° My money is   *a pack follower*
almost spent; I have been tonight exceedingly well cud-
geled; and I think the issue will be I shall have so

360 much° experience for my pains, and so, with no money   *only this much*
at all and a little more wit, return again to Venice.

IAGO How poor are they that have not patience!
What wound did ever heal but by degrees?
Thou know'st we work by wit and not by witchcraft,

365 And wit depends on dilatory° time.   *gradually unfolding*
Does't not go well? Cassio hath beaten thee,

---

1. Black, sticky substance used as a snare.

And thou by that small hurt hath cashiered° Cassio.   *dismissed*
Though other things grow fair against the sun,
Yet fruits that blossom first will first be ripe.[2]
Content thyself awhile. By the Mass,° 'tis morning!   *(a mild oath)*
Pleasure and action make the hours seem short.
Retire thee; go where thou art billeted.
Away! I say; thou shalt know more hereafter.
Nay, get thee gone!   *Exit* RODERIGO
        Two things are to be done:
My wife must move for Cassio to her mistress—
I'll set her on—
Myself a while to draw the Moor apart
And bring him jump° when he may Cassio find   *exactly*
Soliciting his wife. Ay, that's the way!
Dull not device by coldness and delay.[3]   *Exit*

3.1

    Enter CASSIO, MUSICIANS, *and* CLOWN

CASSIO Masters, play here—I will content° your pains—   *reward*
  Something that's brief; and bid "Good morrow, general."
CLOWN Why, masters, have your instruments been in
  Naples, that they speak i'th' nose thus?[1]
MUSICIAN How, sir? how?
CLOWN Are these, I pray you, wind instruments?[2]
MUSICIAN Ay, marry, are they, sir.
CLOWN O, thereby hangs a tail!
MUSICIAN Whereby hangs a tale, sir?
CLOWN Marry, sir, by many a wind instrument that I know.
  But, masters, here's money for you; and the general so
  likes your music that he desires you for love's sake to
  make no more noise with it.
MUSICIAN Well, sir, we will not.
CLOWN If you have any music that may not° be heard, to't   *cannot*
  again. But, as they say, to hear music the general does
  not greatly care.
MUSICIAN We have none such, sir.
CLOWN Then put up your pipes in your bag, for I'll away.
  Go! Vanish into air, away!   *Exeunt* MUSICIANS
CASSIO Dost thou hear, mine honest friend?
CLOWN No, I hear not your honest friend: I hear you.
CASSIO Prithee keep up thy quillets.[3] There's a poor piece
  of gold for thee. If the gentlewoman that attends the
  general be stirring, tell her there's one Cassio entreats
  her a little favor of speech. Wilt thou do this?

---

2. I.e., although others may appear to be prosper-
ing, your plan will be successful soonest because
it was set in motion first.
3. Don't let sluggishness and slowness to act
weaken the plot.
3.1 Location: Outside Othello and Desdemona's
room.

1. That they sound so nasal; perhaps a reference
to venereal disease, often associated with Naples,
or a phallic or anal joke.
2. The exchange that follows depends on the connections among wind instruments, flatulence,
and "tale/tail."
3. Pack up your puns.

CLOWN   She is stirring, sir. If she will stir hither, I shall
   seem° to notify unto her.   *arrange*
CASSIO   Do, good my friend.   *Exit* CLOWN
   Enter IAGO   In happy time,° Iago.   *well met*
30 IAGO   You have not been abed then?
CASSIO   Why, no; the day had broke before we parted.
   I have made bold, Iago, to send in to your wife.
   My suit to her is that she will to virtuous Desdemona
   Procure me some access.
IAGO   I'll send her to you presently;°   *immediately*
35 And I'll devise a mean to draw the Moor
   Out of the way, that your converse and business
   May be more free.
CASSIO   I humbly thank you for't.   *Exit* [IAGO]
                    I never knew
   A Florentine more kind and honest.
   Enter EMILIA
40 EMILIA   Good morrow, good lieutenant. I am sorry
   For your displeasure, but all will sure° be well.   *surely*
   The general and his wife are talking of it,
   And she speaks for you stoutly. The Moor replies
   That he you hurt is of great fame in Cyprus
45 And great affinity,° and that in wholesome wisdom   *well connected*
   He might not but refuse you; but he protests he loves you
   And needs no other suitor but his likings
   To bring you in again.
CASSIO   Yet I beseech you,
   If you think fit, or that it may be done,
50 Give me advantage of some brief discourse
   With Desdemon alone.
EMILIA   Pray you come in.
   I will bestow you where you shall have time
   To speak your bosom° freely.   *heart*
CASSIO   I am much bound to you.
                    Exeunt

3.2

   Enter OTHELLO, IAGO, *and* GENTLEMEN
OTHELLO   These letters give, Iago, to the pilot,
   And by him do my duties° to the senate.   *send my respects*
   That done, I will be walking on the works;°   *fortifications*
   Repair° there to me.   *come*
IAGO   Well, my good lord; I'll do't.
5 OTHELLO   This fortification, gentlemen, shall we see't?
GENTLEMAN   We'll wait upon your lordship.   *Exeunt*

3.3

   Enter DESDEMONA, CASSIO, *and* EMILIA
DESDEMONA   Be thou assured, good Cassio, I will do

3.2 Location: The citadel.
3.3 Location: The citadel's garden.

All my abilities in thy behalf.

EMILIA   Good madam, do. I warrant it grieves my husband
    As if the cause were his.

DESDEMONA   O, that's an honest fellow. Do not doubt,
    Cassio,
    But I will have my lord and you again
    As friendly as you were.

CASSIO   Bounteous madam,
    Whatever shall become of Michael Cassio,
    He's never anything but your true servant.

DESDEMONA   I know't; I thank you. You do love my lord;
    You have known him long; and be you well assured
    He shall in strangeness stand no farther off
    Than in a politic distance.[1]

CASSIO   Ay, but, lady,
    That policy may either last so long,
    Or feed upon such nice and wat'rish diet,
    Or breed itself so out of circumstances,[2]
    That—I being absent, and my place supplied°—   *filled*
    My general will forget my love and service.

DESDEMONA   Do not doubt° that. Before Emilia here,   *fear*
    I give thee warrant° of thy place. Assure thee,   *assurance*
    If I do vow a friendship, I'll perform it
    To the last article. My lord shall never rest:
    I'll watch him tame and talk him out of patience;[3]
    His bed shall seem a school, his board a shrift;°   *confessional*
    I'll intermingle everything he does
    With Cassio's suit. Therefore be merry, Cassio,
    For thy solicitor° shall rather die   *advocate*
    Than give thy cause away.°   *up*
        Enter OTHELLO *and* IAGO

EMILIA   Madam, here comes my lord.

CASSIO   Madam, I'll take my leave.

DESDEMONA   Why, stay and hear me speak.

CASSIO   Madam, not now: I am very ill at ease,
    Unfit for mine own purposes.

DESDEMONA   Well, do your discretion.   *Exit Cassio*

IAGO   Ha! I like not that.

OTHELLO   What dost thou say?

IAGO   Nothing, my lord; or if . . . I know not what.

OTHELLO   Was not that Cassio parted from my wife?

IAGO   Cassio, my lord? No, sure, I cannot think it
    That he would steal away so guilty-like,
    Seeing your coming.

OTHELLO   I do believe 'twas he.

DESDEMONA   How now, my lord?
    I have been talking with a suitor here,

---

1. He will distance himself from you only as
much as good diplomacy requires.
2. "Or feed . . . circumstances": or persist based
on such unimportant and poor justifications, or

continue by chance.
3. I'll keep him awake until he obeys me, and
talk to him beyond his endurance.

A man that languishes in your displeasure.

OTHELLO   Who is't you mean?

45   DESDEMONA   Why, your lieutenant, Cassio. Good my lord,
If I have any grace or power to move you,
His present reconciliation take;°   accept him now
For if he be not one that truly loves you,
That errs in ignorance and not in cunning,°   not knowingly
50   I have no judgment in an honest face.
I prithee call him back.

OTHELLO   Went he hence now?

DESDEMONA   Yes, faith; so humbled
That he hath left part of his grief with me
To suffer with him. Good love, call him back.

55   OTHELLO   Not now, sweet Desdemon; some other time.

DESDEMONA   But shall't be shortly?

OTHELLO   The sooner, sweet, for you.

DESDEMONA   Shall't be tonight, at supper?

OTHELLO   No, not tonight.

DESDEMONA   Tomorrow dinner° then?   midday meal

OTHELLO   I shall not dine at home;
I meet the captains at the citadel.

60   DESDEMONA   Why then, tomorrow night, on Tuesday morn,
On Tuesday noon or night, on Wednesday morn.
I prithee name the time, but let it not
Exceed three days. In faith, he's penitent;
And yet his trespass, in our common reason°—   normal judgment
65   Save that, they say, the wars must make example
Out of her° best—is not almost a fault   (war's)
T'incur a private check.[4] When shall he come?
Tell me, Othello. I wonder in my soul
What you would ask me that I should deny,
70   Or stand so mamm'ring° on? What? Michael Cassio,   hesitating
That came a-wooing with you? and so many a time,
When I have spoke of you dispraisingly,
Hath ta'en your part—to have so much to do
To bring him in?° By'r Lady, I could do much—[5]   into favor
75   OTHELLO   Prithee, no more. Let him come when he will:
I will deny thee nothing.

DESDEMONA   Why, this is not a boon;
'Tis as I should entreat you wear your gloves,
Or feed on nourishing dishes, or keep you warm,
Or sue to you to do a peculiar° profit   particular
80   To your own person. Nay, when I have a suit
Wherein I mean to touch your love indeed,
It shall be full of poise° and difficult weight,   balanced judgment
And fearful to be granted.

OTHELLO   I will deny thee nothing.
Whereon I do beseech thee grant me this,

---

4. Is barely worth even private criticism.
5. Do much to make you regret your reluctance (?).

To leave me but a little to myself.

DESDEMONA   Shall I deny you? No. Farewell, my lord.

OTHELLO   Farewell, my Desdemona; I'll come to thee
    straight.°   *immediately*

DESDEMONA   Emilia, come. [*To* OTHELLO] Be as your
    fancies teach° you.   *as your whims lead*
    Whate'er you be, I am obedient.

                              Exeunt DESDEMONA *and* EMILIA

OTHELLO   Excellent wretch!° Perdition catch my soul   *(affectionate)*
    But I do love thee! and when I love thee not,
    Chaos is come again.

IAGO   My noble lord . . .

OTHELLO   What dost thou say, Iago?

IAGO   Did Michael Cassio, when you wooed my lady,
    Know of your love?

OTHELLO   He did, from first to last.
    Why dost thou ask?

IAGO   But for a satisfaction of my thought,
    No further harm.

OTHELLO   Why of thy thought, Iago?

IAGO   I did not think he had been acquainted with her.

OTHELLO   O yes, and went between us very oft.

IAGO   Indeed?

OTHELLO   Indeed? Ay, indeed. Discern'st thou aught in that?
    Is he not honest?

IAGO   Honest, my lord?

OTHELLO   Honest? Ay, honest.

IAGO   My lord, for aught I know.

OTHELLO   What dost thou think?

IAGO   Think, my lord?

OTHELLO   "Think, my lord?" By heaven, thou echo'st me
    As if there were some monster in thy thought
    Too hideous to be shown. Thou dost mean something:
    I heard thee say even now thou lik'st not that,
    When Cassio left my wife. What didst not like?
    And when I told thee he was of my counsel,°   *in my confidence*
    Of my whole course of wooing, thou cried'st "Indeed?"
    And didst contract and purse thy brow together
    As if thou then hadst shut up in thy brain
    Some horrible conceit.° If thou dost love me,   *thought*
    Show me thy thought.

IAGO   My lord, you know I love you.

OTHELLO   I think thou dost;
    And for° I know thou'rt full of love and honesty,   *since*
    And weigh'st thy words before thou giv'st them breath,
    Therefore these stops° of thine fright me the more: *reluctances*
    For such things in a false disloyal knave
    Are tricks of custom;° but in a man that's just,   *habitual*
    They're close dilations,[6] working from the heart

---

6. I.e., involuntary revelations of interior, close-kept secrets.

That passion cannot rule.°   *control*

IAGO   For Michael Cassio,
    I dare be sworn I think that he is honest.

OTHELLO   I think so too.

IAGO   Men should be what they seem,

130   Or those that be not, would they might seem none.[7]

OTHELLO   Certain, men should be what they seem.

IAGO   Why then, I think Cassio's an honest man.

OTHELLO   Nay, yet there's more in this.
    I prithee speak to me as to thy thinkings,

135   As thou dost ruminate, and give thy worst of thoughts
    The worst of words.

IAGO   Good my lord, pardon me.
    Though I am bound to every act of duty,
    I am not bound to that all slaves are free to:[8]
    Utter my thoughts? Why, say they are vile and false—

140   As where's that palace whereinto foul things
    Sometimes intrude not? Who has that breast so pure
    But some uncleanly apprehensions
    Keep leets and law-days, and in sessions sit
    With meditations lawful?[9]

145 OTHELLO   Thou dost conspire against thy friend,° Iago,   *(Othello)*
    If thou but think'st him wronged and mak'st his ear
    A stranger to thy thoughts.

IAGO   I do beseech you,
    Though I perchance am vicious° in my guess   *mistaken*
    (As I confess it is my nature's plague

150   To spy into abuses, and oft my jealousy
    Shapes faults that are not), that your wisdom
    From one that so imperfectly conceits°   *imagines*
    Would take no notice, nor build yourself a trouble
    Out of his scattering° and unsure observance.   *incoherent*

155   It were not for your quiet, nor your good,
    Nor for my manhood, honesty, and wisdom,
    To let you know my thoughts.

OTHELLO   What dost thou mean?

IAGO   Good name in man and woman, dear my lord,
    Is the immediate jewel of their souls;

160   Who steals my purse steals trash: 'tis something, nothing;
    'Twas mine, 'tis his, and has been slave to thousands.
    But he that filches from me my good name
    Robs me of that which not enriches him
    And makes me poor indeed.

OTHELLO   By heaven, I'll know thy
    thoughts!

165 IAGO   You cannot, if my heart were in your hand,

---

7. "Or . . . none": if only those who are not what
they seem didn't seem to be what they are not.
8. I.e., I am not obligated to reveal my inner
thoughts, something about which even slaves
have a choice.

9. "Uncleanly . . . lawful": illegitimate thoughts
meet in court ("leets") from time to time (on "law-
days") and debate (in court "sessions") with legitimate ones.

Nor shall not, whilst 'tis in my custody.

OTHELLO   Ha?

IAGO   O, beware, my lord, of jealousy!
It is the green-eyed monster, which doth mock
The meat it feeds on.[1] That cuckold lives in bliss
Who, certain of his fate, loves not his wronger;[2]
But O, what damnèd minutes tells he o'er
Who dotes yet doubts, suspects yet strongly loves!

OTHELLO   O misery!

IAGO   Poor and content is rich, and rich enough,
But riches fineless° is as poor as winter   *boundless*
To him that ever fears he shall be poor.
Good God, the souls of all my tribe defend
From jealousy!

OTHELLO   Why, why is this?
Think'st thou I'd make a life of jealousy,
To follow still the changes of the moon°   *i.e., to renew endlessly*
With fresh suspicions? No! To be once in doubt
Is once to be resolved.° Exchange me for a goat   *to be finally settled*
When I shall turn the business of my soul
To such exsufflicate and blowed° surmises,   *inflated and blown up*
Matching thy inference. 'Tis not to make me jealous
To say my wife is fair, feeds well, loves company,
Is free of speech, sings, plays, and dances:
Where virtue is, these are more virtuous.
Nor from mine own weak merits will I draw
The smallest fear or doubt of her revolt,°   *or fear of her betrayal*
For she had eyes and chose me. No, Iago,
I'll see before I doubt; when I doubt, prove;
And on the proof there is no more but this:
Away at once with love or jealousy!

IAGO   I am glad of this; for now I shall have reason
To show the love and duty that I bear you
With franker spirit. Therefore, as I am bound,
Receive it from me. I speak not yet of proof.
Look to your wife; observe her well with Cassio;
Wear your eyes thus: not jealous, nor secure.
I would not have your free and noble nature
Out of self-bounty be abused.[3] Look to't.
I know our country disposition well:
In Venice they do let God see the pranks
They dare not show their husbands; their best
    conscience
Is not to leave't undone, but keep't unknown.

OTHELLO   Dost thou say so?

IAGO   She did deceive her father, marrying you,
And when she seemed to shake, and fear your looks,

---

1. I.e., tortures, as it consumes, the heart of the jealous person.
2. Who, knowing it is his fate to be cuckolded, doesn't love his wife.
3. Be deceived on account of your own goodness.

She loved them most.

OTHELLO   And so she did.

210 IAGO   Why, go to° then.   *that's it*
She that, so young, could give out such a seeming
To seel her father's eyes up close as oak,[4]
He thought 'twas witchcraft . . . ; but I am much to
    blame.
I humbly do beseech you of your pardon
For too much loving you.

215 OTHELLO   I am bound to thee forever.

IAGO   I see this hath a little dashed your spirits.

OTHELLO   Not a jot, not a jot.

IAGO   I'faith, I fear it has.
I hope you will consider what is spoke
Comes from my love. But I do see you're moved.

220 I am to pray you not to strain my speech
To grosser issues° nor to larger reach   *greater conclusions*
Than to suspicion.

OTHELLO   I will not.

IAGO   Should you do so, my lord,
My speech should fall into such vile success

225 Which my thoughts aimed not. Cassio's my worthy
    friend—
My lord, I see you're moved.

OTHELLO   No, not much moved;
I do not think but Desdemona's honest.

IAGO   Long live she so! and long live you to think so!

OTHELLO   And yet how nature, erring from itself—

230 IAGO   Ay, there's the point! as to be bold with you,
Not to affect° many proposed matches   *desire*
Of her own clime, complexion, and degree,
Whereto we see in all things nature tends—
Foh! one may smell in such a will most rank,

235 Foul disproportions, thoughts unnatural.
But, pardon me, I do not in position°   *argument*
Distinctly speak of her, though I may fear
Her will,° recoiling° to her better judgment,   *desire / submitting*
May fall to match you with her country forms,[5]
And happily° repent.   *perhaps*

240 OTHELLO   Farewell, farewell.
If more thou dost perceive, let me know more.
Set on thy wife to observe. Leave me, Iago.

IAGO [*going*]   My lord, I take my leave.

OTHELLO   Why did I marry? This honest creature,
    doubtless,

245 Sees and knows more, much more, than he unfolds.

IAGO [*returning*]   My lord, I would I might entreat your
    honor

---

4. Perhaps: to cover ("seel" means "to blind") her father's eyes as tightly as oak (a fine-grained wood).
5. May happen to compare you with Venetian standards.

To scan this thing no farther; leave it to time.
Although 'tis fit that Cassio have his place
(For sure he fills it up with great ability),
Yet if you please to hold him off awhile,
You shall by that perceive him and his means.[6]
Note if your lady strain his entertainment°   *urge his reception*
With any strong or vehement importunity;
Much will be seen in that. In the meantime
Let me be thought too busy° in my fears   *meddlesome*
(As worthy cause I have to fear I am),
And hold her free,° I do beseech your honor.   *believe her innocent*

OTHELLO   Fear not my government.°   *self-conduct*

IAGO   I once more take my leave.   *Exit*

OTHELLO   This fellow's of exceeding honesty,
And knows all qualities° with a learned spirit   *(human) types*
Of human dealings. If I do prove her haggard,°   *wild (from falconry)*
Though that her jesses were my dear heartstrings,
I'd whistle her off and let her down the wind
To prey at fortune.[7] Haply for° I am black,   *perhaps because*
And have not those soft parts of conversation°   *easy manners*
That chamberers° have, or for I am declined   *gallants*
Into the vale of years—yet that's not much—
She's gone, I am abused,° and my relief   *deceived*
Must be to loathe her. O curse of marriage!
That we can call these delicate creatures ours
And not their appetites! I had rather be a toad
And live upon the vapor of a dungeon
Than keep a corner in the thing I love
For others' uses. Yet 'tis the plague of great ones:
Prerogatived° are they less than the base;°   *privileged / lowborn*
'Tis destiny unshunnable, like death;
Even then this forkèd plague is fated to us
When we do quicken.[8]
                    Enter DESDEMONA *and* EMILIA
                         Look where she comes!
If she be false, O then heaven mocks itself;
I'll not believe't.

DESDEMONA   How now, my dear Othello?
Your dinner, and the generous° islanders   *noble*
By you invited, do attend° your presence.   *wait for*

OTHELLO   I am to blame.

DESDEMONA   Why do you speak so faintly?
Are you not well?

OTHELLO   I have a pain upon my forehead, here.°   *(from cuckold's horns)*

DESDEMONA   Faith, that's with watching;° 'twill away   *from lack of sleep*
   again.
Let me but bind it hard, within this hour

---

6. Method (for restoring himself to favor).
7. "Though . . . fortune": even if what tied her
("jesses" were leg straps put on a hawk) were my
own heartstrings, I'd set her loose downwind

forever to hunt on her own.
8. "Even . . . quicken": the "plague" of horns
(imagined to grow from the forehead of a cuckold)
is our fate as soon as we live.

It will be well.

OTHELLO   Your napkin° is too little;   *handkerchief*

[*The handkerchief is dropped*]

290   Let it alone. Come, I'll go in with you.

DESDEMONA   I am very sorry that you are not well.

Exeunt OTHELLO *and* DESDEMONA

EMILIA   I am glad I have found this napkin;

This was her first remembrance° from the Moor.   *keepsake*

My wayward husband hath a hundred times

295   Wooed me to steal it. But she so loves the token

(For he conjured her° she should ever keep it)   *made her swear*

That she reserves it evermore about her

To kiss and talk to. I'll have the work ta'en out,°   *embroidery copied*

And giv't Iago; what he will do with it

300   Heaven knows, not I:

I nothing° but to please his fantasy.   *intend nothing*

Enter Iago

IAGO   How now? What do you here alone?

EMILIA   Do not you chide; I have a thing for you.

IAGO   You have a thing for me? It is a common thing—⁹

305   EMILIA   Ha?

IAGO   To have a foolish wife.

EMILIA   O, is that all? What will you give me now

For that same handkerchief?

IAGO   What handkerchief?

EMILIA   What handkerchief?

310   Why, that the Moor first gave to Desdemona,

That which so often you did bid me steal.

IAGO   Hast stolen it from her?

EMILIA   No, faith; she let it drop by negligence,

And to th'advantage° I, being here, took't up.   *taking the occasion*

Look, here 'tis.

315   IAGO   A good wench! Give it me.

EMILIA   What will you do with't, that you have been so

earnest

To have me filch it?

IAGO [*taking it*]   Why, what is that to you?

EMILIA   If it be not for some purpose of import,

Giv' me again. Poor lady, she'll run mad

When she shall lack it.

320   IAGO   Be not acknown on't;°   *don't let it be known*

I have use for it. Go—leave me!   *Exit* EMILIA

I will in Cassio's lodging lose this napkin

And let him find it. Trifles light as air

Are to the jealous confirmations strong

325   As proofs of holy writ. This may do something.

The Moor already changes with my poison:

Dangerous conceits° are in their natures poisons,   *ideas*

Which at the first are scarce found to distaste,

---

9. It is a vagina ("thing") available to all.

But with a little act° upon the blood   *effect*
Burn like the mines of sulphur.[1]
    Enter OTHELLO   I did say so—
Look where he comes! Not poppy nor mandragora[2]
Nor all the drowsy syrups of the world
Shall ever medicine thee to that sweet sleep
Which thou owedst° yesterday.   *owned*
OTHELLO   Ha! ha! false to me?
IAGO   Why, how now, general? No more of that!
OTHELLO   Avaunt! be gone! Thou hast set me on the rack.
   I swear 'tis better to be much abused°   *mistreated; deceived*
   Than but to know't a little.
IAGO   How now, my lord?
OTHELLO   What sense had I of her stol'n hours of lust?
   I saw't not, thought it not; it harmed not me;
   I slept the next night well, fed well, was free and merry;
   I found not Cassio's kisses on her lips.
   He that is robbed, not wanting° what is stol'n,   *missing*
   Let him not know't, and he's not robbed at all.
IAGO   I am sorry to hear this.
OTHELLO   I had been happy if the general camp,
   Pioneers° and all, had tasted her sweet body,   *manual laborers*
   So° I had nothing known. O, now forever   *if*
   Farewell the tranquil mind! farewell content!
   Farewell the plumèd troops and the big wars
   That makes ambition virtue! O, farewell!
   Farewell the neighing steed and the shrill trump,°   *trumpet*
   The spirit-stirring drum, th'ear-piercing fife,
   The royal banner and all quality,°   *aspects*
   Pride,° pomp, and circumstance° of glorious war!   *magnificence / ceremony*
   And O you mortal engines° whose rude throats   *deadly cannons*
   Th'immortal Jove's dread clamors° counterfeit,   *thunderclaps*
   Farewell! Othello's occupation's gone!
IAGO   Is't possible, my lord?
OTHELLO   [*grabs* IAGO *by the throat*] Villain, be sure
   thou prove my love a whore!
   Be sure of it, give me the ocular proof,
   Or by the worth of mine eternal soul,
   Thou hadst been better have been born a dog
   Than answer my waked wrath.
IAGO   Is't come to this?
OTHELLO   Make me to see't, or at the least so prove it
   That the probation° bear no hinge nor loop   *proof*
   To hang a doubt on, or woe upon thy life!
IAGO   My noble lord—
OTHELLO   If thou dost slander her and torture me,
   Never pray more; abandon all remorse;

---

1. Pliny the Elder (23/24–79 C.E.) describes two islands of sulfur between mainland Italy and Sicily that were rumored to be always on fire.

2. A sleep-inducing substance made from the mandrake root.

On horror's head horrors accumulate;
Do deeds to make heaven weep, all earth amazed;
For nothing canst thou to damnation add
Greater than that.

IAGO   O grace! O heaven forgive me!

375   Are you a man? Have you a soul? or sense?
God buy you; take mine office.[3] O wretched fool,°   (to himself)
That lov'st to make thine honesty a vice!°   fault
O monstrous world! Take note, take note, O world:
To be direct and honest is not safe.

380   I thank you for this profit,° and from hence   profitable lesson
I'll love no friend, sith° love breeds such offense.   since

OTHELLO   Nay, stay; thou shouldst be honest.

IAGO   I should be wise; for honesty's a fool
And loses that° it works for.   what

OTHELLO   By the world,[4]

385   I think my wife be honest, and think she is not;
I think that thou art just, and think thou art not.
I'll have some proof. My name, that was as fresh
As Dian's[5] visage, is now begrimed and black
As mine own face. If there be cords or knives,

390   Poison, or fire, or suffocating streams,
I'll not endure it. Would I were satisfied!

IAGO   I see you are eaten up with passion;
I do repent me that I put it to you.
You would be satisfied?

OTHELLO   Would? Nay, and I will.

395   IAGO   And may . . . but how? how satisfied, my lord?
Would you, the supervisor,° grossly gape on?   observer
Behold her topped?

OTHELLO   Death and damnation! O!

IAGO   It were a tedious° difficulty, I think,   painful
To bring them to that prospect. Damn them then,

400   If ever mortal eyes do see them bolster°   share a pillow
More° than their own.° What then? How then?   other / own eyes
What shall I say? Where's satisfaction?
It is impossible you should see this,
Were they as prime° as goats, as hot as monkeys,   lustful

405   As salt as wolves in pride,[6] and fools as gross
As ignorance made drunk. But yet, I say,
If imputation and strong circumstances[7]
Which lead directly to the door of truth
Will give you satisfaction, you might have't.

410   OTHELLO   Give me a living° reason she's disloyal.   sustainable; valid

IAGO   I do not like the office.°   task

---

3. Good-bye, I resign my official position (ensign).
4. Othello's speech (lines 384–91) does not appear in Q.
5. Diana, goddess of chastity and of the (pale) moon. The Second Quarto (1630) replaces "My"

(line 387) with "Her," a plausible but arguably less powerful reading that lacks textual authority.
6. As lecherous as wolves in heat.
7. If inference and strong circumstantial evidence.

But sith I am entered in this cause so far,
Pricked to't° by foolish honesty and love,   *prodded on*
I will go on. I lay with Cassio lately,
And being troubled with a raging tooth,
I could not sleep. There are a kind of men
So loose of soul that in their sleeps will mutter
Their affairs; one of this kind is Cassio.
In sleep I heard him say "Sweet Desdemona,
Let us be wary, let us hide our loves!"
And then, sir, would he gripe° and wring my hand,   *grip*
Cry "O sweet creature!" then kiss me hard,
As if he plucked up kisses by the roots
That grew upon my lips, lay his leg o'er my thigh,
And sigh, and kiss, and then cry "Cursèd fate
That gave thee to the Moor!"
OTHELLO   O monstrous! monstrous!
IAGO   Nay, this was but his
    dream.
OTHELLO   But this denoted a foregone conclusion;°   *an earlier event*
'Tis a shrewd doubt,° though it be but a dream.[8]   *reasonable fear*
IAGO   And this may help to thicken other proofs
    That do demonstrate thinly.
OTHELLO   I'll tear her all to pieces!
IAGO   Nay, yet be wise; yet we see nothing done;
    She may be honest yet. Tell me but this:
    Have you not sometimes seen a handkerchief
    Spotted with strawberries in your wife's hand?
OTHELLO   I gave her such a one; 'twas my first gift.
IAGO   I know not that; but such a handkerchief—
    I am sure it was your wife's—did I today
    See Cassio wipe his beard with.
OTHELLO   If it be that—
IAGO   If it be that, or any that was hers,
    It speaks against her with the other proofs.
OTHELLO   O that the slave° had forty thousand lives!   *(Cassio)*
    One is too poor, too weak for my revenge.
    Now do I see 'tis true. Look here, Iago:
    All my fond love thus do I blow to heaven.
    'Tis gone.
    Arise, black vengeance, from the hollow hell!
    Yield up, O love, thy crown and hearted throne°   *rule of the heart*
    To tyrannous hate! Swell, bosom, with thy fraught,°   *burden*
    For 'tis of aspics'° tongues!   *poisonous snakes'*
IAGO   Yet be content.
OTHELLO   O, blood! blood! blood!
IAGO   Patience, I say; your mind may change.
OTHELLO   Never, Iago. Like to the Pontic Sea,°   *Black Sea*
    Whose icy current and compulsive course
    Ne'er keeps retiring ebb but keeps due on

---

8. Q gives this line to Iago.

To the Propontic and the Hellespont,[9]
Even so my bloody thoughts with violent pace
Shall ne'er look back, ne'er ebb to humble love,
Till that a capable° and wide revenge   *capacious*
Swallow them up.   OTHELLO *kneels*
460   Now, by yond marble heaven,
In the due reverence of a sacred vow,
I here engage my words.
IAGO   Do not rise yet.   IAGO *kneels*
Witness, you ever-burning lights above,
You elements that clip° us round about,   *embrace*
465 Witness that here Iago doth give up
The execution° of his wit, hands, heart,   *command*
To wrongèd Othello's service. Let him command,
And to obey shall be in me remorse,°   *pity (for Othello)*
What bloody business ever.°   [*They rise*]   *soever*
OTHELLO   I greet thy love,
470 Not with vain thanks but with acceptance bounteous,
And will upon the instant put thee to't.°   *immediately test it*
Within these three days let me hear thee say
That Cassio's not alive.
IAGO   My friend is dead;
'Tis done at your request. But let her live.
OTHELLO   Damn her, lewd minx!° O, damn her! damn   *wanton*
475   her!
Come, go with me apart; I will withdraw
To furnish me with some swift means of death
For the fair devil. Now art thou my lieutenant.
IAGO   I am your own forever.   *Exeunt*

3.4

    Enter DESDEMONA, EMILIA, *and* CLOWN
DESDEMONA   Do you know, sirrah,[1] where Lieutenant Cas-
  sio lies?
CLOWN   I dare not say he lies anywhere.
DESDEMONA   Why, man?
5 CLOWN   He's a soldier, and for me to say a soldier lies, 'tis
  stabbing.
DESDEMONA   Go to; where lodges he?
CLOWN   To tell you where he lodges is to tell you where
  I lie.
10 DESDEMONA   Can anything be made of this?
CLOWN   I know not where he lodges, and for me to devise
  a lodging and say he lies here or he lies there were to lie in
  mine own throat.°   *lie outrageously*
DESDEMONA   Can you inquire him out and be edified by
15   report?

---

9. The Propontic was the body of water bounded
by the straits of Bosphorus and the Dardanelles
(Hellespont), the latter strait leading to the
Aegean.
3.4 Location: Before the citadel.
1. A form of address to an inferior.

CLOWN   I will catechize the world for him—that is, make
    questions and by them answer.
DESDEMONA   Seek him, bid him come hither. Tell him I
    have moved° my lord on his behalf and hope all will be   *petitioned*
    well.
CLOWN   To do this is within the compass° of man's wit,   *scope*
    and therefore I will attempt the doing it.   *Exit* CLOWN
DESDEMONA   Where should° I lose the handkerchief,   *did*
    Emilia?
EMILIA   I know not, madam.
DESDEMONA   Believe me, I had rather have lost my purse
    Full of crusadoes,° and but° my noble Moor   *gold coins / except that*
    Is true of mind and made of no such baseness
    As jealous creatures are, it were enough
    To put him to ill-thinking.
EMILIA   Is he not jealous?
DESDEMONA   Who, he? I think the sun where he was born
    Drew all such humors from him.[2]
        Enter OTHELLO
EMILIA   Look where he comes.
DESDEMONA [*aside*]   I will not leave him now till Cassio be
    Called to him.—How is't with you, my lord?
OTHELLO   Well, my good lady. [*Aside*] O, hardness to dissemble!—
    How do you, Desdemona?
DESDEMONA   Well, my good lord.
OTHELLO   Give me your hand. This hand is moist, my lady.
DESDEMONA   It hath felt no age nor known no sorrow.
OTHELLO   This argues fruitfulness and liberal heart.[3]
    Hot, hot and moist. This hand of yours requires
    A sequester from liberty: fasting and prayer,
    Much castigation, exercise devout;
    For here's a young and sweating devil here
    That commonly rebels. 'Tis a good hand,
    A frank° one.   *(sexually) open*
DESDEMONA   You may indeed say so,
    For 'twas that hand that gave away my heart.
OTHELLO   A liberal hand. The hearts of old gave hands,
    But our new heraldry is hands, not hearts.[4]
DESDEMONA   I cannot speak of this. Come now, your promise.
OTHELLO   What promise, chuck?°   *woodchuck (affectionate)*
DESDEMONA   I have sent to bid Cassio come speak with you.
OTHELLO   I have a salt and sorry rheum° offends me;   *badly watering eyes*
    Lend me thy handkerchief.
DESDEMONA   Here, my lord.
OTHELLO   That which I gave you.

---

2. As if the African sun dried up the bodily fluids
("humors") that produce jealousy.
3. This demonstrates fertility (perhaps, by implication, lust) and a generous (hinting at "loose")
heart. A moist hand was thought to be a sign of
active desire.
4. I.e., these days the joining of hands doesn't
signify the joining of hearts.

DESDEMONA   I have it not about me.
OTHELLO   Not?
DESDEMONA   No, faith, my lord.
OTHELLO   That's a fault. That
55   handkerchief
         Did an Egyptian to my mother give.
         She was a charmer° and could almost read   sorceress
         The thoughts of people. She told her, while she kept it,
         'Twould make her amiable° and subdue my father   desirable
60   Entirely to her love; but if she lost it
         Or made a gift of it, my father's eye
         Should hold her loathèd, and his spirits should hunt
         After new fancies. She, dying, gave it me,
         And bid me, when my fate would have me wived,
65   To give it her.° I did so; and—take heed on't!—   to my wife
         Make it a darling like your precious eye.
         To lose't or give't away were such perdition°   loss; damnation
         As nothing else could match.
DESDEMONA   Is't possible?
OTHELLO   'Tis true. There's magic in the web of it:
70   A sibyl° that had numbered in the world   female prophet
         The sun to course two hundred compasses,⁵
         In her prophetic fury° sewed the work;   rapture
         The worms were hallowed that did breed the silk,
         And it was dyed in mummy,⁶ which the skillful
         Conserved of° maidens' hearts.   preserved out of
75 DESDEMONA   I'faith? Is't true?
OTHELLO   Most veritable; therefore look to't well.
DESDEMONA   Then would to God that I had never seen't!
OTHELLO   Ha? wherefore?
DESDEMONA   Why do you speak so startingly and rash?°   fitfully and urgently
80 OTHELLO   Is't lost? Is't gone? Speak, is't out o'th'way?
DESDEMONA   Heaven bless us!
OTHELLO   Say you?
DESDEMONA   It is not lost; but what an if° it were?   an if = if
OTHELLO   How?
85 DESDEMONA   I say it is not lost.
OTHELLO   Fetch't, let me see't!
DESDEMONA   Why, so I can; but I will not now.
         This is a trick to put me from my suit.
         Pray you let Cassio be received again.
90 OTHELLO   Fetch me the handkerchief, my mind misgives—
DESDEMONA   Come, come!
         You'll never meet a more sufficient° man—   complete
OTHELLO   The handkerchief!
DESDEMONA   I pray, talk me of Cassio.
OTHELLO   The handkerchief!⁷

5. "That . . . compasses": who was two hundred
years old.
6. Fluid drained from mummified bodies, supposedly magical.
7. Desdemona's "I pray, talk me of Cassio" and
Othello's "The handkerchief!" are only in Q.

DESDEMONA   A man that all his time
  Hath founded his good fortunes on your love,
  Shared dangers with you—
OTHELLO   The handkerchief!
DESDEMONA   I'faith, you are to blame.
OTHELLO   'Swounds!   *Exit* OTHELLO
EMILIA   Is not this man jealous?
DESDEMONA   I ne'er saw this before.
  Sure, there's some wonder in this handkerchief;
  I am most unhappy in the loss of it.
EMILIA   'Tis not a year or two shows us a man.[8]
  They are all but° stomachs, and we all but food;   *nothing but*
  They eat us hungerly, and when they are full
  They belch us.
      Enter IAGO *and* CASSIO
            Look you, Cassio and my husband.
IAGO   There is no other way; 'tis she must do't;
  And lo the happiness![9] go and importune her.
DESDEMONA   How now, good Cassio, what's the news
  with you?
CASSIO   Madam, my former suit. I do beseech you
  That by your virtuous means I may again
  Exist and be a member of his love
  Whom I, with all the office° of my heart,   *duty; loyal service*
  Entirely honor. I would not be delayed.
  If my offense be of such mortal° kind   *deadly*
  That nor° my service past nor present sorrows   *neither*
  Nor purposed merit in futurity
  Can ransom me into his love again,
  But to know so° must be my benefit;   *even to know this*
  So° shall I clothe me in a forced content   *if so*
  And shut° myself up in some other course   *give*
  To fortune's alms.
DESDEMONA   Alas, thrice-gentle Cassio,
  My advocation is not now in tune.[1]
  My lord is not my lord, nor should I know him,
  Were he in favor° as in humor° altered.   *appearance / mood*
  So help me every spirit sanctified
  As I have spoken for you all my best
  And stood within the blank[2] of his displeasure
  For my free speech. You must awhile be patient.
  What I can do I will, and more I will
  Than for myself I dare. Let that suffice you.
IAGO   Is my lord angry?
EMILIA   He went hence but now,
  And certainly in strange unquietness.
IAGO   Can he be angry? I have seen the cannon

---

8. I.e., it doesn't take long to see what a man is.
9. What a happy coincidence (seeing Desdemona).
1. My advocacy isn't working properly.

2. The "blank" was the white spot at the center
of a target.

135 When it hath blown his ranks into the air
And, like the devil, from his very arm
Puffed his own brother[3]—and is he angry?
Something of moment then. I will go meet him;
There's matter in't indeed if he be angry.

DESDEMONA   I prithee do so.   *Exit* [IAGO]

140   Something sure of state[4]—
Either from Venice, or some unhatched practice°   unfinished plot
Made demonstrable here in Cyprus to him—
Hath puddled his clear spirit; and in such cases
Men's natures wrangle with inferior things,

145 Though great ones are their object. 'Tis even so.
For let our finger ache, and it endues°   induces
Our other, healthful members even to a sense
Of pain. Nay, we must think men are not gods,
Nor of them look for such observancy°   careful attention

150 As fits the bridal.°—Beshrew me° much, Emilia.   wedding / (mild curse)
I was, unhandsome° warrior as I am,   unskilled
Arraigning his unkindness with my soul;
But now I find I had suborned the witness,
And he's indicted falsely.[5]

EMILIA   Pray heaven it be

155 State matters, as you think, and no conception
Nor no jealous toy° concerning you.   whim

DESDEMONA   Alas the day! I never gave him cause.

EMILIA   But jealous souls will not be answered so;
They are not ever jealous for the cause,

160 But jealous for they're jealous. It is a monster
Begot upon itself, born on itself.

DESDEMONA   Heaven keep the monster from Othello's
     mind!

EMILIA   Lady, amen!

DESDEMONA   I will go seek him; Cassio, walk here about.

165 If I do find him fit, I'll move your suit
And seek to effect it to my uttermost.

CASSIO   I humbly thank your ladyship.

                         Exeunt DESDEMONA *and* EMILIA
          Enter BIANCA[6]

BIANCA   Save you,° friend Cassio!   God save you

CASSIO   What make° you from   brings
     home?
How is't with you, my most fair Bianca?

170 I'faith, sweet love, I was coming to your house.

BIANCA   And I was going to your lodging, Cassio.
What? keep a week away? seven days and nights?
Eightscore-eight hours? And lovers' absent hours

---

3. Blew up his own brother (and Othello wasn't
angry even then).
4. Surely some official business.
5. Made the witness lie and so accused Othello

falsely.
6. "Bianca" means "white" in Italian—an ironic
reversal of conventional color imagery, given that
Bianca is a "customer" (courtesan, 4.1.119).

More tedious than the dial eightscore times![7]
O weary reckoning!°   *calculating*
CASSIO   Pardon me, Bianca;
  I have this while with leaden thoughts been pressed,
  But I shall in a more continuate° time   *opportune*
  Strike off° this score of absence. Sweet Bianca,   *make up*
            [*Gives her* DESDEMONA'S *handkerchief*]
  Take me this work out.°   *copy this embroidery*
BIANCA   O, Cassio! whence came this?
  This is some token from a newer friend;
  To the felt absence now I feel a cause.
  Is't come to this? Well, well.
CASSIO   Go to,° woman!   *stop it*
  Throw your vile guesses in the devil's teeth,
  From whence you have them. You are jealous now
  That this is from some mistress some remembrance;
  No, by my faith, Bianca.
BIANCA   Why, whose is it?
CASSIO   I know not neither; I found it in my chamber.
  I like the work well; ere it be demanded,°   *sought out*
  As like° enough it will, I would have it copied.   *likely*
  Take it and do't, and leave me for this time.
BIANCA   Leave you? Wherefore?
CASSIO   I do attend here on the general,
  And think it no addition,° nor my wish,   (*to my cause*)
  To have him see me womaned.
BIANCA   Why, I pray you?
CASSIO   Not that I love you not.
BIANCA   But that you do not love me.
  I pray you bring me on the way a little,
  And say if I shall see you soon at night.
CASSIO   'Tis but a little way that I can bring you,
  For I attend here; but I'll see you soon.
BIANCA   'Tis very good—I must be circumstanced.[8]
                                                          Exeunt

4.1

    Enter OTHELLO *and* IAGO
IAGO   Will you think so?
OTHELLO   Think so, Iago?
IAGO   What,
  To kiss in private?
OTHELLO   An unauthorized kiss!
IAGO   Or to be naked with her friend in bed
  An hour or more, not meaning any harm?
OTHELLO   Naked in bed, Iago, and not mean harm?
  It is hypocrisy against the devil.[1]

---

7. "Lovers' . . . times": each hour lovers are parted
is eightscore (160) times more tedious than normal clock time.
8. Content with what circumstances offer.

4.1 Location: Before the citadel.
1. I.e., by appearing to act sinfully while actually being good.

They that mean virtuously, and yet do so,
The devil their virtue tempts, and they tempt heaven.[2]
IAGO   If they do nothing, 'tis a venial slip;°   *an excusable sin*
10   But if I give my wife a handkerchief—
OTHELLO   What then?
IAGO   Why then, 'tis hers, my lord; and being hers,
She may, I think, bestow't on any man.
OTHELLO   She is protectress of her honor too;
15   May she give that?
IAGO   Her honor is an essence that's not seen;
They° have it very oft that have it not.   *they are reputed to*
But for the handkerchief—
OTHELLO   By heaven, I would most gladly have forgot it!
20   Thou said'st—O, it comes o'er my memory
As doth the raven o'er the infectious house,[3]
Boding to all!—he had my handkerchief.
IAGO   Ay, what of that?
OTHELLO   That's not so good now.
IAGO   What if I had said I had seen him do you wrong?
25   Or heard him say—as knaves be such abroad[4]
Who (having by their own importunate suit
Or voluntary dotage° of some mistress   *doting*
Convincèd or supplied° them) cannot choose   *seduced or satisfied*
But they must blab—
OTHELLO   Hath he said anything?
30   IAGO   He hath, my lord, but be you well assured,
No more than he'll unswear.
OTHELLO   What hath he said?
IAGO   Faith, that he did . . . I know not what he did.
OTHELLO   What? What?
IAGO   Lie . . .
OTHELLO   With her?
IAGO   With her, on her; what you will.
35   OTHELLO   Lie with her? lie on her? We say lie on her when
they belie° her. Lie with her? 'Swounds, that's ful-   *slander*
some.°— Handkerchief! confessions! handkerchief!—To[5]   *nauseating*
confess, and be hanged for his labor. First to be hanged,
and then to confess: I tremble at it. Nature would not
40   invest herself in such shadowing passion without some
instruction.[6] It is not words that shakes me thus. Pish!
Noses, ears, and lips! Is't possible? Confess? Handkerchief? O devil!   *Falls in a trance*
IAGO   Work on;
45   My medicine works! Thus credulous fools are caught,
And many worthy and chaste dames even thus,
All guiltless, meet reproach.—What ho! my lord!

---

2. "They . . . heaven": those who mean well ("virtuously") but act in this lascivious fashion ("so")
open themselves to temptation by the devil, and
they tempt heaven (to give them over). "Thou
shalt not tempt the Lord thy God" (Matthew 4.7).
3. The raven was thought to be an ill omen and a
carrier of plague. "Infectious": plague-infested.

4. As such knaves do exist in the world.
5. The rest of the speech does not appear in Q.
6. "Nature . . . instruction": it isn't natural that I
would feel such overwhelming ("shadowing")
emotion (jealousy) unless there were some cause
for it.

My lord, I say! Othello!
  Enter CASSIO
       How now, Cassio?
CASSIO What's the matter?
IAGO My lord is fallen into an epilepsy.
 This is his second fit; he had one yesterday.
CASSIO Rub him about the temples.
IAGO   No, forbear.
 The lethargy° must have his° quiet course;   *trance / its*
 If not, he foams at mouth and by and by
 Breaks out to savage madness. Look, he stirs.
 Do you withdraw yourself a little while;
 He will recover straight.° When he is gone,   *immediately*
 I would on great occasion° speak with you. *important matters*
       [*Exit* CASSIO]
 How is it, general? Have you not hurt your head?[7]
OTHELLO Dost thou mock me?
IAGO   I mock you not, by heaven.
 Would you would bear your fortune like a man!
OTHELLO A hornèd man's a monster and a beast.
IAGO There's many a beast then in a populous city,
 And many a civil° monster.   *city-dwelling*
OTHELLO Did he confess it?
IAGO   Good sir, be a man:
 Think every bearded fellow that's but yoked
 May draw with you.[8] There's millions now alive
 That nightly lie in those unproper beds
 Which they dare swear peculiar.[9] Your case is better.
 O, 'tis the spite of hell, the fiend's arch-mock,° *devil's greatest mock*
 To lip° a wanton in a secure° couch *kiss / an unsuspected*
 And to suppose her chaste. No, let me know;
 And knowing what I am,° I know what she shall be. *(a cuckold)*
OTHELLO O, thou art wise, 'tis certain.
IAGO   Stand you a while
 apart,
 Confine yourself but in a patient list.°   *boundary*
 Whilst you were here, o'er-whelmèd with your grief—
 A passion most unsuiting such a man—
 Cassio came hither. I shifted him away
 And laid good 'scuses upon your ecstasy,°   *for your fit*
 Bade him anon return and here speak with me,
 The which he promised. Do but encave° yourself, *hide*
 And mark the fleers,° the gibes, and notable scorns *sneers*
 That dwell in every region of his face;
 For I will make him tell the tale anew:
 Where, how, how oft, how long ago, and when
 He hath and is again to cope° your wife. *copulate with*
 I say, but mark his gesture. Marry, patience!

7. Othello takes this as suggesting that he has grown cuckold's horns.
8. Every married man ("yoked," like an ox, to his wife and hence to cuckoldry) labors ("draws") under the same fate.
9. Who lie in beds that don't belong entirely to them but that they would swear are exclusively their own.

Or I shall say you're all in all in spleen,°   *completely impulsive*
And nothing of a man.
OTHELLO   Dost thou hear, Iago?
90   I will be found most cunning in my patience;
But—dost thou hear?—most bloody.
IAGO   That's not amiss,
But yet keep time° in all. Will you withdraw?   *maintain control*
               [OTHELLO *withdraws*]
Now will I question Cassio of Bianca,
A huswife° that by selling her desires   *hussy*
95   Buys herself bread and cloth. It is a creature
That dotes on Cassio—as 'tis the strumpet's plague
To beguile many and be beguiled by one.
He, when he hears of her, cannot restrain
From the excess of laughter. Here he comes.
     Enter CASSIO
100   As he shall smile, Othello shall go mad;
And his unbookish° jealousy must conster°   *ignorant / construe*
Poor Cassio's smiles, gestures, and light behaviors
Quite in the wrong. How do you, lieutenant?
CASSIO   The worser that you give me the addition°   *title*
105   Whose want even kills me.
IAGO   Ply Desdemona well, and you are sure on't.
Now if this suit lay in Bianca's power,
How quickly should you speed!
CASSIO   Alas, poor caitiff!°   *wretch*
OTHELLO   Look how he laughs already!
110 IAGO   I never knew woman love man so.
CASSIO   Alas, poor rogue! I think, i'faith, she loves me.
OTHELLO   Now he denies it faintly and laughs it out.
IAGO   Do you hear, Cassio?
OTHELLO   Now he importunes him
To tell it o'er. Go to! well said, well said!
115 IAGO   She gives it out that you shall marry her.
Do you intend it?
CASSIO   Ha, ha, ha!
OTHELLO   Do ye triumph, Roman?[1] do you triumph?
CASSIO   I marry? What! a customer?° Prithee bear some   *courtesan*
120   charity to my wit;° do not think it so unwholesome. Ha, ha,   *sense*
ha!
OTHELLO   So, so, so, so! they laugh that wins.
IAGO   Faith, the cry goes that you marry her.
CASSIO   Prithee say true.
125 IAGO   I am a very villain else.°   *if it's not true*
OTHELLO   Have you scored° me? Well.   *scored off*
CASSIO   This is the monkey's own giving out.[2] She is per-
suaded I will marry her out of her own love and flattery,
not out of my promise.

---

1. Othello draws on associations either with Rome's imperial successes (and subsequent collapse) or with the Roman practice of holding cel-ebratory processions (called triumphs) for military victors.
2. I.e., this is Bianca's own story.

OTHELLO   Iago beckons me; now he begins the story.

                               [OTHELLO *draws closer*]

CASSIO   She was here even now; she haunts me in every
   place. I was the other day talking on the sea-bank with
   certain Venetians, and thither comes the bauble° and   *toy*
   falls me thus about my neck—

OTHELLO   Crying "O dear Cassio!" as it were: his gesture
   imports° it.   *indicates*

CASSIO   So hangs and lolls and weeps upon me, so shakes
   and pulls me. Ha, ha, ha!

OTHELLO   Now he tells how she plucked him to my cham
   ber. O, I see that nose of yours, but not that dog I shall
   throw it to.[3]

CASSIO   Well, I must leave her company.

IAGO   Before me! look where she comes!

      Enter BIANCA

CASSIO   'Tis such another fitchew![4] marry, a perfumed one!
   What do you mean by this haunting of me?

BIANCA   Let the devil and his dam° haunt you! What did   *mother*
   you mean by that same handkerchief you gave me even
   now? I was a fine fool to take it. I must take out° the   *copy*
   work? A likely piece of work,[5] that you should find it in
   your chamber and know not who left it there! This is
   some minx's token, and I must take out the work? There,
   give it your hobby-horse!° Wheresoever you had it, I'll *mountable woman*
   take out no work on't.

CASSIO   How now, my sweet Bianca?
   How now? how now?

OTHELLO   By heaven, that should° be my handkerchief!   *must*

BIANCA   If you'll come to supper tonight, you may; if you
   will not, come when you are next prepared for.[6]   *Exit*

IAGO   After her, after her!

CASSIO   Faith, I must; she'll rail in the streets else.

IAGO   Will you sup there?

CASSIO   Faith, I intend so.

IAGO   Well, I may chance to see you, for I would very
   fain speak with you.

CASSIO   Prithee come, will you?

IAGO   Go to; say no more.   *Exit* CASSIO

OTHELLO [*comes forward*]   How shall I murder him, Iago?

IAGO   Did you perceive how he laughed at his vice?

OTHELLO   O Iago!

IAGO   And did you see the handkerchief?

OTHELLO   Was that mine?

IAGO   Yours, by this hand! and to see how he prizes the
   foolish woman, your wife! She gave it him, and he hath
   given it his whore.

---

3. I.e., I'm envisioning my revenge, but the time
is not yet quite right.
4. Polecat, associated with prostitutes because

of its bad smell and supposed lecherousness.
5. An implausible story.
6. Come next time I prepare for you (never).

175   OTHELLO   I would have him nine years a-killing![7]—A fine
      woman, a fair woman, a sweet woman!

      IAGO   Nay, you must forget that.

      OTHELLO   Ay, let her rot and perish and be damned
      tonight, for she shall not live! No, my heart is turned to
180   stone; I strike it, and it hurts my hand.—O, the world
      hath not a sweeter creature! She might lie by an emper-
      or's side and command him tasks.

      IAGO   Nay, that's not your way.°   *(the way to think)*

      OTHELLO   Hang her!—I do but say what she is: so delicate
185   with her needle; an admirable musician (O, she will sing
      the savageness out of a bear!); of so high and plenteous
      wit and invention!°   *imagination*

      IAGO   She's the worse for all this.

      OTHELLO   O, a thousand, a thousand times!—And then of
190   so gentle° a condition!   *highly born*

      IAGO   Ay, too gentle.°   *generous (sexually)*

      OTHELLO   Nay, that's certain.—But yet the pity of it, Iago!
      O Iago, the pity of it, Iago!

      IAGO   If you are so fond° over her iniquity, give her patent°   *foolish / license*
195   to offend; for if it touch not you, it comes near nobody.

      OTHELLO   I will chop her into messes!° Cuckold me!   *pieces of food*

      IAGO   O, 'tis foul in her.

      OTHELLO   With mine officer!

      IAGO   That's fouler.

200   OTHELLO   Get me some poison, Iago, this night. I'll not
      expostulate with her, lest her body and beauty unprovide
      my mind° again. This night, Iago.   *weaken my resolve*

      IAGO   Do it not with poison. Strangle her in her bed, even
      the bed she hath contaminated.

205   OTHELLO   Good, good! The justice of it pleases. Very
      good!

      IAGO   And for Cassio, let me be his undertaker.° You shall   *murderer*
      hear more by midnight.

      OTHELLO   Excellent good!

          A trumpet [within]

210   What trumpet is that same?

      IAGO   I warrant something from Venice.

          Enter LODOVICO, DESDEMONA, *and attendants*

      'Tis Lodovico; this comes from the duke.

      See, your wife's with him.

      LODOVICO   God save you, worthy general.

215   OTHELLO   With all my heart,° sir.   *thank you*

      LODOVICO   The duke and the senators of Venice greet you.

                     [Gives him a letter]

      OTHELLO   I kiss the instrument° of their pleasures.°   *bearer / commands*

                     [Opens the letter and reads]

      DESDEMONA   And what's the news, good cousin Lodovico?

---

7. I would like to spend nine years killing him.

IAGO I am very glad to see you, signor.
　Welcome to Cyprus.
LODOVICO I thank you. How does Lieutenant Cassio?
IAGO Lives, sir.
DESDEMONA Cousin, there's fallen between him and my
　lord
　An unkind° breach; but you shall make all well.　　　　　　　*unnatural*
OTHELLO Are you sure of that?
DESDEMONA My lord?
OTHELLO [*reads*] "This fail you not to do, as you will . . ."
LODOVICO He did not call: he's busy in the paper.
　Is there division 'twixt my lord and Cassio?
DESDEMONA A most unhappy one; I would do much
　T'atone° them, for the love I bear to Cassio.　　　　　　*to reconcile*
OTHELLO Fire and brimstone!
DESDEMONA　　　　　　　　My lord?
OTHELLO　　　　　　　　　　Are you wise?
DESDEMONA What, is he angry?
LODOVICO　　　　　　　　　May be the letter moved him;
　For, as I think, they do command him home,
　Deputing Cassio in his government.°　　　　　　*official position*
DESDEMONA By my troth, I am glad on't.
OTHELLO　　　　　　　　　　Indeed!
DESDEMONA　　　　　　　　　　　My lord?
OTHELLO I am glad to see you mad.[8]
DESDEMONA　　　　　　　　　Why, sweet Othello?
OTHELLO Devil!　　　　　　　　[*Strikes her*]
DESDEMONA I have not deserved this.
LODOVICO My lord, this would not be believed in Venice,
　Though I should swear I saw't. 'Tis very much;°　　　*going too far*
　Make her amends—she weeps.
OTHELLO　　　　　　　　O devil, devil!
　If that the earth could teem with° woman's tears,　*become pregnant by*
　Each drop she falls would prove a crocodile.[9]
　Out of my sight!
DESDEMONA　　　　　I will not stay to offend you.
LODOVICO Truly obedient lady!
　I do beseech your lordship call her back.
OTHELLO Mistress!
DESDEMONA My lord?
OTHELLO What would you° with her, sir?　　　　　　*do you wish*
LODOVICO　　　　　　　　Who, I, my lord?
OTHELLO Ay, you did wish that I would make her turn.°　*return*
　Sir, she can turn, and turn,° and yet go on　　　　*(sexually)*
　And turn again. And she can weep, sir, weep.
　And she's obedient; as you say, obedient,
　Very obedient.—Proceed you in your tears.—

8. Othello is pleased that Desdemona is rejoicing in Cassio's promotion and thus revealing their adulterous affair, which she would be "mad" to do in public and in front of him.

9. Each drop would cause the earth to conceive a crocodile (crocodiles proverbially wept false tears for their victims).

Concerning this, sir—O well-painted passion!—
I am commanded home.—Get you away!
I'll send for you anon.—Sir, I obey the mandate
And will return to Venice.—Hence, avaunt!°   *begone*

[*Exit* DESDEMONA]

260   Cassio shall have my place. And, sir, tonight
I do entreat that we may sup together.
You are welcome, sir, to Cyprus.—Goats and monkeys!¹

Exit

LODOVICO   Is this the noble Moor whom our full senate
Call all-in-all sufficient? Is this the nature
265   Whom passion could not shake? whose solid virtue
The shot of accident nor dart of chance
Could neither graze nor pierce?

IAGO   He is much changed.

LODOVICO   Are his wits safe? Is he not light of brain?

IAGO   He's that he is; I may not breathe my censure.
270   What he might be—if what he might he is not—
I would to heaven he were.

LODOVICO   What! Strike his wife?

IAGO   'Faith, that was not so well; yet would I knew
That stroke would prove the worst.

LODOVICO   Is it his use?°   *custom*
Or did the letters work upon his blood°   *passions*
And new create his fault?

275   IAGO   Alas, alas!
It is not honesty in me to speak
What I have seen and known. You shall observe him,
And his own courses° will denote him so   *actions*
That I may save my speech. Do but go after
280   And mark how he continues.

LODOVICO   I am sorry that I am deceived in him.

Exeunt

4.2

Enter OTHELLO *and* EMILIA

OTHELLO   You have seen nothing then?

EMILIA   Nor ever heard, nor ever did suspect.

OTHELLO   Yes, you have seen Cassio and she together.

EMILIA   But then I saw no harm, and then I heard
5   Each syllable that breath made up between them.

OTHELLO   What, did they never whisper?

EMILIA   Never, my lord.

OTHELLO   Nor send you out o'th' way?

EMILIA   Never.

OTHELLO   To fetch her fan, her gloves, her mask, nor nothing?

10   EMILIA   Never, my lord.

OTHELLO   That's strange.

EMILIA   I durst, my lord, to wager she is honest,

---

1. Symbols of lust.
4.2 Location: The citadel.

Lay down my soul at stake. If you think other,
Remove your thought; it doth abuse your bosom.
If any wretch have put this in your head,
Let heaven requite it with the serpent's curse,[1]
For if she be not honest, chaste, and true,
There's no man happy. The purest of their wives
Is foul as slander.

OTHELLO   Bid her come hither—go. *Exit* EMILIA
She says enough; yet she's a simple bawd
That cannot say as much.[2] This is a subtle whore:
A closet lock and key° of villainous secrets;   *a hider*
And yet she'll kneel and pray; I have seen her do't.

Enter DESDEMONA *and* EMILIA

DESDEMONA   My lord, what is your will?
OTHELLO   Pray you, chuck,
    come hither.
DESDEMONA   What is your pleasure?
OTHELLO   Let me see your eyes.
    Look in my face.
DESDEMONA   What horrible fancy's this?
OTHELLO [*to* EMILIA]   Some of your function,[3] mistress:
    Leave procreants° alone and shut the door;   *copulators*
    Cough or cry "hem" if anybody come.
    Your mystery, your mystery!° Nay, dispatch! *Exit* EMILIA   *profession*
DESDEMONA   Upon my knees, what doth your speech
    import?
    I understand a fury in your words,
    But not the words.
OTHELLO   Why? What art thou?
DESDEMONA   Your wife, my lord, your true and loyal wife.
OTHELLO   Come, swear it! damn thyself!
    Lest, being° like one of heaven, the devils themselves   *appearing*
    Should fear to seize thee. Therefore be double-damned:
    Swear thou art honest!
DESDEMONA   Heaven doth truly know it.
OTHELLO   Heaven truly knows that thou art false as hell.
DESDEMONA   To whom, my lord? With whom? How am I
    false?
OTHELLO   Ah, Desdemon! away, away, away!
DESDEMONA   Alas the heavy day! Why do you weep?
    Am I the motive of these tears, my lord?
    If haply° you my father do suspect   *perhaps*
    An instrument of this your calling back,
    Lay not your blame on me. If you have lost him,
    I have lost him too.
OTHELLO   Had it pleased heaven
    To try me with affliction, had they rained
    All kind of sores and shames on my bare head,
    Steeped me in poverty to the very lips,

1. In Genesis, the curse that God laid on the
serpent who deceived Eve.
2. Yet it would be a simpleminded go-between
who couldn't say as much as she did.
3. Fulfill your bawd's function by guarding the
door.

Given to captivity me and my utmost hopes,
I should have found in some place of my soul
A drop of patience. But, alas, to make me
The fixèd figure for the time of scorn
55 To point his slow and moving finger at!⁴
Yet could I bear that too—well, very well;
But there where I have garnered° up my heart,   stored
Where either I must live or bear no life,
The fountain from the which my current runs
60 Or else dries up; to be discarded thence,
Or keep it as a cistern for foul toads
To knot and gender⁵ in!—Turn thy complexion there,
Patience,⁶ thou young and rose-lipped cherubin;
Ay, here look grim as hell!
65 DESDEMONA   I hope my noble lord esteems me honest.
OTHELLO   O, ay, as summer flies are in the shambles,°   slaughterhouse
That quicken even with blowing.⁷ O thou weed,
Who art so lovely fair and smell'st so sweet
That the sense aches at thee,
70 Would thou hadst never been born!
DESDEMONA   Alas, what ignorant sin have I committed?
OTHELLO   Was this fair paper, this most goodly book,
Made to write "whore" upon? What committed?
Committed?⁸ O, thou public commoner!°   prostitute
75 I should make very forges of my cheeks
That would to cinders burn up modesty
Did I but speak thy deeds. What committed?
Heaven stops the nose at it, and the moon winks;°   closes its eyes
The bawdy° wind that kisses all it meets   promiscuous
80 Is hushed within the hollow mine of earth°   within a cave
And will not hear't. What committed?
DESDEMONA   By heaven, you do me wrong!
OTHELLO   Are not you a strumpet?
DESDEMONA   No, as I am a Christian!
If to preserve this vessel for my lord
85 From any other foul unlawful touch
Be not to be a strumpet, I am none.
OTHELLO   What, not a whore?
DESDEMONA   No, as I shall be saved!
OTHELLO   Is't possible?
DESDEMONA   O, heaven forgive us!
OTHELLO   I cry you mercy° then.   I beg your pardon
90 I took you for that cunning whore of Venice
That married with Othello.—You! Mistress!
That have the office opposite to Saint Peter

---

4. The designated object of scorn for this scorn-ful time to point (as on a clock face) its slowly moving hand at.
5. To couple and engender.
6. Change color at the thought of that, Patience.
7. Who come to life (or bring their offspring to life and hence make the meat foul) as soon as the eggs are deposited. The point seems to be the speed of breeding, inferred from Desdemona's supposed infidelity.
8. Lines 74–77 do not appear in Q.

And keeps the gate of hell. You, you!
    Enter EMILIA
                           Ay, you.
We have done our course;° [*giving her money*] there's   *business*
  money for your pains;
I pray you turn the key and keep our counsel.   *Exit*
EMILIA   Alas, what does this gentleman conceive?°   *believe*
  How do you, madam? how do you, my good lady?
DESDEMONA   Faith, half asleep.
EMILIA   Good madam, what's the matter with my lord?
DESDEMONA   With who?
EMILIA   Why, with my lord, madam.
DESDEMONA   Who is thy lord?
EMILIA   He that is yours, sweet lady.
DESDEMONA   I have none. Do not talk to me, Emilia;
  I cannot weep, nor answers have I none
  But what should go by water.° Prithee tonight   *appear in tears*
  Lay on my bed my wedding sheets, remember;
  And call thy husband hither.
EMILIA   Here's a change indeed!
                             Exit
DESDEMONA   'Tis meet° I should be used so, very meet.   *fitting*
  How have I been behaved that he might stick
  The small'st opinion on my least misuse?⁹
    Enter IAGO *and* EMILIA
IAGO   What is your pleasure, madam? How is't with you?
DESDEMONA   I cannot tell. Those that do teach young babes
  Do it with gentle means and easy tasks.
  He might have chid me so; for in good faith
  I am a child to chiding.
IAGO   What is the matter, lady?
EMILIA   Alas, Iago, my lord hath so bewhored her,°   *called her a whore*
  Thrown such despite° and heavy terms upon her,   *spite*
  That true hearts cannot bear it.
DESDEMONA   Am I that name, Iago?
IAGO   What name, fair lady?
DESDEMONA   Such as she said my lord did say I was.
EMILIA   He called her whore. A beggar in his drink
  Could not have laid such terms upon his callet.°   *whore*
IAGO   Why did he so?
DESDEMONA   I do not know; I am sure I am none such.
IAGO   Do not weep, do not weep. Alas the day!
EMILIA   Hath she forsook so many noble matches,
  Her father and her country and her friends,
  To be called whore? Would it not make one weep?
DESDEMONA   It is my wretched fortune.
IAGO   Beshrew° him for't!   *curse*
  How comes this trick° upon him?   *behavior*
DESDEMONA   Nay, heaven doth know.

---

9. "That . . . misuse": that would cause him to suspect even slightly the least fault (?).

130 EMILIA   I will be hanged if some eternal villain,
      Some busy° and insinuating rogue,   *meddling*
      Some cogging,° cozening° slave, to get some office,   *deceiving / cheating*
      Have not devised this slander. I will be hanged else.
   IAGO   Fie! there is no such man; it is impossible.
135 DESDEMONA   If any such there be, heaven pardon him.
   EMILIA   A halter° pardon him, and hell gnaw his bones!   *hangman's noose*
      Why should he call her whore? Who keeps her company?
      What place? what time? what form? what likelihood?
      The Moor's abused by some most villainous knave,
140   Some base notorious knave, some scurvy fellow.
      O heaven, that such companions thou'dst unfold,°   *reveal*
      And put in every honest hand a whip
      To lash the rascals naked through the world
      Even from the east to th' west!
   IAGO   Speak within door.°   *more softly*
145 EMILIA   O, fie upon them! Some such squire° he was   *fellow*
      That turned your wit the seamy side without°   *wrong side out*
      And made you to suspect me with the Moor.
   IAGO   You are a fool; go to.
   DESDEMONA   O God,[1] Iago,
      What shall I do to win my lord again?
150   Good friend, go to him; for by this light of heaven,
      I know not how I lost him. Here I kneel:[2]
      If e'er my will did trespass 'gainst his love,
      Either in discourse of thought or actual deed,
      Or that mine eyes, mine ears, or any sense
155   Delighted them in any other form,[3]
      Or that I do not yet,° and ever did,   *still*
      And ever will (though he do shake me off
      To beggarly divorcement) love him dearly—
      Comfort forswear me!° Unkindness may do much,   *deny me divine solace*
160   And his unkindness may defeat my life,
      But never taint my love.   [*She rises*]
                      I cannot say "whore."
      It does abhor[4] me now I speak the word.
      To do the act that might the addition° earn,   *label*
      Not the world's mass of vanity° could make me.   *all worldly splendor*
165 IAGO   I pray you be content; 'tis but his humor;°   *mood*
      The business of the state does him offense.
   DESDEMONA   If 'twere no other—
   IAGO   It is but so, I warrant.
                      [*Trumpets within*]
      Hark how these instruments summon to supper.
      The messengers of Venice stays the meat;°   *are waiting to eat*
170   Go in, and weep not; all things shall be well.
                Exeunt DESDEMONA *and* EMILIA
      Enter RODERIGO

1. The folio reads "Alas," in keeping with the
censorship of oaths that led to many changes from
the quarto text. Q's reading here, "O Good," is
probably a misprint for "O God."
2. Lines 151–64 (beginning with "Here") do not

appear in Q.
3. Took pleasure in anyone but him.
4. Fill me with abhorrence; make me abhorrent,
with a pun on "ab-whore."

How now, Roderigo?

RODERIGO I do not find that thou deal'st justly with me.

IAGO What in the contrary?

RODERIGO Every day thou doff'st me with some device,[5]
Iago, and rather, as it seems to me now, keep'st from me
all conveniency° than suppliest me with the least advan-   *opportunity*
tage of hope. I will indeed no longer endure it. Nor am I
yet persuaded to put up in peace what already I have
foolishly suffered.

IAGO Will you hear me, Roderigo?

RODERIGO Faith, I have heard too much; and your words
and performances are no kin together.

IAGO You charge me most unjustly.

RODERIGO With naught but truth. I have wasted myself
out of my means. The jewels you have had from me to
deliver Desdemona would half have corrupted a votarist.°   *nun*
You have told me she hath received them, and returned
me expectations and comforts of sudden respect and
acquaintance, but I find none.

IAGO Well, go to, very well.

RODERIGO "Very well"! "go to"! I cannot go to,° man, nor   *succeed sexually*
'tis not very well. Nay, I think it is scurvy, and begin to
find myself fopped° in it.   *made a fool*

IAGO Very well.

RODERIGO I tell you 'tis not very well. I will make myself
known to Desdemona. If she will return me my jewels, I
will give over my suit and repent my unlawful solicitation. If not, assure yourself I will seek satisfaction of
you.

IAGO You have said° now.   *finished*

RODERIGO Ay, and said nothing but what I protest intend-
ment of doing.

IAGO Why, now I see there's mettle in thee, and even
from this instant do build on thee a better opinion than
ever before. Give me thy hand, Roderigo. Thou hast taken
against me a most just exception, but yet I protest I have
dealt most directly in thy affair.

RODERIGO It hath not appeared.

IAGO I grant indeed it hath not appeared, and your suspi
cion is not without wit and judgment. But, Roderigo, if
thou hast that in thee indeed which I have greater reason to believe now than ever—I mean purpose, courage,
and valor—this night show it. If thou the next night following enjoy not Desdemona, take me from this world
with treachery and devise engines for° my life.   *plots against*

RODERIGO Well, what is it? Is it within reason and
compass?°   *possibility*

IAGO Sir, there is especial commission come from Venice
to depute Cassio in Othello's place.

5. You put me off with some trick.

220 RODERIGO Is that true? Why, then Othello and Desdemona
return again to Venice.
IAGO O no; he goes into Mauritania[6] and taketh away
with him the fair Desdemona, unless his abode be lingered here by some accident; wherein none can be so
225 determinate° as the removing of Cassio.   *effectual*
RODERIGO How do you mean "removing" him?
IAGO Why, by making him uncapable of Othello's place—
knocking out his brains.
RODERIGO And that you would have me to do.
230 IAGO Ay, if you dare do yourself a profit and a right. He
sups tonight with a harlotry, and thither will I go to him.
He knows not yet of his honorable fortune.° If you will   *his promotion*
watch his going thence, which I will fashion° to fall out   *arrange*
between twelve and one, you may take him at your plea-
235 sure. I will be near to second your attempt, and he shall
fall between us. Come, stand not amazed at it, but go
along with me. I will show you such a necessity in his
death that you shall think yourself bound to put it on
him. It is now high suppertime, and the night grows to
240 waste. About it!
RODERIGO I will hear further reason for this.
IAGO And you shall be satisfied.   *Exeunt*

4.3

Enter OTHELLO, LODOVICO, DESDEMONA, EMILIA, *and*
attendants

LODOVICO I do beseech you, sir, trouble yourself no
further.
OTHELLO O, pardon me; 'twill do me good to walk.
LODOVICO [*to* DESDEMONA] Madam, good night. I humbly
thank your ladyship.
DESDEMONA Your honor is most welcome.
OTHELLO   Will you walk, sir?
5 O, Desdemona—
DESDEMONA My lord?
OTHELLO Get you to bed on th'instant. I will be returned
forthwith. Dismiss your attendant there. Look't be done.
DESDEMONA I will, my lord.
Exeunt [OTHELLO *with* LODOVICO *and attendants*]
10 EMILIA How goes it now? He looks gentler than he did.
DESDEMONA He says he will return incontinent,°   *immediately*
And hath commanded me to go to bed,
And bid me to dismiss you.
EMILIA   Dismiss me?
DESDEMONA It was his bidding; therefore, good Emilia,
15 Give me my nightly wearing, and adieu.
We must not now displease him.

6. Country in the western Sahara.
4.3 Location: Scene continues.

EMILIA   I would you had never seen him.
DESDEMONA   So would not I: my love doth so approve him
That even his stubbornness, his checks, his frowns—
Prithee unpin[1] me—have grace and favor in them.
[EMILIA *helps* DESDEMONA *undress*]
EMILIA   I have laid those sheets you bade me on the bed.
DESDEMONA   All's one.° Good faith, how foolish are our   *it doesn't matter*
    minds!
If I do die before thee, prithee shroud me
In one of these same sheets.
EMILIA   Come, come—you talk.
DESDEMONA   My mother had a maid called Barbary;
She was in love, and he she loved proved mad
And did forsake her. She had a Song of "Willow"—
An old thing 'twas, but it expressed her fortune—
And she died singing it. That song tonight
Will not go from my mind; I[2] have much to do
But to[3] go hang my head all at one side
And sing it, like poor Barbary. Prithee dispatch.°   *make haste*
EMILIA   Shall I go fetch your nightgown?
DESDEMONA   No. Unpin me here.
This Lodovico is a proper man.
EMILIA   A very handsome man.
DESDEMONA   He speaks well.
EMILIA   I know a lady in Venice would have walked barefoot
to Palestine for a touch of his nether° lip.   *lower*
DESDEMONA [*sings*]
    The poor soul sat sighing by a sycamore tree,
        Sing all a green willow;[4]
    Her hand on her bosom, her head on her knee,
        Sing willow, willow, willow.
    The fresh streams ran by her and murmured her moans,
        Sing willow, willow, willow;
    Her salt tears fell from her and softened the stones,
        Sing willow—
[*to* EMILIA] Lay by these.°   *put these things aside*
[*sings*]
                willow, willow.
[*to* EMILIA] Prithee hie° thee—he'll come anon.°   *hurry / straightaway*
[*sings*]
        Sing all a green willow must be my garland.
        Let nobody blame him, his scorn I approve.
Nay, that's not next. Hark, who is't that knocks?
EMILIA   It's the wind.
DESDEMONA [*sings*]
    I called my love false love, but what said he then?[5]
        Sing willow, willow, willow;
    If I court more women, you'll couch with more men.

---

1. To "unpin" a woman was to undo her dress, by the removal of pins.
2. Lines 30–52 ("I . . . next") do not appear in Q.
3. I can barely bring myself not to.
4. A conventional symbol of disappointed love.
5. Lines 54–56 do not appear in Q.

[*to* EMILIA] So, get thee gone, good night. Mine eyes do
   itch—
Doth that bode° weeping?   *foretell*
EMILIA   'Tis neither here nor there.
DESDEMONA   I have heard it said so. O, these men, these
   men!⁶

60   Dost thou in conscience think—tell me, Emilia—
That there be women do abuse their husbands
In such gross kind?°   *fashion*
EMILIA   There be some such, no question.
DESDEMONA   Wouldst thou do such a deed for all the world?
EMILIA   Why, would not you?
DESDEMONA   No, by this heavenly light!
65   EMILIA   Nor I neither, by this heavenly light:
I might do't as well i'th' dark.
DESDEMONA   Wouldst thou do such a deed for all the
   world?
EMILIA   The world's a huge thing: it is a great price for a
   small vice.
DESDEMONA   In troth, I think thou wouldst not.
70   EMILIA   In troth, I think I should—and undo't when I had
   done. Marry, I would not do such a thing for a joint
   ring,⁷ nor for measures of lawn,° nor for gowns, petti-   *linen*
   coats, nor caps, nor any petty exhibition.° But for all the   *gift*
   whole world—'Uds° pity! who would not make her hus-   *God's*
75   band a cuckold to make him a monarch? I should venture
   purgatory for't.
DESDEMONA   Beshrew me if I would do such a wrong for
   the whole world!
EMILIA   Why, the wrong is but a wrong i'th' world; and
80   having the world for your labor, 'tis a wrong in your own
   world, and you might quickly make it right.
DESDEMONA   I do not think there is any such woman.
EMILIA   Yes, a dozen; and as many to'th' vantage as
   would store the world they played for.⁸
85   But I do think it is their husbands' faults⁹
If wives do fall. Say that they slack their duties°   *marital duties*
And pour our treasures into foreign laps;¹
Or else break out in peevish jealousies,
Throwing restraint upon us; or say they strike us,
90   Or scant our former having in despite.²
Why, we have galls;° and though we have some grace,³   *tempers*
Yet have we some revenge. Let husbands know
Their wives have sense like them. They see, and smell,
And have their palates both for sweet and sour,
95   As husbands have. What is it that they do

6. Lines 59–62 do not appear in Q.
7. A cheap ring in separable halves.
8. And as many more as it would take to popu-
late the world they gained by doing it.
9. Lines 85–102 do not appear in Q.

1. And give the semen that belongs to us to other
women.
2. Or reduce our allowances out of spite.
3. Capacity for goodness, forgiveness.

When they change us for others? Is it sport?
I think it is. And doth affection° breed it?   *lust*
I think it doth. Is't frailty that thus errs?
It is so too. And have not we affections,
Desires for sport, and frailty, as men have?
Then let them use us well; else let them know,
The ills we do, their ills instruct us so.
DESDEMONA   Good night, good night. God me such uses°   *habits*
    send,
Not to pick bad from bad, but by bad, mend!⁴   *Exeunt*

5.1

    Enter IAGO *and* RODERIGO
IAGO   Here, stand behind this bulk,° straight¹ will he   *shop stall*
    come.
Wear thy good rapier bare, and put it home.°   *drive it into him*
Quick, quick, fear nothing! I'll be at thy elbow.
It makes us or it mars us; think on that
And fix most firm thy resolution.
RODERIGO   Be near at hand; I may miscarry in't.
IAGO   Here, at thy hand. Be bold, and take thy stand.
                               [*Stands aside*]
RODERIGO   I have no great devotion to the deed,
And yet he hath given me satisfying reasons;
'Tis but a man gone. Forth my sword: he dies!
IAGO   I have rubbed this young quat° almost to the sense,²   *pimple*
And he grows angry. Now, whether he kill Cassio
Or Cassio him, or each do kill the other,
Every way makes my gain. Live Roderigo,°   *if Roderigo lives*
He calls me to a restitution large
Of gold and jewels that I bobbed from him°   *defrauded him of*
As gifts to Desdemona.
It must not be. If Cassio do remain,
He hath a daily beauty in his life
That makes me ugly; and besides, the Moor
May unfold° me to him; there stand I in much peril.   *reveal*
No, he must die. But so—I hear him coming.
    Enter CASSIO
RODERIGO   I know his gait; 'tis he. Villain, thou diest!
                          [*Thrusts at* CASSIO]
CASSIO   That thrust had been mine enemy indeed,
But that my coat is better° than thou know'st.   *thicker; more armored*
I will make proof of° thine.   [*Wounds* RODERIGO]   *test*
RODERIGO   O, I am slain!
       [IAGO *wounds* CASSIO *in the leg and exits*]
CASSIO   I am maimed forever! Help, ho! murder! murder!
    Enter OTHELLO

4. Not to take bad behavior as an example to be   1. Right away.
followed, but to learn from it what to avoid.   2. To the quick.
5.1 Location: A street in Cyprus.

OTHELLO   The voice of Cassio. Iago keeps his word.
RODERIGO   O, villain that I am!
OTHELLO   It is even so.
30 CASSIO   O, help ho! light! a surgeon!
OTHELLO   'Tis he. O brave Iago, honest and just,
   That hast such noble sense of thy friend's wrong!
   Thou teachest me. Minion,° your dear lies dead,   *hussy (Desdemona)*
   And your unblest fate hies.° Strumpet, I come.   *damnation hurries on*
35   Forth of° my heart those charms, thine eyes, are blotted.   *out of*
   Thy bed, lust-stained, shall with lust's blood be spotted.
                                     Exit OTHELLO
       Enter LODOVICO *and* GRATIANO
CASSIO   What ho! no watch? no passage?° Murder, murder!   *passerby*
GRATIANO   'Tis some mischance; the voice is very direful.
CASSIO   O help!
40 LODOVICO   Hark!
RODERIGO   O wretched villain!
LODOVICO   Two or three groan. 'Tis heavy° night;   *dark*
   These may be counterfeits; let's think't unsafe
   To come into° the cry without more help.   *go near*
45 RODERIGO   Nobody come? Then shall I bleed to death.
       Enter IAGO *with a light*
LODOVICO   Hark.
GRATIANO   Here's one comes in his shirt, with light and
   weapons.
IAGO   Who's there? Whose noise is this that cries on murder?
LODOVICO   We do not know.
IAGO   Do not you hear a cry?
CASSIO   Here, here! for heaven's sake, help me!
50 IAGO   What's the matter?
GRATIANO   This is Othello's ancient, as I take it.
LODOVICO   The same indeed, a very valiant fellow.
IAGO   What are you here that cry so grievously?
CASSIO   Iago? O, I am spoiled, undone by villains!
55   Give me some help.
IAGO   O me, lieutenant! What villains have done this?
CASSIO   I think that one of them is hereabout
   And cannot make away.
IAGO   O treacherous villains!
   [*to* LODOVICO *and* GRATIANO] What are you there? Come
   in, and give some help.
60 RODERIGO   O, help me there!
CASSIO   That's one of them.
IAGO   O murd'rous slave! O villain!
                      [*Stabs* RODERIGO]
RODERIGO   O damned Iago! O inhuman dog!
IAGO   Kill men i'th' dark?—Where be these bloody
   thieves?—
   How silent is this town!—Ho, murder, murder!—
   [*to* LODOVICO *and* GRATIANO] What may you be? Are you
65   of good or evil?
LODOVICO   As you shall prove us, praise us.

IAGO   Signor Lodovico?
LODOVICO   He, sir.
IAGO   I cry you mercy. Here's Cassio hurt by villains.
GRATIANO   Cassio?
IAGO   How is't, brother?
CASSIO   My leg is cut in two.
IAGO   Marry, heaven forbid!
  Light, gentlemen. I'll bind it with my shirt.
      Enter BIANCA
BIANCA   What is the matter, ho? Who is't that cried?
IAGO   Who is't that cried?
BIANCA   O, my dear Cassio!
  My sweet Cassio! O Cassio, Cassio, Cassio!
IAGO   O notable strumpet! Cassio, may you suspect
  Who they should be that have thus mangled you?
CASSIO   No.
GRATIANO   I am sorry to find you thus; I have been to
    seek you.
IAGO   Lend me a garter.³ So . . . O for a chair°   *litter*
  To bear him easily hence!
BIANCA   Alas, he faints! O Cassio, Cassio, Cassio!
IAGO   Gentlemen all, I do suspect this trash
  To be a party in this injury.—
  Patience awhile, good Cassio.—Come, come!
  Lend me a light. Know we this face or no?
  Alas! my friend and my dear countryman,
  Roderigo! No—yes, sure! O heaven, Roderigo!
GRATIANO   What, of Venice?
IAGO   Even he, sir. Did you know him?
GRATIANO   Know him? Ay.
IAGO   Signor Gratiano? I cry your gentle pardon.
  These bloody accidents must excuse my manners
  That so neglected you.
GRATIANO   I am glad to see you.
IAGO   How do you, Cassio? O, a chair, a chair!
GRATIANO   Roderigo?
IAGO   He, he, 'tis he.   [*Enter attendants with a litter*]
                O, that's well said, the chair.
  Some good man bear him carefully from hence;
  I'll fetch the general's surgeon.—For you, mistress,
  Save you your labor.—He that lies slain here, Cassio,
  Was my dear friend. What malice was between you?
CASSIO   None in the world, nor do I know the man.
IAGO [*to* BIANCA]   What, look you pale? [*To attendants*] O,
    bear him out o'th'air.⁴
           [*Exeunt attendants with* CASSIO *in the
               litter and with* RODERIGO's *body*]
  Stay you, good gentlemen.—Look you pale, mistress?—
  Do you perceive the gastness° of her eye?—   *terror*

---

3. A band worn as a sash or belt. Iago wants to use one as a tourniquet.
4. Out of the open air (thought to be bad for wounds).

Nay, if you stare, we shall hear more anon.—
Behold her well; I pray you look upon her.
Do you see, gentlemen? Nay, guiltiness will speak
Though tongues were out of use.
      Enter EMILIA

EMILIA   Alas, what is the matter? what is the matter, hus-
110   band?
IAGO   Cassio hath here been set on in the dark
  By Roderigo and fellows that are scaped.
  He's almost slain, and Roderigo quite dead.
EMILIA   Alas, good gentleman! alas, good Cassio!
115 IAGO   This is the fruits of whoring. Prithee, Emilia,
  Go know of Cassio where he supped tonight.—
  What, do you shake at that?
BIANCA   He supped at my house, but I therefore shake not.
IAGO   O did he so? I charge you go with me.
120 EMILIA   O fie upon thee, strumpet!
BIANCA   I am no strumpet, but of life as honest
  As you that thus abuse me.
EMILIA   As I? Fie upon thee!
IAGO   Kind gentlemen, let's go see poor Cassio dressed.[5]—
  Come, mistress, you must tell's another tale.
125   Emilia, run you to the citadel
  And tell my lord and lady what hath happed.
                            [Exit EMILIA*]*
  Will you go on afore?   *Exeunt [all but* IAGO*]*
          This is the night
  That either makes me or fordoes° me quite.   *[Exit]*   *undoes*

5.2

    Enter OTHELLO *with a light,* DESDEMONA *in her bed*
    [asleep]
OTHELLO   It is the cause,[1] it is the cause, my soul.
  Let me not name it to you, you chaste stars.
  It is the cause. Yet I'll not shed her blood,
  Nor scar that whiter skin of hers than snow,
5   And smooth as monumental alabaster.°   *stone used in tombs*
  Yet she must die, else she'll betray more men.
  Put out the light, and then put out the light.[2]
  If I quench thee, thou flaming minister,°   *light that serves me*
  I can again thy former light restore,
10   Should I repent me. But once put out thy light,
  Thou cunning'st pattern of excelling nature,[3]
  I know not where is that Promethean heat[4]
  That can thy light relume.° When I have plucked thy rose   *relight*
  I cannot give it vital growth again;

---

5. I.e., see his wound dressed.
5.2 Location: Desdemona and Othello's bedroom.
1. I.e., Desdemona's infidelity is the "cause" of—
the thing that demands—justice, which Othello
sees himself as being required to execute.
2. This and the following lines compare the light
of Othello's lamp or torch to Desdemona's "light"

of life.
3. You most cleverly wrought example of nature's
surpassing work.
4. Life-giving fire. In Greek mythology, Prometheus stole fire from heaven to give it to
humankind; in a different tradition, he is credited
with animating humankind from clay.

It needs must wither. I'll smell thee on the tree.

[He smells, then kisses her]

O balmy breath, that dost almost persuade
Justice to break her sword! One more; one more.

[He kisses her]

Be thus when thou art dead, and I will kill thee
And love thee after. One more, and that's the last.

He kisses her

So sweet was ne'er so fatal. I must weep,
But they are cruel tears. This sorrow's heavenly:
It strikes where it doth love.[5] She wakes.

DESDEMONA Who's there? Othello?

OTHELLO   Ay, Desdemona.

DESDEMONA Will you come to bed, my lord?

OTHELLO Have you prayed tonight, Desdemon?

DESDEMONA   Ay, my lord.

OTHELLO If you bethink yourself of any crime
  Unreconciled as yet to heaven and grace,
  Solicit° for it straight.   *ask forgiveness*

DESDEMONA Alack, my lord, what may you mean by that?

OTHELLO Well, do it, and be brief; I will walk by.
  I would not kill thy unpreparèd spirit.
  No, heavens forfend! I would not kill thy soul.

DESDEMONA Talk you of killing?

OTHELLO   Ay, I do.

DESDEMONA   Then heaven
  Have mercy on me!

OTHELLO   Amen, with all my heart!

DESDEMONA If you say so, I hope you will not kill me.

OTHELLO Humh.

DESDEMONA And yet I fear you, for you're fatal then
  When your eyes roll so. Why I should fear, I know not,
  Since guiltiness I know not; but yet I feel I fear.

OTHELLO Think on thy sins.

DESDEMONA   They are loves I bear to you.

OTHELLO Ay, and for that thou diest.

DESDEMONA That death's unnatural that kills for loving.
  Alas, why gnaw you so your nether lip?
  Some bloody passion shakes your very frame.
  These are portents; but yet I hope, I hope,
  They do not point on me.

OTHELLO   Peace, and be still.

DESDEMONA I will so. What's the matter?

OTHELLO   That handkerchief,
  Which I so loved and gave thee, thou gav'st to Cassio.

DESDEMONA No, by my life and soul! Send for the man
  And ask him.

OTHELLO Sweet soul, take heed; take heed of perjury;
  Thou art on thy deathbed.

DESDEMONA Ay, but not yet to die.

---

5. See Hebrews 12.6: "For whom the Lord loveth, he chasteneth."

OTHELLO   Presently.°   *immediately*
　　Therefore confess thee freely of thy sin;
55　For to deny each article with oath
　　Cannot remove nor choke the strong conception
　　That I do groan withal.⁶ Thou art to die.
DESDEMONA Then Lord have mercy on me!
OTHELLO   I say amen.
DESDEMONA And have you mercy too! I never did
60　Offend you in my life, never loved Cassio
　　But with such general warranty of heaven
　　As I might love. I never gave him token.
OTHELLO By heaven, I saw my handkerchief in's hand!
　　O perjured woman! thou dost stone° my heart,   *harden*
65　And makes me call what I intend to do
　　A murder, which I thought a sacrifice.
　　I saw the handkerchief.
DESDEMONA   He found it then.
　　I never gave it him. Send for him hither.
　　Let him confess a truth.
OTHELLO   He hath confessed.
70　DESDEMONA What, my lord?
OTHELLO That he hath used thee.
DESDEMONA   How? unlawfully?
OTHELLO   Ay.
DESDEMONA He will not say so.
OTHELLO   No, his mouth is stopped.
　　Honest Iago hath ta'en order for't.
DESDEMONA O, my fear interprets! What, is he dead?
75　OTHELLO Had all his hairs been lives, my great revenge
　　Had stomach for them all.
DESDEMONA [*weeping*] Alas, he is betrayed and I undone!
OTHELLO Out, strumpet! Weep'st thou for him to my
　　face?
DESDEMONA O banish me, my lord, but kill me not!
80　OTHELLO [*attacking her*] Down, strumpet!
DESDEMONA Kill me tomorrow, let me live tonight!
OTHELLO Nay, if you strive—
DESDEMONA But half an hour!
OTHELLO   Being done, there is no
　　pause.⁷
DESDEMONA But while I say one prayer!
OTHELLO   It is too late.
　　　　　　　　　　　　　　　　Smothers her
85　DESDEMONA O Lord, Lord, Lord!
EMILIA *calls within* My lord, my lord! What ho! My lord,
　　my lord!
OTHELLO What noise is this? Not dead? not yet quite dead?
　　I that am cruel am yet merciful;

6. Cannot change the strong conviction I have of
your guilt (or the firm plan to kill you), which
makes me groan so. The metaphor is from

childbirth.
7. Now that I've started, there's no stopping.

I would not have thee linger in thy pain.
So, so.

EMILIA *within*   What ho? my lord, my lord!

OTHELLO   Who's there?

EMILIA [*within*]   O good my lord, I would speak a word
    with you.

OTHELLO [*calling*]   Yes.—'Tis Emilia.—[*calling*] By and
    by.°—She's dead.   *in a moment*
    'Tis like she comes to speak of Cassio's death.
    The noise was high.° Ha, no more moving?   *commotion was loud*
    Still as the grave. Shall she come in? Were't good?
    I think she stirs again. No. What's best to do?
    If she come in, she'll sure speak to my wife.
    My wife, my wife! What wife? I have no wife.
    O insupportable! O heavy hour!
    Methinks it should be now a huge eclipse
    Of sun and moon, and that th'affrighted globe
    Should yawn at alteration.[8]

EMILIA [*within*]   I do beseech you
    That I may speak with you. O good my lord!

OTHELLO   I had forgot thee. O, come in, Emilia.
    Soft,° by and by; let me the curtains draw.   *quiet*
                    [*He closes the bed curtains*]
    Where art thou? What's the matter with thee now?
                [*He unlocks the door.*] Enter EMILIA

EMILIA   O my good lord, yonder's foul murders done!

OTHELLO   What? now?

EMILIA   But° now, my lord.   *just*

OTHELLO   It is the very error° of the moon;   *deviation*
    She comes more nearer earth than she was wont
    And makes men mad.

EMILIA   Cassio, my lord, hath killed
    A young Venetian called Roderigo.

OTHELLO   Roderigo killed? and Cassio killed?

EMILIA   No, Cassio is not killed.

OTHELLO   Not Cassio killed? Then murder's out of tune,
    And sweet revenge grows harsh.

DESDEMONA   O falsely, falsely murdered!

EMILIA   O Lord! what cry is that?

OTHELLO   That? What?

EMILIA   Out and alas! that was my lady's voice.
                [*She opens the bed curtains*]
    Help, help ho, help! O, lady, speak again!
    Sweet Desdemona, O sweet mistress, speak!

DESDEMONA   A guiltless death I die.

EMILIA   O, who hath done this deed?

DESDEMONA   Nobody. I myself. Farewell.
    Commend me to my kind lord. O, farewell!   [*She dies*]

OTHELLO   Why, how should she be murdered?

8. Should gape at the change. Earthquakes were associated with eclipses.

EMILIA   Alas, who
    knows?
130   OTHELLO   You heard her say herself it was not I.

EMILIA   She said so; I must needs report the truth.

OTHELLO   She's like a liar gone to burning hell!
    'Twas I that killed her!

EMILIA   O, the more angel she,
    And you the blacker devil!

135   OTHELLO   She turned to folly,° and she was a whore.   *wantonness*

EMILIA   Thou dost belie her, and thou art a devil.

OTHELLO   She was false as water.

EMILIA   Thou art rash as fire to say
    That she was false. O, she was heavenly true!

OTHELLO   Cassio did top her. Ask thy husband else.°   *if you doubt it*

140   O, I were damned beneath all depth in hell
    But that I did proceed upon just grounds
    To this extremity! Thy husband knew it all.

EMILIA   My husband?

OTHELLO   Thy husband.

145   EMILIA   That she was false to wedlock?

OTHELLO   Ay, with Cassio. Had she been true,
    If heaven would make me such another world
    Of one entire and perfect chrysolite,°   *topaz*
    I'd not have sold her for it.

EMILIA   My husband?

150   OTHELLO   Ay, 'twas he that told me on her first.
    An honest man he is, and hates the slime
    That sticks on filthy deeds.

EMILIA   My husband?

OTHELLO   What needs this iterance,° woman?   *repetition*
    I say, thy husband.

155   EMILIA   O mistress, villainy hath made mocks with° love![9]   *at*
    My husband say she was false?

OTHELLO   He, woman;
    I say, thy husband; dost understand the word?
    My friend, thy husband; honest, honest Iago.

EMILIA   If he say so, may his pernicious soul
160   Rot half a grain a day! He lies to th'heart.
    She was too fond of her most filthy bargain.[1]

OTHELLO   Ha?

EMILIA   Do thy worst.
    This deed of thine is no more worthy heaven
    Than thou wast worthy her.

165   OTHELLO   Peace, you were best!°   *it would be best for you*

EMILIA   Thou hast not half that power to do me harm
    As I have to be hurt. O gull,° O dolt!   *fool*
    As ignorant as dirt! Thou hast done a deed—
                       [*He draws his sword*]
    I care not for thy sword; I'll make thee known,

---

9. Lines 155–58 do not appear in Q.
1. I.e., her marriage, or her husband.

Though I lost twenty lives. Help, help, ho, help!
The Moor hath killed my mistress! Murder, murder!
    Enter MONTANO, GRATIANO, IAGO, *and others*
MONTANO   What is the matter? How now, general?
EMILIA   O, are you come, Iago? You have done well,
That men must lay their murders on your neck.
GRATIANO   What is the matter?
EMILIA [*to* IAGO]   Disprove this villain, if thou be'st a man.
He says thou told'st him that his wife was false.
I know thou didst not; thou'rt not such a villain.
Speak, for my heart is full.
IAGO   I told him what I thought, and told no more
Than what he found himself was apt and true.
EMILIA   But did you ever tell him she was false?
IAGO   I did.
EMILIA   You told a lie, an odious damnèd lie!
Upon my soul, a lie! a wicked lie!
She false with Cassio? Did you say with Cassio?
IAGO   With Cassio, mistress! Go to, charm° your tongue!   *silence*
EMILIA   I will not charm my tongue; I am bound to speak:
My mistress here lies murdered in her bed—²
ALL   O heavens forfend!—
EMILIA [*to* IAGO]   And your reports have set the murder on.
OTHELLO   Nay, stare not, masters; it is true indeed.
GRATIANO   'Tis a strange truth.
MONTANO   O monstrous act!
EMILIA   Villainy, villainy, villainy!
I think upon't, I think I smell't. O villainy!
I thought so then.—I'll kill myself for grief!
O villainy! villainy!
IAGO   What, are you mad? I charge you get you home!
EMILIA   Good gentlemen, let me have leave to speak.
'Tis proper I obey him, but not now.
Perchance, Iago, I will ne'er go home.
OTHELLO   O! O! O!   *Falls on the bed*
EMILIA   Nay, lay thee down and roar,
For thou hast killed the sweetest innocent
That e'er did lift up eye.°   *(to heaven)*
OTHELLO [*rising*]   O, she was foul!
    [*To* GRATIANO] I scarce did know you, uncle. There lies
      your niece,
Whose breath, indeed, these hands have newly stopped.
I know this act shows° horrible and grim.   *appears*
GRATIANO   Poor Desdemon, I am glad thy father's dead;
Thy match° was mortal to him, and pure grief   *marriage*
Shore his old thread in twain.³ Did he live now,
This sight would make him do a desperate turn;°   *act*
Yea, curse his better angel from his side

2. Lines 189–98 do not appear in Q.
3. Cut the thread of his life.

215   And fall to reprobance.⁴

    OTHELLO   'Tis pitiful; but yet Iago knows
      That she with Cassio hath the act of shame
      A thousand times committed. Cassio confessed it,
      And she did gratify his amorous works

220   With that recognizance° and pledge of love   *token*
      Which I first gave her. I saw it in his hand;
      It was a handkerchief, an antique token
      My father gave my mother.

    EMILIA   O God! O heavenly God!

    IAGO   'Swounds, hold your peace!

225   EMILIA   'Twill out, 'twill out! I peace?
      No, I will speak as liberal as the north;⁵
      Let heaven and men and devils, let them all,
      All, all cry shame against me, yet I'll speak!

    IAGO   Be wise, and get you home.

                 [IAGO *threatens* EMILIA *with his sword*]

    EMILIA   I will not!

230   GRATIANO   Fie! Your sword upon a woman?

    EMILIA   O thou dull Moor, that handkerchief thou speak'st of
      I found by fortune and did give my husband;
      For often with a solemn earnestness—
      More than indeed belonged to such a trifle—
      He begged of me to steal't.

235   IAGO   Villainous whore!

    EMILIA   She give it Cassio? No, alas, I found it,
      And I did giv't my husband.

    IAGO   Filth, thou liest!

    EMILIA   By heaven, I do not! I do not, gentlemen.—
      O murderous coxcomb!° What should such a fool   *fool*
      Do with so good a wife?

240   OTHELLO   Are there no stones° in heaven   *thunderbolts*
      But what serves for the thunder? Precious° villain!   *absolute*

        The Moor runs at IAGO. [MONTANO *disarms* OTHELLO.]
        IAGO [*stabs*] *his wife*

    GRATIANO   The woman falls; sure he hath killed his wife.

    EMILIA   Ay, ay. O lay me by my mistress' side.   *Exit* IAGO

    GRATIANO   He's gone, but his wife's killed.

245   MONTANO   'Tis a notorious villain. Take you this weapon,
      Which I have here recovered from the Moor.
      Come, guard the door without; let him not pass,
      But kill him rather. I'll after that same villain,
      For 'tis a damnèd slave.

        Exeunt MONTANO, GRATIANO [*and all but* OTHELLO
        and EMILIA]

    OTHELLO   I am not valiant neither,

250   But every puny whipster° gets my sword.   *insignificant person*
    But why should honor outlive honesty?⁶
    Let it go all.

---

4. Suicide, the unforgivably sinful act of despair.
5. As freely as the north wind.

6. Why should military reputation outlive integrity?

EMILIA   What did thy song bode, lady?[7]
  Hark, canst thou hear me? I will play the swan,
  And die in music. [*Sings*] "Willow, willow, willow."
  Moor, she was chaste. She loved thee, cruel Moor.
  So come my soul to bliss as I speak true!
  So speaking as I think, alas, I die.   *She dies*
OTHELLO   I have another weapon in this chamber;
  It was a sword of Spain, the ice-brook's temper.°   *tempered in icy water*
  O, here it is.—Uncle, I must come forth.
GRATIANO [*within*]   If thou attempt it, it will cost thee dear;
  Thou hast no weapon and perforce must suffer.
OTHELLO   Look in upon me then and speak with me,
  Or, naked° as I am, I will assault thee.   *unarmed*
    [*Enter* GRATIANO]
GRATIANO   What is the matter?
OTHELLO   Behold, I have a weapon;
  A better never did itself sustain
  Upon a soldier's thigh. I have seen the day
  That with this little arm and this good sword
  I have made my way through more impediments
  Than twenty times your stop.° But O, vain boast!   *power to stop*
  Who can control his fate? 'Tis not so now.
  Be not afraid, though you do see me weaponed.[8]
  Here is my journey's end, here is my butt°   *destination*
  And very seamark° of my utmost sail.   *beacon*
  Do you go back dismayed? 'Tis a lost° fear.   *an unnecessary*
  Man but a rush° against Othello's breast   *aim even a reed*
  And he retires.° Where should Othello go?   *falls back*
  [*To* DESDEMONA] Now, how dost thou look now? O
    ill-starred wench,
  Pale as thy smock. When we shall meet at count,°   *Judgment Day*
  This look of thine will hurl my soul from heaven,
  And fiends will snatch at it.
              [*He touches her*]
          Cold, cold, my girl?
  Even like thy chastity. O cursèd, cursèd slave!
  Whip me, ye devils,
  From the possession of this heavenly sight!
  Blow me about in winds, roast me in sulphur,
  Wash me in steep-down gulfs of liquid fire!
  O Desdemon! dead Desdemon; dead. O, O!
    Enter LODOVICO, CASSIO *in a chair,* MONTANO, *and*
    IAGO, *with officers*
LODOVICO   Where is this rash and most unfortunate man?
OTHELLO   That's he that was Othello; here I am.
LODOVICO   Where is that viper? Bring the villain forth.
OTHELLO   I look down towards his feet,[9] but that's a fable;
  If that thou be'st a devil, I cannot kill thee.
             [*Wounds* IAGO]
LODOVICO   Wrench his sword from him.

---

7. Lines 252–54 ("What . . . willow.'") do not   8. Lines 272–78 do not appear in Q.
appear in Q.   9. To look for the devil's cloven feet.

IAGO   I bleed, sir, but not
  killed.
OTHELLO   I am not sorry, neither; I'd have thee live,
295   For in my sense° 'tis happiness to die.   *state of feeling*
LODOVICO   O thou Othello, that was once so good,
  Fallen in the practice° of a cursèd slave,   *plot*
  What shall be said to thee?
OTHELLO   Why, anything:
  An honorable murderer, if you will;
300   For naught I did in hate, but all in honor.
LODOVICO   This wretch hath part confessed his villainy.
  Did you and he consent in Cassio's death?
OTHELLO   Ay.
CASSIO   Dear general, I never gave you cause.
305   OTHELLO   I do believe it, and I ask your pardon.
  Will you, I pray, demand° that demi-devil   *ask*
  Why he hath thus ensnared my soul and body?
IAGO   Demand me nothing. What you know, you know.
  From this time forth I never will speak word.
LODOVICO   What, not to pray?
310   GRATIANO   Torments° will ope your lips.   *tortures*
OTHELLO   Well, thou dost best.
LODOVICO   Sir, you shall understand what hath befall'n,
  Which, as I think, you know not. Here is a letter
  Found in the pocket of the slain Roderigo,
315   And here another. The one of them imports
  The death of Cassio, to be undertook
  By Roderigo.
OTHELLO   O villain!
CASSIO   Most heathenish and most gross!°   *monstrous*
LODOVICO   Now here's another discontented paper
320   Found in his pocket too; and this, it seems,
  Roderigo meant t'have sent this damnèd villain,
  But that, belike,° Iago in the interim   *most likely*
  Came in and satisfied him.
OTHELLO   O thou pernicious caitiff!°—   *wretch*
  How came you, Cassio, by that handkerchief
  That was my wife's?
325   CASSIO   I found it in my chamber;
  And he himself confessed it, but even now,
  That there he dropped it for a special purpose
  Which wrought to his desire.
OTHELLO   O fool, fool, fool!
CASSIO   There is besides in Roderigo's letter
330   How he upbraids Iago that he made him
  Brave° me upon the watch, whereon it came   *defy*
  That I was cast;° and even but now he spake,   *dismissed*
  After long seeming dead, Iago hurt him,
  Iago set him on.
LODOVICO [*to* OTHELLO]   You must forsake this room and
335   go with us.

Your power and your command is taken off,
And Cassio rules in Cyprus. For this slave,
If there be any cunning cruelty
That can torment him much and hold him° long,   *(alive)*
It shall be his. You shall close° prisoner rest   *tightly confined*
Till that the nature of your fault be known
To the Venetian state. [*To officers*] Come, bring away.
OTHELLO   Soft you;° a word or two before you go.   *wait*
I have done the state some service, and they know't;
No more of that. I pray you, in your letters,
When you shall these unlucky deeds relate,
Speak of me as I am. Nothing extenuate,
Nor set down aught in malice. Then must you speak
Of one that loved not wisely but too well;
Of one not easily jealous but, being wrought,
Perplexed in the extreme; of one whose hand,
Like the base Judean,[1] threw a pearl away
Richer than all his tribe, of one whose subdued° eyes,   *(by grief)*
Albeit unusèd to the melting mood,
Drops tears as fast as the Arabian trees
Their medicinable gum.° Set you down this;   *myrrh*
And say besides that in Aleppo once,
Where a malignant and a turbaned Turk
Beat a Venetian and traduced the state,
I took by th'throat the circumcisèd dog
And smote him—thus!   *He stabs himself*
LODOVICO   O bloody period!°   *conclusion*
GRATIANO   All that is spoke is marred.
OTHELLO [*to* DESDEMONA]   I kissed thee ere I killed thee.
   No way but this,
Killing myself, to die upon a kiss.
            He [*kisses* DESDEMONA *and*] *dies*
CASSIO   This did I fear, but thought he had no weapon;
For he was great of heart.
LODOVICO [*to* IAGO]   O Spartan dog,[2]
More fell° than anguish, hunger, or the sea,   *cruel*
Look on the tragic loading of this bed:
This is thy work. The object poisons sight;
Let it be hid. Gratiano, keep the house
And seize upon the fortunes of the Moor,
For they succeed on you. [*To* CASSIO] To you, lord
   governor,
Remains the censure° of this hellish villain;   *sentence*
The time, the place, the torture—O, enforce it!
Myself will straight aboard, and to the state
This heavy act with heavy heart relate.   *Exeunt*

---

1. Probably alludes to Judas Iscariot, betrayer of Jesus. "Base Indian," in the quarto, suggests naïve gullibility rather than malice.
2. "Spartan dog": a bloodhound; hence a relentless, bloodthirsty man. Also the people of ancient Sparta were reputed to be inhumane and unfeeling.

The Early Seventeenth Century 1603–1660

1603: Death of Elizabeth I; accession of James I, first Stuart king of England

1605: The Gunpowder Plot, a failed effort by Catholic extremists to blow up Parliament and the king

1607: Establishment of first permanent English colony in the New World at Jamestown, Virginia

1625: Death of James I; accession of Charles I

1642: Outbreak of civil war; theaters closed

1649: Execution of Charles I; beginning of Commonwealth and Protectorate, known inclusively as the Interregnum (1649–60)

1660: End of the Protectorate; restoration of Charles II

Queen Elizabeth died on March 24, 1603, after ruling England for more than four decades. The Virgin Queen had not, of course, produced a child to inherit her throne, but her kinsman, the thirty-six-year-old James Stuart, James VI of Scotland, succeeded her as James I without the violence that many had feared. Many welcomed the accession of a man in the prime of life, supposing that he would prove more decisive than his notoriously vacillating predecessor. Worries over the succession, which had plagued the reigns of the Tudor monarchs since Henry VIII, could finally subside: James already had several children with his queen, Anne of Denmark. Writers and scholars jubilantly noted that their new ruler had literary inclinations. He was the author of

Sacred and Profane Love (detail), ca. 1515, Titian. For more information about this image, see the color insert in this volume.

treatises on government and witchcraft, and some youthful efforts at poetry.

Nonetheless, there were grounds for disquiet. James had come to maturity in Scotland, in the seventeenth century a foreign land with a different church, different customs, and different institutions of government. Two of his books, *The True Law of Free Monarchies* (1598) and *Basilikon Doron* (1599), expounded authoritarian theories of kingship: James's views seemed incompatible with the English tradition of "mixed" government, in which power was shared by the monarch, the House of Lords, and the House of Commons. As Thomas Howard wrote in 1611, while Elizabeth "did talk of her subjects' love and good affection," James "talketh of his subjects' fear and subjection." James liked to imagine himself as a modern version of the wise, peace-loving Roman Augustus Caesar, who autocratically governed a vast empire. The Romans had deified their emperors, and while the Christian James could not expect the same, he insisted on his closeness to divinity. Kings, he believed, derived their powers from God rather than from the people. As God's specially chosen delegate, surely he deserved his subjects' reverent, unconditional obedience.

Yet unlike the charismatic Elizabeth, James was personally unprepossessing. One contemporary, Anthony Weldon, provides a barbed description: "His tongue too large for his mouth, which ever made him speak full in the mouth, and drink very uncomely as if eating his drink . . . he never washed his hands . . . his walk was ever circular, his fingers ever in that walk fiddling about his codpiece." Unsurprisingly, James did not always inspire in his subjects the deferential awe to which he thought himself entitled.

The relationship between the monarch and his people and the relationship between England and Scotland would be sources of friction throughout James's reign. James had hoped to unify his domains as a single nation, "the empire of Britain." But the two realms' legal and ecclesiastical systems proved difficult to reconcile, and the English Parliament, traditionally a sporadically convened advisory body to the monarch, offered robustly xenophobic opposition. The failure of unification was only one of several clashes with the English Parliament, especially with the House of Commons, which had authority over taxation. After James died in 1625 and his son, Charles I, succeeded him, tensions persisted and intensified. Charles, indeed, attempted to rule without summoning Parliament at all between 1629 and 1638. By 1642 England was up in arms, in a civil war between the king's forces and armies loyal to the House of Commons. The conflict ended with Charles's defeat and beheading in 1649.

Although in the early 1650s the monarchy as an institution seemed as dead as the man who had last worn the crown, an adequate replacement proved difficult to devise. Executive power devolved upon a "Lord Protector," Oliver Cromwell, former general of the parliamentary forces, who wielded power nearly as autocratically as Charles had done. Yet without an institutionally sanctioned method of transferring power upon Cromwell's death in 1658, the attempt to fashion a commonwealth without a hereditary monarch eventually failed. In 1660 Parliament invited the eldest son of the old king home from exile. He succeeded to the throne as King Charles II.

As James's accession marks the beginning of "the early seventeenth century," his grandson's marks the end. Literary periods often fail to correlate neatly with the reigns of monarchs, and the period 1603–60 can seem especially arbitrary. Many of the most important cultural trends in seventeenth-century Europe neither began nor ended in these years but were in the process of unfolding slowly, over several centuries. The Protestant Reformation of the sixteenth century was still ongoing in the seventeenth, and still producing turmoil. The printing press, invented in the fifteenth century, made books ever more widely available, contributing to an expansion of literacy and to a changed conception of authorship. Although the English economy remained primarily agrarian, its manufacturing and trade sectors were expanding rapidly. England was beginning to establish itself as a colonial power and as a leading maritime nation. From 1550 on, London grew explosively as a center of population, trade, and literary endeavor. All these important developments got under way before James came to the throne, and many of them would continue after the 1714 death of James's great-granddaughter Queen Anne, the last of the Stuarts to reign in England.

From a literary point of view, 1603 can seem a particularly capricious dividing line because at the accession of James I so many writers happened to be in midcareer. The professional lives of William Shakespeare, Ben Jonson, John Donne, Francis Bacon, Walter Ralegh, and many less important writers—Thomas Dekker, George Chapman, Samuel Daniel, Michael Drayton, and Thomas Heywood, for instance—straddle the reigns of Elizabeth and James. The Restoration of Charles II, with which this section ends, is likewise a more significant political than literary milestone: John Milton completed *Paradise Lost* and wrote two other major poems in the 1660s. Nonetheless, recognizing the years 1603–60 as a period sharpens our awareness of some important political, intellectual, cultural, and stylistic currents that bear directly upon literary production. It helps focus attention too upon the seismic shift in national consciousness that, in 1649, could permit the formal trial, conviction, and execution of an anointed king at the hands of his former subjects.

STATE AND CHURCH, 1603–40

In James's reign, the most pressing difficulties were apparently financial, but money troubles were merely symptoms of deeper quandaries about the proper relationship between the king and the people. Compared to James's native Scotland, England seemed a prosperous nation, but James was less wealthy than he believed. Except in times of war, the Crown was supposed to fund the government not through regular taxation but through its own extensive land revenues and by exchanging Crown prerogatives, such as the collection of taxes on luxury imports, in return for money or services. Yet the Crown's independent income had declined throughout the sixteenth century as inflation eroded the value of land rents. Meanwhile, innovations in military technology and shipbuilding dramatically increased the expense of port security and other defenses, a traditional Crown responsibility. Elizabeth had responded to straitened finances with parsimony, transferring much of the expense of her court, for instance, onto wealthy subjects, whom she visited for extended periods on her annual "progresses." She kept a tight lid on honorific titles too, creating new knights or peers very rarely, even though the years of her reign saw considerable upward social mobility. In consequence, by 1603 there was considerable pent-up pressure both for "honors" and for more tangible rewards for government officials. As soon as James came to power, he was immediately besieged with supplicants.

James responded with what seemed to him appropriate royal munificence, knighting and ennobling many of his courtiers and endowing them with opulent gifts. His expenses were unavoidably higher than Elizabeth's, because he had to maintain not only his own household, but also separate establishments for his queen and for the heir apparent, Prince Henry. Yet he quickly became notorious for his financial heedlessness. Compared to Elizabeth's, his court was disorderly and wasteful, marked by hard drinking, gluttonous feasting, and a craze for hunting. "It is not possible for a king of England . . . to be rich or safe, but by frugality," warned James's lord treasurer, Robert Cecil, but James seemed unable to restrain himself. Soon he was deep in debt and unable to convince Parliament to bankroll him by raising taxes.

The king's financial difficulties set his authoritarian assertions about the monarch's supremacy at odds with Parliament's control over taxation. How were his prerogatives as a ruler to coexist with the rights of his subjects? Particularly disturbing to many was James's tendency to bestow high offices upon favorites apparently chosen for good looks rather than for good judgment. James's openly romantic attachment first to Robert Carr, Earl of Somerset, and then to George Villiers, Duke of Buckingham, gave rise to widespread rumors of homosexuality at court. The period had complex attitudes toward same-sex relationships; on the one hand, "sodomy" was a capital crime (though it was very rarely prosecuted); on the other hand, passionately intense male friendship, sometimes suffused with eroticism, constituted an important cultural ideal. In James's case, at least, contemporaries considered his susceptibility to lovely, expensive youths more a political than a moral calamity. For his critics, it crystallized what was wrong with unlimited royal power: the ease with which a king could confuse his own whim with a divine mandate.

Despite James's ungainly demeanor, his frictions with Parliament, and his chronic problems of self-management, he was politically astute. Often, like Elizabeth, he succeeded not through decisiveness but through canny inaction. Cautious by temperament, he characterized himself as a peacemaker and, for many years, successfully kept England out of the religious wars raging on the Continent. His 1604 peace treaty with England's old enemy, Spain, made the Atlantic safe for English ships, a prerequisite for the colonization of the New World and for regular long-distance trading expeditions into the Mediterranean and down the African coast into the Indian Ocean. During James's reign the first permanent English settlements were established in North America, first at Jamestown, then in Bermuda, at Plymouth, and in the Caribbean. In 1611 the East India Company established England's first foothold in India. Even when expeditions ended disastrously, as did Henry Hudson's 1611 attempt to find the Northwest Passage and Walter Ralegh's 1617 expedition to Guiana, they often asserted territorial claims that England would exploit in later decades.

Although the Crown's deliberate attempts to manage the economy were often misguided, its frequent inattention or refusal to interfere had the unintentional effect of stimulating growth. Early seventeenth-century entrepreneurs undertook a wide variety of schemes for industrial or agricultural improvement. Some ventures were almost as loony as Sir Politic Would-be's ridiculous moneymaking notions in Ben Jonson's *Volpone* (1606), but others were serious, profitable enterprises. In the south, domestic industries began manufacturing goods like pins and light woolens that had previously been imported. In the north, newly developed coal mines provided fuel for England's growing cities. In the east, landowners drained wetlands, producing more arable land to feed England's rapidly growing population. These endeavors gave rise to a new respect for the practical arts, a faith in technology as a means of improving human life, and a conviction that the future might be better than the past: all important influences upon the scientific theories of Francis Bacon and his seventeenth-century followers. Economic growth in this period owed more to the initiative of individuals and small groups than to government policy, a factor that encouraged a reevaluation of the role of self-interest, the profit motive, and the role of business contracts in the betterment of the community. This reevaluation was a prerequisite for the secular, contractual political theories proposed by Thomas Hobbes and John Locke later in the seventeenth century.

On the vexations faced by the Church of England, James was likewise often most successful when he was least activist. Since religion cemented sociopolitical order, it seemed necessary to English rulers that all of their subjects belong to a single church. Yet how could they do so when the Reformation had discredited many familiar religious practices and had bred disagreement over many theological issues? Sixteenth- and seventeenth-century English people argued over many religious topics. How should public worship be conducted, and what sorts of qualifications should ministers possess? How should Scripture be understood? How should people pray? What did the sacrament of Communion mean? What happened to people's souls after they died? Elizabeth's government had needed to devise a common religious practice when actual consensus was impossible. Sensibly, it sought a middle ground between traditional and reformed views. Everyone was legally required to attend Church of England services, and the form of the services themselves was mandated in the Elizabethan Book of Common Prayer. Yet the Book of Common Prayer deliberately avoided addressing abstruse theological controversies. The language of the English church service was carefully chosen to be open to several interpretations and acceptable to both Protestant- and Catholic-leaning subjects.

The Elizabethan compromise effectively tamed many of the Reformation's divisive energies and proved acceptable to the majority of Elizabeth's subjects. To staunch Catholics on one side and ardent Protestants on the other, however, the Elizabethan church seemed to have sacrificed truth to political expediency. Catholics wanted to return England to the Roman fold; while some of them were loyal subjects of the queen, others advocated invasion by a foreign Catholic power. Meanwhile the Puritans, as they were disparagingly called, pressed for more thoroughgoing reformation in doctrine, ritual, and church government, urging the elimination of "popish" elements from worship services and "idolatrous" religious images from churches. Some, the Presbyterians, wanted to separate lay and clerical power in the national church, so that church leaders would be appointed by other ministers, not by secular authorities. Others, the separatists, advocated abandoning a national church in favor of small congregations of the "elect."

The resistance of religious minorities to Elizabeth's established church opened them to state persecution. In the 1580s and 1590s, Catholic priests and the laypeople who harbored them were executed for treason, and radical Protestants for heresy. Both groups greeted James's accession enthusiastically; his mother had been the Catholic Mary, Queen of Scots, while his upbringing had been in the strict Reformed tradition of the Scottish Presbyterian Kirk.

James began his reign with a conference at Hampton Court, one of his palaces, at which advocates of a variety of religious views could openly debate them. Yet the Puritans failed to persuade him to make any substantive reforms. Practically speaking, the Puritan belief that congregations should choose their leaders diminished the monarch's power by stripping him of authority over ecclesiastical appointments. More generally, allowing people to choose their leaders in any sphere of life threatened to subvert the entire system of deference and hierarchy upon which the institution of monarchy itself seemed to rest. "No bishop, no king," James famously remarked.

Nor did Catholics fare well in the new reign. Initially inclined to lift Elizabeth's sanctions against them, James hesitated when he realized how entrenched was the opposition to toleration. Then, in 1605, a small group of disaffected Catholics packed a cellar adjacent to the Houses of Parliament with gunpowder, intending to detonate it on the day that the king formally opened Parliament, with Prince Henry, the Houses of Lords and Commons, and the leading justices in attendance. The conspirators were arrested before they could effect their plan. If the "Gunpowder Plot" had succeeded, it would have eliminated much of England's ruling class in a single tremendous explosion, leaving the land vulnerable to invasion by a foreign, Catholic power. Not surprisingly, the Gunpowder Plot dramatically heightened anti-Catholic paranoia in England, and its apparently

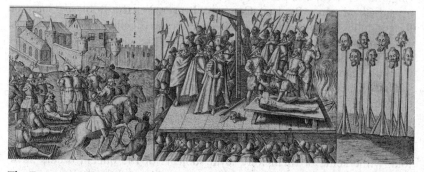

The Execution of the Gunpowder Plot Conspirators. This engraving by the Dutch artist Crispijn van de Passe shows the execution of the Gunpowder Conspirators for treason in January 1606. The punishment for treason was deliberately "cruel and unusual": the traitor was sentenced to be dragged through town on a wicker hurdle "at horse's tail," hanged but cut down while still conscious, and then castrated, disemboweled, beheaded, and his body cut into four pieces and parboiled. Though the punishment was often commuted to simple beheading or hanging, in the case of the Gunpowder Conspirators it was carried out in its entirety. On the left, the condemned men are taken to the place of execution. In the middle, the heart of one of the conspirators is being torn out, to be thrown into the fire. On the right, the heads of the conspirators are mounted on poles for display.

miraculous revelation was widely seen as a sign of God's care for England's Protestant governors.

By and large, then, James's ecclesiastical policies continued along the lines laid down by Elizabeth. By appointing bishops of varying doctrinal views, he restrained any single faction from controlling church policy. The most important religious event of James's reign was a newly commissioned translation of the Bible. First published in 1611, it was a typically moderating document. A much more graceful rendering than its predecessor, the Geneva version produced by Puritan expatriates in the 1550s, the King James Bible immediately became the standard English Scripture. Its impressive rhythms and memorable phrasing would influence writers for centuries. On the one hand, the new translation contributed to the Protestant aim of making the Bible widely available to every reader in the vernacular. On the other hand, unlike the Geneva Bible, the King James Version translated controversial and ambiguous passages in ways that bolstered conservative preferences for a ceremonial church and for a hierarchically organized church government.

James's moderation was not universally popular. Some Protestants yearned for a more confrontational policy toward Catholic powers, particularly toward Spain, England's old enemy. In the first decade of James's reign, this party clustered around James's eldest son and heir apparent, Prince Henry, who cultivated a militantly Protestant persona. When Henry died of typhoid fever in 1612, those who favored his policies were forced to seek avenues of power outside the royal court. By the 1620s, the House of Commons was developing a vigorous sense of its own independence, debating policy agendas often quite at odds with the Crown's and openly attempting to use its power to approve taxation as a means of exacting concessions from the king.

James's second son, Prince Charles, came to the throne upon James's death in 1625. Unlike his father, Charles was not a theorist of royal absolutism, but he acted on that principle with an inflexibility that his father had never been able to muster. By 1629 he had dissolved Parliament three times in frustration with its recalcitrance, and he then began more than a decade of "personal rule" without Parliament. Charles was more prudent in some respects than his father had been—he not only restrained the costs of his own court, but paid off his father's staggering debts by the early 1630s. Throughout his reign, he conscientiously applied himself to the business of government. Yet his refusal to involve powerful individuals and factions in the workings of the state inevitably alienated them, even while it cut him off dangerously from important channels of information about the reactions of his people. Money was a constant problem, too. Even a relatively frugal king required some funds for ambitious government initiatives; but without parliamentary approval, any taxes Charles imposed were widely perceived as illegal. As a result, even wise policies, such as Charles's effort to build up the English navy, spawned misgivings among many of his subjects.

Religious conflicts intensified. Charles's queen, the French princess Henrietta Maria, supported an entourage of Roman Catholic priests, protected English Catholics, and encouraged several noblewomen in her court to convert to the Catholic faith. While Charles remained a staunch member of the Church of England, he loved visual splendor and majestic ceremony in all aspects of life, spiritual and otherwise—proclivities that led his Puritan subjects to suspect him of popish sympathies. Charles's profound attachment to his wife, so different from James's neglect of Anne, only deepened their qualms. Like many fellow Puritans, Lucy Hutchinson blamed the entire debacle of Charles's reign on his wife's influence.

Charles's appointment of William Laud as archbishop of Canterbury, the ecclesiastical head of the English Church, further alienated Puritans. Laud subscribed to a theology that most Puritans rejected. As followers of the sixteenth-century reformer John Calvin, Puritans held that salvation depended upon faith in Christ, not "works." Works were meaningless because the deeds of sinful human beings could not be sanctified in the absence of faith; moreover, the Fall had so thoroughly corrupted human beings that they could not muster this faith without the help of God's grace. God chose (or refused) to extend grace to particular individuals on grounds that human beings were incapable of comprehending, and his decision had been made from eternity, before the individuals concerned were even born. In other words, Puritans believed, God predestined people to be saved or damned, and Christ's redemptive sacrifice was designed only for the saved group, the "elect." Laud, by contrast, advocated the Arminian doctrine that through Christ, God made redemption freely available to all human beings. Individuals could choose whether or not to respond to God's grace, and they could work actively toward their salvation by acts of charity, ritual devotion, and generosity to the church.

Although Laud's theology appears more generously inclusive than the Calvinist alternative, his ecclesiastical policies were uncompromising. Stripping many Puritan ministers of their posts, Laud aligned the doctrine and ceremonies of the English church with Roman Catholicism, which like Arminianism held works in high regard. In an ambitious project of church renovation, Laud installed religious paintings and images in churches; he thought they promoted reverence in worshippers, but the Puritans believed they encouraged idolatry. He rebuilt and resituated altars, making them more ornate and prominent: another change that dismayed Puritans, since it implied that the Eucharist rather than the sermon was the central element of a worship service. In the 1630s thousands of Puritans departed for the New England colonies, but many more remained at home, deeply discontented.

As the 1630s drew to a close, Archbishop Laud and Charles attempted to impose a version of the English liturgy and episcopal organization upon Presbyterian Scotland. Unlike his father, Charles had little acquaintance with his northern realm, and he drastically underestimated the difficulties involved. The Scots objected both on nationalist and on religious grounds, and they were not shy about expressing their objections: the bishop of Brechin, obliged to conduct divine service in the prescribed English style, mounted the pulpit armed with two pistols against his unruly congregation, while his wife, stationed on the floor below, backed him up with a blunderbuss. In the conflict that followed, the Bishops' Wars of 1639 and 1640, Charles's forces met with abject defeat. Exacerbating the situation, Laud was simultaneously insisting upon greater conformity within the English church. Riots in the London streets and the Scots' occupation of several northern English cities forced Charles to call the so-called Long Parliament, which would soon be managing a revolution.

LITERATURE AND CULTURE, 1603–40

Old Ideas and New

In the first part of the seventeenth century, exciting new scientific theories were in the air, but the older ways of thinking about the nature of things had not yet been superseded. Writers such as John Donne, Robert Burton, and Ben Jonson often invoked an inherited body of concepts even though they were aware that those concepts were being questioned or displaced. The Ptolemaic universe, with its fixed earth and circling sun, moon, planets, and stars, was a rich source of poetic imagery. So were the four elements—fire, earth, water, and air—that together were thought to comprise all matter, and the four bodily humors—choler, blood, phlegm, and black bile—which were supposed to determine a person's temperament and to cause physical and mental disease when out of balance. Late Elizabethans and Jacobeans (so called from *Jacobus*, Latin for James) considered themselves especially prone to melancholy, an ailment of scholars and thinkers stemming from an excess of black bile. Shakespeare's Hamlet is melancholic, as is Bosola in John Webster's *Duchess of Malfi* and Milton's title figure in "Il Penseroso" ("the serious-minded one"). In his panoramic *Anatomy of Melancholy*, Burton argued that melancholy was universal.

Key concepts of the inherited system of knowledge were analogy and order. Donne was especially fond of drawing parallels between the macrocosm, or "big world," and the microcosm, or "little world," of the individual human being. Also widespread were versions of the "chain of being" that linked and ordered various kinds of beings in hierarchies. The order of nature, for instance, put God above angels, angels above human beings, human beings above animals, animals above plants, plants above rocks. The social order installed the king over his nobles, nobles over the gentry, gentry over yeomen, yeomen over common laborers. The order of the family set husband above wife, parents above children, master and mistress above servants, the elderly above the young. Each level had its peculiar function, and each was connected to those above and beneath in a tight network of obligation and dependency. Items that occupied similar positions in different hierarchies were related by analogy: thus a monarch was like God, and he was also like a father, the head of the family, or like a lion, most majestic of beasts, or like the sun, the most excellent of heavenly bodies. A medieval or Renaissance poet who calls a king a sun or a lion, then, imagines himself not to be forging a metaphor in his own creative imagination, but to be describing something like an obvious fact of nature. Many Jacobean tragedies, Shakespeare's *King Lear* perhaps most comprehensively, depict the catastrophes that ensue when these hierarchies rupture, and both the social order and the natural order disintegrate.

Yet this conceptual system was itself beginning to crumble. Francis Bacon advocated rooting out of the mind all the intellectual predilections that had made the old ideas so attractive: love of ingenious correlations, reverence for tradition, and a priori assumptions about what was possible in nature. Instead, he argued, groups of collaborators ought to design controlled experiments to find the truths of nature by empirical means. Even as Bacon was promoting his views in *The Advancement of Learning*, *Novum Organum*, and *The New Atlantis*, actual experiments and discoveries were calling the

The Great Chain of Being. This illustration of the "Great Chain of Being" shows the hierarchy of the universe according to Christian orthodoxy. God is at the top of the diagram surrounded by angels, with the blessed souls in heaven sitting on clouds just beneath; below them is the layer of humans, with Eve emerging from Adam's rib in the center; below that are layers of birds, fish, and beasts; below that is a layer of plants upon the earth. All these layers are connected by a chain running down the middle, imagined as connecting all of God's creation. At the bottom, detached from the Great Chain, are Satan and his rebel angels, who can be seen falling from heaven into hell in the right margin.

old verities into question. From the far-flung territories England was beginning to colonize or to trade with, collectors brought animal, plant, and ethnological novelties, many of which were hard to subsume under old categories of understanding. William Harvey's discovery that blood circulated in the body shook received views on the function of blood, casting doubt on the theory of the humors. Galileo's telescope provided evidence confirming

Copernican astronomical theory, which dislodged the earth from its stable central position in the cosmos and, in defiance of all ordinary observation, set it whirling around the sun. Galileo found evidence as well of change in the heavens, which were supposed to be perfect and incorruptible above the level of the moon. Donne, like other writers of his age, responded with a mixture of excitement and anxiety to such novel ideas as these:

> And new philosophy calls all in doubt:
> The element of fire is quite put out;
> The sun is lost, and the earth, and no man's wit
> Can well direct him where to look for it.

Several decades later, however, Milton embraced the new science, proudly recalling a visit during his European tour to "the famous Galileo, grown old, a prisoner to the Inquisition for thinking in astronomy otherwise than the Franciscan and Dominican licensers thought." In *Paradise Lost*, he would make complex poetic use of the astronomical controversy, considering how, and how far, humans should pursue scientific knowledge.

Patrons, Printers, and Acting Companies

The social institutions, customs, and practices that had supported and regulated writers in Tudor times changed only gradually before 1640. As it had under Elizabeth, the church promoted writing of several kinds: devotional treatises; guides to meditation; controversial tracts; "cases of conscience," which work out difficult moral issues in complex situations; and especially sermons. Since everyone was required to attend church, everyone heard sermons at least once and often twice on Sunday, as well as on religious or national holidays. The essence of a sermon, Protestants agreed, was the careful exposition of Scripture, and its purpose was to instruct and to move. Yet styles varied; while some preachers, like Donne, strove to enthrall their congregations with all the resources of artful rhetoric, others, especially many Puritans, sought an undecorated style that would display God's word in its own splendor. Printing made it easy to circulate many copies of sermons, blurring the line between oral delivery and written text and enhancing the role of printers and booksellers in disseminating God's word.

Many writers of the period depended in one way or another upon literary patronage. A Jacobean or Caroline aristocrat, like his medieval forebears, was expected to reward dependents in return for services and homage. Indeed, his status was gauged partly on the size of his entourage (that is one reason why in *King Lear* the hero experiences his daughters' attempts to dismiss his retainers as so intensely humiliating). In the early seventeenth century, although commercial relationships were rapidly replacing feudal ones, patronage pervaded all walks of life: governing relationships between landlords and tenants, masters and servants, kings and courtiers. Writers were assimilated into this system partly because their works reflected well on the patron, and partly because their all-around intelligence made them useful members of a great man's household. Important patrons of the time included the royal family—especially Queen Anne, who sponsored the court masques, and Prince Henry—the members of the intermarried Sidney/Herbert family, and the Countess of Bedford, Queen Anne's confidante.

Because the patronage relationship often took the form of an exchange of favors rather than a simple financial transaction, its terms were very variable and are difficult to recover with any precision at this historical remove. A poet might dedicate a poem or a work to a patron in the expectation of a simple cash payment. But a patron might provide a wide range of other benefits: a place to live; employment as a secretary, tutor, or household servant; or gifts of clothing (textiles were valuable commodities). Donne, for instance, received inexpensive lodging from the Drury family, for whom he wrote the *Anniversaries*; a suit of clerical attire from Lucy Russell, Countess of Bedford, when he took orders in the Church of England; and advancement in the church from King James. Ben Jonson lived for several years at the country estates of Lord Aubigny and of Robert Sidney, in whose honor he wrote "To Penshurst"; he received a regular salary from the king in return for writing court masques; and he served as chaperone to Sir Walter Ralegh's son on a Continental tour. Aemilia Lanyer apparently resided for some time in the household of Margaret Clifford, Countess of Cumberland. Andrew Marvell lived for two years with Thomas Fairfax, tutored his daughter and wrote "Upon Appleton House" for him. All these quite different relationships and forms of remuneration fall under the rubric of patronage.

The patronage system required the poets involved to hone their skills at eulogizing their patrons. Jonson's epigrams and many of Lanyer's dedicatory poems evoke communities of virtuous poets and patrons joined by bonds of mutual respect and affection. Like the line between sycophantic flattery and truthful depiction, the line between patronage and friendship could be a thin one. Literary manuscripts circulated among circles of acquaintances and supporters, many of whom were, at least occasionally, writers as well as readers. Jonson esteemed Mary Wroth both as a fellow poet and as a member of the Sidney family to whom he owed so much. Donne became part of a coterie around Queen Anne's closest confidante, Lucy Russell, Countess of Bedford, who was also an important patron for Ben Jonson, Michael Drayton, and Samuel Daniel. The countess evidently wrote poems herself, although only one attributed to her has apparently survived.

Presenting a poem to a patron, or circulating it among the group of literary people who surrounded the patron, did not require printing it. In early-seventeenth-century England, the reading public for sophisticated literary works was tiny and concentrated in a few social settings: the royal court, the universities, and the Inns of Court or law schools. In these circumstances, manuscript circulation could be an effective way of reaching one's audience. So a great deal of writing remained in manuscript in early-seventeenth-century England. The collected works of many important writers of the period—most notably John Donne, George Herbert, William Shakespeare, and Andrew Marvell—appeared in print only posthumously, in editions produced by friends or admirers. Other writers, like Robert Herrick, collected and printed their own works long after they were written and (probably) circulated in manuscript. In consequence, it is often difficult to date accurately the composition of a seventeenth-century poem. In addition, when authors do not participate in the printing of their own works, editorial problems multiply—when, for instance, the printed version of a poem is inconsistent with a surviving manuscript copy.

Nonetheless, the printing of all kinds of literary works was becoming more common. Writers such as Francis Bacon or Robert Burton, who hoped to reach large numbers of readers with whom they were not acquainted, usually arranged for the printing of their texts soon after they were composed. The sense that the printing of lyric poetry, in particular, was a bit vulgar began to fade when the famous Ben Jonson collected his own works in a grand folio edition.

Until 1640 the Stuart kings kept in place the strict controls over print publication originally instituted by Henry VIII, in response to the ideological threat posed by the Reformation. King Henry had given the members of London's Stationer's Company a monopoly on all printing; in return for their privilege, they were supposed to submit texts to prepublication censorship. In the latter part of the sixteenth century, presses associated with the universities at Oxford and Cambridge would begin operation as well, but they were largely concerned with scholarly and theological books. As a result, with a very few exceptions (such as George Herbert's *The Temple*, published by Cambridge University Press), almost all printed literary texts were produced in London. Most of them were sold there as well, in the booksellers' stalls set up outside St. Paul's Cathedral.

The licensing system located not only primary responsibility for a printed work, but its ownership, with the printer rather than with the author. Printers typically paid writers a onetime fee for the use of their work, but the payment was scanty, and the authors of popular texts realized no royalties from the many copies sold. As a result, no one could make a living as a writer in the early seventeenth century by producing best sellers. The first writer formally to arrange for royalties was apparently John Milton, who received five pounds up front for *Paradise Lost*, and another five pounds and two hundred copies at the end of each of the first three impressions. Still, legal ownership of and control over a printed work remained with the printer: authorial copyright would not become a reality until the early eighteenth century.

In monetary terms, a more promising outlet for writers was the commercial theater, which provided the first literary market in English history. Profitable and popular acting companies, established successfully in London in Elizabeth's time, continued to play a very important cultural role under James and Charles. Because the acting companies staged a large number of different plays and paid for them at a predictable, if not generous, rate, they enabled a few hardworking writers to support themselves as full-time professionals. One of them, Thomas Dekker, commented bemusedly on the novelty of being paid for the mere products of one's imagination: "the theater," he wrote, "is your poet's Royal Exchange upon which their muses—that are now turned to merchants—meeting, barter away that light commodity of words." In James's reign, Shakespeare was at the height of his powers: *Othello, King Lear, Macbeth, Antony and Cleopatra, The Winter's Tale, The Tempest,* and other important plays were first staged during these years. So were Jonson's major comedies: *Volpone, Epicene, The Alchemist,* and *Bartholomew Fair.* The most important new playwright was John Webster, whose dark tragedies *The White Devil* and *The Duchess of Malfi* combined gothic horror with stunningly beautiful poetry.

Just as printers were legally the owners of the texts they printed, so theater companies, not playwrights, were the owners of the texts they performed. Typically, companies guarded their scripts closely, permitting them to be printed only in times of financial distress or when they were so old that printing them seemed unlikely to reduce the paying audience. As a result, many Jacobean and Caroline plays are lost to us or available only in corrupt or posthumous versions. For contemporaries, though, a play was "published" not by being printed but by being performed. Aware of the dangerous potential of plays in arousing the sentiments of large crowds of onlookers, the Stuarts, like the Tudors before them, instituted tight controls over dramatic performances. Acting companies, like printers, were obliged to submit works to the censor before public presentation.

Authors, printers, and acting companies who flouted the censorships laws were subject to imprisonment, fines, or even bodily mutilation. Queen Elizabeth cut off the hand of a man who disagreed in print with her marriage plans, King Charles the ears of a man who inveighed against court masques. Jonson and his collaborators found themselves in prison for ridiculing King James's broad Scots accent in one of their comedies. The effects of censorship on writers' output were therefore far reaching across literary genres. Since overt criticism or satire of the great was so dangerous, political writing was apt to be oblique and allegorical. Writers often employed animal fables, tales of distant lands, or long-past historical events to comment upon contemporary issues.

While the commercial theaters were profitable businesses that made most of their money from paying audiences, several factors combined to bring writing for the theater closer to the Stuart court than it had been in Elizabeth's time. The Elizabethan theater companies had been officially associated with noblemen who guaranteed their legitimacy (in contrast to unsponsored traveling players, who were subject to punishment as vagrants). Early in his reign, James brought the major theater companies under royal auspices. Shakespeare's company, the most successful of the day, became the King's Men: it performed not only all of Shakespeare's plays but also *Volpone* and *The Duchess of Malfi*. Queen Anne, Prince Henry, Prince Charles, and Princess Elizabeth sponsored other companies of actors. Royal patronage, which brought with it tangible rewards and regular court performances, naturally encouraged the theater companies to pay more attention to courtly taste. Shakespeare's *Macbeth* put onstage Scots history and witches, two of James's own interests; in *King Lear*, the hero's disastrous division of his kingdom may reflect controversies over the proposed union of Scotland and England. In the first four decades of the seventeenth century, court-affiliated theater companies such as the King's Men increasingly cultivated audiences markedly more affluent than the audiences they had sought in the 1580s and 1590s, performing in intimate, expensive indoor theaters instead of, or as well as, in the cheap popular amphitheaters. *The Duchess of Malfi*, for instance, was probably written with the King's Men's indoor theater at Blackfriars in mind, because several scenes depend for their effect upon a control over lighting that is impossible outdoors. Partly because the commercial theaters seemed increasingly to cater to the affluent and courtly elements of society, they attracted the ire of the king's opponents when civil war broke out in the 1640s.

Jacobean Writers and Genres

The era saw important changes in poetic fashion. Some major Elizabethan genres fell out of favor—long allegorical or mythological narratives, sonnet sequences, and pastoral poems. The norm was coming to be short, concentrated, often witty poems. Poets and prose writers alike often preferred the jagged rhythms of colloquial speech to the elaborate ornamentation and near-musical orchestration of sound that many Elizabethans had sought. The major poets of these years, Jonson, Donne, and Herbert, led this shift and also promoted a variety of "new" genres: love elegy and satire after the classical models of Ovid and Horace, epigram, verse epistle, meditative religious lyric, and country-house poem. Although these poets differed enormously from one another, all three exercised an important influence on the poets of the next generation.

A native Londoner, Jonson first distinguished himself as an acute observer of urban manners in a series of early, controversial satiric plays. Although he wrote two of his most moving poems to his dead children, Jonson focused rather rarely on the dynamics of the family relationships that so profoundly concerned his contemporary Shakespeare. When generational and dynastic matters do figure in his poetry, as they do at the end of "To Penshurst," they seem part of the agrarian, feudal order that Jonson may have romanticized but that he suspected was rapidly disappearing. By and large, Jonson interested himself in relationships that seemed to be negotiated by the participants, often in a bustling urban or courtly world in which blood kinship no longer decisively determined one's social place. Jonson's poems of praise celebrate and exemplify classical and humanist ideals of friendship: like-minded men and women elect to join in a community that fosters wisdom, generosity, civic responsibility, and mutual respect. In the plays and satiric poems, Jonson stages the violation of those values with such riotous comprehensiveness that the very survival of such ideals seem endangered: the plays swarm with voracious swindlers and their eager victims, social climbers both adroit and inept, and a dizzying assortment of morons and misfits. In many of Jonson's plays, rogues or wits collude to victimize others; their stormy, self-interested alliances, apparently so different from the virtuous friendships of the poems of praise, in fact resemble them in one respect: they are connections entered into by choice, not by law, inheritance, or custom.

Throughout his life, Jonson earned his living entirely from his writing, composing plays for the public theater while also attracting patronage as a poet and a writer of court masques. His acute awareness of his audience was partly, then, a sheerly practical matter. Yet Jonson's yearning for recognition ran far beyond any desire for material reward. A gifted poet, Jonson argued, was a society's proper judge and teacher, and he could only be effective if his audience understood and respected the poet's exalted role. Jonson set out unabashedly to create that audience and to monumentalize himself as a great English author. In 1616 he took the unusual step, for his time, of collecting his poems, plays, and masques in an elegant folio volume.

Jonson's influence upon the next generation of writers, and through them into the Restoration and the eighteenth century, was an effect both of his poetic mastery of his chosen modes and of his powerful personal example. Jonson mentored a group of younger poets, known as the Tribe, or Sons, of Ben, meeting regularly with some of them in the Apollo Room of the Devil

Tavern in London. Many of the royalist, or Cavalier, poets—Robert Herrick, Thomas Carew, Richard Lovelace, Sir John Suckling, Edmund Waller, Henry Vaughan in his secular verse—proudly acknowledged their relationship to Jonson or gave some evidence of it in their verse. Most of them absorbed too Jonson's attitude toward print and in later decades supervised the publication of their own poems.

Donne, like Jonson, spent most of his life in or near London, often in the company of other writers and intellectuals—indeed, in the company of many of the same writers and intellectuals, since the two men were friends and shared some of the same patrons. Yet, unlike Jonson's, most of Donne's poetry concerns itself not with a crowded social panorama, but with a dyad—with the relationship between the speaker and one single other being, a woman or God—that in its intensity blots out the claims of lesser relationships. Love for Donne encompasses an astonishing range of emotional experiences, from the lusty impatience of "To His Mistress Going to Bed" to the cheerful promiscuity of "The Indifferent"; to the mysterious platonic telepathy of "Air and Angels," from the vengeful wit of "The Apparition" to the postcoital tranquility of "The Good Morrow." While for Jonson the shared meal among friends often becomes an emblem of communion, for Donne sexual consummation has something of the same highly charged symbolic character, a moment in which the isolated individual can, however temporarily, escape the boundaries of selfhood in union with another:

> The phoenix riddle hath more with
> By us: we two being one, are it.
> So, to one neutral thing both sexes fit.

In the religious poems, where Donne both yearns for a physical relationship with God and knows it is impossible, he does not abandon his characteristic bodily metaphors. The doctrine of the Incarnation—God's taking material form in the person of Jesus Christ—and the doctrine of the bodily resurrection of the dead at the Last Day are Christian teachings that fascinate Donne, to which he returns again and again in his poems, sermons, and devotional writings. While sexual and religious love had long shared a common vocabulary, Donne delights in making that overlap seem new and shocking. He likens conjoined lovers to saints; demands to be raped by God; speculates, after his wife's death, that God killed her because He was jealous of Donne's divided loyalty; imagines Christ encouraging his Bride, the church, to "open" herself to as many men as possible.

Throughout Donne's life, his faith, like his intellect, was anything but quiet. Born into a family of devout Roman Catholics just as the persecution of Catholics was intensifying in Elizabethan England, Donne eventually became a member of the Church of England. If "Satire 3" is any indication, the conversion was attended by profound doubts and existential crisis. Donne's restless mind can lead him in surprising and sometimes unorthodox directions. At the same time, overwhelmed with a sense of his own unworthiness, he courts God's punishment, demanding to be spat upon, flogged, burnt, broken down, in the expectation that suffering at God's hand will restore him to grace and favor.

In both style and content, Donne's poems were addressed to a select few rather than to the public at large. His style is demanding, characterized by learned terms, audaciously far-fetched analogies, and an intellectually sophisticated play of ironies. Even Donne's sermons, attended by large crowds, share the knotty difficulty of the poems, and something too of their quality of intimate address. Donne circulated his poems in manuscript and largely avoided print publication (most of his poems were printed after his death in 1631). By some critics Donne has been regarded as the founder of a Metaphysical school of poetry. We find echoes of Donne's style in many later poets: in Thomas Carew, who praised Donne as a "monarch of wit," George Herbert, Richard Crashaw, John Cleveland, Sir John Suckling, Abraham Cowley, and Andrew Marvell.

Herbert, the younger son of a wealthy, cultivated, and well-connected family, seemed destined in early adulthood for a brilliant career as a diplomat or government servant. Yet he turned his back on worldly greatness to be ordained a priest in the Church of England. Moreover, eschewing a highly visible career as an urban preacher, he spent the remaining years of his short life ministering to the tiny rural parish of Bemerton. Herbert's poetry is shot through with the difficulty and joy of this renunciation, with all it entailed for him. Literary ambition—pride in one's independent creativity—appears to Herbert a temptation that must be resisted, whether it takes the form of Jonson's openly competitive aspiration for literary preeminence or Donne's brilliantly ironic self-displaying performances. Instead, Herbert seeks other models for poetic agency: the secretary taking dictation from a master, the musician playing in harmonious consort with others, the member of a church congregation who speaks with and for a community.

Herbert destroyed his secular verse in English and he turned his volume of religious verse over to a friend only on his deathbed, desiring him to print it if he thought it would be useful to "some dejected poor soul," but otherwise to burn it. The 177 lyrics contained in that volume, *The Temple*, display a complex religious sensibility and great artistic subtlety in an amazing variety of stanza forms. Herbert was the major influence on the next generation of religious lyric poets and was explicitly recognized as such by Henry Vaughan and Richard Crashaw.

The Jacobean period saw the emergence of what would become a major prose genre, the familiar essay. The works of the French inventor of the form, Michel de Montaigne, appeared in English translation in 1603, influencing Shakespeare as well such later writers as Sir Thomas Browne. Yet the first essays in English, the work of Francis Bacon, attorney general under Elizabeth and eventually lord chancellor under James, bear little resemblance to Montaigne's intimate, tentative, conversational pieces. Bacon's essays present pithy, sententious, sometimes provocative claims in a tone of cool objectivity, tempering moral counsel with an awareness of the importance of prudence and expediency in practical affairs. In *Novum Organum* Bacon adapts his deliberately discontinuous mode of exposition to outline a new scientific method, holding out the tantalizing prospect of eventual mastery over the natural world and boldly articulating the ways in which science might improve the human condition. In his fictional Utopia, described in *The New Atlantis*, Bacon imagines a society that realizes his dream of carefully orchestrated collaborative research, so different from the erratic, uncoordinated efforts of alchemists and amateurs in his own day. Bacon's philosophically revolutionary approach to the natural world profoundly impacted scientifically minded people over the next several generations. His writings influenced the materialist philosophy of his erstwhile secretary, Thomas Hobbes, encouraged Oliver Cromwell to attempt a large-scale overhaul of the university curriculum during the 1650s, and inspired the formation of the Royal Society, an organization of experimental scientists, after the Restoration.

The reigns of the first two Stuart kings mark the entry of Englishwomen, in some numbers, into authorship and publication. Most female writers of the period were from the nobility or gentry; all were much better educated than most women of the period, many of whom remained illiterate. In 1611 Aemilia Lanyer was the first Englishwoman to publish a substantial volume of original poems. It contained poetic dedications, a long poem on Christ's passion, and a country-house poem, all defending women's interests and importance. In 1613 Elizabeth Cary, Lady Falkland, was the first Englishwoman to publish a tragedy, *Mariam*, a closet drama that probes the situation of a queen subjected to her husband's domestic and political tyranny. In 1617 Rachel Speght, the first female polemicist who can be securely identified, published a defense of her sex in response to a notorious attack upon "Lewd, Idle, Froward, and Unconstant Women"; she was also the author of a long dream-vision poem. Lady Mary Wroth, niece of Sir Philip Sidney and the Countess of Pembroke, wrote a long prose romance, *Urania* (1612), which presents a range of women's experiences as lovers, rulers, counselors, scholars, storytellers, poets, and seers. Her Petrarchan sonnet sequence *Pamphilia to Amphilanthus*, published with *Urania*, gives poetic voice to the female in love.

THE CAROLINE ERA, 1625–40

When King Charles came to the throne in 1625, "the fools and bawds, mimics and catamites of the former court grew out of fashion," as the Puritan Lucy Hutchinson recalled. The changed style of the court directly affected the arts and literature of the Caroline period (so called after *Carolus*, Latin for Charles). Charles and his queen, Henrietta Maria, were art collectors on a large scale and patrons of such painters as Peter Paul Rubens and Sir Anthony Van Dyke; the latter portrayed Charles as a heroic figure of knightly romance, mounted on a splendid stallion. The conjunction of chivalric virtue and divine beauty or love, symbolized in the union of the royal couple, was the dominant theme of Caroline court masques, which were even more extravagantly hyperbolic than their Jacobean predecessors. Even as Henrietta Maria encouraged an artistic and literary cult of platonic love, several courtier-poets, such as Carew and Suckling, wrote playful, sophisticated love lyrics that both alluded to this fashion and sometimes urged a more licentiously physical alternative.

The religious tensions between the Caroline court's Laudian church and the Puritan opposition produced something of a culture war. In 1633 Charles reissued the *Book of Sports*, originally published by his father in 1618, prescribing traditional holiday festivities and Sunday sports in every parish. Like his father, he saw these recreations as the rural, downscale equivalent of the court masque: harmless, healthy diversions for people who otherwise spent most of their waking hours hard at work. Puritans regarded masques and rustic dances alike as occasions for sin, the Maypole as a vestige of pagan phallus worship, and Sunday sports as a profanation of the Sabbath. In 1632 William Prynne staked out the most extreme Puritan position, publishing a tirade of over one thousand pages against stage plays, court masques, Maypoles, Laudian church rituals, stained-glass windows, mixed dancing, and other outrages, all of which he associated with licentiousness, effeminacy, and the seduction of popish idolatry. For this cultural critique, Prynne was stripped of his academic degrees, ejected from the legal profession, set in the pillory, sentenced to life imprisonment, and had his books burned and his ears cut off. The severity of the punishments indicates the perceived danger of the book and the inextricability of literary and cultural affairs from politics.

King Charles at Prayer. This frontispiece from *Eikon Basilike* represents the praying king as a Christlike martyr surrounded by allegorical representations of virtue under trial. The left background shows a rock besieged by waves in a storm, surmounted with a Latin caption reading "unmoved I triumph." The left foreground displays palm trees with weights hung to their branches, which was supposed to make them grow more vigorously; the Latin caption reads "Virtue grows under burdens." A shaft of light pierces the stormclouds to illuminate Charles's head, with the caption "More clear out of the shadows." Wearing his coronation robes, Charles is nonetheless shown turning away from this turmoil, having cast aside an earthly crown, labeled "Vanity," to grasp a crown of thorns, labeled "Grace." Set before him is a "treatise of Christ" and a Bible reading "In Your Words, My Hope." Charles is receiving a vision from heaven of the immortal crown, "blessed and eternal," with which his supporters believed God would reward him.

Milton's astonishingly virtuosic early poems also respond to the tensions of the 1630s. Milton repudiated both courtly aesthetics and also Prynne's wholesale prohibitions, developing reformed versions of pastoral, masque, and hymn. In "On the Morning of Christ's Nativity," the birth of Christ coincides with a casting out of idols and a flight of false gods, stanzas that suggest contemporary Puritan resistance to Archbishop Laud's policies. Milton's magnificent funeral elegy "Lycidas" firmly rejects the poetic career of the Cavalier poet, who disregards high artistic ambition to "sport with Amaryllis in the shade / Or with the tangles of Neaera's hair." The poem also vehemently denounces the establishment clergy, ignorant and greedy "blind mouths" who rob their flocks of spiritual nourishment.

THE REVOLUTIONARY ERA, 1640–60

Early in the morning on January 30, 1649, Charles Stuart, the dethroned king Charles I, set off across St. James Park for his execution, surrounded by a heavy guard. He wore two shirts because the weather was frigid, and he did not want to look as if he were shivering with fear to the thousands who had gathered to watch him be beheaded. The black-draped scaffold had been erected just outside James I's elegant Banqueting House, inside of which so many court masques, in earlier decades, had celebrated the might of the Stuart monarchs and assured them of their people's love and gratitude. To those who could not attend, newsbooks provided eyewitness accounts of the dramatic events of the execution, as they had of Charles's trial the week before. Andrew Marvell also memorably describes the execution scene in "An Horatian Ode."

The execution of Charles I was understood at the time, and is still seen by many historians today, as a watershed event in English history. How did it come to pass? Historians do not agree over what caused "the English revolution," or, as it is alternatively called, the English civil war. One group argues that long-term changes in English society and the English economy led to rising social tensions and eventually to violent conflict. New capitalist modes of production in agriculture, industry, and trade were often incompatible with older feudal norms. The gentry, an affluent, highly educated class below the nobility but above the artisans, mechanics, and yeomen, played an increasingly important part in national affairs, as did the rich merchants in London; but the traditional social hierarchies failed to grant them the economic, political, and religious freedoms they believed they deserved. Another group of historians, the "revisionists," emphasize instead short-term and avoidable causes of the war—unlucky chances, personal idiosyncrasies, and poor decisions made by a small group of individuals.

Whatever caused the outbreak of hostilities, there is no doubt that the twenty-year period between 1640 and 1660 saw the emergence of concepts central to bourgeois liberal thought for centuries to come: religious toleration, separation of church and state, freedom from press censorship, and popular sovereignty. These concepts developed out of bitter disputes centering on three fundamental questions: What is the ultimate source of political power? What kind of church government is laid down in Scripture, and therefore ought to be settled in England? What should be the relation between the church and the state? The theories that evolved in response to these questions contained the seeds of much that is familiar in modern thought, mixed with much that is forbiddingly alien. It is vital to recognize that the participants in the disputes were not haphazardly attempting to predict the shape of modern liberalism, but were responding powerfully to the most important problems of their day. The need to find right answers seemed particularly urgent for the Millenarians among them, who, interpreting the upheavals of the time through the lens of the apocalyptic Book of Revelation, believed that their day was very near to being the last day of all.

When the so-called Long Parliament convened in 1640, it did not plan to execute a monarch or even to start a war. It did, however, want to secure its rights in the face of King Charles's perceived absolutist tendencies. Refusing merely to approve taxes and go home, as Charles would have wished, Parliament insisted that it could remain in session until its members agreed to disband. Then it set about abolishing extralegal taxes and courts, reining in the bishops' powers, and arresting (and eventually trying and executing) the king's ministers, the Earl of Strafford and Archbishop Laud. The collapse of effective royal government meant that the machinery of press censorship, which had been a Crown responsibility, no longer restrained the printing of explicit commentary on contemporary affairs of state. As Parliament debated, therefore, presses poured forth a flood of treatises arguing vociferously on all sides of the questions about church and state, creating a lively public forum for political discussion where none had existed before. The suspension of censorship permitted the development of weekly newsbooks that reported, and editorialized on, current domestic events from varying political and religious perspectives.

As the rift widened between Parliament and the king in 1641, Charles sought to arrest five members of Parliament for treason, and Londoners rose in arms against him. The king fled to York, while the queen escaped to the Continent. Negotiations for compromise broke down over the issues that would derail them at every future stage: control of the army and the church. On July 12, 1642, Parliament voted to raise an army, and on August 22 the king stood before a force of two thousand horse and foot at Nottingham, unfurled his royal standard, and summoned his liege men to his aid. Civil war had begun. Regions of the country, cities, towns, social classes, and even families found themselves painfully divided. The king set up court and an alternative parliament in Oxford, to which many in the House of Lords and some in the House of Commons transferred their allegiance.

In the First Civil War (1642–46), Parliament and the Presbyterian clergy that supported it had limited aims. They hoped to secure the rights of the House of Commons, to limit the king's power over the army and the church—but not to depose him—and to settle Presbyterianism as the national established church. As Puritan armies moved through the country, fighting at Edgehill, Marston Moor, Naseby, and elsewhere, they also undertook a crusade to stamp out idolatry in English churches, smashing religious images and stained-glass windows and lopping off the heads of statues as an earlier generation had done at the time of the English Reformation. Their ravages are still visible in English churches and cathedrals.

The Puritans were not, however, a homogeneous group, as the 1643 Toleration Controversy revealed. The Presbyterians wanted a national Presbyterian church, with dissenters punished and silenced as before. But Congregationalists, Independents, Baptists, and other separatists opposed a national church and pressed for some measure of toleration, for themselves at least. The religious radical Roger Williams, just returned from New England, argued that Christ mandated the complete separation of church and state and the civic toleration of all religions, even Roman Catholics, Jews, and Muslims. Yet to most people, the civil war itself seemed to confirm that people of different faiths could not coexist peacefully. Thus even as sects continued to proliferate—Seekers, Finders, Antinomians, Fifth Monarchists, Quakers, Muggletonians, Ranters—even the most broad-minded of the age often attempted to draw a line between what was acceptable and what was not. Predictably, their lines failed to coincide. In *Areopagitica* (1644), John Milton argues vigorously against press censorship and for toleration of most Protestants—but for him, Catholics are beyond the pale. Robert Herrick and Sir Thomas Browne regarded Catholic rites, and even some pagan ones, indulgently but could not stomach Puritan zeal.

In 1648, after a period of negotiation and a brief Second Civil War, the king's army was definitively defeated. His supporters were captured or fled into exile, losing position and property. Yet Charles, imprisoned on the Isle of Wight, remained a threat. He was a natural rallying point for those disillusioned by parliamentary rule—many people disliked Parliament's legal but heavy taxes even more than they had the king's illegal but lighter ones. Charles repeatedly attempted to escape and was accused of trying to open the realm to a foreign invasion. Some powerful leaders of the victorious New Model Army took drastic action. They expelled royalists and Presbyterians, who still wanted to come to an accommodation with the king, from the House of Commons and abolished the House of Lords. With consensus assured by the purgation of dissenting viewpoints, the army brought the king to trial for high treason in the Great Hall of Westminster.

After the king's execution, the Rump Parliament, the part of the House of Commons that had survived the purge, immediately established a new government "in the way of a republic, without king or House of Lords." The new state was extremely fragile. Royalists and Presbyterians fiercely resented their exclusion from power and pronounced the execution of the king a sacrilege. The Rump Parliament and the army were at odds, with the army rank and file arguing that voting rights ought not be restricted to men of property. The Levelers, led by John Lilburne, called for suffrage for all adult males. An associated but more radical group, called the Diggers or True Levelers, pushed for economic reforms to match the political ones. Their spokesman, Gerrard Winstanley, wrote eloquent manifestos developing a Christian communist program. Meanwhile, Millenarians and Fifth Monarchists wanted political power vested in the regenerate "saints" in preparation for the thousand-year reign of Christ on earth foretold in the biblical Book of Revelation. Quakers defied both state and church authority by refusing to take oaths and by preaching incendiary sermons in open marketplaces. Most alarming of all, out of proportion to their scant numbers, were the Ranters, who believed that because God dwelt in them none of their acts could be sinful. Notorious for sexual license and for public nudity, they got their name from their deliberate blaspheming and their penchant for rambling prophecy. In addition to internal disarray, the new state faced serious external threats. After Charles I's execution, the Scots and the Irish—who had not been consulted about the trial—immediately

Cromwell. This depiction of Oliver Cromwell, published in 1658, shows him in armor, surrounded by emblems symbolizing his military prowess, civic authority, piety, and divine favor.

proclaimed his eldest son, Prince Charles, the new king. The prince, exiled on the Continent, was attempting to enlist the support of a major European power for an invasion.

The formidable Oliver Cromwell, now undisputed leader of the army, crushed external threats, suppressing rebellions in Ireland and Scotland. The Irish war was especially bloody, as Cromwell's army massacred the Catholic natives in a frenzy of religious hatred. When trade rivalries erupted with the Dutch over control of shipping lanes in the North Sea and the English Channel, the new republic was again victorious. Yet the domestic situation remained unstable. Given popular disaffection and the unresolved disputes between Parliament and the army, the republic's leaders dared not call new elections. In 1653 power effectively devolved upon Cromwell, who was sworn in as Lord Protector for life under England's first written constitution. Many property owners considered Cromwell the only hope for stability, while others, including Milton, saw him as a champion of religious liberty. Although persecution of Quakers and Ranters continued, Cromwell sometimes intervened to mitigate the lot of the Quakers. He also began a program to readmit Jews to England, partly in the interests of trade but also to open the way for their conversion, supposedly a precursor of the Last Day as prophesied in the Book of Revelation.

The problem of succession remained unresolved, however. When Oliver Cromwell died in 1658, his son, Richard, was appointed in his place, but he had inherited none of his father's leadership qualities. In 1660 General George Monck succeeded in calling elections for a new "full and free" parliament, open to supporters of the monarchy as well as of the republic. The new Parliament immediately recalled the exiled prince, officially proclaiming him King Charles II on May 8, 1660. The period that followed, therefore, is called the Restoration: it saw the restoration of the monarchy and with it the royal court, the established Church of England, and the professional theater.

Over the next few years, the new regime executed some of the regicides that had participated in Charles I's trial and execution and harshly repressed radical Protestants (the Baptist John Bunyan wrote *Pilgrim's Progress* in prison). Yet Charles II, who came to the throne at Parliament's invitation, could not lay claim to absolute power as his father had done. After his accession, Parliament retained its legislative supremacy and complete power over taxation, and exercised some control over the king's choice of counselors. It assembled by its own authority, not by the king's mandate. During the Restoration years, the journalistic commentary and political debates that had first flourished in the 1640s remained forceful and open, and the first modern political parties developed out of what had been the royalist and republican factions in the civil war. In London and in other cities, the merchant classes, filled with dissenters, retained their powerful economic leverage. Although the English revolution was apparently dismantled in 1660, its long-term effects profoundly changed English institutions and English society.

LITERATURE AND CULTURE, 1640–60

The English civil war was disastrous for the English theater. One of Parliament's first acts after hostilities began in 1642 was to abolish public plays and sports, as "too commonly expressing lascivious mirth and levity." Some drama continued to be written and published, but performances were rare and would-be theatrical entrepreneurs had to exploit loopholes in the prohibitions by describing their works as "operas" or presenting their productions in semiprivate circumstances.

As the king's government collapsed, the patronage relationships centered upon the court likewise disintegrated. Many leading poets were staunch royalists, or Cavaliers, who suffered considerably in the war years. Robert Herrick lost his position; Richard Lovelace was imprisoned; Margaret Cavendish went into exile. With their usual networks of manuscript circulation disrupted, many royalist writers printed their verse. Volumes of poetry by Thomas Carew, John Denham, Richard Lovelace, and Robert Herrick appeared in the 1640s. Their poems, some dating from the 1620s or 1630s, celebrate the courtly ideal "of the good life: good food, plenty of wine, good verse, hospitality, and high-spirited loyalty, especially to the king. One characteristic genre is the elegant love lyric, often with a carpe diem theme. In

Herrick's case especially, apparent ease and frivolity masks a frankly political subtext. The Puritans excoriated May Day celebrations, harvest-home festivities, and other time-honored holidays and "sports" as unscriptural, idolatrous, or frankly pagan. For Herrick, they sustained a community that strove neither for ascetic perfection nor for equality among social classes, but that knew the value of pleasure in cementing social harmony and that incorporated everyone—rich and poor, unlettered and learned—as the established church had traditionally tried to do.

During the 1640s and 1650s, as they faced defeat, the Cavaliers wrote movingly of the relationship between love and honor, of fidelity under duress, of like-minded friends sustaining one another in a hostile environment. They presented themselves as amateurs, writing verse in the midst of a life devoted to more important matters: war, love, the king's service, the endurance of loss. Rejecting the radical Protestant emphasis on the "inner light," which they considered merely a pretext for presumptuousness and violence, the Cavalier poets often cultivated a deliberately unidiosyncratic, even self-deprecating poetic persona. Thus the poems of Richard Lovelace memorably express sentiments that he represents not as the unique insights of an isolated genius, but as principles easily grasped by all honorable men. When in "The Vine" Herrick relates a wet dream, he not only laughs at himself but at those who mistake their own fantasies for divine inspiration.

During the 1650s, royalists wrote lyric poems in places far removed from the hostile centers of parliamentary power. In Wales, Henry Vaughan wrote religious verse expressing his intense longing for past eras of innocence and for the perfection of heaven or the millennium. Also in Wales, Katherine Philips wrote and circulated in manuscript poems that celebrate female friends in terms normally reserved for male friendships. The publication of her poems after the Restoration brought Philips some celebrity as "the Matchless Orinda." Richard Crashaw, an exile in Paris and Rome and a convert to Roman Catholicism, wrote lush religious poetry that attempted to reveal the spiritual by stimulating the senses. Margaret Cavendish, also in exile, with the queen in Paris, published two collections of lyrics when she returned to England in 1653; after the Restoration she published several dramas and a remarkable Utopian romance, *The Blazing World*.

Several prose works by royalist sympathizers have become classics in their respective genres. Thomas Hobbes, the most important English philosopher of the period, another exile in Paris, developed his materialist philosophy and psychology there and, in *Leviathan* (1651), his unflinching defense of absolute sovereignty based on a theory of social contract. Some royalist writing seems to have little to do with the contemporary scene, but in fact carries a political charge. In *Religio Medici* (1642–43), Sir Thomas Browne presents himself as a genial, speculative doctor who loves ritual and ceremony not for complicated theological reasons, but because they move him emotionally. While he can sympathize with all Christians, even Roman Catholics, and while he recognizes in himself many idiosyncratic views, he willingly submits his judgment to the Church of England, in sharp contrast to Puritans bent on ridding the church of its errors. Izaak Walton's treatise on fishing, *The Complete Angler* (1653), presents a dialogue between Walton's persona, Piscator the angler, and Venator the hunter. Piscator, speaking like many Cavalier poets for the values of warmheartedness, charity, and inclusiveness, converts the busy, warlike Venator, a figure for the Puritan, to the tranquil and contemplative pursuit of fishing.

The revolutionary era gave new impetus to women's writing. The circumstances of war placed women in novel, occasionally dangerous situations, giving them unusual events to describe and prompting self-discovery. The autobiographies of royalists Lady Anne Halkett and Margaret Cavendish, Duchess of Newcastle, published after the Restoration, report their experiences and their sometimes daring activities during those trying days. Lucy Hutchinson's memoir of her husband, Colonel John Hutchinson, first published in 1806, narrates much of the history of the times from a republican point of view. Leveler women offered petitions and manifestos in support of their cause and of their imprisoned husbands. The widespread belief that the Holy Spirit was moving in unexpected ways encouraged a number of female prophets: Anna Trapnel, Mary Cary, and Lady Eleanor Davies. Their published prophecies often carried a strong political critique of Charles or of Cromwell. Quaker women came into their own as preachers and sometimes as writers of tracts, authorized by the Quaker belief in the spiritual equality of women and men, and by the conviction that all persons should testify to whatever the inner light communicates to them. Many of their memoirs, such as Dorothy Waugh's "Relation," were originally published both to call attention to their sufferings and to inspire other Quakers to similar feats of moral fortitude.

While most writers during this period were royalists, two of the best, Andrew Marvell and John Milton, sided with the republic. Marvell wrote most of the poems for which he is still remembered while at Nunappleton in the early 1650s, tutoring the daughter of the retired parliamentary general Thomas Fairfax; in 1657 he joined his friend Milton in the office of Cromwell's Latin Secretariat. In Marvell's love poems and pastorals, older convictions about ordered harmony give way to wittily unresolved or unresolvable oppositions, some playful, some painful. Marvell's conflictual worldview seems unmistakably the product of the unsettled civil war decades. In his country-house poem "Upon Appleton House," even agricultural practices associated with regular changes of the season, like the flooding of fallow fields, become emblems of unpredictability, reversal, and category confusion. In other poems Marvell eschews an authoritative poetic persona in favor of speakers that seem limited or even a bit unbalanced: a mower who argues for the values of pastoral with disconcerting belligerence, a nymph who seems to exemplify virginal innocence but also immature self-absorption and possibly unconscious sexual perversity. Marvell's finest political poem, "An Horatian Ode upon Cromwell's Return from Ireland," celebrates Cromwell's providential victories even while inviting sympathy for the executed king and warning about the potential dangers of Cromwell's meteoric rise to power.

A promising, prolific young poet in the 1630s, Milton committed himself to the English republic as soon as the conflict between the king and Parliament began to take shape. His loyalty to the revolution remained unwavering despite his disillusion when it failed to realize his ideals: religious toleration for all Protestants and the free circulation of ideas without prior censorship. First as a self-appointed adviser to the state, then as its official defender, he addressed the great issues at stake in the 1640s and the 1650s. In a series of treatises he argued for church disestablishment and for the removal of bishops, for a republican government based on natural law and popular sovereignty, for the right of the people to dismiss from office and even execute their rulers, and, most controversial even to his usual allies, in favor of divorce on the grounds of incompatibility. Milton was a Puritan, but both his theological heterodoxies and his poetic vision mark him as a distinctly unusual one.

During his years as a political polemicist, Milton also wrote several sonnets, revising that small, love-centered genre to accommodate large private and public topics: a Catholic massacre of proto-Protestants in the foothills of Italy, the agonizing questions posed by his blindness, various threats to intellectual and religious liberty. In 1645 he published his collected English and Latin poems as a counterstatement to the royalist volumes of the 1640s. Yet his most ambitious poetry remained to be written. Milton probably wrote some part of *Paradise Lost* in the late 1650s and completed it after the Restoration, encompassing in it all he had thought, read, and experienced of tyranny, political controversy, evil, deception, love, and the need for companionship. This cosmic blank-verse epic assimilates and critiques the epic tradition and Milton's entire intellectual and literary heritage, classical and Christian. Yet it centers not on martial heroes but on a domestic couple who must discover how to live a good life day by day, in Eden and later in the fallen world, amid intense emotional pressures and the seductions of evil.

Seventeenth-century poetry, prose, and drama retains its hold on readers because so much of it is so very good, fusing intellectual power, emotional passion, and extraordinary linguistic artfulness. Poetry in this period ranges over an astonishing variety of topics and modes: highly erotic celebrations of sexual desire, passionate declarations of faith and doubt, lavishly embroidered paeans to friends and benefactors, tough-minded assessments of social and political institutions. English dramatists were at the height of their powers, situating characters of unprecedented complexity in plays sometimes remorselessly satiric, sometimes achingly moving. In these years English prose becomes a highly flexible instrument, suited to informal essays, scientific treatises, religious meditation, political polemic, biography and autobiography, and journalistic reportage. Literary forms evolve for the exquisitely modulated representation of the self: dramatic monologues, memoirs, spiritual autobiographies, sermons in which the preacher takes himself for an example. Finally, we have in Milton an epic poet who assumed the role of inspired prophet, envisioning a world created by God but shaped by human choice and imagination.

The Early Seventeenth Century

TEXTS	CONTEXTS
1603 James I, *Basilikon Doron* reissued	**1603** Death of Elizabeth I; accession of James I. Plague
1604 William Shakespeare, *Othello*	
1605 Shakespeare, *King Lear*. Ben Jonson, *The Masque of Blackness*. Francis Bacon, *The Advancement of Learning*	**1605** Gunpowder Plot, failed effort by Roman Catholic extremists to blow up Parliament
1606 Jonson, *Volpone*. Shakespeare, *Macbeth*	
	1607 Founding of Jamestown colony in Virginia
1609 Shakespeare, *Sonnets*	**1609** Galileo begins observing the heavens with a telescope
1611 "King James" Bible (Authorized Version). Shakespeare, *The Tempest*. John Donne, *The First Anniversary*. Aemilia Lanyer, *Salve Deus Rex Judaeorum*	
1612 Donne, *The Second Anniversary*	**1612** Death of Prince Henry
1613 Elizabeth Cary, *The Tragedy of Mariam*	
1614 John Webster, *The Duchess of Malfi*	
1616 Jonson, *Works*. James I, *Works*	**1616** Death of Shakespeare
	1618 Beginning of the Thirty Years War
	1619 First African slaves in North America exchanged by Dutch frigate for food and supplies at Jamestown
1620 Bacon, *Novum Organum*	**1620** Pilgrims land at Plymouth
1621 Mary Wroth, *The Countess of Montgomery's Urania* and *Pamphilia to Amphilanthus*. Robert Burton, *The Anatomy of Melancholy*	**1621** Donne appointed dean of St. Paul's Cathedral
1623 Shakespeare, First Folio	
1625 Bacon, *Essays*	**1625** Death of James I; accession of Charles I; Charles I marries Henrietta Maria
	1629 Charles I dissolves Parliament
1633 Donne, *Poems*. George Herbert, *The Temple*	**1633** Galileo forced by the Inquisition to recant the Copernican theory
1637 John Milton, "Lycidas"	
1640 Thomas Carew, *Poems*	**1640** Long Parliament called (1640–53). Archbishop Laud impeached
1642 Thomas Browne, *Religio Medici*. Milton, *The Reason of Church Government*	**1642** First Civil War begins (1642–46). Parliament closes the theaters
1643 Milton, *The Doctrine and Discipline of Divorce*	**1643** Accession of Louis XIV of France
1644 Milton, *Areopagitica*	
1645 Milton, *Poems*. Edmund Waller, *Poems*	**1645** Archbishop Laud executed. Royalists defeated at Naseby

TEXTS	CONTEXTS
1648 Robert Herrick, *Hesperides* and *Noble Numbers*	**1648** Second Civil War. "Pride's Purge" of Parliament
1649 Milton, *The Tenure of Kings and Magistrates* and *Eikonoklastes*	**1649** Trial and execution of Charles I. Republic declared. Milton becomes Latin Secretary (1649–59)
1650 Henry Vaughan, *Silex Scintillans* (Part II, 1655)	
1651 Thomas Hobbes, *Leviathan*. Andrew Marvell, "Upon Appleton House" (unpublished)	
	1652 Anglo-Dutch War (1652–54)
	1653 Cromwell made Lord Protector
	1658 Death of Cromwell; his son Richard made Protector
1660 Milton, *Ready and Easy Way to Establish a Free Commonwealth*	**1660** Restoration of Charles II to throne. Royal Society founded
	1662 Charles II marries Catherine of Braganza
	1665 The Great Plague
1666 Margaret Cavendish, *The Blazing World*	**1666** The Great Fire
1667 Milton, *Paradise Lost* (in ten books). Katherine Philips, *Collected Poems*. John Dryden, *Annus Mirabilis*	
1671 Milton, *Paradise Regained* and *Samson Agonistes*	
1674 Milton, *Paradise Lost* (in twelve books)	**1674** Death of Milton
1681 Marvell, *Poems*, published posthumously	

JOHN DONNE
1572-1631

Lovers' eyeballs threaded on a string. A god who assaults the human heart with a battering ram. A teardrop that encompasses and drowns the world. John Donne's poems abound with startling images, some of them exalting and others grotesque. With his strange and playful intelligence, expressed in puns, paradoxes, and the elaborately sustained metaphors known as "conceits," Donne has enthralled and sometimes enraged readers from his day to our own. The tired clichés of love poetry—cheeks like roses, hearts pierced by the arrows of love—emerge reinvigorated and radically transformed, demanding from the reader an unprecedented level of mental alertness and engagement. Donne prided himself on his wit and displayed it not only in his conceits but in his grasp of learned discourses ranging from theology to alchemy, from cosmology to law. Yet for all their ostentatious intellectuality Donne's poems never give the impression of being academic exercises. Rather, they are intense dramatic monologues in which the speaker's ideas and feelings shift and evolve from one line to the next. Donne's prosody is equally dramatic, its jagged rhythms capturing the effect of speech (and eliciting from his classically minded contemporary Ben Jonson the gruff observation that "Donne, for not keeping of accent deserved hanging").

Donne began life as an outsider, and in some respects remained one until death. He was born in London in 1572 into a devout Roman Catholic household. The family was prosperous, but, as the poet later remarked, none had suffered more heavily for its loyalty to the Catholic Church: "I have been ever kept awake in a meditation of martyrdom." Donne was distantly related to the great Catholic humanist and martyr Sir Thomas More. Two of Donne's uncles, Jesuit priests, were forced to flee the realm; Donne's brother Henry, arrested for harboring a priest, died in prison of the plague. As a Catholic in Protestant England, growing up in decades when anti-Roman feeling reached new heights, Donne could not expect any kind of public career, nor could he receive a university degree (he left Oxford without one and studied law for a time at the Inns of Court). What he could reasonably expect instead was prejudice, official harassment, and crippling financial penalties. He chose not to live under such conditions. At some point in the 1590s, having returned to London after travels abroad, and having devoted some years to studying theological issues, Donne converted to the English church.

The poems that belong with certainty to this period of his life—the five satires and most of the elegies—reveal a man both fascinated by and keenly critical of English society. Four of the satires treat commonplace Elizabethan topics—foppish and obsequious courtiers, bad poets, corrupt lawyers and a corrupt court—but are unique both in their visceral revulsion and in their intellectual excitement. Donne uses striking images of pestilence, vomit, excrement, and pox to create a unique satiric world, busy, vibrant, and corrupt, in which his dramatic speakers have only to step outside the door to be inundated by all the fools and knaves in Christendom. By contrast, the third satire treats the quest for true religion—the question that preoccupied him above all others in these years—in terms that are serious, passionately witty, and deeply felt. Donne argues that honest doubting search is better than the facile acceptance of any religious tradition, epitomizing that point brilliantly in the image of Truth on a craggy hill, very difficult to climb. Society's values are of no help whatsoever to the individual seeker—none will escape the final judgment by pleading that "A Harry, or a Martin taught [them] this." In the love elegies Donne seems intent on making up for his social powerlessness through witty representations of mastery in the bedroom and of adventurous travel. In "Elegy 16" he imagines his speaker embarking on a journey "O'er the white Alps" and with mingled tenderness and condescension argues down a naive mistress's proposal to accompany him. In "Elegy 19," his fondling of a naked lover becomes in a famous conceit the equivalent of exploration in America. Donne's interest in satire and elegy—classical Roman genres, which he helped introduce to English verse—is itself significant. He wrote in English, but he reached out to other traditions.

If Donne's conversion to the Church of England promised him security, social acceptance, and the possibility of a public career, that promise was soon to be cruelly withdrawn. In 1596–97 he participated in the Earl of Essex's military expeditions against Catholic Spain in Cádiz and the Azores (the experience prompted two remarkable descriptive poems of life at sea, "The Storm" and "The Calm") and upon his return became secretary to Sir Thomas Egerton, Lord Keeper of the Great Seal. This should have been the beginning of a successful public career. But his secret marriage in 1601 to Egerton's seventeen-year-old niece Ann More enraged Donne's employer and the bride's wealthy father; Donne was briefly imprisoned and dismissed from service. The poet was reduced to a retired country life beset by financial insecurity and a rapidly increasing family; Ann bore twelve children (not counting miscarriages) by the time she died at age thirty-three. At one point, Donne wrote despairingly that while the death of a child would mean one less mouth to feed, he could not afford the burial expenses. In this bleak period, he wrote but dared not publish *Biathanatos,* a paradoxical defense of suicide.

As his family grew, Donne made every effort to reinstate himself in the favor of the great. To win the approval of James I, he penned *Pseudo-Martyr* (1610), defending the king's insistence that Catholics take the Oath of Allegiance. This set an irrevocable public stamp on his renunciation of Catholicism, and Donne followed up with a witty satire on the Jesuits, *Ignatius His Conclave* (1611). In the same period he was producing a steady stream of occasional poems for friends and patrons such as Somerset (the king's favorite), the Countess of Bedford, and Magdalen Herbert, and for small coteries of courtiers and ladies. Like most gentlemen of his era, Donne saw poetry as a polite accomplishment rather than as a trade or vocation, and in consequence he circulated his poems in manuscript but left most of them uncollected and unpublished. In 1611 and 1612, however, he published the first and second *Anniversaries* on the death of the daughter of his patron Sir Robert Drury.

For some years King James had urged an ecclesiastical career on Donne, denying him any other means of advancement. In 1615 Donne finally consented, overcoming his sense of unworthiness and the pull of other ambitions. He was ordained in the Church of England and entered upon a distinguished career as court preacher, reader in divinity at Lincoln's Inn, and dean of St. Paul's. Donne's metaphorical style, bold erudition, and dramatic wit established him as a great preacher in an age that appreciated learned sermons powerfully delivered. Some 160 of his sermons survive, preached to monarchs and courtiers, lawyers and London magistrates, city merchants and trading companies. As a distinguished clergyman in the Church of England, Donne had traveled an immense distance from the religion of his childhood and the adventurous life of his twenties. Yet in his sermons and late poems we find the same brilliant and idiosyncratic mind at work, refashioning his profane conceits to serve a new and higher purpose. In "Expostulation 19" he praises God as the greatest of literary stylists: "a figurative, a metaphorical God," imagining God as a conceit-maker like himself. In poems, meditations, and sermons, Donne came increasingly to be engaged in anxious contemplation of his own mortality. In "Hymn to God My God, in My Sickness," Donne imagines himself spread out on his deathbed like a map showing the route to the next world. Only a few days before his death he preached "Death's Duel," a terrifying analysis of all life as a decline toward death and dissolution, which contemporaries termed his own funeral sermon. On his deathbed, according to his contemporary biographer Izaak Walton,

Donne had a portrait made of himself in his shroud and meditated on it daily. Meditations upon skulls as emblems of mortality were common in the period, but nothing is more characteristic of Donne than to find a way to meditate on his own skull.

Given the shape of Donne's career, it is no surprise that his poems and prose works display an astonishing variety of attitudes, viewpoints, and feelings on the great subjects of love and religion. Yet this variety cannot be fully explained in biographical terms. The poet's own attempt to distinguish between Jack Donne, the young rake, and Dr. Donne, the grave and religious dean of St. Paul's, is (perhaps intentionally) misleading. We do not know the time and circumstances for most of Donne's verses, but it is clear that many of his finest religious poems predate his ordination, and it is possible that he continued to add to the love poems known as his "songs and sonnets" after he entered the church. Theological language abounds in his love poetry, and daringly erotic images in his religious verse.

Donne's "songs and sonnets" have been the cornerstone of his reputation almost since their publication in 1633. The title *Songs and Sonnets* associates them with the popular miscellanies of love poems and sonnet sequences in the Petrarchan tradition, but they directly challenge the popular Petrarchan sonnet sequences of the 1590s. The collection contains only one formal sonnet, the "songs" are not notably lyrical, and Donne draws upon and transforms a whole range of literary traditions concerned with love. Like Petrarch, Donne can present himself as the despairing lover of an unattainable lady ("The Funeral"); like Ovid he can be lighthearted, witty, cynical, and frankly lustful ("The Flea," "The Indifferent"); like the Neoplatonists, he espouses a theory of transcendent love, but he breaks from them with his insistence in many poems on the union of physical and spiritual love. What binds these poems together and grants them enduring power is their compelling immediacy. The speaker is always in the throes of intense emotion, and that emotion is not static but constantly shifting with the turns of the poet's thought. Donne seems supremely present in these poems, standing behind their various speakers. Where Petrarchan poets exhaustively catalogue their beloved's physical features (though in highly conventional terms), Donne's speakers tell us little or nothing about the loved woman, or about the male friends imagined as the audience for many poems. Donne's repeated insistence that the private world of lovers is superior to the wider public world, or that it somehow contains all of that world, is understandable in light of the many disappointments of his career. Yet this was also a poet who threw himself headlong into life, love, and sexuality, and later into the very visible role of court and city preacher.

Donne was long grouped with Herbert, Vaughan, Crashaw, Marvell, Traherne, and Cowley under the heading of "Metaphysical poets." The expression was first employed by critics like Samuel Johnson and William Hazlitt, who found the intricate conceits and self-conscious learning of these poets incompatible with poetic beauty and sincerity. Early in the twentieth century, T. S. Eliot sought to restore their reputation, attributing to them a unity of thought and feeling that had since their time been lost. There was, however, no formal "school" of Metaphysical poetry, and the characteristics ascribed to it by later critics pertain chiefly to Donne. Like Ben Jonson, John Donne immensely influenced the succeeding generation, but he remains a singularity.

FROM SONGS AND SONNETS[1]

The Flea[2]

Mark but this flea, and mark in this,
How little that which thou deniest me is;
Me it sucked first, and now sucks thee,
And in this flea our two bloods mingled be;
5   Thou know'st that this cannot be said
A sin, or shame, or loss of maidenhead,°   *virginity*
  Yet this enjoys before it woo,
  And pampered° swells with one blood made of two,[3]   *overfed*
And this, alas, is more than we would do.

10 Oh stay, three lives in one flea spare,
Where we almost, nay more than married are.
This flea is you and I, and this
Our marriage bed and marriage temple is;
Though parents grudge, and you, we are met,
15 And cloistered[4] in these living walls of jet.°   *black*
  Though use° make you apt to kill me,[5]   *habit*
  Let not to that, self-murder added be,
And sacrilege, three sins in killing three.

Cruel and sudden, hast thou since
20 Purpled thy nail in blood of innocence?
Wherein could this flea guilty be,
Except in that drop which it sucked from thee?
Yet thou triumph'st, and say'st that thou
Find'st not thy self nor me the weaker now;
25 'Tis true; then learn how false fears be:
Just so much honor, when thou yield'st to me,
Will waste, as this flea's death took life from thee.

1633

The Good-Morrow°   *morning greeting*

I wonder, by my troth,° what thou and I   *good faith*
Did, till we loved? Were we not weaned till then,
But sucked on country pleasures, childishly?

1, Donne's love poems were written over nearly two decades, beginning around 1595; they were not published in Donne's lifetime but circulated widely in manuscript. The title *Songs and Sonnets* was supplied in the second edition (1635), which grouped the poems by kind, but neither this arrangement nor the more haphazard organization of the first edition (1633) is Donne's own. In Donne's time the term "sonnet" often meant simply "love lyric," and in fact there is only one formal sonnet in this collection. For the poems we present we follow the 1635 edition, beginning with the extremely popular poem "The Flea."
2. This insect afforded a popular erotic theme for poets all over Europe, deriving from a pseudo-Ovidian medieval poem in which a lover envies the flea for the liberties it takes with his mistress's body.
3. The swelling suggests pregnancy.
4. As in a convent or monastery.
5. By denying me sexual gratification.

Or snorted° we in the seven sleepers' den?[1]   *snored*
5   'Twas so; but° this, all pleasures fancies be.   *except for*
If ever any beauty I did see,
Which I desired, and got, 'twas but a dream of thee.

And now good morrow to our waking souls,
Which watch not one another out of fear;
10   For love all love of other sights controls,
And makes one little room an everywhere.
Let sea-discoverers to new worlds have gone,
Let maps to others, worlds on worlds have shown:
Let us possess one world;[2] each hath one, and is one.

15   My face in thine eye, thine in mine appears,
And true plain hearts do in the faces rest;
Where can we find two better hemispheres,
Without sharp North, without declining West?
Whatever dies was not mixed equally;[3]
20   If our two loves be one, or thou and I
Love so alike that none do slacken, none can die.

                                                            1633

Song

Go and catch a falling star,
    Get with child a mandrake root,[1]
Tell me where all past years are,
    Or who cleft the Devil's foot,
5   Teach me to hear mermaids° singing,   *sirens*
Or to keep off envy's stinging,
        And find
        What wind
Serves to advance an honest mind.

10   If thou beest born to strange sights,
        Things invisible to see,
Ride ten thousand days and nights,
        Till age snow white hairs on thee,
Thou, when thou return'st, wilt tell me
15   All strange wonders that befell thee,
        And swear
        No where
Lives a woman true, and fair.

1. Cave in Ephesus where, according to legend,
seven Christian youths hid from pagan persecutors and slept for 187 years.
2. "Our world" in many manuscripts.
3. Scholastic philosophy taught that when the
elements were imperfectly mixed ("not mixed
equally"), matter was mutable and mortal; conversely, when the elements were perfectly mixed,
matter was immutable and hence immortal.
1. The mandrake root, or mandragora, is forked
like the lower part of the human body. It was
thought to shriek when pulled from the ground
and to kill all humans who heard it; it was also
(paradoxically) thought to help women conceive.

If thou find'st one, let me know,
20   Such a pilgrimage were sweet;
Yet do not, I would not go,
      Though at next door we might meet;
Though she were true when you met her,
And last till you write your letter,
25   Yet she
          Will be
False, ere I come, to two, or three.

1633

The Undertaking

I have done one braver° thing   *more glorious*
      Than all the Worthies[1] did,
And yet a braver thence doth spring,
      Which is, to keep that hid.

5   It were but madness now t' impart
      The skill of specular stone,[2]
When he which can have learned the art
      To cut it, can find none.

So, if I now should utter this,
10   Others (because no more
Such stuff to work upon, there is)
      Would love but as before.

But he who loveliness within
      Hath found, all outward loathes,
15   For he who color loves, and skin,
      Loves but their oldest clothes.

If, as I have, you also do
      Virtue attired in woman see,
And dare love that, and say so too,
20   And forget the He and She;

And if this love, though placèd so,
      From profane men you hide,
Which will no faith on this bestow,
      Or, if they do, deride;

1. According to medieval legend, the Nine Worthies, or supreme heroes of history, included three Jews (Joshua, David, Judas Maccabaeus), three pagans (Hector, Alexander, Julius Caesar), and three Christians (Arthur, Charlemagne, Godfrey of Boulogne).
2. A transparent or translucent material, reputed to have been used in antiquity for windows, but no longer known. Great skill was needed to cut it.

25 Then you have done a braver thing
Than all the Worthies did;
And a braver thence will spring,
Which is, to keep that hid.

1633

The Sun Rising

Busy old fool, unruly sun,
Why dost thou thus
Through windows and through curtains call on us?
Must to thy motions lovers' seasons run?
5 Saucy pedantic wretch, go chide
Late schoolboys and sour prentices,
Go tell court huntsmen that the king will ride,[1]
Call country ants to harvest offices;[2]
Love, all alike, no season knows nor clime,
10 Nor hours, days, months, which are the rags of time.

Thy beams, so reverend and strong
Why shouldst thou think?
I could eclipse and cloud them with a wink,
But that I would not lose her sight so long;
15 If her eyes have not blinded thine,
Look, and tomorrow late, tell me,
Whether both th' Indias of spice and mine[3]
Be where thou leftst them, or lie here with me.
Ask for those kings whom thou saw'st yesterday,
20 And thou shalt hear, All here in one bed lay.

She is all states,° and all princes I,   *nations*
Nothing else is.
Princes do but play us; compared to this,
All honor's mimic, all wealth alchemy.
25 Thou, sun, art half as happy as we,
In that the world's contracted thus;
Thine age asks ease, and since thy duties be
To warm the world, that's done in warming us.
Shine here to us, and thou art everywhere;
30 This bed thy center is, these walls thy sphere.[4]

1633

---

1. King James was very fond of hunting.
2. Autumn chores. "Country ants": farm drudges.
3. The India of "spice" is the East Indies; that of "mine" (gold), the West Indies.

4. According to the old Ptolemaic astronomy, the earth was the center of the sun's orbit, and the sun's motion was contained within its sphere.

The Indifferent

I can love both fair and brown,[1]
Her whom abundance melts, and her whom want betrays,
Her who loves loneness best, and her who masks and plays,
Her whom the country formed, and whom the town,
5 Her who believes, and her who tries,°   *tests*
Her who still° weeps with spongy eyes,   *always*
And her who is dry cork, and never cries;
I can love her, and her, and you, and you,
I can love any, so she be not true.

10 Will no other vice content you?
Will it not serve your turn to do as did your mothers?
Or have you all old vices spent, and now would find out others?
Or doth a fear that men are true torment you?
O we are not, be not you so;
15 Let me, and do you, twenty know.
Rob me, but bind me not, and let me go.
Must I, who came to travail thorough[2] you,
Grow your fixed subject, because you are true?

Venus heard me sigh this song,
20 And by love's sweetest part, variety, she swore,
She heard not this till now; and that it should be so no more.
She went, examined, and returned ere long,
And said, Alas, some two or three
Poor heretics in love there be,
25 Which think to 'stablish dangerous constancy.
But I have told them, Since you will be true,
You shall be true to them who are false to you.

               1633

The Canonization[1]

For God's sake hold your tongue, and let me love,
 Or chide my palsy, or my gout,
My five gray hairs, or ruined fortune, flout,
 With wealth your state, your mind with arts improve,
5 Take you a course, get you a place,[2]
  Observe His Honor, or His Grace,[3]
Or the king's real, or his stampèd face[4]
 Contemplate; what you will, approve,°   *try, test*
  So you will let me love.

1. Both blonde and brunette.
2. Through. "Travail": grief.
1. The poem plays off against the Roman Catholic process of determining that certain persons are saints, proper objects of veneration and prayer.

2. An appointment, at court or elsewhere. "Take you a course": follow some career.
3. Pay court to some lord or bishop.
4. On coins; "real" (royal) refers also to a particular Spanish coin.

10   Alas, alas, who's injured by my love?
        What merchant's ships have my sighs drowned?
    Who says my tears have overflowed his ground?
        When did my colds a forward° spring remove?[5]   *early*
        When did the heats which my veins fill
15   Add one man to the plaguy bill?[6]
    Soldiers find wars, and lawyers find out still
        Litigious men, which quarrels move,
        Though she and I do love.

    Call us what you will, we are made such by love;
20   Call her one, me another fly,
    We're tapers too, and at our own cost die,[7]
    And we in us find the eagle and the dove.
        The phoenix riddle hath more wit
        By us: we two being one, are it.[8]
25   So, to one neutral thing both sexes fit.
        We die and rise the same, and prove
        Mysterious by this love.

    We can die by it, if not live by love,
        And if unfit for tombs and hearse
30   Our legend be, it will be fit for verse;
        And if no piece of chronicle we prove,
        We'll build in sonnets pretty rooms;[9]
        As well a well-wrought urn becomes°   *befits*
    The greatest ashes, as half-acre tombs,
35   And by these hymns,[1] all shall approve°   *confirm*
        Us canonized for love:

    And thus invoke us: You whom reverend love
        Made one another's hermitage;
    You, to whom love was peace, that now is rage;
40   Who did the whole world's soul contract,[2] and drove
        Into the glasses of your eyes
        (So made such mirrors, and such spies,°   *spyglasses, telescopes*
    That they did all to you epitomize)
        Countries, towns, courts:[3] Beg from above
45   A pattern of your love!

                                        1633

---

5. Petrarchan lovers traditionally sigh, weep, and are frozen because of their mistresses' neglect.
6. Deaths from the plague, which raged in summer, were recorded by parish in weekly lists.
7. Flies were emblems of transience and lustfulness; tapers (candles) attract flies to their death and also consume themselves. "Die" in the punning terminology of the period means to experience orgasm, and there was a superstition that intercourse shortened life.
8. The eagle signifies strength and vision; the dove, meekness and mercy. The phoenix was a mythic Arabian bird, only one of which existed at any one time. After living five hundred years, it was consumed by fire, then rose triumphantly from its ashes a new bird. Thus it was a symbol of immortality and sometimes associated with Christ. "Eagle" and "dove" are also alchemical terms for processes leading to the rise of "phoenix," a stage in the transmutation of metals to gold.
9. "Rooms" (punning on the Italian meaning of "stanza") will contain their exploits, as prose chronicle histories contain great deeds done in the world.
1. The lover's own poems.
2. An alternative meaning is "extract."
3. "Countries, towns, courts" are objects of the verb "drove." The notion is that eyes both see and reflect the outside world, and so can contain all of it.

Air and Angels

Twice or thrice had I loved thee,
Before I knew thy face or name;
So in a voice, so in a shapeless flame,
Angels affect us oft, and worshipped be;
5   Still° when, to where thou wert, I came,   *always*
Some lovely glorious nothing[1] I did see.
    But since my soul, whose child love is,
Takes limbs of flesh, and else could nothing do,[2]
    More subtle° than the parent is   *rarefied*
10 Love must not be, but take a body too;
    And therefore what thou wert, and who,
      I bid love ask, and now
That it assume thy body I allow,
And fix itself in thy lip, eye, and brow.
15 Whilst thus to ballast love I thought,
    And so more steadily to have gone,
With wares which would sink° admiration,   *overwhelm*
I saw I had love's pinnace° overfraught;°   *small boat / overloaded*
    Every thy hair for love to work upon
20 Is much too much, some fitter must be sought;
    For, nor in nothing, nor in things
Extreme and scatt'ring° bright, can love inhere.   *dazzling*
    Then as an angel, face and wings
Of air, not pure as it, yet pure doth wear,[3]
25   So thy love may be my love's sphere;[4]
      Just such disparity
As is 'twixt air and angels' purity,
'Twixt women's love and men's will ever be.

                  1633

Break of Day[1]

'Tis true, 'tis day; what though it be?
O wilt thou therefore rise from me?
Why should we rise because 'tis light?
Did we lie down because 'twas night?
5 Love, which in spite of darkness brought us hither,
Should in despite of light keep us together.

---

1. Spiritual beauty, the true object of love in Neoplatonic philosophy.
2. My soul could not function unless it were in a body.
3. It was commonly believed that angels, when they appeared to humans, assumed a body of air which, though pure, was less so than the angel's spiritual essence.

4. Each sphere in the cosmos was thought to be governed by an angel (an intelligence).
1. An aubade, or song of the lovers' parting at dawn, this poem is unusual for Donne in having a female speaker. The poem was given a musical setting and published in 1622, in William Corkine's *Second Book of Ayers*.

Light hath no tongue, but is all eye;
If it could speak as well as spy,
This were the worst that it could say,
10   That being well, I fain° would stay,   gladly
And that I loved my heart and honor so
That I would not from him, that had them, go.

Must business thee from hence remove?
O, that's the worst disease of love.
15   The poor, the foul, the false, love can
Admit, but not the busied man.
He which hath business, and makes love, doth do
Such wrong, as when a married man doth woo.

                                                        1622, 1633

A Valediction:[1] Of Weeping

Let me pour forth
My tears before thy face whilst I stay here,
For thy face coins them, and thy stamp° they bear,   image
And by this mintage they are something worth,
5   For thus they be
         Pregnant of thee;
Fruits of much grief they are, emblems° of more—   symbols
When a tear falls, that thou falls which it bore,
So thou and I are nothing then, when on a diverse° shore.   different

10   On a round ball
A workman that hath copies by can lay
An Europe, Afric, and an Asia,
And quickly make that, which was nothing, all;[2]
         So doth each tear
15   Which thee doth wear,[3]
A globe, yea world, by that impression grow,
Till thy tears mixed with mine do overflow
This world; by waters sent from thee, my heaven dissolvèd so.

         O more than moon,
20   Draw not up seas to drown me in thy sphere;[4]
Weep me not dead in thine arms, but forbear
To teach the sea what it may do too soon.
         Let not the wind
         Example find
25   To do me more harm than it purposeth;
Since thou and I sigh one another's breath,
Whoe'er sighs most is cruelest, and hastes the other's death.

                                                              1633

1. A farewell poem, one of four so titled in the
Songs and Sonnets. Another is "A Valediction:
Forbidding Mourning," pp. 679–80.
2. I.e., on a blank globe one can place maps of
the continents and so convert "nothing" into the
whole world ("all").
3. Which bears your image.
4. A star or planet with more power of attraction
than the moon might not only affect tides but
draw the very seas unto itself.

Love's Alchemy

Some that have deeper digged love's mine than I,
Say where his centric° happiness doth lie: *central*
    I have loved, and got, and told,
But should I love, get, tell, till I were old,
5   I should not find that hidden mystery;
     O, 'tis imposture all:
And as no chemic° yet the elixir[1] got,   *alchemist*
    But glorifies his pregnant pot[2]
    If by the way to him befall
10 Some odoriferous thing, or medicinal;
    So lovers dream a rich and long delight,
    But get a winter-seeming summer's night.[3]

Our ease, our thrift, our honor, and our day,
Shall we for this vain bubble's shadow pay?
15   Ends love in this, that my man°   *servant*
Can be as happy as I can, if he can
Endure the short scorn of a bridegroom's play?
    That loving wretch that swears
'Tis not the bodies marry, but the minds,
20   Which he in her angelic finds,
    Would swear as justly that he hears,
In that day's rude hoarse minstrelsy, the spheres.[4]
   Hope not for mind in women; at their best
Sweetness and wit, they are but mummy, possessed.[5]

1633

A Nocturnal upon Saint Lucy's Day, Being the Shortest Day[1]

'Tis the year's midnight and it is the day's,
Lucy's, who scarce seven hours herself unmasks;
   The sun is spent, and now his flasks[2]
   Send forth light squibs,° no constant rays.   *small fireworks*
5   The world's whole sap is sunk;
   The general balm th' hydroptic[3] earth hath drunk,

1. A magic medicine sought by alchemists and reputed to heal all ills.
2. A fertile (and womb-shaped) retort, calling up the common analogy between producing the elixir of life and human generation.
3. A night cold as in winter and short as in summer.
4. The perfect harmony of the planets, moving in concentric crystalline "spheres," is contrasted with the boisterous serenade of pots, pans, and trumpets performed on the wedding night.
5. The syntax of the last two lines is unclear, and they are punctuated differently in various copies. The 1633 edition reads: "at their best, / Sweetnesse, and wit they'are, but, *mummy*, possesst." Many modern editors punctuate as we do

here. "Mummy" suggests a corpselike body, without mind or spirit.
1. The nocturne, or night office of the Roman Catholic Church, is a service held in the primitive church at midnight. St. Lucy's Day fell on December 13 according to the old calendar still in use in England at the time, and its vigil (the previous day and night) was the winter solstice, the shortest day of the year. At this time of the year, the sun rises after 8 A.M. in the latitude of London and sets well before 4 P.M.
2. The stars are "flasks," thought to store up light from the sun.
3. Dropsical, thus insatiably thirsty. "General balm": the supposedly life-preserving essence of all things.

Whither, as to the bed's feet, life is shrunk,
Dead and interred; yet all these seem to laugh,
Compared with me, who am their epitaph.

10   Study me, then, you who shall lovers be
At the next world, that is, at the next spring;
    For I am every dead thing
    In whom love wrought new alchemy.
      For his art did express°   *extract*
15   A quintessence[4] even from nothingness,
From dull privations and lean emptiness.
He ruined me, and I am re-begot
Of absence, darkness, death: things which are not.

All others from all things draw all that's good,
20   Life, soul, form, spirit, whence they being have;
    I, by love's limbeck,[5] am the grave
    Of all that's nothing. Oft a flood
      Have we two wept, and so
Drowned the whole world, us two; oft did we grow
25   To be two chaoses when we did show
Care to aught° else; and often absences   *anything*
Withdrew our souls, and made us carcasses.

But I am by her death (which word wrongs her)
Of the first nothing the elixir grown;[6]
30   Were I a man, that I were one
    I needs must know; I should prefer,
      If I were any beast,
Some ends, some means; yea plants, yea stones detest
And love.[7] All, all some properties invest.
35   If I an ordinary nothing were,
As shadow, a light and body must be here.

But I am none; nor will my sun renew.
You lovers, for whose sake the lesser sun
    At this time to the Goat[8] is run
40   To fetch new lust and give it you,
      Enjoy your summer all.
Since she enjoys her long night's festival,
Let me prepare towards her, and let me call
This hour her vigil and her eve, since this
45   Both the year's and the day's deep midnight is.

1633

4. The reputed fifth essence, a celestial element beyond the mundane four elements (earth, water, air, fire), thought to be latent in all things and to be a universal cure. Alchemists sought to extract it.
5. Alembic; a vessel used in distilling.
6. I.e., the quintessence of that absolute noth-ingness that existed before the creation.
7. Beasts have intentions; plants and even stones (like lodestones) have attractions and antipathies.
8. The sign of Capricorn, which the sun enters at the winter solstice; the goat is an emblem of sexual vigor.

The Apparition

When by thy scorn, O murderess, I am dead,
    And that thou thinkst thee free
    From all solicitation from me,
Then shall my ghost come to thy bed,
5   And thee, feigned vestal,[1] in worse arms shall see;
Then thy sick taper will begin to wink,°   *flicker*
And he whose thou art then, being tired before,
Will, if thou stir, or pinch to wake him, think
        Thou call'st for more,
10 And in false sleep will from thee shrink,
And then, poor aspen wretch,[2] neglected thou
Bathed in a cold quicksilver sweat[3] wilt lie
    A verier° ghost than I;   *truer*
What I will say, I will not tell thee now,
15 Lest that preserve thee; and since my love is spent,
I had rather thou shouldst painfully repent,
Than by my threatenings rest still innocent.

                                      1633

A Valediction: Forbidding Mourning[1]

As virtuous men pass mildly away,
    And whisper to their souls to go,
Whilst some of their sad friends do say
    The breath goes now, and some say, No;

5 So let us melt, and make no noise,
    No tear-floods, nor sigh-tempests move;
'Twere profanation° of our joys   *desecration*
    To tell the laity our love.

Moving of th' earth brings harms and fears,
10   Men reckon what it did and meant;
But trepidation of the spheres,
    Though greater far, is innocent.[2]

Dull sublunary[3] lovers' love
    (Whose soul is sense) cannot admit

---

1. Virgins consecrated to the Roman goddess Vesta.
2. Aspen leaves flutter in the slightest breeze.
3. Sweating in terror; quicksilver (mercury) was a stock prescription for venereal disease, and sweating was part of the cure.
1. For "valediction" see p. 676, n. 1. Izaak Walton speculated that this poem was addressed to Donne's wife on the occasion of his trip to the Continent in 1611, but there is no proof of that.
2. Earthquakes cause damage and were thought to be portentous. "Trepidation" (in the Ptolemaic cosmology) is an oscillation of the ninth or crystalline sphere imparted to all the inner spheres. Though a much more violent motion than an earthquake, it is neither destructive nor sinister.
3. Beneath the moon, therefore earthly, sensual, and subject to change.

15   Absence, because it doth remove
      Those things which elemented° it.   *composed*

But we, by a love so much refined
    That ourselves know not what it is,
Inter-assurèd of the mind,
20   Care less, eyes, lips, and hands to miss.

Our two souls therefore, which are one,
    Though I must go, endure not yet
A breach, but an expansion,
    Like gold to airy thinness beat.

25   If they be two, they are two so
      As stiff twin compasses[4] are two;
Thy soul, the fixed foot, makes no show
    To move, but doth, if th' other do.

And though it in the center sit,
30   Yet when the other far doth roam,
It leans and hearkens after it,
    And grows erect, as that comes home.

Such wilt thou be to me, who must,
    Like th' other foot, obliquely run;
35   Thy firmness makes my circle just,
    And makes me end where I begun.

1633

The Ecstasy[1]

Where, like a pillow on a bed,
    A pregnant bank swelled up to rest
The violet's reclining head,
    Sat we two, one another's best.

5   Our hands were firmly cemented
      With a fast balm° which thence did spring,   *perspiration*
Our eye-beams[2] twisted, and did thread
    Our eyes upon one double string;

So to intergraft our hands, as yet
10   Was all our means to make us one,
And pictures in our eyes[3] to get°   *beget*
    Was all our propagation.

4. The two legs of a geometer's or draftsman's compass.
1. From *ekstasis* (Greek), a movement of the soul outside of the body.
2. Invisible shafts of light, thought of as going out of the eyes and thereby enabling one to see things.
3. Reflections of each in the other's eyes, often called "making babies."

As 'twixt two equal armies Fate
   Suspends uncertain victory,
15 Our souls (which to advance their state
   Were gone out) hung 'twixt her and me;

And whilst our souls negotiate there,
   We like sepulchral statues lay;
All day the same our postures were,
20   And we said nothing all the day.

If any, so by love refined
   That he soul's language understood,
And by good love were grown all mind,
   Within convenient distance stood,

25 He (though he knew not which soul spake,
   Because both meant, both spake the same)
Might thence a new concoction[4] take,
   And part far purer than he came.

This ecstasy doth unperplex,
30   We said, and tell us what we love;
We see by this it was not sex;
   We see we saw not what did move;°   *motivate us*

But as all several° souls contain   *separate*
   Mixture of things, they know not what,
35 Love these mixed souls doth mix again,
   And makes both one, each this and that.

A single violet transplant,
   The strength, the color, and the size
(All which before was poor and scant)
40   Redoubles still,° and multiplies.   *continually*

When love with one another so
   Interinanimates two souls,
That abler soul, which thence doth flow,
   Defects of loneliness controls.

45 We then, who are this new soul, know
   Of what we are composed and made,
For th' atomies° of which we grow   *components*
   Are souls, whom no change can invade.

But O alas, so long, so far
50   Our bodies why do we forbear?
They are ours, though they are not we; we are
   The intelligences, they the sphere.[5]

---

4. In the alchemical sense of sublimation or purification.
5. In Ptolemaic astronomy, each planet, set in a transparent "sphere" that revolved and so carried it around the earth, was inhabited by a controlling angelic "intelligence."

We owe them thanks because they thus
  Did us to us at first convey,
55 Yielded their forces, sense, to us,
  Nor are dross to us, but allay.[6]

On man heaven's influence works not so
  But that it first imprints the air:[7]
So soul into the soul may flow,
60 Though it to body first repair.°   *go*

As our blood labors to beget
  Spirits[8] as like souls as it can,
Because such fingers need° to knit   *are needed*
  That subtle knot which makes us man,

65 So must pure lovers' souls descend
  T' affections, and to faculties
Which sense may reach and apprehend;
  Else a great prince in prison lies.

To our bodies turn we then, that so
70 Weak men on love revealed may look;
Love's mysteries[9] in souls do grow,
  But yet the body is his book.

And if some lover, such as we,
  Have heard this dialogue of one,[1]
75 Let him still mark° us; he shall see   *observe*
  Small change when we are to bodies gone.

                                    1633

The Funeral

Whoever comes to shroud me, do not harm
  Nor question much
That subtle wreath of hair which crowns my arm;
The mystery, the sign you must not touch,
5   For 'tis my outward soul,
Viceroy to that, which then to heaven being gone,
  Will leave this to control,
And keep these limbs, her[1] provinces, from dissolution.

For if the sinewy thread[2] my brain lets fall
10   Through every part

---

6. "Dross" is an impurity that weakens metal; "allay" (alloy) strengthens it.
7. Astrological influences were thought to work on people through the medium of the surrounding air.
8. Subtle substances thought to be produced by the blood to serve as intermediaries between body and soul.

9. The implied comparison is with God's mysteries, which are revealed and may be read in the book of Nature and the book of Scripture.
1. "Dialogue of one" because "both meant, both spake the same" (line 26).
1. The soul's, but also the mistress's (cf. "she," line 14).
2. The nervous system.

Can tie those parts and make me one of all,
These hairs which upward grew, and strength and art
    Have from a better brain,
Can better do it; except° she meant that I   *unless*
15   By this should know my pain,
As prisoners then are manacled, when they're condemned to die.

Whate'er she meant by it, bury it with me,
    For since I am
Love's martyr, it might breed idolatry,
20   If into others' hands these relics[3] came:
    As 'twas humility
To afford to it all that a soul can do,
    So 'tis some bravery,
That since you would save[4] none of me, I bury some of you.

                                        1633

The Relic

When my grave is broke up again
Some second guest to entertain
(For graves have learned that woman-head°   *female trait*
To be to more than one a bed),[1]
5   And he that digs it spies
A bracelet of bright hair about the bone,
    Will he not let us alone,
And think that there a loving couple lies,
Who thought that this device might be some way
10 To make their souls, at the last busy day,°   *Judgment Day*
Meet at this grave, and make a little stay?

If this fall° in a time, or land,   *happen*
Where mis-devotion[2] doth command,
Then he that digs us up will bring
15   Us to the bishop and the king,
    To make us relics; then
Thou shalt be a Mary Magdalen, and I
    A something else thereby;
All women shall adore us, and some men;
20 And since at such times, miracles are sought,
I would have that age by this paper taught
What miracles we harmless lovers wrought.

    First, we loved well and faithfully,
    Yet knew not what we loved, nor why,

3. Body parts or other objects belonging to a saint, venerated by Roman Catholics.
4. All the early printed texts read "have" (which carries sexual connotations), while many manuscripts read "save."

1. Graves were often used to inter successive corpses, the bones of previous occupants being deposited in charnel houses.
2. False devotion, superstition, i.e., Roman Catholicism.

25   Difference of sex no more we knew,
        Than our guardian angels do;
          Coming and going, we
      Perchance might kiss, but not between those meals;[3]
        Our hands ne'er touched the seals°   *sexual organs*
30 Which nature, injured by late law, sets free:[4]
      These miracles we did: but now, alas,
      All measure and all language I should pass,
      Should I tell what a miracle she was.

                                                                                  1633

_____

Elegy[1] 16. On His Mistress

        By our first strange and fatal interview,
        By all desires which thereof did ensue,
        By our long starving hopes, by that remorse°   *pity*
        Which my words' masculine persuasive force
5   Begot in thee, and by the memory
        Of hurts which spies and rivals threatened me,
        I calmly beg; but by thy father's wrath,
        By all pains which want and divorcement hath,
        I conjure thee; and all the oaths which I
10   And thou have sworn to seal joint constancy
        Here I unswear and overswear them thus:
        Thou shalt not love by ways so dangerous.
        Temper, oh fair love, love's impetuous rage;
        Be my true mistress still, not my feigned page.[2]
15   I'll go, and, by thy kind leave, leave behind
        Thee, only worthy to nurse in my mind
        Thirst to come back. Oh, if thou die before,
        My soul from other lands to thee shall soar.
        Thy (else almighty) beauty cannot move
20   Rage from the seas, nor thy love teach them love,
        Nor tame wild Boreas' harshness.[3] Thou hast read
        How roughly he in pieces shiverèd
        Fair Orithea, whom he swore he loved.
        Fall ill or good, 'tis madness to have proved°   *sought out*
25   Dangers unurged; feed on this flattery,
        That absent lovers one in th' other be.
        Dissemble nothing, not a boy, nor change
        Thy body's habit,° nor mind's; be not strange   *clothing*
        To thyself only; all will spy in thy face

_____

3. The kisses of salutation and parting.
4. Human law forbids the free love permitted by
nature. "Late": recent (comparatively speaking).
1. In Latin poetry, an elegy is a discursive or
reflective poem written in "elegiacs" (unrhymed
couplets of alternating dactylic hexameters and
pentameters). This meter was used for funeral
laments and especially for love poetry. The most
famous classical elegist was the Roman poet
Ovid; his *Amores*, a collection of witty and sen-

sual love poems, deeply influenced Donne's erotic
poetry.
2. The speaker's mistress wanted to accompany
him abroad, disguised as a page boy. Such esca-
pades occasionally took place in real life; in 1605,
Elizabeth Southwell, disguised as a page, went
abroad with Sir Robert Dudley.
3. God of the north wind; in *Metamorphoses* 6
Ovid describes the wild force with which Boreas
abducted Orithea.

A blushing womanly discovering grace.
Richly clothed apes are called apes, and as soon
Eclipsed as bright we call the moon the moon.
Men of France, changeable chameleons,
Spitals° of diseases, shops of fashions,   *hospitals*
35 Love's fuelers[4] and the rightest company
Of players which upon the world's stage be,
Will quickly know thee, and know thee; and alas![5]
Th' indifferent° Italian, as we pass   *bisexual*
His warm land, well content to think thee page,
40 Will hunt thee with such lust and hideous rage
As Lot's fair guests were vexed.[6] But none of these
Nor spongy, hydroptic[7] Dutch shall thee displease
If thou stay here. O stay here, for, for thee,
England is only a worthy gallery
45 To walk in expectation, till from thence
Our greatest king call thee to his presence.[8]
When I am gone, dream me some happiness,
Nor let thy looks our long-hid love confess;
Nor praise nor dispraise me, bless nor curse
50 Openly love's force, nor in bed fright thy nurse
With midnight's startings, crying out "Oh, oh!
Nurse, oh my love is slain, I saw him go
O'er the white Alps alone; I saw him, I,
Assailed, fight, taken, stabbed, bleed, fall, and die."
55 Augur me better chance, except dread Jove
Think it enough for me t' have had thy love.

1635

Elegy 19. To His Mistress Going to Bed

Come, Madam, come, all rest my powers defy,
Until I labor, I in labor lie.[1]
The foe ofttimes having the foe in sight,
Is tired with standing though he never fight.
5 Off with that girdle,° like heaven's zone° glistering,   *belt / zodiac*
But a far fairer world encompassing.
Unpin that spangled breastplate[2] which you wear
That th' eyes of busy fools may be stopped there.
Unlace yourself, for that harmonious chime
10 Tells me from you that now it is bed-time.
Off with that happy busk,° which I envy,   *bodice*
That still° can be and still can stand so nigh.   *always*

---

4. Providers of aphrodisiacs.
5. May pun on "a lass." "Know": in the sexual sense.
6. The inhabitants of Sodom tried to rape two angels who visited Lot in the guise of men to warn the city's impending destruction (Genesis 19.1–11).
7. Dropsical, thus insatiably thirsty.

8. Throne rooms commonly had antechambers (galleries) where visitors waited until the monarch was ready to see them.
1. "Labor" in the dual sense of "get to work (sexually)" and "distress."
2. The stomacher, an ornamental, often jeweled, covering for the chest, worn under the lacing of the bodice.

Your gown going off, such beauteous state reveals
As when from flowery meads th' hill's shadow steals.
15 Off with that wiry coronet and show
The hairy diadem which on you doth grow;
Now off with those shoes, and then safely tread
In this love's hallowed temple, this soft bed.
In such white robes, heaven's angels used to be
20 Received by men; thou, angel, bring'st with thee
A heaven like Mahomet's paradise;[3] and though
Ill spirits walk in white, we easily know
By this these angels from an evil sprite,
Those set our hairs, but these our flesh upright.
25 License my roving hands, and let them go
Before, behind, between, above, below.
O my America! my new-found-land,
My kingdom, safeliest when with one man manned,
My mine of precious stones, my empery,°   empire
30 How blest am I in this discovering thee!
To enter in these bonds is to be free;
There where my hand is set, my seal shall be.[4]
Full nakedness! All joys are due to thee.
As souls unbodied, bodies unclothed must be,
35 To taste whole joys. Gems which you women use
Are like Atalanta's balls,[5] cast in men's views,
That when a fool's eye lighteth on a gem,
His earthly soul may covet theirs, not them.
Like pictures, or like books' gay coverings, made
40 For laymen, are all women thus arrayed;
Themselves are mystic books, which only we
(Whom their imputed grace will dignify)
Must see revealed.[6] Then since that I may know,
As liberally as to a midwife show
45 Thyself: cast all, yea, this white linen hence,
Here is no penance, much less innocence.[7]
To teach thee, I am naked first; why then
What need'st thou have more covering than a man?

1669

Satire 3   In satire the author holds a subject up to ridicule. Like his elegies, Donne's five verse satires were written in his twenties and are in the forefront of an effort in the 1590s (by Donne, Ben Jonson, Joseph Hall, and John Marston) to naturalize those classical forms in England. While elements of satire figure in many different kinds of literature, the great models for formal verse satire were the Roman

3. A place of sensual pleasure, thought to be populated by seductive houris for the delectation of the faithful.
4. The jokes mingle law with sex: where he has signed a document (placed his hand) he will now place his seal; and in the bonds of her arms he will find freedom.
5. Atalanta, running a race against her suitor Hippomenes, was beaten when he dropped golden apples ("balls") for her to pick up. Donne reverses the story.

6. By granting favors to their lovers, women impute to them grace that they don't deserve, as God, in Calvinist doctrine, imputes grace to undeserving sinners. Laymen can only look at the covers of mystic books (clothed women), but "we" elect can read them (see women naked).
7. Some manuscripts read: "There is no penance due to innocence." White garments would be appropriate either for the innocent virgin or for the sinner doing formal penance.

poets Horace and Juvenal, the former for an urbanely witty style, the latter for an indignant or angry manner. While Donne's other satires call on these models, his third satire more nearly resembles those of a third Roman satirist, Persius, known for an abstruse style and moralizing manner. This work is a strenuous discussion of an acute theological problem, for the age and for Donne himself: How may one discover the true Christian church among so many claimants to that role? At the time Donne wrote "Satire 3," he was in the process of leaving the Roman Catholic Church of his heritage for the Church of England.

Satire 3

Kind pity chokes my spleen;[1] brave° scorn forbids   *defiant*
Those tears to issue which swell my eyelids;
I must not laugh, nor weep° sins, and be wise: *lament*
Can railing then cure these worn maladies?
5   Is not our mistress, fair Religion,
As worthy of all our souls' devotion
As virtue was to the first blinded age?[2]
Are not heaven's joys as valiant to assuage
Lusts, as earth's honor was to them?° Alas,   *pagans*
10   As we do them in means, shall they surpass
Us in the end, and shall thy father's spirit
Meet blind philosophers in heaven, whose merit
Of strict life may be imputed faith,[3] and hear
Thee, whom he taught so easy ways and near
15   To follow, damned? O, if thou dar'st, fear this;
This fear great courage and high valor is.
Dar'st thou aid mutinous Dutch,[4] and dar'st thou lay
Thee in ships, wooden sepulchers, a prey
To leaders' rage, to storms, to shot, to dearth?°   *famine*
20   Dar'st thou dive seas and dungeons° of the earth?   *mines, caves*
Hast thou courageous fire to thaw the ice
Of frozen north discoveries?[5] And thrice
Colder than salamanders, like divine
Children in the oven,[6] fires of Spain and the line,
25   Whose countries limbecks to our bodies be,
Canst thou for gain bear?[7] And must every he
Which cries not "Goddess!" to thy mistress, draw,°   *fight a duel*
Or eat thy poisonous words? Courage of straw!
O desperate coward, wilt thou seem bold, and
30   To thy foes and His° (who made thee to stand   *God's*
Sentinel in his world's garrison) thus yield,

1. The seat of bile, hence scorn and ridicule.
2. The age of paganism, blind to Christianity but capable of natural morality ("virtue").
3. Donne's formulation wittily turns on its head the key concept of Protestant theology—that salvation is to be achieved only by imputing Christ's merits to Christians through faith—by suggesting that virtuous pagans might be saved by imputing faith to them on the basis of their moral life.
4. English volunteers took frequent part with the Dutch in their wars against Spain. Donne himself had sailed in two raiding expeditions against the

Spanish.
5. Many explorers tried to find a northwest passage to the Pacific.
6. In the biblical story (Daniel 3), Shadrach, Meshach, and Abednego were rescued from a fiery furnace. The salamander (a lizardlike creature) was thought to be so cold-blooded that it could live in fire.
7. The object of "bear" is "fires of Spain and the line"—inquisitorial and equatorial heats, which roast people as chemists heat materials in "limbecks" (alembics, or vessels for distilling).

And for forbidden wars leave th' appointed field?[8]
Know thy foes: The foul Devil (whom thou
Strivest to please) for hate, not love, would allow
35 Thee fain° his whole realm to be quit;° and as   *gladly / to satisfy you*
The world's all parts wither away and pass,[9]
So the world's self, thy other loved foe, is
In her decrepit wane, and thou, loving this,
Dost love a withered and worn strumpet; last,
40 Flesh (itself's death) and joys which flesh can taste
Thou lovest; and thy fair goodly soul, which doth
Give this flesh power to taste joy, thou dost loathe.
Seek true religion. O, where? Mirreus,[1]
Thinking her unhoused here, and fled from us,
45 Seeks her at Rome; there, because he doth know
That she was there a thousand years ago.
He loves her rags so, as we here obey
The statecloth[2] where the prince sat yesterday.
Crantz to such brave loves will not be enthralled,
50 But loves her only, who at Geneva is called
Religion—plain, simple, sullen, young,
Contemptuous, yet unhandsome; as among
Lecherous humors,° there is one that judges   *temperaments*
No wenches wholesome but coarse country drudges.
55 Graius stays still at home here, and because
Some preachers, vile ambitious bawds, and laws
Still new, like fashions, bid him think that she
Which dwells with us is only perfect, he
Embraceth her whom his godfathers will
60 Tender to him, being tender, as wards still
Take such wives as their guardians offer, or
Pay values.[3] Careless Phrygius doth abhor
All, because all cannot be good, as one
Knowing some women whores, dares marry none.
65 Graccus loves all as one, and thinks that so
As women do in divers countries go
In divers habits,° yet are still one kind,   *styles of clothing*
So doth, so is religion; and this blind-
ness too much light breeds;[4] but unmoved thou
70 Of force° must one, and forced but one allow;   *necessity*
And the right; ask thy father which is she,
Let him ask his; though truth and falsehood be
Near twins, yet truth a little elder is;
Be busy to seek her, believe me this,
75 He's not of none, nor worst, that seeks the best.[5]
To adore, or scorn an image, or protest,
May all be bad; doubt wisely; in strange way

8. Of moral struggle.
9. The common belief that the world was growing old and becoming decrepit.
1. The satiric types in this passage represent
different creeds: "Mirreus" is a Roman Catholic;
"Crantz," an austere Calvinist Presbyterian of
Geneva; "Graius" a Church of England Erastian
who believes in any religion sponsored by the
state; "Phrygius," a skeptic; and "Graccus," a complete relativist.

2. The royal canopy, a symbol of kingly power.
3. If minors in care of a guardian (in wardship)
rejected the wives offered ("tendered") to them
they had to pay fines ("values").
4. I.e., Graccus considers the differences between
religions merely incidental, like womens' clothes,
but his apparently tolerant, "enlightened" attitude
is itself a form of blindness.
5. The person who seeks the best church is neither an unbeliever nor the worst sort of believer.

To stand inquiring right, is not to stray;
To sleep, or run wrong, is. On a huge hill,
80 Cragged and steep, Truth stands, and he that will
Reach her, about must, and about must go,
And what the hill's suddenness resists, win so;
Yet strive so, that before age, death's twilight,
Thy soul rest, for none can work in that night.[6]
85 To will° implies delay, therefore now do.   *intend a future act*
Hard deeds, the body's pains; hard knowledge too
The mind's endeavors reach,° and mysteries   *achieve*
Are like the sun, dazzling, yet plain to all eyes.
Keep the truth which thou hast found; men do not stand
90 In so ill case here, that God hath with his hand
Signed kings' blank charters to kill whom they hate,
Nor are they vicars, but hangmen to fate.[7]
Fool and wretch, wilt thou let thy soul be tied
To man's laws, by which she shall not be tried
95 At the last day? O, will it then boot° thee   *profit*
To say a Philip, or a Gregory,
A Harry, or a Martin taught thee this?[8]
Is not this excuse for mere° contraries   *complete*
Equally strong? Cannot both sides say so?
100 That thou mayest rightly obey power, her bounds know;
Those passed, her nature and name is changed; to be
Then humble to her is idolatry.
As streams are, power is; those blest flowers that dwell
At the rough stream's calm head, thrive and prove well,
105 But having left their roots, and themselves given
To the stream's tyrannous rage, alas, are driven
Through mills, and rocks, and woods, and at last, almost
Consumed in going, in the sea are lost:
So perish souls, which more choose men's unjust
110 Power from God claimed, than God himself to trust.

1633

From Holy Sonnets[1]

1

Thou hast made me, and shall thy work decay?
Repair me now, for now mine end doth haste;
I run to death, and death meets me as fast,
And all my pleasures are like yesterday.

---

6. Echoes John 9.4, "the night cometh, when no man can work."
7. Kings are not God's vicars on earth, with license ("blank charters") to persecute or kill whomever they wish on grounds of religion.
8. "Philip" is Philip II of Spain, "Gregory" is Pope Gregory XIII or XIV, "Harry" is England's Henry VIII, and "Martin" is Martin Luther.
1. Donne wrote a variety of religious poems (called "Divine Poems"), including a group of nineteen "Holy sonnets" that reflect his interest in Jesuit and Protestant meditative procedures. He probably began writing them about 1609, a decade or so after leaving the Catholic Church. Our selections follow the traditional numbering established in Sir Herbert Grierson's influential edition, since for most of these sonnets we cannot tell when they were written or in what order they were intended to appear.

5   I dare not move my dim eyes any way,
    Despair behind, and death before doth cast
    Such terror, and my feeble flesh doth waste
    By sin in it, which it towards hell doth weigh.°   *incline, weigh down*
    Only thou art above, and when towards thee
10   By thy leave I can look, I rise again;
    But our old subtle foe so tempteth me
    That not one hour myself I can sustain.
    Thy grace may wing° me to prevent° his art,   *give wings to / forestall*
    And thou like adamant° draw mine iron heart.   *magnetic lodestone*

                          1635

5

    I am a little world[2] made cunningly
    Of elements, and an angelic sprite;°   *spirit, soul*
    But black sin hath betrayed to endless night
    My world's both parts, and O, both parts must die.
5   You which beyond that heaven which was most high
    Have found new spheres, and of new lands can write,[3]
    Pour new seas in mine eyes, that so I might
    Drown my world with my weeping earnestly,
    Or wash it if it must be drowned no more.[4]
10   But O, it must be burnt! Alas, the fire
    Of lust and envy have burnt it heretofore,
    And made it fouler; let their flames retire,
    And burn me, O Lord, with a fiery zeal
    Of thee and thy house, which doth in eating heal.[5]

                          1635

7

    At the round earth's imagined corners,[6] blow
    Your trumpets, angels; and arise, arise
    From death, you numberless infinities
    Of souls, and to your scattered bodies go:
5   All whom the flood did, and fire[7] shall, o'erthrow,
    All whom war, dearth,° age, agues,° tyrannies,   *famine / fevers*
    Despair, law, chance hath slain, and you whose eyes
    Shall behold God, and never taste death's woe.[8]
    But let them sleep, Lord, and me mourn a space;
10   For, if above all these, my sins abound,
    'Tis late to ask abundance of thy grace
    When we are there. Here on this lowly ground,

2. The traditional idea of the human being as microcosm (a "little world"), containing in miniature all the features of the macrocosm, or great world.
3. Astronomers, especially Galileo, and explorers.
4. God promised Noah (Genesis 9.11) never to flood the earth again.
5. See Psalm 69.9: "For the zeal of thine house hath eaten me up." These lines refer to three kinds of flame—those of the Last Judgment, those of lust and envy, and those of zeal, which alone save.
6. Cf. Revelation 7.1: "I saw four angels standing on the four corners of the earth."
7. Noah's flood, and the universal conflagration at the end of the world (Revelation 6.11).
8. Those who will be alive at the Second Coming (cf. Luke 9.27).

Teach me how to repent; for that's as good
As if thou hadst sealed my pardon with thy blood.

1633

9

If poisonous minerals, and if that tree[9]
Whose fruit threw death on else-immortal us,
If lecherous goats, if serpents envious[1]
Cannot be damned, alas! why should I be?
5   Why should intent or reason, born in me,
Make sins, else equal, in me more heinous?
And, mercy being easy and glorious
To God, in his stern wrath why threatens he?
But who am I that dare dispute with thee
10 O God? Oh, of thine only worthy blood
And my tears, make a heavenly Lethean[2] flood,
And drown in it my sin's black memory.
That thou remember them some claim as debt;
I think it mercy if thou wilt forget.[3]

1633

10

Death, be not proud, though some have callèd thee
Mighty and dreadful, for thou art not so;
For those whom thou think'st thou dost overthrow
Die not, poor Death, nor yet canst thou kill me.
5   From rest and sleep, which but thy pictures be,
Much pleasure; then from thee much more must flow,
And soonest our best men with thee do go,
Rest of their bones, and soul's delivery.[4]
Thou art slave to fate, chance, kings, and desperate men,
10 And dost with poison, war, and sickness dwell,
And poppy° or charms can make us sleep as well   *opium*
And better than thy stroke; why swell'st° thou then?   *puff with pride*
One short sleep past, we wake eternally
And death shall be no more; Death, thou shalt die.[5]

1633

13

What if this present were the world's last night?
Mark in my heart, O soul, where thou dost dwell,

---

9. The Tree of Knowledge of Good and Evil, whose fruit was forbidden to Adam and Eve in Eden.
1. Traits commonly associated with these creatures.
2. In classical mythology, the waters of the river Lethe in the underworld caused total forgetfulness.

3. Cf. Jeremiah 31.34: "I will forgive their iniquity, and I will remember their sins no more."
4. I.e., to find rest for their bones and freedom ("delivery") for their souls.
5. Cf. 1 Corinthians 15.26: "The last enemy that shall be destroyed is death."

The picture of Christ crucified, and tell
Whether that countenance can thee affright.
5 Tears in his eyes quench the amazing light,
Blood fills his frowns, which from his pierced head fell;
And can that tongue adjudge thee unto hell
Which prayed forgiveness for his foes' fierce spite?
No, no; but as in my idolatry
10 I said to all my profane° mistresses,   *secular*
Beauty of pity, foulness only is
A sign of rigor:[6] so I say to thee,
To wicked spirits are horrid shapes assigned,
This beauteous form assures a piteous mind.

1633

14

Batter my heart, three-personed God; for you
As yet but knock, breathe, shine, and seek to mend;
That I may rise and stand, o'erthrow me, and bend
Your force to break, blow, burn, and make me new.
5 I, like an usurped town, to another due,
Labor to admit you, but O, to no end;
Reason, your viceroy[7] in me, me should defend,
But is captived, and proves weak or untrue.
Yet dearly I love you, and would be loved fain,°   *gladly*
10 But am betrothed[8] unto your enemy.
Divorce me, untie or break that knot again;
Take me to you, imprison me, for I,
Except° you enthrall me, never shall be free,   *unless*
Nor ever chaste, except you ravish[9] me.

1633

18

Show me, dear Christ, thy spouse[1] so bright and clear.
What! is it she which on the other shore
Goes richly painted? or which, robbed and tore,
Laments and mourns in Germany and here?[2]
5 Sleeps she a thousand, then peeps up one year?
Is she self-truth, and errs? now new, now outwore?
Doth she, and did she, and shall she evermore
On one, on seven, or on no hill appear?[3]

---

6. In Neoplatonic theory, beautiful features are the sign of a compassionate mind, while ugliness signifies the contrary.
7. The governor in your stead.
8. Humanity's relationship with God has been described in terms of marriage and adultery from the time of the Hebrew prophets.
9. Rape, also overwhelm with wonder. "Enthrall": enslave, also enchant.
1. The church is commonly called the bride of Christ. Cf. Revelation 19.7–8: "The marriage of

the Lamb is come, and his wife hath made herself ready. / And to her was granted that she should be arrayed in fine linen, clean and white."
2. I.e., the painted woman (the Church of Rome) or the ravished virgin (the Lutheran and Calvinist churches in Germany and England).
3. The church on one hill is probably Solomon's temple on Mount Moriah; that on seven hills is the Church of Rome; that on no hill is the Presbyterian church of Geneva.

Dwells she with us, or like adventuring knights
10 First travel we to seek, and then make love?
Betray, kind husband, thy spouse to our sights,
And let mine amorous soul court thy mild dove,
Who is most true and pleasing to thee then
When she is embraced and open to most men.[4]

1899

19

Oh, to vex me, contraries meet in one:
Inconstancy unnaturally hath begot
A constant habit; that when I would not
I change in vows, and in devotion.
5   As humorous° is my contrition   subject to whim
As my profane love, and as soon forgot:
As riddlingly distempered, cold and hot,[5]
As praying, as mute, as infinite, as none.
I durst not view heaven yesterday; and today
10 In prayers and flattering speeches I court God:
Tomorrow I quake with true fear of his rod.
So my devout fits come and go away
Like a fantastic ague:[6] save° that here   except
Those are my best days, when I shake with fear.

1899

Good Friday, 1613. Riding Westward

Let man's soul be a sphere, and then, in this,
The intelligence that moves, devotion is,[1]
And as the other spheres, by being grown
Subject to foreign motions, lose their own,
5   And being by others hurried every day,
Scarce in a year their natural form[2] obey;
Pleasure or business, so, our souls admit
For° their first mover, and are whirled by it.   instead of
Hence is 't, that I am carried towards the West
10 This day, when my soul's form bends toward the East.
There I should see a Sun[3] by rising, set,
And by that setting endless day beget:

---

4. The final lines wittily rework, with startling sexual associations, Song of Solomon 5.2: "Open to me, my sister, my love, my dove, my undefiled." That biblical book was often interpreted as the song of love between Christ and the church.
5. Arising from the unbalanced humors, inexplicably changeable.
6. A fever, attended with paroxysms of hot and cold and trembling fits. "Fantastic": capricious, extravagant.
1. As angelic intelligences guide the celestial spheres, so devotion is or should be the guiding

principle of the soul.
2. Their true moving principle or intelligence. The orbit of the celestial spheres was thought to be governed by an unmoving outermost sphere, the primum mobile, or first mover (line 8), but sometimes outside influences ("foreign motions," line 4) deflected the spheres from their correct orbits.
3. The "sun" / "Son" pun was an ancient one. Christ the Son of God "set" when he rose on the Cross, and that setting (death) gave rise to the Christian era and the promise of immortality.

But that Christ on this cross did rise and fall,
Sin had eternally benighted all.
15 Yet dare I almost be glad I do not see
That spectacle, of too much weight for me.
Who sees God's face, that is self-life, must die;[4]
What a death were it then to see God die?
It made his own lieutenant,° Nature, shrink;   *deputy*
20 It made his footstool crack, and the sun wink.[5]
Could I behold those hands which span the poles,
And tune[6] all spheres at once, pierced with those holes?
Could I behold that endless height which is
Zenith to us, and t'our antipodes,[7]
25 Humbled below us? Or that blood which is
The seat° of all our souls, if not of his,   *dwelling place*
Make dirt of dust, or that flesh which was worn
By God for his apparel, ragg'd and torn?
If on these things I durst not look, durst I
30 Upon his miserable mother cast mine eye,
Who was God's partner here, and furnished thus
Half of that sacrifice which ransomed us?
Though these things, as I ride, be from° mine eye,   *away from*
They are present yet unto my memory,
35 For that looks towards them; and thou look'st towards me,
O Savior, as thou hang'st upon the tree.
I turn my back to thee but to receive
Corrections,[8] till thy mercies bid thee leave.°   *cease*
O think me worth thine anger; punish me;
40 Burn off my rusts and my deformity;
Restore thine image so much, by thy grace,
That thou may'st know me, and I'll turn my face.

1633

Hymn to God My God, in My Sickness[1]

Since I am coming to that holy room
    Where, with thy choir of saints for evermore,
I shall be made thy music; as I come
    I tune the instrument here at the door,
5   And what I must do then, think now before.[2]

Whilst my physicians by their love are grown
    Cosmographers, and I their map, who lie

4. God told Moses, "Thou canst not see my face, for there shall no man see me, and live" (Exodus 33.20).
5. An earthquake and eclipse supposedly accompanied the Crucifixion (Matthew 27.45, 51). Cf. Isaiah 66.1: "Thus saith the Lord, The heaven is my throne, and the earth is my footstool."
6. Some manuscripts read "turn."
7. God is at once the highest point for us and for our "antipodes," those who live on the opposite side of the earth.
8. Suggests a flogging.
1. Though Izaak Walton, Donne's friend and biographer, assigns this poem to the last days of his life, it was probably written during another illness, in December 1623.
2. This and the previous poem are less hymns (songs of praise) than meditations preparing (tuning the instrument) for such hymns.

Flat on this bed, that by them may be shown
 That this is my southwest discovery[3]
10 *Per fretum febris*,[4] by these straits to die,

I joy, that in these straits, I see my West;
 For, though their currents yield return to none,
What shall my West hurt me? As West and East
 In all flat maps (and I am one) are one,[5]
15 So death doth touch the resurrection.

Is the Pacific Sea my home? Or are
 The Eastern riches?° Is Jerusalem?   *Cathay, China*
Anyan,[6] and Magellan, and Gibraltar,
 All straits, and none but straits, are ways to them,
20 Whether where Japhet dwelt, or Cham, or Shem.[7]

We think that Paradise and Calvary,
 Christ's cross and Adam's tree, stood in one place;
Look, Lord and find both Adams[8] met in me;
 As the first Adam's sweat surrounds my face,
25 May the last Adam's blood my soul embrace.

So, in his purple wrapped,[9] receive me, Lord;
 By these his thorns° give me his other crown;   *crown of thorns*
And, as to others' souls I preached thy word,
 Be this my text, my sermon to mine own:
30 Therefore that he may raise the Lord throws down.

1635

A Hymn to God the Father[1]

Wilt thou forgive that sin where I begun,
 Which is my sin, though it were done before?[2]
Wilt thou forgive that sin through which I run,
 And do run still, though still I do deplore?
5 When thou hast done,[3] thou hast not done,
 For I have more.

3. South is the region of heat, west the region of sunset and death.
4. Through the straits of fever, with a pun on straits as sufferings, rigors, and a geographical reference to the Strait of Magellan.
5. If a flat map is pasted on a round globe, west and east meet.
6. Anian, a strait on the west coast of America, shown on early maps as separating America from Asia.
7. The three sons of Noah by whom the world was repopulated after the Flood (Genesis 10). The descendants of Japhet were thought to inhabit Europe; those of Cham (Ham), Africa; and those of Shem, Asia.

8. Adam and Christ. Legend had it that Christ's cross was erected on the spot, or at least in the region, where the tree forbidden to Adam in Eden had stood.
9. In his blood, also in his kingly robes.
1. This hymn was used as a congregational hymn. Walton tells us that Donne wrote it during his illness of 1623, had it set to music, and was delighted to hear it performed (as it frequently was) by the choir of St. Paul's Cathedral.
2. I.e., he inherits the original sin of Adam and Eve.
3. In the refrains, Donne puns on his own name and may pun on his wife's maiden name, Ann More.

Wilt thou forgive that sin by which I have won
Others to sin? and made my sin their door?
Wilt thou forgive that sin which I did shun
10   A year or two, but wallowed in a score?
          When thou hast done, thou hast not done,
          For I have more.

I have a sin of fear, that when I have spun
My last thread, I shall perish on the shore;
15   Swear by thy self, that at my death thy Son
Shall shine as he shines now and heretofore;
          And, having done that, thou hast done,
          I fear[4] no more.

1633

From Devotions upon Emergent Occasions[1]

Meditation 4

Medicusque vocatur.
The physician is sent for.[2]

It is too little to call man a little world; except God, man is a diminutive to nothing.[3] Man consists of more pieces, more parts, than the world; than the world doth, nay, than the world is. And if those pieces were extended and stretched out in man as they are in the world, man would be the giant and the world the dwarf; the world but the map, and the man the world. If all the veins in our bodies were extended to rivers, and all the sinews to veins of mines, and all the muscles that lie upon one another to hills, and all the bones to quarries of stones, and all the other pieces to the proportion of those which correspond to them in the world, the air would be too little for this orb of man to move in, the firmament would be but enough for this star. For as the whole world hath nothing to which something in man doth not answer,[4] so hath man many pieces of which the whole world hath no representation. Enlarge this meditation upon this great world, man, so far as to consider the immensity of the creatures this world produces. Our creatures are our thoughts, creatures that are born giants, that reach from east to west, from earth to heaven, that do not only bestride all the sea and land, but span the sun and firmament at once: my thoughts reach all, comprehend all.

---

4. Some manuscripts read "have."
1. Donne's *Devotions* were composed in the aftermath of his serious illness in the winter of 1623, though Donne characteristically writes as if the events of the illness were happening as he describes them. The *Devotions* recount in twenty-three sections the stages ("emergent occasions") of the illness and recovery: the term associates the exercise with a popular kind of Protestant meditation on the occasions that daily life presents to us. Each section contains a "meditation upon our human condition," an "expostulation and debate-

ment with God," and a prayer to God. The book was published almost immediately, offering its meditation on an intensely personal experience as exemplary for others.
2. Donne's Latin epigraphs are followed by his English translations, often quite free.
3. This meditation is based on the notion that each human being is a microcosm, a little world, analogous in every respect to the macrocosm, or great world. But in playing with this notion, Donne paradoxically reverses it.
4. Correspond.

Inexplicable mystery! I their creator am in a close prison, in a sick bed, anywhere, and any one of my creatures, my thoughts, is with the sun, and beyond the sun, overtakes the sun, and overgoes the sun in one pace, one step, everywhere. And then as the other world produces serpents and vipers, malignant and venomous creatures, and worms and caterpillars, that endeavor to devour that world which produces them, and monsters compiled and complicated[5] of divers parents and kinds, so this world, our selves, produces all these in us, in producing diseases and sicknesses of all those sorts; venomous and infectious diseases, feeding and consuming diseases, and manifold and entangled diseases made up of many several ones. And can the other world name so many venomous, so many consuming, so many monstrous creatures, as we can diseases of all these kinds? O miserable abundance, O beggarly riches! How much do we lack of having remedies for every disease, when as yet we have not names for them?

But we have a Hercules against these giants, these monsters: that is the physician. He musters up all the forces of the other world to succor this, all nature to relieve man. We have the physician but we are not the physician. Here we shrink in our proportion, sink in our dignity in respect of very mean creatures who are physicians to themselves. The hart that is pursued and wounded, they say, knows an herb which, being eaten, throws off the arrow: a strange kind of vomit.[6] The dog that pursues it, though he be subject to sickness, even proverbially knows his grass that recovers him. And it may be true that the drugger is as near to man as to other creatures; it may be that obvious and present simples,[7] easy to be had, would cure him; but the apothecary is not so near him, nor the physician so near him, as they two are to other creatures.[8] Man hath not that innate instinct to apply these natural medicines to his present danger, as those inferior creatures have. He is not his own apothecary, his own physician, as they are. Call back therefore thy meditation again, and bring it down.[9] What's become of man's great extent and proportion, when himself shrinks himself and consumes himself to a handful of dust? What's become of his soaring thoughts, his compassing thoughts, when himself brings himself to the ignorance, to the thoughtlessness, of the grave? His diseases are his own, but the physician is not; he hath them at home, but he must send for the physician.

Meditation 17

Nunc lento sonitu dicunt, morieris.
Now this bell tolling softly for another, says to me,
Thou must die.

Perchance he for whom this bell[1] tolls may be so ill as that he knows not it tolls for him; and perchance I may think myself so much better than I am, as that they who are about me and see my state may have caused it to toll for me, and I know not that. The church is catholic, universal, so are all her actions; all that she does belongs to all. When she baptizes a child, that

---

5. Mixed.
6. Deer supposedly expelled arrows wounding them by eating the herb dittany.
7. Medicinal plants.
8. One who administers drugs might do this for man as well as for other creatures, but one who sells drugs ("the apothecary") and the physician do not know how to prescribe for man as well as for other creatures.
9. I.e., apply it to the present situation.
1. The "passing bell" for the dying.

action concerns me; for that child is thereby connected to that head which is my head too, and ingrafted into that body[2] whereof I am a member. And when she buries a man, that action concerns me: all mankind is of one author and is one volume; when one man dies, one chapter is not torn out of the book, but translated[3] into a better language; and every chapter must be so translated. God employs several translators; some pieces are translated by age, some by sickness, some by war, some by justice; but God's hand is in every translation, and his hand shall bind up all our scattered leaves again for that library where every book shall lie open to one another. As therefore the bell that rings to a sermon calls not upon the preacher only, but upon the congregation to come, so this bell calls us all; but how much more me, who am brought so near the door by this sickness. There was a contention as far as a suit[4] (in which piety and dignity, religion and estimation,[5] were mingled) which of the religious orders should ring to prayers first in the morning; and it was determined that they should ring first that rose earliest. If we understand aright the dignity of this bell that tolls for our evening prayer, we would be glad to make it ours by rising early, in that application, that it might be ours as well as his whose indeed it is. The bell doth toll for him that thinks it doth; and though it intermit again, yet from that minute that that occasion wrought upon him, he is united to God. Who casts not up his eye to the sun when it rises? But who takes off his eye from a comet when that breaks out? Who bends not his ear to any bell which upon any occasion rings? But who can remove it from that bell which is passing a piece of himself out of this world? No man is an island, entire of itself; every man is a piece of the continent, a part of the main.[6] If a clod be washed away by the sea, Europe is the less, as well as if a promontory were, as well as if a manor of thy friend's or of thine own were. Any man's death diminishes me, because I am involved in mankind; and therefore never send to know for whom the bell tolls; it tolls for thee.[7] Neither can we call this a begging of misery or a borrowing of misery, as though we were not miserable enough of ourselves but must fetch in more from the next house, in taking upon us the misery of our neighbors. Truly it were an excusable covetousness if we did; for affliction is a treasure, and scarce any man hath enough of it. No man hath affliction enough that is not matured and ripened by it, and made fit for God by that affliction. If a man carry treasure in bullion, or in a wedge of gold, and have none coined into current moneys, his treasure will not defray[8] him as he travels. Tribulation is treasure in the nature of it, but it is not current money in the use of it, except we get nearer and nearer our home, heaven, by it. Another man may be sick too, and sick to death, and this affliction may lie in his bowels as gold in a mine and be of no use to him; but this bell that tells me of his affliction digs out and applies that gold to me, if by this consideration of another's danger I take mine own into contemplation and so secure myself by making my recourse to my God, who is our only security.

1624

---

2. The church.
3. Punning on the literal sense, "carried across."
4. Controversy that went as far as a lawsuit.
5. Self-esteem.

6. Mainland.
7. This phrase gave Hemingway the title for his novel *For Whom the Bell Tolls*.
8. Meet his expenses.

AEMILIA LANYER
1569–1645

Aemilia Lanyer was the first Englishwoman to publish a substantial volume of original poems and the first to make an overt bid for patronage. She was daughter to an Italian family of court musicians who came to England in the reign of Henry VIII; they may have been Christianized Jews or, alternatively, Protestants forced to flee Catholic persecution in their native land. Some information about Lanyer's life has come down to us from the notebooks of the astrologer and fortune-teller Simon Forman, whom Lanyer consulted in 1597. Educated in the aristocratic household of the Countess of Kent, in her late teens and early twenties Lanyer was the mistress of Queen Elizabeth's lord chamberlain, Henry Carey, Lord Hunsdon. The wealthy Hunsdon, forty-five years her senior, was a notable patron of the arts—Shakespeare's company performed under his auspices in the 1590s—and he maintained his mistress in luxury. Yet when she became pregnant by Hunsdon at age twenty-three, she was married off to Alfonso Lanyer, one of another family of gentleman musicians attached to the courts of Elizabeth I and James I. Lanyer's fortunes declined after her marriage. Lanyer's poetry suggests that she resided for some time in the bookish and cultivated household of Margaret Clifford, Countess of Cumberland, and Margaret's young daughter Anne. Lanyer reports receiving there encouragement in learning, piety, and poetry, as well as, perhaps, some support in the unusual venture of offering her poems for publication. Yet her efforts to find some niche at the Jacobean court came to nothing.

Lanyer's single volume of poems, *Salve Deus Rex Judaeorum* (1611) has a decided feminist thrust. A series of dedicatory poems to former and would-be patronesses praises them as a community of contemporary good women. The title poem, a meditation on Christ's Passion that at times invites comparison with Donne and Crashaw, contrasts the good women in the Passion story with the weak, evil men portrayed there. It also incorporates a defense of Eve and all women. That defense and Lanyer's prose epistle, "To the Virtuous Reader," are spirited contributions to the so-called *querelle des femmes*, or "debate about women," a massive body of writings in several genres and languages: some examples include Chaucer's Wife of Bath's Prologue and Tale, Shakespeare's *Taming of the Shrew*, Joseph Swetnam's attack on "lewd, idle, froward, and unconstant women" and Rachel Speght's reply. The final poem in Lanyer's volume, "The Description of Cookham," celebrates in elegiac mode the Crown estate occasionally occupied by the Countess of Cumberland, portraying it as an Edenic paradise of women, now lost. The poem may or may not have been written before Ben Jonson's "To Penshurst"—commonly thought to have inaugurated the "country-house" genre in English literature—but Lanyer's poem can claim priority in publication. The poems' different conceptions of the role of women in the ideal social order make an instructive comparison.

From Salve Deus Rex Judaeorum[1]

To the Doubtful Reader[2]

Gentle Reader, if thou desire to be resolved, why I give this title, *Salve Deus Rex Judaeorum*, know for certain, that it was delivered unto me in sleep many years before I had any intent to write in this manner, and was quite out of my memory, until I had written the Passion of Christ, when immediately it came into my remembrance, what I had dreamed long before. And thinking it a significant token[3] that I was appointed to perform this work, I gave the very same words I received in sleep as the fittest title I could devise for this book.

Eve's Apology in Defense of Women[4]

 Now Pontius Pilate is to judge the cause°   *case*
 Of faultless Jesus, who before him stands,
 Who neither hath offended prince, nor laws,
 Although he now be brought in woeful bands.
5 O noble governor, make thou yet a pause,
 Do not in innocent blood inbrue° thy hands;   *stain*
  But hear the words of thy most worthy wife,
  Who sends to thee, to beg her Savior's life.[5]

 Let barb'rous cruelty far depart from thee,
10 And in true justice take affliction's part;
 Open thine eyes, that thou the truth may'st see.
 Do not the thing that goes against thy heart,
 Condemn not him that must thy Savior be;
 But view his holy life, his good desert.
15 Let not us women glory in men's fall,[6]
  Who had power given to overrule us all.

 Till now your indiscretion sets us free.
 And makes our former fault much less appear;
 Our mother Eve, who tasted of the tree,
20 Giving to Adam what she held most dear,
 Was simply good, and had no power to see;[7]
 The after-coming harm did not appear:
  The subtle serpent that our sex betrayed
  Before our fall so sure a plot had laid.

1. "Hail God, King of the Jews," a variant of the inscription affixed to Christ's cross.
2. Lanyer placed this explanation at the end of her volume, not the beginning, as a further authorizing gesture. Invoking the familiar genre of the dream vision, she lays claim to poetic, even divine, inspiration. "Doubtful": doubting.
3. Sign.
4. Lanyer supplies the title for this subsection of the *Salve Deus* on her title page. Eve is not, however, the speaker; rather, the narrator presents Eve's "Apology" (defense of her actions), which is also a defense of all women. She does so by means of an apostrophe (impassioned address) to Pilate, the Roman official who authorized the

crucifixion of Jesus. Lanyer makes Pilate and Adam representatives of the male gender, whereas Eve and Pilate's wife represent womankind.
5. Pilate's wife wrote her husband a letter urging Pilate to spare Jesus, about whom she had a warning dream (Matthew 27.19).
6. The fall of Adam, and the prospective fall of Pilate.
7. In Eden, Eve ate the forbidden fruit first, at the serpent's bidding. Genesis commentary usually emphasized Eve's full knowledge that God had forbidden them on pain of death and banishment from Eden to eat the fruit of the Tree of Knowledge of Good and Evil. Her action was usually ascribed to intemperance, pride, and ambition.

25   That undiscerning ignorance perceived
No guile or craft that was by him intended;
For had she known of what we were bereaved,[8]
To his request she had not condescended.°   *consented*
But she, poor soul, by cunning was deceived;

30   No hurt therein her harmless heart intended:
For she alleged° God's word, which he° denies,   *asserted / serpent*
That they should die, but even as gods be wise.

But surely Adam cannot be excused;
Her fault though great, yet he was most to blame;

35   What weakness offered, strength might have refused,
Being lord of all, the greater was his shame.
Although the serpent's craft had her abused,
God's holy word ought all his actions frame,°   *determine*
For he was lord and king of all the earth,

40   Before poor Eve had either life or breath,

Who being framed° by God's eternal hand   *fashioned*
The perfectest man that ever breathed on earth;
And from God's mouth received that strait° command,   *strict*
The breach whereof he knew was present death;

45   Yea, having power to rule both sea and land,
Yet with one apple won to lose that breath[9]
Which God had breathed in his beauteous face,
Bringing us all in danger and disgrace.

And then to lay the fault on Patience' back,

50   That we (poor women) must endure it all.
We know right well he did discretion lack,
Being not persuaded thereunto at all.
If Eve did err, it was for knowledge sake;
The fruit being fair persuaded him to fall:

55   No subtle serpent's falsehood did betray him;
If he would eat it, who had power to stay° him?   *prevent*

Not Eve, whose fault was only too much love,
Which made her give this present to her dear,
That what she tasted he likewise might prove,°   *experience*

60   Whereby his knowledge might become more clear;
He never sought her weakness to reprove
With those sharp words which he of God did hear;
Yet men will boast of knowledge, which he took
From Eve's fair hand, as from a learned book.

65   If any evil did in her remain,
Being made of him,[1] he was the ground of all.

8. Deprived, specifically of eternal life. In Genesis 3, Eve was enticed by the serpent to eat the forbidden fruit; she in turn enticed her husband. God expelled them from Eden, condemning Adam to hard labor, Eve to pain in childbirth and subjection to her husband, and both to suffering and death.
9. The breath of life, which would have been eternal.
1. Genesis 2.21–22 reports God's creation of Eve from Adam's rib.

If one of many worlds[2] could lay a stain
Upon our sex, and work so great a fall
To wretched man by Satan's subtle train,[3]
70 What will so foul a fault amongst you all?
Her weakness did the serpent's words obey,
But you in malice God's dear Son betray,

Whom, if unjustly you condemn to die,
Her sin was small to what you do commit;
75 All mortal sins[4] that do for vengeance cry
Are not to be compared unto it.
If many worlds would altogether try
By all their sins the wrath of God to get,
This sin of yours surmounts them all as far
80 As doth the sun another little star.[5]

Then let us have our liberty again,
And challenge° to yourselves no sovereignty.   claim
You came not in the world without our pain,
Make that a bar against your cruelty;
85 Your fault being greater, why should you disdain
Our being your equals, free from tyranny?
If one weak woman simply did offend,
This sin of yours hath no excuse nor end,

To which, poor souls, we never gave consent.
90 Witness, thy wife, O Pilate, speaks for all,
Who did but dream, and yet a message sent
That thou shouldest have nothing to do at all
With that just man° which, if thy heart relent,   Christ
Why wilt thou be a reprobate° with Saul[6]   damned
95 To seek the death of him that is so good,
For thy soul's health to shed his dearest blood?

1611

The Description of Cookham[1]

Farewell, sweet Cookham, where I first obtained
Grace[2] from that grace where perfect grace remained;
And where the muses gave their full consent,

2. May allude to the commonplace that man is a little world, applying it here to woman.
3. Tradition identifies Satan with the serpent, although that identification is not made in Genesis.
4. Sins punishable by damnation.
5. In the Ptolemaic system, the sun was larger than the other planets and the fixed stars.
6. King of Israel who sought the death of God's annointed prophet-king, David. The parallel is with Pilate, who sought Christ's death.
1. The poem was written in honor of Margaret Clifford, Countess of Cumberland, and celebrates a royal estate leased to her brother, at which the countess occasionally resided. The poem

should be compared with Jonson's "To Penshurst" (pp. 714–16). Lanyer's poem is based on a familiar classical topic, the "farewell to a place," which had its most famous development in Virgil's *Eclogue* 1. Lanyer makes extensive use of the common pastoral motif of nature's active sympathy with and response to human emotion—which later came to be called the "pathetic fallacy."
2. Here, both God's grace and the favor of Her Grace, the Countess of Cumberland. Lanyer attributes both her religious conversion and her vocation as poet to a period of residence at Cookham in the countess's household. We do not know how long or under what circumstances Lanyer resided there.

I should have power the virtuous to content;
5   Where princely palace willed me to indite,°   *write*
The sacred story of the soul's delight.[3]
Farewell, sweet place, where virtue then did rest,
And all delights did harbor in her breast;
Never shall my sad eyes again behold
10 Those pleasures which my thoughts did then unfold.
Yet you, great lady, mistress of that place,
From whose desires did spring this work of grace;
Vouchsafe° to think upon those pleasures past,   *be willing*
As fleeting worldly joys that could not last,
15 Or, as dim shadows of celestial pleasures,
Which are desired above all earthly treasures.
Oh how, methought, against° you thither came,   *in preparation for*
Each part did seem some new delight to frame!
The house received all ornaments to grace it,
20 And would endure no foulness to deface it.
And walks put on their summer liveries,[4]
And all things else did hold like similes:[5]
The trees with leaves, with fruits, with flowers clad,
Embraced each other, seeming to be glad,
25 Turning themselves to beauteous canopies,
To shade the bright sun from your brighter eyes;
The crystal streams with silver spangles graced,
While by the glorious sun they were embraced;
The little birds in chirping notes did sing,
30 To entertain both you and that sweet spring.
And Philomela[6] with her sundry lays,
Both you and that delightful place did praise.
Oh how me thought each plant, each flower, each tree
Set forth their beauties then to welcome thee!
35 The very hills right humbly did descend,
When you to tread on them did intend.
And as you set your feet, they still did rise,
Glad that they could receive so rich a prize.
The gentle winds did take delight to be
40 Among those woods that were so graced by thee,
And in sad murmur uttered pleasing sound,
That pleasure in that place might more abound.
The swelling banks delivered all their pride
When such a phoenix[7] once they had espied.
45 Each arbor, bank, each seat, each stately tree,
Thought themselves honored in supporting thee.
The pretty birds would oft come to attend thee,
Yet fly away for fear they should offend thee;
The little creatures in the burrow by

3. Apparently a reference to the countess as her patron, commissioning her Passion poem.
4. Distinctive garments worn by persons in the service of great families, to indicate whose servants they were.
5. Behaved in similar fashion.
6. In myth, Philomela was raped by her brother-in-law Tereus, who also tore out her tongue; the gods transformed her into a nightingale. Here the bird's song is joyous but later mournful (line 189), associating her own woes with those of Cookham at the women's departure.
7. Mythical bird that lived alone of its kind for five hundred years, then was consumed in flame and reborn from its own ashes; metaphorically, a person of rare excellence. "All their pride": fish (cf. "To Penshurst," lines 31–36).

50 Would come abroad to sport them in your eye,
  Yet fearful of the bow in your fair hand,
  Would run away when you did make a stand.
  Now let me come unto that stately tree,
  Wherein such goodly prospects you did see;
55 That oak that did in height his fellows pass,
  As much as lofty trees, low growing grass,
  Much like a comely cedar straight and tall,
  Whose beauteous stature far exceeded all.
  How often did you visit this fair tree,
60 Which seeming joyful in receiving thee,
  Would like a palm tree spread his arms abroad,
  Desirous that you there should make abode;
  Whose fair green leaves much like a comely veil,
  Defended Phoebus° when he would assail;   *resisted the sun*
65 Whose pleasing boughs did yield a cool fresh air,
  Joying° his happiness when you were there.   *enjoying*
  Where being seated, you might plainly see
  Hills, vales, and woods, as if on bended knee
  They had appeared, your honor to salute,
70 Or to prefer some strange unlooked-for suit;[8]
  All interlaced with brooks and crystal springs,
  A prospect fit to please the eyes of kings.
  And thirteen shires appeared all in your sight,
  Europe could not afford much more delight.
75 What was there then but gave you all content,
  While you the time in meditation spent
  Of their Creator's power, which there you saw,
  In all his creatures held a perfect law;
  And in their beauties did you plain descry°   *perceive*
80 His beauty, wisdom, grace, love, majesty.
  In these sweet woods how often did you walk,
  With Christ and his apostles there to talk;
  Placing his holy writ in some fair tree
  To meditate what you therein did see.
85 With Moses you did mount his holy hill
  To know his pleasure, and perform his will.[9]
  With lowly David you did often sing
  His holy hymns to heaven's eternal King.[1]
  And in sweet music did your soul delight
90 To sound his praises, morning, noon, and night.
  With blessed Joseph you did often feed
  Your pined brethren, when they stood in need.[2]
  And that sweet lady sprung from Clifford's race,
  Of noble Bedford's blood, fair stem of grace,[3]
95 To honorable Dorset now espoused,[4]

8. To urge some unexpected petition, as to a monarch.
9. You sought out and followed God's law, like Moses, who received the Ten Commandments on Mount Sinai.
1. You often sang David's psalms.
2. Like Joseph, who fed the starving Israelites in Egypt, you fed the hungry.

3. Main line of the family tree. Anne Clifford, only surviving child of the seaman-adventurer George Clifford, third Earl of Cumberland, and the countess, a Russell (of "Bedford's blood").
4. Anne Clifford was married to Richard Sackville, third Earl of Dorset, on February 25, 1609; the reference helps date Lanyer's poem.

In whose fair breast true virtue then was housed,
Oh what delight did my weak spirits find
In those pure parts° of her well framéd mind.   *qualities*
And yet it grieves me that I cannot be
100 Near unto her, whose virtues did agree
With those fair ornaments of outward beauty,
Which did enforce from all both love and duty.
Unconstant Fortune, thou art most to blame,
Who casts us down into so low a frame
105 Where our great friends we cannot daily see,
So great a difference is there in degree.[5]
Many are placéd in those orbs of state,
Parters[6] in honor, so ordained by Fate,
Nearer in show, yet farther off in love,
110 In which, the lowest always are above.[7]
But whither am I carried in conceit,°   *thought, fancy*
My wit too weak to conster° of the great.   *construe*
Why not? Although we are but born of earth,
We may behold the heavens, despising death;
115 And loving heaven that is so far above,
May in the end vouchsafe us entire love.[8]
Therefore sweet memory do thou retain
Those pleasures past, which will not turn again:
Remember beauteous Dorset's[9] former sports,
120 So far from being touched by ill reports,
Wherein myself did always bear a part,
While reverend love presented my true heart.
Those recreations let me bear in mind,
Which her sweet youth and noble thoughts did find,
125 Whereof deprived, I evermore must grieve,
Hating blind Fortune, careless to relieve.
And you sweet Cookham, whom these ladies leave,
I now must tell the grief you did conceive
At their departure, when they went away,
130 How everything retained a sad dismay.
Nay long before, when once an inkling came,
Methought each thing did unto sorrow frame:
The trees that were so glorious in our view,
Forsook both flowers and fruit, when once they knew
135 Of your depart, their very leaves did wither,
Changing their colors as they grew together.
But when they saw this had no power to stay you,
They often wept, though, speechless, could not pray you,
Letting their tears in your fair bosoms fall,
140 As if they said, Why will ye leave us all?
This being vain, they cast their leaves away

5. These lines and lines 117–25 probably exaggerate Lanyer's former familiarity with Anne Clifford.
6. Separators, i.e., the various honorific ranks ("orbs of state") act to separate person from person.
7. An egalitarian sentiment playing on the Christian notion that in spiritual things—love and charity—the poor and lowly surpass the great ones.
8. I.e., we (lowly) may also love God and enjoy God's love, and hence are equal to anyone.
9. As was common, Anne Clifford is here referred to by her husband's title.

Hoping that pity would have made you stay:
Their frozen tops, like age's hoary hairs,
Shows their disasters, languishing in fears.
145 A swarthy riveled rind° all over spread,   bark
Their dying bodies half alive, half dead.
But your occasions called you so away[1]
That nothing there had power to make you stay.
Yet did I see a noble grateful mind
150 Requiting each according to their kind,
Forgetting not to turn and take your leave
Of these sad creatures, powerless to receive
Your favor, when with grief you did depart,
Placing their former pleasures in your heart,
155 Giving great charge to noble memory
There to preserve their love continually.
But specially the love of that fair tree,
That first and last you did vouchsafe to see,
In which it pleased you oft to take the air
160 With noble Dorset, then a virgin fair,
Where many a learned book was read and scanned,
To this fair tree, taking me by the hand,
You did repeat the pleasures which had passed,
Seeming to grieve they could no longer last.
165 And with a chaste, yet loving kiss took leave,
Of which sweet kiss I did it soon bereave,°   soon take from it
Scorning a senseless creature should possess
So rare a favor, so great happiness.
No other kiss it could receive from me,
170 For fear to give back what it took of thee,
So I ungrateful creature did deceive it
Of that which you in love vouchsafed to leave it.
And though it oft had given me much content,
Yet this great wrong I never could repent;
175 But of the happiest made it most forlorn,
To show that nothing's free from Fortune's scorn,
While all the rest with this most beauteous tree
Made their sad comfort sorrow's harmony.
The flowers that on the banks and walks did grow,
180 Crept in the ground, the grass did weep for woe.
The winds and waters seemed to chide together
Because you went away they knew not whither;
And those sweet brooks that ran so fair and clear,
With grief and trouble wrinkled did appear.
185 Those pretty birds that wonted° were to sing,   accustomed
Now neither sing, nor chirp, nor use their wing,
But with their tender feet on some bare spray,
Warble forth sorrow, and their own dismay.
Fair Philomela leaves her mournful ditty,
190 Drowned in deep sleep, yet can procure no pity.
Each arbor, bank, each seat, each stately tree

---

1. After her husband's death (1605) Margaret Clifford chiefly resided in her dower properties in the
north; Anne Clifford was married in 1609.

Looks bare and desolate now for want of thee,
Turning green tresses into frosty gray,
While in cold grief they wither all away.
195 The sun grew weak, his beams no comfort gave,
While all green things did make the earth their grave.
Each briar, each bramble, when you went away
Caught fast your clothes, thinking to make you stay;
Delightful Echo wonted to reply
200 To our last words, did now for sorrow die;
The house cast off each garment that might grace it,
Putting on dust and cobwebs to deface it.
All desolation then there did appear,
When you were going whom they held so dear.
205 This last farewell to Cookham here I give,
When I am dead thy name in this may live,
Wherein I have performed her noble hest°   *commission*
Whose virtues lodge in my unworthy breast,
And ever shall, so long as life remains,
210 Tying my life to her by those rich chains.°   *her virtues*

1611

BEN JONSON
1572–1637

I n 1616 Ben Jonson published his *Works*, to the derision of those astounded to see mere plays and poems collected under the same title the king gave to his political treatises. Many of Jonson's contemporaries shied away from publication, either because, like Donne, they wrote for small coterie audiences or because, like Shakespeare, they wrote for theater companies that preferred not to let go of the scripts. Jonson knew and admired both Donne and Shakespeare and more than any Jacobean belonged to both of their very different worlds, but in publishing his *Works* he laid claim to higher literary status. He had risen from humble beginnings to become England's unofficial poet laureate, with a pension from the king and honorary degrees from both Oxford and Cambridge. If he was not the first professional author in England, he was the first to invest that role with dignity and respectability. His published *Works*, over which he labored with painstaking care, testify to an extraordinary feat of self-transformation.

Jonson's early life was tough and turbulent. The posthumous son of a London clergyman, he was educated at Westminster School under the great antiquarian scholar William Camden. There he developed his love of classical learning, but lacking the resources to continue his education, Jonson was forced to turn to his stepfather's trade of bricklaying, a life he "could not endure." He escaped by joining the English forces in Flanders, where, as he later boasted, he killed a man in single combat before the eyes of two armies. Back in London, his attempt to make a living as an actor and playwright almost ended in early disaster. He was imprisoned in 1597 for collaborating with Thomas Nashe on the scandalous play *The Isle of Dogs*

Jonson's 1616 *Works*. This title page makes a strong claim for the importance of Jonson's literary achievement and for the significance of English drama in general. The columned portico suggests Jonson's connection to the classical tradition, and the figures within it represent his mastery of various genres; they represent, clockwise from the top, Tragicomedy, Pastoral, Comedy, Tragedy, and Satire. Underneath Tragedy is a cart of the sort medieval traveling players would have used; underneath Comedy is an ancient Greek amphitheater. Centered just beneath Tragicomedy is a depiction of the English public theaters for which Jonson wrote many of his plays.

(now lost), and shortly after his release he killed one of his fellow actors in a duel. Jonson escaped the gallows by pleading benefit of clergy (a medieval privilege exempting felons who could read Latin from the death penalty). His learning had saved his life, but he emerged from captivity branded on the thumb, and with another mark against him as well. Under the influence of a priest imprisoned with him, he had converted to Catholicism. Jonson was now more than ever a marginal figure, distrusted by the society that he satirized brilliantly in his early plays.

Jonson's fortunes improved with the accession of James I, though not at once. In 1603 he was called before the Privy Council to answer charges of "popery and treason" found in his play *Sejanus*. Little more than a year later he was in jail again for his part in the play *Eastward Ho*, which openly mocked the king's Scots accent and propensity for selling knighthoods. Yet Jonson was now on the way to establishing himself at the new court. In 1605 he received the commission to organize the Twelfth Night entertainment, or masque; eventually he would produce twenty-four masques for the court, most of them in collaboration with the architect and scene designer Inigo Jones. In the same years that he was writing the masques he produced his greatest works for the public theater. His first successful play, *Every Man in His Humor* (1598), had inaugurated the so-called comedy of humors, which ridicules the eccentricities or passions of the characters, thought to be caused by physiological imbalance. He capitalized on this success with the comedies *Volpone* (1606), *Epicene* (1609), *The Alchemist* (1610), and *Bartholomew Fair* (1614). Jonson preserved the detached, satiric perspective of an outsider, but he was rising in society and making accommodations where necessary. In 1605, when suspicion fell upon him as a Catholic following the exposure of the Gunpowder Plot, he showed his loyalty by agreeing to serve as a spy for the Privy Council. Five years later he would return to the Church of England.

Although he rose to a position of eminent respectability, Jonson retained a quarrelsome spirit all his life. Much of his best work emerged out of fierce tensions with collaborators and contemporaries. At the turn of the century he became embroiled in the so-called War of the Theaters, in which he satirized and was satirized by his fellow playwrights John Marston and Thomas Dekker. Later, his long partnership with Inigo Jones was marked by ever more bitter rivalry over the relative importance of words and scenery in the masques. Jonson also poured invective on the theater audiences when they failed, in his view, to appreciate his plays. The failure of his play *The New Inn* elicited his "Ode to Himself" (1629), a disgusted farewell to the "loathed stage." Yet even after a stroke in 1629 left him partially paralyzed and confined to his home, Jonson continued to write, and was at work on a new play when he died in 1637.

In spite of his antagonistic nature, Jonson had a great capacity for friendship. His friends included Shakespeare, Donne, Francis Bacon, and John Selden. In later years he gathered about himself a group of admiring younger men known as the "Sons of Ben," whose numbers included Robert Herrick, Thomas Carew, and Sir John Suckling. He was a fascinating and inexhaustible conversationalist, as recorded by his friend William Drummond of Hawthornden, who carefully noted down Jonson's remarks on a wide variety of subjects, ranging from his fellow poets to his sexual predilections. Jonson also moved easily among the great of the land. His patrons included Lady Mary Wroth and other members of the Sidney and Herbert families. In "To Penshurst," a celebration of Robert Sidney's country estate, Jonson offers an ideal image of a social order in which a virtuous patriarchal governor offers ready hospitality to guests of all stations, from poets to kings.

"To Penshurst," together with Aemilia Lanyer's "Description of Cookham," inaugurated the small genre of the "country-house poem" in England. Jonson tried his hand, usually with success, at a wide range of poetic genres, including epitaph and epigram, love and funeral elegy, verse satire and verse letter, song and ode. More often than not he looked back to classical precedents. From the Roman poets Horace and Martial he derived not only generic models but an ideal vision of the artist and society against which he measured himself and the court he served. In many poems he adopted the persona of a witty, keenly perceptive, and scrupulously honest judge of men and women. The classical values Jonson most admired are enumerated in "Inviting a Friend to Supper," which describes a dinner party characterized by moderation, civility, graciousness, and pleasure that delights without enslaving— all contrasting sharply with the excess and licentiousness that marked the banquets and entertainments of imperial Rome and Stuart England. Yet the poet who produced this image of moderation was a man of immense appetites, which found expression in his art as well as in his life. His best works seethe with an almost uncontrollable imaginative energy and lust for abundance. Even his profound classical learning manifests this impulse. The notes and references to learned authorities that spill across the margins of his *Works* can be seen as the literary equivalent of food and drink piled high on the poet's table. Years of hardship had taught Jonson to seek his feasts in his imagination, and he could make the most mundane object the basis for flights of high fancy. As he told Drummond, he once "consumed a whole night in lying looking to his great toe, about which he had seen Tartars and Turks, Romans and Carthaginians fight in his imagination." In Drummond's view, Jonson was "oppressed with fantasy." Perhaps it was so—but Jonson's capacity for fantasy also produced a wide variety of plays, masques, and poems, in styles ranging from witty comedy to delicate lyricism.

FROM EPIGRAMS[1]

To My Book

It will be looked for, book, when some but see
  Thy title, *Epigrams*, and named of me,
Thou should'st be bold, licentious, full of gall,
  Wormwood° and sulphur, sharp and toothed[2] withal,   *bitter-tasting plant*
5 Become a petulant thing, hurl ink and wit
  As madmen stones, not caring whom they hit.
Deceive their malice who could wish it so,
  And by thy wiser temper let men know
Thou art not covetous of least self-fame
10 Made from the hazard of another's shame[3]—
Much less with lewd, profane, and beastly phrase
  To catch the world's loose laughter or vain gaze.
He that departs° with his own honesty   *parts*
  For vulgar praise, doth it too dearly buy.

1616

On My First Daughter[1]

Here lies, to each her parents' ruth,°   *grief*
Mary, the daughter of their youth;
Yet all heaven's gifts being heaven's due,
It makes the father less to rue.°   *regret*
5 At six months' end she parted hence

---

1. Epigrams are commonly thought of as brief, witty, incisive poems of personal invective, often with a surprise turn at the end. But Jonson uses the word in a more liberal sense. His "Epigrams," a separate section in his collected *Works* of 1616, include not only sharp, satiric poems but many complimentary ones to friends and patrons, as well as memorial epitaphs and a verse letter, "Inviting a Friend to Supper."

2. The distinction between toothed (biting) and toothless (general) satires was a commonplace.

3. Here, as often elsewhere, Jonson echoes the greatest Roman epigrammatist, Martial.

1. Probably written in the late 1590s, in Jonson's Roman Catholic period (ca. 1598–1610).

With safety of her innocence;
Whose soul heaven's queen,° whose name she bears,   *Mary*
In comfort of her mother's tears,
Hath placed amongst her virgin-train:
10   Where, while that severed doth remain,
This grave partakes the fleshly birth;°   *the body*
Which cover lightly, gentle earth![2]

1616

To John Donne

Donne, the delight of Phoebus° and each Muse,   *god of poetry*
Who, to thy one, all other brains refuse;[1]
Whose every work, of thy most early wit,
Came forth example[2] and remains so yet;
5   Longer a-knowing than most wits do live,
And which no affection praise enough can give.
To it[3] thy language, letters, arts, best life,
Which might with half mankind maintain a strife.
All which I meant to praise, and yet I would,
10   But leave, because I cannot as I should.

1616

On My First Son

Farewell, thou child of my right hand,[1] and joy;
My sin was too much hope of thee, loved boy.
Seven years thou wert lent to me, and I thee pay,
Exacted by thy fate, on the just day.
5   O could I lose all father now! For why
Will man lament the state he should envy,
To have so soon 'scaped world's and flesh's rage,
And, if no other misery, yet age?
Rest in soft peace, and asked, say, "Here doth lie
10   Ben Jonson his best piece of poetry."[2]
For whose sake henceforth all his vows be such
As what he loves may never like too much.[3]

1616

---

2. A common sentiment in Latin epitaphs.
1. I.e., the muses shower their favors exclusively on you.
2. A pattern for others to imitate.
3. In addition to your wit.
1. A literal translation of the Hebrew name "Benjamin," which implies the meaning "dexter-

ous" or "fortunate." The boy was born in 1596 and died on his birthday in 1603.
2. Poet and father are both "makers," Jonson's favorite term for the poet.
3. The obscure grammar of the last lines allows for various readings; "like" may carry the sense of "please."

On Lucy, Countess of Bedford[1]

This morning, timely rapt with holy fire,
I thought to form unto my zealous muse,
What kind of creature I could most desire,
To honor, serve, and love; as poets use.[2]
5   I meant to make her fair, and free, and wise,
Of greatest blood, and yet more good than great;
I meant the day-star° should not brighter rise,   the sun
Nor lend like influence[3] from his lucent seat.
I meant she should be courteous, facile,° sweet,   affable
10 Hating that solemn vice of greatness, pride;
I meant each softest virtue, there should meet,
Fit in that softer bosom to reside.
Only a learnèd, and a manly soul
I purposed her; that should, with even powers,
15 The rock, the spindle, and the shears[4] control
Of destiny, and spin her own free hours.
Such when I meant to feign, and wished to see,
My muse bad, *Bedford* write, and that was she.

1616

Inviting a Friend to Supper

Tonight, grave sir, both my poor house and I
  Do equally desire your company:
Not that we think us worthy such a guest,
  But that your worth will dignify our feast
5   With those that come; whose grace may make that seem
  Something, which else could hope for no esteem.
It is the fair acceptance, sir, creates
  The entertainment perfect: not the cates.°   food
Yet shall you have, to rectify your palate,
10   An olive, capers, or some better salad
Ushering the mutton; with a short-legged hen,
  If we can get her, full of eggs, and then
Lemons and wine for sauce; to° these, a coney°   besides / rabbit
  Is not to be despaired of for our money;
15 And though fowl now be scarce, yet there are clerks,°   scholars
  The sky not falling, think we may have larks.
I'll tell you of more, and lie, so you will come:
  Of partridge, pheasant, woodcock, of which some
May yet be there; and godwit if we can,

---

1. Lucy Russell, Countess of Bedford, was a famous patroness of the age, to whom Jonson, Donne, and many other poets addressed poems of compliment.
2. This elegant epigram of praise plays off against the Pygmalion story, in which the sculptor molds a statue of his ideal woman and she then comes to life.
3. Stars were supposed to emit an ethereal fluid, or "influence," that affected the affairs of mortals, for good or ill.
4. Emblems of the three Fates: Clotho spun the thread of life, Lachesis decided its length, and Atropos cut the thread to end life.

20   Knot, rail, and ruff, too.¹ Howsoe'er, my man°   *servant*
        Shall read a piece of Virgil, Tacitus,
            Livy, or of some better book to us,
        Of which we'll speak our minds amidst our meat;°   *food (of any kind)*
        And I'll profess° no verses to repeat: *promise*
25   To this,° if aught appear which I not know of,   *on this point*
            That will the pastry, not my paper, show of.²
        Digestive cheese and fruit there sure will be;
            But that which most doth take my muse and me
        Is a pure cup of rich canary wine,
30   Which is the Mermaid's now, but shall be mine;
        Of which, had Horace or Anacreon³ tasted,
            Their lives, as do their lines, till now had lasted.
        Tobacco, nectar, or the Thespian spring
            Are all but Luther's beer to this I sing.⁴
35   Of this we will sup free but moderately,
            And we will have no Pooly or Parrot⁵ by;
        Nor shall our cups make any guilty men,
            But at our parting we will be as when
        We innocently met. No simple word
40   That shall be uttered at our mirthful board
        Shall make us sad next morning, or affright
            The liberty that we'll enjoy tonight.

                                          1616

Epitaph on S. P., a Child of Queen Elizabeth's Chapel¹

        Weep with me, all you that read
            This little story;
        And know for whom a tear you shed,
            Death's self is sorry.
5   'Twas a child that so did thrive
            In grace and feature,
        As Heaven and Nature seemed to strive
            Which owned the creature.
        Years he numbered scarce thirteen
10   When Fates turned cruel,
        Yet three filled zodiacs had he been
            The stage's jewel;²
        And did act (what now we moan)
            Old men so duly,°   *aptly*

---

1. All these are edible birds.
2. Paper-lined pans were used to keep pies from sticking; the writing sometimes rubbed off on the piecrust.
3. Horace and Anacreon (one in Latin, the other in Greek) wrote many poems in praise of wine. The Mermaid tavern was a favorite haunt of the poets; sweet wine from the Canary Islands was popular in England.
4. Tobacco was an expensive New World novelty in Jonson's time. Nectar is the drink of the gods. The Thespian spring, on Mount Helicon, is a legendary source of poetic inspiration. Compared with canary, these intoxicants are no better than inferior German beer.
5. Pooly and Parrot were government spies. As a Roman Catholic, Jonson had reason to be wary of undercover agents.
1. Salomon Pavy, a boy actor in the troupe known as the Children of Queen Elizabeth's Chapel, who had appeared in several of Jonson's plays; he died in 1602.
2. He had been on the stage for three seasons.

15 As, sooth,° the Parcae° thought him one,   *in truth / Fates*
    He played so truly.
So, by error, to his fate
    They all consented;
But, viewing him since (alas, too late),
20   They have repented,
And have sought (to give new birth)
    In baths[3] to steep him;
But, being so much too good for earth,
    Heaven vows to keep him.

1616

FROM THE FOREST[1]

To Penshurst[2]

Thou art not, Penshurst, built to envious show,
    Of touch[3] or marble; nor canst boast a row
Of polished pillars, or a roof of gold;
    Thou hast no lantern° whereof tales are told,   *cupola*
5 Or stair, or courts; but stand'st an ancient pile,°   *edifice*
    And, these grudged at,[4] art reverenced the while.
Thou joy'st in better marks, of soil, of air,
    Of wood, of water; therein thou art fair.
Thou hast thy walks for health, as well as sport;
10   Thy mount, to which the dryads° do resort,   *wood nymphs*
Where Pan and Bacchus their high feasts have made,
    Beneath the broad beech and the chestnut shade;
That taller tree, which of a nut was set
    At his great birth where all the Muses met.[5]
15 There in the writhèd bark are cut the names
    Of many a sylvan,° taken with his flames;   *countryman*
And thence the ruddy satyrs oft provoke
    The lighter fauns[6] to reach thy Lady's Oak.[7]
Thy copse° too, named of Gamage[8] thou hast there,   *little woods*
20   That never fails to serve thee seasoned deer
When thou wouldst feast or exercise thy friends.
    The lower land, that to the river bends,
Thy sheep, thy bullocks, kine,° and calves do feed;   *cattle*
    The middle grounds thy mares and horses breed.

3. Perhaps such magic baths as that of Medea, which restored Jason's father to his first youth (Ovid, *Metamorphoses* 7).

1. In the 1616 *Works*, Jonson grouped some of his nonepigrammatic poems under the heading "The Forest," a translation of the term *Sylvae*, meaning a poetic miscellany. "To Penshurst" and the two following poems are from that group.

2. Penshurst, in Kent, was the estate of Robert Sidney, Viscount Lisle (later, Earl of Leicester), a younger brother of the poet Sir Philip Sidney. Along with Lanyer's "The Description of Cookham" (pp. 702–7), this poem inaugurated the small genre of English "country-house" poems, which includes Marvell's *Upon Appleton House*.

3. Touchstone, an expensive black basalt.

4. More pretentious houses attract envy.

5. Sir Philip Sidney was born at Penshurst.

6. Satyrs and fauns were woodland spirits. Satyrs had the bodies of men and the legs (and horns) of goats. "Provoke": challenge to a race.

7. Named after a lady of the house who went into labor under its branches.

8. Lady Barbara (Gamage) Sidney, wife of Sir Robert.

25   Each bank doth yield thee conies;° and the tops,°   *rabbits / high ground*
      Fertile of wood, Ashore and Sidney's copse,
To crown thy open table, doth provide
      The purpled pheasant with the speckled side;
The painted partridge lies in every field,
30   And for thy mess° is willing to be killed.   *table*
And if the high-swollen Medway[9] fail thy dish,
      Thou hast thy ponds, that pay thee tribute fish:
Fat agèd carps that run into thy net,
      And pikes, now weary their own kind to eat,
35   As loath the second draft or cast to stay,
      Officiously° at first themselves betray;   *dutifully*
Bright eels that emulate them, and leap on land
      Before the fisher, or into his hand.
Then hath thy orchard fruit, thy garden flowers,
40   Fresh as the air, and new as are the hours.
The early cherry, with the later plum,
      Fig, grape, and quince, each in his time doth come;
The blushing apricot and woolly peach
      Hang on thy walls, that every child may reach.
45   And though thy walls be of the country stone,
      They're reared with no man's ruin, no man's groan;
There's none that dwell about them wish them down;
      But all come in, the farmer and the clown,°   *peasant*
And no one empty-handed, to salute
50   Thy lord and lady, though they have no suit.°   *request to make*
Some bring a capon, some a rural cake,
      Some nuts, some apples; some that think they make
The better cheeses bring them, or else send
      By their ripe daughters, whom they would commend
55   This way to husbands, and whose baskets bear
      An emblem of themselves in plum or pear.
But what can this (more than express their love)
      Add to thy free provisions, far above
The need of such? whose liberal board doth flow
60   With all that hospitality doth know;
Where comes no guest but is allowed to eat,
      Without his fear, and of thy lord's own meat;°   *food*
Where the same beer and bread, and selfsame wine,
      That is his lordship's shall be also mine,[1]
65   And I not fain to sit (as some this day
      At great men's tables), and yet dine away.
Here no man tells° my cups; nor, standing by,   *counts*
      A waiter doth my gluttony envy,°   *resent*
But gives me what I call, and lets me eat;
70   He knows below° he shall find plenty of meat.   *in the servants' quarters*
Thy tables hoard not up for the next day;
      Nor, when I take my lodging, need I pray
For fire, or lights, or livery;° all is there,   *provisions*
      As if thou then wert mine, or I reigned here:

---

9. The local river.
1. Different courses might be served to different guests, depending on their social status. The lord would have the best food.

75 There's nothing I can wish, for which I stay.°   *wait*
      That found King James when, hunting late this way
    With his brave son, the Prince,[2] they saw thy fires
      Shine bright on every hearth, as the desires
    Of thy Penates° had been set on flame   *Roman household gods*
80   To entertain them; or the country came
    With all their zeal to warm their welcome here.
      What (great I will not say, but) sudden cheer
    Didst thou then make 'em! And what praise was heaped
      On thy good lady then, who therein reaped
85 The just reward of her high housewifery;
      To have her linen, plate, and all things nigh,
    When she was far; and not a room but dressed
      As if it had expected such a guest!
    These, Penshurst, are thy praise, and yet not all.
90   Thy lady's noble, fruitful, chaste withal.
    His children thy great lord may call his own,
      A fortune in this age but rarely known.
    They are, and have been, taught religion; thence
      Their gentler spirits have sucked innocence.
95 Each morn and even they are taught to pray,
      With the whole household, and may, every day,
    Read in their virtuous parents' noble parts°   *attributes*
      The mysteries of manners,° arms, and arts.   *moral behavior*
    Now, Penshurst, they that will proportion° thee   *compare*
100   With other edifices, when they see
    Those proud, ambitious heaps, and nothing else,
      May say, their lords have built, but thy lord dwells.

                                                                          1616

From Underwood[1]

From A Celebration of Charis in Ten Lyric Pieces[2]

4. *Her Triumph*[3]

    See the chariot at hand here of Love,
      Wherein my lady rideth!
    Each that draws is a swan or a dove,[4]
      And well the car Love guideth.
5   As she goes, all hearts do duty
          Unto her beauty;
    And enamored do wish, so they might
          But enjoy such a sight,
    That they still° were to run by her side,   *always*
10 Through swords, through seas, whither she would ride.

2. Prince Henry, the heir apparent, who died in November 1612.
1. Preparing a second edition of his *Works* (published posthumously in 1640–41), Jonson added a third section of poems, "Underwood," "out of the analogy they hold to *The Forest* in my former book."

2. The Greek word *charis*, from which Jonson's lady takes her name, means "grace" or "loveliness."
3. Following Petrarch, many Renaissance poets used the figure of the triumphal procession to celebrate a person or concept—time, chastity, fame, etc. Metrically, this poem is highly complex.
4. Venus's birds.

Do but look on her eyes, they do light
    All that Love's world compriseth!
Do but look on her hair, it is bright
    As Love's star° when it riseth!   *Venus, the morning star*
15 Do but mark,° her forehead's smoother   *observe*
        Than words that soothe her!
And from her archèd brows, such a grace
        Sheds itself through the face,
As alone there triumphs to the life
20 All the gain, all the good, of the elements' strife.[5]

Have you seen but a bright lily grow,
    Before rude hands have touched it?
Have you marked but the fall o' the snow,
    Before the soil hath smutched it?
25 Have you felt the wool o' the beaver,
        Or swan's down ever?
Or have smelt o' the bud o' the briar,
        Or the nard[6] i' the fire?
Or have tasted the bag o' the bee?
30 O so white! O so soft! O so sweet is she!

                             1640–41

Queen and Huntress[1]

    Queen and huntress, chaste and fair,
    Now the sun is laid to sleep,
    Seated in thy silver chair,
    State in wonted° manner keep;   *accustomed*
5   Hesperus entreats thy light,
    Goddess excellently bright.

    Earth, let not thy envious shade
    Dare itself to interpose;[2]
    Cynthia's shining orb was made
10   Heaven to clear, when day did close.
    Bless us then with wishèd sight,
    Goddess excellently bright.

    Lay thy bow of pearl apart,
    And thy crystal-shining quiver;
15   Give unto the flying hart
    Space to breathe, how short soever.
    Thou that mak'st a day of night,
    Goddess excellently bright.

                             1600

5. The four elements—earth, water, air, fire—
were thought to be in perpetual conflict.
6. Spikenard, an aromatic ointment.
1. Also from *Cynthia's Revels* (4.3), this song is
sung by Hesperus, the evening star, to Cynthia,
or Diana, goddess of chastity and the moon—
with whom Queen Elizabeth was constantly
compared.
2. Eclipses were thought to portend evil.

To the Memory of My Beloved, The Author, Mr. William Shakespeare, and What He Hath Left Us[1]

To draw no envy, Shakespeare, on thy name,
  Am I thus ample° to thy book and fame,   *copious*
While I confess thy writings to be such
  As neither man nor muse can praise too much.
5 'Tis true, and all men's suffrage.° But these ways   *admission*
  Were not the paths I meant unto thy praise;
For silliest° ignorance on these may light,   *simplest*
  Which, when it sounds at best, but echoes right;
Or blind affection, which doth ne'er advance
10   The truth, but gropes, and urgeth all by chance;
Or crafty malice might pretend this praise,
  And think to ruin where it seemed to raise.
These are as° some infamous bawd or whore   *as though*
  Should praise a matron. What could hurt her more?
15 But thou art proof against them, and, indeed,
  Above th' ill fortune of them, or the need.
I therefore will begin. Soul of the age!
  The applause! Delight! The wonder of our stage!
My Shakespeare, rise; I will not lodge thee by
20   Chaucer or Spenser, or bid Beaumont lie
A little further to make thee a room:[2]
  Thou art a monument without a tomb,
And art alive still while thy book doth live,
  And we have wits to read and praise to give.
25 That I not mix thee so, my brain excuses,
  I mean with great, but disproportioned° Muses;   *not comparable*
For, if I thought my judgment were of years,
  I should commit thee surely with thy peers,
And tell how far thou didst our Lyly outshine,
30   Or sporting Kyd, or Marlowe's mighty line.[3]
And though thou hadst small Latin and less Greek,[4]
  From thence to honor thee I would not seek°   *lack*
For names, but call forth thund'ring Aeschylus,
  Euripides, and Sophocles to us,
35 Pacuvius, Accius, him of Cordova dead,[5]
  To life again, to hear thy buskin° tread   *symbol of tragedy*
And shake a stage; or, when thy socks° were on,   *symbol of comedy*
  Leave thee alone for the comparison
Of all that insolent Greece or haughty Rome
40   Sent forth, or since did from their ashes come.
Triumph, my Britain; thou hast one to show
  To whom all scenes° of Europe homage owe.   *stages*

---

1. This poem was prefixed to the first folio of Shakespeare's plays (1623).
2. Chaucer, Spenser, and Francis Beaumont were buried in Westminster Abbey; Shakespeare, in Stratford.
3. John Lyly, Thomas Kyd, and Christopher Marlowe were Elizabethan dramatists contemporary or nearly contemporary with Shakespeare.

4. Shakespeare's Latin was pretty good, but Jonson is judging by the standard of his own remarkable scholarship.
5. Marcus Pacuvius, Lucius Accius (2nd century B.C.E.), and "him of Cordova" (1st century C.E.), were Latin tragedians. Seneca's tragedies had a large influence on Elizabethan revenge tragedy.

He was not of an age, but for all time!
    And all the Muses still were in their prime
45 When like Apollo° he came forth to warm   *god of poetry*
    Our ears, or like a Mercury° to charm.   *god of eloquence*
Nature herself was proud of his designs,
    And joyed to wear the dressing of his lines,
Which were so richly spun, and woven so fit,
50 As, since, she will vouchsafe° no other wit: *grant*
The merry Greek, tart Aristophanes,
    Neat Terence, witty Plautus[6] now not please,
But antiquated and deserted lie,
    As they were not of Nature's family.
55 Yet must I not give nature all; thy art,
    My gentle Shakespeare, must enjoy a part.
For though the poet's matter° nature be,   *subject matter*
    His art doth give the fashion;° and that he   *form, style*
Who casts° to write a living line must sweat   *undertakes*
60 (Such as thine are) and strike the second heat
Upon the Muses' anvil; turn the same,
    And himself with it, that he thinks to frame,
Or for° the laurel he may gain a scorn;   *instead of*
    For a good poet's made as well as born,
65 And such wert thou. Look how the father's face
    Lives in his issue;° even so the race   *offspring*
Of Shakespeare's mind and manners brightly shines
    In his well-turnèd and true-filèd lines,
In each of which he seems to shake a lance,[7]
70 As brandished at the eyes of ignorance.
Sweet swan of Avon, what a sight it were
    To see thee in our waters yet appear,
And make those flights upon the banks of Thames
    That so did take Eliza and our James![8]
75 But stay; I see thee in the hemisphere
    Advanced and made a constellation there![9]
Shine forth, thou star of poets, and with rage
    Or influence[1] chide or cheer the drooping stage,
Which, since thy flight from hence, hath mourned like night,
80 And despairs day, but for thy volume's light.

1623

---

6. Aristophanes, an ancient Greek satirist and writer of comedy; Terence and Plautus (2nd and 3rd centuries B.C.E.), Roman writers of comedy.
7. Pun on Shake-speare.
8. Queen Elizabeth and King James.
9. Heroes and demigods were typically exalted after death to a place among the stars.

MARY WROTH
1587–1651?

L ady Mary Wroth was the most prolific, self-conscious, and impressive female
author of the Jacobean era. Her published work (1621) includes two firsts for an
Englishwoman: a 558-page romance, *The Countess of Montgomery's Urania*, which
includes more than fifty poems, and appended to it a Petrarchan lyric sequence that
had circulated some years in manuscript, 103 sonnets and elegant songs titled *Pamphilia to Amphilanthus*. Wroth left unpublished a very long but unfinished continuation
of the *Urania* and a pastoral drama, *Love's Victory*, also a first for an Englishwoman.
Her achievement was fostered by her strong sense of identity as a Sidney, heir to the
literary talent and cultural role of her famous uncle Sir Philip Sidney, her famous aunt
Mary Sidney Herbert, Countess of Pembroke, who may have served as mentor to her;
and her father Robert Sidney, Viscount Lisle, author of a recently discovered sonnet
sequence. But she used that heritage transgressively to replace heroes with heroines in
genres employed by the male Sidney authors—notably Philip Sidney's *Astrophil and
Stella* and *The Countess of Pembroke's Arcadia*—transforming their gender politics
and exploring the poetics and situation of women writers.

As Robert Sidney's eldest daughter, she lived and was educated at Penshurst, the
Sidney country house celebrated by Ben Jonson, and was often at her aunt's "little
college" at Wilton. She was married (incompatibly) at age seventeen to Sir Robert
Wroth of Durrance and Loughton Manor, whose office it was to facilitate the king's
hunting; and she was patron to several poets, including Jonson. He celebrated her in
two epigrams and in a verse letter honoring her husband, dedicated his great comedy
The Alchemist to her, and claimed in his only sonnet that the artistry and erotic
power of her sonnets had made him "a better lover, and much better poet." After her
husband's death she carried on a long-standing love affair with her married first
cousin, William Herbert, Earl of Pembroke, himself a poet, a powerful courtier, and
a patron of the theater and of literature. That relationship produced two children
and occasioned some scandal.

The significant names in the title of Wroth's Petrarchan sequence, *Pamphilia* ("all-
loving") *to Amphilanthus* ("lover of two"), are from characters in her romance who at
times shadow Wroth and her lover Pembroke. The Petrarchan lyric sequence had
long served as the major genre for analyzing a male lover's passions, frustrations, and
fantasies (and sometimes his career anxieties). So although the sonnet sequence was
becoming passé by Wroth's time, it was an obvious choice for a woman poet undertaking the construction of subjectivity in a female lover-speaker. Wroth does not,
however, simply reverse roles. Pamphilia addresses very few sonnets to Amphilanthus
and seldom assumes the Petrarchan lover's position of abject servitude to a cruel
beloved. Instead, she proclaims subjection to Cupid, usually identified with the force
of her own desire. This radical revision identifies female desire as the source and
center of the love relationship and celebrates the woman lover-poet's movement from
the bondage of chaotic passion to the freedom of self-chosen constancy.

Wroth's romance, *Urania*, breaks the romance convention of a plot centered on
courtship, portraying instead married heroines and their love relationships, both
inside and outside of marriage. It is in part an idealizing fantasy: the principal characters are queens, kings, and emperors, with the power and comparative freedom
such positions allow. However, the landscape is not Arcadia or Fairyland but wartorn
Europe and Asia. The romance fantasy, with Spenserian symbolic places and knights
fighting evil tyrants and monsters, only partially overlays a rigidly patriarchal Jaco-

Lady Mary Wroth, with archlute (artist unknown). The image represents Mary Wroth in a conventional pose and role, holding the archlute, which indicates that she has been educated in the graceful arts that an aristocratic woman was expected to know. But the massive archlute, emblem of song-making, also points to her Sidney heritage—as niece of the poets Sir Philip Sidney and the Countess of Pembroke, and as daughter of Sir Robert Sidney of Penshurst, also a poet—and to her own unconventional role as female poet.

bean world rife with rape, incest, arranged or forced marriages, jealous husbands, tortured women, and endangered children. Those perils, affecting all women from shepherdesses to queens, are rendered in large part through the numerous stories interpolated in romance fashion within the principal plots. The male heroes are courageous fighters and attractive lovers, but all are flawed by inconstancy. For Wroth, true heroism consists of integrity in love despite social constraints and psychological pressures. A few women are heroic in this sense: Pamphilia, the good queen and pattern of constancy; Urania, the wise counselor who wins self-knowledge and makes wise choices in love; and Veralinda, who weds her true lover after great trials. Almost all Wroth's female characters define themselves through storytelling and making poems. The women compose twice as many of the poems as the men do. Pamphilia, Wroth's surrogate, is singled out as a poet by vocation, both by the number of her poems and by their recognized excellence.

Many contemporaries assumed that the *Urania* was a scandalous roman à clef, alluding not only to Sidney-Pembroke-Wroth affairs but to notable personages of the Jacobean court. A public outcry from one of them, Lord Edward Denny, elicited a spirited satiric response from Wroth. Although she suggested to the king's minister Buckingham that she withdraw the work from circulation, there is no evidence that she actually did so. The uproar, however, may have discouraged her from publishing part 2 of the romance and her pastoral drama.

From Pamphilia to Amphilanthus[1]

1

When night's black mantle could most darkness prove,
  And sleep, death's image, did my senses hire
From knowledge of myself, then thoughts did move
  Swifter than those most swiftness need require.
5 In sleep, a chariot drawn by winged desire
  I saw, where sat bright Venus, Queen of Love,
And at her feet, her son,° still adding fire   Cupid
  To burning hearts, which she did hold above.
But one heart flaming more than all the rest
10 The goddess held, and put it to my breast.
"Dear son, now shut,"[2] said she: "thus must we win."
He her obeyed, and martyred my poor heart.
  I, waking, hoped as dreams it would depart:
  Yet since, O me, a lover I have been.

16

Am I thus conquered? Have I lost the powers
  That to withstand, which joys to ruin me?[3]
Must I be still while it my strength devours,
  And captive leads me prisoner, bound, unfree?
5 Love first shall leave men's fancies to them free,[4]
  Desire shall quench Love's flames, spring hate sweet showers,
Love shall loose all his darts, have sight, and see
  His shame, and wishings hinder happy hours.
Why should we not Love's purblind° charms resist?   completely blind
10 Must we be servile, doing what he list?°   what pleases him
  No, seek some host to harbor thee: I fly
Thy babish tricks, and freedom do profess.
  But O my hurt makes my lost heart confess
  I love, and must: So farewell liberty.

40

False hope which feeds but to destroy, and spill[5]
  What it first breeds; unnatural to the birth
Of thine own womb; conceiving but to kill,
  And plenty gives to make the greater dearth,[6]

---

1. Pamphilia ("all-loving") is the protagonist of
Urania. Her unfaithful beloved's name means
"lover of two." These characters are first cousins,
like Mary Wroth and William Herbert; their
names adumbrate the main theme of both the
romance and the appended sonnet sequence,
constancy in the face of unfaithfulness.
Pamphilia to Amphilanthus is broken into several
separately numbered series (the first of which
includes forty-eight sonnets, with songs inserted
after every sixth sonnet except the last). In Josephine A. Roberts's edition of Wroth's poetry, the
poems are numbered consecutively throughout

the work; we have adopted this convenient
renumbering.
2. I.e., shut the burning heart into Pamphilia's
breast.
3. I.e., have I lost the power to withstand love
("That"), which takes pleasure in ruining me?
4. I.e., this and the other impossibilities that follow will occur before I surrender to love.
5. Kill. The image is of miscarriage or infanti-
cide.
6. Gives abundance only to make scarcity more
painful afterward.

5 So tyrants do who falsely ruling earth
    Outwardly grace them,[7] and with profits fill,
    Advance those who appointed are to death,
    To make their greater fall to please their will.
Thus shadow° they their wicked vile intent,   *conceal*
10   Coloring evil with a show of good
    While in fair shows their malice so is spent;[8]
    Hope kills the heart, and tyrants shed the blood.
For hope deluding brings us to the pride
    Of our desires the farther down to slide.

68

My pain, still smothered in my grievèd breast,
    Seeks for some ease, yet cannot passage find
To be discharged of this unwelcome guest:
    When most I strive, most fast his burdens bind,
5 Like to a ship on Goodwin's[9] cast by wind,
    The more she strives, more deep in sand is pressed,
    Till she be lost; so am I, in this kind,°   *manner*
    Sunk, and devoured, and swallowed by unrest,
Lost, shipwrecked, spoiled, debarred of smallest hope,
10   Nothing of pleasure left; save thoughts have scope,
    Which wander may. Go then, my thoughts, and cry
"Hope's perished, love tempest-beaten, joy lost:
    Killing despair hath all these blessings crossed."
    Yet faith still cries, "love will not falsify."

74

SONG

Love a child is ever crying,
    Please him, and he straight is flying;
    Give him, he the more is craving,
    Never satisfied with having.

5 His desires have no measure,
    Endless folly is his treasure;
    What he promiseth he breaketh:
    Trust not one word that he speaketh.

He vows nothing but false matter,
10   And to cozen° you he'll flatter.   *cheat*
    Let him gain the hand,° he'll leave you,   *the upper hand*
    And still glory to deceive you.

He will triumph in your wailing,
    And yet cause be of your failing:

---

7. I.e., those whom they mean to destroy (see next line).
8. Expended, employed. "Shows": appearances.
9. Goodwin Sands, a line of shoals at the entrance to the Strait of Dover.

15 These his virtues are, and slighter
    Are his gifts, his favors lighter.

    Feathers are as firm in staying,
    Wolves no fiercer in their preying.
    As a child then leave him crying,
20 Nor seek him, so given to flying.

From *A Crown of Sonnets Dedicated to Love*[1]

77

In this strange labyrinth how shall I turn?
    Ways° are on all sides, while the way I miss: *paths*
    If to the right hand, there in love I burn;
    Let me go forward, therein danger is;
5 If to the left, suspicion hinders bliss,
    Let me° turn back, shame cries I ought return,   *if I*
    Nor faint though crosses[2] with my fortunes kiss;
    Stand still is harder, although sure to mourn.[3]
Then let me take the right- or left-hand way;
10 Go forward, or stand still, or back retire;
    I must these doubts endure without allay°   *abatement*
    Or help, but travail find for my best hire.[4]
Yet that which most my troubled sense doth move
Is to leave all, and take the thread of love.[5]

1. The "crown" is a difficult poetic form (originally Italian and usually known by its Italian
name, corona) in which the last line of each
poem serves as the first line of the next, until a
circle is completed by the last line of the final
poem, which is the same as the first line of the
first one. The number of poems varies from
seven to (as in Wroth's corona) fourteen.
In contrast to the errant-child Cupid of the preceding part of the sequence, Love in this series is
a mature and just monarch, whose true service

ennobles lovers. The crown is in part a recanta-
tion of the harsh judgment of love earlier in the
sequence. But Pamphilia relapses into melancholy afterward.
2. Troubles, adversity. "Faint": lose heart.
3. I.e., certain to make me mourn.
4. I.e., I find travail (with a pun on "travel," the
spelling in the 1621 edition) is my only reward.
5. Ariadne gave Theseus a thread to follow so as
to find his way out of the Labyrinth, after killing
the Minotaur at its center.

THOMAS HOBBES
1588–1679

The English civil war and its aftermath raised fundamental questions about the
nature and legitimacy of state power. In 1651 Thomas Hobbes attempted to answer
those questions in his ambitious masterwork of political philosophy, *Leviathan*. He
grounded his political vision upon a comprehensive philosophy of nature and knowledge. Hobbes held that everything in the universe is composed only of matter; spirit
does not exist. All knowledge is gained through sensory impressions, which are

nothing but matter in motion. What we call the self is, for Hobbes, simply a tissue of sensory impressions—clear and immediate in the presence of the objects that evoke them, vague and less vivid in their absence. As a result, an iron determinism of cause and effect governs everything in the universe, including human action.

Because, Hobbes argues, all humans are roughly equal mentally and physically, they possess equal hopes of attaining goods, as well as equal fears of danger from others. In the state of nature, before the foundation of some sovereign power to keep them in awe, everyone is continually at war with everyone else, and life, in Hobbes's memorable phrase, is "solitary, poor, nasty, brutish, and short." To escape this ghastly strife, humans covenant with one another to establish a sovereign government over all of them. That sovereign power—which need not be a king but is always indivisible— incorporates the wills and individuality of them all, so that the people no longer have rights or liberties apart from the sovereign's will. The sovereign's dominion over his subjects extends to the right to pronounce on all matters of religion.

While other versions of covenant theory, for instance Milton's *Tenure of Kings and Magistrates*, insisted that the power transferred by the people to the sovereign could be limited or revoked, in Hobbes's system, the founding political covenant must be a permanent one, since no tyranny can be so evil as the state of war that the sovereign power prevents. Yet if the sovereign power should be overthrown, the individual ruler has no further claim, and the people, for their safety, must accept the new sovereign unconditionally. Hobbes was generally associated with the royalist cause, as a tutor to the Cavendish family and as an exile in Paris from 1640 to 1651, where he tutored the future Charles II. Yet his argument made no distinction between a legitimate monarch and a successful usurper, like Oliver Cromwell. Moreover, Hobbes's philosophical materialism led many to suspect him of atheism; after the Restoration, the publication of many of his books, including a history of the civil war entitled *Behemoth*, was prohibited for a number of years. Undeterred, Hobbes continued to write on a variety of psychological, political, and mathematical topics, completing a translation of Homer's *Iliad* and *Odyssey* at the age of eighty-six.

Hobbes's political theory did not fit easily into the established patterns of English thought partly because his perspective was essentially cosmopolitan. Educated at Oxford as a classicist, Hobbes traveled widely in Europe between 1610 and 1660 as a companion and tutor of noblemen, often remaining abroad for years at a time. During these lengthy sojourns he became acquainted with many of the leading intellectuals and scientists on the Continent, including Galileo, Descartes, and the prominent French mathematician Pierre Gassendi, who argued that the universe was governed entirely by mechanical principles. The most important political philosophers for Hobbes were also Continental figures: the Italian Niccolò Machiavelli, who saw human beings as naturally competitive and power hungry, and Jean Bodin, a French theorist of indivisible, absolute monarchy. One English writer who did influence Hobbes profoundly was Francis Bacon, whose amanuensis Hobbes had been in Bacon's last years. Ironically, Hobbes was not invited to join the Royal Society, established after the Restoration on Baconian principles, because his religious views were suspect and because he had quarreled with several of the society's founders. Yet Hobbes is truly Bacon's heir, sharing Bacon's utter lack of sentimentality and a memorably astringent prose style.

From Leviathan[1]

From *Part 1. Of Man*

CHAPTER 13. OF THE NATURAL CONDITION OF MANKIND AS CONCERNING THEIR FELICITY AND MISERY

Nature hath made men so equal in the faculties of body and mind as that, though there be found one man sometimes manifestly stronger in body or of quicker mind than another, yet when all is reckoned together, the difference between man and man is not so considerable as that one man can thereupon claim to himself any benefit, to which another may not pretend as well as he. For as to the strength of body, the weakest has strength enough to kill the strongest, either by secret machination, or by confederacy[2] with others that are in the same danger with himself.

And as to the faculties of the mind—setting aside the arts grounded upon words, and especially that skill of proceeding upon general and infallible rules, called science; which very few have, and but in few things; as being not a native faculty, born with us; nor attained, as prudence, while we look after somewhat else—I find yet a greater equality amongst men than that of strength. For prudence is but experience, which equal time equally bestows on all men, in those things they equally apply themselves unto. That which may perhaps make such equality incredible is but a vain conceit of one's own wisdom, which almost all men think they have in a greater degree than the vulgar—that is, than all men but themselves and a few others, whom by fame, or for concurring with themselves, they approve. For such is the nature of men, that howsoever they may acknowledge many others to be more witty, or more eloquent, or more learned, yet they will hardly believe there be many so wise as themselves; for they see their own wit at hand, and other men's at a distance. But this proveth rather that men are in that point equal, than unequal. For there is not ordinarily a greater sign of the equal distribution of anything than that every man is contented with his share.

From this equality of ability ariseth equality of hope in the attaining of our ends. And therefore if any two men desire the same thing, which nevertheless they cannot both enjoy, they become enemies; and in the way to their end (which is principally their own conservation, and sometimes their delectation[3] only) endeavor to destroy or subdue one another. And from hence it comes to pass, that where an invader hath no more to fear than another man's single power, if one plant, sow, build, or possess a convenient seat, others may probably be expected to come prepared with forces united, to dispossess and deprive him, not only of the fruit of his labor, but also of his life or liberty. And the invader again is in the like danger of another.

And from this diffidence[4] of one another, there is no way for any man to secure himself so reasonable as anticipation; that is, by force or wiles to master the persons of all men he can, so long, till he see no other power

---

1. The title refers to the primordial sea creature Leviathan, described in Job 41 as the prime evidence of and analogue to God's power, beyond all human measure and comprehension. Hobbes takes him as figure for the sovereign power in the state. Leviathan was also sometimes taken as a figure for Satan, on the basis of Job 41.34: "he is a king over all the children of pride."
2. Alliance.
3. Pleasure.
4. Lack of faith, mistrust.

Leviathan. Abraham Bosse's frontispiece for *Leviathan* was based on a sketch by Hobbes. The "Leviathan" or commonwealth is shown as a gigantic human figure holding a scepter and a sword; the figure is made up of many tiny individual humans who have joined together in the social contract. Hobbes's royalist sympathies are betrayed in the figure's face, which is that of King Charles. The small pictures in the lower part of the engraving display the various attributes of civil power on the left, and ecclesiastical power on the right.

great enough to endanger him; and this is no more than his own conservation requireth, and is generally allowed. Also because there be some, that taking pleasure in contemplating their own power in the acts of conquest, which they pursue farther than their security requires; if others that otherwise would be glad to be at ease within modest bounds, should not by invasion increase their power, they would not be able long time, by standing only on their defense, to subsist. And by consequence, such augmentation of dominion over men being necessary to a man's conservation, it ought to be allowed him.

Again, men have no pleasure, but on the contrary a great deal of grief, in keeping company, where there is no power able to overawe them all. For every man looketh that his companion should value him at the same rate he sets upon himself; and upon all signs of contempt, or undervaluing, naturally endeavors, as far as he dares (which amongst them that have no common power to keep them in quiet, is far enough to make them destroy each other), to extort a greater value from his contemners[5] by damage, and from others by the example.

So that in the nature of man, we find three principal causes of quarrel. First, competition; secondly, diffidence; thirdly, glory.

The first maketh men invade for gain; the second, for safety; and the third, for reputation. The first use violence to make themselves masters of other men's persons, wives, children, and cattle; the second, to defend them; the third, for trifles, as a word, a smile, a different opinion, and any other sign of undervalue, either direct in their persons, or by reflection in their kindred, their friends, their nation, their profession, or their name.

Hereby it is manifest that during the time men live without a common power to keep them all in awe, they are in that condition which is called war; and such a war as is of every man against every man. For war consisteth not in battle only, or the act of fighting, but in a tract of time wherein the will to contend by battle is sufficiently known; and therefore the notion of time is to be considered in the nature of war, as it is in the nature of weather. For as the nature of foul weather lieth not in a shower or two of rain, but in an inclination thereto of many days together; so the nature of war consisteth not in actual fighting, but in the known disposition thereto, during all the time there is no assurance to the contrary. All other time is peace.

Whatsoever therefore is consequent to a time of war, where every man is enemy to every man, the same is consequent to the time wherein men live without other security than what their own strength and their own invention shall furnish them withal. In such condition there is no place for industry, because the fruit thereof is uncertain, and consequently no culture of the earth; no navigation, nor use of the commodities that may be imported by sea; no commodious building; no instruments of moving, and removing, such things as require much force; no knowledge of the face of the earth; no account of time; no arts; no letters; no society; and, which is worst of all, continual fear, and danger of violent death; and the life of man, solitary, poor, nasty, brutish, and short.

It may seem strange to some man that has not well weighed these things, that nature should thus dissociate and render men apt to invade and destroy one another; and he may therefore, not trusting to this inference, made from the passions, desire perhaps to have the same confirmed by experience. Let him therefore consider with himself, when taking a journey, he arms himself and seeks to go well accompanied; when going to sleep, he locks his doors; when even in his house he locks his chests; and this when he knows there be laws, and public officers, armed, to revenge all injuries shall be done him; what opinion he has of his fellow subjects, when he rides armed; of his fel-

5. Scorners.

low citizens, when he locks his doors; and of his children and servants, when he locks his chests. Does he not there as much accuse mankind by his actions, as I do by my words? But neither of us accuse man's nature in it. The desires and other passions of man are in themselves no sin. No more are the actions that proceed from those passions, till they know a law that forbids them, which, till laws be made, they cannot know; nor can any law be made, till they have agreed upon the person that shall make it.

It may peradventure be thought there was never such a time nor condition of war as this; and I believe it was never generally so, over all the world; but there are many places where they live so now. For the savage people in many places of America, except the government of small families, the concord whereof dependeth on natural lust, have no government at all and live at this day in that brutish manner as I said before. Howsoever, it may be perceived what manner of life there would be, where there were no common power to fear, by the manner of life which men that have formerly lived under a peaceful government use to degenerate into in a civil war.[6]

But though there had never been any time wherein particular men were in a condition of war one against another, yet in all times, kings and persons of sovereign authority, because of their independency, are in continual jealousies, and in the state and posture of gladiators; having their weapons pointing, and their eyes fixed on one another; that is, their forts, garrisons, and guns upon the frontiers of their kingdoms, and continual spies upon their neighbors, which is a posture of war. But because they uphold thereby the industry of their subjects, there does not follow from it that misery which accompanies the liberty of particular men.

To this war of every man against every man, this also is consequent: that nothing can be unjust. The notions of right and wrong, justice and injustice, have there no place. Where there is no common power, there is no law; where no law, no injustice. Force and fraud are in war the two cardinal virtues. Justice and injustice are none of the faculties neither of the body nor mind. If they were, they might be in a man that were alone in the world, as well as his senses and passions. They are qualities that relate to men in society, not in solitude. It is consequent also to the same condition that there be no propriety,[7] no dominion, no *mine* and *thine* distinct; but only that to be every man's, that he can get; and for so long as he can keep it. And thus much for the ill condition which man by mere nature is actually placed in; though with a possibility to come out of it, consisting partly in the passions, partly in his reason.

The passions that incline men to peace are fear of death, desire of such things as are necessary to commodious living, and a hope by their industry to obtain them. And reason suggesteth convenient articles of peace, upon which men may be drawn to agreement. These articles are they which otherwise are called the Laws of Nature, whereof I shall speak more particularly in the two following chapters.

1651

---

6. Hobbes is thinking of the recent civil wars in England, and perhaps also of the Greek civil wars described by Thucydides (whom he translated).
7. Property.

GEORGE HERBERT
1593–1633

George Herbert's style in his volume of religious poetry, *The Temple*, is deceptively simple and graceful, especially compared to the learned, witty style of his
friend John Donne. But it is also marked by self-irony, a remarkable intellectual and
emotional range, and an artistry evident in the poems' tight construction, exact diction, perfect control of tone, and enormously varied stanzaic forms and rhythmic
patterns. These poems reflect Herbert's struggle to define his relationship to God
through biblical metaphors invested with the tensions of relationships familiar in
his own society: king and subject, lord and courtier, master and servant, father and
child, bridegroom and bride, friends of unequal status. None of Herbert's secular
English poems survives, so his reputation rests on this single volume, published
posthumously. *The Temple* contains a long prefatory poem, "The Church-Porch,"
and a long concluding poem, "Church Militant," which together enclose a collection
of 177 short lyrics entitled *The Church*, among which are sonnets, songs, hymns,
laments, meditative poems, dialogue poems, acrostic poems, emblematic poems, and
more. Herbert's own description of the collection is apt: "a picture of the many spiritual conflicts that have passed between God and my soul." Izaak Walton reports that
Herbert gave the manuscript to his friend Nicholas Farrar, head of a quasi-monastic
community at Little Gidding, with instructions to publish it if he thought it would
"turn to the advantage of any dejected poor soul" and otherwise to burn it. Fortunately, Farrar chose to publish, and *The Temple* became the major influence on the
religious lyric poets of the Caroline age: Henry Vaughan, Richard Crashaw, Thomas
Traherne, and even Edward Taylor, the American colonial poet.

The fifth son of an eminent Welsh family, Herbert (and his nine siblings) had an
upbringing carefully monitored by his mother, Magdalen Herbert, patron and friend
of Donne and several other scholars and poets. Herbert was educated at Westminster
School and at Trinity College, Cambridge, where he subsequently held a fellowship
and wrote Latin poetry: elegies on the death of Prince Henry (1612), witty epigrams,
poems on Christ's Passion and death, and poems defending the rites of the English
church. In 1620 he was appointed "public orator," the official spokesman and correspondent for the university. This was a step toward a career at court or in public service, as was his election as the member of Parliament from Montgomery in 1624. But
that route was closed off by the death of influential patrons and the change of monarchs. Like Donne, Herbert hesitated for some years before being ordained, but in
1630 he took up pastoral duties in the small country parish at Bemerton in Wiltshire.
Whereas Donne preached to monarchs and statesmen, Herbert ministered to a few
cottagers, and none of his sermons survive. His small book on the duties of his new
life, *A Priest to the Temple; or, The Country Parson*, testifies to the earnestness and
joy, but also to the aristocratic uneasiness, with which he embraced that role. In
chronic bad health, he lived only three more years—performing pastoral duties
assiduously, writing and revising his poems, playing music, and listening to the organ
and choir at nearby Salisbury Cathedral.

Herbert locates himself in the church through many poems that treat church
liturgy, architecture, and art—e.g., "Church Monuments" and "The Windows"—
but his primary emphasis is always on the soul's inner architecture. Unlike Donne,
Herbert does not voice fears about his salvation or about his desperate sins; his
anxieties center rather on his relationship with Christ, most often represented as
that of friend with friend. Many poems register the speaker's distress over the vacil-

lations and regressions in this relationship, over his lack of "fruition" in God's service, and over the instability of his own nature. In several dialogic poems the speaker's difficulties are alleviated by the voice of a divine friend heard within or recalled through a Scripture text (as in "The Collar"). In poem after poem he has to come to terms with the fact that his relationship with Christ is always radically unequal, that Christ must both initiate it and enable his own response. Herbert struggles constantly with the paradox that, as the works of a Christian poet, his poems ought to give fit praise to God but cannot possibly do so—an issue explored in "The Altar," the two "Jordan" poems, "Easter," "The Forerunners," and many more.

His recourse is to develop a biblical poetics that renounces conventional poetic styles—"fiction and false hair"—to depend instead on God's "art" wrought in his own soul and displayed in the language and

George Herbert. This engraving by Robert White was made from a portrait, now lost, painted during Herbert's lifetime and showing the poet in clerical garb. It was published in Isaak Walton's *Life of George Herbert* (1674).

symbolism of the Bible. He makes scant use of Donnean learned imagery, but his scriptural allusions carry profound significances. A biblical metaphor provides the unifying motif for the volume: the New Testament temple in the human heart (1 Corinthians 3.16). Another recurring biblical metaphor represents the Christian as plant or tree or flower in God's garden, needing pruning, rain, and nurture. Herbert was profoundly influenced by the genre of the emblem, which typically associated mysterious but meaningful pictures and mottoes with explanatory text. Shaped poems like "The Altar" or "Easter Wings" present image and picture at once; others, like "The Windows," resemble emblem commentary. Other poems allude to typological symbolism, which reads persons and events in the Old Testament as types or foreshadowings of Christ, the fulfillment or antitype.

From The Temple[1]

The Altar[2]

A broken A L T A R , Lord, thy servant rears,
Made of a heart, and cemented with tears:
Whose parts are as thy hand did frame;
No workman's tool hath touched the same.[3]

5   A H E A R T alone
Is such a stone,
As nothing but
Thy power doth cut.
Wherefore each part
10   Of my hard heart
Meets in this frame,
To praise thy Name:

That, if I chance to hold my peace,
These stones to praise thee may not cease.[4]
15 Oh let thy blessed S A C R I F I C E be mine,
And sanctify this A L T A R to be thine.

Redemption[1]

Having been tenant long to a rich lord,
   Not thriving, I resolvèd to be bold,
And make a suit unto him, to afford
   A new small-rented lease, and cancel th' old.[2]

5 In heaven at his manor I him sought:
   They told me there that he was lately gone
About some land which he had dearly bought
   Long since on earth, to take possession.

I straight° returned, and knowing his great birth,   *at once*
10   Sought him accordingly in great resorts—
In cities, theaters, gardens, parks, and courts:
   At length I heard a ragged noise and mirth

Of thieves and murderers; there I him espied,
   Who straight, "Your suit is granted," said, and died.

1. The title of Herbert's volume sets his poems in relation to David's psalms for the Temple at Jerusalem; his are "psalms" for the New Testament temple in the heart. All of the following poems come from this volume, published in 1633.
2. A variety of emblem poem. Emblems customarily have three parts: a picture, a motto, and a poem. This kind collapses picture and poem into one, presenting the emblem image by its very shape. Shaped poems have been used by authors from Hellenistic times to Dylan Thomas.
3. A reference to Exodus 20.25, in which the Lord enjoins Moses to build an altar of uncut stones, not touched by any tool, and also to Psalm 51.17: "a broken and a contrite heart, O God, thou wilt not despise."
4. A reference to Luke 19.40: "I tell you that, if these should hold their peace, the stones would immediately cry out." Herbert's poems obtain much of their resonance from their biblical echoes.
1. Literally, "buying back." In this beautifully concise sonnet Herbert figures God as a landlord, himself as a discontented tenant.
2. I.e., to ask him for a new lease, with a smaller rent; the figure points to the New Testament supplanting the Old.

Easter Wings[1]

Lord, who createdst man in wealth and store,°   *abundance*
Though foolishly he lost the same,
Decaying more and more
Till he became
Most poor:
With thee
O let me rise
As larks, harmoniously,
And sing this day thy victories:
Then shall the fall further the flight in me.[2]

My tender age in sorrow did begin:
And still with sicknesses and shame
Thou didst so punish sin,
That I became
Most thin.
With thee
Let me combine,
And feel this day thy victory;
For, if I imp[3] my wing on thine,
Affliction shall advance the flight in me.

5
10
15
20

Prayer (1)[1]

Prayer, the church's banquet; angels' age,
   God's breath in man returning to his birth;
The soul in paraphrase,[2] heart in pilgrimage;
   The Christian plummet,[3] sounding heaven and earth;

5   Engine against th' Almighty, sinner's tower,
   Reversèd thunder, Christ-side-piercing spear,
The six-days' world transposing[4] in an hour;
   A kind of tune which all things hear and fear:

Softness and peace and joy and love and bliss;
10   Exalted manna,[5] gladness of the best;
Heaven in ordinary,[6] man well dressed,
   The milky way, the bird of paradise,

Church bells beyond the stars heard, the soul's blood,
   The land of spices; something understood.

---

1. Another emblem poem whose shape presents the emblem picture; the lines, increasing and decreasing, imitate flight, and also the spiritual experience of falling and rising. Early editions printed the poem with the lines running vertically, making the wing shape more apparent.
2. Refers to the "Fortunate Fall," which brought humankind so great a redeemer.
3. In falconry, to insert feathers in a bird's wing.
1. This extraordinary sonnet is a series of epithets without a main verb, defining prayer by metaphor.
2. Clarifying by expansion.
3. A weight used to measure ("sound") the depth of water.
4. A musical term indicating sounds produced at another pitch from the original.
5. The food God supplied to the Israelites in the wilderness.
6. I.e., everyday heaven.

Jordan (1)[1]

Who says that fictions only and false hair
Become a verse? Is there in truth no beauty?
Is all good structure in a winding stair?
May no lines pass, except they do their duty°   *pay reverence*
5   Not to a true, but painted chair?[2]

Is it no verse, except enchanted groves
And sudden arbors shadow coarse-spun lines?[3]
Must purling° streams refresh a lover's loves?   *rippling*
Must all be veiled,[4] while he that reads, divines,
10   Catching the sense at two removes?

Shepherds[5] are honest people: let them sing;
Riddle who list,° for me, and pull for prime:[6]   *wishes*
I envy no man's nightingale or spring;
Nor let them punish me with loss of rhyme,
15   Who plainly say, *My God, My King.*[7]

The Windows[1]

Lord, how can man preach thy eternal word?
    He is a brittle, crazy° glass,   *flawed, distorting*
Yet in thy temple thou dost him afford
    This glorious and transcendent place,
5   To be a window through thy grace.

But when thou dost anneal in glass[2] thy story,
    Making thy life to shine within
The holy preachers, then the light and glory
    More reverend grows, and more doth win,
10   Which else shows wat'rish, bleak, and thin.

Doctrine and life, colors and light, in one
    When they combine and mingle, bring
A strong regard and awe; but speech alone
    Doth vanish like a flaring thing,
15   And in the ear, not conscience, ring.

1. The river Jordan, which the Israelites crossed to enter the Promised Land, was also taken as a symbol for baptism.
2. It was the custom for men to bow before a throne, whether it was occupied or not (see Donne, "Satire 3," lines 47–48, p. 1396), but to require bowing before a throne in a painting would be ridiculous.
3. "Sudden," i.e., that appear unexpectedly (an artificial effect much sought after in landscape gardening). "Shadow": shade.
4. As in allegory.

5. Conventional pastoral poets.
6. To draw a lucky card in the game of primero. "For me": as far as I am concerned.
7. Echoes Psalm 145.1: "my God, O king."
1. From his little parish at Bemerton, Herbert used to walk twice a week across Salisbury Plain to the great cathedral, where he delighted not only in the music but in the stained-glass windows. This poem explores how the preacher himself may become such a window.
2. To burn colors into glass.

Time

Meeting with Time, "Slack thing," said I,[1]
"Thy scythe is dull; whet it for shame."
"No marvel, sir," he did reply,
"If it at length deserve some blame;
5   But where one man would have me grind it,
Twenty for one too sharp do find it."

"Perhaps some such of old did pass,
Who above all things loved this life;
To whom thy scythe a hatchet was,
10   Which now is but a pruning knife.[2]
Christ's coming hath made man thy debtor,
Since by thy cutting he grows better.

"And in his blessing thou art blessed,
For where thou only wert before
15   An executioner at best,
Thou art a gardener now, and more,
An usher to convey our souls
Beyond the utmost stars and poles.

"And this is that makes life so long,
20   While it detains us from our God.
Ev'n pleasures here increase the wrong,
And length of days lengthens the rod.°   *used for blows*
Who wants° the place where God doth dwell   *lacks*
Partakes already half of hell.

25   "Of what strange length must that needs be,
Which ev'n eternity excludes!"—
Thus far Time heard me patiently,
Then chafing said, "This man deludes:
What do I here before his door?
30   He doth not crave less time, but more."

The Collar[1]

I struck the board[2] and cried, "No more;
    I will abroad!
What? Shall I ever sigh and pine?
My lines and life are free, free as the road,
5   Loose as the wind, as large as store.
    Shall I be still in suit?[3]

1. Herbert's speaker reports his dialogue with Time.
2. A hatchet kills, a pruning knife improves growing things.
1. The emblematic title suggests a clerical collar that has become a slave's collar; also, punningly, the speaker's choler (anger) and, perhaps, the caller that he at last hears.
2. Table, with an allusion to the Communion table.
3. Always in attendance, waiting on someone for a favor.

Have I no harvest but a thorn
To let me blood, and not restore
What I have lost with cordial° fruit?   *restorative to the heart*
10   Sure there was wine
Before my sighs did dry it; there was corn°   *grain*
Before my tears did drown it.
Is the year only lost to me?
Have I no bays[4] to crown it,
15   No flowers, no garlands gay? All blasted?
All wasted?
Not so, my heart; but there is fruit,
And thou hast hands.
Recover all thy sigh-blown age
20   On double pleasures: leave thy cold dispute
Of what is fit and not. Forsake thy cage,
Thy rope of sands,
Which petty thoughts have made, and made to thee
Good cable,[5] to enforce and draw,
25   And be thy law,
While thou didst wink and wouldst not see.
Away! Take heed;
I will abroad.
Call in thy death's-head[6] there; tie up thy fears.
30   He that forbears
To suit and serve his need,
Deserves his load."
But as I raved and grew more fierce and wild
At every word,
35   Methoughts I heard one calling, *Child!*[7]
And I replied, *My Lord.*

The Pulley[1]

When God at first made man,
Having a glass of blessings standing by,
"Let us," said he, "pour on him all we can:
Let the world's riches, which dispersèd lie,
5   Contract into a span."

So strength first made a way;
Then beauty flowed, then wisdom, honor, pleasure.
When almost all was out, God made a stay,
Perceiving that, alone of all his treasure,
10   Rest° in the bottom lay.   *repose*

---

4. The poet's laurel wreath, a symbol of recognized accomplishment.
5. Christian restrictions on behavior, which the "petty thoughts" of the docile believer have made into strong bonds.
6. Skull, emblem of human mortality, and often used as an object for meditation.

7. The call "Child!" reminds the speaker of Paul's words (Romans 8.14–17) that Christians are not in "bondage again to fear" but are children of God, "and if children, then heirs."
1. The poem inverts the legend of Pandora's box, which released all manner of evils when opened but left Hope trapped inside.

"For if I should," said He,
"Bestow this jewel also on my creature,
He would adore my gifts instead of me,
And rest in Nature, not the God of Nature;
15   So both should losers be.

"Yet let him keep the rest,[2]
But keep them with repining restlessness:
Let him be rich and weary, that at least,
If goodness lead him not, yet weariness
20   May toss him to my breast."

The Flower

How fresh, O Lord, how sweet and clean
Are thy returns! even as the flowers in spring,
      To which, besides their own demesne,°   *domain, demeanor*
The late-past frosts tributes of pleasure bring.
5   Grief melts away
            Like snow in May,
      As if there were no such cold thing.

Who would have thought my shriveled heart
Could have recovered greenness? It was gone
10   Quite underground; as flowers depart
To see their mother-root, when they have blown,°   *bloomed*
            Where they together
            All the hard weather,
      Dead to the world, keep house unknown.

15   These are thy wonders, Lord of power,
Killing and quickening, bringing down to hell
      And up to heaven in an hour,
Making a chiming of a passing-bell.[1]
            We say amiss
20   This or that is:
      Thy word is all, if we could spell.°   *read*

O that I once past changing were,
Fast in thy Paradise, where no flower can wither!
      Many a spring I shoot up fair,
25   Offering° at heaven, growing and groaning thither;   *aiming*
            Nor doth my flower
            Want a spring shower,°   *tears of contrition*
      My sins and I joining together.

But while I grow in a straight line,
30   Still upwards bent,° as if heaven were mine own,   *directed*

---

2. "Rest" has two senses here: "remainder" and
"repose."
1. The "passing-bell," intended to mark the death
of a parishioner, is tolled in a monotone; a
"chiming" bell offers pleasant variety.

Thy anger comes, and I decline:
What frost to that? What pole is not the zone
    Where all things burn,
    When thou dost turn,
35 And the least frown of thine is shown?[2]

And now in age I bud again,
After so many deaths I live and write;
    I once more smell the dew and rain,
And relish versing. O my only light,
40   It cannot be
            That I am he
On whom thy tempests fell all night.

These are thy wonders, Lord of love,
To make us see we are but flowers that glide;°   *slip silently away*
45 Which when we once can find and prove,°   *experience*
Thou hast a garden for us where to bide;
        Who would be more,
        Swelling through store,
Forfeit their Paradise by their pride.

Love (3)

Love bade me welcome: yet my soul drew back,
        Guilty of dust and sin.
But quick-eyed Love, observing me grow slack°   *hesitant*
        From my first entrance in,
5 Drew nearer to me, sweetly questioning
        If I lacked anything.[1]

"A guest," I answered, "worthy to be here":
        Love said, "You shall be he."
"I, the unkind, ungrateful? Ah, my dear,
10   I cannot look on thee."
Love took my hand, and smiling did reply,
        "Who made the eyes but I?"

"Truth, Lord; but I have marred them; let my shame
        Go where it doth deserve."
15 "And know you not," says Love, "who bore the blame?"
        "My dear, then I will serve."
"You must sit down," says Love, "and taste my meat."
        So I did sit and eat.[2]

---

2. I.e., compared with God's wrath, what polar chill would not seem like the heat of the equator?
1. The first question of tavern waiters to an entering customer would be "What d'ye lack?" (i.e., want).

2. In addition to the sacrament of Communion, the reference is especially to the banquet in heaven, when the Lord "shall gird himself, and make them to sit down to meat, and will come forth and serve them" (Luke 12.37).

ROBERT HERRICK
1591–1674

Robert Herrick was the most devoted of the Sons of Ben, though his epigrams and lyrics (like Jonson's) also show the direct influence of classical poets: Horace, Anacreon, Catullus, Tibullus, Ovid, and Martial. Born in London the son of a goldsmith and apprenticed for some years in that craft, Herrick took B.A. and M.A. degrees at Cambridge and consorted in the early 1620s with Jonson and his "tribe," who met regularly at the Apollo Room. After his ordination in 1623, he apparently served as chaplain to various noblemen and in that role joined Buckingham's failed military expedition to rescue French Protestants at Rhé in 1627. In 1630 he was installed as the vicar of Dean Prior in Devonshire. Expelled as a royalist in 1647, he apparently lived in London until the Restoration, when he was reinstated at Dean Prior and remained there until his death.

Herrick's single volume of poems, *Hesperides* (1648), with its appended book of religious poems, *Noble Numbers*, contains over four hundred short poems. Many are love poems on the carpe diem theme—seize the day, time is fleeting, make love now; a famous example is the elegant song "To the Virgins, to Make Much of Time." But Herrick's range is much wider than is sometimes recognized. He moves from the pastoral to the cynical, from an almost rococo elegance to coarse, even vulgar, epigrams, and from the didactic to the dramatic. Also, he derives mythic energy and power from certain recurring motifs. One is metamorphosis, "times transshifting," the transience of all natural things. Another is celebration—festivals and feasts—evoking the social, ritualistic, and even anthropological significances and energies contained in rural harvest festivals ("The Hock Cart") or the May Day rituals described in what is perhaps his finest poem, "Corinna's Going A-Maying." Yet another is the classical but also perennial ideal of the "good life," defined in his terms as "cleanly wantonness." For Herrick this involves love devoid of high passion (the several mistresses he addresses seem interchangeable and not very real); the pleasures of food, drink, and song; delight in the beauty of surfaces (as in "Upon Julia's Clothes"); and, finally, the creation of poetry as bulwark against the ravages of time.

Published just months before the execution of Charles I, these poems seem merely playful and charming, almost oblivious to the catastrophes of the war. But they are not. Poems celebrating rural feasts and festivals, ceremonial social occasions, and the rituals of good fellowship reinforce the conservative values of social stability, tradition, and order threatened by the Puritans. Several poems that draw upon the Celtic mythology of fairy folk make their feasts, temples, worship, and ceremonies stand in for the forbidden ceremonies of the Laudian church and a life governed by ritual. Still other poems, like "The Hock Cart" and "Corinna's Going A-Maying," celebrate the kind of rural festivals that were at the center of the culture wars between royalists and Puritans. Both James I and Charles I urged such activities in their *Book of Sports* as a means of reinforcing traditional institutions in the countryside and deflecting discontent, while Puritans vigorously opposed them as occasions for drunkenness and licentiousness.

FROM HESPERIDES[1]

The Argument[2] of His Book

I sing of brooks, of blossoms, birds, and bowers,
Of April, May, of June, and July flowers.
I sing of Maypoles, hock carts, wassails, wakes,[3]
Of bridegrooms, brides, and of their bridal cakes.
5   I write of youth, of love, and have access
By these to sing of cleanly wantonness.
I sing of dews, of rains, and, piece by piece,
Of balm, of oil, of spice, and ambergris.[4]
I sing of times trans-shifting,° and I write   *changing*
10   How roses first came red and lilies white.
I write of groves, of twilights, and I sing
The court of Mab and of the fairy king.[5]
I write of hell; I sing (and ever shall)
Of heaven, and hope to have it after all.

The Vine

I dreamed this mortal part of mine
Was metamorphosed to a vine,
Which, crawling one and every way,
Enthralled my dainty Lucia.[1]
5   Methought, her long small legs and thighs
I with my tendrils did surprise;
Her belly, buttocks, and her waist
By my soft nervelets were embraced.
About her head I writhing hung,
10   And with rich clusters (hid among
The leaves) her temples I behung,
So that my Lucia seemed to me
Young Bacchus ravished by his tree.°   *the grapevine*
My curls about her neck did crawl,
15   And arms and hands they did enthrall,
So that she could not freely stir
(All parts there made one prisoner).
But when I crept with leaves to hide
Those parts which maids keep unespied,
20   Such fleeting pleasures there I took

1. In myth, the Hesperides, or Western Maidens, guarded an orchard and garden, also called Hesperides, in which grew a tree bearing golden apples. Herrick's title suggests that his poems are golden apples from his residence in western Devonshire; the following poems are all from that volume published in 1648.
2. Subject matter, theme.
3. Festive, not funerary, occasions, to celebrate the dedication of a new church. "Hock carts" carried home the last load of the harvest, so they were adorned and celebrated. "Wassails" were Twelfth Night celebrations.
4. A secretion of the sperm whale that is used in making perfume—hence it suggests something rare and delectable.
5. Mab was queen of the fairies and wife of their king, Oberon.
1. For the sake of both rhyme and meter, the name of this lady is given three syllables here; in line 12 it has only two.

The Middle Ages (to ca. 1485)

Scepter, from the Sutton Hoo Treasure, ca. 625 C.E.

Discovered in 1939, among other items (jewelry, pottery, fragments of a helmet and shield), in a funeral ship buried in a mound near the coast of East Anglia, the scepter—probably a symbol of royal authority—consists of a massive ceremonial whetstone carved with faces and attached to a ring of twisted bronze wires mounted by an intricately carved stag. The treasure suggests the one laden on Scyld's funeral ship in *Beowulf* (lines 26–52; p. 42) and the material world imagined throughout the poem; the scepter evokes the "gold standard . . . / high above [the king's] head." THE BRITISH MUSEUM, LONDON, UK / BRIDGEMAN ART LIBRARY.

Annunciation to the Shepherds; the Magi before Herod, ca. 1150

Stories of the Nativity figure prominently both in the mystery plays and in medieval Psalters such as this one. The Latin text on the angels' scrolls is from Luke 2.11: "Natus est nobis hodie salvator qui est Christus Dominus in civitate David" (Unto us is born in the city of David a savior who is Christ the Lord). Herod's scroll gives his instructions to the Magi from Matthew 2.8: "ite et interrogate diligenter de puero" (go and inquire diligently about the child). The caption above each image is in French. THE BRITISH LIBRARY, COTTON NERO C. IV, FOLIO 11.

Noah urging his wife to board the ark, ca. 1290

Noah's trouble getting his wife to board the ark was a popular subject in medieval drama and art (See Chaucer, *The Miller's Tale*, lines 430–35; pp. 273–74). In this illustration from a Psalter, Noah admonishes his wife with his left hand and grabs her wrist with the right, urging her to come aboard. Concealed, riding piggyback on the wife, a winged devil comes along as a stowaway. Below, he exits through the hull among drowned bodies on the seafloor. Other manuscripts show the serpent plugging the hole with his tail. THE PIERPONT MORGAN LIBRARY / ART RESOURCE, NY.

Plowing, the Luttrell Psalter, ca. 1330

The Psalter made for Sir Geoffrey Luttrell is sumptuously illustrated with idealized depictions of family, servants, workers, animals, and their activities (plowing, sowing, harvesting, feasting, playing) on the lord's estate; it is also elaborately decorated with foliage and grotesques. The Plowman here is a symbolic figure of order like Chaucer's Plowman (p. 256) and Langland's Piers Plowman (p. 373). The image echoes line 6 of the Psalm above: "Si dicebam motus est pes meus, misericordia tua, domine, adiuvabat me" (If I said: My foot is moved: thy mercy, Lord, helped me); "pes" (foot) anticipates the plow foot that moves the soil. THE BRITISH LIBRARY, FOLIO 170R FROM THE LUTTRELL PSALTER, MS ADDITIONAL 42130.

The Wilton Diptych,
Flemish school,
1395–96

Richard II commissioned this double-panel painting, both pious and political, not long before his deposition. In it he is portrayed as a boy, perhaps ten years old, the age at which he became king. Two English kings, St. Edmund and St. Edward "the Confessor," and John the Baptist, Richard's patron saint, present the young king to the Virgin and Child, who are surrounded by angels. The Christ Child blesses the red-cross standard of St. George (the patron saint of England), about to be given into the kneeling king's open hands. Richard's robe and the angels' sleeves display his personal emblem, a white hart (punning on *riche-hart*). NATIONAL GALLERY, LONDON, GREAT BRITAIN / ART RESOURCE, NY.

The Crucifixion, Lapworth Missal, 1398

This late medieval manuscript illumination typically portrays the humanity of Christ: frail, eyes closed, head inclining on his shoulder. At the sides stand the Virgin mother, who swoons in the arms of Mary Magdalene, and St. John the evangelist. The skull signifies Golgotha (place of skulls), the site of the Crucifixion. According to medieval legend, the tree of knowledge had stood on the same site and Adam was buried there: thus the skull is that of Adam, whose original sin is being redeemed by the blood that the angels are collecting. The sun and moon symbolize the New and Old Testaments: as the sun illuminates the moon, the light of the New Testament reveals the hidden truths of the Old. Symbols of the four evangelists appear in the corners of the intricately decorated frame. Corpus Christi College, University of Oxford, Ms 394.

Portrait of Chaucer, ca. 1411

In his poem *The Regiment of Princes*, Hoccleve, a younger disciple of Chaucer, memorializes "My maistir Chaucer, flour of eloquence, / Mirour of fructuous entendement, / O universel fadir in science!" One manuscript preserves a small portrait of Chaucer that Hoccleve placed in the margin so "That they that han of him lost thought and mynde / By this peynture may ageyn him fynde." Chaucer holds a rosary in his left hand; attached to his gown, a penknife (formerly used for making and mending quill pens) or pen case functions as a symbol of authorship. THE BRITISH LIBRARY, MS HARLEY 4866, FOLIO 88.

Manuscript illumination of pilgrims leaving Canterbury, ca. 1420

Chaucer's pilgrims never get to Canterbury, but they do in the prologue to John Lydgate's *The Siege of Thebes*. In the prologue, Lydgate, a monk of Bury St. Edmund's and an enthusiastic follower of Chaucer, tells how on his own pilgrimage to Canterbury he encounters Chaucer's pilgrims. The Host invites the monk to join the company on their return journey and calls on him to tell the first tale. Lydgate is the middle figure in a monk's cowl, costumed more soberly than Chaucer's Monk (pp. 247–48). The cathedral and walls of Canterbury appear in the background. THE BRITISH LIBRARY, MS ROYAL 18 D II, FOLIO 148.

Three hunting scenes, *Le Mireur du Monde,* French manuscript, ca. 1475

The medieval nobility regarded the hunt as both a sport and an art—a test of the skill and endurance of men, dogs, and quarry. These scenes of hunters stalking the deer, breaking up the carcass, and pursuing the boar correspond to the *Gawain* poet's elaborate descriptions of the first two hunts (pp. 209ff., 213ff., 219ff.). The stylized rhetoric describing the hunts both parallels and contrasts with the stylized exchanges between Gawain and the lady in the interspersed bedroom scenes where she is the hunter and he the quarry. Bodleian Library, University of Oxford, MS Douce 338, folio 60, 56, 78.

The Sixteenth Century
(1485–1603)

St. George and the Dragon (London version), Paolo Uccello, ca. 1455–60

A depiction by the Florentine artist Uccello of the legend that was to inspire Edmund Spenser in Book 1 of *The Faerie Queene*. Already held on a leash by the elegant lady—as if the struggle's outcome were not in doubt—the dragon submits to the knight's lance (thrust through the nose in a gesture that better recalls the domestication of cattle than the thwarting of an enemy). The desolate cave is strangely conjoined with the formal garden and the lady's elegant court dress: the story is imagined as located at once in the wilderness and at the very center of civilization. NATIONAL GALLERY, LONDON, GREAT BRITAIN / ART RESOURCE, NY.

Thomas More, Hans Holbein, 1527

Painted on the eve of More's great conflict with Henry VIII over the validity of the king's marriage to Catherine of Aragon, Holbein's portrait emphasizes both the chancellor's importance and his strength of character. More wears the heavy gold chain and rich dress of high office, which he had satirized a decade earlier in *Utopia*. In all probability, if early biographies of More can be believed, he also wears a hair shirt under the velvet and fur, a hidden, painful reminder of the vulnerable flesh that he secretly mortified. COPYRIGHT THE FRICK COLLECTION, NEW YORK.

Edward VI and the Pope: An Allegory of the Reformation, English school, ca. 1568–71

The dying Henry VIII hands over the mandate for church reform to his young son and heir, Prince Edward. This is a polemical attempt to depict the religious revolution that had a deep impact on English society and literature. The open book, proclaiming the Protestant emphasis on the Word of God in vernacular translation, crushes the pope and the taglines of Catholic corruption that surround him. The Council of Regency (appointed to guide the king, who was only nine when he ascended the throne) is in attendance; to the left, two monks flee the pope's downfall. In the upper right, a painting (or view from the window?) heralds the collapse of the Old Church and the breaking of its "idols." Several places in the painting are intended for inscriptions, but for unknown reasons these were never completed. NATIONAL PORTRAIT GALLERY, LONDON, UK / BRIDGEMAN ART LIBRARY.

The Wife and Daughter of a Chief,
John White, 1585

Accompanying Thomas Hariot's *Brief and
True Report of the New-found Land of
Virginia,* John White's watercolors chronicle Algonkian life as seen by the English
voyagers. Here, a girl "of the age of 8 or
10 yeares" carries a European doll, dressed
in full Elizabethan costume, that she has
clearly been given as a gift by the strange
visitors. The presentation of small gifts
was a regular English practice, frequently
alternating with murderous violence.
White's drawing manages to convey both
the exoticism and the dignity that Hariot
and others perceived in the American
natives. THE BRITISH MUSEUM.

*Portrait of a Melancholy Young
Man,* Isaac Oliver, ca. 1590–95

Equally fashionable in attitude and
dress, Oliver's young man displays
the fascination of the English elite
with the "melancholy humour." In
addition to the sad expression, the
black clothes and crossed arms are
conventional markers of melancholy.
Men in love, like Sidney's Astrophil
(p. 1084) and Duke Orsino in *Twelfth
Night* (p. 1188), found it particularly
glamorous to parade their pensive
dispositions. The romance of this
"disease" figures in the couple just
walking into the labyrinth-garden on
the right. THE ROYAL COLLECTION
© 2003, HER MAJESTY QUEEN
ELIZABETH II.

Captain Thomas Lee, Marcus Gheeraerts the Younger, 1594

Restless, ambitious Thomas Lee was executed in 1601 for participating in the rebellion against the queen led by the Earl of Essex, but in 1594 he was in the midst of his bid for the position of chief negotiator between Ireland and the English Crown. His appearance refers both to his military service in Ireland and to his status at home: Lee sports the bare legs and open shirt of a "kerne," or Irish footsoldier, along with the rich brocade and armor of a wealthy English nobleman. Lee, whose hand had been injured in a skirmish, wishes to be compared with the Roman Gaius Mucius Scaevola, who demonstrated to the enemy Etruscans his resolution and indifference to pain by thrusting his right hand into a fire. Scaevola so impressed the Etruscans that their leader, Porsena, sued for peace. Painted in the tree to Lee's right is a quotation from Livy attributed to Scaevola: "Both to act and to suffer with fortitude is a Roman's part" (trans. Karen Hearn, ed. *Dynasties*). Tate Gallery, London / Art Resource, NY.

The Life and Death of Sir Henry Unton, anonymous, ca. 1597

A masque of musicians and dancers performs for a dinner party of Unton's friends. Theatrical life in this period, which often included music and dancing, was not restricted to the playhouse; it extended into other social settings, such as this one. Theater here is depicted as incidental entertainment: some guests turn their backs on the pageant; the actors are considerably smaller than their patrons, an index of relative social importance. BY COURTESY OF THE NATIONAL PORTRAIT GALLERY, LONDON.

The "Chandos" Portrait of William Shakespeare, anonymous, date unknown

The formal portrait of the playwright that appears in the First Folio edition of his works depicts him stiffly posed in a brocade jacket and a heavily starched collar. Here, in a portrait named after its owner, the Duke of Chandos, Shakespeare is presented less formally and more as his friends and colleagues may have known him. The artist is unknown, but some speculate that it may have been Shakespeare's fellow actor Richard Burbage. BY COURTESY OF THE NATIONAL PORTRAIT GALLERY, LONDON.

A Young Man, Nicholas Hilliard, ca. 1600

This tiny painting from a playing card approximately two inches square represents the "other side" of Elizabethan love poetry: passion replaces languor. The image of the lover tormented by the "fire" of his mistress's eyes or the hellish inner torment of desire was common. Though Sidney's Astrophil lives "in blackest winter night," he feels "the flames of hottest summer day" (p. 1099), while even disillusioned lovers in Shakespeare's sonnets do not know how "To shun the heaven that leads men to this hell" (p. 1183). The locket held by the young man presumably contains another miniature: a portrait of the beloved. VICTORIA & ALBERT MUSEUM, LONDON / ART RESOURCE, NY.

Elizabeth I in Procession, attributed to Robert Peake, ca. 1600

Carried on a litter like an image of the Virgin in the religious processions of previous centuries, the gorgeously arrayed Queen Elizabeth is shown here as a time-defying icon of purity and power. When the painting was executed, the queen was sixty-seven years old. Until the end of her life she continued her custom of going on "Progresses" through the realm: surrounded by her courtiers and ladies in waiting, she would venture forth to show herself to her people, many of whom nearly bankrupted themselves to entertain her in style. THE STAPLETON COLLECTION / BRIDGEMAN ART LIBRARY.

Henry Wriothesley, Third Earl of Southampton, John de Critz, 1603

Henry Wriothesley, the third Earl of Southampton, was nearly executed for his part in the rebellion against Queen Elizabeth led by his friend the Earl of Essex in 1601. Though he was eventually pardoned, Southampton was imprisoned for two years in the Tower of London, where he is here depicted along with his favorite cat. Tradition has it that the cat found its way to him in prison and reached him by coming down the chimney. An early patron of Shakespeare, the wealthy earl may be the "Mr. W. H." (his initials reversed) to whom the first edition of the sonnets is dedicated (p. 1170). On the eve of the Essex rebellion, Southampton seems to have instigated a performance of *Richard II* by Shakespeare's company to put the people of London in mind of deposition. The painting was clearly commissioned after his release, the date of which is painted on the tablet, along with the proud inscription "In Vinculis / Invictus" (Though in chains, unconquered). PRIVATE COLLECTION / BRIDGEMAN ART LIBRARY.

The Early Seventeenth Century
(1603–1660)

The Expulsion from Paradise, Masaccio, ca. 1427–28

This striking fresco shows an agonized Adam and Eve being driven from Eden by a sword-wielding angel. Adam is so overcome he buries his face in his hands; Eve's face is a mask of despair. They do not touch: each seems imprisoned in his or her own pain. Milton's representation of the expulsion at the end of Book 12 of *Paradise Lost* is very different, and the comparison is instructive (see pp. 2173ff.). SCALA / ART RESOURCE, NY.

The Three Graces (detail), *The Primavera*, Sandro Botticelli, ca. 1481

The Graces are a prominent allusive feature of seventeenth-century poetry and masques. At times they carry the allegorical significance suggested in Botticelli's portrayal of them as extensions of Venus, goddess of love and beauty, and as manifestations of the beauty, joy, and freshness of spring. Milton's "L'Allegro" (p. 1909) is couched as a literary hymn honoring Euphrosyne, the Grace who signifies youthful mirth; her sisters are Aglaia, splendor, and Thalia, abundance or pleasure. Their linked hands and postures are said to symbolize the giving and receiving of joy, bounty, and pleasure. ERICH LESSING / ART RESOURCE, NY.

Sacred and Profane Love, Titian, ca. 1515

This image might almost serve as an emblem for the two kinds of love celebrated and often contrasted in seventeenth-century verse. In Titian's Neoplatonic program, the nude figure bearing the torch is the celestial Venus, the principle of universal and eternal beauty and love; the clothed figure is the earthly Venus, who creates the perishable images of beauty in humans, flowers and trees, gold and gems, and works of art. Cupid is placed between them but somewhat closer to the terrestrial Venus. SCALA / ART RESOURCE, NY.

God Creating the Animals, Tintoretto, 1550–52

A remarkable rendering of the scene, with God the Father depicted as an immense figure, exuding power and energy, actively calling forth many varieties of animals. The conception invites comparison with Milton's rendering of the Genesis creation story in *Paradise Lost*, Book 7 (p. 2063). CAMARAPHOTO / ART RESOURCE, NY.

John Donne, anonymous, ca. 1595

This portrait presents Donne in the guise of a melancholy lover fond of self-display; the signs are his broad-brimmed black hat, soulful eyes, sensual lips, delicate hands, and united but expensive lace collar. Parts of Donne's *Songs and Sonnets* (pp. 1373ff.) date from this period. Melancholy, supposedly caused by an excess of black bile and often associated with the scholarly and artistic temperament, was identified in Robert Burton's massive and very popular *Anatomy of Melancholy* as a well-nigh universal attribute of the period. It is the temperament of many literary characters, among them Hamlet, Duke Orsino (in *Twelfth Night*, p. 1188), Jacques in *As You Like It*, and Milton's II Penseroso (p. 1913). PRIVATE COLLECTION / BRIDGEMAN ART LIBRARY.

Lady Sidney and Six of Her Children, Marcus Gheeraerts the Younger, ca. 1596

This portrait of Barbara (Gamage) Sidney, wife of Sir Robert Sidney of Penshurst, provides an insight into domestic relations in the period, as well as an illuminating comment on Ben Jonson's poem "To Penshurst" (p. 1546). Robert Sidney (brother of Sir Philip Sidney) is absent, serving as governor of the English stronghold in Flushing. Lady Sidney is portrayed as a fruitful, fostering mother. Her hands rest on her two sons—both still in skirts, though the heir wears a sword; the four daughters are arranged in two pairs, the elder of each pair imitating her mother's nurturing gesture. The eldest daughter will become Lady Mary Wroth, author of *Urania* and the sonnet sequence *Pamphilia to Amphilanthus* (pp. 1560ff.). REPRODUCED BY KIND PERMISSION OF VISCOUNT DE L'ISLE, FROM HIS PRIVATE COLLECTION AT PENSHURST PLACE.

Lucy, Countess of Bedford, as a Masquer, attributed to John de Critz, ca. 1606

Lucy (Harrington) Russell, Countess of Bedford, prominent courtier, favorite of Queen Anne, patron of Donne and Jonson, and frequent planner of and participant in court masques, is shown in masquing costume for the wedding masque *Hymenaei*, by Ben Jonson and Inigo Jones. Jonson describes the masquing ladies as "attired richly and alike in the most celestial colors" associated with the rainbow, with elaborate headdresses and shoes, "all full of splendor, sovereignty, and riches." Their masque dances were "fully of subtlety and device." Woburn Abbey, Bedfordshire, UK / Bridgeman Art Library.

The Garden of Eden with the Fall of Man, Jan Brueghel the Elder and Peter Paul Rubens, ca. 1615

Possibly foreshadowing Milton's portrayal of Eden in *Paradise Lost,* the painting presents an idyllic scene with cavorting animals in a lush landscape and a graceful human pair—perhaps just enjoying the garden's fruit, but at least intimating the moment of the Fall as a seductive Eve hands Adam an apple and a snake looks on. A favorite painter of Charles I, Rubens designed and painted for the king the splendid ceiling of Whitehall, portraying King James in apotheosis, as a supporter of wisdom, justice, concord, and peace. SCALA / ART RESOURCE, NY.

Charles I on Horseback, Sir Anthony Van Dyck, 1637–38

One of Charles I's court painters, knighted and pensioned by the king, Van Dyck produced several portraits of the royal family and their circle at court. This magnificent equestrian portrait of the king in armor presents him as hero and warrior, in a pose that looks back to portraits and statues of Roman emperors on horseback. It was painted to be hung at the end of the Long Gallery in St. James Palace. NATIONAL GALLERY, LONDON, UK / BRIDGEMAN ART LIBRARY, NY.

The Penitent Magdalen, Georges de la Tour, ca. 1638–43

This remarkable image of a young woman in meditative pose, her face lit by candlelight and her hand touching a skull, can serve as an emblem for the extensive meditative literature of the period—the poetry and prose of Donne, Herbert, Vaughan, and Traherne, among others—on such topics as sickness, human mortality, the transience of life and beauty, and the inevitability of death. RÉUNION DES MUSÉES NATIONAUX / ART RESOURCE, NY.

The Restoration and the Eighteenth Century (1660–1785)

Landscape with Apollo and the Muses, Claude Lorrain, 1652

Claude's poetic landscapes inspired many British landscape gardens. In this painting, a river god sprawls by the Castalian spring under Mount Parnassus; the white swans are sacred to Apollo. On the terrace to the left, Apollo plays his lyre, surrounded by the nine Muses, while four poets approach through the woods. At the upper left, below a temple, the fountain of Hippocrene pours forth its inspiring waters. The dreamlike distance of the figures in this mysterious, luminous scene is intended to draw the viewer in. Similarly, in landscape gardens visitors were invited to stroll amid temples, inscriptions, swans, and statues, gradually comprehending the master plan. NATIONAL GALLERY OF SCOTLAND, EDINBURGH, SCOTLAND / BRIDGEMAN ART LIBRARY.

Great Fire of London,
Dutch school, 1666

The fire of London,
described by Dryden in
Annus Mirabilis and by
Pepys in his diary, destroyed
most of the central city. In
the foreground of this
panorama, huddled refugees
carry their goods away from
the city. Under a pall of
smoke across the Thames,
St. Paul's Cathedral blazes
in the center, with London
Bridge on the far left and
the Tower on the far right.
The fire raged for four days,
after which a new city
eventually rose from the
ashes. MUSEUM OF LONDON,
UK / BRIDGEMAN ART
LIBRARY.

Embarkment for Cythera,
Jean Antoine Watteau, 1717

Cythera is one of the names of Venus, and in this painting elegant pilgrims visit an island of love to pay homage to Venus (whose statue is on the far right). Paired off, these lovers pass through a romantic, erotic dreamscape, related to the visionary landscape of Pope's *Eloisa to Abelard* (lines 155 ff., p. 2709). A ship of love waits on the left to carry the couples away. Are they going or coming to Cythera? In the grip of love, is the prevailing mood one of joy and anticipation, or of melancholy and surfeit? Critics differ; this painting does not reveal all its secrets. RÉUNION DES MUSÉES NATIONAUX / ART RESOURCE, NY.

Bristol Docks and
anonymous, early
eighteenth centur

Bristol, in southwe
England, profited
enormously from t
expansion of the s
trade. From this p
merchants sent tri
guns, and rum to V
Africa in exchange
slaves, who were tr
ported to North A
and the West Indie
exchange for mone
sugar. This paintin
shows a bustling m
olis whose trade m
possible the busy s
the right and the g
houses in the back
ground. BRISTOL C
MUSEUM AND ART
GALLERY, UK /
BRIDGEMAN ART L

Gulliver Taking Leave of the Houyhnhnms, Sawrey Gilpin, 1769

In part 4 of *Gulliver's Travels* (pp. 2587 ff.), Swift cleverly makes use of the eighteenth-century British love of horses. Gulliver's infatuation with the dignity and nobility of the Houyhnhnms reflects the feelings of many hunters mounted for the chase or of gentlefolk promenading in the park; some preferred horses to human beings. Commercially, "horse painters" found eager and wealthy buyers, while Sawrey Gilpin tried to elevate horse painting by placing his horses against rich landscapes and in historical settings. PRIVATE COLLECTION / BRIDGEMAN ART LIBRARY.

The Beggar's Opera, act 3, scene 11, William Hogarth, 1729

The highwayman Macheath, in leg irons, stands at the center, flanked by the women between whom he cannot choose. To the left, Lucy kneels before the jailer Lockit; to the right, Polly kneels before her father, Peachum. In the rear, a group of prisoners waits for its cue. But the setting is not so much a prison as the theater; spectators are seated on each side of the stage. Hogarth connects the audience with the actors just as *The Beggar's Opera* does, suggesting corruption "through all the employments of life." Behind Peachum, John Gay confers with his producer, John Rich. Below them, seated at the far right, the duke of Bolton (note his Star of the Garter) exchanges a rapt gaze with Polly; a satyr points down at him. On opening night, the duke fell in love with the actor who played Polly, Lavinia Fenton. He returned every night, until she became his mistress—and, two decades later, his wife. TATE GALLERY, LONDON / ART RESOURCE, NY.

Garrick between T
and Comedy, Josh
Reynolds, 1762

Sir Joshua Reynold
cialized in portrait
characterized his s
by alluding to class
erature and art. He
great actor David C
is torn between Co
on the left, and Tra
on the right. The p
parodies a well-kno
image, *Hercules bet*
Virtue and Pleasure
alludes to Guido Re
(Tragedy) and Cor
(Comedy). Exalted
edy urges Garrick t
low her, but darling
Comedy drags him
SOMERSET MAUGHA
THEATRE COLLECT
LONDON, UK / BRID
ART LIBRARY.

A Philosopher Giving That Lecture on the Orrery, in Which a Lamp Is Put in Place
of the Sun, Joseph Wright, 1766

Joseph Wright came from the English Midlands, where an intense interest in science helped
spark the industrial revolution. The orrery, a mechanism that represents the movements of the
planets around the sun, was one of many devices that taught the public to appreciate the wonders
and pleasures of science. In this picture, the philosopher at the center bears a striking resemblance to portraits of Sir Isaac Newton, who had cast light on the solar system. Wright specialized in "candlelight pictures." Strong effects of light and shade play over the faces around the
lamp, as if to reflect the literal meaning of enlightenment. GIRAUDON / ART RESOURCE, NY.

e Death of General Wolfe, Benjamin West, 1771

story painting—pictures that represent a famous legend or historical event—was the most
estigious genre of eighteenth-century art. West's painting of Wolfe, who fell on the day that he
ptured Quebec, revolutionized the genre by dressing the figures in contemporary clothes, not
ssical togas. Twelve years after his death, Wolfe had become an icon; the composition draws on
ages of mourners around the dead Christ. The poetic shading is also appropriate to Wolfe. The
ght before he died, he is supposed to have said of Gray's "Elegy" (p. 3051) that he "would rather
ve been the author of that piece than beat the French tomorrow"; and in his copy of the poem, he
rked one passage: "The paths of glory lead but to the grave." PRIVATE COLLECTION / PHILLIPS,
NE ART AUCTIONEERS, NY / BRIDGEMAN ART LIBRARY.

The Parting of Abelard from Heloise,
Angelika Kauffmann, ca. 1778

Angelika Kauffmann, born in
Switzerland in 1741, was a child
prodigy; at eleven she made a
name in Italy for her portraits.
From 1766 to 1781 she lived in
England, where she was admired
both as a singer and as a painter.
During the eighteenth century the
affair of Abelard and Heloise,
which Pope depicted as a struggle
between God and Eros, softened
into a sentimental love story.
Rousseau's novel *The New Heloise*
(1761) helped transform the
heroine into a saint of love. In an
Age of Sensibility, Kauffmann
portrays a youthful and feminized
Abelard, not a wounded middle-
aged scholar, and pathos, not
repentance, marks this tender
parting. COPYRIGHT © 2003 STATE
HERMITAGE MUSEUM,
ST. PETERSBURG, RUSSIA.

Inside the illustration, the text panel reads:

50   ODE ON THE DEATH

Her coat, that with the tortoife vies,
Her ears of jet, and emerald eyes,
   She faw; and purr'd applaufe.

Still had fhe gaz'd; but 'midft the tide
Two angel forms were feen to glide,
   The Genii of the ftream:
Their fcaly armour's Tyrian hue,
Thro' richeft purple to the view
   Betray'd a golden gleam.

The haplefs nymph with wonder faw:
A whifker firft, and then a claw,
   With many an ardent wifh,
She ftretch'd, in vain, to reach the prize.
What female heart can gold defpife?
   What cat's averfe to fifh?

                                    Prefump-

Illustration for Gray's "Ode on the Death of a Favourite Cat," William Blake, 1798

In 1797, as a birthday gift for his wife, Nancy, the sculptor John Flaxman commissioned Blake to illustrate Gray's poems. These designs, in pen and watercolor, view the art of Gray through Blake's own vision. The charm of Gray's ode depends on picturing Selima both as a cat who tumbles for goldfish and as a "nymph" or "maid" who falls for gold. Blake mixes the two together in a cat and turns the goldfish (or "genii of the stream") into fleeing, finny human forms. Meanwhile, a lurking Fate cuts the thread of Selima's life, reminding us, in this interpretation of Gray, that perverted desires can be deadly. © YALE CENTER FOR BRITISH ART, PAUL MELLON COLLECTION, USA / BRIDGEMAN ART LIBRARY.

That with the fancy I awoke,
And found (ah me!) this flesh of mine
More like a stock° than like a vine.   *hard stalk*

Delight in Disorder[1]

A sweet disorder in the dress
Kindles in clothes a wantonness.
A lawn° about the shoulders thrown   *fine linen scarf*
Into a fine distractiòn;
5   An erring° lace, which here and there   *wandering*
Enthralls the crimson stomacher;[2]
A cuff neglectful, and thereby
Ribbons to flow confusedly;
A winning wave, deserving note,
10   In the tempestuous petticoat;
A careless shoestring, in whose tie
I see a wild civility:
Do more bewitch me than when art
Is too precise[3] in every part.

Corinna's Going A-Maying

Get up! Get up for shame! The blooming morn
Upon her wings presents the god unshorn.[1]
    See how Aurora throws her fair
    Fresh-quilted colors through the air:[2]
5   Get up, sweet slug-a-bed, and see
    The dew bespangling herb and tree.
Each flower has wept and bowed toward the east
Above an hour since, yet you not dressed;
    Nay, not so much as out of bed?
10   When all the birds have matins° said,   *morning prayer*
    And sung their thankful hymns, 'tis sin,
    Nay, profanation° to keep in,   *impiety*
Whenas a thousand virgins on this day
Spring, sooner than the lark, to fetch in May.[3]

15   Rise, and put on your foliage, and be seen
To come forth, like the springtime, fresh and green,
    And sweet as Flora.[4] Take no care

---

1. One of several poems in this period in which women's dress is a means by which to explore the relation of nature and art.
2. An ornamental covering of the chest, worn under the laces of the bodice.
3. "Precise" and "precision" were terms used satirically about Puritans. Herrick, in praising feminine disarray, is at one level praising the "sprezzatura," or careless grace, of Cavalier art.

1. Apollo, the sun god; sunbeams are seen as his flowing locks.
2. Aurora is goddess of the dawn.
3. On May Day morning, it was the custom to gather whitethorn blossoms and trim the house with them.
4. Flora, Italian goddess of flowers, had her festival in the spring.

For jewels for your gown or hair;
Fear not; the leaves will strew
20 Gems in abundance upon you;
Besides, the childhood of the day has kept,
Against° you come, some orient pearls[5] unwept;   *until*
     Come and receive them while the light
     Hangs on the dew-locks of the night,
25   And Titan° on the eastern hill   *the sun*
     Retires himself, or else stands still
Till you come forth. Wash, dress, be brief in praying:
Few beads[6] are best when once we go a-Maying.

Come, my Corinna, come; and, coming, mark
30 How each field turns° a street, each street a park   *turns into*
     Made green and trimmed with trees; see how
     Devotion gives each house a bough
     Or branch: each porch, each door ere this,
     An ark, a tabernacle is,[7]
35 Made up of whitethorn neatly interwove,
As if here were those cooler shades of love.
     Can such delights be in the street
     And open fields, and we not see 't?
     Come, we'll abroad; and let's obey
40   The proclamation[8] made for May,
And sin no more, as we have done, by staying;
But, my Corinna, come, let's go a-Maying.

There's not a budding boy or girl this day
But is got up and gone to bring in May;
45   A deal of youth, ere this, is come
     Back, and with whitethorn laden, home.
     Some have dispatched their cakes and cream
     Before that we have left to dream;
And some have wept, and wooed, and plighted troth,[9]
50 And chose their priest, ere we can cast off sloth.
     Many a green gown[1] has been given,
     Many a kiss, both odd and even;[2]
     Many a glance, too, has been sent
     From out the eye, love's firmament;°   *sky*
55 Many a jest told of the keys betraying
This night, and locks picked; yet we're not a-Maying.

Come, let us go while we are in our prime,
And take the harmless folly of the time.
     We shall grow old apace, and die
60   Before we know our liberty.

---

5. Pearls from the Orient were especially lustrous, like drops of dew.
6. Rosary beads of the "old" Catholic religion, but more generally, a casual term for prayers.
7. The doorways, ornamented with whitethorn, are like the Hebrew Ark of the Covenant or the sanctuary that housed it (Leviticus 23.40–42:

"Ye shall take you on the first day the boughs of goodly trees . . .").
8. Probably a reference to Charles I's "Declaration to his subjects concerning lawful sports."
9. Engaged themselves to marry.
1. Got by rolling in the grass.
2. Kisses are odd and even in kissing games.

Our life is short, and our days run
As fast away as does the sun;
And, as a vapor or a drop of rain,
Once lost, can ne'er be found again,
65   So when or you or I are made
A fable, song, or fleeting shade,
All love, all liking, all delight
Lies drowned with us in endless night.[3]
Then while time serves, and we are but decaying,
70   Come, my Corinna, come, let's go a-Maying.

To the Virgins, to Make Much of Time

Gather ye rosebuds while ye may,
    Old time is still° a-flying;[1]   *always*
And this same flower that smiles today,
    Tomorrow will be dying.

5   The glorious lamp of heaven, the sun,
        The higher he's a-getting,
    The sooner will his race be run,
        And nearer he's to setting.

    That age is best which is the first,
10   When youth and blood are warmer;
    But being spent, the worse, and worst
        Times still succeed the former.

    Then be not coy, but use your time,
        And while ye may, go marry;
15 For having lost but once your prime,
        You may forever tarry.

Upon Julia's Clothes

Whenas in silks my Julia goes,°   *walks*
Then, then, methinks, how sweetly flows
That liquefaction of her clothes.

Next, when I cast mine eyes and see
5   That brave° vibration each way free,   *splendid*
Oh, how that glittering taketh me!

---

3. Some echoes of the apocryphal book Wisdom of Solomon 2.1–8: "For the ungodly said . . . the breath of our nostrils is as smoke, and a little spark . . . and our life shall pass away as the trace of a cloud. . . . Come on therefore . . . Let us crown ourselves with rose buds before they be withered." This carpe diem sentiment is a frequent theme in classical love poetry.
1. Translates the Latin *tempus fugit*.

RICHARD LOVELACE
1618–1657

The quintessential Cavalier, Richard Lovelace was described by a contemporary as "the most amiable and beautiful person that ever eye beheld." Born into a wealthy Kentish family, he was educated at Oxford and fought for Charles I in Scotland (in both expeditions, 1639 and 1640). He shared with his king a serious interest in art, especially the paintings of Rubens, Van Dyck, and Lely. He was imprisoned for a few months in 1642 for supporting the "Kentish Petition" that urged restoration of the king to his ancient rights; in "To Althea, from Prison," he finds freedom from external bondage in the Cavalier ideals of women, wine, and royalism. During 1643–46 he fought in Holland and France and in the king's armies in England and was wounded abroad. In a general roundup of known royalists in 1648 he was imprisoned for ten months, and while there prepared his poems for publication under the title *Lucasta* (1649). Besides witty and charming love songs, the volume includes the plaintive ballad about the conflict between love and honor, "To Lucasta, Going to the Wars," and also "The Grasshopper," a poem that presents the Cavalier ideal at its most attractive. Like that emblematic summer creature, the once-carefree Cavalier suffers in the Puritan "winter," but Lovelace finds in the fellowship of Cavalier friends a nobler version of the good life. After 1649 he endured years of penury, largely dependent on the largesse of his friend and fellow royalist, Charles Cotton. His remaining poems appeared in 1659 as *Lucasta: Postume Poems*.

From Lucasta

To Lucasta, Going to the Wars

Tell me not, sweet, I am unkind,
  That from the nunnery
Of thy chaste breast and quiet mind
  To war and arms I fly.

5 True, a new mistress now I chase,
  The first foe in the field;
And with a stronger faith embrace
  A sword, a horse, a shield.

Yet this inconstancy is such
10 As you too shall adore;
I could not love thee, dear, so much,
  Loved I not honor more.

1649

To Althea, from Prison

When Love with unconfinèd wings
 Hovers within my gates,
And my divine Althea brings
 To whisper at the grates;
5 When I lie tangled in her hair
 And fettered to her eye,
The gods[1] that wanton° in the air   *play*
 Know no such liberty.

When flowing cups run swiftly round,
10 With no allaying Thames,[2]
Our careless heads with roses bound,
 Our hearts with loyal flames;
When thirsty grief in wine we steep,
 When healths and drafts go free,
15 Fishes that tipple in the deep
 Know no such liberty.

When, like committed linnets,° I   *caged finches*
 With shriller throat shall sing
The sweetness, mercy, majesty,
20 And glories of my king;
When I shall voice aloud how good
 He is, how great should be,
Enlargèd winds, that curl the flood,
 Know no such liberty.

25 Stone walls do not a prison make,
 Nor iron bars a cage;
Minds innocent and quiet take
 That for an hermitage.
If I have freedom in my love,
30 And in my soul am free,
Angels alone, that soar above,
 Enjoy such liberty.

1649

---

1. Some versions read "birds" instead of "gods."
2. No mixture of water (as from the river Thames) in the wine.

KATHERINE PHILIPS
1632–1664

The best-known woman poet of her own and the next generation, Katherine Philips was honored as "the Matchless Orinda," the classical name she chose for herself in her poetic addresses to a coterie of chiefly female friends, especially Mary Aubrey (M. A.) and Anne Owen (Lucasia). Sometimes reminiscent of Donne's love lyrics and sometimes of the ancient Greek Sappho's erotic lyrics to women, these poems develop an exalted ideal of female friendship as a Platonic union of souls. Born to a well-to-do Presbyterian family and educated at Mrs. Salmon's Presbyterian School, Philips was taken to Wales when her mother remarried. In 1648, at age seventeen, she was married to James Philips, a prominent member of Parliament. They lived together twelve years, chiefly in the small Welsh town of Cardigan, and had two children: Hector, whose death a few days after birth prompted one of her most moving poems, and Katherine, who lived to adulthood. A royalist despite her Puritan family connections, Philips forged connections with other displaced royalists. Her poems circulated in manuscript and elicited high praise from Vaughan in *Olor Iscanus*. They include elegies, epitaphs, poems at parting, and friendship poems to women and men, but also poetry on political themes: a denunciation of the regicide, "Upon the Double Murder of King Charles," and panegyrics on the restored Stuarts. After the Restoration, James Philips barely escaped execution as a regicide, had his estates confiscated, and lost his seat in Parliament, but Katherine became a favorite at court, promoted by her friend Sir Charles Cotterell ("Poliarchus"), who was master of ceremonies. In Ireland attempting (unsuccessfully) to redeem an investment, she translated Corneille's *Pompey* and her friend the Earl of Orrery produced and printed it in Dublin in 1663. The first edition of her poems, apparently pirated, appeared in 1664, the same year she died of smallpox. Her friend Cotterell brought out an authorized edition in 1667.

A Married State[1]

A married state affords but little ease
The best of husbands are so hard to please.
This in wives' careful° faces you may spell°   *full of cares / read*
Though they dissemble their misfortunes well.
5   A virgin state is crowned with much content;[2]
It's always happy as it's innocent.
No blustering husbands to create your fears;
No pangs of childbirth to extort your tears;
No children's cries for to offend your ears;
10   Few worldly crosses to distract your prayers:
Thus are you freed from all the cares that do

1. In a manuscript (Orielton MSS Box 24 at the National Library of Wales) this poem appears with another by Philips, addressed to Anne Barlow (whom she probably met in 1646); this one is probably also for Barlow. Both are signed by her maiden name, C. Fowler, so were evidently written before her marriage in 1648.
2. Praise of the single life is a common topic in women's poetry.

Attend on matrimony and a husband too.
Therefore Madam, be advised by me
Turn, turn apostate to love's levity,
15　Suppress wild nature if she dare rebel.
There's no such thing as leading apes in hell.[3]

ca. 1646　　　　　　　　　　　　　　　　　　　　Ms; 1988

Upon the Double Murder of King Charles

In Answer to a Libelous Rhyme made by V. P.[1]

I think not on the state, nor am concerned
Which way soever that great helm[2] is turned,
But as that son whose father's danger nigh
Did force his native dumbness, and untie
5　His fettered organs: so here is a cause
That will excuse the breach of nature's laws.[3]
Silence were now a sin: nay passion now
Wise men themselves for merit would allow.[4]
What noble eye could see (and careless pass)
10　The dying lion kicked by every ass?
Hath Charles so broke God's laws, he must not have
A quiet crown, nor yet a quiet grave?
Tombs have been sanctuaries; thieves lie here
Secure from all their penalty and fear.
15　Great Charles his double misery was this,
Unfaithful friends, ignoble enemies;
Had any heathen been this prince's foe,
He would have wept to see him injured so.
His title was his crime, they'd reason good
20　To quarrel at the right they had withstood.
He broke God's laws, and therefore he must die,
And what shall then become of thee and I?
Slander must follow treason; but yet stay,
Take not our reason with our king away.
25　Though you have seized upon all our defense,
Yet do not sequester° our common sense.　　　　　　　*confiscate*
But I admire° not at this new supply:　　　　　　　*wonder*
No bounds will hold those who at scepters fly.
Christ will be King, but I ne'er understood,
30　His subjects built his kingdom up with blood
(Except their own) or that he would dispense
With his commands, though for his own defense.

---

3. Proverbially, the fate of spinsters.
1. The itinerant Welsh preacher Vavasour Powell was a Fifth Monarchist and an ardent republican who justified the regicide on the ground that Christ's second coming was imminent, when he would rule with his saints, putting down all earthly kings. His poem and Philips's answer were likely written shortly after Charles I's execution (January 30, 1649). Powell's poem has been pub-lished by Elizabeth H. Hageman in *English Manu-script Studies*.
2. Steering wheel for the "ships" of state.
3. Breaking the supposed law of nature that excludes women from speaking about public affairs.
4. Wise men, especially Stoic philosophers, nor-mally counsel the firm control or elimination of passions.

Oh! to what height of horror are they come
Who dare pull down a crown, tear up a tomb![5]

1649?   1664

Friendship's Mystery, To My Dearest *Lucasia*[1]

1

Come, my Lucasia, since we see
   That miracles men's faith do move,
By wonder and by prodigy
   To the dull angry world let's prove
5   There's a religion in our love.

2

For though we were designed t' agree,
   That fate no liberty destroys,
But our election is as free
   As angels, who with greedy choice
10   Are yet determined to their joys.[2]

3

Our hearts are doubled by the loss,
   Here mixture is addition grown;
We both diffuse,° and both engross:°   *spread out / collect*
   And we whose minds are so much one,
15   Never, yet ever are alone.

4

We court our own captivity
   Than thrones more great and innocent:
'Twere banishment to be set free,
   Since we wear fetters whose intent
20   Not bondage is, but ornament.

5

Divided joys are tedious found,
   And griefs united easier grow:
We are selves but by rebound,

5. Their slanders tear up Charles's tomb after his death.
1. This poem was first printed, with a musical setting by the royalist musician and composer Henry Lawes, as "Mutual Affection betweene *Orinda* and *Lucasia*" in Lawes's *The Second Book of Ayres* (1655); our text is from *Poems by*

the Most Deservedly Admired Mrs. Katherine Philips, the Matchless Orinda (1667). Lucasia is Philips's name for her friend Anne Owen.
2. Angels, though created with free will, were thought to have become fixed in goodness when they turned toward God in the first moments after their creation.

And all our titles shuffled so,
25   Both princes, and both subjects too.[3]

6

Our hearts are mutual victims laid,
    While they (such power in friendship lies)
Are altars, priests, and off'rings made:
    And each heart which thus kindly° dies,   *benevolently, naturally*
30   Grows deathless by the sacrifice.

1655, 1664

On the Death of My First and Dearest Child, Hector Philips[1]

Twice forty months in wedlock[2] I did stay,
    Then had my vows crowned with a lovely boy.
And yet in forty days[3] he dropped away;
    O swift vicissitude of human joy!

5   I did but see him, and he disappeared,
    I did but touch the rosebud, and it fell;
A sorrow unforeseen and scarcely feared,
    So ill can mortals their afflictions spell.°   *discern*

And now, sweet babe, what can my trembling heart
10   Suggest to right my doleful fate or thee?
Tears are my muse, and sorrow all my art,
    So piercing groans must be thy elegy.

Thus whilst no eye is witness of my moan,
    I grieve thy loss (ah, boy too dear to live!),
15   And let the unconcernèd world alone,
    Who neither will, nor can, refreshment give.

An off'ring too for thy sad tomb I have,
    Too just a tribute to thy early hearse.
Receive these gasping numbers to thy grave,
20   The last of thy unhappy mother's verse.[4]

1655   1667

3. Compare Donne, "The Sun Rising", line 21: "She is all states, and all princes, I" (p. 672).
1. In Philips's manuscript the subtitle reads, "born the 23d of April, and died the 2d of May 1655. Set by Mr. Lawes." The musical setting has been published by Joan Applegate in *English Manuscript Studies*.
2. Philips was married in August 1648.

3. The subtitle indicates that he lived barely ten days; the change here is clearly for the parallelism.
4. This was not in fact Philips's last poem, but the sentiment is both true to human feeling and common in elegy. She had one other child, a year later—a daughter, Katherine, who survived her.

ANDREW MARVELL
1621–1678

A ndrew Marvell's finest poems are second to none in this or any other period. He wrote less than Donne, Jonson, and Herbert did, but his range was in some ways greater, as he claimed both the private worlds of love and religion and the public worlds of political and satiric poetry and prose. His overriding concern with art, his elegant, well-crafted, limpid style, and the cool balance and reserve of some poems align him with Jonson. Yet his paradoxes and complexities of tone, his use of dramatic monologue, and his witty, dialectical arguments associate him with Donne. Above all, he is a supremely original poet, so complex and elusive that it is often hard to know what he really thought about the subjects he treated. Many of his poems were published posthumously in 1681, some thirty years after they were written, by a woman who claimed to be his widow but was probably his housekeeper. So their date and order of composition is often in doubt, as is his authorship of some anonymous works.

The son of a Church of England clergyman, Marvell grew up in Yorkshire, attended Trinity College, Cambridge (perhaps deriving the persistent strain of Neoplatonism in his poetry from the academics known as the Cambridge Platonists), ran off to London, and converted to Roman Catholicism until his father put an end to both ventures. He returned to Cambridge, took his degree in 1639, and stayed on as a scholar until his father's death in 1641. During the years of the civil wars (1642–48), he traveled in France, Italy, Holland, and Spain; much later he said of the Puritan "Good Old Cause" that it was "too good to have been fought for." While his earliest poems associate him with royalists, those after 1649 celebrate the Commonwealth and Oliver Cromwell; although he is sometimes ambivalent, Marvell recognizes divine providence in the political changes. From 1650 to 1652 he lived at Nunappleton as tutor to the twelve-year-old daughter of Thomas Fairfax, who had given over his command of the parliamentary army to Cromwell because he was unwilling to invade Scotland. In these years of retirement and ease, Marvell probably wrote most of his love lyrics and pastorals as well as *Upon Appleton House*. Subsequently he was tutor to Cromwell's ward, William Dutton, and traveled with him on the Continent; in 1657 he joined the blind Milton, at Milton's request, in the post of Latin secretary to Cromwell's Council of State. Marvell accepted the Restoration but maintained his own independent vision and his abiding belief in religious toleration, a mixed state, and constitutional government. He helped his friend Milton avoid execution for his revolutionary polemics and helped negotiate Milton's release from a brief imprisonment. Elected a member of Parliament in 1659 from his hometown, Hull, in Yorkshire, he held that post until 1678, focusing his attention on the needs of his district; on two occasions he went on diplomatic missions—to Holland and Russia. His (necessarily anonymous) antiroyalist polemics of these years include several verse satires on Charles II and his ministers, as well as his best-known prose work, *The Rehearsal Transprosed* (1672–73), which defends Puritan dissenters and denounces censorship with verve and wit. He also wrote a brilliant poem of criticism and interpretation on Milton's *Paradise Lost* that was prefixed to the second edition (1674).

Many of Marvell's poems explore the human condition in terms of fundamental dichotomies that resist resolution. In religious or philosophical poems like "The Coronet" or "The Dialogue Between the Soul and Body," the conflict is between nature and grace, or body and soul, or poetic creation and sacrifice. In love poems such as "The Definition of Love" or "To His Coy Mistress," it is often between flesh and spirit, or physical sex and platonic love, or idealizing courtship and the ravages of time. In pastorals like the Mower poems and "The Garden," the opposition is between nature and art, or the fallen and the Edenic state, or violent passion and contentment. Marvell's most subtle and complex political poem, "An Horatian Ode upon Cromwell's Return from Ireland," sets stable traditional order and ancient right against providential revolutionary change, and the goods and costs of retirement and peace against those of action and war. *Upon Appleton House* also opposes the attractions of various kinds of retirement to the duties of action and reformation.

Marvell experimented with style and genre to striking effect. Many of his dramatic monologues are voiced by named, naive personas—the Mower, the Nymph—who stand at some remove from the author. "To His Coy Mistress," perhaps the best known of the century's carpe diem poems, is voiced by a witty and urbane speaker in balanced and artful couplets. But its rapid shifts from the world of fantasy to the charnal house of reality raise questions as to whether this is a clever seduction poem or a probing of existential angst, and whether Marvell intends to endorse or critique this speaker's view of passion and sex. In *Upon Appleton House* Marvell transforms the static, mythic features of Jonson's country-house poem "To Penshurst" to create a poem that incorporates history and the conflicts of contemporary society. It assimilates to the course of providential history the topographical features of the Fairfax estate, the Fairfax family myth of origin, the experiences of the poet-tutor on his progress around the estate, and the activities and projected future of the daughter of the house. In the poem's rich symbolism, biblical events—Eden, the first temptation, the Fall, the wilderness experience of the Israelites—find echoes in the experiences of the Fairfax family, the speaker, the history of the English Reformation, and the wanton destruction of the recent civil wars.

From Poems[1]

To His Coy Mistress

> Had we but world enough, and time,
> This coyness, lady, were no crime.
> We would sit down, and think which way
> To walk, and pass our long love's day.
> 5 Thou by the Indian Ganges' side
> Shouldst rubies find; I by the tide
> Of Humber would complain.[2] I would
> Love you ten years before the Flood,
> And you should, if you please, refuse
> 10 Till the conversion of the Jews.[3]
> My vegetable love should grow
> Vaster than empires, and more slow;
> An hundred years should go to praise
> Thine eyes, and on thy forehead gaze;
> 15 Two hundred to adore each breast,

1. Marvell's lyrics were published posthumously in 1681.
2. The exotic river Ganges in India is on one side of the world, the Humber River flows past Marvell's city, Hull, on the opposite side. Complaints are poems of plaintive, unavailing love.
3. Popular belief had it that the Jews were to be converted just before the Last Judgment. The exaggerated offers in this stanza play off against conventional hyperbolic declarations of love in Petrarchan poetry.

But thirty thousand to the rest:
An age at least to every part,
And the last age should show your heart.
For, lady, you deserve this state,°   dignity
20   Nor would I love at lower rate.
        But at my back I always hear
Time's wingèd chariot hurrying near;
And yonder all before us lie
Deserts of vast eternity.
25   Thy beauty shall no more be found,
Nor, in thy marble vault, shall sound
My echoing song; then worms shall try
That long-preserved virginity,
And your quaint⁴ honor turn to dust,
30   And into ashes all my lust:
The grave's a fine and private place,
But none, I think, do there embrace.
        Now therefore, while the youthful hue
Sits on thy skin like morning dew,⁵
35   And while thy willing soul transpires
At every pore with instant fires,⁶
Now let us sport us while we may,
And now, like amorous birds of prey,
Rather at once our time devour
40   Than languish in his slow-chapped⁷ power.
Let us roll all our strength and all
Our sweetness up into one ball,
And tear our pleasures with rough strife
Thorough° the iron gates of life:⁸   through
45   Thus, though we cannot make our sun
Stand still, yet we will make him run.⁹

ca. 1650–52   1681

The Definition of Love

My Love is of a birth as rare
As 'tis, for object, strange and high;
It was begotten by Despair
Upon Impossibility.

5   Magnanimous Despair alone
Could show me so divine a thing,
Where feeble Hope could ne'er have flown
But vainly flapped its tinsel wing.

---

4. "Quaint" puns on "out of date" and *queynte*, a term for the female genitals.
5. The text reads "glew," which could be correct, but "dew" is a common emendation.
6. Urgent, sudden enthusiasm. "Transpires": breathes forth.

7. Slowly devouring jaws.
8. One manuscript reads "grates," a somewhat different figure for the sexual act proposed.
9. The sun stood still for Joshua (Joshua 10.12) in his war against Gibeon; see the very different resolution in Donne's "The Sun Rising" (p. 672).

And yet I quickly might arrive
10   Where my extended soul is fixed;[1]
But Fate does iron wedges drive,
And always crowds itself betwixt.

For Fate with jealous eye does see
Two perfect loves, nor lets them close;°   *unite*
15   Their union would her ruin be,
And her tyrannic power depose.[2]

And therefore her decrees of steel
Us as the distant poles have placed
(Though Love's whole world on us doth wheel),[3]
20   Not by themselves to be embraced,

Unless the giddy heaven fall,
And earth some new convulsion tear,
And, us to join, the world should all
Be cramped into a planisphere.[4]

25   As lines, so loves oblique may well
Themselves in every angle greet;[5]
But ours, so truly parallel,
Though infinite, can never meet.

Therefore the Love which us doth bind,
30   But Fate so enviously debars,
Is the conjunction of the mind,
And opposition of the stars.[6]

ca. 1650–52   1681

The Mower to the Glowworms

Ye living lamps, by whose dear light
The nightingale does sit so late,
And studying all the summer night
Her matchless songs does meditate,

5   Ye country comets, that portend
No war nor prince's funeral,
Shining unto no higher end
Than to presage the grass's fall;

---

1. The soul has extended itself from the speaker's body and fixed itself to his lover.
2. Two perfections, united, would not be subject to change and thereby to Fate.
3. Rotates as on its axis.
4. A two-dimensional map of the world; Marvell images a round globe collapsed into a flat pancake shape, top to bottom, which would bring the two poles together.
5. Oblique lines can touch in angles, as might "oblique" lovers that (in one meaning of the term) "deviate from right conduct or thought."
6. "Conjunction" is the coming together of two heavenly bodies in the same sign of the zodiac; "opposition" places them at diametrical opposites.

Ye glowworms, whose officious° flame   *helpful*
10   To wand'ring mowers shows the way,
That in the night have lost their aim,
And after foolish fires° do stray;   *will-o'-the-wisps*

Your courteous fires in vain you waste,
Since Juliana here is come,
15   For she my mind hath so displaced
That I shall never find my home.

ca. 1650–52   1681

The Mower's Song

My mind was once the true survey
Of all these meadows fresh and gay,
And in the greenness of the grass
Did see its hopes[1] as in a glass;°   *mirror*
5   When Juliana came, and she,
What I do to the grass, does to my thoughts and me.[2]

But these, while I with sorrow pine,
Grew more luxuriant still and fine,
That not one blade of grass you spied
10   But had a flower on either side;
When Juliana came, and she,
What I do to the grass, does to my thoughts and me.

Unthankful meadows, could you so
A fellowship so true forego,
15   And in your gaudy May-games[3] meet,
While I lay trodden under feet?
When Juliana came, and she,
What I do to the grass, does to my thoughts and me.

But what you in compassion ought
20   Shall now by my revenge be wrought,
And flowers, and grass, and I, and all,
Will in one common ruin fall;
For Juliana comes, and she,
What I do to the grass, does to my thoughts and me.

25   And thus ye meadows, which have been
Companions of my thoughts more green,
Shall now the heraldry become
With which I shall adorn my tomb;

1. Green is the color of hope.
2. The alexandrine (twelve-syllable line) used here is the only example of a refrain in Marvell.

3. Festivals and merrymaking marked the first of May, May Day.

For Juliana comes, and she,
30   What I do to the grass, does to my thoughts and me.

ca. 1650–52   1681

The Garden

How vainly men themselves amaze°   *bewilder*
To win the palm, the oak, or bays,[1]
And their uncessant labors see
Crowned from some single herb or tree,
5 Whose short and narrow-vergèd° shade   *edged*
Does prudently their toils upbraid;°   *reprove*
While all flowers and all trees do close°   *unite, agree*
To weave the garlands of repose!

Fair Quiet, have I found thee here,
10 And Innocence, thy sister dear?
Mistaken long, I sought you then
In busy companies of men.
Your sacred plants, if here below,°   *on earth*
Only among the plants will grow;
15 Society is all but rude,
To° this delicious solitude.   *compared to*

No white nor red[2] was ever seen
So amorous as this lovely green.
Fond lovers, cruel as their flame,
20 Cut in these trees their mistress' name:
Little, alas, they know or heed
How far these beauties hers exceed!
Fair trees, wheresoe'er your barks I wound,
No name shall but your own be found.[3]

25 When we have run our passion's heat,
Love hither makes his best retreat.
The gods, that mortal beauty chase,
Still° in a tree did end their race: *always*
Apollo hunted Daphne so,
30 Only that she might laurel grow;
And Pan did after Syrinx speed,
Not as a nymph, but for a reed.[4]

What wondrous life is this I lead!
Ripe apples drop about my head;
35 The luscious clusters of the vine
Upon my mouth do crush their wine;

---

1. Honors, respectively, for military, civic, and poetic achievement.
2. Colors traditionally associated with female beauty.
3. Marvell proposes to carve in the bark of trees not "Sylvia" or "Laura," but "Beech" and "Oak."

4. Apollo, the god of poetry, chased Daphne until she turned into a laurel (the emblematic reward of poets); Pan pursued Syrinx until she became a reed, out of which he made panpipes. The gods' motives were, of course, sexual, not horticultural.

The nectarine and curious° peach   *exquisite*
Into my hands themselves do reach;
Stumbling on melons[5] as I pass,
40   Ensnared with flowers, I fall on grass.

Meanwhile the mind, from pleasure less,
Withdraws into its happiness;
The mind, that ocean where each kind
Does straight° its own resemblance find;[6]   *immediately*
45   Yet it creates, transcending these,
Far other worlds and other seas,
Annihilating all that's made
To a green thought in a green shade.

Here at the fountain's sliding foot,
50   Or at some fruit tree's mossy root,
Casting the body's vest° aside,   *garment*
My soul into the boughs does glide:
There like a bird it sits and sings,
Then whets° and combs its silver wings,   *preens*
55   And, till prepared for longer flight,
Waves in its plumes the various light.[7]

Such was that happy garden-state,
While man there walked without a mate:
After a place so pure and sweet,
60   What other help could yet be meet![8]
But 'twas beyond a mortal's share
To wander solitary there:
Two paradises 'twere in one
To live in paradise alone.

65   How well the skillful gardener drew
Of flowers and herbs this dial new,[9]
Where from above the milder sun
Does through a fragrant zodiac run;
And as it works, th' industrious bee
70   Computes its time[1] as well as we!
How could such sweet and wholesome hours
Be reckoned but with herbs and flowers?

ca. 1650–52   1681

---

5. "Melons," with etymological roots in the Greek word for "apple," may recall the apple over which all humankind stumbled.
6. As the ocean supposedly contained a counterpart of every creature on land, so the ocean of the mind holds the innate ideas of all things (in Neoplatonic philosophy).

7. The multicolored light of this world, contrasted with the white radiance of eternity.
8. Genesis 2.18 recounts the Lord's decision to make a "help meet" for Adam, Eve.
9. The garden itself is laid out as a sundial.
1. With a pun on "thyme."

The Execution of Charles I. A German print illustrates the beheading of Charles I before an enormous crowd, on a scaffold erected in front of the Banqueting House. At the top of the picture small portraits of General Fairfax and Cromwell, leaders of the Parliamentary forces, flank a portrait of King Charles, to whom an angel in the clouds is extending a heavenly crown. In the lower right corner, a woman faints.

An Horatian Ode

Upon Cromwell's Return from Ireland[1]

The forward° youth that would appear   *eager, ambitious*
Must now forsake his Muses dear,
    Nor in the shadows sing
    His numbers languishing:

5 'Tis time to leave the books in dust
And oil th' unusèd armor's rust,
    Removing from the wall
    The corselet° of the hall.[2]   *upper body armor*

1. Oliver Cromwell, the general primarily responsible for Parliament's victory in the civil war, returned from conquering Ireland in May 1650, about eighteen months after the execution of Charles I. The two events were persistently connected: Cromwell's success in Ireland was taken as a sign of God's favor to the new republican regime and to Cromwell as his chosen instrument. Pindaric odes (like Jonson's Cary-Morison ode) are heroic and ecstatic; Horatian odes are poems of cool and balanced judgment, as this one is in its representations of Cromwell, Charles I, and the issues of power and providence.
2. Here as elsewhere there are allusions to Lucan's *Pharsalia*, a poem of civil war whose sympathies are with Pompey, Cato, and the Roman Republic against Caesar and the empire. The poem's allusions to Caesar are most often to Charles I, but sometimes to Cromwell.

So restless Cromwell could not cease
10   In the inglorious arts of peace,
        But through adventurous war
        Urgèd his active star;[3]

And, like the three-forked lightning, first
    Breaking the clouds where it was nursed,
15   Did through his own side
        His fiery way divide:[4]

For 'tis all one to courage high,
    The emulous, or enemy;
        And with such, to enclose
20   Is more than to oppose.

Then burning through the air he went,
    And palaces and temples rent;
        And Caesar's head at last
        Did through his laurels blast.[5]

25 'Tis madness to resist or blame
    The force of angry heaven's flame;
        And if we would speak true,
        Much to the man is due,

Who from his private gardens, where
30   He lived reservèd and austere
        (As if his highest plot
        To plant the bergamot),[6]

Could by industrious valor climb
    To ruin the great work of time,
35   And cast the kingdom old
        Into another mold;

Though Justice against Fate complain,
    And plead the ancient rights in vain:
        But those do hold or break,
40   As men are strong or weak.

Nature that hateth emptiness,
    Allows of penetration less,[7]
        And therefore must make room
        Where greater spirits come.

---

3. Normally the stars are thought to control men's fates, but Cromwell presses his own star forward.
4. The "three-forked lightning" identifies him with Zeus, suggesting the elemental force by which he surpassed all those in his own party ("side") of radical Independents; the imagery of giving birth to himself also suggests going Caesar (born by cesarean section) one better.
5. Royal crowns were made of laurel because they were supposed to protect from lightning.
6. A pear-shaped orange (from the Turkish, "prince's pear").
7. Nature abhors a vacuum, but even more, the penetration of one body's space by another body.

45   What field of all the civil wars
Where his were not the deepest scars?
     And Hampton shows what part
     He had of wiser art;[8]

Where, twining subtle fears with hope,
50   He wove a net of such a scope
     That Charles himself might chase
     To Caresbrooke's narrow case,

That thence the royal actor[9] borne,
The tragic scaffold might adorn;
55   While round the armèd bands
     Did clap their bloody hands.

He nothing common did or mean
Upon that memorable scene,
     But with his keener eye
60   The ax's edge[1] did try;

Nor called the gods with vulgar spite
To vindicate his helpless right;
     But bowed his comely head
     Down, as upon a bed.

65   This was that memorable hour,
Which first assured the forcèd power;
     So when they did design
     The Capitol's first line,

A bleeding head where they begun
70   Did fright the architects to run;
     And yet in that the state
     Foresaw its happy fate.[2]

And now the Irish are ashamed
To see themselves in one year tamed;
75   So much one man can do,
     That does both act and know.

They can affirm his praises best,
And have, though overcome, confessed

---

8. Charles was confined at Hampton Court after his defeat, as Parliament attempted to negotiate terms for his restoration. Cromwell was rumored to have connived at his escape to Carisbrooke Castle, on the Isle of Wight, in order to convince Parliament that he could not be trusted and must be executed. Cromwell has shown himself master of the two "arts" of rule defined by Machiavelli, namely, force and craft.
9. The theater metaphors used for Charles are even more powerful because the "tragic scaf-

fold" was erected outside Whitehall, where so many royal masques were produced. See a depiction of the king's execution on p. 757.
1. A play on the Latin *acies*, which means the edge of a sword or ax, a keen glance, and the vanguard of a battle.
2. Livy and Pliny record that the workmen digging the foundations for a temple of Jupiter at Rome uncovered a bloody head which they were persuaded to take as an omen that Rome would be head (*caput*) of a great empire; the temple and the hill took the name Capitoline from that event.

How good he is, how just,
80   And fit for highest trust.[3]

Nor yet grown stiffer with command,
But still in the republic's hand—
       How fit he is to sway,
       That can so well obey.[4]

85 He to the Commons' feet presents
A kingdom for his first year's rents;
       And, what he may, forbears
       His fame to make it theirs;[5]

And has his sword and spoils ungirt,
90 To lay them at the public's skirt:
       So, when the falcon high
       Falls heavy from the sky,

She, having killed, no more does search,
But on the next green bough to perch;
95   Where, when he first does lure,
       The falconer has her sure.

What may not then our isle presume,
While victory his crest does plume!
       What may not others fear,
100   If thus he crown each year!

A Caesar he ere long to Gaul,
To Italy an Hannibal,
       And to all states not free,
       Shall climactèric be.[6]

105 The Pict no shelter now shall find
Within his parti-colored mind,
       But from this valor sad,°   severe, solemn
       Shrink underneath the plaid;[7]

Happy if in the tufted brake
110 The English hunter him mistake,
       Nor lay his hounds in near
       The Caledonian° deer.   Scottish

3. Cromwell conducted a particularly brutal campaign in Ireland, and the Irish had no such testimonials for him; the lines are deeply equivocal.
4. The maxim about obedience fitting one to rule is a commonplace. The implications of "yet" and "still," along with the next stanza, suggest a Caesar figure who has not—but might—cross the Rubicon and defy the Republic, as Julius Caesar did.
5. Thus far, Cromwell gives the Republic credit for his victories.
6. It was thought that Cromwell's military acumen might subdue France and Italy (which threatened to attack the new republic to restore Charles II), just as did Caesar and Hannibal of old. "Climacteric": a period of crucial, epochal change—here, the expectation that the example of a successful English republic would topple absolute monarchs abroad.
7. Early Scots were called Picts (from the Latin pictus, painted), because the warriors painted themselves many colors; contemporary Scots are "parti-colored" (divided into many factions) like a scotch plaid. Cromwell was about to go to subdue Scotland, which had declared for Charles II.

But thou, the war's and Fortune's son,
March indefatigably on;
115   And for the last effect,
        Still keep thy sword erect;

Besides the force it has to fright
The spirits of the shady night,[8]
        The same arts that did gain
120   A power must it maintain.[9]

1650   1681

8. A sword carried with the blade upright evokes the classical tradition that underworld spirits (here, the slain king and his followers) are frightened off by raised weapons.

9. The maxim alludes to Machiavelli's advice that a kingdom won by force must for some time be maintained by force.

MARGARET CAVENDISH
1623–1673

M argaret (Lucas) Cavendish, Duchess of Newcastle, wrote and published numerous works during the Interregnum and Restoration era, in a great variety of genres: poetry (*Poems and Fancies*, 1653); essays (*Philosophical Fancies*, 1653; *The World's Olio*, 1655), short fiction (*Nature's Pictures*, 1656), autobiography (*A True Relation of My Birth, Breeding, and Life*, 1656), Utopian romance (*The Blazing World*, 1666), scientific essays chiefly critical of the new science, letters, a biography of her husband (*The Life of . . . William Cavendish*, 1667), and some eighteen plays, of which one, *The Forced Marriage*, was produced in 1670. Most were published in lavish editions at the Newcastles' own expense. At the time they elicited more derision than praise: for a woman, especially an aristocratic woman, to publish works dealing so intimately with her desires, opinions, personal circumstances, and aspirations to fame and authorship seemed to many disgraceful. Samuel Pepys concluded, after reading her life of her husband the duke, that she was "a mad, conceited, ridiculous woman, and he an ass to suffer [her] to write what she writes to him and of him." Her fantastic dress and sometimes idiosyncratic behavior abetted that characterization: she took pride in "singularity" and even paid a visit to the all-male Royal Society. But the philosopher Thomas Hobbes thought well of her, and her rediscoverers in recent decades have praised her works and her self-construction as a female author.

Cavendish's autobiography analyzes her responses to the circumstances of her life. Born into a wealthy royalist family that encouraged her disposition to read and write, she became maid of honor to Queen Henrietta Maria, whom she followed into exile in Paris. There she married, in 1645, the widowed William Cavendish, thirty years her senior, who was one of Charles I's generals and later Duke of Newcastle. Exiled for fifteen years on the Continent, where (his estates having been sequestered) they ran up exorbitant debts, they were restored to status and fortune after the Restoration. The duke, who was himself a poet, playwright, and philosopher, supported and promoted Margaret's literary endeavors, for which she was profoundly grateful.

In polemical prefaces to her several works, she develops a fragmentary poetics, trenchantly defends her right to publish and to participate in contemporary intellectual exchange, defends women's rational powers, and decries their educational disadvantages and exclusion from the public domain.

The Blazing World   Part romance, part utopia, and part science fiction, *The Blazing World* is also an idealized version of Cavendish's own fantasies in that it portrays the effortless rise of a woman to absolute power. It begins in the vein of romance: a young woman is abducted and miraculously saved as a tempest carries the abductors' boat to the North Pole and on to another universe, the Blazing World, whose emperor promptly marries her and turns over the entire government of the realm to her. It takes on a utopian character, as the new empress learns from the fantastically diverse inhabitants about their numerous scientific experiments and about the royalist politics and religious uniformity of the place. The empress then brings Margaret Cavendish to be her scribe and returns with Margaret (in the state of disembodied spirits and Platonic friends) to visit and learn about Margaret's world; she also puts down a rebellion at home and subjects other nations to her beneficent rule. Cavendish's preface makes a bold claim for authorial self-sufficiency, equating her creation of and rule over her textual world with the conquering and ruling of empires by Caesar and Alexander. She emphasizes the satisfactions of authorship, but in doing so she also underscores the social and political restrictions on women that have confined her sphere of action to an imagined world.

The Description of a New World, Called The Blazing World[1]

To the Reader

* * *This is the reason, why I added this piece of fancy to my philosophical observations, and joined them as two worlds at the ends of their poles; both for my own sake, to divert my studious thoughts, which I employed in the contemplation thereof, and to delight the reader with variety, which is always pleasing. But lest my fancy should stray too much, I chose such a fiction as would be agreeable to the subject treated of in the former parts; it is a description of a new world, not such as Lucian's or the French-man's world in the moon;[2] but a world of my own creating, which I call the Blazing World: the first part whereof is romantical, the second philosophical, and the third is merely fancy, or (as I may call it) fantastical, which if it add any satisfaction to you, I shall account myself a happy creatoress; if not, I must be content to live a melancholy life in my own world; I cannot call it a poor world, if poverty be only want of gold, silver, and jewels; for there is more gold in it than all the chemists ever did, and (as I verily believe) will ever be able to make. As for the rocks of diamonds, I wish with all my soul they might be shared amongst my noble female friends, and upon that condition, I would willingly quit my part; and of the gold I should only desire so

---

1. *The Blazing World* was published in 1666 and 1668, together with Newcastle's *Observations upon Experimental Philosophy*, a critique of the new science emphasizing the limitations of experiment founded on human perception and such instruments as the microscope and the telescope.

2. Cyrano de Bergerac (1619–1655), author of *Histoire comique des états et empires de la lune* (1656). The Greek satirist Lucian of Samosata (125–200? C.E.) wrote dialogues about an imaginary voyage, translated in 1634.

much as might suffice to repair my noble lord and husband's losses:[3] for I am not covetous, but as ambitious as ever any of my sex was, is, or can be; which makes, that though I cannot be Henry the Fifth, or Charles the Second, yet I endeavor to be Margaret the First; and although I have neither power, time nor occasion to conquer the world as Alexander and Caesar did; yet rather than not to be mistress of one, since fortune and the fates would give me none, I have made a world of my own: for which nobody, I hope, will blame me, since it is in everyone's power to do the like.

---

* * *No sooner was the lady brought before the emperor, but he conceived her to be some goddess, and offered to worship her; which she refused, telling him, (for by that time she had pretty well learned their language) that although she came out of another world, yet was she but a mortal; at which the emperor rejoicing, made her his wife, and gave her an absolute power to rule and govern all that world as she pleased. But her subjects, who could hardly be persuaded to believe her mortal, tendered her all the veneration and worship due to a deity. . . .

Their priests and governors were princes of the imperial blood, and made eunuchs for that purpose; and as for the ordinary sort of men in that part of the world where the emperor resided, they were of several complexions; not white, black, tawny, olive or ash-colored; but some appeared of an azure, some of a deep purple, some of a grass-green, some of a scarlet, some of an orange color, etc. Which colors and complexions, whether they were made by the bare reflection of light, without the assistance of small particles, or by the help of well-ranged and ordered atoms; or by a continual agitation of little globules; or by some pressing and reacting motion, I am not able to determine. The rest of the inhabitants of that world, were men of several different sorts, shapes, figures, dispositions, and humors, as I have already made mention heretofore; some were bear-men, some worm-men, some fish- or mear-men,[4] otherwise called sirens; some bird-men, some fly-men, some ant-men, some geese-men, some spider-men, some lice-men, some fox-men, some ape-men, some jackdaw-men, some magpie-men, some parrot-men, some satyrs, some giants, and many more, which I cannot all remember; and of these several sorts of men, each followed such a profession as was most proper for the nature of their species, which the empress encouraged them in, especially those that had applied themselves to the study of several arts and sciences; for they were as ingenious and witty in the invention of profitable and useful arts, as we are in our world, nay, more; and to that end she erected schools, and founded several societies. The bear-men were to be her experimental philosophers, the bird-men her astronomers, the fly-, worm-, and fish-men her natural philosophers, the ape-men her chemists, the satyrs her Galenic physicians, the fox-men her politicians, the spider- and lice-men her mathematicians, the jackdaw-, magpie-, and parrot-men her orators and logicians, the giants her architects, etc. But before all things, she having got a sovereign power from the emperor over all the world, desired to be informed both of the manner of their religion and government, and to that end she

---

3. Cavendish's husband, William, was formally banished from England and his estates confiscated in 1649; they were all restored after the Restoration. During his banishment Margaret estimated that he suffered financial losses of around £940,000.

4. Mermen, the male counterparts of mermaids.

called the priests and statesmen, to give her an account of either. Of the statesmen she inquired, first, why they had so few laws? To which they answered, that many laws made many divisions, which most commonly did breed factions, and at last break out into open wars. Next, she asked, why they preferred the monarchical form of government before any other? They answered, that as it was natural for one body to have but one head, so it was also natural for a politic body to have but one governor; and that a commonwealth, which had many governors, was like a monster with many heads: besides, said they, a monarchy is a divine form of government, and agrees most with our religion; for as there is but one God, whom we all unanimously worship and adore with one faith, so we are resolved to have but one emperor, to whom we all submit with one obedience.

Then the empress seeing that the several sorts of her subjects had each their churches apart, asked the priests whether they were of several religions? They answered Her Majesty, that there was no more but one religion in all that world, nor no diversity of opinions in that same religion; for though there were several sorts of men, yet had they all but one opinion concerning the worship and adoration of God. The empress asked them, whether they were Jews, Turks, or Christians? We do not know, said they, what religions those are; but we do all unanimously acknowledge, worship, and adore the only, omnipotent, and eternal God, with all reverence, submission, and duty. Again, the empress inquired, whether they had several forms of worship? They answered, no: for our devotion and worship consists only in prayers, which we frame according to our several necessities, in petitions, humiliations, thanksgiving, etc. Truly, replied the empress, I thought you had been either Jews, or Turks, because I never perceived any women in your congregations; but what is the reason, you bar them from your religious assemblies? It is not fit, said they, that men and women should be promiscuously together in time of religious worship; for their company hinders devotion, and makes many, instead of praying to God, direct their devotion to their mistresses. But, asked the empress, have they no congregation of their own, to perform the duties of divine worship, as well as men? No, answered they: but they stay at home, and say their prayers by themselves in their closets.[5] Then the empress desired to know the reason why the priests and governors of their world were made eunuchs? They answered, to keep them from marriage: for women and children most commonly make disturbance both in church and state. But, said she, women and children have no employment in church or state. 'Tis true, answered they; but although they are not admitted to public employments, yet are they so prevalent[6] with their husbands and parents, that many times by their importunate persuasions, they cause as much, nay, more mischief secretly, than if they had the management of public affairs.

* * *

[THE EMPRESS BRINGS THE DUCHESS OF NEWCASTLE TO THE BLAZING WORLD]

After some time, when the spirits had refreshed themselves in their own vehicles, they sent one of their nimblest spirits, to ask the empress, whether

---

5. Private chambers.   6. I.e., they prevail so much.

she would have a scribe.* * * Then the spirit asked her, whether she would
have the soul of a living or a dead man? Why, said the empress, can the soul
quit a living body, and wander or travel abroad? Yes, answered he, for
according to Plato's doctrine, there is a conversation of souls, and the souls
of lovers live in the bodies of their beloved. Then I will have, answered she,
the soul of some ancient famous writer, either of Aristotle, Pythagoras,
Plato, Epicurus,[7] or the like. The spirit said, that those famous men were
very learned, subtle, and ingenious writers, but they were so wedded to their
own opinions, that they would never have the patience to be scribes. Then,
said she, I'll have the soul of one of the most famous modern writers, as
either of Galileo, Gassendus, Descartes, Helmont, Hobbes, H. More,[8] etc.
The spirit answered, that they were fine ingenious writers, but yet so self-
conceited, that they would scorn to be scribes to a woman. But, said he,
there's a lady, the Duchess of Newcastle, which although she is not one of
the most learned, eloquent, witty, and ingenious, yet is she a plain and rational writer, for the principle of her writings, is sense and reason, and she will
without question, be ready to do you all the service she can. This lady then,
said the empress, will I choose for my scribe, neither will the emperor have
reason to be jealous, she being one of my own sex. In truth, said the spirit,
husbands have reason to be jealous of platonic lovers, for they are very dangerous, as being not only very intimate and close, but subtle and insinuating.
You say well, replied the empress; wherefore I pray send me the Duchess of
Newcastle's soul; which the spirit did; and after she came to wait on the
empress, at her first arrival the empress embraced and saluted her with a
spiritual kiss.

* * *

[THE DUCHESS WANTS A WORLD TO RULE]

Well, said the duchess, setting aside this dispute, my ambition is, that I
would fain be as you are, that is, an empress of a world, and I shall never be
at quiet until I be one. I love you so well, replied the empress, that I wish
with all my soul, you had the fruition of your ambitious desire, and I shall
not fail to give you my best advice how to accomplish it; the best informers
are the immaterial spirits, and they'll soon tell you, whether it be possible
to obtain your wish. But, said the duchess, I have little acquaintance with
them, for I never knew any before the time you sent for me. They know you,
replied the empress; for they told me of you, and were the means and
instrument of your coming hither: wherefore I'll confer with them, and
inquire whether there be not another world, whereof you may be empress as
well as I am of this. No sooner had the empress said this, but some immaterial spirits came to visit her, of whom she inquired, whether there were but
three worlds in all, to wit, the Blazing World where she was in, the world
which she came from, and the world where the duchess lived? The spirits

---

7. Classical philosophers and founders, respectively, of schools of philosophy: the Peripatetics,
the Pythagoreans, the Academics, the Epicureans.
8. Galileo Galilei (1564–1642), Italian astronomer
and defender of the Copernican system; Pierre
Gassendi (1592–1655), proponent of a mechanistic
theory of matter; René Descartes (1596–1650),

French mathematician and philosopher who had a
major influence on the new science; Jan Baptista
van Helmont (1579–1644), Flemish chemist;
Thomas Hobbes, English mechanistic philosopher
and political scientist, author of Leviathan; Henry
More (1614–1687), one of the antimaterialist Cambridge Platonists.

answered, that there were more numerous worlds than the stars which appeared in these three mentioned worlds. Then the empress asked, whether it was not possible, that her dearest friend the Duchess of Newcastle, might be empress of one of them.[9] Although there be numerous, nay, infinite worlds, answered the spirits, yet none is without government. But is none of these worlds so weak, said she, that it may be surprised or conquered? The spirits answered, that Lucian's world of lights, had been for some time in a snuff,[1] but of late years one Helmont had got it, who since he was emperor of it, had so strengthened the immortal parts thereof with mortal outworks, as it was for the present impregnable. Said the empress, if there be such an infinite number of worlds, I am sure, not only my friend, the duchess, but any other might obtain one. Yes, answered the spirits, if those worlds were uninhabited; but they are as populous as this, your majesty governs. Why, said the empress, it is not impossible to conquer a world. No, answered the spirits, but, for the most part, conquerors seldom enjoy their conquest, for they being more feared than loved, most commonly come to an untimely end. If you will but direct me, said the duchess to the spirits, which world is easiest to be conquered, her Majesty will assist me with means, and I will trust to fate and fortune; for I had rather die in the adventure of noble achievements, than live in obscure and sluggish security; since by the one, I may live in a glorious fame, and by the other I am buried in oblivion. The spirits answered, that the lives of fame were like other lives; for some lasted long, and some died soon. 'Tis true, said the duchess; but yet the shortest-lived fame lasts longer than the longest life of man. But, replied the spirits, if occasion does not serve you, you must content yourself to live without such achievements that may gain you a fame: but we wonder, proceeded the spirits, that you desire to be empress of a terrestrial world, whenas you can create yourself a celestial world if you please. What, said the empress, can any mortal be a creator? Yes, answered the spirits; for every human creature can create an immaterial world fully inhabited by immaterial creatures, and populous of immaterial subjects, such as we are, and all this within the compass of the head or skull; nay, not only so, but he may create a world of what fashion and government he will, and give the creatures thereof such motions, figures, forms, colors, perceptions, etc. as he pleases, and make whirlpools, lights, pressures, and reactions, etc. as he thinks best; nay, he may make a world full of veins, muscles, and nerves, and all these to move by one jolt or stroke: also he may alter that world as often as he pleases, or change it from a natural world, to an artificial; he may make a world of ideas, a world of atoms, a world of lights, or whatsoever his fancy leads him to. And since it is in your power to create such a world, what need you to venture life, reputation and tranquility, to conquer a gross material world? . . . You have converted me, said the duchess to the spirits, from my ambitious desire; wherefore I'll take your advice, reject and despise all the worlds without me, and create a world of my own.

* * *

9. Speculation about multiple inhabited worlds was an occasional topic in texts on the new astronomy. Milton's Raphael introduces the idea to Adam (*Paradise Lost* 8.140–58).
1. On the point of extinction.

The Epilogue to the Reader

By this poetical description, you may perceive, that my ambition is not only to be empress, but authoress of a whole world; and that the worlds I have made, both the Blazing and the other Philosophical World, mentioned in the first part of this description, are framed and composed of the most pure, that is, the rational parts of matter, which are the parts of my mind; which creation was more easily and suddenly effected, than the conquests of the two famous monarchs of the world, Alexander and Caesar:[2] neither have I made such disturbances, and caused so many dissolutions of particulars, otherwise named deaths, as they did; for I have destroyed but some few men in a little boat, which died through the extremity of cold, and that by the hand of justice, which was necessitated to punish their crime of stealing away a young and beauteous lady.[3] And in the formation of those worlds, I take more delight and glory, than ever Alexander or Caesar did in conquering this terrestrial world; and though I have made my Blazing World, a peaceable world, allowing it but one religion, one language, and one government; yet could I make another world, as full of factions, divisions, and wars, as this is of peace and tranquility; and the rational figures of my mind might express as much courage to fight, as Hector and Achilles had; and be as wise as Nestor, as eloquent as Ulysses, and as beautiful as Helen.[4] But I esteeming peace before war, wit before policy,[5] honesty before beauty; instead of the figures of Alexander, Caesar, Hector, Achilles, Nestor, Ulysses, Helen, etc. chose rather the figure of honest Margaret Newcastle, which now I would not change for all this terrestrial world; and if any should like the world I have made, and be willing to be my subjects, they may imagine themselves such, and they are such, I mean, in their minds, fancies, or imaginations; but if they cannot endure to be subjects, they may create worlds of their own, and govern themselves as they please: but yet let them have a care, not to prove unjust usurpers, and to rob me of mine; for concerning the Philosophical World, I am empress of it myself; and as for the Blazing World, it having an empress already, who rules it with great wisdom and conduct, which empress is my dear platonic friend; I shall never prove so unjust, treacherous, and unworthy to her, as to disturb her government, much less to depose her from her imperial throne, for the sake of any other; but rather choose to create another world for another friend.

1666, 1668

---

2. Alexander the Great and Julius Caesar were both famed as conquerors of much of the world known to them.

3. A reference to the romancelike incident with which The Blazing World begins, the abduction of a young woman by a party of adventurers whose boat is blown in a tempest to the North Pole, where they perish (except for the woman, who enters into the Blazing World).

4. Hector the Trojan and Achilles the Greek are the principal heroes of Homer's Iliad; Nestor, wise adviser to the Greeks; Ulysses, hero of Homer's Odyssey, Helen, the one whose beauty caused the Trojan War, as it prompted the Trojan Paris to steal her away from her Greek husband, Menelaus.

5. Intelligence before cunning.

JOHN MILTON
1608–1674

As a young man, John Milton proclaimed himself the future author of a great
English epic. He promised a poem devoted to the glory of the nation, centering
on the deeds of King Arthur or some other ancient hero. When Milton finally published his epic thirty years later, readers found instead a poem about the Fall of
Satan and humankind, set in Heaven, Hell, and the Garden of Eden, in which traditional heroism is denigrated and England not once mentioned. What lay between
the youthful promise and the eventual fulfillment was a career marked by private
tragedy and public controversy.

In his poems and prose tracts Milton often alludes to crises in his own life: his
choice of a vocation, the early death of friends, painful disappointment in marriage, and the catastrophe of blindness. At the same time, no other major English
poet has been so deeply involved in the great questions and political crises of his
times. His works reflect upon and help develop some basic Western concepts that
were taking modern form in his lifetime: companionate marriage, the new science,
freedom of the press, religious liberty and toleration, republicanism, and more. It is
scarcely possible to treat Milton's career separately from the history of England in
his lifetime, not only because he was an active participant in affairs of church and
state, but also because when he signed himself, as he often did, "John Milton,
Englishman," he was presenting himself as England's prophetic bard. He considered himself the spokesman for the nation as a whole even when he found himself
in a minority of one.

No English poet before Milton fashioned himself quite so self-consciously as
an author. The young Milton deliberately set out to follow the steps of the ideal
poetic career—beginning with pastoral (the mode of several of his early poems) and
ending with epic. His models for this progression were Virgil and Spenser: he called
the latter "a better teacher than Scotus or Aquinas." In his systematic approach to
his vocation he stood at the opposite end of the spectrum from such Cavalier contemporaries as Richard Lovelace, who turned to verse with an air of studied carelessness. Milton resembles Spenser especially in his constant use of myth and
archetype and also in his readiness to juxtapose biblical and classical stories. He is
everywhere concerned with the conventions of genre, yet he infused every genre he
used with new energy, transforming it for later practitioners. The Western literary
and intellectual heritage impinged on his writing as immediately and directly as the
circumstances of his own life, but he continually reconceived the ideas, literary
forms, and values of this heritage to make them relevant to himself and to his age.

Milton's family was bourgeois, cultured, and staunchly Protestant. His father was
a scrivener—a combination solicitor, investment adviser, and moneylender—as well
as an amateur composer with some reputation in musical circles. Milton had a
younger brother, Christopher, who practiced law, and an elder sister, Anne. At age
seventeen he wrote a funeral elegy for the death of Anne's infant daughter and later
educated her two sons, Edward and John (Edward wrote his biography). Milton had
private tutors at home and also attended one of the finest schools in the land, St.
Paul's. At school he began a close friendship with Charles Diodati, with whom he
exchanged Latin poems and letters over several years, and for whose death in 1638
he wrote a moving Latin elegy. Milton's excellent early education gave him special
facility in languages (Latin, Greek, Hebrew and its dialects, Italian, and French;
later he learned Spanish and Dutch).

In 1625 Milton entered Christ's College, Cambridge. He was briefly suspended during his freshman year over some dispute with his tutor, but he graduated in 1629 and was made Master of Arts three years later. As his surviving student orations indicate, he was profoundly disappointed in his university education, reviling the scholastic logic and Latin rhetorical exercises that still formed its core as "futile and barren controversies and wordy disputes" that "stupefy and benumb the mind." He went to university with the serious intention of taking orders in the Church of England—the obvious vocation for a young man of his scholarly and religious bent—but became increasingly disenchanted with the lack of reformation in the church under Archbishop William Laud, and in

Milton.

the hindsight of 1642 he proclaimed himself "church-outed by the prelates." No doubt his change of direction was also linked to the fastidious contempt he expressed for the ignorant and clownish clergymen-in-the-making who were his fellow students at Cambridge: "They thought themselves gallant men, and I thought them fools." Those students retaliated by dubbing Milton "the Lady of Christ's College."

Above all, Milton came to believe more and more strongly that he was destined to serve his language, his country, and his God as a poet. He began by writing occasional poetry in Latin, the usual language for collegiate poets and for poets who sought a European audience. Milton wrote some of the century's best Latin poems, but as early as 1628 he announced to a university audience his determination to glorify England and the English language in poetry. In his first major English poem (at age twenty-one), the hymn "On the Morning of Christ's Nativity," Milton already portrayed himself as a prophetic bard. This poem is very different from Richard Crashaw's Nativity hymn, with its Spenserian echoes, its allusion to Roman Catholic and Laudian "idolatry" in the long passage on the expulsion of the pagan gods, and its stunning moves from the Creation to Doomsday, from the manger at Bethlehem to the cosmos, and from the shepherd's chatter to the music of the spheres. Two or three years later, probably, Milton wrote the companion poems "L'Allegro" and "Il Penseroso," achieving a stylistic tour de force by creating from the same meter (octosyllabic couplets) entirely different sound qualities, rhythmic effects, and moods. These poems celebrate, respectively, Mirth and Melancholy, defining them by their ancestry, lifestyles, associates, landscapes, activities, music, and literature. In 1634, at the invitation of his musician friend Henry Lawes, he wrote the masque called *Comus*, in which the villain is portrayed as a refined, seductive, and dissolute Cavalier. *Comus* challenges the absolutist politics of previous court masques by locating true virtue and good pleasure in the households of the country aristocracy rather than at court.

After university, as part of his preparation for a poetic career, Milton undertook a six-year program of self-directed reading in ancient and modern theology, philosophy, history, science, politics, and literature. He was profoundly grateful to his father for sparing him the grubby business of making money and for financing these years of private study, followed by a fifteen-month "grand tour" of France, Italy, and Switzerland. In 1638 Milton contributed the pastoral elegy "Lycidas" to a Cambridge volume lamenting the untimely death of a college contemporary. This greatest of English funeral elegies explores Milton's deep anxieties about poetry as a vocation, confronts the terrors of mortality in language of astonishing resonance and power, and incorporates a furious apocalyptic diatribe on the corrupt Church of England clergy. Nonetheless, while he was in Italy he exchanged verses and learned compliments with various Catholic intellectuals and men of letters, some of whom became his friends. Milton could always maintain friendships and family relationships across ideological divides. In 1645 his English and Latin poems were published together in a two-part volume, *Poems of Mr. John Milton*.

Upon his return to England, Milton opened a school and was soon involved in Presbyterian efforts to depose the bishops and reform church liturgy, writing five "antiprelatical tracts" denouncing and satirizing bishops. These were the first in a series of political interventions Milton produced over the next twenty years, characterized by remarkable courage and independence of thought. He wrote successively on church government, divorce, education, freedom of the press, regicide, and republicanism. From the outbreak of the Civil War in 1642 until his death, Milton allied himself with the Puritan cause, but his religious opinions developed throughout his life, from relative orthodoxy in his youth to ever more heretical positions in his later years. And while his family belonged to the class that benefited most directly from Europe's first bourgeois revolution, his brother, Christopher, fought on the royalist side. The Milton brothers, like most of their contemporaries, did not see these wars as a confrontation of class interests, but as a conflict between radically differing theories of government and, above all, religion.

Some of Milton's treatises were prompted by personal concerns. He interrupted his polemical tract, *The Reason of Church Government Urged Against Prelaty* (1642), to devote several pages to a discussion of his poetic vocation and the great works he hoped to produce in the future. His tracts about divorce, which can hardly have seemed the most pressing of issues in the strife-torn years 1643–45, were motivated by his own disastrous marriage. Aged thirty-three, inexperienced with women, and idealistic about marriage as in essence a union of minds and spirits, he married a young woman of seventeen, Mary Powell, who returned to her royalist family just a few months after the wedding. In response, Milton wrote several tracts vigorously advocating divorce on the grounds of incompatibility and with the right to remarry—a position almost unheard of at the time and one that required a boldly antiliteral reading of the Gospels. The fact that these tracts could not be licensed and were roundly denounced in Parliament, from pulpits, and in print prompted him to write *Areopagitica* (1644), an impassioned defense of a free press and the free commerce in ideas against a Parliament determined to restore effective censorship. He saw these personal issues—reformed poetry, domestic liberty achieved through needful divorce, and a free press—as vital to the creation of a reformed English culture.

In 1649, just after Charles I was executed, Milton published *The Tenure of Kings and Magistrates* (see the supplemental ebook for extracts from the *Tenure*), which defends the revolution and the regicide and was of considerable importance in developing a "contract theory" of government based on the inalienable sovereignty of the people—a version of contract very different from that of Thomas Hobbes. Milton was appointed Latin Secretary to the Commonwealth government (1649–53) and to Oliver Cromwell's Protectorate (1654–58), which meant that he wrote the official letters—mostly in Latin—to foreign governments and heads of state. He also wrote polemical defenses of the new government: *Eikonoklastes* (1649), to counter the powerful emotional effect of *Eikon Basilike*, supposedly written by the king just before his death (an excerpt is included in the supplemental ebook), and two Latin *Defenses* upholding the regicide and the new republic to European audiences.

During these years Milton suffered a series of agonizing tragedies. Mary Powell returned to him in 1645 but died in childbirth in 1652, leaving four children; the only son, John, died a few months later. That same year Milton became totally blind; he thought his boyhood habit of reading until midnight had weakened his eyesight and that writing his first *Defense* to answer the famous French scholar Claudius Salmasius had destroyed it. Milton married again in 1656, apparently happily, but his new wife, Katherine Woodcock, was dead two years later, along with their infant daughter. Katherine is probably the subject of his sonnet "Methought I Saw My Late Espoused Saint," a moving dream vision poignant with the sense of loss—both of sight and of love. Milton had little time for poetry in these years, but his few sonnets revolutionized the genre, overlaying the Petrarchan metrical structure with an urgent rhetorical voice and using the small sonnet form, hitherto confined mainly to matters of love, for new and grand subjects: praises of Cromwell and other statesmen mixed with admonition and political advice; a prophetic denunciation calling down God's vengeance for Protestants massacred in Piedmont; and an emotion-filled account of his continuing struggle to come to terms with his blindness as part of God's providence.

Cromwell's death in 1658 led to mounting chaos and a growing belief that a restored Stuart monarchy was inevitable. Milton held out against that tide. His several tracts of 1659–60 developed radical arguments for broad toleration, church disestablishment, and republican government. And just as he was among the first to attack the power of the bishops, so he was virtually the last defender of the "Good Old Cause" of the Revolution; the second edition of his *Ready and Easy Way to Establish a Free Commonwealth* appeared in late April 1660, scarcely two weeks before the monarchy was restored. For several months after that event, Milton was in hiding, his life in danger. Friends, especially the poet Andrew Marvell, managed to secure his pardon and later his release from a brief imprisonment. He lived out his last years in reduced circumstances, plagued by ever more serious attacks of gout but grateful for the domestic comforts provided by his third wife, Elizabeth Minshull, whom he married in 1663 and who survived him.

In such conditions, dismayed by the defeat of his political and religious cause, totally blind and often ill, threatened by the horrific plague of 1665 and the great fire of 1666, and entirely dependent on amanuenses and friends to transcribe his dictation, he completed his great epic poem. *Paradise Lost* (1667/74) radically reconceives the epic genre and epic heroism, choosing as protagonists a domestic couple rather than martial heroes and degrading the military glory celebrated in epic tradition in favor of "the better fortitude / Of patience and heroic martyrdom." It offers a sweeping imaginative vision of Hell, Chaos, and Heaven; prelapsarian life in Eden; the power of the devil's political rhetoric; the psychology of Satan, Adam, and Eve; and the high drama of the Fall and its aftermath.

In his final years, Milton published works on grammar and logic chiefly written during his days as a schoolmaster, a history of Britain (1670) from the earliest times to the Norman Conquest, and a treatise urging toleration for Puritan dissenters (1673). He also continued work on his *Christian Doctrine*, a Latin treatise that reveals how far he had moved from the orthodoxies of his day. The work denies the Trinity (making the Son and the Holy Spirit much inferior to God the Father), insists upon free will against Calvinist predestination, and privileges the inspiration of the Spirit even above the Scriptures and the Ten Commandments. Such radical and heterodox positions could not be made public in his lifetime, certainly not in the repressive conditions of the Restoration, and Milton's *Christian Doctrine* was subsequently lost to view for over 150 years.

In 1671 Milton published two poems that resonated with the harsh repression and the moral and political challenges all Puritan dissenters faced after the Restoration. *Paradise Regained*, a brief epic in four books, treats Jesus' Temptation in the Wilderness as an intellectual struggle through which the hero comes to understand both himself and his mission and through which he defeats Satan by renouncing the whole panoply of faulty versions of the good life and of God's kingdom. *Samson Agonistes*, a classical tragedy, is the more harrowing for the resemblances between its tragic hero and its author. The deeply flawed, pain-wracked, blind, and defeated Samson struggles, in dialogues with his visitors, to gain self-knowledge, discovering at last a desperate way to triumph over his captors and offer his people a chance to regain their freedom. (The tragedy in its entirety is available in the supplemental ebook.) In these last poems Milton sought to educate his readers in moral and political wisdom and virtue. Only through such inner transformation, Milton now firmly believed, would men and women come to value—and so perhaps reclaim— the intellectual, religious, and political freedom he so vigorously promoted in his prose and poetry.

FROM POEMS

On Shakespeare[1]

What needs my Shakespeare for his honored bones
The labor of an age in pilèd stones,
Or that his hallowed relics should be hid
Under a star-ypointing[2] pyramid?
5 Dear son of memory,[3] great heir of fame,
What° need'st thou such weak witness of thy name?   *why*
Thou in our wonder and astonishment
Hast built thyself a livelong° monument.   *enduring*
For whilst to th' shame of slow-endeavoring art
10 Thy easy numbers° flow, and that each heart   *verses*
Hath from the leaves of thy unvalued° book   *invaluable*
Those Delphic[4] lines with deep impression took,
Then thou, our fancy of itself bereaving,
Dost make us marble with too much conceiving;[5]
15 And so sepùlchered in such pomp dost lie,
That kings for such a tomb would wish to die.

1630   1632

L'Allegro[1]

Hence loathèd Melancholy,[2]
Of Cerberus[3] and blackest midnight born,
In Stygian[4] cave forlorn

---

1. This tribute, Milton's first published poem, appeared in the Second Folio of Shakespeare's plays (1632).
2. A Spenserian archaism.
3. As "son of memory" Shakespeare is a brother of the Muses, who are the daughters of Mnemosyne (Memory).
4. Apollo, god of poetry, had his oracle at Delphi.
5. Shakespeare's mesmerized readers are themselves his ("marble") monument.
1. The companion poems "L'Allegro" and "Il Penseroso" are both written in tetrameter couplets, except for the first ten lines, but Milton's virtuosity produces entirely different tempos and sound qualities in the two poems. The Italian titles name, respectively, the cheerful, mirthful man and the melancholy, contemplative man.

The poems are carefully balanced and their different values celebrated, though "Il Penseroso's" greater length and final coda may intimate that life's superiority. Mirth, the presiding deity of "L'Allegro," is described in terms that evoke Botticelli's presentation of the Grace Euphrosyne (youthful mirth) and her sisters in his *Primavera.*
2. The black melancholy recognized and here exorcized by Mirth's man is a disease leading to madness. "Il Penseroso" celebrates "white" melancholy as the temperament of the scholarly, contemplative man, represented in Dürer's famous engraving *Melancholy.* Burton's *Anatomy of Melancholy* treats the entire range of possibilities.
3. The three-headed hellhound of classical mythology.
4. Near the river Styx, in the underworld.

'Mongst horrid shapes, and shrieks, and sights unholy,
5   Find out some uncouth° cell,   desolate
         Where brooding Darkness spreads his jealous wings,
And the night raven sings;
         There under ebon shades and low-browed rocks,
As ragged as thy locks,
10   In dark Cimmerian⁵ desert ever dwell.
But come thou goddess fair and free,
In heaven yclept Euphrosyne,⁶
And by men, heart-easing Mirth,
Whom lovely Venus at a birth
15   With two sister Graces more
To ivy-crownèd Bacchus bore;
Or whether (as some sager sing)
The frolic wind that breathes the spring,
Zephyr with Aurora playing,
20   As he met her once a-Maying,
There on beds of violets blue,
And fresh-blown° roses washed in dew,   newly opened
Filled her with thee a daughter fair,
So buxom,° blithe, and debonair.   lively
25   Haste thee nymph, and bring with thee
Jest and youthful Jollity,
Quips° and Cranks,° and wanton Wiles,   witty sayings / jokes
Nods, and Becks,° and wreathèd Smiles,   beckonings
Such as hang on Hebe's⁷ cheek,
30   And love to live in dimple sleek;
Sport that wrinkled Care derides,
And Laughter holding both his sides.
Come, and trip it° as ye go   dance
On the light fantastic toe,
35   And in thy right hand lead with thee
The mountain nymph, sweet Liberty;
And if I give thee honor due,
Mirth, admit me of thy crew
To live with her and live with thee,
40   In unreprovèd° pleasures free;   irreproachable
To hear the lark begin his flight,
And, singing, startle the dull night,
From his watch tower in the skies,
Till the dappled dawn doth rise;
45   Then to come in spite of° sorrow,   in defiance of
And at my window bid good morrow,
Through the sweetbriar or the vine,
Or the twisted eglantine.
While the cock with lively din
50   Scatters the rear of darkness thin,

---

5. Homer's Cimmereans (*Odyssey* 11.13–19) live on the outer edge of the world, in perpetual darkness.
6. The three Graces—Euphrosyne (four syllables) figuring Youthful Mirth; Aglaia, Brilliance; and Thalia, Bloom—were commonly taken to be offspring of Venus (Love and Beauty) and Bacchus (god of wine). Milton proceeds, however, to devise another, more innocent parentage for Euphrosyne (ascribing it to "some sager," lines 17–24): Zephyr, the West Wind, and Aurora, goddess of the Dawn.
7. Goddess of youth and cupbearer to the gods.

And to the stack or the barn door,
Stoutly struts his dames before;
Oft listening how the hounds and horn
Cheerly rouse the slumbering morn,
55 From the side of some hoar° hill,   *ancient*
Through the high wood echoing shrill.
Sometime walking not unseen
By hedgerow elms, on hillocks green,
Right against the eastern gate,
60 Where the great sun begins his state,[8]
Robed in flames and amber light,
The clouds in thousand liveries dight;°   *dressed*
While the plowman near at hand
Whistles o'er the furrowed land,
65 And the milkmaid singeth blithe,
And the mower whets his scythe,
And every shepherd tells his tale
Under the hawthorn in the dale.
Straight° mine eye hath caught new pleasures   *immediately*
70 Whilst the landscape round it measures,
Russet lawns and fallows° gray,   *plowed land*
Where the nibbling flocks do stray,
Mountains on whose barren breast
The laboring clouds do often rest;
75 Meadows trim with daisies pied,°   *multicolored*
Shallow brooks, and rivers wide.
Towers and battlements it sees
Bosomed high in tufted trees,
Where perhaps some beauty lies,
80 The cynosure[9] of neighboring eyes.
Hard by, a cottage chimney smokes
From betwixt two agèd oaks,
Where Corydon and Thyrsis met
Are at their savory dinner set
85 Of herbs and other country messes,
Which the neat-handed° Phyllis dresses;   *dexterous*
And then in haste her bower she leaves,
With Thestylis[1] to bind the sheaves;
Or if the earlier season lead
90 To the tanned° haycock in the mead.   *sun-dried*
Sometimes with secure° delight   *careless*
The upland hamlets will invite,
When the merry bells ring round
And the jocund rebecks[2] sound
95 To many a youth and many a maid,
Dancing in the checkered shade;
And young and old come forth to play
On a sunshine holiday,

8. Stately procession, as by a monarch.
9. Literally, the bright polestar, or North Star,
by which mariners steer; here, a splendid object,
much gazed at.
1. Milton uses traditional names from classical

pastoral—Corydon, Thyrsis, Phyllis, Thestylis—
for his rustic English shepherds.
2. A small three-stringed fiddle. "Jocund": merry,
sprightly.

Till the livelong daylight fail;
100 Then to the spicy nut-brown ale,
With stories told of many a feat,
How fairy Mab the junkets[3] eat;
She was pinched and pulled, she said,
And he, by friar's lantern led,
105 Tells how the drudging goblin[4] sweat
To earn his cream bowl duly set,
When in one night, ere glimpse of morn,
His shadowy flail hath threshed the corn
That ten day laborers could not end;
110 Then lies him down the lubber fiend,[5]
And stretched out all the chimney's° length,   *fireplace's*
Basks at the fire his hairy strength;
And crop-full° out of doors he flings   *satiated*
Ere the first cock his matin rings.
115 Thus done the tales, to bed they creep,
By whispering winds soon lulled asleep.
Towered cities please us then,
And the busy hum of men,
Where throngs of knights and barons bold
120 In weeds of peace high triumphs[6] hold,
With store of ladies, whose bright eyes
Rain influence,[7] and judge the prize
Of wit or arms, while both contend
To win her grace, whom all commend.
125 There let Hymen[8] oft appear
In saffron robe, with taper clear,
And pomp and feast and revelry,
With masque and antique° pageantry;   *ancient, also antic*
Such sights as youthful poets dream
130 On summer eves by haunted stream.
Then to the well-trod stage anon,
If Jonson's learned sock be on,
Or sweetest Shakespeare, fancy's child,
Warble his native woodnotes wild.[9]
135 And ever against eating cares;[1]
Lap me in soft Lydian airs,[2]
Married to immortal verse
Such as the meeting soul may pierce
In notes with many a winding bout°   *circuit*
140 Of linkèd sweetness long drawn out,

3. Sweetmeats, especially with cream. Queen Mab is the fairy queen, consort of Oberon. "She" and "he" in the next two lines are country folk telling of their experiences with fairies.
4. Robin Goodfellow, alias Puck, Pook, or Hobgoblin. "Friar's lantern": will-o'-the-wisp.
5. Puck, here identified with the folktale goblin, Lob-lie-by-the-fire. Robin traditionally did all manner of drudging work for people, to be rewarded with a bowl of cream.
6. Pageants. "Weeds of peace": courtly raiment.
7. The ladies' eyes are stars and so have astrological influence over the men.
8. Roman god of marriage. An orange-yellow

("saffron") robe and a torch are his attributes.
9. It was conventional to contrast Jonson as a "learned" poet and Shakespeare as a "natural" one, but L'Allegro's views and choices of literature also suits with his nature. "Sock": the comedian's low-heeled slipper, contrasted with the tragedian's buskin, a high-heeled boot.
1. "Eating cares" (Horace, *Odes* 2.11.18) is one of many classical echoes in the poem.
2. Plato considered "Lydian airs" to be enervating, soft, and sensual; he preferred the solemn Doric mode. Some others thought Lydian airs relaxing and delightful.

With wanton heed and giddy cunning,
The melting voice through mazes running,
Untwisting all the chains that tie
The hidden soul of harmony;
145   That Orpheus' self may heave his head
From golden slumber on a bed
Of heaped Elysian flowers, and hear
Such strains as would have won the ear
Of Pluto, to have quite set free
150   His half-regained Eurydice.[3]
These delights if thou canst give,
Mirth, with thee I mean to live.[4]

ca. 1631   1645

Il Penseroso[1]

Hence vain deluding joys,[2]
   The brood of Folly without father bred,
How little you bestead,°   *avail*
   Or fill the fixèd mind with all your toys°   *trifles*
5   Dwell in some idle brain,
   And fancies fond° with gaudy shapes possess,   *foolish*
As thick and numberless
   As the gay motes that people the sunbeams,
Or likest hovering dreams,
10   The fickle pensioners of Morpheus'[3] train.
But hail thou Goddess sage and holy,
Hail, divinest Melancholy,
Whose saintly visage is too bright
To hit° the sense of human sight,   *suit*
15 And therefore to our weaker view
O'erlaid with black, staid wisdom's hue;[4]
Black, but such as in esteem,
Prince Memnon's sister[5] might beseem,
Or that starred Ethiope queen[6] that strove
20 To set her beauty's praise above
The sea nymphs, and their powers offended.

---

3. Orpheus's music so moved Pluto that he agreed to release Orpheus's dead wife Eurydice (four syllables, accent on the second) from the underworld (Elysium), but he violated the condition set—that he not look back at her—and so lost her again. Milton often uses Orpheus as a figure for the poet.
4. The final lines echo Marlowe's "The Passionate Shepherd to His Love" (pp. 499–500): "If these delights thy mind may move, / Then live with me and be my love."
1. Il Penseroso whose name is Italian for "the thoughtful one," celebrates a melancholy that does not produce madness but the scholarly temperament, ruled by Saturn. See note 2 on p. 772 to "L'Allegro."

2. In "Il Penseroso," Mirth is not the innocent joys of "L'Allegro," but "vain deluding joys."
3. Morpheus is the god of sleep. "Pensioners": followers.
4. The melancholy humor, caused by black bile, was thought to make the face dark or saturnine—from the ancient god Saturn, allegorized in Neoplatonic philosophy as "the collective angelic mind."
5. Memnon, in *Odyssey* 11, was a handsome Ethiopian prince; his sister Himera's beauty was mentioned by later commentators. Cf. Song of Solomon 1.5, "I am black but comely."
6. Cassiopeia was turned into a constellation ("starred") for bragging that she was more beautiful than the sea nymphs.

Yet thou art higher far descended;
Thee bright-haired Vesta long of yore
To solitary Saturn bore;[7]
25 His daughter she (in Saturn's reign
Such mixture was not held a stain).
Oft in glimmering bowers and glades
He met her, and in secret shades
Of woody Ida's inmost grove,
30 While yet there was no fear of Jove.
Come pensive nun, devout and pure,
Sober, steadfast, and demure,
All in a robe of darkest grain,°   color
Flowing with majestic train,
35 And sable stole[8] of cypress lawn
Over thy decent° shoulders drawn.   comely, modestly covered
Come, but keep thy wonted° state,°   usual / dignity
With even step and musing gait,
And looks commercing with the skies,
40 Thy rapt soul sitting in thine eyes:
There held in holy passion still,
Forget thyself to marble,[9] till
With a sad° leaden downward cast°   grave, dignified / glance
Thou fix them on the earth as fast.
45 And join with thee calm Peace and Quiet,
Spare Fast, that oft with gods doth diet,
And hears the Muses in a ring
Aye° round about Jove's altar sing.   continually
And add to these retired Leisure,
50 That in trim gardens takes his pleasure;
But first, and chiefest, with thee bring
Him that yon soars on golden wing,
Guiding the fiery-wheelèd throne,
The cherub Contemplatiòn;[1]
55 And the mute Silence hist° along,   summon
'Less Philomel[2] will deign a song,
In her sweetest, saddest plight,°   mood
Smoothing the rugged brow of night,
While Cynthia[3] checks her dragon yoke
60 Gently o'er th' accustomed oak;
Sweet bird that shunn'st the noise of folly,
Most musical, most melancholy!
Thee chantress oft the woods among
I woo to hear thy evensong;[4]

---

7. Vesta, daughter of Saturn, was goddess of the household and a virgin, as were her priestesses. Milton invented the story of her sexual congress with Saturn on Mount Ida, resulting in Melancholy's birth. Saturn ruled the gods and the world during the Golden Age, which ended when he was murdered by his son Jove.
8. A delicate black cloth.
9. Still as a statue.
1. The special function of cherubim is contemplation of God; Milton alludes also (line 53) to their identification with the wheels of the mystical chariot/throne of God described by Eze-

kiel (Ezekiel 10).
2. The nightingale (the bird into which Philomela was transformed after her rape by her brother-in-law Tereus) traditionally sings a mournful song. "'Less": unless.
3. Goddess of the moon, also associated with Hecate, goddess of the underworld, who drives a pair of sleepless dragons.
4. The evening liturgy traditionally sung by cloistered monks and nuns ("chantress" evokes such a singer); "L'Allegro's" cock, by contrast, calls hearers to the morning liturgy, "matins" (line 114).

65　And missing thee, I walk unseen
　　On the dry smooth-shaven green,
　　To behold the wandering moon,
　　Riding near her highest noon,
　　Like one that had been led astray
70　Through the heaven's wide pathless way;
　　And oft as if her head she bowed,
　　Stooping through a fleecy cloud.
　　Oft on a plat° of rising ground,　　　　　　　*plot, open field*
　　I hear the far-off curfew sound
75　Over some wide-watered shore,
　　Swinging slow with sullen° roar;　　　　　　*deep, mournful*
　　Or if the air will not permit,
　　Some still removèd place will fit,
　　Where glowing embers through the room
80　Teach light to counterfeit a gloom,
　　Far from all resort of mirth,
　　Save the cricket on the hearth,
　　Or the bellman's[5] drowsy charm,
　　To bless the doors from nightly harm;
85　Or let my lamp at midnight hour
　　Be seen in some high lonely tower,
　　Where I may oft outwatch the Bear,[6]
　　With thrice-great Hermes, or unsphere
　　The spirit of Plato[7] to unfold
90　What words or what vast regions hold
　　The immortal mind that hath forsook
　　Her mansion in this fleshly nook;
　　And of those demons[8] that are found
　　In fire, air, flood, or underground,
95　Whose power hath a true consent°　　　　　　*agreement*
　　With planet, or with element.
　　Sometime let gorgeous Tragedy
　　In sceptered pall[9] come sweeping by,
　　Presenting Thebes, or Pelops' line,
100　Or the tale of Troy divine,[1]
　　Or what (though rare) of later age
　　Ennobled hath the buskined[2] stage.
　　But, O sad virgin, that thy power
　　Might raise Musaeus[3] from his bower,
105　Or bid the soul of Orpheus[4] sing
　　Such notes as, warbled to the string,
　　Drew iron tears down Pluto's cheek,

5. Night watchman who rang a bell to mark the hours.
6. The Great Bear constellation never sets in northern skies.
7. Various esoteric books (actually written in the 3rd and 4th centuries) were attributed to an ancient Egyptian, Hermes Trismegistus ("thrice great"). Neoplatonists made him the father of all knowledge; later he became a patron of magicians and alchemists. To "unsphere" Plato is to bring him magically back to earth from whatever sphere he now inhabits—in practical terms, by reading his books.

8. Demons (daemons), halfway between gods and men, preside over the four elements.
9. Royal robe, worn by tragic actors.
1. Tragedies about Thebes include Sophocles' *Oedipus* cycle, those about the line of Pelops, Aeschylus's *Oresteia*, and those about Troy, Euripedes' *Trojan Women*.
2. The buskin (high boot) of tragedy, contrasted with the "sock" of comedy ("L'Allegro," line 132).
3. Mythical poet-priest of the pre-Homeric age, supposedly a son or pupil of Orpheus.
4. For the story of Orpheus, see "L'Allegro," line 145, and note 3 (on line 150).

And made Hell grant what love did seek.
Or call up him[5] that left half told
110 The story of Cambuscan bold,
Of Camball and of Algarsife,
And who had Canacee to wife,
That owned the virtuous° ring and glass,   *having magical*
And of the wondrous horse of brass,   *powers*
115 On which the Tartar king did ride;
And if aught° else great bards beside   *anything*
In sage and solemn tunes have sung,
Of tourneys and of trophies hung,
Of forests and enchantments drear,
120 Where more is meant than meets the ear.[6]
Thus, Night, oft see me in thy pale career,
Till civil-suited Morn appear,
Not tricked and frounced as she was wont
With the Attic boy to hunt,[7]
125 But kerchiefed in a comely cloud,
While rocking winds are piping loud,
Or ushered with a shower still,°   *gentle*
When the gust hath blown his fill,
Ending on the rustling leaves,
130 With minute drops from off the eaves.
And when the sun begins to fling
His flaring beams, me, Goddess, bring
To archèd walks of twilight groves,
And shadows brown that Sylvan[8] loves
135 Of pine or monumental oak,
Where the rude ax with heavèd stroke
Was never heard the nymphs to daunt,
Or fright them from their hallowed haunt.
There in close covert° by some brook,   *hidden place*
140 Where no profaner eye may look,
Hide me from day's garish eye,
While the bee with honeyed thigh,
That at her flowery work doth sing,
And the waters murmuring
145 With such consort° as they keep,   *musical harmony*
Entice the dewy-feathered sleep;
And let some strange mysterious dream
Wave at his wings in airy stream
Of lively portraiture displayed
150 Softly on my eyelids laid.
And as I wake, sweet music breathe
Above, about, or underneath,
Sent by some spirit to mortals good,
Or th' unseen genius° of the wood.   *guardian deity*
155 But let my due feet never fail
To walk the studious cloister's pale,°   *enclosure*

---

5. Chaucer, whose Squire's Tale is unfinished.
6. A capsule definition of allegory.
7. The now soberly dressed Aurora, goddess of the dawn, once fell in love with Cephalus ("the

Attic boy") and hunted with him. "Tricked and frounced": adorned and with frizzled hair.
8. Roman god of woodlands.

And love the high embowèd roof,
With antic pillars massy proof,[9]
And storied windows richly dight,[1]
160   Casting a dim religious light.
There let the pealing organ blow
To the full-voiced choir below,
In service high and anthems clear,
As may with sweetness, through mine ear,
165   Dissolve me into ecstasies,
And bring all heaven before mine eyes.
And may at last my weary age
Find out the peaceful hermitage,
The hairy gown and mossy cell,
170   Where I may sit and rightly spell°   study
Of every star that heaven doth shew,
And every herb that sips the dew,
Till old experience do attain
To something like prophetic strain.
175   These pleasures, Melancholy, give,[2]
And I with thee will choose to live.

ca. 1631   1645

Lycidas   Milton wrote this pastoral elegy for a volume of Latin, Greek, and English poems, *Justa Eduourdo King Naufrago* (1638), commemorating the death by shipwreck of his college classmate Edward King, three years younger than himself. King was not a close friend, but Milton's deepest emotions, anxieties, and fears are engaged here because, as poet and minister, King could serve Milton as a kind of alter ego. Still engaged in preparing himself, at the age of twenty-nine, for his projected poetic career, Milton was forced to recognize the uncertainty of all human endeavors. King's death posed the problem of mortality in its most agonizing form: the death of the young, the unfulfilled, the good seems to deny all meaning to life, to demonstrate the uselessness of exceptional talent, lofty ambition, and noble ideals of service to God.

While the poem expresses Milton's anxieties, it also serves as an announcement of his grand ambitions. Like Edmund Spenser, Milton saw mastery of the pastoral mode as the first step in a great poetic career. In "Lycidas" that mastery is complete. In the tradition that Milton received from classical and Renaissance predecessors, including Theocritus, Virgil, Petrarch, and Spenser, the pastoral landscape was invested with profound significances that had little indeed to do with the hard life of agricultural labor. In lines 25–36, Milton evokes the conventional pastoral topic of carefree shepherds who engage in singing contests, watch contentedly over their grazing sheep, fall in love, and write poetry, offering an image of human life in harmony with nature and the seasonal processes of fruition and mellowing before the winter of death. That classical image of the shepherd as poet is mingled with the Christian understanding of the shepherd as pastor (Christ is the Good Shepherd), and sometimes as the prophet called to his mission from the fields, like David or Isaiah. Milton calls on all these associations, along with other motifs specific to pastoral funeral elegy: the recollection of past friendship, a questioning of destiny

---

9. Massive and strong. "Antic": covered with quaint or grotesque carvings, also antique.
1. Dressed. "Storied windows": stained-glass windows depicting biblical stories.

2. Compare "L'Allegro," lines 151–52 (p. 776), and the final lines of Marlowe's "Passionate Shepherd" (pp. 499–500).

for cutting short this life, a procession of mourners (often mythological figures), and a "flower passage" in which nature pays tribute to the dead shepherd.

"Lycidas" uses but continually tests and challenges the assumptions and conventions of pastoral elegy, making for profound tensions and clashes of tone. The pastoral "oaten flute" is interrupted by divine pronouncements and bitter invective; nature seems rife with examples of meaningless waste and early death; the "blind Fury" often cuts off the poet's "thin-spun life" before he can win fame; good pastors die young while corrupt "Blind mouths" remain; and Nature cannot even pay her tribute of flowers to Lycidas's funeral bier since he welters in the deep, his bones hurled to the "bottom of the monstrous world." In response to these fierce challenges come pronouncements by Apollo and St. Peter, and images of protection and resurrection in nature and myth, culminating in a new vision of pastoral: in heaven Lycidas enjoys a perfected pastoral existence, and in the coda the consoled shepherd arises and carries his song to "pastures new." Milton's questioning leads to a final reassertion of confidence in his calling as national poet. Moreover, in the headnote added in the 1645 volume of his *Poems*, he lays claim to prophetic authority, for the Church of England clergy he denounced as corrupt in 1638 had mostly been expelled from their livings by Puritan reformers in 1645.

Lycidas

In this monody[1] the author bewails a learned friend, unfortunately drowned in his passage from Chester on the Irish seas, 1637. And by occasion foretells the ruin of our corrupted clergy, then in their height.

    Yet once more, O ye laurels, and once more
Ye myrtles brown, with ivy never sere,[2]
I come to pluck your berries harsh and crude,°   *unripe*
And with forced fingers rude,°   *unskilled*
5 Shatter your leaves before the mellowing year.
Bitter constraint, and sad occasion dear,°   *heartfelt, also dire*
Compels me to disturb your season due;
For Lycidas is dead, dead ere his prime,[3]
Young Lycidas, and hath not left his peer.
10   Who would not sing for Lycidas? He knew
Himself to sing, and build the lofty rhyme.[4]
He must not float upon his watery bier
Unwept, and welter° to the parching wind,   *be tossed about*
Without the meed° of some melodious tear.°   *reward / elegy*
15   Begin then, sisters of the sacred well[5]
That from beneath the seat of Jove doth spring,
Begin, and somewhat loudly sweep the string.
Hence with denial vain, and coy excuse;
So may some gentle muse[6]

1. A dirge sung by a single voice, though this one incorporates several other voices. Milton added this headnote in the edition of 1645; it identifies Milton as a prophet in the passage denouncing the clergy in this 1638 poem (lines 112–31) and invites the reader to remember Milton's 1641–42 polemics against the English bishops and church government (now dismantled).
2. "Laurels," associated with Apollo and poetry; "myrtle," associated with Venus and love; "ivy,"

associated with Bacchus and frenzy (also learning). All three are evergreens ("never sere") linked to poetic inspiration.
3. King was twenty-five.
4. King had written several poems of compliment in the patronage mode, chiefly on members of the royal family.
5. The nine (sister) Muses called (probably) from the fountain Aganippe, near Mount Helicon.
6. Here, some kindly poet.

20   With lucky words favor my destined urn,
     And as he passes turn,
     And bid fair peace be to my sable shroud.
     For we were nursed upon the selfsame hill,
     Fed the same flock, by fountain, shade, and rill.

25   Together both, ere the high lawns° appeared   *upland pastures*
     Under the opening eyelids of the morn,
     We drove afield, and both together heard
     What time the grayfly winds her sultry horn,[7]
     Battening° our flocks with the fresh dews of night,   *feeding fat*
30   Oft till the star that rose at evening bright[8]
     Toward heaven's descent had sloped his westering wheel.
     Meanwhile the rural ditties were not mute,
     Tempered to th' oaten flute,[9]
     Rough satyrs danced, and fauns with cloven heel
35   From the glad sound would not be absent long,
     And old Damoetas[1] loved to hear our song.

     But O the heavy change, now thou art gone,
     Now thou art gone, and never must return!
     Thee, shepherd, thee the woods and desert caves,
40   With wild thyme and the gadding° vine o'ergrown,   *wandering*
     And all their echoes mourn.
     The willows and the hazel copses° green   *thickets of trees*
     Shall now no more be seen,
     Fanning their joyous leaves to thy soft lays.
45   As killing as the canker° to the rose,   *cankerworm*
     Or taint-worm[2] to the weanling herds that graze,
     Or frost to flowers that their gay wardrobe wear
     When first the white-thorn blows;[3]
     Such, Lycidas, thy loss to shepherd's ear.

50   Where were ye, nymphs,[4] when the remorseless deep
     Closed o'er the head of your loved Lycidas?
     For neither were ye playing on the steep
     Where your old bards, the famous Druids,[5] lie,
     Nor on the shaggy top of Mona high,
55   Nor yet where Deva spreads her wizard stream:[6]
     Ay me! I fondly dream—
     Had ye been there—for what could that have done?
     What could the Muse[7] herself that Orpheus bore,
     The Muse herself, for her enchanting[8] son
60   Whom universal Nature did lament,
     When by the rout that made the hideous roar
     His gory visage down the stream was sent,

---

7. I.e., heard the grayfly when she buzzes.
8. Hesperus, the evening star.
9. Panpipes, played traditionally by shepherds in pastoral.
1. A type name from pastoral poetry, possibly referring to some particular tutor at Cambridge. "Satyrs": goat-legged woodland creatures, Pan's boisterous attendants.
2. Internal parasite fatal to newly weaned lambs.
3. Hawthorn blooms.
4. Nature deities.
5. Priestly poet-kings of Celtic Britain, who wor-shipped the forces of nature. They are buried on the mountain ("steep") Kerig-y-Druidion in Wales.
6. Mona is the island of Anglesey. Deva, the river Dee in Cheshire, was magic ("wizard") because its shifting stream foretold prosperity or dearth for the land. All these places are in the West Country, near where King drowned.
7. Calliope, Muse of epic poetry, was the mother of Orpheus.
8. Implies both song and magic; the root word survives in "incantation."

Down the swift Hebrus to the Lesbian shore?[9]
    Alas! What boots° it with incessant care   *profits*
65 To tend the homely slighted shepherd's trade,
And strictly meditate the thankless muse?[1]
Were it not better done as others use,
To sport with Amaryllis in the shade,
Or with the tangles of Neaera's hair?[2]
70 Fame is the spur that the clear spirit doth raise
(That last infirmity of noble mind)
To scorn delights, and live laborious days;
But the fair guerdon° when we hope to find,   *reward*
And think to burst out into sudden blaze,
75 Comes the blind Fury[3] with th' abhorrèd shears,
And slits the thin-spun life. "But not the praise,"
Phoebus replied, and touched my trembling ears;[4]
"Fame is no plant that grows on mortal soil,
Nor in the glistering foil[5]
80 Set off to th' world, nor in broad rumor lies,
But lives and spreads aloft by those pure eyes,
And perfect witness of all-judging Jove;
As he pronounces lastly on each deed,
Of so much fame in heaven expect thy meed."°   *reward*
85   O fountain Arethuse, and thou honored flood,
Smooth-sliding Mincius, crowned with vocal reeds,
That strain I heard was of a higher mood.[6]
But now my oat° proceeds,   *pastoral flute*
And listens to the herald of the sea[7]
90 That came in Neptune's plea.
He asked the waves, and asked the felon° winds,   *savage*
"What hard mishap hath doomed this gentle swain?"° *shepherd*
And questioned every gust of rugged° wings   *stormy*
That blows from off each beakèd promontory;
95 They knew not of his story,
And sage Hippotades[8] their answer brings,
That not a blast was from his dungeon strayed;
The air was calm, and on the level brine,
Sleek Panope[9] with all her sisters played.
100 It was that fatal and perfidious bark,
Built in th' eclipse,[1] and rigged with curses dark,
That sunk so low that sacred head of thine.

---

9. Orpheus's song was drowned out by the screams of a mob ("rout") of Thracian women, the Bacchantes, who then were able to tear him to pieces and throw his gory head into the river Hebrus, which carried it—still singing—to the island of Lesbos, bringing that island the gift of poetry.
1. I.e., study to write poetry (a Virgilian phrase).
2. "Amaryllis" and "Neaera" (*Nee-eye-ra*), conventional names for pretty shepherdesses wooed in song by pastoral shepherds.
3. Atropos, one of the three Fates, whose scissors cuts the thread of human life after her sisters spin and measure it. Milton makes her a savage, and blind, Fury.
4. Phoebus Apollo, god of poetic inspiration. In

Eclogue 6.3–4 he plucked Virgil's ears, warning him against impatient ambition.
5. Flashy, glittering metal foil, set under a gem to enhance its brilliance.
6. Arethusa was a fountain in Sicily associated with Greek pastoral poetry (Theocritus), Mincius a river in Lombardy associated with Latin pastoral (Virgil); Milton invokes them as a return to the pastoral after the "higher mood" of Apollo's speech.
7. Triton, who comes gathering evidence about the accident for Neptune's court.
8. Aeolus, god of winds.
9. The chief Nereid, or sea nymph.
1. Eclipses were taken as evil omens.

Next Camus,[2] reverend sire, went footing slow,
His mantle hairy, and his bonnet sedge,°   *formed of reeds*
105 Inwrought with figures dim, and on the edge
Like to that sanguine flower inscribed with woe.[3]
"Ah! who hath reft," quoth he, "my dearest pledge?"
Last came and last did go
The pilot of the Galilean lake;[4]
110 Two massy keys he bore of metals twain
(The golden opes, the iron shuts amain).°   *forever*
He shook his mitered locks, and stern bespake:
"How well could I have spared for° thee, young swain,   *in place of*
Enow° of such as for their bellies' sake   *enough (plural)*
115 Creep and intrude and climb into the fold![5]
Of other care they little reckoning make,
Than how to scramble at the shearers' feast,[6]
And shove away the worthy bidden guest.
Blind mouths![7] that scarce themselves know how to hold
120 A sheep-hook, or have learned aught else the least
That to the faithful herdsman's art belongs!
What recks it them? What need they? They are sped;[8]
And when they list,° their lean° and flashy songs   *choose / meager*
Grate on their scrannel° pipes of wretched straw.   *harsh, thin*
125 The hungry sheep look up, and are not fed,
But swol'n with wind, and the rank mist they draw,°   *inhale*
Rot inwardly,[9] and foul contagion spread,
Besides what the grim wolf with privy paw[1]
Daily devours apace, and nothing said.
130 But that two-handed engine at the door[2]
Stands ready to smite once, and smite no more."
Return, Alpheus,[3] the dread voice is past,
That shrunk thy streams; return, Sicilian muse,
And call the vales, and bid them hither cast
135 Their bells and flowerets of a thousand hues.[4]
Ye valleys low where the mild whispers use,°   *frequent*

2. God of the river Cam, representing Cambridge University.
3. Like the *AI AI* cry of grief supposedly found on the hyacinth, a "sanguine flower" sprung from the blood of the youth Hyacinthus, beloved of Apollo and accidentally killed by him.
4. St. Peter, originally a fisherman on the sea of Galilee, was Christ's chief apostle; his keys open and shut the gates of heaven. He wears a bishop's miter (line 112): Milton in his "antiprelatical tracts" allows for a special role for apostles but denies any distinction in office between bishops and ministers in the later church.
5. Cf. John 10.1: "He that entereth not by the door into the sheepfold, but climbeth up some other way, the same is a thief and a robber."
6. Festive suppers for the sheepshearers (hence, the material rewards of their ministry). "Worthy bidden guest" (next line): cf. Matthew 22.8, the parable of the marriage feast, "they which were bidden were not worthy."
7. Collapsing blindness with greed, this audacious metaphor accuses churchmen of shirking oversight (*episcopus*, bishop, means "supervision") and of glutting themselves, although pastors ought to feed their flocks. "Sheep-hook"

(next line): the bishop's staff is in the form of a shepherd's crook.
8. Provided for. "What recks it them?": what do they care?
9. Sheep rot is used as an allegory of church corruption by both Petrarch and Dante.
1. I.e., Roman Catholicism, whole agents operated in secret ("privy"). Conversions in the court of the Roman Catholic queen Henrietta Maria were notorious.
2. A celebrated crux, variously explained as the two houses of Parliament, St. Peter's keys, the two-edged sword of the Book of Revelation, a sword wielded by two hands, and by other guesses; what is clear is the denunciation of impending, apocalyptic vengeance. In Matthew 24.33 the Last Judgment is said to be "even at the doors."
3. A river in Arcadia, fabled to pass unmixed through the sea before mixing its waters with the "fountain Arethuse" in Sicily, again reviving the pastoral mode after the fierce denunciation of Peter (see lines 85–87).
4. A catalogue of flowers was a common pastoral topic. "Bells": bell-shaped flowers.

Of shades and wanton winds, and gushing brooks,
On whose fresh lap the swart star[5] sparely looks,
Throw hither all your quaint enameled eyes,[6]
140 That on the green turf suck the honeyed showers,
And purple all the ground with vernal flowers.
Bring the rathe° primrose that forsaken dies,   *early*
The tufted crow-toe, and pale jessamine,[7]
The white pink, and the pansy freaked° with jet,   *flecked*
145 The glowing violet,
The musk rose, and the well-attired woodbine,
With cowslips wan° that hang the pensive head,   *pale*
And every flower that sad embroidery wears:
Bid amaranthus[8] all his beauty shed,
150 And daffadillies fill their cups with tears,
To strew the laureate hearse° where Lycid lies.   *laurel-decked bier*
For so to interpose a little ease,
Let our frail thoughts dally with false surmise.[9]
Ay me! whilst thee the shores and sounding seas
155 Wash far away, where'er thy bones are hurled,
Whether beyond the stormy Hebrides,[1]
Where thou perhaps under the whelming° tide *roaring, overwhelming*
Visit'st the bottom of the monstrous world;
Or whether thou, to our moist vows denied,
160 Sleep'st by the fable of Bellerus old,[2]
Where the great vision of the guarded mount
Looks toward Namancos and Bayona's hold;[3]
Look homeward angel now, and melt with ruth:°   *pity*
And, O ye dolphins,[4] waft the hapless youth.
165   Weep no more, woeful shepherds, weep no more,
For Lycidas your sorrow is not dead,
Sunk though he be beneath the wat'ry floor;
So sinks the daystar° in the ocean bed,   *the sun*
And yet anon repairs his drooping head,
170 And tricks° his beams, and with new-spangled ore   *adorns, trims*
Flames in the forehead of the morning sky:
So Lycidas sunk low, but mounted high,
Through the dear might of him that walked the waves,[5]
Where, other groves and other streams along,[6]
175 With nectar pure his oozy° locks he laves,   *moist*

---

5. The Dog Star, Sirius, associated with the heats of late summer.
6. Flowers curiously patterned and adorned with many colors.
7. White jasmine. "Tufted crow-toe": hyacinth or buttercup, growing in clusters. "Woodbine" (line 146): honeysuckle.
8. In Greek, "unfading," a legendary flower of immortality, one that never fades.
9. False, because Lycidas's body is not here to receive floral and poetic tributes.
1. Islands off the coast of Scotland, the northern terminus of the Irish Sea.
2. A fabulous giant invented by Milton as the origin of the Latin name for Land's End in Cornwall, *Bellerium.* "Monstrous world" (line 158): filled with monsters, also, immense.

3. "The guarded mount" is St. Michael's Mount in Cornwall, where the archangel was said to have appeared to fishermen in 495, and from which he is envisioned as looking over the Atlantic toward a region and fortress ("Bayona's hold") in northern Spain, thereby guarding Protestant England against the continuing Roman Catholic threat.
4. Dolphins brought the Greek poet Arion safely ashore, for love of his verse, and also performed other sea rescues.
5. Christ, who rescued Peter when he tried and failed to walk on the Sea of Galilee (Matthew 14.25–31).
6. See Revelation 22.1–2, on the "pure river of water of life," and the "tree of life, which bare twelve manner of fruits."

And hears the unexpressive nuptial song,[7]
In the blest kingdoms meek of joy and love.
There entertain him all the saints above,
In solemn troops and sweet societies
180   That sing, and singing in their glory move,
And wipe the tears forever from his eyes.
Now, Lycidas, the shepherds weep no more;
Henceforth thou art the Genius[8] of the shore,
In thy large recompense, and shalt be good
185   To all that wander in that perilous flood.
        Thus sang the uncouth swain[9] to th' oaks and rills,
While the still morn went out with sandals gray;
He touched the tender stops of various quills,[1]
With eager thought warbling his Doric[2] lay:
190   And now the sun had stretched out all the hills,
And now was dropped into the western bay;
At last he rose, and twitched his mantle blue:[3]
Tomorrow to fresh woods, and pastures new.

November 1637   1638

Areopagitica   This passionate, trenchant defense of intellectual liberty has
had a powerful influence on the evolving liberal conception of freedom of speech,
press, and thought. Milton's specific target is the Press Ordinance of June 14, 1643,
Parliament's attempt to crack down on the flood of pamphlets (including Milton's
own controversial treatises on divorce) that poured forth both from legal and from
underground presses as the Civil War raged. Like Tudor and Stuart censorship laws,
Parliament's ordinance demanded that works be registered with the stationers and
licensed by the censors before publication, and that both author and publisher be
identified, on pain of fines and imprisonment for both. Milton vigorously protests the
prepublication licensing of books, arguing that such measures have only been used
by, and are only fit for, degenerate cultures. In the regenerate English nation, now
"rousing herself like a strong man after sleep," men and women must be allowed to
develop in virtue by participating in the clash and conflict of ideas. Truth will always
overcome falsehood in reasoned debate. Thus, in opposition to the Presbyterians
then in power, Milton defends widespread religious toleration, though with restrictions on Roman Catholicism, which, like most of his Protestant contemporaries, he
viewed as a political threat and a tyranny binding individual conscience to the pope.
    The title associates the tract with the speech of the Greek orator Isocrates to the
Areopagus, the Council of the Wise in Athens. Learned readers would have recognized the irony of this. While Isocrates instructed the council to reform Athens by
careful supervision of the private lives of citizens, Milton argues that only liberty and
removal of censorship can advance reformation. This association explains the oratori-
cal tone of the tract, which was, in fact, subtitled "A Speech." In this most literary of
his tracts, Milton's style is elevated, eloquent, dense with poetic figures, and ranges in
tone from satire and ridicule to urgent pleading and florid praise. His arguments and
principles are often couched in striking images and phrases. One example is his passionate testimony to the potency and inestimable value of books: "As good almost kill

---

7. Inexpressible hymn of joy sung at "the marriage supper of the Lamb" (Revelation 19).
8. Local guardian spirit.
9. Another voice now seems to take over from
the previously heard voice of the "uncouth
swain" (unknown, unskilled shepherd).

1. The oaten stalks of panpipes.
2. Rustic, the dialect of Theocritus and other
famous Greek pastoral poets.
3. The color of hope. "Twitched": pulled up
around his shoulders.

a man as kill a good book . . . ." Most memorable is his ringing credo that echoes down the centuries to protest every new tyranny: "Give me the liberty to know, to utter, and to argue freely according to conscience, above all liberties."

From Areopagitica

I deny not, but that it is of greatest concernment in the church and commonwealth, to have a vigilant eye how books demean[1] themselves as well as men; and thereafter to confine, imprison, and do sharpest justice on them as malefactors:[2] For books are not absolutely dead things, but do contain a potency of life in them to be as active as that soul was whose progeny they are; nay they do preserve as in a vial the purest efficacy and extraction of that living intellect that bred them. I know they are as lively, and as vigorously productive, as those fabulous dragon's teeth; and being sown up and down, may chance to spring up armed men.[3] And yet on the other hand unless wariness be used, as good almost kill a man as kill a good book; who kills a man kills a reasonable creature, God's image; but he who destroys a good book, kills reason itself, kills the image of God, as it were in the eye. Many a man lives a burden to the earth; but a good book is the precious lifeblood of a master spirit, embalmed and treasured up on purpose to a life beyond life. 'Tis true, no age can restore a life, whereof perhaps there is no great loss; and revolutions of ages do not oft recover the loss of a rejected truth, for the want of which whole nations fare the worse. We should be wary therefore what persecution we raise against the living labors of public men, how we spill that seasoned life of man preserved and stored up in books; since we see a kind of massacre, whereof the execution ends not in the slaying of an elemental life, but strikes at that ethereal and fifth essence,[4] the breath of reason itself, slays an immortality rather than a life. But lest I should be condemned of introducing licence, while I oppose licensing, I refuse not the pains to be so much historical, as will serve to show what hath been done by ancient and famous commonwealths, against this disorder, till the very time that this project of licensing crept out of the Inquisition,[5] was catched up by our prelates, and hath caught some of our presbyters.[6] * * *

* * *Good and evil we know in the field of this world grow up together almost inseparably; and the knowledge of good is so involved and interwoven with the knowledge of evil, and in so many cunning resemblances hardly to be discerned, that those confused seeds which were imposed on Psyche as an incessant labor to cull out and sort asunder were not more intermixed.[7] It was from out the rind of one apple tasted, that the knowledge

1. Behave.
2. Milton allows that books may be called to account after publication, if they are proved to contain libels or other manifest crimes (he leaves this quite vague).
3. After Cadmus killed a dragon on his way to founding Thebes, on a god's advice he sowed the dragon's teeth, which sprang up as an army, the belligerent forefathers of Sparta.
4. Quintessence, a pure, mystical substance above the four elements (fire, air, water, earth).
5. The Roman Catholic institution for suppressing heresy, especially strong in Spain.

6. The Presbyterians, powerful in the Parliament, were striving to establish theirs as the national church and suppress others. Milton, who began by supporting them in The Reason of Church Government and his other antiprelatical tracts (1641–42), now rejects them, in large part because they seek to supplant one repressive church with another.
7. Angry at her son Cupid's love for Psyche, Venus set the girl many trials, among them to sort out a vast mound of mixed seeds, but the ants took pity on her and did the work.

of good and evil, as two twins cleaving together, leaped forth into the world. And perhaps this is that doom which Adam fell into of knowing good and evil, that is to say of knowing good by evil.

As therefore the state of man now is, what wisdom can there be to choose, what continence to forbear, without the knowledge of evil? He that can apprehend and consider vice with all her baits and seeming pleasures, and yet abstain, and yet distinguish, and yet prefer that which is truly better, he is the true wayfaring[8] Christian. I cannot praise a fugitive and cloistered virtue, unexercised and unbreathed,[9] that never sallies out and sees her adversary, but slinks out of the race where that immortal garland is to be run for, not without dust and heat. Assuredly we bring not innocence into the world, we bring impurity much rather; that which purifies us is trial, and trial is by what is contrary. That virtue therefore which is but a youngling in the contemplation of evil, and knows not the utmost that vice promises to her followers, and rejects it, is but a blank virtue, not a pure; her whiteness is but an excremental[1] whiteness; which was the reason why our sage and serious poet Spenser (whom I dare be known to think a better teacher than Scotus or Aquinas), describing true temperance under the person of Guyon, brings him in with his Palmer through the Cave of Mammon and the Bower of Earthly Bliss,[2] that he might see and know, and yet abstain.

Since therefore the knowledge and survey of vice is in this world so necessary to the constituting of human virtue, and the scanning of error to the confirmation of truth, how can we more safely, and with less danger, scout into the regions of sin and falsity than by reading all manner of tractates and hearing all manner of reason? And this is the benefit which may be had of books promiscuously read.

But of the harm that may result hence, three kinds are usually reckoned. First is feared the infection that may spread; but then all human learning and controversy in religious points must remove out of the world, yea, the Bible itself; for that ofttimes relates blasphemy not nicely,[3] it describes the carnal sense of wicked men not unelegantly, it brings in holiest men passionately murmuring against providence through all the arguments of Epicurus;[4] in other great disputes it answers dubiously and darkly to the common reader.[5]

* * *

To sequester out of the world into Atlantic and Utopian politics,[6] which never can be drawn into use, will not mend our condition, but to ordain wisely as in

---

8. The printed text reads "wayfaring," calling up the image of the Christian pilgrim; several presentation copies correct it (by hand) to "warfaring," calling up the image of the Christian warrior. Both suit the passage.

9. Not forced by exertion to breathe hard. "Immortal garland" (next line): the prize for the winner of a race, as figure for the "crown of life" promised to those who endure temptation (James 1.12).

1. Exterior only.

2. John Duns Scotus and Thomas Aquinas, major Scholastic theologians. Guyon (following), the hero of Book 2 of the *Faerie Queene*, passes through the Cave of Mammon (symbolic of all worldly goods and honors) without his Palmer-guide, but that figure does accompany

him through the Bower of Bliss.

3. Daintily.

4. Greek philosopher (342–270 B.C.E.) who taught that happiness is the greatest good, and that virtue should be practiced because it brings happiness; some of his followers equated happiness with sensual enjoyment. Milton may be thinking of the biblical book of Ecclesiastes.

5. Milton goes on to argue that a fool can find material for folly in the best books, and a wise person material for wisdom in the worst. Also, one cannot remove evil by censoring books without also censoring ballads, fiddlers, clothing, conversation, and all social life.

6. Milton alludes to More's *Utopia* and Bacon's *New Atlantis*.

this world of evil, in the midst whereof God hath placed us unavoidably. . . . Impunity and remissness, for certain, are the bane of a commonwealth; but here the great art lies, to discern in what the law is to bid restraint and punishment, and in what things persuasion only is to work. If every action which is good or evil in man at ripe years were to be under pittance[7] and prescription and compulsion, what were virtue but a name, what praise could be then due to well-doing, what gramercy[8] to be sober, just, or continent?

Many there be that complain of divine providence for suffering Adam to transgress; foolish tongues! When God gave him reason, he gave him freedom to choose, for reason is but choosing; he had been else a mere artificial Adam, such an Adam as he is in the motions.[9] We ourselves esteem not of that obedience, or love, or gift, which is of force: God therefore left him free, set before him a provoking object, ever almost in his eyes; herein consisted his merit, herein the right of his reward, the praise of his abstinence.[1] Wherefore did he create passions within us, pleasures round about us, but that these rightly tempered are the very ingredients of virtue? They are not skillful considerers of human things, who imagine to remove sin by removing the matter of sin; for, besides that it is a huge heap increasing under the very act of diminishing, though some part of it may for a time be withdrawn from some persons, it cannot from all, in such a universal thing as books are; and when this is done, yet the sin remains entire. Though ye take from a covetous man all his treasure, he has yet one jewel left: ye cannot bereave him of his covetousness. Banish all objects of lust, shut up all youth into the severest discipline that can be exercised in any hermitage, ye cannot make them chaste that came not thither so: such great care and wisdom is required to the right managing of this point.

Suppose we could expel sin by this means; look how much we thus expel of sin, so much we expel of virtue: for the matter of them both is the same; remove that, and ye remove them both alike. This justifies the high providence of God, who, though he commands us temperance, justice, continence, yet pours out before us, even to a profuseness, all desirable things, and gives us minds that can wander beyond all limit and satiety. Why should we then affect a rigor contrary to the manner of God and of nature, by abridging or scanting those means, which books freely permitted are, both to the trial of virtue and the exercise of truth? It would be better done to learn that the law must needs be frivolous which goes to restrain things uncertainly and yet equally working to good and to evil. And were I the chooser, a dram of well-doing should be preferred before many times as much the forcible hindrance of evil-doing. For God sure esteems the growth and completing of one virtuous person more than the restraint of ten vicious.

✳ ✳ ✳

What advantage is it to be a man over it is to be a boy at school, if we have only scaped the ferula to come under the fescue of an *imprimatur*;[2] if serious and elaborate writings, as if they were no more than the theme of a

---

7. Rationing.
8. Reward, thanks.
9. Puppet shows.
1. Compare Milton's representation of Adam and Eve in Eden in *Paradise Lost.*
2. "Ferula": a schoolmaster's rod; "fescue": a

pointer, "imprimatur": "it may be printed" (Latin), appears on the title page of books approved by the Roman Catholic censors. Milton's keen sense of the affront to scholars and scholarship, and to himself, is evident in this passage.

grammarlad under his pedagogue, must not be uttered without the cursory eyes of a temporizing and extemporizing licenser?[3] He who is not trusted with his own actions, his drift not being known to be evil, and standing to the hazard of law and penalty, has no great argument to think himself reputed, in the commonwealth wherein he was born, for other than a fool or a foreigner.

When a man writes to the world, he summons up all his reason and deliberation to assist him; he searches, meditates, is industrious, and likely consults and confers with his judicious friends, after all which done he takes himself to be informed in what he writes, as well as any that writ before him. If in this the most consummate act of his fidelity and ripeness, no years, no industry, no former proof of his abilities can bring him to that state of maturity as not to be still mistrusted and suspected (unless he carry all his considerate diligence, all his midnight watchings, and expense of Palladian[4] oil, to the hasty view of an unleisured licenser, perhaps much his younger, perhaps far his inferior in judgment, perhaps one who never knew the labor of book-writing), and if he be not repulsed, or slighted, must appear in print like a puny[5] with his guardian, and his censor's hand on the back of his title to be his bail and surety that he is no idiot, or seducer; it cannot be but a dishonor and derogation to the author, to the book, to the privilege and dignity of learning.* * *

And how can a man teach with authority, which is the life of teaching, how can he be a doctor[6] in his book as he ought to be, or else had better be silent, whenas all he teaches, all he delivers, is but under the tuition, under the correction of his patriarchal[7] licenser to blot or alter what precisely accords not with the hide-bound humor which he calls his judgment? When every acute reader upon the first sight of a pedantic license, will be ready with these like words to ding the book a quoit's[8] distance from him: "I hate a pupil teacher, I endure not an instructor that comes to me under the wardship of an overseeing fist. I know nothing of the licenser, but that I have his own hand here for his arrogance; who shall warrant me his judgment?"

"The state, sir," replies the stationer,[9] but has a quick return: "The state shall be my governors, but not my critics; they may be mistaken in the choice of a licenser, as easily as this licenser may be mistaken in an author."

* * *

Well knows he who uses to consider, that our faith and knowledge thrives by exercise, as well as our limbs and complexion.[1] Truth is compared in Scripture to a streaming fountain;[2] if her waters flow not in a perpetual progression, they sicken into a muddy pool of conformity and tradition. A man may be a heretic in the truth; and if he believe things only because his pastor says so, or the Assembly[3] so determines, without knowing other reason, though his belief be true, yet the very truth he holds becomes his heresy.

---

3. He temporizes in following the times, and acts by whim (extemporizes).
4. Pertaining to Pallas Athena, goddess of wisdom.
5. A minor, hence, young, unseasoned.
6. Teacher.
7. Taking on the role of a father; also, standing in for ecclesiastical patriarchs or prelates (like Archbishop Laud).
8. A flat disc of stone or metal, thrown as an exer-

cise of strength or skill.
9. Printer, who was responsible for submitting books before publication to the "licenser" (censor).
1. Constitution, the proper mingling of qualities in the body.
2. In Psalm 85.11.
3. The Westminster Assembly, convened by Parliament in 1643 to reorganize the English church along Presbyterian lines.

* * *

Truth indeed came once into the world with her Divine Master, and was a perfect shape most glorious to look on: but when he ascended, and his apostles after him were laid asleep, then straight arose a wicked race of deceivers, who, as that story goes of the Egyptian Typhon with his conspirators, how they dealt with the good Osiris,[4] took the virgin Truth, hewed her lovely form into a thousand pieces, and scattered them to the four winds. From that time ever since, the sad friends of Truth, such as durst appear, imitating the careful search that Isis made for the mangled body of Osiris, went up and down gathering up limb by limb, still as they could find them. We have not yet found them all, Lords and Commons, nor ever shall do, till her Master's second coming; he shall bring together every joint and member, and shall mold them into an immortal feature of loveliness and perfection. Suffer not these licensing prohibitions to stand at every place of opportunity, forbidding and disturbing them that continue seeking, that continue to do our obsequies[5] to the torn body of our martyred saint.

We boast our light; but if we look not wisely on the sun itself, it smites us into darkness. Who can discern those planets that are oft combust,[6] and those stars of brightest magnitude that rise and set with the sun, until the opposite motion of their orbs bring them to such a place in the firmament where they may be seen evening or morning? The light which we have gained was given us, not to be ever staring on, but by it to discover onward things more remote from our knowledge. It is not the unfrocking of a priest, the unmitering of a bishop, and the removing him from off the Presbyterian shoulders, that will make us a happy nation. No, if other things as great in the church, and in the rule of life both economical and political, be not looked into and reformed, we have looked so long upon the blaze that Zwinglius and Calvin[7] hath beaconed up to us, that we are stark blind.

There be who perpetually complain of schisms and sects, and make it such a calamity that any man dissents from their maxims. 'Tis their own pride and ignorance which causes the disturbing, who neither will hear with meekness, nor can convince; yet all must be suppressed which is not found in their syntagma.[8] They are the troublers, they are the dividers of unity, who neglect and permit not others to unite those dissevered pieces which are yet wanting to the body of Truth. To be still searching what we know not by what we know, still closing up truth to truth as we find it (for all her body is homogeneal and proportional), this is the golden rule in theology as well as in arithmetic, and makes up the best harmony in a church; not the forced and outward union of cold and neutral and inwardly divided minds.

Lords and Commons of England, consider what nation it is whereof ye are, and whereof ye are the governors: a nation not slow and dull, but of a quick, ingenious, and piercing spirit, acute to invent, subtle and sinewy to discourse, not beneath the reach of any point the highest that human capacity can soar to. Therefore the studies of learning in her deepest sciences have been so ancient and so eminent among us, that writers of good antiquity

---

4. Plutarch tells, in "Isis and Osiris," of Typhon's scattering the fragments of his brother Osiris and of Isis's efforts to recover them.
5. Funeral or commemorative rites.
6. Burned up; in astrology, so close to the sun as

not to be visible.
7. Zwingli and Calvin, famous Protestant reformers, were mainstays of the Presbyterian cause. "Economical": domestic.
8. Compilations of beliefs, creeds.

and ablest judgment have been persuaded that even the school of Pythagoras and the Persian wisdom took beginning from the old philosophy of this island.[9] And that wise and civil Roman, Julius Agricola,[1] who governed once here for Caesar, preferred the natural wits of Britain before the labored studies of the French. Nor is it for nothing that the grave and frugal Transylvanian[2] sends out yearly from as far as the mountainous borders of Russia, and beyond the Hercynian wilderness, not their youth, but their staid men, to learn our language and our theologic arts.

Yet that which is above all this, the favor and the love of heaven we have great argument to think in a peculiar manner propitious and propending[3] towards us. Why else was this nation chosen before any other, that out of her, as out of Zion,[4] should be proclaimed and sounded forth the first tidings and trumpet of Reformation to all Europe? And had it not been the obstinate perverseness of our prelates against the divine and admirable spirit of Wycliffe to suppress him as a schismatic and innovator, perhaps neither the Bohemian Huss and Jerome,[5] no, nor the name of Luther or of Calvin, had been ever known: the glory of reforming all our neighbors had been completely ours. But now, as our obdurate clergy have with violence demeaned the matter, we are become hitherto the latest and the backwardest scholars of whom[6] God offered to have made us the teachers.

Now once again by all concurrence of signs, and by the general instinct of holy and devout men, as they daily and solemnly express their thoughts, God is decreeing to begin some new and great period in his church, even to the reforming of Reformation itself; what does he then but reveal himself to his servants, and as his manner is, first to his Englishmen? I say, as his manner is, first to us, though we mark not the method of his counsels, and are unworthy. Behold now this vast city: a city of refuge,[7] the mansion house of liberty, encompassed and surrounded with his protection; the shop of war hath not there more anvils and hammers waking, to fashion out the plates[8] and instruments of armed justice in defense of beleaguered truth, than there be pens and heads there, sitting by their studious lamps, musing, searching, revolving new notions and ideas wherewith to present, as with their homage and their fealty, the approaching Reformation: others as fast reading, trying all things, assenting to the force of reason and convincement.

What could a man require more from a nation so pliant and so prone to seek after knowledge? What wants there to such a towardly and pregnant[9] soil, but wise and faithful laborers, to make a knowing people, a nation of prophets,[1] of sages, and of worthies? We reckon more than five months yet

---

9. Some speculation existed as to whether the Pythagorean notion of the transmigration of souls might trace back to the Druids, but the notion was mostly denied.

1. The "civil" (cultured, civilized) Agricola's opinion of the British intellect is found in Tacitus's *Life of Agricola*. Transylvania (following; now Romania) was an independent Protestant country whose citizens sometimes came to England to study. "Hercynian wilderness": Roman name for a forested and mountainous region of Germany.

2. The Protestant princes of Transylvania encouraged their theologians and humanist scholars to study at English universities.

3. Inclining, favorable. "Argument": reason.

4. Mount Zion, in Jerusalem, the site of the Temple.

5. John Wycliffe was a 14th-century English reformer and translator of the Bible, whose books were forbidden by Pope Alexander V in 1409. John Huss spread Wycliffe's doctrines on the Continent; he was burned at the stake in 1415, as was (the next year) his follower Jerome of Prague.

6. Of those whom. "Demeaned": conducted, degraded.

7. Numbers 35 instructs the Jews to establish "cities of refuge" where those accused of crimes will be protected from "revengers of blood."

8. Plate mail, for armor.

9. Favorable and fertile.

1. In Numbers 11.29 Moses reproaches Joshua, who complained of the presence of other prophets: "Enviest thou for my sake? Would God that all the Lord's people were prophets."

to harvest; there need not be five weeks; had we but eyes to lift up, the fields are white already.[2] Where there is much desire to learn, there of necessity will be much arguing, much writing, many opinions; for opinion in good men is but knowledge in the making. Under these fantastic terrors of sect and schism we wrong the earnest and zealous thirst after knowledge and understanding which God hath stirred up in this city.

What some lament of, we rather should rejoice at, should rather praise this pious forwardness among men, to reassume the ill-deputed care of their religion into their own hands again. A little generous prudence, a little forbearance of one another, and some grain of charity might win all these diligences to join, and unite into one general and brotherly search after truth; could we but forgo this prelatical tradition of crowding free consciences and Christian liberties into canons and precepts of men. I doubt not, if some great and worthy stranger should come among us, wise to discern the mold and temper of a people, and how to govern it, observing the high hopes and aims, the diligent alacrity of our extended thoughts and reasonings in the pursuance of truth and freedom, but that he would cry out as Pyrrhus did, admiring the Roman docility and courage: "If such were my Epirots, I would not despair the greatest design that could be attempted, to make a church or kingdom happy."[3] Yet these are the men cried out against for schismatics and sectaries;[4] as if, while the temple of the Lord was building, some cutting, some squaring the marble, others hewing the cedars, there should be a sort of irrational men, who could not consider there must be many schisms and many dissections[5] made in the quarry and in the timber, ere the house of God can be built. And when every stone is laid artfully together, it cannot be united into a continuity, it can but be contiguous in this world; neither can every piece of the building be of one form; nay rather the perfection consists in this, that out of many moderate varieties and brotherly dissimilitudes that are not vastly disproportional, arises the goodly and the graceful symmetry that commends the whole pile and structure. Let us therefore be more considerate builders, more wise in spiritual architecture, when great reformation is expected. For now the time seems come, wherein Moses the great prophet may sit in heaven rejoicing to see that memorable and glorious wish of his fulfilled, when not only our seventy elders, but all the Lord's people, are become prophets.[6]

*   *   *

Methinks I see in my mind a noble and puissant nation rousing herself like a strong man after sleep, and shaking her invincible locks:[7] methinks I see her as an eagle mewing her mighty youth, and kindling her undazzled eyes at the full midday beam;[8] purging and unsealing her long-abused sight at the fountain itself of heavenly radiance; while the whole noise of timorous

---

2. Milton is paraphrasing Christ's words to his disciples (John 4.35): "Lift up your eyes, and look on the fields: for they are white already to harvest."
3. Though King Pyrrhus of Epirus beat the Roman armies at Heraclea in 280 B.C.E., he was much impressed by their discipline.
4. "Schismatics": those who cut up or divide the church; "sectaries": members of Protestant communions outside the national church.
5. Milton is playing on the literal meaning of "schism," cutting up or dividing.

6. Again alluding to Numbers 11.29, Milton equates the English assembly of clergy to set doctrine and church order (the Westminster Assembly) with the Jewish Sanhedrin of seventy elders.
7. The allusion is to Samson, whose uncut hair made him invincible, when he frustrated the first three attempts of Delilah and the Philistines to subdue him in sleep (Judges 16.6–14).
8. Eagles were thought to be able to look directly at the sun. "Mewing": molting, when the eagle sheds it feathers and thereby renews its coat.

and flocking birds, with those also that love the twilight, flutter about, amazed at what she means, and in their envious gabble would prognosticate[9] a year of sects and schisms.

What should ye do then, should ye suppress all this flowery crop of knowledge and new light sprung up and yet springing daily in this city? Should ye set an oligarchy of twenty engrossers[1] over it, to bring a famine upon our minds again, when we shall know nothing but what is measured to us by their bushel? Believe it, Lords and Commons, they who counsel ye to such a suppressing do as good as bid ye suppress yourselves; and I will soon show how.[2]

* * *

And now the time in special is by privilege to write and speak what may help to the further discussing of matters in agitation. The temple of Janus with his two controversial faces might now not unsignificantly be set open.[3] And though all the winds of doctrine were let loose to play upon the earth, so Truth be in the field, we do injuriously by licensing and prohibiting to misdoubt her strength. Let her and Falsehood grapple; who ever knew Truth put to the worse in a free and open encounter? Her[4] confuting is the best and surest suppressing. He who hears what praying there is for light and clearer knowledge to be sent down among us would think of other matters to be constituted beyond the discipline of Geneva framed and fabriced already to our hands.[5]

Yet when the new light which we beg for shines in upon us, there be who envy and oppose if it come not first in at their casements. What a collusion is this, whenas we are exhorted by the wise man to use diligence, to seek for wisdom as for hidden treasures early and late,[6] that another order shall enjoin us to know nothing but by statute. When a man hath been laboring the hardest labor in the deep mines of knowledge, hath furnished out his findings in all their equipage, drawn forth his reasons as it were a battle[7] ranged, scattered and defeated all objections in his way, calls out his adversary into the plain, offers him the advantage of wind and sun if he please, only that he may try the matter by dint of argument; for his opponents then to skulk, to lay ambushments, to keep a narrow bridge of licensing where the challenger should pass, though it be valor enough in soldiership, is but weakness and cowardice in the wars of Truth.

For who knows not that Truth is strong, next to the Almighty? She needs no policies nor stratagems nor licensings to make her victorious—those are the shifts and the defenses that error uses against her power. Give her but room, and do not bind her when she sleeps, for then she speaks not true, as the old Proteus[8] did, who spake oracles only when he was caught and bound, but then rather she turns herself into all shapes except her own, and perhaps

---

9. Predict.

1. Engrossers, much hated in the English countryside, bought up great quantities of grain and held it for times of famine, selling it at high prices; Milton equates them with the twenty authorized printers, the stationers.

2. Milton goes on to argue that Parliament, by its own liberalizing reforms to date, has created the vigorous and inquiring minds it now seeks to suppress.

3. Janus, as god of beginnings and endings, had two faces looking in opposite directions; a door dedicated to him in Rome was kept open in time

of war, closed in time of peace.

4. I.e., Falsehood's.

5. Milton was already disenchanted with Genevan "Discipline" (Presbyterian church government) and within a year or so would be writing "New *presbyter* is but old *priest*, writ large." "Fabriced": fabricated.

6. Solomon's advice in Proverbs 8.11.

7. Line of battle. Wind and sun (below) were significant advantages in a fight with swords.

8. The sea god who could change shape at will, to avoid capture (*Odyssey* 4).

tunes her voice according to the time, as Micaiah did before Ahab,[9] until she be adjured into her own likeness.

Yet it is not impossible that she may have more shapes than one. What else is all that rank of things indifferent, wherein Truth may be on this side or on the other without being unlike herself? What but a vain shadow else is the abolition of those ordinances, that handwriting nailed to the cross?[1] What great purchase is this Christian liberty which Paul so often boasts of? His doctrine is that he who eats or eats not, regards a day or regards it not, may do either to the Lord.[2] How many other things might be tolerated in peace and left to conscience, had we but charity, and were it not the chief stronghold of our hypocrisy to be ever judging one another? I fear yet this iron yoke of outward conformity hath left a slavish print upon our necks; the ghost of a linen decency[3] yet haunts us. We stumble and are impatient at the least dividing of one visible congregation from another, though it be not in fundamentals; and through our forwardness to suppress and our backwardness to recover any enthralled piece of truth out of the grip of custom, we care not[4] to keep truth separated from truth, which is the fiercest rent and disunion of all. We do not see that while we still affect by all means a rigid and external formality, we may as soon fall again into a gross conforming stupidity, a stark and dead congealment of "wood and hay and stubble,"[5] forced and frozen together, which is more to the sudden degenerating of a church than many subdichotomies of petty schisms.

Not that I can think well of every light separation, or that all in a church is to be expected "gold and silver and precious stones." It is not possible for man to sever the wheat from the tares, the good fish from the other fry; that must be the angels' ministry at the end of mortal things.[6] Yet if all cannot be of one mind—as who looks they should be?—this doubtless is more wholesome, more prudent, and more Christian, that many be tolerated rather than all compelled. I mean not tolerated popery and open superstition, which, as it extirpates all religions and civil supremacies, so itself should be extirpate, provided first that all charitable and compassionate means be used to win and regain the weak and the misled; that also which is impious or evil absolutely, either against faith or manners,[7] no law can possibly permit that intends not to unlaw itself; but those neighboring differences or rather indifferences are what I speak of, whether in some point of doctrine or of discipline, which though they may be many yet need not interrupt "the unity of spirit," if we could but find among us the "bond of peace."[8]

In the meanwhile, if anyone would write and bring his helpful hand to the slow-moving reformation which we labor under, if truth have spoken to him before others, or but seemed at least to speak, who hath so bejesuited[9]

9. Micaiah, a prophet of God, tried for a time to disguise an unpleasant prophecy from King Ahab but then spoke truth when adjured to do so (1 Kings 22.10–28).
1. The locution, from Colossians 2.14, implies that the Crucifixion canceled all the rules and penalties of the Mosaic law. Paul's doctrine of Christian liberty (below) is expressed in Galatians 5 and elsewhere.
2. In the Lord's service.
3. White bands around the necks of clergymen are made emblems of formal piety.
4. Scruple not.
5. The contrast between "wood and hay and stubble" and "gold and silver and precious stones" (next paragraph) is from 1 Corinthians 3.12.
6. In Matthew 13.24–30, 36–43, Christ in a parable tells his disciples to let the wheat and tares (weeds) grow up together till harvest time.
7. Morals.
8. The quoted phrases are from Ephesians 4.3.
9. Imposed on us Jesuit ideas (of censorship).

us that we should trouble that man with asking license to do so worthy a deed? And not consider this, that if it come to prohibiting, there is not aught more likely to be prohibited than truth itself; whose first appearance to our eyes bleared and dimmed with prejudice and custom is more unsightly and unplausible than many errors, even as the person is of many a great man slight and contemptible to see to. And what do they tell us vainly of new opinions, when this very opinion of theirs, that none must be heard but whom they like, is the worst and newest opinion of all others, and is the chief cause why sects and schisms do so much abound, and true knowledge is kept at distance from us; besides yet a greater danger which is in it. For when God shakes a kingdom[1] with strong and healthful commotions to a general reforming, it is not untrue that many sectaries and false teachers are then busiest in seducing; but yet more true it is that God then raises to his own work men of rare abilities and more than common industry, not only to look back and revise what hath been taught heretofore, but to gain further and go on some new enlightened steps in the discovery of truth.

1644

Sonnets   Milton wrote twenty-four sonnets between 1630 and 1658. Five in Italian constitute a mini-Petrarchan sequence on a perhaps imaginary Italian lady. The rest, in English, are individual poems on a wide variety of topics and occasions, though not on the usual sonnet topics (love, as in the sequences of Sidney, Spenser, and Shakespeare, or religious devotion, as in that of Donne). Milton writes sometimes about personal crises (his blindness, the death of his wife), sometimes about political issues or personages (Cromwell, the persecuting Parliament), sometimes about friends and friendship (Cyriack Skinner, Lady Margaret Ley), sometimes about historical events (a threatened royalist attack on London, the massacre of Protestants in Piedmont). His tone ranges from Jonsonian urbanity to prophetic denunciation. The form of the sonnets is Petrarchan (see "Poetic Forms and Literary Terminology," in the appendices to this volume), but in the later sonnets especially (e.g., the Blindness and Piedmont sonnets) the sense runs on from line to line, overriding the expected end-stopped lines and the octave/sestet shift. There is some precedent for this in the Italian sonneteer Giovanni della Casa, but not for the powerful tension Milton creates as meaning and emotion strive within and against the formal metrics of the Petrarchan sonnet. Milton's new ways with the sonnet had a profound and acknowledged influence on the Romantic poets, especially Wordsworth and Shelley.

SONNETS

How Soon Hath Time

How soon hath Time, the subtle thief of youth,
    Stol'n on his wing my three and twentieth year!
    My hasting days fly on with full career,

---

1. Milton alludes to Haggai 2.7: "I will shake all nations, and the desire of all nations shall come, and I will fill this house with glory, saith the Lord of hosts."

But my late spring no bud or blossom shew'th.
5 Perhaps my semblance might deceive[1] the truth,
That I to manhood am arrived so near,
And inward ripeness doth much less appear,
That some more timely-happy spirits endu'th.°   *endows*
Yet be it less or more, or soon or slow,
10   It shall be still in strictest measure even[2]
To that same lot, however mean or high,
Toward which Time leads me, and the will of Heaven;
All is, if I have grace to use it so,
As ever in my great Taskmaster's eye.[3]

1632?   1645

When I Consider How My Light Is Spent[1]

When I consider how my light is spent,°   *extinguished*
Ere half my days,[2] in this dark world and wide,
And that one talent which is death to hide[3]
Lodged with me useless, though my soul more bent
5 To serve therewith my Maker, and present
My true account, lest he returning chide;
"Doth God exact day-labor, light denied?"[4]
I fondly° ask; but Patience to prevent°   *foolishly / forestall*
That murmur, soon replies, "God doth not need
10   Either man's work or his own gifts; who best
Bear his mild yoke, they serve him best. His state°   *splendor*
Is kingly.[5] Thousands at his bidding speed
And post o'er land and ocean without rest:
They also serve who only stand and wait."

1652?   1673

1. Misrepresent. "Semblance": appearance.
2. Equal, adequate. "It": Milton's inner growth.
"Even / To that same lot": conformed to my
appointed destiny.
3. The final lines allow for various readings.
"Taskmaster" identifies God with the parable
(Matthew 20.1–16) in which a vineyard keeper
takes on workers throughout the day, paying the
same wages to those hired at the first and at the
eleventh hour.
1. Apparently written soon after Milton lost his
sight entirely in 1652.
2. Milton was forty-three in 1652; he is obviously not thinking of the biblical lifespan of seventy, but perhaps of that of his father, who died
at eighty-four.
3. In the parable of the talents (Matthew 25.14–
30), a crucial text for Puritans, the servants who

put their master's money ("talents") to earn
interest for him were praised, while the servant
who buried the single talent he was given was
deprived of it and cast into outer darkness. Milton puns on "literary talent." "Useless" (line 4)
carries a pun on "usury," the return expected by
the Master.
4. Milton alludes here to the parable of the vineyard keeper (see "How Soon Hath Time," note 3),
and also to John 9.4, spoken by Jesus before curing a blind man: "I must work the works of him
that sent me, while it is day: the night cometh,
when no man can work."
5. The changed metaphor for God—from master
who needs to profit from his workers to king—
allows the inference that those who "stand and
wait" may be placed nearest the throne.

On the Late Massacre in Piedmont[1]

Avenge,[2] O Lord, thy slaughtered saints, whose bones
    Lie scattered on the Alpine mountains cold;
    Even them who kept thy truth so pure of old
    When all our fathers worshipped stocks and stones,[3]
5 Forget not: in thy book[4] record their groans
    Who were thy sheep and in their ancient fold
    Slain by the bloody Piemontese that rolled
    Mother with infant down the rocks. Their moans
The vales redoubled to the hills, and they
10   To heaven. Their martyred blood and ashes sow
    O'er all th' Italian fields, where still doth sway
The triple tyrant:[5] that from these may grow
A hundredfold, who having learnt thy way
Early may fly the Babylonian woe.[6]

1655   1673

Methought I Saw My Late Espousèd Saint[1]

Methought I saw my late espousèd saint
    Brought to me like Alcestis[2] from the grave,
    Whom Jove's great son to her glad husband gave,
    Rescued from death by force though pale and faint.
5 Mine, as whom[3] washed from spot of childbed taint,
    Purification in the old law did save,[4]

1. The Waldensians (or Vaudois) were a proto-Protestant sect dating to the 12th century who lived in the valleys of northern Italy (the Piedmont) and southern France; Protestants considered them a remnant retaining apostolic purity, free of Catholic superstitions and graven images ("stocks and stones," line 4). The treaty that had allowed them freedom of worship was bypassed in 1655 when the armies of the Catholic duke of Savoy conducted a massacre, razing villages, committing unspeakable atrocities, and hurling women and children from the mountaintops. Protestant Europe was outraged, and in his capacity as Cromwell's Latin secretary Milton translated and wrote several letters about the episode. The sonnet incorporates details from such letters and the contemporary newsbooks. Here Milton transforms the sonnet into a prophetic denunciation.
2. Cf. Revelation 6.9–10: "the souls of them that were slain for the word of God . . . cried with a loud voice, saying, 'How long, O Lord, holy and true, dost thou not judge and avenge our blood . . . ?'"
3. Pagan gods of wood and stone, but with allusion to Roman Catholic "idols."
4. Cf. Revelation 20.12: "the dead were judged out of those things which were written in the books, according to their works." "Sheep" (next line) echoes Romans 8.36: "we are accounted as

sheep for the slaughter."
5. The pope, wearing his tiara with three crowns. The passage alludes to Tertullian's maxim that "the blood of the martyrs is the seed of the church"; also to the parable of the sower (Matthew 13.3), some of whose seed brought forth fruit "an hundredfold" (see next line); and also to Cadmus, who sowed dragon's teeth that sprang forth armed men.
6. Protestants often identified the Roman Church with the whore of Babylon (Revelation 17–18).
1. There is some debate as to whether this poem refers to Milton's first wife, Mary Powell, who died in May 1652, three days after giving birth to her third daughter, or his second wife, Katherine Woodcock, who died in February 1658, after giving birth (in October 1657) to a daughter. The text can support either, but the latter seems more likely. The sonnet is couched as a dream vision.
2. In Euripides' Alcestis, Alcestis, wife of Admetus, is rescued from the underworld by Hercules ("Jove's great son," next line) and restored, veiled, to Admetus; he is overjoyed when he lifts the veil, but she must remain silent until she is ritually cleansed.
3. As one whom.
4. The Mosaic Law (Leviticus 12.2–8) prescribed periods for the purification of women after childbirth (eighty days for a daughter).

And such, as yet once more I trust to have
    Full sight of her in heaven without restraint,
    Came vested all in white, pure as her mind.
10   Her face was veiled, yet to my fancied sight[5]
    Love, sweetness, goodness, in her person shined
So clear, as in no face with more delight.
    But O, as to embrace me she inclined,
    I waked, she fled, and day brought back my night.

1658   1673

Paradise Lost   The setting of Milton's great epic encompasses Heaven, Hell, primordial Chaos, and the planet earth. It features battles among immortal spirits, voyages through space, and lakes of fire. Yet its protagonists are a married couple living in a garden, and its climax consists in the eating of a piece of fruit. *Paradise Lost* is ultimately about the human condition, the Fall that caused "all our woe," and the promise and means of restoration. It is also about knowing and choosing, about free will. In the opening passages of Books 1, 3, 7, and 9, Milton highlights the choices and difficulties he faced in creating his poem. His central characters— Satan, Beelzebub, Abdiel, Adam, and Eve—are confronted with hard choices under the pressure of powerful desires and sometimes devious temptations. Milton's readers, too, are continually challenged to choose and to reconsider their most basic assumptions about freedom, heroism, work, pleasure, language, nature, and love. The great themes of *Paradise Lost* are intimately linked to the political questions at stake in the English Revolution and the Restoration, but the connection is by no means simple or straightforward. This is a poem in which Satan leads a revolution against an absolute monarch and in which questions of tyranny, servitude, and liberty are debated in a parliament in Hell. Milton's readers are hereby challenged to rethink these topics and, like Abdiel debating with Satan in Books 5 and 6, to make crucial distinctions between God as monarch and earthly kings.

In Milton's time, the conventions of epic poetry followed a familiar recipe. The action was to begin *in medias res* (in the middle of things), following the poet's statement of his theme and invocation of his Muse. The reader could expect grand battles and love affairs, supernatural intervention, a descent into the underworld, catalogues of warriors, and epic similes. Milton had absorbed the epic tradition in its entirety, and his poem abounds with echoes of Homer and Virgil, the fifteenth-century Italians Tasso and Ariosto, and the English Spenser. But in *Paradise Lost* he at once heightens epic conventions and values and utterly transforms them. This is the epic to end all epics. Milton gives us the first and greatest of all wars (between God and Satan) and the first and greatest of love affairs (between Adam and Eve). His theme is the destiny of the entire human race, caught up in the temptation and Fall of our first "grand parents."

Milton challenges his readers in *Paradise Lost*, at once fulfilling and defying all of our expectations. Nothing in the epic tradition or in biblical interpretation can prepare us for the Satan who hurtles into view in Book 1, with his awesome energy and defiance, incredible fortitude, and, above all, magnificent rhetoric. For some readers, including Blake and Shelley, Satan is the true hero of the poem. But Milton is engaged in a radical reevaluation of epic values, and Satan's version of heroism must be contrasted with those of the loyal Abdiel and the Son of God. Moreover, the poem's truly epic action takes place not on the battlefield but in the moral and

---

5. She is veiled like Alcestis, and Milton's sight of her is only "fancied"; he never saw the face of his second wife, Katherine, because of his blindness.

domestic arena. Milton's Adam and Eve are not conventional epic heroes, but neither are they the conventional Adam and Eve. Their state of innocence is not childlike, tranquil, and free of sexual desire. Instead, the first couple enjoy sex, experience tension and passion, make mistakes of judgment, and grow in knowledge. Their task is to prune what is unruly in their own natures as they prune the vegetation in their garden, for both have the capacity to grow wild. Their relationship exhibits gender hierarchy, but Milton's early readers may have been surprised by the fullness and complexity of Eve's character and the centrality of her role, not only in the Fall but in the promised restoration.

We expect in epics a grand style, and Milton's style engulfs us from the outset with its energy and power, as those rushing, enjambed, blank-verse lines propel us along with only a few pauses for line endings or grammar (there is only one full stop in the first twenty-six lines). The elevated diction and complex syntax, the sonorities and patternings make a magnificent music. But that music is an entire orchestra of tones, including the high political rhetoric of Satan in Books 1 and 2, the evocative sensuousness of the descriptions of Eden, the delicacy of Eve's love lyric to Adam in Book 4, the relatively plain speech of God in Book 3, and the speech rhythms of Adam and Eve's marital quarrel in Book 9. This majestic achievement depends on the poet's rejection of heroic couplets, the norm for epic and tragedy in the Restoration, vigorously defended by Dryden but denounced by Milton in his note on "The Verse." The choice of verse form was, like so many other things in Milton's life, in part a question of politics. Milton's terms associate the "troublesome and modern bondage of rhyming" with Restoration monarchy and the repression of dissidents and present his use of unrhymed blank verse as a recovery of "ancient liberty."

The first edition (1667) presented *Paradise Lost* in ten books; the second (1674) recast it into twelve books, after the Virgilian model, splitting the original Books 7 and 10.

FROM PARADISE LOST

SECOND EDITION (1674)

The Verse

The measure is English heroic verse without rhyme, as that of Homer in Greek and of Virgil in Latin; rhyme being no necessary adjunct or true ornament of poem or good verse, in longer works especially, but the invention of a barbarous age, to set off wretched matter[1] and lame meter; graced indeed since by the use of some famous modern poets,[2] carried away by custom, but much to their own vexation, hindrance, and constraint to express many things otherwise, and for the most part worse than else they would have expressed them. Not without cause therefore some both Italian[3] and Spanish poets of prime note have rejected rhyme both in longer and shorter works, as have also long since our best English tragedies, as a thing of itself, to all judicious ears, trivial and of no true musical delight; which consists only in apt numbers,[4] fit quantity of syllables, and the sense variously drawn out from one verse into another, not in the jingling sound of like endings, a

---

1. Perhaps the bawdy content of the Latin songs composed by goliardic poets of the Middle Ages; they learned rhyme from medieval hymns.
2. Notably, Dryden. See his *Essay of Dramatic*

Poesy.
3. Trissino and Tasso.
4. Appropriate rhythm.

fault avoided by the learned ancients both in poetry and all good oratory. This neglect then of rhyme so little is to be taken for a defect, though it may seem so perhaps to vulgar readers, that it rather is to be esteemed an example set, the first in English, of ancient liberty recovered to heroic poem from the troublesome and modern bondage of rhyming.

Book 1

The Argument[1]

This first book proposes, first in brief, the whole subject, man's disobedience, and the loss thereupon of Paradise wherein he was placed: then touches the prime cause of his fall, the Serpent, or rather Satan in the Serpent; who revolting from God, and drawing to his side many legions of angels, was by the command of God driven out of Heaven with all his crew into the great deep. Which action passed over, the poem hastes into the midst of things,[2] presenting Satan with his angels now fallen into Hell, described here, not in the center[3] (for Heaven and Earth may be supposed as yet not made, certainly not yet accursed) but in a place of utter darkness, fitliest called Chaos: here Satan with his angels lying on the burning lake, thunderstruck and astonished, after a certain space recovers, as from confusion, calls up him who next in order and dignity lay by him; they confer of their miserable fall. Satan awakens all his legions, who lay till then in the same manner confounded; they rise, their numbers, array of battle, their chief leaders named, according to the idols known afterwards in Canaan and the countries adjoining. To these Satan directs his speech, comforts them with hope yet of regaining Heaven, but tells them lastly of a new world and new kind of creature to be created, according to an ancient prophecy or report in Heaven; for that angels were long before this visible creation, was the opinion of many ancient Fathers.[4] To find out the truth of this prophecy, and what to determine[5] thereon he refers to a full council. What his associates thence attempt. Pandemonium the palace of Satan rises, suddenly built out of the deep: the infernal peers there sit in council.

Of man's first disobedience, and the fruit[1]
Of that forbidden tree, whose mortal° taste   *deadly*
Brought death into the world, and all our woe,
With loss of Eden, till one greater Man[2]
Restore us, and regain the blissful seat,
Sing Heav'nly Muse,[3] that on the secret top

---

1. *Paradise Lost* appeared originally without any sort of prose aid to the reader, but the printer asked Milton for some "Arguments," or summary explanations of the action in the various books, and these were prefixed to later issues of the poem. We reprint the "Argument" for the first book.
2. According to Horace, the epic poet should begin, "in medias res."
3. I.e., of the earth.
4. Church Fathers, the Christian writers of the first centuries.

5. I.e., what action to take.
1. Eve's apple, and all the consequences of eating it. This first proem (lines 1–26) combines the epic statement of theme and invocation.
2. Christ, the second Adam.
3. In Greek mythology, Urania, Muse of astronomy; here, however, by the references to Oreb (Horeb) and Sinai (following), identified with the Muse who inspired Moses ("that shepherd") to write Genesis and the other four books of the Pentateuch for the instruction of the Jews ("the chosen seed").

Of Oreb, or of Sinai, didst inspire
That shepherd, who first taught the chosen seed,
In the beginning how the heav'ns and earth
10   Rose out of Chaos: or if Sion hill[4]
Delight thee more, and Siloa's brook that flowed
Fast by the oracle of God; I thence
Invoke thy aid to my advent'rous song,
That with no middle flight intends to soar
15   Above th' Aonian mount,[5] while it pursues
Things unattempted yet in prose or rhyme.[6]
And chiefly thou O Spirit,[7] that dost prefer
Before all temples th' upright heart and pure,
Instruct me, for thou know'st; thou from the first
20   Wast present, and with mighty wings outspread
Dove-like sat'st brooding[8] on the vast abyss
And mad'st it pregnant: what in me is dark
Illumine, what is low raise and support;
That to the height of this great argument°   *subject, theme*
25   I may assert Eternal Providence,
And justify° the ways of God to men.   *show the justice of*
    Say first, for Heav'n hides nothing from thy view
Nor the deep tract of Hell, say first what cause[9]
Moved our grand parents in that happy state,
30   Favored of Heav'n so highly, to fall off
From their Creator, and transgress his will
For° one restraint, lords of the world besides?°   *because of / otherwise*
Who first seduced them to that foul revolt?
Th' infernal Serpent; he it was, whose guile
35   Stirred up with envy and revenge, deceived
The mother of mankind, what time° his pride   *when*
Had cast him out from Heav'n, with all his host
Of rebel angels, by whose aid aspiring
To set himself in glory above his peers,°   *equals*
40   He trusted to have equaled the Most High,
If he opposed; and with ambitious aim
Against the throne and monarchy of God
Raised impious war in Heav'n and battle proud
With vain attempt. Him the Almighty Power
45   Hurled headlong flaming from th' ethereal sky
With hideous ruin and combustion down
To bottomless perdition, there to dwell
In adamantine[1] chains and penal fire,
Who durst defy th' Omnipotent to arms.

---

4. Mount Zion: the site of Solomon's Temple. "Siloa's brook" (next line): a spring near the Temple where Christ cured a blind man.
5. Helicon, home of the classical Muses. Milton will attempt to surpass Homer and Virgil.
6. Paradoxically, Milton vaunts his originality in a translated line from Ariosto's *Orlando Furioso* 1.2. The allusion also challenges the romantic epic in Ariosto's tradition.
7. Here identified with God's creating power.
8. A composite of phrases and ideas from Gene-

sis 1.2 ("And the earth was without form, and void, and darkness was upon the face of the deep. And the Spirit of God moved upon the face of the waters"). Only a small number of Milton's many allusions to the Bible (in many versions) can be indicated in the notes. Milton's brooding dove image comes from the Latin (Tremellius) Bible version, *incubabat*, "incubated."
9. An opening question like this is an epic convention.
1. A mythical substance of great hardness.

Nine times the space[2] that measures day and night
To mortal men, he with his horrid crew
Lay vanquished, rolling in the fiery gulf
Confounded though immortal: but his doom
Reserved him to more wrath; for now the thought
Both of lost happiness and lasting pain
Torments him; round he throws his baleful° eyes   *malignant*
That witnessed huge affliction and dismay
Mixed with obdúrate pride and steadfast hate:
At once as far as angels' ken° he views   *range of sight*
The dismal situation waste and wild,
A dungeon horrible, on all sides round
As one great furnace flamed, yet from those flames
No light, but rather darkness visible
Served only to discover sights of woe,
Regions of sorrow, doleful shades, where peace
And rest can never dwell, hope never comes
That comes to all;[3] but torture without end
Still urges,° and a fiery deluge, fed   *always provokes*
With ever-burning sulphur unconsumed:
Such place Eternal Justice had prepared
For those rebellious, here their prison ordained
In utter darkness, and their portion set
As far removed from God and light of Heav'n
As from the center thrice to th' utmost pole.[4]
O how unlike the place from whence they fell!
There the companions of his fall, o'erwhelmed
With floods and whirlwinds of tempestuous fire,
He soon discerns, and welt'ring° by his side   *rolling in the waves*
One next himself in power, and next in crime,
Long after known in Palestine, and named
Beëlzebub.[5] To whom th' Arch-Enemy,
And thence in Heav'n called Satan,[6] with bold words
Breaking the horrid silence thus began.
 "If thou beest he; but O how fall'n![7] how changed
From him, who in the happy realms of light
Clothed with transcendent brightness didst outshine
Myriads though bright: if he whom mutual league,
United thoughts and counsels, equal hope
And hazard in the glorious enterprise,
Joined with me once, now misery hath joined
In equal ruin: into what pit thou seest
From what height fall'n, so much the stronger proved

2. Extent of time.
3. The phrase alludes to Dante ("All hope abandon, ye who enter here").
4. Milton makes use of various images of the cosmos in *Paradise Lost*: (1) the earth is the center of the (Ptolemaic) cosmos of ten concentric spheres; (2) the earth and the whole cosmos are an appendage hanging from Heaven by a golden chain; (3) the cosmos seems Copernican from the angels' perspective (see Book 8). Here, the fall from Heaven to Hell is described as thrice as far as the distance from the center (earth) to the

outermost sphere.
5. A Phoenician deity, or Baal (the name means "Lord of Flies"). He is called the prince of devils in Matthew 12.24. As with the other fallen angels, his angelic name has been obliterated, and he is now called by the name he will bear as a pagan deity. That literary strategy evokes all the evil associations attaching to those names in human history.
6. In Hebrew the name means "adversary."
7. Alludes to Isaiah 14.12: "How art thou fallen from heaven, O Lucifer, Son of the morning."

He with his thunder:° and till then who knew   *thunderbolt*
The force of those dire arms? Yet not for those,
95 Nor what the potent victor in his rage
Can else inflict, do I repent or change,
Though changed in outward luster, that fixed mind
And high disdain, from sense of injured merit,
That with the mightiest raised me to contend,
100 And to the fierce contention brought along
Innumerable force of spirits armed
That durst dislike his reign, and me preferring,
His utmost power with adverse power opposed
In dubious° battle on the plains of Heav'n,   *of uncertain outcome*
105 And shook his throne. What though the field be lost?
All is not lost; the unconquerable will,
And study° of revenge, immortal hate,   *intense consideration*
And courage never to submit or yield:
And what is else not to be overcome?[8]
110 That glory never shall his wrath or might
Extort from me. To bow and sue for grace
With suppliant knee, and deify his power
Who from the terror of this arm so late
Doubted° his empire, that were low indeed,   *feared for*
115 That were an ignominy and shame beneath
This downfall; since by fate the strength of gods[9]
And this empyreal substance cannot fail,°   *cease to exist*
Since through experience of this great event
In arms not worse, in foresight much advanced,
120 We may with more successful hope resolve
To wage by force or guile eternal war
Irreconcilable, to our grand foe,
Who now triúmphs, and in th' excess of joy
Sole reigning holds the tyranny of Heav'n."
125 So spake th' apostate angel, though in pain,
Vaunting aloud, but racked with deep despair:
And him thus answered soon his bold compeer.°   *comrade*
  "O Prince, O Chief of many thronéd Powers,
That led th' embattled Seraphim[1] to war
130 Under thy conduct, and in dreadful deeds
Fearless, endangered Heav'ns perpetual King;
And put to proof his high supremacy,
Whether upheld by strength, or chance, or fate;
Too well I see and rue the dire event,°   *outcome*
135 That with sad overthrow and foul defeat
Hath lost us Heav'n, and all this mighty host
In horrible destruction laid thus low,
As far as gods and heav'nly essences
Can perish: for the mind and spirit remains
140 Invincible, and vigor soon returns,

---

8. I.e., what else does it mean not to be overcome?
9. A term commonly used in the poem for angels. But to Satan and his followers it means more, as Satan claims the position of a god, subject to fate but nothing else. Their substance is "empyreal" (next line), of the empyrean.

1. According to tradition, there were nine orders of angels, arranged hierarchically—seraphim, cherubim, thrones, dominions, virtues, powers, principalities, archangels, and angels. The poem makes use of some of these titles but does not keep this hierarchy.

Though all our glory extinct, and happy state
Here swallowed up in endless misery.
But what if he our conqueror (whom I now
Of force° believe almighty, since no less   *necessarily*
Than such could have o'erpow'red such force as ours)
Have left us this our spirit and strength entire
Strongly to suffer and support our pains,
That we may so suffice° his vengeful ire,   *satisfy*
Or do him mightier service as his thralls
By right of war, whate'er his business be
Here in the heart of Hell to work in fire,
Or do his errands in the gloomy deep;
What can it then avail though yet we feel
Strength undiminished, or eternal being
To undergo eternal punishment?"
Whereto with speedy words th' Arch-Fiend replied.
      "Fall'n Cherub, to be weak is miserable
Doing or suffering: but of this be sure,
To do aught° good never will be our task,   *anything*
But ever to do ill our sole delight,
As being the contrary to his high will
Whom we resist. If then his providence
Out of our evil seek to bring forth good,
Our labor must be to pervert that end,
And out of good still to find means of evil;
Which ofttimes may succeed, so as perhaps
Shall grieve him, if I fail° not, and disturb   *err*
His inmost counsels from their destined aim.
But see the angry victor hath recalled
His ministers of vengeance and pursuit
Back to the gates of Heav'n: the sulphurous hail
Shot after us in storm, o'erblown hath laid°   *calmed*
The fiery surge, that from the precipice
Of Heav'n received us falling, and the thunder,
Winged with red lightning and impetuous rage,
Perhaps hath spent his shafts, and ceases now
To bellow through the vast and boundless deep.
Let us not slip° th' occasion, whether scorn,   *let slip*
Or satiate fury yield it from our foe.
Seest thou yon dreary plain, forlorn and wild,
The seat of desolation, void of light,
Save what the glimmering of these livid° flames   *bluish*
Casts pale and dreadful? Thither let us tend
From off the tossing of these fiery waves,
There rest, if any rest can harbor there,
And reassembling our afflicted powers,°   *armies*
Consult how we may henceforth most offend°   *harm, vex*
Our enemy, our own loss how repair,
How overcome this dire calamity,
What reinforcement we may gain from hope,
If not what resolution from despair."[2]
      Thus Satan talking to his nearest mate

2. Five of the last nine lines of Satan's speech rhyme.

With head uplift above the wave, and eyes
That sparkling blazed, his other parts besides
195 Prone on the flood, extended long and large
Lay floating many a rood,[3] in bulk as huge
As whom° the fables name of monstrous size,   *as those whom*
Titanian, or Earth-born, that warred on Jove,
Briareos or Typhon,[4] whom the den
200 By ancient Tarsus held, or that sea-beast
Leviathan,[5] which God of all his works
Created hugest that swim th' ocean stream:
Him haply° slumb'ring on the Norway foam   *perhaps*
The pilot of some small night-foundered° skiff,   *overcome by night*
205 Deeming some island, oft, as seamen tell,[6]
With fixèd anchor in his scaly rind
Moors by his side under the lee,° while night   *out of the wind*
Invests° the sea, and wishèd morn delays: *covers*
So stretched out huge in length the Arch-Fiend lay
210 Chained on the burning lake, nor ever thence
Had ris'n or heaved his head, but that the will
And high permission of all-ruling Heaven
Left him at large to his own dark designs,
That with reiterated crimes he might
215 Heap on himself damnation, while he sought
Evil to others, and enraged might see
How all his malice served but to bring forth
Infinite goodness, grace, and mercy shown
On man by him seduced, but on himself
220 Treble confusion, wrath, and vengeance poured.
Forthwith upright he rears from off the pool
His mighty stature; on each hand the flames
Driv'n backward slope their pointing spires,° and rolled   *points of flames*
In billows, leave i' th' midst a horrid° vale.   *dreadful, bristling*
225 Then with expanded wings he steers his flight
Aloft, incumbent on° the dusky air   *resting on*
That felt unusual weight, till on dry land
He lights,° if it were land that ever burned   *alights*
With solid, as the lake with liquid fire,
230 And such appeared in hue; as when the force
Of subterranean wind transports a hill
Torn from Pelorus, or the shattered side
Of thund'ring Etna,[7] whose combustible
And fueled entrails thence conceiving fire,
235 Sublimed° with mineral fury, aid the winds,   *vaporized*
And leave a singèd bottom all involved°   *enveloped*

---

3. An old unit of measure, between six and eight yards.
4. Both the Titans, led by Briareos (said to have had a hundred hands), and the earth-born Giants, represented by Typhon (who lived in Cilicea near Tarsus and was said to have had a hundred heads), fought with Jove. They were punished by being thrown into the underworld. Christian mythographers found in these stories an analogy to Satan's revolt and punishment.

5. The whale, often identified with the great sea monster and enemy of the Lord in Isaiah 17.1 and the crocodile-like dragon of Job 41. Both were also identified with Satan.
6. The story of the deceived sailor and the illusory island was a commonplace, but the reference to Norway suggests a 16th-century version by Olaus Magnus, a Swedish historian.
7. Pelorus and Etna are volcanic mountains in Sicily.

With stench and smoke: such resting found the sole
Of unblest feet. Him followed his next mate,
Both glorying to have scaped the Stygian° flood   Styxlike, hellish
As gods, and by their own recovered strength,
Not by the sufferance° of supernal power.   permission
   "Is this the region, this the soil, the clime,"
Said then the lost Archangel, "this the seat°   estate
That we must change for Heav'n, this mournful gloom
For that celestial light? Be it so, since he
Who now is sov'reign can dispose and bid
What shall be right: farthest from him is best
Whom reason hath equaled, force hath made supreme
Above his equals. Farewell happy fields
Where joy forever dwells: Hail horrors, hail
Infernal world, and thou profoundest Hell
Receive thy new possessor: one who brings
A mind not to be changed by place or time.
The mind is its own place, and in itself
Can make a Heav'n of Hell, a Hell of Heav'n.[8]
What matter where, if I be still the same,
And what I should be, all but less than° he   barely less than
Whom thunder hath made greater? Here at least
We shall be free; th' Almighty hath not built
Here for his envy,[9] will not drive us hence:
Here we may reign secure, and in my choice
To reign is worth ambition though in Hell:
Better to reign in Hell, than serve in Heav'n.[1]
But wherefore let we then our faithful friends,
Th' associates and copartners of our loss
Lie thus astonished° on th' oblivious pool,[2]   stunned
And call them not to share with us their part
In this unhappy mansion, or once more
With rallied arms to try what may be yet
Regained in Heav'n, or what more lost in Hell?"
   So Satan spake, and him Beëlzebub
Thus answered. "Leader of those armies bright,
Which but th' Omnipotent none could have foiled,
If once they hear that voice, their liveliest pledge
Of hope in fears and dangers, heard so oft
In worst extremes, and on the perilous edge°   front lines
Of battle when it raged, in all assaults
Their surest signal, they will soon resume
New courage and revive, though now they lie
Groveling and prostrate on yon lake of fire,
As we erewhile, astounded and amazed,
No wonder, fall'n such a pernicious highth."
   He scarce had ceased when the superior Fiend
Was moving toward the shore; his ponderous shield

8. Compare Satan's soliloquy, 4.32–113.
9. I.e., because he desires this place.
1. An ironic echo of *Odyssey* 11.489–91, where
the shade of Achilles tells Odysseus that it is better to be a farmhand on earth than king among

the dead.
2. The epithet "oblivious" is transferred from
the fallen angels to the pool into which they have
fallen.

285   Ethereal temper,[3] massy, large and round,
      Behind him cast; the broad circumference
      Hung on his shoulders like the moon, whose orb
      Through optic glass the Tuscan artist views[4]
      At evening from the top of Fesole,
290   Or in Valdarno, to descry new lands,
      Rivers or mountains in her spotty globe.
      His spear, to equal which the tallest pine
      Hewn on Norwegian hills, to be the mast
      Of some great ammiral,° were but a wand   *admiral's ship*
295   He walked with to support uneasy steps
      Over the burning marl,° not like those steps   *soil*
      On heaven's azure; and the torrid clime
      Smote on him sore besides, vaulted with fire;
      Nathless° he so endured, till on the beach   *nevertheless*
300   Of that inflamed° sea, he stood and called   *flaming*
      His legions, angel forms, who lay entranced
      Thick as autumnal leaves that strow the brooks
      In Vallombrosa,[5] where th' Etrurian shades
      High overarched embow'r;° or scattered sedge°   *form bowers / seaweed*
305   Afloat, when with fierce winds Orion armed
      Hath vexed the Red Sea coast,[6] whose waves o'erthrew
      Busiris[7] and his Memphian chivalry,
      While with perfidious hatred they pursued
      The sojourners of Goshen, who beheld
310   From the safe shore their floating carcasses
      And broken chariot wheels; so thick bestrown
      Abject and lost lay these, covering the flood,
      Under amazement of their hideous change.
      He called so loud, that all the hollow deep
315   Of Hell resounded. "Princes, Potentates,
      Warriors, the flow'r of Heav'n, once yours, now lost,
      If such astonishment as this can seize
      Eternal Spirits: or have ye chos'n this place
      After the toil of battle to repose
320   Your wearied virtue,° for the ease you find   *strength, valor*
      To slumber here, as in the vales of Heav'n?
      Or in this abject posture have ye sworn
      To adore the conqueror? who now beholds
      Cherub and Seraph rolling in the flood
325   With scattered arms and ensigns,° till anon   *battle flags*
      His swift pursuers from Heav'n gates discern
      Th' advantage, and descending tread us down
      Thus drooping, or with linkèd thunderbolts

---

3. I.e., tempered in celestial fire.
4. Galileo, who looked through a telescope ("optic glass") from the hill town of Fiesole, outside Florence, in the valley of the Arno River ("Valdarno," val d'Arno, line 290). In 1610 he published a book describing the mountains on the moon.
5. The name means "shady valley" and refers to a region high in the Apennines, about twenty miles from Florence, in Tuscany ("Etruria"). Similes comparing the numberless dead to falling leaves

are frequent in epic (e.g., *Aeneid* 6.309–10).
6. Orion is a constellation whose rising near sunset in late summer and autumn was associated with storms in the Red Sea.
7. Mythical Egyptian pharaoh, whom Milton associates with the pharaoh of Exodus 14, who pursued the Israelites ("sojourners of Goshen," line 309) into the Red Sea, which God parted for them. His "chivalry" (following) are horsemen from Memphis.

Transfix us to the bottom of this gulf.
Awake, arise, or be forever fall'n."
   They heard, and were abashed, and up they sprung
Upon the wing, as when men wont° to watch   *accustomed*
On duty, sleeping found by whom they dread,
Rouse and bestir themselves ere well awake.
Nor did they not perceive the evil plight
In which they were, or the fierce pains not feel;[8]
Yet to their general's voice they soon obeyed
Innumerable. As when the potent rod
Of Amram's son[9] in Egypt's evil day
Waved round the coast, up called a pitchy cloud
Of locusts, warping° on the eastern wind,   *swarming*
That o'er the realm of impious Pharaoh hung
Like night, and darkened all the land of Nile:
So numberless were those bad angels seen
Hovering on wing under the cope° of Hell   *roof*
'Twixt upper, nether, and surrounding fires;
Till, as a signal giv'n, th' uplifted spear
Of their great Sultan[1] waving to direct
Their course, in even balance down they light
On the firm brimstone, and fill all the plain;
A multitude, like which the populous north
Poured never from her frozen loins, to pass
Rhene or the Danaw, when her barbarous sons
Came like a deluge on the south, and spread
Beneath Gibraltar to the Libyan sands.[2]
Forthwith from every squadron and each band
The heads and leaders thither haste where stood
Their great commander; godlike shapes and forms
Excelling human, princely dignities,
And powers that erst° in Heaven sat on thrones;   *formerly*
Though of their names in heav'nly records now
Be no memorial, blotted out and razed°   *erased*
By their rebellion, from the Books of Life.
Nor had they yet among the sons of Eve
Got them new names, till wand'ring o'er the earth,
Through God's high sufferance for the trial of man,
By falsities and lies the greatest part
Of mankind they corrupted to forsake
God their Creator, and th' invisible
Glory of him that made them, to transform
Oft to the image of a brute, adorned
With gay religions° full of pomp and gold,   *showy rites*
And devils to adore for deities:
Then were they known to men by various names,
And various idols through the heathen world. ⌒
   Say, Muse, their names then known, who first, who last,[3]

---

8. The double negatives make a positive: they did perceive both plight and pain.
9. Moses, who drew down a plague of locusts on Egypt (Exodus 10.12–15).
1. A first use of this description of Satan as an Oriental despot.

2. The barbarian invasions of Rome began with crossings of the Rhine ("Rhene") and Danube ("Danaw") rivers and spread across Spain, via Gibraltar, to North Africa.
3. The catalogue of gods here is an epic convention; Homer catalogues ships; Virgil, warriors.

Roused from the slumber on that fiery couch,
At their great emperor's call, as next in worth
Came singly° where he stood on the bare strand,   *one at a time*
380   While the promiscuous° crowd stood yet aloof.   *mixed*
     The chief were those who from the pit of Hell
Roaming to seek their prey on earth, durst fix
Their seats long after next the seat of God,[4]
Their altars by his altar, gods adored
385   Among the nations round, and durst abide
Jehovah thund'ring out of Zion, throned
Between the Cherubim;[5] yea, often placed
Within his sanctuary itself their shrines,
Abomination; and with cursèd things
390   His holy rites, and solemn feasts profaned,
And with their darkness durst affront his light.
First Moloch,[6] horrid king besmeared with blood
Of human sacrifice, and parents' tears,
Though for the noise of drums and timbrels° loud   *tambourines*
395   Their children's cries unheard, that passed through fire
To his grim idol. Him the Ammonite[7]
Worshipped in Rabba and her wat'ry plain,
In Argob and in Basan, to the stream
Of utmost Arnon. Nor content with such
400   Audacious neighborhood, the wisest heart
Of Solomon he led by fraud to build
His temple right against the temple of God
On that opprobrious hill, and made his grove
The pleasant valley of Hinnom, Tophet thence
405   And black Gehenna called, the type of Hell.[8]
Next Chemos,[9] th' obscene dread of Moab's sons,
From Aroer to Nebo, and the wild
Of southmost Abarim; in Hesebon
And Horanaim, Seon's realm, beyond
410   The flow'ry dale of Sibma clad with vines,
And Elealè to th' Asphaltic Pool.[1]
Peor[2] his other name, when he enticed
Israel in Sittim on their march from Nile
To do him wanton rites, which cost them woe.
415   Yet thence his lustful orgies he enlarged
Even to that hill of scandal,[3] by the grove
Of Moloch homicide, lust hard by° hate;   *close by*

4. The first group of devils come from the Middle East, close neighbors of Jehovah "throned" in his sanctuary in Jerusalem.
5. Golden cherubim adorned opposite ends of the gold cover on the Ark of the Covenant.
6. Moloch was a sun god, sometimes represented as a roaring bull or with a calf's head, within whose brazen image living children were supposedly burned as sacrifices.
7. The Ammonites lived east of the Jordan River. "Rabba" (next line) is modern Amman, in Jordan; "Argob," "Basan," "utmost Arnon" (lines 398–99) are lands east of the Dead Sea.
8. The rites of Moloch on "that opprobrious hill" (the Mount of Olives), just opposite the Jewish temple, and in the valley of Hinnom so polluted those places that they were turned into

the refuse dump of Jerusalem. Under the name "Tophet" and "Gehenna," Hinnom became a type of Hell.
9. Chemos, or Chemosh, associated with Moloch in 1 Kings 11.7, was the god of the Moabites, whose lands (many drawn from Isaiah 15–16) are mentioned in the following lines.
1. The Dead Sea.
2. The story of Peor seducing the Israelites in Sittim is told in Numbers 25.
3. The Mount of Olives, where Solomon built temples for Chemos and Moloch (1 Kings 11.7); epithets were commonly attached to the names of gods, as in the next line, Moloch "homicide." Josiah (following line) destroyed pagan idols in Jerusalem and other cities (2 Chronicles 34).

Till good Josiah drove them thence to Hell.
With these came they, who from the bord'ring flood
Of old Euphrates to the brook that parts
Egypt from Syrian ground,[4] had general names
Of Baalim and Ashtaroth, those male,
These feminine.[5] For Spirits when they please
Can either sex assume, or both; so soft
And uncompounded is their essence pure,
Not tied or manacled with joint or limb,
Nor founded on the brittle strength of bones,
Like cumbrous flesh; but in what shape they choose
Dilated or condensed, bright or obscure,
Can execute their airy purposes,
And works of love or enmity fulfill.
For those the race of Israel oft forsook
Their Living Strength, and unfrequented left
His righteous altar, bowing lowly down
To bestial gods; for which their heads as low
Bowed down in battle, sunk before the spear
Of despicable foes. With these in troop
Came Astoreth, whom the Phoenicians called
Astartè, queen of Heav'n, with crescent horns;
To whose bright image nightly by the moon
Sidonian virgins[6] paid their vows and songs,
In Sion also not unsung, where stood
Her temple on th' offensive mountain,[7] built
By that uxorious king, whose heart though large,
Beguiled by fair idolatresses, fell
To idols foul. Thammuz[8] came next behind,
Whose annual wound in Lebanon allured
The Syrian damsels to lament his fate
In amorous ditties all a summer's day,
While smooth Adonis[9] from his native work
Ran purple to the sea, supposed with blood
Of Thammuz yearly wounded: the love-tale
Infected Sion's daughters with like heat,
Whose wanton passions in the sacred porch
Ezekiel[1] saw, when by the vision led
His eye surveyed the dark idolatries
Of alienated Judah. Next came one
Who mourned in earnest, when the captive ark
Maimed his brute image, head and hands lopped off
In his own temple, on the grunsel edge,[2]

---

4. Palestine lies between the Euphrates and "the brook Besor" (1 Samuel 30.10).
5. Plural forms, masculine and feminine, respectively, denoting aspects of the sun god Baal and the moon goddess Astarte (called "Astoreth" in line 438, below).
6. Sidon and Tyre were the chief cities of Phoenicia.
7. The Mount of Olives again. "That uxorious king" (next line) is Solomon, who "loved many strange women" (2 Kings 11.1–8).
8. A Syrian god, supposedly killed by a boar in Lebanon; his Greek form was Adonis, beloved of

Aphrodite and god of the solar year. Annual festivals mourned his death and celebrated his revival as signifying the death and rebirth of vegetation.
9. Here, the Lebanese river named for the deity because every spring it turned bloodred from sedimentary mud.
1. The prophet complained that Jewish women were worshipping Thammuz (Ezekiel 8.14).
2. When the Philistines stole the ark of God, they placed it in the temple of their sea god, Dagon, but in the morning the mutilated statue of Dagon was found on the threshhold ("grunsel edge") (1 Samuel 5.1–5).

Where he fell flat, and shamed his worshippers:
Dagon his name, sea monster, upward man
And downward fish: yet had his temple high
Reared in Azotus, dreaded through the coast
465   Of Palestine, in Gath and Ascalon
And Accaron and Gaza's³ frontier bounds.
Him followed Rimmon,⁴ whose delightful seat
Was fair Damascus, on the fertile banks
Of Abbana and Pharphar, lucid streams.
470   He also against the house of God was bold:
A leper once he lost and gained a king,
Ahaz his sottish conqueror, whom he drew
God's altar to disparage and displace
For one of Syrian mode,⁵ whereon to burn
475   His odious off'rings, and adore the gods
Whom he had vanquished. After these appeared
A crew who under names of old renown,
Osiris, Isis, Orus⁶ and their train
With monstrous shapes and sorceries abused
480   Fanatic Egypt and her priests, to seek
Their wand'ring gods disguised in brutish forms
Rather than human. Nor did Israel scape
Th' infection when their borrowed gold composed
The calf in Oreb:⁷ and the rebel king
485   Doubled that sin in Bethel and in Dan,
Lik'ning his Maker to the grazèd ox,⁸
Jehovah, who in one night when he passed
From Egypt marching, equaled° with one stroke   *leveled*
Both her firstborn and all her bleating gods.⁹
490   Belial came last,¹ than whom a spirit more lewd
Fell not from Heaven, or more gross to love
Vice for itself: to him no temple stood
Or altar smoked; yet who more oft than he
In temples and at altars, when the priest
495   Turns atheist, as did Eli's sons,² who filled
With lust and violence the house of God.
In courts and palaces he also reigns
And in luxurious cities, where the noise
Of riot ascends above their loftiest tow'rs,

---

3. The five chief cities of the Philistines, sites of Dagon's worship.
4. A Phoenician god whose temple was in Damascus.
5. A Syrian general, Naaman, was cured of leprosy and converted from worship of Rimmon by the waters of the Jordan (2 Kings 5), while King Ahaz, an Israelite monarch who conquered Damascus, was converted there to Rimmon's worship.
6. The second group of devils includes the Egyptian gods driven from Heaven by the revolt of the giants (Ovid, *Metamorphoses* 5) and forced to wander in "monstrous" (next line) animal disguises.
7. In the wilderness of Egypt, while Moses was receiving the Law, Aaron made a golden calf,

thought to be an idol of the Egyptian god Apis and made of ornaments brought out of Egypt (Exodus 32).
8. Jeroboam, "the rebel king" who led the ten tribes of Israel in revolt against Solomon's son, Rehoboam; he doubled Aaron's sin by making two golden calves (1 Kings 12.25–30).
9. Jehovah smote the firstborn of all Egyptian families as well as their gods (Exodus 12.12).
1. Belial was never worshipped as a god; his name means "wickedness," but its use in phrases like "sons of Belial" encouraged personification.
2. Priests who were termed "sons of Belial" because they seized for themselves offerings made to God and lay with women who assembled at the door of the tabernacle (1 Samuel 2.12–22).

And injury and outrage: and when night
Darkens the streets, then wander forth the sons
Of Belial, flown° with insolence and wine.[3]   *flushed*
Witness the streets of Sodom, and that night
In Gibeah, when the hospitable door
Exposed a matron to avoid worse rape.[4]
    These were the prime in order and in might;
The rest were long to tell, though far renowned,
Th' Ionian gods, of Javan's issue held
Gods, yet confessed later than Heav'n and Earth
Their boasted parents;[5] Titan Heav'n's firstborn
With his enormous brood, and birthright seized
By younger Saturn, he from mightier Jove,
His own and Rhea's son, like measure found;
So Jove usurping reigned:[6] these first in Crete
And Ida known, thence on the snowy top
Of cold Olympus ruled the middle air
Their highest heav'n; or on the Delphian cliff,
Or in Dodona, and through all the bounds
Of Doric land;[7] or who with Saturn old
Fled over Adria to th' Hesperian fields,
And o'er the Celtic roamed the utmost isles.[8]
    All these and more came flocking; but with looks
Downcast and damp,° yet such wherein appeared   *depressed, dazed*
Obscure some glimpse of joy, to have found their chief
Not in despair, to have found themselves not lost
In loss itself; which on his count'nance cast
Like doubtful hue:[9] but he his wonted° pride   *accustomed*
Soon recollecting, with high words, that bore
Semblance of worth, not substance, gently raised
Their fainting courage, and dispelled their fears.
    Then straight° commands that at the warlike sound   *immediately*
Of trumpets loud and clarions be upreared
His mighty standard; that proud honor claimed
Azazel[1] as his right, a Cherub tall:
Who forthwith from the glittering staff unfurled
Th' imperial ensign, which full high advanced
Shone like a meteor streaming to the wind
With gems and golden luster rich emblazed,
Seraphic arms and trophies:[2] all the while

3. This passage, with its present-tense verbs, invites application to current examples—at court and in Restoration London.
4. Lot begged the Sodomites to rape his daughters rather than his (male) angel guests (Genesis 19); in Gibeah a Levite avoided "worse" (homosexual) rape by surrendering his concubine to riotous "sons of Belial" (Judges 19.21–30).
5. The Ionian Greeks ("Javan's issue," i.e., of the line of Javan, grandson of Noah) regarded the Titans as gods; their supposed parents were Heaven (Uranus) and Earth (Gaia).
6. The Titan Cronos, or Saturn, deposed his father, married his sister Rhea, and ruled until he was deposed by his son, Zeus (Jove), who had been reared in secret on Mount Ida in Crete.

7. Zeus and the other Olympian gods had their seat on Mount Olympus, in "middle air"; they were worshipped in Delphi, Dodona, and throughout Greece ("Doric lands").
8. Saturn, after his downfall, fled over "Adria" (the Adriatic Sea) to the "Hesperian fields" (Italy), crossed the "Celtic" fields of France, and thence to Britain, the "utmost isles."
9. Satan's face reflected the same mixed emotions.
1. Traditionally, one of the four standard-bearers in Satan's army. "Clarions" (line 532): small, shrill trumpets.
2. Their flags bear the heraldic arms of the various orders of angels and memorials of their battles.

540 Sonorous metal° blowing martial sounds: *trumpets*
    At which the universal host upsent
    A shout that tore Hell's concave,° and beyond   *vault*
    Frighted the reign of Chaos and old Night.³
    All in a moment through the gloom were seen
545 Ten thousand banners rise into the air
    With orient° colors waving: with them rose   *lustrous*
    A forest huge of spears: and thronging helms
    Appeared, and serried° shields in thick array   *pushed close together*
    Of depth immeasurable: anon they move
550 In perfect phalanx to the Dorian⁴ mood
    Of flutes and soft recorders; such as raised
    To highth of noblest temper heroes old
    Arming to battle, and instead of rage
    Deliberate valor breathed, firm and unmoved
555 With dread of death to flight or foul retreat,
    Nor wanting power to mitigate and swage°   *assuage*
    With solemn touches, troubled thoughts, and chase
    Anguish and doubt and fear and sorrow and pain
    From mortal or immortal minds. Thus they
560 Breathing united force with fixèd thought
    Moved on in silence to soft pipes that charmed
    Their painful steps o'er the burnt soil; and now
    Advanced in view they stand, a horrid° front   *bristling with spears*
    Of dreadful length and dazzling arms, in guise
565 Of warriors old with ordered spear and shield,
    Awaiting what command their mighty chief
    Had to impose. He through the armèd files
    Darts his experienced eye, and soon traverse°   *across*
    The whole battalion views, their order due,
570 Their visages and stature as of gods,
    Their number last he sums. And now his heart
    Distends with pride, and hard'ning in his strength
    Glories: for never since created man⁵
    Met such embodied force, as named° with these   *composed*
575 Could merit more than that small infantry
    Warred on by cranes:⁶ though all the giant brood
    Of Phlegra with th' heroic race were joined
    That fought at Thebes and Ilium,⁷ on each side
    Mixed with auxiliar° gods; and what resounds   *allied*
580 In fable or romance of Uther's son
    Begirt with British and Armoric knights;
    And all who since, baptized or infidel
    Jousted in Aspramont or Montalban,
    Damasco, or Morocco, or Trebisond,
585 Or whom Biserta sent from Afric shore

---

3. In *Paradise Lost* 2.894–909, 959–70 Chaos and Night rule the region of unformed matter between Heaven and earth.
4. Severe, martial music used by the Spartans marching to battle. "Phalanx": battle formation.
5. I.e., since the creation of man.
6. Pygmies (little people, with a pun, in "infantry" on "infants") had periodic fights with the cranes, in Pliny's account. Compared with Satan's forces, all other armies are puny.
7. In Greek mythology, the Giants fought the gods at Phlegra in Macedonia; in Roman myth, it was at Phlegra in Italy. Satan's forces surpass them, even if joined with the Seven who fought against Thebes and the whole Greek host that besieged Troy ("Ilium").

When Charlemagne with all his peerage fell
By Fontarabia.[8] Thus far these beyond
Compare of mortal prowess, yet observed°   *obeyed*
Their dread commander: he above the rest
In shape and gesture proudly eminent
Stood like a tow'r; his form had yet not lost
All her[9] original brightness, nor appeared
Less than Archangel ruined, and th' excess
Of glory obscured: as when the sun new-ris'n
Looks through the horizontal° misty air   *on the horizon*
Shorn of his beams, or from behind the moon
In dim eclipse disastrous° twilight sheds   *ill-starred*
On half the nations, and with fear of change
Perplexes monarchs. Darkened so, yet shone
Above them all th' Archangel: but his face
Deep scars of thunder had intrenched,° and care   *furrowed*
Sat on his faded cheek, but under brows
Of dauntless courage, and considerate° pride   *conscious, deliberate*
Waiting revenge: cruel his eye, but cast
Signs of remorse and passion° to behold   *compassion, pain*
The fellows of his crime, the followers rather
(Far other once beheld in bliss) condemned
Forever now to have their lot in pain,
Millions of Spirits for his fault amerced°   *deprived*
Of Heav'n, and from eternal splendors flung
For his revolt, yet faithful how they stood,
Their glory withered: as when Heaven's fire
Hath scathed° the forest oaks, or mountain pines,   *damaged*
With singèd top their stately growth though bare
Stands on the blasted heath. He now prepared
To speak; whereat their doubled ranks they bend
From wing to wing, and half enclose him round
With all his peers: attention held them mute.
Thrice he essayed,° and thrice, in spite of scorn,   *attempted*
Tears such as angels weep burst forth: at last
Words interwove with sighs found out their way.
    "O myriads of immortal Spirits, O Powers
Matchless, but with th' Almighty, and that strife
Was not inglorious, though th' event° was dire,   *outcome*
As this place testifies, and this dire change
Hateful to utter: but what power of mind
Foreseeing or presaging, from the depth
Of knowledge past or present, could have feared,
How such united force of gods, how such
As stood like these, could ever know repulse?
For who can yet believe, though after loss,
That all these puissant° legions, whose exile   *potent, powerful*
Hath emptied Heav'n, shall fail to reascend

---

8. Satan's forces also surpass the "British and Armoric" (from Brittany) knights who fought with King Arthur ("Uther's son") and all the romance knights who fought at the famous named sites in the following lines. Roncesvalles, near Fontara-bia, was the place where Charlemagne's "peerage," including his best knight, Roland, were defeated in battle (though not Charlemagne himself).
9. *Forma* in Latin is feminine.

Self-raised, and repossess their native seat?
635   For me, be witness all the host of Heav'n,
If counsels different,° or danger shunned   *contradictory*
By me, have lost our hopes. But he who reigns
Monarch in Heav'n, till then as one secure
Sat on his throne, upheld by old repute,
640   Consent or custom, and his regal state
Put forth at full, but still° his strength concealed,   *always*
Which tempted our attempt, and wrought our fall.
Henceforth his might we know, and know our own
So as not either to provoke, or dread
645   New war, provoked; our better part remains
To work in close design, by fraud or guile
What force effected not: that he no less
At length from us may find, who overcomes
By force, hath overcome but half his foe.
650   Space may produce new worlds; whereof so rife°   *common*
There went a fame° in Heav'n that he ere long   *rumor*
Intended to create, and therein plant
A generation, whom his choice regard
Should favor equal to the sons of Heaven:
655   Thither, if but to pry, shall be perhaps
Our first eruption,° thither or elsewhere: *breaking out*
For this infernal pit shall never hold
Celestial Spirits in bondage, not th' abyss
Long under darkness cover. But these thoughts
660   Full counsel must mature: peace is despaired,
For who can think submission? War then, war
Open or understood° must be resolved."   *covert*
     He spake: and to confirm his words, out flew
Millions of flaming swords, drawn from the thighs
665   Of mighty Cherubim; the sudden blaze
Far round illumined Hell: highly they raged
Against the Highest, and fierce with graspèd arms
Clashed on their sounding shields the din of war,[1]
Hurling defiance toward the vault of Heav'n.
670   There stood a hill not far whose grisly top
Belched fire and rolling smoke; the rest entire
Shone with a glossy scurf,° undoubted sign   *crust*
That in his womb was hid metallic ore,
The work of sulphur.[2] Thither winged with speed
675   A numerous brígade hastened. As when bands
Of pioneers° with spade and pickax armed   *military engineers*
Forerun the royal camp, to trench a field,
Or cast a rampart. Mammon[3] led them on,
Mammon, the least erected Spirit that fell
680   From Heav'n, for ev'n in Heav'n his looks and thoughts

1. Like Roman legionnaires, the fallen angels applaud by beating swords on shields.
2. Sulfur and mercury were considered the basic substances of all metals.
3. "Mammon," an abstract word for riches, came to be personified and associated with the god of wealth, Plutus, and so with Pluto, god of the underworld. Cf. Matthew 6.24: "Ye cannot serve God and mammon."

Were always downward bent, admiring more
The riches of Heav'n's pavement, trodden gold,
Than aught divine or holy else enjoyed
In vision beatific: by him first
Men also, and by his suggestion taught,
Ransacked the center, and with impious hands
Rifled the bowels of their mother earth
For treasures better hid. Soon had his crew
Opened into the hill a spacious wound
And digged out ribs of gold. Let none admire°   *wonder*
That riches grow in Hell; that soil may best
Deserve the precious bane.° And here let those   *poison*
Who boast in mortal things, and wond'ring tell
Of Babel, and the works of Memphian kings,[4]
Learn how their greatest monuments of fame,
And strength and art are easily outdone
By Spirits reprobate, and in an hour
What in an age they with incessant toil
And hands innumerable scarce perform.
Nigh on the plain in many cells prepared,
That underneath had veins of liquid fire
Sluiced from the lake, a second multitude
With wondrous art founded° the massy ore,   *melted*
Severing° each kind, and scummed the bullion dross:° *separating / boiling dregs*
A third as soon had formed within the ground
A various mold, and from the boiling cells
By strange conveyance filled each hollow nook,
As in an organ from one blast of wind
To many a row of pipes the soundboard breathes.
Anon out of the earth a fabric huge
Rose like an exhalation, with the sound
Of dulcet symphonies and voices sweet,
Built like a temple,[5] where pilasters° round   *columns set in a wall*
Were set, and Doric pillars[6] overlaid
With golden architrave; nor did there want
Cornice or frieze, with bossy° sculptures grav'n;   *embossed*
The roof was fretted° gold. Not Babylon,   *richly ornamented*
Nor great Alcairo such magnificence
Equaled in all their glories, to enshrine
Belus or Serapis[7] their gods, or seat
Their kings, when Egypt with Assyria strove
In wealth and luxury. Th' ascending pile
Stood fixed° her stately height, and straight° the doors *complete / at once*
Opening their brazen folds discover° wide   *reveal*
Within, her ample spaces, o'er the smooth
And level pavement: from the archèd roof

4. The Tower of Babel and the pyramids of Egypt.
5. After melting the gold with fire from the lake and pouring it into molds, the devils cause their building to rise as by magic, to the sounds of marvelous music.
6. Doric pillars are severe and plain. The devils' palace combines classical architectural features with elaborate ornamentation, suggesting, perhaps, St. Peter's in Rome.
7. At Babylon, in Assyria, there were temples to "Belus" or Baal; at Alcairo (modern Cairo, ancient Memphis), in Egypt, they were to Osiris ("Serapis").

Pendent by subtle magic many a row
Of starry lamps and blazing cressets[8] fed
With naphtha and asphaltus yielded light
730 As from a sky. The hasty multitude
Admiring entered, and the work some praise
And some the architect: his hand was known
In Heav'n by many a towered structure high,
Where sceptered angels held their residence,
735 And sat as princes, whom the Súpreme King
Exalted to such power, and gave to rule,
Each in his hierarchy, the orders bright.
Nor was his name unheard or unadored
In ancient Greece and in Ausonian land
740 Men called him Mulciber[9] and how he fell
From Heav'n, they fabled, thrown by angry Jove
Sheer o'er the crystal battlements: from morn
To noon he fell, from noon to dewy eve,
A summer's day; and with the setting sun
745 Dropped from the zenith like a falling star,
On Lemnos th' Aégean isle: thus they relate,
Erring; for he with this rebellious rout
Fell long before; nor aught availed him now
To have built in Heav'n high tow'rs; nor did he scape
750 By all his engines, but was headlong sent
With his industrious crew to build in Hell.
   Meanwhile the wingèd heralds by command
Of sov'reign power, with awful ceremony
And trumpet's sound throughout the host proclaim
755 A solemn council forthwith to be held
At Pandemonium,[1] the high capitol
Of Satan and his peers:° their summons called   *nobles*
From every band and squarèd regiment
By place° or choice° the worthiest; they anon   *rank / election*
760 With hundreds and with thousands trooping came
Attended: all access was thronged, the gates
And porches wide, but chief the spacious hall
(Though like a covered field, where champions bold
Wont ride in armed, and at the soldan's° chair   *sultan's*
765 Defied the best of paynim° chivalry   *pagan*
To mortal combat or career with lance)
Thick swarmed, both on the ground and in the air,
Brushed with the hiss of rustling wings. As bees
In springtime, when the sun with Taurus rides,[2]
770 Pour forth their populous youth about the hive
In clusters; they among fresh dews and flowers
Fly to and fro, or on the smoothèd plank,
The suburb of their straw-built citadel,

8. Basketlike lamps, hung from the ceiling.
9. Hephaestus, or Vulcan, was sometimes known in "Ausonian land" (Italy) as "Mulciber." The story of Jove's tossing him out of Heaven (see following lines) is told in Book 1 of the *Iliad*.

1. "Pandemonium" (a Miltonic coinage) means literally "all demons," an inversion of "pantheon," "all gods."
2. The sun is in the zodiacal sign of Taurus from about April 19 to May 20.

New rubbed with balm, expatiate and confer[3]
Their state affairs. So thick the aery crowd
Swarmed and were straitened; till the signal giv'n,
Behold a wonder! They but now who seemed
In bigness to surpass Earth's giant sons
Now less than smallest dwarfs, in narrow room
Throng numberless, like that Pygmean race
Beyond the Indian mount,[4] or fairy elves,
Whose midnight revels, by a forest side
Or fountain some belated peasant sees,
Or dreams he sees, while overhead the moon
Sits arbitress,° and nearer to the earth   *witness*
Wheels her pale course: they on their mirth and dance
Intent, with jocund° music charm his ear;[5]   *merry*
At once with joy and fear his heart rebounds.
Thus incorporeal Spirits to smallest forms
Reduced their shapes immense, and were at large,
Though without number still amidst the hall
Of that infernal court. But far within
And in their own dimensions like themselves
The great Seraphic Lords and Cherubim
In close recess and secret conclave sat,
A thousand demigods on golden seats,
Frequent and full.[6] After short silence then
And summons read, the great consult[7] began.

Book 2

High on a throne of royal state, which far
Outshone the wealth of Ormus and of Ind,[1]
Or where the gorgeous East with richest hand
Show'rs on her kings barbaric pearl and gold,
Satan exalted sat, by merit raised
To that bad eminence; and from despair
Thus high uplifted beyond hope, aspires
Beyond thus high, insatiate to pursue
Vain war with Heav'n, and by success° untaught   *the outcome*
His proud imaginations° thus displayed.   *schemes*
    "Powers and Dominions,[2] deities of Heaven,
For since no deep within her gulf can hold
Immortal vigor, though oppressed and fall'n,
I give not Heav'n for lost. From this descent
Celestial Virtues rising, will appear
More glorious and more dread than from no fall,

---

3. Spread out and discuss. Bee similes were common in epic from Homer on; also, the bees' (royalist) society was often cited in political argument. The simile prepares for the sudden contraction of the devils, who can shrink or dilate at will.
4. The pygmies were supposed to live beyond the Himalayas.
5. The belated peasant's.
6. Crowded together, and in full complement.
7. Consultation, often secret and seditious.
1. India. "Ormus": an island in the Persian Gulf, modern Hormuz, famous for pearls.
2. Angelic orders.

And trust themselves to fear no second fate.
Me though just right, and the fixed laws of Heav'n
Did first create your leader, next, free choice,
20   With what besides, in counsel or in fight,
Hath been achieved of merit, yet this loss
Thus far at least recovered, hath much more
Established in a safe unenvied throne
Yielded with full consent. The happier state
25   In Heav'n, which follows dignity, might draw
Envy from each inferior; but who here
Will envy whom the highest place exposes
Foremost to stand against the Thunderer's aim
Your bulwark, and condemns to greatest share
30   Of endless pain? Where there is then no good
For which to strive, no strife can grow up there
From faction; for none sure will claim in Hell
Precédence, none, whose portion is so small
Of present pain, that with ambitious mind
35   Will covet more. With this advantage then
To union, and firm faith, and firm accord,
More than can be in Heav'n, we now return
To claim our just inheritance of old,
Surer to prosper than prosperity
40   Could have assured us;[3] and by what best way,
Whether of open war or covert guile,[4]
We now debate; who can advise, may speak."
     He ceased, and next him Moloch, sceptered king
Stood up, the strongest and the fiercest Spirit
45   That fought in Heav'n; now fiercer by despair:
His trust was with th' Eternal to be deemed
Equal in strength, and rather than be less
Cared not to be at all; with that care lost
Went all his fear: of God, or Hell, or worse
50   He recked° not, and these words thereafter spake.   *cared*
     "My sentence° is for open war: of wiles,   *judgment*
More unexpért,° I boast not: them let those   *less experienced*
Contrive who need, or when they need, not now.
For while they sit contriving, shall the rest,
55   Millions that stand in arms, and longing wait
The signal to ascend, sit lingering here
Heav'n's fugitives, and for their dwelling place
Accept this dark opprobrious den of shame,
The prison of his tyranny who reigns
60   By our delay? No, let us rather choose
Armed with Hell flames and fury all at once
O'er Heav'n's high tow'rs to force resistless way,
Turning our tortures into horrid° arms   *bristling, horrifying*
Against the Torturer; when to meet the noise
65   Of his almighty engine° he shall hear   *the thunderbolt*
Infernal thunder, and for lightning see

---

3. Note the play on "surer," "prosper," "prosperity," "assured," a favorite device of Milton's.
4. A typical epic convention (in Homer, Virgil,

Tasso, and elsewhere) involved councils debating
war or peace, with spokesmen on each side. Satan
offers only the option of war, open or covert.

Black fire and horror shot with equal rage
Among his angels; and his throne itself
Mixed with Tartarean[5] sulfur, and strange fire,
His own invented torments. But perhaps
The way seems difficult and steep to scale
With upright wing against a higher foe.
Let such bethink them, if the sleepy drench°   *large draught*
Of that forgetful° lake benumb not still,   *causing oblivion*
That in our proper° motion we ascend   *natural to us*
Up to our native seat: descent and fall
To us is adverse. Who but felt of late
When the fierce foe hung on our broken rear
Insulting,[6] and pursued us through the deep,
With what compulsion and laborious flight
We sunk thus low? Th' ascent is easy then;
Th' event° is feared; should we again provoke   *outcome*
Our stronger, some worse way his wrath may find
To our destruction: if there be in Hell
Fear to be worse destroyed: what can be worse
Than to dwell here, driven out from bliss, condemned
In this abhorrèd deep to utter woe;
Where pain of unextinguishable fire
Must exercise° us without hope of end   *vex, afflict*
The vassals[7] of his anger, when the scourge
Inexorably, and the torturing hour
Calls us to penance? More destroyed than thus
We should be quite abolished and expire.
What fear we then? What° doubt we to incense   *why*
His utmost ire? which to the height enraged,
Will either quite consume us, and reduce
To nothing this essential,° happier far   *essence*
Than miserable to have eternal being:
Or if our substance be indeed divine,
And cannot cease to be, we are at worst
On this side nothing;[8] and by proof we feel
Our power sufficient to disturb his Heav'n,
And with perpetual inroads to alarm,
Though inaccessible, his fatal[9] throne:
Which if not victory is yet revenge."
  He ended frowning, and his look, denounced°   *portended*
Desperate revenge, and battle dangerous
To less than gods. On th' other side up rose
Belial, in act more graceful and humane;°   *civil, polite*
A fairer person lost not Heav'n; he seemed
For dignity composed and high exploit:
But all was false and hollow; though his tongue
Dropped manna, and could make the worse appear
The better reason,[1] to perplex and dash°   *confuse*

---

5. Tartarus is a classical name for hell.
6. With the Latin sense of stamping on; also, triumphantly scorning.
7. Servants, but perhaps also vessels. See Romans 9.22: "vessels of wrath fitted to destruction."
8. I.e., we cannot be worse off than we are now, and still live.

9. Established by Fate; also, deadly.
1. The Sophists, mercenary teachers of rhetoric in ancient Greece, were denounced by Plato for making "the worse appear / The better reason." "His tongue / Dropped manna": his honeyed words seemed like the manna supplied to the Israelites in the desert.

115 Maturest counsels: for his thoughts were low;
    To vice industrious, but to nobler deeds
    Timorous and slothful: yet he pleased the ear,
    And with persuasive accent thus began.
    "I should be much for open war, O Peers,
120 As not behind in hate; if what was urged
    Main reason to persuade immediate war,
    Did not dissuade me most, and seem to cast
    Ominous conjecture on the whole success:
    When he who most excels in fact° of arms,   *feat*
125 In what he counsels and in what excels
    Mistrustful, grounds his courage on despair
    And utter dissolution, as the scope
    Of all his aim, after some dire revenge.
    First, what revenge? The tow'rs of Heav'n are filled
130 With armèd watch, that render all access
    Impregnable; oft on the bordering deep
    Encamp their legions, or with óbscure wing
    Scout far and wide into the realm of Night,
    Scorning surprise. Or could we break our way
135 By force, and at our heels all Hell should rise
    With blackest insurrection, to confound
    Heav'n's purest light, yet our great enemy
    All incorruptible would on his throne
    Sit unpolluted, and th' ethereal mold[2]
140 Incapable of stain would soon expel
    Her mischief, and purge off the baser fire
    Victorious. Thus repulsed, our final hope
    Is flat despair: we must exasperate
    Th' almighty victor to spend all his rage,
145 And that must end us, that must be our cure,
    To be no more; sad cure; for who would lose,
    Though full of pain, this intellectual being,
    Those thoughts that wander through eternity,
    To perish rather, swallowed up and lost
150 In the wide womb of uncreated night,
    Devoid of sense and motion? And who knows,
    Let this be good, whether our angry foe
    Can give it, or will ever? How he can
    Is doubtful; that he never will is sure.
155 Will he, so wise, let loose at once his ire,
    Belike° through impotence, or unaware,   *perhaps*
    To give his enemies their wish, and end
    Them in his anger, whom his anger saves
    To punish endless? 'Wherefore cease we then?'
160 Say they who counsel war, 'We are decreed,
    Reserved and destined to eternal woe;
    Whatever doing, what can we suffer more,
    What can we suffer worse?' Is this then worst,
    Thus sitting, thus consulting, thus in arms?
165 What when we fled amain,° pursued and strook°   *headlong / struck*

2. Heavenly substance, derived from "ether," the fifth and purest element, thought to be incorruptible.

With Heav'n's afflicting thunder, and besought
The deep to shelter us? This Hell then seemed
A refuge from those wounds. Or when we lay
Chained on the burning lake? That sure was worse.
What if the breath that kindled those grim fires
Awaked should blow them into sevenfold rage
And plunge us in the flames? Or from above
Should intermitted° vengeance arm again   *suspended*
His red right hand to plague us? What if all
Her° stores were opened, and this firmament°   *Hell's / sky*
Of Hell should spout her cataracts° of fire,   *cascades*
Impendent[3] horrors, threat'ning hideous fall
One day upon our heads; while we perhaps
Designing or exhorting glorious war,
Caught in a fiery tempest shall be hurled
Each on his rock transfixed, the sport and prey
Of racking whirlwinds, or forever sunk
Under yon boiling ocean, wrapped in chains;
There to converse with everlasting groans,
Unrespited, unpitied, unreprieved,
Ages of hopeless end; this would be worse.
War therefore, open or concealed, alike
My voice dissuades; for what can force or guile[4]
With him, or who deceive his mind, whose eye
Views all things at one view? He from Heav'n's high
All these our motions° vain, sees and derides;   *proposals*
Not more almighty to resist our might
Than wise to frustrate all our plots and wiles.
Shall we then live thus vile, the race of Heav'n
Thus trampled, thus expelled to suffer here
Chains and these torments? Better these than worse
By my advice; since fate inevitable
Subdues us, and omnipotent decree,
The victor's will. To suffer, as to do,
Our strength is equal, nor the law unjust
That so ordains: this was at first resolved,
If we were wise, against so great a foe
Contending, and so doubtful what might fall.
I laugh, when those who at the spear are bold
And vent'rous, if that fail them, shrink and fear
What yet they know must follow, to endure
Exile, or ignominy, or bonds, or pain,
The sentence of their conqueror: This is now
Our doom; which if we can sustain and bear,
Our Súpreme Foe in time may much remit
His anger, and perhaps thus far removed
Not mind us not offending, satisfied
With what is punished; whence these raging fires
Will slacken, if his breath stir not their flames.
Our purer essence then will overcome

3. In the Latin sense, hanging down, threatening.
4. The verb "accomplish" or "achieve" is understood.

Their noxious vapor, or inured° not feel,   *accustomed*
Or changed at length, and to the place conformed
In temper and in nature, will receive
Familiar the fierce heat, and void of pain;
220 This horror will grow mild, this darkness light,
Besides what hope the never-ending flight
Of future days may bring, what chance, what change
Worth waiting, since our present lot appears
For happy though but ill, for ill not worst,[5]
225 If we procure not to ourselves more woe."
  Thus Belial, with words clothed in reason's garb,
Counseled ignoble ease and peaceful sloth,
Not peace: and after him thus Mammon spake.
  "Either to disenthrone the King of Heav'n
230 We war, if war be best, or to regain
Our own right lost: him to unthrone we then
May hope when everlasting Fate shall yield
To fickle Chance, and Chaos judge the strife:
The former vain to hope argues° as vain   *proves*
235 The latter: for what place can be for us
Within Heav'n's bound, unless Heav'n's Lord supreme
We overpower? Suppose he should relent
And publish grace to all, on promise made
Of new subjection; with what eyes could we
240 Stand in his presence humble, and receive
Strict laws imposed, to celebrate his throne
With warbled hymns, and to his Godhead sing
Forced hallelujahs; while he lordly sits
Our envied Sov'reign, and his altar breathes
245 Ambrosial° odors and ambrosial flowers, *fragrant, immortal*
Our servile offerings. This must be our task
In Heav'n, this our delight; how wearisome
Eternity so spent in worship paid
To whom we hate. Let us not then pursue
250 By force impossible, by leave obtained
Unácceptable, though in Heav'n, our state
Of splendid vassalage,° but rather seek   *servitude*
Our own good from ourselves, and from our own
Live to ourselves, though in this vast recess,
255 Free, and to none accountable, preferring
Hard liberty before the easy yoke
Of servile pomp. Our greatness will appear
Then most conspicuous, when great things of small,
Useful of hurtful, prosperous of adverse
260 We can create, and in what place soe'er
Thrive under evil, and work ease out of pain
Through labor and endurance. This deep world
Of darkness do we dread? How oft amidst
Thick clouds and dark doth Heav'n's all-ruling Sire
265 Choose to reside, his glory unobscured,
And with the majesty of darkness round

---

5. I.e., from the point of view of happiness, the devils are in an ill state, but it could be worse.

Covers his throne; from whence deep thunders roar
Must'ring their rage, and Heav'n resembles Hell?
As he our darkness, cannot we his light
Imitate when we please? This desert soil
Wants° not her hidden luster, gems and gold;   *lacks*
Nor want we skill or art, from whence to raise
Magnificence; and what can Heav'n show more?
Our torments also may in length of time
Become our elements, these piercing fires
As soft as now severe, our temper° changed   *constitution*
Into their temper; which must needs remove
The sensible of pain.[6] All things invite
To peaceful counsels, and the settled state
Of order, how in safety best we may
Compose° our present evils, with regard   *come to terms with*
Of what we are and where, dismissing quite
All thoughts of war: ye have what I advise."
   He scarce had finished, when such murmur filled
Th' assembly, as when hollow rocks retain
The sound of blust'ring winds, which all night long
Had roused the sea, now with hoarse cadence lull
Seafaring men o'erwatched,° whose bark by chance   *worn out from watching*
Or pinnace° anchors in a craggy bay   *boat*
After the tempest: such applause was heard
As Mammon ended, and his sentence pleased,
Advising peace: for such another field°   *battlefield*
They dreaded worse than Hell: so much the fear
Of thunder and the sword of Michaël[7]
Wrought still within them; and no less desire
To found this nether empire, which might rise
By policy,° and long process of time,   *statecraft*
In emulation opposite to Heav'n.
Which then Beëlzebub perceived, than whom,
Satan except, none higher sat, with grave
Aspect he rose, and in his rising seemed
A pillar of state; deep on his front° engraven   *brow*
Deliberation sat and public care;
And princely counsel in his face yet shone,
Majestic though in ruin: sage he stood
With Atlantean[8] shoulders fit to bear
The weight of mightiest monarchies; his look
Drew audience and attention still as night
Or summer's noontide air, while thus he spake.
   "Thrones and imperial Powers, offspring of Heav'n
Ethereal Virtues; or these titles[9] now
Must we renounce, and changing style° be called   *title*
Princes of Hell? for so the popular vote
Inclines, here to continue, and build up here
A growing empire. Doubtless! while we dream,

---

6. Pain felt by the senses.
7. The warrior angel, chief of the angelic armies.
8. Worthy of Atlas, the Titan who as a punish-ment for rebellion was condemned to hold up the heavens on his shoulders.
9. The official titles of angelic orders.

And know not that the King of Heav'n hath doomed
This place our dungeon, not our safe retreat
Beyond his potent arm, to live exempt
From Heav'n's high jurisdiction, in new league
320 Banded against his throne, but to remain
In strictest bondage, though thus far removed,
Under th' inevitable curb, reserved
His captive multitude: for he, be sure,
In height or depth, still first and last will reign
325 Sole King, and of his kingdom lose no part
By our revolt, but over Hell extend
His empire, and with iron scepter rule
Us here, as with his golden those in Heav'n.
What° sit we then projecting peace and war?   *why*
330 War hath determined us,[1] and foiled with loss
Irreparable; terms of peace yet none
Vouchsafed° or sought; for what peace will be giv'n   *granted*
To us enslaved, but custody severe,
And stripes, and arbitrary punishment
335 Inflicted? And what peace can we return,
But, to our power,[2] hostility and hate,
Untamed reluctance,° and revenge though slow,   *resistance*
Yet ever plotting how the conqueror least
May reap his conquest, and may least rejoice
340 In doing what we most in suffering feel?
Nor will occasion want,° nor shall we need   *be lacking*
With dangerous expedition to invade
Heav'n, whose high walls fear no assault or siege,
Or ambush from the deep. What if we find
345 Some easier enterprise? There is a place
(If ancient and prophetic fame° in Heav'n   *rumor*
Err not) another world, the happy seat
Of some new race called Man, about this time
To be created like to us, though less
350 In power and excellence, but favored more
Of him who rules above; so was his will
Pronounced among the gods, and by an oath,
That shook Heav'n's whole circumference, confirmed.
Thither let us bend all our thoughts, to learn
355 What creatures there inhabit, of what mold,
Or substance, how endued,° and what their power,   *endowed*
And where their weakness, how attempted° best,   *attacked, tempted*
By force or subtlety. Though Heav'n be shut,
And Heav'n's high arbitrator sit secure
360 In his own strength, this place may lie exposed,
The utmost border of his kingdom, left
To their defense who hold it:[3] here perhaps
Some advantageous act may be achieved
By sudden onset, either with hellfire
365 To waste° his whole creation, or possess   *lay waste*

---

1. I.e., war has decided the question for us, but   2. I.e., to the best of our power.
also limited us.   3. To be defended by the occupants.

All as our own, and drive as we were driven,
The puny habitants, or if not drive,
Seduce them to our party, that their God
May prove their foe, and with repenting hand
Abolish his own works.[4] This would surpass
Common revenge, and interrupt his joy
In our confusion, and our joy upraise
In his disturbance; when his darling sons
Hurled headlong to partake with us, shall curse
Their frail original,° and faded bliss,   *originator, parent*
Faded so soon. Advise° if this be worth   *consider*
Attempting, or to sit in darkness here
Hatching vain empires." Thus Beëlzebub
Pleaded his devilish counsel, first devised
By Satan, and in part proposed: for whence,
But from the author of all ill could spring
So deep a malice, to confound° the race   *ruin*
Of mankind in one root,[5] and earth with Hell
To mingle and involve, done all to spite
The great Creator? But their spite still serves
His glory to augment. The bold design
Pleased highly those infernal States,° and joy   *nobles*
Sparkled in all their eyes; with full assent
They vote: whereat his speech he thus renews.
    "Well have ye judged, well ended long debate,
Synod of gods, and like to what ye are,
Great things resolved, which from the lowest deep
Will once more lift us up, in spite of fate,
Nearer our ancient seat; perhaps in view
Of those bright confines, whence with neighboring arms
And opportune excursion we may chance
Reenter Heav'n; or else in some mild zone
Dwell not unvisited of Heav'n's fair light
Secure, and at the bright'ning orient° beam   *lustrous*
Purge off this gloom; the soft delicious air,
To heal the scar of these corrosive fires
Shall breathe her balm. But first whom shall we send
In search of this new world, whom shall we find
Sufficient? Who shall tempt° with wand'ring feet   *attempt, venture*
The dark unbottomed infinite abyss
And through the palpable obscure[6] find out
His uncouth° way, or spread his aery flight   *unknown*
Upborne with indefatigable wings
Over the vast abrupt,[7] ere he arrive
The happy isle? What strength, what art can then
Suffice, or what evasion bear him safe
Through the strict senteries° and stations thick   *sentries*
Of angels watching round? Here he had need

---

4. Cf. Genesis 6.7: "And the Lord said, 'I will destroy man [and all other creatures]; for it repenteth me that I have made them.'"
5. Adam, the first man, is the "root" of the human race.

6. Darkness so thick it can be felt (cf. Exodus 10.21).
7. Chaos, a striking example of sound imitating sense.

All circumspection, and we now no less
415 Choice° in our suffrage; for on whom we send,   *discrimination*
The weight of all and our last hope relies."
        This said, he sat; and expectation held
His look suspense,⁸ awaiting who appeared
To second, or oppose, or undertake
420 The perilous attempt: but all sat mute,
Pondering the danger with deep thoughts; and each
In other's count'nance read his own dismay
Astonished. None among the choice and prime
Of those Heav'n-warring champions could be found
425 So hardy as to proffer or accept
Alone the dreadful voyage; till at last
Satan, whom now transcendent glory raised
Above his fellows, with monarchal pride
Conscious of highest worth, unmoved thus spake.
430   "O progeny of Heav'n, empyreal Thrones,
With reason hath deep silence and demur°   *hesitation*
Seized us, though undismayed: long is the way
And hard, that out of Hell leads up to light;
Our prison strong, this huge convex of fire,
435 Outrageous to devour, immures us round
Ninefold,⁹ and gates of burning adamant
Barred over us prohibit all egress.
These passed, if any pass, the void profound
Of unessential Night receives him next
440 Wide gaping, and with utter loss of being
Threatens him, plunged in that abortive gulf.¹
If thence he scape into whatever world,
Or unknown region, what remains him less°   *awaits him except*
Than unknown dangers and as hard escape?
445 But I should ill become this throne, O Peers,
And this imperial sov'reignty, adorned
With splendor, armed with power, if aught proposed
And judged of public moment,° in the shape   *importance*
Of difficulty or danger could deter
450 Me from attempting. Wherefore do I assume
These royalties, and not refuse to reign,
Refusing° to accept as great a share   *if I refuse*
Of hazard as of honor, due alike
To him who reigns, and so much to him due
455 Of hazard more, as he above the rest
High honored sits? Go therefore mighty Powers,
Terror of Heav'n, though fall'n; intend° at home,   *consider*
While here shall be our home, what best may ease
The present misery, and render Hell
460 More tolerable; if there be cure or charm
To respite or deceive, or slack the pain
Of this ill mansion: intermit no watch

---

8. I.e., he sat waiting in suspense.
9. Hell's fiery walls and gates have nine thick-
nesses (see lines 645ff.). "Adamant" (following):
a fabulously hard metal.

1. Chaos is a womb in which all potential forms
fragment (see lines 895ff.) "Unessential" (line
439): i.e., having no real essence.

Against a wakeful foe, while I abroad
Through all the coasts° of dark destruction seek   *districts*
Deliverance for us all: this enterprise
None shall partake with me." Thus saying rose
The monarch, and prevented° all reply,   *forestalled*
Prudent, lest from his resolution raised°   *roused*
Others among the chief might offer now
(Certain to be refused) what erst° they feared;   *formerly*
And so refused might in opinion stand
His rivals, winning cheap the high repute
Which he through hazard huge must earn. But they
Dreaded not more th' adventure than his voice
Forbidding; and at once with him they rose;
Their rising all at once was as the sound
Of thunder heard remote. Towards him they bend
With awful° reverence prone; and as a god   *full of awe*
Extol him equal to the Highest in Heav'n:
Nor failed they to express how much they praised,
That for the general safety he despised
His own: for neither do the Spirits damned
Lose all their virtue; lest bad men should boast
Their specious° deeds on earth, which glory excites,   *pretending to worth*
Or close° ambition varnished o'er with zeal.   *secret*
    Thus they their doubtful consultations dark
Ended rejoicing in their matchless chief:
As when from mountaintops the dusky clouds
Ascending, while the north wind sleeps, o'erspread
Heav'n's cheerful face, the louring element°   *threatening sky*
Scowls o'er the darkened landscape snow, or show'r;
If chance the radiant sun with farewell sweet
Extend his evening beam, the fields revive,
The birds their notes renew, and bleating herds
Attest their joy, that hill and valley rings.
O shame to men! Devil with devil damned
Firm concord holds, men only disagree
Of creatures rational, though under hope
Of heavenly grace: and God proclaiming peace,
Yet live in hatred, enmity, and strife
Among themselves, and levy cruel wars,
Wasting the earth, each other to destroy:
As if (which might induce us to accord)
Man had not hellish foes enow° besides,   *enough*
That day and night for his destruction wait.
    The Stygian° council thus dissolved; and forth   *Styx-like, hellish*
In order came the grand infernal peers:
Midst came their mighty paramount,° and seemed   *supreme ruler*
Alone th' antagonist of Heav'n, nor less
Than Hell's dread emperor with pomp supreme,
And godlike imitated state; him round
A globe° of fiery Seraphim enclosed   *band, circle*
With bright emblazonry and horrent[2] arms.

2. Bristling. "Emblazonry": decorated shields.

Then of their session ended they bid cry
515 With trumpet's regal sound the great result:
Toward the four winds four speedy Cherubim
Put to their mouths the sounding alchemy[3]
By herald's voice explained; the hollow abyss
Heard far and wide, and all the host of Hell
520 With deaf'ning shout, returned them loud acclaim.
Thence more at ease their minds and somewhat raised
By false presumptuous hope, the rangèd° powers   *arrayed in ranks*
Disband, and wand'ring, each his several way
Pursues, as inclination or sad choice
525 Leads him perplexed, where he may likeliest find
Truce to his restless thoughts, and entertain
The irksome hours, till his great chief return.
Part on the plain, or in the air sublime°   *aloft*
Upon the wing, or in swift race contend,
530 As at th' Olympian games or Pythian fields;[4]
Part curb their fiery steeds, or shun the goal[5]
With rapid wheels, or fronted° brígades form.   *confronting*
As when to warn proud cities war appears
Waged in the troubled sky, and armies rush
535 To battle in the clouds,[6] before each van°   *vanguard*
Prick° forth the aery knights, and couch their spears   *spur*
Till thickest legions close; with feats of arms
From either end of Heav'n the welkin° burns.   *sky*
Others with vast Typhoean[7] rage more fell°   *fierce*
540 Rend up both rocks and hills, and ride the air
In whirlwind; Hell scarce holds the wild uproar.
As when Alcides from Oechalia crowned
With conquest, felt th' envenomed robe, and tore
Through pain up by the roots Thessalian pines,
545 And Lichas from the top of Oeta threw
Into th' Euboic sea.[8] Others more mild,
Retreated in a silent valley, sing
With notes angelical to many a harp
Their own heroic deeds and hapless fall
550 By doom of battle; and complain that fate
Free virtue should enthrall to force or chance.
Their song was partial,° but the harmony   *prejudiced*
(What could it less when Spirits immortal sing?)
Suspended° Hell, and took with ravishment   *held in suspense*
555 The thronging audience. In discourse more sweet
(For eloquence the soul, song charms the sense)
Others apart sat on a hill retired,
In thoughts more elevate, and reasoned high
Of providence, foreknowledge, will, and fate,

---

3. Trumpets (made of the goldlike alloy brass).
4. The Olympic games were held at Olympia, the Pythian games at Delphi. Games celebrating a (usually dead) hero are an epic convention.
5. To drive a chariot as close as possible around a column without hitting it.
6. The appearance of warfare in the skies, reported before several notable battles, portends trouble on earth.
7. Like that of Typhon, the hundred-headed Titan (see 1.199).
8. Wearing a poisoned robe given him in a deception, Hercules ("Alcides") in his dying agonies threw his beloved companion Lichas, along with a good part of Mount Oeta, into the Euboean Sea, near Thermopylae.

Fixed fate, free will, foreknowledge absolute,
And found no end, in wand'ring mazes lost.
Of good and evil much they argued then,
Of happiness and final misery,
Passion and apathy,[9] and glory and shame,
Vain wisdom all, and false philosophy:
Yet with a pleasing sorcery could charm
Pain for a while or anguish, and excite
Fallacious hope, or arm th' obdurèd° breast   hardened
With stubborn patience as with triple steel.
Another part in squadrons and gross° bands,   solid, dense
On bold adventure to discover wide
That dismal world, if any clime perhaps
Might yield them easier habitation, bend
Four ways their flying march, along the banks
Of four infernal rivers that disgorge
Into the burning lake their baleful streams:[1]
Abhorrèd Styx the flood of deadly hate,
Sad Acheron of sorrow, black and deep;
Cocytus, named of lamentation loud
Heard on the rueful stream; fierce Phlegethon
Whose waves of torrent fire inflame with rage.
Far off from these a slow and silent stream,
Lethe the river of oblivion rolls
Her wat'ry labyrinth, whereof who drinks,
Forthwith his former state and being forgets,
Forgets both joy and grief, pleasure and pain.
Beyond this flood a frozen continent
Lies dark and wild, beat with perpetual storms
Of whirlwind and dire hail, which on firm land
Thaws not, but gathers heap,[2] and ruin seems
Of ancient pile; all else deep snow and ice,
A gulf profound as that Serbonian bog[3]
Betwixt Damiata and Mount Casius old,
Where armies whole have sunk: the parching air
Burns frore,° and cold performs th' effect of fire.   frozen
Thither by harpy-footed[4] Furies haled,°   driven
At certain revolutions° all the damned   recurring times
Are brought: and feel by turns the bitter change
Of fierce extremes, extremes by change more fierce,
From beds of raging fire to starve° in ice   make numb
Their soft ethereal warmth, and there to pine
Immovable, infixed, and frozen round,
Periods of time; thence hurried back to fire.
They ferry over this Lethean sound
Both to and fro, their sorrow to augment,

9. The Stoic goal of freedom from passion.
1. These four rivers are traditional in hellish
geography. Milton distinguishes them by the original meanings of their Greek names: Styx means
"hateful," Acheron "woeful," etc. Lethe is "far
off" and quite different from the others, oblivion
being a desired state in Hell.
2. In a heap, resembling the ruin of an old build-

ing ("ancient pile," next line).
3. Lake Serbonis, once famous for its quick-
sands, lies near the city of Damietta ("Damiata,"
next line), just east of the Nile.
4. Taloned. In Greek mythology the Harpies
(monsters with women's faces) carried off individuals to the Furies, who avenged crimes.

And wish and struggle, as they pass, to reach
The tempting stream, with one small drop to lose
In sweet forgetfulness all pain and woe,
All in one moment, and so near the brink;
610 But fate withstands, and to oppose th' attempt
Medusa[5] with Gorgonian terror guards
The ford, and of itself the water flies
All taste of living wight,° as once it fled   *creature*
The lip of Tantalus.[6] Thus roving on
615 In cónfused march forlorn, th' advent'rous bands
With shudd'ring horror pale, and eyes aghast
Viewed first their lamentable lot, and found
No rest: through many a dark and dreary vale
They passed, and many a region dolorous,
620 O'er many a frozen, many a fiery alp,°   *volcano*
Rocks, caves, lakes, fens, bogs, dens, and shades of death,
A universe of death, which God by curse
Created evil, for evil only good,
Where all life dies, death lives, and nature breeds,
625 Perverse, all monstrous, all prodigious things,
Abominable, inutterable, and worse
Than fables yet have feigned, or fear conceived,
Gorgons and Hydras, and Chimeras[7] dire.
    Meanwhile the Adversary[8] of God and man,
630 Satan, with thoughts inflamed of highest design,
Puts on swift wings,° and towards the gates of Hell   *flies swiftly*
Explores his solitary flight; sometimes
He scours the right-hand coast, sometimes the left,
Now shaves with level wing the deep, then soars
635 Up to the fiery concave° tow'ring high.   *vault*
As when far off at sea a fleet descried
Hangs on the clouds, by equinoctial° winds   *from the equator*
Close sailing from Bengala,° or the isles   *Bengal*
Of Ternate and Tidore,[9] whence merchants bring
640 Their spicy drugs: they on the trading flood
Through the wide Ethiopian to the Cape
Ply stemming nightly toward the pole:[1] so seemed
Far off the flying Fiend. At last appear
Hell bounds high reaching to the horrid roof,
645 And thrice threefold the gates; three folds were brass,
Three iron, three of adamantine rock,
Impenetrable, impaled with circling fire,
Yet unconsumed. Before the gates there sat
On either side a formidable shape;[2]

---

5. One of the three Gorgons, women with snaky
hair, scaly bodies, and boar's tusks, the sight of
whose faces changed men to stone.
6. Tantalus, afflicted with a raging thirst, stood in
the middle of a lake, the water of which always
receded when he tried to drink (hence, "tantalize").
7. The Hydra was a serpent whose multiple heads
grew back when severed; the Chimera was a fire-
breathing creature, part lion, part dragon, part
goat.
8. *Satan* in Hebrew means "adversary."
9. Two of the Moluccas, or Spice Islands, mod-

ern Indonesia.
1. The South Pole. "Ethiopian": the Indian
Ocean. "The Cape" is the Cape of Good Hope.
2. The allegorical figures of Sin and Death are
founded on James 1.15: "Then when lust hath
conceived, it bringeth forth sin: and sin, when it is
finished, bringeth forth death." But the incestu-
ous relations of Sin and Death are Milton's own
invention. Physically, Sin is modeled on Virgil's or
Ovid's Scylla, with some touches adopted from
Spenser's Error. Death is a traditional figure,
vague and vast.

The one seemed woman to the waist, and fair,
But ended foul in many a scaly fold
Voluminous and vast, a serpent armed
With mortal sting: about her middle round
A cry° of hellhounds never ceasing barked   *pack*
With wide Cerberean[3] mouths full loud, and rung
A hideous peal: yet, when they list,° would creep,   *wish*
If aught disturbed their noise, into her womb,
And kennel there, yet there still barked and howled,
Within unseen. Far less abhorred than these
Vexed Scylla[4] bathing in the sea that parts
Calabria from the hoarse Trinacrian shore:
Nor uglier follow the night-hag,[5] when called
In secret, riding through the air she comes
Lured with the smell of infant blood, to dance
With Lapland witches, while the laboring° moon   *troubled*
Eclipses at their charms.° The other shape,   *magic*
If shape it might be called that shape had none
Distinguishable in member, joint, or limb,
Or substance might be called that shadow seemed,
For each seemed either; black it stood as night,
Fierce as ten Furies, terrible as hell,
And shook a dreadful dart; what seemed his head
The likeness of a kingly crown had on.
Satan was now at hand, and from his seat
The monster moving onward came as fast
With horrid strides. Hell trembled as he strode.
Th' undaunted Fiend what this might be admired,°   *wondered*
Admired, not feared; God and his Son except,
Created thing naught valued he nor shunned;
And with disdainful look thus first began.
     "Whence and what art thou, execrable shape,
That dar'st, though grim and terrible, advance
Thy miscreated front° athwart my way   *misshapen face*
To yonder gates? Through them I mean to pass,
That be assured, without leave asked of thee:
Retire, or taste° thy folly, and learn by proof,   *experience*
Hell-born, not to contend with Spirits of Heav'n."
     To whom the goblin full of wrath replied:
"Art thou that traitor angel, art thou he,
Who first broke peace in Heav'n and faith, till then
Unbroken, and in proud rebellious arms
Drew after him the third part of Heav'n's sons
Conjured° against the Highest, for which both thou   *sworn together*
And they outcast from God, are here condemned
To waste eternal days in woe and pain?
And reckon'st thou thyself with Spirits of Heav'n,
Hell-doomed, and breath'st defiance here and scorn,

---

3. Like Cerberus, the multiheaded hound of Hell.
4. Circe, out of jealousy, threw poison into the water where Scylla bathed, in the straits between Calabria and Sicily ("Trinacria," next line); the poison caused Scylla to develop a ring of barking, snapping dogs around her waist.
5. Hecate (three syllables), goddess of sorcery. She attends orgies of witches in Lapland (line 665, famous for witchcraft), drawn by the blood of babies sacrificed for the occasion.

Where I reign king, and to enrage thee more,
Thy king and lord? Back to thy punishment,
700 False fugitive, and to thy speed add wings,
Lest with a whip of scorpions I pursue
Thy ling'ring, or with one stroke of this dart
Strange horror seize thee, and pangs unfelt before."
        So spake the grisly terror, and in shape,
705 So speaking and so threat'ning, grew tenfold
More dreadful and deform: on th' other side
Incensed with indignation Satan stood
Unterrified, and like a comet burned
That fires the length of Ophiuchus[6] huge
710 In th' arctic sky, and from his horrid° hair   *bristling*
Shakes pestilence and war. Each at the head
Leveled his deadly aim; their fatal hands
No second stroke intend, and such a frown
Each cast at th' other, as when, two black clouds
715 With Heav'n's artillery fraught,[7] come rattling on
Over the Caspian,[8] then stand front to front
Hov'ring a space, till winds the signal blow
To join their dark encounter in mid-air:
So frowned the mighty combatants, that Hell
720 Grew darker at their frown, so matched they stood;
For never but once more was either like
To meet so great a foe.[9] And now great deeds
Had been achieved, whereof all Hell had rung,
Had not the snaky sorceress that sat
725 Fast by Hell gate, and kept the fatal key,
Ris'n, and with hideous outcry rushed between.
        "O father, what intends thy hand," she cried,
"Against thy only son?[1] What fury O son,
Possesses thee to bend that mortal dart
730 Against thy father's head? And know'st for whom;
For him who sits above and laughs the while
At thee ordained his drudge, to execute
Whate'er his wrath, which he calls justice, bids,
His wrath which one day will destroy ye both."
735   She spake, and at her words the hellish pest
Forbore, then these to her Satan returned.
        "So strange thy outcry, and thy words so strange
Thou interposest, that my sudden hand
Prevented° spares to tell thee yet by deeds   *forestalled*
740 What it intends; till first I know of thee,
What thing thou art, thus double-formed, and why
In this infernal vale first met thou call'st
Me father, and that phantasm call'st my son?
I know thee not, nor ever saw till now
745 Sight more detestable than him and thee."

---

6. A vast northern constellation, "the Serpent
Bearer."
7. Loaded with thunderbolts.
8. The Caspian is a particularly stormy area.

9. I.e., the Son of God.
1. Sin, Death, and Satan, in their various inter-
relations, parody obscenely the relations between
God and the Son, Adam and Eve.

    T' whom thus the portress of Hell gate replied:
"Hast thou forgot me then, and do I seem
Now in thine eye so foul, once deemed so fair
In Heav'n, when at th' assembly, and in sight
Of all the Seraphim with thee combined
In bold conspiracy against Heav'n's King,
All on a sudden miserable pain
Surprised thee, dim thine eyes, and dizzy swum
In darkness, while thy head flames thick and fast
Threw forth, till on the left side op'ning wide,
Likest to thee in shape and count'nance bright,
Then shining heav'nly fair, a goddess armed
Out of thy head I sprung:[2] amazement seized
All th' host of Heav'n; back they recoiled afraid
At first, and called me Sin, and for a sign
Portentous held me; but familiar grown,
I pleased, and with attractive graces won
The most averse, thee chiefly, who full oft
Thyself in me thy perfect image viewing
Becam'st enamored, and such joy thou took'st
With me in secret, that my womb conceived
A growing burden. Meanwhile war arose,
And fields were fought in Heav'n; wherein remained
(For what could else) to our almighty foe
Clear victory, to our part loss and rout
Through all the empyrean: down they fell
Driv'n headlong from the pitch° of Heaven, down   *summit*
Into this deep, and in the general fall
I also; at which time this powerful key
Into my hand was giv'n, with charge to keep
These gates forever shut, which none can pass
Without my op'ning. Pensive here I sat
Alone, but long I sat not, till my womb
Pregnant by thee, and now excessive grown
Prodigious motion felt and rueful throes.
At last this odious offspring whom thou seest
Thine own begotten, breaking violent way
Tore through my entrails, that with fear and pain
Distorted, all my nether shape thus grew
Transformed: but he my inbred enemy
Forth issued, brandishing his fatal dart
Made to destroy: I fled, and cried out 'Death';
Hell trembled at the hideous name, and sighed
From all her caves, and back resounded 'Death.'
I fled, but he pursued (though more, it seems,
Inflamed with lust than rage) and swifter far,
Me overtook his mother all dismayed,
And in embraces forcible and foul
Engend'ring with me, of that rape begot
These yelling monsters that with ceaseless cry
Surround me, as thou saw'st, hourly conceived

---

2. As Athena sprang full grown from the head of Zeus.

And hourly born, with sorrow infinite
To me, for when they list,° into the womb   *wish*
That bred them they return, and howl and gnaw
800 My bowels, their repast; then bursting forth
Afresh with conscious terrors vex me round,
That rest or intermission none I find.
Before mine eyes in opposition sits
Grim Death my son and foe, who sets them on,
805 And me his parent would full soon devour
For want of other prey, but that he knows
His end with mine involved; and knows that I
Should prove a bitter morsel, and his bane,°   *poison*
Whenever that shall be; so fate pronounced.
810 But thou O father, I forewarn thee, shun
His deadly arrow; neither vainly hope
To be invulnerable in those bright arms,
Though tempered heav'nly, for that mortal dint,°   *blow*
Save he who reigns above, none can resist."
815   She finished, and the subtle Fiend his lore°   *lesson*
Soon learned, now milder, and thus answered smooth.
"Dear daughter, since thou claim'st me for thy sire,
And my fair son here show'st me, the dear pledge
Of dalliance had with thee in Heav'n, and joys
820 Then sweet, now sad to mention, through dire change
Befall'n us unforeseen, unthought of, know
I come no enemy, but to set free
From out this dark and dismal house of pain,
Both him and thee, and all the heav'nly host
825 Of Spirits that in our just pretenses° armed   *claims*
Fell with us from on high: from them I go
This uncouth errand[3] sole, and one for all
Myself expose, with lonely steps to tread
Th' unfounded° deep, and through the void immense   *bottomless*
830 To search with wand'ring quest a place foretold
Should be, and, by concurring signs, ere now
Created vast and round, a place of bliss
In the purlieus° of Heav'n, and therein placed   *outskirts*
A race of upstart creatures, to supply
835 Perhaps our vacant room, though more removed,
Lest Heav'n surcharged° with potent multitude   *overcrowded*
Might hap to move new broils:° be this or aught   *controversies*
Than this more secret now designed, I haste
To know, and this once known, shall soon return,
840 And bring ye to the place where thou and Death
Shall dwell at ease, and up and down unseen
Wing silently the buxom° air, embalmed°   *yielding / made fragrant*
With odors; there ye shall be fed and filled
Immeasurably, all things shall be your prey."
845 He ceased, for both seemed highly pleased, and Death
Grinned horrible a ghastly smile, to hear
His famine° should be filled, and blessed his maw°   *ravenous hunger / belly*

3. Unknown journey—a parody of Christ's errand on earth (3.236–65).

Destined to that good hour: no less rejoiced
His mother bad, and thus bespake her sire.
   "The key of this infernal pit by due,
And by command of Heav'n's all-powerful King
I keep, by him forbidden to unlock
These adamantine gates; against all force
Death ready stands to interpose his dart,
Fearless to be o'ermatched by living might.
But what owe I to his commands above
Who hates me, and hath hither thrust me down
Into this gloom of Tartarus profound,
To sit in hateful office here confined,
Inhabitant of Heav'n, and heav'nly-born,
Here in perpetual agony and pain,
With terrors and with clamors compassed round
Of mine own brood, that on my bowels feed?
Thou art my father, thou my author, thou
My being gav'st me; whom should I obey
But thee, whom follow? Thou wilt bring me soon
To that new world of light and bliss, among
The gods who live at ease, where I shall reign
At thy right hand voluptuous,[4] as beseems
Thy daughter and thy darling, without end."
   Thus saying, from her side the fatal key,
Sad instrument of all our woe, she took;
And towards the gate rolling her bestial train,[5]
Forthwith the huge portcullis high up drew,
Which but herself not all the Stygian powers°   *armies of Hell*
Could once have moved; then in the keyhole turns
Th' intrícate wards, and every bolt and bar
Of massy iron or solid rock with ease
Unfastens: on a sudden open fly
With impetuous recoil and jarring sound
Th' infernal doors, and on their hinges grate
Harsh thunder, that the lowest bottom shook
Of Erebus.° She opened, but to shut   *Hell*
Excelled° her power; the gates wide open stood,   *exceeded*
That with extended wings a bannered host
Under spread ensigns° marching might pass through   *flags, standards*
With horse and chariots ranked in loose array;
So wide they stood, and like a furnace mouth
Cast forth redounding° smoke and ruddy flame.   *billowing*
Before their eyes in sudden view appear
The secrets of the hoary° deep, a dark   *ancient*
Illimitable° ocean without bound,   *without limit*
Without dimension, where length, breadth, and height,
And time and place are lost; where eldest Night
And Chaos, ancestors of Nature, hold
Eternal anarchy, amidst the noise
Of endless wars, and by confusion stand.

---

4. As the Son sits at God's right hand, Sin will at
Satan's, a blasphemous parody of the Apostles'

Creed and of *Paradise Lost* 3.250–80.
5. I.e. propelling her yelping offspring.

For Hot, Cold, Moist, and Dry, four champions fierce
Strive here for mastery, and to battle bring
900 Their embryon atoms;[6] they around the flag
Of each his faction, in their several clans,
Light-armed or heavy, sharp, smooth, swift or slow,
Swarm populous, unnumbered as the sands
Of Barca or Cyrene's torrid soil,[7]
905 Levied to side with warring winds, and poise[8]
Their lighter wings. To whom these most adhere,
He rules a moment; Chaos[9] umpire sits,
And by decision more embroils the fray
By which he reigns: next him high arbiter
910 Chance governs all. Into this wild abyss,
The womb of Nature and perhaps her grave,
Of neither sea, nor shore, nor air, nor fire,
But all these in their pregnant causes° mixed   seeds
Confus'dly, and which thus must ever fight,
915 Unless th' Almighty Maker them ordain
His dark materials to create more worlds,
Into this wild abyss the wary Fiend
Stood on the brink of Hell and looked a while,
Pondering his voyage; for no narrow frith°   channel, firth
920 He had to cross. Nor was his ear less pealed°   dinned
With noises loud and ruinous (to compare
Great things with small) than when Bellona[1] storms,
With all her battering engines bent to raze
Some capital city; or less than if this frame°   structure
925 Of Heav'n were falling, and these elements
In mutiny had from her axle torn
The steadfast earth. At last his sail-broad vans°   wings
He spreads for flight, and in the surging smoke
Uplifted spurns the ground, thence many a league
930 As in a cloudy chair ascending rides
Audacious, but that seat soon failing, meets
A vast vacuity: all unawares
Flutt'ring his pennons[2] vain plumb down he drops
Ten thousand fathom deep, and to this hour
935 Down had been falling, had not by ill chance
The strong rebuff° of some tumultuous cloud   counterblast
Instinct° with fire and niter° hurried him   filled / saltpeter
As many miles aloft: that fury stayed,
Quenched in a boggy Syrtis,[3] neither sea,
940 Nor good dry land: nigh foundered° on he fares,   drowned
Treading the crude consistence, half on foot,
Half flying; behoves° him now both oar and sail.   befits
As when a griffin through the wilderness

6. These subatomic qualities combine together in nature to form the four elements, fire, earth, water, and air, but they struggle endlessly in Chaos, where the atoms of these elements remain undeveloped (in "embryo").
7. Cities built on the shifting sands of North Africa.
8. Give weight to. "Levied": both enlisted and raised up.
9. Chaos is both the place where confusion reigns and personified confusion itself.
1. Goddess of war.
2. Useless wings ("pinions").
3. Quicksand in North African gulfs, famous for their shifting sandbars.

With wingèd course o'er hill or moory° dale,   *marshy*
Pursues the Arimaspian, who by stealth
Had from his wakeful custody purloined
The guarded gold:[4] so eagerly the Fiend
O'er bog or steep, through strait, rough, dense, or rare,
With head, hands, wings, or feet pursues his way,
And swims or sinks, or wades, or creeps, or flies:
At length a universal hubbub wild
Of stunning sounds and voices all confused
Borne through the hollow dark assaults his ear
With loudest vehemence: thither he plies,
Undaunted to meet there whatever Power
Or Spirit of the nethermost abyss
Might in that noise reside, of whom to ask
Which way the nearest coast of darkness lies
Bordering on light; when straight behold the throne
Of Chaos, and his dark pavilion spread
Wide on the wasteful deep; with him enthroned
Sat sable-vested Night, eldest of things,
The consort of his reign; and by them stood
Orcus and Ades,[5] and the dreaded name
Of Demogorgon,[6] Rumor next and Chance,
And Tumult and Confusion all embroiled,
And Discord with a thousand various mouths.
   T' whom Satan turning boldly, thus. "Ye Powers
And Spirits of this nethermost abyss,
Chaos and ancient Night, I come no spy,
With purpose to explore or to disturb
The secrets of your realm, but by constraint
Wand'ring this darksome desert, as my way
Lies through your spacious empire up to light,
Alone, and without guide, half lost, I seek
What readiest path leads where your gloomy bounds
Confine with° Heav'n; or if some other place   *border on*
From your dominion won, th' Ethereal King
Possesses lately, thither to arrive
I travel this profound;° direct my course;   *deep pit*
Directed, no mean recompense it brings
To your behoof,° if I that region lost,   *on your behalf*
All usurpation thence expelled, reduce
To her original darkness and your sway
(Which is my present journey)[7] and once more
Erect the standard there of ancient Night;
Yours be th' advantage all, mine the revenge."
   Thus Satan; and him thus the anarch[8] old
With falt'ring speech and visage incomposed°   *disordered*
Answered. "I know thee, stranger, who thou art,
That mighty leading angel, who of late

---

4. Griffins, mythical creatures, half-eagle, half-lion, hoarded gold that was stolen from them by the one-eyed Arimaspians.
5. Latin and Greek names of Pluto, god of Hell.
6. A mysterious deity associated with Fate; Mil-ton elsewhere identifies him with Chaos.
7. The purpose of my present journey.
8. Chaos is not monarch of his realm but, appropriately, "anarch," nonruler.

Made head against Heav'n's King, though overthrown.
I saw and heard, for such a numerous host
Fled not in silence through the frighted deep
995 With ruin upon ruin, rout on rout,
Confusion worse confounded; and Heav'n gates
Poured out by millions her victorious bands
Pursuing. I upon my frontiers here
Keep residence; if all I can will serve,
1000 That little which is left so to defend,
Encroached on still° through our intestine broils°   *constantly / civil wars*
Weak'ning the scepter of old Night: first Hell
Your dungeon stretching far and wide beneath;
Now lately heaven and earth,[9] another world
1005 Hung o'er my realm, linked in a golden chain
To that side Heav'n from whence your legions fell:
If that way be your walk, you have not far;
So much the nearer danger; go and speed;
Havoc and spoil and ruin are my gain."
1010 He ceased; and Satan stayed not to reply,
But glad that now his sea should find a shore,
With fresh alacrity and force renewed
Springs upward like a pyramid of fire
Into the wild expanse, and through the shock
1015 Of fighting elements, on all sides round
Environed wins his way; harder beset
And more endangered, than when Argo passed
Through Bosporus betwixt the justling rocks:[1]
Or when Ulysses on the larboard shunned
1020 Charybdis, and by th' other whirlpool steered.[2]
So he with difficulty and labor hard
Moved on, with difficulty and labor he;
But he once passed, soon after when man fell,
Strange alteration! Sin and Death amain°   *at full speed*
1025 Following his track, such was the will of Heav'n,
Paved after him a broad and beaten way
Over the dark abyss, whose boiling gulf
Tamely endured a bridge of wondrous length
From Hell continued reaching th' utmost orb[3]
1030 Of this frail world; by which the Spirits perverse
With easy intercourse pass to and fro
To tempt or punish mortals, except whom
God and good angels guard by special grace.
But now at last the sacred influence
1035 Of light appears, and from the walls of Heav'n
Shoots far into the bosom of dim Night
A glimmering dawn; here Nature first begins
Her farthest verge,° and Chaos to retire   *threshold*

9. The cosmos, with its own "heaven" (not the empyrean, the Heaven of God and the angels).
1. Jason and his fifty Argonauts, sailing through the Bosporus to the Black Sea in pursuit of the Golden Fleece, had to pass through the Symplegades, or clashing rocks.
2. Homer's Ulysses, sailing where Italy almost touches Sicily, had to pass between Charybdis, a whirlpool, and Scylla, a monster who devoured six of his men (not another whirlpool, as used here).
3. The bridge ends on the outermost sphere of the ten concentric spheres making up the universe.

As from her outmost works a broken foe
With tumult less and with less hostile din,
That° Satan with less toil, and now with ease   *so that*
Wafts on the calmer wave by dubious light
And like a weather-beaten vessel holds°   *makes for*
Gladly the port, though shrouds and tackle torn;
Or in the emptier waste, resembling air
Weighs° his spread wings, at leisure to behold   *balances*
Far off th' empyreal Heav'n, extended wide
In circuit, undetermined square or round,
With opal tow'rs and battlements adorned
Of living sapphire, once his native seat;
And fast by hanging in a golden chain
This pendent world,° in bigness as a star   *universe*
Of smallest magnitude close by the moon.
Thither full fraught with mischievous revenge,
Accursed, and in a cursèd hour, he hies.

From Book 3

[THE INVOCATION, THE COUNCIL IN HEAVEN,
AND THE CONCLUSION OF SATAN'S JOURNEY]

Hail holy Light, offspring of Heav'n firstborn,
Or of th' Eternal coeternal beam
May I express thee unblamed?[1] Since God is light,
And never but in unapproachèd light
Dwelt from eternity, dwelt then in thee,
Bright effluence of bright essence increate.°   *uncreated, eternal*
Or hear'st thou rather[2] pure ethereal stream,
Whose fountain who shall tell? Before the sun,
Before the heavens thou wert, and at the voice
Of God, as with a mantle, didst invest°   *cover*
The rising world of waters dark and deep,
Won from the void and formless infinite.
Thee I revisit now with bolder wing,
Escaped the Stygian pool, though long detained
In that obscure sojourn, while in my flight
Through utter and through middle darkness[3] borne
With other notes than to th' Orphéan lyre[4]
I sung of Chaos and eternal Night,
Taught by the Heav'nly Muse[5] to venture down
The dark descent, and up to reascend,
Though hard and rare: thee I revisit safe,

1. This second proem or invocation (3.1–55) is a hymn to Light, addressed either as the first creature of God or as coeternal with God, with allusion to 1 John 1.5, "God is Light, and in him is no darkness at all."
2. I.e., would you rather be called (a Latinism).
3. Hell is "utter" (i.e., outer) darkness; Chaos is middle darkness.
4. One of the so-called Orphic hymns is "To Night," and Orpheus himself visited the underworld. But Milton's song, Christian and epic, is of a different kind.
5. Urania (though not named until 7.1).

And feel thy sov'reign vital lamp; but thou
Revisit'st not these eyes, that roll in vain
To find thy piercing ray, and find no dawn;
25 So thick a drop serene hath quenched their orbs,
Or dim suffusion[6] veiled. Yet not the more
Cease I to wander where the Muses haunt
Clear spring, or shady grove, or sunny hill,
Smit with the love of sacred song; but chief
30 Thee Sion[7] and the flow'ry brooks beneath
That wash thy hallowed feet, and warbling flow,
Nightly I visit: nor sometimes forget°   always remember
Those other two equaled with me in fate,[8]
So were I equaled with them in renown,
35 Blind Thamyris and blind Maeonides,
And Tiresias and Phineus prophets old,[9]
Then feed on thoughts, that voluntary move
Harmonious numbers;° as the wakeful bird°   verses / nightingale
Sings darkling,° and in shadiest covert hid   in the dark
40 Tunes her nocturnal note. Thus with the year
Seasons return, but not to me returns
Day, or the sweet approach of ev'n or morn,
Or sight of vernal bloom, or summer's rose,
Or flocks, or herds, or human face divine;
45 But cloud instead, and ever-during° dark   everlasting
Surrounds me, from the cheerful ways of men
Cut off, and for the book of knowledge° fair   Book of Nature
Presented with a universal blank
Of nature's works to me expunged and razed,°   erased
50 And wisdom at one entrance quite shut out.
So much the rather thou celestial Light
Shine inward, and the mind through all her powers
Irradiate, there plant eyes, all mist from thence
Purge and disperse, that I may see and tell
55 Of things invisible to mortal sight.
        Now had the Almighty Father from above,
From the pure empyrean° where he sits   Heaven
High throned above all height, bent down his eye,
His own works and their works at once to view:
60 Above him all the sanctities° of Heaven   angels
Stood thick as stars, and from his sight received
Beatitude past utterance; on his right
The radiant image of his glory sat,
His only Son; on earth he first beheld
65 Our two first parents, yet the only two
Of mankind, in the happy garden placed,
Reaping immortal fruits of joy and love,
Uninterrupted joy, unrivaled love
In blissful solitude; he then surveyed

---

6. Cataract—*suffusio nigra*. "Drop serene": *gutta serena*, the medical term for Milton's kind of blindness.
7. The mountain of scriptural inspiration, with its brooks Siloa and Kidron.

8. I.e., blind like me.
9. Thamyris was a blind Thracian poet who lived before Homer; "Maeonides" is an epithet of Homer; Tiresias was the blind prophet of Thebes; Phineus was a blind king and seer (*Aeneid* 3).

Hell and the gulf between, and Satan there
Coasting the wall of Heav'n on this side Night
In the dun° air sublime,° and ready now   *dusky / aloft*
To stoop° with wearied wings, and willing feet   *swoop down*
On the bare outside of this world,° that seemed   *universe*
Firm land embosomed without firmament,°   *atmosphere*
Uncertain which, in ocean or in air.
Him God beholding from his prospect high,
Wherein past, present, future he beholds,
Thus to his only Son foreseeing spake.
   "Only begotten Son, seest thou what rage
Transports our Adversary, whom no bounds
Prescribed, no bars of Hell, nor all the chains
Heaped on him there, nor yet the main° abyss   *vast*
Wide interrupt[1] can hold; so bent he seems
On desperate revenge, that shall redound°   *flow back*
Upon his own rebellious head. And now
Through all restraint broke loose he wings his way
Not far off Heav'n, in the precincts of light,
Directly towards the new-created world,
And man there placed, with purpose to essay°   *try*
If him by force he can destroy, or worse,
By some false guile pervert; and shall pervert;
For man will hearken to his glozing° lies,   *flattering*
And easily transgress the sole command,
Sole pledge of his obedience: so will fall
He and his faithless progeny: whose fault?
Whose but his own? Ingrate, he had of me
All he could have; I made him just and right,
Sufficient to have stood, though free to fall.
Such I created all th' ethereal Powers
And Spirits, both them who stood and them who failed;
Freely they stood who stood, and fell who fell.
Not free, what proof could they have giv'n sincere
Of true allegiance, constant faith or love,
Where only what they needs must do, appeared,
Not what they would? What praise could they receive?
What pleasure I from such obedience paid,
When will and reason (reason also is choice)
Useless and vain, of freedom both despoiled,
Made passive both, had served necessity,
Not me. They therefore as to right belonged,
So were created, nor can justly accuse
Their Maker, or their making, or their fate,
As if predestination overruled
Their will, disposed by absolute decree
Or high foreknowledge; they themselves decreed
Their own revolt, not I: if I foreknew,
Foreknowledge had no influence on their fault,
Which had no less proved certain unforeknown.[2]

---

1. Forming a wide breach between Heaven and Hell.   2. I.e., if I had not foreknown it.

120 So without least impulse or shadow of fate,
    Or aught by me immutably foreseen,
    They trespass, authors to themselves in all
    Both what they judge and what they choose; for so
    I formed them free, and free they must remain,
125 Till they enthrall themselves: I else must change
    Their nature, and revoke the high decree
    Unchangeable, eternal, which ordained
    Their freedom, they themselves ordained their fall.
    The first sort[3] by their own suggestion fell,
130 Self-tempted, self-depraved: man falls deceived
    By the other first: man therefore shall find grace,
    The other none: in mercy and justice both,
    Through Heav'n and earth, so shall my glory excel,
    But mercy first and last shall brightest shine."
135   Thus while God spake, ambrosial° fragrance filled   *fragrant, immortal*
    All Heav'n, and in the blessèd Spirits elect°   *unfallen*
    Sense of new joy ineffable° diffused: *inexpressible*
    Beyond compare the Son of God was seen
    Most glorious, in him all his Father shone
140 Substantially expressed, and in his face
    Divine compassion visibly appeared,
    Love without end, and without measure grace,
    Which uttering thus he to his Father spake.
        "O Father, gracious was that word which closed
145 Thy sov'reign sentence, that man should find grace;
    For which both Heav'n and earth shall high extol
    Thy praises, with th' innumerable sound
    Of hymns and sacred songs, wherewith thy throne
    Encompassed shall resound thee ever blessed.
150 For should man finally be lost, should man
    Thy creature late so loved, thy youngest son
    Fall circumvented thus by fraud, though joined
    With his own folly? That be from thee far,
    That far be from thee, Father, who art judge
155 Of all things made, and judgest only right.[4]
    Or shall the Adversary thus obtain
    His end, and frustrate thine, shall he fulfill
    His malice, and thy goodness bring to naught,
    Or proud return though to his heavier doom,
160 Yet with revenge accomplished, and to Hell
    Draw after him the whole race of mankind,
    By him corrupted? Or wilt thou thyself
    Abolish thy creation, and unmake,
    For him, what for thy glory thou hast made?
165 So should thy goodness and thy greatness both
    Be questioned and blasphemed° without defense."   *profaned*
        To whom the great Creator thus replied.
    "O Son, in whom my soul hath chief delight,

---

3. Satan and his crew.
4. The Son echoes (or rather foreshadows) Abraham pleading with the Lord to spare Sodom: "That be far from thee to do after this manner, to slay the righteous with the wicked . . . that be far from thee: Shall not the Judge of all the earth do right?" (Genesis 18.25).

Son of my bosom, Son who art alone
My Word, my wisdom, and effectual might,[5]
All hast thou spoken as my thoughts are, all
As my eternal purpose hath decreed:
Man shall not quite be lost, but saved who will,
Yet not of will in him, but grace in me
Freely vouchsafed;° once more I will renew   *bestowed*
His lapsèd powers, though forfeit and enthralled
By sin to foul exorbitant desires;
Upheld by me, yet once more he shall stand
On even ground against his mortal foe,
By me upheld, that he may know how frail
His fall'n condition is, and to me owe
All his deliv'rance, and to none but me.
Some I have chosen of peculiar grace
Elect above the rest;[6] so is my will:
The rest shall hear me call, and oft be warned°   *warned about*
Their sinful state, and to appease betimes
Th' incensèd Deity, while offered grace
Invites; for I will clear their senses dark,
What may suffice, and soften stony hearts
To pray, repent, and bring obedience due.
To prayer, repentance, and obedience due,
Though but endeavored with sincere intent,
Mine ear shall not be slow, mine eye not shut.
And I will place within them as a guide
My umpire conscience, whom if they will hear,
Light after light well used they shall attain,[7]
And to the end persisting, safe arrive.
This my long sufferance and my day of grace
They who neglect and scorn, shall never taste;
But hard be hardened, blind be blinded more,
That they may stumble on, and deeper fall;
And none but such from mercy I exclude.
But yet all is not done; man disobeying,
Disloyal breaks his fealty, and sins
Against the high supremacy of Heav'n,
Affecting° Godhead, and so losing all,   *aspiring to*
To expiate his treason hath naught left,
But to destruction sacred and devote,°   *consecrated*
He with his whole posterity must die,
Die he or justice must; unless for him
Some other able, and as willing, pay
The rigid satisfaction, death for death.
Say heav'nly Powers, where shall we find such love,
Which of ye will be mortal to redeem

---

5. God's speech is rhythmic and sometimes rhymed.
6. In this speech, Milton's God rejects the Calvinist doctrine that he had from the beginning predestined the damnation or salvation of each individual soul; he claims rather that grace sufficient for salvation is offered to all, enabling everyone, if they choose to do so, to believe and persevere. He does, however, assert his right to give special grace to some.
7. By using the light of conscience well they will gain more light.

215 Man's mortal crime,[8] and just th' unjust to save,
Dwells in all Heaven charity so dear?"
    He asked, but all the heav'nly choir stood mute,[9]
And silence was in Heav'n; on man's behalf
Patron or intercessor none appeared,
220 Much less that durst upon his own head draw
The deadly forfeiture, and ransom set.
And now without redemption all mankind
Must have been lost, adjudged to death and Hell
By doom severe, had not the Son of God,
225 In whom the fullness dwells of love divine,
His dearest mediation° thus renewed.   *intercession*
    "Father, thy word is passed, man shall find grace;
And shall grace not find means, that finds her way,
The speediest of thy wingèd messengers,
230 To visit all thy creatures, and to all
Comes unprevented,° unimplored, unsought,   *unanticipated*
Happy for man, so coming; he her aid
Can never seek, once dead in sins and lost;
Atonement for himself or offering meet,°   *fitting*
235 Indebted and undone, hath none to bring:
Behold me then, me for him, life for life
I offer, on me let thine anger fall;
Account me man; I for his sake will leave
Thy bosom, and this glory next to thee
240 Freely put off, and for him lastly die
Well pleased, on me let Death wreak all his rage;
Under his gloomy power I shall not long
Lie vanquished; thou hast giv'n me to possess
Life in myself forever, by thee I live,
245 Though now to Death I yield, and am his due
All that of me can die, yet that debt paid,
Thou wilt not leave me in the loathsome grave
His prey, nor suffer my unspotted soul
Forever with corruption there to dwell;
250 But I shall rise victorious, and subdue
My vanquisher, spoiled of his vaunted spoil;
Death his death's wound shall then receive, and stoop
Inglorious, of his mortal sting disarmed.
I through the ample air in triumph high
255 Shall lead Hell captive maugre° Hell, and show   *in spite of*
The powers of darkness bound. Thou at the sight
Pleased, out of Heaven shalt look down and smile,
While by thee raised I ruin[1] all my foes,
Death last, and with his carcass glut the grave:
260 Then with the multitude of my redeemed
Shall enter Heaven long absent, and return,
Father, to see thy face, wherein no cloud
Of anger shall remain, but peace assured,

8. "Mortal" means "human" in line 214, but   2.420–26.
"deadly" in line 215.   1. In the Latin sense, throw down.
9. Compare the devils in the Great Consult,

And reconcilement; wrath shall be no more
Thenceforth, but in thy presence joy entire."
   His words here ended, but his meek aspéct
Silent yet spake, and breathed immortal love
To mortal men, above which only shone
Filial obedience: as a sacrifice
Glad to be offered, he attends the will
Of his great Father. Admiration° seized   *wonder*
All Heav'n, what this might mean, and whither tend
Wond'ring; but soon th' Almighty thus replied:
   "O thou in Heav'n and earth the only peace
Found out for mankind under wrath, O thou
My sole complacence!° well thou know'st how dear   *pleasure, delight*
To me are all my works, nor man the least
Though last created, that for him I spare
Thee from my bosom and right hand, to save,
By losing thee a while, the whole race lost.
Thou therefore whom² thou only canst redeem,
Their nature also to thy nature join;
And be thyself man among men on earth,
Made flesh, when time shall be, of virgin seed,
By wondrous birth: be thou in Adam's room
The head of all mankind, though Adam's son.³
As in him perish all men, so in thee
As from a second root shall be restored,
As many as are restored, without thee none.
His crime makes guilty all his sons; thy merit
Imputed shall absolve them who renounce
Their own both righteous and unrighteous deeds,
And live in thee transplanted, and from thee
Receive new life.⁴ So man, as is most just,
Shall satisfy for man, be judged and die,
And dying rise, and rising with him raise
His brethren, ransomed with his own dear life.
So heav'nly love shall outdo hellish hate,
Giving to death, and dying to redeem,
So dearly to redeem what hellish hate
So easily destroyed, and still destroys
In those who, when they may, accept not grace.
Nor shalt thou by descending to assume
Man's nature, lessen or degrade thine own.
Because thou hast, though throned in highest bliss
Equal to God, and equally enjoying
Godlike fruition,° quitted all to save   *pleasurable possession*
A world from utter loss, and hast been found
By merit more than birthright Son of God,⁵

---

2. The antecedent of "whom" is, loosely construed, the "their nature" that follows it.
3. The Son of God, who long antedates the creation of Adam and who is actually the first created being (3.383), is later incarnated in Jesus Christ; he is called Second Adam and Son of Man by reason of his descent from the first man, Adam. Cf. 1 Corinthians 15.22: "For as in Adam all die, even so in Christ shall all be made alive."
4. The merit of Christ attributed vicariously ("imputed") to human beings frees from original sin those who renounce their own deeds, good and bad, and hope to be saved by faith.
5. A heterodox doctrine, that Christ was Son of God by merit. Compare with Satan (2.5).

310 Found worthiest to be so by being good,
Far more than great or high; because in thee
Love hath abounded more than glory abounds.
Therefore thy humiliation shall exalt
With thee thy manhood also to this throne;
315 Here shalt thou sit incarnate, here shalt reign
Both God and man, Son both of God and man,
Anointed[6] universal King; all power
I give thee, reign forever, and assume
Thy merits; under thee as Head Supreme
320 Thrones, Princedoms, Powers, Dominions[7] I reduce:
All knees to thee shall bow, of them that bide
In Heaven, or earth, or under earth in Hell;
When thou attended gloriously from Heav'n
Shalt in the sky appear, and from thee send
325 The summoning Archangels to proclaim
Thy dread tribunal: forthwith from all winds°   directions
The living, and forthwith the cited° dead   summoned
Of all past ages to the general doom°   judgment
Shall hasten, such a peal shall rouse their sleep.
330 Then all thy saints assembled, thou shalt judge
Bad men and angels, they arraigned° shall sink   accursed
Beneath thy sentence; Hell, her numbers full,
Thenceforth shall be forever shut. Meanwhile
The world shall burn, and from her ashes spring
335 New heav'n° and earth, wherein the just shall dwell,[8]   sky, cosmos
And after all their tribulations long
See golden days, fruitful of golden deeds,
With joy and love triumphing, and fair truth.
Then thou thy regal scepter shalt lay by,
340 For regal scepter then no more shall need,°   be needed
God shall be all in all. But all ye gods,°   angels
Adore him, who to compass all this dies,
Adore the Son, and honor him as me."
   No sooner had th' Almighty ceased, but all
345 The multitude of angels with a shout
Loud as from numbers without number, sweet
As from blest voices, uttering joy, Heav'n rung[9]
With jubilee, and loud hosannas filled
Th' eternal regions: lowly reverent
350 Towards either throne[1] they bow, and to the ground
With solemn adoration down they cast
Their crowns inwove with amarant[2] and gold,
Immortal amarant, a flow'r which once
In Paradise, fast by the Tree of Life
355 Began to bloom, but soon for man's offense
To Heav'n removed where first it grew, there grows,

---

6. In Hebrew "Messiah" means "the anointed one."
7. Orders of angels.
8. Milton's description of the Last Judgment draws on several biblical texts, including Matthew 24.30–31 and 25.31–32; the account of the burning and re-creation of the heavens and earth is from 2 Peter 3.12–13.
9. "Multitude" (line 345) is the subject of the sentence, "rung" the verb, and "Heav'n" the object.
1. Thrones of God and the Son.
2. In Greek, "unfading," a legendary immortal flower.

And flow'rs aloft shading the Fount of Life,
And where the river of bliss through midst of Heav'n
Rolls o'er Elysian[3] flow'rs her amber stream;
With these that never fade the Spirits elect
Bind their resplendent locks inwreathed with beams,
Now in loose garlands thick thrown off, the bright
Pavement that like a sea of jasper shone
Impurpled with celestial roses smiled.
Then crowned again their golden harps they took,
Harps ever tuned, that glittering by their side
Like quivers hung, and with preamble sweet
Of charming symphony they introduce
Their sacred song, and waken raptures high;
No voice exempt,° no voice but well could join   excluded
Melodious part, such concord is in Heav'n.
    Thee Father first they sung omnipotent,
Immutable, immortal, infinite,
Eternal King; thee Author of all being,
Fountain of light, thyself invisible
Amidst the glorious brightness where thou sitt'st
Throned inaccessible, but° when thou shad'st   except
The full blaze of thy beams, and through a cloud
Drawn round about thee like a radiant shrine,[4]
Dark with excessive bright thy skirts appear,
Yet dazzle Heav'n, that brightest Seraphim
Approach not, but with both wings veil their eyes.
Thee next they sang of all creation first,[5]
Begotten Son, Divine Similitude,
In whose conspicuous count'nance, without cloud
Made visible, th' Almighty Father shines,
Whom else no creature can behold;[6] on thee
Impressed th' effulgence of his glory abides,
Transfused on thee his ample spirit rests.
He Heav'n of heavens and all the Powers therein
By thee created, and by thee threw down
Th' aspiring Dominations.[7] Thou that day
Thy Father's dreadful thunder didst not spare,
Nor stop thy flaming chariot wheels, that shook
Heav'n's everlasting frame, while o'er the necks
Thou drov'st of warring angels disarrayed.
Back from pursuit thy Powers° with loud acclaim   angels
Thee only extolled, Son of thy Father's might,
To execute fierce vengeance on his foes,
Not so on man; him through their malice fall'n,
Father of mercy and grace, thou didst not doom
So strictly, but much more to pity incline:
No sooner did thy dear and only Son
Perceive thee purposed not to doom° frail man   judge

---

3. Milton draws freely, for his Christian Heaven, on descriptions of the classical paradisal place, the Elysian Fields.
4. The turn from theological debate to images that evoke a more mystical aspect of God.

5. The Son is not eternal, as in Trinitarian doctrine, but rather, God's first creation.
6. If it were not for the Son who is God's image, no creature could see God.
7. The rebel angels.

405 So strictly, but much more to pity inclined,
He to appease thy wrath, and end the strife
Of mercy and justice in thy face discerned,
Regardless of the bliss wherein he sat
Second to thee, offered himself to die
410 For man's offense. O unexampled love,
Love nowhere to be found less than divine!
Hail Son of God, Savior of men, thy name
Shall be the copious matter of my[8] song
Henceforth, and never shall my harp thy praise
415 Forget, nor from thy Father's praise disjoin.
    Thus they in Heav'n, above the starry sphere,
Their happy hours in joy and hymning spent.
Meanwhile upon the firm opacous° globe   *opaque*
Of this round world, whose first convex divides
420 The luminous inferior orbs, enclosed
From Chaos and th' inroad of Darkness old,
Satan alighted walks:[9] a globe far off
It seemed, now seems a boundless continent
Dark, waste, and wild, under the frown of Night
425 Starless exposed, and ever-threatening storms
Of Chaos blust'ring round, inclement sky;
Save on that side which from the wall of Heav'n
Though distant far some small reflection gains
Of glimmering air less vexed with tempest loud:
430 Here walked the Fiend at large in spacious field.
As when a vulture on Imaus bred,
Whose snowy ridge the roving Tartar bounds,[1]
Dislodging from a region scarce of prey
To gorge the flesh of lambs or yeanling° kids   *newborn*
435 On hills where flocks are fed, flies toward the springs
Of Ganges or Hydaspes, Indian streams;[2]
But in his way lights on the barren plains
Of Sericana, where Chineses drive
With sails and wind their cany wagons light:
440 So on this windy sea of land, the Fiend
Walked up and down alone bent on his prey,
Alone, for other creature in this place
Living or lifeless to be found was none,
None yet, but store hereafter from the earth
445 Up hither like aërial vapors flew
Of all things transitory and vain, when sin
With vanity had filled the works of men:
Both all things vain, and all who in vain things
Built their fond° hopes of glory or lasting fame,   *foolish*
450 Or happiness in this or th' other life;
All who have their reward on earth, the fruits

8. Either Milton here quotes the angels singing as a single chorus, or he associates himself with their song, or both.
9. Satan is on the outermost of the ten concentric spheres that make up the cosmos.
1. Imaus, a ridge of mountains beyond the modern Himalayas, runs north through Asia from modern Afghanistan to the Arctic Circle.
2. Both the Ganges and the Hydaspes (a tributary of the Indus) rise from the mountains of northern India. Sericana (line 438) is a region in northwest China.

Of painful superstition and blind zeal,
Naught seeking but the praise of men, here find
Fit retribution, empty as their deeds;
All th' unaccomplished° works of nature's hand,   *imperfect*
Abortive, monstrous, or unkindly° mixed,   *unnaturally*
Dissolved on earth, fleet° hither, and in vain,   *float*
Till final dissolution, wander here,
Not in the neighboring moon, as some[3] have dreamed;
Those argent° fields more likely habitants,   *silver*
Translated saints,[4] or middle Spirits hold
Betwixt th' angelical and human kind:
Hither of ill-joined sons and daughters born
First from the ancient world those giants came
With many a vain exploit, though then renowned:[5]
The builders next of Babel on the plain
Of Sennaär,[6] and still with vain design
New Babels, had they wherewithal, would build:
Others came single; he who to be deemed
A god, leaped fondly° into Etna flames,   *foolishly*
Empedocles, and he who to enjoy
Plato's Elysium, leaped into the sea,
Cleombrotus, and many more too long,[7]
Embryos and idiots, eremites° and friars   *hermits*
White, black, and gray, with all their trumpery.[8]
Here pilgrims roam, that strayed so far to seek
In Golgotha[9] him dead, who lives in Heav'n;
And they who to be sure of paradise
Dying put on the weeds° of Dominic,   *garments*
Or in Franciscan think to pass disguised;[1]
They pass the planets seven, and pass the fixed,
And that crystalline sphere whose balance weighs
The trepidation talked, and that first moved;[2]
And now Saint Peter at Heav'n's wicket seems
To wait them with his keys, and now at foot
Of Heav'n's ascent they lift their feet, when lo
A violent crosswind from either coast
Blows them transverse ten thousand leagues awry
Into the devious° air. Then might ye see   *erratic*
Cowls, hoods, and habits[3] with their wearers tossed

---

3. Milton's Paradise of Fools (named in line 496) was inspired by Ariosto's Limbo of Vanity in *Orlando Furioso* (Book 34, lines 73ff.); Milton's region is reserved for deluded victims of misplaced devotion, chiefly Roman Catholics.
4. Holy men like Enoch and Elijah, transported to Heaven while yet alive. (Genesis 5.24; 2 Kings 2.11–12).
5. Giants, born of unnatural marriages between the "sons of God" and the daughters of men (Genesis 6.4), are creatures unkindly mixed.
6. Shinar, the plain of Babel (Genesis 11.2–9); the Tower of Babel is an emblem of human pride and folly.
7. I.e., it would take too long to name them. Both Empedocles and Cleombrotus foolishly carried piety to the point of suicide.
8. Religious paraphernalia. The white friars are

Carmelites; the black, Dominicans; and the gray, Franciscans.
9. Place where Christ was crucified.
1. Some try to trick God into granting them salvation by wearing on their deathbeds the garb of various religious orders.
2. Milton follows their souls through the spheres of the moon and sun, the five then-known planets, the fixed stars, and the sphere responsible for the "trepidation" (a periodic corrective shudder of the cosmos), up to the primum mobile, or prime mover. The next step seems to be the empyreal Heaven.
3. The dress of religious orders, together with (next lines) saints' relics, rosary beads, various kinds of pardon for sins, and papal decrees ("bulls").

And fluttered into rags; then relics, beads,
Indulgences, dispenses, pardons, bulls,
The sport of winds: all these upwhirled aloft
Fly o'er the backside° of the world far off   *rump*
495 Into a limbo large and broad, since called
The Paradise of Fools, to few unknown
Long after, now unpeopled, and untrod;
All this dark globe the Fiend found as he passed,
And long he wandered, till at last a gleam
500 Of dawning light turned thitherward in haste
His traveled° steps; far distant he descries   *travel-weary*
Ascending by degrees° magnificent   *steps*
Up to the wall of Heaven a structure high,
At top whereof, but far more rich appeared
505 The work as of a kingly palace gate
With frontispiece° of diamond and gold   *pediment*
Embellished; thick with sparkling orient° gems *lustrous*
The portal shone, inimitable on earth,
By model, or by shading pencil drawn.
510 The stairs were such as whereon Jacob saw
Angels ascending and descending, bands
Of guardians bright, when he from Esau fled
To Padan-Aram in the field of Luz,
Dreaming by night under the open sky,
515 And waking cried, "This is the gate of Heav'n."[4]
Each stair mysteriously was meant, nor stood
There always, but drawn up to Heav'n sometimes
Viewless,° and underneath a bright sea flowed *invisible*
Of jasper, or of liquid pearl, whereon
520 Who after came from earth, sailing arrived,
Wafted by angels, or flew o'er the lake
Rapt in a chariot drawn by fiery steeds.[5]
The stairs were then let down, whether to dare
The Fiend by easy ascent, or aggravate
525 His sad exclusion from the doors of bliss.
Direct against which opened from beneath,
Just o'er the blissful seat of Paradise,
A passage down to th' earth, a passage wide,[6]
Wider by far than that of aftertimes
530 Over Mount Zion, and, though that were large,
Over the Promised Land to God so dear,
By which, to visit oft those happy tribes,
On high behests his angels to and fro
Passed frequent, and his eye with choice° regard *discriminating*
535 From Paneas the fount of Jordan's flood
To Beërsaba, where the Holy Land
Borders on Egypt and the Arabian shore;[7]
So wide the op'ning seemed, where bounds were set

---

4. The story of Jacob's vision is summarized from Genesis 28.1–19; the stairs of the ladder (next line) allegorically ("mysteriously") represent stages of spiritual growth.
5. Elijah was wafted to heaven in a chariot.

6. A passage through the crystalline spheres, otherwise impenetrable.
7. From Paneas (or Dan) in northern Palestine to Beersaba, or Beersheba, near the Egyptian border—the entire land of Israel.

To darkness, such as bound the ocean wave.
Satan from hence now on the lower stair
That scaled by steps of gold to Heaven gate
Looks down with wonder at the sudden view
Of all this world at once. As when a scout
Through dark and desert ways with peril gone
All night; at last by break of cheerful dawn
Obtains° the brow of some high-climbing hill,   *gains*
Which to his eye discovers unaware
The goodly prospect of some foreign land
First seen, or some renowned metropolis
With glistering spires and pinnacles adorned,
Which now the rising sun gilds with his beams.
Such wonder seized, though after Heaven seen,
The Spirit malign, but much more envy seized
At sight of all this world beheld so fair.
Round he surveys, and well might, where he stood
So high above the circling canopy
Of night's extended shade; from eastern point
Of Libra to the fleecy star that bears
Andromeda far off Atlantic seas[8]
Beyond th' horizon; then from pole to pole
He views in breadth, and without longer pause
Down right into the world's first region throws
His flight precipitant, and winds with ease
Through the pure marble° air his oblique way   *sparkling*
Amongst innumerable stars, that shone
Stars distant, but nigh hand seemed other worlds,
Or other worlds they seemed, or happy isles,
Like those Hesperian gardens famed of old,
Fortunate fields, and groves and flow'ry vales,[9]
Thrice happy isles, but who dwelt happy there
He stayed not to inquire: above them all
The golden sun in splendor likest Heaven
Allured his eye: thither his course he bends
Through the calm firmament;° but up or down   *sky*
By center, or eccentric, hard to tell,
Or longitude,[1] where the great luminary
Aloof the vulgar constellations thick,
That from his lordly eye keep distance due,
Dispenses light from far; they as they move
Their starry dance in numbers that compute
Days, months, and years, towards his all-cheering lamp
Turn swift their various motions, or are turned
By his magnetic beam, that gently warms
The universe, and to each inward part
With gentle penetration, though unseen,
Shoots invisible virtue° even to the deep: *influence, strength*
So wondrously was set his station bright.

8. In the zodiac, Libra is diametrically opposite Aries, or the Ram ("the fleecy star"), which seems to carry the constellation Andromeda on its back. 9. The gardens of the Hesperides and the "fortu- nate isles" of Greek mythology, classical versions of paradise, lay far out in the Atlantic. 1. The passage leaves open whether the sun or the earth is at the center of the cosmos.

Summary　Landing on the bright orb of the sun, Satan disguises himself as a youthful cherub and approaches the solar guardian, the archangel Uriel. Pretending interest in the new great works of God, he gets directions to Earth and Adam's bower, then spirals down and lands on Mount Niphates (in modern Iran), overlooking the site of Paradise.

From Book 4

[SATAN'S ENTRY INTO PARADISE; ADAM AND EVE IN THEIR BOWER]

O for that warning voice, which he who saw
Th' Apocalypse, heard cry in Heaven aloud,
Then when the Dragon, put to second rout,
Came furious down to be revenged on men,
5 "Woe to the inhabitants on earth!"[1] that now,
While time was, our first parents had been warned
The coming of their secret foe, and scaped
Haply° so scaped his mortal° snare; for now　　　　　　　　*perhaps / deadly*
Satan, now first inflamed with rage, came down,
10 The tempter ere° th' accuser of mankind,　　　　　　　　*before being*
To wreak° on innocent frail man his loss　　　　　　　　*avenge*
Of that first battle, and his flight to Hell:
Yet not rejoicing in his speed, though bold,
Far off and fearless, nor with cause to boast,
15 Begins his dire attempt, which nigh the birth
Now rolling, boils in his tumultuous breast,
And like a devilish engine back recoils
Upon himself; horror and doubt distract
His troubled thoughts, and from the bottom stir
20 The Hell within him, for within him Hell
He brings, and round about him, nor from Hell
One step no more than from himself can fly
By change of place: now conscience wakes despair
That slumbered, wakes the bitter memory
25 Of what he was, what is, and what must be
Worse; of worse deeds worse sufferings must ensue.
Sometimes towards Eden which now in his view
Lay pleasant, his grieved look he fixes sad,
Sometimes towards Heav'n and the full-blazing sun,
30 Which now sat high in his meridian tow'r:[2]
Then much revolving,° thus in sighs began.　　　　　　　　*pondering*
　　"O thou that with surpassing glory crowned,[3]
Look'st from thy sole dominion like the god
Of this new world: at whose sight all the stars
35 Hide their diminished heads; to thee I call,
But with no friendly voice, and add thy name
O sun, to tell thee how I hate thy beams

---

1. John of Patmos, in Revelation 12.3–12, hears such a cry during a second war in Heaven, between the Dragon and the angels.
2. At midday, the height of noon.

3. Milton's nephew, Edward Phillips, said that this soliloquy was written "several years before the poem was begun," and was intended to begin a drama on the topic, *Adam Unparadised.*

That bring to my remembrance from what state
I fell, how glorious once above thy sphere;
Till pride and worse ambition threw me down
Warring in Heav'n against Heav'n's matchless King:
Ah wherefore! he deserved no such return
From me, whom he created what I was
In that bright eminence, and with his good
Upbraided[4] none, nor was his service hard.
What could be less than to afford him praise,
The easiest recompense, and pay him thanks,
How due! yet all his good proved ill in me,
And wrought but malice; lifted up so high
I 'sdained° subjection, and thought one step higher   disdained
Would set me highest, and in a moment quit°   pay
The debt immense of endless gratitude,
So burthensome still° paying, still to owe;   always
Forgetful what from him I still received,
And understood not that a grateful mind
By owing owes not, but still pays, at once
Indebted and discharged; what burden then?
O had his powerful destiny ordained
Me some inferior angel, I had stood
Then happy; no unbounded hope had raised
Ambition. Yet why not? some other Power°   angel
As great might have aspired, and me though mean
Drawn to his part; but other Powers as great
Fell not, but stand unshaken, from within
Or from without, to all temptations armed.
Hadst thou[5] the same free will and power to stand?
Thou hadst: whom hast thou then or what to accuse,
But Heav'n's free love dealt equally to all?
Be then his love accursed, since love or hate,
To me alike, it deals eternal woe.
Nay cursed be thou; since against his thy will
Chose freely what it now so justly rues.
Me miserable![6] which way shall I fly
Infinite wrath, and infinite despair?
Which way I fly is Hell; myself am Hell;[7]
And in the lowest deep a lower deep
Still threat'ning to devour me opens wide,
To which the Hell I suffer seems a Heav'n.
O then at last relent! is there no place
Left for repentance, none for pardon left?
None left but by submission; and that word
Disdain forbids me, and my dread of shame
Among the Spirits beneath, whom I seduced
With other promises and other vaunts
Than to submit, boasting I could subdue
Th' Omnipotent. Ay me, they little know

---

4. Reproached (James 1.5).
5. Compare Satan's address to himself here with Adam's soliloquy in parallel circumstances (10.758ff.).
6. A Latinism, *me miserum!*
7. Compare Satan's earlier claim that "the mind is its own place" (1.254).

How dearly I abide° that boast so vain,   *pay the penalty far*
Under what torments inwardly I groan:
While they adore me on the throne of Hell,
90 With diadem and scepter high advanced
The lower still I fall, only supreme
In misery; such joy ambition finds.
But say I could repent and could obtain
By act of grace[8] my former state; how soon
95 Would heighth recall high thoughts, how soon unsay
What feigned submission swore: ease would recant
Vows made in pain, as violent° and void.   *forced*
For never can true reconcilement grow
Where wounds of deadly hate have pierced so deep:
100 Which would but lead me to a worse relapse,
And heavier fall: so should I purchase dear
Short intermission bought with double smart.
This knows my punisher; therefore as far
From granting he, as I from begging peace:
105 All hope excluded thus, behold instead
Of us outcast, exiled, his new delight,
Mankind created, and for him this world.
So farewell hope, and with hope farewell fear,
Farewell remorse: all good to me is lost;
110 Evil be thou my good; by thee at least
Divided empire with Heav'n's King I hold
By thee, and more than half perhaps will reign;
As man ere long, and this new world shall know."
  Thus while he spake, each passion dimmed his face
115 Thrice changed with pale,° ire, envy, and despair, *pallor*
Which marred his borrowed visage, and betrayed
Him counterfeit, if any eye beheld.
For heav'nly minds from such distempers foul
Are ever clear. Whereof he soon aware,
120 Each perturbation smoothed with outward calm,
Artificer of fraud; and was the first
That practiced falsehood under saintly show,
Deep malice to conceal, couched° with revenge: *hidden*
Yet not enough had practiced to deceive
125 Uriel once warned; whose eye pursued him down
The way he went, and on th' Assyrian mount°   *Niphates*
Saw him disfigured, more than could befall
Spirit of happy sort: his gestures fierce
He marked and mad demeanor, then alone,
130 As he supposed, all unobserved, unseen.
  So on he fares, and to the border comes
Of Eden, where delicious Paradise,[9]
Now nearer, crowns with her enclosure green,
As with a rural mound the champaign head° *open summit*
135 Of a steep wilderness, whose hairy sides
With thicket overgrown, grotesque[1] and wild,

8. The technical term for a formal pardon. land of Eden.
9. Paradise is a delightful ("delicious") garden 1. Characterized by interwoven, tangled vines
on top of a steep hill situated in the east of the and branches.

Access denied; and overhead up grew
Insuperable heighth of loftiest shade,
Cedar, and pine, and fir, and branching palm,
A sylvan scene, and as the ranks ascend
Shade above shade, a woody theater[2]
Of stateliest view. Yet higher than their tops
The verdurous wall of Paradise up sprung:
Which to our general sire gave prospect large
Into his nether empire neighboring round.
And higher than that wall a circling row
Of goodliest trees loaden with fairest fruit,
Blossoms and fruits at once of golden hue
Appeared, with gay enameled° colors mixed: *bright*
On which the sun more glad impressed his beams
Than in fair evening cloud, or humid bow,°   *rainbow*
When God hath show'red the earth; so lovely seemed
That landscape: and of pure now purer air[3]
Meets his approach, and to the heart inspires°   *infuses*
Vernal delight and joy, able to drive°   *drive out*
All sadness but despair: now gentle gales
Fanning their odoriferous° wings dispense   *fragrance-bearing*
Native perfumes, and whisper whence they stole
Those balmy spoils. As when to them who sail
Beyond the Cape of Hope,° and now are past   *Cape of Good Hope*
Mozambic, off at sea northeast winds blow
Sabean odors from the spicy shore
Of Araby the Blest,[4] with such delay
Well pleased they slack their course, and many a league
Cheered with the grateful° smell old Ocean smiles.   *pleasing*
So entertained those odorous sweets the Fiend
Who came their bane,° though with them better pleased   *poison*
Than Asmodeus with the fishy fume,
That drove him, though enamored, from the spouse
Of Tobit's son, and with a vengeance sent
From Media post to Egypt, there fast bound.[5]
    Now to th'ascent of that steep savage° hill   *wooded, wild*
Satan had journeyed on, pensive and slow;
But further way found none, so thick entwined,
As one continued brake,° the undergrowth   *thicket*
Of shrubs and tangling bushes had perplexed
All path of man or beast that passed that way:
One gate there only was, and that looked east
On th' other side: which when th' arch-felon saw
Due entrance he disdained, and in contempt,
At one slight bound high overleaped all bound
Of hill or highest wall, and sheer within
Lights on his feet. As when a prowling wolf,
Whom hunger drives to seek new haunt for prey,

2. As if in a Greek amphitheater, the trees are set row on row.
3. The air becomes still purer.
4. *Arabia Felix* (modern Yemen). "Sabean": the biblical Sheba.
5. The Apocryphal book of Tobit tells of Tobias, Tobit's son, who married Sara and avoided the fate of her previous seven husbands (killed on their wedding night by the demon Asmodeus) by following the instructions of the angel Raphael and making a fishy smell to drive him off; Asmodeus then fled to Egypt, where Raphael bound him.

185 Watching where shepherds pen their flocks at eve
In hurdled cotes° amid the field secure,   *pens of woven reeds*
Leaps o'er the fence with ease into the fold:
Or as a thief bent to unhoard the cash
Of some rich burgher, whose substantial doors,
190 Cross-barred and bolted fast, fear no assault,
In at the window climbs, or o'er the tiles;
So clomb° this first grand thief into God's fold: *climbed*
So since into his church lewd hirelings[6] climb.
Thence up he flew, and on the Tree of Life,
195 The middle tree and highest there that grew,
Sat like a cormorant;[7] yet not true life
Thereby regained, but sat devising death
To them who lived; nor on the virtue° thought   *power*
Of that life-giving plant, but only used
200 For prospect,° what well used had been the pledge   *as a lookout*
Of immortality. So little knows
Any, but God alone, to value right
The good before him, but perverts best things
To worst abuse, or to their meanest use.
205   Beneath him with new wonder now he views
To all delight of human sense exposed
In narrow room nature's whole wealth, yea more,
A heav'n on earth: for blissful Paradise
Of God the garden was, by him in the east
210 Of Eden planted; Eden stretched her line
From Auran eastward to the royal tow'rs
Of great Seleucia, built by Grecian kings,
Or where the sons of Eden long before
Dwelt in Telassar:[8] in this pleasant soil
215 His far more pleasant garden God ordained;
Out of the fertile ground he caused to grow
All trees of noblest kind for sight, smell, taste;
And all amid them stood the Tree of Life,
High eminent, blooming ambrosial° fruit   *divinely fragrant*
220 Of vegetable gold; and next to life
Our death the Tree of Knowledge grew fast by,
Knowledge of good bought dear by knowing ill.
Southward through Eden went a river large,[9]
Nor changed his course, but through the shaggy hill
225 Passed underneath engulfed, for God had thrown
That mountain as his garden mold° high raised   *rich earth*
Upon the rapid current, which through veins
Of porous earth with kindly° thirst up drawn,   *natural*
Rose a fresh fountain, and with many a rill
230 Watered the garden; thence united fell
Down the steep glade, and met the nether flood,

---

6. Base men interested only in money; Milton would have clergymen not paid by required tithes or by the state, to ensure their purity of motive.
7. A sea bird, noted for gluttony.
8. Auran is the province of Hauran on the eastern border of Israel. Selucia, a powerful city on the

Tigris, near modern Baghdad, was founded by one of Alexander's generals ("built by Grecian kings"). Telassar is another Near Eastern kingdom.
9. The Tigris (identified at 9.71) flowed under the hill.

Which from his darksome passage now appears,
And now divided into four main streams,
Runs diverse, wand'ring many a famous realm
And country whereof here needs no account,
But rather to tell how, if art could tell,
How from that sapphire fount the crispèd° brooks,   *wavy, rippling*
Rolling on orient pearl and sands of gold,
With mazy error[1] under pendent shades
Ran nectar, visiting each plant, and fed
Flow'rs worthy of Paradise which not nice° art   *fastidious*
In beds and curious knots, but nature boon°   *bounteous*
Poured forth profuse on hill and dale and plain,
Both where the morning sun first warmly smote
The open field, and where the unpierced shade
Embrowned° the noontide bow'rs. Thus was this place,   *darkened*
A happy rural seat of various view,[2]
Groves whose rich trees wept odorous gums and balm,
Others whose fruit burnished with golden rind
Hung amiable,° Hesperian fables true,[3]   *lovely*
If true, here only, and of delicious taste:
Betwixt them lawns, or level downs,° and flocks   *uplands*
Grazing the tender herb, were interposed,
Or palmy hillock, or the flow'ry lap
Of some irriguous° valley spread her store,   *well-watered*
Flow'rs of all hue, and without thorn the rose:
Another side, umbrageous° grots and caves   *shady*
Of cool recess, o'er which the mantling° vine   *enveloping*
Lays forth her purple grape, and gently creeps
Luxuriant; meanwhile murmuring waters fall
Down the slope hills, dispersed, or in a lake,
That to the fringèd bank with myrtle crowned,
Her crystal mirror holds, unite their streams.
The birds their choir apply; airs,[4] vernal airs,
Breathing the smell of field and grove, attune
The trembling leaves, while universal Pan[5]
Knit° with the Graces and the Hours in dance   *clasping hands*
Led on th' eternal spring. Not that fair field
Of Enna, where Proserpine gathering flow'rs
Herself a fairer flow'r by gloomy Dis
Was gathered, which cost Ceres all that pain
To seek her through the world; nor that sweet grove
Of Daphne by Orontes, and th' inspired
Castalian spring, might with this Paradise
Of Eden strive;[6] nor that Nyseian isle
Girt with the river Triton, where old Cham,

---

1. From Latin *errare*, wandering.
2. Like a country estate, with a variety of prospects.
3. These were real golden apples, by contrast to those feigned golden apples of the Hesperides, fabled paradisal islands in the Western Ocean.
4. Both breezes and melodies. "Their choir apply": practice their songs.
5. The god of all nature—*pan* in Greek means "all."
6. Milton compares Paradise with famous beauty spots of antiquity. Enna in Sicily was a lovely meadow from which Proserpine was kidnapped by "gloomy Dis" (i.e., Pluto); her mother Ceres sought her throughout the world. The grove of Daphne, near Antioch and the Orontes River in the Near East, had a spring called "Castalia" after the Muses' fountain near Parnassus.

Whom Gentiles Ammon call and Libyan Jove,
Hid Amalthea and her florid° son _wine-flushed_
Young Bacchus from his stepdame Rhea's eye;[7]
280 Nor where Abassin kings their issue guard,
Mount Amara,[8] though this by some supposed
True Paradise under the Ethiop line° _equator_
By Nilus'° head, enclosed with shining rock, _Nile's_
A whole day's journey high, but wide remote
285 From this Assyrian garden,° where the Fiend _Eden_
Saw undelighted all delight, all kind
Of living creatures new to sight and strange:
   Two of far nobler shape erect and tall,
Godlike erect, with native honor clad
290 In naked majesty seemed lords of all,
And worthy seemed, for in their looks divine
The image of their glorious Maker shone,
Truth, wisdom, sanctitude severe and pure,
Severe but in true filial freedom placed;
295 Whence true authority in men;[9] though both
Not equal, as their sex not equal seemed;
For contemplation he and valor formed,
For softness she and sweet attractive grace,
He for God only, she for God in him:[1]
300 His fair large front° and eye sublime declared _forehead_
Absolute rule; and hyacinthine[2] locks
Round from his parted forelock manly hung
Clust'ring, but not beneath his shoulders broad:
She as a veil down to the slender waist
305 Her unadorned golden tresses wore
Disheveled, but in wanton° ringlets waved _unrestrained_
As the vine curls her tendrils,[3] which implied
Subjection, but required° with gentle sway,° _requested / persuasion_
And by her yielded, by him best received,
310 Yielded with coy° submission, modest pride, _shyly reserved_
And sweet reluctant amorous delay.
Nor those mysterious parts were then concealed,
Then was not guilty shame, dishonest° shame _unchaste_
Of nature's works, honor dishonorable,
315 Sin-bred, how have ye troubled all mankind
With shows instead, mere shows of seeming pure,
And banished from man's life his happiest life,
Simplicity and spotless innocence.
So passed they naked on, nor shunned the sight
320 Of God or angel, for they thought no ill:
So hand in hand they passed, the loveliest pair

7. The isle of Nysa in the river Triton in Tunisia was where Ammon (an Egyptian god, identified with Cham, the son of Noah) hid Bacchus, his child by Amalthea (who later became the god of wine), away from the eyes of his wife Rhea.
8. Atop Mount Amara, the "Abassin" (Abyssinian) king had a splendid palace in a paradisal garden.
9. This phrase underscores Milton's idea that true freedom involves obedience to natural supe-

riors (i.e., God).
1. The phrase has as its context 1 Corinthians 11.3: "The head of every man is Christ; and the head of the woman is the man."
2. A classical metaphor for hair curled in the form of hyacinth petals, and perhaps also implying dark or flowing.
3. Eve's hair is curly, abundant, not subjected to rigid control, like the vegetation in Paradise.

That ever since in love's embraces met,
Adam the goodliest man of men since born
His sons, the fairest of her daughters Eve.
Under a tuft of shade that on a green
Stood whispering soft, by a fresh fountain side
They sat them down, and after no more toil
Of their sweet gard'ning labor than sufficed
To recommend cool Zephyr,[4] and made ease
More easy, wholesome thirst and appetite
More grateful, to their supper fruits they fell,
Nectarine° fruits which the compliant boughs   *sweet as nectar*
Yielded them, sidelong as they sat recline
On the soft downy bank damasked with flow'rs:
The savory pulp they chew, and in the rind
Still as they thirsted scoop the brimming stream;
Nor gentle purpose,° nor endearing smiles   *conversation*
Wanted,° nor youthful dalliance as beseems   *lacked*
Fair couple, linked in happy nuptial league,
Alone as they. About them frisking played
All beasts of th' earth, since wild, and of all chase°   *game animals*
In wood or wilderness, forest or den;
Sporting the lion ramped,° and in his paw   *stood on hind legs*
Dandled the kid; bears, tigers, ounces,° pards°   *lynxes / leopards*
Gamboled before them; th' unwieldy elephant
To make them mirth used all his might, and wreathed
His lithe proboscis;° close the serpent sly   *trunk*
Insinuating,° wove with Gordian twine   *writhing, twisting*
His braided train,[5] and of his fatal guile
Gave proof unheeded; others on the grass
Couched, and now filled with pasture gazing sat,
Or bedward ruminating:° for the sun   *chewing the cud*
Declined was hasting now with prone° career   *sinking*
To th' Ocean Isles,° and in th' ascending scale   *the Azores*
Of Heav'n the stars that usher evening rose:
When Satan still in gaze, as first he stood,
Scarce thus at length failed speech recovered sad.
   "O Hell! what do mine eyes with grief behold,
Into our room of bliss thus high advanced
Creatures of other mold, earth-born perhaps,
Not Spirits, yet to heav'nly Spirits bright
Little inferior; whom my thoughts pursue
With wonder, and could love, so lively shines
In them divine resemblance, and such grace
The hand that formed them on their shape hath poured.
Ah gentle pair, ye little think how nigh
Your change approaches, when all these delights
Will vanish and deliver ye to woe,
More woe, the more your taste is now of joy;
Happy, but for so happy° ill secured   *such happiness*
Long to continue, and this high seat your heav'n

---

4. I.e., to make a cool breeze welcome.   convoluted as the Gordian knot that Alexander
5. Checkered body. "Gordian twine": cords as   the Great had to cut with his sword.

Ill fenced for Heav'n to keep out such a foe
As now is entered; yet no purposed foe
To you whom I could pity thus forlorn
375 Though I unpitied: league with you I seek,
And mutual amity so strait,° so close,   *intimate*
That I with you must dwell, or you with me
Henceforth; my dwelling haply° may not please   *perhaps*
Like this fair Paradise, your sense, yet such
380 Accept your Maker's work; he gave it me,
Which I as freely give; Hell shall unfold,
To entertain you two, her widest gates,
And send forth all her kings; there will be room,
Not like these narrow limits, to receive
385 Your numerous offspring; if no better place,
Thank him who puts me loath to this revenge
On you who wrong me not for° him who wronged.   *in place of*
And should I at your harmless innocence
Melt, as I do, yet public reason just,
390 Honor and empire with revenge enlarged
By conquering this new world, compels me now
To do what else though damned I should abhor."⁶
      So spake the Fiend, and with necessity,
The tyrant's plea, excused his devilish deeds.
395 Then from his lofty stand on that high tree
Down he alights among the sportful herd
Of those four-footed kinds, himself now one,
Now other, as their shape served best his end
Nearer to view his prey, and unespied
400 To mark what of their state he more might learn
By word or action marked: about them round
A lion now he stalks with fiery glare,
Then as a tiger, who by chance hath spied
In some purlieu° two gentle fawns at play,   *outskirts of a forest*
405 Straight° couches close, then rising changes oft   *at once*
His couchant watch, as one who chose his ground
Whence rushing he might surest seize them both
Gripped in each paw: when Adam first of men
To first of women Eve thus moving speech
410 Turned him all ear to hear new utterance flow:
      "Sole partner and sole° part of all these joys,   *chief*
Dearer thyself than all; needs must the Power
That made us, and for us this ample world
Be infinitely good, and of his good
415 As liberal and free as infinite,
That raised us from the dust and placed us here
In all this happiness, who at his hand
Have nothing merited, nor can perform
Aught whereof he hath need, he who requires
420 From us no other service than to keep
This one, this easy charge, of all the trees

---

6. Satan's excuse—reason of state, public interest, empire, etc.—is called "the tyrant's plea" in line 394.

In Paradise that bear delicious fruit
So various, not to taste that only Tree
Of Knowledge, planted by the Tree of Life,
So near grows death to life, whate'er death is,
Some dreadful thing no doubt; for well thou know'st
God hath pronounced it death to taste that Tree,
The only sign of our obedience left
Among so many signs of power and rule
Conferred upon us, and dominion giv'n
Over all other creatures that possess
Earth, air, and sea. Then let us not think hard
One easy prohibition, who enjoy
Free leave so large to all things else, and choice
Unlimited of manifold delights:
But let us ever praise him, and extol
His bounty, following our delightful task
To prune these growing plants, and tend these flow'rs,
Which were it toilsome, yet with thee were sweet."
    To whom thus Eve replied. "O thou for whom
And from whom I was formed flesh of thy flesh,
And without whom am to no end, my guide
And head, what thou hast said is just and right.
For we to him indeed all praises owe,
And daily thanks, I chiefly who enjoy
So far the happier lot, enjoying thee
Preeminent by so much odds,° while thou   *advantage*
Like consort to thyself canst nowhere find.
That day I oft remember, when from sleep
I first awaked, and found myself reposed°   *resting*
Under a shade on flowers, much wond'ring where
And what I was, whence thither brought, and how.
Not distant far from thence a murmuring sound
Of waters issued from a cave and spread
Into a liquid plain, then stood unmoved
Pure as th' expanse of Heav'n; I thither went
With unexperienced thought, and laid me down
On the green bank, to look into the clear
Smooth lake, that to me seemed another sky.
As I bent down to look, just opposite,
A shape within the wat'ry gleam appeared
Bending to look on me, I started back,
It started back, but pleased I soon returned,
Pleased it returned as soon with answering looks
Of sympathy and love; there I had fixed
Mine eyes till now, and pined with vain° desire,[7]   *futile*
Had not a voice thus warned me, 'What thou seest,
What there thou seest fair creature is thyself,
With thee it came and goes: but follow me,
And I will bring thee where no shadow stays°   *hinders*
Thy coming, and thy soft embraces, he

---

7. Eve's experience reprises (but with significant differences) the story of Narcissus, who fell in love with his own reflection and was transformed into a flower.

Whose image thou art, him thou shall enjoy
Inseparably thine, to him shalt bear
Multitudes like thyself, and thence be called
475 Mother of human race': what could I do,
But follow straight° invisibly thus led?   *at once*
Till I espied thee, fair indeed and tall,
Under a platan,° yet methought less fair,   *plane tree*
Less winning soft, less amiably mild,
480 Than that smooth wat'ry image; back I turned,
Thou following cried'st aloud, 'Return fair Eve,
Whom fli'st thou? Whom thou fli'st, of him thou art,
His flesh, his bone; to give thee being I lent
Out of my side to thee, nearest my heart
485 Substantial life, to have thee by my side
Henceforth an individual° solace dear;   *inseparable, distinct*
Part of my soul I seek thee, and thee claim
My other half': with that thy gentle hand
Seized mine, I yielded, and from that time see
490 How beauty is excelled by manly grace
And wisdom, which alone is truly fair."
    So spake our general mother, and with eyes
Of conjugal attraction unreproved,
And meek surrender, half embracing leaned
495 On our first father, half her swelling breast
Naked met his under the flowing gold
Of her loose tresses hid: he in delight
Both of her beauty and submissive charms
Smiled with superior love, as Jupiter
500 On Juno smiles, when he impregns° the clouds   *impregnates*
That shed May flowers; and pressed her matron lip
With kisses pure: aside the Devil turned
For envy, yet with jealous leer malign
Eyed them askance, and to himself thus plained.°   *complained*
505   "Sight hateful, sight tormenting! thus these two
Imparadised in one another's arms
The happier Eden, shall enjoy their fill
Of bliss on bliss, while I to Hell am thrust,
Where neither joy nor love, but fierce desire,
510 Among our other torments not the least,
Still° unfulfilled with pain of longing pines;   *always*
Yet let me not forget what I have gained
From their own mouths; all is not theirs it seems:
One fatal tree there stands of Knowledge called,
515 Forbidden them to taste: knowledge forbidden?
Suspicious, reasonless. Why should their Lord
Envy° them that? Can it be sin to know,   *begrudge*
Can it be death? And do they only stand
By ignorance, is that their happy state,
520 The proof of their obedience and their faith?
O fair foundation laid whereon to build
Their ruin! Hence I will excite their minds
With more desire to know, and to reject
Envious commands, invented with design

To keep them low whom knowledge might exalt
Equal with gods; aspiring to be such,
They taste and die: what likelier can ensue?
But first with narrow search I must walk round
This garden, and no corner leave unspied;
A chance, but chance[8] may lead where I may meet
Some wand'ring Spirit of Heav'n, by fountain side,
Or in thick shade retired, from him to draw
What further would be learnt. Live while ye may,
Yet happy pair; enjoy, till I return,
Short pleasures, for long woes are to succeed."
   So saying, his proud step he scornful turned,
But with sly circumspection, and began
Through wood, through waste, o'er hill, o'er dale his roam.°   *act of wandering*
Meanwhile in utmost longitude, where heav'n°   *the sky*
With earth and ocean meets, the setting sun
Slowly descended, and with right aspéct
Against the eastern gate of Paradise
Leveled his evening rays.[9] It was a rock
Of alabaster,[1] piled up to the clouds,
Conspicuous far, winding with one ascent
Accessible from earth, one entrance high;
The rest was craggy cliff, that overhung
Still as it rose, impossible to climb.
Betwixt these rocky pillars Gabriel[2] sat
Chief of th' angelic guards, awaiting night;
About him exercised heroic games
Th' unarmèd youth of Heav'n, but nigh at hand
Celestial armory, shields, helms, and spears
Hung high with diamond flaming, and with gold.
Thither came Uriel, gliding through the even
On a sunbeam, swift as a shooting star
In autumn thwarts° the night, when vapors fired   *passes across*
Impress the air, and shows the mariner
From what point of his compass to beware
Impetuous winds:[3] he thus began in haste.
   "Gabriel, to thee thy course by lot hath giv'n
Charge and strict watch that to this happy place
No evil thing approach or enter in;
This day at height of noon came to my sphere
A Spirit, zealous, as he seemed, to know
More of th' Almighty's works, and chiefly man
God's latest image: I described° his way   *descried, observed*
Bent all on speed, and marked his airy gait;°   *path*
But in the mount that lies from Eden north,
Where he first lighted, soon discerned his looks
Alien from Heav'n, with passions foul obscured:
Mine eye pursued him still, but under shade°   *trees*

8. An opportunity, even if only by luck.
9. Setting in the west, the sun struck the eastern gate from the inside, at a ninety-degree angle.
1. White, translucent marble veined with colors.
2. In Hebrew, "strength of God." A tradition (cf. 1 Enoch 20.7) gave Gabriel charge of Paradise.
3. Shooting stars were thought to indicate by the direction of their fall the source of oncoming storms. "Vapors fired": heat lightning.

Lost sight of him; one of the banished crew
I fear, hath ventured from the deep, to raise
575 New troubles; him thy care must be to find."
      To whom the winged warrior thus returned:
"Uriel, no wonder if thy perfect sight,
Amid the sun's bright circle where thou sitt'st,
See far and wide. In at this gate none pass
580 The vigilance here placed, but such as come
Well known from Heav'n; and since meridian hour°   *noon*
No creature thence: if Spirit of other sort,
So minded, have o'erleaped these earthy bounds
On purpose, hard thou know'st it to exclude
585 Spiritual substance with corporeal bar.
But if within the circuit of these walks,
In whatsoever shape he lurk, of whom
Thou tell'st, by morrow dawning I shall know."
      So promised he, and Uriel to his charge
590 Returned on that bright beam, whose point now raised
Bore him slope downward to the sun now fall'n
Beneath th' Azorès; whether the prime orb,
Incredible how swift, had thither rolled
Diurnal,° or this less volúble° earth   *daily / swift-turning*
595 By shorter flight to th' east,[4] had left him there
Arraying with reflected purple and gold
The clouds that on his western throne attend.
Now came still evening on, and twilight gray
Had in her sober livery all things clad;
600 Silence accompanied, for beast and bird,
They to their grassy couch, these to their nests
Were slunk, all but the wakeful nightingale;
She all night long her amorous descant° sung;   *melody*
Silence was pleased: now glowed the firmament
605 With living sapphires: Hesperus[5] that led
The starry host, rode brightest, till the moon
Rising in clouded majesty, at length
Apparent° queen unveiled her peerless light,   *clearly seen*
And o'er the dark her silver mantle threw.
610   When Adam thus to Eve: "Fair consort, th' hour
Of night, and all things now retired to rest
Mind us of like repose, since God hath set
Labor and rest, as day and night to men
Successive, and the timely dew of sleep
615 Now falling with soft slumbrous weight inclines
Our eyelids; other creatures all day long
Rove idle unemployed, and less need rest;
Man hath his daily work of body or mind
Appointed, which declares his dignity,
620 And the regard of Heav'n on all his ways;
While other animals unactive range,

---

4. Here and elsewhere Milton leaves open the
question of whether the sun moves around the
earth, or vice versa.

5. Called Venus when it appears in the evening
sky.

And of their doings God takes no account.
Tomorrow ere fresh morning streak the east
With first approach of light, we must be ris'n,
And at our pleasant labor, to reform
Yon flow'ry arbors, yonder alleys green,
Our walk at noon, with branches overgrown,
That mock our scant manuring,° and require   *cultivating*
More hands than ours to lop their wanton° growth: *luxuriant*
Those blossoms also, and those dropping gums,
That lie bestrown unsightly and unsmooth,
Ask riddance,° if we mean to tread with ease;"   *need to be cleared*
Meanwhile, as nature wills, night bids us rest."
  To whom thus Eve with perfect beauty adorned.
"My author and disposer, what thou bidd'st
Unargued I obey; so God ordains,
God is thy law, thou mine: to know no more
Is woman's happiest knowledge and her praise.
With thee conversing I forget all time.
All seasons° and their change, all please alike.   *times of day*
Sweet[6] is the breath of morn, her rising sweet,
With charm[7] of earliest birds; pleasant the sun
When first on this delightful land he spreads
His orient° beams, on herb, tree, fruit, and flow'r, *lustrious, eastern*
Glist'ring with dew; fragrant the fertile earth
After soft showers; and sweet the coming on
Of grateful evening mild, then silent night
With this her solemn bird° and this fair moon,   *the nightingale*
And these the gems of heav'n, her starry train:
But neither breath of morn when she ascends
With charm of earliest birds, nor rising sun
On this delightful land, nor herb, fruit, flow'r,
Glist'ring with dew, nor fragrance after showers,
Nor grateful evening mild, nor silent night
With this her solemn bird, nor walk by moon,
Or glittering starlight without thee is sweet.
But wherefore all night long shine these, for whom
This glorious sight, when sleep hath shut all eyes?"
  To whom our general ancestor replied.
"Daughter of God and man, accomplished[8] Eve,
Those have their course to finish, round the earth,
By morrow evening, and from land to land
In order, though to nations yet unborn,
Minist'ring light prepared, they set and rise;
Lest total darkness should by night regain
Her old possession, and extinguish life
In nature and all things, which these soft° fires   *agreeable*
Not only enlighten, but with kindly° heat   *natural, benevolent*
Of various influence foment° and warm,   *foster*

---

6. With this embedded lyric, beginning here, Eve displays her literary talents in an elegant love song, sonnetlike and replete with striking rhetorical figures of circularity and repetition.

7. Blended singing of many birds.

8. Having many talents and achievements; perfect, complete.

670 Temper or nourish, or in part shed down
Their stellar virtue on all kinds that grow
On earth, made hereby apter to receive
Perfection from the sun's more potent ray.[9]
These then, though unbeheld in deep of night,
675 Shine not in vain, nor think, though men were none,
That heav'n would want° spectators, God want praise;   *lack*
Millions of spiritual creatures walk the earth
Unseen, both when we wake, and when we sleep:
All these with ceaseless praise his works behold
680 Both day and night: how often from the steep
Of echoing hill or thicket have we heard
Celestial voices to the midnight air,
Sole, or responsive each to other's note
Singing their great Creator: oft in bands
685 While they keep watch, or nightly rounding walk,
With heav'nly touch of instrumental sounds
In full harmonic number joined, their songs
Divide[1] the night, and lift our thoughts to Heaven."
    Thus talking hand in hand alone they passed
690 On to their blissful bower; it was a place
Chos'n by the sov'reign Planter, when he framed°   *fashioned*
All things to man's delightful use; the roof
Of thickest covert was inwoven shade
Laurel and myrtle, and what higher grew
695 Of firm and fragrant leaf; on either side
Acanthus, and each odorous bushy shrub
Fenced up the verdant wall; each beauteous flow'r,
Iris all hues, roses, and jessamine°   *jasmine*
Reared high their flourished° heads between, and wrought   *flowering*
700 Mosaic; underfoot the violet,
Crocus, and hyacinth with rich inlay
Broidered the ground, more colored than with stone
Of costliest emblem:° other creature here   *inlaid work*
Beast, bird, insect, or worm durst enter none,
705 Such was their awe of man. In shadier bower
More sacred and sequestered,° though but feigned,   *secluded*
Pan or Silvanus never slept, nor nymph,
Nor Faunus[2] haunted. Here in close recess
With flowers, garlands, and sweet-smelling herbs
710 Espousèd Eve decked first her nuptial bed,
And heav'nly choirs the hymenean° sung,   *wedding song*
What day the genial[3] angel to our sire
Brought her in naked beauty more adorned,
More lovely than Pandora, whom the gods
715 Endowed with all their gifts, and O too like
In sad event,° when to the unwiser son   *outcome*
Of Japhet brought by Hermes, she ensnared
Mankind with her fair looks, to be avenged

---

9. The stars were thought to have their own occult influence, and also to moderate that of the sun.
1. Mark the watches of the night; also, perform musical "divisions," elaborate melodic passages.
2. Forest and field divinities of classical mythology.
3. Presiding over marriage and generation.

On him who had stole Jove's authentic fire.[4]
    Thus at their shady lodge arrived, both stood,
Both turned, and under open sky adored
The God that made both sky, air, earth, and heav'n
Which they beheld, the moon's resplendent globe
And starry pole:° "Thou also mad'st the night,   *sky*
Maker Omnipotent, and thou the day,
Which we in our appointed work employed
Have finished happy in our mutual help
And mutual love, the crown of all our bliss
Ordained by thee, and this delicious place
For us too large, where thy abundance wants
Partakers, and uncropped falls to the ground.
But thou hast promised from us two a race
To fill the earth, who shall with us extol
Thy goodness infinite, both when we wake,
And when we seek, as now, thy gift of sleep."
    This said unanimous, and other rites
Observing none, but adoration pure
Which God likes best,[5] into their inmost bow'r
Handed° they went; and eased° the putting off   *hand in hand / spared*
These troublesome disguises which we wear,
Straight side by side were laid, nor turned I ween°   *surmise*
Adam from his fair spouse, nor Eve the rites
Mysterious[6] of connubial love refused:
Whatever hypocrites austerely talk
Of purity and place and innocence,
Defaming as impure what God declares
Pure, and commands to some, leaves free to all.
Our Maker bids increase,[7] who bids abstain
But our destroyer, foe to God and man?
Hail wedded Love, mysterious law, true source
Of human offspring, sole propriety°   *private property*
In Paradise of all things common else.
By thee adulterous lust was driv'n from men
Among the bestial herds to range, by thee
Founded in reason, loyal, just, and pure,
Relations dear, and all the charities°   *loves*
Of father, son, and brother first were known.
Far be it, that I should write thee sin or blame,
Or think thee unbefitting holiest place,
Perpetual fountain of domestic sweets,
Whose bed is undefiled and chaste pronounced,
Present, or past, as saints and patriarchs used.[8]

---

4. Pandora (the name means "all gifts") was an artificial woman, molded of clay, bestowed by the gods on Epimetheus, brother of Prometheus (who angered Jove by stealing fire from heaven). She brought a box that foolish Epimetheus opened, releasing all the ills of the human race, leaving only hope inside. The brothers were sons of Iapetos, whom Milton identifies with Japhet, Noah's third son. The Eve-Pandora parallel was often noted.

5. Like many Puritans, Milton objected to set forms of prayer, so Adam and Eve pray spontane-ously (therefore sincerely), but also, paradoxically, together. Their prayer develops variations on Psalm 104.20–24.

6. Ephesians 5.32 calls the union of man and woman a "mystery" paralleling that of Christ and the church.

7. Genesis 1.28: "Be fruitful and multiply, and replenish the earth."

8. Throughout history ("present or past"), Old and New Testament worthies have "used" matrimony as a noble estate.

Here Love his golden shafts employs,[9] here lights
His constant lamp, and waves his purple wings,
765 Reigns here and revels; not in the bought smile
Of harlots, loveless, joyless, unendeared,
Casual fruition, nor in court amours,
Mixed dance, or wanton masque, or midnight ball,
Or serenade, which the starved° lover sings   deprived
770 To his proud fair, best quitted with disdain.
These lulled by nightingales embracing slept,
And on their naked limbs the flow'ry roof
Show'red roses, which the morn repaired.° Sleep on,   replaced
Blest pair; and O yet happiest if ye seek
775 No happier state, and know to know no more.[1]

Summary   Fulfilling his promise to Uriel, Gabriel divides his night watch into
search parties, assigning Ithuriel and Zephon to guard closely the bower of Adam
and Eve. They find Satan in the bower, whispering in the ear of the sleeping Eve, and
bring him before Gabriel. A battle impends, but is averted by a heavenly signal, and
Satan flees out of Paradise.

From Book 5

[EVE'S DREAM; TROUBLE IN PARADISE]

Now Morn her rosy steps in th' eastern clime
Advancing, sowed the earth with orient pearl,°   sparkling dew
When Adam waked, so customed, for his sleep
Was aery light, from pure digestion bred,
5 And temperate vapors bland,° which th' only sound   gentle, balmy
Of leaves and fuming rills, Aurora's fan,[1]
Lightly dispersed, and the shrill matin° song   morning
Of birds on every bough; so much the more
His wonder was to find unwakened Eve
10 With tresses discomposed, and glowing cheek,
As through unquiet rest: he on his side
Leaning half-raised, with looks of cordial° love   heartfelt
Hung over her enamored, and beheld
Beauty, which whether waking or asleep,
15 Shot forth peculiar° graces; then with voice   its own
Mild, as when Zephyrus on Flora[2] breathes,
Her hand soft touching, whispered thus: "Awake
My fairest, my espoused, my latest found,
Heav'n's last best gift, my ever new delight,
20 Awake, the morning shines, and the fresh field
Calls us, we lose the prime, to mark how spring

9. The "golden shafts" (arrows) of Cupid produce true love, his lead-tipped arrows, hate.
1. Know enough to be content with what you
know.

1. Rustling leaves and streams ("rills") stirred by
Aurora, goddess of the dawn.
2. Zephyrus is god of the gentle west wind, Flora
goddess of flowers.

Our tended plants, how blows° the citron grove,   *blooms*
What drops the myrrh, and what the balmy reed,°   *balsam*
How nature paints her colors, how the bee
Sits on the bloom extracting liquid sweet."³
    Such whispering waked her, but with startled eye
On Adam, whom embracing, thus she spake:
    "O sole in whom my thoughts find all repose,
My glory, my perfection, glad I see
Thy face, and morn returned, for I this night,
Such night till this I never passed, have dreamed,
If dreamed, not as I oft am wont,° of thee,   *accustomed*
Works of day past, or morrow's next design,
But of offense and trouble, which my mind
Knew never till this irksome night. Methought
Close at mine ear one called me forth to walk
With gentle voice, I thought it thine; it said,
'Why sleep'st thou Eve? Now is the pleasant time,
The cool, the silent, save where silence yields
To the night-warbling bird, that now awake
Tunes sweetest his love-labored song; now reigns
Full-orbed the moon, and with more pleasing light
Shadowy sets off the face of things, in vain,
If none regard; heav'n wakes with all his eyes,°   *stars*
Whom to behold but thee, nature's desire,
In whose sight all things joy, with ravishment
Attracted by thy beauty still° to gaze.'   *continually*
I rose as at thy call, but found thee not;
To find thee I directed then my walk;
And on, me thought, alone I passed through ways
That brought me on a sudden to the tree
Of interdicted knowledge: fair it seemed,
Much fairer to my fancy than by day:
And as I wond'ring looked, beside it stood
One shaped and winged like one of those from Heav'n
By us oft seen; his dewy locks distilled
Ambrosia;° on that tree he also gazed;   *heavenly fragrance*
And 'O fair plant,' said he, 'with fruit surcharged,°   *overburdened*
Deigns none to ease thy load and taste thy sweet,
Nor god,° nor man? Is knowledge so despised?   *angel*
Or envy, or what reserve forbids to taste?⁴
Forbid who will, none shall from me withhold
Longer thy offered good, why else set here?'
This said he paused not, but with vent'rous arm
He plucked, he tasted; me damp horror chilled
At such bold words vouched with° a deed so bold: *backed by*
But he thus overjoyed, 'O fruit divine,
Sweet of thyself, but much more sweet thus cropped,
Forbidden here, it seems, as only fit

---

3. Adam sings a morning love song (*aubade*) to
Eve, which works variations on Song of Solomon
2.10–12: "Rise up, my love, my fair one, and come
away. . . . The flowers appear on the earth; the
time of the singing of birds is come." Compare

Satan's serenade (5.38–47), a parody of Adam's
aubade and the Song of Solomon. "Prime" (line
21): first hour of the day.
4. I.e., does envy or some other barrier ("reserve")
forbid your being tasted?

70 For gods, yet able to make gods of men:
And why not gods of men, since good, the more
Communicated, more abundant grows,
The author not impaired,° but honored more?   injured, diminished
Here, happy creature, fair angelic Eve,
75 Partake thou also; happy though thou art,
Happier thou may'st be, worthier canst not be:
Taste this, and be henceforth among the gods
Thyself a goddess, not to earth confined,
But sometimes in the air, as we, sometimes
80 Ascend to Heav'n, by merit thine, and see
What life the gods live there, and such live thou.'
So saying, he drew nigh, and to me held,
Even to my mouth of that same fruit held part
Which he had plucked; the pleasant savory smell
85 So quickened appetite, that I, methought,
Could not but taste. Forthwith up to the clouds
With him I flew, and underneath beheld
The earth outstretched immense, a prospect wide
And various: wond'ring at my flight and change
90 To this high exaltation: suddenly
My guide was gone, and I, methought, sunk down,
And fell asleep; but O how glad I waked
To find this but a dream!" Thus Eve her night
Related, and thus Adam answered sad.°   gravely, soberly
95 "Best image of myself and dearer half,
The trouble of thy thoughts this night in sleep
Affects me equally; nor can I like
This uncouth° dream, of evil sprung I fear;   strange, unpleasant
Yet evil whence? In thee can harbor none,
100 Created pure. But know that in the soul
Are many lesser faculties⁵ that serve
Reason as chief; among these fancy next
Her office holds; of all external things,
Which the five watchful senses represent,
105 She forms imaginations,° aery shapes,   images
Which reason joining or disjoining, frames
All what we affirm or what deny, and call
Our knowledge or opinion; then retires
Into her private cell when nature rests.
110 Oft in her absence mimic fancy wakes
To imitate her; but misjoining shapes,
Wild work produces oft, and most in dreams,
Ill matching words and deeds long past or late.
Some such resemblances methinks I find
115 Of our last evening's talk in this thy dream,⁶
But with addition strange; yet be not sad.
Evil into the mind of god⁷ or man

5. Adam's explanation of the dream (lines 100–
116) summarizes the orthodox faculty psychology and dream theory of Milton's time—one
among many kinds of knowledge with which
unfallen man was endowed.

6. Adam recalls his own words in 4.411–39.
7. Probably "angel" as elsewhere, but perhaps
God, whose omniscience must encompass knowledge of evil as well as good.

May come and go, so unapproved,[8] and leave
No spot or blame behind: which gives me hope
That what in sleep thou didst abhor to dream,
Waking thou never wilt consent to do.
Be not disheartened then, nor cloud those looks
That wont to be° more cheerful and serene   *usually are*
Than when fair morning first smiles on the world,
And let us to our fresh employments rise
Among the groves, the fountains, and the flow'rs
That open now their choicest bosomed smells
Reserved from night, and kept for thee in store."
    So cheered he his fair spouse, and she was cheered,
But silently a gentle tear let fall
From either eye, and wiped them with her hair;
Two other precious drops that ready stood,
Each in their crystal sluice, he ere they fell
Kissed as the gracious signs of sweet remorse
And pious awe, that feared to have offended.

Summary Before going to work at their rural tasks, Adam and Eve recite their spontaneous morning prayers. God, seeing and pitying their unprotected innocence, dispatches Raphael to warn them of approaching dangers. The affable archangel enters the bower just about noontime and is promptly invited to join the midday meal, an invitation that he gladly accepts.

[A VISIT WITH THE ANGEL. THE SCALE OF NATURE]

* * * So to the sylvan lodge
They came, that like Pomona's[9] arbor smiled
With flow'rets decked° and fragrant smells; but Eve   *covered*
Undecked, save with herself more lovely fair
Than wood nymph, or the fairest goddess feigned
Of three that in Mount Ida naked strove,[1]
Stood to entertain her guest from Heav'n; no veil
She needed, virtue-proof,° no thought infirm   *armored in virtue*
Altered her cheek. On whom the Angel "Hail"
Bestowed, the holy salutation used
Long after to blest Mary, second Eve.[2]
    "Hail mother of mankind, whose fruitful womb
Shall fill the world more numerous with thy sons
Than with these various fruits the trees of God
Have heaped this table." Raised of grassy turf
Their table was, and mossy seats had round,
And on her ample square from side to side
All autumn piled, though spring and autumn here
Danced hand in hand. A while discourse they hold;

---

8. If not willed (approved of) or not acted on (put to the proof).
9. The Roman goddess of fruit trees.
1. On Mount Ida, Venus, Juno, and Minerva "strove" naked for the title of the most beautiful; Paris awarded the prize (the apple of discord) to

Venus, which led to the rape of Helen and the Trojan War.
2. Cf. the angel's words to Mary announcing that she would bear a son, Jesus (Luke 1.28): "Hail, thou that art highly favored, the Lord is with thee: blessed art thou among women."

No fear lest dinner cool; when thus began
Our author:° "Heav'nly stranger, please to taste   *forefather*
These bounties which our Nourisher, from whom
All perfect good unmeasured out, descends,
400 To us for food and for delight hath caused
The earth to yield; unsavory food perhaps
To spiritual natures; only this I know,
That one Celestial Father gives to all."
     To whom the angel: "Therefore what he gives
405 (Whose praise be ever sung) to man in part
Spiritual, may of° purest Spirits be found   *by*
No ingrateful food: and food alike those pure
Intelligential substances require[3]
As doth your rational; and both contain
410 Within them every lower faculty
Of sense, whereby they hear, see, smell, touch, taste,
Tasting concoct, digest, assimilate,[4]
And corporeal to incorporeal turn.
For know, whatever was created, needs
415 To be sustained and fed; of elements
The grosser feeds the purer, earth the sea,
Earth and the sea feed air, the air those fires
Ethereal, and as lowest first the moon;
Whence in her visage round those spots, unpurged
420 Vapors not yet into her substance turned.[5]
Nor doth the moon no nourishment exhale
From her moist continent to higher orbs.[6]
The sun that light imparts to all, receives
From all his alimental° recompense   *nourishing*
425 In humid exhalations, and at even
Sups with the ocean:[7] though in Heav'n the trees
Of life ambrosial° fruitage bear, and vines   *divinely fragrant*
Yield nectar,[8] though from off the boughs each morn
We brush mellifluous° dews, and find the ground   *honey-flowing*
430 Covered with pearly grain; yet God hath here
Varied his bounty so with new delights,
As may compare with Heaven; and to taste
Think not I shall be nice."° So down they sat,   *fastidious, finicky*
And to their viands fell, nor seemingly°   *in show*
435 The angel, nor in mist, the common gloss°   *explanation*
Of theologians, but with keen dispatch
Of real hunger, and concoctive° heat   *digestive*
To transubstantiate;[9] what redounds, transpires

---

3. Milton's angels ("intelligential substances") require real food, even as "rational" men do (see below, lines 430–38). As a monist (believer that all creation is of one matter), Milton denied the more common (dualistic) idea that angels are pure spirit, holding instead that they are of a very highly refined material substance.

4. Three stages in digestion.

5. Here Raphael describes lunar spots as still-undigested vapors (in keeping with his exposition of the universal need of nourishment); in 1.287–91 he referred to moon spots in Galileo's terms, as landscape features.

6. A double negative: the moon does exhale such nourishment to other planets.

7. Milton explains evaporation as the sun dining off moisture exhaled from the oceans.

8. Ambrosia is the food and nectar the drink of the classical gods; Milton adds "pearly grain" (line 430), like the manna showered on the Israelites in the desert (Exodus 16.14–15).

9. In common theological use, transubstantiation is the Roman Catholic doctrine that the bread and wine of the Eucharist become the body and blood of Christ. Milton vigorously denied that doctrine, but he describes the angels' trans-

Through Spirits with ease; nor wonder, if by fire
Of sooty coal the empiric° alchemist   *experimental*
Can turn, or holds it possible to turn
Metals of drossiest ore to perfect gold
As from the mine. Meanwhile at table Eve
Ministered naked, and their flowing cups
With pleasant liquors crowned.° O innocence   *filled to the brim*
Deserving Paradise! if ever, then,
Then had the Sons of God excuse t' have been
Enamored at that sight,[1] but in those hearts
Love unlibidinous° reigned, nor jealousy   *without lust*
Was understood, the injured lover's hell.
    Thus when with meats and drinks they had sufficed,
Not burdened nature, sudden mind arose
In Adam, not to let th' occasion pass
Given him by this great conference to know
Of things above his world, and of their being
Who dwell in Heav'n, whose excellence he saw
Transcend his own so far, whose radiant forms
Divine effulgence,° whose high power so far   *shining forth*
Exceeded human, and his wary speech
Thus to th' empyreal minister he framed:
    "Inhabitant with God, now know I well
Thy favor, in this honor done to man,
Under whose lowly roof thou hast vouchsafed
To enter and these earthly fruits to taste,
Food not of angels, yet accepted so,
As that more willingly thou couldst not seem
At Heav'n's high feasts t' have fed: yet what compare?"
    To whom the wingèd hierarch° replied: *authority*
"O Adam, one Almighty is, from whom
All things proceed, and up to him return,
If not depraved from good, created all
Such to perfection, one first matter all,[2]
Endued with various forms, various degrees
Of substance, and in things that live, of life;
But more refined, more spiritous, and pure,
As nearer to him placed or nearer tending
Each in their several active spheres assigned,
Till body up to spirit work, in bounds
Proportioned to each kind.[3] So from the root
Springs lighter the green stalk, from thence the leaves
More airy, last the bright consummate flow'r

---

forming of earthly food into their more highly refined spiritual substance as a true transubstantiation. The excess ("what redounds") is exhaled ("transpires") through angelic pores.
1. Genesis 6.2 tells of the marriage of "the daughters of men" with "the sons of God," usually identified as sons of Seth, but a patristic tradition (alluded to here) identifies them as angels.
2. Milton held that the universe was created out of Chaos, not out of nothing: the primal matter of Chaos had its origin in God, who subsequently created all things from that matter (see 7.168–73, 210–42). This materialist "monism" denies sharp distinctions between angels and men, spirit and matter: all beings are of one substance, of varying degrees of refinement and life.
3. Milton's version of the chain of being qualifies natural hierarchy by allowing for movement up or down; beings may become increasingly spiritual ("more spiritous") or increasingly gross (as the rebel angels do), depending on their moral choices—"nearer tending."

Spirits odorous breathes:[4] flow'rs and their fruit
Man's nourishment, by gradual scale sublimed°   *purified*
To vital spirits aspire, to animal,
485 To intellectual, give both life and sense,
Fancy° and understanding, whence the soul   *imagination*
Reason receives, and reason is her being,
Discursive, or intuitive;[5] discourse
Is oftest yours, the latter most is ours,
490 Differing but in degree, of kind the same.
Wonder not then, what God for you saw good
If I refuse not, but convert, as you,
To proper° substance; time may come when men   *our own*
With angels may participate, and find
495 No inconvenient diet, nor too light fare:
And from these corporal nutriments perhaps
Your bodies may at last turn all to spirit,
Improved by tract° of time, and winged ascend   *passage*
Ethereal as we, or may at choice
500 Here or in heav'nly paradises dwell;
If ye be found obedient, and retain
Unalterably firm his love entire
Whose progeny you are. Meanwhile enjoy
Your fill what happiness this happy state
505 Can comprehend, incapable° of more."   *unable to contain*
    To whom the patriarch of mankind replied:
"O favorable Spirit, propitious guest,
Well hast thou taught the way that might direct
Our knowledge, and the scale of nature set
510 From center to circumference, whereon
In contemplation of created things
By steps we may ascend to God. * * *

Summary   After this mingled explanation and warning, Raphael, by way of
emphasizing the danger that threatens Adam and Eve, enters upon the story of
Satan's revolt and fall. Satan, pretending that God's exaltation of the Son was an
offense to angelic dignity, persuaded the angels under his command—a third of the
heavenly host—to go off and set up a camp in the north of Heaven. When he revealed
his rebellious purpose, however, one of these angels refused to embrace it. The seraph Abdiel, though scorned by Satan and all his legions, denounced the rebellion and
returned, heroically alone, to the ranks of God's followers.

Book 6 Summary   Continuing the story of the war in Heaven, Raphael
describes the assembling of the armies and a first skirmish in which Satan is both
insulted and wounded by Abdiel. After the first day's battle, the evil angels retire

4. The plant figure—root, stalk, leaves, flowers,
and fruit—provides an illustration of the dyna-
mism of being in the universe and further
explains why Raphael can eat the fruit. Such
food is then transformed (next lines) into various
orders of "spirits"—"vital," "animal," and "intellectual" (fluids in the blood that sustain life, sensation, motion, and finally intellect and its
functions, "fancy," "understanding," and "rea-

son"), indicating that the soul is also material.
5. Traditionally, on the dualist assumption that
angels are pure spirit and humans a combination
of matter and spirit, angelic intuition (immediate apprehension of truth) was absolutely distinguished from human "discourse" of reason
(arguing from premises to conclusions). Milton,
denying that assumption, makes the distinction
only relative, a matter of "degree" (line 490).

discomfited; but overnight Satan invents cannon, with which, on the second day, the good angels are put to some disorder. In the fury of the fight, however, they pull up mountains by the roots and bury the cannon beneath them; thus the issue remains inconclusive. On the third day, God withdraws all His armies and sends the Son alone into battle; the Son drives His enemies over the wall of Heaven, and after falling nine days through Chaos they are swallowed up in Hell.

From Book 7

[THE INVOCATION]

Descend from Heav'n Urania,[1] by that name
If rightly thou art called, whose voice divine
Following, above th' Olympian hill I soar,
Above the flight of Pegasean wing.[2]
The meaning, not the name I call: for thou
Nor of the muses nine, nor on the top
Of old Olympus dwell'st, but heav'nly born
Before the hills appeared, or fountain flowed,
Thou with eternal Wisdom[3] didst converse,°   *associate*
Wisdom thy sister, and with her didst play
In presence of th' Almighty Father, pleased
With thy celestial song. Up led by thee
Into the Heav'n of Heav'ns I have presumed,
An earthly guest, and drawn empyreal air,
Thy temp'ring;° with like safety guided down   *made suitable by thee*
Return me to my native element:
Lest from this flying steed unreined (as once
Bellerophon,[4] though from a lower clime)°   *region*
Dismounted, on th' Aleian field I fall
Erroneous° there to wander and forlorn.   *straying*
Half yet remains unsung, but narrower bound
Within the visible diurnal sphere;[5]
Standing on earth, not rapt° above the pole,   *transported, enraptured*
More safe I sing with mortal voice, unchanged
To hoarse or mute, though fall'n on evil days,
On evil days though fall'n, and evil tongues;
In darkness, and with dangers compassed round,[6]
And solitude; yet not alone, while thou
Visit'st my slumbers nightly, or when morn

1. Urania, the Greek Muse of astronomy, had been made into the Muse of Christian poetry by du Bartas and other religious poets. Milton, however, constructs another derivation for her (line 5ff.). Milton begins Book 7 with a third proem (lines 1–39).
2. Pegasus, the flying horse of inspired poetry, suggests (in connection with Bellerophon, line 18) Milton's sense of perilous audacity in writing this poem.
3. In Proverbs 8.24–31 Wisdom tells of her activities before the Creation: "Then I was by him [God], as one brought up with him: and I was daily his delight, rejoicing always before him." Milton describes "eternal Wisdom" as a daughter of God (personification of his wisdom) and devises a myth in which the Muse of divine poetry ("celestial song," line 12) is Wisdom's "sister"—also, thereby, originating from God.
4. Bellerophon incurred the gods' anger when he tried to fly to heaven upon Pegasus; Zeus sent an insect to sting the horse, and Bellerophon fell down to the "Aleian field" (plain of error), where he wandered alone and blind until his death.
5. The universe, which appears to rotate daily.
6. After the Restoration of Charles II (May 1660) and until the passage of the Act of Oblivion (August 1660), Milton was in danger of death and dismemberment (like Orpheus, lines 34–35); several of his republican colleagues were hanged, disembowelled, and quartered for their part in the revolution and regicide.

30   Purples the east: still govern thou my song,
      Urania, and fit audience find, though few.
      But drive far off the barbarous dissonance
      Of Bacchus and his revelers, the race
      Of that wild rout that tore the Thracian bard
35   In Rhodope, where woods and rocks had ears
      To rapture, till the savage clamor drowned
      Both harp and voice;[7] nor could the Muse defend
      Her son.[8] So fail not thou, who thee implores:
      For thou art heav'nly, she an empty dream.

Summary   At Adam's request, Raphael continues his narration and describes how God, to replace the fallen angels, created the world, its creatures, and finally man, in the course of six days; the story of the creation concludes, on the seventh day, with a chorus of thanksgiving by the angels.

From Book 8

Summary   Adam, to prolong his visit with Raphael, asks why so many and such splendid stars seem to be at the service of the earth, which appears smaller and less noble than they. At this point Eve discreetly takes her leave. Replying to Adam's question, Raphael proposes various astronomical possibilities, but gives no conclusive answer, advising Adam to concern himself with matters closer to home. The angel, on the other hand, is much interested to hear the story, which Adam proposes to tell, of his own creation.

[ADAM DESCRIBES HIS OWN CREATION AND THAT OF EVE;
HAVING REPEATED HIS WARNING, THE ANGEL DEPARTS]

    So spake the godlike Power, and thus our sire:
250   "For man to tell how human life began
      Is hard; for who himself beginning knew?[1]
      Desire with thee still longer to converse
      Induced me. As new-waked from soundest sleep
      Soft on the flow'ry herb I found me laid
255   In balmy sweat, which with his beams the sun
      Soon dried, and on the reeking° moisture fed.   *steaming*
      Straight toward heav'n my wond'ring eyes I turned,
      And gazed a while the ample sky, till raised
      By quick instinctive motion up I sprung
260   As thitherward endeavoring, and upright
      Stood on my feet; about me round I saw
      Hill, dale, and shady woods, and sunny plains,

---

7. The music of the "Thracian bard" Orpheus, type of the poet, charmed even "woods and rocks," but his song was drowned out by the Bacchantes, a "wild rout" of screaming women who murdered and dismembered him and threw his body parts into the Hebrus River, which rises in the "Rhodope" mountains. Milton fears that a similar "barbarous dissonance" unleashed by the Restoration will drown out his voice and threaten his life.
8. Orpheus's mother is Calliope, Muse of epic poetry.
1. Compare Satan's inability to remember his origins (5.856–63), from which he infers self-creation, whereas Adam infers a Maker (line 278).

And liquid lapse° of murmuring streams; by these,   *flow*
Creatures that lived, and moved, and walked, or flew,
Birds on the branches warbling; all things smiled,
With fragrance and with joy my heart o'erflowed.
Myself I then perused, and limb by limb
Surveyed, and sometimes went,° and sometimes ran   *walked*
With supple joints, as lively vigor led:
But who I was, or where, or from what cause,
Knew not; to speak I tried, and forthwith spake,
My tongue obeyed and readily could name
Whate'er I saw.² 'Thou sun,' said I, 'fair light,
And thou enlightened earth, so fresh and gay,
Ye hills and dales, ye rivers, woods, and plains,
And ye that live and move, fair creatures, tell,
Tell, if ye saw, how came I thus, how here?
Not of myself; by some great Maker then,
In goodness and in power preeminent;
Tell me, how may I know him, how adore,
From whom I have that thus I move and live,
And feel that I am happier than I know.'
While thus I called, and strayed I knew not whither,
From where I first drew air, and first beheld
This happy light, when answer none returned,
On a green shady bank profuse of flow'rs
Pensive I sat me down; there gentle sleep
First found me, and with soft oppression seized
My drowsèd sense, untroubled, though I thought
I then was passing to my former state
Insensible, and forthwith to dissolve:
When suddenly stood at my head a dream,
Whose inward apparition gently moved
My fancy to believe I yet had being,
And lived: one came, methought, of shape divine,
And said, 'Thy mansion° wants° thee, Adam, rise,   *habitation / lacks*
First man, of men innumerable ordained
First father, called by thee I come thy guide
To the garden of bliss, thy seat° prepared.'   *residence*
So saying, by the hand he took me raised,
And over fields and waters, as in air
Smooth sliding without step, last led me up
A woody mountain whose high top was plain,
A circuit wide, enclosed, with goodliest trees
Planted, with walks, and bowers, that what I saw
Of earth before scarce pleasant seemed. Each tree
Load'n with fairest fruit, that hung to the eye
Tempting, stirred in me sudden appetite
To pluck and eat; whereat I waked, and found
Before mine eyes all real, as the dream
Had lively° shadowed: here had new begun   *vividly*
My wand'ring, had not he who was my guide
Up hither, from among the trees appeared,

---

2. Adam's ability to name the creatures was said to signify his intuitive understanding of their natures.

Presence Divine. Rejoicing, but with awe
315 In adoration at his feet I fell
Submiss:° he reared me, and 'Whom thou sought'st I am,'   *submissive*
Said mildly, 'Author of all this thou seest
Above, or round about thee or beneath.
This Paradise I give thee, count it thine
320 To till and keep,° and of the fruit to eat: *care for*
Of every tree that in the garden grows
Eat freely with glad heart; fear here no dearth:
But of the tree whose operation° brings   *action*
Knowledge of good and ill, which I have set
325 The pledge of thy obedience and thy faith,
Amid the garden by the Tree of Life,
Remember what I warn thee, shun to taste,
And shun the bitter consequence: for know,
The day thou eat'st thereof, my sole command
330 Transgressed, inevitably thou shalt die;
From that day mortal, and this happy state
Shalt lose, expelled from hence into a world
Of woe and sorrow.'³ Sternly he pronounced
The rigid interdiction,° which resounds   *prohibition*
335 Yet dreadful in mine ear, though in my choice
Not to incur; but soon his clear aspéct°   *untroubled expression*
Returned and gracious purpose° thus renewed: *speech*
'Not only these fair bounds, but all the earth
To thee and to thy race I give; as lords
340 Possess it, and all things that therein live,
Or live in sea, or air, beast, fish, and fowl.
In sign whereof each bird and beast behold
After their kinds; I bring them to receive
From thee their names, and pay thee fealty
345 With low subjection; understand the same
Of fish within their wat'ry residence,
Not hither summoned, since they cannot change
Their element to draw the thinner air.'
As thus he spake, each bird and beast behold
350 Approaching two and two, these° cow'ring low   *the beasts*
With blandishment,° each bird stooped on his wing.   *flattering gesture*
I named them, as they passed, and understood
Their nature, with such knowledge God endued
My sudden apprehension:⁴ but in these
355 I found not what methought I wanted still;
And to the heav'nly Vision thus presumed:
"'O by what name, for thou above all these,
Above mankind, or aught than mankind higher,
Surpassest far my naming,⁵ how may I
360 Adore thee, Author of this universe,

---

3. Compare God's commands to Adam (Genesis 1.28–30, 2.16–17) with Milton's elaboration here.
4. Adam had already begun naming the sun and features of the earth (lines 272–74), but here he names (and thereby shows he understands) all living creatures.
5. Adam reasons, as the Scholastics did, from the creatures to the fact of a Creator, but he cannot name (and so indicates that he cannot understand) God, except as God reveals himself.

And all this good to man, for whose well-being
So amply, and with hands so liberal
Thou hast provided all things: but with me
I see not who partakes. In solitude
What happiness, who can enjoy alone,
Or all enjoying, what contentment find?'
Thus I presumptuous; and the Vision bright,
As with a smile more brightened, thus replied:
    "'What call'st thou solitude? Is not the earth
With various living creatures, and the air
Replenished,° and all these at thy command   *fully stocked*
To come and play before thee? Know'st thou not
Their language and their ways? They also know,°   *have understanding*
And reason not contemptibly; with these
Find pastime, and bear rule; thy realm is large.'
So spake the Universal Lord, and seemed
So ordering. I with leave of speech implored,
And humble deprecation thus replied:
    "'Let not my words offend thee, Heav'nly Power,
My Maker, be propitious while I speak.
Hast thou not made me here thy substitute,
And these inferior far beneath me set?
Among unequals what society
Can sort,° what harmony or true delight?   *agree*
Which must be mutual, in proportion due
Giv'n and received; but in disparity
The one intense, the other still remiss
Cannot well suit with either,[6] but soon prove
Tedious alike. Of fellowship I speak
Such as I seek, fit to participate°   *partake of*
All rational delight, wherein the brute
Cannot be human consort; they rejoice
Each with their kind, lion with lioness;
So fitly them in pairs thou hast combined;
Much less can bird with beast, or fish with fowl
So well converse, nor with the ox the ape;
Worse then can man with beast, and least of all.'
    "Whereto th' Almighty answered, not displeased:
'A nice° and subtle happiness I see   *fastidious*
Thou to thyself proposest, in the choice
Of thy associates, Adam, and wilt taste
No pleasure, though in pleasure, solitary.
What think'st thou then of me, and this my state?
Seem I to thee sufficiently possessed
Of happiness, or not? who am alone
From all eternity, for none I know
Second to me or like, equal much less.
How have I then with whom to hold converse
Save with the creatures which I made, and those
To me inferior, infinite descents

6. As with poorly matched musical instruments, Adam's string is too taut ("intense") and the animals'
is too slack ("remiss") to be in harmony ("suit").

Beneath what other creatures are to thee?'
   "He ceased, I lowly answered: 'To attain
The height and depth of thy eternal ways
All human thoughts come short, Supreme of things;
415   Thou in thyself art perfect, and in thee
Is no deficience found; not so is man,
But in degree, the cause of his desire
By conversation with his like to help,
Or solace his defects.[7] No need that thou
420   Shouldst propagate, already infinite;
And through all numbers absolute, though One;
But man by number is to manifest
His single imperfection, and beget
Like of his like, his image multiplied,
425   In unity defective,[8] which requires
Collateral° love, and dearest amity.   *mutual*
Thou in thy secrecy° although alone,   *seclusion*
Best with thyself accompanied, seek'st not
Social communication, yet so pleased,
430   Canst raise thy creature to what height thou wilt
Of union or communion, deified;
I by conversing cannot these erect
From prone, nor in their ways complacence° find.'   *satisfaction*
Thus I emboldened spake, and freedom used
435   Permissive,° and acceptance found, which gained   *permitted*
This answer from the gracious Voice Divine:
   "'Thus far to try thee, Adam, I was pleased,
And find thee knowing not of beasts alone,
Which thou hast rightly named, but of thyself,
440   Expressing well the spirit within thee free,
My image, not imparted to the brute,
Whose fellowship therefore unmeet° for thee   *unsuitable*
Good reason was thou freely shouldst dislike,
And be so minded still. I, ere thou spak'st,
445   Knew it not good for man to be alone,
And no such company as then thou saw'st
Intended thee, for trial only brought,
To see how thou couldst judge of fit and meet:
What next I bring shall please thee, be assured,
450   Thy likeness, thy fit help, thy other self,
Thy wish, exactly to thy heart's desire.'[9]
   "He ended, or I heard no more, for now
My earthly by his heav'nly overpowered,
Which it had long stood under,° strained to the height   *been exposed to*
455   In that celestial colloquy sublime,
As with an object that excels° the sense,   *exceeds*
Dazzled and spent, sunk down, and sought repair

---

7. God is absolutely perfect, man only relatively so ("in degree"), and thereby needs companionship with a fit mate to assuage ("solace") the "defects" arising from solitude.

8. God, "though One," (line 421), contains all numbers, but man has to remedy the "imperfec-tion" of being single (line 423) by procreating and thereby multiplying his single and thereby "defective" image (line 425).

9. Compare the account in Genesis 2.18 with Milton's elaboration.

Of sleep, which instantly fell on me, called
By nature as in aid, and closed mine eyes.
Mine eyes he closed, but open left the cell
Of fancy° my internal sight, by which   *imagination*
Abstract° as in a trance methought I saw,   *withdrawn*
Though sleeping, where I lay, and saw the shape
Still glorious before whom awake I stood;
Who stooping opened my left side, and took
From thence a rib, with cordial° spirits warm,   *from the heart*
And lifeblood streaming fresh; wide was the wound,
But suddenly with flesh filled up and healed:
The rib he formed and fashioned with his hands;
Under his forming hands a creature grew,[1]
Manlike, but different sex, so lovely fair
That what seemed fair in all the world seemed now
Mean, or in her summed up, in her contained
And in her looks, which from that time infused
Sweetness into my heart, unfelt before,
And into all things from her air° inspired   *mien, look*
The spirit of love and amorous delight.
She disappeared, and left me dark, I waked
To find her, or forever to deplore
Her loss, and other pleasures all abjure:
When out of hope, behold her, not far off,
Such as I saw her in my dream, adorned
With what all earth or heaven could bestow
To make her amiable:° on she came,   *lovely*
Led by her heav'nly Maker, though unseen,[2]
And guided by his voice, nor uninformed
Of nuptial sanctity and marriage rites:
Grace was in all her steps, Heav'n in her eye,
In every gesture dignity and love.
I overjoyed could not forbear aloud:
    "'This turn hath made amends; thou hast fulfilled
Thy words, Creator bounteous and benign,
Giver of all things fair, but fairest this
Of all thy gifts, nor enviest.° I now see   *given reluctantly*
Bone of my bone, flesh of my flesh, my self
Before me; woman is her name, of man
Extracted; for this cause he shall forgo
Father and mother, and to his wife adhere;
And they shall be one flesh, one heart, one soul.'[3]
    "She heard me thus, and though divinely brought,
Yet innocence and virgin modesty,
Her virtue and the conscience° of her worth   *consciousness*
That would be wooed, and not unsought be won,
Not obvious,° not obtrusive,° but retired,   *bold / forward*
The more desirable, or to say all,
Nature herself, though pure of sinful thought,

---

1. Go to the online StudySpace to see the *Creation of Eve* by the Italian painter Paolo Veronese (1528–1588).
2. Compare Eve's version of these events (4.440–91).
3. Compare the account in Genesis 2.23–24.

Wrought in her so that, seeing me, she turned;
I followed her, she what was honor knew,
And with obsequious° majesty approved   compliant
510 My pleaded reason. To the nuptial bow'r
I led her blushing like the morn: all heav'n,
And happy constellations on that hour
Shed their selectest influence; the earth
Gave sign of gratulation,° and each hill;   rejoicing, congratulation
515 Joyous the birds; fresh gales and gentle airs[4]
Whispered it to the woods, and from their wings
Flung rose, flung odors from the spicy shrub,
Disporting,° till the amorous bird of night°   frolicking / nightingale
Sung spousal, and bid haste the evening star°   Venus
520 On his hill top, to light the bridal lamp.
    Thus I have told thee all my state, and brought
My story to the sum of earthly bliss
Which I enjoy, and must confess to find
In all things else delight indeed, but such
525 As used or not, works in the mind no change,
Nor vehement desire, these delicacies
I mean of taste, sight, smell, herbs, fruits, and flow'rs,
Walks, and the melody of birds; but here
Far otherwise, transported° I behold,   enraptured
530 Transported touch; here passion first I felt,
Commotion° strange, in all enjoyments else   mental agitation
Superior and unmoved, here only weak
Against the charm of beauty's powerful glance.
Or° nature failed in me, and left some part   either
535 Not proof enough such object to sustain,°   withstand
Or from my side subducting,° took perhaps   subtracting
More than enough; at least on her bestowed
Too much of ornament, in outward show
Elaborate, of inward less exact.
540 For well I understand in the prime end
Of nature her th' inferior, in the mind
And inward faculties, which most excel,
In outward also her resembling less
His image who made both, and less expressing
545 The character of that dominion giv'n
O'er other creatures; yet when I approach
Her loveliness, so absolute° she seems   perfect, independent
And in herself complete, so well to know
Her own, that what she wills to do or say,
550 Seems wisest, virtuousest, discreetest, best;
All higher knowledge in her presence falls
Degraded, wisdom in discourse with her
Loses discount'nanced,° and like folly shows;   disconcerted, abashed
Authority and reason on her wait,
555 As one intended first, not after made
Occasionally;° and to consúmmate all,   incidentally
Greatness of mind and nobleness their seat

4. Both breezes and melodies. "Gales": winds.

Build in her loveliest, and create an awe
About her, as a guard angelic placed."
To whom the angel with contracted brow:
  "Accuse not nature, she hath done her part;
Do thou but thine, and be not diffident°   *mistrustful*
Of wisdom, she deserts thee not, if thou
Dismiss not her, when most thou need'st her nigh,
By áttributing overmuch to things
Less excellent, as thou thyself perceiv'st.
For what admir'st thou, what transports thee so,
An outside? Fair no doubt, and worthy well
Thy cherishing, thy honoring, and thy love,
Not thy subjection: weigh with her thyself;
Then value: ofttimes nothing profits more
Than self-esteem, grounded on just and right
Well managed; of that skill the more thou know'st,
The more she will acknowledge thee her head,[5]
And to realities yield all her shows:
Made so adorn for thy delight the more,
So awful,° that with honor thou may'st love   *awe-inspiring*
Thy mate, who sees when thou art seen least wise.
But if the sense of touch whereby mankind
Is propagated seem such dear delight
Beyond all other, think the same vouchsafed
To cattle and each beast; which would not be
To them made common and divulged,° if aught   *imparted generally*
Therein enjoyed were worthy to subdue
The soul of man, or passion in him move.
What higher in her society thou find'st
Attractive, human, rational, love still;
In loving thou dost well, in passion not,
Wherein true love consists not; love refines
The thoughts, and heart enlarges, hath his seat
In reason, and is judicious, is the scale[6]
By which to heav'nly love thou may'st ascend,
Not sunk in carnal pleasure, for which cause
Among the beasts no mate for thee was found."
  To whom thus half abashed Adam replied.
"Neither her outside formed so fair, nor aught
In procreation common to all kinds
(Though higher of the genial[7] bed by far,
And with mysterious reverence I deem)
So much delights me, as those graceful acts,
Those thousand decencies° that daily flow   *fitting acts*
From all her words and actions, mixed with love
And sweet compliance, which declare unfeigned
Union of mind, or in us both one soul;

---

5. See 1 Corinthians 11.3: "the head of every man is Christ; and the head of the woman is the man; and the head of Christ is God."

6. The ladder of love, a Neoplatonic concept for the movement from sensual love to higher forms, and ultimately to love of God.

7. Both "nuptial" and "generative." Adam takes respectful issue with the apparent denigration of human sex in Raphael's account of the Neoplatonic ladder, which prompts his question about angelic sex (lines 615–17).

605 Harmony to behold in wedded pair
More grateful than harmonious sound to the ear.
Yet these subject not; I to thee disclose
What inward thence I feel, not therefore foiled,°   overcome
Who meet with various objects, from the sense
610 Variously representing;[8] yet still free
Approve the best, and follow what I approve.
To love thou blam'st me not, for love thou say'st
Leads up to Heav'n, is both the way and guide;
Bear with me then, if lawful what I ask;
615 Love not the heav'nly Spirits, and how their love
Express they, by looks only, or do they mix
Irradiance, virtual or immediate° touch?"   actual
    To whom the angel with a smile that glowed
Celestial rosy red, love's proper hue,[9]
620 Answered. "Let it suffice thee that thou know'st
Us happy, and without love no happiness.
Whatever pure thou in the body enjoy'st
(And pure thou wert created) we enjoy
In eminence,° and obstacle find none   higher degree
625 Of membrane, joint, or limb, exclusive bars:
Easier than air with air, if Spirits embrace,
Total they mix, union of pure with pure
Desiring; nor restrained conveyance need
As flesh to mix with flesh, or soul with soul.
630 But I can now no more; the parting sun
Beyond the earth's green cape and verdant isles
Hesperian sets,[1] my signal to depart.
Be strong, live happy, and love, but first of all
Him whom to love is to obey, and keep
635 His great command; take heed lest passion sway
Thy judgment to do aught, which else free will
Would not admit;° thine and of all thy sons   permit
The weal or woe in thee is placed; beware.
I in thy persevering shall rejoice,
640 And all the blest: stand fast; to stand or fall
Free in thine own arbitrament° it lies.   determination
Perfect within, no outward aid require;°   depend on
And all temptation to transgress repel."
    So saying, he arose; whom Adam thus
645 Followed with benediction. "Since to part,
Go heavenly guest, ethereal messenger,
Sent from whose sov'reign goodness I adore.
Gentle to me and affable hath been
Thy condescension, and shall be honored ever
650 With grateful memory: thou to mankind
Be good and friendly still,° and oft return."   always
    So parted they, the angel up to Heav'n
From the thick shade, and Adam to his bow'r.

---

8. I.e., various objects, variously represented to me by my senses.
9. This is not likely to be an embarrassed blush: red is the color traditionally associated with Seraphim, who burn with ardor. Raphael's smile also glows with friendship for Adam and appreciation of his perceptive inference about angelic love.
1. Cape Verde, near Dakar, and the islands off that coast are the westernmost ("Hesperian") points of Africa.

Book 9

No more of talk where God or angel guest
With man, as with his friend, familiar used
To sit indulgent, and with him partake
Rural repast, permitting him the while
Venial° discourse unblamed: I now must change   *permissible*
Those notes to tragic; foul distrust, and breach
Disloyal on the part of man, revolt,
And disobedience: on the part of Heav'n
Now alienated, distance and distaste,°   *aversion*
Anger and just rebuke, and judgment giv'n,
That brought into this world a world of woe,
Sin and her shadow Death, and misery
Death's harbinger:° sad task, yet argument°   *forerunner / subject*
Not less but more heroic than the wrath
Of stern Achilles on his foe pursued
Thrice fugitive about Troy wall; or rage
Of Turnus for Lavinia disespoused,
Or Neptune's ire or Juno's, that so long
Perplexed the Greek and Cytherea's son;[1]
If answerable° style I can obtain   *fitting*
Of my celestial patroness, who deigns
Her nightly visitation unimplored,[2]
And dictates to me slumb'ring, or inspires
Easy my unpremeditated verse:
Since first this subject for heroic song
Pleased me long choosing, and beginning late;
Not sedulous° by nature to indite   *eager*
Wars, hitherto the only argument°   *subject*
Heroic deemed, chief mastery to dissect
With long and tedious havoc fabled knights
In battles feigned; the better fortitude
Of patience and heroic martyrdom
Unsung; or to describe races and games,
Or tilting furniture, emblazoned shields,
Impresses quaint, caparisons and steeds;
Bases[3] and tinsel trappings, gorgeous knights
At joust and tournament; then marshaled feast
Served up in hall with sewers,° and seneschals;°   *waiters / stewards*
The skill of artifice° or office mean,   *mechanic art*
Not that which justly gives heroic name
To person or to poem. Me of these

---

1. In this fourth proem (lines 1–47), after signaling his change from pastoral to tragic mode (lines 1–6), Milton emphasizes tragic elements in several classical epics: Achilles pursuing Hector three times around the wall of Troy before killing him (*Iliad* 22); Turnus fighting Aeneas over the loss of his betrothed Lavinia, and then killed by Aeneas; Odysseus ("the Greek") and Aeneas ("Cytherea's son," i.e., Venus's son) tormented ("perplexed") by Neptune (Poseidon) and Juno, respectively.
2. Milton does not here invoke the Muse but testifies to her customary nightly visits. Milton's nephew reports that he often awoke in the morning with lines of poetry fully formed in his head, ready to dictate them to a scribe.
3. Cloth coverings for horses; "tilting furniture": equipment for jousting; "impresses quaint": cunningly designed heraldic devices on shields; "caparisons": ornamental trappings or armor for horses. After rejecting the classical epic subjects, Milton here rejects the familiar topics of romance.

Nor skilled nor studious, higher argument
Remains,[4] sufficient of itself to raise
That name, unless an age too late, or cold
45 Climate, or years damp my intended wing
Depressed, and much they may, if all be mine,
Not hers who brings it nightly to my ear.
    The sun was sunk, and after him the star
Of Hesperus,[5] whose office is to bring
50 Twilight upon the earth, short arbiter
'Twixt day and night, and now from end to end
Night's hemisphere had veiled the horizon round:
When Satan who late° fled[6] before the threats   *recently*
Of Gabriel out of Eden, now improved°   *increased*
55 In meditated fraud and malice, bent
On man's destruction, maugre what might hap
Of heavier on himself,[7] fearless returned.
By night he fled, and at midnight returned
From compassing the earth, cautious of day,
60 Since Uriel regent of the sun descried
His entrance, and forewarned the Cherubim
That kept their watch; thence full of anguish driv'n,
The space of seven continued nights he rode
With darkness, thrice the equinoctial line°   *equator*
65 He circled, four times crossed the car of Night
From pole to pole, traversing each colure;[8]
On the eighth returned, and on the coast averse°   *turned away*
From entrance on Cherubic watch, by stealth
Found unsuspected way. There was a place,
70 Now not, though sin, not time, first wrought the change,
Where Tigris at the foot of Paradise
Into a gulf shot underground, till part
Rose up a fountain by the Tree of Life;
In with the river sunk, and with it rose
75 Satan involved° in rising mist, then sought   *enveloped*
Where to lie hid. Sea he had searched and land
From Eden over Pontus,[9] and the pool
Maeotis, up beyond the river Ob;
Downward as far Antarctic; and in length
80 West from Orontes to the ocean barred
At Darien, thence to the land where flows
Ganges and Indus: thus the orb he roamed
With narrow° search; and with inspection deep   *strict*

4. For a heroic poem. He proceeds to recap worries he has voiced before: that the times might not be receptive to such poems ("age too late"), that the "cold Climate" of England or his own advanced age might "damp" (benumb, dampen) his "intended wing / Depressed" (poetic flights held down, kept from soaring).
5. Venus, the evening star.
6. At the end of Book 4.
7. I.e., despite ("maugre") what might result in heavier punishments for himself.
8. The colures are two great circles that intersect at right angles at the poles. By circling the globe from east to west at the equator and then

over the north and south poles, Satan can remain in darkness, keeping the earth between himself and the sun. "Car of Night" (line 65): the earth's shadow, imagined as the chariot of the goddess Night.
9. The Black Sea. Satan's journey (lines 77–82) takes him from there to the Sea of Azov in Russia ("Maeotis"), beyond the river "Ob" in Siberia, which flows into the Arctic Ocean, then south to Antarctica; thence west from "Orontes" (a river in Syria) across the Atlantic to "Darien" (the Isthmus of Panama), then across the Pacific and Asia to India where the "Ganges" and "Indus" rivers flow.

Considered every creature, which of all
Most opportune might serve his wiles, and found
The serpent subtlest beast of all the field.[1]
Him after long debate, irresolute°   *undecided*
Of° thoughts revolved, his final sentence° chose   *among / decision*
Fit vessel, fittest imp° of fraud, in whom   *offshoot*
To enter, and his dark suggestions hide
From sharpest sight: for in the wily snake,
Whatever sleights° none would suspicious mark,   *artifices*
As from his wit and native subtlety
Proceeding, which in other beasts observed
Doubt° might beget of diabolic pow'r   *suspicion*
Active within beyond the sense of brute.
Thus he resolved, but first from inward grief
His bursting passion into plaints thus poured:
        "O earth, how like to Heav'n, if not preferred
More justly, seat worthier of gods, as built
With second thoughts, reforming what was old!
For what God after better worse would build?
Terrestrial heav'n, danced round by other heav'ns
That shine, yet bear their bright officious° lamps,   *dutiful*
Light above light, for thee alone, as seems,[2]
In thee concent'ring all their precious beams
Of sacred influence: as God in Heav'n
Is center, yet extends to all, so thou
Centring receiv'st from all those orbs; in thee,
Not in themselves, all their known virtue appears
Productive in herb, plant, and nobler birth
Of creatures animate with gradual life
Of growth, sense, reason,[3] all summed up in man.
With what delight could I have walked thee round,
If I could joy in aught, sweet interchange
Of hill and valley, rivers, woods and plains,
Now land, now sea, and shores with forest crowned,
Rocks, dens, and caves; but I in none of these
Find place or refuge; and the more I see
Pleasures about me, so much more I feel
Torment within me, as from the hateful siege°   *conflict*
Of contraries; all good to me becomes
Bane,° and in Heav'n much worse would be my state.   *poison*
But neither here seek I, no nor in Heav'n
To dwell, unless by mastering Heav'n's Supreme;
Nor hope to be myself less miserable
By what I seek, but others to make such
As I, though thereby worse to me redound:
For only in destroying I find ease
To my relentless thoughts; and him[4] destroyed,
Or won to what may work his utter loss,

---

1. The serpent is so described in Genesis 3.1.
2. Like Adam (8.15ff.) and Eve (4.657–58) but
not Raphael (8.114–78), Satan assumes a Ptolemaic universe centered on the earth and humankind.

3. Graduated in steps ("gradual," 112) from vegetable to animal to rational forms (souls); cf.
5.469–90.
4. Adam. "This" (line 132): the universe.

For whom all this was made, all this will soon
Follow, as to him linked in weal or woe:
In woe then; that destruction wide may range:

135   To me shall be the glory sole among
The infernal Powers, in one day to have marred
What he Almighty styled,° six nights and days   *called*
Continued making, and who knows how long
Before had been contriving, though perhaps

140   Not longer than since I in one night freed
From servitude inglorious well-nigh half
Th' angelic name, and thinner left the throng
Of his adorers. He to be avenged,
And to repair his numbers thus impaired,

145   Whether such virtue° spent of old now failed   *power*
More angels to create, if they at least
Are his created, or to spite us more,
Determined to advance into our room
A creature formed of earth, and him endow,

150   Exalted from so base original,°   *origin*
With Heav'nly spoils, our spoils: what he decreed
He effected; man he made, and for him built
Magnificent this world, and earth his seat,
Him lord pronounced, and, O indignity!

155   Subjected to his service angel wings,
And flaming ministers to watch and tend
Their earthy charge: of these the vigilance
I dread, and to elude, thus wrapped in mist
Of midnight vapor glide obscure, and pry

160   In every bush and brake, where hap° may find   *luck*
The serpent sleeping, in whose mazy folds
To hide me, and the dark intent I bring.
O foul descent! that I who erst contended
With gods to sit the highest, am now constrained

165   Into a beast, and mixed with bestial slime,
This essence to incarnate and imbrute,[5]
That to the height of deity aspired;
But what will not ambition and revenge
Descend to? Who aspires must down as low

170   As high he soared, obnoxious° first or last   *exposed*
To basest things. Revenge, at first though sweet,
Bitter ere long back on itself recoils;
Let it; I reck° not, so it light well aimed,   *care*
Since higher I fall short, on him who next

175   Provokes my envy, this new favorite
Of Heav'n, this man of clay, son of despite,
Whom us the more to spite his Maker raised
From dust: spite then with spite is best repaid."
    So saying, through each thicket dank or dry,

180   Like a black mist low creeping, he held on
His midnight search, where soonest he might find

---

5. Satan "imbruting" himself in a snake parodies, grotesquely, the Son's incarnation in human form, as Christ.

The serpent: him fast sleeping soon he found
In labyrinth of many a round self-rolled,
His head the midst, well stored with subtle wiles:
Not yet in horrid shade or dismal den,
Nor nocent° yet, but on the grassy herb   *harmful, guilty*
Fearless unfeared he slept: in at his mouth
The Devil entered, and his brutal° sense,   *animal*
In heart or head, possessing soon inspired
With act intelligential: but his sleep
Disturbed not, waiting close° th' approach of morn.   *hidden*
Now whenas sacred light began to dawn
In Eden on the humid flow'rs, that breathed
Their morning incense, when all things that breathe,
From th' earth's great altar send up silent praise
To the Creator, and his nostrils fill
With grateful° smell, forth came the human pair   *pleasing*
And joined their vocal worship to the choir
Of creatures wanting° voice; that done, partake   *lacking*
The season, prime° for sweetest scents and airs: *best*
Then cómmune how that day they best may ply
Their growing work; for much their work outgrew
The hands' dispatch of two gard'ning so wide.
And Eve first to her husband thus began:
     "Adam, well may we labor still° to dress   *continually*
This garden, still to tend plant, herb, and flow'r,
Our pleasant task enjoined, but till more hands
Aid us, the work under our labor grows,
Luxurious° by restraint; what we by day   *luxuriant*
Lop overgrown, or prune, or prop, or bind,
One night or two with wanton° growth derides,   *unrestrained*
Tending to wild. Thou therefore now advise
Or hear what to my mind first thoughts present,
Let us divide our labors, thou where choice
Leads thee, or where most needs, whether to wind
The woodbine round this arbor, or direct
The clasping ivy where to climb, while I
In yonder spring° of roses intermixed   *growth*
With myrtle, find what to redress° till noon: *set upright*
For while so near each other thus all day
Our task we choose, what wonder if so near
Looks intervene and smiles, or object new
Casual discourse draw on, which intermits°   *interrupts*
Our day's work brought to little, though begun
Early, and th' hour of supper comes unearned."
     To whom mild answer Adam thus returned:
"Sole Eve, associate sole,[6] to me beyond
Compare above all living creatures dear,
Well hast thou motioned,° well thy thoughts employed   *proposed*
How we might best fulfill the work which here
God hath assigned us, nor of me shalt pass
Unpraised: for nothing lovelier can be found

6. Adam puns on "sole" as "unrivaled" and "only" (cf. 4.411).

In woman, than to study household good,
And good works in her husband to promote.[7]
235   Yet not so strictly hath our Lord imposed
Labor, as to debar us when we need
Refreshment, whether food, or talk between,
Food of the mind, or this sweet intercourse
Of looks and smiles, for smiles from reason flow,
240   To brute denied, and are of love the food,
Love not the lowest end of human life.
For not to irksome toil, but to delight
He made us, and delight to reason joined.
These paths and bowers doubt not but our joint hands
245   Will keep from wilderness with ease, as wide
As we need walk, till younger hands ere long
Assist us: but if much convérse perhaps
Thee satiate, to short absence I could yield.
For solitude sometimes is best society,
250   And short retirement urges sweet return.
But other doubt possesses me, lest harm
Befall thee severed from me; for thou know'st
What hath been warned us, what malicious foe
Envying our happiness, and of his own
255   Despairing, seeks to work us woe and shame
By sly assault; and somewhere nigh at hand
Watches, no doubt, with greedy hope to find
His wish and best advantage, us asunder,
Hopeless to circumvent us joined, where each
260   To other speedy aid might lend at need;
Whether his first design be to withdraw
Our fealty° from God, or to disturb   allegiance
Conjugal love, than which perhaps no bliss
Enjoyed by us excites his envy more;
265   Or° this, or worse, leave not the faithful side   whether
That gave thee being, still shades thee and protects.
The wife, where danger or dishonor lurks,
Safest and seemliest by her husband stays,
Who guards her, or with her the worst endures."
270   To whom the virgin[8] majesty of Eve,
As one who loves, and some unkindness meets,
With sweet austere composure thus replied.
   "Offspring of Heav'n and earth, and all earth's lord,
That such an enemy we have, who seeks
275   Our ruin, both by thee informed I learn,
And from the parting angel overheard
As in a shady nook I stood behind,
Just then returned at shut of evening flow'rs.[9]
But that thou shouldst my firmness therefore doubt

---

7. Adam's compliments resemble the praises of a good wife in Proverbs 31.
8. The term here means unspotted or peerless; Milton has insisted at the end of Books 4 and 8 that Adam and Eve have sex.
9. Somewhat confusing, since Eve heard the full story of the war in Heaven and Raphael's earlier warnings; Raphael's parting words (8.630–43) overheard by Eve do not specifically mention Satan but warn Adam to resist his passion for Eve. He does, however, reiterate the charge to obey the "great command" and repel temptation.

To God or thee, because we have a foe
May tempt it, I expected not to hear.
His violence thou fear'st not, being such,
As we, not capable of death or pain,
Can either not receive, or can repel.
His fraud is then thy fear, which plain infers
Thy equal fear that my firm faith and love
Can by his fraud be shaken or seduced;
Thoughts, which how found they harbor in thy breast,
Adam, misthought of° her to thee so dear?"   misapplied to
      To whom with healing words Adam replied.
"Daughter of God and man, immortal Eve,
For such thou art, from sin and blame entire:°   untouched
Not diffident° of thee do I dissuade   distrustful
Thy absence from my sight, but to avoid
Th' attempt itself, intended by our foe.
For he who tempts, though in vain, at least asperses°   bespatters
The tempted with dishonor foul, supposed
Not incorruptible of faith, not proof
Against temptation: thou thyself with scorn
And anger wouldst resent the offered wrong,
Though ineffectual found; misdeem not then,
If such affront I labor to avert
From thee alone, which on us both at once
The enemy, though bold, will hardly dare,
Or daring, first on me th' assault shall light.
Nor thou his malice and false guile contemn;°   despise
Subtle he needs must be, who could seduce
Angels, nor think superfluous others' aid.
I from the influence of thy looks receive
Access° in every virtue, in thy sight   increase
More wise, more watchful, stronger, if need were
Of outward strength; while shame, thou looking on,
Shame to be overcome or overreached°   outwitted
Would utmost vigor raise, and raised unite.
Why shouldst not thou like sense within thee feel
When I am present, and thy trial choose
With me, best witness of thy virtue tried."
      So spake domestic Adam in his care
And matrimonial love; but Eve, who thought
Less° attribúted to her faith sincere,   too little
Thus her reply with accent sweet renewed.
      "If this be our condition, thus to dwell
In narrow circuit straitened° by a foe,   confined
Subtle or violent, we not endued
Single with like defense, wherever met,
How are we happy, still° in fear of harm?   always
But harm precedes not sin: only our foe
Tempting affronts us with his foul esteem
Of our integrity: his foul esteem
Sticks no dishonor on our front,° but turns   forehead
Foul on himself; then wherefore shunned or feared
By us? who rather double honor gain

From his surmise proved false, find peace within,
Favor from Heav'n, our witness from th' event.°   *outcome*
335 And what is faith, love, virtue unassayed
Alone, without exterior help sustained?[1]
Let us not then suspect our happy state
Left so imperfect by the Maker wise,
As not secure to single° or combined.   *one alone*
340 Frail is our happiness, if this be so,
And Eden were no Eden thus exposed."
    To whom thus Adam fervently replied.
"O woman, best are all things as the will
Of God ordained them, his creating hand
345 Nothing imperfect or deficient left
Of all that he created, much less man,
Or aught that might his happy state secure,
Secure from outward force; within himself
The danger lies, yet lies within his power:
350 Against his will he can receive no harm.
But God left free the will, for what obeys
Reason, is free, and reason he made right,[2]
But bid her well beware, and still erect,°   *ever-alert*
Lest by some fair appearing good surprised
355 She dictate false, and misinform the will
To do what God expressly hath forbid.
Not then mistrust, but tender love enjoins,
That I should mind° thee oft, and mind thou me.   *remind, pay heed to*
Firm we subsist,° yet possible to swerve,   *stand, exist*
360 Since reason not impossibly may meet
Some specious° object by the foe suborned,   *deceptively attractive*
And fall into deception unaware,
Not keeping strictest watch, as she was warned.
Seek not temptation then, which to avoid
365 Were better, and most likely if from me
Thou sever not: trial will come unsought.
Wouldst thou approve° thy constancy, approve   *prove*
First thy obedience; th' other who can know,
Not seeing thee attempted, who attest?
370 But if thou think, trial unsought may find
Us both securer° than thus warned thou seem'st,   *overconfident*
Go; for thy stay, not free, absents thee more;
Go in thy native innocence, rely
On what thou hast of virtue, summon all,
375 For God towards thee hath done his part, do thine."
    So spake the patriarch of mankind, but Eve
Persisted, yet submiss, though last, replied:
    "With thy permission then, and thus forewarned
Chiefly by what thy own last reasoning words
380 Touched only, that our trial, when least sought,
May find us both perhaps far less prepared,

---

1. Compare and contrast *Areopagitica*, pp. 786–96.
2. Right reason, a classical concept accommo-

dated to Christian thought, is the God-given power to apprehend truth and moral law.

The willinger I go, nor much expect
A foe so proud will first the weaker seek;
So bent, the more shall shame him his repulse."
Thus saying, from her husband's hand her hand
Soft she withdrew, and like a wood nymph light[3]
Oread or Dryad, or of Delia's train,
Betook her to the groves, but Delia's self
In gait surpassed and goddess-like deport,°   *bearing*
Though not as she with bow and quiver armed,
But with such gardening tools as art yet rude,
Guiltless of fire[4] had formed, or angels brought.
To Pales, or Pomona, thus adorned,
Likest she seemed Pomona when she fled
Vertumnus, or to Ceres in her prime,
Yet virgin of Proserpina from Jove.[5]
Her long with ardent look his eye pursued
Delighted, but desiring more her stay.
Oft he to her his charge of quick return
Repeated, she to him as oft engaged
To be returned by noon amid the bow'r,
And all things in best order to invite
Noontide repast, or afternoon's repose.
O much deceived, much failing,° hapless° Eve,   *erring / unlucky*
Of thy presumed return! event° perverse!   *outcome*
Thou never from that hour in Paradise
Found'st either sweet repast, or sound repose;
Such ambush hid among sweet flow'rs and shades
Waited with hellish rancor imminent
To intercept thy way, or send thee back
Despoiled of innocence, of faith, of bliss.
For now, and since first break of dawn the Fiend,
Mere serpent in appearance, forth was come,
And on his quest, where likeliest he might find
The only two of mankind, but in them
The whole included race, his purposed prey.
In bow'r and field he sought, where any tuft
Of grove or garden plot more pleasant lay,
Their tendance or plantation for delight,[6]
By fountain or by shady rivulet
He sought them both, but wished his hap° might find   *luck*
Eve separate; he wished, but not with hope
Of what so seldom chanced, when to his wish,
Beyond his hope, Eve separate he spies,
Veiled in a cloud of fragrance, where she stood,

3. Light-footed, with overtones of "fickle" or
"frivolous." "Oread" (next line): a mountain
nymph. "Dryad": a wood nymph. "Delia": Diana,
born on the isle of Delos, hunted with a "train"
of nymphs.
4. Having no experience of fire, not needed in
Paradise. Milton may be alluding to the guilt of
Prometheus, who stole fire from heaven.
5. These goddesses, like Eve, are associated with
agriculture (lines 393–96)—Pales, with flocks

and pastures; Pomona, with fruit trees; Ceres,
with harvests—and the latter two foreshadow
Eve's situation. Pomona was chased by the wood
god "Vertumnus" in many guises before surrendering to him; Ceres was impregnated by Jove
with Proserpina—later carried off to Hades by
Pluto.
6. I.e., which they had cultivated or planted for
their pleasure.

Half spied, so thick the roses bushing round
About her glowed, oft stooping to support
Each flow'r of slender stalk, whose head though gay
Carnation, purple, azure, or specked with gold,
430 Hung drooping unsustained, them she upstays
Gently with myrtle band, mindless° the while,   *heedless*
Herself, though fairest unsupported flow'r
From her best prop so far, and storm so nigh.[7]
Nearer he drew, and many a walk traversed
435 Of stateliest covert, cedar, pine, or palm,
Then voluble° and bold, now hid, now seen   *undulating*
Among thick-woven arborets° and flow'rs   *small trees*
Embordered on each bank, the hand° of Eve: *handiwork*
Spot more delicious than those gardens feigned
440 Or° of revived Adonis, or renowned   *either*
Alcinous, host of old Laertes' son,
Or that, not mystic, where the sapient king
Held dalliance with his fair Egyptian spouse.[8]
Much he the place admired, the person more.
445 As one who long in populous city pent,
Where houses thick and sewers annoy° the air,   *make noisome, befoul*
Forth issuing on a summer's morn to breathe
Among the pleasant villages and farms
Adjoined, from each thing met conceives delight,
450 The smell of grain, or tedded grass, or kine,[9]
Or dairy, each rural sight, each rural sound;
If chance with nymph-like step fair virgin pass,
What pleasing seemed, for° her now pleases more,   *because of*
She most, and in her look sums all delight.
455 Such pleasure took the Serpent to behold
This flow'ry plat,° the sweet recess° of Eve   *plot / retreat*
Thus early, thus alone; her heav'nly form
Angelic, but more soft, and feminine,
Her graceful innocence, her every air°   *manner*
460 Of gesture or least action overawed
His malice, and with rapine sweet[1] bereaved
His fierceness of the fierce intent it brought:
That space the Evil One abstracted° stood   *withdrawn*
From his own evil, and for the time remained
465 Stupidly good,° of enmity disarmed,   *good because stupefied*
Of guile, of hate, of envy, of revenge;
But the hot hell that always in him burns,
Though in mid-Heav'n, soon ended his delight,
And tortures him now more, the more he sees
470 Of pleasure not for him ordained: then soon
Fierce hate he recollects, and all his thoughts

---

7. The conceit of the flower-gatherer who is herself gathered evokes the story of Proserpina, to whom it was applied in 4.269–71.
8. The gardens of Adonis were beauty spots named for the lovely youth loved by Venus, killed by a boar, and subsequently revived; Odysseus ("Laertes' son") was entertained by Alcinous in his beautiful gardens; Solomon ("the sapient king") entertained his "fair Egyptian spouse," the Queen of Sheba, in a real garden (not "mystic," or "feigned," as the others were).
9. Cattle. "Tedded": spread out to dry, like hay.
1. From Latin *rapere*, to seize, the root of both "rape" and "rapture," underscoring the paradox of the ravisher (temporarily) ravished.

Of mischief gratulating,° thus excites: *greeting*
 "Thoughts, whither have ye led me, with what sweet
Compulsion thus transported to forget
What hither brought us, hate, not love, nor hope
Of Paradise for Hell, hope here to taste
Of pleasure, but all pleasure to destroy,
Save what is in destroying, other joy
To me is lost. Then let me not let pass
Occasion which now smiles, behold alone
The woman, opportune° to all attempts,   *open*
Her husband, for I view far round, not nigh,
Whose higher intellectual more I shun,
And strength, of courage haughty,° and of limb   *exalted*
Heroic built, though of terrestrial° mold,   *earthly*
Foe not informidable, exempt from wound,
I not; so much hath Hell debased, and pain
Enfeebled me, to what I was in Heav'n.
She fair, divinely fair, fit love for gods,
Not terrible,° though terror be in love   *terrifying*
And beauty, not° approached by stronger hate,   *unless*
Hate stronger, under show of love well feigned,
The way which to her ruin now I tend."
 So spake the Enemy of mankind, enclosed
In serpent, inmate bad, and toward Eve
Addressed his way, not with indented° wave,   *zigzag*
Prone on the ground, as since, but on his rear,
Circular base of rising folds, that tow'red
Fold above fold a surging maze, his head
Crested aloft, and carbuncle° his eyes;   *deep red*
With burnished neck of verdant° gold, erect   *green*
Amidst his circling spires,° that on the grass   *coils*
Floated redundant:° pleasing was his shape, *in swelling waves*
And lovely, never since of serpent kind
Lovelier, not those that in Illyria changed
Hermione and Cadmus, or the god
In Epidaurus;[2] nor to which transformed
Ammonian Jove, or Capitoline was seen,
He with Olympias, this with her who bore
Scipio, the height of Rome.[3] With tract° oblique *course*
At first, as one who sought accéss, but feared
To interrupt, sidelong he works his way.
As when a ship by skillful steersman wrought
Nigh river's mouth or foreland, where the wind
Veers oft, as oft so steers, and shifts her sail;
So varied he, and of his tortuous train°   *twisting length*
Curled many a wanton° wreath in sight of Eve, *luxuriant, sportive*
To lure her eye; she busied heard the sound

2. The legendary founder of Thebes, Cadmus, and his wife Harmonia (Milton's "Hermione") were changed to serpents when they went to Illyria in old age; Aesculapius, god of healing, sometimes came forth as a serpent from his temple in Epidaurus.

3. Jupiter Ammon ("Ammonian Jove") made love to Olympias in the form of a snake and sired Alexander the Great; the Jupiter worshipped in Rome ("Capitoline"), also in serpent form, sired Scipio Africanus, the savior and great leader ("height") of Rome.

Of rustling leaves, but minded not, as used
520 To such disport before her through the field,
From every beast, more duteous at her call,
Than at Circean call the herd disguised.[4]
He bolder now, uncalled before her stood;
But as in gaze admiring: oft he bowed
525 His turret crest, and sleek enameled° neck,　　　　　　　　*multicolored*
Fawning, and licked the ground whereon she trod.
His gentle dumb expression turned at length
The eye of Eve to mark his play; he glad
Of her attention gained, with serpent tongue
530 Organic, or impulse of vocal air,[5]
His fraudulent temptation thus began.
　　"Wonder not, sovereign mistress, if perhaps
Thou canst, who art sole wonder, much less arm
Thy looks, the heav'n of mildness, with disdain,
535 Displeased that I approach thee thus, and gaze
Insatiate, I thus single, nor have feared
Thy awful° brow, more awful thus retired.　　　　　　　　*awe-inspiring*
Fairest resemblance of thy Maker fair,
Thee all things living gaze on, all things thine
540 By gift, and thy celestial beauty adore
With ravishment beheld, there best beheld
Where universally admired; but here
In this enclosure wild, these beasts among,
Beholders rude, and shallow to discern
545 Half what in thee is fair, one man except,
Who sees thee? (and what is one?) who shouldst be seen
A goddess among gods, adored and served
By angels numberless, thy daily train."[6]
　　So glozed° the Tempter, and his proem° tuned;　　　*flattered / prelude*
550 Into the heart of Eve his words made way,
Though at the voice much marveling; at length
Not unamazed she thus in answer spake.
"What may this mean? Language of man pronounced
By tongue of brute, and human sense expressed?
555 The first at least of these I thought denied
To beasts, whom God on their creation day
Created mute to all articulate sound;
The latter I demur,° for in their looks　　　　　　　　*hesitate about*
Much reason, and in their actions oft appears.
560 Thee, Serpent, subtlest beast of all the field
I knew, but not with human voice endued;°　　　　　　　*endowed*
Redouble then this miracle, and say,
How cam'st thou speakable° of mute, and how　　　　　*able to speak*
To me so friendly grown above the rest
565 Of brutal kind, that daily are in sight?
Say, for such wonder claims attention due."
　　To whom the guileful Tempter thus replied:

---

4. Circe, in the *Odyssey*, transformed men to beasts and was attended by an obedient herd.
5. Satan either used the actual tongue of the serpent or impressed the air with his own voice.
6. Satan's entire speech is couched in the extravagant praises of the Petrarchan love convention.

"Empress of this fair world, resplendent Eve,
Easy to me it is to tell thee all
What thou command'st, and right thou shouldst be obeyed:
I was at first as other beasts that graze
The trodden herb, of abject thoughts and low,
As was my food, nor aught but food discerned
Or sex, and apprehended nothing high:
Till on a day roving the field, I chanced
A goodly tree far distant to behold
Loaden with fruit of fairest colors mixed,
Ruddy and gold: I nearer drew to gaze;
When from the boughs a savory odor blown,
Grateful to appetite, more pleased my sense
Than smell of sweetest fennel, or the teats
Of ewe or goat dropping with milk at ev'n,[7]
Unsucked of lamb or kid, that tend their play.
To satisfy the sharp desire I had
Of tasting those fair apples, I resolved
Not to defer;° hunger and thirst at once,   *delay*
Powerful persuaders, quickened at the scent
Of that alluring fruit, urged me so keen.
About the mossy trunk I wound me soon,
For high from ground the branches would require
Thy utmost reach or Adam's: round the tree
All other beasts that saw, with like desire
Longing and envying stood, but could not reach.
Amid the tree now got, where plenty hung
Tempting so nigh, to pluck and eat my fill
I spared° not, for such pleasure till that hour   *refrained*
At feed or fountain never had I found.
Sated at length, ere long I might perceive
Strange alteration in me, to degree
Of reason in my inward powers, and speech
Wanted° not long, though to this shape retained.[8]   *lacked*
Thenceforth to speculations high or deep
I turned my thoughts, and with capacious mind
Considered all things visible in Heav'n,
Or earth, or middle,° all things fair and good;   *regions between*
But all that fair and good in thy divine
Semblance, and in thy beauty's heav'nly ray
United I beheld; no fair° to thine   *beauty*
Equivalent or second, which compelled
Me thus, though importune° perhaps, to come   *inopportunely*
And gaze, and worship thee of right declared
Sov'reign of creatures, universal dame."[9]
    So talked the spirited[1] sly snake; and Eve

---

7. According to Pliny, serpents ate fennel to aid in shedding their skins and to sharpen their eyesight; folklore had it that they drank the milk of sheep and goats.
8. There is no precedent in Genesis or the interpretative tradition for Satan's powerfully persuasive argument by analogy based on the snake's supposed experience of attaining to reason and speech by eating the forbidden fruit.
9. Satan continues his Petrarchan language of courtship.
1. Both inspired by and possessed by an evil spirit, Satan.

Yet more amazed unwary thus replied:
615   "Serpent, thy overpraising leaves in doubt
The virtue° of that fruit, in thee first proved: *power*
But say, where grows the tree, from hence how far?
For many are the trees of God that grow
In Paradise, and various, yet unknown
620 To us, in such abundance lies our choice,
As leaves a greater store of fruit untouched,
Still hanging incorruptible, till men
Grow up to their provision,[2] and more hands
Help to disburden nature of her birth."
625   To whom the wily adder, blithe and glad:
"Empress, the way is ready, and not long,
Beyond a row of myrtles, on a flat,
Fast by° a fountain, one small thicket past   *close by*
Of blowing myrrh and balm;[3] if thou accept
630 My conduct,° I can bring thee thither soon."   *guidance*
   "Lead then," said Eve. He leading swiftly rolled
In tangles, and made intricate seem straight,
To mischief swift. Hope elevates, and joy
Brightens his crest, as when a wand'ring fire,°   *will-o'-the-wisp*
635 Compact° of unctuous° vapor, which the night *composed / oily*
Condenses, and the cold environs round,
Kindled through agitation to a flame,
Which oft, they say, some evil spirit attends,
Hovering and blazing with delusive light,
640 Misleads th' amazed° night-wanderer from his way   *bewildered*
To bogs and mires, and oft through pond or pool,
There swallowed up and lost, from succor far.
So glistered the dire snake, and into fraud
Led Eve our credulous mother, to the tree
645 Of prohibition, root of all our woe;
Which when she saw, thus to her guide she spake:
   "Serpent, we might have spared our coming hither,
Fruitless to me, though fruit be here to excess,
The credit of whose virtue° rest with thee,   *power*
650 Wondrous indeed, if cause of such effects.
But of this tree we may not taste nor touch;
God so commanded, and left that command
Sole daughter of his voice;[4] the rest, we live
Law to ourselves, our reason is our law."
655   To whom the Tempter guilefully replied:
"Indeed? hath God then said that of the fruit
Of all these garden trees ye shall not eat,
Yet lords declared of all in earth or air?"
   To whom thus Eve yet sinless: "Of the fruit
660 Of each tree in the garden we may eat,
But of the fruit of this fair tree amidst

---

2. I.e., until the numbers of the human race are such as to consume the food God has provided.
3. Blooming trees that exude the aromatic gums myrrh and balm (balsam).
4. God's only direct commandment (in Hebrew,

Bath Kol, "daughter of a voice" from heaven). Otherwise (see following), they follow the moral law of nature, known to them perfectly by their unfallen reason, "our reason is our law."

The garden, God hath said, 'Ye shall not eat
Thereof, nor shall ye touch it, lest ye die.'"[5]
   She scarce had said, though brief, when now more bold
The Tempter, but with show of zeal and love
To man, and indignation at his wrong,
New part puts on, and as to passion moved,
Fluctuates disturbed, yet comely, and in act
Raised,[6] as of some great matter to begin.
As when of old some orator renowned
In Athens or free Rome, where eloquence
Flourished, since mute, to some great cause addressed,
Stood in himself collected, while each part,
Motion, each act won audience ere the tongue,°   *before speaking*
Sometimes in height began, as no delay
Of preface brooking[7] through his zeal of right.
So standing, moving, or to high upgrown
The Tempter all impassioned thus began:
   "O sacred, wise, and wisdom-giving plant,
Mother of science,° now I feel thy power   *knowledge*
Within me clear, not only to discern
Things in their causes, but to trace the ways
Of highest agents, deemed however wise.
Queen of this universe, do not believe
Those rigid threats of death; ye shall not die:
How should ye? By the fruit? It gives you life
To knowledge.[8] By the Threat'ner? Look on me,
Me who have touched and tasted, yet both live,
And life more perfect have attained than fate
Meant me, by vent'ring higher than my lot.
Shall that be shut to man, which to the beast
Is open? Or will God incense his ire
For such a petty trespass, and not praise
Rather your dauntless virtue,° whom the pain   *courage*
Of death denounced,° whatever thing death be,   *threatened*
Deterred not from achieving what might lead
To happier life, knowledge of good and evil;
Of good, how just?[9] Of evil, if what is evil
Be real, why not known, since easier shunned?
God therefore cannot hurt ye, and be just;
Not just, not God; not feared then,[1] nor obeyed:
Your fear itself of death removes the fear.
Why then was this forbid? Why but to awe,
Why but to keep ye low and ignorant,
His worshippers; he knows that in the day

---

5. Eve's formulation indicates her "sufficient" understanding of the prohibition and the conditions of life in Eden. See 3.98–101.
6. Drawn up to full dignity. Satan as the snake takes on the role of a Greek or Roman orator defending liberty (lines 670–72), a Demosthenes or a Cicero.
7. Bursting into the middle of his speech without a preface, and "upgrown" to the impassioned high style ("high") at once (lines 675–78).

8. I.e., life as well as knowledge, and a better life enhanced by knowledge, which Satan in the snake presents as a magical property of the tree.
9. I.e., how can it be just to forbid the knowledge of good?
1. Satan's sophism invites atheism: if God forbids knowledge of good and evil he is not just, therefore not God, therefore his threat of death need not be feared.

Ye eat thereof, your eyes that seem so clear,
Yet are but dim, shall perfectly be then
Opened and cleared, and ye shall be as gods,[2]
Knowing both good and evil as they know.
710 That ye should be as gods, since I as man,
Internal man, is but proportion meet,
I of brute human, ye of human gods.[3]
So ye shall die perhaps, by putting off
Human, to put on gods, death to be wished,
715 Though threatened, which no worse than this can bring.
And what are gods that man may not become
As they, participating° godlike food?   *partaking of*
The gods are first, and that advantage use
On our belief, that all from them proceeds;
720 I question it, for this fair earth I see,
Warmed by the sun, producing every kind,
Them nothing: if they all° things, who enclosed   *produce all*
Knowledge of good and evil in this tree,
That whoso eats thereof, forthwith attains
725 Wisdom without their leave? And wherein lies
Th' offense, that man should thus attain to know?
What can your knowledge hurt him, or this tree
Impart against his will if all be his?
Or is it envy, and can envy dwell
730 In heav'nly breasts? These, these and many more
Causes import° your need of this fair fruit.   *prove*
Goddess humane,[4] reach then, and freely taste."
    He ended, and his words replete with guile
Into her heart too easy entrance won:
735 Fixed on the fruit she gazed, which to behold
Might tempt alone, and in her ears the sound
Yet rung of his persuasive words, impregned°   *impregnated*
With reason, to her seeming, and with truth;
Meanwhile the hour of noon drew on, and waked
740 An eager appetite, raised by the smell
So savory of that fruit, which with desire,
Inclinable now grown to touch or taste,
Solicited her longing eye; yet first
Pausing a while, thus to herself she mused:
745 "Great are thy virtues,° doubtless, best of fruits,   *powers*
Though kept from man, and worthy to be admired,
Whose taste, too long forborne, at first assay°   *try*
Gave elocution to the mute, and taught
The tongue not made for speech to speak thy praise:
750 Thy praise he also who forbids thy use,
Conceals not from us, naming thee the Tree
Of Knowledge, knowledge both of good and evil;
Forbids us then to taste, but his forbidding
Commends thee more, while it infers° the good   *implies*
755 By thee communicated, and our want:°   *lack*

2. Hereafter, Satan speaks of "gods," not God.
3. Satan invites the aspiration to divinity, based
on analogy to the supposed experience of the
snake.
4. Both "human" and "gracious" or "kindly."

For good unknown, sure is not had, or had
And yet unknown, is as not had at all.
In plain° then, what forbids he but to know,   *in plain words*
Forbids us good, forbids us to be wise?
Such prohibitions bind not. But if death
Bind us with after-bands,° what profits then   *later bonds*
Our inward freedom? In the day we eat
Of this fair fruit, our doom is, we shall die.
How dies the serpent? He hath eat'n and lives,
And knows, and speaks, and reasons, and discerns,
Irrational till then. For us alone
Was death invented? Or to us denied
This intellectual food, for beasts reserved?
For beasts it seems: yet that one beast which first
Hath tasted, envies° not, but brings with joy   *begrudges*
The good befall'n him, author unsuspect,[5]
Friendly to man, far from deceit or guile.
What fear I then, rather what know to fear
Under this ignorance of good and evil,
Of God or death, of law or penalty?
Here grows the cure of all, this fruit divine,
Fair to the eye, inviting to the taste,
Of virtue° to make wise: what hinders then   *power*
To reach, and feed at once both body and mind?"
    So saying, her rash hand in evil hour
Forth reaching to the fruit, she plucked, she eat.[6]
Earth felt the wound, and nature from her seat
Sighing through all her works gave signs of woe,
That all was lost. Back to the thicket slunk
The guilty serpent, and well might, for Eve
Intent now wholly on her taste, naught else
Regarded, such delight till then, as seemed,
In fruit she never tasted, whether true
Or fancied so, through expectation high
Of knowledge, nor was godhead from her thought.
Greedily she engorged without restraint,
And knew not eating death:[7] satiate at length,
And heightened as with wine, jocund° and boon,°   *merry / jolly*
Thus to herself she pleasingly began:
    "O sov'reign, virtuous, precious of all trees
In Paradise, of operation blest
To sapience, hitherto obscured, infamed,[8]
And thy fair fruit let hang, as to no end
Created; but henceforth my early care,
Not without song, each morning, and due praise
Shall tend thee, and the fertile burden ease
Of thy full branches offered free to all;
Till dieted by thee I grow mature
In knowledge, as the gods who all things know;

---

5. An authority or informant beyond suspicion.
6. Ate: an accepted past tense, pronounced *et*.
7. I.e., she is eating death and doesn't know it, or experience it yet, but also, punning, death is eating her too.
8. Slandered. "Sapience": both knowledge and tasting (Latin *sapere*).

805 Though others envy what they cannot give;
For had the gift been theirs,[9] it had not here
Thus grown. Experience, next to thee I owe,
Best guide; not following thee, I had remained
In ignorance, thou open'st wisdom's way,
810 And giv'st accéss, though secret° she retire.   *hidden*
And I perhaps am secret;° Heav'n is high,   *unseen*
High and remote to see from thence distinct
Each thing on earth; and other care perhaps
May have diverted from continual watch
815 Our great Forbidder, safe with all his spies
About him. But to Adam in what sort°   *guise*
Shall I appear? Shall I to him make known
As yet my change, and give him to partake
Full happiness with me, or rather not,
820 But keep the odds° of knowledge in my power   *advantage*
Without copartner? so to add what wants°   *lacks*
In female sex, the more to draw his love,
And render me more equal, and perhaps,
A thing not undesirable, sometime
825 Superior; for inferior who is free?[1]
This may be well: but what if God have seen,
And death ensue? Then I shall be no more,
And Adam wedded to another Eve,
Shall live with her enjoying, I extinct;
830 A death to think. Confirmed then I resolve,
Adam shall share with me in bliss or woe:
So dear I love him, that with him all deaths
I could endure, without him live no life."
    So saying, from the tree her step she turned,
835 But first low reverence done, as to the power
That dwelt within,[2] whose presence had infused
Into the plant sciential° sap, derived   *knowledge-producing*
From nectar, drink of gods. Adam the while
Waiting desirous her return, had wove
840 Of choicest flow'rs a garland to adorn
Her tresses, and her rural labors crown,
As reapers oft are wont° their harvest queen.   *accustomed*
Great joy he promised to his thoughts, and new
Solace in her return, so long delayed;
845 Yet oft his heart, divine of° something ill,   *foreboding*
Misgave him; he the falt'ring measure° felt;   *heartbeat*
And forth to meet her went, the way she took
That morn when first they parted; by the Tree
Of Knowledge he must pass; there he her met,
850 Scarce from the tree returning; in her hand
A bough of fairest fruit that downy smiled,
New gathered, and ambrosial° smell diffused.   *fragrant*
To him she hasted, in her face excuse
Came prologue,[3] and apology to prompt,

---

9. Like Satan, Eve now conflates gods and God, ascribing envy but also lack of power to "them."
1. Cf. Satan, 1.248–63, 5.790–97.
2. Eve ends with idolatry, worship of the tree.

3. I.e., excuse came like the prologue in a play, and apology (justification, self-defense) served as prompter.

Which with bland° words at will she thus addressed.   *mild, coaxing*
　"Hast thou not wondered, Adam, at my stay?
Thee I have missed, and thought it long, deprived
Thy presence, agony of love till now
Not felt, nor shall be twice, for never more
Mean I to try, what rash untried I sought,
The pain of absence from thy sight. But strange
Hath been the cause, and wonderful to hear:
This tree is not as we are told, a tree
Of danger tasted,° nor to evil unknown   *if tasted*
Op'ning the way, but of divine effect
To open eyes, and make them gods who taste;
And hath been tasted such: the serpent wise,
Or° not restrained as we, or not obeying,   *either*
Hath eaten of the fruit, and is become,
Not dead, as we are threatened, but thenceforth
Endued with human voice and human sense,
Reasoning to admiration,° and with me   *wonderfully well*
Persuasively° hath so prevailed, that I   *by persuasion*
Have also tasted, and have also found
Th' effects to correspond, opener mine eyes,
Dim erst,° dilated spirits, ampler heart,   *before*
And growing up to godhead; which for thee
Chiefly I sought, without thee can despise.
For bliss, as thou hast part, to me is bliss,
Tedious, unshared with thee, and odious soon.
Thou therefore also taste, that equal lot
May join us, equal joy, as equal love;
Lest thou not tasting, different degree°   *rank*
Disjoin us, and I then too late renounce
Deity for thee, when fate will not permit."[4]
　　Thus Eve with count'nance blithe her story told;
But in her cheek distemper[5] flushing glowed.
On th' other side, Adam, soon as he heard
The fatal trespass done by Eve, amazed,°   *stunned*
Astonied° stood and blank, while horror chill   *petrified*
Ran through his veins, and all his joints relaxed;
From his slack hand the garland wreathed for Eve
Down dropped, and all the faded roses shed:
Speechless he stood and pale, till thus at length
First to himself he inward silence broke:
　"O fairest of creation, last and best
Of all God's works, creature in whom excelled
Whatever can to sight or thought be formed,
Holy, divine, good, amiable, or sweet!
How art thou lost, how on a sudden lost,
Defaced, deflow'red, and now to death devote?°   *doomed*
Rather how hast thou yielded to transgress
The strict forbiddance, how to violate
The sacred° fruit forbidd'n! Some cursèd fraud   *consecrated*

4. Compare Eve in soliloquy, lines 817–33.
5. I.e., disorder arising from disturbance of the balance of humors in the body, intoxication.

905   Of enemy hath beguiled thee, yet unknown,
      And me with thee hath ruined, for with thee
      Certain my resolution is to die;
      How can I live without thee, how forgo
      Thy sweet converse and love so dearly joined,
910   To live again in these wild woods forlorn?
      Should God create another Eve, and I
      Another rib afford, yet loss of thee
      Would never from my heart; no no, I feel
      The link of nature draw me: flesh of flesh,
915   Bone of my bone thou art,[6] and from thy state
      Mine never shall be parted, bliss or woe."
            So having said, as one from sad dismay
      Recomforted, and after thoughts disturbed
      Submitting to what seemed remédiless,
920   Thus in calm mood his words to Eve he turned:
            "Bold deed thou hast presumed, advent'rous Eve,
      And peril great provoked, who thus hast dared
      Had it been only coveting to eye
      That sacred fruit, sacred° to abstinence,   set apart
925   Much more to taste it under ban to touch.
      But past who can recall, or done undo?
      Not God omnipotent, nor fate; yet so
      Perhaps thou shalt not die, perhaps the fact°   deed
      Is not so heinous now, foretasted fruit,
930   Profaned first by the serpent, by him first
      Made common and unhallowed ere our taste;
      Nor yet on him found deadly, he yet lives,
      Lives, as thou saidst, and gains to live as man
      Higher degree of life, inducement strong
935   To us, as likely tasting to attain
      Proportional ascent, which cannot be
      But to be gods, or angels demigods.
      Nor can I think that God, Creator wise,
      Though threat'ning, will in earnest so destroy
940   Us his prime creatures, dignified so high,
      Set over all his works, which in our fall,
      For us created, needs with us must fail,
      Dependent made; so God shall uncreate,
      Be frustrate, do, undo, and labor lose,
945   Not well conceived of God, who though his power
      Creation could repeat, yet would be loath
      Us to abolish, lest the Adversary°   Satan
      Triumph and say; 'Fickle their state whom God
      Most favors, who can please him long? Me first
950   He ruined, now mankind; whom will he next?'
      Matter of scorn, not to be given the Foe.
      However I with thee have fixed my lot,
      Certain° to undergo like doom; if death   resolved
      Consort° with thee, death is to me as life;   associate
955   So forcible within my heart I feel

6. Adam echoes Genesis 2.23–24.

The bond of nature draw me to my own,
My own in thee, for what thou art is mine;
Our state cannot be severed, we are one,
One flesh; to lose thee were to lose myself."
    So Adam, and thus Eve to him replied:
"O glorious trial of exceeding[7] love,
Illustrious evidence, example high!
Engaging me to emulate, but short
Of thy perfection, how shall I attain,
Adam, from whose dear side I boast me sprung,
And gladly of our union hear thee speak,
One heart, one soul in both; whereof good proof
This day affords, declaring thee resolved,
Rather than death or aught° than death more dread   *anything other*
Shall separate us, linked in love so dear,
To undergo with me one guilt, one crime,
If any be, of tasting this fair fruit,
Whose virtue,° for of good still good proceeds,   *power*
Direct, or by occasion° hath presented   *indirectly*
This happy trial of thy love, which else
So eminently never had been known.
Were it° I thought death menaced would ensue°   *if / result from*
This my attempt, I would sustain alone
The worst, and not persuade thee, rather die
Deserted, than oblige° thee with a fact°   *bind / deed*
Pernicious to thy peace, chiefly assured
Remarkably so late of thy so true,
So faithful love unequaled;[8] but I feel
Far otherwise th' event,° not death, but life   *result*
Augmented, opened eyes, new hopes, new joys,
Taste so divine, that what of sweet before
Hath touched my sense, flat seems to this, and harsh.
On my experience, Adam, freely taste,
And fear of death deliver to the winds."
    So saying, she embraced him, and for joy
Tenderly wept, much won that he his love
Had so ennobled, as of choice to incur
Divine displeasure for her sake, or death.
In recompense (for such compliance bad
Such recompense best merits) from the bough
She gave him of that fair enticing fruit
With liberal hand: he scrupled not to eat
Against his better knowledge, not deceived,[9]
But fondly° overcome with female charm.   *foolishly*
Earth trembled from her entrails, as again
In pangs, and nature gave a second groan;
Sky loured, and muttering thunder, some sad drops
Wept at completing of the mortal sin

---

7. The word, which Eve intends as praise, carries the implication of "excessive."
8. I.e., since I have so recently been assured of your unparalleled love.

9. Cf. 1 Timothy 2.14: "And Adam was not deceived, but the woman being deceived was in the transgression."

Original;[1] while Adam took no thought,
1005 Eating his fill, nor Eve to iterate°   repeat
Her former trespass feared, the more to soothe
Him with her loved society, that now
As with new wine intoxicated both
They swim in mirth, and fancy that they feel
1010 Divinity within them breeding wings
Wherewith to scorn the earth: but that false fruit
Far other operation first displayed,
Carnal desire inflaming, he on Eve
Began to cast lascivious eyes, she him
1015 As wantonly repaid; in lust they burn:
Till Adam thus 'gan Eve to dalliance move:
    "Eve, now I see thou art exact of taste,
And elegant, of sapience[2] no small part,
Since to each meaning savor we apply,
1020 And palate call judicious; I the praise
Yield thee, so well this day thou hast purveyed.°   provided
Much pleasure we have lost, while we abstained
From this delightful fruit, nor known till now
True relish, tasting; if such pleasure be
1025 In things to us forbidden, it might be wished,
For this one tree had been forbidden ten.
But come, so well refreshed, now let us play,
As meet° is, after such delicious fare;   appropriate
For never did thy beauty since the day
1030 I saw thee first and wedded thee, adorned
With all perfections, so inflame my sense
With ardor to enjoy thee, fairer now
Than ever, bounty of this virtuous tree."
    So said he, and forbore not glance or toy°   caress
1035 Of amorous intent, well understood
Of° Eve, whose eye darted contagious fire.   by
Her hand he seized, and to a shady bank,
Thick overhead with verdant roof embow'red
He led her nothing loath; flow'rs were the couch,
1040 Pansies, and violets, and asphodel,
And hyacinth, earth's freshest softest lap.
There they their fill of love and love's disport
Took largely, of their mutual guilt the seal,
The solace of their sin, till dewy sleep
1045 Oppressed them, wearied with their amorous play.
Soon as the force of that fallacious fruit,
That with exhilarating vapor bland°   pleasing
About their spirits had played, and inmost powers
Made err, was now exhaled, and grosser sleep
1050 Bred of unkindly fumes,° with conscious dreams   unnatural vapors
Encumbered,° now had left them, up they rose   oppressed
As from unrest, and each the other viewing,

1. The theological doctrine that all Adam's descendants are stained by Adam's sin and are thereby subject to physical death and (unless saved by grace) to damnation.

2. Adam commends Eve for her fine ("exact") and discriminating ("elegant") taste, as a part of "sapience," which means both "taste" and "wisdom."

Soon found their eyes how opened, and their minds
How darkened; innocence, that as a veil
Had shadowed them from knowing ill, was gone,
Just confidence, and native righteousness,
And honor from about them, naked left
To guilty shame: he° covered, but his robe   *shame*
Uncovered more. So rose the Danite strong
Hercúlean Samson from the harlot-lap
Of Philistéan Dálilah, and waked
Shorn of his strength,[3] they destitute and bare
Of all their virtue: silent, and in face
Confounded long they sat, as strucken mute,
Till Adam, though not less than Eve abashed,
At length gave utterance to these words constrained:° *forced*
 "O Eve, in evil[4] hour thou didst give ear
To that false worm, of whomsoever taught
To counterfeit man's voice, true in our fall,
False in our promised rising; since our eyes
Opened we find indeed, and find we know
Both good and evil, good lost and evil got,[5]
Bad fruit of knowledge, if this be to know,
Which leaves us naked thus, of honor void,
Of innocence, of faith, of purity,
Our wonted° ornaments now soiled and stained, *accustomed*
And in our faces evident the signs
Of foul concupiscence;[6] whence evil store;
Even shame, the last of evils; of the first
Be sure then. How shall I behold the face
Henceforth of God or angel, erst with joy
And rapture so oft beheld? Those heav'nly shapes
Will dazzle now this earthly, with their blaze
Insufferably bright. O might I here
In solitude live savage, in some glade
Obscured, where highest woods impenetrable
To star or sunlight, spread their umbrage° broad, *shadow, foliage*
And brown as evening: cover me ye pines,
Ye cedars, with innumerable boughs
Hide me, where I may never see them more.
But let us now, as in bad plight, devise
What best may for the present serve to hide
The parts of each from other, that seem most
To shame obnoxious,° and unseemliest seen,   *exposed*
Some tree whose broad smooth leaves together sewed,
And girded on our loins, may cover round
Those middle parts, that this newcomer, shame,
There sit not, and reproach us as unclean."

---

3. Samson, of the tribe of Dan, told the "harlot" Philistine Delilah that the secret of his strength (like that of Hercules) lay in his hair; she sheared it off while he slept, and when he awoke he was easily captured and blinded by his enemies.
4. Adam's bitter pun—Eve, evil—repudiates the actual etymology of Eve, "life," which Adam will later reaffirm (11.159–61).

5. Milton, like most commentators, derives the tree's name from the event (4.222, 11.84–89).
6. The theological term for the unruly human passions and desires seen as one effect of the Fall, a sign of abundance ("store") of evils. If "shame" (see following lines) is the "last" evil, the "first" is probably the guiltiness that produces it, according to Milton's *Christian Doctrine* (1.12).

So counseled he, and both together went
1100 Into the thickest wood, there soon they chose
The fig tree,[7] not that kind for fruit renowned,
But such as at this day to Indians known
In Malabar or Deccan spreads her arms
Branching so broad and long, that in the ground
1105 The bended twigs take root, and daughters grow
About the mother tree, a pillared shade
High overarched, and echoing walks between;
There oft the Indian herdsman shunning heat
Shelters in cool, and tends his pasturing herds
1110 At loopholes cut through thickest shade: those leaves
They gathered, broad as Amazonian targe,°   *shields*
And with what skill they had, together sewed,
To gird their waist, vain covering if to hide
Their guilt and dreaded shame. O how unlike
1115 To that first naked glory. Such of late
Columbus found th' American so girt
With feathered cincture,° naked else and wild,   *belt*
Among the trees on isles and woody shores.
Thus fenced, and as they thought, their shame in part
1120 Covered, but not at rest or ease of mind,
They sat them down to weep, nor only tears
Rained at their eyes, but high winds worse within
Began to rise, high passions, anger, hate,
Mistrust, suspicion, discord, and shook sore
1125 Their inward state of mind, calm region once
And full of peace, now tossed and turbulent:
For understanding ruled not, and the will
Heard not her lore, both in subjection now
To sensual appetite, who from beneath
1130 Usurping over sov'reign reason claimed
Superior sway: from thus distempered breast,[8]
Adam, estranged° in look and altered style,   *unlike himself*
Speech intermitted° thus to Eve renewed: *interrupted*
   "Would thou hadst hearkened to my words, and stayed
1135 With me, as I besought thee, when that strange
Desire of wand'ring this unhappy morn,
I know not whence possessed thee; we had then
Remained still happy, not as now, despoiled
Of all our good, shamed, naked, miserable.
1140 Let none henceforth seek needless cause to approve°   *prove*
The faith they owe; when earnestly they seek
Such proof, conclude, they then begin to fail."
   To whom soon moved with touch of blame thus Eve:
"What words have passed thy lips, Adam severe,
1145 Imput'st thou that to my default, or will
Of wand'ring, as thou call'st it, which who knows
But might as ill have happened thou being by,

---

7. The banyan, or Indian fig, has small leaves, but the account Milton draws on from Gerard's *Herbal* (1597) contains the details of lines 1104–11; Malabar and Deccan (line 1103) are in southern India.

8. The immediate psychological effects of the Fall are evident in the subjection of reason to the lower faculties of sensual appetite.

Or to thyself perhaps: hadst thou been there,
Or here th' attempt, thou couldst not have discerned
Fraud in the serpent, speaking as he spake;
No ground of enmity between us known,
Why he should mean me ill, or seek to harm.
Was I to have never parted from thy side?
As good have grown there still a lifeless rib.
Being as I am, why didst not thou the head
Command me absolutely not to go,
Going into such danger as thou saidst?
Too facile° then thou didst not much gainsay,°   *easy, mild / oppose*
Nay didst permit, approve, and fair dismiss.
Hadst thou been firm and fixed in thy dissent,
Neither had I transgressed, nor thou with me."
   To whom then first incensed Adam replied.
"Is this the love, is this the recompense
Of mine to thee, ingrateful Eve, expressed°   *demonstrated*
Immutable when thou wert lost, not I,
Who might have lived and joyed immortal bliss,
Yet willingly chose rather death with thee:
And am I now upbraided, as the cause
Of thy transgressing? not enough severe,
It seems, in thy restraint: what could I more?
I warned thee, I admonished thee, foretold
The danger, and the lurking enemy
That lay in wait; beyond this had been force,
And force upon free will hath here no place.
But confidence then bore thee on, secure°   *self-assured*
Either to meet no danger, or to find
Matter of glorious trial; and perhaps
I also erred in overmuch admiring
What seemed in thee so perfect, that I thought
No evil durst attempt thee, but I rue
That error now, which is become my crime,
And thou th' accuser. Thus it shall befall
Him who to worth in women overtrusting
Lets her will rule; restraint she will not brook,°   *accept*
And left to herself, if evil thence ensue,
She first his weak indulgence will accuse."
   Thus they in mutual accusation spent
The fruitless hours, but neither self-condemning,
And of their vain contést appeared no end.

From Book 10

Summary   When it is known in Heaven that man has fallen, God sends his Son to pass judgment on the sinners. Having found them in the garden, he hears their confession and passes instant sentence, cursing the serpent, condemning Eve to the pains of childbirth and Adam to those of daily toil; but in mercy, he clothes the human couple both outwardly with skins of beasts and inwardly with his righteousness. Meanwhile Sin and Death, sitting by Hell-gate, feel new strength, and pass across Chaos, leaving a great bridge behind them. On their way they meet with their parent, Satan, learn of his success on Earth, and press eagerly forward in hopes of destroying humankind altogether. Satan, on the other hand, continues his flight back toward Hell, where he is to report to his constituents.

[CONSEQUENCES OF THE FALL]

>   * * * Th' other way Satan went down
> The causey° to Hell gate; on either side   *causeway*
> Disparted Chaos over-built exclaimed,
> And with rebounding surge the bars assailed,
> That scorned his indignation.[1] Through the gate,
> Wide open and unguarded, Satan passed,
> And all about found desolate; for those[2]
> Appointed to sit there, had left their charge,
> Flown to the upper world; the rest were all
> Far to the inland retired, about the walls
> Of Pandemonium, city and proud seat
> Of Lucifer, so by allusion° called,   *metaphor*
> Of that bright star to Satan paragoned.[3]
> There kept their watch the legions, while the grand[4]
> In council sat, solicitous° what chance   *anxious*
> Might intercept their emperor sent, so he
> Departing gave command, and they observed.
> As when the Tartar from his Russian foe
> By Astracan over the snowy plains
> Retires, or Bactrian Sophi from the horns
> Of Turkish crescent, leaves all waste beyond
> The realm of Aladule, in his retreat
> To Tauris or Casbeen:[5] so these the late
> Heav'n-banished host, left desert utmost Hell
> Many a dark league, reduced° in careful watch   *drawn together*
> Round their metropolis, and now expecting
> Each hour their great adventurer from the search
> Of foreign worlds: he through the midst unmarked,°   *unnoticed*
> In show plebeian angel militant
> Of lowest order, passed; and from the door
> Of that Plutonian[6] hall, invisible
> Ascended his high throne, which under state°   *canopy*
> Of richest texture spread, at th' upper end
> Was placed in regal luster. Down a while
> He sat, and round about him saw unseen:
> At last as from a cloud his fulgent head
> And shape star-bright appeared, or brighter, clad

Line numbers: 415, 420, 425, 430, 435, 440, 445, 450

1. Chaos is the instinctive enemy of all order, so hostile to the bridge built over it.
2. Sin and Death.
3. Satan before his fall was Lucifer, the Light-bringer, and the morning star is named Lucifer because it is compared ("paragoned") to him.
4. The "grand infernal peers" who govern (cf. 2.507).
5. The simile, begun in line 431, compares the fallen angels, withdrawn from other regions of Hell to guard their metropolis, to Tartars retir-
ing before attacking Russians and Persians retreating before the attacking Turks. "Astra-can": a region west of the Caspian Sea inhabited by Russia and defended against Turks and Tartars; "Aladule": the region of Armenia, from which the last Persian ruler, called Anadule, a "Bactrian Sophi" (Persian shah), was forced to retreat from the Turks, to Tabriz ("Tauris") and Kazvin ("Casbeen").
6. Pertaining to Pluto, ruler of the classical underworld.

With what permissive° glory since his fall *permitted*
Was left him, or false glitter: all amazed
At that so sudden blaze the Stygian[7] throng
Bent their aspéct, and whom they wished beheld,
Their mighty chief returned: loud was th' acclaim:
Forth rushed in haste the great consulting peers,
Raised from their dark divan,[8] and with like joy
Congratulant approached him, who with hand
Silence, and with these words attention won:
    "Thrones, Dominations, Princedoms, Virtues, Powers,
For in possession such, not only of right,
I call ye[9] and declare ye now, returned
Successful beyond hope, to lead ye forth
Triumphant out of this infernal pit
Abominable, accurst, the house of woe,
And dungeon of our tyrant: now possess,
As lords, a spacious world, to our native Heaven
Little inferior, by my adventure hard
With peril great achieved. Long were to tell
What I have done, what suffered, with what pain
Voyaged th' unreal,° vast, unbounded deep *unformed*
Of horrible confusion, over which
By Sin and Death a broad way now is paved
To expedite your glorious march; but I
Toiled out my uncouth° passage, forced to ride *strange*
Th' untractable abyss, plunged in the womb
Of unoriginal[1] Night and Chaos wild,
That jealous of their secrets fiercely opposed
My journey strange, with clamorous uproar
Protesting Fate[2] supreme; thence how I found
The new-created world, which fame in Heav'n
Long had foretold, a fabric wonderful
Of absolute perfection, therein man
Placed in a paradise, by our exile
Made happy: him by fraud I have seduced
From his Creator, and the more to increase
Your wonder, with an apple. He thereat
Offended, worth your laughter, hath giv'n up
Both his beloved man and all his world,
To Sin and Death a prey, and so to us,
Without our hazard, labor, or alarm,
To range in, and to dwell, and over man
To rule, as over all he should have ruled.
True is, me also he hath judged, or rather
Me not, but the brute serpent in whose shape
Man I deceived; that which to me belongs,
Is enmity, which he will put between
Me and mankind; I am to bruise his heel;

---

7. Of the river Styx in Hades, the river of hate.
8. The Turkish Council of State.
9. I.e., you now have these titles not only by right

but by possession (from the conquest on earth).
1. Having no origin, uncreated.
2. Protesting both to and against Fate.

His seed, when is not set, shall bruise my head:
500 A world who would not purchase with a bruise,
Or much more grievous pain? Ye have th' account
Of my performance: what remains, ye gods,
But up and enter now into full bliss."[3]
 So having said, a while he stood, expecting
505 Their universal shout and high applause
To fill his ear, when contrary he hears
On all sides, from innumerable tongues
A dismal universal hiss, the sound
Of public scorn; he wondered, but not long
510 Had leisure, wond'ring at himself now more;
His visage drawn he felt to sharp and spare,
His arms clung to his ribs, his legs entwining
Each other, till supplanted° down he fell   tripped up
A monstrous serpent on his belly prone,
515 Reluctant,° but in vain, a greater power   struggling
Now ruled him, punished in the shape he sinned,
According to his doom: he would have spoke,
But hiss for hiss returned with forkèd tongue
To forkèd tongue, for now were all transformed
520 Alike, to serpents[4] all as accessories
To his bold riot:° dreadful was the din   revolt
Of hissing through the hall, thick swarming now
With complicated° monsters, head and tail,   tangled
Scorpion and asp, and amphisbaena dire,
525 Cerastes horned, hydrus, and ellops drear,
And dipsas[5] (not so thick swarmed once the soil
Bedropped with blood of Gorgon, or the isle
Ophiusa)[6] but still greatest he the midst,
Now dragon grown, larger than whom the sun
530 Engendered in the Pythian vale on slime,
Huge Python,[7] and his power no less he seemed
Above the rest still to retain; they all
Him followed issuing forth to th' open field,
Where all yet left of that revolted rout
535 Heav'n-fall'n, in station stood or just array,[8]
Sublime° with expectation when to see   raised up
In triumph issuing forth their glorious chief;
They saw, but other sight instead, a crowd
Of ugly serpents; horror on them fell,
540 And horrid sympathy; for what they saw,

3. Ironically, the final word of Satan's proud, triumphal speech rhymes with and so prepares for the "hiss" (line 508) that will soon greet him, as his would-be triumph is turned by God to abject humiliation.
4. The scene recalls Dante's vivid description of the thieves metamorphosed to snakes in *Inferno* 24–25.
5. The "scorpion" has a venomous sting at the tip of the tail; "asp" is a small Egyptian viper; "amphisbaena" supposedly had a head at each end; "Cerastes" is an asp with horny projections over each eye; "hydrus" and "ellops" were mythical water snakes; "dipsas" was a mythical snake whose bite caused raging thirst.
6. Drops of blood from the Gorgon Medusa's severed head turned into snakes; "Ophiusa" in Greek means "isle of snakes."
7. A gigantic serpent engendered from the slime left by Deucalion's flood; Apollo slew him and appropriated the "Pythian" vale and shrine at Delphi.
8. I.e., at their posts or on parade.

They felt themselves now changing; down their arms,
Down fell both spear and shield, down they as fast,
And the dire hiss renewed, and the dire form
Catched by contagion, like in punishment,
As in their crime. Thus was th' applause they meant,
Turned to exploding hiss, triumph to shame
Cast on themselves from their own mouths. There stood
A grove hard by, sprung up with this their change,
His will who reigns above, to aggravate
Their penance,° laden with fair fruit, like that   *punishment*
Which grew in Paradise, the bait of Eve
Used by the Tempter: on that prospect strange
Their earnest eyes they fixed, imagining
For one forbidden tree a multitude
Now ris'n, to work them further woe or shame;
Yet parched with scalding thirst and hunger fierce,
Though to delude them sent, could not abstain,
But on they rolled in heaps, and up the trees
Climbing, sat thicker than the snaky locks
That curled Megaera:[9] greedily they plucked
The fruitage fair to sight, like that which grew
Near that bituminous lake where Sodom flamed;[1]
This more delusive, not the touch, but taste
Deceived; they fondly° thinking to allay   *foolishly*
Their appetite with gust,° instead of fruit   *relish*
Chewed bitter ashes, which th' offended taste
With spattering noise rejected: oft they assayed,°   *attempted*
Hunger and thirst constraining, drugged as oft,
With hatefulest disrelish writhed their jaws
With soot and cinders filled; so oft they fell
Into the same illusion, not as man
Whom they triumphed once lapsed.[2] Thus were they plagued
And worn with famine, long and ceaseless hiss,
Till their lost shape, permitted, they resumed,[3]
Yearly enjoined, some say, to undergo
This annual humbling certain numbered days,
To dash their pride, and joy for man seduced.
However some tradition they dispersed
Among the heathen of their purchase° got,   *plunder*
And fabled how the serpent, whom they called
Ophion with Eurynome, the wide-
Encroaching Eve perhaps, had first the rule
Of high Olympus, thence by Saturn driv'n
And Ops, ere yet Dictaean Jove was born.[4]

---

9. One of three Furies with snaky hair.
1. Sodom apples reputedly grew on the spot where the accursed city once stood, now the Dead Sea ("that bituminous lake"); the apples look good but dissolve into ashes when eaten.
2. Unlike man who fell once, they try to eat the dissolving apples over and over again.
3. God permitted them to regain their "lost shape" as fallen angels; but they are undergoing a slower, natural metamorphosis into grosser substance by their continuing commitment to and choice of evil.
4. The Titan Ophion (whose name means "snake") and his wife Eurynome ("the wide-reacher") ruled Olympus until driven away by "Saturn" and his wife Ops, who were in turn overthrown by Jove, who lived on the mountain Dicte. Milton suggests that these may represent versions of the story transmitted by the fallen angels to the pagans (lines 578–79).

Summary Sin and Death proceed without further interruption to Earth, and enter into possession of it. God sees their arrival and declines to interfere, but prophesies that their triumph will be only temporary; in due course they will be forced back to Hell again, and forever. Meanwhile, the angels are ordered to twist the Earth on its axis, disorder the planets so their influence will in future be bad as well as good, and rearrange the cosmos generally. In consequence, the temperate climate of Paradise at once gives way to extremes of heat and cold, and furious winds begin to blow across the ruined planet.

[ADAM, EVE, AND THE FIRST STEPS TO REDEMPTION]

* * * Thus began
Outrage from lifeless things; but Discord first
Daughter of Sin, among th' irrational,
Death introduced through fierce antipathy:[5]
710 Beast now with beast gan war, and fowl with fowl,
And fish with fish; to graze the herb° all leaving,   *grass*
Devour'd each other; nor stood much in awe
Of man, but fled him, or with count'nance grim
Glared on him passing: these were from without
715 The growing miseries, which Adam saw
Already in part, though hid in gloomiest shade,
To sorrow abandoned, but worse felt within,
And in a troubled sea of passion tossed,
Thus to disburden sought with sad complaint:
720   "O miserable of happy![6] Is this the end
Of this new glorious world, and me so late
The glory of that glory, who now become
Accurst of blessèd, hide me from the face
Of God, whom to behold was then my height
725 Of happiness: yet well, if here would end
The misery, I deserved it, and would bear
My own deservings; but this will not serve;
All that I eat or drink, or shall beget,
Is propagated[7] curse. O voice once heard
730 Delightfully, 'Increase and multiply,'
Now death to hear! For what can I increase
Or multiply, but curses on my head?
Who of all ages to succeed, but feeling
The evil on him brought by me, will curse
735 My head: 'Ill fare our ancestor impure,
For this we may thank Adam'; but his thanks
Shall be the execration; so besides
Mine own that bide upon me, all from me
Shall with a fierce reflux on me redound,
740 On me as on their natural center light
Heavy, though in their place.[8] O fleeting joys

5. Discord (personified as daughter of Sin) introduced Death among the animals ("th' irrational") by stirring up "antipathy" among them.
6. Adam's complaint begins with the classical formula for a tragic fall, or *peripeteia*, the change from happiness to misery.
7. Handed down from one generation to the next.

8. I.e., Adam's "own" curse will remain ("bide") with him, and the curse ("execration") of "all" who descend from him will "redound" on him as to their "natural center"; objects so placed ("in their place") were thought to be weightless ("light"), but these curses will be "heavy."

Of Paradise, dear bought with lasting woes!
Did I request thee, Maker, from my clay
To mold me man, did I solicit thee
From darkness to promote me, or here place
In this delicious garden? As my will
Concurred not to my being, it were but right
And equal° to reduce me to my dust,   *just*
Desirous to resign, and render back
All I received, unable to perform
Thy terms too hard, by which I was to hold
The good I sought not. To the loss of that,
Sufficient penalty, why hast thou added
The sense of endless woes? Inexplicable
Thy justice seems; yet to say truth, too late
I thus contest; then should have been refused
Those terms whatever, when they were proposed:
Thou⁹ didst accept them; wilt thou enjoy the good,
Then cavil° the conditions? And though God   *object frivolously to*
Made thee without thy leave, what if thy son
Prove disobedient, and reproved, retort,
'Wherefore didst thou beget me? I sought it not':
Wouldst thou admit for his contempt of thee
That proud excuse? Yet him not thy election,°   *choice*
But natural necessity begot.
God made thee of choice his own, and of his own
To serve him, thy reward was of his grace,
Thy punishment then justly is at his will.
Be it so, for I submit, his doom is fair,
That dust I am, and shall to dust return:
O welcome hour whenever! Why delays
His hand to execute what his decree
Fixed on this day? Why do I overlive,
Why am I mocked with death, and lengthened out
To deathless pain? How gladly would I meet
Mortality my sentence, and be earth
Insensible, how glad would lay me down
As in my mother's lap! There I should rest
And sleep secure; his dreadful voice no more
Would thunder in my ears, no fear of worse
To me and to my offspring would torment me
With cruel expectation. Yet one doubt
Pursues me still, lest all I° cannot die,   *all of me*
Lest that pure breath of life, the spirit of man
Which God inspired, cannot together perish
With this corporeal clod; then in the grave,
Or in some other dismal place, who knows
But I shall die a living death? O thought
Horrid, if true! Yet why? It was but breath
Of life that sinned; what dies but what had life
And sin? The body properly hath neither.

9. Adam turns from addressing God to address himself.

All of me then shall die:[1] let this appease
The doubt, since human reach no further knows.
For though the Lord of all be infinite,
795   Is his wrath also? Be it, man is not so,
But mortal doomed. How can he exercise
Wrath without end on man whom death must end?
Can he make deathless death? That were to make
Strange contradiction, which to God himself
800   Impossible is held, as argument
Of weakness, not of power. Will he draw out,
For anger's sake, finite to infinite
In punished man, to satisfy his rigor
Satisfied never; that were to extend
805   His sentence beyond dust and nature's law,
By which all causes else according still
To the reception of their matter act,
Not to th' extent of their own sphere.[2] But say
That death be not one stroke, as I supposed,
810   Bereaving° sense, but endless misery   *taking away*
From this day onward, which I feel begun
Both in me, and without° me, and so last   *outside of*
To perpetuity; ay me, that fear
Comes thund'ring back with dreadful revolution°   *return*
815   On my defenseless head; both Death and I
Am found eternal, and incorporate° both,   *made one body*
Nor I on my part single, in me all
Posterity stands cursed: fair patrimony
That I must leave ye, sons; O were I able
820   To waste it all myself, and leave ye none!
So disinherited how would ye bless
Me now your curse! Ah, why should all mankind
For one man's fault thus guiltless be condemned,
If guiltless? But from me what can proceed,
825   But all corrupt, both mind and will depraved,
Not to do° only, but to will the same   *act*
With me? How can they then acquitted stand
In sight of God? Him after all disputes
Forced I absolve: all my evasions vain
830   And reasonings, though through mazes, lead me still
But to my own conviction: first and last
On me, me only, as the source and spring
Of all corruption, all the blame lights due;
So might the wrath.[3] Fond° wish! Couldst thou support *foolish*
835   That burden heavier than the earth to bear,
Than all the world much heavier, though divided

---

1. After debating the matter, Adam concludes that the soul dies with the body; Milton in his *Christian Doctrine* worked out this "mortalist" doctrine, with its corollary, that both soul and body rise at the Last Judgment.
2. Adam convinces himself that "finite" matter (line 802) cannot suffer "infinite" punishment by an axiom of traditional philosophy, that by "nature's law" (line 805) the actions of agents are limited by the nature of the object they act upon.
3. Cf. the Son's offer to accept all humankind's guilt (3.236–41), and Eve's similar offer (10.933–36).

With that bad woman? Thus what thou desir'st,
And what thou fear'st, alike destroys all hope
Of refuge, and concludes thee miserable
Beyond all past example and future,
To Satan only like both crime and doom.
O conscience, into what abyss of fears
And horrors hast thou driv'n me; out of which
I find no way, from deep to deeper plunged!"
    Thus Adam to himself lamented loud
Through the still night, not now, as ere man fell,
Wholesome and cool, and mild, but with black air
Accompanied, with damps° and dreadful gloom,   *noxious vapors*
Which to his evil conscience represented
All things with double terror: on the ground
Outstretched he lay, on the cold ground, and oft
Cursed his creation, Death as oft accused
Of tardy execution, since denounced°   *pronounced*
The day of his offense: "Why comes not Death,"
Said he, "with one thrice-ácceptáble stroke
To end me? Shall Truth fail to keep her word,
Justice divine not hasten to be just?
But Death comes not at call, Justice divine
Mends not her slowest pace for prayers or cries.
O woods, O fountains, hillocks, dales, and bow'rs,
With other echo late I taught your shades
To answer, and resound far other song."⁴
Whom thus afflicted when sad Eve beheld,
Desolate where she sat, approaching nigh,
Soft words to his fierce passion she assayed;°   *attempted*
But her with stern regard he thus repelled:
    "Out of my sight, thou serpent,⁵ that name best
Befits thee with him leagued, thyself as false
And hateful; nothing wants,° but that thy shape,   *is lacking*
Like his, and color serpentine may show
Thy inward fraud, to warn all creatures from thee
Henceforth; lest that too heav'nly form, pretended⁶
To hellish falsehood, snare them. But° for thee   *except*
I had persisted happy, had not thy pride
And wand'ring vanity, when least was safe,
Rejected my forewarning, and disdained
Not to be trusted, longing to be seen
Though by the Devil himself, him overweening°   *overconfident*
To overreach, but with the serpent meeting
Fooled and beguiled, by him thou, I by thee,
To trust thee from my side, imagined wise,
Constant, mature, proof against all assaults,
And understood not all was but a show
Rather than solid virtue, all but a rib
Crooked by nature, bent, as now appears,

---

4. Cf. their morning hymn (5.153–208).   name Eve, aspirated, means "serpent."
5. Adam's bitter, misogynistic outcry begins   6. Held in front, as a cover or mask.
with reference to the patristic notion that the

More to the part sinister° from me drawn,   *the left side*
Well if thrown out, as supernumerary
To my just number found.[7] O why did God,
Creator wise, that peopled highest heav'n
890 With Spirits masculine,[8] create at last
This novelty on earth, this fair defect
Of nature,[9] and not fill the world at once
With men as angels without feminine,
Or find some other way to generate
895 Mankind? This mischief had not then befall'n,
And more that shall befall, innumerable
Disturbances on earth through female snares,
And strait conjunction[1] with this sex: for either
He never shall find out fit mate, but such
900 As some misfortune brings him, or mistake,
Or whom he wishes most shall seldom gain
Through her perverseness, but shall see her gained
By a far worse, or if she love, withheld
By parents, or his happiest choice too late
905 Shall meet, already linked and wedlock-bound
To a fell° adversary, his hate or shame: *bitter*
Which infinite calamity shall cause
To human life, and household peace confound."
    He added not, and from her turned, but Eve
910 Not so repulsed, with tears that ceased not flowing,
And tresses all disordered, at his feet
Fell humble, and embracing them, besought
His peace, and thus proceeded in her plaint:
    "Forsake me not thus, Adam, witness Heav'n
915 What love sincere, and reverence in my heart
I bear thee, and unweeting° have offended,   *unintentionally*
Unhappily deceived; thy suppliant
I beg, and clasp thy knees;[2] bereave me not,
Whereon I live, thy gentle looks, thy aid,
920 Thy counsel in this uttermost distress,
My only strength and stay: forlorn of thee,
Whither shall I betake me, where subsist?
While yet we live, scarce one short hour perhaps,
Between us two let there be peace, both joining,
925 As joined in injuries, one enmity
Against a foe by doom express° assigned us,   *explicit judgment*
That cruel serpent: on me exercise not
Thy hatred for this misery befall'n,
On me already lost, me than thyself
930 More miserable; both have sinned, but thou

---

7. It was supposed that Adam had thirteen ribs on the left side, so he could spare one for the creation of Eve and still retain the proper ("just") number, twelve.
8. The Miltonic bard indicated that angels can assume at will "either sex . . . or both" (1.424).
9. Aristotle had claimed that the female is a defective male.
1. Close, hard-pressing, binding union: Adam then projects the problems of future marriages.
2. Eve assumes the posture of the classical suppliant, clasping the knees of the one she begs from.

Against God only, I against God and thee,
And to the place of judgment will return,
There with my cries importune Heaven, that all
The sentence from thy head removed may light
On me, sole cause to thee of all this woe,
Me me only just object of his ire."[3]
    She ended weeping, and her lowly plight,°   *posture*
Immovable till peace obtained from fault
Acknowledged and deplored, in Adam wrought
Commiseration; soon his heart relented
Towards her, his life so late and sole delight,
Now at his feet submissive in distress,
Creature so fair his reconcilement seeking,
His counsel whom she had displeased, his aid;
As one disarmed, his anger all he lost,
And thus with peaceful words upraised her soon:
    "Unwary, and too desirous, as before,
So now of what thou know'st not, who desir'st
The punishment all on thyself; alas!
Bear thine own first, ill able to sustain
His full wrath whose thou feel'st as yet least part,
And my displeasure bear'st so ill.[4] If prayers
Could alter high decrees, I to that place
Would speed before thee, and be louder heard,
That on my head all might be visited,
Thy frailty and infirmer sex forgiv'n,
To me committed and by me exposed.
But rise, let us no more contend, nor blame
Each other, blamed enough elsewhere, but strive
In offices of love, how we may light'n
Each other's burden in our share of woe;
Since this day's death denounced, if aught I see,
Will prove no sudden, but a slow-paced evil,
A long day's dying to augment our pain,
And to our seed (O hapless seed!) derived."°   *passed on*
    To whom thus Eve, recovering heart, replied:
"Adam, by sad experiment I know
How little weight my words with thee can find,
Found so erroneous, thence by just event°   *consequence*
Found so unfortunate; nevertheless,
Restored by thee, vile as I am, to place
Of new acceptance, hopeful to regain
Thy love, the sole contentment of my heart
Living or dying, from thee I will not hide
What thoughts in my unquiet breast are ris'n,
Tending to some relief of our extremes,
Or end, though sharp and sad, yet tolerable,
As in our evils, and of easier choice.

---

3. Eve also echoes the Son's offer (3.236–41).
Cf. Adam's cry (10.832–34).
4. I.e., you could hardly bear God's "full wrath"
since you are so distraught when you feel only
the smallest part of it, and you can "ill" bear my
displeasure.

If care of our descent perplex us most,[5]
980 Which must be born to certain woe, devoured
By Death at last, and miserable it is
To be to others cause of misery,
Our own begotten, and of our loins to bring
Into this cursèd world a woeful race,
985 That after wretched life must be at last
Food for so foul a monster, in thy power
It lies, yet ere conception to prevent
The race unblest, to being yet unbegot.
Childless thou art, childless remain; so Death
990 Shall be deceived° his glut, and with us two   *cheated of*
Be forced to satisfy his rav'nous maw.
But if thou judge it hard and difficult,
Conversing, looking, loving, to abstain
From love's due rites, nuptial embraces sweet,
995 And with desire to languish without hope,
Before the present object[6] languishing
With like desire, which would be misery
And torment less than none of what we dread,
Then both ourselves and seed at once to free
1000 From what we fear for both, let us make short,°   *lose no time*
Let us seek Death, or he not found, supply
With our own hands his office on ourselves;
Why stand we longer shivering under fears,
That show no end but death, and have the power,
1005 Of many ways to die the shortest choosing,
Destruction with destruction to destroy."
      She ended here, or vehement despair
Broke off the rest; so much of death her thoughts
Had entertained, as dyed her cheeks with pale.
1010 But Adam with such counsel nothing swayed,
To better hopes his more attentive mind
Laboring had raised, and thus to Eve replied.
      "Eve thy contempt of life and pleasure seems
To argue in thee something more sublime
1015 And excellent than what thy mind contemns;°   *despises*
But self-destruction therefore sought, refutes
That excellence thought in thee, and implies,
Not thy contempt, but anguish and regret
For loss of life and pleasure overloved.
1020 Or if thou covet death, as utmost end
Of misery, so thinking to evade
The penalty pronounced, doubt not but God
Hath wiselier armed his vengeful ire than so
To be forestalled; much more I fear lest death
1025 So snatched will not exempt us from the pain
We are by doom to pay: rather such acts
Of contumácy° will provoke the Highest   *contempt*

---

5. I.e., if concern for our descendants most torment ("perplex") us.

6. I.e., Eve herself, who then projects her own frustrated desire if they were to forgo sex.

To make death in us live. Then let us seek
Some safer resolution, which methinks
I have in view, calling to mind with heed
Part of our sentence, that thy seed shall bruise
The serpent's head; piteous amends, unless
Be meant, whom I conjecture, our grand foe
Satan, who in the serpent hath contrived
Against us this deceit: to crush his head
Would be revenge indeed; which will be lost
By death brought on ourselves, or childless days
Resolved, as thou proposest; so our foe
Shall scape his punishment ordained, and we
Instead shall double ours upon our heads.
No more be mentioned then of violence
Against ourselves, and willful barrenness,
That cuts us off from hope, and savors only
Rancor and pride, impatience and despite,
Reluctance° against God and his just yoke   resistance
Laid on our necks. Remember with what mild
And gracious temper he both heard and judged
Without wrath or reviling; we expected
Immediate dissolution, which we thought
Was meant by death that day, when lo, to thee
Pains only in childbearing were foretold,
And bringing forth, soon recompensed with joy,
Fruit of thy womb:[7] on me the curse aslope
Glanced on the ground,[8] with labor I must earn
My bread; what harm? Idleness had been worse;
My labor will sustain me; and lest cold
Or heat should injure us, his timely care
Hath unbesought provided, and his hands
Clothed us unworthy, pitying while he judged;
How much more, if we pray him, will his ear
Be open, and his heart to pity incline,
And teach us further by what means to shun
Th' inclement seasons, rain, ice, hail, and snow,
Which now the sky with various face begins
To show us in this mountain, while the winds
Blow moist and keen, shattering° the graceful locks   scattering
Of these fair spreading trees; which bids us seek
Some better shroud,° some better warmth to cherish   shelter
Our limbs benumbed, ere this diurnal star°   the sun
Leave cold the night, how we his gathered beams
Reflected, may with matter sere° foment,   dry
Or by collision of two bodies grind
The air attrite to fire,[9] as late the clouds

---

7. Adam's prophetic echo of Elizabeth's address to Mary, mother of Jesus (Luke 1.41–42), "blessed is the fruit of thy womb," lays the ground for their fuller understanding of the promise about the "seed" of the woman.

8. I.e., the curse, like a spear that almost missed its target, glanced aside and hit the ground.

9. Adam projects the invention of fire: they might, by striking two bodies together, rub ("attrite") the air into fire by friction; or else (lines 1070–71) focus reflected sunbeams (through some equivalent of glass) on dry ("sere") matter.

Justling or pushed with winds rude in their shock
1075 Tine° the slant lightning, whose thwart° flame driv'n down   *ignite / slanting*
Kindles the gummy bark of fir or pine,
And sends a comfortable heat from far,
Which might supply° the sun: such fire to use,   *take the place of*
And what may else be remedy or cure
1080 To evils which our own misdeeds have wrought,
He will instruct us praying, and of grace
Beseeching him, so as we need not fear
To pass commodiously this life, sustained
By him with many comforts, till we end
1085 In dust, our final rest and native home.
What better can we do, than to the place
Repairing where he judged us, prostrate fall
Before him reverent, and there confess
Humbly our faults, and pardon beg, with tears
1090 Watering the ground, and with our sighs the air
Frequenting,° sent from hearts contrite, in sign   *filling*
Of sorrow unfeigned, and humiliation meek.
Undoubtedly he will relent and turn
From his displeasure; in whose look serene,
1095 When angry most he seemed and most severe,
What else but favor, grace, and mercy shone?"
   So spake our father penitent, nor Eve
Felt less remorse: they forthwith to the place
Repairing where he judged them prostrate fell
1100 Before him reverent, and both confessed
Humbly their faults, and pardon begged, with tears
Watering the ground, and with their sighs the air
Frequenting, sent from hearts contrite, in sign
Of sorrow unfeigned, and humiliation meek.[1]

Book 11 *Summary*   The prayers of Adam and Eve prove acceptable to God.
But while humankind may now hope for ultimate redemption, humans may no longer dwell in Paradise; and Michael, the warrior archangel, is dispatched to explain the sentence, offer some hope for the future, and dismiss Adam and Eve from the happy garden. Adam is at first overcome with grief; but the angel encourages him, and while Eve is put in a trance, Adam is raised to the peak of a high hill and shown in a vision the future of humankind as far as the flood of Noah.

From Book 12

Summary   Continuing his instruction of Adam, Michael relates the history of the world from the time of Noah through the coming of Christ, whose ascent into Heaven and triumph over Death after the Crucifixion he describes.

---

1. The final six lines repeat, almost word for word, lines 1086–92, as the poet describes Adam's proposed gesture of repentance carried out in every detail.

[THE DEPARTURE FROM EDEN]

So spake th' Archangel Michaël, then paused,
As at the world's great period;° and our sire   *consummation*
Replete with joy and wonder thus replied:
"O goodness infinite, goodness immense!
That all this good of evil shall produce,
And evil turn to good; more wonderful
Than that which by creation first brought forth
Light out of darkness! Full of doubt I stand,
Whether I should repent me now of sin
By me done and occasioned, or rejoice
Much more, that much more good thereof shall spring,
To God more glory, more good will to men
From God, and over wrath grace shall abound.[1]
But say, if our Deliverer up to Heav'n
Must reascend, what will betide the few
His faithful, left among th' unfaithful herd,
The enemies of truth; who then shall guide
His people, who defend? Will they not deal
Worse with his followers than with him they dealt?"
   "Be sure they will," said th' angel; "but from Heav'n
He to his own a Comforter will send,[2]
The promise of the Father, who shall dwell
His Spirit within them, and the law of faith
Working through love, upon their hearts shall write,
To guide them in all truth, and also arm
With spiritual armor, able to resist
Satan's assaults, and quench his fiery darts,[3]
What° man can do against them, not afraid,   *as much as*
Though to the death, against such cruelties
With inward consolations recompensed,
And oft supported so as shall amaze
Their proudest persecutors: for the Spirit
Poured first on his apostles, whom he sends
To evangelize the nations, then on all
Baptized, shall them with wondrous gifts endue°   *endow*
To speak all tongues, and do all miracles,
As did their Lord before them. Thus they win
Great numbers of each nation to receive
With joy the tidings brought from Heav'n: at length
Their ministry performed, and race well run,
Their doctrine and their story written left,[4]
They die; but in their room, as they forewarn,

---

1. These lines do not formulate the medieval idea of the *felix culpa*—that the Fall was fortunate in bringing humans greater happiness than they would otherwise have enjoyed—only that the Fall has provided God an occasion to bring still greater good out of evil. The poem makes clear that Adam and Eve would have grown in perfection and advanced to Heaven had they not sinned.
2. The Holy Spirit, who for Milton is much subordinate to both Father and Son.
3. Cf. Ephesians 6.11–16: "Put on the whole armor of God, that ye may be able to stand against the wiles of the devil. . . . Above all, taking the shield of faith, wherewith ye shall be able to quench all the fiery darts of the wicked." The subsequent history (lines 493–507) is that of the early Christian church in apostolic times.
4. I.e., in the Gospels and Epistles.

Wolves shall succeed for teachers, grievous wolves,
Who all the sacred mysteries of Heav'n
510 To their own vile advantages shall turn
Of lucre° and ambition, and the truth   *wealth*
With superstitions and traditions taint,[5]
Left only in those written records pure,
Though not but by the Spirit understood.
515 Then shall they seek to avail themselves of names,°   *honors*
Places° and titles, and with these to join   *offices*
Secular power, though feigning still to act
By spiritual, to themselves appropriating
The Spirit of God, promised alike and giv'n
520 To all believers; and from that pretense,
Spiritual laws by carnal° power shall force   *fleshly, worldly*
On every conscience;[6] laws which none shall find
Left them enrolled, or what the Spirit within
Shall on the heart engrave.[7] What will they then
525 But force the Spirit of Grace itself, and bind
His consort Liberty; what, but unbuild
His living temples,[8] built by faith to stand,
Their own faith not another's: for on earth
Who against faith and conscience can be heard
530 Infallible?[9] Yet many will presume:
Whence heavy persecution shall arise
On all who in the worship persevere
Of Spirit and Truth; the rest, far greater part,
Will deem in outward rites and specious forms
535 Religion satisfied; Truth shall retire
Bestuck with sland'rous darts, and works of faith
Rarely be found: so shall the world go on,
To good malignant, to bad men benign,
Under her own weight groaning, till the day
540 Appear of respiration° to the just,   *respite*
And vengeance to the wicked, at return
Of him so lately promised to thy aid,
The Woman's Seed,[1] obscurely then foretold,
Now amplier known thy Savior and thy Lord,
545 Last in the clouds from Heav'n to be revealed
In glory of the Father, to dissolve
Satan with his perverted world, then raise

---

5. The history summarized in lines 508–40 is of the corruption of the Christian church by superstitions, traditions, and persecutions of conscience in patristic times under the popes and the Christian emperors, but also extending to the Last Day. The terms point especially to what Milton saw as the revival of "popish" superstitions in the English church of the Restoration and to the fierce persecution of dissenters.
6. These lines affirm the Protestant principle of every Christian's right to interpret Scripture according to the "inner light" of the Spirit, and denounce (as Milton consistently did in his tracts) the use of civil ("carnal") power to enforce orthodoxy.

7. I.e., there is nothing in Scripture or in the Spirit's inner teaching that sanctions persecution for conscience.
8. Cf. 1 Corinthians 3.16: "Know ye not that ye are the temple of God?" "His consort Liberty": Milton typically insists that Christ's gospel and the Spirit of God teach liberty, religious and civil, alluding as here to 2 Corinthians 3.17: "where the Spirit of the Lord is, there is liberty."
9. An attack on papal claims to infallibility, asserted though not yet proclaimed as doctrine.
1. Michael's story ends with the full explication of the promised "Woman's Seed" as Christ, and with the renewal of all things after the Last Judgment (lines 545–51).

From the conflagrant mass,° purged and refined,   *the burning world*
New heav'ns, new earth, ages of endless date
Founded in righteousness and peace of love,
To bring forth fruits joy and eternal bliss."
   He ended; and thus Adam last replied:
"How soon hath thy prediction, seer blest,
Measured this transient world, the race of time,
Till time stand fixed: beyond is all abyss,
Eternity, whose end no eye can reach.
Greatly instructed I shall hence depart,
Greatly in peace of thought, and have my fill
Of knowledge, what° this vessel can contain;   *as much as*
Beyond which was my folly to aspire.
Henceforth I learn, that to obey is best,
And love with fear the only God, to walk
As in his presence, ever to observe
His providence, and on him sole depend,
Merciful over all his works, with good
Still overcoming evil, and by small
Accomplishing great things, by things deemed weak
Subverting worldly strong, and worldly wise
By simply meek; that suffering for truth's sake
Is fortitude to highest victory,
And to the faithful death the gate of life;
Taught this by his example whom I now
Acknowledge my Redeemer ever blest."
   To whom thus also th' angel last replied:
"This having learnt, thou hast attained the sum
Of wisdom; hope no higher, though all the stars
Thou knew'st by name,[2] and all th' ethereal powers,
All secrets of the deep, all nature's works,
Or works of God in heav'n, air, earth, or sea,
And all the riches of this world enjoy'dst,
And all the rule, one empire; only add
Deeds to thy knowledge answerable,° add faith,   *corresponding*
Add virtue, patience, temperance, add love,
By name to come called charity, the soul
Of all the rest: then wilt thou not be loath
To leave this Paradise, but shalt possess
A paradise within thee, happier far.
Let us descend now therefore from this top
Of speculation;° for the hour precise   *hill of speculation*
Exacts° our parting hence; and see the guards,   *requires*
By me encamped on yonder hill, expect
Their motion,° at whose front a flaming sword,   *await their orders*
In signal of remove, waves fiercely round;
We may no longer stay: go, waken Eve;
Her also I with gentle dreams have calmed
Portending good, and all her spirits composed

---

2. Michael glances back at Raphael's warning in Book 8 that Adam should concern himself first with matters pertaining to his own life and world, rather than speculating overmuch about the cosmos.

To meek submission: thou at season fit
Let her with thee partake what thou hast heard,
Chiefly what may concern her faith to know,
600 The great deliverance by her seed to come
(For by the Woman's Seed) on all mankind.
That ye may live, which will be many days,
Both in one faith unanimous though sad,
With cause for evils past, yet much more cheered
605 With meditation on the happy end."
    He ended, and they both descend the hill;
Descended, Adam to the bow'r where Eve
Lay sleeping ran before, but found her waked;
And thus with words not sad she him received:
610   "Whence thou return'st, and whither went'st, I know;
For God is also in sleep, and dreams advise,[3]
Which he hath sent propitious, some great good
Presaging, since with sorrow and heart's distress
Wearied I fell asleep: but now lead on;
615 In me is no delay; with thee to go,
Is to stay here; without thee here to stay,
Is to go hence unwilling; thou to me
Art all things under heav'n, all places thou,[4]
Who for my willful crime art banished hence.
620 This further consolation yet secure
I carry hence; though all by me is lost,
Such favor I unworthy am vouchsafed,
By me the promised Seed shall all restore."
    So spake our mother Eve, and Adam heard
625 Well pleased, but answered not; for now too nigh
Th' Archangel stood, and from the other hill
To their fixed station, all in bright array
The Cherubim descended; on the ground
Gliding metéorous,° as evening mist   *like a meteor*
630 Ris'n from a river o'er the marish° glides,   *marsh*
And gathers ground fast at the laborer's heel
Homeward returning. High in front advanced,
The brandished sword of God before them blazed
Fierce as a comet; which with torrid heat,
635 And vapor° as the Libyan air adust,°   *smoke / parched*
Began to parch that temperate clime; whereat
In either hand the hast'ning angel caught
Our ling'ring parents, and to th' eastern gate
Led them direct, and down the cliff as fast
640 To the subjected° plain; then disappeared.   *low-lying*
They looking back, all th' eastern side beheld
Of Paradise, so late their happy seat,°   *estate*
Waved over by that flaming brand,° the gate   *sword*

---

3. The lines suggest that Eve's dream has provided her a parallel (if lesser) prophecy to Adam's visions and instruction. Cf. Numbers 12.6: "If there be a prophet among you, I the Lord will make myself known unto him in a vision, and will speak unto him in a dream."
4. Eve's lines—the final speech in the poem—recall her prelapsarian love song to Adam (4.641ff.) and Ruth's promise to accompany her mother-in-law, Naomi (Ruth 1.16).

With dreadful faces thronged and fiery arms:
Some natural tears they dropped, but wiped them soon;
The world was all before them, where to choose
Their place of rest, and Providence their guide:
They hand in hand with wand'ring steps and slow,
Through Eden took their solitary way.

1674

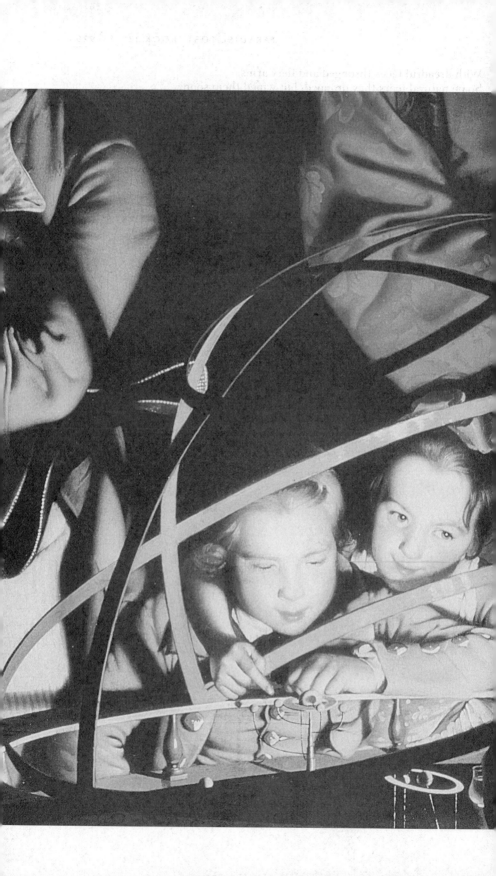

The Restoration and the Eighteenth Century 1660–1785

1660:	Charles II restored to the English throne
1688–89:	The Glorious Revolution: deposition of James II and accession of William of Orange
1700:	Death of John Dryden
1707:	Act of Union unites Scotland and England, creating the nation of "Great Britain"
1714:	Rule by House of Hanover begins with accession of George I
1744–45:	Deaths of Alexander Pope and Jonathan Swift
1784:	Death of Samuel Johnson

The Restoration and the eighteenth century brought vast changes to the island of Great Britain, which became a single nation after 1707, when the Act of Union joined Scotland to England and Wales. After the prolonged civil and religious strife of the seventeenth century, Britain attained political stability and unprecedented commercial vigor. The countryside kept its seemingly timeless agricultural rhythms, even as the nation's great families consolidated their control over the land and those who worked it. Change came most dramatically to cities, which absorbed much of a national population that nearly doubled in the period, to ten million. Britons came together in civil society—the public but nongovernmental institutions and practices that became newly powerful in the period. The theaters (reopened at the Restoration), coffeehouses, concert halls, pleasure gardens, lending

A Philosopher Giving That Lecture on the Orrery, in Which a Lamp Is Put in Place of the Sun (detail), 1766, Joseph Wright. For more information about this painting, see the color insert in this volume.

libraries, picture exhibitions, and shopping districts gave life in London and elsewhere a feeling of bustle and friction. Reflecting and stimulating this activity, an expanding assortment of printed works vied to interest literate women and men, whose numbers grew to include most of the middle classes and many among the poor. Civil society also linked people to an increasingly global economy, as they shopped for diverse goods from around the world. The rich and even the moderately well off could profit or go broke from investments in joint-stock companies, which controlled much of Britain's international trade, including its lucrative traffic in slaves. At home, new systems of canals and turnpikes stimulated domestic trade, industry, and travel, bringing distant parts of the country closer together. The cohesion of the nation also depended on ideas of social order—some old and clear, many subtle and new. An ethos of politeness came to prevail, a standard of social behavior to which more and more could aspire yet that served to distinguish the privileged sharply from the rude and vulgar. This and other ideas, of order and hierarchy, of liberty and rights, of sentiment and sympathy, helped determine the ways in which an expanding diversity of people could seek to participate in Britain's thriving cultural life.

RELIGION AND POLITICS

The Restoration of 1660—the return of Charles Stuart and, with him, the monarchy to England—brought hope to a divided nation, exhausted by years of civil war and political turmoil. Almost all of Charles's subjects welcomed him home. After the abdication of Richard Cromwell in 1659 the country had seemed at the brink of chaos, and Britons were eager to believe that their king would bring order and law and a spirit of mildness back into the national life. But no political settlement could be stable until the religious issues had been resolved. The restoration of the monarchy meant that the established church would also be restored, and though Charles was willing to pardon or ignore many former enemies (such as Milton), the bishops and Anglican clergy were less tolerant of dissent. When Parliament reimposed the Book of Common Prayer in 1662 and then in 1664 barred Nonconformists from religious meetings outside the established church, thousands of clergymen resigned their livings, and the jails were filled with preachers like John Bunyan who refused to be silenced. In 1673 the Test Act required all holders of civil and military offices to take the sacrament in an Anglican church and to deny belief in transubstantiation. Thus Protestant Dissenters and Roman Catholics were largely excluded from public life; for instance, Alexander Pope, a Catholic, could not attend a university, own land, or vote. The scorn of Anglicans for Nonconformist zeal or "enthusiasm" (a belief in private revelation) bursts out in Samuel Butler's popular *Hudibras* (1663), a caricature of Presbyterians and Independents. And English Catholics were widely regarded as potential traitors and (wrongly) thought to have set the Great Fire that destroyed much of London in 1666.

Yet the triumph of the established church did not resolve the constitutional issues that had divided Charles I and Parliament. Charles II had promised to govern through Parliament but slyly tried to consolidate royal power. Steering away from crises, he hid his Catholic sympathies and avoided a test of strength with Parliament—except on one occasion. In 1678 the report of the Popish

Plot, in which Catholics would rise and murder their Protestant foes, terrified London; and though the charge turned out to be a fraud, the House of Commons exploited the fear by trying to force Charles to exclude his Catholic brother, James, duke of York, from succession to the throne. The turmoil of this period is captured brilliantly by Dryden's *Absalom and Achitophel* (1681). Finally, Charles defeated the Exclusion Bill by dissolving Parliament. But the crisis resulted in a basic division of the country between two new political parties: the Tories, who supported the king, and the Whigs, the king's opponents.

Neither party could live with James II. After he came to the throne in 1685, he claimed the right to make his own laws, suspended the Test Act, and began to fill the army and government with fellow Catholics. The birth of James's son in 1688 brought matters to a head, confronting the nation with the prospect of a Catholic dynasty. Secret negotiations paved the way for the Dutchman William of Orange, a champion of Protestantism and the husband of James's Protestant daughter Mary. William landed with a small army in southwestern England and marched toward London. As he advanced the king's allies melted away, and James fled to a permanent exile in France. But the house of Stuart would be heard from again. For more than half a century some loyal Jacobites (from the Latin *Jacobus,* "James"), especially in Scotland, supported James, his son ("the Old Pretender"), and his grandson ("the Young Pretender" or "Bonnie Prince Charlie") as the legitimate rulers of Britain. Moreover, a good many writers, from Aphra Behn and Dryden (and arguably Pope and Johnson) to Robert Burns, privately sympathized with Jacobitism. But after the failure of one last rising in 1745, the cause would dwindle gradually into a wistful sentiment. In retrospect, the coming of William and Mary in 1688—the Glorious, or Bloodless, Revolution— came to be seen as the beginning of a stabilized, unified Great Britain.

A number of innovations made this stability possible. In 1689 a Bill of Rights revoked James's actions; it limited the powers of the Crown, reaffirmed the supremacy of Parliament, and guaranteed some individual rights. The same year the Toleration Act relaxed the strain of religious conflict by granting a limited freedom of worship to Dissenters (although not to Catholics or Jews) so long as they swore allegiance to the Crown. This proved to be a workable compromise. The passage of the Act of Settlement in 1701 seemed finally to resolve the difficult problem of succession that had bedeviled the monarchy. Sophia, the electress of Hanover, and her descendants were put in line for the throne. As the granddaughter of James I, she was the closest Protestant relative of Princess Anne, James II's younger daughter (whose sole surviving child died in that year). The principles established in these years endured unaltered in essentials until the Reform Bill of 1832.

But the political rancor that often animates contests for power did not vanish, and during Anne's reign (1702–14), new tensions embittered the nation. In the War of the Spanish Succession (1702–13), England and its allies defeated France and Spain. As these commercial rivals were weakened and war profits flowed in, the Whig lords and London merchants supporting the war grew rich. The spoils included new colonies and the *asiento,* a contract to supply slaves to the Spanish Empire. The hero of the war, Captain-General John Churchill, duke of Marlborough, won the famous victory of Blenheim; was showered with honors and wealth; and, with his duchess, dominated the queen until 1710. But the Whigs and Marlborough pushed their luck too hard. When the Whigs tried to reward the Dissenters for their loyalty by removing the Test, Anne fought back to defend the established church. She dismissed her Whig ministers and the Marlboroughs and called in Robert Harley and the brilliant young Henry St. John to form a Tory ministry. These ministers employed prominent writers like Defoe and Swift and commissioned Matthew Prior to negotiate the Peace of Utrecht (1713). But to Swift's despair—he later burlesqued events at court in *Gulliver's Travels*—a bitter rivalry broke out between Harley (now earl of Oxford) and St. John (now Viscount Bolingbroke). Though Bolingbroke succeeded in ousting Oxford, the death of Anne in 1714 reversed his fortunes. The Whigs returned to power, and George I (Sophia's son) became the first Hanoverian king (he would reign until 1727). Harley was imprisoned in the Tower of London until 1717; and Bolingbroke, charged with being a Jacobite traitor, fled to France. Government was now securely in the hands of the Whigs.

The political principles of the Whig and Tory parties, which bring so much fire to eighteenth-century public debate, evolved through the period to address changing circumstances. Now we tend to think of Tories as conservative and Whigs as liberal. (Members of today's Conservative Party in the United Kingdom are sometimes called Tories.) During the Exclusion Crisis of the 1680s the Whigs asserted the liberties of the English subject against the royal prerogatives of Charles II, whom Tories such as Dryden supported. After both parties survived the 1688 Glorious Revolution, the Tories guarded the preeminence of the established church (sometimes styling themselves the Church Party), while Whigs tended to support toleration of Dissenters. Economically, too, Tories defined themselves as traditionalists, affirming landownership as the proper basis of wealth, power, and privilege (though most thought trade honorable), whereas the Whigs came to be seen as supporting a new "moneyed interest" (as Swift called it): managers of the Bank of England (founded 1694), contrivers of the system of public credit, and investors in the stock market. But conservatism and liberalism did not exist as ideological labels in the period, and the vicissitudes of party dispute offer many surprises. When Bolingbroke returned to England in 1724 after being pardoned, he led a Tory opposition that decried the "ministerial tyranny" of the Whig government. This opposition patriotically hailed liberty in a manner recalling the Whig rhetoric of earlier decades, appealed to both landed gentry and urban merchants, and anticipated the antigovernment radicalism of the end of the eighteenth century. Conversely, the Whigs sought to secure a centralized fiscal and military state machine and a web of financial interdependence controlled by the wealthiest aristocrats.

The great architect of this Whig policy was Robert Walpole, who came to power as a result of the "South Sea bubble" (1720), a stock market crash. His ability to restore confidence and keep the country running smoothly, as well as to juggle money, would mark his long ascendancy. Coming to be known as Britain's first "prime" minister, he consolidated his power during the reign of George II (1727–60). More involved in British affairs than his essentially German father, George II came to appreciate the efficient administration of the patronage system under Walpole, who installed dependents in government offices and controlled the House of Commons by financially rewarding its members. Many great writers found these methods offensive and embraced Bolingbroke's new Tory rhetoric extolling the Englishman's fierce independence from the corrupting power of centralized government and concentrations of wealth. Gay's *Beggar's Opera* (1728) and Fielding's *Jonathan*

Wild (1743) draw parallels between great criminals and great politicians, and Pope's *Dunciad* uses Walpole as an emblem of the venal commercialization of the whole social fabric. This distaste, however, did not prevent Pope himself from marketing his poems as cleverly as he wrote them.

Walpole fell in 1742 because he was unwilling to go to war against the French and Spanish, a war he thought would cost too much but that many perceived would enhance Britain's wealth still further. The next major English statesman, William Pitt the Elder, appealed to a spirit of patriotism and called for the expansion of British power and commerce overseas. The defeat of the French in the Seven Years' War (1756–63), especially in North America, was largely his doing. The long reign of George III (1760–1820) was dominated by two great concerns: the emergence of Britain as a colonial power and the cry for a new social order based on liberty and radical reform. In 1763 the Peace of Paris consolidated British rule over Canada and India, and not even the later loss of the American colonies could stem the rise of the empire. Great Britain was no longer an isolated island but a nation with interests and responsibilities around the world.

At home, however, there was discontent. The wealth brought to England by industrialism and foreign trade had not spread to the great mass of the poor. For much of the century, few had questioned the idea that those at the top of the social hierarchy rightfully held power. Rich families' alliances and rivalries, national and local, dominated politics; while male property owners could vote in Parliamentary elections, they and others of the middle classes and the poor had mostly followed the powerful people who could best help them thrive or at least survive. But toward the end of the century it seemed to many that the bonds of custom that once held people together had finally broken, and now money alone was respected. Protestants turned against Catholics; in 1780 the Gordon Riots put London temporarily under mob rule. The king was popular with his subjects and tried to take government into his own hands, rising above partisanship, but his efforts often backfired—as when the American colonists took him for a tyrant. From 1788 to the end of his life, moreover, an inherited disease (porphyria) periodically unhinged his mind, as in a memorable scene described by Frances Burney. Meanwhile, reformers such as John Wilkes, Richard Price, and Catherine Macaulay called for a new political republic. Fear of their radicalism would contribute to the British reaction against the French Revolution. In the last decades of the century British authors would be torn between two opposing attitudes: loyalty to the old traditions of subordination, mutual obligations, and local self-sufficiency, and yearning for a new dispensation founded on principles of liberty, the rule of reason, and human rights.

THE CONTEXT OF IDEAS

Much of the most powerful writing after 1660 exposed divisions in the nation's thinking inherited from the tumult of earlier decades. As the possibility of a Christian Commonwealth receded, the great republican John Milton published *Paradise Lost* (final version, 1674), and John Bunyan's immensely popular masterwork *Pilgrim's Progress* (1679) expressed the conscience of a Nonconformist. Conversely, an aristocratic culture, led by Charles II himself, aggressively celebrated pleasure and the right of the elite to behave as they wished. Members of the court scandalized respectable London citizens and considered their wives and daughters fair game. The court's hero, the earl of Rochester, became a celebrity for enacting the creed of a libertine and rake. The delights of the court also took more refined forms. French and Italian musicians, as well as painters from the Low Countries, migrated to England; and playhouses—closed by the Puritans since 1642—sprang back to life. In 1660 Charles authorized two new companies of actors, the King's Players and the Duke's; their repertory included witty, bawdy comedies written and acted by women as well as men. But as stark as the contrasts were during the Restoration between libertine and religious intellectuals, royalists and republicans, High Churchmen and Nonconformists, the court and the rest of the country, a spirit of compromise was brewing.

Perhaps the most widely shared intellectual impulse of the age was a distrust of dogmatism. Nearly everybody blamed it for the civil strife through which the nation had recently passed. Opinions varied widely about which dogmatism was most dangerous—Puritan enthusiasm, papal infallibility, the divine right of kings, medieval scholastic or modern Cartesian philosophy—but these were denounced in remarkably similar terms. As far apart intellectually and temperamentally as Rochester and Milton were, both portray overconfidence in human reasoning as the supreme disaster. It is the theme of Butler's *Hudibras* and much of the work of Dryden. Many philosophers, scientists, and divines began to embrace a mitigated skepticism, which argued that human beings could readily achieve a sufficient degree of necessary knowledge (sometimes called "moral certainty") but also contended that the pursuit of absolute certainty was vain, mad, and socially calamitous. If, as the commentator Martin Clifford put it in *A Treatise of Humane Reason* (1675), "in this vast latitude of probabilities," a person thinks "there is none can lead one to salvation, but the path wherein he treads himself, we may see the evident and necessary consequence of eternal troubles and confusions." Such writers insist that a distrust of human capacities is fully compatible with religious faith: for them the inability of reason and sensory evidence to settle important questions reveals our need to accept Christian mysteries as our intellectual foundation. Dryden's poem *Religio Laici* (1682) explains: "So pale grows reason in religion's sight; / So dies, and so dissolves in supernatural light."

Far from inhibiting fresh thinking, however, the distrust of old dogmas inspired new theories, projects, and explorations. In *Leviathan* (1651), Thomas Hobbes jettisoned the notion of a divine basis for kingly authority, proposing instead a naturalistic argument for royal absolutism begun from the claim that mere "matter in motion" composes the universe: if not checked by an absolute sovereign, mankind's "perpetual and restless desire of power after power" could lead to civic collapse. Other materialist philosophies derived from ancient Epicurean thought, which was Christianized by the French philosopher Pierre Gassendi (1592–1655). The Epicurean doctrine that the universe consists only of minuscule atoms and void unnerved some thinkers—Swift roundly mocks it in *A Tale of a Tub*—but it also energized efforts to examine the world with deliberate, acute attention. This new scientific impulse advanced Francis Bacon's program of methodical experimentation and inductive reasoning formulated earlier in the century.

Charles II gave official approval to the scientific revolution by chartering the Royal Society of London for the Improving of Natural Knowledge in

Frontispiece to Thomas Sprat's *History of the Royal Society*;
Wenceslaus Hollar, engraving, London, 1667. A bust of King
Charles II, called the "author and patron of the Royal Society"
(Latin), is being crowned by Fame. To the left is the Royal Society's
president, Lord Bruckner; to the right, Francis Bacon, pointing to
mathematical and military technology. On the left side are shelves
full of books, and in the background, more scientific instruments,
including Robert Boyle's air pump (center left).

1662. But observations of nature advanced both formally and informally in an
eclectic range of areas: the specialized, professional "scientist" we know today
did not yet exist. And new features of the world were disclosed to everyone
who had the chance to look. Two wonderful inventions, the microscope and
telescope, had begun to reveal that nature is more extravagant—teeming
with tiny creatures and boundless galaxies—than anyone had ever imagined. One book that stayed popular for more than a century, Fontenelle's
Conversations on the Plurality of Worlds (1686; translated from French by
Behn and later by Burney), suggested that an infinite number of alternate
worlds and living creatures might exist, not only in outer space but under
our feet, invisibly small. Travels to unfamiliar regions of the globe also
enlarged understandings of what nature could do: Behn's classifying and
collecting of South American flora and fauna in *Oroonoko* show how the
appetite for wondrous facts kept pace with the economic motives of world
exploration and colonization. Encounters with hitherto little known societies
in the Far East, Africa, and the Americas enlarged Europeans' understanding

of human norms as well. In *Gulliver's Travels*, Swift shows the comical, painful ways in which the discovery of new cultures forces one average Briton to reexamine his own.

Scientific discovery and exploration also affected religious attitudes. Alongside "natural history" (the collection and description of facts of nature) and "natural philosophy" (the study of the causes of what happens in nature), thinkers of the period placed "natural religion" (the study of nature as a book written by God). Newly discovered natural laws, such as Newton's laws of optics and celestial mechanics, seemed evidence of a universal order in creation, which implied God's hand in the design of the universe, as a watch implies a watchmaker. Expanded knowledge of peoples around the world who had never heard of Christianity led theologians to formulate supposedly universal religious tenets available to all rational beings. Some intellectuals embraced Deism, the doctrine that religion need not depend on mystery or biblical truths and could rely on reason alone, which recognized the goodness and wisdom of natural law and its creator. Natural religion could not, however, discern an active God who punished vice and rewarded virtue in this life; evidently the First Cause had withdrawn from the universe He set in motion. Many orthodox Christians shuddered at the vision of a vast, impersonal machine of nature. Instead they rested their faith on the revelation of Scripture, the scheme of salvation in which Christ died to redeem our sins. Other Christians, such as Pope in *An Essay on Man* and Thomson in *The Seasons*, espoused arguments for natural religion that they felt did not conflict with or diminish orthodox belief.

Some people began to argue that the achievements of modern inquiry had eclipsed those of the ancients (and the fathers of the church), who had not known about the solar system, the New World, microscopic organisms, or the circulation of the blood. The school curriculum still began with years of Latin and Greek, inculcating a long-established humanistic tradition cherished by many authors, including Swift and Pope. A battle of the books erupted in the late seventeenth century between champions of ancient and of modern learning. Swift crusaded fiercely in this battle: *Gulliver's Travels* denounces the pointlessness and arrogance he saw in experiments of the Royal Society, while "A Modest Proposal" depicts a peculiar new cruelty and indifference to moral purpose made possible by statistics and economics (two fields pioneered by Royal Society member Sir William Petty). But as sharp as such disagreements were, accommodation was also possible. Even as works such as Newton's *Principia* (1687) and *Opticks* (1704) revolutionized previously held views of the world, Newton himself maintained a seemly diffidence, comparing himself to "a boy playing on the sea-shore" "whilst the great ocean of truth lay all undiscovered before me." He and other modest modern inquirers such as Locke won the admiration of Pope and many ardent defenders of the past.

The widespread devotion to the direct observation of experience established empiricism as the dominant intellectual attitude of the age, which would become Britain's great legacy to world philosophy. Locke and his heirs George Berkeley and David Hume pursue the experiential approach in widely divergent directions. But even when they reach conclusions shocking to common sense, they tend to reassert the security of our prior knowledge. Berkeley insists we know the world only through our senses and thus cannot prove that any material thing exists, but he uses that argument to demonstrate the necessity of faith, because reality amounts to no more than a perception in the mind of God. Hume's famous argument about causation—that "causes and effects are discoverable, not by reason but by experience"—grounds our sense of the world not on rational reflection but on spontaneous, unreflective beliefs and feelings. Perhaps Locke best expresses the temper of his times in the *Essay Concerning Human Understanding* (1690):

> If by this inquiry into the nature of the understanding, I can discover the powers thereof; how far they reach; to what things they are in any degree proportionate; and where they fail us, I suppose it may be of use, to prevail with the busy mind of man to be more cautious in meddling with things exceeding its comprehension; to stop when it is at the utmost extent of its tether; and to sit down in a quiet ignorance of those things which, upon examination, are found to be beyond the reach of our capacities. . . . Our business here is not to know all things, but those which concern our conduct.

Such a position is Swift's, when he inveighs against metaphysics, abstract logical deductions, and theoretical science. It is similar to Pope's warning against human presumption in *An Essay on Man*. It prompts Johnson to talk of "the business of living" and to restrain the flights of unbridled imagination. And it helps account for the Anglican clergy's dislike of emotion and "enthusiasm" in religion and for their emphasis on good works, rather than faith, as the way to salvation. Locke's attitudes pervaded eighteenth-century British thought on politics, education, and morals as well as philosophy; Johnson's great *Dictionary* (1755) uses more than fifteen hundred illustrations from his writings.

Yet one momentous new idea at the turn of the eighteenth century was set against Lockean thinking. The groundbreaking intellectual Mary Astell, in *A Serious Proposal to the Ladies* (1694) and *Some Reflections upon Marriage* (1700, 1706), initiated a powerful strain of modern feminism, arguing for the establishment of women's educational institutions and decrying the tyranny that husbands legally exercised over their wives. She nonetheless mocked the calls for political rights and liberty by Locke and other Whig theorists, rights that pointedly did not extend to women. Instead, she and other early feminists, including Sarah Fyge Egerton and Mary, Lady Chudleigh, embraced the Tory principle of obedience to royal and church authority. Women's advocates had to fight "tyrant Custom" (in Egerton's words), rooted in ancient traditions of domestic power and enshrined in the Bible and mythic human prehistory. This struggle seemed distinct from public political denunciations of the tyranny of some relatively recent Charles or James. Astell feared that the doctrines of male revolutionaries could produce civil chaos and so jeopardize the best that women could hope for in her day: the freedom to become fully educated, practice their religion, and marry (or not) according to their own enlightened judgment.

Other thinkers, male and female, began to advocate improving women's education as part of a wider commitment to enhancing and extending sociability. Richard Steele's periodical *The Tatler* satirized Astell as "Madonella" because she seemed to recommend women to a nun-like, "recluse life." In *The Spectator* (1711–12; 1714), conversely, Steele and Joseph Addison encouraged women to learn to participate in an increasingly sociable, intellectually

Robert Dighton, *Mr. Deputy Dumpling and Family Enjoying a Summer Afternoon*, 1781. A family of the middling sort, the father self-important, the mother beaming, visit Bagnigge Wells, one of many resorts in London catering to specific classes.

sophisticated, urbane world, where all sorts of people could mingle, as in the streets, parks, and pleasure grounds of a thriving city like London. Such periodicals sought to teach as large a readership as possible to think and behave politely. On a more aristocratic plane, the *Characteristics of Men, Manners, Opinions, and Times* (1711) by the third earl of Shaftesbury similarly asserted the naturally social meaning of human character and meditated on the affections, the witty intercourse, and the standards of politeness that bind people together. Such ideas led to the popularity around mid-century of a new word, *sentimental,* which locates the bases of social conduct in instinctual feeling rather than divinely sanctioned moral codes. Religion itself, according to Laurence Sterne, might be a "Great Sensorium," a sort of central nervous system that connects the feelings of all living creatures in one great benevolent soul. And people began to feel exquisite pleasure in the exercise of charity. The cult of sensibility fostered a philanthropy that led to social reforms seldom envisioned in earlier times—to the improvement of jails, the relief of imprisoned debtors, the establishment of foundling hospitals and of homes for penitent prostitutes, and ultimately the abolition of the slave trade. And it also loosed a ready flow of sympathetic responses to the joys and sorrows of fellow human beings.

As they cultivated fine feelings, Britons also pursued their fascination with the material world. Scientific discoveries increasingly found practical applications in industry, the arts, and even entertainment. By the late 1740s, as knowledge of electricity advanced, public experiments offered fashionable British crowds the opportunity to electrocute themselves. Amateurs everywhere amused themselves with air pumps and chemical explosions. Birmingham became famous as a center where science and manufacturing were combining to change the world: in the early 1760s Matthew Boulton (1728–1809) established the most impressive factory of the age just outside town, producing vast quantities of pins, buckles, and buttons; in subsequent decades, his applications and manufacture of the new steam engine invented by Scotsman James Watt (1736–1819) helped build an industry to drive all others. Practical chemistry also led to industrial improvements: domestic porcelain production became established in the 1750s; and from the 1760s Josiah Wedgwood (1730–1795) developed glazing, manufacturing, and marketing techniques that enabled British ceramics to compete with China for fashionable taste. (In 1765 he named his creamware "Queen's ware" to remind customers of its place on Queen Charlotte's table.) Wedgwood and others answered an ever-increasing demand in Britain for beautiful objects. Artist William Hogarth satirized this appetite of the upper and middle classes for the accumulation of finery: a chaotic collection of china figurines crowds the mantel in Plate 2 of *Marriage A-la-Mode* (1743–45). Yet the images that made Hogarth famous would soon decorate English ceramic teapots and plates and be turned into porcelain figurines themselves.

New forms of religious devotion sprang up amid Britain's spectacular material success. The evangelical revival known as Methodism began in the 1730s, led by three Oxford graduates: John Wesley (1703–1791), his brother Charles (1707–1788), and George Whitefield (1714–1770). The Methodists took their gospel to the common people, warning that all were sinners and damned, unless they accepted "amazing grace," salvation through faith. Often denied the privilege of preaching in village churches, evangelicals preached to thousands in barns or the open fields. The emotionalism of such revival meetings repelled the somnolent Anglican Church and the upper classes, who feared that the fury and zeal of the Puritan sects were returning. Methodism was sometimes related to madness; convinced that he was damned forever, the poet William Cowper broke down and became a recluse. But the religious awakening persisted and affected many clergymen and laymen within the Establishment, who reanimated the church and promoted unworldliness and piety. Nor did the insistence of Methodists on faith over works as the way to salvation prevent them or their Anglican allies from fighting for social reforms. The campaign to abolish slavery and the slave trade was driven largely by a passion to save souls.

Sentimentalism, evangelicalism, and the pursuits of wealth and luxury in different ways all placed a new importance on individuals—the gratification of their tastes and ambitions or their yearning for personal encounters with each other or a personal God. Diary keeping, elaborate letter writing, and the novel also testified to the growing importance of the private, individual life. Few histories of kings or nations could rival Richardson's novel *Clarissa* in length, popularity, or documentary detail: it was subtitled "the History of a Young Lady." The older hierarchical system had tended to subordinate individuals to their social rank or station. In the eighteenth century that fixed system began to break down, and people's sense of themselves began to change. By the end of the century many issues of politics and the law revolve around rights, not traditions. The modern individual had been invented; no product of the age is more enduring.

CONDITIONS OF LITERARY PRODUCTION

Publishing boomed as never before in eighteenth-century Britain, as the number of titles appearing annually and the periodicals published in London and the provincial towns dramatically increased. This expansion in part resulted from a loosening of legal restraints on printing. Through much of the previous three centuries, the government had licensed the texts deemed suitable for publication and refused to license those it wanted suppressed (a practice called "prior restraint"). After the Restoration, the new Printing Act (1662) tightened licensing controls, though unlike his Stuart predecessors Charles II now shared this power with Parliament. But in 1695, during the reign of William III, the last in a series of printing acts was not renewed. Debate in Parliament on the matter was more practical than idealistic: it was argued that licensing fettered the printing trades and was ineffective at preventing obnoxious publications anyway, which could be better constrained after publication by enforcing laws against seditious libel, obscenity, and treason. As the two-party system consolidated, both Whigs and Tories seemed to realize that prepublication censorship could bite them when their own side happened to be out of power. Various governments attempted to revive licensing during political crises throughout the eighteenth century, but it was gone for good.

This did not end the legal liabilities, and the prosecutions, of authors. Daniel Defoe, for instance, was convicted of seditious libel and faced the pillory and jail for his satirical pamphlet "The Shortest Way with the Dissenters" (1702), which imitated High Church zeal so extravagantly that it provoked both the Tories and the Dissenters he had set about to defend. And licensing of the stage returned: irritated especially by Henry Fielding's antigovernment play *The Historical Register for the Year 1736*, Robert Walpole pushed the Stage Licensing Act through Parliament in 1737, which authorized the Lord Chamberlain to license all plays and reduced the number of London theaters to two (Drury Lane and Covent Garden), closing Fielding's New Theatre in the Haymarket and driving him to a new career as a novelist. But despite such constraints, Hume could begin his essay "Of the Liberty of the Press" (1741) by citing "the extreme liberty we enjoy in this country of communicating whatever we please to the public" as an internationally recognized commonplace. This freedom allowed eighteenth-century Britain to build an exemplary version of what historians have called "the public sphere": a cultural arena, free of direct government control, consisting of not just published comment on matters of national interest but also the public venues—coffeehouses, clubs, taverns—where readers circulated, discussed, and conceived responses to it. The first regular daily London newspaper, the *Daily Courant*, appeared in 1702; in 1731, the first magazine, the *Gentleman's Magazine*. The latter was followed both by imitations and by successful literary journals like the *Monthly Review* (1749) and the *Critical Review* (1756). Each audience attracted some periodical tailored to it, as with the *Female Tatler* (1709) and Eliza Haywood's *Female Spectator* (1744–46).

After 1695, the legal status of printed matter became ambiguous, and in 1710 Parliament enacted the Statute of Anne—"An Act for the Encouragement of Learning by Vesting the Copies of Printed Books in the Authors or Purchasers of Such Copies"—the first copyright law in British history not tied to government approval of works' contents. Typically, these copyrights were held by booksellers, who operated much as publishers do today (in the eighteenth century, *publisher* referred to one who distributed books). A bookseller paid an author for a work's copyright and, after registering the work with the Stationers' Company for a fee, had exclusive right for fourteen years to publish it; if alive when this term expired, he owned it another fourteen years. Payments to authors for copyright varied. Pope got £15 for the 1714 version of *The Rape of the Lock*, while Samuel Johnson's *Rasselas* earned him £100. The Statute of Anne spurred the book trade by enhancing booksellers' control over works and hence their chance to profit by them. But the government soon introduced a new constraint. In 1712, the first Stamp Act put a tax on all newspapers, advertisements, paper, and pamphlets (effectively any work under a hundred pages or so): all printed matter had to carry the stamp indicating the taxes had been paid. Happily for Anne and her ministry, the act both raised government revenue and drove a number of the more irresponsible, ephemeral newspapers out of business, though the *Spectator* simply doubled its price and thrived. Stamp Acts were in effect throughout the century, and duties tended to increase when the government needed to raise money and rein in the press, as during the Seven Years' War in 1757.

But such constraints were not heavy enough to hold back the publishing market, which began to sustain the first true professional class of authors in British literary history. The lower echelon of the profession was called "Grub Street," which was, as Johnson's *Dictionary* explains, "originally the name of a street in Moorfields in London, much inhabited by writers of small histories, dictionaries, and temporary poems." The market increasingly motivated the literary elite too, and Johnson himself came to remark that "no man but a blockhead ever wrote, except for money." As a young writer, he sold articles to the *Gentleman's Magazine*, and many other men and women struggled to survive doing piecework for periodicals. The enhanced opportunity to sell their works on the open market meant that fewer authors needed to look to aristocratic patrons for support. But a new practice, publication by subscription, blended elements of patronage and literary capitalism and created the century's most spectacular authorial fortunes. Wealthy readers could subscribe to a work in progress, usually by agreeing to pay the author half in advance and half upon receipt of the book. Subscribers were rewarded with an edition more sumptuous than the common run and the appearance of their names in a list in the book's front pages. Major works by famous authors, such as Dryden's translation of Virgil (1697) and the 1718 edition of Prior's poems, generated the most subscription sales; the grandest success was Pope's translation of Homer's *Iliad* (1715–20), which gained him about £5000; his *Odyssey* (1725–26) raised nearly that much. But smaller projects deemed to need special encouragement also sold by subscription, including nearly all books of poetry by women, such as Mary Leapor's poems (1751).

Not all entered the literary market with equal advantages; and social class played a role, though hardly a simple one, in preparing authors for success. The better educated were better placed to be taken seriously: many eminent male writers, including Dryden, Locke, Addison, Swift, Hume, Johnson, Burke—the list could go on and on—had at least some university education, either at Oxford or Cambridge or at Scottish or Irish universities, where attendance by members of the laboring classes was virtually nil. Also, universities were officially closed to non-Anglicans. Some important writers attended the Dissenting academies that sprang up to fulfill Nonconformists' educational aspirations: Defoe went to an excellent one at Newington Green. A few celebrated authors such as Rochester and Henry Fielding had aristocratic backgrounds, but many came from the "middle class," though those in this category show how heterogeneous it was. Pope, a Catholic, obtained his education privately, and his father was a linen wholesaler, but he eventually became intimate with earls and viscounts, whereas Richardson, who had a family background in trade and (as he said) "only common school-learning," was a successful printer before he became a novelist. Both were middle class in a sense and made their own fortunes in eighteenth-century print culture, yet they inhabited vastly different social worlds.

Despite the general exclusion of the poor from education and other means of social advancement, some self-educated writers of the laboring classes fought their way into print. A few became celebrities, aided by the increasing popularity of the idea, famously expressed by Gray in his "Elegy Written in a Country Churchyard," that there must be unknown geniuses among the poor. Stephen Duck, an agricultural worker from Wiltshire, published his popular *Poems on Several Subjects* in 1730, which included "The Thresher's Labor" (he became known as the Thresher Poet). Queen Caroline herself retained him to be keeper of her library in Richmond. Several authors of the "common sort" followed in Duck's wake, including Mary Collier, whose poem "The Woman's Labor: An Epistle to Mr. Duck" (1739) defended country women against charges of idleness. Apart from such visible successes, eighteenth-century print culture afforded work for many from lower socio-economic levels, if not as authors, then as hawkers of newspapers on city streets and singers of political ballads (who were often illiterate and female), bookbinders, papermakers, and printing-press workers. The vigor of the literary market demanded the labor of all classes.

As all women were barred from universities and faced innumerable other disadvantages and varieties of repression, the story of virtually every woman author in the period is one of self-education, courage, and extraordinary initiative. Yet women did publish widely for the first time in the period, and the examples that can be assembled are as diverse as they are impressive. During the Restoration and early eighteenth century, a few aristocratic women poets were hailed as marvelous exceptions and given fanciful names: the poems of Katherine Philips (1631–1664), "the matchless Orinda," were published posthumously in 1667; and others, including Anne Finch, Anne Killigrew, and later, Lady Mary Wortley Montagu, printed poems or circulated them in manuscript among fashionable circles. A more broadly public sort of female authorship was more ambivalently received. Though Aphra Behn built a successful career in the theater and in print, her sexually frank works were sometimes denounced as unbecoming a woman. Many women writers of popular literature after her in the early eighteenth century assumed "scandalous"

Richard Samuel, *Portraits in the Characters of the Muses in the Temple of Apollo* (*The Nine Living Muses of Great Britain*), 1778. A mythological depiction of some "bluestockings," women who made outstanding contributions to British literature and culture after the mid-18th century. *Standing, left to right*: Elizabeth Carter, Anna Barbauld, Elizabeth Sheridan, Hannah More, and Charlotte Lennox; *seated, left to right*: Angelica Kauffmann, Catherine Macaulay, Elizabeth Montagu, and Elizabeth Griffith.

public roles. Delarivier Manley published transparent fictionalizations of the doings of the Whig nobility, including *The New Atalantis* (1709), while Eliza Haywood produced stories about seduction and sex (though her late works, including *The History of Miss Betsy Thoughtless*, 1751, courted a rising taste for morality). Male defenders of high culture found it easy to denounce these women and their works as affronts simultaneously to sexual decency and to good literary taste: Pope's *Dunciad* (1728) awards Haywood as the prize in a pissing contest between scurrilous male booksellers.

Many women writers after midcentury were determined to be more moral than their predecessors. Around 1750, intellectual women established clubs of their own under the leadership of Elizabeth Vesey and Elizabeth Montagu, cousin to Lady Mary. Proclaiming a high religious and intellectual standard, these women came to be called "bluestockings" (after the inelegant worsted hose of an early member). Eminent men joined the bluestockings for literary conversation, including Samuel Johnson, Samuel Richardson, Horace Walpole (novelist, celebrated letter writer, and son of the prime minister), and David Garrick, preeminent actor of his day. The literary accomplishments of bluestockings ranged widely: in 1758 Elizabeth Carter published her translation of the Greek philosopher Epictetus, while

Hannah More won fame as a poet, abolitionist, and educational theorist. Some of the most considerable literary achievements of women after mid-century came in the novel, a form increasingly directed at women readers, often exploring the moral difficulties of young women approaching marriage. The satirical novel *The Female Quixote* (1752) by Charlotte Lennox describes one such heroine deluded by the extravagant romances she reads, while Frances Burney's *Evelina* (1778) unfolds the sexual and other dangers besetting its naïve but good-hearted heroine.

Readers' abilities and inclinations to consume literature helped determine the volume and variety of published works. While historians disagree about how exactly the literacy rate changed in Britain through the early modern period, there is widespread consensus that by 1800 between 60 and 70 percent of adult men could read, in contrast to 25 percent in 1600. Since historians use the ability to sign one's name as an indicator of literacy, the evidence is even sketchier for women, who were less often parties to legal contracts: perhaps a third of women could read by the mid-eighteenth century. Reading was commoner among the relatively well off than among the very poor, and among the latter, more prevalent in urban centers than the countryside. Most decisively, cultural commentators throughout the century portrayed literacy as a good in itself: everyone in a Protestant country such as Britain, most thought, would benefit from direct access to the Bible and devotional works, and increasingly employers found literacy among servants and other laborers useful, especially those working in cities. Moral commentators did their best to steer inexperienced readers away from the frivolous and idle realm of popular imaginative literature, though literacy could not but give its new possessors freedom to explore their own tastes and inclinations.

Cost placed another limit on readership: few of the laboring classes would have disposable income to buy a cheap edition of Milton (around two shillings at mid-century) or even a copy of the *Gentleman's Magazine* (six pence), let alone the spare time or sense of entitlement to peruse such things. Nonetheless, reading material was widely shared (Addison optimistically calculated "twenty readers to every paper" of the *Spectator*), and occasionally servants were given access to the libraries of their employers or the rich family of the neighborhood. In the 1740s, circulating libraries began to emerge in cities and towns throughout Britain. Though the yearly fee they usually charged put them beyond the reach of the poor, these libraries gave the middle classes access to a wider array of books than they could afford to assemble on their own. Records of such libraries indicate that travels, histories, letters, and novels were most popular, though patrons borrowed many specialized, technical works as well. One fascinating index of change in the character of the reading public was the very look of words on the page. In the past, printers had rather capriciously capitalized many nouns—words as common as *Wood* or *Happiness*—and frequently italicized various words for emphasis. But around the middle of the eighteenth century, new conventions arose: initial capitals were reserved for proper names, and the use of italics was reduced. Such changes indicate that the reading public was becoming sophisticated enough not to require such overt pointing to the meanings of what they read. The modern, eighteenth-century reader had come to expect that all English writing, no matter how old or new, on any topic, in any genre, would be printed in the same consistent, uncluttered style. No innovation of the eighteenth-century culture of reading more immediately demonstrates its linkage to our own.

LITERARY PRINCIPLES

The literature appearing between 1660 and 1785 divides conveniently into three shorter periods of about forty years each. The first, extending to the death of Dryden in 1700, is characterized by an effort to bring a new refinement to English literature according to sound critical principles of what is fitting and right; the second, ending with the deaths of Pope in 1744 and Swift in 1745, extends that effort to a wider circle of readers, with special satirical attention to what is unfitting and wrong; the third, concluding with the death of Johnson in 1784 and the publication of Cowper's *The Task* in 1785, confronts the old principles with revolutionary ideas that would come to the fore in the Romantic movement of the late eighteenth and early nineteenth centuries.

A sudden change of taste seemed to occur around 1660. The change had been long prepared, however, by a trend in European culture, especially in seventeenth-century France: the desire for an elegant simplicity. Reacting against the difficulty and occasional extravagance of late Renaissance literature, writers and critics called for a new restraint, clarity, regularity, and good sense. Donne's "metaphysics" and Milton's bold storming of heaven, for instance, seemed overdone to some Restoration readers. Hence Dryden and Andrew Marvell both were tempted to revise *Paradise Lost*, smoothing away its sublime but arduous idiosyncrasies. As daring and imaginative as Dryden's verse is, he tempers even its highly dramatic moments with an ease and sense of control definitive of the taste of his times.

This movement produced in France an impressive body of classical literature that distinguished the age of Louis XIV. In England it produced a literature often termed "Augustan," after the writers who flourished during the reign of Augustus Caesar, the first Roman emperor. Rome's Augustan Age reestablished stability after the civil war that followed the assassination of Julius Caesar. Its chief poets, Virgil, Horace, and Ovid, addressed their polished works to a sophisticated aristocracy among whom they looked for patrons. Dryden's generation took advantage of the analogy between post–civil war England and Augustan Rome. Later generations would be suspicious of that analogy; after 1700 most writers stressed that Augustus had been a tyrant who thought himself greater than the law. But in 1660 there was hope that Charles would be a better Augustus, bringing England the civilized virtues of an Augustan age without its vices.

Charles and his followers brought back from exile an admiration of French literature as well as French fashions, and the theoretical "correctness" of such writers as Pierre Corneille, René Rapin, and Nicolas Boileau came into vogue. England also had a native tradition of classicism, derived from Ben Jonson and his followers, whose couplets embodied a refinement Dryden eagerly inherited and helped codify. The effort to formulate rules of good writing appealed to many critics of the age. Even Shakespeare had sometimes been careless; and although writers could not expect to surpass his genius, they might hope to avoid his faults. But "neoclassical" English literature aimed to be not only classical but *new*. Rochester and Dryden drew on literary traditions of variety, humor, and freewheeling fancy represented by Chaucer, Spenser, Shakespeare, Jonson, and Milton to infuse fresh life into Greek or Latin or French classical models.

Above all, the new simplicity of style aimed to give pleasure to readers—to express passions that everyone could recognize in language that everyone could understand. According to Dryden, Donne's amorous verse misguidedly "perplexes the minds of the fair sex with nice speculations of philosophy, when he should engage their hearts, and entertain them with the softnesses of love." Dryden's poems would not make that mistake; like subsequent English critics, he values poetry according to its power to move an audience. Thus Timotheus, in Dryden's "Alexander's Feast," is not only a musician but an archetypal poet who can make Alexander tearful or loving or angry at will. Readers, in turn, were supposed to cooperate with authors through the exercise of their own imaginations, creating pictures in the mind. When Timotheus describes vengeful ghosts holding torches, Alexander halluci-nates in response and seizes a torch "with zeal to destroy." Much eighteenth-century poetry demands to be visualized. A phrase from Horace's *Art of Poetry*, *ut pictura poesis* (as in painting, so in poetry), was interpreted to mean that poetry ought to be a visual as well as verbal art. Pope's "Eloisa to Abe-lard," for instance, begins by picturing two rival female personifications: "heavenly-pensive contemplation" and "ever-musing melancholy" (in the older typographical style, the nouns would be capitalized). Readers were expected to *see* these figures: Contemplation, in the habit of a nun, whose eyes roll upward toward heaven; and the black goddess Melancholy, in wings and drapery, who broods upon the darkness. These two competing visions fight for Eloisa's soul throughout the poem, which we see entirely through her perspective. Eighteenth-century readers knew how to translate words into pictures, and modern readers can share their pleasure by learning to see poetic images in the mind's eye.

What poets most tried to see and represent was *Nature*—a word of many meanings. The Augustans focused especially on one: Nature as the universal and permanent elements in human experience. External nature, the land-scape, attracted attention throughout the eighteenth century as a source of pleasure and an object of inquiry. But as Finch muses on the landscape, in "A Nocturnal Reverie," it is her own soul she discovers. Pope's injunction to the critic, "First follow Nature," has primarily *human* nature in view. Nature consists of the enduring, general truths that have been, are, and will be true for everyone in all times, everywhere. Hence the business of the poet, accord-ing to Johnson's *Rasselas*, is "to examine, not the individual, but the species; to remark general properties and large appearances . . . to exhibit in his por-traits of nature such prominent and striking features as recall the original to every mind." Yet if human nature was held to be uniform, human beings were known to be infinitely varied. Pope praises Shakespeare's characters as "Nature herself," but continues that "every single character in Shakespeare is as much an individual as those in life itself; it is . . . impossible to find any two alike." The general need not exclude the particular. In *The Vanity of Human Wishes*, Johnson describes the sorrows of an old woman: "Now kindred Merit fills the sable Bier, / Now lacerated Friendship claims a tear." Here "kindred Merit" refers particularly to a worthy relative who has died, and "lacerated Friendship" refers to a friend who has been wasted by violence or disease. Yet Merit and Friendship are also personifications, and the lines imply that the woman may be mourning the passing of goodness like her own or a broken friendship; values and sympathies can die as well as people. This play on words is not a pun. Rather, it indicates a state of mind in which life assumes the form of a perpetual allegory and some abiding truth shines through each circumstance as it passes. The particular is already the general, in good eighteenth-century verse.

To study Nature was also to study the ancients. Nature and Homer, according to Pope, were the same; and both Pope and his readers applied Horace's satires on Rome to their own world, because Horace had expressed the perennial forms of life. Moreover, modern writers could learn from the ancients how to practice their craft. If a poem is an object to be made, the *poet* (a word derived from the Greek for "maker") must make the object to proper specifications. Thus poets were taught to plan their works in one of the classical "kinds" or genres—epic, tragedy, comedy, pastoral, satire, or ode—to choose a language appropriate to that genre, and to select the right style and tone and rhetorical figures. The rules of art, as Pope had said, "are Nature methodized." At the same time, however, writers needed *wit*: quickness of mind, inventiveness, a knack for conceiving images and metaphors and for perceiving resemblances between things apparently unlike. Shakespeare had surpassed the ancients themselves in wit, and no one could deny that Pope was witty. Hence a major project of the age was to combine good method with wit, or judgment with fancy. Nature intended them to be one, and the role of judgment was not to suppress passion, energy, and originality but to make them more effective through discipline: "The winged courser, like a generous horse, / Shows most true mettle when you check his course."

The test of a poet's true mettle is language. When Wordsworth, in the preface to *Lyrical Ballads* (1800), declared that he wrote "in a selection of the language really used by men," he went on to attack eighteenth-century poets for their use of an artificial and stock "poetic diction." Many poets did employ a special language. It is characterized by personification, representing a thing or abstraction in human form, as when an "Ace of Hearts steps forth" or "Melancholy frowns"; by periphrasis (a roundabout way of avoiding homely words: "finny tribes" for *fish*, or "household feathery people" for *chickens*); by stock phrases such as "shining sword," "verdant mead," "bounding main," and "checkered shade"; by words used in their original Latin sense, such as "genial," "gelid," and "horrid"; and by English sentences forced into Latin syntax ("Here rests his head upon the lap of Earth / A youth to Fortune and to Fame unknown," where *youth* is the subject of the verb *rests*). This language originated in the attempt of Renaissance poets to rival the elegant diction of Virgil and other Roman writers, and Milton depended on it to help him obtain "answerable style" for the lofty theme of *Paradise Lost*. When used mechanically it could become a mannerism. But Thomas Gray contrives subtle, expressive effects from artificial diction and syntax, as in the ironic inflation of "Ode on the Death of a Favorite Cat" or a famous stanza from "Elegy Written in a Country Churchyard":

> The boast of heraldry, the pomp of power,
> And all that beauty, all that wealth e'er gave,
> Awaits alike the inevitable hour.
> The paths of glory lead but to the grave.

It is easy to misread the first sentence. What is the subject of *awaits*? The answer must be *hour* (the only available singular noun), which lurks at the end of the sentence, ready to spring a trap not only on the reader but on all those aristocratic, powerful, beautiful, wealthy people who forget that their hour will come. Moreover, the intricacy of that sentence sets off the simplicity of the next, which says the same thing with deadly directness. The artful mix in the "Elegy" of a special poetic language—a language that nobody speaks—with sentiments that everybody feels helps account for the poem's enduring popularity.

Versification also tests a poet's skill. The heroic couplet was brought to such perfection by Pope, Johnson thought, that "to attempt any further improvement of versification will be dangerous." Pope's couplets, in rhymed iambic pentameter, typically present a complete statement, closed by a punctuation mark. Within the binary system of these two lines, a world of distinctions can be compressed. The second line of the couplet might closely parallel the first in structure and meaning, for instance, or the two lines might antithetically play against each other. Similarly, because a slight pause called a "caesura" often divides the typical pentameter line ("Know then

"Here rests his head . . ." Through a crumbling Gothic arch appears a youth reading the epitaph on a tombstone that concludes Thomas Gray's "Elegy Written in a Country Churchyard." Illustration, *Designs by Mr. R. Bentley for Six Poems by Mr. T. Gray* (1753).

thyself, presume not God to scan"), one part of the line can be made parallel with or antithetical to the other or even to one part of the following line. An often quoted and parodied passage of Sir John Denham's "Cooper's Hill" (1642) illustrates these effects. The poem addresses the Thames and builds up a witty comparison between the flow of a river and the flow of verse (italics are added to highlight the terms compared):

	O could I flow like thee, │ and make thy stream
Parallelism:	*My great example*, │ as it is *my theme!*
Double balance:	Though *deep*, yet *clear*, │ though *gentle*, yet not *dull*,
Double balance:	*Strong* without *rage*, │ without *o'erflowing, full.*

Once Dryden and Pope had bound such passages more tightly together with alliteration and assonance, the typical metrical-rhetorical wit of the new age had been perfected. For most of the eighteenth century its only metrical rival was blank verse: iambic pentameter that does not rhyme and is not closed in couplets. Milton's blank verse in *Paradise Lost* provided one model, and the dramatic blank verse of Shakespeare and Dryden provided another. This more expansive form appealed to poets who cared less for wit than for stories and thoughts with plenty of room to develop. Blank verse was favored as the best medium for descriptive and meditative poems, from Thomson's *Seasons* (1726–30) to Cowper's *The Task* (1785), and the tradition continued in Wordsworth's "Tintern Abbey" and *Prelude.*

Yet not all poets chose to compete with Pope's wit or Milton's heroic striving. Ordinary people also wrote and read verse, and many of them neither knew nor regarded the classics. Only a minority of men, and very few women, had the chance to study Latin and Greek, but that did not keep a good many from playing with verse as a pastime or writing about their own lives. Hence the eighteenth century is the first age to reflect the modern tension between "high" and "low" art. While the heroic couplet was being perfected, doggerel also thrived, and Milton's blank verse was sometimes reduced to describing a drunk or an oyster. Burlesque and broad humor characterize the common run of eighteenth-century verse. As the audience for poetry became more diversified, so did the subject matter. No readership was too small to address; Isaac Watts, and later Anna Laetitia Barbauld and William Blake, wrote songs for children. The rise of unconventional forms and topics of verse subverted an older poetic ideal: the Olympian art that only a handful of the elect could possibly master. The eighteenth century brought poetry down to earth. In the future, art that claimed to be high would have to find ways to distinguish itself from the low.

RESTORATION LITERATURE, 1660–1700

Dryden brought England a *modern* literature between 1660 and 1700. He combined a cosmopolitan outlook on the latest European trends with some of the richness and variety he admired in Chaucer and Shakespeare. In most of the important contemporary forms—occasional verse, comedy, tragedy, heroic play, ode, satire, translation, and critical essay—both his example and his precepts influenced others. As a critic, he spread the word that English literature, particularly his own, could vie with the best of the past. As a translator, he made such classics as Ovid and Virgil available to a wide public; for the first time, a large number of women and men without a formal education could feel included in the literary world.

Restoration prose clearly indicated the desire to reach a new audience. The styles of Donne's sermons, Milton's pamphlets, or Browne's treatises now seemed too elaborate and rhetorical for simple communication. By contrast, Pepys and Behn head straight to the point, informally and unself-consciously. The Royal Society asked its members to employ a plain, utilitarian prose style that spelled out scientific truths; rhetorical flourishes and striking metaphors might be acceptable in poetry, which engaged the emotions, but they had no place in rational discourse. In polite literature, exemplified by Cowley, Dryden, and Sir William Temple, the ideal of good prose came to be a style with the ease and poise of well-bred urbane conversation. This is a social prose for a sociable age. Later, it became the mainstay of essayists like Addison and Steele, of eighteenth-century novelists, and of the host of brilliant eighteenth-century letter writers, including Montagu, Horace Walpole, Gray, Cowper, and Burney, who still give readers the sense of being their intimate friends.

Yet despite its broad appeal to the public, Restoration literature kept its ties to an aristocratic heroic ideal. The "fierce wars and faithful loves" of epic poems were expected to offer patterns of virtue for noble emulation. These ideals lived on in popular French prose romances and in Behn's *Oroonoko*. But the ideal was most fully expressed in heroic plays like those written by Dryden, which push to extremes the conflict between love and honor in the hearts of impossibly valiant heroes and impossibly high-minded and attractive heroines. Dryden's best serious drama, however, was his blank verse tragedy *All for Love* (produced 1677), based on the story of Antony and Cleopatra. Instead of Shakespeare's worldwide panorama, his rapid shifts of scene and complex characters, this version follows the unities of time, place, and action, compressing the plot to the tragic last hours of the lovers. Two other tragic playwrights were celebrated in the Restoration and for a long time to come: Nathaniel Lee (ca. 1649–1692), known for violent plots and wild ranting, and the passionately sensitive Thomas Otway (1652–1685).

But comedy was the real distinction of Restoration drama. The best plays of Sir George Etherege (*The Man of Mode*, 1676), William Wycherley (*The Country Wife*, 1675, available complete in the supplemental ebook), Aphra Behn (*The Rover*, 1677), William Congreve (*Love for Love*, 1695, available complete in the supplemental ebook; *The Way of the World*, 1700), and later George Farquhar (*The Beaux' Stratagem*, 1707) can still hold the stage today. These "comedies of manners" pick social behavior apart, exposing the nasty struggles for power among the upper classes, who use wit and manners as weapons. Human nature in these plays often conforms to the worst fears of Hobbes; sensual, false-hearted, selfish characters prey on each other. The male hero lives for pleasure and for the money and women that he can conquer. The object of his game of sexual intrigue is a beautiful, witty, pleasure-loving, and emancipated lady, every bit his equal in the strategies of love. What makes the favored couple stand out is the true wit and well-bred grace with which they step through the minefield of the plot. But during the 1690s "Societies for the Reformation of Manners" began to attack the blasphemy and obscenity they detected in such plays, and they sometimes brought offenders to trial. When Dryden died in 1700, a more respectable society was coming into being.

EIGHTEENTH-CENTURY LITERATURE, 1700-1745

Early in the eighteenth century a new and brilliant group of writers emerged: Swift, with *A Tale of a Tub* (1704–10); Addison, with *The Campaign* (1705), a poetic celebration of the battle of Blenheim; Prior, with *Poems on Several Occasions* (1707); Steele, with the *Tatler* (1709); and the youthful Pope, in the same year, with his *Pastorals*. These writers consolidate and popularize the social graces of the previous age. Determined to preserve good sense and civilized values, they turn their wit against fanaticism and innovation. Hence this is a great age of satire. Deeply conservative but also playful, their finest works often cast a strange light on modern times by viewing them through the screen of classical myths and classical forms. Thus Pope exposes the frivolity of fashionable London, in *The Rape of the Lock*, through the incongruity of verse that casts the idle rich as epic heroes. Similarly, Swift uses epic similes to mock the moderns in *The Battle of the Books*, and John Gay's *Trivia, or the Art of Walking the Streets of London* (1716) uses mock georgics to order his tour of the city. Such incongruities are not entirely negative. They also provide a fresh perspective on things that had once seemed too low for poetry to notice—for instance, in *The Rape of the Lock*, a girl putting on her makeup. In this way a parallel with classical literature can show not only how far the modern world has fallen but also how fascinating and magical it is when seen with "quick, poetic eyes."

The Augustans' effort to popularize and enforce high literary and social values was set against the new mass and multiplicity of writings that responded more spontaneously to the expanding commercial possibilities of print. The array of popular prose genres—news, thinly disguised political allegories, biographies of notorious criminals, travelogues, gossip, romantic tales—often blended facts and patently fictional elements, cemented by a rich lode of exaggeration, misrepresentations, and outright lies. Out of this matrix the modern novel would come to be born. The great master of such works was Daniel Defoe, producing first-person accounts such as *Robinson Crusoe* (1719), the famous castaway, and *Moll Flanders* (1722), mistress of lowlife crime. Claims that such works present (as the "editor" of *Crusoe* says) "a just history of fact," believed or not, sharpened the public's avidity for them. Defoe shows his readers a world plausibly like the one they know, where ordinary people negotiate familiar, entangled problems of financial, emotional, and spiritual existence. Jane Barker, Mary Davys, and many others brought women's work and daily lives as well as love affairs to fiction. Such stories were not only amusing but also served as models of conduct; they influenced the stories that real people told about themselves.

The theater also began to change its themes and effects to appeal to a wider audience. The clergyman Jeremy Collier had vehemently taken Dryden, Wycherley, and Congreve to task in *A Short View of the Immorality and Profaneness of the English Stage* (1698), which spoke for the moral outrage of the pious middle classes. The wits retreated. The comedy of manners was replaced by a new kind, later called "sentimental" not only because goodness triumphs over vice but also because it deals in high moral sentiments rather than witty dialogue and because the embarrassments of its heroines and heroes move the audience not to laughter but to tears. Virtue refuses to bow to aristocratic codes. In one crucial scene of Steele's influential play *The*

Conscious Lovers (1722) the hero would rather accept dishonor than fight a duel with a friend. Piety and middle-class values typify tragedies such as George Lillo's *London Merchant* (1731). One luxury invented in eighteenth-century Europe was the delicious pleasure of weeping, and comedies as well as tragedies brought that pleasure to playgoers through many decades. Some plays resisted the tide. Gay's cynical *Beggar's Opera* (1728) was a tremendous success, and later in the century the comedies of Goldsmith and Sheridan proved that sentiment is not necessarily an enemy to wit and laughter (for the complete text of Sheridan's masterpiece *The School for Scandal*, see the supplemental ebook). Yet larger and larger audiences responded more to spectacles and special effects than to sophisticated writing. Although the *stage* prospered during the eighteenth century, and the star system produced idolized actors and actresses (such as David Garrick and Sarah Siddons), the authors of *drama* tended to fade to the background.

Despite the sociable impulses of much the period's writing, readers also craved less crowded, more meditative works. Since the seventeenth century, no poems had been more popular than those about the pleasures of retirement, which invited the reader to dream about a safe retreat in the country or to meditate, like Finch, on scenery and the soul. But after 1726, when Thomson published *Winter*, the first of his cycle on the seasons, the poetry of natural description came into its own. A taste for gentle, picturesque beauty found expression not only in verse but in the elaborate, cultivated art of landscape gardening, and finally in the cherished English art of landscape painting in watercolor or oils (often illustrating Thomson's *Seasons*). Many readers also learned to enjoy a thrilling pleasure or fear in the presence of the sublime in nature: rushing waters, wild prospects, and mountains shrouded in mist. Whether enthusiasts went to the landscape in search of God or merely of heightened sensations, they came back feeling that they had been touched by something beyond the life they knew, by something that could hardly be expressed. Tourists as well as poets roamed the countryside, frequently quoting verse as they gazed at some evocative scene. A partiality for the sublime passed from Thomson to Collins to inspire the poetry of the Romantic age to come.

THE EMERGENCE OF NEW LITERARY THEMES AND MODES, 1740–85

When Matthew Arnold called the eighteenth century an "age of prose," he meant to belittle its poetry, but he also stated a significant fact: great prose does dominate the age. Until the 1740s, poetry tended to set the standards of literature. But the growth of new kinds of prose took the initiative away from verse. Novelists became better known than poets. Intellectual prose also flourished, with the achievements of Johnson in the essay and literary criticism, of Boswell in biography, of Hume in philosophy, of Burke in politics, of Edward Gibbon in history, of Sir Joshua Reynolds in aesthetics, of Gilbert White in natural history, and of Adam Smith in economics. Each of these authors is a master stylist, whose effort to express himself clearly and fully demands an art as carefully wrought as poetry. Other writers of prose were more informal. The memoirs of such women as Laetitia Pilkington, Charlotte Charke, Hester Thrale Piozzi, and Frances Burney bring each reader into their private lives and also remind us that the new print culture created celebrities, who wrote not only about themselves but about other celebrities they knew. The interest of readers in Samuel Johnson helped sell his own books as well as a host of books that quoted his sayings. But the prose of the age also had to do justice to difficult and complicated ideas. An unprecedented effort to formulate the first principles of philosophy, history, psychology, and art required a new style of persuasion.

Johnson helped codify that language, not only with his writings but with the first great English *Dictionary* (1755). This work established him as a national man of letters; eventually the period would be known as "the Age of Johnson." But his dominance was based on an ideal of service to others. The *Dictionary* illustrates its definitions with more than 114,000 quotations from the best English writers, thus building a bridge from past to present usage; and Johnson's essays, poems, and criticism also reflect his desire to preserve the lessons of the past. Yet he looks to the future as well, trying both to reach and to mold a nation of readers. If Johnson speaks for his age, one reason is his faith in common sense and the common reader. "By the common sense of readers uncorrupted with literary prejudices," he wrote in the last of his *Lives of the Poets* (1781), "must be finally decided all claim to poetical honors." A similar respect for the good judgment of ordinary people, and for standards of taste and behavior that anyone can share, marks many writers of the age. Both Burke, the great conservative statesman and author, and Thomas Paine, his radical adversary, proclaim themselves apostles of common sense.

No prose form better united availability to the common reader and seriousness of artistic purpose than the novel in the hands of two of its early masters, Samuel Richardson and Henry Fielding. Like many writers of fiction earlier in the century, Richardson initially did not set out to entertain the public with an avowedly invented tale: he conceived *Pamela, or Virtue Rewarded* (1740) while compiling a little book of model letters. The letters grew into a story about a captivating young servant who resists her master's base designs on her virtue until he gives up and marries her. The combination of a high moral tone with sexual titillation and a minute analysis of the heroine's emotions and state of mind proved irresistible to readers, in Britain and in Europe at large. Richardson topped *Pamela*'s success with *Clarissa* (1747–48), another epistolary novel, which explored the conflict between the libertine Lovelace, an attractive and diabolical aristocrat, and the angelic Clarissa, a middle-class paragon who struggles to stay pure. The sympathy that readers felt for Clarissa was magnified by a host of sentimental novels, including Frances Sheridan's *Memoirs of Miss Sidney Bidulph* (1761), Rousseau's *Julie, or The New Heloise* (1761), and Henry Mackenzie's *The Man of Feeling* (1771).

Henry Fielding made his entrance into the novel by turning *Pamela* farcically upside-down, as the hero of *Joseph Andrews* (1742), Pamela's brother, defends his chastity from the lewd advances of Lady Booby. Fielding's true model, however, is Cervantes's great *Don Quixote* (1605–15), from which he took an ironic, antiromantic style; a plot of wandering around the countryside; and an idealistic central character (Parson Adams) who keeps mistaking appearances for reality. The ambition of writing what Fielding called "a comic epic-poem in prose" went still further in *The History of Tom Jones, a Foundling* (1749). Crowded with incidents and comments on the state of England, the novel contrasts a good-natured, generous, wayward hero (who needs to learn prudence) with cold-hearted people who use moral codes and the law for their own selfish interests. This emphasis on instinctive virtue and vice, instead of Richardson's devotion to good principles, put off respectable readers like Johnson and Burney. But Coleridge thought that *Tom Jones* (along with *Oedipus Rex* and Jonson's *Alchemist*) was one of "the three most perfect plots ever planned."

An age of great prose can burden its poets. To Gray, Collins, Mark Akenside, and the brothers Joseph and Thomas Warton, it seemed that the spirit of poetry might be dying, driven out by the spirit of prose, by uninspiring truth, by the end of superstitions that had once peopled the land with poetic fairies and demons. In an age barren of magic, they ask, where has poetry gone? That question haunts many poems, suffusing them with melancholy. Poets who muse in silence are never far from thoughts of death, and a morbid fascination with suicide and the grave preoccupies many at midcentury. Such an attitude has little in common with that of poets like Dryden and Pope, social beings who live in a crowded world and seldom confess their private feelings in public. Pope's *Essay on Man* had taken a sunny view of providence; Edward Young's *The Complaint: or Night Thoughts on Life, Death, and Immortality* (1742–46), an immensely long poem in blank verse, is darkened by Christian fear of the life to come.

Often the melancholy poet withdraws into himself and yearns to be living in some other time and place. In his "Ode to Fancy" (1746), Joseph Warton associated "fancy" with visions in the wilderness and spontaneous passions; the true poet was no longer defined as a craftsman or maker but as a seer or nature's priest. "The public has seen all that art can do," William Shenstone wrote in 1761, welcoming James Macpherson's *Ossian*, "and they want the more striking efforts of wild, original, enthusiastic genius." Macpherson filled the bill. His primitive, sentimental epics, supposedly translated from an ancient Gaelic warrior-bard, won the hearts of readers around the world; Napoleon and Thomas Jefferson, for instance, both thought that Ossian was greater than Homer. Poets began to cultivate archaic language and antique forms. Inspired by Thomas Percy's edition of *Reliques of Ancient English Poetry* (1765), Thomas Chatterton passed off his own ballads as medieval; he died at seventeen, soon after his forgeries were exposed, but the Romantics later idolized his precocious genius.

The most remarkable consequence of the medieval revival, however, was the invention of the Gothic novel. Horace Walpole set *The Castle of Otranto* (1765), a dreamlike tale of terror, in a simulacrum of Strawberry Hill, his own tiny, pseudo-medieval castle, which helped revive a taste for Gothic architecture. Walpole created a mode of fiction that retains its popularity to the present day. In a typical Gothic romance, amid the glooms and secret passages of some remote castle, the laws of nightmare replace the laws of probability. Forbidden themes—incest, murder, necrophilia, atheism, and the torments of sexual desire—are allowed free play. Most such romances, like William Beckford's *Vathek* (1786) and Matthew Lewis's *The Monk* (1796), revel in sensationalism and the grotesque. The Gothic vogue suggested that classical canons of taste—simplicity and harmonious balance—might count for less than the pleasures of fancy—intricate puzzles and a willful excess. But Gothicism also resulted in works, like Ann Radcliffe's, that temper romance with reality as well as in serious novels of social purpose, like William Godwin's *Caleb Williams* (1794) and Mary

Wollstonecraft's *Maria, or The Wrongs of Woman* (1798); and Mary Shelley, the daughter of Wollstonecraft and Godwin, eventually composed a romantic nightmare, *Frankenstein* (1818), that continues to haunt our dreams.

The century abounded in other remarkable experiments in fiction, anticipating many of the forms that novelists still use today. Tobias Smollett's picaresque *Roderick Random* (1748) and *Humphry Clinker* (1771) delight in coarse practical jokes, the freaks and strong odors of life. But the most *novel* novelist of the age was Laurence Sterne, a humorous, sentimental clergyman who loves to play tricks on his readers. *The Life and Opinions of Tristram Shandy* (1760–67) abandons clock time for psychological time, whimsically follows chance associations, interrupts its own stories, violates the conventions of print by putting chapters 18 and 19 after chapter 25, sneaks in double entendres, and seems ready to go on forever. And yet these games get us inside the characters' minds,

Bertie Greatheed, *Diego and Jaquez Frightened by the Giant Foot*, 1791. A scene from Horace Walpole's Gothic novel *The Castle of Otranto* (1764), showing servants terrified by the supernatural appearance of an oversize stone foot in the castle.

as if the world were as capricious as our thoughts. Sterne's self-conscious art implies that people's private obsessions shape their lives—or help create reality itself. As unique as Sterne's fictional world is, his interest in private life matched the concerns of the novel toward the end of the century: depictions of characters' intimate feelings dominated the tradition of domestic fiction that included Burney, Radcliffe, and, later, Maria Edgeworth, culminating in the masterworks of Jane Austen. A more "masculine" orientation emerged at the beginning of the next century, as Walter Scott's works, with their broad historical scope and outdoor scenes of men at work and war, appealed to a large readership. Yet the copious, acute, often ironic attention to details of private life by Richardson, Sterne, and Austen continued to influence the novel profoundly through its subsequent history.

CONTINUITY AND REVOLUTION

The history of eighteenth-century literature was first composed by the Romantics, who wrote it to serve their own interests. Prizing originality, they naturally preferred to stress how different they were from writers of the previous age. Later historians have tended to follow their lead, competing to prove that everything changed in 1776, or 1789, or 1798. This revolutionary view of history accounts for what happened to the word *revolution*. The older meaning referred to a movement around a point, a recurrence or cycle, as in the revolutions of the planets; the newer meaning signified a violent break with the past, an overthrow of the existing order, as in the Big Bang or the French Revolution. Romantic rhetoric made heavy use of such dramatic upheavals. Yet every history devoted to truth must take account of both sorts of revolution, of continuities as well as changes. The ideals that many Romantics made their own—the passion for liberty and equality, the founding of justice on individual rights, the distrust of institutions, the love of nature, the reverence for imagination, and even the embrace of change— grew from seeds that had been planted long before. Nor did Augustan literature abruptly vanish on that day in 1798 when Wordsworth and Coleridge anonymously published a small and unsuccessful volume of poems called *Lyrical Ballads*. Even when they rebel against the work of Pope and Johnson and Gray, Romantic writers incorporate much of their language and values.

What Restoration and eighteenth-century literature passed on to the future, in fact, was chiefly a set of unresolved problems. The age of Enlightenment was also, in England, an age that insisted on holding fast to older beliefs and customs; the age of population explosion was also an age of individualism; the age that developed the slave trade was also the age that gave rise to the abolitionist movement; the age that codified rigid standards of conduct for women was also an age when many women took the chance to read and write and think for themselves; the age of reason was also the age when sensibility flourished; the last classical age was also the first modern age. These contradictions are far from abstract; writers were forced to choose their own directions. When young James Boswell looked for a mentor whose biography he might write, he considered not only Samuel Johnson but also David Hume, whose skeptical views of morality, truth, and religion were everything Johnson abhorred. The two writers seem to inhabit different worlds, yet Boswell traveled freely between them. That was exciting and also instructive. "Without Contraries is no progression," according to one citizen of Johnson's London, William Blake, who also thought that "Opposition is true Friendship." Good conversation was a lively eighteenth-century art, and sharp disagreements did not keep people from talking. The conversations the period started have not ended yet.

The Restoration and
The Eighteenth Century

TEXTS	CONTEXTS
1660 Samuel Pepys begins his diary	1660 Charles II restored to the throne. Reopening of the theaters
1662 Samuel Butler, *Hudibras*, part 1	1662 Act of Uniformity requires all clergy to obey the Church of England. Chartering of the Royal Society
	1664–66 Great Plague of London
	1666 Fire destroys the City of London
1667 John Milton, *Paradise Lost*	
1668 John Dryden, *Essay of Dramatic Poesy*	1668 Dryden becomes poet laureate
	1673 Test Act requires all officeholders to swear allegiance to Anglicanism
1678 John Bunyan, *Pilgrim's Progress*, part 1	1678 The "Popish Plot" inflames anti-Catholic feeling
1681 Dryden, *Absalom and Achitophel*	1681 Charles II dissolves Parliament
	1685 Death of Charles II. James II, his Catholic brother, takes the throne
1687 Sir Isaac Newton, *Principia Mathematica*	
1688 Aphra Behn, *Oroonoko*	1688–89 The Glorious Revolution. James II exiled and succeeded by his Protestant daughter, Mary, and her husband, William of Orange
1690 John Locke, *An Essay Concerning Human Understanding*	
1700 William Congreve, *The Way of the World*. Mary Astell, *Some Reflections upon Marriage*	
	1702 War of the Spanish Succession begins. Death of William III. Succession of Anne (Protestant daughter of James II)
1704 Jonathan Swift, *A Tale of a Tub*. Newton, *Opticks*	
	1707 Act of Union with Scotland
	1710 Tories take power
1711 Alexander Pope, *An Essay on Criticism*. Joseph Addison and Sir Richard Steele, *Spectator* (1711–12, 1714)	
	1713 Treaty of Utrecht ends War of the Spanish Succession
	1714 Death of Queen Anne. George I (great-grandson of James I) becomes the first Hanoverian king. Tory government replaced by Whigs
1716 Lady Mary Wortley Montagu writes her letters from Turkey (1716–18)	
1717 Pope, *The Rape of the Lock* (final version)	

TEXTS	CONTEXTS
1719 Daniel Defoe, *Robinson Crusoe*	
	1720 South Sea Bubble collapses
	1721 Robert Walpole comes to power
1726 Swift, *Gulliver's Travels*	
	1727 George I dies. George II succeeds
1728 John Gay, *The Beggar's Opera*	
1733 Pope, *An Essay on Man*	
	1737 Licensing Act censors the stage
1740 Samuel Richardson, *Pamela*	
1742 Henry Fielding, *Joseph Andrews*	1742 Walpole resigns
1743 Pope, *The Dunciad* (final version). William Hogarth, *Marriage A-la-Mode*	
1746 William Collins's *Odes*	1746 Charles Edward Stuart's defeat at Culloden ends the last Jacobite rebellion
1747 Richardson, *Clarissa*	
1749 Fielding, *Tom Jones*	
1751 Thomas Gray, "Elegy Written in a Country Churchyard"	1751 Robert Clive seizes Arcot, the prelude to English control of India
1755 Samuel Johnson, *Dictionary*	
	1756 Beginning of Seven Years' War
1759 Johnson, *Rasselas.* Voltaire, *Candide*	1759 James Wolfe's capture of Quebec ensures British control of Canada
1760 Laurence Sterne, *Tristram Shandy* (1760–67)	1760 George III succeeds to the throne
1765 Johnson's edition of Shakespeare	
	1768 Captain James Cook voyages to Australia and New Zealand
1770 Oliver Goldsmith, "The Deserted Village"	
	1775 American Revolution (1775–83). James Watt produces steam engines
1776 Adam Smith, *The Wealth of Nations*	
1778 Frances Burney, *Evelina*	
1779 Johnson, *Lives of the Poets* (1779–81)	
	1780 Gordon Riots in London
1783 George Crabbe, *The Village*	1783 William Pitt becomes prime minister
1785 William Cowper, *The Task*	

JOHN DRYDEN
1631–1700

Although John Dryden's parents seem to have sided with Parliament against the king, there is no evidence that the poet grew up in a strict Puritan family. His father, a country gentleman of moderate fortune, gave his son a gentleman's education at Westminster School, under the renowned Dr. Richard Busby, who used the rod as a pedagogical aid in imparting a sound knowledge of the learned languages and literatures to his charges (among others John Locke and Matthew Prior). From Westminster, Dryden went to Trinity College, Cambridge, where he took his A.B. in 1654. His first important poem, "Heroic Stanzas" (1659), was written to commemorate the death of Cromwell. The next year, however, in "Astraea Redux," Dryden joined his countrymen in celebrating the return of Charles II to his throne. During the rest of his life Dryden was to remain entirely loyal to Charles and to his successor, James II.

Dryden is the commanding literary figure of the last four decades of the seventeenth century. Every important aspect of the life of his times—political, religious, philosophical, artistic—finds expression somewhere in his writings. Dryden is the least personal of poets. He is not at all the solitary, subjective poet listening to the murmur of his own voice and preoccupied with his own feelings but rather a citizen of the world commenting publicly on matters of public concern.

From the beginning to the end of his literary career, Dryden's nondramatic poems are most typically occasional poems, which commemorate particular events of a public character—a coronation, a military victory, a death, or a political crisis. Such poems are social and often ceremonial, written not for the self but for the nation. Dryden's principal achievements in this form are the two poems on the king's return and his coronation; *Annus Mirabilis* (1667), which celebrates the English naval victory over the Dutch and the fortitude of the people of London and the king during the Great Fire, both events of that "wonderful year," 1666; the political poems; the lines on the death of Oldham (1684); and odes such as "Alexander's Feast."

Between 1664 and 1681, however, Dryden was mainly a playwright. The newly chartered theaters needed a modern repertory, and he set out to supply the need. Dryden wrote his plays, as he frankly confessed, to please his audiences, which were not heterogeneous like Shakespeare's but were largely drawn from the court and from people of fashion. In the style of the time, he produced rhymed heroic plays, in which incredibly noble heroes and heroines face incredibly difficult choices between love and honor; comedies, in which male and female rakes engage in intrigue and bright repartee; and later, libretti for the newly introduced dramatic form, the opera. His one great tragedy, *All for Love* (1677), in blank verse, adapts Shakespeare's *Antony and Cleopatra* to the unities of time, place, and action. As his *Essay of Dramatic Poesy* (1668) shows, Dryden had studied the works of the great playwrights of Greece and Rome, of the English Renaissance, and of contemporary France, seeking sound theoretical principles on which to construct the new drama that the age demanded. Indeed, his fine critical intelligence always supported his creative powers, and, because he took literature seriously and enjoyed discussing it, he became, almost casually, what Samuel Johnson called him: "the father of English criticism." His abilities as both poet and dramatist brought him to the attention of the king, who in 1668 made him poet laureate. Two years later the post of historiographer royal was added to the laureateship at a combined stipend of £200, enough money to live comfortably on.

Between 1678 and 1681, when he was nearing fifty, Dryden discovered his great gift for writing formal verse satire. A quarrel with the playwright Thomas Shadwell prompted the mock-heroic episode "Mac Flecknoe," probably written in 1678 or 1679 but not published until 1682. Out of the stresses occasioned by the Popish Plot (1678) and its political aftermath came his major political satires, *Absalom and Achitophel* (1681), and "The Medal" (1682), his final attack on the villain of *Absalom and Achitophel*, the earl of Shaftesbury. Twenty years' experience as poet and playwright had prepared him technically for the triumph of *Absalom and Achitophel*. He had mastered the heroic couplet, having fashioned it into an instrument suitable in his hands for every sort of discourse from the thrust and parry of quick logical argument, to lyric feeling, rapid narrative, or forensic declamation. Thanks to this long discipline, he was able in one stride to rival the masters of verse satire: Horace, Juvenal, Persius, in ancient Rome, and Boileau, his French contemporary.

The consideration of religious and political questions that the events of 1678–81 forced on Dryden brought a new seriousness to his mind and works. In 1682 he published *Religio Laici*, a poem in which he examined the grounds of his religious faith and defended the middle way of the Anglican Church against the rationalism of Deism on the one hand and the authoritarianism of Rome on the other. But he had moved closer to Rome than he perhaps realized when he wrote the poem. Charles II died in 1685 and was succeeded by his Catholic brother, James II. Within a year Dryden and his two sons converted to Catholicism. Though his enemies accused him of opportunism, he proved his sincerity by his steadfast loyalty to the Roman Church after James abdicated and the Protestant William and Mary came in; as a result he was to lose his offices and their much-needed stipends. From his new position as a Roman Catholic, Dryden wrote in 1687 *The Hind and the Panther*, in which a milk-white Hind (the Roman Church) and a spotted Panther (the Anglican Church) eloquently debate theology. The Hind has the better of the argument, but Dryden already knew that James's policies were failing, and with them the Catholic cause in England.

Dryden was now nearing sixty, with a family to support on a much-diminished income. To earn a living, he resumed writing plays and turned to translations. In 1693 appeared his versions of Juvenal and Persius, with a long dedicatory epistle on satire; and in 1697, his greatest achievement in this mode, the works of Virgil. At the very end, two months before his death, came the *Fables Ancient and Modern*, prefaced by one of the finest of his critical essays and made up of translations from Ovid, Boccaccio, and Chaucer.

Dryden's foremost achievement was to bring the pleasures of literature to the ever-increasing reading public of Britain. As a critic and translator, he made many classics available to men and women who lacked a classical education. His canons of taste and theoretical principles would set the standard for the next generation. As a writer of prose, he helped establish a popular new style, shaped to the cadences of good conversation. Johnson praised its apparent artlessness: "every word seems to drop by chance, though it falls into its proper place. Nothing is cold or languid; the whole is airy, animated, and vigorous . . . though all is easy, nothing is feeble; though all seems careless, there is nothing harsh." Although Dryden's plays went out of fashion, his poems did not. His satire inspired the most brilliant verse satirist of the next century, Alexander Pope, and the energy and variety of his metrics launched the long-standing vogue of heroic couplets. Augustan style is at its best in his poems: lively, dignified, precise, and always musical—a flexible instrument of public speech. "By him we were taught *sapere et fari*, to think naturally and express forcibly," Johnson concluded. "What was said of Rome, adorned by Augustus, may be applied by an easy metaphor to English poetry embellished by Dryden, *lateritiam invenit, marmoream reliquit*, he found it brick, and he left it marble."

For more of Dryden's poetry and criticism, see the supplemental ebook.

Absalom and Achitophel In 1678 a dangerous crisis, both religious and political, threatened to undo the Restoration settlement and to precipitate England once again into civil war. The Popish Plot and its aftermath not only whipped up extreme anti-Catholic passions, but led between 1679 and 1681 to a bitter political struggle between Charles II (whose adherents came to be called Tories) and the earl of Shaftesbury (whose followers were termed Whigs). The issues were nothing less than the prerogatives of the crown and the possible exclusion of the king's Catholic brother, James, duke of York, from his position as heir-presumptive to the throne. Charles's cool courage and brilliant, if unscrupulous, political genius saved the throne for his brother and gave at least temporary peace to his people.

Charles was a Catholic at heart—he received the last rites of that church on his deathbed—and was eager to do what he could do discreetly for the relief of his Catholic subjects, who suffered severe civil and religious disabilities imposed by their numerically superior Protestant compatriots. James openly professed the Catholic religion, an awkward fact politically, for he was next in line of succession because Charles had no legitimate children. The household of the duke, as well as that of Charles's neglected queen, Catherine of Braganza, inevitably became the center of Catholic life and intrigue at court and consequently of Protestant prejudice and suspicion.

No one understood, however, that the situation was explosive until 1678, when Titus Oates (a renegade Catholic convert of infamous character) offered sworn testimony of the existence of a Jesuit plot to assassinate the king, burn London, massacre Protestants, and reestablish the Roman Church.

The country might have kept its head and come to realize (what no historian has doubted) that Oates and his confederates were perjured rascals, as Charles himself quickly perceived. But panic was created by the discovery of the body of a prominent London justice of the peace, Sir Edmund Berry Godfrey, who a few days before had received for safekeeping a copy of Oates's testimony. The murder, immediately ascribed to the Catholics, has never been solved. Fear and indignation reached a hysterical pitch when the seizure of the papers of the duke of York's secretary revealed that he had been in correspondence with the confessor of Louis XIV regarding the reestablishment of the Roman Church in England. Before the terror subsided many innocent men were executed on the increasingly bold and always false evidence of Oates and his accomplices.

The earl of Shaftesbury, the duke of Buckingham, and others quickly took advantage of the situation. With the support of the Commons and the City of London, they moved to exclude the duke of York from the succession. Between 1679 and 1681 Charles and Shaftesbury were engaged in a mighty struggle. The Whigs found a candidate of their own in the king's favorite illegitimate son, the handsome and engaging duke of Monmouth, whom they advanced as a proper successor to his father. They urged Charles to legitimize him, and when he refused, they whispered that there was proof that the king had secretly married Monmouth's mother. The young man allowed himself to be used against his father. He was sent on a triumphant progress, through western England, where he was enthusiastically received. Twice an Exclusion Bill nearly passed both houses. But by early 1681 Charles had secured his own position by secretly accepting from Louis XIV a three-year subsidy that made him independent of Parliament, which had tried to force his hand by refusing to vote him funds. He summoned Parliament to meet at Oxford in the spring of 1681, and a few moments after the Commons had passed the Exclusion Bill, in a bold stroke he abruptly dissolved Parliament, which never met again during his reign. Already, as Charles was aware, a reaction had set in against the violence of the Whigs. In midsummer, when he felt it safe to move against his enemies, Shaftesbury was sent to the Tower of London, charged with high treason. In November, the grand jury, packed with Whigs, threw out the indictment, and the earl was free, but his power was broken, and he lived only two more years.

Shortly before the grand jury acted, Dryden published anonymously the first part of *Absalom and Achitophel*, apparently hoping to influence their verdict. The issues in question were grave; the chief actors, the most important men in the realm. Dryden, therefore, could not use burlesque and caricature as had Butler, or the mock heroic as he himself had done in "Mac Flecknoe." Only a heroic style and manner were appropriate to his weighty material, and the poem is most original in its blending of the heroic and the satiric. Dryden's task called for all his tact and literary skill; he had to mention, but to gloss over, the king's faults: his indolence and love of pleasure; his neglect of his wife, and his devotion to his mistresses—conduct that had left him with many children, but no heir except his Catholic brother. He had to deal gently with Monmouth, whom Charles still loved. And he had to present, or appear to present, the king's case objectively.

The remarkable parallels between the rebellion of Absalom against his father, King David (2 Samuel 13–18), had already been remarked in sermons, satires, and pamphlets. Dryden took the hint and gave contemporary events a due distance and additional dignity by approaching them indirectly through their biblical analogues. The poem is famous for its brilliant portraits of the king's enemies and friends, but equally admirable are the temptation scene (which, like other passages, is indebted to *Paradise Lost*) and the remarkably astute analysis of the Popish Plot itself.

A second part of *Absalom and Achitophel* appeared in 1682. Most of it is the work of Nahum Tate, but lines 310–509, which include the devastating portraits of Doeg and Og (two Whig poets, Elkanah Settle and Thomas Shadwell), are certainly by Dryden.

Absalom and Achitophel: A Poem

    In pious times, ere priestcraft[1] did begin,
Before polygamy was made a sin;
When man on many multiplied his kind,
Ere one to one was cursedly confined;
5   When nature prompted and no law denied
Promiscuous use of concubine and bride;
Then Israel's monarch after Heaven's own heart,[2]
His vigorous warmth did variously impart
To wives and slaves; and, wide as his command,
10   Scattered his Maker's image through the land.
Michal,[3] of royal blood, the crown did wear,
A soil ungrateful to the tiller's care:
Not so the rest; for several mothers bore
To godlike David several sons before.
15   But since like slaves his bed they did ascend,
No true succession could their seed attend.
Of all this numerous progeny was none
So beautiful, so brave, as Absalom:[4]
Whether, inspired by some diviner lust,
20   His father got him with a greater gust,°   *relish, pleasure*
Or that his conscious destiny made way,
By manly beauty, to imperial sway.
Early in foreign fields he won renown,

1. "Religious frauds; management of wicked priests to gain power" (Johnson's *Dictionary*).
2. David ("a man after [God's] own heart," according to 1 Samuel 13.14) represents Charles II.
3. One of David's wives, who represents the childless queen, Catherine of Braganza.
4. James Scott, duke of Monmouth (1649–1685).

With kings and states allied to Israel's crown:[5]
25 In peace the thoughts of war he could remove,
And seemed as he were only born for love.
Whate'er he did, was done with so much ease,
In him alone 'twas natural to please;
His motions all accompanied with grace;
30 And paradise was opened in his face.
With secret joy indulgent David viewed
His youthful image in his son renewed:
To all his wishes nothing he denied;
And made the charming Annabel[6] his bride.
35 What faults he had (for who from faults is free?)
His father could not, or he would not see.
Some warm excesses which the law forbore,
Were cònstrued youth that purged by boiling o'er:
And Amnon's murther,[7] by a specious name,
40 Was called a just revenge for injured fame.
Thus praised and loved the noble youth remained,
While David, undisturbed, in Sion° reigned.   *London*
But life can never be sincerely° blest;   *wholly*
Heaven punishes the bad, and proves° the best.   *tests*
45 The Jews,° a headstrong, moody, murmuring race,   *English*
As ever tried the extent and stretch of grace;
God's pampered people, whom, debauched with ease,
No king could govern, nor no God could please
(Gods they had tried of every shape and size
50 That god-smiths could produce, or priests devise);[8]
These Adam-wits, too fortunately free,
Began to dream they wanted liberty;[9]
And when no rule, no precedent was found,
Of men by laws less circumscribed and bound,
55 They led their wild desires to woods and caves,
And thought that all but savages were slaves.
They who, when Saul was dead, without a blow,
Made foolish Ishbosheth[1] the crown forgo;
Who banished David did from Hebron[2] bring,
60 And with a general shout proclaimed him king:
Those very Jews, who, at their very best,
Their humor° more than loyalty expressed,   *caprice*
Now wondered why so long they had obeyed
An idol monarch, which their hands had made;
65 Thought they might ruin him they could create,
Or melt him to that golden calf,[3] a state.°   *republic*

---

5. Monmouth had won repute as a soldier fighting for France against Holland and for Holland against France.

6. Anne Scott, duchess of Buccleuch (pronounced *Bue-cloo*), a beauty and a great heiress.

7. Absalom killed his half-brother Amnon, who had raped Absalom's sister Tamar (2 Samuel 13.28–29). The parallel with Monmouth is vague. He is known to have committed acts of violence in his youth, but certainly not fratricide.

8. Dryden recalls the political and religious controversies that, since the Reformation, had divided England and finally caused civil wars.

9. Adam rebelled because he felt that he lacked ("wanted") liberty, because he was forbidden to eat the fruit of one tree.

1. Saul's son. He stands for Richard Cromwell, who succeeded his father as lord protector. "Saul": Oliver Cromwell.

2. Where David reigned over Judah after the death of Saul and before he became king of Israel (2 Samuel 1–5). Charles had been crowned in Scotland in 1651.

3. The image worshiped by the children of Israel during the period that Moses spent on Mount Sinai, receiving the law from God.

But these were random bolts;° no formed design   *shots*
Nor interest made the factious crowd to join:
The sober part of Israel, free from stain,
70   Well knew the value of a peaceful reign;
And, looking backward with a wise affright,
Saw seams of wounds, dishonest° to the sight: *disgraceful*
In contemplation of whose ugly scars
They cursed the memory of civil wars.
75   The moderate sort of men, thus qualified,°   *assuaged*
Inclined the balance to the better side;
And David's mildness managed it so well,
The bad found no occasion to rebel.
But when to sin our biased⁴ nature leans,
80   The careful Devil is still at hand with means;
And providently pimps for ill desires:
The Good Old Cause⁵ revived, a plot requires.
Plots, true or false, are necessary things,
To raise up commonwealths and ruin kings.
85   The inhabitants of old Jerusalem
Were Jebusites;⁶ the town so called from them;
And theirs the native right.
But when the chosen people° grew more strong,   *Protestants*
The rightful cause at length became the wrong;
90   And every loss the men of Jebus bore,
They still were thought God's enemies the more.
Thus worn and weakened, well or ill content,
Submit they must to David's government:
Impoverished and deprived of all command,
95   Their taxes doubled as they lost their land;
And, what was harder yet to flesh and blood,
Their gods disgraced, and burnt like common wood.⁷
This set the heathen priesthood° in a flame;   *Roman Catholic clergy*
For priests of all religions are the same:
100   Of whatsoe'er descent their godhead be,
Stock, stone, or other homely pedigree,
In his defense his servants are as bold,
As if he had been born of beaten gold.
The Jewish rabbins,° though their enemies,   *Anglican clergy*
105   In this conclude them honest men and wise:
For 'twas their duty, all the learned think,
To espouse his cause, by whom they eat and drink.
From hence began that Plot, the nation's curse,
Bad in itself, but represented worse;
110   Raised in extremes, and in extremes decried;
With oaths affirmed, with dying vows denied;
Not weighed or winnowed by the multitude;
But swallowed in the mass, unchewed and crude.
Some truth there was, but dashed° and brewed with lies,   *adulterated*
115   To please the fools, and puzzle all the wise.
Succeeding times did equal folly call,

---

4. Inclined (cf. "Mac Flecknoe," line 189 and n. 5, p. 990).
5. The Commonwealth. Dryden stigmatizes the Whigs by associating them with subversion.

6. Roman Catholics. The original name of Jerusalem (here, London) was Jebus.
7. Such oppressive laws against Roman Catholics date from the time of Elizabeth I.

Believing nothing, or believing all.
The Egyptian rites the Jebusites embraced,
Where gods were recommended by their taste.[8]

120   Such savory deities must needs be good,
As served at once for worship and for food.
By force they could not introduce these gods,
For ten to one in former days was odds;
So fraud was used (the sacrificer's trade):

125   Fools are more hard to conquer than persuade.
Their busy teachers mingled with the Jews,
And raked for converts even the court and stews:°   *brothels*
Which Hebrew priests the more unkindly took,
Because the fleece accompanies the flock.[9]

130   Some thought they God's anointed° meant to slay   *the king*
By guns, invented since full many a day:
Our author swears it not; but who can know
How far the Devil and Jebusites may go?
This Plot, which failed for want of common sense,

135   Had yet a deep and dangerous consequence:
For, as when raging fevers boil the blood,
The standing lake soon floats into a flood,
And every hostile humor,[1] which before
Slept quiet in its channels, bubbles o'er;

140   So several factions from this first ferment
Work up to foam, and threat the government.
Some by their friends, more by themselves thought wise,
Opposed the power to which they could not rise.
Some had in courts been great, and thrown from thence,

145   Like fiends were hardened in impenitence;
Some, by their monarch's fatal mercy, grown
From pardoned rebels kinsmen to the throne,
Were raised in power and public office high;
Strong bands, if bands ungrateful men could tie.

150   Of these the false Achitophel[2] was first;
A name to all succeeding ages cursed:
For close designs, and crooked counsels fit;
Sagacious, bold, and turbulent of wit;°   *unruly imagination*
Restless, unfixed in principles and place;

155   In power unpleased, impatient of disgrace:
A fiery soul, which, working out its way, ⎫
Fretted the pygmy body to decay,   ⎬
And o'er-informed the tenement of clay.[3] ⎭
A daring pilot in extremity;

8. Here Dryden sneers at the doctrine of transubstantiation. "Egyptian": French, therefore Catholic.
9. Dryden charges that the Anglican clergy ("Hebrew priests") resented proselytizing by Catholics chiefly because they stood to lose their tithes ("fleece").
1. Bodily fluid. Such fluids were thought to determine health and temperament.
2. Anthony Ashley Cooper, first earl of Shaftesbury (1621–1683). He had served in the parliamentary army and been a member of Cromwell's council of state. He later helped bring back

Charles and, in 1670, was made a member of the notorious Cabal Ministry, which formed an alliance with Louis XIV in which England betrayed her ally, Holland, and joined France in war against that country. In 1672 he became lord chancellor, but with the dissolution of the cabal in 1673, he was removed from office. Lines 146–49 apply perfectly to him.
3. The soul is thought of as the animating principle, the force that puts the body in motion. Shaftesbury's body seemed too small to house his fiery, energetic soul.

160   Pleased with the danger, when the waves went high,
     He sought the storms; but, for a calm unfit,
     Would steer too nigh the sands, to boast his wit.
     Great wits° are sure to madness near allied,[4]   *men of genius*
     And thin partitions do their bounds divide;
165   Else why should he, with wealth and honor blest,
     Refuse his age the needful hours of rest?
     Punish a body which he could not please;
     Bankrupt of life, yet prodigal of ease?
     And all to leave what with his toil he won,
170   To that unfeathered two-legged thing,[5] a son;
     Got, while his soul did huddled° notions try;   *confused, hurried*
     And born a shapeless lump, like anarchy.
     In friendship false, implacable in hate,
     Resolved to ruin or to rule the state.
175   To compass this the triple bond[6] he broke, ⎫
     The pillars of the public safety shook,   ⎬
     And fitted Israel for a foreign yoke;   ⎭
     Then seized with fear, yet still affecting fame,
     Usurped a patriot's all-atoning name.
180   So easy still it proves in factious times,
     With public zeal to cancel private crimes.
     How safe is treason, and how sacred ill,
     Where none can sin against the people's will!
     Where crowds can wink, and no offense be known,
185   Since in another's guilt they find their own!
     Yet fame deserved, no enemy can grudge;
     The statesman we abhor, but praise the judge.
     In Israel's courts ne'er sat an Abbethdin[7]
     With more discerning eyes, or hands more clean;
190   Unbribed, unsought, the wretched to redress;
     Swift of dispatch, and easy of access.
     Oh, had he been content to serve the crown,
     With virtues only proper to the gown°   *judge's robe*
     Or had the rankness of the soil been freed
195   From cockle,° that oppressed the noble seed;   *weeds*
     David for him his tuneful harp had strung,
     And Heaven had wanted one immortal song.[8]
     But wild Ambition loves to slide, not stand,
     And Fortune's ice prefers to Virtue's land.
200   Achitophel, grown weary to possess
     A lawful fame, and lazy happiness,
     Disdained the golden fruit to gather free,
     And lent the crowd his arm to shake the tree.
     Now, manifest of° crimes contrived long since,   *detected in*

---

4. That genius and madness are akin is a very old idea.

5. Cf. Plato's definition of a human: "a featherless biped."

6. The triple alliance of England, Sweden, and Holland against France, 1668. Shaftesbury helped bring about the war against Holland in 1672.

7. The chief of the seventy elders who composed the Jewish supreme court. The allusion is to Shaftesbury's serving as lord chancellor from 1672 to 1673. Dryden's praise of Shaftesbury's integrity in this office, by suggesting a balanced judgment, makes his condemnation of the statesman more effective than it might otherwise have been.

8. I.e., David would have had occasion to write one fewer song of praise to heaven. The reference may be to 2 Samuel 22 or to Psalm 4.

205 He stood at bold defiance with his prince;
Held up the buckler of the people's cause
Against the crown, and skulked behind the laws.
The wished occasion of the Plot he takes;
Some circumstances finds, but more he makes.
210 By buzzing emissaries fills the ears
Of listening crowds with jealousies° and fears   suspicions
Of arbitrary counsels brought to light,
And proves the king himself a Jebusite.
Weak arguments! which yet he knew full well
215 Were strong with people easy to rebel.
For, governed by the moon, the giddy Jews
Tread the same track when she the prime renews;
And once in twenty years, their scribes record,[9]
By natural instinct they change their lord.
220 Achitophel still wants a chief, and none
Was found so fit as warlike Absalom:
Not that he wished his greatness to create
(For politicians neither love nor hate),
But, for he knew his title not allowed,
225 Would keep him still depending on the crowd,
That° kingly power, thus ebbing out, might be   so that
Drawn to the dregs of a democracy.[1]
Him he attempts with studied arts to please,
And sheds his venom in such words as these:
230   "Auspicious prince, at whose nativity
Some royal planet[2] ruled the southern sky;
Thy longing country's darling and desire;
Their cloudy pillar and their guardian fire:
Their second Moses, whose extended wand
235 Divides the seas, and shows the promised land;[3]
Whose dawning day in every distant age
Has exercised the sacred prophet's rage:
The people's prayer, the glad diviners' theme,
The young men's vision, and the old men's dream![4]
240 Thee, savior, thee, the nation's vows[5] confess,
And, never satisfied with seeing, bless:
Swift unbespoken° pomps thy steps proclaim,   spontaneous
And stammering babes are taught to lisp thy name.
How long wilt thou the general joy detain,
245 Starve and defraud the people of thy reign?
Content ingloriously to pass thy days
Like one of Virtue's fools that feeds on praise;
Till thy fresh glories, which now shine so bright,
Grow stale and tarnish with our daily sight.

9. The moon "renews her prime" when its several phases recur on the same day of the solar calendar (i.e., complete a cycle) as happens approximately every twenty years. The crisis between Charles I and Parliament began to grow acute about 1640; Charles II returned in 1660; it is now 1680 and a full cycle has been completed.
1. I.e., mob rule. To Dryden, *democracy* meant popular government.
2. A planet whose influence destines him to

kingship.
3. After their exodus from Egypt under the leadership of Moses, whose "extended wand" separated the waters of the Red Sea so that they crossed over on dry land, the Israelites were led in their forty-year wandering in the wilderness by a pillar of cloud by day and a pillar of fire by night (Exodus 13–14).
4. Cf. Joel 2.28.
5. Solemn promises of fidelity.

250 Believe me, royal youth, thy fruit must be
    Or gathered ripe, or rot upon the tree.
    Heaven has to all allotted, soon or late,
    Some lucky revolution of their fate;
    Whose motions if we watch and guide with skill
255 (For human good depends on human will),
    Our Fortune rolls as from a smooth descent,
    And from the first impression takes the bent;
    But, if unseized, she glides away like wind,
    And leaves repenting Folly far behind.
260 Now, now she meets you with a glorious prize,
    And spreads her locks before her as she flies.[6]
    Had thus old David, from whose loins you spring,
    Not dared, when Fortune called him, to be king,
    At Gath[7] an exile he might still remain,
265 And heaven's anointing[8] oil had been in vain.
    Let his successful youth your hopes engage;
    But shun the example of declining age;
    Behold him setting in his western skies,
    The shadows lengthening as the vapors rise.
270 He is not now, as when on Jordan's sand[9]
    The joyful people thronged to see him land,
    Covering the beach, and blackening all the strand;
    But, like the Prince of Angels, from his height
    Comes tumbling downward with diminished light;[1]
275 Betrayed by one poor plot to public scorn
    (Our only blessing since his cursed return),
    Those heaps of people which one sheaf did bind,
    Blown off and scattered by a puff of wind.
    What strength can he to your designs oppose,
280 Naked of friends, and round beset with foes?
    If Pharaoh's[2] doubtful succor he should use,
    A foreign aid would more incense the Jews:
    Proud Egypt would dissembled friendship bring;
    Foment the war, but not support the king:
285 Nor would the royal party e'er unite
    With Pharaoh's arms to assist the Jebusite;
    Or if they should, their interest soon would break,
    And with such odious aid make David weak.
    All sorts of men by my successful arts,
290 Abhorring kings, estrange their altered hearts
    From David's rule: and 'tis the general cry,
    'Religion, commonwealth, and liberty.'[3]
    If you, as champion of the public good,
    Add to their arms a chief of royal blood,

6. Achitophel gives to Fortune the traditional attributes of the allegorical personification of Opportunity: bald except for a forelock, she can be seized only as she approaches.
7. Brussels, where Charles spent his last years in exile. David took refuge from Saul in Gath (1 Samuel 27.4).
8. After God rejected Saul, he sent Samuel to anoint the boy David, as a token that he should

finally come to the throne (1 Samuel 16.1–13).
9. The seashore at Dover, where Charles landed (May 25, 1660).
1. Cf. the fall of Satan in *Paradise Lost* 1.50–124, which dims the brightness of the archangel. The choice of the undignified word *tumbling* is deliberate.
2. Pharaoh is Louis XIV of France.
3. Cf. line 82 and n. 5.

295 What may not Israel hope, and what applause
Might such a general gain by such a cause?
Not barren praise alone, that gaudy flower
Fair only to the sight, but solid power;
And nobler is a limited command,
300 Given by the love of all your native land,
Than a successive title,[4] long and dark,
Drawn from the moldy rolls of Noah's ark."
    What cannot praise effect in mighty minds,
When flattery soothes, and when ambition blinds!
305 Desire of power, on earth a vicious weed,
Yet, sprung from high, is of celestial seed:
In God 'tis glory; and when men aspire,
'Tis but a spark too much of heavenly fire.
The ambitious youth, too covetous of fame,
310 Too full of angels' metal[5] in his frame,
Unwarily was led from virtue's ways,
Made drunk with honor, and debauched with praise.
Half loath, and half consenting to the ill
(For loyal blood within him struggled still),
315 He thus replied: "And what pretense have I
To take up arms for public liberty?
My father governs with unquestioned right;
The faith's defender, and mankind's delight,
Good, gracious, just, observant of the laws:
320 And heaven by wonders has espoused his cause.
Whom has he wronged in all his peaceful reign?
Who sues for justice to his throne in vain?
What millions has he pardoned of his foes,
Whom just revenge did to his wrath expose?
325 Mild, easy, humble, studious of our good,
Inclined to mercy, and averse from blood;
If mildness ill with stubborn Israel suit,
His crime is God's beloved attribute.
What could he gain, his people to betray,
330 Or change his right for arbitrary sway?
Let haughty Pharaoh curse, with such a reign
His fruitful Nile, and yoke a servile train.
If David's rule Jerusalem displease,
The Dog Star[6] heats their brains to this disease.
335 Why then should I, encouraging the bad,
Turn rebel and run popularly mad?
Were he a tyrant, who, by lawless might
Oppressed the Jews, and raised the Jebusite,
Well might I mourn; but nature's holy bands
340 Would curb my spirits and restrain my hands:
The people might assert° their liberty,   *claim*
But what was right in them were crime in me.

---

4. A title to the crown based on succession.
5. An alternative spelling of *mettle* (i.e., spirit).
But a pun on *metal* is intended, as is obvious from
the pun *angel* (a purely intellectual being and a
coin). Ambition caused the revolt of the angels in
heaven.
6. Sirius, which in midsummer rises and sets
with the sun and is thus associated with the
maddening heat of the "dog days."

His favor leaves me nothing to require;
Prevents my wishes, and outruns desire.
345   What more can I expect while David lives?
All but his kingly diadem he gives:
And that"—But there he paused; then sighing, said—
"Is justly destined for a worthier head.
For when my father from his toils shall rest
350   And late augment the number of the blest,
His lawful issue shall the throne ascend,
Or the collateral line,[7] where that shall end.
His brother, though oppressed with vulgar spite,[8]
Yet dauntless, and secure of native right,
355   Of every royal virtue stands possessed;
Still dear to all the bravest and the best.
His courage foes, his friends his truth proclaim;
His loyalty the king, the world his fame.
His mercy even the offending crowd will find,
360   For sure he comes of a forgiving kind.[9]
Why should I then repine at heaven's decree,
Which gives me no pretense to royalty?
Yet O that fate, propitiously inclined,
Had raised my birth, or had debased my mind;
365   To my large soul not all her treasure lent,
And then betrayed it to a mean descent!
I find, I find my mounting spirits bold,
And David's part disdains my mother's mold.
Why am I scanted by a niggard birth?[1]
370   My soul disclaims the kindred of her earth;
And, made for empire, whispers me within,
'Desire of greatness is a godlike sin.'"
    Him staggering so when hell's dire agent found,
While fainting Virtue scarce maintained her ground,
375   He pours fresh forces in, and thus replies:
    "The eternal god, supremely good and wise,
Imparts not these prodigious gifts in vain:
What wonders are reserved to bless your reign!
Against your will, your arguments have shown,
380   Such virtue's only given to guide a throne.
Not that your father's mildness I contemn,
But manly force becomes the diadem.
'Tis true he grants the people all they crave;
And more, perhaps, than subjects ought to have:
385   For lavish grants suppose a monarch tame,
And more his goodness than his wit° proclaim.   intelligence
But when should people strive their bonds to break,
If not when kings are negligent or weak?
Let him give on till he can give no more,
390   The thrifty Sanhedrin[2] shall keep him poor;
And every shekel which he can receive,

---

7. In the event of Charles's dying without legitimate issue, the throne would constitutionally pass to his brother, James, or his descendants, the "collateral line."
8. Anger of the common people.
9. Race, in the sense of family.
1. I.e., why does my mean birth impose such limits on me?
2. The highest judicial counsel of the Jews, here, Parliament.

Shall cost a limb of his prerogative.[3]
To ply him with new plots shall be my care;
Or plunge him deep in some expensive war;
395 Which when his treasure can no more supply,
He must, with the remains of kingship, buy.
His faithful friends our jealousies and fears
Call Jebusites, and Pharaoh's pensioners;
Whom when our fury from his aid has torn,
400 He shall be naked left to public scorn.
The next successor, whom I fear and hate,
My arts have made obnoxious to the state;
Turned all his virtues to his overthrow,
And gained our elders[4] to pronounce a foe.
405 His right, for sums of necessary gold,
Shall first be pawned, and afterward be sold;
Till time shall ever-wanting David draw,
To pass your doubtful title into law:
If not, the people have a right supreme
410 To make their kings; for kings are made for them.
All empire is no more than power in trust,
Which, when resumed,° can be no longer just.   *taken back*
Succession, for the general good designed,
In its own wrong a nation cannot bind;
415 If altering that the people can relieve,
Better one suffer than a nation grieve.
The Jews well know their power: ere Saul they chose,[5]
God was their king, and God they durst depose.
Urge now your piety,[6] your filial name,
420 A father's right and fear of future fame;
The public good, that universal call,
To which even heaven submitted, answers all.
Nor let his love enchant your generous mind;
'Tis Nature's trick to propagate her kind.
425 Our fond begetters, who would never die,
Love but themselves in their posterity.
Or let his kindness by the effects be tried,
Or let him lay his vain pretense aside.
God said he loved your father; could he bring
430 A better proof than to anoint him king?
It surely showed he loved the shepherd well,
Who gave so fair a flock as Israel.
Would David have you thought his darling son?
What means he then, to alienate[7] the crown?
435 The name of godly he may blush to bear:
'Tis after God's own heart[8] to cheat his heir.
He to his brother gives supreme command;

3. The Whigs hoped to limit the special privileges of the Crown (the royal "prerogative") by
refusing to vote money to Charles. He circumvented them by living on French subsidies and
refusing to summon Parliament.
4. The chief magistrates and rulers of the Jews.
Shaftesbury had won over ("gained") country gentlemen and nobles to his hostile view of James.
5. Before Saul, the first king of Israel, came to

the throne, the Jews were governed by judges.
Similarly Oliver Cromwell as lord protector took
over the reins of government, after he had dissolved the Rump Parliament in 1653.
6. Dutifulness to a parent.
7. In law, to convey the title to property to another
person.
8. An irony (cf. line 7 and n. 2).

To you a legacy of barren land,[9]
Perhaps the old harp, on which he thrums his lays,
440   Or some dull Hebrew ballad in your praise.
Then the next heir, a prince severe and wise,
Already looks on you with jealous eyes;
Sees through the thin disguises of your arts,
And marks your progress in the people's hearts.
445   Though now his mighty soul its grief contains,
He meditates revenge who least complains;
And, like a lion, slumbering in the way,
Or sleep dissembling, while he waits his prey,
His fearless foes within his distance draws,
450   Constrains his roaring, and contracts his paws;
Till at the last, his time for fury found,
He shoots with sudden vengeance from the ground;
The prostrate vulgar° passes o'er and spares,   *common people*
But with a lordly rage his hunters tears.
455   Your case no tame expedients will afford:
Resolve on death, or conquest by the sword,
Which for no less a stake than life you draw;
And self-defense is nature's eldest law.
Leave the warm people no considering time;
460   For then rebellion may be thought a crime.
Prevail yourself of what occasion gives,
But try your title while your father lives;
And that your arms may have a fair pretense,°   *pretext*
Proclaim you take them in the king's defense;
465   Whose sacred life each minute would expose
To plots, from seeming friends, and secret foes.
And who can sound the depth of David's soul?
Perhaps his fear his kindness may control.
He fears his brother, though he loves his son,
470   For plighted vows too late to be undone.
If so, by force he wishes to be gained,
Like women's lechery, to seem constrained.°   *forced*
Doubt not; but when he most affects the frown,
Commit a pleasing rape upon the crown.
475   Secure his person to secure your cause:
They who possess the prince, possess the laws."
    He said, and this advice above the rest
With Absalom's mild nature suited best:
Unblamed of life (ambition set aside),
480   Not stained with cruelty, nor puffed with pride,
How happy had he been, if destiny
Had higher placed his birth, or not so high!
His kingly virtues might have claimed a throne,
And blest all other countries but his own.
485   But charming greatness since so few refuse,
'Tis juster to lament him than accuse.
Strong were his hopes a rival to remove,

---

9. James was given the title of generalissimo in   withdrew to Holland.
1678. In 1679 Monmouth was banished and

With blandishments to gain the public love;
To head the faction while their zeal was hot,
490 And popularly prosecute the Plot.
To further this, Achitophel unites
The malcontents of all the Israelites;
Whose differing parties he could wisely join,
For several ends, to serve the same design:
495 The best (and of the princes some were such),
Who thought the power of monarchy too much;
Mistaken men, and patriots in their hearts;
Not wicked, but seduced by impious arts.
By these the springs of property were bent,
500 And wound so high, they cracked the government.
The next for interest sought to embroil the state,
To sell their duty at a dearer rate;
And make their Jewish markets of the throne,
Pretending public good, to serve their own.
505 Others thought kings an useless heavy load,
Who cost too much, and did too little good.
These were for laying honest David by,
On principles of pure good husbandry.°   economy
With them joined all the haranguers of the throng,
510 That thought to get preferment by the tongue.
Who follow next, a double danger bring,
Not only hating David, but the king:
The Solymaean rout,[1] well-versed of old
In godly faction, and in treason bold;
515 Cowering and quaking at a conqueror's sword,
But lofty to a lawful prince restored;
Saw with disdain an ethnic[2] plot begun,
And scorned by Jebusites to be outdone.
Hot Levites[3] headed these; who, pulled before
520 From the ark, which in the Judges' days they bore,
Resumed their cant, and with a zealous cry
Pursued their old beloved theocracy:
Where Sanhedrin and priest enslaved the nation,
And justified their spoils by inspiration:
525 For who so fit for reign as Aaron's race,[4]
If once dominion they could found in grace?
These led the pack; though not of surest scent,
Yet deepest-mouthed[5] against the government.
A numerous host of dreaming saints[6] succeed,
530 Of the true old enthusiastic breed:

---

1. I.e., London rabble. Solyma was a name for
Jerusalem.
2. Gentile; here, Roman Catholic.
3. I.e., Presbyterian clergymen. The tribe of Levi,
assigned to duties in the tabernacle, carried the
Ark of the Covenant during the forty-year sojourn
in the wilderness (Numbers 4). Under the Commonwealth ("in the Judges' days") Presbyterianism
became the state religion, and its clergy, therefore,
"bore the ark." The Act of Uniformity (1662)
forced the Presbyterian clergy out of their livings:
in short, before the Popish Plot, they had been

"pulled from the ark." They are represented here
as joining the Whigs in the hope of restoring the
commonwealth, "their old beloved theocracy."
4. Priests had to be descendants of Aaron (Exodus 28.1, Numbers 18.7).
5. Loudest. The phrase is applied to hunting
dogs. "Pack" and "scent" sustain the image.
6. Term used by certain Dissenters for those
elected to salvation. The extreme fanaticism of
the "saints" and their claims to inspiration are
characterized as a form of religious madness
("enthusiastic," line 530).

'Gainst form and order they their power employ,
Nothing to build, and all things to destroy.
But far more numerous was the herd of such,
Who think too little, and who talk too much.
535 These out of mere instinct, they knew not why,
Adored their fathers' God and property;
And, by the same blind benefit of fate,
The Devil and the Jebusite did hate:
Born to be saved, even in their own despite,
540 Because they could not help believing right.
Such were the tools; but a whole Hydra more
Remains, of sprouting heads too long to score.°   count
Some of their chiefs were princes of the land:
In the first rank of these did Zimri[7] stand;
545 A man so various, that he seemed to be
Not one, but all mankind's epitome:
Stiff in opinions, always in the wrong;
Was everything by starts, and nothing long;
But, in the course of one revolving moon,
550 Was chymist,° fiddler, statesman, and buffoon: chemist
Then all for women, painting, rhyming, drinking,
Besides ten thousand freaks that died in thinking.
Blest madman, who could every hour employ,
With something new to wish, or to enjoy!
555 Railing° and praising were his usual themes;   reviling, abusing
And both (to show his judgment) in extremes:
So over-violent, or over-civil,
That every man, with him, was God or Devil.
In squandering wealth was his peculiar art:
560 Nothing went unrewarded but desert.
Beggared by fools, whom still° he found° too late,   constantly / found out
He had his jest, and they had his estate.
He laughed himself from court; then sought relief
By forming parties, but could ne'er be chief;
565 For, spite of him, the weight of business fell
On Absalom and wise Achitophel:
Thus, wicked but in will, of means bereft,
He left not faction, but of that was left.
   Titles and names 'twere tedious to rehearse
570 Of lords, below the dignity of verse.
Wits, warriors, Commonwealth's men, were the best;
Kind husbands, and mere nobles, all the rest.
And therefore, in the name of dullness, be
The well-hung Balaam and cold Caleb, free;
575 And canting Nadab let oblivion damn,

7. George Villiers, second duke of Buckingham (1628–1687), wealthy, brilliant, dissolute, and unstable. He had been an influential member of the cabal, but after 1673 had joined Shaftesbury in opposition to the court party. This is the least political of the satirical portraits in the poem. Buckingham had been the chief author of *The Rehearsal* (1671), the play that satirized heroic tragedy and ridiculed Dryden in the character of Mr. Bayes. Politics gave Dryden an opportunity to retaliate. He comments on this portrait in his "A Discourse Concerning the Original and Progress of Satire." Dryden had two biblical Zimris in mind: the Zimri destroyed for his lustfulness and blasphemy (Numbers 25) and the conspirator and regicide of 1 Kings 16.8–20 and 2 Kings 9.31.

Who made new porridge for the paschal lamb.[8]
Let friendship's holy band some names assure;
Some their own worth, and some let scorn secure.
Nor shall the rascal rabble here have place,
580   Whom kings no titles gave, and God no grace:
Not bull-faced Jonas,[9] who could statutes draw
To mean rebellion, and make treason law.
But he, though bad, is followed by a worse,
The wretch who heaven's anointed dared to curse:
585   Shimei,[1] whose youth did early promise bring
Of zeal to God and hatred to his king,
Did wisely from expensive sins refrain,
And never broke the Sabbath, but for gain;
Nor ever was he known an oath to vent,
590   Or curse, unless against the government.
Thus heaping wealth, by the most ready way
Among the Jews, which was to cheat and pray,
The city, to reward his pious hate
Against his master, chose him magistrate.
595   His hand a vare° of justice did uphold;   *staff*
His neck was loaded with a chain of gold.
During his office, treason was no crime;
The sons of Belial[2] had a glorious time;
For Shimei, though not prodigal of pelf,
600   Yet loved his wicked neighbor as himself.
When two or three were gathered to declaim ⎤
Against the monarch of Jerusalem,   ⎬
Shimei was always in the midst of them; ⎦
And if they cursed the king when he was by,
605   Would rather curse than break good company.
If any durst his factious friends accuse,
He packed a jury of dissenting Jews;
Whose fellow-feeling in the godly cause
Would free the suffering saint from human laws.
610   For laws are only made to punish those
Who serve the king, and to protect his foes.
If any leisure time he had from power
(Because 'tis sin to misemploy an hour),
His business was, by writing, to persuade
615   That kings were useless, and a clog to trade;
And, that his noble style he might refine,

---

8. The lamb slain during Passover; here, Christ. The identities of Balaam, Caleb, and Nadab have not been certainly established, although various Whig nobles have been suggested. For Balaam see Numbers 22–24; for Caleb, Numbers 13–14; and for Nadab, Leviticus 10.1–2. "Well-hung": fluent of speech or sexually potent or both. "Cold": contrasts with the second meaning of *well-hung.* "Canting": points to a Nonconformist, as does "new porridge," for Dissenters referred to the Book of Common Prayer contemptuously as "porridge," a hodgepodge, unsubstantial stuff.
9. Sir William Jones, attorney general, had been largely responsible for the passage of the first Exclusion Bill by the House of Commons. He prosecuted the accused in the Popish Plot.
1. Shimei cursed and stoned David when he fled into the wilderness during Absalom's revolt (2 Samuel 16.5–14). His name is used here for one of the two sheriffs of London: Slingsby Bethel, a Whig, former republican, and virulent enemy of Charles. He packed juries with Whigs and so secured the acquittal of enemies of the court, among them Shaftesbury himself.
2. Sons of wickedness (cf. Milton, *Paradise Lost* 1.490–505). Dryden probably intended a pun on Balliol, the Oxford college in which leading Whigs stayed during the brief and fateful meeting of Parliament at Oxford in 1681.

No Rechabite[3] more shunned the fumes of wine.
Chaste were his cellars, and his shrieval board[4]
The grossness of a city feast abhorred:
620 His cooks, with long disuse, their trade forgot;
Cool was his kitchen, though his brains were hot,
Such frugal virtue malice may accuse,
But sure 'twas necessary to the Jews:
For towns once burnt[5] such magistrates require
625 As dare not tempt God's providence by fire.
With spiritual food he fed his servants well,
But free from flesh that made the Jews rebel;
And Moses' laws he held in more account,
For forty days of fasting in the mount.[6]
630 To speak the rest, who better are forgot,
Would tire a well-breathed witness of the Plot.
Yet, Corah,[7] thou shalt from oblivion pass:
Erect thyself, thou monumental brass,
High as the serpent of thy metal made,[8]
635 While nations stand secure beneath thy shade.
What though his birth were base, yet comets rise
From earthy vapors, ere they shine in skies.
Prodigious actions may as well be done
By weaver's issue,[9] as by prince's son.
640 This arch-attestor for the public good
By that one deed ennobles all his blood.
Who ever asked the witnesses' high race
Whose oath with martyrdom did Stephen[1] grace?
Ours was a Levite, and as times went then,
645 His tribe were God Almighty's gentlemen.
Sunk were his eyes, his voice was harsh and loud,
Sure signs he neither choleric° was nor proud: prone to anger
His long chin proved his wit; his saintlike grace
A church vermilion, and a Moses' face.[2]
650 His memory, miraculously great,
Could plots, exceeding man's belief, repeat;
Which therefore cannot be accounted lies,
For human wit could never such devise.
Some future truths are mingled in his book;
655 But where the witness failed, the prophet spoke:
Some things like visionary flights appear;
The spirit caught him up, the Lord knows where,
And gave him his rabbinical degree,
Unknown to foreign university.[3]

3. An austere Jewish sect that drank no wine (Jeremiah 35.2–19).
4. Sheriff's dinner table.
5. London burned in 1666.
6. Mount Sinai, where, during a fast of forty days, Moses received the law (Exodus 34.28).
7. Or Korah, a rebellious Levite, swallowed up by the earth because of his crimes (Numbers 16). Corah is Titus Oates, the self-appointed, perjured, and "well-breathed" (long-winded) witness of the plot.
8. Moses erected a brazen serpent to heal the

Jews bitten by fiery serpents (Numbers 21.4–9). *Brass* also means impudence or shamelessness.
9. Oates's father, a clergyman, belonged to an obscure family of ribbon weavers.
1. The first Christian martyr, accused by false witnesses (Acts 6–7).
2. Moses' face shone when he came down from Mount Sinai with the tables of the law (Exodus 34.29–30). Oates's face suggests high living, not spiritual illumination.
3. Oates falsely claimed to be a doctor of divinity in the University of Salamanca.

660 His judgment yet his memory did excel;
    Which pieced his wondrous evidence so well,
    And suited to the temper of the times,
    Then groaning under Jebusitic crimes.
    Let Israel's foes suspect his heavenly call,
665 And rashly judge his writ apocryphal;[4]
    Our laws for such affronts have forfeits made:
    He takes his life, who takes away his trade.
    Were I myself in witness Corah's place,
    The wretch who did me such a dire disgrace
670 Should whet my memory, though once forgot,
    To make him an appendix of my plot.
    His zeal to heaven made him his prince despise,
    And load his person with indignities;
    But zeal peculiar privilege affords,
675 Indulging latitude to deeds and words;
    And Corah might for Agag's[5] murder call,
    In terms as coarse as Samuel used to Saul.
    What others in his evidence did join
    (The best that could be had for love or coin),
680 In Corah's own predicament will fall;
    For *witness* is a common name to all.
      Surrounded thus with friends of every sort,
    Deluded Absalom forsakes the court:
    Impatient of high hopes, urged with renown,
685 And fired with near possession of a crown.
    The admiring crowd are dazzled with surprise,
    And on his goodly person feed their eyes:
    His joy concealed, he sets himself to show,
    On each side bowing popularly[6] low;
690 His looks, his gestures, and his words he frames,
    And with familiar ease repeats their names.
    Thus formed by nature, furnished out with arts,
    He glides unfelt into their secret hearts.
    Then, with a kind compassionating look,
695 And sighs, bespeaking pity ere he spoke,
    Few words he said; but easy those and fit,
    More slow than Hybla-drops,[7] and far more sweet.
      "I mourn, my countrymen, your lost estate;
    Though far unable to prevent your fate:
700 Behold a banished man, for your dear cause
    Exposed a prey to arbitrary laws!
    Yet oh! that I alone could be undone,
    Cut off from empire, and no more a son!
    Now all your liberties a spoil are made;
705 Egypt° and Tyrus° intercept your trade,   *France / Holland*
    And Jebusites your sacred rites invade.

---

4. Not inspired and hence excluded from Holy Writ.
5. Agag is probably one of the five Catholic peers executed for the Popish Plot in 1680, most likely Lord Stafford, against whom Oates fabricated testimony. He is almost certainly not, as is usually suggested, Sir Edmund Berry Godfrey. "Agag's murder" and Samuel's coarse terms to Saul are in 1 Samuel 15.
6. "So as to please the crowd" (Johnson's *Dictionary*).
7. The famous honey of Hybla in Sicily.

My father, whom with reverence yet I name,
Charmed into ease, is careless of his fame;
And, bribed with petty sums of foreign gold,
710 Is grown in Bathsheba's[8] embraces old;
Exalts his enemies, his friends destroys;
And all his power against himself employs.
He gives, and let him give, my right away;
But why should he his own, and yours betray?
715 He only, he can make the nation bleed,
And he alone from my revenge is freed.
Take then my tears (with that he wiped his eyes),
'Tis all the aid my present power supplies:
No court-informer can these arms accuse;
720 These arms may sons against their fathers use:
And 'tis my wish, the next successor's reign
May make no other Israelite complain."
    Youth, beauty, graceful action seldom fail;
But common interest always will prevail;
725 And pity never ceases to be shown
To him who makes the people's wrongs his own.
The crowd (that still believe their kings oppress)
With lifted hands their young Messiah bless:
Who now begins his progress to ordain
730 With chariots, horsemen, and a numerous train;
From east to west his glories he displays,[9]
And, like the sun, the promised land surveys.
Fame runs before him as the morning star,
And shouts of joy salute him from afar:
735 Each house receives him as a guardian god,
And consecrates the place of his abode:
But hospitable treats did most commend
Wise Issachar,[1] his wealthy western friend.
This moving court, that caught the people's eyes,
740 And seemed but pomp, did other ends disguise:
Achitophel had formed it, with intent
To sound the depths, and fathom, where it went,
The people's hearts; distinguish friends from foes,
And try their strength, before they came to blows.
745 Yet all was colored with a smooth pretense
Of specious love, and duty to their prince.
Religion, and redress of grievances,
Two names that always cheat and always please,
Are often urged; and good King David's life
750 Endangered by a brother and a wife.[2]
Thus, in a pageant show, a plot is made,
And peace itself is war in masquerade.
O foolish Israel! never warned by ill,

8. Bathsheba is the woman with whom David committed adultery (2 Samuel 11). Here, Charles II's French mistress, Louise de Keroualle, duchess of Portsmouth.
9. In 1680 Monmouth made a progress through the west of England, seeking popular support for his cause.

1. Thomas Thynne of Longleat. He entertained Monmouth on his journey in the west. *Wise* is, of course, ironic.
2. Titus Oates had sworn that both James, duke of York, and the queen were involved in a similar plot to poison Charles II.

Still the same bait, and circumvented still!
755 Did ever men forsake their present ease,
In midst of health imagine a disease;
Take pains contingent mischiefs to foresee,
Make heirs for monarchs, and for God decree?
What shall we think! Can people give away
760 Both for themselves and sons, their native sway?
Then they are left defenseless to the sword
Of each unbounded, arbitrary lord:
And laws are vain, by which we right enjoy,
If kings unquestioned can those laws destroy.
765 Yet if the crowd be judge of fit and just,
And kings are only officers in trust,
Then this resuming covenant was declared
When kings were made, or is forever barred.
If those who gave the scepter could not tie
770 By their own deed their own posterity,
How then could Adam bind his future race?
How could his forfeit on mankind take place?
Or how could heavenly justice damn us all,
Who ne'er consented to our father's fall?
775 Then kings are slaves to those whom they command,
And tenants to their people's pleasure stand.
Add, that the power for property allowed
Is mischievously seated in the crowd;
For who can be secure of private right,
780 If sovereign sway may be dissolved by might?
Nor is the people's judgment always true:
The most may err as grossly as the few;
And faultless kings run down, by common cry,
For vice, oppression, and for tyranny.
785 What standard is there in a fickle rout,
Which, flowing to the mark,° runs faster out?   highwater mark
Nor only crowds, but Sanhedrins may be
Infected with this public lunacy,[3]
And share the madness of rebellious times,
790 To murder monarchs for imagined crimes.[4]
If they may give and take whene'er they please,
Not kings alone (the Godhead's images),
But government itself at length must fall
To nature's state, where all have right to all.
795 Yet, grant our lords the people kings can make,
What prudent men a settled throne would shake?
For whatsoe'er their sufferings were before,
That change they covet makes them suffer more.
All other errors but disturb a state,
800 But innovation is the blow of fate.
If ancient fabrics nod, and threat to fall,
To patch the flaws, and buttress up the wall,
Thus far 'tis duty; but here fix the mark;

3. The fickle crowd flows and ebbs like the tide, which is pulled back and forth by the moon (hence "lunacy," after the Latin *luna*, or "moon").
4. An allusion to the execution of Charles I.

For all beyond it is to touch our ark.[5]
805 To change foundations, cast the frame anew,
Is work for rebels, who base ends pursue,
At once divine and human laws control,
And mend the parts by ruin of the whole.
The tampering world is subject to this curse,
810 To physic their disease into a worse.
　　　Now what relief can righteous David bring?
How fatal 'tis to be too good a king!
Friends he has few, so high the madness grows:
Who dare be such, must be the people's foes:
815 Yet some there were, even in the worst of days;
Some let me name, and naming is to praise.
　　　In this short file Barzillai[6] first appears;
Barzillai, crowned with honor and with years:
Long since, the rising rebels he withstood
820 In regions waste, beyond the Jordan's flood:
Unfortunately brave to buoy the State;
But sinking underneath his master's fate:
In exile with his godlike prince he mourned;
For him he suffered, and with him returned.
825 The court he practiced, not the courtier's art:
Large was his wealth, but larger was his heart:
Which well the noblest objects knew to choose,
The fighting warrior, and recording Muse.
His bed could once a fruitful issue boast;
830 Now more than half a father's name is lost.
His eldest hope,[7] with every grace adorned,
By me (so Heaven will have it) always mourned,
And always honored, snatched in manhood's prime
By unequal fates, and Providence's crime:
835 Yet not before the goal of honor won, ⎫
All parts fulfilled of subject and of son; ⎬
Swift was the race, but short the time to run. ⎭
O narrow circle, but of power divine,
Scanted in space, but perfect in thy line!
840 By sea, by land, thy matchless worth was known,
Arms thy delight, and war was all thy own:
Thy force, infused, the fainting Tyrians° propped;　　　*the Dutch*
And haughty Pharaoh found his fortune stopped.
Oh ancient honor! Oh unconquered hand,
845 Whom foes unpunished never could withstand!
But Israel was unworthy of thy name:
Short is the date of all immoderate fame.
It looks as Heaven our ruin had designed,
And durst not trust thy fortune and thy mind.
850 Now, free from earth, thy disencumbered soul

5. Uzzah was struck dead because he sacrilegiously touched the Ark of the Covenant (2 Samuel 6.6–7).
6. James Butler, duke of Ormond (1610–1688). He was famous for his loyalty to the Stuart cause. He fought for Charles I in Ireland, and when that cause was hopeless, he joined Charles II in his exile abroad. He spent a large fortune on behalf of the king and continued to serve him loyally after the Restoration. Six of his ten children were dead (see line 830). Cf. 2 Samuel 19.31–39.
7. Ormond's son, Thomas, earl of Ossory (1634–1680), a famous soldier and, like his father, devoted to Charles II.

Mounts up, and leaves behind the clouds and starry pole:
From thence thy kindred legions mayst thou bring,
To aid the guardian angel of thy king.
Here stop my Muse, here cease thy painful flight;
855 No pinions can pursue immortal height:
Tell good Barzillai thou canst sing no more,
And tell thy soul she should have fled before:
Or fled she with his life, and left this verse
To hang on her departed patron's hearse?
860 Now take thy steepy flight from heaven, and see
If thou canst find on earth another *he*:
Another *he* would be too hard to find;
See then whom thou canst see not far behind.
Zadoc the priest, whom, shunning power and place,
865 His lowly mind advanced to David's grace:
With him the Sagan[8] of Jerusalem,
Of hospitable soul, and noble stem;
Him of the western dome, whose weighty sense
Flows in fit words and heavenly eloquence.
870 The prophets' sons,[9] by such example led,
To learning and to loyalty were bred:
For colleges on bounteous kinds depend,
And never rebel was to arts a friend.
To these succeed the pillars of the laws,
875 Who best could plead, and best can judge a cause.
Next them a train of loyal peers ascend;
Sharp-judging Adriel,[1] the Muses' friend,
Himself a Muse—in Sanhedrin's debate
True to his prince, but not a slave of state:
880 Whom David's love with honors did adorn,
That from his disobedient son were torn.
Jotham[2] of piercing wit, and pregnant thought,
Indued by nature, and by learning taught
To move assemblies, who but only tried
885 The worse a while, then chose the better side;
Nor chose alone, but turned the balance too;
So much the weight of one brave man can do.
Hushar,[3] the friend of David in distress,
In public storms, of manly steadfastness:
890 By foreign treaties he informed his youth,
And joined experience to his native truth.
His frugal care supplied the wanting throne,
Frugal for that, but bounteous of his own:
'Tis easy conduct when exchequers flow,
895 But hard the task to manage well the low;
For sovereign power is too depressed or high,
When kings are forced to sell, or crowds to buy.
Indulge one labor more, my weary Muse,

---

8. Henry Compton, bishop of London. "Zadoc":
William Sancroft, archbishop of Canterbury.
9. The boys of Westminster School, which Dryden
had attended. "Him of the western dome": John

Dolben, dean of Westminster.
1. John Sheffield, earl of Mulgrave.
2. George Savile, marquis of Halifax.
3. Laurence Hyde, earl of Rochester.

For Amiel:[4] who can Amiel's praise refuse?
900   Of ancient race by birth, but nobler yet
In his own worth, and without title great:
The Sanhedrin long time as chief he ruled,
Their reason guided, and their passion cooled:
So dexterous was he in the crown's defense,
905   So formed to speak a loyal nation's sense,
That, as their band was Israel's tribes in small,
So fit was he to represent them all.
Now rasher charioteers the seat ascend,
Whose loose careers his steady skill commend°:   *set off to advantage*
910   They like the unequal ruler of the day,
Misguide the seasons, and mistake the way;
While he withdrawn at their mad labor smiles,
And safe enjoys the sabbath of his toils.
    These were the chief, a small but faithful band ⎤
915   Of worthies, in the breach who dared to stand, ⎬
And tempt the united fury of the land. ⎦
With grief they viewed such powerful engines bent,
To batter down the lawful government:
A numerous faction, with pretended frights,
920   In Sanhedrins to plume° the regal rights;   *pluck, plunder*
The true successor from the court removed:[5]
The Plot, by hireling witnesses, improved.
These ills they saw, and, as their duty bound,
They showed the king the danger of the wound:
925   That no concessions from the throne would please,
But lenitives° fomented the disease;   *pain relievers*
That Absalom, ambitious of the crown,
Was made the lure to draw the people down;
That false Achitophel's pernicious hate
930   Had turned the Plot to ruin Church and State:
The council violent, the rabble worse;
That Shimei taught Jerusalem to curse.
    With all these loads of injuries oppressed,
And long revolving, in his careful breast,
935   The event of things, at last, his patience tired,
Thus from his royal throne, by Heaven inspired,
The godlike David spoke: with awful fear
His train their Maker in their master hear.
    "Thus long have I, by native mercy swayed,
940   My wrongs dissembled, my revenge delayed:
So willing to forgive the offending age,
So much the father did the king assuage.
But now so far my clemency they slight,
The offenders question my forgiving right.
945   That one was made for many, they contend;
But 'tis to rule; for that's a monarch's end.
They call my tenderness of blood, my fear;
Though manly tempers can the longest bear.

---

4. Edward Seymour, speaker of the House of Commons.

5. The duke of York had been banished from England.

Yet, since they will divert my native course,
950 'Tis time to show I am not good by force.
Those heaped affronts that haughty subjects bring,
Are burdens for a camel, not a king:
Kings are the public pillars of the State,
Born to sustain and prop the nation's weight:
955 If my young Samson will pretend a call
To shake the column, let him share the fall:[6]
But, oh, that yet he would repent and live!
How easy 'tis for parents to forgive!
With how few tears a pardon might be won
960 From nature, pleading for a darling son!
Poor pitied youth, by my paternal care
Raised up to all the height his frame could bear:
Had God ordained his fate for empire born,
He would have given his soul another turn:
965 Gulled° with a patriot's name, whose modern sense   *deceived*
Is one that would by law supplant his prince:
The people's brave,° the politician's tool;   *bully*
Never was patriot yet, but was a fool.
Whence comes it that religion and the laws
970 Should more be Absalom's than David's cause?
His old instructor,[7] ere he lost his place,
Was never thought indued with so much grace.
Good heavens, how faction can a patriot paint!
My rebel ever proves my people's saint:
975 Would *they* impose an heir upon the throne?
Let Sanhedrins be taught to give their own.
A king's at least a part of government,
And mine as requisite as their consent;
Without my leave a future king to choose,
980 Infers a right the present to depose:
True, they petition me to approve their choice;
But Esau's hands suit ill with Jacob's voice.[8]
My pious subjects for my safety pray,
Which to secure, they take my power away.
985 From plots and treasons Heaven preserve my years,
But save me most from my petitioners.
Unsatiate as the barren womb or grave;
God cannot grant so much as they can crave.
What then is left but with a jealous eye
990 To guard the small remains of royalty?
The law shall still direct my peaceful sway,
And the same law teach rebels to obey:
Votes shall no more established power control—
Such votes as make a part exceed the whole:
995 No groundless clamors shall my friends remove,
Nor crowds have power to punish ere they prove:
For gods and godlike kings, their care express,
Still to defend their servants in distress.

---

6. Judges 16.   8. Genesis 27.22.
7. The earl of Shaftesbury.

O that my power to saving were confined:

1000 Why am I forced, like Heaven, against my mind, ⎫
To make examples of another kind? ⎬
Must I at length the sword of justice draw? ⎭
O curst effects of necessary law!
How ill my fear they by my mercy scan°!   *judge*

1005 Beware the fury of a patient man.
Law they require, let Law then show her face;
They could not be content to look on Grace,
Her hinder parts, but with a daring eye
To tempt the terror of her front and die.[9]

1010 By their own arts, 'tis righteously decreed,
Those dire artificers of death shall bleed.
Against themselves their witnesses will swear,
Till viper-like their mother Plot they tear:
And suck for nutriment that bloody gore,

1015 Which was their principle of life before.
Their Belial with their Belzebub[1] will fight;
Thus on my foes, my foes shall do me right:
Nor doubt the event; for factious crowds engage,
In their first onset, all their brutal rage.

1020 Then let 'em take an unresisted course,
Retire and traverse,° and delude their force: *thwart*
But when they stand all breathless, urge the fight,
And rise upon 'em with redoubled might:
For lawful power is still superior found,

1025 When long driven back, at length it stands the ground."
He said. The Almighty, nodding, gave consent;
And peals of thunder shook the firmament.
Henceforth a series of new time began,
The mighty years in long procession ran:

1030 Once more the godlike David was restored,
And willing nations knew their lawful lord.

1681

Mac Flecknoe

The target of this superb satire, which is cast in the form of a mock-heroic episode, is Thomas Shadwell (1640–1692), the playwright, with whom Dryden had been on good terms for a number of years, certainly as late as March 1678. Shadwell considered himself the successor of Ben Jonson and the champion of the type of comedy that Jonson had written, the "comedy of humors," in which each character is presented under the domination of a single psychological trait or eccentricity, his humor. His plays are not without merit, but they are often clumsy and prolix and certainly much inferior to Jonson's. For many years he had conducted a public argument with Dryden on the merits of Jonson's comedies, which he thought Dryden undervalued. Exactly what moved Dryden to attack him is a matter of conjecture: he may simply have grown progressively bored and irritated by Shadwell and his tedious argument. The poem seems to have been written in late 1678 or 1679 and to have circulated only in manuscript until it was printed in 1682 in a pirated edition by an obscure publisher. By that time, the two playwrights were alienated by

---

9. Moses was not allowed to see the countenance of Jehovah (Exodus 33.20–23).

1. A god of the Philistines. "Belial": the incarnation of all evil.

politics as well as by literary quarrels. Shadwell was a violent Whig and the reputed author of a sharp attack on Dryden as the Tory author of *Absalom and Achitophel* and "The Medal." It was probably for this reason that the printer added the subtitle referring to Shadwell's Whiggism in the phrase "true-blue-Protestant poet." Political passions were running high, and sales would be helped if the poem seemed to refer to the events of the day.

Whereas Butler had debased and degraded his victims by using burlesque, caricature, and the grotesque, Dryden exposed Shadwell to ridicule by using the devices of mock epic, which treats the low, mean, or absurd in the grand language, lofty style, and solemn tone of epic poetry. The obvious disparity between subject and style makes the satiric point. In 1678, a prolific, untalented writer, Richard Flecknoe, died. Dryden conceived the idea of presenting Shadwell (the self-proclaimed heir of Ben Jonson, the laureate) as the son and successor of Flecknoe (an irony also because Flecknoe was a Catholic priest)—hence *Mac* (son of) *Flecknoe*—from whom he inherits the throne of dullness. Flecknoe in the triple role of king, priest, and poet hails his successor, pronounces a panegyric on his perfect fitness for the throne, anoints and crowns him, foretells his glorious reign, and as he sinks (leaden dullness cannot soar), leaves his mantle to fall symbolically on Shadwell's shoulders. The poem abounds in literary allusions—to Roman legend and history and to the *Aeneid*, to Cowley's fragmentary epic *The Davideis*, to *Paradise Lost*, and to Shadwell's own plays. Biblical allusions add an unexpected dimension of incongruous dignity to the low scene. The coronation takes place in the City, to the plaudits of the citizens, who are fit to admire only what is dull. In 217 lines, Dryden created an image of Shadwell that has fixed his reputation to this day.

Mac Flecknoe

Or a Satire upon the True-Blue-Protestant Poet, T. S.

All human things are subject to decay,
And when fate summons, monarchs must obey.
This Flecknoe found, who, like Augustus,[1] young
Was called to empire, and had governed long;
5   In prose and verse, was owned, without dispute,
Through all the realms of Nonsense, absolute.
This aged prince, now flourishing in peace,
And blest with issue of a large increase,
Worn out with business, did at length debate
10   To settle the succession of the state;
And, pondering which of all his sons was fit
To reign, and wage immortal war with wit,
Cried: "'Tis resolved; for nature pleads that he
Should only rule, who most resembles me.
15   Sh——[2] alone my perfect image bears,
Mature in dullness from his tender years:
Sh———alone, of all my sons, is he
Who stands confirmed in full stupidity.
The rest to some faint meaning make pretense,

1. In 31 B.C.E. Octavian became the first Roman emperor, at the age of thirty-two. He assumed the title Augustus in 27 B.C.E.
2. Thomas Shadwell. The initial and second letter of the name followed by a dash give the appearance, but only the appearance, of protecting Dryden's victim by concealing his name. A common device in the satire of the period.

20   But Sh—— never deviates into sense.
     Some beams of wit on other souls may fall,
     Strike through, and make a lucid interval;
     But Sh——'s genuine night admits no ray,
     His rising fogs prevail upon the day.
25   Besides, his goodly fabric[3] fills the eye,
     And seems designed for thoughtless majesty:
     Thoughtless as monarch oaks that shade the plain,
     And, spread in solemn state, supinely reign.
     Heywood and Shirley were but types of thee,[4]
30   Thou last great prophet of tautology.[5]
     Even I, a dunce of more renown than they,
     Was sent before but to prepare thy way;
     And, coarsely clad in Norwich drugget,° came   *coarse woolen cloth*
     To teach the nations in thy greater name.[6]
35   My warbling lute, the lute I whilom° strung,   *formerly*
     When to King John of Portugal[7] I sung,
     Was but the prelude to that glorious day,
     When thou on silver Thames didst cut thy way,
     With well-timed oars before the royal barge,
40   Swelled with the pride of thy celestial charge;
     And big with hymn, commander of a host,
     The like was ne'er in Epsom blankets tossed.[8]
     Methinks I see the new Arion[9] sail,
     The lute still trembling underneath thy nail.
45   At thy well-sharpened thumb from shore to shore
     The treble squeaks for fear, the basses roar;
     Echoes from Pissing Alley Sh—— call,
     And Sh—— they resound from Aston Hall.
     About thy boat the little fishes throng,
50   As at the morning toast° that floats along.   *sewage*
     Sometimes, as prince of thy harmonious band,
     Thou wield'st thy papers in thy threshing hand,
     St. André's[1] feet ne'er kept more equal time,
     Not ev'n the feet of thy own *Psyche's* rhyme;
55   Though they in number as in sense excel:
     So just, so like tautology, they fell,
     That, pale with envy, Singleton[2] forswore
     The lute and sword, which he in triumph bore, ⎤
     And vowed he ne'er would act Villerius[3] more." ⎦

3. His body. Shadwell was a corpulent man.
4. Thomas Heywood (ca. 1570–1641) and James Shirley (1596–1666), playwrights popular before the closing of the theaters in 1642 but now out of fashion. They are introduced here as "types" (i.e., prefigurings) of Shadwell, in the sense that Solomon was regarded as an Old Testament prefiguring of Christ, the "last [final] great prophet."
5. Unnecessary repetition of meaning in different words.
6. The parallel between Flecknoe, as forerunner of Shadwell, and John the Baptist, as forerunner of Jesus, is made plain in lines 32–34 by the use of details and even words taken from Matthew 3.3–4 and John 1.23.
7. Flecknoe boasted of the patronage of the Por-
tuguese king.
8. A reference to Shadwell's comedy *Epsom Wells* and to the farcical scene in his *Virtuoso*, in which Sir Samuel Hearty is tossed in a blanket.
9. A legendary Greek poet. Returning home by sea, he was robbed and thrown overboard by the sailors, but was saved by a dolphin that had been charmed by his music.
1. A French dancer who designed the choreography of Shadwell's opera *Psyche* (1675). Dryden's sneer at the mechanical metrics of the songs in *Psyche* is justified.
2. John Singleton (d. 1686), a musician at the Theatre Royal.
3. A character in Sir William Davenant's *Siege of Rhodes* (1656), the first English opera.

60   Here stopped the good old sire, and wept for joy
     In silent raptures of the hopeful boy.
     All arguments, but most his plays, persuade,
     That for anointed dullness[4] he was made.
        Close to the walls which fair Augusta° bind   *London*
65   (The fair Augusta much to fears inclined),[5]
     An ancient fabric,° raised to inform the sight,   *building*
     There stood of yore, and Barbican it hight:°   *was called*
     A watchtower once; but now, so fate ordains,
     Of all the pile an empty name remains.
70   From its old ruins brothel houses rise,
     Scenes of lewd loves, and of polluted joys,
     Where their vast courts the mother-strumpets keep,
     And, undisturbed by watch, in silence sleep.
     Near these a Nursery[6] erects its head,
75   Where queens are formed, and future heroes bred;
     Where unfledged actors learn to laugh and cry, ⎫
     Where infant punks° their tender voices try, ⎬   *prostitutes*
     And little Maximins[7] the gods defy. ⎭
     Great Fletcher never treads in buskins here,
80   Nor greater Jonson dares in socks[8] appear;
     But gentle Simkin[9] just reception finds
     Amidst this monument of vanished minds:
     Pure clinches° the suburbian Muse affords,   *puns*
     And Panton[1] waging harmless war with words.
85   Here Flecknoe, as a place to fame well known,
     Ambitiously design'd his Sh——'s throne;
     For ancient Dekker[2] prophesied long since, ⎫
     That in this pile would reign a mighty prince, ⎬
     Born for a scourge of wit, and flail of sense; ⎭
90   To whom true dullness should some *Psyches* owe,
     But worlds of *Misers* from his pen should flow;
     Humorists and *Hypocrites*[3] it should produce,
     Whole Raymond families, and tribes of Bruce.
        Now Empress Fame had published the renown
95   Of Sh——'s coronation through the town.
     Roused by report of Fame, the nations meet,
     From near Bunhill, and distant Watling Street.[4]
     No Persian carpets spread the imperial way,
     But scattered limbs of mangled poets lay;
100 From dusty shops neglected authors come,

---

4. The anticipated phrase is "anointed *majesty*." English kings are anointed with oil at their coronations.

5. This line alludes to the fears excited by the Popish Plot (cf. *Absalom and Achitophel*, p. 963).

6. The name of a training school for young actors.

7. Maximin is the cruel emperor, in Dryden's *Tyrannic Love* (1669), notorious for his bombast.

8. "Buskins" and "socks" were the symbols of tragedy and comedy, respectively. John Fletcher (1579–1625), the playwright and collaborator with Francis Beaumont (ca. 1584–1616).

9. A popular character in low farces.

1. Said to have been a celebrated punster.

2. Thomas Dekker (ca. 1572–1632), the playwright, whom Jonson had satirized in *The Poetaster*.

3. Three of Shadwell's plays; *The Hypocrite*, a failure, was not published. "Raymond" and "Bruce" (line 93) are characters in *The Humorists* and *The Virtuoso*, respectively.

4. Because Bunhill is about a quarter mile and Watling Street little more than a half mile from the site of the Nursery, where the coronation is held, Shadwell's fame is narrowly circumscribed. Moreover, his subjects live in the heart of the City, regarded by men of wit and fashion as the abode of bad taste and middle-class vulgarity.

Martyrs of pies, and relics of the bum.[5]
Much Heywood, Shirley, Ogilby[6] there lay,
But loads of Sh—— almost choked the way.
Bilked stationers for yeomen stood prepared,
105 And Herringman was captain of the guard.[7]
The hoary prince in majesty appeared,
High on a throne of his own labors reared.
At his right hand our young Ascanius sate,
Rome's other hope, and pillar of the state.
110 His brows thick fogs, instead of glories, grace,
And lambent dullness played around his face.[8]
As Hannibal did to the altars come,
Sworn by his sire a mortal foe to Rome,[9]
So Sh—— swore, nor should his vow be vain,
115 That he till death true dullness would maintain;
And, in his father's right, and realm's defense,
Ne'er to have peace with wit, nor truce with sense.
The king himself the sacred unction[1] made,
As king by office, and as priest by trade.
120 In his siníster° hand, instead of ball,   left
He placed a mighty mug of potent ale;
Love's Kingdom to his right he did convey,
At once his scepter, and his rule of sway;
Whose righteous lore the prince had practiced young,
125 And from whose loins recorded *Psyche* sprung.
His temples, last, with poppies were o'erspread,
That nodding seemed to consecrate his head.[2]
Just at that point of time, if fame not lie,
On his left hand twelve reverend owls did fly.[3]
130 So Romulus, 'tis sung, by Tiber's brook,
Presage of sway from twice six vultures took.
The admiring throng loud acclamations make,
And omens of his future empire take.
The sire then shook the honors[4] of his head,
135 And from his brows damps of oblivion shed
Full on the filial dullness: long he stood, ⎫
Repelling from his breast the raging god; ⎬
At length burst out in this prophetic mood: ⎭
    "Heavens bless my son, from Ireland let him reign
140 To far Barbadoes on the western main;[5]

---

5. Unsold books were used to line pie plates and as toilet paper.
6. John Ogilby, a translator of Homer and Virgil, ridiculed by both Dryden and Pope as a bad poet.
7. "Bilked stationers": cheated publishers, acting as "yeomen" of the guard, led by Henry Herringman, who until 1679 was the publisher of both Shadwell and Dryden.
8. Ascanius, or Iulus, was the son of Aeneas. Virgil referred to him as *"spes altera Romae"* ("Rome's other hope," *Aeneid* 12.168). As Troy fell, he was marked as favored by the gods when a flickering ("lambent") flame played round his head (*Aeneid* 2.680–84).
9. Hannibal, who almost conquered Rome in 216 B.C.E., during the second Punic War, took this oath at the age of nine (Livy 21.1).

1. The sacramental oil, used in the coronation.
2. During the coronation a British monarch holds two symbols of the throne: a globe ("ball") representing the world in the left hand and a scepter in the right. Shadwell's symbols of monarchy are a mug of ale; Flecknoe's dreary play *Love's Kingdom*; and a crown of poppies, which suggest heaviness, dullness, and drowsiness. The poppies also refer obliquely to Shadwell's addiction to opium.
3. Birds of night. Appropriate substitutes for the twelve vultures whose flight confirmed to Romulus the destined site of Rome, of which he was founder and king.
4. Ornaments, hence locks.
5. Shadwell's empire is vast but empty.

Of his dominion may no end be known,
And greater than his father's be his throne;
Beyond *Love's Kingdom* let him stretch his pen!"
He paused, and all the people cried, "Amen."
145 Then thus continued he: "My son, advance
Still in new impudence, new ignorance.
Success let others teach, learn thou from me
Pangs without birth, and fruitless industry.
Let *Virtuosos* in five years be writ;
150 Yet not one thought accuse thy toil of wit.
Let gentle George[6] in triumph tread the stage,
Make Dorimant betray, and Loveit rage;
Let Cully, Cockwood, Fopling, charm the pit,
And in their folly show the writer's wit.
155 Yet still thy fools shall stand in thy defense,
And justify their author's want of sense.
Let 'em be all by thy own model made
Of dullness, and desire no foreign aid;
That they to future ages may be known,
160 Not copies drawn, but issue of thy own.
Nay, let thy men of wit too be the same,
All full of thee, and differing but in name.
But let no alien S—dl—y[7] interpose,
To lard with wit[8] thy hungry *Epsom* prose.
165 And when false flowers of rhetoric thou wouldst cull,
Trust nature, do not labor to be dull;
But write thy best, and top; and, in each line,
Sir Formal's[9] oratory will be thine:
Sir Formal, though unsought, attends thy quill,
170 And does thy northern dedications[1] fill.
Nor let false friends seduce thy mind to fame,
By arrogating Jonson's hostile name.
Let father Flecknoe fire thy mind with praise,
And uncle Ogilby thy envy raise.
175 Thou art my blood, where Jonson has no part:
What share have we in nature, or in art?
Where did his wit on learning fix a brand,
And rail at arts he did not understand?
Where made he love in Prince Nicander's vein,[2]
180 Or swept the dust in *Psyche's* humble strain?
Where sold he bargains, 'whip-stitch,[3] kiss my arse,'
Promised a play and dwindled to a farce?[4]
When did his Muse from Fletcher scenes purloin,
As thou whole Eth'rege dost transfuse to thine?

6. Sir George Etherege (ca. 1635–1691), a writer of brilliant comedies. In the next couplet Dryden names characters from his plays.
7. Sir Charles Sedley (1638–1701), wit, rake, poet, and playwright. Dryden hints that he contributed more than the prologue to Shadwell's *Epsom Wells*.
8. This phrase recalls a sentence in Burton's *Anatomy of Melancholy:* "They lard their lean books with the fat of others' works."
9. Sir Formal Trifle, the ridiculous and vapid

orator in *The Virtuoso.*
1. Shadwell frequently dedicated his works to the duke of Newcastle and members of his family.
2. In *Psyche.*
3. A nonsense word frequently used by Sir Samuel Hearty in *The Virtuoso.* "Sell bargains": to answer an innocent question with a coarse or indecent phrase, as in this line.
4. Low comedy that depends largely on situation rather than wit, consistently condemned by Dryden and other serious playwrights.

185　But so transfused, as oil on water's flow,
　　His always floats above, thine sinks below.
　　This is thy province, this thy wondrous way,
　　New humors to invent for each new play:
　　This is that boasted bias⁵ of thy mind,
190　By which one way, to dullness, 'tis inclined;
　　Which makes thy writings lean on one side still,
　　And, in all changes, that way bends thy will.
　　Nor let thy mountain-belly make pretense
　　Of likeness; thine's a tympany⁶ of sense.
195　A tun° of man in thy large bulk is writ,　　　　　　　*large cask*
　　But sure thou'rt but a kilderkin° of wit.　　　　　　*small cask*
　　Like mine, thy gentle numbers feebly creep;
　　Thy tragic Muse gives smiles, thy comic sleep.
　　With whate'er gall thou sett'st thyself to write,
200　Thy inoffensive satires never bite.
　　In thy felonious heart though venom lies,
　　It does but touch thy Irish pen,⁷ and dies.
　　Thy genius calls thee not to purchase fame
　　In keen iambics,° but mild anagram.　　　　　　　　*sharp satire*
205　Leave writing plays, and choose for thy command
　　Some peaceful province in acrostic land.
　　There thou may'st wings display and altars raise,⁸
　　And torture one poor word ten thousand ways.
　　Or, if thou wouldst thy different talent suit,
210　Set thy own songs, and sing them to thy lute."
　　　He said: but his last words were scarcely heard ⎤
　　For Bruce and Longville had a trap prepared,　　⎬
　　And down they sent the yet declaiming bard.⁹　　⎦
　　Sinking he left his drugget robe behind,
215　Borne upwards by a subterranean wind.
　　The mantle fell to the young prophet's part,¹
　　With double portion of his father's art.

ca. 1679　　　　　　　　　　　　　　　　　　　　　　1682

To the Memory of Mr. Oldham¹

Farewell, too little, and too lately known,
Whom I began to think and call my own:
For sure our souls were near allied, and thine

---

5. In bowling, the spin given to the bowl that causes it to swerve. Dryden closely parodies a passage in Shadwell's epilogue to *The Humorists*.
6. A swelling in some part of the body caused by wind.
7. Dryden accuses Flecknoe and his "son" of being Irish. Ireland suggested only poverty, superstition, and barbarity to 17th-century Londoners.
8. "Wings" and "altars" refer to poems in the shape of these objects as in George Herbert's "Easter Wings" (p. 733) and "The Altar" (p. 732). "Anagram": the transposition of letters in a word so as to make a new one. "Acrostic": a poem in which the first letter of each line, read downward, makes up the name of the person or thing that is the subject

of the poem. Dryden is citing instances of triviality and overingenuity in literature.
9. In *The Virtuoso*, Bruce and Longville play this trick on Sir Formal Trifle while he makes a speech.
1. When the prophet Elijah was carried to heaven in a chariot of fire borne on a whirlwind, his mantle fell on his successor, the younger prophet Elisha (2 Kings 2.8–14). Flecknoe, prophet of dullness, naturally cannot ascend, but must sink.
1. John Oldham (1653–1683), the young poet whose *Satires upon the Jesuits* (1681), which Dryden admired, were written in 1679, before Dryden's major satires appeared (see line 8). This elegy was published in Oldham's *Remains in Verse and Prose* (1684).

Cast in the same poetic mold with mine.
5   One common note on either lyre did strike,
And knaves and fools[2] we both abhorred alike.
To the same goal did both our studies drive;
The last set out the soonest did arrive.
Thus Nisus fell upon the slippery place,
10 While his young friend[3] performed and won the race.
O early ripe! to thy abundant store
What could advancing age have added more?
It might (what nature never gives the young)
Have taught the numbers° of thy native tongue.   metrics, verse
15 But satire needs not those, and wit will shine
Through the harsh cadence of a rugged line.[4]
A noble error, and but seldom made,
When poets are by too much force betrayed.
Thy generous fruits, though gathered ere their prime,
20 Still showed a quickness;[5] and maturing time
But mellows what we write to the dull sweets of rhyme.
Once more, hail and farewell;[6] farewell, thou young,
But ah too short, Marcellus[7] of our tongue;
Thy brows with ivy, and with laurels bound;[8]
25 But fate and gloomy night encompass thee around.

1684

A Song for St. Cecilia's Day[1]

1

From harmony, from heavenly harmony
    This universal frame began:
When Nature underneath a heap
    Of jarring atoms lay,
5   And could not heave her head,
The tuneful voice was heard from high:
    "Arise, ye more than dead."

2. Objects of satire.
3. Nisus, on the point of winning a footrace, slipped in a pool of blood. His "young friend" was Euryalus (Virgil's *Aeneid* 5.315–39).
4. Dryden repeats the Renaissance idea that the satirist should avoid smoothness and affect rough meters ("harsh cadence").
5. Sharpness of flavor.
6. Dryden echoes the famous words that conclude Catullus's elegy to his brother: *"Atque in perpetuum, frater, ave atque vale"* (And forever, brother, hail and farewell!).
7. The nephew of Augustus, adopted by him as his successor. After winning military fame as a youth, he died at the age of twenty. Virgil celebrated him in the *Aeneid* 6.854–86. The last line of Dryden's poem is a reminiscence of *Aeneid* 6.866.
8. The poet's wreath (cf. Milton's *Lycidas*, lines 1–2, p. 781).
1. St. Cecilia, a Roman lady, was an early Chris-

tian martyr. She has long been regarded as the patroness of music and the supposed inventor of the organ. Celebrations of her festival day (November 22) in England were usually devoted to music and the praise of music, and from about 1683 to 1703 the Musical Society in London annually commemorated it with a religious service and a public concert. This concert always included an ode written and set to music for the occasion, of which the two by Dryden ("A Song for St. Cecilia's Day," 1687, and "Alexander's Feast," 1697) are the most distinguished. G. B. Draghi, an Italian brought to England by Charles II, set this ode to music; but Handel's fine score, composed in 1739, has completely obscured the original setting. This is an irregular ode in the manner of Cowley. In stanzas 3–6, Dryden boldly attempted to suggest in the sounds of his words the characteristic tones of the instruments mentioned.

Then cold, and hot, and moist, and dry,[2]
In order to their stations leap,
10   And Music's power obey.
From harmony, from heavenly harmony
        This universal frame began:
        From harmony to harmony
Through all the compass of the notes it ran,
15 The diapason[3] closing full in man.

2

What passion cannot Music raise and quell![4]
        When Jubal struck the corded shell,[5]
        His listening brethren stood around,
        And, wondering, on their faces fell
20   To worship that celestial sound.
Less than a god they thought there could not dwell
        Within the hollow of that shell
        That spoke so sweetly and so well.
What passion cannot Music raise and quell!

3

25   The trumpet's loud clangor
            Excites us to arms,
        With shrill notes of anger,
            And mortal alarms.
        The double double double beat
30   Of the thundering drum
Cries: "Hark! the foes come;
Charge, charge, 'tis too late to retreat."

4

        The soft complaining flute
        In dying notes discovers
35   The woes of hopeless lovers,
Whose dirge is whispered by the warbling lute.

5

        Sharp violins[6] proclaim
        Their jealous pangs, and desperation,

2. "Nature": created nature, ordered by the Divine
Wisdom out of chaos, which Dryden, adopting
the physics of the Greek philosopher Epicurus,
describes as composed of the warring and dis-
cordant ("jarring") atoms of the four elements:
earth, fire, water, and air ("cold," "hot," "moist,"
and "dry").
3. The entire compass of tones in the scale.
Dryden is thinking of the Chain of Being, the
ordered creation from inanimate nature up to
humans, God's latest and final work. The just gradations of notes in a scale are analogous to the
equally just gradations in the ascending scale of
created beings. Both are the result of harmony.

4. The power of music to describe, evoke, or
subdue emotion ("passion") is a frequent theme
in 17th-century literature. In stanzas 2–6, the
poet considers music as awakening religious awe,
warlike courage, sorrow for unrequited love, jealousy and fury, and the impulse to worship God.
5. According to Genesis 4.21, Jubal was the
inventor of the lyre and the pipe. Dryden imagines Jubal's lyre to have been made of a tortoiseshell ("corded shell").
6. A reference to the bright tone of the modern
violin, introduced into England at the Restoration.
The tone of the old-fashioned viol is much duller.

Fury, frantic indignation,
40 Depth of pains, and height of passion,
    For the fair, disdainful dame.

6

    But O! what art can teach,
    What human voice can reach,
      The sacred organ's praise?
45   Notes inspiring holy love,
    Notes that wing their heavenly ways
      To mend the choirs above.

7

Orpheus[7] could lead the savage race;
And trees unrooted left their place,
50   Sequacious of° the lyre;   *following*
But bright Cecilia raised the wonder higher:
When to her organ vocal breath was given,
An angel heard, and straight appeared,[8]
    Mistaking earth for heaven.

GRAND CHORUS

55   *As from the power of sacred lays*
     The spheres began to move,
   And sung the great Creator's praise[9]
     To all the blest above;
   So, when the last and dreadful hour
60   *This crumbling pageant*[1] *shall devour,*
   The trumpet shall be heard on high,
   The dead shall live, the living die,
   And Music shall untune the sky.[2]

1687

7. Legendary poet, son of one of the Muses, who played so wonderfully on the lyre that wild beasts ("the savage race") grew tame and followed him, as did even rocks and trees.
8. According to the legend, it was Cecilia's piety, not her music, that brought an angel to visit her.
9. As it was harmony that ordered the universe, so it was angelic song ("sacred lays") that put the celestial bodies ("spheres") in motion. The harmonious chord that results from the traditional "music of the spheres" is a hymn of "praise" sung by created nature to its "Creator."
1. The universe, the stage on which the drama of human salvation has been acted out.
2. The "last trump" of 1 Corinthians 15.52, which will announce the Resurrection and the Last Judgment.

CRITICISM

Dryden's impulse to write criticism came from his practical urge to explain and justify his own writings; his attraction to clear, ordered theoretical principles; and his growing sense of himself as a leader of English literary taste and judgment. The Elizabethans, largely impelled by the example of Italian humanists, had produced an interesting but unsystematic body of critical writings. Dryden could look back to such pioneer works as George Puttenham's *Art of English Poesy* (1589), Sir Philip Sidney's *Defense of Poesy* (1595), Samuel Daniel's *Defense of Rhyme* (ca. 1603), and Ben Jonson's *Timber, or Discoveries* (1641). These and later writings Dryden knew, as he knew the ancients and the important contemporary French critics, notably Pierre Corneille, René Rapin, and Nicolas Boileau. Taken as a whole, his critical prefaces and dedications, which appeared between 1664 and 1700, are the work of a man of independent mind who has made his own synthesis of critical canons from wide reading, a great deal of thinking, and the constant practice of the art of writing. As a critic he is no one's disciple, and he has the saving grace of being always willing to change his mind.

All but a very few of Dryden's critical works (most notably *An Essay of Dramatic Poesy*) grew out of the works to which they served as prefaces: comedies, heroic plays, tragedies, translations, and poems of various sorts. Each work posed problems that Dryden was eager to discuss with his readers, and the topics that he treated proved to be important in the development of the new literature of which he was the principal apologist. He dealt with the processes of literary creation, the poet's relation to tradition, the forms of modern drama, the craft of poetry, and above all the genius of earlier poets: Shakespeare, Jonson, Chaucer, Juvenal, Horace, Homer, and Virgil. For nearly forty years this voice was heard in the land; and when it was finally silenced, a set of critical standards had come into existence and a new age had been given its direction.

From An Essay of Dramatic Poesy[1]

[SHAKESPEARE AND BEN JONSON COMPARED][2]

"To begin, then, with Shakespeare. He was the man who of all modern, and perhaps ancient poets, had the largest and most comprehensive soul. All the images of Nature were still present to him, and he drew them, not laboriously, but luckily; when he describes anything, you more than see it, you feel it too. Those who accuse him to have wanted learning, give him the greater commendation: he was naturally learned; he needed not the spectacles of books to read Nature; he looked inwards, and found her there. I cannot say he is everywhere alike; were he so, I should do him injury to compare him with the greatest of mankind. He is many times flat, insipid; his comic wit degenerating into clenches, his serious swelling into bombast. But he is always great when some great occasion is presented to him; no man can say he ever had a fit subject for his wit and did not then raise himself as high above the rest of poets,

1. With the reopening of the theaters in 1660, older plays were revived, but despite their power and charm, they seemed old-fashioned. Although new playwrights, ambitious to create a modern English drama, soon appeared, they were uncertain of their direction. What, if anything, useful could they learn from the dramatic practice of the ancients? Should they ignore the English dramatists of the late 16th and early 17th centuries? Should they make their example the vigorous contemporary drama of France? Dryden addresses himself to these and other problems in this essay, his first extended piece of criticism. Its purpose, he tells us, was "chiefly to vindicate the honor of our English writers from the censure of those who unjustly prefer the French before them." Its method is skeptical: Dryden presents several points of view, but imposes none. The form is a dialogue among friends, like the *Tuscu-*

lan Disputations or the *Brutus* of Cicero. Crites praises the drama of the ancients; Eugenius protests against their authority and argues for the idea of progress in the arts; Lisideius urges the excellence of French plays; and Neander, speaking in the climactic position, defends the native tradition and the greatness of Shakespeare, Fletcher, and Jonson. The dialogue takes place on June 3, 1665, in a boat on the Thames. The four friends are rowed downstream to listen to the cannonading of the English and Dutch fleets, engaged in battle off the Suffolk coast. As the gunfire recedes they are assured of victory and order their boatman to return to London, and naturally enough they fall to discussing the number of bad poems that the victory will evoke.

2. Neander's contrast of Shakespeare and Jonson introduces an extended commentary on the latter's play *Epicoene; or the Silent Woman*.

Quantum lenta solent inter viburna cupressi[3]

The consideration of this made Mr. Hales[4] of Eton say that there was no subject of which any poet ever writ, but he would produce it much better treated of in Shakespeare; and however others are now generally preferred before him, yet the age wherein he lived, which had contemporaries with him Fletcher and Jonson, never equaled them to him in their esteem: and in the last king's court, when Ben's reputation was at highest, Sir John Suckling,[5] and with him the greater part of the courtiers, set our Shakespeare far above him. . . .

"As for Jonson, to whose character I am now arrived, if we look upon him while he was himself (for his last plays were but his dotages), I think him the most learned and judicious writer which any theater ever had. He was a most severe judge of himself, as well as others. One cannot say he wanted wit, but rather that he was frugal of it. In his works you find little to retrench[6] or alter. Wit, and language, and humor also in some measure, we had before him; but something of art[7] was wanting to the drama till he came. He managed his strength to more advantage than any who preceded him. You seldom find him making love in any of his scenes or endeavoring to move the passions; his genius was too sullen and saturnine[8] to do it gracefully, especially when he knew he came after those who had performed both to such an height. Humor was his proper sphere: and in that he delighted most to represent mechanic people.[9] He was deeply conversant in the ancients, both Greek and Latin, and he borrowed boldly from them: there is scarce a poet or historian among the Roman authors of those times whom he has not translated in *Sejanus* and *Catiline*.[1] But he has done his robberies so openly, that one may see he fears not to be taxed by any law. He invades authors like a monarch; and what would be theft in other poets is only victory in him. With the spoils of these writers he so represents old Rome to us, in its rites, ceremonies, and customs, that if one of their poets had written either of his tragedies, we had seen less of it than in him. If there was any fault in his language, 'twas that he weaved it too closely and laboriously, in his serious plays:[2] perhaps, too, he did a little too much Romanize our tongue, leaving the words which he translated almost as much Latin as he found them: wherein, though he learnedly followed the idiom of their language, he did not enough comply with the idiom of ours. If I would compare him with Shakespeare, I must acknowledge him the more correct poet, but Shakespeare the greater wit.[3] Shakespeare was the Homer, or father of our dramatic poets; Jonson was the Virgil, the pattern of elaborate writing; I admire him, but I love Shakespeare. To conclude of him; as he has given us the most correct plays, so in the precepts which he has laid down in his *Discoveries,* we have as many and profitable rules for perfecting the stage, as any wherewith the French can furnish us."

1668

---

3. As do cypresses among the bending shrubs (Latin; Virgil's *Eclogues* 1.25).
4. The learned John Hales (1584–1656), provost of Eton. He is reputed to have said this to Jonson himself.
5. Courtier, poet, playwright, much admired in Dryden's time for his wit and the easy naturalness of his style. "King's court": that of Charles I.
6. Delete.
7. Craftsmanship.
8. Heavy.

9. I.e., artisans. In Jonson's comedies the characters are seen under the domination of some psychological trait, ruling passion, or affectation—i.e., some "humor"—that makes them unique and ridiculous.
1. Jonson's two Roman plays, dated 1605 and 1611, respectively.
2. This is the reading of the first edition. Curiously enough, in the second edition Dryden altered the phrase to "in his comedies especially."
3. Genius.

From A Discourse Concerning the Original and Progress of Satire[1]

[THE ART OF SATIRE]

* * * How easy is it to call rogue and villain, and that wittily! But how hard to make a man appear a fool, a blockhead, or a knave without using any of those opprobrious terms! To spare the grossness of the names, and to do the thing yet more severely, is to draw a full face, and to make the nose and cheeks stand out, and yet not to employ any depth of shadowing.[2] This is the mystery of that noble trade, which yet no master can teach to his apprentice; he may give the rules, but the scholar is never the nearer in his practice. Neither is it true that this fineness of raillery[3] is offensive. A witty man is tickled while he is hurt in this manner, and a fool feels it not. The occasion of an offense may possibly be given, but he cannot take it. If it be granted that in effect this way does more mischief; that a man is secretly wounded, and though he be not sensible himself, yet the malicious world will find it out for him; yet there is still a vast difference betwixt the slovenly butchering of a man, and the fineness of a stroke that separates the head from the body, and leaves it standing in its place. A man may be capable, as Jack Ketch's[4] wife said of his servant, of a plain piece of work, a bare hanging; but to make a malefactor die sweetly was only belonging to her husband. I wish I could apply it to myself, if the reader would be kind enough to think it belongs to me. The character of Zimri in my *Absalom*[5] is, in my opinion, worth the whole poem: it is not bloody, but it is ridiculous enough; and he, for whom it was intended, was too witty to resent it as an injury. If I had railed,[6] I might have suffered for it justly; but I managed my own work more happily, perhaps more dexterously. I avoided the mention of great crimes, and applied myself to the representing of blindsides, and little extravagancies; to which, the wittier a man is, he is generally the more obnoxious.[7] It succeeded as I wished; the jest went round, and he was laughed at in his turn who began the frolic. * * *

1693

---

1. This passage is an excerpt from the long and rambling preface that served as the dedication of a translation of the satires of the Roman satirists Juvenal and Persius to Charles Sackville, sixth earl of Dorset. The translations were made by Dryden and other writers, among them William Congreve. Dryden traces the origin and development of verse satire in Rome and in a very fine passage contrasts Horace and Juvenal as satiric poets. It is plain that he prefers the "tragic" satire of Juvenal to the urbane and laughing satire of Horace. But in the passage printed here, he praises his own satiric character of Zimri (the duke of Buckingham) in *Absalom and Achitophel*

for the very reason that it is modeled on Horatian "raillery," not Juvenalian invective.
2. Early English miniaturists prided themselves on the art of giving roundness to the full face without painting in shadows.
3. Satirical mirth, good-natured satire.
4. A notorious public executioner of Dryden's time (d. 1686). His name later became a generic term for all members of his profession.
5. *Absalom and Achitophel,* lines 544–68 (p. 976).
6. Reviled, abused. Observe that the verb differed in meaning from its noun, defined above.
7. Liable.

JOHN WILMOT, SECOND
EARL OF ROCHESTER
1647–1680

John Wilmot, second earl of Rochester, was the precocious son of one of Charles II's most loyal followers in exile. He won the king's favor at the Restoration and, in 1664, after education at Oxford and on the Continent, took a place at court, at the age of seventeen. There he soon distinguished himself as "the man who has the most wit and the least honor in England." For one escapade, the abduction of Elizabeth Malet, an heiress, he was imprisoned in the Tower of London. But he regained his position by courageous service in the naval war against the Dutch, and in 1667 he married Malet. The rest of his career was no less stormy. His satiric wit, directed not only at ordinary mortals but at Dryden and Charles II himself, embroiled him in constant quarrels and exiles; his practical jokes, his affairs, and his dissipation were legendary. He circulated his works, always intellectually daring and often obscene, to a limited court readership in manuscripts executed by professional scribes—a common way of handling writing deemed too ideologically or morally scandalous for print. An early printed collection of his poems did appear in 1680, though the title page read "Antwerp," probably to hide its London origin. The air of scandal and disguise surrounding his writing only intensified his notoriety as the exemplar of the dissolute, libertine ways of court culture. He told his biographer, Gilbert Burnet, that "for five years together he was continually drunk." Just before his death, however, he was converted to Christian repentance, and for posterity, Rochester became a favorite moral topic: the libertine who had seen the error of his ways.

Wit, in the Restoration, meant not only a clever turn of phrase but mental capacity and intellectual power. Rochester was famous for both kinds of wit. His fierce intelligence, impatient of sham and convention, helped design a way of life based on style, cleverness, and self-interest—a way of life observable in Restoration plays (Dorimant, in Etherege's *The Man of Mode,* strongly resembles Rochester; for another famous example of libertine comedy of the Restoration, see William Wycherley's *The Country Wife* in the supplemental ebook). Stylistically, Rochester infuses forms such as the heroic couplet with a volatility that contrasts with the pointed and balanced manner of its other masters. From the very first line of "A Satire against Reason and Mankind"—"Were I (who to my cost already am"—he plunges the reader into a couplet mode energized by speculation, self-interruption, and enjambment; and he frequently employs extravagant effects (such as the alliterations "love's lesser lightning" and "balmy brinks of bliss" in "The Imperfect Enjoyment") to flaunt his delight in dramatizing situations, sensations, and himself. "The Disabled Debauchee," composed in "heroic stanzas" like those of Dryden's *Annus Mirabilis,* subverts the very notion of heroism by turning conventions upside down. Philosophically, Rochester is daring and destabilizing. In "A Satire," he rejects high-flown, theoretical reason and consigns its "misguided follower" to an abyss of doubt. The poem's speaker himself happily embraces the "right reason" of instinct, celebrating the life of a "natural man." The poem thus accords with Hobbes's doctrine that all laws, even our notions of good and evil, are artificial social checks on natural human desires. Yet it remains unclear, in Rochester's world of intellectual risk and conflict, whether he thinks humanity's paradoxical predicament can ever finally be escaped. Often called a skeptic himself, he seems to hint that the doubt raised by reason's collapse may surge to engulf him too.

The Disabled Debauchee

As some brave admiral, in former war
    Deprived of force, but pressed with courage still,
Two rival fleets appearing from afar,
    Crawls to the top of an adjacent hill;

5   From whence, with thoughts full of concern, he views
    The wise and daring conduct of the fight,
And each bold action to his mind renews
    His present glory and his past delight;

From his fierce eyes flashes of fire he throws,
10   As from black clouds when lightning breaks away;
Transported, thinks himself amidst his foes,
    And absent, yet enjoys the bloody day;

So, when my days of impotence approach,
    And I'm by pox° and wine's unlucky chance   *syphilis*
15 Forced from the pleasing billows of debauch
    On the dull shore of lazy temperance,

My pains at least some respite shall afford
    While I behold the battles you maintain
When fleets of glasses sail about the board,°   *table*
20   From whose broadsides[1] volleys of wit shall rain.

Nor shall the sight of honorable scars,
    Which my too forward valor did procure,
Frighten new-listed° soldiers from the wars: *newly enlisted*
    Past joys have more than paid what I endure.

25   Should any youth (worth being drunk) prove nice,°   *coy, fastidious*
    And from his fair inviter meanly shrink,
'Twill please the ghost of my departed vice
    If, at my counsel, he repent and drink.

Or should some cold-complexioned sot forbid,
30   With his dull morals, our bold night-alarms,
I'll fire his blood by telling what I did
    When I was strong and able to bear arms.

I'll tell of whores attacked, their lords at home;
    Bawds' quarters beaten up, and fortress won;
35 Windows demolished, watches° overcome;   *watchmen*
    And handsome ills by my contrivance done.

Nor shall our love-fits, Chloris, be forgot,
    When each the well-looked linkboy[2] strove t' enjoy,

---

1. The sides of the table; artillery on a ship; sheets on which satirical verses were printed.

2. Good-looking boy employed to light the way with a link or torch.

And the best kiss was the deciding lot
40   Whether the boy used³ you, or I the boy.

With tales like these I will such thoughts inspire
        As to important mischief shall incline:
I'll make him long some ancient church to fire,
        And fear no lewdness he's called to by wine.

45 Thus, statesmanlike, I'll saucily impose,
        And safe from action, valiantly advise;
Sheltered in impotence, urge you to blows,
        And being good for nothing else, be wise.

                                                1680

The Imperfect Enjoyment¹

Naked she lay, clasped in my longing arms,
I filled with love, and she all over charms;
Both equally inspired with eager fire,
Melting through kindness, flaming in desire.
5 With arms, legs, lips close clinging to embrace,
She clips° me to her breast, and sucks me to her face.   hugs
Her nimble tongue, Love's lesser lightning, played
Within my mouth, and to my thoughts conveyed
Swift orders that I should prepare to throw
10 The all-dissolving thunderbolt below.
My fluttering soul, sprung² with the pointed kiss,
Hangs hovering o'er her balmy brinks of bliss.
But whilst her busy hand would guide that part
Which should convey my soul up to her heart,
15 In liquid raptures I dissolve all o'er,
Melt into sperm, and spend at every pore.
A touch from any part of her had done 't:
Her hand, her foot, her very look's a cunt.
        Smiling, she chides in a kind murmuring noise,
20 And from her body wipes the clammy joys,
When, with a thousand kisses wandering o'er
My panting bosom, "Is there then no more?"
She cries. "All this to love and rapture's due;
Must we not pay a debt to pleasure too?"
25   But I, the most forlorn, lost man alive,
To show my wished obedience vainly strive:
I sigh, alas! and kiss, but cannot swive.°   screw

---

3. The meaning of "used," which appears in the first printed version and many manuscript versions, includes but extends beyond that of "fucked," another prevalent alternative and one preferred by most modern editors.
1. The genre of poems about the downfall of male

"pride"—not only a swelled head but an erection—derives from Ovid's *Amores* 3.7. For a woman's treatment of this situation, see Aphra Behn's "The Disappointment" (p. 1006).
2. Startled from cover, like a game bird.

Eager desires confound my first intent,
Succeeding shame does more success prevent,
30   And rage at last confirms me impotent.
Ev'n her fair hand, which might bid heat return
To frozen age, and make cold hermits burn,
Applied to my dead cinder, warms no more
Than fire to ashes could past flames restore.
35   Trembling, confused, despairing, limber, dry,
A wishing, weak, unmoving lump I lie.
This dart of love, whose piercing point, oft tried,
With virgin blood ten thousand maids have dyed;
Which nature still directed with such art
40   That it through every cunt reached every heart—
Stiffly resolved, 'twould carelessly invade
Woman or man, nor aught° its fury stayed: *anything*
Where'er it pierced, a cunt it found or made—
Now languid lies in this unhappy hour,
45   Shrunk up and sapless like a withered flower.
    Thou treacherous, base deserter of my flame,
False to my passion, fatal to my fame,
Through what mistaken magic dost thou prove
So true to lewdness, so untrue to love?
50   What oyster-cinder-beggar-common whore
Didst thou e'er fail in all thy life before?
When vice, disease, and scandal lead the way,
With what officious haste dost thou obey!
Like a rude, roaring hector° in the streets   *bully*
55   Who scuffles, cuffs, and justles all he meets,
But if his King or country claim his aid,
The rakehell villain shrinks and hides his head;
Ev'n so thy brutal valor is displayed,
Breaks every stew,[3] does each small whore invade,
60   But when great Love the onset does command,
Base recreant to thy prince, thou dar'st not stand.
Worst part of me, and henceforth hated most,
Through all the town a common fucking post,
On whom each whore relieves her tingling cunt
65   As hogs on gates do rub themselves and grunt,
Mayst thou to ravenous chancres be a prey,
Or in consuming weepings waste away;
May strangury and stone[4] thy days attend;
May'st thou ne'er piss, who didst refuse to spend
70   When all my joys did on false thee depend.
    And may ten thousand abler pricks agree
    To do the wronged Corinna right for thee.

1680

---

3. Breaks into every brothel.
4. "Strangury" and "stone" cause slow and pain-

ful urination. "Chancres" and "weepings" are
signs of venereal disease.

Upon Nothing

Nothing, thou elder brother even to shade,
Thou hadst a being ere the world was made
And (well fixed) art alone of ending not afraid.

Ere time and place were, time and place were not,
5   When primitive Nothing Something straight begot,
Then all proceeded from the great united *What*.

Something, the general attribute of all,
Severed from thee, its sole original,
Into thy boundless self must undistinguished fall.

10   Yet Something did thy mighty power command
And from thy fruitful emptiness's hand
Snatched men, beasts, birds, fire, water, air, and land.

Matter, the wick'dst offspring of thy race,
By form assisted, flew from thy embrace,
15   And rebel light obscured thy reverend dusky face.

With form and matter, time and place did join,
Body thy foe, with these did leagues combine[1]
To spoil thy peaceful realm and ruin all thy line.

But turncoat time assists the foe in vain
20   And bribed by thee destroys their short-lived reign
And to thy hungry womb drives back thy slaves again.

Though mysteries are barred from laic eyes[2]
And the divine alone with warrant pries
Into thy bosom where thy truth in private lies,

25   Yet this of thee the wise may truly say:
Thou from the virtuous, nothing tak'st away,[3]
And to be part of thee, the wicked wisely pray.

Great negative, how vainly would the wise
Enquire, define, distinguish, teach, devise,
30   Didst thou not stand to point° their blind philosophies.   *expose*

Is or Is Not, the two great ends of fate,
And true or false, the subject of debate
That perfect or destroy the vast designs of state,

When they have racked the politician's breast,
35   Within thy bosom most securely rest
And when reduced to thee are least unsafe and best.

---

1. Form, matter, time, and place combined in
alliances against Nothing.
2. I.e., the eyes of the laity, who are uninitiated
in Nothing's mysteries.
3. You, Nothing, do not take anything away from
the virtuous.

But Nothing, why does Something still permit
That sacred monarchs should at council sit
With persons highly thought, at best, for nothing fit;

40   Whilst weighty Something modestly abstains
From princes' coffers[4] and from statesmen's brains
And Nothing there like stately Something reigns?

Nothing, who dwellst with fools in grave disguise,
For whom they reverend shapes and forms devise,
45   Lawn-sleeves and furs and gowns,[5] when they like thee look wise;

French truth, Dutch prowess, British policy,
Hibernian° learning, Scotch civility,   *Irish*
Spaniards' dispatch, Danes' wit[6] are mainly seen in thee;

The great man's gratitude to his best friend,
50   Kings' promises, whores' vows, towards thee they bend,
Flow swiftly into thee and in thee ever end.

1679

APHRA BEHN
1640?–1689

"A woman wit has often graced the stage," Dryden wrote in 1681. Soon after actresses first appeared in English public theaters, there was an even more striking debut by a woman writer who boldly signed her plays and talked back to her critics. In a dozen years, Aphra Behn turned out at least that many plays, discovering fresh dramatic possibilities in casts that included women with warm bodies and clever heads. She also drew attention as a warm and witty poet of love. When writing for the stage became less profitable, she turned to the emerging field of prose fiction, composing a pioneering epistolary novel, *Love Letters between a Nobleman and His Sister,* and diverse short tales—not to mention a raft of translations from the French, pindarics to her beloved Stuart rulers, compilations, prologues, complimentary verses, all the piecework and puffery that were the stock in trade of the Restoration town wit. She worked in haste and with flair for nearly two decades and more than held her own as a professional writer. In the end, no author of her time—except Dryden himself—proved more versatile, more alive to new currents of thought, or more inventive in recasting fashionable forms.

Much of Behn's life remains a mystery. Although her books have been accompanied—and often all but buried—by volumes of rumor, hard facts are elu-

4. Charles II's coffers were notably empty, and he was forced to declare bankruptcy in 1672.
5. "Furs and gowns" were worn by judges. "Lawn": a fine linen or cotton fabric, worn by bishops.

6. All proverbial deficiencies of the various nationalities mentioned, many of them exposed during the Anglo-Dutch war (1672–74).

sive. She was almost certainly from East Kent; she may well have been named John-son. But she herself seems to have left no record of her date and place of birth, her family name and upbringing, or the identity of the shadowy Mr. Behn whom she reportedly married. Her many references to nuns and convents, as well as praise for prominent Catholic lords (*Oroonoko* is dedicated to one), have prompted speculation that she may have been raised as a Catholic and educated in a convent abroad. With-out doubt, she drew on a range of worldly experience that would be closed to women in the more genteel ages to come. The circumstantial detail of *Oroonoko* supports her claim that she was in the new sugar colony of Surinam early in 1664. Perhaps she exaggerated her social position to enhance her tale, but many particulars—from dialect words and the location of plantations to methods of selling and torturing slaves—can be authenticated. During the trade war that broke out in 1665—which left her "vast and charming world" a Dutch prize—Behn traveled to the Low Coun-tries on a spying mission for King Charles II. The king could be lax about payment, however, and Behn had to petition desperately to escape debtor's prison. In 1670 she brought out her first plays, "forced to write for bread," she confessed, "and not ashamed to own it."

In London, Behn flourished in the cosmopolitan world of the playhouse and the court. Dryden and other wits encouraged her; she mixed with actresses and manag-ers and playwrights and exchanged verses with a lively literary set that she called her "cabal." Surviving letters record a passionate, troubled attachment to a lawyer named John Hoyle, a bisexual with libertine views. She kept up with the most advanced thinking and joined public debates with pointed satire against the Whigs. But the festivity of the Restoration world was fading out in bitter party acrimony. In 1682 Behn was placed under arrest for "abusive reflections" on the king's illegitimate son, the Whig duke of Monmouth (Dryden's Absalom). Her Royalist opinions and the immodesty of her public role made her a target; gleeful lampoons declared that she was aging and ill and once again poor. She responded by bringing out her works at a still faster rate, composing *Oroonoko*, her dedication claims, "in a few hours . . . for I never rested my pen a moment for thought." In some last works she recorded her hope that her writings would live: "I value fame as much as if I had been born a hero." When she died she was buried in Westminster Abbey.

"All women together ought to let flowers fall upon the grave of Aphra Behn," Vir-ginia Woolf wrote, "for it was she who earned them the right to speak their minds." Behn herself spoke her mind. She scorned hypocrisy and calculation in her society and commented freely on religion, science, and philosophy. Moreover, she spoke as a woman. Denied the classical education of most male authors, she dismissed "musty rules" and lessons and relished the immediate human appeal of popular forms. Her first play, *The Forced Marriage*, exposes the bondage of matches arranged for money and status, and many later works invoke the powerful natural force of love, whose energy breaks through conventions. In a range of genres, from simple pastoral songs to complex plots of intrigue, she candidly explores the sexual feelings of women, their schooling in disguise, their need to "love upon the honest square" (for this her work was later denounced as coarse and impure). *Oroonoko* represents another departure for Behn and prose fiction. It achieves something new both in its narrative form and in extending some of her favorite themes to an original subject: the destiny of a black male hero on a world historical stage.

Oroonoko cannot be classified as fact or fiction, realism or romance. In the still unshaped field of prose narrative—where a "history" could mean any story, true or false—Behn combined the attractions of three older forms. First, she presents the work as a memoir, a personal account of what she has heard and seen. According to a friend, Behn had told this tale over and over; perhaps that explains the conversa-tional ease with which she turns back and forth, interpreting faraway scenes for her readers at home. Second, *Oroonoko* is a travel narrative in three parts. It turns west to a new world often extolled as a paradise, then east to Africa and the amorous intrigues of a corrupt old-world court (popular reading fare), then finally west again with its hero across the infamous "Middle Passage"—over which millions of slaves would be transported during the next century—to the conflicts of a raw colonial world. Exotic scenes fascinate Behn, but she wants even more to talk to people and learn about their ways of life. As in imaginary voyages, from Sir Thomas More's *Utopia* to *Gulliver's Travels* and *Rasselas,* encounters with foreign cultures sharply challenge Europeans to reexamine themselves. Behn's primitive Indians and noble Africans live by a code of virtue, by principles of fidelity and honor, that "civilized" Christians often ignore or betray. Oroonoko embodies this code. Above all, the book is his biography. Courageous, high-minded, and great hearted, he rivals the heroes of classical epics and Plutarch's *Lives* and is equally worthy of fame. Nor does he lack gentler virtues. Like the heroes of seventeenth-century heroic dramas and romances, he shines in the company of women and proves his nobility by his passionate and constant love for Imoinda, his ideal counterpart. Yet finally a contradiction dooms Oroonoko: he is at once prince and chattel, a "royal slave."

Behn handles her forms dynamically, drawing out their inner discords and tensions. In the biography, Oroonoko's deepest values are turned against him. His trust in friendship and scrupulous truth to his word expose him to the treachery of Europeans who calculate human worth on a yardstick of profit. A hero cannot survive in such a world. His self-respect demands action, even when he can find no clear path through the tangle of assurances and lies. Moreover, the colony too seems tangled in contradictions. Behn's travel narrative reveals a broken paradise where, in the absence of secure authority, the settlers descend into a series of unstable alliances, improvised power relations, and escalating suspicions. Here every term—friend and foe, tenderness and brutality, savagery and civilization—can suddenly turn into its opposite. And the author also seems caught between worlds. The cultivated Englishwoman who narrates and acts in this memoir thinks highly of her hero's code of honor and shares his contempt for the riffraff who plague him. Yet her own role is ambiguous: she lacks the power to save Oroonoko and might even be viewed as implicated in his downfall. Only as a writer can she take control, preserving the hero in her work.

The story of Oroonoko did not end with Behn. Compassion for the royal slave and outrage at his fate were enlisted in the long battle against the slave trade. Reprinted, translated, serialized, dramatized, and much imitated, *Oroonoko* helped teach a mass audience to feel for all victims of the brutal commerce in human beings. A hundred years later, the popular writer Hannah More testified to the widening influence of the story: "No individual griefs my bosom melt, / For millions feel what Oroonoko felt." Women especially identified with the experience of personal injustice and everyday indignity—the pain of being treated as something less than fully human. Perhaps it is appropriate that the writer who made the suffering of the royal slave famous had known the pride and lowliness of being "a female pen."

The Disappointment[1]

One day the amorous Lysander,
By an impatient passion swayed,
Surprised fair Cloris, that loved maid,
Who could defend herself no longer.

---

1. This variation on the "imperfect enjoyment" genre compares with Rochester's (p. 1001); it first appeared in a collection of his poems. But Behn gives the theme of impotence her own twist. Freely translating a French poem, Cantenac's "The Lost Chance Recovered," she cuts the conclusion, in which the French lover regained his potency, and she highlights the woman's feelings as well as the man's.

5 All things did with his love conspire;
    The gilded planet of the day,°   *the sun*
    In his gay chariot drawn by fire,
    Was now descending to the sea,
    And left no light to guide the world
10 But what from Cloris' brighter eyes was hurled.

    In a lone thicket made for love,
    Silent as yielding maid's consent,
    She with a charming languishment,
    Permits his force, yet gently strove;
15 Her hands his bosom softly meet,
    But not to put him back designed,
    Rather to draw 'em on inclined:
    Whilst he lay trembling at her feet,
    Resistance 'tis in vain to show:
20 She wants° the power to say—*Ah! what d'ye do?*   *lacks*

    Her bright eyes sweet and yet severe,
    Where love and shame confusedly strive,
    Fresh vigor to Lysander give;
    And breathing faintly in his ear,
25 She cried—*Cease, cease—your vain desire,*
    Or I'll call out—what would you do?
    My dearer honor even to you
    I cannot, must not give—Retire,
    Or take this life, whose chiefest part
30 *I gave you with the conquest of my heart.*

    But he as much unused to fear,
    As he was capable of love,
    The blessed minutes to improve
    Kisses her mouth, her neck, her hair;
35 Each touch her new desire alarms;
    His burning, trembling hand he pressed
    Upon her swelling snowy breast,
    While she lay panting in his arms.
    All her unguarded beauties lie
40 The spoils and trophies of the enemy.

    And now without respect or fear
    He seeks the object of his vows
    (His love no modesty allows)
    By swift degrees advancing—where
45 His daring hand that altar seized,
    Where gods of love do sacrifice:
    That awful throne, that paradise
    Where rage is calmed, and anger pleased;
    That fountain where delight still flows,
50 And gives the universal world repose.

    Her balmy lips encountering his,
    Their bodies, as their souls, are joined;

Where both in transports unconfined
Extend themselves upon the moss.
55 Cloris half dead and breathless lay;
Her soft eyes cast a humid light
Such as divides the day and night;
Or falling stars, whose fires decay:
And now no signs of life she shows,
60 But what in short-breathed sighs returns and goes.

He saw how at her length she lay;
He saw her rising bosom bare;
Her loose thin robes, through which appear
A shape designed for love and play;
65 Abandoned by her pride and shame
She does her softest joys dispense,
Offering her virgin innocence
A victim to love's sacred flame;
While the o'er-ravished shepherd lies
70 Unable to perform the sacrifice.

Ready to taste a thousand joys,
The too transported hapless swain
Found the vast pleasure turned to pain;
Pleasure which too much love destroys:
75 The willing garments by he laid,[2]
And heaven all opened to his view.
Mad to possess, himself he threw
On the defenseless lovely maid.
But oh what envying god conspires
80 To snatch his power, yet leave him the desire!

Nature's support (without whose aid
She can no human being give)
Itself now wants the art[3] to live;
Faintness its slackened nerves invade:
85 In vain th'enraged youth essayed
To call its fleeting vigor back;
No motion 'twill from motion take;
Excess of love his love betrayed:
In vain he toils, in vain commands:
90 The insensible[4] fell weeping in his hand.

In this so amorous cruel strife,
Where love and fate were too severe,
The poor Lysander in despair
Renounced his reason with his life:
95 Now all the brisk and active fire
That should the nobler part inflame
Served to increase his rage and shame,
And left no spark for new desire:

---

2. He took off her compliant clothes.
3. Lacks the capacity.

4. Devoid of feeling and too small to be noticed.

Not all her naked charms could move
100 Or calm that rage that had debauched his love.

Cloris returning from the trance
Which love and soft desire had bred,
Her timorous hand she gently laid
(Or guided by design or chance)
105 Upon that fabulous Priapus,[5]
That potent god, as poets feign:
But never did young shepherdess,
Gathering the fern upon the plain,
More nimbly draw her fingers back,
110 Finding beneath the verdant leaves a snake,

Than Cloris her fair hand withdrew,
Finding that god of her desires
Disarmed of all his awful fires,
And cold as flowers bathed in the morning dew.
115 Who can the nymph's confusion guess?
The blood forsook the hinder place,
And strewed with blushes all her face,
Which both disdain and shame expressed:
And from Lysander's arms she fled,
120 Leaving him fainting on the gloomy bed.

Like lightning through the grove she hies,
Or Daphne from the Delphic god;[6]
No print upon the grassy road
She leaves, to instruct pursuing eyes.
125 The wind that wantoned in her hair
And with her ruffled garments played,
Discovered in the flying maid
All that the gods e'er made, if fair.
So Venus, when her love[7] was slain,
130 With fear and haste flew o'er the fatal plain.

The nymph's resentments none but I
Can well imagine or condole:
But none can guess Lysander's soul,
But those who swayed his destiny.
135 His silent griefs swell up to storms,
And not one god his fury spares;
He cursed his birth, his fate, his stars;
But more the shepherdess's charms,
Whose soft bewitching influence
140 Had damned him to the hell of impotence.[8]

1680

---

5. Phallus. The ancient god Priapus is always pictured with an outstanding erection.
6. Apollo, from whom the Greek nymph Daphne fled until she turned into a laurel tree.

7. Adonis, who was killed by a boar.
8. Blaming the woman for an imperfect enjoyment is typical of the genre.

Oroonoko; or, The Royal Slave[1]

I do not pretend, in giving you the history of this royal slave, to entertain my reader with the adventures of a feigned hero, whose life and fortunes fancy may manage at the poet's pleasure; nor in relating the truth, design to adorn it with any accidents but such as arrived in earnest to him. And it shall come simply into the world, recommended by its own proper merits and natural intrigues, there being enough of reality to support it, and to render it diverting, without the addition of invention.

I was myself an eyewitness to a great part of what you will find here set down, and what I could not be witness of, I received from the mouth of the chief actor in this history, the hero himself, who gave us the whole transactions of his youth; and though I shall omit for brevity's sake a thousand little accidents of his life, which, however pleasant to us, where history was scarce and adventures very rare, yet might prove tedious and heavy to my reader, in a world where he finds diversions for every minute, new and strange. But we who were perfectly charmed with the character of this great man were curious to gather every circumstance of his life.

The scene of the last part of his adventures lies in a colony in America called Surinam,[2] in the West Indies.

But before I give you the story of this gallant slave, 'tis fit I tell you the manner of bringing them to these new colonies, for those they make use of there are not natives of the place; for those we live with in perfect amity, without daring to command 'em, but on the contrary caress 'em with all the brotherly and friendly affection in the world, trading with 'em for their fish, venison, buffaloes, skins, and little rarities; as marmosets, a sort of monkey as big as a rat or weasel but of a marvelous and delicate shape, and has face and hands like a human creature, and *cousheries*,[3] a little beast in the form and fashion of a lion, as big as a kitten, but so exactly made in all parts like that noble beast, that it is it in miniature. Then for little parakeetoes, great parrots, macaws, and a thousand other birds and beasts of wonderful and surprising forms, shapes, and colors. For skins of prodigious snakes, of which there are some threescore yards in length, as is the skin of one that may be seen at his Majesty's antiquaries'; where are also some rare flies[4] of amazing forms and colors, presented to 'em by myself, some as big as my fist, some less, and all of various excellencies, such as art cannot imitate. Then we trade for feathers, which they order into all shapes, make themselves little short habits of 'em, and glorious wreaths for their heads, necks, arms and legs, whose tinctures are unconceivable. I had a set of these presented to me, and I gave 'em to the King's theater, and it was the dress of the Indian Queen,[5] infinitely admired by persons of quality, and were unimitable. Besides these,

---

1. The text, prepared by Joanna Lipking, is based on the 1688 edition, the sole edition published during Behn's lifetime. The critical edition of G. C. Duchovnay (diss., Indiana, 1971), which collates the four 17th-century editions, has been consulted.
2. A British sugar colony on the South American coast east of Venezuela; later Dutch Guiana, now the Republic of Suriname.
3. A name appearing in local descriptions, but the animal is not clearly identified; probably the lion-headed marmoset or perhaps the *cujara* (Portuguese), a rodent known as the rice rat. "Buffaloes": wild oxen of various species.
4. Butterflies. "Antiquaries": probably the natural history museum of the Royal Society.
5. The title character in the 1664 heroic play by Sir Robert Howard and John Dryden, which was noted for its lavish production. There are contemporary records of "speckled plumes" and feather headdresses.

a thousand little knacks and rarities in nature, and some of art, as their baskets, weapons, aprons, et cetera. We dealt with 'em with beads of all colors,
knives, axes, pins and needles, which they used only as tools to drill holes
with in their ears, noses, and lips, where they hang a great many little things,
as long beads, bits of tin, brass, or silver beat thin, and any shining trinket.
The beads they weave into aprons about a quarter of an ell long, and of the
same breadth,[6] working them very prettily in flowers of several colors of
beads; which apron they wear just before 'em, as Adam and Eve did the fig
leaves, the men wearing a long stripe of linen which they deal with us for.
They thread these beads also on long cotton threads and make girdles to tie
their aprons to, which come twenty times or more about the waist, and then
cross, like a shoulder belt, both ways, and round their necks, arms, and
legs. This adornment, with their long black hair, and the face painted in
little specks or flowers here and there, makes 'em a wonderful figure to
behold.

Some of the beauties which indeed are finely shaped, as almost all are,
and who have pretty features, are very charming and novel; for they have all
that is called beauty, except the color, which is a reddish yellow; or after a
new oiling, which they often use to themselves, they are of the color of a new
brick, but smooth, soft, and sleek. They are extreme[7] modest and bashful,
very shy and nice of being touched. And though they are all thus naked, if
one lives forever among 'em there is not to be seen an indecent action or
glance; and being continually used to see one another so unadorned, so like
our first parents before the Fall, it seems as if they had no wishes; there
being nothing to heighten curiosity, but all you can see you see at once, and
every moment see, and where there is no novelty there can be no curiosity.
Not but I have seen a handsome young Indian dying for love of a very beautiful young Indian maid; but all his courtship was to fold his arms, pursue her
with his eyes, and sighs were all his language; while she, as if no such lover
were present, or rather, as if she desired none such, carefully guarded her
eyes from beholding him, and never approached him but she looked down
with all the blushing modesty I have seen in the most severe and cautious of
our world. And these people represented to me an absolute idea of the first
state of innocence, before man knew how to sin. And 'tis most evident and
plain that simple Nature is the most harmless, inoffensive, and virtuous mistress. 'Tis she alone, if she were permitted, that better instructs the world
than all the inventions of man. Religion would here but destroy that tranquillity they possess by ignorance, and laws would but teach 'em to know offense,
of which now they have no notion. They once made mourning and fasting
for the death of the English governor, who had given his hand to come on
such a day to 'em and neither came nor sent, believing when once a man's
word was passed, nothing but death could or should prevent his keeping it.
And when they saw he was not dead, they asked him what name they had for
a man who promised a thing he did not do. The governor told them, such a
man was a liar, which was a word of infamy to a gentleman. Then one of 'em
replied, "Governor, you are a liar, and guilty of that infamy." They have a
native justice which knows no fraud, and they understand no vice or cunning, but when they are taught by the white men. They have plurality of
wives, which, when they grow old, they serve those that succeed 'em, who are

6. About a foot square.   7. Extremely.

young, but with a servitude easy and respected; and unless they take slaves in war, they have no other attendants.

Those on that continent where I was had no king, but the oldest war captain was obeyed with great resignation. A war captain is a man who has led them on to battle with conduct[8] and success, of whom I shall have occasion to speak more hereafter, and of some other of their customs and manners, as they fall in my way.

With these people, as I said, we live in perfect tranquillity and good understanding, as it behooves us to do, they knowing all the places where to seek the best food of the country and the means of getting it, and for very small and unvaluable trifles, supply us with what 'tis impossible for us to get; for they do not only in the wood and over the savannas, in hunting, supply the parts of hounds, by swiftly scouring through those almost impassable places, and by the mere activity of their feet run down the nimblest deer and other eatable beasts; but in the water one would think they were gods of the rivers, or fellow citizens of the deep, so rare an art they have in swimming, diving, and almost living in water, by which they command the less swift inhabitants of the floods. And then for shooting, what they cannot take, or reach with their hands, they do with arrows, and have so admirable an aim that they will split almost a hair; and at any distance that an arrow can reach, they will shoot down oranges and other fruit, and only touch the stalk with the dart's point, that they may not hurt the fruit. So that they being, on all occasions, very useful to us, we find it absolutely necessary to caress 'em as friends, and not to treat 'em as slaves; nor dare we do other, their numbers so far surpassing ours in that continent.

Those then whom we make use of to work in our plantations of sugar are Negroes, black slaves altogether, which are transported thither in this manner. Those who want slaves make a bargain with a master or captain of a ship and contract to pay him so much apiece, a matter of twenty pound a head for as many as he agrees for, and to pay for 'em when they shall be delivered on such a plantation. So that when there arrives a ship laden with slaves, they who have so contracted go aboard and receive their number by lot; and perhaps in one lot that may be for ten, there may happen to be three or four men, the rest women and children. Or be there more or less of either sex, you are obliged to be contented with your lot.

Coramantien,[9] a country of blacks so called, was one of those places in which they found the most advantageous trading for these slaves, and thither most of our great traders in that merchandise trafficked; for that nation is very warlike and brave, and having a continual campaign, being always in hostility with one neighboring prince or other, they had the fortune to take a great many captives; for all they took in battle were sold as slaves, at least those common men who could not ransom themselves. Of these slaves so taken, the general only has all the profit; and of these generals, our captains and masters of ships buy all their freights.

The King of Coramantien was himself a man of a hundred and odd years old, and had no son, though he had many beautiful black wives; for most

8. Capacity to lead.
9. Not a country but a British-held fort and slave market on the Gold Coast of Africa, in modern-day Ghana. As the slave trade expanded, the slaves and workers shipped out from the region (who came to be called Cormantines) impressed many European observers by their beauty and bearing, their fierceness in war, and their extreme dignity under captivity or torture.

certainly there are beauties that can charm of that color. In his younger years he had had many gallant men to his sons, thirteen of which died in battle, conquering when they fell; and he had only left him for his successor one grandchild, son to one of these dead victors, who, as soon as he could bear a bow in his hand and a quiver at his back, was sent into the field, to be trained up by one of the oldest generals to war; where, from his natural inclination to arms and the occasions given him, with the good conduct of the old general, he became, at the age of seventeen, one of the most expert captains and bravest soldiers that ever saw the field of Mars. So that he was adored as the wonder of all that world, and the darling of the soldiers. Besides, he was adorned with a native beauty so transcending all those of his gloomy race that he struck an awe and reverence even in those that knew not his quality; as he did in me, who beheld him with surprise and wonder, when afterwards he arrived in our world.

He had scarce arrived at his seventeenth year, when fighting by his side, the general was killed with an arrow in his eye, which the Prince Oroonoko (for so was this gallant Moor[1] called) very narrowly avoided; nor had he, if the general, who saw the arrow shot, and perceiving it aimed at the Prince, had not bowed his head between, on purpose to receive it in his own body rather than it should touch that of the Prince, and so saved him.

'Twas then, afflicted as Oroonoko was, that he was proclaimed general in the old man's place; and then it was, at the finishing of that war, which had continued for two years, that the Prince came to court, where he had hardly been a month together from the time of his fifth year to that of seventeen; and 'twas amazing to imagine where it was he learned so much humanity; or to give his accomplishments a juster name, where 'twas he got that real greatness of soul, those refined notions of true honor, that absolute generosity, and that softness that was capable of the highest passions of love and gallantry, whose objects were almost continually fighting men, or those mangled or dead; who heard no sounds but those of war and groans. Some part of it we may attribute to the care of a Frenchman of wit and learning, who, finding it turn to very good account to be a sort of royal tutor to this young black, and perceiving him very ready, apt, and quick of apprehension, took a great pleasure to teach him morals, language, and science, and was for it extremely beloved and valued by him. Another reason was, he loved, when he came from war, to see all the English gentlemen that traded thither, and did not only learn their language but that of the Spaniards also, with whom he traded afterwards for slaves.

I have often seen and conversed with this great man, and been a witness to many of his mighty actions, and do assure my reader the most illustrious courts could not have produced a braver man, both for greatness of courage and mind, a judgment more solid, a wit more quick, and a conversation more sweet and diverting. He knew almost as much as if he had read much. He had heard of and admired the Romans; he had heard of the late civil wars in England, and the deplorable death of our great monarch,[2] and would discourse of it with all the sense and abhorrence of the injustice imaginable.

1. Loosely used for any dark-skinned person.
2. Charles I, beheaded in 1649 during the civil wars between Royalists and Parliamentarians. In 1688 this remark and others would have signaled

Behn's ardent support of James II, the last of the Stuart kings, who would be forced into exile within the year.

He had an extreme good and graceful mien, and all the civility of a well-bred great man. He had nothing of barbarity in his nature, but in all points addressed himself as if his education had been in some European court.

This great and just character of Oroonoko gave me an extreme curiosity to see him, especially when I knew he spoke French and English, and that I could talk with him. But though I had heard so much of him, I was as greatly surprised when I saw him as if I had heard nothing of him, so beyond all report I found him. He came into the room and addressed himself to me, and some other women, with the best grace in the world. He was pretty tall, but of a shape the most exact that can be fancied. The most famous statuary[3] could not form the figure of a man more admirably turned from head to foot. His face was not of that brown, rusty black which most of that nation are, but a perfect ebony or polished jet. His eyes were the most awful that could be seen, and very piercing, the white of 'em being like snow, as were his teeth. His nose was rising and Roman, instead of African and flat; his mouth the finest shaped that could be seen, far from those great turned lips which are so natural to the rest of the Negroes. The whole proportion and air of his face was so noble and exactly formed that, bating[4] his color, there could be nothing in nature more beautiful, agreeable, and handsome. There was no one grace wanting that bears the standard of true beauty. His hair came down to his shoulders by the aids of art; which was by pulling it out with a quill and keeping it combed, of which he took particular care. Nor did the perfections of his mind come short of those of his person, for his discourse was admirable upon almost any subject; and whoever had heard him speak would have been convinced of their errors, that all fine wit is confined to the white men, especially to those of Christendom, and would have confessed that Oroonoko was as capable even of reigning well, and of governing as wisely, had as great a soul, as politic[5] maxims, and was as sensible of power, as any prince civilized in the most refined schools of humanity and learning, or the most illustrious courts.

This prince, such as I have described him, whose soul and body were so admirably adorned, was (while yet he was in the court of his grandfather), as I said, as capable of love as 'twas possible for a brave and gallant man to be; and in saying that, I have named the highest degree of love, for sure, great souls are most capable of that passion.

I have already said, the old general was killed by the shot of an arrow, by the side of this prince, in battle, and that Oroonoko was made general. This old dead hero had one only daughter left of his race, a beauty that, to describe her truly, one need say only she was female to the noble male, the beautiful black Venus to our young Mars, as charming in her person as he, and of delicate virtues. I have seen an hundred white men sighing after her, and making a thousand vows at her feet, all vain and unsuccessful. And she was, indeed, too great for any but a prince of her own nation to adore.

Oroonoko coming from the wars (which were now ended), after he had made his court to his grandfather, he thought in honor he ought to make a visit to Imoinda, the daughter of his foster-father, the dead general; and to

3. Sculptor.
4. Except for. The singling out of Africans with European looks or moral values is by no means unique to Behn; for example, Edward Long's 1774 *History of Jamaica* reports of the Cormantines that

"their features are very different from the rest of the African Negroes, being smaller, and more of the European turn."
5. Shrewd, sagacious.

make some excuses to her, because his preservation was the occasion of her father's death; and to present her with those slaves that had been taken in this last battle, as the trophies of her father's victories. When he came, attended by all the young soldiers of any merit, he was infinitely surprised at the beauty of this fair queen of night, whose face and person was so exceeding all he had ever beheld; that lovely modesty with which she received him; that softness in her look, and sighs, upon the melancholy occasion of this honor that was done by so great a man as Oroonoko, and a prince of whom she had heard such admirable things: the awfulness[6] wherewith she received him, and the sweetness of her words and behavior while he stayed, gained a perfect conquest over his fierce heart, and made him feel the victor could be subdued. So that having made his first compliments, and presented her a hundred and fifty slaves in fetters, he told her with his eyes that he was not insensible of her charms; while Imoinda, who wished for nothing more than so glorious a conquest, was pleased to believe she understood that silent language of newborn love, and from that moment put on all her additions to beauty.

The Prince returned to court with quite another humor than before; and though he did not speak much of the fair Imoinda, he had the pleasure to hear all his followers speak of nothing but the charms of that maid, insomuch that, even in the presence of the old king, they were extolling her and heightening, if possible, the beauties they had found in her. So that nothing else was talked of, no other sound was heard in every corner where there were whisperers, but "Imoinda! Imoinda!"

'Twill be imagined Oroonoko stayed not long before he made his second visit, nor, considering his quality, not much longer before he told her he adored her. I have often heard him say that he admired by what strange inspiration he came to talk things so soft and so passionate, who never knew love, nor was used to the conversation[7] of women; but (to use his own words) he said, most happily some new and till then unknown power instructed his heart and tongue in the language of love, and at the same time, in favor of him, inspired Imoinda with a sense of his passion. She was touched with what he said, and returned it all in such answers as went to his very heart, with a pleasure unknown before. Nor did he use those obligations[8] ill that love had done him, but turned all his happy moments to the best advantage; and as he knew no vice, his flame aimed at nothing but honor, if such a distinction may be made in love; and especially in that country, where men take to themselves as many as they can maintain, and where the only crime and sin with woman is to turn her off, to abandon her to want, shame, and misery. Such ill morals are only practiced in Christian countries, where they prefer the bare name of religion, and, without virtue or morality, think that's sufficient. But Oroonoko was none of those professors, but as he had right notions of honor, so he made her such propositions as were not only and barely such; but contrary to the custom of his country, he made her vows she should be the only woman he would possess while he lived; that no age or wrinkles should incline him to change, for her soul would be always fine and always young, and he should have an eternal idea in his mind of the charms

---

6. Reverence.
7. Company. "Admired": marveled.
8. Benefits.

she now bore, and should look into his heart for that idea when he could find it no longer in her face.

After a thousand assurances of his lasting flame, and her eternal empire over him, she condescended to receive him for her husband, or rather, received him as the greatest honor the gods could do her.

There is a certain ceremony in these cases to be observed, which I forgot to ask him how performed; but 'twas concluded on both sides that, in obedience to him, the grandfather was to be first made acquainted with the design, for they pay a most absolute resignation to the monarch, especially when he is a parent also.

On the other side, the old king, who had many wives and many concubines, wanted not court flatterers to insinuate in his heart a thousand tender thoughts for this young beauty, and who represented her to his fancy as the most charming he had ever possessed in all the long race of his numerous years. At this character his old heart, like an extinguished brand, most apt to take fire, felt new sparks of love and began to kindle; and now grown to his second childhood, longed with impatience to behold this gay thing, with whom, alas! he could but innocently play. But how he should be confirmed she was this wonder, before he used his power to call her to court (where maidens never came, unless for the King's private use), he was next to consider; and while he was so doing, he had intelligence brought him that Imoinda was most certainly mistress to the Prince Oroonoko. This gave him some chagrin; however, it gave him also an opportunity, one day when the Prince was a-hunting, to wait on a man of quality, as his slave and attendant, who should go and make a present to Imoinda as from the Prince; he should then, unknown, see this fair maid, and have an opportunity to hear what message she would return the Prince for his present, and from thence gather the state of her heart and degree of her inclination. This was put in execution, and the old monarch saw, and burned. He found her all he had heard, and would not delay his happiness, but found he should have some obstacle to overcome her heart; for she expressed her sense of the present the Prince had sent her in terms so sweet, so soft and pretty, with an air of love and joy that could not be dissembled, insomuch that 'twas past doubt whether she loved Oroonoko entirely. This gave the old king some affliction, but he salved it with this, that the obedience the people pay their king was not at all inferior to what they paid their gods; and what love would not oblige Imoinda to do, duty would compel her to.

He was therefore no sooner got to his apartment but he sent the royal veil to Imoinda, that is, the ceremony of invitation: he sends the lady he has a mind to honor with his bed a veil, with which she is covered, and secured for the King's use; and 'tis death to disobey, besides held a most impious disobedience.

'Tis not to be imagined the surprise and grief that seized this lovely maid at this news and sight. However, as delays in these cases are dangerous and pleading worse than treason, trembling, and almost fainting, she was obliged to suffer herself to be covered and led away.

They brought her thus to court; and the King, who had caused a very rich bath to be prepared, was led into it, where he sat under a canopy, in state, to receive this longed-for virgin; whom he having commanded should be brought to him, they (after disrobing her) led her to the bath, and making fast the doors, left her to descend. The King, without more courtship, bade her throw off her mantle and come to his arms. But Imoinda, all in tears, threw herself on the marble, on the brink of the bath, and besought him to hear her. She told him, as she was a maid, how proud of the divine glory she should have been, of having it in her power to oblige her king; but as by the laws he could not, and from his royal goodness would not, take from any man his wedded wife, so she believed she should be the occasion of making him commit a great sin, if she did not reveal her state and condition, and tell him she was another's, and could not be so happy to be his.

The King, enraged at this delay, hastily demanded the name of the bold man that had married a woman of her degree without his consent. Imoinda, seeing his eyes fierce and his hands tremble (whether with age or anger, I know not, but she fancied the last), almost repented she had said so much, for now she feared the storm would fall on the Prince. She therefore said a thousand things to appease the raging of his flame, and to prepare him to hear who it was with calmness; but before she spoke, he imagined who she meant, but would not seem to do so, but commanded her to lay aside her mantle and suffer herself to receive his caresses; or by his gods, he swore that happy man whom she was going to name should die, though it were even Oroonoko himself. "Therefore," said he, "deny this marriage, and swear thyself a maid." "That," replied Imoinda, "by all our powers I do, for I am not yet known to my husband." "'Tis enough," said the King; "'tis enough to satisfy both my conscience and my heart." And rising from his seat, he went and led her into the bath, it being in vain for her to resist.

In this time the Prince, who was returned from hunting, went to visit his Imoinda, but found her gone; and not only so, but heard she had received the royal veil. This raised him to a storm, and in his madness they had much ado to save him from laying violent hands on himself. Force first prevailed, and then reason. They urged all to him that might oppose his rage, but nothing weighed so greatly with him as the King's old age, uncapable of injuring him with Imoinda. He would give way to that hope, because it pleased him most, and flattered best his heart. Yet this served not altogether to make him cease his different passions, which sometimes raged within him, and sometimes softened into showers. 'Twas not enough to appease him, to tell him his grandfather was old and could not that way injure him, while he retained that awful duty which the young men are used there to pay to their grave relations. He could not be convinced he had no cause to sigh and mourn for the loss of a mistress he could not with all his strength and courage retrieve. And he would often cry, "O my friends! Were she in walled cities or confined from me in fortifications of the greatest strength, did enchantments or monsters detain her from me, I would venture through any hazard to free her. But here, in the arms of a feeble old man, my youth, my violent love, my trade in arms, and all my vast desire of glory avail me nothing. Imoinda is as irrecoverably lost to me as if she were snatched by the cold arms of Death. Oh! she is never to be retrieved. If I would wait tedious years, till fate should bow the old king to his grave, even that would not leave me Imoinda free; but still that custom that makes it so vile a crime for a son to marry his father's wives or mistresses would hinder my happiness, unless I would either ignobly set an ill precedent to my successors, or abandon my country and fly with her to some unknown world, who never heard our story."

But it was objected to him that his case was not the same; for Imoinda being his lawful wife, by solemn contract, 'twas he was the injured man and might if he so pleased take Imoinda back, the breach of the law being on his grandfather's side; and that if he could circumvent him and redeem her from the Otan, which is the palace of the King's women, a sort of seraglio, it was both just and lawful for him so to do.

This reasoning had some force upon him, and he should have been entirely comforted, but for the thought that she was possessed by his grandfather. However, he loved so well that he was resolved to believe what most favored his hope, and to endeavor to learn from Imoinda's own mouth what only she could satisfy him in, whether she was robbed of that blessing which was only due to his faith and love. But as it was very hard to get a sight of the women (for no men ever entered into the Otan but when the King went to entertain himself with some one of his wives or mistresses, and 'twas death at any other time for any other to go in), so he knew not how to contrive to get a sight of her.

While Oroonoko felt all the agonies of love, and suffered under a torment the most painful in the world, the old king was not exempted from his share of affliction. He was troubled for having been forced by an irresistible passion to rob his son[9] of a treasure he knew could not but be extremely dear to him, since she was the most beautiful that ever had been seen, and had besides all the sweetness and innocence of youth and modesty, with a charm of wit surpassing all. He found that, however she was forced to expose her lovely person to his withered arms, she could only sigh and weep there, and think of Oroonoko; and oftentimes could not forbear speaking of him, though her life were, by custom, forfeited by owning her passion. But she spoke not of a lover only, but of a prince dear to him to whom she spoke, and of the praises of a man who, till now, filled the old man's soul with joy at every recital of his bravery, or even his name. And 'twas this dotage on our young hero that gave Imoinda a thousand privileges to speak of him without offending, and this condescension in the old king that made her take the satisfaction of speaking of him so very often.

Besides, he many times inquired how the Prince bore himself; and those of whom he asked, being entirely slaves to the merits and virtues of the Prince, still answered what they thought conduced best to his service; which was to make the old king fancy that the Prince had no more interest in Imoinda, and had resigned her willingly to the pleasure of the King; that he diverted himself with his mathematicians, his fortifications, his officers, and his hunting.

This pleased the old lover, who failed not to report these things again to Imoinda, that she might, by the example of her young lover, withdraw her heart, and rest better contented in his arms. But however she was forced to receive this unwelcome news, in all appearance with unconcern and content, her heart was bursting within, and she was only happy when she could get alone, to vent her griefs and moans with sighs and tears.

What reports of the Prince's conduct were made to the King, he thought good to justify as far as possibly he could by his actions, and when he appeared in the presence of the King, he showed a face not at all betraying his heart. So that in a little time, the old man being entirely convinced that he was no longer a lover of Imoinda, he carried him with him in his train to the Otan, often to banquet with his mistress. But as soon as he entered, one

9. I.e., grandson.

day, into the apartment of Imoinda with the King, at the first glance from
her eyes, notwithstanding all his determined resolution, he was ready to sink
in the place where he stood, and had certainly done so but for the support of
Aboan, a young man who was next to him; which, with his change of countenance, had betrayed him, had the King chanced to look that way. And
I have observed, 'tis a very great error, in those who laugh when one says
a Negro can change color, for I have seen 'em as frequently blush, and look
pale, and that as visibly as ever I saw in the most beautiful white. And 'tis
certain that both these changes were evident, this day, in both these lovers.
And Imoinda, who saw with some joy the change in the Prince's face, and
found it in her own, strove to divert the King from beholding either by a
forced caress, with which she met him, which was a new wound in the heart
of the poor dying Prince. But as soon as the King was busied in looking on
some fine thing of Imoinda's making, she had time to tell the Prince with
her angry but love-darting eyes that she resented his coldness, and bemoaned
her own miserable captivity. Nor were his eyes silent, but answered hers
again, as much as eyes could do, instructed by the most tender and most
passionate heart that ever loved. And they spoke so well and so effectually,
as Imoinda no longer doubted but she was the only delight and the darling of
that soul she found pleading in 'em its right of love, which none was more
willing to resign than she. And 'twas this powerful language alone that in an
instant conveyed all the thoughts of their souls to each other, that[1] they both
found there wanted but opportunity to make them both entirely happy. But
when he saw another door opened by Onahal, a former old wife of the King's
who now had charge of Imoinda, and saw the prospect of a bed of state
made ready with sweets and flowers for the dalliance of the King, who
immediately led the trembling victim from his sight into that prepared
repose, what rage, what wild frenzies seized his heart! which forcing to keep
within bounds, and to suffer without noise, it became the more insupportable, and rent his soul with ten thousand pains. He was forced to retire to
vent his groans, where he fell down on a carpet and lay struggling a long
time, and only breathing now and then, "—O Imoinda!"

When Onahal had finished her necessary affair within, shutting the door,
she came forth to wait till the King called; and hearing someone sighing in
the other room, she passed on, and found the Prince in that deplorable
condition, which she thought needed her aid. She gave him cordials, but all
in vain, till finding the nature of his disease by his sighs and naming Imoinda.
She told him, he had not so much cause as he imagined to afflict himself, for
if he knew the King so well as she did, he would not lose a moment in jealousy, and that she was confident that Imoinda bore, at this minute, part in
his affliction. Aboan was of the same opinion, and both together persuaded
him to reassume his courage; and all sitting down on the carpet, the Prince
said so many obliging things to Onahal that he half persuaded her to be of his
party. And she promised him she would thus far comply with his just desires,
that she would let Imoinda know how faithful he was, what he suffered, and
what he said.

This discourse lasted till the King called, which gave Oroonoko a certain
satisfaction, and with the hope Onahal had made him conceive, he assumed
a look as gay as 'twas possible a man in his circumstances could do; and pres-

---

1. So that.

ently after, he was called in with the rest who waited without. The King commanded music to be brought, and several of his young wives and mistresses came all together by his command to dance before him; where Imoinda performed her part with an air and grace so passing all the rest as her beauty was above 'em, and received the present ordained as a prize. The Prince was every moment more charmed with the new beauties and graces he beheld in this fair one. And while he gazed, and she danced, Onahal was retired to a window with Aboan.

This Onahal, as I said, was one of the cast mistresses of the old king; and 'twas these (now past their beauty) that were made guardians or governants[2] to the new and the young ones, and whose business it was to teach them all those wanton arts of love with which they prevailed and charmed heretofore in their turn; and who now treated the triumphing happy ones with all the severity, as to liberty and freedom, that was possible, in revenge of those honors they rob them of; envying them those satisfactions, those gallantries and presents, that were once made to themselves, while youth and beauty lasted, and which they now saw pass regardless by, and paid only to the bloomings. And certainly nothing is more afflicting to a decayed beauty than to behold in itself declining charms that were once adored, and to find those caresses paid to new beauties to which once she laid a claim; to hear 'em whisper as she passes by, "That once was a delicate woman." These abandoned ladies therefore endeavor to revenge all the despites[3] and decays of time on these flourishing happy ones. And 'twas this severity that gave Oroonoko a thousand fears he should never prevail with Onahal to see Imoinda. But, as I said, she was now retired to a window with Aboan.

This young man was not only one of the best quality,[4] but a man extremely well made and beautiful; and coming often to attend the King to the Otan, he had subdued the heart of the antiquated Onahal, which had not forgot how pleasant it was to be in love. And though she had some decays in her face, she had none in her sense and wit; she was there agreeable still, even to Aboan's youth, so that he took pleasure in entertaining her with discourses of love. He knew also that to make his court to these she-favorites was the way to be great, these being the persons that do all affairs and business at court. He had also observed that she had given him glances more tender and inviting than she had done to others of his quality. And now, when he saw that her favor could so absolutely oblige the Prince, he failed not to sigh in her ear and to look with eyes all soft upon her, and give her hope that she had made some impressions on his heart. He found her pleased at this, and making a thousand advances to him; but the ceremony ending and the King departing broke up the company for that day, and his conversation.

Aboan failed not that night to tell the Prince of his success, and how advantageous the service of Onahal might be to his amour with Imoinda. The Prince was overjoyed with this good news and besought him, if it were possible, to caress her so as to engage her entirely, which he could not fail to do, if he complied with her desires. "For then," said the Prince, "her life lying at your mercy, she must grant you the request you make in my behalf." Aboan understood him, and assured him he would make love so effectually that he would defy the most expert mistress of the art to find out whether he dissembled it or had it really. And 'twas with impatience they waited the next opportunity of going to the Otan.

The wars came on, the time of taking the field approached, and 'twas impossible for the Prince to delay his going at the head of his army to encounter the enemy. So that every day seemed a tedious year till he saw his Imoinda, for he believed he could not live if he were forced away without being so happy. 'Twas with impatience, therefore, that he expected the next visit the King would make, and according to his wish, it was not long.

The parley of the eyes of these two lovers had not passed so secretly but an old jealous lover could spy it; or rather, he wanted not flatterers who told him they observed it. So that the Prince was hastened to the camp, and this was the last visit he found he should make to the Otan; he therefore urged Aboan to make the best of this last effort, and to explain himself so to Onahal that she, deferring her enjoyment of her young lover no longer, might make way for the Prince to speak to Imoinda.

The whole affair being agreed on between the Prince and Aboan, they attended the King, as the custom was, to the Otan, where, while the whole company was taken up in beholding the dancing and antic postures the women-royal made to divert the King, Onahal singled out Aboan, whom she found most pliable to her wish. When she had him where she believed she could not be heard, she sighed to him, and softly cried, "Ah, Aboan! When will you be sensible of my passion? I confess it with my mouth, because I would not give my eyes the lie; and you have but too much already perceived they have confessed my flame. Nor would I have you believe that because I am the abandoned mistress of a king, I esteem myself altogether divested of charms. No, Aboan; I have still a rest[5] of beauty enough engaging, and have learned to please too well not to be desirable. I can have lovers still, but will have none but Aboan." "Madam," replied the half-feigning youth, "you have already, by my eyes, found you can still conquer, and I believe 'tis in pity of me you condescend to this kind confession. But, Madam, words are used to be so small a part of our country courtship, that 'tis rare one can get so happy an opportunity as to tell one's heart, and those few minutes we have are forced to be snatched for more certain proofs of love than speaking and sighing; and such I languish for."

He spoke this with such a tone that she hoped it true, and could not forbear believing it; and being wholly transported with joy, for having subdued the finest of all the King's subjects to her desires, she took from her ears two large pearls and commanded him to wear 'em in his. He would have refused 'em, crying, "Madam, these are not the proofs of your love that I expect; 'tis opportunity, 'tis a lone hour only, that can make me happy." But forcing the pearls into his hand, she whispered softly to him, "Oh! Do not fear a woman's invention, when love sets her a-thinking." And pressing his hand, she cried, "This night you shall be happy. Come to the gate of the orange groves behind the Otan, and I will be ready, about midnight, to receive you." 'Twas thus agreed, and she left him, that no notice might be taken of their speaking together.

The ladies were still dancing, and the King, laid on a carpet, with a great deal of pleasure was beholding them, especially Imoinda, who that day appeared more lovely than ever, being enlivened with the good tidings

5. Remnant.

Onahal had brought her of the constant passion the Prince had for her. The Prince was laid on another carpet at the other end of the room, with his eyes fixed on the object of his soul; and as she turned or moved, so did they, and she alone gave his eyes and soul their motions. Nor did Imoinda employ her eyes to any other use than in beholding with infinite pleasure the joy she produced in those of the Prince. But while she was more regarding him than the steps she took, she chanced to fall, and so near him as that, leaping with extreme force from the carpet, he caught her in his arms as she fell; and 'twas visible to the whole presence[6] the joy wherewith he received her. He clasped her close to his bosom, and quite forgot that reverence that was due to the mistress of a king, and that punishment that is the reward of a bold-ness of this nature; and had not the presence of mind of Imoinda (fonder of his safety than her own) befriended him, in making her spring from his arms and fall into her dance again, he had at that instant met his death; for the old king, jealous to the last degree, rose up in rage, broke all the diver-sion, and led Imoinda to her apartment, and sent out word to the Prince to go immediately to the camp, and that if he were found another night in court he should suffer the death ordained for disobedient offenders.

You may imagine how welcome this news was to Oroonoko, whose unsea-sonable transport and caress of Imoinda was blamed by all men that loved him; and now he perceived his fault, yet cried that for such another moment, he would be content to die.

All the Otan was in disorder about this accident; and Onahal was par-ticularly concerned, because on the Prince's stay depended her happiness, for she could no longer expect that of Aboan. So that ere they departed, they contrived it so that the Prince and he should come both that night to the grove of the Otan, which was all of oranges and citrons, and that there they should wait her orders.

They parted thus, with grief enough, till night, leaving the King in pos-session of the lovely maid. But nothing could appease the jealousy of the old lover. He would not be imposed on, but would have it that Imoinda made a false step on purpose to fall into Oroonoko's bosom, and that all things looked like a design on both sides; and 'twas in vain she protested her inno-cence. He was old and obstinate, and left her more than half assured that his fear was true.

The King going to his apartment sent to know where the Prince was, and if he intended to obey his command. The messenger returned and told him, he found the Prince pensive and altogether unpreparing for the campaign, that he lay negligently on the ground, and answered very little. This con-firmed the jealousy of the King, and he commanded that they should very narrowly and privately watch his motions, and that he should not stir from his apartment but one spy or other should be employed to watch him. So that the hour approaching wherein he was to go to the citron grove, and taking only Aboan along with him, he leaves his apartment, and was watched to the very gate of the Otan, where he was seen to enter, and where they left him, to carry back the tidings to the King.

Oroonoko and Aboan were no sooner entered but Onahal led the Prince to the apartment of Imoinda, who, not knowing anything of her happiness, was laid in bed. But Onahal only left him in her chamber, to make the best of

6. Company.

his opportunity, and took her dear Aboan to her own, where he showed the heighth of complaisance for his prince, when, to give him an opportunity, he suffered himself to be caressed in bed by Onahal.

The Prince softly wakened Imoinda, who was not a little surprised with joy to find him there; and yet she trembled with a thousand fears. I believe he omitted saying nothing to this young maid that might persuade her to suffer him to seize his own, and take the rights of love; and I believe she was not long resisting those arms where she so longed to be; and having opportunity, night and silence, youth, love and desire, he soon prevailed, and ravished in a moment what his old grandfather had been endeavoring for so many months.

'Tis not to be imagined the satisfaction of these two young lovers; nor the vows she made him that she remained a spotless maid till that night, and that what she did with his grandfather had robbed him of no part of her virgin honor, the gods in mercy and justice having reserved that for her plighted lord, to whom of right it belonged. And 'tis impossible to express the transports he suffered, while he listened to a discourse so charming from her loved lips, and clasped that body in his arms for whom he had so long languished; and nothing now afflicted him but his sudden departure from her; for he told her the necessity and his commands, but should depart satisfied in this, that since the old king had hitherto not been able to deprive him of those enjoyments which only belonged to him, he believed for the future he would be less able to injure him; so that abating the scandal of the veil, which was no otherwise so than that she was wife to another, he believed her safe, even in the arms of the King, and innocent; yet would he have ventured at the conquest of the world, and have given it all, to have had her avoided that honor of receiving the royal veil. 'Twas thus, between a thousand caresses, that both bemoaned the hard fate of youth and beauty, so liable to that cruel promotion. 'Twas a glory that could well have been spared here, though desired and aimed at by all the young females of that kingdom.

But while they were thus fondly employed, forgetting how time ran on, and that the dawn must conduct him far away from his only happiness, they heard a great noise in the Otan, and unusual voices of men; at which the Prince, starting from the arms of the frighted Imoinda, ran to a little battle-ax he used to wear by his side, and having not so much leisure as to put on his habit, he opposed himself against some who were already opening the door; which they did with so much violence that Oroonoko was not able to defend it, but was forced to cry out with a commanding voice, "Whoever ye are that have the boldness to attempt to approach this apartment thus rudely, know that I, the Prince Oroonoko, will revenge it with the certain death of him that first enters. Therefore stand back, and know, this place is sacred to love and me this night; tomorrow 'tis the King's."

This he spoke with a voice so resolved and assured that they soon retired from the door, but cried, "'Tis by the King's command we are come; and being satisfied by thy voice, O Prince, as much as if we had entered, we can report to the King the truth of all his fears, and leave thee to provide for thy own safety, as thou art advised by thy friends."

At these words they departed, and left the Prince to take a short and sad leave of his Imoinda, who, trusting in the strength of her charms, believed she should appease the fury of a jealous king by saying she was surprised, and that it was by force of arms he got into her apartment. All her concern now was for his life, and therefore she hastened him to the camp, and with much ado prevailed on him to go. Nor was it she alone that prevailed; Aboan and Onahal both pleaded, and both assured him of a lie that should be well enough contrived to secure Imoinda. So that at last, with a heart sad as death, dying eyes, and sighing soul, Oroonoko departed and took his way to the camp.

It was not long after the King in person came to the Otan, where, beholding Imoinda with rage in his eyes, he upbraided her wickedness and perfidy, and threatening her royal lover, she fell on her face at his feet, bedewing the floor with her tears and imploring his pardon for a fault which she had not with her will committed, as Onahal, who was also prostrate with her, could testify; that unknown to her, he had broke into her apartment, and ravished her. She spoke this much against her conscience, but to save her own life 'twas absolutely necessary she should feign this falsity. She knew it could not injure the Prince, he being fled to an army that would stand by him against any injuries that should assault him. However, this last thought of Imoinda's being ravished changed the measures of his revenge; and whereas before he designed to be himself her executioner, he now resolved she should not die. But as it is the greatest crime in nature amongst 'em to touch a woman after having been possessed by a son, a father, or a brother, so now he looked on Imoinda as a polluted thing, wholly unfit for his embrace; nor would he resign her to his grandson, because she had received the royal veil. He therefore removes her from the Otan, with Onahal; whom he put into safe hands, with order they should be both sold off as slaves to another country, either Christian or heathen; 'twas no matter where.

This cruel sentence, worse than death, they implored might be reversed; but their prayers were vain, and it was put in execution accordingly, and that with so much secrecy that none, either without or within the Otan, knew anything of their absence or their destiny.

The old king, nevertheless, executed this with a great deal of reluctancy; but he believed he had made a very great conquest over himself, when he had once resolved, and had performed what he resolved. He believed now that his love had been unjust, and that he could not expect the gods, or Captain of the Clouds (as they call the unknown power), should suffer a better consequence from so ill a cause. He now begins to hold Oroonoko excused, and to say he had reason for what he did. And now everybody could assure the King how passionately Imoinda was beloved by the Prince; even those confessed it now, who said the contrary before his flame was abated. So that the King being old, and not able to defend himself in war, and having no sons of all his race remaining alive but only this, to maintain him on his throne; and looking on this as a man disobliged, first by the rape of his mistress, or rather wife; and now by depriving of him wholly of her, he feared, might make him desperate and do some cruel thing, either to himself or his old grandfather, the offender: he began to repent him extremely of the contempt he had, in his rage, put on Imoinda. Besides, he considered he ought in honor to have killed her for this offense, if it had been one. He ought to have had so much value and consideration for a maid of her quality as to have nobly put her to death, and not to have sold her like a common slave, the greatest revenge and the most disgraceful of any; and to which they a thousand times prefer death, and implore it, as Imoinda did, but could not obtain that honor. Seeing therefore it was certain that Oroonoko would highly resent this affront, he thought good to make some excuse for his rashness to him; and to that end he sent a messenger to the camp, with orders to treat with him about the matter, to gain his pardon, and to endeavor to mitigate his grief; but that by no means he should tell him she was sold, but secretly put to death, for he knew he should never obtain his pardon for the other.

When the messenger came, he found the Prince upon the point of engaging with the enemy; but as soon as he heard of the arrival of the messenger, he commanded him to his tent, where he embraced him and received him with joy; which was soon abated by the downcast looks of the messenger, who was instantly demanded the cause by Oroonoko, who, impatient of delay, asked a thousand questions in a breath, and all concerning Imoinda. But there needed little return, for he could almost answer himself of all he demanded, from his sighs and eyes. At last, the messenger casting himself at the Prince's feet, and kissing them with all the submission of a man that had something to implore which he dreaded to utter, he besought him to hear with calmness what he had to deliver to him, and to call up all his noble and heroic courage to encounter with his words, and defend himself against the ungrateful[7] things he must relate. Oroonoko replied, with a deep sigh and a languishing voice, "I am armed against their worst efforts—; for I know they will tell me, Imoinda is no more—and after that, you may spare the rest." Then, commanding him to rise, he laid himself on a carpet, under a rich pavilion, and remained a good while silent, and was hardly heard to sigh. When he was come a little to himself, the messenger asked him leave to deliver that part of his embassy which the Prince had not yet divined. And the Prince cried, "I permit thee—." Then he told him the affliction the old king was in, for the rashness he had committed in his cruelty to Imoinda; and how he deigned to ask pardon for his offense, and to implore the Prince would not suffer that loss to touch his heart too sensibly, which now all the gods could not restore him, but might recompense him in glory, which he begged he would pursue; and that Death, that common revenger of all injuries, would soon even the account between him and a feeble old man.

Oroonoko bade him return his duty to his lord and master, and to assure him, there was no account of revenge to be adjusted between them; if there were, 'twas he was the aggressor, and that Death would be just and, maugre[8] his age, would see him righted; and he was contented to leave his share of glory to youths more fortunate and worthy of that favor from the gods. That henceforth he would never lift a weapon or draw a bow, but abandon the small remains of his life to sighs and tears, and the continual thoughts of what his lord and grandfather had thought good to send out of the world, with all that youth, that innocence, and beauty.

After having spoken this, whatever his greatest officers and men of the best rank could do, they could not raise him from the carpet, or persuade him to action and resolutions of life; but commanding all to retire, he shut himself into his pavilion all that day, while the enemy was ready to engage; and wondering at the delay, the whole body of the chief of the army then addressed themselves to him, and to whom they had much ado to get admittance. They fell on their faces at the foot of his carpet, where they lay and besought him with earnest prayers and tears to lead 'em forth to battle, and not let the enemy take advantages of them; and implored him to have regard to his glory, and to the world, that depended on his courage and conduct. But he made no

---

7. Offensive.
8. In spite of. Oroonoko is saying that he will die before the king does.

other reply to all their supplications but this, that he had now no more business for glory; and for the world, it was a trifle not worth his care. "Go," continued he, sighing, "and divide it amongst you; and reap with joy what you so vainly prize, and leave me to my more welcome destiny."

They then demanded what they should do, and whom he would constitute in his room, that the confusion of ambitious youth and power might not ruin their order and make them a prey to the enemy. He replied, he would not give himself the trouble—; but wished 'em to choose the bravest man amongst 'em, let his quality or birth be what it would. "For, O my friends!" said he, "it is not titles make men brave or good, or birth that bestows courage and generosity, or makes the owner happy. Believe this, when you behold Oroonoko, the most wretched and abandoned by fortune of all the creation of the gods." So turning himself about, he would make no more reply to all they could urge or implore.

The army, beholding their officers return unsuccessful, with sad faces and ominous looks that presaged no good luck, suffered a thousand fears to take possession of their hearts, and the enemy to come even upon 'em, before they would provide for their safety by any defense; and though they were assured by some, who had a mind to animate 'em, that they should be immediately headed by the Prince, and that in the meantime Aboan had orders to command as general, yet they were so dismayed for want of that great example of bravery that they could make but a very feeble resistance; and at last downright fled before the enemy, who pursued 'em to the very tents, killing 'em. Nor could all Aboan's courage, which that day gained him immortal glory, shame 'em into a manly defense of themselves. The guards that were left behind about the Prince's tent, seeing the soldiers flee before the enemy and scatter themselves all over the plain, in great disorder, made such outcries as roused the Prince from his amorous slumber, in which he had remained buried for two days without permitting any sustenance to approach him. But in spite of all his resolutions, he had not the constancy of grief to that degree, as to make him insensible of the danger of his army; and in that instant he leaped from his couch and cried, "—Come, if we must die, let us meet Death the noblest way; and 'twill be more like Oroonoko to encounter him at an army's head, opposing the torrent of a conquering foe, than lazily on a couch to wait his lingering pleasure, and die every moment by a thousand wrecking[9] thoughts; or be tamely taken by an enemy, and led a whining, lovesick slave to adorn the triumphs of Jamoan, that young victor, who already is entered beyond the limits I had prescribed him."

While he was speaking, he suffered his people to dress him for the field, and sallying out of his pavilion, with more life and vigor in his countenance than ever he showed, he appeared like some divine power descended to save his country from destruction; and his people had purposely put on him all things that might make him shine with most splendor, to strike a reverend awe into the beholders. He flew into the thickest of those that were pursuing his men, and being animated with despair, he fought as if he came on purpose to die, and did such things as will not be believed that human strength could perform, and such as soon inspired all the rest with new courage and new order. And now it was that they began to fight indeed, and so as if they would not be outdone even by their adored hero; who, turning the tide of the

9. Racking.

victory, changing absolutely the fate of the day, gained an entire conquest; and Oroonoko having the good fortune to single out Jamoan, he took him prisoner with his own hand, having wounded him almost to death.

This Jamoan afterwards became very dear to him, being a man very gallant and of excellent graces and fine parts; so that he never put him amongst the rank of captives, as they used to do, without distinction, for the common sale or market; but kept him in his own court, where he retained nothing of the prisoner but the name, and returned no more into his own country, so great an affection he took for Oroonoko; and by a thousand tales and adventures of love and gallantry flattered[1] his disease of melancholy and languishment, which I have often heard him say had certainly killed him, but for the conversation of this prince and Aboan, and the French governor he had from his childhood, of whom I have spoken before, and who was a man of admirable wit, great ingenuity and learning, all which he had infused into his young pupil. This Frenchman was banished out of his own country for some heretical notions he held, and though he was a man of very little religion, he had admirable morals and a brave soul.

After the total defeat of Jamoan's army, which all fled, or were left dead upon the place, they spent some time in the camp, Oroonoko choosing rather to remain a while there in his tents than enter into a palace or live in a court where he had so lately suffered so great a loss. The officers, therefore, who saw and knew his cause of discontent, invented all sorts of diversions and sports to entertain their prince; so that what with those amusements abroad and others at home, that is, within their tents, with the persuasions, arguments, and care of his friends and servants that he more peculiarly prized, he wore off in time a great part of that chagrin and torture of despair which the first efforts of Imoinda's death had given him. Insomuch as having received a thousand kind embassies from the King, and invitations to return to court, he obeyed, though with no little reluctancy; and when he did so, there was a visible change in him, and for a long time he was much more melancholy than before. But time lessens all extremes, and reduces 'em to mediums and unconcern; but no motives or beauties, though all endeavored it, could engage him in any sort of amour, though he had all the invitations to it, both from his own youth and others' ambitions and designs.

Oroonoko was no sooner returned from this last conquest, and received at court with all the joy and magnificence that could be expressed to a young victor, who was not only returned triumphant but beloved like a deity, when there arrived in the port an English ship.

This person[2] had often before been in these countries and was very well known to Oroonoko, with whom he had trafficked for slaves, and had used to do the same with his predecessors.

This commander was a man of a finer sort of address and conversation, better bred and more engaging than most of that sort of men are, so that he seemed rather never to have been bred out of a court than almost all his life at sea. This captain therefore was always better received at court than most of the traders to those countries were; and especially by Oroonoko, who was more civilized, according to the European mode, than any other had been, and took more delight in the white nations, and above all men of parts and

---

1. Soothed.   2. The ship's captain.

wit. To this captain he sold abundance of his slaves, and for the favor and esteem he had for him, made him many presents, and obliged him to stay at court as long as possibly he could. Which the captain seemed to take as a very great honor done him, entertaining the Prince every day with globes and maps, and mathematical discourses and instruments; eating, drinking, hunting, and living with him with so much familiarity that it was not to be doubted but he had gained very greatly upon the heart of this gallant young man. And the captain, in return of all these mighty favors, besought the Prince to honor his vessel with his presence, some day or other, to dinner, before he should set sail; which he condescended to accept, and appointed his day. The captain, on his part, failed not to have all things in a readiness, in the most magnificent order he could possibly. And the day being come, the captain in his boat, richly adorned with carpets and velvet cushions, rowed to the shore to receive the Prince, with another longboat where was placed all his music and trumpets, with which Oroonoko was extremely delighted; who met him on the shore attended by his French governor, Jamoan, Aboan, and about a hundred of the noblest of the youths of the court. And after they had first carried the Prince on board, the boats fetched the rest off; where they found a very splendid treat, with all sorts of fine wines, and were as well entertained as 'twas possible in such a place to be.

The Prince, having drunk hard of punch and several sorts of wine, as did all the rest (for great care was taken they should want nothing of that part of the entertainment), was very merry, and in great admiration of the ship, for he had never been in one before; so that he was curious of beholding every place where he decently might descend. The rest, no less curious, who were not quite overcome with drinking, rambled at their pleasure fore and aft, as their fancies guided 'em. So that the captain, who had well laid his design before, gave the word, and seized on all his guests; they clapping great irons suddenly on the Prince, when he was leaped down in the hold to view that part of the vessel, and locking him fast down, secured him. The same treachery was used to all the rest; and all in one instant, in several places of the ship, were lashed fast in irons, and betrayed to slavery. That great design over, they set all hands to work to hoise[3] sail; and with as treacherous and fair a wind, they made from the shore with this innocent and glorious prize, who thought of nothing less than such an entertainment.

Some have commended this act as brave in the captain; but I will spare my sense of it, and leave it to my reader to judge as he pleases.

It may be easily guessed in what manner the Prince resented this indignity, who may be best resembled to a lion taken in a toil; so he raged, so he struggled for liberty, but all in vain; and they had so wisely managed his fetters that he could not use a hand in his defense, to quit himself of a life that would by no means endure slavery, nor could he move from the place where he was tied to any solid part of the ship, against which he might have beat his head, and have finished his disgrace that way. So that being deprived of all other means, he resolved to perish for want of food. And pleased at last with that thought, and toiled and tired by rage and indignation, he laid himself down, and sullenly resolved upon dying, and refused all things that were brought him.

---

3. Hoist.

This did not a little vex the captain, and the more so because he found almost all of 'em of the same humor; so that the loss of so many brave slaves, so tall and goodly to behold, would have been very considerable. He therefore ordered one to go from him (for he would not be seen himself) to Oroonoko, and to assure him he was afflicted for having rashly done so unhospitable a deed, and which could not be now remedied, since they were far from shore; but since he resented it in so high a nature, he assured him he would revoke his resolution, and set both him and his friends ashore on the next land they should touch at; and of this the messenger gave him his oath, provided he would resolve to live. And Oroonoko, whose honor was such as he never had violated a word in his life himself, much less a solemn asseveration, believed in an instant what this man said, but replied, he expected for a confirmation of this to have his shameful fetters dismissed. This demand was carried to the captain, who returned him answer that the offense had been so great which he had put upon the Prince that he durst not trust him with liberty while he remained in the ship, for fear lest by a valor natural to him, and a revenge that would animate that valor, he might commit some outrage fatal to himself and the King his master, to whom his vessel did belong. To this Oroonoko replied, he would engage his honor to behave himself in all friendly order and manner, and obey the command of the captain, as he was lord of the King's vessel and general of those men under his command.

This was delivered to the still doubting captain, who could not resolve to trust a heathen, he said, upon his parole,[4] a man that had no sense or notion of the God that he worshipped. Oroonoko then replied, he was very sorry to hear that the captain pretended to the knowledge and worship of any gods who had taught him no better principles than not to credit as he would be credited; they told him the difference of their faith occasioned that distrust. For the captain had protested to him upon the word of a Christian, and sworn in the name of a great god, which if he should violate, he would expect eternal torment in the world to come. "Is that all the obligation he has to be just to his oath?" replied Oroonoko. "Let him know I swear by my honor; which to violate, would not only render me contemptible and despised by all brave and honest men, and so give myself perpetual pain, but it would be eternally offending and diseasing all mankind, harming, betraying, circumventing and outraging all men; but punishments hereafter are suffered by one's self, and the world takes no cognizances whether this god have revenged 'em or not, 'tis done so secretly and deferred so long. While the man of no honor suffers every moment the scorn and contempt of the honester world, and dies every day ignominiously in his fame, which is more valuable than life. I speak not this to move belief, but to show you how you mistake, when you imagine that he who will violate his honor will keep his word with his gods." So turning from him with a disdainful smile, he refused to answer him, when he urged him to know what answer he should carry back to his captain; so that he departed without saying any more.

The captain pondering and consulting what to do, it was concluded that nothing but Oroonoko's liberty would encourage any of the rest to eat, except the Frenchman, whom the captain could not pretend to keep prisoner, but only told him he was secured because he might act something in favor of the Prince, but that he should be freed as soon as they came to land. So that they

4. Word of honor.

concluded it wholly necessary to free the Prince from his irons, that he might show himself to the rest; that they might have an eye upon him, and that they could not fear a single man.

This being resolved, to make the obligation the greater, the captain himself went to Oroonoko; where after many compliments, and assurances of what he had already promised, he receiving from the Prince his parole and his hand for his good behavior, dismissed his irons and brought him to his own cabin; where after having treated and reposed him a while, for he had neither eat[5] nor slept in four days before, he besought him to visit those obstinate people in chains, who refused all manner of sustenance, and entreated him to oblige 'em to eat, and assure 'em of their liberty the first opportunity.

Oroonoko, who was too generous not to give credit to his words, showed himself to his people, who were transported with excess of joy at the sight of their darling prince, falling at his feet and kissing and embracing 'em, believing, as some divine oracle, all he assured 'em. But he besought 'em to bear their chains with that bravery that became those whom he had seen act so nobly in arms; and that they could not give him greater proofs of their love and friendship, since 'twas all the security the captain (his friend) could have, against the revenge, he said, they might possibly justly take for the injuries sustained by him. And they all with one accord assured him, they could not suffer enough, when it was for his repose and safety.

After this they no longer refused to eat, but took what was brought 'em, and were pleased with their captivity, since by it they hoped to redeem the Prince, who, all the rest of the voyage, was treated with all the respect due to his birth, though nothing could divert his melancholy; and he would often sigh for Imoinda, and think this a punishment due to his misfortune, in having left that noble maid behind him that fatal night, in the Otan, when he fled to the camp.

Possessed with a thousand thoughts of past joys with this fair young person, and a thousand griefs for her eternal loss, he endured a tedious voyage, and at last arrived at the mouth of the river of Surinam, a colony belonging to the King of England, and where they were to deliver some part of their slaves. There the merchants and gentlemen of the country going on board to demand those lots of slaves they had already agreed on, and, amongst those, the overseers of those plantations where I then chanced to be, the captain, who had given the word, ordered his men to bring up those noble slaves in fetters whom I have spoken of; and having put 'em some in one and some in other lots, with women and children (which they call pickaninnies), they sold 'em off as slaves to several merchants and gentlemen; not putting any two in one lot, because they would separate 'em far from each other, not daring to trust 'em together, lest rage and courage should put 'em upon contriving some great action, to the ruin of the colony.

Oroonoko was first seized on, and sold to our overseer, who had the first lot, with seventeen more of all sorts and sizes, but not one of quality with him. When he saw this, he found what they meant, for, as I said, he understood English pretty well; and being wholly unarmed and defenseless, so as it was in vain to make any resistance, he only beheld the captain with a look

5. The past form of *eat*.

all fierce and disdainful, upbraiding him with eyes that forced blushes on his guilty cheeks; he only cried, in passing over the side of the ship, "Farewell, sir. 'Tis worth my suffering, to gain so true a knowledge both of you and of your gods by whom you swear." And desiring those that held him to forbear their pains, and telling 'em he would make no resistance, he cried, "Come, my fellow slaves; let us descend, and see if we can meet with more honor and honesty in the next world we shall touch upon." So he nimbly leaped into the boat, and showing no more concern, suffered himself to be rowed up the river with his seventeen companions.

The gentleman that bought him was a young Cornish gentleman whose name was Trefry, a man of great wit and fine learning, and was carried into those parts by the Lord——, Governor,[6] to manage all his affairs. He reflecting on the last words of Oroonoko to the captain, and beholding the richness of his vest,[7] no sooner came into the boat but he fixed his eyes on him; and finding something so extraordinary in his face, his shape and mien, a greatness of look and haughtiness in his air, and finding he spoke English, had a great mind to be inquiring into his quality and fortune; which, though Oroonoko endeavored to hide, by only confessing he was above the rank of common slaves, Trefry soon found he was yet something greater than he confessed, and from that moment began to conceive so vast an esteem for him that he ever after loved him as his dearest brother, and showed him all the civilities due to so great a man.

Trefry was a very good mathematician and a linguist, could speak French and Spanish; and in the three days they remained in the boat (for so long were they going from the ship to the plantation) he entertained Oroonoko so agreeably with his art and discourse, that he was no less pleased with Trefry than he was with the Prince; and he thought himself at least fortunate in this, that since he was a slave, as long as he would suffer himself to remain so, he had a man of so excellent wit and parts for a master. So that before they had finished their voyage up the river, he made no scruple of declaring to Trefry all his fortunes, and most part of what I have here related, and put himself wholly into the hands of his new friend, whom he found resenting all the injuries were done him, and was charmed with all the greatness of his actions; which were recited with that modesty and delicate sense as wholly vanquished him, and subdued him to his interest. And he promised him on his word and honor, he would find the means to reconduct him to his own country again, assuring him, he had a perfect abhorrence of so dishonorable an action, and that he would sooner have died than have been the author of such a perfidy. He found the Prince was very much concerned to know what became of his friends, and how they took their slavery; and Trefry promised to take care about the inquiring after their condition, and that he should have an account of 'em.

Though, as Oroonoko afterwards said, he had little reason to credit the words of a *backearary*,[8] yet he knew not why, but he saw a kind of sincerity and awful truth in the face of Trefry; he saw an honesty in his eyes, and he found him wise and witty enough to understand honor; for it was one of his maxims, a man of wit could not be a knave or villain.

---

6. Lord Willoughby of Parham, coproprietor of Surinam by royal grant. John Treffry was his plantation overseer.
7. An outer garment or robe.

8. White person or master; a variant of *backra*, from an Ibo word transported with the slaves to Surinam and the Caribbean.

In their passage up the river they put in at several houses for refreshment, and ever when they landed, numbers of people would flock to behold this man; not but their eyes were daily entertained with the sight of slaves, but the fame of Oroonoko was gone before him, and all people were in admiration of his beauty. Besides, he had a rich habit on, in which he was taken, so different from the rest, and which the captain could not strip him of, because he was forced to surprise his person in the minute he sold him. When he found his habit made him liable, as he thought, to be gazed at the more, he begged Trefry to give him something more befitting a slave, which he did, and took off his robes. Nevertheless, he shone through all; and his osenbrigs (a sort of brown holland[9] suit he had on) could not conceal the graces of his looks and mien, and he had no less admirers than when he had his dazzling habit on. The royal youth appeared in spite of the slave, and people could not help treating him after a different manner, without designing it. As soon as they approached him, they venerated and esteemed him; his eyes insensibly commanded respect, and his behavior insinuated it into every soul. So that there was nothing talked of but this young and gallant slave, even by those who yet knew not that he was a prince.

I ought to tell you that the Christians never buy any slaves but they give 'em some name of their own, their native ones being likely very barbarous and hard to pronounce; so that Mr. Trefry gave Oroonoko that of Caesar, which name will live in that country as long as that (scarce more) glorious one of the great Roman; for 'tis most evident, he wanted[1] no part of the personal courage of that Caesar, and acted things as memorable, had they been done in some part of the world replenished with people and historians that might have given him his due. But his misfortune was to fall in an obscure world, that afforded only a female pen to celebrate his fame; though I doubt not but it had lived from others' endeavors, if the Dutch, who immediately after his time took that country,[2] had not killed, banished, and dispersed all those that were capable of giving the world this great man's life, much better than I have done. And Mr. Trefry, who designed it, died before he began it, and bemoaned himself for not having undertook it in time.

For the future, therefore, I must call Oroonoko Caesar, since by that name only he was known in our western world, and by that name he was received on shore at Parham House, where he was destined a slave. But if the King himself (God bless him) had come ashore, there could not have been greater expectations by all the whole plantation, and those neighboring ones, than was on ours at that time; and he was received more like a governor than a slave. Notwithstanding, as the custom was, they assigned him his portion of land, his house, and his business, up in the plantation. But as it was more for form than any design to put him to his task, he endured no more of the slave but the name, and remained some days in the house, receiving all visits that were made him, without stirring towards that part of the plantation where the Negroes were.

At last he would needs go view his land, his house, and the business assigned him. But he no sooner came to the houses of the slaves, which are like a little town by itself, the Negroes all having left work, but they all came

9. Coarse cotton or linen, sometimes called osna-burg, after a German cloth-manufacturing town.
1. Lacked.

2. In 1667 the Dutch attacked and conquered Surinam, and England ceded it by treaty in exchange for New York.

forth to behold him, and found he was that prince who had, at several times, sold most of 'em to these parts; and from a veneration they pay to great men, especially if they know 'em, and from the surprise and awe they had at the sight of him, they all cast themselves at his feet, crying out in their language, "Live, O King! Long live, O King!" and kissing his feet, paid him even divine homage.

Several English gentlemen were with him; and what Mr. Trefry had told 'em was here confirmed, of which he himself before had no other witness than Caesar himself. But he was infinitely glad to find his grandeur confirmed by the adoration of all the slaves.

Caesar, troubled with their over-joy and over-ceremony, besought 'em to rise and to receive him as their fellow slave, assuring them he was no better. At which they set up with one accord a most terrible and hideous mourning and condoling, which he and the English had much ado to appease; but at last they prevailed with 'em, and they prepared all their barbarous music, and everyone killed and dressed something of his own stock (for every family has their land apart, on which, at their leisure times, they breed all eatable things), and clubbing it together,[3] made a most magnificent supper, inviting their *Grandee Captain,* their prince, to honor it with his presence; which he did, and several English with him; where they all waited on him, some playing, others dancing before him all the time, according to the manners of their several nations, and with unwearied industry endeavoring to please and delight him.

While they sat at meat Mr. Trefry told Caesar that most of these young slaves were undone in love with a fine she-slave, whom they had had about six months on their land. The Prince, who never heard the name of love without a sigh, nor any mention of it without the curiosity of examining further into that tale, which of all discourses was most agreeable to him, asked how they came to be so unhappy as to be all undone for one fair slave. Trefry, who was naturally amorous and loved to talk of love as well as anybody, proceeded to tell him, they had the most charming black that ever was beheld on their plantation, about fifteen or sixteen years old, as he guessed; that for his part, he had done nothing but sigh for her ever since she came, and that all the white beauties he had seen never charmed him so absolutely as this fine creature had done; and that no man, of any nation, ever beheld her that did not fall in love with her; and that she had all the slaves perpetually at her feet, and the whole country resounded with the fame of Clemene, "for so," said he, "we have christened her. But she denies us all with such a noble disdain, that 'tis a miracle to see that she, who can give such eternal desires, should herself be all ice and all unconcern. She is adorned with the most graceful modesty that ever beautified youth; the softest sigher—that, if she were capable of love, one would swear she languished for some absent happy man; and so retired, as if she feared a rape even from the god of day,[4] or that the breezes would steal kisses from her delicate mouth. Her task of work some sighing lover every day makes it his petition to perform for her, which she accepts blushing and with reluctance, for fear he will ask her a look for a recompense, which he dares not presume to hope, so great an awe she strikes into the hearts of her admirers." "I do not wonder," replied the Prince, "that Clemene should refuse slaves, being as you say so beautiful, but wonder how she escapes those who can entertain her as you can do; or why, being your slave, you do not oblige her to yield." "I confess," said Trefry, "when I have, against her will, entertained her with love so long as to be transported with my passion, even above decency, I have been ready to make use of those advantages of strength and force nature has given me. But oh! she disarms me with that modesty and weeping, so tender and so moving that I retire, and thank my stars she overcame me." The company laughed at his civility to a slave, and Caesar only applauded the nobleness of his passion and nature, since that slave might be noble or, what was better, have true notions of honor and virtue in her. Thus passed they this night, after having received from the slaves all imaginable respect and obedience.

The next day Trefry asked Caesar to walk, when the heat was allayed, and designedly carried him by the cottage of the fair slave, and told him she whom he spoke of last night lived there retired. "But," says he, "I would not wish you to approach, for I am sure you will be in love as soon as you behold her." Caesar assured him he was proof against all the charms of that sex, and that if he imagined his heart could be so perfidious to love again, after Imoinda, he believed he should tear it from his bosom. They had no sooner spoke, but a little shock dog⁵ that Clemene had presented her, which she took great delight in, ran out; and she, not knowing anybody was there, ran to get it in again, and bolted out on those who were just speaking of her. When seeing them, she would have run in again, but Trefry caught her by the hand and cried, "Clemene, however you fly a lover, you ought to pay some respect to this stranger" (pointing to Caesar). But she, as if she had resolved never to raise her eyes to the face of a man again, bent 'em the more to the earth when he spoke, and gave the Prince the leisure to look the more at her. There needed no long gazing or consideration to examine who this fair creature was; he soon saw Imoinda all over her; in a minute he saw her face, her shape, her air, her modesty, and all that called forth his soul with joy at his eyes, and left his body destitute of almost life; it stood without motion, and for a minute knew not that it had a being; and I believe he had never come to himself, so oppressed he was with over-joy, if he had not met with this allay, that he perceived Imoinda fall dead in the hands of Trefry. This awakened him, and he ran to her aid and caught her in his arms, where by degrees she came to herself; and 'tis needless to tell with what transports, what ecstasies of joy, they both a while beheld each other, without speaking; then snatched each other to their arms; then gaze again, as if they still doubted whether they possessed the blessing they grasped; but when they recovered their speech, 'tis not to be imagined what tender things they expressed to each other, wondering what strange fate had brought 'em again together. They soon informed each other of their fortunes, and equally bewailed their fate; but at the same time they mutually protested that even fetters and slavery were soft and easy, and would be supported with joy and pleasure, while they could be so happy to possess each other and to be able to make good their vows. Caesar swore he disdained the empire of the world while he could behold his Imoinda; and she despised grandeur and pomp, those vanities of her sex, when she could gaze on Oroonoko. He adored the very cottage where she resided, and

5. A long-haired dog or poodle, especially associated with women of fashion.

said that little inch of the world would give him more happiness than all the universe could do; and she vowed it was a palace, while adorned with the presence of Oroonoko.

Trefry was infinitely pleased with this novel,[6] and found this Clemene was the fair mistress of whom Caesar had before spoke; and was not a little satisfied that heaven was so kind to the Prince as to sweeten his misfortunes by so lucky an accident; and leaving the lovers to themselves, was impatient to come down to Parham House (which was on the same plantation) to give me an account of what had happened. I was as impatient to make these lovers a visit, having already made a friendship with Caesar, and from his own mouth learned what I have related; which was confirmed by his Frenchman, who was set on shore to seek his fortunes, and of whom they could not make a slave, because a Christian, and he came daily to Parham Hill to see and pay his respects to his pupil prince. So that concerning and interesting myself in all that related to Caesar, whom I had assured of liberty as soon as the Governor arrived, I hasted presently to the place where the lovers were, and was infinitely glad to find this beautiful young slave (who had already gained all our esteems, for her modesty and her extraordinary prettiness) to be the same I had heard Caesar speak so much of. One may imagine then we paid her a treble respect; and though, from her being carved in fine flowers and birds all over her body, we took her to be of quality before, yet when we knew Clemene was Imoinda, we could not enough admire her.

I had forgot to tell you that those who are nobly born of that country are so delicately cut and rased[7] all over the forepart of the trunk of their bodies, that it looks as if it were japanned, the works being raised like high point round the edges of the flowers. Some are only carved with a little flower or bird at the sides of the temples, as was Caesar; and those who are so carved over the body resemble our ancient Picts,[8] that are figured in the chronicles, but these carvings are more delicate.

From that happy day Caesar took Clemene for his wife, to the general joy of all people; and there was as much magnificence as the country would afford at the celebration of this wedding: and in a very short time after she conceived with child, which made Caesar even adore her, knowing he was the last of his great race. This new accident made him more impatient of liberty, and he was every day treating with Trefry for his and Clemene's liberty, and offered either gold or a vast quantity of slaves, which should be paid before they let him go, provided he could have any security that he should go when his ransom was paid. They fed him from day to day with promises, and delayed him till the Lord Governor should come; so that he began to suspect them of falsehood, and that they would delay him till the time of his wife's delivery and make a slave of that too, for all the breed is theirs to whom the parents belong. This thought made him very uneasy, and his sullenness gave them some jealousies[9] of him; so that I was obliged, by some persons who feared a mutiny (which is very fatal sometimes in those colonies, that abound so with slaves that they exceed the whites in vast numbers), to discourse with Caesar, and to give him all the satisfaction I possibly could; they knew he and Clemene were scarce an hour in a day from my

---

6. I.e., novel event or piece of news.
7. Incised. The carving is likened to figured lacquerwork in the Japanese style and to elaborate "high point" lace.
8. A North British people appearing in histories of England and Scotland.
9. Suspicions.

lodgings, that they eat with me, and that I obliged 'em in all things I was capable of. I entertained him with the lives of the Romans, and great men, which charmed him to my company, and her with teaching her all the pretty works[1] that I was mistress of, and telling her stories of nuns, and endeavoring to bring her to the knowledge of the true God. But of all discourses Caesar liked that the worst, and would never be reconciled to our notions of the Trinity, of which he ever made a jest; it was a riddle, he said, would turn his brain to conceive, and one could not make him understand what faith was. However, these conversations failed not altogether so well to divert him that he liked the company of us women much above the men, for he could not drink, and he is but an ill companion in that country that cannot. So that obliging him to love us very well, we had all the liberty of speech with him, especially myself, whom he called his Great Mistress; and indeed my word would go a great way with him. For these reasons, I had opportunity to take notice to him that he was not well pleased of late as he used to be; was more retired and thoughtful; and told him I took it ill he should suspect we would break our words with him, and not permit both him and Clemene to return to his own kingdom, which was not so long a way but when he was once on his voyage he would quickly arrive there. He made me some answers that showed a doubt in him, which made me ask him what advantage it would be to doubt. It would but give us a fear of him, and possibly compel us to treat him so as I should be very loath to behold; that is, it might occasion his confinement. Perhaps this was not so luckily spoke of me, for I perceived he resented that word, which I strove to soften again in vain. However, he assured me that whatsoever resolutions he should take, he would act nothing upon the white people; and as for myself and those upon that plantation where he was, he would sooner forfeit his eternal liberty, and life itself, than lift his hand against his greatest enemy on that place. He besought me to suffer no fears upon his account, for he could do nothing that honor should not dictate; but he accused himself for having suffered slavery so long; yet he charged that weakness on Love alone, who was capable of making him neglect even glory itself, and for which now he reproaches himself every moment of the day. Much more to this effect he spoke, with an air impatient enough to make me know he would not be long in bondage; and though he suffered only the name of a slave, and had nothing of the toil and labor of one, yet that was sufficient to render him uneasy; and he had been too long idle, who used to be always in action and in arms. He had a spirit all rough and fierce, and that could not be tamed to lazy rest; and though all endeavors were used to exercise himself in such actions and sports as this world afforded, as running, wrestling, pitching the bar, hunting and fishing, chasing and killing tigers of a monstrous size, which this continent affords in abundance, and wonderful snakes, such as Alexander is reported to have encountered at the river of Amazons,[2] and which Caesar took great delight to overcome, yet these were not actions great enough for his large soul, which was still panting after more renowned action.

Before I parted that day with him, I got, with much ado, a promise from him to rest yet a little longer with patience, and wait the coming of the Lord

---

1. Decorative needlework or other handiwork.
2. Alexander the Great is supposed to have encountered both snakes and Amazons in a campaign against India. "Pitching the bar": game in which players compete in throwing a heavy bar or rod. "Tigers": wild cats, including the South American jaguar and cougar.

Governor, who was every day expected on our shore; he assured me he would, and this promise he desired me to know was given perfectly in complaisance to me, in whom he had an entire confidence.

After this, I neither thought it convenient to trust him much out of our view, nor did the country, who feared him; but with one accord it was advised to treat him fairly, and oblige him to remain within such a compass, and that he should be permitted as seldom as could be to go up to the plantations of the Negroes or, if he did, to be accompanied by some that should be rather in appearance attendants than spies. This care was for some time taken, and Caesar looked upon it as a mark of extraordinary respect, and was glad his discontent had obliged 'em to be more observant to him. He received new assurance from the overseer, which was confirmed to him by the opinion of all the gentlemen of the country, who made their court to him. During this time that we had his company more frequently than hitherto we had had, it may not be unpleasant to relate to you the diversions we entertained him with, or rather he us.

My stay was to be short in that country, because my father died at sea, and never arrived to possess the honor was designed him (which was lieutenant general of six and thirty islands, besides the continent[3] of Surinam) nor the advantages he hoped to reap by them; so that though we were obliged to continue on our voyage, we did not intend to stay upon the place. Though, in a word, I must say thus much of it, that certainly had his late Majesty, of sacred memory, but seen and known what a vast and charming world he had been master of in that continent, he would never have parted so easily with it to the Dutch. 'Tis a continent whose vast extent was never yet known, and may contain more noble earth than all the universe besides, for, they say, it reaches from east to west, one way as far as China and another to Peru. It affords all things both for beauty and use; 'tis there eternal spring, always the very months of April, May, and June; the shades are perpetual, the trees bearing at once all degrees of leaves and fruit, from blooming buds to ripe autumn: groves of oranges, lemons, citrons, figs, nutmegs, and noble aromatics, continually bearing their fragrancies. The trees appearing all like nosegays adorned with flowers of different kinds; some are all white, some purple, some scarlet, some blue, some yellow; bearing, at the same time, ripe fruit and blooming young, or producing every day new. The very wood of all these trees has an intrinsic value above common timber, for they are, when cut, of different colors, glorious to behold, and bear a price considerable, to inlay withal. Besides this they yield rich balm and gums, so that we make our candles of such an aromatic substance as does not only give a sufficient light, but, as they burn, they cast their perfumes all about. Cedar is the common firing, and all the houses are built with it. The very meat we eat, when set on the table, if it be native, I mean of the country, perfumes the whole room; especially a little beast called an armadilly, a thing which I can liken to nothing so well as a rhinoceros; 'tis all in white armor, so jointed that it moves as well in it as if it had nothing on; this beast is about the bigness of a pig of six weeks old. But it were endless to give an account of all the diverse wonderful and strange things that country affords, and which we took a very great delight to go in search of, though those adventures are often-

3. "Land not disjoined by the sea from other lands" (Johnson's *Dictionary*).

times fatal and at least dangerous. But while we had Caesar in our company on these designs we feared no harm, nor suffered any.

As soon as I came into the country, the best house in it was presented me, called St. John's Hill. It stood on a vast rock of white marble, at the foot of which the river ran a vast depth down, and not to be descended on that side; the little waves still dashing and washing the foot of this rock made the softest murmurs and purlings in the world; and the opposite bank was adorned with such vast quantities of different flowers eternally blowing,[4] and every day and hour new, fenced behind 'em with lofty trees of a thousand rare forms and colors, that the prospect was the most ravishing that fancy can create. On the edge of this white rock, towards the river, was a walk or grove of orange and lemon trees, about half the length of the Mall[5] here, whose flowery and fruit-bearing branches met at the top and hindered the sun, whose rays are very fierce there, from entering a beam into the grove; and the cool air that came from the river made it not only fit to entertain people in, at all the hottest hours of the day, but refreshed the sweet blossoms and made it always sweet and charming; and sure the whole globe of the world cannot show so delightful a place as this grove was. Not all the gardens of boasted Italy can produce a shade to outvie this, which nature had joined with art to render so exceeding fine; and 'tis a marvel to see how such vast trees, as big as English oaks, could take footing on so solid a rock and in so little earth as covered that rock; but all things by nature there are rare, delightful, and wonderful. But to our sports.

Sometimes we would go surprising,[6] and in search of young tigers in their dens, watching when the old ones went forth to forage for prey; and oftentimes we have been in great danger and have fled apace for our lives when surprised by the dams. But once, above all other times, we went on this design, and Caesar was with us, who had no sooner stolen a young tiger from her nest but, going off, we encountered the dam, bearing a buttock of a cow which he[7] had torn off with his mighty paw, and going with it towards his den. We had only four women, Caesar, and an English gentleman, brother to Harry Martin, the great Oliverian;[8] we found there was no escaping this enraged and ravenous beast. However, we women fled as fast as we could from it; but our heels had not saved our lives if Caesar had not laid down his cub, when he found the tiger quit her prey to make the more speed towards him, and taking Mr. Martin's sword, desired him to stand aside, or follow the ladies. He obeyed him, and Caesar met this monstrous beast of might, size, and vast limbs, who came with open jaws upon him; and fixing his awful stern eyes full upon those of the beast, and putting himself into a very steady and good aiming posture of defense, ran his sword quite through his breast down to his very heart, home to the hilt of the sword. The dying beast stretched forth her paw, and going to grasp his thigh, surprised with death in that very moment, did him no other harm than fixing her long nails in his flesh very deep, feebly wounded him, but could not grasp the flesh to tear off any. When he had done this, he hallooed to us to return, which, after some assurance of his victory, we did, and

4. Blooming.
5. Fashionable walk in St. James's Park in London.
6. A military term for making sudden raids.
7. The jarring mixture of pronouns in the two accounts of the tigers (wild cats) may suggest a reluctance to use a feminine pronoun in moments of extreme violence. The first account was left uncorrected in all four 17th-century editions.
8. Supporter of Oliver Cromwell.

found him lugging out the sword from the bosom of the tiger, who was laid in her blood on the ground; he took up the cub, and with an unconcern that had nothing of the joy or gladness of a victory, he came and laid the whelp at my feet. We all extremely wondered at his daring, and at the bigness of the beast, which was about the heighth of a heifer but of mighty, great, and strong limbs.

Another time, being in the woods, he killed a tiger which had long infested that part, and borne away abundance of sheep and oxen, and other things that were for the support of those to whom they belonged; abundance of people assailed this beast, some affirming they had shot her with several bullets quite through the body at several times, and some swearing they shot her through the very heart, and they believed she was a devil rather than a mortal thing. Caesar had often said he had a mind to encounter this monster, and spoke with several gentlemen who had attempted her, one crying, "I shot her with so many poisoned arrows," another with his gun in this part of her, and another in that; so that he, remarking all these places where she was shot, fancied still he should overcome her by giving her another sort of a wound than any had yet done; and one day said (at the table), "What trophies and garlands, ladies, will you make me, if I bring you home the heart of this ravenous beast that eats up all your lambs and pigs?" We all promised he should be rewarded at all our hands. So taking a bow, which he choosed out of a great many, he went up in the wood, with two gentlemen, where he imagined this devourer to be; they had not passed very far in it but they heard her voice, growling and grumbling, as if she were pleased with something she was doing. When they came in view, they found her muzzling in the belly of a new ravished sheep, which she had torn open; and seeing herself approached, she took fast hold of her prey with her forepaws and set a very fierce raging look on Caesar, without offering to approach him, for fear at the same time of losing what she had in possession. So that Caesar remained a good while, only taking aim, and getting an opportunity to shoot her where he designed; 'twas some time before he could accomplish it, and to wound her and not kill her would but have enraged her more, and endangered him. He had a quiver of arrows at his side, so that if one failed he could be supplied; at last, retiring a little, he gave her opportunity to eat, for he found she was ravenous, and fell to as soon as she saw him retire, being more eager of her prey than of doing new mischiefs. When he going softly to one side of her, and hiding his person behind certain herbage that grew high and thick, he took so good aim that, as he intended, he shot her just into the eye, and the arrow was sent with so good a will and so sure a hand that it stuck in her brain, and made her caper and become mad for a moment or two; but being seconded by another arrow, he fell dead upon the prey. Caesar cut him open with a knife, to see where those wounds were that had been reported to him, and why he did not die of 'em. But I shall now relate a thing that possibly will find no credit among men, because 'tis a notion commonly received with us, that nothing can receive a wound in the heart and live; but when the heart of this courageous animal was taken out, there were seven bullets of lead in it, and the wounds seamed up with great scars, and she lived with the bullets a great while, for it was long since they were shot. This heart the conqueror brought up to us, and 'twas a very great curiosity, which all the country came to see, and which gave Caesar occasion of many fine discourses, of accidents in war and strange escapes.

At other times he would go a-fishing; and discoursing on that diversion, he found we had in that country a very strange fish, called a numb eel[9] (an eel of which I have eaten), that while it is alive, it has a quality so cold, that those who are angling, though with a line of never so great a length with a rod at the end of it, it shall, in the same minute the bait is touched by this eel, seize him or her that holds the rod with benumbedness, that shall deprive 'em of sense for a while; and some have fallen into the water, and others dropped as dead on the banks of the rivers where they stood, as soon as this fish touches the bait. Caesar used to laugh at this, and believed it impossible a man could lose his force at the touch of a fish, and could not understand that philoso-phy,[1] that a cold quality should be of that nature. However, he had a great curiosity to try whether it would have the same effect on him it had on others, and often tried, but in vain. At last the sought for fish came to the bait, as he stood angling on the bank; and instead of throwing away the rod or giving it a sudden twitch out of the water, whereby he might have caught both the eel and have dismissed the rod, before it could have too much power over him, for experiment sake he grasped it but the harder, and faint-ing fell into the river; and being still possessed of the rod, the tide carried him, senseless as he was, a great way, till an Indian boat took him up, and perceived when they touched him a numbness seize them, and by that knew the rod was in his hand; which with a paddle (that is, a short oar) they struck away, and snatched it into the boat, eel and all. If Caesar were almost dead with the effect of this fish, he was more so with that of the water, where he had remained the space of going a league, and they found they had much ado to bring him back to life. But at last they did, and brought him home, where he was in a few hours well recovered and refreshed, and not a little ashamed to find he should be overcome by an eel, and that all the people who heard his defiance would laugh at him. But we cheered him up; and he being convinced, we had the eel at supper, which was a quarter of an ell about and most deli-cate meat, and was of the more value, since it cost so dear as almost the life of so gallant a man.

About this time we were in many mortal fears about some disputes the English had with the Indians, so that we could scarce trust ourselves, without great numbers, to go to any Indian towns or place where they abode, for fear they should fall upon us, as they did immediately after my coming away; and that it was in the possession of the Dutch, who used 'em not so civilly as the English, so that they cut in pieces all they could take, getting into houses and hanging up the mother and all her children about her, and cut a footman I left behind me all in joints, and nailed him to trees.

This feud began while I was there, so that I lost half the satisfaction I proposed, in not seeing and visiting the Indian towns. But one day, bemoan-ing of our misfortunes upon this account, Caesar told us we need not fear, for if we had a mind to go, he would undertake to be our guard. Some would, but most would not venture; about eighteen of us resolved and took barge, and after eight days arrived near an Indian town. But approaching it, the hearts of some of our company failed, and they would not venture on shore; so we polled who would and who would not. For my part, I said if Caesar

9. Electric eel.
1. "Hypothesis or system upon which natural effects are explained" (Johnson's *Dictionary*).

would, I would go; he resolved; so did my brother and my woman, a maid of good courage. Now none of us speaking the language of the people, and imagining we should have a half diversion in gazing only and not knowing what they said, we took a fisherman that lived at the mouth of the river, who had been a long inhabitant there, and obliged him to go with us. But because he was known to the Indians, as trading among 'em, and being by long living there become a perfect Indian in color, we, who resolved to surprise 'em by making 'em see something they never had seen (that is, white people), resolved only myself, my brother and woman should go; so Caesar, the fisherman, and the rest, hiding behind some thick reeds and flowers that grew on the banks, let us pass on towards the town, which was on the bank of the river all along. A little distant from the houses, or huts, we saw some dancing, others busied in fetching and carrying of water from the river. They had no sooner spied us but they set up a loud cry, that frighted us at first; we thought it had been for those that should kill us, but it seems it was of wonder and amazement. They were all naked, and we were dressed so as is most commode for the hot countries, very glittering and rich, so that we appeared extremely fine; my own hair was cut short, and I had a taffety cap with black feathers on my head; my brother was in a stuff[2] suit, with silver loops and buttons and abundance of green ribbon. This was all infinitely surprising to them, and because we saw them stand still till we approached 'em, we took heart and advanced, came up to 'em, and offered 'em our hands; which they took, and looked on us round about, calling still for more company; who came swarming out, all wondering and crying out *"Tepeeme,"* taking their hair up in their hands and spreading it wide to those they called out to, as if they would say (as indeed it signified) "Numberless wonders," or not to be recounted, no more than to number the hair of their heads. By degrees they grew more bold, and from gazing upon us round, they touched us, laying their hands upon all the features of our faces, feeling our breasts and arms, taking up one petticoat, then wondering to see another; admiring our shoes and stockings, but more our garters, which we gave 'em, and they tied about their legs, being laced with silver lace at the ends, for they much esteem any shining things. In fine, we suffered 'em to survey us as they pleased, and we thought they would never have done admiring us. When Caesar and the rest saw we were received with such wonder, they came up to us; and finding the Indian trader whom they knew (for 'tis by these fishermen, called Indian traders, we hold a commerce with 'em, for they love not to go far from home, and we never go to them), when they saw him therefore they set up a new joy, and cried, in their language, "Oh! here's our *tiguamy,* and we shall now know whether those things can speak." So advancing to him, some of 'em gave him their hands and cried, *"Amora tiguamy,"* which is as much as, "How do you?" or "Welcome, friend," and all with one din began to gabble to him, and asked if we had sense and wit; if we could talk of affairs of life and war, as they could do; if we could hunt, swim, and do a thousand things they use. He answered 'em, we could. Then they invited us into their houses, and dressed venison and buffalo for us; and going out, gathered a leaf of a tree called a *sarumbo* leaf, of six yards long, and spread it on the ground for a tablecloth; and cutting another in pieces instead of plates, setting us on little

2. Woven fabric, worsted. "Commode": suitable.

bow Indian stools, which they cut out of one entire piece of wood and paint in a sort of japan work. They serve everyone their mess[3] on these pieces of leaves, and it was very good, but too high seasoned with pepper. When we had eat, my brother and I took out our flutes and played to 'em, which gave 'em new wonder; and I soon perceived, by an admiration that is natural to these people, and by the extreme ignorance and simplicity of 'em, it were not difficult to establish any unknown or extravagant religion among them, and to impose any notions or fictions upon 'em. For seeing a kinsman of mine set some paper afire with a burning glass, a trick they had never before seen, they were like to have adored him for a god, and begged he would give them the characters or figures of his name, that they might oppose it against winds and storms; which he did, and they held it up in those seasons, and fancied it had a charm to conquer them, and kept it like a holy relic. They are very superstitious, and called him the great *Peeie,* that is, prophet. They showed us their Indian *Peeie,* a youth of about sixteen years old, as handsome as nature could make a man. They consecrate a beautiful youth from his infancy, and all arts are used to complete him in the finest manner, both in beauty and shape. He is bred to all the little arts and cunning they are capable of, to all the legerdemain tricks and sleight of hand, whereby he imposes upon the rabble, and is both a doctor in physic[4] and divinity; and by these tricks makes the sick believe he sometimes eases their pains, by drawing from the afflicted part little serpents, or odd flies, or worms, or any strange thing; and though they have besides undoubted good remedies for almost all their diseases, they cure the patient more by fancy than by medicines, and make themselves feared, loved, and reverenced. This young *Peeie* had a very young wife, who seeing my brother kiss her, came running and kissed me; after this they kissed one another, and made it a very great jest, it being so novel; and new admiration and laughing went round the multitude, that they never will forget that ceremony, never before used or known. Caesar had a mind to see and talk with their war captains, and we were conducted to one of their houses, where we beheld several of the great captains, who had been at council. But so frightful a vision it was to see 'em no fancy can create; no such dreams can represent so dreadful a spectacle. For my part I took 'em for hobgoblins or fiends rather than men; but however their shapes appeared, their souls were very humane and noble; but some wanted their noses, some their lips, some both noses and lips, some their ears, and others cut through each cheek with long slashes, through which their teeth appeared; they had other several formidable wounds and scars, or rather dismemberings. They had *comitias* or little aprons before 'em, and girdles of cotton, with their knives naked, stuck in it; a bow at their backs and a quiver of arrows on their thighs; and most had feathers on their heads of diverse colors. They cried *"Amora tiguamy"* to us at our entrance, and were pleased we said as much to 'em; they seated us, and gave us drink of the best sort, and wondered, as much as the others had done before, to see us. Caesar was marveling as much at their faces, wondering how they should all be so wounded in war; he was impatient to know how they all came by those frightful marks of rage or malice, rather than wounds got in noble battle. They told us, by our interpreter, that when any war was waging, two men chosen out by some old captain whose fighting was past, and who could only

3. Meal.

4. Medicine.

teach the theory of war, these two men were to stand in competition for the generalship, or great war captain; and being brought before the old judges, now past labor, they are asked what they dare do to show they are worthy to lead an army. When he who is first asked, making no reply, cuts off his nose, and throws it contemptibly[5] on the ground; and the other does something to himself that he thinks surpasses him, and perhaps deprives himself of lips and an eye; so they slash on till one gives out, and many have died in this debate. And 'tis by a passive valor they show and prove their activity, a sort of courage too brutal to be applauded by our black hero; nevertheless he expressed his esteem of 'em.

In this voyage Caesar begot so good an understanding between the Indians and the English that there were no more fears or heart-burnings during our stay, but we had a perfect, open, and free trade with 'em. Many things remarkable and worthy reciting we met with in this short voyage, because Caesar made it his business to search out and provide for our entertainment, especially to please his dearly adored Imoinda, who was a sharer in all our adventures; we being resolved to make her chains as easy as we could, and to compliment the Prince in that manner that most obliged him.

As we were coming up again, we met with some Indians of strange aspects; that is, of a larger size and other sort of features than those of our country. Our Indian slaves that rowed us asked 'em some questions, but they could not understand us; but showed us a long cotton string with several knots on it, and told us, they had been coming from the mountains so many moons as there were knots. They were habited in skins of a strange beast, and brought along with 'em bags of gold dust, which, as well as they could give us to understand, came streaming in little small channels down the high mountains when the rains fell; and offered to be the convoy to any body or persons that would go to the mountains. We carried these men up to Parham, where they were kept till the Lord Governor came. And because all the country was mad to be going on this golden adventure, the Governor by his letters commanded (for they sent some of the gold to him) that a guard should be set at the mouth of the river of Amazons[6] (a river so called, almost as broad as the river of Thames) and prohibited all people from going up that river, it conducting to those mountains of gold. But we going off for England before the project was further prosecuted, and the Governor being drowned in a hurricane, either the design died, or the Dutch have the advantage of it. And 'tis to be bemoaned what his Majesty lost by losing that part of America.

Though this digression is a little from my story, however since it contains some proofs of the curiosity and daring of this great man, I was content to omit nothing of his character.

It was thus for some time we diverted him; but now Imoinda began to show she was with child, and did nothing but sigh and weep for the captivity of her lord, herself, and the infant yet unborn, and believed if it were so hard to gain the liberty of two, 'twould be more difficult to get that for three. Her griefs were so many darts in the great heart of Caesar; and taking his opportunity one Sunday when all the whites were overtaken in drink, as there were abundance of several trades and slaves for four years[7] that

---

5. With contempt.
6. The mouth of the Amazon, in Brazil, is far distant from Surinam.

7. Whites who, for crimes or debt, were indentured for a fixed period. "Trades": tradesman.

inhabited among the Negro houses, and Sunday was their day of debauch (otherwise they were a sort of spies upon Caesar), he went pretending out of goodness to 'em to feast amongst 'em; and sent all his music, and ordered a great treat for the whole gang, about three hundred Negroes; and about a hundred and fifty were able to bear arms, such as they had, which were sufficient to do execution[8] with spirits accordingly. For the English had none but rusty swords that no strength could draw from a scabbard, except the people of particular quality, who took care to oil 'em and keep 'em in good order. The guns also, unless here and there one, or those newly carried from England, would do no good or harm; for 'tis the nature of that country to rust and eat up iron, or any metals but gold and silver. And they are very unexpert at the bow, which the Negroes and Indians are perfect masters of.

Caesar, having singled out these men from the women and children, made an harangue to 'em of the miseries and ignominies of slavery, counting up all their toils and sufferings, under such loads, burdens, and drudgeries as were fitter for beasts than men, senseless brutes than human souls. He told 'em, it was not for days, months, or years, but for eternity; there was no end to be of their misfortunes. They suffered not like men, who might find a glory and fortitude in oppression, but like dogs that loved the whip and bell,[9] and fawned the more they were beaten. That they had lost the divine quality of men and were become insensible asses, fit only to bear; nay, worse: an ass, or dog, or horse, having done his duty, could lie down in retreat and rise to work again, and while he did his duty endured no stripes; but men, villainous, senseless men such as they, toiled on all the tedious week till Black Friday;[1] and then, whether they worked or not, whether they were faulty or meriting, they promiscuously, the innocent with the guilty, suffered the infamous whip, the sordid stripes, from their fellow slaves, till their blood trickled from all parts of their body, blood whose every drop ought to be revenged with a life of some of those tyrants that impose it. "And why," said he, "my dear friends and fellow sufferers, should we be slaves to an unknown people? Have they vanquished us nobly in fight? Have they won us in honorable battle? And are we by the chance of war become their slaves? This would not anger a noble heart, this would not animate a soldier's soul; no, but we are bought and sold like apes or monkeys, to be the sport of women, fools, and cowards, and the support of rogues, runagades,[2] that have abandoned their own countries for rapine, murders, thefts, and villainies. Do you not hear every day how they upbraid each other with infamy of life, below the wildest savages; and shall we render obedience to such a degenerate race, who have no one human virtue left to distinguish 'em from the vilest creatures? Will you, I say, suffer the lash from such hands?" They all replied, with one accord, "No, no, no; Caesar has spoke like a great captain, like a great king."

After this he would have proceeded, but was interrupted by a tall Negro of some more quality than the rest; his name was Tuscan; who bowing at the feet of Caesar, cried, "My lord, we have listened with joy and attention to what you have said, and, were we only men, would follow so great a leader

---

8. Harm, slaughter.
9. Proverbial for something that distracts from comfort or pleasure, from the protective charm on chariots of triumphing generals in ancient Rome.

1. Here a day of customary beating; more widely, a Friday bringing some notable disaster, from students' slang for examination day.
2. Renegades or fugitives.

through the world. But oh! consider, we are husbands and parents too, and have things more dear to us than life, our wives and children, unfit for travel in these unpassable woods, mountains, and bogs; we have not only difficult lands to overcome, but rivers to wade, and monsters to encounter, ravenous beasts of prey—." To this, Caesar replied that honor was the first principle in nature that was to be obeyed; but as no man would pretend to that, without all the acts of virtue, compassion, charity, love, justice, and reason, he found it not inconsistent with that to take an equal care of their wives and children as they would of themselves; and that he did not design, when he led them to freedom and glorious liberty, that they should leave that better part of themselves to perish by the hand of the tyrant's whip. But if there were a woman among them so degenerate from love and virtue to choose slavery before the pursuit of her husband, and with the hazard of her life to share with him in his fortunes, that such a one ought to be abandoned, and left as a prey to the common enemy.

To which they all agreed—and bowed. After this, he spoke of the impassable woods and rivers, and convinced 'em, the more danger, the more glory. He told them that he had heard of one Hannibal, a great captain, had cut his way through mountains of solid rocks;[3] and should a few shrubs oppose them, which they could fire before 'em? No, 'twas a trifling excuse to men resolved to die or overcome. As for bogs, they are with a little labor filled and hardened; and the rivers could be no obstacle, since they swam by nature, at least by custom, from their first hour of their birth. That when the children were weary they must carry them by turns, and the woods and their own industry would afford them food. To this they all assented with joy.

Tuscan then demanded what he would do. He said, they would travel towards the sea, plant a new colony, and defend it by their valor; and when they could find a ship, either driven by stress of weather or guided by Providence that way, they would seize it and make it a prize, till it had transported them to their own countries; at least, they should be made free in his kingdom, and be esteemed as his fellow sufferers, and men that had the courage and the bravery to attempt, at least, for liberty; and if they died in the attempt it would be more brave than to live in perpetual slavery.

They bowed and kissed his feet at this resolution, and with one accord vowed to follow him to death. And that night was appointed to begin their march; they made it known to their wives, and directed them to tie their hamaca[4] about their shoulder and under their arm like a scarf, and to lead their children that could go, and carry those that could not. The wives, who pay an entire obedience to their husbands, obeyed, and stayed for 'em where they were appointed. The men stayed but to furnish themselves with what defensive arms they could get; and all met at the rendezvous, where Caesar made a new encouraging speech to 'em, and led 'em out.

But as they could not march far that night, on Monday early, when the overseers went to call 'em all together to go to work, they were extremely surprised to find not one upon the place, but all fled with what baggage they had. You may imagine this news was not only suddenly spread all over the plantation, but soon reached the neighboring ones; and we had by noon

---

3. The Carthaginian general and his troops literally hacked their way down the Alps into Italy   to attack Rome.
4. Hammock.

about six hundred men they call the militia of the county, that came to assist us in the pursuit of the fugitives. But never did one see so comical an army march forth to war. The men of any fashion would not concern themselves, though it were almost the common cause; for such revoltings are very ill examples, and have very fatal consequences oftentimes in many colonies. But they had a respect for Caesar, and all hands were against the Parhamites, as they called those of Parham plantation, because they did not, in the first place, love the Lord Governor, and secondly they would have it that Caesar was ill used, and baffled with;[5] and 'tis not impossible but some of the best in the country was of his counsel in this flight, and depriving us of all the slaves; so that they of the better sort would not meddle in the matter. The deputy governor,[6] of whom I have had no great occasion to speak, and who was the most fawning fair-tongued fellow in the world and one that pretended the most friendship to Caesar, was now the only violent man against him; and though he had nothing, and so need fear nothing, yet talked and looked bigger than any man. He was a fellow whose character is not fit to be mentioned with the worst of the slaves. This fellow would lead his army forth to meet Caesar, or rather to pursue him; most of their arms were of those sort of cruel whips they call cat with nine tails; some had rusty useless guns for show, others old basket hilts[7] whose blades had never seen the light in this age, and others had long staffs and clubs. Mr. Trefry went along, rather to be a mediator than a conqueror in such a battle; for he foresaw and knew, if by fighting they put the Negroes into despair, they were a sort of sullen fellows that would drown or kill themselves before they would yield; and he advised that fair means was best. But Byam was one that abounded in his own wit and would take his own measures.

It was not hard to find these fugitives; for as they fled they were forced to fire and cut the woods before 'em, so that night or day they pursued 'em by the light they made and by the path they had cleared. But as soon as Caesar found he was pursued, he put himself in a posture of defense, placing all the women and children in the rear, and himself with Tuscan by his side, or next to him, all promising to die or conquer. Encouraged thus, they never stood to parley, but fell on pell-mell upon the English, and killed some and wounded a good many, they having recourse to their whips as the best of their weapons. And as they observed no order, they perplexed the enemy so sorely with lashing 'em in the eyes; and the women and children seeing their husbands so treated, being of fearful cowardly dispositions, and hearing the English cry out, "Yield and live, yield and be pardoned," they all run in amongst their husbands and fathers, and hung about 'em, crying out, "Yield, yield; and leave Caesar to their revenge"; that by degrees the slaves abandoned Caesar, and left him only Tuscan and his heroic Imoinda; who, grown big as she was, did nevertheless press near her lord, having a bow and a quiver full of poisoned arrows, which she managed with such dexterity that she wounded several, and shot the governor[8] into the shoulder; of which wound he had like to have died, but that an Indian woman, his mistress, sucked the wound and cleansed it from the venom. But however, he stirred not from the place till he had parleyed with Caesar, who he found was

5. Cheated.
6. William Byam. There are recorded complaints against him for high-handedness and from him

about insubordination by settlers and slaves.
7. Swords with protective hilt guards.
8. I.e., Byam, the deputy governor.

resolved to die fighting, and would not be taken; no more would Tuscan, or Imoinda. But he, more thirsting after revenge of another sort than that of depriving him of life, now made use of all his art of talking and dissembling, and besought Caesar to yield himself upon terms which he himself should propose, and should be sacredly assented to and kept by him. He told him, it was not that he any longer feared him, or could believe the force of two men, and a young heroine, could overcome all them, with all the slaves now on their side also; but it was the vast esteem he had for his person, the desire he had to serve so gallant a man, and to hinder himself from the reproach hereafter of having been the occasion of the death of a prince whose valor and magnanimity deserved the empire of the world. He protested to him, he looked upon this action as gallant and brave, however tending to the prejudice of his lord and master, who would by it have lost so considerable a number of slaves; that this flight of his should be looked on as a heat of youth, and rashness of a too forward courage, and an unconsidered impatience of liberty, and no more; and that he labored in vain to accomplish that which they would effectually perform as soon as any ship arrived that would touch on his coast. "So that if you will be pleased," continued he, "to surrender yourself, all imaginable respect shall be paid you; and yourself, your wife, and child, if it be here born, shall depart free out of our land."

But Caesar would hear of no composition;[9] though Byam urged, if he pursued and went on in his design, he would inevitably perish, either by great snakes, wild beasts, or hunger; and he ought to have regard to his wife, whose condition required ease, and not the fatigues of tedious travel, where she could not be secured from being devoured. But Caesar told him, there was no faith in the white men or the gods they adored, who instructed 'em in principles so false that honest men could not live amongst 'em; though no people professed so much, none performed so little; that he knew what he had to do when he dealt with men of honor, but with them a man ought to be eternally on his guard, and never to eat and drink with Christians without his weapon of defense in his hand; and for his own security, never to credit one word they spoke. As for the rashness and inconsiderateness of his action, he would confess the governor is in the right; and that he was ashamed of what he had done, in endeavoring to make those free who were by nature slaves, poor wretched rogues, fit to be used as Christians' tools; dogs, treacherous and cowardly, fit for such masters; and they wanted only but to be whipped into the knowledge of the Christian gods to be the vilest of all creeping things, to learn to worship such deities as had not power to make 'em just, brave, or honest. In fine, after a thousand things of this nature, not fit here to be recited, he told Byam he had rather die than live upon the same earth with such dogs. But Trefry and Byam pleaded and protested together so much that Trefry, believing the governor to mean what he said, and speaking very cordially himself, generously put himself into Caesar's hands, and took him aside and persuaded him, even with tears, to live, by surrendering himself, and to name his conditions. Caesar was overcome by his wit and reasons, and in consideration of Imoinda; and demanding what he desired, and that it should be ratified by their hands in writing, because he had perceived that was the common way of contract between man and man, amongst the whites. All this was performed, and Tuscan's pardon was put in, and they surrender

9. Settlement.

to the governor, who walked peaceably down into the plantation with 'em, after giving order to bury their dead. Caesar was very much toiled with the bustle of the day, for he had fought like a fury; and what mischief was done he and Tuscan performed alone, and gave their enemies a fatal proof that they durst do anything and feared no mortal force.

But they were no sooner arrived at the place where all the slaves receive their punishments of whipping, but they laid hands on Caesar and Tuscan, faint with heat and toil; and surprising them, bound them to two several stakes, and whipped them in a most deplorable and inhuman manner, rending the very flesh from their bones; especially Caesar, who was not perceived to make any moan or to alter his face, only to roll his eyes on the faithless governor, and those he believed guilty, with fierceness and indignation; and to complete his rage, he saw every one of those slaves, who but a few days before adored him as something more than mortal, now had a whip to give him some lashes, while he strove not to break his fetters; though if he had, it were impossible. But he pronounced a woe and revenge from his eyes, that darted fire that 'twas at once both awful and terrible to behold.

When they thought they were sufficiently revenged on him, they untied him, almost fainting with loss of blood from a thousand wounds all over his body, from which they had rent his clothes, and led him bleeding and naked as he was, and loaded him all over with irons; and then rubbed his wounds, to complete their cruelty, with Indian pepper, which had like to have made him raving mad; and in this condition made him so fast to the ground that he could not stir, if his pains and wounds would have given him leave. They spared Imoinda, and did not let her see this barbarity committed towards her lord, but carried her down to Parham and shut her up; which was not in kindness to her, but for fear she should die with the sight, or miscarry, and then they should lose a young slave and perhaps the mother.

You must know, that when the news was brought on Monday morning that Caesar had betaken himself to the woods and carried with him all the Negroes, we were possessed with extreme fear, which no persuasions could dissipate, that he would secure himself till night, and then that he would come down and cut all our throats. This apprehension made all the females of us fly down the river, to be secured; and while we were away they acted this cruelty. For I suppose I had authority and interest enough there, had I suspected any such thing, to have prevented it; but we had not gone many leagues but the news overtook us that Caesar was taken and whipped like a common slave. We met on the river with Colonel Martin, a man of great gallantry, wit, and goodness, and whom I have celebrated in a character of my new comedy[1] by his own name, in memory of so brave a man. He was wise and eloquent and, from the fineness of his parts, bore a great sway over the hearts of all the colony. He was a friend to Caesar, and resented this false dealing with him very much. We carried him back to Parham, thinking to have made an accommodation; when we came, the first news we heard was that the governor was dead of a wound Imoinda had given him; but it was not so well. But it seems he would have the pleasure of beholding the revenge he took on Caesar, and before the cruel ceremony was finished, he dropped down; and then they perceived the wound he had on his shoulder was by

---

1. *The Younger Brother; or, The Amorous Jilt,* not produced until 1696 despite this piece of promotion.

a venomed arrow, which, as I said, his Indian mistress healed by sucking the wound.

We were no sooner arrived but we went up to the plantation to see Caesar, whom we found in a very miserable and unexpressible condition; and I have a thousand times admired how he lived, in so much tormenting pain. We said all things to him that trouble, pity, and good nature could suggest, protesting our innocency of the fact and our abhorrence of such cruelties; making a thousand professions of services to him and begging as many pardons for the offenders, till we said so much that he believed we had no hand in his ill treatment; but told us he could never pardon Byam; as for Trefry, he confessed he saw his grief and sorrow for his suffering, which he could not hinder, but was like to have been beaten down by the very slaves for speaking in his defense. But for Byam, who was their leader, their head—and should, by his justice and honor, have been an example to 'em—for him, he wished to live, to take a dire revenge of him, and said, "It had been well for him if he had sacrificed me, instead of giving me the contemptible[2] whip." He refused to talk much, but begging us to give him our hands, he took 'em, and protested never to lift up his to do us any harm. He had a great respect for Colonel Martin, and always took his counsel like that of a parent, and assured him he would obey him in anything but his revenge on Byam. "Therefore," said he, "for his own safety, let him speedily dispatch me; for if I could dispatch myself I would not, till that justice were done to my injured person,[3] and the contempt of a soldier. No, I would not kill myself, even after a whipping, but will be content to live with that infamy, and be pointed at by every grinning slave, till I have completed my revenge; and then you shall see that Oroonoko scorns to live with the indignity that was put on Caesar." All we could do could get no more words from him; and we took care to have him put immediately into a healing bath to rid him of his pepper, and ordered a chirurgeon[4] to anoint him with healing balm, which he suffered; and in some time he began to be able to walk and eat. We failed not to visit him every day, and to that end had him brought to an apartment at Parham.

The governor was no sooner recovered, and had heard of the menaces of Caesar, but he called his council; who (not to disgrace them, or burlesque the government there) consisted of such notorious villains as Newgate[5] never transported; and possibly originally were such who understood neither the laws of God or man, and had no sort of principles to make 'em worthy the name of men; but at the very council table would contradict and fight with one another, and swear so bloodily that 'twas terrible to hear and see 'em. (Some of 'em were afterwards hanged when the Dutch took possession of the place, others sent off in chains.) But calling these special rulers of the nation together, and requiring their counsel in this weighty affair, they all concluded that (Damn 'em) it might be their own cases; and that Caesar ought to be made an example to all the Negroes, to fright 'em from daring to threaten their betters, their lords and masters; and at this rate no man was safe from his own slaves; and concluded, *nemine contradicente*,[6] that Caesar should be hanged.

Trefry then thought it time to use his authority, and told Byam his command did not extend to his lord's plantation, and that Parham was as much

---

2. Showing contempt.
3. Body or character.
4. Surgeon.

5. The major London prison, from which criminals were transported to the colonies.
6. No one disagreeing (Latin).

exempt from the law as Whitehall,[7] and that they ought no more to touch the servants of the Lord——(who there represented the King's person) than they could those about the King himself; and that Parham was a sanctuary; and though his lord were absent in person, his power was still in being there, which he had entrusted with him as far as the dominions of his particular plantations reached, and all that belonged to it; the rest of the country, as Byam was lieutenant to his lord, he might exercise his tyranny upon. Trefry had others as powerful, or more, that interested themselves in Caesar's life, and absolutely said he should be defended. So turning the governor and his wise council out of doors (for they sat at Parham House), they set a guard upon our landing place, and would admit none but those we called friends to us and Caesar.

The governor having remained wounded at Parham till his recovery was completed, Caesar did not know but he was still there; and indeed, for the most part his time was spent there, for he was one that loved to live at other people's expense; and if he were a day absent, he was ten present there, and used to play and walk and hunt and fish with Caesar. So that Caesar did not at all doubt, if he once recovered strength, but he should find an opportunity of being revenged on him. Though after such a revenge, he could not hope to live, for if he escaped the fury of the English mobile,[8] who perhaps would have been glad of the occasion to have killed him, he was resolved not to survive his whipping; yet he had, some tender hours, a repenting softness, which he called his fits of coward, wherein he struggled with Love for the victory of his heart, which took part with his charming Imoinda there; but for the most part his time was passed in melancholy thought and black designs. He considered, if he should do this deed and die, either in the attempt or after it, he left his lovely Imoinda a prey, or at best a slave, to the enraged multitude; his great heart could not endure that thought. "Perhaps," said he, "she may be first ravished by every brute, exposed first to their nasty lusts and then a shameful death." No; he could not live a moment under that apprehension, too insupportable to be borne. These were his thoughts and his silent arguments with his heart, as he told us afterwards; so that now resolving not only to kill Byam but all those he thought had enraged him, pleasing his great heart with the fancied slaughter he should make over the whole face of the plantation, he first resolved on a deed, that (however horrid it at first appeared to us all), when we had heard his reasons, we thought it brave and just. Being able to walk and, as he believed, fit for the execution of his great design, he begged Trefry to trust him into the air, believing a walk would do him good, which was granted him; and taking Imoinda with him, as he used to do in his more happy and calmer days, he led her up into a wood, where, after (with a thousand sighs, and long gazing silently on her face, while tears gushed, in spite of him, from his eyes) he told her his design first of killing her, and then his enemies, and next himself, and the impossibility of escaping, and therefore he told her the necessity of dying, he found the heroic wife faster pleading for death than he was to propose it, when she found his fixed resolution, and on her knees besought him not to leave her a prey to his enemies. He (grieved to death) yet pleased at her noble resolution, took her up, and embracing her with all the passion

7. The king's palace in London. Trefry stands as Lord Willoughby's deputy on his private land, Byam in the colony at large.
8. Common people or mob.

and languishment of a dying lover, drew his knife to kill this treasure of his soul, this pleasure of his eyes; while tears trickled down his cheeks, hers were smiling with joy she should die by so noble a hand, and be sent in her own country (for that's their notion of the next world) by him she so tenderly loved and so truly adored in this; for wives have a respect for their husbands equal to what any other people pay a deity, and when a man finds any occasion to quit his wife, if he love her, she dies by his hand; if not, he sells her, or suffers some other to kill her. It being thus, you may believe the deed was soon resolved on; and 'tis not to be doubted but the parting, the eternal leave-taking of two such lovers, so greatly born, so sensible,[9] so beautiful, so young, and so fond, must be very moving, as the relation of it was to me afterwards.

C. Grignion, after J. Barralet, *Mr. Savigny in the Character of Oroonoko*; engraving, 1785. Through the 18th century, the story of *Oroonoko* was known mostly in a 1696 play adapted from Behn's work by Thomas Southerne. His version makes Imoinda white, as this scene from a 1775 production shows. The actor plays Oroonoko in blackface, here on the verge of killing Imoinda. In *Oroonoko. A tragedy. Written by Thomas Southern, Marked with the variations in the manager's book, at the Theatre-Royal in Drury-Lane* (1785).

All that love could say in such cases being ended, and all the intermitting irresolutions being adjusted, the lovely, young, and adored victim lays herself down before the sacrificer; while he, with a hand resolved and a heart breaking within, gave the fatal stroke; first cutting her throat, and then severing her yet smiling face from that delicate body, pregnant as it was with fruits of tenderest love. As soon as he had done, he laid the body decently on leaves and flowers, of which he made a bed, and concealed it under the same coverlid of nature; only her face he left yet bare to look on. But when he found she was dead and past all retrieve, never more to bless him with her eyes and soft language, his grief swelled up to rage; he tore, he raved, he roared, like some monster of the wood, calling on the loved name of Imoinda. A thousand times he turned the fatal knife that did the deed toward his own heart, with a resolution to go immediately after her; but dire revenge, which now was a thousand times more fierce in his soul than before, prevents him; and he would cry out, "No; since I have sacrificed Imoinda to my revenge, shall I lose that glory which I have purchased so dear as at the price of the fairest, dearest, softest creature

9. Sensitive.

that ever nature made? No, no!" Then, at her name, grief would get the ascendant of rage, and he would lie down by her side and water her face with showers of tears, which never were wont to fall from those eyes. And however bent he was on his intended slaughter, he had not power to stir from the sight of this dear object, now more beloved and more adored than ever.

He remained in this deploring condition for two days, and never rose from the ground where he had made his sad sacrifice. At last, rousing from her side, and accusing himself with living too long now Imoinda was dead, and that the deaths of those barbarous enemies were deferred too long, he resolved now to finish the great work; but offering to rise, he found his strength so decayed that he reeled to and fro, like boughs assailed by contrary winds; so that he was forced to lie down again, and try to summon all his courage to his aid. He found his brains turned round, and his eyes were dizzy, and objects appeared not the same to him they were wont to do; his breath was short, and all his limbs surprised with a faintness he had never felt before. He had not eat in two days, which was one occasion of this feebleness, but excess of grief was the greatest; yet still he hoped he should recover vigor to act his design, and lay expecting it yet six days longer, still mourning over the dead idol of his heart, and striving every day to rise, but could not.

In all this time you may believe we were in no little affliction for Caesar and his wife; some were of opinion he was escaped never to return; others thought some accident had happened to him. But however, we failed not to send out an hundred people several ways to search for him; a party of about forty went that way he took, among whom was Tuscan, who was perfectly reconciled to Byam. They had not gone very far into the wood but they smelt an unusual smell, as of a dead body; for stinks must be very noisome that can be distinguished among such a quantity of natural sweets as every inch of that land produces. So that they concluded they should find him dead, or somebody that was so. They passed on towards it, as loathsome as it was, and made such a rustling among the leaves that lie thick on the ground, by continual falling, that Caesar heard he was approached; and though he had during the space of these eight days endeavored to rise, but found he wanted strength, yet looking up and seeing his pursuers, he rose and reeled to a neighboring tree, against which he fixed his back; and being within a dozen yards of those that advanced and saw him, he called out to them and bid them approach no nearer, if they would be safe. So that they stood still, and hardly believing their eyes, that would persuade them that it was Caesar that spoke to 'em, so much was he altered, they asked him what he had done with his wife, for they smelt a stink that almost struck them dead. He, pointing to the dead body, sighing, cried, "Behold her there." They put off the flowers that covered her with their sticks, and found she was killed, and cried out, "Oh, monster! that hast murdered thy wife." Then asking him why he did so cruel a deed, he replied, he had no leisure to answer impertinent questions. "You may go back," continued he, "and tell the faithless governor he may thank fortune that I am breathing my last, and that my arm is too feeble to obey my heart in what it had designed him." But his tongue faltering, and trembling, he could scarce end what he was saying. The English, taking advantage by his weakness, cried, "Let us take him alive by all means." He heard 'em; and as if he had revived from a fainting, or a dream, he cried out, "No, gentlemen, you are deceived; you will find no more Caesars to be whipped, no more find a faith in me. Feeble as you think me, I have strength yet left to secure me from a second indignity." They swore all anew, and he only shook his head and beheld them with scorn. Then they cried out, "Who will venture on this single man? Will nobody?" They stood all silent while Caesar replied, "Fatal will be the attempt to the first adventurer, let him assure himself," and at that word, held up his knife in a menacing posture. "Look ye, ye faithless crew," said he, "'tis not life I seek, nor am I afraid of dying," and at that word cut a piece of flesh from his own throat, and threw it at 'em; "yet still I would live if I could, till I had perfected my revenge. But oh! it cannot be; I feel life gliding from my eyes and heart, and if I make not haste, I shall yet fall a victim to the shameful whip." At that, he ripped up his own belly, and took his bowels and pulled 'em out, with what strength he could; while some, on their knees imploring, besought him to hold his hand. But when they saw him tottering, they cried out, "Will none venture on him?" A bold English cried, "Yes, if he were the devil" (taking courage when he saw him almost dead); and swearing a horrid oath for his farewell to the world, he rushed on him; Caesar, with his armed hand, met him so fairly as stuck him to the heart, and he fell dead at his feet. Tuscan, seeing that, cried out, "I love thee, O Caesar, and therefore will not let thee die, if possible." And running to him, took him in his arms; but at the same time warding a blow that Caesar made at his bosom, he received it quite through his arm; and Caesar having not the strength to pluck the knife forth, though he attempted it, Tuscan neither pulled it out himself nor suffered it to be pulled out, but came down with it sticking in his arm; and the reason he gave for it was, because the air should not get into the wound. They put their hands across, and carried Caesar between six of 'em, fainted as he was, and they thought dead, or just dying; and they brought him to Parham, and laid him on a couch, and had the chirurgeon immediately to him, who dressed his wounds and sewed up his belly, and used means to bring him to life, which they effected. We ran all to see him, and if before we thought him so beautiful a sight, he was now so altered that his face was like a death's head blacked over, nothing but teeth and eyeholes. For some days we suffered nobody to speak to him, but caused cordials to be poured down his throat, which sustained his life; and in six or seven days he recovered his senses. For you must know that wounds are almost to a miracle cured in the Indies, unless wounds in the legs, which rarely ever cure.

When he was well enough to speak, we talked to him, and asked him some questions about his wife, and the reasons why he killed her; and he then told us what I have related of that resolution, and of his parting; and he besought us we would let him die, and was extremely afflicted to think it was possible he might live; he assured us if we did not dispatch him, he would prove very fatal to a great many. We said all we could to make him live, and gave him new assurances; but he begged we would not think so poorly of him, or of his love to Imoinda, to imagine we could flatter him to life again; but the chirurgeon assured him he could not live, and therefore he need not fear. We were all (but Caesar) afflicted at this news; and the sight was gashly;[1] his discourse was sad, and the earthly smell about him so strong that I was persuaded to leave the place for some time (being myself but sickly, and very apt to fall into fits of dangerous illness upon any extraordinary melancholy). The servants

---

1. Ghastly.

and Trefry and the chirurgeons promised all to take what possible care they could of the life of Caesar, and I, taking boat, went with other company to Colonel Martin's, about three days' journey down the river; but I was no sooner gone, but the governor taking Trefry about some pretended earnest business a day's journey up the river, having communicated his design to one Banister, a wild Irishman and one of the council, a fellow of absolute barbarity, and fit to execute any villainy, but was rich: he came up to Parham, and forcibly took Caesar, and had him carried to the same post where he was whipped; and causing him to be tied to it, and a great fire made before him, he told him he should die like a dog, as he was. Caesar replied, this was the first piece of bravery that ever Banister did, and he never spoke sense till he pronounced that word; and if he would keep it, he would declare, in the other world, that he was the only man of all the whites that ever he heard speak truth. And turning to the men that bound him, he said, "My friends, am I to die, or to be whipped?" And they cried, "Whipped! No, you shall not escape so well." And then he replied, smiling, "A blessing on thee," and assured them they need not tie him, for he would stand fixed like a rock, and endure death so as should encourage them to die. "But if you whip me," said he, "be sure you tie me fast."

He had learned to take tobacco; and when he was assured he should die, he desired they would give him a pipe in his mouth, ready lighted, which they did; and the executioner came, and first cut off his members,[2] and threw them into the fire; after that, with an ill-favored knife, they cut his ears, and his nose, and burned them; he still smoked on, as if nothing had touched him. Then they hacked off one of his arms, and still he bore up, and held his pipe; but at the cutting off the other arm, his head sunk, and his pipe dropped, and he gave up the ghost, without a groan or a reproach. My mother and sister were by him all the while, but not suffered to save him, so rude and wild were the rabble, and so inhuman were the justices, who stood by to see the execution, who after paid dearly enough for their insolence. They cut Caesar in quarters, and sent them to several of the chief plantations. One quarter was sent to Colonel Martin, who refused it, and swore he had rather see the quarters of Banister and the governor himself than those of Caesar on his plantations, and that he could govern his Negroes without terrifying and grieving them with frightful spectacles of a mangled king.

Thus died this great man, worthy of a better fate, and a more sublime wit than mine to write his praise; yet, I hope, the reputation of my pen is considerable enough to make his glorious name to survive to all ages, with that of the brave, the beautiful, and the constant Imoinda.

1688

---

2. Genitals.

JONATHAN SWIFT
1667–1745

J onathan Swift—a posthumous child—was born of English parents in Dublin. Through the generosity of an uncle he was educated at Kilkenny School and Trinity College, Dublin, but before he could fix on a career, the troubles that followed upon James II's abdication and subsequent invasion of Ireland drove Swift along with other Anglo-Irish to England. Between 1689 and 1699 he was more or less continuously a member of the household of his kinsman Sir William Temple, an urbane, civilized man, a retired diplomat, and a friend of King William. During these years Swift read widely, rather reluctantly decided on the church as a career and so took orders, and discovered his astonishing gifts as a satirist. About 1696–97 he wrote his powerful satires on corruptions in religion and learning, A Tale of a Tub and The Battle of the Books, which were published in 1704 and reached their final form only in the fifth edition of 1710. These were the years in which he slowly came to maturity. When, at the age of thirty-two, he returned to Ireland as chaplain to the lord justice, the earl of Berkeley, he had a clear sense of his genius.

For the rest of his life, Swift devoted his talents to politics and religion—not clearly separated at the time—and most of his works in prose were written to further a specific cause. As a clergyman, a spirited controversialist, and a devoted supporter of the Anglican Church, he was hostile to all who seemed to threaten it: Deists, freethinkers, Roman Catholics, Nonconformists, or merely Whig politicians. In 1710 he abandoned the Whigs, because he opposed their indifference to the welfare of the Anglican Church in Ireland and their desire to repeal the Test Act, which required all holders of offices of state to take the Sacrament according to the Anglican rites, thus excluding Roman Catholics and Dissenters. Welcomed by the Tories, he became the most brilliant political journalist of the day, serving the government of Oxford and Bolingbroke as editor of the party organ, the Examiner, and as author of its most powerful articles as well as writing longer pamphlets in support of important policies, such as that favoring the Peace of Utrecht (1713). He was greatly valued by the two ministers, who admitted him to social intimacy, although never to their counsels. The reward of his services was not the English bishopric that he had a right to expect, but the deanship of St. Patrick's Cathedral in Dublin, which came to him in 1713, a year before the death of Queen Anne and the fall of the Tories put an end to all his hopes of preferment in England.

In Ireland, where he lived unwillingly, he became not only an efficient ecclesiastical administrator but also, in 1724, the leader of Irish resistance to English oppression. Under the pseudonym "M. B. Drapier," he published the famous series of public letters that aroused the country to refuse to accept £100,000 in new copper coins (minted in England by William Wood, who had obtained his patent through court corruption), which, it was feared, would further debase the coinage of the already poverty-stricken kingdom. Although his authorship of the letters was known to all Dublin, no one could be found to earn the £300 offered by the government for information as to the identity of the drapier. Swift is still venerated in Ireland as a national hero. He earned the right to refer to himself in the epitaph that he wrote for his tomb as a vigorous defender of liberty.

His last years were less happy. Swift had suffered most of his adult life from what we now recognize as Ménière's disease, which affects the inner ear, causing dizziness, nausea, and deafness. After 1739, when he was seventy-two years old, his infirmities cut him off from his duties as dean, and from then on his social life dwindled. In 1742 guardians were appointed to administer his affairs, and his last three years were spent in gloom and lethargy. But this dark ending should not put his earlier life, so full of energy and humor, into a shadow. The writer of the satires was a man in full control of great intellectual powers.

He also had a gift for friendship. Swift was admired and loved by many of the distinguished men of his time. His friendships with Joseph Addison, Alexander Pope, John Arbuthnot, John Gay, Matthew Prior, Lord Oxford, and Lord Bolingbroke, not to mention those in his less brilliant but amiable Irish circle, bear witness to his moral integrity and social charm. Nor was he, despite some of his writings, indifferent to women. Esther Johnson (Swift's "Stella") was the daughter of Temple's steward, and when Swift first knew her, she was little more than a child. He educated her, formed her character, and came to love her as he was to love no other person. After Temple's death she moved to Dublin, where she and Swift met constantly, but never alone. While working with the Tories in London, he wrote letters to her, later published as *The Journal to Stella* (1766), and they exchanged poems as well. Whether they were secretly married or never married—and in either case why—has been often debated. A marriage of any sort seems most unlikely; and however perplexing their relationship was to others, it seems to have satisfied them. Not even the violent passion that Swift awakened, no doubt unwittingly, in the much younger woman Hester Vanhomrigh (pronounced *Van-úm-mery*)—with her pleadings and reproaches and early death—could unsettle his devotion to Stella. An enigmatic account of his relations with "Vanessa," as he called Vanhomrigh, is given in his poem "Cadenus and Vanessa."

For all his involvement in public affairs, Swift seems to stand apart from his contemporaries—a striking figure among the statesmen of the time, a writer who towered above others by reason of his imagination, mordant wit, and emotional intensity. He has been called a misanthrope, a hater of humanity, and *Gulliver's Travels* has been considered an expression of savage misanthropy. It is true that Swift proclaimed himself a misanthrope in a letter to Pope, declaring that, though he loved individuals, he hated "that animal called man" in general and offering a new definition of the species not as *animal rationale* ("a rational animal") but as merely *animal rationis capax* ("an animal *capable* of reason"). This, he declared, is the "great foundation" on which his "misanthropy" was erected. Swift was stating not his hatred of his fellow creatures but his antagonism to the current optimistic view that human nature is essentially good. To the "philanthropic" flattery that sentimentalism and Deistic rationalism were paying to human nature, Swift opposed a more ancient view: that human nature is deeply and permanently flawed and that we can do nothing with or for the human race until we recognize its moral and intellectual limitations. In his epitaph he spoke of the "fierce indignation" that had torn his heart, an indignation that found superb expression in his greatest satires. It was provoked by the constant spectacle of creatures capable of reason, and therefore of reasonable conduct, steadfastly refusing to live up to their capabilities.

Swift is a master of prose. He defined a good style as "proper words in proper places," a more complex and difficult saying than at first appears. Clear, simple, concrete diction; uncomplicated syntax; and economy and conciseness of language mark all his writings. His is a style that shuns ornaments and singularity of all kinds, a style that grows more tense and controlled the more fierce the indignation that it is called on to express. The virtues of his prose are those of his poetry, which shocks us with its hard look at the facts of life and the body. It is unpoetic poetry, devoid of, indeed as often as not mocking at, inspiration, romantic love, cosmetic beauty, easily assumed literary attitudes, and conventional poetic language. Like the prose, it is predominantly satiric in purpose, but not without its moments of comedy and lightheartedness, though most often written less to divert than to agitate the reader.

For more prose by Swift, including "Abolishing Christianity in England," see the supplemental ebook.

A Description of a City Shower

Careful observers may foretell the hour
(By sure prognostics) when to dread a shower:
While rain depends,[1] the pensive cat gives o'er
Her frolics, and pursues her tail no more.
5 Returning home at night, you'll find the sink°   sewer
Strike your offended sense with double stink.
If you be wise, then go not far to dine;
You'll spend in coach hire more than save in wine.
A coming shower your shooting corns presage,
10 Old achés throb, your hollow tooth will rage.
Sauntering in coffeehouse is Dulman seen;
He damns the climate and complains of spleen.[2]
    Meanwhile the South, rising with dabbled wings,
A sable cloud athwart the welkin flings,
15 That swilled more liquor than it could contain,
And, like a drunkard, gives it up again.
Brisk Susan whips her linen from the rope,
While the first drizzling shower is borne aslope:
Such is that sprinkling which some careless quean°   wench, slut
20 Flirts on you from her mop, but not so clean:
You fly, invoke the gods; then turning, stop
To rail; she singing, still whirls on her mop.
Not yet the dust had shunned the unequal strife,
But, aided by the wind, fought still for life,
25 And wafted with its foe by violent gust,
'Twas doubtful which was rain and which was dust.
Ah! where must needy poet seek for aid,
When dust and rain at once his coat invade?
Sole coat, where dust cemented by the rain
30 Erects the nap,[3] and leaves a mingled stain.
    Now in contiguous drops the flood comes down,
Threatening with deluge this devoted town.
To shops in crowds the daggled° females fly,   mud-spattered
Pretend to cheapen° goods, but nothing buy.   bargain for
35 The Templar spruce, while every spout's abroach,[4]
Stays till 'tis fair, yet seems to call a coach.
The tucked-up sempstress walks with hasty strides,
While streams run down her oiled umbrella's sides.
Here various kinds, by various fortunes led,
40 Commence acquaintance underneath a shed.
Triumphant Tories and desponding Whigs
Forget their feuds,[5] and join to save their wigs.
Boxed in a chair° the beau impatient sits,   sedan chair
While spouts run clattering o'er the roof by fits,

1. Impends, is imminent. An example of elevated
diction used frequently throughout the poem.
2. The English tendency to melancholy ("the
spleen") was often attributed to the rainy climate.
"Dulman": a type name (from "dull man"), like
Congreve's "Petulant" or "Witwoud."
3. Stiffens the coat's surface.

4. Pouring out water. "The Templar": a young man
engaged in studying law.
5. The Whig ministry had just fallen and the
Tories, led by Harley and St. John, were forming
the government with which Swift was to be
closely associated until the death of the queen in
1714.

45   And ever and anon with frightful din
     The leather sounds;[6] he trembles from within.
     So when Troy chairmen bore the wooden steed,
     Pregnant with Greeks impatient to be freed
     (Those bully Greeks, who, as the moderns do,
50   Instead of paying chairmen, run them through),[7]
     Laocoön struck the outside with his spear,
     And each imprisoned hero quaked for fear.[8]
       Now from all parts the swelling kennels[9] flow,
     And bear their trophies with them as they go:
55   Filth of all hues and odors seem to tell
     What street they sailed from, by their sight and smell.
     They, as each torrent drives with rapid force,
     From Smithfield or St. Pulchre's shape their course,
     And in huge confluence joined at Snow Hill ridge,
60   Fall from the conduit prone to Holborn Bridge.[1]
     Sweepings from butchers' stalls, dung, guts, and blood,
     Drowned puppies, stinking sprats,[2] all drenched in mud, } *small*
     Dead cats, and turnip tops, come tumbling down the flood.[3] } *herrings*

1710

Gulliver's Travels

Gulliver's Travels is Swift's most enduring satire. Although full of allusions to recent and current events, it still rings true today, for its objects are human failings and the defective political, economic, and social institutions that they call into being. Swift adopts an ancient satirical device: the imaginary voyage. Lemuel Gulliver, the narrator, is a ship's surgeon, a moderately well educated man, kindly, resourceful, cheerful, inquiring, patriotic, truthful, and rather unimaginative—in short, a reasonably decent example of humanity, with whom a reader can readily identify. He undertakes four voyages, all of which end disastrously among "several remote nations of the world." In the first, Gulliver is shipwrecked in the empire of Lilliput, where he finds himself a giant among a diminutive people, charmed by their miniature city and amused by their toylike prettiness. But in the end they prove to be treacherous, malicious, ambitious, vengeful, and cruel. As we read we grow disenchanted with the inhabitants of this fanciful kingdom, and then gradually we begin to recognize our likeness to them, especially in the disproportion between our natural pettiness and our boundless and destructive passions. In the second voyage, Gulliver is abandoned by his shipmates in Brobdingnag, a land of giants, creatures ten times as large as Europeans. Though he fears that such monsters must be brutes, the reverse proves to be the case. Brobdingnag is something of a utopia, governed by a humane and enlightened prince who is the embodiment of moral and political wisdom. In the long interview in which Gulliver pridefully enlarges on the glories of England and its political institutions, the king reduces him to resentful silence by asking questions that reveal the difference between what England is and what it ought to be. In Brobdingnag, Gulliver finds himself a Lilliputian, his pride humbled

---

6. The roof of the sedan chair was made of leather.
7. I.e., with their swords.
8. *Aeneid* 2.40–53.
9. The open gutters in the middle of the street.
1. An accurate description of the drainage system of this part of London—the eastern edge of Holborn and West Smithfield, which lie outside the old walls west and east of Newgate. The great cattle and sheep markets were in Smithfield. The church of St. Sepulchre ("St. Pulchre's") stood opposite Newgate Prison. Holborn Conduit was

at the foot of Snow Hill. It drained into Fleet Ditch, an evil-smelling open sewer, at Holborn Bridge.
2. Small herrings.
3. In Faulkner's edition of Swift's *Works* (Dublin, 1735) a note almost certainly suggested by Swift points to the concluding triplet, with its resonant final alexandrine, as a burlesque of a mannerism of Dryden and other Restoration poets and claims that Swift's ridicule banished the triplet from contemporary poetry.

by his helpless state and his human vanity diminished by the realization that his body must have seemed as disgusting to the Lilliputians as do the bodies of the Brobdingnagians to him.

In the third voyage, to Laputa, Swift is chiefly concerned with attacking extremes of theoretical and speculative reasoning, whether in science, politics, or economics. Much of this voyage is an allegory of political life under the administration of the Whig minister, Sir Robert Walpole. The final voyage sets Gulliver between a race of horses, Houyhnhnms (prounced *Hwín-ims*), who live entirely by reason except for a few well-controlled and muted social affections, and their slaves, the Yahoos, whose bodies are obscene caricatures of the human body and who have no glimmer of reason but are mere creatures of appetite and passion.

When *Gulliver's Travels* first appeared, everyone read it—children for the story and politicians for the satire of current affairs—and ever since it has retained a hold on readers of every kind. Almost unique in world literature, it is simple enough for children, complex enough to carry adults beyond their depth. Swift's art works on many levels. First of all, there is the sheer playfulness of the narrative. Through Gulliver's eyes, we gaze on marvel after marvel: a tiny girl who threads an invisible needle with invisible silk or a white mare who threads a needle between pastern and hoof. The travels, like a fairy story, transport us to imaginary worlds that function with a perfect, fantastic logic different from our own; Swift exercises our sense of vision. But beyond that, he exercises our perceptions of meaning. In *Gulliver's Travels*, things are seldom what they seem; irony, probing or corrosive, underlies almost every word. In the last chapter, Gulliver insists that the example of the Houyhnhnms has made him incapable of telling a lie—but the oath he swears is quoted from Sinon, whose lies to the Trojans persuaded them to accept the Trojan *horse*. Swift trains us to read alertly, to look beneath the surface. Yet on its deepest level, the book does not offer final meanings, but a question: What is a human being? Voyaging through imaginary worlds, we try to find ourselves. Are we prideful insects or lords of creation? brutes or reasonable beings? In the last voyage, Swift pushes such questions, and Gulliver himself, almost beyond endurance; hating his own humanity, Gulliver forgets who he is. For the reader, however, the outcome cannot be so clear. Swift does not set out to satisfy our minds but to vex and unsettle them. And he leaves us at the moment when the mixed face of humanity—the pettiness of the Lilliputians, the savagery of the Yahoos, the innocence of Gulliver himself—begins to look strangely familiar, like our own faces in a mirror.

Swift's full title for this work was *Travels into Several Remote Nations of the World. In Four Parts. By Lemuel Gulliver, First a Surgeon, and then a Captain of several Ships.* In the first edition (1726), either the bookseller or Swift's friends Charles Ford, Pope, and others, who were concerned in getting the book anonymously into print, altered and omitted so much of the original manuscript (because of its dangerous political implications) that Swift was seriously annoyed. When, in 1735, the Dublin bookseller George Faulkner brought out an edition of Swift's works, the dean seems to have taken pains, surreptitiously, to see that a more authentic version of the work was published. This text is the basis of modern editions.

From Gulliver's Travels

A Letter from Captain Gulliver to His Cousin Sympson[1]

I hope you will be ready to own publicly, whenever you shall be called to it, that by your great and frequent urgency you prevailed on me to publish a very

---

1. In this letter, first published in 1735, Swift complains, among other matters, of the alterations in his original text made by the publisher, Benjamin Motte, in the interest of what he considered political discretion.

loose and uncorrect account of my travels; with direction to hire some young gentlemen of either University to put them in order, and correct the style, as my Cousin Dampier[2] did by my advice, in his book called *A Voyage round the World*. But I do not remember I gave you power to consent that anything should be omitted, and much less that anything should be inserted: therefore, as to the latter, I do here renounce everything of that kind; particularly a paragraph about her Majesty the late Queen Anne, of most pious and glorious memory; although I did reverence and esteem her more than any of human species. But you, or your interpolator, ought to have considered that as it was not my inclination, so was it not decent to praise any animal of our composition before my master Houyhnhnm; and besides, the fact was altogether false; for to my knowledge, being in England during some part of her Majesty's reign, she did govern by a chief Minister; nay, even by two successively; the first whereof was the Lord of Godolphin, and the second the Lord of Oxford; so that you have made me *say the thing that was not*. Likewise, in the account of the Academy of Projectors, and several passages of my discourse to my master Houyhnhnm, you have either omitted some material circumstances, or minced or changed them in such a manner, that I do hardly know mine own work. When I formerly hinted to you something of this in a letter, you were pleased to answer that you were afraid of giving offense; that people in power were very watchful over the press; and apt not only to interpret, but to punish everything which looked like an *innuendo* (as I think you called it). But pray, how could that which I spoke so many years ago, and at above five thousand leagues distance, in another reign, be applied to any of the Yahoos, who now are said to govern the herd; especially, at a time when I little thought on or feared the unhappiness of living under them. Have not I the most reason to complain, when I see these very Yahoos carried by Houyhnhnms in a vehicle, as if these were brutes, and those the rational creatures? And, indeed, to avoid so monstrous and detestable a sight was one principal motive of my retirement hither.[3]

Thus much I thought proper to tell you in relation to yourself, and to the trust I reposed in you.

I do in the next place complain of my own great want of judgment, in being prevailed upon by the intreaties and false reasonings of you and some others, very much against mine own opinion, to suffer my travels to be published. Pray bring to your mind how often I desired you to consider, when you insisted on the motive of public good, that the Yahoos were a species of animals utterly incapable of amendment by precepts or examples; and so it hath proved; for instead of seeing a full stop put to all abuses and corruptions, at least in this little island, as I had reason to expect, behold, after above six months warning, I cannot learn that my book hath produced one single effect according to mine intentions; I desired you would let me know by a letter, when party and faction were extinguished; judges learned and upright; pleaders honest and modest, with some tincture of common sense; and Smithfield blazing with pyramids of law books; the young nobility's education entirely changed; the physicians banished; the female Yahoos abounding in virtue, honor, truth, and good sense; courts and levees of great ministers thoroughly weeded and swept; wit, merit, and learning rewarded;

2. William Dampier (1652–1715), the explorer, whose account of his circumnavigation of the globe Swift had read.

3. To Nottinghamshire.

all disgracers of the press in prose and verse, condemned to eat nothing but their own cotton,[4] and quench their thirst with their own ink. These, and a thousand other reformations, I firmly counted upon by your encouragement; as indeed they were plainly deducible from the precepts delivered in my book. And, it must be owned that seven months were a sufficient time to correct every vice and folly to which Yahoos are subject; if their natures had been capable of the least disposition to virtue or wisdom; yet so far have you been from answering mine expectation in any of your letters, that on the contrary, you are loading our carrier every week with libels, and keys, and reflections, and memoirs, and second parts; wherein I see myself accused of reflecting upon great statesfolk; of degrading human nature (for so they have still the confidence to style it) and of abusing the female sex. I find likewise, that the writers of those bundles are not agreed among themselves; for some of them will not allow me to be author of mine own travels; and others make me author of books to which I am wholly a stranger.

I find likewise that your printer hath been so careless as to confound the times, and mistake the dates of my several voyages and returns; neither assigning the true year, or the true month, or day of the month; and I hear the original manuscript is all destroyed, since the publication of my book. Neither have I any copy left; however, I have sent you some corrections, which you may insert, if ever there should be a second edition; and yet I cannot stand to them, but shall leave that matter to my judicious and candid readers, to adjust it as they please.

I hear some of our sea Yahoos find fault with my sea language, as not proper in many parts, nor now in use. I cannot help it. In my first voyages, while I was young, I was instructed by the oldest mariners, and learned to speak as they did. But I have since found that the sea Yahoos are apt, like the land ones, to become new fangled in their words; which the latter change every year; insomuch, as I remember upon each return to mine own country, their old dialect was so altered, that I could hardly understand the new. And I observe, when any Yahoo comes from London out of curiosity to visit me at mine own house, we neither of us are able to deliver our conceptions in a manner intelligible to the other.[5]

If the censure of Yahoos could any way affect me, I should have great reason to complain that some of them are so bold as to think my book of travels a mere fiction out of mine own brain; and have gone so far as to drop hints that the Houyhnhnms, and Yahoos have no more existence than the inhabitants of Utopia.

Indeed I must confess that as to the people of Lilliput, Brobdingrag (for so the word should have been spelled, and not erroneously Brobdingnag) and Laputa, I have never yet heard of any Yahoo so presumptuous as to dispute their being, or the facts I have related concerning them; because the truth immediately strikes every reader with conviction. And, is there less probability in my account of the Houyhnhnms or Yahoos, when it is manifest as to the latter, there are so many thousands even in this city, who only differ from their brother brutes in Houyhnhnmland, because they use a sort of a jabber, and do not go naked. I wrote for their amendment, and not their approbation. The united praise of the whole race would be of less consequence to

---

4. Presumably their paper. "Pleaders": lawyers. Smithfield was a part of London containing many bookshops. "Levees": morning receptions.

5. Swift was the inveterate enemy of slang.

me, than the neighing of those two degenerate Houyhnhnms I keep in my stable; because, from these, degenerate as they are, I still improve in some virtues, without any mixture of vice.

Do these miserable animals presume to think that I am so far degenerated as to defend my veracity; Yahoo as I am, it is well known through all Houyhnhnmland, that by the instructions and example of my illustrious master, I was able in the compass of two years (although I confess with the utmost difficulty) to remove that infernal habit of lying, shuffling, deceiving, and equivocating, so deeply rooted in the very souls of all my species; especially the Europeans.

I have other complaints to make upon this vexatious occasion; but I forbear troubling myself or you any further. I must freely confess that since my last return, some corruptions of my Yahoo nature have revived in me by conversing with a few of your species, and particularly those of mine own family, by an unavoidable necessity; else I should never have attempted so absurd a project as that of reforming the Yahoo race in this kingdom; but I have now done with all such visionary schemes for ever.

1727?   1735

The Publisher to the Reader

The author of these travels, Mr. Lemuel Gulliver, is my ancient and intimate friend; there is likewise some relation between us by the mother's side. About three years ago Mr. Gulliver, growing weary of the concourse of curious people coming to him at his house in Redriff,[6] made a small purchase of land, with a convenient house, near Newark, in Nottinghamshire, his native country; where he now lives retired, yet in good esteem among his neighbors.

Although Mr. Gulliver were born in Nottinghamshire, where his father dwelt, yet I have heard him say his family came from Oxfordshire; to confirm which, I have observed in the churchyard at Banbury, in that county, several tombs and monuments of the Gullivers.

Before he quitted Redriff, he left the custody of the following papers in my hands, with the liberty to dispose of them as I should think fit. I have carefully perused them three times; the style is very plain and simple; and the only fault I find is that the author, after the manner of travelers, is a little too circumstantial. There is an air of truth apparent through the whole; and indeed the author was so distinguished for his veracity, that it became a sort of proverb among his neighbors at Redriff, when anyone affirmed a thing, to say, it was as true as if Mr. Gulliver had spoke it.

By the advice of several worthy persons, to whom, with the author's permission, I communicated these papers, I now venture to send them into the world; hoping they may be, at least for some time, a better entertainment to our young noblemen, than the common scribbles of politics and party.

This volume would have been at least twice as large, if I had not made bold to strike out innumerable passages relating to the winds and tides, as well as to the variations and bearings in the several voyages; together with the minute descriptions of the management of the ship in storms, in the style of sailors; likewise the account of the longitudes and latitudes, wherein I have

---

6. Rotherhithe, a district in southern London, below Tower Bridge, then frequented by sailors.

reason to apprehend that Mr. Gulliver may be a little dissatisfied; but I was resolved to fit the work as much as possible to the general capacity of readers. However, if my own ignorance in sea affairs shall have led me to commit some mistakes, I alone am answerable for them; and if any traveler hath a curiosity to see the whole work at large, as it came from the hand of the author, I will be ready to gratify him.

As for any further particulars relating to the author, the reader will receive satisfaction from the first pages of the book.

RICHARD SYMPSON

Part 1. A *Voyage to Lilliput*

CHAPTER 1. *The author gives some account of himself and family; his first inducements to travel. He is shipwrecked, and swims for his life; gets safe on shore in the country of Lilliput; is made a prisoner, and carried up the country.*

My father had a small estate in Nottinghamshire; I was the third of five sons. He sent me to Emanuel College in Cambridge, at fourteen years old, where I resided three years, and applied myself close to my studies: but the charge of maintaining me (although I had a very scanty allowance) being too great for a narrow fortune, I was bound apprentice to Mr. James Bates, an eminent surgeon in London, with whom I continued four years; and my father now and then sending me small sums of money, I laid them out in learning navigation, and other parts of the mathematics, useful to those who intend to travel, as I always believed it would be some time or other my fortune to do. When I left Mr. Bates, I went down to my father; where, by the assistance of him and my uncle John, and some other relations, I got forty pounds, and a promise of thirty pounds a year to maintain me at Leyden:[7] there I studied physic two years and seven months, knowing it would be useful in long voyages.

Soon after my return from Leyden, I was recommended by my good master Mr. Bates, to be surgeon to the *Swallow*, Captain Abraham Pannell commander; with whom I continued three years and a half, making a voyage or two into the Levant[8] and some other parts. When I came back, I resolved to settle in London, to which Mr. Bates, my master, encouraged me; and by him I was recommended to several patients. I took part of a small house in the Old Jury; and being advised to alter my condition, I married Mrs.[9] Mary Burton, second daughter to Mr. Edmond Burton, hosier, in Newgate Street, with whom I received four hundred pounds for a portion.

But, my good master Bates dying in two years after, and I having few friends, my business began to fail; for my conscience would not suffer me to imitate the bad practice of too many among my brethren. Having therefore consulted with my wife, and some of my acquaintance, I determined to go again to sea. I was surgeon successively in two ships, and made several voyages, for six years, to the East and West Indies; by which I got some addition to my fortune. My hours of leisure I spent in reading the best authors, ancient and modern, being always provided with a good number of books; and when I was ashore, in observing the manners and dispositions of the people, as well as learning their language; wherein I had a great facility by the strength of my memory.

The last of these voyages not proving very fortunate, I grew weary of the sea, and intended to stay at home with my wife and family. I removed from the Old Jury to Fetter Lane, and from thence to Wapping, hoping to get business among the sailors; but it would not turn to account. After three years' expectation that things would mend, I accepted an advantageous offer from Captain William Prichard, master of the *Antelope,* who was making a voyage to the South Sea. We set sail from Bristol, May 4th, 1699, and our voyage at first was very prosperous.

It would not be proper, for some reasons, to trouble the reader with the particulars of our adventures in those seas: let it suffice to inform him, that in our passage from thence to the East Indies we were driven by a violent storm to the northwest of Van Diemen's Land.[1] By an observation, we found ourselves in the latitude of 30 degrees 2 minutes south. Twelve of our crew were dead by immoderate labor, and ill food, the rest were in a very weak condition. On the fifth of November, which was the beginning of summer in those parts, the weather being very hazy, the seamen spied a rock, within half a cable's length[2] of the ship; but the wind was so strong, that we were driven directly upon it, and immediately split. Six of the crew, of whom I was one, having let down the boat into the sea, made a shift to get clear of the ship, and the rock. We rowed by my computation about three leagues, till we were able to work no longer, being already spent with labor while we were in the ship. We therefore trusted ourselves to the mercy of the waves; and in about half an hour the boat was overset by a sudden flurry from the north. What became of my companions in the boat, as well as of those who escaped on the rock, or were left in the vessel, I cannot tell; but conclude they were all lost. For my own part, I swam as fortune directed me, and was pushed forward by wind and tide. I often let my legs drop, and could feel no bottom; but when I was almost gone, and able to struggle no longer, I found myself within my depth; and by this time the storm was much abated. The declivity was so small, that I walked near a mile before I got to the shore, which I conjectured was about eight o'clock in the evening. I then advanced forward near half a mile, but could not discover any sign of houses or inhabitants; at least I was in so weak a condition, that I did not observe them. I was extremely tired, and with that, and the heat of the weather, and about half a pint of brandy that I drank as I left the ship, I found myself much inclined to sleep. I lay down on the grass, which was very short and soft, where I slept sounder than ever I remember to have done in my life, and as I reckoned, above nine hours; for when I awaked, it was just daylight. I attempted to rise, but was not able to stir: for as I happened to lie on my back, I found my arms and legs were strongly fastened on each side to the ground; and my hair, which was long and thick, tied down in the same manner. I likewise felt several slender ligatures across my body, from my armpits to my thighs. I could only look upwards; the sun began to grow hot, and the light offended my eyes. I heard a confused noise about me, but in the posture I lay, could

1. Tasmania.
2. A cable is about six hundred feet (one hundred fathoms).

see nothing except the sky. In a little time I felt something alive moving on my left leg, which advancing gently forward over my breast, came almost up to my chin; when bending my eyes downwards as much as I could, I perceived it to be a human creature not six inches high,[3] with a bow and arrow in his hands, and a quiver at his back. In the meantime, I felt at least forty more of the same kind (as I conjectured) following the first. I was in the utmost astonishment, and roared so loud, that they all ran back in a fright; and some of them, as I was afterwards told, were hurt with the falls they got by leaping from my sides upon the ground. However, they soon returned; and one of them, who ventured so far as to get a full sight of my face, lifting up his hands and eyes by way of admiration,[4] cried out in a shrill, but distinct voice, *Hekinah Degul*: the others repeated the same words several times, but I then knew not what they meant. I lay all this while, as the reader may believe, in great uneasiness; at length, struggling to get loose, I had the fortune to break the strings, and wrench out the pegs that fastened my left arm to the ground; for, by lifting it up to my face, I discovered the methods they had taken to bind me; and, at the same time, with a violent pull, which gave me excessive pain, I a little loosened the strings that tied down my hair on the left side; so that I was just able to turn my head about two inches. But the creatures ran off a second time, before I could seize them; whereupon there was a great shout in a very shrill accent; and after it ceased, I heard one of them cry aloud, *Tolgo phonac*; when in an instant I felt above an hundred arrows discharged on my left hand, which pricked me like so many needles; and besides they shot another flight into the air, as we do bombs in Europe, whereof many, I suppose, fell on my body (though I felt them not) and some on my face, which I immediately covered with my left hand. When this shower of arrows was over, I fell a groaning with grief and pain; and then striving again to get loose, they discharged another volley larger than the first, and some of them attempted with spears to stick me in the sides; but, by good luck, I had on me a buff jerkin,[5] which they could not pierce. I thought it the most prudent method to lie still; and my design was to continue so till night, when, my left hand being already loose, I could easily free myself: and as for the inhabitants, I had reason to believe I might be a match for the greatest armies they could bring against me, if they were all of the same size with him that I saw. But fortune disposed otherwise of me. When the people observed I was quiet, they discharged no more arrows: but by the noise increasing, I knew their numbers were greater; and about four yards from me, over-against my right ear, I heard a knocking for above an hour, like people at work; when turning my head that way, as well as the pegs and strings would permit me, I saw a stage erected about a foot and a half from the ground, capable of holding four of the inhabitants, with two or three ladders to mount it: from whence one of them, who seemed to be a person of quality, made me a long speech, whereof I understood not one syllable. But I should have mentioned, that before the principal person began his oration, he cried out three times, *Langro Dehul san*: (these words and the former were afterwards repeated and explained to me). Whereupon immediately about fifty of the inhabitants came, and cut the strings that fastened the left side of my head, which gave me the liberty of turning it to the right,

---

3. Lilliput is scaled, fairly consistently, at one-twelfth of Gulliver's world.
4. Wonderment.
5. Leather jacket.

and of observing the person and gesture of him who was to speak. He appeared to be of a middle age, and taller than any of the other three who attended him; whereof one was a page who held up his train, and seemed to be somewhat longer than my middle finger; the other two stood one on each side to support him. He acted every part of an orator, and I could observe many periods[6] of threatenings, and others of promises, pity and kindness. I answered in a few words, but in the most submissive manner, lifting up my left hand and both my eyes to the sun, as calling him for a witness; and being almost famished with hunger, having not eaten a morsel for some hours before I left the ship, I found the demands of nature so strong upon me, that I could not forbear showing my impatience (perhaps against the strict rules of decency) by putting my finger frequently on my mouth, to signify that I wanted food. The *Hurgo* (for so they call a great lord, as I afterwards learned) understood me very well. He descended from the stage, and commanded that several ladders should be applied to my sides, on which above an hundred of the inhabitants mounted, and walked towards my mouth, laden with baskets full of meat, which had been provided and sent thither by the King's orders upon the first intelligence he received of me. I observed there was the flesh of several animals, but could not distinguish them by the taste. There were shoulders, legs, and loins shaped like those of mutton, and very well dressed, but smaller than the wings of a lark. I eat them by two or three at a mouthful, and took three loaves at a time, about the bigness of musket bullets. They supplied me as fast as they could, showing a thousand marks of wonder and astonishment at my bulk and appetite. I then made another sign that I wanted drink. They found by my eating that a small quantity would not suffice me; and being a most ingenious people, they slung up with great dexterity one of their largest hogsheads; then rolled it towards my hand, and beat out the top; I drank it off at a draught, which I might well do, for it hardly held half a pint, and tasted like a small wine of Burgundy, but much more delicious. They brought me a second hogshead, which I drank in the same manner, and made signs for more, but they had none to give me. When I had performed these wonders, they shouted for joy, and danced upon my breast, repeating several times as they did at first, *Hekinah Degul*. They made me a sign that I should throw down the two hogsheads, but first warned the people below to stand out of the way, crying aloud, *Borach Mivola*, and when they saw the vessels in the air, there was an universal shout of *Hekinah Degul*. I confess I was often tempted, while they were passing backwards and forwards on my body, to seize forty or fifty of the first that came in my reach, and dash them against the ground. But the remembrance of what I had felt, which probably might not be the worst they could do; and the promise of honor I made them, for so I interpreted my submissive behavior, soon drove out those imaginations. Besides, I now considered myself as bound by the laws of hospitality to a people who had treated me with so much expense and magnificence. However, in my thoughts I could not sufficiently wonder at the intrepidity of these diminutive mortals, who durst venture to mount and walk on my body, while one of my hands was at liberty, without trembling at the very sight of so prodigious a creature as I must appear to them. After some time, when they observed that I made no more demands for meat, there appeared before

---

6. In rhetoric, complete, well-constructed sentences.

me a person of high rank from his Imperial Majesty. His Excellency, having mounted on the small of my right leg, advanced forwards up to my face, with about a dozen of his retinue. And producing his credentials under the Signet Royal, which he applied[7] close to my eyes, spoke about ten minutes, without any signs of anger, but with a kind of determinate resolution; often pointing forwards, which, as I afterwards found, was towards the capital city, about half a mile distant, whither it was agreed by his Majesty in council that I must be conveyed. I answered in a few words, but to no purpose, and made a sign with my hand that was loose, putting it to the other (but over his Excellency's head, for fear of hurting him or his train) and then to my own head and body, to signify that I desired my liberty. It appeared that he understood me well enough; for he shook his head by way of disapprobation, and held his hand in a posture to show that I must be carried as a prisoner. However, he made other signs to let me understand that I should have meat and drink enough, and very good treatment. Whereupon I once more thought of attempting to break my bonds; but again, when I felt the smart of their arrows upon my face and hands, which were all in blisters, and many of the darts still sticking in them; and observing likewise that the number of my enemies increased; I gave tokens to let them know that they might do with me what they pleased. Upon this the *Hurgo* and his train withdrew, with much civility and cheerful countenances. Soon after I heard a general shout, with frequent repetitions of the words, *Peplom Selan*, and I felt great numbers of the people on my left side relaxing the cords to such a degree, that I was able to turn upon my right, and to ease myself with making water; which I very plentifully did, to the great astonishment of the people, who conjecturing by my motions what I was going to do, immediately opened to the right and left on that side, to avoid the torrent which fell with such noise and violence from me. But before this, they had daubed my face and both my hands with a sort of ointment very pleasant to the smell, which in a few minutes removed all the smart of their arrows. These circumstances, added to the refreshment I had received by their victuals and drink, which were very nourishing, disposed me to sleep. I slept about eight hours, as I was afterwards assured; and it was no wonder; for the physicians, by the Emperor's order, had mingled a sleeping potion in the hogsheads of wine.

It seems that upon the first moment I was discovered sleeping on the ground after my landing, the Emperor had early notice of it by an express; and determined in council that I should be tied in the manner I have related (which was done in the night while I slept), that plenty of meat and drink should be sent me, and a machine prepared to carry me to the capital city.

This resolution perhaps may appear very bold and dangerous, and I am confident would not be imitated by any prince in Europe on the like occasion; however, in my opinion it was extremely prudent as well as generous. For supposing these people had endeavored to kill me with their spears and arrows while I was asleep; I should certainly have awaked with the first sense of smart, which might so far have roused my rage and strength, as to enable me to break the strings wherewith I was tied; after which, as they were not able to make resistance, so they could expect no mercy.

These people are most excellent mathematicians, and arrived to a great perfection in mechanics by the countenance and encouragement of the

7. Brought.

Emperor, who is a renowned patron of learning. This prince hath several machines fixed on wheels, for the carriage of trees and other great weights. He often builds his largest men of war, whereof some are nine foot long, in the woods where the timber grows, and has them carried on these engines[8] three or four hundred yards to the sea. Five hundred carpenters and engineers were immediately set at work to prepare the greatest engine they had. It was a frame of wood raised three inches from the ground, about seven foot long and four wide, moving upon twenty-two wheels. The shout I heard was upon the arrival of this engine, which it seems set out in four hours after my landing. It was brought parallel to me as I lay. But the principal difficulty was to raise and place me in this vehicle. Eighty poles, each of one foot high, were erected for this purpose, and very strong cords of the bigness of packthread were fastened by hooks to many bandages, which the workmen had girt round my neck, my hands, my body, and my legs. Nine hundred of the strongest men were employed to draw up these cords by many pulleys fastened on the poles; and thus, in less than three hours, I was raised and slung into the engine, and there tied fast. All this I was told, for while the whole operation was performing, I lay in a profound sleep, by the force of that soporiferous[9] medicine infused into my liquor. Fifteen hundred of the Emperor's largest horses, each about four inches and a half high, were employed to draw me towards the metropolis, which, as I said, was half a mile distant.

About four hours after we began our journey, I awaked by a very ridiculous accident; for, the carriage being stopped a while to adjust something that was out of order, two or three of the young natives had the curiosity to see how I looked when I was asleep; they climbed up into the engine, and advancing very softly to my face, one of them, an officer in the guards, put the sharp end of his half-pike a good way up into my left nostril, which tickled my nose like a straw, and made me sneeze violently: whereupon they stole off unperceived, and it was three weeks before I knew the cause of my awaking so suddenly. We made a long march the remaining part of the day, and rested at night with five hundred guards on each side of me half with torches, and half with bows and arrows, ready to shoot me if I should offer to stir. The next morning at sunrise we continued our march, and arrived within two hundred yards of the city gates about noon. The Emperor and all his court came out to meet us, but his great officers would by no means suffer his Majesty to endanger his person by mounting on my body.

At the place where the carriage stopped, there stood an ancient temple, esteemed to be the largest in the whole kingdom, which having been polluted some years before by an unnatural murder,[1] was, according to the zeal of those people, looked on as profane, and therefore had been applied to common use, and all the ornaments and furniture carried away. In this edifice it was determined I should lodge. The great gate fronting to the north was about four foot high, and almost two foot wide, through which I could easily creep. On each side of the gate was a small window not above six inches from the ground: into that on the left side, the King's smiths conveyed fourscore and eleven chains, like those that hang to a lady's watch in Europe, and almost as large, which were locked to my left leg with six and thirty padlocks. Over against this temple, on the other side of the great high-

8. Contrivances.
9. Inducing unnatural sleep.

1. Presumably a reference to the execution of Charles I, who was sentenced in Westminster Hall.

way, at twenty foot distance, there was a turret at least five foot high. Here the Emperor ascended with many principal lords of his court, to have an opportunity of viewing me, as I was told, for I could not see them. It was reckoned that above an hundred thousand inhabitants came out of the town upon the same errand; and in spite of my guards, I believe there could not be fewer than ten thousand, at several times, who mounted upon my body by the help of ladders. But a proclamation was soon issued to forbid it upon pain of death. When the workmen found it was impossible for me to break loose, they cut all the strings that bound me; whereupon I rose up with as melancholy a disposition as ever I had in my life. But the noise and astonishment of the people at seeing me rise and walk are not to be expressed. The chains that held my left leg were about two yards long, and gave me not only the liberty of walking backwards and forwards in a semicircle; but, being fixed within four inches of the gate, allowed me to creep in, and lie at my full length in the temple.

CHAPTER 2. *The Emperor of Lilliput, attended by several of the nobility, comes to see the author in his confinement. The Emperor's person and habit described. Learned men appointed to teach the author their language. He gains favor by his mild disposition. His pockets are searched, and his sword and pistols taken from him.*

When I found myself on my feet, I looked about me, and must confess I never beheld a more entertaining prospect. The country round appeared like a continued garden, and the inclosed fields, which were generally forty foot square, resembled so many beds of flowers. These fields were intermingled with woods of half a stang,[2] and the tallest trees, as I could judge, appeared to be seven foot high. I viewed the town on my left hand, which looked like the painted scene of a city in a theater.

I had been for some hours extremely pressed by the necessities of nature; which was no wonder, it being almost two days since I had last disburthened myself. I was under great difficulties between urgency and shame. The best expedient I could think on, was to creep into my house, which I accordingly did; and shutting the gate after me, I went as far as the length of my chain would suffer; and discharged my body of that uneasy load. But this was the only time I was ever guilty of so uncleanly an action; for which I cannot but hope the candid reader will give some allowance, after he hath maturely and impartially considered my case, and the distress I was in. From this time my constant practice was, as soon as I rose, to perform that business in open air, at the full extent of my chain, and due care was taken every morning before company came, that the offensive matter should be carried off in wheelbarrows by two servants appointed for that purpose. I would not have dwelt so long upon a circumstance, that perhaps at first sight may appear not very momentous, if I had not thought it necessary to justify my character in point of cleanliness to the world; which I am told some of my maligners have been pleased, upon this and other occasions, to call in question.

When this adventure was at an end, I came back out of my house, having occasion for fresh air. The Emperor was already descended from the tower,

2. A quarter of an acre.

and advancing on horseback towards me, which had like to have cost him dear; for the beast, although very well trained, yet wholly unused to such a sight, which appeared as if a mountain moved before him, reared up on his hinder feet: but that prince, who is an excellent horseman, kept his seat, until his attendants ran in, and held the bridle, while his Majesty had time to dismount. When he alighted, he surveyed me round with great admiration, but kept beyond the length of my chains. He ordered his cooks and butlers, who were already prepared, to give me victuals and drink, which they pushed forward in a sort of vehicles upon wheels until I could reach them. I took these vehicles, and soon emptied them all; twenty of them were filled with meat, and ten with liquor; each of the former afforded me two or three good mouthfuls, and I emptied the liquor of ten vessels, which was contained in earthen vials, into one vehicle, drinking it off at a draught; and so I did with the rest. The Empress, and young princes of the blood, of both sexes, attended by many ladies, sat at some distance in their chairs; but upon the accident that happened to the Emperor's horse, they alighted, and came near his person; which I am now going to describe. He is taller, by almost the breadth of my nail, than any of his court, which alone is enough to strike an awe into the beholders. His features are strong and masculine, with an Austrian lip, and arched nose, his complexion olive, his countenance[3] erect, his body and limbs well proportioned, all his motions graceful, and his deportment majestic. He was then past his prime, being twenty-eight years and three quarters old, of which he had reigned about seven, in great felicity, and generally victorious. For the better convenience of beholding him, I lay on my side, so that my face was parallel to his, and he stood but three yards off: however, I have had him since many times in my hand, and therefore cannot be deceived in the description. His dress was very plain and simple, the fashion of it between the Asiatic and the European; but he had on his head a light helmet of gold, adorned with jewels, and a plume on the crest. He held his sword drawn in his hand, to defend himself, if I should happen to break loose; it was almost three inches long, the hilt and scabbard were gold enriched with diamonds. His voice was shrill, but very clear and articulate, and I could distinctly hear it when I stood up. The ladies and courtiers were all most magnificently clad, so that the spot they stood upon seemed to resemble a petticoat spread on the ground, embroidered with figures of gold and silver. His Imperial Majesty spoke often to me, and I returned answers, but neither of us could understand a syllable. There were several of his priests and lawyers present (as I conjectured by their habits) who were commanded to address themselves to me, and I spoke to them in as many languages as I had the least smattering of, which were High and Low Dutch, Latin, French, Spanish, Italian, and Lingua Franca;[4] but all to no purpose. After about two hours the court retired, and I was left with a strong guard, to prevent the impertinence, and probably the malice of the rabble, who were very impatient to crowd about me as near as they durst; and some of them had the impudence to shoot their arrows at me as I sat on the ground by the door of my house, whereof one very narrowly missed my left eye. But the colonel ordered six of the ringleaders to be seized, and

---

3. Bearing, appearance. Swift may be satirically idealizing George I, whom most of the British thought gross.

4. A jargon, based on Italian, used by traders in the Mediterranean. "High and Low Dutch": German and Dutch, respectively.

thought no punishment so proper as to deliver them bound into my hands, which some of his soldiers accordingly did, pushing them forwards with the butt-ends of their pikes into my reach; I took them all in my right hand, put five of them into my coat-pocket; and as to the sixth, I made a countenance as if I would eat him alive. The poor man squalled terribly, and the colonel and his officer were in much pain, especially when they saw me take out my penknife: but I soon put them out of fear; for, looking mildly, and immediately cutting the strings he was bound with, I set him gently on the ground, and away he ran. I treated the rest in the same manner, taking them one by one out of my pocket, and I observed both the soldiers and people were highly obliged at this mark of my clemency, which was represented very much to my advantage at court.

Towards night I got with some difficulty into my house, where I lay on the ground, and continued to do so about a fortnight; during which time the Emperor gave orders to have a bed prepared for me. Six hundred beds of the common measure were brought in carriages, and worked up in my house; an hundred and fifty of their beds sewn together made up the breadth and length, and these were four double, which however kept me but very indifferently from the hardness of the floor, that was of smooth stone. By the same computation they provided me with sheets, blankets, and coverlets, tolerable enough for one who had been so long enured to hardships as I.

As the news of my arrival spread through the kingdom, it brought prodigious numbers of rich, idle, and curious people to see me; so that the villages were almost emptied, and great neglect of tillage and household affairs must have ensued, if his Imperial Majesty had not provided by several proclamations and orders of state against this inconveniency. He directed that those who had already beheld me should return home, and not presume to come within fifty yards of my house without license from court; whereby the secretaries of state got considerable fees.

In the mean time, the Emperor held frequent councils to debate what course should be taken with me; and I was afterwards assured by a particular friend, a person of great quality, who was as much in the secret as any, that the court was under many difficulties concerning me. They apprehended[5] my breaking loose, that my diet would be very expensive, and might cause a famine. Sometimes they determined to starve me, or at least to shoot me in the face and hands with poisoned arrows, which would soon dispatch me: but again they considered, that the stench of so large a carcass might produce a plague in the metropolis, and probably spread through the whole kingdom. In the midst of these consultations, several officers of the army went to the door of the great council chamber; and two of them being admitted, gave an account of my behavior to the six criminals above-mentioned; which made so favorable an impression in the breast of his Majesty, and the whole board, in my behalf, that an imperial commission was issued out, obliging all the villages nine hundred yards round the city to deliver in every morning six beeves, forty sheep, and other victuals for my sustenance; together with a proportionable quantity of bread and wine, and other liquors: for the due payment of which his Majesty gave assignments[6] upon his treasury. For this prince lives chiefly upon his own demesnes; seldom except upon great occasions raising any subsidies upon his subjects, who are bound

---

5. Anticipated with fear.   6. Formal mandates of revenue.

to attend him in his wars at their own expense. An establishment was also made of six hundred persons to be my domestics, who had board-wages allowed for their maintenance, and tents built for them very conveniently on each side of my door. It was likewise ordered, that three hundred tailors should make me a suit of clothes after the fashion of the country: that six of his Majesty's greatest scholars should be employed to instruct me in their language: and, lastly, that the Emperor's horses, and those of the nobility, and troops of guards, should be exercised in my sight, to accustom themselves to me. All these orders were duly put in execution; and in about three weeks I made a great progress in learning their language; during which time the Emperor frequently honored me with his visits, and was pleased to assist my masters in teaching me. We began already to converse together in some sort; and the first words I learned, were to express my desire that he would please to give me my liberty; which I every day repeated on my knees.[7] His answer, as I could apprehend, was, that this must be a work of time, not to be thought on without the advice of his council; and that first I must *Lumos kelmin pesso desmar lon emposo;* that is, swear a peace with him and his kingdom. However, that I should be used with all kindness; and he advised me to acquire by my patience and discreet behavior, the good opinion of himself and his subjects. He desired I would not take it ill, if he gave orders to certain proper officers to search me; for probably I might carry about me several weapons, which must needs be dangerous things, if they answered the bulk of so prodigious a person.[8] I said, his Majesty should be satisfied, for I was ready to strip myself, and turn up my pockets before him. This I delivered part in words, and part in signs. He replied, that by the laws of the kingdom, I must be searched by two of his officers; that he knew this could not be done without my consent and assistance; that he had so good an opinion of my generosity and justice, as to trust their persons in my hands; that whatever they took from me should be returned when I left the country, or paid for at the rate which I would set upon them. I took up the two officers in my hands, put them first into my coat-pockets, and then into every other pocket about me, except my two fobs, and another secret pocket which I had no mind should be searched, wherein I had some little necessaries of no consequence to any but myself. In one of my fobs there was a silver watch, and in the other a small quantity of gold in a purse. These gentlemen, having pen, ink, and paper about them, made an exact inventory of everything they saw; and when they had done, desired I would set them down, that they might deliver it to the Emperor. This inventory I afterwards translated into English, and is word for word as follows.

Imprimis,[9] In the right coat-pocket of the Great Man-Mountain (for so I interpret the words *Quinbus Flestrin*) after the strictest search, we found only one great piece of coarse cloth, large enough to be a foot-cloth for your Majesty's chief room of state. In the left pocket, we saw a huge silver chest, with a cover of the same metal, which we the searchers were not able to lift. We desired it should be opened; and one of us, stepping into it, found himself up to the mid leg in a sort of dust, some part

---

7. Gulliver's plea for liberty and the threat of starvation or rebellion he represents to his captors suggest the situation of Ireland with respect to England.
8. When the Whigs came into power in 1715, the leading Tories, who included Swift's friends Oxford and Bolingbroke (Robert Harley and Henry St. John) as well as Swift himself, were investigated by a committee of secrecy.
9. In the first place (Latin).

whereof flying up to our faces, set us both a sneezing for several times together. In his right waistcoat-pocket, we found a prodigious bundle of white thin substances, folded one over another, about the bigness of three men, tied with a strong cable, and marked with black figures; which we humbly conceive to be writings; every letter almost half as large as the palm of our hands. In the left there was a sort of engine, from the back of which were extended twenty long poles, resembling the palisados[1] before your Majesty's court; wherewith we conjecture the Man-Mountain combs his head; for we did not always trouble him with questions, because we found it a great difficulty to make him understand us. In the large pocket on the right side of his middle cover (so I translate the word *ranfu-lo,* by which they meant my breeches) we saw a hollow pillar of iron, about the length of a man, fastened to a strong piece of timber, larger than the pillar; and upon one side of the pillar were huge pieces of iron sticking out, cut into strange figures; which we know not what to make of. In the left pocket, another engine of the same kind. In the smaller pocket on the right side, were several round flat pieces of white and red metal, of different bulk; some of the white, which seemed to be silver, were so large and heavy, that my comrade and I could hardly lift them. In the left pocket were two black pillars irregularly shaped: we could not, without difficulty, reach the top of them as we stood at the bottom of his pocket. One of them was covered, and seemed all of a piece; but at the upper end of the other, there appeared a white round substance, about twice the bigness of our heads. Within each of these was inclosed a prodigious plate of steel; which, by our orders, we obliged him to show us, because we apprehended they might be dangerous engines. He took them out of their cases, and told us, that in his own country his practice was to shave his beard with one of these, and to cut his meat with the other. There were two pockets which we could not enter: these he called his fobs; they were two large slits cut into the top of his middle cover, but squeezed close by the pressure of his belly. Out of the right fob hung a great silver chain, with a wonderful kind of engine at the bottom. We directed him to draw out whatever was at the end of the chain, which appeared to be a globe, half silver, and half of some transparent metal: for on the transparent side we saw certain strange figures circularly drawn, and thought we could touch them, until we found our fingers stopped with that lucid substance. He put this engine to our ears, which made an incessant noise like that of a water-mill. And we conjecture it is either some unknown animal, or the god that he worships: but we are more inclined to the latter opinion, because he assured us (if we understood him right, for he expressed himself very imperfectly), that he seldom did any thing without consulting it. He called it his oracle, and said it pointed out the time for every action of his life. From the left fob he took out a net almost large enough for a fisher-man, but contrived to open and shut like a purse, and served him for the same use: we found therein several massy pieces of yellow metal, which if they be of real gold, must be of immense value.

Having thus, in obedience to your Majesty's commands, diligently searched all his pockets, we observed a girdle[2] about his waist made of

---

1. Fences of stakes.　　　　2. Belt.

the hide of some prodigious animal; from which, on the left side, hung a sword of the length of five men; and on the right, a bag or pouch divided into cells; each cell capable of holding three of your Majesty's subjects. In one of these cells were several globes or balls of a most ponderous metal, about the bigness of our heads, and required a strong hand to lift them: the other cell contained a heap of certain black grains, but of no great bulk or weight, for we could hold above fifty of them in the palms of our hands.

This is an exact inventory of what we found about the body of the Man-Mountain; who used us with great civility, and due respect to your Majesty's commission. Signed and sealed on the fourth day of the eighty-ninth moon of your Majesty's auspicious reign.

CLEFREN FRELOCK, MARSI FRELOCK.

When this inventory was read over to the Emperor, he directed me to deliver up the several particulars. He first called for my scimitar, which I took out, scabbard and all. In the meantime he ordered three thousand of his choicest troops (who then attended him) to surround me at a distance, with their bows and arrows just ready to discharge: but I did not observe it; for my eyes were wholly fixed upon his Majesty. He then desired me to draw my scimitar, which, although it had got some rust by the sea water, was in most parts exceeding bright. I did so, and immediately all the troops gave a shout between terror and surprise; for the sun shone clear, and the reflection dazzled their eyes, as I waved the scimitar to and fro in my hand. His Majesty, who is a most magnanimous[3] prince, was less daunted than I could expect; he ordered me to return it into the scabbard, and cast it on the ground as gently as I could, about six foot from the end of my chain. The next thing he demanded was one of the hollow iron pillars, by which he meant my pocket-pistols. I drew it out, and at his desire, as well as I could, expressed to him the use of it, and charging it only with powder, which by the closeness of my pouch happened to escape wetting in the sea (an inconvenience that all prudent mariners take special care to provide against), I first cautioned the Emperor not to be afraid; and then I let it off in the air. The astonishment here was much greater than at the sight of my scimitar. Hundreds fell down as if they had been struck dead; and even the Emperor, although he stood his ground, could not recover himself in some time. I delivered up both my pistols in the same manner as I had done my scimitar, and then my pouch of powder and bullets; begging him that the former might be kept from fire; for it would kindle with the smallest spark, and blow up his imperial palace into the air. I likewise delivered up my watch, which the Emperor was very curious to see; and commanded two of his tallest yeomen of the guards to bear it on a pole upon their shoulders, as draymen in England do a barrel of ale. He was amazed at the continual noise it made, and the motion of the minute-hand, which he could easily discern; for their sight is much more acute than ours: he asked the opinions of his learned men about him, which were various and remote, as the reader may well imagine without my repeating; although indeed I could not very perfectly understand them. I then gave up my silver and copper money, my purse with nine large pieces of gold,

---

3. Courageous, great-spirited. Magnanimity, the relation (direct or inverse) between the size of the body and the soul, is a central concern of the first two parts of the *Travels*.

and some smaller ones; my knife and razor, my comb and silver snuffbox, my handkerchief and journal book. My scimitar, pistols, and pouch, were conveyed in carriages to his Majesty's stores; but the rest of my goods were returned me.

I had, as I before observed, one private pocket which escaped their search, wherein there was a pair of spectacles (which I sometimes use for the weakness of my eyes), a pocket perspective,[4] and several other little conveniences; which, being of no consequence to the Emperor, I did not think myself bound in honor to discover, and I apprehended they might be lost or spoiled if I ventured them out of my possession.

CHAPTER 3. *The author diverts the Emperor and his nobility of both sexes in a very uncommon manner. The diversions of the court of Lilliput described. The author hath his liberty granted him upon certain conditions.*

My gentleness and good behavior had gained so far on the Emperor and his court, and indeed upon the army and people in general, that I began to conceive hopes of getting my liberty in a short time. I took all possible methods to cultivate this favorable disposition. The natives came by degrees to be less apprehensive of any danger from me. I would sometimes lie down, and let five or six of them dance on my hand. And at last the boys and girls would venture to come and play at hide-and-seek in my hair. I had now made a good progress in understanding and speaking their language. The Emperor had a mind one day to entertain me with several of the country shows; wherein they exceed all nations I have known, both for dexterity and magnificence. I was diverted with none so much as that of the rope-dancers, performed upon a slender white thread, extended about two foot, and twelve inches from the ground. Upon which I shall desire liberty, with the reader's patience, to enlarge a little.

This diversion is only practiced by those persons who are candidates for great employments, and high favor, at court. They are trained in this art from their youth, and are not always of noble birth, or liberal education. When a great office is vacant either by death or disgrace (which often happens) five or six of those candidates petition the Emperor to entertain his Majesty and the court with a dance on the rope; and whoever jumps the highest without falling, succeeds in the office. Very often the chief ministers themselves are commanded to show their skill, and to convince the Emperor that they have not lost their faculty. Flimnap,[5] the Treasurer, is allowed to cut a caper on the strait rope, at least an inch higher than any other lord in the whole empire. I have seen him do the summerset several times together upon a trencher[6] fixed on the rope, which is no thicker than a common packthread in England. My friend Reldresal, Principal Secretary for Private Affairs, is, in my opinion, if I am not partial, the second after the Treasurer; the rest of the great officers are much upon a par.

These diversions are often attended with fatal accidents, whereof great numbers are on record. I myself have seen two or three candidates break a limb. But the danger is much greater when the ministers themselves are commanded to show their dexterity; for, by contending to excel themselves

---

4. Telescope.
5. Sir Robert Walpole, the Whig head of the government, was notorious in Swift's circle for his political acrobatics.
6. Plate. "Summerset": somersault.

and their fellows, they strain so far, that there is hardly one of them who hath not received a fall; and some of them two or three. I was assured, that a year or two before my arrival, Flimnap would have infallibly broke his neck, if one of the King's cushions,[7] that accidentally lay on the ground, had not weakened the force of his fall.

There is likewise another diversion, which is only shown before the Emperor and Empress, and first minister, upon particular occasions. The Emperor lays on a table three fine silken threads of six inches long. One is blue, the other red, and the third green.[8] These threads are proposed as prizes for those persons whom the Emperor hath a mind to distinguish by a peculiar mark of his favor. The ceremony is performed in his Majesty's great chamber of state; where the candidates are to undergo a trial of dexterity very different from the former, and such as I have not observed the least resemblance of in any other country of the old or the new world. The Emperor holds a stick in his hands, both ends parallel to the horizon, while the candidates, advancing one by one, sometimes leap over the stick, sometimes creep under it backwards and forwards several times, according as the stick is advanced or depressed. Sometimes the Emperor holds one end of the stick, and his first minister the other; sometimes the minister has it entirely to himself. Whoever performs his part with most agility, and holds out the longest in *leaping* and *creeping*, is rewarded with the blue-colored silk; the red is given to the next, and the green to the third, which they all wear girt twice round about the middle; and you see few great persons about this court who are not adorned with one of these girdles.

The horses of the army, and those of the royal stables, having been daily led before me, were no longer shy, but would come up to my very feet, without starting. The riders would leap them over my hand as I held it on the ground; and one of the Emperor's huntsmen, upon a large courser, took[9] my foot, shoe and all; which was indeed a prodigious leap. I had the good fortune to divert the Emperor one day after a very extraordinary manner. I desired he would order several sticks of two foot high, and the thickness of an ordinary cane, to be brought me; whereupon his Majesty commanded the master of his woods to give directions accordingly; and the next morning six woodmen arrived with as many carriages, drawn by eight horses to each. I took nine of these sticks, and fixing them firmly in the ground in a quadrangular figure, two foot and a half square, I took four other sticks, and tied them parallel at each corner, about two foot from the ground; then I fastened my handkerchief to the nine sticks that stood erect, and extended it on all sides till it was as tight as the top of a drum; and the four parallel sticks, rising about five inches higher than the handkerchief, served as ledges on each side. When I had finished my work, I desired the Emperor to let a troop of his best horse, twenty-four in number, come and exercise upon this plain. His Majesty approved of the proposal, and I took them up one by one in my hands, ready mounted and armed, with the proper officers to exercise them. As soon as they got into order, they divided into two parties, performed mock skirmishes, discharged blunt arrows, drew their swords, fled and pursued, attacked and retired; and in short discovered the best military discipline I ever beheld. The parallel sticks secured them and their

7. A mistress of George I was supposed to have helped restore Walpole to office in 1721.
8. The Orders of the Garter, the Bath, and the

Thistle, conferred for services to the king.
9. Jumped over.

horses from falling over the stage; and the Emperor was so much delighted, that he ordered this entertainment to be repeated several days; and once was pleased to be lifted up, and give the word of command; and, with great difficulty, persuaded even the Empress herself to let me hold her in her close chair[1] within two yards of the stage, from whence she was able to take a full view of the whole performance. It was my good fortune that no ill accident happened in these entertainments, only once a fiery horse that belonged to one of the captains pawing with his hoof struck a hole in my handkerchief, and his foot slipping, he overthrew his rider and himself; but I immediately relieved them both; for covering the hole with one hand, I set down the troop with the other, in the same manner as I took them up. The horse that fell was strained in the left shoulder, but the rider got no hurt, and I repaired my handkerchief as well as I could; however, I would not trust to the strength of it any more in such dangerous enterprises.

About two or three days before I was set at liberty, as I was entertaining the court with these kinds of feats, there arrived an express to inform his Majesty that some of his subjects, riding near the place where I was first taken up, had seen a great black substance lying on the ground, very oddly shaped, extending its edges round as wide as his Majesty's bedchamber, and rising up in the middle as high as a man; that it was no living creature, as they at first apprehended, for it lay on the grass without motion, and some of them had walked round it several times; that by mounting upon each other's shoulders, they had got to the top, which was flat and even; and stamping upon it they found it was hollow within; that they humbly conceived it might be something belonging to the Man-Mountain, and if his Majesty pleased, they would undertake to bring it with only five horses. I presently[2] knew what they meant; and was glad at heart to receive this intelligence. It seems upon my first reaching the shore after our shipwreck, I was in such confusion, that before I came to the place where I went to sleep, my hat, which I had fastened with a string to my head while I was rowing, and had stuck on all the time I was swimmings, fell off after I came to land; the string, as I conjecture, breaking by some accident which I never observed, but thought my hat had been lost at sea. I intreated his Imperial Majesty to give orders it might be brought to me as soon as possible, describing to him the use and the nature of it: and the next day the wagoners arrived with it, but not in a very good condition; they had bored two holes in the brim, within an inch and half of the edge, and fastened two hooks in the holes; these hooks were tied by a long cord to the harness, and thus my hat was dragged along for above half an English mile: but the ground in that country being extremely smooth and level, it received less damage than I expected.

Two days after this adventure, the Emperor, having ordered that part of his army which quarters in and about his metropolis to be in a readiness, took a fancy of diverting himself in a very singular manner. He desired I would stand like a colossus, with my legs as far asunder as I conveniently could. He then commanded his general (who was an old experienced leader, and a great patron of mine) to draw up the troops in close order, and march them under me; the foot[3] by twenty-four in a breast, and the horse by sixteen, with drums beating, colors flying, and pikes advanced. This body consisted of three thousand

1. An enclosed or sedan chair.
2. Immediately.

3. Foot soldiers or infantry.

foot, and a thousand horse. His Majesty gave orders, upon pain of death, that every soldier in his march should observe the strictest decency with regard to my person; which, however, could not prevent some of the younger officers from turning up their eyes as they passed under me. And, to confess the truth, my breeches were at that time in so ill a condition, that they afforded some opportunities for laughter and admiration.

I had sent so many memorials and petitions for my liberty, that his Majesty at length mentioned the matter first in the cabinet, and then in a full council; where it was opposed by none, except Skyresh Bolgolam,[4] who was pleased, without any provocation, to be my mortal enemy. But it was carried against him by the whole board, and confirmed by the Emperor. That minister was *Galbet*, or Admiral of the Realm; very much in his master's confidence, and a person well versed in affairs, but of a morose and sour complexion.[5] However, he was at length persuaded to comply; but prevailed that the articles and conditions upon which I should be set free, and to which I must swear, should be drawn up by himself. These articles were brought to me by Skyresh Bolgolam in person, attended by two under-secretaries, and several persons of distinction. After they were read, I was demanded to swear to the performance of them; first in the manner of my own country, and afterwards in the method prescribed by their laws; which was to hold my right foot in my left hand, to place the middle finger of my right hand on the crown of my head, and my thumb on the tip of my right ear. But because the reader may perhaps be curious to have some idea of the style and manner of expression peculiar to that people, as well as to know the articles upon which I recovered my liberty, I have made a translation of the whole instrument,[6] word for word, as near as I was able; which I here offer to the public.

GOLBASTO MOMAREN EVLAME GURDILO SHEFIN MULLY ULLY GUE, most mighty Emperor of Lilliput, delight and terror of the universe, whose dominions extend five thousand blustrugs (about twelve miles in circumference) to the extremities of the globe; Monarch of all Monarchs; taller than the sons of men; whose feet press down to the center, and whose head strikes against the sun; at whose nod the princes of the earth shake their knees; pleasant as the spring, comfortable as the summer, fruitful as autumn, dreadful as winter. His most sublime Majesty proposeth to the Man-Mountain, lately arrived at our celestial dominions, the following articles, which by a solemn oath he shall be obliged to perform.

First, The Man-Mountain shall not depart from our dominions, without our license under our great seal.

Secondly, He shall not presume to come into our metropolis, without our express order; at which time the inhabitants shall have two hours warning, to keep within their doors.

Thirdly, The said Man-Mountain shall confine his walks to our principal high roads; and not offer to walk or lie down in a meadow, or field of corn.

Fourthly, As he walks the said roads, he shall take the utmost care not to trample upon the bodies of any of our loving subjects, their horses, or

---

4. The earl of Nottingham, an enemy of Swift.   6. A formal legal document.
5. Disposition.

carriages, nor take any of our said subjects into his hands, without their own consent.

Fifthly, If an express require extraordinary dispatch, the Man-Mountain shall be obliged to carry in his pocket the messenger and horse, a six days' journey once in every moon, and return the said messenger back (if so required) safe to our Imperial Presence.

Sixthly, He shall be our ally against our enemies in the island of Blefuscu, and do his utmost to destroy their fleet, which is now preparing to invade us.

Seventhly, That the said Man-Mountain shall, at his times of leisure, be aiding and assisting to our workmen, in helping to raise certain great stones, towards covering the wall of the principal park, and other our royal buildings.

Eighthly, That the said Man-Mountain shall, in two moons' time, deliver in an exact survey of the circumference of our dominions by a computation of his own paces round the coast.

Lastly, That upon his solemn oath to observe all the above articles, the said Man-Mountain shall have a daily allowance of meat and drink sufficient for the support of 1,728 of our subjects; with free access to our Royal Person, and other marks of our favor. Given at our palace at Belfaborac the twelfth day of the ninety-first moon of our reign.

I swore and subscribed to these articles with great cheerfulness and content, although some of them were not so honorable as I could have wished; which proceeded wholly from the malice of Skyresh Bolgolam the High Admiral: whereupon my chains were immediately unlocked, and I was at full liberty: the Emperor himself in person did me the honor to be by at the whole ceremony. I made my acknowledgements by prostrating myself at his Majesty's feet: but he commanded me to rise; and after many gracious expressions, which, to avoid the censure of vanity, I shall not repeat, he added, that he hoped I should prove a useful servant, and well deserve all the favors he had already conferred upon me, or might do for the future.

The reader may please to observe, that in the last article for the recovery of my liberty, the Emperor stipulates to allow me a quantity of meat and drink, sufficient for the support of 1,728 Lilliputians. Some time after, asking a friend at court how they came to fix on that determinate number, he told me, that his Majesty's mathematicians, having taken the height of my body by the help of a quadrant, and finding it to exceed theirs in the proportion of twelve to one, they concluded from the similarity of their bodies, that mine must contain at least 1,728 of theirs, and consequently would require as much food as was necessary to support that number of Lilliputians. By which, the reader may conceive an idea of the ingenuity of that people, as well as the prudent and exact economy of so great a prince.

CHAPTER 4. *Mildendo, the metropolis of Lilliput, described, together with the Emperor's palace. A conversation between the author and a principal secretary, concerning the affairs of that empire; the author's offers to serve the Emperor in his wars.*

The first request I made after I had obtained my liberty, was, that I might have license to see Mildendo, the metropolis; which the Emperor easily granted me, but with a special charge to do no hurt, either to the inhabitants, or their houses. The people had notice by proclamation of my design to visit the town. The wall which encompassed it is two foot and an half high, and at least eleven inches broad, so that a coach and horses may be driven very safely round it; and it is flanked with strong towers at ten foot distance. I stepped over the great western gate, and passed very gently, and sideling[7] through the two principal streets, only in my short waistcoat, for fear of damaging the roofs and eaves of the houses with the skirts of my coat. I walked with the utmost circumspection, to avoid treading on any stragglers, who might remain in the streets, although the orders were very strict, that all people should keep in their houses, at their own peril. The garret windows and tops of houses were so crowded with spectators, that I thought in all my travels I had not seen a more populous place. The city is an exact square, each side of the wall being five hundred foot long. The two great streets, which run cross and divide it into four quarters, are five foot wide. The lanes and alleys, which I could not enter, but only viewed them as I passed, are from twelve to eighteen inches. The town is capable of holding five hundred thousand souls. The houses are from three to five stories. The shops and markets well provided.

The Emperor's palace is in the center of the city, where the two great streets meet. It is enclosed by a wall of two foot high, and twenty foot distant from the buildings. I had his Majesty's permission to step over this wall; and the space being so wide between that and the palace, I could easily view it on every side. The outward court is a square of forty foot, and includes two other courts: in the inmost are the royal apartments, which I was very desirous to see, but found it extremely difficult; for the great gates, from one square into another, were but eighteen inches high, and seven inches wide. Now the buildings of the outer court were at least five foot high; and it was impossible for me to stride over them, without infinite damage to the pile, although the walls were strongly built of hewn stone, and four inches thick. At the same time the Emperor had a great desire that I should see the magnificence of his palace; but this I was not able to do till three days after, which I spent in cutting down with my knife some of the largest trees in the royal park, about an hundred yards distance from the city. Of these trees I made two stools, each about three foot high, and strong enough to bear my weight. The people having received notice a second time, I went again through the city to the palace, with my two stools in my hands. When I came to the side of the outer court, I stood upon one stool, and took the other in my hand: this I lifted over the roof, and gently set it down on the space between the first and second court, which was eight foot wide. I then stepped over the buildings very conveniently from one stool to the other, and drew up the first after me with a hooked stick. By this contrivance I got into the inmost court; and lying down upon my side, I applied my face to the windows of the middle stories, which were left open on purpose, and discovered the most splendid apartments that can be imagined. There I saw the Empress, and the young princes in their several lodgings, with their chief attendants about them. Her Imperial Majesty was pleased to smile very graciously upon me and gave me out of the window her hand to kiss.

But I shall not anticipate the reader with farther descriptions of this kind, because I reserve them for a greater work, which is now almost ready

---

7. Sideways.

for the press; containing a general description of this empire, from its first erection, through a long series of princes, with a particular account of their wars and politics, laws, learning, and religion; their plants and animals, their peculiar manners and customs, with other matters very curious and useful; my chief design at present being only to relate such events and transactions as happened to the public, or to myself, during a residence of about nine months in that empire.

One morning, about a fortnight after I had obtained my liberty, Reldresal, Principal Secretary (as they style him) of Private Affairs, came to my house, attended only by one servant. He ordered his coach to wait at a distance, and desired I would give him an hour's audience; which I readily consented to, on account of his quality, and personal merits, as well as of the many good offices he had done me during my solicitations at court. I offered to lie down, that he might the more conveniently reach my ear; but he chose rather to let me hold him in my hand during our conversation. He began with compliments on my liberty, said he might pretend to some merit in it; but, however, added, that if it had not been for the present situation of things at court, perhaps I might not have obtained it so soon. For, said he, as flourishing a condition as we appear to be in to foreigners, we labor under two mighty evils; a violent faction at home, and the danger of an invasion by a most potent enemy from abroad. As to the first, you are to understand, that for above seventy moons past, there have been two struggling parties in the empire, under the names of *Tramecksan*, and *Slamecksan*,[8] from the high and low heels on their shoes, by which they distinguish themselves.

It is alleged indeed, that the high heels are most agreeable to our ancient constitution: but however this be, his Majesty hath determined to make use of only low heels in the administration of the government and all offices in the gift of the crown; as you cannot but observe; and particularly, that his Majesty's imperial heels are lower at least by a *drurr* than any of his court; (*drurr* is a measure about the fourteenth part of an inch). The animosities between these two parties run so high, that they will neither eat nor drink, nor talk with each other. We compute the *Tramecksan*, or High-Heels, to exceed us in number; but the power is wholly on our side. We apprehend his Imperial Highness, the heir to the crown, to have some tendency towards the High-Heels; at least we can plainly discover one of his heels higher than the other, which gives him a hobble in his gait.[9] Now, in the midst of these intestine disquiets, we are threatened with an invasion from the island of Blefuscu,[1] which is the other great empire of the universe, almost as large and powerful as this of his Majesty. For as to what we have heard you affirm, that there are other kingdoms and states in the world, inhabited by human creatures as large as yourself, our philosophers are in much doubt; and would rather conjecture that you dropped from the moon, or one of the stars; because it is certain, that an hundred mortals of your bulk would, in a short time, destroy all the fruits and cattle of his Majesty's dominions. Besides, our histories of six thousand moons make no mention of any other regions, than the two great empires of Lilliput and Blefuscu. Which two mighty powers have, as I was going to tell you, been engaged in a most obstinate war for six and thirty moons past. It began upon the following occasion.

8. Tory (High Church) and Whig (Low Church), respectively.
9. The prince of Wales (later George II) had

friends in both parties.
1. France.

It is allowed on all hands, that the primitive way of breaking eggs before we eat them, was upon the larger end: but his present Majesty's grandfather, while he was a boy, going to eat an egg, and breaking it according to the ancient practice, happened to cut one of his fingers. Whereupon the Emperor his father published an edict, commanding all his subjects, upon great penalties, to break the smaller end of their eggs. The people so highly resented this law, that our histories tell us there have been six rebellions raised on that account; wherein one emperor lost his life, and another his crown.[2] These civil commotions were constantly fomented by the monarchs of Blefuscu; and when they were quelled, the exiles always fled for refuge to that empire. It is computed, that eleven thousand persons have, at several times, suffered death, rather than submit to break their eggs at the smaller end. Many hundred large volumes have been published upon this controversy: but the books of the Big-Endians have been long forbidden, and the whole party rendered incapable by law of holding employments.[3] During the course of these troubles, the emperors of Blefuscu did frequently expostulate by their ambassadors, accusing us of making a schism in religion, by offending against a fundamental doctrine of our great prophet Lustrog, in the fifty-fourth chapter of the *Brundecral* (which is their Alcoran[4]). This, however, is thought to be a mere strain upon the text: for the words are these; *That all true believers shall break their eggs at the convenient end*: and which is the convenient end, seems, in my humble opinion, to be left to every man's conscience, or at least in the power of the chief magistrate[5] to determine. Now the Big-Endian exiles have found so much credit in the Emperor of Blefuscu's court, and so much private assistance and encouragement from their party here at home, that a bloody war hath been carried on between the two empires for six and thirty moons with various success;[6] during which time we have lost forty capital ships, and a much greater number of smaller vessels, together with thirty thousand of our best seamen and soldiers; and the damage received by the enemy is reckoned to be somewhat greater than ours. However, they have now equipped a numerous fleet, and are just preparing to make a descent upon us; and his Imperial Majesty, placing great confidence in your valor and strength, hath commanded me to lay this account of his affairs before you.

I desired the Secretary to present my humble duty to the Emperor, and to let him know, that I thought it would not become me, who was a foreigner, to interfere with parties; but I was ready, with the hazard of my life, to defend his person and state against all invaders.

CHAPTER 5. *The author by an extraordinary stratagem prevents an invasion. A high title of honor is conferred upon him. Ambassadors arrive from the Emperor of Blefuscu, and sue for peace. The Empress's apartment on fire by an accident; the author instrumental in saving the rest of the palace.*

The empire of Blefuscu is an island situated to the north north-east side of Lilliput, from whence it is parted only by a channel of eight hundred yards

---

2. Swift's satirical allegory of the strife between Catholics (Big-Endians) and Protestants (Little-Endians) touches on Henry VIII (who "broke" with the Pope), Charles I (who lost his life), and James II (who lost his crown).
3. The Test Act (1673) prevented Catholics and Nonconformists from holding office unless they accepted the Anglican Sacrament.
4. Koran.
5. Ruler, sovereign. Swift himself accepted the right of the king to determine religious observances.
6. Reminiscent of the War of the Spanish Succession (1702–13).

wide. I had not yet seen it, and upon this notice of an intended invasion, I avoided appearing on that side of the coast, for fear of being discovered by some of the enemy's ships, who had received no intelligence of me; all intercourse between the two empires having been strictly forbidden during the war, upon pain of death; and an embargo laid by our Emperor upon all vessels whatsoever. I communicated to his Majesty a project I had formed of seizing the enemy's whole fleet; which, as our scouts assured us, lay at anchor in the harbor ready to sail with the first fair wind. I consulted the most experienced seamen upon the depth of the channel, which they had often plumbed; who told me, that in the middle at high water it was seventy *glumgluffs* deep, which is about six foot of European measure; and the rest of it fifty *glumgluffs* at most. I walked to the northeast coast over against Blefuscu; where, lying down behind a hillock, I took out my small pocket perspective glass, and viewed the enemy's fleet at anchor, consisting of about fifty men of war, and a great number of transports: I then came back to my house, and gave order (for which I had a warrant) for a great quantity of the strongest cable and bars of iron. The cable was about as thick as packthread and the bars of the length and size of a knitting-needle. I trebled the cable to make it stronger, and for the same reason I twisted three of the iron bars together, bending the extremities into a hook. Having thus fixed fifty hooks to as many cables, I went back to the northeast coast, and putting off my coat, shoes, and stockings, walked into the sea in my leathern jerkin, about half an hour before high water. I waded with what haste I could, and swam in the middle about thirty yards until I felt the ground; I arrived at the fleet in less than half an hour. The enemy was so frighted when they saw me, that they leaped out of their ships, and swam to shore, where there could not be fewer than thirty thousand souls. I then took my tackling, and fastening a hook to the hole at the prow of each, I tied all the cords together at the end. While I was thus employed, the enemy discharged several thousand arrows, many of which stuck in my hands and face; and besides the excessive smart, gave me much disturbance in my work. My greatest apprehension was for my eyes, which I should have infallibly lost, if I had not suddenly thought of an expedient. I kept, among other little necessaries, a pair of spectacles in a private pocket, which, as I observed before, had escaped the Emperor's searchers. These I took out, and fastened as strongly as I could upon my nose; and thus armed went on boldly with my work in spite of the enemy's arrows; many of which struck against the glasses of my spectacles, but without any other effect, further than a little to discompose them. I had now fastened all the hooks, and taking the knot in my hand, began to pull; but not a ship would stir, for they were all too fast by their anchors, so that the boldest part of my enterprise remained. I therefore let go the cord, and leaving the hooks fixed to the ships, I resolutely cut with my knife the cables that fastened the anchors, receiving about two hundred shots in my face and hands; then I took up the knotted end of the cables to which my hooks were tied; and with great ease drew fifty of the enemy's largest men-of-war after me.

The Blefuscudians, who had not the least imagination of what I intended, were at first confounded with astonishment. They had seen me cut the cables, and thought my design was only to let the ships run adrift, or fall foul on each other: but when they perceived the whole fleet moving in order, and saw me pulling at the end, they set up such a scream of grief and despair, that it is almost impossible to describe or conceive. When I had got out of danger, I stopped a while to pick out the arrows that stuck in my hands and face, and rubbed on some of the same ointment that was given me at my first arrival, as I have formerly mentioned. I then took off my spectacles, and waiting about an hour until the tide was a little fallen, I waded through the middle with my cargo, and arrived safe at the royal port of Lilliput.

The Emperor and his whole court stood on the shore, expecting the issue of this great adventure. They saw the ships move forward in a large half-moon, but could not discern me, who was up to my breast in water. When I advanced to the middle of the channel, they were yet more in pain, because I was under water to my neck. The Emperor concluded me to be drowned, and that the enemy's fleet was approaching in a hostile manner: but he was soon eased of his fears, for the channel growing shallower every step I made, I came in a short time within hearing; and holding up the end of the cable by which the fleet was fastened, I cried in a loud voice, Long live the most puissant Emperor of Lilliput! This great prince received me at my landing with all possible encomiums, and created me a *Nardac* upon the spot, which is the highest title of honor among them.

His Majesty desired I would take some other opportunity of bringing all the rest of his enemy's ships into his ports. And so unmeasurable is the ambition of princes, that he seemed to think of nothing less than reducing the whole empire of Blefuscu into a province, and governing it by a viceroy; of destroying the Big-Endian exiles, and compelling that people to break the smaller end of their eggs, by which he would remain sole monarch of the whole world. But I endeavored to divert him from this design, by many arguments drawn from the topics of policy as well as justice: and I plainly protested, that I would never be an instrument of bringing a free and brave people into slavery. And when the matter was debated in council, the wisest part of the ministry were of my opinion.

This open bold declaration of mine was so opposite to the schemes and politics of his Imperial Majesty, that he could never forgive me; he mentioned it in a very artful manner at council, where I was told that some of the wisest appeared, at least by their silence, to be of my opinion; but others, who were my secret enemies, could not forbear some expressions, which by a side-wind[7] reflected on me. And from this time began an intrigue between his Majesty and a junta of ministers maliciously bent against me, which broke out in less than two months, and had like to have ended in my utter destruction. Of so little weight are the greatest services to princes, when put into the balance with a refusal to gratify their passions.[8]

About three weeks after this exploit, there arrived a solemn embassy from Blefuscu, with humble offers of a peace; which was soon concluded upon conditions very advantageous to our Emperor; wherewith I shall not trouble the reader. There were six ambassadors, with a train of about five hundred persons; and their entry was very magnificent, suitable to the grandeur of their master, and the importance of their business. When their treaty was finished, wherein I did them several good offices by the credit I now had, or at least appeared to have at court, their Excellencies, who were privately told how much I had been their friend, made me a visit in form. They began with many compliments upon my valor and generosity; invited me to that king-

---

7. Indirectly.
8. After a series of British naval victories, the Treaty of Utrecht (1713) had ended the war with France, but the Tory ministers who engineered the peace were subsequently accused of having sold out to the enemy.

dom in the Emperor their master's name; and desired me to show them some proofs of my prodigious strength, of which they had heard so many wonders; wherein I readily obliged them, but shall not interrupt the reader with the particulars.

When I had for some time entertained their Excellencies to their infinite satisfaction and surprise, I desired they would do me the honor to present my most humble respects to the Emperor their master, the renown of whose virtues had so justly filled the whole world with admiration, and whose royal person I resolved to attend before I returned to my own country. Accordingly, the next time I had the honor to see our Emperor, I desired his general license to wait on the Blefuscudian monarch, which he was pleased to grant me, as I could plainly perceive, in a very cold manner; but could not guess the reason, till I had a whisper from a certain person, that Flimnap and Bolgolam had represented my intercourse with those ambassadors as a mark of disaffection, from which I am sure my heart was wholly free. And this was the first time I began to conceive some imperfect idea of courts and ministers.

It is to be observed, that these ambassadors spoke to me by an interpreter; the languages of both empires differing as much from each other as any two in Europe, and each nation priding itself upon the antiquity, beauty, and energy of their own tongues, with an avowed contempt for that of their neighbor; yet our Emperor, standing upon the advantage he had got by the seizure of their fleet, obliged them to deliver their credentials, and make their speech, in the Lilliputian tongue. And it must be confessed, that from the great intercourse of trade and commerce between both realms, from the continual reception of exiles, which is mutual among them, and from the custom in each empire to send their young nobility and richer gentry to the other, in order to polish themselves, by seeing the world, and understanding men and manners, there are few persons of distinction, or merchants, or seamen, who dwell in the maritime parts, but what can hold conversation in both tongues; as I found some weeks after, when I went to pay my respects to the Emperor of Blefuscu, which in the midst of great misfortunes, through the malice of my enemies, proved a very happy adventure to me, as I shall relate in its proper place.

The reader may remember, that when I signed those articles upon which I recovered my liberty, there were some which I disliked upon account of their being too servile, neither could any thing but an extreme necessity have forced me to submit. But being now a *Nardac*, of the highest rank in that empire, such offices[9] were looked upon as below my dignity, and the Emperor (to do him justice) never once mentioned them to me. However, it was not long before I had an opportunity of doing his Majesty, at least as I then thought, a most signal service. I was alarmed at midnight with the cries of many hundred people at my door; by which being suddenly awaked, I was in some kind of terror. I heard the word *burglum* repeated incessantly; several of the Emperor's court, making their way through the crowd, intreated me to come immediately to the palace, where her Imperial Majesty's apartment was on fire, by the carelessness of a maid of honor, who fell asleep while she was reading a romance. I got up in an instant; and orders being given to clear the way before me, and it being likewise a moonshine night, I made a shift to get to the palace without trampling on any of the

9. Duties.

people. I found they had already applied ladders to the walls of the apartment, and were well provided with buckets, but the water was at some distance. These buckets were about the size of a large thimble, and the poor people supplied me with them as fast as they could; but the flame was so violent, that they did little good. I might easily have stifled it with my coat, which I unfortunately left behind me for haste, and came away only in my leathern jerkin. The case seemed wholly desperate and deplorable; and this magnificent palace would have infallibly been burnt down to the ground, if, by a presence of mind, unusual to me, I had not suddenly thought of an expedient. I had the evening before drank plentifully of a most delicious wine, called *glimigrim* (the Blefuscudians call it *flunec*, but ours is esteemed the better sort), which is very diuretic. By the luckiest chance in the world, I had not discharged myself of any part of it. The heat I had contracted by coming very near the flames, and by my laboring to quench them, made the wine begin to operate by urine; which I voided in such a quantity, and applied so well to the proper places, that in three minutes the fire was wholly extinguished; and the rest of that noble pile, which had cost so many ages in erecting, preserved from destruction.

It was now daylight, and I returned to my house, without waiting to congratulate with the Emperor; because, although I had done a very eminent piece of service, yet I could not tell how his Majesty might resent the manner by which I had performed it: for, by the fundamental laws of the realm, it is capital[1] in any person, of what quality soever, to make water within the precincts of the palace. But I was a little comforted by a message from his Majesty, that he would give orders to the Grand Justiciary for passing my pardon in form; which, however, I could not obtain. And I was privately assured, that the Empress, conceiving the greatest abhorrence of what I had done,[2] removed to the most distant side of the court, firmly resolved that those buildings should never be repaired for her use; and, in the presence of her chief confidents, could not forbear vowing revenge.

CHAPTER 6. *Of the inhabitants of Lilliput; their learning, laws, and customs, the manner of educating their children. The author's way of living in that country. His vindication of a great lady.*

Although I intend to leave the description of this empire to a particular treatise, yet in the mean time I am content to gratify the curious reader with some general ideas. As the common size of the natives is somewhat under six inches, so there is an exact proportion in all other animals, as well as plants and trees: for instance, the tallest horses and oxen are between four and five inches in height, the sheep an inch and a half, more or less; their geese about the bigness of a sparrow; and so the several gradations downwards, till you come to the smallest, which, to my sight, were almost invisible; but nature hath adapted the eyes of the Lilliputians to all objects proper for their view: they see with great exactness, but at no great distance. And to show the sharpness of their sight towards objects that are near, I have been much pleased with observing a cook pulling[3] a lark, which was not so large

---

1. Punishable by death.
2. Queen Anne, whom Swift called "a royal prude," strongly objected to the coarseness of A

Tale of a Tub.
3. Plucking.

as a common fly; and a young girl threading an invisible needle with invisible silk. Their tallest trees are about seven foot high; I mean some of those in the great royal park, the tops whereof I could but just reach with my fist clinched. The other vegetables[4] are in the same proportion; but this I leave to the reader's imagination.

I shall say but little at present of their learning, which for many ages hath flourished in all its branches among them: but their manner of writing is very peculiar; being neither from the left to the right, like the Europeans; nor from the right to the left, like the Arabians; nor from up to down, like the Chinese; nor from down to up, like the Cascagians;[5] but aslant from one corner of the paper to the other, like ladies in England.

They bury their dead with their heads directly downwards; because they hold an opinion that in eleven thousand moons they are all to rise again; in which period, the earth (which they conceive to be flat) will turn upside down, and by this means they shall, at their resurrection, be found ready standing on their feet. The learned among them confess the absurdity of this doctrine; but the practice still continues, in compliance to the vulgar.[6]

There are some laws and customs in this empire very peculiar; and if they were not so directly contrary to those of my own dear country, I should be tempted to say a little in their justification. It is only to be wished, that they were as well executed. The first I shall mention relateth to informers. All crimes against the state are punished here with the utmost severity; but if the person accused make his innocence plainly to appear upon his trial, the accuser is immediately put to an ignominious death; and out of his goods or lands, the innocent person is quadruply recompensed for the loss of his time, for the danger he underwent, for the hardship of his imprisonment, and for all the charges he hath been at in making his defense. Or, if that fund be deficient, it is largely[7] supplied by the crown. The Emperor doth also confer on him some public mark of his favor; and proclamation is made of his innocence through the whole city.

They look upon fraud as a greater crime than theft, and therefore seldom fail to punish it with death; for they allege, that care and vigilance, with a very common understanding, may preserve a man's goods from thieves; but honesty hath no fence against superior cunning: and since it is necessary that there should be a perpetual intercourse of buying and selling, and dealing upon credit, where fraud is permitted or connived at, or hath no law to punish it, the honest dealer is always undone, and the knave gets the advantage. I remember when I was once interceding with the King for a criminal who had wronged his master of a great sum of money, which he had received by order, and ran away with; and happening to tell his Majesty, by way of extenuation, that it was only a breach of trust, the Emperor thought it monstrous in me to offer, as a defense, the greatest aggravation of the crime: and truly, I had little to say in return, farther than the common answer, that different nations had different customs; for, I confess, I was heartily ashamed.

Although we usually call reward and punishment the two hinges upon which all government turns, yet I could never observe this maxim to be put in practice by any nation, except that of Lilliput. Whoever can there bring sufficient proof that he hath strictly observed the laws of his country for

---

4. Plants.
5. Swift's invention.

6. The (beliefs of the) common people.
7. Fully.

seventy-three moons, hath a claim to certain privileges, according to his quality[8] and condition of life, with a proportionable sum of money out of a fund appropriated for that use: he likewise acquires the title of *Snilpall*, or *Legal*, which is added to his name, but doth not descend to his posterity. And these people thought it a prodigious defect of policy among us, when I told them that our laws were enforced only by penalties, without any mention of reward. It is upon this account that the image of Justice, in their courts of judicature, is formed with six eyes, two before, as many behind, and on each side one, to signify circumspection; with a bag of gold open in her right hand, and a sword sheathed in her left, to show she is more disposed to reward than to punish.

In choosing persons for all employments, they have more regard to good morals than to great abilities; for, since government is necessary to mankind, they believe that the common size of human understandings is fitted to some station or other; and that Providence never intended to make the management of public affairs a mystery, to be comprehended only by a few persons of sublime genius, of which there seldom are three born in an age: but they suppose truth, justice, temperance, and the like, to be in every man's power; the practice of which virtues, assisted by experience and a good intention, would qualify any man for the service of his country, except where a course of study is required. But they thought the want of moral virtues was so far from being supplied by superior endowments of the mind, that employments could never be put into such dangerous hands as those of persons so qualified; and at least, that the mistakes committed by ignorance in a virtuous disposition would never be of such fatal consequence to the public weal, as the practices of a man whose inclinations led him to be corrupt, and had great abilities to manage, to multiply, and defend his corruptions.

In like manner, the disbelief of a divine Providence renders a man uncapable of holding any public station; for since kings avow themselves to be the deputies of Providence, the Lilliputians think nothing can be more absurd than for a prince to employ such men as disown the authority under which he acteth.

In relating these and the following laws, I would only be understood to mean the original institutions, and not the most scandalous corruptions into which these people are fallen by the degenerate nature of man. For as to that infamous practice of acquiring great employments by dancing on the ropes, or badges of favor and distinction by leaping over sticks, and creeping under them, the reader is to observe, that they were first introduced by the grandfather of the Emperor now reigning; and grew to the present height by the gradual increase of party and faction.

Ingratitude is among them a capital crime, as we read it to have been in some other countries; for they reason thus, that whoever makes ill returns to his benefactor, must needs be a common enemy to the rest of mankind, from whom he hath received no obligation; and therefore such a man is not fit to live.

Their notions relating to the duties of parents and children differ extremely from ours. For, since the conjunction of male and female is founded upon the great law of nature, in order to propagate and continue the species, the Lilliputians will needs have it, that men and women are joined together like

8. Social position.

other animals, by the motives of concupiscence; and that their tenderness towards their young proceedeth from the like natural principle: for which reason they will never allow, that a child is under any obligation to his father for begetting him, or to his mother for bringing him into the world; which, considering the miseries of human life, was neither a benefit in itself, nor intended so by his parents, whose thoughts in their love-encounters were otherwise employed. Upon these, and the like reasonings, their opinion is, that parents are the last of all others to be trusted with the education of their own children: and therefore they have in every town public nurseries, where all parents, except cottagers[9] and laborers, are obliged to send their infants of both sexes to be reared and educated when they come to the age of twenty moons; at which time they are supposed to have some rudiments of docility. These schools are of several kinds, suited to different qualities, and to both sexes. They have certain professors[1] well skilled in preparing children for such a condition of life as befits the rank of their parents, and their own capacities as well as inclinations. I shall first say something of the male nurseries, and then of the female.

The nurseries for males of noble or eminent birth are provided with grave and learned professors, and their several deputies. The clothes and food of the children are plain and simple. They are bred up in the principles of honor, justice, courage, modesty, clemency, religion, and love of their country; they are always employed in some business, except in the times of eating and sleeping, which are very short, and two hours for diversions, consisting of bodily exercises. They are dressed by men until four years of age, and then are obliged to dress themselves, although their quality be ever so great; and the women attendants, who are aged proportionably to ours at fifty, perform only the most menial offices. They are never suffered to converse with servants, but go together in small or greater numbers to take their diversions, and always in the presence of a professor, or one of his deputies; whereby they avoid those early bad impressions of folly and vice to which our children are subject. Their parents are suffered to see them only twice a year; the visit is not to last above an hour; they are allowed to kiss the child at meeting and parting; but a professor, who always standeth by on those occasions, will not suffer them to whisper, or use any fondling expressions, or bring any presents of toys, sweetmeats, and the like.

The pension from each family for the education and entertainment[2] of a child, upon failure of due payment, is levied by the Emperor's officers.

The nurseries for children of ordinary gentlemen, merchants, traders, and handicrafts, are managed proportionably after the same manner; only those designed for trades are put out apprentices at seven years old; whereas those of persons of quality continue in their exercises until fifteen, which answers to one and twenty with us: but the confinement is gradually lessened for the last three years.

In the female nurseries, the young girls of quality are educated much like the males, only they are dressed by orderly servants of their own sex, but always in the presence of a professor or deputy, until they come to dress themselves, which is at five years old. And if it be found that these nurses ever presume to entertain the girls with frightful or foolish stories, or the

---

9. Agricultural workers, peasants.
1. Professional teachers.
2. Sustenance.

common follies practiced by chambermaids among us, they are publicly whipped thrice about the city, imprisoned for a year, and banished for life to the most desolate parts of the country. Thus the young ladies there are as much ashamed of being cowards and fools as the men; and despise all personal ornaments beyond decency and cleanliness: neither did I perceive any difference in their education, made by their difference of sex, only that the exercises of the females were not altogether so robust; and that some rules were given them relating to domestic life, and a smaller compass of learning was enjoined them: for their maxim is, that among people of quality, a wife should be always a reasonable and agreeable companion, because she cannot always be young. When the girls are twelve years old, which among them is the marriageable age, their parents or guardians take them home, with great expressions of gratitude to the professors, and seldom without tears of the young lady and her companions.

In the nurseries of females of the meaner sort, the children are instructed in all kinds of works proper for their sex, and their several degrees:[3] those intended for apprentices are dismissed at seven years old, the rest are kept to eleven.

The meaner families who have children at these nurseries are obliged, besides their annual pension, which is as low as possible, to return to the steward of the nursery a small monthly share of their gettings, to be a portion for the child; and therefore all parents are limited in their expenses by the law. For the Lilliputians think nothing can be more unjust, than that people, in subservience to their own appetites, should bring children into the world, and leave the burthen of supporting them on the public. As to persons of quality, they give security to appropriate a certain sum for each child, suitable to their condition; and these funds are always managed with good husbandry, and the most exact justice.

The cottagers and laborers keep their children at home, their business being only to till and cultivate the earth; and therefore their education is of little consequence to the public; but the old and diseased among them are supported by hospitals: for begging is a trade unknown in this empire.

And here it may perhaps divert the curious reader, to give some account of my domestic,[4] and my manner of living in this country, during a residence of nine months and thirteen days. Having a head mechanically turned, and being likewise forced by necessity, I had made for myself a table and chair convenient enough, out of the largest trees in the royal park. Two hundred sempstresses were employed to make me shirts, and linen for my bed and table, all of the strongest and coarsest kind they could get; which, however, they were forced to quilt together in several folds; for the thickest was some degrees finer than lawn. Their linen is usually three inches wide, and three foot make a piece. The sempstresses took my measure as I lay on the ground, one standing at my neck, and another at my mid-leg, with a strong cord extended, that each held by the end, while the third measured the length of the cord with a rule of an inch long. Then they measured my right thumb, and desired no more; for by a mathematical computation, that twice round the thumb is one round the wrist, and so on to the neck and the waist; and by the help of my old shirt, which I displayed on the ground before them for a pattern, they fitted me exactly. Three hundred tailors were employed in the

3. Various social ranks. 4. Household.

same manner to make me clothes; but they had another contrivance for taking my measure. I kneeled down, and they raised a ladder from the ground to my neck; upon this ladder one of them mounted, and let fall a plumb-line from my collar to the floor, which just answered the length of my coat; but my waist and arms I measured myself. When my clothes were finished, which was done in my house (for the largest of theirs would not have been able to hold them), they looked like the patchwork made by the ladies in England, only that mine were all of a color.

I had three hundred cooks to dress my victuals, in little convenient huts built about my house, where they and their families lived, and prepared me two dishes apiece. I took up twenty waiters in my hand, and placed them on the table; an hundred more attended below on the ground, some with dishes of meat, and some with barrels of wine, and other liquors, slung on their shoulders; all which the waiters above drew up as I wanted, in a very ingenious manner, by certain cords, as we draw the bucket up a well in Europe. A dish of their meat was a good mouthful, and a barrel of their liquor a reasonable draught. Their mutton yields to ours, but their beef is excellent. I have had a sirloin so large, that I have been forced to make three bites of it; but this is rare. My servants were astonished to see me eat it bones and all, as in our country we do the leg of a lark. Their geese and turkeys I usually eat at a mouthful, and I must confess they far exceed ours. Of their smaller fowl I could take up twenty or thirty at the end of my knife.

One day his Imperial Majesty, being informed of my way of living, desired that himself and his royal consort, with the young princes of the blood of both sexes, might have the happiness (as he was pleased to call it) of dining with me. They came accordingly, and I placed them upon chairs of state on my table, just over against me, with their guards about them. Flimnap the Lord High Treasurer attended there likewise, with his white staff; and I observed he often looked on me with a sour countenance, which I would not seem to regard, but eat more than usual, in honor to my dear country, as well as to fill the court with admiration. I have some private reasons to believe, that this visit from his Majesty gave Flimnap an opportunity of doing me ill offices to his master. That minister had always been my secret enemy, although he outwardly caressed me more than was usual to the moroseness of his nature. He represented to the Emperor the low condition of his treasury; that he was forced to take up money at great discount; that exchequer bills[5] would not circulate under nine per cent below par; that I had cost his Majesty above a million and a half of *sprugs* (their greatest gold coin, about the bigness of a spangle); and upon the whole, that it would be advisable in the Emperor to take the first fair occasion of dismissing me.

I am here obliged to vindicate the reputation of an excellent lady, who was an innocent sufferer upon my account. The Treasurer took a fancy to be jealous of his wife, from the malice of some evil tongues, who informed him that her Grace had taken a violent affection for my person; and the court-scandal ran for some time that she once came privately to my lodging. This I solemnly declare to be a most infamous falsehood, without any grounds, farther than that her Grace was pleased to treat me with all innocent marks of freedom and friendship. I own she came often to my house, but always publicly, nor ever without three more in the coach, who were usually her

---

5. Government bills of credit. Walpole was noted as a canny financier.

sister and young daughter, and some particular acquaintance; but this was common to many other ladies of the court. And I still appeal to my servants round, whether they at any time saw a coach at my door without knowing what persons were in it. On those occasions, when a servant had given me notice, my custom was to go immediately to the door; and, after paying my respects, to take up the coach and two horses very carefully in my hands (for if there were six horses, the postillion always unharnessed four) and place them on a table, where I had fixed a moveable rim quite round, of five inches high, to prevent accidents. And I have often had four coaches and horses at once on my table full of company, while I sat in my chair leaning my face towards them; and when I was engaged with one set, the coachmen would gently drive the others round my table. I have passed many an afternoon very agreeably in these conversations. But I defy the Treasurer, or his two informers (I will name them, and let them make their best of it) Clustril and Drunlo, to prove that any person ever came to me *incognito*, except the Secretary Reldresal, who was sent by express command of his Imperial Majesty, as I have before related. I should not have dwelt so long upon this particular, if it had not been a point wherein the reputation of a great lady is so nearly concerned, to say nothing of my own; although I had the honor to be a *Nardac*, which the Treasurer himself is not; for all the world knows he is only a *Clumglum*, a title inferior by one degree, as that of a marquis is to a duke in England; yet I allow he preceded me in right of his post. These false informations, which I afterwards came to the knowledge of, by an accident not proper to mention, made the Treasurer show his lady for some time an ill countenance, and me a worse; for although he was at last undeceived and reconciled to her, yet I lost all credit with him; and found my interest decline very fast with the Emperor himself, who was indeed too much governed by that favorite.

CHAPTER 7. *The author, being informed of a design to accuse him of high treason, makes his escape to Blefuscu. His reception there.*

Before I proceed to give an account of my leaving this kingdom, it may be proper to inform the reader of a private intrigue which had been for two months forming against me.

I had been hitherto all my life a stranger to courts, for which I was unqualified by the meanness of my condition. I had indeed heard and read enough of the dispositions of great princes and ministers; but never expected to have found such terrible effects of them in so remote a country, governed, as I thought, by very different maxims from those in Europe.

When I was just preparing to pay my attendance on the Emperor of Blefuscu, a considerable person at court (to whom I had been very serviceable at a time when he lay under the highest displeasure of his Imperial Majesty) came to my house very privately at night in a close chair, and without sending his name, desired admittance. The chairmen were dismissed; I put the chair, with his Lordship in it, into my coat-pocket; and giving orders to a trusty servant to say I was indisposed and gone to sleep, I fastened the door of my house, placed the chair on the table, according to my usual custom, and sat down by it. After the common salutations were over, observing his Lordship's countenance full of concern, and enquiring into the reason, he desired I would hear him with patience, in a matter that highly concerned my honor and my life. His speech was to the following effect, for I took notes of it as soon as he left me.

You are to know, said he, that several committees of council have been lately called in the most private manner on your account: and it is but two days since his Majesty came to a full resolution.

You are very sensible that Skyresh Bolgolam (*Galbet*, or High Admiral) hath been your mortal enemy almost ever since your arrival. His original reasons I know not; but his hatred is much increased since your great success against Blefuscu, by which his glory, as Admiral, is obscured. This lord, in conjunction with Flimnap the High Treasurer, whose enmity against you is notorious on account of his lady, Limtoc the General, Lalcon the Chamberlain, and Balmuff the Grand Justiciary, have prepared articles of impeachment against you, for treason, and other capital crimes.[6]

This preface made me so impatient, being conscious of my own merits and innocence, that I was going to interrupt; when he entreated me to be silent, and thus proceeded.

Out of gratitude for the favors you have done me, I procured information of the whole proceedings, and a copy of the articles, wherein I venture my head for your service.

Articles of Impeachment against *Quinbus Flestrin* (the Man-Mountain).

ARTICLE 1

Whereas, by a statute made in the reign of his Imperial Majesty Calin Deffar Plune, it is enacted, that whoever shall make water within the precincts of the royal palace shall be liable to the pains and penalties of high treason: notwithstanding, the said Quinbus Flestrin, in open breach of the said law, under color of extinguishing the fire kindled in the apartment of his Majesty's most dear imperial consort, did maliciously, traitorously, and devilishly, by discharge of his urine, put out the said fire kindled in the said apartment, lying and being within the precincts of the said royal palace; against the statute in that case provided, etc., against the duty, etc.

ARTICLE 2

That the said Quinbus Flestrin, having brought the imperial fleet of Blefuscu into the royal port, and being afterwards commanded by his Imperial Majesty to seize all the other ships of the said empire of Blefuscu, and reduce that empire to a province, to be governed by a viceroy from hence; and to destroy and put to death not only all the Big-Endian exiles, but likewise all the people of that empire who would not immediately forsake the Big-Endian heresy: he, the said Flestrin, like a false traitor against his most auspicious, serene, Imperial Majesty, did petition to be excused from the said service, upon pretense of unwillingness to force the consciences, or destroy the liberties and lives of an innocent people.

---

6. After the Whigs had investigated Oxford and Bolingbroke, both were impeached for high treason, on charges of being sympathetic to the Jacobites and the French.

ARTICLE 3

That, whereas certain ambassadors arrived from the court of Blefuscu to sue for peace in his Majesty's court: he the said Flestrin did, like a false traitor, aid, abet, comfort, and divert the said ambassadors; although he knew them to be servants to a prince who was lately an open enemy to his Imperial Majesty, and in open war against his said Majesty.

ARTICLE 4

That the said Quinbus Flestrin, contrary to the duty of a faithful subject, is now preparing to make a voyage to the court and empire of Blefuscu, for which he hath received only verbal license from his Imperial Majesty; and under color of the said license, doth falsely and traitorously intend to take the said voyage, and thereby to aid, comfort, and abet the Emperor of Blefuscu, so late an enemy, and in open war with his Imperial Majesty aforesaid.

There are some other articles, but these are the most important, of which I have read you an abstract.

In the several debates upon this impeachment, it must be confessed that his Majesty gave many marks of his great *lenity*, often urging the services you had done him, and endeavoring to extenuate your crimes. The Treasurer and Admiral insisted that you should be put to the most painful and ignominious death, by setting fire on your house at night; and the General was to attend with twenty thousand men armed with poisoned arrows, to shoot you on the face and hands. Some of your servants were to have private orders to strew a poisonous juice on your shirts and sheets, which would soon make you tear your own flesh, and die in the utmost torture. The General came into the same opinion; so that for a long time there was a majority against you. But his Majesty resolving, if possible, to spare your life, at last brought off[7] the Chamberlain.

Upon this incident, Reldresal, Principal Secretary for Private Affairs, who always approved[8] himself your true friend, was commanded by the Emperor to deliver his opinion, which he accordingly did; and therein justified the good thoughts you have of him. He allowed your crimes to be great; but that still there was room for mercy, the most commendable virtue in a prince, and for which his Majesty was so justly celebrated. He said, the friendship between you and him was so well known to the world, that perhaps the most honorable board might think him partial: however, in obedience to the command he had received, he would freely offer his sentiments. That if his Majesty, in consideration of your services, and pursuant to his own merciful disposition, would please to spare your life, and only give order to put out both your eyes, he humbly conceived, that by this expedient justice might in some measure be satisfied, and all the world would applaud the *lenity* of the Emperor, as well as the fair and generous proceedings of those who have the honor to be his counselors. That the loss of your eyes would be no impediment to your bodily strength, by which you might still be useful to his Majesty. That blindness is an addition to courage, by concealing dangers from us; that the fear you had for your eyes was the greatest difficulty in bringing

---

7. Won over.   8. Proved.

over the enemy's fleet; and it would be sufficient for you to see by the eyes of the ministers, since the greatest princes do no more.

This proposal was received with the utmost disapprobation by the whole board. Bolgolam, the Admiral, could not preserve his temper; but rising up in fury, said, he wondered how the Secretary durst presume to give his opinion for preserving the life of a traitor: that the services you had performed were, by all true reasons of state, the great aggravation of your crimes; that you, who were able to extinguish the fire by discharge of urine in her Majesty's apartment (which he mentioned with horror), might, at another time, raise an inundation by the same means, to drown the whole palace; and the same strength which enabled you to bring over the enemy's fleet might serve, upon the first discontent, to carry it back: that he had good reasons to think you were a Big-Endian in your heart; and as treason begins in the heart before it appears in overt acts, so he accused you as a traitor on that account, and therefore insisted you should be put to death.

The Treasurer was of the same opinion; he showed to what straits his Majesty's revenue was reduced by the charge of maintaining you, which would soon grow insupportable: that the Secretary's expedient of putting out your eyes was so far from being a remedy against this evil, that it would probably increase it; as it is manifest from the common practice of blinding some kind of fowl, after which they fed the faster, and grew sooner fat: that his sacred Majesty, and the council, who are your judges, were in their own consciences fully convinced of your guilt; which was a sufficient argument to condemn you to death, without the formal proofs required by the strict letter of the law.

But his Imperial Majesty, fully determined against capital punishment, was graciously pleased to say, that since the council thought the loss of your eyes too easy a censure, some other may be inflicted hereafter. And your friend the Secretary humbly desiring to be heard again, in answer to what the Treasurer had objected concerning the great charge his Majesty was at in maintaining you, said, that his Excellency, who had the sole disposal of the Emperor's revenue, might easily provide against this evil, by gradually lessening your establishment; by which, for want of sufficient food, you would grow weak and faint, and lose your appetite, and consequently decay and consume in a few months; neither would the stench of your carcass be then so dangerous, when it should become more than half diminished; and immediately upon your death, five or six thousand of his Majesty's subjects might, in two or three days, cut your flesh from your bones, take it away by cart-loads, and bury it in distant parts to prevent infection; leaving the skeleton as a monument of admiration to posterity.

Thus by the great friendship of the Secretary, the whole affair was compromised. It was strictly enjoined, that the project of starving you by degrees should be kept a secret; but the sentence of putting out your eyes was entered on the books; none dissenting except Bolgolam the Admiral, who being a creature of the Empress, was perpetually instigated by her Majesty to insist upon your death; she having borne perpetual malice against you, on account of that infamous and illegal method you took to extinguish the fire in her apartment.

In three days your friend the Secretary will be directed to come to your house, and read before you the articles of impeachment; and then to signify the great lenity and favor of his Majesty and council; whereby you are only condemned to the loss of your eyes, which his Majesty doth not question you will gratefully and humbly submit to; and twenty of his Majesty's surgeons will attend, in order to see the operation well performed, by discharging very sharp-pointed arrows into the balls of your eyes, as you lie on the ground.

I leave to your prudence what measures you will take; and to avoid suspicion, I must immediately return in as private a manner as I came.

His Lordship did so, and I remained alone, under many doubts and perplexities of mind.

It was a custom introduced by this prince and his ministry (very different, as I have been assured, from the practices of former times), that after the court had decreed any cruel execution, either to gratify the monarch's resentment, or the malice of a favorite, the Emperor always made a speech to his whole council, expressing his great lenity and tenderness, as qualities known and confessed by all the world. This speech was immediately published through the kingdom; nor did any thing terrify the people so much as those encomiums on his Majesty's mercy; because it was observed, that the more these praises were enlarged and insisted on, the more inhuman was the punishment, and the sufferer more innocent. Yet as to myself, I must confess, having never been designed for a courtier, either by my birth or education, I was so ill a judge of things, that I could not discover the lenity and favor of this sentence, but conceived it (perhaps erroneously) rather to be rigorous than gentle. I sometimes thought of standing my trial; for although I could not deny the facts alleged in the several articles, yet I hoped they would admit of some extenuations. But having in my life perused many state trials, which I ever observed to terminate as the judges thought fit to direct, I durst not rely on so dangerous a decision, in so critical a juncture, and against such powerful enemies. Once I was strongly bent upon resistance: for while I had liberty, the whole strength of that empire could hardly subdue me, and I might easily with stones pelt the metropolis to pieces; but I soon rejected that project with horror, by remembering the oath I had made to the Emperor, the favors I received from him, and the high title of *Nardac* he conferred upon me. Neither had I so soon learned the gratitude of courtiers, to persuade myself that his Majesty's present severities acquitted me of all past obligations.

At last I fixed upon a resolution, for which it is probable I may incur some censure, and not unjustly; for I confess I owe the preserving my eyes, and consequently my liberty, to my own great rashness and want of experience: because if I had then known the nature of princes and ministers, which I have since observed in many other courts, and their methods of treating criminals less obnoxious than myself, I should with great alacrity and readiness have submitted to so *easy* a punishment. But hurried on by the precipitancy of youth, and having his Imperial Majesty's license to pay my attendance upon the Emperor of Blefuscu, I took this opportunity, before the three days were elapsed, to send a letter to my friend the Secretary, signifying my resolution of setting out that morning for Blefuscu,[9] pursuant to the leave I had got; and without waiting for an answer, I went to that side of the island where our fleet lay. I seized a large man of war, tied a cable to the prow, and lifting up the anchors, I stripped myself, put my clothes (together with my coverlet, which I carried under my arm) into the vessel; and drawing it after me, between wading and swimming, arrived at the royal port of Blefuscu, where

9. Before his trial for treason could be held, Bolingbroke had escaped to France.

the people had long expected me. They lent me two guides to direct me to the capital city, which is of the same name; I held them in my hands until I came within two hundred yards of the gate; and desired them to signify my arrival to one of the secretaries, and let him know, I there waited his Majesty's commands. I had an answer in about an hour, that his Majesty, attended by the royal family, and great officers of the court, was coming out to receive me. I advanced a hundred yards; the Emperor, and his train, alighted from their horses, the Empress and ladies from their coaches; and I did not perceive they were in any fright or concern. I lay on the ground to kiss his Majesty's and the Empress's hand. I told his Majesty that I was come according to my promise, and with the license of the Emperor my master, to have the honor of seeing so mighty a monarch, and to offer him any service in my power, consistent with my duty to my own prince; not mentioning a word of my disgrace, because I had hitherto no regular information of it, and might suppose myself wholly ignorant of any such design; neither could I reasonably conceive that the Emperor would discover the secret while I was out of his power: wherein, however, it soon appeared I was deceived.

I shall not trouble the reader with the particular account of my reception at this court, which was suitable to the generosity of so great a prince; nor of the difficulties I was in for want of a house and bed, being forced to lie on the ground, wrapped up in my coverlet.

CHAPTER 8. *The author, by a lucky accident, finds means to leave Blefuscu; and, after some difficulties, returns safe to his native country.*

Three days after my arrival, walking out of curiosity to the northeast coast of the island, I observed, about half a league off, in the sea, somewhat that looked like a boat overturned. I pulled off my shoes and stockings, and wading two or three hundred yards, I found the object to approach nearer by force of the tide; and then plainly saw it to be a real boat, which I supposed might, by some tempest, have been driven from a ship. Whereupon I returned immediately towards the city, and desired his Imperial Majesty to lend me twenty of the tallest vessels he had left after the loss of his fleet, and three thousand seamen under the command of his Vice Admiral. This fleet sailed round, while I went back the shortest way to the coast where I first discovered the boat; I found the tide had driven it still nearer; the seamen were all provided with cordage, which I had beforehand twisted to a sufficient strength. When the ships came up, I stripped myself, and waded till I came within an hundred yards of the boat; after which I was forced to swim till I got up to it. The seamen threw me the end of the cord, which I fastened to a hole in the forepart of the boat, and the other end to a man of war: but I found all my labor to little purpose; for being out of my depth, I was not able to work. In this necessity, I was forced to swim behind, and push the boat forwards as often as I could, with one of my hands; and the tide favoring me, I advanced so far, that I could just hold up my chin and feel the ground. I rested two or three minutes, and then gave the boat another shove, and so on till the sea was no higher than my armpits. And now the most laborious part being over, I took out my other cables which were stowed in one of the ships, and fastening them first to the boat, and then to nine of the vessels which attended me, the wind being favorable, the seamen towed, and I shoved till we arrived within forty yards of the shore; and waiting till the tide was out, I got dry to the boat, and by the assistance of two thousand men, with ropes and engines, I made a shift to turn it on its bottom, and found it was but little damaged.

I shall not trouble the reader with the difficulties I was under by the help of certain paddles, which cost me ten days making, to get my boat to the royal port of Blefuscu; where a mighty concourse of people appeared upon my arrival, full of wonder at the sight of so prodigious a vessel. I told the Emperor that my good fortune had thrown this boat in my way, to carry me to some place from whence I might return into my native country; and begged his Majesty's orders for getting materials to fit it up, together with license to depart; which, after some kind expostulations, he was pleased to grant.

I did very much wonder, in all this time, not to have heard of any express relating to me from our Emperor to the court of Blefuscu. But I was afterwards given privately to understand, that his Imperial Majesty, never imagining I had the least notice of his designs, believed I was only gone to Blefuscu in performance of my promise, according to the license he had given me, which was well known at our court; and would return in a few days when that ceremony was ended. But he was at last in pain at my long absence; and, after consulting with the Treasurer, and the rest of that cabal, a person of quality was dispatched with the copy of the articles against me. This envoy had instructions to represent to the monarch of Blefuscu the great lenity of his master, who was content to punish me no further than with the loss of my eyes; that I had fled from justice, and if I did not return in two hours, I should be deprived of my title of *Nardac*, and declared a traitor. The envoy further added, that in order to maintain the peace and amity between both empires, his master expected, that his brother of Blefuscu would give orders to have me sent back to Lilliput, bound hand and foot, to be punished as a traitor.

The Emperor of Blefuscu, having taken three days to consult, returned an answer consisting of many civilities and excuses. He said, that as for sending me bound, his brother knew it was impossible; that although I had deprived him of his fleet, yet he owed great obligations to me for many good offices I had done him in making the peace. That however, both their Majesties would soon be made easy; for I had found a prodigious vessel on the shore, able to carry me on the sea, which he had given order to fit up with my own assistance and direction; and he hoped in a few weeks both empires would be freed from so insupportable an incumbrance.

With this answer the envoy returned to Lilliput, and the monarch of Blefuscu related to me all that had passed, offering me at the same time (but under the strictest confidence) his gracious protection, if I would continue in his service; wherein although I believed him sincere, yet I resolved never more to put any confidence in princes or ministers, where I could possibly avoid it; and therefore, with all due acknowledgements for his favorable intentions, I humbly begged to be excused. I told him, that since fortune, whether good or evil, had thrown a vessel in my way, I was resolved to venture myself in the ocean, rather than be an occasion of difference between two such mighty monarchs. Neither did I find the Emperor at all displeased; and I discovered by a certain accident, that he was very glad of my resolution, and so were most of his ministers.

These considerations moved me to hasten my departure somewhat sooner than I intended; to which the court, impatient to have me gone, very readily contributed. Five hundred workmen were employed to make two sails to my boat, according to my directions, by quilting thirteen fold of their strongest linen together. I was at the pains of making ropes and cables, by twisting ten, twenty or thirty of the thickest and strongest of theirs. A great stone that I happened to find, after a long search by the seashore, served me for an anchor. I had the tallow of three hundred cows for greasing my boat, and other uses. I was at incredible pains in cutting down some of the largest timber trees for oars and masts, wherein I was, however, much assisted by his Majesty's ship-carpenters, who helped me in smoothing them, after I had done the rough work.

In about a month, when all was prepared, I sent to receive his Majesty's commands, and to take my leave. The Emperor and royal family came out of the palace; I lay down on my face to kiss his hand, which he very graciously gave me: so did the Empress, and young princes of the blood. His Majesty presented me with fifty purses of two hundred *sprugs* apiece, together with his picture at full length, which I put immediately into one of my gloves, to keep it from being hurt. The ceremonies at my departure were too many to trouble the reader with at this time.

I stored the boat with the carcasses of an hundred oxen, and three hundred sheep, with bread and drink proportionable, and as much meat ready dressed as four hundred cooks could provide. I took with me six cows and two bulls alive, with as many ewes and rams, intending to carry them into my own country, and propagate the breed. And to feed them on board, I had a good bundle of hay, and a bag of corn.[1] I would gladly have taken a dozen of the natives; but this was a thing the Emperor would by no means permit; and besides a diligent search into my pockets, his Majesty engaged my honor not to carry away any of his subjects, although with their own consent and desire.

Having thus prepared all things as well as I was able, I set sail on the twenty-fourth day of September, 1701, at six in the morning; and when I had gone about four leagues to the northward, the wind being at southeast, at six in the evening, I descried a small island about half a league to the northwest. I advanced forward, and cast anchor on the lee-side of the island, which seemed to be uninhabited. I then took some refreshment, and went to my rest. I slept well, and as I conjecture at least six hours; for I found the day broke in two hours after I awaked. It was a clear night; I eat my breakfast before the sun was up; and heaving anchor, the wind being favorable, I steered the same course that I had done the day before, wherein I was directed by my pocket compass. My intention was to reach, if possible, one of those islands which I had reason to believe lay to the northeast of Van Diemen's Land. I discovered nothing all that day; but upon the next, about three in the afternoon, when I had by my computation made twenty-four leagues from Blefuscu, I descried a sail steering to the southeast; my course was due east. I hailed her, but could get no answer; yet I found I gained upon her, for the wind slackened. I made all the sail I could, and in half an hour she spied me, then hung out her ancient,[2] and discharged a gun. It is not easy to express the joy I was in upon the unexpected hope of once more seeing my beloved country, and the dear pledges[3] I had left in it. The ship slackened her sails, and I came up with her between five and six in the evening,

---

1. Generic term for any cereal or grain crop (here, wheat).

2. Flag.

3. Hostages (i.e., his family).

September 26; but my heart leapt within me to see her English colors. I put my cows and sheep into my coat-pockets and got on board with all my little cargo of provisions. The vessel was an English merchantman, returning from Japan by the North and South Seas;[4] the captain, Mr. John Biddel of Deptford, a very civil man, and an excellent sailor. We were now in the latitude of 30 degrees south; there were about fifty men in the ship; and here I met an old comrade of mine, one Peter Williams, who gave me a good character to the captain. This gentleman treated me with kindness, and desired I would let him know what place I came from last, and whither I was bound; which I did in few words; but he thought I was raving, and that the dangers I underwent had disturbed my head; whereupon I took my black cattle and sheep out of my pocket, which, after great astonishment, clearly convinced him of my veracity. I then showed him the gold given me by the Emperor of Blefuscu, together with his Majesty's picture at full length, and some other rarities of that country. I gave him two purses of two hundred *sprugs* each, and promised, when we arrived in England, to make him a present of a cow and a sheep big with young.

I shall not trouble the reader with a particular account of this voyage; which was very prosperous for the most part. We arrived in the Downs[5] on the 13th of April, 1702. I had only one misfortune, that the rats on board carried away one of my sheep; I found her bones in a hole, picked clean from the flesh. The rest of my cattle I got safe on shore, and set them a grazing in a bowling-green at Greenwich, where the fineness of the grass made them feed very heartily, though I had always feared the contrary; neither could I possibly have preserved them in so long a voyage, if the captain had not allowed me some of his best biscuit, which rubbed to powder, and mingled with water, was their constant food. The short time I continued in England, I made a considerable profit by showing my cattle to many persons of quality, and others: and before I began my second voyage, I sold them for six hundred pounds. Since my last return, I find the breed is considerably increased, especially the sheep; which I hope will prove much to the advantage of the woolen manufacture, by the fineness of the fleeces.

I stayed but two months with my wife and family; for my insatiable desire of seeing foreign countries would suffer me to continue no longer. I left fifteen hundred pounds with my wife, and fixed her in a good house at Redriff. My remaining stock I carried with me, part in money, and part in goods, in hopes to improve my fortunes. My eldest uncle, John, had left me an estate in land, near Epping, of about thirty pounds a year; and I had a long lease of the Black Bull in Fetter Lane, which yielded me as much more: so that I was not in any danger of leaving my family upon the parish.[6] My son Johnny, named so after his uncle, was at the grammar school, and a towardly[7] child. My daughter Betty (who is now well married, and has children) was then at her needlework. I took leave of my wife, and boy and girl, with tears on both sides; and went on board the *Adventure*, a merchant-ship of three hundred tons, bound for Surat, Captain John Nicholas of Liverpool, Commander. But my account of this voyage must be referred to the second part of my *Travels*.

---

4. North and South Pacific.
5. A rendezvous for ships off the southeast coast of England.
6. On welfare (living on charity given by the parish).
7. Promising.

Part 2. A Voyage to Brobdingnag

CHAPTER 1. *A great storm described. The longboat sent to fetch water; the Author goes with it to discover the country. He is left on shore, is seized by one of the natives, and carried to a farmer's house. His reception there, with several accidents that happened there. A description of the inhabitants.*

Having been condemned by nature and fortune to an active and restless life, in ten months after my return I again left my native country, and took shipping in the Downs on the 20th day of June, 1702, in the *Adventure*, Captain John Nicholas, a Cornish man, Commander, bound for Surat.[8] We had a very prosperous gale till we arrived at the Cape of Good Hope, where we landed for fresh water, but discovering a leak we unshipped our goods and wintered there; for the Captain falling sick of an ague, we could not leave the Cape till the end of March. We then set sail, and had a good voyage till we passed the Straits of Madagascar; but having got northward of that island, and to about five degrees south latitude, the winds, which in those seas are observed to blow a constant equal gale between the north and west from the beginning of December to the beginning of May, on the 19th of April began to blow with much greater violence and more westerly than usual, continuing so far twenty days together, during which time we were driven a little to the east of the Molucca Islands and about three degrees northward of the Line, as our Captain found by an observation he took the 2nd of May, at which time the wind ceased, and it was a perfect calm, whereat I was not a little rejoiced. But he, being a man well experienced in the navigation of those seas, bid us all prepare against a storm, which accordingly happened the day following: for a southern wind, called the southern monsoon, began to set in.

Finding it was likely to overblow,[9] we took in our spritsail, and stood by to hand the foresail; but making foul weather, we looked the guns were all fast, and handed the mizzen. The ship lay very broad off, so we thought it better spooning before the sea, than trying or hulling. We reefed the foresail and set him, we hauled aft the foresheet; the helm was hard aweather. The ship wore bravely. We belayed the fore-downhaul; but the sail was split, and we hauled down the yard and got the sail into the ship, and unbound all the things clear of it. It was a very fierce storm; the sea broke strange and dangerous. We hauled off upon the lanyard of the whipstaff, and helped the man at helm. We would not get down our topmast, but let all stand, because she scudded before the sea very well, and we knew that the topmast being aloft, the ship was the wholesomer, and made better way through the sea, seeing we had searoom. When the storm was over, we set foresail and mainsail, and brought the ship to. Then we set the mizzen, main topsail and the fore topsail. Our course was east-northeast, the wind was at southwest. We got the starboard tacks aboard, we cast off our weather braces and lifts; we set in the lee braces, and hauled forward by the weather bowlings, and

8. In India. The geography of the voyage (described next) is simple: The *Adventure*, after sailing up the east coast of Africa to about five degrees south of the equator (the "Line"), is blown past India into the Malay Archipelago, north of the islands of Buru and Ceram. The storm then drives the ship northward and eastward, away from the coast of Siberia ("Great Tartary") into the northeast Pacific, at that time unexplored. Brobdingnag lies somewhere in the vicinity of Alaska.
9. This paragraph is taken almost literally from Samuel Sturmy's *Mariner's Magazine* (1669). Swift is ridiculing the use of technical terms by writers of popular voyages.

hauled them tight, and belayed them, and hauled over the mizzen tack to windward, and kept her full and by as near as she would lie.

During this storm, which was followed by a strong wind west-southwest, we were carried by my computation about five hundred leagues to the east, so that the oldest sailor on board could not tell in what part of the world we were. Our provisions held out well, our ship was staunch, and our crew all in good health; but we lay in the utmost distress for water. We thought it best to hold on the same course rather than turn more northerly, which might have brought us to the northwest parts of Great Tartary, and into the frozen sea.

On the 16th day of June, 1703, a boy on the topmast discovered land. On the 17th we came in full view of a great island or continent (for we knew not whether) on the south side whereof was a small neck of land jutting out into the sea, and a creek[1] too shallow to hold a ship of above one hundred tons. We cast anchor within a league of this creek, and our Captain sent a dozen of his men well armed in the longboat, with vessels for water if any could be found. I desired his leave to go with them that I might see the country and make what discoveries I could. When we came to land we saw no river or spring, nor any sign of inhabitants. Our men therefore wandered on the shore to find out some fresh water near the sea, and I walked alone about a mile on the other side, where I observed the country all barren and rocky. I now began to be weary, and seeing nothing to entertain my curiosity, I returned gently down towards the creek; and the sea being full in my view, I saw our men already got into the boat, and rowing for life to the ship. I was going to hollow after them, although it had been to little purpose, when I observed a huge creature walking after them in the sea as fast as he could; he waded not much deeper than his knees and took prodigious strides, but our men had the start of him half a league, and the sea thereabouts being full of sharp-pointed rocks, the monster was not able to overtake the boat. This I was afterwards told, for I durst not stay to see the issue of that adventure, but ran as fast as I could the way I first went, and then climbed up a steep hill, which gave me some prospect of the country. I found it fully cultivated; but that which first surprised me was the length of the grass, which, in those grounds that seemed to be kept for hay, was about twenty foot high.[2]

I fell into a highroad, for so I took it to be, although it served to the inhabitants only as a footpath through a field of barley. Here I walked on for some time, but could see little on either side, it being now near harvest, and the corn[3] rising at least forty foot. I was an hour walking to the end of this field, which was fenced in with a hedge of at least one hundred and twenty foot high, and the trees so lofty that I could make no computation of their altitude. There was a stile to pass from this field into the next: it had four steps, and a stone to cross over when you came to the utmost. It was impossible for me to climb this stile, because every step was six foot high, and the upper stone above twenty. I was endeavoring to find some gap in the hedge when I discovered one of the inhabitants in the next field advancing towards the stile, of the same size with him whom I saw in the sea pursuing our boat. He appeared as tall as an ordinary spire-steeple, and took about ten yards at every stride, as near as I could guess. I was struck with the utmost fear and

---

1. A small bay or cove, affording anchorage.
2. Swift's intention, not always carried out accurately, is that everything in Brobdingnag should be, in relation to our familiar world, on a scale of ten to one.
3. Here, barley.

astonishment, and ran to hide myself in the corn, from whence I saw him at the top of the stile, looking back into the next field on the right hand; and heard him call in a voice many degrees louder than a speaking trumpet; but the noise was so high in the air that at first I certainly thought it was thunder. Whereupon seven monsters like himself came towards him with reaping hooks in their hands, each hook about the largeness of six scythes. These people were not so well clad as the first, whose servants or laborers they seemed to be. For, upon some words he spoke, they went to reap the corn in the field where I lay. I kept from them at as great a distance as I could, but was forced to move with extreme difficulty, for the stalks of the corn were sometimes not above a foot distant, so that I could hardly squeeze my body betwixt them. However, I made a shift to go forward till I came to a part of the field where the corn had been laid by the rain and wind; here it was impossible for me to advance a step, for the stalks were so interwoven that I could not creep through, and the beards of the fallen ears so strong and pointed that they pierced through my clothes into my flesh. At the same time I heard the reapers not above an hundred yards behind me. Being quite dispirited with toil, and wholly overcome by grief and despair, I lay down between two ridges and heartily wished I might there end my days. I bemoaned my desolate widow and fatherless children; I lamented my own folly and willfulness in attempting a second voyage against the advice of all my friends and relations. In this terrible agitation of mind, I could not forbear thinking of Lilliput, whose inhabitants looked upon me as the greatest prodigy that ever appeared in the world; where I was able to draw an imperial fleet in my hand, and perform those other actions which will be recorded forever in the chronicles of that empire, while posterity shall hardly believe them, although attested by millions. I reflected what a mortification it must prove to me to appear as inconsiderable in this nation as one single Lilliputian would be among us. But this I conceived was to be the least of my misfortunes; for as human creatures are observed to be more savage and cruel in proportion to their bulk, what could I expect but to be a morsel in the mouth of the first among these enormous barbarians who should happen to seize me? Undoubtedly philosophers are in the right when they tell us that nothing is great or little otherwise than by comparison. It might have pleased fortune to let the Lilliputians find some nation where the people were as diminutive with respect to them as they were to me. And who knows but that even this prodigious race of mortals might be equally overmatched in some distant part of the world, whereof we have yet no discovery?

Scared and confounded as I was, I could not forbear going on with these reflections; when one of the reapers approaching within ten yards of the ridge where I lay, made me apprehend that with the next step I should be squashed to death under his foot, or cut in two with his reaping hook. And therefore when he was again about to move, I screamed as loud as fear could make me. Whereupon the huge creature trod short, and looking round about under him for some time, at last espied me as I lay on the ground. He considered a while with the caution of one who endeavors to lay hold on a small dangerous animal in such a manner that it shall not be able either to scratch or to bite him, as I myself have sometimes done with a weasel in England. At length he ventured to take me up behind by the middle between his forefinger and thumb, and brought me within three yards of his eyes, that he might behold my shape more perfectly. I guessed his meaning, and my good fortune gave me so much presence of mind that I resolved not to struggle in the least as he held me in the air about sixty foot from the ground, although he grievously pinched my sides, for fear I should slip through his fingers. All I ventured was to raise mine eyes towards the sun, and place my hands together in a supplicating posture, and to speak some words in an humble melancholy tone, suitable to the condition I then was in. For I apprehended every moment that he would dash me against the ground, as we usually do any little hateful animal which we have a mind to destroy. But my good star would have it that he appeared pleased with my voice and gestures, and began to look upon me as a curiosity, much wondering to hear me pronounce articulate words, although he could not understand them. In the meantime I was not able to forbear groaning and shedding tears and turning my head towards my sides, letting him know, as well as I could, how cruelly I was hurt by the pressure of his thumb and finger. He seemed to apprehend my meaning; for, lifting up the lappet[4] of his coat, he put me gently into it, and immediately ran along with me to his master, who was a substantial farmer, and the same person I had first seen in the field.

The farmer having (as I supposed by their talk) received such an account of me as his servant could give him, took a piece of a small straw about the size of a walking staff, and therewith lifted up the lappets of my coat, which it seems he thought to be some kind of covering that nature had given me. He blew my hairs aside to take a better view of my face. He called his hinds[5] about him, and asked them (as I afterwards learned) whether they had ever seen in the fields any little creature that resembled me. He then placed me softly on the ground upon all four; but I got immediately up, and walked slowly backwards and forwards, to let those people see I had no intent to run away. They all sat down in a circle about me, the better to observe my motions. I pulled off my hat, and made a low bow towards the farmer; I fell on my knees, and lifted up my hands and eyes, and spoke several words as loud as I could; I took a purse of gold out of my pocket, and humbly presented it to him. He received it on the palm of his hand, then applied it close to his eye to see what it was, and afterwards turned it several times with the point of a pin (which he took out of his sleeve), but could make nothing of it. Whereupon I made a sign that he should place his hand on the ground; I then took the purse, and opening it, poured all the gold into his palm. There were six Spanish pieces of four pistoles each, beside twenty or thirty smaller coins. I saw him wet the tip of his little finger upon his tongue, and take up one of my largest pieces, and then another; but he seemed to be wholly ignorant what they were. He made me a sign to put them again into my purse, and the purse again into my pocket, which after offering to him several times, I thought it best to do.

The farmer by this time was convinced I must be a rational creature. He spoke often to me, but the sound of his voice pierced my ears like that of a water mill, yet his words were articulate enough. I answered as loud as I could in several languages, and he often laid his ear within two yards of me, but all in vain, for we were wholly unintelligible to each other. He then sent his servants to their work, and taking his handkerchief out of his pocket, he doubled and spread it on his hand, which he placed flat on the ground with the palm upwards, making me a sign to step into it, as I could easily do, for

---

4. Flap or fold.   5. Farm servants.

it was not above a foot in thickness. I thought it my part to obey, and for fear of falling, laid myself at full length upon the handkerchief, with the remainder of which he lapped me up to the head for further security, and in this manner carried me home to his house. There he called his wife, and showed me to her; but she screamed and ran back as women in England do at the sight of a toad or a spider. However, when she had a while seen my behavior, and how well I observed the signs her husband made, she was soon reconciled, and by degrees grew extremely tender of me.

It was about twelve at noon, and a servant brought in dinner. It was only one substantial dish of meat (fit for the plain condition of an husbandman) in a dish of about four-and-twenty foot diameter. The company were the farmer and his wife, three children, and an old grandmother. When they were sat down, the farmer placed me at some distance from him on the table, which was thirty foot high from the floor. I was in a terrible fright, and kept as far as I could from the edge, for fear of falling. The wife minced a bit of meat, then crumbled some bread on a trencher, and placed it before me. I made her a low bow, took out my knife and fork, and fell to eat; which gave them exceeding delight. The mistress sent her maid for a small dram cup, which held about two gallons, and filled it with drink; I took up the vessel with much difficulty in both hands, and in a most respectful manner drank to her ladyship's health, expressing the words as loud as I could in English; which made the company laugh so heartily that I was almost deafened with the noise. This liquor tasted like a small cider,[6] and was not unpleasant. Then the master made me a sign to come to his trencher side; but as I walked on the table, being in great surprise all the time, as the indulgent reader will easily conceive and excuse, I happened to stumble against a crust, and fell flat on my face, but received no hurt. I got up immediately, and observing the good people to be in much concern, I took my hat (which I held under my arm out of good manners) and waving it over my head, made three huzzas to show I had got no mischief by my fall. But advancing forwards toward my master (as I shall henceforth call him), his youngest son who sat next him, an arch boy of about ten years old, took me up by the legs, and held me so high in the air that I trembled every limb; but his father snatched me from him, and at the same time gave him such a box on the left ear as would have felled an European troop of horse to the earth, ordering him to be taken from the table. But being afraid the boy might owe me a spite, and well remembering how mischievous all children among us naturally are to sparrows, rabbits, young kittens, and puppy dogs, I fell on my knees, and pointing to the boy, made my master to understand, as well as I could, that I desired his son might be pardoned. The father complied, and the lad took his seat again; whereupon I went to him and kissed his hand, which my master took, and made him stroke me gently with it.

In the midst of dinner, my mistress's favorite cat leaped into her lap. I heard a noise behind me like that of a dozen stocking weavers at work; and turning my head, I found it proceeded from the purring of this animal, who seemed to be three times larger than an ox, as I computed by the view of her head and one of her paws, while her mistress was feeding and stroking her. The fierceness of this creature's countenance altogether discomposed me, although I stood at the farther end of the table, about fifty foot off, and

6. I.e., weak cider.

although my mistress held her fast for fear she might give a spring and seize me in her talons. But it happened there was no danger, for the cat took not the least notice of me when my master placed me within three yards of her. And as I have been always told, and found true by experience in my travels, that flying or discovering[7] fear before a fierce animal is a certain way to make it pursue or attack you, so I resolved in this dangerous juncture to show no manner of concern. I walked with intrepidity five or six times before the very head of the cat, and came within half a yard of her; whereupon she drew herself back, as if she were more afraid of me. I had less apprehension concerning the dogs, whereof three or four came into the room, as it is usual in farmers' houses; one of which was a mastiff, equal in bulk to four elephants, and a greyhound, somewhat taller than the mastiff, but not so large.

When dinner was almost done, the nurse came in with a child of a year old in her arms, who immediately spied me, and began a squall that you might have heard from London Bridge to Chelsea, after the usual oratory of infants, to get me for a plaything. The mother out of pure indulgence took me up, and put me towards the child, who presently seized me by the middle, and got my head in his mouth, where I roared so loud that the urchin was frighted and let me drop; and I should infallibly have broke my neck if the mother had not held her apron under me. The nurse to quiet her babe made use of a rattle, which was a kind of hollow vessel filled with great stones, and fastened by a cable to the child's waist: but all in vain, so that she was forced to apply the last remedy by giving it suck. I must confess no object ever disgusted me so much as the sight of her monstrous breast, which I cannot tell what to compare with so as to give the curious reader an idea of its bulk, shape, and color. It stood prominent six foot, and could not be less than sixteen in circumference. The nipple was about half the bigness of my head, and the hue both of that and the dug so varified with spots, pimples, and freckles that nothing could appear more nauseous: for I had a near sight of her, she sitting down the more conveniently to give suck, and I standing on the table. This made me reflect upon the fair skins of our English ladies, who appear so beautiful to us, only because they are of our own size, and their defects not to be seen but through a magnifying glass, where we find by experiment that the smoothest and whitest skins look rough and coarse and ill colored.

I remember when I was at Lilliput, the complexion of those diminutive people appeared to me the fairest in the world; and talking upon this subject with a person of learning there, who was an intimate friend of mine, he said that my face appeared much fairer and smoother when he looked on me from the ground than it did upon a nearer view when I took him up in my hand and brought him close, which he confessed was at first a very shocking sight. He said he could discover great holes in my skin; that the stumps of my beard were ten times stronger than the bristles of a boar, and my complexion made up of several colors altogether disagreeable: although I must beg leave to say for myself that I am as fair as most of my sex and country and very little sunburnt by all my travels. On the other side, discoursing of the ladies in that Emperor's court, he used to tell me one had freckles, another too wide a mouth, a third too large a nose; nothing of which I was able to distinguish. I confess this reflection was obvious enough; which however I could not forbear, lest the reader might think those vast creatures

_____

7. Revealing.

were actually deformed: for I must do them justice to say they are a comely race of people; and particularly the features of my master's countenance, although he were but a farmer, when I beheld him from the height of sixty foot, appeared very well proportioned.

When dinner was done, my master went out to his laborers; and as I could discover by his voice and gesture, gave his wife a strict charge to take care of me. I was very much tired and disposed to sleep, which my mistress perceiving, she put me on her own bed, and covered me with a clean white handkerchief, but larger and coarser than the mainsail of a man-of-war.

I slept about two hours, and dreamed I was at home with my wife and children, which aggravated my sorrows when I awaked and found myself alone in a vast room, between two and three hundred foot wide, and above two hundred high, lying in a bed twenty yards wide. My mistress was gone about her household affairs, and had locked me in. The bed was eight yards from the floor. Some natural necessities required me to get down; I durst not presume to call, and if I had, it would have been in vain with such a voice as mine at so great a distance from the room where I lay to the kitchen where the family kept. While I was under these circumstances, two rats crept up the curtains, and ran smelling backwards and forwards on the bed. One of them came up almost to my face; whereupon I rose in a fright, and drew out my hanger[8] to defend myself. These horrible animals had the boldness to attack me on both sides, and one of them held his forefeet at my collar; but I had the good fortune to rip up his belly before he could do me any mischief. He fell down at my feet; and the other seeing the fate of his comrade, made his escape, but not without one good wound on the back, which I gave him as he fled, and made the blood run trickling from him. After this exploit I walked gently to and fro on the bed, to recover my breath and loss of spirits. These creatures were of the size of a large mastiff, but infinitely more nimble and fierce; so that if I had taken off my belt before I went to sleep, I must have infallibly been torn to pieces and devoured. I measured the tail of the dead rat, and found it to be two yards long, wanting an inch; but it went against my stomach to drag the carcass off the bed, where it lay still bleeding; I observed it had yet some life, but with a strong slash cross the neck, I thoroughly dispatched it.

Soon after, my mistress came into the room, who seeing me all bloody, ran and took me up in her hand. I pointed to the dead rat, smiling and making other signs to show I was not hurt, whereat she was extremely rejoiced, calling the maid to take up the dead rat with a pair of tongs, and throw it out of the window. Then she set me on a table, where I showed her my hanger all bloody, and wiping it on the lappet of my coat, returned it to the scabbard. I was pressed to do more than one thing, which another could not do for me, and therefore endeavored to make my mistress understand that I desired to be set down on the floor; which after she had done, my bashfulness would not suffer me to express myself farther than by pointing to the door, and bowing several times. The good woman with much difficulty at last perceived what I would be at, and taking me up again in her hand, walked into the garden, where she set me down. I went on one side about two hundred yards; and beckoning to her not to look or to follow me, I hid myself between two leaves of sorrel, and there discharged the necessities of nature.

8. A short, broad sword.

I hope the gentle reader will excuse me for dwelling on these and the like particulars, which however insignificant they may appear to groveling vulgar minds, yet will certainly help a philosopher[9] to enlarge his thoughts and imagination, and apply them to the benefit of public as well as private life, which was my sole design in presenting this and other accounts of my travels to the world; wherein I have been chiefly studious of truth, without affecting any ornaments of learning or of style. But the whole scene of this voyage made so strong an impression on my mind, and is so deeply fixed in my memory, that in committing it to paper I did not omit one material circumstance; however, upon a strict review, I blotted out several passages of less moment which were in my first copy, for fear of being censured as tedious and trifling, whereof travelers are often, perhaps not without justice, accused.

CHAPTER 2. *A description of the farmer's daughter. The Author carried to a market town, and then to the metropolis. The particulars of his journey.*

My mistress had a daughter of nine years old, a child of towardly parts for her age, very dexterous at her needle, and skillful in dressing her baby.[1] Her mother and she contrived to fit up the baby's cradle for me against night: the cradle was put into a small drawer of a cabinet, and the drawer placed upon a hanging shelf for fear of the rats. This was my bed all the time I stayed with those people, although made more convenient by degrees as I began to learn their language, and make my wants known. This young girl was so handy, that after I had once or twice pulled off my clothes before her, she was able to dress and undress me, although I never gave her that trouble when she would let me do either myself. She made me seven shirts, and some other linen of as fine cloth as could be got, which indeed was coarser than sackcloth, and these she constantly washed for me with her own hands. She was likewise my schoolmistress to teach me the language: when I pointed to anything, she told me the name of it in her own tongue, so that in a few days I was able to call for whatever I had a mind to. She was very good-natured, and not above forty foot high, being little for her age. She gave me the name of *Grildrig*, which the family took up, and afterwards the whole kingdom. The word imports what the Latins call *nanunculus*, the Italian *homunceletino*, and the English *mannikin*.[2] To her I chiefly owe my preservation in that country: we never parted while I was there; I called her my *Glumdalclitch*, or little nurse: and I should be guilty of great ingratitude if I omitted this honorable mention of her care and affection towards me, which I heartily wish it lay in my power to requite as she deserves, instead of being the innocent but unhappy instrument of her disgrace, as I have too much reason to fear.

It now began to be known and talked of in the neighborhood that my master had found a strange animal in the field, about the bigness of a *splacknuck*, but exactly shaped in every part like a human creature, which it likewise imitated in all its actions: seemed to speak in a little language of its own, had already learned several words of theirs, went erect upon two legs, was tame and gentle, would come when it was called, do whatever it was bid,

---

9. Scientist, in contrast to the "vulgar" (commonplace, uncultivated).
1. Doll. "Towardly parts": promising abilities.
2. Little man, dwarf. The Latin and Italian words are Swift's own coinages, as, of course, are the various words from the Brobdingnagian language.

had the finest limbs in the world, and a complexion fairer than a nobleman's daughter of three years old. Another farmer who lived hard by, and was a particular friend of my master, came on a visit on purpose to inquire into the truth of this story. I was immediately produced, and placed upon a table, where I walked as I was commanded, drew my hanger, put it up again, made my reverence to my master's guest, asked him in his own language how he did, and told him he was welcome, just as my little nurse had instructed me. This man, who was old and dimsighted, put on his spectacles to behold me better, at which I could not forbear laughing very heartily, for his eyes appeared like the full moon shining into a chamber at two windows. Our people, who discovered the cause of my mirth, bore me company in laughing, at which the old fellow was fool enough to be angry and out of countenance. He had the character of a great miser, and to my misfortune he well deserved it by the cursed advice he gave my master to show me as a sight upon a market day in the next town, which was half an hour's riding, about two and twenty miles from our house. I guessed there was some mischief contriving when I observed my master and his friend whispering long together, sometimes pointing at me; and my fears made me fancy that I overheard and understood some of their words. But the next morning Glumdalclitch, my little nurse, told me the whole matter, which she had cunningly picked out from her mother. The poor girl laid me on her bosom, and fell a weeping with shame and grief. She apprehended some mischief would happen to me from rude vulgar folks, who might squeeze me to death, or break one of my limbs by taking me in their hands. She had also observed how modest I was in my nature, how nicely I regarded my honor, and what an indignity I should conceive it to be exposed for money as a public spectacle to the meanest of the people. She said her papa and mamma had promised that Grildrig should be hers; but now she found they meant to serve her as they did last year, when they pretended to give her a lamb, and yet, as soon as it was fat, sold it to a butcher. For my own part, I may truly affirm that I was less concerned than my nurse. I had a strong hope, which never left me, that I should one day recover my liberty; and as to the ignominy of being carried about for a monster, I considered myself to be a perfect stranger in the country, and that such a misfortune could never be charged upon me as a reproach, if ever I should return to England; since the King of Great Britain himself, in my condition, must have undergone the same distress.

My master, pursuant to the advice of his friend, carried me in a box the next market day to the neighboring town, and took along with him his little daughter, my nurse, upon a pillion[3] behind him. The box was close on every side, with a little door for me to go in and out, and a few gimlet holes to let in air. The girl had been so careful to put the quilt of her baby's bed into it, for me to lie down on. However, I was terribly shaken and discomposed in this journey, although it were but of half an hour. For the horse went about forty foot at every step, and trotted so high that the agitation was equal to the rising and falling of a ship in a great storm, but much more frequent. Our journey was somewhat further than from London to St. Albans.[4] My master alighted at an inn which he used to frequent; and after consulting a while with the innkeeper, and making some necessary preparations, he

---

3. A pad attached to the hinder part of a saddle, on which a second person, usually a woman, could ride.
4. About twenty miles.

hired the *Grultrud*, or crier, to give notice through the town of a strange creature to be seen at the Sign of the Green Eagle, not so big as a *splacknuck* (an animal in that country very finely shaped, about six foot long), and in every part of the body resembling an human creature; could speak several words and perform an hundred diverting tricks.

I was placed upon a table in the largest room of the inn, which might be near three hundred foot square. My little nurse stood on a low stool close to the table, to take care of me, and direct what I should do. My master, to avoid a crowd, would suffer only thirty people at a time to see me. I walked about on the table as the girl commanded; she asked me questions as far as she knew my understanding of the language reached, and I answered them as loud as I could. I turned about several times to the company, paid my humble respects, said they were welcome, and used some other speeches I had been taught. I took up a thimble filled with liquor, which Glumdalclitch had given me for a cup, and drank their health. I drew out my hanger, and flourished with it after the manner of fencers in England. My nurse gave me part of a straw, which I exercised as pike, having learned the art in my youth. I was that day shown to twelve sets of company, and as often forced to go over again with the same fopperies, till I was half dead with weariness and vexation. For those who had seen me made such wonderful reports that the people were ready to break down the doors to come in. My master for his own interest would not suffer anyone to touch me except my nurse; and, to prevent danger, benches were set round the table at such a distance as put me out of everybody's reach. However, an unlucky schoolboy aimed a hazel-nut directly at my head, which very narrowly missed me; otherwise, it came with so much violence that it would have infallibly knocked out my brains, for it was almost as large as a small pumpion:[5] but I had the satisfaction to see the young rogue well beaten, and turned out of the room.

My master gave public notice that he would show me again the next market day, and in the meantime he prepared a more convenient vehicle for me, which he had reason enough to do; for I was so tired with my first journey, and with entertaining company for eight hours together, that I could hardly stand upon my legs or speak a word. It was at least three days before I recovered my strength; and that I might have no rest at home, all the neighboring gentlemen from an hundred miles round, hearing of my fame, came to see me at my master's own house. There could not be fewer than thirty persons with their wives and children (for the country is very populous); and my master demanded the rate of a full room whenever he showed me at home, although it were only to a single family. So that for some time I had but little ease every day of the week (except Wednesday, which is their Sabbath) although I were not carried to the town.

My master finding how profitable I was like to be, resolved to carry me to the most considerable cities of the kingdom. Having therefore provided himself with all things necessary for a long journey, and settled his affairs at home, he took leave of his wife; and upon the 17th of August, 1703, about two months after my arrival, we set out for the metropolis, situated near the middle of that empire, and about three thousand miles distance from our house. My master made his daughter Glumdalclitch ride behind him. She carried me on her lap in a box tied about her waist. The girl had lined it on

5. Pumpkin.

all sides with the softest cloth she could get, well quilted underneath, furnished it with her baby's bed, provided me with linen and other necessaries, and made everything as convenient as she could. We had no other company but a boy of the house, who rode after us with the luggage.

My master's design was to show me in all the towns by the way, and to step out of the road for fifty or an hundred miles to any village or person of quality's house where he might expect custom. We made easy journeys of not above seven or eight score miles a day: for Glumdalclitch, on purpose to spare me, complained she was tired with the trotting of the horse. She often took me out of my box at my own desire, to give me air and show me the country, but always held me fast by leading strings.[6] We passed over five or six rivers many degrees broader and deeper than the Nile or the Ganges; and there was hardly a rivulet so small as the Thames at London Bridge. We were ten weeks in our journey, and I was shown in eighteen large towns, besides many large villages and private families.

On the 26th day of October, we arrived at the metropolis, called in their language *Lorbrulgrud*, or Pride of the Universe. My master took a lodging in the principal street of the city, not far from the royal palace, and put out bills in the usual form, containing an exact description of my person and parts. He hired a large room between three and four hundred foot wide. He provided a table sixty foot in diameter, upon which I was to act my part, and palisadoed it round three foot from the edge, and as many high, to prevent my falling over. I was shown ten times a day to the wonder and satisfaction of all people. I could now speak the language tolerably well, and perfectly understood every word that was spoken to me. Besides, I had learned their alphabet, and could make a shift to explain a sentence here and there; for Glumdalclitch had been my instructor while we were at home, and at leisure hours during our journey. She carried a little book in her pocket, not much larger than a Sanson's *Atlas*;[7] it was a common treatise for the use of young girls, giving a short account of their religion: out of this she taught me my letters, and interpreted the words.

CHAPTER 3. *The Author sent for to Court. The Queen buys him of his master, the farmer, and presents him to the King. He disputes with his Majesty's great scholars. An apartment at Court provided for the Author. He is in high favor with the Queen. He stands up for the honor of his own country. His quarrels with the Queen's dwarf.*

The frequent labors I underwent every day made in a few weeks a very considerable change in my health: the more my master got by me, the more unsatiable he grew. I had quite lost my stomach, and was almost reduced to a skeleton. The farmer observed it, and concluding I soon must die, resolved to make as good a hand of me as he could. While he was thus reasoning and resolving with himself, a *Slardral*, or Gentleman Usher, came from Court, commanding my master to carry me immediately thither for the diversion of the Queen and her ladies. Some of the latter had already been to see me and reported strange things of my beauty, behavior, and good sense. Her Majesty and those who attended her were beyond measure delighted with my demeanor. I fell on my knees and begged the honor of kissing her Imperial

---

6. Used to guide children learning to walk.   7. I.e., over two feet long and about two feet wide.

foot; but this gracious princess held out her little finger towards me (after I was set on a table), which I embraced in both my arms, and put the tip of it, with the utmost respect, to my lip. She made me some general questions about my country and my travels, which I answered as distinctly and in as few words as I could. She asked whether I would be content to live at Court. I bowed down to the board of the table, and humbly answered that I was my master's slave, but if I were at my own disposal, I should be proud to devote my life to her Majesty's service. She then asked my master whether he were willing to sell me at a good price. He, who apprehended I could not live a month, was ready enough to part with me, and demanded a thousand pieces of gold, which were ordered him on the spot, each piece being about the bigness of eight hundred moidores;[8] but, allowing for the proportion of all things between that country and Europe, and the high price of gold among them, was hardly so great a sum as a thousand guineas would be in England. I then said to the Queen, since I was now her Majesty's most humble creature and vassal, I must beg the favor that Glumdalclitch, who had always tended me with so much care and kindness, and understood to do it so well, might be admitted into her service, and continue to be my nurse and instructor. Her Majesty agreed to my petition, and easily got the farmer's consent, who was glad enough to have his daughter preferred at Court; and the poor girl herself was not able to hide her joy. My late master withdrew, bidding me farewell, and saying he had left me in a good service; to which I replied not a word, only making him a slight bow.

The Queen observed my coldness, and when the farmer was gone out of the apartment, asked me the reason. I made bold to tell her Majesty that I owed no other obligation to my late master than his not dashing out the brains of a poor harmless creature found by chance in his field; which obligation was amply recompensed by the gain he had made in showing me through half the kingdom, and the price he had now sold me for. That the life I had since led was laborious enough to kill an animal of ten times my strength. That my health was much impaired by the continual drudgery of entertaining the rabble every hour of the day; and that if my master had not thought my life in danger, her Majesty perhaps would not have got so cheap a bargain. But as I was out of all fear of being ill treated under the protection of so great and good an Empress, the Ornament of Nature, the Darling of the World, the Delight of her Subjects, the Phoenix of the Creation; so I hoped my late master's apprehensions would appear to be groundless, for I already found my spirits to revive by the influence of her most august presence.

This was the sum of my speech, delivered with great improprieties and hesitation; the latter part was altogether framed in the style peculiar to that people, whereof I learned some phrases from Glumdalclitch, while she was carrying me to Court.

The Queen, giving great allowance for my defectiveness in speaking, was however surprised at so much wit and good sense in so diminutive an animal. She took me in her own hand, and carried me to the King, who was then retired to his cabinet.[9] His Majesty, a prince of much gravity, and austere countenance, not well observing my shape at first view, asked the Queen after a cold manner how long it was since she grew fond of a *splacknuck*; for such it seems he took me to be, as I lay upon my breast in her Majesty's right

---

8. Portuguese coins.   9. Private apartment.

hand. But this princess, who hath an infinite deal of wit and humor, set me gently on my feet upon the scrutore,[1] and commanded me to give his Majesty an account of myself, which I did in a very few words; and Glumdalclitch, who attended at the cabinet door, and could not endure I should be out of her sight, being admitted, confirmed all that had passed from my arrival at her father's house.

The King, although he be as learned a person as any in his dominions, had been educated in the study of philosophy and particularly mathematics; yet when he observed my shape exactly, and saw me walk erect, before I began to speak, conceived I might be a piece of clockwork (which is in that country arrived to a very great perfection) contrived by some ingenious artist. But when he heard my voice, and found what I delivered to be regular and rational, he could not conceal his astonishment. He was by no means satisfied with the relation I gave him of the manner I came into his kingdom, but thought it a story concerted between Glumdalclitch and her father, who had taught me a set of words to make me sell at a higher price. Upon this imagination he put several other questions to me, and still received rational answers, no otherwise defective than by a foreign accent, and an imperfect knowledge in the language, with some rustic phrases which I had learned at the farmer's house, and did not suit the polite style of a court.

His Majesty sent for three great scholars who were then in their weekly waiting (according to the custom in that country). These gentlemen, after they had a while examined my shape with much nicety, were of different opinions concerning me. They all agreed that I could not be produced according to the regular laws of nature, because I was not framed with a capacity of preserving my life, either by swiftness, or climbing of trees, or digging holes in the earth. They observed by my teeth, which they viewed with great exactness, that I was a carnivorous animal; yet most quadrupeds being an overmatch for me, and field mice, with some others, too nimble, they could not imagine how I should be able to support myself, unless I fed upon snails and other insects; which they offered, by many learned arguments, to evince that I could not possibly do. One of them seemed to think that I might be an embryo, or abortive birth. But this opinion was rejected by the other two, who observed my limbs to be perfect and finished, and that I had lived several years, as it was manifested from my beard, the stumps whereof they plainly discovered through a magnifying glass. They would not allow me to be a dwarf, because my littleness was beyond all degrees of comparison; for the Queen's favorite dwarf, the smallest ever known in that kingdom, was nearly thirty foot high. After much debate, they concluded unanimously that I was only *relplum scalcath*, which is interpreted literally, *lusus naturae*; a determination exactly agreeable to the modern philosophy of Europe, whose professors, disdaining the old evasion of *occult causes*, whereby the followers of Aristotle endeavor in vain to disguise their ignorance, have invented this wonderful solution of all difficulties, to the unspeakable advancement of human knowledge.[2]

After this decisive conclusion, I entreated to be heard a word or two. I applied myself to the King, and assured his Majesty that I came from a

1. Writing desk.
2. Swift had contempt for both the medieval Schoolmen, who discussed "occult causes," the unknown causes of observable effects, and mod-

ern scientists, who, he believed, often concealed their ignorance by using equally meaningless terms. "*Lusus naturae*": one of nature's sports, or roughly, freaks.

country which abounded with several millions of both sexes, and of my own stature, where the animals, trees, and houses were all in proportion, and where by consequence I might be as able to defend myself, and to find sustenance, as any of his Majesty's subjects could do here; which I took for a full answer to those gentlemen's arguments. To this they only replied with a smile of contempt, saying that the farmer had instructed me very well in my lesson. The King, who had a much better understanding, dismissing his learned men, sent for the farmer, who by good fortune was not yet gone out of town; having therefore first examined him privately, and then confronted him with me and the young girl, his Majesty began to think that what we told him might possibly be true. He desired the Queen to order that a particular care should be taken of me, and was of opinion that Glumdalclitch should still continue in her office of tending me, because he observed we had a great affection for each other. A convenient apartment was provided for her at Court; she had a sort of governess appointed to take care of her education, a maid to dress her, and two other servants for menial offices; but the care of me was wholly appropriated to herself. The Queen commanded her own cabinetmaker to contrive a box that might serve me for a bedchamber, after the model that Glumdalclitch and I should agree upon. This man was a most ingenious artist, and according to my directions, in three weeks finished for me a wooden chamber of sixteen foot square and twelve high, with sash windows, a door, and two closets, like a London bedchamber. The board that made the ceiling was to be lifted up and down by two hinges, to put in a bed ready furnished by her Majesty's upholsterer, which Glumdalclitch took out every day to air, made it with her own hands, and letting it down at night, locked up the roof over me. A nice[3] workman, who was famous for little curiosities, undertook to make me two chairs, with backs and frames, of a substance not unlike ivory, and two tables, with a cabinet to put my things in. The room was quilted on all sides, as well as the floor and the ceiling, to prevent any accident from the carelessness of those who carried me, and to break the force of a jolt when I went in a coach. I desired a lock for my door to prevent rats and mice from coming in: the smith, after several attempts, made the smallest that ever was seen among them, for I have known a larger at the gate of a gentleman's house in England. I made a shift[4] to keep the key in a pocket of my own, fearing Glumdalclitch might lose it. The Queen likewise ordered the thinnest silks that could be gotten, to make me clothes, not much thicker than an English blanket, very cumbersome till I was accustomed to them. They were after the fashion of the kingdom, partly resembling the Persian, and partly the Chinese, and are a very grave, decent habit.

The Queen became so fond of my company that she could not dine without me. I had a table placed upon the same at which her Majesty ate, just at her left elbow, and a chair to sit on. Glumdalclitch stood upon a stool on the floor, near my table, to assist and take care of me. I had an entire set of silver dishes and plates, and other necessaries, which, in proportion to those of the Queen, were not much bigger than what I have seen of the same kind in a London toyshop,[5] for the furniture of a baby-house: these my little nurse kept in her pocket in a silver box and gave me at meals as I wanted them, always cleaning them herself. No person dined with the Queen but the two

3. Exact.
4. Contrived.

5. A shop for selling knickknacks.

Princesses Royal, the elder sixteen years old, and the younger at that time thirteen and a month. Her Majesty used to put a bit of meat upon one of my dishes, out of which I carved for myself; and her diversion was to see me eat in miniature. For the Queen (who had indeed but a weak stomach) took up at one mouthful as much as a dozen English farmers could eat at a meal, which to me was for some time a very nauseous sight. She would craunch the wing of a lark, bones and all, between her teeth, although it were nine times as large as that of a full-grown turkey; and put a bit of bread into her mouth as big as two twelve-penny loaves. She drank out of a golden cup, above a hogshead at a draught. Her knives were twice as long as a scythe set straight upon the handle. The spoons, forks, and other instruments were all in the same proportion. I remember when Glumdalclitch carried me out of curiosity to see some of the tables at Court, where ten or a dozen of these enormous knives and forks were lifted up together, I thought I had never till then beheld so terrible a sight.

It is the custom that every Wednesday (which, as I have before observed, was their Sabbath) the King and Queen, with the royal issue of both sexes, dine together in the apartment of his Majesty, to whom I was now become a favorite; and at these times my little chair and table were placed at his left hand, before one of the salt-cellars. This prince took a pleasure in conversing with me, inquiring into the manners, religion, laws, government, and learning of Europe; wherein I gave him the best account I was able. His apprehension was so clear, and his judgment so exact, that he made very wise reflections and observations upon all I said. But I confess that after I had been a little too copious in talking of my own beloved country, of our trade and wars by sea and land, of our schisms in religion and parties in the state, the prejudices of his education prevailed so far that he could not forbear taking me up in his right hand, and stroking me gently with the other, after an hearty fit of laughing, asked me whether I were a Whig or a Tory. Then turning to his first minister, who waited behind him with a white staff, near as tall as the mainmast of the *Royal Sovereign*,[6] he observed how contemptible a thing was human grandeur, which could be mimicked by such diminutive insects as I: "and yet," said he, "I dare engage, these creatures have their titles and distinctions of honor; they contrive little nests and burrows, that they call houses and cities; they make a figure in dress and equipage; they love, they fight, they dispute, they cheat, they betray." And thus he continued on, while my color came and went several times with indignation to hear our noble country, the mistress of arts and arms, the scourge of France, the arbitress of Europe, the seat of virtue, piety, honor, and truth, the pride and envy of the world, so contemptuously treated.

But as I was not in a condition to resent injuries, so, upon mature thoughts, I began to doubt whether I were injured or no. For, after having been accustomed several months to the sight and converse of this people, and observed every object upon which I cast my eyes to be of proportionable magnitude, the horror I had first conceived from their bulk and aspect was so far worn off that if I had then beheld a company of English lords and ladies in their finery and birthday clothes,[7] acting their several parts in the most courtly manner of strutting and bowing and prating, to say the truth, I should have been strongly tempted to laugh as much at them as this King and his grandees did

6. One of the largest ships in the Royal Navy. At the English court the lord treasurer bore a "white staff" as the symbol of his office.

7. Courtiers dressed with special splendor on the monarch's birthday.

at me. Neither indeed could I forbear smiling at myself when the Queen used to place me upon her hand towards a looking glass, by which both our persons appeared before me in full view together; and there could be nothing more ridiculous than the comparison; so that I really began to imagine myself dwindled many degrees below my usual size.

Nothing angered and mortified me so much as the Queen's dwarf, who being of the lowest stature that was ever in that country (for I verily think he was not full thirty foot high) became so insolent at seeing a creature so much beneath him that he would always affect to swagger and look big as he passed by me in the Queen's antechamber, while I was standing on some table talking with the lords or ladies of the court; and he seldom failed of a smart word or two upon my littleness, against which I could only revenge myself by calling him brother, challenging him to wrestle, and such repartees as are usual in the mouths of Court pages. One day at dinner this malicious little cub was so nettled with something I had said to him that, raising himself upon the frame of Her Majesty's chair, he took me up by the middle, as I was sitting down, not thinking any harm, and let me drop into a large silver bowl of cream, and then ran away as fast as he could. I fell over head and ears, and if I had not been a good swimmer, it might have gone very hard with me; for Glumdalclitch in that instant happened to be at the other end of the room, and the Queen was in such a fright that she wanted presence of mind to assist me. But my little nurse ran to my relief, and took me out, after I had swallowed above a quart of cream. I was put to bed; however, I received no other damage than the loss of a suit of clothes, which was utterly spoiled. The dwarf was soundly whipped, and as further punishment, forced to drink up the bowl of cream into which he had thrown me; neither was he ever restored to favor: for soon after the Queen bestowed him to a lady of high quality, so that I saw him no more, to my very great satisfaction; for I could not tell to what extremity such a malicious urchin might have carried his resentment.

He had before served me a scurvy trick, which set the Queen a laughing, although at the same time she were heartily vexed, and would have immediately cashiered him, if I had not been so generous as to intercede. Her Majesty had taken a marrow bone upon her plate, and after knocking out the marrow, placed the bone again in the dish, erect as it stood before; the dwarf watching his opportunity, while Glumdalclitch was gone to the sideboard, mounted upon the stool she stood on to take care of me at meals, took me up in both hands, and squeezing my legs together, wedged them into the marrow bone above my waist, where I stuck for some time, and made a very ridiculous figure. I believe it was near a minute before anyone knew what was become of me, for I thought it below me to cry out. But, as princes seldom get their meat hot, my legs were not scalded, only my stockings and breeches in a sad condition. The dwarf at my entreaty had no other punishment than a sound whipping.

I was frequently rallied by the Queen upon account of my fearfulness, and she used to ask me whether the people of my country were as great cowards as myself. The occasion was this. The kingdom is much pestered with flies in summer, and these odious insects, each of them as big as a Dunstable lark, hardly gave me any rest while I sat at dinner, with their continual humming and buzzing about my ears. They would sometimes alight upon my victuals, and leave their loathsome excrement or spawn behind, which to me was very visible, although not to the natives of that country, whose large optics were not so acute as mine in viewing smaller objects. Sometimes they would fix upon my nose or forehead, where they stung me to the quick, smelling very offensively; and I could easily trace that viscous matter, which our naturalists tell us enables those creatures to walk with their feet upwards upon a ceiling. I had much ado to defend myself against these detestable animals, and could not forbear starting when they came on my face. It was the common practice of the dwarf to catch a number of these insects in his hand, as schoolboys do among us, and let them out suddenly under my nose, on purpose to frighten me, and divert the Queen. My remedy was to cut them in pieces with my knife as they flew in the air, wherein my dexterity was much admired.

I remember one morning when Glumdalclitch had set me in my box upon a window, as she usually did in fair days to give me air (for I durst not venture to let the box be hung on a nail out of the window, as we do with cages in England), after I had lifted up one of my sashes, and sat down at my table to eat a piece of sweet cake for my breakfast, above twenty wasps, allured by the smell, came flying into the room, humming louder than the drones of as many bagpipes. Some of them seized my cake, and carried it piecemeal away; others flew about my head and face, confounding me with the noise, and putting me in the utmost terror of their stings. However, I had the courage to rise and draw my hanger, and attack them in the air. I dispatched four of them, but the rest got away, and I presently shut my window. These insects were as large as partridges; I took out their stings, found them an inch and a half long, and as sharp as needles. I carefully preserved them all, and having since shown them with some other curiosities in several parts of Europe, upon my return to England I gave three of them to Gresham College,[8] and kept the fourth for myself.

CHAPTER 4. *The country described. A proposal for correcting modern maps. The King's palace, and some account of the metropolis. The Author's way of traveling. The chief temple described.*

I now intend to give the reader a short description of this country, as far as I had traveled in it, which was not above two thousand miles round Lorbrulgrud the metropolis. For the Queen, whom I always attended, never went further when she accompanied the King in his progresses, and there stayed till his Majesty returned from viewing his frontiers. The whole extent of this prince's dominions reacheth about six thousand miles in length, and from three to five in breadth. From whence I cannot but conclude that our geographers of Europe are in a great error by supposing nothing but sea between Japan and California: for it was ever my opinion that there must be a balance of earth to counterpoise the great continent of Tartary; and therefore they ought to correct their maps and charts by joining this vast tract of land to the northwest parts of America, wherein I shall be ready to lend them my assistance.

The kingdom is a peninsula, terminated to the northeast by a ridge of mountains thirty miles high, which are altogether impassable by reason of the volcanoes upon the tops. Neither do the most learned know what sort of mortals inhabit beyond those mountains, or whether they be inhabited at

8. The Royal Society, in its earliest years, met in Gresham College.

all. On the three other sides it is bounded by the ocean. There is not one sea-port in the whole kingdom; and those parts of the coasts into which the rivers issue are so full of pointed rocks, and the sea generally so rough, that there is no venturing with the smallest of their boats; so that these people are wholly excluded from any commerce with the rest of the world. But the large rivers are full of vessels, and abound with excellent fish, for they seldom get any from the sea, because the sea fish are of the same size with those in Europe, and consequently not worth catching; whereby it is manifest that nature, in the production of plants and animals of so extraordinary a bulk, is wholly con-fined to this continent, of which I leave the reasons to be determined by phi-losophers. However, now and then they take a whale that happens to be dashed against the rocks, which the common people feed on heartily. These whales I have known so large that a man could hardly carry one upon his shoulders; and sometimes for curiosity they are brought in hampers to Lor-brulgrud: I saw one of them in a dish at the King's table, which passed for a rarity, but I did not observe he was fond of it; for I think indeed the bigness disgusted him, although I have seen one somewhat larger in Greenland.

The country is well inhabited, for it contains fifty-one cities, near an hundred walled towns, and a great number of villages. To satisfy my curi-ous reader, it may be sufficient to describe Lorbrulgrud. This city stands upon almost two equal parts on each side the river that passes through. It contains above eight thousand houses, and about six hundred thousand inhabitants. It is in length three *glonglungs* (which make about fifty-four English miles) and two and a half in breadth, as I measured it myself in the royal map made by the King's order, which was laid on the ground on pur-pose for me, and extended an hundred feet; I paced the diameter and cir-cumference several times barefoot, and computing by the scale, measured it pretty exactly.

The King's palace is no regular edifice, but an heap of buildings about seven miles round: the chief rooms are generally two hundred and forty foot high, and broad and long in proportion. A coach was allowed to Glumdal-clitch and me, wherein her governess frequently took her out to see the town, go among the shops; and I was always of the party, carried in my box, although the girl at my own desire would often take me out, and hold me in her hand, that I might more conveniently view the houses and the people as we passed along the streets. I reckoned our coach to be about a square of Westminster Hall,[9] but not altogether so high; however, I cannot be very exact. One day the governess ordered our coachman to stop at several shops, where the beggars, watching their opportunity, crowded to the sides of the coach, and gave me the most horrible spectacles that ever an English eye beheld. There was a woman with a cancer in her breast, swelled to a mon-strous size, full of holes, in two or three of which I could have easily crept, and covered my whole body. There was a fellow with a wen in his neck, larger than five woolpacks, and another with a couple of wooden legs, each about twenty foot high. But the most hateful sight of all was the lice crawling on their clothes. I could see distinctly the limbs of these vermin with my naked eye, much better than those of an European louse through a microscope, and their snouts with which they rooted like swine. They were the first I had ever

9. The ancient hall, now incorporated into the Houses of Parliament, where the law courts then sat. Swift presumably means the square of its breadth (just under sixty-eight feet).

beheld; and I should have been curious enough to dissect one of them if I had proper instruments (which I unluckily left behind me in the ship), although indeed the sight was so nauseous that it perfectly turned my stomach.

Besides the large box in which I was usually carried, the Queen ordered a smaller one to be made for me, of about twelve foot square and ten high, for the convenience of traveling, because the other was somewhat too large for Glumdalclitch's lap, and cumbersome in the coach; it was made by the same artist, whom I directed in the whole contrivance. This traveling closet was an exact square with a window in the middle of three of the squares, and each window was latticed with iron wire on the outside, to prevent accidents in long journeys. On the fourth side, which had no windows, two strong staples were fixed, through which the person that carried me, when I had a mind to be on horseback, put in a leathern belt, and buckled it about his waist. This was always the office of some grave trusty servant in whom I could confide, whether I attended the King and Queen in their progresses, or were disposed to see the gardens, or pay a visit to some great lady or minister of state in the court, when Glumdalclitch happened to be out of order: for I soon began to be known and esteemed among the greatest officers, I suppose more upon account of their Majesties' favor than any merit of my own. In journeys, when I was weary of the coach, a servant on horseback would buckle my box, and place it on a cushion before him; and there I had a full prospect of the country on three sides from my three windows. I had in this closet a field bed[1] and a hammock hung from the ceiling, two chairs and a table, neatly screwed to the floor to prevent being tossed about by the agitation of the horse or the coach. And having been long used to sea voyages, those motions, although sometimes very violent, did not much discompose me.

When I had a mind to see the town, it was always in my traveling closet, which Glumdalclitch held in her lap in a kind of open sedan, after the fashion of the country, borne by four men, and attended by two others in the Queen's livery. The people, who had often heard of me, were very curious to crowd about the sedan; and the girl was complaisant enough to make the bearers stop, and to take me in her hand that I might be more conveniently seen.

I was very desirous to see the chief temple, and particularly the tower belonging to it, which is reckoned the highest in the kingdom. Accordingly one day my nurse carried me thither, but I may truly say I came back disappointed; for the height is not above three thousand foot, reckoning from the ground to the highest pinnacle top; which, allowing for the difference between the size of those people and us in Europe, is no great matter for admiration, nor at all equal in proportion (if I rightly remember) to Salisbury steeple.[2] But, not to detract from a nation to which during my life I shall acknowledge myself extremely obliged, it must be allowed that whatever this famous tower wants in height is amply made up in beauty and strength. For the walls are near an hundred foot thick, built of hewn stone, whereof each is about forty foot square, and adorned on all sides with statues of gods and emperors cut in marble larger than the life, placed in their several niches. I measured a little finger which had fallen down from one of these statues,

1. Folding bed, cot.
2. One of the most beautiful Gothic steeples in

England is that of Salisbury Cathedral, 404 feet high.

and lay unperceived among some rubbish, and found it exactly four foot and an inch in length. Glumdalclitch wrapped it up in a handkerchief, and carried it home in her pocket to keep among other trinkets, of which the girl was very fond, as children at her age usually are.

The King's kitchen is indeed a noble building, vaulted at top, and about six hundred foot high. The great oven is not so wide by ten paces as the cupola at St. Paul's:[3] for I measured the latter on purpose after my return. But if I should describe the kitchen grate, the prodigious pots and kettles, the joints of meat turning on the spits, with many other particulars, perhaps I should be hardly believed; at least a severe critic would be apt to think I enlarged a little, as travelers are often suspected to do. To avoid which censure, I fear I have run too much into the other extreme, and that if this treatise should happen to be translated into the language of Brobdingnag (which is the general name of that kingdom) and transmitted thither, the King and his people would have reason to complain that I had done them an injury by a false and diminutive representation.

His Majesty seldom keeps above six hundred horses in his stables: they are generally from fifty-four to sixty foot high. But when he goes abroad on solemn days, he is attended for state by a militia guard of five hundred horse, which indeed I thought was the most splendid sight that could be ever beheld, till I saw part of his army in battalia,[4] whereof I shall find another occasion to speak.

CHAPTER 5. *Several adventures that happened to the Author. The execution of a criminal. The Author shows his skill in navigation.*

I should have lived happy enough in that country if my littleness had not exposed me to several ridiculous and troublesome accidents, some of which I shall venture to relate. Glumdalclitch often carried me into the gardens of the court in my smaller box, and would sometimes take me out of it and hold me in her hand, or set me down to walk. I remember, before the dwarf left the Queen, he followed us one day into those gardens; and my nurse having set me down, he and I being close together near some dwarf apple trees, I must needs show my wit by a silly allusion between him and the trees, which happens to hold in their language as it doth in ours. Whereupon, the malicious rogue watching his opportunity, when I was walking under one of them, shook it directly over my head, by which a dozen apples, each of them near as large as a Bristol barrel, came tumbling about my ears; one of them hit me on the back as I chanced to stoop, and knocked me down flat on my face, but I received no other hurt; and the dwarf was pardoned at my desire, because I had given the provocation.

Another day Glumdalclitch left me on a smooth grassplot to divert myself while she walked at some distance with her governess. In the meantime there suddenly fell such a violent shower of hail that I was immediately by the force of it struck to the ground: and when I was down, the hailstones gave me such cruel bangs all over the body as if I had been pelted with tennis balls;[5] however I made a shift to creep on all four, and shelter myself by lying on my face

---

3. The cupola of St. Paul's Cathedral in London is 108 feet in diameter.
4. Battle array.

5. Eighteenth-century tennis balls, unlike the modern, were very hard.

on the lee side of a border of lemon thyme, but so bruised from head to foot that I could not go abroad in ten days. Neither is this at all to be wondered at, because nature in that country observing the same proportion through all her operations, a hailstone is near eighteen hundred times as large as one in Europe; which I can assert upon experience, having been so curious to weigh and measure them.

But a more dangerous accident happened to me in the same garden when my little nurse, believing she had put me in a secure place, which I often entreated her to do that I might enjoy my own thoughts, and having left my box at home to avoid the trouble of carrying it, went to another part of the garden with her governess and some ladies of her acquaintance. While she was absent and out of hearing, a small white spaniel belonging to one of the chief gardeners, having got by accident into the garden, happened to range near the place where I lay. The dog following the scent, came directly up, and taking me in his mouth, ran straight to his master, wagging his tail, and set me gently on the ground. By good fortune he had been so well taught that I was carried between his teeth without the least hurt, or even tearing my clothes. But the poor gardener, who knew me well, and had a great kindness for me, was in a terrible fright. He gently took me up in both his hands, and asked me how I did; but I was so amazed and out of breath that I could not speak a word. In a few minutes I came to myself, and he carried me safe to my little nurse, who by this time had returned to the place where she left me, and was in cruel agonies when I did not appear nor answer when she called; she severely reprimanded the gardener on account of his dog. But the thing was hushed up and never known at court; for the girl was afraid of the Queen's anger; and truly, as to myself, I thought it would not be for my reputation that such a story should go about.

This accident absolutely determined Glumdalclitch never to trust me abroad for the future out of her sight. I had been long afraid of this resolution, and therefore concealed from her some little unlucky adventures that happened in those times when I was left by myself. Once a kite hovering over the garden made a stoop[6] at me, and if I had not resolutely drawn my hanger, and run under a thick espalier, he would have certainly carried me away in his talons. Another time walking to the top of a fresh molehill, I fell to my neck in the hole through which that animal had cast up the earth, and coined some lie, not worth remembering, to excuse myself for spoiling my clothes. I likewise broke my right shin against the shell of a snail, which I happened to stumble over, as I was walking alone, and thinking on poor England.

I cannot tell whether I were more pleased or mortified to observe in those solitary walks that the smaller birds did not appear to be at all afraid of me; but would hop about within a yard distance, looking for worms and other food with as much indifference and security as if no creature at all were near them. I remember a thrush had the confidence to snatch out of my hand with his bill a piece of cake that Glumdalclitch had just given me for my breakfast. When I attempted to catch any of these birds, they would boldly turn against me, endeavoring to pick my fingers, which I durst not venture within their reach; and then they would hop back unconcerned to hunt for worms or snails, as they did before. But one day I took a thick cudgel, and threw it with all my strength so luckily at a linnet that I knocked

6. Swoop. "Kite": a bird of prey.

him down, and seizing him by the neck with both my hands, ran with him in triumph to my nurse. However, the bird, who had only been stunned, recovering himself, gave me so many boxes with his wings on both sides of my head and body, though I held him at arm's length, and was out of the reach of his claws, that I was twenty times thinking to let him go. But I was soon relieved by one of our servants, who wrung off the bird's neck, and I had him next day for dinner, by the Queen's command. This linnet, as near as I can remember, seemed to be somewhat larger than an English swan.

The Maids of Honor often invited Glumdalclitch to their apartments, and desired she would bring me along with her, on purpose to have the pleasure of seeing and touching me. They would often strip me naked from top to toe and lay me at full length in their bosoms; wherewith I was much disgusted, because, to say the truth, a very offensive smell came from their skins, which I do not mention or intend to the disadvantage of those excellent ladies, for whom I have all manner of respect; but I conceive that my sense was more acute in proportion to my littleness, and that those illustrious persons were no more disagreeable to their lovers, or to each other, than people of the same quality are with us in England. And, after all, I found their natural smell was much more supportable than when they used perfumes, under which I immediately swooned away. I cannot forget that an intimate friend of mine in Lilliput took the freedom in a warm day, when I had used a good deal of exercise, to complain of a strong smell about me, although I am as little faulty that way as most of my sex: but I suppose his faculty of smelling was as nice with regard to me as mine was to that of this people. Upon this point, I cannot forbear doing justice to the Queen, my mistress, and Glumdalclitch, my nurse, whose persons were as sweet as those of any lady in England.

That which gave me most uneasiness among these Maids of Honor, when my nurse carried me to visit them, was to see them use me without any manner of ceremony, like a creature who had no sort of consequence. For they would strip themselves to the skin and put on their smocks in my presence, while I was placed on their toilet[7] directly before their naked bodies; which, I am sure, to me was very far from being a tempting sight, or from giving me any other emotions than those of horror and disgust. Their skins appeared so coarse and uneven, so variously colored, when I saw them near, with a mole here and there as broad as a trencher, and hairs hanging from it thicker than packthreads, to say nothing further concerning the rest of their persons. Neither did they at all scruple, while I was by, to discharge what they had drunk, to the quantity of at least two hogsheads, in a vessel that held above three tuns. The handsomest among these Maids of Honor, a pleasant frolicsome girl of sixteen, would sometimes set me astride upon one of her nipples, with many other tricks, wherein the reader will excuse me for not being over particular. But I was so much displeased that I entreated Glumdalclitch to contrive some excuse for not seeing that young lady any more.

One day a young gentleman, who was nephew to my nurse's governess, came and pressed them both to see an execution. It was of a man who had murdered one of that gentleman's intimate acquaintance. Glumdalclitch was prevailed on to be of the company, very much against her inclination,

7. Toilet table.

for she was naturally tender-hearted: and as for myself, although I abhorred such kind of spectacles, yet my curiosity tempted me to see something that I thought must be extraordinary. The malefactor was fixed in a chair upon a scaffold erected for the purpose, and his head cut off at a blow with a sword of about forty foot long. The veins and arteries spouted up such a prodigious quantity of blood, and so high in the air, that the great *jet d'eau* at Versailles was not equal for the time it lasted; and the head, when it fell on the scaffold floor, gave such a bounce,[8] as made me start, although I were at least half an English mile distant.

The Queen, who often used to hear me talk of my sea voyages, and took all occasions to divert me when I was melancholy, asked me whether I understood how to handle a sail or an oar, and whether a little exercise of rowing might not be convenient for my health. I answered that I understood both very well. For although my proper employment had been to be surgeon or doctor to the ship, yet often, upon a pinch, I was forced to work like a common mariner. But I could not see how this could be done in their country, where the smallest wherry was equal to a first-rate man-of-war among us, and such a boat as I could manage would never live in any of their rivers. Her Majesty said, if I would contrive a boat, her own joiner should make it, and she would provide a place for me to sail in. The fellow was an ingenious workman and, by my instructions, in ten days finished a pleasure boat with all its tackling, able conveniently to hold eight Europeans. When it was finished, the Queen was so delighted that she ran with it in her lap to the King, who ordered it to be put in a cistern full of water, with me in it, by way of trial; where I could not manage my two sculls, or little oars, for want of room. But the Queen had before contrived another project. She ordered the joiner to make a wooden trough of three hundred foot long, fifty broad, and eight deep; which being well pitched to prevent leaking, was placed on the floor along the wall in an outer room of the palace. It had a cock near the bottom to let out the water when it began to grow stale, and two servants could easily fill it in half an hour. Here I often used to row for my own diversion, as well as that of the Queen and her ladies, who thought themselves well entertained with my skill and agility. Sometimes I would put up my sail, and then my business was only to steer, while the ladies gave me a gale with their fans; and when they were weary, some of the pages would blow my sail forward with their breath, while I showed my art by steering starboard or larboard as I pleased. When I had done, Glumdalclitch always carried my boat into her closet, and hung it on a nail to dry.

In this exercise I once met an accident which had like to have cost me my life. For one of the pages having put my boat into the trough, the governess who attended Glumdalclitch very officiously lifted me up to place me in the boat; but I happened to slip through her fingers, and should have infallibly fallen down forty foot upon the floor, if by the luckiest chance in the world I had not been stopped by a corking-pin that stuck in the good gentlewoman's stomacher;[9] the head of the pin passed between my shirt and the waistband of my breeches, and thus I was held by the middle in the air until Glumdalclitch ran to my relief.

8. A sudden noise. "*Jet d'eau* at Versailles": this fountain rose over forty feet in the air.
9. An ornamental covering for the front and upper part of the body. "Officiously": kindly, dutifully. "Corking-pin": a pin of the largest size.

Another time, one of the servants, whose office it was to fill my trough every third day with fresh water, was so careless to let a huge frog (not perceiving it) slip out of his pail. The frog lay concealed till I was put into my boat, but then seeing a resting place, climbed up, and made it lean so much on one side that I was forced to balance it with all my weight on the other, to prevent overturning. When the frog was got in, it hopped at once half the length of the boat, and then over my head, backwards and forwards, daubing my face and clothes with its odious slime. The largeness of its features made it appear the most deformed animal that can be conceived. However, I desired Glumdalclitch to let me deal with it alone. I banged it a good while with one of my sculls, and at last forced it to leap out of the boat.

But the greatest danger I ever underwent in that kingdom was from a monkey, who belonged to one of the clerks of the kitchen. Glumdalclitch had locked me up in her closet, while she went somewhere upon business or a visit. The weather being very warm, the closet window was left open, as well as the windows in the door of my bigger box, in which I usually lived, because of its largeness and conveniency. As I sat quietly meditating at my table, I heard something bounce in at the closet window, and skip about from one side to the other, whereat, although I was much alarmed, yet I ventured to look out, but stirred not from my seat; and then I saw this frolicsome animal, frisking and leaping up and down, till at last he came to my box, which he seemed to view with great pleasure and curiosity, peeping in at the door and every window. I retreated to the farther corner of my room, or box, but the monkey looking in at every side, put me into such a fright that I wanted presence of mind to conceal myself under the bed, as I might easily have done. After some time spent in peeping, grinning, and chattering, he at last espied me, and reaching one of his paws in at the door, as a cat does when she plays with a mouse, although I often shifted place to avoid him, he at length seized the lappet of my coat (which, being made of that country cloth, was very thick and strong) and dragged me out. He took me up in his right forefoot, and held me as a nurse does a child she is going to suckle, just as I have seen the same sort of creature do with a kitten in Europe: and when I offered to struggle, he squeezed me so hard that I thought it more prudent to submit. I have good reason to believe that he took me for a young one of his own species, by his often stroking my face very gently with his other paw. In these diversions he was interrupted by a noise at the closet door, as if somebody were opening it, whereupon he suddenly leaped up to the window at which he had come in, and thence upon the leads and gutters, walking upon three legs, and holding me in the fourth, till he clambered up to a roof that was next to ours. I heard Glumdalclitch give a shriek at the moment he was carrying me out. The poor girl was almost distracted: that quarter of the palace was all in an uproar; the servants ran for ladders; the monkey was seen by hundreds in the court, sitting upon the ridge of a building, holding me like a baby in one of his forepaws and feeding me with the other, by cramming into my mouth some victuals he had squeezed out of the bag on one side of his chaps, and patting me when I would not eat; whereat many of the rabble below could not forebear laughing; neither do I think they justly ought to be blamed, for without question the sight was ridiculous enough to everybody but myself. Some of the people threw up stones, hoping to drive the monkey down; but this was strictly forbidden, or else very probably my brains had been dashed out.

The ladders were now applied, and mounted by several men; which the monkey observing, and finding himself almost encompassed, not being able to make speed enough with his three legs, let me drop on a ridge tile, and made his escape. Here I sat for some time three hundred yards from the ground, expecting every moment to be blown down by the wind, or to fall by my own giddiness, and come tumbling over and over from the ridge to the eaves. But an honest lad, one of my nurse's footmen, climbed up, and putting me into his breeches pocket, brought me down safe.

I was almost choked with the filthy stuff the monkey had crammed down my throat; but my dear little nurse picked it out of my mouth with a small needle, and then I fell a vomiting, which gave me great relief. Yet I was so weak and bruised in the sides with the squeezes given me by this odious animal that I was forced to keep my bed a fortnight. The King, Queen, and all the Court sent every day to inquire after my health, and her Majesty made me several visits during my sickness. The monkey was killed, and an order made that no such animal should be kept about the palace.

When I attended the King after my recovery, to return him thanks for his favors, he was pleased to rally me a good deal upon this adventure. He asked me what my thoughts and speculations were while I lay in the monkey's paw, how I liked the victuals he gave me, his manner of feeding, and whether the fresh air on the roof had sharpened my stomach. He desired to know what I would have done upon such an occasion in my own country. I told his Majesty that in Europe we had no monkeys, except such as were brought for curiosities from other places, and so small that I could deal with a dozen of them together, if they presumed to attack me. And as for that monstrous animal with whom I was so lately engaged (it was indeed as large as an elephant), if my fears had suffered me to think so far as to make use of my hanger (looking fiercely and clapping my hand upon the hilt as I spoke) when he poked his paw into my chamber, perhaps I should have given him such a wound as would have made him glad to withdraw it with more haste than he put it in. This I delivered in a firm tone, like a person who was jealous lest his courage should be called in question. However, my speech produced nothing else besides a loud laughter, which all the respect due to his Majesty from those about him could not make them contain. This made me reflect how vain an attempt it is for a man to endeavor doing himself honor among those who are out of all degree of equality or comparison with him. And yet I have seen the moral of my own behavior very frequent in England since my return, where a little contemptible varlet, without the least title to birth, person, wit, or common sense, shall presume to look with importance, and put himself upon a foot with the greatest persons of the kingdom.

I was every day furnishing the court with some ridiculous story; and Glumdalclitch, although she loved me to excess, yet was arch enough to inform the Queen whenever I committed any folly that she thought would be diverting to her Majesty. The girl, who had been out of order,[1] was carried by her governess to take the air about an hour's distance, or thirty miles from town. They alighted out of the coach near a small footpath in a field, and Glumdalclitch setting down my traveling box, I went out of it to walk. There was a cow dung in the patch, and I must needs try my activity by attempting to leap over it. I took a run, but unfortunately jumped short, and

1. Not feeling well.

found myself just in the middle up to my knees. I waded through with some difficulty, and one of the footmen wiped me as clean as he could with his handkerchief; for I was filthily bemired, and my nurse confined me to my box till we returned home, where the Queen was soon informed of what had passed and the footmen spread it about the Court, so that all the mirth, for some days, was at my expense.

CHAPTER 6. *Several contrivances of the Author to please the King and Queen. He shows his skill in music. The King inquires into the state of Europe, which the Author relates to him. The King's observations thereon.*

I used to attend the King's levee once or twice a week, and had often seen him under the barber's hand, which indeed was at first very terrible to behold. For the razor was almost twice as long as an ordinary scythe. His Majesty, according to the custom of the country, was only shaved twice a week. I once prevailed on the barber to give me some of the suds or lather, out of which I picked forty or fifty of the strongest stumps of hair. I then took a piece of fine wood, and cut it like the back of a comb, making several holes in it at equal distance with as small a needle as I could get from Glumdalclitch. I fixed in the stumps so artificially,[2] scraping and sloping them with my knife towards the points, that I made a very tolerable comb; which was a seasonable supply, my own being so much broken in the teeth that it was almost useless; neither did I know any artist in that country so nice and exact as would undertake to make me another.

And this puts me in mind of an amusement wherein I spent many of my leisure hours. I desired the Queen's woman to save for me the combings of her Majesty's hair, whereof in time I got a good quantity; and consulting with my friend the cabinetmaker, who had received general orders to do little jobs for me, I directed him to make two chair frames, no larger than those I had in my box, and then to bore little holes with a fine awl round those parts where I designed the backs and seats; through these holes I wove the strongest hairs I could pick out, just after the manner of cane chairs in England. When they were finished, I made a present of them to her Majesty, who kept them in her cabinet, and used to show them for curiosities, as indeed they were the wonder of every one that beheld them. The Queen would have made me sit upon one of these chairs, but I absolutely refused to obey her, protesting I would rather die a thousand deaths than place a dishonorable part of my body on those precious hairs that once adorned her Majesty's head. Of these hairs (as I had always a mechanical genius) I likewise made a neat little purse above five foot long, with her Majesty's name deciphered in gold letters, which I gave to Glumdalclitch by the Queen's consent. To say the truth, it was more for show than use, being not of strength to bear the weight of the larger coins; and therefore she kept nothing in it but some little toys[3] that girls are fond of.

The King, who delighted in music, had frequent consorts[4] at court, to which I was sometimes carried, and set in my box on a table to hear them; but the noise was so great that I could hardly distinguish the tunes. I am confident that all the drums and trumpets of a royal army, beating and sounding

2. Skillfully.
3. Trifles.
4. Concerts.

together just at your ears, could not equal it. My practice was to have my box removed from the places where the performers sat, as far as I could, then to shut the doors and windows of it, and draw the window curtains, after which I found their music not disagreeable.

I had learned in my youth to play a little upon the spinet. Glumdalclitch kept one in her chamber, and a master attended twice a week to teach her: I call it a spinet, because it somewhat resembled that instrument, and was played upon in the same manner. A fancy came into my head that I would entertain the King and Queen with an English tune upon this instrument. But this appeared extremely difficult: for the spinet was near sixty foot long, each key being almost a foot wide; so that, with my arms extended, I could not reach to above five keys, and to press them down required a good smart stroke with my fist, which would be too great a labor and to no purpose. The method I contrived was this: I prepared two round sticks about the bigness of common cudgels; they were thicker at one end than the other, and I covered the thicker ends with a piece of a mouse's skin, that by rapping on them I might neither damage the tops of the keys, nor interrupt the sound. Before the spinet a bench was placed, about four foot below the keys, and I was put upon the bench. I ran sideling upon it that way and this, as fast as I could, banging the proper keys with my two sticks; and made a shift to play a jig, to the great satisfaction of both their Majesties: but it was the most violent exercise I ever underwent, and yet I could not strike above sixteen keys, nor, consequently, play the bass and treble together, as other artists do; which was a great disadvantage to my performance.

The King, who, as I before observed, was a prince of excellent understanding, would frequently order that I should be brought in my box and set upon the table in his closet. He would then command me to bring one of my chairs out of the box, and sit down within three yards distance upon the top of the cabinet, which brought me almost to a level with his face. In this manner I had several conversations with him. I one day took the freedom to tell his Majesty that the contempt he discovered towards Europe, and the rest of the world, did not seem answerable to those excellent qualities of mind that he was master of. That reason did not extend itself with the bulk of the body: on the contrary, we observed in our country that the tallest persons were usually least provided with it. That among other animals, bees and ants had the reputation of more industry, art, and sagacity than many of the larger kinds; and that, as inconsiderable as he took me to be, I hoped I might live to do his Majesty some signal service. The King heard me with attention, and began to conceive a much better opinion of me than he had before. He desired I would give him as exact an account of the government of England as I possibly could; because, as fond as princes commonly are of their own customs (for so he conjectured of other monarchs, by my former discourses), he should be glad to hear of anything that might deserve imitation.

Imagine with thyself, courteous reader, how often I then wished for the tongue of Demosthenes or Cicero,[5] that might have enabled me to celebrate the praise of my own dear native country in a style equal to its merits and felicity.

I began my discourse by informing his Majesty that our dominions consisted of two islands, which composed three mighty kingdoms under one

5. Great orators of Athens and Rome, respectively.

sovereign, beside our plantations in America. I dwelt long upon the fertility of our soil, and the temperature of our climate. I then spoke at large upon the constitution of an English Parliament, partly made up of an illustrious body called the House of Peers,[6] persons of the noblest blood, and of the most ancient and ample patrimonies. I described that extraordinary care always taken of their education in arts and arms, to qualify them for being counselors born to the king and kingdom; to have a share in the legislature, to be members of the highest Court of Judicature, from whence there could be no appeal; and to be champions always ready for the defense of their prince and country, by their valor, conduct, and fidelity. That these were the ornament and bulwark of the kingdom, worthy followers of their most renowned ancestors, whose honor had been the reward of their virtue, from which their posterity were never once known to degenerate. To these were joined several holy persons, as part of that assembly, under the title of Bishops, whose peculiar business it is to take care of religion, and of those who instruct the people therein. These were searched and sought out through the whole nation, by the prince and his wisest counselors, among such of the priesthood as were most deservedly distinguished by the sanctity of their lives and the depth of their erudition, who were indeed the spiritual fathers of the clergy and the people.

That the other part of the Parliament consisted of an assembly called the House of Commons, who were all principal gentlemen, freely picked and culled out by the people themselves, for their great abilities and love of their country, to represent the wisdom of the whole nation. And these two bodies make up the most august assembly in Europe, to whom, in conjunction with the prince, the whole legislature is committed.

I then descended to the Courts of Justice, over which the Judges, those venerable sages and interpreters of the law, presided, for determining the disputed rights and properties of men, as well as for the punishment of vice, and protection of innocence. I mentioned the prudent management of our treasury, the valor and achievements of our forces by sea and land. I computed the number of our people, by reckoning how many millions there might be of each religious sect, or political party among us. I did not omit even our sports and pastimes, or any other particular which I thought might redound to the honor of my country. And I finished all with a brief historical account of affairs and events in England for about an hundred years past.

This conversation was not ended under five audiences, each of several hours, and the King heard the whole with great attention, frequently taking notes of what I spoke, as well as memorandums of several questions he intended to ask me.

When I had put an end to these long discourses, his Majesty in a sixth audience consulting his notes, proposed many doubts, queries, and objections, upon every article. He asked what methods were used to cultivate the minds and bodies of our young nobility, and in what kind of business they commonly spent the first and teachable part of their lives. What course was taken to supply that assembly when any noble family became extinct. What qualifications were necessary in those who were to be created new lords. Whether the humor[7] of the prince, a sum of money to a Court lady or a prime

---

6. The House of Lords. "Temperature": temperateness.   7. Whim.

minister, or a design of strengthening a party opposite to the public interest, ever happened to be motives in those advancements. What share of knowledge these lords had in the laws of their country, and how they came by it, so as to enable them to decide the properties of their fellow subjects in the last resort. Whether they were always so free from avarice, partialities, or want that a bribe or some other sinister view could have no place among them. Whether those holy lords I spoke of were constantly promoted to that rank upon account of their knowledge in religious matters, and the sanctity of their lives; had never been compliers with the times while they were common priests, or slavish prostitute chaplains to some nobleman, whose opinions they continued servilely to follow after they were admitted into that assembly.

He then desired to know what arts were practiced in electing those whom I called Commoners. Whether a stranger with a strong purse might not influence the vulgar voters to choose him before their own landlord or the most considerable gentleman in the neighborhood. How it came to pass that people were so violently bent upon getting into this assembly, which I allowed to be a great trouble and expense, often to the ruin of their families, without any salary or pension: because this appeared such an exalted strain of virtue and public spirit that his Majesty seemed to doubt it might possibly not be always sincere; and he desired to know whether such zealous gentlemen could have any views of refunding themselves for the charges and trouble they were at, by sacrificing the public good to the designs of a weak and vicious prince in conjunction with a corrupted ministry. He multiplied his questions, and sifted me thoroughly upon every part of this head, proposing numberless inquiries and objections, which I think it not prudent or convenient to repeat.

Upon what I said in relation to our Courts of Justice, his Majesty desired to be satisfied in several points: and this I was the better able to do, having been formerly almost ruined by a long suit in chancery, which was decreed for me with costs. He asked what time was usually spent in determining between right and wrong, and what degree of expense. Whether advocates and orators had liberty to plead in causes manifestly known to be unjust, vexatious, or oppressive. Whether party in religion or politics were observed to be of any weight in the scale of justice. Whether those pleading orators were persons educated in the general knowledge of equity, or only in provincial, national, and other local customs. Whether they or their judges had any part in penning those laws which they assumed the liberty of interpreting and glossing upon at their pleasure. Whether they had ever at different times pleaded for and against the same cause, and cited precedents to prove contrary opinions. Whether they were a rich or a poor corporation. Whether they received any pecuniary reward for pleading or delivering their opinions. And particularly whether they were ever admitted as members in the lower senate.

He fell next upon the management of our treasury, and said he thought my memory had failed me, because I computed our taxes at about five or six millions a year, and when I came to mention the issues,[8] he found they sometimes amounted to more than double, for the notes he had taken were very particular in this point; because he hoped, as he told me, that the knowledge of our conduct might be useful to him, and he could not be deceived

---

8. Expenditures.

in his calculations. But if what I told him were true, he was still at a loss how a kingdom could run out of its estate like a private person. He asked me, who were our creditors? and where we should find money to pay them? He wondered to hear me talk of such chargeable and extensive wars; that certainly we must be a quarrelsome people, or live among very bad neighbors, and that our generals must needs be richer than our kings.[9] He asked what business we had out of our own islands, unless upon the score of trade or treaty or to defend the coasts with our fleet. Above all, he was amazed to hear me talk of a mercenary standing army[1] in the midst of peace, and among a free people. He said if we were governed by our own consent in the persons of our representatives, he could not imagine of whom we were afraid, or against whom we were to fight; and would hear my opinion whether a private man's house might not better be defended by himself, his children, and family, than by half a dozen rascals picked up at a venture[2] in the streets for small wages, who might get an hundred times more by cutting their throats.

He laughed at my odd kind of arithmetic (as he was pleased to call it) in reckoning the numbers of our people by a computation drawn from the several sects among us in religion and politics. He said he knew no reason why those who entertain opinions prejudicial to the public should be obliged to change, or should not be obliged to conceal them. And as it was tyranny in any government to require the first, so it was weakness not to enforce the second: for a man may be allowed to keep poisons in his closet, but not to vend them about for cordials.[3]

He observed that among the diversions of our nobility and gentry I had mentioned gaming. He desired to know at what age this entertainment was usually taken up, and when it was laid down; how much of their time it employed; whether it ever went so high as to affect their fortunes; whether mean, vicious people, by their dexterity in that art, might not arrive at great riches, and sometimes keep our very nobles in dependence, as well as habituate them to vile companions, wholly take them from the improvement of their minds, and force them, by the losses they received, to learn and practice that infamous dexterity upon others.

He was perfectly astonished with the historical account I gave him of our affairs during the last century, protesting it was only an heap of conspiracies, rebellions, murders, massacres, revolutions, banishments, the very worst effects that avarice, faction, hypocrisy, perfidiousness, cruelty, rage, madness, hatred, envy, lust, malice, or ambition could produce.

His Majesty in another audience was at the pains to recapitulate the sum of all I had spoken; compared the questions he made with the answers I had given; then taking me into his hands, and stroking me gently, delivered himself in these words, which I shall never forget, nor the manner he spoke them in. "My little friend Grildrig, you have made a most admirable panegyric upon your country. You have clearly proved that ignorance, idleness, and vice are the proper ingredients for qualifying a legislator. That laws are best explained, interpreted, and applied by those whose interests and abilities lie

---

9. An allusion to the enormous fortune gained by the duke of Marlborough, formerly captain-general of the army, whom Swift detested.
1. Since the declaration of the Bill of Rights (1689), a standing army without authorization by Parliament had been illegal. Swift and the Tories

in general were vigilant in their opposition to such an army.
2. By chance.
3. Medicines to stimulate the heart, or, equally commonly, liqueurs.

in perverting, confounding, and eluding them. I observe among you some lines of an institution which in its original might have been tolerable; but these half erased, and the rest wholly blurred and blotted by corruptions. It doth not appear from all you have said how any one virtue is required towards the procurement of any one station among you; much less that men are ennobled on account of their virtue, that priests are advanced for their piety or learning, soldiers for their conduct or valor, judges for their integrity, senators for the love of their country, or counselors for their wisdom. As for yourself," continued the King, "who have spent the greatest part of your life in traveling, I am well disposed to hope you may hitherto have escaped many vices of your country. But by what I have gathered from your own relation, and the answers I have with much pains wringed and extorted from you, I cannot but conclude the bulk of your natives to be the most pernicious race of little odious vermin that nature ever suffered to crawl upon the surface of the earth."

CHAPTER 7. *The Author's love of his country. He makes a proposal of much advantage to the King; which is rejected. The King's great ignorance in politics. The learning of that country very imperfect and confined. Their laws, and military affairs, and parties in the State.*

Nothing but an extreme love of truth could have hindered me from concealing this part of my story. It was in vain to discover my resentments, which were always turned into ridicule: and I was forced to rest with patience while my noble and most beloved country was so injuriously treated. I am heartily sorry as any of my readers can possibly be that such an occasion was given, but this prince happened to be so curious and inquisitive upon every particular that it could not consist either with gratitude or good manners to refuse giving him what satisfaction I was able. Yet thus much I may be allowed to say in my own vindication: that I artfully eluded many of his questions, and gave to every point a more favorable turn by many degrees than the strictness of truth would allow. For I have always borne that laudable partiality to my own country, which Dionysius Halicarnassensis[4] with so much justice recommends to an historian. I would hide the frailties and deformities of my political mother, and place her virtues and beauties in the most advantageous light. This was my sincere endeavor in those many discourses I had with that mighty monarch, although it unfortunately failed of success.

But great allowances should be given to a King who lives wholly secluded from the rest of the world, and must therefore be altogether unacquainted with the manners and customs that most prevail in other nations: the want of which knowledge will ever produce many *prejudices*, and a certain *narrowness of thinking*, from which we and the politer countries of Europe are wholly exempted. And it would be hard indeed if so remote a prince's notions of virtue and vice were to be offered as a standard for all mankind.

To confirm what I have now said, and further to show the miserable effects of a *confined education*, I shall here insert a passage which will hardly obtain belief. In hopes to ingratiate myself farther into his Majesty's favor, I told him of an invention discovered between three and four hundred

---

4. A Greek rhetorician and historian, who flourished ca. 25 B.C.E. His history of Rome was written to reconcile the Greeks to their Roman masters.

years ago, to make a certain powder, into an heap of which the smallest spark of fire falling would kindle the whole in a moment, although it were as big as a mountain, and make it all fly up in the air together, with a noise and agitation greater than thunder. That a proper quantity of this powder rammed into an hollow tube of brass or iron, according to its bigness, would drive a ball of iron or lead with such violence and speed as nothing was able to sustain its force. That the largest balls thus discharged would not only destroy whole ranks of an army at once, but batter the strongest walls to the ground; sink down ships with a thousand men in each, to the bottom of the sea; and, when linked together by a chain, would cut through masts and rigging; divide hundreds of bodies in the middle, and lay all waste before them. That we often put this powder into large hollow balls of iron, and discharged them by an engine into some city we were besieging; which would rip up the pavements, tear the houses to pieces, burst and throw splinters on every side, dashing out the brains of all who came near. That I knew the ingredients very well, which were cheap and common; I understood the manner of compounding them, and could direct his workmen how to make those tubes of a size proportionable to all other things in his Majesty's kingdom, and the largest need not be above two hundred foot long; twenty or thirty of which tubes, charged with the proper quantity of powder and balls, would batter down the walls of the strongest town in his dominions in a few hours; or destroy the whole metropolis, if ever it should pretend to dispute his absolute commands. This I humbly offered to his Majesty as a small tribute of acknowledgement in return of so many marks that I had received of his royal favor and protection.

The King was struck with horror at the description I had given of those terrible engines and the proposal I had made. He was amazed how so impotent and groveling an insect as I (these were his expressions) could entertain such inhuman ideas, and in so familiar a manner as to appear wholly unmoved at all the scenes of blood and desolation which I had painted as the common effects of those destructive machines; whereof he said some evil genius, enemy to mankind, must have been the first contriver. As for himself, he protested that although few things delighted him so much as new discoveries in art or in nature, yet he would rather lose half his kingdom than be privy to such a secret, which he commanded me, as I valued my life, never to mention any more.

A strange effect of *narrow principles* and *short views!* that a prince possessed of every quality which procures veneration, love, and esteem; of strong parts, great wisdom, and profound learning; endued with admirable talents for government, and almost adored by his subjects; should from a *nice, unnecessary scruple,* whereof in Europe we can have no conception, let slip an opportunity put into his hands that would have made him absolute master of the lives, the liberties, and the fortunes of his people. Neither do I say this with the least intention to detract from the many virtues of that excellent King, whose character I am sensible will on this account be very much lessened in the opinion of an English reader: but I take this defect among them to have risen from their ignorance; they not having hitherto reduced politics into a science, as the more acute wits of Europe have done. For I remember very well, in a discourse one day with the King, when I happened to say there were several thousand books among us written upon the art of government, it gave him (directly contrary to my intention) a very mean opinion of our understandings. He professed both to abominate and despise all *mystery, refinement,* and *intrigue,* either in a prince or a minister. He could not tell what I meant by *secrets of state,* where an enemy or some rival nation were not in the case. He confined the knowledge of governing within very *narrow bounds:* to common sense and reason, to justice and lenity, to the speedy determination of civil and criminal causes, with some other obvious topics which are not worth considering. And he gave it for his opinion that whoever could make two ears of corn or two blades of grass to grow upon a spot of ground where only one grew before would deserve better of mankind and do more essential service to his country than the whole race of politicians[5] put together.

The learning of this people is very defective, consisting only in morality, history, poetry, and mathematics; wherein they must be allowed to excel. But the last of these is wholly applied to what may be useful in life, to the improvement of agriculture and all mechanical arts; so that among us it would be little esteemed. And as to ideas, entities, abstractions, and transcendentals,[6] I could never drive the least conception into their heads.

No law of that country must exceed in words the number of letters in their alphabet, which consists only in two and twenty. But indeed few of them extend even to that length. They are expressed in the most plain and simple terms, wherein those people are not mercurial enough to discover above one interpretation. And to write a comment upon any law is a capital crime. As to the decision of civil causes, or proceedings against criminals, their precedents are so few that they have little reason to boast of any extraordinary skill in either.

They have had the art of printing as well as the Chinese, time out of mind. But their libraries are not very large; for that of the King's, which is reckoned the biggest, doth not amount to above a thousand volumes, placed in a gallery of twelve hundred foot long, from whence I had liberty to borrow what books I pleased. The Queen's joiner had contrived in one of the Glumdalclitch's rooms a kind of wooden machine five and twenty foot high, formed like a standing ladder; the steps were each fifty foot long. It was indeed a movable pair of stairs, the lowest end placed at ten foot distance from the wall of the chamber. The book I had a mind to read was put up leaning against the wall. I first mounted to the upper step of the ladder, and turning my face towards the book began at the top of the page, and so walking to the right and left about eight or ten paces according to the length of the lines, till I had gotten a little below the level of mine eyes, and then descending gradually till I came to the bottom: after which I mounted again, and began the other page in the same manner, and so turned over the leaf, which I could easily do with both my hands, for it was as thick and stiff as a pasteboard, and in the largest folios not above eighteen or twenty foot long.

Their style is clear, masculine, and smooth, but not florid; for they avoid nothing more than multiplying unnecessary words or using various expressions. I have perused many of their books, especially those in history and morality. Among the rest, I was much diverted with a little old treatise, which always lay in Glumdalclitch's bedchamber, and belonged to her governess, a grave elderly gentlewoman, who dealt in writings of morality and devotion.

5. Swift means something like our modern political scientists or theorists.

6. In Swift's time, *transcendental* was practically synonymous with *metaphysical.*

The book treats of the weakness of human kind, and is in little esteem, except among the women and the vulgar. However, I was curious to see what an author of that country could say upon such a subject. This writer went through all the usual topics of European moralists: showing how diminutive, contemptible, and helpless an animal was man in his own nature; how unable to defend himself from the inclemencies of the air, or the fury of wild beasts; how much he was excelled by one creature in strength, by another in speed, by a third in foresight, by a fourth in industry. He added that nature was degenerated in these latter declining ages of the world, and could now produce only small abortive births in comparison of those in ancient times. He said it was very reasonable to think, not only that the species of men were originally much larger, but also that there must have been giants in former ages; which, as it is asserted by history and tradition, so it hath been confirmed by huge bones and skulls casually dug up in several parts of the kingdom, far exceeding the common dwindled race of man in our days. He argued that the very laws of nature absolutely required we should have been made in the beginning of a size more large and robust, not so liable to destruction from every little accident of a tile falling from a house, or a stone cast from the hand of a boy, or of being drowned in a little brook. From this way of reasoning, the author drew several moral applications useful in the conduct of life, but needless here to repeat. For my own part, I could not avoid reflecting how universally this talent was spread, of drawing lectures in morality, or indeed rather matter of discontent and repining, from the quarrels we raise with nature. And I believe, upon a strict inquiry, those quarrels might be shown as ill grounded among us as they are among that people.

As to their military affairs, they boast that the King's army consists of an hundred and seventy-six thousand foot and thirty-two thousand horse: if that may be called an army which is made up of tradesmen in the several cities, and farmers in the country, whose commanders are only the nobility and gentry, without pay or reward. They are indeed perfect enough in their exercises, and under very good discipline, wherein I saw no great merit; for how should it be otherwise, where every farmer is under the command of his own landlord, and every citizen under that of the principal men in his own city, chosen after the manner of Venice by ballot?

I have often seen the militia of Lorbrulgrud drawn out to exercise in a great field near the city, of twenty miles square. They were in all not above twenty-five thousand foot, and six thousand horse; but it was impossible for me to compute their number, considering the space of ground they took up. A cavalier mounted on a large steed might be about an hundred foot high. I have seen this whole body of horse, upon a word of command, draw their swords at once, and brandish them in the air. Imagination can figure nothing so grand, so surprising, and so astonishing. It looked as if ten thousand flashes of lightning were darting at the same time from every quarter of the sky.

I was curious to know how this prince, to whose dominions there is no access from any other country, came to think of armies, or to teach his people the practice of military discipline. But I was soon informed, both by conversation and reading their histories. For in the course of many ages they have been troubled with the same disease to which the whole race of mankind is subject: the nobility often contending for power, the people for liberty, and the King for absolute dominion. All which, however happily tempered by the laws of the kingdom, have been sometimes violated by each of the three parties, and have more than once occasioned civil wars, the last whereof was happily put an end to by this prince's grandfather in a general composition;[7] and the militia, then settled with common consent, hath been ever since kept in the strictest duty.

CHAPTER 8. *The King and Queen make a progress to the frontiers. The Author attends them. The manner in which he leaves the country very particularly related. He returns to England.*

I had always a strong impulse that I should some time recover my liberty, though it were impossible to conjecture by what means, or to form any project with the least hope of succeeding. The ship in which I sailed was the first ever known to be driven within sight of that coast; and the King had given strict orders that if at any time another appeared, it should be taken ashore, and with all its crew and passengers brought in a tumbrel[8] to Lorbrulgrud. He was strongly bent to get me a woman of my own size, by whom I might propagate the breed: but I think I should rather have died than undergone the disgrace of leaving a posterity to be kept in cages like tame canary birds, and perhaps in time sold about the kingdom to persons of quality for curiosities. I was indeed treated with much kindness: I was the favorite of a great King and Queen, and the delight of the whole Court, but it was upon such a foot as ill became the dignity of human kind. I could never forget those domestic pledges I had left behind me. I wanted to be among people with whom I could converse upon even terms, and walk about the streets and fields without fear of being trod to death like a frog or a young puppy. But my deliverance came sooner than I expected, and in a manner not very common; the whole story and circumstances of which I shall faithfully relate.

I had now been two years in this country; and about the beginning of the third, Glumdalclitch and I attended the King and Queen in progress to the south coast of the kingdom. I was carried as usual in my traveling box, which, as I have already described, was a very convenient closet of twelve foot wide. I had ordered a hammock to be fixed by silken ropes from the four corners at the top, to break the jolts when a servant carried me before him on horseback, as I sometimes desired; and would often sleep in my hammock while we were upon the road. On the roof of my closet, set not directly over the middle of the hammock, I ordered the joiner to cut out a hole of a foot square to give me air in hot weather as I slept, which hole I shut at pleasure with a board that drew backwards and forwards through a groove.

When we came to our journey's end, the King thought proper to pass a few days at a palace he hath near Flanflasnic, a city within eighteen English miles of the seaside. Glumdalclitch and I were much fatigued; I had gotten a small cold, but the poor girl was so ill as to be confined to her chamber. I longed to see the ocean, which must be the only scene of my escape, if ever it should happen. I pretended to be worse than I really was, and desired leave to take the fresh air of the sea with a page whom I was very fond of, and who had sometimes been trusted with me. I shall never forget with what

7. A political settlement based on general agreement of all parties.   8. A farm wagon.

unwillingness Glumdalclitch consented, nor the strict charge she gave the page to be careful of me, bursting at the same time into a flood of tears, as if she had some foreboding of what was to happen. The boy took me out in my box about half an hour's walk from the palace, towards the rocks on the seashore. I ordered him to set me down, and lifting up one of my sashes, cast many a wistful melancholy look towards the sea. I found myself not very well, and told the page that I had a mind to take a nap in my hammock, which I hoped would do me good. I got in, and the boy shut the window close down, to keep out the cold. I soon fell asleep: and all I can conjecture is that while I slept, the page, thinking no danger could happen, went among the rocks to look for birds' eggs; having before observed him from my window searching about, and picking up one or two in the clefts. Be that as it will, I found myself suddenly awaked with a violent pull upon the ring which was fastened at the top of my box for the conveniency of carriage. I felt my box raised very high in the air, and then borne forward with prodigious speed. The first jolt had like to have shaken me out of my hammock, but afterwards the motion was easy enough. I called out several times as loud as I could raise my voice, but all to no purpose. I looked towards my windows, and could see nothing but the clouds and sky. I heard a noise just over my head like the clapping of wings, and then began to perceive the woeful condition I was in; that some eagle had got the ring of my box in his beak, with an intent to let it fall on a rock, like a tortoise in a shell, and then pick out my body and devour it. For the sagacity and smell of this bird enable him to discover his quarry at a great distance, although better concealed than I could be within a two-inch board.

In a little time I observed the noise and flutter of wings to increase very fast, and my box was tossed up and down like a signpost in a windy day. I heard several bangs or buffets, as I thought, given to the eagle (for such I am certain it must have been that held the ring of my box in his beak), and then all on a sudden felt myself falling perpendicularly down for above a minute, but with such incredible swiftness that I almost lost my breath. My fall was topped by a terrible squash, that sounded louder to mine ears than the cataract of Niagara; after which I was quite in the dark for another minute, and then my box began to rise so high that I could see light from the tops of my windows. I now perceived that I was fallen into the sea. My box, by the weight of my body, the goods that were in, and the broad plates of iron fixed for strength at the four corners of the top and bottom, floated above five foot deep in water. I did then and do now suppose that the eagle which flew away with my box was pursued by two or three others, and forced to let me drop while he was defending himself against the rest, who hoped to share in the prey. The plates of iron fastened at the bottom of the box (for those were the strongest) preserved the balance while it fell, and hindered it from being broken on the surface of the water. Every joint of it was well grooved, and the door did not move on hinges, but up and down like a sash; which kept my closet so tight that very little water came in. I got with much difficulty out of my hammock, having first ventured to draw back the slip-board on the roof already mentioned, contrived on purpose to let in air, for want of which I found myself almost stifled.

How often did I then wish myself with my dear Glumdalclitch, from whom one single hour had so far divided me! And I may say with truth that in the midst of my own misfortune, I could not forbear lamenting my poor nurse, the grief she would suffer for my loss, the displeasure of the Queen, and the ruin of her fortune. Perhaps many travelers have not been under greater difficulties and distress than I was at this juncture, expecting every moment to see my box dashed in pieces, or at least overset by the first violent blast or a rising wave. A breach in one single pane of glass would have been immediate death, nor could anything have preserved the windows but the strong lattice wires placed on the outside against accidents in traveling. I saw the water ooze in at several crannies, although the leaks were not considerable, and I endeavored to stop them as well as I could. I was not able to lift up the roof of my closet, which otherwise I certainly should have done, and sat on the top of it, where I might at least preserve myself from being shut up, as I may call it, in the hold. Or, if I escaped these dangers for a day or two, what could I expect but a miserable death of cold and hunger! I was four hours under these circumstances, expecting and indeed wishing every moment to be my last.

I have already told the reader that there were two strong staples fixed upon that side of my box which had no window and into which the servant, who used to carry me on horseback, would put a leathern belt, and buckle it about his waist. Being in this disconsolate state, I heard, or at least thought I heard, some kind of grating noise on that side of my box where the staples were fixed; and soon after I began to fancy that the box was pulled or towed along in the sea; for I now and then felt a sort of tugging, which made the waves rise near the tops of my windows, leaving me almost in the dark. This gave me some faint hopes of relief, although I was not able to imagine how it could be brought about. I ventured to unscrew one of my chairs, which were always fastened to the floor; and having made a hard shift to screw it down again directly under the slipping-board that I had lately opened, I mounted on the chair, and putting my mouth as near as I could to the hole, I called for help in a loud voice, and in all the languages I understood. I then fastened my handkerchief to a stick I usually carried, and thrusting it up the hole, waved it several times in the air, that if any boat or ship were near, the seamen might conjecture some unhappy mortal to be shut up in the box.

I found no effect from all I could do, but plainly perceived my closet to be moved along; and in the space of an hour or better, that side of the box where the staples were, and had no window, struck against something that was hard. I apprehended it to be a rock, and found myself tossed more than ever. I plainly heard a noise upon the cover of my closet, like that of a cable, and the grating of it as it passed through the ring. I then found myself hoisted up by degrees at least three foot higher than I was before. Whereupon I again thrust up my stick and handkerchief, calling for help till I was almost hoarse. In return to which, I heard a great shout repeated three times, giving me such transports of joy as are not to be conceived but by those who feel them. I now heard a trampling over my head, and somebody calling through the hole with a loud voice in the English tongue: "If there be anybody below, let them speak." I answered, I was an Englishman, drawn by ill fortune into the greatest calamity that ever any creature underwent, and begged, by all that was moving, to be delivered out of the dungeon I was in. The voice replied, I was safe, for my box was fastened to their ship; and the carpenter should immediately come and saw an hole in the cover, large enough to pull me out. I answered, that was needless and would take up too much time, for there was no more to be done but let one of the crew put his finger into the ring, and take the box out of the sea into the ship, and so into the captain's cabin. Some of them, upon hearing me talk so wildly, thought I was mad; others laughed; for indeed it never came into my head that I was now got among people of my own stature and strength. The carpenter came, and in a few minutes sawed a passage about four foot square; then let down a small ladder, upon which I mounted, and from thence was taken into the ship in a very weak condition.

The sailors were all in amazement, and asked me a thousand questions, which I had no inclination to answer. I was equally confounded at the sight of so many pygmies, for such I took them to be, after having so long accustomed my eyes to the monstrous objects I had left. But the Captain, Mr. Thomas Wilcocks, an honest, worthy Shropshire man, observing I was ready to faint, took me into his cabin, gave me a cordial to comfort me, and made me turn in upon his own bed, advising me to take a little rest, of which I had great need. Before I went to sleep I gave him to understand that I had some valuable furniture in my box, too good to be lost, a fine hammock, an handsome field bed, two chairs, a table, and a cabinet; that my closet was hung on all sides, or rather quilted with silk and cotton; that if he would let one of the crew bring my closet into his cabin, I would open it before him and show him my goods. The Captain, hearing me utter these absurdities, concluded I was raving; however (I suppose to pacify me), he promised to give order as I desired, and going upon deck, sent some of his men down into my closet, from whence (as I afterwards found) they drew up all my goods and stripped off the quilting; but the chairs, cabinet, and bedstead, being screwed to the floor, were much damaged by the ignorance of the seamen, who tore them up by force. Then they knocked off some of the boards for the use of the ship; and when they had got all they had a mind for, let the hulk drop into the sea, which, by reason of many breaches made in the bottom and sides, sunk to rights.[9] And indeed I was glad not to have been a spectator of the havoc they made, because I am confident it would have sensibly touched me, by bringing former passages into my mind, which I had rather forget.

I slept some hours, but perpetually disturbed with dreams of the place I had left, and the dangers I had escaped. However, upon waking, I found myself much recovered. It was now about eight o'clock at night, and the Captain ordered supper immediately, thinking I had already fasted too long. He entertained me with great kindness, observing me not to look wildly, or talk inconsistently; and when we were left alone, desired I would give him a relation of my travels, and by what accident I came to be set adrift in that monstrous wooden chest. He said that about twelve o'clock at noon, as he was looking through his glass, he spied it at a distance, and thought it was a sail, which he had a mind to make,[1] being not much out of his course, in hopes of buying some biscuit, his own beginning to fall short. That, upon coming nearer, and finding his error, he sent out his longboat to discover what I was; that his men came back in a fright, swearing they had seen a swimming house. That he laughed at their folly, and went himself in the boat, ordering his men to take a strong cable along with them. That the weather being calm, he rowed round me several times, observed my windows, and the wire lattices that defended them. That he discovered two staples upon one side, which was all of boards, without any passage for light. He then commanded his men to row up to that side, and fastening a cable to one of the staples, ordered his men to tow my chest (as he called it) towards the ship. When it was there, he gave directions to fasten another cable to the ring fixed in the cover, and to raise up my chest with pulleys, which all the sailors were not able to do above two or three foot. He said they saw my stick and handkerchief thrust out of the hole, and concluded that some unhappy man must be

9. At once, altogether.   1. Overtake.

shut up in the cavity. I asked whether he or the crew had seen any prodigious birds in the air about the time he first discovered me. To which he answered that, discoursing this matter with the sailors while I was asleep, one of them said he had observed three eagles flying towards the north, but remarked nothing of their being larger than the usual size (which I suppose must be imputed to the great height they were at), and he could not guess the reason of my question. I then asked the Captain how far he reckoned we might be from land; he said, by the best computation he could make, we were at least an hundred leagues. I assured him that he must be mistaken by almost half; for I had not left the country from whence I came above two hours before I dropped into the sea. Whereupon he began again to think that my brain was disturbed, of which he gave me a hint, and advised me to go to bed in a cabin he had provided. I assured him I was well refreshed with his good entertainment and company, and as much in my senses as ever I was in my life. He then grew serious and desired to ask me freely whether I were not troubled in mind by the consciousness of some enormous crime, for which I was punished at the command of some prince, by exposing me in that chest, as great criminals in other countries have been forced to sea in a leaky vessel without provisions; for although he should be sorry to have taken so ill[2] a man into his ship, yet he would engage his word to set me safe on shore in the first port where we arrived. He added that his suspicions were much increased by some very absurd speeches I had delivered at first to the sailors, and afterwards to himself, in relation to my closet or chest, as well as by my odd looks and behavior while I was at supper.

I begged his patience to hear me tell my story, which I faithfully did from the last time I left England to the moment he first discovered me. And as truth always forceth its way into rational minds, so this honest, worthy gentleman, who had some tincture of learning, and very good sense, was immediately convinced of my candor and veracity. But further to confirm all I had said, I entreated him to give order that my cabinet should be brought, of which I kept the key in my pocket (for he had already informed me how the seamen disposed of my closet). I opened it in his presence and showed him the small collection of rarities I made in the country from whence I had been so strangely delivered. There was the comb I had contrived out of the stumps of the King's beard, and another of the same materials, but fixed into a paring of her Majesty's thumbnail, which served for the back. There was a collection of needles and pins from a foot to half a yard long; four wasp-stings, like joiners' tacks; some combings of the Queen's hair; a gold ring which one day she made me a present of in a most obliging manner, taking it from her little finger, and throwing it over my head like a collar. I desired the Captain would please to accept this ring in return for his civilities, which he absolutely refused. I showed him a corn that I had cut off with my own hand from a Maid of Honor's toe; it was about the bigness of a Kentish pippin, and grown so hard that, when I returned to England, I got it hollowed into a cup and set in silver. Lastly, I desired him to see the breeches I had then on, which were made of a mouse's skin.

I could force nothing on him but a footman's tooth, which I observed him to examine with great curiosity, and found he had a fancy for it. He received it with abundance of thanks, more than such a trifle could deserve. It was drawn by an unskillful surgeon in a mistake from one of Glumdalclitch's men, who was afflicted with the toothache; but it was as sound as any in his

2. Evil.

head. I got it cleaned, and put it into my cabinet. It was about a foot long, and four inches in diameter.

The Captain was very well satisfied with this plain relation I had given him, and said he hoped when we returned to England I would oblige the world by putting it in paper and making it public. My answer was that I thought we were already overstocked with books of travels; that nothing could now pass which was not extraordinary; wherein I doubted some authors less consulted truth than their own vanity or interest, or the diversion of ignorant readers. That my story could contain little besides common events, without those ornamental descriptions of strange plants, trees, birds, and other animals, or the barbarous customs and idolatry of savage people, with which most writers abound. However, I thanked him for his good opinion, and promised to take the matter into my thoughts.

He said he wondered at one thing very much, which was to hear me speak so loud, asking me whether the King or Queen of that country were thick of hearing. I told him it was what I had been used to for above two years past, and that I admired[3] as much at the voices of him and his men, who seemed to me only to whisper, and yet I could hear them well enough. But, when I spoke in that country, it was like a man talking in the street to another looking out from the top of a steeple, unless when I was placed on a table, or held in any person's hand. I told him I had likewise observed another thing: that when I first got into the ship, and the sailors stood all about me, I thought they were the most little contemptible creatures I had ever beheld. For indeed while I was in that prince's country, I could never endure to look in a glass after my eyes had been accustomed to such prodigious objects, because the comparison gave me so despicable a conceit[4] of myself. The Captain said that while we were at supper he observed me to look at everything with a sort of wonder, and that I often seemed hardly able to contain my laughter; which he knew not well how to take, but imputed it to some disorder in my brain. I answered, it was very true; and I wondered how I could forbear, when I saw his dishes of the size of a silver threepence, a leg of pork hardly a mouthful, a cup not so big as a nutshell; and so I went on, describing the rest of his household stuff and provisions after the same manner. For, although the Queen had ordered a little equipage of all things necessary for me while I was in her service, yet my ideas were wholly taken up with what I saw on every side of me, and I winked at my own littleness, as people do at their own faults. The Captain understood my raillery very well, and merrily replied with the old English proverb, that he doubted[5] my eyes were bigger than my belly, for he did not observe my stomach so good, although I had fasted all day; and continuing in his mirth, protested he would have gladly given an hundred pounds to have seen my closet in the eagle's bill, and afterwards in its fall from so great an height into the sea; which would certainly have been a most astonishing object, worthy to have the description of it transmitted to future ages: and the comparison of Phaeton[6] was so obvious, that he could not forbear applying it, although I did not much admire the conceit.

The Captain having been at Tonquin,[7] was in his return to England driven northeastward to the latitude of 44 degrees, and of longitude 143. But meet-

3. Wondered.
4. Notion.
5. Feared.
6. Son of Helios, the sun god, whose unsuccessful attempt to drive his father's chariot led to his death, when he lost control and was hurled by Zeus from the sky, falling into the river Eridanus, where he drowned.
7. Tonkin, now in Vietnam.

ing a trade wind two days after I came on board him, we sailed southward a long time, and coasting New Holland[8] kept our course west-southwest, and then south-southwest till we doubled the Cape of Good Hope. Our voyage was very prosperous, but I shall not trouble the reader with a journal of it. The Captain called in at one or two ports, and sent in his longboat for provisions and fresh water; but I never went out of the ship till we came into the Downs, which was on the third day of June, 1706, about nine months after my escape. I offered to leave my goods in security for payment of my freight; but the Captain protested he would not receive one farthing. We took kind leave of each other, and I made him promise he would come to see me at my house in Redriff. I hired a horse and guide for five shillings, which I borrowed of the Captain.

As I was on the road, observing the littleness of the houses, the trees, the cattle, and the people, I began to think myself in Lilliput. I was afraid of trampling on every traveler I met, and often called aloud to have them stand out of the way, so that I had like to have gotten one or two broken heads for my impertinence.

When I came to my own house, for which I was forced to inquire, one of the servants opening the door, I bent down to go in (like a goose under a gate) for fear of striking my head. My wife ran out to embrace me, but I stooped lower than her knees, thinking she could otherwise never be able to reach my mouth. My daughter kneeled to ask my blessing, but I could not see her till she arose, having been so long used to stand with my head and eyes erect to above sixty foot; and then I went to take her up with one hand by the waist. I looked down upon the servants and one or two friends who were in the house, as if they had been pygmies and I a giant. I told my wife she had been too thrifty; for I found she had starved herself and her daughter to nothing. In short, I behaved myself so unaccountably that they were all of the Captain's opinion when he first saw me, and concluded I had lost my wits. This I mention as an instance of the great power of habit and prejudice.

In a little time I and my family and friends came to a right understanding; but my wife protested I should never go to sea any more, although my evil destiny so ordered that she had not power to hinder me; as the reader may know hereafter. In the meantime I here conclude the second part of my unfortunate voyages.

From *Part 3. A Voyage to Laputa, Balnibarbi, Glubbdubdrib, Luggnagg, and Japan*

* * *

[THE FLYING ISLAND OF LAPUTA][9]

CHAPTER 2. *The humors and dispositions of the Laputans described. An account of their learning. Of the King and his court. The author's reception there. The inhabitants subject to fears and disquietudes. An account of the women.*

At my alighting I was surrounded by a crowd of people, but those who stood nearest seemed to be of better quality. They beheld me with all the

---

8. Australia.
9. In the first chapter of part 3 Gulliver starts on his third voyage, but is captured by pirates and set adrift. Just as he is about to despair, a vast flying island appears in the sky, and the inhabitants draw him up with pulleys.

marks and circumstances of wonder; neither indeed was I much in their debt, having never till then seen a race of mortals so singular in their shapes, habits, and countenances. Their heads were all reclined to the right, or the left; one of their eyes turned inward, and the other directly up to the zenith. Their outward garments were adorned with the figures of suns, moons, and stars, interwoven with those of fiddles, flutes, harps, trumpets, guitars, harpsichords, and many more instruments of music, unknown to us in Europe.[1] I observed here and there many in the habits of servants, with a blown bladder fastened like a flail to the end of a short stick, which they carried in their hands. In each bladder was a small quantity of dried pease or little pebbles (as I was afterwards informed). With these bladders they now and then flapped the mouths and ears of those who stood near them, of which practice I could not then conceive the meaning. It seems, the minds of these people are so taken up with intense speculations, that they neither can speak, or attend to the discourses of others, without being roused by some external taction[2] upon the organs of speech and hearing; for which reason those persons who are able to afford it always keep a flapper (the original is *climenole*) in their family, as one of their domestics; nor ever walk abroad or make visits without him. And the business of this officer is, when two or more persons are in company, gently to strike with his bladder the mouth of him who is to speak, and the right ear of him or them to whom the speaker addresseth himself. This flapper is likewise employed diligently to attend his master in his walks, and upon occasion to give him a soft flap on his eyes, because he is always so wrapped up in cogitation, that he is in manifest danger of falling down every precipice, and bouncing his head against every post; and in the streets, of jostling others, or being jostled himself into the kennel.[3]

It was necessary to give the reader this information, without which he would be at the same loss with me, to understand the proceedings of these people, as they conducted me up the stairs to the top of the island, and from thence to the royal palace. While we were ascending, they forgot several times what they were about, and left me to myself, till their memories were again roused by their flappers; for they appeared altogether unmoved by the sight of my foreign habit and countenance, and by the shouts of the vulgar, whose thoughts and minds were more disengaged.

At last we entered the palace, and proceeded into the chamber of presence; where I saw the King seated on his throne, attended on each side by persons of prime quality. Before the throne was a large table filled with globes and spheres, and mathematical instruments of all kinds. His Majesty took not the least notice of us, although our entrance was not without sufficient noise, by the concourse of all persons belonging to the court. But he was then deep in a problem, and we attended at least an hour before he could solve it. There stood by him on each side a young page, with flaps in their hands, and when they saw he was at leisure, one of them gently struck his mouth, and the other his right ear; at which he started like one awaked on the sudden, and looking towards me, and the company I was in, recollected the occasion of our coming, whereof he had been informed before. He spoke some words, whereupon immediately a young man with a flap

---

1. The Laputans represent contemporary speculation, deplored by Swift, about abstract theories of science, mathematics, and music. Both the Royal Society and Sir Isaac Newton took an inter-est in the mathematical basis of music.
2. Touch.
3. Gutter.

came up to my side, and flapped me gently on the right ear; but I made signs as well as I could, that I had no occasion for such an instrument; which as I afterwards found gave his Majesty and the whole court a very mean opinion of my understanding. The King, as far as I could conjecture, asked me several questions, and I addressed myself to him in all the languages I had. When it was found that I could neither understand nor be understood, I was conducted by his order to an apartment in his palace (this prince being distinguished above all his predecessors for his hospitality to strangers),[4] where two servants were appointed to attend me. My dinner was brought, and four persons of quality, whom I remembered to have seen very near the King's person, did me the honor to dine with me. We had two courses, of three dishes each. In the first course there was a shoulder of mutton, cut into an equilateral triangle; a piece of beef into a rhomboid; and a pudding into a cycloid. The second course was two ducks, trussed up into the form of fiddles; sausages and pudding resembling flutes and haut-boys,[5] and a breast of veal in the shape of a harp. The servants cut our bread into cones, cylinders, parallelograms, and several other mathematical figures.

While we were at dinner, I made bold to ask the names of several things in their language, and those noble persons, by the assistance of their flappers, delighted to give me answers, hoping to raise my admiration of their great abilities, if I could be brought to converse with them. I was soon able to call for bread and drink, or whatever else I wanted.

After dinner my company withdrew, and a person was sent to me by the King's order, attended by a flapper. He brought with him pen, ink, and paper, and three or four books; giving me to understand by signs, that he was sent to teach me the language. We sat together four hours, in which time I wrote down a great number of words in columns, with the translations over against them. I likewise made a shift to learn several short sentences. For my tutor would order one of my servants to fetch something, to turn about, to make a bow, to sit, or stand, or walk, and the like. Then I took down the sentence in writing. He showed me also in one of his books the figures of the sun, moon, and stars, the zodiac, the tropics and polar circles, together with the denominations of many figures of planes and solids. He gave me the names and descriptions of all the musical instruments, and the general terms of art in playing on each of them. After he had left me, I placed all my words with their interpretations in alphabetical order. And thus in a few days, by the help of a very faithful memory, I got some insight into their language.

The word, which I interpret the *Flying* or *Floating Island*, is in the original *Laputa*; whereof I could never learn the true etymology. *Lap* in the old obsolete language signifieth *high*, and *untuh* a *governor*; from which they say by corruption was derived *Laputa*, from *Lapuntuh*. But I do not approve of this derivation, which seems to be a little strained. I ventured to offer to the learned among them a conjecture of my own, that *Laputa* was *quasi Lap outed*; *Lap* signifying properly the dancing of the sunbeams in the sea, and *outed* a wing, which however I shall not obtrude, but submit to the judicious reader.[6]

Those to whom the King had entrusted me, observing how ill I was clad, ordered a tailor to come next morning, and take my measure for a suit of

4. George I, a patron of music and science, had filled his court with Hanoverians when he came to England in 1714.

5. Oboes.

6. Gulliver overlooks a likelier etymology: Spanish *la puta*, "the whore."

clothes. This operator did his office after a different manner from those of his trade in Europe. He first took my altitude by a quadrant, and then, with rule and compasses, described the dimensions and outlines of my whole body; all which he entered upon paper, and in six days brought my clothes very ill made, and quite out of shape, by happening to mistake a figure in the calculation. But my comfort was, that I observed such accidents very frequent, and little regarded.

During my confinement for want of clothes, and by an indisposition that held me some days longer, I much enlarged my dictionary; and when I went next to court, was able to understand many things the King spoke, and to return him some kind of answers. His Majesty had given orders that the island should move northeast and by east, to the vertical point over Lagado, the metropolis of the whole kingdom, below upon the firm earth. It was about ninety leagues distant, and our voyage lasted four days and a half. I was not in the least sensible of the progressive motion made in the air by the island. On the second morning, about eleven o'clock, the King himself in person, attended by his nobility, courtiers, and officers, having prepared all their musical instruments, played on them for three hours without intermission, so that I was quite stunned with the noise; neither could I possibly guess the meaning, till my tutor informed me. He said, that the people of their island had their ears adapted to hear the music of the spheres, which always played at certain periods; and the court was now prepared to bear their part in whatever instrument they most excelled.

In our journey towards Lagado, the capital city, his Majesty ordered that the island should stop over certain towns and villages, from whence he might receive the petitions of his subjects. And to this purpose, several pack-threads were let down with small weights at the bottom. On these pack-threads the people strung their petitions, which mounted up directly like the scraps of paper fastened by schoolboys at the end of the string that holds their kite.[7] Sometimes we received wine and victuals from below, which were drawn up by pulleys.

The knowledge I had in mathematics gave me great assistance in acquiring their phraseology, which depended much upon that science and music; and in the latter I was not unskilled. Their ideas are perpetually conversant in lines and figures. If they would, for example, praise the beauty of a woman, or any other animal, they describe it by rhombs, circles, parallelograms, ellipses, and other geometrical terms; or else by words of art drawn from music, needless here to repeat. I observed in the King's kitchen all sorts of mathematical and musical instruments, after the figures of which they cut up the joints that were served to his Majesty's table.

Their houses are very ill built, the walls bevil, without one right angle in any apartment; and this defect ariseth from the contempt they bear for practical geometry; which they despise as vulgar and mechanic, those instructions they give being too refined for the intellectuals of their workmen; which occasions perpetual mistakes. And although they are dextrous enough upon a piece of paper, in the management of the rule, the pencil, and the divider, yet in the common actions and behavior of life I have not seen a more clumsy, awkward, and unhandy people, nor so slow and perplexed in their concep-

7. Petitioners, that is, might as well go fly a kite. Throughout this section Swift satirizes the "distance" of George I (who spent much of his time in Hanover) from his British subjects.

tions upon all other subjects, except those of mathematics and music. They are very bad reasoners, and vehemently given to opposition, unless when they happen to be of the right opinion, which is seldom their case. Imagination, fancy, and invention, they are wholly strangers to, nor have any words in their language by which those ideas can be expressed; the whole compass of their thoughts and mind being shut up within the two forementioned sciences.

Most of them, and especially those who deal in the astronomical part, have great faith in judicial astrology, although they are ashamed to own it publicly. But what I chiefly admired,[8] and thought altogether unaccountable, was the strong disposition I observed in them towards news and politics; perpetually enquiring into public affairs, giving their judgments in matters of state; and passionately disputing every inch of a party opinion. I have indeed observed the same disposition among most of the mathematicians I have known in Europe; although I could never discover the least analogy between the two sciences; unless those people suppose, that because the smallest circle hath as many degrees as the largest, therefore the regulation and management of the world require no more abilities than the handling and turning of a globe. But I rather take this quality to spring from a very common infirmity of human nature, inclining us to be more curious and conceited in matters where we have least concern, and for which we are least adapted either by study or nature.

These people are under continual disquietudes, never enjoying a minute's peace of mind; and their disturbances proceed from causes which very little affect the rest of mortals. Their apprehensions arise from several changes they dread in the celestial bodies. For instance; that the earth, by the continual approaches of the sun towards it, must in course of time be absorbed or swallowed up. That the face of the sun will by degrees be encrusted with its own effluvia,[9] and give no more light to the world. That the earth very narrowly escaped a brush from the tail of the last comet, which would have infallibly reduced it to ashes; and that the next, which they have calculated for one and thirty years hence, will probably destroy us.[1] For, if in its perihelion it should approach within a certain degree of the sun (as by their calculations they have reason to dread), it will conceive a degree of heat ten thousand times more intense than that of red-hot glowing iron; and in its absence from the sun, carry a blazing tail ten hundred thousand and fourteen miles long; through which if the earth should pass at the distance of one hundred thousand miles from the nucleus, or main body of the comet, it must in its passage be set on fire, and reduced to ashes. That the sun daily spending its rays without any nutriment to supply them, will at last be wholly consumed and annihilated; which must be attended with the destruction of this earth, and of all the planets that receive their light from it.

They are so perpetually alarmed with the apprehensions of these and the like impending dangers, that they can neither sleep quietly in their beds, nor have any relish for the common pleasures or amusements of life. When they meet an acquaintance in the morning, the first question is about the sun's health, how he looked at his setting and rising, and what hopes they have to avoid the stroke of the approaching comet. This conversation they are

8. Wondered at.
9. Sunspots.
1. Halley's comet, some astronomers had feared, might strike the earth on its next appearance

(1758). All the disasters that disquiet the Laputans had occurred to English scientists as possible implications of Newtonian theory.

apt to run into with the same temper that boys discover in delighting to hear terrible stories of sprites and hobgoblins, which they greedily listen to, and dare not go to bed for fear.

The women of the island have abundance of vivacity; they contemn their husbands, and are exceedingly fond of strangers, whereof there is always a considerable number from the continent below, attending at court, either upon affairs of the several towns and corporations, or their own particular occasions; but are much despised, because they want[2] the same endowments. Among these the ladies choose their gallants: but the vexation is, that they act with too much ease and security; for the husband is always so rapt in speculation, that the mistress and lover may proceed to the greatest familiarities before his face, if he be but provided with paper and implements, and without his flapper at his side.

The wives and daughters lament their confinement to the island, although I think it the most delicious spot of ground in the world; and although they live here in the greatest plenty and magnificence, and are allowed to do whatever they please, they long to see the world, and take the diversions of the metropolis, which they are not allowed to do without a particular license from the King; and this is not easy to be obtained, because the people of quality have found by frequent experience, how hard it is to persuade their women to return from below. I was told that a great court lady, who had several children, is married to the prime minister, the richest subject in the kingdom, a very graceful person, extremely fond of her, and lives in the finest palace of the island, went down to Lagado, on the pretense of health, there hid herself for several months, till the King sent a warrant to search for her, and she was found in an obscure eating-house all in rags, having pawned her clothes to maintain an old deformed footman, who beat her every day, and in whose company she was taken much against her will. And although her husband received her with all possible kindness, and without the least reproach, she soon after contrived to steal down again with all her jewels, to the same gallant, and hath not been heard of since.

This may perhaps pass with the reader rather for an European or English story, than for one of a country so remote. But he may please to consider, that the caprices of womankind are not limited by any climate or nation; and that they are much more uniform than can be easily imagined.

In about a month's time I had made a tolerable proficiency in their language, and was able to answer most of the King's questions, when I had the honor to attend him. His Majesty discovered not the least curiosity to enquire into the laws, government, history, religion, or manners of the countries where I had been; but confined his questions to the state of mathematics, and received the account I gave him with great contempt and indifference, though often roused by his flapper on each side.[3]

* * *

2. Lack. "Corporations": municipal authorities.
3. In the omitted chapters, Gulliver visits countries that show the consequences of modern learning. After an account of the Flying Island, whose power of motion (derived from a giant magnet or lodestone) allows it to dominate the regions below, he descends to Balnibarbi, a once fertile land now ruined by the fanciful projects of impractical scientists. In the Grand Academy of Lagado he meets many professors who are contriving such perverse "improvements" as making clothes from cobwebs or breeding naked sheep. Then he visits the part of the academy devoted to speculative learning.

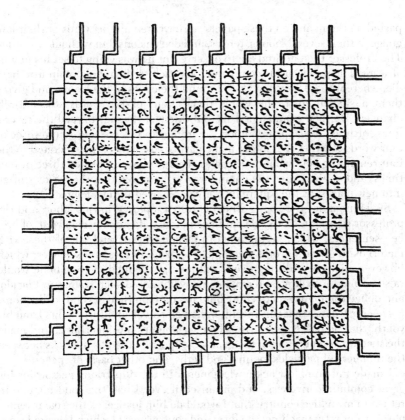

[THE ACADEMY OF LAGADO]⁴
FROM CHAPTER 5.

The first professor I saw was in a very large room, with forty pupils about him. After salutation, observing me to look earnestly upon a frame, which took up the greatest part of both the length and breadth of the room, he said, perhaps I might wonder to see him employed in a project for improving speculative knowledge by practical and mechanical operations. But the world would soon be sensible⁵ of its usefulness, and he flattered himself that a more noble, exalted thought never sprang in any other man's head. Everyone knew how laborious the usual method is of attaining to arts and sciences; whereas by his contrivance the most ignorant person at a reasonable charge, and with a little bodily labor, may write books in philosophy, poetry, politics, law, mathematics, and theology, without the least assistance from genius or study. He then led me to the frame, about the sides whereof all his pupils stood in ranks. It was twenty foot square, placed in the middle of the room. The superficies⁶ was composed of several bits of wood, about the bigness of a die, but some larger than others. They were all linked together by slender wires. These bits of wood were covered on every square with papers

4. The Grand Academy of Lagado satirizes the Royal Society of London, an organization founded in 1662 to encourage the pursuit of scientific knowledge. Some of the projects described by

Swift resemble the experiments or speculations of British scientists at the time.
5. Aware.
6. Surface.

pasted on them; and on these papers were written all the words of their language in their several moods, tenses, and declensions, but without any order. The professor then desired me to observe, for he was going to set his engine at work. The pupils at his command took each of them hold of an iron handle, whereof there were forty fixed round the edges of the frame; and giving them a sudden turn, the whole disposition[7] of the words was entirely changed. He then commanded six and thirty of the lads to read the several lines softly as they appeared upon the frame; and where they found three or four words together that might make part of a sentence, they dictated to the four remaining boys who were scribes. This work was repeated three or four times, and at every turn the engine was so contrived that the words shifted into new places, as the square bits of wood moved upside down.

Six hours a day the young students were employed in this labor; and the professor showed me several volumes in large folio already collected, of broken sentences, which he intended to piece together, and out of those rich materials to give the world a complete body of all arts and sciences; which however might be still improved, and much expedited, if the public would raise a fund for making and employing five hundred such frames in Lagado, and oblige the managers to contribute in common their several[8] collections.

He assured me, that this invention had employed all his thoughts from his youth, that he had emptied the whole vocabulary into his frame, and made the strictest computation of the general proportion there is in books between the numbers of particles, nouns, and verbs, and other parts of speech.

I made my humblest acknowledgments to this illustrious person for his great communicativeness, and promised if ever I had the good fortune to return to my native country, that I would do him justice, as the sole inventor of this wonderful machine; the form and contrivance of which I desired leave to delineate upon paper as in the figure here annexed. I told him, although it were the custom of our learned in Europe to steal inventions from each other, who had thereby at least this advantage, that it became a controversy which was the right owner, yet I would take such caution, that he should have the honor entire without a rival.

We next went to the school of languages, where three professors sat in consultation upon improving that of their own country.[9]

The first project was to shorten discourse by cutting polysyllables into one, and leaving out verbs and participles, because in reality all things imaginable are but nouns.

The other was a scheme for entirely abolishing all words whatsoever; and this was urged as a great advantage in point of health as well as brevity. For it is plain, that every word we speak is in some degree a diminution of our lungs by corrosion, and consequently contributes to the shortening of our lives. An expedient was therefore offered, that since words are only names for *things*, it would be more convenient for all men to carry about them such *things* as were necessary to express the particular business they are to discourse on. And this invention would certainly have taken place, to the great ease as well as health of the subject, if the women in conjunction with the vulgar and illiterate had not threatened to raise a rebellion, unless they

7. Arrangement.
8. Separate.
9. Many contemporary scientists had proposed a philosophical language that would eliminate the treacherous disparity between words and things and thus allow accurate scientific discourse.

might be allowed the liberty to speak with their tongues, after the manner of their forefathers. Such constant irreconcilable enemies to science[1] are the common people. However, many of the most learned and wise adhere to the new scheme of expressing themselves by *things,* which hath only this inconvenience attending it, that if a man's business be very great, and of various kinds, he must be obliged in proportion to carry a greater bundle of *things* upon his back, unless he can afford one or two strong servants to attend him. I have often beheld two of those sages almost sinking under the weight of their packs, like pedlars among us, who when they met in the streets would lay down their loads, open their sacks, and hold conversation for an hour together, then put up their implements, help each other to resume their burdens, and take their leave.

But for short conversations a man may carry implements in his pockets and under his arms, enough to supply him, and in his house he cannot be at a loss; therefore the room where company meet who practice this art is full of all *things* ready at hand, requisite to furnish matter for this kind of artificial converse.[2]

Another great advantage proposed by this invention was that it would serve as an universal language to be understood in all civilized nations, whose goods and utensils are generally of the same kind, or nearly resembling, so that their uses might easily be comprehended. And thus, ambassadors would be qualified to treat with foreign princes or ministers of state to whose tongues they were utter strangers.

I was at the mathematical school, where the master taught his pupils after a method scarce imaginable to us in Europe. The proposition and demonstration were fairly written on a thin wafer, with ink composed of a cephalic tincture.[3] This the student was to swallow upon a fasting stomach, and for three days following eat nothing but bread and water. As the wafer digested, the tincture mounted to his brain, bearing the proposition along with it. But the success hath not hitherto been answerable, partly by some error in the *quantum* or composition, and partly by the perverseness of lads, to whom this bolus[4] is so nauseous that they generally steal aside, and discharge it upwards before it can operate; neither have they been yet persuaded to use so long an abstinence as the prescription requires.[5]

* * *

[THE STRULDBRUGGS]

CHAPTER 10. *The Luggnaggians commended. A particular description of the struldbruggs, with many conversations between the author and some eminent persons upon that subject.*

The Luggnaggians are a polite[6] and generous people, and although they are not without some share of that pride which is peculiar to all eastern countries, yet they show themselves courteous to strangers, especially such

1. Knowledge.
2. The Royal Society had sponsored a collection intended to contain one specimen of every thing in the world.
3. A solution or dye directed toward the head.
4. A large pill. *"Quantum"*: amount.
5. In the omitted chapters Gulliver hears projects for improving politics and offers some of his own. He sails to Glubbdubdrib, the Island of Sorcerers, where he talks with the spirits of the dead; he learns that history is a pack of lies and that humanity has degenerated since ancient times. He is then received by the king of Luggnagg.
6. Refined, cultivated.

who are countenanced by the court. I had many acquaintance among persons of the best fashion, and being always attended by my interpreter, the conversation we had was not disagreeable.

One day in much good company, I was asked by a person of quality, whether I had seen any of their *struldbruggs* or *immortals*. I said I had not; and desired he would explain to me what he meant by such an appellation, applied to a mortal creature. He told me, that sometimes, although very rarely, a child happened to be born in a family with a red circular spot in the forehead, directly over the left eyebrow, which was an infallible mark that it should never die. The spot, as he described it, was about the compass of a silver threepence, but in the course of time grew larger, and changed its color; for at twelve years old it became green, so continued till five and twenty, then turned to a deep blue; at five and forty it grew coal black, and as large as an English shilling; but never admitted any farther alteration. He said these births were so rare, that he did not believe there could be above eleven hundred *struldbruggs* of both sexes in the whole kingdom, of which he computed about fifty in the metropolis, and among the rest a young girl born about three years ago. That these productions were not peculiar to any family, but a mere effect of chance; and the children of the *struldbruggs* themselves were equally mortal with the rest of the people.

I freely own myself to have been struck with inexpressible delight upon hearing this account: and the person who gave it me happening to understand the Balnibarbian language, which I spoke very well, I could not forbear breaking out into expressions perhaps a little too extravagant. I cried out as in a rapture: Happy nation, where every child hath at least a chance for being immortal! Happy people who enjoy so many living examples of ancient virtue, and have masters ready to instruct them in the wisdom of all former ages! But happiest beyond all comparison are those excellent *struldbruggs*, who being born exempt from that universal calamity of human nature, have their minds free and disengaged, without the weight and depression of spirits caused by the continual apprehension of death. I discovered my admiration that I had not observed any of these illustrious persons at court; the black spot on the forehead being so remarkable a distinction, that I could not have easily overlooked it; and it was impossible that his Majesty, a most judicious prince, should not provide himself with a good number of such wise and able counselors. Yet perhaps the virtue of those reverend sages was too strict for the corrupt and libertine manners of a court. And we often find by experience that young men are too opinionative[7] and volatile to be guided by the sober dictates of their seniors. However, since the King was pleased to allow me access to his royal person, I was resolved upon the very first occasion to deliver my opinion to him on this matter freely, and at large by the help of my interpreter; and whether he would please to take my advice or no, yet in one thing I was determined, that his Majesty having frequently offered me an establishment in this country, I would with great thankfulness accept the favor, and pass my life here in the conversation of those superior beings the *struldbruggs*, if they would please to admit me.

The gentleman to whom I addressed my discourse, because (as I have already observed) he spoke the language of Balnibarbi, said to me with a

---

7. Speculative, impractical.

sort of a smile, which usually ariseth from pity to the ignorant, that he was glad of any occasion to keep me among them, and desired my permission to explain to the company what I had spoke. He did so; and they talked together for some time in their own language, whereof I understood not a syllable, neither could I observe by their countenances what impression my discourse had made on them. After a short silence the same person told me, that his friends and mine (so he thought fit to express himself) were very much pleased with the judicious remarks I had made on the great happiness and advantages of immortal life; and they were desirous to know in a particular manner, what scheme of living I should have formed to myself, if it had fallen to my lot to have been born a *struldbrugg*.

I answered, it was easy to be eloquent on so copious and delightful a subject, especially to me who have been often apt to amuse myself with visions of what I should do if I were a king, a general, or a great lord; and upon this very case I had frequently run over the whole system how I should employ myself, and pass the time if I were sure to live forever.

That, if it had been my good fortune to come into the world a *struldbrugg*, as soon as I could discover my own happiness by understanding the difference between life and death, I would first resolve by all arts and methods whatsoever to procure myself riches: in the pursuit of which, by thrift and management, I might reasonably expect in about two hundred years to be the wealthiest man in the kingdom. In the second place, I would from my earliest youth apply myself to the study of arts and sciences, by which I should arrive in time to excel all others in learning. Lastly, I would carefully record every action and event of consequence that happened in the public, impartially draw the characters of the several successions of princes, and great ministers of state; with my own observations on every point. I would exactly set down the several changes in customs, languages, fashions of dress, diet and diversions. By all which acquirements, I should be a living treasury of knowledge and wisdom, and certainly become the oracle of the nation.

I would never marry after threescore, but live in an hospitable manner, yet still on the saving side. I would entertain myself in forming and directing the minds of hopeful young men, by convincing them from my own remembrance, experience and observation, fortified by numerous examples, of the usefulness of virtue in public and private life. But my choice and constant companions should be a set of my own immortal brotherhood, among whom I would elect a dozen from the most ancient down to my own contemporaries. Where any of these wanted fortunes, I would provide them with convenient lodges round my own estate, and have some of them always at my table, only mingling a few of the most valuable among you mortals, whom length of time would harden me to lose with little or no reluctance, and treat your posterity after the same manner; just as a man diverts himself with the annual succession of pinks and tulips in his garden, without regretting the loss of those which withered the preceding year.

These *struldbruggs* and I would mutually communicate our observations and memorials[8] through the course of time; remark the several gradations by which corruption steals into the world, and oppose it in every step, by giving perpetual warning and instruction to mankind; which, added to the

---

8. Memories.

strong influence of our own example, would probably prevent that continual degeneracy of human nature, so justly complained of in all ages.

Add to all this, the pleasure of seeing the various revolutions of states and empires; the changes in the lower and upper world;[9] ancient cities in ruins; and obscure villages become the seats of kings. Famous rivers lessening into shallow brooks; the ocean leaving one coast dry, and overwhelming another; the discovery of many countries yet unknown. Barbarity overrunning the politest nations, and the most barbarous becoming civilized. I should then see the discovery of the longitude, the perpetual motion, the universal medicine,[1] and many other great inventions brought to the utmost perfection.

What wonderful discoveries should we make in astronomy, by outliving and confirming our own predictions, by observing the progress and returns of comets, with the changes of motion in the sun, moon and stars.

I enlarged upon many other topics, which the natural desire of endless life and sublunary happiness could easily furnish me with. When I had ended, and the sum of my discourse had been interpreted as before to the rest of the company, there was a good deal of talk among them in the language of the country, not without some laughter at my expense. At last the same gentleman who had been my interpreter said, he was desired by the rest to set me right in a few mistakes, which I had fallen into through the common imbecility[2] of human nature, and upon that allowance was less answerable for them. That this breed of *struldbruggs* was peculiar to their country, for there were no such people either in Balnibarbi or Japan, where he had the honor to be ambassador from his Majesty, and found the natives in both those kingdoms very hard to believe that the fact was possible; and it appeared from my astonishment when he first mentioned the matter to me, that I received it as a thing wholly new, and scarcely to be credited. That in the two kingdoms above mentioned, where during his residence he had conversed very much, he observed long life to be the universal desire and wish of mankind. That whoever had one foot in the grave was sure to hold back the other as strongly as he could. That the oldest had still hopes of living one day longer, and looked on death as the greatest evil, from which nature always prompted him to retreat; only in this island of Luggnagg the appetite for living was not so eager, from the continual example of the *struldbruggs* before their eyes.

That the system of living contrived by me was unreasonable and unjust, because it supposed a perpetuity of youth, health, and vigor, which no man could be so foolish to hope, however extravagant he might be in his wishes. That the question therefore was not whether a man would choose to be always in the prime of youth, attended with prosperity and health; but how he would pass a perpetual life under all the usual disadvantages which old age brings along with it. For although few men will avow their desires of being immortal upon such hard conditions, yet in the two kingdoms before mentioned of Balnibarbi and Japan, he observed that every man desired to put off death for some time longer, let it approach ever so late; and he rarely heard of any man who died willingly, except he were incited by the extremity of grief or torture. And he appealed to me whether in those countries

---

9. Earth and heaven; figuratively, common people and the ruling class. "Revolutions": cycles.
1. The *elixir vitae*, an alchemical formula to preserve life forever, was considered by Swift an

impossible dream, like a method for calculating longitude at sea, or a perpetual motion machine.
2. Weakness.

I had traveled, as well as my own, I had not observed the same general disposition.

After this preface he gave me a particular account of the *struldbruggs* among them. He said they commonly acted like mortals, till about thirty years old, after which by degrees they grew melancholy and dejected, increasing in both till they came to fourscore. This he learned from their own confession; for otherwise there not being above two or three of that species born in an age, they were too few to form a general observation by. When they came to fourscore years, which is reckoned the extremity of living in this country, they had not only all the follies and infirmities of other old men, but many more which arose from the dreadful prospect of never dying. They were not only opinionative, peevish, covetous, morose, vain, talkative; but uncapable of friendship, and dead to all natural affection, which never descended below their grandchildren. Envy and impotent desires are their prevailing passions. But those objects against which their envy seems principally directed, are the vices of the younger sort, and the deaths of the old. By reflecting on the former, they find themselves cut off from all possibility of pleasure; and whenever they see a funeral, they lament and repine that others are gone to an harbor of rest, to which they themselves never can hope to arrive. They have no remembrance of anything but what they learned and observed in their youth and middle age, and even that is very imperfect. And for the truth or particulars of any fact, it is safer to depend on common traditions than upon their best recollections. The least miserable among them appear to be those who turn to dotage, and entirely lose their memories; these meet with more pity and assistance, because they want many bad qualities which abound in others.

If a *struldbrugg* happen to marry one of his own kind, the marriage is dissolved of course by the courtesy of the kingdom, as soon as the younger of the two comes to be fourscore. For the law thinks it a reasonable indulgence, that those who are condemned without any fault of their own to a perpetual continuance in the world, should not have their misery doubled by the load of a wife.

As soon as they have completed the term of eighty years, they are looked on as dead in law; their heirs immediately succeed to their estates, only a small pittance is reserved for their support; and the poor ones are maintained at the public charge. After that period they are held incapable of any employment of trust or profit; they cannot purchase land, or take leases, neither are they allowed to be witnesses in any cause, either civil or criminal, not even for the decision of meers[3] and bounds.

At ninety they lose their teeth and hair; they have at that age no distinction of taste, but eat and drink whatever they can get, without relish or appetite. The diseases they were subject to still continue without increasing or diminishing. In talking they forget the common appellation of things, and the names of persons, even of those who are their nearest friends and relations. For the same reason they never can amuse themselves with reading, because their memory will not serve to carry them from the beginning of a sentence to the end, and by this defect they are deprived of the only entertainment whereof they might otherwise be capable.

The language of this country being always upon the flux, the *struldbruggs* of one age do not understand those of another; neither are they able after

---

3. Boundaries.

two hundred years to hold any conversation (farther than by a few general words) with their neighbors the mortals; and thus they lie under the disadvantage of living like foreigners in their own country.

This was the account given me of the *struldbruggs*, as near as I can remember. I afterwards saw five or six of different ages, the youngest not above two hundred years old, who were brought to me at several times by some of my friends; but although they were told that I was a great traveler, and had seen all the world, they had not the least curiosity to ask me a question; only desired I would give them *slumskudask*, or a token of remembrance; which is a modest way of begging, to avoid the law that strictly forbids it, because they are provided for by the public, although indeed with a very scanty allowance.

They are despised and hated by all sorts of people; when one of them is born, it is reckoned ominous, and their birth is recorded very particularly; so that you may know their age by consulting the registry, which however hath not been kept above a thousand years past, or at least hath been destroyed by time or public disturbances. But the usual way of computing how old they are, is by asking them what kings or great persons they can remember, and then consulting history; for infallibly the last prince in their mind did not begin his reign after they were fourscore years old.

They were the most mortifying sight I ever beheld; and the women more horrible than the men. Besides the usual deformities in extreme old age, they acquired an additional ghastliness in proportion to their number of years, which is not to be described; and among half a dozen I soon distinguished which was the oldest, although there were not above a century or two between them.

The reader will easily believe, that from what I had heard and seen, my keen appetite for perpetuity of life was much abated. I grew heartily ashamed of the pleasing visions I had formed; and thought no tyrant could invent a death into which I would not run with pleasure from such a life. The King heard of all that had passed between me and my friends upon this occasion, and rallied[4] me very pleasantly; wishing I would send a couple of *struldbruggs* to my own country, to arm our people against the fear of death; but this it seems is forbidden by the fundamental laws of the kingdom; or else I should have been well content with the trouble and expense of transporting them.

I could not but agree, that the laws of this kingdom relating to the *struldbruggs*, were founded upon the strongest reasons, and such as any other country would be under the necessity of enacting in the like circumstances. Otherwise, as avarice is the necessary consequent of old age, those immortals would in time become proprietors of the whole nation, and engross[5] the civil power; which, for want of abilities to manage, must end in the ruin of the public.[6]

* * *

---

4. Ridiculed.
5. Absorb, monopolize.
6. In the omitted chapter, Gulliver sails to Japan, where a Dutch ship provides him passage back to Europe.

Part 4. A Voyage to the Country of the Houyhnhnms[7]

CHAPTER 1. *The Author sets out as Captain of a ship. His men conspire against him, confine him a long time to his cabin, set him on shore in an unknown land. He travels up into the country. The Yahoos, a strange sort of animal, described. The Author meets two Houyhnhnms.*

I continued at home with my wife and children about five months in a very happy condition, if I could have learned the lesson of knowing when I was well. I left my poor wife big with child, and accepted an advantageous offer made me to be Captain of the *Adventure*, a stout merchantman of 350 tons; for I understood navigation well, and being grown weary of a surgeon's employment at sea, which however I could exercise upon occasion, I took a skillful young man of that calling, one Robert Purefoy, into my ship. We set sail from Portsmouth upon the 7th day of September, 1710; on the 14th we met with Captain Pocock of Bristol, at Tenariff, who was going to the Bay of Campeachy[8] to cut logwood. On the 16th he was parted from us by a storm; I heard since my return that his ship foundered and none escaped, but one cabin boy. He was an honest man and a good sailor, but a little too positive in his own opinions, which was the cause of his destruction, as it hath been of several others. For if he had followed my advice, he might at this time have been safe at home with his family as well as myself.

I had several men died in my ship of calentures,[9] so that I was forced to get recruits out of Barbadoes and the Leeward Islands, where I touched by the direction of the merchants who employed me; which I had soon too much cause to repent, for I found afterwards that most of them had been buccaneers. I had fifty hands on board; and my orders were that I should trade with the Indians in the South Sea, and make what discoveries I could. These rogues whom I had picked up debauched my other men, and they all formed a conspiracy to seize the ship and secure me; which they did one morning, rushing into my cabin, and binding me hand and foot, threatening to throw me overboard, if I offered to stir. I told them I was their prisoner, and would submit. This they made me swear to do, and then unbound me, only fastening one of my legs with a chain near my bed, and placed a sentry at my door with his piece charged, who was commanded to shoot me dead if I attempted my liberty. They sent me down victuals and drink, and took the government of the ship to themselves. Their design was to turn pirates and plunder the Spaniards, which they could not do, till they got more men. But first they resolved to sell the goods in the ship, and then go to Madagascar for recruits, several among them having died since my confinement. They sailed many weeks, and traded with the Indians; but I knew not what course they took, being kept close prisoner in my cabin, and expecting nothing less than to be murdered, as they often threatened me.

Upon the 9th day of May, 1711, one James Welch came down to my cabin; and said he had orders from the Captain to set me ashore. I expostulated with him, but in vain; neither would he so much as tell me who their new Captain was. They forced me into the longboat, letting me put on my best

---

7. Pronounced *hwin-ims*. The word suggests the neigh characteristic of a horse.
8. Campeche, in the Gulf of Mexico. Teneriffe is one of the Canary Islands.

9. "A distemper peculiar to sailors, in hot climates; wherein they imagine the sea to be green fields, and will throw themselves into it, if not restrained" (Johnson's *Dictionary*).

suit of clothes, which were as good as new, and a small bundle of linen, but no arms except my hanger; and they were so civil as not to search my pockets, into which I conveyed what money I had, with some other little necessaries. They rowed about a league, and then set me down on a strand. I desired them to tell me what country it was; they all swore, they knew no more than myself, but said that the Captain (as they called him) was resolved, after they had sold the lading, to get rid of me in the first place where they discovered land. They pushed off immediately, advising me to make haste, for fear of being overtaken by the tide, and bade me farewell.

In this desolate condition I advanced forward, and soon got upon firm ground, where I sat down on a bank to rest myself, and consider what I had best to do. When I was a little refreshed, I went up into the country, resolving to deliver myself to the first savages I should meet, and purchase my life from them by some bracelets, glass rings, and other toys, which sailors usually provide themselves with in those voyages, and whereof I had some about me. The land was divided by long rows of trees, not regularly planted, but naturally growing; there was great plenty of grass, and several fields of oats. I walked very circumspectly for fear of being surprised, or suddenly shot with an arrow from behind, or on either side. I fell into a beaten road, where I saw many tracks of human feet, and some of cows, but most of horses. At last I beheld several animals in a field, and one or two of the same kind sitting in trees. Their shape was very singular, and deformed, which a little discomposed me, so that I lay down behind a thicket to observe them better. Some of them coming forward near the place where I lay, gave me an opportunity of distinctly marking their form. Their heads and breasts were covered with a thick hair, some frizzled and others lank; they had beards like goats, and a long ridge of hair down their backs, and the fore parts of their legs and feet; but the rest of their bodies were bare, so that I might see their skins, which were of a brown buff color. They had no tails, nor any hair at all on their buttocks, except about the anus; which, I presume Nature had placed there to defend them as they sat on the ground; for this posture they used, as well as lying down, and often stood on their hind feet. They climbed high trees, as nimbly as a squirrel, for they had strong extended claws before and behind, terminating in sharp points, and hooked. They would often spring, and bound, and leap with prodigious agility. The females were not so large as the males; they had long lank hair on their heads, and only a sort of down on the rest of their bodies, except about the anus, and pudenda. Their dugs hung between their forefeet, and often reached almost to the ground as they walked. The hair of both sexes was of several colors, brown, red, black, and yellow. Upon the whole, I never beheld in all my travels so disagreeable an animal, or one against which I naturally conceived so strong an antipathy. So that thinking I had seen enough, full of contempt and aversion, I got up and pursued the beaten road, hoping it might direct me to the cabin of some Indian. I had not gone far when I met one of these creatures full in my way, and coming up directly to me. The ugly monster, when he saw me, distorted several ways every feature of his visage, and stared as at an object he had never seen before; then approaching nearer, lifted up his forepaw, whether out of curiosity or mischief, I could not tell; but I drew my hanger, and gave him a good blow with the flat side of it; for I durst not strike him with the edge, fearing the inhabitants might be provoked against me, if they should come to know that I had killed or maimed any of their cattle. When the beast felt the smart, he drew back, and roared so loud, that a herd of at least forty came flocking about me from the near field, howling and making odious faces; but I ran to the body of a tree, and leaning my back against it, kept them off, by waving my hanger. Several of this cursed brood getting hold of the branches behind, leaped up into the tree, from whence they began to discharge their excrements on my head; however, I escaped pretty well, by sticking close to the stem of the tree, but was almost stifled with the filth, which fell about me on every side.

In the midst of this distress, I observed them all to run away on a sudden as fast as they could; at which I ventured to leave the tree, and pursue the road, wondering what it was that could put them into this fright. But looking on my left hand, I saw a horse walking softly in the field; which my persecutors having sooner discovered, was the cause of their flight. The horse started a little when he came near me, but soon recovering himself, looked full in my face with manifest tokens of wonder; he viewed my hands and feet, walking round me several times. I would have pursued my journey, but he placed himself directly in the way, yet looking with a very mild aspect, never offering the least violence. We stood gazing at each other for some time; at last I took the boldness, to reach my hand towards his neck, with a design to stroke it; using the common style and whistle of jockies when they are going to handle a strange horse. But this animal, seeming to receive my civilities with disdain, shook his head, and bent his brows, softly raising up his left forefoot to remove my hand. Then he neighed three or four times, but in so different a cadence, that I almost began to think he was speaking to himself in some language of his own.

While he and I were thus employed, another horse came up; who applying himself to the first in a very formal manner, they gently struck each other's right hoof before, neighing several times by turns, and varying the sound, which seemed to be almost articulate. They went some paces off, as if it were to confer together, walking side by side, backward and forward, like persons deliberating upon some affair of weight; but often turning their eyes towards me, as it were to watch that I might not escape. I was amazed to see such actions and behavior in brute beasts; and concluded with myself that if the inhabitants of this country were endued with a proportionable degree of reason, they must needs be the wisest people upon earth. This thought gave me so much comfort, that I resolved to go forward until I could discover some house or village, or meet with any of the natives, leaving the two horses to discourse together as they pleased. But the first, who was a dapple grey, observing me to steal off, neighed after me in so expressive a tone that I fancied myself to understand what he meant; whereupon I turned back, and came near him, to expect his farther commands; but concealing my fear as much as I could; for I began to be in some pain, how this adventure might terminate; and the reader will easily believe I did not much like my present situation.

The two horses came up close to me, looking with great earnestness upon my face and hands. The grey steed rubbed my hat all round with his right fore hoof, and discomposed it so much that I was forced to adjust it better, by taking it off, and settling it again; whereat both he and his companion (who was a brown bay) appeared to be much surprised; the latter felt the lappet of my coat, and finding it to hang loose about me, they both looked with new signs of wonder. He stroked my right hand, seeming to admire the softness, and color; but he squeezed it so hard between his hoof and his pastern, that I was forced to roar; after which they both touched me with all possible tenderness. They were under great perplexity about my shoes and stockings, which they felt very often, neighing to each other, and using various gestures, not unlike those of a philosopher, when he would attempt to solve some new and difficult phenomenon.

Upon the whole, the behavior of these animals was so orderly and rational, so acute and judicious, that I at last concluded, they must needs be magicians, who had thus metamorphosed themselves upon some design; and seeing a stranger in the way, were resolved to divert themselves with him; or perhaps were really amazed at the sight of a man so very different in habit, feature, and complexion from those who might probably live in so remote a climate. Upon the strength of this reasoning, I ventured to address them in the following manner: "Gentlemen, if you be conjurers, as I have good cause to believe, you can understand any language; therefore I make bold to let your worships know that I am a poor distressed Englishman, driven by his misfortunes upon your coast; and I entreat one of you, to let me ride upon his back, as if he were a real horse, to some house or village, where I can be relieved. In return of which favor, I will make you a present of this knife and bracelet" (taking them out of my pocket). The two creatures stood silent while I spoke, seeming to listen with great attention; and when I had ended, they neighed frequently towards each other, as if they were engaged in serious conversation. I plainly observed, that their language expressed the passions very well, and the words might with little pains be resolved into an alphabet more easily than the Chinese.

I could frequently distinguish the word Yahoo,[1] which was repeated by each of them several times; and although it were impossible for me to conjecture what it meant, yet while the two horses were busy in conversation, I endeavored to practice this word upon my tongue; and as soon as they were silent, I boldly pronounced "Yahoo" in a loud voice, imitating, at the same time, as near as I could, the neighing of a horse; at which they were both visibly surprised, and the grey repeated the same word twice, as if he meant to teach me the right accent, wherein I spoke after him as well as I could, and found myself perceivably to improve every time, although very far from any degree of perfection. Then the bay tried me with a second word, much harder to be pronounced; but reducing it to the English orthography, may be spelt thus, Houyhnhnm. I did not succeed in this so well as the former, but after two or three farther trials, I had better fortune; and they both appeared amazed at my capacity.

After some farther discourse, which I then conjectured might relate to me, the two friends took their leaves, with the same compliment of striking each other's hoof; and the grey made me signs that I should walk before him; wherein I thought it prudent to comply, till I could find a better director. When I offered to slacken my pace, he would cry, "Hhuun, Hhuun"; I guessed his meaning, and gave him to understand, as well as I could that I was weary, and not able to walk faster; upon which, he would stand a while to let me rest.

CHAPTER 2. *The Author conducted by a Houyhnhnm to his house. The house described. The Author's reception. The food of the Houyhnhnms. The Author*

---

1. Perhaps compounded from two expressions of disgust, *yah* and *ugh* (or *hoo*), common in the 18th century.

in distress for want of meat is at last relieved. His manner of feeding in that country.

Having traveled about three miles, we came to a long kind of building, made of timber, stuck in the ground, and wattled across; the roof was low, and covered with straw. I now began to be a little comforted, and took out some toys, which travelers usually carry for presents to the savage Indians of America and other parts, in hopes the people of the house would be thereby encouraged to receive me kindly. The horse made me a sign to go in first; it was a large room with a smooth clay floor, and a rack and manger extending the whole length on one side. There were three nags, and two mares, not eating, but some of them sitting down upon their hams, which I very much wondered at; but wondered more to see the rest employed in domestic business. The last seemed but ordinary cattle; however this confirmed my first opinion, that a people who could so far civilize brute animals must needs excel in wisdom all the nations of the world. The grey came in just after, and thereby prevented any ill treatment, which the others might have given me. He neighed to them several times in a style of authority, and received answers.

Beyond this room there were three others, reaching the length of the house, to which you passed through three doors, opposite to each other, in the manner of a vista; we went through the second room towards the third; here the grey walked in first, beckoning me to attend.[2] I waited in the second room, and got ready my presents, for the master and mistress of the house; they were two knives, three bracelets of false pearl, a small looking glass and a bead necklace. The horse neighed three or four times, and I waited to hear some answers in a human voice, but I heard no other returns than in the same dialect, only one or two a little shriller than his. I began to think that this house must belong to some person of great note among them, because there appeared so much ceremony before I could gain admittance. But, that a man of quality should be served all by horses, was beyond my comprehension. I feared my brain was disturbed by my sufferings and misfortunes; I roused myself, and looked about me in the room where I was left alone; this was furnished as the first, only after a more elegant manner. I rubbed my eyes often, but the same objects still occurred. I pinched my arms and sides, to awaken myself, hoping I might be in a dream. I then absolutely concluded that all these appearances could be nothing else but necromancy and magic. But I had no time to pursue these reflections; for the grey horse came to the door, and made me a sign to follow him into the third room; where I saw a very comely mare, together with a colt and foal, sitting on their haunches, upon mats of straw, not unartfully made, and perfectly neat and clean.

The mare soon after my entrance, rose from her mat, and coming up close, after having nicely observed my hands and face, gave me a most contemptuous look; then turning to the horse, I heard the word Yahoo often repeated betwixt them; the meaning of which word I could not then comprehend, although it were the first I had learned to pronounce; but I was soon better informed, to my everlasting mortification: for the horse beckoning to me with his head, and repeating the word, "Hhuun, Hhuun," as he did upon

2. To wait. "Vista": a long, open corridor.

the road, which I understood was to attend him, led me out into a kind of court, where was another building at some distance from the house. Here we entered, and I saw three of those detestable creatures, which I first met after my landing, feeding upon roots, and the flesh of some animals, which I afterwards found to be that of asses and dogs, and now and then a cow dead by accident or disease. They were all tied by the neck with strong withes,[3] fastened to a beam; they held their food between the claws of their forefeet, and tore it with their teeth.

The master horse ordered a sorrel nag, one of his servants, to untie the largest of these animals, and take him into a yard. The beast and I were brought close together; and our countenances diligently compared, both by master and servant, who thereupon repeated several times the word "Yahoo." My horror and astonishment are not to be described, when I observed, in this abominable animal, a perfect human figure; the face of it indeed was flat and broad, the nose depressed, the lips large, and the mouth wide; but these differences are common to all savage nations, where the lineaments of the countenance are distorted by the natives suffering their infants to lie groveling on the earth, or by carrying them on their backs, nuzzling with their face against the mother's shoulders. The forefeet of the Yahoo differed from my hands in nothing else but the length of the nails, the coarseness and brownness of the palms, and the hairiness on the backs. There was the same resemblance between our feet, with the same differences, which I knew very well, although the horses did not, because of my shoes and stockings; the same in every part of our bodies, except as to hairiness and color, which I have already described.

The great difficulty that seemed to stick with the two horses was to see the rest of my body so very different from that of a Yahoo, for which I was obliged to my clothes, whereof they had no conception; the sorrel nag offered me a root, which he held (after their manner, as we shall describe in its proper place) between his hoof and pastern; I took it in my hand, and having smelled it, returned it to him again as civilly as I could. He brought out of the Yahoo's kennel a piece of ass's flesh, but it smelled so offensively that I turned from it with loathing; he then threw it to the Yahoo, by whom it was greedily devoured. He afterwards showed me a wisp of hay, and a fetlock full of oats; but I shook my head, to signify that neither of these were food for me. And indeed, I now apprehended that I must absolutely starve, if I did not get to some of my own species; for as to those filthy Yahoos, although there were few greater lovers of mankind, at that time, than myself, yet I confess I never saw any sensitive being so detestable on all accounts; and the more I came near them, the more hateful they grew, while I stayed in that country. This the master horse observed by my behavior, and therefore sent the Yahoo back to his kennel. He then put his forehoof to his mouth, at which I was much surprised, although he did it with ease, and with a motion that appeared perfectly natural; and made other signs to know what I would eat; but I could not return him such an answer as he was able to apprehend; and if he had understood me, I did not see how it was possible to contrive any way for finding myself nourishment. While we were thus engaged, I observed a cow passing by; whereupon I pointed to her, and expressed a desire to let me go and milk her. This had its effect; for he led

---

3. Slender, flexible branches.

me back into the house, and ordered a mare-servant to open a room, where a good store of milk lay in earthen and wooden vessels, after a very orderly and cleanly manner. She gave me a large bowl full, of which I drank very heartily, and found myself well refreshed.

About noon I saw coming towards the house a kind of vehicle, drawn like a sledge by four Yahoos. There was in it an old steed, who seemed to be of quality; he alighted with his hind feet forward, having by accident got a hurt in his left forefoot. He came to dine with our horse, who received him with great civility. They dined in the best room, and had oats boiled in milk for the second course, which the old horse eat warm, but the rest cold. Their mangers were placed circular in the middle of the room, and divided into several partitions, round which they sat on their haunches upon bosses[4] of straw. In the middle was a large rack with angles answering to every partition of the manger. So that each horse and mare eat their own hay, and their own mash of oats and milk, with much decency and regularity. The behavior of the young colt and foal appeared very modest; and that of the master and mistress extremely cheerful and complaisant to their guest. The grey ordered me to stand by him; and much discourse passed between him and his friend concerning me, as I found by the stranger's often looking on me, and the frequent repetition of the word Yahoo.

I happened to wear my gloves; which the master grey observing, seemed perplexed; discovering signs of wonder what I had done to my forefeet; he put his hoof three or four times to them, as if he would signify, that I should reduce them to their former shape, which I presently did, pulling off both my gloves, and putting them into my pocket. This occasioned farther talk, and I saw the company was pleased with my behavior, whereof I soon found the good effects. I was ordered to speak the few words I understood; and while they were at dinner, the master taught me the names for oats, milk, fire, water, and some others which I could readily pronounce after him, having from my youth a great facility in learning languages.

When dinner was done, the master horse took me aside, and by signs and words made me understand the concern he was in that I had nothing to eat. Oats in their tongue are called *hlunnh*. This word I pronounced two or three times; for although I had refused them at first, yet upon second thoughts, I considered that I could contrive to make a kind of bread, which might be sufficient with milk to keep me alive, till I could make my escape to some other country, and to creatures of my own species. The horse immediately ordered a white mare-servant of his family to bring me a good quantity of oats in a sort of wooden tray. These I heated before the fire as well as I could, and rubbed them till the husks came off, which I made a shift to winnow from the grain; I ground and beat them between two stones, then took water, and made them into a paste or cake, which I toasted at the fire, and eat warm with milk. It was at first a very insipid diet, although common enough in many parts of Europe, but grew tolerable by time; and having been often reduced to hard fare in my life, this was not the first experiment I had made how easily nature is satisfied. And I cannot but observe that I never had one hour's sickness, while I staid in this island. It is true, I sometimes made a shift to catch a rabbit, or bird, by springes[5] made of Yahoos' hairs; and I often gathered wholesome herbs, which I boiled, or eat as salads

4. Seats of bundled grasses.   5. Snares.

with my bread; and now and then, for a rarity, I made a little butter, and drank the whey. I was at first at a great loss for salt; but custom soon reconciled the want of it; and I am confident that the frequent use of salt among us is an effect of luxury, and was first introduced only as a provocative to drink; except where it is necessary for preserving of flesh in long voyages, or in places remote from great markets. For we observe no animal to be fond of it but man;[6] and as to myself, when I left this country, it was a great while before I could endure the taste of it in anything that I eat.

This is enough to say upon the subject of my diet, wherewith other travelers fill their books, as if the readers were personally concerned whether we fare well or ill. However, it was necessary to mention this matter, lest the world should think it impossible that I could find sustenance for three years in such a country, and among such inhabitants.

When it grew towards evening, the master horse ordered a place for me to lodge in; it was but six yards from the house, and separated from the stable of the Yahoos. Here I got some straw, and covering myself with my own clothes, slept very sound. But I was in a short time better accommodated, as the reader shall know hereafter, when I come to treat more particularly about my way of living.

CHAPTER 3. *The Author studious to learn the language, the Houyhnhnm his master assists in teaching him. The language described. Several Houyhnhnms of quality come out of curiosity to see the Author. He gives his master a short account of his voyage.*

My principal endeavor was to learn the language, which my master (for so I shall henceforth call him) and his children, and every servant of his house were desirous to teach me. For they looked upon it as a prodigy, that a brute animal should discover such marks of a rational creature. I pointed to everything, and enquired the name of it, which I wrote down in my journal book when I was alone, and corrected my bad accent, by desiring those of the family to pronounce it often. In this employment, a sorrel nag, one of the under servants, was very ready to assist me.

In speaking, they pronounce through the nose and throat, and their language approaches nearest to the High Dutch or German, of any I know in Europe; but is much more graceful and significant. The Emperor Charles V made almost the same observation, when he said, that if he were to speak to his horse, it should be in High Dutch.[7]

The curiosity and impatience of my master were so great, that he spent many hours of his leisure to instruct me. He was convinced (as he afterwards told me) that I must be a Yahoo, but my teachableness, civility, and cleanliness astonished him; which were qualities altogether so opposite to those animals. He was most perplexed about my clothes, reasoning sometimes with himself whether they were a part of my body; for I never pulled them off till the family were asleep, and got them on before they waked in the morning. My master was eager to learn from whence I came; how I acquired those appearances of reason, which I discovered in all

---

6. Gulliver is, of course, in error; many animals require salt.
7. The emperor is supposed to have said that he would speak to his God in Spanish, to his mistress in Italian, and to his horse in German.

my actions; and to know my story from my own mouth, which he hoped he should soon do by the great proficiency I made in learning and pronouncing their words and sentences. To help my memory, I formed all I learned into the English alphabet, and writ the words down with the translations. This last, after some time, I ventured to do in my master's presence. It cost me much trouble to explain to him what I was doing; for the inhabitants have not the least idea of books or literature.

In about ten weeks time I was able to understand most of his questions; and in three months could give him some tolerable answers. He was extremely curious to know from what part of the country I came, and how I was taught to imitate a rational creature; because the Yahoos (whom he saw I exactly resembled in my head, hands, and face, that were only visible) with some appearance of cunning, and the strongest disposition to mischief, were observed to be the most unteachable of all brutes. I answered that I came over the sea, from a far place, with many others of my own kind, in a great hollow vessel made of the bodies of trees; that my companions forced me to land on this coast, and then left me to shift for myself. It was with some difficulty, and by the help of many signs, that I brought him to understand me. He replied that I must needs be mistaken, or that I *said the thing which was not.* (For they have no word in their language to express lying or falsehood.) He knew it was impossible that there could be a country beyond the sea, or that a parcel of brutes could move a wooden vessel whither they pleased upon water. He was sure no Houyhnhnm alive could make such a vessel, or would trust Yahoos to manage it.

The word Houyhnhnm, in their tongue, signifies a Horse; and in its etymology, the Perfection of Nature. I told my master that I was at a loss for expression, but would improve as fast as I could; and hoped in a short time I should be able to tell him wonders. He was pleased to direct his own mare, his colt, and foal, and the servants of the family to take all opportunities of instructing me; and every day for two or three hours, he was at the same pains himself. Several horses and mares of quality in the neighborhood came often to our house, upon the report spread of a wonderful Yahoo, that could speak like a Houyhnhnm, and seemed in his words and actions to discover some glimmerings of reason. These delighted to converse with me; they put many questions, and received such answers as I was able to return. By all which advantages, I made so great a progress, that in five months from my arrival, I understood whatever was spoke, and could express myself tolerably well.

The Houyhnhnms who came to visit my master, out of a design of seeing and talking with me, could hardly believe me to be a right Yahoo, because my body had a different covering from others of my kind. They were astonished to observe me without the usual hair or skin, except on my head, face, and hands; but I discovered that secret to my master, upon an accident, which happened about a fortnight before.

I have already told the reader, that every night when the family were gone to bed, it was my custom to strip and cover myself with my clothes; it happened one morning early, that my master sent for me, by the sorrel nag, who was his valet; when he came, I was fast asleep, my clothes fallen off on one side, and my shirt above my waist. I awaked at the noise he made, and observed him to deliver his message in some disorder; after which he went to my master, and in a great fright gave him a very confused account of what he had seen. This I presently discovered; for going as soon as I was dressed, to pay my attendance upon his honor, he asked me the meaning of what his servant had reported; that I was not the same thing when I slept as I appeared to be at other times; that his valet assured him, some part of me was white, some yellow, at least not so white, and some brown.

I had hitherto concealed the secret of my dress, in order to distinguish myself as much as possible, from that cursed race of Yahoos; but now I found it in vain to do so any longer. Besides, I considered that my clothes and shoes would soon wear out, which already were in a declining condition, and must be supplied by some contrivance from the hides of Yahoos, or other brutes; whereby the whole secret would be known. I therefore told my master, that in the country from whence I came, those of my kind always covered their bodies with the hairs of certain animals prepared by art, as well for decency, as to avoid inclemencies of air both hot and cold; of which, as to my own person I would give him immediate conviction, if he pleased to command me; only desiring his excuse, if I did not expose those parts that Nature taught us to conceal. He said, my discourse was all very strange, but especially the last part; for he could not understand why Nature should teach us to conceal what Nature had given. That neither himself nor family were ashamed of any parts of their bodies; but however I might do as I pleased. Whereupon, I first unbuttoned my coat, and pulled it off. I did the same with my waistcoat; I drew off my shoes, stockings, and breeches. I let my shirt down to my waist, and drew up the bottom, fastening it like a girdle about my middle to hide my nakedness.

My master observed the whole performance with great signs of curiosity and admiration. He took up all my clothes in his pastern, one piece after another, and examined them diligently; he then stroked my body very gently, and looked round me several times; after which he said, it was plain I must be a perfect Yahoo; but that I differed very much from the rest of my species, in the whiteness and smoothness of my skin, my want of hair in several parts of my body, the shape and shortness of my claws behind and before, and my affectation of walking continually on my two hinder feet. He desired to see no more; and gave me leave to put on my clothes again, for I was shuddering with cold.

I expressed my uneasiness at his giving me so often the appellation of Yahoo, an odious animal, for which I had so utter an hatred and contempt. I begged he would forbear applying that word to me, and take the same order in his family, and among his friends whom he suffered to see me. I requested likewise, that the secret of my having a false covering to my body might be known to none but himself, at least as long as my present clothing should last; for as to what the sorrel nag his valet had observed, his honor might command him to conceal it.

All this my master very graciously consented to; and thus the secret was kept till my clothes began to wear out, which I was forced to supply by several contrivances, that shall hereafter be mentioned. In the meantime, he desired I would go on with my utmost diligence to learn their language, because he was more astonished at my capacity for speech and reason, than at the figure of my body, whether it were covered or no; adding that he waited with some impatience to hear the wonders which I promised to tell him.

From thenceforward he doubled the pains he had been at to instruct me; he brought me into all company, and made them treat me with civility, because, as he told them privately, this would put me into good humor, and make me more diverting.

Every day when I waited on him, beside the trouble he was at in teaching, he would ask me several questions concerning myself, which I answered as well as I could; and by those means he had already received some general ideas, although very imperfect. It would be tedious to relate the several steps, by which I advanced to a more regular conversation, but the first account I gave of myself in any order and length was to this purpose:

That, I came from a very far country, as I already had attempted to tell him, with about fifty more of my own species; that we traveled upon the seas, in a great hollow vessel made of wood, and larger than his honor's house. I described the ship to him in the best terms I could; and explained by the help of my handkerchief displayed, how it was driven forward by the wind. That, upon a quarrel among us, I was set on shore on this coast, where I walked forward without knowing whither, till he delivered me from the persecution of those execrable Yahoos. He asked me who made the ship, and how it was possible that the Houyhnhnms of my country would leave it to the management of brutes? My answer was that I durst proceed no farther in my relation, unless he would give me his word and honor that he would not be offended; and then I would tell him the wonders I had so often promised. He agreed; and I went on by assuring him, that the ship was made by creatures like myself, who in all the countries I had traveled, as well as in my own, were the only governing, rational animals; and that upon my arrival hither, I was as much astonished to see the Houyhnhnms act like rational beings, as he or his friends could be in finding some marks of reason in a creature he was pleased to call a Yahoo; to which I owned my resemblance in every part, but could not account for their degenerate and brutal nature. I said farther, that if good fortune ever restored me to my native country, to relate my travels hither, as I resolved to do, everybody would believe that I *said the thing which was not*, that I invented the story out of my own head; and with all possible respect to himself, his family, and friends, and under his promise of not being offended, our countrymen would hardly think it probable, that a Houyhnhnm should be the presiding creature of a nation, and a Yahoo the brute.

CHAPTER 4. *The Houyhnhnms' notion of truth and falsehood. The Author's discourse disapproved by his master. The Author gives a more particular account of himself, and the accidents of his voyage.*

My master heard me with great appearances of uneasiness in his countenance; because *doubting* or *not believing* are so little known in this country, that the inhabitants cannot tell how to behave themselves under such circumstances. And I remember in frequent discourses with my master concerning the nature of manhood, in other parts of the world, having occasion to talk of *lying* and *false representation*, it was with much difficulty that he comprehended what I meant; although he had otherwise a most acute judgment. For he argued thus: that the use of speech was to make us understand one another, and to receive information of facts; now if anyone *said the thing which was not*, these ends were defeated; because I cannot properly be said to understand him; and I am so far from receiving information, that he leaves me worse than in ignorance; for I am led to believe a thing *black* when it is *white*, and *short* when it is *long*. And these were all the notions he had concerning the faculty of *lying*, so perfectly well understood, and so universally practiced among human creatures.

To return from this digression; when I asserted that the Yahoos were the only governing animals in my country, which my master said was altogether past his conception, he desired to know, whether we had Houyhnhnms among us, and what was their employment. I told him we had great numbers; that in summer they grazed in the fields, and in winter were kept in houses, with hay and oats, where Yahoo servants were employed to rub their skins smooth, comb their manes, pick their feet, serve them with food, and make their beds. "I understand you well," said my master; "it is now very plain from all you have spoken, that whatever share of reason the Yahoos pretend to, the Houyhnhnms are your masters; I heartily wish our Yahoos would be so tractable." I begged his honor would please to excuse me from proceeding any farther, because I was very certain that the account he expected from me would be highly displeasing. But he insisted in commanding me to let him know the best and the worst; I told him he should be obeyed. I owned that the Houyhnhnms among us, whom we called Horses, were the most generous[8] and comely animal we had; that they excelled in strength and swiftness; and when they belonged to persons of quality, employed in traveling, racing, and drawing chariots, they were treated with much kindness and care, till they fell into diseases, or became foundered in the feet; but then they were sold, and used to all kind of drudgery till they died; after which their skins were stripped and sold for what they were worth, and their bodies left to be devoured by dogs and birds of prey. But the common race of horses had not so good fortune, being kept by farmers and carriers, and other mean people, who put them to greater labor, and feed them worse. I described as well as I could, our way of riding; the shape and use of a bridle, a saddle, a spur, and a whip; of harness and wheels. I added, that we fastened plates of a certain hard substance called iron at the bottom of their feet, to preserve their hoofs from being broken by the stony ways on which we often traveled.

My master, after some expressions of great indignation, wondered how we dared to venture upon a Houyhnhnm's back; for he was sure, that the weakest servant in his house would be able to shake off the strongest Yahoo; or by lying down, and rolling upon his back, squeeze the brute to death. I answered that our horses were trained up from three or four years old to the several uses we intended them for; that if any of them proved intolerably vicious, they were employed for carriages; that they were severely beaten while they were young for any mischievous tricks; that the males, designed for the common use of riding or draught, were generally castrated about two years after their birth, to take down their spirits, and make them more tame and gentle; that they were indeed sensible of rewards and punishments; but his honor would please to consider that they had not the least tincture of reason any more than the Yahoos in this country.

It put me to the pains of many circumlocutions to give my master a right idea of what I spoke; for their language doth not abound in variety of words, because their wants and passions are fewer than among us. But it is impossible to express his noble resentment at our savage treatment of the Houyhnhnm race; particularly after I had explained the manner and use of castrating horses among us, to hinder them from propagating their kind, and to render them more servile. He said, if it were possible there could be any country where Yahoos alone were endued with reason, they certainly

---

8. Noble.

must be the governing animal, because reason will in time always prevail against brutal strength. But, considering the frame of our bodies, and especially of mine, he thought no creature of equal bulk was so ill-contrived for employing that reason in the common offices of life; whereupon he desired to know whether those among whom I lived resembled me or the Yahoos of his country. I assured him that I was as well shaped as most of my age; but the younger and the females were much more soft and tender, and the skins of the latter generally as white as milk. He said I differed indeed from other Yahoos, being much more cleanly, and not altogether so deformed; but in point of real advantage, he thought I differed for the worse. That my nails were of no use either to my fore or hinder feet; as to my forefeet, he could not properly call them by that name, for he never observed me to walk upon them; that they were too soft to bear the ground; that I generally went with them uncovered, neither was the covering I sometimes wore on them of the same shape, or so strong as that on my feet behind. That I could not walk with any security; for if either of my hinder feet slipped, I must inevitably fall. He then began to find fault with other parts of my body; the flatness of my face, the prominence of my nose, my eyes placed directly in front, so that I could not look on either side without turning my head; that I was not able to feed myself without lifting one of my forefeet to my mouth; and therefore nature had placed those joints to answer that necessity. He knew not what could be the use of those several clefts and divisions in my feet behind; that these were too soft to bear the hardness and sharpness of stones without a covering made from the skin of some other brute; that my whole body wanted a fence against heat and cold, which I was forced to put on and off every day with tediousness and trouble. And lastly, that he observed every animal in his country naturally to abhor the Yahoos, whom the weaker avoided, and the stronger drove from them. So that supposing us to have the gift of reason, he could not see how it were possible to cure that natural antipathy which every creature discovered against us; nor consequently, how we could tame and render them serviceable. However, he would (as he said) debate the matter no farther, because he was more desirous to know my own story, the country where I was born, and the several actions and events of my life before I came hither.

I assured him how extremely desirous I was that he should be satisfied in every point; but I doubted much whether it would be possible for me to explain myself on several subjects whereof his honor could have no conception, because I saw nothing in his country to which I could resemble them. That however, I would do my best, and strive to express myself by similitudes, humbly desiring his assistance when I wanted proper words; which he was pleased to promise me.

I said, my birth was of honest parents, in an island called England, which was remote from this country, as many days journey as the strongest of his honor's servants could travel in the annual course of the sun. That I was bred a surgeon, whose trade it is to cure wounds and hurts in the body, got by accident or violence. That my country was governed by a female man, whom we called a queen. That I left it to get riches, whereby I might maintain myself and family when I should return. That in my last voyage, I was Commander of the ship and had about fifty Yahoos under me, many of which died at sea, and I was forced to supply them by others picked out from several nations. That our ship was twice in danger of being sunk; the first time by a great storm, and the second, by striking against a rock. Here my master interposed, by asking me, how I could persuade strangers out of different countries to venture with me, after the losses I had sustained, and the hazards I had run. I said, they were fellows of desperate fortunes, forced to fly from the places of their birth, on account of their poverty or their crimes. Some were undone by lawsuits; others spent all they had in drinking, whoring, and gaming; others fled for treason; many for murder, theft, poisoning, robbery, perjury, forgery, coining false money; for committing rapes or sodomy; for flying from their colors, or deserting to the enemy; and most of them had broken prison. None of these durst return to their native countries for fear of being hanged, or of starving in a jail; and therefore were under a necessity of seeking a livelihood in other places.

During this discourse, my master was pleased often to interrupt me. I had made use of many circumlocutions in describing to him the nature of the several crimes, for which most of our crew had been forced to fly their country. This labor took up several days conversation before he was able to comprehend me. He was wholly at a loss to know what could be the use or necessity of practicing those vices. To clear up which I endeavored to give him some ideas of the desire of power and riches; of the terrible effects of lust, intemperance, malice, and envy. All this I was forced to define and describe by putting of cases, and making suppositions. After which, like one whose imagination was struck with something never seen or heard of before, he would lift up his eyes with amazement and indignation. Power, government, war, law, punishment, and a thousand other things had no terms, wherein that language could express them; which made the difficulty almost insuperable to give my master any conception of what I meant; but being of an excellent understanding, much improved by contemplation and converse, he at last arrived at a competent knowledge of what human nature in our parts of the world is capable to perform; and desired I would give him some particular account of that land, which we call Europe, especially, of my own country.

CHAPTER 5. *The Author, at his master's commands, informs him of the state of England. The causes of war among the princes of Europe. The Author begins to explain the English Constitution.*

The reader may please to observe that the following extract of many conversations I had with my master contains a summary of the most material points, which were discoursed at several times for above two years; his honor often desiring fuller satisfaction as I farther improved in the Houyhnhnm tongue. I laid before him, as well as I could, the whole state of Europe; I discoursed of trade and manufactures, of arts and sciences; and the answers I gave to all the questions he made, as they arose upon several subjects, were a fund of conversation not to be exhausted. But I shall here only set down the substance of what passed between us concerning my own country, reducing it into order as well as I can, without any regard to time or other circumstances, while I strictly adhere to truth. My only concern is that I shall hardly be able to do justice to my master's arguments and expressions; which must needs suffer by my want of capacity, as well as by a translation into our barbarous English.

In obedience therefore to his honor's commands, I related to him the Revolution under the Prince of Orange; the long war with France entered into by the said Prince, and renewed by his successor the present queen; wherein the greatest powers of Christendom were engaged, and which still continued. I computed at his request, that about a million of Yahoos might have been killed in the whole progress of it; and perhaps a hundred or more cities taken, and five times as many ships burned or sunk.[9]

He asked me what were the usual causes or motives that made one country to go to war with another. I answered, they were innumerable; but I should only mention a few of the chief. Sometimes the ambition of princes, who never think they have land or people enough to govern; sometimes the corruption of ministers, who engage their master in a war in order to stifle or divert the clamor of the subjects against their evil administration. Difference in opinions hath cost many millions of lives; for instance, whether flesh be bread, or bread be flesh; whether the juice of a certain berry be blood or wine; whether whistling be a vice or a virtue; whether it be better to kiss a post, or throw it into the fire; what is the best color for a coat, whether black, white, red, or grey; and whether it should be long or short, narrow or wide, dirty or clean;[1] with many more. Neither are any wars so furious and bloody, or of so long continuance, as those occasioned by difference in opinion, especially if it be in things indifferent.[2]

Sometimes the quarrel between two princes is to decide which of them shall dispossess a third of his dominions, where neither of them pretend to any right. Sometimes one prince quarreleth with another, for fear the other should quarrel with him. Sometimes a war is entered upon, because the enemy is too strong, and sometimes because he is too weak. Sometimes our neighbors want the things which we have, or have the things which we want; and we both fight, till they take ours or give us theirs. It is a very justifiable cause of war to invade a country after the people have been wasted by famine, destroyed by pestilence, or embroiled by factions amongst themselves. It is justifiable to enter into a war against our nearest ally, when one of his towns lies convenient for us, or a territory of land, that would render our dominions round and compact. If a prince send forces into a nation, where the people are poor and ignorant, he may lawfully put half of them to death, and make slaves of the rest, in order to civilize and reduce them from their barbarous way of living. It is a very kingly, honorable, and frequent practice, when one prince desires the assistance of another to secure him against an invasion, that the assistant, when he hath driven out the invader, should seize on the dominions himself, and kill, imprison, or banish the prince he came to relieve. Alliance by blood or marriage is a sufficient cause of war between princes; and the nearer the kindred is, the greater is their disposition to quarrel. Poor nations are hungry, and rich nations are proud; and pride and hunger will ever be at variance. For these reasons, the trade of a soldier is held the most honorable of all others: because a soldier is a Yahoo hired to kill in cold blood as many of his own species, who have never offended him, as possibly he can.

There is likewise a kind of beggarly princes in Europe, not able to make war by themselves, who hire out their troops to richer nations for so much

---

9. Gulliver relates recent English history: the Glorious Revolution (1688–89) and the War of Spanish Succession (1701–13). He greatly exaggerates the casualties in the war.
1. Gulliver refers to the religious controversies of

the Reformation and Counter-Reformation: the doctrine of transubstantiation, the use of music in church services, the veneration of the crucifix, and the wearing of priestly vestments.
2. Of little consequence.

a day to each man; of which they keep three fourths to themselves, and it is the best part of their maintenance; such are those in many northern parts of Europe.[3]

"What you have told me," said my master, "upon the subject of war, doth indeed discover most admirably the effects of that reason you pretend to. However, it is happy that the shame is greater than the danger; and that Nature hath left you utterly uncapable of doing much mischief; for your mouths lying flat with your faces, you can hardly bite each other to any purpose, unless by consent. Then, as to the claws upon your feet before and behind, they are so short and tender, that one of our Yahoos would drive a dozen of yours before him. And therefore in recounting the numbers of those who have been killed in battle, I cannot but think that you have *said the thing which is not*."

I could not forbear shaking my head and smiling a little at his ignorance. And, being no stranger to the art of war, I gave him a description of cannons, culverins, muskets, carabines, pistols, bullets, powder, swords, bayonets, battles, sieges, retreats, attacks, undermines, countermines, bombardments, sea fights; ships sunk with a thousand men; twenty thousand killed on each side; dying groans, limbs flying in the air; smoke, noise, confusion, trampling to death under horses' feet; flight, pursuit, victory; fields strewed with carcasses left for food to dogs, and wolves, and birds of prey; plundering, stripping, ravishing, burning, and destroying. And, to set forth the valor of my own dear countrymen, I assured him that I had seen them blow up a hundred enemies at once in a siege, and as many in a ship; and beheld the dead bodies drop down in pieces from the clouds, to the great diversion of all the spectators.

I was going on to more particulars, when my master commanded me silence. He said, whoever understood the nature of Yahoos might easily believe it possible for so vile an animal, to be capable of every action I had named, if their strength and cunning equaled their malice. But, as my discourse had increased his abhorrence of the whole species, so he found it gave him a disturbance in his mind, to which he was wholly a stranger before. He thought his ears being used to such abominable words, might by degrees admit them with less detestation. That, although he hated the Yahoos of this country, yet he no more blamed them for their odious qualities, than he did a *gnnayh* (a bird of prey) for its cruelty, or a sharp stone for cutting his hoof. But, when a creature pretending to reason could be capable of such enormities, he dreaded lest the corruption of that faculty might be worse than brutality itself. He seemed therefore confident, that instead of reason, we were only possessed of some quality fitted to increase our natural vices; as the reflection from a troubled stream returns the image of an ill-shapen body, not only larger, but more distorted.

He added that he had heard too much upon the subject of war, both in this and some former discourses. There was another point which a little perplexed him at present. I had said that some of our crew left their country on account of being ruined by law: that I had already explained the meaning of the word; but he was at a loss how it should come to pass, that the law which was intended for every man's preservation, should be any man's ruin. Therefore he desired to be farther satisfied what I meant by law, and the dispensers thereof, according to the present practice in my own country;

3. A satiric glance at George I, who, as elector of Hanover, had dealt in this trade.

because he thought Nature and Reason were sufficient guides for a reasonable animal, as we pretended to be, in showing us what we ought to do, and what to avoid.

I assured his honor that law was a science wherein I had not much conversed, further than by employing advocates, in vain, upon some injustices that had been done me. However, I would give him all the satisfaction I was able.

I said there was a society of men among us, bred up from their youth in the art of proving by words multiplied for the purpose, that white is black, and black is white, according as they are paid. To this society all the rest of the people are slaves.

"For example. If my neighbor hath a mind to my cow, he hires a lawyer to prove that he ought to have my cow from me. I must then hire another to defend my right; it being against all rules of law that any man should be allowed to speak for himself. Now in this case, I who am the true owner lie under two great disadvantages. First, my lawyer being practiced almost from his cradle in defending falsehood is quite out of his element when he would be an advocate for justice, which as an office unnatural, he always attempts with great awkwardness, if not with ill-will. The second disadvantage is that my lawyer must proceed with great caution, or else he will be reprimanded by the judges, and abhorred by his brethren, as one who would lessen the practice of the law. And therefore I have but two methods to preserve my cow. The first is to gain over my adversary's lawyer with a double fee; who will then betray his client, by insinuating that he hath justice on his side. The second way is for my lawyer to make my cause appear as unjust as he can; by allowing the cow to belong to my adversary; and this if it be skillfully done, will certainly bespeak the favor of the bench.

"Now, your honor is to know that these judges are persons appointed to decide all controversies of property, as well as for the trial of criminals; and picked out from the most dextrous lawyers who are grown old or lazy; and having been biased all their lives against truth and equity, lie under such a fatal necessity of favoring fraud, perjury, and oppression, that I have known some of them to have refused a large bribe from the side where justice lay, rather than injure the faculty,[4] by doing anything unbecoming their nature or their office.

"It is a maxim among these lawyers, that whatever hath been done before may legally be done again; and therefore they take special care to record all the decisions formerly made against common justice and the general reason of mankind. These, under the name of *precedents*, they produce as authorities to justify the most iniquitous opinions; and the judges never fail of directing accordingly.

"In pleading, they studiously avoid entering into the merits of the cause; but are loud, violent, and tedious in dwelling upon all circumstances which are not to the purpose. For instance, in the case already mentioned, they never desire to know what claim or title my adversary hath to my cow; but whether the said cow were red or black; her horns long or short; whether the field I graze her in be round or square; whether she were milked at home or abroad; what diseases she is subject to, and the like. After which they consult

4. Profession.

precedents, adjourn the cause, from time to time, and in ten, twenty, or thirty years come to an issue.

"It is likewise to be observed, that this society hath a peculiar cant and jargon of their own, that no other mortal can understand, and wherein all their laws are written, which they take special care to multiply; whereby they have wholly confounded the very essence of truth and falsehood, of right and wrong; so that it will take thirty years to decide whether the field, left me by my ancestors for six generations, belong to me, or to a stranger three hundred miles off.

"In the trial of persons accused for crimes against the state, the method is much more short and commendable: the judge first sends to sound the disposition of those in power; after which he can easily hang or save the criminal, strictly preserving all the forms of law."

Here my master interposing said it was a pity that creatures endowed with such prodigious abilities of mind as these lawyers, by the description I gave of them, must certainly be, were not rather encouraged to be instructors of others in wisdom and knowledge. In answer to which, I assured his honor that in all points out of their own trade, they were usually the most ignorant and stupid generation among us, the most despicable in common conversation, avowed enemies to all knowledge and learning; and equally disposed to pervert the general reason of mankind, in every other subject of discourse as in that of their own profession.

CHAPTER 6. *A continuation of the state of England, under Queen Anne. The character of a first minister in the courts of Europe.*

My master was yet wholly at a loss to understand what motives could incite this race of lawyers to perplex, disquiet, and weary themselves by engaging in a confederacy of injustice, merely for the sake of injuring their fellow animals; neither could he comprehend what I meant in saying they did it for hire. Whereupon I was at much pains to describe to him the use of money, the materials it was made of, and the value of the metals; that when a Yahoo had got a great store of this precious substance, he was able to purchase whatever he had a mind to; the finest clothing, the noblest houses, great tracts of land, the most costly meats and drinks; and have his choice of the most beautiful females. Therefore since money alone was able to perform all these feats, our Yahoos thought they could never have enough of it to spend or to save, as they found themselves inclined from their natural bent either to profusion or avarice. That the rich man enjoyed the fruit of the poor man's labor, and the latter were a thousand to one in proportion to the former. That the bulk of our people was forced to live miserably, by laboring every day for small wages to make a few live plentifully. I enlarged myself much on these and many other particulars to the same purpose, but his honor was still to seek,[5] for he went upon a supposition that all animals had a title to their share in the productions of the earth; and especially those who presided over the rest. Therefore he desired I would let him know what these costly meats were, and how any of us happened to want them. Whereupon I enumerated as many sorts as came into my head, with the various methods of dressing them, which could not be done without sending vessels by sea to every part of

---

5. Still did not understand.

the world, as well for liquors to drink, as for sauces, and innumerable other conveniencies. I assured him, that this whole globe of earth must be at least three times gone round, before one of our better female Yahoos could get her breakfast, or a cup to put it in. He said, "That must needs be a miserable country which cannot furnish food for its own inhabitants." But what he chiefly wondered at, was how such vast tracts of ground as I described, should be wholly without fresh water, and the people put to the necessity of sending over the sea for drink. I replied that England (the dear place of my nativity) was computed to produce three times the quantity of food, more than its inhabitants are able to consume, as well as liquors extracted from grain, or pressed out of the fruit of certain trees, which made excellent drink; and the same proportion in every other convenience of life. But, in order to feed the luxury and intemperance of the males, and the vanity of the females, we sent away the greatest part of our necessary things to other countries, from whence in return we brought the materials of diseases, folly, and vice, to spend among ourselves. Hence it follows of necessity, that vast numbers of our people are compelled to seek their livelihood by begging, robbing, stealing, cheating, pimping, forswearing, flattering, suborning, forging, gaming, lying, fawning, hectoring, voting, scribbling, star gazing, poisoning, whoring, canting, libeling, freethinking, and the like occupations; every one of which terms, I was at much pains to make him understand.

That, wine was not imported among us from foreign countries, to supply the want of water or other drinks, but because it was a sort of liquid which made us merry, by putting us out of our senses; diverted all melancholy thoughts, begat wild extravagant imaginations in the brain, raised our hopes, and banished our fears; suspended every office of reason for a time, and deprived us of the use of our limbs, until we fell into a profound sleep; although it must be confessed, that we always awaked sick and dispirited; and that the use of this liquor filled us with diseases, which made our lives uncomfortable and short.

But beside all this, the bulk of our people supported themselves by furnishing the necessities or conveniencies of life to the rich, and to each other. For instance, when I am at home and dressed as I ought to be, I carry on my body the workmanship of an hundred tradesmen; the building and furniture of my house employ as many more; and five times the number to adorn my wife.

I was going on to tell him of another sort of people, who get their livelihood by attending the sick; having upon some occasions informed his honor that many of my crew had died of diseases. But here it was with the utmost difficulty that I brought him to apprehend what I meant. He could easily conceive that a Houyhnhnm grew weak and heavy a few days before his death; or by some accident might hurt a limb. But that nature, who worketh all things to perfection, should suffer any pains to breed in our bodies, he thought impossible; and desired to know the reason of so unaccountable an evil. I told him, we fed on a thousand things which operated contrary to each other; that we eat when we were not hungry, and drank without the provocation of thirst; that we sat whole nights drinking strong liquors without eating a bit, which disposed us to sloth, inflamed our bodies, and precipitated or prevented digestion. That, prostitute female Yahoos acquired a certain malady, which bred rottenness in the bones of those who fell into their embraces; that this and many other diseases were propagated from father to son; so that great numbers come into the world with complicated maladies upon them; that it would be endless to give him a catalogue of all diseases incident to human bodies; for they could not be fewer than five or six hundred, spread over every limb, and joint; in short, every part, external and intestine, having diseases appropriated to each. To remedy which, there was a sort of people bred up among us, in the profession or pretense of curing the sick. And because I had some skill in the faculty, I would in gratitude to his honor let him know the whole mystery and method by which they proceed.

Their fundamental is that all diseases arise from repletion; from whence they conclude, that a great evacuation of the body is necessary, either through the natural passage, or upwards at the mouth. Their next business is, from herbs, minerals, gums, oils, shells, salts, juices, seaweed, excrements, barks of trees, serpents, toads, frogs, spiders, dead men's flesh and bones, birds, beasts and fishes, to form a composition for smell and taste the most abominable, nauseous, and detestable, that they can possibly contrive, which the stomach immediately rejects with loathing, and this they call a vomit. Or else from the same storehouse, with some other poisonous additions, they command us to take in at the orifice above or below (just as the physician then happens to be disposed) a medicine equally annoying and disgustful to the bowels; which relaxing the belly, drives down all before it; and this they call a purge, or a clyster. For nature (as the physicians allege) having intended the superior anterior orifice only for the intromission of solids and liquids, and the inferior posterior for ejection, these artists ingeniously considering that in all diseases nature is forced out of her seat; therefore to replace her in it, the body must be treated in a manner directly contrary, by interchanging the use of each orifice; forcing solids and liquids in at the anus, and making evacuations at the mouth.

But, besides real diseases, we are subject to many that are only imaginary, for which the physicians have invented imaginary cures; these have their several names, and so have the drugs that are proper for them; and with these our female Yahoos are always infested.

One great excellency in this tribe is their skill at prognostics, wherein they seldom fail; their predictions in real diseases, when they rise to any degree of malignity, generally portending death, which is always in their power, when recovery is not, and therefore, upon any unexpected signs of amendment, after they have pronounced their sentence, rather than be accused as false prophets, they know how to approve[6] their sagacity to the world by a seasonable dose.

They are likewise of special use to husbands and wives, who are grown weary of their mates; to eldest sons, to great ministers of state, and often to princes.

I had formerly upon occasion discoursed with my master upon the nature of government in general, and particularly of our own excellent constitution, deservedly the wonder and envy of the whole world. But having here accidently mentioned a minister of state, he commanded me some time after to inform him what species of Yahoo I particularly meant by that appellation.

I told him that a first or chief minister of state, whom I intended to describe, was a creature wholly exempt from joy and grief, love and hatred,

6. Prove.

pity and anger; at least makes use of no other passions but a violent desire of wealth, power, and titles; that he applies his words to all uses, except to the indication of his mind; that he never tells a truth, but with an intent that you should take it for a lie; nor a lie, but with a design that you should take it for a truth; that those he speaks worst of behind their backs are in the surest way to preferment; and whenever he begins to praise you to others or to yourself, you are from that day forlorn. The worst mark you can receive is a promise, especially when it is confirmed with an oath; after which every wise man retires, and gives over all hopes.

There are three methods by which a man may rise to be chief minister: the first is by knowing how with prudence to dispose of a wife, a daughter, or a sister; the second, by betraying or undermining his predecessor; and the third is by a furious zeal in public assemblies against the corruptions of the court. But a wise prince would rather choose to employ those who practice the last of these methods; because such zealots prove always the most obsequious and subservient to the will and passions of their master. That, these ministers having all employments at their disposal, preserve themselves in power by bribing the majority of a senate or great council; and at last by an expedient called an Act of Indemnity[7] (whereof I described the nature to him) they secure themselves from after reckonings, and retire from the public, laden with the spoils of the nation.

The palace of a chief minister is a seminary to breed up others in his own trade; the pages, lackies, and porter, by imitating their master, become ministers of state in their several districts, and learn to excel in the three principal ingredients, of insolence, lying, and bribery. Accordingly, they have a subaltern court paid to them by persons of the best rank; and sometimes by the force of dexterity and impudence, arrive through several gradations to be successors to their lord.

He is usually governed by a decayed wench, or favorite footman, who are the tunnels through which all graces are conveyed, and may properly be called, in the last resort, the governors of the kingdom.

One day, my master, having heard me mention the nobility of my country, was pleased to make me a compliment which I could not pretend to deserve: that, he was sure, I must have been born of some noble family, because I far exceeded in shape, color, and cleanliness, all the Yahoos of his nation, although I seemed to fail in strength, and agility, which must be imputed to my different way of living from those other brutes; and besides, I was not only endowed with the faculty of speech, but likewise with some rudiments of reason, to a degree, that with all his acquaintance I passed for a prodigy.

He made me observe, that among the Houyhnhnms, the white, the sorrel, and the iron grey were not so exactly shaped as the bay, the dapple grey, and the black; nor born with equal talents of mind, or a capacity to improve them; and therefore continued always in the condition of servants, without ever aspiring to match out of their own race, which in that country would be reckoned monstrous and unnatural.

I made his honor my most humble acknowledgments for the good opinion he was pleased to conceive of me; but assured him at the same time, that my birth was of the lower sort, having been born of plain, honest parents, who

---

7. An act passed at each session of Parliament to protect ministers of state who in good faith might have acted illegally.

were just able to give me a tolerable education; that, nobility among us was altogether a different thing from the idea he had of it; that, our young noblemen are bred from their childhood in idleness and luxury; that, as soon as years will permit, they consume their vigor, and contract odious diseases among lewd females; and when their fortunes are almost ruined, they marry some woman of mean birth, disagreeable person, and unsound constitution, merely for the sake of money, whom they hate and despise. That, the productions of such marriages are generally scrofulous, rickety or deformed children; by which means the family seldom continues above three generations, unless the wife take care to provide a healthy father among her neighbors, or domestics, in order to improve and continue the breed. That a weak diseased body, a meager countenance, and sallow complexion are the true marks of noble blood; and a healthy robust appearance is so disgraceful in a man of quality, that the world concludes his real father to have been a groom or a coachman. The imperfections of his mind run parallel with those of his body; being a composition of spleen, dullness, ignorance, caprice, sensuality, and pride.

Without the consent of this illustrious body, no law can be enacted, repealed, or altered, and these nobles have likewise the decision of all our possessions without appeal.

CHAPTER 7. *The Author's great love of his native country. His master's observations upon the constitution and administration of England, as described by the Author, with parallel cases and comparisons. His master's observations upon human nature.*

The reader may be disposed to wonder how I could prevail on myself to give so free a representation of my own species, among a race of mortals who were already too apt to conceive the vilest opinion of humankind, from that entire congruity betwixt me and their Yahoos. But I must freely confess that the many virtues of those excellent quadrupeds placed in opposite view to human corruptions had so far opened my eyes, and enlarged my understanding, that I began to view the actions and passions of man in a very different light; and to think the honor of my own kind not worth managing;[8] which, besides, it was impossible for me to do before a person of so acute a judgment as my master, who daily convinced me of a thousand faults in myself, whereof I had not the least perception before, and which with us would never be numbered even among human infirmities. I had likewise learned from his example an utter detestation of all falsehood or disguise; and truth appeared so amiable to me, that I determined upon sacrificing everything to it.

Let me deal so candidly with the reader as to confess that there was yet a much stronger motive for the freedom I took in my representation of things. I had not been a year in this country, before I contracted such a love and veneration for the inhabitants, that I entered on a firm resolution never to return to humankind, but to pass the rest of my life among these admirable Houyhnhnms in the contemplation and practice of every virtue; where I could have no example or incitement to vice. But it was decreed by fortune, my perpetual enemy, that so great a felicity should not fall to my share. However, it is now some comfort to reflect that in what I said of my countrymen,

8. Taking care of.

I extenuated their faults as much as I durst before so strict an examiner; and upon every article, gave as favorable a turn as the matter would bear. For, indeed, who is there alive that will not be swayed by his bias and partiality to the place of his birth?

I have related the substance of several conversations I had with my master, during the greatest part of the time I had the honor to be in his service; but have indeed for brevity sake omitted much more than is here set down.

When I had answered all his questions, and his curiosity seemed to be fully satisfied; he sent for me one morning early, and commanding me to sit down at some distance (an honor which he had never before conferred upon me), he said he had been very seriously considering my whole story, as far as it related both to myself and my country; that, he looked upon us as a sort of animals to whose share, by what accident he could not conjecture, some small pittance of reason had fallen, whereof we made no other use than by its assistance to aggravate our natural corruptions, and to acquire new ones which nature had not given us. That we disarmed ourselves of the few abilities she had bestowed; had been very successful in multiplying our original wants, and seemed to spend our whole lives in vain endeavors to supply them by our own inventions. That, as to myself, it was manifest I had neither the strength or agility of a common Yahoo; that I walked infirmly on my hinder feet; had found out a contrivance to make my claws of no use or defense, and to remove the hair from my chin, which was intended as a shelter from the sun and the weather. Lastly, that I could neither run with speed, nor climb trees like my brethren (as he called them) the Yahoos in this country.

That our institutions of government and law were plainly owing to our gross defects in reason, and by consequence, in virtue; because reason alone is sufficient to govern a rational creature; which was therefore a character we had no pretense to challenge, even from the account I had given of my own people; although he manifestly perceived, that in order to favor them, I had concealed many particulars, and often *said the thing which was not.*

He was the more confirmed in this opinion, because he observed that I agreed in every feature of my body with other Yahoos, except where it was to my real disadvantage in point of strength, speed, and activity, the shortness of my claws, and some other particulars where Nature had no part; so, from the representation I had given him of our lives, our manners, and our actions, he found as near a resemblance in the disposition of our minds. He said the Yahoos were known to hate one another more than they did any different species of animals; and the reason usually assigned was the odiousness of their own shapes, which all could see in the rest, but not in themselves. He had therefore begun to think it not unwise in us to cover our bodies, and by that invention, conceal many of our deformities from each other, which would else be hardly supportable. But he now found he had been mistaken; and that the dissensions of those brutes in his country were owing to the same cause with ours, as I had described them. For, if (said he) you throw among five Yahoos as much food as would be sufficient for fifty, they will instead of eating peaceably, fall together by the ears, each single one impatient to have all to itself; and therefore a servant was usually employed to stand by while they were feeding abroad, and those kept at home were tied at a distance from each other. That, if a cow died of age or accident, before a Houyhnhnm could secure it for his own Yahoos, those in the neighborhood would come in herds to seize it, and then would ensue such a battle as I had described, with terrible wounds made by their claws on both sides, although they seldom were able to kill one another, for want of such convenient instruments of death as we had invented. At other times the like battles have been fought between the Yahoos of several neighborhoods without any visible cause; those of one district watching all opportunities to surprise the next before they are prepared. But if they find their project hath miscarried, they return home, and for want of enemies, engage in what I call a civil war among themselves.

That, in some fields of his country, there are certain shining stones of several colors, whereof the Yahoos are violently fond; and when part of these stones are fixed in the earth, as it sometimes happeneth, they will dig with their claws for whole days to get them out, and carry them away, and hide them by heaps in their kennels; but still looking round with great caution, for fear their comrades should find out their treasure. My master said he could never discover the reason of this unnatural appetite, or how these stones could be of any use to a Yahoo; but now he believed it might proceed from the same principle of avarice, which I had ascribed to mankind. That he had once, by way of experiment, privately removed a heap of these stones from the place where one of his Yahoos had buried it, whereupon, the sordid animal missing his treasure, by his loud lamenting brought the whole herd to the place, there miserably howled, then fell to biting and tearing the rest; began to pine away, would neither eat nor sleep, nor work, till he ordered a servant privately to convey the stones into the same hole, and hide them as before; which when his Yahoo had found, he presently recovered his spirits and good humor; but took care to remove them to a better hiding place; and hath ever since been a very serviceable brute.

My master farther assured me, which I also observed myself, that in the fields where these shining stones abound, the fiercest and most frequent battles are fought, occasioned by perpetual inroads of the neighboring Yahoos.

He said it was common when two Yahoos discovered such a stone in a field, and were contending which of them should be the proprietor, a third would take the advantage, and carry it away from them both; which my master would needs contend to have some resemblance with our suits at law; wherein I thought it for our credit not to undeceive him; since the decision he mentioned was much more equitable than many decrees among us; because the plaintiff and defendant there lost nothing beside the stone they contended for; whereas our courts of equity would never have dismissed the cause while either of them had anything left.

My master continuing his discourse said there was nothing that rendered the Yahoos more odious, than their undistinguished appetite to devour everything that came in their way, whether herbs, roots, berries, corrupted flesh of animals, or all mingled together; and it was peculiar in their temper, that they were fonder of what they could get by rapine or stealth at a greater distance, than much better food provided for them at home. If their prey held out, they would eat till they were ready to burst, after which nature had pointed out to them a certain root that gave them a general evacuation.

There was also another kind of root very juicy, but something rare and difficult to be found, which the Yahoos sought for with much eagerness, and would suck it with great delight; it produced the same effects that wine hath upon us. It would make them sometimes hug, and sometimes tear one another; they would howl and grin, and chatter, and reel, and tumble, and then fall asleep in the mud.

I did indeed observe that the Yahoos were the only animals in this country subject to any diseases; which however, were much fewer than horses have among us, and contracted not by any ill treatment they meet with, but by the nastiness and greediness of that sordid brute. Neither has their language any more than a general appellation for those maladies; which is borrowed from the name of the beast, and called *Hnea Yahoo,* or the Yahoo's Evil; and the cure prescribed is a mixture of their own dung and urine, forcibly put down the Yahoo's throat. This I have since often known to have been taken with success, and do here freely recommend it to my countrymen, for the public good, as an admirable specific[9] against all diseases produced by repletion.

As to learning, government, arts, manufactures, and the like, my master confessed he could find little or no resemblance between the Yahoos of that country and those in ours. For he only meant to observe what parity there was in our natures. He had heard indeed some curious Houyhnhnms observe that in most herds there was a sort of ruling Yahoo (as among us there is generally some leading or principal stag in a park) who was always more deformed in body, and mischievous in disposition, than any of the rest. That this leader had usually a favorite as like himself as he could get, whose employment was to lick his master's feet and posteriors, and drive the female Yahoos to his kennel; for which he was now and then rewarded with a piece of ass's flesh. This favorite is hated by the whole herd; and therefore to protect himself, keeps always near the person of his leader. He usually continues in office till a worse can be found; but the very moment he is discarded, his successor, at the head of all the Yahoos in that district, young and old, male and female, come in a body, and discharge their excrements upon him from head to foot. But how far this might be applicable to our courts and favorites, and ministers of state, my master said I could best determine.

I durst make no return to this malicious insinuation, which debased human understanding below the sagacity of a common hound, who hath judgment enough to distinguish and follow the cry of the ablest dog in the pack, without being ever mistaken.

My master told me there were some qualities remarkable in the Yahoos, which he had not observed me to mention, or at least very slightly, in the accounts I had given him of humankind. He said, those animals, like other brutes, had their females in common; but in this they differed, that the she-Yahoo would admit the male while she was pregnant; and that the hes would quarrel and fight with the females as fiercely as with each other. Both which practices were such degrees of infamous brutality, that no other sensitive creature ever arrived at.

Another thing he wondered at in the Yahoos was their strange disposition to nastiness and dirt; whereas there appears to be a natural love of cleanliness in all other animals. As to the two former accusations, I was glad to let them pass without any reply, because I had not a word to offer upon them in defense of my species, which otherwise I certainly had done from my own inclinations. But I could have easily vindicated humankind from the imputation of singularity upon the last article, if there had been any swine in that country (as unluckily for me there were not) which although it may be a

9. Remedy.

sweeter quadruped than a Yahoo, cannot I humbly conceive in justice pretend to more cleanliness; and so his honor himself must have owned, if he had seen their filthy way of feeding, and their custom of wallowing and sleeping in the mud.

My master likewise mentioned another quality, which his servants had discovered in several Yahoos, and to him was wholly unaccountable. He said, a fancy would sometimes take a Yahoo, to retire into a corner, to lie down and howl, and groan, and spurn away all that came near him, although he were young and fat, and wanted neither food nor water; nor did the servants imagine what could possibly ail him. And the only remedy they found was to set him to hard work, after which he would infallibly come to himself. To this I was silent out of partiality to my own kind; yet here I could plainly discover the true seeds of spleen,[1] which only seizeth on the lazy, the luxurious, and the rich; who, if they were forced to undergo the same regimen, I would undertake for the cure.

His Honor had farther observed, that a female Yahoo would often stand behind a bank or a bush, to gaze on the young males passing by, and then appear, and hide, using many antic gestures and grimaces; at which time it was observed, that she had a most offensive smell; and when any of the males advanced, would slowly retire, looking back, and with a counterfeit show of fear, run off into some convenient place where she knew the male would follow her.

At other times, if a female stranger came among them, three or four of her own sex would get about her, and stare and chatter, and grin, and smell her all over; and then turn off with gestures that seemed to express contempt and disdain.

Perhaps my master might refine a little in these speculations, which he had drawn from what he observed himself, or had been told by others; however, I could not reflect without some amazement, and much sorrow, that the rudiments of lewdness, coquetry, censure, and scandal, should have place by instinct in womankind.

I expected every moment that my master would accuse the Yahoos of those unnatural appetites in both sexes, so common among us. But Nature it seems hath not been so expert a schoolmistress; and these politer pleasures are entirely the productions of art and reason, on our side of the globe.

CHAPTER 8. *The Author relateth several particulars of the Yahoos. The great virtues of the Houyhnhnms. The education and exercises of their youth. Their general assembly.*

As I ought to have understood human nature much better than I supposed it possible for my master to do, so it was easy to apply the character he gave of the Yahoos to myself and my countrymen; and I believed I could yet make farther discoveries from my own observation. I therefore often begged his honor to let me go among the herds of Yahoos in the neighborhood; to which he always very graciously consented, being perfectly convinced that the hatred I bore those brutes would never suffer me to be corrupted by them; and his honor ordered one of his servants, a strong sorrel nag, very honest and good-natured, to be my guard; without whose protection I durst not

1. Depression.

undertake such adventures. For I have already told the reader how much I was pestered by those odious animals upon my first arrival. I afterwards failed very narrowly three or four times of falling into their clutches, when I happened to stray at any distance without my hanger. And I have reason to believe, they had some imagination that I was of their own species, which I often assisted myself, by stripping up my sleeves, and shewing my naked arms and breast in their sight, when my protector was with me; at which times they would approach as near as they durst, and imitate my actions after the manner of monkeys, but ever with great signs of hatred; as a tame jackdaw with cap and stockings is always persecuted by the wild ones, when he happens to be got among them.

They are prodigiously nimble from their infancy; however, I once caught a young male of three years old, and endeavored by all marks of tenderness to make it quiet; but the little imp fell a squalling, scratching, and biting with such violence, that I was forced to let it go; and it was high time, for a whole troop of old ones came about us at the noise; but finding the cub was safe (for away it ran) and my sorrel nag being by, they durst not venture near us. I observed the young animal's flesh to smell very rank, and the stink was somewhat between a weasel and a fox, but much more disagreeable. I forgot another circumstance (and perhaps I might have the reader's pardon, if it were wholly omitted) that while I held the odious vermin in my hands, it voided its filthy excrements of a yellow liquid substance, all over my clothes; but by good fortune there was a small brook hard by, where I washed myself as clean as I could; although I durst not come into my master's presence until I were sufficiently aired.

By what I could discover, the Yahoos appear to be the most unteachable of all animals, their capacities never reaching higher than to draw or carry burdens. Yet I am of opinion, this defect ariseth chiefly from a perverse, restive disposition. For they are cunning, malicious, treacherous and revengeful. They are strong and hardy, but of a cowardly spirit, and by consequence insolent, abject, and cruel. It is observed that the red-haired of both sexes are more libidinous and mischievous than the rest, whom yet they much exceed in strength and activity.

The Houyhnhnms keep the Yahoos for present use in huts not far from the house; but the rest are sent abroad to certain fields, where they dig up roots, eat several kinds of herbs, and search about for carrion, or sometimes catch weasels and *luhimuhs* (a sort of wild rat) which they greedily devour. Nature hath taught them to dig deep holes with their nails on the side of a rising ground, wherein they lie by themselves; only the kennels of the females are larger, sufficient to hold two or three cubs.

They swim from their infancy like frogs, and are able to continue long under water, where they often take fish, which the females carry home to their young. And upon this occasion, I hope the reader will pardon my relating an odd adventure.

Being one day abroad with my protector the sorrel nag, and the weather exceeding hot, I entreated him to let me bathe in a river that was near. He consented, and I immediately stripped myself stark naked, and went down softly into the stream. It happened that a young female Yahoo standing behind a bank, saw the whole proceeding; and inflamed by desire, as the nag and I conjectured, came running with all speed, and leaped into the water within five yards of the place where I bathed. I was never in my life so terribly frighted; the nag was grazing at some distance, not suspecting any harm. She embraced me after a most fulsome manner; I roared as loud as I could, and the nag came galloping towards me, whereupon she quitted her grasp, with the utmost reluctancy, and leaped upon the opposite bank, where she stood gazing and howling all the time I was putting on my clothes.

This was matter of diversion to my master and his family, as well as of mortification to myself. For now I could no longer deny that I was a real Yahoo, in every limb and feature, since the females had a natural propensity to me as one of their own species; neither was the hair of this brute of a red color (which might have been some excuse for an appetite a little irregular) but black as a sloe, and her countenance did not make an appearance altogether so hideous as the rest of the kind; for I think, she could not be above eleven years old.

Having already lived three years in this country, the reader I suppose will expect that I should, like other travelers, give him some account of the manners and customs of its inhabitants, which it was indeed my principal study to learn.

As these noble Houyhnhnms are endowed by Nature with a general disposition to all virtues, and have no conceptions or ideas of what is evil in a rational creature; so their grand maxim is to cultivate reason, and to be wholly governed by it. Neither is reason among them a point problematical as with us, where men can argue with plausibility on both sides of a question; but strikes you with immediate conviction; as it must needs do where it is not mingled, obscured, or discolored by passion and interest. I remember it was with extreme difficulty that I could bring my master to understand the meaning of the word "opinion," or how a point could be disputable; because reason taught us to affirm or deny only where we are certain; and beyond our knowledge we cannot do either. So that controversies, wranglings, disputes, and positiveness in false or dubious propositions are evils unknown among the Houyhnhnms. In the like manner when I used to explain to him our several systems of natural philosophy,[2] he would laugh that a creature pretending to reason should value itself upon the knowledge of other people's conjectures, and in things, where that knowledge, if it were certain, could be of no use. Wherein he agreed entirely with the sentiments of Socrates, as Plato delivers them, which I mention as the highest honor I can do that prince of philosophers. I have often since reflected what destruction such a doctrine would make in the libraries of Europe; and how many paths to fame would be then shut up in the learned world.

Friendship and benevolence are the two principal virtues among the Houyhnhnms; and these not confined to particular objects, but universal to the whole race. For a stranger from the remotest part is equally treated with the nearest neighbor, and wherever he goes, looks upon himself as at home. They preserve decency and civility in the highest degrees, but are altogether ignorant of ceremony. They have no fondness for their colts or foals; but the care they take in educating them proceedeth entirely from the dictates of reason. And I observed my master to show the same affection to his neighbor's issue that he had for his own. They will have it that Nature teaches them to love the whole species, and it is reason only that maketh a distinction of persons, where there is a superior degree of virtue.

2. Science.

When the matron Houyhnhnms have produced one of each sex, they no longer accompany with their consorts, except they lose one of their issue by some casualty, which very seldom happens; but in such a case they meet again; or when the like accident befalls a person whose wife is past bearing, some other couple bestows on him one of their own colts, and then go together a second time, until the mother be pregnant. This caution is necessary to prevent the country from being overburdened with numbers. But the race of inferior Houyhnhnms bred up to be servants is not so strictly limited upon this article; these are allowed to produce three of each sex, to be domestics in the noble families.

In their marriages they are exactly careful to choose such colors as will not make any disagreeable mixture in the breed. Strength is chiefly valued in the male, and comeliness in the female; not upon the account of love, but to preserve the race from degenerating; for, where a female happens to excel in strength, a consort is chosen with regard to comeliness. Courtship, love, presents, jointures, settlements, have no place in their thoughts, or terms whereby to express them in their language. The young couple meet and are joined, merely because it is the determination of their parents and friends; it is what they see done every day; and they look upon it as one of the necessary actions in a reasonable being. But the violation of marriage, or any other unchastity, was never heard of; and the married pair pass their lives with the same friendship and mutual benevolence that they bear to all others of the same species who come in their way, without jealousy, fondness, quarreling, or discontent.

In educating the youth of both sexes, their method is admirable, and highly deserveth our imitation. These are not suffered to taste a grain of oats, except upon certain days, till eighteen years old; nor milk, but very rarely; and in summer they graze two hours in the morning, and as many in the evening, which their parents likewise observe; but the servants are not allowed above half that time; and a great part of the grass is brought home, which they eat at the most convenient hours when they can be best spared from work.

Temperance, industry, exercise, and cleanliness are the lessons equally enjoined to the young ones of both sexes; and my master thought it monstrous in us to give the females a different kind of education from the males, except in some articles of domestic management; whereby, as he truly observed, one half of our natives were good for nothing but bringing children into the world; and to trust the care of their children to such useless animals, he said was yet a greater instance of brutality.

But the Houyhnhnms train up their youth to strength, speed, and hardiness, by exercising them in running races up and down steep hills, or over hard stony grounds; and when they are all in a sweat, they are ordered to leap over head and ears into a pond or a river. Four times a year the youth of certain districts meet to show their proficiency in running, and leaping, and other feats of strength or agility; where the victor is rewarded with a song made in his or her praise. On this festival the servants drive a herd of Yahoos into the field, laden with hay, and oats, and milk for a repast to the Houyhnhnms; after which these brutes are immediately driven back again, for fear of being noisome to the assembly.

Every fourth year, at the vernal equinox, there is a representative council of the whole nation, which meets in a plain about twenty miles from our house, and continueth about five or six days. Here they inquire into the state and condition of the several districts; whether they abound or be deficient in hay or oats, or cows or Yahoos? And wherever there is any want (which is but seldom) it is immediately supplied by unanimous consent and contribution. Here likewise the regulation of children is settled: as for instance, if a Houyhnhnm hath two males, he changeth one of them with another who hath two females, and when a child hath been lost by any casualty, where the mother is past breeding, it is determined what family in the district shall breed another to supply the loss.

CHAPTER 9. *A grand debate at the general assembly of the Houyhnhnms, and how it was determined. The learning of the Houyhnhnms. Their buildings. Their manner of burials. The defectiveness of their language.*

One of these grand assemblies was held in my time, about three months before my departure, whither my master went as the representative of our district. In this council was resumed their old debate, and indeed, the only debate that ever happened in their country; whereof my master after his return gave me a very particular account.

The question to be debated was whether the Yahoos should be exterminated from the face of the earth. One of the members for the affirmative offered several arguments of great strength and weight, alleging that, as the Yahoos were the most filthy, noisome, and deformed animal which nature ever produced, so they were the most restive and indocible,[3] mischievous, and malicious; they would privately suck the teats of the Houyhnhnms' cows; kill and devour their cats, trample down their oats and grass, if they were not continually watched; and commit a thousand other extravagancies. He took notice of a general tradition, that Yahoos had not been always in their country, but that many ages ago, two of these brutes appeared together upon a mountain; whether produced by the heat of the sun upon corrupted mud and slime, or from the ooze and froth of the sea, was never known. That these Yahoos engendered, and their brood in a short time grew so numerous as to overrun and infest the whole nation. That the Houyhnhnms to get rid of this evil, made a general hunting, and at last enclosed the whole herd; and destroying the older, every Houyhnhnm kept two young ones in a kennel, and brought them to such a degree of tameness as an animal so savage by nature can be capable of acquiring, using them for draught and carriage. That there seemed to be much truth in this tradition, and that those creatures could not be *ylnhniamshy* (or aborigines of the land) because of the violent hatred the Houyhnhnms as well as all other animals bore them; which although their evil disposition sufficiently deserved, could never have arrived at so high a degree, if they had been aborigines, or else they would have long since been rooted out. That the inhabitants taking a fancy to use the service of the Yahoos, had very imprudently neglected to cultivate the breed of asses, which were a comely animal, easily kept, more tame and orderly, without any offensive smell, strong enough for labor, although they yield to the other in agility of body; and if their braying be no agreeable sound, it is far preferable to the horrible howlings of the Yahoos.

Several others declared their sentiments to the same purpose, when my master proposed an expedient to the assembly, whereof he had indeed bor-

3. Unteachable.

rowed the hint from me. He approved of the tradition, mentioned by the honorable member, who spoke before; and affirmed, that the two Yahoos said to be first seen among them, had been driven thither over the sea; that coming to land, and being forsaken by their companions, they retired to the mountains, and degenerating by degrees, became in process of time much more savage than those of their own species in the country from whence these two originals came. The reason of his assertion was that he had now in his possession a certain wonderful Yahoo (meaning myself) which most of them had heard of, and many of them had seen. He then related to them how he first found me; that my body was all covered with an artificial composure of the skins and hairs of other animals; that I spoke in a language of my own, and had thoroughly learned theirs; that I had related to him the accidents which brought me thither; that when he saw me without my covering, I was an exact Yahoo in every part, only of a whiter color, less hairy and with shorter claws. He added how I had endeavored to persuade him that in my own and other countries the Yahoos acted as the governing, rational animal, and held the Houyhnhnms in servitude; that he observed in me all the qualities of a Yahoo, only a little more civilized by some tincture of reason, which however was in a degree as far inferior to the Houyhnhnm race as the Yahoos of their country were to me; that among other things, I mentioned a custom we had of castrating Houyhnhnms when they were young, in order to render them tame; that the operation was easy and safe; that it was no shame to learn wisdom from brutes, as industry is taught by the ant, and building by the swallow (for so I translate the world *lyhannh*, although it be a much larger fowl). That this invention might be practiced upon the younger Yahoos here, which, besides rendering them tractable and fitter for use, would in an age put an end to the whole species without destroying life. That in the meantime the Houyhnhnms should be exhorted to cultivate the breed of asses, which, as they are in all respects more valuable brutes, so they have this advantage, to be fit for service at five years old, which the other are not till twelve.

This was all my master thought fit to tell me at that time, of what passed in the grand council. But he was pleased to conceal one particular, which related personally to myself, whereof I soon felt the unhappy effect, as the reader will know in its proper place, and from whence I date all the succeeding misfortunes of my life.

The Houyhnhnms have no letters, and consequently, their knowledge is all traditional. But there happening few events of any moment among a people so well united, naturally disposed to every virtue, wholly governed by reason, and cut off from all commerce with other nations, the historical part is easily preserved without burdening their memories. I have already observed that they are subject to no diseases, and therefore can have no need of physicians. However, they have excellent medicines composed of herbs, to cure accidental bruises and cuts in the pastern or frog[4] of the foot by sharp stones, as well as other maims and hurts in the several parts of the body.

They calculate the year by the revolution of the sun and the moon, but use no subdivisions into weeks. They are well enough acquainted with the motions of those two luminaries, and understand the nature of eclipses; and this is the utmost progress of their astronomy.

4. Sole.

In poetry they must be allowed to excel all other mortals; wherein the justness of their similes, and the minuteness, as well as exactness of their descriptions, are indeed inimitable. Their verses abound very much in both of these, and usually contain either some exalted notions of friendship and benevolence, or the praises of those who were victors in races and other bodily exercises. Their buildings, although very rude and simple, are not inconvenient, but well contrived to defend them from all injuries of cold and heat. They have a kind of tree, which at forty years old loosens in the root, and falls with the first storm; it grows very straight, and being pointed like stakes with a sharp stone (for the Houyhnhnms know not the use of iron), they stick them erect in the ground about ten inches asunder, and then weave in oat straw, or sometimes wattles, betwixt them. The roof is made after the same manner, and so are the doors.

The Houyhnhnms use the hollow part between the pastern and the hoof of their forefeet as we do our hands, and this with greater dexterity than I could at first imagine. I have seen a white mare of our family thread a needle (which I lent her on purpose) with that joint. They milk their cows, reap their oats, and do all the work which requires hands in the same manner. They have a kind of hard flints, which by grinding against other stones they form into instruments that serve instead of wedges, axes, and hammers. With tools made of these flints, they likewise cut their hay, and reap their oats, which there groweth naturally in several fields. The Yahoos draw home the sheaves in carriages, and the servants tread them in certain covered huts, to get out the grain, which is kept in stores. They make a rude kind of earthen and wooden vessels, and bake the former in the sun.

If they can avoid casualties, they die only of old age, and are buried in the obscurest places that can be found, their friends and relations expressing neither joy nor grief at their departure; nor does the dying person discover the least regret that he is leaving the world, any more than if he were upon returning home from a visit to one of his neighbors; I remember my master having once made an appointment with a friend and his family to come to his house upon some affair of importance; on the day fixed, the mistress and her two children came very late; she made two excuses, first for her husband, who, as she said, happened that very morning to *lhnuwnh*. The word is strongly expressive in their language, but not easily rendered into English; it signifies, *to retire to his first Mother*. Her excuse for not coming sooner was that her husband dying late in the morning, she was a good while consulting her servants about a convenient place where his body should be laid; and I observed she behaved herself at our house, as cheerfully as the rest. She died about three months after.

They live generally to seventy or seventy-five years, very seldom to four-score; some weeks before their death they feel a gradual decay, but without pain. During this time they are much visited by their friends, because they cannot go abroad with their usual ease and satisfaction. However, about ten days before their death, which they seldom fail in computing, they return the visits that have been made by those who are nearest in the neighborhood, being carried in a convenient sledge drawn by Yahoos; which vehicle they use, not only upon this occasion, but when they grow old, upon long journeys, or when they are lamed by any accident. And therefore when the dying Houyhnhnms return those visits, they take a solemn leave of their friends, as if they were going to some remote part of the country, where they designed to pass the rest of their lives.

I know not whether it may be worth observing, that the Houyhnhnms have no word in their language to express anything that is evil, except what they borrow from the deformities or ill qualities of the Yahoos. Thus they denote the folly of a servant, an omission of a child, a stone that cuts their feet, a continuance of foul or unseasonable weather, and the like, by adding to each the epithet of Yahoo. For instance, *hhnm Yahoo, whnaholm Yahoo, ynlhmnd-wihlma Yahoo,* and an ill-contrived house, *ynholmhnmrohlnw Yahoo.*

I could with great pleasure enlarge farther upon the manners and virtues of this excellent people; but intending in a short time to publish a volume by itself expressly upon that subject, I refer the reader thither. And in the meantime, proceed to relate my own sad catastrophe.

CHAPTER 10. *The Author's economy, and happy life among the Houyhnhnms. His great improvement in virtue, by conversing with them. Their conversations. The Author hath notice given him by his master that he must depart from the country. He falls into a swoon for grief, but submits. He contrives and finishes a canoe, by the help of a fellow servant, and puts to sea at a venture.*

I had settled my little economy to my own heart's content. My master had ordered a room to be made for me after their manner, about six yards from the house; the sides and floors of which I plastered with clay, and covered with rush mats of my own contriving; I had beaten hemp, which there grows wild, and made of it a sort of ticking; this I filled with the feathers of several birds I had taken with springes made of Yahoos' hairs, and were excellent food. I had worked two chairs with my knife, the sorrel nag helping me in the grosser and more laborious part. When my clothes were worn to rags, I made myself others with the skins of rabbits, and of a certain beautiful animal about the same size, called *nnuhnoh,* the skin of which is covered with a fine down. Of these I likewise made very tolerable stockings. I soled my shoes with wood which I cut from a tree, and fitted to the upper leather, and when this was worn out, I supplied it with the skins of Yahoos, dried in the sun. I often got honey out of hollow trees, which I mingled with water, or eat it with my bread. No man could more verify the truth of these two maxims, that *Nature is very easily satisfied*; and, that *Necessity is the mother of invention.* I enjoyed perfect health of body, and tranquility of mind; I did not feel the treachery or inconstancy of a friend, nor the inquiries of a secret or open enemy. I had no occasion of bribing, flattering, or pimping to procure the favor of any great man, or of his minion. I wanted no fence against fraud or oppression; here was neither physician to destroy my body, nor lawyer to ruin my fortune; no informer to watch my words and actions, or forge accusations against me for hire; here were no gibers, censurers, backbiters, pickpockets, highwaymen, housebreakers, attorneys, bawds, buffoons, gamesters, politicians, wits, splenetics, tedious talkers, controvertists, ravishers, murderers, robbers, virtuosos;[5] no leaders or followers of party and faction; no encouragers to vice, by seducement or examples; no dungeons, axes, gibbets, whipping posts, or pillories; no cheating shopkeepers or mechanics; no pride, vanity or affectation; no fops, bullies, drunkards, strolling whores, or poxes; no ranting, lewd, expensive wives; no stupid, proud pedants; no importunate, overbearing, quarrelsome, noisy, roaring, empty, conceited, swearing companions; no scoundrels raised from the dust upon the merit of their vices; or nobility

5. Those who pursue special interests in the arts or sciences.

thrown into it on account of their virtues; no lords, fiddlers, judges, or dancing masters.

I had the favor of being admitted to several Houyhnhnms, who came to visit or dine with my master; where his honor graciously suffered me to wait in the room, and listen to their discourse. Both he and his company would often descend to ask me questions, and receive my answers. I had also sometimes the honor of attending my master in his visits to others. I never presumed to speak, except in answer to a question; and then I did it with inward regret, because it was a loss of so much time for improving myself; but I was infinitely delighted with the station of an humble auditor in such conversations, where nothing passed but what was useful, expressed in the fewest and most significant words; where (as I have already said) the greatest decency was observed, without the least degree of ceremony; where no person spoke without being pleased himself, and pleasing his companions; where there was no interruption, tediousness, heat, or difference of sentiments. They have a notion, that when people are met together, a short silence doth much improve conversation; this I found to be true; for during those little intermissions of talk, new ideas would arise in their minds, which very much enlivened the discourse. Their subjects are generally on friendship and benevolence; on order and economy; sometimes upon the visible operations of nature, or ancient traditions; upon the bounds and limits of virtue; upon the unerring rules of reason; or upon some determinations, to be taken at the next great assembly; and often upon the various excellencies of poetry. I may add, without vanity, that my presence often gave them sufficient matter for discourse, because it afforded my master an occasion of letting his friends into the history of me and my country, upon which they were all pleased to descant in a manner not very advantageous to human kind; and for that reason I shall not repeat what they said; only I maybe allowed to observe that his honor, to my great admiration, appeared to understand the nature of Yahoos much better than myself. He went through all our vices and follies, and discovered many which I had never mentioned to him; by only supposing what qualities a Yahoo of their country, with a small proportion of reason, might be capable of exerting; and concluded, with too much probability, how vile as well as miserable such a creature must be.

I freely confess, that all the little knowledge I have of any value was acquired by the lectures I received from my master, and from hearing the discourses of him and his friends; to which I should be prouder to listen, than to dictate to the greatest and wisest assembly in Europe. I admired the strength, comeliness, and speed of the inhabitants; and such a constellation of virtues in such amiable persons produced in me the highest veneration. At first, indeed, I did not feel that natural awe which the Yahoos and all other animals bear towards them; but it grew upon me by degrees, much sooner than I imagined, and was mingled with a respectful love and gratitude, that they would condescend to distinguish me from the rest of my species.

When I thought of my family, my friends, my countrymen, or human race in general, I considered them as they really were, Yahoos in shape and disposition, perhaps a little more civilized, and qualified with the gift of speech; but making no other use of reason than to improve and multiply those vices, whereof their brethren in this country had only the share that nature allotted them. When I happened to behold the reflection of my own form in a lake or fountain, I turned away my face in horror and detestation of myself, and could better endure the sight of a common Yahoo than of my own person. By conversing with the Houyhnhnms, and looking upon them with delight, I fell to imitate their gait and gesture, which is now grown into a habit; and my friends often tell me in a blunt way, that I trot like a horse; which, however, I take for a great compliment. Neither shall I disown, that in speaking I am apt to fall into the voice and manner of the Houyhnhnms, and hear myself ridiculed on that account without the least mortification.

In the midst of this happiness, when I looked upon myself to be fully settled for life, my master sent for me one morning a little earlier than his usual hour. I observed by his countenance that he was in some perplexity, and at a loss how to begin what he had to speak. After a short silence, he told me, he did not know how I would take what he was going to say; that, in the last general assembly, when the affair of the Yahoos was entered upon, the representatives had taken offense at his keeping a Yahoo (meaning myself) in his family more like a Houyhnhnm than a brute animal. That he was known frequently to converse with me, as if he could receive some advantage of pleasure in my company; that such a practice was not agreeable to reason or nature, or a thing ever heard of before among them. The assembly did therefore exhort him, either to employ me like the rest of my species, or command me to swim back to the place from whence I came. That the first of these expedients was utterly rejected by all the Houyhnhnms who had ever seen me at his house or their own; for, they alleged, that because I had some rudiments of reason, added to the natural pravity[6] of those animals, it was to be feared, I might be able to seduce them into the woody and mountainous parts of the country, and bring them in troops by night to destroy the Houyhnhnms' cattle, as being naturally of the ravenous kind, and averse from labor.

My master added that he was daily pressed by the Houyhnhnms of the neighborhood to have the assembly's exhortation executed, which he could not put off much longer. He doubted[7] it would be impossible for me to swim to another country; and therefore wished I would contrive some sort of vehicle resembling those I had described to him, that might carry me on the sea; in which work I should have the assistance of his own servants, as well as those of his neighbors. He concluded that for his own part he could have been content to keep me in his service as long as I lived; because he found I had cured myself of some bad habits and dispositions, by endeavoring, as far as my inferior nature was capable, to imitate the Houyhnhnms.

I should here observe to the reader, that a decree of the general assembly in this country is expressed by the word *hnhloayn*, which signifies an exhortation, as near as I can render it; for they have no conception how a rational creature can be compelled, but only advised, or exhorted; because no person can disobey reason without giving up his claim to be a rational creature.

I was struck with the utmost grief and despair at my master's discourse; and being unable to support the agonies I was under, I fell into a swoon at his feet; when I came to myself, he told me that he concluded I had been dead (for these people are subject to no such imbecilities of nature). I answered, in a faint voice, that death would have been too great an happiness; that although I could not blame the assembly's exhortation, or the urgency of his friends; yet in my weak and corrupt judgment, I thought it

6. Corruption.   7. Feared.

might consist with reason to have been less rigorous. That I could not swim a league, and probably the nearest land to theirs might be distant above an hundred; that many materials, necessary for making a small vessel to carry me off, were wholly wanting in this country, which, however, I would attempt in obedience and gratitude to his honor, although I concluded the thing to be impossible, and therefore looked on myself as already devoted to destruction. That the certain prospect of an unnatural death was the least of my evils; for, supposing I should escape with life by some strange adventure, how could I think with temper[8] of passing my days among Yahoos, and relapsing into my old corruptions, for want of examples to lead and keep me within the paths of virtue. That I knew too well upon what solid reasons all the determinations of the wise Houyhnhnms were founded, not to be shaken by arguments of mine, a miserable Yahoo; and therefore after presenting him with my humble thanks for the offer of his servants' assistance in making a vessel, and desiring a reasonable time for so difficult a work, I told him I would endeavor to preserve a wretched being; and, if ever I returned to England, was not without hopes of being useful to my own species by celebrating the praises of the renowned Houyhnhnms, and proposing their virtues to the imitation of mankind.

My master in a few words made me a very gracious reply, allowed me the space of two months to finish my boat, and ordered the sorrel nag, my fellow servant (for so at this distance I may presume to call him), to follow my instructions, because I told my master that his help would be sufficient, and I knew he had a tenderness for me.

In his company my first business was to go to that part of the coast where my rebellious crew had ordered me to be set on shore. I got upon a height, and looking on every side into the sea, fancied I saw a small island towards the northeast; I took out my pocket glass, and could then clearly distinguish it about five leagues off, as I computed; but it appeared to the sorrel nag to be only a blue cloud; for, as he had no conception of any country besides his own, so he could not be as expert in distinguishing remote objects at sea, as we who so much converse in that element.

After I had discovered this island, I considered no farther; but resolved, it should, if possible, be the first place of my banishment, leaving the consequence to fortune.

I returned home, and consulting with the sorrel nag, we went into a copse at some distance, where I with my knife, and he with a sharp flint fastened very artificially,[9] after their manner, to a wooden handle, cut down several oak wattles about the thickness of a walking staff, and some larger pieces. But I shall not trouble the reader with a particular description of my own mechanics; let it suffice to say, that in six weeks time, with the help of the sorrel nag, who performed the parts that required most labor, I finished a sort of Indian canoe; but much larger, covering it with the skins of Yahoos, well stitched together, with hempen threads of my own making. My sail was likewise composed of the skins of the same animal; but I made use of the youngest I could get, the older being too tough and thick; and I likewise provided myself with four paddles. I laid in a stock of boiled flesh, of rabbits and fowls; and took with me two vessels, one filled with milk, and the other with water.

8. Equanimity. "Devoted": doomed.   9. Artfully.

I tried my canoe in a large pond near my master's house, and then corrected in it what was amiss, stopping all the chinks with Yahoo's tallow, till I found it staunch, and able to bear me and my freight. And when it was as complete as I could possibly make it, I had it drawn on a carriage very gently by Yahoos, to the seaside, under the conduct of the sorrel nag and another servant.

When all was ready, and the day came for my departure, I took leave of my master and lady, and the whole family, my eyes flowing with tears and my heart quite sunk with grief.[1] But his honor, out of curiosity, and perhaps (if I may speak it without vanity) partly out of kindness, was determined to see me in my canoe; and got several of his neighboring friends to accompany him. I was forced to wait above an hour for the tide, and then observing the wind very fortunately bearing towards the island to which I intended to steer my course, I took a second leave of my master; but as I was going to prostrate myself to kiss his hoof, he did me the honor to raise it gently to my mouth. I am not ignorant how much I have been censured for mentioning this last particular. Detractors are pleased to think it improbable that so illustrious a person should descend to give so great a mark of distinction to a creature so inferior as I. Neither have I forgot how apt some travelers are to boast of extraordinary favors they have received. But, if these censurers were better acquainted with the noble and courteous disposition of the Houyhnhnms, they would soon change their opinion. I paid my respects to the rest of the Houyhnhnms in his honor's company; then getting into my canoe, I pushed off from shore.

CHAPTER 11. *The Author's dangerous voyage. He arrives at New Holland, hoping to settle there. Is wounded with an arrow by one of the natives. Is seized and carried by force into a Portuguese ship. The great civilities of the Captain. The Author arrives at England.*

I began this desperate voyage on February 15, 1714/5,[2] at 9 o'clock in the morning. The wind was very favorable; however, I made use at first only of my paddles; but considering I should soon be weary, and that the wind might probably chop about, I ventured to set up my little sail, and thus, with the help of the tide, I went at the rate of a league and a half an hour, as near as I could guess. My master and his friends continued on the shore, till I was almost out of sight; and I often heard the sorrel nag (who always loved me) crying out, *"Hnuy illa nyha maiah Yahoo"* ("Take care of thyself, gentle Yahoo").

My design was, if possible, to discover some small island uninhabited, yet sufficient by my labor to furnish me with necessaries of life, which I would have thought a greater happiness than to be first minister in the politest court of Europe, so horrible was the idea I conceived of returning to live in the society and under the government of Yahoos. For in such a solitude as I desired, I could at least enjoy my own thoughts, and reflect with delight on the virtues of those inimitable Houyhnhnms, without any opportunity of degenerating into the vices and corruptions of my own species.

The reader may remember what I related when my crew conspired against me, and confined me to my cabin, how I continued there several weeks,

---

1. For a depiction of this scene by Sawrey Gilpin, see the color insert in this volume.

2. I.e., 1715, by modern dating. The year began on March 25.

without knowing what course we took; and when I was put ashore in the longboat, how the sailors told me with oaths, whether true or false, that they knew not in what part of the world we were. However, I did then believe us to be about 10 degrees southward of the Cape of Good Hope, or about 45 degrees southern latitude, as I gathered from some general words I overheard among them, being I supposed to the southeast in their intended voyage to Madagascar. And although this were but little better than conjecture, yet I resolved to steer my course eastward, hoping to reach the southwest coast of New Holland, and perhaps some such island as I desired, lying westward of it. The wind was full west, and by six in the evening I computed I had gone eastward at least eighteen leagues; when I spied a very small island about half a league off, which I soon reached. It was nothing but a rock with one creek, naturally arched by the force of tempests. Here I put in my canoe, and climbing a part of the rock, I could plainly discover land to the east, extending from south to north. I lay all night in my canoe; and repeating my voyage early in the morning, I arrived in seven hours to the southeast point of New Holland. This confirmed me in the opinion I have long entertained, that the maps and charts place this country at least three degrees more to the east than it really is; which thought I communicated many years ago to my worthy friend Mr. Herman Moll,[3] and gave him my reasons for it, although he hath rather chosen to follow other authors.

I saw no inhabitants in the place where I landed; and being unarmed, I was afraid of venturing far into the country. I found some shellfish on the shore, and eat them raw, not daring to kindle a fire, for fear of being discovered by the natives. I continued three days feeding on oysters and limpets, to save my own provisions; and I fortunately found a brook of excellent water, which gave me great relief.

On the fourth day, venturing out early a little too far, I saw twenty or thirty natives upon a height, not above five hundred yards from me. They were stark naked, men, women, and children round a fire, as I could discover by the smoke. One of them spied me, and gave notice to the rest; five of them advanced towards me, leaving the women and children at the fire. I made what haste I could to the shore, and getting into my canoe, shoved off; the savages observing me retreat, ran after me; and before I could get far enough into the sea, discharged an arrow, which wounded me deeply on the inside of my left knee. (I shall carry the mark to my grave.) I apprehended the arrow might be poisoned; and paddling out of the reach of their darts (being a calm day) I made a shift to suck the wound, and dress it as well as I could.

I was at a loss what to do, for I durst not return to the same landing place, but stood to the north, and was forced to paddle; for the wind, although very gentle, was against me, blowing northwest. As I was looking about for a secure landing place, I saw a sail to the north northeast, which appearing every minute more visible, I was in some doubt whether I should wait for them or no; but at last my detestation of the Yahoo race prevailed; and turning my canoe, I sailed and paddled together to the south, and got into the same creek from whence I set out in the morning, choosing rather to trust myself among these barbarians than live with European Yahoos. I drew up my canoe as close as I could to the shore, and hid myself behind a stone by the little brook, which, as I have already said, was excellent water.

---

3. A famous contemporary map maker.

The ship came within half a league of this creek, and sent out her long-boat with vessels to take in fresh water (for the place it seems was very well known), but I did not observe it until the boat was almost on shore; and it was too late to seek another hiding place. The seamen at their landing observed my canoe, and rummaging it all over, easily conjectured that the owner could not be far off. Four of them well armed searched every cranny and lurking hole, till at last they found me flat on my face behind the stone. They gazed a while in admiration at my strange uncouth dress; my coat made of skins, my wooden-soled shoes, and my furred stockings; from whence, however, they concluded I was not a native of the place, who all go naked. One of the seamen in Portuguese bid me rise, and asked who I was. I understood that language very well, and getting upon my feet, said I was a poor Yahoo, banished from the Houyhnhnms, and desired they would please to let me depart. They admired to hear me answer them in their own tongue, and saw by my complexion I must be an European; but were at a loss to know what I meant by Yahoos and Houyhnhnms, and at the same time fell a laughing at my strange tone in speaking, which resembled the neighing of a horse. I trembled all the while betwixt fear and hatred; I again desired leave to depart, and was gently moving to my canoe; but they laid hold on me, desiring to know what country I was of? whence I came? with many other questions. I told them I was born in England, from whence I came about five years ago, and then their country and ours was at peace. I therefore hoped they would not treat me as an enemy, since I meant them no harm, but was a poor Yahoo, seeking some desolate place where to pass the remainder of his unfortunate life.

When they began to talk, I thought I never heard or saw any thing so unnatural; for it appeared to me as monstrous as if a dog or a cow should speak in England, or a Yahoo in Houyhnhnmland. The honest Portuguese were equally amazed at my strange dress, and the odd manner of delivering my words, which however they understood very well. They spoke to me with great humanity, and said they were sure their Captain would carry me *gratis* to Lisbon, from whence I might return to my own country; that two of the seamen would go back to the ship, to inform the Captain of what they had seen, and receive his orders; in the meantime, unless I would give my solemn oath not to fly, they would secure me by force. I thought it best to comply with their proposal. They were very curious to know my story, but I gave them very little satisfaction; and they all conjectured, that my misfortunes had impaired my reason. In two hours the boat, which went laden with vessels of water, returned with the Captain's commands to fetch me on board. I fell on my knees to preserve my liberty; but all was in vain, and the men having tied me with cords, heaved me into the boat, from whence I was taken into the ship, and from thence into the Captain's cabin.

His name was Pedro de Mendez; he was a very courteous and generous person; he entreated me to give some account of myself, and desired to know what I would eat or drink; said I should be used as well as himself, and spoke so many obliging things, that I wondered to find such civilities from a Yahoo. However, I remained silent and sullen; I was ready to faint at the very smell of him and his men. At last I desired something to eat out of my own canoe; but he ordered me a chicken and some excellent wine, and then directed that I should be put to bed in a very clean cabin. I would not undress myself, but lay on the bedclothes; and in half an hour stole out, when I thought the crew was at dinner; and getting to the side of the ship, was going to leap into the sea, and swim for my life, rather than continue among Yahoos. But one of the seamen prevented me, and having informed the Captain, I was chained to my cabin.

After dinner Don Pedro came to me, and desired to know my reason for so desperate an attempt; assured me he only meant to do me all the service he was able; and spoke so very movingly, that at last I descended to treat him like an animal which had some little portion of reason. I gave him a very short relation of my voyage; of the conspiracy against me by my own men; of the country where they set me on shore, and of my five years residence there. All which he looked upon as if it were a dream or a vision; whereat I took great offense; for I had quite forgot the faculty of lying, so peculiar to Yahoos in all countries where they preside, and consequently the disposition of suspecting truth in others of their own species. I asked him whether it were the custom of his country to *say the thing that was not?* I assured him I had almost forgot what he meant by falsehood; and if I had lived a thousand years in Houyhnhnmland, I should never have heard a lie from the meanest servant. That I was altogether indifferent whether he believed me or no; but however, in return for his favors, I would give so much allowance to the corruption of his nature, as to answer any objection he would please to make; and he might easily discover the truth.

The Captain, a wise man, after many endeavors to catch me tripping in some part of my story, at last began to have a better opinion of my veracity. But he added that since I professed so inviolable an attachment to truth, I must give him my word of honor to bear him company in this voyage without attempting anything against my life; or else he would continue me a prisoner till we arrived at Lisbon. I gave him the promise he required; but at the same time protested that I would suffer the greatest hardships rather than return to live among Yahoos.

Our voyage passed without any considerable accident. In gratitude to the Captain I sometimes sat with him at his earnest request, and strove to conceal my antipathy against humankind, although it often broke out; which he suffered to pass without observation. But the greatest part of the day, I confined myself to my cabin, to avoid seeing any of the crew. The Captain had often entreated me to strip myself of my savage dress, and offered to lend me the best suit of clothes he had. This I would not be prevailed on to accept, abhorring to cover myself with anything that had been on the back of a Yahoo. I only desired he would lend me two clean shirts, which having been washed since he wore them, I believed would not so much defile me. These I changed every second day, and washed them myself.

We arrived at Lisbon, Nov. 5, 1715. At our landing, the Captain forced me to cover myself with his cloak, to prevent the rabble from crowding about me. I was conveyed to his own house; and at my earnest request, he led me up to the highest room backwards.[4] I conjured him to conceal from all persons what I had told him of the Houyhnhnms; because the least hint of such a story would not only draw numbers of people to see me, but probably put me in danger of being imprisoned, or burned by the Inquisition. The Captain persuaded me to accept a suit of clothes newly made; but I would not suffer the tailor to take my measure; however, Don Pedro being almost of my

4. At the rear.

size, they fitted me well enough. He accoutered me with other necessaries, all new, which I aired for twenty-four hours before I would use them.

The Captain had no wife, nor above three servants, none of which were suffered to attend at meals; and his whole deportment was so obliging, added to very good human understanding, that I really began to tolerate his company. He gained so far upon me, that I ventured to look out of the back window. By degrees I was brought into another room, from whence I peeped into the street, but drew my head back in a fright. In a week's time he seduced me down to the door. I found my terror gradually lessened, but my hatred and contempt seemed to increase. I was at last bold enough to walk the street in his company, but kept my nose well stopped with rue, or sometimes with tobacco.

In ten days, Don Pedro, to whom I had given some account of my domestic affairs, put it upon me as a point of honor and conscience that I ought to return to my native country, and live at home with my wife and children. He told me there was an English ship in the port just ready to sail, and he would furnish me with all things necessary. It would be tedious to repeat his arguments, and my contradictions. He said it was altogether impossible to find such a solitary island as I had desired to live in; but I might command in my own house, and pass my time in a manner as recluse as I pleased.

I complied at last, finding I could not do better. I left Lisbon the 24th day of November, in an English merchantman, but who was the Master I never inquired. Don Pedro accompanied me to the ship, and lent me twenty pounds. He took kind leave of me, and embraced me at parting; which I bore as well as I could. During this last voyage I had no commerce with the Master, or any of his men; but pretending I was sick kept close in my cabin. On the fifth of December, 1715, we cast anchor in the Downs about nine in the morning, and at three in the afternoon I got safe to my house at Redriff.

My wife and family received me with great surprise and joy, because they concluded me certainly dead; but I must freely confess, the sight of them filled me only with hatred, disgust, and contempt; and the more, by reflecting on the near alliance I had to them. For although since my unfortunate exile from the Houyhnhnm country, I had compelled myself to tolerate the sight of Yahoos, and to converse with Don Pedro de Mendez; yet my memory and imaginations were perpetually filled with the virtues and ideas of those exalted Houyhnhnms. And when I began to consider that by copulating with one of the Yahoo species, I had become a parent of more, it struck me with the utmost shame, confusion, and horror.

As soon as I entered the house, my wife took me in her arms, and kissed me; at which, having not been used to the touch of that odious animal for so many years, I fell in a swoon for almost an hour. At the time I am writing, it is five years since my last return to England. During the first year I could not endure my wife or children in my presence, the very smell of them was intolerable; much less could I suffer them to eat in the same room. To this hour they dare not presume to touch my bread, or drink out of the same cup; neither was I ever able to let one of them take me by the hand. The first money I laid out was to buy two young stone-horses,[5] which I keep in a good stable, and next to them the groom is my greatest favorite; for I feel my spirits revived by the smell he contracts in the stable. My horses understand me

5. Stallions.

tolerably well; I converse with them at least four hours every day. They are strangers to bridle or saddle; they live in great amity with me, and friendship to each other.

CHAPTER 12. *The Author's veracity. His design in publishing this work. His censure of those travelers who swerve from the truth. The Author clears himself from any sinister ends in writing. His native country commended. The right of the crown to those countries described by the Author is justified. The difficulty of conquering them. The Author takes his last leave of the reader; proposeth his manner of living for the future; gives good advice, and concludeth.*

Thus gentle reader, I have given thee a faithful history of my travels for sixteen years, and above seven months; wherein I have not been so studious of ornament as of truth. I could perhaps like others have astonished thee with strange improbable tales; but I rather chose to relate plain matter of fact in the simplest manner and style; because my principal design was to inform, and not to amuse thee.

It is easy for us who travel into remote countries, which are seldom visited by Englishmen or other Europeans, to form descriptions of wonderful animals both at sea and land. Whereas a traveler's chief aim should be to make men wiser and better, and to improve their minds by the bad as well as good example of what they deliver concerning foreign places.

I could heartily wish a law were enacted, that every traveler, before he were permitted to publish his voyages, should be obliged to make oath before the Lord High Chancellor that all he intended to print was absolutely true to the best of his knowledge; for then the world would no longer be deceived as it usually is, while some writers, to make their works pass the better upon the public, impose the grossest falsities on the unwary reader. I have perused several books of travels with great delight in my younger days; but, having since gone over most parts of the globe, and been able to contradict many fabulous accounts from my own observation, it hath given me a great disgust against this part of reading, and some indignation to see the credulity of mankind so impudently abused. Therefore, since my acquaintance were pleased to think my poor endeavors might not be unacceptable to my country, I imposed on myself as a maxim, never to be swerved from, that I would *strictly adhere to truth*; neither indeed can I be ever under the least temptation to vary from it, while I retain in my mind the lectures and example of my noble master, and the other illustrious Houyhnhnms, of whom I had so long the honor to be an humble hearer.

——*Nec si miserum Fortuna Sinonem*
Finxit, vanum etiam, mendacemque improba finget.[6]

I know very well how little reputation is to be got by writings which require neither genius nor learning, nor indeed any other talent, except a good memory, or an exact journal. I know likewise, that writers of travels, like dictionary-makers, are sunk into oblivion by the weight and bulk of those who come last, and therefore lie uppermost. And it is highly probable that such travelers who shall hereafter visit the countries described in this work of mine, may be detecting my errors (if there be any) and adding many

---

6. Nor if Fortune had molded Sinon for misery, will she also in spite mold him as false and lying (Latin; Virgil's *Aeneid* 2.79–80).

new discoveries of their own, jostle me out of vogue, and stand in my place, making the world forget that ever I was an author. This indeed would be too great a mortification if I wrote for fame; but, as my sole intention was the PUBLIC GOOD, I cannot be altogether disappointed. For, who can read the virtues I have mentioned in the glorious Houyhnhnms, without being ashamed of his own vices, when he considers himself as the reasoning, governing animal of his country? I shall say nothing of those remote nations where Yahoos preside; amongst which the least corrupted are the Brobdingnagians, whose wise maxims in morality and government it would be our happiness to observe. But I forbear descanting further, and rather leave the judicious reader to his own remarks and applications.

I am not a little pleased that this work of mine can possibly meet with no censurers; for what objections can be made against a writer who relates only plain facts that happened in such distant countries, where we have not the least interest with respect either to trade or negotiations? I have carefully avoided every fault with which common writers of travels are often too justly charged. Besides, I meddle not the least with any party, but write without passion, prejudice, or ill-will against any man or number of men whatsoever. I write for the noblest end, to inform and instruct mankind, over whom I may, without breach of modesty, pretend to some superiority, from the advantages I received by conversing so long among the most accomplished Houyhnhnms. I write without any view towards profit or praise. I never suffer a word to pass that may look like a reflection,[7] or possibly give the least offense even to those who are most ready to take it. So that, I hope, I may with justice pronounce myself an Author perfectly blameless; against whom the tribes of answerers, considerers, observers, reflectors, detecters, remarkers will never be able to find matter for exercising their talents.

I confess it was whispered to me that I was bound in duty as a subject of England, to have given in a memorial[8] to a secretary of state, at my first coming over; because, whatever lands are discovered by a subject, belong to the Crown. But I doubt whether our conquests in the countries I treat of would be as easy as those of Ferdinando Cortez over the naked Americans. The Lilliputians, I think, are hardly worth the charge of a fleet and army to reduce them; and I question whether it might be prudent or safe to attempt the Brobdingnagians; or, whether an English army would be much at their ease with the Flying Island over their heads. The Houyhnhnms, indeed, appear not to be so well prepared for war, a science to which they are perfect strangers, and especially against missive weapons. However, supposing myself to be a minister of state, I could never give my advice for invading them. Their prudence, unanimity, unacquaintedness with fear, and their love of their country would amply supply all defects in the military art. Imagine twenty thousand of them breaking into the midst of an European army, confounding the ranks, overturning the carriages, battering the warriors' faces into mummy, by terrible yerks from their hinder hoofs: for they would well deserve the character given to Augustus, *Recalcitrat undique tutus*.[9] But instead of proposals for conquering that magnanimous nation, I rather wish they were in a capacity or disposition to send a sufficient number of their inhabitants for civilizing Europe; by teaching us the first principles of Honor, Justice, Truth, Temperance, Public Spirit, Fortitude, Chastity, Friendship, Benevolence, and Fidelity. The

7. Censure, criticism.
8. Statement of facts for government use.
9. He kicks backward, at every point on his guard (Latin; Horace's *Satires* 2.1.20). "Mummy": pulp. "Yerks": kicks.

names of all which virtues are still retained among us in most languages, and are to be met with in modern as well as ancient authors, which I am able to assert from my own small reading.

But I had another reason which made me less forward to enlarge his majesty's dominions by my discoveries: to say the truth, I had conceived a few scruples with relation to the distributive justice of princes upon those occasions. For instance, a crew of pirates are driven by a storm they know not whither; at length a boy discovers land from the topmast; they go on shore to rob and plunder; they see an harmless people, are entertained with kindness, they give the country a new name, they take formal possession of it for the king, they set up a rotten plank or a stone for a memorial, they murder two or three dozen of the natives, bring away a couple more by force for a sample, return home, and get their pardon. Here commences a new dominion acquired with a title by Divine Right. Ships are sent with the first opportunity; the natives driven out or destroyed, their princes tortured to discover their gold; a free license given to all acts of inhumanity and lust; the earth reeking with the blood of its inhabitants: and this execrable crew of butchers employed in so pious an expedition is a *modern colony* sent to convert and civilize an idolatrous and barbarous people.

But this description, I confess, doth by no means affect the British nation, who may be an example to the whole world for their wisdom, care, and justice in planting colonies; their liberal endowments for the advancement of religion and learning; their choice of devout and able pastors to propagate Christianity; their caution in stocking their provinces with people of sober lives and conversations from this the Mother Kingdom; their strict regard to the distribution of justice, in supplying the civil administration through all their colonies with officers of the greatest abilities, utter strangers to corruption: and to crown all, by sending the most vigilant and virtuous governors, who have no other views than the happiness of the people over whom they preside, and the honor of the king their master.

But, as those countries which I have described do not appear to have any desire of being conquered, and enslaved, murdered, or driven out by colonies, nor abound either in gold, silver, sugar, or tobacco, I did humbly conceive they were by no means proper objects of our zeal, our valor, or our interest. However, if those whom it may concern, think fit to be of another opinion, I am ready to depose, when I shall be lawfully called, that no European did ever visit these countries before me. I mean, if the inhabitants ought to be believed.

But, as to the formality of taking possession in my sovereign's name, it never came once into my thoughts; and if it had, yet as my affairs then stood, I should perhaps in point of prudence and self-preservation have put it off to a better opportunity.

Having thus answered the only objection that can be raised against me as a traveler, I here take a final leave of my courteous readers, and return to enjoy my own speculations in my little garden at Redriff; to apply those excellent lessons of virtue which I learned among the Houyhnhnms; to instruct the Yahoos of my own family as far as I shall find them docible animals; to behold my figure often in a glass, and thus if possible habituate myself by time to tolerate the sight of a human creature; to lament the brutality of Houyhnhnms in my own country, but always treat their persons with respect, for the sake of my noble master, his family, his friends, and the whole Houyhnhnm race, whom these of ours have the honor to resemble in all their lineaments, however their intellectuals came to degenerate.

I began last week to permit my wife to sit at dinner with me, at the farthest end of a long table; and to answer (but with the utmost brevity) the few questions I ask her. Yet the smell of a Yahoo continuing very offensive, I always keep my nose well stopped with rue, lavender, or tobacco leaves. And although it be hard for a man late in life to remove old habits, I am not altogether out of hopes in some time to suffer a neighbor Yahoo in my company, without the apprehensions I am yet under of his teeth or his claws.

My reconcilement to the Yahoo kind in general might not be so difficult, if they would be content with those vices and follies only which nature hath entitled them to. I am not in the least provoked at the sight of a lawyer, a pickpocket, a colonel, a fool, a lord, a gamester, a politician, a whoremonger, a physician, an evidence,[1] a suborner, an attorney, a traitor, or the like: this is all according to the due course of things. But when I behold a lump of deformity, and diseases both in body and mind, smitten with *pride,* it immediately breaks all the measures of my patience; neither shall I be ever able to comprehend how such an animal and such a vice could tally together. The wise and virtuous Houyhnhnms, who abound in all excellencies that can adorn a rational creature, have no name for this vice in their language, which hath no terms to express anything that is evil, except those whereby they describe the detestable qualities of their Yahoos, among which they were not able to distinguish this of pride, for want of thoroughly understanding human nature, as it showeth itself in other countries, where that animal presides. But I, who had more experience, could plainly observe some rudiments of it among the wild Yahoos.

But the Houyhnhnms, who live under the government of reason, are no more proud of the good qualities they possess, than I should be for not wanting a leg or an arm, which no man in his wits would boast of, although he must be miserable without them. I dwell the longer upon this subject from the desire I have to make the society of an English Yahoo by any means not insupportable; and therefore I here entreat those who have any tincture of this absurd vice, that they will not presume to appear in my sight.

1726, 1735

A Modest Proposal[1]

FOR PREVENTING THE CHILDREN OF POOR PEOPLE IN IRELAND FROM BEING A BURDEN TO THEIR PARENTS OR COUNTRY, AND FOR MAKING THEM BENEFICIAL TO THE PUBLIC

It is a melancholy object to those who walk through this great town[2] or travel in the country, when they see the streets, the roads, and cabin doors, crowded

---

1. Witness.

1. "A Modest Proposal" is an example of Swift's favorite satiric devices used with superb effect. Irony (from the deceptive adjective *modest* in the title to the very last sentence) pervades the piece. A rigorous logic deduces ghastly arguments from a premise so quietly assumed that readers assent before they are aware of what that assent implies. Parody, at which Swift is adept, allows him to glance sardonically at the by then familiar figure of the benevolent humanitarian (forerunner of the modern sociologist, social worker, and economic planner) concerned to correct a social evil by means of a theoretically conceived plan. The proposer, as naive as he is apparently logical and kindly, ignores and therefore emphasizes for the reader the enormity of his plan. The whole is an elaboration of a rather trite metaphor: "The English are devouring the Irish." But there is nothing trite about the pamphlet, which expresses in Swift's most controlled style his revulsion at the contemporary state of Ireland and his indignation at the rapacious English absentee landlords, who were bleeding the country white with the silent approbation of Parliament, ministers, and the crown.

2. Dublin.

with beggars of the female sex, followed by three, four, or six children, all in rags and importuning every passenger for an alms. These mothers, instead of being able to work for their honest livelihood, are forced to employ all their time in strolling to beg sustenance for their helpless infants, who, as they grow up, either turn thieves for want of work, or leave their dear native country to fight for the Pretender in Spain, or sell themselves to the Barbadoes.[3]

I think it is agreed by all parties that this prodigious number of children in the arms, or on the backs, or at the heels of their mothers, and frequently of their fathers, is in the present deplorable state of the kingdom a very great additional grievance; and therefore whoever could find out a fair, cheap, and easy method of making these children sound, useful members of the commonwealth would deserve so well of the public as to have his statue set up for a preserver of the nation.

But my intention is very far from being confined to provide only for the children of professed beggars; it is of a much greater extent, and shall take in the whole number of infants at a certain age who are born of parents in effect as little able to support them as those who demand our charity in the streets.

As to my own part, having turned my thoughts for many years upon this important subject, and maturely weighed the several schemes of other projectors,[4] I have always found them grossly mistaken in their computation. It is true, a child just dropped from its dam may be supported by her milk for a solar year, with little other nourishment; at most not above the value of two shillings, which the mother may certainly get, or the value in scraps, by her lawful occupation of begging; and it is exactly at one year old that I propose to provide for them in such a manner as instead of being a charge upon their parents or the parish, or wanting food and raiment for the rest of their lives, they shall on the contrary contribute to the feeding, and partly to the clothing, of many thousands.

There is likewise another great advantage in my scheme, that it will prevent those voluntary abortions, and that horrid practice of women murdering their bastard children, alas, too frequent among us, sacrificing the poor innocent babes, I doubt, more to avoid the expense than the shame, which would move tears and pity in the most savage and inhuman breast.

The number of souls in this kingdom[5] being usually reckoned one million and a half, of these I calculate there may be about two hundred thousand couple whose wives are breeders; from which number I subtract thirty thousand couples who are able to maintain their own children, although I apprehend there cannot be so many under the present distresses of the kingdom; but this being granted, there will remain an hundred and seventy thousand breeders. I again subtract fifty thousand for those women who miscarry, or whose children die by accident or disease within the year. There only remain an hundred and twenty thousand children of poor parents annually born. The question therefore is, how this number shall be reared and provided for, which, as I have already said, under the present situation of affairs, is utterly impossible by all the methods hitherto proposed. For we can neither employ them in handicraft or agriculture; we neither build houses (I mean in the

3. James Francis Edward Stuart (1688–1766), the son of James II, was claimant ("Pretender") to the throne of England from which the Glorious Revolution had barred his succession. Catholic Ireland was loyal to him, and Irishmen joined him in his exile on the Continent. Because of the poverty in Ireland, many Irishmen emigrated to the West Indies and other British colonies in America; they paid their passage by binding themselves to work for a stated period for one of the planters.
4. Devisers of schemes.
5. Ireland.

country) nor cultivate land. They can very seldom pick up a livelihood by stealing till they arrive at six years old, except where they are of towardly parts;[6] although I confess they learn the rudiments much earlier, during which time they can however be looked upon only as probationers, as I have been informed by a principal gentleman in the county of Cavan, who protested to me that he never knew above one or two instances under the ages of six, even in a part of the kingdom so renowned for the quickest proficiency in that art.

I am assured by our merchants that a boy or a girl before twelve years old is no salable commodity; and even when they come to this age they will not yield above three pounds, or three pounds and half a crown at most on the Exchange; which cannot turn to account either to the parents or the kingdom, the charge of nutriment and rags having been at least four times that value.

I shall now therefore humbly propose my own thoughts, which I hope will not be liable to the least objection.

I have been assured by a very knowing American of my acquaintance in London, that a young healthy child well nursed is at a year old a most delicious, nourishing, and wholesome food, whether stewed, roasted, baked, or boiled; and I make no doubt that it will equally serve in a fricassee or a ragout.[7]

I do therefore humbly offer it to public consideration that of the hundred and twenty thousand children, already computed, twenty thousand may be reserved for breed, whereof only one fourth part to be males, which is more than we allow to sheep, black cattle, or swine; and my reason is that these children are seldom the fruits of marriage, a circumstance not much regarded by our savages, therefore one male will be sufficient to serve four females. That the remaining hundred thousand may at a year old be offered in sale to the persons of quality and fortune through the kingdom, always advising the mother to let them suck plentifully in the last month, so as to render them plump and fat for a good table. A child will make two dishes at an entertainment for friends; and when the family dines alone, the fore or hind quarter will make a reasonable dish, and seasoned with a little pepper or salt will be very good boiled on the fourth day, especially in winter.

I have reckoned upon a medium that a child just born will weigh twelve pounds, and in a solar year if tolerably nursed increaseth to twenty-eight pounds.

I grant this food will be somewhat dear, and therefore very proper for landlords, who, as they have already devoured most of the parents, seem to have the best title to the children.

Infant's flesh will be in season throughout the year, but more plentiful in March, and a little before and after. For we are told by a grave author, an eminent French physician,[8] that fish being a prolific diet, there are more children born in Roman Catholic countries about nine months after Lent than at any other season; therefore, reckoning a year after Lent, the markets will be more glutted than usual, because the number of popish infants is at least three to one in this kingdom; and therefore it will have one other collateral advantage, by lessening the number of Papists among us.

I have already computed the charge of nursing a beggar's child (in which list I reckon all cottagers, laborers, and four fifths of the farmers) to be about two shillings per annum, rags included; and I believe no gentleman

6. Promising abilities.
7. A highly seasoned meat stew.

8. François Rabelais (ca. 1494–1553), a humorist and satirist, by no means grave.

would repine to give ten shillings for the carcass of a good fat child, which, as I have said, will make four dishes of excellent nutritive meat, when he hath only some particular friend or his own family to dine with him. Thus the squire will learn to be a good landlord, and grow popular among the tenants; the mother will have eight shillings net profit, and be fit for the work till she produces another child.

Those who are more thrifty (as I must confess the times require) may flay the carcass; the skin of which artificially[9] dressed will make admirable gloves for ladies, and summer boots for fine gentlemen.

As to our city of Dublin, shambles[1] may be appointed for this purpose in the most convenient parts of it, and butchers we may be assured will not be wanting; although I rather recommend buying the children alive, and dressing them hot from the knife as we do roasting pigs.

A very worthy person, a true lover of his country, and whose virtues I highly esteem, was lately pleased in discoursing on this matter to offer a refinement upon my scheme. He said that many gentlemen of this kingdom, having of late destroyed their deer, he conceived that the want of venison might be well supplied by the bodies of young lads and maidens, not exceeding fourteen years of age nor under twelve, so great a number of both sexes in every county being now ready to starve for want of work and service; and these to be disposed of by their parents, if alive, or otherwise by their nearest relations. But with due deference to so excellent a friend and so deserving a patriot, I cannot be altogether in his sentiments; for as to the males, my American acquaintance assured me from frequent experience that their flesh was generally tough and lean, like that of our schoolboys, by continual exercise, and their taste disagreeable; and to fatten them would not answer the charge. Then as to the females, it would, I think with humble submission, be a loss to the public, because they soon would become breeders themselves; and besides, it is not improbable that some scrupulous people might be apt to censure such a practice (although indeed very unjustly) as a little bordering upon cruelty; which I confess, hath always been with me the strongest objection against any project, how well soever intended.

But in order to justify my friend, he confessed that this expedient was put into his head by the famous Psalmanazar,[2] a native of the island Formosa, who came from thence to London above twenty years ago, and in conversation told my friend that in his country when any young person happened to be put to death, the executioner sold the carcass to persons of quality as a prime dainty; and that in his time the body of a plump girl of fifteen, who was crucified for an attempt to poison the emperor, was sold to his Imperial Majesty's prime minister of state, and other great mandarins of the court, in joints from the gibbet, at four hundred crowns. Neither indeed can I deny that if the same use were made of several plump young girls in this town, who without one single groat to their fortunes cannot stir abroad without a chair, and appear at the playhouse and assemblies in foreign fineries which they never will pay for, the kingdom would not be the worse.

Some persons of a desponding spirit are in great concern about that vast number of poor people who are aged, diseased, or maimed, and I have been

---

9. Skillfully.
1. Slaughterhouses.
2. George Psalmanazar (ca. 1679–1763), a famous impostor. A Frenchman, he imposed himself on

English bishops, noblemen, and scientists as a Formosan. He wrote an entirely fictitious account of Formosa, in which he described human sacrifices and cannibalism.

desired to employ my thoughts what course may be taken to ease the nation of so grievous an encumbrance. But I am not in the least pain upon that matter, because it is very well known that they are every day dying and rotting by cold and famine, and filth and vermin, as fast as can be reasonably expected. And as to the younger laborers, they are now in almost as hopeful a condition. They cannot get work, and consequently pine away for want of nourishment to a degree that if at any time they are accidentally hired to common labor, they have not strength to perform it; and thus the country and themselves are happily delivered from the evils to come.

I have too long digressed, and therefore shall return to my subject. I think the advantages by the proposal which I have made are obvious and many, as well as of the highest importance.

For first, as I have already observed, it would greatly lessen the number of Papists, with whom we are yearly overrun, being the principal breeders of the nation as well as our most dangerous enemies; and who stay at home on purpose to deliver the kingdom to the Pretender, hoping to take their advantage by the absence of so many good Protestants, who have chosen rather to leave their country than stay at home and pay tithes against their conscience to an Episcopal curate.[3]

Secondly, the poorer tenants will have something valuable of their own, which by law may be made liable to distress,[4] and help to pay their landlord's rent, their corn and cattle being already seized and money a thing unknown.

Thirdly, whereas the maintenance of an hundred thousand children, from two years old and upwards, cannot be computed at less than ten shillings a piece per annum, the nation's stock will be thereby increased fifty thousand pounds per annum, besides the profit of a new dish introduced to the tables of all gentlemen of fortune in the kingdom who have any refinement in taste. And the money will circulate among ourselves, the goods being entirely of our own growth and manufacture.

Fourthly, the constant breeders, besides the gain of eight shillings sterling per annum by the sale of their children, will be rid of the charge of maintaining them after the first year.

Fifthly, this food would likewise bring great custom to taverns, where the vintners will certainly be so prudent as to procure the best receipts[5] for dressing it to perfection, and consequently have their houses frequented by all the fine gentlemen, who justly value themselves upon their knowledge in good eating; and a skillful cook, who understands how to oblige his guests, will contrive to make it as expensive as they please.

Sixthly, this would be a great inducement to marriage, which all wise nations have either encouraged by rewards or enforced by laws and penalties. It would increase the care and tenderness of mothers toward their children, when they were sure of a settlement for life to the poor babes, provided in some sort by the public, to their annual profit instead of expense. We should see an honest emulation among the married women, which of them could bring the fattest child to the market. Men would become as fond of their wives during the time of their pregnancy as they are now of their mares

3. Ireland had many Protestant sectarians who did not support the "Episcopal" (Anglican) Church of Ireland.
4. Distraint, i.e., the seizing, through legal action, of property for the payment of debts and other obligations. "Corn": grain.
5. Recipes.

in foal, their cows in calf, or sows when they are ready to farrow; nor offer to beat or kick them (as is too frequent a practice) for fear of a miscarriage.

Many other advantages might be enumerated. For instance, the addition of some thousand carcasses in our exportation of barreled beef, the propagation of swine's flesh, and improvement in the art of making good bacon, so much wanted among us by the great destruction of pigs, too frequent at our tables, which are no way comparable in taste or magnificence to a well-grown, fat, yearling child, which roasted whole will make a considerable figure at a lord mayor's feast or any other public entertainment. But this and many others I omit, being studious of brevity.

Supposing that one thousand families in this city would be constant customers for infants' flesh, besides others who might have it at merry meetings, particularly weddings and christenings, I compute that Dublin would take off annually about twenty thousand carcasses, and the rest of the kingdom (where probably they will be sold somewhat cheaper) the remaining eighty thousand.

I can think of no one objection that will probably be raised against this proposal, unless it should be urged that the number of people will be thereby much lessened in the kingdom. This I freely own, and it was indeed one principal design in offering it to the world. I desire the reader will observe, that I calculate my remedy for this one individual kingdom of Ireland and for no other that ever was, is, or I think ever can be upon earth. Therefore let no man talk to me of other expedients: of taxing our absentees at five shillings a pound: of using neither clothes nor household furniture except what is of our own growth and manufacture: of utterly rejecting the materials and instruments that promote foreign luxury: of curing the expensiveness of pride, vanity, idleness, and gaming in our women: of introducing a vein of parsimony, prudence, and temperance: of learning to love our country, in the want of which we differ even from Laplanders and the inhabitants of Topinamboo:[6] of quitting our animosities and factions, nor acting any longer like the Jews, who were murdering one another at the very moment their city was taken:[7] of being a little cautious not to sell our country and conscience for nothing: of teaching landlords to have at least one degree of mercy toward their tenants: lastly, of putting a spirit of honesty, industry, and skill into our shopkeepers; who, if a resolution could now be taken to buy only our native goods, would immediately unite to cheat and exact upon us in the price, the measure, and the goodness, nor could ever yet be brought to make one fair proposal of just dealing, though often and earnestly invited to it.[8]

Therefore I repeat, let no man talk to me of these and the like expedients, till he hath at least some glimpse of hope that there will ever be some hearty and sincere attempt to put them in practice.

But as to myself, having been wearied out for many years with offering vain, idle, visionary thoughts, and at length utterly despairing of success, I fortunately fell upon this proposal, which, as it is wholly new, so it hath something solid and real, of no expense and little trouble, full in our own

---

6. I.e., even Laplanders love their frozen, infertile country and the savage tribes of Brazil love their jungle more than the Anglo-Irish love Ireland.
7. During the siege of Jerusalem by the Roman Titus (later emperor), who captured and destroyed the city in 70 C.E., bloody fights broke out between fanatical factions among the defenders.
8. Swift himself had made all these proposals in various pamphlets. In editions printed during his lifetime the various proposals were italicized to indicate Swift's support for them.

power, and whereby we can incur no danger in disobliging England. For this kind of commodity will not bear exportation, the flesh being of too tender a consistence to admit a long continuance in salt, although perhaps I could name a country which would be glad to eat up our whole nation without it.[9]

After all, I am not so violently bent upon my own opinion as to reject any offer proposed by wise men, which shall be found equally innocent, cheap, easy, and effectual. But before something of that kind shall be advanced in contradiction to my scheme, and offering a better, I desire the author or authors will be pleased maturely to consider two points. First, as things now stand, how they will be able to find food and raiment for an hundred thousand useless mouths and backs. And secondly, there being a round million of creatures in human figure throughout this kingdom, whose sole subsistence put into a common stock would leave them in debt two millions of pounds sterling, adding those who are beggars by profession to the bulk of farmers, cottagers, and laborers, with their wives and children who are beggars in effect; I desire those politicians who dislike my overture, and may perhaps be so bold to attempt an answer, that they will first ask the parents of these mortals whether they would not at this day think it a great happiness to have been sold for food at a year old in the manner I prescribe, and thereby have avoided such a perpetual sense of misfortunes as they have since gone through by the oppression of landlords, the impossibility of paying rent without money or trade, the want of common sustenance, with neither house nor clothes to cover them from the inclemencies of the weather, and the most inevitable prospect of entailing the like or greater miseries upon their breed forever.

I profess, in the sincerity of my heart, that I have not the least personal interest in endeavoring to promote this necessary work, having no other motive than the public good of my country, by advancing our trade, providing for infants, relieving the poor, and giving some pleasure to the rich. I have no children by which I can propose to get a single penny; the youngest being nine years old, and my wife past childbearing.

1729

9. England.

ALEXANDER POPE
1688–1744

Alexander Pope is the only important writer of his generation who was solely a man of letters. Because he could not, as a Roman Catholic, attend a university, vote, or hold public office, he was excluded from the sort of patronage that was bestowed by statesmen on many writers during the reign of Anne. This disadvantage he turned into a positive good, for the translation of Homer's *Iliad* and *Odyssey*, which he undertook for profit as well as for fame, gave him ample means to live the life of an independent suburban gentleman. After 1718 he lived hospitably in his villa by the

Thames at Twickenham (then pronounced *Twit'nam*), entertaining his friends and converting his five acres of land into a diminutive landscape garden. Almost exactly a century earlier, William Shakespeare had earned enough to retire to a country estate at Stratford—but he had been an actor-manager as well as a playwright; Pope was the first English writer to build a lucrative, lifelong career by publishing his works.

Ill health plagued Pope almost from birth. Crippled early by tuberculosis of the bone, he never grew taller than four and a half feet. In later life he suffered from violent headaches and required constant attention from servants. But Pope did not allow his infirmities to hold him back; he was always a master at making the best of what he had. Around 1700 his father, a well-to-do, retired London merchant, moved to a small property at Binfield in Windsor Forest. There, in rural surroundings, young Pope completed his education by reading whatever he pleased, "like a boy gathering flowers in the woods and fields just as they fall in his way"; and there, encouraged by his father, he began to write verse. He was already an accomplished poet in his teens; no English poet has ever been more precocious.

Pope's first striking success as a poet was *An Essay on Criticism*. (1711), which brought him Joseph Addison's approval and an intemperate personal attack from the critic John Dennis, who was angered by a casual reference to himself in the poem. *The Rape of the Lock*, both in its original shorter version of 1712 and in its more elaborate version of 1714, proved the author a master not only of metrics and of language but also of witty, urbane satire. In *An Essay on Criticism*, Pope had excelled all his predecessors in writing a didactic poem after the example of Horace; in the *Rape*, he had written the most brilliant mock epic in the language. But there was another vein in Pope's youthful poetry, a tender concern with natural beauty and love. The *Pastorals* (1709), his first publication, and *Windsor Forest* (1713; much of it was written earlier) abound in visual imagery and descriptive passages of ideally ordered nature; they remind us that Pope was an amateur painter. The "Elegy to the Memory of an Unfortunate Lady" and *Eloisa to Abelard*, published in the collected poems of 1717, dwell on the pangs of unhappy lovers (Pope himself never married). And even the long task of translating Homer, the "dull duty" of editing Shakespeare, and, in middle age, his dedication to ethical and satirical poetry did not make less fine his keen sense of beauty in nature and art.

Pope's early poetry brought him to the attention of literary men, with whom he began to associate in the masculine world of coffeehouse and tavern, where he liked to play the rake. Between 1706 and 1711 he came to know, among many others, William Congreve; William Walsh, the critic and poet; and Richard Steele and Joseph Addison. As it happened, all were Whigs. Pope could readily ignore politics in the excitement of taking his place among the leading wits of the town. But after the fall of the Whigs in 1710 and the formation of the Tory government under Robert Harley (later the earl of Oxford) and Henry St. John (later Viscount Bolingbroke), party loyalties bred bitterness among the wits as among the politicians. By 1712, Pope had made the acquaintance of another group of writers, all Tories, who were soon his intimate friends: Jonathan Swift, by then the close associate of Harley and St. John and the principal propagandist for their policies; Dr. John Arbuthnot, physician to the queen, a learned scientist, a wit, and a man of humanity and integrity; John Gay, the poet, who in 1728 was to create *The Beggar's Opera*, the greatest theatrical success of the century; and the poet Thomas Parnell. Through them he became the friend and admirer of Oxford and later the intimate of Bolingbroke. In 1714 this group, at the instigation of Pope, formed a club for satirizing all sorts of false learning. The friends proposed to write jointly the biography of a learned fool whom they named Martinus Scriblerus (Martin the Scribbler), whose life and opinions would be a running commentary on educated nonsense. Some amusing episodes were later rewritten and published as the *Memoirs of Martinus Scriblerus* (1741). The real importance of the club, however, is that it fostered a satiric temper that would be expressed in such mature works of the friends as *Gulliver's Travels*, *The Beggar's Opera*, and *The Dunciad*.

"The life of a wit is a warfare on earth," said Pope, generalizing from his own experience. His very success as a poet (and his astonishing precocity brought him success very early) made enemies who were to plague him in pamphlets, verse satires, and squibs in the journals throughout his entire literary career. He was attacked for his writings, his religion, and his physical deformity. Although he smarted under the jibes of his detractors, he was a fighter who struck back, always giving better than he got. Pope's literary warfare began in 1713, when he announced his intention of translating the *Iliad* and sought subscribers to a deluxe edition of the work. Subscribers came in droves, but the Whig writers who surrounded Addison at Button's Coffee House did all they could to discredit the venture. The eventual success of the first published installment of his *Iliad* in 1715 did not obliterate Pope's resentment against Addison and his "little senate"; and he took his revenge in the damaging portrait of Addison (under the name of Atticus), which was later included in the *Epistle to Dr. Arbuthnot* (1735), lines 193–214. The not unjustified attacks on Pope's edition of Shakespeare (1725) by the learned Shakespeare scholar Lewis Theobald (Pope always spelled and pronounced the name "Tibbald" in his satires) led to Theobald's appearance as king of the dunces in *The Dunciad* (1728). In this impressive poem Pope stigmatized his literary enemies as agents of all that he disliked and feared in the tendencies of his time—the vulgarization of taste and the arts consequent on the rapid growth of the reading public and the development of journalism, magazines, and other popular and cheap publications, which spread scandal, sensationalism, and political partisanship—in short the new commercial spirit of the nation that was corrupting not only the arts but, as Pope saw it, the national life itself.

In the 1730s Pope moved on to philosophical, ethical, and political subjects in *An Essay on Man*, the *Epistles to Several Persons*, and the *Imitations of Horace*. The reigns of George I and George II appeared to him, as to Swift and other Tories, a period of rapid moral, political, and cultural deterioration. The agents of decay fed on the rise of moneyed (as opposed to landed) wealth, which accounted for the political corruption encouraged by Sir Robert Walpole and the court party and the corruption of all aspects of the national life by a vulgar class of *nouveaux riches*. Pope assumed the role of the champion of traditional values: of right reason, humanistic learning, sound art, good taste, and public virtue. It was fortunate that many of his enemies happened to illustrate various degrees of unreason, pedantry, bad art, vulgar taste, and at best, indifferent morals.

The satirist traditionally deals in generally prevalent evils and generally observable human types, not with particular individuals. So too with Pope; the bulk of his satire can be read and enjoyed without much biographical information. Usually he used fictional or type names, although he most often had an individual in mind—Sappho, Atossa, Atticus, Sporus—and when he named individuals (as he consistently did in *The Dunciad*), his purpose was to raise his victims to emblems of folly and vice. To judge and censure the age, Pope also created the *I* of the satires (not identical with Alexander Pope of Twickenham). This semifictional figure is the detached observer, somewhat removed from the City, town, and court, the centers of corruption; he is the friend of the virtuous, whose friendship for him testifies to his integrity; he is fond of peace, country life, the arts, morality, and truth; and he detests their opposites that flourish in the great world. In such an age, Pope implies, it is impossible for such a man—honest, truthful, blunt—not to write satire.

Pope was a master of style. From first to last, his verse is notable for its rhythmic variety, despite the apparently rigid metrical unit—the heroic couplet—in which he wrote; for the precision of meaning and the harmony (or expressive disharmony) of his language; and for the union of maximum conciseness with maximum complexity. Variety and harmony can be observed in even so short a passage as lines 71–76 of the pastoral "Summer" (1709), lines so lyrical that, in *Semele*, Handel set them to music. In the passage quoted below (as also in the quotation that follows), only those rhetorical stresses that distort the normal iambic flow of the verse have been marked; these distortions often stem from a slight emphasis given to "you," Summer, the addressee of the passage, on the off beat. Internal pauses within the line are indicated by single and double bars, alliteration and assonance by italics.

> Óh déign to visit our *f*orsaken se*a*ts,
>
> The mossy *f*ountains || and the *gr*een re*tr*eats!
>
> Where'er yóu wálk || cóol gáles shall *f*an the *gl*ade,
>
> Trées whére yóu sít || shall cro*w*d into a sha*d*e:
>
> Where'er yóu tŕead || the blu*sh*ing *fl*o*w*ers shall rise,
>
> And all thíngs *fl*óurish where yóu túrn your eyes.

Pope has attained metrical variety by the free substitution of trochees and spond- ees for the normal iambs; he has achieved rhythmic variety by arranging phrases and clauses (units of syntax and logic) of different lengths within single lines and couplets, so that the passage moves with the sinuous fluency of thought and feel- ing; and he not only has chosen musical combinations of words but has also subtly modulated the harmony of the passage by unobtrusive patterns of alliteration and assonance.

Contrast with this pastoral passage lines 16–25 of the "Epilogue to the Satires, Dialogue 2" (1738), in which Pope is not making music but imitating actual conver- sation so realistically that the metrical pattern and the integrity of the couplet and individual line seem to be destroyed (although in fact they remain in place). In a dialogue with a friend who warns him that his satire is too personal, indeed mere libel, the poet-satirist replies:

> Yé státesmen, | priests of one religion all!
>
> Yé trádesmen vile || in army, court, or hall!
>
> Yé réverend atheists. || F. Scandal! | name them, | Who?
>
> P. Why that's the thing you bid me not to do.
>
> Whó stárved a sister, || who foreswore a debt,
>
> Í néver named; || the town's inquiring yet.
>
> The poisoning dame—| F. Yóu méan—| P. I don't—| F. Yóu dó.
>
> P. Sée, nów Í kéep the secret, || and nót yóu!
>
> The bribing statesman—| F. Hóld, || tóo hígh you go.
>
> P. The bribed elector—|| F. There you stoop tóo lów.

In such a passage the language and rhythms of poetry merge with the language and rhythms of impassioned living speech.

A fine example of Pope's ability to derive the maximum of meaning from the most economic use of language and image is the description of the manor house in which lives old Cotta, the miser (*Epistle to Lord Bathurst*, lines 187–96):

> Like some lone Chartreuse stands the good old Hall,
> Silence without, and fasts within the wall;
> No raftered roofs with dance and tabor sound,
> No noontide bell invites the country round;
> Tenants with sighs the smokeless towers survey,
> And turn the unwilling steeds another way;
> Benighted wanderers, the forest o'er,
> Curse the saved candle and unopening door;
> While the gaunt mastiff growling at the gate,
> Affrights the beggar whom he longs to eat.

The first couplet of this passage associates the "Hall," symbol of English rural hospitality, with the Grande Chartreuse, the monastery in the French Alps, which, although a place of "silence" and "fasts" for the monks, afforded food and shelter to all travelers. Then the dismal details of Cotta's miserly dwelling provide a stark contrast, and the meaning of the scene is concentrated in the grotesque image of the last couplet: the half-starved watchdog and the frightened beggar confronting each other in mutual hunger.

But another sort of variety derives from Pope's respect for the idea that the different kinds of literature have their different and appropriate styles. Thus *An Essay on Criticism*, an informal discussion of literary theory, is written, like Horace's *Art of Poetry* (a similarly didactic poem), in a plain style, the easy language of well-bred talk. *The Rape of the Lock*, "a heroi-comical poem" (that is, a comic poem that treats trivial material in an epic style), employs the lofty heroic language that John Dryden had perfected in his translation of Virgil and introduces amusing parodies of passages in *Paradise Lost*, parodies later raised to truly Miltonic sublimity and complexity by the conclusion of *The Dunciad*. *Eloisa to Abelard* renders the brooding, passionate voice of its heroine in a declamatory language, given to sudden outbursts and shifts of tone, that recalls the stage. The grave epistles that make up *An Essay on Man*, a philosophical discussion of such majestic themes as the Creator and His creation, the universe, human nature, society, and happiness, are written in a stately forensic language and tone and constantly employ the traditional rhetorical figures. The *Imitations of Horace* and, above all, the *Epistle to Dr. Arbuthnot*, his finest poem "in the Horatian way," reveal Pope's final mastery of the plain style of Horace's epistles and satires and support his image of himself as the heir of the Roman poet. In short, no other poet of the century can equal Pope in the range of his materials, the diversity of his poetic styles, and the wizardry of his technique.

For more poems by Pope, see the supplemental ebook.

An Essay on Criticism

There is no pleasanter introduction to the canons of taste in the English Augustan age than Pope's *An Essay on Criticism*. As Addison said in his review in *Spectator* 253, it assembles the "most known and most received observations on the subject of literature and criticism." Pope was attempting to do for his time what Horace, in his *Art of Poetry*, and what Nicolas Boileau (French poet, of the age of Louis XIV), in his *L'Art Poétique*, had done for theirs. Horace is Pope's model not only for principles of criticism but also for style, especially in the simple, conversational language and the tone of well-bred ease.

In framing his critical creed, Pope did not try for novelty: he wished merely to give to generally accepted doctrines pleasing and memorable expression and make them useful to modern poets. Here one meets the key words of neoclassical criticism: *wit*, *Nature*, *ancients*, *rules*, and *genius*. *Wit* in the poem is a word of many meanings—a clever remark or the person who makes it, a conceit, liveliness of mind, inventiveness, fancy, genius, a genius, and poetry itself, among others. *Nature* is an equally ambiguous word, meaning not "things out there" or "the outdoors" but most important that which is representative, universal, permanent in human experience as opposed to the idiosyncratic, the individual, the temporary. In line 21, *Nature* comes close to meaning "intuitive knowledge." In line 52, it means that half-personified power manifested in the cosmic order, which in its modes of working is a model for art. The reverence felt by most Augustans for the great writers of ancient Greece and Rome raised the question how far the authority of these *ancients* extended. Were their works to be received as models to be conscientiously imitated? Were the *rules* received from them or deducible from their works to be accepted as prescriptive laws or merely convenient guides? Was individual *genius* to be bound by what has been conventionally held to be *Nature*, by the authority of the *ancients*, and by the legalistic pedantry of *rules*? Or could it go its own way?

In part 1 of the *Essay*, Pope constructs a harmonious system in which he effects a compromise among all these conflicting forces—a compromise that is typical of his times. Part 2 analyzes the causes of faulty criticism. Part 3 characterizes the good critic and praises the great critics of the past.

An Essay on Criticism

Part 1

'Tis hard to say, if greater want of skill
Appear in writing or in judging ill;
But of the two less dangerous is the offense
To tire our patience than mislead our sense.
5   Some few in that, but numbers err in this,
Ten censure° wrong for one who writes amiss;   *judge*
A fool might once himself alone expose,
Now one in verse makes many more in prose.
   'Tis with our judgments as our watches, none
10   Go just alike, yet each believes his own.
In poets as true genius is but rare,
True taste as seldom is the critic's share;
Both must alike from Heaven derive their light,
These born to judge, as well as those to write.
15   Let such teach others who themselves excel,
And censure freely who have written well.
Authors are partial to their wit, 'tis true,
But are not critics to their judgment too?
   Yet if we look more closely, we shall find
20   Most have the seeds of judgment in their mind:
Nature affords at least a glimmering light;
The lines, though touched but faintly, are drawn right.
But as the slightest sketch, if justly traced, ⎫
Is by ill coloring but the more disgraced, ⎬
25   So by false learning is good sense defaced: ⎭
Some are bewildered in the maze of schools,
And some made coxcombs[1] Nature meant but fools.
In search of wit these lose their common sense,
And then turn critics in their own defense:
30   Each burns alike, who can, or cannot write,
Or with a rival's or an eunuch's spite.
All fools have still an itching to deride,
And fain would be upon the laughing side.
If Maevius[2] scribble in Apollo's spite,
35   There are who judge still worse than he can write.
   Some have at first for wits, then poets passed,
Turned critics next, and proved plain fools at last.
Some neither can for wits nor critics pass,
As heavy mules are neither horse nor ass.
40   Those half-learn'd witlings, numerous in our isle,
As half-formed insects on the banks of Nile;[3]

---

1. Superficial pretenders to learning.
2. A silly poet alluded to contemptuously by Virgil in *Eclogue* 3 and by Horace in *Epode* 10.
3. The ancients believed that many forms of life were spontaneously generated in the fertile mud of the Nile.

Unfinished things, one knows not what to call,
Their generation's so equivocal:
To tell° them would a hundred tongues require,   reckon, count
45   Or one vain wit's, that might a hundred tire.
      But you who seek to give and merit fame,
And justly bear a critic's noble name,
Be sure yourself and your own reach to know,
How far your genius, taste, and learning go;
50   Launch not beyond your depth, but be discreet,
And mark that point where sense and dullness meet.
      Nature to all things fixed the limits fit,
And wisely curbed proud man's pretending° wit.   aspiring
As on the land while here the ocean gains,
55   In other parts it leaves wide sandy plains;
Thus in the soul while memory prevails,
The solid power of understanding fails;
Where beams of warm imagination play,
The memory's soft figures melt away.
60   One science° only will one genius fit,   branch of learning
So vast is art, so narrow human wit.
Not only bounded to peculiar arts,
But oft in those confined to single parts.
Like kings we lose the conquests gained before,
65   By vain ambition still to make them more;
Each might his several province well command,
Would all but stoop to what they understand.
      First follow Nature, and your judgment frame
By her just standard, which is still the same;
70   Unerring Nature, still divinely bright,
One clear, unchanged, and universal light,
Life, force, and beauty must to all impart,
At once the source, and end, and test of art.
Art from that fund each just supply provides,
75   Works without show, and without pomp presides.
In some fair body thus the informing soul
With spirits feeds, with vigor fills the whole,
Each motion guides, and every nerve sustains;
Itself unseen, but in the effects remains.
80   Some, to whom Heaven in wit has been profuse,
Want as much more to turn it to its use;
For wit and judgment often are at strife,
Though meant each other's aid, like man and wife.
'Tis more to guide than spur the Muse's steed,
85   Restrain his fury than provoke his speed;
The wingèd courser,[4] like a generous° horse,   spirited, highly bred
Shows most true mettle when you check his course.
      Those rules of old discovered, not devised,
Are Nature still, but Nature methodized;
90   Nature, like liberty, is but restrained
By the same laws which first herself ordained.
      Hear how learn'd Greece her useful rules indites,
When to repress and when indulge our flights:

4. Pegasus, associated with the Muses and poetic inspiration.

High on Parnassus' top her sons she showed,
95 And pointed out those arduous paths they trod;
Held from afar, aloft, the immortal prize,
And urged the rest by equal steps to rise.
Just precepts thus from great examples given,
She drew from them what they derived from Heaven.
100 The generous critic fanned the poet's fire,
And taught the world with reason to admire.
Then criticism the Muse's handmaid proved,
To dress her charms, and make her more beloved:
But following wits from that intention strayed,
105 Who could not win the mistress, wooed the maid;
Against the poets their own arms they turned,
Sure to hate most the men from whom they learned.
So modern 'pothecaries, taught the art
By doctors's bills° to play the doctor's part,   *prescriptions*
110 Bold in the practice of mistaken rules,
Prescribe, apply, and call their masters fools.
Some on the leaves of ancient authors prey,
Nor time nor moths e'er spoiled so much as they.
Some dryly plain, without invention's aid,
115 Write dull receipts⁵ how poems may be made.
These leave the sense their learning to display,
And those explain the meaning quite away.
    You then whose judgment the right course would steer,
Know well each ancient's proper character;
120 His fable,⁶ subject, scope° in every page;   *aim, purpose*
Religion, country, genius of his age:
Without all these at once before your eyes,
Cavil you may, but never criticize.
Be Homer's works your study and delight,
125 Read them by day, and meditate by night;
Thence form your judgment, thence your maxims bring,
And trace the Muses upward to their spring.
Still with itself compared, his text peruse;
And let your comment be the Mantuan Muse.
130   When first young Maro⁷ in his boundless mind
A work to outlast immortal Rome designed,
Perhaps he seemed above the critic's law,
And but from Nature's fountains scorned to draw;
But when to examine every part he came,
135 Nature and Homer were, he found, the same.
Convinced, amazed, he checks the bold design, ⎤
And rules as strict his labored work confine   ⎬
As if the Stagirite⁸ o'erlooked each line.   ⎦
Learn hence for ancient rules a just esteem;
140 To copy Nature is to copy them.

5. Formulas for preparing a dish; recipes. Pope himself wrote an amusing burlesque, "Receipt to Make an Epic Poem," first published in the *Guardian* 78 (1713).
6. Plot or story of a play or poem.
7. Virgil, who was born in a village adjacent to Mantua in Italy, hence "Mantuan Muse." His epic, the *Aeneid*, was modeled on Homer's *Iliad* and *Odyssey* and was considered to be a refinement, of the Greek poems. Thus it could be thought of as a commentary ("comment") on Homer's poems.
8. Aristotle, a native of Stagira, from whose *Poetics* later critics formulated strict rules for writing tragedy and the epic.

Some beauties yet no precepts can declare,
For there's a happiness as well as care.[9]
Music resembles poetry, in each ⎱
Are nameless graces which no methods teach, ⎰
145   And which a master hand alone can reach.
If, where the rules not far enough extend
(Since rules were made but to promote their end)
Some lucky license answers to the full
The intent proposed, that license is a rule.
150   Thus Pegasus, a nearer way to take,
May boldly deviate from the common track.
Great wits sometimes may gloriously offend,
And rise to faults true critics dare not mend;
From vulgar bounds with brave disorder part,
155   And snatch a grace beyond the reach of art,
Which, without passing through the judgment, gains
The heart, and all its end at once attains.
In prospects thus, some objects please our eyes, ⎱
Which out of Nature's common order rise, ⎰
160   The shapeless rock, or hanging precipice.
But though the ancients thus their rules invade°   *violate*
(As kings dispense with laws themselves have made)
Moderns, beware! or if you must offend
Against the precept, ne'er transgress its end;
165   Let it be seldom, and compelled by need;
And have at least their precedent to plead.
The critic else proceeds without remorse,
Seizes your fame, and puts his laws in force.
   I know there are, to whose presumptuous thoughts
170   Those freer beauties, even in them, seem faults.[1]
Some figures monstrous and misshaped appear,
Considered singly, or beheld too near,
Which, but proportioned to their light or place,
Due distance reconciles to form and grace.
175   A prudent chief not always must display
His powers in equal ranks and fair array,
But with the occasion and the place comply,
Conceal his force, nay seem sometimes to fly.
Those oft are stratagems which errors seem,
180   Nor is it Homer nods, but we that dream.
   Still green with bays each ancient altar stands
Above the reach of sacrilegious hands,
Secure from flames, from envy's fiercer rage,
Destructive war, and all-involving age.
185   See, from each clime the learn'd their incense bring!
Here in all tongues consenting° paeans ring!   *agreeing, concurring*
In praise so just let every voice be joined,[2]
And fill the general chorus of mankind.
Hail, bards triumphant! born in happier days,
190   Immortal heirs of universal praise!

9. I.e., no rules ("precepts") can explain ("declare")
some beautiful effects in a work of art that can be
the result only of inspiration or good luck ("happiness"), not of painstaking labor ("care").
1. Pronounced *fawts*.
2. Pronounced *jined*.

Whose honors with increase of ages grow,
As streams roll down, enlarging as they flow;
Nations unborn your mighty names shall sound,
And worlds applaud that must not yet be found!
195 Oh, may some spark of your celestial fire,
The last, the meanest of your sons inspire
(That on weak wings, from far, pursues your flights,
Glows while he reads, but trembles as he writes)
To teach vain wits a science little known,
200 To admire superior sense, and doubt their own!

Part 2

Of all the causes which conspire to blind
Man's erring judgment, and misguide the mind,
What the weak head with strongest bias rules,
Is pride, the never-failing vice of fools.
205 Whatever Nature has in worth denied,
She gives in large recruits° of needful pride;   *supplies*
For as in bodies, thus in souls, we find
What wants in blood and spirits, swelled with wind:
Pride, where wit fails, steps in to our defense,
210 And fills up all the mighty void of sense.
If once right reason drives that cloud away,
Truth breaks upon us with resistless day.
Trust not yourself: but your defects to know,
Make use of every friend—and every foe.
215 A little learning is a dangerous thing;
Drink deep, or taste not the Pierian spring.[3]
There shallow draughts intoxicate the brain,
And drinking largely sobers us again.
Fired at first sight with what the Muse imparts,
220 In fearless youth we tempt° the heights of arts,   *attempt*
While from the bounded level of our mind
Short views we take, nor see the lengths behind;
But more advanced, behold with strange surprise
New distant scenes of endless science rise!
225 So pleased at first the towering Alps we try,
Mount o'er the vales, and seem to tread the sky,
The eternal snows appear already past,
And the first clouds and mountains seem the last;
But, those attained, we tremble to survey
230 The growing labors of the lengthened way,
The increasing prospect tires our wandering eyes,
Hills peep o'er hills, and Alps on Alps arise!
A perfect judge will read each work of wit
With the same spirit that its author writ:
235 Survey the whole, nor seek slight faults to find
Where Nature moves, and rapture warms the mind;
Nor lose, for that malignant dull delight,
The generous pleasure to be charmed with wit.

3. The spring in Pieria on Mount Olympus, sacred to the Muses.

But in such lays as neither ebb nor flow,
240 Correctly cold, and regularly low,
That, shunning faults, one quiet tenor keep,
We cannot blame indeed—but we may sleep.
In wit, as nature, what affects our hearts
Is not the exactness of peculiar° parts;   *particular*
245 'Tis not a lip, or eye, we beauty call,
But the joint force and full result of all.
Thus when we view some well-proportioned dome[4]
(The world's just wonder, and even thine, O Rome!),
No single parts unequally surprise,
250 All comes united to the admiring eyes:
No monstrous height, or breadth, or length appear;
The whole at once is bold and regular.
　　Whoever thinks a faultless piece to see,
Thinks what ne'er was, nor is, nor e'er shall be.
255 In every work regard the writer's end,
Since none can compass more than they intend;
And if the means be just, the conduct true,
Applause, in spite of trivial faults, is due.
As men of breeding, sometimes men of wit,
260 To avoid great errors must the less commit,
Neglect the rules each verbal critic lays,
For not to know some trifles is a praise.
Most critics, fond of some subservient art,
Still make the whole depend upon a part:
265 They talk of principles, but notions prize,
And all to one loved folly sacrifice.
　　Once on a time La Mancha's knight,[5] they say,
A certain bard encountering on the way,
Discoursed in terms as just, with looks as sage,
270 As e'er could Dennis,[6] of the Grecian stage;
Concluding all were desperate sots and fools
Who durst depart from Aristotle's rules.
Our author, happy in a judge so nice,
Produced his play, and begged the knight's advice;
275 Made him observe the subject and the plot,
The manners, passions, unities; what not?
All which exact to rule were brought about,
Were but a combat in the lists left out.
"What! leave the combat out?" exclaims the knight.
280 "Yes, or we must renounce the Stagirite."
"Not so, by Heaven!" he answers in a rage,
"Knights, squires, and steeds must enter on the stage."
"So vast a throng the stage can ne'er contain."
"Then build a new, or act it in a plain."
285 　　Thus critics of less judgment than caprice,
Curious,° not knowing, not exact, but nice,°   *laborious / fussy*

4. The dome of St. Peter's, designed by Michelangelo.
5. Don Quixote. The story comes not from Cervantes's novel, but from a spurious sequel to it by Don Alonzo Fernandez de Avellaneda.
6. John Dennis (1657–1734), although one of

the leading critics of the time, was frequently ridiculed by the wits for his irascibility and pomposity. Pope apparently did not know Dennis personally, but his jibe at him in part 3 of this poem made him a bitter enemy.

Form short ideas, and offend in arts
(As most in manners), by a love to parts.
　　Some to conceit[7] alone their taste confine,
290　And glittering thoughts struck out at every line;
Pleased with a work where nothing's just or fit,
One glaring chaos and wild heap of wit.
Poets, like painters, thus unskilled to trace
The naked nature and the living grace,
295　With gold and jewels cover every part,
And hide with ornaments their want of art.
True wit is Nature to advantage dressed,
What oft was thought, but ne'er so well expressed;
Something whose truth convinced at sight we find,
300　That gives us back the image of our mind.
As shades more sweetly recommend the light,
So modest plainness sets off sprightly wit;
For works may have more wit than does them good,
As bodies perish through excess of blood.
305　　Others for language all their care express,
And value books, as women men, for dress.
Their praise is still—the style is excellent;
The sense they humbly take upon content.°　　　　　*mere acquiescence*
Words are like leaves; and where they most abound,
310　Much fruit of sense beneath is rarely found.
False eloquence, like the prismatic glass,
Its gaudy colors spreads on every place;[8]
The face of Nature we no more survey,
All glares alike, without distinction gay.
315　But true expression, like the unchanging sun,⎫
Clears and improves whate'er it shines upon;　⎬
It gilds all objects, but it alters none.　　　　⎭
Expression is the dress of thought, and still
Appears more decent as more suitable.
320　A vile conceit in pompous words expressed
Is like a clown° in regal purple dressed:　　　　*country bumpkin*
For different styles with different subjects sort,
As several garbs with country, town, and court.
Some by old words to fame have made pretense,
325　Ancients in phrase, mere moderns in their sense.
Such labored nothings, in so strange a style,
Amaze the unlearn'd, and make the learned smile;
Unluck as Fungoso[9] in the play,　　　　　　⎫
These sparks with awkward vanity display　　⎬
330　What the fine gentleman wore yesterday;　　⎭
And but so mimic ancient wits at best,
As apes our grandsires in their doublets dressed.
In words as fashions the same rule will hold,
Alike fantastic if too new or old:

---

7. Pointed wit, ingenuity and extravagance, or affectation in the use of figures, especially similes and metaphors.
8. A very up-to-date scientific reference. Newton's *Opticks*, which dealt with the prism and the

spectrum, had been published in 1704, although his theories had been known earlier.
9. A character in Ben Jonson's comedy *Every Man out of His Humor* (1599).

335   Be not the first by whom the new are tried,
     Nor yet the last to lay the old aside.
        But most by numbers° judge a poet's song,   *versification*
     And smooth or rough with them is right or wrong.
     In the bright Muse though thousand charms conspire,
340   Her voice is all these tuneful fools admire,
     Who haunt Parnassus but to please their ear, ⎫
     Not mend their minds; as some to church repair, ⎬
     Not for the doctrine, but the music there. ⎭
     These equal syllables alone require,
345   Though oft the ear the open vowels tire,[1]
     While expletives[2] their feeble aid do join,
     And ten low words oft creep in one dull line:
     While they ring round the same unvaried chimes,
     With sure returns of still expected rhymes;
350   Where'er you find "the cooling western breeze,"
     In the next line, it "whispers through the trees";
     If crystal streams "with pleasing murmurs creep,"
     The reader's threatened (not in vain) with "sleep";
     Then, at the last and only couplet fraught
355   With some unmeaning thing they call a thought,
     A needless Alexandrine[3] ends the song
     That, like a wounded snake, drags its slow length along.
     Leave such to tune their own dull rhymes, and know
     What's roundly smooth or languishingly slow;
360   And praise the easy vigor of a line
     Where Denham's strength and Waller's sweetness join.[4]
     True ease in writing comes from art, not chance,
     As those move easiest who have learned to dance.
     'Tis not enough no harshness gives offense,
365   The sound must seem an echo to the sense.
     Soft is the strain when Zephyr gently blows,
     And the smooth stream in smoother numbers flows;
     But when loud surges lash the sounding shore,
     The hoarse, rough verse should like the torrent roar.
370   When Ajax strives some rock's vast weight to throw,
     The line too labors, and the words move slow;
     Not so when swift Camilla[5] scours the plain,
     Flies o'er the unbending corn, and skims along the main.
     Hear how Timotheus'[6] varied lays surprise,
375   And bid alternate passions fall and rise!
     While at each change the son of Libyan Jove°   *Alexander the Great*
     Now burns with glory, and then melts with love;
     Now his fierce eyes with sparkling fury glow,
     Now sighs steal out, and tears begin to flow:

1. In lines 345–57 Pope cleverly contrives to make his own metrics or diction illustrate the faults that he is exposing.
2. Words used merely to achieve the necessary number of feet in a line of verse.
3. A line of verse containing six iambic feet; it is illustrated in the next line.
4. Dryden, whom Pope echoes here, considered Sir John Denham (1615–1669) and Edmund Waller (1606–1687) to have been the principal shapers of the closed pentameter couplet. He had distinguished the "strength" of the one and the "sweetness" of the other.
5. Fleet-footed virgin warrior (*Aeneid* 7, 11).
6. The musician in Dryden's "Alexander's Feast." Pope retells the story of that poem in the following lines.

380 Persians and Greeks like turns of nature[7] found
And the world's victor stood subdued by sound!
The power of music all our hearts allow,
And what Timotheus was, is Dryden now.
    Avoid extremes; and shun the fault of such
385 Who still are pleased too little or too much.
At every trifle scorn to take offense:
That always shows great pride, or little sense.
Those heads, as stomachs, are not sure the best,
Which nauseate all, and nothing can digest.
390 Yet let not each gay turn thy rapture move;
For fools admire,° but men of sense approve:[8]   wonder
As things seem large which we through mists descry,
Dullness is ever apt to magnify.
    Some foreign writers, some our own despise;
395 The ancients only, or the moderns prize.
Thus wit, like faith, by each man is applied
To one small sect, and all are damned beside.
Meanly they seek the blessing to confine,
And force that sun but on a part to shine,
400 Which not alone the southern wit sublimes,°   raises up, purifies
But ripens spirits in cold northern climes;
Which from the first has shone on ages past,
Enlights the present, and shall warm the last;
Though each may feel increases and decays,
405 And see now clearer and now darker days.
Regard not then if wit be old or new,
But blame the false and value still the true.
    Some ne'er advance a judgment of their own,
But catch the spreading notion of the town;
410 They reason and conclude by precedent,
And own° stale nonsense which they ne'er invent.   lay claim to
Some judge of authors' names, not works, and then
Nor praise nor blame the writings, but the men.
Of all this servile herd the worst is he
415 That in proud dullness joins with quality,[9]
A constant critic at the great man's board,
To fetch and carry nonsense for my lord.
What woeful stuff this madrigal would be
In some starved hackney sonneteer° or me!   hireling poet
420 But let a lord once own the happy lines,
How the wit brightens! how the style refines!
Before his sacred name flies every fault,
And each exalted stanza teems with thought!
    The vulgar thus through imitation err;
425 As oft the learn'd by being singular;
So much they scorn the crowd, that if the throng
By chance go right, they purposely go wrong.
So schismatics[1] the plain believers quit,

---

7. Alternations of feelings.
8. Judge favorably only after due deliberation.
9. People of high rank.
1. Those who have divided the church on points

of theology. Pope stressed the first syllable, the
pronunciation approved by Johnson in his *Dictionary*.

And are but damned for having too much wit.
430   Some praise at morning what they blame at night,
But always think the last opinion right.
A Muse by these is like a mistress used,
This hour she's idolized, the next abused;
While their weak heads like towns unfortified,
435   'Twixt sense and nonsense daily change their side.
Ask them the cause; they're wiser still, they say;
And still tomorrow's wiser than today.
We think our fathers fools, so wise we grow;
Our wiser sons, no doubt, will think us so.
440   Once school divines[2] this zealous isle o'erspread;
Who knew most sentences[3] was deepest read.
Faith, Gospel, all seemed made to be disputed,
And none had sense enough to be confuted.
Scotists and Thomists now in peace remain
445   Amidst their kindred cobwebs in Duck Lane.[4]
If faith itself has different dresses worn,
What wonder modes in wit should take their turn?
Oft, leaving what is natural and fit,
The current folly proves the ready wit;
450   And authors think their reputation safe,
Which lives as long as fools are pleased to laugh.
    Some valuing those of their own side or mind,
Still make themselves the measure of mankind:
Fondly° we think we honor merit then,   *foolishly*
455   When we but praise ourselves in other men.
Parties in wit attend on those of state,
And public faction doubles private hate.
Pride, Malice, Folly against Dryden rose,
In various shapes of parsons, critics, beaux;
460   But sense survived, when merry jests were past;
For rising merit will buoy up at last.
Might he return and bless once more our eyes,
New Blackmores and new Milbourns[5] must arise.
Nay, should great Homer lift his awful head,
465   Zoilus[6] again would start up from the dead.
Envy will merit, as its shade, pursue,
But like a shadow, proves the substance true;
For envied wit, like Sol eclipsed, makes known
The opposing body's grossness, not its own.
470   When first that sun too powerful beams displays,
It draws up vapors which obscure its rays;
But even those clouds at last adorn its way,
Reflect new glories, and augment the day.
    Be thou the first true merit to befriend;
475   His praise is lost who stays till all commend.

---

2. The medieval theologians, such as the followers of Duns Scotus and St. Thomas Aquinas, mentioned below.
3. Allusion to Peter Lombard's *Book of Sentences*, a book esteemed by Scholastic philosophers.
4. Street where publishers' remainders and secondhand books were sold.

5. Luke Milbourn had attacked Dryden's translation of Virgil. Sir Richard Blackmore, physician and poet, had attacked Dryden for the immorality of his plays.
6. A Greek critic of the 4th century B.C.E. who wrote a book of carping criticism of Homer.

Short is the date, alas! of modern rhymes,
And 'tis but just to let them live betimes.°   *for a brief time*
No longer now that golden age appears,
When patriarch wits survived a thousand years:
480 Now length of fame (our second life) is lost,
And bare threescore is all even that can boast;
Our sons their fathers' failing language see,
And such as Chaucer is, shall Dryden be.[7]
So when the faithful pencil has designed
485 Some bright idea of the master's mind,
Where a new world leaps out at his command,
And ready Nature waits upon his hand;
When the ripe colors soften and unite,
And sweetly melt into just shade and light;
490 When mellowing years their full perfection give,
And each bold figure just begins to live,
The treacherous colors the fair art betray,
And all the bright creation fades away!
　　Unhappy° wit, like most mistaken things,   *ill-fated*
495 Atones not for that envy which it brings.
In youth alone its empty praise we boast,
But soon the short-lived vanity is lost;
Like some fair flower the early spring supplies,
That gaily blooms, but even in blooming dies.
500 What is this wit, which must our cares employ?
The owner's wife, that other men enjoy;
Then most our trouble still when most admired,
And still the more we give, the more required;
Whose fame with pains we guard, but lose with ease,
505 Sure some to vex, but never all to please;
'Tis what the vicious fear, the virtuous shun,
By fools 'tis hated, and by knaves undone!
　　If wit so much from ignorance undergo,
Ah, let not learning too commence its foe!
510 Of old those met rewards who could excel,
And such were praised who but endeavored well;
Though triumphs were to generals only due,
Crowns were reserved to grace the soldiers too.[8]
Now they who reach Parnassus' lofty crown
515 Employ their pains to spurn° some others down;   *kick*
And while self-love each jealous writer rules,
Contending wits become the sport of fools;
But still the worst with most regret commend,
For each ill author is as bad a friend.
520 To what base ends, and by what abject ways,
Are mortals urged through sacred° lust of praise![9]   *accursed*
Ah, ne'er so dire a thirst of glory boast,
Nor in the critic let the man be lost!

---

7. The radical changes that took place in the
English language between the death of Chaucer
in 1400 and the death of Dryden in 1700 suggested that in another three hundred years
Dryden would be unintelligible.

8. To celebrate Roman victories, valiant soldiers
were decorated with a variety of crowns.
9. The phrase imitates Virgil's *auri sacra famis*,
"accursed hunger for gold" (*Aeneid* 3.57).

Good nature and good sense must ever join;
525   To err is human, to forgive divine.
          But if in noble minds some dregs remain
       Not yet purged off, of spleen° and sour disdain,   rancor
       Discharge that rage on more provoking crimes,
       Nor fear a dearth in these flagitious° times.   scandalously wicked
530   No pardon vile obscenity should find,
       Though wit and art conspire to move your mind;
       But dullness with obscenity must prove
       As shameful sure as impotence in love.
       In the fat age of pleasure, wealth, and ease
535   Sprung the rank weed, and thrived with large increase:
       When love was all an easy monarch's[1] care,
       Seldom at council, never in a war;
       Jilts[2] ruled the state, and statesmen farces writ;
       Nay, wits had pensions, and young lords had wit;
540   The fair sat panting at a courtier's play,
       And not a mask[3] went unimproved away;
       The modest fan was lifted up no more,
       And virgins smiled at what they blushed before.
       The following license of a foreign reign
545   Did all the dregs of bold Socinus[4] drain;
       Then unbelieving priests reformed the nation,
       And taught more pleasant methods of salvation;
       Where Heaven's free subjects might their rights dispute,
       Lest God himself should seem too absolute;
550   Pulpits their sacred satire learned to spare,
       And Vice admired° to find a flatterer there!   wondered
       Encouraged thus, wit's Titans braved the skies,
       And the press groaned with licensed blasphemies.
       These monsters, critics! with your darts engage,
555   Here point your thunder, and exhaust your rage!
       Yet shun their fault, who, scandalously nice,°   subtle
       Will needs mistake an author into vice;
       All seems infected that the infected spy,
       As all looks yellow to the jaundiced eye.

Part 3

560   Learn then what morals critics ought to show,
       For 'tis but half a judge's task, to know.
       'Tis not enough, taste, judgment, learning, join;
       In all you speak, let truth and candor° shine: kindness, impartiality
       That not alone what to your sense is due
565   All may allow; but seek your friendship too.
          Be silent always when you doubt your sense;
       And speak, though sure, with seeming diffidence:
       Some positive, persisting fops we know,

1. Charles II. The concluding lines of part 2 discuss the corruption of wit and poetry under this monarch.
2. Mistresses of the king.
3. A woman wearing a mask.

4. The name of two Italian theologians of the 16th century who denied the divinity of Jesus. Pope charges that freethinkers attained the upper hand during the "foreign reign" of William III, a Dutchman.

Who, if once wrong, will needs be always so;
570   But you, with pleasure own your errors past,
And make each day a critic° on the last.   *critique*
      'Tis not enough, your counsel still be true;
Blunt truths more mischief than nice falsehoods do;
Men must be taught as if you taught them not,
575   And things unknown proposed as things forgot.
Without good breeding, truth is disapproved;
That only makes superior sense beloved.
      Be niggards of advice on no pretense;
For the worst avarice is that of sense.
580   With mean complacence⁵ ne'er betray your trust,
Nor be so civil as to prove unjust.
Fear not the anger of the wise to raise;
Those best can bear reproof, who merit praise.
      'Twere well might critics still this freedom take;
585   But Appius reddens at each word you speak,
And stares, tremendous! with a threatening eye,
Like some fierce tyrant in old tapestry.⁶
Fear most to tax an honorable fool,
Whose right it is, uncensured to be dull;
590   Such, without wit, are poets when they please,
As without learning they can take degrees.⁷
Leave dangerous truths to unsuccessful satyrs,°   *satires*
And flattery to fulsome dedicators,
Whom, when they praise, the world believes no more,
595   Than when they promise to give scribbling o'er.
'Tis best sometimes your censure to restrain,
And charitably let the dull be vain:
Your silence there is better than your spite,
For who can rail so long as they can write?
600   Still humming on, their drowsy course they keep,
And lashed so long, like tops, are lashed asleep.⁸
False steps but help them to renew the race,
As, after stumbling, jades° will mend their pace.   *worn-out horses*
What crowds of these, impenitently bold,
605   In sounds and jingling syllables grown old,
Still run on poets, in a raging vein,
Even to the dregs and squeezings of the brain,
Strain out the last dull droppings of their sense,
And rhyme with all the rage of impotence.
610   Such shameless bards we have, and yet 'tis true,
There are as mad, abandoned critics too.
The bookful blockhead, ignorantly read,
With loads of learned lumber° in his head,   *rubbish*
With his own tongue still edifies his ears,

---

5. Softness of manners; desire of pleasing.
6. "This picture was taken to himself by John Dennis, a furious old critic by profession, who, upon no other provocation, wrote against this Essay and its author, in a manner perfectly lunatic" [Pope's note, 1744]. Pope *did* intend to ridicule Dennis, whose *Appius and Virginia* had failed on

the stage in 1709 and who was known for his stare and his use of the word *tremendous* (see line 270).
7. Honorary degrees were granted to unqualified men of rank.
8. Tops "sleep" when they spin so rapidly that they seem not to move.

615 And always listening to himself appears.
    All books he reads, and all he reads assails,
    From Dryden's *Fables* down to Durfey's *Tales*.[9]
    With him, most authors steal their works, or buy;
    Garth did not write his own *Dispensary*.[1]
620 Name a new play, and he's the poet's friend,
    Nay showed his faults—but when would poets mend?
    No place so sacred from such fops is barred,
    Nor is Paul's church more safe than Paul's churchyard:[2]
    Nay, fly to altars; *there* they'll talk you dead:
625 For fools rush in where angels fear to tread.
    Distrustful sense with modest caution speaks,   ⎫
    It still looks home, and short excursions makes; ⎬
    But rattling nonsense in full volleys breaks,   ⎭
    And never shocked, and never turned aside,
630 Bursts out, resistless, with a thundering tide.
        But where's the man, who counsel can bestow,
    Still pleased to teach, and yet not proud to know?
    Unbiased, or° by favor, or by spite: *either*
    Not dully prepossessed, nor blindly right;
635 Though learned, well-bred; and though well-bred, sincere;
    Modestly bold, and humanly severe:
    Who to a friend his faults can freely show,
    And gladly praise the merit of a foe?
    Blessed with a taste exact, yet unconfined;
640 A knowledge both of books and humankind;
    Gen'rous converse;[3] a soul exempt from pride;
    And love to praise, with reason on his side?
        Such once were critics; such the happy few,
    Athens and Rome in better ages knew.
645 The mighty Stagirite° first left the shore,   *Aristotle*
    Spread all his sails, and durst the deeps explore;
    He steered securely, and discovered far,
    Led by the light of the Maeonian star.[4]
    Poets, a race long unconfined, and free,
650 Still fond and proud of savage liberty,
    Received his laws; and stood convinced 'twas fit,
    Who conquered nature, should preside o'er wit.
        Horace still charms with graceful negligence,
    And without method talks us into sense;
655 Will, like a friend, familiarly convey
    The truest notions in the easiest° way.   *least formal*
    He, who supreme in judgment, as in wit,
    Might boldly censure, as he boldly writ,
    Yet judged with coolness, though he sung with fire;
660 His precepts teach but what his works inspire.

---

9. Thomas D'Urfey's *Tales* (1704) were notorious potboilers. Dryden's *Fables* (1700), a set of translations, were among his most admired works.
1. Samuel Garth (1661–1719), who had been accused of plagiarizing his mock-epic poem *The Dispensary* (1699), was admired and defended by Pope.

2. Booksellers' district near St. Paul's Cathedral, whose aisles were used as a place to meet and do business.
3. Well-bred conversation.
4. Homer, who was supposed to have been born in Maeonia.

Our critics take a contrary extreme,
They judge with fury, but they write with fle'me.°   *phlegmatically*
Nor suffers Horace more in wrong translations
By wits, than critics[5] in as wrong quotations.
665   See Dionysius[6] Homer's thoughts refine,
And call new beauties forth from every line!
Fancy and art in gay Petronius[7] please,
The scholar's learning, with the courtier's ease.
In grave Quintilian's[8] copious work, we find
670   The justest rules, and clearest method joined:
Thus useful arms in magazines° we place,   *storehouses, arsenals*
All ranged in order, and disposed with grace,
But less to please the eye, than arm the hand,
Still fit for use, and ready at command.
675   Thee, bold Longinus![9] all the nine° inspire,   *Muses*
And bless their critic with a poet's fire.
An ardent judge, who, zealous in his trust,
With warmth gives sentence, yet is always just;
Whose own example strengthens all his laws,
680   And is himself that great sublime he draws.
Thus long succeeding critics justly reigned,
License repressed, and useful laws ordained.
Learning and Rome alike in empire grew;
And arts still followed where her eagles[1] flew;
685   From the same foes, at last, both felt their doom,
And the same age saw learning fall, and Rome.
With tyranny, then superstition joined,
As that the body, this enslaved the mind;
Much was believed, but little understood,
690   And to be dull was construed to be good;
A second deluge learning thus o'errun,
And the monks finished what the Goths begun.[2]
At length Erasmus, that great, injured name
(The glory of the priesthood, and the shame!),[3]
695   Stemmed the wild torrent of a barb'rous age,
And drove those holy Vandals off the stage.
But see! each Muse, in Leo's golden days,
Starts from her trance, and trims her withered bays![4]
Rome's ancient Genius, o'er its ruins spread,
700   Shakes off the dust, and rears his reverend head.
Then sculpture and her sister-arts revive;
Stones leaped to form, and rocks began to live;

---

5. I.e., than by critics. Phrases from Horace's *Art of Poetry* were quoted incessantly by critics.
6. Dionysius of Halicarnassus (1st century B.C.E.) wrote an important treatise on the artistic arrangement of words.
7. Author of the *Satyricon* (1st century C.E.).
8. Author of the *Institutio Oratorio* (ca. 95 C.E.), a famous treatise on rhetoric. Here as elsewhere, Pope's terms of praise are drawn from the author he is praising.
9. Supposed author of the influential treatise *On the Sublime* (1st century C.E.), greatly in vogue at the time of Pope.

1. Emblems on the standards of the Roman army.
2. Pope thought that the Scholastic theologians of the Middle Ages were "holy Vandals" who had "sacked" learning as the Goths and Vandals had sacked Rome.
3. Erasmus (1466–1536), the great humanist scholar, was the "glory of the priesthood" because of his goodness and learning and its "shame" because he was persecuted.
4. The wreath of poetry. Leo X, pope from 1513 to 1521, was notable for his encouragement of artists.

With sweeter notes each rising temple rung;
A Raphael painted, and a Vida[5] sung.
705 Immortal Vida: on whose honored brow
The poet's bays and critic's ivy grow:
Cremona now shall ever boast thy name,
As next in place to Mantua, next in fame![6]
    But soon by impious arms from Latium[7] chased,
710 Their ancient bounds the banished Muses passed;
Thence arts o'er all the northern world advance,
But critic-learning flourished most in France:
The rules a nation, born to serve, obeys;
And Boileau still in right of Horace sways.[8]
715 But we, brave Britons, foreign laws despised,
And kept unconquered—and uncivilized;
Fierce for the liberties of wit, and bold,
We still defied the Romans, as of old.
Yet some there were, among the sounder few
720 Of those who less presumed, and better knew,
Who durst assert the juster ancient cause,
And here restored wit's fundamental laws.
Such was the Muse, whose rules and practice tell,
"Nature's chief masterpiece is writing well."[9]
725 Such was Roscommon,[1] not more learned than good,
With manners gen'rous as his noble blood;
To him the wit of Greece and Rome was known,
And every author's merit, but his own.
Such late was Walsh—the Muse's[2] judge and friend,
730 Who justly knew to blame or to commend;
To failings mild, but zealous for desert;
The clearest head, and the sincerest heart.
This humble praise, lamented shade! receive,
This praise at least a grateful Muse may give:
735 The Muse, whose early voice you taught to sing,
Prescribed her heights, and pruned her tender wing,
(Her guide now lost) no more attempts to rise,
But in low numbers° short excursions tries: *humble verses*
Content, if hence the unlearned their wants may view,
740 The learned reflect on what before they knew:
Careless of° censure, nor too fond of fame;   *unconcerned at*
Still pleased to praise, yet not afraid to blame;
Averse alike to flatter, or offend;
Not free from faults, nor yet too vain to mend.

1709   1711

---

5. "M. Hieronymus Vida, an excellent Latin poet, who writ an Art of Poetry in verse. He flourished in the time of Leo the Tenth" [Pope's note]. Raphael (1483–1520) painted many of his greatest works under the patronage of Leo X.
6. Vida came from Cremona, near Mantua, the birthplace of Virgil, his favorite poet.
7. Italy. German and Spanish troops sacked Rome in 1527.
8. Boileau's *L'Art Poétique* (1674) regularized and modernized the lessons of Horace's *Art of Poetry*.
9. Quoted from an *Essay on Poetry* by John Sheffield, duke of Buckingham (1648–1721), who had befriended the young Pope.
1. Wentworth Dillon, earl of Roscommon, wrote the important *Essay on Translated Verse* (1684).
2. Here, Pope himself. William Walsh (1663–1708), whom Dryden once called "the best critic of our nation," had advised Pope to work at becoming the first great "correct" poet in English.

The Rape of the Lock

The Rape of the Lock is based on an actual episode that provoked a quarrel between two prominent Catholic families. Pope's friend John Caryll, to whom the poem is addressed (line 3), suggested that Pope write it, in the hope that a little laughter might serve to soothe ruffled tempers. Lord Petre had cut off a lock of hair from the head of the lovely Arabella Fermor (often spelled "Farmer" and doubtless so pronounced), much to the indignation of the lady and her relatives. In its original version of two cantos and 334 lines, published in 1712, *The Rape of the Lock* was a great success. In 1713 a new version was undertaken against the advice of Addison, who considered the poem perfect as it was first written. Pope greatly expanded the earlier version, adding the delightful "machinery" (i.e., the supernatural agents in epic action) of the Sylphs, Belinda's toilet, the card game, and the visit to the Cave of Spleen in canto 4. In 1717, with the addition of Clarissa's speech on good humor, the poem assumed its final form.

With delicate fancy and playful wit, Pope elaborated the trivial episode that occasioned the poem into the semblance of an epic in miniature, the most nearly perfect heroicomical poem in English. The verse abounds in parodies and echoes of the *Iliad*, the *Aeneid*, and *Paradise Lost*, thus constantly forcing the reader to compare small things with great. The familiar devices of epic are observed, but the incidents or characters are beautifully proportioned to the scale of mock epic. The *Rape* tells of war, but it is the drawing-room war between the sexes; it has its heroes and heroines, but they are beaux and belles; it has its supernatural characters ("machinery"), but they are Sylphs (borrowed, as Pope tells us in his dedicatory letter, from Rosicrucian lore)—creatures of the air, the souls of dead coquettes, with tasks appropriate to their nature—or the Gnome Umbriel, once a prude on earth; it has its epic game, played on the "velvet plain" of the card table, its feasting heroes, who sip coffee and gossip, and its battle, fought with the clichés of compliment and conceits, with frowns and angry glances, with snuff and bodkin; it has the traditional epic journey to the underworld—here the Cave of Spleen, emblematic of the ill nature of female hypochondriacs. And Pope creates a world in which these actions take place, a world that is dense with beautiful objects: brocades, ivory and tortoiseshell, cosmetics and diamonds, lacquered furniture, silver teapot, delicate chinaware. It is a world that is constantly in motion and that sparkles and glitters with light, whether the light of the sun or of Belinda's eyes or that light into which the "fluid" bodies of the Sylphs seem to dissolve as they flutter in shrouds and around the mast of Belinda's ship. Pope laughs at this world, its ritualized triviality, its irrational, upper-class women and feminized men—and remembers that a grimmer, darker world surrounds it (3.19–24 and 5.145–48); but he also makes us aware of its beauty and charm.

The epigraph may be translated, "I was unwilling, Belinda, to ravish your locks; but I rejoice to have conceded this to your prayers" (Martial's *Epigrams* 12.84.1–2). Pope substituted his heroine for Martial's Polytimus. The epigraph is intended to suggest that the poem was published at Miss Fermor's request.

The Rape of the Lock

An Heroi-Comical Poem

Nolueram, Belinda, tuos violare capillos;
sed juvat hoc precibus me tribuisse tuis.
—MARTIAL

TO MRS. ARABELLA FERMOR

MADAM,

It will be in vain to deny that I have some regard for this piece, since I dedicate it to you. Yet you may bear me witness, it was intended only to divert a few young ladies, who have good sense and good humor enough to laugh not only at their sex's little unguarded follies, but at their own. But as it was communicated with the air of a secret, it soon found its way into the world. An imperfect copy having been offered to a bookseller, you had the good nature for my sake to consent to the publication of one more correct; this I was forced to, before I had executed half my design, for the machinery was entirely wanting to complete it.

The machinery, Madam, is a term invented by the critics, to signify that part which the deities, angels, or demons are made to act in a poem; for the ancient poets are in one respect like many modern ladies: let an action be never so trivial in itself, they always make it appear of the utmost importance. These machines I determined to raise on a very new and odd foundation, the Rosicrucian[1] doctrine of spirits.

I know how disagreeable it is to make use of hard words before a lady; but 'tis so much the concern of a poet to have his works understood, and particularly by your sex, that you must give me leave to explain two or three difficult terms.

The Rosicrucians are a people I must bring you acquainted with. The best account I know of them is in a French book called *Le Comte de Gabalis*,[2] which both in its title and size is so like a novel, that many of the fair sex have read it for one by mistake. According to these gentlemen, the four elements are inhabited by spirits, which they call Sylphs, Gnomes, Nymphs, and Salamanders. The Gnomes or Demons of earth delight in mischief; but the Sylphs, whose habitation is in the air, are the best-conditioned creatures imaginable. For they say, any mortals may enjoy the most intimate familiarities with these gentle spirits, upon a condition very easy to all true adepts, an inviolate preservation of chastity.

As to the following cantos, all the passages of them are as fabulous as the vision at the beginning, or the transformation at the end (except the loss of your hair, which I always mention with reverence). The human persons are as fictitious as the airy ones; and the character of Belinda, as it is now managed, resembles you in nothing but in beauty.

If this poem had as many graces as there are in your person, or in your mind, yet I could never hope it should pass through the world half so uncensured as you have done. But let its fortune be what it will, mine is happy

---

1. A system of arcane philosophy introduced into England from Germany in the 17th century.

2. By the Abbé de Montfaucon de Villars, published in 1670.

enough, to have given me this occasion of assuring you that I am, with the truest esteem,

MADAM,
Your most obedient, humble servant,
A. POPE

Canto 1

What dire offense from amorous causes springs,
What mighty contests rise from trivial things,
I sing—This verse to Caryll, Muse! is due:
This, even Belinda may vouchsafe to view:
5 Slight is the subject, but not so the praise,
If she inspire, and he approve my lays.
    Say what strange motive, Goddess! could compel
A well-bred lord to assault a gentle belle?
Oh, say what stranger cause, yet unexplored,
10 Could make a gentle belle reject a lord?
In tasks so bold can little men engage,
And in soft bosoms dwells such mighty rage?
    Sol through white curtains shot a timorous ray,
And oped those eyes that must eclipse the day.
15 Now lapdogs give themselves the rousing shake,
And sleepless lovers, just at twelve, awake:
Thrice rung the bell, the slipper knocked the ground,
And the pressed watch[3] returned a silver sound.
Belinda still her downy pillow pressed,
20 Her guardian Sylph prolonged the balmy rest.
'Twas he had summoned to her silent bed
The morning dream that hovered o'er her head.
A youth more glittering than a birthnight beau[4]
(That even in slumber caused her cheek to glow)
25 Seemed to her ear his winning lips to lay,
And thus in whispers said, or seemed to say:
    "Fairest of mortals, thou distinguished care
Of thousand bright inhabitants of air!
If e'er one vision touched thy infant thought,
30 Of all the nurse and all the priest have taught,
Of airy elves by moonlight shadows seen,
The silver token, and the circled green,[5]
Or virgins visited by angel powers,
With golden crowns and wreaths of heavenly flowers,
35 Hear and believe! thy own importance know,
Nor bound thy narrow views to things below.
Some secret truths, from learned pride concealed,
To maids alone and children are revealed:
What though no credit doubting wits may give?

3. A watch that chimes the hour and the quarter hour when the stem is pressed down. "Knocked the ground": summons to a maid.
4. Courtiers wore especially fine clothes on the sovereign's birthday.
5. Rings of bright green grass, which are common in England even in winter, were held to be caused by the round dances of fairies. According to popular belief, fairies skim off the cream from jugs of milk left standing overnight and leave a coin ("silver token") in payment.

40 The fair and innocent shall still believe.
Know, then, unnumbered spirits round thee fly,
The light militia of the lower sky:
These, though unseen, are ever on the wing,
Hang o'er the box, and hover round the Ring.[6]
45 Think what an equipage thou hast in air,
And view with scorn two pages and a chair.°   *sedan chair*
As now your own, our beings were of old,
And once enclosed in woman's beauteous mold;
Thence, by a soft transition, we repair
50 From earthly vehicles to these of air.
Think not, when woman's transient breath is fled,
That all her vanities at once are dead:
Succeeding vanities she still regards,
And though she plays no more, o'erlooks the cards.
55 Her joy in gilded chariots, when alive,
And love of ombre,[7] after death survive.
For when the Fair in all their pride expire,
To their first elements[8] their souls retire:
The sprites of fiery termagants in flame
60 Mount up, and take a Salamander's[9] name.
Soft yielding minds to water glide away,
And sip, with Nymphs, their elemental tea.[1]
The graver prude sinks downward to a Gnome,
In search of mischief still on earth to roam.
65 The light coquettes in Sylphs aloft repair,
And sport and flutter in the fields of air.
 "Know further yet; whoever fair and chaste
Rejects mankind, is by some Sylph embraced:
For spirits, freed from mortal laws, with ease
70 Assume what sexes and what shapes they please.[2]
What guards the purity of melting maids,
In courtly balls, and midnight masquerades,
Safe from the treacherous friend, the daring spark,
The glance by day, the whisper in the dark,
75 When kind occasion prompts their warm desires,
When music softens, and when dancing fires?
'Tis but their Sylph, the wise Celestials° know, *heavenly beings*
Though Honor is the word with men below.
 "Some nymphs[3] there are, too conscious of their face,
80 For life predestined to the Gnomes' embrace.
These swell their prospects and exalt their pride,
When offers are disdained, and love denied:
Then gay ideas° crowd the vacant brain,   *showy images*

6. The "box" in the theater and the fashionable
circular drive ("Ring") in Hyde Park.
7. The popular card game (see n. 1, p. 1234).
8. The four elements out of which all things were
believed to have been made were fire, water, earth,
and air. One or another of these elements was supposed to be predominant in both the physical and
the psychological makeup of each human being.
In this context they are spoken of as "humors."
9. A lizardlike animal, in antiquity believed to

live in fire. Each element was inhabited by a
spirit, as the following lines explain. "Termagants": shrewish or overbearing women.
1. Pronounced *tay*.
2. Cf. *Paradise Lost* 1.427–31; this is one of
many allusions to that poem in the *Rape*.
3. Here and after, a fanciful name for a young
woman, to be distinguished from the "Nymphs"
(water spirits) in line 62.

While peers, and dukes, and all their sweeping train,
85 And garters, stars, and coronets[4] appear,
And in soft sounds, 'your Grace'° salutes their ear.   *a duchess*
'Tis these that early taint the female soul,
Instruct the eyes of young coquettes to roll,
Teach infant cheeks a bidden blush to know,
90 And little hearts to flutter at a beau.
    "Oft, when the world imagine women stray,
The Sylphs through mystic mazes guide their way,
Through all the giddy circle they pursue,
And old impertinence° expel by new.   *trifle*
95 What tender maid but must a victim fall
To one man's treat, but for another's ball?
When Florio speaks, what virgin could withstand,
If gentle Damon did not squeeze her hand?
With varying vanities, from every part,
100 They shift the moving toyshop[5] of their heart;
Where wigs with wigs, with sword-knots sword-knots strive,
Beaux banish beaux, and coaches coaches drive.
This erring mortals levity may call;
Oh, blind to truth! the Sylphs contrive it all.
105   "Of these am I, who thy protection claim,
A watchful sprite, and Ariel is my name.
Late, as I ranged the crystal wilds of air,
In the clear mirror of thy ruling star
I saw, alas! some dread event impend,
110 Ere to the main this morning sun descend,
But Heaven reveals not what, or how, or where:
Warned by thy Sylph, O pious maid, beware!
This to disclose is all thy guardian can:
Beware of all, but most beware of Man!"
115   He said; when Shock,[6] who thought she slept too long,
Leaped up, and waked his mistress with his tongue.
'Twas then, Belinda, if report say true,
Thy eyes first opened on a billet-doux;
Wounds, charms, and ardors were no sooner read,
120 But all the vision vanished from thy head.
    And now, unveiled, the toilet stands displayed,
Each silver vase in mystic order laid.
First, robed in white, the nymph intent adores,
With head uncovered, the cosmetic powers.
125 A heavenly image in the glass appears;
To that she bends, to that her eyes she rears.
The inferior priestess, at her altar's side,
Trembling begins the sacred rites of Pride.
Unnumbered treasures ope at once, and here
130 The various offerings of the world appear;
From each she nicely culls with curious toil,
And decks the goddess with the glittering spoil.
This casket India's glowing gems unlocks,

---

4. Emblems of nobility.
5. A shop stocked with baubles and trifles.

6. A long-haired poodle, Belinda's lapdog.

And all Arabia breathes from yonder box.
135 The tortoise here and elephant unite,
Transformed to combs, the speckled and the white.
Here files of pins extend their shining rows,
Puffs, powders, patches, Bibles,[7] billet-doux.
Now awful° Beauty puts on all its arms;   *awe-inspiring*
140 The fair each moment rises in her charms,
Repairs her smiles, awakens every grace,
And calls forth all the wonders of her face;
Sees by degrees a purer blush arise,
And keener lightnings quicken in her eyes.
145 The busy Sylphs surround their darling care,
These set the head, and those divide the hair,
Some fold the sleeve, whilst others plait the gown;
And Betty's[8] praised for labors not her own.

Canto 2

Not with more glories, in the ethereal plain,
The sun first rises o'er the purpled main,
Than, issuing forth, the rival of his beams
Launched on the bosom of the silver Thames.
5 Fair nymphs and well-dressed youths around her shone,
But every eye was fixed on her alone.
On her white breast a sparkling cross she wore,
Which Jews might kiss, and infidels adore.
Her lively looks a sprightly mind disclose,
10 Quick as her eyes, and as unfixed as those:
Favors to none, to all she smiles extends;
Oft she rejects, but never once offends.
Bright as the sun, her eyes the gazers strike,
And, like the sun, they shine on all alike.
15 Yet graceful ease, and sweetness void of pride,
Might hide her faults, if belles had faults to hide:
If to her share some female errors fall,
Look on her face, and you'll forget 'em all.
This nymph, to the destruction of mankind,
20 Nourished two locks which graceful hung behind
In equal curls, and well conspired to deck
With shining ringlets her smooth ivory neck.
Love in these labyrinths his slaves detains,
And mighty hearts are held in slender chains.
25 With hairy springes[9] we the birds betray,
Slight lines of hair surprise the finny prey,
Fair tresses man's imperial race ensnare,
And beauty draws us with a single hair.
The adventurous Baron the bright locks admired,
30 He saw, he wished, and to the prize aspired.
Resolved to win, he meditates the way,

7. It has been suggested that Pope intended here not "Bibles," but "bibelots" (trinkets), but this interpretation has not gained wide acceptance.

8. Belinda's maid, the "inferior priestess" mentioned in line 127.

9. Snares (pronounced *sprin-jez*).

By force to ravish, or by fraud betray;
For when success a lover's toil attends,
Few ask if fraud or force attained his ends.
35   For this, ere Phoebus° rose, he had implored   *the sun*
Propitious Heaven, and every power adored,
But chiefly Love—to Love an altar built,
Of twelve vast French romances, neatly gilt.
There lay three garters, half a pair of gloves,
40   And all the trophies of his former loves.
With tender billet-doux he lights the pyre,
And breathes three amorous sighs to raise the fire.
Then prostrate falls, and begs with ardent eyes
Soon to obtain, and long possess the prize:
45   The powers gave ear, and granted half his prayer,
The rest the winds dispersed in empty air.
      But now secure the painted vessel glides,
The sunbeams trembling on the floating tides,
While melting music steals upon the sky,
50   And softened sounds along the waters die.
Smooth flow the waves, the zephyrs gently play,
Belinda smiled, and all the world was gay.
All but the Sylph—with careful thoughts oppressed,
The impending woe sat heavy on his breast.
55   He summons straight his denizens of air;
The lucid squadrons round the sails repair:
Soft o'er the shrouds aërial whispers breathe
That seemed but zephyrs to the train beneath.
Some to the sun their insect-wings unfold,
60   Waft on the breeze, or sink in clouds of gold.
Transparent forms too fine for mortal sight,
Their fluid bodies half dissolved in light,
Loose to the wind their airy garments flew,
Thin glittering textures of the filmy dew,
65   Dipped in the richest tincture of the skies,
Where light disports in ever-mingling dyes,
While every beam new transient colors flings,
Colors that change whene'er they wave their wings.
Amid the circle, on the gilded mast,
70   Superior by the head was Ariel placed;
His purple[1] pinions opening to the sun,
He raised his azure wand, and thus begun:
      "Ye Sylphs and Sylphids, to your chief give ear!
Fays, Fairies, Genïi, Elves, and Daemons, hear!
75   Ye know the spheres and various tasks assigned
By laws eternal to the aërial kind.
Some in the fields of purest ether play,
And bask and whiten in the blaze of day.
Some guide the course of wandering orbs on high,
80   Or roll the planets through the boundless sky.
Some less refined, beneath the moon's pale light

---

1. In 18th-century poetic diction the word might mean bloodred, purple, or simply (as is likely here) brightly colored. The word derives from Virgil's *Eclogue* 9.40, *purpureum.* An example of the Latinate nature of some poetic diction of the period.

Pursue the stars that shoot athwart the night,
Or suck the mists in grosser air below,
Or dip their pinions in the painted bow,°   *rainbow*
85 Or brew fierce tempests on the wintry main,
Or o'er the glebe° distill the kindly rain.   *cultivated field*
Others on earth o'er human race preside,
Watch all their ways, and all their actions guide:
Of these the chief the care of nations own,
90 And guard with arms divine the British Throne.
  "Our humbler province is to tend the Fair,
Not a less pleasing, though less glorious care:
To save the powder from too rude a gale,
Nor let the imprisoned essences° exhale;   *perfumes*
95 To draw fresh colors from the vernal flowers;
To steal from rainbows e'er they drop in showers
A brighter wash;° to curl their waving hairs, *cosmetic lotion*
Assist their blushes, and inspire their airs,
Nay oft, in dreams invention we bestow,
100 To change a flounce, or add a furbelow.
  "This day black omens threat the brightest fair,
That e'er deserved a watchful spirit's care;
Some dire disaster, or by force or slight,
But what, or where, the Fates have wrapped in night:
105 Whether the nymph shall break Diana's[2] law,
Or some frail china jar receive a flaw,
Or stain her honor, or her new brocade,
Forget her prayers, or miss a masquerade,
Or lose her heart, or necklace, at a ball;
110 Or whether Heaven has doomed that Shock must fall.
Haste, then, ye spirits! to your charge repair:
The fluttering fan be Zephyretta's care;
The drops[3] to thee, Brillante, we consign;
And, Momentilla, let the watch be thine;
115 Do thou, Crispissa,[4] tend her favorite Lock;
Ariel himself shall be the guard of Shock.
  "To fifty chosen Sylphs, of special note,
We trust the important charge, the petticoat;
Oft have we known that sevenfold fence to fail,
120 Though stiff with hoops, and armed with ribs of whale.[5]
Form a strong line about the silver bound,
And guard the wide circumference around.
  "Whatever spirit, careless of his charge,
His post neglects, or leaves the fair at large,
125 Shall feel sharp vengeance soon o'ertake his sins,
Be stopped in vials, or transfixed with pins,
Or plunged in lakes of bitter washes lie,
Or wedged whole ages in a bodkin's[6] eye;
Gums and pomatums shall his flight restrain,
130 While clogged he beats his silken wings in vain,

---

2. Diana was the goddess of chastity.
3. Diamond earrings. Observe the appropriateness of the names of the Sylphs to their assigned functions.
4. From Latin *crispere*, "to curl."

5. Corsets and the hoops of hoopskirts were made of whalebone.
6. A blunt needle with a large eye used for drawing ribbon through eyelets in the edging of women's garments.

Or alum styptics with contracting power
Shrink his thin essence like a riveled[7] flower:
Or, as Ixion[8] fixed, the wretch shall feel
The giddy motion of the whirling mill,
135   In fumes of burning chocolate shall glow,
And tremble at the sea that froths below!"
    He spoke; the spirits from the sails descend;
Some, orb in orb, around the nymph extend;
Some thread the mazy ringlets of her hair;
140   Some hang upon the pendants of her ear:
With beating hearts the dire event they wait,
Anxious, and trembling for the birth of Fate.

Canto 3

    Close by those meads, forever crowned with flowers,
Where Thames with pride surveys his rising towers,
There stands a structure of majestic frame,
Which from the neighboring Hampton[9] takes its name.
5   Here Britain's statesmen oft the fall foredoom
Of foreign tyrants and of nymphs at home;
Here thou, great Anna! whom three realms obey,
Dost sometimes counsel take—and sometimes tea.
    Hither the heroes and the nymphs resort,
10   To taste awhile the pleasures of a court;
In various talk the instructive hours they passed,
Who gave the ball, or paid the visit last;
One speaks the glory of the British Queen,
And one describes a charming Indian screen;
15   A third interprets motions, looks, and eyes;
At every word a reputation dies.
Snuff, or the fan, supply each pause of chat,
With singing, laughing, ogling, and all that.
    Meanwhile, declining from the noon of day,
20   The sun obliquely shoots his burning ray;
The hungry judges soon the sentence sign,
And wretches hang that jurymen may dine;
The merchant from the Exchange returns in peace,
And the long labors of the toilet cease.
25   Belinda now, whom thirst of fame invites,
Burns to encounter two adventurous knights,
At ombre[1] singly to decide their doom,
And swells her breast with conquests yet to come.

---

7. To "rivel" is to "contract into wrinkles and corrugations" (Johnson's *Dictionary*).
8. In the Greek myth, he was punished in the underworld by being bound on an everturning wheel.
9. Hampton Court, the royal palace, about fifteen miles up the Thames from London.
1. The game of ombre that Belinda plays against the baron and another young man is too complicated for complete explication here. Pope has carefully arranged the cards so that Belinda wins. The baron's hand is strong enough to be a threat, but the third player's is of little account. The hand is played exactly according to the rules of ombre, and Pope's description of the cards is equally accurate. Each player holds nine cards (line 30). The "Matadores" (line 33), when spades are trump, are "Spadillio" (line 49), the ace of spades; "Manillio" (line 51), the two of spades; and "Basto" (line 53), the ace of clubs. Belinda holds all three of these. (For a more complete description of ombre, see *The Rape of the Lock and Other Poems*, ed. Geoffrey Tillotson, in the Twickenham Edition of Pope's poems, vol. 2, Appendix C.)

Straight the three bands prepare in arms to join,
30   Each band the number of the sacred nine.
Soon as she spreads her hand, the aërial guard
Descend, and sit on each important card:
First Ariel perched upon a Matadore,
Then each according to the rank they bore;
35   For Sylphs, yet mindful of their ancient race,
Are, as when women, wondrous fond of place.
    Behold, four Kings in majesty revered,
With hoary whiskers and a forky beard;
And four fair Queens whose hands sustain a flower,
40   The expressive emblem of their softer power;
Four Knaves in garbs succinct,° a trusty band,   girded up
Caps on their heads, and halberts in their hand;
And parti-colored troops, a shining train,
Draw forth to combat on the velvet plain.
45   The skillful nymph reviews her force with care;
"Let Spades be trumps!" she said, and trumps they were.
    Now move to war her sable Matadores,
In show like leaders of the swarthy Moors.
Spadillio first, unconquerable lord!
50   Led off two captive trumps, and swept the board.
As many more Manillio forced to yield,
And marched a victor from the verdant field.
Him Basto followed, but his fate more hard
Gained but one trump and one plebeian card.
55   With his broad saber next, a chief in years,
The hoary Majesty of Spades appears,
Puts forth one manly leg, to sight revealed,
The rest his many-colored robe concealed.
The rebel Knave, who dares his prince engage,
60   Proves the just victim of his royal rage.
Even mighty Pam,[2] that kings and queens o'erthrew
And mowed down armies in the fights of loo,
Sad chance of war! now destitute of aid,
Falls undistinguished by the victor Spade.
65   Thus far both armies to Belinda yield;
Now to the Baron fate inclines the field.
His warlike amazon her host invades,
The imperial consort of the crown of Spades.
The Club's black tyrant first her victim died,
70   Spite of his haughty mien and barbarous pride.
What boots° the regal circle on his head,   avails
His giant limbs, in state unwieldy spread?
That long behind he trails his pompous robe,
And of all monarchs only grasps the globe?[3]
75   The Baron now his Diamonds pours apace;
The embroidered King who shows but half his face,
And his refulgent Queen, with powers combined,
Of broken troops an easy conquest find.

2. The knave of clubs, the highest trump in the   3. In the English deck, only the king of clubs
game of loo.   holds an imperial orb.

Clubs, Diamonds, Hearts, in wild disorder seen,
80 With throngs promiscuous strew the level green.
Thus when dispersed a routed army runs,
Of Asia's troops, and Afric's sable sons,
With like confusion different nations fly,
Of various habit, and of various dye,
85 The pierced battalions disunited fall
In heaps on heaps; one fate o'erwhelms them all.
    The Knave of Diamonds tries his wily arts,
And wins (oh, shameful chance!) the Queen of Hearts.
At this, the blood the virgin's cheek forsook,
90 A livid paleness spreads o'er all her look;
She sees, and trembles at the approaching ill,
Just in the jaws of ruin, and Codille.[4]
And now (as oft in some distempered state)
On one nice trick depends the general fate.
95 An Ace of Hearts steps forth: the King unseen
Lurked in her hand, and mourned his captive Queen.
He springs to vengeance with an eager pace,
And falls like thunder on the prostrate Ace.
The nymph exulting fills with shouts the sky,
100 The walls, the woods, and long canals reply.
    O thoughtless mortals! ever blind to fate,
Too soon dejected, and too soon elate:
Sudden these honors shall be snatched away,
And cursed forever this victorious day.
105   For lo! the board with cups and spoons is crowned,
The berries crackle, and the mill turns round;[5]
On shining altars of Japan[6] they raise
The silver lamp; the fiery spirits blaze:
From silver spouts the grateful liquors glide,
110 While China's earth receives the smoking tide.
At once they gratify their scent and taste,
And frequent cups prolong the rich repast.
Straight hover round the fair her airy band;
Some, as she sipped, the fuming liquor fanned,
115 Some o'er her lap their careful plumes displayed,
Trembling, and conscious of the rich brocade.
Coffee (which makes the politician wise,
And see through all things with his half-shut eyes)
Sent up in vapors to the Baron's brain
120 New stratagems, the radiant Lock to gain.
Ah, cease, rash youth! desist ere 'tis too late,
Fear the just Gods, and think of Scylla's[7] fate!
Changed to a bird, and sent to flit in air,
She dearly pays for Nisus' injured hair!
125   But when to mischief mortals bend their will,

---

4. The term applied to losing a hand at cards.
5. I.e., coffee is roasted and ground.
6. I.e., small, lacquered tables. "Altars" suggests the ritualistic character of coffee drinking in Belinda's world.
7. Scylla, daughter of Nisus, was turned into a sea bird because, for the sake of her love for Minos of Crete, who was besieging her father's city of Megara, she cut from her father's head the purple lock on which his safety depended. She is not the Scylla of "Scylla and Charybdis."

How soon they find fit instruments of ill!
Just then, Clarissa drew with tempting grace
A two-edged weapon from her shining case:
So ladies in romance assist their knight,
130 Present the spear, and arm him for the fight.
He takes the gift with reverence, and extends
The little engine on his fingers' ends;
This just behind Belinda's neck he spread,
As o'er the fragrant steams she bends her head.
135 Swift to the Lock a thousand sprites repair,
A thousand wings, by turns, blow back the hair,
And thrice they twitched the diamond in her ear,
Thrice she looked back, and thrice the foe drew near.
Just in that instant, anxious Ariel sought
140 The close recesses of the virgin's thought;
As on the nosegay in her breast reclined,
He watched the ideas rising in her mind,
Sudden he viewed, in spite of all her art,
An earthly lover lurking at her heart.
145 Amazed, confused, he found his power expired,
Resigned to fate, and with a sigh retired.
    The Peer now spreads the glittering forfex° wide,   *scissors*
To enclose the Lock; now joins it, to divide.
Even then, before the fatal engine closed,
150 A wretched Sylph too fondly interposed;
Fate urged the shears, and cut the Sylph in twain
(But airy substance soon unites again):
The meeting points the sacred hair dissever
From the fair head, forever and forever!
155   Then flashed the living lightning from her eyes,
And screams of horror rend the affrighted skies.
Not louder shrieks to pitying heaven are cast,
When husbands, or when lapdogs breathe their last;
Or when rich china vessels fallen from high,
160 In glittering dust and painted fragments lie!
"Let wreaths of triumph now my temples twine,"
The victor cried, "the glorious prize is mine!
While fish in streams, or birds delight in air,
Or in a coach and six the British fair,
165 As long as *Atalantis*[8] shall be read,
Or the small pillow grace a lady's bed,
While visits shall be paid on solemn days,
When numerous wax-lights in bright order blaze,
While nymphs take treats,° or assignations give,   *free refreshments*
170 So long my honor, name, and praise shall live!
    "What time would spare, from steel receives its date,
And monuments, like men, submit to fate!
Steel could the labor of the Gods destroy,
And strike to dust the imperial towers of Troy;
175 Steel could the works of mortal pride confound,

---

8. Delarivier Manley's *New Atalantis* (1709) was notorious for its thinly concealed allusions to contemporary scandals.

And hew triumphal arches to the ground.
What wonder then, fair nymph! thy hairs should feel,
The conquering force of unresisted steel?"

Canto 4

But anxious cares the pensive nymph oppressed,
And secret passions labored in her breast.
Not youthful kings in battle seized alive,
Not scornful virgins who their charms survive,
5   Not ardent lovers robbed of all their bliss,
Not ancient ladies when refused a kiss,
Not tyrants fierce that unrepenting die,
Not Cynthia when her manteau's° pinned awry,   *wrap*
E'er felt such rage, resentment, and despair,
10   As thou, sad virgin! for thy ravished hair.
For, that sad moment, when the Sylphs withdrew
And Ariel weeping from Belinda flew,
Umbriel,[9] a dusky, melancholy sprite
As ever sullied the fair face of light,
15   Down to the central earth, his proper scene,
Repaired to search the gloomy Cave of Spleen.°   *Ill Humor*
Swift on his sooty pinions flits the Gnome,
And in a vapor reached the dismal dome.
No cheerful breeze this sullen region knows,
20   The dreaded east is all the wind that blows.
Here in a grotto, sheltered close from air,
And screened in shades from day's detested glare,
She sighs forever on her pensive bed,
Pain at her side, and Megrim° at her head.   *headache*
25   Two handmaids wait the throne: alike in place
But differing far in figure and in face.
Here stood Ill-Nature like an ancient maid,
Her wrinkled form in black and white arrayed;
With store of prayers for mornings, nights, and noons,
30   Her hand is filled; her bosom with lampoons.
There Affectation, with a sickly mien,
Shows in her cheek the roses of eighteen,
Practiced to lisp, and hang the head aside,
Faints into airs, and languishes with pride,
35   On the rich quilt sinks with becoming woe,
Wrapped in a gown, for sickness and for show.
The fair ones° feel such maladies as these,   *women*
When each new nightdress gives a new disease.
A constant vapor[1] o'er the palace flies,
40   Strange phantoms rising as the mists arise;
Dreadful as hermit's dreams in haunted shades,
Or bright as visions of expiring maids.
Now glaring fiends, and snakes on rolling spires,°   *coils*
Pale specters, gaping tombs, and purple fires;

9. The name suggests shade and darkness.
1. Emblematic of "the vapors," a fashionable hypochondria, melancholy, or peevishness.

45   Now lakes of liquid gold, Elysian scenes,
    And crystal domes, and angels in machines.[2]
       Unnumbered throngs on every side are seen
    Of bodies changed to various forms by Spleen.
    Here living teapots stand, one arm held out,
50   One bent; the handle this, and that the spout:
    A pipkin° there, like Homer's tripod,[3] walks;   *earthen pot*
    Here sighs a jar, and there a goose pie talks;
    Men prove with child, as powerful fancy works,
    And maids, turned bottles, call aloud for corks.
55   Safe passed the Gnome through this fantastic band,
    A branch of healing spleenwort[4] in his hand.
    Then thus addressed the Power: "Hail, wayward Queen!
    Who rule the sex to fifty from fifteen:
    Parent of vapors and of female wit,
60   Who give the hysteric or poetic fit,
    On various tempers act by various ways,
    Make some take physic,° others scribble plays;   *medicine*
    Who cause the proud their visits to delay,
    And send the godly in a pet to pray.
65   A nymph there is that all your power disdains,
    And thousands more in equal mirth maintains.
    But oh! if e'er thy Gnome could spoil a grace,
    Or raise a pimple on a beauteous face,
    Like citron-waters[5] matrons' cheeks inflame,
70   Or change complexions at a losing game;
    If e'er with airy horns[6] I planted heads,
    Or rumpled petticoats, or tumbled beds,
    Or caused suspicion when no soul was rude,
    Or discomposed the headdress of a prude,
75   Or e'er to costive lapdog gave disease,
    Which not the tears of brightest eyes could ease,
    Hear me, and touch Belinda with chagrin:°   *ill humor*
    That single act gives half the world the spleen."
      The Goddess with a discontented air
80   Seems to reject him though she grants his prayer.
    A wondrous bag with both her hands she binds,
    Like that where once Ulysses held the winds;[7]
    There she collects the force of female lungs,
    Sighs, sobs, and passions, and the war of tongues.
85   A vial next she fills with fainting fears,
    Soft sorrows, melting griefs, and flowing tears.
    The Gnome rejoicing bears her gifts away,
    Spreads his black wings, and slowly mounts to day.

2. Mechanical devices used in the theaters for spectacular effects. The catalog of hallucinations draws on the sensational stage effects popular with contemporary audiences.
3. In the *Iliad* (18.373–77), Vulcan furnishes the gods with self-propelling "tripods" (three-legged stools).
4. An herb, efficacious against diseases of the spleen. Pope alludes to the golden bough that Aeneas and the Cumaean sibyl carry with them for protection into the underworld in *Aeneid* 6.

5. Brandy flavored with orange or lemon peel.
6. The symbol of the cuckold, the man whose wife has been unfaithful to him; here "airy," because they exist only in the jealous suspicions of the husband, the victim of the mischievous Umbriel.
7. Aeolus (later conceived of as god of the winds) gave Ulysses a bag containing all the winds adverse to his voyage home. When his ship was in sight of Ithaca, his companions opened the bag and the storms that ensued drove Ulysses far away (*Odyssey* 10.19ff.).

Sunk in Thalestris'[8] arms the nymph he found,
90 Her eyes dejected and her hair unbound.
Full o'er their heads the swelling bag he rent,
And all the Furies issued at the vent.
Belinda burns with more than mortal ire,
And fierce Thalestris fans the rising fire.
95 "O wretched maid!" she spread her hands, and cried
(While Hampton's echoes, "Wretched maid!" replied),
"Was it for this you took such constant care
The bodkin, comb, and essence to prepare?
For this your locks in paper durance bound,
100 For this with torturing irons wreathed around?
For this with fillets strained your tender head,
And bravely bore the double loads of lead?[9]
Gods! shall the ravisher display your hair,
While the fops envy, and the ladies stare!
105 Honor forbid! at whose unrivaled shrine
Ease, pleasure, virtue, all, our sex resign.
Methinks already I your tears survey,
Already hear the horrid things they say,
Already see you a degraded toast,
110 And all your honor in a whisper lost!
How shall I, then, your helpless fame defend?
'Twill then be infamy to seem your friend!
And shall this prize, the inestimable prize,
Exposed through crystal to the gazing eyes,
115 And heightened by the diamond's circling rays,
On that rapacious hand forever blaze?
Sooner shall grass in Hyde Park Circus grow,
And wits take lodgings in the sound of Bow;[1]
Sooner let earth, air, sea, to chaos fall,
120 Men, monkeys, lapdogs, parrots, perish all!"
She said; then raging to Sir Plume repairs,
And bids her beau demand the precious hairs
(Sir Plume of amber snuffbox justly vain,
And the nice conduct of a clouded° cane).   *marbled, veined*
125 With earnest eyes, and round unthinking face,
He first the snuffbox opened, then the case,
And thus broke out—"My Lord, why, what the devil!
Z—ds! damn the lock! 'fore Gad, you must be civil!
Plague on 't! 'tis past a jest—nay prithee, pox!
130 Give her the hair"—he spoke, and rapped his box.
"It grieves me much," replied the Peer again,
"Who speaks so well should ever speak in vain.
But by this Lock, this sacred Lock I swear
(Which never more shall join its parted hair;
135 Which never more its honors shall renew,
Clipped from the lovely head where late it grew),
That while my nostrils draw the vital air,

---

8. The name is borrowed from a queen of the Amazons, hence a fierce and warlike woman.
9. The frame on which the elaborate coiffures of the day were arranged.

1. A person born within sound of the bells of St. Mary-le-Bow in Cheapside is said to be a cockney. No fashionable wit would have so vulgar an address.

This hand, which won it, shall forever wear."
He spoke, and speaking, in proud triumph spread
140 The long-contended honors² of her head.
    But Umbriel, hateful Gnome, forbears not so;
He breaks the vial whence the sorrows flow.
Then see! the nymph in beauteous grief appears,
Her eyes half languishing, half drowned in tears;
145 On her heaved bosom hung her drooping head,
Which with a sigh she raised, and thus she said:
    "Forever cursed be this detested day,
Which snatched my best, my favorite curl away!
Happy! ah, ten times happy had I been,
150 If Hampton Court these eyes had never seen!
Yet am not I the first mistaken maid,
By love of courts to numerous ills betrayed.
Oh, had I rather unadmired remained
In some lone isle, or distant northern land;
155 Where the gilt chariot never marks the way,
Where none learn ombre, none e'er taste bohea!³
There kept my charms concealed from mortal eye,
Like roses that in deserts bloom and die.
What moved my mind with youthful lords to roam?
160 Oh, had I stayed, and said my prayers at home!
'Twas this the morning omens seemed to tell;
Thrice from my trembling hand the patch box⁴ fell;
The tottering china shook without a wind,
Nay, Poll sat mute, and Shock was most unkind!
165 A Sylph too warned me of the threats of fate,
In mystic visions, now believed too late!
See the poor remnants of these slighted hairs!
My hands shall rend what e'en thy rapine spares.
These in two sable ringlets taught to break,
170 Once gave new beauties to the snowy neck.
The sister lock now sits uncouth, alone,
And in its fellow's fate foresees its own;
Uncurled it hangs, the fatal shears demands,
And tempts once more thy sacrilegious hands.
175 Oh, hadst thou, cruel! been content to seize
Hairs less in sight, or any hairs but these!"

Canto 5

    She said: the pitying audience melt in tears.
But Fate and Jove had stopped the Baron's ears.
In vain Thalestris with reproach assails,
For who can move when fair Belinda fails?
5 Not half so fixed the Trojan⁵ could remain,
While Anna begged and Dido raged in vain.

2. Ornaments, hence locks; a Latinism.
3. A costly sort of tea.
4. To hold the ornamental patches of court plaster worn on the face by both sexes.
5. Aeneas, who forsook Dido at the bidding of the gods, despite her reproaches and the supplications of her sister Anna. Virgil compares him to a steadfast oak that withstands a storm (*Aeneid* 4.437–43).

Then grave Clarissa graceful waved her fan;
Silence ensued, and thus the nymph began:
"Say, why are beauties praised and honored most,
10 The wise man's passion, and the vain man's toast?
Why decked with all that land and sea afford,
Why angels called, and angel-like adored?
Why round our coaches crowd the white-gloved beaux,
Why bows the side box from its inmost rows?
15 How vain are all these glories, all our pains,
Unless good sense preserve what beauty gains;
That men may say when we the front box grace,
'Behold the first in virtue as in face!'
Oh! if to dance all night, and dress all day,
20 Charmed the smallpox, or chased old age away,
Who would not scorn what housewife's cares produce,
Or who would learn one earthly thing of use?
To patch, nay ogle, might become a saint,
Nor could it sure be such a sin to paint.
25 But since, alas! frail beauty must decay,
Curled or uncurled, since locks will turn to gray;
Since painted, or not painted, all shall fade,
And she who scorns a man must die a maid;
What then remains but well our power to use,
30 And keep good humor still whate'er we lose?
And trust me, dear, good humor can prevail
When airs, and flights, and screams, and scolding fail.
Beauties in vain their pretty eyes may roll;
Charms strike the sight, but merit wins the soul."[6]
35   So spoke the dame, but no applause ensued;
Belinda frowned, Thalestris called her prude.
"To arms, to arms!" the fierce virago cries,
And swift as lightning to the combat flies.
All side in parties, and begin the attack;
40 Fans clap, silks rustle, and tough whalebones crack;
Heroes' and heroines' shouts confusedly rise,
And bass and treble voices strike the skies.
No common weapons in their hands are found,
Like Gods they fight, nor dread a mortal wound.
45   So when bold Homer makes the Gods engage,
And heavenly breasts with human passions rage;
'Gainst Pallas, Mars; Latona, Hermes arms;
And all Olympus rings with loud alarms:
Jove's thunder roars, heaven trembles all around,
50 Blue Neptune storms, the bellowing deeps resound:
Earth shakes her nodding towers, the ground gives way,
And the pale ghosts start at the flash of day!
Triumphant Umbriel on a sconce's[7] height
Clapped his glad wings, and sat to view the fight:
55 Propped on the bodkin spears, the sprites survey

---

6. The speech is a close parody of Pope's own translation of the speech of Sarpedon to Glaucus, first published in 1709 and slightly revised in his version of the *Iliad* (12.371–96).

7. A sconce is a candlestick fastened on the wall.

The growing combat, or assist the fray.
   While through the press enraged Thalestris flies,
And scatters death around from both her eyes,
A beau and witling perished in the throng,
60 One died in metaphor, and one in song.
"O cruel nymph! a living death I bear,"
Cried Dapperwit, and sunk beside his chair.
A mournful glance Sir Fopling upwards cast,
"Those eyes are made so killing"—was his last.
65 Thus on Maeander's flowery margin lies
The expiring swan,[8] and as he sings he dies.
   When bold Sir Plume had drawn Clarissa down,
Chloe stepped in, and killed him with a frown;
She smiled to see the doughty hero slain,
70 But, at her smile, the beau revived again.
   Now Jove suspends his golden scales in air,
Weighs the men's wits against the lady's hair;
The doubtful beam long nods from side to side;
At length the wits mount up, the hairs subside.
75 See, fierce Belinda on the Baron flies,
With more than usual lightning in her eyes;
Nor feared the chief the unequal fight to try,
Who sought no more than on his foe to die.
   But this bold lord with manly strength endued,
80 She with one finger and a thumb subdued:
Just where the breath of life his nostrils drew,
A charge of snuff the wily virgin threw;
The Gnomes direct, to every atom just,
The pungent grains of titillating dust.
85 Sudden, with starting tears each eye o'erflows,
And the high dome re-echoes to his nose.
   "Now meet thy fate," incensed Belinda cried,
And drew a deadly bodkin[9] from her side.
(The same, his ancient personage to deck,
90 Her great-great-grandsire wore about his neck,
In three seal rings; which after, melted down,
Formed a vast buckle for his widow's gown:
Her infant grandame's whistle next it grew,
The bells she jingled, and the whistle blew;
95 Then in a bodkin graced her mother's hairs,
Which long she wore, and now Belinda wears.)
   "Boast not my fall," he cried, "insulting foe!
Thou by some other shalt be laid as low.
Nor think to die dejects my lofty mind:
100 All that I dread is leaving you behind!
Rather than so, ah, let me still survive,
And burn in Cupid's flames—but burn alive."
   "Restore the Lock!" she cries; and all around
"Restore the Lock!" the vaulted roofs rebound.
105 Not fierce Othello in so loud a strain

8. The Maeander, a river in Asia Minor, was famous in mythology for its swans.

9. Here, an ornamental hairpin shaped like a dagger.

Roared for the handkerchief that caused his pain.[1]
But see how oft ambitious aims are crossed,
And chiefs contend till all the prize is lost!
The lock, obtained with guilt, and kept with pain,
110 In every place is sought, but sought in vain:
With such a prize no mortal must be blessed,
So Heaven decrees! with Heaven who can contest?
   Some thought it mounted to the lunar sphere,
Since all things lost on earth are treasured there.
115 There heroes' wits are kept in ponderous vases,
And beaux' in snuffboxes and tweezer cases.
There broken vows and deathbed alms are found,
And lovers' hearts with ends of riband bound,
The courtier's promises, and sick man's prayers,
120 The smiles of harlots, and the tears of heirs,
Cages for gnats, and chains to yoke a flea,
Dried butterflies, and tomes of casuistry.
   But trust the Muse—she saw it upward rise,
Though marked by none but quick, poetic eyes
125 (So Rome's great founder to the heavens withdrew,[2]
To Proculus alone confessed in view);
A sudden star, it shot through liquid air,
And drew behind a radiant trail of hair.
Not Berenice's locks first rose so bright,[3]
130 The heavens bespangling with disheveled light.
The Sylphs behold it kindling as it flies,
And pleased pursue its progress through the skies.
   This the beau monde shall from the Mall[4] survey,
And hail with music its propitious ray.
135 This the blest lover shall for Venus take,
And send up vows from Rosamonda's Lake.[5]
This Partridge[6] soon shall view in cloudless skies,
When next he looks through Galileo's eyes;°   *telescope*
And hence the egregious wizard shall foredoom
140 The fate of Louis, and the fall of Rome.
   Then cease, bright nymph! to mourn thy ravished hair,
Which adds new glory to the shining sphere!
Not all the tresses that fair head can boast
Shall draw such envy as the Lock you lost.
145 For, after all the murders of your eye,
When, after millions slain, yourself shall die:
When those fair suns shall set, as set they must,
And all those tresses shall be laid in dust,
This Lock the Muse shall consecrate to fame,
150 And 'midst the stars inscribe Belinda's name.

1712   1714, 1717

1. *Othello* 3.4.
2. Romulus, the "founder" and first king of Rome, was snatched to heaven in a storm cloud while reviewing his army in the Campus Martius (Livy 1.16).
3. Berenice, the wife of Ptolemy III, dedicated a lock of her hair to the gods to ensure her husband's safe return from war. It was turned into a constellation.
4. A walk laid out by Charles II in St. James's Park (London), a resort for strollers of all sorts.
5. In St. James's Park; associated with unhappy lovers.
6. John Partridge, an astrologer whose annually published predictions (among them that Louis XIV and the Catholic Church would fall) had been amusingly satirized by Swift and other wits in 1708.

An Essay on Man

An Essay on Man Pope's philosophical poem *An Essay on Man* represents the beginnings of an ambitious but never completed plan for what he called his "ethic work," intended to be a large survey of human nature, society, and morals. He dedicated the *Essay* to Henry St. John (pronounced *Sín-jun*), Viscount Bolingbroke (1678–1751), the brilliant, erratic secretary of state in the Tory ministry of 1710–14. After the accession of George I, Bolingbroke fled to France, but he was allowed to return in 1723, settling near Pope at Dawley Farm. The two formed a close friendship and talked through the ideas expressed in the *Essay* and in Bolingbroke's own philosophical writings (some of which are addressed to Pope). But Pope's poem has many sources in the thought of his times and the philosophical tradition at large, and he says himself in the poem's little preface that his intention is to formulate a widely acceptable system of obvious, familiar truths. Pope's "optimism"—his insistence that everything must be "RIGHT" in a universe created and superintended by God—skips over the tragic elements of experience that much great literary, philosophical, and religious expression confronts. But the strains and contradictions of the poem are themselves deeply revealing about the thinking of Pope and his age, as he both presents and withholds a comprehensive view of the universe and reasons out reason's drastic limitations.

Pope's purpose is to "vindicate the ways of God to man," a phrase that consciously echoes *Paradise Lost* 1.26. Like John Milton, Pope faces the problem of the existence of evil in a world presumed to be the creation of a good god. *Paradise Lost* is biblical in content, Christian in doctrine; *An Essay on Man* avoids all specifically Christian doctrines, not because Pope disbelieved them but because "man," the subject of the poem, includes millions who never heard of Christianity and Pope is concerned with the universal. Milton tells a Judeo-Christian story. Pope writes in abstract terms.

The *Essay* is divided into four epistles. In the first Pope asserts the essential order and goodness of the universe and the rightness of our place in it. The other epistles deal with how we may emulate in our nature and in society the cosmic harmony revealed in the first epistle. The second seeks to show how we may attain a psychological harmony that can become the basis of a virtuous life through the cooperation of self-love and the passions (both necessary to our complete humanity) with reason, the controller and director. The third is concerned with the individual in society, which, it teaches, was created through the cooperation of self-love (the egoistic drives that motivate us) and social love (our dependence on others, our inborn benevolence). The fourth is concerned with happiness, which lies within the reach of all for it is dependent on virtue, which becomes possible when—though only when—self-love is transmuted into love of others and love of God. Such, in brief summary, are Pope's main ideas, expressed in many phrases so memorable that they have detached themselves from the poem and become part of daily speech.

From An Essay on Man

TO HENRY ST. JOHN, LORD BOLINGBROKE

Epistle 1. Of the Nature and State of Man,
with Respect to the Universe

> Awake, my St. John! leave all meaner things
> To low ambition, and the pride of kings.
> Let us (since life can little more supply
> Than just to look about us and to die)
> 5   Expatiate free° o'er all this scene of man;   *range freely*
> A mighty maze! but not without a plan;

A wild, where weeds and flowers promiscuous shoot,
Or garden, tempting with forbidden fruit.
Together let us beat this ample field,[1]
10 Try what the open, what the covert yield;
The latent tracts, the giddy heights, explore
Of all who blindly creep, or sightless soar;
Eye Nature's walks, shoot folly as it flies,
And catch the manners living as they rise;
15 Laugh where we must, be candid° where we can;   *favorably disposed*
But vindicate the ways of God to man.

    1. Say first, of God above, or man below,
What can we reason, but from what we know?
Of man, what see we but his station here,
20 From which to reason, or to which refer?
Through worlds unnumbered though the God be known,
'Tis ours to trace him only in our own.
He, who through vast immensity can pierce,
See worlds on worlds compose one universe,
25 Observe how system into system runs,
What other planets circle other suns,
What varied being peoples every star,
May tell why Heaven has made us as we are.
But of this frame° the bearings, and the ties,   *the universe*
30 The strong connections, nice dependencies,
Gradations just, has thy pervading soul
Looked through? or can a part contain the whole?
    Is the great chain, that draws all to agree,
And drawn supports, upheld by God, or thee?[2]

35   2. Presumptuous man! the reason wouldst thou find,
Why formed so weak, so little, and so blind?
First, if thou canst, the harder reason guess,
Why formed no weaker, blinder, and no less!
Ask of thy mother earth, why oaks are made
40 Taller or stronger than the weeds they shade?
Or ask of yonder argent fields above,
Why Jove's satellites[3] are less than Jove?
    Of systems possible, if 'tis confessed
That Wisdom Infinite must form the best,
45 Where all must full or not coherent be,
And all that rises, rise in due degree;
Then, in the scale of reasoning life, 'tis plain,
There must be, somewhere, such a rank as man:
And all the question (wrangle e'er so long)
50 Is only this, if God has placed him wrong?
    Respecting man, whatever wrong we call,
May, must be right, as relative to all.
In human works, though labored on with pain,

---

1. Pope and Bolingbroke will try to drive truth
into the open, like hunters beating the bushes
for game.

2. For the chain of being, see lines 207–58.
3. In his *Dictionary*, Johnson notes and condemns
Pope's giving this word four syllables, as in Latin.

A thousand movements scarce one purpose gain;
55 In God's, one single can its end produce;
Yet serves to second too some other use.
So man, who here seems principal alone,
Perhaps acts second to some sphere unknown,
Touches some wheel, or verges to some goal;
60 'Tis but a part we see, and not a whole.
When the proud steed shall know why man restrains
His fiery course, or drives him o'er the plains;
When the dull ox, why now he breaks the clod,
Is now a victim, and now Egypt's god:[4]
65 Then shall man's pride and dullness comprehend
His actions', passions', being's use and end;
Why doing, suffering, checked, impelled; and why
This hour a slave, the next a deity.
Then say not man's imperfect, Heaven in fault;
70 Say rather, man's as perfect as he ought;
His knowledge measured to his state and place,
His time a moment, and a point his space.
If to be perfect in a certain sphere,[5]
What matter, soon or late, or here or there?
75 The blest today is as completely so,
As who began a thousand years ago.

3. Heaven from all creatures hides the book of Fate,
All but the page prescribed, their present state:
From brutes what men, from men what spirits know:
80 Or who could suffer being here below?
The lamb thy riot° dooms to bleed today,   *feast*
Had he thy reason, would he skip and play?
Pleased to the last, he crops the flowery food,
And licks the hand just raised to shed his blood.
85 O blindness to the future! kindly given,
That each may fill the circle marked by Heaven:
Who sees with equal eye, as God of all,
A hero perish, or a sparrow fall,
Atoms or systems° into ruin hurled,   *solar systems*
90 And now a bubble burst, and now a world.
Hope humbly then; with trembling pinions soar;
Wait the great teacher Death, and God adore!
What future bliss, he gives not thee to know,
But gives that hope to be thy blessing now.
95 Hope springs eternal in the human breast:
Man never is, but always to be blest:
The soul, uneasy and confined from home,
Rests and expatiates in a life to come.
Lo! the poor Indian, whose untutored mind
100 Sees God in clouds, or hears him in the wind;
His soul proud Science never taught to stray
Far as the solar walk, or milky way;
Yet simple Nature to his hope has given,

---

4. The Egyptians worshiped a bull called Apis. 5. I.e., in one's "state and place."

Behind the cloud-topped hill, an humbler heaven;
105　Some safer world in depth of woods embraced,
Some happier island in the watery waste,
Where slaves once more their native land behold,
No fiends torment, no Christians thirst for gold!
To be, contents his natural desire,
110　He asks no angel's wing, no seraph's fire;
But thinks, admitted to that equal° sky,　　　　　　*impartial*
His faithful dog shall bear him company.

4. Go, wiser thou! and, in thy scale of sense,
Weigh thy opinion against Providence;
115　Call imperfection what thou fancy'st such,
Say, here he gives too little, there too much;
Destroy all creatures for thy sport or gust,[6]
Yet cry, if man's unhappy, God's unjust;
If man alone engross not Heaven's high care,
120　Alone made perfect here, immortal there:
Snatch from his hand the balance and the rod,[7]
Rejudge his justice, be the God of God!
In pride, in reasoning pride, our error lies;
All quit their sphere, and rush into the skies.
125　Pride still is aiming at the blest abodes,
Men would be angels, angels would be gods.
Aspiring to be gods, if angels fell,
Aspiring to be angels, men rebel:
And who but wishes to invert the laws
130　Of order, sins against the Eternal Cause.

5. Ask for what end the heavenly bodies shine,
Earth for whose use? Pride answers, "'Tis for mine:
For me kind Nature wakes her genial power,
Suckles each herb, and spreads out every flower;
135　Annual for me, the grape, the rose renew
The juice nectareous, and the balmy dew;
For me, the mine a thousand treasures brings;
For me, health gushes from a thousand springs;
Seas roll to waft me, suns to light me rise;
140　My footstool earth, my canopy the skies."
But errs not Nature from this gracious end,
From burning suns when livid deaths descend,
When earthquakes swallow, or when tempests sweep
Towns to one grave, whole nations to the deep?
145　"No," 'tis replied, "the first Almighty Cause
Acts not by partial, but by general laws;
The exceptions few; some change since all began,
And what created perfect?"—Why then man?
If the great end be human happiness,
150　Then Nature deviates; and can man do less?
As much that end a constant course requires
Of showers and sunshine, as of man's desires;
As much eternal springs and cloudless skies,

---

6. "Sense of tasting" (Johnson's *Dictionary*).　　　7. Symbols of judgment and punishment.

As men forever temperate, calm, and wise.
155 If plagues or earthquakes break not Heaven's design,
Why then a Borgia, or a Catiline?[8]
Who knows but he whose hand the lightning forms,
Who heaves old ocean, and who wings the storms,
Pours fierce ambition in a Caesar's mind,
160 Or turns young Ammon° loose to scourge mankind?   *Alexander the*
From pride, from pride, our very reasoning springs;   *Great*
Account for moral, as for natural things:
Why charge we Heaven in those, in these acquit?
In both, to reason right is to submit.
165   Better for us, perhaps, it might appear,
Were there all harmony, all virtue here;
That never air or ocean felt the wind;
That never passion discomposed the mind:
But ALL subsists by elemental strife;
170 And passions are the elements of life.
The general ORDER, since the whole began,
Is kept in Nature, and is kept in man.

     6. What would this man? Now upward will he soar,
And little less than angel, would be more;
175 Now looking downwards, just as grieved appears
To want the strength of bulls, the fur of bears.
Made for his use all creatures if he call,
Say what their use, had he the powers of all?
Nature to these, without profusion, kind,
180 The proper organs, proper powers assigned;
Each seeming want compènsated of course,°   *as a matter of course*
Here with degrees of swiftness, there of force;
All in exact proportion to the state;
Nothing to add, and nothing to abate.
185 Each beast, each insect, happy in its own;
Is Heaven unkind to man, and man alone?
Shall he alone, whom rational we call,
Be pleased with nothing, if not blessed with all?
     The bliss of man (could pride that blessing find)
190 Is not to act or think beyond mankind;
No powers of body or of soul to share,
But what his nature and his state can bear.
Why has not man a microscopic eye?
For this plain reason, man is not a fly.
195 Say what the use, were finer optics given,
To inspect a mite, not comprehend the heaven?
Or touch, if tremblingly alive all o'er,
To smart and agonize at every pore?
Or quick effluvia[9] darting through the brain,

8. The Italian Renaissance family the Borgias was notorious for its ruthless lust for power, cruelty, rapaciousness, treachery, and murder (especially by poisoning). Cesare Borgia (1476–1507), son of Pope Alexander VI, is here referred to. Lucius Sergius Catiline (ca. 108–62 B.C.E.), an ambitious, greedy, and cruel conspirator against the Roman state, was denounced in Cicero's famous orations before the senate and in the Forum.
9. According to the philosophy of Epicurus (adopted by Robert Boyle, the chemist, and other 17th-century scientists), the senses are stirred to perception by being bombarded through the pores by steady streams of "effluvia," incredibly thin and tiny—but material—images of the objects that surround us.

200 Die of a rose in aromatic pain?
If nature thundered in his opening ears,
And stunned him with the music of the spheres,
How would he wish that Heaven had left him still
The whispering zephyr, and the purling rill?
205 Who finds not Providence all good and wise,
Alike in what it gives, and what denies?

7. Far as creation's ample range extends,
The scale of sensual,° mental powers ascends: *sensory*
Mark how it mounts, to man's imperial race,
210 From the green myriads in the peopled grass:
What modes of sight betwixt each wide extreme,
The mole's dim curtain, and the lynx's beam:[1]
Of smell, the headlong lioness between,
And hound sagacious° on the tainted green: *quick of scent*
215 Of hearing, from the life that fills the flood,
To that which warbles through the vernal wood:
The spider's touch, how exquisitely fine!
Feels at each thread, and lives along the line:
In the nice° bee, what sense so subtly true   *exact, accurate*
220 From poisonous herbs extracts the healing dew:
How instinct varies in the groveling swine,
Compared, half-reasoning elephant, with thine!
'Twixt that, and reason, what a nice barrier,[2]
Forever separate, yet forever near!
225 Remembrance and reflection how allied;
What thin partitions sense from thought divide:
And middle natures, how they long to join,
Yet never pass the insuperable line!
Without this just gradation, could they be
230 Subjected, these to those, or all to thee?
The powers of all subdued by thee alone,
Is not thy reason all these powers in one?

8. See, through this air, this ocean, and this earth,
All matter quick, and bursting into birth.
235 Above, how high progressive life may go!
Around, how wide! how deep extend below!
Vast Chain of Being! which from God began,
Natures ethereal, human, angel, man,
Beast, bird, fish, insect, what no eye can see,
240 No glass can reach! from Infinite to thee,
From thee to nothing.—On superior powers
Were we to press, inferior might on ours:
Or in the full creation leave a void,
Where, one step broken, the great scale's destroyed:
245 From Nature's chain whatever link you strike,
Tenth or ten thousandth, breaks the chain alike.
And, if each system in gradation roll

---

1. One of several early theories of vision held
that the eye casts a beam of light that makes
objects visible.
2. Pronounced *ba-réer.*

Alike essential to the amazing whole,
The least confusion but in one, not all
250　That system only, but the whole must fall.
Let earth unbalanced from her orbit fly,
Planets and suns run lawless through the sky,
Let ruling angels from their spheres be hurled,
Being on being wrecked, and world on world,
255　Heaven's whole foundations to their center nod,
And Nature tremble to the throne of God:
All this dread ORDER break—for whom? for thee?
Vile worm!—oh, madness, pride, impiety!

　　9. What if the foot, ordained the dust to tread,
260　Or hand, to toil, aspired to be the head?
What if the head, the eye, or ear repined
To serve mere engines to the ruling Mind?[3]
Just as absurd, for any part to claim
To be another, in this general frame.
265　Just as absurd, to mourn the tasks or pains,
The great directing MIND of ALL ordains.
　　All are but parts of one stupendous whole,
Whose body Nature is, and God the soul;
That, changed through all, and yet in all the same,
270　Great in the earth, as in the ethereal frame,
Warms in the sun, refreshes in the breeze,
Glows in the stars, and blossoms in the trees,
Lives through all life, extends through all extent,
Spreads undivided, operates unspent,
275　Breathes in our soul, informs our mortal part,
As full, as perfect, in a hair as heart;
As full, as perfect, in vile man that mourns,
As the rapt seraph that adores and burns;
To him no high, no low, no great, no small;
280　He fills, he bounds, connects, and equals all.

　　10. Cease then, nor ORDER imperfection name:
Our proper bliss depends on what we blame.
Know thy own point: this kind, this due degree
Of blindness, weakness, Heaven bestows on thee.
285　Submit—In this, or any other sphere,
Secure to be as blest as thou canst bear:
Safe in the hand of one disposing Power,
Or in the natal, or the mortal hour.
All Nature is but art, unknown to thee;
290　All chance, direction, which thou canst not see;
All discord, harmony not understood;
All partial evil, universal good:
And, spite of pride, in erring reason's spite,
One truth is clear: Whatever IS, is RIGHT.

3. Cf. 1 Corinthians 12.14–26.

*From Epistle 2. Of the Nature and State of Man
with Respect to Himself, as an Individual*

1. Know then thyself, presume not God to scan;°   *judge*
The proper study of mankind is Man.
Placed on this isthmus of a middle state,
A being darkly wise, and rudely great:
5 With too much knowledge for the skeptic side,
With too much weakness for the Stoic's pride,
He hangs between; in doubt to act, or rest,
In doubt to deem himself a god, or beast;
In doubt his mind or body to prefer,
10 Born but to die, and reasoning but to err;
Alike in ignorance, his reason such,
Whether he thinks too little, or too much:
Chaos of thought and passion, all confused;
Still by himself abused, or disabused;
15 Created half to rise, and half to fall;
Great lord of all things, yet a prey to all;
Sole judge of truth, in endless error hurled:
The glory, jest, and riddle of the world!

*   *   *

1733

Epistle to Dr. Arbuthnot   Dr. John Arbuthnot (1667–1735), to whom Pope

addressed his best-known verse epistle, was distinguished both as a physician and
as a man of wit. He had been one of the liveliest members of the Martinus Scriblerus Club, helping his friends create the character and shape the career of the
learned pedant whose memoirs the club had undertaken to write.

Pope had long been meditating such a poem, which was to be both an attack on his
detractors and a defense of his own character and career. In his usual way, he had
jotted down hints, lines, couplets, and fragments over a period of two decades, but
the poem might never have been completed had it not been for two events: Arbuthnot, from his deathbed, wrote to urge Pope to continue his abhorrence of vice and to
express it in his writings and, during 1733, Pope was the victim of two bitter attacks
by "persons of rank and fortune," as the Advertisement has it. The "Verses Addressed
to the Imitator of Horace" was the work of Lady Mary Wortley Montagu, helped by
her friend Lord Hervey (pronounced *Harvey*), a close friend and confidant of Queen
Caroline. "An Epistle to a Doctor of Divinity from a Nobleman at Hampton Court"
was the work of Lord Hervey alone. Montagu had provocation enough, especially in
Pope's recent reference to her in "The First Satire of the Second Book of Horace,"
lines 83–84; but Hervey had little to complain of beyond occasional covert references
to him as "Lord Fanny." At any rate, the two scurrilous attacks goaded Pope into
action, and he completed the poem by the end of the summer of 1734.

The *Epistle* is the most brilliant and daring execution of the techniques that Pope
used in many of the autobiographical poems of the 1730s. He presents himself in a
theatrical array of postures: the comically exaggerating complainer, the admired
man of genius, the true friend, the unpretentiously honest man, the satirist-hero of
his country, the "manly" defender of virtue, the tender son mothering his own
mother. Part of what cements this mixture is the verve with which he modulates
from role to role, implying that none of them exhaustively defines him. Pope tries to
force the reader to take sides, for him and what he claims to represent, or against
him. Thus reading becomes an ethical exercise; readers must make up their own

minds about his moral superiority, his exquisitely crafted portraits of his enemies, his social self-positioning, or his self-righteous politics. Pope solicits our judgment of his character and his professed ideals, and no other poet in English does so with so much artistic energy, resourcefulness, and success.

It is not clear that Pope intended the poem to be thought of as a dialogue, as it has usually been printed since Warburton's edition of 1751. The original edition, while suggesting interruptions in the flow of the monologue, kept entirely to the form of a letter. The introduction of the friend, who speaks from time to time, converts the original letter into a dramatic dialogue.

Epistle to Dr. Arbuthnot

Advertisement

TO THE FIRST PUBLICATION OF THIS *Epistle*

This paper is a sort of bill of complaint, begun many years since, and drawn up by snatches, as the several occasions offered. I had no thoughts of publishing it, till it pleased some persons of rank and fortune (the authors of *Verses to the Imitator of Horace*, and of an *Epistle to a Doctor of Divinity from a Nobleman at Hampton Court*) to attack, in a very extraordinary manner, not only my writings (of which, being public, the public is judge) but my person, morals, and family, whereof, to those who know me not, a truer information may be requisite. Being divided between the necessity to say something of myself, and my own laziness to undertake so awkward a task, I thought it the shortest way to put the last hand[1] to this epistle. If it have anything pleasing, it will be that by which I am most desirous to please, the truth and the sentiment; and if anything offensive, it will be only to those I am least sorry to offend, the vicious or the ungenerous.

Many will know their own pictures in it, there being not a circumstance but what is true; but I have, for the most part, spared their names, and they may escape being laughed at, if they please.

I would have some of them know, it was owing to the request of the learned and candid friend to whom it is inscribed, that I make not as free use of theirs as they have done of mine. However, I shall have this advantage, and honor, on my side, that whereas, by their proceeding, any abuse may be directed at any man, no injury can possibly be done by mine, since a nameless character can never be found out, but by its truth and likeness. P.

> P. Shut, shut the door, good John![2] (fatigued, I said),
> Tie up the knocker, say I'm sick, I'm dead.
> The Dog Star[3] rages! nay 'tis past a doubt
> All Bedlam,[4] or Parnassus, is let out:
> 5   Fire in each eye, and papers in each hand,
> They rave, recite, and madden round the land.
>   What walls can guard me, or what shades can hide?
> They pierce my thickets, through my grot[5] they glide,

---

1. Finish.
2. John Serle, Pope's gardener.
3. Sirius, associated with the period of greatest heat (and hence of madness) because it sets with the sun in late summer. August, in ancient Rome, was the season for reciting poetry.
4. Bethlehem Hospital for the insane, in London.
5. The subterranean passage under the road that separated his house at Twickenham from his garden became, in Pope's hands, a romantic grotto ornamented with shells and mirrors.

By land, by water, they renew the charge,
10 They stop the chariot, and they board the barge.
No place is sacred, not the church is free;
Even Sunday shines no Sabbath day to me:
Then from the Mint[6] walks forth the man of rhyme,
Happy! to catch me just at dinner time.
15   Is there a parson, much bemused in beer,
A maudlin poetess, a rhyming peer,
A clerk foredoomed his father's soul to cross,
Who pens a stanza when he should engross?[7]
Is there who, locked from ink and paper,[8] scrawls
20 With desperate charcoal round his darkened walls?
All fly to Twit'nam,[9] and in humble strain
Apply to me to keep them mad or vain.
Arthur,[1] whose giddy son neglects the laws,
Imputes to me and my damned works the cause:
25 Poor Cornus[2] sees his frantic wife elope,
And curses wit, and poetry, and Pope.
        Friend to my life (which did not you prolong,
The world had wanted° many an idle song)   *missed*
What drop or nostrum° can this plague remove?   *medicine*
30 Or which must end me, a fool's wrath or love?
A dire dilemma! either way I'm sped,°   *killed*
If foes, they write, if friends, they read me dead.
Seized and tied down to judge, how wretched I!
Who can't be silent, and who will not lie.
35 To laugh were want of goodness and of grace,
And to be grave exceeds all power of face.
I sit with sad civility, I read
With honest anguish and an aching head,
And drop at last, but in unwilling ears,
40 This saving counsel, "Keep your piece nine years."[3]
        "Nine years!" cries he, who high in Drury Lane,[4]
Lulled by soft zephyrs through the broken pane,
Rhymes ere he wakes, and prints before term[5] ends,
Obliged by hunger and request of friends:
45 "The piece, you think, is incorrect? why, take it,
I'm all submission, what you'd have it, make it."
        Three things another's modest wishes bound,
My friendship, and a prologue,[6] and ten pound.
        Pitholeon[7] sends to me: "You know his Grace,
50 I want a patron; ask him for a place."

---

6. A place in Southwark where debtors were free from arrest (they could not be arrested anywhere on Sundays).
7. Write out legal documents.
8. Is there some madman who, locked up without ink or paper . . . ?
9. I.e., Twickenham, Pope's villa on the bank of the Thames; a few miles above Hampton Court.
1. Arthur Moore, whose son, James Moore Smythe, dabbled in literature. Moore Smythe had earned Pope's enmity by using in one of his plays some unpublished lines from Pope's "Epistle 2. To a Lady" in spite of Pope's objections.
2. Latin for "horn," the traditional emblem of

the cuckold.
3. The advice of Horace in *Art of Poetry* (line 388).
4. I.e., living in a garret in Drury Lane, site of one of the theaters and the haunt of the profligate.
5. One of the four annual periods in which the law courts are in session and with which the publishing season coincided.
6. Famous poets helped playwrights by contributing prologues to their plays.
7. "A foolish poet of Rhodes, who pretended much to Greek" [Pope's note]. He is Leonard Welsted, who translated Longinus and had attacked and slandered Pope (see line 375).

Pitholeon libeled me—"but here's a letter
Informs you, sir, 'twas when he knew no better.
Dare you refuse him? Curll[8] invites to dine,
He'll write a *Journal,* or he'll turn divine."[9]
55 Bless me! a packet.—"'Tis a stranger sues,°   *asks for help*
A virgin tragedy, an orphan Muse."
If I dislike it, "Furies, death, and rage!"
If I approve, "Commend it to the stage."
There (thank my stars) my whole commission ends,
60 The players and I are, luckily, no friends.
Fired that the house° reject him, "'Sdeath, I'll print it,   *playhouse*
And shame the fools—Your interest, sir, with Lintot!"[1]
Lintot, dull rogue, will think your price too much.
"Not, sir, if you revise it, and retouch."
65 All my demurs but double his attacks;
At last he whispers, "Do; and we go snacks."°   *shares*
Glad of a quarrel, straight I clap the door,
"Sir, let me see your works and you no more."
    'Tis sung, when Midas' ears began to spring
70 (Midas, a sacred person and a king),
His very minister who spied them first,
(Some say his queen) was forced to speak, or burst.[2]
And is not mine, my friend, a sorer case,
When every coxcomb perks them in my face?
75   A. Good friend, forbear! you deal in dangerous things.
I'd never name queens, ministers, or kings;
Keep close to ears,° and those let asses prick;   *whisper*
'Tis nothing——P. Nothing? if they bite and kick?
Out with it, *Dunciad!* let the secret pass,
80 That secret to each fool, that he's an ass:
The truth once told (and wherefore should we lie?)
The queen of Midas slept, and so may I.
    You think this cruel? take it for a rule,
No creature smarts so little as a fool.
85 Let peals of laughter, Codrus![3] round thee break,
Thou unconcerned canst hear the mighty crack.
Pit, box, and gallery in convulsions hurled,
Thou stand'st unshook amidst a bursting world.
Who shames a scribbler? break one cobweb through,
90 He spins the slight, self-pleasing thread anew:
Destroy his fib or sophistry, in vain;
The creature's at his dirty work again,
Throned in the center of his thin designs,
Proud of a vast extent of flimsy lines.
95 Whom have I hurt? has poet yet or peer

8. Edmund Curll, shrewd and disreputable book-seller, published pirated works, works falsely ascribed to reputable writers, scandalous biographies, and other ephemera. Pope had often attacked him and had assigned to him a low role in *The Dunciad.*
9. I.e., he will attack Pope in the *London Journal* or write a treatise on theology, as Welsted in fact did.
1. Bernard Lintot, publisher of Pope's Homer and other early works.
2. Midas, king of ancient Lydia, had the bad taste to prefer the flute-playing of Pan to that of Apollo, whereupon the god endowed him with ass's ears. It was his barber (not his wife or his minister) who discovered the secret and whispered it into a hole in the earth. The reference to "queen" and "minister" makes it plain that Pope is alluding to George II, Queen Caroline, and Walpole.
3. Poet ridiculed by Virgil and Juvenal.

Lost the arched eyebrow or Parnassian sneer?
And has not Colley still his lord and whore?
His butchers Henley?[4] his freemasons Moore?
Does not one table Bavius still admit?
100 Still to one bishop Philips[5] seem a wit?
Still Sappho[6]——A. Hold! for god's sake—you'll offend.
No names—be calm—learn prudence of a friend.
I too could write, and I am twice as tall;
But foes like these!——P. One flatterer's worse than all.
105 Of all mad creatures, if the learn'd are right,
It is the slaver kills, and not the bite.
A fool quite angry is quite innocent:
Alas! 'tis ten times worse when they repent.

One dedicates in high heroic prose,
110 And ridicules beyond a hundred foes;
One from all Grub Street[7] will my fame defend,
And, more abusive, calls himself my friend.
This prints my letters,[8] that expects a bribe,
And others roar aloud, "Subscribe, subscribe!"[9]
115 There are, who to my person pay their court:
I cough like Horace,[1] and, though lean, am short;
Ammon's great son[2] one shoulder had too high,
Such Ovid's nose,[3] and "Sir! you have an eye—"
Go on, obliging creatures, make me see
120 All that disgraced my betters met in me.
Say for my comfort, languishing in bed,
"Just so immortal Maro° held his head":   *Virgil*
And when I die, be sure you let me know
Great Homer died three thousand years ago.

125 Why did I write? what sin to me unknown
Dipped me in ink, my parents', or my own?
As yet a child, nor yet a fool to fame,
I lisped in numbers,° for the numbers came.   *verses*
I left no calling for this idle trade,
130 No duty broke, no father disobeyed.
The Muse but served to ease some friend, not wife,
To help me through this long disease, my life,
To second, Arbuthnot! thy art and care,
And teach the being you preserved, to bear.°   *endure*
135 A. But why then publish? P. Granville the polite,

---

4. John Henley, known as "Orator" Henley, an independent preacher of marked eccentricity, was popular among the common people, especially for his elocution. Colley Cibber, the poet laureate.
5. The "bishop" is Hugh Boulter, bishop of Armagh. He had employed as his secretary Ambrose Philips (1674–1749), whose insipid simplicity of manner in poetry earned him the nickname of "Namby-Pamby." Bavius, the bad poet alluded to in Virgil's *Eclogue* 3.
6. Lady Mary Wortley Montagu.
7. A term denoting the whole society of literary, political, and journalistic hack writers.

8. In 1726 Curll had surreptitiously acquired and published without permission some of Pope's letters to Henry Cromwell.
9. To ensure the financial success of a work, wealthy readers were often asked to "subscribe" to it before printing was undertaken. Pope's Homer was published in this manner.
1. Horace, who mentions a cough in a few poems, was plump and short.
2. Alexander the Great, whose head inclined to his left shoulder, resembling Pope's hunchback.
3. Ovid's family name, Naso, suggests the Latin word *nasus* ("nose"), hence the pun.

And knowing Walsh, would tell me I could write;
Well-natured Garth inflamed with early praise,
And Congreve loved, and Swift endured my lays;
The courtly Talbot, Somers, Sheffield, read;
140 Even mitered Rochester would nod the head,
And St. John's self (great Dryden's friends before)
With open arms received one poet more.[4]
Happy my studies, when by these approved!
Happier their author, when by these beloved!
145 From these the world will judge of men and books,
Not from the Burnets, Oldmixons, and Cookes.[5]
    Soft were my numbers; who could take offense
While pure description held the place of sense?
Like gentle Fanny's[6] was my flowery theme,
150 A painted mistress, or a purling stream.
Yet then did Gildon draw his venal quill;[7]
I wished the man a dinner, and sat still.
Yet then did Dennis[8] rave in furious fret;
I never answered, I was not in debt.
155 If want provoked, or madness made them print,
I waged no war with Bedlam or the Mint.
    Did some more sober critic come abroad?
If wrong, I smiled; if right, I kissed the rod.
Pains, reading, study are their just pretense,
160 And all they want is spirit, taste, and sense.
Commas and points they set exactly right,
And 'twere a sin to rob them of their mite.
Yet ne'er one sprig of laurel graced these ribalds,
From slashing Bentley down to piddling Tibbalds.[9]
165 Each wight who reads not, and but scans and spells,
Each word-catcher that lives on syllables,
Even such small critics some regard may claim,
Preserved in Milton's or in Shakespeare's name.
Pretty! in amber to observe the forms
170 Of hairs, or straws, or dirt, or grubs, or worms!
The things, we know, are neither rich nor rare,
But wonder how the devil they got there.
    Were others angry? I excused them too;
Well might they rage; I gave them but their due.
175 A man's true merit 'tis not hard to find;

4. The purpose of this list is to establish Pope as the successor of Dryden and thus to place him far above his Grub Street persecutors. George Granville, Lord Lansdowne, poet, and statesman; William Walsh, poet and critic; Sir Samuel Garth, physician and mock-epic poet; William Congreve, the playwright; Charles Talbot, duke of Shrewsbury, Lord Sommers; John Sheffield, duke of Buckinghamshire; and Francis Atterbury, bishop of Rochester, statesmen, had all been associated with Dryden in his later years and had all encouraged the young Pope.
5. Thomas Burnet, John Oldmixon, and Thomas Cooke: Pope identifies them in a note as "authors of secret and scandalous history."
6. John, Lord Hervey, whom Pope satirizes in the character of Sporus (lines 305–33).

7. Charles Gildon, minor critic and scribbler, who, Pope believed, early attacked him at the instigation of Addison; hence "venal quill."
8. John Dennis (see An Essay on Criticism, n. 6, p. 1215).
9. Lewis Theobald (1688–1744), whose minute learning in Elizabethan literature had enabled him to expose Pope's defects as an editor of Shakespeare in 1726. Pope made him king of the Dunces in The Dunciad of 1728. Richard Bentley (1662–1742), the eminent classical scholar, seemed to both Pope and Swift the perfect type of the pedant: he is called "slashing" because, in his edition of Paradise Lost (1732), he had set in square brackets all passages that he disliked on the grounds they had been slipped into the poem without the blind poet's knowledge.

But each man's secret standard in his mind,
That casting weight[1] pride adds to emptiness,
This, who can gratify? for who can guess?
The bard[2] whom pilfered pastorals renown,
180 Who turns a Persian tale for half a crown,
Just writes to make his barrenness appear,
And strains from hard-bound brains eight lines a year:
He, who still wanting, though he lives on theft,
Steals much, spends little, yet has nothing left;
185 And he who now to sense, now nonsense leaning,
Means not, but blunders round about a meaning:
And he whose fustian's so sublimely bad,
It is not poetry, but prose run mad:
All these, my modest satire bade translate,
190 And owned that nine such poets made a Tate.[3]
How did they fume, and stamp, and roar, and chafe!
And swear, not Addison himself was safe.
    Peace to all such! but were there one whose fires
True Genius kindles, and fair Fame inspires;
195 Blessed with each talent and each art to please,
And born to write, converse, and live with ease:
Should such a man, too fond to rule alone,
Bear, like the Turk, no brother near the throne;[4]
View him with scornful, yet with jealous eyes,
200 And hate for arts that caused himself to rise;
Damn with faint praise, assent with civil leer,
And without sneering, teach the rest to sneer;
Willing to wound, and yet afraid to strike,
Just hint a fault, and hesitate dislike;
205 Alike reserved to blame or to commend,
A timorous foe, and a suspicious friend;
Dreading even fools; by flatterers besieged,
And so obliging that he ne'er obliged;
Like Cato, give his little senate[5] laws,
210 And sit attentive to his own applause;
While wits and Templars° every sentence raise,   law students
And wonder with a foolish face of praise—
Who but must laugh, if such a man there be?
Who would not weep, if Atticus[6] were he?
215   What though my name stood rubric° on the walls   in red letters
Or plastered posts, with claps,° in capitals?   posters
Or smoking forth, a hundred hawkers' load,

1. The weight that turns the scale; here, the "deciding factor."
2. Philips, Pope's rival in pastoral poetry in 1709, when their pastorals were published in Tonson's 6th *Miscellany*. Philips had also translated some Persian tales (see line 100 and n. 5, p. 1256).
3. Nahum Tate, poet laureate from 1692 to 1715. His popular rewriting of Shakespeare's *King Lear* provided a happy ending; he wrote most of part 2 of *Absalom and Achitophel*. The line refers to the old adage that it takes nine tailors to make one man.
4. Turkish monarchs proverbially killed off their nearest rivals.
5. Addison's tragedy *Cato* had been a sensational success in 1713. Pope had written the prologue, in which occurs the line, "While Cato gives his little senate laws." The satirical reference here is to Addison in the role of arbiter of taste among his friends and admirers, mostly Whigs, at Button's Coffee House. This group worked against the success of Pope's Homer.
6. Pope's satiric pseudonym for Addison. Atticus (109–32 B.C.E.), a wealthy man of letters and a friend of Cicero, was known as wise and disinterested.

On wings of winds came flying all abroad?
I sought no homage from the race that write;
220 I kept, like Asian monarchs, from their sight:
Poems I heeded (now berhymed so long)
No more than thou, great George! a birthday song.
I ne'er with wits or witlings passed my days
To spread about the itch of verse and praise;
225 Nor like a puppy daggled through the town
To fetch and carry sing-song up and down;
Nor at rehearsals sweat, and mouthed, and cried,
With handkerchief and orange at my side;
But sick of fops, and poetry, and prate,
230 To Bufo left the whole Castalian⁷ state.
      Proud as Apollo on his forkèd hill,⁸
Sat full-blown Bufo, puffed° by every quill;°   *flattered / pen*
Fed with soft dedication all day long,
Horace and he went hand in hand in song.
235 His library (where busts of poets dead
And a true Pindar stood without a head)
Received of wits an undistinguished race,
Who first his judgment asked, and then a place:
Much they extolled his pictures, much his seat,⁹
240 And flattered every day, and some days eat:
Till grown more frugal in his riper days,
He paid some bards with port, and some with praise;
To some a dry rehearsal was assigned,
And others (harder still) he paid in kind.
245 Dryden alone (what wonder?) came not nigh;
Dryden alone escaped this judging eye:
But still the great have kindness in reserve;
He helped to bury whom he helped to starve.
      May some choice patron bless each gray goose quill!
250 May every Bavius have his Bufo still!
So when a statesman wants a day's defense,
Or envy holds a whole week's war with sense,
Or simple pride for flattery makes demands,
May dunce by dunce be whistled off my hands!
255 Blessed be the great! for those they take away,
And those they left me—for they left me Gay;¹
Left me to see neglected genius bloom,
Neglected die, and tell it on his tomb;
Of all thy blameless life the sole return
260 My verse, and Queensberry weeping o'er thy urn!
Oh, let me live my own, and die so too!
("To live and die is all I have to do")²

---

7. The Castalian spring on Mount Parnassus was sacred to Apollo and the Muses. "Bufo": a type of tasteless patron of the arts. (*Bufo* means "toad" in Latin.)
8. Mount Parnassus had two peaks, one sacred to Apollo, one to Bacchus.
9. Estate. Pronounced *sate* and rhymed in next line with "eat" (*ate*).
1. John Gay (1685–1732), author of *The Beggar's*

Opera, dear friend of Swift and Pope. His failure to obtain patronage from the court intensified Pope's hostility to the Whig administration and the queen. Gay spent the last years of his life under the protection of the duke and duchess of Queensberry. Pope wrote his epitaph.
2. A quotation from John Denham's poem "Of Prudence."

Maintain a poet's dignity and ease,
And see what friends, and read what books I please;
265 Above a patron, though I condescend
Sometimes to call a minister my friend.
I was not born for courts or great affairs;
I pay my debts, believe, and say my prayers,
Can sleep without a poem in my head,
270 Nor know if Dennis be alive or dead.
    Why am I asked what next shall see the light?
Heavens! was I born for nothing but to write?
Has life no joys for me? or (to be grave)
Have I no friend to serve, no soul to save?
275 "I found him close with Swift"—"Indeed? no doubt"
Cries prating Balbus,[3] "something will come out."
'Tis all in vain, deny it as I will.
"No, such a genius never can lie still,"
And then for mine obligingly mistakes
280 The first lampoon Sir Will or Bubo[4] makes.
Poor guiltless I! and can I choose but smile,
When every coxcomb knows me by my style?
    Cursed be the verse, how well soe'er it flow,
That tends to make one worthy man my foe,
285 Give virtue scandal, innocence a fear,
Or from the soft-eyed virgin steal a tear!
But he who hurts a harmless neighbor's peace,
Insults fallen worth, or beauty in distress,
Who loves a lie, lame slander helps about,
290 Who writes a libel, or who copies out:
That fop whose pride affects a patron's name,
Yet absent, wounds an author's honest fame;
Who can your merit selfishly approve,
And show the sense of it without the love;
295 Who has the vanity to call you friend,
Yet wants the honor, injured, to defend;
Who tells whate'er you think, whate'er you say,
And, if he lie not, must at least betray:
Who to the dean and silver bell can swear,
300 And sees at Cannons what was never there:[5]
Who reads but with a lust to misapply,
Make satire a lampoon, and fiction, lie:
A lash like mine no honest man shall dread,
But all such babbling blockheads in his stead.
305   Let Sporus[6] tremble——A. What? that thing of silk,
Sporus, that mere white curd of ass's milk?[7]
Satire or sense, alas! can Sporus feel?

---

3. Latin for *stammering*.
4. Sir William Yonge, Whig politician and poet-aster. George Bubb ("Bubo") Dodington, a Whig patron of letters.
5. Pope's enemies had accused him of satirizing Cannons, the ostentatious estate of the duke of Chandos, in his description of Timon's villa in the *Epistle to Burlington*. This Pope quite justly denied. The bell of Timon's chapel was of silver,
and there preached a dean who "never mentions Hell to ears polite."
6. John, Lord Hervey, effeminate courtier and confidant of Queen Caroline (see headnote, p. 1252). The original Sporus was a boy, whom the emperor Nero publicly married (see Suetonius's life of Nero in *The Twelve Caesars*).
7. Drunk by invalids.

Who breaks a butterfly upon a wheel?
   p. Yet let me flap this bug with gilded wings,
310 This painted child of dirt, that stinks and stings;
Whose buzz the witty and the fair annoys,
Yet wit ne'er tastes, and beauty ne'er enjoys;
So well-bred spaniels civilly delight
In mumbling of the game they dare not bite.
315 Eternal smiles his emptiness betray,
As shallow streams run dimpling all the way.
Whether in florid impotence he speaks,
And, as the prompter breathes, the puppet squeaks;
Or at the ear of Eve,[8] familiar toad,
320 Half froth, half venom, spits himself abroad,
In puns, or politics, or tales, or lies,
Or spite, or smut, or rhymes, or blasphemies.
His wit all seesaw between *that* and *this*,
Now high, now low, now master up, now miss,
325 And he himself one vile antithesis.
Amphibious thing! that acting either part,
The trifling head or the corrupted heart,
Fop at the toilet, flatterer at the board,
Now trips a lady, and now struts a lord.
330 Eve's tempter thus the rabbins[9] have expressed,
A cherub's face, a reptile all the rest;
Beauty that shocks you, parts that none will trust,
Wit that can creep, and pride that licks the dust.
   Not fortune's worshiper, nor fashion's fool,
335 Not lucre's madman, nor ambition's tool,
Not proud, nor servile, be one poet's praise,
That if he pleased, he pleased by manly ways:
That flattery, even to kings, he held a shame,
And thought a lie in verse or prose the same:
340 That not in fancy's maze he wandered long,
But stooped[1] to truth, and moralized his song:
That not for fame, but virtue's better end,
He stood the furious foe, the timid friend,
The damning critic, half approving wit,
345 The coxcomb hit, or fearing to be hit;
Laughed at the loss of friends he never had,
The dull, the proud, the wicked, and the mad;
The distant threats of vengeance on his head,
The blow unfelt, the tear he never shed;
350 The tale revived, the lie so oft o'erthrown,
The imputed trash, and dullness not his own;
The morals blackened when the writings 'scape,
The libeled person, and the pictured shape;[2]
Abuse on all he loved, or loved him, spread,
355 A friend in exile, or a father dead;
The whisper, that to greatness still too near,

---

8. The queen; the allusion is to *Paradise Lost* (4.799–809).
9. Scholars of and authorities on Jewish law and doctrine.

1. The falcon is said to "stoop" to its prey when it swoops down and seizes it in flight.
2. Pope's deformity was frequently ridiculed and occasionally caricatured.

Perhaps yet vibrates on his Sovereign's ear—
Welcome for thee, fair virtue! all the past:
For thee, fair virtue! welcome even the last!
360   A. But why insult the poor, affront the great?
P. A knave's a knave to me in every state:
Alike my scorn, if he succeed or fail,
Sporus at court, or Japhet[3] in a jail,
A hireling scribbler, or a hireling peer,
365 Knight of the post[4] corrupt, or of the shire,
If on a pillory, or near a throne,
He gain his prince's ear, or lose his own.[5]
    Yet soft by nature, more a dupe than wit,
Sappho° can tell you how this man was bit:°   *Montagu / deceived*
370 This dreaded satirist Dennis will confess
Foe to his pride, but friend to his distress:[6]
So humble, he has knocked at Tibbald's door,
Has drunk with Cibber, nay, has rhymed for Moore.
Full ten years slandered, did he once reply?
375 Three thousand suns went down on Welsted's lie.[7]
To please a mistress one aspersed his life;
He lashed him not, but let her be his wife.
Let Budgell charge low Grub Street on his quill,
And write whate'er he pleased, except his will;[8]
380 Let the two Curlls of town and court,[9] abuse
His father, mother, body, soul, and muse.
Yet why? that father held it for a rule,
It was a sin to call our neighbor fool;
That harmless mother thought no wife a whore:
385 Hear this, and spare his family, James Moore!
Unspotted names, and memorable long,
If there be force in virtue, or in song.
    Of gentle blood (part shed in honor's cause,
While yet in Britain honor had applause)
390 Each parent sprung——A. What fortune, pray?——P. Their own,
And better got than Bestia's[1] from the throne.
Born to no pride, inheriting no strife,
Nor marrying discord in a noble wife,
Stranger to civil and religious rage,
395 The good man walked innoxious through his age.
No courts he saw, no suits would ever try,
Nor dared an oath,[2] nor hazarded a lie.
Unlearn'd, he knew no schoolman's subtle art,
No language but the language of the heart.

3. Japhet Crook, a notorious forger.
4. One who lives by selling false evidence.
5. Those punished in the pillory often also had their ears cropped.
6. Pope wrote the prologue to Cibber's *Provoked Husband* (1728) when that play was performed for Dennis's benefit, shortly before the old critic died.
7. "This man had the impudence to tell in print that Mr. P. had occasioned a Lady's death, and to name a person he had never heard of" [Pope's note].
8. Eustace Budgell attacked the *Grub Street Journal* for publishing what he took to be a squib by

Pope charging him with having forged the will of Dr. Matthew Tindal.
9. I.e., the publisher and Lord Hervey.
1. Probably the duke of Marlborough, whose vast fortune was made through the favor of Queen Anne. The actual Bestia was a corrupt Roman consul.
2. As a Catholic, Pope's father refused to take the Oaths of Allegiance and Supremacy and the oath against the pope. He thus rendered himself vulnerable to the many repressive anti-Catholic laws then in force.

400 By nature honest, by experience wise,
     Healthy by temperance, and by exercise;
     His life, though long, to sickness passed unknown,
     His death was instant, and without a groan.
     Oh, grant me thus to live, and thus to die!
405 Who sprung from kings shall know less joy than I.
        O friend! may each domestic bliss be thine!
     Be no unpleasing melancholy mine:
     Me, let the tender office long engage,
     To rock the cradle of reposing age,
410 With lenient arts extend a mother's breath,
     Make languor smile, and smooth the bed of death,
     Explore the thought, explain the asking eye,
     And keep a while one parent from the sky![3]
     On cares like these if length of days attend,
415 May Heaven, to bless those days, preserve my friend,
     Preserve him social, cheerful, and serene,
     And just as rich as when he served a Queen![4]
        A. Whether that blessing be denied or given,
     Thus far was right—the rest belongs to Heaven.

                                                    1735

The Dunciad: Book the Fourth

The fourth book of *The Dunciad*, Pope's last major work, was originally intended as a continuation of *An Essay on Man*. To Jonathan Swift, the spiritual ancestor of the poem, Pope confided in 1736 that he was at work on a series of epistles on the uses of human reason and learning, to conclude with "a satire against the misapplication of all these, exemplified by pictures, characters, and examples." But the epistles never appeared; instead, the satire grew until it took their place. As Pope surveyed England in his last years, the complex literary and social order that had sustained him seemed to be crumbling. It was a time for desperate measures, for satire. And the means of retribution was at hand, in the structure of Pope's own *Dunciad*, the long work that had already impaled so many enemies.

The first *Dunciad*, published in three books in 1728, is a mock-epic reply to Pope's critics and other petty authors. Its hero and victim, Lewis Theobald, had attacked Pope's edition of Shakespeare (1725); other victims had offended Pope either by personal abuse or simply by ineptitude. Inspired by Dryden's "Mac Flecknoe," *The Dunciad* celebrates the triumph of the hordes of Grub Street. Indeed, so many obscure hacks were mentioned that a *Dunciad Variorum* (1729) was soon required, in which mock-scholarly notes identify the victims, "since it is only in this monument that they must expect to survive." But a modern reader need not catch every reference to enjoy the dazzling wit of the poem, or the sheer sense of fun with which Pope remakes the London literary world into a tiny insane fairground of his own.

The New Dunciad (1742), however, plays a far more serious game: here Pope takes aim at the rot of the whole social fabric. The satire goes deep and works at many levels, which for convenience may be divided into four. (1) Politics: From 1721 to 1742 England had been ruled by the Whig supremacy of Robert Walpole, first minister. To Pope and his circle, the immensely powerful Walpole (no friend of poets) seemed

---

3. Pope was a tender and devoted son. His mother had died in 1733. The earliest version of these lines dates from 1731, when the poet was nursing her through a serious illness.

4. Pope alludes to the fact that Arbuthnot, a man of strict probity, left the queen's service no wealthier than when he entered it.

crass and greedy, like his monarch George II. It is no accident, in the kingdom of *The Dunciad*, that Dulness personified sits on a throne. (2) Society: Just as the action of the *Aeneid* had been the removal of the empire of Troy to Latium, the action of *The Dunciad*, according to Pope, is "the removal of the empire of Dulness from the City of London to the polite world, Westminster"; that is, the abdication of civility in favor of commerce and financial interests. In modern England, authors write for money, and ministers govern for profit; conspicuous consumption (especially the consumption of paper by scribblers) has replaced the old values of the yeoman and the aristocrat. In 1743 Pope revised the original *Dunciad*, substituting the actor and poet laureate Colley Cibber for Theobald as the hero and incorporating *The New Dunciad* as the fourth book (the version printed here). Dulness, he implies, has achieved her final triumph; Cibber is laureate in England. (3) Education: The word *dunce* is derived from the Scholastic philosopher John Duns Scotus (ca. 1265–1308), whose name had come to stand for silly and useless subtlety, logical hairsplitting. Pope, as an heir of the Renaissance, believes that the central subject of education must always be its relevance for human behavior: "The proper study of mankind is Man," and moral philosophy, the relation of individuals to each other and to the world, should be the teacher's first and last concern. By contrast, Dunces waste their time on grammar (words alone) or the "science" of the collector (things alone); they never comprehend that word and thing, like spirit and matter, are essentially dead unless they join. (4) Religion: At its deepest level, the subject of *The Dunciad* is the undoing of God's creation. Many passages from the fourth book echo *Paradise Lost,* and one of Pope's starting places seems to be Satan's threat to return the world to its original darkness, chaos, and ancient night (*Paradise Lost* 2.968–87). *The Dunciad* ends in a great apocalypse, with a yawn that signals the death of *Logos;* as words have become meaningless, so has the whole creation, which the Lord called forth with words. Here Pope invokes, with sublime intensity, the old idea that God was the first poet, one whose poem was the world, and suggests that the sickness of the word has infected all nature. Such a cosmic collapse allows Pope to realize in full the aim of his satirical poetry: to depict the evil of his enemies in all its excessive might and magnitude. As matter without spirit and substance without essence prevail in the final *Dunciad* over Pope's own ideals, the poem perversely confirms his poetic power, and the destruction of art permits his ultimate artistic triumph.

From The Dunciad

From *Book the Fourth*

Yet, yet a moment, one dim ray of light
Indulge, dread Chaos, and eternal Night!
Of darkness visible[1] so much be lent,
As half to show, half veil the deep intent.
5   Ye Powers![2] whose mysteries restored I sing,
To whom Time bears me on his rapid wing,
Suspend a while your force inertly strong,
Then take at once the poet and the song.
    Now flamed the Dog-star's[3] unpropitious ray,
10 Smote every brain, and withered every bay,[4]

1. Cf. *Paradise Lost* 1.63.
2. Chaos and Night, invoked in place of the Muse, because "the restoration of their empire is the action of the poem" [Pope's note].
3. Sirius, associated with the heat of summer and the madness of poets (see *Epistle to Dr. Arbuthnot,* line 3, p. 1253).
4. The laurel, whose garlands are bestowed on poets.

Sick was the sun, the owl forsook his bower,
The moon-struck prophet felt the madding hour:
Then rose the seed[5] of Chaos, and of Night,
To blot out Order, and extinguish Light,
15 Of dull and venal a new world to mold,
And bring Saturnian days of lead and gold.[6]
　　She mounts the throne: her head a cloud concealed,
In broad effulgence all below revealed,
('Tis thus aspiring Dulness ever shines)
20 Soft on her lap her Laureate son[7] reclines.
　　Beneath her foot-stool, Science groans in chains,
And Wit dreads exile, penalties and pains.
There foamed rebellious Logic, gagged and bound,
There, stripped, fair Rhetoric languished on the ground;
25 His blunted arms by Sophistry are borne,
And shameless Billingsgate[8] her robes adorn.
Morality, by her false guardians drawn,
Chicane in furs, and Casuistry in lawn,[9]
Gasps, as they straighten at each end the cord,
30 And dies, when Dulness gives her Page[1] the word.

*　*　*

[THE EDUCATOR]

135　　Now crowds on crowds around the Goddess press,
Each eager to present the first address.[2]
Dunce scorning dunce beholds the next advance,
But fop shows fop superior complaisance.
When lo! a specter[3] rose, whose index-hand
140 Held forth the virtue of the dreadful wand;
His beavered brow a birchen garland wears,[4]
Dropping with infant's blood, and mother's tears.
O'er every vein a shuddering horror runs,
Eton and Winton shake through all their sons.
145 All flesh is humbled, Westminster's bold race[5]
Shrink, and confess the Genius[6] of the place:
The pale boy-Senator yet tingling stands,
And holds his breeches close with both his hands.
　　Then thus. "Since Man from beast by words is known,
150 Words are Man's province, words we teach alone.
When reason doubtful, like the Samian letter,[7]

---

5. The Goddess Dulness.
6. Saturn ruled during the golden age; the new age of "gold" will be reestablished by the dull and venal.
7. Colley Cibber, the poet laureate.
8. Fishmarket slang, which now covers the noble science of rhetoric.
9. Chicanery (legal trickery) wears the ermine robe of a judge. Casuistry wears the linen ("lawn") sleeves of a bishop.
1. Sir Francis Page, a notorious hanging judge; or court page, used to strangle criminals in Turkey; or page of writing on which a dull author "kills" moral sentiments.
2. The goddess, newly enthroned, is receiving petitions and congratulations.
3. The ghost of Dr. Busby, stern headmaster of Westminster School.
4. He wears a hat (beaver) and a garland of birch twigs, used for flogging. "Wand": cane used for beating.
5. Alumni of Westminster School, with a play on the justices and members of Parliament who meet at Westminster Hall.
6. I.e., admit that Dr. Busby is the presiding deity (Genius).
7. The letter Y, which Pythagoras (a native of Samos) used as an emblem of the different roads of virtue and vice.

Points him two ways, the narrower is the better.
Placed at the door of learning, youth to guide,
We never suffer it to stand too wide.
155　To ask, to guess, to know, as they commence,
As fancy opens the quick springs of sense,
We ply the memory, we load the brain,
Bind rebel wit, and double chain on chain,
Confine the thought, to exercise the breath;[8]
160　And keep them in the pale of words till death.
Whate'er the talents, or howe'er designed,
We hang one jingling padlock on the mind:
A poet the first day, he dips his quill;
And what the last? a very poet still.
165　Pity! the charm works only in our wall,
Lost, lost too soon in yonder House or Hall."[9]

*　*　*

[THE TRIUMPH OF DULNESS]

　　Then blessing all,[1] "Go children of my care!
580　To practice now from theory repair.
All my commands are easy, short, and full:
My sons! be proud, be selfish, and be dull.
Guard my prerogative, assert my throne:
This nod confirms each privilege your own.
585　The cap and switch be sacred to his Grace;[2]
With staff and pumps[3] the Marquis lead the race;
From stage to stage the licensed[4] Earl may run,
Paired with his fellow-charioteer the sun;
The learned baron butterflies design,
590　Or draw to silk Arachne's subtle line;°　　　　　　　　*spiderweb*
The Judge to dance his brother Sergeant[5] call;
The Senator at cricket urge the ball;
The Bishop stow (pontific luxury!)
An hundred souls of turkeys in a pie;[6]
595　The sturdy squire to Gallic masters° stoop,　　　　　　*French chefs*
And drown his lands and manors in a soup.
Others import yet nobler arts from France,
Teach kings to fiddle, and make senates dance.
Perhaps more high some daring son may soar,[7]
600　Proud to my list to add one monarch more;
And nobly conscious, Princes are but things
Born for First Ministers, as slaves for kings,

8. Students are taught only to recite the classic poets by heart.
9. The House of Commons and Westminster Hall, where law cases were heard. The eloquence learned by rote disappears on occasions for public speaking.
1. Having conferred her titles, Dulness bids each eminent dunce to indulge in the triviality closest to his heart.
2. His Grace, a duke who loves horse racing, is to use the cap and switch of a jockey.

3. Footmen, who wore pumps (low-cut shoes for running), were matched in races.
4. The license required by the owner of a stage-coach; also privileged or licentious.
5. A lawyer or legislative officer. Formal ceremonies at the Inns of Court are said to have resembled a country dance.
6. According to Pope, a hundred turkeys had been "not unfrequently deposited in one Pye in the Bishopric of Durham."
7. A bold, direct attack on Walpole.

Tyrant supreme! shall three estates command,
And MAKE ONE MIGHTY DUNCIAD OF THE LAND!"

605 More she had spoke, but yawned—All Nature nods:
What mortal can resist the yawn of Gods?
Churches and chapels instantly it reached;
(St. James's first, for leaden Gilbert[8] preached)
Then catched the schools; the Hall scarce kept awake;

610 The Convocation gaped,[9] but could not speak:
Lost was the Nation's Sense,° nor could be found,   *Parliament*
While the long solemn unison went round:
Wide, and more wide, it spread o'er all the realm;
Even Palinurus[1] nodded at the helm:

615 The vapor mild o'er each committee crept;
Unfinished treaties in each office slept;
And chiefless armies dozed out the campaign;
And navies yawned for orders on the main.
  O Muse! relate (for you can tell alone,

620 Wits have short memories, and dunces none)
Relate, who first, who last resigned to rest;
Whose heads she partly, whose completely blessed;
What charms could faction, what ambition lull,
The venal quiet, and entrance the dull;

625 'Till drowned was sense, and shame, and right, and wrong—
O sing, and hush the nations with thy song!
. . . .

In vain, in vain,—the all-composing Hour
Resistless falls: The Muse obeys the Power.
She comes! she comes![2] the sable throne behold

630 Of Night primeval, and of Chaos old!
Before her, Fancy's gilded clouds decay,
And all its varying rainbows die away.
Wit shoots in vain its momentary fires,
The meteor drops, and in a flash expires.

635 As one by one, at dread Medea's strain,
The sickening stars fade off the ethereal plain;[3]
As Argus' eyes by Hermes' wand oppressed,
Closed one by one to everlasting rest;[4]
Thus at her felt approach, and secret might,

640 Art after Art goes out, and all is Night.
See skulking Truth to her old cavern fled,[5]
Mountains of casuistry heaped o'er her head!
Philosophy, that leaned on Heaven before,
Shrinks to her second cause,[6] and is no more.

---

8. Dr. John Gilbert, dean of Exeter.
9. The Convocation, an assembly of clergy consulting on ecclesiastical affairs, had been adjourned since 1717.
1. The pilot of Aeneas's ship; here Walpole.
2. Having triumphed in the contemporary world of affairs, Dulness (like her antitype Christ) has a Second Coming, a prophetic vision in which she extinguishes the light of the arts and sciences.
3. In Seneca's *Medea*, the stars obey the curse of Medea, a magician and avenger.

4. Argus, Hera's hundred-eyed watchman, was charmed to sleep and slain by Hermes.
5. Alluding to the saying of Democritus, that Truth lay at the bottom of a deep well [Pope's note].
6. Science (philosophy) no longer accepts God as the first cause or final explanation of how all things came to be; instead, it accepts only the second or material cause and tries to account for all things by physical principles alone.

645 Physic[7] of Metaphysic begs defense,
And Metaphysic calls for aid on Sense!
See Mystery[8] to Mathematics fly!
In vain! they gaze, turn giddy, rave, and die.
Religion blushing veils her sacred fires,
650 And unawares Morality expires.
Nor public flame, nor private, dares to shine;
Nor human spark is left, nor glimpse divine!
Lo! thy dread Empire, CHAOS! is restored;
Light dies before thy uncreating word:[9]
655 Thy hand, great Anarch! lets the curtain fall;
And Universal Darkness buries All.

1743

7. Natural science in general.
8. A religious truth known only through divine revelation.
9. Cf. God's first creating words in Genesis, "Let there be light."

LADY MARY WORTLEY MONTAGU
1689–1762

In her early teens Lady Mary Pierrepont did something that well-bred young women were not supposed to do: she secretly taught herself Latin. The act reveals many of the traits that would also characterize her as a mature woman: curiosity, love of learning, intelligence, ambition, and independence of mind. The eldest daughter of a wealthy Whig peer (he later became marquess of Dorchester), she grew up amid a glittering London circle that included Addison, Steele, Congreve, and later Pope and Gay. But she was not content to live the life of a dutiful aristocratic daughter. Unlike most women in her time, she married for love, and when her husband, Edward Wortley Montagu, was appointed ambassador to Constantinople in 1716, she took advantage of the opportunity by traveling through Europe and studying the language and customs of Turkey. Returning home in 1718, she spent unhappy years that included bitter political quarrels with Pope and the gradual failure of her marriage. Then, in middle age, she fell in love with a young Italian author, Francesco Algarotti. In 1739 she traveled to Italy hoping to see him; but the passion that had kindled in their letters was soon quenched when he failed to join her. The rest of her life was passed abroad, in Avignon, France, and in Brescia and Venice, Italy. She died soon after her return to London, in 1762.

In a century that included many of the great letter writers in English—Gray, Horace Walpole, William Cowper, and others—Montagu is one of the greatest. She had saved her correspondence from 1716 to 1718, which centered on her experiences in the Ottoman empire, and in the year before she died, she deposited a manuscript version with a Protestant clergyman, intending it to be published. *Letters Written During Her Travels* appeared, posthumously, in 1763. "What fire, what ease, what knowledge of Europe and Asia!" the eminent historian Edward Gibbon exclaimed of the work. Montagu had traveled as a young woman with the deliberate ambition to gain such knowledge. Before arriving in Turkey, she undertook the project of understanding its culture in conversations with an Islamic scholar in Belgrade, and her curiosity led her to a multitude of revealing, provocative situations, on which she reflects with acuity and wit. She approvingly describes the liberties given to women by Turkish customs and institutions, such as the veils that rendered a woman incognito in the street (the better, she thought, to conduct secret love affairs). Letter XXXI explains the technique of smallpox inoculation in Turkey. Montagu would earn a place in medical history for her brave introduction of the practice to Britain on her return (her son and daughter were among the first to be inoculated), arousing resistance from doctors (as she predicts) and from fearful people in general. The admiring frankness of Montagu's description of the communal nudity of women in Turkish baths, in Letter XXVI, disturbed and shocked readers when the letters were finally published. Her correspondence presents two subjects to which many British readers at the time were unaccustomed: a complex, formidable civilization beyond Europe's borders, and the independent, brilliant perceptions of a woman able to view the norms of her own society critically in light of those of another.

From an early age Montagu had tried her hand at other literary forms as well: essays, poems, fiction, and even a translated play. In her own time she was especially admired as a poet. When Pope, after their quarrel, gave her the name "Sappho" [(see *Epistle 2. To a Lady*, lines 24–26)], he was doubtless betraying the nervousness that many men felt in the presence of intelligent women (the Greek poet Sappho, after all, preferred women to men); yet Pope was also associating her with the classic author of lyric verse. Montagu's poems, although often casual, reveal the mind of a woman who is not willing to accept the stereotypes imposed on her by men. Like her friend Mary Astell, Montagu puts her trust in education and reason, not in the opinions of others, and she insists on preserving her freedom of choice. A woman, her poems suggest, need not defer to a man who is less than her equal; she must look to her own satisfaction before she looks to his, and she retains the right to say no. The verse demands respect by virtue of its sexual candor and punishing wit. Like Montagu herself, it is never dull, and at its best it places her in that ideal community defined by E. M. Forster: "Not an aristocracy of power, based upon rank and influence, but an aristocracy of the sensitive, the considerate, and the plucky."

From Letters of the Right Honorable Lady M—y W——y M——e: Written During Her Travels in Europe, Asia and Africa, to Persons of Distinction [The Turkish Embassy Letters]

Letter XXVI, To Lady ——, *Adrianople,*[1] *1 April 1717*

["THE WOMEN'S COFFEE HOUSE"; OR, THE TURKISH BATHS]

I am now got into a new world, where every thing I see appears to me a change of scene; and I write to your ladyship with some content of mind, hoping, at least, that you will find the charm of novelty in my letters, and no longer reproach me that I tell you nothing extraordinary. I won't trouble you with a relation of our tedious journey; but I must not omit what I saw remarkable at Sophia,[2] one of the most beautiful towns in the Turkish empire and famous for its hot baths, that are resorted to both for diversion and health. I stopped here one day on purpose to see them; and designing to go *incognito*,

1. A city in western Turkey, named after the Roman emperor Hadrian and now called Edirne.

2. Sofia, now the capital of Bulgaria.

Unknown artist, *Mary Wortley Montagu in the Turkish Bath*, 1781. The scene in Montagu's *Letters* that most fascinated her European readers: the visit to the Turkish baths. From the frontispiece of *Letters . . . Written during her Travels in Europe, Asia, and Africa to Persons of Distinction, Men of Letters, &c. . . . which Contain . . . Accounts of the Policy & Manners of the Turks* (Berlin, 1781).

I hired a Turkish coach. These voitures[3] are not at all like ours, but much more convenient for the country, the heat being so great that glasses[4] would be very troublesome. They are made a good deal in the manner of the Dutch coaches, having wooden lattices painted and gilded; the inside being painted with baskets and nosegays of flowers, intermixed commonly with little poetical mottos. They are covered all over with scarlet cloth, lined with silk, and very often richly embroidered and fringed. This covering entirely hides the persons in them, but may be thrown back at pleasure, and thus permit the ladies to peep through the lattices. They hold four people very conveniently, seated on cushions, but not raised.

In one of these covered wagons, I went to the bagnio[5] about ten o'clock. It was already full of women. It is built of stone, in the shape of a dome, with no windows but in the roof, which gives light enough. There were five of these domes joined together, the outmost being less[6] than the rest, and serving only as a hall, where the portress stood at the door. Ladies of quality generally give this woman the value of a crown or ten shillings, and I did not forget that ceremony. The next room is a very large one, paved with marble, and all round it raised two sofas of marble, one above another. There were four fountains of cold water in this room, falling first into marble basins, and then running on the floor in little channels made for that purpose, which carried

3. Carriages.
4. Windowpanes.

5. Bathhouse.
6. Smaller.

the streams into the next room, something less than this, with the same sort of marble sofas, but so hot with steams of sulphur proceeding from the baths joining to it, 'twas impossible to stay there with one's clothes on. The two other domes were the hot baths, one of which had cocks[7] of cold water turning into it, to temper it to what degree of warmth the bathers pleased to have.

I was in my traveling habit, which is a riding dress, and certainly appeared very extraordinary to them. Yet there was not one of them that showed the least surprise or impertinent curiosity, but received me with all the obliging civility possible. I know no European court where the ladies would have behaved themselves in so polite a manner to such a stranger. I believe, upon the whole, there were two hundred women, and yet none of those disdainful smiles or satirical whispers that never fail in our assemblies when anybody appears that is not dressed exactly in fashion. They repeated over and over to me, "Uzelle, pek uzelle," which is nothing but "charming, very charming."—The first sofas were covered with cushions and rich carpets, on which sat the ladies; and on the second, their slaves behind them, but without any distinction of rank by their dress, all being in the state of nature, that is, in plain English, stark naked, without any beauty or defect concealed. Yet there was not the least wanton smile or immodest gesture amongst them. They walked and moved with the same majestic grace which Milton describes our General Mother[8] with. There were many amongst them as exactly proportioned as ever any goddess was drawn by the pencil of Guido or Titian,[9] and most of their skins shiningly white, only adorned by their beautiful hair, divided into many tresses hanging on their shoulders, braided either with pearl or ribbon, perfectly representing the figures of the graces.[1]

I was here convinced of the truth of a reflection I had often made, that if it were the fashion to go naked, the face would be hardly observed. I perceived that the ladies of the most delicate skins and finest shapes had the greatest share of my admiration, though their faces were sometimes less beautiful than those of their companions. To tell you the truth, I had wickedness enough to wish secretly that Mr. Gervase[2] could have been there invisible. I fancy it would have very much improved his art to see so many fine women naked in different postures, some in conversation, some working, others drinking coffee or sherbet, and many negligently lying on their cushions while their slaves (generally pretty girls of seventeen or eighteen) were employed in braiding their hair in several pretty fancies. In short, 'tis the women's coffee house, where all the news of the town is told, scandal invented, etc. They generally take this diversion once a week, and stay there at least four or five hours without getting cold, by immediate coming out of the hot bath into the cool room, which was very surprising to me. The lady that seemed the most considerable amongst them entreated me to sit by her, and would fain have undressed me for the bath. I excused myself with some difficulty. They being however all so earnest in persuading me, I was at last forced to open my skirt and show them my stays,[3] which satisfied them very well, for I saw they believed

---

7. Faucets.
8. Eve. See *Paradise Lost*, 4.492 and 8.42–43.
9. Guido Reni, Italian painter (1575–1642). Titian, Italian painter (ca. 1488–1576).
1. Three goddesses, daughters of Zeus, personi-

fying grace and beauty.
2. Charles Jervas (1675–1739), English portrait painter, friend of Montagu, Pope, and Swift.
3. Corset stiffened with strips of whalebone.

I was locked up in that machine, and that it was not in my own power to open it, which contrivance they attributed to my husband. I was charmed with their civility and beauty and should have been very glad to pass more time with them, but Mr. W[ortley] resolving to pursue his journey the next morning early, I was in haste to see the ruins of Justinian's church,[4] which did not afford me so agreeable a prospect as I had left, being little more than a heap of stones.

Adieu, Madam. I am sure I have now entertained you with an account of such a sight as you never saw in your life, and what no book of travels could inform you of, as 'tis no less than death for a man to be found in one of these places.

Letter XXXI, To Mrs. S. C. [Sarah Chiswell], Adrianople, 1 April 1717

[THE TURKISH METHOD OF INOCULATION FOR THE SMALL POX]

* * *

Apropos of distempers,[5] I am going to tell you a thing that will make you wish yourself here. The small pox, so fatal and so general amongst us, is here entirely harmless by the invention of engrafting, which is the term they give it. There is a set of old women who make it their business to perform the operation, every autumn, in the month of September, when the great heat is abated. People send to one another to know if any of their family has a mind to have the small pox; they make parties for this purpose, and when they are met (commonly fifteen or sixteen together) the old woman comes with a nutshell full of the matter of the best sort of small pox,[6] and asks what veins you please to have opened. She immediately rips open that you offer to her, with a large needle (which gives you no more pain than a common scratch) and puts into the vein as much matter as can lie upon the head of her needle, and after that, binds up the little wound with a hollow bit of shell, and in this manner opens four or five veins. The Grecians have commonly the superstition of opening one in the middle of the forehead, one in each arm, and one on the breast to mark the sign of the cross; but this has a very ill effect, all these wounds leaving little scars, and is not done by those that are not superstitious, who choose to have them in the legs, or that part of the arm that is concealed. The children or young patients play together all the rest of the day and are in perfect health to the eighth. Then the fever begins to seize them, and they keep their beds two days, very seldom three. They have very rarely above twenty or thirty in their faces, which never mark, and in eight days' time they are as well as before their illness. Where they are wounded, there remains running sores during the distemper, which I don't doubt is a great relief to it. Every year thousands undergo this operation, and the French ambassador says pleasantly that they take the small pox here by way of diversion, as they take the waters in other countries. There is no example of anyone that has died in it, and you may believe I am very

---

4. Roman emperor Justinian (483–565) built St. Sofia Church in the middle of the 6th century.
5. Montagu has just described a mild outbreak of the plague in the area.
6. In inoculation or variolation, the milder form of the smallpox virus (*Variola minor*) is introduced to the skin of a healthy person; the localized nature of this infection stimulates the immune system in time for the body both to terminate it and to protect itself against the virus in the future.

well satisfied of the safety of this experiment, since I intend to try it on my dear little son. I am patriot enough to take pains to bring this useful invention into fashion in England, and I should not fail to write to some of our doctors very particularly about it, if I knew any one of them that I thought had virtue enough to destroy such a considerable branch of their revenue, for the good of mankind. But that distemper is too beneficial to them, not to expose to all their resentment the hardy wight[7] that should undertake to put an end to it. Perhaps if I live to return, I may, however, have courage to war with them. Upon this occasion, admire the heroism in the heart of your friend, etc.

1717   1763

Epistle from Mrs. Yonge to Her Husband[1]

Think not this paper comes with vain pretense
To move your pity, or to mourn th' offense.
Too well I know that hard obdurate heart;
No softening mercy there will take my part,
5   Nor can a woman's arguments prevail,
When even your patron's wise example fails.[2]
But this last privilege I still retain;
Th' oppressed and injured always may complain.
      Too, too severely laws of honor bind
10   The weak submissive sex of womankind.
If sighs have gained or force compelled our hand,
Deceived by art, or urged by stern command,
Whatever motive binds the fatal tie,
The judging world expects our constancy.
15   Just heaven! (for sure in heaven does justice reign,
Though tricks below that sacred name profane)
To you appealing I submit my cause,
Nor fear a judgment from impartial laws.
All bargains but conditional° are made;   *only conditionally*
20   The purchase void, the creditor unpaid;
Defrauded servants are from service free;
A wounded slave regains his liberty.

7. Archaic word meaning "person," often implying misfortune.

1. In 1724 the notorious libertine William Yonge, separated from his wife, Mary, discovered that she (like him) had committed adultery. He sued her lover, Colonel Norton, for damages and collected £1500. Later that year, according to the law of the time, he petitioned the Houses of Parliament for a divorce. The case was tried in public, Mrs. Yonge's love letters were read aloud, and two men testified that they had found her and Norton "together in naked bed." Yonge was granted the divorce, his wife's dowry, and the greater part of her fortune.

Although the "Epistle" is obviously based on this sensational affair, it is also a work of imagination. Like Pope's *Eloisa to Abelard*—to which the author himself called Montagu's attention—it takes the form of a heroic epistle, the passionate outcry of an abandoned woman. The poet, entering into the feelings of Mary Yonge, justifies her conduct with reasons both of the heart and of the head. The objects of her attack include the institution of marriage, which binds wives in "eternal chains"; the double standard of morality, which requires chastity from women but not men; the hypocrisy of society, which condemns the very behavior it secretly lusts after; and the craven greed and cruelty of the husband himself. But 18th-century women seldom dared to speak like this in public, and the "Epistle" was not published until the 1970s.

2. Sir Robert Walpole, William Yonge's friend at court, was rumored to tolerate his own wife's infidelities.

For wives ill used no remedy remains,
To daily racks condemned, and to eternal chains.
25   From whence is this unjust distinction grown?
Are we not formed with passions like your own?
Nature with equal fire our souls endued,
Our minds as haughty, and as warm our blood;
O'er the wide world your pleasures you pursue,
30   The change is justified by something new;
But we must sigh in silence—and be true.
Our sex's weakness you expose and blame
(Of every prattling fop the common theme),
Yet from this weakness you suppose is due
35   Sublimer virtue than your Cato[3] knew.
Had heaven designed us trials so severe,
It would have formed our tempers them to bear.
     And I have borne (oh what have I not borne!)
The pang of jealousy, the insults of scorn.
40   Wearied at length, I from your sight remove,
And place my future hopes in secret love.
In the gay bloom of glowing youth retired,
I quit the woman's joy to be admired,
With that small pension your hard heart allows,
45   Renounce your fortune, and release your vows.
To custom (though unjust) so much is due;
I hide my frailty from the public view.
My conscience clear, yet sensible of shame,
My life I hazard, to preserve my fame.
50   And I prefer this low inglorious state
To vile dependence on the thing I hate—
But you pursue me to this last retreat.
Dragged into light, my tender crime is shown
And every circumstance of fondness known.
55   Beneath the shelter of the law you stand,
And urge my ruin with a cruel hand,
While to my fault thus rigidly severe,
Tamely submissive to the man you fear.[4]
     This wretched outcast, this abandoned wife,
60   Has yet this joy to sweeten shameful life:
By your mean conduct, infamously loose,
You are at once my accuser and excuse.
Let me be damned by the censorious prude
(Stupidly dull, or spiritually lewd),
65   My hapless case will surely pity find
From every just and reasonable mind.
When to the final sentence I submit,
The lips condemn me, but their souls acquit.
     No more my husband, to your pleasures go,
70   The sweets of your recovered freedom know.
Go: court the brittle friendship of the great,

---

3. The asceticism and self-discipline of the
Roman statesman Cato were emphasized in
Addison's famous tragedy *Cato* (1713).

4. I.e., Walpole. Montagu suggests that the whole
political establishment of England takes sides
against Mary Yonge.

Smile at his board,° or at his levee[5] wait; *dining table*
And when dismissed, to madam's toilet[6] fly,
More than her chambermaids, or glasses,° lie, *mirrors*
75   Tell her how young she looks, how heavenly fair,
Admire the lilies and the roses there.
Your high ambition may be gratified,
Some cousin of her own be made your bride,
And you the father of a glorious race
80   Endowed with Ch—l's strength and Low—r's face.[7]

1724   1972

5. Morning reception of visitors.
6. It was fashionable for women like Lady Walpole to receive visitors during the last stages of
dressing (their "toilet").
7. General Churchill was rumored to have had an
affair with Lady Walpole. Antony Lowther was a

notorious gallant. The author implies that William Yonge's next wife may be as untrue as his
first. Mary Yonge remarried immediately after her
divorce; five years later Yonge himself (whose
divorce had made him rich) married the daughter
of a baron.

WILLIAM HOGARTH
1697–1764

William Hogarth was a Londoner born and bred; the life of the city, both high and low, fills all his work. His early life was hard. When his father, a writer and teacher, failed in business, the family was confined to the area of the Fleet, the debtor's prison. Hogarth never forgot "the cruel treatment" of his father by booksellers, and he resolved to make his living without relying on dealers; he would always be aggressively independent. Apprenticed as an engraver, he trained himself to sketch scenes quickly or catch them in memory. He also learned to paint, studying with the Serjeant Painter to the King, Sir James Thornhill, whose daughter he married (late in life Hogarth himself would become Serjeant Painter). Gradually he won a reputation for portraits and conversation pieces—group portraits in which members of a family or assembly interact in a social situation. But his popular fame was forged by sets of pictures that told a story: *A Harlot's Progress* (1731–32), *A Rake's Progress* (1734–35), and *Marriage A-la-Mode* (1743–45). First Hogarth painted these Modern Moral Subjects (as he called them), then prints were made and sold in large editions. He also found new ways to market and protect his work; a copyright bill to ban cheap imitations of prints was known as "Hogarth's Act." Despite this success, however, his ambition to redefine British standards of art led to frustration. The high regard and high prices for continental old masters were too well entrenched to be undermined. Hogarth did not get prestigious commissions, and his *Analysis of Beauty* (1753), an effort to fix "the fluctuating ideas of taste" by appealing to practical observations, not academic rules, was poorly received. Political and aesthetic controversies embittered his final years.

Writers have always loved Hogarth's satiric art, and many have claimed him as one of their own. Swift, Fielding, and Sterne associated their work with his; Horace Walpole considered him more "a writer of comedy with a pencil" than a painter;

Charles Lamb compared him to Shakespeare; and William Hazlitt included him among the great English comic writers. This emphasis may slight Hogarth's importance in the history of art. His attempts to found a British school that looked at life and nature directly, not through a haze of ideas or reverence for the past, and to give pleasure to common people, not only to critics and connoisseurs, opened the eyes of many artists to come. But Hogarth is also a great storyteller, someone to *read*. Like novels and plays, his pictures have plots and morals; they ask us not only to look but also to think. Yet looking and thinking are always intertwined. The mind delights in riddles, according to Hogarth; and as he revised his work he stuffed in more and more clues, like a mystery writer. A feast of interpretation draws the reader in. So many expressive details crowd the pictures, so many keys to character and meaning, that viewers often become obsessed with figuring them out. Even inanimate objects can speak; playwrights rely on words, as Walpole pointed out, but "it was reserved to Hogarth to write a scene of furniture."

The furniture is particularly eloquent in *Marriage A-la-Mode*; note, for example, the fallen chairs in Plates 2 and 6. Hogarth took special pains with this series. The audience at which he aimed, as well as the subject matter, belonged to high society; and the art too is highly refined. A sinuous line weaves through each picture, leading the reader on, and each piece of bric-a-brac carries a message of lavish excess. Yet the story itself is brutally straightforward. A disastrous forced marriage stands at the center: a rich but miserly merchant buys the worthless son of an aristocrat for his restless daughter, and with nothing in common the couple destroy one another. The crisis of values that Hogarth depicts was bringing about radical changes in English life. In the tension between a fading aristocracy, both morally and financially bankrupt, and an upwardly mobile middle class, greedy for power but culturally insecure, the marriage reflects a society that has lost all sense of right and wrong. The artist plays no favorites. The aristocratic Squanderfields are not only vain, effete, and dissipated but also lacking in taste; the wan mythological paintings on their walls are just the sort of pretentious, overpriced art that Hogarth hates. But the vulgar Dutch art on the merchant's walls (in Plate 6) seems even worse, and his daughter falls for every extravagant, spurious fashion (in Plate 4). Nor do the parasites who live off these easy marks offer any hope. Lawyer and doctor, bawd and servant pave the road to ruin. Hogarth's satire warns against the spreading corruption of modern times, when self-interest eats into marriage and old values die. Look hard, he tells the public. These objects make up the world we live in. We might become these people.

Many commentaries have been written on Hogarth's pictures. The notes printed here were supplied by the editors of this volume.

Marriage A-la-Mode

Plate 1. *The Marriage Contract*.   Lord Squanderfield points to the family tree, going back to William the Conquerer, that his son will bring to the marriage. Coronets are blazed all over the room, from the top of the canopy at the upper left to the side of the prostrate dog on the lower right. The earl, though hobbled by gout, is proud. But he has run out of money: construction has stopped on the Palladian mansion seen through the window. Sitting across from him, a squinting merchant grasps the marriage settlement. Some of the coins and banknotes he has placed on the table have been taken up by a scrawny usurer, who hands the earl a mortgage in return. At the right the betrothed sit back to back, uncaring as the dogs chained to each other below. The vacuous viscount pinches snuff and gazes at himself in a mirror, which ominously reflects the image of lawyer Silvertongue, who sharpens his pen as he bends unctuously over the bride-to-be. Pouting, she twirls her wedding ring in a handkerchief. Disasters from mythology cover the walls. A bombastic portrait of the earl as Jupiter, astride a cannon, dominates the room; and in a candle sconce on the right Medusa glowers over the scene.

Plate 2. **After the Marriage**.   By now the couple are used to ignoring each other. The morning after a spree, the rumpled, exhausted viscount slouches in a chair. His broken sword has dropped on the carpet, and a lapdog sniffs at a woman's cap in his pocket—souvenirs of the night. Lolling and stretching in an unladylike pose, his wife too is half asleep. She has spent the night home but not alone. *Hoyle on Whist* lies before her, cards are scattered on the floor, and the overturned chair, book of music, and violin cases suggest that some player may have departed in haste. A steward carries away a sheaf of bills—only one paid—and the household ledger; a Methodist (*Regeneration* is in his pocket), he petitions heaven to look down on these heathens. Oriental idols decorate the mantel over the fireplace, surmounted by a broken-nosed Roman bust that frowns like the steward and a painting of Cupid playing the bagpipes. On the left, amid the shrubbery of a rococo clock, a cat leers over fish and a Buddha smiles. In the next room, a dozing servant fails to notice that a candle has set fire to a chair. Next to a row of saints, a curtain does not quite cover a bawdy painting from which a naked foot peeps.

Plate 3. *The Scene with the Quack.*   The husband has come to this chamber of medical horrors in search of a cure. The pillbox he holds toward the quack has not done its job, and he raises his cane as if with a playful threat. Evidently the little girl who stands between his legs is infected. She dabs a sore on her lip, and her ageless face may hint that she is not as young and pure as she looks. Her cap resembles the cap in Plate 2; she is the husband's mistress. Perhaps the beauty spot on his neck also covers a sore. The bowlegged Monsieur de la Pillule comfortably wipes his glasses; he has seen all this before. Between the two men an angry woman, fortified by a massive hoop skirt, opens a knife. She may be the wife of the quack, defending her man, or else a bawd who resents the charge that her girls are damaged goods. Medical oddities and monstrosities clutter the room, along with portents of death. The viscount's cane points to a cabinet where a wigged head looks at a skeleton that seems to be groping a cadaver; the tripod above evokes a gallows tree. At the far left, in front of a laboratory door, are two of the doctor's inventions: machines for setting bones and uncorking bottles. Their similarity to instruments of torture hints at how useful the doctor's assistance will be.

Plate 4. *The Countess's Levee.*   In her bedchamber at rising (*levée*; French), the countess receives some guests and puts on a show. Her husband is now earl (note the coronets), and they have a child (note the rattle on her chair). While a hairdresser curls her locks, she hangs on the words of Silvertongue, who makes himself at home (note his portrait on the upper right wall). Tonight they will be going to a masquerade ball, like the one on the screen he gestures toward; his left hand holds the tickets. At the far right a puffy, bedizened castrato sings, accompanied by a flute. His audience includes a self-absorbed dandy in curl-papers; a man who appreciatively smirks and opens his hand, from which a fan dangles; a snoring husband, holding his riding-crop like a baton; and his enraptured wife, who leans forward as if about to swoon. Unobserved by the others, a black servant, bearing a cup of chocolate, smiles in amazement at these precious airs. At the lower left another black servant, a boy in a turban, grins at gewgaws purchased at an auction. His finger points both to Actaeon's horns, the sign of a cuckold, and to the couple as they arrange their tryst. Wall paintings illustrate unnatural sex: Lot's seduction by his daughters, Jupiter embracing Io, and the rape of Ganymede.

Plate 5. ***The Death of the Earl.*** The melodramatic tableau at the center, as the earl totters toward death and the countess kneels to beg forgiveness, imitates paintings of Christ descending from the cross while Mary Magdalen mourns. But the surroundings are sordid. At a house of ill repute, the Turk's Head Bagnio, the countess and Silvertongue have been surprised in bed. The earl has broken in (key and socket on the floor) and drawn his sword, and the lawyer has run him through. As the horrified owner and constable enter, under a watchman's lantern, the killer, still in his nightshirt, flees through a window. A fire, outside the picture on the lower right, casts lurid light on the victim; the shadow of the tongs encircles the murder weapon. Costumed as a nun and friar, the lovers have come from a masquerade, and their discarded masks and clothes show they were in haste. Pills (presumably mercury, prescribed for venereal disease) have spilled from an overturned table on the right, beside an advertisement for the bagnio, a corset, and a bundle of firewood. The portrait of a streetwalker, a squirrel perched on her hand, leers over the countess; on the wall behind the earl an uplifted blade is about to sever a child, in the Judgment of Solomon. At the top left St. Luke, the patron of artists, inscribes these transgressions.

Plate 6. *The Death of the Countess.* "Counseller Silvertongues Last Dying Speech," a paper on the floor announces, and a bottle of laudanum has dropped beside it. News of her lover's execution has driven the countess to poison herself. Slumped in a chair, she is already dead; on the far right a doctor steals away. Her father calmly slides the ring from her finger. This is his house; a window with cobwebs and broken panes opens on London Bridge, in the heart of the City. No luxury here. The furnishings are sparse, the floor is bare, and the dining table holds only one egg and a few leftovers, including a pathetic boar's head from which a starving hound is tearing scraps. The art is equally cheap: a pissing boy, a jumbled still life, a pipe set alight by the glowing nose of a drunk. At the center, beneath a coatrack, a stout apothecary (stomach pump and julep in his pocket) points toward the empty bottle in reproof and pokes the servant who brought it—an idiot wearing a coat many sizes too large, the merchant's hand-me-down. The service staff is completed by a withered old woman who holds out the countess's little child for one last hug and kiss. But the mark on the child's cheek and the brace on its leg imply that disease has passed to the next generation. This noble family will have no heir.

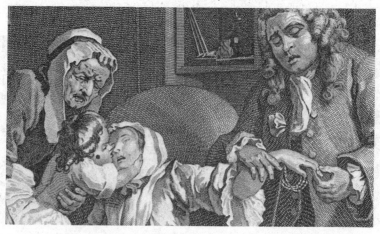

SAMUEL JOHNSON
1709–1784

Samuel Johnson was famous as a talker in his own time, and his conversation (preserved by James Boswell and others) has been famous ever since. But his wisdom survives above all in his writings: a few superb poems; the grave *Rambler* essays, which established his reputation as a stylist and a moralist; the lessons about life in *Rasselas* and the *Lives of the Poets*; and literary criticism that ranks among the best in English. The virtues of the talk and the writings are the same. They come hot from a mind well stored with knowledge, searingly honest, humane, and quick to seize the unexpected but appropriate image of truth. Johnson's wit is timeless, for it deals with the great facts of human experience, with hope and happiness and loss and duty and the fear of death. Whatever topic he addresses, whatever the form in which he writes, he holds to one commanding purpose: to see life as it is.

Two examples must suffice here. When Anna Williams wondered why a man should make a beast of himself through drunkenness, Johnson answered that "he who makes a beast of himself gets rid of the pain of being a man." In this reply Williams's tired metaphor is so charged with an awareness of the dark aspects of human life that it comes almost unbearably alive. Such moments characterize Johnson's writings as well. For instance, in reviewing the book of a fatuous would-be philosopher who blandly explained away the pains of poverty by declaring that a kindly providence compensates the poor by making them more hopeful, more healthy, more easily pleased, and less sensitive than the rich, Johnson retorted: "The poor indeed are insensible of many little vexations which sometimes embitter the possessions and pollute the enjoyments of the rich. They are not pained by casual incivility, or mortified by the mutilation of a compliment; but this happiness is like that of a malefactor who ceases to feel the cords that bind him when the pincers are tearing his flesh."

Johnson had himself known the pains of poverty. During his boyhood and youth in Lichfield, his father's bookshop and other businesses plunged into debt, so that he was forced to leave Oxford before he had taken a degree. An early marriage to a well-to-do widow, Elizabeth ("Tetty") Porter, more than twenty years older than he, enabled him to open a school. But the school failed, and he moved to London to make his way as a writer. The years between 1737, when he first arrived there with his pupil David Garrick (who later became the leading actor of his generation), and 1755, when the publication of the *Dictionary* established his reputation, were often difficult. He supported himself at first as best he could by doing hack work for the *Gentleman's Magazine*, but gradually his own original writings began to attract attention.

In 1747 Johnson published the Plan of his *Dictionary*, and he spent the next seven years compiling it—although he had expected to finish it in three. When in 1748 Dr. Adams, a friend from Oxford days, questioned his ability to carry out such a work alone so fast and reminded him that the *Dictionary* of the French Academy had needed forty academicians working for forty years, Johnson replied with humorous jingoism: "Sir, thus it is. This is the proportion. Let me see; forty times forty is sixteen hundred. As three to sixteen hundred, so is the proportion of an Englishman to a Frenchman."

Johnson's achievement in compiling the *Dictionary* seems even greater when we realize that he was writing some of his best essays and poems during the same period. Although the booksellers who published the *Dictionary* paid him what was then the large sum of £1575, it was not enough to enable him to support his household, buy materials, and pay the wages of the six assistants whom he employed year by year until the task was accomplished. He therefore had to earn more money by writing. In 1749, his early tragedy *Irene* (pronounced *I-re-nĕ*) was produced at long last by his old friend Garrick, by then the manager of Drury Lane. The play was not a success, although Johnson made some profit from it. In the same year appeared his finest poem, "The Vanity of Human Wishes." With the *Rambler* (1750–52) and the *Idler* (1758–60), two series of periodical essays, Johnson found a devoted audience, but his pleasure was tempered by the death of his wife in 1752. He never remarried.

Boswell said of the *Rambler* essays that "in no writings whatever can be found more bark and steel [i.e., quinine and iron] for the mind." Moral strength and health; the importance of applying reason to experience; the test of virtue by what we do, not what we say or "feel"; faith in God: these are the centers to which Johnson's moral writings always return. What Johnson uniquely offers us is the quality of his understanding of the human condition, based on wide reading but always ultimately referred to his own passionate and often anguished experience. Such understanding had to be fought for again and again.

Johnson is thought of as the great generalizer, but what gives his generalizations strength is that they are rooted in the particulars of his self-knowledge. He had constantly to fight against what he called "filling the mind" with illusions to avoid the call of duty, his own black melancholy, and the realities of life. The portrait (largely a self-portrait) of Sober in *Idler* 31 is revealing: he occupies his idle hours with crafts and hobbies and has now taken up chemistry—he "sits and counts the drops as they come from his retort, and forgets that, whilst a drop is falling, a moment flies away."

His theme of themes is expressed in the title "The Vanity of Human Wishes": the dangerous but all-pervasive power of wishful thinking, the feverish intrusion of desires and hopes that distort reality and lead to false expectations. Almost all of Johnson's major writings—verse satire, moral essay, or the prose fable *Rasselas* (1759)—express this theme. In *Rasselas* it is called "the hunger of imagination, which preys upon life," picturing things as one would like them to be, not as they are. The travelers who are the fable's protagonists pursue some formula for happiness; they reflect our naive hope, against the lessons of experience, that one choice of life will make us happy forever.

Johnson also developed a style of his own: balanced, extended sentences, phrases, or clauses moving to carefully controlled rhythms, in language that is characteristically general, often Latinate, and frequently polysyllabic. This style is far from Swift's simplicity or Addison's neatness, but it never becomes obscure or turgid, for even a very complex sentence reveals—as it should—the structure of the thought, and the learned words are always precisely used. While reading early scientists to collect words for the *Dictionary*, Johnson developed a new vocabulary: for example, *obtund, exuberate, fugacity,* and *frigorific.* But he used many of these strange words in conversation as well as in his writings, often with a peculiarly Johnsonian felicity, describing the operations of the mind with a scientific precision.

After Johnson received his pension in 1762, he no longer had to write for a living, and because he held that "no man but a blockhead" ever wrote for any other reason, he produced as little as he decently could during the last twenty years of his life. His edition of Shakespeare, long delayed, was published in 1765, with a fine preface and fascinating notes. His last important work is the *Lives of the Poets*, which came out in two parts in 1779 and 1781. These biographical and critical prefaces were commissioned by a group of booksellers who had joined together to publish a large collection of the English poets and who wished to give their venture the prestige that Johnson would lend it. The poets to be included (except for four insisted on by Johnson) were selected by the booksellers according to current fashions. Therefore the collection begins with Abraham Cowley and John Milton and ends with Thomas Gray, and it omits such standard poets as Chaucer, Spenser, Sidney, Donne, and Marvell.

In the *Lives of the Poets* and in the earlier *Life of Richard Savage* (1744), Johnson did much to advance the art of biography in England. Biography had long been associated with panegyrics or scandalous memoirs; and therefore, Johnson's insistence on truth, even about the subject's defects, and on concrete, often minute, details was a new departure. "The biographical part of literature is what I love most," Johnson said, for he found every biography useful in revealing the human nature that all of us share. His insistence on truth in biography (and knowing that Boswell intended to write his life, he insisted that he should write it truthfully) was owing to his conviction that only a truthful work can be trusted to help us with the business of living.

The ideal poet, according to Johnson, has a genius for making the things we see every day seem new. The same might be said of Johnson himself as a critic. Johnson is our great champion, in criticism, of common sense and the common reader. Without denying the right of the poet to flights of imagination, he also insists that poems must make sense, please readers, and help us not only understand the world but cope with it. Johnson holds poems to the truth, as he sees it: the principles of nature, logic, religion, and morality. Not even Shakespeare can be excused when "he sacrifices virtue to convenience" and "seems to write without any moral purpose." Yet Johnson is no worshiper of authority or mere "correctness." As a critic he is always the empiricist, testing theory by practice. His determination to judge literature by its truth to life, not by abstract rules, is perfectly illustrated by his treatment of the doctrine of the three unities in the Preface to Shakespeare. Johnson is never afraid to state the obvious, whether the lack of human interest in *Paradise Lost* or Shakespeare's temptation by puns. But at its best, as in the praise of Milton or Shakespeare, his criticism engages some of the deepest questions about literature: why it endures, and how it helps us endure.

For more on Johnson's prose, see the supplemental ebook.

The Vanity of Human Wishes   This poem is an imitation of Juvenal's *Satire 10*. Although it closely follows the order and the ideas of the Latin poem, it remains a very personal work, for Johnson has used the Roman Stoic's satire as a means of expressing his own sense of the tragic and comic in human life. He has tried to reproduce in English verse the qualities he thought especially Juvenalian: stateliness, pointed sentences, and declamatory grandeur. The poem is difficult because of the extreme compactness of the style: every line is forced to convey the greatest possible amount of meaning. Johnson believed that "great thoughts are always general," but he certainly did not intend that the general should fade into the abstract: observe, for example, how he makes personified nouns concrete, active, and dramatic by using them as subjects of active and dramatic verbs: "Hate *dogs* their flight, and Insult *mocks* their end" (line 78). But the difficulty of the poem is also related to its theme, the difficulty of seeing anything clearly on this earth. In a world of blindness and illusion, human beings must struggle to find a point of view that will not deceive them, and a happiness that can last.

The Vanity of Human Wishes

In Imitation of the Tenth Satire of Juvenal

> Let Observation, with extensive view,
> Survey mankind, from China to Peru;
> Remark each anxious toil, each eager strife,
> And watch the busy scenes of crowded life;
> 5   Then say how hope and fear, desire and hate
> O'erspread with snares the clouded maze of fate,
> Where wavering man, betrayed by venturous Pride
> To tread the dreary paths without a guide,

As treacherous phantoms in the mist delude,
10   Shuns fancied ills, or chases airy good.
How rarely Reason guides the stubborn choice,
Rules the bold hand, or prompts the suppliant voice;
How nations sink, by darling schemes oppressed,
When Vengeance listens to the fool's request.
15   Fate wings with every wish the afflictive dart,
Each gift of nature, and each grace of art;
With fatal heat impetuous courage glows,
With fatal sweetness elocution flows,
Impeachment stops the speaker's powerful breath,
20   And restless fire precipitates on death.
    But scarce observed, the knowing and the bold
Fall in the general massacre of gold;
Wide-wasting pest! that rages unconfined,
And crowds with crimes the records of mankind;
25   For gold his sword the hireling ruffian draws,
For gold the hireling judge distorts the laws;
Wealth heaped on wealth, nor truth nor safety buys,
The dangers gather as the treasures rise.
    Let History tell where rival kings command,
30   And dubious title° shakes the madded land,   *claim of right*
When statutes glean the refuse of the sword,
How much more safe the vassal than the lord;
Low skulks the hind° beneath the rage of power,   *peasant*
And leaves the wealthy traitor in the Tower,[1]
35   Untouched his cottage, and his slumbers sound,
Though Confiscation's vultures hover round.
    The needy traveler, serene and gay,
Walks the wild heath, and sings his toil away.
Does envy seize thee? crush the upbraiding joy,
40   Increase his riches and his peace destroy;
New fears in dire vicissitude invade,
The rustling brake° alarms, and quivering shade,   *thicket*
Nor light nor darkness bring his pain relief,
One shows the plunder, and one hides the thief.
45   Yet still one general cry the skies assails,
And gain and grandeur load the tainted gales;
Few know the toiling statesman's fear or care,
The insidious rival and the gaping heir.
    Once more, Democritus,[2] arise on earth,
50   With cheerful wisdom and instructive mirth,
See motley life in modern trappings dressed,
And feed with varied fools the eternal jest:
Thou who couldst laugh where Want enchained Caprice,
Toil crushed Conceit, and man was of a piece;
55   Where Wealth unloved without a mourner died;
And scarce a sycophant was fed by Pride;
Where ne'er was known the form of mock debate,

---

1. I.e., the Tower of London, which served as a prison. Johnson first wrote "bonny traitor," recalling the Jacobite uprising of 1745 and the execution of four of its Scot leaders.

2. A Greek philosopher of the late 5th century B.C.E., remembered as the "laughing philosopher" because men's follies only moved him to mirth.

Or seen a new-made mayor's unwieldy state;[3]
Where change of favorites made no change of laws,
60 And senates heard before they judged a cause;
How wouldst thou shake at Britain's modish tribe,
Dart the quick taunt, and edge the piercing gibe?
Attentive truth and nature to descry,
And pierce each scene with philosophic eye.
65 To thee were solemn toys or empty show
The robes of pleasure and the veils of woe:
All aid the farce, and all thy mirth maintain,
Whose joys are causeless, or whose griefs are vain.
    Such was the scorn that filled the sage's mind,
70 Renewed at every glance on human kind;
How just that scorn ere yet thy voice declare,
Search every state, and canvass every prayer.
    Unnumbered suppliants crowd Preferment's gate,
Athirst for wealth, and burning to be great;
75 Delusive Fortune hears the incessant call,
They mount, they shine, evaporate,[4] and fall.
On every stage the foes of peace attend,
Hate dogs their flight, and Insult mocks their end.
Love ends with hope, the sinking statesman's door
80 Pours in the morning worshiper no more;[5]
For growing names the weekly scribbler lies,
To growing wealth the dedicator flies;
From every room descends the painted face,
That hung the bright palladium[6] of the place;
85 And smoked in kitchens, or in auctions sold,
To better features yields the frame of gold;
For now no more we trace in every line
Heroic worth, benevolence divine:
The form distorted justifies the fall,
90 And Detestation rids the indignant wall.
    But will not Britain hear the last appeal,
Sign her foes' doom, or guard her favorites' zeal?
Through Freedom's sons no more remonstrance rings,
Degrading nobles and controlling kings;
95 Our supple tribes repress their patriot throats,
And ask no questions but the price of votes;
With weekly libels and septennial ale,[7]
Their wish is full to riot and to rail.
    In full-blown dignity, see Wolsey[8] stand,
100 Law in his voice, and fortune in his hand:
To him the church, the realm, their powers consign,
Through him the rays of regal bounty shine;

3. Pomp. Mayors organized costly processions.
4. Disperse in vapors, like fireworks.
5. Statesmen gave interviews and received friends and petitioners at levees, or morning receptions.
6. An image of Pallas Athena, that fell from heaven and was preserved at Troy. Not until it was stolen by Diomedes could the city fall to the Greeks.
7. Ministers and even the king freely bought support by bribing members of Parliament, who in turn won elections by buying votes. "Weekly libels": politically motivated lampoons published in the weekly newspapers. "Septennial ale": the ale given away by candidates at parliamentary elections, held at least every seven years.
8. Thomas Cardinal Wolsey (ca. 1475–1530), lord chancellor and favorite of Henry VIII. Shakespeare dramatized his fall in Henry VIII.

Turned by his nod the stream of honor flows,
His smile alone security bestows:
105 Still to new heights his restless wishes tower,
Claim leads to claim, and power advances power;
Till conquest unresisted ceased to please,
And rights submitted, left him none to seize.
At length his sovereign frowns—the train of state
110 Mark the keen glance, and watch the sign to hate.
Where'er he turns, he meets a stranger's eye,
His suppliants scorn him, and his followers fly;
At once is lost the pride of awful state,
The golden canopy, the glittering plate,
115 The regal palace, the luxurious board,
The liveried army, and the menial lord.
With age, with cares, with maladies oppressed,
He seeks the refuge of monastic rest.
Grief aids disease, remembered folly stings,
120 And his last sighs reproach the faith of kings.
    Speak thou, whose thoughts at humble peace repine,
Shall Wolsey's wealth, with Wolsey's end be thine?
Or liv'st thou now, with safer pride content,
The wisest justice on the banks of Trent?
125 For why did Wolsey, near the steeps of fate,
On weak foundations raise the enormous weight?
Why but to sink beneath misfortune's blow,
With louder ruin to the gulfs below?
    What gave great Villiers⁹ to the assassin's knife,
130 And fixed disease on Harley's closing life?
What murdered Wentworth, and what exiled Hyde,
By kings protected, and to kings allied?
What but their wish indulged in courts to shine,
And power too great to keep or to resign?
135   When first the college rolls receive his name,
The young enthusiast quits his ease for fame;
Through all his veins the fever of renown
Burns from the strong contagion of the gown:¹
O'er Bodley's dome his future labors spread,
140 And Bacon's² mansion trembles o'er his head.
Are these thy views? proceed, illustrious youth,
And Virtue guard thee to the throne of Truth!
Yet should thy soul indulge the generous heat,
Till captive Science° yields her last retreat;   *knowledge*
145 Should Reason guide thee with her brightest ray,
And pour on misty Doubt resistless day;

9. George Villiers, first duke of Buckingham, favorite of James I and Charles I, was assassinated in 1628. Mentioned in the following lines: Robert Harley, earl of Oxford, chancellor of the exchequer and later lord treasurer under Queen Anne (1710–14), impeached and imprisoned by the Whigs in 1715. Thomas Wentworth, earl of Strafford, intimate and adviser of Charles I, impeached by the Long Parliament and executed in 1641. Edward Hyde, earl of Clarendon ("to

kings allied" because his daughter married James, duke of York), lord chancellor under Charles II (impeached in 1667, he fled to the Continent).
1. Academic robe; here associated with the poisoned shirt that tormented Hercules.
2. Roger Bacon (ca. 1214–1294), scientist and philosopher, taught at Oxford, where his study, according to tradition, would collapse if a man greater than he should appear at Oxford. "Bodley's dome": the Bodleian Library, Oxford.

Should no false kindness lure to loose delight,
Nor praise relax, nor difficulty fright;
Should tempting Novelty thy cell refrain,
150 And Sloth effuse her opiate fumes in vain;
Should Beauty blunt on fops her fatal dart,
Nor claim the triumph of a lettered heart;
Should no disease thy torpid veins invade,
Nor Melancholy's phantoms haunt thy shade;
155 Yet hope not life from grief or danger free,
Nor think the doom of man reversed for thee:
Deign on the passing world to turn thine eyes,
And pause a while from letters, to be wise;
There mark what ills the scholar's life assail,
160 Toil, envy, want, the patron,[3] and the jail.
See nations slowly wise, and meanly just,
To buried merit raise the tardy bust.
If dreams yet flatter, once again attend,
Hear Lydiat's life, and Galileo's[4] end.
165   Nor deem, when Learning her last prize bestows,
The glittering eminence exempt from foes;
See when the vulgar 'scapes, despised or awed,
Rebellion's vengeful talons seize on Laud.[5]
From meaner minds, though smaller fines content,
170 The plundered palace or sequestered rent;[6]
Marked out by dangerous parts° he meets   *accomplishments*
     the shock,
And fatal Learning leads him to the block:
Around his tomb let Art and Genius weep,
But hear his death, ye blockheads, hear and sleep.
175   The festal blazes, the triumphal show,
The ravished standard, and the captive foe,
The senate's thanks, the gazette's pompous tale,
With force resistless o'er the brave prevail.
Such bribes the rapid Greek° o'er Asia whirled,   *Alexander the Great*
180 For such the steady Romans shook the world;
For such in distant lands the Britons shine,
And stain with blood the Danube or the Rhine;
This power has praise that virtue scarce can warm,
Till fame supplies the universal charm.
185 Yet Reason frowns on War's unequal game,
Where wasted nations raise a single name,
And mortgaged states their grandsires' wreaths regret
From age to age in everlasting debt;
Wreaths which at last the dear-bought right convey
190 To rust on medals, or on stones decay.
     On what foundation stands the warrior's pride?

---

3. In the first edition, "garret."
4. Famous astronomer (1564–1642) who was imprisoned as a heretic by the Inquisition in 1633; he died blind. Thomas Lydiat (1572–1646), Oxford scholar, died impoverished because of his Royalist sympathies.
5. Appointed archbishop of Canterbury by

Charles I, William Laud followed rigorously High Church policies and was executed by order of the Long Parliament in 1645.
6. During the Commonwealth, the estates of many Royalists were pillaged and their incomes confiscated ("sequestered") by the state.

How just his hopes, let Swedish Charles[7] decide;
A frame of adamant, a soul of fire,
No dangers fright him, and no labors tire;
195 O'er love, o'er fear, extends his wide domain,
Unconquered lord of pleasure and of pain;
No joys to him pacific scepters yield,
War sounds the trump, he rushes to the field;
Behold surrounding kings their powers combine,
200 And one capitulate, and one resign;[8]
Peace courts his hand, but spreads her charms in vain;
"Think nothing gained," he cries, "till naught remain,
On Moscow's walls till Gothic standards fly,
And all be mine beneath the polar sky."
205 The march begins in military state,
And nations on his eye suspended wait;
Stern Famine guards the solitary coast,
And Winter barricades the realms of Frost;
He comes, nor want nor cold his course delay—
210 Hide, blushing Glory, hide Pultowa's day:
The vanquished hero leaves his broken bands,
And shows his miseries in distant lands;
Condemned a needy supplicant to wait,
While ladies interpose, and slaves debate.
215 But did not Chance at length her error mend?
Did no subverted empire mark his end?
Did rival monarchs give the fatal wound?
Or hostile millions press him to the ground?
His fall was destined to a barren strand,
220 A petty fortress, and a dubious hand;[9]
He left the name at which the world grew pale,
To point a moral, or adorn a tale.
    All times their scenes of pompous woes afford,
From Persia's tyrant to Bavaria's lord.[1]
225 In gay hostility, and barbarous pride,
With half mankind embattled at his side,
Great Xerxes comes to seize the certain prey,
And starves exhausted regions in his way;
Attendant Flattery counts his myriads o'er,
230 Till counted myriads soothe his pride no more;
Fresh praise is tried till madness fires his mind,
The waves he lashes, and enchains the wind;[2]
New powers are claimed, new powers are still bestowed,
Till rude resistance lops the spreading god;
235 The daring Greeks deride the martial show,

---

7. Charles XII of Sweden (1682–1718). Defeated by the Russians at Pultowa (1709), he escaped to Turkey and tried to form an alliance against Russia with the sultan. Returning to Sweden, he attacked Norway and was killed in the attack on Fredrikshald.
8. Frederick IV of Denmark capitulated to Charles in 1700. Augustus II of Poland resigned his throne to Charles in 1704.
9. It was disputed whether Charles was shot by the enemy or by his own aide-de-camp.
1. The Elector Charles Albert caused the War of the Austrian Succession (1740–48) when he contested the crown of the empire with Maria Theresa ("Fair Austria" in line 245). "Persia's tyrant": Xerxes invaded Greece and was totally defeated in the sea battle off Salamis, 480 B.C.E.
2. When storms destroyed Xerxes' boats, he commanded his men to punish the wind and sea.

And heap their valleys with the gaudy foe;
The insulted sea with humbler thoughts he gains,
A single skiff to speed his flight remains;
The encumbered oar scarce leaves the dreaded coast
240   Through purple billows and a floating host.
       The bold Bavarian, in a luckless hour,
Tries the dread summits of Caesarean power,
With unexpected legions bursts away,
And sees defenseless realms receive his sway;
245   Short sway! fair Austria spreads her mournful charms,
The queen, the beauty, sets the world in arms;
From hill to hill the beacon's rousing blaze
Spreads wide the hope of plunder and of praise;
The fierce Croatian, and the wild Hussar,[3]
250   With all the sons of ravage crowd the war;
The baffled prince in honor's flattering bloom
Of hasty greatness finds the fatal doom,
His foes' derision, and his subjects' blame,
And steals to death from anguish and from shame.
255   Enlarge my life with multitude of days!
In health, in sickness, thus the suppliant prays;
Hides from himself his state, and shuns to know,
That life protracted is protracted woe.
Time hovers o'er, impatient to destroy,
260   And shuts up all the passages of joy;
In vain their gifts the bounteous seasons pour,
The fruit autumnal, and the vernal flower;
With listless eyes the dotard views the store,
He views, and wonders that they please no more;
265   Now pall the tasteless meats, and joyless wines,
And Luxury with sighs her slave resigns.
Approach, ye minstrels, try the soothing strain,
Diffuse the tuneful lenitives of pain:°   *painkillers*
No sounds, alas! would touch the impervious ear,
270   Though dancing mountains witnessed Orpheus[4] near;
Nor lute nor lyre his feeble powers attend,
Nor sweeter music of a virtuous friend,
But everlasting dictates crowd his tongue,
Perversely grave, or positively wrong.
275   The still returning tale, and lingering jest,
Perplex the fawning niece and pampered guest,
While growing hopes scarce awe the gathering sneer,
And scarce a legacy can bribe to hear;
The watchful guests still hint the last offense,
280   The daughter's petulance, the son's expense,
Improve° his heady rage with treacherous skill,   *increase*
And mold his passions till they make his will.
       Unnumbered maladies his joints invade,
Lay siege to life and press the dire blockade;
285   But unextinguished avarice still remains,

---

3. Hungarian light cavalry.
4. A legendary poet who played on the lyre so beautifully that even stones were moved.

And dreaded losses aggravate his pains;
He turns, with anxious heart and crippled hands,
His bonds of debt, and mortgages of lands;
Or views his coffers with suspicious eyes,
290   Unlocks his gold, and counts it till he dies.
        But grant, the virtues of a temperate prime
Bless with an age exempt from scorn or crime;
An age that melts with unperceived decay,
And glides in modest innocence away;
295   Whose peaceful day Benevolence endears,
Whose night congratulating Conscience cheers;
The general favorite as the general friend:
Such age there is, and who shall wish its end?
        Yet even on this her load Misfortune flings,
300   To press the weary minutes' flagging wings;
New sorrow rises as the day returns,
A sister sickens, or a daughter mourns.
Now kindred Merit fills the sable bier,
Now lacerated Friendship claims a tear;
305   Year chases year, decay pursues decay,
Still drops some joy from withering life away;
New forms arise, and different views engage,
Superfluous lags the veteran[5] on the stage,
Till pitying Nature signs the last release,
310   And bids afflicted Worth retire to peace.
        But few there are whom hours like these await,
Who set unclouded in the gulfs of Fate.
From Lydia's monarch[6] should the search descend,
By Solon cautioned to regard his end,
315   In life's last scene what prodigies surprise,
Fears of the brave, and follies of the wise!
From Marlborough's eyes the streams of dotage flow,
And Swift[7] expires a driveler and a show.
        The teeming mother, anxious for her race,°   *family*
320   Begs for each birth the fortune of a face:
Yet Vane could tell what ills from beauty spring;
And Sedley[8] cursed the form that pleased a king.
Ye nymphs of rosy lips and radiant eyes,
Whom Pleasure keeps too busy to be wise,
325   Whom Joys with soft varieties invite,
By day the frolic, and the dance by night;
Who frown with vanity, who smile with art,
And ask the latest fashion of the heart;
What care, what rules your heedless charms shall save,
330   Each nymph your rival, and each youth your slave?
Against your fame with Fondness Hate combines,

---

5. I.e., of life, not of war.
6. Croesus, the wealthy and fortunate king, was warned by Solon not to count himself happy until he ceased to live. He lost his crown to Cyrus the Great of Persia.
7. Jonathan Swift, who passed the last four years of his life in utter senility. John Churchill, Duke

of Marlborough, England's brilliant general during most of the War of the Spanish Succession (1702–13).
8. Catherine Sedley, mistress of James II. Anne Vane, mistress of Frederick, Prince of Wales (son of George II).

The rival batters, and the lover mines.[9]
With distant voice neglected Virtue calls,
Less heard and less, the faint remonstrance falls;
335 Tired with contempt, she quits the slippery reign,
And Pride and Prudence take her seat in vain.
In crowd at once, where none the pass defend,
The harmless freedom, and the private friend.
The guardians yield, by force superior plied:
340 To Interest, Prudence; and to Flattery, Pride.
Now Beauty falls betrayed, despised, distressed,
And hissing Infamy proclaims the rest.
    Where then shall Hope and Fear their objects find?
Must dull Suspense° corrupt the stagnant mind?   *uncertainty*
345 Must helpless man, in ignorance sedate,
Roll darkling down the torrent of his fate?
Must no dislike alarm, no wishes rise,
No cries invoke the mercies of the skies?
Inquirer, cease; petitions yet remain,
350 Which Heaven may hear, nor deem religion vain.
Still raise for good the supplicating voice,
But leave to Heaven the measure and the choice.
Safe in his power, whose eyes discern afar
The secret ambush of a specious prayer.
355 Implore his aid, in his decisions rest,
Secure, whate'er he gives, he gives the best.
Yet when the sense of sacred presence fires,
And strong devotion to the skies aspires,
Pour forth thy fervors for a healthful mind,
360 Obedient passions, and a will resigned;
For love, which scarce collective man can fill;[1]
For patience sovereign o'er transmuted ill;
For faith, that panting for a happier seat,
Counts death kind Nature's signal of retreat:
365 These goods for man the laws of Heaven ordain,
These goods he grants, who grants the power to gain;
With these celestial Wisdom calms the mind,
And makes the happiness she does not find.

1749

Rasselas Johnson wrote *Rasselas* in January 1759 during the evenings of one week, a remarkable instance of his ability to write rapidly and brilliantly under the pressure of necessity. His mother lay dying in Lichfield. Her son, famous for his *Dictionary*, was nonetheless oppressed by poverty and in great need of ready money with which to make her last days comfortable, pay her funeral expenses, and settle her small debts. He was paid £100 for the first edition of *Rasselas*, but not in time to attend her deathbed or her funeral.

Rasselas is a philosophical fable cast in the popular form of an Oriental tale, a type of fiction that owed its popularity to the vogue of the *Arabian Nights*, first translated

9. Plants mines beneath, as in the siege of a fortress.

1. Which humankind as a whole can hardly over-task.

into English in the early eighteenth century. Because the work is a fable, we should not approach it as a novel: psychologically credible characters and a series of intricately involved actions that lead to a necessary resolution and conclusion are not to be found in *Rasselas*. Instead we are meant to reflect on the ideas and to savor the melancholy resonance and intelligence of the stately prose that expresses them. Johnson arranges the incidents of the fable to test a variety of possible solutions to a problem: What choice of life will bring us happiness? (*The Choice of Life* was his working title for the book.) Many ways of life are examined in turn, and each is found wanting. Johnson does not pretend to have solved the problem. Rather, he locates the sources of discontent in a basic principle of human nature: the "hunger of imagination which preys incessantly upon life" (chapter 32) and which lures us to "listen with credulity to the whispers of fancy and pursue with eagerness the phantoms of hope" (chapter 1). The tale is a gentle satire on one of the perennial topics of satirists: the folly of all of us who stubbornly cling to our illusions despite the evidence of experience. *Rasselas* is not all darkness and gloom, for Johnson's theme invites comic as well as tragic treatment, and some of the episodes evoke that laughter of the mind that is the effect of high comedy. In its main theme, however—the folly of cherishing the dream of ever attaining unalloyed happiness in a world that can never wholly satisfy our desires—and in many of the sayings of its characters, especially of the sage Imlac, *Rasselas* expresses some of Johnson's own deepest convictions.

From The History of Rasselas, Prince of Abyssinia

Chapter 1. Description of a Palace in a Valley

Ye who listen with credulity to the whispers of fancy, and pursue with eagerness the phantoms of hope; who expect that age will perform the promises of youth, and that the deficiencies of the present day will be supplied by the morrow—attend to the history of Rasselas, prince of Abyssinia.

Rasselas was the fourth son of the mighty emperor in whose dominions the Father of Waters[1] begins his course; whose bounty pours down the streams of plenty, and scatters over half the world the harvests of Egypt.

According to the custom which has descended from age to age among the monarchs of the torrid zone, Rasselas was confined in a private palace, with the other sons and daughters of Abyssinian royalty, till the order of succession should call him to the throne.

The place which the wisdom or policy of antiquity had destined for the residence of the Abyssinian princes was a spacious valley[2] in the kingdom of Amhara, surrounded on every side by mountains, of which the summits overhang the middle part. The only passage by which it could be entered was a cavern that passed under a rock, of which it has long been disputed whether it was the work of nature or of human industry. The outlet of the cavern was concealed by a thick wood, and the mouth which opened into the valley was closed with gates of iron, forged by the artificers of ancient days, so massy that no man could, without the help of engines, open or shut them.

From the mountains on every side rivulets descended that filled all the valley with verdure and fertility, and formed a lake in the middle, inhabited by fish of every species, and frequented by every fowl whom nature has taught to

1. The Nile.
2. Johnson had read of the Happy Valley in the Portuguese Jesuit Father Lobo's book on Abyssinia, which he translated in 1735. This descrip-

tion also owes something to the description of the Garden in *Paradise Lost* 4, and Coleridge's "Kubla Khan" may owe something to it.

dip the wing in water. This lake discharged its superfluities by a stream, which entered a dark cleft of the mountain on the northern side, and fell with dreadful noise from precipice to precipice till it was heard no more.

The sides of the mountains were covered with trees, the banks of the brooks were diversified with flowers; every blast[3] shook spices from the rocks, and every month dropped fruits upon the ground. All animals that bite the grass, or browse the shrub, whether wild or tame, wandered in this extensive circuit, secured from beasts of prey by the mountains which confined them. On one part were flocks and herds feeding in the pastures, on another all the beasts of chase frisking in the lawns; the sprightly kid was bounding on the rocks, the subtle monkey frolicking in the trees, and the solemn elephant reposing in the shade. All the diversities of the world were brought together, the blessings of nature were collected, and its evils extracted and excluded.

The valley, wide and fruitful, supplied its inhabitants with the necessaries of life, and all delights and superfluities were added at the annual visit which the emperor paid his children, when the iron gate was opened to the sound of music, and during eight days everyone that resided in the valley was required to propose whatever might contribute to make seclusion pleasant, to fill up the vacancies of attention, and lessen the tediousness of time. Every desire was immediately granted. All the artificers of pleasure were called to gladden the festivity; the musicians exerted the power of harmony, and the dancers showed their activity before the princes, in hope that they should pass their lives in this blissful captivity, to which those only were admitted whose performance was thought able to add novelty to luxury. Such was the appearance of security and delight which this retirement afforded, that they to whom it was new always desired that it might be perpetual; and as those on whom the iron gate had once closed were never suffered to return, the effect of longer experience could not be known. Thus every year produced new schemes of delight and new competitors for imprisonment.

The palace stood on an eminence, raised about thirty paces[4] above the surface of the lake. It was divided into many squares or courts, built with greater or less magnificence according to the rank of those for whom they were designed. The roofs were turned into arches of massy stone, joined with a cement that grew harder by time, and the building stood from century to century, deriding the solstitial rains and equinoctial hurricanes, without need of reparation.

This house, which was so large as to be fully known to none but some ancient officers, who successively inherited the secrets of the place, was built as if suspicion herself had dictated the plan. To every room there was an open and secret passage; every square had a communication with the rest, either from the upper stories by private galleries, or by subterranean passages from the lower apartments. Many of the columns had unsuspected cavities, in which a long race of monarchs had reposited their treasures. They then closed up the opening with marble, which was never to be removed but in the utmost exigencies of the kingdom, and recorded their accumulations in a book, which was itself concealed in a tower, not entered but by the emperor, attended by the prince who stood next in succession.

3. "A gust or puff of wind" (Johnson's *Dictionary*).   4. About 150 feet.

Chapter 2. The Discontent of Rasselas in the Happy Valley

Here the sons and daughters of Abyssinia lived only to know the soft vicissitudes of pleasure and repose, attended by all that were skillful to delight, and gratified with whatever the senses can enjoy. They wandered in gardens of fragrance, and slept in the fortresses of security. Every art was practiced to make them pleased with their own condition. The sages who instructed them told them of nothing but the miseries of public life, and described all beyond the mountains as regions of calamity, where discord was always raging, and where man preyed upon man.

To heighten their opinion of their own felicity, they were daily entertained with songs, the subject of which was the *happy valley*. Their appetites were excited by frequent enumerations of different enjoyments, and revelry and merriment was the business of every hour, from the dawn of morning to the close of even.

These methods were generally successful; few of the princes had ever wished to enlarge their bounds, but passed their lives in full conviction that they had all within their reach that art or nature could bestow, and pitied those whom fate had excluded from this seat of tranquility, as the sport of chance and the slaves of misery.

Thus they rose in the morning and lay down at night, pleased with each other and with themselves; all but Rasselas, who, in the twenty-sixth year of his age, began to withdraw himself from their pastimes and assemblies, and to delight in solitary walks and silent meditation. He often sat before tables covered with luxury, and forgot to taste the dainties that were placed before him; he rose abruptly in the midst of the song, and hastily retired beyond the sound of music. His attendants observed the change, and endeavored to renew his love of pleasure. He neglected their officiousness, repulsed their invitations, and spent day after day on the banks of rivulets sheltered with trees, where he sometimes listened to the birds in the branches, sometimes observed the fish playing in the stream, and anon cast his eyes upon the pastures and mountains filled with animals, of which some were biting the herbage, and some sleeping among the bushes.

This singularity of his humor made him much observed. One of the sages, in whose conversation he had formerly delighted, followed him secretly, in hope of discovering the cause of his disquiet. Rasselas, who knew not that anyone was near him, having for some time fixed his eyes upon the goats that were browsing among the rocks, began to compare their condition with his own.

"What," said he, "makes the difference between man and all the rest of the animal creation? Every beast that strays beside me has the same corporal necessities with myself; he is hungry, and crops the grass, he is thirsty, and drinks the stream, his thirst and hunger are appeased, he is satisfied, and sleeps; he rises again, and he is hungry, he is again fed, and is at rest. I am hungry and thirsty like him, but when thirst and hunger cease, I am not at rest; I am, like him, pained with want, but am not, like him, satisfied with fullness. The intermediate hours are tedious and gloomy; I long again to be hungry that I may again quicken my attention. The birds peck the berries or the corn, and fly away to the groves, where they sit in seeming happiness on the branches, and waste their lives in tuning one unvaried series of sounds. I likewise can call the lutanist and the singer, but the sounds that pleased me yesterday weary me today, and will grow yet more wearisome tomorrow. I can discover within me no power of perception which is not glutted with its proper pleasure, yet I do not feel myself delighted. Man has surely some latent sense for which this place affords no gratification, or he has some desires distinct from sense, which must be satisfied before he can be happy."

After this he lifted up his head, and seeing the moon rising, walked towards the palace. As he passed through the fields, and saw the animals around him, "Ye," said he, "are happy, and need not envy me that walk thus among you, burthened with myself; nor do I, ye gentle beings, envy your felicity, for it is not the felicity of man. I have many distresses from which ye are free; I fear pain when I do not feel it; I sometimes shrink at evils recollected, and sometimes start at evils anticipated. Surely the equity of Providence has balanced peculiar sufferings with peculiar enjoyments."

With observations like these the prince amused himself as he returned, uttering them with a plaintive voice, yet with a look that discovered[5] him to feel some complacence in his own perspicacity, and to receive some solace of the miseries of life from consciousness of the delicacy with which he felt, and the eloquence with which he bewailed them. He mingled cheerfully in the diversions of the evening, and all rejoiced to find that his heart was lightened.

Chapter 3. *The Wants of Him That Wants Nothing*

On the next day his old instructor, imagining that he had now made himself acquainted with his disease of mind, was in the hope of curing it by counsel, and officiously sought an opportunity of conference, which the prince, having long considered him as one whose intellects were exhausted, was not very willing to afford. "Why," said he, "does this man thus intrude upon me; shall I be never suffered to forget those lectures which pleased only while they were new, and to become new again must be forgotten?" He then walked into the wood, and composed himself to his usual meditations; when, before his thoughts had taken any settled form, he perceived his pursuer at his side, and was at first prompted by his impatience to go hastily away; but, being unwilling to offend a man whom he had once reverenced and still loved, he invited him to sit down with him on the bank.

The old man, thus encouraged, began to lament the change which had been lately observed in the prince, and to inquire why he so often retired from the pleasures of the palace, to loneliness and silence. "I fly from pleasure," said the prince, "because pleasure has ceased to please; I am lonely because I am miserable, and am unwilling to cloud with my presence the happiness of others." "You, sir," said the sage, "are the first who has complained of misery in the *happy valley.* I hope to convince you that your complaints have no real cause. You are here in full possession of all that the emperor of Abyssinia can bestow; here is neither labor to be endured nor danger to be dreaded, yet here is all that labor or danger can procure or purchase. Look round and tell me which of your wants is without supply; if you want nothing, how are you unhappy?"

5. Showed.

"That I want nothing," said the prince, "or that I know not what I want, is the cause of my complaint; if I had any known want, I should have a certain wish; that wish would excite endeavor, and I should not then repine to see the sun move so slowly towards the western mountain, or lament when the day breaks, and sleep will no longer hide me from myself. When I see the kids and the lambs chasing one another, I fancy that I should be happy if I had something to pursue. But, possessing all that I can want, I find one day and one hour exactly like another, except that the latter is still more tedious than the former. Let your experience inform me how the day may now seem as short as in my childhood, while nature was yet fresh and every moment showed me what I never had observed before. I have already enjoyed too much; give me something to desire."

The old man was surprised at this new species of affliction and knew not what to reply, yet was unwilling to be silent. "Sir," said he, "if you had seen the miseries of the world you would know how to value your present state." "Now," said the prince, "you have given me something to desire. I shall long to see the miseries of the world, since the sight of them is necessary to happiness."[6]

*   *   *

Chapter 6. A Dissertation on the Art of Flying

Among the artists that had been allured into the happy valley, to labor for the accommodation and pleasure of its inhabitants, was a man eminent for his knowledge of the mechanic powers, who had contrived many engines[7] both of use and recreation. By a wheel, which the stream turned, he forced the water into a tower, whence it was distributed to all the apartments of the palace. He erected a pavillion in the garden, around which he kept the air always cool by artificial showers. One of the groves appropriated to the ladies, was ventilated by fans, to which the rivulet that run through it gave a constant motion; and instruments of soft music were placed at proper distances, of which some played by the impulse of the wind, and some by the power of the stream.

This artist was sometimes visited by Rasselas, who was pleased with every kind of knowledge, imagining that the time would come when all his acquisitions should be of use to him in the open world. He came one day to amuse himself in his usual manner, and found the master busy in building a sailing chariot: he saw that the design was practicable upon a level surface, and with expressions of great esteem solicited its completion. The workman was pleased to find himself so much regarded by the prince, and resolved to gain yet higher honors. "Sir," said he, "you have seen but a small part of what the mechanic sciences can perform. I have been long of opinion, that, instead of the tardy conveyance of ships and chariots, man might use the swifter migration of wings; that the fields of air are open to knowledge, and that only ignorance and idleness need crawl upon the ground."

This hint rekindled the prince's desire of passing the mountains; having seen what the mechanist had already performed, he was willing to fancy that

---

6. In chapters 4 and 5, Rasselas dreams about escaping the valley.

7. Machines. "Mechanic powers": the forces that cause things to move.

he could do more; yet resolved to inquire further before he suffered hope to afflict him by disappointment. "I am afraid," said he to the artist, "that your imagination prevails over your skill, and that you now tell me rather what you wish than what you know. Every animal has his element assigned him; the birds have the air, and man and beasts the earth." "So," replied the mechanist, "fishes have the water, in which yet beasts can swim by nature, and men by art. He that can swim needs not despair to fly: to swim is to fly in a grosser fluid, and to fly is to swim in a subtler.[8] We are only to proportion our power of resistance to the different density of the matter through which we are to pass. You will be necessarily upborn by the air, if you can renew any impulse upon it, faster than the air can recede from the pressure."

"But the exercise of swimming," said the prince, "is very laborious; the strongest limbs are soon wearied; I am afraid the act of flying will be yet more violent, and wings will be of no great use, unless we can fly further than we can swim."

"The labor of rising from the ground," said the artist, "will be great, as we see it in the heavier domestic fowls; but, as we mount higher, the earth's attraction, and the body's gravity, will be gradually diminished, till we shall arrive at a region where the man will float in the air without any tendency to fall: no care will then be necessary, but to move forwards, which the gentlest impulse will effect. You, Sir, whose curiosity is so extensive, will easily conceive with what pleasure a philosopher, furnished with wings, and hovering in the sky, would see the earth, and all its inhabitants, rolling beneath him, and presenting to him successively, by its diurnal motion, all the countries within the same parallel. How must it amuse the pendent spectator to see the moving scene of land and ocean, cities and deserts! To survey with equal security the marts of trade, and the fields of battle; mountains infested by barbarians, and fruitful regions gladdened by plenty, and lulled by peace! How easily shall we then trace the Nile through all his passage; pass over to distant regions, and examine the face of nature from one extremity of the earth to the other!"

"All this," said the prince, "is much to be desired, but I am afraid that no man will be able to breathe in these regions of speculation and tranquility. I have been told, that respiration is difficult upon lofty mountains, yet from these precipices, though so high as to produce great tenuity of the air, it is very easy to fall: therefore I suspect, that from any height, where life can be supported, there may be danger of too quick descent."

"Nothing," replied the artist, "will ever be attempted, if all possible objections must be first overcome. If you will favor my project I will try the first flight at my own hazard. I have considered the structure of all volant[9] animals, and find the folding continuity of the bat's wings most easily accommodated to the human form. Upon this model I shall begin my task tomorrow, and in a year expect to tower into the air beyond the malice or pursuit of man. But I will work only on this condition, that the art shall not be divulged, and that you shall not require me to make wings for any but ourselves."

"Why," said Rasselas, "should you envy others so great an advantage? All skill ought to be exerted for universal good; every man has owed much to others, and ought to repay the kindness that he has received."

"If men were all virtuous," returned the artist, "I should with great alacrity teach them all to fly. But what would be the security of the good, if the bad

8. Thinner.   9. Able to fly.

Unknown engraver, *Rasselas*, 1787. Rasselas pulls the artist to shore. *The History of Rasselas, Prince of Abissinia, a tale, in two volumes.*

could at pleasure invade them from the sky? Against an army sailing through the clouds neither walls, nor mountains, nor seas, could afford any security. A flight of northern savages might hover in the wind, and light at once with irresistible violence upon the capital of a fruitful region that was rolling under them. Even this valley, the retreat of princes, the abode of happiness, might be violated by the sudden descent of some of the naked nations that swarm on the coast of the southern sea."

The prince promised secrecy, and waited for the performance, not wholly hopeless of success. He visited the work from time to time, observed its progress, and remarked many ingenious contrivances to facilitate motion, and unite levity with strength. The artist was every day more certain that he should leave vultures and eagles behind him, and the contagion of his confidence seized upon the prince.

In a year the wings were finished, and, on a morning appointed, the maker appeared furnished for flight on a little promontory: he waved his pinions a while to gather air, then leaped from his stand, and in an instant dropped into the lake. His wings, which were of no use in the air, sustained him in the water, and the prince drew him to land, half dead with terror and vexation.[1]

* * *

Chapter 10. Imlac's History Continued. A Dissertation upon Poetry

"Wherever I went, I found that poetry was considered as the highest learning, and regarded with a veneration somewhat approaching to that which man would pay to the angelic nature. And yet it fills me with wonder that, in almost all countries, the most ancient poets are considered as the best: whether it be that every other kind of knowledge is an acquisition gradually attained, and poetry is a gift conferred at once; or that the first poetry of every nation surprised them as a novelty, and retained the credit by consent which it received by accident at first; or whether, as the province of poetry is

---

1. In chapters 7–9, Rasselas comes to know Imlac, a scholar and poet who knows the great world outside the valley and who tells the story of his life.

to describe nature and passion, which are always the same, the first writers took possession of the most striking objects for description and the most probable occurrences for fiction, and left nothing to those that followed them, but transcription of the same events, and new combinations of the same images—whatever be the reason, it is commonly observed that the early writers are in possession of nature, and their followers of art; that the first excel in strength and invention, and the latter in elegance and refinement.

"I was desirous to add my name to this illustrious fraternity. I read all the poets of Persia and Arabia, and was able to repeat by memory the volumes that are suspended in the mosque of Mecca.[2] But I soon found that no man was ever great by imitation. My desire of excellence impelled me to transfer my attention to nature and to life. Nature was to be my subject, and men to be my auditors: I could never describe what I had not seen; I could not hope to move those with delight or terror, whose interests and opinions I did not understand.

"Being now resolved to be a poet, I saw everything with a new purpose; my sphere of attention was suddenly magnified; no kind of knowledge was to be overlooked. I ranged mountains and deserts for images and resemblances, and pictured upon my mind every tree of the forest and flower of the valley. I observed with equal care the crags of the rock and the pinnacles of the palace. Sometimes I wandered along the mazes of the rivulet, and sometimes watched the changes of the summer clouds. To a poet nothing can be useless. Whatever is beautiful, and whatever is dreadful, must be familiar to his imagination; he must be conversant with all that is awfully[3] vast or elegantly little. The plants of the garden, the animals of the wood, the minerals of the earth, and meteors of the sky, must all concur to store his mind with inexhaustible variety: for every idea[4] is useful for the enforcement or decoration of moral or religious truth; and he who knows most will have most power of diversifying his scenes, and of gratifying his reader with remote allusions and unexpected instruction.

"All the appearances of nature I was therefore careful to study, and every country which I have surveyed has contributed something to my poetical powers."

"In so wide a survey," said the prince, "you must surely have left much unobserved. I have lived till now within the circuit of these mountains, and yet cannot walk abroad without the sight of something which I have never beheld before, or never heeded."

"The business of a poet," said Imlac, "is to examine, not the individual, but the species; to remark general properties and large appearances; he does not number the streaks of the tulip, or describe the different shades in the verdure of the forest. He is to exhibit in his portraits of nature such prominent and striking features as recall the original to every mind, and must neglect the minuter discriminations, which one may have remarked and another have neglected, for those characteristics which are alike obvious to vigilance and carelessness.

"But the knowledge of nature is only half the task of a poet; he must be acquainted likewise with all the modes of life. His character requires that he

2. In the 7th century, seven peerless Arabic poems were supposed to have been transcribed in gold and hung up in a mosque.

3. Awe-inspiringly.
4. Mental image.

estimate the happiness and misery of every condition; observe the power of all the passions in all their combinations, and trace the changes of the human mind, as they are modified by various institutions and accidental influences of climate or custom, from the sprightliness of infancy to the despondence of decrepitude. He must divest himself of the prejudices of his age or country; he must consider right and wrong in their abstracted and invariable state; he must disregard present laws and opinions, and rise to general and transcendental[5] truths, which will always be the same. He must, therefore, content himself with the slow progress of his name, contemn the applause of his own time, and commit his claims to the justice of posterity. He must write as the interpreter of nature and the legislator of mankind, and consider himself as presiding over the thoughts and manners of future generations, as a being superior to time and place.

"His labor is not yet at an end; he must know many languages and many sciences; and, that his style may be worthy of his thoughts, must by incessant practice familiarize to himself every delicacy of speech and grace of harmony."

Chapter 11. Imlac's Narrative Continued. A Hint on Pilgrimage

Imlac now felt the enthusiastic fit, and was proceeding to aggrandize his own profession, when the prince cried out: "Enough! thou hast convinced me that no human being can ever be a poet. Proceed with thy narration."

"To be a poet," said Imlac, "is indeed very difficult." "So difficult," returned the prince, "that I will at present hear no more of his labors. Tell me whither you went when you had seen Persia."

"From Persia," said the poet, "I traveled through Syria, and for three years resided in Palestine, where I conversed with great numbers of the northern and western nations of Europe, the nations which are now in possession of all power and all knowledge, whose armies are irresistible, and whose fleets command the remotest parts of the globe. When I compared these men with the natives of our own kingdom, and those that surround us, they appeared almost another order of beings. In their countries it is difficult to wish for anything that may not be obtained; a thousand arts, of which we never heard, are continually laboring for their convenience and pleasure; and whatever their own climate has denied them is supplied by their commerce."

"By what means," said the prince, "are the Europeans thus powerful, or why, since they can so easily visit Asia and Africa for trade or conquest, cannot the Asiatics and Africans invade their coasts, plant colonies in their ports, and give laws to their natural princes? The same wind that carries them back would bring us thither."

"They are more powerful, sir, than we," answered Imlac, "because they are wiser; knowledge will always predominate over ignorance, as man governs the other animals. But why their knowledge is more than ours, I know not what reason can be given, but the unsearchable will of the Supreme Being."

"When," said the prince with a sigh, "shall I be able to visit Palestine, and mingle with this mighty confluence of nations? Till that happy moment shall arrive, let me fill up the time with such representations as thou canst give me. I am not ignorant of the motive that assembles such numbers in that

---

5. "General; pervading many particulars" (Johnson's *Dictionary*).

place, and cannot but consider it as the center of wisdom and piety, to which the best and wisest men of every land must be continually resorting."

"There are some nations," said Imlac, "that send few visitants to Palestine; for many numerous and learned sects in Europe concur to censure pilgrimage as superstitious, or deride it as ridiculous."

"You know," said the prince, "how little my life has made me acquainted with diversity of opinions. It will be too long to hear the arguments on both sides; you, that have considered them, tell me the result."

"Pilgrimage," said Imlac, "like many other acts of piety, may be reasonable or superstitious, according to the principles upon which it is performed. Long journeys in search of truth are not commanded. Truth, such as is necessary to the regulation of life, is always found where it is honestly sought. Change of place is no natural cause of the increase of piety, for it inevitably produces dissipation of mind. Yet, since men go every day to view the fields where great actions have been performed, and return with stronger impressions of the event, curiosity of the same kind may naturally dispose us to view that country whence our religion had its beginning; and I believe no man surveys those awful scenes without some confirmation of holy resolutions. That the Supreme Being may be more easily propitiated in one place than in another is the dream of idle superstition, but that some places may operate upon our own minds in an uncommon manner is an opinion which hourly experience will justify. He who supposes that his vices may be more successfully combated in Palestine, will, perhaps, find himself mistaken, yet he may go thither without folly; he who thinks they will be more freely pardoned, dishonors at once his reason and religion."

"These," said the prince, "are European distinctions. I will consider them another time. What have you found to be the effect of knowledge? Are those nations happier than we?"

"There is so much infelicity," said the poet, "in the world that scarce any man has leisure from his own distresses to estimate the comparative happiness of others. Knowledge is certainly one of the means of pleasure, as is confessed by the natural desire which every mind feels of increasing its ideas. Ignorance is mere privation, by which nothing can be produced; it is a vacuity in which the soul sits motionless and torpid for want of attraction; and, without knowing why, we always rejoice when we learn, and grieve when we forget. I am therefore inclined to conclude that if nothing counteracts the natural consequence of learning, we grow more happy as our minds take a wider range.

"In enumerating the particular comforts of life, we shall find many advantages on the side of the Europeans. They cure wounds and diseases with which we languish and perish. We suffer inclemencies of weather which they can obviate. They have engines for the despatch of many laborious works, which we must perform by manual industry. There is such communication between distant places that one friend can hardly be said to be absent from another. Their policy removes all public inconveniences; they have roads cut through their mountains, and bridges laid upon their rivers. And, if we descend to the privacies of life, their habitations are more commodious, and their possessions are more secure."

"They are surely happy," said the prince, "who have all these conveniencies, of which I envy none so much as the facility with which separated friends interchange their thoughts."

"The Europeans," answered Imlac, "are less unhappy than we, but they are not happy. Human life is everywhere a state in which much is to be endured, and little to be enjoyed."[6]

* * *

Chapter 15. The Prince and Princess Leave the Valley, and See Many Wonders

The prince and princess had jewels sufficient to make them rich whenever they came into a place of commerce, which, by Imlac's direction, they hid in their clothes, and, on the night of the next full moon, all left the valley. The princess was followed only by a single favorite, who did not know whither she was going.

They clambered through the cavity, and began to go down on the other side. The princess and her maid turned their eyes towards every part, and, seeing nothing to bound their prospect, considered themselves as in danger of being lost in a dreary vacuity. They stopped and trembled. "I am almost afraid," said the princess, "to begin a journey of which I cannot perceive an end, and to venture into this immense plain where I may be approached on every side by men whom I never saw." The prince felt nearly the same emotions, though he thought it more manly to conceal them.

Imlac smiled at their terrors, and encouraged them to proceed; but the princess continued irresolute till she had been imperceptibly drawn forward too far to return.

In the morning they found some shepherds in the field, who set milk and fruits before them. The princess wondered that she did not see a palace ready for her reception, and a table spread with delicacies; but, being faint and hungry, she drank the milk and ate the fruits, and thought them of a higher flavor than the products of the valley.

They traveled forward by easy journeys, being all unaccustomed to toil or difficulty, and knowing, that though they might be missed, they could not be pursued. In a few days they came into a more populous region, where Imlac was diverted with the admiration which his companions expressed at the diversity of manners, stations and employments.

Their dress was such as might not bring upon them the suspicion of having any thing to conceal, yet the prince, wherever he came, expected to be obeyed, and the princess was frighted, because those that came into her presence did not prostrate themselves before her. Imlac was forced to observe them with great vigilance, lest they should betray their rank by their unusual behavior, and detained them several weeks in the first village to accustom them to the sight of common mortals.

By degrees the royal wanderers were taught to understand that they had for a time laid aside their dignity, and were to expect only such regard as liberality and courtesy could procure. And Imlac, having, by many admonitions, prepared them to endure the tumults of a port, and the ruggedness of the commercial race, brought them down to the seacoast.

The prince and his sister, to whom every thing was new, were gratified equally at all places, and therefore remained for some months at the port

---

6. In Chapters 12–14, Rasselas and Imlac, assisted by Nakayah, Rasselas's sister, succeed in making a tunnel through the mountain.

without any inclination to pass further. Imlac was content with their stay, because he did not think it safe to expose them, unpracticed in the world, to the hazards of a foreign country.

At last he began to fear lest they should be discovered, and proposed to fix a day for their departure. They had no pretensions to judge for themselves, and referred the whole scheme to his direction. He therefore took passage in a ship to Suez; and, when the time came, with great difficulty prevailed on the princess to enter the vessel. They had a quick and prosperous voyage, and from Suez traveled by land to Cairo.

Chapter 16. They Enter Cairo, and Find Every Man Happy

As they approached the city, which filled the strangers with astonishment, "This," said Imlac to the prince, "is the place where travelers and merchants assemble from all the corners of the earth. You will here find men of every character and every occupation. Commerce is here honorable. I will act as a merchant, and you shall live as strangers, who have no other end of travel than curiosity. It will soon be observed that we are rich; our reputation will procure us access to all whom we shall desire to know; you will see all the conditions of humanity, and enable yourself at leisure to make your *choice of life.*"

They now entered the town, stunned by the noise, and offended by the crowds. Instruction had not yet so prevailed over habit, but that they wondered to see themselves pass undistinguished along the street, and met by the lowest of the people without reverence or notice. The princess could not at first bear the thought of being leveled with the vulgar,[7] and for some days continued in her chamber, where she was served by her favorite, Pekuah, as in the palace of the valley.

Imlac, who understood traffic,[8] sold part of the jewels the next day, and hired a house, which he adorned with such magnificence that he was immediately considered as a merchant of great wealth. His politeness attracted many acquaintance, and his generosity made him courted by many dependents. His table was crowded by men of every nation, who all admired his knowledge, and solicited his favor. His companions, not being able to mix in the conversation, could make no discovery[9] of their ignorance or surprise, and were gradually initiated in the world as they gained knowledge of the language.

The prince had, by frequent lectures, been taught the use and nature of money; but the ladies could not for a long time comprehend what the merchants did with small pieces of gold and silver, or why things of so little use should be received as equivalent to the necessaries of life.

They studied the language two years, while Imlac was preparing to set before them the various ranks and conditions of mankind. He grew acquainted with all who had anything uncommon in their fortune or conduct. He frequented the voluptuous and the frugal, the idle and the busy, the merchants and the men of learning.

The prince being now able to converse with fluency, and having learned the caution necessary to be observed in his intercourse with strangers, began to accompany Imlac to places of resort, and to enter into all assemblies, that he might make his *choice of life.*

7. Ordinary people.
8. Commerce.

9. Exposure.

For some time he thought choice needless, because all appeared to him equally happy. Wherever he went he met gaiety and kindness, and heard the song of joy or the laugh of carelessness. He began to believe that the world overflowed with universal plenty, and that nothing was withheld either from want or merit; that every hand showered liberality, and every heart melted with benevolence: "And who then," says he, "will be suffered to be wretched?"

Imlac permitted the pleasing delusion, and was unwilling to crush the hope of inexperience, till one day, having sat awhile silent, "I know not," said the prince, "what can be the reason that I am more unhappy than any of our friends. I see them perpetually and unalterably cheerful, but feel my own mind restless and uneasy. I am unsatisfied with those pleasures which I seem most to court; I live in the crowds of jollity, not so much to enjoy company as to shun myself, and am only loud and merry to conceal my sadness."

"Every man," said Imlac, "may, by examining his own mind, guess what passes in the minds of others; when you feel that your own gaiety is counterfeit, it may justly lead you to suspect that of your companions not to be sincere. Envy is commonly reciprocal. We are long before we are convinced that happiness is never to be found, and each believes it possessed by others, to keep alive the hope of obtaining it for himself. In the assembly where you passed the last night, there appeared such sprightliness of air, and volatility of fancy, as might have suited beings of an higher order, formed to inhabit serener regions, inaccessible to care or sorrow; yet, believe me, prince, there was not one who did not dread the moment when solitude should deliver him to the tyranny of reflection."

"This," said the prince, "may be true of others, since it is true of me; yet, whatever be the general infelicity of man, one condition is more happy than another, and wisdom surely directs us to take the least evil in the *choice of life*."

"The causes of good and evil," answered Imlac, "are so various and uncertain, so often entangled with each other, so diversified by various relations, and so much subject to accidents which cannot be foreseen, that he who would fix his condition upon incontestable reasons of preference must live and die inquiring and deliberating."

"But, surely," said Rasselas, "the wise men, to whom we listen with reverence and wonder, chose that mode of life for themselves which they thought most likely to make them happy."

"Very few," said the poet, "live by choice. Every man is placed in his present condition by causes which acted without his foresight, and with which he did not always willingly cooperate; and therefore you will rarely meet one who does not think the lot of his neighbor better than his own."

"I am pleased to think," said the prince, "that my birth has given me at least one advantage over others, by enabling me to determine for myself. I have here the world before me. I will review it at leisure; surely happiness is somewhere to be found."

Chapter 17. *The Prince Associates with Young Men of Spirit and Gaiety*

Rasselas rose next day, and resolved to begin his experiments upon life. "Youth," cried he, "is the time of gladness: I will join myself to the young men, whose only business is to gratify their desires, and whose time is all spent in a succession of enjoyments."

To such societies he was readily admitted, but a few days brought him back weary and disgusted. Their mirth was without images,[1] their laughter without motive; their pleasures were gross and sensual, in which the mind had no part; their conduct was at once wild and mean; they laughed at order and at law, but the frown of power dejected, and the eye of wisdom abashed them.

The prince soon concluded, that he should never be happy in a course of life of which he was ashamed. He thought it unsuitable to a reasonable being to act without a plan, and to be sad or cheerful only by chance. "Happiness," said he, "must be something solid and permanent, without fear and without uncertainty."

But his young companions had gained so much of his regard by their frankness and courtesy, that he could not leave them without warning and remonstrance. "My friends," said he, "I have seriously considered our manners and our prospects, and find that we have mistaken our own interest. The first years of man must make provision for the last. He that never thinks never can be wise. Perpetual levity must end in ignorance; and intemperance, though it may fire the spirits for an hour, will make life short or miserable. Let us consider that youth is of no long duration, and that in maturer age, when the enchantments of fancy shall cease, and phantoms of delight dance no more about us, we shall have no comforts but the esteem of wise men, and the means of doing good. Let us, therefore, stop, while to stop is in our power: let us live as men who are sometime to grow old, and to whom it will be the most dreadful of all evils not to count their past years but by follies, and to be reminded of their former luxuriance of health only by the maladies which riot has produced."

They stared a while in silence one upon another, and, at last, drove him away by a general chorus of continued laughter.

The consciousness that his sentiments were just, and his intentions kind, was scarcely sufficient to support him against the horror of derision. But he recovered his tranquillity, and pursued his search.

Chapter 18. The Prince Finds a Wise and Happy Man

As he was one day walking in the street, he saw a spacious building which all were, by the open doors, invited to enter: he followed the stream of people, and found it a hall or school of declamation, in which professors read lectures to their auditory.[2] He fixed his eye upon a sage raised above the rest, who discoursed with great energy on the government of the passions. His look was venerable, his action graceful, his pronunciation clear, and his diction elegant. He showed with great strength of sentiment and variety of illustration that human nature is degraded and debased, when the lower faculties predominate over the higher; that when fancy, the parent of passion, usurps the dominion of the mind, nothing ensues but the natural effect of unlawful government, perturbation, and confusion; that she betrays the fortresses of the intellect to rebels, and excites her children to sedition against reason, their lawful sovereign. He compared reason to the sun, of which the light is constant, uniform and lasting; and fancy to a meteor, of bright but transitory luster, irregular in its motion, and delusive in its direction.

1. Ideas.   2. Audience.

He then communicated the various precepts given from time to time for the conquest of passion, and displayed the happiness of those who had obtained the important victory, after which man is no longer the slave of fear, nor the fool of hope; is no more emaciated by envy, inflamed by anger, emasculated by tenderness, or depressed by grief; but walks on calmly through the tumults or the privacies of life, as the sun pursues alike his course through the calm or the stormy sky.

He enumerated many examples of heroes immovable by pain or pleasure, who looked with indifference on those modes or accidents to which the vulgar give the names of good and evil. He exhorted his hearers to lay aside their prejudices, and arm themselves against the shafts of malice or misfortune, by invulnerable patience; concluding that this state only was happiness, and that this happiness was in everyone's power.

Rasselas listened to him with the veneration due to the instructions of a superior being, and, waiting for him at the door, humbly implored the liberty of visiting so great a master of true wisdom. The lecturer hesitated a moment, when Rasselas put a purse of gold into his hand, which he received with a mixture of joy and wonder.

"I have found," said the prince at his return to Imlac, "a man who can teach all that is necessary to be known; who, from the unshaken throne of rational fortitude, looks down on the scenes of life changing beneath him. He speaks, and attention watches his lips. He reasons, and conviction closes his periods.[3] This man shall be my future guide; I will learn his doctrines, and imitate his life."

"Be not too hasty," said Imlac, "to trust or to admire the teachers of morality: they discourse like angels, but they live like men."

Rasselas, who could not conceive how any man could reason so forcibly without feeling the cogency of his own arguments, paid his visit in a few days, and was denied admission. He had now learned the power of money, and made his way by a piece of gold to the inner apartment, where he found the philosopher in a room half darkened, with his eyes misty and his face pale. "Sir," said he, "you are come at a time when all human friendship is useless; what I suffer cannot be remedied, what I have lost cannot be supplied. My daughter, my only daughter, from whose tenderness I expected all the comforts of my age, died last night of a fever. My views, my purposes, my hopes are at an end; I am now a lonely being, disunited from society."

"Sir," said the prince, "mortality is an event by which a wise man can never be surprised; we know that death is always near, and it should therefore always be expected." "Young man," answered the philosopher, "you speak like one that has never felt the pangs of separation." "Have you then forgot the precepts," said Rasselas, "which you so powerfully enforced? Has wisdom no strength to arm the heart against calamity? Consider that external things are naturally variable, but truth and reason are always the same." "What comfort," said the mourner, "can truth and reason afford me? Of what effect are they now, but to tell me that my daughter will not be restored?"

The prince, whose humanity would not suffer him to insult misery with reproof, went away, convinced of the emptiness of rhetorical sound, and the inefficacy of polished periods and studied sentences.[4]

---

3. Completed sentences.   4. Maxims or moral axioms.

Chapter 19. A Glimpse of Pastoral Life

He was still eager upon the same inquiry; and having heard of a hermit that lived near the lowest cataract of the Nile, and filled the whole country with the fame of his sanctity, resolved to visit his retreat, and inquire whether that felicity which public life could not afford was to be found in solitude; and whether a man whose age and virtue made him venerable could teach any peculiar art of shunning evils, or enduring them.

Imlac and the princess agreed to accompany him, and, after the necessary preparations, they began their journey. Their way lay through fields, where shepherds tended their flocks and the lambs were playing upon the pasture. "This," said the poet, "is the life which has been often celebrated for its innocence and quiet; let us pass the heat of the day among the shepherds' tents, and know whether all our searches are not to terminate in pastoral simplicity."

The proposal pleased them, and they induced the shepherds, by small presents and familiar questions, to tell their opinion of their own state. They were so rude and ignorant, so little able to compare the good with the evil of the occupation, and so indistinct in their narratives and descriptions, that very little could be learned from them. But it was evident that their hearts were cankered with discontent; that they considered themselves as condemned to labor for the luxury of the rich, and looked up with stupid malevolence toward those that were placed above them.

The princess pronounced with vehemence that she would never suffer these envious savages to be her companions, and that she should not soon be desirous of seeing any more specimens of rustic happiness; but could not believe that all the accounts of primeval pleasures were fabulous, and was yet in doubt whether life had anything that could be justly preferred to the placid gratifications of fields and woods. She hoped that the time would come, when, with a few virtuous and elegant companions, she could gather flowers planted by her own hand, fondle the lambs of her own ewe, and listen, without care, among brooks and breezes, to one of her maidens reading in the shade.

Chapter 20. The Danger of Prosperity

On the next day they continued their journey, till the heat compelled them to look round for shelter. At a small distance they saw a thick wood, which they no sooner entered than they perceived that they were approaching the habitations of men. The shrubs were diligently cut away to open walks where the shades were darkest; the boughs of opposite trees were artificially interwoven; seats of flowery turf were raised in vacant spaces, and a rivulet, that wantoned along the side of a winding path, had its banks sometimes opened into small basins, and its stream sometimes obstructed by little mounds of stone heaped together to increase its murmurs.

They passed slowly through the wood, delighted with such unexpected accommodations, and entertained each other with conjecturing what, or who, he could be, that, in those rude and unfrequented regions, had leisure and art for such harmless luxury.

As they advanced, they heard the sound of music, and saw youths and virgins dancing in the grove; and, going still further, beheld a stately palace built upon a hill surrounded with woods. The laws of eastern hospitality allowed them to enter, and the master welcomed them like a man liberal and wealthy.

He was skilful enough in appearances soon to discern that they were no common guests, and spread his table with magnificence. The eloquence of Imlac caught his attention, and the lofty courtesy of the princess excited his respect. When they offered to depart he entreated their stay, and was the next day still more unwilling to dismiss them than before. They were easily persuaded to stop, and civility grew up in time to freedom and confidence.

The prince now saw all the domestics cheerful, and all the face of nature smiling round the place, and could not forbear to hope that he should find here what he was seeking; but when he was congratulating the master upon his possessions, he answered with a sigh, "My condition has indeed the appearance of happiness, but appearances are delusive. My prosperity puts my life in danger; the Bassa[5] of Egypt is my enemy, incensed only by my wealth and popularity. I have been hitherto protected against him by the princes of the country; but, as the favor of the great is uncertain, I know not how soon my defenders may be persuaded to share the plunder with the Bassa. I have sent my treasures into a distant country, and, upon the first alarm, am prepared to follow them. Then will my enemies riot in my mansion, and enjoy the gardens which I have planted."

They all joined in lamenting his danger, and deprecating his exile; and the princess was so much disturbed with the tumult of grief and indignation, that she retired to her apartment. They continued with their kind inviter a few days longer, and then went forward to find the hermit.

Chapter 21. The Happiness of Solitude. The Hermit's History

They came on the third day, by the direction of the peasants, to the hermit's cell: it was a cavern in the side of a mountain, over-shadowed with palm-trees; at such a distance from the cataract, that nothing more was heard than a gentle uniform murmur, such as composed the mind to pensive meditation, especially when it was assisted by the wind whistling among the branches. The first rude essay of nature had been so much improved by human labor, that the cave contained several apartments, appropriated to different uses, and often afforded lodging to travelers, whom darkness or tempests happened to overtake.

The hermit sat on a bench at the door, to enjoy the coolness of the evening. On one side lay a book with pens and papers, on the other mechanical instruments of various kinds. As they approached him unregarded, the princess observed that he had not the countenance of a man that had found, or could teach, the way to happiness.

They saluted him with great respect, which he repaid like a man not unaccustomed to the forms of courts. "My children," said he, "if you have lost your way, you shall be willingly supplied with such conveniencies for the night as this cavern will afford. I have all that nature requires, and you will not expect delicacies in a hermit's cell."

They thanked him, and, entering, were pleased with the neatness and regularity of the place. The hermit set flesh and wine before them, though he

5. Pasha: a Turkish viceroy.

fed only upon fruits and water. His discourse was cheerful without levity, and pious without enthusiasm.[6] He soon gained the esteem of his guests, and the princess repented of her hasty censure.

At last Imlac began thus: "I do not now wonder that your reputation is so far extended; we have heard at Cairo of your wisdom, and came hither to implore your direction for this young man and maiden in the *choice of life.*"

"To him that lives well," answered the hermit, "every form of life is good; nor can I give any other rule for choice, than to remove from all apparent evil."

"He will remove most certainly from evil," said the prince, "who shall devote himself to that solitude which you have recommended by your example."

"I have indeed lived fifteen years in solitude," said the hermit, "but have no desire that my example should gain any imitators. In my youth I professed arms, and was raised by degrees to the highest military rank. I have traversed wide countries at the head of my troops, and seen many battles and sieges. At last, being disgusted by the preferment of a younger officer, and feeling that my vigor was beginning to decay, I resolved to close my life in peace, having found the world full of snares, discord, and misery. I had once escaped from the pursuit of the enemy by the shelter of this cavern, and therefore chose it for my final residence. I employed artificers to form it into chambers, and stored it with all that I was likely to want.

"For some time after my retreat, I rejoiced like a tempest-beaten sailor at his entrance into the harbor, being delighted with the sudden change of the noise and hurry of war, to stillness and repose. When the pleasure of novelty went away, I employed my hours in examining the plants which grow in the valley, and the minerals which I collected from the rocks. But that inquiry is now grown tasteless and irksome. I have been for some time unsettled and distracted: my mind is disturbed with a thousand perplexities of doubt, and vanities of imagination, which hourly prevail upon me, because I have no opportunities of relaxation or diversion. I am sometimes ashamed to think that I could not secure myself from vice, but by retiring from the exercise of virtue, and begin to suspect that I was rather impelled by resentment, than led by devotion, into solitude. My fancy riots in scenes of folly, and I lament that I have lost so much, and have gained so little. In solitude, if I escape the example of bad men, I want likewise the counsel and conversation of the good. I have been long comparing the evils with the advantages of society, and resolve to return into the world tomorrow. The life of a solitary man will be certainly miserable, but not certainly devout."

They heard his resolution with surprise, but, after a short pause, offered to conduct him to Cairo. He dug up a considerable treasure which he had hid among the rocks, and accompanied them to the city, on which, as he approached it, he gazed with rapture.

Chapter 22. *The Happiness of a Life Led According to Nature*

Rasselas went often to an assembly of learned men, who met at stated times to unbend their minds and compare their opinions. Their manners were

---

6. "A vain belief of private revelation; a vain confidence of divine favor or communication" (Johnson's *Dictionary*).

somewhat coarse, but their conversation was instructive, and their disputations acute, though sometimes too violent, and often continued till neither controvertist remembered upon what question they began. Some faults were almost general among them; everyone was desirous to dictate to the rest, and everyone was pleased to hear the genius or knowledge of another depreciated.

In this assembly Rasselas was relating his interview with the hermit, and the wonder with which he heard him censure a course of life which he had so deliberately chosen, and so laudably followed. The sentiments of the hearers were various. Some were of opinion that the folly of his choice had been justly punished by condemnation to perpetual perseverance. One of the youngest among them, with great vehemence, pronounced him an hypocrite. Some talked of the right of society to the labor of individuals, and considered retirement as a desertion of duty. Others readily allowed that there was a time when the claims of the public were satisfied, and when a man might properly sequester himself, to review his life and purify his heart.

One, who appeared more affected with the narrative than the rest, thought it likely that the hermit would in a few years go back to his retreat, and perhaps, if shame did not restrain, or death intercept him, return once more from his retreat into the world. "For the hope of happiness," said he, "is so strongly impressed that the longest experience is not able to efface it. Of the present state, whatever it be, we feel and are forced to confess the misery; yet when the same state is again at a distance, imagination paints it as desirable. But the time will surely come when desire will be no longer our torment, and no man shall be wretched but by his own fault."

"This," said a philosopher who had heard him with tokens of great impatience, "is the present condition of a wise man. The time is already come when none are wretched but by their own fault. Nothing is more idle than to inquire after happiness, which nature has kindly placed within our reach. The way to be happy is to live according to nature, in obedience to that universal and unalterable law with which every heart is originally impressed; which is not written on it by precept, but engraven by destiny, not instilled by education, but infused at our nativity. He that lives according to nature will suffer nothing from the delusions of hope, or importunities of desire; he will receive and reject with equability of temper, and act or suffer as the reason of things shall alternately prescribe. Other men may amuse themselves with subtle definitions, or intricate ratiocination. Let them learn to be wise by easier means; let them observe the hind of the forest, and the linnet of the grove; let them consider the life of animals, whose motions are regulated by instinct; they obey their guide, and are happy. Let us therefore, at length, cease to dispute, and learn to live; throw away the encumbrance of precepts, which they who utter them with so much pride and pomp do not understand, and carry with us this simple and intelligible maxim, that deviation from nature is deviation from happiness."

When he had spoken, he looked round him with a placid air, and enjoyed the consciousness of his own beneficence. "Sir," said the prince with great modesty, "as I, like all the rest of mankind, am desirous of felicity, my closest attention has been fixed upon your discourse. I doubt not the truth of a position which a man so learned has so confidently advanced. Let me only know what it is to live according to nature."

"When I find young men so humble and so docile," said the philosopher, "I can deny them no information which my studies have enabled me to afford.

To live according to nature, is to act always with due regard to the fitness arising from the relations and qualities of causes and effects; to concur with the great and unchangeable scheme of universal felicity; to co-operate with the general disposition and tendency of the present system of things."

The prince soon found that this was one of the sages whom he should understand less as he heard him longer. He therefore bowed and was silent; and the philosopher, supposing him satisfied, and the rest vanquished, rose up and departed with the air of a man that had co-operated with the present system.[7]

* * *

Chapter 26. The Princess Continues Her Remarks upon Private Life

Nekayah, perceiving her brother's attention fixed, proceeded in her narrative.

"In families where there is or is not poverty, there is commonly discord. If a kingdom be, as Imlac tells us, a great family, a family likewise is a little kingdom, torn with factions and exposed to revolutions. An unpracticed observer expects the love of parents and children to be constant and equal; but this kindness seldom continues beyond the years of infancy: in a short time the children become rivals to their parents. Benefits are allayed[8] by reproaches, and gratitude debased by envy.

"Parents and children seldom act in concert; each child endeavors to appropriate the esteem or fondness of the parents, and the parents, with yet less temptation, betray each other to their children. Thus, some place their confidence in the father, and some in the mother, and by degrees the house is filled with artifices and feuds.

"The opinions of children and parents, of the young and the old, are naturally opposite, by the contrary effects of hope and despondence, of expectation and experience, without crime or folly on either side. The colors of life in youth and age appear different, as the face of nature in spring and winter. And how can children credit the assertions of parents, which their own eyes show them to be false?

"Few parents act in such a manner as much to enforce their maxims by the credit of their lives. The old man trusts wholly to slow contrivance and gradual progression; the youth expects to force his way by genius, vigor, and precipitance. The old man pays regard to riches, and the youth reverences virtue. The old man deifies prudence; the youth commits himself to magnanimity and chance. The young man, who intends no ill, believes that none is intended, and therefore acts with openness and candor; but his father, having suffered the injuries of fraud, is impelled to suspect, and too often allured to practice it. Age looks with anger on the temerity of youth, and youth with contempt on the scrupulosity[9] of age. Thus parents and children, for the greatest part, live on to love less and less; and, if those whom nature has thus closely united are the torments of each other, where shall we look for tenderness and consolation?"

---

7. In chapters 23–25, Rasselas examines court life; and Nekayah, domestic life. She reports her findings to him.
8. To allay is "to join anything to another, so as to abate its predominant qualities" (Johnson's *Dictionary*).
9. "Fear of acting in any manner" (Johnson's *Dictionary*).

"Surely," said the prince, "you must have been unfortunate in your choice of acquaintance: I am unwilling to believe that the most tender of all relations is thus impeded in its effects by natural necessity."

"Domestic discord," answered she, "is not inevitably and fatally necessary, but yet is not easily avoided. We seldom see that a whole family is virtuous; the good and evil cannot well agree, and the evil can yet less agree with one another. Even the virtuous fall sometimes to variance, when their virtues are of different kinds, and tending to extremes. In general, those parents have most reverence who most deserve it; for he that lives well cannot be despised.

"Many other evils infest private life. Some are the slaves of servants whom they have trusted with their affairs. Some are kept in continual anxiety to the caprice of rich relations, whom they cannot please, and dare not offend. Some husbands are imperious, and some wives perverse; and, as it is always more easy to do evil than good, though the wisdom or virtue of one can very rarely make many happy, the folly or vice of one may often make many miserable."

"If such be the general effect of marriage," said the prince, "I shall for the future think it dangerous to connect my interest with that of another, lest I should be unhappy by my partner's fault."

"I have met," said the princess, "with many who live single for that reason; but I never found that their prudence ought to raise envy. They dream away their time without friendship, without fondness, and are driven to rid themselves of the day, for which they have no use, by childish amusements, or vicious delights. They act as beings under the constant sense of some known inferiority that fills their minds with rancor, and their tongues with censure. They are peevish at home, and malevolent abroad; and, as the outlaws of human nature, make it their business and their pleasure to disturb that society which debars them from its privileges. To live without feeling or exciting sympathy, to be fortunate without adding to the felicity of others, or afflicted without tasting the balm of pity, is a state more gloomy than solitude; it is not retreat but exclusion from mankind. Marriage has many pains, but celibacy has no pleasures."

"What then is to be done?" said Rasselas; "the more we inquire, the less we can resolve. Surely he is most likely to please himself that has no other inclination to regard."[1]

* * *

Chapter 29. *The Debate on Marriage Continued*

"The good of the whole," says Rasselas, "is the same with the good of all its parts. If marriage be best for mankind it must be evidently best for individuals, or a permanent and necessary duty must be the cause of evil, and some must be inevitably sacrificed to the convenience of others. In the estimate which you have made of the two states, it appears that the incommodities of a single life are, in a great measure, necessary and certain, but those of the conjugal state accidental and avoidable.

---

1. In chapters 27–29, Rasselas reports on the unhappiness of court life, and he and Nekayah debate whether marriage leads to happiness or misery.

"I cannot forbear to flatter myself that prudence and benevolence will make marriage happy. The general folly of mankind is the cause of general complaint. What can be expected but disappointment and repentance from a choice made in the immaturity of youth, in the ardor of desire, without judgment, without foresight, without inquiry after conformity of opinions, similarity of manners, rectitude of judgment, or purity of sentiment.

"Such is the common process of marriage. A youth and maiden meeting by chance, or brought together by artifice, exchange glances, reciprocate civilities, go home, and dream of one another. Having little to divert attention, or diversify thought, they find themselves uneasy when they are apart, and therefore conclude that they shall be happy together. They marry, and discover what nothing but voluntary blindness had before concealed; they wear out life in altercations, and charge nature with cruelty.

"From those early marriages proceeds likewise the rivalry of parents and children: the son is eager to enjoy the world before the father is willing to forsake it, and there is hardly room at once for two generations. The daughter begins to bloom before the mother can be content to fade, and neither can forbear to wish for the absence of the other.

"Surely all these evils may be avoided by that deliberation and delay which prudence prescribes to irrevocable choice. In the variety and jollity of youthful pleasures life may be well enough supported without the help of a partner. Longer time will increase experience, and wider views will allow better opportunities of inquiry and selection: one advantage, at least, will be certain; the parents will be visibly older than their children."

"What reason cannot collect," said Nekayah, "and what experiment has not yet taught, can be known only from the report of others. I have been told that late marriages are not eminently happy. This is a question too important to be neglected, and I have often proposed it to those, whose accuracy of remark, and comprehensiveness of knowledge, made their suffrages[2] worthy of regard. They have generally determined that it is dangerous for a man and woman to suspend their fate upon each other, at a time when opinions are fixed, and habits are established; when friendships have been contracted on both sides, when life has been planned into method, and the mind has long enjoyed the contemplation of its own prospects.

"It is scarcely possible that two traveling through the world under the conduct of chance should have been both directed to the same path, and it will not often happen that either will quit the track which custom has made pleasing. When the desultory levity of youth has settled into regularity, it is soon succeeded by pride ashamed to yield, or obstinacy delighting to contend. And even though mutual esteem produces mutual desire to please, time itself, as it modifies unchangeably the external mien, determines likewise the direction of the passions, and gives an inflexible rigidity to the manners. Long customs are not easily broken: he that attempts to change the course of his own life very often labors in vain; and how shall we do that for others which we are seldom able to do for ourselves?"

"But surely," interposed the prince, "you suppose the chief motive of choice forgotten or neglected. Whenever I shall seek a wife, it shall be my first question, whether she be willing to be led by reason?"

2. Opinions.

"Thus it is," said Nekayah, "that philosophers are deceived. There are a thousand familiar[3] disputes which reason never can decide; questions that elude investigation, and make logic ridiculous; cases where something must be done, and where little can be said. Consider the state of mankind, and inquire how few can be supposed to act upon any occasions, whether small or great, with all the reasons of action present to their minds. Wretched would be the pair above all names of wretchedness, who should be doomed to adjust by reason every morning all the minute detail of a domestic day.

"Those who marry at an advanced age will probably escape the encroachments of their children; but, in diminution of this advantage, they will be likely to leave them, ignorant and helpless, to a guardian's mercy: or, if that should not happen, they must at least go out of the world before they see those whom they love best either wise or great.

"From their children, if they have less to fear, they have less also to hope, and they lose, without equivalent, the joys of early love, and the convenience of uniting with manners pliant and minds susceptible of new impressions, which might wear away their dissimilitudes by long cohabitation, as soft bodies, by continual attrition, conform their surfaces to each other.

"I believe it will be found that those who marry late are best pleased with their children, and those who marry early with their partners."

"The union of these two affections," said Rasselas, "would produce all that could be wished. Perhaps there is a time when marriage might unite them, a time neither too early for the father, nor too late for the husband."

"Every hour," answered the princess, "confirms my prejudice in favor of the position so often uttered by the mouth of Imlac, 'That nature sets her gifts on the right hand and on the left.' Those conditions, which flatter hope and attract desire, are so constituted that, as we approach one, we recede from another. There are goods so opposed that we cannot seize both, but, by too much prudence, may pass between them at too great a distance to reach either. This is often the fate of long consideration; he does nothing who endeavors to do more than is allowed to humanity. Flatter not yourself with contrarieties of pleasure. Of the blessings set before you make your choice, and be content. No man can taste the fruits of autumn, while he is delighting his scent with the flowers of the spring: no man can, at the same time, fill his cup from the source and from the mouth of the Nile."[4]

*　*　*

Chapter 31. They Visit the Pyramids

The resolution being thus taken, they set out the next day. They laid tents upon their camels, being resolved to stay among the pyramids till their curiosity was fully satisfied. They traveled gently, turned aside to everything remarkable, stopped from time to time and conversed with the inhabitants, and observed the various appearances of towns ruined and inhabited, of wild and cultivated nature.

When they came to the great pyramid, they were astonished at the extent of the base, and the height of the top. Imlac explained to them the principles

3. Domestic.
4. In chapter 30, Imlac proposes a visit to the pyramids.

upon which the pyramidal form was chosen for a fabric intended to coextend its duration with that of the world; he showed that its gradual diminution gave it such stability as defeated all the common attacks of the elements, and could scarcely be overthrown by earthquakes themselves, the least resistible of natural violence. A concussion that should shatter the pyramid would threaten the dissolution of the continent.

They measured all its dimensions, and pitched their tents at its foot. Next day they prepared to enter its interior apartments, and having hired the common guides, climbed up to the first passage, when the favorite of the princess, looking into the cavity, stepped back and trembled. "Pekuah," said the princess, "of what art thou afraid?" "Of the narrow entrance," answered the lady, "and of the dreadful gloom. I dare not enter a place which must surely be inhabited by unquiet souls. The original possessors of these dreadful vaults will start up before us, and perhaps shut us in forever." She spoke, and threw her arms round the neck of her mistress.

"If all your fear be of apparitions," said the prince, "I will promise you safety. There is no danger from the dead; he that is once buried will be seen no more."

"That the dead are seen no more," said Imlac, "I will not undertake to maintain, against the concurrent and unvaried testimony of all ages, and of all nations. There is no people, rude or learned, among whom apparitions of the dead are not related and believed. This opinion, which perhaps prevails as far as human nature is diffused, could become universal only by its truth; those that never heard of one another would not have agreed in a tale which nothing but experience can make credible. That it is doubted by single cavilers can very little weaken the general evidence; and some who deny it with their tongues confess it by their fears.

"Yet I do not mean to add new terrors to those which have already seized upon Pekuah. There can be no reason why specters should haunt the pyramid more than other places, or why they should have power or will to hurt innocence and purity. Our entrance is no violation of their privileges; we can take nothing from them, how then can we offend them?"

"My dear Pekuah," said the princess, "I will always go before you, and Imlac shall follow you. Remember that you are the companion of the princess of Abyssinia."

"If the princess is pleased that her servant should die," returned the lady, "let her command some death less dreadful than enclosure in this horrid cavern. You know I dare not disobey you; I must go if you command me, but if I once enter, I never shall come back."

The princess saw that her fear was too strong for expostulation or reproof, and, embracing her, told her that she should stay in the tent till their return. Pekuah was yet not satisfied, but entreated the princess not to pursue so dreadful a purpose as that of entering the recesses of the pyramid. "Though I cannot teach courage," said Nekayah, "I must not learn cowardice, nor leave at last undone what I came hither only to do."

Chapter 32. They Enter the Pyramid

Pekuah descended to the tents, and the rest entered the pyramid. They passed through the galleries, surveyed the vaults of marble, and examined the chest in which the body of the founder is supposed to have been reposited.

They then sat down in one of the most spacious chambers to rest a while before they attempted to return.

"We have now," said Imlac, "gratified our minds with an exact view of the greatest work of man, except the wall of China.

"Of the wall it is very easy to assign the motive. It secured a wealthy and timorous nation from the incursions of barbarians, whose unskillfulness in arts made it easier for them to supply their wants by rapine than by industry, and who from time to time poured in upon the habitations of peaceful commerce, as vultures descend upon domestic fowl. Their celerity and fierceness made the wall necessary, and their ignorance made it efficacious.

"But for the pyramids, no reason has ever been given adequate to the cost and labor of the work. The narrowness of the chambers proves that it could afford no retreat from enemies, and treasures might have been reposited at far less expense with equal security. It seems to have been erected only in compliance with that hunger of imagination which preys incessantly upon life, and must be always appeased by some employment. Those who have already all that they can enjoy must enlarge their desires. He that has built for use till use is supplied, must begin to build for vanity, and extend his plan to the utmost power of human performance, that he may not be soon reduced to form another wish.

"I consider this mighty structure as a monument of the insufficiency of human enjoyments. A king, whose power is unlimited, and whose treasures surmount all real and imaginary wants, is compelled to solace, by the erection of a pyramid, the satiety of dominion and tastelessness of pleasures, and to amuse the tediousness of declining life by seeing thousands laboring without end, and one stone, for no purpose, laid upon another. Whoever thou art, that, not content with a moderate condition, imaginest happiness in royal magnificence, and dreamest that command or riches can feed the appetite of novelty with perpetual gratifications, survey the pyramids, and confess thy folly!"[5]

*　*　*

Chapter 40. The History of a Man of Learning

They returned to Cairo, and were so well pleased at finding themselves together, that none of them went much abroad. The prince began to love learning, and one day declared to Imlac, that he intended to devote himself to science,[6] and pass the rest of his days in literary solitude.

"Before you make your final choice," answered Imlac, "you ought to examine its hazards, and converse with some of those who are grown old in the company of themselves. I have just left the observatory of one of the most learned astronomers in the world, who has spent forty years in unwearied attention to the motions and appearances of the celestial bodies, and has drawn out his soul in endless calculations. He admits a few friends once a month to hear his deductions and enjoy his discoveries. I was introduced as a man of knowledge worthy of his notice. Men of various ideas and fluent conversation are commonly welcome to those whose thoughts have been long

5. In chapters 33–39, Pekuah—while her friends are not in the pyramid—is abducted by a troop of Arabs. The chief is tempted to keep her, but eventually accepts a ransom and returns her unharmed.
6. Knowledge.

fixed upon a single point, and who find the images of other things stealing away. I delighted him with my remarks, he smiled at the narrative of my travels, and was glad to forget the constellations, and descend for a moment into the lower world.

"On the next day of vacation[7] I renewed my visit, and was so fortunate as to please him again. He relaxed from that time the severity of his rule, and permitted me to enter at my own choice. I found him always busy, and always glad to be relieved. As each knew much which the other was desirous of learning, we exchanged our notions with great delight. I perceived that I had every day more of his confidence, and always found new cause of admiration in the profundity of his mind. His comprehension is vast, his memory capacious and retentive, his discourse is methodical, and his expression clear.

"His integrity and benevolence are equal to his learning. His deepest researches and most favorite studies are willingly interrupted for any opportunity of doing good by his counsel or his riches. To his closest retreat,[8] at his most busy moments, all are admitted that want his assistance: 'For though I exclude idleness and pleasure, I will never,' says he, 'bar my doors against charity. To man is permitted the contemplation of the skies, but the practice of virtue is commanded.'"

"Surely," said the princess, "this man is happy."

"I visited him," said Imlac, "with more and more frequency, and was every time more enamored of his conversation: he was sublime without haughtiness, courteous without formality, and communicative without ostentation. I was at first, great princess, of your opinion, thought him the happiest of mankind, and often congratulated him on the blessing that he enjoyed. He seemed to hear nothing with indifference but the praises of his condition, to which he always returned a general answer, and diverted the conversation to some other topic.

"Amidst this willingness to be pleased, and labor to please, I had quickly reason to imagine that some painful sentiment pressed upon his mind. He often looked up earnestly towards the sun, and let his voice fall in the midst of his discourse. He would sometimes, when we were alone, gaze upon me in silence with the air of a man who longed to speak what he was yet resolved to suppress. He would often send for me with vehement injunctions of haste, though, when I came to him, he had nothing extraordinary to say. And sometimes, when I was leaving him, he would call me back, pause a few moments and then dismiss me.

Chapter 41. The Astronomer Discovers the Cause of His Uneasiness

"At last the time came when the secret burst his reserve. We were sitting together last night in the turret of his house, watching the emersion of a satellite of Jupiter. A sudden tempest clouded the sky, and disappointed our observation. We sat a while silent in the dark, and then he addressed himself to me in these words: 'Imlac, I have long considered thy friendship as the greatest blessing of my life. Integrity without knowledge is weak and useless, and knowledge without integrity is dangerous and dreadful. I have found in thee all the qualities requisite for trust, benevolence, experience, and fortitude. I have long discharged an office which I must soon quit at

---

7. Leisure.   8. Most secluded place of privacy.

the call of nature, and shall rejoice in the hour of imbecility[9] and pain to devolve it upon thee.'

"I thought myself honored by this testimony, and protested that whatever could conduce to his happiness would add likewise to mine.

"'Hear, Imlac, what thou wilt not without difficulty credit. I have possessed for five years the regulation of weather, and the distribution of the seasons: the sun has listened to my dictates, and passed from tropic to tropic by my direction; the clouds, at my call, have poured their waters, and the Nile has overflowed at my command; I have restrained the rage of the dog-star, and mitigated the fervors of the crab.[1] The winds alone, of all the elemental powers, have hitherto refused my authority, and multitudes have perished by equinoctial tempests which I found myself unable to prohibit or restrain. I have administered this great office with exact justice, and made to the different nations of the earth an impartial dividend of rain and sunshine. What must have been the misery of half the globe, if I had limited the clouds to particular regions, or confined the sun to either side of the equator?'

Chapter 42. The Opinion of the Astronomer Is Explained and Justified

"I suppose he discovered in me, through the obscurity of the room, some tokens of amazement and doubt, for, after a short pause, he proceeded thus:

"'Not to be easily credited will neither surprise nor offend me; for I am, probably, the first of human beings to whom this trust has been imparted. Nor do I know whether to deem this distinction a reward or punishment; since I have possessed it I have been far less happy than before, and nothing but the consciousness of good intention could have enabled me to support the weariness of unremitted vigilance.'

"'How long, Sir,' said I, 'has this great office been in your hands?'

"'About ten years ago,' said he, 'my daily observations of the changes of the sky led me to consider, whether, if I had the power of the seasons, I could confer greater plenty upon the inhabitants of the earth. This contemplation fastened on my mind, and I sat days and nights in imaginary dominion, pouring upon this country and that the showers of fertility, and seconding every fall of rain with a due proportion of sunshine. I had yet only the will to do good, and did not imagine that I should ever have the power.

"'One day as I was looking on the fields withering with heat, I felt in my mind a sudden wish that I could send rain on the southern mountains, and raise the Nile to an inundation. In the hurry of my imagination I commanded rain to fall, and, by comparing the time of my command, with that of the inundation, I found that the clouds had listened to my lips.'

"'Might not some other cause,' said I, 'produce this concurrence? the Nile does not always rise on the same day.'

"'Do not believe,' said he with impatience, 'that such objections could escape me: I reasoned long against my own conviction, and labored against truth with the utmost obstinacy. I sometimes suspected myself of madness, and should not have dared to impart this secret but to a man like you, capable of distinguishing the wonderful from the impossible, and the incredible from the false.'

"'Why, Sir,' said I, 'do you call that incredible, which you know, or think you know, to be true?'

---

9. Feebleness.
1. The fourth sign of the zodiac (Cancer). "The dog-star": Sirius was supposed to cause the heat ("dog days") of summer.

"'Because,' said he, 'I cannot prove it by any external evidence; and I know too well the laws of demonstration to think that my conviction ought to influence another, who cannot, like me, be conscious of its force. I therefore shall not attempt to gain credit by disputation. It is sufficient that I feel this power, that I have long possessed, and every day exerted it. But the life of man is short, the infirmities of age increase upon me, and the time will soon come when the regulator of the year must mingle with the dust. The care of appointing a successor has long disturbed me; the night and the day have been spent in comparisons of all the characters which have come to my knowledge, and I have yet found none so worthy as thyself.

Chapter 43. The Astronomer Leaves Imlac His Directions

"'Hear therefore, what I shall impart, with attention, such as the welfare of a world requires. If the task of a king be considered as difficult, who has the care only of a few millions, to whom he cannot do much good or harm, what must be the anxiety of him, on whom depends the action of the elements, and the great gifts of light and heat!—Hear me therefore with attention.

"'I have diligently considered the position of the earth and sun, and formed innumerable schemes in which I changed their situation. I have sometimes turned aside the axis of the earth, and sometimes varied the ecliptic of the sun: but I have found it impossible to make a disposition by which the world may be advantaged; what one region gains, another loses by any imaginable alteration, even without considering the distant parts of the solar system with which we are unacquainted. Do not, therefore, in thy administration of the year, indulge thy pride by innovation; do not please thyself with thinking that thou canst make thyself renowned to all future ages, by disordering the seasons. The memory of mischief is no desirable fame. Much less will it become thee to let kindness or interest prevail. Never rob other countries of rain to pour it on thine own. For us the Nile is sufficient.'

"I promised that when I possessed the power, I would use it with inflexible integrity, and he dismissed me, pressing my hand. 'My heart,' said he, 'will be now at rest, and my benevolence will no more destroy my quiet: I have found a man of wisdom and virtue, to whom I can cheerfully bequeath the inheritance of the sun.'"

The prince heard this narration with very serious regard, but the princess smiled, and Pekuah convulsed herself with laughter. "Ladies," said Imlac, "to mock the heaviest of human afflictions is neither charitable nor wise. Few can attain this man's knowledge, and few practice his virtues; but all may suffer his calamity. Of the uncertainties of our present state, the most dreadful and alarming is the uncertain continuance of reason."

The princess was recollected, and the favorite was abashed. Rasselas, more deeply affected, inquired of Imlac, whether he thought such maladies of the mind frequent, and how they were contracted.

Chapter 44. The Dangerous Prevalence[2] of Imagination

"Disorders of intellect," answered Imlac, "happen much more often than superficial observers will easily believe. Perhaps, if we speak with rigorous

2. Predominance.

exactness, no human mind is in its right state. There is no man whose imagination does not sometimes predominate over his reason, who can regulate his attention wholly by his will, and whose ideas will come and go at his command. No man will be found in whose mind airy notions do not sometimes tyrannize, and force him to hope or fear beyond the limits of sober probability. All power of fancy over reason is a degree of insanity; but while this power is such as we can control and repress, it is not visible to others, nor considered as any depravation of the mental faculties; it is not pronounced madness but when it comes ungovernable, and apparently influences speech or action.

"To indulge the power of fiction, and send imagination out upon the wing, is often the sport of those who delight too much in silent speculation. When we are alone we are not always busy; the labor of excogitation is too violent to last long; the ardor of inquiry will sometimes give way to idleness or satiety. He who has nothing external that can divert him must find pleasure in his own thoughts, and must conceive himself what he is not; for who is pleased with what he is? He then expatiates in boundless futurity, and culls from all imaginable conditions that which for the present moment he should most desire, amuses his desires with impossible enjoyments, and confers upon his pride unattainable dominion. The mind dances from scene to scene, unites all pleasures in all combinations, and riots in delights which nature and fortune, with all their bounty, cannot bestow.

"In time, some particular train of ideas fixes the attention; all other intellectual gratifications are rejected; the mind, in weariness or leisure, recurs constantly to the favorite conception, and feasts on the luscious falsehood, whenever she is offended with the bitterness of truth. By degrees the reign of fancy is confirmed; she grows first imperious, and in time despotic. Then fictions begin to operate as realities, false opinions fasten upon the mind, and life passes in dreams of rapture or of anguish.

"This, sir, is one of the dangers of solitude, which the hermit has confessed not always to promote goodness, and the astronomer's misery has proved to be not always propitious to wisdom."

"I will no more," said the favorite, "imagine myself the queen of Abyssinia. I have often spent the hours which the princess gave to my own disposal, in adjusting ceremonies and regulating the court; I have repressed the pride of the powerful, and granted the petitions of the poor; I have built new palaces in more happy situations, planted groves upon the tops of mountains, and have exulted in the beneficence of royalty, till, when the princess entered, I had almost forgotten to bow down before her."

"And I," said the princess, "will not allow myself any more to play the shepherdess in my waking dreams. I have often soothed my thoughts with the quiet and innocence of pastoral employments, till I have in my chamber heard the winds whistle, and the sheep bleat; sometimes freed the lamb entangled in the thicket, and sometimes with my crook encountered the wolf. I have a dress like that of the village maids, which I put on to help my imagination, and a pipe on which I play softly, and suppose myself followed by my flocks."

"I will confess," said the prince, "an indulgence of fantastic delight more dangerous than yours. I have frequently endeavored to image the possibility of a perfect government, by which all wrong should be restrained, all vice reformed, and all the subjects preserved in tranquility and innocence. This thought produced innumerable schemes of reformation, and dictated many useful regulations and salutary edicts. This has been the sport, and sometimes the labor, of my solitude; and I start, when I think with how little anguish I once supposed the death of my father and my brothers."

"Such," says Imlac, "are the effects of visionary schemes; when we first form them, we know them to be absurd, but familiarize them by degrees, and in time lose sight of their folly."

Chapter 45. They Discourse with an Old Man

The evening was now far past, and they rose to return home. As they walked along the bank of the Nile, delighted with the beams of the moon quivering on the water, they saw at a small distance an old man, whom the prince had often heard in the assembly of the sages. "Yonder," said he, "is one whose years have calmed his passions, but not clouded his reason. Let us close the disquisitions of the night by inquiring what are his sentiments of his own state, that we may know whether youth alone is to struggle with vexation, and whether any better hope remains for the latter part of life."

Here the sage approached and saluted them. They invited him to join their walk, and prattled a while, as acquaintance that had unexpectedly met one another. The old man was cheerful and talkative, and the way seemed short in his company. He was pleased to find himself not disregarded, accompanied them to their house, and, at the prince's request, entered with them. They placed him in the seat of honor, and set wine and conserves before him.

"Sir," said the princess, "an evening walk must give to a man of learning like you pleasures which ignorance and youth can hardly conceive. You know the qualities and the causes of all that you behold, the laws by which the river flows, the periods in which the planets perform their revolutions. Everything must supply you with contemplation, and renew the consciousness of your own dignity."

"Lady," answered he, "let the gay and the vigorous expect pleasure in their excursions; it is enough that age can obtain ease. To me the world has lost its novelty; I look round, and see what I remember to have seen in happier days. I rest against a tree, and consider that in the same shade I once disputed upon the annual overflow of the Nile with a friend who is now silent in the grave. I cast my eyes upward, fix them on the changing moon, and think with pain on the vicissitudes of life. I have ceased to take much delight in physical truth; for what have I to do with those things which I am soon to leave?"

"You may at least recreate[3] yourself," said Imlac, "with the recollection of an honorable and useful life, and enjoy the praise which all agree to give you."

"Praise," said the sage with a sigh, "is to an old man an empty sound. I have neither mother to be delighted with the reputation of her son, nor wife to partake the honors of her husband. I have outlived my friends and my rivals. Nothing is now of much importance; for I cannot extend my interest beyond myself. Youth is delighted with applause, because it is considered as the earnest of some future good, and because the prospect of life is far extended; but to me, who am now declining to decrepitude, there is little to be feared from

---

3. Refresh.

the malevolence of men, and yet less to be hoped from their affection or esteem. Something they may yet take away, but they can give me nothing. Riches would now be useless, and high employment would be pain. My retrospect of life recalls to my view many opportunities of good neglected, much time squandered upon trifles, and more lost in idleness and vacancy. I leave many great designs unattempted, and many great attempts unfinished. My mind is burthened with no heavy crime, and therefore I compose myself to tranquility; endeavor to abstract my thoughts from hopes and cares which, though reason knows them to be vain, still try to keep their old possession of the heart; expect,[4] with serene humility, that hour which nature cannot long delay; and hope to possess, in a better state, that happiness which here I could not find, and that virtue which here I have not attained."

He arose and went away, leaving his audience not much elated with the hope of long life. The prince consoled himself with remarking that it was not reasonable to be disappointed by this account; for age had never been considered as the season of felicity, and if it was possible to be easy in decline and weakness, it was likely that the days of vigor and alacrity might be happy; that the noon of life might be bright, if the evening could be calm.

The princess suspected that age was querulous and malignant, and delighted to repress the expectations of those who had newly entered the world. She had seen the possessors of estates look with envy on their heirs, and known many who enjoy pleasure no longer than they can confine it to themselves.

Pekuah conjectured that the man was older than he appeared, and was willing to impute his complaints to delirious dejection; or else supposed that he had been unfortunate, and was therefore discontented. "For nothing," said she, "is more common than to call our own condition the condition of life."

Imlac, who had no desire to see them depressed, smiled at the comforts which they could so readily procure to themselves, and remembered that, at the same age, he was equally confident of unmingled prosperity, and equally fertile of consolatory expedients. He forbore to force upon them unwelcome knowledge, which time itself would too soon impress. The princess and her lady retired; the madness of the astronomer hung upon their minds, and they desired Imlac to enter upon his office, and delay next morning the rising of the sun.[5]

* * *

Chapter 48. Imlac Discourses on the Nature of the Soul

"What reason," said the prince, "can be given, why the Egyptians should thus expensively preserve those carcasses which some nations consume with fire, others lay to mingle with the earth, and all agree to remove from their sight, as soon as decent rites can be performed?"

"The original of ancient customs," said Imlac, "is commonly unknown; for the practice often continues when the cause has ceased; and concerning

4. Await.
5. In chapters 46 and 47, Nekayah, Pekuah, and Rasselas befriend the astronomer and gradually wean him from madness. In search of diversion, all of them visit the catacombs.

superstitious ceremonies it is vain to conjecture; for what reason did not dictate reason cannot explain. I have long believed that the practice of embalming arose only from tenderness to the remains of relations or friends, and to this opinion I am more inclined, because it seems impossible that this care should have been general: had all the dead been embalmed, their repositories must in time have been more spacious than the dwellings of the living. I suppose only the rich or honorable were secured from corruption, and the rest left to the course of nature.

"But it is commonly supposed that the Egyptians believed the soul to live as long as the body continued undissolved, and therefore tried this method of eluding death."

"Could the wise Egyptians," said Nekayah, "think so grossly of the soul? If the soul could once survive its separation, what could it afterwards receive or suffer from the body?"

"The Egyptians would doubtless think erroneously," said the astronomer, "in the darkness of heathenism, and the first dawn of philosophy. The nature of the soul is still disputed amidst all our opportunities of clearer knowledge: some yet say, that it may be material, who, nevertheless, believe it to be immortal."

"Some," answered Imlac, "have indeed said that the soul is material, but I can scarcely believe that any man has thought it, who knew how to think; for all the conclusions of reason enforce the immateriality of mind, and all the notices of sense and investigations of science concur to prove the unconsciousness of matter.

"It was never supposed that cogitation is inherent in matter, or that every particle is a thinking being. Yet if any part of matter be devoid of thought, what part can we suppose to think? Matter can differ from matter only in form, density, bulk, motion, and direction of motion: to which of these, however varied or combined, can consciousness be annexed? To be round or square, to be solid or fluid, to be great or little, to be moved slowly or swiftly one way or another, are modes of material existence, all equally alien from the nature of cogitation. If matter be once without thought, it can only be made to think by some new modification, but all the modifications which it can admit are equally unconnected with cogitative powers."

"But the materialists," said the astronomer, "urge that matter may have qualities with which we are unacquainted."

"He who will determine," returned Imlac, "against that which he knows, because there may be something which he knows not; he that can set hypothetical possibility against acknowledged certainty, is not to be admitted among reasonable beings. All that we know of matter is, that matter is inert, senseless and lifeless; and if this conviction cannot be opposed but by referring us to something that we know not, we have all the evidence that human intellect can admit. If that which is known may be overruled by that which is unknown, no being, not omniscient, can arrive at certainty."

"Yet let us not," said the astronomer, "too arrogantly limit the Creator's power."

"It is no limitation of omnipotence," replied the poet, "to suppose that one thing is not consistent with another, that the same proposition cannot be at once true and false, that the same number cannot be even and odd, that cogitation cannot be conferred on that which is created incapable of cogitation."

"I know not," said Nekayah, "any great use of this question. Does that immateriality, which, in my opinion, you have sufficiently proved, necessarily include eternal duration?"

"Of immateriality," said Imlac, "our ideas are negative, and therefore obscure. Immateriality seems to imply a natural power of perpetual duration as a consequence of exemption from all causes of decay: whatever perishes, is destroyed by the solution of its contexture,[6] and separation of its parts; nor can we conceive how that which has no parts, and therefore admits no solution, can be naturally corrupted or impaired."

"I know not," said Rasselas, "how to conceive anything without extension: what is extended must have parts, and you allow, that whatever has parts may be destroyed."

"Consider your own conceptions," replied Imlac, "and the difficulty will be less. You will find substance without extension. An ideal form is no less real than material bulk: yet an ideal form has no extension. It is no less certain, when you think on a pyramid, that your mind possesses the idea of a pyramid, than that the pyramid itself is standing. What space does the idea of a pyramid occupy more than the idea of a grain of corn? or how can either idea suffer laceration? As is the effect such is the cause; as thought is, such is the power that thinks; a power impassive and indiscerptible."[7]

"But the Being," said Nekayah, "whom I fear to name, the Being which made the soul, can destroy it."

"He, surely, can destroy it," answered Imlac, "since, however unperishable, it receives from a superior nature its power of duration. That it will not perish by any inherent cause of decay, or principle of corruption, may be shown by philosophy; but philosophy can tell no more. That it will not be annihilated by him that made it, we must humbly learn from higher authority."

The whole assembly stood a while silent and collected. "Let us return," said Rasselas, "from this scene of mortality. How gloomy would be these mansions of the dead to him who did not know that he shall never die; that what now acts shall continue its agency, and what now thinks shall think on for ever. Those that lie here stretched before us, the wise and the powerful of ancient times, warn us to remember the shortness of our present state: they were, perhaps, snatched away while they were busy, like us, in the choice of life."

"To me," said the princess, "the choice of life is become less important; I hope hereafter to think only on the choice of eternity."

They then hastened out of the caverns, and, under the protection of their guard, returned to Cairo.

Chapter 49. The Conclusion, in Which Nothing Is Concluded

It was now the time of the inundation of the Nile: a few days after their visit to the catacombs, the river began to rise.

They were confined to their house. The whole region being under water gave them no invitation to any excursions, and being well supplied with materials for talk, they diverted themselves with comparisons of the different forms of life which they had observed, and with various schemes of happiness which each of them had formed.

---

6. Dissolution of its structure.   7. Not to be separated.

Pekuah was never so much charmed with any place as the convent of St. Anthony, where the Arab restored her to the princess, and wished only to fill it with pious maidens, and to be made prioress of the order; she was weary of expectation and disgust,[8] and would gladly be fixed in some unvariable state.

The princess thought that, of all sublunary things, knowledge was the best: she desired first to learn all sciences, and then purposed to found a college of learned women, in which she would preside, that, by conversing with the old and educating the young, she might divide her time between the acquisition and communication of wisdom, and raise up for the next age models of prudence, and patterns of piety.

The prince desired a little kingdom, in which he might administer justice in his own person, and see all the parts of government with his own eyes; but he could never fix the limits of his dominion, and was always adding to the number of his subjects.

Imlac and the astronomer were contented to be driven along the stream of life, without directing their course to any particular port.

Of these wishes that they had formed, they well knew that none could be obtained. They deliberated a while what was to be done, and resolved, when the inundation should cease, to return to Abyssinia.[9]

1759

Rambler No. 4

[ON FICTION]

Saturday, March 31, 1750

Simul et jucunda et idonea dicere vitae.
—HORACE, *Art of Poetry*, 334

And join both profit and delight in one.
—CREECH

The works of fiction with which the present generation seems more particularly delighted are such as exhibit life in its true state, diversified only by accidents that daily happen in the world, and influenced by passions and qualities which are really to be found in conversing with mankind.

This kind of writing may be termed, not improperly, the comedy of romance, and is to be conducted nearly by the rules of comic poetry. Its province is to bring about natural events by easy means, and to keep up curiosity without the help of wonder: it is therefore precluded from the machines[1] and expedients of the heroic romance, and can neither employ giants to snatch away a lady from the nuptial rites, nor knights to bring her back from captivity; it can neither bewilder its personages in deserts, nor lodge them in imaginary castles.

I remember a remark made by Scaliger upon Pontanus,[2] that all his writings are filled with the same images; and that if you take from him his lilies

8. Aversion.
9. Probably not to the Happy Valley, which they earlier fled. Their future remains uncertain.
1. The technical term in neoclassical critical theory for the supernatural agents who intervene in human affairs in epic and tragedy.
2. Julius Caesar Scaliger (1484–1558) criticized the Latin poems of the Italian poet Jovianus Pontanus (1426–1503).

and his roses, his satyrs and his dryads, he will have nothing left that can be called poetry. In like manner, almost all the fictions of the last age will vanish if you deprive them of a hermit and a wood, a battle and a shipwreck.

Why this wild strain of imagination found reception so long in polite and learned ages, it is not easy to conceive; but we cannot wonder that while readers could be procured, the authors were willing to continue it; for when a man had by practice gained some fluency of language, he had no further care than to retire to his closet, let loose his invention, and heat his mind with incredibilities; a book was thus produced without fear of criticism, without the toil of study, without knowledge of nature, or acquaintance with life.

The task of our present writers is very different; it requires, together with that learning which is to be gained from books, that experience which can never be attained by solitary diligence, but must arise from general converse and accurate observation of the living world. Their performances have, as Horace expresses it, *plus oneris quanto veniae minus*,[3] little indulgence, and therefore more difficulty. They are engaged in portraits of which everyone knows the original, and can detect any deviation from exactness of resemblance. Other writings are safe, except from the malice of learning, but these are in danger from every common reader; as the slipper ill executed was censured by a shoemaker who happened to stop in his way at the Venus of Apelles.[4]

But the fear of not being approved as just copiers of human manners is not the most important concern that an author of this sort ought to have before him. These books are written chiefly to the young, the ignorant, and the idle, to whom they serve as lectures of conduct, and introductions into life. They are the entertainment of minds unfurnished with ideas, and therefore easily susceptible of impressions; not fixed by principles, and therefore easily following the current of fancy; not informed by experience, and consequently open to every false suggestion and partial account.

That the highest degree of reverence should be paid to youth, and that nothing indecent should be suffered to approach their eyes or ears, are precepts extorted by sense and virtue from an ancient writer by no means eminent for chastity of thought.[5] The same kind, though not the same degree, of caution, is required in everything which is laid before them, to secure them from unjust prejudices, perverse opinions, and incongruous combinations of images.

In the romances formerly written, every transaction and sentiment was so remote from all that passes among men that the reader was in very little danger of making any applications to himself; the virtues and crimes were equally beyond his sphere of activity; and he amused himself with heroes and with traitors, deliverers and persecutors, as with beings of another species, whose actions were regulated upon motives of their own, and who had neither faults nor excellencies in common with himself.

But when an adventurer is leveled with the rest of the world, and acts in such scenes of the universal drama as may be the lot of any other man, young spectators fix their eyes upon him with closer attention, and hope, by

---

3. *Epistles* 2.1.170.
4. According to Pliny the Younger (*Naturalis Historia* 35.85), the Greek painter Apelles of Kos (4th century B.C.E.) corrected the drawing of a sandal after hearing a shoemaker criticize it as faulty, but when the flattered artisan dared to find fault with the drawing of a leg, the artist bade him "stick to his last."
5. Juvenal's *Satires* 14.1–58.

observing his behavior and success, to regulate their own practices when they shall be engaged in the like part.

For this reason these familiar histories may perhaps be made of greater use than the solemnities of professed morality, and convey the knowledge of vice and virtue with more efficacy than axioms and definitions. But if the power of example is so great as to take possession of the memory by a kind of violence, and produce effects almost without the intervention of the will, care ought to be taken that when the choice is unrestrained, the best examples only should be exhibited; and that which is likely to operate so strongly should not be mischievous or uncertain in its effects.

The chief advantage which these fictions have over real life is that their authors are at liberty, though not to invent, yet to select objects, and to cull from the mass of mankind those individuals upon which the attention ought most to be employed; as a diamond, though it cannot be made, may be polished by art, and placed in such situation as to display that luster which before was buried among common stones.

It is justly considered as the greatest excellency of art to imitate nature; but it is necessary to distinguish those parts of nature which are most proper for imitation: greater care is still required in representing life, which is so often discolored by passion or deformed by wickedness. If the world be promiscuously[6] described, I cannot see of what use it can be to read the account; or why it may not be as safe to turn the eye immediately upon mankind as upon a mirror which shows all that presents itself without discrimination.

It is therefore not a sufficient vindication of a character that it is drawn as it appears, for many characters ought never to be drawn; nor of a narrative that the train of events is agreeable to observation and experience, for that observation which is called knowledge of the world will be found much more frequently to make men cunning than good. The purpose of these writings is surely not only to show mankind, but to provide that they may be seen hereafter with less hazard; to teach the means of avoiding the snares which are laid by Treachery for Innocence, without infusing any wish for that superiority with which the betrayer flatters his vanity; to give the power of counteracting fraud without the temptation to practice it; to initiate youth by mock encounters in the art of necessary defense, and to increase prudence without impairing virtue.

Many writers, for the sake of following nature, so mingle good and bad qualities in their principal personages that they are both equally conspicuous; and as we accompany them through their adventures with delight, and are led by degrees to interest ourselves in their favor, we lose the abhorrence of their faults because they do not hinder our pleasure, or perhaps regard them with some kindness for being united with so much merit.[7]

There have been men indeed splendidly wicked, whose endowments threw a brightness on their crimes, and whom scarce any villainy made perfectly detestable because they never could be wholly divested of their excellencies; but such have been in all ages the great corrupters of the world, and their resemblance ought no more to be preserved than the art of murdering without pain.

---

6. Indiscriminately.
7. Johnson is probably thinking of such popular novels as Tobias Smollett's *Roderick Random* (1748) and Henry Fielding's *Tom Jones* (1749), as opposed to the model of virtue provided by Samuel Richardson's *Clarissa* (1747–48).

Some have advanced, without due attention to the consequences of this notion, that certain virtues have their correspondent faults, and therefore that to exhibit either apart is to deviate from probability. Thus men are observed by Swift to be "grateful in the same degree as they are resentful." This principle, with others of the same kind, supposes man to act from a brute impulse, and pursue a certain degree of inclination without any choice of the object; for, otherwise, though it should be allowed that gratitude and resentment arise from the same constitution of the passions, it follows not that they will be equally indulged when reason is consulted; yet, unless that consequence be admitted, this sagacious maxim becomes an empty sound, without any relation to practice or to life.

Nor is it evident that even the first motions to these effects are always in the same proportion. For pride, which produces quickness of resentment, will obstruct gratitude by unwillingness to admit that inferiority which obligation implies; and it is very unlikely that he who cannot think he receives a favor will acknowledge or repay it.

It is of the utmost importance to mankind that positions of this tendency should be laid open and confuted; for while men consider good and evil as springing from the same root, they will spare the one for the sake of the other, and in judging, if not of others at least of themselves, will be apt to estimate their virtues by their vices. To this fatal error all those will contribute who confound the colors of right and wrong, and, instead of helping to settle their boundaries, mix them with so much art that no common mind is able to disunite them.

In narratives where historical veracity has no place, I cannot discover why there should not be exhibited the most perfect idea of virtue; of virtue not angelical, nor above probability (for what we cannot credit, we shall never imitate), but the highest and purest that humanity can reach, which, exercised in such trials as the various revolutions of things shall bring upon it, may, by conquering some calamities and enduring others, teach us what we may hope, and what we can perform. Vice (for vice is necessary to be shown) should always disgust; nor should the graces of gaiety, nor the dignity of courage, be so united with it as to reconcile it to the mind. Wherever it appears, it should raise hatred by the malignity of its practices, and contempt by the meanness of its stratagems: for while it is supported by either parts[8] or spirit, it will be seldom heartily abhorred. The Roman tyrant was content to be hated if he was but feared;[9] and there are thousands of the readers of romances willing to be thought wicked if they may be allowed to be wits. It is therefore to be steadily inculcated that virtue is the highest proof of understanding, and the only solid basis of greatness; and that vice is the natural consequence of narrow thoughts; that it begins in mistake, and ends in ignominy.

8. Abilities.
9. The emperor Tiberius (see Suetonius's *Lives of the Caesars*).

Rambler No. 60

[BIOGRAPHY]

Saturday, October 13, 1750

—*Quid sit pulchrum, quid turpe, quid utile, quid non,*
Plenius ac melius Chrysippo et Crantore dicit.
—HORACE, *Epistles*, 1.2.3–4

> Whose works the beautiful and base contain,
> Of vice and virtue more instructive rules,
> Than all the sober sages of the schools.
> —FRANCIS

All joy or sorrow for the happiness or calamities of others is produced by an act of the imagination, that realizes the event, however fictitious, or approximates it,[1] however remote, by placing us, for a time, in the condition of him whose fortune we contemplate; so that we feel, while the deception lasts, whatever motions would be excited by the same good or evil happening to ourselves.

Our passions are therefore more strongly moved, in proportion as we can more readily adopt the pains or pleasure proposed to our minds, by recognizing them as once our own, or considering them as naturally incident to our state of life. It is not easy for the most artful writer to give us an interest in happiness or misery, which we think ourselves never likely to feel, and with which we have never yet been made acquainted. Histories of the downfall of kingdoms, and revolutions of empires, are read with great tranquility; the imperial tragedy pleases common auditors only by its pomp of ornament, and grandeur of ideas; and the man whose faculties have been engrossed by business, and whose heart never fluttered but at the rise or fall of stocks, wonders how the attention can be seized, or the affections agitated, by a tale of love.

Those parallel circumstances, and kindred images to which we readily conform our minds, are, above all other writings, to be found in narratives of the lives of particular persons; and therefore no species of writing seems more worthy of cultivation than biography, since none can be more delightful or more useful, none can more certainly enchain the heart by irresistible interest, or more widely diffuse instruction to every diversity of condition.

The general and rapid narratives of history, which involve a thousand fortunes in the business of a day, and complicate[2] innumerable incidents in one great transaction, afford few lessons applicable to private life, which derives its comforts and its wretchedness from the right or wrong management of things, which nothing but their frequency makes considerable, *Parva si non fiunt quotidie*, says Pliny,[3] and which can have no place in those relations which never descend below the consultation of senates, the motions of armies, and the schemes of conspirators.

I have often thought that there has rarely passed a life of which a judicious and faithful narrative would not be useful. For, not only every man has in the

---

1. Brings it near.
2. Join.

3. Pliny the Younger's *Epistles* 3.1. Johnson translates the phrase in the preceding clause.

mighty mass of the world great numbers in the same condition with himself, to whom his mistakes and miscarriages, escapes and expedients, would be of immediate and apparent use; but there is such an uniformity in the state of man, considered apart from adventitious and separable decorations and disguises, that there is scarce any possibility of good or ill, but is common to humankind. A great part of the time of those who are placed at the greatest distance by fortune, or by temper, must unavoidably pass in the same manner; and though, when the claims of nature are satisfied, caprice, and vanity, and accident, begin to produce discriminations and peculiarities, yet the eye is not very heedful or quick, which cannot discover the same causes still[4] terminating their influence in the same effects, though sometimes accelerated, sometimes retarded, or perplexed by multiplied combinations. We are all prompted by the same motives, all deceived by the same fallacies, all animated by hope, obstructed by danger, entangled by desire, and seduced by pleasure.

It is frequently objected to relations of particular lives, that they are not distinguished by any striking or wonderful vicissitudes. The scholar who passed his life among his books, the merchant who conducted only his own affairs, the priest whose sphere of action was not extended beyond that of his duty, are considered as no proper objects of public regard, however they might have excelled in their several stations, whatever might have been their learning, integrity, and piety. But this notion arises from false measures of excellence and dignity, and must be eradicated by considering, that in the esteem of uncorrupted reason, what is of most use is of most value.

It is, indeed, not improper to take honest advantages of prejudice, and to gain attention by a celebrated name; but the business of the biographer is often to pass slightly over those performances and incidents, which produce vulgar greatness, to lead the thoughts into domestic privacies, and display the minute details of daily life, where exterior appendages are cast aside, and men excel each other only by prudence and by virtue. The account of Thuanus[5] is, with great propriety, said by its author to have been written, that it might lay open to posterity the private and familiar character of that man, *cujus ingenium et candorem ex ipsius scriptis sunt olim semper miraturi*, whose candor and genius will to the end of time be by his writings preserved in admiration.

There are many invisible circumstances which, whether we read as inquirers after natural or moral knowledge, whether we intend to enlarge our science, or increase our virtue, are more important than public occurrences. Thus Sallust, the great master of nature, has not forgot, in his account of Catiline,[6] to remark that *his walk was now quick, and again slow*, as an indication of a mind revolving something with violent commotion. Thus the story of Melancthon[7] affords a striking lecture on the value of time, by informing us that when he made an appointment, he expected not only the hour, but the minute to be fixed, that the day might not run out in the idleness of suspense; and all the plans and enterprises of De Witt are now of less impor-

---

4. Always.

5. Jacques-Auguste de Thou (1553–1617), an important French historian, of whom Nicholas Rigault wrote a brief biography, a sentence of which Johnson quotes and translates below.

6. Sallust, a Roman historian of the 1st century B.C.E., wrote an account of Catiline's conspiracy against the Roman state.

7. Camerarius wrote a life of Melancthon, a German theologian of the 16th century.

tance to the world, than that part of his personal character, which represents him as careful of his health, and negligent of his life.[8]

But biography has often been allotted to writers who seem very little acquainted with the nature of their task, or very negligent about the performance. They rarely afford any other account than might be collected from public papers, but imagine themselves writing a life when they exhibit a chronological series of actions or preferments; and so little regard the manners or behavior of their heroes, that more knowledge may be gained of a man's real character, by a short conversation with one of his servants, than from a formal and studied narrative, begun with his pedigree, and ended with his funeral.

If now and then they condescend to inform the world of particular facts, they are not always so happy as to select the most important. I know not well what advantage posterity can receive from the only circumstance by which Tickell has distinguished Addison from the rest of mankind, the irregularity of his pulse:[9] nor can I think myself overpaid for the time spent in reading the life of Malherbe, by being enabled to relate, after the learned biographer,[1] that Malherbe had two predominant opinions; one, that the looseness of a single woman might destroy all her boast of ancient descent; the other, that the French beggars made use very improperly and barbarously of the phrase *noble gentleman*, because either word included the sense of both.

There are, indeed, some natural reasons why these narratives are often written by such as were not likely to give much instruction or delight, and why most accounts of particular persons are barren and useless. If a life be delayed till interest and envy are at an end, we may hope for impartiality, but must expect little intelligence;[2] for the incidents which give excellence to biography are of a volatile and evanescent kind, such as soon escape the memory, and are rarely transmitted by tradition. We know how few can portray a living acquaintance, except by his most prominent and observable particularities, and the grosser features of his mind; and it may be easily imagined how much of this little knowledge may be lost in imparting it, and how soon a succession of copies will lose all resemblance of the original.

If the biographer writes from personal knowledge, and makes haste to gratify the public curiosity, there is danger lest his interest, his fear, his gratitude, or his tenderness, overpower his fidelity, and tempt him to conceal, if not to invent. There are many who think it an act of piety to hide the faults or failings of their friends, even when they can no longer suffer by their detection; we therefore see whole ranks of characters adorned with uniform panegyric, and not to be known from one another, but by extrinsic and casual circumstances. "Let me remember," says Hale, "when I find myself inclined to pity a criminal, that there is likewise a pity due to the country."[3] If we owe regard to the memory of the dead, there is yet more respect to be paid to knowledge, to virtue, and to truth.

8. Sir William Temple, characterizing the Dutch statesman John De Witt.
9. From Thomas Tickell's preface to Addision's *Works* (1721).
1. The life of the French poet François de Malherbe (1555–1628) was written by Honorat de Racan.
2. Information.
3. From Gilbert Burnet's *Life and Death of Sir Matthew Hale* (1682).

A Dictionary of the English Language   Before Johnson, no standard dictionary of the English language existed. The lack had troubled speakers of English for some time, both because Italian and French academies had produced major dictionaries of their own tongues and because, in the absence of any authority, English seemed likely to change utterly from one generation to another. Many eighteenth-century authors feared that their own language would soon become obsolete: as Alexander Pope wrote in *An Essay on Criticism,*

> Our sons their fathers' failing language see,
> And such as Chaucer is, shall Dryden be.

A dictionary could help retard such change, and commercially it would be a book that everyone would need to buy. In 1746 a group of London publishers commissioned Johnson, still an unknown author, to undertake the project. He hoped to finish it in three years; it took him nine. But the quantity and quality of work he accomplished, aided only by six part-time assistants, made him famous as "Dictionary Johnson." The *Dictionary* remained a standard reference book for one hundred years.

Johnson's achievement is notable in three respects: its size (forty thousand words), the wealth of illustrative quotations, and the excellence of the definitions. No earlier English dictionary rivaled the scope of Johnson's two large folio volumes. About 114,000 quotations, gathered from the best English writers from Sidney to the eighteenth century, exemplify the usage of words as well as their meanings. Above all, it was the definitions, however, that established the authority of Johnson's *Dictionary.* A small selection is only too likely to concentrate on a few amusing or notorious definitions, but the great majority are full, clear, and totally free from eccentricity. Indeed, many of them are still repeated in modern dictionaries. Language, Johnson knew, cannot be fixed once and for all; many of the words he defines have radically changed meaning since the eighteenth century. Yet Johnson did more than any other person of his time to preserve the ideal of a standard English.

From A Dictionary of the English Language

From *Preface*

* * *

A large work is difficult because it is large, even though all its parts might singly be performed with facility; where there are many things to be done, each must be allowed its share of time and labor, in the proportion only which it bears to the whole; nor can it be expected that the stones which form the dome of a temple should be squared and polished like the diamond of a ring.

Of the event of this work, for which, having labored it with so much application, I cannot but have some degree of parental fondness, it is natural to form conjectures. Those who have been persuaded to think well of my design will require that it should fix our language, and put a stop to those alterations which time and chance have hitherto been suffered to make in it without opposition. With this consequence I will confess that I flattered myself for a while;[1] but now begin to fear that I have indulged expectation which neither reason nor experience can justify. When we see men grow old and die at a

---

1. Johnson's Plan (1747) had called for "a dictionary by which the pronunciation of our language may be fixed, and its attainment facilitated; by which its purity may be preserved, its use ascertained, and its duration lengthened."

certain time one after another, from century to century, we laugh at the elixir that promises to prolong life to a thousand years; and with equal justice may the lexicographer be derided, who being able to produce no example of a nation that has preserved their words and phrases from mutability, shall imagine that his dictionary can embalm his language and secure it from corruption and decay, that it is in his power to change sublunary nature, or clear the world at once from folly, vanity, and affectation.

With this hope, however, academies have been instituted, to guard the avenues of their languages, to retain fugitives, and repulse intruders; but their vigilance and activity have hitherto been vain; sounds are too volatile and subtle for legal restraints; to enchain syllables, and to lash the wind, are equally the undertakings of pride, unwilling to measure its desires by its strength. The French language has visibly changed under the inspection of the academy;[2] the style of Amelot's translation of father Paul is observed by Le Courayer to be *un peu passé;*[3] and no Italian will maintain that the diction of any modern writer is not perceptibly different from that of Boccace, Machiavel, or Caro.[4]

Total and sudden transformations of a language seldom happen; conquests and migrations are now very rare: but there are other causes of change, which, though slow in their operation, and invisible in their progress, are perhaps as much superior to human resistance as the revolutions of the sky, or intumescence[5] of the tide. Commerce, however necessary, however lucrative, as it depraves the manners, corrupts the language; they that have frequent intercourse with strangers, to whom they endeavor to accommodate themselves, must in time learn a mingled dialect, like the jargon which serves the traffickers[6] on the Mediterranean and Indian coasts. This will not always be confined to the exchange, the warehouse, or the port, but will be communicated by degrees to other ranks of the people, and be at last incorporated with the current speech.

There are likewise internal causes equally forcible. The language most likely to continue long without alteration would be that of a nation raised a little, and but a little, above barbarity, secluded from strangers, and totally employed in procuring the conveniencies of life; either without books, or, like some of the Mahometan countries, with very few: men thus busied and unlearned, having only such words as common use requires, would perhaps long continue to express the same notions by the same signs. But no such constancy can be expected in a people polished by arts, and classed by subordination, where one part of the community is sustained and accommodated by the labor of the other. Those who have much leisure to think, will always be enlarging the stock of ideas, and every increase of knowledge, whether real or fancied, will produce new words, or combinations of words. When the mind is unchained from necessity, it will range after convenience; when it is left at large in the fields of speculation, it will shift opinions; as any custom is disused, the words that expressed it must

2. The French academy, founded to purify the French language, had produced a dictionary in 1694; but revisions were necessary within a few years.

3. A bit old-fashioned (French). Le Courayer's translation (1736) of Father Paolo Sarpi's *History of the Council of Trent* superseded Amelot's (1683).

4. Like Boccaccio (1313–1375) and Machiavelli (1469–1527), Annibale Caro (1507–1566) was a classic Italian stylist whose work had preceded the dictionary published in 1612 by the Italian academy.

5. Swelling.

6. Traders.

perish with it; as any opinion grows popular, it will innovate speech in the same proportion as it alters practice.

As by the cultivation of various sciences, a language is amplified, it will be more furnished with words deflected from their original sense; the geometrician will talk of a courtier's zenith, or the eccentric virtue of a wild hero, and the physician of sanguine expectations and phlegmatic delays.[7] Copiousness of speech will give opportunities to capricious choice, by which some words will be preferred, and others degraded; vicissitudes of fashion will enforce the use of new, or extend the signification of known terms. The tropes[8] of poetry will make hourly encroachments, and the metaphorical will become the current sense: pronunciation will be varied by levity or ignorance, and the pen must at length comply with the tongue; illiterate writers will at one time or other, by public infatuation, rise into renown, who, not knowing the original import of words, will use them with colloquial licentiousness, confound distinction, and forget propriety. As politeness increases, some expressions will be considered as too gross and vulgar for the delicate, others as too formal and ceremonious for the gay and airy; new phrases are therefore adopted, which must, for the same reasons, be in time dismissed. Swift, in his petty treatise on the English language,[9] allows that new words must sometimes be introduced, but proposes that none should be suffered to become obsolete. But what makes a word obsolete, more than general agreement to forbear it? and how shall it be continued, when it conveys an offensive idea, or recalled again into the mouths of mankind, when it has once by disuse become unfamiliar, and by unfamiliarity unpleasing.

There is another cause of alteration more prevalent than any other, which yet in the present state of the world cannot be obviated. A mixture of two languages will produce a third distinct from both, and they will always be mixed, where the chief part of education, and the most conspicuous accomplishment, is skill in ancient or in foreign tongues. He that has long cultivated another language, will find its words and combinations crowd upon his memory; and haste or negligence, refinement or affectation, will obtrude borrowed terms and exotic expressions.

The great pest of speech is frequency of translation. No book was ever turned from one language into another, without imparting something of its native idiom; this is the most mischievous and comprehensive innovation; single words may enter by thousands, and the fabric of the tongue continue the same, but new phraseology changes much at once; it alters not the single stones of the building, but the order[1] of the columns. If an academy should be established for the cultivation of our style, which I, who can never wish to see dependence multiplied, hope the spirit of English liberty will hinder or destroy, let them, instead of compiling grammars and dictionaries, endeavor with all their influence to stop the license of translators, whose idleness and ignorance, if it be suffered to proceed, will reduce us to babble a dialect of France.

---

7. "Sanguine" and "phlegmatic" once referred only to the physiological predominance of blood or phlegm. "Zenith" (the point of the sky directly overhead) and "eccentric" (deviating from the center) were originally astronomical and geometrical terms.
8. "A change of a word from its original significa-

tion" (Johnson's *Dictionary*).
9. "A Proposal for Correcting, Improving, and Ascertaining the English Tongue" (1712). "Petty": little.
1. Architectural mode (Doric, etc.), which determines the style and proportions of columns.

If the changes that we fear be thus irresistible, what remains but to acquiesce with silence, as in the other insurmountable distresses of humanity? It remains that we retard what we cannot repel, that we palliate what we cannot cure. Life may be lengthened by care, though death cannot be ultimately defeated: tongues, like governments, have a natural tendency to degeneration; we have long preserved our constitution, let us make some struggles for our language.

In hope of giving longevity to that which its own nature forbids to be immortal, I have devoted this book, the labor of years, to the honor of my country, that we may no longer yield the palm of philology without a contest to the nations of the continent. The chief glory of every people arises from its authors: whether I shall add anything by my own writings to the reputation of English literature, must be left to time. Much of my life has been lost under the pressures of disease; much has been trifled away; and much has always been spent in provision for the day that was passing over me; but I shall not think my employment useless or ignoble, if by my assistance foreign nations, and distant ages, gain access to the propagators of knowledge, and understand the teachers of truth; if my labors afford light to the repositories of science, and add celebrity to Bacon, to Hooker, to Milton, and to Boyle.[2]

When I am animated by this wish, I look with pleasure on my book, however defective; and deliver it to the world with the spirit of a man that has endeavored well. That it will immediately become popular I have not promised to myself: a few wild blunders and risible absurdities, from which no work of such multiplicity was ever free, may for a time furnish folly with laughter, and harden ignorance in contempt; but useful diligence will at last prevail, and there never can be wanting some who distinguish desert;[3] who will consider that no dictionary of a living tongue ever can be perfect, since while it is hastening to publication, some words are budding, and some falling away; that a whole life cannot be spent upon syntax and etymology, and that even a whole life would not be sufficient; that he, whose design includes whatever language can express, must often speak of what he does not understand; that a writer will sometimes be hurried by eagerness to the end, and sometimes faint with weariness under a task, which Scaliger compares to the labors of the anvil and the mine;[4] that what is obvious is not always known, and what is known is not always present; that sudden fits of inadvertency will surprise vigilance, slight avocations[5] will reduce attention, and casual eclipses of the mind will darken learning; and that the writer shall often in vain trace his memory at the moment of need, for that which yesterday he knew with intuitive readiness, and which will come uncalled into his thoughts tomorrow.

In this work, when it shall be found that much is omitted, let it not be forgotten that much likewise is performed; and though no book was ever spared out of tenderness to the author, and the world is little solicitous to know whence proceeded the faults of that which it condemns; yet it may gratify

2. Leading physicist and chemist (1627–1691). "Science": knowledge. Richard Hooker wrote *The Laws of Ecclesiastical Polity* (1594–97), a famous defense of the Church of England.
3. Merit.

4. Joseph Justus Scaliger (1540–1609), a great scholar and lexicographer, wrote Latin verses suggesting that criminals should be condemned to lexicography.
5. Whatever calls one aside.

curiosity to inform it, that the *English Dictionary* was written with little assistance of the learned, and without any patronage of the great;[6] not in the soft obscurities of retirement, or under the shelter of academic bowers, but amidst inconvenience and distraction, in sickness and in sorrow: and it may repress the triumph of malignant criticism to observe, that if our language is not here fully displayed, I have only failed in an attempt which no human powers have hitherto completed. If the lexicons of ancient tongues, now immutably fixed, and comprised in a few volumes, be yet, after the toil of successive ages, inadequate and delusive; if the aggregated knowledge and cooperating diligence of the Italian academicians did not secure them from the censure of Beni;[7] if the embodied critics of France, when fifty years had been spent upon their work, were obliged to change its economy,[8] and give their second edition another form, I may surely be contented without the praise of perfection, which, if I could obtain, in this gloom of solitude, what would it avail me? I have protracted my work till most of those whom I wished to please have sunk into the grave,[9] and success and miscarriage are empty sounds: I therefore dismiss it with frigid tranquility, having little to fear or hope from censure or from praise.

[SOME DEFINITIONS: A SMALL ANTHOLOGY][1]

ANTHO'LOGY. *n.*

1. A collection of flowers.

To CANT. *v.*

  To talk in the jargon of particular professions, or in any kind of formal affected language, or with a peculiar and studied tone of voice.

  > Men *cant* endlessly about *materia forma;* and hunt chimeras by rules of
  > art, or dress up ignorance in words of bulk or sound, which may stop
  > up the mouth of inquiry.—*Glanville's Scepsis Scientifica.*

ENTHU'SIASM. *n.*

1. A vain belief of private revelation; a vain confidence of divine favor or communication.

  > *Enthusiasm* is founded neither on reason nor divine revelation, but
  > rises from the conceits of a warmed or overweening brain.—*Locke.*

GE'NIUS. *n.*

1. The protecting or ruling power of men, places, or things.

  > And as I awake, sweet music breathe,
  > Sent by some spirit to mortals good,
  > Or th' unseen *genius* of the wood.—*Milton.*

2. A man endowed with superior faculties.

3. Mental power or faculties.

4. Disposition of nature by which anyone is qualified for some peculiar employment.

5. Nature; disposition.

IMA'GINATION, *n.*

1. Fancy; the power of forming ideal pictures; the power of representing things absent to one's self or others.

---

6. See Johnson's letter to Lord Chesterfield in Boswell's *Life of Johnson* (pp. 1363–64).
7. Paolo Beni's *L'Anticrusca* (1612) violently attacked the first edition of the *Vocabolario* (the Italian dictionary).

8. Organization.
9. Johnson's wife had died three years earlier.
1. Johnson's definitions include etymologies and illustrative quotations, some of which are omitted in this selection.

2. Conception; image in the mind; idea.

3. Contrivance; scheme.

LEXICO'GRAPHER. *n.*

A writer of dictionaries; a harmless drudge, that busies himself in tracing the original, and detailing the signification of words.

MELANCHO'LY. *n.*

1. A disease, supposed to proceed from a redundance of black bile.

2. A kind of madness, in which the mind is always fixed on one object.

3. A gloomy, pensive, discontented temper.

NA'TURE. *n.*

1. An imaginary being supposed to preside over the material and animal world.

> Thou, *nature*, art my goddess; to thy law
> My services are bound.—*Shakespeare.*

2. The native state or properties of anything, by which it is discriminated from others.

3. The constitution of an animated body.

4. Disposition of mind; temper.

5. The regular course of things.

6. The compass of natural existence.

7. Natural affection, or reverence; native sensations.

8. The state or operation of the material world.

9. Sort; species.

10. Sentiments or images adapted to nature, or comfortable to truth and reality.

11. Physics; the science which teaches the qualities of things.

> *Nature* and *nature's* laws lay hid in night,
> God said, Let Newton be, and all was light.—*Pope.*

NE'TWORK. *n.*

Anything reticulated or decussated, at equal distances, with interstices between the intersections.

OATS. *n.*

A grain, which in England is generally given to horses, but in Scotland supports the people.

PA'STERN. *n.*

1. The knee of an horse.[2]

PA'TRON. *n.*

1. One who countenances, supports, or protects. Commonly a wretch who supports with insolence, and is paid with flattery.

PE'NSION. *n.*

An allowance made to anyone without an equivalent. In England it is generally understood to mean pay given to a state hireling for treason to his country.[3]

SA'TIRE. *n.*

A poem in which wickedness or folly is censured. Proper *satire* is distinguished, by the generality of the reflections, from a *lampoon*, which is aimed against a particular person; but they are too frequently confounded.

---

2. "A lady once asked him how he came to define *Pastern* the *knee* of a horse: instead of making an elaborate defense, as she expected, he at once answered, 'Ignorance, Madam, pure ignorance'" (Boswell).

3. In 1762 Johnson was awarded a pension, but he did not revise the definition in later editions.

TO'RY. *n.*

One who adheres to the ancient constitution of the state, and the apostolical hierarchy of the church of England, opposed to a whig.

> The knight is more a *tory* in the country than the town, because it more advances his interest.—*Addison.*

WHIG. *n.*

2. The name of a faction.

> Whoever has a true value for church and state, should avoid the extremes of *whig* for the sake of the former, and the extremes of tory on the account of the latter.—*Swift.*

WIT. *n.*

1. The powers of the mind; the mental faculties; the intellects. This is the original signification.

2. Imagination; quickness of fancy.

3. Sentiments produced by quickness of fancy.

4. A man of fancy.

5. A man of genius.

6. Sense; judgment.

7. In the plural. Sound mind; intellect not crazed.

8. Contrivance; stratagem; power of expedients.

1755

The Preface to Shakespeare This is the finest piece of Shakespeare criticism in the eighteenth century; it culminates a critical tradition that began with John Dryden's remarks on Shakespeare and continued as the plays were edited by Nicholas Rowe, Alexander Pope, Lewis Theobald, and William Warburton. Johnson addresses the standard topics: Shakespeare is the poet of nature, not learning; the creator of characters who spring to life; and a writer whose works express the full range of human passions. But the Preface also takes a fresh look not only at the plays but at the first principles of criticism. Resisting "bardolatry"—uncritical worship of Shakespeare—Johnson points out his faults as well as his virtues and finds that his truth to life, or "just representations of general nature," surpasses that of all other modern writers. The Preface is most original when it attacks the long-standing critical reverence for the unities of time and place. What seems real on the stage, Johnson argues, does not depend on artificial rules but on what the mind is willing to imagine.

Johnson's edition of Shakespeare also contained footnotes and brief introductions to each of the plays. Reprinted here is his afterword to *Othello.*

From The Preface to Shakespeare

[SHAKESPEARE'S EXCELLENCE, GENERAL NATURE]

That praises are without reason lavished on the dead, and that the honors due only to excellence are paid to antiquity, is a complaint likely to be always continued by those who, being able to add nothing to truth, hope for eminence from the heresies of paradox; or those who, being forced by disappointment upon consolatory expedients, are willing to hope from posterity what the present age refuses, and flatter themselves that the regard which is yet denied by envy will be at last bestowed by time.

Antiquity, like every other quality that attracts the notice of mankind, has undoubtedly votaries that reverence it not from reason but from prejudice. Some seem to admire indiscriminately whatever has been long preserved, without considering that time has sometimes cooperated with chance; all perhaps are more willing to honor past than present excellence; and the mind contemplates genius through the shades of age, as the eye surveys the sun through artificial opacity. The great contention of criticism is to find the faults of the moderns and the beauties of the ancients. While an author is yet living we estimate his powers by his worst performance; and when he is dead we rate them by his best.

To works, however, of which the excellence is not absolute and definite, but gradual and comparative; to works not raised upon principles demonstrative and scientific, but appealing wholly to observation and experience, no other test can be applied than length of duration and continuance of esteem. What mankind have long possessed they have often examined and compared; and if they persist to value the possession, it is because frequent comparisons have confirmed opinion in its favor. As among the works of nature no man can properly call a river deep or a mountain high, without the knowledge of many mountains and many rivers; so in the productions of genius, nothing can be styled excellent till it has been compared with other works of the same kind. Demonstration[1] immediately displays its power and has nothing to hope or fear from the flux of years; but works tentative and experimental must be estimated by their proportion to the general and collective ability of man, as it is discovered in a long succession of endeavors. Of the first building that was raised, it might be with certainty determined that it was round or square, but whether it was spacious or lofty must have been referred to time. The Pythagorean scale of numbers[2] was at once discovered to be perfect; but the poems of Homer we yet know not to transcend the common limits of human intelligence, but by remarking that nation after nation, and century after century, has been able to do little more than transpose his incidents, new name his characters, and paraphrase his sentiments.

The reverence due to writings that have long subsisted arises, therefore, not from any credulous confidence in the superior wisdom of past ages, or gloomy persuasion of the degeneracy of mankind, but is the consequence of acknowledged and indubitable positions, that what has been longest known has been most considered, and what is most considered is best understood.

The poet of whose works I have undertaken the revision may now begin to assume the dignity of an ancient and claim the privilege of established fame and prescriptive veneration. He has long outlived his century, the term commonly fixed as the test of literary merit.[3] Whatever advantages he might once derive from personal allusions, local customs, or temporary opinions, have for many years been lost; and every topic of merriment or motive of sorrow which the modes of artificial life afforded him now only obscure the scenes which they once illuminated. The effects of favor and competition are at an end; the tradition of his friendships and his enmities has perished; his works

---

1. "The highest degree of deducible or argumental evidence" (Johnson's *Dictionary*).
2. Pythagoras discovered the ratios that determine the principal intervals of the musical scale.
3. Horace's *Epistles* 2.1.39.

support no opinion with arguments nor supply any faction with invectives; they can neither indulge vanity nor gratify malignity; but are read without any other reason than the desire of pleasure, and are therefore praised only as pleasure is obtained; yet, thus unassisted by interest or passion, they have passed through variations of taste and changes of manners, and, as they devolved from one generation to another, have received new honors at every transmission.

But because human judgment, though it be gradually gaining upon certainty, never becomes infallible, and approbation, though long continued, may yet be only the approbation of prejudice or fashion, it is proper to inquire by what peculiarities of excellence Shakespeare has gained and kept the favor of his countrymen.

Nothing can please many, and please long, but just representations of general nature. Particular manners can be known to few, and therefore few only can judge how nearly they are copied. The irregular combinations of fanciful invention may delight awhile by that novelty of which the common satiety of life sends us all in quest; but the pleasures of sudden wonder are soon exhausted, and the mind can only repose on the stability of truth.

Shakespeare is, above all writers, at least above all modern writers, the poet of nature, the poet that holds up to his readers a faithful mirror of manners and of life. His characters are not modified by the customs of particular places, unpracticed by the rest of the world; by the peculiarities of studies or professions, which can operate but upon small numbers; or by the accidents of transient fashions or temporary opinions: they are the genuine progeny of common humanity, such as the world will always supply and observation will always find. His persons act and speak by the influence of those general passions and principles by which all minds are agitated and the whole system of life is continued in motion. In the writings of other poets a character is too often an individual: in those of Shakespeare it is commonly a species.

It is from this wide extension of design that so much instruction is derived. It is this which fills the plays of Shakespeare with practical axioms and domestic wisdom. It was said of Euripides[4] that every verse was a precept; and it may be said of Shakespeare that from his works may be collected a system of civil and economical prudence. Yet his real power is not shown in the splendor of particular passages, but by the progress of his fable[5] and the tenor of his dialogue; and he that tries to recommend him by select quotations will succeed like the pedant in Hierocles[6] who, when he offered his house to sale, carried a brick in his pocket as a specimen.

It will not easily be imagined how much Shakespeare excels in accommodating his sentiments to real life but by comparing him with other authors. It was observed of the ancient schools of declamation that the more diligently they were frequented, the more was the student disqualified for the world, because he found nothing there which he should ever meet in any other place. The same remark may be applied to every stage but that of Shake-

4. The Greek tragic poet (ca. 480–406 B.C.E.). The observation is Cicero's.
5. Plot. "The series or contexture of events which constitute a poem epic or dramatic" (Johnson's *Dictionary*).
6. Hierocles of Alexandria, a Greek philosopher of the 5th century C.E.

speare. The theater, when it is under any other direction, is peopled by such characters as were never seen, conversing in a language which was never heard, upon topics which will never arise in the commerce of mankind. But the dialogue of this author is often so evidently determined by the incident which produces it, and is pursued with so much ease and simplicity, that it seems scarcely to claim the merit of fiction, but to have been gleaned by diligent selection out of common conversation and common occurrences.

Upon every other stage the universal agent is love, by whose power all good and evil is distributed and every action quickened or retarded. To bring a lover, a lady, and a rival into the fable; to entangle them in contradictory obligations, perplex them with oppositions of interest, and harass them with violence of desires inconsistent with each other; to make them meet in rapture, and part in agony; to fill their mouths with hyperbolical joy and outrageous sorrow; to distress them as nothing human ever was distressed; to deliver them as nothing human ever was delivered, is the business of a modern dramatist. For this, probability is violated, life is misrepresented, and language is depraved. But love is only one of many passions; and as it has no great influence upon the sum of life, it has little operation in the dramas of a poet who caught his ideas from the living world and exhibited only what he saw before him. He knew that any other passion, as it was regular or exorbitant, was a cause of happiness or calamity.

Characters thus ample and general were not easily discriminated and preserved; yet perhaps no poet ever kept his personages more distinct from each other. I will not say with Pope that every speech may be assigned to the proper speaker,[7] because many speeches there are which have nothing characteristical; but perhaps though some may be equally adapted to every person, it will be difficult to find that any can be properly transferred from the present possessor to another claimant. The choice is right when there is reason for choice.

Other dramatists can only gain attention by hyperbolical or aggravated characters, by fabulous and unexampled excellence or depravity, as the writers of barbarous romances invigorated the reader by a giant and a dwarf; and he that should form his expectations of human affairs from the play or from the tale would be equally deceived. Shakespeare has no heroes; his scenes are occupied only by men, who act and speak as the reader thinks that he should himself have spoken or acted on the same occasion; even where the agency is supernatural, the dialogue is level with life. Other writers disguise the most natural passions and most frequent incidents so that he who contemplates them in the book will not know them in the world: Shakespeare approximates[8] the remote, and familiarizes the wonderful; the event which he represents will not happen, but, if it were possible, its effects would probably be such as he has assigned; and it may be said that he has not only shown human nature as it acts in real exigencies, but as it would be found in trials to which it cannot be exposed.

This therefore is the praise of Shakespeare, that his drama is the mirror of life; that he who has mazed his imagination in following the phantoms which other writers raise up before him, may here be cured of his delirious ecstasies by reading human sentiments in human language, by scenes from

7. In the preface to his edition of Shakespeare's plays (1725).
8. Brings near.

which a hermit may estimate the transactions of the world, and a confessor predict the progress of the passions.

[SHAKESPEARE'S FAULTS. THE THREE DRAMATIC UNITIES]

Shakespeare with his excellencies has likewise faults, and faults sufficient to obscure and overwhelm any other merit. I shall show them in the proportion in which they appear to me, without envious malignity or superstitious veneration. No question can be more innocently discussed than a dead poet's pretensions to renown; and little regard is due to that bigotry which sets candor[9] higher than truth.

His first defect is that to which may be imputed most of the evil in books or in men. He sacrifices virtue to convenience, and is so much more careful to please than to instruct that he seems to write without any moral purpose. From his writings indeed a system of social duty may be selected, for he that thinks reasonably must think morally, but his precepts and axioms drop casually from him; he makes no just distribution of good or evil, nor is always careful to show in the virtuous a disapprobation of the wicked; he carries his persons indifferently through right and wrong, and at the close dismisses them without further care, and leaves their examples to operate by chance. This fault the barbarity of his age cannot extenuate; for it is always a writer's duty to make the world better, and justice is a virtue independent on time or place.

The plots are often so loosely formed that a very slight consideration may improve them, and so carelessly pursued that he seems not always fully to comprehend his own design. He omits opportunities of instructing or delighting which the train of his story seems to force upon him, and apparently rejects those exhibitions which would be more affecting for the sake of those which are more easy.

It may be observed that in many of his plays the latter part is evidently neglected. When he found himself near the end of his work, and in view of his reward, he shortened the labor to snatch the profit. He therefore remits his efforts where he should most vigorously exert them, and his catastrophe is improbably produced or imperfectly represented.

He had no regard to distinction of time or place, but gives to one age or nation, without scruple, the customs, institutions, and opinions of another, at the expense not only of likelihood but of possibility. These faults Pope has endeavored, with more zeal than judgment, to transfer to his imagined interpolators. We need not wonder to find Hector quoting Aristotle, when we see the loves of Theseus and Hippolyta combined with the Gothic mythology of fairies.[1] Shakespeare, indeed, was not the only violator of chronology, for in the same age Sidney, who wanted not the advantages of learning, has, in his *Arcadia*, confounded the pastoral with the feudal times, the days of innocence, quiet, and security with those of turbulence, violence, and adventure.

In his comic scenes he is seldom very successful when he engages his characters in reciprocations of smartness and contests of sarcasm; their jests are commonly gross, and their pleasantry licentious; neither his gentlemen nor his ladies have much delicacy, nor are sufficiently distinguished from his clowns[2]

---

9. Kindness.
1. In *Troilus and Cressida* 2.2.166 and in *A Mid-*

summer Night's Dream, respectively.
2. Rustics.

by any appearance of refined manners. Whether he represented the real conversation of his time is not easy to determine: the reign of Elizabeth is commonly supposed to have been a time of stateliness, formality, and reserve; yet perhaps the relaxations of that severity were not very elegant. There must, however, have been always some modes of gaiety preferable to others, and a writer ought to choose the best.

In tragedy his performance seems constantly to be worse as his labor is more. The effusions of passion, which exigence forces out, are for the most part striking and energetic; but whenever he solicits his invention, or strains his faculties, the offspring of his throes is tumor,[3] meanness, tediousness, and obscurity.

In narration he affects a disproportionate pomp of diction and a wearisome train of circumlocution, and tells the incident imperfectly in many words which might have been more plainly delivered in few. Narration in dramatic poetry is naturally tedious, as it is unanimated and inactive, and obstructs the progress of the action; it should therefore always be rapid and enlivened by frequent interruption. Shakespeare found it an encumbrance, and instead of lightening it by brevity, endeavored to recommend it by dignity and splendor.

His declamations or set speeches are commonly cold and weak, for his power was the power of nature; when he endeavored, like other tragic writers, to catch opportunities of amplification and, instead of inquiring what the occasion demanded, to show how much his stores of knowledge could supply, he seldom escapes without the pity or resentment of his reader.

It is incident to him to be now and then entangled with an unwieldy sentiment which he cannot well express, and will not reject; he struggles with it awhile, and, if it continues stubborn, comprises it in words such as occur, and leaves it to be disentangled and evolved[4] by those who have more leisure to bestow upon it.

Not that always where the language is intricate the thought is subtle, or the image always great where the line is bulky; the equality of words to things is very often neglected, and trivial sentiments and vulgar[5] ideas disappoint the attention, to which they are recommended by sonorous epithets and swelling figures.

But the admirers of this great poet have most reason to complain when he approaches nearest to his highest excellence, and seems fully resolved to sink them in dejection and mollify them with tender emotions by the fall of greatness, the danger of innocence, or the crosses of love. What he does best, he soon ceases to do. He is not long soft and pathetic without some idle conceit or contemptible equivocation. He no sooner begins to move than he counteracts himself; and terror and pity, as they are rising in the mind, are checked and blasted by sudden frigidity.

A quibble[6] is to Shakespeare what luminous vapors are to the traveler: he follows it at all adventures; it is sure to lead him out of his way, and sure to engulf him in the mire. It has some malignant power over his mind, and its fascinations are irresistible. Whatever be the dignity or profundity of his disquisitions, whether he be enlarging knowledge or exalting affection, whether he be amusing[7] attention with incidents, or enchaining it in suspense, let but

3. Inflated grandeur, false magnificence.
4. Unfolded.
5. "Mean; low; being of the common rate" (Johnson's *Dictionary*).

6. Pun.
7. "To entertain with tranquility; to fill with thoughts that engage the mind, without distracting it" (Johnson's *Dictionary*).

a quibble spring up before him, and he leaves his work unfinished. A quibble is the golden apple for which he will always turn aside from his career[8] or stoop from his elevation. A quibble, poor and barren as it is, gave him such delight that he was content to purchase it by the sacrifice of reason, propriety, and truth. A quibble was to him the fatal Cleopatra for which he lost the world, and was content to lose it.

It will be thought strange that in enumerating the defects of this writer, I have not yet mentioned his neglect of the unities; his violation of those laws which have been instituted and established by the joint authority of poets and critics.

For his other deviations from the art of writing, I resign him to critical justice without making any other demand in his favor than that which must be indulged to all human excellence: that his virtues be rated with his failings. But from the censure which this irregularity may bring upon him I shall, with due reverence to that learning which I must oppose, adventure to try how I can defend him.

His histories, being neither tragedies nor comedies, are not subject to any of their laws; nothing more is necessary to all the praise which they expect than that the changes of action be so prepared as to be understood; that the incidents be various and affecting, and the characters consistent, natural, and distinct. No other unity is intended, and therefore none is to be sought.

In his other works he has well enough preserved the unity of action. He has not, indeed, an intrigue regularly perplexed and regularly unraveled: he does not endeavor to hide his design only to discover it, for this is seldom the order of real events, and Shakespeare is the poet of nature: but his plan has commonly what Aristotle requires,[9] a beginning, a middle, and an end; one event is concatenated with another, and the conclusion follows by easy consequence. There are, perhaps, some incidents that might be spared, as in other poets there is much talk that only fills up time upon the stage; but the general system makes gradual advances, and the end of the play is the end of expectation.

To the unities of time and place he has shown no regard; and perhaps a nearer view of the principles on which they stand will diminish their value and withdraw from them the veneration which, from the time of Corneille,[1] they have very generally received, by discovering that they have given more trouble to the poet than pleasure to the auditor.

The necessity of observing the unities of time and place arises from the supposed necessity of making the drama credible. The critics hold it impossible that an action of months or years can be possibly believed to pass in three hours; or that the spectator can suppose himself to sit in the theater while ambassadors go and return between distant kings, while armies are levied and towns besieged, while an exile wanders and returns, or till he whom they saw courting his mistress shall lament the untimely fall of his son. The mind revolts from evident falsehood, and fiction loses its force when it departs from the resemblance of reality.

8. Course of action; the ground on which a race is run. In Greek legend Atalanta refused to marry any man who could not defeat her in a foot race. Hippomenes won her by dropping, as he ran, three of the golden apples of the Hesperides, which she paused to pick up.
9. *Poetics* 7.
1. Pierre Corneille (1606–1684), the French playwright, discussed the unities in his *Discours des trois unités* (1660).

From the narrow limitation of time necessarily arises the contraction of place. The spectator who knows that he saw the first act at Alexandria cannot suppose that he sees the next at Rome, at a distance to which not the dragons of Medea[2] could, in so short a time, have transported him; he knows with certainty that he has not changed his place; and he knows that place cannot change itself, that what was a house cannot become a plain, that what was Thebes can never be Persepolis.

Such is the triumphant language with which a critic exults over the misery of an irregular poet, and exults commonly without resistance or reply. It is time, therefore, to tell him by the authority of Shakespeare that he assumes, as an unquestionable principle, a position which, while his breath is forming it into words, his understanding pronounces to be false. It is false that any representation is mistaken for reality; that any dramatic fable in its materiality was ever credible or, for a single moment, was ever credited.

The objection arising from the impossibility of passing the first hour at Alexandria and the next at Rome supposes that when the play opens the spectator really imagines himself at Alexandria, and believes that his walk to the theater has been a voyage to Egypt, and that he lives in the days of Antony and Cleopatra. Surely he that imagines this may imagine more. He that can take the stage at one time for the palace of the Ptolemies may take it in half an hour for the promontory of Actium. Delusion, if delusion be admitted, has no certain limitation; if the spectator can be once persuaded that his old acquaintances are Alexander and Caesar, that a room illuminated with candles is the plain of Pharsalia or the bank of Granicus, he is in a state of elevation above the reach of reason or of truth, and from the heights of empyrean poetry may despise the circumscriptions of terrestrial nature. There is no reason why a mind thus wandering in ecstasy should count the clock, or why an hour should not be a century in that calenture[3] of the brain that can make the stage a field.

The truth is that the spectators are always in their senses, and know, from the first act to the last, that the stage is only a stage, and that the players are only players. They came to hear a certain number of lines recited with just gesture and elegant modulation. The lines relate to some action, and an action must be in some place; but the different actions that complete a story may be in places very remote from each other; and where is the absurdity of allowing that space to represent first Athens, and then Sicily, which was always known to be neither Sicily nor Athens but a modern theater?

By supposition, as place is introduced, time may be extended; the time required by the fable elapses, for the most part, between the acts; for, of so much of the action as is represented, the real and poetical duration is the same. If, in the first act, preparations for war against Mithridates are represented to be made in Rome, the event of the war may, without absurdity, be represented, in the catastrophe, as happening in Pontus; we know that there is neither war nor preparation for war; we know that we are neither in Rome nor Pontus, that neither Mithridates nor Lucullus are before us. The drama exhibits successive imitations of successive actions; and why may not the second imitation represent an action that happened years after the first,

---

2. According to legend, Medea fled the scene of her crimes in a chariot drawn by dragons.
3. A delirium produced by tropical heat, which causes sailors to leap into the sea under the delusion that it is a green field.

if it be so connected with it that nothing but time can be supposed to intervene? Time is, of all modes of existence, most obsequious[4] to the imagination; a lapse of years is as easily conceived as a passage of hours. In contemplation we easily contract the time of real actions, and therefore willingly permit it to be contracted when we only see their imitation.

It will be asked how the drama moves if it is not credited. It is credited with all the credit due to a drama. It is credited, whenever it moves, as a just picture of a real original; as representing to the auditor what he would himself feel if he were to do or suffer what is there feigned to be suffered or to be done. The reflection that strikes the heart is not that the evils before us are real evils, but that they are evils to which we ourselves may be exposed. If there be any fallacy, it is not that we fancy the players, but that we fancy ourselves, unhappy for a moment; but we rather lament the possibility than suppose the presence of misery, as a mother weeps over her babe when she remembers that death may take it from her. The delight of tragedy proceeds from our consciousness of fiction; if we thought murders and treasons real, they would please no more.

Imitations produce pain or pleasure, not because they are mistaken for realities, but because they bring realities to mind. When the imagination is recreated[5] by a painted landscape, the trees are not supposed capable to give us shade or the fountains coolness; but we consider how we should be pleased with such fountains playing beside us and such woods waving over us. We are agitated in reading the history of *Henry the Fifth;* yet no man takes his book for the field of Agincourt. A dramatic exhibition is a book recited with concomitants that increase or diminish its effect. Familiar[6] comedy is often more powerful on the theater than in the page; imperial tragedy is always less. The humor of Petruchio may be heightened by grimace; but what voice or what gesture can hope to add dignity or force to the soliloquy of Cato?[7]

A play read affects the mind like a play acted. It is therefore evident that the action is not supposed to be real; and it follows that between the acts a longer or shorter time may be allowed to pass, and that no more account of space or duration is to be taken by the auditor of a drama than by the reader of a narrative, before whom may pass in an hour the life of a hero or the revolutions of an empire.

Whether Shakespeare knew the unities and rejected them by design or deviated from them by happy ignorance, it is, I think, impossible to decide and useless to inquire. We may reasonably suppose that, when he rose to notice, he did not want[8] the counsels and admonitions of scholars and critics, and that he at last deliberately persisted in a practice which he might have begun by chance. As nothing is essential to the fable but unity of action, and as the unities of time and place arise evidently from false assumptions, and, by circumscribing the extent of the drama, lessen its variety, I cannot think it much to be lamented that they were not known by him, or not observed: nor, if such another poet could arise, should I very vehemently reproach him that his first act passed at Venice and his next in Cyprus.[9] Such violations of rules merely positive[1] become the comprehensive genius

4. "Obedient; compliant" (Johnson's *Dictionary*).
5. Delighted.
6. Domestic.
7. In Addison's tragedy *Cato* (5.1), the hero soliloquizes on immortality shortly before committing

suicide. Petruchio is the hero of Shakespeare's comedy *The Taming of the Shrew.*
8. Lack.
9. As is the case in *Othello.*
1. Arbitrary; not natural.

of Shakespeare, and such censures are suitable to the minute and slender criticism of Voltaire.

> Non usque adeo permiscuit imis
> Longus summa dies, ut non, si voce Metelli
> Serventur leges, malint a Caesare tolli.[2]

Yet when I speak thus slightly of dramatic rules, I cannot but recollect how much wit and learning may be produced against me; before such authorities I am afraid to stand: not that I think the present question one of those that are to be decided by mere authority, but because it is to be suspected that these precepts have not been so easily received but for better reasons than I have yet been able to find. The result of my inquiries, in which it would be ludicrous to boast of impartiality, is that the unities of time and place are not essential to a just drama, that though they may sometimes conduce to pleasure, they are always to be sacrificed to the nobler beauties of variety and instruction; and that a play written with nice observation of critical rules is to be contemplated as an elaborate curiosity, as the product of superfluous and ostentatious art, by which is shown rather what is possible than what is necessary.

He that without diminution of any other excellence shall preserve all the unities unbroken deserves the like applause with the architect who shall display all the orders of architecture in a citadel without any deduction for its strength; but the principal beauty of a citadel is to exclude the enemy, and the greatest graces of a play are to copy nature and instruct life. * * *

[OTHELLO]

The beauties of this play impress themselves so strongly upon the attention of the reader that they can draw no aid from critical illustration. The fiery openness of Othello, magnanimous, artless, and credulous, boundless in his confidence, ardent in his affection, inflexible in his resolution, and obdurate in his revenge; the cool malignity of Iago, silent in his resentment, subtle in his designs, and studious at once of his interest and his vengeance; the soft simplicity of Desdemona, confident of merit and conscious of innocence, her artless perseverance in her suit, and her slowness to suspect that she can be suspected are such proofs of Shakespeare's skill in human nature as, I suppose, it is vain to seek in any modern writer. The gradual progress which Iago makes in the Moor's conviction and the circumstances which he employs to inflame him are so artfully natural that, though it will perhaps not be said of him as he says of himself that he is "a man not easily jealous," yet we cannot but pity him when at last we find him "perplexed in the extreme."

There is always danger lest wickedness conjoined with abilities should steal upon[3] esteem, though it misses of approbation; but the character of Iago is so conducted that he is from the first scene to the last hated and despised.

Even the inferior characters of this play would be very conspicuous in any other piece, not only for their justness but their strength. Cassio is

---

2. Lucan's *Pharsalia* 3.138–40: "The course of time has not wrought such confusion that the laws would not rather be trampled on by Caesar than saved by Metellus."
3. Imperceptibly gain.

brave, benevolent, and honest, ruined only by his want of stubbornness to resist an insidious invitation. Roderigo's suspicious credulity and impatient submission to the cheats which he sees practiced upon him and which by persuasion he suffers to be repeated exhibit a strong picture of a weak mind betrayed by unlawful desires to a false friend; and the virtue of Emilia is such as we often find worn loosely but not cast off, easy to commit small crimes but quickened and alarmed at atrocious villainies.

The scenes from the beginning to the end are busy, varied by happy interchanges[4], and regularly promoting the progression of the story; and the narrative in the end[5], though it tells but what is known already, yet is necessary to produce the death of Othello.

Had the scene opened in Cyprus and the preceding incidents been occasionally[6] related, there had been little wanting to a drama of the most exact and scrupulous regularity.[7]

1765

FROM LIVES OF THE POETS

From Milton[1]

["LYCIDAS"]

One of the poems on which much praise has been bestowed is *Lycidas;* of which the diction is harsh, the rhymes uncertain, and the numbers[2] unpleasing. What beauty there is, we must therefore seek in the sentiments and images. It is not to be considered as the effusion of real passion; for passion runs not after remote allusions and obscure opinions. Passion plucks no berries from the myrtle and ivy, nor calls upon Arethuse and Mincius, nor tells of "rough satyrs and fauns with cloven heel." Where there is leisure for fiction there is little grief.

In this poem there is no nature, for there is no truth; there is no art, for there is nothing new. Its form is that of a pastoral, easy, vulgar, and therefore disgusting:[3] whatever images it can supply are long ago exhausted; and its inherent improbability always forces dissatisfaction on the mind. When Cowley tells of Hervey that they studied together,[4] it is easy to suppose how much he must miss the companion of his labors and the partner of his discoveries; but what image of tenderness can be excited by these lines!

> We drove afield, and both together heard
> What time the grayfly winds her sultry horn,
> Battening our flocks with the fresh dews of night.

---

4. Apt successions of actions and events.
5. Concluding explanation to Othello of Iago's plots.
6. When the chance arose.
7. Adherence to rules of good drama.
1. Johnson's treatment of Milton as man and poet offended many ardent Miltonians in his own day and damaged his reputation as a critic in the following century. He did not admire Milton's character, and he detested his politics and religion.

But no one has praised *Paradise Lost* more handsomely. Especially offensive in the 19th century was his attack on "Lycidas." Johnson disliked modern pastorals, believing that the tradition had been worn threadbare. His views on the genre may be read in *Rambler* no. 36 and no. 37.
2. Versification.
3. Distasteful, because too facile and common.
4. Cowley's "On the Death of Mr. William Hervey" (1656).

We know that they never drove afield, and that they had no flocks to batten; and though it be allowed that the representation may be allegorical, the true meaning is so uncertain and remote that it is never sought because it cannot be known when it is found.

Among the flocks and copses and flowers appear the heathen deities, Jove and Phoebus, Neptune and Aeolus, with a long train of mythological imagery, such as a college easily supplies. Nothing can less display knowledge or less exercise invention than to tell how a shepherd has lost his companion and must now feed his flocks alone, without any judge of his skill in piping; and how one god asks another god what is become of Lycidas, and how neither god can tell. He who thus grieves will excite no sympathy; he who thus praises will confer no honor.

This poem has yet a grosser fault. With these trifling fictions are mingled the most awful and sacred truths, such as ought never to be polluted with such irreverent combinations. The shepherd likewise is now a feeder of sheep, and afterwards an ecclesiastical pastor, a superintendent of a Christian flock. Such equivocations are always unskillful; but here they are indecent,[5] and at least approach to impiety, of which, however, I believe the writer not to have been conscious.

Such is the power of reputation justly acquired that its blaze drives away the eye from nice examination. Surely no man could have fancied that he read *Lycidas* with pleasure had he not known its author.

[*PARADISE LOST*]

Those little pieces may be dispatched without much anxiety; a greater work calls for greater care. I am now to examine *Paradise Lost*, a poem which, considered with respect to design, may claim the first place, and with respect to performance the second, among the productions of the human mind.

By the general consent of critics the first praise of genius is due to the writer of an epic poem, as it requires an assemblage of all the powers which are singly sufficient for other compositions. Poetry is the art of uniting pleasure with truth, by calling imagination to the help of reason. Epic poetry undertakes to teach the most important truths by the most pleasing precepts, and therefore relates some great event in the most affecting manner. History must supply the writer with the rudiments of narration, which he must improve and exalt by a nobler art, must animate by dramatic energy, and diversify by retrospection and anticipation; morality must teach him the exact bounds and different shades of vice and virtue; from policy and the practice of life he has to learn the discriminations of character and the tendency of the passions, either single or combined; and physiology[6] must supply him with illustrations and images. To put these materials to poetical use is required an imagination capable of painting nature and realizing fiction. Nor is he yet a poet till he has attained the whole extension of his language, distinguished all the delicacies of phrase, and all the colors of words, and learned to adjust their different sounds to all the varieties of metrical modulation.

Bossu is of opinion that the poet's first work is to find a *moral*, which his fable is afterwards to illustrate and establish.[7] This seems to have been the

---

5. Unbecoming, lacking in decorum.
6. "The doctrine of the constitution of the works of nature" (Johnson's *Dictionary*).

7. René le Bossu's treatise on the epic poem, *Traité du Poëme Épique*, 1675, was much admired in the late 17th and early 18th centuries.

process only of Milton: the moral of other poems is incidental and consequent; in Milton's only it is essential and intrinsic. His purpose was the most useful and the most arduous: "to vindicate the ways of God to man";[8] to show the reasonableness of religion, and the necessity of obedience to the Divine Law.

To convey this moral there must be a *fable*, a narration artfully constructed, so as to excite curiosity and surprise expectation. In this part of his work Milton must be confessed to have equaled every other poet. He has involved in his account of the Fall of Man the events which preceded, and those that were to follow it: he has interwoven the whole system of theology with such propriety that every part appears to be necessary, and scarcely any recital is wished shorter for the sake of quickening the progress of the main action.

The subject of an epic poem is naturally an event of great importance. That of Milton is not the destruction of a city, the conduct of a colony, or the foundation of an empire. His subject is the fate of worlds, the revolutions of heaven and of earth; rebellion against the Supreme King raised by the highest order of created beings; the overthrow of their host and the punishment of their crime; the creation of a new race of reasonable creatures; their original happiness and innocence, their forfeiture of immortality, and their restoration to hope and peace.

Great events can be hastened or retarded only by persons of elevated dignity. Before the greatness displayed in Milton's poem all other greatness shrinks away. The weakest of his agents are the highest and noblest of human beings, the original parents of mankind; with whose actions the elements consented; on whose rectitude or deviation of will depended the state of terrestrial nature and the condition of all the future inhabitants of the globe.

Of the other agents in the poem, the chief are such as it is irreverence to name on slight occasions. The rest were lower powers;

> of which the least could wield
> Those elements, and arm him with the force
> Of all their regions;[9]

powers which only the control of Omnipotence restrains from laying creation waste, and filling the vast expanse of space with ruin and confusion. To display the motives and actions of beings thus superior, so far as human reason can examine them or human imagination represent them, is the task which this mighty poet has undertaken and performed.

In the examination of epic poems much speculation is commonly employed upon the *characters*. The characters in the *Paradise Lost* which admit of examination are those of angels and of man; of angels good and evil, of man in his innocent and sinful state.

Among the angels the virtue of Raphael is mild and placid, of easy condescension and free communication; that of Michael is regal and lofty, and, as may seem, attentive to the dignity of his own nature. Abdiel and Gabriel appear occasionally, and act as every incident requires; the solitary fidelity of Abdiel is very amiably painted.[1]

---

8. Milton wrote "justify," not "vindicate" (*Paradise Lost* 1.26). It was Pope, in *An Essay on Man* 1.16, who used "vindicate."

9. *Paradise Lost* 6.221.
1. *Paradise Lost* 5.803ff.

Of the evil angels the characters are more diversified. To Satan, as Addison observes, such sentiments are given as suit "the most exalted and most depraved being."[2] Milton has been censured by Clarke for the impiety which sometimes breaks from Satan's mouth. For there are thoughts, as he justly remarks, which no observation of character can justify, because no good man would willingly permit them to pass, however transiently, through his own mind.[3] To make Satan speak as a rebel, without any such expressions as might taint the reader's imagination, was indeed one of the great difficulties in Milton's undertaking, and I cannot but think that he has extricated himself with great happiness. There is in Satan's speeches little that can give pain to a pious ear. The language of rebellion cannot be the same with that of obedience. The malignity of Satan foams in haughtiness and obstinacy; but his expressions are commonly general, and no otherwise offensive than as they are wicked.

The other chiefs of the celestial rebellion are very judiciously discriminated in the first and second books; and the ferocious character of Moloch appears, both in the battle and the council, with exact consistency.

To Adam and Eve are given during their innocence such sentiments as innocence can generate and utter. Their love is pure benevolence and mutual veneration; their repasts are without luxury and their diligence without toil. Their addresses to their Maker have little more than the voice of admiration and gratitude. Fruition left them nothing to ask, and Innocence left them nothing to fear.

But with guilt enter distrust and discord, mutual accusation, and stubborn self-defense; they regard each other with alienated minds, and dread their Creator as the avenger of their transgression. At last they seek shelter in his mercy, soften to repentance, and melt in supplication. Both before and after the Fall the superiority of Adam is diligently sustained.

Of the *probable* and the *marvelous*,[4] two parts of a vulgar epic poem which immerge the critic in deep consideration, the *Paradise Lost* requires little to be said. It contains the history of a miracle, of Creation and Redemption; it displays the power and the mercy of the Supreme Being: the probable therefore is marvelous, and the marvelous is probable. The substance of the narrative is truth; and as truth allows no choice, it is, like necessity, superior to rule. To the accidental or adventitious parts, as to every thing human, some slight exceptions may be made. But the main fabric is immovably supported.

It is justly remarked by Addison[5] that this poem has, by the nature of its subject, the advantage above all others, that it is universally and perpetually interesting. All mankind will, through all ages, bear the same relation to Adam and to Eve, and must partake of that good and evil which extend to themselves.

Of the *machinery*, so called from *theòs apò mēkhanēs*,[6] by which is meant the occasional interposition of supernatural power, another fertile topic of critical remarks, here is no room to speak, because every thing is done under the immediate and visible direction of Heaven; but the rule is so far observed that no part of the action could have been accomplished by any other means.

---

2. *Spectator* 303.
3. John Clarke's *Essay upon Study* (1731).
4. Actions in an epic poem that are wonderful because they exceed the probable.

5. *Spectator* 273.
6. Aristotle's *Poetics* 15.10. *Deus ex machina*, the intervention of supernatural powers into the affairs of humans.

Of *episodes*[7] I think there are only two, contained in Raphael's relation of the war in heaven and Michael's prophetic account of the changes to happen in this world. Both are closely connected with the great action; one was necessary to Adam as a warning, the other as a consolation.

To the completeness or *integrity* of the design nothing can be objected; it has distinctly and clearly what Aristotle requires, a beginning, a middle, and an end. There is perhaps no poem of the same length from which so little can be taken without apparent mutilation. Here are no funeral games, nor is there any long description of a shield. The short digressions at the beginning of the third, seventh, and ninth books might doubtless be spared; but superfluities so beautiful who would take away? or who does not wish that the author of the *Iliad* had gratified succeeding ages with a little knowledge of himself? Perhaps no passages are more frequently or more attentively read than those extrinsic paragraphs; and since the end of poetry is pleasure, that cannot be unpoetical with which all are pleased.

The questions, whether the action of the poem be strictly *one*,[8] whether the poem can be properly termed *heroic*, and who is the hero, are raised by such readers as draw their principles of judgment rather from books than from reason. Milton, though he entitled *Paradise Lost* only a "poem," yet calls it himself "heroic song."[9] Dryden, petulantly and indecently, denies the heroism of Adam because he was overcome; but there is no reason why the hero should not be unfortunate except established practice, since success and virtue do not go necessarily together. Cato is the hero of Lucan, but Lucan's authority will not be suffered by Quintilian to decide. However, if success be necessary, Adam's deceiver was at last crushed; Adam was restored to his Maker's favor, and therefore may securely resume his human rank.

After the scheme and fabric of the poem must be considered its component parts, the sentiments, and the diction.

The *sentiments*, as expressive of manners or appropriated to characters, are for the greater part unexceptionably just. Splendid passages containing lessons of morality or precepts of prudence occur seldom. Such is the original formation of this poem that as it admits no human manners till the Fall, it can give little assistance to human conduct. Its end is to raise the thoughts above sublunary cares or pleasures. Yet the praise of that fortitude, with which Abdiel maintained his singularity of virtue against the scorn of multitudes, may be accommodated to all times; and Raphael's reproof of Adam's curiosity after the planetary motions, with the answer returned by Adam, may be confidently opposed to any rule of life which any poet has delivered.[1]

The thoughts which are occasionally called forth in the progress are such as could only be produced by an imagination in the highest degree fervid and active, to which materials were supplied by incessant study and unlimited curiosity. The heat of Milton's mind might be said to sublimate his learning, to throw off into his work the spirit of science,[2] unmingled with its grosser parts.

He had considered creation in its whole extent, and his descriptions are therefore learned. He had accustomed his imagination to unrestrained

7. Incidental but related narratives within an epic poem. Johnson is citing *Paradise Lost* 5.577ff. and 11.334ff.
8. I.e., a single action dealing with a single character.
9. *Paradise Lost* 9.25.
1. *Paradise Lost* 8.65ff.
2. Knowledge.

indulgence, and his conceptions therefore were extensive. The characteristic quality of his poem is sublimity. He sometimes descends to the elegant, but his element is the great. He can occasionally invest himself with grace; but his natural port is gigantic loftiness. He can please when pleasure is required; but it is his peculiar power to astonish.

He seems to have been well acquainted with his own genius, and to know what it was that Nature had bestowed upon him more bountifully than upon others; the power of displaying the vast, illuminating the splendid, enforcing the awful, darkening the gloomy, and aggravating the dreadful: he therefore chose a subject on which too much could not be said, on which he might tire his fancy without the censure of extravagance.

* * *

The defects and faults of *Paradise Lost*, for faults and defects every work of man must have, it is the business of impartial criticism to discover. As in displaying the excellence of Milton I have not made long quotations, because of selecting beauties there had been no end, I shall in the same general manner mention that which seems to deserve censure; for what Englishman can take delight in transcribing passages, which, if they lessen the reputation of Milton, diminish in some degree the honor of our country?

* * *

The plan of *Paradise Lost* has this inconvenience, that it comprises neither human actions nor human manners. The man and woman who act and suffer are in a state which no other man or woman can ever know. The reader finds no transaction in which he can be engaged, beholds no condition in which he can by any effort of imagination place himself; he has, therefore, little natural curiosity or sympathy.

We all, indeed, feel the effects of Adam's disobedience; we all sin like Adam, and like him must all bewail our offenses; we have restless and insidious enemies in the fallen angels, and in the blessed spirits we have guardians and friends; in the Redemption of mankind we hope to be included: in the description of heaven and hell we are surely interested, as we are all to reside hereafter either in the regions of horror or of bliss.

But these truths are too important to be new: they have been taught to our infancy; they have mingled with our solitary thoughts and familiar conversation, and are habitually interwoven with the whole texture of life. Being therefore not new they raise no unaccustomed emotion in the mind: what we knew before, we cannot learn; what is not unexpected, cannot surprise.

Of the ideas suggested by these awful scenes, from some we recede with reverence, except when stated hours require their association; and from others we shrink with horror, or admit them only as salutary inflictions, as counterpoises to our interests and passions. Such images rather obstruct the career of fancy than incite it.

Pleasure and terror are indeed the genuine sources of poetry; but poetical pleasure must be such as human imagination can at least conceive, and poetical terror such as human strength and fortitude may combat. The good and evil of Eternity are too ponderous for the wings of wit; the mind sinks under them in passive helplessness, content with calm belief and humble adoration.

Known truths however may take a different appearance, and be conveyed to the mind by a new train of intermediate images. This Milton has undertaken, and performed with pregnancy and vigor of mind peculiar to himself. Whoever considers the few radical[3] positions which the Scriptures afforded him will wonder by what energetic operation he expanded them to such extent and ramified them to so much variety, restrained as he was by religious reverence from licentiousness of fiction.

Here is a full display of the united force of study and genius; of a great accumulation of materials, with judgment to digest and fancy to combine them: Milton was able to select from nature or from story, from ancient fable or from modern science, whatever could illustrate or adorn his thoughts. An accumulation of knowledge impregnated his mind, fermented by study and exalted by imagination.

*   *   *

But original deficience cannot be supplied. The want of human interest is always felt. *Paradise Lost* is one of the books which the reader admires and lays down, and forgets to take up again. None ever wished it longer than it is. Its perusal is a duty rather than a pleasure. We read Milton for instruction, retire harassed and overburdened, and look elsewhere for recreation; we desert our master, and seek for companions.

*   *   *

Dryden remarks that Milton has some flats among his elevations.[4] This is only to say that all the parts are not equal. In every work one part must be for the sake of others; a palace must have passages, a poem must have transitions. It is no more to be required that wit should always be blazing than that the sun should always stand at noon. In a great work there is a vicissitude[5] of luminous and opaque parts, as there is in the world a succession of day and night. Milton, when he has expatiated in the sky, may be allowed sometimes to revisit earth; for what other author ever soared so high or sustained his flight so long?

*   *   *

The highest praise of genius is original invention. Milton cannot be said to have contrived the structure of an epic poem, and therefore owes reverence to that vigor and amplitude of mind to which all generations must be indebted for the art of poetical narration, for the texture of the fable, the variation of incidents, the interposition of dialogue, and all the stratagems that surprise and enchain attention. But of all the borrowers from Homer Milton is perhaps the least indebted. He was naturally a thinker for himself, confident of his own abilities and disdainful of help or hindrance; he did not refuse admission to the thoughts or images of his predecessors, but he did not seek them. From his contemporaries he neither courted nor received support; there is in his writings nothing by which the pride of other authors might be gratified or favor gained, no exchange of praise or solicitation of support. His great works were performed under discountenance and in blindness, but difficulties vanished at his touch; he was born for whatever is arduous; and his work is not the greatest of heroic poems, only because it is not the first.

1779

---

3. Original or primary.
4. Preface to *Sylvae*.

5. Regular change.

JAMES BOSWELL
1740–1795

The discovery of a vast number of James Boswell's personal papers (believed until 1925 to have been destroyed by his literary executors) has made it possible to know the author of *The Life of Samuel Johnson* as well as we can know anybody, dead or living. His published letters and journals have made modern readers aware of the serious and absurd, the charming and repellent sides of his character. At twenty-two, when he met Johnson, he had already trained himself to listen, to observe, and to remember until he found time to write it all down. Only rarely did he take notes while a conversation was in progress, since to do so would of course have been a serious breach of basic social etiquette. His unusual memory and disciplined art enabled him to re-create and vividly preserve the many "scenes" that distinguish his journals as they do the *Life*.

Boswell was the eldest son and heir of Alexander Boswell of Auchinleck (pronounced *Affléck*) in Ayrshire, a judge who bore the courtesy title of Lord Auchinleck. As a member of an ancient family and heir to its large estate, Boswell was in the technical sense of the term a gentleman, with entrée into the best circles of Edinburgh and London. By temperament he was unstable, emotionally and sexually skittish. After attending the universities of Edinburgh and Glasgow and studying law in Holland, he made the grand tour of Europe; in Switzerland he met and succeeded in captivating the two foremost French men of letters, Jean-Jacques Rousseau and Voltaire. He visited the beleaguered hero of Corsica, General Pasquale de Paoli, whose revolt against Genoa seemed to European liberals to embody all the civic and military virtues of Republican Rome. Upon returning to England, Boswell wrote *An Account of Corsica* (1768). It was promptly translated into Dutch, German, French, and Italian, and its young author found himself with a considerable European reputation.

By 1769, Boswell was established in what was to prove a successful law practice in Edinburgh and had married his cousin, Margaret Montgomerie. But he kept his ties to London and Johnson. In 1733, he fulfilled a plan first suggested by Johnson ten years earlier to tour the Scottish Highlands and Hebrides together. Almost every aspect of the adventure should have made it impossible. Johnson, nearing his sixty-fourth birthday and after years of sedentary city living, found himself astride a horse in wild country or in open boats in autumn weather. As a devout Anglican, he was an outspoken enemy of the Presbyterian church. As a lover of London, he was a stranger to the primitive life of the Highlands. Moreover, for many years he had half-jestingly, half-seriously, made Scots the butt of his wit. But such were Boswell's social tact and Johnson's vigor and curiosity that the tour was a great success. Johnson's *Journey to the Western Islands of Scotland* (1775) is a thoughtful account of the way that people live in the Hebrides (though some Scots were offended). Boswell's *Journal of a Tour to the Hebrides* (1785), a preliminary study for the *Life*, is a lively and entertaining diary that amused Johnson himself.

In 1786, four years after Johnson's death, Boswell abandoned his Scottish practice; moved to London; was admitted to the English bar (but never actually practiced); and, often depressed and drunken, began the *Life*. Fortunately he had the help and encouragement of the distinguished literary scholar Edmond Malone, without whose guidance he might never have finished his task.

Boswell had an overwhelming amount of material to deal with: his own journals, all of Johnson's letters that he could find, Johnson's voluminous writings, and every scrap of information that his friends would furnish—all of which had to be collected, verified, and somehow reduced to unity. The *Life* is a record not of Johnson alone but of literary England during the last half of the century. But Boswell wrote with his eye on the object, and that object was Samuel Johnson, toward whom such eminent persons as Sir Joshua Reynolds, Edmund Burke, Oliver Goldsmith, Lord Chesterfield—even the king himself—always face. Individual episodes are designed to reveal the great protagonist in a variety of aspects, and the world that Boswell created and populated is sustained by the vitality of his hero.

Boswell's gift is not only narrative but also dramatic. A gifted mimic, he often writes like a theatrical improviser, creating scenes with living people and playing simultaneously the roles of contriver of the dialogue, director of the plot, actor in the drama, and applauding audience—for Boswell kept an eye on his own performance. The quintessence of Boswell as both a social genius and a literary artist is to be found in his description of his visit to Voltaire: "I placed myself by him. I touched the keys in unison with his imagination. I wish you had heard the music."

Although the Johnson of popular legend is largely Boswell's creation, there was much in his life about which Boswell had no firsthand knowledge. At their first meeting, Johnson was fifty-four, a widower, already established as "Dictionary" Johnson and the author of the *Rambler*, and pensioned by the crown. Boswell knew nothing at firsthand of the long, hard years during which Johnson made his way painfully up from obscurity to fame. Hence the *Life* is the portrait of a sage. Its chief glory is conversation: the talk of a man who has experienced broadly, read widely, and observed and reflected on his observations; whose ideas are constantly brought to the test of experience; and whose experience is habitually transmuted into ideas. The book is as large as life and as human as its central character.

From The Life of Samuel Johnson, LL.D.

[PLAN OF THE *LIFE*]

* * * Had Dr. Johnson written his own life, in conformity with the opinion which he has given, that every man's life may be best written by himself;[1] had he employed in the preservation of his own history, that clearness of narration and elegance of language in which he has embalmed so many eminent persons, the world would probably have had the most perfect example of biography that was ever exhibited. But although he at different times, in a desultory manner, committed to writing many particulars of the progress of his mind and fortunes, he never had persevering diligence enough to form them into a regular composition. Of these memorials a few have been preserved; but the greater part was consigned by him to the flames, a few days before his death.

As I had the honor and happiness of enjoying his friendship for upwards of twenty years; as I had the scheme of writing his life constantly in view; as he was well apprised of this circumstance, and from time to time obligingly satisfied my inquiries, by communicating to me the incidents of his early years; as I acquired a facility in recollecting, and was very assiduous in recording, his conversation, of which the extraordinary vigor and vivacity constituted one of the first features of his character; and as I have spared no pains in obtaining materials concerning him, from every quarter where I could discover that they were to be found, and have been favored with the most liberal communications by his friends; I flatter myself that few biographers have entered upon such a work as this with more advantages; independent of literary abilities, in which I am not vain enough to compare myself with some great names who have gone before me in this kind of writing. * * *

Instead of melting down my materials into one mass, and constantly speaking in my own person, by which I might have appeared to have more merit in

1. *Idler* 84.

the execution of the work, I have resolved to adopt and enlarge upon the excellent plan of Mr. Mason, in his *Memoirs of Gray*.[2] Wherever narrative is necessary to explain, connect, and supply, I furnish it to the best of my abilities; but in the chronological series of Johnson's life, which I trace as distinctly as I can, year by year, I produce, wherever it is in my power, his own minutes, letters, or conversation, being convinced that this mode is more lively, and will make my readers better acquainted with him than even most of those were who actually knew him, but could know him only partially; whereas there is here an accumulation of intelligence from various points, by which his character is more fully understood and illustrated.

Indeed I cannot conceive a more perfect mode of writing any man's life than not only relating all the most important events of it in their order, but interweaving what he privately wrote, and said, and thought; by which mankind are enabled as it were to see him live, and to "live o'er each scene"[3] with him, as he actually advanced through the several stages of his life. Had his other friends been as diligent and ardent as I was, he might have been almost entirely preserved. As it is, I will venture to say that he will be seen in this work more completely than any man who has ever yet lived.

And he will be seen as he really was; for I profess to write, not his panegyric, which must be all praise, but his Life; which, great and good as he was, must not be supposed to be entirely perfect. To be as he was, is indeed subject of panegyric enough to any man in this state of being; but in every picture there should be shade as well as light, and when I delineate him without reserve, I do what he himself recommended, both by his precept and his example. * * *

I am fully aware of the objections which may be made to the minuteness on some occasions of my detail of Johnson's conversation, and how happily it is adapted for the petty exercise of ridicule, by men of superficial understanding and ludicrous fancy; but I remain firm and confident in my opinion, that minute particulars are frequently characteristic, and always amusing, when they relate to a distinguished man. I am therefore exceedingly unwilling that anything, however slight, which my illustrious friend thought it worth his while to express, with any degree of point, should perish. * * *

Of one thing I am certain, that considering how highly the small portion which we have of the table-talk and other anecdotes of our celebrated writers is valued, and how earnestly it is regretted that we have not more, I am justified in preserving rather too many of Johnson's sayings, than too few; especially as from the diversity of dispositions it cannot be known with certainty beforehand, whether what may seem trifling to some, and perhaps to the collector himself, may not be most agreeable to many; and the greater number that an author can please in any degree, the more pleasure does there arise to a benevolent mind. * * *

[JOHNSON'S EARLY YEARS, MARRIAGE AND LONDON]

[*1709*] Samuel Johnson was born at Lichfield, in Staffordshire, on the 18th of September, N.S.,[4] 1709; and his initiation into the Christian Church was not delayed; for his baptism is recorded, in the register of St. Mary's parish in

2. William Mason, poet and dramatist, published his life of Thomas Gray in 1774:
3. Pope's Prologue to Addison's *Cato*, line 4.
4. New Style. In 1752, Great Britain adopted the Gregorian calendar, introduced in 1582 by Pope Gregory XIII, to correct the accumulated inaccuracies of Julius Caesar's calendar, which had been in use since 46 B.C.E. By 1752, the error amounted to eleven days. Dates before September 2, 1752, must, therefore, be corrected by adding eleven days or by using the Julian date, followed by "O.S." (Old Style).

that city, to have been performed on the day of his birth. His father is there styled *Gentleman*, a circumstance of which an ignorant panegyrist has praised him for not being proud; when the truth is, that the appellation of Gentleman, though now lost in the indiscriminate assumption of *Esquire*, was commonly taken by those who could not boast of gentility. His father was Michael Johnson, a native of Derbyshire, of obscure extraction, who settled in Lichfield as a bookseller and stationer. His mother was Sarah Ford, descended of an ancient race of substantial yeomanry in Warwickshire. They were well advanced in years when they married, and never had more than two children, both sons; Samuel, their first-born, who lived to be the illustrious character whose various excellence I am to endeavor to record, and Nathanael, who died in his twenty-fifth year.

Mr. Michael Johnson was a man of a large and robust body, and of a strong and active mind; yet, as in the most solid rocks veins of unsound substance are often discovered, there was in him a mixture of that disease, the nature of which eludes the most minute inquiry, though the effects are well known to be a weariness of life, an unconcern about those things which agitate the greater part of mankind, and a general sensation of gloomy wretchedness. From him then his son inherited, with some other qualities, "a vile melancholy," which in his too strong expression of any disturbance of the mind, "made him mad all his life, at least not sober." Michael was, however, forced by the narrowness of his circumstances to be very diligent in business, not only in his shop, but by occasionally resorting to several towns in the neighborhood, some of which were at a considerable distance from Lichfield. At that time booksellers' shops in the provincial towns of England were very rare, so that there was not one even in Birmingham, in which town old Mr. Johnson used to open a shop every market day. He was a pretty good Latin scholar, and a citizen so creditable as to be made one of the magistrates of Lichfield; and, being a man of good sense, and skill in his trade, he acquired a reasonable share of wealth, of which however he afterwards lost the greatest part, by engaging unsuccessfully in a manufacture of parchment. He was a zealous highchurch man and royalist, and retained his attachment to the unfortunate house of Stuart, though he reconciled himself, by casuistical arguments of expediency and necessity, to take the oaths imposed by the prevailing power. * * *

Johnson's mother was a woman of distinguished understanding. I asked his old schoolfellow, Mr. Hector,[5] surgeon of Birmingham, if she was not vain of her son. He said, "She had too much good sense to be vain, but she knew her son's value." Her piety was not inferior to her understanding; and to her must be ascribed those early impressions of religion upon the mind of her son, from which the world afterwards derived so much benefit. He told me that he remembered distinctly having had the first notice of Heaven, "a place to which good people went," and hell, "a place to which bad people went," communicated to him by her, when a little child in bed with her; and that it might be the better fixed in his memory, she sent him to repeat it to Thomas Jackson, their manservant; he not being in the way, this was not done; but there was no occasion for any artificial aid for its preservation. * * *

[1728] That a man in Mr. Michael Johnson's circumstances should think of sending his son to the expensive University of Oxford, at his own charge,

---

5. Edmund Hector, a lifelong friend of Johnson.

seems very improbable. The subject was too delicate to question Johnson upon. But I have been assured by Dr. Taylor[6] that the scheme never would have taken place had not a gentleman of Shropshire, one of his schoolfellows, spontaneously undertaken to support him at Oxford, in the character of his companion; though, in fact, he never received any assistance whatever from that gentleman.

He, however, went to Oxford, and was entered a Commoner of Pembroke College on the 31st of October, 1728, being then in his nineteenth year.

The Reverend Dr. Adams,[7] who afterwards presided over Pembroke College with universal esteem, told me he was present, and gave me some account of what passed on the night of Johnson's arrival at Oxford. On that evening, his father, who had anxiously accompanied him, found means to have him introduced to Mr. Jorden, who was to be his tutor. * * *

His father seemed very full of the merits of his son, and told the company he was a good scholar, and a poet, and wrote Latin verses. His figure and manner appeared strange to them; but he behaved modestly and sat silent, till upon something which occurred in the course of conversation, he suddenly struck in and quoted Macrobius; and thus he gave the first impression of that more extensive reading in which he had indulged himself.

His tutor, Mr. Jorden, fellow of Pembroke, was not, it seems, a man of such abilities as we should conceive requisite for the instructor of Samuel Johnson, who gave me the following account of him. "He was a very worthy man, but a heavy man, and I did not profit much by his instructions. Indeed, I did not attend him much. The first day after I came to college I waited upon him, and then stayed away four. On the sixth, Mr. Jorden asked me why I had not attended. I answered I had been sliding in Christ Church meadow. And this I said with as much *nonchalance* as I am now talking to you. I had no notion that I was wrong or irreverent to my tutor." BOSWELL: "That, Sir, was great fortitude of mind." JOHNSON: "No, Sir; stark insensibility." * * *

[1729] The "morbid melancholy," which was lurking in his constitution, and to which we may ascribe those particularities and that aversion to regular life, which, at a very early period, marked his character, gathered such strength in his twentieth year as to afflict him in a dreadful manner. While he was at Lichfield, in the college vacation of the year 1729, he felt himself overwhelmed with an horrible hypochondria,[8] with perpetual irritation, fretfulness, and impatience; and with a dejection, gloom, and despair, which made existence misery. From this dismal malady he never afterwards was perfectly relieved; and all his labors, and all his enjoyments, were but temporary interruptions of its baleful influence. He told Mr. Paradise[9] that he was sometimes so languid and inefficient that he could not distinguish the hour upon the town-clock. * * *

To Johnson, whose supreme enjoyment was the exercise of his reason, the disturbance or obscuration of that faculty was the evil most to be dreaded. Insanity, therefore, was the object of his most dismal apprehension; and he fancied himself seized by it, or approaching to it, at the very time when he was giving proofs of a more than ordinary soundness and vigor of judgment. That his own diseased imagination should have so far deceived him, is

6. A well-to-do clergyman who had been Johnson's schoolfellow in Lichfield.
7. The Reverend William Adams, D.D., elected master of Pembroke in 1775.

8. Depression.
9. John Paradise, a member of the Essex Head Club, which Johnson founded in 1783.

strange; but it is stranger still that some of his friends should have given credit to his groundless opinion, when they had such undoubted proofs that it was totally fallacious; though it is by no means surprising that those who wish to depreciate him should, since his death, have laid hold of this circumstance, and insisted upon it with very unfair aggravation. * * *

Dr. Adams told me that Johnson, while he was at Pembroke College, "was caressed and loved by all about him, was a gay and frolicsome fellow, and passed there the happiest part of his life." But this is a striking proof of the fallacy of appearances, and how little any of us know of the real internal state even of those whom we see most frequently; for the truth is, that he was then depressed by poverty, and irritated by disease. When I mentioned to him this account as given me by Dr. Adams, he said, "Ah, Sir, I was mad and violent. It was bitterness which they mistook for frolic. I was miserably poor, and I thought to fight my way by my literature and my wit; so I disregarded all power and all authority." * * *

[1734] In a man whom religious education has secured from licentious indulgences, the passion of love, when once it has seized him, is exceedingly strong; being unimpaired by dissipation,[1] and totally concentrated in one object. This was experienced by Johnson, when he became the fervent admirer of Mrs. Porter, after her first husband's death. Miss Porter told me that when he was first introduced to her mother, his appearance was very forbidding: he was then lean and lank, so that his immense structure of bones was hideously striking to the eye, and the scars of the scrofula were deeply visible. He also wore his hair,[2] which was straight and stiff, and separated behind: and he often had, seemingly, convulsive starts and odd gesticulations, which tended to excite at once surprise and ridicule. Mrs. Porter was so much engaged by his conversation that she overlooked all these external disadvantages, and said to her daughter, "This is the most sensible man that I ever saw in my life."

[1735] Though Mrs. Porter was double the age of Johnson, and her person and manner, as described to me by the late Mr. Garrick,[3] were by no means pleasing to others, she must have had a superiority of understanding and talents, as she certainly inspired him with a more than ordinary passion; and she having signified her willingness to accept of his hand, he went to Lichfield to ask his mother's consent to the marriage, which he could not but be conscious was a very imprudent scheme, both on account of their disparity of years and her want of fortune. But Mrs. Johnson knew too well the ardor of her son's temper, and was too tender a parent to oppose his inclinations.

I know not for what reason the marriage ceremony was not performed at Birmingham; but a resolution was taken that it should be at Derby, for which place the bride and bridegroom set out on horseback, I suppose in very good humor. But though Mr. Topham Beauclerk[4] used archly to mention Johnson's having told him, with much gravity, "Sir, it was a love marriage on both sides," I have had from my illustrious friend the following curious account of their journey to church upon the nuptial morn:

9th July: "Sir, she had read the old romances, and had got into her head the fantastical notion that a woman of spirit should use her lover like a dog.

---

1. Scattered attention.
2. I.e., he wore no wig.
3. David Garrick (1717–1779), the most famous actor of his day. In 1736 he was one of Johnson's

three pupils in an unsuccessful school at Edial.
4. Pronounced *bo-clare*. A descendant of Charles II and the actress Nell Gwynn, he was brilliant and dissolute.

So, Sir, at first she told me that I rode too fast, and she could not keep up with me; and, when I rode a little slower, she passed me, and complained that I lagged behind. I was not to be made the slave of caprice; and I resolved to begin as I meant to end. I therefore pushed on briskly, till I was fairly out of her sight. The road lay between two hedges, so I was sure she could not miss it; and I contrived that she should soon come up with me. When she did, I observed her to be in tears." * * *

[1737] Johnson now thought of trying his fortune in London, the great field of genius and exertion, where talents of every kind have the fullest scope and the highest encouragement. It is a memorable circumstance that his pupil David Garrick went thither at the same time, with intention to complete his education, and follow the profession of the law, from which he was soon diverted by his decided preference for the stage.[5] * * *

[1744] * * * He produced one work this year, fully sufficient to maintain the high reputation which he had acquired. This was *The Life of Richard Savage*;[6] a man of whom it is difficult to speak impartially without wondering that he was for some time the intimate companion of Johnson; for his character was marked by profligacy, insolence, and ingratitude: yet, as he undoubtedly had a warm and vigorous, though unregulated mind, had seen life in all its varieties, and been much in the company of the statesmen and wits of his time, he could communicate to Johnson an abundant supply of such materials as his philosophical curiosity most eagerly desired; and as Savage's misfortunes and misconduct had reduced him to the lowest state of wretchedness as a writer for bread, his visits to St. John's Gate[7] naturally brought Johnson and him together.

It is melancholy to reflect that Johnson and Savage were sometimes in such extreme indigence that they could not pay for a lodging; so that they have wandered together whole nights in the streets. Yet in these almost incredible scenes of distress, we may suppose that Savage mentioned many of the anecdotes with which Johnson afterwards enriched the life of his unhappy companion, and those of other poets.

He told Sir Joshua Reynolds that one night in particular, when Savage and he walked round St. James's Square for want of a lodging, they were not at all depressed by their situation; but in high spirits and brimful of patriotism, traversed the square for several hours, inveighed against the minister, and "resolved they would *stand by their country*." * * *

[1752] That there should be a suspension of his literary labors during a part of the year 1752[8] will not seem strange when it is considered that soon after closing his *Rambler*, he suffered a loss which, there can be no doubt,

---

5. Johnson had hoped to complete his tragedy *Irene* and to get it produced, but this was not accomplished until Garrick staged it in 1749. Meanwhile Johnson struggled against poverty, at first as a writer and translator for Edward Cave's *Gentleman's Magazine*. He gradually won recognition but was never financially secure until he was pensioned in 1762. Garrick succeeded in the theater much more rapidly than did Johnson in literature.

6. The poet Richard Savage courted and gained notoriety by claiming to be the illegitimate son of Earl Rivers and the Countess of Macclesfield, whose husband had divorced her because of her unfaithfulness with Rivers. Savage publicized his claim and persecuted his alleged mother. Johnson and many others believed Savage's story and resented what they considered the lady's inhumanity. Savage was a gifted man, but he lived in poverty as a hack writer, although he was long assisted by Pope and others. He died in a debtor's prison in Bristol in 1743.

7. Where Cave published the *Gentleman's Magazine*.

8. Johnson's important works written before the publication of the *Dictionary* are the poems "London" (1738) and "The Vanity of Human Wishes" (1749), the *Life of Savage* (1744), and the essays that made up his periodical the *Rambler* (1750–52).

affected him with the deepest distress. For on the 17th of March, O.S., his wife died. * * *

The following very solemn and affecting prayer was found, after Dr. Johnson's decease, by his servant, Mr. Francis Barber, who delivered it to my worthy friend the Reverend Mr. Strahan, Vicar of Islington, who at my earnest request has obligingly favored me with a copy of it, which he and I compared with the original:

"April 26, 1752, being after 12 at night of the 25th.

"O Lord! Governor of heaven and earth, in whose hands are embodied and departed spirits, if thou hast ordained the souls of the dead to minister to the living, and appointed my departed wife to have care of me, grant that I may enjoy the good effects of her attention and ministration, whether exercised by appearance, impulses, dreams or in any other manner agreeable to thy government. Forgive my presumption, enlighten my ignorance, and however meaner agents are employed, grant me the blessed influences of thy holy Spirit, through Jesus Christ our Lord. Amen." * * *

One night when Beauclerk and Langton[9] had supped at a tavern in London, and sat till about three in the morning, it came into their heads to go and knock up Johnson, and see if they could prevail on him to join them in a ramble. They rapped violently at the door of his chambers in the Temple,[1] till at last he appeared in his shirt, with his little black wig on the top of his head, instead of a nightcap, and a poker in his hand, imagining, probably, that some ruffians were coming to attack him. When he discovered who they were, and was told their errand, he smiled, and with great good humor agreed to their proposal: "What, is it you, you dogs! I'll have a frisk with you." He was soon dressed, and they sallied forth together into Covent Garden, where the greengrocers and fruiterers were beginning to arrange their hampers, just come in from the country. Johnson made some attempts to help them; but the honest gardeners stared so at his figure and manner and odd interference, that he soon saw his services were not relished. They then repaired to one of the neighboring taverns, and made a bowl of that liquor called *Bishop*,[2] which Johnson had always liked; while in joyous contempt of sleep, from which he had been roused, he repeated the festive lines,

> Short, O short then be thy reign,
> And give us to the world again![3]

They did not stay long, but walked down to the Thames, took a boat, and rowed to Billingsgate. Beauclerk and Johnson were so well pleased with their amusement that they resolved to persevere in dissipation for the rest of the day: but Langton deserted them, being engaged to breakfast with some young ladies. Johnson scolded him for "leaving his social friends, to go and sit with a set of wretched *un-idea'd* girls." Garrick being told of this ramble, said to him smartly, "I heard of your frolic t' other night. You'll be

9. Bennet Langton. As a boy he so much admired the *Rambler* that he sought Johnson's acquaintance. They became lifelong friends.
1. Because Johnson lived in Inner Temple Lane between 1760 and 1765, the "frisk" could not have taken place in the year of his wife's death, where

Boswell, for his own convenience, placed it.
2. A drink made of wine, sugar, and either lemon or orange.
3. Misquoted from Lansdowne's "Drinking Song to Sleep."

in the *Chronicle*." Upon which Johnson afterwards observed, "*He* durst not do such a thing. His *wife* would not *let* him!" * * *

[THE LETTER TO CHESTERFIELD]

[1754] Lord Chesterfield,[4] to whom Johnson had paid the high compliment of addressing to his Lordship the *Plan* of his *Dictionary*, had behaved to him in such a manner as to excite his contempt and indignation. The world has been for many years amused with a story confidently told, and as confidently repeated with additional circumstances, that a sudden disgust was taken by Johnson upon occasion of his having been one day kept long in waiting in his Lordship's antechamber, for which the reason assigned was that he had company with him; and that at last, when the door opened, out walked Colley Cibber;[5] and that Johnson was so violently provoked when he found for whom he had been so long excluded, that he went away in a passion, and never would return. I remember having mentioned this story to George Lord Lyttelton, who told me he was very intimate with Lord Chesterfield; and holding it as a well-known truth, defended Lord Chesterfield, by saying, that Cibber, who had been introduced familiarly by the back stairs, had probably not been there above ten minutes. It may seem strange even to entertain a doubt concerning a story so long and so widely current, and thus implicitly adopted, if not sanctioned, by the authority which I have mentioned; but Johnson himself assured me that there was not the least foundation for it. He told me that there never was any particular incident which produced a quarrel between Lord Chesterfield and him; but that his Lordship's continued neglect was the reason why he resolved to have no connection with him. When the *Dictionary* was upon the eve of publication, Lord Chesterfield, who, it is said, had flattered himself with expectations that Johnson would dedicate the work to him, attempted, in a courtly manner, to soothe, and insinuate himself with the sage, conscious, as it should seem, of the cold indifference with which he had treated its learned author; and further attempted to conciliate him, by writing two papers in *The World*, in recommendation of the work; and it must be confessed that they contain some studied compliments, so finely turned, that if there had been no previous offense, it is probable that Johnson would have been highly delighted. Praise, in general, was pleasing to him; but by praise from a man of rank and elegant accomplishments, he was peculiarly gratified. * * *

This courtly device failed of its effect. Johnson, who thought that "all was false and hollow,"[6] despised the honeyed words, and was even indignant that Lord Chesterfield should, for a moment, imagine that he could be dupe of such an artifice. His expression to me concerning Lord Chesterfield, upon this occasion, was, "Sir, after making great professions, he had, for many years, taken no notice of me; but when my *Dictionary* was coming out, he fell a-scribbling in *The World* about it. Upon which, I wrote him a letter expressed in civil terms, but such as might show him that I did not mind what he said or wrote, and that I had done with him."

4. Philip Dormer Stanhope, earl of Chesterfield (1694–1773), statesman; wit, man of fashion. His *Letters*, written for the guidance of his natural son, are famous for their worldly good sense and for their expression of the ideal of an 18th-century gentleman.

5. Cibber (1671–1757), playwright, comic actor, and (after 1730) poet laureate. A fine actor but a very bad poet, Cibber was a constant object of ridicule by the wits of the town. Pope made him king of the Dunces in the *Dunciad* of 1743.
6. *Paradise Lost* 2.112.

This is that celebrated letter of which so much has been said, and about which curiosity has been so long excited, without being gratified. I for many years solicited Johnson to favor me with a copy of it, that so excellent a composition might not be lost to posterity. He delayed from time to time to give it me; till at last in 1781, when we were on a visit at Mr. Dilly's,[7] at Southill in Bedfordshire, he was pleased to dictate it to me from memory. He afterwards found among his papers a copy of it, which he had dictated to Mr. Baretti,[8] with its title and corrections, in his own handwriting. This he gave to Mr. Langton; adding that if it were to come into print, he wished it to be from that copy. By Mr. Langton's kindness, I am enabled to enrich my work with a perfect transcript of what the world has so eagerly desired to see.

[A MEMORABLE YEAR: BOSWELL MEETS JOHNSON]

[1763] This is to me a memorable year; for in it I had the happiness to obtain the acquaintance of that extraordinary man whose memoirs I am now writing; an acquaintance which I shall ever esteem as one of the most fortunate circumstances in my life. * * *

Mr. Thomas Davies the actor, who then kept a bookseller's shop in Russel Street, Covent Garden, told me that Johnson was very much his friend, and came frequently to his house, where he more than once invited me to meet him; but by some unlucky accident or other he was prevented from coming to us. * * *

At last, on Monday the 16th of May, when I was sitting in Mr. Davies's back parlor, after having drunk tea with him and Mrs. Davies, Johnson unexpectedly came into the shop; and Mr. Davies having perceived him through the glass door in the room in which we were sitting, advancing towards us— he announced his awful approach to me, somewhat in the manner of an actor in the part of Horatio, when he addresses Hamlet on the appearance of his father's ghost, "Look, my Lord, it comes." I found that I had a very perfect idea of Johnson's figure, from the portrait of him painted by Sir Joshua Reynolds soon after he had published his *Dictionary*, in the attitude of sitting in his easy chair in deep meditation, which was the first picture his friend did for him, which Sir Joshua very kindly presented to me, and from which an engraving has been made for this work. Mr. Davies mentioned my name, and respectfully introduced me to him. I was much agitated; and recollecting his prejudice against the Scotch, of which I had heard much, I said to Davies, "Don't tell where I come from."—"From Scotland," cried Davies roguishly. "Mr. Johnson," said I, "I do indeed come from Scotland, but I cannot help it." I am willing to flatter myself that I meant this as light pleasantry to soothe and conciliate him, and not as an humiliating abasement at the expense of my country. But however that might be, this speech was somewhat unlucky; for with that quickness of wit for which he was so remarkable, he seized the expression "come from Scotland," which I used in the sense of being of that country; and, as if I had said that I had come away from it, or left it, retorted, "That, Sir, I find, is what a very great many of your countrymen cannot help." This stroke stunned me a good deal; and when we had sat down, I felt myself

---

7. Southill was the country home of Charles and Edward Dilly, publishers. The firm published all of Boswell's serious works and shared in the publication of Johnson's *Lives of the Poets* (1779–81).

8. Giuseppe Baretti, an Italian writer and lexicographer whom Johnson introduced into his circle.

not a little embarrassed, and apprehensive of what might come next. He then addressed himself to Davies: "What do you think of Garrick? He has refused me an order for the play for Miss Williams,[9] because he knows the house will be full, and that an order would be worth three shillings." Eager to take any opening to get into conversation with him, I ventured to say, "O Sir, I cannot think Mr. Garrick would grudge such a trifle to you." "Sir," said he, with a stern look, "I have known David Garrick longer than you have done: and I know no right you have to talk to me on the subject." Perhaps I deserved this check; for it was rather presumptuous in me, an entire stranger, to express any doubt of the justice of his animadversion upon his old acquaintance and pupil. I now felt myself much mortified, and began to think that the hope which I had long indulged of obtaining his acquaintance was blasted. And, in truth, had not my ardor been uncommonly strong, and my resolution uncommonly persevering, so rough a reception might have deterred me forever from making any further attempts. Fortunately, however, I remained upon the field not wholly discomfited. * * *

I was highly pleased with the extraordinary vigor of his conversation, and regretted that I was drawn away from it by an engagement at another place. I had, for a part of the evening, been left alone with him, and had ventured to make an observation now and then, which he received very civilly; so that I was satisfied that though there was a roughness in his manner, there was no ill nature in his disposition. Davies followed me to the door, and when I complained to him a little of the hard blows which the great man had given me, he kindly took upon him to console me by saying, "Don't be uneasy. I can see he likes you very well."

A few days afterwards I called on Davies, and asked him if he thought I might take the liberty of waiting on Mr. Johnson at his chambers in the Temple. He said I certainly might, and that Mr. Johnson would take it as a compliment. So upon Tuesday the 24th of May, after having been enlivened by the witty sallies of Messieurs Thornton, Wilkes, Churchill, and Lloyd,[1] with whom I had passed the morning, I boldly repaired to Johnson. His chambers were on the first floor of No. 1, Inner Temple Lane, and I entered them with an impression given me by the Reverend Dr. Blair,[2] of Edinburgh, who had been introduced to him not long before, and described his having "found the giant in his den"; an expression, which, when I came to be pretty well acquainted with Johnson, I repeated to him, and he was diverted at this picturesque account of himself. Dr. Blair had been presented to him by Dr. James Fordyce.[3] At this time the controversy concerning the pieces published by Mr. James Macpherson, as translations of *Ossian*, was at its height.[4] Johnson had all along denied their authenticity; and, what was still more provoking to their admirers, maintained that they had no merit. The subject

---

9. Mrs. Anna Williams (1706–1783), a blind poet and friend of Mrs. Johnson. She continued to live in Johnson's house after his wife's death and habitually sat up to make tea for him whenever he came home.
1. Robert Lloyd, poet and essayist. Bonnell Thornton, journalist. Charles Churchill, satirist. John Wilkes, journalist. The four were bound together by a common love of wit and dissipation. Boswell enjoyed their company in 1763.
2. The Reverend Hugh Blair (1718–1800), Scot-

tish divine and professor of rhetoric and *belles lettres* at the University of Edinburgh.
3. A Scottish preacher.
4. Macpherson had imposed on most of his contemporaries, Scottish and English, by convincing them of the genuineness of prose poems that he had concocted but that he claimed to have translated from the original Gaelic of Ossian, a blind epic poet of the 3rd century. The vogue of the poems both in Europe and in America was enormous.

having been introduced by Dr. Fordyce, Dr. Blair, relying on the internal evidence of their antiquity, asked Dr. Johnson whether he thought any man of a modern age could have written such poems? Johnson replied, "Yes, Sir, many men, many women, and many children." Johnson, at this time, did not know that Dr. Blair had just published a dissertation, not only defending their authenticity, but seriously ranking them with the poems of Homer and Virgil; and when he was afterwards informed of this circumstance, he expressed some displeasure at Dr. Fordyce's having suggested the topic, and said, "I am not sorry that they got thus much for their pains. Sir, it was like leading one to talk of a book when the author is concealed behind the door."

He received me very courteously; but, it must be confessed that his apartment, and furniture, and morning dress, were sufficiently uncouth. His brown suit of clothes looked very rusty; he had on a little old shriveled unpowdered wig, which was too small for his head; his shirt neck and knees of his breeches were loose; his black worsted stockings ill drawn up; and he had a pair of unbuckled shoes by way of slippers. But all these slovenly particularities were forgotten the moment that he began to talk. Some gentlemen, whom I do not recollect, were sitting with him; and when they went away, I also rose; but he said to me, "Nay, don't go." "Sir," said I, "I am afraid that I intrude upon you. It is benevolent to allow me to sit and hear you." He seemed pleased with this compliment, which I sincerely paid him, and answered, "Sir, I am obliged to any man who visits me." I have preserved the following short minute of what passed this day:

"Madness frequently discovers itself merely by unnecessary deviation from the usual modes of the world. My poor friend Smart showed the disturbance of his mind by falling upon his knees, and saying his prayers in the street, or in any other unusual place. Now although, rationally speaking, it is greater madness not to pray at all than to pray as Smart did, I am afraid there are so many who do not pray, that their understanding is not called in question."

Concerning this unfortunate poet, Christopher Smart, who was confined in a madhouse, he had, at another time, the following conversation with Dr. Burney:[5] BURNEY. "How does poor Smart do, Sir; is he likely to recover?" JOHNSON. "It seems as if his mind had ceased to struggle with the disease; for he grows fat upon it." BURNEY. "Perhaps, Sir, that may be from want of exercise." JOHNSON. "No, Sir; he has partly as much exercise as he used to have, for he digs in the garden. Indeed, before his confinement, he used for exercise to walk to the ale house; but he was *carried* back again. I did not think he ought to be shut up. His infirmities were not noxious to society. He insisted on people praying with him; and I'd as lief pray with Kit Smart as anyone else. Another charge was that he did not love clean linen; and I have no passion for it."—Johnson continued. "Mankind have a great aversion to intellectual labor; but even supposing knowledge to be easily attainable, more people would be content to be ignorant than would take even a little trouble to acquire it."

Talking of Garrick, he said, "He is the first man in the world for sprightly conversation."

When I rose a second time he again pressed me to stay, which I did. * * *

---

5. Dr. Charles Burney (1726–1814), historian of music and father of the novelist and diarist Frances Burney, whom Johnson befriended in his old age.

[FEAR OF DEATH]

[*1769*] When we were alone, I introduced the subject of death, and endeavored to maintain that the fear of it might be got over. I told him that David Hume said to me, he was no more uneasy to think he should *not be* after this life, than that he *had not been* before he began to exist. JOHNSON. "Sir, if he really thinks so, his perceptions are disturbed; he is mad: if he does not think so, he lies. He may tell you, he holds his finger in the flame of a candle, without feeling pain; would you believe him? When he dies, he at least gives up all he has." BOSWELL. "Foote,[6] Sir, told me, that when he was very ill he was not afraid to die." JOHNSON. "It is not true, Sir. Hold a pistol to Foote's breast, or to Hume's breast, and threaten to kill them, and you'll see how they behave." BOSWELL. "But may we not fortify our minds for the approach of death?" Here I am sensible I was in the wrong, to bring before his view what he ever looked upon with horror; for although when in a celestial frame, in his *Vanity of Human Wishes*, he has supposed death to be "kind Nature's signal for retreat," from this stage of being to "a happier seat," his thoughts upon this awful change were in general full of dismal apprehensions. His mind resembled the vast amphitheater, the Colosseum at Rome. In the center stood his judgment, which, like a mighty gladiator, combated those apprehensions that, like the wild beasts of the arena, were all around in cells, ready to be let out upon him. After a conflict, he drove them back into their dens; but not killing them, they were still assailing him. To my question, whether we might not fortify our minds for the approach of death, he answered, in a passion, "No, Sir, let it alone. It matters not how a man dies, but how he lives. The act of dying is not of importance, it lasts so short a time." He added (with an earnest look), "A man knows it must be so, and submits. It will do him no good to whine."

I attempted to continue the conversation. He was so provoked that he said, "Give us no more of this"; and was thrown into such a state of agitation that he expressed himself in a way that alarmed and distressed me; showed an impatience that I should leave him, and when I was going away, called to me sternly, "Don't let us meet tomorrow." * * *

[JOHNSON FACES DEATH]

As Johnson had now very faint hopes of recovery, and as Mrs. Thrale was no longer devoted to him, it might have been supposed that he would naturally have chosen to remain in the comfortable house of his beloved wife's daughter,[7] and end his life where he began it. But there was in him an animated and lofty spirit, and however complicated diseases might depress ordinary mortals, all who saw him, beheld and acknowledged the *invictum animum Catonis*.[8] Such was his intellectual ardor even at this time that he said to one friend, "Sir, I look upon every day to be lost, in which I do not make a new acquaintance"; and to another, when talking of his illness, "I will be conquered; I will not capitulate." And such was his love of London, so high a relish had he of its magnificent extent, and variety of intellectual entertainment, that he languished when absent from it, his mind having become quite luxurious from the long habit of enjoying the metropolis; and, therefore,

6. Samuel Foote, actor and dramatist, famous for his wit and his skill in mimicry.
7. Lucy Porter.
8. The unconquered soul of Cato (Latin). An adaptation of a phrase in Horace's *Odes* 2.1.24.

although at Lichfield, surrounded with friends, who loved and revered him, and for whom he had a very sincere affection, he still found that such conversation as London affords, could be found nowhere else. These feelings, joined, probably, to some flattering hopes of aid from the eminent physicians and surgeons in London, who kindly and generously attended him without accepting fees, made him resolve to return to the capital. * * * Death had always been to him an object of terror; so that, though by no means happy, he still clung to life with an eagerness at which many have wondered. At any time when he was ill, he was very much pleased to be told that he looked better. An ingenious member of the Eumelian Club[9] informs me that upon one occasion when he said to him that he saw health returning to his cheek, Johnson seized him by the hand and exclaimed, "Sir, you are one of the kindest friends I ever had." * * *

Dr. Heberden, Dr. Brocklesby, Dr. Warren, and Dr. Butter, physicians, generously attended him, without accepting any fees, as did Mr. Cruikshank, surgeon; and all that could be done from professional skill and ability was tried, to prolong a life so truly valuable. He himself, indeed, having, on account of his very bad constitution, been perpetually applying himself to medical inquiries, united his own efforts with those of the gentlemen who attended him; and imagining that the dropsical collection of water which oppressed him might be drawn off by making incisions in his body, he, with his usual resolute defiance of pain, cut deep, when he thought that his surgeon had done it too tenderly.

About eight or ten days before his death, when Dr. Brocklesby paid him his morning visit, he seemed very low and desponding, and said, "I have been as a dying man all night." He then emphatically broke out in the words of Shakespeare:

> "Canst thou not minister to a mind diseased;
> Pluck from the memory a rooted sorrow,
> Raze out the written troubles of the brain,
> And with some sweet oblivious antidote
> Cleanse the stuffed bosom of that perilous stuff
> Which weighs upon the heart?"

To which Dr. Brocklesby readily answered, from the same great poet:

> "—Therein the patient
> Must minister to himself."[1]

Johnson expressed himself much satisfied with the application. * * *

Amidst the melancholy clouds which hung over the dying Johnson, his characteristical manner showed itself on different occasions.

When Dr. Warren, in the usual style, hoped that he was better; his answer was, "No, Sir; you cannot conceive with what acceleration I advance towards death."

A man whom he had never seen before was employed one night to sit up with him. Being asked next morning how he liked his attendant, his answer was, "Not at all, Sir: the fellow's an idiot; he is as awkward as a turnspit[2] when first put into the wheel, and as sleepy as a dormouse."

9. A club to which Boswell and Reynolds belonged.
1. *Macbeth* 5.3.40–46.

2. "A dog kept to turn the roasting-spit by running within a tread-wheel connected to it" (*OED*).

Mr. Windham[3] having placed a pillow conveniently to support him, he thanked him for his kindness, and said, "That will do—all that a pillow can do." * * *

Johnson, with that native fortitude, which, amidst all his bodily distress and mental sufferings, never forsook him, asked Dr. Brocklesby, as a man in whom he had confidence, to tell him plainly whether he could recover. "Give me," said he, "a direct answer." The Doctor having first asked him if he could bear the whole truth, which way soever it might lead, and being answered that he could, declared that, in his opinion, he could not recover without a miracle. "Then," said Johnson, "I will take no more physic, not even my opiates; for I have prayed that I may render up my soul to God unclouded." In this resolution he persevered, and, at the same time, used only the weakest kinds of sustenance. Being pressed by Mr. Windham to take somewhat more generous nourishment, lest too low a diet should have the very effect which he dreaded, by debilitating his mind, he said, "I will take anything but inebriating sustenance."

The Reverend Mr. Strahan,[4] who was the son of his friend, and had been always one of his great favorites, had, during his last illness, the satisfaction of contributing to soothe and comfort him. That gentleman's house, at Islington, of which he is Vicar, afforded Johnson, occasionally and easily, an agreeable change of place and fresh air; and he attended also upon him in town in the discharge of the sacred offices of his profession.

Mr. Strahan has given me the agreeable assurance that, after being in much agitation, Johnson became quite composed, and continued so till his death.

Dr. Brocklesby, who will not be suspected of fanaticism, obliged me with the following account:

> "For some time before his death, all his fears were calmed and absorbed by the prevalence of his faith, and his trust in the merits and *propitiation* of Jesus Christ." * * *

Johnson having thus in his mind the true Christian scheme, at once rational and consolatory, uniting justice and mercy in the Divinity, with the improvement of human nature, previous to his receiving the Holy Sacrament in his apartment, composed and fervently uttered this prayer:

> "Almighty and most merciful Father, I am now as to human eyes, it seems, about to commemorate, for the last time, the death of thy Son Jesus Christ, our Saviour and Redeemer. Grant, O Lord, that my whole hope and confidence may be in his merits, and thy mercy; enforce and accept my imperfect repentance; make this commemoration available to the confirmation of my faith, the establishment of my hope, and the enlargement of my charity; and make the death of thy Son Jesus Christ effectual to my redemption. Have mercy upon me, and pardon the multitude of my offenses. Bless my friends; have mercy upon all men. Support me, by thy Holy Spirit, in the days of weakness, and at the hour of death; and receive me, at my death, to everlasting happiness, for the sake of Jesus Christ. Amen."

3. William Windham, one of Johnson's younger friends, later a member of Parliament.
4. The Reverend George Strahan (pronounced *Strawn*), who later published Johnson's *Prayers and Meditations*.

Having * * * made his will on the 8th and 9th of December, and settled all his worldly affairs, he languished till Monday, the 13th of that month, when he expired, about seven o'clock in the evening, with so little apparent pain that his attendants hardly perceived when his dissolution took place. * * *

1791

FRANCES BURNEY
1752–1840

People have often made the mistake of underestimating Frances Burney. In person, as in her writing, she seemed a proper, self-effacing lady. Many readers still call her "Fanny," as if familiarity could make her harmless. But she saw through such poses. Sir Joshua Reynolds said that "if he was conscious to himself of any trick, or any affectation, there is nobody he should so much fear as this little Burney!" And Samuel Johnson teased her by claiming that "your shyness, & slyness, & pretending to know nothing, never took *me* in, whatever you may do with others. *I* always knew you for a *toadling!*" (according to legend, little toads may look submissive but actually carry poison). Although her writing crackles with humor, it can be relentless—and sometimes cruel—in exposing bad manners or a selfish heart.

She learned quite young how to hide in a crowd. A devoted daughter of Charles Burney, a popular teacher and historian of music, Frances grew up in a large family that gave her many opportunities to study character and mix discreetly in society. Her first novel, *Evelina, or A Young Lady's Entrance into the World* (1778), was written in secret and published anonymously. But delighted readers, including Johnson, Burke, and Hester Thrale, soon found her out and sang her praises; and a second novel, *Cecilia* (1782), confirmed her reputation. Her home life was less happy, however; she and her stepmother disliked each other, and she fell in love with a young clergyman who never got around to proposing. In 1786, to please her father, she accepted a place as a lady-in-waiting at court, where the paralyzing etiquette and lack of independence tormented her for the next five years, until she finally managed to resign. At forty-one she married a French émigré, General Alexandre-Gabriel-Jean-Baptiste d'Arblay. Despite the disapproval of her father—d'Arblay was penniless, Catholic, and politically liberal—the marriage was happy. Madame d'Arblay soon bore a son, and her novel *Camilla* (1796) brought in good money. After she joined her husband in France, in 1802, the Napoleonic wars prevented them from returning to England for ten years; the pain of an outcast dominates her last novel, *The Wanderer, or Female Difficulties* (1814). But she never stopped writing, producing a doctored version of her father's *Memoirs* (1832) and more of the diaries and letters that, edited after her death by a niece, made her famous again.

Burney wrote all her life—not only novels and plays but perpetual letters and journals, recording whatever she saw for friends and family as well as herself. Even the most informal pages display her gifts: a knack for catching character, a wonderful ear for dialogue, wry humor, and a swift pace that carries the reader along from moment to moment. Her special subject is embarrassment—often her own. In scenes like her flight from the king, where she is torn between opposite notions of the right thing to do, shame and comedy mingle. These trepidations can also be incredibly painful, as in her gripping account of a mastectomy. Despite her propriety, Burney looks at the world and its institutions with the clear eyes of an outsider, aware of the gaps between what people say and what they do. She frees herself to write with utter honesty by pretending, at first, that nobody is going to read her. But her private thoughts are reported so fully and faithfully that, in the end, every reader can share them.

From The Journal and Letters

[FIRST JOURNAL ENTRY]

Poland Street, London, March 27, 1768[1]

To have some account of my thoughts, manners, acquaintance and actions, when the hour arrives at which time is more nimble than memory, is the reason which induces me to keep a journal: a journal in which I must confess my *every* thought, must open my whole heart! But a thing of this kind ought to be addressed to somebody—I must imagine myself to be talking— talking to the most intimate of friends—to one in whom I should take delight in confiding, and feel remorse in concealment: but who must this friend be?—to make choice of one to whom I can but *half* rely, would be to frustrate entirely the intention of my plan. The only one I could wholly, totally confide in, lives in the same house with me, and not only never *has*, but never *will*, leave me one secret *to* tell her.[2] To whom, then *must* I dedicate my wonderful, surprising and interesting adventures?—to *whom* dare I reveal my private opinion of my nearest relations? the secret thoughts of my dearest friends? my own hopes, fears, reflections and dislikes—Nobody!

To Nobody, then, will I write my Journal! since To Nobody can I be wholly unreserved—to Nobody can I reveal every thought, every wish of my heart, with the most unlimited confidence, the most unremitting sincerity to the end of my life! For what chance, what accident can end my connections with Nobody? No secret *can* I conceal from No—body, and to No— body can I be *ever* unreserved. Disagreement cannot stop our affection, Time itself has no power to end our friendship. The love, the esteem I entertain for Nobody, No-body's self has not power to destroy. From Nobody I have nothing to fear, the secrets sacred to friendship, Nobody will not reveal, when the affair is doubtful, Nobody will not look towards the side least favourable.—

I will suppose you, then, to be my best friend; tho' God forbid you ever should! my dearest companion—and a romantick girl, for mere oddity may perhaps be more sincere—more *tender*—than if you were a friend in propria personae[3]—in as much as imagination often exceeds reality. In your breast my errors may create pity without exciting contempt; may raise your compassion, without eradicating your love.

From this moment, then, my dear girl—but why, permit me to ask, must a *female* be made Nobody? Ah! my dear, what were this world good for, *were* Nobody a female? And now I have done with *perambulation*.

---

1. This is the first page of Burney's first journal, begun when she was fifteen.
2. Burney's younger sister Susanna. In 1773, when Burney spent the summer away from home,

she began a journal for her sister, continuing it off and on until 1800, when Susanna died.
3. As a real person.

["DOWN WITH HER, BURNEY"]

Streatham, September 15, 1778[4]

I was then looking over the "Life of Cowley," which he[5] had himself given me to read, at the same time that he gave to Mrs. Thrale that of Waller. They are now printed, though they will not be published for some time. But he bade me put it away.

"Do," cried he, "put away that now, and prattle with us; I can't make this little Burney prattle, and I am sure she prattles well; but I shall teach her another lesson than to sit thus silent before I have done with her."

"To talk," cried I, "is the only lesson I shall be backward to learn from you, sir."

* * *

Mrs. Thrale. "To morrow, Sir, Mrs. Montagu[6] dines here! and then you will have talk enough."

Dr. Johnson began to seesaw, with a countenance strongly expressive of *inward fun*,—and, after enjoying it some time in silence, he suddenly, and with great animation, turned to me, and cried *"Down* with her, Burney!—*down* with her!—spare her not! attack her, fight her, and *down* with her at once!—*You* are a *rising* wit,—*she* is at the *top*,—and when *I* was beginning the world, and was nothing and nobody, the joy of my life was to fire at all the established wits!—and then, every body loved to hallow[7] me on;—but there is no game *now*, and *now*, every body would be glad to see me *conquered*: but *then*, when I was *new*,—to vanquish the great ones was all the delight of my poor little dear soul!—So at her, Burney!—at her, and *down* with her!"

O how we were all amused! By the way, I must tell you that Mrs. Montagu is in very great estimation here, even with Dr. Johnson himself, when others do not praise her *improperly*: Mrs Thrale ranks her as the *first of women*, in the literary way.

* * *

I should have told you that Miss Gregory, daughter of the Gregory who wrote the "Letters," or, "Legacy of Advice,"[8] lives with Mrs. Montagu, and was invited to accompany her.

"Mark, now," said Dr. Johnson, "if I contradict her tomorrow. I am determined, let her say what she will, that I will not contradict her."

Mrs. T.—Why, to be sure, sir, you did put her a little out of countenance last time she came. Yet you were neither rough, nor cruel, nor ill-natured; but still, when a lady changes color, we imagine her feelings are not quite composed.

Dr. J.—Why, madam, I won't answer that I shan't contradict her again, if she provokes me as she did then; but a less provocation I will withstand. I believe I am not high in her good graces already; and I begin (added he,

---

4. *Evelina* was published in January 1778 and enthusiastically received. After her authorship became known, Burney was invited to Streatham Park, the country house of Henry and Hester Lynch Thrale. Samuel Johnson spent much of his time there and was then writing his *Lives of the Poets.* He and Hester Thrale became fond of Burney.
5. Johnson.

6. Elizabeth Montagu, known as "Queen of the Blues" (or bluestockings), a group of intellectual women, was probably the most respected literary woman in England; she had written the famous *Essay on Shakespear* (1769).
7. A cry inciting hunters to the chase.
8. John Gregory, *A Father's Legacy to His Daughters* (1774).

laughing heartily) to tremble for my admission into her new house. I doubt I shall never see the inside of it.

(Mrs. Montagu is building a most superb house.)

Mrs. T.—Oh, I warrant you, she fears you, indeed; but that, you know, is nothing uncommon; and dearly I love to hear your disquisitions; for certainly she is the first woman for literary knowledge in England, and if in England, I hope I may say in the world.

Dr. J.—I believe you may, madam. She diffuses more knowledge in her conversation than any woman I know, or, indeed, almost any man.

Mrs. T.—I declare I know no man equal to her, take away yourself and Burke, for that art. And you who love magnificence, won't quarrel with her, as everybody else does, for her love of finery.

Dr. J.—No, I shall not quarrel with her upon that topic. (Then, looking earnestly at me,) "Nay," he added, "it's very handsome!"

"What, sir?" cried I, amazed.

"Why, your cap:—I have looked at it some time, and I like it much. It has not that vile bandeau[9] across it, which I have so often cursed."

Did you ever hear anything so strange? nothing escapes him. My Daddy Crisp[4] is not more minute in his attentions: nay, I think he is even less so.

Mrs. T.—Well, sir, that bandeau you quarreled with was worn by every woman at court the last birthday,[1] and I observed that all the men found fault with it.

Dr. J.—The truth is, women, take them in general, have no idea of grace. Fashion is all they think of. I don't mean Mrs. Thrale and Miss Burney, when I talk of women!—they are goddesses!—and therefore I except them.

Mrs. T.—Lady Ladd never wore the bandeau, and said she never would, because it is unbecoming.

Dr. J.—(Laughing.) Did not she? then is Lady Ladd a charming woman, and I have yet hopes of entering into engagements with her!

Mrs. T.—Well, as to that I can't say; but to be sure, the only similitude I have yet discovered in you, is in size: there you agree mighty well.

Dr. J.—Why, if anybody could have worn the bandeau, it must have been Lady Ladd; for there is enough of her to carry it off; but you are too little for anything ridiculous; that which seems nothing upon a Patagonian,[2] will become very conspicuous upon a Lilliputian, and of you there is so little in all, that one single absurdity would swallow up half of you.

Some time after, when we had all been a few minutes wholly silent, he turned to me and said:

"Come, Burney, shall you and I study our parts against[3] Mrs. Montagu comes?"

"Miss Burney," cried Mr. Thrale, "you must get up your courage for this encounter! I think you should begin with Miss Gregory; and down with her first."

Dr. J.—No, no, always fly at the eagle! down with Mrs. Montagu herself! I hope she will come full of "Evelina"!

9. A narrow headband.
1. June 4, the king's birthday.
2. The Indians of Patagonia, whose average height was more than six feet, were commonly thought to be giants.
3. Before.

[ENCOUNTERING THE KING]

Kew Palace, Monday February 2, 1789

What an adventure had I this morning! one that has occasioned me the severest personal terror I ever experienced in my life.

Sir Lucas Pepys still persisting that exercise and air were absolutely necessary to save me from illness, I have continued my walks, varying my gardens from Richmond to Kew, according to the accounts I received of the movements of the King. For this I had her majesty's permission, on the representation of Sir Lucas.

This morning, when I received my intelligence of the king, from Dr. John Willis,[4] I begged to know where I might walk in safety? In Kew Garden, he said, as the king would be in Richmond.

"Should any unfortunate circumstance," I cried, "at any time, occasion my being seen by his majesty, do not mention my name, but let me run off, without call or notice."

This he promised. Everybody, indeed, is ordered to keep out of sight.

Taking, therefore, the time I had most at command, I strolled into the garden; I had proceeded, in my quick way, nearly half the round, when I suddenly perceived, through some trees, two or three figures. Relying on the instructions of Dr. John, I concluded them to be workmen, and gardeners;—yet tried to look sharp,—and in so doing, as they were less shaded, I thought I saw the person of his majesty!

Alarmed past all possible expression, I waited not to know more, but turning back, ran off with all my might—But what was my terror to hear myself pursued!—to hear the voice of the king himself, loudly and hoarsely calling after me "Miss Burney! Miss Burney!—"

I protest I was ready to die;—I knew not in what state he might be at the time; I only knew the orders to keep out of his way were universal; that the queen would highly disapprove any unauthorised meeting, and that the very action of my running away might deeply, in his present irritable state, offend him.

Nevertheless, on I ran,—too terrified to stop, and in search of some short passage, for the garden is full of little labyrinths, by which I might escape.

The steps still pursued me, and still the poor hoarse and altered voice rang in my ears:—more and more footsteps resounded frightfully behind me,—the attendants all running, to catch their eager master, and the voices of the two Doctor Willises loudly exhorting him not to heat himself so unmercifully.

Heavens how I ran!—I do not think I should have felt the hot lava from Vesuvius,—at least not the hot cinders, had I so ran during its eruption. My feet were not sensible that they even touched the ground.

Soon after, I heard other voices, shriller though less nervous, call out "Stop! Stop!—Stop!—"

I could by no means consent,—I knew not what was purposed,—but I recollected fully my agreement with Dr. John that very morning, that I should decamp if surprised, and not be named.

---

4. In 1788, two years after Burney joined the court, George III began to have fits of madness or delirium (today diagnosed as resulting from por- phyria, a hereditary disease). He was kept in isolation at Kew, under the control of two physicians, Francis and John Willis.

My own fears and repugnance, also, after a flight and disobedience like this, were doubled in the thought of not escaping; I knew not to what I might be exposed, should the malady be then high, and take the turn of resentment.

Still, therefore, on I flew,—and such was my speed, so almost incredible to relate, or recollect, that I fairly believe no one of the whole party could have overtaken me, if these words, from one of the attendants, had not reached me: "Dr. Willis begs you to stop!—"

"I cannot!—I cannot!—" I answered, still flying on,—when he called out "You *must*, ma'am, it hurts the king to run.—"

Then, indeed, I stopt!—in a state of fear really amounting to agony!—I turned round,—I saw the two doctors had got the king between them, and about 8 attendants of Dr. Willis's were hovering about. They all slacked their pace, as they saw me stand still,—but such was the excess of my alarm, that I was wholly insensible to the effects of a race which, at any other time, would have required an hour's recruit.[5]

As they approached, some little presence of mind happily came to my command; it occurred to me that, to appease the wrath of my flight, I must now show some confidence; I therefore faced them as undauntedly as I was able,—only charging the nearest of the attendants to stand by my side.

When they were within a few yards of me, the king called out "Why did you run away?—"

Shocked at a question impossible to answer, yet a little assured by the mild tone of his voice, I instantly forced myself forward, to meet him—though the internal sensation which satisfied me this was a step the most proper, to appease his suspicions and displeasure, was so violently combated by the tremor of my nerves, that I fairly think I may reckon it the greatest effort of personal courage I have ever made.

The effort answered,—I looked up, and met all his wonted benignity of countenance, though something still of wildness in his eyes. Think, however, of my surprise, to feel him put both his hands round my two shoulders, and then kiss my cheek!—I wonder I did not really sink, so exquisite was my affright when I saw him spread out his arms!—Involuntarily, I concluded he meant to crush me:—but the Willises, who have never seen him till this fatal illness, not knowing how very extraordinary an action this was from him, simply smiled and looked pleased, supposing, perhaps, it was his customary salutation!

I have reason, however, to believe it was but the joy of a heart unbridled, now, by the forms and proprieties of established custom, and sober reason. He looked almost in *rapture* at the meeting, from the moment I advanced; and to see any of his household thus by accident, seemed such a near approach to liberty and recovery, that who can wonder it should serve rather to elate[6] than lessen what yet remains of his disorder?—

He now spoke in such terms of his pleasure in seeing me, that I soon lost the whole of my terror, though it had threatened to almost lose *me*: astonishment to find him so nearly *well*, and gratification to see him so pleased, removed every uneasy feeling, and the joy that succeeded, in my conviction of his recovery, made me ready to throw myself at his feet to express it.

5. Renewal of strength.   6. Heighten.

What a conversation followed!—when he saw me fearless, he grew more and more alive, and made me walk close by his side, away from the attendants, and even the Willises themselves, who, to indulge him, retreated. I own myself not completely *composed*, but *alarm* I could entertain no more.—

Everything that came uppermost in his mind he mentioned; he seemed to have just such remains of his flightiness, as heated his imagination, without deranging his reason, and robbed him of all control over his speech, though nearly in his perfect state of mind as to his opinions.

What did he not say!—He opened his whole heart to me,—expounded all his sentiments, and acquainted me with all his intentions.

*   *   *

He next talked to me a great deal of my dear father, and made a thousand inquiries concerning his history of music. This brought him to his favorite theme, Handel;[7] and he told me innumerable anecdotes of him, and particularly that celebrated tale of Handel's saying of himself, when a boy, "While that boy lives, my music will never want a protector—" And this, he said, I might relate to my father.

Then he ran over most of his oratorios, attempting to sing the subjects of several airs and choruses, but so dreadfully hoarse, that the sound was terrible.

Dr. Willis, quite alarmed at this exertion, feared he would do himself harm, and again proposed a separation. "No! no! no!" he exclaimed, "not yet,—I have something I must just mention first."

Dr. Willis, delighted to comply, even when uneasy at compliance, again gave way.

The good king then greatly affected me,—he began upon my revered old friend, Mrs. Delany![8]—and he spoke of her with such warmth, such kindness:—"She was my *friend*!" he cried, "and I *loved* her as a friend!—I have made a memorandum when I lost her!—I will show it you—"

He pulled out a pocketbook, and rummaged some time, but to no purpose—

The tears stood in his eyes,—he wiped them,—and Dr. Willis again became very anxious,—"Come, sir," he cried, "now do you come in, and let the lady go on her walk,—come, now you have talked a long while,—so will go in,—if your majesty pleases."

"No!—no!—" he cried, "I want to ask her a few questions,—I have lived so long out of the world, I know nothing!—"

This touched me to the heart.

*   *   *

What a scene! how variously was I affected by it!—but, upon the whole, how inexpressibly thankful to see him so nearly himself! so little removed from recovery.

---

7. From childhood, George III had been a devotee of George Frideric Handel (1685–1759), the great German-English composer. George III, who loved German music, took a keen interest in Charles Burney's pioneering work, *A General History of Music*; the third and fourth volumes were just about to be published.

8. Mary Delany, a figure at court and accomplished artist of works in cut paper, was regarded by Burney as "the pattern of a perfect fine lady," and had died the previous year.

[A MASTECTOMY]

Paris, March 22, 1812[9]

Separated as I have now so long—long been from my dearest father—brothers—sisters—nieces, and native friends, I would spare, at least, their kind hearts any grief for me but what they must inevitably feel in reflecting upon the sorrow of such an absence to one so tenderly attached to all her first and forever so dear and regretted ties—nevertheless, if they should hear that I have been dangerously ill from any hand but my own, they might have doubts of my perfect recovery which my own alone can obviate. And how can I hope they will escape hearing what has reached Seville to the south, and Constantinople to the east? from both I have had messages—yet nothing could urge me to this communication till I heard that M. de Boinville[1] had written it to his wife, without any precaution, because in ignorance of my plan of silence. Still I must hope it may never travel to my dearest father—But to you, my beloved Esther, who, living more in the world, will surely hear it ere long, to you I will write the whole history, certain that, from the moment you know any evil has befallen me your kind kind heart will be constantly anxious to learn its extent and its circumstances, as well as its termination.

About August, in the year 1810, I began to be annoyed by a small pain in my breast, which went on augmenting from week to week, yet, being rather heavy than acute, without causing me any uneasiness with respect to consequences: Alas, "what was the ignorance?" The most sympathizing of partners, however, was more disturbed: not a start, not a wry face, not a movement that indicated pain was unobserved, and he early conceived apprehensions to which I was a stranger. He pressed me to see some surgeon; I revolted from the idea, and hoped, by care and warmth, to make all succor unnecessary. Thus passed some months, during which Madame de Maisonneuve, my particularly intimate friend, joined with M. d'Arblay to press me to consent to an examination. I thought their fears groundless, and could not make so great a conquest over my repugnance. I relate this false confidence, now, as a warning to my dear Esther—my sisters and nieces, should any similar sensations excite similar alarm. M. d'Arblay now revealed his uneasiness to another of our kind friends, Mme. de Tracy, who wrote to me a long and eloquent letter upon the subject, that began to awaken very unpleasant surmises; and a conference with her ensued, in which her urgency and representations, aided by her long experience of disease, and most miserable existence by art, subdued me, and, most painfully and reluctantly, I ceased to object, and M. d'Arblay summoned a physician—M. Bourdois? Maria will cry;—No, my dear Maria, I would not give your beau frere[2] that trouble; not him, but Dr. Jouart, the physician of Miss Potts. Thinking but slightly of my statement, he gave me some directions that produced no fruit—on the contrary, I grew worse, and M. d'Arblay now would take no denial to my consulting M. Dubois, who had already attended and cured me in an abscess of which Maria, my dearest Esther, can give you the history.

---

9. Burney (now Madame D'Arblay) sent this letter to Esther Burney, her sister; it describes an operation performed the previous September.
1. Because Chastel de Boinville's wife was English, it was likely that news of the illness would spread to the Burney family in England.
2. Brother-in-law. Maria (or Marianne), Esther Burney's daughter, had married Antoine Bourdois, whose brother was a prominent French physician.

M. Dubois, the most celebrated surgeon of France, was then appointed accoucheur to the empress, and already lodged in the Tuilleries,[3] and in constant attendance: but nothing could slacken the ardour of M. d'Arblay to obtain the first advice. Fortunately for his kind wishes, M. Dubois had retained a partial regard for me from the time of his former attendance, and, when applied to through a third person, he took the first moment of liberty, granted by a *promenade* taken by the empress, to come to me. It was now I began to perceive my real danger, M. Dubois gave me a prescription to be pursued for a month, during which time he could not undertake to see me again, and pronounced nothing—but uttered so many charges to me to be tranquil, and to suffer no uneasiness, that I could not but suspect there was room for terrible inquietude. My alarm was increased by the nonappearance of M. d'Arblay after his departure. They had remained together some time in the book room, and M. d'Arblay did not return—till, unable to bear the suspense, I begged him to come back. He, also, sought then to tranquilize me— but in words only; his looks were shocking! his features, his whole face displayed the bitterest woe. I had not, therefore, much difficulty in telling myself what he endeavored not to tell me—that a small operation would be necessary to avert evil consequences!—Ah, my dearest Esther, for this I felt no courage—my dread and repugnance, from a thousand reasons *besides* the pain, almost shook all my faculties, and, for some time, I was rather confounded and stupified than affrighted.—Direful, however, was the effect of this interview; the pains became quicker and more violent, and the hardness of the spot affected increased. I took, but vainly, my proscription, and every symptom grew more serious.

* * *

A physician was now called in, Dr. Moreau, to hear if he could suggest any new means: but Dr. Larrey[4] had left him no resources untried. A formal consultation now was held, of Larrey, Ribe, and Moreau—and, in fine, I was formally condemned to an operation by all three. I was as much astonished as disappointed—for the poor breast was no where discoloured, and not much larger than its healthy neighbor. Yet I felt the evil to be deep, so deep, that I often thought if it could not be dissolved, it could only with life be extirpated. I called up, however, all the reason I possessed, or could assume, and told them that—if they saw no other alternative, I would not resist their opinion and experience:—the good Dr. Larrey, who, during his long attendance had conceived for me the warmest friendship, had now tears in his eyes; from my dread he had expected resistance.

* * *

All hope of escaping this evil now at an end, I could only console or employ my mind in considering how to render it less dreadful to M. d'Arblay. M. Dubois had pronounced "il faut s'attendre à souffrir, Je ne veux pas vous tromper—Vous souffrirez—vous souffrirez *beaucoup*!—"[5] M. Ribe had *charged* me to cry! to withhold or restrain myself might have seriously

3. The royal palace in Paris. "Accoucheur": obstetrician.
4. Dominique-Jean Larrey, "Napoleon's surgeon," is remembered for his courage on the battlefield and his innovative procedures.

5. You must expect to suffer. I do not want to deceive you—you will suffer—you will suffer *greatly* (French). Operations were then performed without anesthetics.

bad consequences, he said. M. Moreau, in echoing this injunction, inquired whether I had cried or screamed at the birth of Alexander—Alas, I told him, it had not been possible to do otherwise; Oh then, he answered, there is no fear!—What terrible inferences were here to be drawn! I desired, therefore, that M. d'Arblay might be kept in ignorance of the day till the operation should be over. To this they agreed, except M. Larrey, with high approbation: M. Larrey looked dissentient, but was silent. M. Dubois protested he would not undertake to act, after what he had seen of the agitated spirits of M. d'Arblay if he were present: nor would he suffer me to know the time myself over night; I obtained with difficulty a promise of 4 hours warning, which were essential to me for sundry regulations.

From this time, I assumed the best spirits in my power, *to meet the coming blow*;—and support my too sympathizing partner.

* * *

Sundry necessary works and orders filled up my time entirely till one o'clock, when all was ready—but Dr. Moreau then arrived, with news that M. Dubois could not attend till three. Dr. Aumont went away—and the coast was clear. This, indeed, was a dreadful interval. I had no longer any thing to do—I had only to think—two hours thus spent seemed never-ending. I would fain have written to my dearest father—to you, my Esther—to Charlotte James—Charles—Amelia Lock—but my arm prohibited me: I strolled to the salon—I saw it fitted with preparations, and I recoiled—But I soon returned; to what effect disguise from myself what I must so soon know?—yet the sight of the immense quantity of bandages, compresses, spunges, lint—made me a little sick:—I walked backwards and forwards till I quieted all emotion, and became by degrees, nearly stupid—torpid, without sentiment or consciousness;—and thus I remained till the clock struck three. A sudden spirit of exertion then returned,—I defied my poor arm, no longer worth sparing, and took my long banished pen to write a few words to M. d'Arblay—and a few more for Alex, in case of a fatal result. These short billets I could only deposit safely, when the cabriolets[6]—one—two—three—four—succeeded rapidly to each other in stopping at the door. Dr. Moreau instantly entered my room, to see if I were alive. He gave me a wine cordial, and went to the salon. I rang for my maid and nurses,—but before I could speak to them, my room, without previous message, was entered by 7 men in black, Dr. Larrey, M. Dubois, Dr. Moreau, Dr. Aumont, Dr. Ribe, and a pupil of Dr. Larrey, and another of M. Dubois. I was now awakened from my stupor—and by a sort of indignation—Why so many? and without leave?—But I could not utter a syllable. M. Dubois acted as commander in chief. Dr. Larrey kept out of sight; M. Dubois ordered a bedstead into the middle of the room. Astonished, I turned to Dr. Larrey, who had promised that an arm chair would suffice; but he hung his head, and would not look at me. Two *old mattresses* M. Dubois then demanded, and an old sheet. I now began to tremble violently, more with distaste and horror of the preparations even than of the pain. These arranged to his liking, he desired me to mount the bedstead. I stood suspended, for a moment, whether I should not abruptly escape—I looked at the door, the windows—I felt desperate—but it was only for a moment, my reason then took the command, and my fears and feelings struggled vainly

6. Carriages.

against it. I called to my maid—she was crying, and the two nurses stood, transfixed, at the door. "Let those women all go!" cried M. Dubois. This order recovered me my voice—"No," I cried, "let them stay! *qu'elles restent!*" This occasioned a little dispute, that re-animated me—The maid, however, and one of the nurses ran off—I charged the other to approach, and she obeyed. M. Dubois now tried to issue his commands *en militaire*,[7] but I resisted all that were resistable—I was compelled, however, to submit to taking off my long robe de chambre,[8] which I had meant to retain—Ah, then, how did I think of my sisters!—not one, at so dreadful an instant, at hand, to protect—adjust—guard me—I regretted that I had refused Mme de Maisonneuve—Mme Chastel—no one upon whom I could rely—my departed angel![9]—how did I think of her!—how did I long—long for my Esther—my Charlotte!—My distress was, I suppose, apparent, though not my wishes, for M. Dubois himself now softened, and spoke soothingly. "Can *you*," I cried, "feel for an operation that, to *you*, must seem so trivial?"—"Trivial?" he repeated—taking up a bit of paper, which he tore, unconsciously, into a million pieces, "*oui—c'est peu de chose—mais—*"[1] he stammered, and could not go on. No one else attempted to speak, but I was softened myself, when I saw even M. Dubois grow agitated, while Dr. Larrey kept always aloof, yet a glance showed me he was pale as ashes. I knew not, positively, then, the immediate danger, but every thing convinced me danger was hovering about me, and that this experiment could alone save me from its jaws. I mounted, therefore, unbidden, the bedstead—and M. Dubois placed me upon the mattress, and spread a cambric handkerchief upon my face. It was transparent, however, and I saw, through it, that the bedstead was instantly surrounded by the 7 men and my nurse. I refused to be held; but when, bright through the cambric, I saw the glitter of polished steel—I closed my eyes. I would not trust to convulsive fear the sight of the terrible incision. A silence the most profound ensued, which lasted for some minutes, during which, I imagine, they took their orders by signs, and made their examination—Oh what a horrible suspension!—I did not breathe—and M. Dubois tried vainly to find any pulse. This pause, at length, was broken by Dr. Larrey, who in a voice of solemn melancholy, said "Qui me tiendra ce sein?—"[2]

No one answered; at least not verbally; but this aroused me from my passively submissive state, for I feared they imagined the whole breast infected—feared it too justly,—for, again through the cambric, I saw the hand of M. Dubois held up, while his forefinger first described a straight line from top to bottom of the breast, secondly a cross, and thirdly a circle; intimating that the whole was to be taken off. Excited by this idea, I started up, threw off my veil, and, in answer to the demand "Qui me tiendra ce sein?" cried "C'est moi, Monsieur!"[3] and I held my hand under it, and explained the nature of my sufferings, which all sprang from one point, though they darted into every part. I was heard attentively, but in utter silence, and M. Dubois then, re-placed me as before, and, as before, spread my veil over my face. How vain, alas, my representation! immediately again I saw the fatal finger describe the cross—and the circle—Hopeless, then, desperate, and self-given

---

7. In military fashion (French). Most of the attending physicians had been army surgeons.
8. Dressing gown.
9. Susanna, Burney's favorite sister, had died in

1800.
1. Yes—it is not much—but— (French).
2. Who will hold this breast for me? (French).
3. *I* will (French).

up, I closed once more my eyes, relinquishing all watching, all resistance, all interference, and sadly resolute to be wholly resigned.

My dearest Esther,—and all my dears to whom she communicates this doleful ditty, will rejoice to hear that this resolution once taken, was firmly adhered to, in defiance of a terror that surpasses all description, and the most torturing pain. Yet—when the dreadful steel was plunged into the breast—cutting through veins—arteries—flesh—nerves—I needed no injunctions not to restrain my cries. I began a scream that lasted unintermittingly during the whole time of the incision—and I almost marvel that it rings not in my ears still! so excruciating was the agony. When the wound was made, and the instrument was withdrawn, the pain seemed undiminished, for the air that suddenly rushed into those delicate parts felt like a mass of minute but sharp and forked poniards,[4] that were tearing the edges of the wound—but when again I felt the instrument—describing a curve—cutting against the grain, if I may so say, while the flesh resisted in a manner so forcible as to oppose and tire the hand of the operator, who was forced to change from the right to the left—then, indeed, I thought I must have expired. I attempted no more to open my eyes,—they felt as if hermetically shut, and so firmly closed, that the eyelids seemed indented into the cheeks. The instrument this second time withdrawn, I concluded the operation over,—Oh no! presently the terrible cutting was renewed—and worse than ever, to separate the bottom, the foundation of this dreadful gland from the parts to which it adhered—Again all description would be baffled—yet again all was not over,—Dr. Larrey rested but his own hand, and—Oh heaven!—I then felt the knife rackling[5] against the breast bone—scraping it!—This performed, while I yet remained in utterly speechless torture, I heard the voice of Mr. Larrey,—(all others guarded a dead silence) in a tone nearly tragic, desire every one present to pronounce if anything more remained to be done; or if he thought the operation complete. The general voice was yes,—but the finger of Mr. Dubois—which I literally *felt* elevated over the wound, though I saw nothing, and though he touched nothing, so indescribably sensitive was the spot—pointed to some further requisition[6]—and again began the scraping!—and, after this, Dr. Moreau thought he discerned a peccant atom—and still, and still, M. Dubois demanded atom after atom—My dearest Esther, not for days, not for weeks, but for months I could not speak of this terrible business without nearly again going through it! I could not *think* of it with impunity! I was sick, I was disordered by a single question—even now, 9 months after it is over, I have a head ache from going on with the account! and this miserable account, which I began 3 months ago, at least, I dare not revise, nor read, the recollection is still so painful.

To conclude, the evil was so profound, the case so delicate, and the precautions necessary for preventing a return so numerous, that the operation, including the treatment and the dressing, lasted 20 minutes! a time, for sufferings so acute, that was hardly supportable—However, I bore it with all the courage I could exert, and never moved, nor stopped them, nor resisted, nor remonstrated, nor spoke—except once or twice, during the dressings, to say "Ah Messieurs! que je vous plains!—"[7] for indeed I was sensible to the feeling

4. Daggers.
5. Raking (?).
6. Necessity. Surgical practice of the time dictated that "the whole diseased structure" be cut out, no matter how long or painful the operation.
7. How I pity you! (French).

concern with which they all saw what I endured, though my speech was principally—*very* principally meant for Dr. Larrey. Except this, I uttered not a
syllable, save, when so often they re-commenced, calling out "Avertissez moi,
Messieurs! avertissez moi!—"[8] Twice, I believe, I fainted; at least, I have two
total chasms in my memory of this transaction, that impede my tying together
what passed. When all was done, and they lifted me up that I might be put to
bed, my strength was so totally annihilated, that I was obliged to be carried,
and could not even sustain my hands and arms, which hung as if I had been
lifeless; while my face, as the nurse has told me, was utterly colorless. This
removal made me open my eyes—and I then saw my good Dr. Larrey, pale
nearly as myself, his face streaked with blood, and its expression depicting
grief, apprehension, and almost horror.

When I was in bed,—my poor M. d'Arblay—who ought to write you him-
selfhisownhistoryofthismorning—wascalledtome—andafterwardsourAlex.—

[M. D'ARBLAY'S POSTSCRIPT]

No! No my dearest and ever more dear friends, I shall not make a *fruitless*
attempt. No language could convey what I felt in the deadly course of these
seven hours. Nevertheless, every one *of you, my dearest dearest friends*, can
guess, must even know it. Alexandre had no less feeling, but showed more
fortitude. He, perhaps, will be more able to describe to you, nearly at least,
the torturing state of my poor heart and soul. Besides, I must own, to you,
that these details which were, till just now, quite unknown to me, have
almost killed me, and I am only able to thank God that this more than half
angel has had the sublime courage to deny herself the comfort I might have
offered her, to spare me, not the sharing of her excruciating pains, that was
impossible, but the witnessing so terrific a scene, and perhaps the remorse to
have rendered it more tragic. For I don't flatter myself I could have got
through it—I must confess it.

Thank heaven! She is now surprisingly well, and in good spirits, and we
hope to have many many still happy days. May that of peace soon arrive, and
enable me to embrace better than with my pen my beloved and ever ever
more dear friends of the town and country. Amen. Amen![9]

---

8. Give me warning! (French).
9. The wound healed without infection. Burney

returned to England later in 1812 and lived for
twenty-eight more years.

OLAUDAH EQUIANO
ca. 1745–1797

---

*T*he *Interesting Narrative of the Life of Olaudah Equiano, or Gustavus Vassa,
the African, Written by Himself*, published in 1789, is the classic story of an
eighteenth-century African's descent into slavery and rise to freedom. It describes
how its author (ca. 1745–1797) was raised in an Ibo village (in modern Nigeria), kid-

napped by African raiders, and sold into slavery. Particularly powerful is its account of the horrors of the Middle Passage to the New World. There, an English naval officer bought him to serve as a cabin boy and renamed him Gustavus Vassa, after a sixteenth-century Swedish hero who freed his people from the Danes (such names concealed the status of a slave, because slavery was frowned on by the British Navy). During years at sea, as well as a period at a London school, Equiano acquired a basic education. He also underwent baptism, a ritual that many slaves expected to make them free. But his hopes were cruelly disappointed when, after six years' service, he was suddenly sold and shipped to the West Indies. There a Quaker merchant, Robert King, purchased him, employed him as a clerk and a seaman, and eventually allowed him, in 1766, to buy his freedom. Equiano went back to England, working first as a hairdresser and later voyaging all over the world, even taking part in an effort to find a passage to India by way of the North Pole. Scholars have raised doubts about the account that the *Interesting Narrative* gives of the early parts of Equiano's life: parish and British naval records indicate he was born not in Africa but in South Carolina and hence did not himself undergo the Middle Passage. Whether fact or fiction—scholars may never determine conclusively—the description of his days in Africa, abduction, and suffering in the slave ship gives a voice to countless Africans who faced such experiences and dramatizes the undeniable realities of the slave trade to a white readership. Equiano's publication of his story is a culmination of his involvement in the abolitionist movement through the 1780s and was an important contribution to that movement, not only for its explicit arguments against the slave trade but also for its demonstration that someone of African descent could be humane, intelligent, a good Christian, and a free and eloquent British subject. The book went through many editions and made Equiano famous. He married an Englishwoman, fathered two daughters, and died in London in 1797.

The *Life of Equiano* combines several literary genres. It is a captivity narrative, a spiritual autobiography, a travel memoir, an adventure story, and an abolitionist tract. The early chapters describe the healthy, cheerful, and virtuous life of Africans, contrasted with European inhumanity, and the later chapters show how much a black man can achieve, when given a chance. Equiano does not disguise the strains of his position as he is pulled between different identities and different worlds. His main

William Blake, **A Coromantyn Free Negro, or Ranger, Armed,** 1796. Blake depicts the strength and independence of one of the African soldiers in Surinam promised their freedom for fighting with whites to suppress a slave rebellion. His scarlet cap signifies liberty. From John Stedman, *Narrative of a Five Years Expedition Against the Revolted Negroes of Surinam . . . from the Year 1772, to 1777* (1796).

purpose, however, is clearly to force his readers to face the ordeals a slave must endure—to live in his skin. If *Oroonoko* taught Europeans to sympathize with Africans, Equiano taught them that a black man could speak for himself.

From The Interesting Narrative of the Life of Olaudah Equiano, or Gustavus Vassa, the African, Written by Himself

[THE MIDDLE PASSAGE][1]

The first object which saluted my eyes when I arrived on the coast was the sea, and a slave ship, which was then riding at anchor, and waiting for its cargo. These filled me with astonishment, which was soon converted into terror when I was carried on board. I was immediately handled and tossed up to see if I were sound by some of the crew; and I was now persuaded that I had gotten into a world of bad spirits, and that they were going to kill me. Their complexions too differing so much from ours, their long hair, and the language they spoke, (which was very different from any I had ever heard) united to confirm me in this belief. Indeed such were the horrors of my views and fears at the moment, that, if ten thousand worlds had been my own, I would have freely parted with them all to have exchanged my condition with that of the meanest slave in my own country. When I looked round the ship too and saw a large furnace of copper boiling, and a multitude of black people of every description chained together, every one of their countenances expressing dejection and sorrow, I no longer doubted of my fate; and, quite overpowered with horror and anguish, I fell motionless on the deck and fainted. When I recovered a little I found some black people about me, who I believe were some of those who brought me on board, and had been receiving their pay; they talked to me in order to cheer me, but all in vain. I asked them if we were not to be eaten by those white men with horrible looks, red faces, and loose hair. They told me I was not; and one of the crew brought me a small portion of spirituous liquor in a wine glass; but, being afraid of him, I would not take it out of his hand. One of the blacks therefore took it from him and gave it to me, and I took a little down my palate, which, instead of reviving me, as they thought it would, threw me into the greatest consternation at the strange feeling it produced, having never tasted any such liquor before. Soon after this the blacks who brought me on board went off, and left me abandoned to despair. I now saw myself deprived of all chance of returning to my native country, or even the least glimpse of hope of gaining the shore, which I now considered as friendly; and I even wished for my former slavery in preference to my present situation, which was filled with horrors of every kind, still heightened by my ignorance of what I was to undergo. I was not long suffered to indulge my grief; I was soon put down under the decks, and there I received such a salutation in my nostrils as I had never experienced in my life; so that, with the loathsomeness of the stench, and crying together, I became so sick and low that I was not able to eat, nor had I the least desire to taste any thing. I now wished for

---

1. After his kidnapping, young Equiano passes from one African master to another. The last of these, a merchant, treats him like a member of the family, until one morning the boy is suddenly wakened and hurried away to the seacoast.

the last friend, death, to relieve me; but soon, to my grief, two of the white men offered me eatables; and, on my refusing to eat, one of them held me fast by the hands, and laid me across I think the windlass, and tied my feet, while the other flogged me severely. I had never experienced any thing of this kind before; and although, not being used to the water, I naturally feared that element the first time I saw it, yet nevertheless, could I have got over the nettings,[2] I would have jumped over the side, but I could not; and, besides, the crew used to watch us very closely who were not chained down to the decks, lest we should leap into the water; and I have seen some of these poor African prisoners most severely cut for attempting to do so, and hourly whipped for not eating. This indeed was often the case with myself. In a little time after, amongst the poor chained men, I found some of my own nation, which in a small degree gave ease to my mind. I inquired of these what was to be done with us; they gave me to understand we were to be carried to these white people's country to work for them. I then was a little revived, and thought, if it were no worse than working, my situation was not so desperate: but still I feared I should be put to death, the white people looked and acted, as I thought, in so savage a manner; for I had never seen among any people such instances of brutal cruelty; and this not only shewn towards us blacks, but also to some of the whites themselves. One white man in particular I saw, when we were permitted to be on deck, flogged so unmercifully with a large rope near the foremast, that he died in consequence of it; and they tossed him over the side as they would have done a brute. This made me fear these people the more; and I expected nothing less than to be treated in the same manner. I could not help expressing my fears and apprehensions to some of my countrymen: I asked them if these people had no country, but lived in this hollow place (the ship): they told me they did not, but came from a distant one. "Then," said I, "how comes it in all our country we never heard of them?" They told me because they lived so very far off. I then asked where were their women? had they any like themselves? I was told they had: "and why," said I, "do we not see them?" they answered, because they were left behind. I asked how the vessel could go? they told me they could not tell; but that there were cloths put upon the masts by the help of the ropes I saw, and then the vessel went on; and the white men had some spell or magic they put in the water when they liked in order to stop the vessel. I was exceedingly amazed at this account, and really thought they were spirits. I therefore wished much to be from amongst them, for I expected they would sacrifice me: but my wishes were vain; for we were so quartered that it was impossible for any of us to make our escape. While we stayed on the coast I was mostly on deck; and one day, to my great astonishment, I saw one of these vessels coming in with the sails up. As soon as the whites saw it, they gave a great shout, at which we were amazed; and the more so as the vessel appeared larger by approaching nearer. At last she came to an anchor in my sight, and when the anchor was let go I and my countrymen who saw it were lost in astonishment to observe the vessel stop; and were now convinced it was done by magic. Soon after this the other ship got her boats out, and they came on board of us, and the people of both ships seemed very glad to see each other. Several of the strangers also shook

---

2. A network of small ropes around the ship kept slaves from jumping overboard.

hands with us black people, and made motions with their hands, signifying I suppose we were to go to their country; but we did not understand them. At last, when the ship we were in had got in all her cargo, they made ready with many fearful noises, and we were all put under deck, so that we could not see how they managed the vessel. But this disappointment was the least of my sorrow. The stench of the hold while we were on the coast was so intolerably loathsome, that it was dangerous to remain there for any time, and some of us had been permitted to stay on the deck for the fresh air; but now that the whole ship's cargo were confined together, it became absolutely pestilential. The closeness of the place, and the heat of the climate, added to the number in the ship, which was so crowded that each had scarcely room to turn himself, almost suffocated us. This produced copious perspirations, so that the air soon became unfit for respiration, from a variety of loathsome smells, and brought on a sickness among the slaves, of which many died, thus falling victims to the improvident avarice, as I may call it, of their purchasers. This wretched situation was again aggravated by the galling of the chains, now become insupportable; and the filth of the necessary tubs,[3] into which the children often fell, and were almost suffocated. The shrieks of the women, and the groans of the dying, rendered the whole a scene of horror almost inconceivable. Happily perhaps for myself I was soon reduced so low here that it was thought necessary to keep me almost always on deck; and from[4] my extreme youth I was not put in fetters. In this situation I expected every hour to share the fate of my companions, some of whom were almost daily brought upon deck at the point of death, which I began to hope would soon put an end to my miseries. Often did I think many of the inhabitants of the deep much more happy than myself. I envied them the freedom they enjoyed, and as often wished I could change my condition for theirs. Every circumstance I met with served only to render my state more painful, and heighten my apprehensions, and my opinion of the cruelty of the whites. One day they had taken a number of fishes; and when they had killed and satisfied themselves with as many as they thought fit, to our astonishment who were on the deck, rather than give any of them to us to eat as we expected, they tossed the remaining fish into the sea again, although we begged and prayed for some as well as we could, but in vain; and some of my countrymen, being pressed by hunger, took an opportunity, when they thought no one saw them, of trying to get a little privately; but they were discovered, and the attempt procured them some very severe floggings.

One day, when we had a smooth sea and moderate wind, two of my wearied countrymen who were chained together (I was near them at the time), preferring death to such a life of misery, somehow made through the nettings and jumped into the sea; immediately another quite dejected fellow, who, on account of his illness, was suffered to be out of irons, also followed their example; and I believe many more would very soon have done the same if they had not been prevented by the ship's crew, who were instantly alarmed. Those of us that were the most active were in a moment put down under the deck, and there was such a noise and confusion amongst the people of the ship as I never heard before, to stop her, and get the boat out

3. Latrines.   4. Because of.

to go after the slaves. However two of the wretches were drowned, but they got the other, and afterwards flogged him unmercifully for thus attempting to prefer death to slavery. In this manner we continued to undergo more hardships than I can now relate, hardships which are inseparable from this accursed trade. Many a time we were near suffocation from the want of fresh air, which we were often without for whole days together. This, and the stench of the necessary tubs, carried off many. During our passage I first saw flying fishes, which surprised me very much: they used frequently to fly across the ship, and many of them fell on the deck. I also now first saw the use of the quadrant; I had often with astonishment seen the mariners make observations with it, and I could not think what it meant. They at last took notice of my surprise; and one of them, willing to increase it, as well as to gratify my curiosity, made me one day look through it. The clouds appeared to me to be land, which disappeared as they passed along. This heightened my wonder; and I was now more persuaded than ever that I was in another world, and that every thing about me was magic. At last we came in sight of the island of Barbados,[5] at which the whites on board gave a great shout, and made many signs of joy to us. We did not know what to think of this; but as the vessel drew nearer we plainly saw the harbor, and other ships of different kinds and sizes; and we soon anchored amongst them off Bridge Town. Many merchants and planters now came on board, though it was in the evening. They put us in separate parcels,[6] and examined us attentively. They also made us jump, and pointed to the land, signifying we were to go there. We thought by this we should be eaten by these ugly men, as they appeared to us; and, when soon after we were all put down under the deck again, there was much dread and trembling among us, and nothing but bitter cries to be heard all the night from these apprehensions, insomuch that at last the white people got some old slaves from the land to pacify us. They told us we were not to be eaten, but to work, and were soon to go on land, where we should see many of our country people. This report eased us much; and sure enough, soon after we were landed, there came to us Africans of all languages. We were conducted immediately to the merchant's yard, where we were pent up altogether like so many sheep in a fold, without regard to sex or age. As every object was new to me, every thing I saw filled me with surprise. What struck me first was that the houses were built with stories, and in every other respect different from those in Africa; but I was still more astonished on seeing people on horseback. I did not know what this could mean; and indeed I thought these people were full of nothing but magical arts. While I was in this astonishment one of my fellow prisoners spoke to a countryman of his about the horses, who said they were the same kind they had in their country. I understood them, though they were from a distant part of Africa, and I thought it odd I had not seen any horses there; but afterwards, when I came to converse with different Africans, I found they had many horses amongst them, and much larger than those I then saw. We were not many days in the merchant's custody before we were sold after their usual manner, which is this:—On a signal given (as the beat of a drum) the buyers rush at once into the yard where the slaves are confined, and make a choice of that parcel they like best. The noise and clamor with which this is

5. The easternmost Caribbean island, then an important center for the trade of sugar and slaves.

6. Groups sorted to be sold as one lot.

attended, and the eagerness visible in the countenances of the buyers, serve not a little to increase the apprehensions of the terrified Africans, who may well be supposed to consider them as the ministers of that destruction to which they think themselves devoted.[7] In this manner, without scruple, are relations and friends separated, most of them never to see each other again. I remember in the vessel in which I was brought over, in the men's apartment, there were several brothers, who, in the sale, were sold in different lots; and it was very moving on this occasion to see and hear their cries at parting. O, ye nominal Christians! might not an African ask you, learned you this from your God, who says unto you, Do unto all men as you would men should do unto you? Is it not enough that we are torn from our country and friends to toil for your luxury and lust of gain? Must every tender feeling be likewise sacrificed to your avarice? Are the dearest friends and relations, now rendered more dear by their separation from their kindred, still to be parted from each other, and thus prevented from cheering the gloom of slavery with the small comfort of being together and mingling their sufferings and sorrows? Why are parents to lose their children, brothers their sisters, or husbands their wives? Surely this is a new refinement in cruelty, which, while it has no advantage to atone for it, thus aggravates distress, and adds fresh horrors even to the wretchedness of slavery.

* * *

[A FREE MAN][8]

Every day now brought me nearer my freedom, and I was impatient till we proceeded again to sea, that I might have an opportunity of getting a sum large enough to purchase it. I was not long ungratified; for, in the beginning of the year 1766, my master bought another sloop, named the *Nancy*, the largest I had ever seen. She was partly laden, and was to proceed to Philadelphia; our Captain had his choice of three, and I was well pleased he chose this, which was the largest; for, from his having a large vessel, I had more room, and could carry a larger quantity of goods with me. Accordingly, when we had delivered our old vessel, the *Prudence*, and completed the lading of the *Nancy*, having made near three hundred per cent, by four barrels of pork I brought from Charlestown, I laid in as large a cargo as I could, trusting to God's providence to prosper my undertaking. With these views I sailed for Philadelphia. On our passage, when we drew near the land, I was for the first time surprised at the sight of some whales, having never seen any such large sea monsters before; and as we sailed by the land one morning I saw a puppy whale close by the vessel; it was about the length of a wherry boat, and it followed us all the day till we got within the Capes. We arrived safe and in good time at Philadelphia, and I sold my goods there chiefly to the Quakers. They always appeared to be a very honest discreet sort of people, and never attempted to impose on me; I therefore liked them, and ever after chose to deal with them in preference to any others.

---

7. Doomed.
8. Frustrated in his hope to be set free in England, Equiano is shipped to Montserrat, a British colony in the Leeward Islands of the West Indies. Robert King, a prosperous Quaker merchant from Philadelphia, buys him, treats him kindly, and values him as a reliable worker. By being useful to a friendly sea captain, Thomas Farmer, Equiano has opportunities to travel and trade goods for money. Eventually King promises to let him purchase his freedom for his original cost: forty pounds sterling.

One Sunday morning while I was here, as I was going to church, I chanced to pass a meeting house. The doors being open, and the house full of people, it excited my curiosity to go in. When I entered the house, to my great surprise, I saw a very tall woman standing in the midst of them, speaking in an audible voice something which I could not understand. Having never seen anything of this kind before, I stood and stared about me for some time, wondering at this odd scene. As soon as it was over I took an opportunity to make inquiry about the place and people, when I was informed they were called Quakers.[9] I particularly asked what that woman I saw in the midst of them had said, but none of them were pleased to satisfy me; so I quitted them, and soon after, as I was returning, I came to a church crowded with people; the church-yard was full likewise, and a number of people were even mounted on ladders, looking in at the windows. I thought this a strange sight, as I had never seen churches, either in England or the West Indies, crowded in this manner before. I therefore made bold to ask some people the meaning of all this, and they told me the Rev. Mr. George Whitfield[1] was preaching. I had often heard of this gentleman, and had wished to see and hear him; but I had never before had an opportunity. I now therefore resolved to gratify myself with the sight, and I pressed in amidst the multitude. When I got into the church I saw this pious man exhorting the people with the greatest fervor and earnestness, and sweating as much as I ever did while in slavery on Montserrat beach. I was very much struck and impressed with this; I thought it strange I had never seen divines exert themselves in this manner before, and I was no longer at a loss to account for the thin congregations they preached to.

When we had discharged our cargo here, and were loaded again, we left this fruitful land once more, and set sail for Montserrat. My traffic had hitherto succeeded so well with me, that I thought, by selling my goods when we arrived at Montserrat, I should have enough to purchase my freedom. But, as soon as our vessel arrived there, my master came on board, and gave orders for us to go to St. Eustatia,[2] and discharge our cargo there, and from thence proceed for Georgia. I was much disappointed at this; but thinking, as usual, it was of no use to murmur at the decrees of fate, I submitted without repining, and we went to St. Eustatia. After we had discharged our cargo there we took in a live cargo, as we call a cargo of slaves. Here I sold my goods tolerably well; but, not being able to lay out all my money in this small island to as much advantage as in many other places, I laid out only part, and the remainder I brought away with me neat.[3] We sailed from hence for Georgia, and I was glad when we got there, though I had not much reason to like the place from my last adventure in Savannah;[4] but I longed to get back to Montserrat and procure my freedom, which I expected to be able to purchase when I returned. As soon as we arrived here I waited on my careful doctor, Mr. Brady, to whom I made the most grateful acknowledgments in my power for his former kindness and attention during my illness.

9. Quaker meetings are not led by clergy; any worshiper who feels inspired by God can rise to speak.
1. Whitefield (1714–1770), a famous evangelist who helped found Methodism, was in Britain, not Philadelphia, in 1766. It is possible that Equiano had heard him preach the previous year, in Savannah, Georgia. Equiano's later conversion to Meth-odism will become a dominant theme of his life story.
2. An island in the Netherlands Antilles (West Indies).
3. Intact.
4. The year before, a drunken slave owner and his servant had beaten Equiano so brutally that he nearly died.

While we were here an odd circumstance happened to the Captain and me, which disappointed us both a good deal. A silversmith, whom we had brought to this place some voyages before, agreed with the Captain to return with us to the West Indies, and promised at the same time to give the Captain a great deal of money, having pretended to take a liking to him, and being, as we thought, very rich. But while we stayed to load our vessel this man was taken ill in a house where he worked, and in a week's time became very bad. The worse he grew the more he used to speak of giving the Captain what he had promised him, so that he expected something considerable from the death of this man, who had no wife or child, and he attended him day and night. I used also to go with the Captain, at his own desire, to attend him; especially when we saw there was no appearance of his recovery; and, in order to recompense me for my trouble, the Captain promised me ten pounds, when he should get the man's property. I thought this would be of great service to me, although I had nearly money enough to purchase my freedom, if I should get safe this voyage to Montserrat. In this expectation I laid out above eight pounds of my money for a suit of superfine clothes to dance with at my freedom, which I hoped was then at hand. We still continued to attend this man, and were with him even on the last day he lived, till very late at night, when we went on board. After we were got to bed, about one or two o'clock in the morning, the Captain was sent for, and informed the man was dead. On this he came to my bed, and, waking me, informed me of it, and desired me to get up and procure a light, and immediately go to him. I told him I was very sleepy, and wished he would take somebody else with him, or else, as the man was dead, and could want no farther attendance, to let all things remain as they were till next morning. "No, no," said he, "we will have the money tonight, I cannot wait till tomorrow; so let us go." Accordingly I got up and struck a light, and away we both went and saw the man as dead as we could wish. The Captain said he would give him a grand burial, in gratitude for the promised treasure; and desired that all the things belonging to the deceased might be brought forth. Among others, there was a nest of trunks of which he had kept the keys whilst the man was ill, and when they were produced we opened them with no small eagerness and expectation; and as there were a great number within one another, with much impatience we took them one out of the other. At last, when we came to the smallest, and had opened it, we saw it was full of papers, which we supposed to be notes; at the sight of which our hearts leapt for joy; and that instant the Captain, clapping his hands, cried out, "Thank God, here it is." But when we took up the trunk, and began to examine the supposed treasure and long-looked-for bounty, (alas! alas! how uncertain and deceitful are all human affairs!) what had we found! While we were embracing a substance we grasped an empty nothing. The whole amount that was in the nest of trunks was only one dollar and a half; and all that the man possessed would not pay for his coffin. Our sudden and exquisite joy was now succeeded by as sudden and exquisite pain; and my Captain and I exhibited, for some time, most ridiculous figures—pictures of chagrin and disappointment! We went away greatly mortified, and left the deceased to do as well as he could for himself, as we had taken so good care of him when alive for nothing. We set sail once more for Montserrat, and arrived there safe; but much out of humor with our friend the silversmith. When we had unladen the vessel, and I had sold my venture, finding myself master of about forty-seven pounds, I consulted my true friend, the Captain, how I should proceed in offering my master the money for my freedom. He told me to come on a certain morning, when he and my master would be at breakfast together. Accordingly, on that morning I went, and met the Captain there, as he had appointed. When I went in I made my obeisance to my master, and with my money in my hand, and many fears in my heart, I prayed him to be as good as his offer to me, when he was pleased to promise me my freedom as soon as I could purchase it. This speech seemed to confound him; he began to recoil; and my heart that instant sank within me. "What," said he, "give you your freedom? Why, where did you get the money? Have you got forty pounds sterling?" "Yes, sir," I answered. "How did you get it?" replied he. I told him, very honestly. The Captain then said he knew I got the money very honestly and with much industry, and that I was particularly careful. On which my master replied, I got money much faster than he did; and said he would not have made me the promise he did if he had thought I should have got money so soon. "Come, come," said my worthy Captain, clapping my master on the back, "Come, Robert" (which was his name), "I think you must let him have his freedom; you have laid your money out very well; you have received good interest for it all this time, and here is now the principal at last. I know Gustavus has earned you more than an hundred a-year, and he will still save you money, as he will not leave you:—Come, Robert, take the money." My master then said, he would not be worse than his promise; and, taking the money, told me to go to the Secretary at the Register Office, and get my manumission[5] drawn up. These words of my master were like a voice from heaven to me: in an instant all my trepidation was turned into unutterable bliss; and I most reverently bowed myself with gratitude, unable to express my feelings, but by the overflowing of my eyes, while my true and worthy friend, the Captain, congratulated us both with a peculiar degree of heartfelt pleasure. As soon as the first transports of my joy were over, and that I had expressed my thanks to these my worthy friends in the best manner I was able, I rose with a heart full of affection and reverence, and left the room, in order to obey my master's joyful mandate of going to the Register Office. As I was leaving the house I called to mind the words of the Psalmist, in the 126th Psalm, and like him, "I glorified God in my heart, in whom I trusted." These words had been impressed on my mind from the very day I was forced from Deptford[6] to the present hour, and I now saw them, as I thought, fulfilled and verified. My imagination was all rapture as I flew to the Register Office, and in this respect, like the apostle Peter[7] (whose deliverance from prison was so sudden and extraordinary, that he thought he was in a vision), I could scarcely believe I was awake. Heavens! who could do justice to my feelings at this moment! Not conquering heroes themselves, in the midst of a triumph—Not the tender mother who had just regained her long-lost infant, and presses it to her heart—Not the weary hungry mariner, at the sight of the desired friendly port—Not the lover, when he once more embraces his beloved mistress, after she had been ravished from his arms!—All within my breast was tumult, wildness, and delirium! My feet scarcely touched the ground, for they were winged with joy, and, like Elijah, as he rose to Heaven,[8] they "were with lightning

---

5. Release from slavery.
6. The port near London from which Equiano was sold by his English master.
7. Acts, chap, xii, ver. 9 [Equiano's note].
8. 2 Kings 2.11.

sped as I went on." Every one I met I told of my happiness, and blazed about the virtue of my amiable master and captain.

When I got to the office and acquainted the Register with my errand he congratulated me on the occasion, and told me he would draw up my manumission for half price, which was a guinea. I thanked him for his kindness; and having received it and paid him, I hastened to my master to get him to sign it, that I might be fully released. Accordingly he signed the manumission that day, so that, before night, I who had been a slave in the morning, trembling at the will of another, was become my own master, and completely free. I thought this was the happiest day I had ever experienced; and my joy was still heightened by the blessings and prayers of the sable race, particularly the aged, to whom my heart had ever been attached with reverence.

As the form of my manumission has something peculiar in it, and expresses the absolute power and dominion one man claims over his fellow, I shall beg leave to present it before my readers at full length:

Montserrat.—To all men unto whom these presents shall come: I Robert King, of the parish of St. Anthony in the said island, merchant, send greeting: Know ye, that I the aforesaid Robert King, for and in consideration of the sum of seventy pounds current money of the said island,[9] to me in hand paid, and to the intent that a negro man-slave, named Gustavus Vassa, shall and may become free, have manumitted, emancipated, enfranchised, and set free, and by these presents do manumit, emancipate, enfranchise, and set free, the aforesaid negro man-slave, named Gustavus Vassa, for ever, hereby giving, granting, and releasing unto him, the said Gustavus Vassa, all right, title, dominion, sovereignty, and property, which, as lord and master over the aforesaid Gustavus Vassa, I had, or now I have, or by any means whatsoever I may or can hereafter possibly have over him the aforesaid negro, for ever. In witness whereof I the above-said Robert King have unto these presents set my hand and seal, this tenth day of July, in the year of our Lord one thousand seven hundred and sixty-six.

ROBERT KING

Signed, sealed, and delivered in the presence of Terrylegay, Montserrat.

Registered the within manumission at full length, this eleventh day of July, 1766, in liber D.[1]

TERRYLEGAY, REGISTER.

In short, the fair as well as black people immediately styled me by a new appellation, to me the most desirable in the world, which was Freeman, and at the dances I gave my Georgia superfine blue clothes made no indifferent appearance, as I thought.

* * *

1789

---

9. The equivalent of forty pounds in British money.

1. Book or register D.

THOMAS GRAY
1716–1771

T he man who wrote the English poem most loved by those whom Samuel Johnson called "the common reader" was a scholarly recluse who lived the quiet life
of a university professor in the stagnant atmosphere of mid-eighteenth-century
Cambridge. Born in London, Thomas Gray was the only one of twelve children to
survive, and his family life was desperately unhappy. At eight he left home for Eton,
where he made intimate friends: Richard West, a fellow poet; Thomas Ashton; and
Horace Walpole, the son of the prime minister. After four years at Cambridge, Gray
left without a degree to take the grand tour of France and Italy as Walpole's guest.
The death of West in 1742 desolated Gray, and memories of West haunt much of his
verse. He spent the rest of his life in Cambridge, pursuing his studies and writing
wonderful letters as well as a handful of poems. Two high-flown Pindaric odes,
"The Progress of Poesy" (1754) and "The Bard" (1757), display his learning and his
love of nature and the sublime.

Most of Gray's poems take part in a contemporary reaction against the wit and
satiric elegance of Pope's couplets; poets sought a new style, at once intimate and
prophetic. Gray was not easily satisfied; he constantly revised his poems and published very little. Because he held that "the language of the age is never the language
of poetry," he often uses archaic words and a word order borrowed from Latin, where
a verb can precede its subject (as in line 35 of the "Elegy Written in a Country
Churchyard": "Awaits alike the inevitable hour"). But the "Elegy" stands alone in his
work. It balances Latinate phrases with living English speech, and the learning of a
scholar with a common humanity that everyone can share. Johnson, who did not usually like Gray's poetry, acknowledged that the "Elegy" would live on:

> The Churchyard abounds with images that find a mirror in every mind, and with
> sentiments to which every bosom returns an echo. The four stanzas beginning
> "Yet even these bones" are to me original: I have never seen the notions in any
> other place; yet he that reads them here, persuades himself that he has always
> felt them. Had Gray written often thus, it had been vain to blame, and useless to
> praise him.

Ode on the Death of a Favorite Cat[1]

Drowned in a Tub of Goldfishes

'Twas on a lofty vase's side,
Where China's gayest art had dyed
   The azure flowers that blow;°   *bloom*
Demurest of the tabby kind,
5 The pensive Selima reclined,
   Gazed on the lake below.

---

1. Selima, one of Horace Walpole's cats, had
recently drowned in a china cistern. Gray wrote
this memorial at Walpole's request. For an illustration of this poem by William Blake, see the
color insert in this volume.

Her conscious tail her joy declared;
The fair round face, the snowy beard,
 The velvet of her paws,
10 Her coat, that with the tortoise vies,
Her ears of jet, and emerald eyes,
 She saw; and purred applause.

Still had she gazed; but 'midst the tide
Two angel forms were seen to glide,
15 The genii of the stream:
Their scaly armor's Tyrian° hue   *purple*
Through richest purple to the view
 Betrayed a golden gleam.

The hapless nymph with wonder saw:
20 A whisker first and then a claw,
 With many an ardent wish,
She stretched in vain to reach the prize.
What female heart can gold despise?
 What cat's averse to fish?

25 Presumptuous maid! with looks intent
Again she stretched, again she bent,
 Nor knew the gulf between.
(Malignant Fate sat by and smiled)
The slippery verge her feet beguiled,
30 She tumbled headlong in.

Eight times emerging from the flood
She mewed to every watery god,
 Some speedy aid to send.
No dolphin came, no nereid° stirred: *sea nymph*
35 Nor cruel Tom, nor Susan[2] heard.
 A favorite has no friend!

From hence, ye beauties, undeceived,
Know, one false step is ne'er retrieved,
 And be with caution bold.
40 Not all that tempts your wandering eyes
And heedless hearts is lawful prize;
 Nor all that glisters gold.

1747   1748

Elegy Written in a Country Churchyard

The curfew[1] tolls the knell of parting day,
 The lowing herd wind slowly o'er the lea,
The plowman homeward plods his weary way,
 And leaves the world to darkness and to me.

2. Servants' names.   1. A bell rung in the evening.

5 Now fades the glimmering landscape on the sight,
     And all the air a solemn stillness holds,
  Save where the beetle wheels his droning flight,
     And drowsy tinklings lull the distant folds;

  Save that from yonder ivy-mantled tower
10   The moping owl does to the moon complain
  Of such, as wandering near her secret bower,
     Molest her ancient solitary reign.

  Beneath those rugged elms, that yew tree's shade,
     Where heaves the turf in many a moldering heap,
15 Each in his narrow cell forever laid,
     The rude° forefathers of the hamlet sleep.   *uneducated*

  The breezy call of incense-breathing Morn,
     The swallow twittering from the straw-built shed,
  The cock's shrill clarion, or the echoing horn,°   *hunter's horn*
20   No more shall rouse them from their lowly bed.

  For them no more the blazing hearth shall burn,
     Or busy housewife ply her evening care;
  No children run to lisp their sire's return,
     Or climb his knees the envied kiss to share.

25 Oft did the harvest to their sickle yield,
     Their furrow oft the stubborn glebe° has broke;   *soil*
  How jocund did they drive their team afield!
     How bowed the woods beneath their sturdy stroke!

  Let not Ambition mock their useful toil,
30   Their homely joys, and destiny obscure;
  Nor Grandeur hear with a disdainful smile
     The short and simple annals of the poor.

  The boast of heraldry,° the pomp of power,   *noble birth*
     And all that beauty, all that wealth e'er gave,
35 Awaits alike the inevitable hour.
     The paths of glory lead but to the grave.

  Nor you, ye proud, impute to these the fault,
     If Memory o'er their tomb no trophies[2] raise,
  Where through the long-drawn aisle and fretted[3] vault
40   The pealing anthem swells the note of praise.

  Can storied urn[4] or animated° bust   *lifelike*
     Back to its mansion call the fleeting breath?
  Can Honor's voice provoke° the silent dust,   *call forth*
     Or Flattery soothe the dull cold ear of Death?

---

2. An ornamental or symbolic group of figures depicting the achievements of the deceased.
3. Decorated with intersecting lines in relief.

4. A funeral urn with an epitaph or pictured story inscribed on it.

45 Perhaps in this neglected spot is laid
    Some heart once pregnant with celestial fire;
Hands that the rod of empire might have swayed,°   *wielded*
    Or waked to ecstasy the living lyre.

But Knowledge to their eyes her ample page
50   Rich with the spoils of time did ne'er unroll;
Chill Penury repressed their noble rage,°   *inspiration*
    And froze the genial° current of the soul.   *creative*

Full many a gem of purest ray serene,
    The dark unfathomed caves of ocean bear:
55 Full many a flower is born to blush unseen,
    And waste its sweetness on the desert air.

Some village Hampden,[5] that with dauntless breast
    The little tyrant of his fields withstood;
Some mute inglorious Milton here may rest,
60   Some Cromwell guiltless of his country's blood.

The applause of listening senates to command,
    The threats of pain and ruin to despise,
To scatter plenty o'er a smiling land,
    And read their history in a nation's eyes,

65 Their lot forbade: nor circumscribed alone
    Their growing virtues, but their crimes confined;
Forbade to wade through slaughter to a throne,
    And shut the gates of mercy on mankind,

The struggling pangs of conscious truth to hide,
70   To quench the blushes of ingenuous shame,
Or heap the shrine of Luxury and Pride
    With incense kindled at the Muse's flame.

Far from the madding crowd's ignoble strife,
    Their sober wishes never learned to stray;
75 Along the cool sequestered vale of life
    They kept the noiseless tenor of their way.

Yet even these bones from insult to protect
    Some frail memorial still erected nigh,
With uncouth rhymes and shapeless sculpture decked,[6]
80   Implores the passing tribute of a sigh.

Their name, their years, spelt by the unlettered Muse,
    The place of fame and elegy supply:
And many a holy text around she strews,
    That teach the rustic moralist to die.

---

5. John Hampden (1594–1643), who, both as a private citizen and as a member of Parliament, zealously defended the rights of the people against the autocratic policies of Charles I.
6. Cf. "storied urn or animated bust" dedicated inside the church to "the proud" (line 41).

85 For who to dumb Forgetfulness a prey,
      This pleasing anxious being e'er resigned,
    Left the warm precincts of the cheerful day,
      Nor cast one longing lingering look behind?

    On some fond breast the parting soul relies,
90   Some pious drops the closing eye requires;
    Even from the tomb the voice of Nature cries,
      Even in our ashes live their wonted fires.

    For thee, who mindful of the unhonored dead
      Dost in these lines their artless tale relate;
95 If chance,° by lonely contemplation led,   *perchance*
      Some kindred spirit shall inquire thy fate,

    Haply some hoary-headed swain may say,
      "Oft have we seen him at the peep of dawn
    Brushing with hasty steps the dews away
100   To meet the sun upon the upland lawn.

    "There at the foot of yonder nodding beech
      That wreathes its old fantastic roots so high,
    His listless length at noontide would he stretch,
      And pore upon the brook that babbles by.

105 "Hard by yon wood, now smiling as in scorn,
      Muttering his wayward fancies he would rove,
    Now drooping, woeful wan, like one forlorn,
      Or crazed with care, or crossed in hopeless love.

    "One morn I missed him on the customed hill,
110   Along the heath and near his favorite tree;
    Another came; nor yet beside the rill,
      Nor up the lawn, nor at the wood was he;

    "The next with dirges due in sad array
      Slow through the churchway path we saw him borne.
115 Approach and read (for thou canst read) the lay,
      Graved on the stone beneath yon aged thorn."

The Epitaph

Here rests his head upon the lap of Earth
  A youth to Fortune and to Fame unknown.
Fair Science° frowned not on his humble birth,   *Learning*
120   *And Melancholy marked him for her own.*

Large was his bounty, and his soul sincere,
  Heaven did a recompense as largely send:
He gave to Misery all he had, a tear,
  He gained from Heaven ('twas all he wished) a friend.

125 *No farther seek his merits to disclose,*
  Or draw his frailties from their dread abode

(There they alike in trembling hope repose),
The bosom of his Father and his God.

ca. 1742–50   1751

WILLIAM COLLINS
1721–1759

William Collins was born in Chichester and was educated at Winchester and Oxford. Coming up to London from the university, he tried to establish himself as an author, but he was given rather to planning than to writing books. He came to know Samuel Johnson, who later remembered him affectionately as a man of learning who "loved fairies, genii, giants, and monsters" and who "delighted to rove through the meanders of enchantment." In 1746 Collins published his *Odes on Several Descriptive and Allegorical Subjects*, his part in an undertaking, with his friend Joseph Warton, to create a new poetry, more lyrical and fanciful than that of Alexander Pope's generation. Collins's *Odes* address personified abstractions (Fear, Pity, the Passions), which are imagined as vivid presences that overwhelm the poet as he calls them to life. In form these poems represent a new version of the Great or Cowleian Ode; Collins returns to Pindar's regularity of structure. But the originality of the *Odes* lies in their intensity of vision, which risks obscurity in quest of the sublime.

To his disappointment, contemporaries preferred his early *Persian Eclogues* to the more difficult *Odes*. Inheriting some money, the poet traveled for a while, but fits of depression gradually deepened into total debility. He spent his last years in Chichester, forgotten by all but a small circle of loyal friends. As the century progressed he gained in reputation. The Romantics admired his poems and felt akin to him. Coleridge said that "Ode on the Poetical Character" "has inspired and whirled me along with greater agitations of enthusiasm than any the most *impassioned* scene in Schiller or Shakespeare."

Ode on the Poetical Character
This ode, long disregarded, has lately been acclaimed by critics as an early, dramatic engagement with one of the central concerns of the Romantic age—the origin and role of the creative imagination and, indeed, of the poet himself.

In the strophe an analogy is drawn between the magic girdle of Venus, which only the chaste can wear, and the cest, or girdle, of Fancy, or the creative imagination. In the epode the creation of the world is presented as an act of the divine imagination. Inspired by God, Fancy gives birth to another sublime creation, the spirit of poetry.

In the antistrophe, John Milton is regarded as the type of poet divinely able to wear the girdle of Fancy. Collins pictures himself pursuing the "guiding steps" (line 71) of Milton, as of Edmund Spenser (in the strophe)—both poet-prophets. His movement away from the elegant school of Edmund Waller (and, by implication, that of Alexander Pope) is "In vain" (line 72), however, for he lives in an uninspired age.

Ode on the Poetical Character

Strophe

As once, if not with light regard,
I read aright that gifted bard
(Him[1] whose school above the rest
His loveliest Elfin Queen has blest),
One, only one, unrivaled fair
Might hope the magic girdle wear,
At solemn tourney hung on high,
The wish of each love-darting eye;[2]
Lo! to each other nymph in turn applied,
    As if, in air unseen, some hovering hand,
Some chaste and angel-friend to virgin-fame,
    With whispered spell had burst the starting band,
It left unblest her loathed dishonored side;
    Happier, hopeless fair, if never
    Her baffled hand with vain endeavor
Had touched that fatal zone° to her denied!   girdle
Young Fancy thus, to me divinest name,
    To whom, prepared and bathed in Heaven
    The cest° of amplest power is given: girdle
    To few the godlike gift assigns,
    To gird their blest, prophetic loins,[3]
And gaze her visions wild, and feel unmixed her flame!

Epode

The band, as fairy legends say,
Was wove on that creating day,
When He,[4] who called with thought to birth
Yon tented sky, this laughing earth,
And dressed with springs, and forests tall,
And poured the main engirting all,
Long by the loved Enthusiast[5] wooed,
Himself in some diviner mood,
Retiring, sate with her alone,
And placed her on his sapphire throne;
The whiles, the vaulted shrine around,
Seraphic wires were heard to sound,
Now sublimest triumph swelling,
Now on love and mercy dwelling;
And she, from out the veiling cloud,
Breathed her magic notes aloud:
And thou, thou rich-haired Youth of Morn,[6]
And all thy subject life was born!

---

1. Edmund Spenser.
2. *The Faerie Queene* 4.5 tells of the contest of many beautiful ladies for the girdle of Venus.
3. Pronounced *lines*.
4. God, on the day of creation.

5. I.e., Fancy; literally, "enthusiast" means "one possessed by a god."
6. Apollo, god of the sun and of poetry, associated with the archetypal poet.

The dangerous Passions kept aloof,
Far from the sainted growing woof:
But near it sate ecstatic Wonder,
Listening the deep applauding thunder:
45 And Truth, in sunny vest arrayed,
By whose the tarsel's° eyes were made;   *falcon's*
All the shadowy tribes of Mind,
In braided dance their murmurs joined,
And all the bright uncounted Powers
50 Who feed on Heaven's ambrosial flowers.
Where is the bard, whose soul can now
Its high presuming hopes avow?
Where he who thinks, with rapture blind,
This hallow'd work[7] for him designed?

Antistrophe

55 High on some cliff, to Heaven up-piled,
Of rude access, of prospect wild,
Where, tangled round the jealous° steep,   *vigilant*
Strange shades o'erbrow the valleys deep,
And holy Genii guard the rock,
60 Its glooms embrown, its springs unlock,
While on its rich ambitious head,
An Eden, like his° own, lies spread: *Milton's*
I view that oak, the fancied glades among,
By which as Milton lay, his evening ear,
65 From many a cloud that dropped ethereal dew,
Nigh sphered in Heaven its native strains could hear:
On which that ancient trump he reached was hung;
    Thither oft, his glory greeting,
    From Waller's[8] myrtle shades retreating,
70 With many a vow from Hope's aspiring tongue,
My trembling feet his guiding steps pursue;
    In vain—such bliss to one alone,°   *Milton*
    Of all the sons of soul was known,
    And Heaven, and Fancy, kindred powers,
75   Have now o'erturned the inspiring bowers,
Or curtained close such scene from every future view.

1746

Ode to Evening[1]

If aught of oaten stop,[2] or pastoral song,
May hope, chaste Eve, to soothe thy modest ear,

7. The girdle of Fancy.
8. Edmund Waller (1606–1687). The myrtle is the symbol of love poetry; Waller's poetry is thought of as trivial compared with Milton's grandeur.
1. Collins borrowed the metrical structure and the rhymeless lines of this ode from Milton's translation of Horace, *Odes* 1.5 (1673). The text printed here is based on the revised version, published in Dodsley's *Miscellany* (1748).
2. Finger hole in a shepherd's flute.

Like thy own solemn springs,
Thy springs and dying gales,
5 O nymph reserved, while now the bright-haired sun
Sits in yon western tent, whose cloudy skirts,
With brede° ethereal wove,   *embroidery*
O'erhang his wavy bed:
Now air is hushed, save where the weak-eyed bat,
10 With short shrill shriek flits by on leathern wing,
Or where the beetle winds
His small but sullen horn,
As oft he rises 'midst the twilight path,
Against the pilgrim borne in heedless hum:
15 Now teach me, maid composed,
To breathe some softened strain,
Whose numbers,° stealing through thy darkening vale,   *measures*
May not unseemly with its stillness suit,
As, musing slow, I hail
20 Thy genial° loved return!   *life-giving*
For when thy folding-star[3] arising shows
His paly circlet, at his warning lamp
The fragrant Hours, and elves
Who slept in flowers the day,
25 And many a nymph who wreaths her brows with sedge,
And sheds the freshening dew, and, lovelier still,
The pensive Pleasures sweet,
Prepare thy shadowy car.
Then lead, calm vot'ress, where some sheety lake
30 Cheers the lone heath, or some time-hallowed pile
Or upland fallows gray
Reflect its last cool gleam.
But when chill blustering winds, or driving rain,
Forbid my willing feet, be mine the hut
35 That from the mountain's side
Views wilds, and swelling floods,
And hamlets brown, and dim-discovered spires,
And hears their simple bell, and marks o'er all
Thy dewy fingers draw
40 The gradual dusky veil.
While Spring shall pour his showers, as oft he wont,
And bathe thy breathing tresses, meekest Eve;
While Summer loves to sport
Beneath thy lingering light;
45 While sallow Autumn fills thy lap with leaves;
Or Winter, yelling through the troublous air,
Affrights thy shrinking train,
And rudely rends thy robes;
So long, sure-found beneath the sylvan shed,
50 Shall Fancy, Friendship, Science, rose-lipped Health,
Thy gentlest influence own,
And hymn thy favorite name!

1746, 1748

---

3. The evening star, which signals the hour for herding the sheep into the sheepfold.

CHRISTOPHER SMART
1722–1771

In 1756 Christopher Smart, who had won prizes at Pembroke College, Cambridge, as a scholar and poet and was known in London as a wit and bon vivant, was seized by religious mania: "a preternatural excitement to prayer," according to Hester Thrale, "which he held it as a duty not to control or repress." If Smart had been content to pray in private, his life might have ended as happily as it began, but he insisted on kneeling down in the streets, in parks, and in assembly rooms. He became a public nuisance, and the public took its revenge. For most of the next seven years Smart was confined, first in St. Luke's hospital, then in a private madhouse. There, severed from his wife, his children, and his friends, he began to write a bold new sort of poetry: vivid, concise, abrupt, syntactically daring. Few of his contemporaries noticed it. After Smart's release from the madhouse (1763) he fell into debt—he had always been profligate—and his masterpiece, A Song to David (1763), was almost completely ignored (for the complete text of A Song to David, see the supplemental ebook). He died, forgotten, in a debtor's prison. But in the nineteenth century his reputation revived, and since the publication of Jubilate Agno in 1939 his poems have become newly famous.

Jubilate Agno (Rejoice in the Lamb), written a few lines at a time during Smart's confinement, is (1) a record of his daily life and thoughts; (2) the notebook of a scholar, crammed with puns and obscure learning, which sets out elaborate correspondences between the world of the Bible and modern England; and (3) a personal testament or book of worship, antiphonally arranged in lines beginning alternately with Let and For, which seeks to join the material and spiritual universes in one unending prayer. It has also come to be recognized, since first published in 1939 by W. F. Stead, as a poem—a poem unique in English for its ecstatic sense of the presence of the divine spirit. The most famous passage describes Smart's cat, Jeoffry, his only companion during the years of confinement: "For I am possessed of a cat, surpassing in beauty, from whom I take occasion to bless Almighty God." At once a real cat, lovingly observed in all its frisks, and visible evidence of the providential plan, Jeoffry celebrates the Maker, as all things do, in his very being.

From Jubilate Agno

[MY CAT JEOFFRY]

For I will consider my Cat Jeoffry.
For he is the servant of the Living God duly and daily serving him.
For at the first glance of the glory of God in the East° he worships in his way.   *sunrise*
For is this done by wreathing his body seven times round with elegant quickness.
5 For then he leaps up to catch the musk, wch is the blessing of God upon his prayer.
For he rolls upon prank° to work it in.   *prankishly*

For having done duty and received blessing he begins to consider himself.

For this he performs in ten degrees.

For first he looks upon his fore-paws to see if they are clean.

10 For secondly he kicks up behind to clear away there.

For thirdly he works it upon stretch with the fore-paws extended.

For fourthly he sharpens his paws by wood.

For fifthly he washes himself.

For Sixthly he rolls upon wash.

15 For Seventhly he fleas himself, that he may not be interrupted upon the beat.

For Eighthly he rubs himself against a post.

For Ninthly he looks up for his instructions.

For Tenthly he goes in quest of food.

For having consider'd God and himself he will consider his neighbor.

20 For if he meets another cat he will kiss her in kindness.

For when he takes his prey he plays with it to give it a chance.

For one mouse in seven escapes by his dallying.

For when his day's work is done his business more properly begins.

For he keeps the Lord's watch in the night against the adversary.

25 For he counteracts the powers of darkness by his electrical skin & glaring eyes.

For he counteracts the Devil, who is death, by brisking about the life.

For in his morning orisons he loves the sun and the sun loves him.

For he is of the tribe of Tiger.

For the Cherub Cat is a term of the Angel Tiger.[1]

30 For he has the subtlety and hissing of a serpent, which in goodness he suppresses.

For he will not do destruction if he is well-fed, neither will he spit without provocation.

For he purrs in thankfulness, when God tells him he's a good Cat.

For he is an instrument for the children to learn benevolence upon.

For every house is incomplete without him & a blessing is lacking in the spirit.

35 For the Lord commanded Moses concerning the cats at the departure of the Children of Israel from Egypt.[2]

For every family had one cat at least in the bag.

For the English Cats are the best in Europe.

For he is the cleanest in the use of his fore-paws of any quadrupede.

For the dexterity of his defence is an instance of the love of God to him exceedingly.

40 For he is the quickest to his mark of any creature.

For he is tenacious of his point.

For he is a mixture of gravity and waggery.

For he knows that God is his Saviour.

For there is nothing sweeter than his peace when at rest.

45 For there is nothing brisker than his life when in motion.

---

1. As a cherub is a small angel, so a cat is a small tiger.

2. No cats are mentioned in the Bible.

For he is of the Lord's poor and so indeed is he called by benevolence
    perpetually—Poor Jeoffry! poor Jeoffry! the rat has bit thy
    throat.
For I bless the name of the Lord Jesus that Jeoffry is better.
For the divine spirit comes about his body to sustain it in compleat
    cat.
For his tongue is exceeding pure so that it has in purity what it wants
    in music.
50   For he is docile and can learn certain things.
For he can set up with gravity which is patience upon approbation.
For he can fetch and carry, which is patience in employment.
For he can jump over a stick which is patience upon proof positive.
For he can spraggle upon waggle[3] at the word of command.
55   For he can jump from an eminence into his master's bosom.
For he can catch the cork and toss it again.
For he is hated by the hypocrite and miser.
For the former is afraid of detection.
For the latter refuses the charge.
60   For he camels his back to bear the first notion of business.
For he is good to think on, if a man would express himself neatly.
For he made a great figure in Egypt for his signal services.
For he killed the Icneumon-rat very pernicious by land.[4]
For his ears are so acute that they sting again.
65   For from this proceeds the passing° quickness of his   *surpassing*
    attention.
For by stroking of him I have found out electricity.
For I perceived God's light about him both wax and fire.
For the Electrical fire is the spiritual substance, which God sends
    from heaven to sustain the bodies both of man and beast.
For God has blessed him in the variety of his movements.
70   For, though he cannot fly, he is an excellent clamberer.
For his motions upon the face of the earth are more than any other
    quadrupede.
For he can tread to all the measures upon the music.
For he can swim for life.
For he can creep.

1759–63   1939

---

3. He can sprawl when his master waggles a finger or stick.
4. The ichneumon, which resembles a weasel,
was venerated and domesticated by the ancient
Egyptians.

WILLIAM COWPER
1731–1800

There are no saner poems in the language than William Cowper's, yet they were written by a man who was periodically insane and who for forty years lived day to day with the possibility of madness. After attempting suicide in 1763, he believed that he was damned for having committed the unforgivable sin, the "sin against the Holy Ghost." From then on, a refugee from life, he looked for hope in Evangelicalism and found shelter first, in 1765, in the pious family of the clergyman Morley Unwin, and after Unwin's death, with his widow, Mary Unwin, who cared for Cowper until her death in 1796. Their move to rural Olney (pronounced *Own-y*) in 1768 brought them under the influence of the strenuous and fervent Evangelical minister John Newton, author of "Amazing Grace." With him Cowper wrote the famous *Olney Hymns*, still familiar to Methodists and other Nonconformists. But a second attack of madness, in 1773, not only frustrated his planned marriage to Mary Unwin but left him for the rest of his life with the assurance that he had been cast out by God. He never again attended services, and the main purpose of his life thereafter was to divert his mind from numb despair by every possible innocent device. He gardened, he kept pets, he walked, he wrote letters (some of the best of the century), he conversed, he read—and he wrote poetry. When it was published, it brought him a measure of fame that his modest nature could never have hoped for.

Cowper's major work is *The Task* (1785), undertaken at the bidding of Lady Austen, a friend who, when he complained that he had no subject, directed him to write about the sofa in his parlor. It began with a mock-heroic account of the development of the sofa from a simple stool, but it grew into a long meditative poem of more than five thousand lines. The poet describes his small world of country, village, garden, and parlor, and from time to time he glances toward the great world to condemn cities and worldliness, war and slavery, luxury and corruption. The tone is muted, the sensibility delicate, the language on the whole precise and clear. Cowper does not strive to be great, yet his contemporaries recognized their own concerns in his pious and humorous musings. Blake, Wordsworth, and Coleridge felt close to him, and so did many literary women. No eighteenth-century poet was more beloved.

The Castaway

Obscurest night involved the sky,
    The Atlantic billows roared,
When such a destined wretch as I,
    Washed headlong from on board,
5   Of friends, of hope, of all bereft,
    His floating home forever left.

No braver chief[1] could Albion boast
    Than he with whom he went,

---

1. George, Lord Anson (1697–1762), in whose *Voyage* (1748) Cowper, years before writing this poem, had read the story of the sailor washed overboard in a storm.

Nor ever ship left Albion's coast,
10   With warmer wishes sent.
He loved them both, but both in vain,
Nor him beheld, nor her again.

Not long beneath the whelming brine,
    Expert to swim, he lay;
15   Nor soon he felt his strength decline,
    Or courage die away;
But waged with death a lasting strife,
Supported by despair of life.

He shouted; nor his friends had failed
20   To check the vessel's course,
But so the furious blast prevailed,
    That, pitiless perforce,
They left their outcast mate behind,
And scudded still before the wind.

25   Some succor yet they could afford;
    And, such as storms allow,
The cask, the coop, the floated cord,
    Delayed not to bestow.
But he (they knew) nor ship, nor shore,
30   Whate'er they gave, should visit more.

Nor, cruel as it seemed, could he
    Their haste himself condemn,
Aware that flight, in such a sea,
    Alone could rescue them;
35   Yet bitter felt it still to die
Deserted, and his friends so nigh.

He long survives, who lives an hour
    In ocean, self-upheld;
And so long he, with unspent power,
40   His destiny repelled;
And ever, as the minutes flew,
Entreated help, or cried, "Adieu!"

At length, his transient respite past,
    His comrades, who before
45   Had heard his voice in every blast,
    Could catch the sound no more.
For then, by toil subdued, he drank
The stifling wave, and then he sank.

No poet wept him; but the page
50   Of narrative sincere,
That tells his name, his worth, his age,
    Is wet with Anson's tear.
And tears by bards or heroes shed
Alike immortalize the dead.

55 I therefore purpose not, or dream,
   Descanting on his fate,
To give the melancholy theme
   A more enduring date:
But misery still delights to trace
60 Its semblance in another's case.

No voice divine the storm allayed,
   No light propitious shone,
When, snatched from all effectual aid,
   We perished, each alone;
65 But I beneath a rougher sea,
And whelmed in deeper gulfs than he.

1799   1803

APPENDIXES

General Bibliography

This bibliography consists of a list of suggested general readings on English literature. Bibliographies for the authors in *The Norton Anthology of English Literature* are available online in the Supplemental Ebook.

Suggested General Readings

Histories of England and of English Literature

Even the most distinguished of the comprehensive general histories written in past generations have come to seem outmoded. Innovative research in social, cultural, and political history has made it difficult to write a single coherent account of England from the Middle Ages to the present, let alone to accommodate in a unified narrative the complex histories of Scotland, Ireland, Wales, and the other nations where writing in English has flourished. Readers who wish to explore the historical matrix out of which the works of literature collected in this anthology emerged are advised to consult the studies of particular periods listed in the appropriate sections of this bibliography. The multivolume *Oxford History of England* and *New Oxford History of England* are useful, as are the three-volume *Peoples of the British Isles: A New History*, ed. Stanford Lehmberg, 1992; the nine-volume *Cambridge Cultural History of Britain*, ed. Boris Ford, 1992; the three-volume *Cambridge Social History of Britain, 1750–1950*, ed. F. M. L. Thompson, 1992; and the multivolume *Penguin History of Britain*, gen. ed. David Cannadine, 1996–. For Britain's imperial history, readers can consult the five-volume *Oxford History of the British Empire*, ed. Roger Louis, 1998–99, as well as *Gender and Empire*, ed. Philippa Levine, 2004. Given the cultural centrality of London, readers may find particular interest in *The London Encyclopaedia*, ed. Ben Weinreb and Christopher Hibbert, rev. ed., 1993; Roy Porter, *London: A Social History*, 1994; and Jerry White, *London in the Nineteenth Century: "A Human Awful Wonder of God,"* 2007, and *London in the Twentieth Century: A City and Its People*, 2001.

Similar observations may be made about literary history. In the light of such initiatives as women's studies, new historicism, and postcolonialism, the range of authors deemed significant has expanded in recent years, along with the geographical and conceptual boundaries of literature in English. Attempts to capture in a unified account the great sweep of literature from *Beowulf* to the early twenty-first century have largely given way to studies of individual genres, carefully delimited time periods, and specific authors. For these more focused accounts, see the listings by period. Among the large-scale literary surveys, *The Cambridge Guide to Literature in English*, 1994, is useful, as is the seven-volume *Penguin History of Literature*, 1993–94. *The Feminist Companion to Literature in English*, ed. Virginia Blain, Isobel Grundy, and Patricia Clements, 1990, is an important resource, and the editorial materials in *The Norton Anthology of Literature by Women*, 3rd ed., 2007, ed. Sandra M. Gilbert and Susan Gubar, constitute a concise history and set of biographies of women authors since the Middle Ages. *Annals of English Literature, 1475–1950*, rev. 1961, lists important publications year by year, together with the significant literary events for each year. Five volumes have been published in the *Oxford English Literary History*, gen. ed. Jonathan Bate, 2002–: James Simpson, *1350–1547: Reform and*

Cultural Revolution; Philip Davis, *1830–1880: The Victorians*; Chris Baldick, *1830–1880: The Modern Movement*; Randall Stevenson, *1960–2000: The Last of England?*; and Bruce King, *1948–2000: The Internationalization of English Literature*. See also *The Cambridge History of Medieval English Literature*, ed. David Wallace, 1999; *The Cambridge History of Early Modern English Literature*, ed. David Loewenstein and Janel Mueller, 2002; *The Cambridge History of English Literature, 1660–1780*, ed. John Richetti, 2005; *The Cambridge History of English Romantic Literature*, ed. James Chandler, 2009; and *The Cambridge History of Twentieth-Century English Literature*, ed. Laura Marcus and Peter Nicholls, 2005.

Helpful treatments and surveys of English meter, rhyme, and stanza forms are Paul Fussell Jr., *Poetic Meter and Poetic Form*, rev. 1979; Donald Wesling, *The Chances of Rhyme: Device and Modernity*, 1980; Charles O. Hartman, *Free Verse: An Essay in Prosody*, 1983; John Hollander, *Rhyme's Reason: A Guide to English Verse*, rev. 1989; Derek Attridge, *Poetic Rhythm: An Introduction*, 1995; Robert Pinsky, *The Sounds of Poetry: A Brief Guide*, 1998; and Mark Strand and Eavan Boland, eds., *The Making of a Poem: A Norton Anthology of Poetic Forms*, 2000.

On the development and functioning of the novel as a form, see Ian Watt, *The Rise of the Novel*, 1957; Gérard Genette, *Narrative Discourse: An Essay in Method*, 1980; Peter Brooks, *Reading for the Plot: Design and Intention in Narrative*, 1984; *The Columbia History of the British Novel*, ed. John Richetti, 1994; Margaret Doody, *The True Story of the Novel*, 1996; *Theory of the Novel: A Historical Approach*, ed. Michael McKeon, 2000; and McKeon, *The Origins of the English Novel, 1600–1740*, 15th anniversary ed., 2002. On women novelists and readers, see Nancy Armstrong, *Desire and Domestic Fiction: A Political History of the Novel*, 1987; and Catherine Gallagher, *Nobody's Story: The Vanishing Acts of Women Writers in the Marketplace, 1670–1820*, 1994.

On the history of playhouse design, see Richard Leacroft, *The Development of the English Playhouse: An Illustrated Survey of Theatre Building in England from Medieval to Modern Times*, 1988. For a survey of the plays that have appeared on these and other stages, see Allardyce Nicoll, *British Drama*, rev. 1962; the eight-volume *Revels History of Drama in English*, gen. eds. Clifford Leech and T. W. Craik, 1975–83; and Alfred Harbage, *Annals of English Drama, 975–1700*, 3rd ed., 1989, rev. S. Schoenbaum and Sylvia Wagonheim.

On some of the key intellectual currents that are at once reflected in and shaped by literature and contemporary literary criticism, Arthur O. Lovejoy's classic studies *The Great Chain of Being*, 1936, and *Essays in the History of Ideas*, 1948, remain valuable, along with such works as Georg Simmel, *The Philosophy of Money*, 1907; Lovejoy and George Boas, *Primitivism and Related Ideas in Antiquity*, 1935; Norbert Elias, *The Civilizing Process*, orig. pub. 1939, English trans. 1969; Ernst Cassirer, *The Philosophy of Symbolic Forms*, 4 vols., 1953–96; Ernst Kantorowicz, *The King's Two Bodies: A Study in Medieval Political Theology*, 1957, new ed. 1997; Richard Popkin, *The History of Skepticism from Erasmus to Descartes*, 1960; M. H. Abrams, *Natural Supernaturalism: Tradition and Revolution in Romantic Literature*, 1971; Michel Foucault, *Madness and Civilization: A History of Insanity in the Age of Reason*, Eng. trans. 1965, and *The Order of Things: An Archaeology of the Human Sciences*, Eng. trans. 1970; Gaston Bachelard, *The Poetics of Space*, Eng. trans. 1969; Martin Jay, *The Dialectical Imagination: A History of the Frankfurt School and the Institute of Social Research, 1923–1950*, 1973, new ed. 1996; Hayden White, *Metahistory*, 1973; Roland Barthes, *The Pleasure of the Text*, Eng. trans. 1975; Jacques Derrida, *Of Grammatology*, Eng. trans. 1976, and *Dissemination*, Eng. trans. 1981; Richard Rorty, *Philosophy and the Mirror of Nature*, 1979; Gilles Deleuze and Félix Guattari, *A Thousand Plateaus* (1980); Raymond Williams, *Keywords: A Vocabulary of Culture and Society*, rev. 1983; Pierre Bourdieu, *Distinction: A Social Critique of the Judgment of Taste*, Eng. trans. 1984; Michel de Certeau, *The Practice of Every-*

day Life, Eng. trans. 1984; Hans Blumenberg, *The Legitimacy of the Modern Age*, Eng. trans. 1985; Jürgen Habermas, *The Philosophical Discourse of Moderntiy*, Eng. trans, 1987; Slavoj Žižek, *The Sublime Object of Ideology*, 1989; and Sigmund Freud, *Writings on Art and Literature*, ed. Neil Hertz, 1997.

Reference Works

The single most important tool for the study of literature in English is the *Oxford English Dictionary*, 2nd ed. 1989, 3rd ed. in process. The most current edition is available online to subscribers. The *OED* is written on historical principles: that is, it attempts not only to describe current word use but also to record the history and development of the language from its origins before the Norman conquest to the present. It thus provides, for familiar as well as archaic and obscure words, the widest possible range of meanings and uses, organized chronologically and illustrated with quotations. The *OED* can be searched as a conventional dictionary arranged a–z and also by subject, usage, region, origin, and timeline (the first appearance of a word). Beyond the *OED* there are many other valuable dictionaries, such as *The American Heritage Dictionary* (4th ed. 2000), *The Oxford Dictionary of Abbreviations*, *The Concise Oxford Dictionary of English Etymology*, *The Oxford Dictionary of English Grammar*, *A New Dictionary of Eponyms*, *The Oxford Essential Dictionary of Foreign Terms in English*, *The Oxford Dictionary of Idioms*, *The Concise Oxford Dictionary of Linguistics*, *The Oxford Guide to World English*, and *The Concise Oxford Dictionary of Proverbs*. Other valuable reference works include *The Cambridge Encyclopedia of the English Language*, ed. David Crystal, 1995; *The Concise Oxford Companion to the English Language*; *Pocket Fowler's Modern English Usage*; and the numerous guides to specialized vocabularies, slang, regional dialects, and the like.

There is a steady flow of new editions of most major and many minor writers in English, along with a ceaseless outpouring of critical appraisals and scholarship. James L. Harner's *Literary Research Guide: An Annotated List of Reference Sources in English Literary Studies* (5th ed., 2008; online ed. at www.mla.org/store/PID335) offers thorough, evaluative annotations of a wide range of sources. For the historical record of scholarship and critical discussion, *The New Cambridge Bibliography of English Literature*, ed. George Watson, 5 vols. (1969–77) and *The Cambridge Bibliography of English Literature*, ed. F. W. Bateson, 5 vols. (1941–57) are useful. The *MLA International Bibliography* (also online) is a key resource for following critical discussion of literatures in English. Ranging from 1926 to the present, it includes journal articles, essays, chapters from collections, books, and dissertations, and covers folklore, linguistics, and film. The *Annual Bibliography of English Language and Literature* (*ABELL*), compiled by the Modern Humanities Research Association, lists monographs, periodical articles, critical editions of literary works, book reviews and collections of essays published anywhere in the world; unpublished doctoral dissertations are covered for the period 1920–99 (available online to subscribers and as part of Literature Online http://lion.chadwyck.com/marketing/index.jsp.)

For compact biographies of English authors, see the multivolume *Oxford Dictionary of National Biography* (*DNB*), ed. H. C. G. Matthew and Brian Harrison, 2004; since 2004 the *DNB* has been extended online with three annual updates. Handy reference books of authors, works, and various literary terms and allusions include many volumes in the *Cambridge Companion* and *Oxford Companion* series (e.g., *The Cambridge Companion to Narrative*, ed David Herman, 2007; *The Oxford Companion to English Literature*, ed. Margaret Drabble, rev. 2009; *The Cambridge Companion to Allegory*, ed. Rita Copeland and Peter Struck, 2010; etc.). *The Oxford Companion to the Theatre*, ed. Phyllis Hartnoll, is available online to subscribers via Oxford Reference Online's Performing Arts collection (www.oxfordreference.com/pub/views/home.html). Likewise, *The New Princeton Encyclopedia of Poetry and Poetics*, ed. Alex Preminger and others, is available online to subscribers in Literature Online (http://lion.chadwyck.com/marketing/index.jsp). Handbooks that define and illustrate literary concepts and terms are *The Penguin Dictionary of Literary Terms and Literary Theory*, ed. J. A. Cuddon, 4th ed., 2000; W. F. Thrall and Addison Hibbard, *A Handbook to Literature*, ed. William Harmon and Hugh Holman, 8th ed., 1999 (companion website http://wps.prenhall.com/hss_harmon_handbook_10); *Critical Terms for Literary Study*, ed. Frank Lentricchia and Thomas McLaughlin, rev. 1995; and M. H. Abrams, *A Glossary of Literary Terms*, 9th ed., 2009. Also useful are Richard Lanham, *A Handlist of Rhetorical Terms*, 2nd ed., 1991; Arthur Quinn, *Figures of Speech: 60 Ways to Turn a Phrase*, 1993; and the *Barnhart Concise Dictionary of Etymology*, ed. Robert K. Barnhart, 1995.

On the Greek and Roman backgrounds, see *The Cambridge History of Classical Literature* (vol. 1: *Greek Literature*, 1982; vol. 2: *Latin Literature*, 1989), both available online; *The Oxford Companion to Classical Literature*, ed. M. C. Howatson, 2nd ed., 1989; Gian Biagio Conte, *Latin Literature: A History*, 1994; *The Oxford Classical Dictionary*, 3rd ed., rev. 2003, also available online; Richard Rutherford, *Classical Literature: A Concise History*, 2005; and Mark P. O. Morford, Robert J. Lenardon, and Michael Sham, *Classical Mythology*, 9th ed., 2010.

Digital resources in the humanities have vastly proliferated since the previous edition of *The Norton Anthology of English Literature* and are continuing to grow rapidly. The NAEL StudySpace (wwnorton.com/nael) is the gateway to an extensive array of annotated texts, images, and other materials especially designed for the readers of this anthology. Among other useful electronic resources for the study of English literature are enormous digital archives, available to subscribers: Early English Books Online (EEBO) http://eebo.chadwyck.com/home; Literature Online http://lion.chadwyck.com/marketing/index.jsp; and Eighteenth Century Collections Online (ECCO) http://mlr.com/DigitalCollections/products/ecco/. There are also numerous free sites of variable quality. Many of the best of these are period or author specific and hence are listed in the subsequent sections of this bibliography. Among the general sites, one of the most useful and wide-ranging is Voice of the Shuttle (http://vox.ucsb.edu), which includes in its aggregation links to Bartleby.com and Project Gutenberg.

Literary Criticism and Theory

Eight volumes of the *Cambridge History of Literary Criticism* have been published, 1989– : *Classical Criticism*, ed. George A. Kennedy; *The Middle Ages*, ed. Alastair Minnis and Ian Johnson; *The Renaissance*, ed. Glyn P. Norton; *The Eighteenth Century*, ed. H. B. Nisbet and Claude Rawson; *Romanticism*, ed. Marshall Brown; *Modernism and the New Criticism*, ed. A. Walton Litz, Louis Menand, and Lawrence Rainey; *From Formalism to Poststructuralism*, ed. Raman Selden; and *Twentieth-Century Historical, Philosophical, and Psychological Perspectives*, ed. Christa Knellwolf and Christopher Norris. See also M. H. Abrams, *The Mirror and the Lamp: Romantic Theory and the Critical Tradition*, 1953; William K. Wimsatt and Cleanth Brooks, *Literary Criticism: A Short History*, 1957; René Wellek, *A History of Modern Criticism: 1750–1950*, 9 vols., 1955–93; Frank Lentricchia, *After the New Criticism*, 1980; and J. Hillis Miller, *On Literature*, 2002. Raman Selden, Peter Widdowson, and Peter Brooker have written *A Reader's Guide to Contemporary Literary Theory*, 1997. Other useful resources include *The Johns Hopkins Guide to Literary Theory and Criticism*, ed. Michael Groden and Martin Kreiswirth, 1994 (also online); *Literary Theory, an Anthology*, ed. Julie Rivkin and Michael Ryan, 1998; and *The Norton Anthology of Theory and Criticism*, 2nd ed., gen. ed. Vincent Leitch, 2010.

Modern approaches to English literature and literary theory were shaped by certain landmark works: William Empson, *Seven Types of Ambiguity*, 1930, 3rd ed.

1953, *Some Versions of Pastoral*, 1935, rpt. 1986, and *The Structure of Complex Words*, 1951; F. R. Leavis, *Revaluation*, 1936, and *The Great Tradition*, 1948; Lionel Trilling, *The Liberal Imagination*, 1950; T. S. Eliot, *Selected Essays*, 3rd ed. 1951, and *On Poetry and Poets*, 1957; Erich Auerbach, *Mimesis: The Representation of Reality in Western Literature*, 1953; William K. Wimsatt, *The Verbal Icon*, 1954; Northrop Frye, *Anatomy of Criticism*, 1957; Wayne C. Booth, *The Rhetoric of Fiction*, 1961, rev. ed. 1983; and W. J. Bate, *The Burden of the Past and the English Poet*, 1970. René Wellek and Austin Warren, *Theory of Literature*, rev. 1970, is a useful introduction to the variety of scholarly and critical approaches to literature up to the time of its publication. Jonathan Culler's *Literary Theory: A Very Short Introduction*, 1997, discusses recurrent issues and debates.

Beginning in the late 1960s, there was a significant intensification of interest in literary theory as a specific field. Certain forms of literary study had already been influenced by the work of the Russian linguist Roman Jakobson and the Russian formalist Viktor Shklovsky and, still more, by conceptions that derived or claimed to derive from Marx and Engels, but the full impact of these theories was not felt until what became known as the "theory revolution" of the 1970s and '80s. For Marxist literary criticism, see Georg Lukacs, *Theory of the Novel*, 1920, trans. 1971; *The Historical Novel*, 1937, trans. 1983; and *Studies in European Realism*, trans. 1964; Walter Benjamin's essays from the 1920s and '30s represented in *Illuminations*, trans. 1986, and *Reflections*, trans. 1986; Mikhail Bakhtin's essays from the 1930s represented in *The Dialogic Imagination*, trans. 1981, and his *Rabelais and His World*, 1941, trans. 1968; *Selections from the Prison Notebooks of Antonio Gramsci*, ed. and trans. Quintin Hoare and Geoffrey Smith, 1971; Raymond Williams, *Marxism and Literature*, 1977; Fredric Jameson, *The Political Unconscious: Narrative as a Socially Symbolic Act*, 1981; and Terry Eagleton, *Literary Theory: An Introduction*, 1983, and *The Ideology of the Aesthetic*, 1990.

Structural linguistics and anthropology gave rise to a flowering of structuralist literary criticism; convenient introductions include Robert Scholes, *Structuralism in Literature: An Introduction*, 1974, and Jonathan Culler, *Structuralist Poetics*, 1975. Poststructuralist challenges to this approach are epitomized in such influential works as Jacques Derrida, *Writing and Difference*, 1967, trans. 1978, and Paul de Man, *Blindness and Insight: Essays in the Rhetoric of Contemporary Criticism*, 1971, 2nd ed., 1983. Poststructuralism is discussed in Jonathan Culler, *On Deconstruction*, 1982; Slavoj Žižek, *The Sublime Object of Ideology*, 1989; Fredric Jameson, *Postmodernism; or the Cultural Logic of Late Capitalism*, 1991; John McGowan, *Postmodernism and Its Critics*, 1991; and *Beyond Structuralism*, ed. Wendell Harris, 1996. A figure who greatly influenced both structuralism and poststructuralism is Roland Barthes, in *Mythologies*, trans. 1972, and *S/Z*, trans. 1974. Among other influential contributions to literary theory are the psychoanalytic approach in Harold Bloom, *The Anxiety of Influence*, 1973; and the reader-response approach in Stanley Fish, *Is There a Text in This Class?: The Authority of Interpretive Communities*, 1980. For a retrospect on the theory decades, see Terry Eagleton, *After Theory*, 2003.

Influenced by these theoretical currents but not restricted to them, modern feminist literary criticism was fashioned by such works as Patricia Meyer Spacks, *The Female Imagination*, 1975; Ellen Moers, *Literary Women*, 1976; Elaine Showalter, *A Literature of Their Own*, 1977; and Sandra Gilbert and Susan Gubar, *The Madwoman in the Attic*, 1979. More recent studies include Jane Gallop, *The Daughter's Seduction: Feminism and Psychoanalysis*, 1982; Luce Irigaray, *This Sex Which Is Not One*, trans. 1985; Gayatri Chakravorty Spivak, *In Other Worlds: Essays in Cultural Politics*, 1987; Sandra Gilbert and Susan Gubar, *No Man's Land: The Place of the Woman Writer in the Twentieth Century*, 3 vols., 1988–94; Barbara Johnson, *A World of Difference*, 1989; Judith Butler, *Gender Trouble*, 1990; and the critical views sampled in Elaine Showalter, *The New Feminist Criticism*, 1985; *The Hélène Cixous Reader*, ed. Susan Sellers, 1994; *Feminist Literary Theory: A Reader*, ed. Mary Eagleton, 2nd ed., 1995; and *Feminisms: An Anthology of Literary Theory and Criticism*, ed. Robyn R. Warhol and Diane Price Herndl, 2nd ed. 1997.

Gay literature and queer studies are represented in *Inside/Out: Lesbian Theories, Gay Theories*, ed. Diana Fuss, 1991; *The Lesbian and Gay Studies Reader*, ed. Henry Abelove, Michele Barale, and David Halperin, 1993; *The Columbia Anthology of Gay Literature: Readings from Western Antiquity to the Present Day*, ed. Byrne R. S. Fone, 1998; and by such books as Eve Sedgwick, *Between Men: English Literature and Male Homosocial Desire*, 1985, and *Epistemology of the Closet*, 1990; Diana Fuss, *Essentially Speaking: Feminism, Nature, and Difference*, 1989; Terry Castle, *The Apparitional Lesbian: Female Homosexuality and Modern Culture*, 1993; Leo Bersani, *Homos*, 1995; Gregory Woods, *A History of Gay Literature: The Male Tradition*, 1998; David Halperin, *How to Do the History of Homosexuality*, 2002; and Judith Halberstam, *In a Queer Time and Place: Transgender Bodies, Subcultural Lives*, 2005.

New historicism is represented in Stephen Greenblatt, *Learning to Curse*, 1990; in the essays collected in *The New Historicism Reader*, ed. Harold Veeser, 1993, and *New Historical Literary Study: Essays on Reproducing Texts, Representing History*, ed. Jeffrey N. Cox and Larry J. Reynolds, 1993; and in Catherine Gallagher and Stephen Greenblatt, *Practicing New Historicism*, 2000. The related social and historical dimension of texts is discussed in Jerome McGann, *Critique of Modern Textual Criticism*, 1983; and *Scholarly Editing: A Guide to Research*, ed. D. C. Greetham, 1995. Characteristic of new historicism is an expansion of the field of literary interpretation still further in cultural studies; for a broad sampling of the range of interests, see Lawrence Grossberg, Cary Nelson, and Paula Treichler, eds., *Cultural Studies*, 1992; *The Cultural Studies Reader*, ed. Simon During, 1993; and *A Cultural Studies Reader: History, Theory, Practice*, ed. Jessica Munns and Gita Rajan, 1997. This expansion of the field is similarly reflected in postcolonial studies: see Frantz Fanon, *Black Skin, White Masks*, 1952, new trans. 2008, and *The Wretched of the Earth*, 1961, new trans. 2004; Edward Said, *Orientalism*, 1978, and *Culture and Imperialism*, 1993; *The Post-Colonial Studies Reader*, ed. Bill Ashcroft, Gareth Griffiths, and Helen Tiffin, 1995; and such influential books as Ranajit Guha and Gayatri Chakravorty Spivak, *Selected Subaltern Studies*, 1988; Homi Bhabha, ed., *Nation and Narration*, 1990, and *The Location of Culture*, 1994; Anne McClintock, *Imperial Leather: Race, Gender, and Sexuality in the Colonial Contest*, 1995; Robert J. C. Young, *Postcolonialism: An Historical Introduction*, 2001; Bill Ashcroft, Gareth Griffiths, and Helen Tiffin, *The Empire Writes Back: Theory and Practice in Post-Colonial Literatures*, 1989, 2nd ed. 2002; Elleke Boehmer, *Colonial and Postcolonial Literature*, 1995, 2nd ed. 2005; and *The Cambridge History of Postcolonial Literature*, ed. Ato Quayson, 2011.

In the wake of the theory revolution, critics have focused on a wide array of topics, which can only be briefly surveyed here. One current of work, focusing on the history of emotion, is represented in Brian Massumi, *Parables for the Virtual*, 2002; Sianne Ngai, *Ugly Feelings*, 2005; and *The Affect Theory Reader*, eds. Melissa Gregg and Gregory J. Seigworth, 2010. A somewhat related current, examining the special role of traumatic memory in literature, is exemplified in Cathy Caruth, *Trauma: Explorations in Memory*, 1995; and Dominic LaCapra, *Writing History, Writing Trauma*, 2000. Work on the literary implications of cognitive science may be glimpsed in *Introduction to Cognitive Cultural Studies*, ed. Lisa Zunshine, 2010. A growing interest in quantitative approaches to literature has been sparked by Franco Moretti, *Graphs, Maps, Trees: Abstract Models for Literary History*, 2005. There is an ongoing flourishing of ecocriticism, or studies of literature and the environment, including *The Ecocriticism Reader: Landmarks in Literary Ecology*, ed. Cheryll Glotfelty and Harold Fromm, 1996; *Writing the Environment*, eds. Richard Kerridge and Neil

Sammells, 1998; and Jonathan Bate, *The Song of the Earth*, 2002. The relationship between literature and law is central to such works as *Interpreting Law and Literature: A Hermeneutic Reader*, ed. Sanford Levinson and Steven Mailloux, 1988; *Law's Stories: Narrative and Rhetoric in the Law*, ed. Peter Brooks and Paul Gerwertz, 1998; and *Literature and Legal Problem Solving: Law and Literature as Ethical Discourse*, Paul J. Heald, 1998. Ethical questions in literature have been usefully explored by, among others, Geoffrey Galt Harpham in *Getting It Right: Language, Literature, and Ethics*, 1997, and Derek Attridge in *The Singularity of Literature*, 2004. Finally, approaches to literature, such as formalism and literary biography, that had seemed superseded in the theoretical ferment of the late twentieth century, have had a powerful resurgence. A renewed interest in form is evident in Susan Stewart, *Poetry and the Fate of the Senses*, 2002, and *Reading for Form*, ed. Susan J. Wolfson and Marshall Brown, 2007. Revitalized interest in the history of the book has been spearheaded by D. F. McKenzie's *Bibliography and the Sociology of Texts*, 1986; and Roger Chartier's *The Order of Books: Readers, Authors, and Libraries in Europe Between the Fourteenth and Eighteenth Centuries*, 1994. See also *The Cambridge History of the Book in Britain*, 6 vols., 1998–2009; and *The Practice and Representation of Reading in England*, ed. James Raven, Helen Small, and Naomi Tadmor, 2007.

Anthologies representing a range of recent approaches include *Modern Criticism and Theory*, ed. David Lodge, 1988; *Contemporary Literary Criticism*, ed. Robert Con Davis and Ronald Schlieffer, rev. ed. 1998; and *The Norton Anthology of Theory and Criticism*, ed. Vincent Leitch, et al., 2nd ed. 2010.

Literary Terminology*

Using simple technical terms can sharpen our understanding and streamline our discussion of literary works. Some terms, such as the ones in section A, help us address the internal style, structure, form, and kind of works. Other terms, such as those in section B, provide insight into the material forms in which literary works have been produced.

In analyzing what they called "rhetoric," ancient Greek and Roman writers determined the elements of what we call "style" and "structure." Our literary terms are derived, via medieval and Renaissance intermediaries, from the Greek and Latin sources. In the definitions that follow, the etymology, or root, of the word is given when it helps illuminate the word's current usage.

Most of the examples are drawn from texts in this anthology.

Words **boldfaced** within definitions are themselves defined in this appendix. Some terms are defined within definitions; such words are *italicized*.

A. Terms of Style, Structure, Form, and Kind

accent (synonym "stress"): a term of **rhythm.** The special force devoted to the voicing of one syllable in a word over others. In the noun "accent," for example, the accent, or stress, is on the first syllable.

act: the major subdivision of a play, usually divided into **scenes.**

aesthetics (from Greek, "to feel, apprehend by the senses"): the philosophy of artistic meaning as a distinct mode of apprehending untranslatable truth, defined as an alternative to rational enquiry, which is purely abstract. Developed in the late eighteenth century by the German philosopher Immanuel Kant especially.

Alexandrine: a term of **meter.** In French verse a line of twelve syllables, and, by analogy, in English verse a line of six stresses. See **hexameter.**

allegory (Greek "saying otherwise"): saying one thing (the "vehicle" of the allegory) and meaning another (the allegory's "tenor"). Allegories may be momentary aspects of a work, as in **metaphor** ("John is a lion"), or, through extended metaphor, may constitute the basis of narrative, as in Bunyan's *Pilgrim's Progress:* this second meaning is the dominant one. See also **symbol** and **type.** Allegory is one of the most significant **figures of thought.**

alliteration (from Latin "litera," alphabetic letter): a **figure of speech.** The repetition of an initial consonant sound or consonant cluster in consecutive or closely positioned words. This pattern is often an inseparable part of the meter in Germanic languages, where the tonic, or accented **syllable,** is usually the first syllable. Thus all Old English poetry and some varieties of Middle English poetry use alliteration as part of their basic metrical practice. *Sir Gawain and the Green Knight,* line 1: "Sithen the sege and the assaut was sesed at Troye" (see vol. 1/A, p. 184). Otherwise used for local effects; Stevie Smith, "Pretty," lines 4–5: "And in the pretty pool the pike stalks / He stalks his prey . . ." (see vol. 2/F, p. 2604).

---

*This appendix was devised and compiled by James Simpson with the collaboration of all the editors. We especially thank Professor Lara Bovilsky of the University of Oregon at Eugene, who helped us reshape this appendix for this edition.

allusion: Literary allusion is a passing but illuminating reference within a literary text to another, well-known text (often biblical or **classical**). Topical allusions are also, of course, common in certain modes, especially **satire.**

anagnorisis (Greek "recognition"): the moment of **protagonist's** recognition in a narrative, which is also often the moment of moral understanding.

anapest: a term of **rhythm.** A three-syllable foot following the rhythmic pattern, in English verse, of two unstressed (uu) syllables followed by one stressed (/). Thus, for example, "Illinois."

anaphora (Greek "carrying back"): a **figure of speech.** The repetition of words or groups of words at the beginning of consecutive sentences, clauses, or phrases. Blake, "London," lines 5–8: "In every cry of every Man, / In every Infant's cry of fear, / In every voice, in every ban . . ." (see vol. 2/D, p. 132); Louise Bennett, "Jamaica Oman," lines 17–20: "Some backa man a push, some side-a / Man a hole him han, / Some a lick sense eena him head, / Some a guide him pon him plan!" (see vol. 2/F, p. 2729).

animal fable: a **genre.** A short narrative of speaking animals, followed by moralizing comment, written in a low style and gathered into a collection. Robert Henryson, "The Cock and the Fox" (see vol. 1/A, p. 501).

antithesis (Greek "placing against"): a **figure of thought.** The juxtaposition of opposed terms in clauses or sentences that are next to or near each other; Milton, *Paradise Lost* 1.777–80: "They but now who seemed / In bigness to surpass Earth's giant sons / Now less than smallest dwarfs, in narrow room / Throng numberless" (see vol. 1/B, p. 1964).

apostrophe (from Greek "turning away"): a **figure of thought.** An address, often to an absent person, a force, or a quality. For example, a poet makes an apostrophe to a Muse when invoking her for inspiration.

apposition: a term of **syntax.** The repetition of elements serving an identical grammatical function in one sentence. The effect of this repetition is to arrest the flow of the sentence, but in doing so to add extra semantic nuance to repeated elements. This is an especially important feature of Old English poetic style. See, for example, Caedmon's *Hymn* (vol. 1/A, p. 30), where the phrases "heaven-kingdom's Guardian," "the Measurer's might," "his mind-plans," and "the work of the Glory-Father" each serve an identical syntactic function as the direct objects of "praise."

assonance (Latin "sounding to"): a **figure of speech.** The repetition of identical or near identical stressed vowel sounds in words whose final consonants differ, producing half-rhyme. Tennyson, "The Lady of Shalott," line 100: "His broad clear brow in sunlight glowed" (see vol. 2/E, p. 1163).

aubade (originally from Spanish "alba," dawn): a **genre.** A lover's dawn song or lyric bewailing the arrival of the day and the necessary separation of the lovers; Donne, "The Sun Rising" (see vol. 1/B, p. 1376). Larkin recasts the genre in "Aubade" (see vol. 2/F, p. 2789).

autobiography (Greek "self-life writing"): a **genre.** A narrative of a life written by the subject; Wordsworth, *The Prelude* (see vol. 2/D, p. 349). There are subgenres, such as the spiritual autobiography, narrating the author's path to conversion and subsequent spiritual trials, as in Bunyan's *Grace Abounding.*

ballad stanza: a **verse form.** Usually a **quatrain** in alternating **iambic tetrameter** and **iambic trimeter** lines, rhyming abcb. See "Sir Patrick Spens" (vol. 2/D, p. 36); Louise Bennett's poems (vol. 2/F, pp. 2726–27); Eliot, "Sweeney among the Nightingales" (vol. 2/F, p. 2528); Larkin, "This Be the Verse" (vol. 2/F, p. 2789).

ballade: a **verse form.** A form consisting usually of three stanzas followed by a four-line envoi (French, "send off"). The last line of the first stanza establishes a **refrain,** which is repeated, or subtly varied, as the last line of each stanza. The form was derived from French medieval poetry; English poets, from the fourteenth to the sixteenth centuries especially, used it with varying stanza forms. Chaucer, "Complaint to His Purse" (see vol. 1/A, p. 345).

bathos (Greek "depth"): a **figure of thought.** A sudden and sometimes ridiculous descent of tone; Pope, *The Rape of the Lock* 3.157–58: "Not louder shrieks to pitying heaven are cast, / When husbands, or when lapdogs breathe their last" (see vol. 1/C, p. 2169).

beast epic: a **genre.** A continuous, unmoralized narrative, in prose or verse, relating the victories of the wholly unscrupulous but brilliant strategist Reynard the Fox over all adversaries. Chaucer arouses, only to deflate, expectations of the genre in *The Nun's Priest's Tale* (see vol. 1/A, p. 326).

biography (Greek "life-writing"): a **genre.** A life as the subject of an extended narrative. Thus Izaak Walton, *The Life of Dr. Donne* (see vol. 1/B, p. 1424).

blank verse: a **verse form.** Unrhymed **iambic pentameter** lines. Blank verse has no stanzas, but is broken up into uneven units (verse paragraphs) determined by sense rather than form. First devised in English by Henry Howard, Earl of Surrey, in his translation of two books of Virgil's *Aeneid* (see vol. 1/B, p. 669), this very flexible verse type became the standard form for dramatic poetry in the seventeenth century, as in most of Shakespeare's plays. Milton and Wordsworth, among many others, also used it to create an English equivalent to **classical epic.**

blazon: strictly, a heraldic shield; in rhetorical usage, a **topos** whereby the individual elements of a beloved's face and body are singled out for **hyperbolic** admiration. Spenser, *Epithalamion,* lines 167–84 (see vol. 1/B, p. 990). For an inversion of the **topos,** see Shakespeare, Sonnet 130 (vol. 1/B, p. 1183).

burlesque (French and Italian "mocking"): a work that adopts the **conventions** of a genre with the aim less of comically mocking the genre than of satirically mocking the society so represented (see **satire**). Thus Pope's *Rape of the Lock* (see vol. 1/C, p. 2157) does not mock **classical epic** so much as contemporary mores.

caesura (Latin "cut") (plural "caesurae"): a term of **meter.** A pause or breathing space within a line of verse, generally occurring between syntactic units; Louise Bennett, "Colonization in Reverse," lines 5–8: "By de hundred, by de tousan, / From country an from town, / By de ship-load, by de plane-load, / Jamaica is Englan boun" (see vol. 2/F, p. 2727), where the caesurae occur in lines 5 and 7.

canon (Greek "rule"): the group of texts regarded as worthy of special respect or attention by a given institution. Also, the group of texts regarded as definitely having been written by a certain author.

catastrophe (Greek "overturning"): the decisive turn in **tragedy** by which the plot is resolved and, usually, the **protagonist** dies.

catharsis (Greek "cleansing"): According to Aristotle, the effect of **tragedy** on its audience, through their experience of pity and terror, was a kind of spiritual cleansing, or catharsis.

character (Greek "stamp, impression"): a person, personified animal, or other figure represented in a literary work, especially in narrative and drama. The more a character seems to generate the action of a narrative, and the less he or she seems merely to serve a preordained narrative pattern, the "fuller," or more "rounded," a character is said to be. A "stock" character, common particularly in many comic genres, will perform a predictable function in different works of a given genre.

chiasmus (Greek "crosswise"): a **figure of speech.** The inversion of an already established sequence. This can involve verbal echoes: Pope, "Eloisa to Abelard," line 104, "The crime was common, common be the pain" (see vol. 1/C, p. 2180); or it can be purely a matter of syntactic inversion: Pope, *Epistle to Dr. Arbuthnot,* line 8: "They pierce my thickets, through my grot they glide" (see vol. 1/C, p. 2195).

classical, classicism, classic: Each term can be widely applied, but in English literary discourse, "classical" primarily describes the works of either Greek or Roman antiquity. "Classicism" denotes the practice of art forms inspired by classical antiquity, in particular the observance of rhetorical norms of **decorum** and balance, as opposed to following the dictates of untutored inspiration, as in Romanticism. "Classic" denotes an especially famous work within a given **canon.**

climax (Greek "ladder"): a moment of great intensity and structural change, especially in drama. Also a **figure of speech** whereby a sequence of verbally linked clauses is made, in which each successive clause is of greater consequence than its predecessor. Bacon, *Of Studies:* "Studies serve for pastimes, for ornaments, and for abilities. Their chief use for pastimes is in privateness and retiring; for ornament, is in discourse; and for ability, is in judgement" (see vol. 1/B, p. 1673).

comedy: a **genre.** A term primarily applied to drama, and derived from ancient drama, in opposition to **tragedy.** Comedy deals with humorously confusing, sometimes ridiculous situations in which the ending is, nevertheless, happy. A comedy often ends in one or more marriages. Shakespeare, *Twelfth Night* (see vol. 1/B, p. 1186).

comic mode: Many genres (e.g., **romance, fabliau, comedy**) involve a happy ending in which justice is done, the ravages of time are arrested, and that which is lost is found. Such genres participate in a comic mode.

connotation: To understand connotation, we need to understand **denotation.** While many words can denote the same concept—that is, have the same basic meaning—those words can evoke different associations, or connotations. Contrast, for example, the clinical-sounding term "depression" and the more colorful, musical, even poetic phrase "the blues."

consonance (Latin "sounding with"): a **figure of speech.** The repetition of final consonants in words or stressed syllables whose vowel sounds are different. Herbert, "Easter," line 13: "Consort, both heart and lute . . ." (see vol. 1/B, p. 1708).

convention: a repeatedly recurring feature (in either form or content) of works, occurring in combination with other recurring formal features, which constitutes a convention of a particular genre.

couplet: a **verse form.** In English verse two consecutive, rhyming lines usually containing the same number of stresses. Chaucer first introduced the **iambic pentameter** couplet into English (*Canterbury Tales*); the form was later used in many types of writing, including drama; imitations and translations of **classical epic** (thus *heroic couplet*); essays; and **satire** (see Dryden and Pope). The *distich* (Greek "two lines") is a couplet usually making complete sense; Aemilia Lanyer, *Salve Deus Rex Judaeorum,* lines 5–6: "Read it fair queen, though it defective be, / Your excellence can grace both it and me" (see vol. 1/B, p. 1431).

dactyl (Greek "finger," because of the finger's three joints): a term of **rhythm.** A three-syllable foot following the rhythmic pattern, in English verse, of one stressed followed by two unstressed syllables. Thus, for example, "Oregon."

decorum (Latin "that which is fitting"): a rhetorical principle whereby each formal aspect of a work should be in keeping with its subject matter and/or audience.

deixis (Greek "pointing"): relevant to **point of view.** Every work has, implicitly or explicitly, a "here" and a "now" from which it is narrated. Words that refer to or imply this point from which the voice of the work is projected (such as "here," "there," "this," "that," "now," "then") are examples of deixis, or "deictics." This technique is especially important in drama, where it is used to create a sense of the events happening as the spectator witnesses them.

denotation: A word has a basic, "prosaic" (factual) meaning prior to the associations it connotes (see **connotation**). The word "steed," for example, might call to mind a horse fitted with battle gear, to be ridden by a warrior, but its denotation is simply "horse."

denouement (French "unknotting"): the point at which a narrative can be resolved and so ended.

dialogue (Greek "conversation"): a **genre.** Dialogue is a feature of many genres, especially in both the **novel** and drama. As a genre itself, dialogue is used in philosophical traditions especially (most famously in Plato's *Dialogues*), as the representation of a conversation in which a philosophical question is pursued among various speakers.

diction, or **"lexis"** (from, respectively, Latin "dictio" and Greek "lexis," each meaning "word"): the actual words used in any utterance—speech, writing, and, for our purposes here, literary works. The choice of words contributes significantly to the style of a given work.

didactic mode (Greek "teaching mode"): **Genres** in a didactic mode are designed to instruct or teach, sometimes explicitly (e.g., sermons, philosophical **discourses, georgic**), and sometimes through the medium of fiction (e.g., **animal fable, parable**).

diegesis (Greek for "narration"): a term that simply means "narration," but is used in literary criticism to distinguish one kind of story from another. In a *mimetic* story, the events are played out before us (see **mimesis**), whereas in diegesis someone recounts the story to us. Drama is for the most part *mimetic*, whereas the novel is for the most part diegetic. In novels the narrator is not, usually, part of the action of the narrative; s/he is therefore extradiegetic.

dimeter (Greek "two measure"): a term of **meter.** A two-stress line, rarely used as the meter of whole poems, though used with great frequency in single poems by Skelton, e.g., "The Tunning of Elinour Rumming" (see vol. 1/B, p. 567). Otherwise used for single lines, as in Herbert, "Discipline," line 3: "O my God" (see vol. 1/B, p. 1724).

discourse (Latin "running to and fro"): broadly, any nonfictional speech or writing; as a more specific genre, a philosophical meditation on a set theme. Thus Newman, *The Idea of a University* (see vol. 2/E, p. 1078).

dramatic irony: a feature of narrative and drama, whereby the audience knows that the outcome of an action will be the opposite of that intended by a **character.**

dramatic monologue (Greek "single speaking"): a **genre.** A poem in which the voice of a historical or fictional **character** speaks, unmediated by any narrator, to an implied though silent audience. See Tennyson, "Ulysses" (vol. 2/E, p. 1170); Browning, "The Bishop Orders His Tomb" (vol. 2/E, p. 1286); Eliot, "The Love Song of J. Alfred Prufrock" (vol. 2/F, p. 2525); Carol Ann Duffy, "Medusa" and "Mrs Lazarus" (vol. 2/F, pp. 3044–45).

ecphrasis (Greek "speaking out"): a **topos** whereby a work of visual art is represented in a literary work. Auden, "Musée des Beaux Arts" (see vol. 2/F, p. 2686).

elegy: a **genre.** In **classical** literature elegy was a form written in elegiac **couplets** (a **hexameter** followed by a **pentameter**) devoted to many possible topics. In Ovidian elegy a lover meditates on the trials of erotic desire (e.g., Ovid's *Amores*). The **sonnet** sequences of both Sidney and Shakespeare exploit this genre, and, while it was still practiced in classical tradition by Donne ("On His Mistress" [see vol. 1/B, p. 1392]), by the later seventeenth century the term came to denote the poetry of loss, especially through the death of a loved person. See Tennyson, *In Memoriam* (vol. 2/E, p. 1187); Yeats, "In Memory of Major Robert Gregory" (vol. 2/F, p. 2034); Auden, "In Memory of W. B. Yeats" (see vol. 2/F, p. 2686); Heaney, "Clearances" (vol. 2/F, p. 2963).

emblem (Greek "an insertion"): a **figure of thought.** A picture allegorically expressing a moral, or a verbal picture open to such interpretation. Donne, "A Hymn to Christ," lines 1–2: "In what torn ship soever I embark, / That ship shall be my emblem of thy ark" (see vol. 1/B, p. 1416).

end-stopping: the placement of a complete syntactic unit within a complete line, fulfilling the metrical pattern; Auden, "In Memory of W. B. Yeats," line 42: "Earth, receive an honoured guest" (see vol. 2/F, p. 2688). Compare **enjambment.**

enjambment (French "striding," encroaching): The opposite of **end-stopping,** enjambment occurs when the syntactic unit does not end with the end of the line and the fulfillment of the metrical pattern. When the sense of the line overflows its meter and, therefore, the line break, we have enjambment; Auden, "In Memory of W. B. Yeats," lines 44–45: "Let the Irish vessel lie / Emptied of its poetry" (see vol. 2/F, p. 2688).

epic (synonym, *heroic poetry*): a **genre.** An extended narrative poem celebrating martial heroes, invoking divine inspiration, beginning in medias res (see **order**), written in a high style (including the deployment of **epic similes;** on high style, see **register**), and divided into long narrative sequences. Homer's *Iliad* and Virgil's *Aeneid* were the prime models for English writers of epic verse. Thus Milton, *Paradise Lost* (see vol. 1/B, p. 1943); Wordsworth, *The Prelude* (see vol. 2/D, p. 349); and Walcott, *Omeros* (see vol. 2/F, p. 2806). With its precise repertoire of stylistic resources, epic lent itself easily to **parodic** and **burlesque** forms, known as **mock epic;** thus Pope, *The Rape of the Lock* (see vol. 1/C, p. 2157).

epigram: a **genre.** A short, pithy poem wittily expressed, often with wounding intent. See Jonson, *Epigrams* (see vol. 1/B, p. 1539).

epigraph (Greek "inscription"): a **genre.** Any formal statement inscribed on stone; also the brief formulation on a book's title page, or a quotation at the beginning of a poem, introducing the work's themes in the most compressed form possible.

epistle (Latin "letter"): a **genre.** The letter can be shaped as a literary form, involving an intimate address often between equals. The *Epistles* of Horace provided a model for English writers from the sixteenth century. Thus Wyatt, "Mine own John Poins" (see vol. 1/B, p. 659), or Pope, "Epistle to a Lady" (vol. 1/C, p. 2245). Letters can be shaped to form the matter of an extended fiction, as the eighteenth-century epistolary **novel** (e.g., Samuel Richardson's *Pamela*).

epitaph: a **genre.** A pithy formulation to be inscribed on a funeral monument. Thus Ralegh, "The Author's Epitaph, Made by Himself" (see vol. 1/B, p. 1030).

epithalamion (Greek "concerning the bridal chamber"): a **genre.** A wedding poem, celebrating the marriage and wishing the couple good fortune. Thus Spenser, *Epithalamion* (see vol. 1/B, p. 990).

epyllion (plural "epyllia") (Greek: "little epic"): a **genre.** A relatively short poem in the meter of epic poetry. See, for example, Marlowe, *Hero and Leander.*

essay (French "trial, attempt"): a **genre.** An informal philosophical meditation, usually in prose and sometimes in verse. The journalistic periodical essay was developed in the early eighteenth century. Thus Addison and Steele, periodical essays (see vol. 1/C, p. 2113); Pope, *An Essay on Criticism* (see vol. 1/C, p. 2141).

euphemism (Greek "sweet saying"): a **figure of thought.** The figure by which something distasteful is described in alternative, less repugnant terms (e.g., "he passed away").

exegesis (Greek "leading out"): interpretation, traditionally of the biblical text, but, by transference, of any text.

exemplum (Latin "example"): an example inserted into a usually nonfictional writing (e.g., sermon or **essay**) to give extra force to an abstract thesis. Thus Johnson's example of "Sober" in his essay "On Idleness" (see vol. 1/C, p. 2326).

fabliau (French "little story," plural *fabliaux*): a **genre.** A short, funny, often bawdy narrative in low style (see **register**) imitated and developed from French models most subtly by Chaucer; see *The Miller's Prologue and Tale* (vol. 1/A, p. 264).

farce (French "stuffing"): a **genre.** A play designed to provoke laughter through the often humiliating antics of stock **characters.** Congreve's *The Way of the World* (see vol. 1/C, p. 1832) draws on this tradition.

figures of speech: Literary language often employs patterns perceptible to the eye and/or to the ear. Such patterns are called "figures of speech"; in classical rhetoric they were called "schemes" (from Greek "schema," meaning "form, figure").

figures of thought: Language can also be patterned conceptually, even outside the rules that normally govern it. Literary language in particular exploits this licensed linguistic irregularity. Synonyms for figures of thought are "trope" (Greek "twisting," referring to the irregularity of use) and "conceit" (Latin "concept," referring to the fact that these figures are perceptible only to the mind). Be careful not to confuse **trope** with **topos** (a common error).

first-person narration: relevant to **point of view,** a narrative in which the voice narrating refers to itself with forms of the first-person pronoun ("I," "me," "my," etc., or possibly "we," "us," "our"), and in which the narrative is determined by the limitations of that voice. Thus Mary Wollstonecraft Shelley, *Frankenstein.*

frame narrative: Some narratives, particularly collections of narratives, involve a frame narrative that explains the genesis of, and/or gives a perspective on, the main narrative or narratives to follow. Thus Chaucer, *Canterbury Tales;* Mary Wollstonecraft Shelley, *Frankenstein;* or Conrad, *Heart of Darkness.*

free indirect style: relevant to **point of view,** a narratorial voice that manages, without explicit reference, to imply, and often implicitly to comment on, the voice of a **character** in the narrative itself. Virginia Woolf, "A Sketch of the Past," where the voice, although strictly that of the adult narrator, manages to convey the child's manner of perception: "—I begin: the first memory. This was of red and purple flowers on a black background—my mother's dress."

genre and mode: The **style,** structure, and, often, length of a work, when coupled with a certain subject matter, raise expectations that a literary work conforms to a certain **genre** (French "kind"). Good writers might upset these expectations, but they remain aware of the expectations and thwart them purposefully. Works in different genres may nevertheless participate in the same **mode,** a broader category designating the fundamental perspectives governing various genres of writing. For mode, see **tragic, comic, satiric,** and **didactic modes.** Genres are fluid, sometimes very fluid (e.g., the **novel**); the word "usually" should be added to almost every account of the characteristics of a given genre!

georgic (Greek "farming"): a **genre.** Virgil's *Georgics* treat agricultural and occasionally scientific subjects, giving instructions on the proper management of farms. Unlike **pastoral,** which treats the countryside as a place of recreational idleness among shepherds, the georgic treats it as a place of productive labor. For an English poem that critiques both genres, see Crabbe, "The Village" (vol. 1/C, p. 1932).

hermeneutics (from the Greek god Hermes, messenger between the gods and humankind): the science of interpretation, first formulated as such by the German philosophical theologian Friedrich Schleiermacher in the early nineteenth century.

heroic poetry: see **epic.**

hexameter (Greek "six measure"): a term of **meter.** The hexameter line (a six-stress line) is the meter of **classical** Latin **epic;** while not imitated in that form for epic verse in English, some instances of the hexameter exist. See, for example, the last line of a Spenserian stanza, *Faerie Queene* 1.1.2: "O help thou my weake wit, and sharpen my dull tong" (vol. 1/B, p. 781), or Yeats, "The Lake Isle of Innisfree," line 1: "I will arise and go now, and go to Innisfree" (vol. 2/F, p. 2088).

homily (Greek "discourse"): a **genre.** A sermon, to be preached in church; *Book of Homilies* (see vol. 1/B, p. 692). Writers of literary fiction sometimes exploit the homily, or sermon, as in Chaucer, *The Pardoner's Tale* (see vol. 1/A, p. 310).

homophone (Greek "same sound"): a **figure of speech.** A word that sounds identical to another word but has a different meaning ("bear" / "bare").

hyperbaton (Greek "overstepping"): a term of **syntax.** The rearrangement, or inversion, of the expected word order in a sentence or clause. Gray, "Elegy Written in a Country Churchyard," line 38: "If Memory o'er their tomb no trophies raise" (vol. 1/C, p. 2524). Poets can suspend the expected syntax over many lines, as in the first sentences of the *Canterbury Tales* (vol. 1/A, p. 243) and of *Paradise Lost* (vol. 1/B, p. 1943).

hyperbole (Greek "throwing over"): a **figure of thought.** Overstatement, exaggeration; Marvell, "To His Coy Mistress," lines 11–12: "My vegetable love would grow / Vaster than empires, and more slow" (see vol. 1/B, p. 1797); Auden, "As I Walked Out One Evening," lines 9–12: "'I'll love you, dear, I'll love you / Till China and Africa meet / And the river jumps over the mountain / And the salmon sing in the street" (see vol. 2/F, p. 2684).

hypermetrical (adj.; Greek "over measured"): a term of **meter;** the word describes a breaking of the expected metrical pattern by at least one extra syllable.

hypotaxis, or **subordination** (respectively Greek and Latin "ordering under"): a term of **syntax.** The subordination, by the use of subordinate clauses, of different elements of a sentence to a single main verb. Milton, *Paradise Lost* 9.513–15: "As when a ship by skillful steersman wrought / Nigh river's mouth or foreland, where the wind / Veers oft, as oft so steers, and shifts her sail; So varied he" (vol. 1/B, p. 2102). The contrary principle to **parataxis.**

iamb: a term of **rhythm.** The basic foot of English verse; two syllables following the rhythmic pattern of unstressed followed by stressed and producing a rising effect. Thus, for example, "Vermont."

imitation: the practice whereby writers strive ideally to reproduce and yet renew the **conventions** of an older form, often derived from **classical** civilization. Such a practice will be praised in periods of classicism (e.g., the eighteenth century) and repudiated in periods dominated by a model of inspiration (e.g., Romanticism).

irony (Greek "dissimulation"): a **figure of thought.** In broad usage, irony designates the result of inconsistency between a statement and a context that undermines the statement. "It's a beautiful day" is unironic if it's a beautiful day; if, however, the weather is terrible, then the inconsistency between statement and context is ironic. The effect is often amusing; the need to be ironic is sometimes produced by censorship of one kind or another. Strictly, irony is a subset of allegory: whereas allegory says one thing and means another, irony says one thing and means its opposite. For an extended example of irony, see Swift's "Modest Proposal." See also **dramatic irony.**

journal (French "daily"): a **genre.** A diary, or daily record of ephemeral experience, whose perspectives are concentrated on, and limited by, the experiences of single days. Thus Pepys, *Diary* (see vol. 1/C, p. 1732).

lai: a **genre.** A short narrative, often characterized by images of great intensity; a French term, and a form practiced by Marie de France (see vol. 1/A, p. 142).

legend (Latin "requiring to be read"): a **genre.** A narrative of a celebrated, possibly historical, but mortal **protagonist.** To be distinguished from **myth.** Thus the "Arthurian legend" but the "myth of Proserpine."

lexical set: Words that habitually recur together (e.g., January, February, March, etc.; or red, white, and blue) form a lexical set.

litotes (from Greek "smooth"): a **figure of thought.** Strictly, understatement by denying the contrary; More, *Utopia:* "differences of no slight import" (see vol. 1/B, p. 575). More loosely, understatement; Swift, "A Tale of a Tub": "Last week I saw a woman flayed, and you will hardly believe how much it altered her person for the worse" (see vol. 1/C, p. 1956). Stevie Smith, "Sunt Leones," lines 11–12: "And if the Christians felt a little blue— / Well people being eaten often do" (see vol. 2/F, p. 2600).

lullaby: a **genre.** A bedtime, sleep-inducing song for children, in simple and regular meter. Adapted by Auden, "Lullaby" (see vol. 2/F, p. 2680).

lyric (from Greek "lyre"): Initially meaning a song, "lyric" refers to a short poetic form, without restriction of meter, in which the expression of personal emotion, often by a voice in the first person, is given primacy over narrative sequence. Thus "The Wife's Lament" (see vol. 1/A, p. 120); Yeats, "The Wild Swans at Coole" (see vol. 2/F, p. 2096).

masque: a **genre.** Costly entertainments of the Stuart court, involving dance, song, speech, and elaborate stage effects, in which courtiers themselves participated.

metaphor (Greek "carrying across," etymologically parallel to Latin "translation"): One of the most significant **figures of thought,** metaphor designates identification or implicit identification of one thing with another with which it is not literally identifiable. Blake, "London," lines 11–12: "And the hapless Soldier's sigh / Runs in blood down Palace walls" (see vol. 2/D, p. 132).

meter: Verse (from Latin "versus," turned) is distinguished from prose (from Latin "prorsus," straightforward) as a more compressed form of expression, shaped by metrical norms. **Meter** (Greek "measure") refers to the regularly recurring sound pattern of verse lines. The means of producing sound patterns across lines differ in different poetic traditions. Verse may be **quantitative,** or determined by the quantities of syllables (set patterns of long and short syllables), as in Latin and Greek poetry. It may be **syllabic,** determined by fixed numbers of syllables in the line, as in the verse of Romance languages (e.g., French and Italian). It may be **accentual,** determined by the number of accents, or stresses in the line, with variable numbers f syllables, as in Old English and some varieties of Middle English alliterative verse. Or it may be **accentual-syllabic**, determined by the numbers of accents, but possessing a regular pattern of stressed and unstressed syllables, so as to produce regular numbers of syllables per line. Since Chaucer, English verse has worked primarily within the many possibilities of accentual-syllabic meter. The unit of meter is the **foot**. In English verse the number of feet per line corresponds to the number of accents in a line. For the types and examples of different meters, see **monometer, dimeter, trimester, tetrameter, pentameter,** and **hexameter.** In the definitions below, "u" designates one unstressed syllable, and "/" one stressed syllable.

metonymy (Greek "change of name"): one of the most significant **figures of thought.** Using a word to **denote** another concept or other concepts, by virtue of habitual association. Thus "The Press," designating printed news media. Fictional names often work by associations of this kind. Closely related to **synecdoche.**

mimesis (Greek for "imitation"): A central function of literature and drama has been to provide a plausible imitation of the reality of the world beyond the literary work; mimesis is the representation and imitation of what is taken to be reality.

mise-en-abyme (French for "cast into the abyss"): Some works of art represent themselves in themselves; if they do so effectively, the represented artifact also represents itself, and so ad infinitum. The effect achieved is called "*mise-en-abyme.*" Hoccleve's *Complaint*, for example, represents a depressed man reading about a depressed man. This sequence threatens to become a *mise-en-abyme.*

monometer (Greek "one measure"): a term of **meter.** An entire line with just one stress; *Sir Gawain and the Green Knight,* line 15, "most (u) grand (/)" (see vol. 1/A, p. 186).

myth: a **genre.** The narrative of **protagonists** with, or subject to, superhuman powers. A myth expresses some profound foundational truth, often by accounting for the origin of natural phenomena. To be distinguished from **legend.** Thus the "Arthurian legend" but the "myth of Proserpine."

novel: an extremely flexible **genre** in both form and subject matter. Usually in prose, giving high priority to narration of events, with a certain expectation of length, novels are preponderantly rooted in a specific, and often complex, social world; sensitive to the realities of material life; and often focused on one **character** or a small circle of central characters. By contrast with chivalric **romance** (the main European narrative genre prior to the novel), novels tend to eschew the marvelous in favor of a recognizable social world and credible action. The novel's openness allows it to participate in all modes, and to be co-opted for a huge variety of subgenres. In English literature the novel dates from the late seventeenth century and has been astonishingly successful in appealing to a huge readership, particularly in the nineteenth and twentieth centuries. The English and Irish tradition of the novel includes, for example, Fielding, Austen, the Brontë sisters, Dickens, George Eliot, Conrad, Woolf, Lawrence, Joyce, to name but a few very great exponents of the genre.

novella: a **genre.** A short **novel,** often characterized by imagistic intensity. Conrad, *Heart of Darkness* (see vol. 2/F, p. 1954).

occupatio (Latin "taking possession"): a **figure of thought.** Denying that one will discuss a subject while actually discussing it; also known as "praeteritio" (Latin "passing by"). See Chaucer, *Nun's Priest's Tale,* lines 414–32 (see vol. 1/A, p. 335).

ode (Greek "song"): a **genre.** A **lyric** poem in elevated, or high style (see **register**), often addressed to a natural force, a person, or an abstract quality. The Pindaric ode in English is made up of **stanzas** of unequal length, while the Horatian ode has stanzas of equal length. For examples of both types, see, respectively, Wordsworth, "Ode: Intimations of Immortality" (vol. 2/D, p. 335); and Marvell, "An Horatian Ode" (vol. 1/B, p. 1806), or Keats, "Ode on Melancholy" (vol. 2/D, p. 931). For a fuller discussion, see the headnote to Jonson's "Ode on Cary and Morison" (vol. 1/B, p. 1551).

omniscient narrator (Latin "all-knowing narrator"): relevant to **point of view**. A narrator who, in the fiction of the narrative, has complete access to both the deeds and the thoughts of all **characters** in the narrative. Thus Thomas Hardy, "On the Western Circuit" (see vol. 2/F, p. 1917).

onomatopoeia (Greek "name making"): a **figure of speech**. Verbal sounds that imitate and evoke the sounds they denote. Hopkins, "Binsey Poplars," lines 10–12 (about some felled trees): "O if we but knew what we do / When we delve [dig] or hew— / Hack and rack the growing green!" (see vol. 2/E, p. 1552).

order: A story may be told in different narrative orders. A narrator might use the sequence of events as they happened, and thereby follow what **classical** rhetoricians called the *natural order;* alternatively, the narrator might reorder the sequence of events, beginning the narration either in the middle or at the end of the sequence of events, thereby following an *artificial order.* If a narrator begins in the middle of events, he or she is said to begin *in medias res* (Latin "in the middle of the matter"). For a brief discussion of these concepts, see Spenser, *Faerie Queene,* "A Letter of the Authors" (vol. 1/B, p. 777). Modern narratology makes a related distinction, between *histoire* (French "story") for the natural order that readers mentally reconstruct, and *discours* (French, here "narration") for the narrative as presented. See also **plot** and **story.**

ottava rima: a **verse form.** An eight-line stanza form, rhyming abababcc, using **iambic pentameter;** Yeats, "Sailing to Byzantium" (see vol. 2/F, p. 2103). Derived from the Italian poet Boccaccio, an eight-line stanza was used by fifteenth-century English poets for inset passages (e.g., Christ's speech from the Cross in Lydgate's *Testament,* lines 754–897). The form in this rhyme scheme was used in English poetry for long narrative by, for example, Byron (*Don Juan;* see vol. 2/D, p. 672).

oxymoron (Greek "sharp blunt"): a **figure of thought.** The conjunction of normally incompatible terms; Milton, *Paradise Lost* 1.63: "darkness visible" (see vol. 1/B, p. 1947).

panegyric: a **genre.** Demonstrative, or epideictic (Greek "showing"), rhetoric was a branch of **classical** rhetoric. Its own two main branches were the rhetoric of praise on the one hand and of vituperation on the other. Panegyric, or eulogy (Greek "sweet speaking"), or encomium (plural *encomia*), is the term used to describe the speeches or writings of praise.

parable: a **genre.** A simple story designed to provoke, and often accompanied by, **allegorical** interpretation, most famously by Christ as reported in the Gospels.

paradox (Greek "contrary to received opinion"): a **figure of thought.** An apparent contradiction that requires thought to reveal an inner consistency. Chaucer, "Troilus's Song," line 12: "O sweete harm so quainte" (see vol. 1/A, p. 344).

parataxis, or **coordination** (respectively Greek and Latin "ordering beside"): a term of **syntax.** The coordination, by the use of coordinating conjunctions, of different main clauses in a single sentence. Malory, "Morte Darthur": "So Sir Lancelot departed and took his sword under his arm, and so he walked in his mantel, that noble knight, and put himself in great jeopardy" (see vol. 1/A, p. 484). The opposite principle to **hypotaxis.**

parody: a work that uses the **conventions** of a particular genre with the aim of comically mocking a **topos,** a genre, or a particular exponent of a genre. Shakespeare parodies the topos of **blazon** in Sonnet 130 (see vol. 1/B, p. 1183).

pastoral (from Latin "pastor," shepherd): a **genre.** Pastoral is set among shepherds, making often refined **allusion** to other apparently unconnected subjects (sometimes politics) from the potentially idyllic world of highly literary if illiterate shepherds. Pastoral is distinguished from **georgic** by representing recreational rural idleness, whereas the georgic offers instruction on how to manage rural labor. English writers had classical models in the *Idylls* of Theocritus in Greek and Virgil's *Eclogues* in Latin. Pastoral is also called bucolic (from the Greek word for "herdsman"). Thus Spenser, *Shepheardes Calender* (see vol. 1/B, p. 769).

pathetic fallacy: the attribution of sentiment to natural phenomena, as if they were in sympathy with human feelings. Thus Milton, *Lycidas*, lines 146–47: "With cowslips wan that hang the pensive head, / And every flower that sad embroidery wears" (see vol. 1/B, p. 1922). For critique of the practice, see Ruskin (who coined the term), "Of the Pathetic Fallacy" (vol. 2/E, p. 1340).

pentameter (Greek "five measure"): a term of **meter.** In English verse, a five-stress line. Between the late fourteenth and the nineteenth centuries, this meter, frequently employing an iambic rhythm, was the basic line of English verse. Chaucer, Shakespeare, Milton, and Wordsworth each, for example, deployed this very flexible line as their primary resource; Milton, *Paradise Lost* 1.128: "O Prince, O Chief of many thronèd Powers" (see vol. 1/B, p. 1949).

performative: Verbal expressions have many different functions. They can, for example, be descriptive, or constative (if they make an argument), or performative, for example. A performative utterance is one that makes something happen in the world by virtue of its utterance. "I hereby sentence you to ten years in prison," if uttered in the appropriate circumstances, itself performs an action; it makes something happen in the world. By virtue of its performing an action, it is called a "performative." See also **speech act.**

peripeteia (Greek "turning about"): the sudden reversal of fortune (in both directions) in a dramatic work.

periphrasis (Greek "declaring around"): a **figure of thought.** Circumlocution; the use of many words to express what could be expressed in few or one; Sidney, *Astrophil and Stella* 39.1–4 (vol. 1/B, p. 1091).

persona (Latin "sound through"): originally the mask worn in the Roman theater to magnify an actor's voice; in literary discourse persona (plural *personae*) refers to the narrator or speaker of a text, whose voice is coherent and whose person need have no relation to the person of the actual author of a text. Eliot, "The Love Song of J. Alfred Prufrock" (see vol. 2/F, p. 2525).

personification, or **prosopopoeia** (Greek "person making"): a **figure of thought.** The attribution of human qualities to nonhuman forces or objects; Shakespeare, *King Lear* 3.2.1: "Blow winds and crack your cheeks, rage! Blow!" (see vol. 1/B, p. 1295).

plot: the sequence of events in a story as narrated, as distinct from **story,** which refers to the sequence of events as we reconstruct them from the plot. See also **order.**

point of view: All of the many kinds of writing involve a point of view from which a text is, or seems to be, generated. The presence of such a point of view may be powerful and explicit, as in many novels, or deliberately invisible, as in much drama. In some genres, such as the **novel,** the narrator does not necessarily tell the story from a position we can predict; that is, the needs of a particular story, not the **conventions** of the genre, determine the narrator's position. In other genres, the narrator's position is fixed by convention; in certain kinds of love poetry, for example, the narrating voice is always that of a suffering lover. Not only does the point of view significantly inform the style of a work, but it also informs the structure of that work.

protagonist (Greek "first actor"): the hero or heroine of a drama or narrative.

pun: a figure of thought. A sometimes irresolvable doubleness of meaning in a single word or expression; Shakespeare, Sonnet 135, line 1: "Whoever hath her wish, thou hast thy *Will*" (see vol. 1/B, p. 1183).

quatrain: a verse form. A stanza of four lines, usually rhyming abcb, abab, or abba. Of many possible examples, see Crashaw, "On the Wounds of Our Crucified Lord" (see vol. 1/B, p. 1746).

refrain: usually a single line repeated as the last line of consecutive stanzas, sometimes with subtly different wording and ideally with subtly different meaning as the poem progresses. See, for example, Wyatt, "Blame not my lute" (vol. 1/B, p. 656).

register: The register of a word is its stylistic level, which can be distinguished by degree of technicality but also by degree of formality. We choose our words from different registers according to context, that is, audience and/or environment. Thus a chemist in a laboratory will say "sodium chloride," a cook in a kitchen "salt." A formal register designates the kind of language used in polite society (e.g., "Mr. President"), while an informal or colloquial register is used in less formal or more relaxed social situations (e.g., "the boss"). In **classical** and medieval rhetoric, these registers of formality were called *high style* and *low style*. A *middle style* was defined as the style fit for narrative, not drawing attention to itself.

rhetoric: the art of verbal persuasion. **Classical** rhetoricians distinguished three areas of rhetoric: the forensic, to be used in law courts; the deliberative, to be used in political or philosophical deliberations; and the demonstrative, or epideictic, to be used for the purposes of public praise or blame. Rhetorical manuals covered all the skills required of a speaker, from the management of style and structure to delivery. These manuals powerfully influenced the theory of poetics as a separate branch of verbal practice, particularly in the matter of style.

rhyme: a figure of speech. The repetition of identical vowel sounds in stressed syllables whose initial consonants differ ("dead" / "head"). In poetry, rhyme often links the end of one line with another. *Masculine rhyme:* full rhyme on the final syllable of the line ("decays" / "days"). *Feminine rhyme:* full rhyme on syllables that are followed by unaccented syllables ("fountains" / "mountains"). *Internal rhyme:* full rhyme within a single line; Coleridge, *The Rime of the Ancient Mariner*, line 7: "The guests are met, the feast is set" (see vol. 2/D, p. 444). *Rhyme riche:* rhyming on **homophones;** Chaucer, *General Prologue*, lines 17–18: "seeke" / "seke." *Off rhyme* (also known as *half rhyme, near rhyme,* or *slant rhyme*): differs from perfect rhyme in changing the vowel sound and/or the concluding consonants expected of perfect rhyme; Byron, "They say that Hope is Happiness," lines 5–7: "most" / "lost." *Pararhyme:* stressed vowel sounds differ but are flanked by identical or similar consonants; Owen, "Miners," lines 9–11: "simmer" / "summer" (see vol. 2/F, p. 2037).

rhyme royal: a verse form. A **stanza** of seven **iambic pentameter** lines, rhyming ababbcc; first introduced by Chaucer and called "royal" because the form was used by James I of Scotland for his *Kingis Quair* in the early fifteenth century. Chaucer, "Troilus's Song" (see vol. 1/A, p. 344).

rhythm: Rhythm is not absolutely distinguishable from **meter.** One way of making a clear distinction between these terms is to say that rhythm (from the Greek "to flow") denotes the patterns of sound within the feet of verse lines and the combination of those feet. Very often a particular meter will raise expectations that a given rhythm will be used regularly through a whole line or a whole poem. Thus in English verse the pentameter regularly uses an iambic rhythm. Rhythm, however, is much more fluid than meter, and many lines within the same poem using a single meter will frequently exploit different rhythmic possibilities. For examples of different rhythms, see **iamb, trochee, anapest, spondee,** and **dactyl.**

romance: a **genre.** From the twelfth to the sixteenth century, the main form of European narrative, in either verse or prose, was that of chivalric romance. Romance, like the later **novel,** is a very fluid genre, but romances are often characterized by (i) a tripartite structure of social integration, followed by disintegration, involving moral tests and often marvelous events, itself the prelude to reintegration in a happy ending, frequently of marriage; and (ii) aristocratic social milieux. Thus *Sir Gawain and the Green Knight* (see vol. 1/A, p. 186); Spenser's (unfinished) *Faerie Queene* (vol. 1/B, p. 775). The immensely popular, fertile genre was absorbed, in both domesticated and undomesticated form, by the novel. For an adaptation of romance, see Chaucer, *Wife of Bath's Tale* (vol. 1/A, p. 282).

sarcasm (Greek "flesh tearing"): a **figure of thought.** A wounding expression, often expressed ironically; Boswell, *Life of Johnson:* Johnson [asked if any man of the modern age could have written the **epic** poem *Fingal*] replied, "Yes, Sir, many men, many women, and many children" (see vol. 1/C, p. 2446).

satire (Latin for "a bowl of mixed fruits"): a **genre.** In Roman literature (e.g., Juvenal), the communication, in the form of a letter between equals, complaining of the ills of contemporary society. The genre in this form is characterized by a first-person narrator exasperated by social ills; the letter form; a high frequency of contemporary reference; and the use of invective in **low-style** language. Pope practices the genre thus in the *Epistle to Dr. Arbuthnot* (see vol. 1/C, p. 2193). Wyatt's "Mine own John Poins" (see vol. 1/B, p. 659) draws ultimately on a gentler, Horatian model of the genre.

satiric mode: Works in a very large variety of genres are devoted to the more or less savage attack on social ills. Thus Swift's travel narrative *Gulliver's Travels* (see vol. 1/C, p. 1959), his **essay** "A Modest Proposal" (vol. 1/C, p. 2105), Pope's mock-**epic** *The Dunciad* (vol. 1/C, p. 2204), and Gay's *Beggar's Opera* (vol. 1/C, p. 2261), to look no further than the eighteenth century, are all within a satiric mode.

scene: a subdivision of an **act,** itself a subdivision of a dramatic performance and/or text. The action of a scene usually occurs in one place.

sensibility (from Latin, "capable of being perceived by the senses"): as a literary term, an eighteenth-century concept derived from moral philosophy that stressed the social importance of fellow feeling and particularly of sympathy in social relations. The concept generated a literature of "sensibility," such as the sentimental **novel** (the most famous of which was Goethe's *Sorrows of the Young Werther* [1774]), or sentimental poetry, such as Cowper's passage on the stricken deer in *The Task* (see vol. 1/C, p. 2546).

short story: a **genre.** Generically similar to, though shorter and more concentrated than, the **novel;** often published as part of a collection. Thus Mansfield, "The Daughters of the Late Colonel" (see vol. 2/F, p. 2569).

simile (Latin "like"): a **figure of thought.** Comparison, usually using the word "like" or "as," of one thing with another so as to produce sometimes surprising analogies. Donne, "The Storm," lines 29–30: "Sooner than you read this line did the gale, / Like feared till felt, our sails assail." Frequently used, in extended form, in **epic** ...etry; Milton, *Paradise Lost* 1.338–46 (see vol. 1/B, p. 1954).

soliloquy (Latin "single speaking"): a **topos** of drama, in which a **character,** alone or thinking to be alone on stage, speaks so as to give the audience access to his or her private thoughts. Thus Viola's soliloquy in Shakespeare, *Twelfth Night* 2.2.17– 41 (vol. 1/B, p. 1205).

sonnet: a verse form. A form combining a variable number of units of rhymed lines to produce a fourteen-line poem, usually in rhyming **iambic pentameter** lines. In English there are two principal varieties: the Petrarchan sonnet, formed by an octave (an eight-line stanza, often broken into two **quatrains** having the same rhyme scheme, typically abba abba) and a sestet (a six-line stanza, typically cdecde or cdcdcd); and the Shakespearean sonnet, formed by three quatrains (abab cdcd efef) and a **couplet** (gg). The declaration of a sonnet can take a sharp turn, or "volta," often at the decisive formal shift from octave to sestet in the Petrarchan sonnet, or in the final couplet of a Shakespearean sonnet, introducing a trenchant counterstatement. Derived from Italian poetry, and especially from the poetry of Petrarch, the sonnet was first introduced to English poetry by Wyatt, and initially used principally for the expression of unrequited erotic love, though later poets used the form for many other purposes. See Wyatt, "Whoso list to hunt" (vol. 1/B, p. 649); Sidney, *Astrophil and Stella* (vol. 1/B, p. 1084); Shakespeare, *Sonnets* (vol. 1/B, p. 1169); Wordsworth, "London, 1802" (vol. 2/D, p. 346); McKay, "If We Must Die" (vol. 2/F, p. 2724); Heaney, "Clearances" (vol. 2/F, p. 2963).

speech act: Words and deeds are often distinguished, but words are often (perhaps always) themselves deeds. Utterances can perform different speech acts, such as promising, declaring, casting a spell, encouraging, persuading, denying, lying, and so on. See also **performative.**

Spenserian stanza: a verse form. The stanza developed by Spenser for *The Faerie Queene;* nine **iambic** lines, the first eight of which are **pentameters,** followed by one **hexameter,** rhyming ababbcbcc. See also, for example, Shelley, *Adonais* (vol. 2/D, p. 839), and Keats, *The Eve of St. Agnes* (vol. 2/D, p. 912).

spondee: a term of **meter.** A two-syllable foot following the rhythmic pattern, in English verse, of two stressed syllables. Thus, for example, "Utah."

stanza (Italian "room"): groupings of two or more lines, though "stanza" is usually reserved for groupings of at least four lines. Stanzas are often joined by rhyme, often in sequence, where each group shares the same metrical pattern and, when rhymed, rhyme scheme. Stanzas can themselves be arranged into larger groupings. Poets often invent new **verse forms,** or they may work within established forms.

story: a narrative's sequence of events, which we reconstruct from those events as they have been recounted by the narrator (i.e., the **plot**). See also **order.**

stream of consciousness: usually a **first-person** narrative that seems to give the reader access to the narrator's mind as it perceives or reflects on events, prior to organizing those perceptions into a coherent narrative. Thus (though generated from a **third-person** narrative) Joyce, *Ulysses*, "Penelope" (see vol. 2/F, p. 2475).

style (from Latin for "writing instrument"): In literary works the manner in which something is expressed contributes substantially to its meaning. The expressions "sun," "mass of helium at the center of the solar system," "heaven's golden orb" all designate "sun," but do so in different manners, or styles, which produce different meanings. The manner of a literary work is its "style," the effect of which is its "tone." We often can intuit the tone of a text; from that intuition of tone we can analyze the stylistic resources by which it was produced. We can analyze the style of literary works through consideration of different elements of style; for example, **diction, figures of thought, figures of speech, meter and rhythm, verse form, syntax, point of view.**

sublime: As a concept generating a literary movement, the sublime refers to the realm of experience beyond the measurable, and so beyond the rational, produced especially by the terrors and grandeur of natural phenomena. Derived especially from the first-century Greek treatise *On the Sublime,* sometimes attributed to Longinus, the notion of the sublime was in the later eighteenth century a spur to Romanticism.

syllable: the smallest unit of sound in a pronounced word. The syllable that receives the greatest stress is called the *tonic* syllable.

symbol (Greek "token"): a **figure of thought.** Something that stands for something else, and yet seems necessarily to evoke that other thing. In Neoplatonic, and there-fore Romantic, theory, to be distinguished from **allegory** thus: whereas allegory involves connections between vehicle and tenor agreed by convention or made explicit, the meanings of a symbol are supposedly inherent to it. For discussion, see Coleridge, "On Symbol and Allegory" (vol. 2/D, p. 502).

synecdoche (Greek "to take with something else"): a **figure of thought.** Using a part to express the whole, or vice versa; e.g., "all hands on deck." Closely related to **metonymy.**

syntax (Greek "ordering with"): Syntax designates the rules by which sentences are constructed in a given language. Discussion of meter is impossible without some reference to syntax, since the overall effect of a poem is, in part, always the product of a subtle balance of meter and sentence construction. Syntax is also essential to the understanding of prose style, since prose writers, deprived of the full shaping possibilities of meter, rely all the more heavily on syntactic resources. A working command of syntactical practice requires an understanding of the parts of speech (nouns, verbs, adjectives, adverbs, conjunctions, pronouns, prepositions, and inter-jections), since writers exploit syntactic possibilities by using particular combina-tions and concentrations of the parts of speech.

taste (from Italian "touch"): Although medieval monastic traditions used eating and tasting as a metaphor for reading, the concept of taste as a personal ideal to be cultivated by, and applied to, the appreciation and judgment of works of art in gen-eral was developed in the eighteenth century.

tercet: a **verse form.** A stanza or group of three lines, used in larger forms such as **terza rima,** the **Petrarchan sonnet,** and the **villanelle.**

terza rima: a **verse form.** A sequence of rhymed **tercets** linked by rhyme thus: aba bcb cdc, etc. first used extensively by Dante in *The Divine Comedy,* the form was adapted in English **iambic pentameters** by Wyatt and revived in the nineteenth century. See Wyatt, "Mine own John Poins" (vol. 1/B, p. 659); Shelley, "Ode to the West Wind" (vol. 2/D, p. 791); and Morris, "The Defence of Guinevere" (vol. 2/E, p. 1513). For modern adaptations see Eliot, lines 78–149 (though unrhymed) of "Little Gidding" (vol. 2/F, pp. 2548); Heaney, "Station Island" (vol. 2/F, p. 2961); Walcott, *Omeros* (vol. 2/F, p. 2806).

tetrameter (Greek "four measure"): a term of **meter.** A line with four stresses. Coleridge, *Christabel,* line 31: "She stole along, she nothing spoke" (see vol. 2/D, p. 462).

theme (Greek "proposition"): In literary criticism the term designates what the work is about; the theme is the concept that unifies a given work of literature.

third-person narration: relevant to **point of view.** A narration in which the narrator recounts a narrative of **characters** referred to explicitly or implicitly by third-person pronouns ("he," she," etc.), without the limitation of a **first-person narration.** Thus Johnson, *The History of Rasselas.*

topographical poem (Greek "place writing"): a **genre.** A poem devoted to the meditative description of particular places. Thus Gray, "Ode on a Distant Prospect of Eton College" (see vol. 1/C, p. 2519).

topos (Greek "place," plural *topoi*): a commonplace in the content of a given kind of literature. Originally, in **classical** rhetoric, the topoi were tried-and-tested stimuli to literary invention: lists of standard headings under which a subject might be investigated. In medieval narrative poems, for example, it was commonplace to begin with a description of spring. Writers did, of course, render the commonplace uncommon, as in Chaucer's spring scene at the opening of *The Canterbury Tales* (see vol. 1/A, p. 243).

tradition (from Latin "passing on"): A literary tradition is whatever is passed on or revived from the past in a single literary culture, or drawn from others to enrich a writer's culture. "Tradition" is fluid in reference, ranging from small to large referents: thus it may refer to a relatively small aspect of texts (e.g., the tradition of **iambic pentameter**), or it may, at the other extreme, refer to the body of texts that constitute a **canon.**

tragedy: a **genre.** A dramatic representation of the fall of kings or nobles, beginning in happiness and ending in catastrophe. Later transferred to other social milieux. The opposite of **comedy,** Shakespeare, *King Lear* (see vol. 1/B, p. 1251).

tragic mode: Many genres (**epic poetry, legend**ary chronicles, **tragedy,** the **novel**) either do or can participate in a tragic mode, by representing the fall of noble **protagonists** and the irreparable ravages of human society and history.

tragicomedy: a **genre.** A play in which potentially tragic events turn out to have a happy, or **comic,** ending. Thus Shakespeare, *Measure for Measure.*

translation (Latin "carrying across"): the rendering of a text written in one language into another.

trimeter (Greek "three measure"): a term of **meter.** A line with three stresses. Herbert, "Discipline," line 1: "Throw away thy rod" (see vol. 1/B, p. 1724).

triplet: a **verse form.** A **tercet** rhyming on the same sound. Pope inserts triplets among heroic **couplets** to emphasize a particular thought; see *Essay on Criticism,* 315–17 (vol. 1/C, p. 2148).

trochee: a term of **rhythm.** A two-syllable foot following the pattern, in English verse, of stressed followed by unstressed syllable, producing a falling effect. Thus, for example, "Texas."

type (Greek "impression, figure"): a **figure of thought** In Christian allegorical interpretation of the Old Testament, pre-Christian figures were regarded as "types," or foreshadowings, of Christ or the Christian dispensation. *Typology* has been the source of much visual and literary art in which the parallelisms between old and new are extended to nonbiblical figures; thus the virtuous plowman in *Piers Plowman* becomes a type of Christ.

unities: According to a theory supposedly derived from Aristotle's *Poetics,* the events represented in a play should have unity of time, place, and action: that the play take up no more time than the time of the play, or at most a day; that the space of action should be within a single city; and that there should be no subplot. See Johnson, *The Preface to Shakespeare* (vol. 1/C, p. 2408).

vernacular (from Latin "verna," servant): the language of the people, as distinguished from learned and arcane languages. From the later Middle Ages especially, the "vernacular" languages and literatures of Europe distinguished themselves from the learned languages and literatures of Latin, Greek, and Hebrew.

verse form: The terms related to **meter** and **rhythm** describe the shape of individual lines. Lines of verse are combined to produce larger groupings, called verse forms. These larger groupings are in the first instance **stanzas.** The combination of a certain meter and stanza shape constitutes the verse form, of which there are many standard kinds.

villanelle: a **verse form.** A fixed form of usually five **tercets** and a **quatrain** employing only two rhyme sounds altogether, rhyming aba for the tercets and abaa for the quatrain, with a complex pattern of two **refrains.** Derived from a French fixed form. Thomas, "Do Not Go Gentle into That Good Night" (see vol. 2/F, p. 2704).

wit: Originally a synonym for "reason" in Old and Middle English, "wit" became a literary ideal in the Renaissance as brilliant play of the full range of mental resources. For eighteenth-century writers, the notion necessarily involved pleasing expression, as in Pope's definition of true wit as "Nature to advantage dressed, / What oft was thought, but ne'er so well expressed" (*Essay on Criticism,* lines 297–98; see vol. 1/C, p. 2147). See also Johnson, *Lives of the Poets,* "Cowley," on "metaphysical wit" (see vol. 1/C, p. 2419). Romantic theory of the imagination deprived wit of its full range of apprehension, whence the word came to be restricted to its modern sense, as the clever play of mind that produces laughter.

zeugma (Greek "a yoking"): a **figure of thought.** A figure whereby one word applies to two or more words in a sentence, and in which the applications are surprising, either because one is unusual, or because the applications are made in very different ways; Pope, *Rape of the Lock* 3.7–8, in which the word "take" is used in two senses: "Here thou, great Anna! whom three realms obey, / Dost sometimes counsel take—and sometimes tea" (see vol. 1/C, p. 2166).

B: Publishing History, Censorship

By the time we read texts in published books, they have already been treated—that is, changed by authors, editors, and printers—in many ways. Although there are differences across history, in each period literary works are subject to pressures of many kinds, which apply before, while, and after an author writes. The pressures might be financial, as in the relations of author and patron; commercial, as in the marketing of books; and legal, as in, during some periods, the negotiation through official and unofficial censorship. In addition, texts in all periods undergo technological processes, as they move from the material forms in which an author produced them to the forms in which they are presented to readers. Some of the terms below designate important material forms in which books were produced, disseminated, and surveyed across the historical span of this anthology. Others designate the skills developed to understand these processes. The anthology's introductions to individual periods discuss the particular forms these phenomena took in different eras.

bookseller: In England, and particularly in London, commercial bookmaking and-selling enterprises came into being in the early fourteenth century. These were loose organizations of artisans who usually lived in the same neighborhoods (around St. Paul's Cathedral in London). A bookseller or dealer would coordinate the production of hand-copied books for wealthy patrons (see **patronage**), who would order books to be custom-made. After the introduction of **printing** in the late fifteenth century, authors generally sold the rights to their work to booksellers, without any further **royalties**. Booksellers, who often had their own shops, belonged to the **Stationers' Company**. This system lasted into the eighteenth century. In 1710, however, authors were for the first time granted **copyright**, which tipped the commercial balance in their favor, against booksellers.

censorship: The term applies to any mechanism for restricting what can be published. Historically, the reasons for imposing censorship are heresy, sedition, blasphemy, libel, or obscenity. External censorship is imposed by institutions having legislative sanctions at their disposal. Thus the pre-Reformation Church imposed the Constitutions of Archbishop Arundel of 1409, aimed at repressing the Lollard "heresy." After the Reformation, some key events in the history of censorship are as follows: 1547, when anti-Lollard legislation and legislation made by Henry VIII concerning treason by writing (1534) were abolished; the Licensing Order of 1643, which legislated that works be licensed, through the Stationers' Company, prior to publication; and 1695, when the last such Act stipulating prepublication licensing lapsed. Postpublication censorship continued in different periods for different reasons. Thus, for example, British publication of D. H. Lawrence's *Lady Chatterley's Lover* (1928) was obstructed (though unsuccessfully) in 1960, under the Obscene Publications Act of 1959. Censorship can also be international: although not published in Iran, Salman Rushdie's *Satanic Verses* (1988) was censored in that country, where the leader, Ayatollah Ruhollah Khomeini, proclaimed a fatwa (religious decree) promising the author's execution. Very often censorship is not imposed externally, however: authors or publishers can censor work in anticipation of what will incur the wrath of readers or the penalties of the law. Victorian and Edwardian publishers of **novels,** for example, urged authors to remove potentially offensive material, especially for serial publication in popular magazines.

codex: the physical format of most modern books and medieval manuscripts, consisting of a series of separate leaves gathered into quires and bound together, often with a cover. In late antiquity, the codex largely replaced the scroll, the standard form of written documents in Roman culture.

copy text: the particular text of a work used by a textual editor as the basis of an edition of that work.

copyright: the legal protection afforded to authors for control of their work's publication, in an attempt to ensure due financial reward. Some key dates in the history of copyright in the United Kingdom are as follows: 1710, when a statute gave authors the exclusive right to publish their work for fourteen years, and fourteen years more if the author were still alive when the first term had expired; 1842, when the period of authorial control was extended to forty-two years; and 1911, when the term was extended yet further, to fifty years after the author's death. In 1995 the period of protection was harmonized with the laws in other European countries to be the life of the author plus seventy years. In the United States no works first published before 1923 are in copyright. Works published since 1978 are, as in the United Kingdom, protected for the life of the author plus seventy years.

folio: the leaf formed by both sides of a single page. Each folio has two sides: a *recto* (the front side of the leaf, on the right side of a double-page spread in an open codex), and a *verso* (the back side of the leaf, on the left side of a double-page spread). Modern book pagination follows the pattern 1, 2, 3, 4, while medieval manuscript pagination follows the pattern 1r, 1v, 2r, 2v. "Folio" can also designate the size of a printed book. Books come in different shapes, depending originally on the number of times a standard sheet of paper is folded. One fold produces a large volume, a *folio* book; two folds produce a *quarto*, four an *octavo*, and six a very small *duodecimo*. Generally speaking, the larger the book, the grander and more expensive. Shakespeare's plays were, for example, first printed in quartos, but were gathered into a folio edition in 1623.

foul papers: versions of a work before an author has produced, if she or he has, a final copy (a "fair copy") with all corrections removed.

incunabulum (plural "incunabula"): any printed book produced in Europe before 1501. Famous incunabula include the Gutenberg Bible, printed in 1455.

manuscript (Latin, "written by hand"): Any text written physically by hand is a manuscript. Before the introduction of **printing** with moveable type in 1476, all texts in England were produced and reproduced by hand, in manuscript. This is an extremely labor-intensive task, using expensive materials (e.g., **vellum,** or **parchment**); the cost of books produced thereby was, accordingly, very high. Even after the introduction of printing, many texts continued to be produced in manuscript. This is obviously true of letters, for example, but until the eighteenth century, poetry written within aristocratic circles was often transmitted in manuscript copies.

paleography (Greek "ancient writing"): the art of deciphering, describing, and dating forms of handwriting.

parchment: animal skin, used as the material for handwritten books before the introduction of paper. See also **vellum.**

patronage, patron (Latin "protector"): Many technological, legal, and commercial supports were necessary before professional authorship became possible. Although some playwrights (e.g., Shakespeare) made a living by writing for the theater, other authors needed, principally, the large-scale reproductive capacities of **printing** and the security of **copyright** to make a living from writing. Before these conditions obtained, many authors had another main occupation, and most authors had to rely on patronage. In different periods, institutions or individuals offered material support, or patronage, to authors. Thus in Anglo-Saxon England, monasteries afforded the conditions of writing to monastic authors. Between the twelfth and the seventeenth centuries, the main source of patronage was the royal court. Authors offered patrons prestige and ideological support in return for financial support. Even as the conditions of professional authorship came into being at the beginning of the eighteenth century, older forms of direct patronage were not altogether displaced until the middle of the century.

periodical: Whereas journalism, strictly, applies to daily writing (from French "jour," day), periodical writing appears at larger, but still frequent, intervals, characteristically in the form of the **essay.** Periodicals were developed especially in the eighteenth century.

printing: Printing, or the mechanical reproduction of books using moveable type, was invented in Germany in the mid-fifteenth century by Johannes Gutenberg; it quickly spread throughout Europe. William Caxton brought printing into England from the Low Countries in 1476. Much greater powers of reproduction at much lower prices transformed every aspect of literary culture.

publisher: the person or company responsible for the commissioning and publicizing of printed matter. In the early period of **printing,** publisher, printer, and bookseller were often the same person. This trend continued in the ascendancy of the **Stationers' Company,** between the middle of the sixteenth and the end of the seventeenth centuries. Toward the end of the seventeenth century, these three functions began to separate, leading to their modern distinctions.

quire: When medieval manuscripts were assembled, a few loose sheets of parchment or paper would first be folded together and sewn along the fold. This formed a quire (also known as a "gathering" or "signature"). Folded in this way, four large sheets of parchment would produce eight smaller manuscript leaves. Multiple quires could then be bound together to form a codex.

royalties: an agreed-upon proportion of the price of each copy of a work sold, paid by the publisher to the author, or an agreed-upon fee paid to the playwright for each performance of a play.

scribe: In **manuscript** culture, the scribe is the copyist who reproduces a text by hand.

scriptorium (plural "scriptoria"): a place for producing written documents and manuscripts.

serial publication: generally referring to the practice, especially common in the nineteenth-century, of publishing novels a few chapters at a time, in periodicals.

Stationers' Company: The Stationers' Company was an English guild incorporating various tradesmen, including printers, publishers, and booksellers, skilled in the production and selling of books. It was formed in 1403, received its royal charter in 1557, and served as a means both of producing and of regulating books. Authors would sell the manuscripts of their books to individual stationers, who incurred the risks and took the profits of producing and selling the books. The stationers entered their rights over given books in the Stationers' Register. They also regulated the book trade and held their monopoly by licensing books and by being empowered to seize unauthorized books and imprison resisters. This system of licensing broke down in the social unrest of the Civil War and Interregnum (1640–60), and it ended in 1695. Even after the end of licensing, the Stationers' Company continued to be an intrinsic part of the **copyright** process, since the 1710 copyright statute directed that copyright had to be registered at Stationers' Hall.

subscription: An eighteenth-century system of bookselling somewhere between direct **patronage** and impersonal sales. A subscriber paid half the cost of a book before publication and half on delivery. The author received these payments directly. The subscriber's name appeared in the prefatory pages.

textual criticism: Works in all periods often exist in many subtly or not so subtly different forms. This is especially true with regard to manuscript textual reproduction, but it also applies to printed texts. Textual criticism is the art, developed from the fifteenth century in Italy but raised to new levels of sophistication from the eighteenth century, of deciphering different historical states of texts. This art involves the analysis of textual **variants,** often with the aim of distinguishing authorial from scribal forms.

variant: differences that appear among different manuscripts or printed editions of the same text.

vellum: animal skin, used as the material for handwritten books before the introduction of paper. See also **parchment.**

watermark: the trademark of a paper manufacturer, impressed into the paper but largely invisible unless held up to light.

Geographic Nomenclature

The **British Isles** refers to the prominent group of islands off the northwest coast of Europe, especially to the two largest, **Great Britain** and **Ireland**. At present these comprise two sovereign states: **the Republic of Ireland**, or **Éire**, and **the United Kingdom of Great Britain and Northern Ireland**—known for short as the **United Kingdom** or the **U.K.** Most of the smaller islands are part of the **U.K.** but a few, like the **Isle of Man** and the tiny **Channel Islands**, are largely independent. The **U.K.** is often loosely referred to as "**Britain**" or "**Great Britain**" and is sometimes called simply, if inaccurately, "**England**." For obvious reasons, the latter usage is rarely heard among the inhabitants of the other countries of the **U.K.**—**Scotland, Wales**, and **Northern Ireland** (sometimes called **Ulster**). England is by far the most populous part of the kingdom, as well as the seat of its capital, London.

From the first to the fifth century C.E. most of what is now **England** and **Wales** was a province of the Roman Empire called **Britain** (in Latin, **Britannia**). After the fall of Rome, much of the island was invaded and settled by peoples from northern Germany and Denmark speaking what we now call Old English. These peoples are collectively known as the Anglo-Saxons, and the word **England** is related to the first element of their name. By the time of the Norman Conquest (1066) most of the kingdoms founded by the Anglo-Saxons and subsequent Viking invaders had coalesced into the kingdom of **England**, which, in the latter Middle Ages, conquered and largely absorbed the neighboring Celtic kingdom of **Wales**. In 1603 James VI of **Scotland** inherited the island's other throne as James I of **England**, and for the next hundred years—except for the brief period of Puritan rule—**Scotland** (both its English-speaking **Lowlands** and its Gaelic-speaking **Highlands**) and **England** (with **Wales**) were two kingdoms under a single king. In 1707 the Act of Union welded them together as **the United Kingdom of Great Britain. Ireland,** where English rule had begun in the twelfth century and been tightened in the sixteenth, was incorporated by the 1800–1801 Act of Union into **the United Kingdom of Great Britain and Ireland**. With the division of Ireland and the establishment of **the Irish Free State** after World War I, this name was modified to its present form, and in 1949 **the Irish Free State** became **the Republic of Ireland**. In 1999 **Scotland** elected a separate parliament it had relinquished in 1707, and **Wales** elected an assembly it lost in 1409; neither Scotland nor Wales ceased to be part of the **United Kingdom**.

The **British Isles** are further divided into counties, which in **Great Britain** are also known as shires. This word, with its vowel shortened in pronunciation, forms the suffix in the names of many counties, such as **Yorkshire, Wiltshire, Somersetshire**.

The Latin names **Britannia (Britain), Caledonia (Scotland)**, and **Hibernia (Ireland)** are sometimes used in poetic diction; so too is **Britain**'s ancient Celtic name, **Albion**. Because of its accidental resemblance to *albus* (Latin for "white"), **Albion** is especially associated with the chalk cliffs that seem to gird much of the English coast like defensive walls.

The **British Empire** took its name from **the British Isles** because it was created not only by the **English** but also by the **Irish, Scots,** and **Welsh**, as well as by civilians and servicemen from other constituent countries of the empire. Some of the empire's **overseas colonies**, or **crown colonies**, were populated largely by settlers of European origin and their descendants. These predominantly white **settler colonies**, such as **Canada, Australia**, and **New Zealand**, were allowed significant self-government in the nineteenth century and recognized as **dominions** in the early twentieth century. The **white dominions** became members of **the Commonwealth of Nations**, also called **the Commonwealth, the British Commonwealth**, and **"the Old Commonwealth"** at different times, an association of sovereign states under the symbolic leadership of the British monarch.

Other **overseas colonies** of the empire had mostly indigenous populations (or, in the Caribbean, the descendants of imported slaves, indentured servants, and others). These **colonies** were granted political independence after World War II, later than the **dominions**, and have often been referred to since as **postcolonial** nations. In South and Southeast Asia, **India** and **Pakistan** gained independence in 1947, followed by other countries including **Sri Lanka** (formerly **Ceylon**), **Burma** (now **Myanmar**), **Malaya** (now **Malaysia**), and **Singapore**. In West and East Africa, the **Gold Coast** was decolonized as **Ghana** in 1957, **Nigeria** in 1960, **Sierra Leone** in 1961, **Uganda** in 1962, **Kenya** in 1963, and so forth, while in southern Africa, the white minority government of **South Africa** was already independent in 1931, though majority rule did not come until 1994. In the Caribbean, **Jamaica** and **Trinidad and Tobago** won independence in 1962, followed by **Barbados** in 1966, and other islands of the British West Indies in the 1970s and '80s. Other regions with nations emerging out of British colonial rule included Central America (**British Honduras**, now **Belize**), South America (**British Guiana**, now **Guyana**), the Pacific islands (**Fiji**), and Europe (**Cyprus, Malta**). After decolonization, many of these nations chose to remain within a newly conceived **Commonwealth** and are sometimes referred to as **"New Commonwealth"** countries. Some nations, such as **Ireland, Pakistan**, and **South Africa,** withdrew from the **Commonwealth**, though **South Africa** and **Pakistan** eventually rejoined, and others, such as **Burma** (**Myanmar**), gained independence outside the **Commonwealth**. Britain's last major overseas colony, **Hong Kong**, was returned to Chinese sovereignty in 1997, but while Britain retains only a handful of dependent territories, such as **Bermuda** and **Montserrat**, the scope of the **Commonwealth** remains vast, with 30 percent of the world's population.

British Money

One of the most dramatic changes to the system of British money came in 1971. In the system previously in place, the pound consisted of 20 shillings, each containing 12 pence, making 240 pence to the pound. Since 1971, British money has been calculated on the decimal system, with 100 pence to the pound. Britons' experience of paper money did not change very drastically: as before, 5- and 10-pound notes constitute the majority of bills passing through their hands (in addition, 20- and 50- pound notes have been added). But the shift necessitated a whole new way of thinking about and exchanging coins and marked the demise of the shilling, one of the fundamental units of British monetary history. Many other coins, still frequently encountered in literature, had already passed. These include the groat, worth 4 pence (the word "groat" is often used to signify a trifling sum); the angel (which depicted the archangel Michael triumphing over a dragon), valued at 10 shillings; the mark, worth in its day two-thirds of a pound or 13 shillings 4 pence; and the sovereign, a gold coin initially worth 22 shillings 6 pence, later valued at 1 pound, last circulated in 1932. One prominent older coin, the guinea, was worth a pound and a shilling; though it has not been minted since 1813, a very few quality items or prestige awards (like the purse in a horse race) may still be quoted in guineas. (The table below includes some other well-known, obsolete coins.) Colloquially, a pound was (and is) called a quid; a shilling a bob; sixpence, a tanner; a copper could refer to a penny, a half-penny, or a farthing (¼ penny).

Old Currency	New Currency
1 pound note	1 pound coin (or note in Scotland)
10 shilling (half-pound note)	50 pence
5 shilling (crown)	
2½ shilling (half crown)	20 pence
2 shilling (florin)	10 pence
1 shilling	5 pence
6 pence	
2½ pence	1 penny
2 pence	
1 penny	
½ penny	
¼ penny (farthing)	

In recent years, the British government and people have been contemplating and debating a change even greater than the shift to the decimal system. Britain, a member of the European Union, may adopt the EU's common currency, the Euro, and eventually see the pound itself become obsolete. More than many other EU-member countries, Britain has resisted this change: many people strongly identify their country with its rich commercial history and tend to view their currency patriotically as a national symbol.

Even more challenging than sorting out the values of obsolete coins is calculating for any given period the purchasing power of money, which fluctuates over time by its very nature. At the beginning of the twentieth century, 1 pound was worth about 5 American dollars, though those bought three to four times what they now do. Now the pound buys anywhere from $1.50 to $1.90. As difficult as it is to generalize, it is clear that money used to be worth much more than it is currently. In Anglo-Saxon times, the most valuable circulating coin was the silver penny: four would buy a sheep. Beyond long-term inflationary trends, prices varied from times of plenty to those marked by poor harvests; from peacetime to wartime; from the country to the metropolis (life in London has always been very expensive); and wages varied according to the availability of labor (wages would sharply rise, for instance, during the devastating Black Death in the fourteenth century). The chart below provides a glimpse of some actual prices of given periods and their changes across time, though all the variables mentioned above prevent them from being definitive. Even from one year to the next, an added tax on gin or tea could drastically raise prices, and a lottery ticket could cost much more the night before the drawing than just a month earlier. Still, the prices quoted below do indicate important trends, such as the disparity of incomes in British society and the costs of basic commodities. In the chart below, the symbol £ is used for pound, s. for shilling, d. for a penny (from Latin *denarius*); a sum would normally be written £2.19.3, i.e., 2 pounds, 19 shillings, 3 pence. (This is Leopold Bloom's budget for the day depicted in Joyce's novel *Ulysses* [1922]; in the new currency, it would be about £2.96.)

circa	1390	1590	1650	1750	1815	1875	1950
food and drink	gallon (8 pints) of ale, 1.5d.	tankard of beer, .5d.	coffee, 1d. a dish	"drunk for a penny, dead drunk for two-pence" (gin shop sign in Hogarth print)	ounce of laudanum, 3d.	pint of beer, 3d.	pint of Guinness stout, 11d.
	gallon (8 pints) of wine, 3 to 4d.	pound of beef, 2s. 5d.	chicken, 1s. 4d.	dinner at a steakhouse, 1s.	ham and potato dinner for two, 7s.	dinner in a good hotel, 5s.	pound of beef, 2s. 2d.
	pound of cinnamon, 1 to 3s.	pound of cinnamon, 10s. 6d.	pound of tea, £3 10s.	pound of tea, 16s.	Prince Regent's dinner party for 2000, £12,000	pound of tea, 2s.	dinner on railway car, 7s. 6d.
entertainment	no cost to watch a cycle play	admission to public theater, 1 to 3d.	falcon, £11s. 5d.	theater tickets, 1 to 5s.	admission to Covent Garden theater, 1 to 7s.	theater tickets, 6d. to 7s.	admission to Old Vic theater, 1s. 6d. to 10s. 6d.
	contributory admission to professional troupe theater	cheap seat in private theater, 6d.	billiard table, £25	admission to Vauxhall Gardens, 1s.	annual subscription to Almack's (exclusive club), 10 guineas	admission to Madam Tussaud's waxworks, 1s.	admission to Odeon cinema, Manchester, 1s. 3d.
	maintenance for royal hounds at Windsor, .75d. a day	"to see a dead Indian" (quoted in *The Tempest*), 1.25d. (ten "doits")	three-quarter length portrait painting, £31	lottery ticket, £20 (shares were sold)	Jane Austen's piano, 30 guineas	annual fees at a gentleman's club, 7 to 10 guineas	tropical fish tank, £4 4s.

circa	1390	1590	1650	1750	1815	1875	1950
reading	cheap romance, 1s.	play quarto, 6d.	pamphlet, 1 to 6d.	issue of The Gentleman's Magazine, 6d.	issue of Edinburgh Review, 6s.	copy of The Times, 3d.	copy of The Times, 3d.
	a Latin Bible, 2 to £4	Shakespeare's First Folio (1623), £1	student Bible, 6s.	cheap edition of Milton, 2s.	membership in circulating library (3rd class), £1 4s. a year	illustrated edition of Through the Looking-glass, 6s.	issue of Eagle comics, 4.5d.
	payment for illuminating a liturgical book, £22 9s.	Foxe's Acts and Monuments, 24s.	Hobbes's Leviathan, 8s.	Johnson's Dictionary, folio, 2 vols., £4 10s.	1st edition of Austen's Pride and Prejudice, 18s.	1st edition of Trollope's The Way We Live Now, 2 vols., £1 1s.	Orwell's Nineteen Eighty Four, paperback, 3s. 6d.
transportation	night's supply of hay for horse, 2d.	wherry (whole boat) across Thames, 1d.	day's journey, coach, 10s.	boat across Thames, 4d.	coach ride, outside, 2 to 3d. a mile; inside, 4 to 5d. a mile	15-minute journey in a London cab, 1s. 6d.	London tube fare, about 2d. a mile
	coach, £8	hiring a horse for a day, 12d.	coach horse, £30	coach fare, London to Edinburgh, £4 10s.	palanquin transport in Madras, 5s. a day	railway, 3rd class, London to Plymouth, 18s.	petrol, 3s. a gallon
						8d. (about 1d. a mile)	
	quality horse, £10	hiring a coach for a day, 10s.	fancy carriage, £170	transport to America, £5	passage, Liverpool to New York, £10	passage to India, 1st class, £50	midsize Austin sedan, £449 plus £188 4s. 2d. tax
clothes	clothing allowance for	shoes with buckles, 8d.	footman's frieze coat, 15s.	working woman's gown	checked muslin	flannel for a	woman's sun

labor/incomes

shoes for gentry wearer, 4d.	woman's gloves, £1 5s.	falconer's hat, 10s.	gentleman's suit, £8	hiring a dressmaker for a pelisse, 8s.	overcoat for an Eton schoolboy, £1 1s.	tweed sports jacket, £3 16s. 6d.
hat for gentry wearer, 10d.	fine cloak, £16	black cloth for mourning household of an earl, £100	very fine wig, £30	ladies silk stockings, 12s.	set of false teeth, £2 10s.	"Teddy boy" drape suit, £20
hiring a skilled building worker, 4d. a day	actor's daily wage during playing season, 1s.	agricultural laborer, 6s. 5d. a week	price of boy slave, £32	lowest-paid sailor on Royal Navy ship, 10s. 9d. a month	seasonal agricultural laborer, 14s. a week	minimum wage, agricultural laborer, £4 14s. per 47-hour week
wage for professional scribe, £2 3s. 4d. a year + cloak	household servant 2 to £5 a year + food, clothing	tutor to noble-man's children, £30 a year	housemaid's wage, £6 to £8 a year	contributor to *Quarterly Review*, 10 guineas per sheet	housemaid's wage, £10 to £25 a year	shorthand typist, £367 a year
minimum income to be called gentleman £10 a year; for knighthood, 40 to £400	minimum income for eligibility for knighthood, £30 a year	Milton's salary as Secretary of Foreign Tongues, £288 a year	Boswell's allowance, £200 a year	minimum income for a "genteel" family, £100 a year	income of the "comfortable" classes, £800 and up a year	middle manager's salary, £1,480 a year
income from land of richest magnates, £3,500 a year	income from land of average earl, £4000 a year	Earl of Bedford's income, £8,000 a year	Duke of New-castle's income, £40,000 a year	Mr. Darcy's income, *Pride and Prejudice*, £10,000	Trollope's income, £4,000 a year	barrister's salary, £2,032 a year

The British Baronage

The English monarchy is in principle hereditary, though at times during the Middle Ages the rules were subject to dispute. In general, authority passes from father to eldest surviving son, from daughters in order of seniority if there is no son, to a brother if there are no children, and in default of direct descendants to collateral lines (cousins, nephews, nieces) in order of closeness. There have been breaks in the order of succession (1066, 1399, 1688), but so far as possible the usurpers have always sought to paper over the break with a legitimate, i.e., hereditary, claim. When a queen succeeds to the throne and takes a husband, he does not become king unless he is in the line of blood succession; rather, he is named prince consort, as Albert was to Victoria. He may father kings, but is not one himself.

The original Saxon nobles were the king's thanes, ealdormen, or earls, who provided the king with military service and counsel in return for booty, gifts, or landed estates. William the Conqueror, arriving from France, where feudalism was fully developed, considerably expanded this group. In addition, as the king distributed the lands of his new kingdom, he also distributed dignities to men who became known collectively as "the baronage." "Baron" in its root meaning signifies simply "man," and barons were the king's men. As the title was common, a distinction was early made between greater and lesser barons, the former gradually assuming loftier and more impressive titles. The first English "duke" was created in 1337; the title of "marquess," or "marquis" (pronounced "markwis"), followed in 1385, and "viscount" ("vyekount") in 1440. Though "earl" is the oldest title of all, an earl now comes between a marquess and a viscount in order of dignity and precedence, and the old term "baron" now designates a rank just below viscount."Baronets" were created in 1611 as a means of raising revenue for the crown (the title could be purchased for about £1000); they are marginal nobility and have never sat in the House of Lords.

Kings and queens are addressed as "Your Majesty," princes and princesses as "Your Highness," the other hereditary nobility as "My Lord" or "Your Lordship." Peers receive their titles either by inheritance (like Lord Byron, the sixth baron of that line) or from the monarch (like Alfred Lord Tennyson, created first Baron Tennyson by Victoria). The children, even of a duke, are commoners unless they are specifically granted some other title or inherit their father's title from him. A peerage can be forfeited by act of attainder, as for example when a lord is convicted of treason; and, when forfeited, or lapsed for lack of a successor, can be bestowed on another family. Thus in 1605 Robert Cecil was made first earl of Salisbury in the third creation, the first creation dating from 1149, the second from 1337, the title having been in abeyance since 1539. Titles descend by right of succession and do not depend on tenure of land; thus, a title does not always indicate where a lord dwells or holds power. Indeed, noble titles do not always refer to a real place at all. At Prince Edward's marriage in 1999, the queen created him earl of Wessex, although the old kingdom of Wessex has had no political existence since the Anglo-Saxon period, and the name was all but forgotten until it was resurrected by Thomas Hardy as the setting of his novels. (This is perhaps but one of many ways in which the world of the aristocracy increasingly resembles the realm of literature.)

The king and queen	(These are all of the royal line.)
Prince and princess	
Duke and duchess	(These may or may not be of the royal line, but are ordinarily remote from the succession.)
Marquess and marchioness	
Earl and countess	
Viscount and viscountess	
Baron and baroness	
Baronet and lady	

Scottish peers sat in the parliament of Scotland, as English peers did in the parliament of England, till at the Act of Union (1707) Scottish peers were granted sixteen seats in the English House of Lords, to be filled by election. (In 1963, all Scottish lords were allowed to sit.) Similarly, Irish peers, when the Irish parliament was abolished in 1801, were granted the right to elect twenty-eight of their number to the House of Lords in Westminster. (Now that the Republic of Ireland is a separate nation, this no longer applies.) Women members (peeresses) were first allowed to sit in the House as nonhereditary Life Peers in 1958 (when that status was created for members of both genders); women first sat by their own hereditary right in 1963. Today the House of Lords still retains some power to influence or delay legislation, but its future is uncertain. In 1999, the hereditary peers (then amounting to 750) were reduced to 92 temporary members elected by their fellow peers. Holders of Life Peerages remain, as do senior bishops of the Church of England and high-court judges (the "Law Lords").

Below the peerage the chief title of honor is "knight." Knighthood, which is not hereditary, is generally a reward for services rendered. A knight (Sir John Black) is addressed, using his first name, as "Sir John"; his wife, using the last name, is "Lady Black"—unless she is the daughter of an earl or nobleman of higher rank, in which case she will be "Lady Arabella." The female equivalent of a knight bears the title of "Dame." Though the word itself comes from the Anglo-Saxon *cniht*, there is some doubt as to whether knighthood amounted to much before the arrival of the Normans. The feudal system required military service as a condition of land tenure, and a man who came to serve his king at the head of an army of tenants required a title of authority and badges of identity—hence the title of knighthood and the coat of arms. During the Crusades, when men were far removed from their land (or even sold it in order to go on crusade), more elaborate forms of fealty sprang up that soon expanded into orders of knighthood. The Templars, Hospitallers, Knights of the Teutonic Order, Knights of Malta, and Knights of the Golden Fleece were but a few of these companionships; not all of them were available at all times in England.

Gradually, with the rise of centralized government and the decline of feudal tenures, military knighthood became obsolete, and the rank largely honorific; sometimes, as under James I, it degenerated into a scheme of the royal government for making money. For hundreds of years after its establishment in the fourteenth century, the Order of the Garter was the only English order of knighthood, an exclusive courtly companionship. Then, during the late seventeenth, the eighteenth, and the nineteenth centuries, a number of additional orders were created, with names such as the Thistle, Saint Patrick, the Bath, Saint Michael and Saint George, plus a number of special Victorian and Indian orders. They retain the terminology, ceremony, and dignity of knighthood, but the military implications are vestigial.

Although the British Empire now belongs to history, appointments to the Order of the British Empire continue to be conferred for services to that empire at home or abroad. Such honors (commonly referred to as "gongs") are granted by the monarch in her New Year's and Birthday lists, but the decisions are now made by the government in power. In recent years there have been efforts to popularize and democratize the dispensation of honors, with recipients including rock stars and actors. But this does not prevent large sectors of British society from regarding both knighthood and the peerage as largely irrelevant to modern life.

The Royal Lines of England and Great Britain

England

SAXONS AND DANES

Egbert, king of Wessex	802–839
Ethelwulf, son of Egbert	839–858
Ethelbald, second son of Ethelwulf	858–860
Ethelbert, third son of Ethelwulf	860–866
Ethelred I, fourth son of Ethelwulf	866–871
Alfred the Great, fifth son of Ethelwulf	871–899
Edward the Elder, son of Alfred	899–924
Athelstan the Glorious, son of Edward	924–940
Edmund I, third son of Edward	940–946
Edred, fourth son of Edward	946–955
Edwy the Fair, son of Edmund	955–959
Edgar the Peaceful, second son of Edmund	959–975
Edward the Martyr, son of Edgar	975–978 (murdered)
Ethelred II, the Unready, second son of Edgar	978–1016
Edmund II, Ironside, son of Ethelred II	1016–1016
Canute the Dane	1016–1035
Harold I, Harefoot, natural son of Canute	1035–1040
Hardecanute, son of Canute	1040–1042
Edward the Confessor, son of Ethelred II	1042–1066
Harold II, brother-in-law of Edward	1066–1066 (died in battle)

HOUSE OF NORMANDY

William I the Conqueror	1066–1087
William II, Rufus, third son of William I	1087–1100 (shot from ambush)
Henry I, Beauclerc, youngest son of William I	1100–1135

HOUSE OF BLOIS

Stephen, son of Adela, daughter of William I	1135–1154

HOUSE OF PLANTAGENET

Henry II, son of Geoffrey Plantagenet by Matilda, daughter of Henry I	1154–1189
Richard I, Coeur de Lion, son of Henry II	1189–1199
John Lackland, son of Henry II	1199–1216
Henry III, son of John	1216–1272
Edward I, Longshanks, son of Henry III	1272–1307
Edward II, son of Edward I	1307–1327 (deposed)
Edward III of Windsor, son of Edward II	1327–1377
Richard II, grandson of Edward III	1377–1399 (deposed)

HOUSE OF LANCASTER

Henry IV, son of John of Gaunt, son of Edward III	1399–1413
Henry V, Prince Hal, son of Henry IV	1413–1422
Henry VI, son of Henry V	1422–1461 (deposed), 1470–1471 (deposed)

HOUSE OF YORK

Edward IV, great-great-grandson of Edward III	1461–1470 (deposed), 1471–1483
Edward V, son of Edward IV	1483–1483 (murdered)
Richard III, Crookback	1483–1485 (died in battle)

HOUSE OF TUDOR

Henry VII, married daughter of Edward IV	1485–1509
Henry VIII, son of Henry VII	1509–1547
Edward VI, son of Henry VIII	1547–1553
Mary I, "Bloody," daughter of Henry VIII	1553–1558
Elizabeth I, daughter of Henry VIII	1558–1603

HOUSE OF STUART

James I (James VI of Scotland)	1603–1625
Charles I, son of James I	1625–1649 (executed)

COMMONWEALTH & PROTECTORATE

Council of State	1649–1653
Oliver Cromwell, Lord Protector	1653–1658
Richard Cromwell, son of Oliver	1658–1660 (resigned)

HOUSE OF STUART (RESTORED)

Charles II, son of Charles I	1660–1685
James II, second son of Charles I	1685–1688

(INTERREGNUM, 11 DECEMBER 1688 TO 13 FEBRUARY 1689)

William III of Orange, by	
Mary, daughter of Charles I	1689–1701
and Mary II, daughter of James II	–1694
Anne, second daughter of James II	1702–1714

Great Britain

HOUSE OF HANOVER

George I, son of Elector of Hanover and	
Sophia, granddaughter of James I	1714–1727
George II, son of George I	1727–1760
George III, grandson of George II	1760–1820
George IV, son of George III	1820–1830
William IV, third son of George III	1830–1837
Victoria, daughter of Edward, fourth son	
of George III	1837–1901

HOUSE OF SAXE-COBURG AND GOTHA

Edward VII, son of Victoria	1901–1910

HOUSE OF WINDSOR (NAME ADOPTED 17 JULY 1917)

George V, second son of Edward VII	1910–1936
Edward VIII, eldest son of George V	1936–1936 (abdicated)
George VI, second son of George V	1936–1952
Elizabeth II, daughter of George VI	1952–

Religions in England

In the sixth century C.E., missionaries from Ireland and the Continent introduced Christianity to the Anglo-Saxons—actually, reintroduced it, since it had briefly flourished in the southern parts of the British Isles during the Roman occupation, and even after the Roman withdrawal had persisted in the Celtic regions of Scotland and Wales. By the time the earliest poems included in the *Norton Anthology* were composed, therefore, the English people had been Christians for hundreds of years; such Anglo-Saxon poems as "The Dream of the Rood" bear witness to their faith. Our knowledge of the religion of pre-Christian Britain is sketchy, but it is likely that vestiges of paganism assimilated into, or coexisted with, the practice of Christianity: fertility rites were incorporated into the celebration of Easter resurrection, rituals commemorating the dead into All-Hallows Eve and All Saints Day, and elements of winter solstice festivals into the celebration of Christmas. In English literature such "folkloric" elements often elicit romantic nostalgia. Geoffrey Chaucer's Wife of Bath looks back to a magical time before the arrival of Christianity in which the land was "fulfilled of fairye." Hundreds of years later, the seventeenth-century writer Robert Herrick honors the amalgamation of Christian and pagan elements in agrarian British culture in such poems as "Corinna's Gone A-Maying" and "The Hock Cart."

Medieval Christianity was fairly uniform across Western Europe—hence called "catholic," or universally shared—and its rituals and expectations, common to the whole community, permeated everyday life. The Catholic Church was also an international power structure. In its hierarchy of pope, cardinals, archbishops, and bishops, it resembled the feudal state, but the church power structure coexisted alongside a separate hierarchy of lay authorities with a theoretically different sphere of social responsibilities. The sharing out of lay and ecclesiastical authority in medieval England was sometimes a source of conflict. Chaucer's pilgrims are on their way to visit the memorial shrine to one victim of such struggle: Thomas a Becket, Archbishop of Canterbury, who opposed the policies of King Henry III, was assassinated on the king's orders in 1120 and later made a saint. As an international organization, the church conducted its business in the universal language of Latin, and thus although statistically in the period the largest segment of literate persons were monks and priests, the clerical contribution to great writing in English was relatively modest. Yet the lay writers of the period reflect the importance of the church as an institution and the pervasiveness of religion in everyday life.

Beginning in 1517 the German monk Martin Luther, in Wittenberg, Germany, openly challenged many aspects of Catholic practice and by 1520 had completely repudiated the authority of the Pope, setting in train the Protestant Reformation. Luther argued that the Roman Catholic Church had strayed far from the pattern of Christianity laid out in scripture. He rejected Catholic doctrines for which no biblical authority was to be found, such as the belief in Purgatory, and translated the Bible into German, on the grounds that the importance of scripture for all Christians made its translation into the vernacular tongue essential. Luther was not the first to advance such views—followers of the Englishman John Wycliffe had translated the Bible in the fourteenth century. But Luther, protected by powerful German rulers, was able to speak out with impunity and convert others to his views, rather than suffer the persecution usually meted out to heretics. Soon other reformers were following in Luther's footsteps: of these, the Swiss Ulrich Zwingli and the French Jean Calvin would be especially influential for English religious thought.

At first England remained staunchly Catholic. Its king, Henry VIII, was so severe to heretics that the Pope awarded him the title "Defender of the Faith," which British monarchs have retained to this day. In 1534, however, Henry rejected the authority of the Pope to prevent his divorce from his queen, Catherine of Aragon, and his marriage to his mistress, Ann Boleyn. In doing so, Henry appropriated to himself ecclesiastical as well as secular authority. Thomas More, author of *Utopia*, was executed for refusing to endorse Henry's right to govern the English church. Over the following six years, Henry consolidated his grip on the ecclesiastical establishment by dissolving the powerful, populous Catholic monasteries and redistributing their massive landholdings to his own lay followers. Yet Henry's church largely retained Catholic doctrine and liturgy. When Henry died and his young son, Edward, came to the throne in 1547, the English church embarked on a more Protestant path, a direction abruptly reversed when Edward died and his older sister Mary, the daughter of Catherine of Aragon, took the throne in 1553 and attempted to reintroduce Roman Catholicism. Mary's reign was also short, however, and her successor, Elizabeth I, the daughter of Ann Boleyn, was a Protestant. Elizabeth attempted to establish a "middle way" Christianity, compromising between Roman Catholic practices and beliefs and reformed ones.

The Church of England, though it laid claim to a national rather than pan-European authority, aspired like its predecessor to be the universal church of all English subjects. It retained the Catholic structure of parishes and dioceses and the Catholic hierarchy of bishops, though the ecclesiastical authority was now the Archbishop of Canterbury and the Church's "Supreme Governor" was the monarch. Yet disagreement and controversy persisted. Some members of the Church of England wanted to retain many of the ritual and liturgical elements of Catholicism. Others, the Puritans, advocated a more thoroughgoing reformation. Most Puritans remained within the Church of England, but a minority, the "Separatists" or "Congregationalists," split from the established church altogether. These dissenters no longer the ideal church thought of as an organization to which everybody belonged; instead, they conceived it as a more exclusive group of likeminded people, one not necessarily attached to a larger body of believers.

In the seventeenth century, the succession of the Scottish king James to the English throne produced another problem. England and Scotland were separate nations, and in the sixteenth century Scotland had developed its own national Presbyterian church, or "kirk," under the leadership of the reformer John Knox. The kirk retained fewer Catholic liturgical elements than did the Church of England, and its authorities, or "presbyters," were elected by assemblies of their fellow clerics, rather than appointed by the king. James I and his son Charles I, especially the latter, wanted to bring the Scottish kirk into conformity with Church of England practices. The Scots violently resisted these efforts, with the collaboration of many English Puritans, in a conflict that eventually developed into the English Civil War in the mid-seventeenth century. The effect of these disputes is visible in the poetry of such writers as John Milton, Robert Herrick, Henry Vaughan, and Thomas Traherne, and in the prose of Thomas Browne, Lucy Hutchinson, and Dorothy Waugh. Just as in the mid-sixteenth century, when a succession of monarchs with different religious commitments destabilized the church, so the seventeenth century endured spiritual whiplash. King Charles I's highly ritualistic Church of England was violently overturned by the Puritan victors in the Civil War—until 1660, after the death of the Puritan leader, Oliver Cromwell, when the Church of England was restored along with the monarchy.

The religious and political upheavals of the seventeenth century produced Christian sects that de-emphasized the ceremony of the established church and rejected as well its top-down authority structure. Some of these groups were ephemeral, but the Baptists (founded in 1608 in Amsterdam by the English expatriate John Smyth) and Quakers, or Society of Friends (founded by George Fox in the 1640s), flourished outside the established church, sometimes despite cruel persecution. John Bunyan, a Baptist, wrote the Christian allegory *Pilgrim's Progress* while in prison. Some dissenters, like the Baptists, shared the reformed reverence for the absolute authority of scripture but interpreted the scriptural texts differently from their fellow Protestants. Others, like the Quakers, favored, even over the authority of the Bible, the "inner light" or voice of individual conscience, which they took to be the working of the Holy Spirit in the lives of individuals.

The Protestant dissenters were not England's only religious minorities. Despite crushing fines and the threat of imprisonment, a minority of Catholics under Elizabeth and James openly refused to give their allegiance to the new church, and others remained secret adherents to the old ways. John Donne was brought up in an ardently Catholic family, and several other writers converted to Catholicism as adults—Ben Jonson for a considerable part of his career, Elizabeth Carey and Richard Crashaw permanently, and at profound personal cost. In the eighteenth century, Catholics remained objects of suspicion as possible agents of sedition, especially after the "Glorious Revolution" in 1688 deposed the Catholic James II in favor of the Protestant William and Mary. Anti-Catholic prejudice affected John Dryden, a Catholic convert, as well as the lifelong Catholic Alexander Pope. By contrast, the English colony of Ireland remained overwhelmingly Roman Catholic, the fervor of its religious commitment at least partly inspired by resistance to English occupation. Starting in the reign of Elizabeth, England shored up its own authority in Ireland by encouraging Protestant immigrants from Scotland to settle in northern Ireland, producing a virulent religious divide the effects of which are still playing out today.

A small community of Jews had moved from France to London after 1066, when the Norman William the Conqueror came to the English throne. Although despised and persecuted by many Christians, they were allowed to remain as moneylenders to the Crown, until the thirteenth century, when the king developed alternative sources of credit. At this point, in 1290, the Jews were expelled from England. In 1655 Oliver Cromwell permitted a few to return, and in the late seventeenth and early eighteenth centuries the Jewish population slowly increased, mainly by immigration from Germany. In the mid-eighteenth century some prominent Jews had their children brought up as Christians so as to facilitate their full integration into English society: thus the nineteenth-century writer and politician Benjamin Disraeli, although he and his father were members of the Church of England, was widely considered a Jew insofar as his ancestry was Jewish.

In the late seventeenth century, as the Church of England reasserted itself, Catholics, Jews, and dissenting Protestants found themselves subject to significant legal restrictions. The Corporation Act, passed in 1661, and the Test Act, passed in 1673, excluded all who refused to take communion in the Church of England from voting, attending university, or working in government or in the professions. Members of religious minorities, as well as Church of England communicants, paid mandatory taxes in support of Church of England ministers and buildings. In 1689 the dissenters gained the right to worship in public, but Jews and Catholics were not permitted to do so.

During the eighteenth century, political, intellectual, and religious history remained closely intertwined. The Church of England came to accommodate a good deal of variety. "Low church" services resembled those of the dissenting Protestant churches, minimizing ritual and emphasizing the sermon; the "high church" retained more elaborate ritual elements, yet its prestige was under attack on several fronts. Many Enlightenment thinkers subjected the Bible to rational critique and found it wanting: the philosopher David Hume, for instance, argued that the "miracles" described therein were more probably lies or errors than real breaches of the laws of nature. Within the Church of England, the "broad church" Latitudinarians welcomed this rationalism, advocating theological openness and an emphasis on ethics rather than dogma. More radically, the Unitarian movement rejected the divinity of Christ while professing to accept his ethical teachings. Taking a different tack, the preacher John Wesley, founder of Methodism, responded to the rationalists' challenge with a newly fervent call to evangelism and personal discipline; his movement was particularly successful in Wales. Revolutions in America and France at the end of the century generated considerable millenarian excitement and fostered more new religious ideas, often in conjunction with a radical social agenda. Many important writers of the Romantic period were indebted to traditions of protestant dissent: Unitarian and rationalist protestant ideas influenced William Hazlitt, Anna Barbauld, Mary Wollstonecraft, and the young Samuel Taylor Coleridge. William Blake created a highly idiosyncratic poetic mythology loosely indebted to radical strains of Christian mysticism. Others were even more heterodox: Lord Byron and Robert Burns, brought up as Scots Presbyterians, rebelled fiercely, and Percy Shelley's writing of an atheistic pamphlet resulted in his expulsion from Oxford.

Great Britain never erected an American-style "wall of separation" between church and state, but in practice religion and secular affairs grew more and more distinct during the nineteenth century. In consequence, members of religious minorities no longer seemed to pose a threat to the commonweal. A movement to repeal the Test Act failed in the 1790s, but a renewed effort resulted in the extension of the franchise to dissenting Protestants in 1828 and to Catholics in 1829. The numbers of Roman Catholics in England were swelled by immigration from Ireland, but there were also some prominent English adherents. Among writers, the converts John Newman and Gerard Manley Hopkins are especially important. The political participation and social integration of Jews presented a thornier challenge. Lionel de Rothschild, repeatedly elected to represent London in Parliament during the 1840s and 1850s, was not permitted to take his seat there because he refused to take his oath of office "on the true faith of a Christian"; finally, in 1858, the Jewish Disabilities Act allowed him to omit these words. Only in 1871, however, were Oxford and Cambridge opened to non-Anglicans.

Meanwhile geological discoveries and Charles Darwin's evolutionary theories increasingly cast doubt on the literal truth of the Creation story, and close philological analysis of the biblical text suggested that its origins were human rather than divine. By the end of the nineteenth century, many writers were bearing witness to a world in which Christianity no longer seemed fundamentally plausible. In his poetry and prose, Thomas Hardy depicts a world devoid of benevolent providence. Matthew Arnold's poem "Dover Beach" is in part an elegy to lost spiritual assurance, as the "Sea of Faith" goes out like the tide: "But now I only hear / Its melancholy, long, withdrawing roar / Retreating." For Arnold, literature must replace religion as a source of spiritual truth, and intimacy between individuals substitute for the lost communal solidarity of the universal church.

The work of many twentieth-century writers shows the influence of a religious upbringing or a religious conversion in adulthood. T. S. Eliot and W. S. Auden embrace Anglicanism, William Butler Yeats spiritualism. James Joyce repudiates Irish Catholicism but remains obsessed with it. Yet religion, or lack of it, is a matter of individual choice and conscience, not social or legal mandate. In the past fifty years, church attendance has plummeted in Great Britain. Although 71 percent of the population still identified itself as "Christian" on the 2000 census, only about 7 percent of these regularly attend religious services of any denomination. Meanwhile, immigration from former British colonies has swelled the ranks of religions once alien to the British Isles—Muslim, Sikh, Hindu, Buddhist—though the numbers of adherents remain small relative to the total population.

THE UNIVERSE ACCORDING TO PTOLEMY

Ptolemy was a Roman astronomer of Greek descent, born in Egypt during the second century C.E.; for nearly fifteen hundred years after his death his account of the design of the universe was accepted as standard. During that time, the basic pattern underwent many detailed modifications and was fitted out with many astrological and pseudoscientific trappings. But in essence Ptolemy's followers portrayed the earth as the center of the universe, with the sun, planets, and fixed stars set in transparent spheres orbiting around it. In this scheme of things, as modified for Christian usage, Hell was usually placed under the earth's surface at the center of the cosmic globe, while Heaven, the abode of the blessed spirits, was in the outermost, uppermost circle, the empyrean. But in 1543 the Polish astronomer Copernicus proposed an alternative hypothesis—that the earth rotates around the sun, not vice versa; and despite theological opposition, observations with the new telescope and careful mathematical calculations insured ultimate acceptance of the new view.

The map of the Ptolemaic universe below is a simplified version of a diagram in Peter Apian's *Cosmography* (1584). In such a diagram, the Firmament is the sphere that contained the fixed stars; the Crystalline Sphere, which contained no heavenly bodies, is a late innovation, included to explain certain anomalies in the observed movement of the heavenly bodies; and the Prime Mover is the sphere that, itself put into motion by God, imparts rotation around the earth to all the other spheres.

Milton, writing in the mid-seventeenth century, used two universes. The Copernican universe, though he alludes to it, was too large, formless, and unfamiliar to be the setting for the war between Heaven and Hell in *Paradise Lost*. He therefore used the Ptolemaic cosmos, but placed Heaven well outside this smaller earth-centered universe, Hell far beneath it, and assigned the vast middle space to Chaos.

The Empyrean
The Prime Mover
The Crystalline Sphere
The Firmament
The Sphere of Saturn
The Sphere of Jupiter
The Sphere of Mars
The Sphere of the Sun
The Sphere of Venus
The Sphere of Mercury
The Sphere of the Moon

PERMISSIONS ACKNOWLEDGMENTS

TEXT CREDITS

Aphra Behn: *The Complete Text of OROONOKO*, edited by Joanna Lipking. Copyright © 1993 by Joanna Lipking and W. W. Norton & Company, Inc. Reprinted by permission of W. W. Norton & Company, Inc.

Beowulf: from BEOWULF, translated by Seamus Heaney. Copyright © 2000 by Seamus Heaney. Used with permission of W. W. Norton & Company, Inc.

Margaret Lucas Cavendish: Extracts from THE BLAZING WORLD are taken from Margaret Cavendish, Duchess of Newcastle, THE DESCRIPTION OF A NEW WORLD CALLED THE BLAZING WORLD AND OTHER WRITINGS, edited by Kate Lilley (London: Pickering & Chatto 1992). Pp.24,132–25, 180–81, 184–86. Reprinted by permission of the publisher.

Geoffrey Chaucer: All excerpts are from CHAUCER'S POETRY: AN ANTHOLOGY FOR THE MODERN READER, 2nd ed., edited by E. T. Donaldson. Copyright © 1958, 1975 by Judith Anderson and Deirdre Donaldson. Used by permission of W. W. Norton & Company, Inc.

Dream of the Rood: translated by Alfred David. Copyright © 2012 by Alfred David. Reprinted by permission of the translator.

Early Irish Lyrics: From EARLY IRISH LYRICS, edited and translated by Gerard Murphy, Four Courts Press, 1998. Reproduced with permission from Gerard Murphy and Four Courts Press.

Queen Elizabeth: *On Monsieur's Departure* from THE POEMS OF QUEEN ELIZABETH I, edited by Leicester Bradner. Copyright © 1964 by Brown University. Reprinted by permission of the University Press of New England. *The Golden Speech* from THE PUBLIC SPEAKING OF QUEEN ELIZABETH: SELECTIONS FROM HER OFFICIAL ADDRESSES, edited by George P. Rice, Jr. (AMS Press, 1966). Reprinted with the permission of AMS Press, Inc.

Thomas Gray: From the manuscript of *Elegy Written in a Country Churchyard*. Transcribed by kind permission of the Provost and Fellows of Eton College.

Stephen Greenblatt et al.: From THE NORTON SHAKESPEARE: BASED ON THE OXFORD EDITION, Second Edition, edited by Stephen Greenblatt. Copyright © 2008, 1997 by W. W. Norton & Company, Inc. Used by permission of W. W. Norton & Company, Inc.

Samuel Johnson: Excerpt from the manuscript of *The Vanity of Human Wishes*. Reprinted with permission.

Julian of Norwich: Excerpts reprinted from Julian of Norwich, A BOOK OF SHOWINGS, edited by Edmund Colledge and James Walsh, by permission of the publisher. Copyright © 1978 by the Pontifical Institute of Medieval Studies, Toronto.

Margery Kempe: All excerpts including bibliographical citation excerpts from THE BOOK OF MARGERY KEMPE, edited by Lynn Staley (Kalamazoo, MI: Medieval Institute Publications). Copyright © 1996 by the Board of The Medieval Institute. Reprinted by permission of the publisher.

Marie de France: Translation of LANVAL by Alfred David. Copyright © 2000 by Alfred David. Reprinted with the permission of the translator.

John Milton: Excerpts from *Areopagitica* from THE COMPLETE POETRY AND MAJOR PROSE OF MILTON, edited by Merritt Y. Hughes, copyright © 1957. Reprinted by permission of Prentice-Hall, Inc., Upper Saddle River, N.J. Complete text and endnotes From PARADISE LOST: A Norton Critical Edition, Second Edition, by John Milton edited by Gordon Teskey. Copyright © 2005 by W. W. Norton & Company, Inc. Reprinted by permission of W. W. Norton & Company, Inc.

Lady Mary Wortley Montagu: Poems from LADY MARY WORTLEY MONTAGU, ESSAYS AND POEMS, 1977, Revised 1993, edited by R. Halsband and I. Grundy. Reprinted with permission.

Mystery Plays: *The Wakefield Second Shepherd's Play* based on the edition by A. C. Cawley and Martin Stevens. Copyright © 1994. By permission of The Council of the Early English Text Society.

Petrarch: Reprinted by permission of the publisher from PETRARCH'S LYRIC POEMS: THE *RIME SPARSE* AND OTHER LYRICS, translated and edited by Robert M. Durling, pp. 284 and 336, Cambridge, Mass.: Harvard University Press, Copyright © 1976 by Robert M. Durling

Katherine Philips: *A Married State* from NLW Orielton Collection, box 24. Courtesy of The National Library of Wales.

William Shakespeare: From OTHELLO: A NORTON CRITICAL EDITION by William Shakespeare, edited by Edward Pechter. Copyright © 2004 by W. W. Norton & Company, Inc. Used by permission of W. W. Norton & Company, Inc.

Sir Gawain and the Green Knight: From SIR GAWAIN AND THE GREEN KNIGHT: A NEW VERSE TRANSLATION translated by Simon Armitage. Copyright © 2007 by Simon Armitage. Used by permission of W. W. Norton & Company, Inc. and Faber and Faber Ltd.

Christopher Smart: *My Cat Jeoffry* from JUBILATE AGNO, edited by W. H. Bond. Reprinted by permission of HarperCollins Publishers Ltd.

Tain Epic: *Cuchulainn's Boyhood Deeds* from THE TAIN translated by Thomas Kinsella. Copyright © 1969 by Thomas Kinsella. Used by permission of the translator.

The Wanderer: translated by Alfred David. Copyright © 2012 by Alfred David. Reprinted by permission of the translator.

The Wife's Lament: translated by Alfred David. Copyright © 2012 by Alfred David. Reprinted by permission of the translator.

Mary Wroth: from THE POEMS OF LADY MARY WROTH, edited by Josephine A. Roberts. Reprinted by permission of Louisiana State University Press.

Every effort has been made to contact the copyright holders of each of the selections. Rights holders of any selections not credited should contact W. W. Norton & Company, Inc., 500 Fifth Avenue, New York, NY 10110, in order for a correction to be made in the next reprinting of our work.

Index